Elements of
Literature

Third Course

correlated to the

Oklahoma Priority
Academic Student Skills

HOLT, RINEHART AND WINSTON

A Harcourt Classroom Education Company

Austin • New York • Orlando • Atlanta • San Francisco • Boston • Dallas • Toronto • London

STAFF CREDITS

Director of Special Projects: Suzanne Thompson

Managing Editor: Joan Marie Lindsay

Senior Editor: Annie Hartnett

Product Analyst: Jimmie Lou Ford

Editorial Assistant: Brian Howell

ISBN 0-03-066942-1
123 048 030201

CORRELATION TO OKLAHOMA PRIORITY ACADEMIC STUDENT SKILLS

The following chart is a correlation of **ELEMENTS OF LITERATURE, Third Course,** to the Oklahoma Priority Academic Student Skills. The format for this correlation follows the same basic format established by the Student Skills, modified to accommodate the addition of page references. The correlation provides a cross-reference between the skills in the Oklahoma Priority Academic Student Skills and representative page numbers where those skills are taught or assessed. In the chart, *PE* refers to the Pupil's Edition, while *ATE* refers to the Annotated Teacher's Edition. The references contained in this correlation reflect Holt, Rinehart and Winston's interpretation of the Language Arts objectives outlined in the Oklahoma curriculum.

I. READING PROCESS: Students will apply a wide range of strategies to comprehend, interpret, evaluate, and appreciate texts.

A. Vocabulary: Knowledge of words and word meanings.

The student will:

1. Continue to build personal vocabulary through word study, the reading of literature, and class discussion (e.g., multiple meanings, dictionary definitions, and meanings in context).

   PE   3, 49, 101, 103, 312, 343, 354, 459, 473, 508, 539, 569, 817, 835, 981, 1030

   ATE   3, 14, 16, 18, 50, 60, 69, 96, 146, 539, 750, 823

2. Apply knowledge of Greek (e.g., tele/phone, micro/phone), Latin (e.g., flex/ible), and Anglo-Saxon (e.g., un/friend/ly) roots and affixes to determine word meanings.

   PE   93, 103, 243, 313, 419, 425, 473, 709, 763, 789, 817, 1032, 1033

   ATE   93, 103, 138, 419, 457, 562, 584

3. Use word meanings within the appropriate context and verify those meanings by definition, restatement, example, comparison, and contrast.

   PE   3, 49, 93, 129, 181, 211, 243, 291, 302, 313, 327, 354, 365, 374, 425, 451, 459, 473, 489, 539, 661, 687, 763, 927, 953, 981

   ATE   12, 16, 50

4. Connect technical and specialized terms with new concepts in content area text.

   PE   200, 418, 485

   ATE   14, 573

5. Understand and explain the implied relationships in word analogies to extend vocabulary development.

   PE   163, 302, 381

   ATE   132, 381

6. Understand and explain shades of meaning in related words (e.g., softly and quietly).

   PE   129, 365, 381, 451, 508, 661, 687, 953, 981

   ATE   204, 565, 566, 822, 830

Additional instruction, practice, and reinforcement for Priority Academic Skill I A can be found in the following ancillaries:

- Lesson Plans, Including Strategies for English-Language Learners
- Words to Own
- Audio CD Library
- Standardized Test Preparation
- Portfolio Management System
- Reading Skills and Strategies: Reaching Struggling Readers
- Visual Connections Videocassette Program

I. READING PROCESS: (CONT.)

B. Comprehension: Ability to interact with the words and concepts on the page to understand what the writer has said.

The student will:

1. Read and comprehend both fiction and nonfiction that is appropriately designed for grade-level reading.

    PE 34-44, 80-91, 126, 144-154, 233-241, 266-275, 279-287, 314-325, 328-330, 339, 356-363, 371, 375, 399, 406-417, 426-431, 460-465, 512, 709, 710-713, 852, 860-862

    ATE 36, 188, 328, 384, 603, 706, 710

2. Preview the material and determine the purpose for reading a specific text.

    "Before You Read" sets a purpose for reading a selection. Examples include:

    PE 12, 50, 120, 144, 166, 202, 232, 348, 446, 524, 632, 888

3. Use prior knowledge to become actively engaged with the reading material and use a range of comprehension skills (e.g., literal, inferential, and evaluative).

    PE 348, 352, 426, 432, 610, 612

    ATE 349, 350, 427, 429

4. Skim text for an overall impression and scan text for particular information.

    PE 120, 263, 278, 289, 404, 491, 620, 817

    ATE 40, 96, 151, 537, 645

5. Use correction strategies when the meaning is not clear (e.g., read on, reread, ask questions, try alternate pronunciations, use resources).

    PE 94, 161, 303, 312, 835

    ATE 14, 37, 85, 96, 99, 140, 206, 305, 321, 510, 523, 593, 637, 669, 819, 821, 826, 838, 841, 844, 846, 848, 850, 861

6. Recognize signal words and their contribution to the meaning of the text (e.g., in spite of, for example, a major force, consequently, expecially relevant).

    PE 118, 400

    ATE 118, 402, 403, 646

7. Vary reading speed and strategies according to the type of material and the purpose for reading.

    PE 127, 182, 241, 417, 426, 458

    ATE 20, 88, 96, 110, 134, 157, 169, 189, 245, 272, 282, 307, 368, 455, 470, 532, 682, 737, 739, 742, 780, 835, 902, 906

Additional instruction, practice, and reinforcement for Priority Academic Skill I B can be found in the following ancillaries:

- Lesson Plans, Including Strategies for English-Language Learners
- Words to Own
- Audio CD Library
- Standardized Test Preparation
- Portfolio Management System
- Reading Skills and Strategies, Reaching Struggling Readers
- Visual Connections Videocassette Program
- High School PASS Practice Test Workbook

I. READING PROCESS: (CONT.)

C. Fluency: Ability to identify words rapidly so that attention is directed at the meaning of the text.

The student will:

1. Increase reading speed and comprehension through daily independent reading.

   PE   111, 193, 249, 331, 385, 437, 477, 613, 715, 863, 957

2. Continue to read with expression, interjecting a sense of feeling, anticipation, or characterization.

   PE   182, 187, 337, 364, 373, 443, 529, 569, 575, 578, 597, 619, 661, 720, 740-741, 867, 875, 952

   ATE   152, 184, 201, 259, 280, 326, 383, 501, 566, 582, 583, 765

Additional instruction, practice, and reinforcement for Priority Academic Skill I C can be found in the following ancillaries:

- Reading Skills and Strategies, Reaching Struggling Readers
- HRW Library
- Audio CD Library
- Cross-Curricular Activities
- Portfolio Management System
- HRW Internet Site

II. RESPONDING TO TEXT: Students read, construct meaning, and respond to a wide variety of literary forms.

The student will:

A. Recall and organize information, make inferences, and draw conclusions by using story structure (e.g., setting, character, goal, plot, conflict, and resolution).

   PE   12, 32-33, 120, 130-131, 161, 165, 166, 179, 210, 219, 229, 242, 263, 266, 276, 380, 426, 451, 458, 626, 627, 628, 716, 816, 834, 862

   ATE   84, 100, 193

B. Compare and evaluate the effectiveness of plot, theme, setting and characterization in selections of American and world literature.

   PE   47, 264-265, 266, 275, 278, 292, 300, 303, 312, 325, 333, 563, 707, 978

   ATE   102, 108, 136, 138, 153

C. Develop an understanding of the effect of history of American literature (e.g., literary movements and periods).

   American literature is presented in *Elements of Literature, Fifth Course.*

II. RESPONDING TO TEXT: (CONT.)

D. Evaluate works of world literature as reflections of time and culture.

Readings in world literature are presented in *Elements of Literature, Fourth Course.*

E. Analyze the recurrence of archetypal characters, settings, and themes in world literature.

Homer's *The Odyssey* provides an opportunity for students to identify archetypal characters, settings, and themes.
PE   888-950
ATE   895, 898, 902, 905, 908, 920, 924, 930, 932, 934, 942

F. Analyze and trace the author's development of time and sequence, including the use of complex literary devices (e.g., foreshadowing and flashbacks).

PE   29, 50, 77, 113, 405, 686, 788, 925, 971
ATE   52, 56, 57, 58, 60, 646, 678

G. Analyze interactions among main and subordinate characters in a literary text (e.g., internal and external conflicts, motivations, relationships, influences) and explain the way those interactions affect the plot.

PE   32-33, 34, 47, 210, 229, 626, 660, 762, 974, 975
ATE   14, 23, 28, 32, 33, 58, 68, 101, 102, 330

H. Use text organization as an aid to comprehension of increasingly difficult content material (e.g., compare/contrast, cause/effect, problem/solution, sequential order).

PE   400
ATE   97, 169, 402, 403, 646, 906

I. Use knowledge of literary genre and text structures to aid comprehension (drama, poetry, short stories, essays, speeches, and novels).

PE   32-33, 130-131, 164-165, 212-213, 264-265, 355, 399, 420, 454, 458, 492-493, 507, 520-521, 554-555, 559-560, 626-630, 730, 878-879
ATE   162, 164, 239, 257, 265

J. Summarize fiction/nonfiction by determining the main idea and supporting details.

PE   278, 289, 366, 375, 380, 454, 468, 472
ATE   37, 57, 67, 70, 105, 216, 285, 286, 368, 370, 371, 379, 455, 456, 463, 470, 471, 475, 791, 824, 853, 921

K. Analyze details for relevancy and accuracy.

ATE   37, 70, 216, 286, 297, 456, 791, 824, 913, 921

L. Discuss underlying theme or message when interpreting fiction and poetry.

PE   47, 264-265, 266, 275, 278, 292, 300, 303, 312, 325, 333, 563, 707, 978
ATE   102, 108, 136, 138, 153

M. Analyze the poet's use of imagery, personification, symbolism, and figures of speech.

PE   90, 140, 379, 471, 490, 499-501, 526-527, 533-534, 536-537, 540-541, 551-552, 555, 556-557, 564, 572-573, 740, 948, 970, 977
ATE   90, 208, 262, 285, 356, 449, 490, 493, 524, 888, 890

N. Explain how the use of sound devices in poetry supports the subject and mood (e.g., rhyme, rhythm, alliteration, and onomatopoeia).

PE   552, 554-555, 558, 559, 560, 561, 563, 564, 566, 569, 572, 575, 587, 967, 968, 973, 975, 976
ATE   183, 284, 383, 511, 524, 559, 560, 566, 572, 573

II. RESPONDING TO TEXT: (CONT.)

O. Support ideas, make inferences, and draw conclusions from evidence presented in text.

PE 120, 127, 232

ATE 135, 136, 149, 153, 154, 158, 235, 262, 282, 329, 346, 358, 361, 435, 475, 589, 602, 647, 679, 682, 691, 697, 706, 737, 744, 815, 938

P. Evaluate, react, and respond to reading material through activities such as discussions, correspondence, family histories, Reader's Theater, and multimedia projects.

PE 92, 242, 364, 373, 443, 489, 539, 553, 558, 575, 582-584, 714, 723, 740-741, 864-867, 875, 926, 938

ATE 48, 54, 165, 201, 230, 259, 280, 288, 326, 582

H. Interpret the use of figurative language and literary devices within text (e.g., metaphor, simile, hyperbole, dialect, and irony).

PE 47, 77, 186, 209, 212-213, 218, 241, 325, 352, 404, 498, 513, 520-521, 544, 556, 586-587, 601, 608, 660, 686, 762, 788, 816, 859, 925

ATE 36, 63, 84, 151

R. Identify the author's writing style.

PE 32-33, 130-131, 164-165, 212-213, 264-265, 355, 399, 420, 454, 458, 492-493, 507, 520-521, 554-555, 559-560, 626-630, 730, 878-879

ATE 162, 164, 239, 257, 265

S. Determine the author's purpose (persuade, inform, entertain) and point of view to evaluate source credibility and reliability.

PE 132, 141, 258, 263, 420, 424

ATE 134, 136, 138, 139, 157, 190, 260, 422, 428

T. Analyze the effect of bias, stereotyping, unsupported inferences, fallacious reasoning, and propaganda techniques in expository text (e.g., flag waving, prestige identification, exigency).

ATE 710

U. Evaluate advertisements, editorials, and feature stories for relationships between intent and factual content.

ATE 710

Additional instruction, practice, and reinforcement for Priority Academic Skill II can be found in the following ancillaries:

• Reading Skills and Strategies, Reaching Struggling Readers
• Literary Elements: Transparencies and Worksheets
• Standardized Test Preparation
• Viewing and Representing: Transparencies and Worksheets
• HRW Library
• Visual Connections Videocassette Program
• Portfolio Management System
• High School PASS Practice Test Workbook

III. INFORMATION AND RESEARCH: Students read widely to acquire knowledge, conduct research, and organize information.

The student will:

A. Use clear research questions and suitable research methods (e.g., library, electronic media, and personal interview) to elicit and present evidence from primary and secondary sources.

PE   48, 78, 180, 210, 276, 312, 353, 432, 450, 458, 472, 485, 569, 597, 609, 621, 723, 763, 789, 817, 856, 857, 868-870, 983-986

ATE   21, 41, 56, 763, 789

B. Analyze, synthesize, evaluate, summarize, or paraphrase relevant information from multiple sources into a written report or summary.

PE   44, 48, 78, 180, 301, 312, 326, 339, 432, 450, 472, 478, 498, 529, 535, 569, 609, 621, 856, 857, 868-870, 956, 960, 983-986

ATE   21, 41, 56, 305

C. Give credit for both quoted and paraphrased information in a bibliography.

PE   276, 869, 871, 986-987, 988-989

ATE   952

D. Interpret information from schedules, letters, catalogs, directories, charts, maps, graphs, tables, diagrams, and directions, as appropriate to content area curriculum.

PE   30, 118, 162, 229, 353, 444, 466, 498, 616, 708, 951, 982

ATE   30, 64, 78, 87, 158, 165, 173, 180, 210, 263, 309

E. Understand technical directions to complete tasks (e.g., home or auto repair, use of computer software, assembling equipment), as appropriate to content area curriculum.

Critical thinking and reading skills and strategies may be applied to content area curriculum documents. Examples include:

PE   979-980

F. Select the best source for a given purpose (e.g., reference books, almanacs, atlases, encyclopedias, dictionaries, thesauruses, electronic card catalogs and databases, tables of contents, glossaries, indexes, magazines, newspapers, and the *Reader's Guide to Periodical Literature*).

PE   78, 103, 210, 312, 326, 343, 354, 459, 473, 485, 508, 529, 551, 569, 621, 817, 869, 981, 983, 1030

ATE   16, 76, 210, 331, 384, 823

G. Compare and contrast the features of consumer materials to gain meaning from the documents (e.g., warranties, contracts, instructional manuals, and product information), as appropriate to content area curriculum.

Critical thinking and reading skills and strategies can be applied to content area curriculum documents. Examples include:

PE   3, 979-980

H. Develop and organize notes from content area text using graphic organizers, note cards, or outlines.

PE   426, 432, 610, 612

ATE   97

I. Use supplementary resources to enhance understanding of content area subjects (e.g., audio/video recordings, print materials, interviews).

PE   78, 312, 432, 459, 485, 508, 529, 551, 621, 869, 874, 983, 984-986

ATE   48, 56, 76, 165, 210, 217, 230, 280, 331, 384, 498

III. INFORMATION AND RESEARCH: (CONT.)

J. Analyze, synthesize, evaluate, summarize, and paraphrase information from multiple sources.

PE 44, 48, 92, 180, 301, 312, 339, 353, 404, 432, 450,
472, 478, 569, 597, 609, 621, 723, 789, 857, 956,
960, 983-986, 986-987

ATE 21, 24, 25, 41, 56

K. Continue to apply test-taking strategies.

PE 991-992

**Additional instruction, practice, and reinforcement for Priority Academic Skill III
can be found in the following ancillaries:**

- Reading Skills and Strategies, Reaching Struggling Readers
- HRW Internet Site
- Writer's Workshop 1 CD-ROM
- Viewing and Representing: HRW Multimedia Presentation Maker
- Workshop Resources: Transparencies and Worksheets
- Portfolio Management System

IV. EFFECTIVE READING HABITS: Students demonstrate the behaviors, habits, and attitudes of an effective reader.

The student will:

A. Participate in daily, independent reading of self-
selected literature (e.g., Sustained Silent Reading/Drop
Everything and Read: 20-30 minutes daily).

PE 111, 193, 249, 331, 385, 437, 477, 613, 715, 863,
957

B. Share and discuss daily books and authors in pairs, in
small groups, and in large groups.

PE 109, 141, 186, 187, 192, 241, 248, 330, 373, 384,
436, 458, 466, 476, 498, 549, 581, 612, 618, 714,
862, 875, 956

ATE 66, 78, 128, 130, 148

C. Respond to oral reading led by teacher through discussion, art, drama, and writing.

PE 29, 179, 186, 209, 229, 275, 300, 312, 325, 363, 372,
458, 660, 707

ATE 29, 179, 186, 209, 229, 275, 300, 312, 325, 363, 372,
458, 660, 707

D. Read for a variety of purposes such as for pleasure,
to gain information, to communicate, or to support an
opinion.

PE 111, 193, 249, 331, 385, 437, 477, 613, 715, 863,
957

E. Read, discuss, and analyze short stories, novels,
essays, speeches, technical documents, and other
works representing diversity (e.g., gender, ethnicity,
and nationality).

PE 104-109, 125, 214-217, 262, 299, 342, 344-346,
361, 362, 403, 416, 426-431, 448-449, 499-501,
524-525, 531, 534, 567, 581, 592, 599

ATE 274

V. WRITING

The student will:

A. Use a writing process to develop and refine composition skills. Students are expected to use prewriting strategies, write and revise multiple drafts, edit, and share their compositions.

PE 112-117, 194-198, 250-255, 332-337, 386-391, 438-443, 478-483, 516-518, 550-552, 614-619, 716-721, 868-873, 958-963

B. Write a variety of narrative, descriptive, expository, persuasive, and reflective compositions that establish and support a central idea with a thesis statement, supporting paragraphs with facts, details, explanations, or examples, and a concluding paragraph that summarizes the points.

PE 112-117, 194-198, 250-255, 332-337, 386-391, 438-443, 478-483, 516-518, 550-552, 614-619, 716-721, 868-873, 958-963

C. Write analytically about literature using appropriate literary terms such as character types and development, plot structure, setting, point of view, and theme.

PE 92, 162, 180, 187, 194-198, 217, 230, 263, 276, 290, 301, 326, 332-337, 516, 597, 600, 605, 609, 614-619, 661, 708, 716-721, 789, 857, 952

ATE 102, 111, 193, 269

D. Write a documented essay using research methods, incorporating the techniques of Modern Language Association or similar parenthetical styles.

PE 44, 78, 92, 102, 180, 210, 276, 301, 312, 353, 404, 438-442, 472, 478-482, 529, 597, 609, 621, 716-720, 857, 868-870, 958-962, 988-989

ATE 21, 24, 25, 102

E. Demonstrate essay test-taking techniques by addressing and analyzing the question and using such methods as comparison/contrast, analysis, exposition, and persuasion.

PE 991-992

F. Select and use reference materials and resources as needed for writing, revising, and editing final drafts.

PE 116, 117, 198, 199, 253, 254, 336, 337, 390, 391, 442, 443, 482, 518, 584, 618, 619, 871, 872, 962, 963

ATE 115, 254, 336, 354

Additional instruction, practice, and reinforcement for Priority Academic Skill V can be found in the following ancillaries:

• Workshop Resources: Transparencies and Worksheets
• Portfolio Management System
• Reading Skills and Strategies, Reaching Struggling Readers
• Writer's Workshop 1 CD-ROM

VI. GRAMMAR/USAGE AND MECHANICS

The student will:

A. Demonstrate appropriate practices in speaking and writing. Students are expected to write using complete sentences and edit for usage, mechanics, and spelling.

PE   31, 79, 93, 117, 143, 163, 181, 199, 211, 232, 255, 277, 313, 337, 354, 365, 374, 419, 433, 443, 451, 459, 467, 483, 619, 789, 858-859, 873, 927

B. Demonstrate correct use of standard English usage.

1. Capitalization and punctuation

PE   116, 231, 243, 337, 354, 425, 433, 473, 564, 720, 864, 1014, 1023-1025, 1026-1028, 1029-1030, 1030-1031

ATE   231, 238, 243, 254, 334, 354, 425, 440

2. Commonly confused terms (e.g., there, their, they're; two, too, to; accept, except; affect, effect)

PE   1035-1039

3. Formation of plurals

PE   1034

ATE   413

4. Pronoun usage, pronoun/antecedent agreement, and clear pronoun reference

PE   231, 993-994, 996-997, 1009, 1029, 1030

ATE   231, 254

5. Subject-verb agreement

PE   93, 994-996

ATE   93

6. Verb forms and tenses

PE   79, 405, 999

ATE   79, 116, 390, 405

7. Sentence structure

PE   93, 117, 619, 1011-1012, 1013, 1014-1015, 1016

ATE   84, 93, 117, 199, 255, 839

8. Parallel structure

PE   467, 721, 1017

ATE   467, 721

9. Spell frequently used and previously studied words correctly.

PE   354, 473, 709, 998, 1004, 1015, 1019, 1031-1034

ATE   468, 469, 471, 472, 531

10. Use reference materials and technology to check and correct spelling.

PE   254, 354, 473, 720

ATE   254, 390, 481, 720

11. Avoid dangling and misplaced modifiers.

PE   143

ATE   143

12. Avoid run-ons and fragments.

PE   199, 337, 1010, 1014-1015

ATE   199, 336, 337

VI. GRAMMAR/USAGE AND MECHANICS: (CONT.)

C. Identify some major influences on language and how language changes. For example, vowel shift and fewer inflections are typical of patterns of change. Changes in politics (glasnost, apartheid) and technology (Internet, laser) are examples of how new words are added to our vocabulary.

ATE   62

Additional instruction, practice, and reinforcement for Priority Academic Skill VI can be found in the following ancillaries:

• Daily Oral Grammar
• Grammar and Language Links
• Workshop Resources: Transparencies, and Worksheets
• Language Handbook Resources
• Language Workshop CD-ROM
• Portfolio Management System
• High School PASS Practice Test Workbook

VII. LISTENING/SPEAKING

The student will:

A. Demonstrate thinking skills in listening, speaking, reading, and writing. For example, students, individually or in groups, will gather information, organize and analyze it, and generate a report that conveys ideas clearly and relates to the background and interest of the audience.

PE   44, 48, 102, 242, 248, 263, 339, 418, 466, 472, 478-482, 485, 609, 614-618, 621, 763, 817, 834, 856, 857, 868-873, 958-962

ATE   102, 180, 265, 287, 432, 503, 614-618, 716-720

B. Prepare, organize, and deliver oral responses to literary works.

1. Summarize significant events and details.

PE   217, 373
ATE   373

2. Articulate an understanding of several ideas and images communicated by literary works.

PE   78, 92, 180, 248, 312, 339, 353, 432, 458, 466, 472, 485, 569, 609, 621, 661, 723, 817, 857, 862, 864-867, 875, 926, 952, 965

ATE   180, 265, 432, 503

3. Use relevant examples or textual evidence from the work to support conclusions.

PE   48, 78, 92, 162, 180, 248, 312, 353, 418, 432, 458, 466, 472, 485, 569, 609, 621, 661, 723, 817, 857, 864-867, 875, 926, 952, 965

ATE   180, 432, 481

C. Understand the major ideas and supporting evidence in informative and persuasive messages, and defend a point of view using precise language and appropriate details.

PE 48, 78, 312, 339, 353, 418, 432, 458, 459, 466, 472, 485, 609, 621, 661, 723, 817, 857, 862, 864-867, 875, 926, 956, 965

ATE 136, 180, 432, 481, 503, 539

D. Present reports using appropriate delivery (volume, rate, enunciation, and movement) and language skills (pronunciation, word choice, and usage).

PE 78, 92, 180, 182, 187, 243, 248, 312, 339, 373, 450, 481, 485, 539, 582-584, 621, 857, 875, 926, 952

ATE 54, 162, 165, 213, 296, 481, 610

E. Analyze purpose, audience, and occasion to choose effective verbal and nonverbal strategies such as pitch and tone of voice, posture, and eye contact.

PE 242, 373, 450, 481, 539, 582-583, 687, 926

F. Determine the purpose for listening (i.e., gaining information, solving problems; or for enjoying, appreciating, recalling, interpreting, applying, analyzing, evaluating, receiving directions, or learning concepts).

PE 582-584, 864-867

ATE 230, 584, 658, 846, 847, 864

G. Recognize and understand barriers to effective listening (i.e., internal and external distractions, personal biases, and conflicting demands).

PE 459, 569, 621, 723

ATE 136, 213, 230, 298, 683

H. Predict, clarify, analyze, and critique a speaker's information and point of view.

PE 582-584, 864-867

I. Distinguish between a speaker's opinion and verifiable facts.

PE 459, 569, 621, 723

ATE 136, 213, 230, 298, 584, 658, 683, 846, 847, 864

J. Evaluate the spoken message in terms of content, credibility, and delivery.

PE 459, 569, 621, 723

ATE 78, 136, 213, 230, 298, 581, 584, 608, 658, 683, 846, 847, 864

K. Show consideration and respect for others.

1. Listen and speak to gain and share knowledge of one's culture, the culture of others, and the common elements of cultures.

PE 109, 141, 186, 187, 241, 248, 330, 353, 364, 373, 380, 384, 386-390, 436, 458, 466, 476, 549, 612, 618, 714, 862, 956

ATE 66, 78, 128, 130, 148, 387-390

2. Speak responsibly to present accurate, truthful, and ethical messages.

PE 30

ATE 213, 270, 276, 277, 280

VII. LISTENING/SPEAKING: (CONT.)

> **Additional instruction, practice, and reinforcement for Priority Academic Skill VII can be found in the following ancillaries:**
>
> • Audio CD Library
> • Visual Connections Videocassette Program
> • Reading Skills and Strategies, Reaching Struggling Readers
> • Cross-Curricular Activities
> • Portfolio Management System

VIII. VISUAL LITERACY

The student will:

A. Distinguish fact, opinion, and fiction in print and non-print media, such as in literature, electronic media, and advertising.

PE   78, 266, 459, 569, 723, 956
ATE   136, 539, 718, 730

B. Interpret and evaluate the various ways visual image makers such as graphic artists, illustrators, and news photographers represent meaning.

PE   459, 723, 789, 952
ATE   155, 213, 718, 730

C. Compare and contrast print, visual, and electronic media, such as film, with a written story.

PE   78, 142, 148
ATE   123, 148, 157, 165, 718

D. Interpret important events and ideas gathered from maps, charts, graphics, video segments, or technology presentations.

PE   30, 118, 162, 229, 301, 333, 353, 444, 446, 466, 498, 616, 708, 875, 951, 982
ATE   21, 30, 64, 78, 87, 158, 165, 173, 180, 230, 263, 267, 309

E. Access information from a variety of media (television, computers, videos, CD-ROMs) and evaluate the quality of material selected.

PE   266, 312, 459, 485, 569, 723, 869, 874, 960, 984-985, 985-986
ATE   718, 730

F. Analyze and evaluate the effectiveness of the techniques used in media messages for a particular audience.

PE   78, 266, 459, 569, 723, 956
ATE   136, 539, 718, 730

> **Additional instruction, practice, and reinforcement for Priority Academic Skill VIII can be found in the following ancillaries:**
>
> • Visual Connections Videocassette Program
> • Viewing and Representing: Fine Art Transparencies
> • Portfolio Management System
> • HRW Internet Site

IX. LITERATURE

The student will:

A. Demonstrate a knowledge of and an appreciation for various forms (genres) of literature, such as short story, novel, drama, narrative and lyric poetry, essay, and informational texts.

PE 29, 179, 186, 209, 229, 275, 300, 312, 325, 363, 372, 458, 660, 707

ATE 29, 179, 186, 209, 229, 275, 300, 312, 325, 363, 372, 458, 660, 707

B. Demonstrate a knowledge of literary elements and techniques and how they affect the development of a literary work. For example, students are expected to recognize and explain plot, character, setting, theme, conflict, symbolism, point of view, imagery, flashback, foreshadowing, irony, tone, and allusion.

PE 33, 34, 132, 220, 230, 258, 292, 303, 325, 363, 626, 707, 762, 816, 857, 974, 978

ATE 23, 51, 58, 87, 101, 138, 139, 316, 330, 349, 350, 586

C. Identify and use figurative language and sound devices in speaking and writing. For example, students are expected to recognize and use analogy, rhyme, metaphor, simile, personification, alliteration, onomatopoeia, and hyperbole.

PE 186, 291, 327, 365, 404, 424, 498, 508, 521, 538, 540, 544, 545, 558, 590, 859, 884, 927, 950

ATE 36, 52, 104, 245, 253, 316, 318, 416, 742, 812

D. Read and respond to historically or culturally significant works of literature. For example, students are expected to find ways to clarify the ideas and make connections between literary works.

PE 856, 956

ATE 76, 90, 100, 185, 208, 262, 288, 299, 311, 351, 362, 371, 423, 449, 459, 464, 470, 471, 496, 506, 569, 593, 852, 853, 854, 935, 940

E. Expand vocabulary through word study, literature, and class discussion. For example, students are expected to distinguish connotation and denotation of words, etymology, levels of usage, and neologisms.

PE 92, 93, 103, 200, 243, 313, 374, 418, 425, 451, 563, 596, 709, 763, 789, 817, 969, 1035

ATE 14, 34, 62, 83, 93, 103, 379, 448, 542, 573, 595

F. Draw inferences such as conclusions or generalizations and support them with text evidence and personal experience.

PE 266, 275

ATE 45, 82, 136, 171, 191, 234, 235, 268, 269, 270, 329, 346, 358, 360, 647, 649, 681, 706, 737, 739, 744, 749, 791, 815, 897, 919, 938

G. Recognize and discuss universal themes (archetypal patterns) in literature.

PE 47, 264-265, 266, 275, 278, 292, 300, 303, 312, 325, 333, 563, 707, 978

ATE 102, 108, 136, 138, 153

H. Analyze characteristics of subgenres, such as satire, parody, allegory, and pastorals, that are used in poetry, prose, plays, novels, short stories, essays, and other basic genres.

PE 132, 141, 976

ATE 133, 134, 135, 136, 138

I. Analyze, evaluate, and explain the thinking or behavior represented in a work of literature from or about various past and/or present cultures and relate it to own culture.

PE 229, 372, 476, 600, 762

ATE 18, 62, 86, 176, 190, 205, 235, 260, 286, 369, 379, 501, 589, 695, 756, 786, 814, 882, 908

IX. LITERATURE: (CONT.)

Additional instruction, practice, and reinforcement for Priority Academic Skill IX can be found in the following ancillaries:

- Lesson Plans, Including Strategies for English-Language Learners
- Audio CD Library
- HRW Library
- Visual Connections Videocassette Program
- Words to Own Worksheets
- Graphic Organizers for Active Reading
- Literary Elements: Transparencies and Worksheets
- Reading Skills and Strategies, Reaching Struggling Readers
- HRW Internet Site
- High School PASS Practice Test Workbook

ELEMENTS OF *Literature*

THIRD COURSE

*W*hen you set out for Ithaca,
pray that your road's a long one,
full of adventure, full of discovery.

— from "Ithaca" by C. P. Cavafy

HOLT, RINEHART AND WINSTON

A Harcourt Education Company

Austin • Orlando • Chicago • New York • Toronto • London • San Diego

Credits

EDITORIAL

Project Director:	Kathleen Daniel
Managing Editors:	Richard Sime, Bill Wahlgren
Project Editor:	Hester Weeden
Book Editor:	Mary R. Bulkot
Editorial Staff:	Steven Fechter, Abigail Winograd, Susan Kent Cakars, Dorothy M. Coe, Edward S. Cohen, Lanie Lee, Christine de Lignières, and Ron Ottaviano; David Knaggs and Sharon Churchin; Vicky Aeschbacher, Jane Archer-Feinstein, Roger Boylan, James Decker, Eric Estlund, Peggy Ferrin, Emily Gavin, Mikki Gibson, Annie Hartnett, Sean Henry, Julie Hoover, Eileen Joyce, Marcia Kelley, Linda Miller, Chi Nguyen, Carla Robinson, Deanna Roy, Tressa Sanders, Errol Smith, Suzanne Thompson, and Stephen Wesson
Editorial Support Staff:	Dan Hunter, Laurie Muir, Su Gordon, Leila Jamal, David Smith, Elizabeth Butler, Ruth Hooker, Kelly Keeley, Marie Price, Margaret Sanchez
Permissions:	Tamara Blanken, Sacha Frey, Mark Hughs
Research and Development:	Joan Burditt

PRODUCTION AND DESIGN

Text Design:	Preface, Inc.
Design Coordinator:	Joseph Padial
Electronic Files:	Preface, Inc., H & S Graphics, Inc.
Production and Manufacturing:	Athena Blackorby
Marketing Design:	Bob Bretz

COVER

Cover Artist:	Greg Geisler
Photo Credits:	Front cover: (Poseidon), from the Artemisium at Cape Sounion, Nimatallah/Art Resource, New York; (rocky coast), David Olsen/Tony Stone Images; (ancient Greek ship), Studio Kontos; (crashing waves), H. Richard Johnston/FPG International; (lighthouse), John Lund/Tony Stone Images. Back cover: (astrolabe), Giraudon/Art Resource, New York.
Quotation on Cover:	From "Ithaca" by C.P. Cavafy, translated by Edmund Keeley and Philip Sherrard, courtesy of Princeton University Press. For the complete poem, see page 948.

Program Authors

Kylene Beers wrote the Reading Matters section of the book and developed the accompanying *Reading Skills and Strategies* component. A former middle school teacher, Dr. Beers has turned her commitment to helping readers having difficulty into the major focus of her research, writing, speaking, and teaching. A clinical associate professor at the University of Houston, Dr. Beers is also currently the editor of the National Council of Teachers of English journal *Voices from the Middle*. She is the author of *When Kids Can't Read: The Reading Handbook for Teachers Grades 6–12* and co-editor of *Into Focus: Understanding and Creating Middle School Readers*. She has served on the review boards of the *English Journal* and *The ALAN Review*. Dr. Beers is a recipient of the NCTE Richard W. Halle Award. She currently serves on the board of directors of the International Reading Association's Special Interest Group on Adolescent Literature.

Robert E. Probst established the pedagogical framework for the 1997, 2000, and current editions of *Elements of Literature*. Dr. Probst is Professor of English Education at Georgia State University. He has taught English in Maryland and been Supervisor of English for the Norfolk, Virginia, Public Schools. He is the author of *Response and Analysis: Teaching Literature in Junior and Senior High School* and has contributed chapters to such books as *Literature Instruction: A Focus on Student Response; Reader Response in the Classroom; Handbook of Research on Teaching the English Language Arts; Transactions with Literature;* and *For Louise M. Rosenblatt*. Dr. Probst has worked on the National Council of Teachers of English Committee on Research, the Commission on Reading, and the Commission on Curriculum. He has also served on the board of directors of the Adolescent Literature Assembly and is a member of the National Conference on Research in Language and Literacy.

Robert Anderson wrote the introductions to "Modern Drama" and "William Shakespeare." He also wrote the instructional materials for *The Miracle Worker* and *Romeo and Juliet*. Mr. Anderson is a playwright, novelist, screenwriter, and teacher. His plays include *Tea and Sympathy; Silent Night, Lonely Night; You Know I Can't Hear You When the Water's Running;* and *I Never Sang for My Father*. His screenplays include *The Nun's Story* and *The Sand Pebbles*. Mr. Anderson has taught at the Writers' Workshop at the University of Iowa, the American Theater Wing Professional Training Program, and the Salzburg Seminar in American Studies. He is a past president of the Dramatists' Guild, a past vice president of the Authors' League of America, and a member of the Theater Hall of Fame.

John Malcolm Brinnin wrote the Elements of Literature essays on poetry, biographies of the poets, and instructional materials on individual poems. Mr. Brinnin is the author of six volumes of poetry, which received many prizes and awards. He was a member of the American Academy and Institute of Arts and Letters. He was also a critic of poetry and a biographer of poets and was for a number of years director of New York's famous Poetry Center. His teaching career, begun at Vassar College, included long terms at the University of Connecticut and Boston University, where he succeeded Robert Lowell as Professor of Creative Writing and Contemporary Letters. Mr. Brinnin's books include *Dylan Thomas in America: An Intimate Journal* and *Sextet: T.S. Eliot & Truman Capote & Others*.

John Leggett wrote the Elements of Literature essays on the short story, biographies of the short-story writers, and instructional materials on individual short stories. Mr. Leggett is a novelist, a biographer, and a former teacher. He went to the Writers' Workshop at the University of Iowa in the spring of 1969, expecting to work there for a single semester. In 1970, he assumed temporary charge of the program, and for the next seventeen years he was its director. Mr. Leggett's novels include *Wilder Stone; The Gloucester Branch; Who Took the Gold Away?; Gulliver House;* and *Making Believe*. He also wrote the highly acclaimed biography *Ross and Tom: Two American Tragedies*.

Special Contributors

Janet Burroway wrote the Elements of Literature essays on nonfiction. She also wrote biographies of the nonfiction writers and instructional materials on nonfiction. Ms. Burroway is a novelist and teacher who has also written children's books and a popular textbook, *Writing Fiction*. Ms. Burroway has taught at the University of Sussex, England; the University of Illinois; and the Writers' Workshop at the University of Iowa. She is currently Robert O. Lawton Distinguished Professor at Florida State University in Tallahassee. Her novels include *The Buzzards* (nominated for the Pulitzer Prize), *Raw Silk* (nominated for the National Book Award), *Opening Nights*, and *Cutting Stone*.

David Adams Leeming wrote the introduction to the *Odyssey* and instruction material on "The Epic." Dr. Leeming was for many years a Professor of English and Comparative Literature at the University of Connecticut. He is the author of several books on mythology, including *Mythology: The Voyage of the Hero; The World of Myths;* and *Encyclopedia of Creation Myths.* For several years Dr. Leeming taught English at Robert College in Istanbul, Turkey. He also served as secretary and assistant to the writer James Baldwin in New York and Istanbul. He has published the biographies *James Baldwin* and *Amazing Grace: A Biography of Beauford Delaney.*

Writers

The writers prepared instructional materials for the text under the supervision of Dr. Probst and the editorial staff.

Mary E. McCurnin
Educational Writer and Editor
Tallahassee, Florida

Carl Morse
Educational Writer and Editor
New York, New York

Carroll Moulton
Former Teacher
Educational Writer and Editor
Southampton, New York

Sandra Riggs
Former Teacher
Educational Writer and Editor
Amherst, Massachusetts

Diane Tasca
Educational Writer and Editor
Palo Alto, California

Acknowledgments

For permission to reprint copyrighted material in the Annotated Teacher's Edition, grateful acknowledgment is made to the following sources:

Curtis Brown Ltd, London, on behalf of the Estate of Daphne du Maurier: From *Enchanted Cornwall: Her Pictorial Memoir* by Daphne du Maurier. Copyright © 1989 by Daphne du Maurier.

Chelsea House Publishers: From *The Crow* by Frederick E. Hoxie. Copyright © 1989 by Chelsea House Publishers, a division of Main Line Book Co.

Doubleday, a division of Random House, Inc.: From *The Power of Myth* by Joseph Campbell with Bill Moyers. Copyright © 1988 by Apostrophe S Productions, Inc., and Bill Moyers and Alfred Van der Marck Editions for itself and the estate of Joseph Campbell.

Farrar, Straus & Giroux, Inc.: From "The Delta Factor" from *The Message in the Bottle* by Walker Percy. Copyright © 1975 by Walker Percy. From *Roald Dahl: A Biography* by Jeremy Treglown. Copyright © 1994 by Jeremy Treglown.

Fitzhenry & Whiteside, Markham, Ontario: From "Romeo and Juliet" from *Northrop Frye on Shakespeare*, edited by Robert Sandler. Copyright © 1986 by Northrop Frye.

The Gale Group: From "Kurt Vonnegut" from *Authors & Artists for Young Adults*, vol. 6, edited by Agnes Garrett and Helga P. McCue. Copyright © 1991 by Gale Research, Inc. All rights reserved. From "Sandra Cisneros" from *Authors & Artists for Young Adults*, vol. 9, edited by Laurie Collier. Copyright © 1992 by Gale Research, Inc. All rights reserved. From "Eugenia Collier" from *Contemporary Authors,* vols. 49-52, edited by Clare D. Kinsman. Copyright © 1975 by Gale Research Company. All rights reserved. From "Nikki Giovanni" from *Contemporary Authors,* vol. 60, edited by Daniel Jones and John D. Jorgenson. Copyright © 1998 by Gale Research, Inc. All rights reserved. From "Cynthia Rylant" from *Something About the Author,* vol. 76, edited by Diane Telgen. Copyright © 1994 by Gale Research, Inc. All rights reserved.

Harcourt Brace & Company: From "Little Gidding" from *Four Quartets* by T. S. Eliot. Copyright 1942 by T. S. Eliot; copyright renewed © 1970 by Esme Valerie Eliot.

Harvard University Press and the Trustees of Amherst College: From "76: Exultation is the going" and from "1255: Longing is like the Seed" from *The Poems of Emily Dickinson,* edited by Thomas H. Johnson. Copyright © 1951, 1955, 1979, 1983 by the President and Fellows of Harvard College. Published by The Belknap Press of Harvard University Press, Cambridge, MA.

David Higham Associates: From "Poison" from *Someone Like You* by Roald Dahl. Copyright 1950 by Roald Dahl. Published by Alfred A. Knopf, Inc.

Knight-Ridder/Tribune Information Services: Quote by David Thomson from "Judging Films by Their Covers: What's Coming As Hollywood Raids the Library" by Stephen Whitty from *San Jose Mercury News,* 1996. Copyright © 1996 by Knight Ridder/Tribune Information Services. All rights reserved.

Macmillan Library Reference USA, a division of Ahsuog, Inc.: Quote by Ray Bradbury from an interview with David Mogen from *Ray Bradbury* by David Mogen. Copyright © 1986 by G. K. Hall & Co.

Manchester University Press: From "Romeo and Juliet" from *Passion Lends Them Power: A Study of Shakespeare's Love Tragedies* by Derick R. C. Marsh. Copyright © 1976 by Derick R. C. Marsh. All rights reserved.

Modern Language Association: From "The Brevity of Friar Laurence" by Bertrand Evans from *PMLA,* LXV, 1950. Copyright © 1950 by the Modern Language Association of America.

Oxford University Press: From "William Shakespeare" by Philip Edwards from *The Oxford Illustrated History of English Literature,* edited by Pat Rogers. Copyright © 1987 by Oxford University Press.

Putnam Berkley, a division of Penguin Putnam Inc., and CineBooks®: From "Romeo and Juliet" from *The Movie Guide* by the editors of CineBooks. Copyright © 1998 by Cinebooks, a division of New American Publications.

St. Martin's Press, Incorporated: Quotes by Diane Ackerman from *Contemporary Poets,* Fourth Edition, edited by James Vinson and D. L. Kirkpatrick. Copyright © 1985 by James Vinson and D. L. Kirkpatrick.

Shakespeare Bulletin: From a review by Justin Shaltz of the *Romeo and Juliet* production at the Illinois Shakespeare Festival, 1994, from *Shakespeare Bulletin,* vol. 12.4, Fall 1994. Copyright © 1994 by Shakespeare Bulletin.

Simon & Schuster Books for Young Readers, an imprint of Simon & Schuster Children's Publishing Division: From Foreword by Lois Duncan from *Trapped!: Cages of Mind and Body,* edited by Lois Duncan. Copyright © 1998 by Lois Duncan.

Stanford University Press: From *Matsuo Bashō* by Makoto Ueda. Copyright © 1992 by the Board of Trustees of the Leland Stanford Junior University. All rights reserved.

Variety, Inc.: From "Hollywood's Fickle Courtship: Showbiz Overtures Remain Mysterious" by Chris Petrikin from *Variety,* vol. 368, no. 8, September 29, 1997. Copyright © 1997 by Cahners Publishing Company. All rights reserved.

SOURCES CITED

Quote by John Barton from "Speaking Shakespeare" by John Lair from *The New Yorker,* vol. LXXIV, no. 26, September 7, 1998.

Quote by Sister Wendy Beckett from "Sharing How Great Thou Art: Britain's Sister Wendy Blesses the Masses with Masterpieces" by Christopher P. Winner, FINA ed., *USA Today,* February 25, 1997.

From *An Introduction to Shakespeare* by Marchette Chute. Published by E. P. Dutton and Company, Inc., New York, 1951.

From "e. e. cummings" from *Poetry Criticism,* vol. 5, edited by Robyn V. Young. Published by Gale Research, Inc., Farmington Hills, MI, 1992.

From *Going Solo* by Roald Dahl. Published by Farrar, Straus & Giroux, Inc., New York, 1986.

From *The Letters of Robert Frost to Louis Untermeyer.* Published by Holt, Rinehart and Winston, New York, 1963.

From *Extra Innings* by Doris Grumbach. Published by W. W. Norton & Company, Inc., New York, 1993.

From "Romeo and Juliet" from *Shakespeare's Tragedies* by Phyllis Rackin. Published by Frederick Ungar Publishing Company, New York, 1978.

From *O. Henry: A Biography of William Sydney Porter* by David Stuart. Published by Scarborough House, Chelsea, MI, 1990.

From *Everyday Use* by Alice Walker, edited by Barbara T. Christian. Published by Rutgers University Press, New Brunswick, NJ, 1994.

Quote by Edmund Wilson from *James Thurber: His Life and Times* by Harrison Kinney. Published by Henry Holt and Company, Inc., New York, 1995.

CONTENTS IN BRIEF

The Poetry Collections

Modern Drama

William Shakespeare

The Epic

Resource Center

CONTENTS

Collection 2
The Human Spirit
COLLECTION PLANNING GUIDE T118A–T118D

COMMUNICATIONS WORKSHOPS

Language/Grammar Links
- Modifiers Make Meanings More Definite 129
- Misplaced Modifiers Are Confusing 143
- Figures of Speech 163
- Vivid Modifiers—A Definite Choice 181

Collection 3
Expect the Unexpected
COLLECTION PLANNING GUIDE T200A–T200D

Language/Grammar Links
• Diction—Ornate or Plain? **211**
• Pronoun Problems **231**
• Dialogue—Who's Talking? **243**

COMMUNICATIONS WORKSHOPS

Collection 4
Discoveries
COLLECTION PLANNING GUIDE T256A–T256D

COMMUNICATIONS WORKSHOPS

The Nonfiction Collections

Collection 5

We Remember
COLLECTION PLANNING GUIDE T346A–T346D

COMMUNICATIONS WORKSHOPS

Collection 6

A Place Called Home

COLLECTION PLANNING GUIDE T392A–T392D

COMMUNICATIONS WORKSHOPS

Collection 7

What I Think

COLLECTION PLANNING GUIDE T444A–T444D

Language/Grammar Links

- Connotations and Loaded Words **451**
- Euphemisms—Language That Covers Up **459**
- Parallel Structure—Keeping Things Balanced **467**
- Homonyms—Words That Sound Alike **473**

COMMUNICATIONS WORKSHOPS

The Poetry Collections

Collection 8

See the Miracles

COLLECTION PLANNING GUIDE T490A–T490D

COMMUNICATIONS WORKSHOP

Collection 9

Imagine

COLLECTION PLANNING GUIDE T518A–T518D

COMMUNICATIONS WORKSHOP

Collection 10

The Ways We Are
COLLECTION PLANNING GUIDE T552A–T552D

COMMUNICATIONS WORKSHOP

Collection 11

Say It!
COLLECTION PLANNING GUIDE T584A–T584D

COMMUNICATIONS WORKSHOPS

Modern Drama

Collection 12

Opening Doors
COLLECTION PLANNING GUIDE T630A–T630D

COMMUNICATIONS WORKSHOPS

William Shakespeare

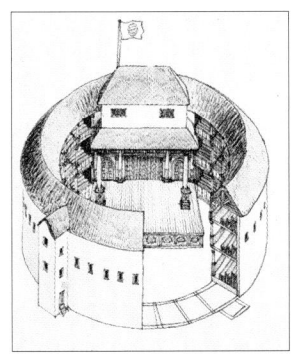

Collection 13

The Destruction of Innocence

COLLECTION PLANNING GUIDE T730A–T730D

COMMUNICATIONS WORKSHOPS

The Epic

Collection 14

The Perilous Journey
COLLECTION PLANNING GUIDE T886A–T886D

Language/Grammar Links

- Figures of Speech—Homeric Similes **927**
- Epithets **953**

COMMUNICATIONS WORKSHOPS

Resource Center

SELECTIONS BY GENRE

Short Story

Nonfiction

Autobiography and Memoir

Editorial and News Feature

Poetry

FEATURES

Elements of Literature

Interviews with Authors

William Shakespeare

The Epic

Connections

Across the Curriculum

Student Models

Extending the Theme

Writer's Workshops

Reading for Life

Learning for Life

SKILLS

Reading Skills and Strategies

Language / Grammar Links

Vocabulary Skills

Speaking and Listening Workshops

Sentence Workshops

ELEMENTS OF *Literature*

© 2003

Building a Foundation for Success in Literature and Reading

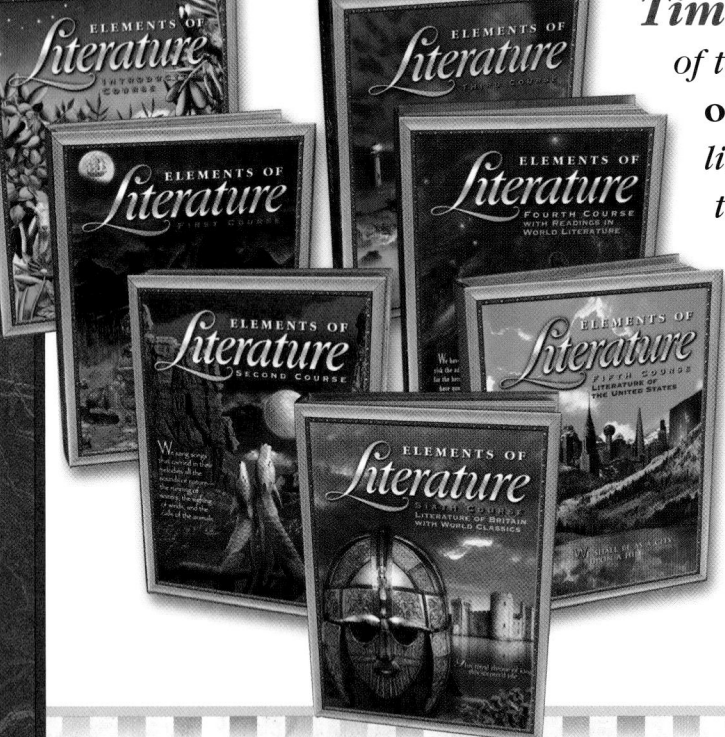

Time-tested and a favorite of teachers around the nation, **Elements of Literature** *has proven itself as the literature and language arts program that gets results and forges strong connections between students' lives and the literature teachers love to teach. Designed to get students actively involved in literature and learning, this unique program combines a student-centered approach to the study of literature with a sharp focus on the development of practical reading, writing, and life skills.*

GRAMMAR, LANGUAGE, AND WRITING RESOURCES

DAILY ORAL GRAMMAR TRANSPARENCIES AND WORKSHEETS
include exercises that review sentence construction, usage, and mechanics skills in the context of literary selections found in the **Student Edition**.

GRAMMAR AND LANGUAGE LINKS WORKSHEETS
provide reinforcement, practice, and extension of the grammar and language skills presented in the **Student Edition**.

AUTHENTIC AUTHORSHIP THAT SPEAKS TO STUDENTS

The success of *Elements of Literature* is due in large part to the team of authors that shaped it. Robert Anderson, John Malcolm Brinnan, and John Leggett, authors since the program's inception, have established the literary framework and have brought to the program a unique, motivational approach to instruction. Dr. Robert Probst has infused the program with a student-centered pedagogy, encouraging students to make the study of literature relevant to their lives and experiences. Renowned reading expert Dr. Kylene Beers has helped to integrate the reading strand in the *Student Edition* with creative, effective ways to reach struggling and reluctant readers. In addition, literacy expert Dr. Richard Vacca has helped to develop the conceptual framework of the reading strand, bringing to the program its strong emphasis on reading skills.

STUDENT EDITION THAT INVITES INVOLVEMENT

Frequent opportunities for skill building, personal and critical response, and writing practice prepare and motivate your students. Activities on **go.hrw.com** help students build literary and life skills. The **Test Smarts** section helps students prepare for standardized tests. The **Reading Matters** section, developed by reading expert Dr. Kylene Beers, helps students build a strong foundation in reading and master state and national standards.

ANNOTATED TEACHER'S EDITION THAT OPTIMIZES LESSONS

The *Annotated Teacher's Edition* helps you make the best use of the textbook with planning charts at point-of-use and references to the *One-Stop Planner® CD-ROM with Test Generator.* Helpful, creative suggestions for addressing the different kinds of learners in your classroom are annotated throughout the book.

ORGANIZATION THAT ENCOURAGES SUCCESS

• Grades 6, 7, and 8 are organized by genres centered around themes.

• Grades 9 and 10 include the study of genres in collections organized by theme.

• Grades 11 and 12 present selections chronologically and focus on themes emerging naturally from each literary period.

• Grade 11, *Literature of the United States with Literature of the Americas,* is available in two volumes.

LANGUAGE HANDBOOK WORKSHEETS
include tests at the end of each section that can be used either for assessment or for review.

WORKSHOP RESOURCES: TRANSPARENCIES AND WORKSHEETS
provide additional practice with the language skills presented in the **Writer's Workshop, Sentence Workshop,** and **Language Workshop** features of the *Student Edition.*

SPANISH RESOURCES

SPANISH RESOURCES help your Spanish-speaking students explore literature with translations of the **Before You Read** feature in the *Student Edition* and the *Graphic Organizers for Active Reading* teaching resource. This package also includes Spanish summaries of the literature selections, reading check questions in Spanish, and the *Visual Connections Videocassette Program* with Spanish soundtrack.

The Building Blocks of Solid Reading Skills

ELEMENTS OF

Literature *helps students become lifelong readers by building skills in reading comprehension, literary response and analysis, and vocabulary development. The cornerstone of the program, this strong emphasis on reading skills is integrated throughout the* **Student Edition** *and in highly effective resource and technology materials.*

READING SUPPORT

Every secondary classroom has students who haven't mastered the skills they need to be competent readers. The resources within the ***Elements of Literature*** program offer a multitude of means—strategies, skill-building exercises, MiniReads,™ graphic organizers, vocabulary and test practice to help students acquire the skills they need to be lifelong readers. Consumable worktexts make the lessons hands-on and easily accessible. Also available on CD-ROM.

HRW LIBRARY

This diverse collection of award-winning **HRW Library** titles builds students' independence and confidence as they become life-long readers. Each full-length work includes **Connections,** related readings such as poems, short stories, essays, memoirs, and interviews that extend themes into other genres, places, and times.

STUDY GUIDES
- background information and historical, cultural, and literary context
- reproducible masters for reading skills, vocabulary activities, and literary elements study
- more information at **www.hrw.com**

CONTENT AREA READERS
- reading selections in the context of the social sciences, science, and mathematics
- informational materials such as newspaper articles, biographies, and excerpts from nonfiction books

ADDITIONAL READING SUPPORT

AUDIO CD LIBRARY
helps struggling readers and auditory learners build comprehension skills with dramatic readings of the literary selections in *Elements of Literature.* In this extensive collection of audio CDs, professional actors read poems, plays, short stories, and essays.

WORDS TO OWN WORKSHEETS build
vocabulary skill and help students make words their own.

GRAPHIC ORGANIZERS FOR ACTIVE READING allow
students to respond to literature visually while mastering program content.

LITERARY ELEMENTS TRANSPARENCIES AND WORKSHEETS
include graphic organizers that help students identify and learn the literary terms presented in the *Student Editions*.

SPELLING AND DECODING WORKSHEETS
(GRADES 6–8) allow students to practice spelling (using words taken from literary selections) and explore sound correspondences and structure patterns.

Solidify Instruction with Planning and Assessment Resources

TEST PREP TOOL KIT

Comprehensive and flexible, the ***Test Prep Tool Kit*** features high-interest activities that keep students involved. The kit consists of 39 activity cards, correlated to state standards, that address the reading and writing objectives typically measured by standardized tests. The cards let students work at their own pace, allowing them to monitor their performance as they work to master a variety of reading and writing skills.

ONE-STOP PLANNER® CD-ROM WITH TEST GENERATOR

With editable lesson plans and an easy-to-use test generator, this convenient planning tool includes all the teaching resources for ***Elements of Literature***. Also included are preview of all teaching resources, of the ***Visual Connections Videocassette Program,*** and of transparencies and worksheets linked to features in the ***Student Edition.*** Point-and-click menu formats make accessing information on the ***One-Stop Planner*** fast and easy in both Macintosh® and Windows® platforms.

MORE FOR PLANNING

LESSON PLANS, INCLUDING STRATEGIES FOR ENGLISH-LANGUAGE LEARNERS include
resource checklists, ideas for teaching literature selections, and strategies for motivating students who are developing English proficiency.

CROSS-CURRICULAR ACTIVITIES engage students
with lessons that encompass literature, science, music, history, geography, and technology.

BLOCK SCHEDULING LESSON PLANS WITH PACING GUIDE help you
manage and pace block-scheduling instruction and activities.

MORE FOR ASSESSMENT

FORMAL ASSESSMENT includes literary-
element tests, reading-application tests, genre tests, and English-language tests.

PORTFOLIO MANAGEMENT SYSTEM
offers ideas for implementing portfolios in the classroom and blackline masters for assessing portfolios and performance on activities from the ***Student Edition.***

STANDARDIZED TEST PREPARATION includes practice tests for
reading along with blackline masters and transparencies for four modes.

PREPARATION FOR COLLEGE ADMISSION EXAMS prepares high school
juniors and seniors for college admission exams with a collection of practice tests.

Reinforce Learning with Internet Resources

ONLINE RESOURCES

GO.HRW.COM

Internet references throughout the **Student Edition** direct you and your students to a Web site dedicated exclusively to content in **Elements of Literature.** From biographical information about authors to help with textbook activities and writing assignments, from historical background to cross-curricular support, this Web site allows your students to link instantly to well-researched resources that support the selections they are studying.

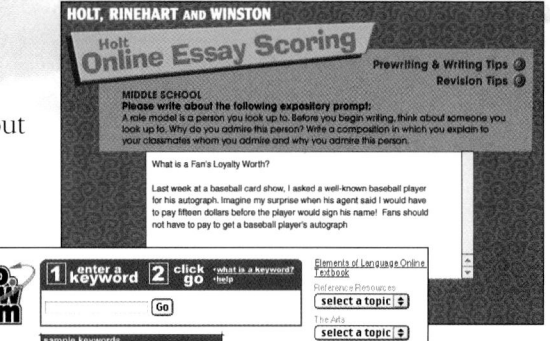

HOLT ONLINE ESSAY SCORING

Help your students improve their writing skills and give them practice with the kinds of prompts typically seen on state writing assessments. The site includes writing prompts, scores based on a four- or six-point holistic scale, and explanations of the scoring criteria.

MORE TECHNOLOGY

AUDIO CD LIBRARY helps struggling readers and auditory learners, build comprehension skills with dramatic readings of the literary selections in **Elements of Literature.** In this extensive collection of audio CDs, professional actors read poems, plays, short stories, and essays.

VISUAL CONNECTIONS VIDEOCASSETTE PROGRAM features biographies, interviews, historical summaries, and cross-curricular connections that enrich and extend instruction. Available with Spanish and English soundtracks.

THE HOLT READER: AN INTERACTIVE WORKTEXT CD-ROM includes literary and informational selections and graphic organizers that guide students to participate actively in reading. This CD-ROM is a convenient alternative to **The Holt Reader: An Interactive WorkText** booklet.

WRITER'S WORKSHOP 1 AND 2 INTERACTIVE MULTIMEDIA CD-ROMS

include a variety of writing assignments featuring step-by-step guidance—from prewriting to publishing—and the ability to share work online. These interactive CD-ROMs also include built-in word processing, a spell checker, and advanced writing tools.

LANGUAGE WORKSHOP INTERACTIVE MULTIMEDIA CD-ROM SOFTWARE

reinforces and extends the grammar and writing lessons in **Elements of Literature** with a complete, interactive course in grammar, usage, and mechanics. (Grades 6–12)

Literature

AN INVITATION TO A DIALOGUE

Dr. Robert Probst, *Georgia State University*

The classroom is the place for students to learn to read and reflect on visions of human possibilities offered them by the great literature and to begin to tell their own visions and stories.

Literature and Life

Surely, of all the arts, literature is most immediately implicated with life itself. The very medium through which the author shapes the text—language—is grounded in the shared lives of human beings. Language is the bloodstream of a common culture, a common history.

— LOUISE ROSENBLATT

Mathematicians, scientists, and engineers build bridges and send people to the moon, statisticians calculate our insurance premiums and life expectancies, and accountants figure our taxes and amortize our house payments, but the poets, dramatists, novelists, and story writers have nonetheless remained at the center of life. They bind us together as a society, and they define us as individuals within that society.

When we're very young we need stories almost as much as we need food and protection. Stories entertain us and help us sleep, but they also teach us how to get through the world. They tell us there are pots of gold waiting for us at the end of the rainbow, and they warn us about the trolls hiding under the bridges. They teach us about hope, fear, courage, and all the other elements

of our lives. As we grow out of childhood, the great stories, poems, and plays of the world's literature encourage us to reflect on the issues that have intrigued men and women for centuries, inviting us into a continuing dialogue about human experience. When we're older, our own stories represent what we've done, capturing for us what we've made of our lives. Some we'll tell happily, some we'll tell with great pain, and some we may not tell at all, but they're all important because they are a way of making sense of our lives.

If literature is the ongoing dialogue about what it means to be human, then the language arts classroom is society's invitation to students to join that conversation. The texts we use represent the reflections of the world's cultures on the nature of human experience, and the writings we elicit from our students are their first efforts to join in that reflection. The classroom is the place for students to learn to read and reflect on visions of human possibilities offered them by the great literature and to begin to tell their own stories.

Literature offers an invitation to reflect, but it doesn't offer formulas to memorize or answers to write dutifully in notes so that later on, when life presents us with problems, we can pull out our tattered old notebooks and find our path sketched out for us. Literature is an invitation to a dialogue.

That, perhaps more than any other reason, is why it's so important that we teach literature and writing well. It's too easy to avoid the responsible thought demanded by the significant issues, too tempting to accept someone else's formulation of the truth. "Life imitates art," Richard Peck said in a speech in New Orleans in 1974, "especially

bad art." By that he meant, I think, that we may too often give in to tempting laziness and allow our lives to be governed by visions of human possibilities that we take from film, television, or graffiti. The problem for teachers, of course, is to lead students not simply to absorb unthinkingly what art offers, but to reflect on it.

This textbook series tries to support teachers' efforts to lead students to think, to feel, and to take responsibility for themselves. It will have much in common with other textbooks. After all, we'd miss "The Raven" if he didn't land croaking on our window sill one morning just before homeroom, and twelfth grade wouldn't be the same without an evening or two around the hearth with Beowulf. But if this series has much in common with other textbooks, it will also have much that differs—including new authors, perhaps authors we haven't met before, exploring lives and circumstances that previously may not have been well represented in the pages of school texts. And similarly, there will be familiar approaches to teaching—perhaps specific activities—that we've all come to rely upon, but there will be other suggestions that emphasize aspects of literary experience, writing, and discussion that may not have been prominent in other books.

Principles of the Program

❶ First among the principles of the program is that *the subject matter of the language arts classroom is human experience comprehended and expressed in language.* The classroom invites the student into the dialogue about the big issues of human experience. The content of literature is the content of our days, and we think and feel about these issues before we enter the classroom and open the text.

When we do finally come to the text, it offers students an opportunity to begin to make sense of experience and to see it captured in the literature.

❷ Implicit in this vision of the language arts is a second principle, *that learning in the English classroom is a creative act,* requiring students to make things with language. Reading literature is a process of engaging the text, weighing it against the experiences readers bring to it.

Similarly, writing isn't simply a matter of learning and applying the rules of grammar and usage or of memorizing the structure and strategies of narratives, descriptions, and arguments.

Literature offers us access to hidden experiences and perceptions.

❸ *The third principle focuses on the encounter between student and content.* It doesn't focus exclusively on the information and skills that have at times provided the framework for our instruction.

Nor, on the other hand, is teaching planned with thought only for the student's interests, needs and desires, and thus organized around whatever concerns happen to predominate at the moment. It is, to borrow Rosenblatt's term, transactional.

❹ For this series, *the integration of the several aspects of the English language arts program* is the fourth governing principle. Literature can't be taught effectively without work in composition. Writing, without the inspiration offered by good literature, remains shallow and undeveloped. Oral language has to be acquired in the context of groups working collaboratively. And so, these texts will suggest ways of interrelating instruction in literature, writing, and language.

Working with the Series

You will find, as you work with selections in this textbook, that students have immediate responses to what they've read. That may be the place to start. The students' responses are very likely to lead you back to the issues you would have wanted to discuss anyway, and so the questions we've suggested might be addressed naturally during the flow of the discussion. Look for the potential in students' reactions and their questions even before turning to the questions in the "First Thoughts" section. Then, the questions in the text can extend or expand the discussion.

The same might be said about the writing. The series has been designed so that experiences with literature, with writing, and with group processes will often be interconnected. We hope that the literature will inspire and shape the students' writing, that their writing will lead back to further reading, and that the discussions and group activities suggested will build a supportive community in which all this work can take place.

The objective in all of this is for students to be able to draw upon their literary heritage and their developing skill with written and spoken language so that, as humane and reasoning people, they may be responsibly engaged with the world around them. If the language arts class helps to achieve that goal, we should be well satisfied with our labors. ✽

Reading Matters

Dr. Richard T. Vacca, *Kent State University*

As is the case with many teachers, I have had my fair share of unforgettable students, the "usual suspects," who have made a difference in the way I think about teaching and learning literature. Two such students quickly come to mind.

Tommy was an English teacher's dream; Johnny, a saboteur-in-training. They were contemporaries, but I'm sure their paths never crossed in school. One was a high achiever; the other, a low achiever. The classroom lessons I learned from each of them changed the way I think about reading and literature in English classrooms.

A Tale of Two Students

Johnny was just three years younger than I when I began teaching in a high school just outside Albany, New York. He was one of the forgotten students at school who went unnoticed until he got into trouble. Johnny couldn't read well, but he knew how to take apart a carburetor and replace a timing belt with his eyes closed. (As it turned out, he dropped out of school on his nineteenth birthday and went to work at his uncle's garage.) He and his cohorts tried to sabotage my teaching plans whenever I initiated the study of literature, no matter how relevant the text was to their lives. If the literature study required reading, Johnny could dismantle the lesson as skillfully as he could dismantle a car engine. I held my ground the best I could, but often to little avail. The more I urged him and others in the class to learn about what it means to be human through literature, the more they resisted.

I was tough on Johnny, always challenging him to do better, and I believe there was a measure of respect between the two of us. Even though it's been more than three decades since I saw him, I won't soon forget our last encounter. I remember running into Johnny at his uncle's garage and telling him that I had resigned my teaching position to go back to school to be a reading specialist. "Man," he said, "you read good already." Then he added somewhat wistfully, somewhat defiantly, "Reading robbed me of my manhood."

I had never heard the inability to read put in such human terms. Johnny helped me to understand how much reading matters, not only in students' literate lives but also in their human lives outside of school. What I learned from Johnny, and from other students who struggle with reading literature, is this: Reading gets in the way of too many students' understanding, enjoyment, and appreciation of literary texts. I made assumptions about Johnny's ability to use reading to learn that, in hindsight, were ill-informed. I assumed, for example, that by the time he reached high school he should be using reading to make meaning with literary texts. Because reading was second nature to me, I often assigned literary texts as if reading were second nature to my students. But I couldn't reach Johnny with literature because he didn't have the skills and strategies of an accomplished reader. I, on the other hand, didn't have the instructional know-how to bridge the gap between potentially difficult texts and the literacy capital that Johnny brought to the classroom and the study of literature.

Tommy, on the other hand, made teaching literature smooth sailing. He was tracked in an above-average class with others who knew how to do school well. I recall that his class was in the midst of reading Thornton Wilder's *Our Town* during the birth of my first (and only) child. I shared with the class every heartfelt moment of my ascent into fatherhood and connected the experience to Wilder's play. Unbeknownst to me, Tommy took it upon himself to write a letter to Thornton Wilder, which he mailed to Wilder's publisher. In the letter he shared how much the play (and my journey into fatherhood) had changed the way he thought about life and about relationships that he would have taken for granted. Several weeks later, Tommy received a letter from Wilder's sister explaining that her brother, who was nearly blind at the time and quite ill, enjoyed having the letter read to him. She went on to say that he insisted that she write to Tommy and apologized for not being able to do so directly. Wilder wanted Tommy to know that the letter brightened his spirits and reaffirmed his reasons for writing *Our Town*. Wilder's sister concluded by telling Tommy that her brother was especially grateful for readers such as Tommy who made writing well worth the effort. I remember Tommy saying, "I'll treasure this letter forever."

Reading matters to accomplished students such as Tommy who know how to use literary texts to explore the significance of what they are reading. Often, they are high achievers who are skillful and thoughtful in their approach to reading. But not all average and above-average students are accomplished readers. What I learned early on as a literature teacher is that many academically oriented students—adolescents who were most like me in high school, promising students who sometimes worked hard and sometimes didn't—struggle with reading literature as much as low-achieving students. In between the Johnnys and the Tommys are students who often go through the motions of reading literary texts but are likely to conceal some of their difficulties. These students have developed the ability to read print smoothly and accurately, but they don't know what to do with texts beyond just reading the words. They appear *skillful* in the mechanics of reading, but they aren't *strategic* in their ability to explore and interpret meaning.

Bringing Literature and Reading Together

Technologically advanced societies like ours value literate behavior and demand that citizens acquire literacy for personal, social, academic, and economic success. The pressure to hold teachers accountable for students' reading development is greater today than at any time in our nation's history. To the extent that texts are an integral part of learning in all content areas, *every* teacher has a role to play in helping students become readers, writers, and oral communicators. Yet the responsibility for teaching literacy usually lies with English teachers and with reading specialists in middle and high schools. English teachers, however, are not reading specialists and shouldn't view their roles as such. Showing students how to use reading strategies in the literature classroom doesn't require the specialized training of a reading specialist. Nor does the development of reading skills and strategies in the context of the literature classroom diminish the teacher's role as a subject matter specialist. It is far more realistic and effective to integrate the skills and strategies that readers actually need. The real value of reading lies in the way it is used. To be literate in literature classrooms, students must learn how to use reading to construct meaning from literary texts. Because literacy use is situational, the most meaningful way for students to develop reading skills and strategies is in the context in which they must be used. A student using reading to find meaning in literature gains confidence in his or her ability to read and to interpret texts.

Scaffolding reading experiences is the key to bringing literature and reading together in the literature classroom. The term *scaffolding* is a metaphor used in teaching and learning to suggest a means by which you help students do what they cannot do at first. In other words, scaffolding reading experiences allows teachers to provide the instructional support and guidance that students need to be successful. Instructional scaffolding allows teachers to support students' efforts to think clearly, critically, and creatively about literary texts *while* showing them how to use skills and strategies that will allow them to read more effectively than if left to their own devices.

Developing Skills and Strategies

Because skills and strategies are best learned through meaningful use, the lesson organization for the literary selections in **Elements of Literature** provides numerous opportunities to scaffold students' exploration and interpretation of literary texts. Each lesson creates an instructional framework that respects the nature of the literary experience while making provisions to scaffold students' use of reading skills and strategies. Instructional scaffolding before reading, for example, demonstrates to students the importance of anticipation, making predictions, raising questions, and other strategies that connect their world to the world of the text.

Students are in a strategic position to learn with literature whenever they use their prior knowledge to construct meaning. Prior knowledge includes the experiences, conceptual understandings, attitudes, values, skills, and strategies the reader brings to a text situation. How readers *activate* prior knowledge is the mechanism by which they connect their world to the world of the text. Prior knowledge, when activated, allows readers to seek, organize, retain, and elaborate meaning. In **Elements of Literature,** features such as *Make the Connection* and *Quickwrites* activate prior knowledge in relation to the issues, problems, conflicts, or themes to be studied through the literary experience. These scaffolds provide students with an imaginative entry into the text by raising expectations, arousing curiosity, and anticipating what is ahead in the literature selection.

Making students aware of *why, how,* and *when* they should use strategies to activate prior knowledge and anticipate content is as important as understanding *what* the strategies are. For example: Why is activating what students already know about a topic through a quickwrite (or any prereading strategy) important? How can students connect what they know to what they are about to read? When should a technique such as quickwrite be used and when shouldn't it? From a strategy-learning perspective, these discussions provide students with a rationale for skill and strategy use and build *procedural knowledge*, which is knowledge about why, how, and what skill and strategy to use.

Providing instructional support during and after reading also encourages struggling readers to develop and use skills and strategies as they explore, clarify, and extend their understandings of the text. A skilled reader recognizes the important parts of a text. A struggling reader doesn't. Instead, the student who struggles with text tends to read each word, each sentence, each paragraph with equal emphasis and reverence.

While readers explore meaning before and during reading, they often need to engage in clarification and elaboration after reading. Postreading questions and activities at the end of each literary selection in **Elements of Literature** create another type of instructional support for students. They help students extend their thinking and evaluate the significance of the literary experience.

In addition to scaffolding reading experiences at the point of use, there are other features of **Elements of Literature** that will help you support and guide students' reading development. For example, the MiniRead lessons in the reading binder, *Reading Skills and Strategies: Reaching Struggling Readers,* are instructional resources that provide *explicit instruction* for students who need additional guidance and support. The MiniRead lessons allow students to share insights and knowledge that they might otherwise never discover. These explicit lessons create a framework that unifies skill and strategy development. They provide methods for struggling readers to become aware of, to use, and to develop control over skills and strategies that can make a difference in their literate lives. ❊

Reaching Struggling Readers

AN INTERVIEW WITH

DR. KYLENE BEERS

Dr. Kylene Beers

from the Editor's Desk

As we have listened to teachers over the past few years, one dominant issue has emerged: How do we teach literature to struggling readers? In our search for an answer, we read the research, attended workshops, and interviewed teachers and students. It was obvious that fill-in-the-blank drill worksheets weren't the answer. It was time for a change, but nothing we encountered seemed to offer a real solution to the problem of teaching literature to struggling readers.

Finally, one day Dr. Robert Probst suggested we contact Dr. Kylene Beers. He told us she knew a great deal about reading and might be the person with the answers. During our first meeting with Dr. Beers, she explained the link between reading skills and strategies and discussed the difference she had seen strategies make in the lives of struggling readers. She made a lot of sense to those of us who can recite whole sections of the *Iliad* but had never heard the words *reading* and *strategy* in the same sentence. A year and a half later we see the results of that first meeting: the *Reading Skills and Strategies: Reaching Struggling Readers* binder. This wasn't the easiest project in the history of publishing. Drill worksheets would have been easier to produce, but it was time for a change—time to turn struggling readers into successful ones.

Here are some of the questions we asked Dr. Beers during the course of this project.

The curriculum demands on English teachers are enormous. Teachers often ask us why they should add reading skills and strategies to an already loaded course.

“I used to ask myself the same thing. Twenty years ago, when I began teaching, I expected that I'd carefully guide excited students through the prose and poetry of literary giants like Whitman, Emerson, Dickinson, Thoreau, Kipling, Joyce, Márquez, Angelou, and well, you know the names. I expected that students would arrive early for literature class and leave late for their next class. I expected I'd never have to worry about teaching someone to read—that was for the elementary teachers. I was going to teach *Literature*. Those expectations changed quickly. First, I didn't have students who loved literature. Most of my students didn't even like literature. Second, I didn't have students who could already read. When I didn't get the students I expected, I didn't know what to do.

Twenty years later, I'm still not getting what I expected when it comes to teaching. But I've learned that if I understand students' strengths and have some ideas about how to address their weaknesses, then they'll often give me more than I ever expected.

I've spent the past twenty years learning how to help these secondary students who can't read and don't like to read become better readers. I've worked with students at all grade levels and all ability levels. I've gone back to school to study how to teach reading, and now I see myself as a reading/literature teacher. The teaching of literature and the teaching of reading are integral to one another, so interconnected that separating them seems an abomination. ”

How can a teacher use a literature anthology with the increasing numbers of students who have serious difficulty reading any text?

“After many years of working with all types of readers, but especially struggling and reluctant readers, I've learned some things that have helped me reach those students. I've found that struggling readers have difficulty reading for a myriad of reasons. Often they don't know a lot of words, so limited vocabulary keeps them from understanding what they've read. Sometimes they lack decoding ability, so they don't know how to get through big words. Other times, they can call words well, but they don't know how to make sense of what they've read. And sometimes, their distaste for reading makes them think reading is meaningless, so they see no reason for putting any effort into it. As I work with students and address those issues, I keep what I call the ABCDE rules in mind. A look at the diagram below will quickly show you what these rules are. ”

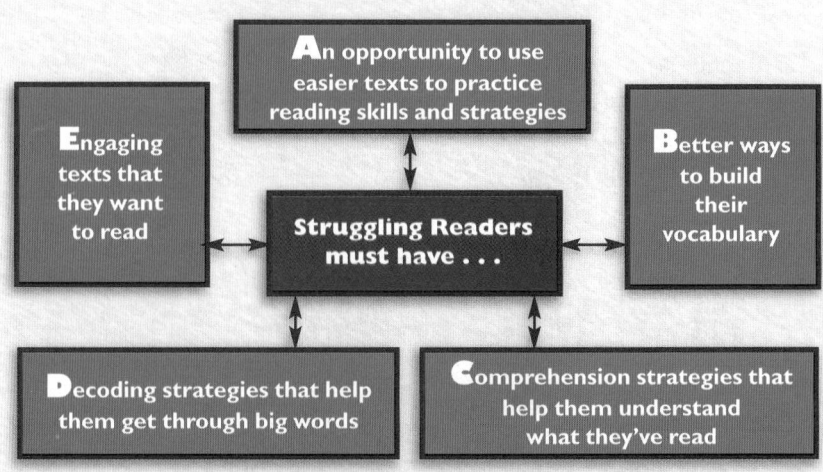

To help provide this ABCDE rule for struggling readers, what should a literature program include?

"A literature program should help teachers with each of those areas, particularly A, B, C, and E. If publishers want to help, they will have to develop specialized materials that complement the basal text. Here's what we did with the *Reading Skills and Strategies* program for *Elements of Literature*:

❶ Easier Selections Provide Practice for Skills and Strategies.

We hired a group of professional writers to write easy fiction and nonfiction pieces. These selections, or MiniReads®, are short texts written at an easier level than the selections in the literature book. The purpose of the MiniReads is to give students the opportunity to practice decoding skills, comprehension strategies, and vocabulary strategies with a text that is not only easier but engaging as well.

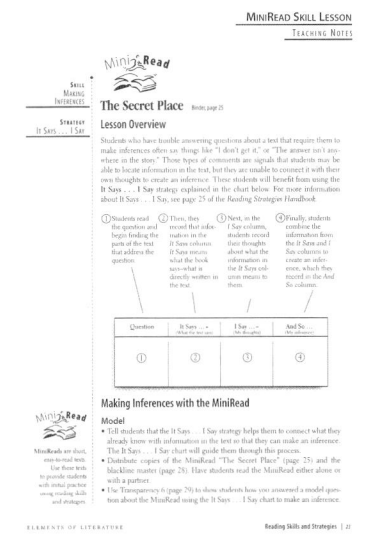

❷ Our MiniRead Lessons Include Modeling.

Each MiniRead includes a complete lesson plan that provides modeling of the skill and strategy. Transparencies help teachers focus students on the strategies. Blackline masters give students a chance to practice the strategies before applying them to selections in the Student Edition.

❸ Reading Skills and Strategies Are Connected to the Selections in *Elements of Literature*.

All skills and strategies are *applied* to selections in the anthology. The detailed lesson plans can be used not only with struggling readers, but with all readers.

❹ The *Handbook* Provides a Thorough Explanation of the Research.

Without research to back them up, the lessons would have no foundation. The *Reading Strategies Handbook* includes transcripts from actual classrooms in which the strategies have been tested with struggling readers. The handbook *shows* rather than just *tells* how to initiate specific strategies, what pitfalls to avoid, and how to document progress. Articles about each of the strategies help teachers become more comfortable with using the strategies with any selection."

DR. KYLENE BEERS

Building a Foundation for Success in Literature

A Foundation for Reading

When the Text Is Tough

Remember the reading you did back in first, second, and third grades? Big print. Short texts. Easy words. Now in high school, however, the texts you read are often filled with small print, long chapters, and complicated plots or topics. Also, you now find yourself reading a variety of material—from your driver's ed handbook to college applications, from notes passed in the hall to graffiti printed on the wall, from job applications to income tax forms, from e-mail to e-zines, from classics to comics, from textbooks to checkbooks.

Doing something every day that you find difficult and tedious isn't much fun—and that includes reading. So, this section of this book is designed for you, to show you what to do when the text gets tough. Let's begin by looking at some *reading* matters—because, after all, reading *matters*.

READING UP CLOSE: HOW TO USE THIS SECTION

- **This section is for you.** Turn to it whenever you need to remind yourself about what to do when the text gets tough. Don't wait for your teacher to assign this section for you to read. It's your handbook. Use it.

- **Read the sections that you need.** You don't have to read every word. Skim the headings and find the information you need.

- **Use this information to help you with reading for other classes,** not just for the reading you do in this book.

- **Don't be afraid to *re-read*** the information you find in Reading Matters. The best readers constantly re-read information.

- **If you need more help, then check the index.** The index will direct you to other pages in this book with information on reading skills and strategies.

Word Recognition

If you have a student with severe word recognition problems, have that student spend some time studying the following word lists. The lists, developed by Dr. Edward Fry, consist of the 600 most common words. Either you or the student can put each word on a flash card (in sets of a hundred); then you can instruct the student to work through the sets of cards daily until he or she can read each word automatically, with no hesitation. The student should master the first hundred words before moving on to the next hundred.

High Frequency Word List
First Hundred Words

the	he	go	who	with	do	man	were
a	I	see	an	it	when	little	before
is	they	then	their	on	so	has	just
you	one	us	she	can	my	them	long
two	good	no	new	will	very	how	here
and	me	him	said	are	all	like	other
we	about	by	did	of	would	our	old
that	had	was	boy	this	any	what	take
in	if	come	three	your	then	know	cat
not	some	get	down	as	out	make	again
for	up	or	work	but	there	which	give
at	her	two	put	be	from	much	after
				have	day	his	many

Second Hundred Words

saw	big	may	fan
home	where	what	five
soon	am	use	read
stand	fall	these	over
box	morning	right	such
upon	live	present	way
first	four	tell	too
came	last	next	shall
girl	color	please	own
house	way	leave	most
find	red	hand	sure
because	friend	more	thing
made	pretty	why	only

Improving Your Comprehension

Have you seen the reruns of an old weekly television show called *Lost in Space*? Perhaps you saw the more recent movie version of it that played in theaters? If so, you probably remember the robot that constantly tried to warn the young boy, Will Robinson, when danger was near by waving his robot arms and announcing loudly, "Danger approaching, Will Robinson!" Then, Will would look up from whatever he was doing, notice whatever evil was moments away, and take evasive action. But until the robot warned him, Will would ignore all warning signs that danger was at hand.

Wouldn't it be nice if when we were reading, something would warn us as we were about to enter a dangerous area—a part of the text that we might not understand. Perhaps our own little robots could pop up in books saying, "Danger, Dear reader! Misunderstandings approaching!" Then we'd know to slow down, pay attention, and carefully study the text we were reading.

Actually, those signs do appear, but not as arm-waving robots in the margins of books. Instead, the signs appear in our minds, as we are reading. However, unless we are paying attention, we often read on past them, not noticing the warnings they offer. What we need to do is learn to recognize the danger signs, so, like Will Robinson, we know when to look up and take action.

READING UP CLOSE

◆ Looking for the Danger Signs

Study each of the signs to the right, and decide what type of danger each could signify while reading. You might want to copy these signs onto stick-on notes to put on your texts as you read.

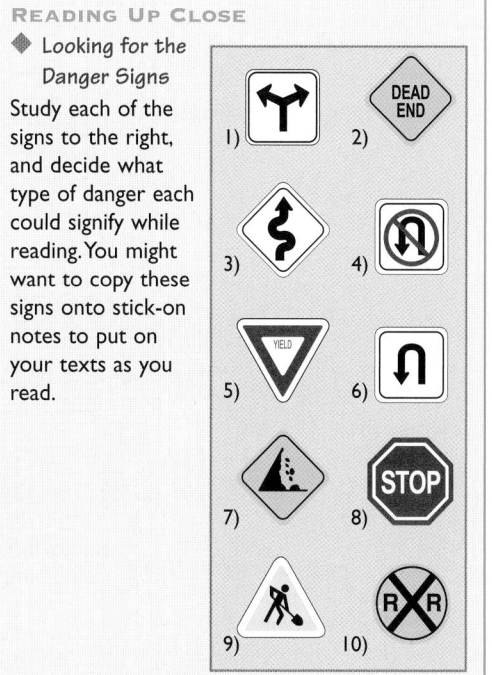

1) 2)
3) 4)
5) 6)
7) 8)
9) 10)

				Third Hundred Words							
could	eat	better	near	ask	hat	off	fire	fly	warm	anything	door
book	want	under	than	small	car	sister	ten	don't	sit	around	clothes
look	year	while	open	yellow	bright	happy	order	fast	dog	close	through
mother	white	should	kind	show	try	once	part	cold	ride	walk	o'clock
run	got	never	must	goes	myself	didn't	early	today	hot	money	second
school	play	each	high	clean	longer	set	that	does	grow	turn	water
people	found	best	bar	buy	those	ground	third	face	cut	might	town
night	left	another	both	think	hold	dress	same	green	seven	hard	took
into	men	seem	end	sleep	full	tell	love	every	woman	along	hair
say	bring	tree	also	letter	carry	wash	hear	brown	funny	fed	now
think	wish	name	until	jump	eight	start	yesterday	coat	yes	fine	keep
back	black	dear	call	help	sing	always	eyes	six	ate	sat	head
								gave	stop	hope	food

41

DANGER SIGN #1
You can't remember what you read.

This happens to all readers occasionally. You read something, and your attention wanders for a moment, but your eyes don't quit moving from word to word. In a few minutes, you realize you are several pages beyond the last point where you can remember thinking about what you were reading. Then, you know you need to back up and start over.

Forgetting what you've read is a danger sign only if it happens to you frequently. If you constantly complete a reading assignment but don't remember anything that you've been reading, then you probably are in the bad habit of letting your mind focus on something else while your eyes are focusing on the words. That's a habit you need to break.

Tips for Staying Focused:
1. Don't read from the beginning of the assignment to the end without pausing. Set up check points for yourself, either every few pages or every five minutes. At those checkpoints, stop reading and ask yourself some basic questions—What's happening now? What do I not understand?
2. As you read, keep paper and pen close by. Take notes as you read, in particular jotting down questions you have about what confuses you, interests you, or perhaps even surprises you.

READING UP CLOSE
◆ Measure Your Attention Quotient
Take the following survey to see what your Attention Quotient is. The lower the score, the less you pay attention to what you are reading.

When I read, I . . .

1. let my mind wander
1   most of the time
2   sometimes
3   almost never

2. forget what I'm reading
1   most of the time
2   sometimes
3   almost never

3. get confused and stay confused
1   most of the time
2   sometimes
3   almost never

4. discover I've turned lots of pages and don't have a clue as to what I've read
1   most of the time
2   sometimes
3   almost never

5. rarely finish whatever I'm supposed to be reading
1   most of the time
2   sometimes
3   almost never

Fourth Hundred Words

told	time	word	wear	bad	large	enough	family
Miss	yet	almost	Mr.	across	few	feet	begin
father	true	thought	side	yard	hit	during	air
children	above	send	poor	winter	cover	gone	young
land	still	receive	lost	table	window	hundred	ago
interest	meet	pay	outside	story	even	week	world
government	since	nothing	wind	sometimes	city	between	airplane
feet	number	need	Mrs.	I'm	together	change	without
garden	state	mean	learn	tired	sun	being	kill
done	matter	late	held	horse	life	care	ready
country	line	half	front	something	street	answer	stay
different	remember	fight	built	brought	party	course	won't
				shoes	suit	against	paper

Fifth Hundred Words

hour	grade	egg	spell
glad	brother	ground	beautiful
follow	remain	afternoon	sick
company	milk	feed	became
believe	several	boat	cry
begin	war	plan	finish
mind	able	question	catch
pass	charge	fish	floor
reach	either	return	stick
month	less	sir	great
point	train	fell	guess
rest	cost	hill	bridge
sent	evening	wood	church

2 DANGER SIGN #2
You don't "see" what you are reading.

The ability to visualize—or see in your mind—what you are reading is important for comprehension. To understand how visualizing makes a difference, try this quick test. When you get home, turn on a television to a program you enjoy. Then, turn your back to the television set. How long will you keep "watching" the program that way? Probably not long. Why not? Because it would be boring if you couldn't see what was happening. The same is true with reading: If you can't "see" in your mind what is happening on the page, then you probably will tune out quickly. You can improve your ability to visualize the text by practicing the following:

1. **Read a few sentences; then pause and describe what is happening on the page.** Forcing yourself to actually describe the scene will take some time at first, but will help in the long run.
2. **On a sheet of paper or a stick-on note, make a graphic representation of what is happening as you are reading.** For instance, if two characters are talking, draw two stick figures with arrows pointing between them to show yourself that they are talking.
3. **Discuss a scene or a part of a chapter with a buddy.** Talk about what you "saw" as you were reading.
4. **Read aloud.** If you are having troubling visualizing the text, it might be because you aren't really "hearing" it. Try reading a portion of your text aloud, using good expression and phrasing. As you hear the words, you may find it easier to see the scenes.

READING UP CLOSE

◆ Visualizing What You Read

Read the following from "Blues Ain't No Mockin Bird" (p. 268), and discuss what you "see."

> "The puddle had frozen over, and me and Cathy went stompin in it. The twins from next door, Tyrone and Terry, were swinging so high out of sight we forgot we were waitin our turn on the tire. Cathy jumped up and came down hard on her heels and started tap-dancin. And the frozen patch splinterin every which way underneath kinda spooky. 'Looks like a plastic spider web,' she said. 'A sort of weird spider, I guess with many mental problems.' But it really looked like the crystal paperweight Granny kept in the parlor."

				Sixth Hundred Words							
talk	note	add	minute	become	herself	demand	aunt	baby	whose	force	twelve
went	past	ice	tomorrow	body	idea	however	system	lady	study	plant	rode
bank	room	chair	snow	chance	drop	figure	line	ring	fear	suppose	uncle
ship	flew	watch	whom	act	river	case	cause	wrote	move	law	labor
business	office	alone	women	die	smile	increase	marry	happen	stood	husband	public
whole	cow	low	among	real	son	enjoy	possible	appear	himself	moment	consider
short	visit	arm	road	speak	bat	rather	supply	heart	strong	person	thus
certain	wait	dinner	farm	already	fact	sound	thousand	swim	knew	result	least
fair	teacher	hair	cousin	doctor	sort	eleven	pen	felt	often	continue	power
reason	spring	service	bread	step	king	music	condition	fourth	toward	price	mark
summer	picture	class	wrong	itself	dark	human	perhaps	I'll	wonder	serve	president
fill	bird	quite	age	nine	themselves	court	produce	kept	twenty	national	voice
								well	important	wife	whether

DANGER SIGN #3
You constantly answer "I don't know" to questions at the end of reading selections.

If you consistently don't know the answers to questions about what you've been reading, then you probably would benefit from the following strategies.

Think Aloud. Comprehension problems don't appear only after you *finish* reading. Confusion occurs *as* you read. Therefore, don't wait until you complete your reading assignment to try to understand the text; instead, work on comprehending while reading by becoming an active reader.

Active readers **predict, connect, clarify, question,** and **visualize** as they read. If you don't do those things, then you need to pause while you read to

- make predictions,
- make connections,
- clarify in your own thoughts what you are reading,
- question what you don't understand, and
- visualize the text and observe key details.

Use the Think-Aloud strategy to practice your active-reading skills. Read a selection of text aloud to a partner. As you read, pause to make comments and ask questions. Your partner's job is to tally your comments and classify each according to the list above.

READING UP CLOSE

◆ **One Student's Think-Aloud**

Here's Jamail's Think-Aloud for "Riding is an Exercise of the Mind" (p. 401).

<u>Page 402, 1st paragraph:</u> "This part here says he moved when he was twelve and the world was a different place, that was like when me and my family, when we moved. Everything was different." **(Connection)**

<u>Page 402, 6th paragraph:</u> "Here it says 'I came to know the land by going out upon it in all seasons' so I bet he's going to live there from now on." **(Prediction)**

<u>Page 402, 8th paragraph:</u> "How is riding an exercise for your mind?" **(Questioning)**

<u>Page 402, 9th paragraph:</u> "Oh, see this part about Billy the Kid being with him when he rides, maybe he's exercising his mind by using his imagination." **(Clarification)**

Retelling. While the Think-Aloud strategy keeps you focused as you read, the Retelling strategy helps you after reading. Read the tips for retelling on the next page, and then practice retelling small portions of your reading assignments. You might ask a friend to listen to you retell what you have read, or you might record yourself as you retell a selection.

Retelling prompts for fiction

1. State what text you are retelling.
2. Give characters' names, and explain who they are.
3. Sequence the events using words like *first, second, third, then, later, next,* or *last.*
4. Identify the conflict in the story.
5. Explain the resolution of the conflict.
6. Tell what you enjoyed or did not enjoy about the text.

Retelling prompts for informational texts

State what text you are retelling, and identify the structure of the text.

- If the structure is a **sequence** (the water cycle), use words like *first, second, third, then, later, afterwards, following that, before,* and *last.*
- If the structure is **comparison and contrast** (the differences between World War I and World War II), use words such as *by comparison, by contrast, on the other hand, yet, but, however, nevertheless, conversely, then again,* or *in opposition.*
- If showing **cause-and-effect relationships,** use words like *reason, motive, basis,* and *grounds* to discuss **causes,** and use words like *outcome, consequence, result,* and *product* to discuss **effects.**

READING UP CLOSE

◆ Evaluate Your Retelling

Listen to your retelling and ask yourself

1. Does my retelling make sense?
2. Does it have enough information?
3. Is the information in the correct order?
4. Could a drawing or a diagram help my retelling?
5. If someone listening to my retelling hadn't read the text, what would that person visualize?
6. To improve my next retelling, should I focus on characters, sequence of events, amount of detail, or general conclusions?

Re-reading and Rewording. The best way to improve your comprehension is simply to **re-read.** The first time you read something, you get the basic idea of the text. The next time you read it, you revise your understanding. Try thinking of your first reading as a draft—just like the first draft of an essay. As you revise your essay, you are improving your writing. As you revise your reading, you are improving your comprehension.

• Sometimes, as you re-read, you find some specific sentences or even passages that you just don't understand. When that's the case, you need to spend some time closely studying those sentences. One effective way to tackle tough text is to **reword** the text:

1. On a sheet of paper, write the sentences that are confusing you.
2. Leave a few blank lines between each line you write.
3. Then, choose the difficult words and reword them in the space above.
4. While you wouldn't want to reword every line of a long text—or even of a short one—this is a powerful way to help you understand key sentences.

Summarizing Narrative Text. Understanding a long piece of text is easier if you can summarize chunks of it. If you are reading a **narrative,** or a story, then use a strategy called **Somebody Wanted But So (SWBS)** to help you write summaries of what you are reading. SWBS is a powerful way to think about the characters in a story and note what each did, what conflict each faced, and what the resolution was. As you write an SWBS statement for different characters within the same story, you are forcing yourself to rethink the story from different **points of view.** By analyzing point of view in this way, you get a better understanding of the impact of the author's choice of narrator.

Here are the steps for writing SWBS statements:

1. Write the words *Somebody, Wanted, But,* and *So* across four column heads.
2. Under the *Somebody* column, write a character's name.
3. Then, under the *Wanted* column, write what that character wanted to do.
4. Next, under the *But* column, explain what happened that kept the character from doing what he or she wanted.
5. Finally, under the *So* column, explain the eventual outcome.
6. If you're making an SWBS chart for a long story or novel, you might need to write several statements at different points in the story.

◆ One Student's SWBS Chart

Here is Ben's SWBS chart for "The Scarlet Ibis" (p. 315).

Somebody	Wanted	But	So
Brother	wanted Doodle to be like other kids,	but Doodle's physical problems kept that from happening,	so Brother pushed Doodle too hard and then had to live with guilt when Doodle died.
Doodle	wanted to please Brother,	but he couldn't do all Brother demanded of him,	so he died.

Summarizing Expository Text.

If summarizing the information in **expository,** or informational, texts is difficult, try a strategy called GIST.

Steps for GIST:

1. Divide the text you want to summarize into three or four sections.
2. Read the first section.
3. Draw twenty blank lines on a sheet of paper.
4. Write a summary of the first section of text using exactly twenty words—one word for each blank.
5. Read the next section of text. In your next set of twenty blanks, write a new summary statement that combines your first summary with whatever you want to add from this second section of text. It's important to note that even though you've now got two chunks of text to cover, you still have only twenty blanks to fill, not forty.
6. Repeat this one or two more times depending on how much more text you have. When you are finished, you have a twenty-word statement that gives you the gist, or overall idea, of what the entire text is about.

◆ One Student's GIST

After reading "Organizing Information in Graphic Form" (p. 118), Erin wrote the following GIST statements.

GIST #1 (for the first column of information)

Graphics illustrate time order (time lines), similarities and differences (Venn diagrams), and cause-and-effect relationships (cause-and-effect charts).

GIST #2 (adding the second column of information)

Signal words like first (time lines), similarly (Venn diagrams), because and consequently (cause-and-effect-charts) signal graphics to use.

GIST #3 (completing the page)

Deciding on which graphic to use happens after reading the information to see which signal words are in the text.

- **Key Words.** Sometimes you don't want to write a summary of what you've been reading. Sometimes you just want to jot down some key words to remind you about a specific topic. To keep your key words organized, don't forget your ABCs. Fill a page with boxes, as in the example below. You can use your computer to make this page or just grab a pencil and notebook paper. Once your boxes are drawn, all you have to do is decide what information to include.

   For instance, Meredith uses her Key Word chart while reading "Thank You, M'am" on page 120. She puts Roger's name in blue at the top of the page and Mrs. Luella Bates Washington Jones's name in red. As Meredith reads the story and thinks of words to describe each character, she puts those key character-description words in the correct box in the correct color. So, she writes "preachy" in red (because she thinks that word describes Mrs. Jones) in the *O–P* box. She writes "ashamed" in blue (because this word is for Roger) in the *A—B* box. When completed, the chart could be a starting point for writing a paper that compares and contrasts Roger and Mrs. Jones.

READING UP CLOSE

◆ Using a Key Word Chart

Here is Meredith's Key Word chart for "Thank You, M'am." Read the story and find more key words to describe the two main characters.

Roger			Mrs. Luella Bates Washington Jones		
A-B	C-D	E-F	G-H	I-J	K-L
ashamed					
M-N	O-P	Q-R	S-T	U-V-W	X-Y-Z
	preachy				

Improving Your Reading Rate

If your reading concerns are more about getting through the words than figuring out the meaning, then this part of Reading Matters is for you.

If you think you are a slow reader, then reading can seem overwhelming. But you can change your reading rate—the pace at which you read. All you have to do is practice. The point isn't to read so fast that you just rush over words—the I'mgoingtoreadsofastthatallthewordsruntogether approach. Instead, the goal is to find a good pace that keeps you moving comfortably through the pages. Why is it important to establish a good reading rate? Let's do a little math to see why your silent reading rate counts.

As you figure out the problem, you see that it takes 100 minutes to read 10 pages at the slowest pace and only 20 minutes at the fastest pace. See the chart for all the times.

> **MATH PROBLEM!**
>
> If you read 40 words per minute (WPM) and there are 400 words on a page, then how long will it take you to read 1 page? 5 pages? 10 pages? How long will it take if you read 80 WPM? 120 WPM? 200 WPM?

	1 page @400 words/page	5 pages @400 words/page	10 pages @400 words/page
40 WPM	10 minutes	50 minutes	100 minutes
80 WPM	5 minutes	25 minutes	50 minutes
120 WPM	3 minutes	17 minutes	34 minutes
200 WPM	2 minutes	10 minutes	20 minutes

Reading Rate and Homework

Now, assume that with literature homework, science homework, and social studies homework, in one night you have 40 pages to read. If you are reading at 40 WPM, you are spending over *6 hours* just reading the information; but at 120 WPM you spend only about 2 –1/4 hours. And at 200 WPM you'd finish in 1 hour and 20 minutes.

> **READING UP CLOSE**
>
> ◆ Tips on Varying Your Reading Rate
>
> • Increasing your rate doesn't matter if your comprehension goes down.
>
> • Don't rush to read fast if that means understanding less. Also, remember that your rate will vary as your purpose for reading varies.
>
> • You'll read more slowly when you are studying for a test than when you are skimming a text.

Figuring Out Your Reading Rate

To determine your silent-reading rate, you'll need three things: a watch with a second hand, a book, and someone who will watch the time for you. Then, do the following:

1. Have your friend time you as you begin reading to yourself.
2. Read at your normal rate. Don't speed just because you're being timed.
3. Stop when your friend tells you one minute is up.
4. Count the number of words you read in that minute. Write down that number.
5. Repeat this process several more times using different passages.
6. Then, add the number of words together and divide by the number of times you timed yourself. That's your average rate.

Example

1st minute	180 words
2nd minute	215 words
3rd minute	190 words
	585 words ÷ 3 = 195 WPM

Reading Rate Reminders

You can improve your reading rate by doing the following:

1. **Make sure you aren't reading just one word at a time, with a pause between each word.** Practice phrasing words in your mind as you read. For instance, look at the sample sentence and pause only where you see the slash marks. One slash (/) means pause a bit. Two slashes (//) mean pause longer.

   Jack and Jill/ went up the hill/ to fetch a pail of water.// Jack fell down/ and broke his crown/ and Jill came tumbling after.//

   Now read it pausing after each word:

   Jack/ and/ Jill/ went/ up/ the/ hill/ to/ fetch/ a/ pail/ of/ water.// Jack/ fell/ down/ and/ broke/ his/ crown/ and/ Jill/ came/ tumbling/ after.//

   Hear the difference? Word-at-a-time reading is much slower than phrase reading. If you are reading one word at a time, you'll want to practice reading by phrases. You can hear good phrasing by listening to a book on tape.

2. **Make sure you aren't sounding out each word.** At this point in school, you need to be able to recognize whole words and save the sounding-out strategy for words you haven't seen before. In other words,

you ought to be able to read *material* as "material" and not "ma-ter-i-al," but you might need to move more slowly through *metacognition* so that you read that word as "met-a-cog-ni-tion."

3. **Make sure when you are reading silently that you really are reading silently.** Don't move your lips or read very softly when reading. These habits slow you down. Remember, if you need to slow down (for instance, the information you are reading is confusing you), then reading aloud to yourself is a smart thing to do. But generally, silent reading means reading silently!

4. **Don't use your finger to point to words as you read.** If you find that you always use your finger to point to words as you read (instead of just occasionally, when you are really concentrating), then you are probably reading one word at a time. Instead, use a bookmark to help yourself stay on the right line and practice your phrase reading.

5. **As you practice your fluency, remember that the single best way to improve your reading rate is simply to read more!** You won't get better at what you never do. Also, always remember that your rate will vary as your purpose for reading varies. So, time yourself, determine your reading rate, start reading more, and remember these *dos* and *don'ts*. Soon, you'll find that reading too slowly isn't a problem any more.

READING UP CLOSE

◆ *Recalculating Your Reading Rate*

After putting into practice some of the advice on improving your reading rate provided above, recalculate your average rate. Once again, use the instructions in Figuring Out Your Reading Rate (page xlii). This time, however, read the following:

1. Page 304: "Helen on Eighty-sixth Street"
2. page 388: "Driver's Ed?"
3. Page 559 : "The Sounds of Poetry"

After you've counted the number of words you read in each passage in one minute, divide by three. The result will be your average rate.

Remember: It's important to slow down your rate when you are confused about what you are reading.

Test Smarts

LESSON 1 Understanding Implied Causes and Effects

Local, state, and national reading tests often check your understanding of implied causes or effects in reading passages. Since the reading passages don't always include **clue words** like *because* or *since* to point out causes or effects, you have to figure out the answer based on how the ideas in the passage are structured.

Here is a typical *reading passage* and its cause-and-effect test question:

> The first permanent colony in the United States, Jamestown, nearly failed from the outset. On the voyage to Virginia, jealousy drove the men to imprison John Smith, the man who would eventually save the colony from starvation.
>
> Once the settlers reached shore, they broke open a chest that the London Company had instructed them to keep sealed until they reached Virginia. The chest contained a list of men chosen to be councilors and leaders of the colony, and the list contained John Smith's name. Those who had imprisoned him were furious. After much discussion, Smith was released and allowed to take his place as a councilor.

> Smith was released from imprisonment because—
> **A.** the men were no longer angry with him
> **B.** the London Company ordered his release
> **C.** he had been appointed councilor
> **D.** they believed he could save them from starvation

Thinking It Through: Answering Cause-and-Effect Questions

■ Keep the following steps in mind as you work through the question:

1. **Read the stem—the beginning of the multiple choice item—carefully.** The stem above contains the word *because* followed by a blank, letting you know that you must look for a cause.

2. **Look for important words in the stem that are the same as, or similar to, words in the passage.** The test question above contains the phrase *Smith was released.* The last sentence of the passage also contains this phrase and says that he was then allowed to take his place as a councilor.

3. **Now try asking yourself these cause-and-effect questions about this sentence:**
   —What happened? (What is the effect?) The settlers released Smith from imprisonment.
   —Why? (What is the cause?) Smith had been appointed councilor.

4. **Select the answer choice that most closely matches your answer to the cause-and-effect question.** The answer is **C**.

Practice

Directions. Read the passage below. On a separate sheet of paper, list the numbers *1* through *5*. Then, for each numbered item, write the letter of the correct response.

Dr. Jonas Salk began researching poliomyelitis in 1942, after the disease had become widespread. Poliomyelitis, or polio, attacks the nervous system, causing pain and stiffness, and often causing paralysis or even death. Salk worked on developing a vaccine to prevent this incurable disease.

First, he studied how polio affects the body. He reasoned that polio is a virus that enters the body through the mouth or nose, eventually reaching the intestines. From there the virus spreads to the central nervous system by means of either blood or nerves. Once the virus enters a nerve cell, it changes how the cell functions. Instead of expelling the virus, the cell reproduces it. The virus then enters the surrounding nerve cells. When enough nerve cells are altered or killed, the nervous system is affected, and paralysis results.

Once Salk knew how the virus spreads through the body, he looked for a substance that would kill it. After lengthy experimentation, he discovered that a formaldehyde solution would destroy the virus. He then developed a vaccine using the dead virus. In 1954, the National Foundation for Infantile Paralysis, the current March of Dimes Foundation, gave him the money that enabled him to test the vaccine. After giving the vaccine to nearly two million schoolchildren and testing the results, he proved that the vaccine was both safe and effective.

1. All of the following are possible effects of polio, *except*—
   A. skin rash
   B. pain
   C. death
   D. stiffness

2. Salk looked into how polio spreads because he wanted to—
   F. see how the virus enters the body
   G. study how nerve cells change
   H. find a way to prevent the disease
   J. discover what causes paralysis from polio

3. Paralysis in people who have been struck with polio occurs when—
   A. the virus kills or alters a sufficient number of nerve cells
   B. the intestines transfer the virus to the central nervous system
   C. the virus causes cells to reproduce it
   D. the blood carries the virus to the brain

4. All of the following are effects of the polio virus entering a nerve cell, *except* —
   F. the cell reproduces the virus
   G. the viruses leave the cell and enter the surrounding nerve cells
   H. the virus changes how the cell functions
   J. the cell expels the virus

5. The National Foundation for Infantile Paralysis affected polio research by—
   A. testing two million schoolchildren
   B. providing Salk with the formaldehyde solution
   C. allowing Salk to develop the vaccine
   D. providing Salk with the money to test the vaccine

TEST SMARTS xlv

PRACTICE
Understanding Implied Causes and Effects
ANSWERS
1. A
2. H
3. A
4. J
5. D

LESSON 2 Responding to Summary Questions

Standardized reading tests often ask you to identify the best summary of a reading passage. Read the passage and sample test question below. Then, use the steps in Thinking It Through to determine the best answer to the question.

A complex series of events occurs before a thunderstorm. First, pockets of warm air must rise from Earth's surface. If a pocket contains enough moisture and if the atmosphere is turbulent, towerlike cumulus clouds result. Sometimes these columns combine to create a mushroom-shaped cumulonimbus cloud, the only type of cloud that can produce a thunderstorm.

Thunderstorms can be tremendously destructive. Each year in the United States alone, lightning from thunderstorms causes hundreds of millions of dollars in property damage and triggers about 10,000 forest fires. Lightning also kills approximately 100 to 200 people every year. In addition, flash floods, high winds, and hail from thunderstorms harm people and property.

Which of the following statements is the best summary of the passage?
A. Lightning kills approximately 100 to 200 people every year.
B. Thunderstorms produce lightning, hail, high winds, and flash floods.
C. Thunderstorms are complex natural events that can cause tremendous destruction to life and property.
D. Thermals, which are pockets of warm air, cause thunderstorms.

Thinking It Through: Responding to Summary Questions

■ Follow these steps to answer summary questions correctly on standardized tests.

1. **Look for the main idea and the most important supporting details as you read the passage slowly and carefully.**

2. **Consider every answer choice,** eliminating those that restate a single detail from the passage, make a general statement about the passage but include no important details, or have little or nothing to do with the passage.

3. **Be sure that the answer you choose covers the *entire* passage by including the main idea and major supporting details. A** is true, but merely restates a single detail. **B** is true, but it also restates a detail. **C** is the best answer. It summarizes the main idea and the most important details, covering the entire passage. **D** is true, but, like **A** and **B,** simply restates a detail.

Practice

Directions. Read the passage below. On a separate sheet of paper, list the numbers *1* through *5*. Then, for each numbered item, write the letter of the correct response.

Some experts predict that rock concerts will create a need in today's teenagers for hearing aids when they are in their fifties. However, there are ways to protect the delicate sense of hearing.

Many rock bands turn up the volume to more than 100 decibels. At that level, permanent damage to hearing occurs in just an hour or two. People who attend loud concerts on a regular basis can experience dramatic hearing loss.

Loud music at rock concerts harms the cochlea, a tiny organ in the ear. Approximately 2/5-inch high and 1/4-inch wide, the cochlea is about the size of the nail on your pinky finger. This organ is affected by everything people hear—from the faintest whisper to a booming electric bass guitar.

The cochlea contains thousands of miniature hair cells. Each cell contains fifty to one hundred hairs called stereocilia. Some stereocilia are surrounded by fluid; when sound waves cause this liquid to vibrate, the stereocilia shake, too. Other stereocilia are jiggled by a membrane that shudders in response to sound. As the bases of the stereocilia shiver, they create nerve signals that travel to the brain.

Repeated exposure to extreme noise damages the delicate stereocilia. Their ability to send nerve impulses to the brain is impaired, causing hearing loss. Once the stereocilia are injured, they cannot be replaced. To protect these sensitive hairs, experts recommend that dedicated rock concert fans sit a good distance from the stage. Even then, hearing damage can occur.

1. Which of the following sentences best summarizes the fourth paragraph?
   A. When stereocilia shake in response to sound, they send nerve signals to the brain.
   B. Some stereocilia are shaken by a membrane that moves in response to sound waves.
   C. The stereocilia are little hairs attached to hair cells inside the cochlea.
   D. Sound waves can cause a liquid around the stereocilia to vibrate.

2. Which of the following details is important enough to be included in a summary of the entire passage?
   F. The cochlea is about 2/5-inch high.
   G. Sensitive hairs in the cochlea, an organ in the ear, are damaged by loud music.
   H. The cochlea is affected by booming electric bass guitars.
   J. Some stereocilia are jiggled by a membrane.

3. Which best describes the author's purpose?
   A. to explain how stereocilia work

   B. to describe the sound of a rock concert
   C. to explain the effects of loud sounds on hearing
   D. to persuade readers to avoid rock concerts

4. Which of the following statements is the best summary of the passage?
   F. Teenagers who frequently attend rock concerts will need hearing aids in their fifties.
   G. Loud music can cause hearing loss by damaging sensitive hairs in the ear.
   H. The tiny hairs inside the cochlea are called stereocilia.
   J. People who attend rock concerts should sit a good distance from the band.

5. Which sentence in the fifth paragraph would not be essential to a summary of that paragraph?
   A. the first sentence
   B. the second sentence
   C. the third sentence
   D. the fifth sentence

PRACTICE
Responding to Summary Questions
ANSWERS
1. A
2. G
3. C
4. G
5. D

Test Smarts

LESSON 3 ▸ Identifying Author's Purpose and Point of View

Standardized reading tests often have questions that ask you to identify an author's **purpose** and **point of view.** To answer, you will have to decide whether the author wants to inform, to entertain, or to persuade readers. Here is a typical reading passage and question about the author's purpose.

Football is no longer the most popular high school sport. According to a recent survey, basketball is now more popular than football. Also, soccer now attracts more new players than football does. Football, however, is the most costly high school sport. It's time to reevaluate the role of this overpriced sport. Today, countless girls begin playing soccer and other sports at an early age and continue to play throughout high school. Furthermore, other sports provide most of the benefits of football while giving students satisfying and exciting exercise. Certainly, football should still be played in high schools, but it should not receive the majority of athletic funding.

> The author wrote this passage to—
> **A.** convince readers that football is dangerous
> **B.** convince readers not to spend any tax dollars on football
> **C.** convince readers that football has value but it receives too much attention and funding
> **D.** convince readers that football should not be offered in high schools because soccer is safer

Thinking It Through: Identifying Purpose and Point of View

■ Keep the following steps in mind as you answer a question about an author's purpose and point of view. The student responses are based on the sample passage and question above.

1. **Examine the passage for words with strong connotations.** Such language is a sure indicator of persuasive purpose. The words *costly, overpriced,* and *satisfying and exciting* are not neutral; therefore, the passage is probably persuasive or expressive.

2. **Check to see if the language is positive or negative.** [topic + word choice = point of view] The negative words *costly* and *overpriced* indicate the writer's point of view.

3. **Look at the first few sentences to find the topic and to see if a topic sentence states the writer's point of view.** In the first four sentences the writer suggests that high school football receives too much attention and funding in comparison with other high school sports.

4. **Look for the choice that best matches your analysis.** The answer that best matches is **C.**

Practice

Directions. Read the passage below. On a separate sheet of paper, list the numbers *1* through *5*. Then, for each numbered item, write the letter of the correct response.

Today at the zoo, I saw protesters holding signs that read "Born Free and Now Caged." One woman told me that wild animals should remain in the wild. A man claimed that caged animals experience stress. While I partially agree with these opinions, I do not think zoos should be eradicated.

Ideally, wild creatures should roam free. However, many zoo inhabitants never were wild. Many were born in a zoo or were recovered from people illegally raising them as pets. Zoos provide a protective environment for such animals.

Zoos also protect many truly wild animals that are losing their habitats. Approximately 5.8 billion people live on our planet, and every ten years nearly another billion are added. People are crowding animals out of their natural habitats. Without zoos, numerous species that are now endangered would probably be extinct.

Throughout the world, zoos are attempting to re-create wild animals' natural environments. Lush, authentic habitats are replacing concrete-floored, bare cages. Although some zoo animals <u>do</u> experience stress from being confined, roaming free is also stressful. Giraffes, for example, sleep just two minutes at a time in the wild because they must watch for predators.

The zoo is neither a prison nor a paradise, but it serves some important purposes in today's world.

1. The author believes that zoos are—
   A. harmful to animals and should be illegal
   B. necessary due to destruction of wild animals' native habitats
   C. an ideal place for wild animals to live
   D. not attempting to improve animals' caged environments

2. What is one of the "important purposes" the author refers to in the last sentence of the article?
   F. protecting and preserving species of animals
   G. providing a place for protesters to complain
   H. understanding the eating habits of wild animals
   J. watching giraffes sleep in their cages

3. All of the following words from the passage have negative connotations except—
   A. *illegally*
   B. *stress*
   C. *endangered*
   D. *environments*

4. In the sentence "Ideally, wild creatures should roam free," the loaded words are—
   F. *should, creatures,* and *wild*
   G. *should, ideally,* and *creatures*
   H. *ideally, wild, roam,* and *free*
   J. *wild, free, world,* and *creatures*

5. The author's point of view is best stated in the—
   A. last paragraph
   B. first sentence of the second paragraph
   C. last sentence of the fourth paragraph
   D. second sentence of the third paragraph

PRACTICE
Identifying Author's Purpose and Point of View
ANSWERS
1. B
2. F
3. D
4. H
5. F

Test Smarts

LESSON 4 Addressing Inference Questions

To test your ability to infer, many reading tests include **inference questions.** These questions ask you to make inferences based on information provided in a reading passage. When you answer an inference question about a reading passage, you should be able to point to evidence in the passage that led you to your answer.

Below is a typical reading passage and an inference test question about it.

Sometimes the smallest action can have a tremendous impact. In Li-Young Lee's poem "The Gift," a father teaches his son about love, trust, and compassion simply by removing a splinter from the boy's hand. To help his son cope with his pain and fear, the father distracts him with a story while pulling the splinter from his palm. The father's soothing voice and gentle, loving hands calm the boy. This simple act plants a seed that flowers many years later in the boy's life. When the speaker is an adult, he removes a splinter from his wife's thumb, using the same tenderness and affection he learned from his father.

> You can reasonably infer from the passage that the father is—
> **A.** a powerful man
> **B.** an experienced surgeon
> **C.** a caring person
> **D.** a helpless onlooker

Thinking It Through: Answering Inference Questions

■ Use the following steps to answer inference questions.

1. **Read the passage slowly and carefully.**

2. **Pick out key words and phrases in the passage on which you might base your inferences.** *Soothing voice, calm,* and *tenderness and affection* are key words.

3. **Consider every answer.** You can usually eliminate one or two right away. Using the steps, you can make the following determinations about the multiple-choice answers provided for the example test question above.

   Answer **A** is incorrect: Nothing in the passage implies that the father is powerful. Answer **B** is incorrect: Removing a splinter does not require the skill of a surgeon, and nothing in the passage implies that the father is a surgeon. Answer **C** is clearly the best answer: The father is obviously a caring person; he distracts his son while removing the splinter from his hand. Answer **D** is incorrect: The father removes the splinter from his son's hand, so he is not a helpless onlooker.

Practice

Directions. Read the passage below. On a separate sheet of paper, list the numbers *1* through *5*. Then, for each numbered item, write the letter of the correct response.

For the speaker of Pat Mora's poem "Legal Alien," being bilingual and bicultural is not entirely a blessing. The speaker, a Mexican American, constantly struggles with the dualities in her life and with the narrow-mindedness of others. She chooses words carefully to communicate precisely her disapproval of both Mexicans' and Anglos' prejudices.

The speaker protests that Anglos view her as "perhaps exotic, perhaps inferior, definitely different." Similarly, she claims that Mexicans think she is an "alien." The negative connotations of these words and others used in the poem underscore the speaker's frustration. She belongs to neither the Anglo nor the Mexican world.

The speaker is able to shift easily between Spanish and English. At a Mexican restaurant, she can order a meal in perfect Spanish, and at her office, she can write a memo in flawless English. Despite this expertise, she is always perceived as being in an odd half-state—neither wholly Mexican nor completely American. She complains that she is "American but hyphenated." To reinforce the concept of being split between two cultures, Mora hyphenates many words in the poem.

In spite of the frustration of her bicultural existence, the speaker smiles to hide her feelings. Her cheerful face is a mask that disguises the "discomfort/of being pre-judged/Bilaterally."

1. It is reasonable to infer, based on details in the passage, that the speaker in the poem—
   A. wants to move to Mexico
   B. is not bothered by being labeled "bicultural"
   C. learned Spanish in public school
   D. is sensitive to people's use of language

2. The writer of the passage infers that the speaker in the poem is irritated by her bicultural duality because the speaker—
   F. wants to be "pre-judged"
   G. dislikes speaking English
   H. uses words with negative connotations
   J. is misunderstood by others

3. Which of the following statements best conveys the way the writer of the passage interprets the poem overall?
   A. The speaker smiles because she does not want anyone to know how she really feels.
   B. The speaker uses precise words with negative connotations.
   C. The speaker's tone is argumentative.
   D. The speaker is critical of how people pre-judge her.

4. The writer infers that Mora hyphenates words because she wants to—
   F. use proper punctuation
   G. divide words at the end of lines
   H. emphasize that the speaker is split between two cultures
   J. draw attention to rhymes in the poem

5. You can reasonably infer from this passage that the speaker—
   A. does not speak up when others annoy her
   B. tells people when they make her feel uncomfortable
   C. thinks that Mexicans are more sympathetic to her than Anglos are
   D. wants to leave America as soon as possible

PRACTICE
Addressing Inference Questions
ANSWERS
1. D
2. H
3. D
4. H
5. A

TEST SMARTS li

Test Smarts

LESSON 5 Applying the S.Qu.A.R.E. Strategy

Local, state, and national writing tests often ask you to write a persuasive essay in response to a question on an issue. You are given a topic in a writing prompt, but you have to decide your opinion, or position, organize your response, write, and proofread—all in a limited amount of time. Thinking of evidence to support an opinion can be the most difficult step on a writing test. Use the following strategy to think of supporting evidence quickly.

Thinking It Through: Using S.Qu.A.R.E. Strategy on a Writing Test

■ The letters in S.Qu.A.R.E. stand for a type of evidence you could use to back up a reason supporting your position. You may not be able to use every type of evidence, but at least some of them will probably apply.

S = Statistic   **Qu = Quotation**   **A = Anecdote**

R = Reasoning/logic   **E = Expert opinion**

1. Memorize what each letter stands for.

2. Ask whether any of the five types of evidence exists to support your reasons.

■ Below is an example of how one student used S.Qu.A.R.E. to generate reasons for a persuasive essay on repairing city roads.

Position: The city should repair the roads in the center of town.

Reason #1: The worse the city allows the road to become, the more it will cost to fix the problem.

S = We left a small leak in our roof unattended. Instead of spending a few dollars early on roofing cement and replacement shingles, we eventually spent <u>hundreds of dollars</u> replacing the bathroom ceiling.

Qu = As the proverb goes, "A stitch in time saves nine."

A = See <u>S</u> above. The statistic is contained within an anecdote.

R = Logic tells you that small holes and cracks, left unattended, will become bigger and bigger.

E = Our neighbor, a lawyer, warned that the city could be sued by drivers whose cars are damaged by driving over the potholes.

Practice

Directions. The graphic organizer below shows six areas you might consider to trigger ideas for reasons supporting your position. Copy the graphic organizer onto a sheet of paper, and complete the following activities on that sheet.

- Choose one of the writing prompts below, and take a position on the issue. Write your position in your graphic organizer.
- Identify two or three reasons that support your position. For each reason, find as many types of evidence as possible, using the graphic organizer below.

PROMPTS

- Some school districts are conducting school year-round. The year is divided into four segments, with a month's break between each. Imagine that you are going to address the school board, which is considering this schedule for your school. What is your position? What supporting reasons can you give?

- Breakfast provides energy to help you think well. Yet many students do not eat or eat poorly before coming to school each day. Could this situation be improved if the school cafeteria offered breakfast as well as lunch? What is your opinion on this issue? What supporting reasons can you give?

Your Position:

	Reason #1	Reason #2
Statistic		
Quotation		
Anecdote		
Reasoning/logic		
Expert opinion		

Applying the S.Qu.A.R.E. Strategy
(Responses will vary. A sample response to the second prompt is provided.)

Reason #1: A school-provided breakfast is sure to be healthier than what many students may choose to eat at home.

S = Of the students that I polled who do eat breakfast, 9 out of 10 said they eat sugar cereals, the sweetest kind on the market, at home.

Qu =

A = I used to eat cereals high in sugar until I noticed that they only gave me short-term energy. By second period, I was ready for a nap.

R =

E = Ms. Muñoz, our school nutritionist, explained that if the school served breakfast, it would be a well-balanced, nutritious meal, low in sugars and fat and high in protein.

Reason #2: Having a ready-to-eat breakfast at school will appeal to students who simply don't have time to prepare their own breakfast at home.

S =

Qu = As one student said, "I don't have time to set up breakfast, eat it, and clean up, so I just skip it."

A =

R = If students walking into school were greeted by the smell of pancakes and eggs, many would be drawn to the cafeteria like a magnet.

E =

61

OBJECTIVES

1. Read short stories centered on the themes "Facing Monsters," "The Human Spirit," "Expect the Unexpected," and "Discoveries"
2. Interpret literary elements in short stories with special emphasis on plot, character, setting, irony, point of view, and theme
3. Apply a variety of reading strategies to short stories with emphasis on ways that readers make meaning from a text
4. Respond to literature using a variety of modes
5. Learn and use new words
6. Plan, draft, revise, edit, proof, and publish a narrative, a character analysis, an evaluation, and a short story analysis
7. Write sentences using models, revise sentence fragments and sentence beginnings, and correct run-on sentences
8. Demonstrate the ability to organize information in graphic form, read memos and e-mail, analyze advertisements, and evaluate an argument
9. Record oral histories

RESPONDING TO THE ART

Many of the works of Iowa-born artist and teacher **Mel Rosas** (1950–   ) show the influence of Surrealists such as Rene Magritte (1898–1967). Here, what at first appears to be a realistic view reveals, on closer inspection, to be an exploration of the line between reality and the imagination.

Activity. Invite students to use their imaginations to construct a story based on what they see in the painting. To get them started, you might ask: Is that a painting, a mirror, or a window on the left-hand page? Who or what is casting the shadow on the wall behind it? Is the number 41 above the doorway a street address? If so, why is it inside the house? What might happen next in this scene? What is the mood?

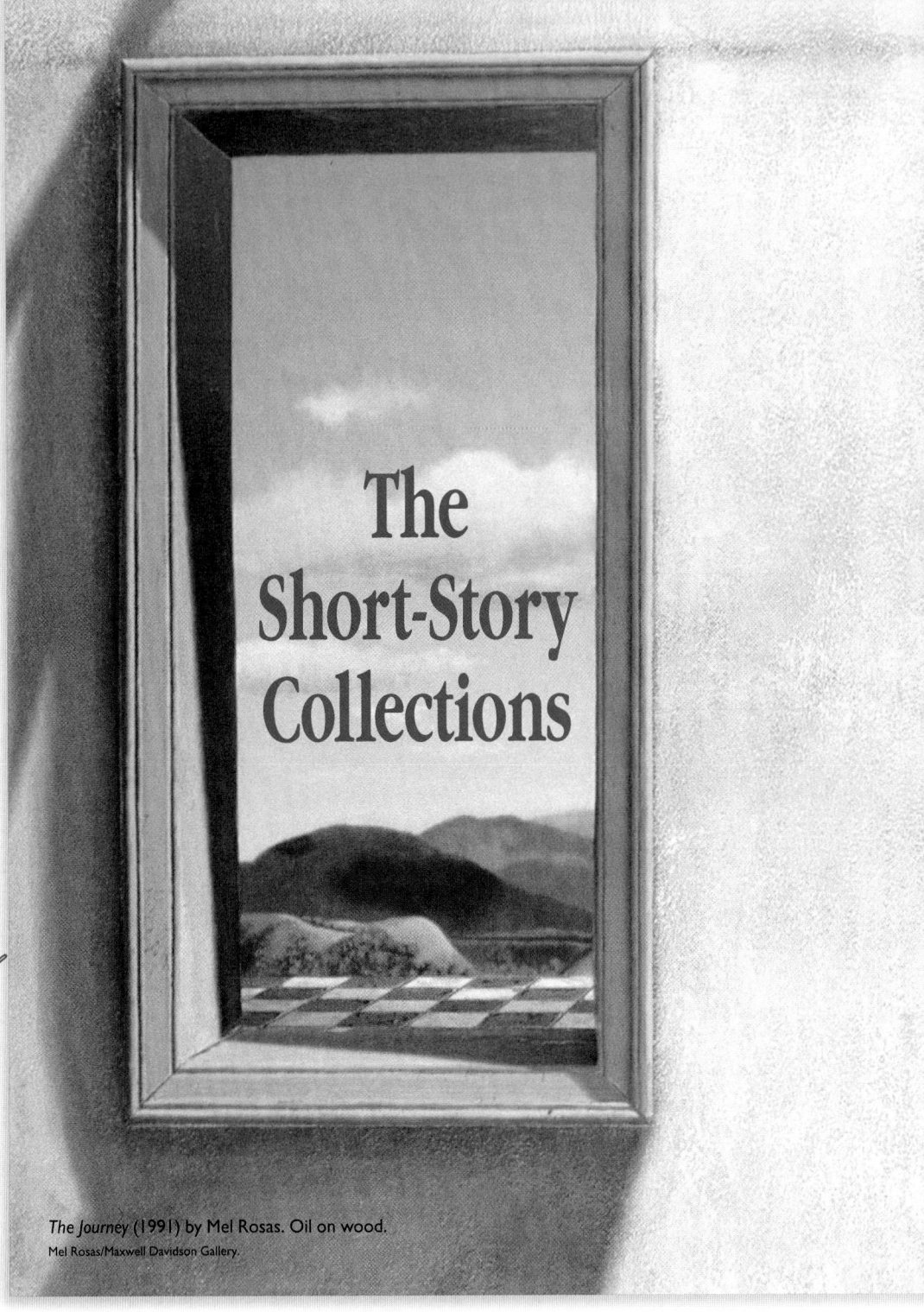

The Short-Story Collections

The Journey (1991) by Mel Rosas. Oil on wood.
Mel Rosas/Maxwell Davidson Gallery.

Selection Readability

This Annotated Teacher's Edition provides a summary of each selection in the student book. Following each Summary heading, you will find one, two, or three small icons. These icons indicate, in an approximate sense, the reading level of the selection.

■ One icon indicates that the selection is easy.

■ ■ Two icons indicate that the selection is on an intermediate reading level.

■ ■ ■ Three icons indicate that the selection is challenging.

There have been great societies that did not use the wheel, but there have been no societies that did not tell stories.

—*Ursula LeGuin*

Responding to the Quotation

Ask students to discuss how often they tell, listen to, read, or watch the dramatization of a story. Encourage students to consider a broad range of "stories," including anecdotes about the weekend, TV sitcoms, courtroom dramas, reminiscences about old times, and talks on the telephone or in the hallway about something that happened during the day. Have students talk about the various types of stories that they might encounter in an average week.

Next, discuss the appeal of stories. Why is it that stories capture people's attention in a way that a mere recital of facts cannot match? Encourage students to discuss these points: Stories weave plots and paint pictures that capture our imaginations; stories tug at our emotions, letting us experience everything from laughter to despair, from terror and suspense to tears and sadness. Stories take us to strange, new, and exciting places; in stories, we meet some unforgettable characters and encounter conflicts we recognize. Stories hold up a mirror in which we may see reflections of ourselves.

A Writer on Storytelling

A CONVERSATION WITH ISAAC BASHEVIS SINGER

As you work through this book, you will be both a reader and a writer. Before you begin, read this interview to see what Isaac Bashevis Singer, a writer whose work was a reflection of his own life, had to say about stories and their meanings. A memoir by Singer about a character from his childhood is on page 188.

Q: What are your "rules" when you write a short story?

Singer: It must be short. A number of writers make their short stories unusually long. Chekhov and Maupassant never did this. Their short stories were really short. Of course, it should have suspense from beginning to end. With bad writers the suspense begins to diminish almost immediately and then evaporates altogether. As for the process itself, first I get the idea or the emotion. Then I need a plot, a story with a beginning, a middle, and an end. . . .

A story to me must have some surprise. The plot should be such that when you read the first page, you don't know what the second will be. When you read the second page, you don't know what the third will be, because this is how life is, full of little surprises.

The second condition is that I must have a passion to write the story. Sometimes I have a very good plot, but somehow the passion to write this story is missing. If this is the case, I would not write it.

And the third condition is the most important. I must be convinced, or at least have the illusion, that I am the only one who could write this particular story or this particular novel.

Now, for a plot you need characters. So instead of inventing characters, I contemplate the people whom I have met in my life who could fit into this story. I sometimes combine two characters and from them make one. I may take a person whom I met in this country and put him in Poland or vice versa. But just the same, I must have a model.

I don't invent characters, because the Almighty has already invented millions and billions of them. Humanity may become a million years old and I'm sure that in all this time there will not be two people who are really alike. Experts at fingerprints do not create fingerprints. They learn how to read them. In the same way the writer reads human characters.

Q: What do you suppose it is that gives readers a sense of enjoyment?

Singer: When people come together—let's say they come to a little party or gathering—you always hear them discuss character. They will say, "This one is a fool, this one is a miser." Gossip makes the conversation. It seems that the analysis of character is the highest human entertainment. And literature does it, unlike gossip, without mentioning specific names—and so it is less malicious. We always love to discuss and reveal character because human character is to us the greatest puzzle. No matter how much you know a human being, you don't know him enough.

Reading Skills and Strategies

Booking space on the Net: Used-book-sellers take a page from other on-line readers. http://www.excite.com/

READING SHORT STORIES: MAKING MEANINGS

As readers, we make meaning. What a story means to us depends, at least in part, on who we are. Because you and I have had different experiences, lived in different places, known different people, we will see things differently. The meaning each of us creates from a text is therefore going to be our own. Take some time to think about what happens as we read.

1. **We connect with the text.** "This reminds me of my sister." "I had an experience like this."

2. **We ask questions.** We ask about situations or statements that puzzle us. We ask about motives. We try to figure out the meanings of unfamiliar words.

3. **We make predictions.** We wonder, "Is this what is going to happen next?" We test our predictions against the text.

4. **We interpret.** We decide what the story means as a whole and how its parts work together.

5. **We extend the text.** We reflect on the meaning of the text and think about its larger significance. We think about how the text can extend to some universal aspect of human life.

6. **We challenge the text.** We might say: "This couldn't possibly happen in real life." "This character seems too good." "I wish the story had a different ending."

HOW TO OWN A WORD

Learning from Context

When you come across an unfamiliar word, you have two resources available: what's already in your head and what's in the text—that is, all the words that surround the unknown word can sometimes give you clues to its meaning.

In the following story one lone man with a rifle lies watching and waiting. He is a sniper. Suppose you are not sure what a sniper is. Here is how you can use context clues to guess at what the word means.

What exactly is a sniper?

(On a rooftop) near O'Connell Bridge, a Republican sniper lay watching. Beside him (lay his rifle) and over his shoulders was slung a pair of (field glasses.) His face was the face of a student, thin and ascetic, but his eyes had the cold gleam of the (fanatic.)

He is in a hidden position.

He is prepared to kill someone.

He's looking for something far away?

He's deadly, dangerous. "Fanatic" suggests he has a cause.

Extending Your Store of Words

What other words does *sniper* make you think of? Is it connected with taking a "snipe" at people or insulting them? Is it related to *snip,* like cutting with scissors? Is it connected with the birds at the shore called *snipes*?

Apply the strategy on the next page. ➡

Reading Skills and Strategies

Mini-Lesson:
Reading Short Stories
Have students set up six pages in their journals with headings listing the six ways readers make meaning from a short story. Students should use the action verbs from the statements on this page as the headings (Connect, Ask Questions, and so on). Have them leave space after each heading to make notes. As students read "The Sniper," they should write their responses under the appropriate categories. As part of post-reading discussion, ask students to share examples of these responses. Students can compare their responses with those in the Dialogue with the Text models shown throughout the selection.

Mini-Lesson:
How to Own a Word
Following the model for the word *sniper* on this page, have students find clues to the meaning of the word *beleaguered,* in the first paragraph of the story on p. 5, or to the meaning of another word in the story that is unfamiliar to them. Have students record the surrounding words and phrases that give clues about the meaning of the word, as well as the conclusions they draw from those context clues. Finally, have students note any other observations they may be able to make with the word they chose.

Getting Students Involved

Cooperative Learning

To emphasize the distinct ways readers make meaning from a text, divide the class into six groups after they have read the short story "The Sniper" (pp. 5–10). Assign each group one of the six ways of making meaning listed above, and ask the members to create two or more illustrations of that thought process. For example, they might draw distinctly different faces and show thought bubbles that indicate a range of responses. Ask students to label their illustrations with the making-meaning category depicted. Divide the duties of artist, writer, and presenter among the group. Have groups share their efforts with the entire class. You can also display the illustrations in the classroom.

T3

Summary ■ ■

The story's setting is Dublin, Ireland, during the civil war in the 1920s. The protagonist is a Republican sniper on a Dublin rooftop who engages an unseen antagonist on the rooftop across the street. They exchange gunfire, and the Republican sniper is wounded, but not fatally. He recovers enough strength to kill his enemy—only to discover that the man he has killed is his own brother. The situational irony is under-scored by the use of a third-person limited point of view. The horrible revelation is presented in a calmly detached objective tone. The "monster" in this story is the war that pits brother against brother.

Resources

Listening
Audio CD Library
For a recording of "The Sniper," see the *Audio CD Library:*
• Disc 1, Track 2

Before You Read

THE SNIPER

Background

This story is set in Dublin, Ireland, in the 1920s. During that time a civil war was taking place in Ireland. On one side were the Republicans; they wanted all of Ireland to become a republic, totally free from British rule. On the other side were the Free Staters; they had compromised with Britain and had agreed to allow the English to continue to rule six counties in the northern province of Ulster. Like all civil wars, this one tore families apart. It pitted children against parents, sister against sister, brother against brother. As you read, notice how the writer helps you feel as if you are right there on a Dublin rooftop.

4 THE SHORT-STORY COLLECTIONS

Reaching All Students

Struggling Readers
The Dialogue with a Text comments can be used to teach students to monitor their reading strategies. For a lesson directly tied to this story that teaches students to monitor reading by using a strategy called Think Aloud, see the *Reading Skills and Strategies* binder:
• MiniRead Skill Lesson, p. 1
• Selection Skill Lesson, p. 217 (Use the "Model" part of the lesson only.)

Advanced Learners
Ask volunteers to provide context for the selection by sharing what they know about the history of the conflict in Northern Ireland. Have students give examples of other works of literature or film that deal with this history, and ask them to describe the themes and plots of these works. Students may also locate and bring to class articles from newspapers or magazines about the conflicts in present-day Ireland.

His eyes had the cold gleam of the fanatic.

The Sniper

Liam O'Flaherty

The long June twilight faded into night. Dublin lay enveloped in darkness but for the dim light of the moon that shone through fleecy clouds, casting a pale light as of approaching dawn over the streets and the dark waters of the Liffey.[1] Around the beleaguered Four Courts[2] the heavy guns roared. Here and there through the city, machine guns and rifles broke the silence of the night, spasmodically, like dogs barking on lone farms. Republicans and Free Staters were waging civil war.

On a rooftop near O'Connell Bridge, a Republican sniper lay watching. Beside him lay his rifle and over his shoulders was slung a pair of field glasses. His face was the face of a student, thin and ascetic,[3] but his eyes had the cold gleam of the fanatic. They were deep and thoughtful, the eyes of a man who is used to looking at death. **Ⓐ**

1. **Liffey:** river that runs through Dublin.
2. **beleaguered** (bē·lē′gərd) **Four Courts:** government buildings in Dublin that were surrounded and under attack.
3. **ascetic** (ə·set′ik): extremely self-disciplined and severe.

Dialogue with the Text

The notes that follow show the thoughts of one reader as she read this short story for the first time. When you read the story yourself for the first time, cover her responses. Track your own responses and then compare your reading with Wendy's.

This captures summer's essence beautifully.

The paragraph contains a huge contrast—between peaceful summer and violent war.

The rooftop of a house?

Wouldn't the eyes of a man used to looking at death be cold and empty? Cold eyes and deep thoughtful eyes disagree with each other.

THE SNIPER 5

Point out to students the critical observation made in the last lines of the model. Discuss the criticism with them. Ask students whether they agree or disagree with this challenge to the text.

Ⓐ Reading Skills and Strategies

Extending the Text

Explain to students that a fanatic is a person whose interest in something or someone is intense and irrational. Ask them to explain why a fanatic's eyes might have a cold gleam. [Possible response: A fanatic's eyes may be cold and unfeeling because a fanatic does not see people as human beings but as part of an exaggerated world view; a fanatic's eyes may gleam, for they are lit by intense interest in a cause.]

Liam O'Flaherty
(1896-1984) 88 yrs.
1917 fought WWI – injured + shell shock
after war joined Communist Party
mental break downs / collapse due to war
+ Novels, Short Stories, Letters
✳ Wrote in Gaelic also

Skill Link

Construct a Graphic Organizer

Explain that a graphic organizer can help keep track of specific types of details in a story. For example, a chart could record the numerous sensory details used by Liam O'Flaherty to convey the experiences of the Republican sniper. Have students make a chart like the one at right and use it to record examples of sensory details in the story. Ask students to note the effect each detail has on them.

Detail		Effect
Sight	p. 5, par. 1, sent. 2	eerie due to poor visibility
Hearing		
Taste		
Touch		
Smell		

Dialogue with the Text

Have students compare their own notes to the questions and observations in the model. Be sure to let them know, however, that there is no correct or incorrect proportion of statements and questions. Encourage students to develop a variety of responses as they read.

Ⓐ Appreciating Language

Figure of Speech

❓ To what does O'Flaherty compare the armored car? [a monster] What other word does he use to make the armored car seem alive? ["panting," to describe its motor]

Ⓑ Reading Skills and Strategies

Making Predictions

Ask students to record their predictions of what will happen next. Remind them to check their predictions after they finish reading the story.

Dialogue with the Text

How can a sniper be watching silently and eating hungrily at the same time?

This guy has never done this job before. He acts carelessly.

This part made me laugh because I knew what would happen if he lit a cigarette.

What does an armored car look like? It reminds me of the vans that pick up money from businesses.

It seems that this guy just wants to shoot at something. Anything.

Wonder how the old woman knew where the sniper was.

He was eating a sandwich hungrily. He had eaten nothing since morning. He had been too excited to eat. He finished the sandwich, and, taking a flask of whiskey from his pocket, he took a short draft. Then he returned the flask to his pocket. He paused for a moment, considering whether he should risk a smoke. It was dangerous. The flash might be seen in the darkness, and there were enemies watching. He decided to take the risk.

Placing a cigarette between his lips, he struck a match, inhaled the smoke hurriedly, and put out the light. Almost immediately, a bullet flattened itself against the parapet[4] of the roof. The sniper took another whiff and put out the cigarette. Then he swore softly and crawled away to the left.

Cautiously he raised himself and peered over the parapet. There was a flash and a bullet whizzed over his head. He dropped immediately. He had seen the flash. It came from the opposite side of the street.

He rolled over the roof to a chimney stack in the rear and slowly drew himself up behind it, until his eyes were level with the top of the parapet. There was nothing to be seen—just the dim outline of the opposite housetop against the blue sky. His enemy was under cover.

Just then an armored car came across the bridge and advanced slowly up the street. It stopped on the opposite side of the street, fifty yards ahead. The sniper could hear the dull panting of the motor. His heart beat faster. It was an enemy car. He wanted to fire, but he knew it was useless. His bullets would never pierce the steel that covered the gray monster.

Then round the corner of a side street came an old woman, her head covered by a tattered shawl. She began to talk to the man in the turret of the car. She was pointing to the roof where the sniper lay. An informer.

4. **parapet** (par′ə·pet′): low wall or railing.

6 THE SHORT-STORY COLLECTIONS

Crossing the Curriculum

Art

Explain that *parapet* and *breastworks* are military architectural terms referring to the types of walls that are constructed to protect troops from a frontal assault by the enemy. Interested students can research military fortifications. They can then use their findings to construct a glossary of terms and present their work to the class accompanied by a set of illustrations.

History

From 1801 to 1922, Ireland was part of the United Kingdom. In the early 1900s, Irish nationalists pressed to end British rule. The 1916 Easter uprising led to civil war. In 1922, the Irish Free State was established, but six northern counties remained under British rule. In 1998, an agreement was reached establishing a new relationship between north and south, and between Britain and Ireland. Ask students to consult reference materials and to create a time line showing the development of the conflict in Ireland. Research should clarify the goals and grievances held by Free Staters and by Republicans, as well as the events that led to dominion and to Ireland's independence. Students may also chronicle more recent events unfolding in Ireland.

The turret opened. A man's head and shoulders appeared, looking toward the sniper. The sniper raised his rifle and fired. The head fell heavily on the turret wall. The woman darted toward the side street. The sniper fired again. The woman whirled round and fell with a shriek into the gutter.

Suddenly from the opposite roof a shot rang out and the sniper dropped his rifle with a curse. The rifle clattered to the roof. The sniper thought the noise would wake the dead. He stooped to pick the rifle up. He couldn't lift it. His forearm was dead. "I'm hit," he muttered.

Dropping flat onto the roof, he crawled back to the parapet. With his left hand he felt the injured right forearm. The blood was oozing through the sleeve of his coat. There was no pain—just a deadened sensation, as if the arm had been cut off.

Quickly he drew his knife from his pocket, opened it on the breastwork[5] of the parapet, and ripped open the sleeve. There was a small hole where the bullet had entered. On the other side there was no hole. The bullet had lodged in the bone. It must have fractured it. He bent the arm below the wound. The arm bent back easily. He ground his teeth to overcome the pain.

Then taking out his field dressing, he ripped open the packet with his knife. He broke the neck of the iodine bottle and let the bitter fluid drip into the wound. A paroxysm[6] of pain swept through him. He placed the cotton wadding over the wound and wrapped the dressing over it. He tied the ends with his teeth.

Then he lay still against the parapet, and, closing his eyes, he made an effort of will to overcome the pain.

In the street beneath all was still. The armored car had

5. **breastwork:** low wall put up as a military defense.
6. **paroxysm** (par′əks·iz′əm): sudden attack; fit.

Dialogue with the Text

The turret of what? The car? How can a car have a turret?

Nice action scene.

All of this makes me cringe! The author's description is so real that I can almost feel the character's pain.

I think I understand what happened earlier now.

THE SNIPER 7

Dialogue with the Text

Ask students in what way the fourth observation is different from earlier comments in the model. [The fourth observation is retrospective; the reader notes the change in her understanding of something that was previously unclear.] Encourage students to record their own responses to the characters and events and the moments when their understanding of the story changes.

C Reading Skills and Strategies
Connecting with the Text

❓ Why do you think the sniper kills the woman? [Possible responses: because she is an informer; because she has put his life in danger.] Ask students to discuss the fairness of the sniper's actions.

D Critical Thinking
Analyzing Details
❓ How does the author make this passage seem real? [He uses figurative language and precise descriptions of the sniper's feelings and actions.]

Using Students' Strengths

Visual Learners
Have students create one or more maps of the island of Ireland. Offer students the following options:
- a map showing the political divisions between the Republic of Ireland and the six northern counties
- a historical map depicting the location of major events in Irish history
- a map illustrating Ireland's topography

Auditory/Musical Learners
Have students create a presentation of Celtic music. Students can bring in recordings of different types of songs and show illustrations of the instruments that are used in the music. They may also be able to locate videos of Irish performers and musicians and play these videos for the class.

Dialogue with the Text

Have students note the reader's question to herself in the first comment in the model on this page. Encourage students to record in their journals any questions generated by their own reading.

A Reading Skills and Strategies

Asking Questions

Ask students to share any questions they have about the situation described in this paragraph. [Sample questions: Why must the sniper leave by morning? Why can't he use the rifle?]

B Critical Thinking

Speculating

? What is the point of the sniper's plan? [He wants to make his enemy think he has been killed.]

RESPONDING TO THE ART

The proclamation at the right, addressed to the people of Ireland, was the declaration of independence signed by leaders of the unsuccessful Easter Rising, which took place on April 24, 1916, and was put down by the British army five days later. The seven men who signed on behalf of the provisional government were later executed by the British. As a result of the executions, feelings in Ireland were aroused as never before, and the men who failed to effect a revolution were seen as martyrs.

Activity. You might have interested students locate a poem that William Butler Yeats wrote about these men, called "Easter 1916."

Dialogue with the Text

Escape from what? The roof?

Suspenseful here, and more interesting.

This is risky. He might need it. Where was he before?

---

retired speedily over the bridge, with the machine gunner's head hanging lifeless over the turret. The woman's corpse lay still in the gutter.

The sniper lay still for a long time nursing his wounded arm and planning escape. Morning must not find him wounded on the roof. The enemy on the opposite roof covered his escape. He must kill that enemy and he could not use his rifle. He had only a revolver to do it. Then he thought of a plan. **A**

Taking off his cap, he placed it over the muzzle of his rifle. Then he pushed the rifle slowly upward over the parapet, until the cap was visible from the opposite side of the street. Almost immediately there was a report, and a bullet pierced the center of the cap. The sniper slanted the rifle forward. The cap slipped down into the street. Then, catching the rifle in the middle, the sniper dropped his left hand over the roof and let it hang, lifelessly. After a few moments he let the rifle drop to the street. Then he sank to the roof, dragging his hand with him. **B**

Crawling quickly to the left, he peered up at the corner of the roof. His ruse had succeeded. The other sniper,

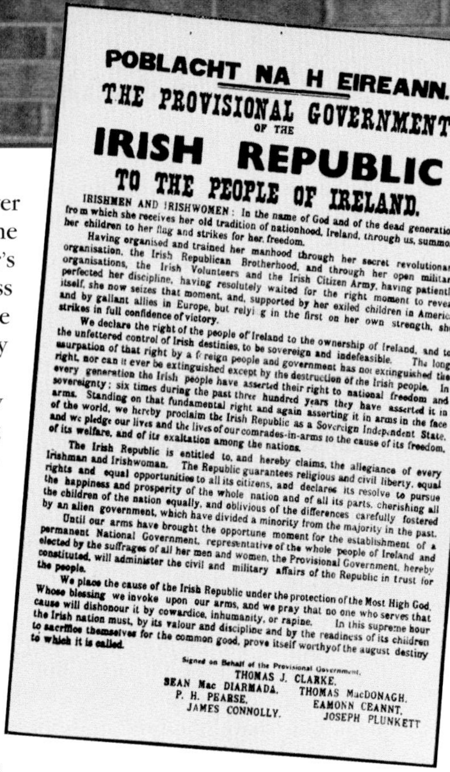

POBLACHT NA H EIREANN.
THE PROVISIONAL GOVERNMENT
OF THE
IRISH REPUBLIC
TO THE PEOPLE OF IRELAND.

IRISHMEN AND IRISHWOMEN: In the name of God and of the dead generations from which she receives her old tradition of nationhood, Ireland, through us, summons her children to her flag and strikes for her freedom.

Having organised and trained her manhood through her secret revolutionary organisation, the Irish Republican Brotherhood, and through her open military organisations, the Irish Volunteers and the Irish Citizen Army, having patiently perfected her discipline, having resolutely waited for the right moment to reveal itself, she now seizes that moment, and, supported by her exiled children in America and by gallant allies in Europe, but relyi g in the first on her own strength, she strikes in full confidence of victory.

We declare the right of the people of Ireland to the ownership of Ireland, and to the unfettered control of Irish destinies, to be sovereign and indefeasible. The long usurpation of that right by a foreign people and government has not extinguished the right, nor can it ever be extinguished except by the destruction of the Irish people. In every generation the Irish people have asserted their right to national freedom and sovereignty; six times during the past three hundred years they have asserted it in arms. Standing on that fundamental right and again asserting it in arms in the face of the world, we hereby proclaim the Irish Republic as a Sovereign Independent State, and we pledge our lives and the lives of our comrades-in-arms to the cause of its freedom, of its welfare, and of its exaltation among the nations.

The Irish Republic is entitled to, and hereby claims, the allegiance of every Irishman and Irishwoman. The Republic guarantees religious and civil liberty, equal rights and equal opportunities to all its citizens, and declares its resolve to pursue the happiness and prosperity of the whole nation and of all its parts, cherishing all the children of the nation equally, and oblivious of the differences carefully fostered by an alien government, which have divided a minority from the majority in the past.

Until our arms have brought the opportune moment for the establishment of a permanent National Government, representative of the whole people of Ireland and elected by the suffrages of all her men and women, the Provisional Government, hereby constituted, will administer the civil and military affairs of the Republic in trust for the people.

We place the cause of the Irish Republic under the protection of the Most High God, Whose blessing we invoke upon our arms, and we pray that no one who serves that cause will dishonour it by cowardice, inhumanity, or rapine. In this supreme hour the Irish nation must, by its valour and discipline and by the readiness of its children to sacrifice themselves for the common good, prove itself worthy of the august destiny to which it is called.

Signed on Behalf of the Provisional Government,
THOMAS J. CLARKE.
SEAN Mac DIARMADA. THOMAS MacDONAGH.
P. H. PEARSE. EAMONN CEANNT.
JAMES CONNOLLY. JOSEPH PLUNKETT

seeing the cap and rifle fall, thought that he had killed his man. He was now standing before a row of chimney pots, looking across, with his head clearly silhouetted against the western sky.

The Republican sniper smiled and lifted his revolver above the edge of the parapet. The distance was about fifty yards—a hard shot in the dim light, and his right arm was paining him like a thousand devils. He took a steady aim. His hand trembled with eagerness. Pressing his lips together, he took a deep breath through his nostrils and fired. He was almost deafened with the report and his arm shook with the recoil.

Then when the smoke cleared he peered across and uttered a cry of joy. His enemy had been hit. He was reeling over the parapet in his death agony. He struggled to keep his feet, but he was slowly falling forward, as if in a dream. The rifle fell from his grasp, hit the parapet, fell over, bounded off the pole of a barber's shop beneath, and then clattered on the pavement.

Then the dying man on the roof crumpled up and fell forward. The body turned over and over in space and hit the ground with a dull thud. Then it lay still.

The sniper looked at his enemy falling and he shuddered. The lust of battle died in him. He became bitten by remorse. The sweat stood out in beads on his forehead. Weakened by his wound and the long summer day of fasting and watching on the roof, he revolted from the sight of the shattered mass of his dead enemy. His teeth chattered, he began to gibber to himself, cursing the war, cursing himself, cursing everybody.

He looked at the smoking revolver in his hand, and with an oath he hurled it to the roof at his feet. The revolver went off with the concussion and the bullet whizzed past the sniper's head. He was frightened back to his senses by the shock. His nerves steadied. The cloud of fear scattered from his mind and he laughed.

Dialogue with the Text

Isn't the other sniper watching him?

I like this author's style. It is descriptive while being concise and suspenseful.

I thought that this man was used to death.

C Wasn't it the night and early morning?

D War is making this man a little crazy and irrational.

Dialogue with the Text

Have students note the reader's observations about the author's style. Ask them to agree or disagree with the comments and to make other observations about the writer's choice of words, sentence length and variety, or pacing of events.

C Critical Thinking
Analyzing Character

? What changes overcome the sniper? [Instead of feeling joy and revenge, he is remorseful, sorry, and sick.] Suggest that students keep track of the different emotions felt by the sniper in the next few paragraphs.

D Reading Skills and Strategies
Challenging the Text

Ask students whether they found the sniper's reaction credible, contrived, or even puzzling. Have them explain why and suggest alternate ways that he might have reacted.

Have students write a sentence or two in their journals speculating on the feelings and thoughts the sniper must have experienced when he discovered the other sniper's identity.

Ⓐ Critical Thinking
Evaluating
❓ How are the two snipers alike?
[Possible responses: They possess similar skills; they are both committed to a cause; they are both used to violence in their day-to-day lives.]

BROWSING IN THE FILES

About the Author. As a young man, Liam O'Flaherty (1896–1984) wandered the world and tried a succession of trades and professions. Trained for the Catholic priesthood, he rejected this vocation for a soldier's life. His military career ended when he was wounded. O'Flaherty later sailed to Rio de Janeiro, Brazil. Over the next few years, he worked in places like Gibraltar, New York, and Smyrna as a deckhand, lumberjack, dishwasher, porter, and bank clerk. His writing illustrates the often difficult struggle to keep alive one's spiritual values in the real world, a struggle he knew well.

A Critic's Comment. Richard J. Thompson wrote that in stories such as "The Sniper," Liam O'Flaherty had a "habit of imposing an oversimplified, chockablock plot . . . forcing home a melodramatic conclusion." Ask students whether they agree or disagree with Thompson's criticism. Did they find the ending to be a powerful surprise, or a melodramatic contrivance?

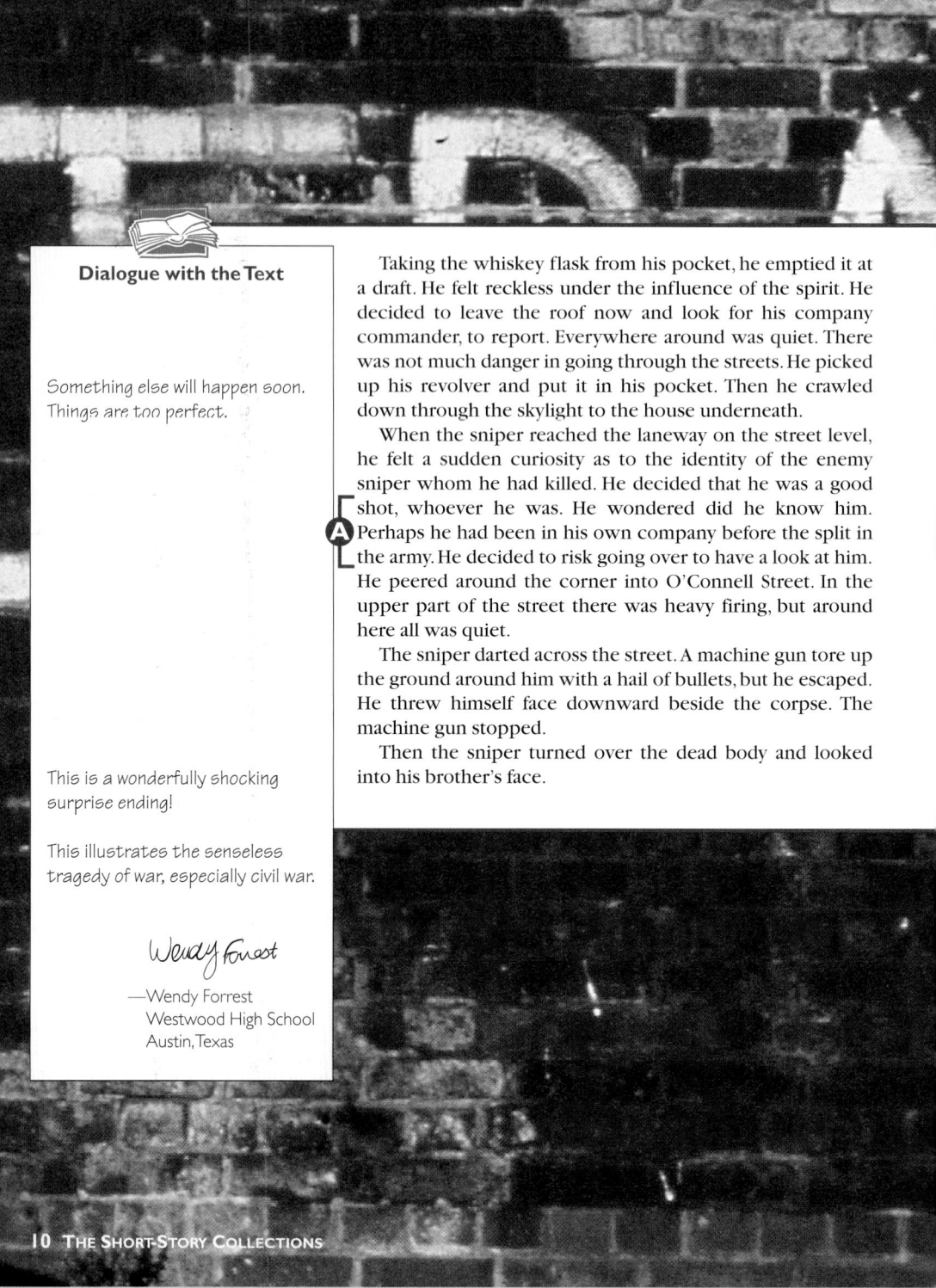

Dialogue with the Text

Something else will happen soon. Things are too perfect.

This is a wonderfully shocking surprise ending!

This illustrates the senseless tragedy of war, especially civil war.

Wendy Forrest

—Wendy Forrest
Westwood High School
Austin, Texas

Taking the whiskey flask from his pocket, he emptied it at a draft. He felt reckless under the influence of the spirit. He decided to leave the roof now and look for his company commander, to report. Everywhere around was quiet. There was not much danger in going through the streets. He picked up his revolver and put it in his pocket. Then he crawled down through the skylight to the house underneath.

When the sniper reached the laneway on the street level, he felt a sudden curiosity as to the identity of the enemy sniper whom he had killed. He decided that he was a good shot, whoever he was. He wondered did he know him. Perhaps he had been in his own company before the split in the army. He decided to risk going over to have a look at him. He peered around the corner into O'Connell Street. In the upper part of the street there was heavy firing, but around here all was quiet.

The sniper darted across the street. A machine gun tore up the ground around him with a hail of bullets, but he escaped. He threw himself face downward beside the corpse. The machine gun stopped.

Then the sniper turned over the dead body and looked into his brother's face.

Assessing Learning

Check Test: Questions and Answers
Answers may vary slightly.
1. Where does the action take place? [on the rooftops of a street in Dublin, Ireland]
2. What happens to the old woman who informs on the sniper? [The sniper kills her.]
3. How is the sniper injured? [The enemy sniper shoots him in the arm.]
4. How does the sniper trick the enemy sniper? [The Republican sniper puts his cap on his rifle, draws fire, and pretends to die. When the enemy sniper stands up, the Republican sniper kills him.]
5. Whom does the sniper discover he has killed? [The sniper has killed his own brother.]

Facing Monsters

Theme

Conflict: The Basis of Storytelling *Conflict is the central element in storytelling. In almost all our stories—from Homer's* Odyssey *to the latest best-seller—conflicts take the shape of struggles with literal or figurative "monsters." The intensity of this conflict in a story is what keeps us turning those pages.*

Reading the Anthology

Reaching Struggling Readers

The *Reading Skills and Strategies: Reaching Struggling Readers* binder provides materials coordinated with the Pupil's Edition (see the Collection Planner, p. T10B) to help students who have difficulty reading and comprehending text, or students who are reluctant readers. The binder for ninth grade is organized around sixteen individual skill areas and offers the following options:

- **MiniRead** MiniReads are short, easy texts that give students a chance to practice a particular skill and strategy before reading selections in the Pupil's Edition. Each MiniRead Skill Lesson can be taught independently or used in conjunction with a Selection Skill Lesson.

- **Selection Skill Lessons** Selection Skill Lessons allow students to apply skills introduced in the MiniReads. Each Selection Skill Lesson provides reading instruction and practice specific to a particular piece of literature in the Pupil's Edition.

Reading Beyond the Anthology

Read On

Each collection in the grade nine book includes an annotated bibliography of books suitable for extended reading. The suggested books are related to works in the collection by theme, by author, or by subject. To preview the Read On for Collection 1, please turn to p. T111.

HRW Library

The *HRW Library* offers novels, plays, works of nonfiction, and short-story collections for extended reading. Each book in the Library includes a major work and thematically or topically related Connections. The Connections are magazine articles, poems, or other pieces of literature. Each book in the *HRW Library* is also accompanied by a Study Guide that provides teaching suggestions and worksheets. The two titles shown here will work well to extend the theme of Collection 1.

TREASURE ISLAND
Robert Louis Stevenson
Treasure Island is the classic adventure tale in which a young boy, Jim Hawkins, discovers the world of pirates and betrayal as he hunts for buried treasure.

THE PIGMAN
Paul Zindel
Two confused teenagers learn about accepting responsibility and protecting friendships through their relationship with Mr. Pignati, the Pigman.

Collection 1 Facing Monsters

Resources for this Collection

Note: All resources for this collection are available for preview on the *One-Stop Planner CD-ROM 1 with Test Generator.* All worksheets and blackline masters may be printed from the CD-ROM.

Internet Resources
go.hrw.com LE0 9-1

Selection or Feature	Reading and Literary Skills	Vocabulary, Language, and Grammar

The Most Dangerous Game
Richard Connell (p.12)
	• *Reading Skills and Strategies: Reaching Struggling Readers*
	  • MiniRead Skill Lesson, p. 1
	  • Selection Skill Lesson, p. 8
	• *Graphic Organizers for Active Reading,* Worksheet p. 1
	• *Literary Elements:* Transparency 1
	  Worksheet p. 4
		• *Words to Own,* Worksheet p. 1
		• *Grammar and Language Links:* Powerful Verbs, Worksheet p. 1
		• *Language Workshop CD-ROM,* Verbs
		• *Daily Oral Grammar,*
		  Transparency 1

Elements of Literature: Plot (p. 32)	• *Literary Elements,* Transparency 1	

A Sound of Thunder
Ray Bradbury (p. 34)
Connections: *from* **Jurassic Park**
Michael Crichton (p. 45)
	• *Reading Skills and Strategies: Reaching Struggling Readers*
	  • MiniRead Skill Lesson, p. 23
	  • Selection Skill Lesson, p. 31
	• *Graphic Organizers for Active Reading,* Worksheet p. 2
		• *Words to Own,* Worksheet p. 2
		• *Grammar and Language Links:* Active and Passive Voice, Worksheet p. 3
		• *Language Workshop CD-ROM,* Active Voice
		• *Daily Oral Grammar,*
		  Transparency 2

The Birds
Daphne du Maurier (p. 50)
Connections: Hundreds of Birds Invade Home in California
(p. 76)
	• *Reading Skills and Strategies: Reaching Struggling Readers*
	  • MiniRead Skill Lesson, p. 35
	  • Selection Skill Lesson, p. 42
	• *Graphic Organizers for Active Reading,* Worksheet p. 3
		• *Words to Own,* Worksheet p. 3
		• *Grammar and Language Links:* Verb Tenses, Worksheet p. 5
		• *Language Workshop CD-ROM,* Verb Tenses
		• *Daily Oral Grammar,*
		  Transparency 3

Poison Roald Dahl (p. 80) **Connections: hate** Tato Laviera (p. 90)	• *Graphic Organizers for Active Reading,* Worksheet p. 4	• *Words to Own,* Worksheet p. 4 • *Grammar and Language Links:* Subject and Verb, Worksheet p. 7 • *Language Workshop CD-ROM,* Subject-Verb Agreement • *Daily Oral Grammar,* Transparency 4
The Interlopers Saki (p. 94) **Connections: The Trapper Trapped** *Vai African traditional, retold by* Roger D. Abrahams (p. 100)	• *Graphic Organizers for Active Reading,* Worksheet p. 5	• *Words to Own,* Worksheet p. 5 • *Grammar and Language Links:* Transitions, Worksheet p. 9 • *Daily Oral Grammar,* Transparency 5
Extending the Theme: *from* **Black Boy** Richard Wright (p. 104)	The Extending the Theme feature provides students with an unstructured opportunity to practice reading strategies using a selection that extends the theme of the collection.	
Writer's Workshop: **Short Narrative** (p. 112)		
Sentence Workshop: **Learning from the Pros** (p. 117)		• *Workshop Resources,* p. 61 • *Language Workshop CD-ROM,* Sentence Structure

(sidebar) **Collection Planner**

Other Resources for this Collection

- *Cross-Curricular Activities*, p. 1
- *Portfolio Management System*, Introduction to Portfolio Assessment, p. 1
- *Test Generator*, Collection Test ⊚

Writing	Listening and Speaking Viewing and Representing	Assessment
• *Portfolio Management System*, Rubrics for Choices, p. 89	• *Audio CD Library*, Disc 1, Track 3 🎧 • *Portfolio Management System*, Rubrics for Choices, p. 89	• *Formal Assessment*, Selection Test, p. 1 • *Test Generator (One-Stop Planner CD-ROM)* ⊚
		• *Formal Assessment*, Literary Elements Test, p. 11
• *Portfolio Management System*, Rubrics for Choices, p. 91	• *Visual Connections:* Videocassette A, Segment 1 📼 • *Audio CD Library*, Disc 2, Track 2 🎧 • *Viewing and Representing:* Fine Art Transparency 1; Worksheet p. 4 📽 • *Portfolio Management System*, Rubrics for Choices, p. 91	• *Formal Assessment*, Selection Test, p. 3 • *Standardized Test Preparation*, p. 10 • *Test Generator (One-Stop Planner CD-ROM)* ⊚
• *Portfolio Management System*, Rubrics for Choices, p. 93	• *Audio CD Library*, Disc 3, Track 2, and Disc 4, Track 2 🎧 • *Viewing and Representing:* Fine Art Transparency 2; Worksheet p. 8 📽 • *Portfolio Management System*, Rubrics for Choices, p. 93	• *Formal Assessment*, Selection Test, p. 5 • *Standardized Test Preparation*, pp. 12, 14 • *Test Generator (One-Stop Planner CD-ROM)* ⊚
• *Portfolio Management System*, Rubrics for Choices, p. 94	• *Audio CD Library*, Disc 5, Track 2 🎧 • *Portfolio Management System*, Rubrics for Choices, p. 94	• *Formal Assessment*, Selection Test, p. 7 • *Test Generator (One-Stop Planner CD-ROM)* ⊚
• *Portfolio Management System*, Rubrics for Choices, p. 95	• *Audio CD Library*, Disc 5, Track 3 🎧 • *Portfolio Management System*, Rubrics for Choices, p. 95	• *Formal Assessment*, Selection Test, p. 9 • *Standardized Test Preparation*, p. 16 • *Test Generator (One-Stop Planner CD-ROM)* ⊚
	• *Audio CD Library*, Disc 5, Track 4 🎧	

• *Workshop Resources*, p. 1		• *Portfolio Management System*
		   • Prewriting, p. 97
		  • Peer Editing, p. 98
		  • Assessment Rubric, p. 99

 Transparency    CD-ROM    Video   🎧 Audio CD

Skills Focus

Skills Focus

Selection or Feature	Reading Skills and Strategies	Elements of Literature	Language/ Grammar	Vocabulary/ Spelling	Writing	Listening/ Speaking	Viewing/ Representing
The Most Dangerous Game Richard Connell (p. 12)	Dialogue with the Text, pp. 12, 29 • Predictions • Double-Entry Journal	Conflict, External and Internal, pp. 12, 30, 32–33 Title, p. 29 Foreshadow, p. 29 Characters, p. 29	Powerful Verbs, p. 31	Word Meanings, p. 31	Identify a Conflict for a Short Narrative, p. 30 Create Sequel, p. 30 Analyze Characters, p. 30	Simulate a Television Discussion, p. 30	Use a Venn Diagram, p. 29 Create a Cluster Diagram, p. 30 Create a Map, p. 30 Create a Chart, p. 30
Elements of Literature: Plot (p. 32)		Plot, p. 32 Conflict, p. 32 Exposition, p. 32 Complication, p. 33 Climax, p. 33 Resolution, p. 33					
A Sound of Thunder Ray Bradbury (p. 34)	Cause and Effect, p. 34 Cause-and-Effect Chain, p. 47 Identify Main Events, p. 48	Climax, pp. 34, 47 Title, p. 47 Figures of Speech, p. 47 Vivid Descriptions, p. 47 Message, p. 47	Active and Passive Verbs, p. 49	Context Clues, p. 49	List Main Events, p. 48 Write a News Report, p. 48 Describe Imaginary Place, p. 48 Describe Dinosaur Encounter, p. 48	Research and Report on Dinosaurs, p. 48	
The Birds Daphne du Maurier (p. 50)	Make Predictions, pp. 50, 77 Evaluate Credibility, p. 77	Foreshadowing, pp. 50, 77 Suspense, p. 77 Conflict, p. 77	Verb Tenses, p. 79	New Words, p. 79	Create a Setting, p. 78 Write a Feature Article, p. 78	Compare a Story and a Movie, p. 78	Research and Create a Sketchbook, p. 78 Use a Credibility Scale, p. 77
Poison Roald Dahl (p. 80)	Monitor Your Reading by Asking Questions, pp. 80, 91	Suspense, pp. 80, 91 Conflicts, p. 91 Historical Context, p. 91	Subject and Verb Agreement, p. 93	Word Maps, p. 93	Use Dialogue, p. 92 Create a Final Scene, p. 92 Research Facts on India, p. 92	Role-play, p. 92 Research and Report on India, p. 92	
The Interlopers Saki (p. 94)	Monitor Your Reading Using Guidelines, pp. 94, 101 Make a Story Map, p. 101	Surprise Endings, pp. 94, 102 Climax, p. 101 Irony, p. 101 Mood, p. 101 Moral, p. 101	Transitions, p. 103	Word Histories/ Etymologies, p. 103	Write a Surprise Ending, p. 102 Write a New Ending, p. 102 Compare Characters, p. 102 Write an Evaluation, p. 102		Make a Storyboard, p. 102
Extending the Theme: *from* **Black Boy** Richard Wright (p. 104)	The Extending the Theme feature provides students with an unstructured opportunity to practice reading strategies using a selection that extends the theme of the collection.						
Writer's Workshop: Short Narrative (p. 112)		Chronological Order, p. 113 Flashback, p. 113	Dialogue, p. 114		Write a Short Narrative, p. 112		Use a Cluster Diagram, p. 112 Use a Story Map, p. 113
Sentence Workshop: Learning from the Pros (p. 117)			Sentence Modeling, p. 117		Revise Sentences, p. 117		
Reading for Life: Organizing Information in Graphic Form (p. 118)	Read a Time Line, Venn Diagram, Cause-and-Effect Chart, p. 118 Identify Signal Words, p. 118						Design a Graphic, p. 118

FACING MONSTERS

WRITING FOCUS: Short Narrative

The oldest of all our stories are about conflicts between people and the monsters—real and imaginary—that threaten them. We can imagine people in prehistoric times huddled around small fires in their dark caves, telling one another stories about terrifying conflicts with monsters that got more and more fantastic as the stories were told and retold. Conflict is still the basic ingredient in our stories. Today, the monsters have disappeared in realistic stories, and characters face more believable problems—floods, bullies at the corner, clashes with friends, viruses in the computer. But perhaps more common today are stories of people who struggle with problems that come from within: anger, prejudice, selfishness, fear. Why is it that so many of our stories deal with conflict? Maybe it's because stories help us absorb the courage, the strength, and the wisdom we need to confront the conflicts we face in our own passage through life.

> *The harder*
> *the conflict,*
> *the more*
> *glorious the*
> *triumph.*
>
> *—Thomas Paine*

Writer's Notebook

Think for a few minutes of all the times in life when you or someone you know struggled with something—something outside, like a hurricane, or something inside, like fear of a big exam or a tough decision. List as many of these conflicts as you can. Write freely; right now you just need to get your ideas down. Keep your notes. You'll return to them for the narrative you'll write for the Writer's Workshop on page 112.

Responding to the Quotation

? Remind students of Thomas Paine's role as a political propagandist during the American Revolution. **How might his words have inspired the colonists in their battle with Great Britain?** [Possible answers: His words might have given them the courage to take on a powerful adversary; his words implied victory.] **Then, ask students whether they agree or disagree with Paine's statement.** [Sample responses: Yes, hard-fought achievements are the most satisfying; no, if the struggle is too hard, no victory is worth the cost.] **What do this quotation and the collection theme suggest about the stories you will read?** [Sample responses: The characters will engage in life-or-death struggles; the characters will stand up to powerful forces and defeat them.]

Writing Focus: Short Narrative

The following **Work in Progress** assignments build to a culminating **Writer's Workshop** at the end of the collection.

• The Most Dangerous Game	Finding a conflict (p. 30)
• A Sound of Thunder	Listing main events (p. 48)
• The Birds	Creating a setting (p. 78)
• Poison	Using dialogue (p. 92)
• The Interlopers	Writing a surprise ending (p. 102)

Writer's Workshop: Narrative Writing / Short Narrative (p. 112)

OBJECTIVES

1. Read and interpret the story
2. Analyze conflict
3. Monitor comprehension
4. Express understanding through critical thinking/speaking, creative writing, analyzing characters, or drawing
5. Identify and use powerful verbs
6. Understand and use new words

SKILLS

Literary
- Analyze conflict

Reading
- Monitor comprehension

Writing
- Diagram details of a conflict
- Write a sequel
- Analyze characters

Critical Thinking/Speaking
- Compare the story with a movie

Drawing
- Map the story's setting

Grammar
- Use vivid verbs

Vocabulary
- Use new words

Viewing/Representing
- Compare a painting with the story (ATE)
- Relate art to the literature (ATE)
- Respond to a painting (ATE)

Planning

- **Block Schedule**
  Block Scheduling Lesson Plans with Pacing Guide
- **Traditional Schedule**
  Lesson Plans Including Strategies for English-Language Learners
- **One-Stop Planner**
  CD-ROM with Test Generator

Before You Read

THE MOST DANGEROUS GAME

Make the Connection

The Chase

The most basic kind of conflict in storytelling pits one person against someone or something else. In movies this conflict is often played out in hair-raising chases in which the hero or heroine is pursued by the villain over rooftops, across rivers, through sewers, down city streets. If the story is told well, we are hooked by the close calls—we keep wanting to know: "What happens next? Will he [or she] escape this time?"

Reading Skills and Strategies

Dialogue with the Text

Before you start this famous chase story, jot down what you **predict** its title might mean. What do you predict the conflict will be? Then, as you read, keep a **double-entry journal,** like the one shown here. On the left, write down comments made by the characters that seem important or controversial. On the right, record your responses to the statements.

Comment	My Response
"The world is made up of two classes—the hunters and the huntees." (page 14)	I'm not a huntee or hunter. This is a really cynical idea.

Elements of Literature

Conflict Makes a Story Go

A character's physical and mental struggles are **conflicts**. If a person is struggling against something outside himself or herself, the conflict is **external**. If the person is fighting to control some inner problem—such as fear, anger, or homesickness—the conflict is **internal**. Pure action stories usually hook us with violent external conflicts. Whatever kind of conflict a story is built on, it must be strong enough to keep us turning those pages—or glued to our seats.

Conflict is a struggle against some outside enemy or some internal problem.

For more on Conflict, see pages 32–33 and the Handbook of Literary Terms.

go.hrw.com
LEO 9-1

Preteaching Vocabulary

Words to Own

Have students read the definitions of the Words to Own listed at the bottom of the selection pages. Then, use these questions to reinforce their knowledge of the words.

1. Would someone who worked **indolently** deserve a raise? [no]
2. Would a **disarming** leader be able to calm an angry crowd? [yes]
3. Are VCRs and answering machines **amenities** in today's world? [yes]
4. Can a **palpable** lump be felt? [yes]
5. Is it **imprudent** for bicyclists to wear helmets? [no]
6. Is someone without **scruples** likely to return a lost wallet? [no]
7. If you are treated **solicitously,** are you treated kindly? [yes]
8. Would loud music be an **opiate** for a tired, crying baby? [no]
9. If a pilot flew **precariously,** would that be **deplorable**? [yes]

THE MOST DANGEROUS GAME

Richard Connell

Summary ▪▪

While traveling by yacht to a big-game hunt, Sanger Rainsford, an expert American hunter, accidentally falls overboard. After battling the sea, he swims to a mysterious island, where he discovers a medieval-style fortress. It is the home of a pleasure-loving Russian, General Zaroff, who is attended by Ivan, a fearsome Cossack manservant, and a pack of fierce hounds. Zaroff confides to Rainsford that his love of hunting has been thwarted by the lack of challenging prey. He boasts that he has stocked his island with the most dangerous and clever game of all—humans. When Rainsford refuses to join Zaroff in a hunt, the Russian general forces his "guest" to become the hunted. Zaroff stalks Rainsford, who must rely on his wits to escape capture and death. After a suspenseful chase, Rainsford outsmarts Zaroff, surprising the general in his bed chamber. The final resolution is not depicted, but it is implied that Zaroff is fed to his hounds.

Resources

Listening

Audio CD Library

For a recording of the short story, see the *Audio CD Library:*
* Disc 1, Track 3

Elements of Literature

Plot

For instruction on creating a plot summary, see *Literary Elements:*
* Transparency 1
* Worksheet, p. 4

Ⓐ Elements of Literature

Setting

What do we know so far about the story's setting? [It is set in the Caribbean.]

"Sailors have a curious dread of the place."

Off there to the right—somewhere—is a large island," said Whitney. "It's rather a mystery——"

"What island is it?" Rainsford asked.

"The old charts call it Ship-Trap Island," Whitney replied. "A suggestive name, isn't it? Sailors have a curious dread of the place. I don't know why. Some superstition——"

"Can't see it," remarked Rainsford, trying to peer through the dank tropical night that was palpable as it pressed its thick warm blackness in upon the yacht.

"You've good eyes," said Whitney, with a laugh, "and I've seen you pick off a moose moving in the brown fall bush at four hundred yards, but even you can't see four miles or so through a moonless Caribbean night."

"Nor four yards," admitted Rainsford. "Ugh! It's like moist black velvet." *← Simile*

"It will be light in Rio," promised Whitney. "We should make it in a few days. I hope the jaguar guns have come from

---

WORDS TO OWN

A **palpable** (pal'pə·bəl) *adj.:* easily felt or touched.

THE MOST DANGEROUS GAME **13**

Resources: Print and Media

Reading
* *Reading Skills and Strategies:*
  MiniRead Skill Lesson, p. 1
  Selection Skill Lesson p. 8
* *Graphic Organizers for Active Reading*, p. 1
* *Words to Own*, p. 1
* *Audio CD Library*,
  Disc 1, Track 3

Elements of Literature
* *Literary Elements*
  Transparency 1
  Worksheet, p. 4

Writing and Language
* *Daily Oral Grammar*
  Transparency 1
* *Grammar and Language Links*
  Worksheet, p. 1
* *Language Workshop CD-ROM*

Assessment
* *Formal Assessment*, p. 1
* *Portfolio Management System*, p. 89
* *Test Generator (One-Stop Planner CD-ROM)*

Internet
* go.hrw.com (keyword: LE0 9-1)

 A Critical Thinking

Expressing an Opinion

❓ Which man do you agree with, Rainsford or Whitney? Why? [Answers will vary.] What does each man's view reveal about him? [Sample response: Whitney shows he has some compassion for animals, but he hunts them anyway, as "great sport." Rainsford is cold and lacking in compassion, but this might make him a better hunter.]

B Reading Skills and Strategies

Dialogue with the Text

Ask students what clues in this dialogue might hint at the coming conflict in the story. Remind students to record important comments made by the characters in their journals and write their own responses to the comments.

Purdey's.[1] We should have some good hunting up the Amazon. Great sport, hunting."

"The best sport in the world," agreed Rainsford.

"For the hunter," amended Whitney. "Not for the jaguar."

"Don't talk rot, Whitney," said Rainsford. "You're a big-game hunter, not a philosopher. Who cares how a jaguar feels?"

"Perhaps the jaguar does," observed Whitney.

"Bah! They've no understanding."

"Even so, I rather think they understand one thing—fear. The fear of pain and the fear of death."

"Nonsense," laughed Rainsford. "This hot weather is making you soft, Whitney. Be a realist. The world is made up of two classes—the hunters and the huntees. Luckily, you and I are the hunters. Do you think we've passed that island yet?"

"I can't tell in the dark. I hope so."

"Why?" asked Rainsford.

"The place has a reputation—a bad one."

"Cannibals?" suggested Rainsford.

"Hardly. Even cannibals wouldn't live in such a Godforsaken place. But it's gotten into sailor lore, somehow. Didn't you notice that the crew's nerves seemed a bit jumpy today?"

"They were a bit strange, now you mention it. Even Captain Nielsen——"

"Yes, even that tough-minded old Swede, who'd go up to the devil himself and ask him for a light. Those fishy blue eyes held a look I never saw there before. All I could get out of him was: 'This place has an evil name among seafaring men, sir.' Then he said to me, very gravely: 'Don't you feel anything?'—as if the air about us was actually poisonous. Now, you mustn't laugh when I tell you this—I did feel something like a sudden chill.

"There was no breeze. The sea was as flat as a plate-glass window. We were drawing near the island then. What I felt was a—a mental chill; a sort of sudden dread."

"Pure imagination," said Rainsford. "One superstitious sailor can taint the whole ship's company with his fear."

"Maybe. But sometimes I think sailors have an extra sense that tells them when they are in danger. Sometimes I think evil is a tangible thing—with wavelengths, just as sound and light have. An evil place can, so to speak, broadcast vibrations of evil. Anyhow, I'm glad we're getting out of this zone. Well, I think I'll turn in now, Rainsford."

"I'm not sleepy," said Rainsford. "I'm going to smoke another pipe on the afterdeck."

"Good night, then, Rainsford. See you at breakfast."

"Right. Good night, Whitney."

There was no sound in the night as Rainsford sat there but the muffled throb of the engine that drove the yacht swiftly through the darkness, and the swish and ripple of the wash of the propeller.

Rainsford, reclining in a steamer chair, indolently puffed on his favorite brier.[2] The sensuous drowsiness of the night was on him. "It's so dark," he thought, "that I could sleep without closing my eyes; the night would be my eyelids——"

An abrupt sound startled him. Off to the right he heard it, and his ears, expert in such matters, could not be mistaken. Again he heard the sound, and again. Somewhere, off in the blackness, someone had fired a gun three times.

Rainsford sprang up and moved quickly to the rail, mystified. He strained his eyes in the direction from which the reports had come, but it was like trying to see through a blanket. He leaped upon the rail and balanced himself there, to get greater elevation; his pipe, striking a rope, was knocked from his mouth. He lunged for it; a short, hoarse cry came from his lips as he realized he had reached too far and had lost his balance. The cry was pinched off short as the blood-warm waters of the Caribbean Sea closed over his head.

---

2. **brier** (brī′ər): tobacco pipe made from the root of a brier bush or tree.

WORDS TO OWN
indolently (in′də·lənt·lē) *adv.:* lazily.

---

1. **Purdey's:** British manufacturer of hunting equipment.

(handwritten note in margin: SIMILE)

Reaching All Students

Struggling Readers

Monitoring Reading Strategies was introduced on page 12. For a lesson directly tied to this story that teaches students to monitor strategies by using a strategy called Think-Aloud, see the *Reading Skills and Strategies* binder:
• MiniRead Skill Lesson, p. 1
• Selection Skill Lesson, p. 8

English Language Learners

Students may be unfamiliar with the story's hunting-related vocabulary, particularly multiple-meaning words such as *game, prey, report,* and *quarry.* Discuss the meanings of these words and others, such as *huntees, twenty-two,* and *caliber.* For additional strategies to supplement instruction for these students, see
• *Lesson Plans Including Strategies for English-Language Learners*

Advanced Learners

Challenge these students to carefully consider the character of the villain, General Zaroff, as they read the story. Do they consider him to be a classic villain? Have them suggest examples of classic villains in other stories they have read or in movies they have seen. Ask them to compare and contrast the characteristics of these villains with those of Zaroff.

He struggled up to the surface and tried to cry out, but the wash from the speeding yacht slapped him in the face and the salt water in his open mouth made him gag and strangle. Desperately he struck out with strong strokes after the receding lights of the yacht, but he stopped before he had swum fifty feet. A certain coolheadedness had come to him; it was not the first time he had been in a tight place. There was a chance that his cries could be heard by someone aboard the yacht, but that chance was slender and grew more slender as the yacht raced on. He wrestled himself out of his clothes and shouted with all his power. The lights of the yacht became faint and ever-vanishing fireflies; then they were blotted out entirely by the night.

METAPHOR

Rainsford remembered the shots. They had come from the right, and doggedly he swam in that direction, swimming with slow, deliberate strokes, conserving his strength. For a seemingly endless time he fought the sea. He began to count his strokes; he could do possibly a hundred more and then——

Rainsford heard a sound. It came out of the darkness, a high screaming sound, the sound of an animal in an extremity of anguish and terror.

He did not recognize the animal that made the sound; he did not try to; with fresh vitality he swam toward the sound. He heard it again; then it was cut short by another noise, crisp, staccato.

"Pistol shot," muttered Rainsford, swimming on.

Ten minutes of determined effort brought another sound to his ears—the most welcome he had ever heard—the muttering and growling of the sea breaking on a rocky shore. He was almost on the rocks before he saw them; on a night less calm he would have been shattered against them. With his remaining strength he dragged himself from the swirling waters. Jagged crags appeared to jut into the opaqueness.[3]

He forced himself upward, hand over hand. Gasping, his hands raw, he reached a flat place at the top. Dense jungle came down to the very edge of the cliffs. What perils that tangle of trees and underbrush might hold for him did not concern Rainsford just then. All he knew was that he was safe from his enemy, the sea, and that utter weariness was on him. He flung himself down at the jungle edge and tumbled headlong into the deepest sleep of his life.

When he opened his eyes he knew from the position of the sun that it was late in the afternoon. Sleep had given him new vigor; a sharp hunger was picking at him. He looked about him, almost cheerfully.

"Where there are pistol shots, there are men. Where there are men, there is food," he thought. But what kind of men, he wondered, in so forbidding a place? An unbroken front of snarled and ragged jungle fringed the shore.

He saw no sign of a trail through the closely knit web of weeds and trees; it was easier to go along the shore, and Rainsford floundered along by the water. Not far from where he had landed, he stopped.

Some wounded thing, by the evidence a large animal, had thrashed about in the underbrush; the jungle weeds were crushed down and the moss was lacerated; one patch of weeds was stained crimson. A small, glittering object not far away caught Rainsford's eye and he picked it up. It was an empty cartridge.

"A twenty-two," he remarked. "That's odd. It must have been a fairly large animal too. The hunter had his nerve with him to tackle it with a light gun. It's clear that the brute put up a fight. I suppose the first three shots I heard was when the hunter flushed his quarry[4] and wounded it. The last shot was when he trailed it here and finished it."

He examined the ground closely and found what he had hoped to find—the print of hunting boots. They pointed along the cliff in the direction he had been going. Eagerly he hurried along, now slipping on a rotten log or a loose stone, but making headway; night was beginning to settle down on the island.

Bleak darkness was blacking out the sea and

---

3. **opaqueness** (ō·pāk′nis): here, darkness. Something opaque does not let light pass through. Milk is an opaque liquid; water is not.

4. **flushed his quarry:** drove the animal he was hunting out of its shelter or hiding place.

C Elements of Literature
Conflict
❓ What is the conflict described here? [It is an external conflict; the conflict is between Rainsford and the sea as he fights to keep from drowning.]

D Critical Thinking
Expressing an Opinion
❓ Would you swim toward such a horrible sound, especially if you didn't recognize it? Why or why not? [Sample responses: Yes, reaching land is the only way to survive; no, the sound could indicate something even more dangerous than the sea.]

E Reading Skills and Strategies
Dialogue with the Text
❓ This passage generates suspense by leaving questions unanswered. What questions do you have? Record them in your journal. [Possible questions: What was killed? Who was the hunter?]

Using Students' Strengths

Visual Learners
Invite these students to work in small groups to create storyboards that illustrate the central events in the plot. Suggest that each group use a 3-inch x 3-inch grid of nine separate panels. The students' first task will be to make a list of the events they want to include, choosing scenes that are essential for telling the story. Students within a group may want to collaborate on creating illustrations of events for the storyboard panels, or they may prefer to designate one or more members to create the illustrations. One student in the group should check that the illustrations accurately depict the story. Ask groups to display their completed storyboards. Discuss differences among the storyboards.

Verbal Learners
Assign students to work with partners. One student will take the role of Zaroff and the other will play Rainsford. Give students about ten minutes to prepare a brief dialogue that did not take place but that would be appropriate in the story. Students should speak in character and refer to events in the story. Have students present their dialogues to the class.

Casanova (1987) by Julio Larraz. Oil on canvas (60″ × 69″).

RESPONDING TO THE ART

Cuban American artist **Julio Larraz** (1944–) has painted primarily in the United States, but his works often refer in some way to his native land.

Activity. Point out to students that this painting, titled *Casanova*, depicts a man without scruples or moral sense who "hunted" women for his own pleasure. You might have students compare the man in the painting with the description of General Zaroff on p. 17. Also, as students continue to read the story, have them look for other comparisons between the two men.

Ⓐ Elements of Literature
Conflict

❓ The writer describes Rainsford's conflict with the sea by personifying it as a creature with greedy lips. Does this comparison make sense? Why or why not? [Possible response: Yes, Rainsford's battle to survive in the sea was so fierce, perhaps he now views the sea as somehow alive and out to get him.]

Ⓑ Reading Skills and Strategies
Dialogue with the Text

Ask students to make a prediction about who this giant man is and about the role he will play in the story. Have them record their predictions in their journals. [Possible predictions: The man is the hunter Rainsford heard or a servant of the hunter's; the man will be Rainsford's adversary.]

jungle when Rainsford sighted the lights. He came upon them as he turned a crook in the coastline, and his first thought was that he had come upon a village, for there were many lights. But as he forged along he saw to his great astonishment that all the lights were in one enormous building—a lofty structure with pointed towers plunging upward into the gloom. His eyes made out the shadowy outlines of a palatial château;[5] it was set on a high bluff, and on three sides of it cliffs dived down to where the sea licked greedy lips in the shadows.

"Mirage," thought Rainsford. But it was no mirage, he found, when he opened the tall spiked iron gate. The stone steps were real enough; the massive door with a leering gargoyle for a knocker was real enough; yet about it all hung an air of unreality.

He lifted the knocker, and it creaked up stiffly, as if it had never before been used. He let it fall, and it startled him with its booming loudness. He thought he heard steps within; the door remained closed. Again Rainsford lifted the heavy knocker and let it fall. The door opened then, opened as suddenly as if it were on a spring, and Rainsford stood blinking in the river of glaring gold light that poured out. The first thing Rainsford's eyes discerned was the largest man Rainsford had ever seen—a gigantic creature, solidly made and blackbearded to the waist. In his hand the man held a long-barreled revolver, and

5. **château** (sha·tō′): large country house.

16 THE SHORT-STORY COLLECTIONS

Skill Link

Using Reference Material

Review with students the use of dictionaries and thesauruses to determine the precise meaning and usage of words. Then, have students work in groups of three, with each group responsible for three Words to Own. Groups should use references to complete a chart like the one at right. Each member should be responsible for one word but help in charting the others.

Word	Meaning	Connotation	Antonym	Sample Sentence
palpable	tangible, noticeable	unnaturally dense	imperceptible	The captured animal's terror became palpable to the onlookers.

he was pointing it straight at Rainsford's heart.

Out of the snarl of beard two small eyes regarded Rainsford.

"Don't be alarmed," said Rainsford, with a smile which he hoped was <u>disarming</u>. "I'm no robber. I fell off a yacht. My name is Sanger Rainsford of New York City."

The menacing look in the eyes did not change. The revolver pointed as rigidly as if the giant were a statue. He gave no sign that he understood Rainsford's words or that he had even heard them. He was dressed in uniform, a black uniform trimmed with gray astrakhan.[6]

"I'm Sanger Rainsford of New York," Rainsford began again. "I fell off a yacht. I am hungry."

The man's only answer was to raise with his thumb the hammer of his revolver. Then Rainsford saw the man's free hand go to his forehead in a military salute, and he saw him click his heels together and stand at attention. Another man was coming down the broad marble steps, an erect, slender man in evening clothes. He advanced to Rainsford and held out his hand.

In a cultivated voice marked by a slight accent that gave it added precision and deliberateness, he said: "It is a very great pleasure and honor to welcome Mr. Sanger Rainsford, the celebrated hunter, to my home."

Automatically Rainsford shook the man's hand.

"I've read your book about hunting snow leopards in Tibet, you see," explained the man. "I am General Zaroff."

Rainsford's first impression was that the man was singularly handsome; his second was that there was an original, almost bizarre quality about the general's face. He was a tall man past middle age, for his hair was a vivid white; but his thick eyebrows and pointed military moustache were as black as the night from which Rainsford had come. His eyes, too, were black and very bright. He had high cheekbones, a sharp-cut nose, a spare, dark face, the face of a man used to giving orders, the face of an aristocrat. Turning to

The menacing look in the eyes did not change.

the giant in uniform, the general made a sign. The giant put away his pistol, saluted, withdrew.

"Ivan is an incredibly strong fellow," remarked the general, "but he has the misfortune to be deaf and dumb. A simple fellow, but, I'm afraid, like all his race, a bit of a savage."

"Is he Russian?"

"He is a Cossack,"[7] said the general, and his smile showed red lips and pointed teeth. "So am I."

"Come," he said, "we shouldn't be chatting here. We can talk later. Now you want clothes, food, rest. You shall have them. This is a most restful spot."

Ivan had reappeared, and the general spoke to him with lips that moved but gave forth no sound.

"Follow Ivan, if you please, Mr. Rainsford," said the general. "I was about to have my dinner when you came. I'll wait for you. You'll find that my clothes will fit you, I think."

It was to a huge, beam-ceilinged bedroom with a canopied bed big enough for six men that Rainsford followed the silent giant. Ivan laid out an evening suit, and Rainsford, as he put it on, noticed that it came from a London tailor who ordinarily cut and sewed for none below the rank of duke.

The dining room to which Ivan conducted him was in many ways remarkable. There was a medieval magnificence about it; it suggested a baronial hall of feudal times, with its oaken panels, its high ceiling, its vast refectory table[8] where two-score men could sit down to eat. About the hall were the mounted heads of many animals—lions, tigers, elephants, moose, bears; larger or more perfect specimens Rainsford had

---

7. **Cossack** (käs′ak′): member of a group from Ukraine, many of whom served as horsemen to the Russian czars and were famed for their fierceness in battle.
8. **refectory table:** long, narrow table, like the tables used in a monastery or college dining hall.

WORDS TO OWN
disarming (dis·ärm′iŋ) *adj.*: removing or lessening suspicions or fears.

---

6. **astrakhan** (as′trə·kən): curly fur of very young lambs.

C **Reading Skills and Strategies**
Dialogue with the Text
? What do you think of the giant's behavior? [Possible responses: It might be normal behavior for people who live in an isolated area; it isn't normal behavior and indicates a sense of paranoia or the fact that the giant has something to hide.]

D **Struggling Readers**
Summarizing
Have students make a list of the dialogue, actions, and descriptive details that the author uses to characterize Zaroff. Then, have them use this list to create a summary of Zaroff's character.

E **Reading Skills and Strategies**
Dialogue with the Text
? Do you find this story to be believable so far? Why or why not? Write your response in your journal. [Some students may say that it is not very believable. How could such a palatial chateau be kept a secret, especially since Zaroff must have hired people to take care of things? Other students may say that it is believable, pointing out that there are occasional news reports about wealthy, eccentric people building odd residences in strange and isolated places.]

Getting Students Involved

Cooperative Learning
The following grouping principles may be useful in helping you to ensure successful cooperative learning activities throughout the year.

- Vary group size from two or three to five or six, depending on the purpose.
- Define the group's task clearly. Students' commitment is enhanced when they know how the work of the group is related to the overall goal.

- Encourage groups, with your help, to assign clearly defined roles to individual members.
- Help students evaluate and recognize the progress they make.
- Provide clear and motivating follow-up activities when the work of the group or partners is completed.

A Historical Connections

In the nineteenth and early twentieth centuries, French was the preferred language of the Russian aristocracy and educated classes. It was spoken at the czar's court and at all aristocratic social gatherings. Zaroff's reference to reading in French, as well as his use of French phrases later in the story, implies that he was a member of the highest levels of Russian society.

B Reading Skills and Strategies

Dialogue with the Text

? Students will probably recognize that this statement by Zaroff is important, because it echoes the title of the story. Have them record their responses in their journals. What "game" might the general be referring to? [Possible answers: some unknown native beast; men.] What words and phrases does the author use to make this passage sound ominous? ["curious red-lipped smile," "same slow tone," "more dangerous game"]

C Critical Thinking

Expressing an Opinion

? Do you agree with the general's assertions here? Why or why not? [Sample responses: No, you are responsible for making your own way in life; no, being a poet is a very different thing from being a beggar or a hunter; yes, fate often plays a role in what you become.]

---

never seen. At the great table the general was sitting, alone.

"You'll have a cocktail, Mr. Rainsford," he suggested. The cocktail was surpassingly good; and, Rainsford noted, the table appointments were of the finest—the linen, the crystal, the silver, the china.

They were eating borscht, the rich red soup with sour cream so dear to Russian palates. Half apologetically General Zaroff said: "We do our best to preserve the amenities of civilization here. Please forgive any lapses. We are well off the beaten track, you know. Do you think the champagne has suffered from its long ocean trip?"

"Not in the least," declared Rainsford. He was finding the general a most thoughtful and affable host, a true cosmopolite.[9] But there was one small trait of the general's that made Rainsford uncomfortable. Whenever he looked up from his plate he found the general studying him, appraising him narrowly.

A "Perhaps," said General Zaroff, "you were surprised that I recognized your name. You see, I read all books on hunting published in English, French, and Russian. I have but one passion in my life, Mr. Rainsford, and it is the hunt."

"You have some wonderful heads here," said Rainsford as he ate a particularly well-cooked filet mignon. "That Cape buffalo is the largest I ever saw."

"Oh, that fellow. Yes, he was a monster."

"Did he charge you?"

"Hurled me against a tree," said the general. "Fractured my skull. But I got the brute."

"I've always thought," said Rainsford, "that the Cape buffalo is the most dangerous of all big game."

B For a moment the general did not reply; he was smiling his curious red-lipped smile. Then he said slowly: "No. You are wrong, sir. The Cape buffalo is not the most dangerous big game." He sipped his wine. "Here in my preserve on this island," he said in the same slow tone, "I hunt more dangerous game."

9. **cosmopolite** (käz·mäp′ə·līt′): knowledgeable citizen of the world.

Rainsford expressed his surprise. "Is there big game on this island?"

The general nodded. "The biggest."

"Really?"

"Oh, it isn't here naturally, of course. I have to stock the island."

"What have you imported, general?" Rainsford asked. "Tigers?"

The general smiled. "No," he said. "Hunting tigers ceased to interest me some years ago. I exhausted their possibilities, you see. No thrill left in tigers, no real danger. I live for danger, Mr. Rainsford."

The general took from his pocket a gold cigarette case and offered his guest a long black cigarette with a silver tip; it was perfumed and gave off a smell like incense.

"We will have some capital hunting, you and I," said the general. "I shall be most glad to have your society."

"But what game——" began Rainsford.

"I'll tell you," said the general. "You will be amused, I know. I think I may say, in all modesty, that I have done a rare thing. I have invented a new sensation. May I pour you another glass of port, Mr. Rainsford?"

"Thank you, general."

C The general filled both glasses and said: "God makes some men poets. Some He makes kings, some beggars. Me He made a hunter. My hand was made for the trigger, my father said. He was a very rich man, with a quarter of a million acres in the Crimea,[10] and he was an ardent sportsman. When I was only five years old, he gave me a little gun, specially made in Moscow for me, to shoot sparrows with. When I shot some of his prize turkeys with it, he did not punish me; he complimented me on my marksmanship. I killed my first bear in the Caucasus[11] when I was ten. My whole life has

10. **Crimea** (krī·mē′ə): peninsula in Ukraine jutting out into the Black Sea.
11. **Caucasus** (kô′kə·səs): mountainous region between southeastern Europe and western Asia.

WORDS TO OWN

amenities (ə·men′ə·tēz) *n*.: comforts and conveniences.

Making the Connections

Cultural Connections

The Essence of Civility. A major character in this story, General Zaroff, describes himself as a "civilized man" and refers to luxuries such as champagne and fine tableware as "amenities of civilization." Ask students to define and discuss the word *civilized*. You might have them look up the words *civilized* ("educated," "brought from a primitive or savage state," "refined") and *civilization* ("an advanced stage of development in

human society with a high level of arts and sciences"). Point out the differences between these words and *civility*, which means "politeness, courtesy." Also, invite students who have knowledge of other languages and cultures to name words with similar meanings. Then, lead students into a discussion of the true qualities of a civilized person. Ask questions such as the following:

- In our culture, which material possessions, actions, or inner human qualities are viewed as evidence of civilization?
- Do you believe that material possessions or human qualities are more important as criteria for being civilized? Explain.
- Do you accept Zaroff's claim that he is a civilized man? Why or why not?

Tropical Storm with Tiger—Surprise (Le Douanier) by Henri Rousseau (1844–1910).

National Gallery, London.

been one prolonged hunt. I went into the army—it was expected of noblemen's sons—and for a time commanded a division of Cossack cavalry, but my real interest was always the hunt. I have hunted every kind of game in every land. It would be impossible for me to tell you how many animals I have killed."

The general puffed at his cigarette.

"After the debacle in Russia[12] I left the country, for it was <u>imprudent</u> for an officer of the czar to stay there. Many noble Russians lost everything. I, luckily, had invested heavily in American securities, so I shall never have to open a tearoom in Monte Carlo[13] or drive a taxi in Paris. Naturally,

I continued to hunt—grizzlies in your Rockies, crocodiles in the Ganges,[14] rhinoceroses in East Africa. It was in Africa that the Cape buffalo hit me and laid me up for six months. As soon as I recovered I started for the Amazon to hunt jaguars, for I had heard they were unusually cunning. They weren't." The Cossack sighed. "They were no match at all for a hunter with his wits about him and a high-powered rifle. I was bitterly disappointed. I was lying in my tent with a splitting headache one night when a terrible thought pushed its way into my mind. Hunting

12. **debacle** (di·bä′kəl) **in Russia:** A debacle is an overwhelming defeat. Zaroff is referring to the Russian Revolution of 1917, in which the czar was overthrown.
13. **Monte Carlo** (mänt′ə kär′lō): gambling resort in Monaco, a country on the Mediterranean Sea.

14. **Ganges** (gan′jēz): river in northern India and Bangladesh.

WORDS TO OWN
imprudent (im·prood′'nt) *adj.:* unwise.

D **Historical Connections**

After the Russian Revolution of 1917, many Russian aristocrats—being French-speaking—fled to France or to French-speaking areas of Europe, where they had to work a variety of jobs in order to earn a living. Zaroff's obvious disdain for his fellow Russian aristocrats reveals a startling lack of sympathy and extreme arrogance.

E **Elements of Literature**

Conflict

? How has the lack of an external conflict led to an internal conflict for General Zaroff? [He is frustrated by the lack of challenging game animals and must now fight against boredom and disappointment.]

RESPONDING TO THE ART

Because he was self-taught, the French painter **Henri Rousseau** (1844–1910) is known as a primitive artist. The childlike simplicity and imaginative power of his works have intrigued millions of viewers. (For more about Rousseau, see the following page.) **Activity.** After students have read the story, ask the following question about this painting: In what ways does Rousseau's *Surprise* remind you of the contest between Rainsford and Zaroff? [Sample responses: The ferocious tiger getting ready to pounce on a victim is like Rainsford ambushing Zaroff; the menacing quality of the painting expresses the mood in the story.]

Using Students' Strengths

Interpersonal Learners

Suggest that students create an "I Am" poem for either Rainsford or Zaroff. Tell students that the poem should consist of several stanzas. Explain that each stanza should be a list of five statements about what the character knows, does, feels, or says (for example, "I want . . ." or "I dream . . ."). Each stanza should conclude with a statement that proclaims "I am . . . ." The statements should reflect the character as he appears in the story. Encourage students to go back through the story to locate vivid language that they can incorporate into their poems. Invite students to share their poems by reading them aloud to the class or to small groups.

A Reading Skills and Strategies

Dialogue with the Text

Make a prediction about what the general is leading up to. Write the prediction in your journal. [Possible answers: He is going to reveal how he came to be on the island, hunting a mysterious beast; he is going to tell how he discovered prey that again made hunting an exciting pursuit.]

Le Charmeuse des serpentes (The Snake Charmer) (detail) (1907) by Henri Rousseau. Oil on canvas (160 cm × 189.5 cm).

Erich Lessing/Art Resource, NY.

was beginning to bore me! And hunting, remember, had been my life. I have heard that in America businessmen often go to pieces when they give up the business that has been their life."

"Yes, that's so," said Rainsford.

The general smiled. "I had no wish to go to **A** pieces," he said. "I must do something. Now, mine is an analytical mind, Mr. Rainsford. Doubtless that is why I enjoy the problems of the chase."

20 THE SHORT-STORY COLLECTIONS

Crossing the Curriculum

Science

Some of the species of wildlife mentioned in the story are extremely endangered. The rhinoceros, for example, has been hunted to near extinction. Hunting for sport isn't the only reason for the rhino's decline. Another is demand for rhinoceros horn—prized in some cultures for its medicinal value—which can command tens of thousands of dollars. Because of hunting and diminished habitat size, the population of the rhino, the third-largest land animal, has shrunk from 65,000 in 1970 to less than 11,000 today. Encourage students interested in wildlife to research one of the animals mentioned as quarry by Zaroff or Rainsford, such as jaguars, crocodiles, grizzly bears, or cape buffalo. Students may investigate the animal's size, habits, habitat, and whether or not it is an endangered or protected species. Alternatively, students can research some of the methods being used in national parks or game reserves in places like East Africa to preserve and protect their wildlife populations. Students can present their research in a visual presentation such as a slide show, web page, or other informative display that includes photos or illustrations of the animal species being discussed.

"No doubt, General Zaroff."

"So," continued the general, "I asked myself why the hunt no longer fascinated me. You are much younger than I am, Mr. Rainsford, and have not hunted as much, but you perhaps can guess the answer."

"What was it?"

"Simply this: Hunting had ceased to be what you call a sporting proposition. It had become too easy. I always got my quarry. Always. There is no greater bore than perfection."

The general lit a fresh cigarette.

"No animal had a chance with me anymore. That is no boast; it is a mathematical certainty. The animal had nothing but his legs and his instinct. Instinct is no match for reason. When I thought of this, it was a tragic moment for me, I can tell you."

Rainsford leaned across the table, absorbed in what his host was saying.

"It came to me as an inspiration what I must do," the general went on.

"And that was?"

The general smiled the quiet smile of one who has faced an obstacle and surmounted it with success. "I had to invent a new animal to hunt," he said.

"A new animal? You're joking."

"Not at all," said the general. "I never joke about hunting. I needed a new animal. I found one. So I bought this island, built this house, and here I do my hunting. The island is perfect for my purposes—there are jungles with a maze of trails in them, hills, swamps——"

"But the animal, General Zaroff?"

"Oh," said the general, "it supplies me with the most exciting hunting in the world. No other hunting compares with it for an instant. Every day I hunt, and I never grow bored now, for I have a quarry with which I can match my wits."

Rainsford's bewilderment showed in his face.

"I wanted the ideal animal to hunt," explained the general. "So I said: 'What are the attributes of an ideal quarry?' And the answer was, of course: 'It must have courage, cunning, and, above all, it must be able to reason.'"

"But no animal can reason," objected Rainsford.

"My dear fellow," said the general, "there is

one that can."

"But you can't mean——" gasped Rainsford.

"And why not?"

"I can't believe you are serious, General Zaroff. This is a grisly joke."

"Why should I not be serious? I am speaking of hunting."

"Hunting? Good God, General Zaroff, what you speak of is murder."

The general laughed with entire good nature. He regarded Rainsford quizzically. "I refuse to believe that so modern and civilized a young man as you seem to be harbors romantic ideas about the value of human life. Surely your experiences in the war——"

"Did not make me condone coldblooded murder," finished Rainsford stiffly.

Laughter shook the general. "How extraordinarily droll you are!" he said. "One does not expect nowadays to find a young man of the educated class, even in America, with such a naive, and, if I may say so, mid-Victorian point of view. It's like finding a snuffbox in a limousine. Ah, well, doubtless you had Puritan ancestors. So many Americans appear to have had. I'll wager you'll forget your notions when you go hunting with me. You've a genuine new thrill in store for you, Mr. Rainsford."

"Thank you, I'm a hunter, not a murderer."

"Dear me," said the general, quite unruffled, "again that unpleasant word. But I think I can show you that your scruples are quite ill-founded."

"Yes?"

"Life is for the strong, to be lived by the strong, and if need be, taken by the strong. The weak of the world were put here to give the strong pleasure. I am strong. Why should I not use my gift? If I wish to hunt, why should I not? I hunt the scum of the earth—sailors from tramp ships—lascars,[15] blacks, Chinese, whites, mongrels—a thoroughbred horse or hound is

---

15. **lascars** (las'kərz): East Indian sailors employed on European ships.

WORDS TO OWN

scruples (skroo'pəlz) *n*.: feelings of doubt or guilt about a suggested action.

B Critical Thinking
Analyzing
❓ Why might a level of perfection be boring? [Sample response: Achieving perfection is the challenge—once you can do something perfectly, it becomes less exciting.]

C Reading Skills and Strategies

Dialogue with the Text
❓ Do you agree with Zaroff's opinion that "instinct is no match for reason"? Explain your answer in your journal. [Possible answers: Yes, instinct does not involve calculation or thought; no, instinct is quicker and often stronger than reason.]

D Elements of Literature
Conflict
❓ Who is in conflict here? [Rainsford and Zaroff] What is the conflict? [They disagree about the idea of hunting men for sport.]

E Advanced Learners
Analyzing Beliefs
❓ Invite students to analyze Zaroff's statements here. Suggest they keep the following questions in mind: What is flawed about Zaroff's interpretation of Darwinian "survival of the fittest"? What would happen if everyone adhered to this philosophy? Are there any historical examples in which this or a similar philosophy was put into practice?

Getting Students Involved

Cooperative Learning
Researching Scientific Theory. Writers often make use of new ideas in science or psychology. In the early part of the twentieth century, the ideas of the English naturalist Charles Darwin (1809–1882) were hotly debated. Darwin formulated a theory of evolution that included a process that he called natural selection. Many people, like General Zaroff in this story, simplified and distorted this idea. They took it to mean that only the

strongest members of a species were worthwhile—which of course is not true at all.

Have interested students work in small groups to investigate Darwin's theory of natural selection. Suggest the following questions for students to research:

- What is natural selection, and what are some common examples?
- What kind of research did Darwin conduct before reaching his conclusions?

- What evidence is there that Darwin was painstaking in his observations?

Have groups present their findings with visual support. Challenge members of the audience to suggest how Zaroff distorted Darwin's theory.

A Critical Thinking

Extending the Text

One of the subthemes of this story is the idea that only point of view distinguishes hunting from murder. Invite students to discuss this idea. Suggest they make a Venn diagram with the headings "Hunting" and "Murder" that compares and contrasts the two.

B Vocabulary Note

Multiple Meanings

Point out the meaning of *game* as Zaroff uses it here: a competition for amusement. Then, remind students of a second definition of the word: animals hunted for sport. Suggest they think back to what they wrote about the story's title and then discuss how the multiple meanings of *game* give the title more resonance.

C Historical Connection

In czarist Russia, men convicted of crimes were subject to a two-part sentence. The first part, known as the punishment phase, was a beating, often a flogging, or knouting. The second phase—if one survived the first—was a prison sentence. Convicted members of the Russian aristocracy did not have to suffer the punishment phase. The reference to knouting here suggests that the author was perhaps implying that Zaroff's views were partly a product of the Russian aristocratic society in which he was raised.

worth more than a score of them."

"But they are men," said Rainsford hotly.

"Precisely," said the general. "That is why I use them. It gives me pleasure. They can reason, after a fashion. So they are dangerous."

"But where do you get them?"

The general's left eyelid fluttered down in a wink. "This island is called Ship-Trap," he answered. "Sometimes an angry god of the high seas sends them to me. Sometimes, when Providence is not so kind, I help Providence a bit. Come to the window with me."

Rainsford went to the window and looked out toward the sea.

"Watch! Out there!" exclaimed the general, pointing into the night. Rainsford's eyes saw only blackness, and then, as the general pressed a button, far out to sea Rainsford saw the flash of lights.

The general chuckled. "They indicate a channel," he said, "where there's none; giant rocks with razor edges crouch like a sea monster with wide-open jaws. They can crush a ship as easily as I crush this nut." He dropped a walnut on the hardwood floor and brought his heel grinding down on it. "Oh, yes," he said, casually, as if in answer to a question, "I have electricity. We try to be civilized here."

"Civilized? And you shoot down men?"

A trace of anger was in the general's black eyes, but it was there for but a second, and he said, in his most pleasant manner: "Dear me, what a righteous young man you are! I assure you I do not do the thing you suggest. That would be barbarous. I treat these visitors with every consideration. They get plenty of good food and exercise. They get into splendid physical condition. You shall see for yourself tomorrow."

"What do you mean?"

"We'll visit my training school," smiled the general. "It's in the cellar. I have about a dozen pupils down there now. They're from the Spanish bark *San Lucar* that had the bad luck to go on the rocks out there. A very inferior lot, I regret to say. Poor specimens and more accustomed to the deck than to the jungle."

He raised his hand, and Ivan, who served as waiter, brought thick Turkish coffee. Rainsford,

with an effort, held his tongue in check.

"It's a game, you see," pursued the general blandly. "I suggest to one of them that we go hunting. I give him a supply of food and an excellent hunting knife. I give him three hours' start. I am to follow, armed only with a pistol of the smallest caliber and range. If my quarry eludes me for three whole days, he wins the game. If I find him"—the general smiled—"he loses."

"Suppose he refuses to be hunted?"

"Oh," said the general, "I give him his option, of course. He need not play that game if he doesn't wish to. If he does not wish to hunt, I turn him over to Ivan. Ivan once had the honor of serving as official knouter[16] to the Great White Czar, and he has his own ideas of sport. Invariably, Mr. Rainsford, invariably they choose the hunt."

"And if they win?"

The smile on the general's face widened. "To date I have not lost," he said.

Then he added, hastily: "I don't wish you to think me a braggart, Mr. Rainsford. Many of them afford only the most elementary sort of problem. Occasionally I strike a tartar.[17] One almost did win. I eventually had to use the dogs."

"The dogs?"

"This way, please. I'll show you."

The general steered Rainsford to a window. The lights from the windows sent a flickering illumination that made grotesque patterns on the courtyard below, and Rainsford could see moving about there a dozen or so huge black shapes; as they turned toward him, their eyes glittered greenly.

"A rather good lot, I think," observed the general. "They are let out at seven every night. If anyone should try to get into my house—or out of it—something extremely regrettable would occur to him." He hummed a snatch of song from the Folies-Bergère.[18]

"And now," said the general, "I want to show

16. **knouter** (nout′ər): person who beats criminals with a knout, a kind of leather whip.
17. **strike a tartar:** get more than one bargained for. A tartar is a violent, unmanageable person.
18. **Folies-Bergère** (fô′lē ber·zher′): famous nightclub in Paris.

Skill Link

Identifying Verbs

You might want to use the following exercise before you teach the Grammar Link exercise on powerful verbs, p. 31. This exercise will help you assess students' skill in identifying verbs. Remind students that verb forms may include a helping verb.

Identify the verb or verbs in each of the following sentences. For a review of verbs, see pp. 993–994 in the Language Handbook.

1. The general played with him. [played]
2. I'll give him a trail to follow. [will give]
3. He forced himself upward, hand over hand. [forced]
4. One superstitious sailor can taint the ship's company with his fear. [can taint]
5. He heard, far off in the jungle, the faint report of a pistol. [heard]
6. I have played the fox; now I must play the cat of the fable. [have played; must play]
7. The general shrugged his shoulders and delicately ate a hothouse grape. [shrugged; ate]
8. The general sensed danger and leaped back with the agility of an ape. [sensed; leaped]
9. Twenty feet below him the sea rumbled and hissed. [rumbled; hissed]

you my new collection of heads. Will you come with me to the library?"

"I hope," said Rainsford, "that you will excuse me tonight, General Zaroff. I'm really not feeling at all well."

"Ah, indeed?" the general inquired solicitously. "Well, I suppose that's only natural, after your long swim. You need a good, restful night's sleep. Tomorrow you'll feel like a new man, I'll wager. Then we'll hunt, eh? I've one rather promising prospect——"

Rainsford was hurrying from the room.

"Sorry you can't go with me tonight," called the general. "I expect rather fair sport—a big, strong black. He looks resourceful—— Well, good night, Mr. Rainsford; I hope you have a good night's rest."

The bed was good and the pajamas of the softest silk, and he was tired in every fiber of his being, but nevertheless Rainsford could not quiet his brain with the opiate of sleep. He lay, eyes wide open. Once he thought he heard stealthy steps in the corridor outside his room. He sought to throw open the door; it would not open. He went to the window and looked out. His room was high up in one of the towers. The lights of the château were out now, and it was dark and silent, but there was a fragment of sallow moon, and by its wan light he could see, dimly, the courtyard; there, weaving in and out in the pattern of shadow, were black, noiseless forms; the hounds heard him at the window and looked up, expectantly, with their green eyes. Rainsford went back to the bed and lay down. By many methods he tried to put himself to sleep. He had achieved a doze when, just as morning began to come, he heard, far off in the jungle, the faint report of a pistol.

General Zaroff did not appear until luncheon. He was dressed faultlessly in the tweeds of a country squire. He was solicitous about the state of Rainsford's health.

"As for me," sighed the general, "I do not feel so well. I am worried, Mr. Rainsford. Last night I detected traces of my old complaint."

To Rainsford's questioning glance the general said: "Ennui. Boredom."

Then, taking a second helping of crêpes suzette,[19] the general explained: "The hunting was not good last night. The fellow lost his head. He made a straight trail that offered no problems at all. That's the trouble with these sailors; they have dull brains to begin with, and they do not know how to get about in the woods. They do excessively stupid and obvious things. It's most annoying. Will you have another glass of Chablis, Mr. Rainsford?"

"General," said Rainsford firmly, "I wish to leave this island at once."

The general raised his thickets of eyebrows; he seemed hurt. "But, my dear fellow," the general protested, "you've only just come. You've had no hunting——"

"I wish to go today," said Rainsford. He saw the dead black eyes of the general on him, studying him. General Zaroff's face suddenly brightened.

He filled Rainsford's glass with venerable Chablis from a dusty bottle.

"Tonight," said the general, "we will hunt—you and I."

Rainsford shook his head. "No, general," he said. "I will not hunt."

The general shrugged his shoulders and delicately ate a hothouse grape. "As you wish, my friend," he said. "The choice rests entirely with you. But may I not venture to suggest that you will find my idea of sport more diverting than Ivan's?"

He nodded toward the corner where the giant stood, scowling, his thick arms crossed on his hogshead of chest.

"You don't mean——" cried Rainsford.

"My dear fellow," said the general, "have I not told you I always mean what I say about

---

19. **crêpes suzette** (krāp soo·zet'): thin pancakes folded in a hot orange-flavored sauce and served in flaming brandy.

WORDS TO OWN

solicitously (sə·lis'ə·təs·lē) *adv.*: in a concerned manner.

opiate (ō'pē·it) *n.*: anything that tends to soothe or calm someone. An opiate may also be a medicine containing opium or a related drug used to relieve pain.

D Reading Skills and Strategies
Analyzing

? What kinds of heads do you think are in Zaroff's new collection? [human heads] What is strange about Zaroff's reply when Rainsford says he doesn't feel well? [Sample answers: Zaroff blames Rainsford's ailment on the swim and doesn't consider the fact that he himself has made Rainsford ill with his revelations; Zaroff is solicitous about Rainsford's feeling ill, but the general has no feelings for his victims.]

E Elements of Literature
Conflict

? What conflict do Rainsford and Zaroff have here? [Zaroff wants Rainsford to hunt with him, but Rainsford doesn't want to.]

F Reading Skills and Strategies
Dialogue with the Text

? What does Zaroff mean? [He is suggesting that Rainsford either be his quarry or submit to Ivan's torture.] Are you surprised by this turn of events? Write your response to Zaroff's words in your journal.

Getting Students Involved

Cooperative Learning

In "The Most Dangerous Game," the hunter Rainsford suddenly and unexpectedly finds himself in the unusual position of being the "huntee." Have students supply examples of other dramatic works (including films) that use similarly ironic role-reversals as a plot device. [Possible responses: *The Prince and the Pauper, Trading Places*.] Discuss with students reasons why these types of ironic reversals are effective plot devices and the dramatic possibilities they allow the author. [Possible response: Role reversals allow the author to show how a character reacts to the experience of being in another's situation. In "The Most Dangerous Game," Rainsford had scoffed at his friend Whitney for suggesting that hunted animals experience pain or fear; the reversal is a dramatic device for teaching Rainsford a lesson in compassion.]

Conflict

? Discuss with students how the conflict changes from clashing viewpoints to physical opposition. Are Rainsford and Zaroff really evenly matched? [No, Zaroff has an advantage because he has a knowledge of the island and will be armed with a pistol; he also has a psychological advantage because he is the one on the offensive rather than the defensive.]

B Elements of Literature

Character

? What does this statement reveal about Zaroff's character? [Sample responses: It emphasizes how unbalanced he really is; it shows that Zaroff loves a dog but cannot feel compassion toward people.]

C Elements of Literature

Conflict

? What feelings or forces within himself must Rainsford control in order to survive? [Possible answers: panic, haste, impulsiveness.]

D Literary Connections

This allusion refers to one of Jean de la Fontaine's fables. In this fable, the fox tries to elude a pack of hounds by trying a hundred holes or hiding places while the cat tries only one—a tree. Rainsford is imitating both the fox and the cat in the fable.

---

hunting? This is really an inspiration. I drink to a foeman worthy of my steel—at last."

The general raised his glass, but Rainsford sat staring at him.

A "You'll find this game worth playing," the general said enthusiastically. "Your brain against mine. Your woodcraft against mine. Your strength and stamina against mine. Outdoor chess! And the stake is not without value, eh?"

"And if I win——" began Rainsford huskily.

"I'll cheerfully acknowledge myself defeated if I do not find you by midnight of the third day," said General Zaroff. "My sloop will place you on the mainland near a town."

The general read what Rainsford was thinking.

"Oh, you can trust me," said the Cossack. "I will give you my word as a gentleman and a sportsman. Of course you, in turn, must agree to say nothing of your visit here."

"I'll agree to nothing of the kind," said Rainsford.

"Oh," said the general, "in that case—— But why discuss that now? Three days hence we can discuss it over a bottle of Veuve Clicquot,[20] unless——"

The general sipped his wine.

Then a businesslike air animated him. "Ivan," he said to Rainsford, "will supply you with hunting clothes, food, a knife. I suggest you wear moccasins; they leave a poorer trail. I suggest too that you avoid the big swamp in the southeast corner of the island. We call it Death Swamp.

B There's quicksand there. One foolish fellow tried it. The deplorable part of it was that Lazarus followed him. You can imagine my feelings, Mr. Rainsford. I loved Lazarus; he was the finest hound in my pack. Well, I must beg you to excuse me now. I always take a siesta after lunch. You'll hardly have time for a nap, I fear. You'll want to start, no doubt. I shall not follow till dusk. Hunting at night is so much more exciting than by day, don't you think? Au revoir, Mr. Rainsford, au revoir."

20. **Veuve Clicquot** (vöv klē·kô'): brand of fine champagne.

General Zaroff, with a deep, courtly bow, strolled from the room.

From another door came Ivan. Under one arm he carried khaki hunting clothes, a haversack of food, a leather sheath containing a long-bladed hunting knife; his right hand rested on a cocked revolver thrust in the crimson sash about his waist. . . .

Rainsford had fought his way through the bush for two hours. "I must keep my nerve. I must keep my nerve," he said through tight teeth.

C He had not been entirely clearheaded when the château gates snapped shut behind him. His whole idea at first was to put distance between himself and General Zaroff, and, to this end, he had plunged along, spurred on by the sharp rowels[21] of something very like panic. Now he had got a grip on himself, had stopped, and was taking stock of himself and the situation.

He saw that straight flight was futile; inevitably it would bring him face to face with the sea. He was in a picture with a frame of water, and his operations, clearly, must take place within that frame.

"I'll give him a trail to follow," muttered Rainsford, and he struck off from the rude paths he had been following into the trackless wilderness. He executed a series of intricate loops; he doubled on his trail again and again, recalling all the lore of the fox hunt and all the dodges of the fox. Night found him leg-weary, with hands and face lashed by the branches, on a thickly wooded ridge. He knew it would be insane to blunder on through the dark, even if he had the strength. His need for rest was imperative and

D he thought: "I have played the fox; now I must play the cat of the fable." A big tree with a thick trunk and outspread branches was nearby, and taking care to leave not the slightest mark, he

21. **rowels** (rou'əlz): small wheels with spurs that horseback riders wear on their heels.

WORDS TO OWN

deplorable (dē·plôr'ə·bəl) *adj.*: regrettable; very bad.

"We call it Death Swamp. There's quicksand there."

Getting Students Involved

Cooperative Learning

"The Most Dangerous Game" Game. Have five or six students work in a small group to create a board game based on the story. Suggest as a possible goal for the game that players successfully negotiate the island within a limited number of turns. Or students may devise their own alternative goals and outcomes. Have them brainstorm rules, the layout of the board, the playing pieces or cards, and so on. Students should all take part in the brainstorming process but should then each take a different role. Each group should have a designer, artist, constructor, scribe, presenter, and perhaps a coordinator to see that individuals complete their tasks and that the group functions as a unit. The presenter can show the finished game to the class while other group members demonstrate how to play it.

climbed up into the crotch and stretching out on one of the broad limbs, after a fashion, rested. Rest brought him new confidence and almost a feeling of security. Even so zealous a hunter as General Zaroff could not trace him there, he told himself; only the devil himself could follow that complicated trail through the jungle after dark. But, perhaps, the general was a devil——

An apprehensive night crawled slowly by like a wounded snake, and sleep did not visit Rainsford, although the silence of a dead world was on the jungle. Toward morning, when a dingy gray was varnishing the sky, the cry of some startled bird focused Rainsford's attention in that direction. Something was coming through the bush, coming slowly, carefully, coming by the same winding way Rainsford had come. He flattened himself down on the limb, and through a screen of leaves almost as thick as tapestry, he watched. The thing that was approaching was a man.

It was General Zaroff. He made his way along with his eyes fixed in utmost concentration on the ground before him. He paused, almost beneath the tree, dropped to his knees and studied the ground. Rainsford's impulse was to hurl himself down like a panther, but he saw the general's right hand held something metallic—a small automatic pistol.

The hunter shook his head several times, as if he were puzzled. Then he straightened up and took from his case one of his black cigarettes; its pungent incenselike smoke floated up to Rainsford's nostrils.

Rainsford held his breath. The general's eyes had left the ground and were traveling inch by inch up the tree. Rainsford froze there, every muscle tensed for a spring. But the sharp eyes of the hunter stopped before they reached the limb where Rainsford lay; a smile spread over his brown face. Very deliberately he blew a smoke ring into the air; then he turned his back on the tree and walked carelessly away, back along the trail he had come. The swish of the underbrush against his hunting boots grew fainter and fainter.

Then pent-up air burst hotly from Rainsford's lungs. His first thought made him feel sick and numb. The general could follow a trail through

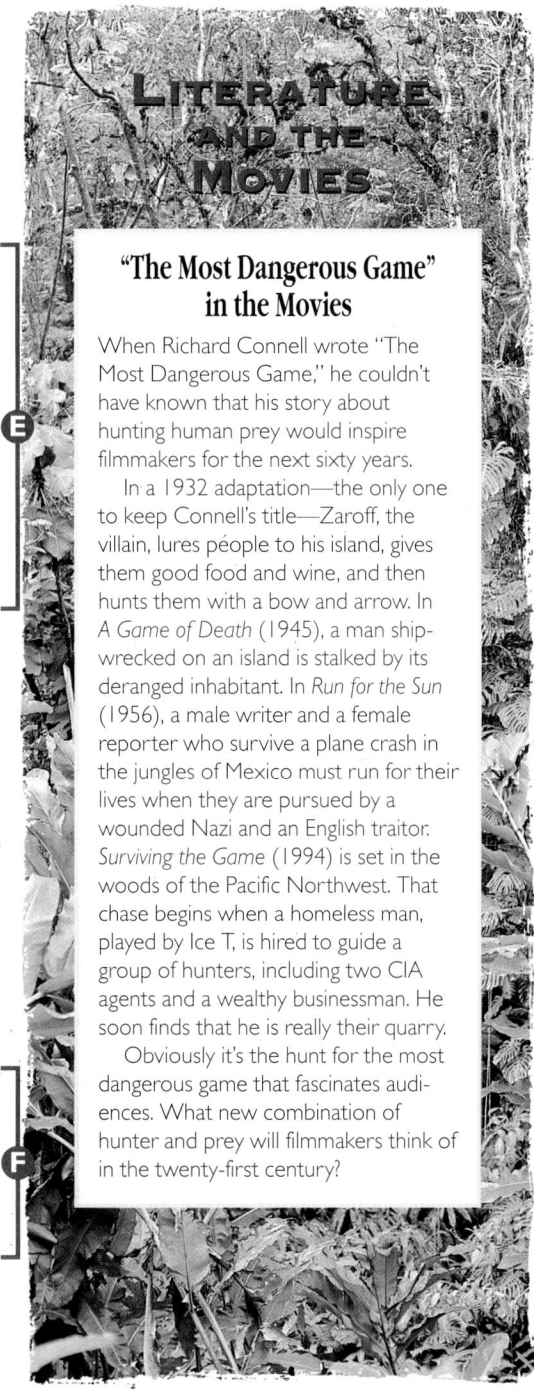

"The Most Dangerous Game" in the Movies

When Richard Connell wrote "The Most Dangerous Game," he couldn't have known that his story about hunting human prey would inspire filmmakers for the next sixty years.

In a 1932 adaptation—the only one to keep Connell's title—Zaroff, the villain, lures people to his island, gives them good food and wine, and then hunts them with a bow and arrow. In *A Game of Death* (1945), a man shipwrecked on an island is stalked by its deranged inhabitant. In *Run for the Sun* (1956), a male writer and a female reporter who survive a plane crash in the jungles of Mexico must run for their lives when they are pursued by a wounded Nazi and an English traitor. *Surviving the Game* (1994) is set in the woods of the Pacific Northwest. That chase begins when a homeless man, played by Ice T, is hired to guide a group of hunters, including two CIA agents and a wealthy businessman. He soon finds that he is really their quarry.

Obviously it's the hunt for the most dangerous game that fascinates audiences. What new combination of hunter and prey will filmmakers think of in the twenty-first century?

THE MOST DANGEROUS GAME **25**

E Reading Skills and Strategies

Dialogue with the Text
❓ How might Rainsford be feeling in this passage? [Possible responses: incredibly apprehensive, scared to death, determined to live.] If you were in Rainsford's position, what would you do? [Answers will vary.] Remind students to record their responses in their journals.

F Elements of Literature
Conflict
❓ Why does Zaroff smile and blow the smoke ring? [Possible answers: He knows Rainsford is in the tree and is playing with him; he thinks he is close to catching Rainsford.] Who seems to have the upper hand in the conflict at this point? [Possible responses: Zaroff, because he is toying with Rainsford. Rainsford; because he has outsmarted Zaroff.]

LITERATURE AND THE MOVIES
Invite students to make a list of other movies they have viewed that have elements in common with "The Most Dangerous Game." They should indicate on the list what element the movie shares with the story. For example, in the movie *The Island of Dr. Moreau* an insane man has created an island (both real and metaphorical) in which cruelty and inhumanity prevail.

Using Students' Strengths

Logical Learners
Students are likely to have strong feelings about the morality of hunting for sport. Form two opposing groups, each comprised of students with likeminded opinions, and use the context of "The Most Dangerous Game" as the focal point for a debate or a panel discussion on whether or not hunting should be allowed. Have students do research to provide evidence with which to support their group's argument.

Naturalist Learners
Islands often possess unique micro-environments, ecosystems easily threatened by tourism, industrial expansion, or the introduction of non-native species. Ask students to choose a specific island or island group (the Hawaiian Islands and the Galápagos Islands are two possibilities) and to research its biodiversity. They can also document threats to an island's ecosystem and the efforts being made to protect it.

Crossing the Curriculum

Music
Students with musical ability may wish to compose and perform a theme song for a movie version of "The Most Dangerous Game." Ask students to include in their compositions sections inspired by each major part of the plot. Other students may wish to select appropriate mood music for each scene to accompany a dramatic reading of the story.

A English Language Learners
Idioms

Explain that Rainsford is referring to the idiom *playing a game of cat and mouse* and that an idiom is a phrase that connotes more than its literal meaning. Suggest that students think about times they have seen a cat chase its prey in real life, in cartoons, or on film. Have them explain why the idiom presents an effective image at this point in the story.

B Critical Thinking
Analyzing

? Zaroff said earlier that the difference between humans and animals is that humans rely on reason and animals rely on instinct. Yet, how does he rely on instinct here? [He senses danger and jumps back.]

C Elements of Literature
Conflict

? Who seems to have won this skirmish in the conflict, Rainsford or Zaroff? [Possible answers: Rainsford, since he has injured Zaroff and caused him to retreat; Zaroff, since he escaped the trap.]

D Appreciating Language
Verbs

Write this passage from the story on the chalkboard, pointing out to students that the verbs have been changed to forms of the verb *pull:* "He tried to pull it back, but the muck pulled viciously at his foot as if it were a giant leech. With a violent effort, he pulled loose." Read the passage aloud. Then, have a volunteer read the sentences from the story. Discuss how the writer's powerful verbs help readers visualize events.

E Historical Connections

Rainsford's mention of digging in France means that he is a veteran of the trench warfare that was a mainstay of World War I. Soldiers would dig trenches in which they lived and battled, sometimes for weeks or months at a time. This type of warfare is generally considered extremely difficult and dangerous, so the reference to it as a "placid pastime" is meant to show the depth of Rainsford's present fear.

---

the woods at night; he could follow an extremely difficult trail; he must have uncanny powers; only by the merest chance had the Cossack failed to see his quarry.

Rainsford's second thought was even more terrible. It sent a shudder of cold horror through his whole being. Why had the general smiled? Why had he turned back?

Rainsford did not want to believe what his reason told him was true, but the truth was as evident as the sun that had by now pushed through the morning mists. The general was playing with him! The general was saving him for another day's sport! The Cossack was the cat; he was the mouse. Then it was that Rainsford knew the full meaning of terror.

"I will not lose my nerve. I will not."

He slid down from the tree and struck off again into the woods. His face was set and he forced the machinery of his mind to function. Three hundred yards from his hiding place he stopped where a huge dead tree leaned precariously on a smaller living one. Throwing off his sack of food, Rainsford took his knife from its sheath and began to work with all his energy.

The job was finished at last, and he threw himself down behind a fallen log a hundred feet away. He did not have to wait long. The cat was coming again to play with the mouse.

Following the trail with the sureness of a bloodhound came General Zaroff. Nothing escaped those searching black eyes, no crushed blade of grass, no bent twig, no mark, no matter how faint, in the moss. So intent was the Cossack on his stalking that he was upon the thing Rainsford had made before he saw it. His foot touched the protruding bough that was the trigger. Even as he touched it, the general sensed his danger and leaped back with the agility of an ape. But he was not quite quick enough; the dead tree, delicately adjusted to rest on the cut living one, crashed down and struck the general a glancing blow on the shoulder as it fell; but for his alertness, he must have been smashed beneath it. He staggered, but he did not fall; nor did he drop his revolver. He stood there, rubbing his injured shoulder, and Rainsford, with fear again gripping his heart, heard the general's mocking laugh ring

through the jungle.

"Rainsford," called the general, "if you are within the sound of my voice, as I suppose you are, let me congratulate you. Not many men know how to make a Malay mancatcher. Luckily for me, I too have hunted in Malacca.[22] You are proving interesting, Mr. Rainsford. I am going now to have my wound dressed; it's only a slight one. But I shall be back. I shall be back."

When the general, nursing his bruised shoulder, had gone, Rainsford took up his flight again. It was flight now, a desperate, hopeless flight, that carried him on for some hours. Dusk came, then darkness, and still he pressed on. The ground grew softer under his moccasins; the vegetation grew ranker, denser; insects bit him savagely. Then, as he stepped forward, his foot sank into the ooze. He tried to wrench it back, but the muck sucked viciously at his foot as if it were a giant leech. With a violent effort, he tore loose. He knew where he was now. Death Swamp and its quicksand.

His hands were tight closed as if his nerve were something tangible that someone in the darkness was trying to tear from his grip. The softness of the earth had given him an idea. He stepped back from the quicksand a dozen feet or so, and, like some huge prehistoric beaver, he began to dig.

Rainsford had dug himself in in France,[23] when a second's delay meant death. That had been a placid pastime compared to his digging now. The pit grew deeper; when it was above his shoulders, he climbed out and from some hard saplings cut stakes and sharpened them to a fine point. These stakes he planted in the bottom of the pit with the points sticking up. With flying fingers he wove a rough carpet of weeds and branches and with it he covered the

---

22. **Malacca** (mə·lak′ə): state in what is now the nation of Malaysia in southeastern Asia.
23. **dug himself in in France:** dug a hole for shelter from gunfire during World War I (1914–1918).

WORDS TO OWN

precariously (prē·ker′ē·əs·lē) *adv.:* unsteadily; in an unstable manner.

Assessing Learning

Ongoing Assessment

Encourage students to maintain reading and writing folders. Reviewing these folders regularly can help you assess the strengths and weaknesses of individuals and plan instruction accordingly. Remind students to date all their work, to arrange the work in chronological order, and to keep everything about a particular selection clipped together. At the end of each grading period, students should review all the reading and writing they have done and select pieces for their portfolios. The process helps students to reflect on themselves as readers and writers and to set or revise learning goals for themselves.

mouth of the pit. Then, wet with sweat and aching with tiredness, he crouched behind the stump of a lightning-charred tree.

He knew his pursuer was coming; he heard the padding sound of feet on the soft earth, and the night breeze brought him the perfume of the general's cigarette. It seemed to Rainsford that the general was coming with unusual swiftness; he was not feeling his way along, foot by foot. Rainsford, crouching there, could not see the general, nor could he see the pit. He lived a year in a minute. Then he felt an impulse to cry aloud with joy, for he heard the sharp crackle of the breaking branches as the cover of the pit gave way; he heard the sharp scream of pain as the pointed stakes found their mark. He leaped up from his place of concealment. Then he cowered back. Three feet from the pit a man was standing, with an electric torch in his hand.

"You've done well, Rainsford," the voice of the general called. "Your Burmese tiger pit has claimed one of my best dogs. Again you score. I think, Mr. Rainsford, I'll see what you can do against my whole pack. I'm going home for a rest now. Thank you for a most amusing evening."

At daybreak Rainsford, lying near the swamp, was awakened by the sound that made him know that he had new things to learn about fear. It was a distant sound, faint and wavering, but he knew it. It was the baying of a pack of hounds.

Rainsford knew he could do one of two things. He could stay where he was and wait. That was suicide. He could flee. That was postponing the inevitable. For a moment he stood there, thinking. An idea that held a wild chance came to him, and, tightening his belt, he headed away from the swamp.

The baying of the hounds drew nearer, then still nearer, nearer, ever nearer. On a ridge Rainsford climbed a tree. Down a watercourse, not a quarter of a mile away, he could see the bush moving. Straining his eyes, he saw the lean figure of General Zaroff; just ahead of him Rainsford made out another figure whose wide shoulders surged through the tall jungle weeds. It was the giant Ivan, and he seemed pulled forward by some unseen force. Rainsford knew that Ivan must be holding the pack in leash.

They would be on him any minute now. His mind worked frantically. He thought of a native trick he had learned in Uganda. He slid down the tree. He caught hold of a springy young sapling and to it he fastened his hunting knife, with the blade pointing down the trail; with a bit of wild grapevine he tied back the sapling. Then he ran for his life. The hounds raised their voices as they hit the fresh scent. Rainsford knew now how an animal at bay feels.

He had to stop to get his breath. The baying of the hounds stopped abruptly, and Rainsford's heart stopped too. They must have reached the knife.

He shinnied excitedly up a tree and looked back. His pursuers had stopped. But the hope that was in Rainsford's brain when he climbed died, for he saw in the shallow valley that General Zaroff was still on his feet. But Ivan was not. The knife, driven by the recoil of the springing tree, had not wholly failed.

"Nerve, nerve, nerve!" he panted, as he dashed along. A blue gap showed between the trees dead ahead. Ever nearer drew the hounds. Rainsford forced himself on toward that gap. He reached it. It was the shore of the sea. Across a cove he could see the gloomy gray stone of the château. Twenty feet below him the sea rumbled and hissed. Rainsford hesitated. He heard the hounds. Then he leaped far out into the sea. . . .

When the general and his pack reached the place by the sea, the Cossack stopped. For some minutes he stood regarding the blue-green expanse of water. He shrugged his shoulders. Then he sat down, took a drink of brandy from a silver flask, lit a perfumed cigarette, and hummed a bit from *Madama Butterfly*.

General Zaroff had an exceedingly good dinner in his great paneled dining hall that

F **Reading Skills and Strategies**

Dialogue with the Text

? What do you think it means to live "a year in a minute"? [Sample responses: Fear, tension, and anxiety make every second vividly felt; the time seems much longer than it actually is.]

G **Cultural Connections**

Zaroff's and Rainsford's knowledge of both the Burmese tiger pit (this page) and the Malay mancatcher (p. 26) suggest that they hunted for sport in colonial Asia. Have students share what they know about colonization. Then, discuss how Zaroff's attitude is an exaggeration of a colonial mindset that deems it acceptable to value certain cultures over others.

H **Reading Skills and Strategies**

Dialogue with the Text

? This contradicts what Rainsford believed at the beginning of the story. What has he learned? [Sample responses: He has learned what it feels like to be hunted; he has learned that a hunted animal experiences pain and fear, as Whitney said.]

I **Appreciating Language**

Style

? How does the author heighten the tension in this passage? [Possible answers: He uses very short sentences that mimic breathlessness and fear; he has the reader experience events through the eyes, ears, and sensations of Rainsford.]

Crossing the Curriculum

Science

The Art of Tracking. Zaroff and Rainsford are both master trackers. They can read every bent twig and crushed blade of grass and follow their quarry wherever it flees. This skill was essential to hunting and gathering societies around the world. Native American hunters, for example, were expert at tracking buffalo, deer, wolverine, and other animals. Tracking game was so important that tribes that spoke different languages developed a sign language to communicate the whereabouts of game. In Africa in the last century, Masai warriors tracked lions, and white hunters such as Zaroff and Rainsford stalked other big game such as rhino, cape buffalo, and elephant.

While tracking requires patience and careful observation, it is an art that you might learn. You could track birds, insects, reptiles, or even machines. Look for tracks in dust, mud, or snow. Once you've found a trail of tracks, keep your eyes peeled for bent grass, broken twigs, and upturned pebbles that show that your prey has passed by. If you like, practice this skill by tracking your cat or dog, your brother's bicycle, etc., and surprise your quarry.

A Elements of Literature
Character
? How do Zaroff's "slight annoyances" show his insanity? [Sample answers: He doesn't mourn Ivan as a normal human would; he is upset that Rainsford has not played his twisted game according to his rules; the fact that he is only "slightly annoyed" after the terrifying events of the day show that he is not a sane human being.]

B Reading Skills and Strategies
Dialogue with the Text
? Suggest that students think about the following questions as they record in their journals their responses to the end of the story. What happens at the end of the story? Who wins? [The details aren't provided, but it can be concluded that Rainsford wins, since he gets to sleep in Zaroff's bed.] What is suggested about Rainsford at the end of the story? [His enjoyment of the bed suggests that perhaps, having killed two people, he himself has become a little bit like Zaroff.] What might the story be suggesting about people in general? [Possible responses: People who kill other beings cannot help being tainted by it; certain "games" can be dangerous in more ways than one.]

Resources

Selection Assessment
Formal Assessment
• Selection Test, p. 1
Test Generator (One-Stop Planner)
• CD-ROM

---

evening. With it he had a bottle of Pol Roger[24] and half a bottle of Chambertin.[25] Two slight annoyances kept him from perfect enjoyment. One was the thought that it would be difficult to replace Ivan; the other was that his quarry had escaped him; of course the American hadn't played the game—so thought the general as he tasted his after-dinner liqueur. In his library he read, to soothe himself, from the works of Marcus Aurelius.[26] At ten he went up to his bedroom. He was deliciously tired, he said to himself as he locked himself in. There was a little moonlight, so before turning on his light, he went to the window and looked down

24. **Pol Roger** (pôl rô·zhā'): brand of champagne.
25. **Chambertin** (shän'ber·tan'): red burgundy wine.
26. **Marcus Aurelius** (mär'kəs ô·rē'lē·əs): emperor of Rome from A.D. 161 to 180, who wrote about the philosophy of Stoicism, which held that people should make themselves indifferent to both pain and pleasure.

at the courtyard. He could see the great hounds, and he called: "Better luck another time," to them. Then he switched on the light.

A man, who had been hiding in the curtains of the bed, was standing there.

"Rainsford!" screamed the general. "How in God's name did you get here?"

"Swam," said Rainsford. "I found it quicker than walking through the jungle."

The general sucked in his breath and smiled. "I congratulate you," he said. "You have won the game."

Rainsford did not smile. "I am still a beast at bay," he said, in a low, hoarse voice. "Get ready, General Zaroff."

The general made one of his deepest bows. "I see," he said. "Splendid! One of us is to furnish a repast for the hounds. The other will sleep in this very excellent bed. On guard, Rainsford. . . ."

He had never slept in a better bed, Rainsford decided.

MEET THE WRITER
Famous for One Story
Richard Connell (1893–1949) started his writing career early. At the age of ten, he began covering baseball games for the newspaper his father edited. He earned ten cents a game. By the age of sixteen he was city editor. As a student at Harvard, Connell edited the humor magazine called the *Lampoon* and the college newspaper. He went on to write novels, hundreds of short stories, and screenplays. Despite Connell's tremendous output, only one story—"The Most Dangerous Game" (1924)—is still in print.

What accounts for the story's enduring popularity? Nothing in it is especially believable—not the characters, not the plot, not even the violence. We are never really afraid that Rainsford will be chewed up by one of those hounds. Perhaps the answer is that "The Most Dangerous Game" is an adventure story, with all the appeal of a Hollywood scare-o-rama, complete with an elegant villain, his huge brute of a manservant, a castle, a dark jungle, bloodthirsty animals, and hideous man-traps. It is a fine example of a macho escape story. When we read it, we escape reality for a short time. We spend an hour or two away from real life and its problems.

Despite its literary flaws, people rarely forget this story.

What do you think of it?

Assessing Learning

Check Test: Questions and Answers
1. How do sailors feel about Ship-Trap Island? [They are scared of the place.]
2. In Whitney's opinion, what one thing do animals understand? [fear]
3. How does Rainsford happen to arrive on the island? [He falls overboard and survives by swimming to land.]
4. Who is Ivan? [Zaroff's butler and bodyguard]
5. What does Zaroff say he has become bored with? [hunting animals]

6. What species has Zaroff now chosen as his prey? [human beings]
7. What are the terms of the game? [The hunted man must elude Zaroff for three days.]
8. Who is the last man Zaroff hunts? [Rainsford]
9. Who is killed in a knife trap? [Ivan]
10. How does Rainsford finally escape Zaroff? [He jumps into the sea.]

Standardized Test Preparation
For practice in proofreading and editing see
• *Daily Oral Grammar,* Transparency 1

First Thoughts

[infer]

1. What do you think happens to Zaroff? What are some possible endings for the story?

Shaping Interpretations

[infer]

2. To hook our curiosity, writers drop clues that **foreshadow,** or hint at, what is going to happen later in a story.

   - What clues at the start of the story foreshadow danger ahead for Rainsford?

   - How does Rainsford's discussion about hunting at the start of the story foreshadow later developments?

   - What details in the description of Zaroff's unusual dental features and lips foreshadow the truth about his nature? (How do these details make him seem like a monster?)

[analyze]

3. Compare and contrast Rainsford and Zaroff. To help you see their **characters,** fill out a Venn diagram like the one here. List the characteristics of each man in his circle. Then list the characteristics they share in the shaded area.

   Rainsford   Zaroff

[synthesize]

4. Based on their characters, decide if Rainsford changes his mind about hunting by the end of the story. (Is it possible that he becomes just like Zaroff?)

Connecting with the Text

[connect]

5. Do the characters in this story make some comments that you felt strongly about? (Check the notes you made as you read the story.) Be sure to evaluate Zaroff's arguments for hunting men, on pages 21–22.

Extending the Text

[apply]

6. Think about Zaroff's civilized tastes and his favorite game. Do "Zaroffs"— people whose manners mask their true nature—exist in real life? Explain.

Challenging the Text

[evaluate]

7. Some stories are so fantastic or contrived that we have to suspend our disbelief. This means that if we do not believe that something in a story is possible, the writer hopes we'll still accept it. Did any details in this story demand that you suspend your disbelief? Share your responses in class.

> ### Reading Check
>
> **a.** Did you predict the meaning of the story's **title?** What is the most dangerous game?
>
> **b.** Why is Zaroff glad that it is Rainsford who has come to the island?
>
> **c.** What happens during the three days of the chase?
>
> **d.** What is Rainsford's **conflict** with Zaroff, and how is it finally resolved?

Reading Check

Answers may vary.

a. Possible responses: Humans are the most dangerous game, in the sense of prey; any game that seriously endangers human life or pits human against human.

b. Initially, Zaroff wants a skilled hunting companion. Later, he is pleased to have challenging prey.

c. Rainsford barely escapes Zaroff the first day. During the next few days, he builds a Malay mancatcher, which wounds Zaroff, a Burmese tiger pit in which one of Zaroff's dogs is killed, and a Ugandan knife trap, which kills Ivan. As a last resort, he dives into the treacherous sea below.

d. The conflict is external; it's a life-or-death hunt. It is resolved when Rainsford swims to shore, hides out in Zaroff's bedroom, and possibly kills Zaroff.

First Thoughts

1. Possible endings: He is killed; he is thrown to the dogs; he is captured by Rainsford and tried in court for his crimes; he escapes.

Shaping Interpretations

2. Responses will vary.
   - The name Ship-Trap Island, its bad reputation among sailors, the discussion of evil, the dread Whitney feels, the three gunshots foreshadow danger for Rainsford.
   - Rainsford arrogantly explains that the world is made up of two classes—hunters and huntees. Then the hunter becomes the huntee. Also, Rainsford claims hunted animals feel neither pain nor fear, but he feels both when he is hunted.
   - Zaroff's very red lips and pointed teeth make him seem bloodthirsty, almost vampirelike.

3. Diagrams will vary. Both: hunters, risk-takers, cunning, adventurous, indifferent to the feelings of their prey. Zaroff: smug, cruel, manipulative, amoral. Rainsford: realistic, respects human life, ethical.

4. Possible answers: Knowing what it's like to be prey, he gives up hunting; having killed two men, he takes to Zaroff's game.

Connecting with the Text

5. Students may respond strongly to the characters' opinions about animals and Zaroff's valuing some human life above others. Students should note that in his arguments, Zaroff distorts logic in order to suit his purpose.

Extending the Text

6. Possible "Zaroffs": ruthless business people, dictators, con artists. These people are able to appear cultured while repudiating the very foundation of culture—respect for humanity.

Challenging the Text

7. Possible responses: one-dimensional characterizations; Rainsford's leaping onto the ship's rail; sources of staff and supplies for the chateau; its presence remaining undetected; the missing part of the plot—what happened between Rainsford's jumping into the sea and his appearing in Zaroff's bedroom.

Grading Timesaver

Rubrics for each Choices assignment appear on p. 89 in the *Portfolio Management System*.

CHOICES: Building Your Portfolio

1. **Writer's Notebook** Remind students to save their work. They can use it as prewriting for the Writer's Workshop on page 112.

2. **Critical Thinking/Speaking** Remind students to choose a movie that has some elements in common with "The Most Dangerous Game." After students fill out the chart, suggest they also use a compare and contrast format in their talk. If possible, videotape your students' TV spots for use as a prereading activity with another class.

3. **Creative Writing** If they wish, allow students to work in pairs to brainstorm ideas for Rainsford's next adventure.

4. **Analyzing Characters** Remind students to include both the physical and mental characteristics of each man. They should also give reasons for their actor recommendations.

5. **Drawing** Suggest that students start by thinking about Rainsford's comment that he is "in a picture with a frame of water." How does that describe the location? Then students should review the story to find details of the setting. Remind them to include a map legend, or key, and a scale of miles, so that others can read their map.

CHOICES: Building Your Portfolio

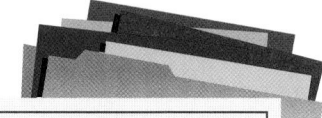

Writer's Notebook

1. Collecting Ideas for a Short Narrative

Finding a conflict. In the Writer's Workshop on page 112, you'll write a short narrative about a conflict. Refer now to the conflicts you listed before you started this collection of stories (see page 11), or make a new list of conflicts you might write about. The conflicts can be real or imaginary. (Rainsford's physical struggle with the sea might give you new ideas.) Highlight or circle any conflict you'd like to elaborate on and do a cluster diagram to see if you have enough material for a short narrative. Save your notes.

Critical Thinking/Speaking

2. Looking at Movies

With a partner, prepare for a five-minute TV spot to talk about how this story compares with current movies. To prepare for your conversation, fill out a chart like the one that follows:

Elements	Connell's Tale	A Movie
1. Hero and his/her values		
2. Villain		
3. Setting		
4. What is at stake?		
5. Hero's exploits		
6. Level of violence		

Creative Writing

3. The Sequel

It is morning. Rainsford has just awakened in Zaroff's excellent bed. What happens next? Write the next episode in Rainsford's adventure. (Does he stay on Ship-Trap Island and turn it into a theme park, or does he go home and work on behalf of endangered species? Or does he do something even more surprising?) You might let Rainsford tell his story, using "I."

Analyzing Characters

4. Roles for Women?

Suppose you've been asked to cast actors for the roles of Zaroff and Rainsford for yet another movie version of the story. The producer wants a written report on the characteristics of each man and suggestions of actors to play their parts. If you filled out a diagram like the one on page 29, refer to it as you draft your report. Could the roles be played by women?

Drawing

5. Map the Chase

As an illustration for this story, prepare a map of the chase. Before you start, list all the features of the island you want to locate. Include geographical features (jagged crags and dense jungle) and man-made features (the château and all the traps).

30 THE SHORT-STORY COLLECTIONS

Using Students' Strengths

Auditory/Musical Learners

To help students match actors with characters for Choice 4, select passages with dialogue for students to reread aloud. Then, ask if there is a famous TV or film character that they think of when they hear Rainsford's or Zaroff's dialogue.

Powerful Verbs

Some of Connell's Verbs

- pressed
- strained
- wrestled
- muttered
- dragged
- flung
- tumbled
- floundered
- thrashed
- hurled
- fluttered
- chuckled
- shrugged
- snapped
- plunged
- flattened
- crashed
- staggered

Verbs help give writing its power and color. Richard Connell's verbs propel his story—they help us visualize very specifically what is happening. Compare Connell's vivid verb choices below to the tamer ones above them.

1. He jumped upon the rail and stood there. . . .
   Connell: "He leaped upon the rail and balanced himself there. . . ."

2. . . . his pipe fell from his mouth. He tried to catch it. . . .
   Connell: ". . . his pipe . . . was knocked from his mouth. He lunged for it. . . ."

3. . . . the wash from the speeding yacht hit him in the face and the salt water in his open mouth made him choke.
   Connell: ". . . the wash from the speeding yacht slapped him in the face and the salt water in his open mouth made him gag and strangle."

Find at least five other passages in the story that use good vivid verbs to help you see very specific actions.

Try It Out

➤ Replace the tame, general verbs in these sentences. Change the wording if you wish.

1. Rainsford went to the cellar.

2. Whitney said something under his breath.

3. Zaroff looked around.

4. An animal called in the night.

➤ You might keep a list of strong verbs in your notebook for use when you revise your own writing. Circle the verbs in your own writing that you think could be made more vivid. Then use your list of verbs to find replacements.

VOCABULARY   HOW TO OWN A WORD

WORD BANK

palpable
indolently
disarming
amenities
imprudent
scruples
solicitously
opiate
deplorable
precariously

Word Meanings

Work with a group to find out how much you already know about the meanings of the Word Bank words. Make up two questions about each word, and organize your answers in a chart. After you have completed charts for all the words, invite another group to answer some of your questions.

palpable	
QUESTIONS	ANSWERS
What are some things in this room that are palpable?	• furniture • people • books
What are some things in this room that aren't palpable?	• air • feelings • ideas

THE MOST DANGEROUS GAME 31

Consider providing a list of powerful verbs from sources such as sports journals or suspense novels. Students can use this list as well as a thesaurus to use vivid verbs in their writing. In a piece of their writing, have them highlight all the "to be" verbs and then replace half of them with more specific verbs.

Try It Out
Possible Answers

1. fled, bounded, sprinted, dashed, raced, slipped down
2. muttered, murmured, grumbled
3. gazed, searched, peered
4. bayed, howled, roared, screeched, growled

VOCABULARY
Sample Questions

- *indolently:* What animals often move indolently? sloths, cats
- *disarming:* What types of people might cultivate disarming smiles? actors, politicians
- *amenities:* Which household items are your favorite amenities? air conditioner, television
- *imprudent:* What kinds of activities are imprudent while driving a car? drinking, being reckless
- *scruples:* In which careers are scruples important? law, medicine, all jobs
- *solicitously:* When do you behave solicitously? when asking for a favor
- *opiate:* Which kinds of music are an opiate for you? jazz, classical
- *deplorable:* What actions of a police officer might be deplorable? beating a suspect, lying under oath
- *precariously:* What things should not be precariously placed? fragile items, hazardous substances

Resources —————

Grammar
- *Grammar and Language Links* Worksheet, p. 1

Vocabulary
- *Words to Own* Worksheet, p. 1

Grammar Link Quick Check

Evaluate the strength of the underlined verb in each of the following sentences. Use these ratings: G = general; V = vivid. Then, replace any general verb with a vivid verb.

___ 1. Rainsford turned away from the trap. [G, possible vivid verb: veered]

___ 2. Ivan held a revolver in his hands. [G, possible vivid verb: clutched]

___ 3. General Zaroff loitered at the base of the tree. [V]

___ 4. Hunters hunt their prey. [G, possible vivid verb: track down]

___ 5. Rainsford disagreed with Zaroff's views on hunting human game. [G, possible vivid verb: contested]

___ 6. Zaroff whirled around to face Rainsford [V]

___ 7. Rainsford sat on a windowsill of the chateau. [G, possible vivid verb: lounged]

OBJECTIVES
1. Identify elements of plot: exposition, complications, climax, and resolution or denouement
2. Distinguish external conflict from internal conflict

Resources

Elements of Literature
Plot
For additional instruction on plot, see
Literary Elements:
• Transparency 1
Formal Assessment
• Literary Elements Test, p. 11

Elements of Literature

This feature focuses on the development of plot in short stories: the basic situation or exposition, the conflict, the complication(s), the climax, and the resolution.

Mini-Lesson:
Plot
Remind students that understanding how a plot develops provides insight into a story, which adds to the reader's enjoyment. Point out that they can apply strategies for understanding plot when they read or listen to stories or view films or television shows.

After students have read the essay, briefly review the elements of plot and the role of conflict. Have volunteers identify the central conflict and provide the plot elements for "The Sniper," or another story, film, or drama your students are all familiar with. Finally, address Leggett's comment that "If one of these bare bones is weak, the story falls apart." Invite students to give examples of stories, novels, or films that lack either a strong basic situation, complication, climax, or resolution/denouement. Have them discuss how the deficiency in plot structure affected their enjoyment of the work.

PLOT: "Hooking" Your Reader's Curiosity

When you talk about stories, plot is the element to start with, for plot is story itself. **Plot** is a series of related events, each event connected to the next, like links in a chain. Each event in a plot "hooks" our curiosity and pulls us forward to the next event, to satisfy that curiosity.

The monster, preparing to paralyze his latest challenger, looked at his victim and saw she was chewing gum.

Right away, we wonder what's going to happen. Why isn't the victim afraid, the way she should be?

The dragon withdrew his venomous talons and asked the young person if she was laughing at him.

Why? the reader wonders. Is the monster especially funny looking? Is he very insecure?

If our curiosity is aroused by these events, we await successive ones with mounting suspense. We want to know: "What happens next?" This buildup of suspense is how a

plot works. A series of related events plants the hook of curiosity in us, making us read to find out: "What happens next?"

> **E**ach event in a plot "hooks" our curiosity and pulls us forward to the next event.

Conflict: The Fuel of Narrative

Usually, we care about what happens next in a story because we're hooked by a **conflict,** or struggle. This struggle might take place between two characters or it might take place between a character and a whole group of people, or it might take place between a character and something nonhuman—a typhoon or a shark or gas in the mine pit or a computer virus. Conflict can also take place within a character's own mind and heart: The desire to be peaceable might conflict with an urge to knock the stuffing out of a bully. A desire to win someone's friendship might conflict with a fear of

rejection. Often, an external conflict results in an internal problem: Facing that typhoon is going to produce fear and perhaps a desire to run away.

When the conflict takes place between a character and another person or between a character and something nonhuman, it is an **external conflict**. When the conflict takes place inside a character's mind, it is an **internal conflict**. Conflict is the fuel of narrative. The greater the conflict, the more we care about the outcome.

> **T**he greater the conflict, the more we care about the outcome.

The "Bare Bones" of a Plot

Stories, like houses and human beings, need a structure or framework to hold them together. Plots are usually built on four major parts, which we might think of as their "bare bones." The first part of a plot can be called the **basic situation**. This is the opening of the story, where the characters and their conflict are usually introduced. (Writers have many names for this part of the story. Some call it **exposition**.)

Using Students' Strengths

Interpersonal Learners
To help students refine their critical judgment of plot, encourage them to work with a partner to take notes on plots for three episodes of their favorite TV drama or situation comedy. As an alternative, ask students to take notes on the plot of another short story. Have them share their notes with the class.

Visual Learners
Diagram on the chalkboard four boxes labeled *Exposition, Complication, Climax,* and *Resolution.* Above these write the word *Conflict.* Have students copy the diagram and then work in groups. After choosing a story or film the group is familiar with, they should discuss its major conflict. Then, members should draw an appropriate scene from the work in each box. Groups should compare and discuss their work.

by John Leggett

Once upon a time there lived a young girl named Cinderella, who was as beautiful as she was good. But she was totally detested by her evil step-mother and two nasty and jealous stepsisters. Cinderella longed to go to the prince's ball—but it was simply out of the question. After all, Cinderella was just a kitchen servant.

The second part of a plot is the **complication**. Now the main character takes some action to resolve the conflict and meets with more problems or complications: danger, hostility, fear, or even a new threatening situation.

A fairy godmother promised to get Cinderella to the ball if she obeyed one rule: "Be home by midnight." Dressed in the most beautiful gown and wearing tiny glass slippers manufactured on the spot by her fairy godmother, Cinderella went to the ball. No one knew who this dazzling beauty was. The prince fell in love with her at first sight, but she had to flee at midnight. One of the dainty glass slippers was left behind as she ran out of the palace.

The third part of a story is the **climax**. This is the key scene of the story—that tense or exciting or terrifying moment when our emotional involvement is greatest. Now we find out what the outcome of the conflict is going to be.

The prince made a house-to-house search for the foot that fit the tiny shoe. The stepsisters shaved off parts of their big feet to try to squeeze into the slipper, but no luck. The prince found that small foot on Cinderella.

The final part of the story is the **resolution**. Sometimes this is called the **denouement** (dā′ nōō·mä*n*′), a French word for "unraveling the knot." The resolution occurs at the end of the story (perhaps it's only a paragraph). Now all the struggles are over, and we know what is going to happen to the people in the story. The resolution "closes" the story.

Cinderella married the prince and they lived happily ever

after. The stepsisters and the cruel stepmother, however, suffered ghastly punishments for their misdeeds.

These four bare bones support a series of events intended to hook our curiosity. If one of these bare bones is weak, the story falls apart. We are not hooked by the characters and their struggle, and we just might not want to finish the story.

> **I**f one of these bare bones is weak, the story falls apart.

"The plot thickened—and then it congealed."

From The Wall Street Journal. Reprinted by permission from Cartoon Features Syndicate.

ELEMENTS OF LITERATURE: PLOT **33**

Reaching All Students

Struggling Readers
Encourage students to come up with their own words and phrases for describing each of the four major parts of a plot. For example, a student might describe the resolution as the portion of a story where "the action winds down" and all "the loose ends are tied up." Use movies or novels that students are already very familiar with as the basis of discussion.

Applying the Element
Have students work in groups of four to analyze the plot development of "The Most Dangerous Game" or another story in this collection. Each student in the group should be responsible for one element: basic situation/exposition, complication(s), climax, or resolution/denouement. Encourage them to discuss whether the key conflict is internal or external and whether elements of the plot are equally important. Remind students before the discussion that differences of opinion about plot and conflict will arise; review with them practical strategies for settling differences.

OBJECTIVES

1. Read and interpret the story
2. Identify a story's climax
3. Understand cause and effect
4. Express understanding through news writing, creative writing, or research/science
5. Distinguish between the active and the passive voice of verbs and use the active voice in writing
6. Understand and use new words
7. Use context clues to infer meaning

SKILLS

Literary
- Identify a story's climax

Reading
- Understand cause and effect

Writing
- List events in order
- Write a news report
- Write an essay
- Write a dinosaur story

Research/Science
- Research and present information about dinosaurs

Grammar
- Use the active voice of verbs

Vocabulary
- Use new words
- Use context clues to infer meaning

Planning

- **Traditional Schedule**
  Lesson Plans Including Strategies for English-Language Learners
- **One-Stop Planner**
  CD-ROM with Test Generator

Before You Read

A SOUND OF THUNDER

Make the Connection

What If . . . ?

Can one small action or decision change a person's life? What if you leave home a fraction of a second too late to cross paths with someone you might have fallen in love with? Or what if you miss your flight to Tokyo the same day a devastating earthquake strikes the city? In the story you're about to read—well, see for yourself.

Quickwrite

This is a story about time travel. Jot down some thoughts about where you'd go if you could travel through time. Would you choose the past or the future? Would you stay in the region where you live or go someplace more distant? How would traveling through time change your life in the present?

go.hrw.com
LEO 9-1

Elements of Literature

The Big Moment: Climax

The moment we look forward to in a story is its **climax**— that highly charged moment when the suspense is greatest, when we finally discover how the conflict is going to work out. In most stories the climax is the moment that brings about some change in the situation, the main character, or both. Often it occurs when the main character makes some dramatic discovery. The climax takes place very near the end of the story. When a climax is especially exciting, we say the story ends with a bang. See how you feel about this one.

> The most emotional moment in a story is the **climax,** when the outcome of the conflict is finally revealed.
>
> *For more on Climax, see pages 32–33 and the Handbook of Literary Terms.*

Reading Skills and Strategies

Cause and Effect: A Chain of Events

A **plot** is a series of related events, like links in a chain. In a well-written story the events that make up the plot are closely related: One event causes another event, which causes another event, and so on. When you ask yourself: "How did that discovery affect the girl in this story?" you are asking a cause-and-effect question. When you ask: "What caused her friend to tell her that secret anyway?" you are asking a cause-and-effect question. When you finish a story, you want to be sure you understand why certain events happened and how they affected the plot or the characters. The story you are about to read is *about* causes and effects.

If you want a crystal-clear model of cause and effect, read Bradbury's paragraph on page 38, beginning " 'So what?' Travis snorted quietly."

Preteaching Vocabulary

Words to Own

Write on the chalkboard the Words to Own listed at the bottom of the selection pages. Review their definitions. Then, have students name the word that fits best in each sentence:

1. On a hot summer day, an ice cream shop may be _____ with people. [teeming]
2. Ocean waves _____. [undulate]
3. After a driver gets too many tickets, the law may _____ his license. [revoke]
4. Bug spray will _____ ants. [annihilate]
5. A time that is even older than ancient times is known as _____. [primeval]
6. You may _____ payment. [remit]
7. Items that are thrown overboard to lighten a load are _____. [expendable]
8. A rubber band is _____. [resilient]
9. Thoughts that lie just below the surface are _____. [subliminal]
10. If a heavy load is light to carry, that is a _____. [paradox]

A SOUND OF THUNDER

Ray Bradbury

The sign on the wall seemed to quaver under a film of sliding warm water. Eckels felt his eyelids blink over his stare, and the sign burned in this momentary darkness:

TIME SAFARI, INC.

Safaris to any
year in the past.

You name the animal.
We take you there.

You shoot it.

*Does this safari guarantee
I come back alive?"*

A SOUND OF THUNDER **35**

Summary ▪▪

This science fiction story begins in the year 2055, the day after an election in which Keith, a democrat, wins out over Deutscher, a fascist. Time travel is possible and Eckels, a wealthy hunter, goes on a prehistoric safari to shoot a dinosaur. As Eckels's party travels back in time, Travis, the leader, warns the hunters not to stray from a prelaid anti-gravity Path, theorizing that the minutest damage to the environment could have serious reverberations for the future. Even the tyrannosaur they are going to shoot is chosen because it would have died minutes later anyway. When the time comes to make the kill, Eckels panics and runs away, stumbling off the Path. Travis is furious. After the party returns to 2055, Eckels notices that things are subtly different. He then discovers a dead butterfly on the sole of his shoe. After finding out that now Deutscher has triumphed over Keith, Eckels realizes the magnitude of his actions—he has changed the course of his country's history. The story's climax comes when Travis shoots Eckels.

Resources

Viewing and Representing
Videocassette A, Segment 1
Available in Spanish and English.
To help generate interest in the collection's theme, show the *Visual Connections* segment "Here There Be Monsters." For full lesson plans and worksheets, see *Visual Connections Teacher's Manual.*

Listening
Audio CD Library
For a recording of "A Sound of Thunder," see the *Audio CD Library:*
• Disc 2, Track 2

Resources: Print and Media

Reading
• *Reading Skills and Strategies*
    MiniRead Skill Lesson, p. 23
    Selection Skill Lesson, p. 31
• *Graphic Organizers for Active Reading,* p. 2
• *Words to Own,* p. 2
• *Audio CD Library,*
    Disc 2, Track 2

Writing and Language
• *Daily Oral Grammar*
    Transparency 2
• *Grammar and Language Links*
    Worksheet, p. 3
• *Language Workshop* CD-ROM

Viewing and Representing
• *Viewing and Representing*
    Fine Art Transparency 1
    Fine Art Worksheet, p. 4

• *Visual Connections*
    Videocassette A, Segment 1

Assessment
• *Formal Assessment,* p. 3
• *Portfolio Management System,* p. 91
• *Standardized Test Preparation,* p. 10
• *Test Generator (One-Stop Planner* CD-ROM)

Internet
• go.hrw.com (keyword: LE0 9–1)

? What do Eckels's actions here reveal about him? [Possible responses: He is scared; he is rich and used to getting guarantees of safety.]

B Appreciating Language

Style

Bradbury is considered by many to be a master of fiction because he indulges in an almost stream-of-consciousness style, which is evident in this passage about the time machine. Help students see that this passage contains a series of images and impressions about the machine, rather than a literal description of it. Discuss whether a description such as this conveys the awe of the machine better than a conventional description would.

C Historical Connection

Point out that in the German language, the name *Deutscher* means "German" (a noun). In post–World War II America, when this story was published, Hitler's Germany was considered the quintessential example of the evils of dictatorship.

D Elements of Literature

Climax

? Based upon what you have read so far, what do you think the climax of this story might be? [Possible responses: The climax will come when Eckels encounters the dinosaur; the climax will be Eckels's killing the dinosaur or the dinosaur killing him.]

A warm phlegm gathered in Eckels's throat; he swallowed and pushed it down. The muscles around his mouth formed a smile as he put his hand slowly out upon the air, and in that hand waved a check for ten thousand dollars to the man behind the desk.

"Does this safari guarantee I come back alive?"

"We guarantee nothing," said the official, "except the dinosaurs." He turned. "This is Mr. Travis, your Safari Guide in the Past. He'll tell you what and where to shoot. If he says no shooting, no shooting. If you disobey instructions, there's a stiff penalty of another ten thousand dollars, plus possible government action, on your return."

Eckels glanced across the vast office at a mass and tangle, a snaking and humming of wires and steel boxes, at an aurora[1] that flickered now orange, now silver, now blue. There was a sound like a gigantic bonfire burning all of Time, all the years and all the parchment calendars, all the hours piled high and set aflame.

A touch of the hand and this burning would, on the instant, beautifully reverse itself. Eckels remembered the wording in the advertisements to the letter. Out of chars and ashes, out of dust and coals, like golden salamanders, the old years, the green years, might leap; roses sweeten the air, white hair turn Irish-black, wrinkles vanish; all, everything fly back to seed, flee death, rush down to their beginnings, suns rise in western skies and set in glorious easts, moons eat themselves opposite to the custom, all and everything cupping one in another like Chinese boxes,[2] rabbits into hats, all and everything returning to the fresh death, the seed death, the green death, to the time before the beginning. A touch of a hand might do it, the merest touch of a hand.

"The Tyrant Lizard, the most incredible monster in history."

"Unbelievable." Eckels breathed, the light of the Machine on his thin face. "A real Time Machine." He shook his head. "Makes you think. If the election had gone badly yesterday, I might be here now running away from the results. Thank God Keith won. He'll make a fine President of the United States."

"Yes," said the man behind the desk. "We're lucky. If Deutscher had gotten in, we'd have the worst kind of dictatorship. There's an anti-everything man for you, a militarist, anti-Christ, anti-human, anti-intellectual. People called us up, you know, joking but not joking. Said if Deutscher became President they wanted to go live in 1492. Of course it's not our business to conduct Escapes, but to form Safaris. Anyway, Keith's President now. All you got to worry about is——"

"Shooting my dinosaur," Eckels finished it for him.

"A *Tyrannosaurus rex*. The Tyrant Lizard, the most incredible monster in history. Sign this release. Anything happens to you, we're not responsible. Those dinosaurs are hungry."

Eckels flushed angrily. "Trying to scare me!"

"Frankly, yes. We don't want anyone going who'll panic at the first shot. Six Safari leaders were killed last year, and a dozen hunters. We're here to give you the severest thrill a *real* hunter ever asked for. Traveling you back sixty million years to bag the biggest game in all of Time. Your personal check's still there. Tear it up."

Mr. Eckels looked at the check. His fingers twitched.

"Good luck," said the man behind the desk. "Mr. Travis, he's all yours."

They moved silently across the room, taking their guns with them, toward the Machine, toward the silver metal and the roaring light.

First a day and then a night and then a day and then a night, then it was day-night-day-night-day. A week, a month, a year, a decade! A.D. 2055. A.D. 2019. 1999! 1957! Gone! The Machine roared.

They put on their oxygen helmets and tested the intercoms.

---

1. **aurora** (ô·rôr′ə): Bradbury is comparing the glow coming from the machine to an aurora, a colorful display of light that appears at night in the skies near the North and South Poles.
2. **Chinese boxes:** set of boxes, each of which fits into the next-largest one.

Reaching All Students

Struggling Readers

Analyzing Cause and Effect was introduced on p. 34. For a lesson directly tied to this story that teaches students to analyze cause and effect by using a strategy called Text Reformulation, see the *Reading and Skills and Strategies* binder:
- MiniRead Skill Lesson, p. 23
- Selection Skill Lesson, p. 31

English Language Learners

Bradbury's prose is not difficult, but the descriptive language (*bats of delirium, night fever*), colloquial phrases (*met my match*), and allusions (*1812, cross the Delaware*) may pose problems for some. Encourage students to ask questions about language or references that they find confusing. For additional strategies, see
- *Lesson Plans Including Strategies for English-Language Learners*

Advanced Learners

Point out that Bradbury is one of the most noted writers in the genre (or category) of science fiction. Invite students to relate what comes to mind when they think of science fiction and list their responses on the chalkboard. Ask students to keep these genre elements in mind as they read Bradbury's story. Afterwards, have them discuss whether or not the story contained the elements they expected from a work of science fiction.

Eckels swayed on the padded seat, his face pale, his jaw stiff. He felt the trembling in his arms, and he looked down and found his hands tight on the new rifle. There were four other men in the Machine. Travis, the Safari Leader; his assistant, Lesperance; and two other hunters, Billings and Kramer. They sat looking at each other, and the years blazed around them.

"Can these guns get a dinosaur cold?" Eckels felt his mouth saying.

"If you hit them right," said Travis on the helmet radio. "Some dinosaurs have two brains, one in the head, another far down the spinal column. We stay away from those. That's stretching luck. Put your first two shots into the eyes, if you can, blind them, and go back into the brain."

The Machine howled. Time was a film run backward. Suns fled and ten million moons fled after them. "Think," said Eckels. "Every hunter that ever lived would envy us today. This makes Africa seem like Illinois."

The Machine slowed; its scream fell to a murmur. The Machine stopped.

The sun stopped in the sky.

The fog that had enveloped the Machine blew away and they were in an old time, a very old time indeed, three hunters and two Safari Heads with their blue metal guns across their knees.

"Christ isn't born yet," said Travis. "Moses has not gone to the mountain to talk with God. The Pyramids are still in the earth, waiting to be cut out and put up. *Remember* that. Alexander,

Caesar, Napoleon, Hitler—none of them exists."

The men nodded.

"That"—Mr. Travis pointed—"is the jungle of sixty million two thousand and fifty-five years before President Keith."

He indicated a metal path that struck off into green wilderness, over streaming swamp, among giant ferns and palms.

"And that," he said, "is the Path, laid by Time Safari for your use. It floats six inches above the earth. Doesn't touch so much as one grass blade, flower, or tree. It's an anti-gravity metal. Its purpose is to keep you from touching this world of the Past in any way. Stay on the Path. Don't go off it. I repeat. *Don't go off.* For *any* reason! If you fall off, there's a penalty. And don't shoot any animal we don't okay."

"Why?" asked Eckels.

They sat in the ancient wilderness. Far birds' cries blew on a wind, and the smell of tar and an old salt sea, moist grasses, and flowers the color of blood.

"We don't want to change the Future. We don't belong here in the Past. The government doesn't *like* us here. We have to pay big graft[3] to keep our franchise. A Time Machine is finicky business. Not knowing it, we might kill an important animal, a small bird, a roach, a flower even, thus destroying an important link in a growing species."

"That's not clear," said Eckels.

"All right," Travis continued, "say we acciden-

3. **graft:** bribes.

Getting Students Involved

Cooperative Learning

Time-Travel Tourism. Have students work in teams of five or six to brainstorm ideas for three trips offered by an agency specializing in time-travel destinations. Team members can take the roles of market researcher, literature researchers, writer, artist and designer, and publicist. To get started, groups could survey friends or classmates to determine which destinations and time periods would be most popular with prospective clients. Survey questions could include activity choices as well as destinations. After selecting the trips that their agencies will offer, group members should research those places and historical periods. Then, challenge them to create brochures with copy describing each adventure, illustrations or photographs depicting the destinations, and complete trip itineraries. Students might also decide what risks are present for voyagers and what types of warnings should be prominently placed in the brochure. Invite the groups' publicists to present and promote their time-travel tours to the class. After all groups have presented their ideas, you might take a class vote to determine the most popular tours.

A Reading Skills and Strategies

Cause and Effect

Travis's explanation is an excellent example of a cause-and-effect chain. To help students better understand the concept of a cause-and-effect sequence of events, you may wish to map out this chain on the chalkboard. Begin with the events below, and have students add to the chain.

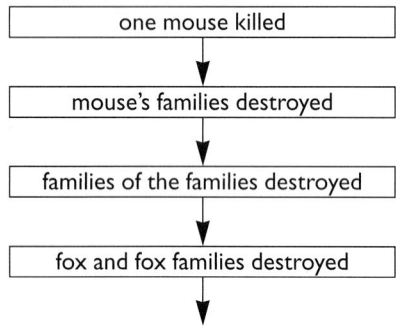

one mouse killed

↓

mouse's families destroyed

↓

families of the families destroyed

↓

fox and fox families destroyed

↓

B Critical Thinking

Expressing an Opinion

❓ Which theory do you agree with? Will killing something in the past change the future a lot, a little, or not at all? Explain. [Sample responses: Travis's theory makes sense—killing something probably would affect the future a lot; Travis's theory is not correct—if it were, then every time someone killed a fly or a cockroach today, they would be dramatically altering the future, which seems highly farfetched.]

---

tally kill one mouse here. That means all the future families of this one particular mouse are destroyed, right?"

"Right."

"And all the families of the families of the families of that one mouse! With a stamp of your foot, you <u>annihilate</u> first one, then a dozen, then a thousand, a million, a *billion* possible mice!"

"So they're dead," said Eckels. "So what?"

"So what?" Travis snorted quietly. "Well, what about the foxes that'll need those mice to survive? For want of ten mice, a fox dies. For want of ten foxes, a lion starves. For want of a lion, all manner of insects, vultures, infinite billions of life forms are thrown into chaos and destruction. Eventually it all boils down to this: Fifty-nine million years later, a cave man, one of a dozen in the *entire world*, goes hunting wild boar or saber-toothed tiger for food. But you, **A** friend, have *stepped* on all the tigers in that region. By stepping on *one* single mouse. So the cave man starves. And the cave man, please note, is not just *any* <u>expendable</u> man, no! He is an *entire future nation*. From his loins would have sprung ten sons. From *their* loins one hundred sons, and thus onward to a civilization. Destroy this one man, and you destroy a race, a people, an entire history of life. It is comparable to slaying some of Adam's grandchildren. The stomp of your foot, on one mouse, could start an earthquake, the effects of which could shake our earth and destinies down through Time, to their very foundations. With the death of that one cave man, a billion others yet unborn are throttled in the womb. Perhaps Rome never rises on its seven hills. Perhaps Europe is forever a dark forest, and only Asia waxes healthy and <u>teeming</u>. Step on a mouse and you crush the Pyramids. Step on a mouse and you leave your print, like a Grand Canyon, across Eternity. Queen Elizabeth might never be born, Washington might not cross the Delaware, there might never be a United States at all. So be careful. Stay on the Path. *Never* step off!"

"I see," said Eckels. "Then it wouldn't pay for

us even to touch the *grass*?"

"Correct. Crushing certain plants could add up infinitesimally. A little error here would multiply in sixty million years, all out of proportion. Of course maybe our theory is wrong. Maybe Time *can't* be changed by us. Or maybe it can be changed only in little subtle ways. A dead mouse here makes an insect imbalance there, a population disproportion later, a bad harvest further on, a depression, mass starvation, and, finally, a change in *social* temperament in far-flung countries. Something much more subtle, like that. Perhaps only a soft breath, a whisper, a hair, pollen on the air, such a **B** slight, slight change that unless you looked close you wouldn't see it. Who knows? Who really can say he knows? We don't know. We're guessing. But until we do know for certain whether our messing around in Time *can* make a big roar or a little rustle in history, we're being careful. This Machine, this Path, your clothing and bodies, were sterilized, as you know, before the journey. We wear these oxygen helmets so we can't introduce our bacteria into an ancient atmosphere."

"How do we know which animals to shoot?"

"They're marked with red paint," said Travis. "Today, before our journey, we sent Lesperance here back with the Machine. He came to this particular era and followed certain animals."

"Studying them?"

"Right," said Lesperance. "I track them through their entire existence, noting which of them lives longest. Very few. How many times they mate. Not often. Life's short. When I find one that's going to die when a tree falls on him, or one that drowns in a tar pit, I note the exact hour, minute, and second. I shoot a paint bomb. It leaves a red patch on his side. We can't miss it.

"Stay on the Path. Never step off!"

WORDS TO OWN

annihilate (ə·nī′ə·lāt′) *v.:* destroy; wipe out.
expendable (ek·spen′də·bəl) *adj.:* worth sacrificing to gain an objective.
teeming (tēm′in) *v.:* used as *adj.:* swarming; overflowing.

Using Students' Strengths

Intrapersonal Learners

After students have read the story, talk about Eckels's reaction when he finally faces the dinosaur. Ask students if they have ever experienced a similar emotional situation—one in which, after getting something they desired, they unexpectedly encountered fear, or the desire to escape the situation into which they had placed themselves. Ask them to write a paragraph describing the situation and the emotions they felt.

Logical/Mathematical Learners

After students have finished reading the story, invite them to think about its conclusion. Ask them to consider how stepping on a butterfly could change the outcome of a presidential campaign 60 million years in the future. Challenge students to come up with plausible answers to this question. Have them work in groups to brainstorm and record some of the possible missing steps in the sequence of events unleashed by Eckels.

Then I correlate our arrival in the Past so that we meet the Monster not more than two minutes before he would have died anyway. This way, we kill only animals with no future, that are never going to mate again. You see how *careful* we are?"

"But if you came back this morning in Time," said Eckels eagerly, "you must've bumped into *us*, our Safari! How did it turn out? Was it successful? Did all of us get through—alive?"

Travis and Lesperance gave each other a look.

"That'd be a paradox," said the latter. "Time doesn't permit that sort of mess—a man meeting himself. When such occasions threaten, Time steps aside. Like an airplane hitting an air pocket. You felt the Machine jump just before we stopped? That was us passing ourselves on the way back to the Future. We saw nothing. There's no way of telling *if* this expedition was a success, *if we* got our monster, or whether all of us—meaning *you*, Mr. Eckels—got out alive."

Eckels smiled palely.

"Cut that," said Travis sharply. "Everyone on his feet!"

They were ready to leave the Machine.

The jungle was high and the jungle was broad and the jungle was the entire world forever and forever. Sounds like music and sounds like flying tents filled the sky, and those were pterodactyls soaring with cavernous gray wings, gigantic bats of delirium and night fever. Eckels, balanced on the narrow Path, aimed his rifle playfully.

"Stop that!" said Travis. "Don't even aim for fun, blast you! If your guns should go off——"

Eckels flushed. "Where's our *Tyrannosaurus*?"

Lesperance checked his wristwatch. "Up ahead. We'll bisect his trail in sixty seconds. Look for the red paint! Don't shoot till we give the word. Stay on the Path. *Stay on the Path!*"

They moved forward in the wind of morning.

"Strange," murmured Eckels. "Up ahead, sixty million years, Election Day over. Keith made President. Everyone celebrating. And here we are, a million years lost, and they don't exist. The things we worried about for months, a lifetime, not even born or thought of yet."

"Safety catches off, everyone!" ordered Travis. "You, first shot, Eckels. Second, Billings. Third, Kramer."

"I've hunted tiger, wild boar, buffalo, elephant, but now, this is *it*," said Eckels. "I'm shaking like a kid."

"Ah," said Travis.

Everyone stopped.

Travis raised his hand. "Ahead," he whispered. "In the mist. There he is. There's His Royal Majesty now."

The jungle was wide and full of twitterings, rustlings, murmurs, and sighs.

Suddenly it all ceased, as if someone had shut a door.

Silence.

A sound of thunder.

Out of the mist, one hundred yards away, came *Tyrannosaurus rex*.

"It," whispered Eckels. "It . . ."

"Sh!"

It came on great oiled, resilient, striding legs. It towered thirty feet above half of the trees, a great evil god, folding its delicate watchmaker's claws close to its oily reptilian chest. Each lower leg was a piston, a thousand pounds of white bone, sunk in thick ropes of muscle, sheathed

---

WORDS TO OWN

paradox (par'ə·däks') *n.*: something that has or seems to have contradictory qualities.

resilient (ri·zil'yənt) *adj.*: elastic; able to return to the original shape quickly after being stretched or compressed. *Resilient* also means "able to recover quickly from misfortune or difficulty."

A Sound of Thunder 39

C **Advanced Learners**
Evaluating the Science in Science Fiction

? Invite students to evaluate Bradbury's idea of a time-travel paradox. Do you think there is scientific merit in the idea that people can't meet themselves during time travel? [Possible response: There is scientific merit to the idea because the same matter can't be in the same place twice.]

D **Elements of Literature**
Climax

? Based on what Eckels says, do you think his encounter with the dinosaur will be the story's climactic event? [Possible responses: Yes, he refers to the encounter as "it"; yes, that encounter is what the story has led up to so far.]

E **Literary Connections**

Here's what Bradbury had to say about his description of the Tyrannosaur: "So Shakespeare has given me the courage —and Melville—to do the aside.... I say to the audience 'I'm going to stop the plot here, okay? . . . and you know what I'm going to do? I'm going to describe a dinosaur as it's never been described. Now watch this.' And then I sit down and write a prose poem about this wonderful creature that comes gliding out of the jungle." Discuss with students why a description like this might be considered a prose poem.

Skill Link

Identifying Past Participles

You might want to use the following exercise before you teach the Grammar Link exercise on verbs in the active and passive voice, on p. 49. Students should recognize that verb phrases in the passive voice include a form of *be* and the past participle of the main verb. This exercise will help you assess students' skill in identifying past participles. For a review of verbs, see pp. 998–1000 in the Language Handbook.

Write (P) next to each sentence that includes the past participle of a verb.

1. Eckels was required to pay a large fee to go on the safari. [P]
2. Travis was not very friendly to his fellow hunters.
3. The hunters were fascinated by the poise and balance of the enormous dinosaurs running toward them. [P]
4. Keith was the original winner of the election.
5. The hunters had been informed in the clearest possible terms that they must never leave the Path. [P]
6. The earth was shaken by the footsteps of the giant reptile. [P]
7. Using the time machine, they rode into the past.
8. Eckels's mistake could never be forgiven by Travis. [P]

T39

LITERATURE AND SCIENCE

Learning that the dinosaurs might have been wiped out after an asteroid or a comet slammed into the earth has generated world-wide anxiety. As movies like *Armageddon* and *Deep Impact* demonstrated, people are becoming more and more concerned with the threat of an impact that could wipe out life as we know it. Certainly the precedent is there: besides the impact that finished off the dinosaurs 65 million years ago, an earlier impact 215 million years ago supposedly wiped out 80 percent of the Earth's species. So, how worried should we be? That depends on whom you ask. Some astronomers claim the threat is extremely small. However, the United States government was worried enough to create the Near Earth Asteroid Tracking (NEAT) program in 1995. Astronomers in the program estimate that eventually they will be able to track 95 percent of the asteroids that pass near Earth in space. No one has yet figured out how to alter an asteroid's course so as to prevent impact, but at least there will be fair warning and many years in which to plan an anti-impact strategy.

How Did They Disappear?

What caused the extinction of the dinosaurs? How could such a dominant, thriving population disappear? Scientists have recently asked whether the extinction was the result of a gradual decline or a sudden catastrophe. Now some geologists think they've found the answer—in rocks.

Geologists know the secret of time travel: They know that layers—or sediments—of rock can reveal the history of the earth. It is in these layers that a team of scientists from the University of California at Berkeley found evidence indicating that the dinosaurs were wiped out after an asteroid or a comet—nobody knows which it was—slammed into the earth sixty-five million years ago. It's a theory that combines some of science fiction's favorite subjects: time travel, asteroids, and dinosaurs.

The rocks tell the story. All over the world the sediment that forms the boundary between the age of the dinosaurs and the age following their extinction contains deposits of iridium, a mineral that is extremely rare on earth but common in outer space. Some scientists believe that the iridium was deposited when a large asteroid or a comet—about six miles across—struck the earth.

Scientists even believe that they have discovered the site where the comet or asteroid hit, in Chicxulub (pronounced chek′shoo·loob′), on the coast of the Yucatán Peninsula in Mexico. The proof is in the rocks, which contain not just deposits of iridium but also all the right minerals and chemicals to prove the theory.

The impact would have caused massive fires, tidal waves, and floods, but the dust created by the impact—composed of iridium and other minerals—caused even bigger problems. The dust blocked the sunlight; the earth became cool and dark, killing plants and devastating the food chain. Eventually the dust settled, but then a greenhouse effect set in, creating temperatures too high to support most life forms. Almost all life on earth vanished. The 150-million-year reign of the dinosaurs had reached its catastrophic end.

Assessing Learning

Self-Assessment

Monitor Your Reading. To help students observe and reflect on their own development as readers, have them copy and complete this scale in their journals after they read the story, rating their response to the selection on a scale from 0 to 10. Ask them to explain why they marked it as they did.

0	10
I don't believe that I understood this story.	I believe that I thoroughly understood this story.

Then, ask students to discuss what they can do when they do not understand a reading assignment. [Identify a troublesome passage, ask questions to clarify, adjust reading rate, reread.] Model some techniques, using a passage from the story. Then, select other passages, and have students model simple strategies.

over in a gleam of pebbled skin like the mail of a terrible warrior. Each thigh was a ton of meat, ivory, and steel mesh. And from the great breathing cage of the upper body those two delicate arms dangled out front, arms with hands which might pick up and examine men like toys, while the snake neck coiled. And the head itself, a ton of sculptured stone, lifted easily upon the sky. Its mouth gaped, exposing a fence of teeth like daggers. Its eyes rolled, ostrich eggs, empty of all expression save hunger. It closed its mouth in a death grin. It ran, its pelvic bones crushing aside trees and bushes, its taloned feet clawing damp earth, leaving prints six inches deep wherever it settled its weight. It ran with a gliding ballet step, far too poised and balanced for its ten tons. It moved into a sunlit arena warily, its beautifully reptilian hands feeling the air.

"Why, why," Eckels twitched his mouth. "It could reach up and grab the moon."

"Sh!" Travis jerked angrily. "He hasn't seen us yet."

"It can't be killed." Eckels pronounced this verdict quietly, as if there could be no argument. He had weighed the evidence and this was his considered opinion. The rifle in his hands seemed a cap gun. "We were fools to come. This is impossible."

"Shut up!" hissed Travis.

"Nightmare."

"Turn around," commanded Travis. "Walk quietly to the Machine. We'll remit one half your fee."

"I didn't realize it would be this *big,*" said Eckels. "I miscalculated, that's all. And now I want out."

"It *sees* us!"

"There's the red paint on its chest!"

The Tyrant Lizard raised itself. Its armored flesh glittered like a thousand green coins. The coins, crusted with slime, steamed. In the slime, tiny insects wriggled, so that the entire body seemed to twitch and undulate, even while the monster itself did not move. It exhaled. The stink of raw flesh blew down the wilderness.

"Get me out of here," said Eckels. "It was never like this before. I was always sure I'd come through alive. I had good guides, good safaris, and safety. This time, I figured wrong. I've met my match and admit it. This is too much for me to get hold of."

"Don't run," said Lesperance. "Turn around. Hide in the Machine."

"Yes." Eckels seemed to be numb. He looked at his feet as if trying to make them move. He gave a grunt of helplessness.

"Eckels!"

He took a few steps, blinking, shuffling.

"Not *that* way!"

The Monster, at the first motion, lunged forward with a terrible scream. It covered one hundred yards in six seconds. The rifles jerked up and blazed fire. A windstorm from the beast's mouth engulfed them in the stench of slime and old blood. The Monster roared, teeth glittering with sun.

Eckels, not looking back, walked blindly to the edge of the Path, his gun limp in his arms, stepped off the Path, and walked, not knowing it, in the jungle. His feet sank into green moss. His legs moved him, and he felt alone and remote from the events behind.

The rifles cracked again. Their sound was lost in shriek and lizard thunder. The great level of the reptile's tail swung up, lashed sideways. Trees exploded in clouds of leaf and branch. The Monster twitched its jeweler's hands down to fondle at the men, to twist them in half, to

---

WORDS TO OWN

remit (ri·mit′) *v.*: here, give back payment.
undulate (un′dyo͞o·lāt′) *v.*: move in waves.

A SOUND OF THUNDER **41**

A **Elements of Literature**
Conflict
? Who is in conflict here? [Eckels and Travis] What is the conflict? [Possible responses: Eckels is overwhelmed by the dinosaur, and Travis thinks Eckels is speaking and acting foolishly; Eckels wants to give up, and Travis fears that Eckels is endangering the expedition.]

B **Elements of Literature**
Climax
? How do you know that this encounter between Eckels and the dinosaur is not the climactic event that Bradbury has set readers up for? [Possible answers: There has been no conflict between Eckels and the dinosaur; Eckels is too scared to do anything to the dinosaur.]

C **Reading Skills and Strategies**

Cause and Effect
? What causes Eckels to step off the Path? [Sample responses: He is overwhelmed by his fear of the Tyrannosaur; he doesn't know what he's doing.] What might be an effect of his stepping off the Path? [Possible answers: He might accidentally crush something and alter the future; the dinosaur might capture him.]

Using Students' Strengths

Visual Learners
After students have finished reading the story, ask them to think of other examples of the "domino effect" described in the story: situations in which a seemingly small incident—such as stepping on an insect—proves to have tremendous implications through a chain of linked events. Have students create posters with illustrations showing how these linked events lead step-by-step to a final result.

Naturalist Learners
Invite interested students to research the prehistoric world and create a "tourist fact-sheet" for time-traveling visitors to the primeval past. Tell students to provide descriptions of the flora and fauna a visitor would encounter, information about the climate and terrain, and other facts that would prepare a Time Safari customer for their primeval adventure.

? Have a student volunteer read this passage aloud and say whether the verbs in it are active or passive. [They are all active.] Then, discuss how Bradbury's use of active verbs makes the death of the tyrannosaur more vivid and immediate. If some of the verbs were switched to the passive voice, would the death of the dinosaur seem as dramatic? [Most students will say that a passive voice would make the death less dramatic.]

B. English Language Learners
Breaking Down Difficult Text

Students may have trouble with the imagery and vocabulary in this passage. Suggest that they read aloud and discuss the passage with partners, explaining the images in their own words. Students should also look up difficult words such as *sac, spleen, locomotive,* and *tonnage* in the dictionary.

C. Elements of Literature
Conflict

? Why is Travis angry at Eckels? [Eckels has stepped off the Path and perhaps jeopardized not only the business but also the future of the world.]

---

crush them like berries, to cram them into its teeth and its screaming throat. Its boulder-stone eyes leveled with the men. They saw themselves mirrored. They fired at the metallic eyelids and the blazing black iris.

A Like a stone idol, like a mountain avalanche, *Tyrannosaurus* fell. Thundering, it clutched trees, pulled them with it. It wrenched and tore the metal Path. The men flung themselves back and away. The body hit, ten tons of cold flesh and stone. The guns fired. The Monster lashed its armored tail, twitched its snake jaws, and lay still. A fount of blood spurted from its throat. Somewhere inside, a sac of fluids burst. Sickening gushes drenched the hunters. They stood, red and glistening.

The thunder faded.

The jungle was silent. After the avalanche, a green peace. After the nightmare, morning.

Billings and Kramer sat on the pathway and threw up. Travis and Lesperance stood with smoking rifles, cursing steadily.

In the Time Machine, on his face, Eckels lay shivering. He had found his way back to the Path, climbed into the Machine.

Travis came walking, glanced at Eckels, took cotton gauze from a metal box, and returned to the others, who were sitting on the Path.

"Clean up."

B They wiped the blood from their helmets. They began to curse too. The Monster lay, a hill of solid flesh. Within, you could hear the sighs and murmurs as the furthest chambers of it died, the organs malfunctioning, liquids running a final instant from pocket to sac to spleen, everything shutting off, closing up forever. It was like standing by a wrecked locomotive or a steam shovel at quitting time, all valves being released or levered tight. Bones cracked; the tonnage of its own flesh, off balance, dead weight, snapped the delicate forearms, caught underneath. The meat settled, quivering.

Another cracking sound. Overhead, a gigantic tree branch broke from its heavy mooring,

The Monster lay, a hill of solid flesh.

fell. It crashed upon the dead beast with finality.

"There." Lesperance checked his watch. "Right on time. That's the giant tree that was scheduled to fall and kill this animal originally." He glanced at the two hunters. "You want the trophy picture?"

"What?"

"We can't take a trophy back to the Future. The body has to stay right here where it would have died originally, so the insects, birds, and bacteria can get at it, as they were intended to. Everything in balance. The body stays. But we *can* take a picture of you standing near it."

The two men tried to think, but gave up, shaking their heads.

They let themselves be led along the metal Path. They sank wearily into the Machine cushions. They gazed back at the ruined Monster, the stagnating mound, where already strange reptilian birds and golden insects were busy at the steaming armor.

A sound on the floor of the Time Machine stiffened them. Eckels sat there, shivering.

C "I'm sorry," he said at last.

"Get up!" cried Travis.

Eckels got up.

"Go out on that Path alone," said Travis. He had his rifle pointed. "You're not coming back in the Machine. We're leaving you here!"

Lesperance seized Travis's arm. "Wait——"

"Stay out of this!" Travis shook his hand away. "This fool nearly killed us. But it isn't *that* so much, no. It's his *shoes*! Look at them! He ran off the Path. That *ruins* us! We'll forfeit! Thousands of dollars of insurance! We guarantee no one leaves the path. He left it. Oh, the fool! I'll have to report to the government. They might <u>revoke</u> our license to travel. Who knows *what* he's done to Time, to History!"

WORDS TO OWN

<u>revoke</u> (ri·vōk′) v.: cancel; withdraw.

Crossing the Curriculum

Science

Was *Tyrannosaurus rex* really the "most incredible monster in history"? If Bradbury were writing his story today, he might have chosen the *Gigantosaurus* instead. In 1994–1995, paleontologists working in Argentina's Patagonia region discovered the skeleton of this prehistoric land predator. The team of paleontologists estimated that the *Gigantosaurus* weighed about 8 tons— 3 more tons than *T. rex*—and measured 47 feet in length (*T. rex* measured between 40 and 50). So is *Gigantosaurus* the undisputed king of dinosaurs? Not necessarily. In Africa, paleontologists have found the skull of yet another species of carnivorous dinosaur, *Carcharodontosaurus*. Its skull alone measured 62 inches in length, almost the same as the skull of *Gigantosaurus*. Without a whole skeleton it is difficult to determine just how big this creature was, but it is estimated to be in the same 40–50 foot range of its two fellow megamonsters. Encourage interested students to prepare a display comparing these and other dinosaur species, using models or illustrations to demonstrate their respective physical attributes and relative sizes.

"Take it easy, all he did was kick up some dirt."

"How do we *know*?" cried Travis. "We don't know anything! It's all a mystery! Get out of here, Eckels!"

Eckels fumbled his shirt. "I'll pay anything. A  hundred thousand dollars!"

Travis glared at Eckels's checkbook and spat. "Go out there. The Monster's next to the Path. Stick your arms up to your elbows in his mouth. Then you can come back with us."

"That's unreasonable!"

"The Monster's dead, you idiot. The bullets! The bullets can't be left behind. They don't belong in the Past; they might change anything. Here's my knife. Dig them out!"

The jungle was alive again, full of the old tremorings and bird cries. Eckels turned slowly to regard the primeval garbage dump, that hill of nightmares and terror. After a long time, like a sleepwalker he shuffled out along the Path.

He returned, shuddering, five minutes later, his arms soaked and red to the elbows. He held out his hands. Each held a number of steel bullets. Then he fell. He lay where he fell, not moving.

"You didn't have to make him do that," said Lesperance.

"Didn't I? It's too early to tell." Travis nudged the still body. "He'll live. Next time he won't go hunting game like this. Okay." He jerked his thumb wearily at Lesperance. "Switch on. Let's go home."

1492. 1776. 1812.

They cleaned their hands and faces. They changed their caking shirts and pants. Eckels was up and around again, not speaking. Travis glared at him for a full ten minutes.

"Don't look at me," cried Eckels. "I haven't done anything."

"Who can tell?"

"Just ran off the Path, that's all, a little mud on my shoes—what do you want me to do—get down and pray?"

"We might need it. I'm warning you, Eckels, I might kill you yet. I've got my gun ready."

"I'm innocent. I've done nothing!"

1999. 2000. 2055.

The Machine stopped.

"Get out," said Travis.

The room was there as they had left it. But not the same as they had left it. The same man sat behind the same desk. But the same man did not quite sit behind the same desk.

Travis looked around swiftly. "Everything okay here?" he snapped.

"Fine. Welcome home!"

Travis did not relax. He seemed to be looking at the very atoms of the air itself, at the way the sun poured through the one high window.

"Okay, Eckels, get out. Don't ever come back."

Eckels could not move.

"You heard me," said Travis. "What're you *staring* at?"

Eckels stood smelling of the air, and there was a thing to the air, a chemical taint so subtle, so slight, that only a faint cry of his subliminal senses warned him it was there. The colors, white, gray, blue, orange, in the wall, in the furniture, in the sky beyond the window, were . . . were . . . And there was a *feel*. His flesh twitched. His hands twitched. He stood drinking the oddness with the pores of his body. Somewhere, someone must have been screaming one of those whistles that only a dog can hear. His body screamed silence in return. Beyond this room, beyond this wall, beyond this man who was not quite the same man seated at this desk that was not quite the same desk . . . lay an entire world of streets and people. What sort of world it was now, there was no telling. He could feel them moving there, beyond the walls, almost, like so many chess pieces blown in a dry wind. . . .

But the immediate thing was the sign painted on the office wall, the same sign he had read earlier today on first entering.

WORDS TO OWN

primeval (prī·mē′vəl) *adj.*: primitive; of the earliest times.
subliminal (sub·lim′ə·nəl) *adj.*: below the level of consciousness.

A SOUND OF THUNDER **43**

D Critical Thinking
Making Judgments
❓ What does Eckels's offer of payment reveal about him? [He thinks money can fix everything.] **Can money fix something like this? Explain.** [Sample answers: Money cannot fix the future; money cannot change what Eckels has done.]

E Historical Connection
Have students identify the historical importance of each date listed here. [1492—Columbus sailed to the Americas; 1776—the Declaration of Independence was written; 1812—the War of 1812 took place]

F Reading Skills and Strategies
Cause and Effect
❓ What does Travis fear might be the effects of Eckels having stepped off the path? [He fears that Eckels might have greatly altered the future.]

G Elements of Literature
Climax
❓ How does this passage build the type of suspense that can lead to the climax of a story? [Possible answers: Bradbury lets the reader know that something is different, but not exactly what; the unidentified change and the conflict between Travis and Eckels indicate that something major is going to happen.]

Crossing the Curriculum

Science and Technology

Like much of Bradbury's fiction, "A Sound of Thunder" displays both a fascination with technology's potential and a warning about unintended consequences that may arise from its use. The time machine liberates people from the present and allows them to explore the past; however, the hunting party's use of the machine has disastrous consequences when they return to the present. Bradbury's ambivalence toward technology is evident in his well-known antipathy toward the automobile, an instrument he feels is often misused. Though the automobile affords transportation benefits to its users, Bradbury believes that it can also make a person "try to prove his machismo, as a result of which he murders other people and murders himself." Ask students to consider the ways in which the technology they use, while designed to improve or facilitate their lives, can also have negative effects. You may wish to have students brainstorm and list on the chalkboard familiar technological devices, such as the cellular phone, the computer, and the Internet. Then, have students list some unintended consequences of the use of those technologies.

A Reading Skills and Strategies

Cause and Effect

❓ What chain of events do the dominoes refer to? [They refer to the way that killing a small creature can set off a chain of events that profoundly affects the future.]

B Elements of Literature

Climax

❓ Why is this the climax of the story? [It is the emotional moment that shows the outcome of the story's conflict.]

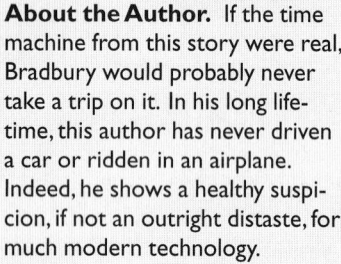

BROWSING IN THE FILES

About the Author. If the time machine from this story were real, Bradbury would probably never take a trip on it. In his long lifetime, this author has never driven a car or ridden in an airplane. Indeed, he shows a healthy suspicion, if not an outright distaste, for much modern technology.

A Critic's Comment. The critic Sam Lundwall claims that "All of Bradbury's works [are] utterly naive and from a scientist's point of view, crazy." How might this criticism pertain to "A Sound of Thunder"?

Resources ——

Selection Assessment

Formal Assessment
• Selection Test, p. 3
Test Generator (One-Stop Planner)
• CD-ROM

Somehow, the sign had changed:

TYME SEFARI INC.

Sefaris tu any yeer en the past.

Yu naim the animall.
Wee taekyuthair.

Yu shoot itt.

Eckels felt himself fall into a chair. He fumbled crazily at the thick slime on his boots. He held up a clod of dirt, trembling, "No, it *can't* be. Not a *little* thing like that. No!"

Embedded in the mud, glistening green and gold and black, was a butterfly, very beautiful and very dead.

"Not a little thing like *that*! Not a butterfly!" cried Eckels.

A It fell to the floor, an exquisite thing, a small thing that could upset balances and knock **B**

---

down a line of small dominoes and then big dominoes and then gigantic dominoes, all down the years across Time. Eckels' mind whirled. It *couldn't* change things. Killing one butterfly couldn't be *that* important! Could it?

His face was cold. His mouth trembled, asking: "Who—who won the presidential election yesterday?"

The man behind the desk laughed. "You joking? You know very well. Deutscher, of course! Who else? Not that fool weakling Keith. We got an iron man now, a man with guts!" The official stopped. "What's wrong?"

Eckels moaned. He dropped to his knees. He scrabbled at the golden butterfly with shaking fingers. "Can't we," he pleaded to the world, to himself, to the officials, to the Machine, "can't we take it *back,* can't we *make* it alive again? Can't we start over? Can't we——"

He did not move. Eyes shut, he waited, shivering. He heard Travis breathe loud in the room; he heard Travis shift his rifle, click the safety catch, and raise the weapon.

B There was a sound of thunder.

MEET THE WRITER
Teller of Tales

Ray Bradbury (1920–   ) calls himself a teller of tales and a magic realist. He also claims to remember everything—every book he's read, every movie he's seen, all the events of his life back to and including his birth, in Waukegan, Illinois, on August 22, 1920. All those memories and a big imagination are the materials for the fiction and poetry he's been writing for more than fifty years. Bradbury gives credit for his writing to his boyhood self:

❝I don't know if I believe in previous lives; I'm not sure I can live forever. But that young boy believed in both, and I have let him have his head. He has written my stories and books for me.❞

Bradbury's work is full of childhood imaginings, fantasies, and nightmares—portraits of Venus and Mars, time travel, ageless children, never-ending rains—but Bradbury the grown-up is a concerned citizen. His fantasy stories are often warnings against blind faith in science, but they're optimistic. By giving strange twists to everyday objects and events, Bradbury challenges his readers to look at them as if for the first time. As a writer, he lets readers see science through the excited eyes of children, but he also informs, suggesting ways adults might use technology more responsibly.

For another Bradbury story, see page 259.

Assessing Learning

Check Test: True-False

1. Time Safari Inc. offers hunting trips into the distant past. [True]
2. Keith, a candidate for president, has dictatorial tendencies. [False]
3. Eckels hopes to shoot a tyrannosaur. [True]
4. Mr. Travis is the group's safari guide. [True]
5. Eckels shows little fear of the giant dinosaur. [False]

6. The hunters are unable to kill their prey. [False]
7. One man is left behind in the world of dinosaurs. [False]
8. Eckels obeys the rule not to step off the Path. [False]
9. The story ends in the distant past. [False]
10. By stepping on a butterfly, Eckels changes the course of history. [True]

Standardized Test Preparation

For practice with standardized test format specific to this selection, see
• *Standardized Test Preparation,* p. 10
For practice in proofreading and editing, see
• *Daily Oral Grammar,* Transparency 2

from Jurassic Park

Michael Crichton

In Michael Crichton's novel Jurassic Park *(1990), John Hammond, a rich corporate executive, hires a team of scientists to clone dinosaurs from DNA and succeeds in bringing the giant reptiles back from extinction. Hammond populates an island reserve, Jurassic Park, with his clones, letting them roam on lands surrounded by electric fences. He plans to have visitors pay to view the monstrous creatures, using Land Cruisers that run on electric tracks throughout the reserve. But before the park's scheduled opening, something goes seriously awry: A park employee trying to enter an off-limits laboratory shuts down portions of the park's electricity. As a result, the power feeding the fences and the tracks fails. The dinosaurs are loose.*

As this excerpt opens, the Land Cruisers stop. In them are two visiting scientists, Dr. Malcolm and Dr. Grant, and Hammond's grandchildren, Tim and his sister, Lex. A tyrannosaur approaches.

The huge head raised back up, jaws open, and then stopped by the side windows. In the glare of lightning, they saw the beady, expressionless reptile eye moving in the socket.

It was looking in the car.

His sister's breath came in ragged, frightened gasps. He reached out and squeezed her arm, hoping she would stay quiet. The dinosaur continued to stare for a long time through the side window. Perhaps the dinosaur couldn't really see them, he thought. Finally the head lifted up, out of view again.

"Timmy . . . ," Lex whispered.

"It's okay," Tim whispered. "I don't think it saw us."

He was looking back toward Dr. Grant when a jolting impact rocked the Land Cruiser and shattered the windshield in a spider web as the tyrannosaur's head crashed against the hood of the Land Cruiser. Tim was knocked flat on the seat. The night-vision goggles slid off his forehead.

He got back up quickly, blinking in the darkness, his mouth warm with blood.

"Lex?"

He couldn't see his sister anywhere.

The tyrannosaur stood near the front of the Land Cruiser, its chest moving as it breathed, the forelimbs making clawing movements in the air.

"Lex!" Tim whispered. Then he heard her groan. She was lying somewhere on the floor under the front seat.

Then the huge head came down, entirely blocking the shattered windshield. The tyrannosaur banged again on the front hood of the Land Cruiser. Tim grabbed the seat as the car rocked on its wheels. The tyrannosaur banged down twice more, denting the metal.

Then it moved around the side of the car. The big raised tail blocked his view out of all the side windows. At the back, the animal snorted, a deep rumbling growl that blended with the

Connections

The idea of contemporary people confronting the prehistoric past has served as an imaginative spring board for many writers. In this excerpt from *Jurassic Park*, Michael Crichton shows how frightening this confrontation might be.

Ⓐ Critical Thinking
Making Connections
❓ Which scene in "A Sound of Thunder" does this remind you of? [Students are likely to mention the scene in which the hunters first meet the tyrannosaur and Travis tries to quiet Eckels.]

Ⓑ Reading Skills and Strategies
Cause and Effect
❓ What causes Tim's mouth to bleed? [The tyrannosaur rocks the Land Cruiser, which shatters the windshield and knocks Tim flat, cutting his mouth.]

Ⓒ Reading Skills and Strategies
Drawing Conclusions
❓ What is the tyrannosaur trying to do? [It's trying to get at the children inside the car.]

Connecting Across Texts

Connecting with "A Sound of Thunder"
Ask students to compare the portrayal of the tyrannosaur in the *Jurassic Park* excerpt with the description of the giant reptile in Bradbury's story. Which depiction did they find more frightening? Why? [Some students may say that descriptive phrases such as "a great evil god" and "stink of raw flesh" made Bradbury's depiction more vivid, and therefore more frightening. Other students may have found that it was easier to visualize and imagine the fear of the passengers trapped in the Land Cruiser.] Many students will be familiar with the film version of *Jurassic Park*. Invite them to discuss whether "A Sound of Thunder" would translate onto the screen as effectively as did Michael Crichton's novel.

A Critical Thinking

Making Connections

Point out that both Crichton and Bradbury use similar images. For example, both writers describe the dinosaur's breath as stinking. Have students discuss whether Crichton may have read "A Sound of Thunder" before writing *Jurassic Park* or whether these images are so obvious that different people could come up with them totally independently.

B Elements of Literature

Climax

❓ Do you think this excerpt reveals the climax of this encounter with the tyrannosaur? Explain. [Possible responses: no, because Tim passes out and we don't know if the tyrannosaur gets the children; yes, the climax comes when the tyrannosaur drops the car, after which readers are just waiting for the resolution.]

thunder. It sank its jaws into the spare tire mounted on the back of the Land Cruiser and, in a single headshake, tore it away. The rear of the car lifted into the air for a moment; then it thumped down with a muddy splash.

"Tim!" Dr. Grant said. "Tim, are you there?"

Tim grabbed the radio. "We're okay," he said. There was a shrill metallic scrape as claws raked the roof of the car. Tim's heart was pounding in his chest. He couldn't see anything out of the windows on the right side except pebbled leathery flesh. The tyrannosaur was leaning against the car, which rocked back and forth with each breath, the springs and metal creaking loudly.

Lex groaned again. Tim put down the radio and started to crawl over into the front seat. The tyrannosaur roared and the metal roof dented downward. Tim felt a sharp pain in his head and tumbled to the floor, onto the transmission hump. He found himself lying alongside Lex, and he was shocked to see that the whole side of her head was covered in blood. She looked unconscious.

There was another jolting impact, and pieces of glass fell all around him. Tim felt rain. He looked up and saw that the front windshield had broken out. There was just a jagged rim of glass and, beyond, the big head of the dinosaur.

Looking down at him.

Tim felt a sudden chill and then the head rushed forward toward him, the jaws open. There was the squeal of metal against teeth, and he felt the hot stinking breath of the animal, and a thick tongue stuck into the car through the windshield opening. The tongue slapped wetly around inside the car—he felt the hot lather of dinosaur saliva—and the tyrannosaur roared—a deafening sound inside the car—

The head pulled away abruptly.

Tim scrambled up, avoiding the dent in the roof. There was still room to sit on the front seat by the passenger door. The tyrannosaur stood in the rain near the front fender. It seemed confused by what had happened to it. Blood dripped freely from its jaws.

The tyrannosaur looked at Tim, cocking its head to stare with one big eye. The head moved

close to the car, sideways, and peered in. Blood splattered on the dented hood of the Land Cruiser, mixing with the rain.

It can't get to me, Tim thought. It's too big.

Then the head pulled away, and in the flare of lightning he saw the hind leg lift up. And the world tilted crazily as the Land Cruiser slammed over on its side, the windows splatting in the mud. He saw Lex fall helplessly against the side window, and he fell down beside her, banging his head. Tim felt dizzy. Then the tyrannosaur's jaws clamped onto the window frame, and the whole Land Cruiser was lifted up into the air and shaken.

"Timmy!" Lex shrieked so near to his ear that it hurt. She was suddenly awake, and he grabbed her as the tyrannosaur crashed the car down again. Tim felt a stabbing pain in his side, and his sister fell on top of him. The car went up again, tilting crazily. Lex shouted "*Timmy!*" and he saw the door give way beneath her, and she fell out of the car into the mud, but Tim couldn't answer because in the next instant everything swung crazily—he saw the trunks of the palm trees sliding downward past him—moving sideways through the air—he glimpsed the ground very far below—the hot roar of the tyrannosaur—the blazing eye—the tops of the palm trees—

And then, with a metallic scraping shriek, the car fell from the tyrannosaur's jaws, a sickening fall, and Tim's stomach heaved in the moment before the world became totally black, and silent.

Crossing the Curriculum

Science

Improbable as it may seem, chickens, pigeons, and parakeets may be cousins to the mighty *Tyrannosaurus rex*. Scientists in China have discovered evidence of feathers on the remains of two 120-million-year-old dinosaurs, creatures related to the terrifying velociraptors that featured prominently in the film version of *Jurassic Park*. These and other findings—such as the presence of a wishbone in a velociraptor skeleton—support the theory that modern birds are direct dinosaur descendants, their family tree branching off during the Jurassic era. Have interested students investigate this subject more thoroughly. Ask them to report their findings to the class, perhaps using visual aids that compare the structures of the two species and listing the evidence that has led scientific researchers to propose this theory.

First Thoughts

[analyze] 1. What happens to Eckels at the end of Bradbury's story? What is the **cause** of the final event?

Shaping Interpretations

[analyze] 2. How does Travis explain the **chain of cause and effect** that he says would occur if a hunter accidentally killed even one mouse (see page 38)? Do you think this might really be possible? Explain.

[connect] 3. Why, in your opinion, does Travis force Eckels to retrieve the steel bullets from the monster's body? What did you think of Travis's demand?

[analyze] 4. What is the significance of the misspellings in the Time Safari, Inc., sign that Eckels sees at the end of the story?

[analyze] 5. How does Eckels change the course of history?

[infer] 6. By the end of the story, what new "monster" is in power?

[infer] 7. What different meanings can you give the story's **title**?

[analyze] 8. Bradbury's writing is lush, full of **figures of speech** and vivid **descriptions**. List all the things that the tyrannosaur is compared with. What descriptive details help you see, hear, and smell Bradbury's fabulous prehistoric swamp?

Extending the Text

[interpret] 9. Do you think this is just an entertaining story, or does it have a serious **message**? Explain your answer.

Challenging the Text

[evaluate] 10. There's no doubt that Bradbury has written what critics would call a blockbuster story. Now, take it apart. Do you find flaws in its logic? How accurate is Bradbury's science? Work in teams, and share your findings. Be sure to consider this last question: Do flaws in the story lessen your enjoyment of it?

Reading Check

Fill in a **cause-and-effect chart** to show the sequence of events in the story. The first event and the last are already filled in. You will have to add other boxes as you need them, to include all the main events.

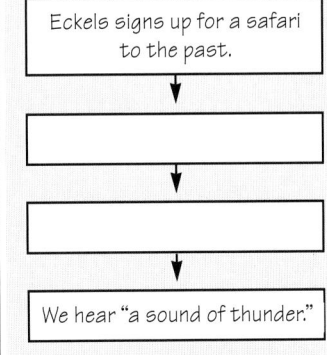

> Eckels signs up for a safari to the past.
>
> ↓
>
> [ ]
>
> ↓
>
> [ ]
>
> ↓
>
> We hear "a sound of thunder."

Put a star beside the event that you think marks the story's **climax**. Be sure to compare your sequences in class.

Reading Check
Sample Response

[first box] Eckels signs up for a safari to the past.
[second box] The hunting party travels to the past and encounters the dinosaur.
[third box] Eckels panics at the sight of the dinosaur and steps off the Path.
[fourth box] When they return to the future, things are different, and Eckels discovers he has killed a butterfly.
[fifth box] Travis aims his gun at Eckels.
*[sixth box] We hear "a sound of thunder."

First Thoughts

1. Travis shoots Eckels and he dies. The cause of this event is the fact that Eckels stepped off the Path and accidentally killed a butterfly, thereby altering the future.

Shaping Interpretations

2. If the mouse is killed, its descendants won't exist. Consequently, a fox will not have mice to eat, a lion will not have foxes to eat, and so on up the food chain to a cave man, who, for lack of game to hunt, will die. Therefore, the entire human race and civilization will eventually die out.

3. Possible responses: Travis knows the bullets don't belong in that time; Travis wants to punish Eckels for straying off the Path.

4. The misspellings show that the course of history has changed.

5. When Eckels strays off the Path, he stomps on a butterfly and kills it, a small change that reverberates into the future.

6. The dictator Deutscher is in power.

7. Possible meanings: The title refers to the blast of Travis's rifle as he kills Eckels; it's a figurative reference to the sound of a momentous historical event; it contains a warning about the dangers of technology.

8. Possible comparisons: "great evil god, terrible warrior," "stone idol, mountain avalanche," "wrecked locomotive," "steam shovel." Possible details: "pterodactyls soaring with cavernous gray wings," "sounds like music and flying tents," "stench of slime and old blood."

Extending the Text

9. Possible response: It has serious messages—the potential harm of technology and the impact of individual action.

Challenging the Text

10. Possible flaws in logic: If changing one thing in the past can have vast repercussions, why doesn't every little change in the present cause great ripples? Also, according to Travis, the butterfly's death should have caused changes that would make their world unrecognizable. Most students will say that the story's flaws did not lessen their enjoyment of it.

Rubrics for each Choices assignment appear on p. 91 in the *Portfolio Management System*.

CHOICES: Building Your Portfolio

1. **Writer's Notebook**   Remind students to save their work. They may use it as prewriting for the Writer's Workshop on p. 112.
2. **News Writing**   Suggest that students work in small groups. Have them hold a newspaper staff meeting to brainstorm what aspects of the story would be of most interest to readers and to develop a range of details to include. Encourage them to consider ways of using details to imply what one might not be able to say under a dictatorship.
3. **Creative Writing**   Invite volunteers to read their essays aloud. You might also combine students' essays to create a time travel brochure or bulletin board.
4. **Research/Science**   Remind students that the Internet can be a great source of current scientific data. Have interested students use a software program to present their findings in electronic form. Students may wish to use video clips and/or music in their presentations.
5. **Creative Writing**   Before they begin writing, suggest that students think about whether or not they want their stories to be in the blockbuster style of *Jurassic Park* and "A Sound of Thunder." Then, as a class, brainstorm a list of blockbuster attributes. You may also wish to encourage students to illustrate their stories, either with their own artwork or with illustrations copied from books, magazines, or newspapers.

CHOICES: Building Your Portfolio

Writer's Notebook

1. Collecting Ideas for a Short Narrative

Listing main events. Bradbury's story might have given you ideas for a short narrative of your own. Before you write *any* narrative, you should have some main events in mind. Suppose you want to write about time travel. First jot down some places in the past or future that you'd like to travel to. Then, list the major events you'd include. You might star the event you'd make the climax. Put your events in chronological order—the order in which they happen. Save your notes for the Writer's Workshop on page 112.

[diagram on notebook paper showing:]
- am warned that trip will be dangerous
- wake up alone on empty, desolate plain
- Time travel to unknown future
- find evidence that others failed to survive
- realize vehicle has malfunctioned*

News Writing

2. And This Just In

Suppose you are a TV news reporter. Word has just come into the newsroom of what happened in the office of Time Safari, Inc. Your assignment is to write an account of what happened to Eckels. In the lead (opening paragraphs) of your news report, answer these questions: Who? What? When? Where? Why? and How? The rest of your report should fill in the details. Remember that you are writing during the rule of a dictator who might not believe in freedom of the press. How honest can you be?

Creative Writing

3. Target a Time

You're entering an essay contest with a grand prize of a time-travel journey to the destination of your choice. Tell exactly where you'd like to go and when (pinpoint a year in the future or the past)—and why. What do you want to accomplish when you reach your destination? Write a few sentences describing what you imagine you will see when you arrive. Check your Quickwrite notes.

Research/Science

4. Dinosaur Data

What do we know about dinosaurs? With a partner, research a limited topic relating to dinosaurs, and share your findings with the class. You might want to illustrate your findings. Here are some possible topics:

- the life and times of one species of dinosaur
- theories of why the dinosaurs disappeared
- what paleontologists (scientists who study fossils) do and how they do it

Creative Writing

5. A Dinosaur Encounter

Both Bradbury's "A Sound of Thunder" and the excerpt from Michael Crichton's *Jurassic Park* (see **Connections** on page 45) portray fictional encounters with dinosaurs. Write your own dinosaur story. What kinds of dinosaurs will you use? What exactly will they look like? No human beings were living during the dinosaur era, so you will have to invent some way for humans and monsters to come together. Help your readers feel they are there—use details to help them **see, smell,** and **hear** the scene.

Using Students' Strengths

Auditory/Musical Learners

Suggest that students create a radio or television news broadcast to deliver their news report for Choice 2. You may wish to have students work in groups, with some students working to "gather the facts" (that is, to answer the who, what, when, where, why, and how questions), others collaborating on the final writing, and another delivering the broadcast.

GRAMMAR LINK `MINI-LESSON`

Language Handbook HELP

See Active and Passive Voice, page 1000.

Technology HELP

See Language Workshop CD-ROM. Key word entry: active voice.

Verbs Play Active and Passive Roles

Like people, action verbs have a voice. A verb in the **active voice** expresses an action performed by its subject: *Tina sent her reply*. A verb in the **passive voice** expresses an action done to its subject: *The reply was sent by Tina*.

Which of these are active verbs, and which are passive?

1. "'Six Safari leaders <u>were killed</u>. . . .'"
2. "The Machine <u>slowed</u>; its scream <u>fell</u> to a murmur."
3. "'This machine, this Path, your clothing and bodies, <u>were sterilized</u>, as you know, before the journey.'"
4. "When such occasions <u>threaten</u>, Time <u>steps</u> aside."

The active voice is strong and direct. A verb in the passive voice sounds weak partly because it always needs a helping verb. The passive voice is useful, however, when the writer doesn't know who or what performed the action (*My bicycle was stolen*) or when the writer doesn't want readers to know who performed the action (*The TV was left on*).

> ### Try It Out
>
> Make each sentence stronger and more direct by changing the verb from the passive voice to the active voice. Notice how the active voice results in shorter, more vigorous sentences.
>
> 1. The idea of hunting the dinosaur was abandoned by Eckels.
> 2. The dinosaur's footsteps could be heard and felt by the hunters.
> 3. The silence was shattered by the dinosaur's terrible scream.
> 4. The story has been reviewed favorably by most students.

VOCABULARY `HOW TO OWN A WORD`

WORD BANK

annihilate
expendable
teeming
paradox
resilient
remit
undulate
revoke
primeval
subliminal

Context Clues

Context clues can help you guess at the meanings of unfamiliar words. Find where the words in the Word Bank are used in the story. See if you can find context clues that hint at their meaning. Put your findings in a diagram, like the one here for *annihilate*.

. . . "Say we accidentally kill one mouse here. That means all the future families of this . . . mouse are destroyed, right?" . . . → verb *kill* used first—one mouse

→ verb *destroyed* used next—all future families

"And all the families of the families of the families of that one mouse! With a stamp of your foot, you annihilate a billion possible mice!" → another clue that *annihilate* means "kill"

→ *Annihilate* is a verb. Probably means "to kill a huge number— a billion!"

A SOUND OF THUNDER 49

GRAMMAR LINK

Have students choose a piece of writing from their portfolios. Ask them to identify all the "to be" verbs in their writing by circling them with a colored pen. Remind them that a sentence written in a passive voice includes a "to be" verb (and sometimes an auxiliary verb like *have* or *has*) and the past participle of the main verb. Ask students to decide if the sentences they identify are in the passive voice. If so, challenge students to work with a partner to change half of the sentences into the active voice.

Try It Out
Possible Answers
1. Eckels abandoned the idea of hunting the dinosaur.
2. The hunters could hear and feel the dinosaur's footsteps.
3. The dinosaur's terrible scream shattered the silence.
4. Most students have reviewed the story favorably.

VOCABULARY
Sample Response
"In the slime, tiny insects wriggled, so that the entire body seemed to twitch and <u>undulate</u>, even while the monster itself did not move."
Context clues including the following words and phrases: "wriggled," "entire body seemed to twitch," "move."

Resources ———
Grammar
• *Grammar and Language Links* Worksheet, p. 3
Vocabulary
• *Words to Own* Worksheet, p. 2

Grammar Link Quick Check

Identify whether the following sentences are in the passive or active voice. Change the sentences that are in the passive voice to the active voice.

1. Eckels was waving a check for ten thousand dollars. [Active]
2. The oxygen masks were put on by the men. [Passive. The men put on oxygen masks.]
3. The sky was filled with pterodactyls and gigantic bats. [Passive. Pterodactyls and gigantic bats filled the sky.]
4. Eckels could not shoot the monster. [Active]
5. The men were engulfed by the stench issuing from the beast. [Passive. The stench issuing from the beast engulfed the men.]
6. The reptile had been brought down by the hunters. [Passive. The hunters brought down the reptile.]
7. The butterfly's death was caused by the stamp of a foot. [Passive. The stamp of a foot caused the butterfly's death.]

OBJECTIVES

1. Read and interpret the story
2. Recognize foreshadowing
3. Make predictions about the story
4. Express understanding through creative writing, research/ science, or speaking and listening
5. Identify verb tenses and use consistent verb tenses in writing
6. Understand and use new words

SKILLS

Literary
- Recognize foreshadowing

Reading
- Make predictions about the story

Writing
- List details of a setting
- Write a feature article
- Compare the story with the film version

Research/Science
- Chart and classify information

Grammar
- Use consistent verb tenses

Vocabulary
- Use new words

Planning

- **Traditional Schedule**
  Lesson Plans Including Strategies for English-Language Learners
- **One-Stop Planner**
  CD-ROM with Test Generator

Before You Read

THE BIRDS

Make the Connection

Nature as a Monster

We human beings have an uneasy relationship with nature. Nature has two faces: We see it as a source of beauty and peace, but we fear its sudden random violence. Extreme weather (hurricanes, droughts, blizzards), volcanoes, earthquakes, even the attacks of tiny creatures (ticks, killer bees, fleas) or viruses can threaten our life on earth. Perhaps this is why, since ancient times, stories have been told about people who find themselves face to face with the dangerous side of nature. In many of these stories, a natural catastrophe threatens to wipe out all evidence of human life on this planet. Such stories reflect our deepest fears, and perhaps for this reason they are, even today, enormously popular.

Quickwrite

Think about this other, darker side of nature. Jot down a few of the ways that nature can threaten

human life. If you have ever personally faced nature in its monstrous forms, you might write briefly about your experience. Save your notes; you'll come back to them later.

Elements of Literature

Danger Signs

Foreshadowing is a technique used by writers to build up suspense, to create anxiety as we read. Foreshadowing hints at what is to come. At the beginning of "The Birds," for example, du Maurier first makes us aware that something might be wrong by saying that the birds are more restless than ever this year. At once we want to know why. Look for other signs of approaching danger as the story continues.

> **F**oreshadowing is the use of clues to hint at events that will occur later.
>
> *For more on Foreshadowing, see the Handbook of Literary Terms.*

Reading Skills and Strategies

Making Predictions: What's Next?

A suspense-filled story is sometimes called a page-turner—we're so eager to find out what happens next that we can barely wait to turn each page. Without even being aware of it, we race ahead, making predictions about what is going to happen next. A **prediction** is a type of inference, a guess based on evidence. When we read, we base our predictions on the following:

- our observations of the characters and their situations
- clues the writer plants that **foreshadow** what's coming next
- our own experience of life
- our understanding of how stories work

We modify our predictions as the story unfolds, but it's always fun at the end to see how right— or wrong—we were.

go.hrw.com
LE0 9-1

Restlessness drove them to the skies again.

Preteaching Vocabulary

Words to Own

Ask students to work with partners to read the Words to Own and their definitions at the bottom of the selection pages. Then, to reinforce their understanding of the words, have the partners complete these exercises together.

1. Use facial expressions to demonstrate the meanings of these words: **fretful, apprehensive, placid, sullen.** Have your partner guess the word.
2. Draw something **garish.**
3. Behave **furtively.**
4. Pick up a pencil in a **deft** motion.
5. Fill in the blanks of this sentence: "It is **imperative** that you _____," said the _____.
6. Describe someone who has a sunny **disposition.**
7. Tell your partner what you have **recounted** to your family or friends about recent school events.

THE BIRDS

Daphne du Maurier

Summary ■■■

The peaceful setting of this story—
a rural village on the coast of Cornwall, England, sometime after World
War II—contrasts with its extraordinary events. As winter approaches,
unusually large flocks of birds attempt
to invade the home of the protagonist
Nat Hocken. He boards up windows
and doors to stop them, but birds of
increasingly greater size and vicious-
ness join the attack. The suspense
builds. All over England, the birds
attack people; planes are downed and
all radio communication ceases. The
story's ambiguous ending maintains the
suspense. The birds wait threateningly
outside as night falls. The Hockens,
huddled fearfully in their cottage, don't
know what will happen.

On December the third, the wind changed overnight, and it was winter. Until then the autumn had been mellow, soft. The leaves had lingered on the trees, golden-red, and the hedgerows were still green. The earth was rich where the plow had turned it.

Nat Hocken, because of a wartime disability, had a pension and did not work full time at the farm. He worked three days a week, and they gave him the lighter jobs: hedging, thatching, repairs to the farm buildings.

Although he was married, with children, his was a solitary disposition; he liked best to work alone. It pleased him when he was given a bank to build up or a gate to mend at the far end of the peninsula, where the sea surrounded the farmland on either side. Then, at midday, he would pause and eat the pasty[1] that his wife had baked for him and, sitting on the cliff's edge, would watch the birds. Autumn was best for this, better than spring. In spring the birds flew inland, purposeful, intent; they knew where they were bound; the rhythm and

ritual of their life brooked no delay. In autumn those that had not migrated overseas but remained to pass the winter were caught up in the same driving urge, but because migration was denied them, followed a pattern of their own. Great flocks of them came to the peninsula, restless, uneasy, spending themselves in motion; now wheeling, circling in the sky, now settling to feed on the rich, new-turned soil; but even when they fed, it was as though they did so without hunger, without desire. Restlessness drove them to the skies again.

Black and white, jackdaw and gull, mingled in strange partnership, seeking some sort of liberation, never satisfied, never still. Flocks of starlings, rustling like silk, flew to fresh pasture, driven by the same necessity of movement, and the smaller birds, the finches and the larks, scattered from tree to hedge as if compelled.

WORDS TO OWN

disposition (dis'pə·zish'ən) *n.*: personality or temperament.

---

1. **pasty (pas'tē):** meat pie.

THE BIRDS 51

Resources ——

Listening
Audio CD Library
A recording of "The Birds" is available
as part of the *Audio CD Library:*
• Disc 3, Track 2

Viewing and Representing
Fine Art Transparency
The transparency of *Portrait of Miles B.
Carpenter* by Uncle Jack Dey will com-
plement your students' reading of the
short story.
• Transparency 2
• Worksheet, p. 8

Resources: Print and Media ——

Reading
• *Reading Skills and Strategies:*
    MiniRead Skill Lesson, p. 35
    Selection Skill Lesson, p. 42
• *Graphic Organizers for Active Reading,* p. 3
• *Words to Own,* p. 3
• *Audio CD Library*
    Disc 3, Track 2

Writing and Language
• *Daily Oral Grammar*
    Transparency 3
• *Grammar and Language Links*
    Worksheets p. 5
• *Language Workshop* CD-ROM

Viewing and Representing
• *Viewing and Representing*
    Fine Art Transparency 2
    Fine Art Worksheet, p. 8

Assessment
• *Formal Assessment,* p. 5
• *Portfolio Management System,* p. 93
• *Standardized Test Preparation,* pp. 12, 14
• *Test Generator (One-Stop Planner* CD-ROM)

Internet
• go.hrw.com (keyword: LE0 9-1)

? What is Nat's attitude towards the birds he watches? [Sample responses: He finds them fascinating and perplexing; he ascribes human qualities to them, so perhaps he feels some kinship with them.]

B Elements of Literature
Foreshadowing

? What might this image foreshadow? [Possible answers: a conflict between people and birds; a flock of birds that will overrun the area.]

C Appreciating Language
Style

Point out how du Maurier uses simple language to create ominous nighttime images. Plainly stated images, such as "east wind, cold and dry," "it sounded hollow in the chimney," "a loose slate rattled on the roof," and "the sea roaring in the bay," make a familiar occurrence, the coming of winter, seem fraught with danger. Since it is night, these images appeal to the senses of touch and hearing rather than sight.

A Nat watched them, and he watched the sea birds too. Down in the bay they waited for the tide. They had more patience. Oystercatchers, redshank, sanderling, and curlew watched by the water's edge; as the slow sea sucked at the shore and then withdrew, leaving the strip of seaweed bare and the shingle[2] churned, the sea birds raced and ran upon the beaches. Then that same impulse to flight seized upon them too. Crying, whistling, calling, they skimmed the placid sea and left the shore. Make haste, make speed, hurry and begone; yet where, and to what purpose? The restless urge of autumn, unsatisfying, sad, had put a spell upon them, and they must flock, and wheel, and cry; they must spill themselves of motion before winter came.

"Perhaps," thought Nat, munching his pasty by the cliff's edge, "a message comes to the birds in autumn, like a warning. Winter is coming. Many of them perish. And like people who, apprehensive of death before their time, drive themselves to work or folly, the birds do likewise."

B The birds had been more restless than ever this fall of the year, the agitation more marked because the days were still. As the tractor traced its path up and down the western hills, the figure of the farmer silhouetted on the driving seat, the whole machine and the man upon it, would be lost momentarily in the great cloud of wheeling, crying birds. There were many more than usual; Nat was sure of this. Always, in autumn, they followed the plow, but not in great flocks like these, nor with such clamor.

Nat remarked upon it when hedging was finished for the day. "Yes," said the farmer, "there are more birds about than usual; I've noticed it too. And daring, some of them, taking no notice of the tractor. One or two gulls came so close to my head this afternoon I thought they'd knock my cap off! As it was, I could scarcely see what I was doing when they were overhead and I had the sun in my eyes. I have a notion the

---

2. **shingle:** beach covered with pebbles.

weather will change. It will be a hard winter. That's why the birds are restless."

Nat, tramping home across the fields and down the lane to his cottage, saw the birds still flocking over the western hills, in the last glow of the sun. No wind, and the gray sea calm and full. Campion in bloom yet in the hedges, and the air mild. The farmer was right, though, and it was **C** that night the weather turned. Nat's bedroom faced east. He woke just after two and heard the wind in the chimney. Not the storm and bluster of a sou'westerly gale, bringing the rain, but east wind, cold and dry. It sounded hollow in the chimney, and a loose slate rattled on the roof. Nat listened, and he could hear the sea roaring in the bay. Even the air in the small bedroom had turned chill: A draft came under the skirting of the door, blowing upon the bed. Nat drew the blanket round him, leaned closer to the back of his sleeping wife, and stayed wakeful, watchful, aware of misgiving without cause.

Then he heard the tapping on the window. There was no creeper on the cottage walls to break loose and scratch upon the pane. He listened, and the tapping continued until, irritated by the sound, Nat got out of bed and went to the window. He opened it, and as he did so something brushed his hand, jabbing at his knuckles, grazing the skin. Then he saw the flutter of the wings and it was gone, over the roof, behind the cottage.

WORDS TO OWN

placid (plas'id) *adj.*: calm; untroubled.
apprehensive (ap'rē·hen'siv) *adj.*: fearful.

Reaching All Students

Struggling Readers
Making predictions was introduced on p. 50. For a lesson directly tied to this story that teaches students to make predictions by using a strategy called Anticipation Guides, see the *Reading Skills and Strategies* binder:
• MiniRead Skill Lesson, p. 35
• Selection Skill Lesson, p. 42

English Language Learners
Given the selection's length, you may wish to place students in study groups. Each group member should have responsibility for summarizing and explaining a single portion of the story. Students can help one another understand challenging passages. For additional strategies, see
• *Lesson Plans Including Strategies for English-Language Learners*

Advanced Learners
Have students discuss the nature of heroism. What makes a hero? What kind of behavior would they classify as heroic? Have students create charts listing three or four heroic qualities such as courage, stamina, wisdom, or leadership. As students read the story, they should consider whether Nat fits their definition of a hero, comparing his qualities to those listed in their charts.

It was a bird; what kind of bird he could not tell. The wind must have driven it to shelter on the sill.

He shut the window and went back to bed but, feeling his knuckles wet, put his mouth to the scratch. The bird had drawn blood. Frightened, he supposed, and bewildered, the bird, seeking shelter, had stabbed at him in the darkness. Once more he settled himself to sleep.

Presently the tapping came again, this time more forceful, more insistent, and now his wife woke at the sound and, turning in the bed, said to him, "See to the window, Nat, it's rattling."

"I've already seen to it," he told her; "there's some bird there trying to get in. Can't you hear the wind? It's blowing from the east, driving the birds to shelter."

"Send them away," she said, "I can't sleep with that noise."

He went to the window for the second time, and now when he opened it, there was not one bird upon the sill but half a dozen; they flew straight into his face, attacking him.

He shouted, striking out at them with his arms, scattering them; like the first one, they flew over the roof and disappeared. Quickly he let the window fall and latched it.

"Did you hear that?" he said. "They went for me. Tried to peck my eyes." He stood by the window, peering into the darkness, and could see nothing. His wife, heavy with sleep, murmured from the bed.

"I'm not making it up," he said, angry at her suggestion. "I tell you the birds were on the sill, trying to get into the room."

Suddenly a frightened cry came from the room across the passage where the children slept.

"It's Jill," said his wife, roused at the sound, sitting up in bed. "Go to her, see what's the matter."

Nat lit the candle, but when he opened the bedroom door to cross the passage the draft blew out the flame.

There came a second cry of terror, this time from both children, and stumbling into their room, he felt the beating of wings about him in the darkness. The window was wide open. Through it came the birds, hitting first the ceiling and the walls, then swerving in midflight, turning to the children in their beds.

"It's all right, I'm here," shouted Nat, and the children flung themselves, screaming, upon him, while in the darkness the birds rose and dived and came for him again.

"What is it, Nat, what's happened?" his wife called from the further bedroom, and swiftly he pushed the children through the door to the passage and shut it upon them, so that he was alone now in their bedroom with the birds.

THE BIRDS 53

D Elements of Literature
Foreshadowing
? What might the fact that the bird drew blood foreshadow? [Sample responses: It might foreshadow that, as the story goes on, birds will draw more blood and harm people; it hints that something unusual and puzzling is starting to happen.]

E Critical Thinking
Speculating
? What is a possible reason for the increase in birds on the sill? [Possible answers: There are more birds in the area than usual, so more of them are seeking shelter; the first bird brought back the others to try to gain entry into the house.]

F Reading Skills and Strategies
Making Predictions
? What do you predict caused the cry from the children's room? [Possible responses: The sound of birds tapping on the window; birds who have actually gotten into the room.]

Getting Students Involved

Cooperative Learning
Concrete Poems. Have students work in pairs to create found poems drawn from this story. Have them first scan the story and jot down words and phrases that describe the birds or other subjects. Then, have partners arrange the text in a design that stresses the poem's meaning. For example, a concrete poem about the birds might be in the shape of a bird. Have students display their work.

T53

A Critical Thinking

Speculating

? Why are the birds attacking Nat?
[Possible answers: They are scared, confused, hungry, or frenzied by the weather.]

B Elements of Literature

Foreshadowing

? What clue in this passage hints at coming dangers? [The fact that different species of birds have banded together for the attack suggests that the situation will be very difficult to control.]

C Reading Skills and Strategies

Interpreting

? What dramatic effect does the sudden disappearance of the birds have?
[Sample responses: The striking absence of birds at dawn is another example of nature turned upside-down; the abrupt disappearance of the birds enhances the nightmarish aspect of their attack and makes the reader anxious about their return.]

D Historical Connections

There have been several references to the east wind already in the story. To today's readers, the east wind seems to symbolize an unnamed yet malevolent force. However, when the story first appeared in the early 1950s, England and the United States were newly engaged in the Cold War struggle against Communism and the Soviet Union. To readers of the time, the east wind may have symbolized that threat.

A He seized a blanket from the nearest bed and, using it as a weapon, flung it to right and left about him in the air. He felt the thud of bodies, heard the fluttering of wings, but they were not yet defeated, for again and again they returned to the assault, jabbing his hands, his head, the little stabbing beaks sharp as pointed forks. The blanket became a weapon of defense; he wound it about his head, and then in greater darkness beat at the birds with his bare hands. He dared not stumble to the door and open it, lest in doing so the birds should follow him.

How long he fought with them in the darkness he could not tell, but at last the beating of the wings about him lessened and then withdrew, and through the density of the blanket he was aware of light. He waited, listened; there was no sound except the fretful crying of one of the children from the bedroom beyond. The fluttering, the whirring of the wings had ceased.

He took the blanket from his head and stared about him. The cold gray morning light exposed the room. Dawn and the open window had called the living birds; the dead lay on the floor. Nat gazed at the little corpses, shocked and horrified. They were all small birds, none of any size; there must have been fifty of them lying there upon the floor. There were robins, finches, sparrows, blue tits, larks, and bramblings, birds B that by nature's law kept to their own flock and their own territory, and now, joining one with another in their urge for battle, had destroyed themselves against the bedroom walls or in the strife had been destroyed by him. Some had lost feathers in the fight; others had blood, his blood, upon their beaks.

Sickened, Nat went to the window and stared out across his patch of garden to the fields.

It was bitter cold, and the ground had all the hard, black look of frost. Not white frost, to

shine in the morning sun, but the black frost that the east wind brings. The sea, fiercer now with the turning tide, white-capped and steep, C broke harshly in the bay. Of the birds there was no sign. Not a sparrow chattered in the hedge beyond the garden gate, no early missel thrush or blackbird pecked on the grass for worms. There was no sound at all but the east wind and the sea.

Nat shut the window and the door of the small bedroom and went back across the passage to his own. His wife sat up in bed, one child asleep beside her, the smaller in her arms, his face bandaged. The curtains were tightly drawn across the window, the candles lit. Her face looked garish in the yellow light. She shook her head for silence.

"He's sleeping now," she whispered, "but only just. Something must have cut him, there was blood at the corner of his eyes. Jill said it was the birds. She said she woke up, and the birds were in the room."

His wife looked up at Nat, searching his face for confirmation. She looked terrified, bewildered, and he did not want her to know that he was also shaken, dazed almost, by the events of the past few hours.

"There are birds in there," he said, "dead birds, nearly fifty of them. Robins, wrens, all the D little birds from hereabouts. It's as though a madness seized them, with the east wind." He sat down on the bed beside his wife and held her hand. "It's the weather," he said; "it must be that, it's the hard weather. They aren't the birds, maybe, from here around. They've been driven down from upcountry."

"But, Nat," whispered his wife, "it's only this night that the weather turned. There's been no snow to drive them. And they can't be hungry

----

WORDS TO OWN
garish (gar'ish) *adj.:* too bright.

54 THE SHORT-STORY COLLECTIONS

Using Students' Strengths

Visual Learners

These students can help themselves and their classmates to visualize the events of the story by drawing a floor plan of the Hockens' cottage. The plan will show the various rooms and features such as doors, windows, and fireplaces. Each room can be labeled with captions that describe the action(s) from the story that occurred there. Students can then use the plan to review or retell the story.

Auditory Learners

Promote understanding of characterization by having students work in pairs to locate and read three dialogues between Nat and his wife. Each partner should first read the part of one character and then switch roles with his or her partner to read the next passage of dialogue. Then each pair should discuss what they have learned from their role playing. Invite partners to share their observations with the class.

yet. There's food for them out there in the fields."

"It's the weather," repeated Nat. "I tell you, it's the weather."

His face, too, was drawn and tired, like hers. They stared at one another for a while without speaking.

"I'll go downstairs and make a cup of tea," he said.

The sight of the kitchen reassured him. The cups and saucers, neatly stacked upon the dresser, the table and chairs, his wife's roll of knitting on her basket chair, the children's toys in a corner cupboard.

He knelt down, raked out the old embers, and relit the fire. The glowing sticks brought normality; the steaming kettle and the brown teapot, comfort and security. He drank his tea, carried a cup up to his wife. Then he washed in the scullery[3] and, putting on his boots, opened the back door.

The sky was hard and leaden, and the brown hills that had gleamed in the sun the day before looked dark and bare. The east wind, like a razor, stripped the trees, and the leaves, crackling and dry, shivered and scattered with the wind's blast. Nat stubbed the earth with his boot. It was frozen hard. He had never known a change so swift and sudden. Black winter had descended in a single night.

The children were awake now. Jill was chattering upstairs and young Johnny crying once again. Nat heard his wife's voice, soothing, comforting. Presently they came down. He had breakfast ready for them, and the routine of the day began.

"Did you drive away the birds?" asked Jill, restored to calm because of the kitchen fire, because of day, because of breakfast.

"Yes, they've all gone now," said Nat. "It was the east wind brought them in. They were frightened and lost; they wanted shelter."

"They tried to peck us," said Jill. "They went for Johnny's eyes."

"Fright made them do that," said Nat. "They

3. **scullery:** room next to the kitchen where dishes are washed.

didn't know where they were in the dark bedroom."

"I hope they won't come again," said Jill. "Perhaps if we put bread for them outside the window they will eat that and fly away."

She finished her breakfast and then went for her coat and hood, her schoolbooks, and her satchel. Nat said nothing, but his wife looked at him across the table. A silent message passed between them.

"I'll walk with her to the bus," he said. "I don't go to the farm today."

And while the child was washing in the scullery he said to his wife, "Keep all the windows closed, and the doors too. Just to be on the safe side. I'll go to the farm. Find out if they heard anything in the night." Then he walked with his small daughter up the lane. She seemed to have forgotten her experience of the night before. She danced ahead of him, chasing the leaves, her face whipped with the cold and rosy under the pixie hood.

"Is it going to snow, Dad?" she said. "It's cold enough."

He glanced up at the bleak sky, felt the wind tear at his shoulders.

"No," he said, "it's not going to snow. This is a black winter, not a white one."

All the while he searched the hedgerows for the birds, glanced over the top of them to the fields beyond, looked to the small wood above the farm where the rooks and jackdaws gathered. He saw none.

The other children waited by the bus stop, muffled, hooded like Jill, the faces white and pinched with cold.

Jill ran to them, waving. "My dad says it won't snow," she called, "it's going to be a black winter."

She said nothing of the birds. She began to push and struggle with another little girl. The bus came ambling up the hill. Nat saw her onto it, then turned and walked back toward the farm. It was not his day for work, but he wanted to satisfy himself that all was well. Jim, the cowman, was clattering in the yard.

"Boss around?" asked Nat.

E Reading Skills and Strategies
Responding to the Text
? Why do you think familiarity brings comfort? [Possible responses: People who are scared of the unfamiliar and unpredictable find comfort in the familiar sights and routines of daily life; familiar places make the world seem normal again.]

F Elements of Literature
Foreshadowing
? What does the swift and sudden change and the dark image of "black winter" portend for the future? [Possible answers: a swift and sudden attack by the birds; a winter of death and destruction.]

G Reading Skills and Strategies
Making Predictions

? Do you think the birds will come again? Explain. [Sample answers: Yes, the birds will return—the story hints at it; yes, the birds will return—there are still many pages of the story left, and since its title is "The Birds," they must show up again.]

Taking a Second Look

Review: Dialogue with the Text
Explain that the strategies readers use to interact with and respond to a text are particularly important when they are reading a longer selection such as "The Birds." Encourage students to carry on an imaginary conversation with the text, mentally saying things like "That's a great description!" or "I wonder what he's going to do." Remind students to:

• Look for places in the text where they can make personal connections with the situation and the characters.

• Stop to ask themselves and others questions about things they don't understand or find confusing.

• Go back and reread a paragraph or passage that is hard to understand or has special significance.

• Make predictions about what will happen next.

Activity
Have students make a three-column chart in their journals with the headings *Connect, Question,* and *Predict.* As they read, they can record their comments, questions, and predictions in the appropriate column. After reading the first third of the story, students can share their charts with a partner and discuss their respective responses. They can repeat the activity after they read the remainder of the selection.

"Gone to market," said Jim. "It's Tuesday, isn't it?"

He clumped off round the corner of a shed. He had no time for Nat. Nat was said to be superior. Read books and the like. Nat had forgotten it was Tuesday. This showed how the events of the preceding night had shaken him. He went to the back door of the farmhouse and heard Mrs. Trigg singing in the kitchen, the wireless[4] making a background to her song.

"Are you there, missus?" called out Nat.

She came to the door, beaming, broad, a good-tempered woman.

"Hullo, Mr. Hocken," she said. "Can you tell me where this cold is coming from? Is it Russia? I've never seen such a change. And it's going on, the wireless says. Something to do with the Arctic Circle."

"We didn't turn on the wireless this morning," said Nat. "Fact is, we had trouble in the night."

"Kiddies poorly?"

"No . . ." He hardly knew how to explain it. Now, in daylight, the battle of the birds would sound absurd.

He tried to tell Mrs. Trigg what had happened, but he could see from her eyes that she thought his story was the result of a nightmare.

"Sure they were real birds," she said, smiling, "with proper feathers and all? Not the funny-shaped kind that the men see after closing hours on a Saturday night?"

"Mrs. Trigg," he said, "there are fifty dead birds, robins, wrens, and such, lying low on the floor of the children's bedroom. They went for me; they tried to go for young Johnny's eyes."

Mrs. Trigg stared at him doubtfully.

"Well there, now," she answered, "I suppose the weather brought them. Once in the bedroom, they wouldn't know where they were to. Foreign birds maybe, from that Arctic Circle."

"No," said Nat, "they were the birds you see about here every day."

"Funny thing," said Mrs. Trigg, "no explaining it, really. You ought to write up and ask the *Guardian*. They'd have some answer for it. Well, I must be getting on."

4. **wireless:** radio.

56 THE SHORT-STORY COLLECTIONS

She nodded, smiled, and went back into the kitchen.

Nat, dissatisfied, turned to the farm gate. Had it not been for those corpses on the bedroom floor, which he must now collect and bury somewhere, he would have considered the tale exaggeration too.

Jim was standing by the gate.

"Had any trouble with the birds?" asked Nat.

"Birds? What birds?"

"We got them up our place last night. Scores of them, came in the children's bedroom. Quite savage they were."

"Oh?" It took time for anything to penetrate Jim's head. "Never heard of birds acting savage," he said at length. "They get tame, like, sometimes. I've seen them come to the windows for crumbs."

"These birds last night weren't tame."

"No? Cold, maybe. Hungry. You put out some crumbs."

Jim was no more interested than Mrs. Trigg had been. It was, Nat thought, like air raids in the war. No one down this end of the country knew what the Plymouth folk had seen and suffered. You had to endure something yourself before it touched you. He walked back along the lane and crossed the stile[5] to his cottage. He found his wife in the kitchen with young Johnny.

"See anyone?" she asked.

"Mrs. Trigg and Jim," he answered. "I don't think they believed me. Anyway, nothing wrong up there."

"You might take the birds away," she said. "I daren't go into the room to make the beds until you do. I'm scared."

5. **stile:** steps over a wall or fence.

Crossing the Curriculum

Science

"Nothing to scare you now," said Nat. "They're dead, aren't they?"

He went up with a sack and dropped the stiff bodies into it, one by one. Yes, there were fifty of them, all told. Just the ordinary, common birds of the hedgerow, nothing as large even as a thrush. It must have been fright that made them act the way they did. Blue tits, wrens—it was incredible to think of the power of their small beaks jabbing at his face and hands the night before. He took the sack out into the garden and was faced now with a fresh problem. The ground was too hard to dig. It was frozen solid, yet no snow had fallen, nothing had happened in the past hours but the coming of the east wind. It was unnatural, queer. The weather prophets must be right. The change was something connected with the Arctic Circle.

The wind seemed to cut him to the bone as he stood there uncertainly, holding the sack. He could see the white-capped seas breaking down under in the bay. He decided to take the birds to the shore and bury them.

When he reached the beach below the headland he could scarcely stand, the force of the east wind was so strong. It hurt to draw breath, and his bare hands were blue. Never had he known such cold, not in all the bad winters he could remember. It was low tide. He crunched his way over the shingle to the softer sand and then, his back to the wind, ground a pit in the sand with his heel. He meant to drop the birds into it, but as he opened up the sack the force of the wind carried them, lifted them, as though in flight again, and they were blown away from him along the beach, tossed like feathers, spread and scattered, the bodies of the fifty frozen birds. There was something ugly in the sight. He did not like it. The dead birds were swept away from him by the wind.

"The tide will take them when it turns," he said to himself.

He looked out to sea and watched the crested breakers, combing green. They rose stiffly, curled, and broke again, and because it was ebb tide the roar was distant, more remote, lacking the sound and thunder of the flood.

Then he saw them. The gulls. Out there, riding the seas.

What he had thought at first to be the white caps of the waves were gulls. Hundreds, thousands, tens of thousands . . . They rose and fell in the trough of the seas, heads to the wind, like a mighty fleet at anchor, waiting on the tide. To eastward and to the west, the gulls were there. They stretched as far as his eye could reach, in close formation, line upon line. Had the sea been still, they would have covered the bay like a white cloud, head to head, body packed to body. Only the east wind, whipping the sea to breakers, hid them from the shore.

Nat turned and, leaving the beach, climbed the steep path home. Someone should know of this. Someone should be told. Something was happening, because of the east wind and the weather, that he did not understand. He wondered if he should go to the call box by the bus stop and ring up the police. Yet what could they do? What could anyone do? Tens of thousands of gulls riding the sea there in the bay because of storm, because of hunger. The police would think him mad, or drunk, or take the statement from him with great calm. "Thank you. Yes, the matter has already been reported. The hard weather is driving the birds inland in great numbers." Nat looked about him. Still no sign of any other bird. Perhaps the cold had sent them all from upcountry? As he drew near to the cottage his wife came to meet him at the door. She called to him, excited. "Nat," she said, "it's on the wireless. They've just read out a special news bulletin. I've written it down."

D **Reading Skills and Strategies**
Finding the Main Idea
❓ Just as ordinary birds have begun to behave in an incredible way, the weather has also taken an unusual turn. How has the weather become a force that seems harmful to Nat? [Nat has never experienced such cold—it hurts him "to draw breath." Nat is not able to bury the birds because the ground is frozen and the wind sweeps them away from his control.]

E **Elements of Literature**
Foreshadowing
❓ To what are the gulls compared? [to "a mighty fleet at anchor" and to a military unit "in close formation"] What do the descriptions suggest for the future? [They suggest that the gulls are like a powerful invading military force; they suggest that the gulls will act in unison against people.]

F **Reading Skills and Strategies**
Making Predictions
❓ What do you think the news bulletin will be about? [Possible response: the unusual situation with the birds; another emergency.]

Skill Link

Identifying Verb Phrases
You may want to use the following exercise before you teach the Grammar Link lesson on verb tenses, on p. 79. This exercise will help you assess students' skill in recognizing a verb phrase. For a review of verb tenses, see pp. 999–1000 in the Language Handbook.

Explain to students that sometimes an auxiliary or helping verb is used with the main verb to form a verb phrase. Use the examples that follow to review the use of single verbs and verb phrases.

Present Tense
Verb: The birds fly.
Verb Phrase: The birds are flying.
Past Tense
Verb: The bird pecked.
Verb Phrase: The bird was pecking.
Future Tense
Verb: The birds will migrate.
Verb Phrase: When will the birds be migrating?

To further assess students' knowledge, have them identify the verb phrases in the following sentences:
1. Was Nat walking when he saw the birds?
2. The birds were trying to break in.
3. The people in need of help are listening, but the radio is silent.
4. The starlings will be uniting with other species of birds for the attack.

T57

A Reading Skills and Strategies
Making Inferences

? Explain to students that the Germans often made their bombing raids during the night. People covered their windows so that the light would not be seen from above and provide enemy planes with an easy target. They also built shelters to hide in during the attacks. What can you infer from this sentence? [Possible responses: Nat's mother was not able to get to the shelter in time when the bombing started; the shelter did not provide enough protection from the air raids.]

B Reading Skills and Strategies
Making Predictions

? Do you think this handiwork will be of any use against the birds, or will it be like Nat's efforts during the war? [Possible responses: No, he cannot protect the house against thousands of attacking birds; yes, it always helps to be prepared.]

C Elements of Literature
Foreshadowing

? This image is particularly ominous, bringing to mind the idea of a whole city with a black cloud hanging over its head. What does this suggest about London's future? [Possible answers: Bad times are ahead for the city; the city will be attacked by birds.]

"What's on the wireless?" he said.

"About the birds," she said. "It's not only here; it's everywhere. In London, all over the country. Something has happened to the birds."

Together they went into the kitchen. He read the piece of paper lying on the table.

"Statement from the Home Office at 11 A.M. today. Reports from all over the country are coming in hourly about the vast quantity of birds flocking above towns, villages, and outlying districts, causing obstruction and damage and even attacking individuals. It is thought that the Arctic airstream, at present covering the British Isles, is causing birds to migrate south in immense numbers and that intense hunger may drive these birds to attack human beings. Householders are warned to see to their windows, doors, and chimneys, and to take reasonable precautions for the safety of their children. A further statement will be issued later."

A kind of excitement seized Nat; he looked at his wife in triumph.

"There you are," he said. "Let's hope they'll hear that at the farm. Mrs. Trigg will know it wasn't any story. It's true. All over the country. I've been telling myself all morning there's something wrong. And just now, down on the beach, I looked out to sea and there are gulls, thousands of them, tens of thousands—you couldn't put a pin between their heads—and they're all out there, riding on the sea, waiting."

"What are they waiting for, Nat?" she asked.

He stared at her, then looked down again at the piece of paper.

"I don't know," he said slowly. "It says here the birds are hungry."

He went over to the drawer where he kept his hammer and tools.

"What are you going to do, Nat?"

"See to the windows and the chimneys too, like they tell you."

"You think they would break in, with the windows shut? Those sparrows and robins and such? Why, how could they?"

He did not answer. He was not thinking of the robins and the sparrows. He was thinking of the gulls. . . .

He went upstairs and worked there the rest of the morning, boarding the windows of the bedrooms, filling up the chimney bases. Good that it was his free day and he was not working at the farm. It reminded him of the old days, at the beginning of the war. He was not married then, and he had made all the blackout boards for his mother's house in Plymouth. Made the shelter too. Not that it had been of any use when the moment came. He wondered if they would take these precautions up at the farm. He doubted it. Too easygoing, Harry Trigg and his missus. Maybe they'd laugh at the whole thing. Go off to a dance or a whist drive.[6]

"Dinner's ready." She called him, from the kitchen.

"All right. Coming down."

He was pleased with his handiwork. The frames fitted nicely over the little panes and at the bases of the chimneys.

When dinner was over and his wife was washing up, Nat switched on the one o'clock news. The same announcement was repeated, the one which she had taken down during the morning, but the news bulletin enlarged upon it. "The flocks of birds have caused dislocation in all areas," read the announcer, "and in London the sky was so dense at ten o'clock this morning that it seemed as if the city was covered by a vast black cloud.

"The birds settled on rooftops, on window ledges, and on chimneys. The species included blackbird, thrush, the common house sparrow, and, as might be expected in the metropolis, a vast quantity of pigeons and starlings and that frequenter of the London river, the black-headed gull. The sight has been so unusual that traffic came to a standstill in many thoroughfares, work was abandoned in shops and offices, and the streets and pavements were crowded with people standing about to watch the birds."

Various incidents were <u>recounted</u>, the suspected reason of cold and hunger stated

6. **whist drive:** card game organized for a large group.

WORDS TO OWN

recounted (ri·kount'id) v.: described in detail; narrated.

---

58 THE SHORT-STORY COLLECTIONS

Reaching All Students

Struggling Readers

To help students better understand the relationship between Nat and his wife, ask them to create a chart like the one at right and to note, as they read, qualities and attitudes that the characters demonstrate. After they have read the story, you might ask students to use their notes as prewriting and to write a brief paragraph analyzing the relationship between these two characters.

Nat	Nat's Wife
1. Likes to observe nature	1. Attentive mother
2.	2.
3.	3.
4.	4.
Characters' Relationship	

T58

D Reading Skills and Strategies

Making Predictions

❓ What do you think will happen to people who don't take the bird threat seriously? [Sample response: They will be attacked and seriously injured or even killed because they did not prepare themselves.]

E Critical Thinking

Speculating

❓ What, if anything, could be done to help people like Nat and his family? [Possible answers: They could be airlifted to underground bunkers or cellars for safety; the government could follow whatever procedures they have for natural disasters like earthquakes or hurricanes; the military could come out to destroy the birds.]

again, and warnings to householders repeated. The announcer's voice was smooth and suave. Nat had the impression that this man, in particular, treated the whole business as he would an elaborate joke. There would be others like him, hundreds of them, who did not know what it was to struggle in darkness with a flock of birds. There would be parties tonight in London, like the ones they gave on election nights. People standing about, shouting and laughing, getting drunk. "Come and watch the birds!"

Nat switched off the wireless. He got up and started work on the kitchen windows. His wife watched him, young Johnny at her heels.

"What, boards for down here too?" she said. "Why, I'll have to light up before three o'clock. I see no call for boards down here."

"Better be sure than sorry," answered Nat. "I'm not going to take any chances."

"What they ought to do," she said, "is to call the Army out and shoot the birds. That would soon scare them off."

"Let them try," said Nat. "How'd they set about it?"

"They have the Army to the docks," she answered, "when the dockers strike. The soldiers go down and unload the ships."

"Yes," said Nat, "and the population of London is eight million or more. Think of all the buildings, all the flats and houses. Do you think they've enough soldiers to go around shooting birds from every roof?"

"I don't know. But something should be done. They ought to do something."

Nat thought to himself that "they" were no doubt considering the problem at that very moment, but whatever "they" decided to do in London and the big cities would not help the people here, three hundred miles away. Each householder must look after his own.

"How are we off for food?" he said.

"Now, Nat, whatever next?"

"Never mind. What have you got in the larder?"

THE BIRDS 59

Crossing the Curriculum

Geography

Although Alfred Hitchcock set his 1963 film version of "The Birds" in California, du Maurier imagined the setting to be the Cornish coast of England. Ask students to research and present an oral report to the class on the people, products, and geography of Cornwall, England. Encourage students to incorporate visual aids in their presentations.

Social Studies

"The Birds" was published in a 1952 issue of *Good Housekeeping* magazine. Have students research the period and, if possible, make photocopies of pages from magazines that show advertisements, clothing styles, and popular culture of the time. Ask students to report on aspects of life and major news events in the United States in that era. Have them discuss how readers of the 1950s might have responded to the story.

Foreshadowing

? Nat notes that there has been no sun all day, with darkness coming in the afternoon, but then he realizes that the presence of the gulls has made the sky dark, just as it was over London. What does this circling of the gulls suggest? [Possible response: They are going to attack soon, since many birds of prey circle before they dive down for the kill.]

B Critical Thinking

Speculating

? Why do you think the mass of birds breaks into groups that fly north, south, east, and west? [Sample responses: The birds are flying off to conquer the entire area; perhaps they are dispersing after all.]

"It's shopping day tomorrow, you know that. I don't keep uncooked food hanging about; it goes off. Butcher doesn't call till the day after. But I can bring back something when I go in tomorrow."

Nat did not want to scare her. He thought it possible that she might not go to town tomorrow. He looked in the larder for himself and in the cupboard where she kept her tins. They would do for a couple of days. Bread was low.

"What about the baker?"

"He comes tomorrow too."

He saw she had flour. If the baker did not call she had enough to bake one loaf.

"We'd be better off in the old days," he said, "when the women baked twice a week, and had pilchards[7] salted, and there was food for a family to last a siege, if need be."

"I've tried the children with tinned fish; they don't like it," she said.

Nat went on hammering the boards across the kitchen windows. Candles. They were low in candles too. That must be another thing she meant to buy tomorrow. Well, it could not be helped. They must go early to bed tonight. That was, if . . .

He got up and went out of the back door and stood in the garden, looking down toward the sea. There had been no sun all day, and now, at barely three o'clock, a kind of darkness had already come, the sky sullen, heavy, colorless like salt. He could hear the vicious sea drumming on the rocks. He walked down the path, halfway to the beach. And then he stopped. He could see the tide had turned. The rock that had shown in midmorning was now covered, but it was not the sea that held his eyes. The gulls had risen. They were circling, hundreds of them, thousands of them, lifting their wings against the wind. It was the gulls that made the darkening of the sky. And they were silent. They made not a sound. They just went on soaring and circling, rising, falling, trying their strength against the wind.

Nat turned. He ran up the path, back to the cottage.

---

7. **pilchards:** fish similar to sardines.

"I'm going for Jill," he said. "I'll wait for her at the bus stop."

"What's the matter?" asked his wife. "You've gone quite white."

"Keep Johnny inside," he said. "Keep the door shut. Light up now, and draw the curtains."

"It's only just gone three," she said.

"Never mind. Do what I tell you."

He looked inside the toolshed outside the back door. Nothing there of much use. A spade was too heavy, and a fork no good. He took the hoe. It was the only possible tool, and light enough to carry.

He started walking up the lane to the bus stop and now and again glanced back over his shoulder.

The gulls had risen higher now; their circles were broader, wider; they were spreading out in huge formation across the sky.

He hurried on; although he knew the bus would not come to the top of the hill before four o'clock, he had to hurry. He passed no one on the way. He was glad of this. No time to stop and chatter.

At the top of the hill he waited. He was much too soon. There was half an hour still to go. The east wind came whipping across the fields from the higher ground. He stamped his feet and blew upon his hands. In the distance he could see the clay hills, white and clean, against the heavy pallor of the sky. Something black rose from behind them, like a smudge at first, then widening, becoming deeper, and the smudge became a cloud, and the cloud divided again into five other clouds, spreading north, east, south, and west, and they were not clouds at all; they were birds. He watched them travel across the sky, and as one section passed overhead, within two or three hundred feet of him, he knew, from their speed, they were bound inland, upcountry; they had no business with the people here on the peninsula. They were rooks, crows, jackdaws, magpies, jays, all birds that usually preyed upon the smaller species;

WORDS TO OWN

sullen (sul'ən) adj.: gloomy.

---

but this afternoon they were bound on some other mission.

"They've been given the towns," thought Nat; "they know what they have to do. We don't matter so much here. The gulls will serve for us. The others go to the towns."

He went to the call box, stepped inside, and lifted the receiver. The exchange would do. They would pass the message on.

"I'm speaking from the highway," he said, "by the bus stop. I want to report large formations of birds traveling upcountry. The gulls are also forming in the bay."

"All right," answered the voice, laconic, weary.

"You'll be sure and pass this message on to the proper quarter?"

"Yes . . . yes . . ." Impatient now, fed up. The buzzing note resumed.

"She's another," thought Nat, "she doesn't care. Maybe she's had to answer calls all day. She hopes to go to the pictures tonight. She'll squeeze some fellow's hand and point up at the sky and say 'Look at all them birds!' She doesn't care."

The bus came lumbering up the hill. Jill climbed out, and three or four other children. The bus went on toward the town.

"What's the hoe for, Dad?"

They crowded around him, laughing, pointing.

"I just brought it along," he said. "Come on now, let's get home. It's cold, no hanging about. Here, you. I'll watch you across the fields, see how fast you can run."

He was speaking to Jill's companions, who came from different families, living in the council houses.[8] A shortcut would take them to the cottages.

"We want to play a bit in the lane," said one of them.

"No, you don't. You go off home or I'll tell your mammy."

They whispered to one another, round-eyed, then scuttled off across the fields. Jill stared at her father, her mouth sullen.

"We always play in the lane," she said.

"Not tonight, you don't," he said. "Come on now, no dawdling."

He could see the gulls now, circling the fields, coming in toward the land. Still silent. Still no sound.

"Look, Dad, look over there, look at all the gulls."

"Yes. Hurry, now."

"Where are they flying to? Where are they going?"

"Upcountry, I dare say. Where it's warmer."

He seized her hand and dragged her after him along the lane.

"Don't go so fast. I can't keep up."

The gulls were copying the rooks and crows. They were spreading out in formation across the sky. They headed, in bands of thousands, to the four compass points.

"Dad, what is it? What are the gulls doing?"

They were not intent upon their flight, as the crows, as the jackdaws had been. They still circled overhead. Nor did they fly so high. It was as though they waited upon some signal. As though some decision had yet to be given. The order was not clear.

8. **council houses:** public housing, built for lower-income families after World War II.

C Critical Thinking
Extending the Text
Here, the birds are personified as armylike, moving in formation on a combat mission. Suggest that students go through the story and list the battle imagery and references to war or wartime. Then have them discuss what du Maurier might be trying to say about World War II or about the Cold War by presenting Nat's conflict with the birds as a war.

D Appreciating Language
Action Verbs
The urgency in this passage is reflected in the number of action verbs. Have students locate at least four of these verbs. [Possibilities include *run, scuttled, hurry, seized,* and *dragged.*]

E Reading Skills and Strategies

Making Predictions
❓ What order do you think the birds are waiting for? [Possible response: a signal or order to attack the town.]

Professional Notes

Two real-life incidents inspired Daphne du Maurier to write "The Birds." The first occurred while she was walking on the beach. Two seagulls flew toward her, tried to bite her dog, then flew directly at her face. The second occurred while she was on a farm, watching a farmer working his fields. Du Maurier recalled, "seagulls chased the tractor, flying down, apparently trying to attack the farmer. Coupled with my other experience, this gave me the idea of birds attacking humans." Discuss du Maurier's experiences with students. Ask them to recall any strange natural occurrences they have witnessed or experienced that they think could be expanded upon as the basis of a short story. Then, have each student choose one experience—their own or one mentioned by another student—and create a brief plot synopsis for a story inspired by the incident.

A English Language Learners

Briticisms

Point out that *pick-a-back* is the British way of saying "piggy back." Students may not be familiar with this or other British terms, particularly older ones that are not in common use today. Suggest that as they read the story, students make a list of unfamiliar British words and phrases. They can share lists with a partner and look up meanings in the dictionary.

B Reading Skills and Strategies

Visualizing

❓ How does the illustration on this page help to convey the child's fright? [Sample answers: The illustration shows the child and father as weak and help-less prey and the gulls as powerful pred-ators; the illustration is from the gulls' perspective, which makes them seem enormous and the people very small.]

C Reading Skills and Strategies

Comparing and Contrasting

❓ How is Mr. Trigg's attitude towards the birds different from Nat's? [He seems amused and excited by the birds, while Nat is worried and fearful of them.] Whose attitude do you find more logical? [Possible answers: Nat's, because the radio has warned that the birds and their actions are menacing, not playful; Mr. Trigg's, because it is too bizarre and unbelievable to think that masses of birds would become attackers.]

A "Do you want me to carry you, Jill? Here, come pick-a-back."

B This way he might put on speed; but he was wrong. Jill was heavy. She kept slipping. And she was crying too. His sense of urgency, of fear, had communicated itself to the child.

"I wish the gulls would go away. I don't like them. They're coming closer to the lane."

He put her down again. He started running, swinging Jill after him. As they went past the farm turning, he saw the farmer backing his car out of the garage. Nat called to him.

"Can you give us a lift?" he said.

"What's that?"

C Mr. Trigg turned in the driving seat and stared at them. Then a smile came to his cheerful, rubicund[9] face.

"It looks as though we're in for some fun," he said. "Have you seen the gulls? Jim and I are going to take a crack at them. Everyone's gone bird crazy, talking of nothing else. I hear you were troubled in the night. Want a gun?"

Nat shook his head.

The small car was packed. There was just room for Jill, if she crouched on top of petrol tins on the back seat.

"I don't want a gun," said Nat, "but I'd be obliged if you'd run Jill home. She's scared of the birds."

9. **rubicund** (rōō′bə·kund′): reddish, rosy.

Making the Connections

Cultural Connections

British English. "The Birds" contains numer-ous unfamiliar British words, such as *pram* and *gib* (footnoted on p. 72), which must be defined to clarify students' understanding. Ask students how U.S. English speakers would say "hire a car" and what a child in the United States might say on a bouncy ride rather than "up-a-down."

Students may already know that the British refer to the trunk of a car as "the boot" and to the hood as "the bonnet." Have volunteers find other examples of vocabulary variation between British and American English, either in this story or in other sources such as British music magazines.

You could use these examples as a bridge into a discussion of regional vocabulary variation within the United States. As a starting point, you might mention the different terms used across the United States for carbonated drinks (*soda, pop, soft drink*).

He spoke briefly. He did not want to talk in front of Jill.

"OK," said the farmer, "I'll take her home. Why don't you stop behind and join the shooting match? We'll make the feathers fly."

Jill climbed in, and turning the car, the driver sped up the lane. Nat followed after. Trigg must be crazy. What use was a gun against a sky of birds?

Now Nat was not responsible for Jill, he had time to look about him. The birds were circling still above the fields. Mostly herring gull, but the black-backed gull amongst them. Usually they kept apart. Now they were united. Some bond had brought them together. It was the black-backed gull that attacked the smaller birds, and even newborn lambs, so he'd heard. He'd never seen it done. He remembered this now, though, looking above him in the sky. They were coming in toward the farm. They were circling lower in the sky, and the black-backed gulls were to the front, the black-backed gulls were leading. The farm, then, was their target. They were making for the farm.

Nat increased his pace toward his own cottage. He saw the farmer's car turn and come back along the lane. It drew up beside him with a jerk.

"The kid has run inside," said the farmer. "Your wife was watching for her. Well, what do you make of it? They're saying in town the Russians have done it. The Russians have poisoned the birds."

"How could they do that?" asked Nat.

"Don't ask me. You know how stories get around. Will you join my shooting match?"

"No, I'll get along home. The wife will be worried else."

"My missus says if you could eat gull there'd be some sense in it," said Trigg. "We'd have roast gull, baked gull, and pickle 'em into the bargain. You wait until I let off a few barrels into the brutes. That'll scare 'em."

"Have you boarded your windows?" asked Nat.

"No. Lot of nonsense. They like to scare you on the wireless. I've had more to do today than to go round boarding up my windows."

"I'd board them now, if I were you."

"Garn. You're windy. Like to come to our place to sleep?"

"No, thanks all the same."

"All right. See you in the morning. Give you a gull breakfast."

The farmer grinned and turned his car to the farm entrance.

Nat hurried on. Past the little wood, past the old barn, and then across the stile to the remaining field.

As he jumped the stile he heard the whir of wings. A black-backed gull dived down at him from the sky, missed, swerved in flight, and rose to dive again. In a moment it was joined by others, six, seven, a dozen, black-backed and herring mixed. Nat dropped his hoe. The hoe was useless. Covering his head with his arms, he ran toward the cottage. They kept coming at him from the air, silent save for the beating wings. The terrible, fluttering wings. He could feel the blood on his hands, his wrists, his neck. Each stab of a swooping beak tore his flesh. If only he could keep them from his eyes. Nothing else mattered. He must keep them from his eyes. They had not learned yet how to cling to a shoulder, how to rip clothing, how to dive in mass upon the head, upon the body. But with each dive, with each attack, they became bolder. And they had no thought for themselves. When they dived low and missed, they crashed, bruised and broken, on the ground. As Nat ran he stumbled, kicking their spent bodies in front of him.

He found the door; he hammered upon it with his bleeding hands. Because of the boarded windows no light shone. Everything was dark.

"Let me in," he shouted, "it's Nat. Let me in."

He shouted loud to make himself heard above the whir of the gulls' wings.

Then he saw the gannet, poised for the dive, above him in the sky. The gulls circled, retired, soared, one after another, against the wind. Only the gannet remained. One single gannet above him in the sky. The wings folded suddenly to its body. It dropped like a stone. Nat screamed, and the door opened. He stumbled

D Critical Thinking
Extending the Text

❓ What might du Maurier be saying about the effectiveness of technology against the forces of nature? [Sample response: Our technology leads us to believe we are superior to anything, but this isn't really true. Our weapons can still be ineffective against nature's powers.]

E Historical Connection

Although the subtext of du Maurier's story may well be about the threat of Communism, this reference to the Russians is above all a sign of the times. In the post–World War II Cold War environment, western nations mistrusted the Soviet Union.

F Reading Skills and Strategies
Making Predictions

❓ What do you think might happen because of Trigg's attitude? [Possible responses: When the birds start attacking, he will not be prepared; he and his farm and family will be harmed or destroyed by the birds.]

G Element of Literature
Conflict

❓ This is the third conflict Nat has had with the birds. What is particularly frightening about this one? [Sample responses: The birds' increasingly more sophisticated attack methods; the birds' willingness to die during attack.]

Skill Link

Analyzing Word Choice

Have students note the author's use of descriptive action verbs throughout the story—words such as *whispered, roared, jammed, flung,* and *clattering.* Ask students to locate several such verbs. You may then wish to focus students' attention on this example from p. 55:"Black winter had descended in a single night." Discuss why the verb *descended* is a more effective choice than a more generic verb, such as *arrived* or *came,* would be. Ask students to

describe the mental pictures the use of the verb *descended* creates in their minds.

Activities

1. Have students locate ten other descriptive verbs used in the story. Ask them to rewrite each sentence using a more generic verb instead. Have students compare the two sentences. Which is more vivid? What mental images does the original verb conjure up?

2. Ask students to choose five verbs from this list: *flew, ran, laughed, ate, talked, wrote, drank.* For each verb, have them think of three more specific verbs they could use instead. Then, ask them to explain the slight differences in image or meaning that each specific verb conveys.

A Elements of Literature
Personification
? What qualities is Nat ascribing to the birds when he claims they waited to attack him? [He is ascribing specific human goals and motivations to the birds; he is expressing his belief that the birds are carrying out planned, deliberate attacks on prechosen targets.]

B Reading Skills and Strategies
Making Predictions
? What do you think the six o'clock news will say? [Sample responses: It will explain what the government is doing to help people; it will explain the birds' unusual and dangerous behavior.]

C Elements of Literature
Foreshadowing
? What does this image suggest? [Possible answers: Like an invading army, the birds will not give up until they find a way into the house. The birds are unstoppable.]

across the threshold, and his wife threw her weight against the door.

They heard the thud of the gannet as it fell.

His wife dressed his wounds. They were not deep. The backs of his hands had suffered most, and his wrists. Had he not worn a cap they would have reached his head. As to the gannet . . . the gannet could have split his skull.

The children were crying, of course. They had seen the blood on their father's hands.

"It's all right now," he told them. "I'm not hurt. Just a few scratches. You play with Johnny, Jill. Mammy will wash these cuts."

He half shut the door to the scullery so that they could not see. His wife was ashen. She began running water from the sink.

"I saw them overhead," she whispered. "They began collecting just as Jill ran in with Mr. Trigg.

I shut the door fast, and it jammed. That's why I couldn't open it at once when you came."

A "Thank God they waited for me," he said. "Jill would have fallen at once. One bird alone would have done it."

Furtively, so as not to alarm the children, they whispered together as she bandaged his hands and the back of his neck.

"They're flying inland," he said, "thousands of them. Rooks, crows, all the bigger birds. I saw them from the bus stop. They're making for the towns."

"But what can they do, Nat?"

"They'll attack. Go for everyone out in the streets. Then they'll try the windows, the chimneys."

"Why don't the authorities do something? Why don't they get the Army, get machine guns, anything?"

B "There's been no time. Nobody's prepared. We'll hear what they have to say on the six o'clock news."

Nat went back into the kitchen, followed by his wife. Johnny was playing quietly on the floor. Only Jill looked anxious.

"I can hear the birds," she said. "Listen, Dad."

C Nat listened. Muffled sounds came from the windows, from the door. Wings brushing the surface, sliding, scraping, seeking a way of entry. The sound of many bodies, pressed together, shuffling on the sills. Now and again came a thud, a crash, as some bird dived and fell. "Some of them will kill themselves that way," he thought, "but not enough. Never enough."

"All right," he said aloud. "I've got boards over the windows, Jill. The birds can't get in."

He went and examined all the windows. His work had been thorough. Every gap was closed. He would make extra certain, however. He found wedges, pieces of old tin, strips of wood and metal, and fastened them at the sides to reinforce the boards. His hammering helped to deafen the sound of the birds, the shuffling, the

WORDS TO OWN
furtively (fur′tiv·lē) *adv.*: stealthily, as if to avoid being seen or heard.

Using Students' Strengths

Naturalist Learners
Invite interested students to prepare a bulletin board that displays illustrations of the different types of bird species (crows, jackdaws, gulls, rooks, etc.) mentioned in the story along with information about each species. Students could also create a map that provides an overview of the bird species that are local to their region or those that fly through the region on their migratory paths.

Interpersonal Learners
Ask students to conduct a survey of classmates, friends, and relatives to find out which types of wildlife people fear the most. Students should first develop a series of survey questions, then conduct their polls. Statistics can be compiled by the class and displayed in chart or graph form. Sample responses in which people explain their fears can be posted alongside the results.

tapping, and more ominous—he did not want his wife or the children to hear it—the splinter of cracked glass.

"Turn on the wireless," he said. "Let's have the wireless."

This would drown the sound also. He went upstairs to the bedrooms and reinforced the windows there. Now he could hear the birds on the roof, the scraping of claws, a sliding, jostling sound.

He decided they must sleep in the kitchen, keep up the fire, bring down the mattresses, and lay them out on the floor. He was afraid of the bedroom chimneys. The boards he had placed at the chimney bases might give way. In the kitchen they would be safe because of the fire. He would have to make a joke of it. Pretend to the children they were playing at camp. If the worst happened, and the birds forced an entry down the bedroom chimneys, it would be hours, days perhaps, before they could break down the doors. The birds would be imprisoned in the bedrooms. They could do no harm there. Crowded together, they would stifle and die.

He began to bring the mattresses downstairs. At the sight of them his wife's eyes widened in apprehension. She thought the birds had already broken in upstairs.

"All right," he said cheerfully, "we'll all sleep together in the kitchen tonight. More cozy here by the fire. Then we shan't be worried by those silly old birds tapping at the windows."

He made the children help him rearrange the furniture, and he took the precaution of moving the dresser, with his wife's help, across the window. It fitted well. It was an added safeguard. The mattresses could now be laid, one beside the other, against the wall where the dresser had stood.

"We're safe enough now," he thought. "We're snug and tight, like an air-raid shelter. We can hold out. It's just the food that worries me. Food, and coal for the fire. We've enough for two or three days, not more. By that time . . ."

No use thinking ahead as far as that. And they'd be giving directions on the wireless. People would be told what to do. And now, in the midst of many problems, he realized that it was dance music only, coming over the air. Not Children's Hour, as it should have been. He glanced at the dial. Yes, they were on the Home Service all right. Dance records. He switched to the Light program. He knew the reason. The usual programs had been abandoned. This only happened at exceptional times. Elections and such. He tried to remember if it had happened in the war, during the heavy raids on London. But of course. The BBC[10] was not stationed in London during the war. The programs were broadcast from other, temporary quarters. "We're better off here," he thought; "we're better off here in the kitchen, with the windows and the doors boarded, than they are up in the towns. Thank God we're not in the towns."

At six o'clock the records ceased. The time signal was given. No matter if it scared the children, he must hear the news. There was a pause after the pips.[11] Then the announcer spoke. His voice was solemn, grave. Quite different from midday.

"This is London," he said. "A national emergency was proclaimed at four o'clock this afternoon. Measures are being taken to safeguard the lives and property of the population, but it must be understood that these are not easy to effect immediately, owing to the unforeseen and unparalleled nature of the present crisis. Every householder must take precautions to his own building, and where several people live together, as in flats and apartments, they must unite to do

10. **BBC:** British Broadcasting Corporation.
11. **pips:** beeping sounds that indicate the exact time.

Taking a Second Look

Review: Cause and Effect
Review cause and effect with students. Make sure they understand that a cause makes something happen and that an effect is what happens as a result of that cause. Remind students that a single event may have multiple causes and multiple effects. Point out that an author may reveal the cause of an event but not its effects, or the effects but not the causes.

When causes and effects are not directly stated by the author, readers must come to their own conclusions. In "The Birds," for example, du Maurier describes numerous effects of the birds' aggressive behavior, but she is not explicit about the causes for it. Tell students that they must use details in the text and their own prior knowledge and experience to figure out the cause-and-effect relationships.

Activities
1. Make a cause-and-effect chain showing how one event in the story has several causes.
2. Make a cause-and-effect diagram showing how one event in the story has multiple effects.
3. Have students use details from the story and their own knowledge and experience to infer possible causes for the behavior of the birds.

A Reading Skills and Strategies

Connecting with the Text

? How does this BBC announcement compare with your own community's emergency broadcast measures? [Answers will vary. Suggest that students unfamiliar with their area's emergency broadcast procedures do research to find out more.]

B Elements of Literature

Personification

? Nat continually personifies the birds. Here, he ascribes to them the ability to reason, the very thing that most people feel separates humans from animals. Why might Nat be imbuing the birds with such human qualities? [Possible responses: It's natural when faced with a foe to personify it; it's easier to see a reason and motive behind an attack than to believe that it's just an unpredictable, uncontrollable act of nature.]

C Reading Skills and Strategies

Making Predictions

? Do you think the planes will get the birds? [Sample responses: Yes, the planes can fire at them and disperse them; no, the planes will be useless against so many birds—they will either crash into the cockpits or become snarled in the engines.]

---

the utmost they can to prevent entry. It is absolutely <u>imperative</u> that every individual stay indoors tonight and that no one at all remain on the streets or roads or anywhere outdoors. The birds, in vast numbers, are attacking anyone on sight and have already begun an assault upon buildings; but these, with due care, should be impenetrable. The population is asked to remain calm and not to panic. Owing to the exceptional nature of the emergency, there will be no further transmission from any broadcasting station until 7 A.M. tomorrow."

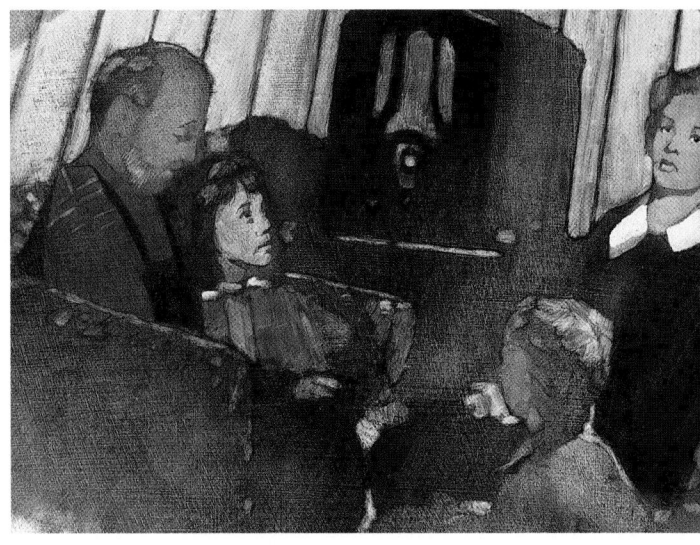

They played the national anthem. Nothing more happened. Nat switched off the set. He looked at his wife. She stared back at him.

"What's it mean?" said Jill. "What did the news say?"

"There won't be any more programs tonight," said Nat. "There's been a breakdown at the BBC."

"Is it the birds?" asked Jill. "Have the birds done it?"

"No," said Nat, "it's just that everyone's very busy, and then of course they have to get rid of the birds, messing everything up, in the towns. Well, we can manage without the wireless for one evening."

"I wish we had a gramophone,"[12] said Jill; "that would be better than nothing."

She had her face turned to the dresser backed against the windows. Try as they did to ignore it, they were all aware of the shuffling, the stabbing, the persistent beating and sweeping of wings.

"We'll have supper early," suggested Nat, "something for a treat. Ask Mammy. Toasted cheese, eh? Something we all like?"

He winked and nodded at his wife. He wanted the look of dread, of apprehension, to go from Jill's face.

He helped with the supper, whistling, singing, making as much clatter as he could, and it seemed to him that the shuffling and the tapping were not so intense as they had been at first. Presently he went up to the bedrooms and listened, and he no longer heard the jostling for place upon the roof.

"They've got reasoning powers," he thought; "they know it's hard to break in here. They'll try elsewhere. They won't waste their time with us."

Supper passed without incident, and then, when they were clearing away, they heard a new sound, droning, familiar, a sound they all knew and understood.

His wife looked up at him, her face alight. "It's planes," she said; "they're sending out planes after the birds. That's what I said they ought to do all along. That will get them. Isn't that gunfire? Can't you hear guns?"

It might be gunfire out at sea. Nat could not

WORDS TO OWN

imperative (im·per′ə·tiv) *adj.:* extremely important; urgent.

---

12. **gramophone:** phonograph; record player.

66 THE SHORT-STORY COLLECTIONS

Crossing the Curriculum

Drama

While Hitchcock's 1963 version of "The Birds" is perhaps the most famous horror film to use animals to inspire fear, it is hardly the only example. The 1954 classic *Them* caused audiences to look at ants in a whole new way; and in the 1990s, viewers of *Arachnaphobia* and *Anaconda* were terrified by monstrous spiders and snakes. Ask students to discuss other films and television programs that use the theme of nature on the attack. Discuss which scenario is more frightening: an attack by creatures that many people are normally afraid of (such as snakes and spiders) or a threat posed by creatures such as birds, which are generally seen as benign and not threatening to human life.

T66

tell. Big naval guns might have an effect upon the gulls out at sea, but the gulls were inland now. The guns couldn't shell the shore because of the population.

"It's good, isn't it," said his wife, "to hear the planes?" And Jill, catching her enthusiasm, jumped up and down with Johnny. "The planes will get the birds. The planes will shoot them."

Just then they heard a crash about two miles distant, followed by a second, then a third. The droning became more distant, passed away out to sea.

"What was that?" asked his wife. "Were they dropping bombs on the birds?"

"I don't know," answered Nat. "I don't think so."

He did not want to tell her that the sound they had heard was the crashing of aircraft. It was, he had no doubt, a venture on the part of the authorities to send out reconnaissance forces, but they might have known the venture was suicidal. What could aircraft do against birds that flung themselves to death against propeller and fuselage but hurtle to the ground themselves? This was being tried now, he supposed, over the whole country. And at a cost. Someone high up had lost his head.

"Where have the planes gone, Dad?" asked Jill.

"Back to base," he said. "Come on, now, time to tuck down for bed."

It kept his wife occupied, undressing the children before the fire, seeing to the bedding, one thing and another, while he went round the cottage again, making sure that nothing had worked loose. There was no further drone of aircraft, and the naval guns had ceased. "Waste of life and effort," Nat said to himself. "We can't

destroy enough of them that way. Cost too heavy. There's always gas. Maybe they'll try spraying with gas, mustard gas. We'll be warned first, of course, if they do. There's one thing, the best brains of the country will be onto it tonight."

Somehow the thought reassured him. He had a picture of scientists, naturalists, technicians, and all those chaps they called the back-room boys, summoned to a council; they'd be working on the problem now. This was not a job for the government, for the chiefs of staff—they would merely carry out the orders of the scientists.

"They'll have to be ruthless," he thought. "Where the trouble's worst they'll have to risk more lives if they use gas. All the livestock, too, and the soil—all contaminated. As long as everyone doesn't panic. That's the trouble. People panicking, losing their heads. The BBC was right to warn us of that."

Upstairs in the bedrooms all was quiet. No **D** further scraping and stabbing at the windows. A lull in battle. Forces regrouping. Wasn't that what they called it in the old wartime bulletins? The wind hadn't dropped, though. He could still hear it roaring in the chimneys. And the sea breaking down on the shore. Then he remembered the tide. The tide would be on the turn. Maybe the lull in battle was because of the tide. There was some law the birds obeyed, and it was all to do with the east wind and the tide.

He glanced at his watch. Nearly eight o'clock. It must have gone high water an hour ago. That explained the lull: The birds attacked with the flood tide. It might not work that way inland, upcountry, but it seemed as if it was so this way on the coast. He reckoned the time limit in his head. They had six hours to go without attack. When the tide **E** turned again, around one-twenty in the morning, the **F** birds would come back. . . .

There were two things he could do. The first to rest, with

D **Critical Thinking**
Interpreting
? How is Nat's opinion about the planes similar to his opinion about Mr. Trigg's guns? [Possible answers: He thinks both will be ineffective; his opinions about both indicate that modern technology is no match against the birds.]

E **Elements of Literature**
Foreshadowing
? Think about the phrase *calm before the storm*. What does this lull in the birds' activity suggest about their next attack? [Their next attack, after six hours of rest, will be even more frenzied and dangerous.]

F **Struggling Readers**
Getting the Main Idea
? What has Nat figured out about the relationship of the tides to the birds' attacks? [The birds attack when the tide is in and retreat when it goes out.] Explain that the tide rises and falls twice within a period of 24 hours and 50 minutes.

Assessing Learning

Ongoing Assessment

Reader's Response Groups. The criteria outlined in the chart at right can help you to assess individuals during their participation in group discussions of literature.

Key: A = Always
S = Sometimes
R = Rarely
N = Never

Characteristic	Date	Rating
Values others' perspectives		
Uses others' ideas to increase interpretive possibilities		
Asks questions		
Seeks help of others to clarify meaning		
Can disagree without disrupting dialogue		

A Elements of Literature

Foreshadowing

? Earlier, the birds swarming the tractor foreshadowed the attacks to come. What do you think the burning aircraft foreshadows? [Possible responses: further death and destruction; the destruction of Trigg's farm.]

B Critical Thinking

Analyzing

? What is Nat doing? [He is using dead birds to keep out living ones.] What details make the passage particularly gruesome? [Details include the birds' clawing and pecking at the dead birds, the warm and bloody bodies, and the feathers matted with blood.]

his wife and the children, and all of them snatch what sleep they could, until the small hours. The second to go out, see how they were faring at the farm, see if the telephone was still working there, so that they might get news from the exchange.

He called softly to his wife, who had just settled the children. She came halfway up the stairs and he whispered to her.

"You're not to go," she said at once, "you're not to go and leave me alone with the children. I can't stand it."

Her voice rose hysterically. He hushed her, calmed her.

"All right," he said, "all right. I'll wait till morning. And we'll get the wireless bulletin then too, at seven. But in the morning, when the tide ebbs again, I'll try for the farm, and they may let us have bread and potatoes, and milk too."

His mind was busy again, planning against emergency. They would not have milked, of course, this evening. The cows would be standing by the gate, waiting in the yard, with the household inside, battened behind boards, as they were here at the cottage. That is, if they had time to take precautions. He thought of the farmer, Trigg, smiling at him from the car. There would have been no shooting party, not tonight.

The children were asleep. His wife, still clothed, was sitting on her mattress. She watched him, her eyes nervous.

"What are you going to do?" she whispered.

He shook his head for silence. Softly, stealthily, he opened the back door and looked outside.

It was pitch dark. The wind was blowing harder than ever, coming in steady gusts, icy, from the sea. He kicked at the step outside the door. It was heaped with birds. There were dead birds everywhere. Under the windows, against the walls. These were the suicides, the divers, the ones with broken necks. Wherever he looked he saw dead birds. No trace of the living. The living had flown seaward with the turn of the tide. The gulls would be riding the seas now, as they had done in the forenoon.

A In the far distance, on the hill where the tractor had been two days before, something was burning. One of the aircraft that had crashed; the fire, fanned by the wind, had set light to a stack.

B He looked at the bodies of the birds, and he had a notion that if he heaped them, one upon the other, on the windowsills they would make added protection for the next attack. Not much, perhaps, but something. The bodies would have to be clawed at, pecked, and dragged aside before the living birds could gain purchase on the sills and attack the panes. He set to work in the darkness. It was queer; he hated touching them. The bodies were still warm and bloody. The blood matted their feathers. He felt his stomach turn, but he went on with his work. He noticed grimly that every windowpane was shattered. Only the boards had kept the birds from breaking in. He stuffed the cracked panes with the bleeding bodies of the birds.

When he had finished he went back into the cottage. He barricaded the kitchen door, made it doubly secure. He took off his bandages, sticky with the birds' blood, not with his own cuts, and put on fresh plaster.

His wife had made him cocoa and he drank it thirstily. He was very tired.

"All right," he said, smiling, "don't worry. We'll get through."

He lay down on his mattress and closed his eyes. He slept at once. He dreamt uneasily, because through his dreams there ran a thread

Making the Connections

Connecting to the Theme: "Facing Monsters"

After students have finished reading the selection, discuss whether or not the characters in the story organize themselves effectively to "face the monster."[They do not; with the exception of Nat, people fail to take the situation seriously.] What does the story say about the failure to take problems seriously, and work together to solve them? [The consequences of this failure can be disastrous.] Ask students to

provide a list of problems in their school and neighborhoods that might be resolved through well-organized effort. Then, divide the class into mixed-ability groups of four or five. Each group should choose one of the problems and make recommendations about how the community could coordinate and solve it. Encourage task allocation and communication.

Alternatively, groups could prepare reports

on real-life situations in which individuals, communities, or nations worked together effectively to respond to a crisis or natural disaster (Midwestern flooding, for example). They could also report on situations in which the lack of a cooperative response to a "monster" was devastating. (For example: Europe's failure to challenge the rise of Fascism before it led to World War II.)

of something forgotten. Some piece of work, neglected, that he should have done. Some precaution that he had known well but had not taken, and he could not put a name to it in his dreams. It was connected in some way with the burning aircraft and the stack upon the hill. He went on sleeping, though; he did not awake. It was his wife shaking his shoulder that awoke him finally.

"They've begun," she sobbed. "They've started this last hour. I can't listen to it any longer alone. There's something smelling bad too, something burning."

Then he remembered. He had forgotten to make up the fire. It was smoldering, nearly out. He got up swiftly and lit the lamp. The hammering had started at the windows and the doors, but it was not that he minded now. It was the smell of singed feathers. The smell filled the kitchen. He knew at once what it was. The birds were coming down the chimney, squeezing their way down to the kitchen range.

He got sticks and paper and put them on the embers, then reached for the can of paraffin.[13]

"Stand back," he shouted to his wife. "We've got to risk this."

He threw the paraffin onto the fire. The flame roared up the pipe, and down upon the fire fell the scorched, blackened bodies of the birds.

The children woke, crying. "What is it?" said Jill. "What's happened?"

Nat had no time to answer. He was raking the bodies from the chimney, clawing them out onto the floor. The flames still roared, and the danger of the chimney catching fire was one he had to take. The flames would send away the living birds from the chimney top. The lower joint was the difficulty, though. This was choked with the smoldering, helpless bodies of the birds caught by fire. He scarcely heeded the attack on the windows and the door: Let them beat their wings, break their beaks, lose their lives in the

13. **paraffin:** British term for "kerosene," a fuel that catches fire easily.

attempt to force an entry into his home. They would not break in. He thanked God he had one of the old cottages, with small windows, stout walls. Not like the new council houses. Heaven help them up the lane in the new council houses.

"Stop crying," he called to the children. "There's nothing to be afraid of, stop crying."

He went on raking at the burning, smoldering bodies as they fell into the fire.

"This'll fetch them," he said to himself, "the draft and the flames together. We're all right, as long as the chimney doesn't catch. I ought to be shot for this. It's all my fault. Last thing, I should have made up the fire. I knew there was something."

Amid the scratching and tearing at the window boards came the sudden homely striking of the kitchen clock. Three A.M. A little more than four hours yet to go. He could not be sure of the exact time of high water. He reckoned it would not turn much before half past seven, twenty to eight.

"Light up the Primus,"[14] he said to his wife. "Make us some tea, and the kids some cocoa. No use sitting around doing nothing."

That was the line. Keep her busy, and the children too. Move about, eat, drink; always best to be on the go.

He waited by the range. The flames were dying. But no more blackened bodies fell from the chimney. He thrust his poker up as far as it could go and found nothing. It was clear. The chimney was clear. He wiped the sweat from his forehead.

"Come on now, Jill," he said, "bring me some more sticks. We'll have a good fire going directly." She wouldn't come near him, though. She was staring at the heaped singed bodies of the birds.

14. **Primus:** small portable stove.

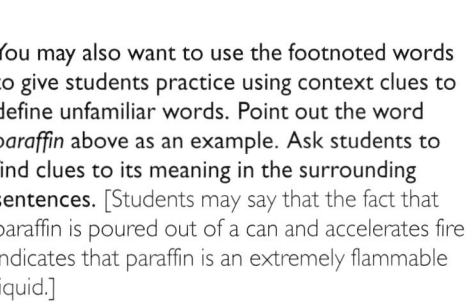

C Reading Skills and Strategies
Making Predictions

❓ What might it be that Nat has forgotten? [Possible responses: He has forgotten to board up some part of the house; he has not put out the aircraft fire, the flames of which could be spread by the wind and set his own house on fire.]

D Appreciating Language
Word Choice

❓ What does the use of the word *clawing* suggest about Nat? [Sample answers: Nat is using bird actions; he has become as ruthless as the birds.]

E Cultural Connections

Throughout this story, Nat, the man of the household, has tried to distract and protect his wife and children from the horror of the birds. Discuss with students how his thoughts and actions reveal the very traditional mindset that was common in both England and the United States in the 1940s and 1950s. Suggest that students speculate about how the division of labor and the defense against the birds might be different in a more modern or less traditional household.

Reaching All Students

Struggling Readers

Review the use of footnotes with students, and be sure they understand that reading the definitions of the footnoted words within the story can help them in their reading. Point out that even though reading the footnotes interrupts the story, they can go back and reread a passage after they have defined an unfamiliar word.

You may also want to use the footnoted words to give students practice using context clues to define unfamiliar words. Point out the word *paraffin* above as an example. Ask students to find clues to its meaning in the surrounding sentences. [Students may say that the fact that paraffin is poured out of a can and accelerates fire indicates that paraffin is an extremely flammable liquid.]

Finally, give students an opportunity to search for context clues. Have them choose five other footnoted words and then locate context clues that would help them define the word if the footnotes did not exist. Ask volunteers to share the words and the context clues that they found with the class. Other students who chose the same words can compare their context clues with those of the presenter.

A **Struggling Readers**

Finding Details

Ask students to name the two things Nat worries about in this passage. [running out of fuel and food] Then, have them identify the details that reveal this. [Details include Nat's deciding to get more fuel from the farm and noticing that they only have half a loaf of bread left.]

B **Critical Thinking**

Speculating

❓ Why do you think Nat's wife is not given a name? [Possible responses: She seems to act mainly as an extension of Nat and is dependent on him; it keeps the reader's attention and sympathy focused on Nat.]

"Never mind them," he said. "We'll put those in the passage when I've got the fire steady."

The danger of the chimney was over. It could not happen again, not if the fire was kept burning day and night.

A "I'll have to get more fuel from the farm tomorrow," he thought. "This will never last. I'll manage, though. I can do all that with the ebb tide. It can be worked, fetching what we need, when the tide's turned. We've just got to adapt ourselves, that's all."

They drank tea and cocoa and ate slices of bread and Bovril.[15] Only half a loaf left, Nat noticed. Never mind, though, they'd get by.

"Stop it," said young Johnny, pointing to the windows with his spoon, "stop it, you old birds."

"That's right," said Nat, smiling, "we don't want the old beggars, do we? Had enough of 'em."

They began to cheer when they heard the thud of the suicide birds.

"There's another, Dad," cried Jill. "He's done for."

"He's had it," said Nat. "There he goes, the blighter."

This was the way to face up to it. This was the spirit. If they could keep this up, hang on like this until seven, when the first news bulletin came through, they would not have done too badly.

"Give us a cigarette," he said to his wife. "A bit of a smoke will clear away the smell of the scorched feathers."

"There's only two left in the packet," she said. "I was going to buy you some from the co-op."

"I'll have one," he said, "t'other will keep for a rainy day."

No sense trying to make the children rest. There was no rest to be got while the tapping and the scratching went on at the windows. He **B** sat with one arm round his wife and the other round Jill, with Johnny on his mother's lap and the blankets heaped about them on the mattress.

"You can't help admiring the beggars," he said; "they've got persistence. You'd think they'd tire of the game, but not a bit of it."

15. **Bovril:** thick, beef-flavored liquid that is spread on bread or used to make broth.

Skill Link

Comparing Reviews with Your Own Response

Discuss with students why it is useful to read reviews of a story, novel, film, or CD, even if the critical comments present opinions that they do not share. [Reviews can point out things that you haven't previously considered or encourage you to find reasons to support your own responses.] Then, share with students the critic Richard Kelly's opinion on du Maurier's decision not to describe the effect of the birds on the world at large. "By limiting the focus of her story upon Nat Hocken and his family du Maurier manages to convey the effect of a believable claustrophobic nightmare. The birds may be attacking people throughout the world, but du Maurier wisely keeps the story within the confines of one person's family.... The Hocken family becomes a microcosm of an apparent worldwide disaster."

Activity

Invite students to compare their own responses to that of the critic. How do they feel about du Maurier's choice? Is the story more effective because of its limited focus or would it be better if the author described what was happening in London and elsewhere? Have students refer to details in the story to support their opinions.

Admiration was hard to sustain. The tapping went on and on and a new rasping note struck Nat's ear, as though a sharper beak than any hitherto had come to take over from its fellows. He tried to remember the names of birds; he tried to think which species would go for this particular job. It was not the tap of the woodpecker. That would be light and frequent. This was more serious because if it continued long the wood would splinter, as the glass had done. Then he remembered the hawks. Could the hawks have taken over from the gulls? Were there buzzards now upon the sills, using talons as well as beaks? Hawks, buzzards, kestrels, falcons—he had forgotten the birds of prey. He had forgotten the gripping power of the birds of prey. Three hours to go, and while they waited, the sound of the splintering wood, the talons tearing at the wood.

Nat looked about him, seeing what furniture he could destroy to fortify the door. The windows were safe because of the dresser. He was not certain of the door. He went upstairs, but when he reached the landing he paused and listened. There was a soft patter on the floor of the children's bedroom. The birds had broken through. . . . He put his ear to the door. No mistake. He could hear the rustle of wings and the light patter as they searched the floor. The other bedroom was still clear. He went into it and began bringing out the furniture, to pile at the head of the stairs should the door of the children's bedroom go. It was a preparation. It might never be needed. He could not stack the furniture against the door, because it opened inward. The only possible thing was to have it at the top of the stairs.

"Come down, Nat, what are you doing?" called his wife.

"I won't be long," he shouted. "Just making everything shipshape up here."

He did not want her to come; he did not want her to hear the pattering of the feet in the children's bedroom, the brushing of those wings against the door.

At five-thirty he suggested breakfast, bacon and fried bread, if only to stop the growing look of panic in his wife's eyes and to calm the <u>fretful</u> children. She did not know about the <u>birds</u> upstairs. The bedroom, luckily, was not over the kitchen. Had it been so, she could not have failed to hear the sound of them up there, tapping the boards. And the silly, senseless thud of the suicide birds, the death and glory boys, who flew into the bedroom, smashing their heads against the walls. He knew them of old, the herring gulls. They had no brains. The blackbacks were different; they knew what they were doing. So did the buzzards, the hawks. . . .

He found himself watching the clock, gazing at the hands that went so slowly round the dial. If his theory was not correct, if the attack did not cease with the turn of the tide, he knew they were beaten. They could not continue through the long day without air, without rest, without more fuel, without . . . His mind raced. He knew there were so many things they needed to withstand siege. They were not fully prepared. They were not ready. It might be that it would be safer in the towns, after all. If he could get a message through on the farm telephone to his cousin, only a short journey by train upcountry, they might be able to hire a car. That would be quicker—hire a car between tides . . .

His wife's voice, calling his name, drove away the sudden, desperate desire for sleep.

"What is it? What now?" he said sharply.

"The wireless," said his wife. "I've been watching the clock. It's nearly seven."

"Don't twist the knob," he said, impatient for the first time. "It's on the Home where it is. They'll speak from the Home."

They waited. The kitchen clock struck seven. There was no sound. No chimes, no music. They waited until a quarter past, switching to the Light. The result was the same. No news bulletin came through.

"We've heard wrong," he said. "They won't be broadcasting until eight o'clock."

They left it switched on, and Nat thought of the battery, wondered how much power was left in it. It was generally recharged when his wife went shopping in the town. If the battery failed, they would not hear the instructions.

WORDS TO OWN

fretful (fret′fəl) *adj.*: irritable and discontented.

Speculating

? This description of the land birds is extremely ominous. What do you think the birds are watching and waiting for? [Possible answers: for the signal to begin attacking again; for Nat to seem even more vulnerable.]

B Reading Skills and Strategies

Drawing Conclusions

? Why does Nat take his family with him? [Sample responses: They are frightened to stay alone; he is worried about leaving them.]

C Reading Skills and Strategies

Making Predictions

? What do you think Nat will find at the farm? [Possible responses: He will find that harm has come to the Triggs because they didn't take precautions against the birds; he will find the family dead.]

"It's getting light," whispered his wife. "I can't see it, but I can feel it. And the birds aren't hammering so loud."

She was right. The rasping, tearing sound grew fainter every moment. So did the shuffling, the jostling for place upon the step, upon the sills. The tide was on the turn. By eight there was no sound at all. Only the wind. The children, lulled at last by the stillness, fell asleep. At half past eight Nat switched the wireless off.

"What are you doing? We'll miss the news," said his wife.

"There isn't going to be any news," said Nat. "We've got to depend upon ourselves."

He went to the door and slowly pulled away the barricades. He drew the bolts and, kicking the bodies from the step outside the door, breathed the cold air. He had six working hours before him, and he knew he must reserve his strength for the right things, not waste it in any way. Food and light and fuel; these were the necessary things. If he could get them in sufficiency, they could endure another night.

He stepped into the garden, and as he did so he saw the living birds. The gulls had gone to ride the sea, as they had done before; they sought sea food and the buoyancy of the tide, before they returned to the attack. Not so the land birds. They waited and watched. Nat saw them, on the hedgerows, on the soil, crowded in the trees, outside in the field, line upon line of birds, all still, doing nothing.

He went to the end of his small garden. The birds did not move. They went on watching him.

"I've got to get food," said Nat to himself. "I've got to go to the farm to find food."

He went back to the cottage. He saw to the windows and the doors. He went upstairs and opened the children's bedroom. It was empty, except for the dead birds on the floor. The living were out there, in the garden, in the fields. He went downstairs.

"I'm going to the farm," he said.

His wife clung to him. She had seen the living birds from the open door.

"Take us with you," she begged. "We can't stay here alone. I'd rather die than stay here alone."

He considered the matter. He nodded.

"Come on, then," he said. "Bring baskets, and Johnny's pram.[16] We can load up the pram."

They dressed against the biting wind, wore gloves and scarves. His wife put Johnny in the pram. Nat took Jill's hand.

"The birds," she whimpered, "they're all out there in the fields."

"They won't hurt us," he said, "not in the light."

They started walking across the field toward the stile, and the birds did not move. They waited, their heads turned to the wind.

When they reached the turning to the farm, Nat stopped and told his wife to wait in the shelter of the hedge with the two children.

"But I want to see Mrs. Trigg," she protested. "There are lots of things we can borrow if they went to market yesterday; not only bread, and . . ."

"Wait here," Nat interrupted. "I'll be back in a moment."

The cows were lowing, moving restlessly in the yard, and he could see a gap in the fence where the sheep had knocked their way through, to roam unchecked in the front garden before the farmhouse. No smoke came from the chimneys. He was filled with misgiving. He did not want his wife or the children to go down to the farm.

"Don't gib[17] now," said Nat, harshly. "Do what I say."

She withdrew with the pram into the hedge, screening herself and the children from the wind.

He went down alone to the farm. He pushed

16. **pram:** baby carriage.
17. **gib:** balk; hesitate.

Crossing the Curriculum

Music

Explain to students that in filming *The Birds,* Alfred Hitchcock made a critical decision—he omitted all music from the sound track. Although he hired the gifted composer Bernard Herrmann (1911–1975) as a sound consultant, Hitchcock used eerie silence and real-life sounds such as the whir of the birds' wings to build suspense. Imagine that you are the director filming a remake of *The Birds.* Would you use music to build suspense, or would you create your own sound track of natural noises? What music would you choose? What sounds would you use? How would you capture the sound of the sea or the scream of the gannet? Choose a suspenseful scene such as the one in which Nat approaches the farm and create your own score or sound track to complement the mood. Have students share their work with the class.

his way through the herd of bellowing cows, which turned this way and that, distressed, their udders full. He saw the car standing by the gate, not put away in the garage. The windows of the farmhouse were smashed. There were many dead gulls lying in the yard and around the house. The living birds perched on the group of trees behind the farm and on the roof of the house. They were quite still. They watched him.

Jim's body lay in the yard . . . what was left of it. When the birds had finished, the cows had trampled him. His gun was beside him. The door of the house was shut and bolted, but, as the windows were smashed, it was easy to lift them and climb through. Trigg's body was close to the telephone. He must have been trying to get through to the exchange when the birds came for him. The receiver was hanging loose, the instrument torn from the wall. No sign of Mrs. Trigg. She would be upstairs. Was it any use going up? Sickened, Nat knew what he would find.

"Thank God," he said to himself, "there were no children."

He forced himself to climb the stairs, but halfway he turned and descended again. He could see her legs protruding from the open bedroom door. Beside her were the bodies of the black-backed gulls and an umbrella, broken.

"It's no use," thought Nat, "doing anything. I've only got five hours, less than that. The Triggs would understand. I must load up with what I can find."

He tramped back to his wife and children.

"I'm going to fill up the car with stuff," he said. "I'll put coal in it, and paraffin for the Primus. We'll take it home and return for a fresh load."

"What about the Triggs?" asked his wife.

"They must have gone to friends," he said.

"Shall I come and help you, then?"

"No; there's a mess down there. Cows and sheep all over the place. Wait, I'll get the car. You can sit in it."

Clumsily he backed the car out of the yard and into the lane. His wife and the children could not see Jim's body from there.

"Stay here," he said, "never mind the pram. The pram can be fetched later. I'm going to load the car."

Her eyes watched his all the time. He believed she understood; otherwise she would have suggested helping him to find the bread and groceries.

They made three journeys altogether, backward and forward between their cottage and the farm, before he was satisfied they had everything they needed. It was surprising, once he started thinking, how many things were necessary. Almost the most important of all was planking for the windows. He had to go round searching for timber. He wanted to renew the boards on all the windows at the cottage. Candles, paraffin, nails, tinned stuff; the list was endless. Besides all that, he milked three of the cows. The rest, poor brutes, would have to go on bellowing.

On the final journey he drove the car to the bus stop, got out, and went to the telephone box. He waited a few minutes, jangling the receiver. No good though. The line was dead. He climbed onto a bank and looked over the countryside, but there was no sign of life at all, nothing in the fields but the waiting, watching birds. Some of them slept—he could see the beaks tucked into the feathers.

"You'd think they'd be feeding," he said to himself, "not just standing in that way."

Then he remembered. They were gorged with food. They had eaten their fill during the night. That was why they did not move this morning. . . .

No smoke came from the chimneys of the council houses. He thought of the children who had run across the fields the night before.

"I should have known," he thought; "I ought to have taken them home with me."

He lifted his face to the sky. It was colorless and gray. The bare trees on the landscape looked bent and blackened by the east wind. The cold did not affect the living birds waiting out there in the fields.

D
E
F

D Critical Thinking
Making Connections
? What might the gun and the damaged telephone next to Jim's and Trigg's bodies suggest? [Sample responses: Technology is useless against the onslaught of the birds; nature's forces are more powerful than technology.]
Where else in the story has a similar idea been suggested? [Possible answers: when Nat had earlier thought the gun was useless; when the planes were sent out.]

E Reading Skills and Strategies
Making Inferences
? What does Nat's wife understand? [that the Triggs are dead]

F Reading Skills and Strategies
Making Inferences
? What does Nat think has happened to the children? [He thinks they are dead.]

Getting Students Involved

Cooperative Learning
What Happens Next? Allow students to provide closure for this open-ended story by having them offer their own original conclusions. Ask small groups of students to pick up the plot where the story ends and extend the story. Group members can collaborate on the basic outline and then take turns contributing sections. Presenters from the groups can share the narratives with the class.

A Elements of Literature

Character

❓ What does this statement by Nat's wife reveal about her character? [Sample responses: She is brave enough to stand the sight of the dead, from which Nat wanted to protect her; she places the protection of Jill over her own feelings.]

B Elements of Literature

Foreshadowing

❓ This image suggests military aircraft taking off. What might the image foreshadow? [Possible responses: another, perhaps more brutal attack by the birds; the birds' overthrow of British military defenses.]

C Critical Thinking

Evaluating

❓ Are manners really important at a time like this? [Possible answers: No, it seems a silly thing to focus on; yes, manners are one of the things that separates people from animals; yes, maintaining standards and normality is important when people are dealing with a crisis.]

D Historical Connection

This mention of America, one of the Cold War superpowers, again suggests the subtext of a communist threat. It is also a reference to the understanding that the U.S. entry into World War II on the side of the United Kingdom was essential to winning the war. It implies that the United States is not coming to the rescue now because it is being devastated by attacking birds.

"This is the time they ought to get them," said Nat; "they're a sitting target now. They must be doing this all over the country. Why don't our aircraft take off now and spray them with mustard gas? What are all our chaps doing? They must know; they must see for themselves."

He went back to the car and got into the driver's seat.

A "Go quickly past that second gate," whispered his wife. "The postman's lying there. I don't want Jill to see."

He accelerated. The little Morris bumped and rattled along the lane. The children shrieked with laughter.

"Up-a-down, up-a-down," shouted young Johnny.

It was a quarter to one by the time they reached the cottage. Only an hour to go.

"Better have cold dinner," said Nat. "Hot up something for yourself and the children, some of that soup. I've no time to eat now. I've got to unload all this stuff."

He got everything inside the cottage. It could be sorted later. Give them all something to do during the long hours ahead. First he must see to the windows and the doors.

He went round the cottage methodically, testing every window, every door. He climbed onto the roof also, and fixed boards across every chimney except the kitchen. The cold was so intense he could hardly bear it, but the job had to be done. Now and again he would look up, searching the sky for aircraft. None came. As he **C** worked he cursed the inefficiency of the authorities.

"It's always the same," he muttered. "They always let us down. Muddle, muddle, from the start. No plan, no real organization. And we don't matter down here. That's what it is. The people upcountry have priority. They're using gas up there, no doubt, and all the aircraft. We've got to **D** wait and take what comes."

He paused, his work on the bedroom chimney finished, and looked out to sea. Something was moving out there. Something gray and white amongst the breakers.

"Good old Navy," he said, "they never let us down. They're coming down-channel; they're turning in the bay."

He waited, straining his eyes, watering in the wind, toward the sea. He was wrong, though. It was not ships. The Navy was not there. The gulls were rising from the sea. **B** The massed flocks in the fields, with ruffled feathers, rose in formation from the ground and, wing to wing, soared upward to the sky.

The tide had turned again.

Nat climbed down the ladder and went inside the kitchen. The family were at dinner. It was a little after two. He bolted the door, put up the barricade, and lit the lamp.

"It's nighttime," said young Johnny.

His wife had switched on the wireless once again, but no sound came from it.

"I've been all round the dial," she said, "foreign stations, and that lot. I can't get anything."

"Maybe they have the same trouble," he said, "maybe it's the same right through Europe."

She poured out a plateful of the Triggs' soup, cut him a large slice of the Triggs' bread, and spread their dripping upon it.

They ate in silence. A piece of the dripping ran down young Johnny's chin and fell onto the table.

"Manners, Johnny," said Jill, "you should learn to wipe your mouth."

The tapping began at the windows, at the door. The rustling, the jostling, the pushing for position on the sills. The first thud of the suicide gulls upon the step.

"Won't America do something?" said his wife. "They've always been our allies, haven't they? Surely America will do something?"

Nat did not answer. The boards were strong against the windows and on the

---

Crossing the Curriculum

Science
Birds have remarkable sensory abilities and powers that humans do not have. Have students work in groups to research and report on various aspects of birds. Possible topics: how migratory birds navigate; how birds fly; the meaning of bird songs; birds' senses of sight, hearing, and smell; how birds nest and care for their young; birds' life processes, such as body temperature, breathing, and heart beat.

Art
Encourage students to explore the works of the world-famous painter of birds, John J. Audubon (1785–1851). He devoted himself to traveling through the American wilderness, studying and sketching the different species of American birds. His *The Birds of America* contains 435 hand-colored plates with 1,065 life-size figures of birds, each shown in its characteristic pose and habitat.

chimneys too. The cottage was filled with stores, with fuel, with all they needed for the next few days. When he had finished dinner he would put the stuff away, stack it neatly, get everything shipshape, handy like. His wife could help him, and the children too. They'd tire themselves out, between now and a quarter to nine, when the tide would ebb; then he'd tuck them down on their mattresses, see that they slept good and sound until three in the morning.

He had a new scheme for the windows, which was to fix barbed wire in front of the boards. He had brought a great roll of it from the farm. The nuisance was, he'd have to work at this in the dark, when the lull came between nine and three. Pity he had not thought of it before. Still, as long as the wife slept, and the kids, that was the main thing.

The smaller birds were at the window now. He recognized the light tap-tapping of their beaks and the soft brush of their wings. The hawks ignored the windows. They concentrated their attack upon the door. Nat listened to the tearing sound of splintering wood and wondered how many million years of memory were stored in those little brains, behind the stabbing beaks, the piercing eyes, now giving them this instinct to destroy mankind with all the deft precision of machines.

"I'll smoke that last cigarette," he said to his wife. "Stupid of me—it was the one thing I forgot to bring back from the farm."

He reached for it, switched on the silent wireless. He threw the empty packet on the fire and watched it burn.

E

WORDS TO OWN

deft *adj.*: skillful in a quick, sure and easy way.

MEET THE WRITER

The Urge to Write

Daphne du Maurier (1907–1989) was born in London, the daughter of a famous actor and theater manager and the grand-daughter of George du Maurier, a writer of popular novels. Although she grew up in a stimulating, well-to-do family, she preferred solitude and reading to the busy social lives her sisters enjoyed.

While she was in her early twenties, du Maurier decided to write a novel and secluded herself in an empty house in Cornwall, on the coast of England. The novel turned out to be a romantic family chronicle which grew to

200,000 words in just ten weeks. As she wrote, she discovered something about writing: "Sometimes my book comes so strongly on me that it's like a restless urge within saying 'Get on! Get on!'"

A Shelfful of Books

Du Maurier's first novel revealed an astonishing gift for storytelling, one that readers have since found irresistible. That book, called *The Loving Spirit* (Avon), not only found a publisher at once but also became a best-seller and the forerunner of a shelfful of others, including the three famous romantic novels: *Rebecca* (Avon), *Jamaica Inn* (Buccaneer), and *Frenchman's Creek* (Dell).

THE BIRDS 75

E Reading Skills and Strategies

Making Predictions

? What do you think will happen to the Hockens? [Possible answers: They will wait out the attacks by supplying themselves from Trigg's farm; their barricades will give way and they will be killed.]

BROWSING IN THE FILES

About the Author. When du Maurier was about twenty, she moved away from her family to live on the rugged Cornish coast. Shortly before her death at age eighty-three, she wrote, "I know that no person will ever get into my blood as a place can, as Cornwall does. People and things pass away but not places."

Writers on Writing. About this story, du Maurier stated, "In the story, the gulls act as one body, bound together by some extra-ordinary power against a human prey so 'civilized' that few can understand, can recognize that in some sinister way the evolutionary tide has turned."

Resources

Selection Assessment
Formal Assessment
• Selection Test, p. 5
Test Generator (One-Stop Planner)
• CD-ROM

Assessing Learning

Check Test: Questions and Answers
Answers may vary slightly.
1. Briefly describe the narrator of the story and his family. [The narrator is Nat Hocken, a part-time farm worker. He has a wife and two small children.]
2. What is Nat's initial explanation for the birds' strange behavior? [The east wind has driven the frightened, lost, and hungry birds to the farm.]

3. How does Nat prepare for the attacks? [He boards up chimneys, windows, and doors; he stuffs dead birds' bodies into broken windows; and he gets supplies from the farm.]
4. What happens to Jim and the Triggs? [They are killed by the birds.]
5. What is Nat's only concern at the end of the story? [He wants to keep his family safe from the birds.]

Standardized Test Preparation
For practice with standardized test format specific to this selection, see
• *Standardized Test Preparation*, pp. 12, 14
For practice in proofreading and editing, see
• *Daily Oral Grammar*, Transparency 3

This news article describes a real-life occurrence similar to the events in du Maurier's story—an invasion of a home in California by hundreds of birds. However, the reason for the invation was more benign; the swifts, flying in foul weather, probably mistook the house's chimney for a tree trunk. They entered the home through the chimney and invaded every corner of the dwelling. As in "The Birds," the flocks came and went and came again. However, unlike the birds in the story, the swifts were harmless, and the Fire Department solved the problem by installing a heavy steel grate over the chimney.

Ⓐ Reading Skills and Strategies

Comparing and Contrasting

❓ What are some similarities and differences between the behavior of the birds described in this newspaper article and the behavior of the birds in the story? [Similarities: Large numbers of birds are swarming, one bird does something and then the rest follow; the birds enter the house through the chimney. Differences: The birds in the article are all one species; they are not as numerous as the birds in the story; they do not attack people.]

Ⓑ Critical Thinking

Making Connections

❓ What two major differences are mentioned here between the Meltons' experience with the birds and the Hockens' experience? [The Meltons had the help of a government agency, the fire department, which the Hockens did not have; according to ornithologists (bird experts), the birds that entered the Meltons' home were unable to bite and scratch people, while the birds in the story viciously attacked Nat Hocken and others.]

Hundreds of Birds Invade Home in California

Ⓐ SANTA PAULA, Calif., May 4 (UPI)—Hundreds of birds swirled "like a tornado" down the chimney of a home twice in one week, creating a fluttering mass invasion reminiscent of the Alfred Hitchcock movie *The Birds,* the home's owners said today.

"They were just swarming around and around," said John Melton, a city councilman in this Ventura County community north of Los Angeles. "Then all of a sudden one went down the chimney. Then they narrowed into a funnel just like a tornado and—shoomp!—right down the chimney."

The birds were identified by ornithologists as Vaux's swifts, now migrating from their winter homes in Mexico and Central America to the Pacific Northwest.

The Meltons returned last Friday from a two-day trip and discovered that the tiny birds had invaded their hillside home by flying down the chimney and through an inch-wide space between the fireplace frame and screen.

"They Were Everywhere"

"They were four deep on our twelve-foot windows," Lucille Melton said. "We walked through the house and they were everywhere. We estimated eight hundred to a thousand birds."

Most of the birds were gone by Saturday afternoon, Mr. Melton said, although the couple continued to find birds "in Kleenex boxes, vases, beneath the kitchen stove, everywhere."

As the family was preparing to go out to dinner Saturday night, a flock of about four hundred swifts returned.

Birds Posed No Danger

The birds finally flew back up the chimney, and the Fire Department installed a heavy steel grate, deterring the flock when they returned a third time Sunday night.

Ornithologists agreed that the Meltons faced no danger from the swifts.

Ⓑ "They couldn't bite you, hurt you, scratch you, if they had to," said Kimball Garrett, bird-collection manager at the Los Angeles County Museum of Natural History.

The birds, flying into foul weather, probably mistook the Meltons' chimney for a tree trunk, their normal roosting place, Mr. Garrett said.

—from *The New York Times*

Connecting Across Texts

Connecting with "The Birds"

Designate a portion of classroom bulletin-board space for articles about unusual occurrences in nature that seem to threaten people. You might suggest that students consider investigating such topics as floods, hurricanes, volcanoes, landslides, plagues of insects, wildlife carriers of disease, and rodent infestations. Students can use the *Reader's Guide to Periodical Literature* or Internet search engines for assistance in finding material. Encourage students to write original stories based on such news events. As they draft their stories, suggest that they review and try to imitate the way du Maurier integrates descriptions of the natural scene with reactions of the characters to the crisis.

MAKING MEANINGS

First Thoughts

[infer] **1.** What do you **predict** will happen next to Nat and his family?

Shaping Interpretations

[infer] **2.** What resolution to the **conflict** do you think might be suggested in the final scene by the silent radio and the burning cigarette package?

[interpret] **3.** Do you think the scene at the Triggs' **foreshadows** what will happen to Nat and his family, or do you think they will survive? In other words, do you read this as a doomsday story (about the end of human life on earth) or as a story in which humans will triumph over nature? Cite details from the text to support your interpretation.

[synthesize] **4.** Find at least five details that suggest that an evil force might be directing the birds to turn against people. What do you imagine this force could be?

Extending the Text

[connect] **5.** In this story du Maurier sometimes seems critical of people and of the way they respond to disaster. Find at least three details that show characters behaving ignorantly or endangering themselves or others. Do you think this is how people really behave?

[synthesize] **6.** Look at your Quickwrite notes about other threats posed by nature. Why do you think du Maurier chose birds to be the attackers in this story?

Challenging the Text

[evaluate] **7.** On just a factual level, do you think nature could suddenly turn on us like this? Give the story a credibility rating on a scale of 1 to 5:

Possible   1   2   3   4   5   Not possible

Be ready to support your rating with details from the text and from your own experience. Be sure to consider the news article "Hundreds of Birds Invade Home in California" (see *Connections* on page 76).

Reading Check

a. On December 3, two apparently minor incidents occur—one involving the farmer, the other involving Nat. What are these incidents, and how do they **foreshadow** what the story's **conflict** will be?

b. In the paragraph beginning "The sky was hard" (page 55), the weather is described. List five details here that strike you as ominous.

c. Nat keeps trying to find a rational explanation for the birds' behavior. What explanations does he think of?

d. How do other people react to the birds—Jim, Mr. Trigg, Jill, Nat's wife?

e. How do the BBC radio announcements create **suspense** as the story progresses?

Reading Check
Answers may vary slightly.

a. Birds swoop close to the farmer's hat; birds attack Nat. These incidents foreshadow the conflict by hinting at the birds' hostility towards humans.

b. The hills are bare, not gleaming; the wind feels like a razor; the dead leaves shiver; the winter is black and sudden; the earth is frozen solid.

c. The sudden change in weather; fierce wind; hunger; need for shelter; the birds are responding to "orders" from an unknown source.

d. Jim ignores Nat's concerns; Mr. Trigg thinks it will be fun to shoot the birds; Jill is afraid; Nat's wife first thinks the birds are a nuisance, but later is terrified.

e. The radio gives official information about the situation but the announcer treats it as a joke. Suspense increases when the announcer is solemn and admits that people are on their own. Then the broadcasts stop.

MAKING MEANINGS

First Thoughts

1. Some students may suggest that the attack suddenly ends and the family survives; others, that the family is killed by the birds.

Shaping Interpretations

2. Students may say that both images seem ominous. The silent radio may suggest that the birds have triumphed in the city and in the world. The burning of the wrapper may suggest the destruction of human civilization.

3. Some students may say that the family will survive because Nat, unlike the Triggs, took precautions and acted wisely. Others may believe that since the birds are so vicious and aggressive, and since there are no signs of other human life, Nat and his family are doomed.

4. Details include "[The birds] were bound on some other mission" (p. 61); "'They've been given the towns'" (p. 61); "It was as though they waited upon some signal" (p. 61); "Some bond had brought them together" (p. 63); "There was some law the birds obeyed" (p. 67). Possible forces include: nuclear fallout; a political enemy; a worldwide weather catastrophe; changes in the sun and moon that affect the tides.

Extending the Text

5. Possible details: Mrs. Trigg and Jim don't believe Nat's story; Trigg wants to shoot the birds for fun; the phone operator doesn't take Nat seriously. Some students may suggest that people don't take emergency warnings seriously, while others will point to natural disasters, such as hurricanes in the United States, to show that they do.

6. Possible answers: Birds seem normal and harmless, yet they have sharp beaks and claws and can fly; birds exist worldwide.

Challenging the Text

7. Possible details that support the story's credibility: the BBC's report of the sudden change in the jet stream; the invasion of the California home in the news article. Details that support lack of credibility: species flocking together; birds turning into carnivores.

Grading Timesaver

Rubrics for each Choices assignment appear on p. 93 in the *Portfolio Management System*.

CHOICES: Building Your Portfolio

1. **Writer's Notebook** Remind students to save their work. They may use it as prewriting for the Writer's Workshop on p. 112.
2. **Creative Writing** To help them recount the events in the order that they occurred, have students work in pairs to create a time line based on the story. Then, suggest that students review the story for possible causes of the birds' behavior and discuss the three best causes with their partners.
3. **Research/Science** Because the story is set in England, some of the birds mentioned may not be familiar to students and may not appear in the bird books available to them. Encourage students to work in pairs or groups and to focus on one type of bird in their research.
4. **Speaking and Listening** Immediately after watching the videotape, have a class discussion in which students talk about their reactions to the film. Then, give them time to compare the specific elements in the story and film and to discuss which they prefer.

CHOICES: Building Your Portfolio

Writer's Notebook

1. Collecting Ideas for a Short Narrative

Creating a setting. Reread the paragraph on page 52 beginning "Nat, tramping home." What details help you picture the isolated farmhouse by the sea, hear the wind, feel you are there with Nat in his chilly house? For the narrative you'll write for the Writer's Workshop on page 112, you'll also want to create a vivid setting to help readers feel they are there. Review the notes you've taken for a narrative of your own. Where will your story be set? List as many details about the setting as you can. Try to focus on sights, sounds, smells, even perhaps taste and touch sensations.

> **Setting for a Narrative**
> Peacefulness of the forest
> Smell of pine trees
> Cheerful chirping of birds
> Crunch of pine needles underfoot
> Bright blue sky showing through the umbrella of trees

Creative Writing

2. Who's in Charge?

Du Maurier tells us that the birds are trying to destroy human life, but we never know what is making them do it. Is it really the weather, as some characters in the story think? Is it an evil force, as du Maurier seems to suggest at times? Suppose you are a historian at some future time studying this famous bird attack. Write a feature article summing up the main events of the historical disaster and offering some possible reasons for the birds' sudden frenzy. Be sure to tell why the murderous birds didn't succeed in wiping out the world. (After all, you as the historian are alive on earth. Or are you somewhere else?)

Research/Science

3. Looking at Birds

Find out how the birds in this story act when they are behaving normally. Review the text to locate the types of birds that are attacking. Then use a bird book or an encyclopedia or database to chart their characteristics, such as size, physical features, feeding habits, and behavior. Classify the birds according to type: land birds, seabirds, birds of prey, or any other categories you can think of. You might sketch some of the birds to show their appearance or behavior: beaks, talons, wingspans, eating habits, ways of swooping or diving. Imagine that the director of a remake of the movie *The Birds* (see below) wants to use your bird book as a resource.

Speaking and Listening

4. Story vs. Movie

Watch a videotape of Alfred Hitchcock's 1963 movie, *The Birds*. Assume the role of talk-show critic and compare the film with du Maurier's story. You should focus on specific elements, such as **setting**, **characters**, or **resolution of the conflict**. Conclude your talk by telling which you prefer, and why: the original story or the film. Be ready to take questions on the telephone from your audience.

Scene from the 1963 film version of *The Birds*.

Reaching All Students

Struggling Readers

If possible, allow students who are working on Choice 4 to watch parts of the film again so they can review points or scenes crucial to their arguments. Students may want to consult one another about their recollections of the film.

Verb Tenses—What Time Is It?

Verbs in English have six tenses:

Tense	Example
present	I give
past	I gave
future	I will give
present perfect	I have given
past perfect	I had given
future perfect	I will have given

Here are three tenses in sentences from "The Birds."

1. "On December the third, the wind changed overnight, and it was winter." [past tense]

2. " 'It will be a hard winter.' " [future tense]

3. " '. . . a message comes to the birds in autumn. . . .' " [present tense]

Fiction is usually written in the past tense. Notice that du Maurier uses the future and the present only in dialogue. It is rare to find stories told in the present tense, though such stories have been written.

> ### Try It Out
> ➤ Choose two narrative paragraphs from the story (try to avoid paragraphs with dialogue) and rewrite them in the present tense. Notice how the change in tense gives the story a "here-and-now" feeling.
>
> ➤ When you are writing, the main problem you are likely to have with verb tenses is keeping them consistent. Take out a piece of your own writing and underline all the verbs. Then label each one according to its tense. Are your tenses consistent?

VOCABULARY | HOW TO OWN A WORD |

> **WORD BANK**
> disposition
> placid
> apprehensive
> garish
> recounted
> sullen
> furtively
> imperative
> fretful
> deft
>
> ### Own It
> 1. Write a pet-wanted ad that uses the word *disposition*.
> 2. Write a description of a park using the word *placid*.
> 3. Write a journal entry using the word *apprehensive*.
> 4. Tell what a *garish* outfit might look like.
> 5. Write the first sentence of a news report using the word *recounted*.
> 6. Use the word *sullen* in a sentence from a counselor's report.
> 7. Describe a burglar's action using the word *furtively*.
> 8. Write a bulletin-board notice using the word *imperative*.
> 9. Describe an annoying incident using the word *fretful*.
> 10. Write two rhyming lines using the words *deft* and *left*.

THE BIRDS 79

GRAMMAR LINK

Have partners read aloud sections of their writing to each other, pausing after each verb; the partner should then identify the tense of the verb. If the listener thinks a verb tense is incorrect, partners should stop and discuss that verb.

Try It Out

After students have labeled the verbs in their own writing, have them rewrite a paragraph, either to make the verbs consistent or to change the tense in which the paragraph was originally written.

VOCABULARY
Possible Answers
1. Wanted: pet with cheerful *disposition.*
2. The park was calm and *placid* on Sunday.
3. Today I am *apprehensive* about the big test.
4. The outfit was *garish*—all orange and red with gold spangles.
5. Today, witnesses *recounted* their experience during the fire.
6. I found the client to be uncooperative and *sullen.*
7. Making sure no one saw him, the burglar *furtively* entered the window.
8. It is *imperative* that residents throw out their own trash.
9. *Fretful* after missing the last bus to school, the child pulled the cat's tail.
10. When I serve with my left, I am not quite as *deft.*

Resources ─────

Grammar
• *Grammar and Language Links* Worksheet, p. 5

Vocabulary
• *Words to Own* Worksheet, p. 3

Grammar Link Quick Check

Label the tenses in the sentences below and rewrite any that do not have a consistent tense.

1. Nat **runs** [present] from the attacking birds and **tried** [past] to open the front door. [runs, tries; or ran, tried]

2. They **were** [past] safe because they **will board** [future] the windows against the birds. [will be, will board; or were, boarded]

3. Because the neighbors **refused** [past] to believe Nat, they **were killed** [past] by the birds.

4. The radio **is** [present] silent, which **made** [past] the family nervous. [was, made; or is, makes]

OBJECTIVES

1. Read and interpret the story
2. Analyze suspense
3. Monitor reading by asking questions
4. Express understanding through creative writing, role-playing, or research/history
5. Identify and practice subject-verb agreement
6. Understand and use new words
7. Research a word's etymology

SKILLS

Literary
- Analyze suspense

Reading
- Monitor reading by asking questions

Writing
- Write dialogue
- Write a paragraph about a character

Role-Playing
- Role-play characters

Research/History
- Research and report on India

Grammar
- Use subject-verb agreement

Vocabulary
- Use new words
- Research a word's etymology

Planning

- **Block Schedule**
  Block Scheduling Lesson Plans with Pacing Guide
- **Traditional Schedule**
  Lesson Plans Including Strategies for English-Language Learners
- **One-Stop Planner**
  CD-ROM with Test Generator

Before You Read

POISON

Make the Connection

Hooking into Our Fears

Three characters confront one another—and danger—in a house in colonial India. As events unfold, we are drawn into their terrible conflicts and their terror. Suppose you were face to face with grave danger. What might the encounter bring out in you: bravery? fear? or perhaps even something you are ashamed of?

Quickwrite

Take notes on your responses to the question above. Can you think of situations in which danger might bring out the worst in people?

Elements of Literature

The Grip of Suspense

A writer holds us in **suspense** by making us uncertain about—but very interested in—what lies ahead. Suspense is what keeps us turning those pages. The word *suspense* is related to the word *suspended*. When we feel suspense, we feel as if we are hanging in midair, like those

characters in a movie who cling by their fingertips to cliffs, their feet kicking out into space. That's suspense—and that's why stories like this one of Dahl's are called cliffhangers.

> **S**uspense is the uncertainty or anxiety we feel about what is going to happen next in a story.
>
> *For more on Suspense, see pages 32–33 and the Handbook of Literary Terms.*

Reading Skills and Strategies

Monitoring Your Reading: Asking Questions

Writers create suspense by planting questions in readers' minds. This story revolves around one big question, but at the end you may find that you're left with additional questions.

Monitor your reading by jotting down any questions you have as you read. You don't have to answer them—the writer will do that for you. (But he may not answer them all.)

Background

This story is set in India when that country was still under British rule.

At one time, the British Empire covered nearly one quarter of the globe. Among the colonies of this powerful empire was the huge subcontinent of India. Many Indians resented the control that the British imposed on all their institutions—their laws, education, army, and government. Religious differences also resulted in conflicts. Most of the Indians were Hindu; a smaller number were Muslim. The English were mostly Christian. Some of the simmering conflicts that eventually resulted in massive bloodshed in India are shown in this story—which is about more than one kind of poison.

go.hrw.com
LE0 9-1

Preteaching Vocabulary

Words to Own

List the Words to Own on the chalkboard, and have volunteers read aloud their definitions (from the bottom of the selection pages). Then, have students decide whether each sentence below makes sense if the boldfaced word is used. If not, have them revise the sentence.

1. The cats were being fed dry food **intravenously** during the week. [No. Sample response: The cats were receiving their medication intravenously.]

2. Through the fog, the pilot was just able to **discern** the runway lights. [Yes]

3. She always found hot August days to be **oppressive**. [Yes]

4. Howard's attitude toward money was **frivolous;** he rarely spent a dime unnecessarily. [No. Sample response: Howard's attitude toward money was frivolous; he often bought worthless trinkets that he rarely used.]

"I haven't been bitten," he whispered. "Not yet."

POISON

Roald Dahl

I t must have been around midnight when I drove home, and as I approached the gates of the bungalow I switched off the headlamps of the car so the beam wouldn't swing in through the window of the side bedroom and wake Harry Pope. But I needn't have bothered. Coming up the drive, I noticed his light was still on, so he was awake anyway—unless perhaps he'd dropped off while reading.

I parked the car and went up the five steps to the balcony, counting each step carefully in the dark so I wouldn't take an extra one which wasn't there, when I got to the top. I crossed the balcony, pushed through the screen doors into the house itself, and switched on the light in the hall. I went across to the door of Harry's room, opened it quietly, and looked in.

He was lying on the bed and I could see he was awake. But he didn't move. He didn't even turn his head toward me, but I heard him say, "Timber, Timber, come here."

He spoke slowly, whispering each word carefully, separately, and I pushed the door right open and started to go quickly across the room.

POISON 81

Summary ■ ■

Set in colonial India, this suspense story explores the conflict between the cultures of Britain and India. Timber Woods, the narrator, comes home late one night to find his housemate, Harry Pope, in bed and in mortal terror of being bitten by a krait, a lethally poisonous Indian snake. Harry believes that the krait is asleep under the sheet on his stomach. The suspense builds as the men anxiously decide upon a course of action. The slightest movement will cause the snake to bite, but doing nothing leaves Harry in the same danger. Timber summons an Indian physician, Dr. Ganderbai, who risks his own life to save Harry. At the end of the story, the men pull back the sheet and discover that there is no krait. The snake either never existed or has fled without anyone being aware. Dr. Ganderbai makes a joke about the situation and, humiliated, Harry turns on Dr. Ganderbai, assaulting him with racial slurs. In an ironic twist, the "poison" in the story turns out to be the bitter, evil prejudice that Harry unleashes on the unsuspecting physician.

Resources ———————

Listening
Audio CD Library
A recording of "Poison" is available as part of the *Audio CD Library:*
• Disc 5, Track 2

Resources: Print and Media

Reading
• *Graphic Organizers for Active Reading,* p. 4
• *Words to Own,* p. 4
• *Audio CD Library*
   Disc 5, Track 2

Writing and Language
• *Daily Oral Grammar*
   Transparency 4
• *Grammar and Language Links*
   Worksheet, p. 7

• *Language Workshop* CD-ROM

Assessment
• *Formal Assessment,* p. 7
• *Portfolio Management System,* p. 94
• *Test Generator (One-Stop Planner* CD-ROM)

Internet
• go.hrw.com (keyword: LE0 9-1)

A Reading Skills and Strategies

Asking Questions

❓ This story opens with an unexplained situation. What questions do you have about it? [Possible questions: What is wrong with Harry? Why is he still awake? Why is he calling out to Timber?]

B Elements of Literature

Suspense

❓ How do Harry's instructions create suspense? [Sample responses: Readers know that something unusual is going on, but they don't know what; Harry's urgency creates a feeling of anxiety about what is wrong.]

C Critical Thinking

Analyzing

Explain to students that this is a reference to Timber's experience during World War II. You may want to discuss with students what purpose this break in the narrative might serve. [It sets the time of the story some time after World War II, and it provides information about a character's background.]

D Reading Skills and Strategies

Drawing Conclusions

❓ What emotion is Harry probably feeling at this point? [Possible answers: terror; anxiety.] What details in the text led you to this conclusion? [Possible responses: the way Harry is speaking; the way he is sweating profusely.]

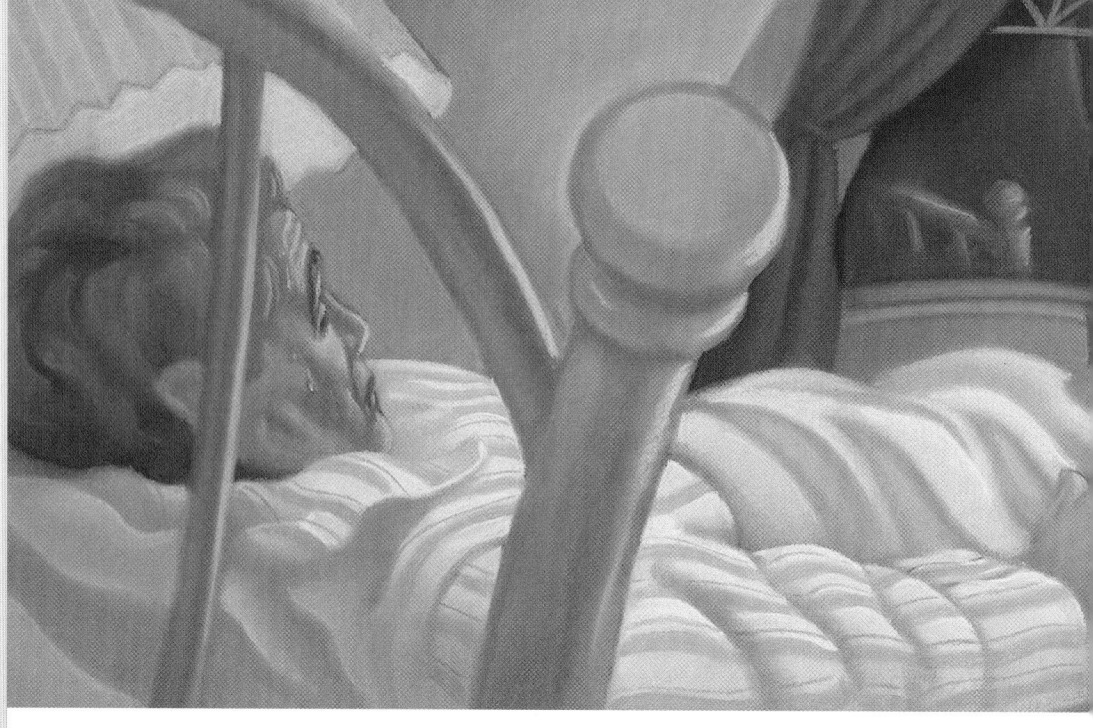

A "Stop. Wait a moment, Timber." I could hardly hear what he was saying. He seemed to be straining enormously to get the words out.

"What's the matter, Harry?"

B "Sshhh!" he whispered. "Sshhh! For God's sake, don't make a noise. Take your shoes off before you come nearer. *Please* do as I say, Timber."

C The way he was speaking reminded me of George Barling after he got shot in the stomach, when he stood leaning against a crate containing a spare airplane engine, holding both hands on his stomach and saying things about the German pilot in just the same hoarse, straining half whisper Harry was using now.

"Quickly, Timber, but take your shoes off first."

I couldn't understand about taking off the shoes but I figured that if he was as ill as he sounded I'd better humor him, so I bent down and removed the shoes and left them in the middle of the floor. Then I went over to his bed.

D "Don't touch the bed! For God's sake, don't touch the bed!" He was still speaking like he'd been shot in the stomach, and I could see him lying there on his back with a single sheet covering three quarters of his body. He was wearing a pair of pajamas with blue, brown, and white stripes, and he was sweating terribly. It was a hot night and I was sweating a little myself, but not like Harry. His whole face was wet, and the pillow around his head was sodden with moisture. It looked like a bad go of malaria[1] to me.

"What is it, Harry?"

"A krait,"[2] he said.

"A *krait*! Oh, my God! Where'd it bite you? How long ago?"

"Shut up," he whispered.

"Listen, Harry," I said, and I leaned forward and touched his shoulder. "We've got to be quick. Come on now, quickly, tell me where it bit you." He was lying there very still and tense

---

1. **malaria** (mə·ler′ē·ə): infectious disease transmitted to humans by the bite of an infected mosquito. Malaria causes frequent sweats and fever.
2. **krait** (krīt): poisonous Asian snake, usually black or dark brown with tan or yellow bands.

82 THE SHORT-STORY COLLECTIONS

Reaching All Students

Struggling Readers

Monitoring Reading was introduced on p. 80. One good strategy to use with monitoring reading is Think-Aloud. For information on using this strategy, see p. 135 of the *Reading Strategies Handbook* in the front of the *Reading Skills and Strategies* binder.

English Language Learners

Pair students who are learning English with fluent readers. Have the pairs pause after reading sections of the story to discuss the events that have occurred. Assess comprehension by having students orally summarize these events. For additional strategies to supplement instruction, see

• *Lesson Plans Including Strategies for English-Language Learners*

E Reading Skills and Strategies
Making Inferences
? What does this statement suggest? [the possibility that there might not be a snake underneath the sheet.]

F Appreciating Language
Style
Point out how Harry's manner of speaking reveals his state of mind. The slowness and softness of his speech shows his increasing fear and agitation as he recounts how the snake came to be lying on his stomach.

G Vocabulary Note
Slang
Inform students that the word *bloody* in this context is British slang. Explain that *bloody* means "cursed" or "miserable" and also "very." It is used for emphasis.

as though he were holding on to himself hard because of sharp pain.

"I haven't been bitten," he whispered. "Not yet. It's on my stomach. Lying there asleep."

I took a quick pace backward; I couldn't help it, and I stared at his stomach or rather at the sheet that covered it. The sheet was rumpled in several places and it was impossible to tell if there was anything underneath.

"You don't really mean there's a krait lying on your stomach now?"

"I swear it."

"How did it get there?" I shouldn't have asked the question because it was easy to see he wasn't fooling. I should have told him to keep quiet.

"I was reading," Harry said, and he spoke very slowly, taking each word in turn and speaking it carefully so as not to move the muscles of his stomach. "Lying on my back reading and I felt something on my chest, behind the book. Sort of tickling. Then out of the corner of my eye saw this little krait sliding over my pajamas. Small, about ten inches. Knew I mustn't move.

Couldn't have anyway. Lay there watching it. Thought it would go over top of the sheet." Harry paused and was silent for a few moments. His eyes looked down along his body toward the place where the sheet covered his stomach, and I could see he was watching to make sure his whispering wasn't disturbing the thing that lay there.

"There was a fold in the sheet," he said, speaking more slowly than ever now and so softly I had to lean close to hear him. "See it, it's still there. It went under that. I could feel it through my pajamas, moving on my stomach. Then it stopped moving and now it's lying there in the warmth. Probably asleep. I've been waiting for you." He raised his eyes and looked at me.

"How long ago?"

"Hours," he whispered. "Hours and bloody hours and hours. I can't keep still much longer. I've been wanting to cough."

There was not much doubt about the truth of Harry's story. As a matter of fact it wasn't a surprising thing for a krait to do. They hang

POISON 83

Getting Students Involved

Cooperative Learning
Handling Negativity Positively. After students have completed the story, have groups discuss Dr. Ganderbai's response to Harry's insulting behavior. Ask whether or not they could have acted in a similarly unemotional manner if faced with such provocation. Ask groups to develop at least two other positive responses to an insult. They may use a chart like the following to gather ideas.

Situation: An acquaintance speaks rudely to you in front of your friends.		**Solution 2** Words: Actions:	Results Expected
Solution 1 Words: Actions:	Results Expected		
		Preferred Solution:	

T83

around people's houses, and they go for the warm places. The surprising thing was that **[A]** Harry hadn't been bitten. The bite is quite deadly except sometimes when you catch it at once, and they kill a fair number of people each year in Bengal, mostly in the villages.

"All right, Harry," I said, and now I was **[B]** whispering too. "Don't move and don't talk anymore unless you have to. You know it won't bite unless it's frightened. We'll fix it in no time."

I went softly out of the room in my stocking feet and fetched a small sharp knife from the kitchen. I put it in my trouser pocket, ready to use instantly in case something went wrong while we were still thinking out a plan. If Harry coughed or moved or did something to frighten the krait and got bitten, I was going to be ready to cut the bitten place and try to suck the venom out. I came back to the bedroom and Harry was still lying there very quiet and sweating all over his face. His eyes followed me as I moved across the room to his bed, and I could see he was wondering what I'd been up to. I stood beside him, trying to think of the best thing to do.

"Harry," I said, and now when I spoke I put my mouth almost on his ear so I wouldn't have to raise my voice above the softest whisper, "I think the best thing to do is for me to draw the sheet back very, very gently. Then we could have a look first. I think I could do that without disturbing it."

"Don't be a fool." There was no expression in his voice. He spoke each word too slowly, too carefully, and too softly for that. The expression was in the eyes and around the corners of the mouth.

"Why not?"

"The light would frighten him. It's dark under there now."

"Then how about whipping the sheet back quick and brushing it off before it has time to strike?"

"Why don't you get a doctor?" Harry said. The way he looked at me told me I should have thought of that myself in the first place.

"A doctor. Of course. That's it. I'll get Ganderbai."

I tiptoed out to the hall, looked up Ganderbai's number in the book, lifted the phone, and told the operator to hurry.

"Doctor Ganderbai," I said. "This is Timber Woods."

"Hello, Mr. Woods. You not in bed yet?"

"Look, could you come round at once? And bring serum—for a krait bite."

"Who's been bitten?" The question came so sharply it was like a small explosion in my ear.

"No one. No one yet. But Harry Pope's in bed, and he's got one lying on his stomach—asleep under the sheet on his stomach."

For about three seconds there was silence on the line. Then speaking slowly, not like an explosion now but slowly, precisely, Ganderbai said, "Tell him to keep quite still. He is not to move or to talk. Do you understand?"

"Of course."

"I'll come at once!" He rang off and I went back to the bedroom. Harry's eyes watched me as I walked across to his bed.

"Ganderbai's coming. He said for you to lie still."

"What does he think I'm doing?"

"Look, Harry, he said no talking. Absolutely no talking. Either of us."

"Why don't you shut up, then?" When he said **[C]** this, one side of his mouth started twitching with rapid little downward movements that continued for a while after he finished speaking. I took out my handkerchief and very gently I wiped the sweat off his face and neck, and I could feel the slight twitching of the muscle—the one he used for smiling—as my fingers passed over it with the handkerchief.

I slipped out to the kitchen, got some ice from the icebox, rolled it up in a napkin, and **[D]** began to crush it small. That business of the mouth, I didn't like that. Or the way he talked, either. I carried the ice pack back to the bedroom and laid it across Harry's forehead.

"Keep you cool."

He screwed up his eyes and drew breath sharply through his teeth. "Take it away," he whispered. "Make me cough." His smiling muscle began to twitch again.

The beam of a headlamp shone through the

84 THE SHORT-STORY COLLECTIONS

T84

window as Ganderbai's car swung around to the front of the bungalow. I went out to meet him, holding the ice pack with both hands.

"How is it?" Ganderbai asked, but he didn't stop to talk; he walked on past me across the balcony and through the screen doors into the hall. "Where is he? Which room?"

He put his bag down on a chair in the hall and followed me into Harry's room. He was wearing soft-soled bedroom slippers and he walked across the floor noiselessly, delicately, like a careful cat. Harry watched him out of the sides of his eyes. When Ganderbai reached the bed he looked down at Harry and smiled, confident and reassuring, nodding his head to tell Harry it was a simple matter and he was not to worry but just to leave it to Doctor Ganderbai. Then he turned and went back to the hall and I followed him.

"First thing is to try to get some serum into him," he said, and he opened his bag and started to make preparations. "Intravenously. But I must do it neatly. Don't want to make him flinch."

We went into the kitchen and he sterilized a needle. He had a hypodermic syringe in one hand and a small bottle in the other, and he stuck the needle through the rubber top of the bottle and began drawing a pale yellow liquid up into the syringe by pulling out the plunger. Then he handed the syringe to me.

"Hold that till I ask for it."

He picked up the bag and together we returned to the room. Harry's eyes were bright now and wide open. Ganderbai bent over Harry and very cautiously, like a man handling sixteenth-century lace, he rolled up the pajama sleeve to the elbow without moving the arm. I noticed he stood well away from the bed.

He whispered, "I'm going to give you an injection. Serum. Just a prick but try not to move. Don't tighten your stomach muscles. Let them go limp."

Harry looked at the syringe.

Ganderbai took a piece of red rubber tubing from his bag and slid one end under and up and around Harry's biceps; then he tied the tubing tight with a knot. He sponged a small area of the bare forearm with alcohol, handed the swab to me, and took the syringe from my hand. He held it up to the light, squinting at the calibrations,[3] squirting out some of the yellow fluid. I stood still beside him, watching. Harry was watching too and sweating all over his face so it shone like it was smeared thick with face cream melting on his skin and running down onto the pillow.

I could see the blue vein on the inside of Harry's forearm, swollen now because of the tourniquet, and then I saw the needle above the vein, Ganderbai holding the syringe almost flat against the arm, sliding the needle in sideways through the skin into the blue vein, sliding it slowly but so firmly it went in smooth as into cheese. Harry looked at the ceiling and closed his eyes and opened them again but he didn't move.

When it was finished, Ganderbai leaned forward, putting his mouth close to Harry's ear. "Now you'll be all right even if you *are* bitten. But don't move. Please don't move. I'll be back in a moment."

He picked up his bag and went out to the hall and I followed.

"Is he safe now?" I asked.

"No."

"How safe is he?"

The little Indian doctor stood there in the hall rubbing his lower lip.

"It must give some protection, mustn't it?" I asked.

He turned away and walked to the screen doors that led onto the veranda. I thought he was going through them, but he stopped this side of the doors and stood looking out into the night.

"Isn't the serum very good?" I asked.

---

3. **calibrations** (kal′ə·brā′shənz): markings on a measuring instrument.

WORDS TO OWN

intravenously (in′trə·vē′nəs·lē) *adv.*: directly into a vein.

POISON 85

krait (p. 82) or when Dr. Ganderbai is about to begin removing the sheet (p. 88).

Elements of Literature
Character
? What does Dr. Ganderbai's manner suggest about his character and his skill as a doctor? [Sample responses: He is kind and gentle; he understands that confidence and unflappability are reassuring to a patient.]

Struggling Readers
Breaking Down Difficult Text
Students may have trouble understanding what happens as they try to follow this long sentence with its many clauses. Suggest they work with other students to break the sentence down into smaller ones, and then list the steps for injecting the serum that are described.

Elements of Literature
Suspense
? How does Dr. Ganderbai's answer add to the suspense of the story? [Possible responses: Readers don't know why Ganderbai gave Harry the serum if it is not an effective antitoxin; the question of whether or not Harry will be saved from the snake is still not answered.]

Taking a Second Look

Review: Making Predictions
Remind students that when making predictions, they should base the predictions on evidence they find in the text combined with their own knowledge and experience.

Activity
Have students pause at suspenseful moments in the story. There are many possible points— for example, just before Harry mentions the krait (p. 82) or when Dr. Ganderbai is about to begin removing the sheet (p. 88). At each point, ask students to write down their predictions about what is going to happen next. Alongside their predictions, students should list evidence from the story and their own knowledge and experience as support for their ideas.

Students can use a chart like the one at right to record their predictions and evidence.

Prediction	
Evidence from the text	
Personal knowledge and experience	

T85

Evaluating

? Dr. Ganderbai told Harry that the serum would protect him even if he was bitten. Now Dr. Ganderbai reveals to Timber that the serum might not save Harry. What do you think of Dr. Ganderbai's strategy of giving Harry a false sense of security? [Sample responses: He is being a good doctor because he is keeping Harry calm; he is wrong to deceive Harry—even though the lie was told to make Harry feel better.]

B Elements of Literature

Conflict

? What is the main conflict so far in the story? [Harry, Timber, and Dr. Ganderbai against the snake.]

C Elements of Literature

Suspense

? How does the narrator build the suspense in this passage? [Possible responses: by describing how slowly and carefully the doctor works; by making readers eager to find out what happens.]

A "Unfortunately not," he answered without turning round. "It might save him. It might not. I am trying to think of something else to do."

"Shall we draw the sheet back quick and brush it off before it has time to strike?"

"Never! We are not entitled to take a risk." He spoke sharply and his voice was pitched a little higher than usual.

"We can't very well leave him lying there," I said. "He's getting nervous."

B "Please! Please!" he said, turning round, holding both hands up in the air. "Not so fast, please. This is not a matter to rush into baldheaded."[4] He wiped his forehead with his handkerchief and stood there, frowning, nibbling his lip.

"You see," he said at last, "there is a way to do this. You know what we must do—we must administer an anesthetic to the creature where it lies."

It was a splendid idea.

"It is not safe," he continued, "because a snake is coldblooded, and anesthetic does not work so well or so quick with such animals, but it is better than any other thing to do. We could use ether . . . chloroform.[5] . . ." He was speaking slowly and trying to think the thing out while he talked.

"Which shall we use?"

"Chloroform," he said suddenly. "Ordinary chloroform. That is best. Now quick!" He took my arm and pulled me toward the balcony. "Drive to my house! By the time you get there, I will have waked up my boy on the telephone and he will show you my poisons cupboard. Here is the key of the cupboard. Take a bottle of chloroform. It has an orange label and the name is printed on it. I'll stay here in case anything happens. Be quick now, hurry! No, no, you don't need your shoes!"

I drove fast and in about fifteen minutes I was back with the bottle of chloroform. Ganderbai came out of Harry's room and met me in the hall.

4. **baldheaded:** without being careful or taking precautions.
5. **ether** (ē′thər) . . . **chloroform** (klôr′ə·fôrm′): anesthetics with very strong, suffocating odors. Anesthetics cause loss of feeling or consciousness.

"You got it?" he said. "Good, good. I've just been telling him what we are going to do. But now we must hurry. It is not easy for him in there like that all this time. I am afraid he might move."

He went back to the bedroom and I followed, carrying the bottle carefully with both hands. Harry was lying on the bed in precisely the same position as before, with the sweat pouring down his cheeks. His face was white and wet. He turned his eyes toward me, and I smiled at him and nodded confidently. He continued to look at me. I raised my thumb, giving him the okay signal. He closed his eyes. Ganderbai was squatted down by the bed, and on the floor beside him was the hollow rubber tube that he had previously used as a tourniquet, and he'd got a small paper funnel fitted into one end of the tube.

C He began to pull a little piece of the sheet out from under the mattress. He was working directly in line with Harry's stomach, about eighteen inches from it, and I watched his fingers as they tugged gently at the edge of the sheet. He worked so slowly it was almost impossible to discern any movement either in his fingers or in the sheet that was being pulled.

Finally he succeeded in making an opening under the sheet and he took the rubber tube and inserted one end of it in the opening so that it would slide under the sheet along the mattress toward Harry's body. I do not know how long it took him to slide that tube in a few inches. It may have been twenty minutes, it may have been forty. I never once saw the tube move. I knew it was going in because the visible part of it grew gradually shorter, but I doubted that the krait could have felt even the faintest vibration. Ganderbai himself was sweating now, large pearls of sweat standing out all over his forehead and along his upper lip. But his hands were steady, and I noticed that his eyes were watching, not the tube in his hands, but the area of crumpled sheet above Harry's stomach.

WORDS TO OWN
discern (di·zurn′) v.: see; detect by looking carefully.

Using Students' Strengths

Visual Learners

Ask students to imagine that a movie has been made of "Poison" and that they must decide what images to include in a preview for the film version. Then, have them work in a small group to create storyboards for such a preview. Students should brainstorm visuals that capture the mood of fear and tension and that reveal the central conflicts and problems in the story.

Making the Connections

Cultural Connections

Discuss with students the pacifist strategies of Mohandas Karamchand Gandhi (1869–1948), known as Mahatma Gandhi, an Indian leader who called for India's independence from Great Britain. He proposed that the Indian people not cooperate with the British in any way, but that this revolutionary effort never be violent. The British put him in prison several times, yet he managed to be very instrumental in negotiating his people's independence. Tragically, after independence, violence broke out over the division of the former British territory into India and Pakistan, and Gandhi was assassinated by a Hindu nationalist. Allow students to comment about whether their view of Dr. Ganderbai's reserve is changed by an awareness of what Gandhi accomplished through nonviolence.

Without looking up, he held out a hand to me for the chloroform. I twisted out the ground-glass stopper and put the bottle right into his hand, not letting go till I was sure he had a good hold on it. Then he jerked his head for me to come closer, and he whispered, "Tell him I'm going to soak the mattress and that it will be very cold under his body. He must be ready for that and he must not move. Tell him now."

I bent over Harry and passed on the message.

"Why doesn't he get on with it?" Harry said.

"He's going to now, Harry. But it'll feel very cold, so be ready for it."

"Oh, get on!" For the first time he raised his voice, and Ganderbai glanced up sharply, watched him for a few seconds, then went back to his business.

Ganderbai poured a few drops of chloroform into the paper funnel and waited while it ran down the tube. Then he poured some more. Then he waited again, and the heavy, sickening smell of chloroform spread out over the room, bringing with it faint unpleasant memories of white-coated nurses and white surgeons standing in a white room around a long white table. Ganderbai was pouring steadily now, and I could see the heavy vapor of the chloroform swirling slowly like smoke above the paper funnel. He paused, held the bottle up to the light, poured one more funnelful, and handed the bottle back to me. Slowly he drew out the rubber tube from under the sheet; then he stood up.

The strain of inserting the tube and pouring the chloroform must have been great, and I recollect that when Ganderbai turned and whispered to me, his voice was small and tired. "We'll give it fifteen minutes. Just to be safe."

I leaned over to tell Harry. "We're going to give it fifteen minutes, just to be safe. But it's probably done for already."

"Then why don't you look and see!" Again he spoke loudly and Ganderbai sprang round, his small brown face suddenly very angry. He had almost pure black eyes and he stared at Harry, and Harry's smiling muscle started to twitch. I took my handkerchief and wiped his wet face, trying to stroke his forehead a little for comfort as I did so.

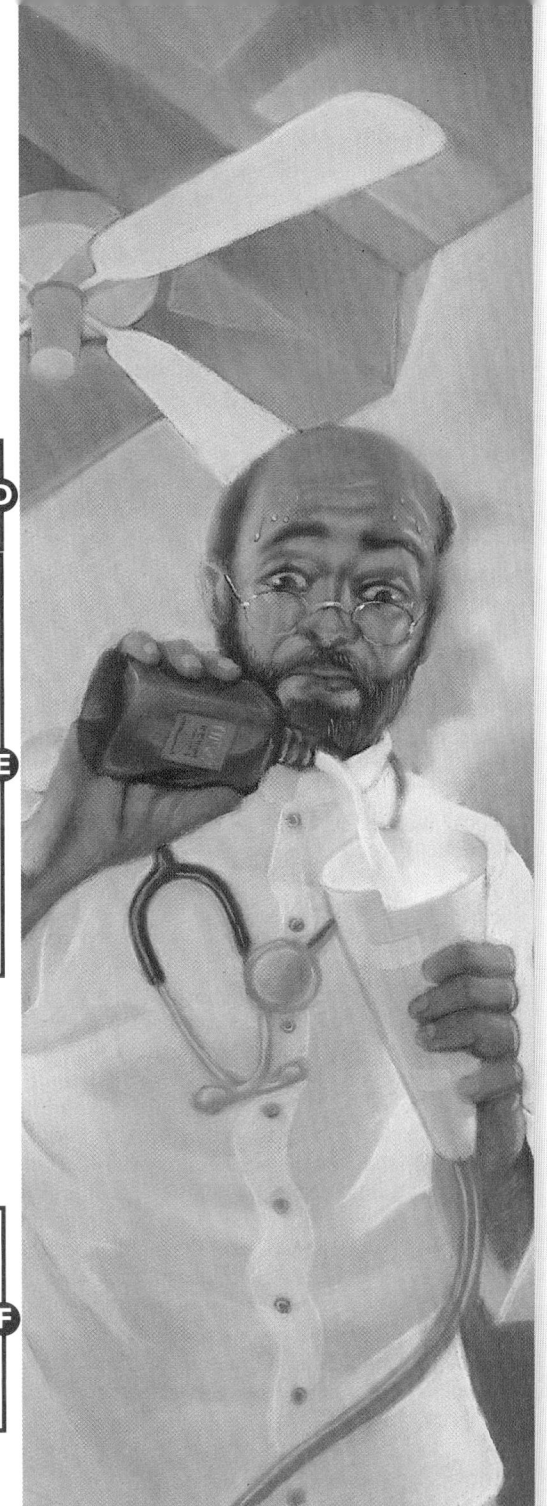

Crossing the Curriculum

Then we stood and waited beside the bed, Ganderbai watching Harry's face all the time in a curious intense manner. The little Indian was concentrating all his willpower on keeping **Ⓐ** Harry quiet. He never once took his eyes from the patient and although he made no sound, he seemed somehow to be shouting at him all the time, saying: Now listen, you've got to listen, you're not going to go spoiling this now, d'you hear me; and Harry lay there twitching his mouth, sweating, closing his eyes, opening them, looking at me, at the sheet, at the ceiling, at me again, but never at Ganderbai. Yet somehow Ganderbai was holding him. The smell of chloroform was <u>oppressive</u> and it made me feel sick, but I couldn't leave the room now.

Ⓑ I had the feeling someone was blowing up a huge balloon and I could see it was going to burst, but I couldn't look away.

At length Ganderbai turned and nodded and I knew he was ready to proceed. "You go over to the other side of the bed," he said. "We will each take one side of the sheet and draw it back together, but very slowly, please, and very quietly."

"Keep still now, Harry," I said, and I went around to the other side of the bed and took hold of the sheet. Ganderbai stood opposite me, and together we began to draw back the sheet, lifting it up clear of Harry's body, taking it back very slowly, both of us standing well away but at the same time bending forward, trying to peer underneath it. The smell of chloroform was awful. I remember trying to hold my breath, and when I couldn't do that any longer, I tried to breathe shallow so the stuff wouldn't get into my lungs.

The whole of Harry's chest was visible now, or rather the striped pajama top which covered it, and then I saw the white cord of his pajama trousers, neatly tied in a bow. A little farther and I saw a button, a mother-of-pearl button, and that was something I had never had on my pajamas, a fly button, let alone a mother-of-pearl **Ⓒ** one. This Harry, I thought, he is very refined.

It is odd how one sometimes has <u>frivolous</u> thoughts at exciting moments, and I <u>distinctly</u> remember thinking about Harry being very refined when I saw that button.

Apart from the button there was nothing on his stomach.

We pulled the sheet back faster then, and when we had uncovered his legs and feet we let the sheet drop over the end of the bed onto the floor.

"Don't move," Ganderbai said, "don't move, Mr. Pope"; and he began to peer around along the side of Harry's body and under his legs.

"We must be careful," he said. "It may be anywhere. It could be up the leg of his pajamas."

When Ganderbai said this, Harry quickly raised his head from the pillow and looked down at his legs. It was the first time he had moved. Then suddenly he jumped up, stood on his bed, and shook his legs one after the other violently in the air. At that moment we both thought he had been bitten, and Ganderbai was already reaching down into his bag for a scalpel and a tourniquet when Harry ceased his caperings and stood still and looked at the mattress he was standing on and shouted, "It's not there!"

Ⓓ Ganderbai straightened up and for a moment he too looked at the mattress; then he looked up at Harry. Harry was all right. He hadn't been bitten and now he wasn't going to get bitten and he wasn't going to be killed and everything was fine. But that didn't seem to make anyone feel any better.

"Mr. Pope, you are of course *quite* sure you saw it in the first place?" There was a note of sarcasm in Ganderbai's voice that he would never have employed in ordinary circumstances. "You don't think you might possibly have been dreaming, do you, Mr. Pope?" The way Ganderbai was looking at Harry, I realized that the sarcasm was not seriously intended. He was only easing up a bit after the strain.

Harry stood on his bed in his striped pajamas, glaring at Ganderbai, and the color began to spread out over his cheeks.

"Are you telling me I'm a liar?" he shouted.

WORDS TO OWN

oppressive (ə·pres′iv) *adj.*: heavy; hard to endure.
frivolous (friv′ə·ləs) *adj.*: silly; not as serious as the occasion requires.

Ⓐ Reading Skills and Strategies
Making Inferences
❓ Why do you think Harry refuses to look at Ganderbai? [Possible answers: He is too terrified to watch what the doctor is doing; he does not want to face the fact that his life is in Dr. Ganderbai's hands; he doesn't like the doctor.]

Ⓑ Elements of Literature
Suspense
❓ Why is this image of a balloon about to burst an effective image of suspense? [Possible responses: Suspense feels like a balloon about to burst; like Timber, readers are gripped, even though they sense that the moment of bursting will be abrupt and shocking.]

Ⓒ Critical Thinking
Speculating
❓ Why do you think Timber is focused on Harry's button? [Sample responses: Perhaps because it explains Harry's behavior by showing that he is wealthy and from the upper-class and, therefore, used to getting his own way and having everything go right for him; perhaps because the refinement of the button contrasts so sharply with the feeling of revulsion that Timber has for the snake he expected to see.]

Ⓓ Elements of Literature
Suspense
❓ Why do none of the characters feel any better? [Possible answer: The fear and suspense has been grueling, and now, instead of being gratified with an outcome, they are left feeling that perhaps the suspense and exertion were all for nothing.]

Professional Notes

In his biography of author Roald Dahl, Jeremy Treglown explains that "in the original version [of "Poison"] Dahl included a more plainly anti-racist paragraph which was obviously based on his time in Tanganyika [now named Tanzania]. The passage both interrupts the tension and, by overanticipating Harry's behavior at the end, weakens its impact. Presumably that is the reason why, although it appeared in the version published by Collier's magazine, Dahl later removed it."

Ganderbai remained absolutely still, watching Harry. Harry took a pace forward on the bed and there was a shining look in his eyes.

"Why, you dirty little sewer rat!"

"Shut up, Harry!" I said.

"You dirty black——"

"Harry!" I called. "Shut up, Harry!" It was terrible, the things he was saying.

Ganderbai went out of the room as though neither of us was there, and I followed him and put my arm around his shoulder as he walked across the hall and out onto the balcony.

"Don't you listen to Harry," I said. "This thing's made him so he doesn't know what he's saying."

We went down the steps from the balcony to the drive and across the drive in the darkness to **E** where his old Morris car was parked. He opened the door and got in.

"You did a wonderful job," I said. "Thank you so very much for coming."

"All he needs is a good holiday," he said **F** quietly, without looking at me; then he started the engine and drove off.

POISON 89

MEET THE WRITER

Fighter Pilot

Roald Dahl (1916–1990) was a fighter pilot with Britain's Royal Air Force during World War II. He suffered serious injuries when his Hurricane fighter plane was shot down over North Africa. Eventually he left flying and went to work for the British Embassy in Washington, D.C. There he was interviewed about his flying experiences for a magazine article. Frustrated that the interview was interfering with his lunch, he volunteered to go home and scribble down some notes instead. In fact, what Dahl did was to sit down and write a perfect short story. *The Saturday Evening Post* published it at once. Dahl went on to write several children's books (including *James and the Giant Peach* and *Charlie and the Chocolate Factory*), as well as many other short stories and an autobiography called *Boy*. When the violence in his books for young children was criticized, Dahl said:

66 Children love to be spooked. . . . They like a touch of the macabre as long as it's funny too. . . . And my nastiness is never gratuitous. It's retribution. Beastly people must be punished. 99

Readers of *Boy* understand some of Dahl's concern about "beastly people." His childhood in an English boarding school was marked by beatings from cruel headmasters.

Like "Poison," Dahl's other short stories almost always place ordinary characters in believable but bizarre situations. Many of his stories have surprise endings—some of them shockers. Several of his stories have been made into TV movies.

Are You Ready for More?

If you'd like to read more by Dahl, take a look at "Dip in the Pool," "Lamb to the Slaughter," and "The Landlady." These three stories are in *The Best of Roald Dahl* (Vintage).

E Critical Thinking
Expressing an Opinion

? Is Harry's reaction expected or unexpected? Explain. [Sample responses: Expected—under such pressure, Harry was bound to lash out at someone; unexpected—he might be hurt about the doctor's needling, but his venom is shocking.]

F Reading Skills and Strategies

Asking Questions

? What questions are you left with at the end of the story? [Possible questions: Why does Ganderbai just take Harry's abuse? What will happen between Harry and Timber later?]

BROWSING IN THE FILES

About the Author. Although Dahl never spent time in colonial India, his experiences in British colonial Tanganyika probably formed the basis for "Poison." In fact, his autobiography *Going Solo* contains several tales of encounters with poisonous snakes, as well as mention of the man who might have inspired the character of Dr. Ganderbai. Dahl writes that "the name of the Indian trader I had to go see in Bagomayo was so wonderful I have never been able to get it out of my mind. . . . He called himself Mister Shankerbai Ganderbai."

Resources

Selection Assessment
Formal Assessment
• Selection Test, p. 7
Test Generator (One-Stop Planner)
• CD-ROM

Assessing Learning

Check Test: Questions and Answers
Answers may vary slightly.

1. Why does Timber find Harry so tense? [There is a poisonous snake asleep on his stomach.]
2. What does Dr. Ganderbai do for Harry? [He reassures him, gets serum, and tries to chloroform the snake.]

3. What do Dr. Ganderbai and Timber discover when they remove the sheet? [that there is no snake on the bed]
4. How does Harry react to Dr. Ganderbai's treatment? [He is impatient and insulting.]

Standardized Test Preparation
For practice in proofreading and editing, see
• *Daily Oral Grammar*, Transparency 4

Connections

The poet issues a terse, metaphorical warning that compares hate to a creature with a poisonous bite.

Ⓐ Critical Thinking
Extending the Text
Discuss with students the different forms of hate that exist in the world today. They should draw upon their knowledge of current events and their own experiences. Then, discuss what each of these has in common with the others. Suggest that students ponder these questions: What is the definition of hatred? How is hate different from dislike?

Ⓑ Critical Thinking
Making Connections
❓What do the poem and "Poison" have in common? [Both compare hate to the poisonous venom of a snake bite.] Would "Hate" be a good title for Dahl's story? [Possible responses: Yes, since that is what it is really about; no, "Poison," with its double meaning, is a much better title.] Could the poem be called "Poison"? [No, because the title is necessary for readers to know what the poem is about.]

Ⓐ hate
Tato Laviera

watch

out

for

the

Ⓑ venom

of

its

first

bite.

Connecting Across Texts

Connecting with "Poison"
After students have read "Poison" and "hate," have them work in groups and go back to the short story to identify the point at which they feel hate takes "its first bite." Groups should share their ideas with the class. Then, discuss the comparison of hate to a snake bite that both authors make. Have students evaluate this comparison with a Venn diagram like the one at right.

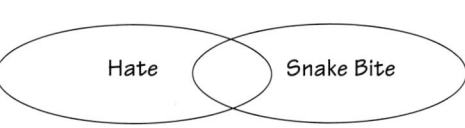

Hate — Snake Bite

MAKING MEANINGS

First Thoughts

[connect]

1. How did each of the characters in "Poison" respond to danger? Compare their responses with those you wrote for your Quickwrite.

Shaping Interpretations

[infer]

2. What is the source of the terrifying **suspense** in this story—that is, what big question does the writer plant in your mind to keep you turning the pages?

[synthesize]

3. Is it possible that there really was a krait under the sheet, or do you think Harry imagined it? What evidence can you find in the text to support each conclusion?

[analyze]

4. The major struggle in the story is an **external conflict**. What **internal conflicts** are also at work?

[analyze]

5. By the story's end, what surprising **conflict** between two of the characters is out in the open?

[synthesize]

6. We might suspect that the **title** of the story refers to more than the venom of the krait. What other kinds of poison is the story about?

[synthesize]

7. Reread the Background on page 80, and then think about the relevance of the time frame. How does knowing the story's **historical context** help you understand Harry's response to the generous Indian doctor?

Extending the Text

[apply]

8. Did Harry's response to Ganderbai remind you of incidents that have occurred in other places when cruelty was revealed by people under great pressure?

[apply]

9. How does the poem "hate" (see *Connections* on page 90) relate to Timber's experience with Harry and Dr. Ganderbai? What wider conflicts in the world could it also apply to?

Challenging the Text

[evaluate]

10. Check your reading notes. Do you have any questions that were not answered by the end of the story? What are they? Talk about whether you found Dahl's resolution effective or disappointing or even puzzling.

Reading Check

a. What clues tell us at once that something is wrong with Harry?

b. At what point do we learn precisely what the **external conflict** is in the story?

c. What plan does Dr. Ganderbai finally put into action to resolve the conflict?

d. What is the outcome of the snake search?

e. What cruel things does Harry say to Dr. Ganderbai at the end?

Reading Check
Answers may vary slightly.
a. Harry is awake but motionless; he whispers slowly and deliberately; he commands Timber to take off his shoes and warns him not to touch the bed.
b. When Harry tells Timber that there is a krait asleep on his stomach.
c. Dr. Ganderbai administers a serum; then he pours chloroform under the sheet; he also has a scalpel and a tourniquet ready in case the chloroform fails.
d. No snake is found.
e. Harry calls the doctor a "dirty little sewer rat" and uses racial slurs.

MAKING MEANINGS

First Thoughts

1. Possible responses: Harry is impatient and selfish; Timber is helpful and loyal; Dr. Ganderbai is competent and forgiving. Comparisons to Quickwrites will vary.

Shaping Interpretations

2. Sample questions: Will Harry survive? Will the snake bite Harry?

3. Possible answers: There really was a krait because Harry's fear and his statement about seeing the krait slither under the sheet seem real; Harry imagined it because no snake was found at the end of the story.

4. The characters struggle internally with their fear, frustration, helplessness, and anger.

5. The conflict, rooted in Harry's prejudice, is between Harry and Dr. Ganderbai.

6. Possible responses: ethnic or racial prejudice; irrational hate.

7. Harry has a colonial mindset and feels Ganderbai has overstepped social boundaries. Harry's awareness that he is out of danger unleashes the bias he kept hidden when he wanted the doctor's help.

Extending the Text

8. Responses will vary. Students might mention wartime situations, or more personal situations they do not mind sharing with others.

9. Connections with the poem: Hatred can be as unexpected and poisonous as a snake bite. Applications to wider conflicts: Students may cite current local, national, and international situations in which hate either gives rise to or fuels a destructive dispute.

Challenging the Text

10. Possible questions: Was the krait ever there? Why does the doctor take Harry's abuse? What will happen later between Harry and Timber? Some students may feel that the ending is disappointing or puzzling because the conflict is not resolved. Others may have found the surprising "bite" at the end effective.

Rubrics for each Choices assignment appear on p. 94 in the *Portfolio Management System.*

CHOICES: Building Your Portfolio

1. **Writer's Notebook**   Remind students to save their work. They can use it as prewriting for the Writer's Workshop on p. 112.
2. **Creative Writing**   Help students understand the significance of Dr. Ganderbai's restraint—that it shows strength of character rather than weakness. Images, words, and symbols in student paragraphs should reflect Ganderbai's strength of character.
3. **Role-Playing**   Remind students to imagine the personality of each character and to keep those traits in mind not only when they occupy the hot seat, but also when they ask a question. For example, would a cautious, indirect method of questioning be more likely to get a calm, thoughtful answer from Harry?
4. **Research/History**   Have students consult the librarian about what resources are available in the school or local community and how they can best access them. Encourage students to develop a multimedia presentation.

Writer's Notebook

1. Collecting Ideas for a Short Narrative

Using dialogue. The three characters in "Poison" move the events of the story along with their dialogue. Dahl gives tense, quick sentences to Harry: "'Take it away,' he whispered. 'Make me cough.'" Ganderbai speaks carefully, trying to keep control: "'It might save him. It might not. I am trying to think of something else to do.'" As you take notes for your own narrative, experiment with dialogue. How will your characters speak? Formally? Informally? In slang? What will they say under stress? Remember that not everyone speaks in the same way.

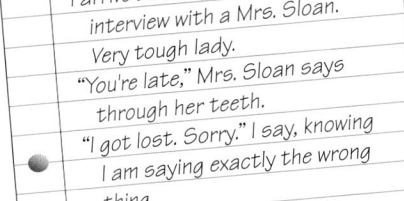

Dialogue: Narrative About a Job Interview

I arrive at doughnut shop for interview with a Mrs. Sloan. Very tough lady.

"You're late," Mrs. Sloan says through her teeth.

"I got lost. Sorry." I say, knowing I am saying exactly the wrong thing.

"Late is bad," replied the stern Sloan. "Late is grounds for firing."

"I'm not even hired," I wail.

Remember also that speakers often use fragments, especially when they are excited. Be sure to provide "tag lines" to tell who is speaking and *how.*

Creative Writing

2. "What's on His Mind?"

Imagine a final scene that takes place with Dr. Ganderbai in his car as he heads for home. What is he thinking? Will he come to the aid of Harry ever again? Does he understand Harry? What does he think *really* happened—does he believe there was a krait under the sheet? Think of images, words, and symbols that you can put in thought bubbles to show what the doctor is thinking. Then write a brief paragraph to explain your look inside Ganderbai's head.

Role-Playing

3. Hot Seat

Get together with a group of classmates and take turns role-playing the characters Timber, Harry, and Dr. Ganderbai. Begin by choosing your character. Then take turns climbing into the "hot seat" and responding to questions—in character—that the rest of the group members ask. Try to find out why a character acted as he did and how a character felt about the night's events. Keep each person in the hot seat for about two minutes. When you've finished the questioning, discuss what you learned about the characters by stepping into their shoes.

Research/History

4. Investigating India

Dahl's story might have made you curious about colonial India—about the source of Harry's rudeness and the reason for Dr. Ganderbai's response. Plan a small research project in which you compile details about life in India in the 1940s, around the time this story takes place. You might focus on these questions or others of your own: How did India become independent? What caused the slaughter in Pakistan? What was Gandhi's role in India's independence? In addition to history books, look at newsmagazines and national newspapers from the time. Your school or local library might have them on microfilm. Present your report in class.

Using Students' Strengths

Kinesthetic Learners
Students may develop the hot-seat responses for Choice 3 into dramatic scenes that can be rehearsed and performed. They can write dramatic dialogue between characters from the story or add script for the human conscience as a character. If equipment is available, have students videotape their scenes for presentation to the entire class.

GRAMMAR LINK

MINI-LESSON

Language Handbook HELP

See Agreement of Subject and Verb, page 994.

Technology HELP

See Language Workshop CD-ROM. *Key word entry: subject-verb agreement.*

An Agreeable Pair—Subject and Verb

Standard American English is the kind of English you most often read in newspapers and hear on the radio and TV. In standard English, verbs agree with their subjects in number—that is, singular subjects take singular verbs, and plural subjects take plural verbs. Subjects and verbs are underlined in these sentences:

1. The krait's <u>bite</u> <u>is</u> quite deadly. [singular subject, singular verb]

2. <u>They</u> <u>kill</u> a fair number of people each year. [plural subject, plural verb]

3. Harry's <u>face</u> and <u>neck</u> <u>were sweating</u>. [compound subject joined by *and*; plural verb]

4. Ganderbai's <u>bag</u> of medical supplies <u>was needed</u>. [singular subject, singular verb. The object of a preposition is never the subject.]

5. <u>Each</u> of the men <u>was</u> tense. [*Each* is singular.]

6. <u>Few</u> of Harry's friends <u>are</u> so refined. [*Few* is plural.]

Try It Out

Be a test maker. Write six sentences that ask for a choice of singular or plural verbs, using the numbered sentences as models. (You might find some sentences in your writing folder that you can use as test items.) Let a partner take your test. Do you both agree on the correct answers?

Tips for writers: The following pronouns are singular: *each, either, neither, one, everyone, everybody, no one, anyone, someone.*

The following pronouns are plural: *several, few, many.*

VOCABULARY

HOW TO OWN A WORD

WORD BANK

intravenously
discern
oppressive
frivolous

Word Maps

Word maps, like the one below, usually include a word's **etymology** (which indicates the origin of each of the word's parts). A word map can also include the word's meaning, related words, and sentences using the word. Work with a partner to produce word maps for the other three words in the Word Bank. You will have to do some research in a dictionary.

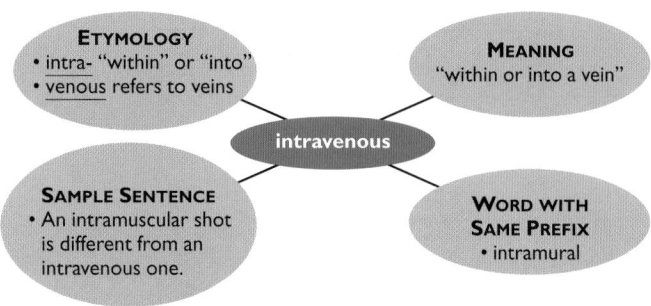

ETYMOLOGY
• intra- "within" or "into"
• venous refers to veins

MEANING
"within or into a vein"

intravenous

SAMPLE SENTENCE
• An intramuscular shot is different from an intravenous one.

WORD WITH SAME PREFIX
• intramural

GRAMMAR LINK

As a proofreading exercise, have students choose a piece of writing from their portfolios and highlight all the subjects in the paper in one color and all the verbs in another. After they have marked their papers, have them work with a partner to make sure that their subjects and verbs agree.

Try It Out

Student tests will vary. Encourage students to work with the tips about the most challenging pronouns. Tell students who disagree with their partners about subject-verb agreement to check pp. 994–996 in the Language Handbook for rules that apply.

VOCABULARY

Sample Answers

discern. Etymology: *dis-*, "apart"; *cern*, "perceive." Meaning: "see; detect." Sample sentence: Can you discern the difference between hatred and hostility? Word with same prefix: discard.

oppressive. Etymology: *ob-*, "against"; *press*, "press down." Meaning: "heavy or hard to endure." Sample sentence: The oppressive British tax laws caused the colonies to rebel. Word with same prefix: oppose.

frivolous. Etymology: *frivol*, "trifle"; *-ous*, "possessing." Meaning: "silly, not serious." Sample sentence: Her frivolous manner dismayed everyone at the memorial service. Word with same suffix: mysterious.

Resources

Grammar
• *Grammar and Language Links* Worksheet, p. 7

Vocabulary
• *Words to Own* Worksheet, p. 4

Grammar Link Quick Check

Circle the subject and underline the verb in each sentence. If the verb agrees with the subject, write a plus (+) at the end of the sentence. If the verb does not agree with the subject, cross it out and correct it.

1. (One) of Roald Dahl's most famous short stories <u>are</u> "Poison." [is]

2. (Neither) the doctor nor Timber <u>are</u> expecting Harry's hateful outburst. [is expecting]

3. (Everybody) in Harry's room <u>face</u> fear of some kind. [faces]

4. The (surprises) in this story <u>leave</u> me with some puzzling questions. [+]

5. Only a (few) characters <u>appears</u> in the story. [appear]

6. Key (conflicts) in "Poison" <u>shows</u> up throughout the story. [show up]

7. (Which) of these <u>prove</u> to be more harmful— the venom of the snake or the poison of Harry's hateful remarks? [proves]

OBJECTIVES

1. Read and interpret the story
2. Analyze a surprise ending
3. Monitor reading
4. Express understanding through creative and critical writing
5. Identify transitional words and phrases and use them in writing
6. Use new words
7. Research word etymology

SKILLS

Literary
- Analyze a surprise ending

Reading
- Monitor reading

Writing
- Collect ideas for a short narrative
- Write a new story ending
- Write an essay comparing characters
- Write an evaluation of the story
- Create a storyboard

Language
- Use transitional words

Vocabulary
- Use new words
- Research word etymology

Viewing/Representing
- Compare a painting with the literature (ATE)
- Analyze a painting (ATE)

Planning

- **Block Schedule**
  Block Scheduling Lesson Plans with Pacing Guide
- **Traditional Schedule**
  Lesson Plans Including Strategies for English-Language Learners
- **One-Stop Planner**
  CD-ROM with Test Generator

Before You Read

THE INTERLOPERS

Make the Connection

My Neighbor, My Enemy

Most arguments can be settled when people agree to talk or compromise, but some arguments become so bitter that they last for generations. Children are carefully taught to hate their relatives' enemies, who are taught to hate them in return. Think of Romeo and Juliet; think of whole regions of the world today that have been locked in conflict for generations.

Quickwrite

Write down a few examples of feuds that have torn families or even countries apart. What keeps such festering hatred alive?

Elements of Literature

Surprise Endings

A great **surprise ending** is one that makes sense but could not have been predicted. In Saki's story the surprise at the end prompts readers to rethink the entire story. The surprise gives new meaning to the events that precede it.

> **A** surprise ending resolves a story's conflict in a totally unexpected—yet logical—way. A surprise ending is a good place to look for a story's meaning.

Reading Skills and Strategies

Monitor Your Reading

Good readers automatically monitor their reading. They know when to seek help, and they know what strategies to use to get through a tough passage. See how good you are at monitoring your reading of Saki's unusual story. Have a notebook or a pad of self-sticking notes handy. Here are some guidelines:

- Ask questions. Modify your predictions as you read.
- When you don't understand a word and it is not defined, look for context clues.
- Break down long sentences into simpler sentences.
- Look for the subject and verb in complicated sentences.
- Stop at the end of a passage you think is important, and summarize it. If you haven't understood a passage, reread it.

HRW go.hrw.com
LEO 9-1

Background

This story is set in a dense forest on the slopes of the Carpathian Mountains, which extend through Poland, Slovakia, Romania, and Ukraine. At the time the story is set, probably at the end of the nineteenth century, aristocratic families owned miles and miles of land—almost entire countries.

A poacher is someone who goes onto private property to fish or hunt illegally. In Europe at one time, someone caught poaching on an estate could be put to death.

Preteaching Vocabulary

Words to Own

Ask volunteers to list on the chalkboard the Words to Own and their definitions, which appear at the bottom of the selection pages. Then, have students answer these questions.

1. Which word could describe gangs who terrorize their neighbors? [marauders]
2. Which word could describe what you do for a friend who fails a test? [succor]
3. Which word could describe a trail that runs up a steep mountain? [precipitous]
4. Which word could describe the action of a brother who agreed to go shopping with his little sister? [acquiesced]
5. Which word could describe the state of someone who is recovering from a serious illness? [languor]

After students have finished, ask them to write their own "Which word?" question for each of the Words to Own. Students can exchange questions with a partner.

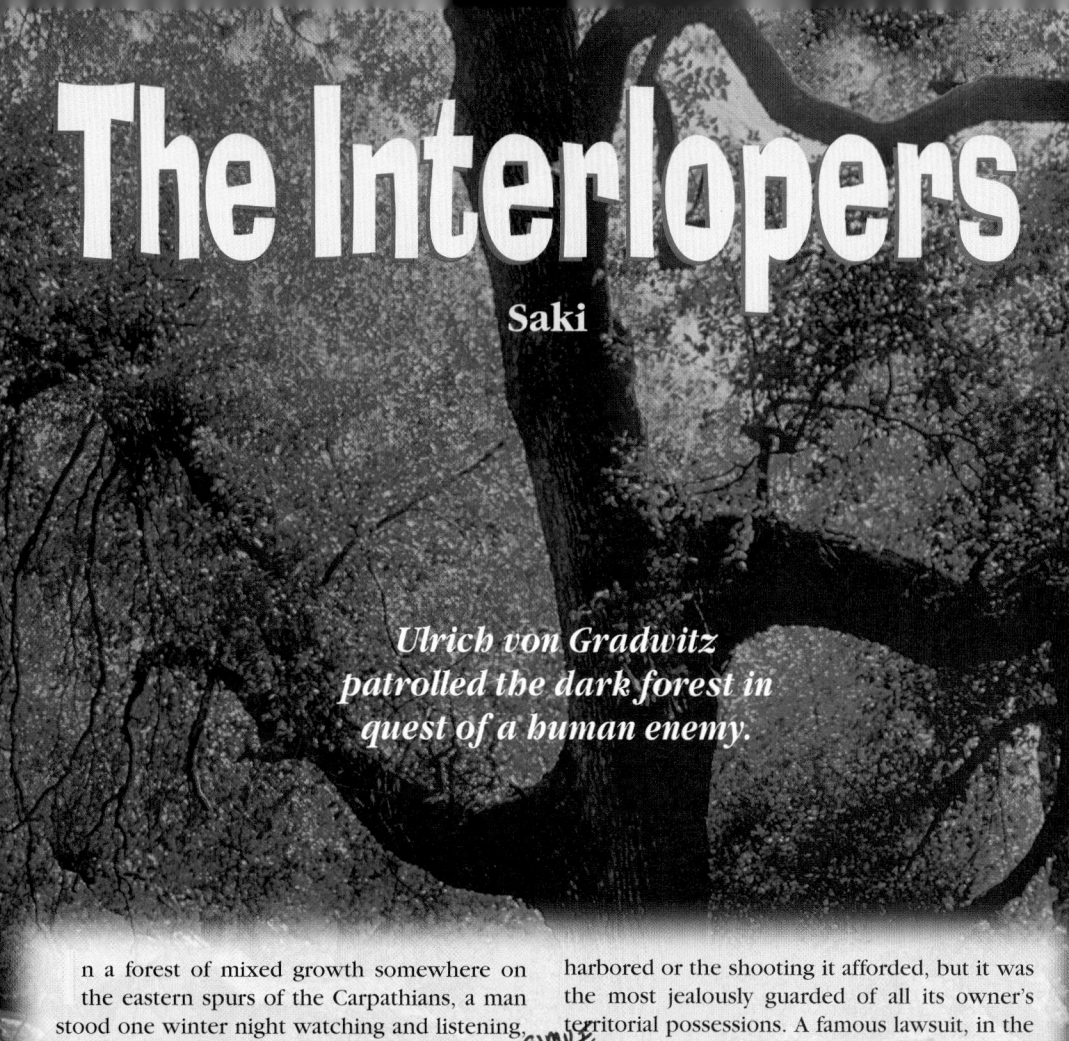

The Interlopers

Saki

Ulrich von Gradwitz patrolled the dark forest in quest of a human enemy.

n a forest of mixed growth somewhere on the eastern spurs of the Carpathians, a man stood one winter night watching and listening, as though he waited for some beast of the woods to come within the range of his vision and, later, of his rifle. But the game for whose presence he kept so keen an outlook was none that figured in the sportsman's calendar as lawful and proper for the chase; Ulrich von Gradwitz patrolled the dark forest in quest of a human enemy.

The forest lands of Gradwitz were of wide extent and well stocked with game; the narrow strip of precipitous woodland that lay on its outskirt was not remarkable for the game it harbored or the shooting it afforded, but it was the most jealously guarded of all its owner's territorial possessions. A famous lawsuit, in the days of his grandfather, had wrested it from the illegal possession of a neighboring family of petty landowners; the dispossessed party had never acquiesced in the judgment of the courts, and a long series of poaching affrays[1] and

A [annotation: *simu[e]*]

----

1. **affrays** (ə·frāz′): noisy quarrels; brawls.

WORDS TO OWN
precipitous (prē·sip′ə·təs) *adj.*: very steep.
acquiesced (ak′wē·est′) *v.* (used with *in*): accepted; complied with.

THE INTERLOPERS **95**

Summary ■ ■

Ulrich von Gradwitz and Georg Znaeym are engaged in a heated feud that dates back in their families for generations. The conflict involves a strip of forest that borders both their properties. One night Ulrich is out patrolling his grounds, hunting for Georg, who he believes is poaching. Suddenly, in a dark, lonely spot in the forest, the two men come face to face, each intent on murdering the other. Before they can shoot, however, a tree falls, pinning both men to the ground. At first, each claims his men will show up first and kill the other. However, as time passes, they begin to realize the folly of their feud. The men make peace and pledge eternal friendship. Together, they call for help. Joyful, Ulrich sees figures approaching who he believes are rescuers. In the surprise ending, however, he soon realizes that they are not rescuers—but wolves.

A **Critical Thinking**
Making Connections
❓ What other story in the collection does this passage remind you of? Why? ["The Most Dangerous Game," because in both stories a hunter searches for human prey]

Resources ————

Listening
Audio CD Library
A recording of "The Interlopers" is available in the *Audio CD Library*:
• Disc 5, Track 3

[handwritten annotations: *Published 1919 posthumously / died @ 46 in 1916 / Written while he served in France. Saki > Victor Munro / was killed by sniper / Saki came from "cupbearer" in his Rubaiyat by Omar Khayyam*]

Resources: Print and Media

Reading
• *Graphic Organizers for Active Reading*, p. 5
• *Words to Own*, p. 5
• *Audio CD Library*
    Disc 5, Track 3

Writing and Language
• *Daily Oral Grammar*
    Transparency 5
• *Grammar and Language Links*
    Worksheet, p. 9

Assessment
• *Formal Assessment*, p. 9
• *Portfolio Management System*, p. 95
• *Standardized Test Preparation*, p. 16
• *Test Generator* (One-Stop Planner CD-ROM)

Internet
• go.hrw.com (keyword: LE0 9-1)

RESPONDING TO THE ART

In *Moon Shadows*, **Louis Dodd** (1927–) uses sharp contrast and a fragmented design to capture the impression of shadows. **Activity.** How does the mood of the painting match the story's mood? [Possible answer: Like the story's stormy mood, the shadows of the trees in the painting have a dark, almost menacing quality that seems to stretch out over the mountain.]

A ## Critical Thinking
Evaluating
❓ Is it normal and healthy to hate as these two men do? Explain. [Possible answers: No, that kind of hatred is unhealthy and obsessive; no, such hatred leaves little energy for anything else.]

B ## Reading Skills and Strategies
Monitor Your Reading
❓ What do you think the word *wont* means? Use context clues to help you. [It means "accustomed." The juxtaposition of "unrest" with "sleep" in the passage implies that sleeping is what the deer are accustomed to doing in the dark.]

C ## Elements of Literature
Suspense
❓ What makes this meeting suspenseful? What questions does it bring to mind? [Sample response: We have read so much about how the two men hate each other that we are anxious about what will happen. Possible questions: Why does Ulrich want no witnesses? What will he do? Who will win the contest?]

D ## Elements of Literature
Conflict
❓ What external conflict has been introduced so far in this story? [the feud between Ulrich and Georg]

Moon Shadows (1992) by Lois Dodd.
Oil on canvas (36″ × 50″).

Courtesy Fischbach Gallery, New York.

similar scandals had embittered the relationships between the families for three generations. The neighbor feud had grown into a personal one since Ulrich had come to be head of his family; if there was a man in the world whom he detested and wished ill to, it was Georg Znaeym, the inheritor of the quarrel and the tireless game snatcher and raider of the disputed border forest. The feud might, perhaps, have died down or been compromised if the personal ill will of the two men had not stood in the way; as boys they had thirsted for one another's blood, as men each prayed that misfortune might fall on the other, and this wind-scourged winter night Ulrich had banded together his foresters to watch the dark forest, not in quest of four-footed quarry, but to keep a lookout for the prowling thieves whom he suspected of being afoot from across the land boundary. The roebuck,[2] which usually kept in the sheltered hollows during a storm wind, were running like driven things tonight, and

there was movement and unrest among the creatures that were wont to sleep through the dark hours. Assuredly there was a disturbing element in the forest, and Ulrich could guess the quarter from whence it came.

He strayed away by himself from the watchers whom he had placed in ambush on the crest of the hill and wandered far down the steep slopes amid the wild tangle of undergrowth, peering through the tree trunks and listening through the whistling and skirling[3] of the wind and the restless beating of the branches for sight or sound of the marauders. If only on this wild night, in this dark, lone spot, he might come across Georg Znaeym, man to man, with none to witness—that was the wish that was uppermost in his thoughts. And as he stepped round the trunk of a huge beech he came face to face with the man he sought.

The two enemies stood glaring at one another for a long silent moment. Each had a rifle in his hand, each had hate in his heart and murder uppermost in his mind. The chance had come to give full play to the passions of a lifetime. But a man who has been brought up under the code of a restraining civilization cannot easily nerve himself to shoot down his neighbor in cold blood and without a word spoken, except for an offense against his hearth

---

3. **skirling:** shrill, piercing sound.

WORDS TO OWN
marauders (mə·rôd′ərz) *n.*: people who roam in search of loot.

---

2. **roebuck:** roe deer, small deer that live in Europe and Asia.

96 THE SHORT-STORY COLLECTIONS

Reaching All Students

Struggling Readers
Monitoring Reading was introduced on p. 94. One good strategy to use with monitoring reading is Say Something. For information on using this strategy, see p. 85 of the *Reading Strategies Handbook* in the front of the *Reading Skills and Strategies* binder.

English Language Learners
Help set a context for students' reading by discussing the concept of a feud. Define and use phrases such as *feuding over, long-standing feud, family feud,* and *blood feud.* Ask volunteers to provide examples of each from history, literature, and film. For additional strategies, see
• *Lesson Plans Including Strategies for English-Language Learners*

and honor. And before the moment of hesitation had given way to action, a deed of Nature's own violence overwhelmed them both. A fierce shriek of the storm had been answered by a splitting crash over their heads, and ere they could leap aside, a mass of falling beech tree had thundered down on them. Ulrich von Gradwitz found himself stretched on the ground, one arm numb beneath him and the other held almost as helplessly in a tight tangle of forked branches, while both legs were pinned beneath the fallen mass. His heavy shooting boots had saved his feet from being crushed to pieces, but if his fractures were not as serious as they might have been, at least it was evident that he could not move from his present position till someone came to release him. The descending twigs had slashed the skin of his face, and he had to wink away some drops of blood from his eyelashes before he could take in a general view of the disaster. At his side, so near that under ordinary circumstances he could almost have touched him, lay Georg Znaeym, alive and struggling, but obviously as helplessly pinioned[4] down as himself. All round them lay a thick-strewn wreckage of splintered branches and broken twigs.

Relief at being alive and exasperation at his captive plight brought a strange medley of pious thank offerings and sharp curses to Ulrich's lips. Georg, who was nearly blinded with the blood which trickled across his eyes, stopped his struggling for a moment to listen, and then gave a short, snarling laugh.

"So you're not killed, as you ought to be, but you're caught, anyway," he cried, "caught fast. Ho, what a jest, Ulrich von Gradwitz snared in his stolen forest. There's real justice for you!"

And he laughed again, mockingly and savagely.

4. **pinioned:** pinned, as if chained or tied up.

"There's real justice for you!"

"I'm caught in my own forest land," retorted Ulrich. "When my men come to release us, you will wish, perhaps, that you were in a better plight than caught poaching on a neighbor's land, shame on you."

Georg was silent for a moment; then he answered quietly:

"Are you sure that your men will find much to release? I have men, too, in the forest tonight, close behind me, and *they* will be here first and do the releasing. When they drag me out from under these branches, it won't need much clumsiness on their part to roll this mass of trunk right over on the top of you. Your men will find you dead under a fallen beech tree. For form's sake I shall send my condolences to your family."

"It is a useful hint," said Ulrich fiercely. "My men had orders to follow in ten minutes' time, seven of which must have gone by already, and when they get me out—I will remember the hint. Only as you will have met your death poaching on my lands, I don't think I can decently send any message of condolence to your family."

"Good," snarled Georg, "good. We fight this quarrel out to the death, you and I and our foresters, with no cursed interlopers to come between us. Death and damnation to you, Ulrich von Gradwitz."

"The same to you, Georg Znaeym, forest thief, game snatcher."

Both men spoke with the bitterness of possible defeat before them, for each knew that it might be long before his men would seek him out or find him; it was a bare matter of chance which party would arrive first on the scene.

Both had now given up the useless struggle to free themselves from the mass of wood that held them down; Ulrich limited his endeavors to an effort to bring his one partially free arm

E Elements of Literature
Conflict

❓ What new external conflict has been introduced? [The new conflict is man against nature—Ulrich and Georg have been trapped and injured by the tree.]

F Critical Thinking
Analyzing

❓ What is ironic about Georg's statement? Why is it the opposite of what might be expected? [He is rejoicing at Ulrich being trapped, but he is trapped also.] What does it reveal about him? [Possible answers: He is so blinded by hatred he cannot seem to recognize his own peril; the defeat of his enemy is more important to him than his own survival.]

G Struggling Readers
Noting Text Organizers

Point out the bold-faced quotation on the page and encourage students to find it in context. Be sure that they realize these "called-out" quotations are either suspenseful or important to the theme of the work. Here the quotation highlights the irony of the situation both men are in.

H Elements of Literature
Surprise Ending

❓ The Before You Read page indicated that the story has a surprise ending. Given what you know about surprise endings, do you think the situation will be resolved as either man predicts? Give a reason for your opinion. [It probably won't be, because to resolve the situation in one of the ways they describe would not be a surprise.]

Crossing the Curriculum

Geography

The Carpathians carve a 900-mile path through Eastern Europe. Though this mountain range is the eastern continuation of the Alps, it is not nearly as high. The tallest peak, Mount Gerlach, is 8,711 feet. Have students find images of the range and research the countries through which it passes. Invite them to use their findings to create a photo essay or bulletin-board display.

Using Students' Strengths

Intrapersonal Learners

Students may recall an experience that caused them to rethink their feelings about someone for whom they previously felt animosity. Encourage students to write a journal entry in which they describe their feelings toward that person both before and after the event. Tell them to identify the reason for the change in their feelings.

A Reading Skills and Strategies

Monitor Your Reading

This is one of the many lengthy sentences in the story that may be difficult for some readers to follow. You may want to suggest that students try to summarize the sentence. If they cannot, suggest that they reread it. [Possible summary: Because the winter has been mild, the trapped men are not suffering greatly from the cold. Even so, as the wine warms Ulrich, he pities his injured enemy and admires him for not complaining.]

B Reading Skills and Strategies

Monitor Your Reading

❓ What is Ulrich's idea? Can you make a prediction about it? [Sample responses: Perhaps he has the idea of ending the feud; perhaps he has an idea for how the men can work together to get free of the tree.]

C Critical Thinking

Speculating

❓ Who are the interlopers Georg talks about? [Possible responses: Perhaps he means other poachers who want to hunt the disputed land—they could happen upon the men and shoot them both; perhaps he means leaders or people from other places who want to stir up trouble or start a war.]

near enough to his outer coat pocket to draw out his wine flask. Even when he had accomplished that operation, it was long before he could manage the unscrewing of the stopper or get any of the liquid down his throat. But what a heaven-sent draft[5] it seemed! It was an open winter,[6] and little snow had fallen as yet, hence the captives suffered less from the cold than might have been the case at that season of the year; nevertheless, the wine was warming and reviving to the wounded man, and he looked across with something like a throb of pity to where his enemy lay, just keeping the groans of pain and weariness from crossing his lips.

"Could you reach this flask if I threw it over to you?" asked Ulrich suddenly. "There is good wine in it, and one may as well be as comfortable as one can. Let us drink, even if tonight one of us dies."

"No, I can scarcely see anything; there is so much blood caked round my eyes," said Georg; "and in any case I don't drink wine with an enemy."

Ulrich was silent for a few minutes and lay listening to the weary screeching of the wind. An idea was slowly forming and growing in his brain, an idea that gained strength every time that he looked across at the man who was fighting so grimly against pain and exhaustion. In the pain and languor that Ulrich himself was feeling, the old fierce hatred seemed to be dying down.

"Neighbor," he said presently, "do as you please if your men come first. It was a fair compact. But as for me, I've changed my mind. If my men are the first to come, you shall be the first to be helped, as though you were my guest. We have quarreled like devils all our lives over this stupid strip of forest, where the trees can't

> 5. **draft:** drink.
> 6. **open winter:** mild winter.

even stand upright in a breath of wind. Lying here tonight, thinking, I've come to think we've been rather fools; there are better things in life than getting the better of a boundary dispute. Neighbor, if you will help me to bury the old quarrel, I—I will ask you to be my friend."

Georg Znaeym was silent for so long that Ulrich thought perhaps he had fainted with the pain of his injuries. Then he spoke slowly and in jerks.

The old fierce hatred seemed to be dying down.

"How the whole region would stare and gabble if we rode into the market square together. No one living can remember seeing a Znaeym and a von Gradwitz talking to one another in friendship. And what peace there would be among the forester folk if we ended our feud tonight. And if we choose to make peace among our people, there is none other to interfere, no interlopers from outside. . . . You would come and keep the Sylvester night[7] beneath my roof, and I would come and feast on some high day at your castle. . . . I would never fire a shot on your land, save when you invited me as a guest; and you should come and shoot with me down in the marshes where the wildfowl are. In all the countryside there are none that could hinder if we willed to make peace. I never thought to have wanted to do other than hate you all my life, but I think I have changed my mind about things too, this last half-hour. And you offered me your wine flask. . . . Ulrich von Gradwitz, I will be your friend."

For a space both men were silent, turning over in their minds the wonderful changes that

> 7. **Sylvester night:** feast day honoring Saint Sylvester (Pope Sylvester I, d. 335), observed on December 31.

WORDS TO OWN
languor (laŋ′gər) *n.:* weakness; weariness.

98 THE SHORT-STORY COLLECTIONS

Skill Link

Identifying Transitional Words

You might want to use the following exercise before you teach the Language Link lesson on how transitions connect ideas, on p. 103. This exercise will help you assess students' skill in identifying transitional words and phrases.

Identify the transitional words and phrases in the following sentences.

1. Although the Gradwitz family had won possession of the land in court, their neighbors also claimed it. [Although; also]

2. Even before Ulrich and Georg were fully grown, they had carried on their families' bitter feud. [Even before]

3. Since Ulrich had become head of the family, the quarrel had escalated. [Since]

4. Now Ulrich stands with his men at the top of a crest. [Now]

5. Below him stretches a steep slope. [Below]

6. Even more important to Ulrich than catching the marauders is coming face to face with his enemy Georg. [Even more important]

7. Georg and Ulrich lie next to each other, pinned beneath a fallen tree. [next to; beneath]

8. After years of hating each other, Georg and Ulrich finally become friends. [After; finally]

9. Of least importance to the two rivals in the end is ownership of the land. [Of least importance; in the end]

10. Rather than men coming to the rescue, the approaching figures are wolves. [Rather than]

T98

this dramatic reconciliation would bring about. In the cold, gloomy forest, with the wind tearing in fitful gusts through the naked branches and whistling round the tree trunks, they lay and waited for the help that would now bring release and succor to both parties. And each prayed a private prayer that his men might be the first to arrive, so that he might be the first to show honorable attention to the enemy that had become a friend.

Presently, as the wind dropped for a moment, Ulrich broke the silence.

"Let's shout for help," he said; "in this lull our voices may carry a little way."

"They won't carry far through the trees and undergrowth," said Georg, "but we can try. Together, then."

The two raised their voices in a prolonged hunting call.

"Together again," said Ulrich a few minutes later, after listening in vain for an answering halloo.

"I heard something that time, I think," said Ulrich.

"I heard nothing but the pestilential[8] wind," said Georg hoarsely.

There was silence again for some minutes, and then Ulrich gave a joyful cry.

"I can see figures coming through the wood. They are following in the way I came down the hillside."

Both men raised their voices in as loud a shout as they could muster.

Chish Yah XV (1992) (detail) by Rick Bartow.
Pastel and graphite on paper (20″ × 40″).

Courtesy of the Froelick Adelhart Gallery, Portland, Oregon.

"They hear us! They've stopped. Now they see us. They're running down the hill toward us," cried Ulrich.

"How many of them are there?" asked Georg.

"I can't see distinctly," said Ulrich; "nine or ten."

"Then they are yours," said Georg; "I had only seven out with me."

"They are making all the speed they can, brave lads," said Ulrich gladly.

"Are they your men?" asked Georg. "Are they your men?" he repeated impatiently, as Ulrich did not answer.

"No," said Ulrich with a laugh, the idiotic chattering laugh of a man unstrung with hideous fear.

"Who are they?" asked Georg quickly, straining his eyes to see what the other would gladly not have seen.

"Wolves."

8. **pestilential:** Strictly speaking, *pestilential* means "deadly; causing disease; harmful." Here, Georg uses the word to mean "cursed."

WORDS TO OWN

succor (suk′ər) *n.*: help given to someone in distress; relief.

THE INTERLOPERS 99

D Reading Skills and Strategies

Monitor Your Reading

❓ How might this sentence read if it were broken down into smaller, simpler ones? [Sample response: The wind tore through the branches of the cold, gloomy forest. It whistled round the tree trunks. The two men waited for others to rescue them.]

E Elements of Literature

Suspense

❓ What creates suspense here? [not knowing why Ulrich doesn't answer the question]

F Elements of Literature

Surprise Ending

Explain why the ending surprised you. [Sample responses: I was expecting rescuers and instead the wolves seal the men's doom; I expected an ending in which one man would triumph over the other in some way.]

RESPONDING TO THE ART

Rick Bartow (1946–   ) is a Native American artist and teacher who lives in the state of Oregon.

Activity. What qualities of the wolf does this artwork stress? [Possible responses: It stresses that the wolf is a carnivorous predator; it stresses the wolf's sharp teeth and its ability to stalk and focus on its prey.]

Assessing Learning

Check Test: True-False

1. The Gradwitz and Znaeym families have a long history of friendship. [False]
2. Ownership of a strip of woodland is in dispute. [True]
3. Ulrich is out in the forest hunting for wild game. [False]
4. Ulrich wants to encounter Georg alone in the forest. [True]
5. Ulrich is accidentally injured by gun fire. [False]
6. Georg helps Ulrich get out from under a fallen tree. [False]
7. Ulrich offers Georg a peace offering of wine. [True]
8. The feelings between Georg and Ulrich change dramatically while they are together in the forest. [True]
9. Together, Georg and Ulrich call for their men. [True]
10. At the end, the men are rescued. [False]

Standardized Test Preparation

For practice with standardized test format specific to this selection, see
• *Standardized Test Preparation,* p. 16

For practice in proofreading and editing, see
• *Daily Oral Grammar,* Transparency 5

Connections

In this traditional African folk tale, Goat and Fox are quarreling. Goat, hoping to gain revenge, plans a trick. However, he is the one who is ultimately the victim. The tale concludes with a moral warning.

Ⓐ Reading Skills and Strategies
Comparing and Contrasting

❓ How is the relationship of Goat and Fox like that of Ulrich and Georg? [Possible responses: Both pairs are feuding; both are competitive relationships in which one party wants to best the other.]

Ⓑ Appreciating Language
Style

❓ Why is the last sentence of the folktale set in italics? [Since the last sentence contains the folktale's message, it is set in italics for emphasis.]

Resources

Selection Assessment
Formal Assessment
• Selection Test, p. 9
Test Generator (One-Stop Planner)
• CD-ROM

MEET THE WRITER
An Exotic Imagination

Hector Hugh Munro (1870–1916) was a mild-mannered Englishman who wrote stories with snappy endings that were either wickedly funny or terrifying. Munro, the youngest of three children, was born in Burma, where his father was an officer in the military police. When his mother died suddenly, the three young children went to live with their grandmother and two stern aunts in a house in England whose windows were never opened. The aunts considered Hector sickly; he played with few children and was not sent to school until he was ten. When he began writing stories, Munro took a foreign pen name, Saki, after the character who served wine to the gods in the then popular poem *The Rubáiyát of Omar Khayyám*. (Omar Khayyám was a Persian poet.)

More Saki Surprises

If you enjoyed "The Interlopers," try "The Open Window," about a young girl with a bizarre imagination, and "The Storyteller," about children who are not what adults think they are.

The Granger Collection, New York.

Connections

A FABLE

The Trapper Trapped
Vai (African) traditional, retold by Roger D. Abrahams

Ⓐ Goat and Fox were quarreling, and Goat told Fox that he intended to get him into trouble so bad he would never be able to get out. Fox said, "All right; you do that, and I will return the favor to you."

Goat went for a walk and saw Leopard. Being frightened, Goat asked, "Auntie, what are you doing here?" "My little one is sick," said Leopard. Then Goat, thinking quickly, said, "Fox has medicine that will make your little one well." Leopard said to call Fox, so Goat went to Fox and said, "They are calling you."

"Who is calling me?" replied Fox. "I don't know," said Goat; "I think it is your friend. Go this way and you will run into him." Fox went down the path and at length came upon Leopard. Fox was frightened, and inquired: "Did you call me?" "Yes, my son. Goat came just a while ago and told me you had medicine that would make my little one well." "Yes," said Fox, "I have medicine that will cure your little one, but I must have a little goat horn to put it in. If you get me a goat horn, I will let you have the medicine." "Which way did Goat go?" asked Leopard. "I left him up there," replied Fox. "You wait here with my little one, and I will bring you the horn," said Leopard, and away she ran. Soon after, Leopard killed Goat and returned with his horns to Fox.

Ⓑ *Beware, lest you fall into the trap you set for someone else.*

Connecting Across Texts

Connecting with "The Interlopers"
Prompt students to make connections between Saki's story and the folk tale with questions such as the following:
• What are the consequences of hatred for the characters in both "The Interlopers" and "The Trapper Trapped"? [Death is the explicit consequence in the folk tale and the implicit outcome in "The Interlopers."]

• In what way does the ending of "The Interlopers" differ from the way one would expect a folk tale or fable to end? [Possible responses: "The Interlopers" has a surprise ending, but endings of folktales are usually predictable and moralistic. In a fable, two enemies who had learned to put aside their differences might be expected to survive. In "The Interlopers," on the other hand, cooperation between the characters only helps to draw the attention of the wolves.]

First Thoughts

[connect]

1. List three adjectives you'd use to describe Saki's story.

Shaping Interpretations

[analyze]

2. What moment is the **climax** of the story?

[analyze]

3. **Irony** is what we feel when something turns out to be different from what we expect or different from what we think is appropriate. We would feel irony, for example, if someone who hates baseball wins season's tickets to the Major League games. What is ironic about the ending of the story—what did you expect would happen? What happens instead?

[infer]

4. What do you think happens next? Is more than one interpretation possible? Elaborate on your answer.

[analyze]

5. Find places in the text where the word *interlopers* is used. What is an interloper? Who are the interlopers in the story? (Could there be several kinds of interlopers in the story?)

[synthesize]

6. What is the weather like on this fateful night? Do you think the story would have had the same **mood** if it had been set on a warm spring afternoon? Why, or why not?

Extending the Text

[interpret]

7. Refer to your Quickwrite notes. Do you think Saki's story has a serious message about the kinds of feuds you described in your notes? Or do you think the story is told just for entertainment? Give reasons for your answer.

[compare]

8. Most fables have a **moral,** a message about how we should live our lives. What is the moral of "The Trapper Trapped" (see *Connections* on page 100)? Do you think that moral is similar to or different from the message of "The Interlopers"? Explain your response.

Challenging the Text

[evaluate]

9. With a partner or a group, discuss your reading of this story. Was it difficult? If so, what presented difficulties for you? What strategies did you use to resolve those difficulties?

Reading Check

Make a story map for "The Interlopers" by filling in these blanks:

Characters:_____

_____

Setting:_____

_____

Conflict:_____

_____

Main events:_____

_____

_____

Climax and resolution:_____

_____

THE INTERLOPERS 101

Reading Check
Sample story map:
Characters: Ulrich von Gradwitz, Georg Znaeym
Setting: a forest in the Carpathian mountains
External conflict: between Ulrich and Georg, between the two men and nature
Internal conflict: Each man mentally struggles with his decision to end the feud.
Main events: Ulrich and Georg meet; they are trapped under a tree; Ulrich offers Georg some wine; they end the feud and become friends;

together, they call for help; wolves come towards them.
Climax and resolution: The conflict between the men reaches a climax when they decide to end the feud and is resolved when they call for help; the conflict between the men and nature reaches a climax when Ulrich realizes that the figures are wolves and is left unresolved when the story ends.

First Thoughts

1. Possible adjectives: surprising, suspenseful, old-fashioned.

Shaping Interpretations

2. There are two possible climaxes: when Georg accepts Ulrich's offer of friendship; when the men realize wolves are approaching.

3. Possible responses: Readers expect the men to be rescued but instead they will probably be eaten by the wolves; readers expect a happy ending when the sworn enemies become friends, but the reverse happens.

4. Possible interpretations: Since the men are expecting rescuers, a group will arrive in time to save them; the horror of Ulrich suggests that the men will be attacked by wolves.

5. Students can find the word on pp. 97 and 98. *Interlopers* means "intruders" or "meddlers in the affairs of others." Possible interlopers: the wolves; the rivals see each other as interlopers; the two men are interlopers in the forest.

6. The weather is dark, stormy, cold, and windy. Pleasant weather would not match the suspenseful mood of the story—the ominous weather is as dangerous and menacing as the threat of guns and wolves.

Extending the Text

7. Possible responses: The story is saying that feuds can cost you your life, which is a serious message; the story's unrealistic coincidences—the men meeting, the tree falling—suggest that it is mainly meant to entertain.

8. The moral of the fable is "Beware, lest you fall into the trap you set for someone else." It is similar to the message of "The Interlopers," since the men, ultimately, are the victims of their wish to best one another.

Challenging the Text

9. Students will cite various difficulties. As strategies, they may cite rereading, summarizing, using context clues for unfamiliar words, identifying subjects and verbs of complicated sentences, and breaking a long sentence into shorter, simpler ones.

Rubrics for each Choices assignment appear on p. 95 in the *Portfolio Management System*.

CHOICES: Building Your Portfolio

1. **Writer's Notebook** Remind students to save their work. They can use it as prewriting for the Writer's Workshop on p. 112.

2. **Creative Writing** Students may wish to work in pairs to add another ending to the story. Challenge them to use a style and vocabulary similar to Saki's.

3. **Comparing Characters** Students may wish to use a Venn Diagram to compare the two characters. Remind them to consider both the internal and external characteristics of each character.

4. **Evaluating a Story** Students may wish to outline their statements before they begin in order to make sure they answer all the points. Once the statements are completed, take a class poll. Would "The Interlopers" have made it into the textbook?

5. **Creative Writing** Before students begin, suggest that they use their story maps (see p. 101) to help them identify the story's events. Then partners can discuss how many camera shots, or scenes, are needed for each of these events.

CHOICES: Building Your Portfolio

Writer's Notebook

1. Collecting Ideas for a Short Narrative

Making up surprise endings.

Saki's **surprise endings** have often been compared with the snappy endings that are the hallmark of the American writer O. Henry. If you like surprise endings, jot down notes for a narrative—true or fictional—that ends with a surprising twist. Often surprise endings are stated in some dramatic way. Notice that Saki's surprise is stated in a new paragraph in a single word in italics. Save your notes for possible use in the Writer's Workshop on page 112.

> **Story Ideas**
>
> Character: me, about 12 years old
>
> Setting: bus
>
> Main events: get on bus, read book, fall asleep
>
> Surprise: Instead of getting on bus to Philadelphia, I am heading for Boston.

Creative Writing

2. The Interlopers, Part 2

What happens next? Refer to your answer to question 4 on page 101. Then, write at least one paragraph in which you add another ending to the story. What happens after Ulrich says *"Wolves"*? Can the story possibly have a happy ending?

Comparing Characters

3. Two "Monsters"?

In a brief essay, compare Ulrich with Zaroff in "The Most Dangerous Game" (page 13). How are the two men alike? How are they different? Remember that when you compare two things, you show how they are alike and, perhaps, how they are different as well.

Evaluating a Story

4. You, the Reviewer

Suppose you are a member of a team of readers deciding whether Saki's story should be included in a textbook. Write a brief statement about the story in which you (a) tell why you think the story will (or will not) appeal to high school students, (b) give at least two reasons for your opinion, and (c) tell how the story compares in appeal

with two other stories you have read (mention the titles and the authors of the other stories). As part of your statement, you might add a rating scale for "The Interlopers." Zero is the lowest rating, and 5 is the highest.

| 0 | 1 | 2 | 3 | 4 | 5 |

Creative Writing

5. Making a Storyboard

Filmmakers use storyboards to plan their camera shots. Imagine that you are the director of a thirty-minute film of "The Interlopers." With a classmate as your cinematographer, create a storyboard showing each scene you will shoot. You may, if you wish, create new scenes that take place before and after the events in the story. First, sketch the major story events on cards, one camera shot per card. Then, arrange the cards in sequence on a sheet of cardboard, and discuss the shots. How do you want to arrange the events? Will they be in chronological order, or will you add flashbacks? Will you have to add or cut scenes? Compare your storyboard with those of your classmates.

Assessing Learning

Peer Assessment

Have students get into the habit of discussing their work with their peers. Encourage them to ask each other questions such as the following: What do you want others to get from your work? What do you hope others will understand about the story through your work? What details of your work make it clear to others that you understand the story?

Making the Connections

Connecting to the Theme: "Facing Monsters"

Ask students to name the "monsters" the two men face in "The Interlopers." [Possible responses: the monster of their own hatred; nature's monstrous power; the wolves.] Ask students to compare these monsters with those faced by other characters in the collection. [Possible responses: the monster of human nature in "The Most Dangerous Game" and "Poison"; the monster of nature in "The Birds."]

Transitions—Bridge Work Ahead

Transitions are words and phrases that connect one idea to another. They are like road signs, guiding readers from one sentence or one paragraph to the next.

What Transitions Can Do
Compare or contrast ideas also, and, both, too, although, but, however, instead, on the other hand
Show cause or effect because, since, for, so, therefore, as a result
Show time or sequence after, before, finally, last, first, now, next
Show place above, below, across, near, next to, through
Show importance mainly, first, last, more important, most important, less important, least important

Try It Out

➤ Make a coherent paragraph by adding transitional words and phrases that show how these statements are related:

Ulrich and Georg are enemies. Their parents and grandparents had been enemies. Ulrich owns the land. Georg disputes his claim. Georg poaches on Ulrich's land. One night they meet in the forest. A tree falls on them. They cannot move. They wait for help. Ulrich offers Georg some wine. He offers his friendship.

In this passage from "The Interlopers," the transitional word is underscored. Notice how it links cause and effect. What other transitional words or phrases could have been used in its place?

"Both men spoke with the bitterness of possible defeat before them, <u>for</u> each knew that it might be long before his men would seek him out or find him. . . ."

VOCABULARY — HOW TO OWN A WORD

WORD BANK
precipitous
acquiesced
marauders
languor
succor

Word Histories

Use a good dictionary to research the origin, or **etymology,** of each word in the Word Bank. This information usually appears in brackets or parentheses following the entry word's pronunciation. The dictionary provides a key to the abbreviations used in an etymology. Use a chart like the one below, which shows the etymology of *precipitous,* to organize your findings.

Word	Language of Origin	Original Word	Derivation
precipitous, "very steep"	Latin (L)	*praeceps,* meaning "head before, or steep"	*prae-* ("before") + *caput* ("head")

THE INTERLOPERS 103

As a proofreading exercise, have partners exchange pieces of writing from their portfolios. Students should circle all transitional words and phrases in their partner's writing and mark sentences that are unclear or lacking transition. Students should then return papers to their partners for revision. Afterwards, have them exchange papers again for a final proofreading.

Try It Out
Possible Answer

Ulrich and Georg are enemies <u>because</u> their parents and grandparents had been enemies. Ulrich owns the land, <u>but</u> Georg disputes his claim <u>and</u> poaches on Ulrich's land. One night, <u>after</u> they meet in the forest, a tree falls on them <u>and</u> they cannot move. While they wait for help, Ulrich offers Georg some wine. <u>Soon afterwards,</u> he offers his friendship.

VOCABULARY
Possible Answers
acquiesced: Latin (L) *acquiescere,* meaning "to yield to" *ad-* ("to") + *quiescere* ("to rest or keep quiet")
marauders: French (Fr) *maraud,* meaning "vagabond"
languor: Latin (L) *languere,* meaning "to be weary"
succor: Latin (L) *succurrere,* meaning "to be useful for" *sub-* ("under") + *currere* ("to run")

Resources

Language
• *Grammar and Language Links* Worksheet, p. 9

Vocabulary
• *Words to Own* Worksheet, p. 5

Language Link Quick Check

Underline the transitional words and phrases in the following sentences and then indicate what they do.

1. The feud was especially bitter <u>because</u> it had lasted for generations. [cause]

2. <u>Finally,</u> the two confronted each other. [sequence]

3. <u>Above</u> their heads, a tree splintered and, <u>before</u> they could move, crashed to the ground. [place; sequence]

4. <u>Although</u> Ulrich's hatred for Georg was strong, it <u>gradually</u> faded when he saw the other man's strength. [contrast; time]

5. <u>More important</u> than their feud was the bond that the men felt <u>after</u> the fallen tree held them captive. [importance; sequence]

6. <u>As a result</u> of their cries for help, the wolves were drawn to the men. [effect]

7. <u>As the story ends,</u> the reader imagines what will happen <u>next.</u> [sequence]

OBJECTIVES

1. Read and interpret the autobiography
2. Find thematic connections across genres
3. Generate relevant and interesting questions for discussion
4. Recognize distinctive and shared characteristics of cultures through reading and discussion

Extending the Theme

When Richard Wright's father disappears, the family goes hungry. His mother goes to work and assigns her young son the task of shopping for food. The first time he goes to the store by himself, a group of boys knock him down and steal his money. On hearing this, his mother gives him more money and sends him back to the store. He is again beaten and robbed. His mother then tells him he must learn to fight for himself. She refuses to let Richard back into the house and gives him a big stick with which to defend himself. She says she will beat him unless he comes back with the groceries. When the boys attack again, he fights with a fury he had not known he possessed, winning the right to walk the streets undisturbed.

Background

This story is from *Black Boy*, an autobiography by the great writer Richard Wright. As this part of his life story opens, Richard and his family are living in a kitchen and bedroom in Memphis, Tennessee, in a run-down tenement. Richard is terrified to go out on the bleak streets alone.

Reading Skills and Strategies

Dialogue with the Text

As you read, remember to pause at least three or four times to jot down your questions and reactions. For ideas, review the model response on pages 5–10.

go.hrw.com
LEO 9-1

Reaching All Students

Struggling Readers

Wright's introductory paragraph, which uses personification to describe hunger, may be difficult for some students. Pair these students with more advanced readers, and ask partners to paraphrase the paragraph in direct and simple written form. Before they begin, you may wish to review some of the words in the paragraph. First, discuss these two multiple-meaning words: *stole*, the past tense of *steal*, which is used here to mean "came secretly," and *still*, which is used as a verb that means "to calm or make quiet." Also be sure students understand the following words: *gauntly, baffled, insistent, clamor, nudging*. You might suggest these synonyms for the words: *bleakly, confused, demanding, protest, pushing*. After partners write their paraphrases, invite them to share their work with the class.

> *I began to wake up at night to find hunger standing at my bedside.*

from Black Boy

Richard Wright

Hunger stole upon me so slowly that at first I was not aware of what hunger really meant. Hunger had always been more or less at my elbow when I played, but now I began to wake up at night to find hunger standing at my bedside, staring at me gauntly. The hunger I had known before this had been no grim, hostile stranger; it had been a normal hunger that had made me beg constantly for bread, and when I ate a crust or two I was satisfied. But this new hunger baffled me, scared me, made me angry and insistent. Whenever I begged for food now, my mother would pour me a cup of tea, which would still the clamor in my stomach for a moment or two; but a little later I would feel hunger nudging my ribs, twisting my empty guts until they ached. I would grow dizzy and my vision would dim. I became less active in my play, and for the first time in my life I had to pause and think of what was happening to me.

"Mama, I'm hungry," I complained one afternoon.

"Jump up and catch a kungry," she said, trying to make me laugh and forget.

"What's a *kungry*?"

"It's what little boys eat when they get hungry," she said.

"What does it taste like?"

"I don't know."

"Then why do you tell me to catch one?"

"Because you said that you were hungry," she said, smiling.

Background

In the following observation, Ralph Ellison, the author of *Invisible Man* (1952), explains why Wright's *Black Boy* makes such a powerful statement about life for African American men in the first half of the twentieth century. "Born on a Mississippi plantation, he was subjected to all those blasting pressures which in a scant eighty years have sent the Negro people hurtling, without clearly defined trajectory, from slavery to emancipation, from log cabin to city tenement, from the white folks' fields and kitchens to factory assembly lines; and which, between two wars, have shattered the wholeness of its folk consciousness into a thousand writhing pieces. *Black Boy* describes this process in the personal terms of one Negro childhood."

Resources

Listening
Audio CD Library
A recording of this excerpt from *Black Boy* is available in the *Audio CD Library:*
- Disc 5, Track 4

Ⓐ Critical Thinking
Analyzing
❓ How does Wright make the hunger so memorable and real? [Possible responses: He personifies it, presenting hunger as a character— a grim, haunting figure that demands attention; he captures the constant ache that characterizes real hunger.]

Ⓑ Reading Skills and Strategies
Finding the Main Idea
❓ Why does Wright's mother respond to him with teasing? [She is trying to entertain and distract him, because there is no food to eat.]

Crossing the Curriculum

History
Richard Wright was one of several notable African American writers, including James Baldwin and Chester Himes, who chose to live in Europe rather than the United States in the post–World War II period. Have students do research to find out more about these expatriate artists. To guide their research, give students the following questions and suggest they try to find the answers:

- What conditions in the United States led these and other writers to make the decision to leave their native country?
- What was it about the political and intellectual climate of Europe that attracted these writers?
- What kind of reception did these artists and their work receive in Europe?

A Reading Skills and Strategies
Making Inferences

❓ Why do you think Wright's mother asks him about his father? [Possible responses: She wants him to figure out what is going on for himself; she cannot bring herself to tell him the truth.] **What might her state of mind be at this time?** [Possible responses: She is probably very upset, hurt, scared, and angry; she is probably feeling very alone and overwhelmed because her husband has left her and abandoned the children, and now she has no way to provide for them.]

B Historical Connections

Point out to students that this episode takes place sometime in the 1910s, before federal programs to help the hungry existed. People without money were left to fend for themselves or rely on private and religious charities for help.

C Reading Skills and Strategies
Monitor Comprehension

You might suggest that students pause at this point to jot down their comments or questions. [Sample responses: Why does Wright use the word *biological* to describe his bitterness? Wright's experience opens up a new understanding of the terrors of hunger and poverty for me.]

I sensed that she was teasing me and it made me angry.

"But I'm hungry. I want to eat."

"You'll have to wait."

"But I want to eat now."

"But there's nothing to eat," she told me.

"Why?"

"Just because there's none," she explained.

"But I want to eat," I said, beginning to cry.

"You'll just have to wait," she said again.

"But why?"

"For God to send some food."

"When is He going to send it?"

"I don't know."

"But I'm hungry!"

She was ironing and she paused and looked at me with tears in her eyes.

"Where's your father?" she asked me.

I stared in bewilderment. Yes, it was true that my father had not come home to sleep for many days now and I could make as much noise as I wanted. Though I had not known why he was absent, I had been glad that he was not there to shout his restrictions at me. But it had never occurred to me that his absence would mean that there would be no food.

"I don't know," I said.

"Who brings food into the house?" my mother asked me.

"Papa," I said. "He always brought food."

"Well, your father isn't here now," she said.

"Where is he?"

"I don't know," she said.

"But I'm hungry," I whimpered, stomping my feet.

"You'll have to wait until I get a job and buy food," she said.

As the days slid past, the image of my father became associated with my pangs of hunger, and whenever I felt hunger, I thought of him with a deep biological bitterness.

My mother finally went to work as a cook and left me and my brother alone in the flat[1] each day with a loaf of bread and a pot of tea. When she returned at evening, she would be tired and

1. **flat:** apartment.

106 THE SHORT-STORY COLLECTIONS

Professional Notes

Because of its shocking realism, raw language, and vivid portrayal of growing up amidst racial oppression in the South, the 1945 publication of *Black Boy* was a literary event that stirred strong feelings. The autobiography surged to the top of the bestseller lists. It drew praise from many of Wright's contemporaries and critics, but it also drew criticism from certain other corners. The following are remarks from Mississippi congressman Thomas Bilbo:

"It is a damnable lie from beginning to end. It is practically all fiction. There is just enough truth to enable him to build his fabulous lies about his experiences in the South. . . . It is the dirtiest, filthiest, lousiest, most obscene piece of writing that I have ever seen in print."

Richard Wright responded: "I think *Black Boy* will be read when Bilbo is dead and his name forgotten." Wright's prediction has proved to be absolutely correct. More than fifty years

after its publication, *Black Boy* continues to be widely read and is recognized as one of the great works of twentieth-century American literature.

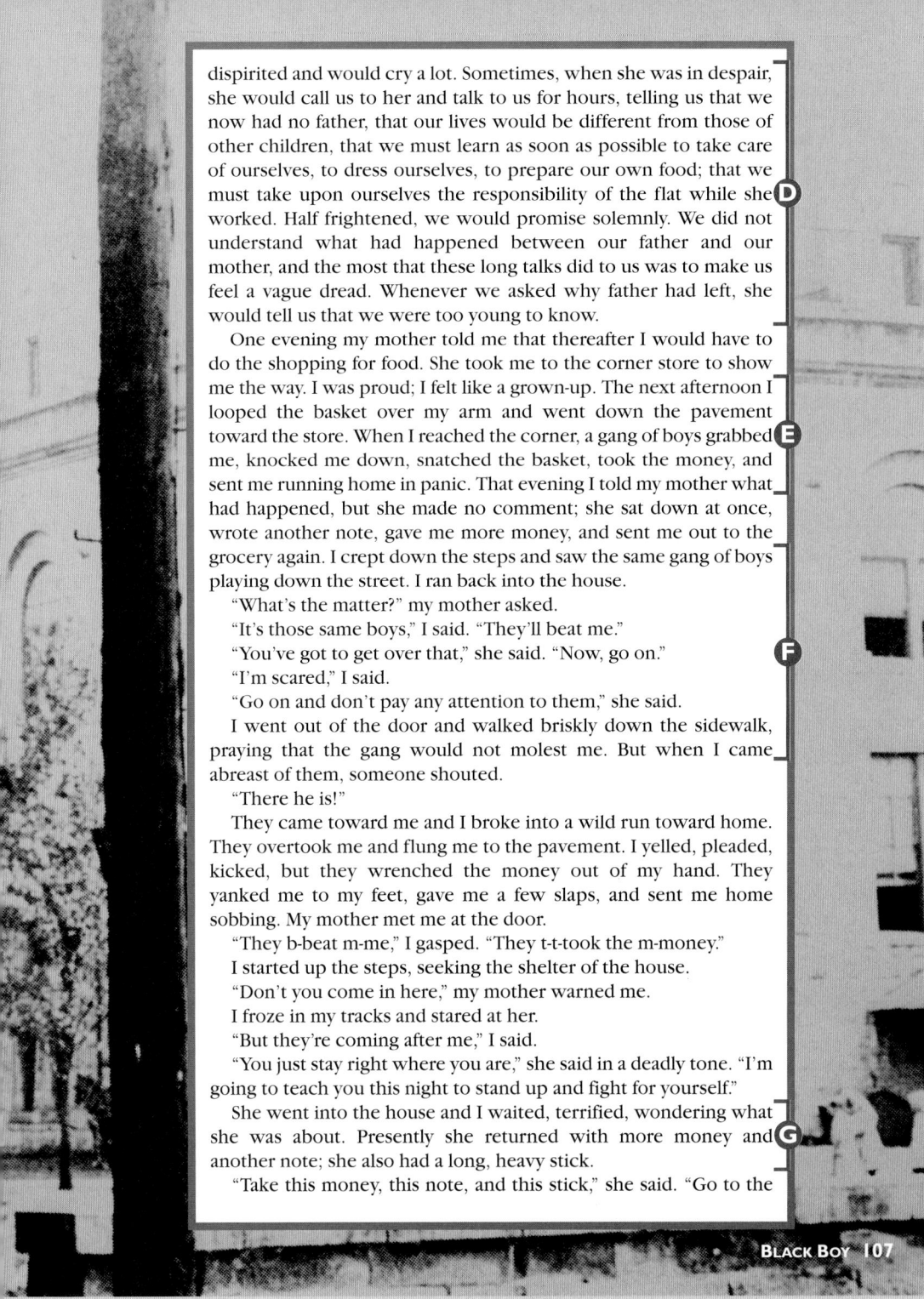

dispirited and would cry a lot. Sometimes, when she was in despair, she would call us to her and talk to us for hours, telling us that we now had no father, that our lives would be different from those of other children, that we must learn as soon as possible to take care of ourselves, to dress ourselves, to prepare our own food; that we must take upon ourselves the responsibility of the flat while she worked. Half frightened, we would promise solemnly. We did not understand what had happened between our father and our mother, and the most that these long talks did to us was to make us feel a vague dread. Whenever we asked why father had left, she would tell us that we were too young to know.

One evening my mother told me that thereafter I would have to do the shopping for food. She took me to the corner store to show me the way. I was proud; I felt like a grown-up. The next afternoon I looped the basket over my arm and went down the pavement toward the store. When I reached the corner, a gang of boys grabbed me, knocked me down, snatched the basket, took the money, and sent me running home in panic. That evening I told my mother what had happened, but she made no comment; she sat down at once, wrote another note, gave me more money, and sent me out to the grocery again. I crept down the steps and saw the same gang of boys playing down the street. I ran back into the house.

"What's the matter?" my mother asked.

"It's those same boys," I said. "They'll beat me."

"You've got to get over that," she said. "Now, go on."

"I'm scared," I said.

"Go on and don't pay any attention to them," she said.

I went out of the door and walked briskly down the sidewalk, praying that the gang would not molest me. But when I came abreast of them, someone shouted.

"There he is!"

They came toward me and I broke into a wild run toward home. They overtook me and flung me to the pavement. I yelled, pleaded, kicked, but they wrenched the money out of my hand. They yanked me to my feet, gave me a few slaps, and sent me home sobbing. My mother met me at the door.

"They b-beat m-me," I gasped. "They t-t-took the m-money."

I started up the steps, seeking the shelter of the house.

"Don't you come in here," my mother warned me.

I froze in my tracks and stared at her.

"But they're coming after me," I said.

"You just stay right where you are," she said in a deadly tone. "I'm going to teach you this night to stand up and fight for yourself."

She went into the house and I waited, terrified, wondering what she was about. Presently she returned with more money and another note; she also had a long, heavy stick.

"Take this money, this note, and this stick," she said. "Go to the

D Critical Thinking
Expressing an Opinion
❓ What do you think of the mother's speaking in this way to the young boys? Explain your response. [Sample responses: Although she may think she is protecting the boys by not explaining what happened, she creates fear by being vague, and the boys probably blame themselves for their father's rejection; her preparing the boys to take responsibility is a good idea, but she ought to show them how to cope, not burden them with her own fears and despair.]

E Elements of Literature
Conflict
❓ What external conflict is introduced? [The conflict is between Wright and a gang of boys who want his money.]

F Elements of Literature
Conflict
❓ What internal conflicts does the young Wright experience? [Possible responses: trying to be a grown-up versus begging his mother for protection; retreating in fear versus defending himself against the gang.]

G Critical Thinking
Speculating
❓ Considering that the family is very poor, why might the mother be willing to risk losing the money rather than go to the store herself? [Sample responses: She is willing to lose the money to have her son learn how to fend for himself, because she knows she can't always protect him; she believes that if you are poor, learning how to fend for yourself on the street is a priceless lesson.]

Assessing Learning

Ongoing Assessment
Reading. Use the following criteria to assess students' responses to literature.
Key: A = always
S = sometimes
R = rarely
N = never

Characteristic	Date	Rating
Asks questions; seeks help to clarify meaning		
Makes reasonable predictions		
Considers multiple interpretations		
Uses text to clarify ideas		

A Critical Thinking

Expressing an Opinion

❓ What is your opinion of the mother's behavior here? [Possible responses: She is just doing what is necessary— if she is soft and comforting Wright will never learn to fend for himself; home and parents should always be a safe haven for children—by being mean, she is hurting him more than she realizes.]

B Elements of Literature

Suspense

❓ What makes this moment suspenseful? [Sample responses: We don't know what Richard will do to defend himself or if it will work; we worry about what will happen to Richard.]

C Elements of Literature

Climax

❓ Why is this the climax of the story? This is the point of greatest interest. This is where we find out what the outcomes of both the internal and external conflicts will be.]

D Critical Thinking

Analyzing

❓ What has Wright won? [Sample responses: respect; freedom to use the streets without fear; some measure of adulthood.] What do you think Wright has lost? [Sample responses: innocence; some of his childhood; the belief that his mother will always protect him.]

---

store and buy those groceries. If those boys bother you, then fight."

I was baffled. My mother was telling me to fight, a thing that she had never done before.

"But I'm scared," I said.

"Don't you come into this house until you've gotten those groceries," she said.

"They'll beat me; they'll beat me," I said.

"Then stay in the streets; don't come back here!"

A I ran up the steps and tried to force my way past her into the house. A stinging slap came on my jaw. I stood on the sidewalk, crying.

"Please, let me wait until tomorrow," I begged.

"No," she said. "Go now! If you come back into this house without those groceries, I'll whip you!"

She slammed the door and I heard the key turn in the lock. I shook with fright. I was alone upon the dark, hostile streets and gangs were after me. I had the choice of being beaten at home or away from home. I clutched the stick, crying, trying to reason. If I were beaten at home, there was absolutely nothing that I could do about it; but if I were beaten in the streets, I had a chance to fight and defend myself. I walked slowly down the sidewalk, coming

B closer to the gang of boys, holding the stick tightly. I was so full of fear that I could scarcely breathe. I was almost upon them now.

"There he is again!" the cry went up.

They surrounded me quickly and began to grab for my hand.

"I'll kill you!" I threatened.

They closed in. In blind fear I let the stick fly, feeling it crack against a boy's skull. I swung again, lamming[2] another skull, then another. Realizing that they would retaliate if I let up for but a second, I fought to lay them low, to knock them cold, to kill them so that they could not strike back at me. I flayed with tears in my eyes, teeth clenched, stark fear making me throw every ounce of my strength behind each blow. I hit again and again, dropping the

C money and the grocery list. The boys scattered, yelling, nursing their heads, staring at me in utter disbelief. They had never seen such frenzy. I stood panting, egging them on, taunting them to come on and fight. When they refused, I ran after them and they tore out for their homes, screaming. The parents of the boys rushed into the streets and threatened me, and for the first time in my life I shouted at grown-ups, telling them that I would give them the same if they bothered me. I finally found my grocery list and the money and went to the store. On my way back I kept my stick poised for

D instant use, but there was not a single boy in sight. That night I won the right to the streets of Memphis.

2. **lamming:** old slang word meaning "beating" or "hitting."

Making the Connections

Connecting to the Theme: "Facing Monsters"

Place students in small groups to fill out a chart like the one at the right. Have them work together to set criteria to rate each story on a scale of 1 (least powerful/memorable) to 5 (most powerful/memorable). Ask each student to write a brief explanation of his or her ratings of the selections.

Selection	"Monster" Faced	Moment of Confrontation	Outcome	Rating
"The Most Dangerous Game"				
"A Sound of Thunder"				
"The Birds"				
"Poison"				
"The Interlopers"				
excerpt from *Black Boy*				

MEET THE WRITER

"Only Through Books . . ."

Richard Wright (1908–1960) began his life in poverty. His father, a share-cropper on a Mississippi farm, abandoned his family when Wright was five; when the boy was twelve, his mother could no longer support her children. Raised by various relatives, Wright early learned the bitter lessons of survival on ghetto streets. He remembered trying alcohol at the age of six, working in a shabby hotel while still a child, living with "the sustained expectation of violence." By borrowing a library card, he was finally able to gain access to books. Later, he wrote:

> **66** . . . it had been only through books . . . that I had managed to keep myself alive. **99**

Black Boy secured Wright's fame and became a best-seller, but in the fifteen years following its publication, Wright, then living abroad, never wrote another book that equaled its success. Wright kept trying to understand the historical and cultural place of black people in the modern world. He visited Africa and recorded his observations. But he felt as alien in Africa as he did in America. Richard Wright died in Paris, where he had found as much of a home as he could.

BROWSING IN THE FILES

About the Author. Characters in the literary works of Richard Wright are often filled with fear or anger, emotions the author experienced as an African American male in the United States prior to the Civil Rights Movement. Though he had spent much of his childhood in the South intent on the idea of escaping to a better life in the North, he found only menial jobs when he arrived in Chicago at age nineteen. Finally joining the ranks of other African American authors, Wright was the first among them to have an impact on a mass audience.

A Critic's Comment. Author Margaret Walker has said that "Wright perhaps consciously strove to make *Black Boy* a symbol of many black lives, of many black boys growing up in America and, thereby, to speak to the conscience of white America. . . . This is not a book of purely factual and verifiable incidents." Discuss how the episode excerpted here might support Walker's statements.

FINDING COMMON GROUND

- Now that you've read the selection, meet in a small group and share the questions and comments you recorded.

1. Select a person to speak for your group.

2. Read aloud your notes (or pass the notes around the table so that everyone can read all of the comments).

3. Identify four or five questions or issues or comments that seem most interesting or most widely shared within your group.

4. Discuss those items, giving a suitable amount of time for each (five to ten minutes).

5. Reconvene as a full class and share the results of your discussion.

BLACK BOY 109

FINDING COMMON GROUND

As its name suggests, this feature requires students through lively discussion to discover areas of agreement about the issues in the literature. To generate equal participation among group members, you might have them take turns sharing observations they have recorded. In response to an observation, other group members may then draw from their own similar or related notes. Suggest that groups fully discuss a single issue before asking another member to share a new observation.

Assessing Learning

Check Test: Questions and Answers
Answers may vary slightly.

1. How does hunger affect Wright physically? [He always has a stomachache; he feels dizzy, has dimmed vision, and cannot play as actively as before.]

2. Why do Wright and his family not have money for food? [Wright's father has left them without support, and his mother does not yet have a job.]

3. How does Wright feel when his mother tells him he will have to do the shopping? [He feels proud and like a grown-up.]

4. Why does Wright's mother lock him out of their home? [She wants him to learn to stand up for himself in the streets.]

5. How does Wright succeed in the street? [He attacks bullies with a stick and yells at adults.]

This brief student piece describes elemental fears—of darkness, faceless attackers, and falling—the universal fears of nightmares. The speaker dreams that she is falling through darkness and that she is saved by her mother's hand.

Ⓐ Critical Thinking
Speculating
❓ Why is the place only identified as "there"? [Sample responses: It is a dream and so the place is never identified; the place doesn't matter as much as the feeling of helplessness the writer is trying to illustrate.]

Ⓑ Reading Skills and Strategies
Comparing and Contrasting
❓ How is this mother's role different from the role of the mother in *Black Boy*? [Here the mother intervenes to save the narrator, whereas in *Black Boy* the mother demands that he save himself.]

Reading Skills and Strategies
Reading Captions
This is a good opportunity to check to see that students read captions carefully. Tell them what a caption is, and ask them how the caption for Brady Dunklee's drawing adds new symbolic meaning to this lighthouse.

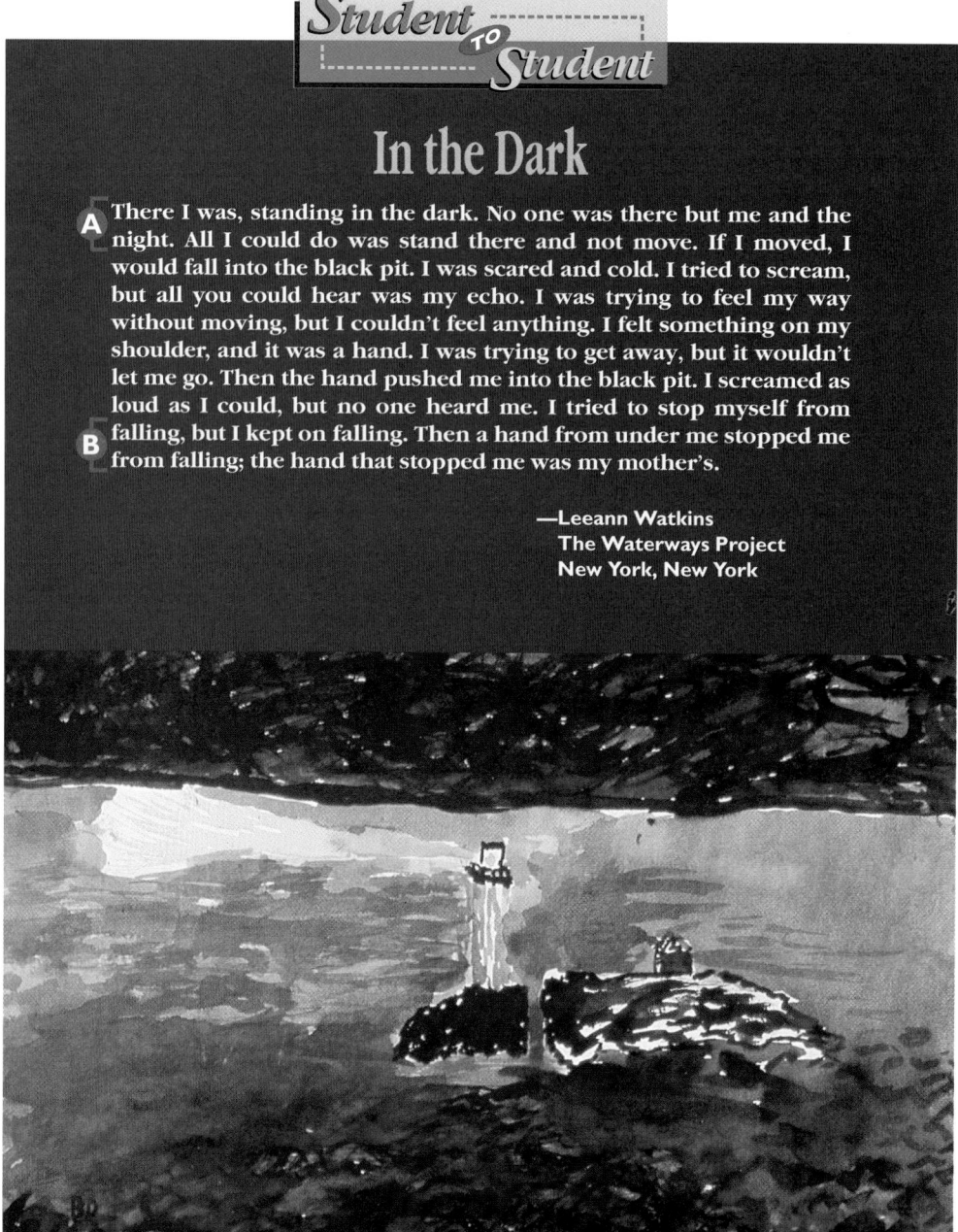

Student to Student

In the Dark

Ⓐ There I was, standing in the dark. No one was there but me and the night. All I could do was stand there and not move. If I moved, I would fall into the black pit. I was scared and cold. I tried to scream, but all you could hear was my echo. I was trying to feel my way without moving, but I couldn't feel anything. I felt something on my shoulder, and it was a hand. I was trying to get away, but it wouldn't let me go. Then the hand pushed me into the black pit. I screamed as loud as I could, but no one heard me. I tried to stop myself from Ⓑ falling, but I kept on falling. Then a hand from under me stopped me from falling; the hand that stopped me was my mother's.

—Leeann Watkins
The Waterways Project
New York, New York

The Lighthouse by Brady Dunklee (U.S.A.). From Yale-New Haven Hospital's collection of international children's art called "Tales of Courage."

READ ON

Just a Little Guy

In J.R.R. Tolkien's fantasy *The Hobbit* (Houghton Mifflin), Bilbo Baggins is just a little guy—a hobbit—who is minding his own business. Then one day, the wizard Gandalf and a gang of thirteen dwarfs arrive at his door and carry him off. So begins Bilbo's great adventure, an adventure with some big challenges for a little guy: bee pastures, giant spiders, icy waterfalls, and the dreaded dragon Smaug.

A Suspense Novel

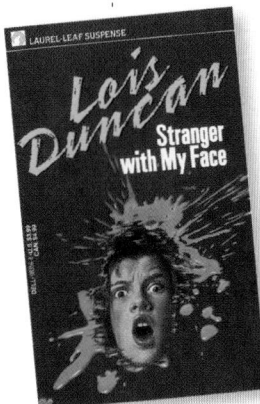

What if you kept feeling that someone was watching you, and your friends blamed you for things you were sure you never did? This happens to a teenage girl in Lois Duncan's *Stranger with My Face* (Dell). The surprise ending of this sinister novel is in the tradition of great writers of suspense like Edgar Allan Poe.

Nobody Said Life Was Fair

You'll get an up-close look at prejudice in Mildred D. Taylor's *Roll of Thunder, Hear My Cry* (Puffin). Too close for comfort—for in this novel, Cassie Logan and her family must fight to hold on to their land and their pride. Emotional and eloquent, Taylor's novel was awarded the Newbery Medal.

READ ON 111

Portfolio Assessment Options
The following projects can help you evaluate and assess students' reading accomplishments outside class. Videotapes or audiotapes of completed projects may be included in students' portfolios.

- **Develop Travel Brochures** Suggest that students create a travel brochure that advertises or highlights settings or landmarks that are important in the book. If possible, bring in sample travel brochures for students to use as models. To illustrate their brochures, students may draw, use pictures from magazines, or use a computer graphics program, if available. Have students present their brochures to the class.

- **Host a Television Book Review Show** Have students who have read the same book work in pairs to script and act out a television book review show. Students should brainstorm criteria for why they would or would not recommend the book to others and should give the book a final rating based on the criteria. If possible, show students a videotape of television movie critics to give them an idea of content and criteria for their own reviews. Have students present their reviews to the class. Videotape them if equipment is available.

- **Translate a Scene to the Screen** Have students rewrite a book's important scenes as a movie script. Remind students that scripts focus more on dialogue and action than on description. Suggest that students read aloud the scene from the book before reading or performing their scripts for the class. Ask the class to identify the differences in the two formats.

Writer's Workshop

ASSIGNMENT

Write a short narrative about a conflict or confrontation that is funny, scary, sad, or just interesting to you. Your story can be a true story or a fictional one.

AIM

To express yourself; to re-create an experience; to give information.

AUDIENCE

Your classmates, family members, or a younger audience. (You choose.)

NARRATIVE WRITING

SHORT NARRATIVE

In stories, as in real life, first one thing happens, then another, then another. Writing that tells about a series of related events that take place over a period of time is called **narrative writing**. In this workshop you'll write a narrative about a true incident or one you make up.

Narration is a very old use of language and is still one of the most popular. You use the techniques of narration when you tell a true story about something that happened to you or someone you know. But you can also use narration in directions for fixing or assembling a machine, in scientific reports, in news stories, in historical writing. You can use narration in short stories and novels, in poems, in speeches, and in biographies and autobiographies.

Prewriting

1. A Head Start: Checking Your Notebook

As you were reading the selections in this collection, you should have been gathering material for a narrative. Review your Writer's Notebook entries: You should have a list of possible conflicts, a list of main events, some notes on setting, some ideas for dialogue, and some notes on a surprise ending. Remember that if you write a true narrative, it should be one you're willing to share.

2. Elaborate, Please

Once you've chosen a topic that interests you, see if you have enough to write about.

- Focus on your topic and **brainstorm** for five minutes, listing every detail that whizzes through your brain. Don't stop to evaluate your ideas—just keep on writing.

- You can collect more details by **freewriting** on the computer or on paper or by making a **cluster diagram** developing your ideas.

- If you are writing about a real experience, consider **interviewing** people who shared your experience. Ask what specific details they recall about the events, people, and setting.

3. Getting Organized

Richard Wright tells about his experience (page 105) in **chronological order,** the order in which the events occurred. Most narratives follow this first-things-first order. But the Student Model on page 114 uses a **flashback.** It begins in the present but then flashes back to an earlier time to explain how the narrator came to be under a car.

A **story map** like the one at the right will help you identify the key events of your narrative. You might circle or highlight events you'll want to elaborate on.

Drafting

1. Show, Don't Tell

The first rule of storytelling is show, don't tell. Include several strong details to help your readers visualize actions and setting; instead of just naming a feeling, *show* it.

EXAMPLES

I was afraid and ran out of the office. [**telling**]

"I burst past her through the half-open door, down the hallway and out into the lobby. A scream exploded from my lungs, a scream of terror and panic. Faces, confused and frightened, snapped up from their magazines. I looked down and realized that I was still only wearing my briefs and ran faster—I was nearly flying now." [**showing**]

—Drake Bennett, from "Coward"

PEANUTS® reprinted by permission of UFS, Inc.

> **Story Map**
>
> **Incident:** When I was four, I ran away from my doctor's office to avoid a needle.
>
> **Who was there:** Me, Mom, the doctor, the nurse.
>
> **Conflict:** Me against the nurse with the needle.
>
> **Main events:** Stripped to my underwear, ⟨waiting for the⟩ ⟨doctor⟩ and needle. Doctor's exam OK. Nurse approaches with needle. I run screaming out of office to ⟨parking lot⟩, hide under a car. ⟨Mom⟩ and ⟨nurse⟩ talk me out from under car. I get needle anyway.

Language/Grammar Link
HELP

Powerful verbs: page 31. Active and passive voice: page 49. Verb tenses: page 79. Subject-verb agreement: page 93. Transitions: page 103.

WRITER'S WORKSHOP **113**

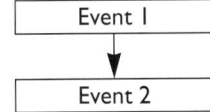

After students have completed their drafts, they may benefit from another look at the Student Model. Have students ask themselves the following questions.

? How does the writer interest the reader at the beginning?

? What details does the writer use to help the reader visualize the event?

? What order does the writer use to explain the events?

? What techniques does this writer use that you might apply in your narrative?

Language Handbook HELP

See Quotation Marks, page 1026.

2. What People Say

Dialogue lets the reader eavesdrop on actual conversations, which are always more interesting than a summary of what people said. Sometimes dialogue plays an essential part in the story. In "Poison" (page 81), for instance, the muffled, clipped dialogue helps us share Harry's terror. Later Dahl uses dialogue to shock us and to give us a glimpse of Harry's true character.

3. A Good Beginning Is Half the Battle

If your opening sentences work well, they'll make readers want to know what's coming next. Look at the Box of Beginnings on page 115. What do these openings tell you immediately? What can you predict about what might happen next? What questions do these openers put in your mind? Here, on the next page, are some strategies for writing a good beginning:

Student Model

FROM COWARD

"Drake, you're making this difficult. You know you're going to have to come out sometime, so you might as well get it over with." Mom's voice had grown impatient. The hard asphalt scraped against my bare body as I turned on my stomach to face her. My nose, pressed against the parking-lot ground, was filled with the dead stench of aging, worn tires and the fumes of burnt gas and dripping oil. I raised my head, hitting it hard on the metal of the muffler above me. A sharp burst of screaming pain shot through my skull. I peered out from under the car at the two sets of feet that imprisoned me. One I recognized immediately: the creased, black leather heels Mom wore to work every day. The white Reebok walking shoes beside them I assumed belonged to the nurse. Mom was wrong. There was no way I was coming out from under that car. It was all that protected me from the pain and terror I had so recently escaped.

The wind picked up, blowing in gusts, skittering freshly fallen leaves across the pavement. A million tiny goose bumps rose all over my body and I shivered. I was cold.

Cold. The bed in the examining room had been cold. The nurse had come into the room and told me to strip down to my underwear and sit on the bed. The

Interesting title.

Opens with dialogue. Makes reader wonder where Drake is.

Shows, doesn't just tell, what his hiding place is like.

Good specific details in this paragraph.

Hooks our interest: Why is he under a car? Why is he in pain and terror?

Makes the setting match his feelings.

Flashes back to an earlier time in the day.

Reaching All Students

Struggling Writers
Students might benefit from writing their first drafts in class with guidance from you. For instance, they may need help with using specific sensory details. Encourage writers to make the action as realistic as possible.

English Language Learners
Students learning English as a second language may prefer to write notes and even to generate a first draft in their native language. Encourage them to write in the language in which they are most comfortable until they have recorded a satisfying introduction and sequence of events. Reassure students that their English versions do not need to be direct translations.

- Start with a bit of dialogue, as the Student Model does and as Richard Connell does in the story on page 13.
- Start with an attention-grabber—a statement that will catch your readers' interest, as Richard Wright does on page 105.
- Start with an especially forceful word or a short, punchy sentence.

Evaluating and Revising
1. Peer Editing

Get together with three or four classmates to read and comment on one another's drafts. Ask yourself: What do I like best about this narrative? What would make this narrative more interesting? (Does it have a good beginning and a satisfying ending? Has the

---

A Box of Beginnings

"By seventh grade I knew better than to spit while girls were around."
—Gary Soto, "The Nile"

"One winter morning in the long-ago, four-year-old days of my life I found myself standing before a fireplace, warming my hands over a mound of glowing coals, listening to the wind whistle past the house outside."
—Richard Wright, *Black Boy*

Evaluating and Revising
- Have students use the Evaluation Criteria on p. 116 to review their drafts and determine needed revisions.
- Point out that the revision phase is the time to add words, phrases, and, sometimes, sentences; to cross out things; to change things; to rearrange sections or paragraphs; and to get help with problem areas.
- Ask students to listen to the "voice" of their writing by reading it aloud. Then, based on the reading, they can make adjustments so that the narrative flows more smoothly.
- For models of sentences by professional writers, refer students to the Sentence Workshop on p. 117.

---

bed had been soft but rubbery, and cold, cold like the blubbery, dead flesh of some huge whale. The paper covering stuck to the backs of my naked thighs, and I rumpled and creased it each time I shifted my weight.

I was only four now, but I could remember coming to Dr. Castor's office twice before, and I knew what to expect. In a few minutes Dr. Castor himself would come in and do all the "checkup" sorts of things: the poking and probing and tapping and weighing and feeling sorts of things. After he finished, he would talk to my mom for a while and then leave. I would wait for a few more minutes.

Then came the part I dreaded, the part that made my checkups with Dr. Castor hellish. The nurse would walk into the room carrying a bottle of alcohol and a cotton swab and a little plastic bag. I would bare my trembling arm and she would wet the swab with alcohol. Noticing my clammy palms and tensed face, she would ask if I was scared. I would shake my head quickly; she would smile, a wide, well-rehearsed smile.

"This will only hurt for a second. . . ."

—Drake Bennett
Phillips Exeter Academy
Exeter, New Hampshire

First appeared in *Merlyn's Pen: The National Magazines of Student Writing.*

Uses vivid figure of speech that creates a sense of disgust.
Flashback again to explain situation.

Good sensory details.

Here is the conflict. This is what the narrative is going to be about.

Crossing the Curriculum

Science
Have students work in small groups to create a comical narrative based on a conflict with a natural phenomenon. One possible title is "Newton Grapples with Gravity." The basic problem and setting should be accurate, but students may take creative liberty with the action and aspects of the characters' personalities.

Proofreading

Have students proofread their own papers first and then exchange them with other students. Suggest that students pay close attention to verb tenses and transitional words and phrases so that the order of events in their narratives will be clear.

If time permits, the final copy should be put aside for at least a day before it is proofread one last time by the author.

Publishing

Encourage students to present their narratives to the audience for whom they were written. Provide a reading forum, or compile a class collection of narratives that can be shared.

Reflecting

Suggest that students reflect on their papers by answering the following questions:

1. What was the most difficult part of writing this narrative?
2. What do I like best about my narrative?
3. What do I want to learn to do better?
4. How can I use what I learned about narration in other forms of writing?

Resources

Peer Editing Forms and Rubrics
• *Portfolio Management System*, p. 98.
Revision Transparencies
• *Workshop Resources*, p. 1

Grading Timesaver

Rubrics for this Writer's Workshop assignment appear on p. 99 of the *Portfolio Management System*.

■ *Evaluation Criteria*

A good narrative

1. *has a beginning that captures the readers' interest*

2. *tells a series of related events*

3. *uses description to show the characters and setting*

4. *uses dialogue*

Communications Handbook
H E L P

See Proofreaders' Marks.

Sentence Workshop
H E L P

Sentence modeling: page 117.

---

writer *shown* me vividly the characters and their setting?)

You might use a colored marker to highlight sentences or passages you think are especially vivid or original. In the margin, write comments and questions that you think will help the writer improve the narrative.

2. Self-Evaluation

You don't have to do everything your peer editors suggest. The story is yours, after all. Make changes that you feel will strengthen and improve your narrative.

Revision Model

	Peer Comments
hard my bare body The asphalt scraped against me as I	*Can you use descriptive words?*
turned on my stomach to face her.	
My nose, pressed against the	*This is great!*
parking-lot ground, was filled with	
aging, worn the dead stench of tires and the	*Add more sensory details like these.*
burnt dripping fumes of gas and oil. I raised my	
head, hitting it hard on the metal of	
A sharp burst of screaming the muffler above me. Pain shot	*Another good spot for sensory details.*
peered through my skull. I looked out from	*Replace with more vivid verbs.*
under the car at the two sets of feet	
imprisoned that held me.	

116 THE SHORT-STORY COLLECTIONS

BUILDING YOUR PORTFOLIO
Sentence Workshop

SENTENCE MODELING: LEARNING FROM THE PROS

To improve your tennis or basketball game, you can watch a tournament or a how-to video made by a pro. You can improve your "writing game" the same way: by analyzing how professional writers put sentences together and by imitating what they do.

In this lesson, you will look at some professionals' sentences and then, for practice, you'll build your own sentences imitating the pros.

In these model sentences, the basic sentence parts (subject + verb + complement, if there is one) are underlined, and additional chunks of meaning (phrases and clauses) are separated by slash marks.

1. "It was a secret place / for us / where nobody else could go / without our permission."
   —Borden Deal, "Antaeus"

2. "Before us / the valley stretched away / into miles / of rocky desolation."
   —James Ramsey Ullman, "Top Man"

3. "In her attic bedroom / Meg regarded Ananda, / who thumped her massive tail / in a friendly manner."
   —Madeleine L'Engle, A Swiftly Tilting Planet

Here are some imitations of these professional sentences. The basic sentence parts in each (subject + verb + complement, if there is one) are underscored.

1. It was a large room, / just for them, / where children could hide / with their books.

2. Before me / the path twisted around / into a maze / of frightening darkness.

3. In the grass, / the snail eyed the cat, / which bared its yellow teeth / in a hungry manner.

Writer's Workshop Follow-up: Revision

Take another look at the narrative you have written for the Writer's Workshop (page 112). Are your sentences interesting? Can you expand any of your sentences with phrases and clauses that will add more specific detail to your story?

Language Handbook HELP

See Sentence Structure, page 1010.

Technology HELP

See Language Workshop CD-ROM. Key word entry: sentence structure.

Try It Out

For each sample below, write your own sentence with the same sentence parts in the same order. Your sentences can be about anything. Exchange your finished sentences with a partner. Underline the basic sentence in your partner's original sentences, and add slashes to separate chunks of meaning. Did you notice any problems?

1. "I remember being startled when I first saw my grandmother rocking away on her porch."
   —Lorraine Hansberry, *To Be Young, Gifted and Black*

2. "When he came back into the room, I was sitting in another machine."
   —Ernest Hemingway, "In Another Country"

3. "She listened to the leaves rustling outside the window."
   —Katherine Anne Porter, "The Jilting of Granny Weatherall"

SENTENCE WORKSHOP 117

OBJECTIVES
1. Improve sentence style by analyzing and imitating sentences written by professional writers
2. Recognize basic structures within sentences

Resources —————
Workshop Resources
• Worksheet, p. 61
Language Workshop CD-ROM
• Sentence Structure

Try It Out
Possible Answers
1. We remember feeling alarmed / when we heard the dog / howling at the moon.
2. As he strolled/ to the corner, / I was watching / from an open window.
3. They worried / about the trains / chugging down the tracks.

Assessing Learning

Quick Check: Basic Sentences
For the following sentences, underline the words that make up the basic sentence.
1. Along the way, / we heard stories / about the old days.
2. Since we had warned her/ of the possible risks, / we felt little sympathy.

3. The smallest children edged close / to have a good look / at the litter of kittens.
4. Though they could not identify the driver, / the witnesses were sure / of the make / of the car.
5. Rain still fell / in the valley / after the sun had come out / in the highlands.

OBJECTIVES

1. Develop strategies for organizing information in graphs
2. Choose the best graphic to organize a particular set of information
3. Construct an informational graphic

Teaching the Lesson

Explain to students that using graphics helps to make information easy to access by separating and highlighting important points. To help students understand the graphics described here, draw examples of each and discuss their strengths.

Time line:

events

time periods

Venn diagram:

differences — simi-larities — differences

Cause-and-effect chart:

cause	event	effect

Using the Strategies

Possible Answers

1. The time line can be used to show when each period began and ended and when each type of dinosaur existed. The Venn diagram will most clearly show the overlap of dinosaur species across two time periods.
2. Time line:

Stegosaurus
Iguanodon
Tyrannosaurus
Ankylosaurus
Torosaurus

Triassic   Jurassic   Cretaceous

Venn diagram:

Stegosaurus (Iguanodon Tyrannosaurus) Ankylo-saurus Torosaurus

Jurassic   Cretaceous

3. No.
4. Answers will vary.

Situation

You've read "A Sound of Thunder," and you are doing research on the major dinosaur families and their era. The information you found is shown in the box on the right. Now you want to display your information on a graph.

> Dinosaurs lived during the Mesozoic era (225 million to 65 million years ago). This era is divided into three periods: the Triassic, the Jurassic, and the Cretaceous. Some kinds of dinosaurs lived through all three periods; others lived only during one or two. For example, the Stegosaurus lived only in the Jurassic period (180 million to 130 million years ago); the Iguanodon and the Tyrannosaurus rex lived in the Jurassic period and the Cretaceous period (130 million to 65 million years ago); the Ankylosaurus and the Torosaurus lived only in the Cretaceous period.
>
> —based on *The World Book Encyclopedia*

Strategies

Different types of graphics show different kinds of relationships among ideas.

- One common kind of graphic, a **time line,** shows the order in which events occur. You can use a time line to chart events in a work of fiction or to track what happens to someone or something over a period of time. See page 456.

- Another graphic, a **Venn diagram,** shows similarities and differences in overlapping circles. It can help you see how two characters (or settings, or other story elements) are alike and how they are different. See page 29.

- A third graphic, a **cause-and-effect chart,** maps the important events in a story and shows their relationships. You can use such a chart to explore *why* characters act as they do and *what happens* as a result of their actions. See page 47.

Search for signal words.

As you read, watch for words and phrases that indicate how ideas are related to one another. Here are some possibilities:

- **Time:** *first, second, before, after, earlier, later, next, then*
- **Cause:** *since, because, for*
- **Effect:** *accordingly, therefore, consequently, as a result*
- **Comparison:** *like, as, in the same way, similarly*
- **Contrast:** *but, yet, however, on the other hand, nevertheless*

Graphics to go.

- You can use graphics to point out connections between stories and within a single story. You can use them as well with nonfiction, poetry, and drama. You can even use them to explore patterns in your own experience. Of course, you may find them handy as study guides and as sources of ideas for papers.

Using the Strategies

1. Which graphic will you use to organize your information about major dinosaur families and their era? Why?
2. Construct and fill in the graphic you selected, using the information above.
3. Review your graphic. Did any dinosaurs live through all three major periods?
4. Did filling in the graphic change the *way* you reviewed your information? If so, how?

Extending the Strategies

Describe two other situations in which you could use one of the graphics described here.

Reaching All Students

Struggling Readers

Pair a student who may need assistance graphically organizing information with a student who is a visual learner. While the struggling student reads the paragraph out loud, the visual learner can model sketching a graphic. Have partners explain why they chose the graphic that they did.

Advanced Learners

Have students find an informational article dealing with a topic in which they have a particular interest: music, history, sports, etc. Then, have each student choose and create a graphic that can be used to organize the article's important points. Have the students present their articles and graphics to the class.

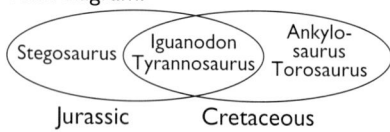

The Human Spirit

Theme

Focus on Character: What Are We Capable Of? *At the center of a conflict is a character, usually a heroic character. We tend to think of heroes as extraordinary, but in this collection, ordinary people struggle with ordinary problems. They teach us that heroism is also found in acts of kindness and unselfishness—even in the mere act of survival in a world that ignores our humanity.*

Reading the Anthology

Reaching Struggling Readers

The *Reading Skills and Strategies: Reaching Struggling Readers* binder provides materials coordinated with the Pupil's Edition (see the Collection Planner, p. T118B) to help students who have difficulty reading and comprehending text, or students who are reluctant readers. The binder for ninth grade is organized around sixteen individual skill areas and offers the following options:

- **MiniRead** MiniReads are short, easy texts that give students a chance to practice a particular skill and strategy before reading selections in the Pupil's Edition. Each MiniRead Skill Lesson can be taught independently or used in conjunction with a Selection Skill Lesson.

- **Selection Skill Lessons** Selection Skill Lessons allow students to apply skills introduced in the MiniReads. Each Selection Skill Lesson provides reading instruction and practice specific to a particular piece of literature in the Pupil's Edition.

Reading Beyond the Anthology

Read On

Each collection in the grade nine book includes an annotated bibliography of books suitable for extended reading. The suggested books are related to works in the collection by theme, by author, or by subject. To preview the Read On for Collection 2, please turn to p. T193.

HRW Library

The *HRW Library* offers novels, plays, works of nonfiction, and short-story collections for extended reading. Each book in the Library includes a major work and thematically or topically related Connections. The Connections are magazine articles, poems, or other pieces of literature. Each book in the *HRW Library* is also accompanied by a Study Guide that provides teaching suggestions and worksheets. The two titles shown here will work well to extend the theme of Collection 2.

A TALE OF TWO CITIES
Charles Dickens
Dickens's story of love and redemption in revolutionary France shows how individuals in times of stress can rise to new levels of gallantry and bravery.

WHERE THE RED FERN GROWS
Wilson Rawls
A grown man recalls the events of his childhood, particularly the lessons of friendship, courage, and determination that he learned from his two dogs.

Collection 2 **The Human Spirit**

Resources for this Collection

Note: All resources for this collection are available for preview on the *One-Stop Planner CD-ROM 1 with Test Generator.* All worksheets and blackline masters may be printed from the CD-ROM.

Internet Resources
go.hrw.com LE0 9-2

Selection or Feature	Reading and Literary Skills	Vocabulary, Language, and Grammar

Thank You, M'am
Langston Hughes (p. 120)
 	
Connections: A Volunteer of Love
Denise Crittendon (p. 126)
	• *Reading Skills and Strategies: Reaching Struggling Readers*
	  • MiniRead Skill Lesson, p. 46
	  • Selection Skill Lesson, p. 54
	• *Graphic Organizers for Active Reading,* Worksheet p. 6
	• *Literary Elements:* Transparency 2
	Worksheet p. 7
		• *Grammar and Language Links:* Modifiers,
		Worksheet p. 11
		
		• *Language Workshop CD-ROM,*
		Modifiers
		
		• *Daily Oral Grammar,*
		Transparency 6

Elements of Literature: **Character** (p. 130)	• *Literary Elements,* Transparency 2	
Harrison Bergeron Kurt Vonnegut (p. 132) **Connections:** **The Lesson of the Moth** Don Marquis (p. 140)	• *Graphic Organizers for Active Reading,* Worksheet p. 7	• *Words to Own,* Worksheet p. 6 • *Grammar and Language Links:* Misplaced Modifiers, Worksheet p. 13 • *Language Workshop CD-ROM,* Misplaced Modifiers • *Daily Oral Grammar,* Transparency 7
A Christmas Memory Truman Capote (p. 144) **Connections:** *from* **A Christmas** **Memory** (screenplay) Truman Capote (p. 155)	• *Graphic Organizers for Active Reading,* Worksheet p. 8 • *Literary Elements:* Transparency 3 Worksheet p. 10	• *Words to Own,* Worksheet p. 7 • *Grammar and Language Links:* Figures of Speech, Worksheet p. 15 • *Daily Oral Grammar,* Transparency 8
Elements of Literature: Setting (p. 164)	• *Literary Elements,* Transparency 3	
A Man Called Horse Dorothy M. Johnson (p. 166)	• *Graphic Organizers for Active Reading,* Worksheet p. 9	• *Words to Own,* Worksheet p. 8 • *Grammar and Language Links:* Vivid Modifiers, Worksheet p. 17 • *Language Workshop CD-ROM,* Modifiers • *Daily Oral Grammar,* Transparency 9
Salvador Late or Early Sandra Cisneros (p. 182) **Connections: who are you, little i** E. E. Cummings (p. 185)	• *Graphic Organizers for Active Reading,* Worksheet p. 10	• *Daily Oral Grammar,* Transparency 10
Extending the Theme: **The Washwoman** Isaac Bashevis Singer (p. 188)	The Extending the Theme feature provides students with an unstructured opportunity to practice reading strategies using a selection that extends the theme of the collection.	
Writer's Workshop: Analyzing a **Character** (p. 194)		
Sentence Workshop: Revising **Sentence Fragments** (p. 199)		• *Workshop Resources,* p. 63 • *Language Workshop CD-ROM,* Sentence Fragments

Collection Planner

Other Resources for this Collection

- *Cross-Curricular Activities,* p. 2
- *Portfolio Management System,* Introduction to Portfolio Assessment, p. 1
- *Test Generator,* Collection Test

Writing	Listening and Speaking Viewing and Representing	Assessment
• *Portfolio Management System,* Rubrics for Choices, p. 100	• *Audio CD Library,* Disc 6, Track 2 • *Viewing and Representing:* Fine Art Transparency 3; Worksheet p. 12 • *Portfolio Management System,* Rubrics for Choices, p. 100	• *Formal Assessment,* Selection Test, p. 13 • *Standardized Test Preparation,* p. 18 • *Test Generator (One-Stop Planner CD-ROM)*
		• *Formal Assessment,* Literary Elements Test, p. 22
• *Portfolio Management System,* Rubrics for Choices, p. 102	• *Audio CD Library,* Disc 6, Track 3 • *Portfolio Management System,* Rubrics for Choices, p. 102	• *Formal Assessment,* Selection Test, p. 15 • *Test Generator (One-Stop Planner CD-ROM)*
• *Portfolio Management System,* Rubrics for Choices, p. 103	• Visual Connections: Videocassette A, Segment 2 • *Audio CD Library,* Disc 6, Track 4 • *Viewing and Representing:* Fine Art Transparency 4; Worksheet p. 16 • *Portfolio Management System,* Rubrics for Choices, p. 103	• *Formal Assessment,* Selection Test, p. 17 • *Standardized Test Preparation,* pp. 20, 22 • *Test Generator (One-Stop Planner CD-ROM)*
		• *Formal Assessment,* Literary Elements Test, p. 24
• *Portfolio Management System,* Rubrics for Choices, p. 104	• *Audio CD Library,* Disc 7, Track 2 • *Portfolio Management System,* Rubrics for Choices, p. 104	• *Formal Assessment,* Selection Test, p. 19 • *Test Generator (One-Stop Planner CD-ROM)*
• *Portfolio Management System,* Rubrics for Choices, p. 105	• *Portfolio Management System,* Rubrics for Choices, p. 105	• *Formal Assessment,* Selection Test, p. 21 • *Standardized Test Preparation,* p. 24 • *Test Generator (One-Stop Planner CD-ROM)*
	• *Audio CD Library,* Disc 7, Track 3	

• *Workshop Resources,* p. 7		• *Portfolio Management System*
		  • Prewriting, p. 107
		  • Peer Editing, p. 108
		  • Assessment Rubric, p. 109

 Transparency    CD-ROM    Video    Audio CD

Collection 2 The Human Spirit

Skills Focus

Skills Focus

Selection or Feature	Reading Skills and Strategies	Elements of Literature	Language/ Grammar	Vocabulary/ Spelling	Writing	Listening/ Speaking	Viewing/ Representing
Thank you, M'am Langston Hughes (p. 120)	Make Inferences, pp. 120, 127 Evaluate a Story's Credibility, p. 127 Identify Main Events, p. 127	Characters, pp. 120, 127 Motivation, p. 127 Setting, p. 127 Image, p. 127	Idioms, p. 128 Specific Modifiers, p. 129	Synonyms, p. 129	Analyze the Words and Actions of a Character, p. 128 Write a Letter from a Character, p. 128 Write a Character Sketch, p. 128 Write a Found Poem, p. 128		Make a Chart, p. 128 Use a Word Map, p. 129
Elements of Literature: Character (p. 130)		Characterization, Direct and Indirect pp. 130–131					
Harrison Bergeron Kurt Vonnegut (p. 132)	Evaluate an Author's Point of View, pp. 132, 141	Satire, pp. 132, 141 Conflict, p. 141	Misplaced Modifiers, p. 143	Word Charts, p. 143 Word Origins, p. 143 Synonyms/Antonyms, p. 143	Compare Characters, p. 142 Evaluate an Author's Position, p. 142 Create a TV Script, p. 142	Write and Perform a TV Script, p. 142	Create a Cartoon Strip, p. 142
A Christmas Memory Truman Capote (p. 144)	Make Inferences About Character, pp. 144, 161	Indirect Characterization, pp. 144, 161 Character, p. 161 Motivation, p. 161 Stereotype, p. 162	Figures of Speech, p. 163	Analogies, p. 163	Judge a Character's Credibility, p. 162 Write a Screenplay, p. 162 Write a Personal Poem, p. 162		Use a Chart, p. 144 Create a Collage, p. 162
Elements of Literature: Setting (p. 164)		Setting, p. 164 Setting and Character, p. 164 Setting and Mood, p. 165					
A Man Called Horse Dorothy M. Johnson (p. 166)	Monitor Comprehension, pp. 166, 179	Setting, pp. 166, 179	Vivid Modifiers, p. 181	Words That Can Be Confused, p. 181	Analyze Changes in a Character, p. 180 Write a Journal Entry for a Character, p. 180 Write a Book Review, p. 180		Create Graphics for a Research Report, p. 180
Salvador Late or Early Sandra Cisneros (p. 182)	Oral Interpretation, pp. 182, 187 • Speed • Pause • Pitch • Emphasis	Character, p. 186 Setting, p. 186 Image, p. 186			Identify Verbs That Define Character, p. 187 Write a Vignette, p. 187 Write a Poem, p. 187	Perform a Dramatic Reading, p. 187 Participate in a Problem-Solving Panel Discussion, p. 187	
Extending the Theme: The Washwoman Isaac Bashevis Singer (p. 188)	Dialogue with a Text, pp. 188, 192 Identify Major Topic, p. 192	The Extending the Theme feature provides students with an unstructured opportunity to practice reading strategies using a selection that extends the theme of the collection.					
Writer's Workshop: Analyzing a Character (p. 194)	Evaluate Character, p. 194				Write an Essay Analyzing a Fictional Character, pp. 194–198		Create a Graphic Organizer, pp. 194–195
Sentence Workshop: Revising Sentence Fragments (p. 199)			Sentence Fragments, p. 199		Proofread for Sentence Fragments, p. 199		
Reading for Life: Reading Memos and E-Mail (p. 200)	Identify the Parts of a Memo, p. 200 Context Clues, p. 200			Technical Terms/Jargon, p. 200	Write a Memo, p. 200		

THE HUMAN SPIRIT
WRITING FOCUS: Analyzing a Character

Most people are neither villains nor heroes. They aren't vicious enough for the one, and life doesn't give them the opportunity for the other, so their lives aren't as full of excitement as the last good movie you saw. Still, they get through each day. They work; they endure; they perform little acts of kindness and generosity. They help one another and console one another. They may even find themselves surprisingly brave. They do it without glory or excitement, without applause or notice, until someone stops to pay attention. Their stories, when they are recorded, reveal much that the human spirit is capable of. They also tell us a great deal about who we are and who we may become.

From what we get,
we can make a living;
what we give,
however, makes a life.

—Arthur Ashe

Writer's Notebook

Think about the characters you know from books and movies and TV shows. Don't stop with the characters you have met recently—think also of characters from the books you read as a child. Then, list those characters that seem especially real to you—just as real as the people you know in school or in your family. Jot down all the qualities that make those fictional characters seem like real people. You might start with "Talks the way real people talk" or "Looks the way I would expect her to look." Save your notes. You might use them later for the assignment in the Writer's Workshop on page 194.

OBJECTIVES

1. Read short stories centered on the theme "The Human Spirit"
2. Interpret literary elements used in short stories, with special emphasis on character and setting
3. Apply a variety of reading strategies to short stories
4. Respond to the literature using a variety of modes
5. Learn and use new words
6. Plan, draft, revise, edit, proof, and publish an essay analyzing a character
7. Revise sentence fragments
8. Demonstrate the ability to read memos and e-mail

Responding to the Quotation

Arthur Ashe (1955–1993) was a great athlete—the first African American tennis player to win the U.S. Open and Wimbledon championships. He is also known as a great American, a fighter for social and political justice. Ask students how making a living is different from making a life. [Possible answer: Making a living relates to money and material things. Making a life relates to emotional and spiritual things and suggests being involved with family, friends, activities, and important issues.] What do you think Arthur Ashe is saying about the difference between giving and getting? [Possible answer: Getting defines what you have, but giving reflects who you are.]

Writer's Notebook

You might have the class brainstorm the most memorable and vivid characters they have encountered from childhood to the present.

Writing Focus: Analyzing a Character

The following **Work in Progress** assignments build to a culminating **Writer's Workshop** at the end of the collection.

• Thank You, M'am	Analyzing words and actions (p. 128)
• Harrison Bergeron	Comparing characters (p. 142)
• A Christmas Memory	Analyzing credibility (p. 162)
• A Man Called Horse	Analyzing how a character changes (p. 180)
• Salvador Late or Early	Analyzing actions (p. 187)

Writer's Workshop: Expository Writing / Analyzing a Character (p. 194)

OBJECTIVES

1. Read and interpret the story
2. Analyze characters
3. Make inferences
4. Express understanding through creative writing or language analysis
5. Identify modifiers and use them in writing
6. Identify and use synonyms

SKILLS

Literary
- Analyze characters

Reading
- Make inferences

Writing
- Analyze characters
- Define and use idioms
- Write a letter from a character's point of view
- Write a character sketch
- Create poetry from prose

Language
- Identify and use modifiers

Vocabulary
- Use synonyms

Viewing/Representing
- Respond to a painting (ATE)
- Analyze an artwork (ATE)

Planning

- **Block Schedule**
  Block Scheduling Lesson Plans with Pacing Guide
- **Traditional Schedule**
  Lesson Plans Including Strategies for English-Language Learners
- **One-Stop Planner**
  CD-ROM with Test Generator

THANK YOU, M'AM

Make the Connection

Way to Go

There's a saying that when the going gets tough, the tough get going. In very tough circumstances, some people do indeed get going. They have a spirit that moves them ahead—that pushes them to do heroic things. What makes these people so tough, so strong in spirit? Why do these people turn out to be good? Why do others go so wrong?

Quickwrite

Before you read "Thank You, M'am," write two or three sentences exploring your feelings about these hard questions. List the factors that you think affect the way people turn out. Keep your notes.

Elements of Literature

Characters Under Stress

People in life and in fiction tend to reveal themselves most dramatically when they are under stress—when they are in a situation that presents a problem they must do something about. In this story two characters have a tense encounter. The writer lets their actions and their words (or their silences) tell us about the kind of people they are—or could be.

> **C**haracters under stress often reveal themselves and their values by what they say and how they act.
>
> *For more on Character, see pages 130–131 and the Handbook of Literary Terms.*

Reading Skills and Strategies

Making Inferences: Educated Guesses

Most good writers don't tell us directly what their characters are like; they allow us to make our own inferences about the kinds of people they are. When you **make an inference,** you take a leap into the unknown. You use your observations and your experience to guess about something you don't know for sure. But an inference isn't just a random guess. It's an educated guess—because it's based on evidence from the text. After you read this story, skim it again, and jot down clues that you think reveal something important about the two characters. Look at what they *say* (or don't say) and at how they *act*.

Thank You, M'am

Langston Hughes

She was a large woman with a large purse that had everything in it but hammer and nails. It had a long strap and she carried it slung across her shoulder. It was about eleven o'clock at night, and she was walking alone, when a boy ran up behind her and tried to snatch her purse. The strap broke with the single tug the boy gave it from behind. But the boy's weight and the

go.hrw.com
LEO 9-2

"Well, you didn't have to snatch my pocketbook to get some suede shoes."

Mom Alice (1944) by William H. Johnson.

The Howard University Gallery of Art, Washington, D.C.

Summary ■

Late one night Roger, who wants a pair of blue suede shoes, tries to snatch Mrs. Jones's purse as she is walking home. The attempt fails, and Mrs. Jones collars the boy, who is no match for his captor. She drags Roger home with her, feeds him, talks to him, and gives him ten dollars to buy the shoes.

Resources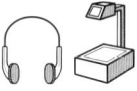

Listening
Audio CD Library
A recording of this story is provided in the *Audio CD Library:*
• Disc 6, Track 2

Viewing and Representing
Fine Art Transparency
For post-reading discussion, introduce the haunting images of city life in the artwork *Urban Faces* by Melissa Grimes. See the *Viewing and Representing Transparencies and Worksheets:*
• Transparency 3
• Worksheet, p. 12

Elements of Literature
Determining Methods of Characterization
For additional instruction on characterization, see *Literary Elements:*
• Transparency 2
• Worksheet, p. 7

> **RESPONDING TO THE ART**
> **William H. Johnson** (1901–1970) is best known for his works that portray the everyday lives of African Americans.
> **Activity.** Ask students to brainstorm adjectives to describe the woman in the painting.

Resources: Print and Media

Reading
• *Reading Skills and Strategies*
  MiniRead Skill Lesson, p. 46
  Selection Skill Lesson, p. 54
• *Graphic Organizers for Active Reading*, p. 6
• *Audio CD Library,*
  Disc 6, Track 2

Elements of Literature
• *Literary Elements*
  Transparency 2
  Worksheet, p. 7

Writing and Language
• *Daily Oral Grammar*
  Transparency 6
• *Grammar and Language Links*
  Worksheet p. 11
• *Language Workshop* CD-ROM

Viewing and Representing
• *Viewing and Representing*
  Fine Art Transparency 3
  Fine Art Worksheet p. 12

Assessment
• *Formal Assessment*, p. 13
• *Portfolio Management System*, p. 100
• *Standardized Test Preparation*, p. 18
• *Test Generator (One-Stop Planner CD-ROM)*

Internet
• go.hrw.com (keyword: LE0 9-2)

A Elements of Literature
Character

❓ What do the woman's actions reveal about her? [Possible answers: She has the strength and will and confidence to respond in a street attack; she has a strong sense of how things should be done and how people should behave; she will allow no one to rob her of her pocketbook or her dignity.]

B Reading Skills and Strategies

Making Inferences

❓ What can you infer about how dangerous or potentially violent this boy is? [Possible answers: The first word out of his mouth is "Yes'm," which suggests he is no hardened criminal but, rather, seems somewhat innocent and childlike; he is sufficiently ashamed or cowed by the situation to offer the half-apology, "I didn't aim to," which makes him seem young and innocent and barely capable of crime.]

C English Language Learners
Dialect

Point out the expression "I got a great mind to...." Tell students that this expression is also commonly phrased as "I have a mind to...." Ask them what they think it means. [Possible answers: "I'm thinking about"; "I plan to"; "I'm determined to."]

D Elements of Literature
Character

❓ What does this action reveal about Roger? [Possible answers: He realizes that the woman will not hurt him and may even help him; he wants to live up to the woman's trust in him; he is too scared to run.]

E Advanced Learners

According to biographer Arnold Rampersad, Langston Hughes lived "a lonely, passed-around childhood . . . [that] left him sensitive about his identity and self-worth." Might Roger in this story also be sensitive, lonely, unsure of his self-worth? Challenge students to prove or disprove this thesis by gathering evidence from the story and making inferences.

---

weight of the purse combined caused him to lose his balance so, instead of taking off full blast as he had hoped, the boy fell on his back on the sidewalk and his legs flew up. The large woman simply turned around and kicked him right square in his blue-jeaned sitter. Then she **(A)** reached down, picked the boy up by his shirt front, and shook him until his teeth rattled.

After that the woman said, "Pick up my pocketbook, boy, and give it here."

She still held him. But she bent down enough to permit him to stoop and pick up her purse. Then she said, "Now ain't you ashamed of yourself?"

Firmly gripped by his shirt front, the boy said, "Yes'm." *— Polite*

The woman said, "What did you want to do it **(B)** for?"

The boy said, "I didn't aim to."

She said, "You a lie!"

By that time two or three people passed, stopped, turned to look, and some stood watching.

"If I turn you loose, will you run?" asked the woman.

"Yes'm," said the boy.

"Then I won't turn you loose," said the woman. She did not release him.

"I'm very sorry, lady, I'm sorry," whispered the boy. *Apology*

"Um-hum! And your face is dirty. I got a great mind to wash your face for you. Ain't you got **(C)** nobody home to tell you to wash your face?" *≈ Dialect*

"No'm," said the boy.

"Then it will get washed this evening," said the large woman starting up the street, dragging the frightened boy behind her.

He looked as if he were fourteen or fifteen, frail and willow-wild, in tennis shoes and blue jeans.

The woman said, "You ought to be my son. I would teach you right from wrong. Least I can do right now is to wash your face. Are you hungry?"

"No'm," said the being-dragged boy. "I just want you to turn me loose."

"Was I bothering *you* when I turned that corner?" asked the woman.

"No'm."

"But you put yourself in contact with *me*," said the woman. "If you think that that contact is not going to last awhile, you got another thought coming. When I get through with you, sir, you are going to remember Mrs. Luella Bates Washington Jones."

Sweat popped out on the boy's face and he began to struggle. Mrs. Jones stopped, jerked him around in front of her, put a half nelson about his neck, and continued to drag him up the street. When she got to her door, she dragged the boy inside, down a hall, and into a large kitchenette-furnished room at the rear of the house. She switched on the light and left the door open. The boy could hear other roomers laughing and talking in the large house. Some of their doors were open, too, so he knew he and the woman were not alone. The woman still had him by the neck in the middle of her room.

She said, "What is your name?"

"Roger," answered the boy.

"Then, Roger, you go to that sink and wash your face," said the woman, whereupon she **(D)** turned him loose—at last. Roger looked at the door—looked at the woman—looked at the door—*and went to the sink.*

"Let the water run until it gets warm," she said. "Here's a clean towel."

"You gonna take me to jail?" asked the boy, bending over the sink.

"Not with that face, I would not take you nowhere," said the woman. "Here I am trying to **(E)** get home to cook me a bite to eat and you snatch my pocketbook! Maybe you ain't been to your supper either, late as it be. Have you?"

"There's nobody home at my house," said the boy.

"Then we'll eat," said the woman. "I believe you're hungry—or been hungry—to try to snatch my pocketbook."

"I wanted a pair of blue suede shoes," said the boy.

"Well, you didn't have to snatch *my* pocketbook to get some suede shoes," said Mrs. Luella Bates Washington Jones. "You could of asked me."

"M'am?"

Reaching All Students

Struggling Readers

Making Inferences was introduced on page 120. For a lesson directly tied to this story that teaches students to make inferences by using a strategy called It Says . . . I Say, see the *Reading Skills and Strategies* binder:

- MiniRead Skill Lesson, p. 46
- Selection Skill Lesson, p. 54

English Language Learners

Help students with the dialect in the story by listing on the chalkboard the standard English equivalents for the following colloquialisms: *Yes'm, didn't aim to, you a lie, gonna, late as it be, could of, I were young, set down,* as well as any other words or phrases you think would be helpful. For strategies for engaging English language learners with the literature, see

- *Lesson Plans Including Strategies for English-Language Learners*

T122

Digestive System (1989) by James Romberger. Pastel on paper (57″ x 60″).

Getting Students Involved

Cooperative Learning

Reading Between the Lines. As in a real conversation, there is plenty in this story's dialogue that is left unsaid. Invite students to work in pairs or small groups to create a more extended subtext for the dialogue in the story. Point out that what the characters say only scratches the surface of what they are thinking, feeling, and communicating. To start students off, suggest that they isolate the dialogue on a page of the story. Then, for everything said, ask them to record what could have been said but wasn't—any thoughts or feelings of the characters that are not directly revealed. Invite groups to present their conjectures in a manner of their choice. For example, student pairs might act out a single character—one reading the dialogue from the story and one reading the below-the-surface dialogue; or they might draw comic book characters whose spoken thoughts are placed in speech balloons emanating from their mouths but whose unspoken thoughts and feelings appear as captions.

T123

The water dripping from his face, the boy looked at her. There was a long pause. A very long pause. After he had dried his face and, not knowing what else to do, dried it again, the boy turned around, wondering what next. The door was open. He could make a dash for it down the hall. He could run, run, run, run, *run*!

The woman was sitting on the daybed. After a while she said, "I were young once and I wanted things I could not get."

A There was another long pause. The boy's mouth opened. Then he frowned, but not knowing he frowned.

The woman said, "Um-hum! You thought I was going to say *but,* didn't you? You thought I was going to say, *but I didn't snatch people's pocketbooks.* Well, I wasn't going to say that." Pause. Silence. "I have done things, too, which I would not tell you, son—neither tell God, if He didn't already know. So you set down while I fix us something to eat. You might run that comb through your hair so you will look presentable."

In another corner of the room behind a screen was a gas plate and an icebox. Mrs. Jones got up and went behind the screen. The woman did not watch the boy to see if he was going to run now, nor did she watch her purse which she left behind her on the daybed. But the boy took care to sit on the far side of the room where he thought she could easily see him out of the corner of her eye, if she wanted to. He did not trust the woman *not* to trust him. And **B** he did not want to be mistrusted now.

"Do you need somebody to go the store," asked the boy, "maybe to get some milk or something?"

Mom Sammy (1938) by Henry Bozeman Jones.

The Howard University Gallery of Art, Washington, D.C.

"Don't believe I do," said the woman, "unless you just want sweet milk yourself. I was going to make cocoa out of this canned milk I got here."

"That will be fine," said the boy.

She heated some lima beans and ham she had in the icebox, made the cocoa, and set the table. The woman did not ask the boy anything about where he lived, or his folks, or anything else that would embarrass him. Instead, as they ate, she told him about her job in a hotel beauty shop that stayed open late, what the work was like, and how all kinds of women came in and out, blondes, redheads, and Spanish. Then she cut him a half of her ten-cent cake.

"Eat some more, son," she said.

When they were finished eating she got up and said, "Now, here, take this ten dollars and buy yourself some blue suede shoes. **C** And next time, do not make the mistake of latching onto *my* pocketbook *nor nobody else's*—because shoes come by devilish like that will burn your feet. I got to get my rest now. But I wish you would behave yourself, son, from here on in."

She led him down the hall to the front door and opened it. "Good night! Behave yourself, boy!" she said, looking out into the street.

The boy wanted to say something else other than "Thank you, m'am" to Mrs. Luella Bates Washington Jones, but he couldn't do so as he **D** turned at the barren stoop and looked back at the large woman in the door. He barely managed to say "Thank you," before she shut the door. And he never saw her again.

Resources ───────

Selection Assessment
Formal Assessment
- Selection Test, p. 13
Test Generator (One-Stop Planner)
- CD-ROM

BROWSING IN THE FILES

About the Author. Although Hughes had written poetry and a novel, he did not start writing short stories until he was in his thirties. While he was on a tour of Russia, a friend lent him a collection of short stories by the English writer D. H. Lawrence. Those stories affected Hughes so deeply that he wrote the first of his own stories. In his short stories, as in much of his poetry, Hughes re-created Harlem again and again. Critic Arthur P. Davis made this observation: "Called the poet laureate of Harlem, Hughes retained all his life a deep love for that colorful city within a city.... To Hughes, Harlem was place, symbol, and on occasion, protagonist."

Writers on Writing. Hughes claimed that the writing of others saved him and that this salvation occurred at a very young age. Beginning at about age seven, said Hughes, he "began to believe in nothing but books and the wonderful world in books—where if people suffered, they suffered in beautiful language, not in monosyllables, as we did in Kansas."

MEET THE WRITER

A Lonely Child

Langston Hughes (1902–1967) was a lonely child who moved often and felt distant from his parents, who eventually divorced. Hughes was born in Joplin, Missouri, graduated from high school in Cleveland, Ohio, and eventually graduated from Lincoln University in Pennsylvania. Early in his adult life Hughes took on a variety of jobs. The man who was later known as one of the great original voices in American literature was at various times a cook, sailor, beachcomber, launderer, doorman, and busboy. Hughes traveled to many parts of the world, but he is chiefly associated with Harlem in New York City. His most creative work was done at his typewriter near a third-floor rear apartment window overlooking a Harlem back yard. We can easily imagine this setting as his inspiration for "Thank You, M'am."

More About Hughes

Hughes has been fortunate in his biographer. Arnold Rampersad, a professor of English at Princeton University, has published two volumes of a very readable biography of Hughes, *I, Too, Sing America* and *I Dream a World* (Oxford University Press).

THANK YOU, M'AM 125

Making the Connections

Connecting to the Theme: "The Human Spirit"

Students will quite readily associate Mrs. Jones with some of the nobler tendencies of the human spirit. But it may be harder for them to relate the character of Roger, and what happens to him, to the theme. Students can discuss the following questions in small groups and then share their best ideas and insights with the class.

- Is Roger a villain in any way? Does he represent a single individual, or do you think he represents a larger segment of society? What universal ideas about being human might he represent?
- In what ways are both Mrs. Jones and Roger almost "all too human"—that is, everyday people with imperfections? In what ways does this interaction between the two of them elevate them both?
- Do you think most people have some version of a "thank you, m'am" story in their own personal history? If so, what forms might that story take?

This magazine article focuses on Fanniedell Peeples, an elderly woman who volunteered her time and her love to take care of infants at a Detroit hospital.

Ⓐ Reading Skills and Strategies

Making Predictions

Encourage students to study the photograph and read the title. Ask them to predict what the article will be about. [Possible answers: The woman shown in the photo is the "volunteer of love"; the feature is about a woman who freely gives her love to help babies who are ill.]

Ⓑ Elements of Literature

Character

❓ What do the woman's actions reveal about her character? [Sample responses: Her gentle voice and manner show that she is loving; her absorption in the baby reveals her generous nature and her commitment to the baby's needs.]

Ⓒ Struggling Readers

Summarizing

❓ What does Peeples give to these babies? [She gives them her time and love and stays with them while they die, so they will not be alone.]

Connections — A NEWS FEATURE

Ⓐ A Volunteer Of Love

DENISE CRITTENDON

Ⓑ An old woman is relaxing in a rocking chair, softly humming a lullaby and holding an infant close to her chest. She stares at the baby, gazing into wide eyes, gently stroking wispy strands of hair. She sings to her; whispers to her.

"I see you fighting sleep. Yes I can," the woman says, her singsongy voice barely above a murmur.

For Fanniedell Peeples, this is a cherished moment. She is one of several Detroit hospital volunteers who take turns caressing the infants who rarely have visitors. Many are crack-cocaine or HIV positive babies. Others are wards of the court, or abandoned children with a host of medical problems. Some have loving family members, some don't. But, says Peeples, "they are human beings and they need human contact."

Ⓒ Peeples won't let them be alone, so sick and so helpless. They won't die alone either. She goes to great lengths to ensure that she is beside her "friends" when they take their final breath. "They feel the love and care and touch you give them because they are sponges of feeling," she explains. "So I stroke and I care and I sing and I rock as they're on their way out. I think that's the least we can do since they have missed so many things. We owe them the dignity to leave as human beings."

—from *The Crisis*

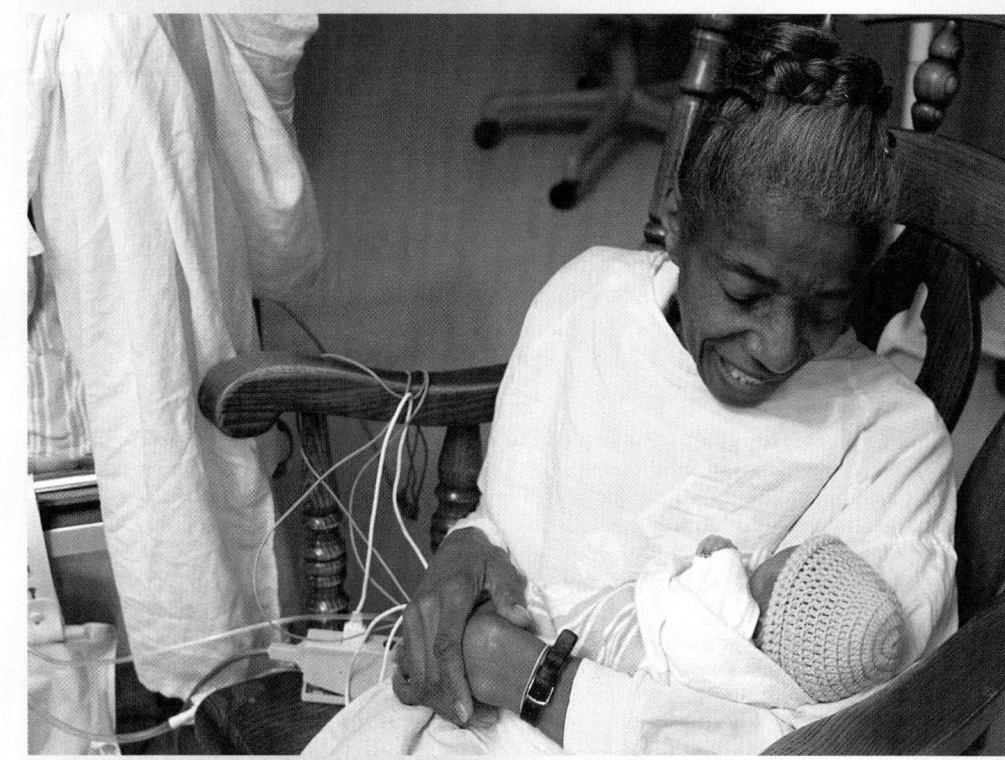

A cherished moment: Fanniedell Peeples with an infant.

Connecting Across Texts

Connecting with "Thank You M'am"

To help students link "A Volunteer of Love" with "Thank You, M'am," have them work in pairs. Ask partners to discuss the following questions:

• Would "A Volunteer of Love" be a good alternate title for "Thank You M'am"? Why or why not?

• What do Mrs. Luella Bates Washington Jones and Fanniedell Peeples have in common? How are they different?

• If Mrs. Jones's encounter with Roger became a news event, how do you think it would be covered? Which story would be more sensational—Peeples's or Jones's? Why?

• What story elements would be needed to turn Fanniedell Peeples into a fictional character and to make this news story into a short story?

Invite partners to share and compare their thoughts with the class.

First Thoughts

[respond]

1. Which **image,** or picture, in Hughes's story stands out most clearly in your mind?

Shaping Interpretations

[infer]

2. **Characters** under stress reveal a lot about themselves. What can we infer about Mrs. Jones and Roger from the ways they react to stress? Draw and fill in a chart like this one to collect your ideas. The last column is where you'll write your inference.

Character	Cause of Stress	Reactions	What Reactions Reveal
Mrs. Jones			
Roger			

[infer]

3. Do you think Roger has stolen before? Go back to the story to see if the writer gives any clues to suggest why Roger has gone wrong. Write down the lines that hint at possible explanations.

[analyze]

4. **Motivation** is the drive that leads a character to act. What do you think motivates Mrs. Jones to give Roger money? Why do you think Mrs. Jones tells Roger that she too has done things she is not proud of?

[infer]

5. What do you think the boy wanted to say, other than "Thank you, m'am"?

[analyze]

6. How does Mrs. Jones's **setting**—her furnished room, the screen with a gas plate and icebox behind it, the ten-cent cake, the noisy tenement—contribute to your sense of the kind of person she is? What details can your imagination add to her surroundings?

Extending the Text

[infer]

7. Some stories leave us with the feeling that there is more to tell. What past can you create for Mrs. Jones? What do you imagine her future holds?

[respond]

8. Think back to your Quickwrite and your ideas about what makes some people turn out to be so good while others go wrong. What do you think made the fictional Mrs. Jones and the real-life Fanniedell Peeples (see *Connections* on page 126) so good?

Challenging the Text

[evaluate]

9. Is the story credible to you—that is, based on your experience, can you believe that these events could happen as Hughes describes them? Why, or why not?

THANK YOU, M'AM 127

Reading Check

Write down the **main events** of this story as if you were reporting them for a newspaper. Answer the questions reporters are told to answer in their news articles: **What** happened? **Whom** did it happen to? **When** and **where** did it happen? **Why** did it happen?

Then compare your lists of events in class. Did you all remember the same details?

Reading Check

Sample answer: As Mrs. Jones is walking home at eleven o'clock at night, a teenage boy named Roger attempts to steal her purse. Mrs. Jones stops him, drags him to her furnished room, and talks with him about her own past, showing that she knows what it's like to be young and in trouble. She "mothers" him, giving him dinner, some good advice, and ten dollars—which she can ill-afford—for his heart's desire: blue suede shoes. They part forever.

First Thoughts

1. Possible responses: the woman dragging the boy; Roger, at the end of the story, looking back at the woman.

Shaping Interpretations

2. Sample responses: For Mrs. Jones, cause of stress—the purse snatching; her reactions—taking Roger home, feeding him, and giving him money; reveals—her compassion, levelheadedness, good judgment. For Roger, causes of stress— lack of money and family, getting caught, being trusted; his reactions—stealing, feeling regret and fear, trying to earn trust; reveals—his desperation, his basic innocence, his need for love and his wish to live up to Mrs. Jones's belief in him.

3. The boy's bungled attempt at stealing and his mumbled apology are evidence that he's not a practiced thief. Clues to his behavior include his replying "No'm" to Luella's question "Ain't you got nobody home to tell you to wash your face?" (p. 122).

4. Mrs. Jones might give Roger money because she realizes how critical his situation is or because someone did the same for her once. She might reveal her own past mistakes to let Roger know that he has worth and is not alone in his misstep or to show him that he can turn his life in the right direction, like she did.

5. Possible responses: He was touched by her kindness; he will not steal again.

6. The surroundings suggest a financial struggle, showing that Mrs. Jones's charity is a true act of generosity. Students may imagine a threadbare carpet or modest belongings.

Extending the Text

7. Possible responses: Her past may include a difficult, impoverished childhood and a misdeed that led to someone helping her change her life; her future may be like the present or may include a new job helping others.

8. Possible answer: Perhaps they have been helped in their own past.

Challenging the Text

9. Possible responses: It is credible because Roger is young enough to be helped and the story takes place before guns were prevalent; it is not credible because a boy like Roger would most likely run away.

T127

Rubrics for each Choices assignment appear on p. 100 in the *Portfolio Management System*

CHOICES: Building Your Portfolio

1. **Writer's Notebook** With each selection, a Writer's Notebook activity appears as the first option in the Choices section. These brief, work-in-progress assignments build toward the writing assignment presented in the Writer's Workshop at the end of the collection. If students save their work for their Writer's Notebook activities as they move through the collection, they should be able to use some of it as starting points for the workshop on p. 194.

2. **Language Analysis** If students have trouble coming up with idioms, remind them that they are listed in the dictionary. One strategy for finding idioms is to look under common verbs such as *give, look,* and *take* and find the idioms listed in each entry.

3. **Creative Writing** Invite students to brainstorm in small groups before they begin writing. They might talk about where the older Roger might live, the job he might have, and the relationships or family he may have in his life.

4. **Creative Writing** Even though students are working from a real-life example, encourage them to give their character a fictional name in order to preserve the person's privacy and prevent any possible misrepresentation.

5. **Creative Writing** In addition to shaping their poems visually, students might work with rhythm by identifying stressed syllables and rearranging the word order.

CHOICES: Building Your Portfolio

Writer's Notebook

1. Collecting Ideas for an Essay Analyzing a Character

Words and actions. Langston Hughes never tells us directly what kind of people Roger and Mrs. Jones are. What do the words (or dialogue) and the actions of these two characters reveal about their true natures? Make a chart like the one below, showing what we learn from each character's words and actions.

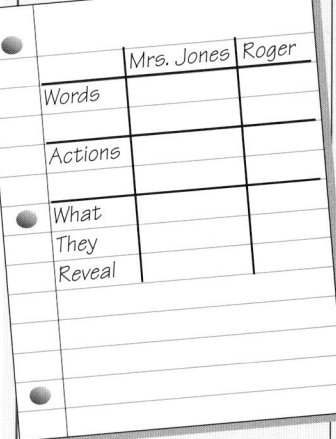

	Mrs. Jones	Roger
Words		
Actions		
What They Reveal		

You might want to refer to the chart you made in answer to question 2 on page 127. Save your notes for the Writer's Workshop on page 194.

Language Analysis

2. Idioms—Don't Take Them Literally

When it's raining cats and dogs, you don't expect creatures to be falling from the sky. Every language has **idioms** like that one, phrases and expressions that mean something different from their literal meaning. How would you explain the following idioms, used in the story, to someone who has just started to learn English?

- take off full blast
- have a bite to eat
- make a dash for it
- latch on to my pocketbook

With a partner, write five entries for a classroom dictionary of English idioms. Use each idiom in a sentence, and then write a definition of it.

Creative Writing

3. A Letter from Roger

What do you think Roger will be like ten years after his encounter with Mrs. Jones? What might he write in a letter to her? Compose a letter from Roger. Write as "I." You will have to write Roger's present address inside your letter. Be sure you state the purpose of his communication after all these years.

Creative Writing

4. Character Up Close

You may not realize it, but the people around you are very interesting. Select a person you know whom you can use as the subject of a character sketch. Think of that person's spirit—how does he or she cope with joy and sorrow, trouble and success? Describe what the person looks like, how he or she acts under stress, how other people respond to him or her. Describe the person's setting. You may want to tell an anecdote, or little story, about the person. Choose your details carefully. Hughes needed only a few details to bring Mrs. Jones to life.

Creative Writing

5. Found Poetry

Sometimes poetry is found embedded in prose paragraphs. Sometimes it's found in news articles, even in weather forecasts or recipes. Find the paragraph from "Thank You, M'am" that begins "In another corner of the room" and reformat it so that it looks like a poem. Break the sentences into lines that seem right to you. Use very short lines for dramatic effect. Change any words you wish to. It will be up to you to decide where to end your poem.

Crossing the Curriculum

Economics

From a Ten-Cent Cake to a Ten-Dollar Bill. Just how generous was Mrs. Jones to Roger? Tell students that her gift of ten dollars was a significant sum for a poor, single, elderly, working-class woman of the time. Explain that this story was first published in *The Langston Hughes Reader* in 1958 and was set in about 1955. What was ten dollars then worth in today's money? Students may find the answer by using resources. One place to look is *The Statistical Abstract of the United States,* in print or online, which has information on consumer prices for things such as food. Counsel students to carefully read all the information about using the tables; point out that statistics are keyed to a base year. Students might also generate and answer other researchable questions about the economy and buying power of the time and place.

LANGUAGE LINK `MINI-LESSON`

Language Handbook HELP

See Using Modifiers, page 1003.

Technology HELP

See Language Workshop CD-ROM. Key word entry: modifiers.

Modifiers Make Meanings More Definite

Modifiers make our writing more specific, more exact, or more definite. Notice how adjectives help us clearly visualize those blue suede shoes that Roger wants so much. Adjectives answer the questions *What kind? Which one? How many?* or *How much?* Adverbs answer the questions *Where? When? How often? In what way?* or *To what extent?* The modifiers in Hughes's sentences that follow are single words, compound words, and phrases.

1. "The <u>large</u> woman <u>simply</u> turned <u>around</u> and kicked him <u>right square</u> in his <u>blue-jeaned</u> sitter."

2. "He looked as if he were <u>fourteen or fifteen</u>, <u>frail</u> and <u>willow-wild</u>, <u>in tennis shoes and blue jeans</u>."

3. ". . . she dragged the boy <u>into a large kitchenette-furnished room in the rear of the house</u>."

Try It Out

➤ Rewrite each sentence at the left three times, replacing the underlined modifiers with words and phrases of your own. Each time, give Mrs. Jones or the boy or the setting a totally different appearance. (For example, you might put Roger in combat boots and a leather jacket.)

➤ When you write a description of a character, look carefully at your modifiers. Try to find very exact adverbs that will make your character's actions clearer. Search for the best adjectives to describe a detail of your character's appearance or setting. Don't overdo it with modifiers, though. Sometimes a simple word is best. Notice that Hughes describes Mrs. Jones's stoop—the stairs to her tenement—with one powerful adjective: The stoop is simply "barren."

VOCABULARY `HOW TO OWN A WORD`

Synonyms

Although a **synonym** is a word that has the same or almost the same meaning as another word, synonyms are not always interchangeable. Often synonyms will have subtle but distinct shades of difference in meaning. Here are three words from the first paragraph of the story: *large, carried,* and *fell.* Find the sentences the words are used in. Then make a map like the one here for each word. Could the synonyms work just as well in each sentence?

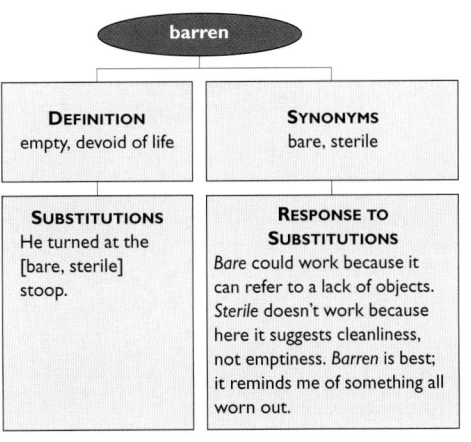

barren

DEFINITION	**SYNONYMS**
empty, devoid of life	bare, sterile
SUBSTITUTIONS	**RESPONSE TO SUBSTITUTIONS**
He turned at the [bare, sterile] stoop.	*Bare* could work because it can refer to a lack of objects. *Sterile* doesn't work because here it suggests cleanliness, not emptiness. *Barren* is best; it reminds me of something all worn out.

LANGUAGE LINK

Ask students to select a piece of writing from their portfolios in which they described people, places, or things. Have them highlight the modifiers they used. Then, have them evaluate whether their modifiers are definite, precise, and exact. Ask them to revise their writing either by replacing an existing modifier with a better choice or by adding or deleting a modifier.

Try It Out
Possible Answers

1. The <u>frail</u> woman <u>sadly</u> turned <u>left</u> and kicked him <u>half-heartedly</u> in his <u>velvet-clad</u> sitter.

2. He looked as if he were <u>nineteen or twenty</u>, <u>strong-boned</u> and <u>cleancut</u>, <u>in dress shoes and a dark suit</u>.

3. . . . she dragged the boy <u>into the enormous entrance hall of the spacious mansion</u>.

VOCABULARY
Possible Answers

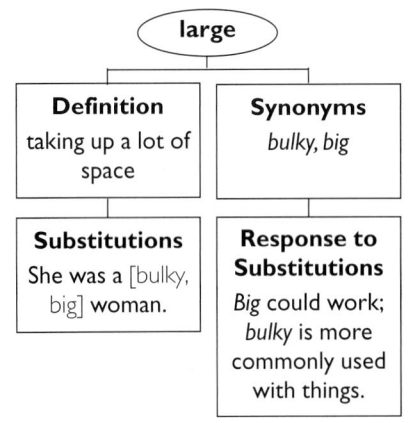

large

Definition	**Synonyms**
taking up a lot of space	*bulky, big*
Substitutions	**Response to Substitutions**
She was a [bulky, big] woman.	*Big* could work; *bulky* is more commonly used with things.

Language Link Quick Check

Circle the modifiers in the following sentences. Tell whether each modifier is an adjective or an adverb. Then, tell whether it is a word, a compound word, or a phrase.

1. In high school, Hughes read works by Carl Sandburg and Vachel Lindsay and began to write poetry. [*In high school*: adverb phrase; *by Carl Sandburg and Vachel Lindsay*: adjective phrase]

2. Once the poet Vachel Lindsay ate dinner in a Washington restaurant. [*Once*: adverb (single word); *in a Washington restaurant*: adverb phrase]

3. Hughes left a few of his own poems on Lindsay's table. [*of his own*: adjective phrase; *on Lindsay's table*: adverb phrase]

4. Lindsay read the poems at his performance later on. [*at his performance*: adverb phrase; *later on*: adverb (compound)]

5. By morning, Hughes was "discovered." [*By morning*: adverb phrase]

OBJECTIVES

1. Recognize methods of characterization such as speech, appearance, thoughts, and actions
2. Identify indirect and direct methods of characterization

Resources

Elements of Literature
Character
For additional instruction on character, see *Literary Elements:*
• Transparency 2

Elements of Literature

This feature focuses on how authors reveal characters through methods of indirect and direct characterization.

Mini-Lesson:
Character

After students have read the feature, ask them to recall "Thank You, M'am." Remind them that they learned that characters under stress may reveal themselves quickly through their actions and words (p. 120). Then, write *indirect characterization* on the board, and ask a student to define it. Call on volunteers to name the five different methods of indirect characterization. As they do, write each method on the board: the character's speech, actions, appearance, and private thoughts; how other characters in the story feel about that character. Next, have students define *direct characterization*. Discuss the types of information likely to be gained through each method of characterization. Ask questions like these:

• What parts of speech might writers rely on to describe a character's appearance? [adjectives, with the nouns they modify] What parts of speech might writers use to describe the way a character speaks or performs an action? [adverbs, along with the verbs they modify]
• Why would information about a character's private thoughts be more revealing than what the character says? [Possible answers: Private thoughts are not guarded because they are not intended for an audience; what characters say may be only an abbreviated or censored form of what they actually think.]

T130

Elements of Literature

CHARACTER: Revealing Human Nature

Creating characters—telling what human beings are like—is the whole point of writing stories. A story is really only interesting to us as readers because of what it tells us about people and how it makes us feel about them.

A magazine editor once told me that all you need to tell a story is a character, an adjective, and a series of choices that the character must make. Let's call our character Adam, give him the adjective *cheap,* have him invite Tina out for her birthday, and see what happens.

If we are told that he has fifty dollars yet walks Tina the sixteen blocks to the concert, pretending not to notice the approaching bus, we know our Adam. We are not surprised when Adam chooses cheap seats in the bleachers. Later, at the restaurant, we know he'll be looking anxiously at the right-hand side of the menu (where the prices are listed).

What we are curious about is how Tina will respond to this cheap character. Suppose that at the restaurant, Adam recommends, instead of the four-dollar hamburger, the ten-dollar steak? A surprise, a change in character! Love, that powerful tonic, has done what no amount of reasoning could do—and we recognize with satisfaction a truth, a revelation of how we and our fellow human beings behave.

Of course, people are much more complex than a single adjective can suggest, and that is the joy, and the difficulty, of storytelling. How does a writer build a character out of words, someone who will seem to become flesh and blood and rise off the page, a fully realized Scarlett O'Hara or Ebenezer Scrooge or Huck Finn?

> **A**ll you need to tell a story is a character, an adjective, and a series of choices that the character must make.

Creating Characters

1. The most obvious method of characterization is the character's **speech**. Think of how you can recognize your friends from what they say—not just from their tone of voice, but also from the kinds of words they use (big inflated words or little punchy ones; formal words or slangy ones). Think of how some people reveal their values by using words that always allude to what things cost, rather than to how pleasurable or beautiful they are. Reading the characters' dialogue in a story is like listening in on a conversation.

2. Writers also use **appearance** to create character. We can tell so much simply from the way a writer describes how a person looks and sounds. Charles Dickens lets us see Scrooge at once:

> The cold within him froze his old features, nipped his pointed nose, shriveled his cheek, stiffened his gait; made his eyes red, his thin lips blue; and spoke out shrewdly in his grating voice. . . .

Clearly, Dickens wants us to think of Scrooge as a character whose cold heart is reflected in his whole appearance.

The kinds of clothes a

Getting Students Involved

Discussion Activity

Write the following list of actions on the chalkboard, and challenge students to work in pairs to come up with at least two characterizations that could account for the action.

1. misplaces something [absent-minded; worried]
2. cheats at cards [compulsive liar; inferiority complex]
3. cooks an elaborate dinner [gourmet; always trying to impress]

4. types all homework [compulsively neat; conscientious]
5. stars in school play [talented actor; class clown]
6. Offers to clean garage [generous; scavenger]
As a follow-up, ask volunteers to suggest how each action listed above might also reveal a character's motive.

by John Leggett

character wears can give us hints too. As readers, we will respond one way to a character wearing a pin-striped suit and carrying a briefcase, and another way to a character wearing faded jeans and carrying a copy of *Of Mice and Men*.

3. In fiction a writer can even take us into the characters' minds to reveal their **private thoughts**. In this sense fiction has an advantage over real life. We might learn that one character detests his brother's drinking or that another one sympathizes with his father for his troubles at his job. We might learn how one character secretly feels when he sees the bully picking on the smallest kid in the schoolyard or how another feels as she watches her grandmother's coffin being lowered into the ground.

4. We can learn about characters by watching **how other characters in the story feel about them**. We might learn, for instance, that a salesman is a good guy in the eyes of his

customers and a generous tipper in the eyes of the local waiter; but he is cranky and selfish in the eyes of his family. Dickens tells us how Scrooge affected other people:

> Nobody ever stopped him in the street to say, with gladsome looks, "My dear Scrooge, how are you? When will you come to see me?" No beggars implored him to bestow a trifle, no children asked him what it was o'clock, no man or woman ever once in all his life inquired the way to such and such a place, of Scrooge. Even the blind men's dogs appeared to know him; and when they saw him coming on, would tug their owners into doorways. . . .

5. Most of all, we understand characters in fiction from their **actions,** from what we see them doing. How would you react to a girl of sixteen who, when you first meet her in a story, is dyeing her hair green? How would you react to another who, at five-thirty in the morning, is out delivering

newspapers? Scrooge, when we first meet him on Christmas Eve, is working on his accounts—an action that instantly reveals his obsession with money.

6. Some writers use **direct characterization** too. This means that a writer tells us directly what a character is like or what a person's motives are. In a famous listing of adjectives, Dickens tells us directly what kind of person Scrooge is:

> Oh, but he was a tightfisted hand at the grindstone, Scrooge! a squeezing, wrenching, grasping, scraping, clutching, covetous old sinner!

Modern writers do not tell us much directly about their characters. They most often use the first five methods listed here, which are called **indirect characterization**. This means that a writer *shows* us a character but allows us to interpret for ourselves the kind of person we are meeting. In fiction, as in life itself, it is much more satisfying to discover for ourselves what characters are truly like.

Applying the Element
To reinforce students' understanding of characterization, ask them these questions about the characters in "Thank You, M'am":

- Does Hughes use direct or indirect characterization? [indirect] Explain your answer. [The characterization is indirect because Hughes does not say outright, for example, that Roger is a neglected, shy kid or that Mrs. Jones is a tough woman who has suffered some guilt of her own. Instead, the reader must infer these things on the basis of what the characters themselves say and do.]
- How does Mrs. Jones's appearance help to characterize her? [Possible answer: The fact that she is big makes her an imposing figure—physically powerful and psychologically impressive.]
- How does Roger's appearance help to characterize him? [Possible answers: The boy's frailness suggests that he is in need of both physical and spiritual "feeding"; it makes him seem vulnerable to the large and imposing Mrs. Jones.]

Resources
Assessment
Formal Assessment
- Literary Elements Test, p. 22

Using Students' Strengths

Kinesthetic Learners
Form a group of these students. Have them each write on a slip of paper a type of character, such as "a fast-talking, finger-snapping teenager," "a smooth and powerful corporate executive," "a fiery elderly politician." Students can then take turns drawing a slip and role-playing the character identified. Other students in the group should identify the method(s) of characterization that the role-player is using.

Verbal Learners
Working together in a small group, have these students skim through the stories the class has already read to try to locate examples of each of the six different methods of characterization (five indirect and one direct). Ask them to create a chart listing each method and an example of its use from one of the stories. Post the chart in the classroom to help all students understand characterization.

OBJECTIVES

1. Read and interpret the story
2. Recognize satire
3. Evaluate the author's point of view
4. Express understanding through critical and creative writing or drawing
5. Identify misplaced modifiers, and place them correctly in writing
6. Understand and use new words
7. Use a dictionary to obtain information about words

SKILLS

Literary
• Recognize satire

Reading
• Evaluate the author's point of view

Writing
• Compare and contrast characters
• Explain a position
• Write a script based on the story

Art
• Draw a cartoon strip

Grammar
• Identify and correct misplaced modifiers

Vocabulary
• Use new words
• Use a dictionary

Viewing/Representing
• Relate artworks to the story (ATE)

Planning

• **Traditional Schedule**
Lesson Plans Including Strategies for English-Language Learners

• **One-Stop Planner**
CD-ROM with Test Generator

Before You Read

HARRISON BERGERON

Make the Connection

Free to Be . . .

Here are three big *what if's:*
What if people were so completely controlled by a powerful government that everyone was just like everyone else? What if all competition were removed from society? What if technology became so advanced that it could read thoughts?

Quickwrite

Take a few minutes to write down your thoughts about these *what-if* questions. Jot down everything that comes to your mind.

Elements of Literature

Laughing at the Ridiculous

You read and hear satire all the time. **Satire** is the use of language or pictures to mock some weakness in individuals or in society or in human nature. Satire is used on late-night talk shows, on TV sitcoms, in the comics, in movies. The methods of satire are mockery and exaggeration: When something is presented to us as ridiculous, its flaws comically exaggerated, we have to laugh.

The satirists hope that this laughter is the first step in bringing about change.

> **S**atire is any kind of writing or speaking or art that ridicules or mocks some weakness in individuals or in society. The main weapon of the satirist is laughter.
>
> *For more on Satire, see the Handbook of Literary Terms.*

Reading Skills and Strategies

Evaluating an Author's Point of View

To discover the satirist's point of view—that is, to understand how the writer feels about the subject—you have to read carefully and trust your instincts. Note where the writer uses exaggeration. Be aware of what the writer wants you to laugh at. "Listen" to the writer's tone. In this story you will notice a satiric point of view in the very first paragraph. What details tell you that Vonnegut doesn't admire this fictional future society? What

does Vonnegut do to make that society seem ridiculous?

You may or may not agree with the writer's point of view. Either way, when you read satire, you must read critically. Think about whether or not you agree—and why or why not.

go.hrw.com
LEO 9-2

Gift of Laila and Thurston Twigg-Smith. Collection of Whitney Museum of American Art, New York. © 1995 Whitney Museum of American Art. 93.139.

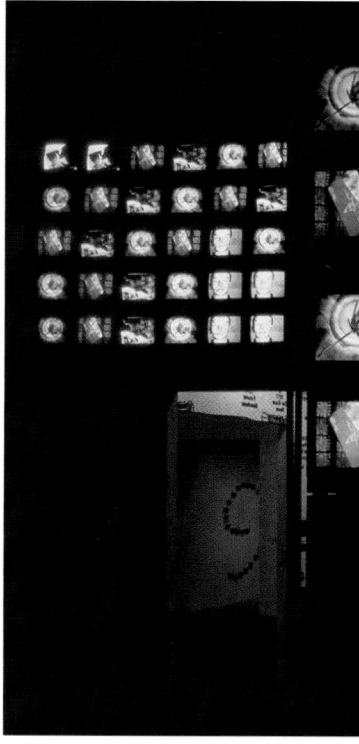

132 THE SHORT-STORY COLLECTIONS

Preteaching Vocabulary

Words to Own

Ask students to work in pairs to read the Words to Own and their definitions at the bottom of the selection pages. Next, have the partners take turns asking and answering questions that include the words. Then, to reinforce their understanding of the words, have students complete each of the following analogies using one of the Words to Own.

1. *Forks* are to *implements* as *handcuffs* are to ____. [hindrances]
2. *Hated* is to *despised* as *cringed* is to ____. [cowered]
3. *Predictable* is to *regularity* as *balanced* is to ____. [symmetry]
4. *Movements* are to *coordinating* as *watches* are to ____. [synchronizing]
5. *Sorrow* is to *grief* as *bewilderment* is to ____. [consternation]

Harrison Bergeron

Kurt Vonnegut

The year was 2081, and everybody was finally equal.

The year was 2081, and everybody was finally equal. They weren't only equal before God and the law. They were equal every which way. Nobody was smarter than anybody else. Nobody was better looking than anybody else. Nobody was stronger or quicker than anybody else. All this equality was due to the 211th, 212th, and 213th Amendments to the Constitution, and to the unceasing vigilance of agents of the United States Handicapper General.

(A)

Fin de Siecle, II (1989) by Nam June Paik.
201 television sets with four laser discs (480″ x 168″ x 60″).

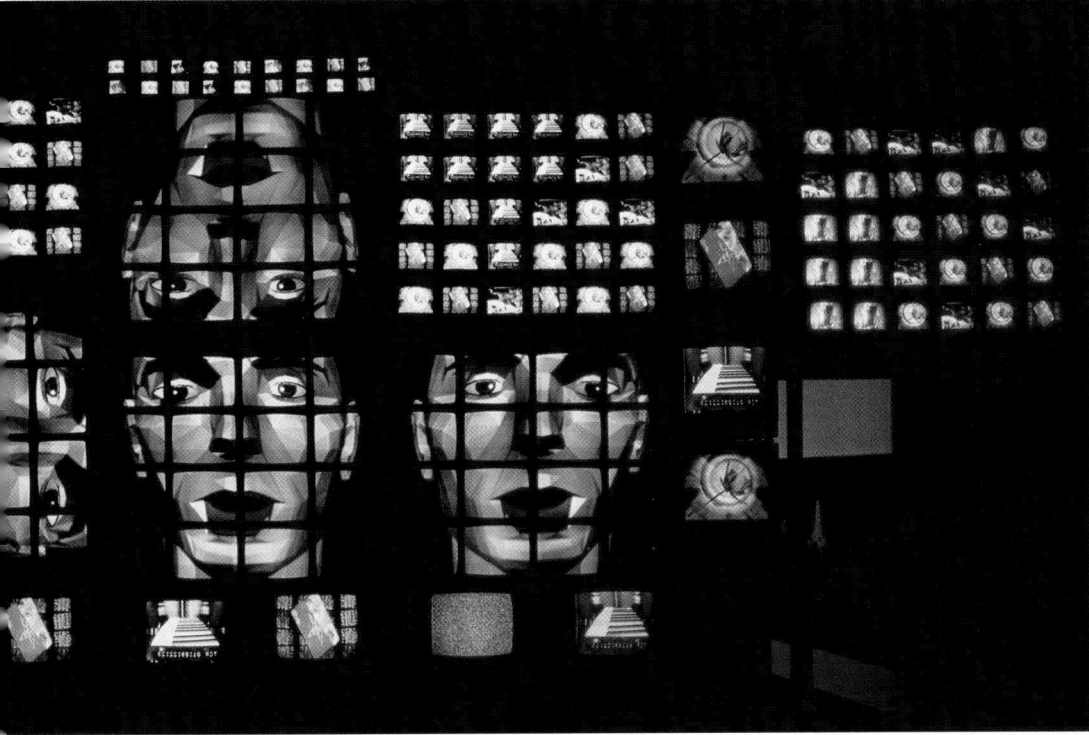

Summary ■ ■

In this satire set in 2081, the government has made everyone equal "every which way" by forcing people with greater talents, intelligence, or beauty to wear handicaps. One night, George and Hazel see their son Harrison, who is handicapped to an extreme degree, disrupt a television show. He removes his handicaps, declares himself the new emperor, and dances with a ballerina. Chaos ensues in the television studio, and—in the story's shocking climax— the audience watches the Handicapper General kill the couple for their defiance. Later, George and Hazel have a vague notion of having seen something sad on television, but their handicaps make the memory dim and hazy.

Resources

Listening
Audio CD Library
A recording of this story is available in the *Audio CD Library:*
• Disc 6, Track 3

(A) Elements of Literature
Satire
? What is funny, in a mocking or critical way, about this opening paragraph? [Possible answers: The very idea that everyone could be precisely equal is ridiculous; the idea that equality in intelligence, looks, and talent could be achieved by constitutional amendments is mockingly funny; the number of amendments is grossly exaggerated and comical.]

RESPONDING TO THE ART
Born in South Korea, **Nam June Paik** (1932–) is best known for his video installations—for example, old TV sets transformed into goldfish bowls or candles or modified to display unusual electronic effects.
Activity. Ask students to speculate about the artist's message. Point out that *fin de siecle* is French for "end of the century." How is his "end of the century" like the near-end of the twenty-first century in "Harrison Bergeron"?

Resources: Print and Media

Reading
• *Graphic Organizers for Active Reading,* p. 7
• *Words to Own,* p. 6
• *Audio CD Library*
  Disc 6, Track 3

Writing and Language
• *Daily Oral Grammar*
  Transparency 7

• *Grammar and Language Links* Worksheet, p. 13
• *Language Workshop CD-ROM*

Assessment
• *Formal Assessment,* p. 15
• *Portfolio Management System,* p. 102
• *Test Generator (One-Stop Planner CD-ROM)*

Internet
• go.hrw.com (keyword: LEO 9-2)

A Struggling Readers

Questioning

Remind students to ask questions as they read. Encourage them to identify questions they could ask at this point. [Possible questions: Who are the H-G men? Why do they take away a fourteen-year-old child?]

B Elements of Literature

Satire

[?] What is the target of the author's satire here? [Through exaggeration, he pokes fun at the average person's supposedly short attention span.]

C Reading Skills and Strategies

Evaluating the Author's Point of View

[?] What opinion do you think the author is expressing about the role of government in this society? [He suggests that the government does not want people to think; this is the reason why it handicaps those who might threaten or challenge it.]

D English Language Learners

Idioms

Tell students that an idiom is an expression that has a meaning different from the literal meaning of the words. Explain that *something the cat drug* [or *dragged*] *in* is an idiom that means "someone that is messy, untidy, or bedraggled." You might point out that the expression comes from the practice cats have of mangling and dragging home their prey. Be sure students understand that the expression is not to be taken literally.

Some things about living still weren't quite right, though. April, for instance, still drove people crazy by not being springtime. And it **A** was in that clammy month that the H-G men took George and Hazel Bergeron's fourteen-year-old son, Harrison, away.

It was tragic, all right, but George and Hazel couldn't think about it very **B** hard. Hazel had a perfectly average intelligence, which meant she couldn't think about anything except in short bursts. And George, while his intelligence was way above normal, had a little mental handicap radio in his ear. He was required by law to wear it at all times. It was tuned to a govern- **C** ment transmitter. Every twenty seconds or so, the transmitter would send out some sharp noise to keep people like George from taking unfair advantage of their brains.

George and Hazel were watching television. There were tears on Hazel's cheeks, but she'd forgotten for the moment what they were about.

On the television screen were ballerinas.

A buzzer sounded in George's head. His thoughts fled in panic, like bandits from a burglar alarm.

"That was a real pretty dance, that dance they just did," said Hazel.

"Huh?" said George.

"That dance—it was nice," said Hazel.

"Yup," said George. He tried to think a little about the ballerinas. They weren't really very good—no better than anybody else would have been, anyway. They were burdened with sash weights and bags of birdshot, and their faces were masked, so that no one, seeing a free and graceful gesture or a pretty face, would feel like

D something the cat drug in. George was toying with the vague notion that maybe dancers shouldn't be handicapped. But he didn't get very far with it before another noise in his ear radio scattered his thoughts.

George winced. So did two out of the eight ballerinas.

Pachuco (1982) by Ed Paschke.

Hazel saw him wince. Having no mental handicap herself, she had to ask George what the latest sound had been.

"Sounded like somebody hitting a milk bottle with a ball-peen hammer,"[1] said George.

1. **ball-peen hammer:** hammer with a ball-shaped head.

134 THE SHORT-STORY COLLECTIONS

Reaching All Students

English Language Learners

Explain that the language in this story, particularly in the dialogue, is informal. Allow these students to work with peer tutors to help them understand such words as *huh, yup, boy,* and *doozy.* For additional strategies for engaging English language learners with the literature, see
• *Lesson Plans Including Strategies for English-Language Learners*

Advanced Learners

When asked about the writing process, Vonnegut said, "It's like making a movie. All sorts of creative things will happen after you've set up the cameras." Students might enjoy cataloging the "sorts of creative things" that happen in this story such as plot events and descriptive details. Students might also work in pairs to speculate on how the creation of one led to the next.

"I'd think it would be real interesting, hearing all the different sounds," said Hazel, a little  envious. "All the things they think up."

"Um," said George.

"Only, if I was Handicapper General, you know what I would do?" said Hazel. Hazel, as a matter of fact, bore a strong resemblance to the

Hazel. "I think I'd make a good Handicapper General."

"Good as anybody else," said George.

"Who knows better'n I do what normal is?" said Hazel.

"Right," said George. He began to think glimmeringly about his abnormal son who was now in jail, about Harrison, but a twenty-one-gun salute in his head stopped that.

"Boy!" said Hazel, "that was a doozy, wasn't it?"

It was such a doozy that George was white and trembling, and tears stood on the rims of his red eyes. Two of the eight ballerinas had collapsed to the studio floor and were holding their temples.

"All of a sudden you look so tired," said Hazel. "Why don't you stretch out on the sofa, so's you can rest your handicap bag on the pillows, honeybunch." She was referring to the forty-seven pounds of birdshot in a canvas bag which was padlocked around George's neck. "Go on and rest the bag for a little while," she said. "I don't care if you're not equal to me for a while."

George weighed the bag with his hands. "I don't mind it," he said. "I don't notice it anymore. It's just a part of me."

"You been so tired lately—kind of wore out," said Hazel.

Handicapper General, a woman named Diana Moon Glampers. "If I was Diana Moon Glampers," said Hazel, "I'd have chimes on Sunday—just chimes. Kind of in honor of religion."

"I could think, if it was just chimes," said George.

"Well—maybe make 'em real loud," said

"If there was just some way we could make a little hole in the bottom of the bag, and just take out a few of them lead balls. Just a few."

"Two years in prison and two thousand dollars fine for every ball I took out," said George. "I don't call that a bargain."

"If you could just take a few out when you came home from work," said Hazel. "I mean—

HARRISON BERGERON **135**

RESPONDING TO THE ART

In this work by **Ed Paschke** (1939–   ), horizontal vibrations in the surface create an effect much like that of a distorted video image.

Activity. What similarities do students notice between the artist's and the satirist's works? [Both distort reality. Both depict chaos. Both are suggestive of a mechanically dominated world.]

E **Elements of Literature**
Character

? What does Hazel's statement reveal about her? [Possible answers: She is extremely simple-minded—she thinks the sounds are interesting when, in fact, they are very painful to George; she has little understanding of the actual situation and, therefore, does not need a mental handicap.]

F **Reading Skills and Strategies**
Making Inferences

? Why do the two ballerinas collapse? [Because they seem to react at the same time and with the same degree of intensity as George, they are probably equipped with the same mental handicap he has; therefore, their collapse was caused by their hearing the twenty-one gun salute.]

G **Elements of Literature**
Satire

? How is the writer mocking Hazel in this passage? [Dimwitted Hazel thinks she is letting George be smarter than she is, which is, on the one hand, humorous and, on the other, pathetic—since George has been denied his natural intelligence.]

Using Students' Strengths

Kinesthetic Learners

Invite students to use found or throwaway objects such as empty cans and common materials such as aluminum foil or construction paper to build a handicap like one in the story. Students might describe the feeling of wearing the handicap and explain how it impairs their activities or thoughts. Ask them to explain how this exercise helps them to understand the impact of such a burden on a character.

Logical Learners

This story has long been a favorite. What does its popularity rest on? Is the society it describes one that could ever exist? Could such handicapping ever occur? Would a goal of government ever be to make everyone equal "every which way"? Invite students to work in small groups to determine what is logical and illogical in the story and to present at least three logical reasons for its continuing appeal.

A Elements of Literature

Satire

❓ What attitude is Vonnegut satirizing in this passage? [He is satirizing passive or uncritical acceptance of the law just because it is the law; he is suggesting that complacency is wrong when it comes to unjust laws, even if they are supposedly in the name of a good cause, like equality.]

B Reading Skills and Strategies

Evaluating the Author's Point of View

❓ Why do you think the author decides to show a character who challenges the government? [Possible answers: He wants to show that such a challenge is possible; he wants to show what can happen when a single individual, instead of an organized group, offers such a challenge; he may wish to show that the government's goal is not achievable after all—there will always be people like Harrison who are not equal.]

C Reading Skills and Strategies

Drawing Conclusions

❓ How does Harrison Bergeron challenge the government's handicap program? [The handicappers cannot create sufficient handicaps to make him "equal," nor can they keep to their usual standards of creating symmetrical, neat handicaps. He is not controllable, and therefore he is dangerous to the equality system, which relies on the government's keeping control.]

---

you don't compete with anybody around here. You just set around."

A "If I tried to get away with it," said George, "then other people'd get away with it—and pretty soon we'd be right back to the Dark Ages again, with everybody competing against everybody else. You wouldn't like that, would you?"

"I'd hate it," said Hazel.

"There you are," said George. "The minute people start cheating on laws, what do you think happens to society?"

If Hazel hadn't been able to come up with an answer to this question, George couldn't have supplied one. A siren was going off in his head.

"Reckon it'd fall all apart," said Hazel.

"What would?" said George blankly.

"Society," said Hazel uncertainly. "Wasn't that what you just said?"

"Who knows?" said George.

The television program was suddenly interrupted for a news bulletin. It wasn't clear at first as to what the bulletin was about, since the announcer, like all announcers, had a serious speech impediment. For about half a minute, and in a state of high excitement, the announcer tried to say, "Ladies and gentlemen——"

He finally gave up, handed the bulletin to a ballerina to read.

"That's all right——" Hazel said of the announcer, "he tried. That's the big thing. He tried to do the best he could with what God gave him. He should get a nice raise for trying so hard."

"Ladies and gentlemen——" said the ballerina, reading the bulletin. She must have been extraordinarily beautiful, because the mask she wore was hideous. And it was easy to see that she was the strongest and most graceful of all the dancers, for her handicap bags were as big as those worn by two-hundred-pound men.

And she had to apologize at once for her voice, which was a very unfair voice for a woman to use. Her voice was a warm, luminous, timeless melody. "Excuse me——" she said, and she began again, making her voice absolutely uncompetitive.

B "Harrison Bergeron, age fourteen," she said in a grackle squawk,[2] "has just escaped from jail,

2. **grackle squawk:** loud, harsh cry, like that of a grackle (blackbird).

where he was held on suspicion of plotting to overthrow the government. He is a genius and an athlete, is under-handicapped, and should be regarded as extremely dangerous."

A police photograph of Harrison Bergeron was flashed on the screen—upside down, then sideways, upside down again, then right side up. The picture showed the full length of Harrison against a background calibrated[3] in feet and inches. He was exactly seven feet tall.

C The rest of Harrison's appearance was Halloween and hardware. Nobody had ever borne heavier handicaps. He had outgrown hindrances faster than the H-G men could think them up. Instead of a little ear radio for a mental handicap, he wore a tremendous pair of earphones, and spectacles with thick wavy lenses. The spectacles were intended not only to make him half blind, but to give him whanging headaches besides.

Scrap metal was hung all over him. Ordinarily, there was a certain symmetry, a military neatness to the handicaps issued to strong people, but Harrison looked like a walking junkyard. In the race of life, Harrison carried three hundred pounds.

And to offset his good looks, the H-G men required that he wear at all times a red rubber ball for a nose, keep his eyebrows shaved off, and cover his even white teeth with black caps at snaggletooth random.

"If you see this boy," said the ballerina, "do not—I repeat, do not—try to reason with him."

There was the shriek of a door being torn from its hinges.

Screams and barking cries of consternation came from the television set. The photograph of Harrison Bergeron on the screen jumped

3. **calibrated** (kal′ə·brāt′id): marked with measurements.

WORDS TO OWN

hindrances (hin′drən·siz) n.: obstacles; things that restrain or prevent an activity.
symmetry (sim′ə·trē) n.: balanced arrangement.
consternation (kän′stər·nā′shən) n.: fear; bewilderment.

Getting Students Involved

Cooperative Learning

To help students understand both character and theme, have them work in groups of four or five to write a skit about the everyday life of people in this futuristic society. Possible topics include a family dinner, a classroom situation, or a workplace scene. Ask group members to brainstorm ideas for their skit and to establish its outline or write a first draft. From that point on, they might establish separate tasks, such as revising the skit, directing it, playing its parts, and procuring or making props. Some students might be responsible for more than one job. After the group has performed its skit for the class, ask the audience to offer constructive critical comments. Then, each student should detail his or her contributions to the group effort and assess the success of the project as a whole.

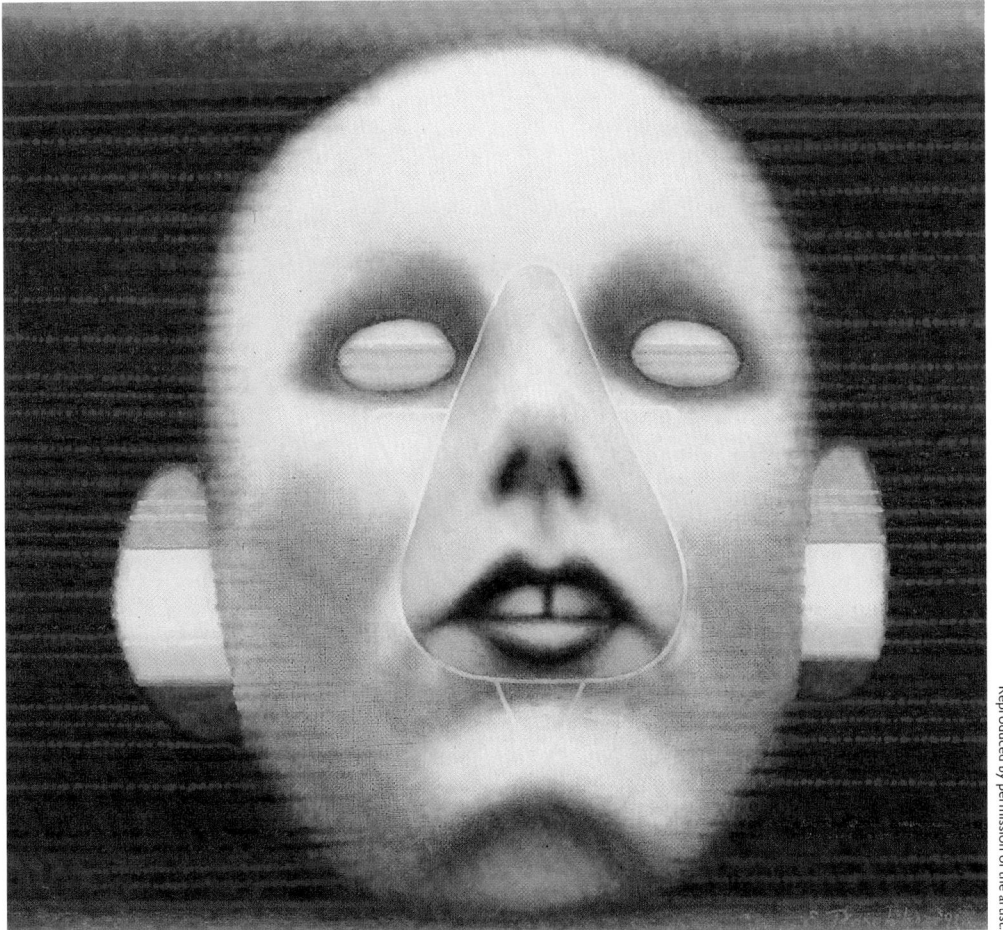

The Triangle (detail) (1991) by Ed Paschke.

Activity. Most students will agree that Ed Paschke's painting is unsettling. Have them talk about the painting to see if they can identify the elements of the work that create that feeling. Ask if this face suggests the limitations put on human achievement that Vonnegut writes about. [The face looks like a mask; there are no eyes or they are closed; the ears look sealed; there is an opening for the nose and mouth. The overall effect is of a hard mask imposed upon a real flesh and blood face. It is suggestive of imprisonment, confinement, censorship, perhaps.]

again and again, as though dancing to the tune of an earthquake.

George Bergeron correctly identified the earthquake, and well he might have—for many was the time his own home had danced to the same crashing tune. "My God—" said George, "that must be Harrison!"

The realization was blasted from his mind instantly by the sound of an automobile collision in his head.

When George could open his eyes again, the photograph of Harrison was gone. A living, breathing Harrison filled the screen.

Clanking, clownish, and huge, Harrison stood in the center of the studio. The knob of the uprooted studio door was still in his hand. Ballerinas, technicians, musicians, and announcers cowered on their knees before him, expecting to die.

"I am the Emperor!" cried Harrison. "Do you hear? I am the Emperor! Everybody must do

WORDS TO OWN

cowered (kou'ərd) v.: drew back or crouched in fear and helplessness.

HARRISON BERGERON   137

D   English Language Learners
Inverted Expressions
Point out the expressions "well he might have" and "many was the time." Students may be puzzled by their uncommon syntax. Explain that these expressions are usually stated as "he might well have" and "there were many times." Tell students that the inverted word order creates a light tone that is in keeping with the humor of the story. Remind students that English syntax has a flexibility that many other languages lack.

E   Appreciating Language
Placement of Modifiers
❓ Call attention to the placement of the modifiers *clanking*, *clownish*, and *huge*. Why are they placed where they are? [Possible answers: By immediately preceding the noun they modify, *Harrison*, the placement is logical and grammatical; by placing the modifiers first, Vonnegut emphasizes Harrison's absurd appearance.]

Crossing the Curriculum

Social Studies
Vonnegut refers to the 211th, 212th, and 213th amendments to the United States Constitution. Have students research the process of amending the Constitution. Ask them also to identify and categorize all amendments to the Constitution that relate to equality or civil rights. Then, have students calculate the rate at which amendments would have to be added to the Constitution if there were to be 211 amendments by the year 2081 (as in the story).

Have them compare this rate with the historical rate at which amendments have been added since the Constitution was written. They might also consider and comment on why amending the Constitution is considered such a serious matter and what a sudden rash of amendments might mean for our government and our society. After their research, suggest that students reread the story to gain new insights into Vonnegut's point of view.

A Reading Skills and Strategies

Evaluating the Author's Point of View

❓ When Harrison takes charge, he scarcely does so with any thoughts of equality. What kind of leader does Harrison wish to be, and why do you think the author presents him in this way? [Possible answer: Harrison wishes to be an emperor or a dictator. This may suggest that the author believes that when a single individual rises up out of a suppressed society, that individual is likely to be dictatorial or absolutist.]

B Elements of Literature

Satire

❓ Why can this sentence be called satirical? [The phrase "much improved" is a ridiculous understatement because Harrison has just manhandled the musicians to make them play better. Small wonder the musicians' music is "much improved."]

C Vocabulary Note

Greek Prefixes and Roots

The word *synchronize* is made up of a Greek prefix *sun-* (written variously as *sym, syn, syl,* and *sy*), meaning, in this case, "same," and the Greek root *khronos,* meaning "time." Ask students how this information helps them understand the word *synchronizing.* [*Synchronizing* means "causing to happen at the same time."] Ask students to think of other words with the prefixes *syn* or *sym* or the root *chronos.* [Sample words: *symmetry, sympathy; chronological, chronometer.*]

what I say at once!" He stamped his foot and the studio shook.

A "Even as I stand here—" he bellowed, "crippled, hobbled, sickened—I am a greater ruler than any man who ever lived! Now watch me become what I *can* become!"

Harrison tore the straps of his handicap harness like wet tissue paper, tore straps guaranteed to support five thousand pounds.

Harrison's scrap-iron handicaps crashed to the floor.

Harrison thrust his thumbs under the bar of the padlock that secured his head harness. The bar snapped like celery. Harrison smashed his headphones and spectacles against the wall.

He flung away his rubber-ball nose, revealed a man that would have awed Thor, the god of thunder.

"I shall now select my Empress!" he said, looking down on the cowering people. "Let the first woman who dares rise to her feet claim her mate and her throne!"

A moment passed, and then a ballerina arose, swaying like a willow.

Harrison plucked the mental handicap from her ear, snapped off her physical handicaps with marvelous delicacy. Last of all, he removed her mask.

She was blindingly beautiful.

"Now—" said Harrison, taking her hand, "shall we show the people the meaning of the word *dance*? Music!" he commanded.

The musicians scrambled back into their chairs, and Harrison stripped them of their handicaps, too. "Play your best," he told them, "and I'll make you barons and dukes and earls."

The music began. It was normal at first— cheap, silly, false. But Harrison snatched two musicians from their chairs, waved them like batons as he sang the music as he wanted it played. He slammed them back into their chairs.

B The music began again and was much improved.

Harrison and his Empress merely listened to

Harrison's scrap-iron handicaps crashed to the floor.

C the music for a while—listened gravely, as though synchronizing their heartbeats with it.

They shifted their weights to their toes.

Harrison placed his big hands on the girl's tiny waist, letting her sense the weightlessness that would soon be hers.

And then, in an explosion of joy and grace, into the air they sprang!

Not only were the laws of the land abandoned, but the law of gravity and the laws of motion as well.

They reeled, whirled, swiveled, flounced, capered, gamboled, and spun.

They leaped like deer on the moon.

The studio ceiling was thirty feet high, but each leap brought the dancers nearer to it.

It became their obvious intention to kiss the ceiling.

They kissed it.

And then, neutralizing gravity with love and pure will, they remained suspended in air inches below the ceiling, and they kissed each other for a long, long time.

It was then that Diana Moon Glampers, the Handicapper General, came into the studio with a double-barreled ten-gauge shotgun. She fired twice, and the Emperor and the Empress were dead before they hit the floor.

Diana Moon Glampers loaded the gun again. She aimed it at the musicians and told them they had ten seconds to get their handicaps back on.

It was then that the Bergerons' television tube burned out.

Hazel turned to comment about the blackout to George. But George had gone out into the kitchen for a can of beer.

George came back in with the beer, paused while a handicap signal shook him up. And then

WORDS TO OWN

synchronizing (siŋ′krə·nī′ziŋ) *v.*: causing to occur at the same rate or time.

Assessing Learning

Check Test: Questions and Answers

1. Who is Harrison Bergeron? [He is the fourteen-year-old son of George and Hazel Bergeron and is seven feet tall, a genius, and an athlete.]

2. What is the purpose of the transmitter George wears? [to interrupt his thoughts every twenty seconds with a loud noise]

3. How are the dancers' grace and beauty hidden? [They must wear masks and weights.]

4. How do Harrison's parents react to his death? [They quickly forget about it.]

Standardized Test Preparation

For practice in proofreading and editing, see
• *Daily Oral Grammar,* Transparency 7

he sat down again. "You been crying?" he said to Hazel.

"Yup," she said.

"What about?" he said.

"I forget," she said. "Something real sad on television."

"What was it?" he said.

"It's all kind of mixed up in my mind," said Hazel.

"Forget sad things," said George.

"I always do," said Hazel.

"That's my girl," said George. He winced. There was the sound of a riveting-gun in his head.

"Gee—I could tell that one was a doozy," said Hazel.

"You can say that again," said George.

"Gee—" said Hazel, "I could tell that one was a doozy."

D

MEET THE WRITER

A Good Citizen

Kurt Vonnegut (1922–   ) is concerned about the way people treat one another in a world of high technology. So he has written novels, mostly social satires, to express his concerns about morality, about human society, about values. "I consider writing an act of good citizenship," he has said. During World War II, Vonnegut was held prisoner in the under-ground meat locker of a slaughterhouse in Dresden, Germany. He used that experience in his most famous novel, *Slaughterhouse Five, or the Children's Crusade* (1969), which carries a strong message against all war.

More by Vonnegut

Welcome to the Monkey House (Bantam/Doubleday) is a collection of Vonnegut's stories and essays that includes "EPICAC," about a computer that falls in love, and "Report on the Barnhouse Effect," about a man with astonishing powers.

HARRISON BERGERON **139**

Making the Connections

Connecting to the Theme: "The Human Spirit"

In this story, societal repression is almost com-plete but not quite. Students might discuss these questions in small groups or as a class.

- When a society is controlled or repressed, are there always people who are waiting to challenge the system for the good of all or waiting to take power for themselves? What

historical examples can you think of? In these instances, were the individuals who revolted acting for the common good, for their own power, or both? What do these acts reveal about the human spirit?

- Do you think it is possible for a humorous story like this to make as serious a statement

about the human spirit as, for example, "Thank You, M'am"? Why or why not?

- What would you say is Vonnegut's belief about the human spirit? Consider in your answer George and Hazel, the Handicapper General, and the bold ballerina, as well as Harrison.

Connections

This famous poem presents the philosophical musings of a cockroach named archy.

Ⓐ Elements of Literature

Satire

❓ What is satirical about this first stanza? [The moth's actions and motives are exaggerated—the moth's instinctive behavior to fly into the light is described as a desire to commit suicide.]

Ⓑ Struggling Readers

Breaking Down Difficult Text

❓ How could you separate these thoughts and phrases to make the whole passage more readable? [Provide struggling readers with a copy of this poem for them to mark. Ask them to place slashes after each unit of meaning that makes sense by itself. Later, students can supply the proper punctuation to show where breaks occur.]

Ⓒ Vocabulary Note

Using Context Clues

❓ What context clues help you understand the word *immolated* (l. 45)? What does it mean? [Sample answer: The words "before I could . . ." suggests the moth did something radical; this action was done with flame; earlier, archy talks about the moth's frying itself. *Immolated* means "killed as a kind of sacrifice."]

Ⓓ Critical Thinking

Interpreting

❓ In your own words, what does archy wish for? [Possible answer: He wishes that something mattered so much to him that he would be willing to give his life for it.]

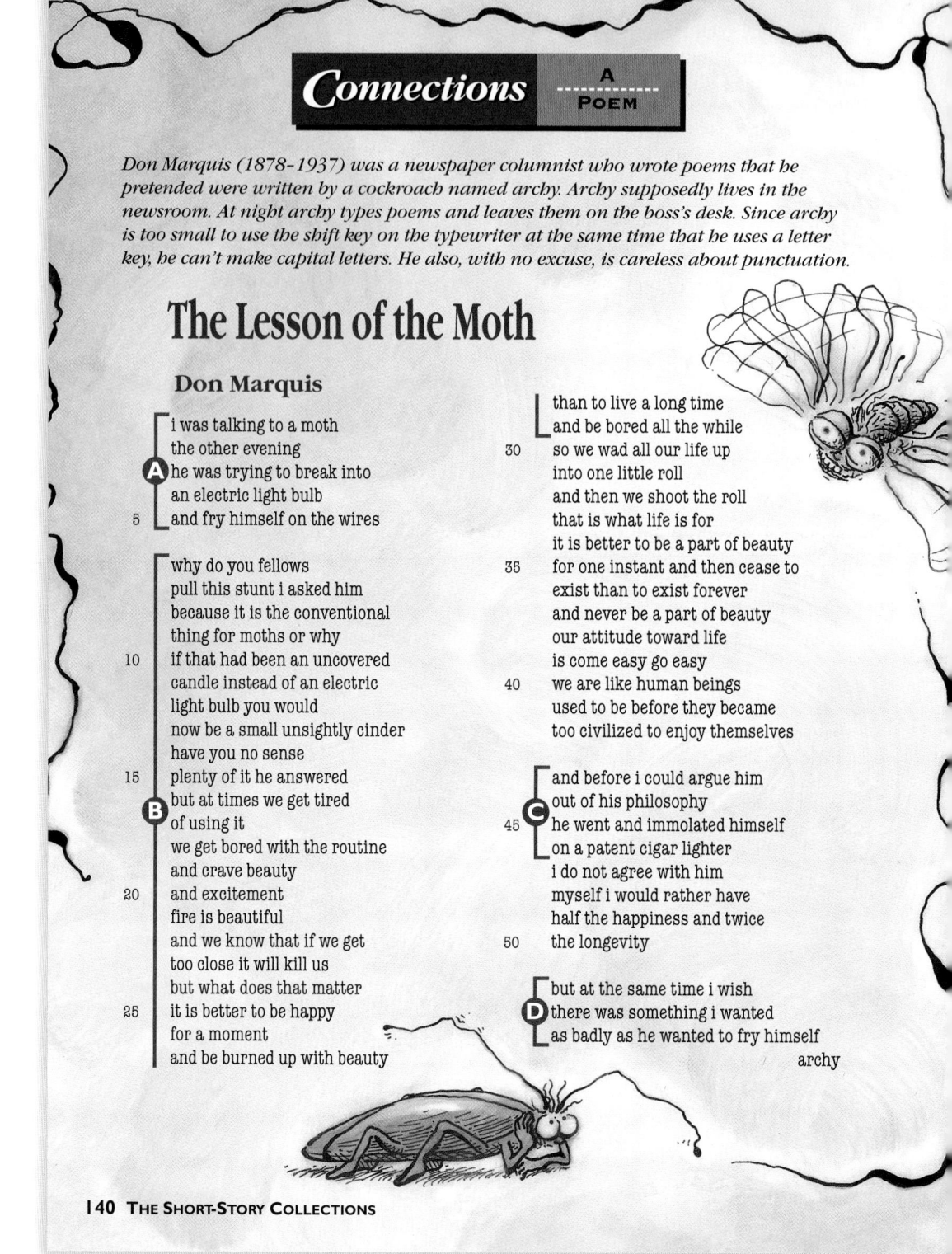

Don Marquis (1878-1937) was a newspaper columnist who wrote poems that he pretended were written by a cockroach named archy. Archy supposedly lives in the newsroom. At night archy types poems and leaves them on the boss's desk. Since archy is too small to use the shift key on the typewriter at the same time that he uses a letter key, he can't make capital letters. He also, with no excuse, is careless about punctuation.

The Lesson of the Moth

Don Marquis

Ⓐ i was talking to a moth
the other evening
he was trying to break into
an electric light bulb
5 and fry himself on the wires

why do you fellows
pull this stunt i asked him
because it is the conventional
thing for moths or why
10 if that had been an uncovered
candle instead of an electric
light bulb you would
now be a small unsightly cinder
have you no sense
15 plenty of it he answered
Ⓑ but at times we get tired
of using it
we get bored with the routine
and crave beauty
20 and excitement
fire is beautiful
and we know that if we get
too close it will kill us
but what does that matter
25 it is better to be happy
for a moment
and be burned up with beauty

than to live a long time
and be bored all the while
30 so we wad all our life up
into one little roll
and then we shoot the roll
that is what life is for
it is better to be a part of beauty
35 for one instant and then cease to
exist than to exist forever
and never be a part of beauty
our attitude toward life
is come easy go easy
40 we are like human beings
used to be before they became
too civilized to enjoy themselves

Ⓒ and before i could argue him
out of his philosophy
45 he went and immolated himself
on a patent cigar lighter
i do not agree with him
myself i would rather have
half the happiness and twice
50 the longevity

Ⓓ but at the same time i wish
there was something i wanted
as badly as he wanted to fry himself

archy

Connecting Across Texts

Connecting with "Harrison Bergeron"
Students might discuss these questions with a partner or write their answers in their journal:
• In what way are both texts humorous? Do they share the same kind of humor?
• Is either the moth's action or Harrison Bergeron's action an act of sacrifice? What, do you think, motivates each action?
• Which work do you prefer? Which work speaks more effectively, forcefully, or memorably about the human spirit? Why?

MAKING MEANINGS

First Thoughts

[respond]
1. At the end of Vonnegut's story, how did you feel about Hazel? George? Harrison?

Shaping Interpretations

[infer]
2. What details in the story make us infer, or guess, that all does not work very smoothly in this society where everyone is equal "every which way"? Do you think this is a realistic prediction of what would happen if all competition were done away with? Why, or why not?

[interpret]
3. What kinds of societies could be the targets of Vonnegut's **satire** in this story? What attitudes is he mocking?

[contrast]
4. What is the difference between believing that people are equals under the law and believing that everyone is the same?

[respond]
5. Poor Hazel says of the bumbling announcer, ". . . he tried. That's the big thing." Should people be rewarded for trying or for actually accomplishing something? Talk about your thoughts on this complicated issue. See if talking it over with other readers affects the way you think.

Extending the Text

[respond]
6. Technology is now more a part of people's lives than ever. Do you think this story has anything to say to us today? Talk over your responses to Vonnegut's point of view.

[extend]
7. This story is a fantasy. What figures from actual life have tried to save a people from repression the way Harrison does?

[compare]
8. What connection can you find between the moth in "The Lesson of the Moth" (see *Connections* on page 140) and the story of Harrison Bergeron?

Challenging the Text

[evaluate]
9. Refer to the Quickwrite you did before reading this story. How do you feel now about these issues? Do you agree with Vonnegut's view of technology, or would you challenge him on some details in the story? Be sure to explain your responses in terms of your own experiences.

> ### Reading Check
> a. When does the story take place?
> b. What kinds of handicaps have been imposed on people with above-average abilities?
> c. Why has Harrison been put in jail?
> d. What action does Harrison take to resolve his **conflict** with the government?
> e. At the story's end, who or what has triumphed?

MAKING MEANINGS

First Thoughts

1. Students may sympathize with George because of his handicaps, with Harrison for his rebellious spirit, and with Hazel because of her stupidity and modicum of sensitivity, or they may feel disgusted with the characters.

Shaping Interpretations

2. Possible details: the monitoring needed to maintain equality; the inability of the announcer to speak; the audience's overhearing the ballerina's real voice; Harrison's escape, his destruction of his handicaps, and his dancing skill. Some students may say that even in a noncompetitive society, people would still be motivated to develop their individual talents or that lack of competition would foster a spirit of cooperation that is not shown here.

3. Possible targets: societies that try to erase differences among people in the interests of greater equality, like those in former Communist nations; totalitarian societies, which dehumanize people while waving the banner of social justice; societies that "dummy down" an entire culture to the lowest common denominator. Vonnegut is mocking extreme attitudes, those that disregard the complexities of real life.

4. Being equal under the law means everyone has the same legal rights and protections. Believing everyone is the same means that no one has more beauty, talent, intelligence, or ability than anyone else.

5. Students may favor a middle ground: encouragement of effort coupled with fair rewards for achievement.

Extending the Text

6. The story may be seen as a warning against totalitarianism or against erasing individual differences or as a criticism of television.

7. Students may cite Mohandas K. Gandhi, Martin Luther King, Jr., or others.

8. Both dislike the ordinary; both die in pursuit of beauty.

Challenging the Text

9. Some students may agree with Vonnegut's fears about the invasion of privacy by new technology or about the government's use of technology to monitor people and impair creative or free thinkers.

Reading Check
Answers may vary slightly.
a. It takes place in 2081.
b. Possible answers: ear radios and wavy-lensed spectacles to reduce intelligence; weights to impede strength and grace; masks, tooth caps, clown noses, and shaved eyebrows to mar beauty.
c. He is suspected of plotting to overthrow the government.
d. He declares himself Emperor, removes his handicaps, names an Empress, and attempts to reclaim beauty, grace, and individual power.
e. The government triumphs by killing Harrison and the dancer and by erasing the event from everyone's memory.

Rubrics for each Choices assignment appear on p. 102 in the *Portfolio Management System*.

CHOICES: Building Your Portfolio

1. **Writer's Notebook** Remind students to save their work. They may use it as prewriting for the Writer's Workshop on p. 194. Another good approach to organizing notes on two characters is to use a two-column chart with sideheads for the characters' thoughts, words, actions, appearance, and other elements of characterization.

2. **Explaining a Position** Students might meet in groups to brainstorm ideas about the effects of eliminating competition in various endeavors. They might also draw conclusions about when and how competition enriches people and societies and when it undermines individuals.

3. **Creative Writing** Before students begin, remind them to make decisions about camera angles and when they want to pan or to zoom in for a close-up. Suggest that they consider the use of a narrator or voice-over to introduce or connect scenes.

4. **Drawing** Bring in samples of comic strips, and have students analyze how the cartoonist builds suspense or irony, conveys humor, and helps the reader make inferences.

CHOICES: Building Your Portfolio

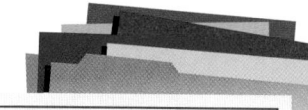

Writer's Notebook

1. Collecting Ideas for an Essay Analyzing a Character

Comparing characters. When you analyze a character, you might find it useful to compare that character with another. If you were analyzing the wise Mrs. Jones in "Thank You, M'am" (page 120), you might compare her with Roger, the boy who tried to mug her. Or you might compare a character in one story with a character in another story. Harrison Bergeron, for example, could be compared with another hero: Superman or King Arthur or *Star Trek*'s Captain Picard. The notes below show how one reader compared

Zaroff in "The Most Dangerous Game" (page 13) with Ulrich von Gradwitz in "The Interlopers" (page 95). (This reader has used a Venn diagram, a helpful device for organizing a comparison-contrast essay.) Take notes on how you might compare Harrison Bergeron or any other character in this book with another character. Save your notes.

Explaining a Position

2. Why Compete?

Even if it were possible to remove all competition from society, would such an act be a good thing? Consider the effects of such a drastic action on sports, business, and education. Present your ideas in the form of a letter to Vonnegut. Open your letter with a general statement telling what you think of Vonnegut's satire.

Creative Writing

3. Made for TV

Work in a small group to rewrite the story of Harrison Bergeron as a TV movie. Block out scenes for a thirty-minute show with three commercial breaks. As you write, remember the network's policy on violence and language. After your script is written, give it to another group for a "table read." This group will read the script aloud, trying out lines and seeing what works and what doesn't. (Part of a TV script for "A Christmas Memory" is on page 155.)

Drawing

4. The Bergerons: A Cartoon Strip

Plan and draw a cartoon strip of this story. Draw the characters as you imagine them, with all their clunky handicaps, and put their words in speech balloons or captions.

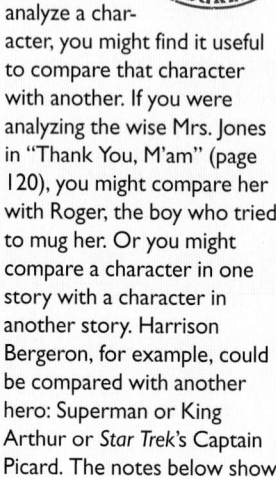

It was 2081, and everyone was finally equal.
But some things weren't quite right.

See Placement of Modifiers, page 1005.

See Language Workshop CD-ROM. *Key word entry:* misplaced modifiers.

See Proofreaders' Marks.

Misplaced Modifiers Are Confusing

For clarity, careful writers place modifying phrases and clauses as close as possible to the words they modify.

Misplaced modifiers can be funny. The comedian Groucho Marx used one in the movie *Animal Crackers*. "One morning I shot an elephant in my pajamas," Groucho said. "How he got in my pajamas, I'll never know."

Below are three examples of how descriptions from "Harrison Bergeron" might sound if modifiers were misplaced.

1. Two of the eight ballerinas had collapsed and were holding their temples to the studio floor. [Where should "to the studio floor" be placed?]

2. The photograph of Harrison Bergeron jumped again and again, as though dancing to the tune of an earthquake on the screen. [Where should "on the screen" be placed?]

3. They remained suspended in air, and they kissed each other inches below the ceiling for a long, long time. [Where should "inches below the ceiling" be placed?]

Try It Out

➤ Rewrite each sentence below so that the misplaced modifier, which is underlined, appears nearer the word it modifies.

1. George wore a mental handicap and seven pounds of bird shot in his ear.

2. Hazel watched the TV set talking happily about nothing.

3. Harrison stood at the center of the studio with a red rubber ball for a nose.

4. The dancers were gunned down by Diana Moon Glampers kissing the ceiling.

➤ As you proofread your writing, make sure you have placed modifying phrases and clauses near the words they modify. You might want to underline modifiers and draw arrows to the words they modify. Can you make the relationship clearer?

VOCABULARY   HOW TO OWN A WORD

WORD BANK

hindrances
symmetry
consternation
cowered
synchronizing

Word Charts: All You Need to Know

This chart organizes some basic information about *hindrances*. With a partner or small group, make similar charts for the other words in the Word Bank. You will have to use a dictionary.

hindrances
• **MEANING:** things that stand in the way or hold back
• **ORIGIN:** Old English, or Anglo-Saxon, "to keep or hold back"
• **SYNONYM OR ANTONYM:** obstacles (synonym)
• **EXAMPLES:** heavy backpack carried on a hike; eye glasses that break just before a test

HARRISON BERGERON 143

GRAMMAR LINK

Have students select a piece of narrative or descriptive writing from their portfolios and assess it for correct placement of modifiers. Ask them to underline each modifier (word or phrase) and draw an arrow connecting the modifier to the word or words that it modifies. If they find sentences in which modifiers are misplaced, have them revise the sentence.

Try It Out
Possible Answers

1. George wore a mental handicap in his ear and seven pounds of birdshot.
2. Talking happily about nothing, Hazel watched the TV set.
3. Harrison, with a red rubber ball for a nose, stood at the center of the studio.
4. The dancers were kissing the ceiling when they were gunned down by Diana Moon Glampers.

VOCABULARY

Sample Response
symmetry
meaning: balanced arrangement
origin: Greek, *sum-,* "like," + *metron,* "measure"
synonym or antonym: balance (synonym)
example: Greek architecture
consternation
meaning: fear; bewilderment
origin: Latin, *com-,* "with," + *sternere,* "to throw down"
synonym or antonym: confusion (synonym)
example: feeling when you fail a test
cowered
meaning: drew back in fear
origin: Middle English, *couren,* "to squat"
synonym or antonym: stood tall (antonym)
example: act of a character in a sci-fi film who encounters an alien
synchronizing
meaning: causing to occur at the same rate or time
origin: Greek, *syn-,* "same," + *khronos,* "time"
synonym or antonym: unifying (synonym)
example: people setting watches for the exact time

Language Link Quick Check

Move each misplaced modifier, which is underlined, nearer the word it modifies.

1. Hazel wanted everyone to be happy with all her heart. [With all her heart, Hazel wanted everyone to be happy.]

2. Harrison rips off straps capable of supporting thousands of pounds with a deft flick of his wrist. [With a deft flick of his wrist, Harrison rips off straps capable of supporting thousands of pounds.]

3. Closer to the ceiling he shows great skill as he jumps. [He shows great skill as he jumps closer to the ceiling.]

4. With a fearful roar he glares at the musicians and announces his intentions. [He glares at the musicians and announces his intentions with a fearful roar.]

5. Life eventually returns for Hazel and George to normal. [Life eventually returns to normal for Hazel and George.]

OBJECTIVES

1. Read and interpret the story
2. Note indirect characterization
3. Make inferences about character
4. Express understanding through writing or art/oral presentation
5. Analyze figures of speech
6. Understand and use new words
7. Analyze analogies

SKILLS

Literary
- Note indirect characterization

Reading
- Make inferences

Writing
- Evaluate a character
- Write a screenplay
- Write a poem

Art
- Create a collage

Language
- Analyze figures of speech

Vocabulary
- Use new words
- Analyze analogies

Viewing/Representing
- Compare techniques of painting and writing (ATE)
- Connect a drawing to the story (ATE)
- Analyze a sculpture (ATE)

Planning

- **Block Schedule**
  Block Scheduling Lesson Plans with Pacing Guide
- **Traditional Schedule**
  Lesson Plans Including Strategies for English-Language Learners
- **One-Stop Planner**
  CD-ROM with Test Generator

Before You Read

A CHRISTMAS MEMORY

Make the Connection

Those Who Give

One of the mysteries of the human spirit is generosity—especially the generosity of those who don't have very much themselves. Here is a story about an unforgettable character, her young cousin, and their rituals of Christmas generosity. The story also reveals something about the nature of friendship and the endurance of love—even when, to the rest of the world, the friendship seems odd and the love is not noticed at all.

Quickwrite

What do friends give each other? Think about your oldest friendship. Why do you think some friendships last and others don't? Jot down your ideas, and save your notes.

Elements of Literature

Characterization—Indirectly

When a writer shows us a character by describing his or her speech, appearance, thoughts, or actions, we say that the characterization is **indirect**. This means that we ourselves have to take all the information we are given about the character and draw our own conclusions about the kind of person we are meeting. Indirect characterization is something like meeting people in real life. In real life, people do not wear T-shirts with slogans explaining what kind of people they are. In real life, we observe people, we listen to what they say, and we watch how they act. Then we draw our own conclusions about them.

> In indirect characterization, a writer reveals what people are like by telling about their speech, their actions, their appearance, their private thoughts, and the ways they affect other characters.
>
> *For more on Character, see pages 130–131 and the Handbook of Literary Terms.*

Reading Skills and Strategies

Making Inferences: Look for the Clues

A graphic organizer like the one on the right will help you analyze the characters you meet in stories. Fill out a similar chart while you read "A Christmas Memory" or when you review the story after your first reading. Once you have gathered your clues, examine your chart carefully. Then, try writing one or two sentences summing up the character of each of the people you have met.

Clues to Characterization
Character's words:
Character's looks:
Character's actions:
Character's thoughts:
Responses of others:
Writer's direct comments:
Setting (where character lives):

144 THE SHORT-STORY COLLECTIONS

Preteaching Vocabulary

Words to Own

Ask pairs of students to read the Words to Own and their definitions. Then, have them use the words to complete these phrases.

1. a cheerful _____ [disposition]
2. bats, balls and other sports _____ [paraphernalia]
3. rowdy behavior that seemed _____ in the temple [sacrilegious]
4. a neutral, _____ remark [noncommittal]
5. a _____ speaker boring his audience with clichés [prosaic]
6. _____ the room with light [suffuse]
7. clearing the _____ from the battlefield [carnage]
8. a company _____ its new hiring policy [inaugurating]
9. rundown and _____ [dilapidated]
10. a steep hill that _____ bikers [exhilarates]

Christmas Morning 1930 by Charles E. Burchfield.
Watercolor on paper (30″ x 22 ⅛″).

Private collection. Photo courtesy of Kennedy Galleries, Inc., New York, and the C. E. Burchfield Foundation.

We are each other's
best friend.

A CHRISTMAS MEMORY

TRUMAN CAPOTE

Imagine a morning in late November. A coming of winter morning more than twenty years ago. Consider the kitchen of a spreading old house in a country town. A great black stove is its main feature; but there is also a big round table and a fireplace with two rocking chairs placed in front of it. Just today the fireplace commenced its seasonal roar.

A woman with shorn white hair is standing at the kitchen window. She is wearing tennis shoes and a shapeless gray sweater over a summery calico dress. She is small and sprightly, like a bantam hen; but, due to a long youthful illness, her shoulders are pitifully hunched. Her face is remarkable—not unlike Lincoln's, craggy like that, and tinted by sun and wind; but it is delicate too, finely boned, and her eyes are sherry-colored and timid. "Oh my," she exclaims, her breath smoking the windowpane, "it's fruitcake weather!"

A CHRISTMAS MEMORY 145

Summary ■ ■ ■

The first-person narrator, Buddy, recalls the final Christmas he spent with his cousin when he was seven and she was in her sixties. The story begins with Buddy's cousin declaring it's "fruit-cake weather." With joy and determination, they scrape together the ingredients to bake their holiday cakes. On Christmas Day they exchange homemade kites. Their intimacy is interrupted only by disapproving relatives, who end the cousins' happiness by sending Buddy to military school. Later, Buddy mourns his cousin's death.

Resources

Viewing and Representing
Videocassette A, Segment 2
Available in Spanish and English. The *Visual Connections* segment "Memories and Celebrations" can help students connect their lives to "A Christmas Memory." The segment focuses on a variety of American celebrations. For full lesson plans and worksheets, see *Visual Connections Teacher's Manual*.

Listening
Audio CD Library
A moving recording of this story is available in the *Audio CD Library*:
• Disc 6, Track 4

Elements of Literature
Analyzing Setting in a Story
For additional instruction on setting, see *Literary Elements*:
• Transparency 3
• Worksheet, p. 10

Resources: Print and Media

Reading
• *Graphic Organizers for Active Reading*, p. 8
• *Words to Own*, p. 7
• *Audio CD Library*
  Disc 6, Track 4

Elements of Literature
• *Literary Elements*
  Transparency 3
  Worksheet, p. 10

Writing and Language
• *Daily Oral Grammar*
  Transparency 8
• *Grammar and Language Links*
  Worksheet, p. 15

Viewing and Representing
• *Viewing and Representing*
  Fine Art Transparency 4
  Fine Art Worksheet, p. 16

• *Visual Connections*
  Videocassette A, Segment 2

Assessment
• *Formal Assessment*, p. 17
• *Portfolio Management System*, p. 103
• *Standardized Test Preparation*, pp. 20, 22
• *Test Generator (One-Stop Planner CD-ROM)*

Internet
• go.hrw.com (keyword: LE0 9-2)

A Elements of Literature

Indirect Characterization

❓ What do the words of the narrator tell you about the character of the woman? [She is in her sixties; she is childlike; she has little real power in her home and is dependent on others.]

B English Language Learners

Multiple-Meaning Words

Explain to students that *buggy* is a word rarely used anymore to refer to a baby carriage. (The word has been replaced by *stroller*.) Tell them that today *buggy* is mainly used to mean "bug-infested," but that it can also refer to a light four-wheeled, horse-drawn carriage.

C Reading Skills and Strategies

Making Inferences

❓ What do these details about the buggy tell you about the lives of those who push it? [Possible answers: The fact that the buggy is old and broken down suggests that they are poor; the many things they do with the buggy, like filling it with flowers or with fishing or picnicking paraphernalia, suggest that they have fun.]

D Elements of Literature

Imagery

❓ What makes the writing in this passage memorable? Ask students to point out words that suggest the sounds they refer to and words that appeal to the senses. [Possible answers: "Caarackle" and "crunch" suggest sounds; "the golden mound of sweet, oily, ivory meat" appeals to the senses of texture, taste, and sight.]

A The person to whom she is speaking is myself. I am seven; she is sixty-something. We are cousins, very distant ones, and we have lived together—well, as long as I can remember. Other people inhabit the house, relatives; and though they have power over us, and frequently make us cry, we are not, on the whole, too much aware of them. We are each other's best friend. She calls me Buddy, in memory of a boy who was formerly her best friend. The other Buddy died in the 1880s, when she was still a child. She is still a child.

"I knew it before I got out of bed," she says, turning away from the window with a purposeful excitement in her eyes. "The courthouse bell sounded so cold and clear. And there were no birds singing; they've gone to warmer country, yes indeed. Oh, Buddy, stop stuffing biscuit and fetch our buggy. Help me find my hat. We've thirty cakes to bake."

It's always the same: A morning arrives in November, and my friend, as though officially <u>inaugurating</u> the Christmas time of year that <u>exhilarates</u> her imagination and fuels the blaze of her heart, announces: "It's fruitcake weather! Fetch our buggy. Help me find my hat."

The hat is found, a straw cartwheel corsaged with velvet roses out-of-doors has faded; it once belonged to a more fashionable relative. **B** Together, we guide our buggy, a <u>dilapidated</u> baby carriage, out to the garden and into a grove of pecan trees. The buggy is mine; that is, it was bought for me when I was born. It is made of wicker, rather unraveled, and the wheels wobble like a drunkard's legs. But it is a faithful object; springtimes, we take it to the woods and fill it with flowers, herbs, wild fern for our porch pots; in the summer, we pile it **C** with picnic <u>paraphernalia</u> and sugar-cane fishing poles and roll it down to the edge of the creek; it has its winter uses, too: as a truck for hauling firewood from the yard to the kitchen, as a warm bed for Queenie, our tough little orange and white rat terrier who has survived distemper and two rattlesnake bites. Queenie is trotting beside it now.

Three hours later we are back in the kitchen hulling a heaping buggyload of windfall pecans.[1] Our backs hurt from gathering them: How hard they were to find (the main crop having been shaken off the trees and sold by the orchard's owners, who are not us) among the concealing leaves, the frosted, deceiving **D** grass. Caarackle! A cheery crunch, scraps of miniature thunder sound as the shells collapse and the golden mound of sweet, oily, ivory meat mounts in the milk-glass bowl. Queenie begs to taste, and now and again my friend sneaks her a mite, though insisting we deprive ourselves. "We mustn't, Buddy. If we start, we won't stop. And there's scarcely enough as there is. For thirty cakes." The kitchen is growing dark. Dusk turns the window into a mirror: Our reflections mingle with the rising moon as we work by the fireside in the firelight. At last, when the moon is quite high, we toss the final hull into the fire and, with joined sighs, watch it catch flame. The buggy is empty; the bowl is brimful.

We eat our supper (cold biscuits, bacon, blackberry jam) and discuss tomorrow. Tomorrow the kind of work I like best begins: buying. Cherries and citron, ginger and vanilla and canned Hawaiian pineapple, rinds and raisins and walnuts and whiskey and oh, so much flour, butter, so many eggs, spices, flavorings: Why, we'll need a pony to pull the buggy home.

But before these purchases can be made, there is the question of money. Neither of us has any. Except for skinflint sums persons in the house occasionally provide (a dime is considered very big money); or what we earn ourselves from various activities: holding

---

1. **windfall pecans:** pecans blown down from the trees by wind.

WORDS TO OWN

inaugurating (in·ô′gyoo·rāt′iŋ) v.: formally beginning.
exhilarates (eg·zil′ə·rāts′) v.: gladdens; excites.
dilapidated (də·lap′ə·dāt′id) adj.: shabby; falling apart.
paraphernalia (par′ə·fər·nāl′yə) n.: equipment; gear.

Reaching All Students

Struggling Readers

Making Inferences was introduced on p. 144. One good strategy to use with making inferences is It Says . . . I Say. For information on using this strategy, see p. 25 of the *Reading Strategies Handbook* in front of the *Reading Skills and Strategies* binder.

English Language Learners

Pair these students with native speakers who can help them with long, descriptive passages. For other strategies for engaging English language learners with the literature, see
• *Lesson Plans Including Strategies for English-Language Learners*

Advanced Learners

Capote said that writing has "laws of perspective, of light and shade, just as painting does." Challenge students to find places in the story where the writing seems to have "light" or where it produces "shade." Also challenge students to find perspective in this story, perhaps by determining how Capote visually focuses on a point in the foreground, yet leads the reader's mind (and feelings) to points and places in the distance.

rummage sales, selling buckets of handpicked blackberries, jars of homemade jam and apple jelly and peach preserves, rounding up flowers for funerals and weddings. Once we won seventy-ninth prize, five dollars, in a national football contest. Not that we know a fool thing about football. It's just that we enter any contest we hear about: At the moment our hopes are centered on the fifty-thousand-dollar Grand Prize being offered to name a new brand of coffee (we suggested "A.M."; and, after some hesitation, for my friend thought it perhaps _sacrilegious_, the slogan "A.M.! Amen!"). To tell the truth, our only _really_ profitable enterprise was the Fun and Freak Museum we conducted  in a backyard woodshed two summers ago. The Fun was a stereopticon[2] with slide views of Washington and New York lent us by a relative who had been to those places (she was furious when she discovered why we'd borrowed it); the Freak was a three-legged biddy chicken[3] hatched by one of our own hens. Everybody hereabouts wanted to see that biddy: We charged grown-ups a nickel, kids two cents. And took in a good twenty dollars before the museum shut down due to the decease of the main attraction.

But one way and another we do each year accumulate Christmas savings, a Fruitcake Fund. These moneys we keep hidden in an ancient bead purse under a loose board under the floor

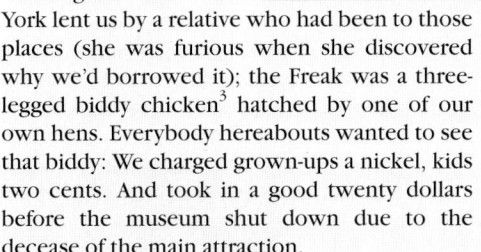
Bouquet and Stove (1929) by Yasuo Kuniyoshi.

under a chamber pot[4] under my friend's bed. The purse is seldom removed from this safe location except to make a deposit, or, as happens every Saturday, a withdrawal; for on Saturdays I am allowed ten cents to go to the picture show. My friend has never been to a picture show, nor does she intend to: "I'd rather hear you tell the story, Buddy. That way I can imagine it more. Besides, a person my age shouldn't squander their eyes. When the Lord comes, let me see Him clear." In addition to never having seen a movie, she has never: eaten in a restaurant, traveled more than five miles from home, received or sent a telegram, read anything except funny papers and the Bible, worn cosmetics, cursed, wished someone harm, told a lie on purpose, let a hungry dog go hungry. Here are a few things she has done, does do: killed with a hoe the biggest rattlesnake ever seen in this county (sixteen rattles), dip snuff[5] (secretly), tame hummingbirds (just try it) till they balance on her finger, tell ghost stories (we both believe in ghosts) so tingling they chill you in July, talk to herself, take walks in the rain, grow the prettiest japonicas[6] in town, know the

4. **chamber pot:** Before indoor plumbing and toilets, people used pots, usually kept in their bedrooms, or chambers.
5. **snuff:** powdered tobacco inhaled by sniffing.
6. **japonicas** (jə·pän′i·kəz): flowering shrubs.

WORDS TO OWN

sacrilegious (sak′rə·lij′əs) _adj._: disrespectful toward religion.

2. **stereopticon** (ster′ē·äp′ti·kən): old-fashioned kind of slide projector.
3. **biddy chicken:** young chicken.

A CHRISTMAS MEMORY **147**

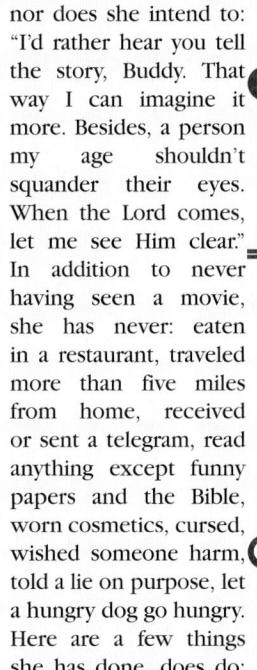

RESPONDING TO THE ART

Yasuo Kuniyoshi (1893–1953) came to the United States from Japan when he was thirteen. **Activity.** The contrast between the colorful, delicate lines of the flowers and the dark, solid mass of the stove emphasizes the qualities of each, enabling the viewer to perceive both stove and flowers more fully. Ask students to compare this visual effect to the literary effect Capote creates by pairing the seven-year-old Buddy with an aging friend.

E Elements of Literature
Setting

❓ What do these details tell you about the story's time and place? What does the setting suggest about the characters' lives? [Possible answers: The details show that the characters live in an isolated, pre-television, rural world; the details indicate that the characters have to make their own fun because manufactured amusements are few and far between.]

F Elements of Literature
Indirect Characterization

❓ What methods of characterization are used in this passage? [The character is shown through her words and actions.] What do these details tell you about her? [Possible answers: She has lived a sheltered life; she has a strong faith in God; she likes to use her imagination.]

G Struggling Readers
Asking Questions

❓ Remind students to ask themselves what these details reveal. For example, what does it say about this woman that she has never eaten in a restaurant or traveled more than five miles from home? [Possible answers: She has led an extremely sheltered life; she has always been poor; she has few wants and needs.]

Using Students' Strengths

Naturalist Learners
Students may enjoy re-creating aspects of the setting of "A Christmas Memory" by displaying natural objects or pictures of natural objects mentioned in the story, such as pecans, rattlesnakes, blackberries, and japonicas. Based on the details given in the story, students might also research other plants and animals found in the same ecosystem but not mentioned in this story.

Intrapersonal Learners
As they read, students can enter into a private dialogue with the narrator by asking him questions and sharing their ideas. They can record in their journals both the questions and the answers they imagine the narrator would give. For example, students might ask the narrator about his unstated thoughts and feelings at a particular moment, or they might tell the narrator how they would have felt or reacted in response to a certain event.

Ask students to discuss the following questions in groups and to report their ideas to the class. Have them consider at least four book-movie combinations.

- Do you, like Buddy's friend, like to use your imagination to visualize the action as you read, or do you prefer to see the movie version?
- Can a story be ruined by being made into a movie? Explain and give examples.
- Can a movie be ruined by being made into a book? Explain and give examples.

A Reading Skills and Strategies

Making Inferences

? What do the characters' actions and the narrator's thoughts tell you about the two characters' relationship to money? [Possible responses: Because they have little money, it is precious to them, as shown by their keeping the money well hidden in a bead purse; the descriptions of the bills and coins suggest the care with which the money has been gathered.]

B Historical Connections

Prohibition

The manufacture, sale, and transportation of intoxicating liquors was prohibited by the Eighteenth Amendment to the U.S. Constitution in 1919. This legislation was the beginning of the prohibition era. It generated a wave of criminal activity, including bootlegging and the existence of the speakeasy, or illegal saloon. Haha Jones plies both of these trades. The amendment was repealed in 1933, and the control of liquor was again relegated to the states.

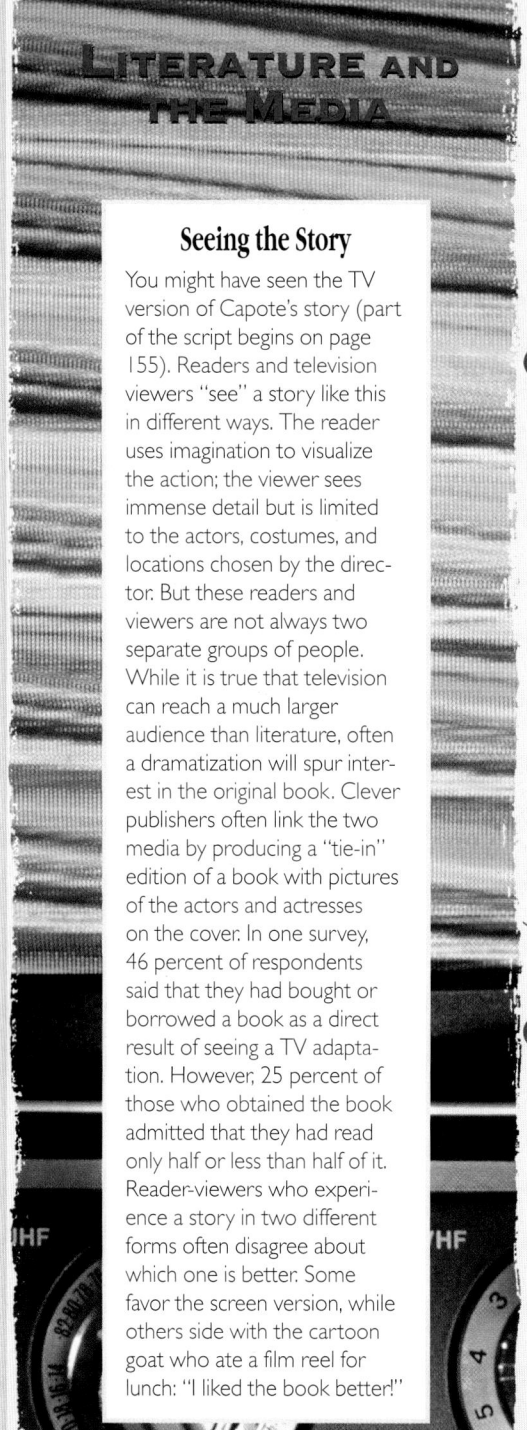

LITERATURE AND
THE MEDIA

Seeing the Story

You might have seen the TV version of Capote's story (part of the script begins on page 155). Readers and television viewers "see" a story like this in different ways. The reader uses imagination to visualize the action; the viewer sees immense detail but is limited to the actors, costumes, and locations chosen by the director. But these readers and viewers are not always two separate groups of people. While it is true that television can reach a much larger audience than literature, often a dramatization will spur interest in the original book. Clever publishers often link the two media by producing a "tie-in" edition of a book with pictures of the actors and actresses on the cover. In one survey, 46 percent of respondents said that they had bought or borrowed a book as a direct result of seeing a TV adaptation. However, 25 percent of those who obtained the book admitted that they had read only half or less than half of it. Reader-viewers who experience a story in two different forms often disagree about which one is better. Some favor the screen version, while others side with the cartoon goat who ate a film reel for lunch: "I liked the book better!"

recipe for every sort of old-time Indian cure, including a magical wart-remover.

Now, with supper finished, we retire to the room in a faraway part of the house where my friend sleeps in a scrap-quilt-covered iron bed painted rose pink, her favorite color. Silently, wallowing in the pleasures of conspiracy, we take the bead purse from its secret place and spill its contents on the scrap quilt. Dollar bills, tightly rolled and green as May buds. Somber fifty-cent pieces, heavy enough to weight a dead man's eyes. Lovely dimes, the liveliest coin, the one that really jingles. Nickels and quarters, worn smooth as creek pebbles. But mostly a hateful heap of bitter-odored pennies. Last summer others in the house contracted to pay us a penny for every twenty-five flies we killed. Oh, the <u>carnage</u> of August: the flies that flew to heaven! Yet it was not work in which we took pride. And, as we sit counting pennies, it is as though we were back tabulating dead flies. Neither of us has a head for figures; we count slowly, lose track, start again. According to her calculations, we have $12.73. According to mine, exactly $13. "I do hope you're wrong, Buddy. We can't mess around with thirteen. The cakes will fall. Or put somebody in the cemetery. Why, I wouldn't dream of getting out of bed on the thirteenth." This is true: She always spends thirteenths in bed. So, to be on the safe side, we subtract a penny and toss it out the window.

Of the ingredients that go into our fruitcakes, whiskey is the most expensive, as well as the hardest to obtain: State laws forbid its sale. But everybody knows you can buy a bottle from Mr. Haha Jones. And the next day, having completed our more <u>prosaic</u> shopping, we set out for Mr. Haha's business address, a "sinful" (to quote public opinion) fish-fry and dancing cafe down by the river. We've been there before, and on the same errand; but in previous

WORDS TO OWN
carnage (kär′nij) *n.*: slaughter.
prosaic (prō·zā′ik) *adj.*: ordinary.

Professional Notes

Best-selling novelist Alice Hoffman expresses one writer's point of view on the process of turning books into movies. She says that the filmmaking process is more collaborative and team-oriented than the process of writing a novel. As she explains, "When you're the novelist, you're the director, star, producer, everything, but the film process is completely different. If you're the screenwriter, you're one of the lesser players. You can't control it as well as you can when writing the book."

San Francisco film historian David Thomson comments on adapting the classics into films. He notes that generally, the greater the book as literature, "the less well it will do as film. If you're taking a book which one treasures for its style, its voice, the actual sensibility in its writing—it's very difficult for the film to get it. If you're going for a book where the strength is the story, the character, the conflict—that's quite a bit easier."

years our dealings have been with Haha's wife, an iodine-dark Indian woman with brassy peroxided hair and a dead-tired <u>disposition</u>. Actually, we've never laid eyes on her husband, though we've heard that he's an Indian too. A giant with razor scars across his cheeks. They call him Haha because he's so gloomy, a man who never laughs. As we approach his cafe (a large log cabin festooned[7] inside and out with chains of garish-gay naked light bulbs and standing by the river's muddy edge under the shade of river trees where moss drifts through the branches like gray mist) our steps slow down. Even Queenie stops prancing and sticks close by. People have been murdered in Haha's cafe. Cut to pieces. Hit on the head. There's a case coming up in court next month. Naturally these goings-on happen at night when the colored lights cast crazy patterns and the Victrola[8] wails. In the daytime Haha's is shabby and deserted. I knock at the door, Queenie barks, my friend calls: "Mrs. Haha, ma'am? Anyone to home?"

Footsteps. The door opens. Our hearts overturn. It's Mr. Haha Jones himself! And he *is* a giant; he *does* have scars; he *doesn't* smile. No, he glowers at us through Satan-tilted eyes and demands to know: "What you want with Haha?"

For a moment we are too paralyzed to tell. Presently my friend half finds her voice, a whispery voice at best: "If you please, Mr. Haha, we'd like a quart of your finest whiskey."

His eyes tilt more. Would you believe it? Haha is smiling! Laughing, too. "Which one of you is a drinkin' man?"

"It's for making fruitcakes, Mr. Haha. Cooking."

This sobers him. He frowns. "That's no way to waste good whiskey." Nevertheless, he retreats into the shadowed cafe and seconds later appears carrying a bottle of daisy-yellow unlabeled liquor. He demonstrates its sparkle in the sunlight and says: "Two dollars."

We pay him with nickels and dimes and pennies. Suddenly, jangling the coins in his hand like a fistful of dice, his face softens. "Tell

7. **festooned** (fes·toond´): decorated.
8. **Victrola** (vik·tro´lə): old term for a record player.

you what," he proposes, pouring the money back into our bead purse, "just send me one of them fruitcakes instead."

"Well," my friend remarks on our way home, "there's a lovely man. We'll put an extra cup of raisins in *his* cake."

The black stove, stoked with coal and firewood, glows like a lighted pumpkin. Eggbeaters whirl, spoons spin round in bowls of butter and sugar, vanilla sweetens the air, ginger spices it; melting, nose-tingling odors saturate the kitchen, <u>suffuse</u> the house, drift out to the world on puffs of chimney smoke. In four days our work is done. Thirty-one cakes, dampened with whiskey, bask on window sills and shelves.

Who are they for?

Friends. Not necessarily neighbor friends: Indeed, the larger share are intended for persons we've met maybe once, perhaps not at all. People who've struck our fancy. Like President Roosevelt. Like the Reverend and Mrs. J. C. Lucey, Baptist missionaries to Borneo who lectured here last winter. Or the little knife grinder who comes through town twice a year. Or Abner Packer, the driver of the six o'clock bus from Mobile, who exchanges waves with us every day as he passes in a dust-cloud whoosh. Or the young Wistons, a California couple whose car one afternoon broke down outside the house and who spent a pleasant hour chatting with us on the porch (young Mr. Wiston snapped our picture, the only one we've ever had taken). Is it because my friend is shy with everyone *except* strangers that these strangers, and merest acquaintances, seem to us our truest friends? I think yes. Also, the scrapbooks we keep of thank-you's on White House stationery, time-to-time communications from California and Borneo, the knife grinder's penny postcards, make us feel connected to eventful worlds beyond the kitchen with its views of a sky that stops.

WORDS TO OWN

disposition (dis´pə·zish´ən) *n.*: usual frame of mind; temperament.
suffuse (sə·fyooz´) *v.*: spread over or through.

A CHRISTMAS MEMORY **149**

C Advanced Learners

Narrative Tension

❓ How is suspense built here, and how is it relieved? [Possible answer: A sinister setting, coupled with allusions to violent "goings-on," builds tension; there is comic relief when Mr. Jones asks which of the two is the "drinkin' man."]

D Elements of Literature

Indirect Characterization

❓ How does the author reveal new information about the character of Haha Jones in this passage? [A kindly side of him is shown through his words and actions and by what Buddy's cousin says about him.]

E Elements of Literature

Setting

❓ How do these details put you in the kitchen? What mood or atmosphere do they create? [Sample answer: The author describes light, warmth, good aromas, and pleasant, purposeful activity. These sensory details help the reader to hear, smell, see, touch, and practically taste the cakes. They create an intimate, homey, cozy atmosphere.]

F Reading Skills and Strategies

Making Inferences

❓ What do these details tell you about Buddy, his cousin, and their motivation? [Possible answers: They do not know many people; they want to reach out and make connections with others; they imagine themselves to be linked through special ties of affection or history to many more people than they actually are.]

Crossing the Curriculum

History

Students might investigate some of the realistic details of the time period that Capote describes in the story. For example, the character of Haha Jones is referred to as an Indian and is portrayed as a bootlegger. Students might research Native American peoples who lived in rural Alabama at this time. (Possibilities include the Choctaw and the Chickasaw.) They might also look into the culture of prohibition, during which the local bootlegger often played a rather prominent, if socially outcast role in the society. Finally, students might investigate the role of the Roosevelts as saviors of the common people during the Depression. Among the thousands of documents that students might explore are hundreds of personal letters from "just plain folks" who wrote to the Roosevelts about their trials and tribulations, their hopes, and their thanks for the New Deal. Ask students to research the effects of the Depression and the New Deal on their own state.

A Elements of Literature
Setting
❓ Why is the time of year important to the message and to the mood of the story? [Possible answers: It is Christmas time, a time of giving; much of the activity in the story revolves around preparing the fruitcakes as Christmas gifts for faraway people; it is a time of seasonal cold and death in nature, and this tinges the story with sadness even at its happiest moments.]

B Vocabulary Note
Using Context Clues
❓ If you don't know what the word *simultaneously* means, what context clues could you use to figure it out? [The context suggests the two are singing together, or at the same time.] What context clues could you use to figure out the meaning of *rollicks*? [This is what the dancing shadow does, which suggests lively, carefree romping.]

C Elements of Literature
Indirect Characterization
❓ What method of characterization is used to show the relatives? [The reader gets only the narrator's impression of them as disembodied voices, scolding eyes and scalding tongues.]

D Reading Skills and Strategies
Making Inferences
❓ This scattering of questions and exclamations is not explained. What inferences can you draw from them? They suggest a history of alcoholism in the family and a family that adheres to stern moral standards.]

A Now a nude December fig branch grates against the window. The kitchen is empty, the cakes are gone; yesterday we carted the last of them to the post office, where the cost of stamps turned our purse inside out. We're broke. That rather depresses me, but my friend insists on celebrating—with two inches of whiskey left in Haha's bottle. Queenie has a spoonful in a bowl of coffee (she likes her coffee chicory-flavored and strong). The rest we divide between a pair of jelly glasses. We're both quite awed at the prospect of drinking straight whiskey; the taste of it brings screwed-up expressions and sour shudders. But by and by we begin to sing, the two of us singing different songs simultaneously. I don't know the words to mine, just: *Come on along, come on along, to the dark-town strut-* **B** *ters' ball.* But I can dance: That's what I mean to be, a tap-dancer in the movies. My dancing shadow rollicks on the walls; our voices rock the chinaware; we giggle as if unseen hands were tickling us. Queenie rolls on her back, her paws plow the air, something like a grin stretches her black lips. Inside myself, I feel warm and sparky as those crumbling logs, carefree as the wind in the chimney. My friend waltzes round the stove, the hem of her poor calico skirt pinched between her fingers as though it were a party dress: *Show me the way to go home,* she sings, her tennis shoes squeaking on the floor. *Show me the way to go home.*

C Enter: two relatives. Very angry. Potent with eyes that scold, tongues that scald. Listen to what they have to say, the words tumbling together into a wrathful tune: "A child of seven! **D** whiskey on his breath! are you out of your mind? feeding a child of seven! must be loony! road to ruination! remember Cousin Kate? Uncle Charlie? Uncle Charlie's brother-in-law? shame! scandal! humiliation! kneel, pray, beg the Lord!"

Queenie sneaks under the stove. My friend gazes at her shoes, her chin quivers, she lifts her skirt and blows her nose and runs to her room. Long after the town has gone to sleep and the house is silent except for the chimings of clocks and the sputter of fading fires, she is weeping

into a pillow already as wet as a widow's handkerchief.

"Don't cry," I say, sitting at the bottom of her bed and shivering despite my flannel night-gown that smells of last winter's cough syrup, "don't cry," I beg, teasing her toes, tickling her

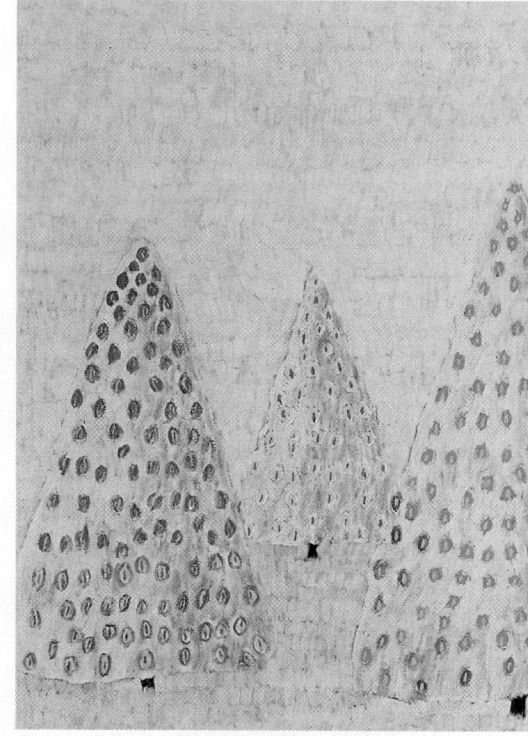

Christmas Trees by Theora Hamblett. Drawing.

feet, "you're too old for that."

"It's because," she hiccups, "I *am* too old. Old and funny."

"Not funny. Fun. More fun than anybody. Listen. If you don't stop crying you'll be so tired tomorrow we can't go cut a tree."

She straightens up. Queenie jumps on the bed (where Queenie is not allowed) to lick her cheeks. "I know where we'll find real pretty trees, Buddy. And holly, too. With berries big as your eyes. It's way off in the woods. Farther than we've ever been. Papa used to bring us

---

Skill Link

Identifying Comparisons
To help assess your students' skill in identifying comparisons, use the following exercise before you teach the Language Link Mini-Lesson on figures of speech, p. 163.

Tell students that to help readers imagine something, writers sometimes describe one thing by comparing it to something else. From each sentence that follows, have students pick out the two things that are being compared.

1. The wrinkles on her face were tracks of time. [wrinkles and tracks]
2. The moon hung in the sky like a silver balloon. [moon and balloon]
3. The coins jingled like sleigh bells. [the sounds of coins and bells]
4. Like the sun after a storm, her smile dispelled the gloom. [the sun and her smile]
5. The faded roses still held a hint of summer. [roses and summer]

Christmas trees from there: carry them on his shoulder. That's fifty years ago. Well, now: I can't wait for morning."

Morning. Frozen rime[9] lusters the grass; the sun, round as an orange and orange as hot-weather moons, balances on the horizon,

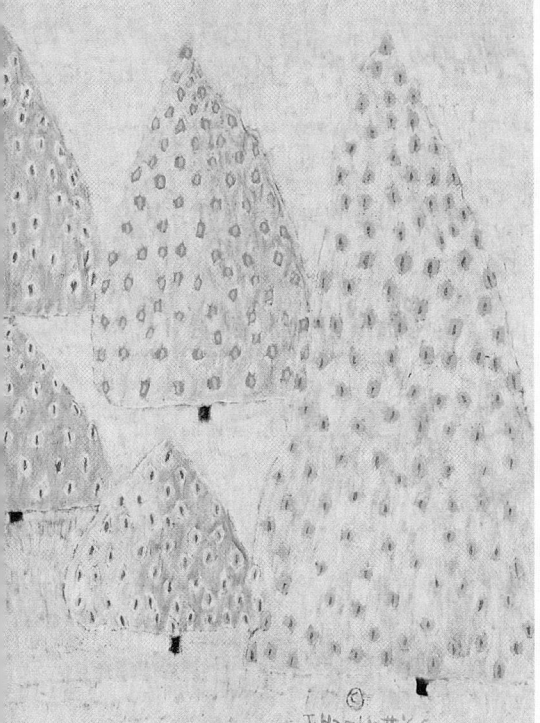

Courtesy of the University Museums, University of Mississippi Cultural Center, University, Mississippi.

burnishes[10] the silvered winter woods. A wild turkey calls. A renegade hog grunts in the undergrowth. Soon, by the edge of knee-deep, rapid-running water, we have to abandon the buggy. Queenie wades the stream first, paddles across, barking complaints at the swiftness of the current, the pneumonia-making coldness of it. We follow, holding our shoes and equipment (a hatchet, a burlap sack) above our heads. A mile more: of chastising thorns, burs and briers that

9. **frozen rime:** frost.
10. **burnishes:** polishes.

catch at our clothes; of rusty pine needles brilliant with gaudy fungus and molted feathers. Here, there, a flash, a flutter, an ecstasy of shrillings remind us that not all the birds have flown south. Always, the path unwinds through lemony sun pools and pitch vine tunnels. Another creek to cross: A disturbed armada[11] of speckled trout froths the water round us, and frogs the size of plates practice belly flops; beaver workmen are building a dam. On the farther shore, Queenie shakes herself and trembles. My friend shivers, too: not with cold but enthusiasm. One of her hat's ragged roses sheds a petal as she lifts her head and inhales the pine-heavy air. "We're almost there; can you smell it, Buddy?" she says, as though we were approaching an ocean.

And, indeed, it is a kind of ocean. Scented acres of holiday trees, prickly-leafed holly. Red berries shiny as Chinese bells: Black crows swoop upon them screaming. Having stuffed our burlap sacks with enough greenery and crimson to garland a dozen windows, we set about choosing a tree. "It should be," muses my friend, "twice as tall as a boy. So a boy can't steal the star." The one we pick is twice as tall as me. A brave, handsome brute that survives thirty hatchet strokes before it keels with a creaking, rending cry. Lugging it like a kill, we commence the long trek out. Every few yards we abandon the struggle, sit down, and pant. But we have the strength of triumphant huntsmen; that and the tree's virile, icy perfume revive us, goad us on. Many compliments accompany our sunset return along the red clay road to town; but my friend is sly and noncommittal when passers-by praise the treasure perched in our buggy: What a fine tree and where did it come from? "Yonderways," she murmurs vaguely. Once a car stops and the rich mill owner's lazy wife leans

— E
— F
— G

11. **armada** (är·mä′də): group, as of warships.

WORDS TO OWN
noncommittal (nän·kə·mit″l) *adj.*: not admitting or committing to any particular purpose or point of view.

A CHRISTMAS MEMORY 151

E Critical Thinking
Analyzing
❓ Why is nature so important in this story? How is it linked to the characters? [Possible answers: It is the setting of the narrator's nostalgic memories of childhood; like the relationship between the cousins, nature is pure and true; they seem most at ease in the beautiful outdoors, enjoying simple pleasures.]

F Elements of Literature
Indirect Characterization
❓ In what ways does Buddy's cousin seem like part of nature here? [Possible answers: She wears part of nature on her hat; like one of nature's creatures might, she smells the holly before she sees it.]

G Elements of Literature
Figures of Speech
❓ To what are the tree and the cutting of it compared? [The tree is first compared to a "brave, handsome brute" and then to a wild animal. Cutting down the tree is compared to hunting and killing a wild animal.]

Taking a Second Look

Review: Monitoring Reading Strategies
Remind students that when they get confused by a long, descriptive passage like the one on this page, or when they are unclear about anything they read, they can reread, question, or use resources to help clarify their understanding. Ask students to work in pairs to do the following:
1. Reread this page, stopping after every six to eight lines.
2. Discuss at each stopping point what exactly they do or do not understand.

3. For things they do not understand, ask students to pinpoint whether the issue is vocabulary, losing track of the plot, a particular sentence, or some other problem.
4. To solve any comprehension problems, have students determine a strategy, such as rereading, consulting with each other, or using a dictionary.

A Elements of Literature

Indirect Characterization

❓ What do you learn about the narrator's cousin from her words and actions here? [Possible answers: She cares little for money and possessions; her last bit of dialogue shows that she has a spiritual respect for living things.]

B English Language Learners

Outdated Usage

Explain that the "five-and-dime" was a variety store once common on every main street of America. These stores sold a broad range of inexpensive merchandise, a great deal of which could be bought for five to ten cents.

C Elements of Literature

Setting

❓ What atmosphere do these details create? [Possible answers: The atmosphere is festive; the details show a bustling happiness.] You might mention that these holiday details form a cheerful surface beneath which a sense of foreboding or sadness lurks.

D Critical Thinking

Making Connections

❓ How do these words relate to the Arthur Ashe quotation on the opening page of the collection (p. 119)? [Possible answers: Buddy's cousin's desire to give is greater than her desire to get, which shows the generosity of her spirit; her life is given meaning by what she can give to those she loves.]

---

out and whines: "Giveya twobits cash for that ol tree." Ordinarily my friend is afraid of saying no; but on this occasion she promptly shakes her head: "We wouldn't take a dollar." The mill owner's wife persists. "A dollar, my foot! Fifty cents. That's my last offer. Goodness, woman, you can get another one." In answer, my friend gently reflects: "I doubt it. There's never two of anything."

Home: Queenie slumps by the fire and sleeps till tomorrow, snoring loud as a human.

A trunk in the attic contains: a shoe box of ermine tails[12] (off the opera cape of a curious lady who once rented a room in the house), coils of frazzled tinsel gone gold with age, one silver star, a brief rope of dilapidated, undoubtedly dangerous candylike light bulbs. Excellent decorations, as far as they go, which isn't far enough: My friend wants our tree to blaze "like a Baptist window," droop with weighty snows of ornament. But we can't afford the made-in-Japan splendors at the five-and-dime. So we do what we've always done: sit for days at the kitchen table with scissors and crayons and stacks of colored paper. I make sketches and my friend cuts them out: lots of cats, fish too (because they're easy to draw), some apples, some watermelons, a few winged angels devised from saved-up sheets of Hershey-bar tinfoil. We use safety pins to attach these creations to the tree; as a final touch, we sprinkle the branches with shredded cotton (picked in August for this purpose). My friend, surveying the effect, clasps her hands together. "Now honest, Buddy. Doesn't it look good enough to eat?" Queenie tries to eat an angel.

After weaving and ribboning holly wreaths for all the front windows, our next project is the fashioning of family gifts. Tie-dye scarves for the ladies, for the men a home-brewed lemon and licorice and aspirin syrup to be taken "at the first Symptoms of a Cold and after Hunting." But

---

12. **ermine** (ʉr′min) **tails:** black-tipped white tails of certain kinds of weasels, used to trim clothes.

---

when it comes time for making each other's gift, my friend and I separate to work secretly. I would like to buy her a pearl-handled knife, a radio, a whole pound of chocolate-covered cherries (we tasted some once and she always swears: "I could live on them, Buddy, Lord yes I could—and that's not taking His name in vain"). Instead, I am building her a kite. She would like to give me a bicycle (she's said so on several million occasions: "If only I could, Buddy. It's bad enough in life to do without something *you* want; but confound it, what gets my goat is not being able to give somebody something you want *them* to have. Only one of these days, I will, Buddy. Locate you a bike. Don't ask how. Steal it, maybe"). Instead, I'm fairly certain that she is building me a kite—the same as last year, and the year before: The year before that we exchanged slingshots. All of which is fine by me. For we are champion kite-fliers who study the wind like sailors; my friend, more accomplished than I, can get a kite aloft when there isn't enough breeze to carry clouds.

Christmas Eve afternoon we scrape together a nickel and go to the butcher's to buy Queenie's traditional gift, a good gnawable beef bone. The bone, wrapped in funny paper, is placed high in the tree near the silver star. Queenie knows it's there. She squats at the foot of the tree, staring up in a trance of greed: When bedtime arrives she refuses to budge. Her excitement is equaled by my own. I kick the covers and turn my pillow as though it were a scorching summer's night. Somewhere a rooster crows: falsely, for the sun is still on the other side of the world.

"Buddy, are you awake?" It is my friend, calling from her room, which is next to mine; and an instant later she is sitting on my bed holding a candle. "Well, I can't sleep a hoot," she declares. "My mind's jumping like a jack rabbit. Buddy, do you think Mrs. Roosevelt will serve our cake at dinner?" We huddle in the bed, and she squeezes my hand I-love-you. "Seems like your hand used to be so much smaller. I guess I hate to see you grow up. When you're grown

---

Getting Students Involved

Cooperative Learning

Reader's Theater. Ask students to work in groups of four or five to present a section of the story as a Reader's Theater project. Remind students that this is a dramatic reenactment in which the actors may read from the book. Explain, however, that they need to add depth and richness to the performances through the use of gestures and through the tone, pitch, and

modulation of their voices. They should also enhance the presentation through the addition of props and/or background music. Three students can take on the roles of the young Buddy, his cousin, and the grown-up Buddy, who serves as the narrator; the remaining student or students can direct the reading and make decisions regarding the use of props and gestures. Since

there is no dialogue for Buddy in the story, students can write lines based on the boy's character. All students should work together to plan the reading and to assess how well it went. Encourage the groups to practice their performances and then present them to the class. Ask the audience to cite positive points about each performance.

up, will we still be friends?" I say always. "But I feel so bad, Buddy. I wanted so bad to give you a bike. I tried to sell my cameo Papa gave me. Buddy—" she hesitates, as though embarrassed. "I made you another kite." Then I confess that I made her one, too; and we laugh. The candle burns too short to hold. Out it goes, exposing the starlight, the stars spinning at the window like a visible caroling that slowly, slowly daybreak silences. Possibly we doze; but the beginnings of dawn splash us like cold water: We're up, wide-eyed and wandering while we wait for others to waken. Quite deliberately my friend drops a kettle on the kitchen floor. I tap-dance in front of closed doors. One by one the household emerges, looking as though they'd like to kill us both; but it's Christmas, so they can't. First, a gorgeous breakfast: just everything you can imagine—from flapjacks and fried squirrel to hominy grits and honey-in-the-comb. Which puts everyone in a good humor except my friend and me. Frankly, we're so impatient to get at the presents we can't eat a mouthful.

Well, I'm disappointed. Who wouldn't be? With socks, a Sunday school shirt, some handkerchiefs, a hand-me-down sweater, and a year's subscription to a religious magazine for children, *The Little Shepherd*. It makes me boil. It really does.

My friend has a better haul. A sack of satsumas,[13] that's her best present. She is proudest, however, of a white wool shawl knitted by her married sister. But she *says* her favorite gift is the kite I built her. And it *is* very beautiful; though not as beautiful as the one she made me, which is blue and scattered with gold and green Good Conduct stars; moreover, my name is painted on it, "Buddy."

"Buddy, the wind is blowing."

The wind is blowing, and nothing will do till we've run to a pasture below the house where Queenie has scooted to bury her bone (and where, a winter hence, Queenie will be buried, too). There, plunging through the healthy,

13. **satsumas** (sat′sə·mäz′): oranges.

waist-high grass, we unreel our kites, feel them twitching at the string like sky fish as they swim into the wind. Satisfied, sun-warmed, we sprawl in the grass and peel satsumas and watch our kites cavort. Soon I forget the socks and hand-me-down sweater. I'm as happy as if we'd already won the fifty-thousand-dollar Grand Prize in that coffee-naming contest.

"My, how foolish I am!" my friend cries, suddenly alert, like a woman remembering too late she has biscuits in the oven. "You know what I've always thought?" she asks in a tone of discovery, and smiling not at me but a point beyond. "I've always thought a body would have to be sick and dying before they saw the Lord. And I imagined that when He came it would be like looking at the Baptist window: pretty as colored glass with the sun pouring through, such a shine you don't know it's getting dark. And it's been a comfort: to think of that shine taking away all the spooky feeling. But I'll wager it never happens. I'll wager at the very end a body realizes the Lord has already shown Himself. That things as they are"— her hand circles in a gesture that gathers clouds and kites and grass and Queenie pawing earth over her bone—"just what they've always seen, was seeing Him. As for me, I could leave the world with today in my eyes."

This is our last Christmas together.

Life separates us. Those who Know Best decide that I belong in a military school. And so follows a miserable succession of bugle-blowing prisons, grim reveille-ridden[14] summer camps. I have a new home too. But it doesn't count. Home is where my friend is, and there I never go.

And there she remains, puttering around the kitchen. Alone with Queenie. Then alone. ("Buddy dear," she writes in her wild hard-to-read script, "yesterday Jim Macy's horse kicked Queenie bad. Be thankful she didn't feel much. I wrapped her in a Fine Linen sheet and rode her

14. **reveille-ridden** (rev′ə·lē rid′'n): ruled by the drum or bugle signal used to rouse sleeping people in a military or summer camp. The writer uses this phrase to suggest a tightly disciplined camp.

E Reading Skills and Strategies
Making Inferences

❓ Why do these presents make Buddy "boil"? [Possible answers: They do not take into account his interests; there is nothing personal about them; they are simply useful—they are not fun or imaginative; they do not seem to reflect the love of the giver.]

F Elements of Literature
Foreshadowing

❓ Foreshadowing is the use of clues to hint at events that will occur later in the plot. Why do you think the author mentions Queenie's eventual death here? [Possible answers: It signals more sadness to come; it suggests the end of these happy times of which Queenie is a part.]

G Literary Connections

❓ The Christian celebration of Epiphany, which occurs shortly after Christmas, commemorates the showing (literally the "manifestation") of the infant Jesus to the Magi, or Three Kings. James Joyce introduced the term *epiphany* in literature to mean a sudden, intuitive revelation. What is the idea that Buddy's friend suddenly comes to understand? [She understands that peace, a sense of harmony, and a knowing of God can be found during life, instead of just at life's end.]

H Appreciating Language
Capitalization

❓ What is the effect of capitalizing the words "Those who Know Best"? [Possible answers: It emphasizes the ironic use of the phrase, which describes relatives who don't seem to have any idea or really care what is best for Buddy and his friend; it underscores the authority Buddy's relatives have over him.]

Making the Connections

Connecting to the Theme: "The Human Spirit"

What does this story have to say about the human spirit? Invite students to discuss these questions:

- The odds seem stacked rather high against the happiness of these two characters, yet they share a sweet companionship that is the subject of the narrator's nostalgia so many years later. What exactly do they share? What makes it so special?

- What is it in the narrator's cousin that allows her to transcend her world of poverty? How would you explain her ability to find joy in such simple tasks?

- What is so worth remembering for this narrator? What does he find in this Christmas memory that he perhaps finds no place else?

A Reading Skills and Strategies

Making Inferences

? Why do you think Buddy's cousin confuses him with the other Buddy? [Possible answers: Both are key friendships in her life; she is mentally confused; in both these friendships, it is not so much individual identity that matters as it is the fact of loving someone, of having a "buddy," or friend.]

B Elements of Literature

Setting

? How does the time of year continue to affect the narrator's feelings? [The December setting, "fruitcake weather," forever recalls the friendship; after Buddy's cousin dies, Christmastime becomes a poignant reminder of his loss.]

Resources ●

Selection Assessment
Formal Assessment
• Selection Test, p. 17
Test Generator (One-Stop Planner)
• CD-ROM

BROWSING IN THE FILES

Writers on Writing. Capote agreed completely with the legions of writers who have said that writing does not come easy: "It's a very excruciating life facing that blank piece of paper every day and having to reach up somewhere into the clouds and bring something down out of them." With even more charm and wit, Capote has said this about characters who take on a life of their own: "You can't blame a writer for what the characters say."

in the buggy down to Simpson's pasture where she can be with all her Bones. . . .") For a few Novembers she continues to bake her fruitcakes single-handed; not as many, but some: And, of course, she always sends me "the best of the batch." Also, in every letter she encloses a dime wadded in toilet paper: "See a picture show and write me the story." But gradually in her letters she tends to confuse me with her other friend, the Buddy who died in the 1880s; more and more, thirteenths are not the only days she stays in bed: A morning arrives in November, a leafless birdless coming of winter morning, when she cannot rouse herself to exclaim: "Oh my, it's fruitcake weather!"

And when that happens, I know it. A message saying so merely confirms a piece of news some secret vein had already received, severing from me an irreplaceable part of myself, letting it loose like a kite on a broken string. That is why, walking across a school campus on this particular December morning, I keep searching the sky. As if I expected to see, rather like hearts, a lost pair of kites hurrying toward heaven.

MEET THE WRITER

"A Turtle on Its Back"

Truman Capote (1924–1984) said he was "sort of dragged up" by assorted elderly relatives who lived in "dirt-road Alabama." He was born in New Orleans, but his father deserted the family, and the boy was shunted about while his mother lived in New York. For several years Capote attended military schools, which he hated. When he was seventeen, he abandoned formal schooling for good and moved to New York City to learn to write. He came to national prominence with the publication of his first novel, *Other Voices, Other Rooms* (1948).

Capote's most famous novel is probably *Breakfast at Tiffany's* (1958). It was made into a movie starring Audrey Hepburn as Holly Golightly, the story's unpredictable and "lost" heroine, who goes to New York from the South to make her fortune. His most talked-about book is not fiction at all, but an account of a mass murder that took place in Kansas. Called *In Cold Blood* (1966), the book took Capote seven years of research and writing and involved him in much controversy. Capote called the book a nonfiction novel—a narrative that reads like a novel but with events that are all true.

In a *New York Times Magazine* interview, Capote once said that his frustrations during his early years made him feel "like a turtle on its back."

❝ I always felt that nobody was going to understand me, going to understand what I felt about things. I guess that's why I started writing. At least on paper I could put down what I thought. ❞

Assessing Learning

Check Test: Questions and Answers

1. Who is Buddy's best friend? [his cousin, a woman in her sixties]
2. What do Buddy and his friend make as gifts for other people? [fruitcakes]
3. From whom do the two friends buy liquor? [Haha Jones]

4. What do the two friends give each other their last Christmas together? [kites]
5. What has happened to Buddy's friend by the end of the story? [She has died.]

Standardized Test Preparation

For practice with standardized test format specific to this selection, see
• *Standardized Test Preparation*, pp. 20, 22
For practice in proofreading and editing, see
• *Daily Oral Grammar*, Transparency 8

Connections
A SCREENPLAY

from A CHRISTMAS MEMORY
Truman Capote

Fade In: A

The dark screen slowly begins to assume color: a pale, pastel, washed-out blue. For several beats it is impossible for us to distinguish what it is we are looking at. Then, slowly, the image begins to resolve—a cloudless, predawn sky which blends with a horizon line made indistinguishable because of the limpidity[1] of the light and the softness of a wispy early-morning ground fog. The sun is about to rise, and as the light increases, we begin to distinguish the graceful shapes of the bare trees of a Southern winter landscape. We see that the grass is rimed with morning frost. The first sound now: A distant but clear tolling bell breaks the still, wintry air. The scene must be one of great beauty, reflecting the pastoral and bucolic[2] innocence of a time and place sweetly recalled.

B
C

1. **limpidity** (lim·pid′·ə·tē): clearness.
2. **bucolic** (byo͞o·käl′·ik): typical of the countryside.

Pages 155–159: Scenes from the television version of *A Christmas Memory,* starring Donnie Melvin and Geraldine Page.
(Above) American Museum of the Moving Image, New York. Photograph by Muky Munkacsi.

A CHRISTMAS MEMORY **155**

Connections

This excerpt from the screenplay of "A Christmas Memory" covers the opening scene of the story (pp. 145–146) where Buddy and his cousin gather pecans for their holiday cakes. If you want to assign students to create a screenplay from any other text in this book, use this screenplay as a model.

A English Language Learners
Technical Language
Be sure students understand the term *fade-in,* which refers to "the gradual appearance from black of a picture on the screen." Also alert them to the use of italics on this page and elsewhere, a signal to the reader that the words are not dialogue but instead are directions for the camera or for the actors.

B Reading Skills and Strategies
Comparing
? How is this opening similar to the opening in the short story? [Possible answers: Readers and viewers are gradually introduced to the setting; the slow fade-in to the setting simulates the way readers are slowly led to picture the opening scene of the story.]

C Elements of Literature
Setting
? In what ways do the details of the setting create an atmosphere, or feeling, that is similar to the feeling in the short story? [Sample answer: The details evoke beauty, innocence, and nostalgia.]

Reaching All Students

Struggling Readers
Preview the text with students, alerting them to the conventions of script-writing, such as the ways in which camera directions are presented in italics and dialogue in indented blocks with no quotation marks.

English Language Learners
Explain the term *voice-over* (a voice commenting or explaining off-camera), and discuss how this technique is used in telling the story. Also define and discuss such terms as *pan* (scan a wide area), *dissolve* (fade away or melt into another picture), *close-up* (a shot close to the subject), and *roll main titles* (the title is superimposed on the picture).

Advanced Learners
Challenge advanced learners to compare camera instructions with descriptive passages in the story to see what is the same and what is changed.

A. Critical Thinking

Speculating

? Why is so much of the screenplay composed of camera directions? [Because film is a visual medium, much of what is described in words in a short story is shown by the camera in a movie.]

B. Struggling Readers

Using Graphic Aids

Tell students that the photographs on this two-page spread are actual frames from the television adaptation of the story. Ask students what type of information the frames on this spread convey. [They show the two main characters, the inside of their home, the buggy, and the scene in the grocery store. Two of the photos convey the intimacy between Buddy and his cousin, and one, with the buggy, shows their joy in nature.]

C. Reading Skills and Strategies

Visualizing

? Do the representations of the main characters in the photos correspond with the mental images of them you created while reading? [Students may say that the woman appears younger, better looking, less frail, less eccentric, or more vibrant than they had imagined. They may have visualized Buddy as a more shy and unkempt looking child than he appears to be in these photos.]

D. Elements of Literature

Setting

? Why does the author want to be sure that the viewer sees a large, warm, old-fashioned kitchen? [Possible answers: He wants to be sure the emotional atmosphere is "warm"; he wants the kitchen to be inviting; he wants to show that the action is quite far in the past; by instructing that it be large, he may want to suggest that the kitchen plays a key role in the memories recounted.]

T156

A *On the horizon comes the first flame of the rising sun, its orange rind in powerful contrast to the blue-gray wash of the landscape. Music gently begins. The sun continues to violate the pellucid³ unity of ground and sky. Now, slowly, CAMERA PANS, losing the sun, to a large, faded, spreading old house. The architectural grace of the house is emphasized by the softness of light and perhaps even the softness of focus with which we might summon and visualize a precious memory of childhood.*

CAMERA begins a slow tracking shot toward the house. We are looking at what must be a kitchen wing. Healthy wood smoke streams from the chimney, while the light from the windows seems warm and inviting. As CAMERA moves closer, music continues and we hear:

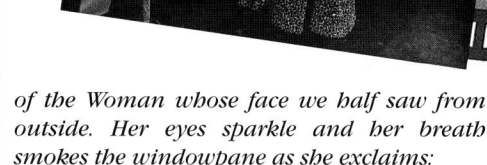

B **NARRATOR** *(softly, voice-over).* A coming of winter morning more than thirty years ago . . .

Now the CAMERA has drawn in on the kitchen window, concentrating on a particular frosted pane which reflects the half-orb of the still-rising sun. Through the frost and behind the window we see a Woman with almost white hair. Her face is remarkable—not unlike Lincoln's, craggy like that, and tinted by sun and wind; but it is delicate too, finely boned,

3. **pellucid** (pə·lōō′sid): clear; transparent.

---

and her eyes are sherry-colored and timid. Much of this we shall see in a moment, as the image of her face now is blurred by the scrim⁴ of the icy windowpane.

CAMERA draws tighter, concentrating on the reflected rising sun. When its orange nearly fills the screen, we LAP DISSOLVE through to an

EXTREME CLOSE-UP of a roaring fire.

NARRATOR *(voice-over).* Just today the fireplace commenced its seasonal roar.

C *CAMERA pulls back to reveal that we are inside the kitchen. Now we PAN to a CLOSE-UP*

of the Woman whose face we half saw from outside. Her eyes sparkle and her breath smokes the windowpane as she exclaims:

WOMAN. Oh my! It's fruitcake weather!

D *CAMERA begins a slow pullback from her face, gradually revealing a warm and enormous old-fashioned kitchen. It includes a great*

4. **scrim:** curtain used in a theater. It is often semi-transparent.

wood stove and a huge fireplace (both functioning in full fettle this early morning), a large wooden white-scrubbed round table, and an atmosphere of faintly impecunious⁵ well-being. As CAMERA continues to pull back it reveals the seated back of a small boy happily involved in eating a large breakfast.

NARRATOR *(voice-over; starts speaking almost immediately after the Woman's line above).* The person to whom she is speaking is myself. I am seven; she is sixty-something. We are cousins, very distant ones, and we have lived together—well, as long as I can remember. Other people inhabit the house, relatives; and though they have power over us, and frequently make us cry, we are not, on the whole, too much aware of them. We are each other's best friend. She calls me Buddy, in memory

of a boy who was formerly her best friend. The other Buddy died in the 1880s, when she was still a child. She is still a child.

During the foregoing, the CAMERA completes a thorough investigation of this warm,

5. **impecunious** (im′pi·kyo͞o′nē·əs): lacking in money.

wonderful room and its two occupants, noting such details as the woman's tennis shoes and her shapeless gray sweater worn over a summery calico dress.

WOMAN *(to the boy, excitedly).* It is! It's fruitcake weather! I knew it before I got out of bed. The courthouse bell sounded so cold and clear. And there were no birds singing. They've gone to warmer country, yes indeed!

She sees Buddy is still happily packing his breakfast away. She crosses to him and snatches his plate.

WOMAN. Oh, Buddy, stop stuffing biscuit and fetch our buggy!

American Museum of the Moving Image, New York. Photograph by Muky Munkacsi. Gift of Ronald A. and Randy P. Munkacsi.

He runs after her, takes the last biscuit off the plate, and puts it in his mouth. The Woman rushes about clearing the table and piling the dishes in the drainboard. Buddy helps her, but, fast as he moves, it isn't fast enough for her. He has the sugar bowl and is opening the cupboard to put it away.

WOMAN. Leave it, Buddy. We've got to go. We've thirty cakes to bake!

Buddy drops the sugar bowl on the counter and runs to the coat rack, hurriedly puts on

E **Critical Thinking**
Speculating
Screenwriters tend to avoid the disruption of an action sequence with a long speech. Why might the writer include this lengthy voice-over narration at this point? [The camera investigates the scene as the voice speaks; this speech supplies important background information and serves as an introduction to the story.]

F **Reading Skills and Strategies**
Determining the Author's Purpose
? What do you think is the author's purpose in repeating the phrase about the fruitcake? [Possible answers: to bring the audience back to the woman's point of view after the camera has wandered around the kitchen and the audience has heard some family history; to show how excited the woman is.]

G **Reading Skills and Strategies**
Making Inferences
? What information does this passage suggest about the relationship of these two friends? [Possible answers: She is the leader, and he is the follower; in some ways, she is like a mother to him; she is the source of his happiness.]

Skill Link

Determining the Writer's Motives
If students have not already noted that Truman Capote wrote this screenplay, as well as the short story on which it is based, be sure they do so now. Discuss the kind of screenplay he was motivated to write by asking students to think about the following questions and then share their responses with the class.

- Where do the words in the screenplay seem especially close to those in the story? Give three examples.
- What examples can you find in the screenplay that show Capote departing from his original story, theme, language, or idea of the characters and their relationship?

- When Capote departs from his original story, why do you think he does so?
- If you had to generalize, would you say Capote wanted to stay close to his original story or create something new and original for television? What makes you think so?

his cap and coat. He takes his long raggedy woolen scarf. The Woman ties it around his neck, the ends hanging down his back.

> **WOMAN.** Raggedy old thing. I've got to knit you a new one.
> **BUDDY** *(anxiously).* Not for my Christmas present?
> **WOMAN.** Would I give you a scarf for *Christmas*? Would I do a thing like that?

He grins and runs out, leaving her still straightening the kitchen.

Buddy comes down the back porch steps and runs to the shed. He opens the door and an instant later comes out wheeling an old rickety wicker baby buggy. Its paint has long ago worn away, and its wheels wobble like a

drunkard's legs. The buggy is half filled with firewood. He takes it out and piles it against the shed and then pushes the buggy at a great rate to the back porch. The Woman is just coming down the steps. She is wearing an old hand-me-down ill-fitting coat and carrying her gloves.

> **BUDDY.** Your hat! You forgot your hat!
> **WOMAN.** Oh goodness, my hat!

She rushes back into the house. She is in a hall. She opens a closet stuffed with the outer clothes of other members of the family, umbrellas, boots on the floor, etc., a clutter of hats, caps, gloves, and scarves on a shelf. She rummages around and finally pulls her hat out from under them. It is a straw cartwheel garlanded with faded velvet roses, some of them hanging loosely by a thread. As she claps it on her head, one of the roses falls off. She picks it up and holds it uncertainly. She is torn by her desire to hurry and yet the rose is precious to her. On the narrow hall table there is a vase of flowers

beneath a dim mirror and perhaps some photographs of relatives. The Woman puts the rose carefully among the flowers in the vase, catches a glimpse of herself in the mirror, straightens the hat from its first crazy angle to another just as odd, and hurries out.

Buddy is down on his hands and knees peering under the house and whistling. Whatever he is whistling at is not answering.

> **WOMAN.** Buddy, Buddy, where are you?
> **BUDDY.** Under here. Queenie won't come out. . . .

Getting Students Involved

WOMAN *(bending down and whistling).* Come on, Queenie, come on, we're going to the pecan grove!

No movement from under the house.

BUDDY. You shouldn't have told her. She knows it's a long way.

WOMAN *(to the dog).* Come on, Queenie, I packed a big bone for your lunch!

Reluctantly, a little orange and white rat terrier crawls out from under the house, and the three of them set off. Buddy and the Woman walk as fast as they can, Queenie trails suspiciously behind them.

Here a series of lovely shots of their pilgrimage. The landscape and surrounding country remain a study in early-morning pastel; in our horizon shots of the three we see the cloudless winter sky still the palest shade of blue. Over this montage we: **E**

ROLL MAIN TITLES.

Final shot of montage brings them to a new barbed-wire fence around the pecan grove, prominently featuring a sign "Callahan's Pecan Farm—Private Property—No Trespass- **F**

ing—Trespassers Will Be Prosecuted to the Fullest Extent of the Law."

EXTREME CLOSE-UP of the "No Trespassing" sign.

REVERSE to the faces of the Woman and Buddy. **D**

They are surveying the fence with dismay.

WOMAN. Buddy, we're going in there!
BUDDY. How?

The Woman steps forward and picks up the top strand of the fence. Buddy gives her a look.

WOMAN. Go on!

G

Buddy looks around. It is clear he is more reluctant about this than she is. Finally he stoops and goes in under the fence. He holds the wire strand for the Woman. She pushes the buggy through and then bends to go under herself. Her sweater catches on a barb. She stops to untangle it.

WOMAN. I simply do not admire a man who puts up a barbed-wire fence.
BUDDY. I don't either.

Pushing the buggy, they walk on into the grove.

A CHRISTMAS MEMORY 159

Connecting Across Texts

Connecting with the Short Story "A Christmas Memory"
Ask students to compare this portion of the screenplay with the short story. Ask the following questions:
- What parts of the short story and the screenplay are identical? [The setting is almost identical, the characters are the same, and the goal of making fruitcakes is the same.]

- How does the screenplay show description? [This tends to be achieved either through voice-over narration or, more consistently, through the camera's eye.]
- Is the story changed in any way in the screenplay? [Most of the story is the same, but there are minor variations, such as the cousin's deliberate decision to trespass.]

Student to Student

In this poem, the student writer juxtaposes images of his grandfather from the past and the present.

Ⓐ Struggling Readers
Summarizing

❓ What is the main idea of these first four lines? [The speaker cannot make the connection between a boy she sees in a photo and her grandfather.]

Ⓑ Critical Thinking
Interpreting

❓ The explicit question in this poem is whether an image of an orphaned little child can actually be the same person that the speaker knows as her grandfather. What more significant—and indirectly stated— question does the speaker ask? [Can this little boy in the photo, who grew up as an orphan, be the same man who is now so intent on keeping his family together?]

RESPONDING TO THE ART

Marisol Escobar (1930–   ) is a Venezuelan artist known simply at Marisol. She became famous in the 1960s for her satirical sculpture and assemblages. Students should note just how big this sculpture is, with its height reaching more than six feet, and how the figures seem comical and serious at the same time.

Activity. How does the sculpture convey the idea that family members are all separate individuals and yet related? [Possible answer: All are part of the same grouping and are cast from the same material, yet each is encased in its own block of wood and looks at its own point on the horizon.]

Photo Album

> Can that skinny little boy with
> the big ears and the rope belt,
> Ⓐ orphaned at seven,
> be my grandfather—
> 5 The grandpa of our loud and boisterous bunch—
> Organizer of family reunions that annually weld
> nineteen cousins from
> Houston,
> Chicago,
> 10 Ⓑ Albany,
> Adirondacks,
> and me
> together—
> and keep his five grown sons and their wives
> 15 unorphaned?

—Gretchen Lund
Highland Park High School
Highland Park, New Jersey

Stephanie's Family (1983)
by Marisol Escobar.
Wood, charcoal, plaster
(74″ x 72″ x 53″).

© Marisol Escobar/Licensed by VAGA, New York, NY.

Connecting Across Texts

Connecting with "A Christmas Memory"
Use the following questions to help students connect this poem to the short story.

• What does the grandfather in this poem have in common with Buddy? [Both are orphaned at an early age; both are seven years old when they are "captured" by the work of art.]

• What effect does being an orphan have on the person in the poem in later years? [It appears to make him value family connections; it makes him want to close the long distances that separate him from his grown children and their families.]

• In the short story the narrator is portrayed as looking back nostalgically to the time when he was seven. How is this different from the way the grandfather is portrayed in this poem? [Possible answers: Nothing about the narrator's current life is portrayed in the short story, while the grandfather is shown as an adult; the grandfather looks to the future, while the narrator looks to the past.]

MAKING MEANINGS

First Thoughts

[respond]

1. Share your responses to Capote's characters and to the ways they are treated by others.

Shaping Interpretations

[interpret]

2. Buddy says on page 146 that his friend is "still a child." What do you think this means? Is this a negative trait or a positive one, and why do you think so?

[analyze]

3. How would you describe the **character** of Buddy's friend? (Refer to the chart you filled out on page 144.) Consider

   • what she says

   • the way her face is described

   • the things she does

   • the things she has never done

   • the ways people respond to her

   • her bedroom

[analyze]

4. **Motivation** refers to the reasons a person does something. When you analyze a character, it's important to think about motivation. In this story, what do you think motivates

   • Buddy's cousin to make fruitcakes for strangers?

   • Mr. Haha to give the money back?

   • Buddy to be so close to his older cousin?

[synthesize]

5. Some people feel that this is a story about two people who are in search of love. How do you feel about this generalization? Explain whether or not you think Buddy and his friend find what they want.

Extending the Text

[compare]

6. If this is a story about love and generosity, could "Thank You, M'am" (page 120) be seen as a story with the same message? With a partner, compare the two stories, and share your conclusions in class.

Challenging the Text

[evaluate]

7. Some readers feel that Buddy's friend is a realistic character, but others feel she is too good to be believable—that people like this don't exist in real life. Which point of view is closer to yours? Why?

A CHRISTMAS MEMORY 161

Reading Check

a. What do you know about the person who is telling this story? What is his relationship to the old woman he calls "my friend"?

b. Why do Buddy and his friend make fruitcakes each year?

c. What obstacles must they overcome to make their gifts?

d. What surprises Buddy and his friend about their visit to Mr. Haha Jones?

e. What does Buddy's friend discover after flying her kite on their last Christmas Day together?

MAKING MEANINGS

MAKING MEANINGS

First Thoughts

1. Students may express warm feelings about the main characters and concern about how they are treated.

Shaping Interpretations

2. Sample responses: Buddy's cousin is childlike in that she is trusting and open to experience. This trait is positive because it enables her to enjoy the simple pleasures of life; this trait is negative because it makes her vulnerable to mistreatment by others and unable to assume adult responsibilities.

3. Her face suggests she has a wisdom separate from the standard experiences of adulthood. Her life has been limited; she has had few opportunities and little experience of the world. She has, however, met some incidents in her life with bravery, such as the encounter with the snake. Those who live with her (except Buddy) seem fed up with her, suggesting she has been the source of problems.

4. Buddy's cousin may be motivated by her sense that Christmas is a time to give and to connect with people; Mr. Haha Jones, by generosity or pity; Buddy, by the need for companionship and love.

5. Some students may find the pair's efforts to connect with strangers rather sad. Others may say that the two seem happy with each other. They may not win the love of strangers with their fruitcakes, but they genuinely love each other.

Extending the Text

6. Both stories portray the positive power of love and generosity; both show the relationship between an older woman and a boy.

Challenging the Text

7. Some students may find her good-natured simplicity and generosity more believable than the facts that she has killed a rattlesnake or never seen a movie. Some students may recognize that since Buddy's friend is seen through the mind and emotions of a child (as recollected by the narrator), she cannot be judged objectively.

Reading Check

Answers may vary slightly.

a. The narrator, Buddy, is a man recalling his special childhood relationship with an older female cousin with whom he lived until he was seven.

b. They make fruitcakes to send to people who seem like friends because they have no other friends; the thank-you letters they receive make them feel connected to the world.

c. They have very little money; they must gather pecans after others have harvested them; they must get illegal whiskey.

d. Buddy and his cousin expect Mr. Haha Jones to be gloomy and sinister. Instead, he cheerfully returns their money and asks instead for a fruitcake.

e. She discovers that the Lord is revealed in everyday objects and events, not just at the end of one's life.

Rubrics for each Choices assignment appear on p. 103 in the *Portfolio Management System.*

CHOICES: Building Your Portfolio

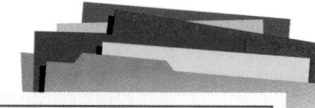

1. **Writer's Notebook** Assure students that because so much is deliberately left unsaid about Buddy's cousin, it is not easy to say definitively whether she is credible or not; nevertheless, it is still possible to evaluate the words and actions provided in the story.

2. **Creating Another Genre** Students should be expected to write only one short scene for whatever story they select and to create explicit camera directions for that scene.

3. **Creative Writing** Suggest that students might also consider using a photo of a family member or even a pet as the basis for their poems.

4. **Art/Oral Presentation** Explain that the collage can present information, convey a mood, or suggest an attitude. It can present concrete images, like pictures of teapots cut from magazines, or abstract ones, like blocks of bold color that collide.

CHOICES: Building Your Portfolio

Writer's Notebook

1. Collecting Ideas for an Essay Analyzing a Character

Are they credible?
When you write an analysis of a character, you might want to include your assessment of the character's believability. That is, does the character behave and talk the way a person in real life would behave and talk? Does the character seem like an individual, or is he or she a **stereotype**—a stock character you find in many other stories? (Another word for believability is *credibility*. You will often hear book and movie critics say, "The characters were not credible.") Take notes now on a character in Capote's story, and evaluate his or her credibility. Note specific details that support your evaluation. The writer of the notes below evaluated the credibility of Zaroff in "The Most Dangerous Game" (page 13). Save your own notes for possible use in the Writer's Workshop on page 194.

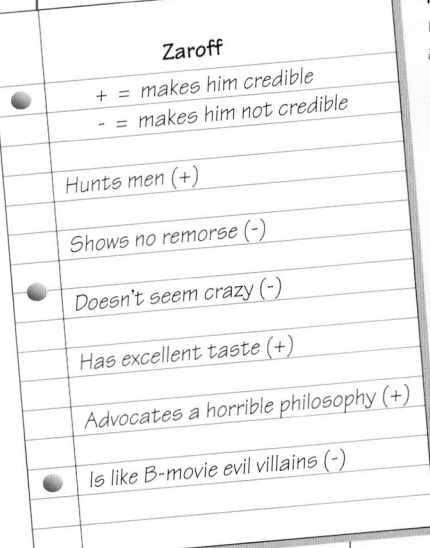

Zaroff

+ = makes him credible
- = makes him not credible

Hunts men (+)

Shows no remorse (-)

Doesn't seem crazy (-)

Has excellent taste (+)

Advocates a horrible philosophy (+)

Is like B-movie evil villains (-)

Creating Another Genre

2. From Print to Screen

In 1966, "A Christmas Memory" was made into a successful TV play that is still shown at Christmastime (see **Connections** on page 155). Use another story from this book as the basis of a screenplay. Before you begin to write, carefully examine the format of the Capote screenplay. Then, block out your story in scenes. Note that you will have to describe exactly what the camera will photograph (see the italicized text in the screenplay).

Creative Writing

3. A Photo of a Friend

In the poem called "Photo Album" on page 160, a writer describes her feelings when she sees a photo of her grandfather as a boy. Write a poem about a photo of a friend of yours. Tell what you see in the photo and what you wonder about. If you imitate "Photo Album," you will write in free verse and not worry about rhyme and a regular meter. You might want to review your Quickwrite notes.

Art/Oral Presentation

4. A Collage of the Cousin

A **collage** is a collection of images, words, or even objects pasted onto a flat surface. The aim is to create an impression—of a place or a person. The words in a collage can come from stories, poems, newspapers, or just your own head. Create a collage of Buddy's cousin, showing her in one of the settings described in the story: the kitchen, the field, Mr. Haha Jones's cafe, the house on Christmas morning, her bedroom. Be prepared to show your collage to the class and explain your choice of objects.

LANGUAGE LINK MINI-LESSON

Handbook of Literary Terms
HELP

See Figure of Speech.

Figures of Speech

Capote's descriptive details help us put our imaginations to work to bring his setting and characters to life. Some of these descriptive details are **figures of speech**—that is, they compare one thing to something else, something very different from it.

In the second paragraph, for example, the narrator compares his friend to a bantam hen. A bantam hen is very different from a human being, but if we use our imaginations, we can picture a person who is small, vigorous, and jumpy, the way a bantam hen is.

As you write your analysis of a character, try to use a few carefully chosen figures of speech to tell your readers what your character reminds you of. You might think of an animal, a plant, even a machine. Test your figures of speech to be sure they "work"—how are these two unlike things alike?

Try It Out

For each figure of speech, tell what is compared to what. Does each figure "work"—that is, how are the two different things alike?

1. ". . . the Christmas time of year . . . fuels the blaze of her heart."
2. "Enter: two relatives. Very angry. Potent with eyes that scold, tongues that scald."
3. ". . . the stars spinning at the window like a visible caroling that slowly, slowly daybreak silences."
4. ". . . the beginnings of dawn splash us like cold water."
5. ". . . we unreel our kites, feel them twitching at the string like sky fish as they swim into the wind."

VOCABULARY HOW TO OWN A WORD

WORD BANK

inaugurating
exhilarates
dilapidated
paraphernalia
sacrilegious
carnage
prosaic
disposition
suffuse
noncommittal

Analogies

An analogy is a comparison between two pairs of words. The words in each pair have the same relationship to each other—for example: "*Toe* is to *foot* as *finger* is to *hand*." Copy these analogies on a piece of paper and fill in each blank with a word from the Word Bank.

1. *Amusing* is to *funny* as _____ is to *everyday*.
2. *Biased* is to *neutral* as _____ is to *dedicated*.
3. *Emotion* is to *feeling* as _____ is to *temperament*.
4. *Opening* is to *closing* as _____ is to *ending*.
5. *Inundate* is to *swamp* as _____ is to *soak*.
6. *Soothes* is to *irritates* as _____ is to *disheartens*.
7. *Pollution* is to *contamination* as _____ is to *slaughter*.
8. *Clothing* is to *outfit* as _____ is to *gear*.
9. *Vain* is to *humble* as _____ is to *reverent*.
10. *Disorganized* is to *orderly* as _____ is to *renovated*.

A CHRISTMAS MEMORY 163

LANGUAGE LINK

Ask students to select a piece of personal, descriptive, narrative, or creative writing from their portfolios. Have them determine whether they have used figures of speech in the writing, and, if so, to underline the things they have compared. If not, ask them to determine a place in the writing where they might effectively add a figure of speech. Then, have them create one and, if necessary, revise the writing to incorporate it.

Try It Out
Possible Answers
1. The cousin's heart is compared to a fire that blazes at Christmastime; both burn brightly.
2. Eyes are compared to harsh criticism; both can be sharp and painful. Tongues are compared to the burning touch of hot liquid; both can leave painful wounds.
3. Stars spinning at the window are compared to people caroling; both stars and carolers appear in groups and are associated with the Christmas season.
4. The beginnings of dawn are compared to a splash of cold water; both awaken the sleepers.
5. Kites are compared to fish because kites "swim" in wind currents.

VOCABULARY
Answers
1. prosaic
2. noncommittal
3. disposition
4. inaugurating
5. suffuse
6. exhilarates
7. carnage
8. paraphernalia
9. sacrilegious
10. dilapidated

Language Link Quick Check

For each phrase below, tell what two things are being compared. Then, tell how the two otherwise different things are alike.
1. "the rising sun, its orange rind" (p. 156) [The arc of the sun is compared to the rind of an orange; both the sun's edge and the rind are bright orange "covers."]
2. "the wheels wobble like a drunkard's legs" (p. 146) [Wobbling wheels are compared to a drunkard's legs because both are shaky.]

3. "Long after the town has gone to sleep" (p. 150) [The town is compared to people sleeping; both are quiet.]
4. "a pillow already as wet as a widow's hand-kerchief" (p. 150) [A wet pillow is compared to a widow's handkerchief, suggesting that the pillow is as wet as a handkerchief soaked with tears of grief.]
5. "A disturbed armada of speckled trout" (p. 151) [A school of trout is compared to a huge group of ships that has been disturbed.]

Resources

Elements of Literature
Setting
For additional instruction on setting, see *Literary Elements:*
• Transparency 3

Elements of Literature

This feature presents the general definition of setting as time and place and explores the ways in which setting helps reveal character and create atmosphere. The feature also discusses how setting is created through word choices and especially through images.

Mini-Lesson:
Setting
After students read the feature, have them brainstorm elements that can be included in a setting, such as the specifics of a location (terrain, buildings, rooms, and furnishings); time period (era, season, time of day); or climate. Ask volunteers to give examples of movies, television series, or stories that are dependent on setting, such as emergency-room or police dramas.

Next, ask students to discuss the relationships between setting and character and between setting and atmosphere. Have them choose one type of setting and suggest the kinds of characters and the atmosphere that might be found there. [Sample response: A big-city hospital might suggest dedicated or ambitious doctors and nurses, and cranky or seriously ill patients. Its atmosphere might be tense, suspenseful, high-pressure.] Then, have students suggest images or sensory elements that could bring their chosen setting to life. [Examples: For a hospital—an antiseptic smell, the sound of emergency buzzers, the sight of steel surgical instruments, a nurse's soothing touch on the forehead of a patient.]

SETTING: Putting Us There

A storyteller, like a travel agent, can help gather us up from wherever we are and put us down in another setting on Earth or, for that matter, on a distant planet. That other setting may be a spot we've always wanted to visit, such as a deluxe hotel in Hawaii, or a place where we don't want to be, such as a sinking ship.

Escape—getting away from the same old sights, smells, and obligations—is certainly one of the easy pleasures of reading. But if that is all that happens, our reading experience is just a diversion. In fact, the term *escape reading* suggests that this kind of reading does not have much to do with our lives in the real world.

> A storyteller, like a travel agent, can help gather us up from wherever we are and put us down in another setting.

Setting as a Background

Setting tells us where and when the story takes place. Setting can include the locale of the story, the weather, the time of day, and the time period (past, present, or future). One purpose of setting is to provide background—a place for the characters to live and act in. A good setting helps to make the story real and believable.

Truman Capote opens his story "A Christmas Memory" (page 145) by telling us to imagine a setting: a morning in late November "more than twenty years ago" (he was referring to the early 1930s), a kitchen in a "spreading" old house in a country town, with a black stove, a round table, a fireplace with two rocking chairs—and in the fireplace, the season's first roaring fire. This setting

provides the backdrop for the story's characters. Because he describes this setting so vividly, Capote helps us to feel that we are there.

Setting and Character

Places where people live and make their homes can reveal a great deal about their characters. In "A Christmas Memory," for example, we learn that Buddy's friend sleeps in a "scrap-quilt-covered iron bed, painted rose pink" and that she grows the "prettiest japonicas in town." To some readers this setting would suggest her simplicity and her yearning for beauty. (How would you feel about her if she slept in a pile of rags that smelled sour, or if her yard was muddy with no flowers?) Capote has put Mr. Haha Jones in a very different setting. His cafe is "festooned inside and out with chains of garish-gay naked light bulbs." It stands by the river's "muddy edge." The moss on the trees is like "gray mist." His cafe is, in daylight, "shabby and deserted." There is something sinister about Haha's setting, as there is about Haha's character (even though he is also kind).

Getting Students Involved

Cooperative Learning
Ask students to work in groups of four or five to develop a short skit that takes place in a specified setting. Provide students with a list of possible settings, such as a ranch in the nineteenth century, a bus station in a large city, a ballroom decorated for a prom, a space shuttle, a sailing ship in the age of discovery, or a newsroom at the moment when news of a war or natural disaster breaks. Invite students to brainstorm additional settings. Then, ask each group to select a setting, place two or more characters in it, and develop a brief skit appropriate to the setting. All group members should collaborate in selecting the setting, but different members can be responsible for drafting the skit, revising it, copying it, directing and coaching it, rehearsing it, performing it, and evaluating its success. After the performance, ask each group member to list his or her contributions to the success of the project.

by John Leggett

Setting and Atmosphere

Setting can also provide **atmosphere** or mood—it can affect the way we feel. Some settings make us feel fear or uneasiness (midnight, a lonely house, the scraping of a branch on the window). Other settings make us feel happy (morning, a garden, the song of a bird). The strange hotel that serves as the setting for Stephen King's novel *The Shining* creates an atmosphere of isolation and terror. We sense that deeds of wickedness can be (and are) committed in the winding, lonely corridors of that huge, old hotel.

How Is Setting Created?

Language is what takes us to King's hotel or to Capote's rural Alabama. One of the wonders of language is that it can summon up a place for us immediately. Language can reach us through our five senses and put us right in the middle of the action, along with the characters themselves.

Like the other elements of storytelling, creating a setting is a skill. To create a believable setting, or one that can make us feel pleasure, mystery, or fear, the writer must select the right details or images. **Images** are words that call forth a response from our senses—sight, smell, touch, hearing, and at times, even taste.

Suppose a writer wants us to imagine a setting as ordinary as the drugstore where Tamara is telling JD she never wants to see him again. We would get tired of a list of all the objects on the shelves. Similarly, we would get tired of a list of all the trees, rocks, and puddles in the mountain pass where the outlaws are waiting for the stagecoach. However, our own imaginations will supply many details if the writer prompts us with the right image. In the drugstore scene, the right image might be a row of bottles, each bearing the label POISON. In the mountain pass the right image might be a circling vulture or the water that seeps into the outlaws'

cracked boots. If we are told that we are landing near a canal on Mars and that the light outside is very harsh, we'll supply not only the glare in the window of the space-ship, but also the intense heat, the dryness of the air, possibly even the sweat trickling down the pilot's back.

When a writer supplies a few right images, we will provide the rest of the scenery. We might draw from our own experience, or we might go beyond our memory into our instincts and into the pool of our subconscious. There we will find all kinds of images—of desert islands, palaces, and planets where, so far as we know, we have never been.

This exercise of our imaginations is what makes fiction a more personal and mind-enhancing experience than, for all their lazy pleasures, the ready-made images of movies and television.

> **O**ne of the wonders of language is that it can summon up a place for us immediately.

ELEMENTS OF LITERATURE: SETTING 165

Applying the Lesson

To help reinforce students' understanding of setting, have them discuss the following questions about "A Christmas Memory."

- Why is the Christmas season an important part of the setting? [Possible answer: Christmas is a time of giving, of connecting with loved ones, and of childhood memories that last for a lifetime—all of which are important strands of the story.]
- What does the setting of the woods, where the characters get their Christmas tree, reveal about the character of Buddy's friend? [Possible answers: It reveals her love and in-depth knowledge of the natural world and her strong feelings of kinship with it; it shows her intimate familiarity with her surroundings.]
- What atmosphere or mood is created by the setting in the woods? [Sample responses: a mood of happiness and excitement; a mood of joy and triumph.]
- What are some of the images that help readers picture that setting? [Sample responses: "the silvered winter woods"; "lemony sun pools"; "an ecstasy of shrillings"; "beaver workmen"; "the pine-heavy air"; "prickly-leafed holly."]

Resources

Assessment

Formal Assessment

- Literary Elements Test, p. 24

Using Students' Strengths

Visual Learners

Students may enjoy using a computer-graphics program to create a setting of their own. They might choose or create a background and add scenery or furnishings from clip-art programs. Students might also add references or images that suggest the time of day or year, or the weather. Invite them to display their work. Ask other students to identify the atmosphere and to suggest the types of characters that might appear in this setting.

Auditory/Musical Learners

In movies and television dramas, aspects of the setting, especially its atmosphere, are often created or enhanced by the soundtrack. Have students create a grid on which they list characters in the first column, a setting in the second column, a conflict in the third column, and a type of music or a range of instrumental sounds to create atmosphere in the fourth column.

Planning

- **Block Schedule**
  Block Scheduling Lesson Plans with Pacing Guide
- **Traditional Schedule**
  Lesson Plans Including Strategies for English-Language Learners
- **One-Stop Planner**
  CD-ROM with Test Generator

A MAN CALLED HORSE

Make the Connection

What We Endure

This is a story of the human spirit, of what it can endure and what it values above all else in life. Jack Schaefer, author of the novel *Shane,* might have been thinking of this story when he said that no one but Dorothy Johnson could write so perceptively about both the white settlers and the Indians—"those displaced persons who saw their lands being taken and their way of life crumbling before the inevitable white advance. Here is no glamorizing, no romantic gilding, of settlers or of Indians. Here is something finer and more gripping, the honest portrayal of good and bad, of strength and frailty, of the admirable and the contemptible, in both white settlements and Indian villages. . . ."

Quickwrite

You've read the title. What do you think this story is about? Jot down your guesses—who is the man called Horse, and what happens to him?

Elements of Literature

Setting Makes It Real

Setting can include the time when the story takes place, its weather, and the customs of the people—how they live, what they do for entertainment, how they dress, what they believe, what they eat. Setting provides background—a place for the characters to live and act. In some stories—as in this one—setting is so crucial that the story could not take place anywhere else.

> **S**etting tells where and when the story takes place.
>
> *For more on Setting, see pages 164–165 and the Handbook of Literary Terms.*

Reading Skills and Strategies

Monitor Your Comprehension

As you read, write down any questions you have about the story and its unusual setting. Record your responses to the characters' actions and ordeals. Note any details that you might want to discuss later—for example, do you think Johnson is fair to all her characters?

Background

Before 1845, most of the West was a frontier and not part of the United States at all. "A Man Called Horse" begins in 1845 and is set in Indian country. The tribe the story brings to vivid life, the Crows, at this time moved frequently to follow the buffalo herds.

Courtesy of the National Museum of the American Indian, Smithsonian Institution, New York. 11/7680.

go.hrw.com
LE0 9-2

Preteaching Vocabulary

Words to Own

Have student partners read the Words to Own and their definitions at the bottom of the selection pages. Then, have each partner use the words he or she is unsure of in a phrase such as "the restive tribe." Finally, have them match each word with its antonym.

1. restive [d]
2. piteously [e]
3. detractor [a]
4. forestalled [b]
5. docile [c]

a. supporter
b. ensured
c. rebellious
d. settled
e. stoically

"I lived with Crows for a while."

A Man Called Horse

Dorothy M. Johnson

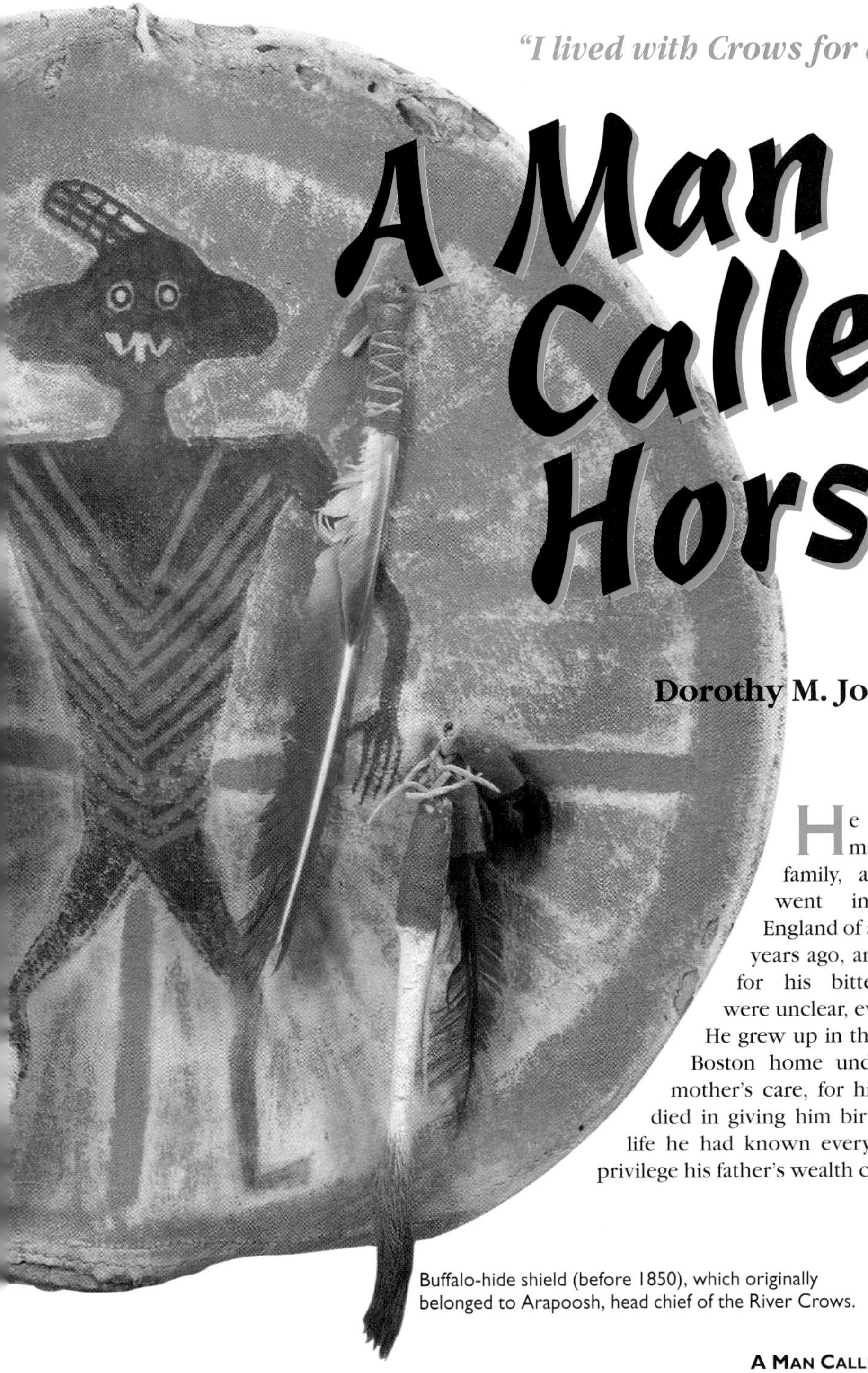

He was a young man of good family, as the phrase went in the New England of a hundred-odd years ago, and the reasons for his bitter discontent were unclear, even to himself. He grew up in the gracious old Boston home under his grand-mother's care, for his mother had died in giving him birth; and all his life he had known every comfort and privilege his father's wealth could provide.

Buffalo-hide shield (before 1850), which originally belonged to Arapoosh, head chief of the River Crows.

A MAN CALLED HORSE 167

Summary ▪▪

In 1845, a young man from Boston, unhappy with his comfortable and safe life, travels west to the fringes of the American frontier. He is taken captive by Crow warriors and brought to their camp as a slave. He tries to retain some dignity by thinking of himself as a horse, a docile and patient bearer of burdens. Adopting the name "Horse," he learns the Crow language, learns to hunt, acquires five horses, and marries (and falls in love with) a young Crow woman. Over time, he recognizes the humanity of the Crow and learns to appreciate his life with them. When his wife dies in childbirth, he voluntarily stays for a while to care for his mother-in-law, who has humbly begged him to stay by calling him "Son." The man accepts by calling her "Mother."

Resources ———

Listening
Audio CD Library
A dramatic reading of this story is available in the *Audio CD Library:*
• Disc 7, Track 2

RESPONDING TO THE ART

Activity. Discuss with students what the decoration on the Buffalo-hide shield suggests about the Crow and about the story they are about to read. [Sample response: It suggests that the Crow are fierce fighters and that the story will contain violence.]

 —— ◉ —— *Resources: Print and Media* —— 🎞️ ——

Reading
• *Graphic Organizers for Active Reading*, p. 9
• *Words to Own*, p. 8
• *Audio CD Library*
   Disc 7, Track 2

Writing and Language
• *Daily Oral Grammar*
   Transparency 9

• *Grammar and Language Links*
   Worksheet, p. 17
• *Language Workshop CD-ROM*

Assessment
• *Formal Assessment*, p. 19
• *Portfolio Management System*, p. 104
• *Test Generator (One-Stop Planner CD-ROM)*

Internet
• go.hrw.com (keyword: LE0 9-2)

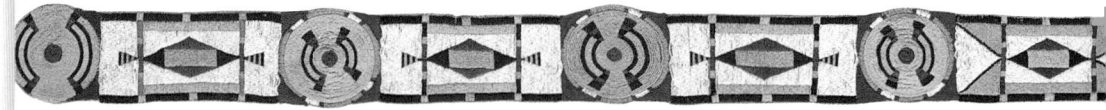

Crow blanket strip (c. 1870–1875). Native American. Buffalo hide, glass beads (63″ x 5.5″). CP-88.

But still there was the discontent, which puzzled him because he could not even define it. He wanted to live among his equals—people who were no better than he and no worse either. That was as close as he could come to describing the source of his unhappiness in Boston and his restless desire to go somewhere else.

In the year 1845, he left home and went out west, far beyond the country's creeping frontier, where he hoped to find his equals. He had the idea that in Indian country, where there was danger, all white men were kings, and he wanted to be one of them. But he found, in the West as in Boston, that the men he respected were still his superiors, even if they could not read, and those he did not respect weren't worth talking to.

He did have money, however, and he could hire the men he respected. He hired four of them, to cook and hunt and guide and be his companions, but he found them not friendly.

They were apart from him and he was still alone. He still brooded about his status in the world, longing for his equals.

On a day in June, he learned what it was to have no status at all. He became a captive of a small raiding party of Crow Indians.

He heard gunfire and the brief shouts of his companions around the bend of the creek just before they died, but he never saw their bodies. He had no chance to fight, because he was naked and unarmed, bathing in the creek, when a Crow warrior seized and held him.

His captor let him go at last, let him run. Then the lot of them rode him down for sport, striking him with their coup sticks. They carried the dripping scalps of his companions, and one had skinned off Baptiste's black beard as well, for a trophy.

They took him along in a matter-of-fact way, as they took the captured horses. He was unshod and naked as the horses were, and like them he had a rawhide thong around his neck.

168 THE SHORT-STORY COLLECTIONS

So long as he didn't fall down, the Crows ignored him.

On the second day they gave him his breeches. His feet were too swollen for his boots, but one of the Indians threw him a pair of moccasins that had belonged to the halfbreed, Henri, who was dead back at the creek. The captive wore the moccasins gratefully. The third day they let him ride one of the

Big Foot's band at Grass Dance on Cheyenne River, August 9, 1890. Photograph.

spare horses so the party could move faster, and on that day they came in sight of their camp.

He thought of trying to escape, hoping he might be killed in flight rather than by slow torture in the camp, but he never had a chance to try. They were more familiar with escape than he was, and knowing what to expect, they forestalled it. The only other time he had tried

WORDS TO OWN
forestalled (fôr·stôld′) v.: prevented by doing something ahead of time.

Reaching All Students

Struggling Readers
Monitoring Comprehension is introduced on p. 166 where students are asked to determine if the author is fair to all her characters. You might use a Semantic Differential Scale to help students think about this. For a description, see p. 93 in the *Reading Strategies Handbook* in the *Reading Skills and Strategies Binder*. The scales could include statements such as:

The author is fair to Greasy Hand.
agree   disagree

Advanced Learners
Challenge students to trace the course of the main character's emotional growth. Have them focus on textual clues relating to equality, the presence and absence of names, comparisons between what is animal and what is human, and the cultural divide that must be crossed to discover the humanity of others.

English Language Learners
Help students understand vocabulary related to the Crow and their culture, such as *teepee* (or *tepee*), *coups sticks, warrior,* and *travois.* Remind students that the photographs provide visual clues to this culture, and then help them link specific vocabulary to what is pictured.
For additional strategies for engaging English language learners with the literature, see
• *Lesson Plans Including Strategies for English-Language Learners*

to escape from anyone, he had succeeded. When he had left his home in Boston, his father had raged and his grandmother had cried, but they could not talk him out of his intention.

The men of the Crow raiding party didn't bother with talk.

D Before riding into camp they stopped and dressed in their regalia and in parts of their victims' clothing; they painted their faces black.

Courtesy of the National Museum of the American Indian, Smithsonian Institution, New York. P7000

Then, leading the white man by the rawhide around his neck as though he were a horse, they rode down toward the tepee circle, shouting and singing, brandishing their weapons. He was unconscious when they got there; he fell and was dragged.

He lay dazed and battered near a tepee while the noisy, busy life of the camp swarmed around him and Indians came to stare. Thirst consumed him, and when it rained he lapped rainwater from the ground like a dog. A scrawny, shrieking, eternally busy old woman with ragged graying hair threw a chunk of meat **E** on the grass, and he fought the dogs for it.

When his head cleared, he was angry, although anger was an emotion he knew he could not afford.

It was better when I was a horse, he thought—when they led me by the rawhide around my neck. I won't be a dog, no matter **F** what!

The hag gave him stinking, rancid grease and let him figure out what it was for. He applied it gingerly to his bruised and sun-seared body.

Now, he thought, *I smell like the rest of them.*

While he was healing, he considered coldly the advantages of being a horse. A man would be humiliated, and sooner or later he would strike back and that would be the end of him. But a horse had only to be <u>docile</u>. Very well, he would learn to do without pride.

He understood that he was the property of the screaming old woman, a fine gift from her son, one that she liked to show off. She did more yelling at him than at anyone else, probably to impress the neighbors so they would not forget what a great and generous man her son was. She was bossy and proud, a dreadful sag of skin and bones, and she was a devilish hard worker.

The white man, who now thought of himself **G** as a horse, forgot sometimes to worry about his danger. He kept making mental notes of things to tell his own people in Boston about this hideous adventure. He would go back a hero, and he would say, "Grandmother, let me fetch your shawl. I've been accustomed to doing little errands for another lady about your age."

Two girls lived in the tepee with the old hag and her warrior son. One of them, the white man concluded, was his captor's wife and the other was his little sister. The daughter-in-law was smug and spoiled. Being beloved, she did not have to be useful. The younger sister had

---

WORDS TO OWN

docile (däs′əl) *adj.*: easy to manage; submissive.

A MAN CALLED HORSE **169**

D Reading Skills and Strategies

Monitor Your Comprehension

? What questions might you want to ask now? [Possible questions: What will the Crow do with this man? What is the man thinking and feeling? Why haven't we yet learned this man's name?]

E Struggling Readers

Finding the Sequence of Events

? What event might you record on a story map at this point? [The man reaches the camp, where he is left on the ground and not harmed.] Tell students that the busy old woman, who has just been introduced, is the second major character.

F Advanced Learners

Interpreting

? In what way is this a turning point for the man? [Possible answers: For the first time, the man shows interest in being more than what he has been reduced to; the man begins to struggle toward an identity that is not assigned to or forced on him but one that he chooses.]

G Cultural Connections

Stereotypes

Tell students that the story, even though written in the third person, presents the man's point of view, and is bound to include his own stereotypes about Native Americans and women. Ask students for reasons why the man might interpret the woman's language as "screaming" and her behavior as "bossy" and that of a "devilish hard worker." [Possible answers: To the man, her language is incomprehensible, so it may seem like shrieking to him even if it would not be so regarded in her culture; the man's background in Boston society accustomed him to "ladylike" (quiet, unaggressive) behavior from women.]

Using Students' Strengths

Visual Learners

Suggest that students plot the story by creating a line of color to indicate the emotional pitch of various scenes. Working from left to right, and labeling their color line, they might, for example, use a bright, hot color to suggest Horse's capture and a dark, dull color to suggest his near abandonment during his early days in the camp. Encourage students to use subtle variations in color, to use contrasting colors to show abrupt shifts, and to make particularly strong statements with primary colors. After students have completed the story and their plot lines, you might have them share their work with the class, retelling the story as they explain their color choices. Students should also find their plot lines useful for answering some of the Making Meanings questions (p. 179) and for the first Choices activity (p. 180).

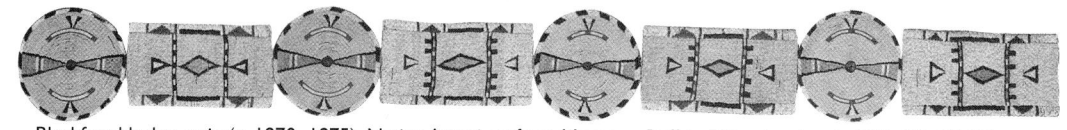

Blackfeet blanket strip (c. 1870–1875). Native American from Montana. Buffalo hide, glass beads (67″ x 7″). CP-87.

A Reading Skills and Strategies
Identifying Cause and Effect
? Why does the man pretend to be a horse? [Possible answers: It gives him an identity as something useful to the Crow and a status that is below the Crow, which, as a captive, he is; choosing this identity helps him to bury his pride, not rebel, and therefore survive.]

B Critical Thinking
Interpreting
? How has the man's idea of loneliness changed? [Possible answers: He thought he was lonely in Boston and when he first came West, but now he has reached a more profound level of loneliness because he has been stripped of his identity and removed from all that is familiar; his loneliness has deepened because there is no communication between him and others.]

C Critical Thinking
Expressing an Opinion
? Do you think that this will be a turning point in the story? Why or why not? [Possible answers: Yes, because now the man will be able to communicate with others; yes, because now the man will be less lonely; yes, because it is language that helps define us as human.]

RESPONDING TO THE ART
Activity. The pair of moccasins points up a universal human impulse—the desire to adorn a utilitarian object. You might ask students how buying new sneakers is similar to Horse's receiving new moccasins. [In each case, the shoes confer a degree of status on the wearer.]

A bright, wandering eyes. Often enough they wandered to the white man who was pretending to be a horse.

The two girls worked when the old woman put them at it, but they were always running off to do something they enjoyed more. There were games and noisy contests, and there was **B** much laughter. But not for the white man. He was finding out what loneliness could be.

That was a rich summer on the plains, with plenty of buffalo for meat and clothing and the making of tepees. The Crows were wealthy in horses, prosperous, and contented. If their men had not been so avid for glory, the white man thought, there would have been a lot more of them. But they went out of their way to court death, and when one of them met it, the whole camp mourned extravagantly and cried to their God for vengeance.

The captive was a horse all summer, a docile bearer of burdens, careful and patient. He kept reminding himself that he had to be better-natured than other horses, because he could not lash out with hoofs or teeth. Helping the old woman load up the horses for travel, he yanked at a pack and said, "Whoa, brother. It goes easier when you don't fight."

The horse gave him a big-eyed stare as if it understood his language—a comforting thought, because nobody else did. But even among the horses he felt unequal. They were able to look out for themselves if they escaped. He would simply starve. He was envious still, even among the horses.

Pair of moccasins.
Courtesy of the National Museum of the American Indian, Smithsonian Institution, New York. 17/8027.

Humbly he fetched and carried. Sometimes he even offered to help, but he had not the skill for the endless work of the women, and he was not trusted to hunt with the men, the providers.

When the camp moved, he carried a pack, trudging with the women. Even the dogs worked then, pulling small burdens on travois[1] of sticks.

The Indian who had captured him lived like a lord, as he had a right to do. He hunted with his peers, attended long ceremonial meetings with much chanting and dancing, and lounged in the shade with his smug bride. He had only two responsibilities: to kill buffalo and to gain glory. The white man was so far beneath him in status that the Indian did not even think of envy.

C One day several things happened that made the captive think he might sometime become a man again. That was the day when he began to understand their language. For four months he had heard it, day and night, the joy and the mourning, the ritual chanting and sung prayers, the squabbles and the deliberations. None of it meant anything to him at all.

But on that important day in early fall the two young women set out for the river, and one of them called over her shoulder to the old woman. The white man was startled. She had said she was going to bathe. His understanding was so sudden that he felt as if his ears had come unstopped. Listening to the racket of the camp, he heard fragments of meaning instead of gabble.

1. **travois** (trə·voiz′): sleds. A travois consists of a net or platform dragged along the ground by two poles.

Skill Link

Chronological Ordering
Remind students that chronological order is time order. Tell them that most stories are organized in chronological order.

1. Have students skim p. 170 to find the two clues to the specific time of year. [In column 1, at the text break, it is summer; in the last paragraph in column 2, it is fall.]
2. Ask students to list the events that occur between those two time markers.
3. Have students examine their lists to see how each event occurs in chronological order. Students might also note that as time passes, the character advances from his animal state to a more human one. (This is already evident before he acquires language but becomes more pronounced in later pages.)

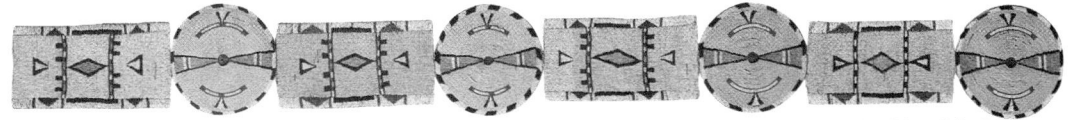

On that same important day the old woman brought a pair of new moccasins out of the tepee and tossed them on the ground before him. He could not believe she would do anything for him because of kindness, but giving him moccasins was one way of looking after her property.

In thanking her, he dared greatly. He picked a little handful of fading fall flowers and took them to her as she squatted in front of her tepee, scraping a buffalo hide with a tool made from a piece of iron tied to a bone. Her hands were hideous—most of the fingers had the first joint missing. He bowed solemnly and offered the flowers.

She glared at him from beneath the short, ragged tangle of her hair. She stared at the flowers, knocked them out of his hand, and went running to the next tepee, squalling the story. He heard her and the other women screaming with laughter.

The white man squared his shoulders and walked boldly over to watch three small boys shooting arrows at a target. He said in English, "Show me how to do that, will you?"

They frowned, but he held out his hand as if there could be no doubt. One of them gave him a bow and one arrow, and they snickered when he missed.

The people were easily amused, except when they were angry. They were amused at him, playing with the little boys. A few days later he asked the hag, with gestures, for a bow that her son had just discarded, a man-sized bow of horn. He scavenged for old arrows. The old woman cackled at his marksmanship and called her neighbors to enjoy the fun.

When he could understand words, he could identify his people by their names. The old woman was Greasy Hand, and her daughter was Pretty Calf. The other young woman's name was not clear to him, for the words were not in his vocabulary. The man who had captured him was Yellow Robe.

Once he could understand, he could begin to talk a little, and then he was less lonely. Nobody

had been able to see any reason for talking to him, since he would not understand anyway. He asked the old woman, "What is my name?" Until he knew it, he was incomplete. She shrugged to let him know he had none.

He told her in the Crow language, "My name is Horse." He repeated it, and she nodded. After that they called him Horse when they called him anything. Nobody cared except the white man himself.

They trusted him enough to let him stray out of camp, so that he might have got away and, by unimaginable good luck, might have reached a trading post or a fort, but winter was too close. He did not dare leave without a horse; he needed clothing and a better hunting weapon than he had and more certain skill in using it. He did not dare steal, for then they would surely have pursued him, and just as certainly they would have caught him. Remembering the warmth of the home that was waiting in Boston, he settled down for the winter.

On a cold night he crept into the tepee after the others had gone to bed. Even a horse might try to find shelter from the wind. The old woman grumbled, but without conviction. She did not put him out.

They tolerated him, back in the shadows, so long as he did not get in the way.

He began to understand how the family that owned him differed from the others. Fate had been cruel to them. In a short, sharp argument among the old women, one of them derided Greasy Hand by sneering, "You have no relatives!" and Greasy Hand raved for minutes of the deeds of her father and uncles and brothers. And she had had four sons, she reminded her detractor—who answered with scorn, "Where are they?"

WORDS TO OWN

detractor (dē·trak'tər) *n.*: one who makes something seem less important or valuable.

A MAN CALLED HORSE 171

D E F G

D Reading Skills and Strategies
Monitor Your Comprehension
? What questions might you ask now? [Possible questions: Will the woman understand the man's gesture? Is the man risking scorn and humiliation? Will their relationship change?]

E Reading Skills and Strategies
Drawing Conclusions
? What change has occurred in the man? [Possible answers: He has begun to take action, and to assert his will; he has begun to be a man again.]

F Critical Thinking
Interpreting
? Why is it important for the man to have a name? [Possible answers: It gives him an identity; it may make the Crow recognize him as a person.]

G Elements of Literature
Setting
? How does the setting help determine the man's actions? [Possible answers: The setting isolates the man; it limits his choices—because he cannot survive in this setting without resources, he must remain with the Crow.]

Taking a Second Look

Review: Analyzing Cause and Effect

Remind students that events in a story are often linked by stated and unstated causes. Part of the job of reading actively is to uncover the underlying causes of events and to link causes with their effects.

Activities

1. Ask students to return to the questions they asked while monitoring their comprehension to see if any of those questions involve cause

and effect. For example, when the old woman gives the white man moccasins, students might ask why she does this and what effect it will have on the relationship between the two of them.

2. Suggest that students work in pairs or groups of three to uncover causes and effects on this page and others. They may find that some causes and effects are stated, while others are implied. For example, on this page the

narration chronicles several cause-effect relationships, as it shows Horse's growing status as a man; yet some of these relationships are not stated directly.

3. When students have finished reading the story, they might isolate a series of causes leading up to and affecting Horse's emotional growth. They might also determine the causes for his change in attitude regarding the Crow and regarding his own identity.

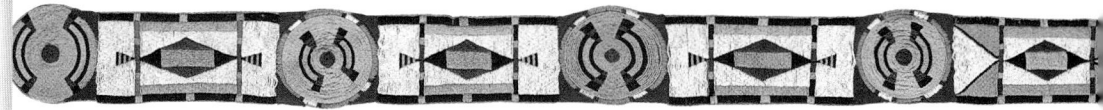

Crow blanket strip (c. 1870–1875). Native American. Buffalo hide, glass beads (63″ x 5.5″). CP-88.

A Reading Skills and Strategies

Monitor Your Comprehension

? How did you respond to this scene? What questions do you have about it? [Possible responses: It is horrifying; it shows brutality on the part of the old woman. Possible questions: Why did the author include this? Is the old woman really that heartless? Could she have done this to Horse?]

B Cultural Connections

? Up to this point, many Crow customs and attitudes have been shown as distasteful or horrifying by white standards. Yet now it seems the Crow would be open-minded enough to let a slave or captive marry into their culture. Would members of Horse's white culture allow such a marriage if the roles were reversed? [Sample answer: Probably not. It seems unlikely, for example, that a Native American woman working as a servant in Horse's Boston home could aspire to marry him.]

C Advanced Learners

Interpreting

? How does this passage reflect a positive change in Horse? [Possible answers: It shows that he is looking to the future rather than to the past; he is recognizing that a person must earn his future rewards.]

D Appreciating Language

Vivid Modifiers

? What modifiers add to the power and precision of this passage? [Possible modifiers: "Moaning" conveys the victim's half-dead state and "lone" underscores his helpless position; the word "eagerly" shows how the boys and Horse regard their prey; the word "sick" underscores that this was scarcely a heroic accomplishment; "small" reminds the reader of the advantage Horse had over his companions; the adjective "still-groaning" emphasizes the horror that is death; the word "hobbled," applied to the horses, points out that the man is no longer restrained.]

Later the white man found her moaning and whimpering to herself, rocking back and forth on her haunches, staring at her mutilated hands. By that time he understood. A mourner often chopped off a finger joint. Old Greasy Hand had mourned often. For the first time he felt a twinge of pity, but he put it aside as another emotion, like anger, that he could not afford. He thought: What tales I will tell when I get home!

He wrinkled his nose in disdain. The camp stank of animals and meat and rancid grease. He looked down at his naked, shivering legs and was startled, remembering that he was still only a horse.

He could not trust the old woman. She fed him only because a starved slave would die and not be worth boasting about. Just how fitful her temper was he saw on the day when she got tired of stumbling over one of the hundred dogs that infested the camp. This was one of her own dogs, a large, strong one that pulled a baggage travois when the tribe moved camp.

Countless times he had seen her kick at the beast as it lay sleeping in front of the tepee, in her way. The dog always moved, with a yelp, but it always got in the way again. One day she gave the dog its usual kick and then stood scolding at it while the animal rolled its eyes sleepily. The old woman suddenly picked up her ax and cut the dog's head off with one blow. Looking well satisfied with herself, she beckoned her slave to remove the body.

It could have been me, he thought, if I were a dog. But I'm a horse.

His hope of life lay with the girl, Pretty Calf. He set about courting her, realizing how desperately poor he was both in property and honor. He owned no horse, no weapon but the old bow and the battered arrows. He had nothing to give away, and he needed gifts, because he did not dare seduce the girl.

One of the customs of courtship involved sending a gift of horses to a girl's older brother and bestowing much buffalo meat upon her mother. The white man could not wait for some far-off time when he might have either horses or meat to give away. And his courtship had to be secret. It was not for him to stroll past the groups of watchful girls, blowing a flute made of an eagle's wing bone, as the flirtatious young men did.

He could not ride past Pretty Calf's tepee, painted and bedizened;[2] he had no horse, no finery.

Back home, he remembered, I could marry just about any girl I'd want to. But he wasted little time thinking about that. A future was something to be earned.

The most he dared do was wink at Pretty Calf now and then, or state his admiration while she giggled and hid her face. The least he dared do to win his bride was to elope with her, but he had to give her a horse to put the seal of tribal approval on that. And he had no horse until he killed a man to get one. . . .

His opportunity came in early spring. He was casually accepted by that time. He did not belong, but he was amusing to the Crows, like a strange pet, or they would not have fed him through the winter.

His chance came when he was hunting small game with three young boys who were his guards as well as his scornful companions. Rabbits and birds were of no account in a camp well fed on buffalo meat, but they made good targets.

His party walked far that day. All of them at once saw the two horses in a sheltered coulee.[3] The boys and the man crawled forward on their bellies, and then they saw an Indian who lay on the ground, moaning, a lone traveler. From the way the boys inched eagerly forward, Horse knew the man was fair prey—a member of some enemy tribe.

This is the way the captive white man acquired wealth and honor to win a bride and

2. **bedizened:** dressed in a showy way.
3. **coulee** (kōō′lē): ravine.

Getting Students Involved

Cooperative Learning

A Found Poem. To help students appreciate the descriptive language in this selection, have them create a "found poem." Assign students to work together in small groups. Have each group choose eight descriptive words or phrases from the story. Then, have students select from their list the four most memorable or poetic words or phrases. Last, have the groups in turn—and without interruption—read one word or phrase from their lists and continue doing so until the lists are exhausted. As they read each word or phrase, write it on the board. The result is a found poem. After students have read and studied the poem, you might want to take suggestions from volunteers about ways to rearrange words and lines in order to improve the rhythm or meaning of the poem.

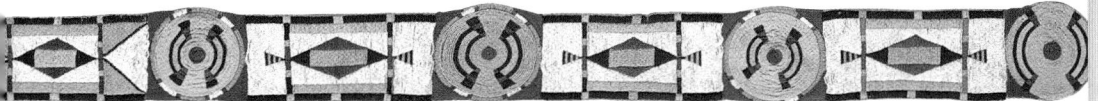
save his life: He shot an arrow into the sick man, a split second ahead of one of his small companions, and dashed forward to strike the still-groaning man with his bow, to count first coup. Then he seized the hobbled horses.

By the time he had the horses secure, and with them his hope for freedom, the boys had followed, counting coup with gestures and shrieks they had practiced since boyhood, and one of them had the scalp. The white man was grimly amused to see the boy double up with sudden nausea when he had the thing in his hand. . . .

There was a hubbub in the camp when they rode in that evening, two of them on each horse. The captive was noticed. Indians who had ignored him as a slave stared at the brave man who had struck first coup and had stolen horses.

The hubbub lasted all night, as fathers boasted loudly of their young sons' exploits. The white man was called upon to settle an argument between two fierce boys as to which of them had struck second coup and which must be satisfied with third. After much talk that went over his head, he solemnly pointed at the nearest boy. He didn't know which boy it was and didn't care, but the boy did.

The white man had watched warriors in their

Bird's Head Shield (1981) by Kevin Red Star.
Courtesy of the National Museum of the American Indian, Smithsonian Institution, New York. 11/7680.

E Elements of Literature
Setting
? Why are horses so important in this time and place? [Possible answers: The distances are vast and cannot be traveled on foot; to get home, Horse needs a horse for transportation; the horse is very important to the Crow culture—without it, the buffalo hunt, on which the Crow depend for survival, is much more difficult.]

F Historical Connections
One influence on the development of the American Northwest was the presence of French traders and trappers. They were among the first Europeans, well before Lewis and Clark, to make contact with Native Americans. This explains why a French word like *coup* is used to describe a Native American custom. It also accounts for the name *Crow.* These Native Americans called themselves *Absaroka,* a word that referred to a large bird. Early French explorers believed that the bird was a crow.

G English Language Learners
Idioms
Point out the common idiom *over his head.* Explain to students that this expression means "beyond his understanding." Help students to see that what was said was incomprehensible to the man because he did not possess the verbal skill or the cultural experience to understand the conversation.

Crossing the Curriculum

Geography
At the time of Horse's adventure, the journey from Boston to what is now Montana would have been extraordinary. Have students plot a possible route he might have taken. Remind them that waterways should play a major role in this route once Horse has gone beyond the established eastern roads, canals, and rails of his day. Also remind students that research will be necessary in order to learn about existing roads and passages used at the time.

Social Studies
Native Americans such as the Crow were very dependent for their livelihood on the buffalo. Suggest that students investigate and report on how the Crow captured and used this animal. Topics to explore include Crow hunting methods and the many uses they made of the parts of the buffalo, like drying its flesh to store as food, forming utensils from its horns, and tanning its hide to make bedding and robes.

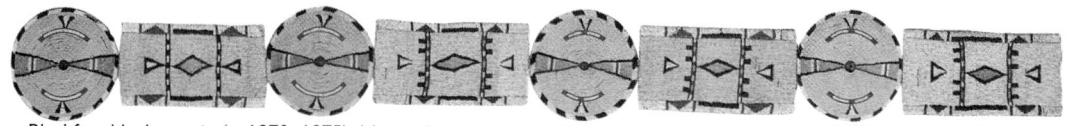

Blackfeet blanket strip (c. 1870–1875). Native American from Montana. Buffalo hide, glass beads (67″x 7″). CP-87.

A Reading Skills and Strategies
Making Inferences

? How is Horse becoming more and more part of Crow culture while still maintaining his original identity? [Possible responses: He boasts loudly of achievements that are important in Crow society while speaking in his original language; he insults the Crow while he follows their customs.]

RESPONDING TO THE ART

Activity. Elaborate ceremonial headdresses such as this one served to associate the wearer with admired qualities of the animal from whose hair, horns, or feathers it was made. Ask students what qualities of the eagle the Crow may have admired and how these qualities relate to the characteristics expected of Crow warriors. [Eagles are noted for their size, strength, swiftness, and hunting prowess—all desirable qualities for a warrior to possess.]

B Critical Thinking
Speculating

? Why does Horse refer to his wife as Freedom? [Horse plans to use his wife as a way to get what he wants—his freedom.] Was he right to marry her? Why or why not? [Possible responses: He was not right—he is treating her unfairly; he was right to use what he has learned of Crow culture to improve his status and try to gain his freedom.]

C Reading Skills and Strategies
Identifying Cause and Effect

? What has caused Horse's transformation? [Possible answers: his marriage; his determination to become an equal in this society; his desire to become human again.]

---

triumph. He knew what to do. Modesty about achievements had no place among the Crow people. When a man did something big, he told about it.

The white man smeared his face with grease and charcoal. He walked inside the tepee circle, **A** chanting and singing. He used his own language.

"You heathens, you savages," he shouted. "I'm going to get out of here someday! I am going to get away!" The Crow people listened respectfully. In the Crow tongue he shouted, "Horse! I am Horse!" and they nodded.

He had a right to boast, and he had two horses. Before dawn, the white man and his bride were sheltered beyond a far hill, and he was telling her, "I love you, little lady. I love you."

She looked at him with her great dark eyes, and he thought she understood his English words— or as much as she needed to understand.

B "You are my treasure," he said, "more precious than jewels, better than fine gold. I am going to call you Freedom."

When they returned to camp two days later, he was bold but worried. His ace, he suspected, might not be high enough in the game he was playing without being sure of the rules. But it served.

Old Greasy Hand raged—but not at him. She complained loudly that her daughter had let herself go too cheap. But the marriage was as good as any Crow marriage. He had paid a horse.

He learned the language faster after that, from Pretty Calf, whom he sometimes called

Crow feather headdress (1890). Native American. Leather, eagle feathers (43.2 cm.). 1988.203.

Photograph © 1995 The Detroit Institute of Arts. Gift of Mr. and Mrs. Richard A. Pohrt. © Robert Hensleigh, photographer, DIA.

Freedom. He learned that his attentive, adoring bride was fourteen years old.

One thing he had not guessed was the difference that being Pretty Calf's husband would make in his relationship to her mother and brother. He had hoped only to make his position a little safer, but he had not expected to be treated with dignity. Greasy Hand no longer spoke to him at all. When the white man spoke to her, his bride murmured in dismay, explaining at great length that he must never do that. There could be no conversation between a man and his mother-in-law. He could not even mention a word that was part of her name.

Having improved his status so magnificently, he felt no need for hurry in getting away. Now that he had a woman, he had as good a chance to be rich as any man. Pretty Calf waited on him; she seldom ran off to play games with other young girls, but took pride in learning from her mother the many women's skills of tanning hides and making clothing and preparing food.

C He was no more a horse but a kind of man, a half-Indian, still poor and unskilled but laden with honors, clinging to the buckskin fringes of Crow society.

Escape could wait until he could manage it in comfort, with fit clothing and a good horse, with hunting weapons. Escape could wait until the camp moved near some trading post. He did not plan how he would get home. He dreamed

174 THE SHORT-STORY COLLECTIONS

Getting Students Involved

Cooperative Learning

Face the Press. If Horse were living today, he certainly would have faced television interviewers after he returned East, and he might have taken part in a news conference. After students finish reading the story, ask them to form groups of five (Horse, an advisor to Horse, and three reporters) to simulate such a conference. Each reporter should prepare three questions on one of these topics:

• Horse's early experiences as a captive

• Horse's courtship, first coup, and marriage
• the deaths of "family members" and Horse's decisions

Reporters should submit the questions to Horse and his advisor before the conference so they can prepare answers. After the conference, ask each group member to assess the quality of their questions and answers, and how well they worked in the actual presentation.

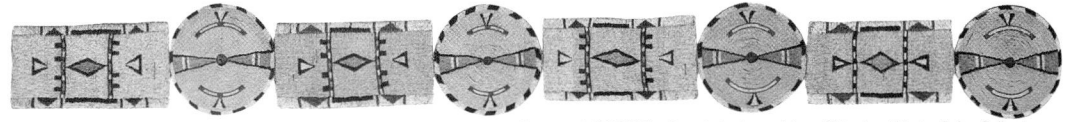

Photograph © 1995 The Detroit Institute of Arts. Richard and Marion Pohrt Collection.

of being there all at once and of telling stories nobody would believe. There was no hurry.

Pretty Calf delighted in educating him. He began to understand tribal arrangements, customs, and why things were as they were. They were that way because they had always been so. His young wife giggled when she told him, in his ignorance, things she had always known. But she did not laugh when her brother's wife was taken by another warrior. She explained that solemnly with words and signs.

Yellow Robe belonged to a society called the Big Dogs. The wife stealer, Cut Neck, belonged to the Foxes. They were fellow tribesmen; they hunted together and fought side by side, but men of one society could take away wives from the other society if they wished, subject to certain limitations.

When Cut Neck rode up to the tepee, laughing and singing, and called to Yellow Robe's wife, "Come out! Come out!" she did as ordered, looking smug as usual, meek and entirely willing. Thereafter she rode beside him in ceremonial processions and carried his coup stick, while his other wife pretended not to care.

"But why?" the white man demanded of his wife, his Freedom. "Why did our brother let his woman go? He sits and smokes and does not speak."

Pretty Calf was shocked at the suggestion. Her brother could not possibly reclaim his woman, she explained. He could not even let her come back if she wanted to—and she probably would want to when Cut Neck tired of her. Yellow Robe could not even admit that his heart was sick. That was the way things were. Deviation meant dishonor.

The woman could have hidden from Cut Neck, she said. She could even have refused to go with him if she had been *ba-wurokee*—a really virtuous woman. But she had been his woman before, for a little while on a berrying expedition, and he had a right to claim her.

There was no sense in it, the white man

insisted. He glared at his young wife. "If you go, I will bring you back!" he promised.

She laughed and buried her head against his shoulder. "I will not have to go," she said. "Horse is my first man. There is no hole in my moccasin."

He stroked her hair and said, "*Ba-wurokee.*"

With great daring, she murmured, "*Hayha,*" and when he did not answer, because he did not know what she meant, she drew away, hurt.

"A woman calls her man that if she thinks he will not leave her. Am I wrong?"

The white man held her closer and lied, "Pretty Calf is not wrong. Horse will not leave her. Horse will not take another woman, either." No, he certainly would not. Parting from this one was going to be harder than getting her had been. "*Hayha,*" he murmured. "Freedom."

His conscience irked him, but not very much. Pretty Calf could get another man easily enough when he was gone, and a better provider. His hunting skill was improving, but he was still awkward.

There was no hurry about leaving. He was used to most of the Crow ways and could stand the rest. He was becoming prosperous. He owned five horses. His place in the life of the tribe was secure, such as it was. Three or four young women, including the one who had belonged to Yellow Robe, made advances to him. Pretty Calf took pride in the fact that her man was so attractive.

By the time he had what he needed for a secret journey, the grass grew yellow on the plains and the long cold was close. He was enslaved by the girl he called Freedom and, before the winter ended, by the knowledge that she was carrying his child. . . .

The Big Dog society held a long ceremony in the spring. The white man strolled with his woman along the creek bank, thinking: When I get home I will tell them about the chants and the drumming. Sometime. Sometime.

Pretty Calf would not go to bed when they went back to the tepee.

A MAN CALLED HORSE 175

D Reading Skills and Strategies
Comparing and Contrasting
? How do Horse's and Yellow Robe's ideas of dishonor differ? [Possible answers: For Yellow Robe, dishonor lies in trying to restrain an unfaithful wife, but for Horse, dishonor lies in allowing such a wife to go; for Yellow Robe, dishonor lies in expressing his grief, but Horse freely expresses his feelings.]

E Appreciating Language
Crow Words
The words *Ba-wurokee* and *Hayha* are in italics because they are non-English words. Ask students why the author uses the Crow language rather than a translation of the words. [Possible answers: Some words cannot be precisely translated—they lose meaning in translation; the use of Crow words shows that Horse is adopting aspects of the Crow culture—a sort of cultural blending is gradually occurring within him.]

F Elements of Literature
Setting
Living among the Crow has influenced how Horse perceives the world around him. Ask students to speculate on how his present definition of *prosperous* differs from the one he would have given in Boston. [In Boston, Horse might have said that a man who was rich and had a large house and servants was prosperous. In this culture, Horse feels prosperous because he owns horses and has a place in community life.]

Professional Notes

Historical Background
In *The Crow*, Frederick E. Hoxie explains warrior societies. "In the 1800s, the Foxes and the Lumpwood were the most prominent societies: others—the Big Dogs, the Muddy Hands, and the Ravens—were of less importance. Each society recruited promising young men, chose its own leaders, and established customs and emblems to represent it. . . . During the spring and summer, the warrior societies competed with each other for prestige and honors. . . . Sometimes members of one society would even capture and marry the wives of those of another. . . . Warrior societies were led by chiefs who had attained this status by performing four types of military exploits: leading a war party, capturing an enemy's horse, being the first to touch an enemy in battle, and snatching an enemy warrior's weapon. The men in each society who accumulated the largest number of these war honors were regarded as the chiefs by general agreement of its members."

Crow blanket strip (c. 1870–1875). Native American. Buffalo hide, glass beads (63″ x 5.5″). CP-88.

A Reading Skills and Strategies

Monitor Your Comprehension

? What questions could you ask yourself at this point in the story? [Possible questions: Who are the Big Dogs? What is happening to Yellow Robe? How will this affect Horse's life? Why are Greasy Hand and Pretty Calf upset?]

B Elements of Literature

Making Inferences

? What do you learn about the values of the Crow in this passage? [Sample responses: The greatest honor is reserved for a successful warrior; facing danger with courage is more important than survival; belief in a spiritual power can strengthen a Crow's resolve.]

C Advanced Learners

Interpreting Word Choice

? Sometimes the author refers to the young man as Horse. Other times she refers to him as "the white man." Why might she refer to him as "the white man" at this point in the story? [Possible responses: At this point, he is a stranger to the customs of the Crow; the phrase "white man" emphasizes the gulf between the cultures, while the name Horse focuses on his Crow identity.]

"Wait and find out about my brother," she urged. "Something may happen."

A So far as Horse could figure out, the Big Dogs were having some kind of election. He pampered his wife by staying up with her by the fire. Even the old woman, who was a great one for getting sleep when she was not working, prowled around restlessly.

The white man was yawning by the time the noise of the ceremony died down. When Yellow Robe strode in, garish and heathen in his paint and feathers and furs, the women cried out. There was conversation, too fast for Horse to follow, and the old woman wailed once, but her son silenced her with a gruff command.

When the white man went to sleep, he thought his wife was weeping beside him.

The next morning she explained.

B "He wears the bearskin belt. Now he can never retreat in battle. He will always be in danger. He will die."

Maybe he wouldn't, the white man tried to convince her. Pretty Calf recalled that some few men had been honored by the bearskin belt, vowed to the highest daring, and had not died. If they lived through the summer, then they were free of it.

"My brother wants to die," she mourned. "His heart is bitter."

Yellow Robe lived through half a dozen clashes with small parties of raiders from hostile tribes. His honors were many. He captured horses in an enemy camp, led two successful raids, counted first coup and snatched a gun from the hand of an enemy tribesman. He wore wolf tails on his moccasins and ermine skins on his shirt, and he fringed his leggings with scalps in token of his glory.

When his mother ventured to suggest, as she did many times, "My son should take a new wife, I need another woman to help me," he ignored her. He spent much time in prayer, alone in the hills or in conference with a medicine man. He fasted and made vows and

kept them. And before he could be free of the heavy honor of the bearskin belt, he went on his last raid.

The warriors were returning from the north just as the white man and two other hunters approached from the south, with buffalo and elk meat dripping from the bloody hides tied on their restive ponies. One of the hunters grunted, and they stopped to watch a rider on the hill north of the tepee circle.

The rider dismounted, held up a blanket and dropped it. He repeated the gesture.

The hunters murmured dismay. "Two! Two men dead!" They rode fast into the camp, where there was already wailing.

A messenger came down from the war party on the hill. The rest of the party delayed to paint their faces for mourning and for victory. One of the two dead men was Yellow Robe. They had put his body in a cave and walled it in with rocks. The other man died later, and his body was in a tree.

There was blood on the ground before the tepee to which Yellow Robe would return no more. His mother, with her hair chopped short, sat in the doorway, rocking back and forth on her haunches, wailing her heartbreak. She cradled one mutilated hand in the other. She had cut off another finger joint.

C Pretty Calf had cut off chunks of her long hair and was crying as she gashed her arms with a knife. The white man tried to take the knife away, but she protested so piteously that he let her do as she wished. He was sickened with the lot of them.

Savages! he thought. Now I will go back! I'll go hunting alone, and I'll keep going.

But he did not go just yet, because he was the

- -

WORDS TO OWN

restive (res′tiv) *adj.*: restless; unsettled.
piteously (pit′ē·əs·lē) *adv.*: in a way that arouses pity or compassion.

- -

Making the Connections

Cultural Connections: Honored Warriors

Tell students that many Plains tribes followed this particular custom of designating a warrior who could never retreat in battle. Among the Crow Owners society of the Lakota Sioux, four members were elected to be sash bearers. During battle, the sash bearers drove wooden stakes through their sashes into the ground, thereby tethering themselves in place. These sash bearers had to remain where they were until they were killed or the enemy retreated. The Mandan Buffalo Bull Society also elected four warriors who swore never to retreat in battle. Such warriors were highly honored and earned the right to wear special emblems and masks and participate in society rituals. Ask students if they know of similar customs in other warrior cultures such as the samurai in Japan or the Spartans of ancient Greece.

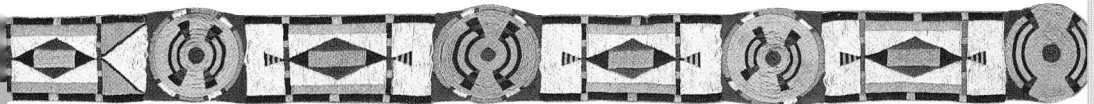

only hunter in the lodge of the two grieving women, one of them old and the other pregnant with his child.

In their mourning, they made him a pauper again. Everything that meant comfort, wealth, and safety they sacrificed to the spirits because of the death of Yellow Robe. The tepee, made of seventeen fine buffalo hides, the furs that should have kept them warm, the white deerskin dress, trimmed with elk teeth, that Pretty Calf loved so well, even their tools and Yellow Robe's weapons—everything but his sacred medicine objects— they left there on the prairie, and the whole camp moved away. Two of his best horses were killed as a sacrifice, and the women gave away the rest.

They had no shelter. They would have no tepee of their own for two months at least of mourning, and then the women would have to tan hides to make it. Meanwhile, they could live in temporary huts made of willows, covered with skins given them in pity by their friends. They could have lived with relatives, but Yellow Robe's women had no relatives.

The white man had not realized until then how terrible a thing it was for a Crow to have no kinfolk. No wonder old Greasy Hand had only stumps for fingers. She had mourned, from one year to the next, for everyone she had ever loved. She had no one left but her daughter, Pretty Calf.

Horse was furious at their foolishness. It had been bad enough for him, a captive, to be naked as a horse and poor as a slave, but that was because his captors had stripped him. These

women had voluntarily given up everything they needed.

He was too angry at them to sleep in the willow hut. He lay under a sheltering tree. And on the third night of the mourning he made his plans. He had a knife and a bow. He would go after meat, taking two horses. And he would not come back. There were, he realized, many things he was not going to tell when he got back home.

In the willow hut, Pretty Calf cried out. He heard rustling there, and the old woman's querulous voice.

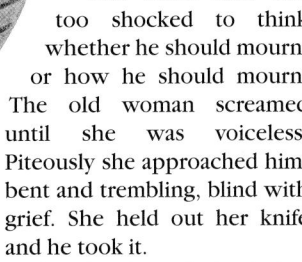

Crow shield with cover (c. 1865).
Buffalo Bill Historical Center, Cody, Wyoming. Chandler-Pohrt Collection, gift of Mr. and Mrs. Edson W. Spencer. NA.108.105.

Some twenty hours later his son was born, two months early, in the tepee of a skilled medicine woman. The child was born without breath, and the mother died before the sun went down.

The white man was too shocked to think whether he should mourn, or how he should mourn. The old woman screamed until she was voiceless. Piteously she approached him, bent and trembling, blind with grief. She held out her knife and he took it.

She spread out her hands and shook her head. If she cut off any more finger joints, she could do no more work. She could not afford any more lasting signs of grief.

The white man said, "All right! All right!" between his teeth. He hacked his arms with the knife and stood watching the blood run down. It was little enough to do for Pretty Calf, for little Freedom.

Now there is nothing to keep me, he realized. When I get home, I must not let them see the scars.

He looked at Greasy Hand, hideous in her

A MAN CALLED HORSE 177

Making the Connections

Connecting to the Theme: "The Human Spirit"

In "Thank You, Ma'm" and in "A Christmas Memory," the theme is conveyed through acts of giving: Mrs. Jones extends both kindness and forgiveness to Roger, while Buddy and his cousin share both concrete and abstract gifts of love and affection. Discuss these questions:

- Is this story also about giving? If so, what is given, and what is received?
- What qualities of the human spirit are celebrated in this story? How does the main

character come to find or recognize these qualities within himself? How are these qualities shown among the people with whom he lives?

- Do you think the author suggests that the human spirit is more likely to prevail or triumph under certain kinds of conditions or when faced with certain kinds of challenges? Explain your answer.

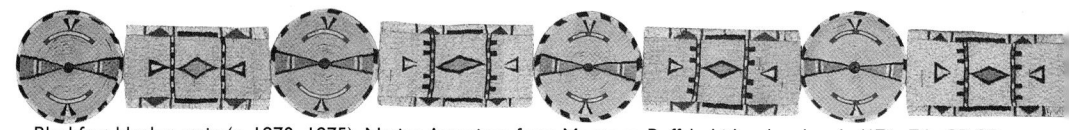

Blackfeet blanket strip (c. 1870–1875). Native American from Montana. Buffalo hide, glass beads (67″x 7″). CP-87.

Photograph © 1995 The Detroit Institute of Arts. Richard and Marion Pohrt Collection.

A Critical Thinking

Interpreting

❓ Think back to the beginning of the story. What is the significance of Horse's calling Greasy Hand "Mother"? [Possible responses: He has accepted responsibility for her; he never knew his own mother and now unselfishly allows someone to take her place.]

B Critical Thinking

Evaluating

Ask students to explain whether this is an appropriate ending for the story. [Possible answers: Yes, because the ending completes the young man's quest for a feeling of worth and belonging; no, because it would have seemed more complete to know about his return to Boston.]

BROWSING IN THE FILES

About the Author. "A Man Called Horse" is representative of the way Dorothy Johnson constructed her stories. According to the critic Judy Alter, Johnson deliberately took a situation, turned it around, and showed it from a different angle. For example, Johnson had done extensive research on the Crow, so much so that she felt she could survive in a Crow camp. She took her knowledge and imagined what life would be like for a man without such knowledge if he found himself captive in a Crow camp; thus, "A Man Called Horse" was born.

Resources

Selection Assessment

Formal Assessment
• Selection Test, p. 19
Test Generator (One-Stop Planner)
• CD-ROM

grief-burdened age, and thought: I really am free now! When a wife dies, her husband has no more duty toward her family. Pretty Calf had told him so, long ago, when he wondered why a certain man moved out of one tepee and into another.

The old woman, of course, would be a scavenger. There was one other with the tribe, an ancient crone who had no relatives, toward whom no one felt any responsibility. She lived on food thrown away by the more fortunate. She slept in shelters that she built with her own knotted hands. She plodded wearily at the end of the procession when the camp moved. When she stumbled, nobody cared. When she died, nobody would miss her.

Tomorrow morning, the white man decided, I will go.

His mother-in-law's sunken mouth quivered. She said one word, questioningly. She said, "*Eero-oshay?*" She said, "Son?"

Blinking, he remembered. When a wife died, her husband was free. But her mother, who had

ignored him with dignity, might if she wished ask him to stay. She invited him by calling him Son, and he accepted by answering Mother.

Greasy Hand stood before him, bowed with years, withered with unceasing labor, loveless and childless, scarred with grief. But with all her burdens, she still loved life enough to beg it from him, the only person she had any right to ask. She was stripping herself of all she had left, her pride.

He looked eastward across the prairie. Two thousand miles away was home. The old woman would not live forever. He could afford to wait, for he was young. He could afford to be magnanimous, for he knew he was a man. He gave her the answer. "*Eegya*," he said. "Mother."

He went home three years later. He explained no more than to say, "I lived with Crows for a while. It was some time before I could leave. They called me Horse."

He did not find it necessary either to apologize or to boast, because he was the equal of any man on earth.

MEET THE WRITER

Kills-Both-Places

Dorothy M. Johnson (1905–1984) grew up in Montana and then moved east. Though she tried hard to be an Easterner, she finally returned to Montana in the 1950s. At this point, according to Jack Schaefer (see his statement on page 166), she began to write "the stories that only Dorothy Johnson could write."

Johnson was welcomed into the Blackfoot tribe in Montana as an honorary member. Her tribal name reflects her double identity as a white woman and a member of the tribe. The Blackfeet called her Kills-Both-Places.

From Print to Film

Johnson's stories "The Hanging Tree," "The Man Who Shot Liberty Valance," and "A Man Called Horse" were all made into movies.

Assessing Learning

Check Test: Questions and Answers

1. Where did the main character originally live? [an upper-class home in Boston in 1845]
2. Who is named Horse—the captive or his captor? [the captive]
3. What does Greasy Hand do to herself to express her grief when a loved one dies? [She cuts off a joint of a finger.]
4. Who does Horse marry? [Pretty Calf]
5. Who asks Horse to stay after his wife dies? [his mother-in-law, Greasy Hand]

Standardized Test Preparation

For practice in proofreading and editing, see
• *Daily Oral Grammar,* Transparency 9

MAKING MEANINGS

First Thoughts

[respond]

1. Did you want Horse to get home to Boston or stay with the Crows? Why?

Shaping Interpretations

[analyze]

2. By the end of the story, Horse has changed. In your own words, explain what he discovers about himself—and other people—in his years with the Crows. How do you think becoming a horse helped him become a man? (How close did you come to predicting all of this?)

[apply]

3. Name at least two incidents in the story that remind us that all people, no matter what their culture, share certain feelings.

[analyze]

4. Which character showed you most forcefully what the human spirit is capable of? Explain.

Connecting with the Text

[respond]

5. How did you respond to the ways the Crows "counted coup" and to how a grieving mother chopped off a joint of one of her fingers for each dead child? How do you think the writer wants you to feel about the Crows? (Be sure to check your reading notes.)

Extending the Text

[extend]

6. This could be described as a story about a clash of cultures. What experiences in today's world might result in similar conflicts? When might a person have to adapt to a new culture? What movies have focused on this theme?

Challenging the Text

[analyze]

7. All that we learn and experience in this story we learn through the perspective of Horse. At what points in the story do you think you are hearing about Horse's prejudices or perceptions, not necessarily the writer's? How would various episodes of the story differ if we were told how Greasy Hand or Pretty Calf thought or felt?

[evaluate]

8. Is the writer fair to all her characters, or did you feel she favors some characters and disapproves of others? Cite passages from the text to support your responses. (Be sure to check your reading notes.)

A MAN CALLED HORSE 179

Reading Check

a. List the few details we are given about the Boston **setting**. Why is the man unhappy there?

b. In contrast to Boston, we are told a great deal about the Crow **setting**. Describe at least five customs of the Crow culture that you learned about in this story.

c. How does the man become a horse?

d. Name the two things that happen one day to make Horse think that he might become a man again.

e. Why does Horse marry Pretty Calf? What happens to his status in the Crow community after his marriage?

MAKING MEANINGS

First Thoughts

1. Sample responses: to stay with the Crows, where he has learned his worth and strength; to return home to prove to himself that he has grown.

Shaping Interpretations

2. Sample responses: Horse learns that he is equal to any human and can survive great hardship; he learns new ideas about respect and status. Being a horse gave him time to heal, to see things from a new point of view, and to learn new customs.

3. Possible answers: Pretty Calf enjoys Horse's attention; Pretty Calf and Greasy Hand mourn the death of Yellow Robe; Greasy Hand mourns the deaths of her daughter and grandchild.

4. Possible responses: Horse, because he survives; Greasy Hand, because she wants to go on living even after everyone she loves dies.

Connecting with the Text

5. Some students may express horror at the violence; others may see the deep emotion expressed by the acts of mourning or the necessity of killing for survival. The writer may want readers to sympathize with the Crows' harsh struggle to survive and their heartfelt observation of old customs.

Extending the Text

6. Similar conflicts might arise when people interact with others from extremely different backgrounds, such as when moving from one country or region to another or from a rural to an urban environment. Movies that focus on this theme include *E.T.* and *The King and I.*

Challenging the Text

7. Possible response: Horse's prejudices are evident when he rages about the women sacrificing their possessions to mourn Yellow Robe. Pretty Calf might have explained that she gave up her possessions to show how great her loss was.

8. Since readers see everything through Horse's eyes, the writer's own opinions are seldom expressed. However, when she describes Greasy Hand's plight at the end of the story, she does seem to express sympathy.

Reading Check

Answers may vary slightly.

a. Horse lives in a gracious Boston home with his wealthy father and grandmother. He feels lonely, alienated, and inferior.

b. Customs include warriors celebrating a victory by wearing ceremonial clothes and face paint; warriors killing and scalping enemies; courting a woman through gifts of horses and buffalo meat; maintaining silence between a husband and his mother-in-law; a man's having no further obligations to his wife's family after her death.

c. He becomes docile and outwardly accepts his status as a slave.

d. Horse begins to understand the Crow language, and Greasy Hand throws him a pair of new moccasins.

e. He marries her to secure his own status and to buy his freedom. After the marriage, he is accepted and treated with dignity.

Rubrics for each Choices assignment appear on p. 104 in the *Portfolio Management System*.

CHOICES: Building Your Portfolio

1. **Writer's Notebook** Remind students to save their work. They may want to use these notes as prewriting for the Writer's Workshop that begins on p. 194.

2. **Creative Writing** Before students begin, they might brainstorm Horse's possible emotional responses to things he will encounter, such as the comforts and luxuries of his home. They might also speculate on how Horse will react to people who express stereotyped views of Indians and Indian life.

3. **Research** Among the crafts objects students may study are the rawhide containers called *parfleches,* quivers, saddles and stirrups, decorated hides, and shields. Additional suggestions for research appear in the Crossing the Curriculum feature at the bottom of this page.

4. **Book Review** Once students have taken notes on a story of captivity, suggest they use a Venn diagram to compare and contrast it with Horse's experience. After they have written their reviews, encourage them to practice reading the review aloud before they tape it.

CHOICES: Building Your Portfolio

Writer's Notebook

1. Collecting Ideas for an Essay Analyzing a Character

What changes?
In the Writer's Workshop on page 194, you'll write an essay analyzing one of the main characters in a story you've read. Focus now on a character in one of the stories you've read in this book. Take notes on these questions:

- Does the character change in an important way?
- What—or who—causes the change?

Save your notes for possible use later.
    Below are one writer's notes on the changes in Buddy in "A Christmas Memory."

> **Narrator of "A Christmas Memory"**
> The character has changed a lot by the time he tells the story. He is older, more mature, and perhaps not as happy.
> **Causes**
> - the passing of time; growing up
> - having been taken away from his friend
> - a new, harsh environment

Creative Writing

2. Horse's Journal

Imagine that the man called Horse is home in Boston and that he writes an entry in his journal describing his first days back in his "own world." What does he think of his own culture now? Is he critical of any customs? Does he miss anything about the Crows? Write a paragraph that Horse might enter in his journal. Have Horse use the first-person pronoun "I."

Research

3. Exploring Crow Culture

Has spending time in a Crow camp made you curious to know more about the Crows? They were not always a nomadic people. They became buffalo hunters only after moving to the Plains in the eighteenth century. Work with a group of classmates to research the history and culture of the Crows (they call themselves Apsaroke). Before you start, narrow your area of interest. For example, you might explore their spiritual beliefs and ceremonies, their distinctive crafts and arts, or the organization of their society. Convert some of the information into a chart or graph, or make drawings based on your research.

Book Review

4. Captivity Stories

Captivity stories have always been popular. Choose a captivity story you know or have read, and share your findings about it in the form of a book review. Summarize the reason for the captivity, the main events of the captivity, and how the captive felt about the jailers. How was this captivity different from Horse's? When you are satisfied with your book review, you might want to tape it for classmates to listen to.

    Instead of a book, you may wish to review a movie that tells a captivity story. Then, compare that story with Horse's experience.

    If you wish to read about an American Indian held in a kind of captivity by whites, try *Ishi in Two Worlds* by Theodora Kroeber (University of California Press).

Crow lance case (c. 1890).
Buffalo Bill Historical Center, Cody, Wyoming. NA 108.95.

Crossing the Curriculum

Social Studies

For Choice 3, here are some possible topics for research: the various ceremonies of the Crow, such as the Sun Dance; the tobacco-planting ritual (which is related to the Crow creation story); the Bear Song Dance; and the Sacred Pipe Dance. Students could also locate and read myths or tales of the Crow and report on what these stories reveal about the culture. One example is the hero tale "Lodge-Boy and Thrown-Away."

Language Handbook
H E L P

See Using Modifiers, page 1003.

Handbook of Literary Terms
H E L P

See Connotation, Imagery.

Technology H E L P

See Language Workshop CD-ROM. *Key word entry: modifiers.*

Vivid Modifiers—A Definite Choice

Using precise, evocative modifiers is often the most immediate way of creating a clear picture of a character's looks and actions. In the following descriptions from "A Man Called Horse," Johnson's precise adjectives and adverbs are the brushstrokes that add detail to her word pictures.

1. "A scrawny, shrieking, eternally busy old woman with ragged graying hair threw a chunk of meat on the grass, and he fought the dogs for it."

2. "He applied it gingerly to his bruised and sun-seared body."

3. "The younger sister had bright, wandering eyes."

Modifiers must be used carefully. Too many modifiers can result in a passage that is "overwritten." (Some critics call such overblown descriptions "purple prose.") For example, Johnson doesn't need a modifier in this sentence to describe how the boys sounded. The verb *snickered* is vivid enough:

"... they snickered when he missed."

In this sentence no adjective is necessary to modify the very precise noun *hag*:

"A few days later he asked the hag, with gestures, for a bow that her son had just discarded. . . ."

Try It Out

➤ Rewrite each of the sentences at the left, replacing Johnson's modifiers with adjectives and adverbs of your own. Try to find modifiers that will give completely different pictures of the characters and their actions. Be sure to compare your descriptions with those of your classmates.

➤ Analyze a piece of your own writing to see how skillfully you have used modifiers. Put a circle around each adjective and adverb, and put a box around each noun or verb that you have left unmodified. Would a modifier help make these nouns and verbs more specific, or do you feel they are vivid enough? Do you have too many circles on your paper—or are you satisfied that those modifiers are just right?

VOCABULARY   HOW TO OWN A WORD

WORD BANK

forestalled
docile
detractor
restive
piteously

What's the Difference? Words That Can Be Confused

Write your answers to these questions. Use a college or unabridged dictionary to look up words you don't know.

1. What is the difference between *restive* and *restful*?
2. What is the difference between *docile* and *domicile*?
3. What is the difference between *forestalled* and *forewarned*?
4. What is the difference between *piteously* and *pityingly*?
5. What is the difference between *detractor* and *retractor*?

A MAN CALLED HORSE 181

LANGUAGE LINK

When students revise one of the pieces of writing in their portfolio, suggest that they try to picture in their minds any people, characters, settings or scenes they have created. Then, have them evaluate the modifiers they used. They should ask themselves: Are the modifiers vivid? Could a string of dull modifiers be replaced by a single, vivid modifier? Do any modifiers need to be added to make the picture come to life?

Try It Out
Possible Answers
1. A plump, quiet, often idle young woman with black curly hair . . .
2. He applied it carelessly to his muscular and sun-tanned body.
3. The younger sister had soft, downcast eyes.

VOCABULARY
Possible Answers
1. *Restive* means "restless"; *restive* and *restful* can be opposites.
2. *Docile* means "obedient"; *domicile* means "home."
3. *Forestalled* means "prevented from happening"; *forewarned* means "warned ahead of time."
4. *Piteously* means "in a way that arouses pity"; *pityingly* means "in a way that shows pity."
5. A *detractor* is a person who belittles something; a *retractor* is a person or utensil that takes or holds something back.

Language Link Quick Check

Have students add modifiers to these sentences to create vivid word pictures. Though students may come up with a variety of responses, possible modifiers are shown after each sentence.

1. The boys hid behind the trees and waited.
[determined boys; dense trees; waited patiently]

2. Pretty Calf smoothed her robe and combed her hair. [gently smoothed; ceremonial robe; perfumed hair]

3. Ignoring the shouts of his father and the pleas of his grandmother, the man closed the door behind him and walked down the stairs.
[angry shouts; tearful pleas; firmly closed; quickly walked]

4. Yellow Robe and his friends circled the buffaloes. [close friends; warily circled; massive buffaloes]

5. He touched the woman's hand and gave her the answer. [lightly touched; mutilated hand]

OBJECTIVES

1. Read and interpret the vignette
2. Orally interpret the vignette
3. Express understanding through creative writing, speaking, or problem solving

SKILLS

Reading
- Orally interpret the vignette

Writing
- Take notes on a character's actions
- Write a vignette
- Write a poem from a character's point of view

Speaking
- Prepare and present a dramatic reading
- Participate in a panel discussion

Planning

- **Block Schedule**
  Block Scheduling Lesson Plans with Pacing Guide
- **Traditional Schedule**
  Lesson Plans Including Strategies for English-Language Learners
- **One-Stop Planner**
  CD-ROM with Test Generator

SALVADOR LATE OR EARLY

Make the Connection

The Invisible Children

Here, Sandra Cisneros gives us just the quickest glimpse of a boy she names Salvador. There are many "Salvadors" in our world. Sometimes people barely notice these children. The impression they make on most of us is as fleeting as this little story itself.

Quickwrite

Write a few notes about any children you can think of—in your neighborhood or in the world news—whose difficult lives or small acts of courage go almost unnoticed.

Reading Skills and Strategies

Oral Interpretation

Practice reading aloud this touching little story until you're satisfied with your interpretation. Here are the vocal elements you should think about: the **speed** at which you read, the places where you **pause** and the length of your pauses, the rise and fall of your voice (**pitch**), and the softness or loudness of your voice (**emphasis**). For more about oral interpretation, see the Speaking and Listening Workshop on page 582.

 go.hrw.com
LE0 9-2

182 THE SHORT-STORY COLLECTIONS

Salvador whose name the teacher cannot remember.

Resources: Print and Media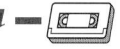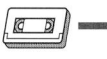

Reading
- *Graphic Organizers for Active Reading*, p. 10

Writing and Language
- *Daily Oral Grammar* Transparency 10

Assessment
- *Formal Assessment*, p. 21
- *Portfolio Management System*, p. 105
- *Standardized Test Preparation*, p. 24
- *Test Generator (One-Stop Planner CD-ROM)*

Internet
- go.hrw.com (keyword: LE0 9-2)

Salvador Late or Early

Sandra Cisneros

Summary ■ ■

In this vignette, Sandra Cisneros uses simple, evocative language to paint a portrait of Salvador, a small boy whose responsibilities—which include getting his little brothers ready for school—far exceed his years. Salvador is a quiet boy whom nobody notices, whose name the teacher can't remember, and whose hope and grief are sealed up in his small body.

Background

In Spanish, the word *salvador* means "rescuer" or "savior"; when capitalized, the word refers to the Christian savior, Jesus Christ.

Ⓐ Critical Thinking
Speculating
❓What are some reasons that a teacher might not remember a student's name? [Possible answers: The student is often absent; the student sits in the back of the class and rarely volunteers; the class is too large for the teacher to get to know every student.]

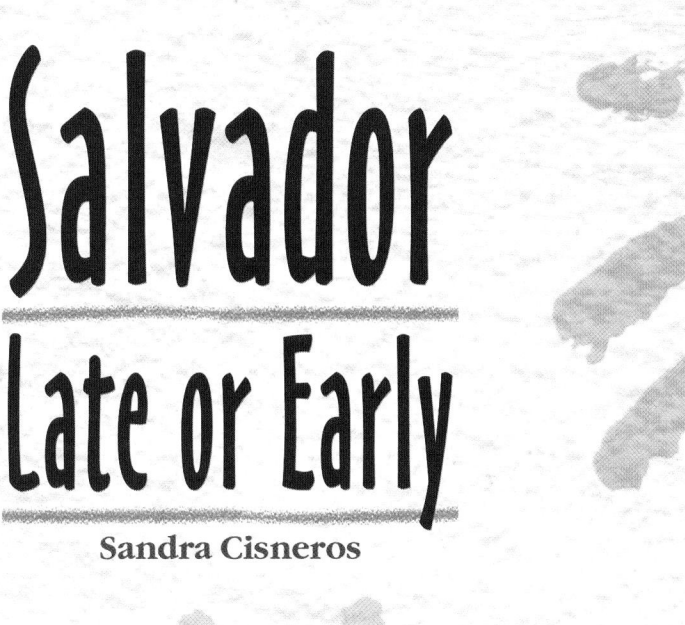

Salvador with eyes the color of caterpillar, Salvador of the crooked hair and crooked teeth, Salvador whose name the teacher cannot remember, is a boy who is no one's friend, runs along somewhere in that vague direction where homes are the color of bad weather, lives behind a raw wood doorway, shakes the sleepy brothers awake, ties their shoes, combs their hair with water, feeds them milk and cornflakes from a tin cup in the dim dark of the morning. Ⓐ

SALVADOR LATE OR EARLY   183

Reaching All Students

Struggling Readers
Remind students to break long sentences into shorter units of meaning. Point out that the first paragraph is one long sentence. Suggest that students stop after each comma and break down the text by creating simple sentences to convey meaning. You might start them off with a couple of examples: Salvador has eyes the color of caterpillar. Salvador has crooked hair and crooked teeth.

English Language Learners
Invite students to listen to the audiotape of the story before they read it for themselves, so they can hear the tone of the writing. Afterwards, they can read the story for meaning. For additional strategies for engaging English language learners with the literature, see
• *Lesson Plans Including Strategies for English-Language Learners*

Advanced Learners
Point out to these students that "Salvador Late or Early" is written in a poetic style. Ask them to look for its poetic elements, such as rhythm, imagery, figures of speech, and alliteration. For example, the first paragraph is one long sentence that has the rhythm of a poem; images such as "homes are the color of bad weather" are poetic; there is alliteration in the phrases the "color of caterpillar" and "the dim dark of the morning."

A Elements of Literature

Character

❓ What character trait of Salvador does this sentence suggest? [Possible answers: He is dependable; he is trustworthy; he is responsible.]

B Reading Skills and Strategies

Oral Interpretation

❓ How might you vary your voice, using pauses, emphasis, speed, and pitch, to interpret this passage? [Possible answers: A reader might pause after "geography of scars" and "history of hurt"; might emphasize the verb "throbs"; might slow down to recite the injustices that begin with "inside that forty-pound body"; might vary pitch to underscore differences between the "hundred balloons of happiness" and the "single guitar of grief."]

C Critical Thinking

Interpreting

❓ What does the ending suggest about the child's significance to the larger world? [Possible answers: People easily forget the pain of a child like Salvador; the world tends to ignore poor children like Salvador.]

Resources ──────

Selection Assessment
Formal Assessment
• Selection Test, p. 21
Test Generator (One-Stop Planner)
• CD-ROM

A Salvador, late or early, sooner or later arrives with the string of younger brothers ready. Helps his mama, who is busy with the business of the baby. Tugs the arms of Cecilio, Arturito, makes them hurry, because today, like yesterday, Arturito has dropped the cigar box of crayons, has let go the hundred little fingers of red, green, yellow, blue, and nub of black sticks that tumble and spill over and beyond the asphalt puddles until the crossing-guard lady holds back the blur of traffic for Salvador to collect them again.

B Salvador inside that wrinkled shirt, inside the throat that must clear itself and apologize each time it speaks, inside that forty-pound body of boy with its geography of scars, its history of hurt, limbs stuffed with feathers and rags, in what part of the eyes, in what part of the heart, in that cage of the chest where something throbs with both fists and knows only what Salvador knows, inside that body too small to contain the hundred balloons of happiness, the single guitar of grief, is a boy like any other disappearing out the door, beside the schoolyard gate, where he has told his brothers they must wait. Collects the hands of Cecilio and Arturito, scuttles off dodging the many schoolyard colors, the elbows and wrists crisscrossing, the several shoes running. Grows small and smaller to the eye, C dissolves into the bright horizon, flutters in the air before disappearing like a memory of kites.

MEET THE WRITER

Swan Keeper

Sandra Cisneros (1954–) was born in inner-city Chicago to a Mexican father and a Mexican American mother. It is no wonder, given her six boisterous brothers, that Cisneros identified with the lone sister in the fairy tale "Six Swans." (The name *Cisneros* means "swan keeper.") Cisneros graduated from Loyola University in Chicago and the Writers' Workshop at the University of Iowa. Most recently, she has lived in San Antonio, Texas.

Cisneros gives readings of her work all over the country. To see her read is to watch an actress at work. Standing alone at the podium, a tiny figure often wearing

Assessing Learning

Check Test: Questions and Answers

1. What detail shows that Salvador is not noticed by people around him? [The teacher does not remember his name.]
2. What is the boy's main task in the morning? [getting his brothers to school]
3. What delays the children's trip to school? [Salvador must pick up all the crayons that his brother drops.]
4. What happens to Salvador at the end? [He vanishes.]

Standardized Test Preparation
For practice with standardized test format specific to this selection, see
• *Standardized Test Preparation,* p. 24
For practice in proofreading and editing, see
• *Daily Oral Grammar,* Transparency 10

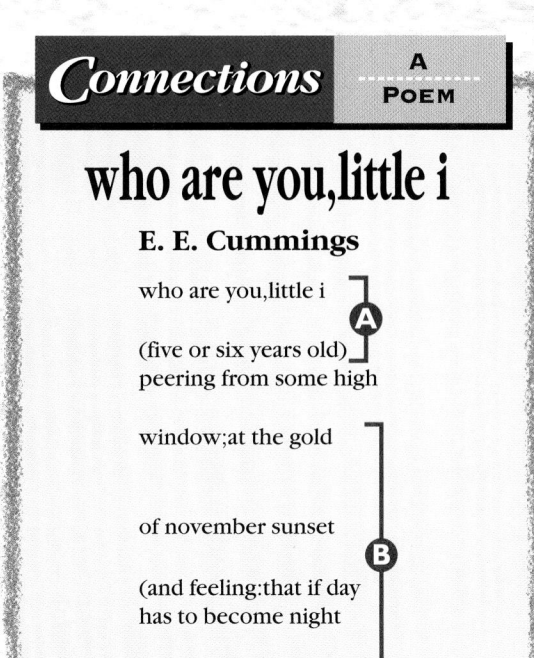

Connections

A POEM

who are you,little i

E. E. Cummings

who are you,little i

Ⓐ

(five or six years old)
peering from some high

window;at the gold

Ⓑ

of november sunset

(and feeling:that if day
has to become night

this is a beautiful way)

---

cowboy boots and huge earrings, Cisneros can "fill" the stage with people who speak in her stories.

When asked about her writing, Cisneros recalled a trip to Falfurrias, Texas, where she visited the shrine of a local healer:

66 While I was visiting the shrine, I discovered all of these little notes that people had pinned there—as thanks for something, or as petitions for something. And I was so overwhelmed by the power of the writing. I mean, mine is a community that supposedly can't write, especially the poor, and here was the most beautiful, most moving writing that I have ever read. These were people who weren't trying to pass an English class, or get their GED—they were just writing from their heart. And when your writing is unselfconscious, when it comes from your heart, that's when it's powerful. **99**

More by Cisneros

If you would like to meet some of the people that fill the stage at a Cisneros reading, read *The House on Mango Street* (Vintage Books). The vignettes in this book read like a series of journal entries written by a young girl named Esperanza. "In English my name means hope," Esperanza remarks in the first entry. "In Spanish it means too many letters." Cisneros' second book, *Woman Hollering Creek* (Random House), is a collection of her short stories, including some about Latino children whose voices are unmistakably authentic and often touchingly funny.

SALVADOR LATE OR EARLY 185

Connections

This brief but memorable poem presents a fleeting impression of a young boy at twilight.

Ⓐ Critical Thinking
Interpreting
? Who might the speaker be? [Possible answers: The speaker seems to be an adult looking back at himself or herself at an earlier age; the speaker is someone who remembers what it's like to be five or six years old.] Whom is the speaker addressing? [Possible answers: "little i"; a younger version of the poet's self.]

Ⓑ Critical Thinking
Determining the Author's Purpose
? Both November, which is near the end of the year, and sunset, which is near the end of the day, suggest the coming of darkness. Do you think that the author intends the ending to be positive or negative? [Sample responses: Positive, because the speaker says that if the end must come at least it comes with beauty; positive, because the speaker suggests that this ending time is golden.]

BROWSING IN THE FILES

About the Author. Cisneros has a strong sense of community responsibility. She is interested in doing "something to make change in the world. I don't think that one could live the kind of life I've lived and witnessed and not take some responsibility.... And the fact that I can do it from my art is so wonderful; I feel really blessed."
Writers on Writing. "Everything I write is true," says Cisneros, "but it didn't all happen to me. I would have to describe it like a cloth in which there are strands which are my own, but there are also strands of other people."

Reaching All Students

Struggling Readers
If students have trouble understanding "who are you,little i," tell them that a poem compresses a great deal of meaning into very few words. Explain that a poem often leaves out words that help form the connection between ideas. Invite students to construct a longer prose version of the poem that supplies some of these missing links. Suggest they start with this sentence: The speaker looks at a child who is five or six years old and asks, "Who are you?"

Connecting Across Texts

Connecting with "Salvador Late or Early"
How is the "little i" in this poem like Salvador in "Salvador Late or Early"? [Possible answers: Like Salvador, the "little i" is a young child; the uncapitalized pronoun suggests that the "little i," like Salvador, is not big and important; there is a poignancy about both characters—one is overburdened and underappreciated, and the other sits and watches the darkness fall in the month of November.]

MAKING MEANINGS

First Thoughts

1. Possible questions: Do you know someone like Salvador? Is this sketch based on a person or people you know? Does Salvador's family have a father? What were Salvador's hurts and scars?

Shaping Interpretations

2. He is rushed, responsible, helpful, poor, self-effacing, sensitive, and solitary when apart from his family. His setting is one of poverty and deprivation.

3. The "scars" and "hurt" may be the figurative wounds of poverty and neglect or the actual wounds of mishaps and abuse.

4. Possible answers: Salvador's actual physical heart; a fighting spirit inside the boy that is uniquely his.

5. Students may feel concern for Salvador if they think of something dull or something that seeks to camouflage and protect itself from possible enemies; they may feel hopeful for him if they think of something jewellike or something on its way to becoming something else. A comparison to "eyes the color of a cloudless sky," for example, might have given the reader a sense of serenity about him.

6. Both stories end in images of free-flying kites. Some students may say that the images have the same effect, for both suggest something fragile. Others may say that the effect of the two is different because one symbolizes the closeness of two human beings while the other symbolizes the alienation of one individual.

Connecting with the Text

7. Responses may range from dismay or anger at the circumstances of this child's life to admiration of his courage and his devotion to duty.

Extending the Text

8. Students may mention children in developing countries or in war-torn areas of the world; homeless children; impoverished or hungry children; children of migrant workers; abused or neglected children of any country, class, or segment of society.

T186

MAKING MEANINGS

First Thoughts

[respond]

1. This little sketch about Salvador leaves a great deal unsaid. What questions would you like to ask Sandra Cisneros if you could talk to her?

Shaping Interpretations

[analyze]

2. What exactly do you know from this little story about the **character** of Salvador and his **setting**?

[infer]

3. What can you infer, or guess, is the cause of Salvador's "geography of scars" and "history of hurt"?

[interpret]

4. What could it be that "throbs with both fists and knows only what Salvador knows"?

[analyze]

5. How does Cisneros make you feel about Salvador when she describes his eyes as being the color of caterpillars? Think of another comparison that would have made you feel differently about Salvador.

[compare]

6. Cisneros' short little story and Capote's longer story (page 145) both end with the same **image**. What are the final images in each story? Do they have the same effect on you? Try to explain why or why not.

Connecting with the Text

[respond]

7. Describe the emotional impact this story had on you. Share your response with your group or with one other reader.

Extending the Text

[compare]

8. Look back at your Quickwrite. What other "invisible children" could be compared with Salvador?

> ### Reading Check
>
> Describe the events of Salvador's morning as if he himself were explaining them to another child or an adult. Start with his first action and continue until you have summed up his school day.

186 THE SHORT-STORY COLLECTIONS

> ### Reading Check
>
> Sample response: I woke my brothers, got them dressed, combed their hair, and gave them milk and cornflakes for breakfast. Then I helped Mama with the baby and hurried Cecilio and Arturito to school. When Arturito dropped the crayons in the street, I picked them up. After school I collected the boys and headed for home with them.

Making the Connections

Connecting to the Theme: "The Human Spirit"

Point out to students that Salvador is a young child who is nearly invisible to the people around him, yet who behaves heroically under very difficult circumstances. Ask students what the story of Salvador says about the human spirit that a story about a pampered or indulged child could never say. How do hardship and invisibility contribute to the portrait of perseverance and triumph that emerges in this story?

CHOICES: Building Your Portfolio

Writer's Notebook

1. Collecting Ideas for an Essay Analyzing a Character

Focus on actions. Salvador seems to be in perpetual motion. If you want to get an idea of the many actions we watch Salvador carrying out, list the verbs that describe him or his movements, beginning with *runs* and continuing in the first paragraph with *lives, shakes, ties, combs, feeds.* In fact, Cisneros eventually drops the subject of her sentences (*Salvador*) and just opens with verbs—Salvador's actions. Take notes on Salvador's important actions and what they tell about the kind of boy he is. Save your

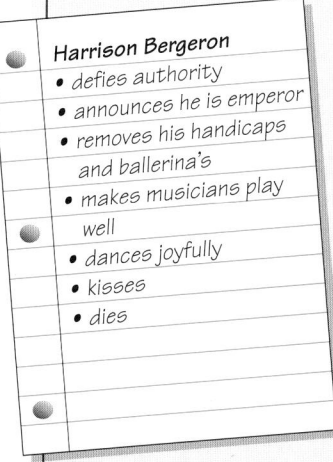

Harrison Bergeron
- defies authority
- announces he is emperor
- removes his handicaps and ballerina's
- makes musicians play well
- dances joyfully
- kisses
- dies

notes for the Writer's Workshop on page 194. (The notes at the bottom of the first column refer to the key actions of another character in this collection.)

Speaking/ A Group Project

2. A Dramatic Reading

In a group of three (one person for each paragraph), prepare Salvador's story for an oral reading. As a reader, you will have to be aware of effective verbal and nonverbal strategies. Decide when you will pause, when you will raise or lower your voice, when you will read fast or slow. You will also have to decide how you will present your reading to the class. Some dramatic readings are done in costume. Some readers sit on stools; others stand. After your presentation, write a brief reflection on your experience.

Creative Writing

3. A Vignette

Using "Salvador Late or Early" as a model, write a vignette—a short literary sketch or portrait—of your own. Think of a character who will catch your readers' interest. Then, put him or her into an interesting

situation. Use colorful verbs to show readers what your character does all day—early and late.

Problem Solving/ Community Extension

4. A Panel Discussion

What responsibilities do communities and schools have to children like Salvador? Working with a group, form a panel of "experts"—a student, a parent, a teacher, and a community member. Plan the panel's agenda: What questions or topics will the panel focus on? How long can each panel member talk? How should each "expert" prepare for the discussion? Someone should record the discussion and summarize its conclusions.

Creative Writing

5. Salvador's Poem

Suppose someone asked Salvador: "who are you, little i"? (See **Connections** on page 185.) Write Salvador's answer. You might have Salvador answer in a poem called "i am salvador," using each letter of his name as the first letter of the first word of each line.

Rubrics for each Choices assignment appear on p. 105 in the *Portfolio Management System.*

CHOICES: Building Your Portfolio

1. **Writer's Notebook** Tell students to list not just the verb but the verb and its direct object or the complete predicate.

2. **Speaking/A Group Project** Suggest that students work together to create a script for their reading. To do so, they might photocopy the selection, underscore those things they plan to emphasize, insert symbols to show places where they will pause, and use different colored highlighters to show variations in pitch and speed.

3. **Creative Writing** Remind students that they need not tell a whole story about their character; instead, they need show only some aspect of what the character does.

4. **Problem Solving/Community Extension** Before students hold the panel discussion, they might talk about the different goals and resources of each member of the panel and talk about what each could contribute to the discussion.

5. **Creative Writing** Suggest that students consider the balloon, guitar, and kite imagery in "Salvador Late or Early." They may want to incorporate these images into their poems or to elaborate on feelings that the images suggest.

Using Students' Strengths

Visual Learners

In "Salvador Late or Early," there are many visual images that help readers picture the face and clothing of the small boy, his home, the time of day, the children's trips to and from school. Ask students to draw or paint an illustration of the story that captures its tone as well as its setting and subject matter. If they prefer, students might instead create a collage based on the imagery.

OBJECTIVES

1. Read and interpret an essay
2. Find thematic connections across genres
3. Generate relevant and interesting discussion
4. Recognize distinctive and shared characteristics of cultures through reading and discussion

Extending the Theme

In this autobiographical essay, the writer describes a remarkable Gentile washwoman who does the laundry for his Jewish family. Old and frail, she walks miles loaded down with laundry. Her meticulous attention to detail wins the admiration of the family. One harsh winter, the washwoman collects the laundry but does not return for more than two months. When she does return, she explains that she had been gravely ill but could not die until her work was done. Leaving, she promises to return to pick up another wash. She never returns. The writer, who is Jewish, says he cannot imagine a Paradise that would not include this Gentile woman.

Resources

Listening

Audio CD Library

A recording of this essay is available in the *Audio CD Library*:

• Disc 7, Track 3

EXTENDING *the theme*

AN ESSAY

Background

The events in this autobiographical essay take place around 1915 in Warsaw, Poland, where most Jews lived in the very old Jewish quarter. At 10 Krochmalna Street, where Isaac Bashevis Singer lived, families shared an outhouse in the courtyard and used kerosene lamps for light.

There was no central heating in the dark, old apartments.

Reading Skills and Strategies

Dialogue with the Text

Be sure to track your responses to this essay as you read. Pay particular attention to passages that seem important or interesting to you. How do details and events in this essay make you feel? What, if anything, does Singer teach you?

go.hrw.com
LEO 9-2

The Washwoman

Isaac Bashevis Singer

The old woman did not want to become a burden.

Our home had little contact with Gentiles.[1] The only Gentile in the building was the janitor. Fridays he would come for a tip, his "Friday money." He remained standing at the door, took off his hat, and my mother gave him six groschen.[2]

Besides the janitor there were also the Gentile washwomen who came to the house to fetch our laundry. My story is about one of these.

She was a small woman, old and wrinkled. When she started washing for us, she was already past seventy. Most Jewish women of her age were sickly, weak, broken in body. All the old women in our street had bent backs and leaned on sticks when they walked. But this washwoman, small and thin as she was, possessed a strength that came from generations of peasant forebears. Mother would count out to her a bundle of laundry that had accumulated over several weeks. She would lift the unwieldy pack, load it on her narrow shoulders, and carry it the long way home. She lived on Krochmalna Street too, but at the other end, near the Wola section. It must have been a walk of an hour and a half.

1. **Gentiles** (jen′tīlz): persons who are not Jewish.
2. **groschen** (grō′shən): European coin or coins.

188 THE SHORT-STORY COLLECTIONS

 *Resources: Print and Media*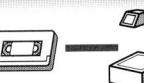

Reading
• *Audio CD Library*
  Disc 7, Track 3

Assessment
• *Test Generator (One-Stop Planner CD-ROM)*

Internet
• go.hrw.com (keyword: LEO 9-2)

Torah binder (1834). Wimpel of Gershon, son of Abraham Seltz (detail 56.341). Germany. Undyed linen, polychrome pigments.

She would bring the laundry back about two weeks later. My mother had never been so pleased with any washwoman. Every piece of linen sparkled like polished silver. Every piece was neatly ironed. Yet she charged no more than the others. She was a real find. Mother always had her money ready, because it was too far for the old woman to come a second time.

Laundering was not easy in those days. The old woman had no faucet where she lived but had to bring in the water from a pump. For the linens to come out so clean, they had to be scrubbed thoroughly in a washtub, rinsed with washing soda, soaked, boiled in an enormous pot, starched, then ironed. Every piece was handled ten times or more. And the drying! It could not be done outside because thieves **Ⓐ** would steal the laundry. The wrung-out wash had to be carried up to the attic and hung on clotheslines. In the winter it would become as brittle as glass and almost break when touched. And there was always a to-do with other housewives and washwomen who wanted the attic clotheslines for their own use. Only God knows all the old woman had to endure each time she did a wash!

She could have begged at the church door or entered a home for the penniless and aged. But there was in her a certain pride and love of labor with which many Gentiles have been blessed. The old woman did not want to become a burden, **Ⓑ** and so she bore her burden.

My mother spoke a little Polish, and the old woman would talk with her about many things. She was especially fond of me and used to say I looked like Jesus. She repeated this every time she came, **Ⓒ** and Mother would frown and whisper to herself, her lips barely moving, "May her words be scattered in the wilderness."

The woman had a son who was rich. I no longer remember what sort of business he had. He was ashamed of his mother, the washwoman, and never came to see her. Nor did he ever give her a groschen. The old woman told this without rancor. One day the son was married. It seemed that he had made a good match. The wedding took place in a church. The son had not invited the old mother to his wedding, but she went to the church and waited at the steps to see her son lead the "young lady" to the altar.

The story of the faithless son left a deep impression on my mother. She talked about it for weeks and months. It was an affront not only to the old woman but to the entire institution of motherhood. Mother would argue, "Nu,

THE WASHWOMAN 189

Reaching All Students

Reading Skills and Strategies

Determining the Author's Purpose

❓ This passage veers away from the topic, the washwoman, to present details about the author's mother. Why is this information included? [Possible answers: The memory of the washwoman helps the writer recall his own mother; he includes it to compare his mother with the washwoman—just as he admires the washwoman for her determination and hard-working spirit, he admires his mother for her determination to do everything for her children, logical or illogical, superstitious or informed.]

B Elements of Literature

Character

❓ What impression of the washwoman do these details combine to create? [Possible answer: She endures all, including old age and freezing weather, without complaint; nothing can stop her; she has no limits except death itself.]

C Cultural Connections

The *tzitzit*, or "twisted cord," is a Jewish man's undergarment (like a long scarf) worn in obedience to a commandment in the Bible. The fringes were once worn attached openly to an outer garment but later, because of persecution, were worn inside. Remind students that the Gentile woman is entrusted with these religious garments.

does it pay to make sacrifices for children? The mother uses up her last strength, and he does not even know the meaning of loyalty."

And she would drop dark hints to the effect that she was not certain of her own children: Who knows what they would do some day? This, however, did not prevent her from dedicating her life to us. If there was any delicacy in the house, she would put it aside for the children and invent all sorts of excuses and reasons why she herself did not want to taste it. She knew charms that went back to ancient times, and she used expressions she had inherited from generations of devoted mothers and grandmothers. If one of the children complained of a pain, she would say, "May I be your ransom and may you outlive my bones!" Or she would say, "May I be the atonement for the least of your fingernails!" When we ate, she used to say, "Health and marrow in your bones!" The day before the new moon she gave us a kind of candy that was said to prevent parasitic worms. If one of us had something in his eye, Mother would lick the eye clean with her tongue. She also fed us rock candy against coughs, and from time to time she would take us to be blessed against the evil eye. This did not prevent her from studying *The Duties of the Heart, The Book of the Covenant,* and other serious philosophic works.

But to return to the washwoman. That winter was a harsh one. The streets were in the grip of a bitter cold. No matter how much we heated our stove, the windows were covered with frostwork and decorated with icicles. The newspapers reported that people were dying of the cold. Coal became dear. The winter had become so severe that parents stopped sending children to cheder,[3] and even the Polish schools were closed.

On one such day the washwoman, now nearly eighty years old, came to our house. A good deal of laundry had accumulated during the past weeks. Mother gave her a pot of tea to warm herself, as well as some bread. The old woman sat on a kitchen chair, trembling and shaking, and warmed her hands against the teapot. Her fingers

3. **cheder** (khā′·dər): Hebrew school for religious instruction.

were gnarled from work, and perhaps from arthritis too. Her fingernails were strangely white. These hands spoke of the stubbornness of mankind, of the will to work not only as one's strength permits but beyond the limits of one's power. Mother counted and wrote down the list: men's undershirts, women's vests, long-legged drawers, bloomers, petticoats, shifts, featherbed covers, pillowcases, sheets, and the men's fringed garments. Yes, the Gentile woman washed these holy garments as well.

The bundle was big, bigger than usual. When the woman placed it on her shoulders, it covered her completely. At first she swayed, as though she were about to fall under the load. But an inner obstinacy seemed to call out: No, you may not fall. A donkey may permit himself to fall under his burden, but not a human being, the crown of creation.

It was fearful to watch the old woman staggering out with the enormous pack, out into the frost, where the snow was dry as salt and the air was filled with dusty white whirlwinds, like goblins dancing in the cold. Would the old woman ever reach Wola?

She disappeared, and Mother sighed and prayed for her.

Usually the woman brought back the wash after two or, at the most, three weeks. But three weeks passed, then four and five, and nothing was heard of the old woman. We remained without linens. The cold had become even more intense. The telephone wires were now as thick as ropes. The branches of the trees looked like glass. So much snow had fallen that the streets had become uneven, and sleds were able to glide down many streets as on the slopes of a hill. Kindhearted people lit fires in the streets for vagrants to warm themselves and roast potatoes in, if they had any to roast.

For us the washwoman's absence was a catastrophe. We needed the laundry. We did not even know the woman's address. It seemed certain that she had collapsed, died. Mother declared she had had a premonition, as the old woman left our house that last time, that we would never see our things again. She found some old torn shirts and washed and mended them. We

Skill Link

Recognize Distinctive and Shared Characteristics of Cultures

While Singer's essay is not primarily about his Jewish culture, it reveals a great deal about it.

1. Ask students to list evidence that places this essay in a particular time, place, and culture. [Among the possibilities: separation of religious groups; Friday as a day for a tip; a stereotyped comment about the Gentile love of labor; the inability of the Jewish mother to speak more than a "little Polish."]

2. List characteristics and actions that unite, rather than divide, these people who are from different cultures. [The washwoman does not hesitate to work for the Jewish family; the Jewish family treats her with kindness, gives her tea on a cold day, respects her, and is concerned for her welfare; the washwoman is fond of the son and is comfortable enough to compliment him and also reveal information about her own son.]

Destruction of the Ghetto, Kiev (1919) by Abraham Manievich. Oil on canvas (198.1 cm. x 188 cm.).

mourned, both for the laundry and for the old, toilworn woman who had grown close to us through the years she had served us so faithfully.

More than two months passed. The frost had subsided, and then a new frost had come, a new wave of cold. One evening, while Mother was sitting near the kerosene lamp mending a shirt, the door opened and a small puff of steam, followed by a gigantic bundle, entered. Under the bundle tottered the old woman, her face as white as a linen sheet. A few wisps of white hair straggled out from beneath her shawl. Mother uttered a half-choked cry. It was as though a corpse had entered the room. I ran toward the old woman and helped her unload her pack. She was even thinner now, more bent. Her face had become more gaunt, and her head shook from side to side as though she were saying no. She could not utter a clear word, but mumbled something with her sunken mouth and pale lips.

After the old woman had recovered somewhat, she told us that she had been ill, very ill. Just what her illness was, I cannot remember. She had been so sick that someone had called a doctor, and the doctor had sent for

a priest. Someone had informed the son, and he had contributed money for a coffin and for the funeral. But the Almighty had not yet wanted to take this pain-racked soul to himself. She began to feel better, she became well, and as soon as she was able to stand on her feet once more, she resumed her washing. Not just ours, but the wash of several other families too.

"I could not rest easy in my bed because of the wash," the old woman explained. "The wash would not let me die."

"With the help of God you will live to be a hundred and twenty," said my mother, as a benediction.

"God forbid! What good would such a long life be? The work becomes harder and harder . . . my strength is leaving me . . . I do not want to be a burden on anyone!" The old woman muttered and crossed herself and raised her eyes toward heaven.

Fortunately there was some money in the house, and Mother counted out what she owed. I had a strange feeling: The coins in the old woman's washed-out hands seemed to become as worn and clean and pious as she herself was. She blew on the coins and tied them in a kerchief. Then she left, promising to return in a few weeks for a new load of wash.

But she never came back. The wash she had returned was her last effort on this earth. She had been driven by an indomitable will to return the property to its rightful owners, to fulfill the task she had undertaken.

And now at last her body, which had long been no more than a shard[4] supported only by the force of honesty and duty, had fallen. Her soul passed into those spheres where all holy souls meet, regardless of the roles they played on this earth, in whatever tongue, of whatever creed. I cannot imagine paradise without this Gentile washwoman. I cannot even conceive of a world where there is no recompense for such effort.

4. **shard** (shärd): fragment, as of a clay pot.

THE WASHWOMAN 191

Assessing Learning

Check Test: Questions and Answers

1. Who is the subject of this essay? [the washwoman]
2. Whom does the washwoman do laundry for? [the writer's family]
3. What keeps the washwoman from dying of her illness? [her sense of duty and honor]
4. What happens to the washwoman after she returns the last load of laundry? [She dies.]

RESPONDING TO THE ART

Kiev is the chief city and capital of the Ukraine. When German forces invaded Kiev in 1941, more than 30,000 Jews, Soviet prisoners of war, and partisans were massacred at Babi Yar, a nearby ravine. Almost all the rest of the Jewish population of Kiev was deported to concentration camps. This painting depicts an earlier pogrom. **Activity.** Describe your response to the painting Destruction of the Ghetto, Kiev. [Sample responses: horror, fear, dread.] **How might Singer's essay help to combat the prejudice that leads to such terror?** [Possible responses: by showing people of two cultures who admire and respect each other; by its concept of universal human salvation.]

D **Critical Thinking**
Analyzing
❓ How does Singer create an air of mystery in this descriptive passage? [Possible answers: The steam and the bundle become apparent before the woman does; the images that precede the washwoman make her seem ghostly or half-alive; the vision of the washwoman frightens Singer's mother, who utters a cry.]

E **Reading Skills and Strategies**
Drawing Conclusions
❓ What does the old woman mean when she says that the wash would not let her die? [Possible answers: Her sense of duty is so strong that she will not let herself die while she has someone else's property; she has made a promise and must fulfill it before she can die.]

F **Cultural Connections**
❓ Singer opens his essay with the distinctions between Jew and Gentile, but he closes it with something that goes well beyond that cultural division. How would you describe the message presented in this final paragraph? [Possible answers: Salvation is universal and not determined by one's creed; there is a paradise in which endurance, hard work, pride, holiness and dignity are rewarded.]

FINDING COMMON GROUND

MEET THE WRITER
The Storyteller

Grandson of two rabbis and son of another, **Isaac Bashevis Singer** (1904–1991) was born in Radzymin, near Warsaw, Poland. Because his family wanted him to continue the tradition, Singer studied to be a rabbi, but he soon discovered that his real love was writing.

He began writing in Hebrew. Later he switched to Yiddish, the language spoken by many Eastern European Jews, and wrote for the Yiddish press in Poland. In 1935, Singer became alarmed at the rise of antisemitism in Europe, and he sailed to America. There he eventually married, became a U.S. citizen, and settled in New York City.

Success as a novelist and short-story writer came late in his life—when he was forty-five. Eventually, in 1978, Singer was awarded the Nobel Prize for literature. Despite his great success as a writer, Singer continued his practice of rewriting. He once told an interviewer that as a writer he considered the wastebasket one of his friends.

Singer saw himself as a storyteller (see also his comments about storytelling on page 2):

66 The idea that literature consists only of a man revealing his inner self and complaining about his complexes is a modern kind of idea, and the truth is that people are not interested. If I sit down and write a book about how unhappy I am that I did not marry my first love, only my second love, and there is no plot, the reader will say 'Who cares?' There has to be a story. 99

No Complaining Here

If you enjoy Singer's storytelling, read the book from which "The Washwoman" is taken, *A Day of Pleasure* (Farrar, Straus & Giroux). Or try *The Family Moskat* (Farrar, Straus & Giroux), a novel about several generations of a Jewish family living in the Warsaw Ghetto.

FINDING COMMON GROUND

1. For you, what was "The Washwoman" about? Take a quick look at this list and make an impulsive decision. Don't reflect; just decide—what was the **major topic** in this story?

work	dignity
acceptance of people who are different	generosity
	faith
pride	God's love for everyone

2. Now take a few minutes to think about the topic you chose. Why did you identify that as the central topic of the essay? Find a passage or two in the story that might have caused you to focus on this idea. Write brief discussion notes elaborating on your thoughts about the passage you identified. Before you write your notes, be sure to check the responses you recorded as you read.

3. Finally, meet with a few other readers and compare your responses. As you talk, be alert for differences of opinion. As the discussion draws to a close, note the questions you've raised and the points you'd like to discuss further with the entire class.

Making the Connections

Connecting to the Theme: "The Human Spirit"

READ ON

The Timeless Classic of Growing Up and the Human Dignity That Unites Us All

TO KILL A MOCKINGBIRD
* Harper Lee *

Crisis in a Small Town

Scout Finch is only a child—eight years old. She's vulnerable and funny. But it is her intelligence and sensitivity that will touch you in Harper Lee's *To Kill a Mockingbird* (Warner). There's a trial in this Pulitzer Prize–winning novel that you're not likely to forget. Set in a small Southern town, Lee's novel is a riveting story of race relations.

A PUFFIN BOOK

The award-winning author's compelling wilderness adventure

WOODSONG
BY GARY PAULSEN

Man's Best Friend

Can you imagine enduring a temperature of –50°F—or lower—on a dog sled that covers a thousand-mile course? Gary Paulsen brings an experience like this to life in his book *Woodsong* (Puffin). In this account of his experiences on the Iditarod, a dog-sled race through Alaska, Paulsen whisks us along on his long and lonely journey. His only friends are a team of dogs, and they turn out to be the best friends he has ever had.

Taking Her Place

CHARLAYNE HUNTER-GAULT

IN MY PLACE

Charlayne Hunter-Gault was the first African American woman to attend the University of Georgia. As you'll see in her autobiography, *In My Place* (Farrar, Straus & Giroux), it wasn't easy. After the triumph of gaining admittance came the pain of prejudice. Even though she was enrolled, there were classmates and professors who didn't want her there. Was it worth the struggle? Hunter-Gault explains why her answer is a definite yes.

Autobiography of a Face
LUCY GREALY

Facing the World

Growing up, most of us think about our looks: our clothes, our hair, our growing bodies, our faces. But Lucy Grealy had a rare type of cancer that made her think about her face even more than most young people do. Her *Autobiography of a Face* (Houghton Mifflin) is the story of a girl who found herself suddenly different at the age of nine. It's the story of a girl struggling to learn to accept and love herself. Lucy Grealy has something to teach the world—about what it values and what it ridicules.

READ ON 193

Writer's Workshop

ASSIGNMENT

Write an essay analyzing a fictional character. The character can be in one of the stories you've read in this book or in a movie or a TV show you have seen or a novel you've enjoyed.

AIM

To use critical thinking skills; to give information.

AUDIENCE

Your teacher and classmates or a student publication that accepts literary reviews.

It may be possible in novel writing to present characters successfully without telling a story; but it is not possible to tell a story successfully without presenting characters.

—Wilkie Collins

EXPOSITORY WRITING

ANALYZING A CHARACTER

Literature helps us learn something about human nature—including ourselves. Laurence Perrine, who taught literature for many years, said that fiction helps us "to know people, to understand them, and to learn compassion for them, as we might not otherwise do."

In this workshop you'll write an essay analyzing a character in a story, novel, TV show, or movie. When you **analyze** something, you examine it closely. You take it apart to see how it was put together and how its parts interact to create meaning.

Prewriting

1. Find a Character

Look back at the notes you've made in your Writer's Notebook. You may have already chosen a character, but it's not too late to change your mind. Choose a character you'd enjoy analyzing. Your character may be the main character or a minor one.

2. Gather Information

- **Make a character profile in graphic form.** Your first task is to find out all you can about your character. Review the essay called "Character: Revealing Human Nature" (pages 130–131). Then, fill out a graphic organizer like the one on the next page. You may be surprised at some of the details you discover. (You won't always be able to fill out every column.) To fill out the "Traits" column, you will have to make inferences based on all the details in the second column. You'll find a useful list of traits in the box on page 195.

- **Ask a few important questions.** What does the character want? Does the character change? If so, what causes the change? Does the character discover something? Jot down your answers to these questions.

- **Evaluate the character.** Is the character believable? Do you like this character, or do you have strong negative feelings about him or her? Jot down reasons for your evaluation.

Resources: Print and Media

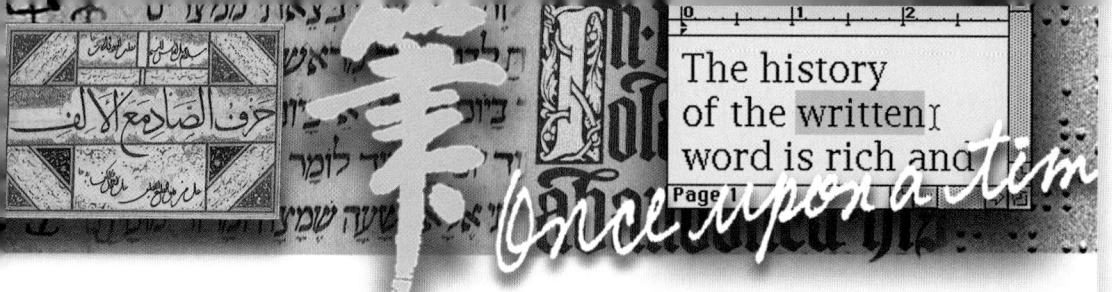

Character Profile of _____		
Clues to Characterization	Details in the Story	Traits
Speech		
Appearance		
Thoughts		
Other characters' responses		
Actions		
Writer's direct comments		

3. Elaborate: Back Up General Statements

Readers will challenge your interpretations and conclusions. They'll ask: "How do you know this?" "Why should I believe you?" To persuade them that you know what you're talking about, support every general statement with evidence from the story— quotations and specific references to the character's actions or speeches.

4. Organize Your Ideas

From your notes, choose two or three aspects of the character you'll want to focus on. Then, figure out what your main points will be, and express each point as a general statement. This statement will serve as the **topic sentence** of a paragraph. Jot down the evidence you'll use to support each general statement. You'll end up with a rough outline that shows your main points and supporting evidence.

   If you haven't already done so, draft a **thesis statement,** a one- or two-sentence summary of your main points about your character.

A Boxful of Character Traits

cruel	kind
proud	humble
lazy	energetic
passive	assertive
selfish	unselfish or generous
timid	courageous
pessimistic	optimistic
silent	talkative
withdrawn	sociable
moody	even-tempered

Framework for an Essay Analyzing a Character

Introduction
Identify character and work (title, author); include thesis statement

Body
• General statement 1 with supporting evidence
• General statement 2 with supporting evidence
[Etc.]

Conclusion

• Have groups of students create lists of memorable or interesting characters from literature, television, or movies. Next to each character's name, students should tell why they regard that character as memorable or interesting.
• Explain that creating believable and interesting characters is crucial for fiction writers. In addition to a character's words and actions, writers use details of speech, appearance, and mannerisms to convey a character's personality.
• Have the groups add to their lists. For each character listed earlier, students should try to name at least one detail of speech, dress, mannerism, gesture, or habit that can be identified with that character.

Teaching the Writer's Workshop

Prewriting

Remind students that they will be asked to give details about the character they choose for their essay. If possible, they should reread the novel or short story or rescreen the television show or movie from which they have taken their character.

Reaching All Students

Struggling Writers

Students who are having difficulty might benefit from working quietly in pairs during several stages of this writing assignment. Have partners work together to search for topic ideas, to brainstorm ideas for filling in their character profiles, and to read their drafts aloud and receive feedback.

English Language Learners

Encourage English language learners to use the language that is most comfortable for them in prewriting. If they choose their native language for prewriting, allow them to write their first draft this way, too. Then, have them select two paragraphs from their essay (the introduction and one other) to translate into standard English. Allow them to complete their entire essay in English as a portfolio option.

Drafting

- Before students begin to write, have them look over the Student Model that appears later in this workshop.
- Remind students to double-space when they write their drafts. They should also leave extra space in the right margin. These blank spaces will be used for comments and editing marks.

Using the Model

After students have completed their drafts, they may benefit from another look at the student model. Have students focus on questions such as these:

- ❓ How does the writer introduce the main character at the beginning of the essay?
- ❓ Does the writer succeed in grabbing your attention?
- ❓ What main points about the character does the writer make in the essay?
- ❓ How does the writer support each main point?
- ❓ What techniques does this writer use that you might incorporate into your paper?

Drafting

1. Be Selective

You've probably collected a pile of notes and ideas. Go over them once more, and discard the weakest material. Choose only your brightest ideas and the strongest support for each one. You're aiming to produce a paper that makes at least two persuasive points about a character.

2. Follow Your Plan

Getting a first draft down on paper is half the battle. With your rough outline before you, start turning your notes into sentences. Think in terms of a paragraph with a topic sentence for each main point. Remember that a draft is just a first version of what you want to say. Focus on the content at first. You'll have time later to go over your draft to improve your sentences and style. To construct your essay, build on a framework like the one on page 195.

Student Model

Luella Bates Washington Jones, in "Thank You, M'am" by Langston Hughes, is a lonely woman. She lives alone in a small apartment building, and she has a job that most likely does not pay well and forces her to work unusual hours. Roger, also lonely, has no one to go home to. It is a fateful night at 11 P.M. that brings these two together for a few significant hours that makes a lonely woman into a one-of-a-kind hero.	*Introduction.*
	Thesis statement.
Here is this young boy, who is roaming the streets deep into the night hours. He sees Luella Jones's huge purse, and motivated by a pair of blue suede shoes, he decides to snatch it. But he fails. Jones holds him and doesn't let him go. By a power that Luella Jones is given, she takes the boy home. He tells her he has no one to go home to. That hits a huge soft spot in Luella's heart.	*Writer refers to story events.*
	Main point 1: She has a soft heart.
Roger is at her house, and she is preparing dinner for the two of them. She tells him to clean up. But that isn't all. At the same time she gives Roger trust—a boy who tried to snatch her purse just moments before. She stuns him so much he does not dare break that trust. She gives him many opportunities to steal or run away, but he doesn't. Luella Bates Washington Jones is a masterpiece of human kindness.	*Writer refers to story events.*
	Main point 2: She is "a masterpiece of human kindness."
When Luella Jones and Roger sit down for dinner, Jones talks to the boy and gives him attention he seems never to have had	

Professional Notes

Block Scheduling

The lengthened class period may allow for productive student writing. If possible, invite a professional writer to visit class on a regular basis when Writer's Workshops are being taught. The writer and you can work with students individually or in small groups to strengthen their writing skills and techniques. Allow time for a class question-and-answer session.

Heterogeneous Grouping

For peer-editing groups it is especially important to mix students of different ability levels. Students who have a verbal facility can often teach their peers effectively. Encourage less skilled students to participate in a positive way by giving them a special role within groups, such as that of timekeeper or distributor of materials.

- **Introduction.** The beginning of the essay must grab readers' attention, identify the work (the title and author) and the character, and include a thesis statement.

THESIS STATEMENT
Roger, a major character in "Thank You, M'am" by Langston Hughes, is a loser whose chances of avoiding a career in crime are slim.

- **Body.** The main points of your analysis are here. Try to make at least two main points. You might refer to them in your thesis statement and use transitions (such as *first, second,* and *finally*) to announce each one. Be specific. Support each general statement with a quotation from the story or with a reference to events or dialogue.

- **Conclusion.** Bring your essay to a strong conclusion by referring to what you said in your introduction or by adding a final thought about the character.

---

before. She does not embarrass him by asking him questions. Instead, she talks about everyday things like her job. They both provide company for each other, but Luella Jones also provides Roger with someone to talk to, someone to sit down and eat dinner with, someone to give him trust and respect.

The dinner is the epitome of her heroic actions. She treats Roger like one of her own kids. She is mad at Roger when they are out in the street, but then she realizes something. Roger needs help. He needs someone there for him. So for a couple of Roger's most important hours, Luella Bates Washington Jones gives him trust, respect, a place to stay, and someone to talk to.

If Roger had never run into Luella Bates Washington Jones, he would have been like every other mistreated child. He would have been in trouble. But for one night, he isn't in trouble, and maybe every night after that. This is all the work of one magnificent woman. Luella Bates Washington Jones tops it all off by giving Roger the money he initially wanted for a pair of blue suede shoes, and then she lets him go. This is truly the work of a hero. She does something most people would never even think of. She gives a young boy a chance.

—Jeff Wulbrecht
A. I. du Pont High School
Wilmington, Delaware

Main point 3: She trusts him and respects him.

The conclusion refers to the thesis statement.

Final thought: She changed Roger's life.

Crossing the Curriculum

History

Historians are often interested in gaining insight into the personalities, thoughts, and beliefs of historical figures. They do this by piecing together information from original source material such as letters, eyewitness and newspaper accounts, and personal narratives. If possible, invite a history teacher to your classroom to discuss with students this aspect of historical research. Afterward, invite comparisons between historians' research of historical figures and students' analyses of characters from fiction.

Evaluating and Revising

Have students use the Evaluation Criteria provided here to review their drafts and determine needed revisions.

Proofreading

Have students proofread their own papers first and then exchange them with another student. For this assignment, remind students to be particularly careful to use quotation marks correctly when including quotations or dialogue.

If time permits, the final copy should be put aside for at least a day before it is proofread one last time by the author. If keeping a proofreading log of recurring problems, the writer should consult the log and then check the essay for evidence of these problems.

Publishing

Have students create a Gallery of Characters. They can combine their essays with drawings or photographs of their characters and display them on a classroom or school bulletin board.

Reflecting

Students may want to consider adding this essay to their portfolios. If so, they should date the final draft and answer the following questions to reflect on their writing experience.

1. What was the most difficult part of writing this essay?
2. What do I like best about the essay?
3. What do I want to learn to do better?

Resources

Peer Editing Forms and Rubrics
• *Portfolio Management System,* p. 108.
Revision Transparencies
• *Workshop Resources,* p. 7

Grading Timesaver

Rubrics for this Writer's Workshop assignment appear on p. 109 of the *Portfolio Management System.*

Sentence Workshop
H E L P

Revising sentence fragments: page 199.

■ *Evaluation Criteria*
A good analysis of a character

1. *has an introduction that identifies the character and the title and author of the work*

2. *contains a thesis statement that presents the paper's focus*

3. *has a body that presents general statements about at least two aspects of the character*

4. *supports all general statements with details and quotations from the text*

5. *has a concluding paragraph that summarizes the main ideas or adds a final thought*

Proofreading Tips

This method is used by professional proofreaders: Cover your essay with a blank sheet of paper, and read one sentence at a time, starting at the bottom of the page.

Communications Handbook
H E L P

See Proofreaders' Marks.

Evaluating and Revising

1. Peer Evaluation

Get together with three or four classmates to read and comment on one another's drafts. (Review the Evaluation Criteria on the left before you begin.) If you don't understand what a writer is saying, ask questions. Be sure that you also comment on the parts of the essay that you think are especially good.

2. Self-Evaluation

Try reading your essay aloud to yourself. Your sentences should flow smoothly, as if you were talking comfortably. Go back and try to tighten your essay: Eliminate padding and wordiness. Add transitions to help your readers follow your ideas.

Revision Model

	Peer Comments
Luella Bates Washington Jones, in	
by Langston Hughes,	
"Thank You, M'am" is a lonely	Who wrote the story?
in a small apartment building,	
woman. She lives alone, and she	
most likely does not pay well and	Can you give
has a job that forces her to work	more details?
, also lonely,	
unusual hours. Roger has no one	
fateful	Do you mean
to go home to. It is a ~~faithful~~ night	"fateful"?
at 11 P.M. that brings these two	
together for a few significant	Where is
that makes a lonely woman into	your thesis
a one-of-a-kind hero.	statement?
hours.	

Sentence Workshop

OBJECTIVES
1. Identify sentence fragments
2. Learn methods of correcting sentence fragments

REVISING SENTENCES: FRAGMENTS

The pros do it. The first sentence of "A Christmas Memory" is followed by "A coming of winter morning more than twenty years ago." That's a **sentence fragment,** not a sentence. Truman Capote uses fragments to help create the narrator's voice, his special way of talking and thinking.

But beware! Fragments probably aren't welcome in the writing you do for school, especially the critical writing. Suppose Capote had decided he wanted to correct his fragments (unlikely). He could have done it in two ways:

1. Attach the fragment to the sentence that is before or after it.

FRAGMENT   "And there she remains, puttering around the kitchen. Alone with Queenie. Then alone."

SENTENCE   There she remains, puttering around the kitchen, alone with Queenie, then alone.

2. Add words to make the fragment a complete sentence.

FRAGMENT   "A coming of winter morning more than twenty years ago."

SENTENCE   It was a coming of winter morning more than twenty years ago.

Writer's Workshop Follow-up: Proofreading

Look again at the essay you wrote for the Writer's Workshop. Check your sentences to be sure each one has a subject and a verb and expresses a complete thought. One way to test your sentences is to draw an arrow from each subject to its verb. If you want to use a fragment for dramatic effect, the way Capote does, consider your audience and be sure your teacher approves.

Basic Ingredients of a Sentence

1. a subject
2. a verb
3. a complete thought

Language Handbook HELP

See Sentence Structure, page 1010.

Technology HELP

See Language Workshop CD-ROM. Key word entry: sentence fragments.

Try It Out

Edit the following paragraph so that all fragments are corrected. Be sure to compare your edited version with a classmate's.

The girl stood on the edge of the high diving board. Her thin arms stretched in front of her. She was nine. Small for her age. She hesitated. Wobbled. Swayed a little. Stared straight ahead of her. Not looking down at the water. Her lips moved. As if she were talking to herself. Angry voices yelled from below. "C'mon, Angie." "Whadya waiting for?" "Jump!" Nothing. After what seemed like hours. She took a deep breath, stepped forward. And plunged into the pool feet first.

Resources ———————

Workshop Resources
• Worksheet, p. 63

Language Workshop CD-ROM
• Sentence Fragments

Try It Out
Possible Answers
• The girl stood on the edge of the high diving board, her thin arms stretched in front of her.
• She was nine and small for her age.
• She hesitated, wobbled, and swayed a little.
• She stared straight ahead of her, not looking down at the water.
• Her lips moved as if she were talking to herself.
• She did nothing.
• Then, after what seemed like hours, she took a deep breath, stepped forward, and plunged into the pool feet first.

SENTENCE WORKSHOP   199

Assessing Learning

Quick Check: Sentence Fragments

Review the following sentences, and correct any fragments by adding subjects or verbs or by attaching the fragment to a sentence that is before or after it.

1. Kurt Vonnegut was the youngest member of his family.
2. An older sister, who was a sculptor, and a brother, who was a scientist. [add "He had"]

3. Vonnegut felt unable to participate in the adult conversation.
4. Started making jokes, at first by accident. [join to sentence 3 with "and"]
5. Technique used in his books. [add "Humor is a"]

Using the Strategies

Answers
1. The sender is Kay Posey; Lee Gomez and Mark Vogt received copies.
2. The assignment is to interview a foreign exchange student and write a feature article. The article is due by 3:00 p.m. Monday, September 27.
3. "Pithy" quotes are interesting statements by the exchange student that the writer can use in the article. "B/W pics" are black-and-white pictures.

Situation

You've signed up to work on the school newspaper. The editor has just sent you, via e-mail, the memo on the right detailing your first assignment. To make sure you understand the message, use these strategies.

Strategies

Head for the header.
- The header tells when the memo was sent, who sent it, and what it's about. Most memos announce the topic with the word *subject* or *re* (short for "in regard to"). An e-mail message will include the sender's and receiver's electronic addresses. A line labeled *cc*, if included, shows who will see a copy of the message.

Dig for the details.
- Read the **body** of the memo carefully to find out exactly what the sender wants you to do: Are you to answer a question, attend a meeting, pass along information?

Examine any attachments.
- If the word *attachment* or *attachments* appears in the memo, additional material accompanies the memo. Be sure to review that material as well. It may contain the information you need in

---

To: leegomez@freenet.khs.edu

From: kayposey@freenet.khs.edu

Subject: Article on New Foreign-Exchange Student

Date: September 14, 1999

cc: markvogt@freenet.khs.edu

Your assignment is to interview our new foreign-exchange student, Signe Rikvold of Norway, and write a 300-word feature article for the October 1 issue. Remember to ask open-ended questions, and try to get some pithy quotes. I will need your copy (manuscript and disk) no later than 3:00 p.m. Monday, September 27. Get together with our staff photographer, Mark Vogt, to schedule a time and place for the interview so that he can get B/W pics at the same time.

---

order to respond to the message.

Clarify and question.
- See if context clues help you interpret the meaning of unfamiliar words, including **technical terms** or **jargon** associated with the field. If context fails to help, look up the words in a dictionary.

Using the Strategies

Answer these questions about the memo above.

1. Who sent the memo, and who received copies of it?

2. What is the assignment? When is it due?

3. What are "pithy" quotes? What are "B/W pics"?

Extending the Strategies

Following the format shown here, write a memo to announce the meeting of a group you belong to or would like to belong to. Try to use some technical terminology. Send your memo by e-mail or deliver it to a classmate. Is your message clear?

Using Students' Strengths

Auditory Learners
Pair auditory learners, and have one of them read the memo aloud while the other takes notes. Then have them change roles, with the listener checking and revising the notes made by his or her partner. The students might prepare a sheet of paper ahead of time, leaving spaces for the memo sender's name, message and other details.

Visual Learners
Give visual learners colored markers and copies of the memo. Have them highlight or underline the various parts of the memo: sender, time and place, required actions, and other details. Students can write clarifying questions directly on their copies, drawing arrows to connect them to the appropriate parts of the memo.

Expect the Unexpected

Theme

Ironic Reversals and Surprises *One of the joys of reading fiction is experiencing the effects of irony. Just as life is forever surprising us with unexpected outcomes, so does fiction continually surprise us. The writers of the stories in this collection are masters of the unanticipated moment, of the unconventional point of view.*

Reading the Anthology

Reaching Struggling Readers

The *Reading Skills and Strategies: Reaching Struggling Readers* binder provides materials coordinated with the Pupil's Edition (see the Collection Planner, p. T200B) to help students who have difficulty reading and comprehending text, or students who are reluctant readers. The binder for ninth grade is organized around sixteen individual skill areas and offers the following options:

*   **MiniRead** MiniReads are short, easy texts that give students a chance to practice a particular skill and strategy before reading selections in the Pupil's Edition. Each MiniRead Skill Lesson can be taught independently or used in conjunction with a Selection Skill Lesson.

*   **Selection Skill Lessons** Selection Skill Lessons allow students to apply skills introduced in the MiniReads. Each Selection Skill Lesson provides reading instruction and practice specific to a particular piece of literature in the Pupil's Edition.

Reading Beyond the Anthology

Read On

Each collection in the grade nine book includes an annotated bibliography of books suitable for extended reading. The suggested books are related to works in the collection by theme, by author, or by subject. To preview the Read On for Collection 3, please turn to p. T249.

HRW Library

The *HRW Library* offers novels, plays, works of nonfiction, and short-story collections for extended reading. Each book in the Library includes a major work and thematically or topically related Connections. The Connections are magazine articles, poems, or other pieces of literature. Each book in the *HRW Library* is also accompanied by a Study Guide that provides teaching suggestions and worksheets. The two titles shown here will work well to extend the theme of Collection 3.

GREAT EXPECTATIONS
Charles Dickens
In *Great Expectations*, Dickens recounts the story of Pip, a young boy whose expectations of a large inheritance alter the course of his life.

JANE EYRE
Charlotte Brontë
This romantic tale traces the surprisingly eventful life of Jane Eyre, an orphan girl employed as a governess by Mr. Rochester, the brooding master of Thornfield Hall.

Collection 3 Expect The Unexpected

Resources for this Collection

Note: All resources for this collection are available for preview on the *One-Stop Planner CD-ROM 1 with Test Generator.* All worksheets and blackline masters may be printed from the CD-ROM.

 **Internet Resources**
go.hrw.com LE0 9-3

Selection or Feature	Reading and Literary Skills	Vocabulary, Language, and Grammar
The Gift of the Magi O. Henry (p. 202) **Connections: When I'm Sixty Four** John Lennon and Paul McCartney (p. 208)	• *Graphic Organizers for Active Reading,* Worksheet p. 11	• *Words to Own,* Worksheet p. 9 • *Grammar and Language Links:* Adapting Diction, Worksheet p. 19 • *Daily Oral Grammar,* Transparency 11
Elements of Literature: Irony **Appointment in Samarra** W. Somerset Maugham (p. 212)	• *Literary Elements,* Transparency 4	
Snow Julia Alvarez (p. 214)	• *Graphic Organizers for Active Reading,* Worksheet p. 12 • *Literary Elements:* Transparency 5 Worksheet p. 16	• *Daily Oral Grammar,* Transparency 12
Elements of Literature: Point of View (p. 218)	• *Literary Elements,* Transparency 5	
The Necklace Guy de Maupassant (p. 220)	• *Reading Skills and Strategies: Reaching Struggling Readers* • MiniRead Skill Lesson, p. 59 • Selection Skill Lesson, p. 66 • *Graphic Organizers for Active Reading,* Worksheet p. 13	• *Words to Own,* Worksheet p. 10 • *Grammar and Language Links:* Pronoun Problems, Worksheet p. 21 • *Language Workshop CD-ROM,* Homonyms • *Daily Oral Grammar,* Transparency 13
The Cask of Amontillado Edgar Allan Poe (p. 232)	• *Reading Skills and Strategies: Reaching Struggling Readers* • MiniRead Skill Lesson, p. 70 • Selection Skill Lesson, p. 76 • *Graphic Organizers for Active Reading,* Worksheet p. 14 • *Literary Elements:* Transparency 4 Worksheet p. 13	• *Words to Own,* Worksheet p. 11 • *Grammar and Language Links:* Dialogue, Worksheet p. 23 • *Language Workshop CD-ROM,* Quotation Marks • *Daily Oral Grammar,* Transparency 14
Extending the Theme: The Princess and the Tin Box James Thurber (p. 244) **The Talking Skull** *A Nigerian folk tale translated by* Leo Frobenius and Douglas G. Fox (p. 247)	The Extending the Theme feature provides students with an unstructured opportunity to practice reading strategies using a selection that extends the theme of the collection.	
Writer's Workshop: Evaluation (p. 250)		
Sentence Workshop: Revising Sentence Beginnings (p. 255)		• *Workshop Resources,* p. 65

Collection Planner

Other Resources for this Collection

- *Cross-Curricular Activities*, p. 3
- *Portfolio Management System*, Introduction to Portfolio Assessment, p. 1
- *Test Generator*, Collection Test 💿

Writing	Listening and Speaking Viewing and Representing	Assessment
• *Portfolio Management System*, Rubrics for Choices, p. 110	• *Audio CD Library*, Disc 8, Track 2 🎧 • *Portfolio Management System*, Rubrics for Choices, p. 110	• *Formal Assessment*, Selection Test, p. 26 • *Test Generator (One-Stop Planner CD-ROM)* 💿
		• *Formal Assessment*, Literary Elements Test, p. 33
• *Portfolio Management System*, Rubrics for Choices, p. 111	• *Viewing and Representing:* Fine Art Transparency 5; Worksheet p. 20 📋 • *Portfolio Management System*, Rubrics for Choices, p. 111	• *Formal Assessment*, Selection Test, p. 28 • *Test Generator (One-Stop Planner CD-ROM)* 💿
		• *Formal Assessment*, Literary Elements Test, p. 35
• *Portfolio Management System*, Rubrics for Choices, p. 112	• *Audio CD Library*, Disc 8, Track 3 🎧 • *Portfolio Management System*, Rubrics for Choices, p. 112	• *Formal Assessment*, Selection Test, p. 29 • *Standardized Test Preparation*, p. 26 • *Test Generator (One-Stop Planner CD-ROM)* 💿
• *Portfolio Management System*, Rubrics for Choices, p. 114	• *Visual Connections:* Videocassette A, Segment 3 📼 • *Audio CD Library*, Disc 9, Track 2 🎧 • *Portfolio Management System*, Rubrics for Choices, p. 114	• *Formal Assessment*, Selection Test, p. 31 • *Standardized Test Preparation*, pp. 28, 30 • *Test Generator (One-Stop Planner CD-ROM)* 💿
	• *Audio CD Library*, Disc 9, Tracks 3, 4 🎧	

• *Workshop Resources*, p. 13
• *Writer's Workshop 2 CD-ROM*, Evaluation 💿
		• *Portfolio Management System*
		  • Prewriting, p. 116
		  • Peer Editing, p. 117
		  • Assessment Rubric, p. 118

 Transparency   💿 CD-ROM   Video   🎧 Audio CD

Collection Planner

Collection 3 Expect the Unexpected

Skills Focus

Selection or Feature	Reading Skills and Strategies	Elements of Literature	Language/ Grammar	Vocabulary/ Spelling	Writing	Listening/ Speaking	Viewing/ Representing
The Gift of the Magi O. Henry (p. 202)	Make Predictions, p. 202 Summarize a Story, p. 209	Ironic Situations, pp. 202, 209 Paradox, p. 209 Irony, p. 209	Diction, p. 211	New Words, p. 211	Analyze Plot, p. 210 Extend a Story, p. 210 Update a Story, p. 210		Research the 1900s to Create a Time Capsule, p. 210
Elements of Literature: Irony **Appointment in Samarra** W. Somerset Maugham (p. 212)		Irony, pp. 212–213 • Verbal • Situational • Dramatic					
Snow Julia Alvarez (p. 214)	Summarize, pp. 214, 217	Narrator, pp. 214, 217 Images, p. 217 Character, p. 217			Evaluate a Character, p. 217	Interview People from Different Cultures, p. 217	
Elements of Literature: Point of View (p. 218)		Point of View, pp. 218–219 • Omniscient • First-Person • Third-Person Limited					
The Necklace Guy de Maupassant (p. 220)	Summarize a Plot, pp. 220, 229	Third-Person Limited Point of View, p. 220 Irony, p. 229 Characters, p. 229	Pronoun Problems, p. 231 Pronoun Contractions, p. 231	Synonyms and Intensity Scales, p. 231	Determine What Makes a Character Believable, p. 230 Extend a Story, p. 230 Determine the Impact of Point of View, p. 230	Participate in a Debate, p. 230 Select a Soundtrack, p. 230	Use a Venn Diagram, p. 229
The Cask of Amontillado Edgar Allan Poe (p. 232)	Draw Conclusions, pp. 232, 241	Unreliable Narrator, pp. 232, 241 Irony, p. 241 Motive, p. 241	Punctuate Dialogue, p. 243	Word Maps, p. 243 Etymology, p. 243 Synonyms/ Antonyms, p. 243	Evaluate an Ending, p. 242 Write a Scene from Another Character's Point of View, p. 242 Explain a Theory, p. 242	Role-Play, p. 242	Design a Stage Set, p. 242
Extending the Theme: The Princess and the Tin Box James Thurber (p. 244) **The Talking Skull** *Nigerian folk tale translated by* Leo Frobenius and Douglas G. Fox (p. 247)		Folk Tale, p. 244	The Extending the Theme feature provides students with an unstructured opportunity to practice reading strategies using a selection that extends the theme of the collection.				
Writer's Workshop: Evaluation (p. 250)				Negative and Positive Judgment Words, p. 253	Write an Essay of Evaluation, pp. 250–254		
Sentence Workshop: Revising Sentence Beginnings (p. 255)			Adverbs, Prepositional Phrases, and Adverbial Clauses, p. 255		Revise for Varied Sentence Beginnings, p. 255		
Reading for Life: Analyzing Advertisements (p. 256)	Analyze an Advertiser's Claims, p. 256 Recognize Emotional Appeals, p. 256			Identify Loaded Words, p. 256			

Skills Focus

EXPECT THE UNEXPECTED

WRITING FOCUS: Evaluation

It ain't over till it's over.

—Yogi Berra, speaking of a ballgame

Things don't always turn out the way we plan them. Sometimes, just when we think that we have taken charge of our lives, we are thrown yet another curveball. Some of us love these surprises; others of us prefer to plan our lives and predict what's going to happen next.

In some ways fiction is just like real life. Fiction is also full of surprises—twists and turns that catch characters unawares and turn their expectations upside down.

The writers of the stories in this collection are not afraid of surprising you with characters whose behavior is unusual, whose motives are sometimes not the best, and whose problems are resolved in ways you least expect.

Writer's Notebook

Every time we read a story (or see a movie) we evaluate it: It was good. It was slow. It was hard to understand. In the Writer's Workshop on page 250, you'll be making judgments like these in order to write an evaluation of a short story. Get started early by thinking of the stories you have read. What did you like about some of them? What did you dislike about others? Exactly what makes an exciting plot or an interesting setting or unforgettable characters? In a cluster diagram, gather your ideas about what makes a good story. Keep your notes, and add to them as you read the stories that follow.

OBJECTIVES

1. Read short stories centered on the theme "Expect the Unexpected"
2. Interpret literary elements used in short stories, with special emphasis on irony and point of view
3. Apply a variety of reading strategies to short stories
4. Respond to the literature using a variety of modes
5. Learn and use new words
6. Plan, draft, revise, edit, proof, and publish an essay of evaluation
7. Revise sentence beginnings
8. Analyze advertisements

Responding to the Quotation

? The oft-quoted Yogi Berra achieved fame as both a player and a manager for major league baseball teams, including the New York Yankees. Why is this quote particularly appropriate coming from someone who made a career in sports? [Possible responses: In many sports, a team that has been winning throughout the game might lose in the last few minutes because of a rally by the other team; in baseball, anything is possible until the final out. An athlete and coach would be very familiar with these scenarios.] Does this quote ring true outside the realm of sports as well? [Possible response: Yes, often in life, things turn out quite differently than you expect.]

Writer's Notebook

Encourage students to share and discuss the stories they write about.

Writing Focus: Evaluation

The following **Work in Progress** assignments build to a culminating **Writer's Workshop** at the end of the collection.

- The Gift of the Magi — Focusing on plot (p. 210)
- Snow — Looking at characters (p. 217)
- The Necklace — Evaluating believability (p. 230)
- The Cask of Amontillado — Focusing on emotional content (p. 242)

Writer's Workshop: Persuasive Writing / Evaluation (p. 250)

OBJECTIVES

1. Read and interpret the story
2. Analyze ironic situations
3. Make predictions
4. Express understanding through creative writing, writing/economics, or research/social studies
5. Rewrite ornate diction
6. Understand and use new words

SKILLS

Literary
• Analyze ironic situations

Reading
• Make predictions

Writing
• Collect ideas for an essay
• Write a paragraph about the story's characters
• Write a modern version of the story

Research/Social Studies
• Research the early 1900s and list objects for a time capsule

Language
• Rewrite ornate diction

Vocabulary
• Use new words

Viewing/Representing
• Use art to tell a story (ATE)
• Use art to help visualize the story's setting (ATE)

Planning

• **Block Schedule**
Block Scheduling Lesson Plans with Pacing Guide

• **Traditional Schedule**
Lesson Plans Including Strategies for English-Language Learners

• **One-Stop Planner**
CD-ROM with Test Generator

Before You Read

THE GIFT OF THE MAGI

Make the Connection

The Perfect Gift

Fiction, like life, brings surprises. O. Henry liked to put a surprise twist or "snapper" in his plots. In "The Gift of the Magi" each character plans to give the other a gift, and because they love each other very much, each one searches for the perfect gift. What happens is not at all what they expected.

Quickwrite

If you could save one item from a disaster— a fire, a flood, an earthquake— what would it be? In a few sentences, describe your most cherished possession, and tell why you treasure it. Was it a gift?

Elements of Literature

Ironic Situations

Often when we read a story, we think one thing will happen, only to be taken by surprise when something entirely different takes place. This is an **ironic situation,** and it reminds us that even though we think we can control our lives, chance or the unexpected often has the last word.

An **ironic situation** is one that turns out to be the opposite of what we expected.

For more on Irony, see pages 212–213 and the Handbook of Literary Terms.

Reading Skills and Strategies

Making Predictions: What Will Happen Next?

Why do we read? One reason is that we are curious. At the start of a story, a writer sets up a situation that raises a lot of questions. We read on because we want to know what happens next.

Read the first paragraph of this story, and then stop and write down a prediction. What do you think will happen next? Stop at least twice more in the story, and write down your predictions. What will happen next? As you do this, be aware of these questions: Is the writer keeping you in suspense? Is he succeeding in surprising you? Keep your notes.

Background

The Magi that O. Henry refers to in the title of this story are the three "wise men" from the East who brought gifts of gold, frankincense, and myrrh to the infant Jesus. Traditionally, these have been regarded as the first Christmas gifts.

go.hrw.com
LE0 9-3

The Gift of the Magi

O. Henry

The Magi, as you know, were wise men.

Preteaching Vocabulary

Words To Own

Have students read the definitions of the Words to Own listed at the bottom of the selection pages. Then, use the following exercises to reinforce students' understanding of the words.

1. Choose the synonym of **instigate**.
   (a) revoke   (b) hesitate   (c) incite [c]

2. Choose the phrase that means the opposite of **scrutiny**. (a) superficial examination (b) careful study   (c) watchful gaze [a]

3. Choose the phrase that means the opposite of **depreciate**. (a) raise the value   (b) purchase cheaply   (c) greatly impress [a]

4. Choose the synonym for **covet**.
   (a) purchase   (b) desire   (c) relinquish [b]

A Woman's Work (1912) by John Sloan (American, 1871–1951).
Oil on canvas (80.3 cm × 65.4 cm).

© The Cleveland Museum of Art, 1995, Gift of Miss Amelia Elizabeth White, 64.160.

O ne dollar and eighty-seven cents. That was all. And sixty cents of it was in
    pennies. Pennies saved one and two at a time by bulldozing the grocer and
the vegetable man and the butcher until one's cheeks burned with the silent imputation of parsimony[1] that such close dealing implied. Three times Della counted it.
One dollar and eighty-seven cents. And the next day would be Christmas.

1. **imputation** (im′pyō̅o̅·tā′shən) **of parsimony** (pär′sə·mō′nē): suggestion of stinginess.

THE GIFT OF THE MAGI **203**

Summary ■ ■ ■

This O. Henry classic, famous for its
characteristic "snapper," or surprise
ending, is a tale of selfless love between
a husband and a wife. At Christmas,
Della sells her long, beautiful hair to
buy her husband, Jim, a platinum fob
chain for his prized watch. Meanwhile,
he has sold his watch to buy an expensive set of combs for her hair.

Resources ———

Listening
Audio CD Library
A recording of "The Gift of the Magi"
is available as part of the *Audio CD
Library*:
• Disc 8, Track 2

RESPONDING TO THE ART
Like Robert Henri (see p. 205),
John Sloan (1871–1951) was a
member of The Eight, a group of
American realist painters who
broke away from the art establishment in 1908. Their work, featuring scenes from everyday urban
life rather than the decorative
scenes then in fashion, roused a
storm of derision; critics labeled
them the Ashcan School.
Activity. Use this painting as a
springboard for oral storytelling.
Ask: Who is the woman in the
painting? What does the setting
suggest about her circumstances?
How does she feel about her
"woman's work"? In what ways is
her life similar to and different
from Della's?

Resources: Print and Media

Reading
• *Graphic Organizers for Active Reading*, p. 11
• *Words to Own* p. 9
• *Audio CD Library*, Disc 8, Track 2

Writing and Language
• *Daily Oral Grammar*
  Transparency 11
• *Grammar and Language Links*,
  Worksheet p. 19

Assessment
• *Formal Assessment*, p. 26
• *Portfolio Management System*, p. 110
• *Test Generator (One-Stop Planner* CD-ROM)

Internet
• go.hrw.com (keyword: LE0 9-3)

FROM THE EDITOR'S DESK
Of course all of us felt sure that
teachers would expect to find
"The Gift of the Magi" in a grade
nine anthology, but it would have
been difficult to pass up the
opportunity to include it in any
event. Not only is it *the* classic
example of irony in storytelling,
but it is a warmhearted and
moving tale.

T203

A Critical Thinking

Expressing an Opinion

? Do you agree with this "moral reflection"? Explain. [Possible answers: Yes, for most people, life is full of hardship, suffering, and sorrow; no, it's too pessimistic—life is what you make of it.]

B Reading Skills and Strategies

Making Inferences

? What do these details tell you about the couple and the setting of the story? [Possible response: The couple is poor, since they have a shabby apartment, their income has shrunk, and they can't afford to fix things. The story takes place in the past, since both the rent and the husband's income are far less than they would be today.]

C Critical Thinking

Interpreting

? What is the narrator saying here? [He is saying Jim and Della value their prized possessions more than riches.]

D Reading Skills and Strategies

Making Predictions

? Where do you think Della is going? [Possible responses: to sell her hair; to take a walk; to find something for Jim that costs no more than $1.87.]

There was clearly nothing to do but flop down on the shabby little couch and howl. So Della did it. Which **instigates** the moral reflection that life is made up of sobs, sniffles, and smiles, with sniffles **predominating**.

While the mistress of the home is gradually **subsiding** from the first stage to the second, take a look at the home. A furnished **flat²** at $8 per week. It did not exactly beggar description, but it certainly had that word on the lookout for the **mendicancy squad.³**

In the **vestibule⁴** below was a letter box into which no letter would go, and an electric button from which no mortal finger could **coax** a ring. Also **appertaining⁵** thereunto was a card bearing the name "Mr. James Dillingham Young."

The "Dillingham" had been flung to the breeze during a former period of prosperity when its possessor was being paid $30 per week. Now, when the income was shrunk to $20, the letters of "Dillingham" looked blurred, as though they were thinking seriously of contracting to a modest and unassuming *D*. But whenever Mr. James Dillingham Young came home and reached his flat above, he was called Jim and greatly hugged by Mrs. James Dillingham Young, already introduced to you as Della. Which is all very good.

Della finished her cry and attended to her cheeks with the powder rag. She stood by the window and looked out dully at a gray cat walking a gray fence in a gray back yard. Tomorrow would be Christmas Day and she had only $1.87 with which to buy Jim a present. She had been saving every penny she could for months, with this result. Twenty dollars a week doesn't go far. Expenses had been greater than she had calculated. They always are. Only $1.87 to buy a present for Jim. Her Jim. Many a happy hour she had spent planning for something nice for him. Something fine and rare and sterling—something just a little bit near to being worthy of the honor of being owned by Jim.

2. **flat:** apartment.
3. **mendicancy** (men′di·kən·sē) **squad:** police who arrested beggars and homeless people.
4. **vestibule:** small entrance hall.
5. **appertaining** (ap′ər·tān′iŋ): belonging.

204 THE SHORT-STORY COLLECTIONS

There was a pier glass⁶ between the windows of the room. Perhaps you have seen a pier glass in an $8 flat. A very thin and very agile person may, by observing his reflection in a rapid sequence of longitudinal strips, obtain a fairly accurate conception of his looks. Della, being slender, had mastered the art.

Suddenly she whirled from the window and stood before the glass. Her eyes were shining brilliantly, but her face had lost its color within twenty seconds. Rapidly she pulled down her hair and let it fall to its full length.

Now, there were two possessions of the James Dillingham Youngs in which they both took a mighty pride. One was Jim's gold watch that had been his father's and his grandfather's. The other was Della's hair. Had the Queen of Sheba lived in the flat across the air shaft,⁷ Della would have let her hair hang out the window some day to dry just to **depreciate** Her Majesty's jewels and gifts. Had King Solomon been the janitor, with all his treasures piled up in the basement, Jim would have pulled out his watch every time he passed, just to see him pluck at his beard from envy.

So now Della's beautiful hair fell about her rippling and shining like a cascade of brown waters. It reached below her knee and made itself almost a garment for her. And then she did it up again nervously and quickly. Once she faltered for a minute and stood still while a tear or two splashed on the worn red carpet.

On went her old brown jacket; on went her old brown hat. With a whirl of skirts and with the brilliant sparkle still in her eyes, she fluttered out the door and down the stairs to the street.

Where she stopped, the sign read: "Mme. Sofronie. Hair Goods of All Kinds." One flight

6. **pier glass:** tall mirror hung between two windows.
7. **air shaft:** narrow gap between two buildings.

WORDS TO OWN

instigates (in′stə·gāts′) *v.*: gives rise to. *Instigates* is generally used to mean "provokes or urges on to some action."

depreciate (dē·prē′shē·āt′) *v.*: belittle; lower the value of.

Reaching All Students

Struggling Readers

Making Predictions was introduced on p. 202. One good strategy to use is Anticipation Guides. For information on using this strategy, see p. 17 in the *Reading Strategies Handbook* in the *Reading Skills and Strategies* binder. Your guide might include statements like:

- People should always give gifts that they can afford, not ones that are too expensive.
- If two people love each other, money doesn't matter.

English Language Learners

Ask students to try using context clues to decipher unfamiliar words in the story. Model the process using this sentence (p. 204): "In the vestibule below was a letter box into which no letter would go...." Ask: Where would you find a letter box, or mailbox? [in an entrance hall or near the front door] For additional strategies, see

- *Lesson Plans Including Strategies for English-Language Learners*

Advanced Learners

To help their peers decipher O. Henry's sometimes difficult vocabulary, students can make a glossary for the selection. Students should include any words they were unfamiliar with upon their first reading of the story. In their glossary, students should include definitions, synonyms, and example sentences for each word selected.

Snow in New York (1902) by Robert Henri. Oil on canvas (32" x 25¾").

Chester Dale Collection, © 1998 Board of Trustees, National Gallery of Art, Washington, D.C.

inside out. It was a platinum fob chain,[8] simple and chaste in design, properly proclaiming its value by substance alone and not by meretricious[9] ornamentation—as all good things should do. It was even worthy of The Watch. As soon as she saw it she knew that it must be Jim's. It was like him. Quietness and value—the description applied to both. Twenty-one dollars they took from her for it, and she hurried home with the 87 cents. With that chain on his watch, Jim might be properly anxious about the time in any company. Grand as the watch was, he sometimes looked at it on the sly on account of the old leather strap that he used in place of a chain.

When Della reached home, her intoxication gave way a little to prudence and reason. She got out her curling irons and lighted the gas and went to work repairing the ravages made by generosity added to love. Which is always a tremendous task, dear friends—a mammoth task.

Within forty minutes her head was covered with tiny, close-lying curls that made her look wonderfully like a truant schoolboy. She looked at her reflection in the mirror long, carefully, and critically.

"If Jim doesn't kill me," she said to herself, "before he takes a second look at me, he'll say I look like a Coney Island chorus girl. But what could I do—oh! what could I do with a dollar and eighty-seven cents?"

At 7 o'clock the coffee was made and the frying pan was on the back of the stove hot and ready to cook the chops.

8. **fob chain:** short chain meant to be attached to a pocket watch.
9. **meretricious** (mer′ə·trish′əs): attractive in a cheap, flashy way.

up Della ran, and collected herself, panting. Madame, large, too white, chilly, hardly looked the "Sofronie."

"Will you buy my hair?" asked Della.

"I buy hair," said Madame. "Take yer hat off and let's have a sight at the looks of it."

Down rippled the brown cascade.

"Twenty dollars," said Madame, lifting the mass with a practiced hand.

"Give it to me quick," said Della.

Oh, and the next two hours tripped by on rosy wings. Forget the hashed metaphor. She was ransacking the stores for Jim's present.

She found it at last. It surely had been made for Jim and no one else. There was no other like it in any of the stores, and she had turned all of them

Ⓔ Appreciating Language
Diction

This paragraph contains highly ornate diction. Have students paraphrase it in plain diction. [Sample paraphrase: When Della got home, her happiness lessened, and her mind turned to practical matters. To fix the damage love and generosity had caused, she tried to curl the hair she had left, but it wasn't easy.]

Ⓕ Elements of Literature
Ironic Situation

❓ How might Della's sacrifice turn out to create an ironic situation? [Possible responses: Jim will be angry at Della; he might prefer her hair short.]

Using Students' Strengths

Intrapersonal Learners

Ask students to name a possession they would find difficult to give up. Have them sketch the item and write ten descriptive words below the picture. Then, have students note in their journals how they would feel about giving it up.

Making the Connections

Cultural Connections

Discuss gift-giving traditions of different cultures. Ask students to share what they know about gift exchanges and donations to the poor associated with the Jewish celebration of Hanuka; the potlatch ceremony among some Native American groups, in which an individual gives away every possession; or the *kula* tradition among Pacific Islanders in Melanesia, in which symbolic exchanges solidify mutual, life-long obligations. Then, ask students how they might characterize birthday, graduation, and wedding customs of gift giving in the United States. Interested students can work in pairs to research and explore another culture's gift-giving traditions. You might have students arrange short reports on and illustrations of their findings in a bulletin-board display.

A Reading Skills and Strategies

Making Predictions

❓ What do you think will happen when Jim sees Della? [Possible responses: He won't care about her hair; he will be angry that she sold her most prized possession just to buy him a present.]

B Critical Thinking

Speculating

❓ Why might Jim be acting so strangely? [Possible responses: He cannot believe her hair is gone; he is confused about what she did.]

C Struggling Readers

Breaking Down Difficult Text

You may wish to discuss this passage to make sure students understand it. If necessary, explain that the author is suggesting that money is not the measure of true love and that the Magi did not bring the gift of self-sacrificing love. Ask students to note how this assertion is clear by the end of the story.

D Elements of Literature

Ironic Situation

❓ Why is this an ironic situation? [Possible responses: With her hair cut so short, Della has no use for the combs; it's ironic because Della sold her hair to buy Jim a gift.]

T206

Jim was never late. Della doubled the fob chain in her hand and sat on the corner of the table near the door that he always entered. Then she heard his step on the stair away down on the first flight, and she turned white for just a moment. She had a habit of saying little silent prayers about the simplest everyday things, and now she whispered: "Please God, make him think I am still pretty."

The door opened and Jim stepped in and closed it. He looked thin and very serious. Poor fellow, he was only twenty-two—and to be burdened with a family! He needed a new overcoat and he was without gloves.

Jim stepped inside the door, as immovable as a setter at the scent of quail. His eyes were fixed upon Della, and there was an expression in them that she could not read, and it terrified her. It was not anger, nor surprise, nor disapproval, nor horror, nor any of the sentiments that she had been prepared for. He simply stared at her fixedly with that peculiar expression on his face.

Della wriggled off the table and went for him.

"Jim, darling," she cried, "don't look at me that way. I had my hair cut off and sold it because I couldn't have lived through Christmas without giving you a present. It'll grow out again—you won't mind, will you? I just had to do it. My hair grows awfully fast. Say 'Merry Christmas!' Jim, and let's be happy. You don't know what a nice—what a beautiful, nice gift I've got for you."

"You've cut off your hair?" asked Jim, laboriously, as if he had not arrived at that patent[10] fact yet even after the hardest mental labor.

"Cut it off and sold it," said Della. "Don't you like me just as well, anyhow? I'm me without my hair, ain't I?"

Jim looked about the room curiously.

"You say your hair is gone?" he said, with an air almost of idiocy.

"You needn't look for it," said Della. "It's sold, I tell you—sold and gone, too. It's Christmas Eve, boy. Be good to me, for it went for you. Maybe the hairs on my head were numbered," she went on with a sudden serious sweetness, "but nobody could ever count my love for you.

---

10. **patent** (păt′'nt): obvious.

206 THE SHORT-STORY COLLECTIONS

Shall I put the chops on, Jim?"

Out of his trance Jim seemed quickly to wake. He enfolded his Della. For ten seconds let us regard with discreet scrutiny some inconsequential object in the other direction. Eight dollars a week or a million a year—what is the difference? A mathematician or a wit would give you the wrong answer. The Magi brought valuable gifts, but that was not among them. This dark assertion will be illuminated later on.

Jim drew a package from his overcoat pocket and threw it upon the table.

"Don't make any mistake, Dell," he said, "about me. I don't think there's anything in the way of a haircut or a shave or a shampoo that could make me like my girl any less. But if you'll unwrap that package, you may see why you had me going awhile at first."

White fingers and nimble tore at the string and paper. And then an ecstatic scream of joy; and then, alas! a quick feminine change to hysterical tears and wails, necessitating the immediate employment of all the comforting powers of the lord of the flat.

For there lay The Combs—the set of combs, side and back, that Della had worshiped for long in a Broadway window. Beautiful combs, pure tortoise shell, with jeweled rims—just the shade to wear in the beautiful vanished hair. They were expensive combs, she knew, and her heart had simply craved and yearned over them without the least hope of possession. And now, they were hers, but the tresses that should have adorned the coveted adornments were gone.

But she hugged them to her bosom, and at length she was able to look up with dim eyes and a smile and say: "My hair grows so fast, Jim!"

And then Della leaped up like a little singed cat and cried, "Oh, oh!"

Jim had not yet seen his beautiful present. She held it out to him eagerly upon her open palm. The dull

WORDS TO OWN

scrutiny (skrōōt′'n·ē) n.: close inspection.
coveted (kuv′it·id) v. used as adj.: longed-for.

Taking a Second Look

Review: Making Inferences About Character

Remind students that when they are trying to decide what a character is like, they should note:

- character's appearance, words, thoughts, actions
- things other characters say and think about the character

Readers can combine these text details about the character with their own knowledge and experience to reach inferences about the character.

Activity

Have students find three details from the story that they think say something important about either Della or Jim. Ask them to consider what these details reveal, keeping in mind their own knowledge and experience with similar details in real life. Then have students share their inferences and explain how they reached them.

precious metal seemed to flash with a reflection of her bright and ardent spirit.

"Isn't it a dandy, Jim? I hunted all over town to find it. You'll have to look at the time a hundred times a day now. Give me your watch. I want to see how it looks on it."

Instead of obeying, Jim tumbled down on the couch and put his hands under the back of his head and smiled.

"Dell," said he, "let's put our Christmas presents away and keep 'em a while. They're too nice to use just at present. I sold the watch to get the money to buy your combs. And now suppose you put the chops on."

The Magi, as you know, were wise men—wonderfully wise men—who brought gifts to the Babe in the manger. They invented the art of giving Christmas presents. Being wise, their gifts were no doubt wise ones, possibly bearing the privilege of exchange in case of duplication. And here I have lamely related to you the uneventful chronicle of two foolish children in a flat who most unwisely sacrificed for each other the greatest treasures of their house. But in a last word to the wise of these days, let it be said that of all who give gifts, these two were the wisest. Of all who give and receive gifts, such as they are wisest. Everywhere they are wisest. They are the Magi.

E **Elements of Literature**
Ironic Situation
? How does this "snapper," or surprise twist, make the situation in the story even more ironic? [Both Della and Jim sacrificed their most cherished possession to buy something for use with the other's most cherished possession.]

F **Critical Thinking**
Making Connections
? How does O. Henry explain his earlier reference to the Magi here? [Possible answer: He is suggesting that the love that inspires sacrifice and generosity is the real gift of the Magi.]

MEET THE WRITER

He ♥ New York

O. Henry (1862–1910), whose real name was William Sydney Porter, was brought up in Greensboro, North Carolina. At the age of twenty, he went to Texas, where he became a rancher, worked as a bank teller, and founded a humorous weekly called *The Rolling Stone*.

When he was accused of stealing a thousand dollars from the First National Bank of Austin, where he was a teller, Porter panicked and fled to Central America. In Honduras he traveled with the outlawed Jennings brothers and helped them spend the loot from a recent robbery. But news of his wife's illness brought him back to Austin. There he was arrested, tried, and sentenced to five years in prison. Ironically, if he had not run away, Porter might have been acquitted. The bank was poorly run, and the loss of money might have been a case of mismanagement, not a crime.

Porter served only three years of his sentence. In prison he wrote more than a dozen stories and absorbed the underworld lore that he would use in stories such as "A Retrieved Reformation." He also may have found his pen name there: One of the prison guards was named Orrin Henry.

Porter left prison in 1901 and went to New York. He loved the city at once, and he wrote about it and its inhabitants for the few years remaining in his life. He once remarked:

66 There are stories in everything. I've got some of my best yarns from park benches, lampposts, and newspaper stands. 99

O. Henry wrote more than six hundred stories altogether—sixty-five in 1904 alone. But he also drank heavily, and tuberculosis killed him when he was only forty-seven. His last words were, "Pull up the shades so I can see New York. I don't want to go home in the dark."

More Snappers by O. Henry

"A Retrieved Reformation"
"The Furnished Room"
"The Ransom of Red Chief"

Pub. 1903 in the New York World

Resources

THE GIFT OF THE MAGI 207

Assessing Learning

Check Test: True-False
1. At the story's beginning, Della does not have nearly enough money for Jim's present. [True]
2. The Youngs have two children to support. [False]
3. Della sells her hair to buy Jim a gift. [True]
4. Jim's watch is a family heirloom passed down to him from his father and grandfather. [True]
5. Jim sells his watch to buy Della a locket. [False]
6. Della buys Jim a fob chain for his watch. [True]

Standardized Test Preparation
For practice in proofreading and editing see
• *Daily Oral Grammar*, Transparency 11

John Lennon and Paul McCartney wrote this song in 1967. They were both young men at that time and popular celebrities. But the lyrics of the song contemplate a far different future. They question the survival of love when the excitement of youth and celebrity are gone. The singer wonders if love will survive quiet days of digging weeds in the garden and knitting by the fireside.

Appreciating Language

Reading Music

The following are instructions on how to read the music:

First verse ("When I get older . . ."): Read until you get to the end of the sixth line of music. The thick vertical line with the two dots at the end of this line means "go back to the beginning to start the second verse."

Second verse ("I could be handy . . ."): Read until you get to the end of the fourth line of music. Then, skip to the seventh line, where the superscript 2 appears. The second verse ends with the words "Vera, Chuck and Dave." Return to the beginning to start the third verse.

Third verse ("Send me a postcard . . ."): Read until you get to the end of the fourth line, where the instruction "3rd time to Coda" appears. Go to the middle of the last line, where the label "Coda" appears. The Coda finishes the song.

A Music Lexicon

Of all the arts, students are probably most personally involved in music. You might use this song to encourage students to think about the structure of music. As a start they could use this song and write a lexicon. Here are some possible entries:

coda (from Latin for "tail"): a more or less independent passage of music added to the end of a section to reinforce the sense of closure.

clef: a symbol written at the beginning of a musical staff to indicate the pitch of the notes. There are many different clefs. This song is written in the G clef. (See the symbol at the start of each staff.)

staff: the horizontal lines on and between which notes are written.

Connections A SONG

When I'm Sixty Four
John Lennon and Paul McCartney

Connecting Across Texts

Connecting with "The Gift of the Magi"

Ask students if they think the characters Della and Jim from "The Gift of the Magi" ever wonder about their future or question whether their love will survive the way the song "When I'm Sixty Four" does. Have them write down some of the questions that Jim or Della might ask and to compare their questions to those in the song. [Some students might feel that Della and Jim would not think about the future or ever question the survival of their love. Some students might think that the quiet activities anticipated in the song more accurately apply to Jim and Della, characters who are poor and already content with simple things, than they do to the songwriters. Others might think Della and Jim hope to be wealthy in the future and that their questions would be far different from those in the song.]

First Thoughts

[respond]

1. What do you think of O. Henry's comments in the last paragraph of this story?

Shaping Interpretations

[predict]

2. Check your reading notes. What predictions did you make as you read the story? (Did you come close to guessing what would happen next?)

[interpret]

3. An **ironic situation** is one that turns out to be just the opposite of what we—or the characters in the story—expect. Describe the situational irony in this story. What lesson about life and love do you think it teaches Della and Jim?

[infer]

4. What is the real "gift" referred to in the **title**? (Notice that O. Henry says "gift," not "gifts.")

[comprehend]

5. A **paradox** is an apparent contradiction that is actually true. It may be a statement or a situation. Explain why the following statement is a paradox: Jim and Della were one of the richest couples on earth.

Reading Check

Suppose you are telling the story of Della and Jim to a group of your friends. Identify the two **characters**, tell what each one **wants** to do, and summarize the **main events**—and the **outcome**—of their story.

Connecting with the Text

[connect]

6. Under what circumstances would you give up a cherished possession—as Jim and Della did? (Be sure to check your Quickwrite notes.)

Extending the Text

[extend]

7. What do you think this little story, written almost a century ago, has to say about our consumer society today? Do you think that we often equate love with money? Consider advertising, the amount of money we spend on gifts, the value placed on having many possessions.

[analyze]

8. O. Henry's poverty-stricken couple is sustained by so much love that it is hard to imagine a cross word coming between the two of them. Suppose a writer with a view of the world different from O. Henry's—someone who viewed human nature as selfish—were to write about this struggling couple. How might the story change?

Challenging the Text

[evaluate]

9. Describe your response to O. Henry's ending—the "snapper." Do you enjoy this kind of **irony** in stories or movies, or does it seem contrived—a trick played on the reader?

THE GIFT OF THE MAGI **209**

First Thoughts

1. Some students will agree with O. Henry's comments; others may disagree, saying that Jim's and Della's love for each other overpowered their common sense.

Shaping Interpretations

2. Responses will vary. Students should be able to confirm or disprove their predictions. Some students may have guessed the story's ending.

3. The situational irony occurs because both Della and Jim expect to delight the other with a gift. Instead, their sacrifices render both gifts useless. Della and Jim may have learned that their love does not need material gifts to survive or that love can lead to unexpected results.

4. Students' wording may vary, but broadly, the real gift is the gift of love. Students will note, too, the values of generosity, unselfishness, and sacrifice.

5. Jim and Della are materially poor, but they are very rich with love.

Connecting with the Text

6. Possible responses: if a loved one needed the item for happiness or survival; if it were the only item owned worth giving.

Extending the Text

7. Possible responses: Modern society is materialistic, and love is often equated with money; not everyone equates love with money—many people volunteer regularly or make donations to charities to honor their loved ones.

8. Possible responses: Another writer might portray selfish characters who become angry or remorseful that they sacrificed; the two characters might blame one another.

Challenging the Text

9. Possible responses: A surprise ending is enjoyable because it makes you see the entire story in a new light; a surprise ending is unsatisfying because it makes you feel tricked.

Reading Check

Possible response: Della has no money to buy her beloved husband Jim a Christmas present. She sells her hair and uses the money to buy Jim a chain for his prized watch. When he comes home in the evening, Jim is stunned to see Della without long hair. He has bought her the fancy hair combs she wanted. He has sold his watch to do so. Neither one can use the gift received, but together the couple have a love more precious than any gift.

Grading Timesaver

Rubrics for each Choices assignment appear on p. 110 in the *Portfolio Management System*.

CHOICES: Building Your Portfolio

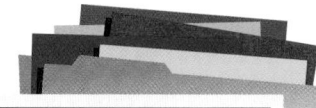

1. **Writer's Notebook** Remind students to save their work. They can use it as prewriting for the Writer's Workshop on p. 250.
2. **Creative Writing** Students may work in pairs, one student writing about Jim's life and the other about Della's life. Using categories such as employment, goals met, and obstacles encountered or overcome, each student may provide input on what the character's life has become.
3. **Creative Writing/Economics** A discussion of current wages and rents in urban and small-town settings will help students generate ideas. Get accurate information by using newspapers or catalogs. Students can also obtain comparative economic data from U.S. government Web sites.
4. **Research/Social Studies** To help students find information about the early 1900s, give them specific topics to research in books and encyclopedias. For instance, they might research the amusement park on Coney Island mentioned in the story or the popular entertainment called vaudeville. Students may wish to work in groups, with each member responsible for a time-capsule artifact from a different aspect of society.

CHOICES: Building Your Portfolio

Writer's Notebook
1. Collecting Ideas for an Essay of Evaluation

Focusing on plot.

What makes a good plot? Apply the following questions to "The Gift of the Magi" or to another story you would like to analyze. Take notes on your responses:

- Is the plot believable? Why?
- Did it create suspense?
- Did it keep you interested?
- Did the writer surprise you?
- Is the plot easy to follow, or is it too complicated?
- Is the ending satisfying?

Save your notes for the Writer's Workshop on page 250.

Plot—"Sound of Thunder"
- *Not believable, but writer makes it seem real. Didn't believe the cause-and-effect part, but it's OK.*
- *Very suspenseful. Couldn't put it down.*
- *Weird ending—not sure I liked that part.*

Creative Writing
2. Life Goes On

The glimpse O. Henry gives us of Della and Jim is of just one brief time in their lives—early in their marriage. But life goes on and people change and grow—sometimes in opposite directions. Suppose you want to provide readers with a glimpse of Della and Jim ten years later. In what ways has each character changed or stayed the same? What is each one doing? Where do they live? Write a paragraph about Della and Jim called "Life Goes On." Do you think they'll be like the couple in the Beatles song (see *Connections* on page 208)?

Creative Writing/Economics
3. Updating the Story

How would the details of O. Henry's love story be different if it were set in Dallas or Los Angeles or some other place (even New York City) today? Consider wages, prices, rents, and living quarters. Would Della have a job?

Work with a partner to write a brief update of the story. Begin with the famous first sentence, but alter the amount of money that Della would have saved and still have found insufficient.

Research/Social Studies
4. Turn of the Century

What was America like in the early 1900s? Suppose you find a time capsule—a collection of objects sealed up at a certain time in history—from that era. What objects are in it? Research the time period and use what you learn to make a list of the capsule's contents. Books, especially those that include illustrations and photographs, and encyclopedias are a good place to start. See what you can find out about the government, economics, communications, and transportation. Will your capsule contain anything that shows what forms of entertainment were popular? You might want to put in your capsule some details about what was happening in Europe, Asia, and South America as Della and Jim were scrimping in New York.

210 THE SHORT-STORY COLLECTIONS

Getting Students Involved

Cooperative Learning
Economics. Have students work in small groups to research economic facts and figures from the time period of the story— the early years of the twentieth century. The prices of many basic items are mentioned on pp. 203–204. They seem incredibly cheap by today's standards. But what were typical salaries back then? What kinds of work did people do? What was the average cost of living? The story mentions that Jim's salary drops from $30 to $20 per week. Was the country undergoing some kind of economic crisis that might have played a factor? Students should begin their research by checking the public library for microfilm of newspapers or magazines from that time period. They can look at the classified advertisement section for such things as employment listings and rents. Groups should present their findings to the class. They can use charts or other graphic organizers to compare economic facts from the past and the present.

T210

Language Handbook HELP

See Improving Sentence Style, page 1017.

Handbook of Literary Terms HELP

See Diction.

Communications Handbook HELP

See Using a Dictionary; Using a Thesaurus.

MINI-LESSON

Diction—Ornate or Plain?

Diction, or word choice, can make a great difference in a piece of writing. A realistic writer might use slang. A science reporter might have to be precise and technical. A romantic might want to be poetic.

O. Henry loved flowery language and ornate diction. In the first paragraph he writes:

> ". . . one's cheeks burned with the silent imputation of parsimony that such close dealing implied."

By using such formal language, O. Henry is showing off his literary skills in a way that was once considered funny. A writer who preferred the plain style might have said:

> . . . you'd blush to think that this haggling over money suggested you were stingy.

Try It Out

➤ Find three ornate sentences in the story and rewrite each of them using plain, straightforward diction, as if you were modernizing the story for today's readers. Compare your edited versions in class.

➤ William Strunk and E. B. White, the authors of a famous writing handbook called *The Elements of Style,* tell writers never to use a twenty-dollar word when a ten-cent word will do just as well. As you work on your writing, think about your diction. Consider the diction that is most appropriate for your characters, for your setting, and for your tone. Can a strong, simple word work just as well as that fancy one?

LANGUAGE LINK

To develop students' proofreading skills, have them select a piece of writing from their portfolio. Ask them to circle three words in their writing that have either a simpler or a more ornate synonym. Then, have students decide whether their original language or a different level of diction would be more effective for their purpose. Have students informally consult one another about their decisions.

Try It Out
Possible Answers

Students' choices of sentences will vary. Here is a sample: The first sentence in paragraph 3, p. 204, might be rewritten as "Down in the entrance hall was a broken mailbox and a doorbell that would not work."

VOCABULARY
Possible Answers

1. Last weekend I *instigated* a discussion with my parents about my curfew.
2. Dents caused by an accident would *depreciate* a car.
3. A guard's *scrutiny* might reveal a concealed weapon.
4. I once *coveted* my older brother's leather jacket.

Resources

Language
• *Grammar and Language Links* Worksheet, p. 19

Vocabulary
• *Words to Own,* Worksheet, p. 9

VOCABULARY — HOW TO OWN A WORD

WORD BANK	In Your Own Words
instigates	1. Describe a time when you instigated something.
depreciate	2. What would depreciate the value of a car?
scrutiny	3. What might an airport guard's scrutiny reveal?
coveted	4. Describe something you once coveted.

PEANUTS® reprinted by permission of UFS, Inc.

THE GIFT OF THE MAGI 211

Language Link Quick Check

Decide whether each of the following sentences is true or false.

1. Ornate diction is characteristic of modern fiction. [False]
2. Using ornate diction means selecting the simplest vocabulary possible. [False]
3. Word choice affects the writer's tone. [True]
4. Diction cannot be controlled by the writer. [False]
5. Diction is important only to professional writers. [False]
6. A simple word sometimes works as well as or better than a fancy word. [True]

Resources

Elements of Literature

Irony

For additional instruction on irony, see *Literary Elements*:
• Transparency 4

Elements of Literature

This lesson focuses on the use of irony—verbal, situational, and dramatic—in short stories.

Mini-Lesson:
Irony

After explaining the characteristics of verbal, situational, and dramatic irony to the class, have groups of students generate a list of examples from well-known stories, TV programs, films, or everyday student life. Each group should cover at least two of the types of irony. Have groups reach a consensus about their best examples, and then ask designated recorders to write the following information on blank paper:

• verbal irony: on side one, what was said; on side two, what was meant
• situational irony: on side one, what was expected; on side two, what actually happened
• dramatic irony: on side one, what happened; on side two, what the audience knew beforehand that the character did not know.

Have group presenters show side one of each example, and let other students try to guess what is on side two and which type of irony is involved. Presenters should then show side two to verify the type of irony.

IRONY: Twists and Surprises

Surprise is often an important ingredient in a good story, just as it is in life itself. In our own lives we are forever expecting events to develop in a certain way, only to see them turn out otherwise. The election is won by an underdog. The firehouse goes up in flames. The shortest kid is the best basketball center. This kind of surprise—the difference between what we expect and what actually happens—is **irony**.

Verbal Irony: Meaning Something Else

The simplest kind of irony is **verbal irony**. You use it yourself every day when you say one thing but mean something else. "Nice clean water you've got here," you might say, standing at the edge of a polluted river. Remember General Zaroff, who hunts and kills other humans in "The Most Dangerous Game" (page 13)? He uses verbal irony when he says: "Oh, yes . . . I have electricity. We try to be civilized here." Zaroff, of course, is anything but civilized.

Situational Irony: Reversing Expectations

Situational irony occurs when a situation turns out to be just the opposite of what we expect. We feel this kind of irony, for example, when the police chief's son turns out to be a thief or when the quietest student in the class turns up on a TV talk show.

A famous example of situational irony is found in O. Henry's story "The Gift of the Magi" (page 202). This situational irony is so important to the story's plot that if we described it we'd be giving away the story. You see this kind of irony in movies. You might remember how, in *The Wizard of Oz*, everyone trembles at the thought of the mighty, terrible ruler of Oz. But when we meet "the wizard," he turns out to be a little con man.

Situational irony cuts deeply into our feelings. When irony is put to work in fiction, it is often what touches us most. Irony can move us toward tears or laughter because we sense we are close to the truth of life. A good example of this kind of irony is Somerset Maugham's retelling of the old tale "Appointment in Samarra." Here it is:

Death speaks: There was a merchant in Baghdad who sent his servant to market to buy provisions, and in a little while the servant came back, white and trembling, and said, "Master, just now when I was in the marketplace I was jostled by a woman in the crowd, and when I turned I saw it was Death that jostled me. She looked at me and made a threatening gesture; now, lend me your horse, and I will ride away from this city and avoid my fate. I will go to Samarra, and there Death will not find me." The merchant lent him his horse, and the

---

"How ironic!"

The election is won by an underdog.

The firehouse goes up in flames.

The shortest kid is the best basketball center.

Using Students' Strengths

Kinesthetic Learners

Have interested students write about a brief incident that includes an ironic situation. Then have them rewrite the incident as a skit and act it out for their classmates. Have the audience discuss the irony they find in the skit.

Visual Learners

Have students think of additional examples of situational irony they have encountered in films, in books, or in their own lives. Then ask them to create a cartoon or picture illustrating one of these ironic situations and to prepare a group bulletin-board display.

by John Leggett

servant mounted it, and he dug his spurs in its flanks, and as fast as the horse could gallop he went. Then the merchant went down to the marketplace and he saw me standing in the crowd and he came to me and said, "Why did you make a threatening gesture to my servant when you saw him this morning?" "That was not a threatening gesture," I said. "It was only a start of surprise. I was astonished to see him in Baghdad, for I had an appointment with him tonight in Samarra."

There is a childish, or perhaps cowardly, logic in the belief that we can avoid the consequences of bad news simply by running away from it. This is what the servant believes when he tries to outwit fate by being out of town when Death calls. But a surprise awaits the servant when he reaches Samarra: He thinks that when he gets there he will have escaped Death. Ironically, just the opposite happens. By running to Samarra, he has actually run to meet Death.

"... the good news is that we now have a phone in the car."

Reprinted from The Saturday Evening Post © 1988.

Dramatic Irony: Withholding Knowledge

Irony comes from the Greek word *eirōneia,* which means "a withholding of knowledge." This is the kind of irony that we see most often in plays, films, and TV programs; we call it **dramatic irony**. We sense this kind of irony when we in the audience know something that characters on stage or screen do *not* know. In a stage comedy, for example, *we* know (but the leading man doesn't know) that the young woman he's flirting with is really his male roommate in disguise. In an action movie, *we* know (but the heroine doesn't know) that one of the cables of the elevator she's about to enter has been cut.

Dramatic irony is used in novels and short stories, too. What about Little Red Riding Hood knocking innocently on Grandma's front door? *We* know about the wolf under the bedclothes wearing Grandma's bonnet, but Little Red is unaware of the toothy surprise that awaits her.

ELEMENTS OF LITERATURE: IRONY 213

Applying the Element

All of the stories in this collection feature one or more types of irony. Ask students to make a chart in their journals with rows labeled *Verbal Irony, Situational Irony,* and *Dramatic Irony.* As they read the stories in the collection, they should record examples of each type of irony they encounter. After students finish reading each selection, have them share their notes and discuss each of the examples they recorded.

Resources ———

Assessment
Formal Assessment
• Literary Elements Test, p. 33

Getting Students Involved

Cooperative Learning

Telephone Talk. Point out that in oral language, tone of voice is a key indicator of verbal irony. Allow volunteers to demonstrate by first speaking statements earnestly, then using tone of voice to indicate irony. Then, have students work in pairs to generate a dialogue for a telephone conversation in which at least three examples of verbal irony are present. After finishing their dialogues, partners can enact their dialogues for other pairs in order to see whether the verbal irony was made clear.

OBJECTIVES
1. Read and interpret the story
2. Identify and analyze first-person narration
3. Summarize the main events of the story
4. Express understanding through writing or interviewing

SKILLS
Literary
- Identify and analyze first-person narration

Reading
- Summarize the main events of the story

Writing
- Evaluate a character

Interviewing
- Interview a student from another country or another part of the United States

Planning

- **Traditional Schedule**
Lesson Plans Including Strategies for English-Language Learners
- **One-Stop Planner**
CD-ROM with Test Generator

Before You Read

Make the Connection

An Unexpected Experience

It might be the sight of a winter sky filled with snow. It might be the feel of the tropical sun in December. Whatever the setting, a new climate can bring surprises. "Snow" is narrated by a girl who has just moved to New York City from the Dominican Republic, a small tropical island southeast of Florida.

Quickwrite

Write about some features of your area that might surprise someone from another country who is new to your school. Think about your climate, customs, food, and clothing. If you are from another country yourself, write about some of the things that surprised you in your new setting.

Elements of Literature

A Character as Narrator

A writer may choose to let one of the characters in a story narrate the events. This **narrator** talks to us directly and uses the first-person pronoun *I*. When the narrator of the story is one of its characters, we can share the person's innermost thoughts and feelings. But there are limits to what we know.

The only information we get about the events in the story is what this narrator tells us.

> The **narrator** is the person telling the story. A **first-person narrator** is a character in the story.
>
> *For more on Point of View, see pages 218–219 and the Handbook of Literary Terms.*

Reading Skills and Strategies

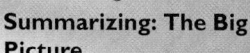

Summarizing: The Big Picture

When you finish a story, you should pause for a few minutes to summarize what happened. You can do this in writing or just in your mind. Sum up who the main characters are and what happens to them. Summarizing helps you to be sure you've gotten all the important details. It also helps you to be sure you understand *why* something happened or what *resulted* from a big event.

Background

The Cuban missile crisis took place in October 1962, when the United States discovered that Soviet missiles had been installed in Cuba, only ninety miles from the U.S. mainland. John F. Kennedy was then president of the United States, and Fidel Castro was prime minister of Cuba. Both Cuba and the Soviet Union had Communist governments, and the missiles were considered a threat to the United States. At times during the crisis, it seemed as if war might break out. Many Americans expected the missiles to be launched against their cities.

go.hrw.com
LE0 9-3

  *Resources: Print and Media*

Reading
- *Graphic Organizers for Active Reading*, p. 12

Elements of Literature
- *Literary Elements*
Transparency 5
Worksheet, p. 16

Writing and Language
- *Daily Oral Grammar*
Transparency 12

Viewing and Representing
- *Viewing and Representing*

Fine Art Transparency 5
Fine Art Worksheet, p.20

Assessment
- *Formal Assessment*, p. 28
- *Portfolio Management System*, p. 111
- *Test Generator (One-Stop Planner CD-ROM)*

Internet
- go.hrw.com (keyword: LE0 9-3)

"Why,
Yolanda dear,
that's snow!"

S☀N☀O☀W

Julia Alvarez

Our first year in New York we rented a small apartment with a Catholic school nearby, taught by the Sisters of Charity, hefty women in long black gowns and bonnets that made them look peculiar, like dolls in mourning. I liked them a lot, especially my grandmotherly fourth-grade teacher, Sister Zoe. I had a lovely name, she said, and she had me teach the whole class how to pronounce it. *Yo-lan-da.* As the only immigrant in my class, I was put in a special seat in the first row by the window, apart from the other children, so that Sister Zoe could tutor me without disturbing

 A

them. Slowly, she enunciated the new words I was to repeat: *laundromat, cornflakes, subway, snow.*

Soon I picked up enough English to understand holocaust[1] was in the air. Sister Zoe explained to a wide-eyed classroom what was happening in Cuba. Russian missiles were being assembled, trained supposedly on New York City. President Kennedy, looking worried too, was on the television at home, explaining we might have to go to war against the Commu-

1. **holocaust** (häl′ə·kôst′): great or total destruction of life.

SNOW **215**

Summary ■

Yolanda, the story's first-person narrator, and her family emigrate from the Dominican Republic to New York City in 1962. During the Cuban missile crisis that fall, the nuns at Yolanda's Catholic school teach the students how to recognize and respond to a nuclear attack. One day in December, looking out the classroom window, Yolanda panics. Having never seen snow before, she thinks that it is radioactive fallout from a nuclear bomb.

Background

Explain that the Cuban missile crisis was one of the major confrontations between the United States and the Soviet Union during the Cold War, which ran from the end of World War II until the collapse of Communism in 1991.

Resources ———

Viewing and Representing
Fine Art Transparency
The fine art transparency of John Sloan's *Backyards, Greenwich Village* will complement students' reading of "Snow."
- Transparency 5
- Worksheet, p. 20

Ⓐ Reading Skills and Strategies
Summarizing
❓ How does Sister Zoe try to make Yolanda feel comfortable in her new school? Summarize the details. [She compliments her name, has Yolanda teach the class how to pronounce her name, places her in a special seat, gives her special tutoring, and helps her learn English.]

Reaching All Students

Struggling Readers
Summarizing was introduced on p. 214. One good strategy to use with summarizing is Most Important Word. This is especially good for summarizing the theme. For information on using this strategy, see p. 45 in the *Reading Strategies Handbook* in front of the *Reading Skills and Strategies* binder.

English Language Learners
After the class has read the selection, encourage students from other countries to share and discuss their own experiences learning the language, adjusting to a new place, and encountering new phenomena. Ask them to compare and contrast their experiences with those of the narrator.
For additional strategies, see
- *Lesson Plans Including Strategies for English-Language Learners*

Advanced Learners
The Cuban missile crisis grew out of antagonism and distrust between the U.S. and the Soviet Union. Have students research the events leading up to the crisis and create a bulletin board with a timeline and copies of historical documents (firsthand accounts and news reports) about the crisis.

A Struggling Readers
Finding Details

Help students make a list of all the nuclear attack-related details in this passage. [Details include air-raid drills, in which a bell would ring, students would file into the hall, fall to the floor, cover their heads, and imagine their hair falling out and their bones going soft; saying a rosary for world peace; and having Sister Zoe explain how an attack would happen.]

B Elements of Literature
Narrator

❓ Why is it significant that the narrator is a child? [A child's grasp of world events is necessarily limited; also, most children are highly impressionable and sensitive to the concerns and fears of the grown-ups around them. Yolanda's innocence is contrasted with the horrible knowledge that war is a possibility.]

C Elements of Literature
Irony

❓ What is ironic about the end of the story? [Possible responses: The irony is that Yolanda expects the "dots" to be nuclear fallout, but they turn out to be harmless crystals of snow; the irony is that to Yolanda, a nuclear attack seems more likely than a snowfall; the irony is that different governments are considering the use of atomic weapons even though such weapons could destroy millions of "beautiful and irreplaceable" human beings.]

Resources

Selection Assessment
Formal Assessment
• Selection Test, p. 28
Test Generator (One-Stop Planner)
• CD-ROM

---

nists. At school, we had air-raid drills: An ominous bell would go off and we'd file into the hall, fall to the floor, cover our heads with our coats, and imagine our hair falling out, the bones in our arms going soft. At home, Mami and my sisters and I said a rosary[2] for world peace. I heard new vocabulary: *nuclear bomb, radioactive fallout, bomb shelter.* Sister Zoe explained how it would happen. She drew a picture of a mushroom on the blackboard and dotted a flurry of chalk marks for the dusty fallout that would kill us all.

The months grew cold, November, December. It was dark when I got up in the morning, frosty when I followed my breath to school.

2. **rosary** (rō'zər·ē): in the Roman Catholic religion, series of prayers counted off on a special set of beads.

One morning, as I sat at my desk daydreaming out the window, I saw dots in the air like the ones Sister Zoe had drawn—random at first, then lots and lots. I shrieked, "Bomb! Bomb!" Sister Zoe jerked around, her full black skirt ballooning as she hurried to my side. A few girls began to cry.

But then Sister Zoe's shocked look faded. "Why, Yolanda dear, that's snow!" She laughed. "Snow."

"Snow," I repeated. I looked out the window warily. All my life I had heard about the white crystals that fell out of American skies in the winter. From my desk I watched the fine powder dust the sidewalk and parked cars below. Each flake was different, Sister Zoe had said, like a person, irreplaceable and beautiful.

MEET THE WRITER
"Listening Closely to Words"

At the age of ten, **Julia Alvarez** (1950–   ) left her home in the Dominican Republic and moved with her family to New York City. The Alvarez children went to Catholic schools and learned English, sometimes with difficulty. "Snow" is from Alvarez's book of fiction called *How the García Girls Lost Their Accents.* The other García girls—besides Yolanda—are Carla, Sandra, and Sofia. Alvarez, who teaches at her alma mater, Middlebury College, in Vermont, has this to say about one of her own teachers:

66 In sixth grade, I had one of the first of a lucky line of great English teachers who began to nurture a love of the language, a love that had been there since a childhood of listening closely to words. Sister Bernadette did not make our class interminably diagram sentences from a workbook or learn a catechism of grammar rules. Instead, she asked us to write little stories imagining we were snowflakes, birds, pianos, a stone in the pavement, a star in the sky. What would it feel like to be a flower with the roots in the ground? If the clouds could talk, what would they say? She had an expressive, dreamy look that was accentuated by her face being framed in a wimple. Supposing, just supposing. My mind would take off, soaring into possibilities, a flower with roots, a star in the sky, a cloud full of sad sad tears, a piano crying out each time its back was tapped, music only to our ears. 99

216 THE SHORT-STORY COLLECTIONS

Crossing the Curriculum

Geography

The Dominican Republic occupies the eastern half of Hispaniola—the second largest island in the West Indies and landing spot of Christopher Columbus in 1492. After students have read the selection, have them work in groups to create a presentation on the country's history, geography, and culture.

Assessing Learning

Check Test: True-False
1. Yolanda likes her teacher. [True]
2. Yolanda can speak English well. [False]
3. Sister Zoe explains that there might be a war. [True]
4. Yolanda has seen snow in her native country. [False]
5. At first, Yolanda thinks the snow is radioactive fallout. [True]

Standardized Test Preparation
For practice in proofreading and editing see
• *Daily Oral Grammar,* Transparency 12

First Thoughts

[visualize]

1. What **images** did you see as you read this story? Describe the image you saw most clearly.

Shaping Interpretations

[infer]

2. Suppose that Sister Zoe was the **narrator** of the story instead of Yolanda. What might she be able to tell you that Yolanda can't?

[compare]

3. Yolanda tells us about two new sets of English words that she learns from Sister Zoe. How do the "war words" differ from the "peacetime words"? How would the "war words" make a child feel?

[infer]

4. As much as anything, this story reveals the **character** of Sister Zoe. What does the last sentence of the story tell you about the way she treats her students?

Extending the Text

[extend]

5. How do you think people today would respond to a crisis like the one in the story? How do you think such situations affect young children?

Reading Check

How would you **summarize** the **main events** in this story for an artist who is going to illustrate it? Be sure the artist understands Yolanda's mix-up and what caused it.

CHOICES: Building Your Portfolio

Writer's Notebook

1. Collecting Ideas for an Essay of Evaluation

Looking at character. When you evaluate almost any story, you'll want to say something about its characters. Take notes on the special character in Yolanda's story, her teacher, Sister Zoe. (You might check your answers to question 4 above.) What do you learn

about Sister Zoe from her actions and from her words to Yolanda? How do you feel about Sister Zoe? Is she a believable character? Is she a good teacher? Save your notes for possible use in the Writer's Workshop on page 250.

Interviewing

2. Cultural Diversity

There may be some students at your school who have

come from other countries or other parts of the United States. Interview one of these students for your school paper. Plan the questions you want to ask. (Use your Quickwrite notes for ideas, if you like.) If you expect to write up your interview in question-and-answer format, you should tape the conversation or take careful notes. (If *you* are the student from another country, you might interview yourself.)

Reading Check

A fourth-grade girl from the Dominican Republic moves to New York City during the Cuban missile crisis. She is so filled with anxiety about nuclear fallout that when she first sees snow, she thinks a bomb has fallen.

First Thoughts

1. Responses will vary. Some students may see images associated with a classroom. Others may see images associated with New York or with cold weather. For many, the clearest image will be the snow.

Shaping Interpretations

2. Possible responses: more about the missile crisis, the humor of Yolanda's misinterpretation of snow, and the concern Sister Zoe has for all of her students.

3. Possible response: Unlike the peacetime words, the war words are scary and overwhelming; they would make most children feel anxious.

4. Sister Zoe treats each student as a unique, beautiful individual, worthy of her attention and respect.

Extending the Text

5. Possible response: People would still have air-raid drills, but the measures to combat fallout might be more advanced. Crisis situations can make young children fearful and uncertain.

Grading Timesaver

Rubrics for each Choices assignment appear on p. 111 in the *Portfolio Management System.*

CHOICES: Building Your Portfolio

1. **Writer's Notebook** Remind students to save their work. They can use it as prewriting for the Writer's Workshop on p. 250.

2. **Interviewing** If it is difficult to find a student subject, students may interview a friend, relative, or community member from another country. You might also suggest finding a peer from another country on the Internet. *You may want to preview any Internet activity that you suggest to students. Because these resources are sometimes public forums, their content can be unpredictable.*

OBJECTIVE
Recognize and distinguish between omniscient, first-person, and third-person limited point of view

Resources

Elements of Literature
Point of View
For additional instruction on point of view, see *Literary Elements*:
• Transparency 5

Elements of Literature
This feature focuses on the three basic points of view used by story writers: omniscient, first-person, and third-person limited.

Mini-Lesson:
Point of View
After reviewing the different points of view, have students write in their own words a definition of each type and the opening sentence of a story for each. Ask questions such as the following ones as you discuss the advantages offered by each type of narration:

• Why might a writer choose the omniscient point of view? [Possible response: It allows the writer to reveal the thoughts, feelings, and actions of all the characters.]

• What are the advantages and disadvantages of the first-person point of view? [Possible responses: The reader experiences the events of a story through the thoughts and the senses of narrator; the reader cannot know what other characters are thinking or feeling.]

POINT OF VIEW: Who's Talking?

Every story has a voice—a **narrator** whose view is the one we share. A writer must decide early on who is going to tell the story. The choice is an important one.

There are three basic points of view available to a writer: **omniscient** (äm·nish'ənt); **first-person;** and **third-person limited**.

The Omniscient Point of View: "All-Knowing"

You are probably most familiar with the omniscient point of view. *Omniscient* means "all-knowing." The all-knowing narrator is not a character in the story and never refers to himself or herself with the first-person pronoun *I*. This omniscient narrator is able to tell us everything about every character (including how each one thinks and feels). Let's look at a story told from the omniscient point of view:

One sunny day, a young woman looked down from her apartment window and saw a young man playing a saxophone. "Cool," she thought as she swayed in time with his tune. Shortly, a large brown dog sauntered up, sat in front of the musician, and howled along with the music.

Then a man in his pajamas yelled from another window. He said that the noise woke him up and he was going to call the police. This man worked the night shift and had to sleep all day and liked cats better than dogs anyway. The young saxophonist left. Soon the young woman appeared in the street and hurried off in the direction taken by the departing horn player. In a year's time, the young woman married the talented saxophonist, he had a hit CD, and they adopted a large brown dog.

The First-Person Point of View: "I" Tells the Story

In the first-person point of view, one of the characters in a story talks to us, using *I*, the first-person pronoun. When a character in the story is the narrator, we can know only what this person sees and hears about events and about other characters. We learn only what "I" chooses—or is able—to tell us. Suppose the saxophonist is

"We can't imagine what a spider thinks, Louisa, because it's a whole different life style."

Drawing by Ziegler; © 1991 The New Yorker Magazine, Inc.

the first-person narrator of the story.

I took the subway to Clancy Street, found a spot in front of Park View Apartments, and started to play my sax. I was hoping to attract an audience and, if I was lucky, earn some money. The morning started out great. This girl opened her window and applauded madly. Later, I had a duet with this big howling dog—what a riot! I had to move on, however, when a guy slammed his window shut and called the police—not a music lover. He said I was disturbing the peace. Give me a break.

Getting Students Involved

Cooperative Learning
Shifting Points of View. Have pairs of students summarize in five to ten sentences the plot of a television episode or movie they have seen recently. They should write from the omniscient point of view, using the textbook example on p. 218 as a model. After an allotted time, have each pair exchange with another pair, and ask students to rewrite the summary they receive from the first-person point of view. Students should then rotate and rewrite summaries one more time, shifting to the third-person limited point of view. Finally, students should return the story summary and the rewrites to the original student pair. Allow students time to read the revisions. Discuss with them the differences between the versions and whether one version seems more effective than another for a particular plot episode, and ask them to express their point-of-view preferences in reading and writing.

by John Leggett

Third-Person Limited: Focus on One Character

The third-person limited point of view means that the story-teller zooms in on just one character. With this point of view, we witness the events of a story just as this one character witnesses them. We share intensely this character's reactions to everything that happens in the story, but what we know about the other characters is limited. Suppose we hear the saxophone story from this point of view, focusing on the man in pajamas.

The man couldn't take any more. It was noon, but he had just fallen asleep, because he had worked the night shift. He had trouble getting to sleep because he was worried—he had just lost his job at the warehouse. And why was he fired? Because he fell asleep on the job. And why had he been so sleepy? Because a barking dog had kept him awake the day before. And here it was again, a barking, howling dog right outside his window! And some beggar playing a horn besides. The man picked up his phone and dialed 911.

Why Is Point of View Important?

The more you think about it, the more you realize what a huge difference point of view makes to a story. When you are reading, ask yourself how the story would differ if someone else were telling it. Whose opinions are being shared? Whose emotions are being expressed? Where do the storyteller's sympathies lie?

While readers are rarely even aware of the techniques of point of view, writers and student writers talk about it constantly, and the best of them are always experimenting with it. In telling the saxophonist's story, they would probably be tempted to let the large brown dog tell it, just to see the difference.

I remember well my sensation as we first entered the house. I knew instantly that something was very wrong. I realized that my father's chair had been sat in, as well as my mother's and my own. The porridge we had left on the table to cool had been partially eaten. None of this, however, prepared me for what we were about to discover upstairs. . . .

ELEMENTS OF LITERATURE: POINT OF VIEW **219**

Applying the Element

Ask students to rewrite a paragraph from "Snow" using a different point of view. Then, ask partners to trade papers and to identify the point of view used. Discuss the following questions with students to help them understand how changing the point of view can give a new slant to a story:

- How does changing the point of view affect the reader's response to the story? [Responses will vary. Students may say that since they no longer share Yolanda's viewpoint, it is more difficult to sense her fears and excitement.]
- How would the story change if it were told by another student in third-person limited point of view? [Responses will vary. Students may say that they would see another child's fears about the possibility of war and that another child might view Yolanda as strange for never having seen snow.]

Resources ━━━━━━

Assessment
Formal Assessment
- Literary Elements Test, p. 35

Using Students' Strengths

Verbal Learners
Choose a familiar children's story, such as "Goldilocks and the Three Bears" or "Jack and the Beanstalk." Have students write a paragraph that summarizes the story from an omniscient point of view. Then, have students retell the story from the first-person point of view, following the example in the textbook. Call on volunteers to read their story versions.

Reaching All Students

Struggling Readers
Use the examples in the textbook lesson to review each type of point of view with students. Then, have student pairs take turns rereading aloud the first several paragraphs from stories in previous collections they are familiar with. After each reading, students should stop and identify the point of view being used.

T219

OBJECTIVES

1. Read and interpret the story
2. Identify and analyze third-person limited point of view
3. Summarize the plot of the story
4. Express understanding through critical and creative writing, debating, or music
5. Correct pronoun problems
6. Understand and use new words
7. Compare synonyms

SKILLS

Literary and Reading
- Analyze point of view
- Summarize a plot

Writing
- Collect ideas for an essay
- Write a story extension
- Analyze points of view

Grammar and Vocabulary
- Correct pronoun problems
- Use new words
- Compare synonyms

Taking a Position/Debating
- Debate an issue generated by the story

Music
- Select music for the story

Viewing/Representing
- Describe a painting's mood (ATE)
- Use fine art to visualize the story's setting (ATE)

Planning

- **Block Schedule**
  Block Scheduling Lesson Plans with Pacing Guide

- **Traditional Schedule**
  Lesson Plans Including Strategies for English-Language Learners

- **One-Stop Planner**
  CD-ROM with Test Generator

Before You Read

THE NECKLACE

Make the Connection

The Grass Is Greener

All of us, at one time or another, have felt that the grass is greener on the other side of the fence—in other words, that someone else's life is better than our own. We believe that having what someone else has will make us happy—until we experience the unexpected results of envy.

Quickwrite

In a few lines, jot down your feelings about this emotion called envy. Have you seen any of its negative effects? Do you know any people who have no envy whatsoever? (Is that possible?)

Elements of Literature

A Limited Point of View

Maupassant was interested in the psychology of his characters, so it's not surprising that he tells this famous story from the limited point of view of Mathilde Loisel. This narrator zooms in at once on Mathilde. We learn in the first seven paragraphs about her past, her dreams, what makes her unhappy, what she envies in other people, what she thinks will make her happy. We follow Mathilde so closely through a crisis in her life that the irony revealed at the story's end hits us almost as powerfully as it strikes the unsuspecting Mathilde.

> **A** third-person **limited** point of view focuses on the thoughts and feelings of a single character in the story.
>
> *For more on Point of View, see pages 218–219 and the Handbook of Literary Terms.*

Reading Skills and Strategies

Summarizing: A Plot Formula

Many short stories and movies have a plot that can be summed up with this formula: **Somebody wants . . . , but . . . , so . . .** The plot begins with **somebody** (the main character) who **wants** something desperately, **but** something or someone stands in the way (the conflict), **so** the character takes steps to overcome the obstacles. Remember that this formula may repeat itself several times in a story until the plot ends. After you finish "The Necklace," see if it fits this formula.

Background

"The Necklace" takes place in Paris in the late 1880s. At that time and in that place, social classes were all-important; people were born into a certain class, and that was usually where they remained. For more information on the kind of world the characters in this story lived in, read "Separate Spheres" on page 223.

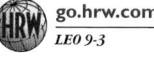

go.hrw.com
LE0 9-3

220 THE SHORT-STORY COLLECTIONS

Preteaching Vocabulary

Words to Own

After students read the definitions, use this exercise. Choose the sentence that correctly uses the word.

1. (a) The boy played his drum **incessantly**.
   (b) The rain fell briefly and then stopped **incessantly**. [a]

2. (a) The pitcher was **disconsolate** after giving up the home run.
   (b) **Disconsolate**, the winner smiled. [a]

3. (a) The **pauper** usually treated his friends.
   (b) Bankruptcy left her a **pauper**. [b]

4. (a) They hoped to withstand the **privations** of a long desert journey.
   (b) Howard was pleased with the holiday **privations**. [a]

5. (a) I refuse to pay the **exorbitant** rates at the new luxury hotel.
   (b) After the race, the runner finally felt **exorbitant**. [a]

T220

THE NECKLACE

Guy de Maupassant

She was one of those pretty and charming girls, born, as if by an accident of fate, into a family of clerks. With no dowry,[1] no prospects, no way of any kind of being met, understood, loved, and married by a man both prosperous and famous, she was finally married to a minor clerk in the Ministry of Education.

She dressed plainly because she could not afford fine clothes, but she was as unhappy as a woman who has come down in the world; for women have no family rank or social class. With them, beauty, grace, and charm take the place of birth and breeding. Their natural poise, their instinctive good taste, and their mental cleverness are the sole guiding principles which make daughters of the common people the equals of ladies in high society.

She grieved incessantly, feeling that she had been born for all the little niceties and luxuries of living. She grieved over the shabbiness of her apartment, the dinginess of the walls, the worn-out appearance of the chairs, the ugliness of the draperies. All these things, which another woman of her class would not even have

She so much longed to please, be envied, be fascinating.

noticed, gnawed at her and made her furious. The sight of the little Breton girl[2] who did her humble housework roused in her disconsolate regrets and wild daydreams. She would dream of silent chambers, draped with Oriental tapestries[3] and lighted by tall bronze floor lamps, and of two handsome butlers in knee breeches, who, drowsy from the heavy warmth cast by the central stove, dozed in large overstuffed armchairs.

She would dream of great reception halls hung with old silks, of fine furniture filled with priceless curios,[4] and of small, stylish, scented sitting rooms just right for the four o'clock chat with intimate friends, with distinguished and sought-after men whose attention every woman envies and longs to attract.

Mathelolie

---

2. **Breton** (bret''n) **girl:** girl from Brittany, a region in northwestern France.
3. **tapestries** (tap'əs·trēz): heavy cloths woven with decorative designs and pictures, used as wall hangings or furniture coverings.
4. **curios** (kyoor'ē·ōz'): unusual items.

WORDS TO OWN

incessantly (in·ses'ənt·lē) adv.: constantly; continually.
disconsolate (dis·kän'sə·lit) adj.: very unhappy.

---

1. **dowry** (dou'rē): property that a woman brings to her husband at marriage.

THE NECKLACE 221

Summary ▪ ▪

This story, told from the third-person limited point of view, begins with Mathilde Loisel's inner conflict. Married to a minor bureaucrat, Loisel is a beautiful woman who despises her life and dreams of wealth and social status. When she gets the chance to attend an elegant reception, she borrows a diamond necklace from a wealthy friend. Mathilde is a sensation at the party but loses the necklace. The Loisels borrow an enormous sum of money to replace it and toil in extreme poverty for ten years to repay the debt. At story's end, Mathilde, haggard and looking old, meets the owner of the necklace by chance and tells her the whole story. The ultimate irony comes when her friend reveals that the original necklace was fake.

Resources ━━━━ 🎧

Listening
Audio CD Library
A recording of "The Necklace" is available as part of the *Audio CD Library*:
• Disc 8, Track 3

FROM THE EDITOR'S DESK
We feel this story's ending truly reflects the collection title, "Expect the Unexpected."

Ⓐ Appreciating Language
Passive Voice
❓ How does the use of passive voice ("of being met," "was . . . married") add to the meaning here? [Possible response: It gives the impression that she has no power or control over her life.]

Resources: Print and Media ━━ 🎧

Reading
• *Reading Skills and Strategies*
   MiniRead Skill Lesson, p. 59
   Selection Skill Lesson, p. 66
• *Graphic Organizers for Active Reading*, p. 13
• *Words to Own*, p. 10
• *Audio CD Library*,
  Disc 8, Track 3

Writing and Language
• *Daily Oral Grammar*
   Transparency 13
• *Grammar and Language Links*,
   Worksheet, p. 21
• *Language Workshop CD-ROM*

Assessment
• *Formal Assessment*, p. 29
• *Portfolio Management System*, p. 112
• *Standardized Test Preparation*, p. 26
• *Test Generator (One-Stop Planner* CD-ROM)

Internet
• go.hrw.com (keyword: LE0 9-3)

A Critical Thinking

Interpreting

? Why would a visit to her friend distress her? [Possible response: because she does not have the life of luxury her friend has, a life she covets and to some extent feels she deserves.]

B Reading Skills and Strategies

Drawing Conclusions

? Why does the invitation upset Mathilde? [Possible response: She does not want to go unless she can impress people.] What does this say about her character and her regard for her husband? [Possible response: She is self-centered and vain and does not seem to care that her husband is trying to please her.]

C Elements of Literature

Third-Person Limited Point of View

? Why might the author step out from Mathilde's limited point of view here? [Possible response: to show the lengths her husband is willing to go to please her, thus shedding light on her spoiled, self-centered nature.]

When dining at the round table, covered for the third day with the same cloth, opposite her husband, who would raise the cover of the soup tureen, declaring delightedly, "Ah! a good stew! There's nothing I like better . . . ," she would dream of fashionable dinner parties, of gleaming silverware, of tapestries making the walls alive with characters out of history and strange birds in a fairyland forest; she would dream of delicious dishes served on wonderful china, of gallant compliments whispered and listened to with a sphinxlike[5] smile as one eats the rosy flesh of a trout or nibbles at the wings of a grouse.

She had no evening clothes, no jewels, nothing. But those were the things she wanted; she felt that was the kind of life for her. She so much longed to please, be envied, be fascinating and sought after.

A She had a well-to-do friend, a classmate of convent-school days whom she would no longer go to see, simply because she would feel so distressed on returning home. And she would weep for days on end from vexation, regret, despair, and anguish.

Then one evening, her husband came home proudly holding out a large envelope.

"Look," he said, "I've got something for you."

She excitedly tore open the envelope and pulled out a printed card bearing these words: "The Minister of Education and Mme. Georges Ramponneau beg M. and Mme. Loisel[6] to do them the honor of attending an evening reception at the Ministerial Mansion on Friday, January 18."

B Instead of being delighted, as her husband had hoped, she scornfully tossed the invitation on the table, murmuring, "What good is that to me?"

"But, my dear, I thought you'd be thrilled to death. You never get a chance to go out, and this is a real affair, a wonderful one! I had an awful time getting a card. Everybody wants one;

---

5. **sphinxlike:** mysterious. The sphinx was a creature in Greek mythology who asked riddles.
6. **Mme. Georges Ramponneau** (mȧ·dȧm′ zhôrzh rȧm′pȯ·nō̂) . . . **M.** (mȯ·syȯr′) . . . **Mme. Loisel** (mȧ·dȧm′ lwä·zel′): M. and Mme. are abbreviations for "Monsieur" and "Madame" and are the French equivalents of Mr. and Mrs.

it's much sought after, and not many clerks have a chance at one. You'll see all the most important people there."

She gave him an irritated glance and burst out impatiently, "What do you think I have to go in?"

He hadn't given that a thought. He stammered, "Why, the dress you wear when we go to the theater. That looks quite nice, I think."

He stopped talking, dazed and distracted to see his wife burst out weeping. Two large tears slowly rolled from the corners of her eyes to the corners of her mouth; he gasped, "Why, what's the matter? What's the trouble?"

By sheer willpower she overcame her outburst and answered in a calm voice while wiping the tears from her wet cheeks, "Oh, nothing. Only I don't have an evening dress and therefore I can't go to that affair. Give the card to some friend at the office whose wife can dress better than I can."

He was stunned. He resumed, "Let's see, Mathilde. How much would a suitable outfit cost—one you could wear for other affairs too—something very simple?"

She thought it over for several seconds, going over her allowance and thinking also of the amount she could ask for without bringing an immediate refusal and an exclamation of dismay from the thrifty clerk.

Finally, she answered hesitatingly, "I'm not sure exactly, but I think with four hundred francs I could manage it."

C He turned a bit pale, for he had set aside just that amount to buy a rifle so that the following summer, he could join some friends who were getting up a group to shoot larks on the plain near Nanterre.[7]

However, he said, "All right. I'll give you four hundred francs. But try to get a nice dress."

As the day of the party approached, Mme. Loisel seemed sad, moody, ill at ease. Her outfit was ready, however. Her husband said to her one evening, "What's the matter? You've been all out of sorts for three days."

---

7. **Nanterre** (nän·ter′): town near Paris.

222 THE SHORT-STORY COLLECTIONS

Reaching All Students

Struggling Readers

Summarizing was introduced on p. 220. For a lesson directly tied to this story that teaches students to summarize by using the Somebody Wanted But So, see the *Reading Skills and Strategies* binder:
- MiniRead Skill Lesson, p. 59
- Selection Skill Lesson, p. 66

English Language Learners

Students may have difficulty with some of Maupassant's complex constructions and descriptive passages. You may wish to place students in mixed-ability pairs for assisted reading. Students can pause to clarify understanding at any time. For additional strategies, see
- *Lesson Plans Including Strategies for English-Language Learners*

Advanced Learners

Students might explore the importance of social class in late nineteenth-century France. Ask students to work with a partner to investigate the class restrictions of the time and to suggest why Mathilde Loisel was unable to marry into a higher class. Students can use their findings to present a panel discussion on the causes and effects of class separation in a society.

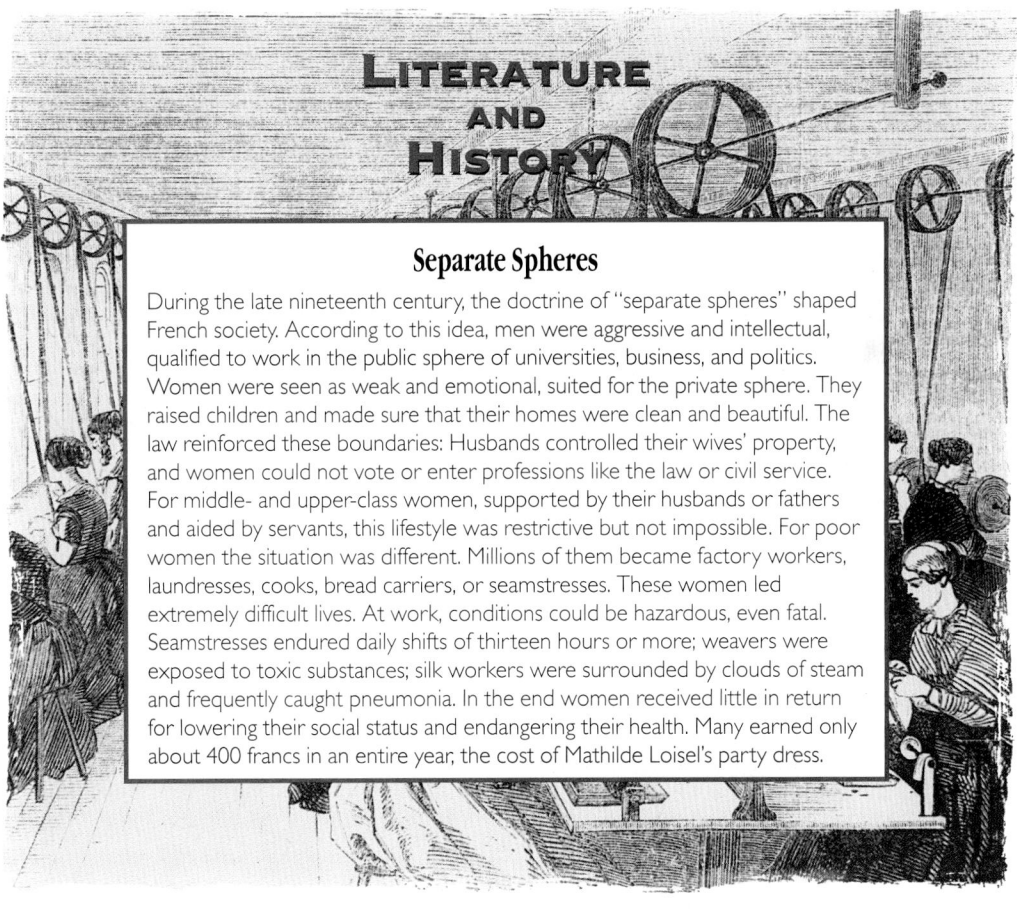

Separate Spheres

During the late nineteenth century, the doctrine of "separate spheres" shaped French society. According to this idea, men were aggressive and intellectual, qualified to work in the public sphere of universities, business, and politics. Women were seen as weak and emotional, suited for the private sphere. They raised children and made sure that their homes were clean and beautiful. The law reinforced these boundaries: Husbands controlled their wives' property, and women could not vote or enter professions like the law or civil service. For middle- and upper-class women, supported by their husbands or fathers and aided by servants, this lifestyle was restrictive but not impossible. For poor women the situation was different. Millions of them became factory workers, laundresses, cooks, bread carriers, or seamstresses. These women led extremely difficult lives. At work, conditions could be hazardous, even fatal. Seamstresses endured daily shifts of thirteen hours or more; weavers were exposed to toxic substances; silk workers were surrounded by clouds of steam and frequently caught pneumonia. In the end women received little in return for lowering their social status and endangering their health. Many earned only about 400 francs in an entire year, the cost of Mathilde Loisel's party dress.

And she answered, "It's embarrassing not to have a jewel or a gem—nothing to wear on my dress. I'll look like a pauper. I'd almost rather not go to the party."

He answered, "Why not wear some flowers? They're very fashionable this season. For ten francs you can get two or three gorgeous roses."

She wasn't at all convinced. "No. . . . There's nothing more humiliating than to look poor among a lot of rich women."

But her husband exclaimed, "My, but you're silly! Go see your friend Mme. Forestier,[8] and ask her to lend you some jewelry. You and she know each other well enough for you to do that."

8. **Forestier** (fô·rəs·tyā′).

She gave a cry of joy. "Why, that's so! I hadn't thought of it."

The next day she paid her friend a visit and told her of her predicament.

Mme. Forestier went toward a large closet with mirrored doors, took out a large jewel box, brought it over, opened it, and said to Mme. Loisel, "Pick something out, my dear."

At first her eyes noted some bracelets, then a pearl necklace, then a Venetian cross, gold and gems, of marvelous workmanship. She tried on these adornments in front of the mirror, but

------

WORDS TO OWN

pauper (pô′pər) n.: very poor person.

THE NECKLACE 223

LITERATURE AND HISTORY

After students have read the story, discuss the roles of women in late nineteenth-century France. Ask students to create a chart like the one below, to compare and contrast those roles with the roles of women in modern U.S. society. Students may use the chart to write an essay.

ROLES OF WOMEN IN SOCIETY	
Nineteenth-Century France	Modern U.S.
1.	1.
2.	2.
3.	3.

D **Elements of Literature**
Character

? What do these comments reveal about Mathilde's character? [She is so vain that she would rather miss a good time than create the wrong impression.]

E **Reading Skills and Strategies**
Summarizing

? How would you use the "Somebody wanted . . . but . . . so . . . " formula to summarize the events so far? [Possible summary: Mathilde Loisel longs to belong to higher society, but she is too poor, so when her husband secures an invitation to a society reception she refuses to go because she doesn't have a suitable dress. To make her happy, he gives her money for a dress, but then she also wants jewelry, so he suggests that she borrow some from a wealthy friend.]

Using Students' Strengths

Interpersonal Learners
Have students work together in small groups to create a story pyramid for this narrative, using the following formula:
1. Name of character
2. Two words describing main character
3. Three words describing setting
4. Four words stating problem
5. Five words describing first event

6. Six words describing second event
7. Seven words describing third event
8. Eight words describing solution
Have students arrange their writing in a pyramid pattern. When cooperative groups have completed their story pyramids, have one group member present the result to the entire class.

Logical Learners
Ask students to brainstorm alternate solutions to Mathilde's conflicts: how she might have originally come to terms with her economic status, how she might better have handled her desire to look pretty at the ball, and how she might have planned her response when the necklace was lost. Students can use these considerations to develop a series of advice-column letters and responses.

RESPONDING TO THE ART

French artist **Jean-Baptiste Camille Corot** (1796–1875) established his reputation as a Neoclassical landscape painter, but he later developed a style that anticipated Impressionism. Corot was particularly interested in capturing the effects of light and in rendering subtle tonal gradations. He is said to have been so generous that he not only allowed younger artists to copy his paintings but also signed some of the copies to make them more valuable.

Activity. Ask students to describe the mood of *Interrupted Reading*. Suggest that they consider the use of light and shadow and speculate about what the young woman might be thinking. Have students ever experienced similar moments of contemplation while reading? Can they describe the sensation?

[Responses will vary. Students might say that the woman looks serious and a little sad. Perhaps, like Mme. Loisel, she is unhappy with her life and tries to escape through reading.]

Interrupted Reading (c. 1870) by Jean-Baptiste Camille Corot (French, 1796–1875). Oil on canvas mounted on board (92.2 cm x 65.1 cm). A detail of this painting appears on page 221.

Taking a Second Look

Review: Oral Interpretation

Review the different ways a reader can convey the meaning of a text through oral interpretation, including varying vocal pitch and tone, facial expressions, body language and posture, and gestures. Then, ask volunteers to read aloud Mme. Loisel's words from this passage (p. 225): "Then she asked, hesitatingly, pleading, 'Could I borrow that, just that and nothing else?'"

Discuss the interpretations. How effectively did the volunteers convey Mme. Loisel's hesitation and pleading?

Activity

Assign each student a section of the story—not more than two or three sentences—for dramatic reading. Any given section may be assigned to two or more students. Then, allow students time to read their sections silently, examining the text for ideas about how it might be spoken and thinking of ways to interpret it effectively. Finally, have students take turns delivering their sections. Remind students that when speaking to any audience, they should make sure to project their voices in order to be heard.

hesitated, unable to decide which to part with and put back. She kept on asking, "Haven't you something else?"

"Oh, yes, keep on looking. I don't know just what you'd like."

All at once she found, in a black satin box, a superb diamond necklace; and her pulse beat faster with longing. Her hands trembled as she took it up. Clasping it around her throat, outside her high-necked dress, she stood in ecstasy looking at her reflection.

Then she asked, hesitatingly, pleading, "Could I borrow that, just that and nothing else?"

"Why, of course."

She threw her arms around her friend, kissed her warmly, and fled with her treasure.

The day of the party arrived. Mme. Loisel was a sensation. She was the prettiest one there, fashionable, gracious, smiling, and wild with joy. All the men turned to look at her, asked who she was, begged to be introduced. All the Cabinet officials wanted to waltz with her. The minister took notice of her.

She danced madly, wildly, drunk with pleasure, giving no thought to anything in the triumph of her beauty, the pride of her success, in a kind of happy cloud composed of all the adulation, of all the admiring glances, of all the awakened longings, of a sense of complete victory that is so sweet to a woman's heart.

She left around four o'clock in the morning. Her husband, since midnight, had been dozing in a small, empty sitting room with three other gentlemen whose wives were having too good a time.

He threw over her shoulders the wraps he had brought for going home, modest garments of everyday life whose shabbiness clashed with the stylishness of her evening clothes. She felt this and longed to escape unseen by the other women, who were draped in expensive furs.

Loisel held her back.

"Hold on! You'll catch cold outside. I'll call a cab."

But she wouldn't listen to him and went rapidly down the stairs. When they were on the street, they didn't find a carriage; and they set out to hunt for one, hailing drivers whom they saw going by at a distance.

They walked toward the Seine,[9] disconsolate and shivering. Finally, on the docks, they found one of those carriages that one sees in Paris only after nightfall, as if they were ashamed to show their drabness during daylight hours.

It dropped them at their door in the Rue des Martyrs,[10] and they climbed wearily up to their apartment. For her, it was all over. For him, there was the thought that he would have to be at the Ministry at ten o'clock.

Before the mirror, she let the wraps fall from her shoulders to see herself once again in all her glory. Suddenly she gave a cry. The necklace was gone.

Her husband, already half undressed, said, "What's the trouble?"

She turned toward him despairingly, "I . . . I . . . I don't have Mme. Forestier's necklace."

"What! You can't mean it! It's impossible!"

They hunted everywhere, through the folds of the dress, through the folds of the coat, in the pockets. They found nothing.

He asked, "Are you sure you had it when leaving the dance?"

"Yes, I felt it when I was in the hall of the Ministry."

"But if you had lost it on the street, we'd have heard it drop. It must be in the cab."

"Yes, quite likely. Did you get its number?"

"No. Didn't you notice it either?"

"No."

They looked at each other aghast. Finally Loisel got dressed again.

"I'll retrace our steps on foot," he said, "to see if I can find it."

And he went out. She remained in her evening clothes, without the strength to go to bed, slumped in a chair in the unheated room, her mind a blank.

Her husband came in around seven o'clock. He had had no luck.

He went to the police station, to the newspapers to post a reward, to the cab companies,

9. **Seine** (sen): river that runs through Paris.
10. **Rue des Martyrs** (rü dā mär·tēr'): street in Paris. The name means "Street of the Martyrs."

A Elements of Literature
Third-Person Limited Point of View
❓ How would the effect of this passage differ if it were told from the first-person point of view by Mme. Loisel? [Sample response: Mme. Loisel would seem to be bragging if she delivered this information herself. Delivered in the third-person point of view, it appears to be an objective observation.]

B Elements of Literature
Plot
❓ What plot complication has arisen? [The Loisels have lost the borrowed necklace.]

C Critical Thinking
Analyzing
❓ Why is Mme. Loisel's mind a blank? [Possible responses: She is so exhausted and worried that she is numb; she can't let herself think about the possibility that they will not recover the necklace.]

Getting Students Involved

Cooperative Learning
Nightly News. Ask students to show their understanding of the plot and setting by generating a human-interest television news feature about the Loisels' plight. Students can watch similar stories on local news programs or national news magazines in order to determine the appropriate tone and style for human-interest journalism.

Have students work in news teams to script and deliver the broadcast. Teams can include a producer, writers, anchors, reporters, and people playing the roles of the Loisels. Teams should deliver their finished "broadcasts" for the class.

Crossing the Curriculum

History/Fashion
Students may criticize the extent of Mme. Loisel's vanity, but many will relate to her desire to appear fashionable and will empathize with her distress at having nothing suitable to wear. Invite students to research clothing styles in vogue in late nineteenth-century France. Students could create a display showing the evolution of styles since that time.

Evaluating

? Is this the best way to deal with the loss of a borrowed item? Explain. [Possible responses: Yes, because it doesn't cause the owner any undue stress or worry; no, it's better to admit the loss and offer to pay for the item.]

B Elements of Literature

Character

? What do Loisel's actions suggest about his character and his love for Mathilde? [Possible response: He has assumed responsibility for his wife's misfortune, so he must love her very much.]

RESPONDING TO THE ART

Sometimes called the father of Impressionism, **Camille Pissaro** (1830–1903) was born in St. Thomas in the Virgin Islands, and moved to France in 1855. His interest in the effects of natural light influenced many of the Impressionists, including Cezanne, Gauguin, and van Gogh. In the late 1880s Pissaro began experimenting with pointillism, in which the paint is applied in small, carefully separated dots, but he later returned to a more Impressionistic approach.

Activity. Explain that Montmartre has long been considered an artists' district. Ask students to describe the atmosphere of this work. [Note the suggestion of lights, crowds, traffic, gaiety.]

---

everywhere the slightest hope drove him.

That evening Loisel returned, pale, his face lined; still he had learned nothing.

A "We'll have to write your friend," he said, "to tell her you have broken the catch and are having it repaired. That will give us a little time to turn around."

She wrote to his dictation.

At the end of a week, they had given up all hope.

And Loisel, looking five years older, declared, "We must take steps to replace that piece of jewelry."

The next day they took the case to the jeweler whose name they found inside. He consulted his records. "I didn't sell that necklace, madame," he said. "I only supplied the case."

Then they went from one jeweler to another hunting for a similar necklace, going over their recollections, both sick with despair and anxiety.

They found, in a shop in Palais Royal,[11] a string of diamonds which seemed exactly like the one they were seeking. It was priced at forty thousand francs. They could get it for thirty-six.

They asked the jeweler to hold it for them for three days. And they reached an agreement that he would take it back for thirty-four thousand if the lost one was found before the end of February.

B Loisel had eighteen thousand francs he had inherited from his father. He would borrow the rest.

He went about raising the money, asking a thousand francs from one, four hundred from another, a hundred here, sixty there. He signed notes, made ruinous deals, did business with loan sharks, ran the whole gamut of money-lenders. He compromised the rest of his life, risked his signature without knowing if he'd be able to honor it, and then, terrified by the outlook of the future, by the blackness of despair about to close around him, by the prospect of all the privations of the body and tortures of the spirit, he went to claim the new necklace with

11. **Palais Royal** (pá·lā′ rwä·yàl′): fashionable shopping district in Paris.

The Boulevard Montmartre at Night (1897) by Camille Pissarro. Oil on canvas (53.3 cm x 64.8 cm).

the thirty-six thousand francs, which he placed on the counter of the shopkeeper.

When Mme. Loisel took the necklace back, Mme. Forestier said to her frostily, "You should have brought it back sooner; I might have needed it."

WORDS TO OWN

privations (prī·vā′shənz) n.: hardships; lack of the things needed for a happy, healthy life.

Skill Link

Apostrophes

You might want to use the following exercise before you teach the Grammar Link exercise on pronoun problems on p. 231. This exercise will help you assess students' skill with apostrophes. Review the following points with students:

• Apostrophes are used to indicate the omitted letters in a contraction—a shortened combination of two words.

I'll (I will)   you're (you are)
she's (she is)   wouldn't (would not)

• Apostrophes are used to indicate possession.
Mathilde's necklace   Loisel's earnings

• Apostrophes are not used with possessive personal pronouns.
Whose necklace is this? The bracelet is yours.

Activity

Write C if the sentence is correct. If not, correct the sentence by adding or deleting apostrophes.

1. Mme. Forestier is a close friend of our's. [ours]
2. She's very upset over her friend's loss. [C]
3. Theyre going to work for many years to pay off the loan. [They're]
4. M. Loisel has no desire to attend any reception of theirs. [C]
5. Well be needing financial aid. [We'll]

For a review of apostrophes, see p. 1029 in the Language Handbook.

She didn't open the case, an action her friend was afraid of. If she had noticed the substitution, what would she have thought? What would she have said? Would she have thought her a thief?

Mme. Loisel experienced the horrible life the needy live. She played her part, however, with sudden heroism. That frightful debt had to be paid. She would pay it. She dismissed her maid; they rented a garret under the eaves.[12]

She learned to do the heavy housework, to

12. **garret under the eaves:** attic under the overhanging lower edges of a roof.

---

perform the hateful duties of cooking. She washed dishes, wearing down her shell-pink nails scouring the grease from pots and pans; she scrubbed dirty linen, shirts, and cleaning rags, which she hung on a line to dry; she took the garbage down to the street each morning, and brought up water, stopping on each landing to get her breath. And, clad like a peasant woman, basket on arm, guarding sou[13] by sou her scanty allowance, she bargained with the fruit dealers, the grocer, the butcher, and was insulted by them.

Each month notes had to be paid, and others renewed to give more time.

Her husband labored evenings to balance a tradesman's accounts, and at night, often, he copied documents at five sous a page.

And this went on for ten years.

Finally, all was paid back, everything including the <u>exorbitant</u> rates of the loan sharks and accumulated compound interest.

Mme. Loisel appeared an old woman now. She became heavy, rough, harsh, like one of the poor. Her hair untended, her skirts askew, her hands red, her voice shrill, she even slopped water on her floors and scrubbed them herself. But, sometimes, while her husband was at work, she would sit near the window and think of that long-ago evening when, at the dance, she had been so beautiful and admired.

What would have happened if she had not lost that necklace? Who knows? Who can say? How strange and unpredictable life is! How little there is between happiness and misery!

Then, one Sunday, when she had gone for a walk on the Champs Élysées[14] to relax a bit from the week's labors, she suddenly noticed a woman strolling with a child. It was Mme. Forestier, still young looking, still beautiful, still charming.

13. **sou** (sōō): old French coin of little value.
14. **Champs Élysées** (shän zā·lē·zā′): famous avenue in Paris.

WORDS TO OWN

exorbitant (eg·zôr′bi·tənt) *adj.:* much too high in price or amount.

C **Elements of Literature**
Irony
? What is ironic about Mathilde's position now and the way she got there? [Possible response: Ironically, her love of finery and the good life has led her to a life in which she is deprived of everything nice.]

D **Reading Skills and Strategies**
Summarizing
? What have the past ten years been like for the Loisels? Use the "Somebody wanted . . . but . . . so" formula to explain. [Possible summary: The Loisels wanted to replace the necklace that had been lost, so they borrowed vast sums of money in order to replace it and sank into a life of poverty.]

E **Elements of Literature**
Third-Person Limited Point of View
? How might this description of Mme. Loisel be different if it were narrated by her in the first person? [Possible responses: She might downplay the loss of her looks; she might be full of self-pity.]

F **Critical Thinking**
Extending the Text
? Can one incident really change the course of a person's life? [Possible responses: Yes, an accident or a hasty decision can ruin a person's life; no, it's not the incident but the way a person responds to it that determines the consequences.]

Assessing Learning

A Critical Thinking

Evaluating

❓ Does this meeting seem contrived? Explain. [Possible responses: Yes, it's artificial that only now, with the debt paid off after ten years, does Mme. Loisel run into her friend; no, their different financial positions would make them unlikely to meet.]

B Elements of Literature

Irony

Help students see the different levels of irony contained in this ending. One is the realization that the necklace the Loisels worked so hard to replace was a fake. Another is that Mathilde, who yearned to be a woman of wealth, was ruined by the loss of fake diamonds. A third is the ironic parallel being drawn between the fake necklace and Mathilde, who was a social fake.

BROWSING IN THE FILES

About the Author. De Maupassant developed the habit of writing to fill the page, regardless of whether he felt he was doing quality work. No matter how hurriedly he composed his prose, Maupassant believed, his literary voice would somehow ring true to and be understood by the reader.

Resources

Selection Assessment
Formal Assessment
• Selection Test, p. 29
Test Generator (One-Stop Planner)
• CD-ROM

A Mme. Loisel felt a rush of emotion. Should she speak to her? Of course. And now that everything was paid off, she would tell her the whole story. Why not?

She went toward her. "Hello, Jeanne."

The other, not recognizing her, showed astonishment at being spoken to so familiarly by this common person. She stammered, "But . . . madame . . . I don't recognize . . . You must be mistaken."

"No, I'm Mathilde Loisel."

Her friend gave a cry, "Oh, my poor Mathilde, how you've changed!"

"Yes, I've had a hard time since last seeing you. And plenty of misfortunes—and all on account of you!"

"Of me . . . How do you mean?"

"Do you remember that diamond necklace you loaned me to wear to the dance at the Ministry?"

"Yes, but what about it?"

"Well, I lost it."

"You lost it! But you returned it."

"I brought you another just like it. And we've been paying for it for ten years now. You can imagine that wasn't easy for us who had nothing. Well, it's over now, and I am glad of it."

Mme. Forestier stopped short. "You mean to say you bought a diamond necklace to replace mine?"

"Yes. You never noticed, then? They were quite alike."

And she smiled with proud and simple joy.

Mme. Forestier, quite overcome, clasped her **B** by the hands. "Oh, my poor Mathilde. But mine was fake. Why, at most it was worth only five hundred francs!"

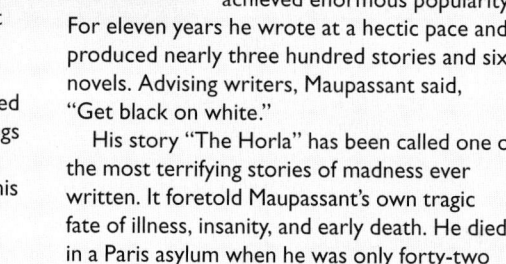

MEET THE WRITER

Hectic Pace

One of the world's greatest short-story writers, **Guy de Maupassant** (gē də mō·pä·sän′) (1850–1893) was born in Normandy, the French province that is the setting for much of his fiction. After his parents separated, Maupassant was raised by his mother, who was a close friend of the great novelist Gustave Flaubert.

Flaubert set out to instruct the young Maupassant in the art of fiction. He explained that good writing depends upon seeing things anew, rather than recording what people before us have thought. Flaubert also gave his student this advice:

❝Whatever you want to say, there is only one word to express it, only one verb to give it movement, only one adjective to qualify it. ❞

For years Maupassant sent Flaubert his writing exercises every week, and then they met to discuss his work over lunch. With the success of his story "Ball of Fat," Maupassant, now aged thirty, quit his job as a clerk with the Naval Ministry and began to put great energy into writing. He quickly achieved enormous popularity. For eleven years he wrote at a hectic pace and produced nearly three hundred stories and six novels. Advising writers, Maupassant said, "Get black on white."

His story "The Horla" has been called one of the most terrifying stories of madness ever written. It foretold Maupassant's own tragic fate of illness, insanity, and early death. He died in a Paris asylum when he was only forty-two years old.

Assessing Learning

Check Test: True-False

1. Mathilde marries into a wealthy family. [False]
2. Until she is invited to the reception, Mathilde is quite satisfied with her position in life. [False]
3. Mathilde borrows a necklace from her friend Mme. Forestier. [True]

4. The Loisels find a replacement necklace for thirty-six thousand francs. [True]
5. The Loisels scrimp for ten years to pay the debts created by the loss of the necklace. [True]
6. Mme. Forestier tells Mathilde the necklace she borrowed years ago was an inexpensive fake. [True]

Standardized Test Preparation

For practice with standardized test format specific to this selection, see
• *Standardized Test Preparation*, p. 26
For practice in proofreading and editing, see
• *Daily Oral Grammar*, Transparency 13

MAKING MEANINGS

MAKING MEANINGS

First Thoughts

[respond]

1. Describe how you felt about Mathilde at the beginning of the story, and how you felt about her by the time the story ended.

> **Reading Check**
>
> Summarize the plot, using the **somebody wants . . . , but . . . , so . . .** formula. (Be sure to compare your summaries in class.)

Shaping Interpretations

[analyze]

2. When Mme. Forestier reveals that the necklace was a fake, the reader feels the force of the **irony**. Explain why her revelation is ironic. How did you respond to this surprise twist in the story?

[infer]

3. What do you think about Mathilde's husband? Consider the things you know about him:

   - his loyalty to Mathilde
   - the way he indulges her
   - his years of sacrifice and hard work
   - his plans to buy something for himself

[interpret]

4. Do you think this story is critical of Mathilde only, or do you think the writer is criticizing the values of a whole society? Tell why you think as you do.

[compare and contrast]

5. Think about the characters and circumstances of two women—Mathilde in "The Necklace" and Della in "The Gift of the Magi" (page 202). Use a diagram like the one at the right to see how the women are alike and how they're different.

   omit

   Mathilde (Both) Della

Connecting with the Text

[connect]

6. Look back at your Quickwrite about envy. Does this story remind you of any experience in your life or in the lives of your friends? Explain.

   omit

Extending the Text

[extend]

7. Could a young woman today be unhappy with her "class," as Mathilde was? What choices do women have today that can help them change their lives?

Challenging the Text

[evaluate]

8. Did you find Maupassant's **plot** believable and the motives of his **characters** convincing? Use specific incidents from the story to support your evaluations.

Reading Check

Summaries will vary.

Mme. Loisel (somebody) desperately (wants) to achieve the lifestyle of the upper class, (but) her relative poverty stands in her way. (So) when she receives an invitation to an elegant reception, she borrows a necklace from a friend in order to appear of higher social standing. After the party, she realizes the necklace is lost. She (somebody) doesn't (want) her friend to learn about the loss, (but) she can't afford to pay for a replacement. (So) she and her husband borrow the money and work for ten years to pay off the loans. Years later, when Mme. Loisel again encounters her friend, she learns that the necklace she worked so hard to replace was merely a fake.

MAKING MEANINGS

First Thoughts

1. Possible responses: Mathilde is self-centered and vain at the beginning, but by the end, she is pitiable because her own pride and envy have destroyed her; hardship causes Mathilde to mature from a selfish, dissatisfied girl into a heroic, justifiably proud woman.

Shaping Interpretations

2. It is ironic because Mathilde and her husband have suffered for ten years to replace a fake necklace with a real one. The ending is overwhelmingly sad; or, the ending seems unbelievable.

3. Possible responses: Mathilde's husband is admirable because he sacrifices his own life for her carelessness; he is foolish because he is the one who made the decision not to tell Mme. Forestier the truth.

4. Possible responses: It is critical of Mathilde only, because if she hadn't been so vain she wouldn't have borrowed the necklace; it is critical of both Mathilde and society because she was a product of a society that measured human worth in terms of wealth.

5. Possible responses: similarities—both dreamers, both lack social standing and wealth, both long for beautiful things; differences— Della is generous and Mathilde is selfish, Della makes the most of what she has while Mathilde is never satisfied, Della sacrifices her appearance for love while Mathilde sacrifices ten years for appearances.

Connecting with the Text

6. Responses will vary. Students should choose an experience that they would not mind sharing with others.

Extending the Text

7. Possible response: Women do have more choices now, but lack of money and education can make it difficult for them to realize their dreams.

Challenging the Text

8. Possible responses: It's hard to believe the punishing workload the Loisels endure to work off their debt; envy is a universal emotion, and chance encounters do occur.

Grading Timesaver

Rubrics for each Choices assignment appear on p. 112 in the *Portfolio Management System.*

CHOICES: Building Your Portfolio

1. **Writer's Notebook** Remind students to save their work. They can use it as prewriting for the Writer's Workshop on p. 250.
2. **Creative Writing** To help students respond to the questions presented here, have them create a chart with two columns. Ask students to write the questions in the first column and their ideas in the second column. They may use these prewriting responses and ideas to create their story extensions.
3. **Analyzing Points of View** Have students reread the story, thinking about how context, diction, and sentence structure, as well as pronouns, would change in first-person point of view.
4. **Taking a Position/Debating** Debate teams may anticipate what their opponents will ask by assigning a member to role-play a member of the other team and to pose questions the other team might ask. To illustrate their positions, students may wish to make electronic presentations, using software to import text, graphics, and video clips.
5. **Music** As students prepare for their presentations, they may work with partners to combine and compare their musical selections. Consider providing a listening station with a cassette player and headphones where students working together can reach consensus.

CHOICES: Building Your Portfolio

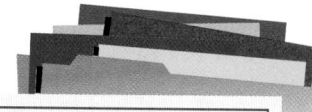

Writer's Notebook

1. Collecting Ideas for an Essay of Evaluation

Are they believable?  You might have listed "believable characters" in your cluster diagram (see page 201). With a partner or a group, brainstorm all the things that you think make a character in a story seem alive. Try to come up with examples (perhaps from stories in this book) of believable characters and of characters who are not at all convincing. As you brainstorm, you might focus on Mathilde in "The Necklace." Save your notes for possible use in the Writer's Workshop on page 250.

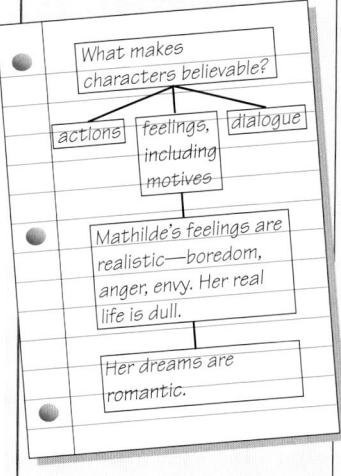

What makes characters believable?
— actions
— feelings, including motives
— dialogue

Mathilde's feelings are realistic—boredom, anger, envy. Her real life is dull.

Her dreams are romantic.

Creative Writing

2. Extending the Story

Write a paragraph telling what might happen after Mme. Forestier reveals that the necklace was a fake. Does she return the difference in value between the original necklace and the one she received as a replacement? Do the Loisels now begin to lead a different kind of life? Is it too late for Mathilde to recapture the past—her beauty and social triumph? Has she learned something during those ten years that makes her unwilling to try?

Analyzing Points of View

3. Another Point of View

Think about this story's **point of view** as if you were Maupassant trying to decide how to tell your story. Write a paragraph telling how the story would change if it were told in the first person by

a. Mathilde's husband

b. Mathilde herself

Be specific. Cite at least two ways in which the story or its effect would differ if a different person told it.

Taking a Position/Debating

4. What's the Difference?

Do you think Mme. Forestier should return the difference in value between the original necklace and the one she received as a replacement? Take one side of this question and write a position statement for or against a payment to the Loisels. Form a debating team and work together to prepare your arguments. Focus on the reasons for your position and try to anticipate what the other team will say. Be ready for them.

Music

5. Mood Music

Suppose you were to make a short film of "The Necklace" and wanted to add songs to the soundtrack as a way of expressing Mathilde's feelings. Select the songs you would use at these three moments: Mathilde at home before learning of the invitation; Mathilde at the party; Mathilde on the Champs Élysées ten years later. Play recordings of the songs you choose, or read the lyrics to the class.

230 THE SHORT-STORY COLLECTIONS

Using Students' Strengths

Auditory Learners

For Choice 3, students may retell the story to a partner. As partners listen, ask them to determine what changes take place in the telling and how the different points of view provide varying insights into the story's plot or the characters' motives.

GRAMMAR LINK · MINI-LESSON

Language Handbook HELP

See Glossary of Usage, page 1035.

Technology HELP

See Language Workshop CD-ROM. *Key word entry:* homonyms.

Words Often Confused

• its, it's
• their, they're
• whose, who's
• your, you're

Pronoun Problems

Some pronouns in English sound exactly like other words: *its* and *it's; their* and *they're; whose* and *who's; your* and *you're.* Words that sound alike are no problem when you are speaking, but they can be troublesome when you are writing. To avoid trouble, you must be aware of the difference between a possessive pronoun and a pronoun contraction.

• A possessive pronoun (such as *its, their, whose, your*) shows ownership or relationship.

• A pronoun contraction (such as *it's, they're, who's,* and *you're*) is a shortened form of a pronoun and another word (*it is, they are, who is,* and *you are*). **A pronoun contraction always has an apostrophe.**

Try It Out

➤ Choose the correct word from the pair in parentheses.

1. "But her husband exclaimed, 'My, but (your, you're) silly!' "

2. " 'Everybody wants one; (its, it's) much sought after, and not many clerks have a chance at one.' "

3. "It dropped them at (their, they're) door in the Rue des Martyrs, and they climbed wearily up to (their, they're) apartment."

4. "The next day they took the case to the jeweler (whose, who's) name they found inside."

➤ Check the pronouns in your writing. Any problems? Highlight any pronoun contractions and then substitute the words they stand for. Do the substitutions make sense? Have you used a possessive where a contraction should be used? Have you spelled a possessive pronoun with an apostrophe?

VOCABULARY · HOW TO OWN A WORD

WORD BANK

incessantly
disconsolate
pauper
privations
exorbitant

Scaling Synonyms

You can reinforce your ownership of a word by comparing the word with other words with similar meanings. One way to compare words is to arrange them on a scale from high to low intensity.

Work with a partner to make an intensity scale for the other four words in the Word Bank. Add at least two words that are synonyms but show an increase or decrease in intensity. Be sure to compare and defend your "intensity scales" in class.

High Intensity	Medium Intensity	Low Intensity
incessantly	constantly	always

THE NECKLACE 231

GRAMMAR LINK

To help students develop pronoun usage skills, ask them to choose any full page of their own writing from their portfolio. Have them form groups and exchange papers. Then, have students circle any words containing apostrophes. Ask them to exchange again within the group and to underline any other pronouns they find. Finally, let students look at their own marked papers to verify their use of pronoun contractions and possessive pronouns.

Try It Out
Answers

1. you're
2. it's
3. their, their
4. whose

VOCABULARY
Possible Answers

High Intensity	Medium Intensity	Low Intensity
disconsolate	saddened	unhappy
pauper	needy	underprivileged person
privations	hardships	shortages
exorbitant	excessive	costly

Resources ——

Grammar
• *Grammar and Language Links* Worksheet, p. 21

Vocabulary
• *Words to Own,* Worksheet, p. 10

Grammar Link Quick Check

For each of the following sentences, write *C* if the pronoun or contraction is correct. Write *I* if it is incorrect.

1. Their going to an evening reception at a fine mansion. [I]

2. Your necklace will be returned next week. [C]

3. Whose going to pay off the loan that we made? [I]

4. We will be arriving before it's time to start dancing. [C]

5. We knew they're mansion was located by the river. [I]

OBJECTIVES

1. Read and interpret the story
2. Evaluate the narrator's reliability
3. Draw conclusions
4. Express understanding through critical and creative writing, critical thinking/role-playing, or drawing
5. Identify and use dialogue conventions
6. Understand and use new words
7. Construct word maps

SKILLS

Literary
• Evaluate the narrator's reliability

Reading
• Draw conclusions

Writing
• Collect ideas for an essay
• Rewrite part of the story

Grammar
• Use dialogue conventions

Vocabulary
• Use new words
• Construct word maps

Explaining a Theory
• Report on a motive for murder

Critical Thinking/Role-Playing
• Write and role-play a courtroom scene

Drawing
• Draw a set design

Planning

• **Block Schedule**
  Block Scheduling Lesson Plans with Pacing Guide

• **Traditional Schedule**
  Lesson Plans Including Strategies for English-Language Learners

• **One-Stop Planner**
  CD-ROM with Test Generator

Before You Read

THE CASK OF AMONTILLADO

Make the Connection

Revenge—Its Grisly Effects

During his brief and tormented life, Edgar Allan Poe searched in vain for love and acceptance. Perhaps to get even with a world that he thought rejected him, Poe became a master at writing stories of revenge. Think about the idea of revenge. What experiences could lead someone to seek revenge? How could an obsession with vengeance lead to tragedy?

Quickwrite

Brainstorm to share your ideas about these questions on revenge. Record your responses. Include any movies, TV programs, and stories that are built around this idea of the avenger.

Elements of Literature

Is the Narrator Reliable?

One of the first questions we ask on reading a story is: Who's telling me this story? or Who's speaking? Poe's story is told by a man who reveals who he is and what he is up to as he and a friend wind through an underground passageway. Over the years since Poe wrote this now-famous story, people have asked: Is the narrator reliable? Is he telling the truth? Are we

being deceived by a liar—or a madman?

An **unreliable narrator** is someone who is not always perceptive about what's going on in a story, or someone who is deliberately not telling the whole truth.
For more on Point of View, see pages 218–219 and the Handbook of Literary Terms.

Reading Skills and Strategies

Drawing Conclusions: Playing Detective

When you read, you're like a detective. You gather evidence from the story and you make all kinds of **conclusions,** or judgments, based on the evidence. Suppose you want to decide if the narrator of Poe's story is unreliable. Look closely at all the narrator *says* and *does.* Then, examine what his enemy Fortunato *says.* Look carefully. What details could support a charge of unreliability—even insanity? You might take notes as you read.

go.hrw.com
LE0 9-3

Background

Centuries ago, in Italy, the early Christians buried their dead in catacombs, which are long, winding underground tunnels. Later, wealthy families built private catacombs beneath their homes. Dark and cool, these chambers were suitable not only for burial but also for the storage of fine wine such as, in this story, amontillado (ə·män′tə·lä′dō). Poe's story happens during carnival, a celebration that still takes place in many countries, including parts of the United States. Carnival is celebrated in February or March, before Ash Wednesday and the start of Lent, the season of penitence. During carnival people wear masks and costumes. They dance and drink on the streets before giving up meat and other pleasures to do penance for their sins.

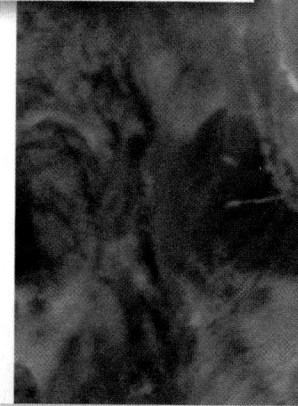

Preteaching Vocabulary

Words to Own
Use this exercise to build understanding. Answer *Yes* or *No* for each question.

1. If you lose your passport, is a trip to Japan **precluded**? [Yes]
2. Should bank robbers be allowed to work with **impunity**? [No]
3. Do you expect **retribution** if you never do your homework? [Yes]
4. Could an earthquake cause the **immolation** of an entire city? [Yes]
5. Would **connoisseurship** of horses help someone recognize a thoroughbred? [Yes]
6. If a guest were to **impose upon** you, would you invite that person again? [No]
7. If a cobra were attacking, would you be **recoiling**? [Yes]
8. If you **endeavored** to do something, did you give up before you started? [No]
9. Is an **obstinate** mule easily moved? [No]
10. Would a **succession** of lost elections please a politician? [No]

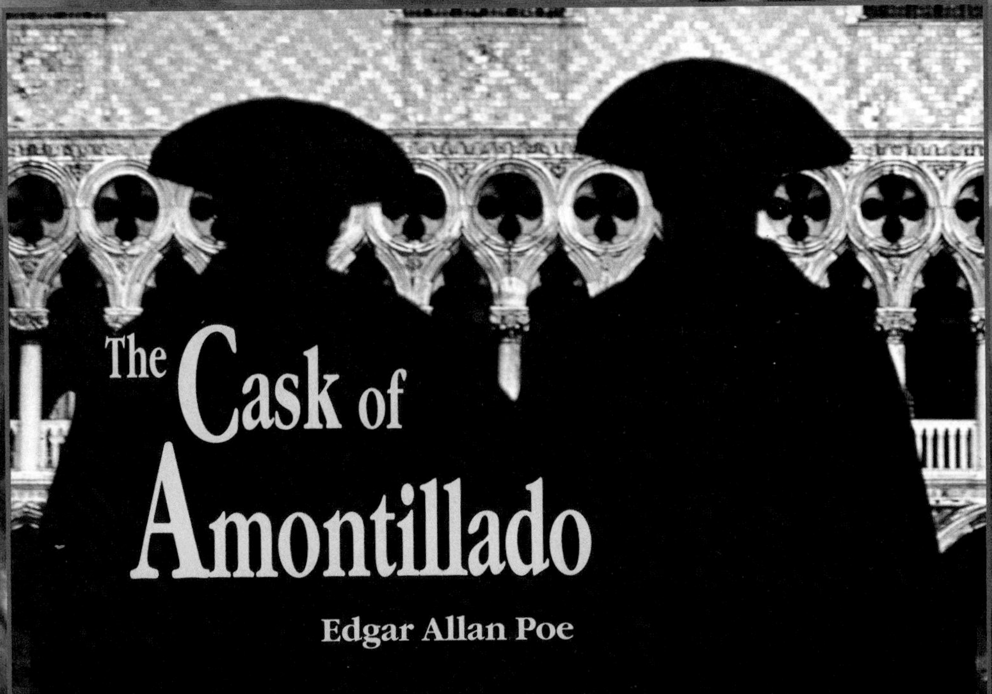

The Cask of Amontillado

Edgar Allan Poe

The thousand injuries of Fortunato I had borne as best I could; but when he ventured upon insult, I vowed revenge. You, who so well know the nature of my soul, will not suppose, however, that I gave utterance to a threat. At length I would be avenged; this was a point definitively settled—but the very definitiveness with which it was resolved precluded the idea of risk. I must not only punish, but punish with impunity. A wrong is unredressed when retribution overtakes its redresser. It is equally unredressed when the avenger fails to make himself felt as such to him who has done the wrong.

WORDS TO OWN
precluded (prē·klood′id) v.: made impossible in advance; prevented.
impunity (im·pyoo′ni·tē) n.: freedom from punishment.
retribution (re′trə·byoo′shən) n.: punishment.

It was about dusk, one evening during the supreme madness of the carnival season.

THE CASK OF AMONTILLADO **233**

Summary ■■■

Montresor, the Italian nobleman who recounts this classic tale of horror, has vowed revenge on Fortunato, who, he claims, has injured and insulted him. Meeting Fortunato during the winter carnival, Montresor hails him with great friendliness and lures him home to taste a cask of amontillado wine that is kept in an underground vault. Once Fortunato is underground, Montresor chains him up and buries him alive. Fifty years later, the crime remains undiscovered. Is Montresor to be believed, or is he an unreliable narrator? Is he lying—or simply mad?

Resources

Viewing and Representing
Videocassette A, Segment 3
Explore the setting of Poe's work with this *Visual Connections* segment.

Listening
Audio CD Library
A recording of "The Cask of Amontillado" is available as part of the *Audio CD Library*:
• Disc 9, Track 2

Elements of Literature
Irony
For additional instruction on identifying irony, see *Literary Elements* booklet:
• Transparency 4
• Worksheet, p. 13

Resources: Print and Media

Reading
• *Reading Skills and Strategies:*
  MiniRead Skill Lesson, p. 70
  Selection Skill Lesson, p. 76
• *Graphic Organizers for Active Reading*, p. 14
• *Words to Own*, p. 11
• *Audio CD Library*, Disc 9, Track 2

Elements of Literature
• *Literary Elements*
  Transparency 4
  Worksheet, p. 13

Writing and Language
• *Daily Oral Grammar*
  Transparency 14
• *Grammar and Language Link*
  Worksheet, p. 23
• *Language Workshop CD-ROM*

Viewing and Representing
• *Visual Connections*
  Videocassette A, Segment 3

Assessment
• *Formal Assessment*, p. 31
• *Portfolio Management System*, p. 114
• *Standardized Test Preparation*, pp. 28, 30
• *Test Generator (One-Stop Planner CD-ROM)*

Internet
• go.hrw.com (keyword: LE0 9-3)

T233

A Elements of Literature
Unreliable Narrator

? What hints do you already have that the narrator may be unreliable? Is this how a normal person would behave in the face of insult? [Possible response: No, most people would confront the insulter and demand an apology. Since the narrator doesn't say what the insult is, readers can't really tell if he is overreacting, but it seems likely that he is.]

B Reading Skills and Strategies

Drawing Conclusions

? Why is the narrator glad to see Fortunato? [Possible response: It gives him an opportunity to exact his revenge.] Is it normal to act pleased and friendly toward someone you hate? [Possible response: No, it shows that the narrator is unbalanced.]

C Cultural Connections

Fortunato's comment notwithstanding, amontillado is in fact a type of sherry. Sherry is a fortified wine originally made in the Andalusia region of Spain. Amontillado is classed as a medium sherry, which means it has been aged.

A It must be understood that neither by word nor deed had I given Fortunato cause to doubt my goodwill. I continued, as was my wont, to smile in his face, and he did not perceive that my smile *now* was at the thought of his immolation.

He had a weak point—this Fortunato—although in other regards he was a man to be respected and even feared. He prided himself on his connoisseurship in wine. Few Italians have the true virtuoso spirit. For the most part their enthusiasm is adopted to suit the time and opportunity—to practice imposture upon the British and Austrian millionaires. In painting and gemmary, Fortunato, like his countrymen, was a quack—but in the matter of old wines he was sincere. In this respect I did not differ from him materially: I was skillful in the Italian vintages myself and bought largely whenever I could.

It was about dusk, one evening during the supreme madness of the carnival season, that I encountered my friend. He accosted me with excessive warmth, for he had been drinking much. The man wore motley.[1] He had on a tight-fitting parti-striped dress, and his head **B** was surmounted by the conical cap and bells. I was so pleased to see him that I thought I should never have done wringing his hand.

I said to him, "My dear Fortunato, you are luckily met. How remarkably well you are looking today! But I have received a pipe[2] of what passes for amontillado, and I have my doubts."

"How?" said he. "Amontillado? A pipe? Impossible! And in the middle of the carnival!"

"I have my doubts," I replied; "and I was silly enough to pay the full amontillado price without consulting you in the matter. You were not to be found, and I was fearful of losing a bargain."

"Amontillado!"

"I have my doubts."

"Amontillado!"

"And I must satisfy them."

"Amontillado!"

"As you are engaged, I am on my way to Luchesi. If anyone has a critical turn, it is he. He will tell me——"

C "Luchesi cannot tell amontillado from sherry."

"And yet some fools will have it that his taste is a match for your own."

"Come, let us go."

"Whither?"

"To your vaults."[3]

---

1. **motley** (mät′lē): multicolored costume worn by a clown or jester.
2. **pipe:** barrel.
3. **vaults** (vôlts): storage cellars.

WORDS TO OWN
immolation (im′ə·lā′shən) *n.*: destruction.
connoisseurship (kän′ə·sur′ship) *n.*: expert knowledge.

Reaching All Students

Struggling Readers
Drawing Conclusions was introduced on p. 232. For a lesson directly tied to this story that teaches students to draw conclusions by using a strategy called Save the Last Word for Me, see the *Reading Skills and Strategies* binder:
• MiniRead Skill Lesson, p. 70
• Selection Skill Lesson, p. 76

English Language Learners
So that all students share in the reading of the story, have them use Echo Reading. Pair students with different levels of proficiency. The more proficient reader should read aloud while the other student follows along, echoing what the first reader says.
For additional strategies, see
• *Lesson Plans Including Strategies for English-Language Learners*

Advanced Learners
Elicit examples of horror stories and novels students have read (such as the works of Stephen King or H. P. Lovecraft), and horror films they have seen. Have students discuss these works and try to reach a consensus on the characteristics of effective horror literature or film. As they read, students can consider which of these characteristics Poe's story illustrates.

"My friend, no; I will not impose upon your good nature. I perceive you have an engagement. Luchesi——"

"I have no engagement; come."

"My friend, no. It is not the engagement, but the severe cold with which I perceive you are afflicted. The vaults are insufferably damp. They are encrusted with niter."[4]

"Let us go, nevertheless. The cold is merely nothing. Amontillado! You have been imposed upon. And as for Luchesi, he cannot distinguish sherry from amontillado."

Thus speaking, Fortunato possessed himself of my arm. Putting on a mask of black silk and drawing a roquelaure[5] closely about my person, I suffered him to hurry me to my *palazzo*.[6]

There were no attendants at home; they had absconded to make merry in honor of the time. I had told them that I should not return until the morning and had given them explicit orders not to stir from the house. These orders were sufficient, I well knew, to ensure their immediate disappearance, one and all, as soon as my back was turned.

I took from their sconces two flambeaux[7] and, giving one to Fortunato, bowed him through several suites of rooms to the archway that led into the vaults. I passed down a long and winding staircase, requesting him to be cautious as he followed. We came at length to the foot of the descent and stood together on the damp ground of the catacombs of the Montresors.

The gait of my friend was unsteady, and the bells upon his cap jingled as he strode.

"The pipe," said he.

"It is farther on," said I; "but observe the white web-work which gleams from these cavern walls."

4. **niter** (nīt'ər): salt deposits.
5. **roquelaure** (räk'ə·lôr'): heavy knee-length cloak.
6. *palazzo* (pä·lät'sô): Italian for "palace."
7. **sconces** (skän'siz): wall fixtures that hold **flambeaux** (flam'bōz'), candlesticks or flaming pieces of wood.

He turned toward me, and looked into my eyes with two filmy orbs that distilled the rheum[8] of intoxication.

"Niter?" he asked, at length.

"Niter," I replied. "How long have you had that cough?"

"Ugh! ugh! ugh!—ugh! ugh! ugh!—ugh! ugh! ugh!—ugh! ugh! ugh!—ugh! ugh! ugh!"

My poor friend found it impossible to reply for many minutes.

"It is nothing," he said, at last.

"Come," I said, with decision, "we will go back; your health is precious. You are rich, respected, admired, beloved; you are happy, as once I was. You are a man to be missed. For me it is no matter. We will go back; you will be ill, and I cannot be responsible. Besides, there is Luchesi——"

"Enough," he said; "the cough is a mere nothing; it will not kill me. I shall not die of a cough."

"True—true," I replied; "and, indeed, I had no intention of alarming you unnecessarily—but you should use all proper caution. A draft of this Médoc[9] will defend us from the damps."

Here I knocked off the neck of a bottle which I drew from a long row of its fellows that lay upon the mold.

"Drink," I said, presenting him the wine.

He raised it to his lips with a leer. He paused and nodded to me familiarly, while his bells jingled.

"I drink," he said, "to the buried that repose around us."

"And I to your long life."

He again took my arm, and we proceeded.

"These vaults," he said, "are extensive."

8. **rheum** (rōōm): watery discharge.
9. **Médoc** (mā·dôk'): type of red wine.

WORDS TO OWN

impose (im·pōz') **upon** v.: take advantage of.

D Reading Skills and Strategies

Drawing Conclusions

❓ What can you conclude about Fortunato's character from his words and actions here? [Possible responses: He is competitive; he considers himself a wine expert; he is disparaging of his rivals.]

E Critical Thinking

Analyzing

❓ What does the narrator's attitude toward his servants reveal about his view of humanity? [Possible responses: He is cynical; he expects people to be disobedient and untrustworthy.]

F Elements of Literature

Unreliable Narrator

❓ What is bizarre about the narrator's reference to Fortunato as his "poor friend"? [Possible response: Since he has vowed revenge on Fortunato, the man is no friend. Also, the "poor" indicates sympathy, an unlikely feeling toward an enemy.]

G Elements of Literature

Irony

❓ Why is the narrator's toast ironic? [Possible response: Montresor actually plans to destroy Fortunato in the immediate future.]

Making the Connections

Cultural Connection

Carnival is a time of merrymaking before the Christian season of Lent, which begins on Ash Wednesday. It is a time of indulgence; people eat, drink, dance, and wear colorful costumes. In the United States, the most famous carnival celebration is Mardi Gras in New Orleans. (The phrase *mardi gras* is French for "fat Tuesday.") There the holiday is celebrated with parades along the city's major streets. At Rio de Janeiro's world-famous carnival celebration, thousands of samba dancers, organized in groups known as schools, compete to be carnival champions. In the West Indies, Trinidad's celebrations include steel band and calypso music competitions. Invite students to research the institution of carnival and to report on its history and how it is marked in different locales. You might also ask students to share what they know about how people spend the days leading up to other periods of atonement, such as Yom Kippur or Ramadan.

This information was drawn from a scholarly paper written by Joseph S. Schick of the University of Chicago and published in the March 1934 volume of *American Literature*, a journal published by Duke University. The paper's title is "The Origin of 'The Cask of Amontillado.'"

The letter writer was Reverend Joel Tyler Headley (1814–1897). The letter was one of several contained in a book by Headley called *Letters from Italy* (1845). Headley was one of the most popular writers of his day; Poe did not share the public's high opinion and was, in fact, critical of Headley's work. Headley's letter, called "A Sketch, a Man Built in a Wall," was published separately in two publications well known to Poe — *The Columbian Magazine* (August 1844) and *The New York Evening Mirror* (July 12, 1845).

When students have finished reading Poe's story, discuss the fact that many well-known works of literature are based upon real life. Make a class list of such stories, books, movies, and plays that students are familiar with, and discuss how accurately the literature follows the true story. (Examples, with varying degrees of accuracy, include the play *The Miracle Worker*, found on p. 632 of this book; the movie *Titanic*; and the novel *To Kill a Mockingbird*.) Suggest that students think about the use of real events as the basis of fiction. How much latitude does a writer have in using actual people and events in storytelling?

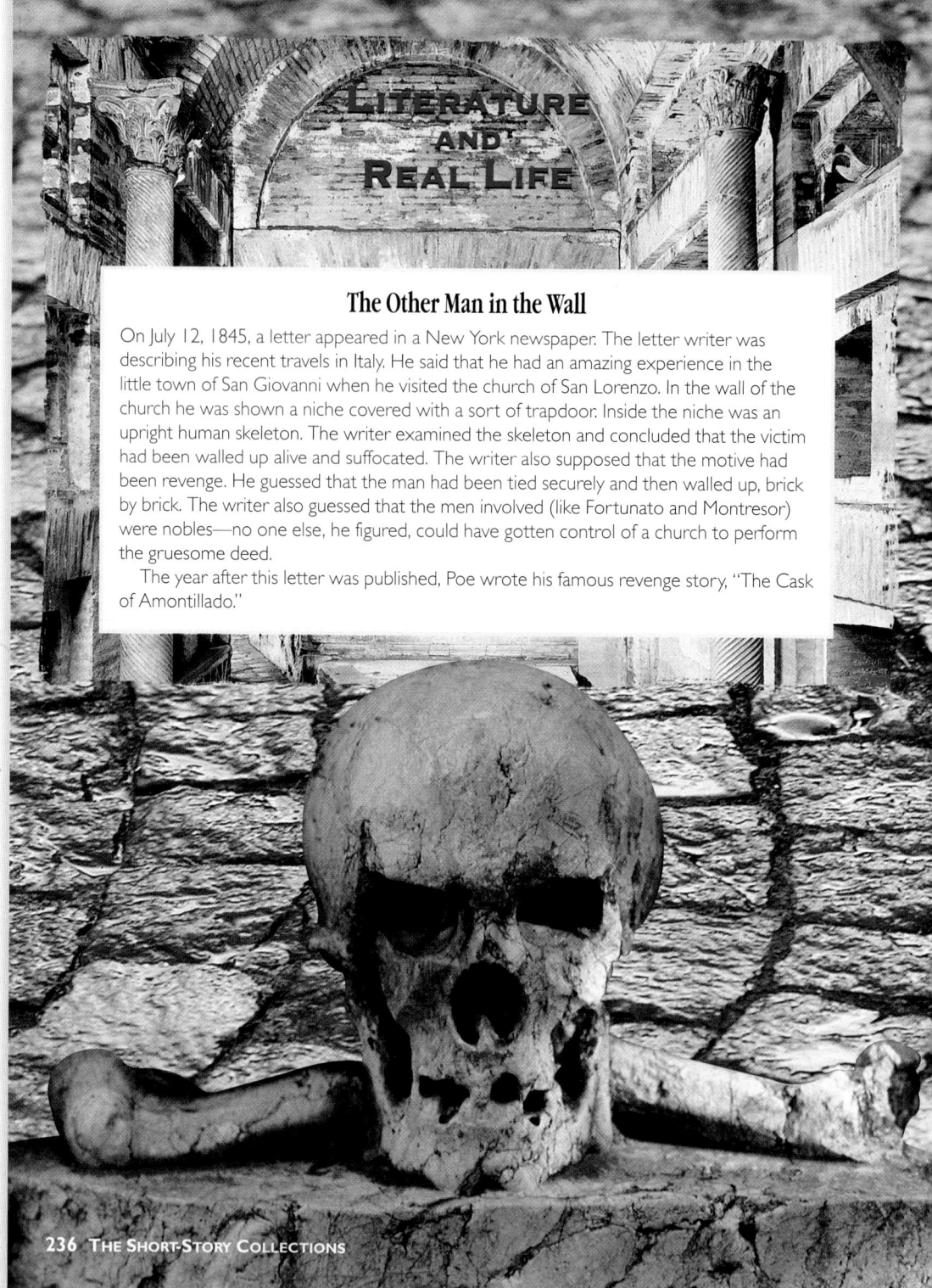

The Other Man in the Wall

On July 12, 1845, a letter appeared in a New York newspaper. The letter writer was describing his recent travels in Italy. He said that he had an amazing experience in the little town of San Giovanni when he visited the church of San Lorenzo. In the wall of the church he was shown a niche covered with a sort of trapdoor. Inside the niche was an upright human skeleton. The writer examined the skeleton and concluded that the victim had been walled up alive and suffocated. The writer also supposed that the motive had been revenge. He guessed that the man had been tied securely and then walled up, brick by brick. The writer also guessed that the men involved (like Fortunato and Montresor) were nobles—no one else, he figured, could have gotten control of a church to perform the gruesome deed.

The year after this letter was published, Poe wrote his famous revenge story, "The Cask of Amontillado."

"The Montresors," I replied, "were a great and numerous family."

"I forget your arms."[10]

"A huge human foot d'or, in a field azure; the foot crushes a serpent rampant whose fangs are embedded in the heel."[11]

"And the motto?"

"Nemo me impune lacessit."[12]

"Good!" he said.

The wine sparkled in his eyes and the bells jingled. My own fancy grew warm with the Médoc. We had passed through walls of piled bones, with casks and puncheons[13] intermingling, into the inmost recesses of the catacombs. I paused again, and this time I made bold to seize Fortunato by an arm above the elbow.

"The niter!" I said. "See, it increases. It hangs like moss upon the vaults. We are below the river's bed. The drops of moisture trickle among the bones. Come, we will go back ere it is too late. Your cough——"

"It is nothing," he said; "let us go on. But first, another draft of the Médoc."

I broke and reached him a flagon of de Grâve.[14] He emptied it at a breath. His eyes flashed with a fierce light. He laughed and threw the bottle upward with a gesticulation I did not understand.

I looked at him in surprise. He repeated the movement—a grotesque one.

"You do not comprehend?" he said.

"Not I," I replied.

"Then you are not of the brotherhood."

"How?"

"You are not of the Masons."[15]

"Yes, yes," I said, "yes, yes."

"You? Impossible! A Mason?"

"A mason," I replied.

"A sign," he said.

"It is this," I answered, producing a trowel from beneath the folds of my roquelaure.

"You jest," he exclaimed, recoiling a few paces. "But let us proceed to the amontillado."

"Be it so," I said, replacing the tool beneath the cloak and again offering him my arm. He leaned upon it heavily. We continued our route in search of the amontillado. We passed through a range of low arches, descended, passed on, and, descending again, arrived at a deep crypt in which the foulness of the air caused our flambeaux rather to glow than flame.

At the most remote end of the crypt there appeared another less spacious. Its walls had been lined with human remains, piled to the vault overhead, in the fashion of the great catacombs of Paris. Three sides of this interior crypt were still ornamented in this manner. From the fourth the bones had been thrown down and lay promiscuously[16] upon the earth, forming at one point a mound of some size. Within the wall thus exposed by the displacing of the bones, we perceived a still interior recess, in depth about four feet, in width three, in height six or seven. It seemed to have been constructed for no especial use within itself, but formed merely the interval between two of the colossal supports of the roof of the catacombs and was backed by one of their circumscribing walls of solid granite.

---

10. arms: coat of arms, a group of symbols used to represent a family.

11. foot d'or . . . heel: The Montresor coat of arms shows a huge golden foot against a blue background, with the foot crushing a snake that is rearing up and biting the heel.

12. *Nemo me impune lacessit* (nā'mō mā im·pōō'nä lä·ke'sit): Latin for "Nobody attacks me without punishment."

13. puncheons (pun'chənz): large wine casks.

14. flagon of de Grâve: narrow-necked bottle with a handle and sometimes a lid, containing a wine from the Graves region of France.

15. Masons (mā'sənz): Freemasons, a secret society of people who believe in brotherhood, giving to the poor, and helping one another. Members use secret signs and gestures to recognize one another.

16. promiscuously (prō·mis'kyōō·əs·lē): randomly; in a disorganized way.

WORDS TO OWN

recoiling (ri·koil'iŋ) *v.* used as *adj.*: moving backward, as if in horror.

Ⓐ Critical Thinking
Analyzing Symbols
❓ What do the images and the motto on the Montresor coat of arms suggest? [Possible response: The Montresors (the foot) always punish those (the snake) who try to wound them.] How does this conversation about the coat of arms heighten the dramatic irony? [Readers are aware that Montresor seeks revenge, but Fortunato is unsuspecting.]

Ⓑ Reading Skills and Strategies
Drawing Conclusions
❓ Why does Montresor profess "concern" for Fortunato's health? [Possible response: He is trying to disarm Fortunato by appearing concerned, so that Fortunato will not suspect that he is actually plotting to harm him.]

Ⓒ Appreciating Language
Word Play/Puns
❓ How is Montresor punning with the word *mason*? [Fortunato means a member of the secret society of Freemasons, but Montresor is referring to himself as a soon-to-be bricklayer, or mason, who uses a trowel.]

Ⓓ Elements of Literature
Unreliable Narrator
❓ How does the phrase "in search of" suggest that Montresor is an unreliable narrator? [Possible response: It implies that he doesn't know where the amontillado is stored (if it even exists), which is highly unlikely.]

Crossing the Curriculum

Social Studies

The Freemasons, the subject of Montresor's punning, are a secret fraternal society that grew out of medieval craft guilds. Founded in London in 1717, it is still the largest secret society in the world. Have students research and report on the Freemasons' rituals and rites and the extent of their influence during the time in which the story is set (the eighteenth or nineteenth century).

Art

Heraldry involves displaying genealogical symbols, as a means of identification, on shields and as coats of arms. Groups can report on heraldry's development during the Crusades and how the use of emblems helped combatants distinguish friend from foe. Have them create a display of various coats of arms, with captions explaining the symbols.

T237

A Reading Skills and Strategies

Drawing Conclusions

❓ What kind of person has Fortunato shown himself to be? [Possible responses: arrogant—he claims to know wine better than anyone else; vain—he refuses to let Montresor seek Luchesi's opinion; mean-spirited—he describes Luchesi as an "ignoramus."]

B Elements of Literature

Irony

❓ What is ironic about Montresor's statement? [Possible response: Since he has chained Fortunato to the wall, it is impossible for Fortunato to return. Also, the phrase "little attentions" usually refers to taking care of someone, but here it clearly means something sinister.]

C Critical Thinking

Interpreting

❓ How does Montresor refer to Fortunato here? [as a "figure," a "chained form"] What does this suggest? [Possible response: He has ceased to see Fortunato as a human being.]

D Elements of Literature

Unreliable Narrator

❓ What is unsettling about Montresor's reference to Fortunato as "noble"? [Possible responses: He has made it clear that he does not think Fortunato is noble, and he is not treating Fortunato nobly; he may be speaking ironically.]

It was in vain that Fortunato, uplifting his dull torch, <u>endeavored</u> to pry into the depth of the recess. Its termination the feeble light did not enable us to see.

"Proceed," I said; "herein is the amontillado. As for Luchesi——"

A "He is an *ignoramus*," interrupted my friend, as he stepped unsteadily forward, while I followed immediately at his heels. In an instant he had reached the extremity of the niche, and finding his progress arrested by the rock, stood stupidly bewildered. A moment more and I had fettered[17] him to the granite. In its surface were two iron staples, distant from each other about two feet horizontally. From one of these depended a short chain, from the other a padlock. Throwing the links about his waist, it was but the work of a few seconds to secure it. He was too much astounded to resist. Withdrawing the key, I stepped back from the recess.

B "Pass your hand," I said, "over the wall; you cannot help feeling the niter. Indeed it is *very* damp. Once more let me *implore* you to return. No? Then I must positively leave you. But I must first render you all the little attentions in my power."

"The amontillado!" ejaculated my friend, not yet recovered from his astonishment.

"True," I replied; "the amontillado."

As I said these words, I busied myself among the pile of bones of which I have before spoken. Throwing them aside, I soon uncovered a quantity of building stone and mortar. With these materials and with the aid of my trowel, I began vigorously to wall up the entrance of the niche.

I had scarcely laid the first tier of the masonry when I discovered that the intoxication of Fortunato had in a great measure worn off. The earliest indication I had of this was a low moaning cry from the depth of the recess. It was *not* the cry of a drunken man. There was then a long and <u>obstinate</u> silence. I laid the second tier, and the third, and the fourth; and then I heard the furious vibrations of the chain. The noise lasted for several minutes, during which, that I might hearken to it with the more satisfaction, I ceased my labors and sat down upon the bones. When at last the clanking subsided, I resumed the trowel and finished without interruption the fifth, the sixth, and the seventh tier. The wall was now nearly upon a level with my breast. I again paused and, holding the flambeaux over the mason-work, threw a few feeble rays upon the figure within.

C A <u>succession</u> of loud and shrill screams, bursting suddenly from the throat of the chained form, seemed to thrust me violently back. For a brief moment I hesitated—I trembled. Unsheathing my rapier,[18] I began to grope with it about the recess; but the thought of an instant reassured me. I placed my hand upon the solid fabric of the catacombs and felt satisfied. I reapproached the wall; I replied to the yells of him who clamored. I reechoed—I aided—I surpassed them in volume and in strength. I did this, and the clamorer grew still.

It was now midnight, and my task was drawing to a close. I had completed the eighth, the ninth, and the tenth tier. I had finished a portion of the last and the eleventh; there remained but a single stone to be fitted and plastered in. I struggled with its weight; I placed it partially in its destined position. But now there came from out the niche a low laugh **D** that erected the hairs upon my head. It was succeeded by a sad voice, which I had difficulty in recognizing as that of the noble Fortunato. The voice said—

"Ha! ha! ha!—he! he! he!—a very good joke indeed—an excellent jest. We will have many a rich laugh about it at the *palazzo*—he! he! he!—over our wine—he! he! he!"

---

17. **fettered** (fet'ərd): chained.

18. **rapier** (rā'pē·ər): slender two-edged sword.

WORDS TO OWN

endeavored (en·dev'ərd) v.: tried.
obstinate (äb'stə·nət) adj.: stubborn.
succession (sək·sesh'ən) n.: series.

Skill Link

Quotations

You might want to use the following exercise before you teach the Grammar Link exercise on dialogue on p. 243. This exercise will help you assess students' skill in understanding the difference between direct and indirect quotations. Ask students what double quotation marks are used for in dialogue. [to enclose a direct quotation—a person's exact words] Discuss the difference between direct and indirect quotations. Students should note that an indirect quotation does not require quotation marks.

Direct quotation:
"Come," I said, with decision, "we will go back; your health is precious."

Indirect quotation:
I urged him to go back, explaining that it was important to protect his health.

Activity

Write *I* if the sentence is an indirect quotation. Punctuate direct quotations.

1. I told Fortunato not to enter the cellar. [*I*]
2. I told Fortunato, "don't enter here."
3. "Please try the amontillado," he said.
4. The gentleman asked me to try the amontillado. [*I*]
5. "The revelers are loud," he replied.

"The amontillado!" I said.

"He! he! he!—he! he! he!—yes, the amontillado. But is it not getting late? Will not they be awaiting us at the *palazzo*—the Lady Fortunato and the rest? Let us be gone."

"Yes," I said, "let us be gone."

"For the love of God, Montresor!"

"Yes," I said, "for the love of God!"

But to these words I hearkened in vain for a reply. I grew impatient. I called aloud—

"Fortunato!"

No answer. I called again—

"Fortunato!"

No answer still. I thrust a torch through the remaining aperture and let it fall within. There came forth in return only a jingling of the bells. My heart grew sick—on account of the dampness of the catacombs. I hastened to make an end of my labor. I forced the last stone into its position; I plastered it up. Against the new masonry I reerected the old rampart[19] of bones. For the half of a century no mortal has disturbed them. *In pace requiescat.*[20]

19. **rampart** (ram′pärt′): wall resembling one built for protection or defense.
20. ***In pace requiescat*** (in pä′chā rā′kwē·es′kät): Latin for "May he rest in peace."

E **Appreciating Language**
Dialogue

? What does this dialogue reveal about the state of mind of the characters at the end of the story? [Possible response: Fortunato's laughter and his disjointed statements, as well as his plea ("For the love of God, Montresor!"), show his growing desperation and terror. Montresor's calm, ironic replies show his calculating, controlled mind-set.]

F **Critical Thinking**
Speculating

? Why does Fortunato never ask why Montresor is burying him alive? [Possible responses: He thinks it's a joke; he is too terrified to think clearly; he still does not really believe that it is happening; he did insult and injure Montresor and so already knows why.]

#3, 4, 6, 7, 15, 20, 26, 27, 28, cask

short story
novel
simile
metaphor
plot
conflict
characters
climax
resolution
setting

Assessing Learning

Observation Assessment: Reading
As students discuss or write their responses to the story, use the following points as the basis for observing and assessing their reading performances and interactions.

Student _____

1=Rarely   2=Sometimes   3=Often

___ Makes personal connections
___ Attends to multiple levels of meaning
___ Uses the text to verify and clarify ideas
___ Challenges the text
___ Makes connections between the text and other works
___ Draws on story elements when explaining meaning

Resources

Selection Assessment
Formal Assessment
- Selection Test, p. 31

Test Generator (One-Stop Planner)
- CD-ROM

MAKING MEANINGS

First Thoughts

1. Possible responses: Montresor is feeling remorseful about the crime; he is gloating about the success of his plan; Montresor hopes that the crime remains undiscovered.

Shaping Interpretations

2. Possible responses: He could be confessing to a priest, perhaps on his deathbed, in search of absolution; he could be unburdening himself—or bragging—to a friend or a relative.

MEET THE WRITER

A Haunted Life

Edgar Allan Poe (1809–1849) was the son of traveling actors. His father deserted the family, and his beautiful young mother died in a theatrical rooming house in Richmond, Virginia, before Edgar was three years old. The little boy was taken in as a foster child by the wealthy and childless Allan family of Richmond.

At first, Edgar's foster parents were pleased with his brilliant scholarship and athletic ability. But later they became angry at his moodiness and irresponsibility with money. Poe went to the University of Virginia but dropped out with heavy gambling debts. (John Allan apparently refused to support him any longer.) Eventually, Poe and his foster father split up completely, and Poe was left penniless. After several failed courtships, Poe married his thirteen-year-old cousin, Virginia Clemm, and moved to New York City. There, in 1837, they set up house, together with Virginia's mother, whom Poe fondly called Muddy.

Poe drank excessively, and he was always in need of money. But he wrote regularly and had increasing success, although his unusual poems and stories were mocked by conservative critics. "The Cask of Amontillado" was published in 1846 during a time when Poe was enduring vicious insults from critics. The story might have been Poe's way of getting even not only with hostile critics but also with his foster father. The Montresors' motto is the motto of Scotland; John Allan was Scottish and, like the hated Fortunato, a businessman and a Mason.

Poe's one refuge in life was threatened when Virginia became ill with tuberculosis. (Almost 25 percent of Americans in the nineteenth century died from tuberculosis.) When she died, Poe broke down completely. Two years later, he was found delirious in a tavern in Baltimore on a rainy election day. The great master of horror died a few days later.

A Second Helping of Poe

If you like Poe, you might also read "The Tell-Tale Heart," "The Masque of the Red Death," and "The Gold Bug." *Pit + pendulum* *Fall of House*

Assessing Learning

Check Test: Questions and Answers

1. Briefly identify the narrator of the story. [Montresor, a European noble living in Italy]
2. How does Montresor describe Fortunato? [Fortunato is to be respected in many things, but he has weaknesses, including excessive pride in his knowledge of wines.]
3. What is amontillado? [a type of wine]
4. What is the Montresor coat of arms? [a human foot that is crushing a snake that is biting it, with a motto that reinforces the idea of revenge]
5. Exactly how does Montresor get revenge? [He buries Fortunato alive behind a wall in a vault.]

Standardized Test Preparation

For practice with standardized test format specific to this selection, see
- *Standardized Test Preparation*, pp. 28, 30

For practice in proofreading and editing, see
- *Daily Oral Grammar*, Transparency 14

T240

MAKING MEANINGS

First Thoughts

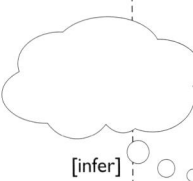

[infer]

1. Draw a head with thought bubbles like the one shown at the left, and fill in the bubbles with words and pictures that show what you think Montresor is thinking as he says *"In pace requiescat."* Be prepared to explain your interpretation.

Shaping Interpretations

[infer]

2. To whom could Montresor be talking, fifty years after the murder, and for what reasons?

[analyze]

3. Part of the story's horrifying effect comes from Poe's use of **irony**. What do *we* know that Fortunato does *not* know about why he has been invited into the vaults? When did *you* figure out what Montresor was up to?

[analyze]

4. Which of Montresor's comments to the unsuspecting Fortunato are **ironic**— that is, which ones mean something different from what they seem to mean?

[respond]

5. The story is full of other examples of **irony**. Think about these uses of irony and how they made you feel:

   - Fortunato's name
   - his costume
   - the fact that a carnival takes place in the streets above the murder

[interpret]

6. Think about whether or not Montresor is a **reliable narrator**. Do any details suggest that he might have imagined "the thousand injuries" and the insult—or even the whole story? Can you find evidence in the story to support Montresor's claim that Fortunato *did* in fact injure and insult him? Talk about your interpretations with a group of classmates.

Extending the Text

[extend]

7. Is this just a gripping horror story told only for entertainment, or do you think it reveals some truth about the way people sometimes behave when they are consumed by a desire for revenge? Give reasons for your opinions.

Challenging the Text

[respond]

8. What do you think of the way the story ends? Consider this question: Do writers have an obligation to punish murderers for their fictional crimes?

[respond]

9. Some people feel that violence in fiction and on TV (like the violence in Poe's story) results in real-life violence. How do you feel about this?

THE CASK OF AMONTILLADO 241

> ### Reading Check
> a. According to Montresor, what makes a perfect crime?
>
> b. How does Montresor lure Fortunato into the catacombs?
>
> c. What does Montresor admit is his **motive** for this crime?
>
> d. According to Montresor, what kind of person is Fortunato?
>
> e. What evidence suggests that Montresor committed the perfect crime?

---

3. The reader knows that Montresor is pretending to be Fortunato's friend in order to lure him to his death. Some will have guessed Montresor's intentions when he reveals that his servants are away, some after reading the "Literature and Real Life" feature, and some when Montresor shows Fortunato the trowel.

4. Nearly all of Montresor's remarks are ironic. Examples include the following ones:
   - "My dear Fortunato. . . . " (p. 234)
   - "[Y]our health is precious." (p.235)
   - "You are a man to be missed." (p. 235)
   - "And I [drink] to your long life." (p. 235)
   - "Once more let me *implore* you to return." (p. 238)

5. It is ironic that a man whose name means "luck" is about to become a murder victim. It is gruesome irony that the victim is dressed up like a clown. The partying above is an ironic contrast to the suffering below.

6. Responses will vary. Some students may point out that Fortunato is quick to insult Luchesi and may have done the same to Montresor; also Fortunato shows contempt for Montresor by forgetting his family's coat of arms. Others may contend that if Fortunato really had insulted Montresor so badly, Fortunato would never have been so unsuspecting in his company.

Extending the Text

7. Possible response: Beyond mere entertainment, the story shows how vengeful impulses can drive people to unspeakable crimes.

Challenging the Text

8. Possible responses: Writers have no such obligation—they should be free to shape their fictional worlds to suit their creative purposes; writers do have such an obligation— their position of influence in society gives them a moral responsibility to uphold society's values.

9. Possible reponses: Fictional violence can incite people who are prone to violence; mentally sound people can read or view fictional violence without becoming violent themselves.

Reading Check
a. A perfect crime is one in which the perpetrator is not caught and the victim realizes that the motive is revenge.

b. Montresor appeals to Fortunato's vanity by suggesting that he will ask Luchesi to taste the amontillado if Fortunato cannot.

c. He says he has vowed to take revenge for Fortunato's insulting him.

d. Montresor portrays Fortunato as arrogant, insulting, and vain.

e. The bones are still undisturbed fifty years after the crime.

Rubrics for each Choices assignment appear on p. 114 in the *Portfolio Management System*.

CHOICES: Building Your Portfolio

1. **Writer's Notebook** Remind students to save their work. They can use it as prewriting for the Writer's Workshop on p. 250.
2. **Creative Writing** Students might benefit from discussing their new beginnings with a partner before writing. Students may try several variations of a beginning told from Fortunato's point of view and then write the one they prefer.
3. **Explaining a Theory** Students may create a chart with two columns to help them organize their thoughts. The first column can list claims made by the detective. The second column can provide details from the story and reasons that support or contradict the detective's interpretation.
4. **Critical Thinking/Role-Playing** Before students write their speeches, have them consult law guides and handbooks written for the general public. Alternately, they could interview a local lawyer.
5. **Drawing** After students have determined a time period, they can visualize their settings by sketching their ideas or using a computer graphics program.

CHOICES: Building Your Portfolio

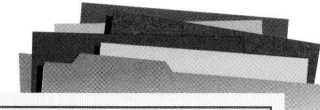

Writer's Notebook

1. Collecting Ideas for an Essay of Evaluation

How did it make you feel?  While reading the stories in this collection, you may have made notes on criteria you can use when you evaluate a story or movie for the Writer's Workshop on page 250. Now, focus on the emotional content of a story. Working with a partner, set up a scale like the one shown below. You may rank the depth of sympathy you feel for a particular character, the effectiveness of the ending, or your feelings about what happened in the story. Remember that when you use a scale like this one, you won't agree with all your classmates. When you write an evaluation, you'll have to support your rating by citing details from the story.

Emotional Scale

effectiveness of ending

```
0   1   2   3   4   5
(not            (very
effective)    powerful)
```

Reasons:

Creative Writing

2. From Fortunato's Point of View

Suppose this story was being told from the point of view of the gullible Fortunato instead of by Montresor. Write a new beginning. Start when the two men meet at dusk, and end when they begin their journey underground. Let the reader know what Fortunato thinks of Montresor. Is he guilty of the thousand injuries and the insult? Tell the story as an omniscient, or all-knowing, narrator who zooms in on Fortunato's thoughts.

Explaining a Theory

3. Finding a Motive

Suppose a detective assigned to the case at the time it happened wrote a report with this theory about the disappearance of Fortunato:

"Montresor is the last member of an old aristocratic Catholic family that lost its money. Fortunato was a businessman who had recently become wealthy and wasn't above cheating to make money. Fortunato also was a member of the Masons, a secret Protestant organization that Catholics cannot join. These facts explain Montresor's hatred of Fortunato. They also supply him with a motive for murder."

Now you are another detective assigned to the still unsolved case a few years later. In a report to your supervisor, explain exactly what you think of this theory. If you agree or disagree, tell why and find reasons in the story to support your case.

Critical Thinking/Role-Playing

4. Crime and Punishment

Suppose the person to whom Montresor is telling his story has turned him over to the police. Montresor's lawyer might argue that his client is insane. The prosecution will argue that Montresor knew exactly what he was doing, even planned it in advance. Write a speech for either lawyer. Then role-play the courtroom scene.

Drawing

5. Designing a Stage Set

Suppose Poe's story is to be dramatized for TV and you are in charge of set design. Before you present your design to your director, decide on an exact time period for the story.

242 THE SHORT-STORY COLLECTIONS

Using Students' Strengths

Visual Learners

Before students create their drawings for Choice 5, suggest that they use the library to research a variety of stage designs. Ask them to consider the different scenes they would choose to show. Have them consider how they can show the revelers above and the labyrinth below simultaneously. How will they convey the clamminess of the catacombs and the niter on the walls?

GRAMMAR LINK   MINI-LESSON

Language Handbook HELP

See Quotation Marks, page 1026.

Technology HELP

See Language Workshop CD-ROM. Key word entry: quotation marks.

Dialogue—Who's Talking?

One way writers make things happen in a story is by using dialogue. Dialogue can advance the plot, reveal the thoughts and words of a character, or even be the tool a writer uses to present important information to a reader. In American usage, dialogue is enclosed in double quotation marks (" "). Usually, a new paragraph lets us know when a different person begins to speak, as in this example from "The Cask of Amontillado":

> "You do not comprehend?" he said.
> "Not I," I replied.
> "Then you are not of the brotherhood."

Most writers use tag lines ("he said," "I replied") to identify the speakers in a dialogue. Some writers do not use tag lines, however. Poe, for example, has written long passages of conversation between Montresor and Fortunato in which neither speaker is directly identified.

Try It Out

Look back at page 234, at the dialogue beginning "Amontillado!," and at page 237, at the dialogue beginning "You do not comprehend?"

1. Get together with a partner and read the dialogues aloud. Use your voices to distinguish one speaker from another.

2. Now add tag lines to Poe's dialogue. Compare your edited versions of Poe's dialogue in class.

3. Finally, look at what Poe's dialogue accomplished. What did you learn about the characters or plot from this exchange?

VOCABULARY   HOW TO OWN A WORD

WORD BANK

precluded
impunity
retribution
immolation
connoisseurship
impose upon
recoiling
endeavored
obstinate
succession

Word Maps

A word map can supply several different kinds of information. It can give the word's **etymology,** or origin. It can give a definition and a sample sentence, and it can list **synonyms** (words with similar meanings) and **antonyms** (words with opposite meanings). With a partner, use a dictionary to make a word map of each word in the Word Bank. (A map of *precluded* appears below.)

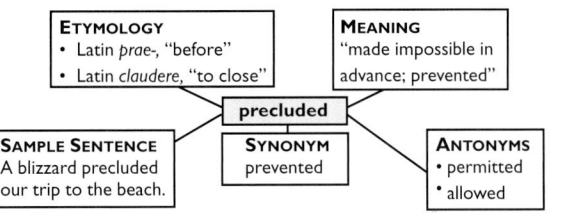

ETYMOLOGY	MEANING
• Latin *prae-*, "before" • Latin *claudere*, "to close"	"made impossible in advance; prevented"

precluded

SAMPLE SENTENCE	SYNONYM	ANTONYMS
A blizzard precluded our trip to the beach.	prevented	• permitted • allowed

THE CASK OF AMONTILLADO   **243**

GRAMMAR LINK

Have students select a portfolio piece that contains narration and involves more than one character. Ask them to write four lines of dialogue to go with the selection and to punctuate it correctly.

Try It Out
Possible Answers
1. Both dialogues begin with Fortunato speaking and alternate between the two men.
2. Tag lines should suit the situation and what is known of the characters.
3. Page 234: Fortunato is astonished that Montresor may have obtained amontillado and scornful of Luchesi's wine connoisseurship; p. 237: Fortunato is a member of the Masons but Montresor is not, and Montresor is carrying a trowel.

VOCABULARY
Word maps will vary. Word etymologies:
impunity L *im-*, "without" + *poena*, "punishment"
retribution L *re-*, "back" + *tribuere*, "to pay"
immolation L *immolatus* or *immolare*, "to sprinkle a victim with sacrificial meal"
connoisseurship L *cognoscere*, "to know"
impose upon L *in-*, "on" + *ponere*, "to put"
recoiling L *re-*, "back" + *cul*, "backside"
endeavored L *in-*, verb-forming prefix + OFr *deveir*, "duty"
obstinate L *ob-*, "against" + *stare*, "to stand"
succession L *succedere*, "to follow after"

Resources ———
Grammar
• *Grammar and Language Links* Worksheet, p. 23
Vocabulary
• *Words to Own*, Worksheet, p. 11

Grammar Link Quick Check

1. How are quotation marks used in dialogue? [to set off the exact words of one character from those of another character]

2. How can tag lines be helpful to a reader? [Tag lines identify the speakers in a dialogue.]

3. How do writers usually indicate when a different person begins to speak? [with a new paragraph]

4. Do writers always use tag lines? [No]

Extending the Theme

To select a husband, a rich, pampered princess must choose which of five princes' gifts she likes best. In a reversal of the traditional fairy-tale ending, she bases her choice on greed rather than romance.

Resources

Listening
Audio CD Library
A recording of this tale is available as part of the *Audio CD Library:*
• Disc 9, Track 3

RESPONDING TO THE ART

Florentine painter **Paolo Uccello** (1397?–1475) apprenticed under sculptor Lorenzo Ghiberti, one of the leading exponents of the Late Gothic style. Later, Uccello's pioneering experiments in foreshortening and linear perspective helped pave the way for the transition to the early Renaissance style.
Activity. Ask students to describe their impression of the young woman in the painting. Does she strike them as friendly or aloof, modest or haughty, tolerant or critical? What qualities, if any, does she seem to share with Thurber's Princess?

Quickwrite

Write a few sentences summing up a folk tale you remember from your childhood. (A **folk tale** is any story passed down by ordinary people through the oral tradition. The story of Cinderella is a popular folk tale. A fairy tale is a type of folk tale.)

Young Lady of Fashion (15th century) by Paolo Uccello.

The Bettmann Archive.

244 THE SHORT-STORY COLLECTIONS

The Princess and the Tin Box

James Thurber

Once upon a time, in a far country, there lived a King whose daughter was the prettiest princess in the world. Her eyes were like the cornflower, her hair was sweeter than the hyacinth, and her throat made the swan look dusty.

From the time she was a year old, the Princess had been showered with presents. Her nursery looked like Cartier's[1] window. Her toys were all made of gold or platinum or diamonds or emeralds. She was not permitted to have wooden blocks or china dolls or rubber dogs or linen books, because such materials were considered cheap for the daughter of a king.

When she was seven, she was allowed to attend the wedding of her brother and throw real pearls at the bride instead of rice. Only the nightingale, with his lyre of gold, was permitted to sing for the Princess. The common blackbird, with his boxwood

1. **Cartier's** (kär′tē·āz): store selling expensive jewelry in New York City.

go.hrw.com
LEO 9-3

Reaching All Students

Struggling Readers
The introductory paragraphs may be particularly challenging for these students, yet they are crucial to an understanding of the Princess's lifestyle and character. Pair mixed-ability students, and have them paraphrase the introduction orally or in writing, using simple, familiar vocabulary.

Using Students' Strengths

Visual Learners
Ask students to sketch on separate pieces of paper a picture of each gift presented to the Princess. Then, read with students just up to the point of the Princess's decision. Have students place their sketches in the order they think would be the princess's preference. Ask volunteers to show their choices to the class and to explain their predictions.

T244

flute, was kept out of the palace grounds. She walked in silver-and-samite[2] slippers to a sapphire-and-topaz bathroom and slept in an ivory bed inlaid with rubies.

On the day the Princess was eighteen, the King sent a royal ambassador to the courts of five neighboring kingdoms to announce that he would give his daughter's hand in marriage to the prince who brought her the gift she liked the most.

The first prince to arrive at the palace rode a swift white stallion and laid at the feet of the Princess an enormous apple made of solid gold which he had taken from a dragon who had guarded it for a thousand years. It was placed on a long ebony table set up to hold the gifts of the Princess' suitors. The second prince, who came on a gray charger, brought her a nightingale made of a thousand diamonds, and it was placed beside the golden apple. The third prince, riding on a black horse, carried a great jewel box made of platinum and sapphires, and it was placed next to the diamond nightingale. The fourth prince, astride a fiery yellow horse, gave the Princess a gigantic heart made of rubies and pierced by an emerald arrow. It was placed next to the platinum-and-sapphire jewel box.

Now the fifth prince was the strongest and handsomest of all the five suitors, but he was the son of a poor king whose realm had been overrun by mice and locusts and wizards and mining engineers so that there was nothing much of value left in it. He came plodding up to the palace of the Princess on a plow horse, and he brought her a small tin box filled with mica and feldspar and hornblende[3] which he had picked up on the way.

The other princes roared with disdainful laughter when they saw the tawdry gift the fifth prince had brought to the Princess. But she examined it with great interest and squealed with delight, for all her life she had been glutted with precious stones and priceless metals, but she had never seen tin before or mica or feldspar or hornblende. The tin box was placed next to

2. **samite** (sam′it): heavy silk fabric.
3. **mica . . . hornblende:** types of ordinary rocks.

the ruby heart pierced with an emerald arrow.

"Now," the King said to his daughter, "you must select the gift you like best and marry the prince that brought it."

The Princess smiled and walked up to the table and picked up the present she liked the most. It was the platinum-and-sapphire jewel box, the gift of the third prince.

"The way I figure it," she said, "is this. It is a very large and expensive box, and when I am married, I will meet many admirers who will give me precious gems with which to fill it to the top. Therefore, it is the most valuable of all the gifts my suitors have brought me, and I like it best."

The Princess married the third prince that very day in the midst of great merriment and high revelry. More than a hundred thousand pearls were thrown at her and she loved it.

Moral: All those who thought that the Princess was going to select the tin box filled with worthless stones instead of one of the other gifts will kindly stay after class and write one hundred times on the blackboard, "I would rather have a hunk of aluminum silicate than a diamond necklace."

Drawing for "The Princess and the Tin Box" (1948) by James Thurber.

A **Elements of Literature**
Simile
? How does this simile let you know that this is not a conventional fairy tale? [A conventional tale wouldn't use a contemporary brand name.]

B **Reading Skills and Strategies**
Making Predictions
? Do you think the Princess will be interested in the fifth prince? Why or why not? [Responses will vary. Some students will predict that she will be attracted to his good looks and strength. They may note that rags-to-riches themes are common in fairy tales and that a poor contender often wins out over wealthier ones. Others may say that given her upbringing, she would not possibly choose a prince whose kingdom is in shambles.]

C **Critical Thinking**
Drawing Conclusions
? Why is the princess so interested in this ordinary gift? [All her life, she has been shielded from contact with ordinary materials.]

D **Elements of Literature**
Irony
? What is the situational irony in the Princess's choice. [Thurber has built up expectations for a traditional romantic fairy-tale ending, one in which the Princess chooses the poor but handsome fifth prince. Instead, the Princess selects the third prince out of decidedly practical considerations.]

Connecting Across Texts

Connecting with "The Princess and the Tin Box" and "The Talking Skull"

After students have read both "The Princess and the Tin Box" and "The Talking Skull," ask them to review their Quickwrite notes and to consider what characteristics their examples have in common. Students may note characteristics such as the following:
• moral lessons
• royalty: kings, queens, princesses, princes

• characters caught in situations of their own making

Then ask them to consider which, if any, of these characteristics are shared by "The Princess and the Tin Box" and "The Talking Skull." Ask: Which of the selections in the text is a more "typical" folk tale? [Students may say

that although both contain royal characters, "The Talking Skull" has more in common with a traditional tale, for the hunter creates trouble for himself when he ignores the talking skull's warning. They may say that Thurber's unconventional tale shows just how unrealistic certain traditional fairy tales are.]

MEET THE WRITER

He Walked into Himself

When he was asked by an editor to write his own biography, **James Thurber** (1894–1961) came up with these details:

66 James Thurber was born on a night of wild portent and high wind in the year 1894, at 147 Parsons Avenue, Columbus, Ohio. The house, which is still standing, bears no tablet or plaque of any description and is never pointed out to visitors. Once Thurber's mother, walking past the place with an old lady from Fostoria, Ohio, said to her, 'My son James was born in that house,' to which the old lady, who was extremely deaf, replied, 'Why, on the Tuesday morning train, unless my sister is worse.' Mrs. Thurber let it go at that.

The infant Thurber was brought into the world by an old practical nurse named Margery Albright, who had delivered the babies of neighbor women before the Civil War. He was, of course, much too young at the time to have been affected by the quaint and homely circumstances of his birth. . . . Not a great deal is known about his earliest years, beyond the fact that he could walk when he was only two years old and was able to speak whole sentences by the time he was four.

Thurber's boyhood (1900–1913) was pretty well devoid of significance. I see no reason why it should take up much of our time. There is no clearly traceable figure or pattern in this phase of his life. If he knew where he was going, it is not apparent from this distance. He fell down a great deal during this period, because of a trick he had of walking into himself. His gold-rimmed glasses forever needed straightening, which gave him the appearance of a person who hears somebody calling but can't make out where the sound is coming from. Because of his badly focused lenses, he saw, not two of everything, but one and a half. Thus, a four-wheeled wagon would not have eight wheels for him, but six. How he succeeded in preventing these two extra wheels from getting into his work, I have no way of knowing.

Thurber's life baffles and irritates the biographer because of its lack of design. One has the disturbing feeling that the man contrived to be some place without actually having gone there. His drawings, for example, sometimes seem to have reached completion by some other route than the common one of intent.

The writing is, I think, different. In his prose pieces he appears always to have started from the beginning and to have reached the end by way of the middle. It is impossible to read any of the stories from the last line to the first without experiencing a definite sensation of going backward. This seems to me to prove that the stories were written and did not, like the drawings, just suddenly materialize.

Thurber's very first bit of writing was a so-called poem entitled 'My Aunt Mrs. John T. Savage's Garden at 185 South Fifth Street, Columbus, Ohio.' It is of no value or importance except insofar as it demonstrates the man's appalling memory for names and numbers. He can tell you to this day the names of all the children who were in the fourth grade when he was. He remembers the phone numbers of several of his high school chums. He knows the birthdays of all his friends and can tell you the date on which any child of theirs was christened. He can rattle off the names of all the persons who attended the lawn fete of the First M.E. Church of Columbus in 1907. This ragbag of precise but worthless information may have helped him in his work, but I don't see how. . . . 99

Assessing Learning

Check Test: True-False

"The Princess and the Tin Box"
1. The Princess is used to being given extravagant gifts. [True]
2. The Princess chooses the box the third prince brings because she anticipates filling it with jewels from future admirers. [True]
3. Thurber's Princess is a traditional fairy-tale heroine. [False]

"The Talking Skull"
1. The hunter doesn't tell anyone about the talking skull. [False]
2. The skull speaks to the guards, but not to the hunter. [False]
3. The hunter learns what talking can lead to. [True]

The Talking Skull

a Nigerian folk tale
translated by
Leo Frobenius *and* Douglas G. Fox

A hunter goes into the bush. He finds an old human skull. The hunter says: "What brought you here?" The skull answers: "Talking brought me here." The hunter runs off. He runs  to the king. He tells the king: "I found a dry human skull in the bush. It asks you how its father and mother are."

The king says: "Never since my mother bore me have I heard that a dead skull can speak." The king summons the Alkali, the Saba, and the Degi and asks them if they have ever heard the like. None of the wise men has heard the like, and they decide to send guards out with the hunter into the bush to find out if his story is true and, if so, to learn the reason for it. The guards accompany the hunter into the bush with the order to kill him on the spot should he have lied.

The guards and the hunter come to the skull. The hunter addresses the skull: "Skull, speak." The skull is silent. The hunter asks as before: "What brought you here?" The skull does not answer. The whole day long the hunter begs the skull to speak, but it does not answer. In the evening the guards tell the hunter to make the skull speak, and when he cannot, the guards kill the hunter in accordance with the king's command.

When the guards are gone, the skull opens its jaws and asks the dead hunter's head: "What brought you here?" The dead hunter's head replies: "Talking brought me here!"

Jimoh Adebisi Okunade, king of a Nigerian (Yoruba) dynasty.

© Phyllis Galembo 1994.

THE TALKING SKULL 247

Making the Connections

Connecting to the Theme:
"Expect the Unexpected"

Discuss with students the range of unexpected twists a text may take. Write the titles of the stories in this collection on the chalkboard, and have students suggest two or three words that describe the effects of the unexpected twists on the reader. [Students may say that they reacted with shock or dismay to the endings of "The Necklace" and "The Cask of Amontillado"; they may say that they reacted with relief or sympathy to the endings of "Snow" and "The Gift of the Magi."] Discuss with students how the unexpected plot twists in Thurber's fable and Halley Wheeless's poem (p. 248) not only create humor but also make serious points about life.

Extending the Theme

In this Nigerian folk tale, a hunter reports his discovery of a talking skull to the King, who sends guards to verify the hunter's story or kill him if he is lying. Not until the guards have executed the hunter does the skull speak—the very words the hunter addressed to it in their first encounter.

Ⓐ Reading Skills and Strategies
Reading Aloud
Point out that folk tales, as stories passed down through the oral tradition, are meant to be recited from memory. Ask a volunteer to read this first paragraph aloud to the class.

Ⓑ Cultural Connections
An *alkali* is a Muslim judge traditionally responsible for administering legal advice and rulings among Nigeria's Hausa people. Encourage interested students to research other folk tales from the diverse cultures of Nigeria, Africa's most populous country.

Ⓒ Elements of Literature
Irony
❓ What is ironic about the ending of the folk tale? [Possible responses: The roles (and dialogue) are reversed; the hunter has learned the hard way what the skull already knew: that talking can be deadly.]

RESPONDING TO THE ART
The main symbol of Yoruba kingship, the beaded crown, is worn by rulers who trace their descent to Ododuwa, the first Yoruba king. The beaded cane, staff, and fly whisk connote the king's spiritual and political force as the representative of his dynasty. What adjectives would you use to describe this man? [Possible responses: majestic, wise, solemn.]

T247

FINDING COMMON GROUND

To help students consider a range of possibilities, ask them to bring books of fairy tales or folk tales from home or from the local library, including tales from a variety of cultures. On the chalkboard, list the possibilities students find. Keep the books accessible so that students can consult them as they illustrate their modernized fairy tales.

Resources ——————————

Listening
Audio CD Library
A recording of this selection is available in the *Audio CD Library*:
• Disc 9, Track 4

FINDING COMMON GROUND

• Work in groups to create your own collection of tales with unexpected endings. Your Quickwrite notes should give you some ideas. Your tales can be takeoffs of fairy tales, like James Thurber's, or they can be traditional, like the Nigerian tale. Here are some more ideas:

1. Retell a fairy tale using a modern setting and modern characters. You might update "Cinderella" or "Red Riding Hood" or "Jack and the Beanstalk."

2. Write a short verse, like the poem below, about a surprise encounter. Put your surprise ending in the last line. You might open with the line "I was walking . . ."

3. Research the folklore of a country or people you are interested in. Look for stories with surprise twists at the end. (Traditional African stories are particularly good for this, as are Native American folk tales.)

4. If there are artists in your group, have them illustrate your story collection. You might want to tell at least one of your tales in the form of cartoon panels.

5. Draw a cartoon that twists a traditional fairy tale. The cartoon on the right is a takeoff on the story of Rapunzel, who let down her long hair so that her beloved could climb up and visit her. You might create a scene from "Sleeping Beauty" in which the princess, who has hacked her way through the brambles, wakes the prince with a kiss.

Drawing by John O'Brien; © 1994 The New Yorker Magazine, Inc.

a chance meeting

i was walking through the forest and came
upon a cockroach
allen, he said
i walked on
i don't talk to cockroaches.

—Halley Wheeless
Worland High School
Worland, Wyoming

Connecting Across Texts

Connecting with "The Princess and the Tin Box" and "The Talking Skull"

Ask students to explain why the final line of "a chance meeting" is ironic. [Possible response: The line is ironic because it assumes that some people *do* talk to cockroaches, which is preposterous—as is the notion that a cockroach can talk.]

Ask them whether they think "a chance meeting" has more in common with the Thurber tale or with "The Talking Skull." [Possible responses: The poem's mock-serious tone is similar to that of "The Princess and the Tin Box"; the poem's matter-of-fact narration of a bizarre encounter is similar to that of the Nigerian folk tale.]

READ ON

New Light on an Old Monster

Was Dr. Frankenstein's creation a monster, a miracle, or just a misunderstood outsider? You might know a monster from the movie version of Mary Shelley's *Frankenstein* (Signet)—a huge creature lurking at the window, wandering the dark lanes. But do you know who the real monster is in this story? You may be in for a surprise when you read the book *Frankenstein*.

Other Worlds

H. G. Wells specializes in fantasy worlds. Once upon a time Wells invented the Time Traveler, put him in a Time Machine, and propelled him from Victorian England thousands of years into the future. If that isn't fantastic enough, another of Wells's stories—about an invasion from Mars—is so convincing that it created a panic when Orson Welles read it on the radio more than forty years after it was first published. Escape to other worlds with Wells's *The Time Machine* and *The War of the Worlds* (Fawcett Premier).

Twilight Zones

A whistling night train and a shrieking dragon just miss crossing each other's path, garbage trucks clean up the aftermath of nuclear annihilation, rainy days on Venus never end. Expect thirty-one excursions into twilight zones when you read Ray Bradbury's *Classic Stories 1* (Bantam Spectra), where everyday life is hauntingly transformed into strange and fantastic tales. You may find your way back from these twilight zones, but the world you knew will never seem the same.

READ ON 249

Writer's Workshop

MAIN OBJECTIVE
Write an evaluation of a short story or a movie

PROCESS OBJECTIVES
1. Use appropriate prewriting techniques to identify and develop a topic
2. Create a first draft
3. Use evaluation criteria as a basis for determining revision strategies
4. Revise the first draft incorporating suggestions generated by self- or peer evaluation
5. Proofread and correct errors
6. Create a final draft
7. Choose an appropriate method of publication
8. Reflect on progress as a writer

Planning

- **Block Schedule**
  Block Scheduling Lesson Plans with Pacing Guide

- **One-Stop Planner**
  CD-ROM with Test Generator

Technology HELP

See Writer's Workshop 2 CD-ROM. *Assignment: Evaluation.*

ASSIGNMENT

Write an essay in which you evaluate one story in this book or a movie you have seen recently.

AIM

To persuade; to inform.

AUDIENCE

Your classmates; readers of the school paper.

PERSUASIVE WRITING

EVALUATION

"I love it." "I hate it." "It's too hard." "It's too silly." Whenever you make a critical assessment, judging whether something is good or bad, successful or unsuccessful (a movie, TV show, pizza, car), you're making an **evaluation**. In this workshop you'll apply evaluation skills and strategies to a short story or a movie. You'll state your opinion and support it with evidence.

Throughout your life you'll face occasions when you must evaluate something: You might have to evaluate job offers, career choices, a new product, perhaps even a proposed piece of legislation, a new management system, or, if you're an English teacher, the writing of your students.

Prewriting

1. Choose a Story

Writing your evaluation will be interesting if you choose a work you feel strongly about. Select one that you either love or hate, one that you'll always remember, or one that you could barely finish.

Don't worry if your choice of best or worst story or movie is different from the choices of your classmates. In your essay you'll have a chance to present evidence to show how you arrived at your judgment.

2. Establish Your Criteria

"I really like this story a lot" is a subjective evaluation—a statement based on personal preference. An objective evaluation, on the other hand, is a judgment based on **objective criteria,** or particular standards of excellence. Your evaluation will have elements of both. Review the criteria you should have listed in your Writer's Notebook. If you feel your criteria aren't well enough developed, get together with your writing group to brainstorm ideas.

When you work on your criteria, ask yourself: What qualities make a short story (or movie) excellent? Then, turn each quality into a statement. What can you say, for example, about the plot

250 THE SHORT-STORY COLLECTIONS

Resources: Print and Media

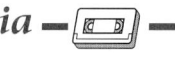

Writing and Language
- *Portfolio Management System*
  - Prewriting, p. 116
  - Peer Editing, p. 117
  - Assessment Rubric, p. 118

- *Workshop Resources*
  - Revision Strategy Teaching Notes, p. 13
  - Revision Strategy Transparencies 7, 8, and 9
- *Writer's Workshop 2 CD-ROM*
  - Evaluation

of an excellent story? If you say the plot is believable, one of your criteria would be *A good short story must have a believable plot.* Compare your group's criteria with those of other groups, and see if you want to revise your list.

3. Apply the Criteria

Once you've established your criteria, apply them to the story or movie you want to focus on. How does the story or movie measure up? Or doesn't it? Dig into your story or movie, using your criteria as a guide for what to take notes on. Complete a chart like the one shown here for "The Necklace" (page 221). On the left side, list all of your criteria. On the right, list the story's or movie's weaknesses and strengths and add details that support your evaluation.

If you wish, give your story or movie a rating: On a scale of zero to ten, ten would be the highest rating.

"The Necklace"		
Criteria	Meets Criteria	Fails to Meet Criteria
Character development: Must be believable and original; motivation must be clear.	Mathilde is believable; how she changes is believable. Reasons for changes are clear.	
Plot: Must not be contrived; must be suspenseful; can't be boring.		
Meaning: Must be important, relevant.		

"The Necklace" = 9.5

Failure as a story ———————— Perfect story

0 —————————————————————— 10

My Rating

4. So, What Do You Think?

After you have listed the ways your story or movie meets the criteria, or fails to, and after you have given your story or movie a rating (if you wish to), draft a **judgment statement** that expresses your overall evaluation. This statement about your

Kinds of Evidence

- your personal reasons
- brief plot summary
- analysis of characters
- analysis of theme
- quotations from the text
- reference to specific scenes and dialogue
- comparison with other stories or movies
- references to (or quotations from) experts' opinions

WRITER'S WORKSHOP **251**

Introducing the Writer's Workshop

- Have students discuss the characteristics that make a five-star movie: believable characters, realistic or interesting dialogue, a suspenseful plot, action, and good directing.
- Share a critical review of a popular film with students, and ask for their reactions to the review.
- Discuss with students how a critical review of a film is similar to or different from an evaluation of a short story. For example, one criterion for a good short story might be a vivid style with interesting, descriptive passages. In a movie a corollary criterion might be the cinematography.
- Ask a volunteer to read the student model on pp. 252-253, or read it to the class yourself.
- Discuss the analysis notes in the side margin.
- Be sure students understand that this is both an objective evaluation—a judgment based on whether or not the work meets certain standards—and an evaluation based on personal preference.

Teaching the Writer's Workshop

Prewriting

- Brainstorm with the students a list of qualities that make a story or movie exciting or dull. Students can use this list and add some of their own criteria. A list of movie elements to help them can be found on p. 252.
- Pick a story students have read in class, and model the drafting of a judgment statement. Remind students that they need to include specific reasons for their opinion in the judgment statement.

Reaching All Students

Struggling Writers

Some students may have difficulty phrasing their opinion statements. If, after filling out their criteria chart, students are still unsure about their *overall* opinion of the story or movie, have them list the good and bad qualities of the movie or story. Their overall opinion will be based on which list is longer. Once the positive or negative stance is determined, a student can begin drafting the essay by writing a general judgment statement.

For example, two viewers might have given these evaluations of the same movie:

Positive: The movie *Homeward Bound* is a must-see for children and adults of all ages.

Negative: The movie *Homeward Bound* was too cute and too simple for anyone over the age of three.

T251

Students should refer to the model while writing their drafts. As they read the model, have students focus on questions such as these:

? How does this evaluation essay match the tone of the movie?

? What details from the movie does the writer mention in the essay?

? How does the organization of this essay take you through the movie?

? How do you know the writer is going to give the movie a "thumbs up" even before the judgment statement?

? What specific details make you want to agree with the judgment statement?

■ *Evaluating a Movie*

If you're reviewing a movie, you might discuss these elements of film:

• *Characters (including quality of acting)*

• *Plot (including action, conflict, suspense)*

• *Setting*

• *Meaning*

• *Tone (humorous, ironic, and so on)*

• *Direction*

• *Cinematography (the way scenes are photographed)*

• *Musical score (if any)*

subject will be the most important part of your introductory paragraph. Note that your judgment statement should cite the work you'll focus on, its author, and your general assessment of the work's effectiveness. The statement can consist of more than one sentence.

EXAMPLE   I think that the popular story "The Most Dangerous Game" by Richard Connell is a fine example of an escape story. It's fun to read; it helps us pass an hour or two. But does it reveal much about human life and the complex world we live in? My answer to that is a strong *no*. I rate this story ten for fun and three for significance.

5. Select the Criteria You Want to Focus On

You might want to avoid any discussion of setting, for example, because in the story or movie you are writing about, you don't feel it's important. You should have at least three strong criteria to apply to your story or movie.

6. Support Your Evaluation

The rest of your essay will support your judgment statement with as many details as you can assemble. An essay of evaluation, like a persuasive essay, should provide sufficient evidence to convince

Student Model

BABE, THE PIG, IS A BLAST

Yes, it's the talking pig, Babe. He's pink, he oinks, and he has his own movie.

The movie starts at a pig farm. The star, Babe (voiced by Christine Cavanaugh), is sitting in his pen with his mother and siblings. Suddenly his mom is swiftly taken to pig paradise.

The little pig is taken to a carnival where Mr. Hoggins wins him and takes him to the Hogginses' farm. While he's on the farm, many different adventures happen to the little pig and his farm friends. Some of his friends include sheep, sheep dogs, ducks, and singing mice.

You may think pigs are considered stinky, muddy, ugly, and stupid. Babe

Opening lines grab readers' attention. Humorous, informal tone is appropriate for evaluation of funny movie written for audience of classmates. Brief plot summary identifies situation, character, setting.

Crossing the Curriculum

Music

Students can apply the evaluation skills they use in this essay in a number of other ways. Have students work in groups to select a list of objective criteria that might be used to evaluate a song. Ask students to think about whether or not they normally use objective criteria to decide whether a song is good, or whether they rely more on subjective criteria or personal preference. Discuss with students the differences between evaluations of music, movies, and literature.

your readers that your opinion is justified. Cite passages or scenes from the story or movie or refer to pages that provide examples to support your general statements.

Drafting

1. Watch Your Tone

Remember that you want your readers to accept your evaluation as a fair one. You'll sound more confident if you avoid "hedge words" like *probably, maybe, perhaps, seems,* and *might.* State your ideas clearly, directly, and positively.

2. Follow a Plan

Organize your essay so that your readers will be able to follow your thoughts easily. Here is one possible way to organize it:

- a forceful introduction that identifies the title and author and contains your judgment statement

- a brief plot summary (no more than three or four sentences)

- a discussion of how the story or movie measures up against three or four criteria (a paragraph for each), with evidence from the text or film to support your points

- a conclusion that restates your evaluation

---

is none of these. He is actually very smart, but because he is young, he doesn't know a lot of things.

As you know, animals don't talk like we do, except in this movie. The animals talk to each other. Apparently the animals were given vocal cords and were taught a very advanced English.

Since this isn't a cartoon, you might not expect it to be a G movie. Well, today is your lucky day. Babe is a G-rated movie; so everyone can go, even adults.

I give this movie a thumbs up because it was funny, made me feel happy, and wasn't what I expected from a G movie.

Gently mocks the movie's lack of realism.

Evaluation of ending, supported by specific reasons.

—Bob Tester
North Middle School
Great Falls, Montana

■ *Evaluation Criteria*

A good essay of evaluation

1. *expresses the writer's judgment clearly and confidently*

2. *supports the judgment with specific examples*

3. *has an interesting beginning and strong conclusion*

Sentence Workshop
H E L P

Varying sentence beginnings: page 255.

A Boxful of Judgment Words	
Positive	*Negative*
gripping	boring
exciting	irritating
intense	contrived
unforgettable	pointless
moving	dull
well crafted	confusing

Communications Handbook
H E L P

See Taking Notes and Documenting Sources.

Drafting

- Students should refer back to the model on pp. 252-253 as they write their paper.
- Remind students to double-space when they write their drafts. They should also leave extra space in the right margin. These blank spaces will be used for comments and editing marks.

Getting Students Involved

Peer Editing

Divide the class into groups of four or five. One member should present his or her evaluation for editing. Make four copies of the paper so the students in the group can follow along as the presenter reads his or her paper. Group members should use the Evaluation Criteria on this page as they assess the presenter's paper.

They may want to use a scale for each of the three criteria:
1 = Not adequate   3 = Adequate
2 = Needs improvement   4 = Good
Have group members discuss assessments with each other and the presenter.

Evaluating and Revising

Have students use the Evaluation Criteria provided on p. 253 to review their drafts and determine needed revisions. You may want students to peer or self-edit using the scale provided in the "Getting Students Involved" feature on p. 253.

Proofreading

Have students proofread their own papers first and then exchange with other students. For this assignment, remind students to be particularly careful of usage problems such as *it's* for *its* or *there* for *they're* or *their*.

If time permits, the final copy should be put aside for at least a day before it is proofread one last time by the author.

Publishing

Many students will be interested in evaluations of stories and movies written by other students. Consider making a bulletin board in your room or in the hall where a different set of evaluations can be hung each week. Add some professional reviews to the display for comparison.

Reflecting

If students are adding their evaluation essays to their portfolios, they should consider these reflection questions:

1. How workable were my criteria? Do they need revising?
2. What writing skills do I need to work on?
3. What did I learn about my own thinking process?

Resources

Peer Editing Forms and Rubrics
• *Portfolio Management System*, p. 117.

Revision Transparencies
• *Workshop Resources*, p. 13

Grading Timesaver

Rubrics for this Writer's Workshop assignment appear on p. 118 of the *Portfolio Management System*.

THE QUIGMANS   by Buddy Hickerson

I'M SORRY, BOB. YOUR WORK OF FICTION LACKS DIRECTION, HAS A GLARING ABSENCE OF CHARACTER DEVELOPMENT, AND NO DISCERNIBLE PLOT.

GREENBACK PUBLISHING COMPANY

IT'S...MY... AUTOBIOGRAPHY.

© B Hickerson, © 1995 Los Angeles Times Syndicate. Reprinted with permission.

Proofreading Tip

If you're writing on a computer, remember that the spelling checker won't tell you if you've used the wrong word. It won't catch *it's* for *its* or *they're* for *there* or *have went* for *have gone*. Proofread your paper carefully.

Language/Grammar Link
H E L P

Diction: page 211. Pronoun problems: page 231. Dialogue: page 243.

Evaluating and Revising

1. Peer Editing

Ask classmates to read and comment on your draft. Have them write suggestions in the margin for improving the paper (see the Evaluation Criteria) and note questions they think you should answer. Peer reviewers should give positive feedback, too. As a peer reviewer, you could highlight sections of your classmates' papers that you think are especially well done.

2. Self-Evaluation

Read your essay aloud to yourself several times. Does the paper sound like you (your own voice)? Check your transitions—words like *also, besides, in addition to, so*—to be sure your ideas are clearly connected.

Revision Model

	Peer Comments
Yes, it's the talking pig, Babe. He's ~~I'm going to write about a~~	*This is a very dull opening. Try to grab readers' attention. "Great" is a cliché.*
pink, he oinks, and he has his own movie. ~~great movie I saw last Saturday~~	
~~night at the Palace. It's called~~	
~~Babe.~~	
The movie starts at a pig	
farm. The star, Babe (voiced by	
Christine Cavanaugh), is sitting	
with his mother and siblings. mom in his pen. Suddenly his mother	*More details, please.*
swiftly taken to pig paradise. is ~~killed~~. ∧	

Sentence Workshop

OBJECTIVES
1. Revise sentences to vary the subject + verb + complement pattern
2. Recognize alternatives for sentence openers

REVISING SENTENCES: BEGINNINGS

The normal word order for English sentences is subject + verb + complement (if there is one), as in this sentence from "The Cask of Amontillado" (page 237).

Language Handbook HELP

See Writing Effective Sentences, page 1015.

<pre>
   S   V   C
</pre>
"He repeated the movement—a grotesque one."

Subject-verb-complement sentences are fine, but a whole series of them, bumper to bumper, dulls a paragraph. A good paragraph has variety, and one way to achieve variety is to vary your sentence beginnings.

   Possible variations. Each of these sentences from "The Gift of the Magi" begins in a different way. To see how the opening word or group of words receives extra emphasis, try rewriting each sentence so that it begins with the subject.

ADVERB	"<u>Suddenly</u> she whirled from the window and stood before the glass." (page 204)
PREPOSITIONAL PHRASES	"<u>With that chain on his watch,</u> Jim might be properly anxious about the time in any company." (page 205)
ADVERB CLAUSE	"<u>When Della reached home,</u> her intoxication gave way a little to prudence and reason." (page 205)

Writer's Workshop Follow-up: Proofreading

   Are your sentences stuck in a rut of the same beginnings? When you revise the essay you've written for the Writer's Workshop (page 250), go over each sentence. Highlight words and phrases that you think could be placed at the beginnings of your sentences to make them more forceful. Then, recast your essay and read it aloud to a partner. Do the sentences sound as if they fit together smoothly?

Try It Out
Rewrite the following sentences so that each one begins with the part specified in parentheses. Is there a change in emphasis?

1. "An arm seems to reach out from behind her and snatch her backward." (prepositional phrase)
   —Alice Walker, "Roselily"
2. "The sight I saw when I entered that large hall was new and strange to me." (adverb clause)
   —Mark Twain, "Life on the Mississippi"
3. "The priest approached the grave slowly, wondering how they had managed to dig into the frozen ground." (adverb)
   —Leslie Marmon Silko, "The Man to Send Rain Clouds"

SENTENCE WORKSHOP 255

Resources
Workshop Resources
• Worksheet, p. 65

Try It Out
Possible Answers
1. From behind her, an arm seems to reach out and snatch her backward.
2. When I entered that large hall, I saw a sight that was new and strange.
3. Slowly, the priest approached the grave, wondering how they had managed to dig into the frozen ground.

Assessing Learning

OBJECTIVES
1. Analyze an advertisement
2. Separate facts from promotional gimmicks
3. Identify emotional appeals

Teaching the Lesson

Examples are an important way for students to understand the emotional appeal of advertisements. You may want students to bring in examples of ads from their favorite magazines or other periodicals. You can also brainstorm a list of television advertisement slogans on the board. Let small groups determine the appeal of several ads and present their findings to the class.

Using the Strategies

Possible Answers

1. Claims: The electronic organizer will make you an organized person. You won't miss important dates. Facts: It has a calendar, phone directory, and is small enough to carry around.
2. Loaded words: *Mother's birthday, in denial, rule, get a grip.*
3. Persuasive techniques: Bandwagon—join the organized people because they "rule."
4. Other sources of information: Magazine product reviews, consumer reports.

Reading for Life

Analyzing Advertisements

Situation

Like Della in "The Gift of the Magi," you want to find the perfect gift for someone you love. You don't want to run all over town to find it, though, so you access an on-line catalog. When you spot the ad on the right, you use these strategies to analyze it.

Strategies

Don't accept an advertiser's claims at face value.

- To make an informed decision about a product, you need hard facts, not just clever copy and a dazzling design. Access other sources, and compare product descriptions and prices. See if you can locate a consumer report on the product.

Read with your head, not with your heart.
Be alert to these emotional appeals:

- **Loaded words:** words and phrases that call up strong feelings. Examples: *all-natural, first-choice, 100% pure.*

- **Bandwagon appeals:** appeals based on the suggestion that you'll be an oddball if you don't do what everyone else is doing. Example: *Everyone's wearing Whooshwalkers. What are you wearing?*

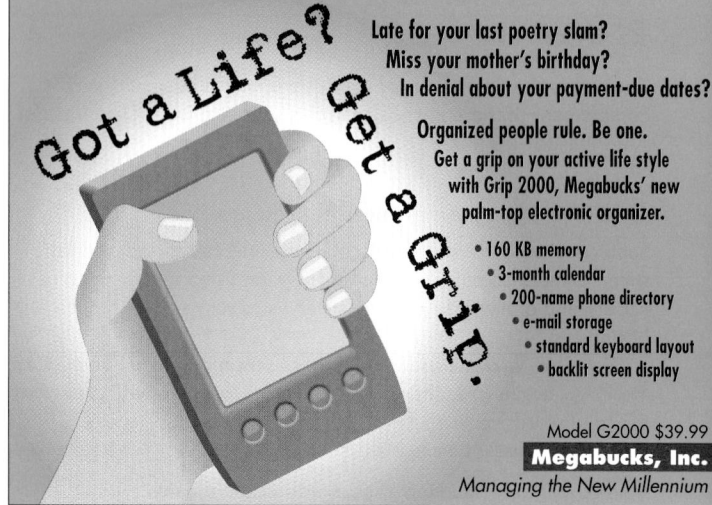

Late for your last poetry slam?
Miss your mother's birthday?
In denial about your payment-due dates?

Organized people rule. Be one.
Get a grip on your active life style with Grip 2000, Megabucks' new palm-top electronic organizer.

- 160 KB memory
- 3-month calendar
- 200-name phone directory
- e-mail storage
- standard keyboard layout
- backlit screen display

Model G2000 $39.99

Megabucks, Inc.
Managing the New Millennium

- **Testimonial:** recommendations made by celebrities who are paid to praise a product. Example: *Hoops star Manley Winch says, "I crave KranKrisps."*

- **"Plain folks":** ordinary-looking actors shown using a product. Example: *We country folks know that for down-home deals, you just can't beat Otto's Oxmobiles.*

Using the Strategies

1. What claims does the ad above make? What facts support those claims?
2. Do any of the words in the ad seem like loaded words to you? What are they?
3. What other persuasive techniques are used?
4. Where might you find objective information about a product of this type?

Extending the Strategies

Find two ads for a particular type of product, and compare their use of persuasive techniques.

256 THE SHORT-STORY COLLECTIONS

Reaching All Students

English Language Learners

Advertisements often contain idioms, slang, or other phrases that do not have a literal meaning and may not translate directly to another language. Use the advertisement from this page to explain how to interpret such phrases. Have the students determine the meaning of the phrases that follow:

- *Got a Life?* (Do you have important things to do and people to see?)
- *Get a Grip.* (Take control of your situation.)

- *poetry slam* (An amateur reading of poetry, often to a rowdy group who approves or disapproves of the poem with cheers or boos.)
- *Organized people rule.* (People who are organized are great.)

Provide an idiom or slang dictionary, if possible. Discuss using the context of the ad to determine the meaning of the phrase.

Discoveries

Theme

Stories as Revelations *Almost every story is about discovery, and in that discovery is the key to the story's theme. The characters in the stories in this collection discover something about themselves or about life itself. They grow up, they learn from their mistakes and disappointments, their eyes are opened to new possibilities. As these characters make their discoveries, we share in their experiences. The truths revealed to them are also revealed to us.*

Reading the Anthology

Reaching Struggling Readers

The *Reading Skills and Strategies: Reaching Struggling Readers* binder provides materials coordinated with the Pupil's Edition (see the Collection Planner, p. T256B) to help students who have difficulty reading and comprehending text, or students who are reluctant readers. The binder for ninth grade is organized around sixteen individual skill areas and offers the following options:

- **MiniRead** MiniReads are short, easy texts that give students a chance to practice a particular skill and strategy before reading selections in the Pupil's Edition. Each MiniRead Skill Lesson can be taught independently or used in conjunction with a Selection Skill Lesson.

- **Selection Skill Lessons** Selection Skill Lessons allow students to apply skills introduced in the MiniReads. Each Selection Skill Lesson provides reading instruction and practice specific to a particular piece of literature in the Pupil's Edition.

Reading Beyond the Anthology

Read On

Each collection in the grade nine book includes an annotated bibliography of books suitable for extended reading. The suggested books are related to works in the collection by theme, by author, or by subject. To preview the Read On for Collection 4, please turn to p. T331.

HRW Library

The *HRW Library* offers novels, plays, works of nonfiction, and short-story collections for extended reading. Each book in the Library includes a major work and thematically or topically related Connections. Each book in the *HRW Library* is also accompanied by a Study Guide that provides teaching suggestions and worksheets.

THE WATSONS GO TO BIRMINGHAM —1963
Christopher Paul Curtis
The Watson family decides to visit Birmingham, Alabama, a trip that will reveal truths about family love and human life.

A SEPARATE PEACE
John Knowles
At prep school, Gene Forrester finds himself in a rivalry with his roommate Phineas. A tragic accident shows Gene the truth about himself.

Collection 4 Discoveries

Resources for this Collection

Note: All resources for this collection are available for preview on the *One-Stop Planner CD-ROM 1 with Test Generator.* All worksheets and blackline masters may be printed from the CD-ROM.

Selection or Feature	Reading and Literary Skills	Vocabulary, Language, and Grammar
The Gift Ray Bradbury (p. 258) **Connections: My Father's Song** Simon J. Ortiz (p. 262)	• *Graphic Organizers for Active Reading,* Worksheet p. 15 • *Literary Elements:* Transparency 6 Worksheet p. 19	• *Daily Oral Grammar,* Transparency 15
Elements of Literature: Theme (p. 264)	• *Literary Elements,* Transparency 6	
Blues Ain't No Mockin Bird Toni Cade Bambara (p. 266)	• *Reading Skills and Strategies: Reaching Struggling Readers* • MiniRead Skill Lesson, p. 80 • Selection Skill Lesson, p. 86 • *Graphic Organizers for Active Reading,* Worksheet p. 16	• *Grammar and Language Links:* Dialect, Worksheet p. 25 • *Daily Oral Grammar,* Transparency 16
Marigolds Eugenia Collier (p. 278) **Connections: Forgive My Guilt** Robert P. Tristram Coffin (p. 288)	• *Graphic Organizers for Active Reading,* Worksheet p. 17	• *Words to Own,* Worksheet p. 12 • *Grammar and Language Links:* Figures of Speech, Worksheet p. 27 • *Daily Oral Grammar,* Transparency 17
American History Judith Ortiz Cofer (p. 292) **Connections: this morning** Lucille Clifton (p. 299)	• *Graphic Organizers for Active Reading,* Worksheet p. 18	• *Words to Own,* Worksheet p. 13 • *Grammar and Language Links:* Clauses, Worksheet p. 29 • *Language Workshop CD-ROM,* Adverb Clauses • *Daily Oral Grammar,* Transparency 18
Helen on Eighty-sixth Street Wendi Kaufman (p. 303)	• *Graphic Organizers for Active Reading,* Worksheet p. 19	• *Words to Own,* Worksheet p. 14 • *Grammar and Language Links:* Coordinating Conjunctions, Worksheet p. 31 • *Language Workshop CD-ROM,* Coordinating Conjunctions • *Daily Oral Grammar,* Transparency 19
The Scarlet Ibis James Hurst (p. 314) **Connections: If There Be Sorrow** Mari Evans (p. 324)	• *Reading Skills and Strategies: Reaching Struggling Readers* • MiniRead Skill Lesson, p. 12 • Selection Skill Lesson, p. 19 • *Graphic Organizers for Active Reading,* Worksheet p. 20	• *Words to Own,* Worksheet p. 15 • *Grammar and Language Links:* Figurative Language, Worksheet p. 33 • *Daily Oral Grammar,* Transparency 20
Extending the Theme: **New Directions** Maya Angelou (p. 328)	The Extending the Theme feature provides students with an unstructured opportunity to practice reading strategies using a selection that extends the theme of the collection.	
Writer's Workshop: Analyzing a **Short Story** (p. 332)		
Sentence Workshop: Stopping in **All the Right Places** (p. 337)		• *Workshop Resources,* p. 67 • *Language Workshop CD-ROM,* Run-on Sentences
Learning for Life: Oral History (p. 339)		

Collection Planner

Other Resources for this Collection

- *Cross-Curricular Activities,* p. 4
- *Portfolio Management System,* Introduction to Portfolio Assessment, p. 1
- *Formal Assessment,* Genre Test, p. 51
- *Test Generator,* Collection Test ⊚

Collection Planner

Writing	Listening and Speaking Viewing and Representing	Assessment
• *Portfolio Management System,* Rubrics for Choices, p. 119	• *Audio CD Library,* Disc 10, Tracks 1, 2 🎧 • *Portfolio Management System,* Rubrics for Choices, p. 119	• *Formal Assessment,* Selection Test, p. 37 • *Standardized Test Preparation,* p. 32 • *Test Generator (One-Stop Planner CD-ROM)* ⊚
		• *Formal Assessment,* Literary Elements Test, p. 49
• *Portfolio Management System,* Rubrics for Choices, p. 120	• *Audio CD Library,* Disc 10, Track 3 🎧 • *Portfolio Management System,* Rubrics for Choices, p. 120	• *Formal Assessment,* Selection Test, p. 39 • *Standardized Test Preparation,* pp. 34, 36 • *Test Generator (One-Stop Planner CD-ROM)* ⊚
• *Portfolio Management System,* Rubrics for Choices, p. 122	• *Audio CD Library,* Disc 10, Tracks 4, 5 🎧 • *Portfolio Management System,* Rubrics for Choices, p. 122	• *Formal Assessment,* Selection Test, p. 41 • *Test Generator (One-Stop Planner CD-ROM)* ⊚
• *Portfolio Management System,* Rubrics for Choices, p. 123	• *Visual Connections:* Videocassette A, Segment 4 📼 • *Audio CD Library,* Disc 11, Track 2 🎧 • *Portfolio Management System,* Rubrics for Choices, p. 123	• *Formal Assessment,* Selection Test, p. 43 • *Test Generator (One-Stop Planner CD-ROM)* ⊚
• *Portfolio Management System,* Rubrics for Choices, p. 125	• *Audio CD Library,* Disc 11, Track 3 🎧 • *Portfolio Management System,* Rubrics for Choices, p. 125	• *Formal Assessment,* Selection Test, p. 45 • *Standardized Test Preparation,* p. 38 • *Test Generator (One-Stop Planner CD-ROM)* ⊚
• *Portfolio Management System,* Rubrics for Choices, p. 126	• *Audio CD Library,* Disc 12, Track 2 🎧 • *Portfolio Management System,* Rubrics for Choices, p. 126	• *Formal Assessment,* Selection Test, p. 47 • *Standardized Test Preparation,* pp. 40, 42 • *Test Generator (One-Stop Planner CD-ROM)* ⊚
	• *Audio CD Library,* Disc 12, Track 3 🎧 • *Viewing and Representing:* Fine Art Transparency 6; Worksheet p. 24	

• Workshop Resources, p. 19
• *Writer's Workshop CD-ROM,* Interpretation ⊚
		• *Portfolio Management System*
		  • Prewriting, p. 128
		  • Peer Editing, p. 129
		  • Assessment Rubric, p. 130

		• *Portfolio Management System,* Rubrics, p. 131

 Transparency    CD-ROM    Video    Audio CD

T256C

Skills Focus

Skills Focus

Selection or Feature	Reading Skills and Strategies	Elements of Literature	Language/ Grammar	Vocabulary/ Spelling	Writing	Listening/ Speaking	Viewing/ Representing
The Gift Ray Bradbury (p. 258)	Find the Writer's Purpose, pp. 258, 263 Compare Texts, p. 263	Climax, pp. 258, 263 Title, p. 263			Freewrite About a Story, p. 263 Write a Proposal for a TV Special, p. 263	Prepare an Oral Report on Traditions, p. 263	Select Images to Illustrate an Oral Report, p. 263
Elements of Literature: Theme (p. 264)		Theme, pp. 264–265 Subject, p. 264					
Blues Ain't No Mockin Bird Toni Cade Bambara (p. 266)	Make Generalizations, pp. 266, 275	Images, p. 275 Theme, pp. 266, 275 Title, pp. 266, 275 Anecdote, p. 275 First-Person Narrator, p. 275 Conflict, p. 275	Dialect, p. 277 • Speech and Character • Regional Speech • Dialect • Idioms		State a Theme, p. 276 Analyze a Character, p. 276 Write a Poem, p. 276 Research Regulations, p. 276 Compare Speakers, p. 276		Use a Graphic Organizer, p. 276
Marigolds Eugenia Collier (p. 278)	Identify Key Passages, pp. 278, 289	Internal Conflict, pp. 278, 289–290	Figures of Speech: Similes and Metaphors, p. 291	New Words, p. 291	Diagram Conflicts, p. 290 Write a Letter to an Agency, p. 290		Create a Chart, p. 290 Create a Collage, p. 290
American History Judith Ortiz Cofer (p. 292)	Dialogue with the Text, pp. 292, 300 Summarize Main Events, p. 300	Theme, pp. 292, 300 Title, p. 300	Adverb Clauses, p. 302 Subordinating Conjunctions, p. 302	Analogies, p. 302	Focus on Setting, p. 301 Write an Oral History, p. 301 Write a Character Sketch, p. 301	Conduct Interviews, p. 301	Create a Graphic Representation of an Idea, p. 301 Interpret a Collage, p. 301
Helen on Eighty-sixth Street Wendi Kaufman (p. 303)	Monitor Comprehension, p. 303 Recognize Allusions, pp. 303, 312 Use Context Clues, p. 303	Theme, pp. 303, 312 Allusion, pp. 303, 312	Coordinating Conjunctions, p. 313	Word Roots, p. 313 Etymologies, p. 313	Analyze a Character, p. 312 Evaluate a Character, p. 312	Research and Deliver a First-Person Oral Report on a Mythological Character, p. 312	
The Scarlet Ibis James Hurst (p. 314)	Dialogue with the Text, pp. 314, 325	Symbols, pp. 314, 325 Theme, p. 325 Similes, p. 327	Figurative Language, p. 327	Malapropisms, p. 327	Determine Point of View, p. 326 Rewrite a Scene, p. 326 Write a Character Analysis, p. 326	Conduct Interviews and Report on Sibling Rivalry, p. 326	Research and Illustrate the Flora of the South, p. 326
Extending the Theme: New Directions Maya Angelou (p. 328)	The Extending the Theme feature provides students with an unstructured opportunity to practice reading strategies using a selection that extends the theme of the collection.						
Writer's Workshop: Analyzing a Short Story (p. 332)		Elements of Literature, p. 333	Transitional Words, p. 334		Write an Essay Analyzing a Short Story, pp. 332–336		
Sentence Workshop: Stopping in All the Right Places (p. 337)			Run-On Sentences, Fused Sentences, and Comma Splices, p. 337		Revise Sentences to Avoid Run-Ons, Comma Splices, or Fused Sentences, p. 337		
Reading for Life: Evaluating Arguments (p. 338)	Inductive and Deductive Reasoning, p. 338 Make Generalizations, p. 338	Argument, p. 338					
Learning for Life: Oral History (p. 339)					Write a Newspaper Article, p. 339	Edit and Share Oral Histories, p. 339	Create a Storyteller's Wall, p. 339

DISCOVERIES

WRITING FOCUS: Analyzing a Short Story

Every once in a while close friends or parents or teachers do something that surprises us. We've been around them a lot and think we know them well. Then a kind and gentle friend reveals a selfish streak, a hard teacher gives us a break, or someone we never trusted comes through for us suddenly. At such moments we discover something about people and life, and the discoveries can be wonderful or painful. More startling still can be the moments when we discover something about ourselves. It may happen when we're suddenly angry at something that never bothered us before or when we finally understand why we're nervous at parties. We might realize that we admire someone we've never noticed before, or want something we never thought we would want. Every story is in some way or other also about a discovery. If the story works, we realize by its end that we, along with the characters, have discovered (or rediscovered) something important about life.

A lie hides the truth.
A story tries to find it.

—Paula Fox

Writer's Notebook

We analyze stories (and movies) all the time, without quite realizing it. We ask: What's happening? What does it mean? Why does this character behave that way? Could that necklace be a symbol? In the Writer's Workshop on page 332, you'll answer questions like these when you write your own analysis of a short story. To get started, jot down some notes now on one or two stories in this book you've already read. Ask this question: What did the main character *discover* by the end of the story? Save your notes.

257

OBJECTIVES

1. Read stories centered on the theme "Discoveries"
2. Identify and analyze literary elements used in the literature with special emphasis on theme
3. Apply a variety of reading strategies to short stories
4. Respond to the literature using a variety of modes
5. Learn and use new words
6. Plan, draft, revise, edit, proof, and publish an analysis of a short story
7. Revise run-on sentences
8. Demonstrate the ability to evaluate an argument
9. Learn how to research and present oral history through a variety of projects

Responding to the Quotation

❓ How can a story present a truth to its readers? [Possible response: It leads them to make discoveries.]

RESPONDING TO THE ART

❓ How does the photograph suggest the theme "Discoveries"? [It shows someone who has climbed a high peak in order to see the world in a new way.]

Writer's Notebook

Write the word *discoveries* on the board. Have the class brainstorm associations or emotions that the word suggests. Explain that there are good discoveries (such as a hidden talent) and bad ones (such as things you might find under a rock). Have students begin a four-column chart in their notebooks to be filled in as they read the stories in the collection. The four columns should contain:

• the title of each story
• its main character
• what the character discovers by the end of the story
• what kind of discovery it is— exciting, sad, or something else

OBJECTIVES
1. Read and interpret the story
2. Identify and interpret the climax
3. Find the writer's purpose
4. Express understanding through writing or an oral report

SKILLS

Literary
- Identify and interpret the climax

Reading
- Find the writer's purpose

Writing
- Describe a response to a story
- Write a proposal for a television special

Speaking/Listening
- Report on holiday traditions

Planning

- **Traditional Schedule**
  Lesson Plans Including Strategies for English-Language Learners
- **One-Stop Planner**
  CD-ROM with Test Generator

Before You Read

THE GIFT

Make the Connection

What Endures

We may not celebrate holidays today in quite the same way our ancestors did. We shop for different gifts, cook with new recipes, and travel in airplanes instead of covered wagons. Still, traditions have a way of enduring—the old meanings are still there. We still choose gifts for people we love and rearrange our schedules to share holidays with them. In Ray Bradbury's "The Gift" the holidays have changed on the outside, but the true meaning of Christmas endures.

Quickwrite

Think for a few minutes about the next holiday in your life. What are your plans? Will you do anything that simply couldn't have been done two hundred years ago—like taking pictures or e-mailing your grandparents? Write for a few minutes about holidays past, present, and future. If things are different today from what they once were, what might they be like in, say, another two hundred years?

Elements of Literature

Climax

The **climax** of a story is its key scene—that tense, terrifying, or just plain exciting moment when our emotional involvement is greatest because we are about to discover the outcome of

> The **climax** is that moment when we realize what the outcome of the story will be.
>
> *For more on Climax, see pages 32–33 and the Handbook of Literary Terms.*

the story's conflict. It's the moment when Cinderella's foot fits into the slipper or when Dorothy clicks her heels together and finds herself back home in Kansas. Very often, at the climax, we readers discover something right along with the characters.

Reading Skills and Strategies

Finding the Writer's Purpose: Making a Point

A short story can be fun to read but still make a serious point. "The Gift" is like that. In fact, the author of this story, Ray Bradbury, says that he "writes for fun," but readers know that his work also contains serious messages. As you read "The Gift," think about the serious points Bradbury makes—about holidays, family, and gift giving. Sometimes readers disagree with a writer's message. How do you feel about Bradbury's? (Be sure to read Bradbury's comments about his writing on page 261.)

go.hrw.com
LE0 9-4

   Resources: Print and Media

Reading
- *Graphic Organizers for Active Reading,* p. 15
- *Audio CD Library*
  Disc 10, Tracks 1, 2

Elements of Literature
- *Literary Elements*
  Transparency 6
  Worksheet, p. 19

Writing and Language
- *Daily Oral Grammar*
  Transparency 15

Assessment
- *Formal Assessment,* p. 37
- *Portfolio Management System,* p. 119
- *Standardized Test Preparation,* p. 32
- *Test Generator (One-Stop Planner CD-ROM)*

Internet
- go.hrw.com (keyword: LE0 9-4)

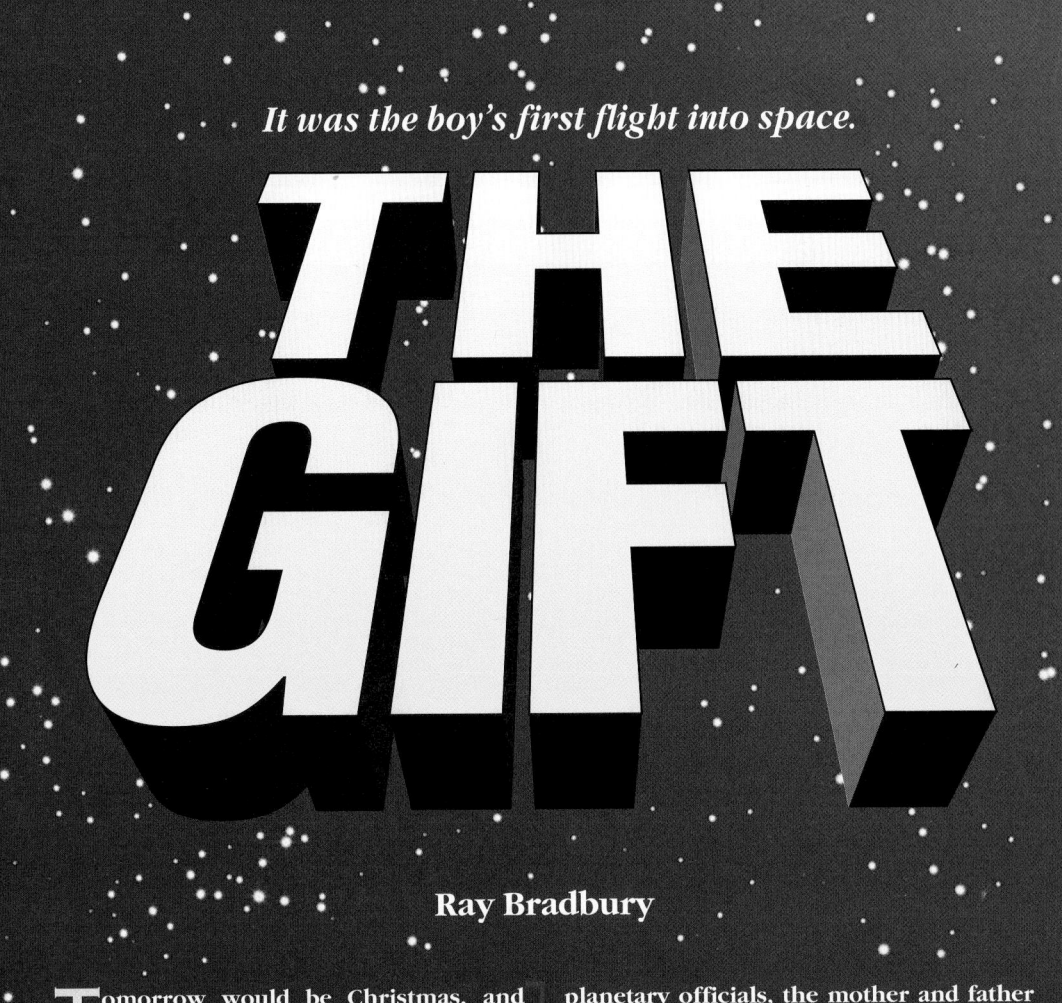

It was the boy's first flight into space.

THE GIFT

Ray Bradbury

Tomorrow would be Christmas, and even while the three of them rode to the rocket port the mother and father were worried. It was the boy's first flight into space, his very first time in a rocket, and they wanted everything to be perfect. So when, at the customs table, they were forced to leave behind his gift, which exceeded the weight limit by no more than a few ounces, and the little tree with the lovely white candles, they felt themselves deprived of the season and their love.

The boy was waiting for them in the Terminal room. Walking toward him, after their unsuccessful clash with the Inter-

planetary officials, the mother and father whispered to each other.

"What shall we do?"

"Nothing, nothing. What *can* we do?"

"Silly rules!"

"And he so wanted the tree!"

The siren gave a great howl and people pressed forward into the Mars Rocket. The mother and father walked at the very last, their small pale son between them, silent.

"I'll think of something," said the father.

"What . . .?" asked the boy.

And the rocket took off and they were flung headlong into dark space.

The rocket moved and left fire behind

THE GIFT **259**

Summary ■

A family of three is traveling aboard the Mars Rocket on Christmas Eve, in the year 2052. Because of customs regulations, the parents have to leave behind the boy's Christmas present and a little tree with white candles. Although they are all disappointed, the father plans a special gift for his son. At midnight he leads his son into a darkened cabin on the ship. At the story's climax the boy sees billions of stars burning like white candles through the cabin's enormous porthole. His father has helped him to discover that the universe itself is a precious gift.

Resources

Listening
Audio CD Library
A reading of this story is provided in the *Audio CD Library*:
• Disc 10, Track 1

Elements of Literature
Theme
For additional instruction on theme, see *Literary Elements*:
• Transparency 6
• Worksheet, p. 19

Ⓐ Elements of Literature
Setting
? What conclusion can you draw about the story's time setting from its opening sentence? [It occurs on December 24 in a future when space travel is available to the general public.]

Ⓑ Elements of Literature
Plot
? What complication has been introduced by the end of the first paragraph? [The boy's parents are concerned because they must leave behind their son's Christmas present and a small Christmas tree.]

Reaching All Students

Struggling Readers
Finding the Author's Purpose was introduced on page 258. One good strategy to use with this skill is Sketch to Stretch. For information on using this strategy, see p. 101 in the *Reading Strategies Handbook* in front of the *Reading Skills and Strategies* binder.

English Language Learners
To help students grasp the story's meaning, ask them to close their eyes and to visualize while you read the climactic scene aloud. Have each student write down two reasons why the sight of billions of stars through the porthole might be a wonderful present. Ask students to share their reasons. For additional strategies for engaging English language learners, see
• *Lesson Plans Including Strategies for English-Language Learners*

Advanced Learners
To expand students' creativity, have them work individually or in small groups to write and illustrate a short story similar to the selection. They might read "The Gift of the Magi" on p. 202 or *A Christmas Carol* for inspiration. Their goal should be to capture the essence of Christmas or another holiday of their choice. Encourage students to choose a setting that appeals to them and to use dialogue. They may wish to read their completed stories to the class.

LITERATURE AND SCIENCE

Have students investigate scientific research, read short stories or novels, or see films about extra-terrestrial life. Some students may wish to research the SETI project. Others may wish to report to the class on films or books like *E.T., Sphere, 2010,* or one of the *Star Trek* or *Star Wars* movies. Have students discuss how fictional depictions of aliens compare with their own visions of life in outer space.

A Reading Skills and Strategies

Finding the Writer's Purpose

? Why do you think the gift matters so much to the boy? What details support your response? [Possible responses: He sounds like a very young child, since little children are the ones who really get excited about gifts and expect that all promises will be fulfilled; he may be ill, since he is described as "pale" and "feverish".] **The boy's questions emphasize material objects. What serious point might Bradbury be making by having the boy equate Christmas with material objects?** [He is reminding the reader that for many people, Christmas means getting things.]

Life in Outer Space?

On October 12, 1992, the 500th anniversary of Columbus's landing in the Americas, the National Aeronautics and Space Administration began a project called SETI, the Search for Extraterrestrial Intelligence. SETI scientists do not hunt for spaceships or little green men; they listen to the static in outer space, hoping to detect a radio signal from an unknown civilization somewhere in the universe. The main tool in this search is the radio telescope, which looks like a huge bowl made of perforated aluminum surrounded by movable antennae. A super computer processes every radio wave that hits the bowl. The computer does billions of tests a second, discarding the random waves given off by stars and carefully scanning any regular patterns. Some scientists dream of discovering an "encyclopedia galactica," a collection of advanced scientific knowledge sent by sophisticated aliens. This dream may be intriguing, but there's no guarantee that humans would be able to recognize or interpret such information if it actually arrived. To date, there is no proof that anyone is out there, and in 1993, Congress ended all federal funding for the project. Still, scientists at three privately supported SETI programs continue to point their telescopes at the stars and to listen.

and left Earth behind on which the date was December 24, 2052, heading out into a place where there was no time at all, no month, no year, no hour. They slept away the rest of the first "day." Near midnight, by their Earth-time New York watches, the boy awoke and said, "I want to go look out the porthole."

There was only one port, a "window" of immensely thick glass of some size, up on the next deck.

"Not quite yet," said the father. "I'll take you up later."

"I want to see where we are and where we're going."

"I want you to wait for a reason," said the father.

He had been lying awake, turning this way and that, thinking of the abandoned gift, the problem of the season, the lost tree and the white candles. And at last, sitting up, no more than five minutes ago, he believed he had found a plan. He need only carry it out and this journey would be fine and joyous indeed.

"Son," he said, "in exactly one half-hour it will be Christmas."

"Oh," said the mother, dismayed that he had mentioned it. Somehow she had rather hoped that the boy would forget.

A The boy's face grew feverish and his lips trembled. "I know, I know. Will I get a present, will I? Will I have a tree? Will I have a tree? You promised——"

"Yes, yes, all that, and more," said the father.

The mother started. "But——"

"I mean it," said the father. "I really mean it. All and more, much more. Excuse me, now. I'll be back."

He left them for about twenty minutes. When he came back, he was smiling. "Almost time."

"Can I hold your watch?" asked the boy, and

260 THE SHORT-STORY COLLECTIONS

Making the Connections

Connecting to the Theme: "Discoveries"

Ask students to consider who has made a discovery in this story. Is it only the boy, who sees his world in a new and unusual way, or have his parents also made a discovery? [Both the boy and the parents discover a new way of viewing the universe, a way that enriches their traditional understanding of Christmas.]

Cultural Connections

Many people associate Christmas with a tree and gift giving, but in some cultures the gifts are given on "Twelfth Night"—January 6, the Christian holiday celebrating the visit of the wise men to Bethlehem. In the Jewish tradition, gifts are given throughout the eight days of Hanukkah, which falls in mid-December. Around the world, Christmas is also connected with a variety of other traditions. In Australia and New Zealand, December is a summer month, and many people go to the beach for a Christmas picnic. A tradition for Mexican children is to break a candy-filled Christmas piñata made of clay or paper. Encourage students to research holiday traditions in various countries and to write a composite article for the school paper. Students from other countries or cultures can report on their traditions.

the watch was handed over and he held it ticking in his fingers as the rest of the hour drifted by in fire and silence and unfelt motion.

"It's Christmas *now*! Christmas! Where's my present?"

"Here we go," said the father and took his boy by the shoulder and led him from the room, down the hall, up a rampway, his wife following.

"I don't understand," she kept saying.

"You will. Here we are," said the father.

They had stopped at the closed door of a large cabin. The father tapped three times and then twice in a code. The door opened and the light in the cabin went out and there was a whisper of voices.

"Go on in, son," said the father.

"It's dark."

"I'll hold your hand. Come on, Mama."

They stepped into the room and the door shut, and the room was very dark indeed. And before them loomed a great glass eye, the porthole, a window four feet high and six feet wide, from which they could look out into space.

The boy gasped.

Behind him, the father and the mother gasped with him, and then in the dark room some people began to sing.

"Merry Christmas, son," said the father.

And the voices in the room sang the old, the familiar carols, and the boy moved slowly until his face was pressed against the cool glass of the port. And he stood there for a long, long time, just looking and looking out into space and the deep night at the burning and the burning of ten billion billion white and lovely candles. . . .

B Elements of Literature
Climax
? What makes this paragraph the climax of the story? [Sample response: It contains a moment of recognition; the boy seems to forget about material things, like his present and the tree, and to realize that Christmas represents something bigger—that joy, sharing, and wonder are more essential to the true meaning of Christmas.]

Resources

Selection Assessment
Formal Assessment
• Selection Test, p. 37
Test Generator (One-Stop Planner)
• CD-ROM

MEET THE WRITER
A Love of Ideas

Ray Bradbury (1920–   ) has been mystifying readers with his tales of the strange and the wonderful for decades. Bradbury credits his large output of stories, novels, and plays to his love of ideas and his taste for good fun:

66 Everything of mine is permeated with my love of ideas—both big and small. It doesn't matter what it is, as long as it grabs me and holds me, fascinates me. And then I'll run out and do something about it. . . . I write for fun. You can't get too serious. I don't pontificate in my work. I have fun with ideas. I play with them. I approach my craft with enthusiasm and respect. If my work sparks serious thought, fine. But I don't write with that in mind. I'm not a serious person, and I don't like serious people. . . . My goal is to entertain myself and others. Hopefully, that will prevent me from taking myself too seriously. **99**

For more biographical information on Ray Bradbury, see page 44.

THE GIFT **261**

Assessing Learning

Check Test: True-False
1. Most of the action in the story takes place on Mars. [False]
2. Rules about weight limits force the boy's parents to leave behind his Christmas gift and a small tree. [True]
3. The father comes up with a plan for a Christmas gift for his son. [True]
4. At midnight on Christmas, the parents light candles on a tree in the captain's cabin. [False]
5. The other passengers on the rocket sing Christmas carols as the boy looks out the porthole. [True]

Standardized Test Preparation
For practice with a standardized test format specific to this selection, see
• *Standardized Test Preparation*, p. 32
For practice in proofreading and editing, see
• *Daily Oral Grammar*, Transparency 15

Connections

The speaker recounts a vivid memory from his childhood. While planting corn with his father, they discover a nest of baby mice. The father moves the mice to safety and this gesture teaches the boy an important lesson about life.

Ⓐ Reading Skills and Strategies
Making Inferences

❓ What is the speaker suggesting here? [He implies that his father has died, which makes the following memory very emotional.]

Ⓑ Critical Thinking
Interpreting

❓ What important lesson do you think the speaker learned from this experience? [Possible response: His father's care for the nest sets an example that teaches the speaker to value life, even in minute forms.]

Resources 🎧

Listening
Audio CD Library
A reading of "My Father's Song" is provided in the *Audio CD Library*:
• Disc 10, Track 2

Connections A POEM

My Father's Song
Simon J. Ortiz

Ⓐ Wanting to say things,
I miss my father tonight.
His voice, the slight catch,
the depth from his thin chest,
5   the tremble of emotion
in something he has just said
to his son, his song:

We planted corn one Spring at Acu——
we planted several times
10 but this one particular time
I remember the soft damp sand
in my hand.

My father had stopped at one point
to show me an overturned furrow;
15 the plowshare had unearthed
the burrow nest of a mouse
in the soft moist sand.

Very gently, he scooped tiny pink animals
into the palm of his hand
20 and told me to touch them.
We took them to the edge
of the field and put them in the shade
of a sand moist clod.

Ⓑ I remember the very softness
25 of cool and warm sand and tiny alive mice
and my father saying things.

Connecting Across Texts

Connecting with "The Gift"
Ortiz's poem, like Bradbury's story, is about a son learning a valuable lesson from his father. The boy in "The Gift" learns to value life by viewing the immensity of the universe. The speaker in "My Father's Song" learns a similar lesson by recognizing the value of tiny mice in a field. Both boys experience a feeling of awe in the presence of the beauty of the natural world.

MAKING MEANINGS

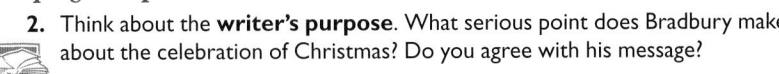

First Thoughts

[interpret]
1. What do you think the family discovers at the **climax** of "The Gift"?

Shaping Interpretations

[interpret]

2. Think about the **writer's purpose**. What serious point does Bradbury make about the celebration of Christmas? Do you agree with his message?

[interpret]
3. What is the gift referred to in the story's **title**?

Extending the Text

[compare]
4. Both "The Gift" and "My Father's Song" (see *Connections* on page 262) are about important childhood experiences. Why are these experiences so important to the children? How are the "gifts" that are exchanged in each selection alike?

CHOICES: Building Your Portfolio

Writer's Notebook

1. Collecting Ideas for an Analysis of a Short Story

WORK IN PROGRESS

Choosing a story. In the Writer's Workshop on page 332, you'll be analyzing—or examining—a short story. Your first task will be to choose your story. Skim the stories you have read so far in this book. Consider especially the stories that have had a great impact on you. Don't forget the ones that you did not enjoy (there was a reason!). Choose one story for practice, and freewrite for a few minutes, describing your general response to it. Keep your notes for possible use later.

Storyboard

2. A TV Special

Your job is to write a proposal for a half-hour television special based on "The Gift." Retell the main events of the story so that it will sound unique and compelling to a TV producer. Describe a few of the special effects that will convey its unusual setting. Which actors do you see in the main roles? Remember, TV producers can be very picky, so give the specific information they'll be looking for:

- What feeling will you be conveying in the special?
- Who will the audience be?
- What time slot would you aim for?
- Who are the characters and what do they want?

- What complications arise?
- How are their problems resolved?

Oral Report

3. Traditions!

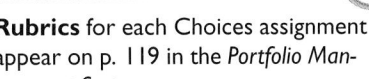

The boy in "The Gift" misses his tree, candles, and gifts because they are part of a tradition he has grown up with. Imagine that you're far away during an important holiday. What would you miss? Gather details about the way you celebrate this holiday. Think of food, events, music, people, clothing, and rituals. Share your traditions with the class. (You might want to use photographs and objects to illustrate your presentation.) Be sure to check your Quickwrite notes.

Using Students' Strengths

Visual/Spatial Learners

For Choice 2, have students order their ideas with a graphic organizer. Have them first create separate boxes or circles for these topics: feeling to be conveyed, audience, time slot, special effects, characters, possible actors, main events, complications, and resolution of the story. Then have them use arrows to indicate how the information in one box or circle relates to another; for example, to show how a certain event elicits a specific feeling.

Grading Timesaver

Rubrics for each Choices assignment appear on p. 119 in the *Portfolio Management System*.

MAKING MEANINGS

First Thoughts

1. Possible responses: The family discovers that lack of a tree or gifts does not take away the meaning of Christmas; they experience joy, sharing, wonder, and love when they look at the stars while their companions sing.

Shaping Interpretations

2. Bradbury's point is that the important thing about Christmas is being with loved ones and sharing a wonderful experience. Most students will agree.

3. The title refers both to the boy's awe-inspiring view of the universe and to his deeper understanding of Christmas.

Extending the Text

4. Although responses will vary, students should understand that sharing and love make these experiences important to the children. The gifts in each selection are not material; both boys are given an insight into nature and a greater feeling of connection to their surroundings.

CHOICES: Building Your Portfolio

1. **Writer's Notebook** Remind students to save their work. They may use it as prewriting for the Writer's Workshop on p. 332.

2. **Storyboard** Before students begin writing their proposals, divide them into small groups to brainstorm ideas. Remind them that their purpose is to convince the TV producer their idea has merit. They might describe the audience, time slot, and feeling of the special and conclude with their reasons for wanting the special produced.

3. **Oral Report** If possible, have students meet with others who share the same holiday traditions and list the food, music, people, clothing, and rituals they associate with the holiday. Then, have students prepare individual reports.

OBJECTIVES
1. Learn how to interpret a story's theme
2. Distinguish theme from subject
3. Learn how to critique the theme of a story

Resources

Elements of Literature

Theme

For additional instruction on theme, see *Literary Elements:*
- Transparency 6

Elements of Literature

This feature focuses on theme. It distinguishes it from the subject of a story and reminds students that sometimes it is wise to question the writer's presentation of a theme.

Mini-Lesson:

Theme

Make sure students understand how to distinguish the theme from the subject, or topic, of a story. A story's theme is its revelation of a truth about human life. A theme is rarely stated directly; usually the writer leads the reader to discover it as the characters discover it. Themes usually reflect a basic conflict in human experience: an awareness of the difference between what *ought to be* and what *is*. The reader should critique the theme offered by the writer: Is it too romantic? too simple? too narrow-minded? Is the writer trying to sell an idea that is false and shoddy? Themes that are weak in any of these ways are characteristic of "slick" or "formula" fiction—stories with smooth, shiny surfaces but little depth.

Elements of Literature

THEME: What Does It Mean?

A story can excel in any number of ways—in the strength of its plot, in the reality of its characters, in the gracefulness of its language. But what often makes us remember a story long after we've read it is the idea on which it's built.

This central idea of a story is called its **theme**. The theme of a story is not the same as its subject. The **subject** is simply the topic of the story. A topic can be stated in one or two words: love, war, growing up. The theme makes some revelation about the subject. A theme is always a statement; it must always be something that can be expressed in at least one sentence.

Revealing a Truth About Human Behavior

Usually, the theme reveals a truth about human behavior. That truth is often one that the writer has discovered from

experience or perhaps in the act of writing—for example, that in certain circumstances it is a mistake to marry only for love; or that as one grows old, death becomes less terrifying. To communicate—perhaps to discover—this idea, the writer tells a story.

The theme is usually not stated directly in the story at all. An essayist often states a theme directly as a way of getting the main idea across clearly, but the fiction writer has a different purpose. The fiction writer can let the story's characters act the idea out for us. The fiction writer hopes that we will feel the characters' experiences so strongly that the truth revealed to them will be revealed to us as well.

When the theme of a story seems fresh and true, we say, "Yes, I see what the writer means, but I hadn't quite thought of it that way before," or "I hadn't felt quite so

> A powerful theme can be the reason that a story gets to our hearts and lingers in our minds.

strongly about it before." Then we have penetrated the surface of human behavior and seen what the writer wants us to recognize about our lives. Although a theme is usually invisible and unstated, it can be the story's most forceful element. A powerful theme can be the reason that a story gets to our hearts and lingers in our minds.

A Conflict Between What Ought to Be and What Is

In previous eras fiction was widely regarded as a way to teach morality—the right and wrong ways to behave. One could usually be sure in those days that a wicked character in a story would be punished and a virtuous one would be rewarded. Today, fiction is not usually regarded as a way to teach morality. Yet that conflict between what we know *would be* in a perfect world and what *is* in a disorderly, imperfect world is still the central business of literature. The theme in a story can be seen as a reflection of this basic conflict in human experience.

Reaching All Students

Struggling Readers

As students read the feature, have them develop an outline of its main points. If a paragraph puzzles them, have them reread it and discuss it with a partner until they can state its main point in their own words. Direct students especially to take notes on the meanings of *subject, theme,* and *"slick"* or *"formula" fiction.*

English Language Learners

To help students recognize theme, have them answer the following questions:
- What is the main subject of "The Gift"? [Christmas on the Mars rocket]
- What does the story say about this subject? [Love and shared experience are often the best gift.]

For additional strategies, see
- *Lesson Plans Including Strategies for English-Language Learners*

Advanced Learners

Ask these students to provide the class with additional examples of popular short stories, novels, or movies, and a statement of the theme of each. They should include stories from their textbooks. Have them present their findings to the class on 3″ x 5″ index cards, each containing a title, a brief summary, and a statement of the theme. Other students can then use these cards as the basis of discussion.

by John Leggett

Thinking Critically About Theme

Sometimes it is wise to question the writer's presentation of a theme. We need to discover whether the writer is presenting a truth about life or trying to force us to accept a view of life that we think is false.

The wise reader makes a judgment about a writer's view of the world and doesn't accept a story's theme as valid just because it's in print. The wise reader asks: Is this story's view of life too romantic? Is it too cynical? Is it too simple? Is it narrow-minded? Is this writer an overzealous salesperson who is trying to get me to buy an idea that is false or shoddy? Is this writer using violent incidents just to sell the story and make money?

Much of the fiction in popular magazines is weak in this way. It is often referred to as "slick" fiction, not only because it is usually found in magazines printed on slick paper, but because such stories have a smooth, shiny surface but little depth.

"Formula fiction" is another way of putting it—many of these stories are written to a plan that satisfies the general preference for happy or upbeat stories over true-to-life ones. Think of the typical romance novel in which a

happy outcome is assured, and you'll have one commercially successful formula.

As wise readers we learn to make our own critical judgments about the fiction we read—just as we do with the television we watch and the movies we see.

> Is this writer an overzealous salesperson who is trying to get me to buy an idea that is false or shoddy?

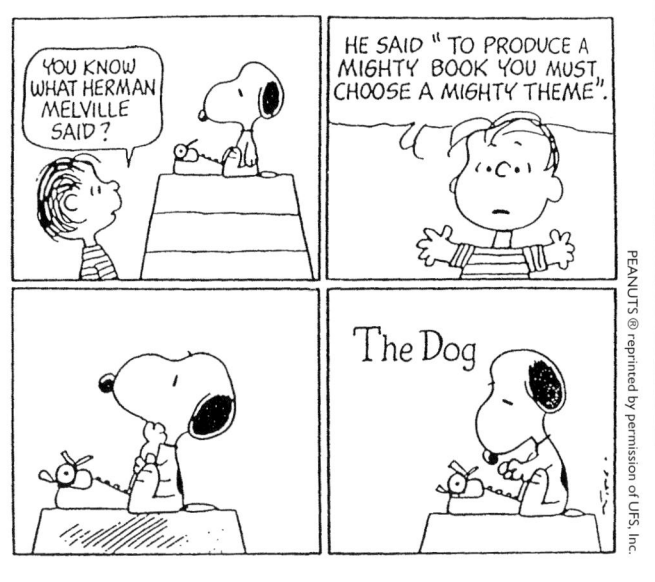

PEANUTS ® reprinted by permission of UFS, Inc.

ELEMENTS OF LITERATURE: THEME **265**

Applying the Element

With your students, compile a list of memorable short stories or novels they have read or movies they have seen. Ask volunteers to offer ideas about what makes one or more of the works memorable. Often these ideas will suggest a theme. For example, students may like the various *Star Trek* spin-offs because they suggest that humankind will, in the future, abandon discrimination and work together. Then have students work in small groups to choose a story, novel, or movie from the list and come to a consensus about its theme. Ask students to evaluate whether or not their theme has something true to say about life, or whether it is a "slick" or "formula" theme that does not address real issues. Have each group present its findings to the class.

Resources ────────

Assessment
Formal Assessment
• Literary Elements Test, p. 49

Getting Students Involved

Cooperative Learning

Topics Ad Lib. To help students better understand the element of theme, prominently display the following topics on the board: future, love, sharing, growing up, holidays, family, gift. Ask for volunteers to select one of the words and use it in a sentence about the theme of "The Gift." Keep going until students have discovered that all of the words can be used in sentences about the theme of the story.

Name That Theme. Have students write a statement of the theme of each story read by the class in recent weeks. Then challenge a small group of students to collect all of the themes and use them to develop a game show quiz that asks participants to name the story to which each theme refers. The group developing the game show will need to select judges to arbitrate disputes, in case a theme can logically be said to apply to more than one story.

OBJECTIVES
1. Read and interpret the story
2. Connect a story's title to its theme
3. Make generalizations
4. Express understanding through critical and creative writing, speaking, or research
5. Identify dialect and rewrite it in standard English

SKILLS

Literary
- Connect a story's title to its theme

Reading
- Make generalizations

Writing
- Make notes on theme
- Write a character analysis
- Write a poem
- Compare the speaker of a poem with a character from the story

Research/Social Studies
- Compile a report on government food stamp programs

Language
- Rewrite dialect

Viewing/Representing
- Compare a painting's subject with the story's narrator (ATE)
- Compare the mood of a painting with the mood of the story (ATE)
- Examine art imagery (ATE)

Planning

- **Block Schedule**
  Block Scheduling Lesson Plans with Pacing Guide
- **Traditional Schedule**
  Lesson Plans Including Strategies for English-Language Learners
- **One-Stop Planner**
  CD-ROM with Test Generator

Before You Read

BLUES AIN'T NO MOCKIN BIRD

Make the Connection

Singing the Blues

The title of this story comes from an old Mississippi blues song sung by African Americans as a response to trouble. The song tells us that the blues are not self-pitying, nor are they songs about death (as the song of the mockingbird is said to be). The blues are really fighting songs. The blues help people get through.

Quickwrite

The grown-ups in this story have plenty of reasons to sing the blues. One of their problems comes from a camera-man who wants to take pictures of them. Jot down quickly your feelings on the ways the media sometimes interfere with people's private lives and private sufferings. Then, think about why people like to watch other people's troubles on television.

Elements of Literature

Title and Theme

The title of a story or novel is part of the text—in fact, it is the first part of the text that we read, though often it is the last thing a writer thinks up. Whatever title the writer chooses, it should bring into sharper focus what the story is about.

> The **title** often gives a clue to a story's theme.
>
> *For more on Theme, see pages 264–265 and the Handbook of Literary Terms.*

Reading Skills and Strategies

Making Generalizations: Big Ideas

People make generalizations—broad statements that can be applied to many situations—all the time. After you read a story, you try to form an idea about its theme. Theme is expressed as a generalization about life, about what we wish for, what we fear, how we should live our lives. You make your generalization based on many details in the text, including, often, its title. Based on its title, which is a full sentence, what do you predict this story will be about?

go.hrw.com
LE0 9-4

"Just people here is what I tend to consider."

(Opposite) *Li'l Sis* (1944)
by William H. Johnson.
Oil on board (26″ x 21¼″).
National Museum of American Art, Washington, D.C.

266 THE SHORT-STORY COLLECTIONS

 *Resources: Print and Media*

Reading
- *Reading Skills and Strategies*
  MiniRead Skill Lesson, p. 80
  Selection Skill Lesson, p. 86
- *Graphic Organizers for Active Reading*, p. 16
- *Audio CD Library*, Disc 10, Track 3

Writing and Language
- *Daily Oral Grammar*, Transparency 16
- *Grammar and Language Links*, Worksheet, p. 25

Assessment
- *Formal Assessment*, p. 39
- *Portfolio Management System*, p. 120
- *Standardized Test Preparation*, pp. 34, 36
- *Test Generator (One-Stop Planner* CD-ROM)

Internet
- go.hrw.com (keyword LE0 9-4)

Blues Ain't No Mockin Bird

Toni Cade Bambara

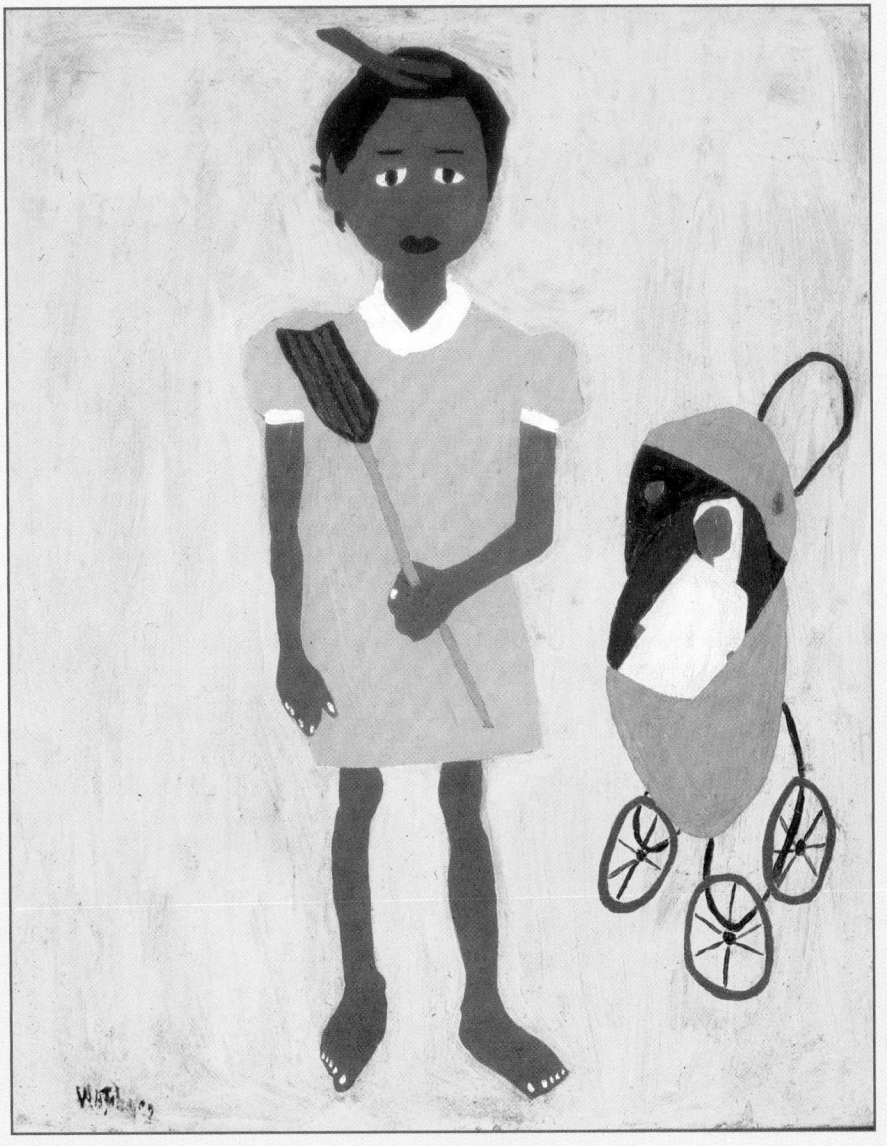

Summary ■■■

Two insensitive filmmakers who are making a documentary about the food stamp program invade the privacy of Granny and Granddaddy Cain, a proud and dignified older couple. The filmmakers have good intentions, but they don't treat the Cains with the proper respect. Without asking for permission they pry into the family's personal life, filming their rural home and disturbing their routine. The narrator and other children watch as Granny and Granddaddy Cain repeatedly but politely rebuff the filmmakers. When Granny Cain finally tells her husband to make the men leave, he resolves the conflict by removing the film from their camera.

Resources ————

Listening
Audio CD Library
Students can hear the dialect in the reading of this story from the *Audio CD Library:*
• Disk 10, Track 3

RESPONDING TO THE ART
For information on **William H. Johnson** see p. T121.
Activity. After students read the story, ask them what similarities with and differences from Bambara's narrator are suggested by this young girl's pose and expression. [Possible responses: The first-person narrator talks directly to the reader, using the pronoun *I*, and the girl in the painting looks directly at the viewer; the narrator is surrounded by other people, but the girl in the painting is alone except for the baby in the carriage.]

Reaching All Students

Struggling Readers
Making Generalizations was introduced on page 266. For a lesson directly tied to this story that teaches students to make generalizations by using a strategy called Sketch to Stretch, see the *Reading Skills and Strategies* binder:
• MiniRead Skill Lesson, p. 80
• Selection Skill Lesson, p. 86

English Language Learners
The dialect in this selection may prove challenging for students learning English. Explain that a dialect varies from standard English in predictable ways. In this story, point out especially the omission of the final *g* on *-ing* forms, the use of double negatives, and the use of *ain't* for *isn't* and *aren't*. For additional strategies, see
• *Lesson Plans Including Strategies for English-Language Learners*

Advanced Learners
After they read the selection, encourage advanced learners to write an imaginary history of the Cain family based on clues provided in the story. Have them develop the motivation for the family's many moves, keeping in mind the smoldering anger within Granny Cain.

T267

Ⓐ Appreciating Language

Dialect

Have students locate the words in the first three sentences that omit the final consonant *g* on *-ing* forms. ["stompin," "swingin," "waitin," "tap-dancin"] Explain that this pattern marks the dialect that is used in the story.

Ⓑ Reading Skills and Strategies

Making Generalizations

❓ What details support the generalization that the family has moved many times? [The narrator speaks about having lived in three other places—"the Judsons' woods," "the Cooper place," and "the dairy."]

Ⓒ Appreciating Language

Dialect

❓ Point out that *ain't* is used in place of standard English *isn't* or *aren't*. Which standard English word is replaced by *ain't* in this sentence? [aren't]

Ⓓ Appreciating Language

Dialect

❓ Cathy uses a double negative, *don't never*. How is this verb form expressed in standard English? [doesn't ever]

Ⓔ Elements of Literature

Conflict and Character

❓ What conflict emerges between Granny and the film crew? [They want to use the Cain home in their film, but Granny doesn't want them on her property.] How can you tell that it never occurred to the filmmakers to ask permission? [Sample response: They just start shooting pictures, and even though one man seems embarrassed, they don't really understand why Granny is so annoyed.] What do Granny's expressions, tone of voice, and words tell you about how she feels? Use details from the story to support your response. [Possible response: She is upset with the filmmakers and wants them to realize they are invading the family's privacy. Details include her smiling "that smile" and the way she interrupts the filmmakers.] What is your overall impression of Granny? [Possible response: She is strong-minded and not afraid to speak up to protect her dignity, her family, and her property.]

Ⓐ The puddle had frozen over, and me and Cathy went stompin in it. The twins from next door, Tyrone and Terry, were swingin so high out of sight we forgot we were waitin our turn on the tire. Cathy jumped up and came down hard on her heels and started tap-dancin. And the frozen patch splinterin every which way underneath kinda spooky. "Looks like a plastic spider web," she said. "A sort of weird spider, I guess, with many mental problems." But really it looked like the crystal paperweight Granny kept in the parlor. She was on the back porch, Granny was, making the cakes drunk. Ⓑ The old ladle dripping rum into the Christmas tins, like it used to drip maple syrup into the pails when we lived in the Judsons' woods, like it poured cider into the vats when we were on the Cooper place, like it used to scoop buttermilk and soft cheese when we lived at the dairy.

Ⓒ "Go tell that man we ain't a bunch of trees."

"Ma'am?"

"I said to tell that man to get away from here with that camera." Me and Cathy look over toward the meadow where the men with the station wagon'd been roamin around all mornin. The tall man with a huge camera lassoed to his shoulder was buzzin our way.

"They're makin movie pictures," yelled Tyrone, stiffenin his legs and twistin so the tire'd come down slow so they could see.

"They're makin movie pictures," sang out Terry.

Ⓓ "That boy don't never have anything original to say," say Cathy grown-up.

By the time the man with the camera had cut across our neighbor's yard, the twins were out of the trees swingin low and Granny was onto the steps, the screen door bammin soft and scratchy against her palms. "We thought we'd get a shot or two of the house and everything Ⓔ and then——"

"Good mornin," Granny cut him off. And smiled that smile.

"Good mornin," he said, head all down the way Bingo does when you yell at him about the bones on the kitchen floor. "Nice place you got here, aunty. We thought we'd take a——"

"Did you?" said Granny with her eyebrows. Cathy pulled up her socks and giggled.

"Nice things here," said the man, buzzin his camera over the yard. The pecan barrels, the sled, me and Cathy, the flowers, the printed stones along the driveway, the trees, the twins, the toolshed.

"I don't know about the thing, the it, and the stuff," said Granny, still talkin with her eyebrows. "Just people here is what I tend to consider."

Camera man stopped buzzin. Cathy giggled into her collar.

"Mornin, ladies," a new man said. He had come up behind us when we weren't lookin. "And gents," discoverin the twins givin him a nasty look. "We're filmin for the county," he said with a smile. "Mind if we shoot a bit around here?"

"I do indeed," said Granny with no smile. Smilin man was smiling up a storm. So was Cathy. But he didn't seem to have another word to say, so he and the camera man backed on out the yard, but you could hear the camera buzzin still. "Suppose you just shut that machine off," said Granny real low through her teeth and took a step down off the porch and then another.

"Now, aunty," Camera said, pointin the thing straight at her.

"Your mama and I are not related."

Smilin man got his notebook out and a chewed-up pencil. "Listen," he said movin back into our yard, "we'd like to have a statement from you . . . for the film. We're filmin for the county, see. Part of the food stamp campaign. You know about the food stamps?"

Granny said nuthin.

"Maybe there's somethin you want to say for the film. I see you grow your own vegetables," he smiled real nice. "If more folks did that, see, there'd be no need——"

Granny wasn't sayin nuthin. So they backed on out, buzzin at our clothesline and the twins' bicycles, then back on down to the meadow. The twins were danglin in the tire, lookin at Granny. Me and Cathy were waitin, too, cause Granny always got somethin to say. She teaches steady with no let-up. "I was on this bridge one

Using Students' Strengths

Auditory Learners

Because of the extensive use of dialect, this story is best heard. If you read it aloud in class, you may wish to assign the main characters' parts to advanced readers: Narrator, Granny, Granddaddy, Cathy, Tyrone, Terry, Camera, and Smilin. Have students familiarize themselves with the rhythms and pronunciations of their parts before they read the story aloud in class.

Kinesthetic Learners

Have kinesthetic learners pantomime the actions of Granny and the two filmmakers as the confrontation scene is read aloud in class. The students should be sure to use any movements, facial expressions, or gestures that are mentioned in the text. Have the whole class discuss how the movements and expressions of the characters add to the meaning of the dialogue.

The Blues—Music of Survival

You know that the "blues ain't no mockin bird," but then what are they? The blues are many things: music, protest, survival, triumph—all these and more.

The first blues songs were sung in the rural South by African Americans—the ancestors of Granny Cain and her family. It wasn't long, though, before the blues had traveled to cities and small towns across the United States and Europe. Today there are different styles of blues, but all blues songs are about hard times and how they make people feel. Blues are not just mournful. They can be hopeful too, even funny. Blues lyrics like the ones below may sound hopeless at first:

> Woke up this morning, feeling sad and blue,
> Woke up this morning, feeling sad and blue,
> Didn't have nobody to tell my troubles to.

> I've got the blues but I'm too darn mean to cry,
> I've got the blues but I'm too darn mean to cry,
> Before I'd cry I'd rather lay down and die.

What sounds hopeless may actually make audiences laugh and rejoice. Blues singers create characters when they sing. The characters may sound as if they've given up, but the singer hasn't—and neither has the audience. By singing and listening to the blues, people keep hope alive. No matter how hard things get—no matter how poor or lonely or heartbroken people are—tomorrow is a new day. Many people believe the first blues songs were the mournful and spiritual songs of slaves working in the fields—hoping for a better day, singing to survive.

The blues and the struggle of African Americans have influenced many American writers, including Toni Cade Bambara. Like the blues singers, her characters in this story are survivors—they defend their way of life against the intrusive eye of the camera.

---

time," she started off. "Was a crowd cause this man was goin to jump, you understand. And a minister was there and the police and some other folks. His woman was there, too."

"What was they doin?" asked Tyrone.

"Tryin to talk him out of it was what they was doin. The minister talkin about how it was a mortal sin, suicide. His woman takin bites out of her own hand and not even knowin it, so nervous and cryin and talkin fast."

"So what happened?" asked Tyrone.

"So here comes . . . this person . . . with a camera, takin pictures of the man and the minister and the woman. Takin pictures of the man in his misery about to jump, cause life so bad and people been messin with him so bad. This person takin up the whole roll of film practically. But savin a few, of course." **F**

"Of course," said Cathy, hatin the person. Me standin there wonderin how Cathy knew it was

---

LITERATURE AND MUSIC

Point out to students that blues music has influenced many rock musicians, including Bob Dylan, Stevie Ray Vaughan, Eric Clapton, Bonnie Raitt, and U2. Ask students to select a blues musician and to explore the themes in his or her songs. Ask students to identify how the characters in the songs, like those in the story, keep fighting and hoping. Students should play a recording for the class of one or two of the songs, and relate the content of the songs to the lives of characters in the story.

F Reading Skills and Strategies

Making Generalizations

? Why was the person with the camera saving some shots? Why does Cathy say, "Of course"? [Somebody insensitive enough to shoot photographs in the first place would save a few in order to capture the person's jump. Cathy is perceptive and understands Granny's point.] **How does Granny's story connect with what is happening in her yard?** [The photographers on her property are equally insensitive.] **What does she want to teach her grandchildren?** [Sample response: She wants them to understand that it is degrading and insensitive to treat people as objects whose lives are of meaning only as a way to excite or entertain others.]

Skill Link

Analyzing Dialect

The Language Link on p. 277 explains what dialect is and how writers use it to reveal character. Dialects differ from standard English in many ways. In the dialect used in this story, characters vary word choice by using expressions like *swallow up the eager* and other idioms common to their culture and region such as *let-ups.* They vary pronunciation by dropping the final consonant *g* on *-ing* words. They use non-standard grammar when they substitute *was* for

were, or use double negatives, such as *don't never* and *can't neither.* They also vary rhythms and sentence structure; for example, they may string a list of descriptive words or phrases at the end of a sentence:"His woman takin bites out of her own hand and not even knowin it, so nervous and cryin and talkin fast."

Activity

Choose a passage of the story for students to rewrite in standard English. They will need to make changes in all of the areas listed above. Passages that work well include:
- the third paragraph on p. 270, beginning "And Granny just stared. . . ."
- the scene in which the filmmakers try to escape the hawk, starting at the bottom of p. 272 and continuing on p. 273

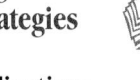

A Reading Skills and Strategies

Making Generalizations

❓ Think about what all of the events described here have in common. Exactly what do people do that disturbs Granny so much? [Sample response: Granny is driven crazy by people's condescension, presumption, insensitivity, and lack of respect for her family's privacy.]

B Elements of Literature

Point of View

Point out that the story is narrated from the first-person point of view, but that this point of view is enlivened and enriched by how the writer makes use of several other characters' observations. The twins make childish but natural comments, often asking obvious questions; Cathy makes sophisticated comments that supplement the narrator's own fresh and humorous insights.

C Appreciating Language

Descriptive Details

❓ What vivid details in this paragraph help you see and hear the action? [Details include: "the shiny black oilskin," "what little left there was of yellows, reds, and oranges," "great white head," "the sound of twigs snapping overhead and underfoot," "tall and quiet and like a king," "drippin red down the back of the oilskin," "the hammerin crackin through the eardrums."]

"of course" when I didn't and it was *my* grand-mother.

After a while Tyrone say, "Did he jump?"

"Yeh, did he jump?" say Terry all eager.

And Granny just stared at the twins till their faces swallow up the eager and they don't even care any more about the man jumpin. Then she goes back onto the porch and lets the screen door go for itself. I'm lookin to Cathy to finish the story cause she knows Granny's whole story before me even. Like she knew how come we move so much and Cathy ain't but a third cousin we picked up on the way last Thanksgivin visitin. But she knew it was on account of people drivin Granny crazy till she'd get up in the night and start packin. Mumblin and packin and wakin everybody up sayin, "Let's get on away from here before I kill me somebody." Like people wouldn't pay her for things like they said they would. Or Mr. Judson bringin us boxes of old clothes and raggedy magazines. Or Mrs. Cooper comin in our kitchen and touchin everything and sayin how clean it all was. Granny goin crazy, and Granddaddy Cain pullin her off the people, sayin, "Now, now, Cora." But next day loadin up the truck, with rocks all in his jaw, madder than Granny in the first place.

"I read a story once," said Cathy soundin like Granny teacher. "About this lady Goldilocks who barged into a house that wasn't even hers. And not invited, you understand. Messed over the people's groceries and broke up the people's furniture. Had the nerve to sleep in the folks' bed."

"Then what happened?" asked Tyrone. "What they do, the folks, when they come in to all this mess?"

"Did they make her pay for it?" asked Terry, makin a fist. "I'd've made her pay me."

I didn't even ask. I could see Cathy actress was very likely to just walk away and leave us in mystery about this story, which I heard was about some bears.

"Did they throw her out?" asked Tyrone, like his father sounds when he's bein extra nasty-plus to the washin-machine man.

"Woulda," said Terry. "I woulda gone upside her head with my fist and——"

"You woulda done whatcha always do—go cry to Mama, you big baby," said Tyrone. So naturally Terry starts hittin on Tyrone, and next thing you know they tumblin out the tire and rollin on the ground. But Granny didn't say a thing or send the twins home or step out on the steps to tell us about how we can't afford to be fightin amongst ourselves. She didn't say nuthin. So I get into the tire to take my turn. And I could see her leanin up against the pantry table, starin at the cakes she was puttin up for the Christmas sale, mumblin real low and grumpy and holdin her forehead like it wanted to fall off and mess up the rum cakes.

Behind me I hear before I can see Grand-daddy Cain comin through the woods in his field boots. Then I twist around to see the shiny black oilskin[1] cuttin through what little left there was of yellows, reds, and oranges. His great white head not quite round cause of this bloody thing high on his shoulder, like he was wearin a cap on sideways. He takes the shortcut through the pecan grove, and the sound of twigs snapping overhead and underfoot travels clear and cold all the way up to us. And here comes Smilin and Camera up behind him like they was goin to do somethin. Folks like to go for him sometimes. Cathy say it's because he's so tall and quiet and like a king. And people just can't stand it. But Smilin and Camera don't hit him in the head or nuthin. They just buzz on him as he stalks by with the chicken hawk slung over his shoulder, squawkin, drippin red down the back of the oilskin. He passes the porch and stops a second for Granny to see he's caught the hawk at last, but she's just starin and mumblin, and not at the hawk. So he nails the bird to the toolshed door, the hammerin crackin through the eardrums. And the bird flappin himself to death and droolin down the door to paint the gravel in the driveway red, then brown, then black. And the two men movin up on tiptoe like they was invisible or we were blind, one.

"Get them persons out of my flower bed,

---

1. **oilskin:** waterproof coat.

Getting Students Involved

Cooperative Learning

Creating a Backdrop. Have students work in groups to create a backdrop for the story. They may paint it on old sheets or large pieces of paper. Remind students to reread descriptions of setting and characters to help them create backdrops that reflect the mood of the story. Show students examples of backdrops in theater books, explaining how the colors and objects represent the mood or symbolize elements of the story or play. Each group should choose an art director, who is responsible for coordinating the project. Other group members should find details about setting and characters in the story. Have each group choose a speaker to present and explain the group's backdrop to the class.

Live Conversations. Have students develop their ear for dialect by asking friends or family members for permission to reproduce one of their conversations in writing. Remind students to listen carefully for pronunciation, special vocabulary, sentence construction, and speech rhythms. Students may wish to tape the conversation and then transcribe it. They should preface their transcriptions with a short paragraph explaining any problems they encountered and what they learned from the activity.

Family (1955) by Charles H. Alston. Oil on canvas (48 ¼" × 35 ¾").

RESPONDING TO THE ART

Charles H. Alston (1907?–1978), an African American painter and sculptor, was among the many artists who found employment with the Federal Art Project (a part of the WPA or Works Progress Administration), which operated from 1935 to 1943. This 1955 work, with its abstractly arranged geometric forms, reveals his interest in Cubism.

Activity. Have students begin by studying the family in the painting. Which figure draws your eye the most strongly? Why? [Possible response: The mother, because she is the largest person in the painting, closest to the front, and painted in the brightest color.] What mood is created by the painting? [Possible response: a somber, serious mood.] Is the mood of the painting similar to the mood in the story? Explain. [Possible response: Yes, although the narrator has a sense of humor, the events in the story are serious.] You might also have students compare this family portrait with the one in *La Primavera* by Romare Bearden, p. 284.

Listening to Music

"Saint Louis Blues" by W. C. Handy, performed by Bessie Smith and many others

Background

Blues, which draw on the musical traditions of Africa, are based on the blues scale, a major scale in which the third and seventh degrees are lowered a half step occasionally, causing the melody to go between a major and a minor mode. Classic blues use a twelve-bar form of three lines of four bars each; the first line is repeated as the second line, and then a third, rhyming line is introduced. Blues had a strong influence on the development of jazz; in fact, many of the early jazz greats, like Louis Armstrong and Fats Waller, got their start playing the blues. Composer and bandmaster William Christopher Handy (1873–1958) helped make the blues successful as popular music. Perhaps the best-known version of his famous "St. Louis Blues" is the one by the great singer Bessie Smith (1894–1937), whose nickname was "Empress of the Blues."

Activity

In conjunction with the Literature and Music feature on p. 269, have students listen to Bessie Smith's famous rendition of Handy's "St. Louis Blues." Point out the typical stanza pattern, with its standard *aab* rhyme scheme. Then have students consider whether the song seems hopeless or in some ways triumphant.

Mister Cain," say Granny, moanin real low like at a funeral.

"How come your grandmother calls her husband Mister Cain all the time?" Tyrone whispers all loud and noisy and from the city and don't know no better. Like his mama, Miss Myrtle, tell us never mind the formality as if we had no better breeding than to call her Myrtle, plain. And then this awful thing—a giant hawk—come wailin up over the meadow, flyin low and tilted and screamin, zigzaggin through the pecan grove, breakin branches and hollerin, snappin past the clothesline, flyin every which way, flyin into things reckless with crazy.

"He's come to claim his mate," say Cathy fast, Ⓐ

and ducks down. We all fall quick and flat into the gravel driveway, stones scrapin my face. I squinch my eyes open again at the hawk on the door, tryin to fly up out of her death like it was just a sack flown into by mistake. Her body holdin her there on that nail, though. The mate beatin the air overhead and clutchin for hair, for heads, for landin space.

The camera man duckin and bendin and runnin and fallin, jigglin the camera and scared. And Smilin jumpin up and down swipin at the huge bird, tryin to bring the hawk down with just his raggedy ole cap. Granddaddy Cain straight up and silent, watchin the circles of the hawk, then aimin the hammer off his wrist. The

Gee's Bend (1947) by Jacob Lawrence. Tempera on gesso on wood (20″ x 24″).

Evansville Museum of Arts and Science, Evansville, Indiana. Courtesy of the artist and the Francine Sedars Gallery, Seattle, Washington.

giant bird fallin, silent and slow. Then here comes Camera and Smilin all big and bad now that the awful screechin thing is on its back and broken, here they come. And Granddaddy Cain looks up at them like it was the first time noticin, but not payin them too much mind B cause he's listenin, we all listenin, to that low groanin music comin from the porch. And we figure any minute, somethin in my back tells me any minute now, Granny gonna bust through that screen with somethin in her hand and murder on her mind. So Granddaddy say above the buzzin, but quiet, "Good day, gentlemen." Just like that. Like he'd invited them in to play cards and they'd stayed too long and all the sandwiches were gone and Reverend Webb was droppin by and it was time to go.

They didn't know what to do. But like Cathy say, folks can't stand Granddaddy tall and silent and like a king. They can't neither. The smile the men smilin is pullin the mouth back and showin the teeth. Lookin like the wolf man, both of them. Then Granddaddy holds his hand out—this huge hand I used to sit in when I was a baby and he'd carry me through the house to my mother like I was a gift on a tray. Like he used to on the trains. They called the other men just waiters. But they spoke of Granddaddy separate and said, The Waiter. And said he had engines in his feet and motors in his hands and couldn't no train throw him off and couldn't nobody turn him round. They were big enough for motors, his hands were. He held that one hand out all still and it gettin to be not at all a hand but a person in itself.

"He wants you to hand him the camera," Smilin whispers to Camera, tiltin his head to talk secret like they was in the jungle or somethin and come upon a native that don't speak the language. The men start untyin the straps, and they put the camera into that great hand speckled with the hawk's blood, all black and crackly now. And the hand don't even drop with the weight, just the fingers move, curl up around the machine. But Granddaddy lookin straight at the men. They lookin at each other and everywhere but at Granddaddy's face.

"We filmin for the county, see," say Smilin. "We puttin together a movie for the food stamp program . . . filmin all around these parts. Uhh, filmin for the county."

"Can I have my camera back?" say the tall man with no machine on his shoulder, but still keepin it high like the camera was still there or needed to be. "Please, sir."

Then Granddaddy's other hand flies up like a sudden and gentle bird, slaps down fast on top of the camera and lifts off half like it was a calabash[2] cut for sharing.

"Hey," Camera jumps forward. He gathers up the parts into his chest and everything unrollin and fallin all over. "Whatcha tryin to do? You'll ruin the film." He looks down into his chest of metal reels and things like he's protectin a kitten from the cold.

"You standin in the missus' flower bed," say E Granddaddy. "This is our own place."

The two men look at him, then at each other, then back at the mess in the camera man's chest, and they just back off. One sayin over and over all the way down to the meadow, "Watch it, Bruno. Keep ya fingers off the film." Then Granddaddy picks up the hammer and jams it into the oilskin pocket, scrapes his boots, and goes into the house. And you can hear the squish of his boots headin through the house. And you can see the funny shadow he throws from the parlor window onto the ground by the string-bean patch. The hammer draggin the pocket of the oilskin out so Granddaddy looked even wider. Granny was hummin now—high, not low and grumbly. And she was doin the cakes again, you could smell the molasses from the rum.

"There's this story I'm goin to write one day," say Cathy dreamer. "About the proper use of the hammer."

"Can I be in it?" Tyrone say with his hand up F like it was a matter of first come, first served.

"Perhaps," say Cathy, climbin onto the tire to pump us up. "If you there and ready."

2. **calabash:** large tropical fruit.

BLUES AIN'T NO MOCKIN BIRD 273

B **Elements of Literature**
  Symbols
❓ The scenes about the suffering hawks take up a good part of the story. How can one or both of the hawks be seen as symbols that stand for some of the characters in the story? [Possible responses: The hawks are like the Cain family in their suffering; the male hawk is like Granny, who fights to protect her family; the male hawk is like the camera crew that keeps buzzing around the property.]

C **Elements of Literature**
  Character
❓ What do you learn about Grand-daddy Cain here? [That even when he is exasperated with people like the film-makers, he can exercise self-control and respond in a polite manner.]

D **Elements of Literature**
  Character
❓ What kind of character traits do Camera and Smilin show? [Sample responses: They are rude, condescend-ing, and presumptuous; they are not sen-sitive to the feelings of others; they are ignorant about how other people live.]

E **Elements of Literature**
  Theme
❓ Granddaddy Cain's words suggest the major theme of the story—a truth about how people should treat each other. In your own words, what is that theme? [People should have respect for the feelings and property of others.]

F **Critical Thinking**
  Analyzing the Text
❓ Who was "there and ready" in the story? [Sample response: Granddaddy Cain, who used his hammer to show that he could end a bird's suffering and also take care of his own family; Granny Cain, who speaks up strongly against the intruders. Both meet the difficulties of life with courage and dignity.]

Making the Connections

Connecting to the Theme: "Discoveries"

The discoveries are less obvious in this story than in "The Gift," yet the narrator and Cathy make discoveries about the characters of Granny and Granddaddy Cain. They also learn how to deal with people who disregard the humanity of others. To lead students to understand these dis-coveries, you might begin by asking them which characters seem *not* to learn or discover anything by the end of the story. [Camera, Smilin, the twins]

Cultural Connections

To help students empathize with the Cain fam-ily's outrage at the filmmakers' invasion of their privacy, conduct a brief discussion based on stu-dents' reactions to having their own privacy invaded. How would they feel if someone went through their personal belongings at home or at school?

Resources ———————
Selection Assessment
Formal Assessment
• Selection Test, p. 39
Test Generator (One-Stop Planner)
• CD-ROM

MEET THE WRITER

Writing on the Upbeat

Toni Cade Bambara (1939–1995) said she wrote upbeat fiction because she was raised on stories of champions: Harriet Tubman, Ida B. Wells, Paul Robeson, and her grandmother Annie. She grew up in Harlem, Brooklyn, and Jersey City, attended schools in New York City and the South, and graduated from Queens College in New York.

In the sixties, Bambara studied theater in Italy and mime in France. When she returned to New York, she became interested in dance but also did social work in local hospitals and community centers. Eventually she turned to teaching, and over the years she taught at various colleges and universities, including Rutgers University in New Brunswick, New Jersey, and Spelman College in Atlanta, Georgia.

"Blues Ain't No Mockin Bird" comes from Bambara's first collection of stories: *Gorilla, My Love* (1972). Many of these stories are told in the voice of a sassy young girl who is tough, compassionate, and brave.

Bambara had her own very definite ideas about writing:

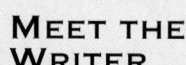

❝ Folks come up to me 'lowing as how since I am a writer I would certainly want to hear blah, blah, blah, blah. They . . . tell me about every ugly overheard and lived-through nightmare imaginable. They've got the wrong writer. The kid can't use it. I straightaway refer them to the neighborhood healer, certain that anyone so intoxicated would surely welcome a cleansing. But they persist— 'Hey, this is for real, square business. The truth.' I don't doubt that the horror tales are factual. I don't even doubt that ugly is a truth for somebody . . . somehow. But I'm not convinced that ugly is *the* truth that can save us, redeem us. The old folks teach that. Be triflin' and ugly and they say, 'Deep down, gal, you know that ain't right,' appealing to a truth about our deep-down nature. Good enough for me. Besides, I can't get happy writing ugly weird. If I'm not laughing while I work, I conclude that I am not communicating nourishment, since laughter is the most sure-fire healant I know. I don't know all my readers, but I know well for whom I write. And I want for them—no less than I want for myself—wholesomeness.

It all sounds so la-di-da and tra-la-la. I can afford to be sunny. I'm but one voice in the chorus. The literature(s) of our time are a collective effort, dependent on so many views, on so many people's productions. There's a lot of work to do, a lot of records to get straight, a lot of living to share, a lot to plumb. This reader wants it all—the oddball, the satiric, the grim, the ludicrous, what have you. As for my own writing, I prefer the upbeat. It pleases me to blow three or four choruses of just sheer energetic fun and optimism. . . . ❞

Assessing Learning

Check Test: True-False

1. Granny Cain welcomes the men who are filming for the county. [False]
2. Granny Cain tells the children about a man she once saw who was threatening to jump from a bridge. [True]

3. Camera and Smilin leave immediately when Granddaddy Cain shows up. [False]
4. Granddaddy Cain tells the filmmakers that they are standing in his wife's flower bed. [True]
5. Granddaddy Cain smashes the film crew's camera. [False]

Standardized Test Preparation

For practice with standardized test format specific to this selection, see
- *Standardized Test Preparation*, pp. 34, 36

For practice in proofreading and editing, see
- *Daily Oral Grammar,* Transparency 16

MAKING MEANINGS

- **First Thoughts**

[respond]

1. Which detail of the story was the most memorable for you? Was it an image, a statement, a character, or something else? Pair up with another student and share your major memory from the story.

Shaping Interpretations

[infer]

2. When Smilin and Camera return to the county office, what do you think they tell their supervisor? How do you think they portray the characters of Granny and Granddaddy Cain?

[interpret]

3. Have you ever said one thing while thinking something else? What do you imagine Granddaddy Cain is thinking when he says, "Good day, gentlemen"? What about when he says, "You standin in the missus' flower bed. This is our own place"?

[interpret]

4. Writers create powerful impressions with concrete dramatic **images**. What do the suffering hawks in the story suggest to you? (Are they like any characters in the story?)

[interpret]

5. State the **theme** of the story in the form of a **generalization** about our lives—that is, what does the story reveal to you about our need for respect and sympathy and privacy? Consider these elements of the story:
   - the **title**
   - the **anecdote**, or little story, Granny tells about the man on the bridge
   - Cathy's **anecdote**, or little story, about Goldilocks

[analyze]

6. What did you learn about the **first-person narrator** in this story? What else would you know if Granny or her husband were narrating the story?

Connecting with the Text

[connect]

7. A family's privacy is invaded in this story. Invasion of privacy has become commonplace in today's media. When have you felt that someone's privacy was invaded by TV cameras or reporters? What would you do if you were in Granny's situation? (Be sure to refer to your Quickwrite notes.)

Challenging the Text

[evaluate]

8. Toni Cade Bambara said she preferred upbeat fiction and liked energetic fun and optimism. Do you think this story is upbeat and optimistic? Why or why not?

Reading Check

a. Which characters play a part in this story's **conflict**? Which ones are onlookers?

b. What details in the story explain why Granny has moved so often?

c. Why do the two men want to film the family?

d. Why does Granny resent the film crew?

e. What action does Granddaddy Cain finally take to **resolve** Granny's conflict with the camera crew?

BLUES AIN'T NO MOCKIN BIRD 275

Reading Check
Answers may vary slightly.

a. Granny and Granddaddy Cain come into conflict with Smilin and Camera. The children—the narrator, Cathy, Tyrone, and Terry—are onlookers.

b. The family has moved because Granny Cain cannot tolerate people not paying her the money they owe her, giving the family charity in the form of used clothing and old magazines,
and acting astonished that she keeps her home clean.

c. They are making a documentary film for the county's food stamp campaign.

d. Granny resents the film crew because they violate her family's privacy.

e. Granddaddy Cain exposes the film in the camera.

MAKING MEANINGS

First Thoughts

1. Possible responses include: Granny's telling the filmmakers to turn off their camera, Granddaddy's arrival home, his killing of the second hawk, or his exposing the film.

Shaping Interpretations

2. Camera and Smilin will most likely blame Granddaddy and Granny for the ruined film. Since they don't recognize their own insensitivity, they will probably portray Granny and Granddaddy as eccentric and belligerent.

3. Responses will vary. He is probably thinking about how angry he is and how he would like to throw the men off his property.

4. Possible response: The hawks fight desperately, suggesting courage and strength. They are like Granddaddy and Granny Cain, who fight to protect their family, property, and privacy.

5. Possible themes: People should respect the privacy and property of others; people can get through troubles with strength and dignity. The title says that the blues, unlike the mockingbird, do not suggest self-pity or death. The anecdote about the man on the bridge reveals Granny's disgust with people who take advantage of the misfortunes of others. Cathy's version of Goldilocks shows an intruder having no respect for the property or privacy of others.

6. The narrator is a young girl who lives with her grandparents. If Granny or her husband told the story, we would know about their inner thoughts when they confront the filmmakers.

Connecting with the Text

7. Students may mention public figures whose personal lives have been made public. In Granny's situation, students might call the family inside and lock the doors, call the police, or react much as Granny does.

Challenging the Text

8. Some students may find the bloody imagery of the hawks downbeat. Others may feel that the ending of the story is optimistic.

T275

Rubrics for each Choices assignment appear on p. 120 in the *Portfolio Management System.*

CHOICES: Building Your Portfolio

1. **Writer's Notebook**   Direct students' attention to the list of themes at the bottom of the page and suggest that they organize their ideas in the same way. Remind students to save their work. They may use it as prewriting for the Writer's Workshop on p. 332.

2. **Analyzing a Character**   Ask students first to write a topic sentence about one of Granny's character traits. Then have them find three examples of the character trait in the story. You may also find it helpful first to have the class brainstorm a list of adjectives that describe people. Write the adjectives on the board or an overhead transparency so that students can refer to them as they work on their character analysis.

3. **Creative Writing/Speaking**   Before students start their poems, have them spend fifteen minutes taking notes from the story on either Granny or Granddaddy Cain. As students write their poems, some may find a tape recorder useful. They can talk out loud as if they were Granny or Granddaddy Cain. Then they can replay the tape and write down the best ideas. Remind students to allow their thoughts to flow freely, but to use each of the beginning phrases.

4. **Research/Social Studies**   Work with the class to make a list of possible information sources on the Federal food stamp program. A review by the school librarian on locating resources in the library might also be helpful.

5. **Comparing Speakers**   Point out to students that the last line of the poem is like Granny's comment that "we ain't a bunch of trees." These lines give clues about the speakers' attitudes toward themselves and how they expect to be treated.

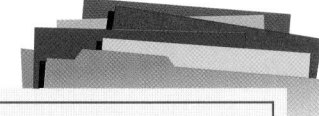

CHOICES: Building Your Portfolio

Writer's Notebook

1. Collecting Ideas for an Analysis of a Short Story

What does it mean? In the Writer's Workshop on page 332, you will be analyzing the way the elements of a short story work to create meaning. The central idea of the story—the theme—is something that you will want to examine. You usually won't find a theme directly stated in a story—finding it will require some thought on your part. Sometimes, though, a title or a key passage will point to the theme. Write down the central idea, or theme, of some stories you have read. Remember that there may be more than one theme in a story and that your statement of the theme may never match anyone else's.

Analyzing a Character

2. Look at Granny

By now you may have speculated on what Smilin and Camera reported to their supervisor about Granny. Suppose you, as an observer, decide the supervisor needs to hear another point of view. Write an analysis of Granny's character as you interpret it. Look in the story for examples of Granny's **words,** her **actions,** and her **effect on others.**

Creative Writing/Speaking

3. "I Am" Poem

Writing as either Granny or Granddaddy Cain, complete the following lines of an "I Am" poem:

I am _____
I wonder _____
I hear _____
I try _____
I wish _____
I dream _____
I see _____
I hope _____

> **Themes**
> "The Gift of The Magi": Love is the best gift in the world. Key passage: p. 207, last paragraph.
>
> "Salvador Late or Early": There are forgotten children in our world who are brave and loving, and no one helps them.

Research/Social Studies

4. Compiling a Report

The two men who came out to Granny's place said they were filming for the county as part of the food stamp program. Food stamps are certificates that are issued by the federal government and traded for food at grocery stores. Do some research of your own. Find out the regulations that govern food stamps and write a summary of your findings. Do most poor people in the United States receive some form of government assistance? Be sure to include a list of your sources.

Comparing Speakers

5. "I'm Not a Wall"

In a paragraph, compare the speaker of the following poem with Granny. The chart below should help you outline their similarities. Fill it out before you write.

> **Silent, but . . .**
> I may be silent, but
> I'm thinking.
> I may not talk, but
> Don't mistake me for a wall.
> —Tsuboi Shigeji

Points of Comparison	Bambara	Shigeji
Line from beginning of story that sounds like line from poem		
How Granny and speaker of poem do **not** want to be treated		
How they **do** want to be treated		

LANGUAGE LINK · MINI-LESSON

Handbook of Literary Terms HELP

See Dialect.

If it doesn't sound right to the ear, if it doesn't come out the way a ranch hand might say it with a pipe in one hand and a cup of coffee in the other, then I change it.
—Louis L'Amour

Dialect Reveals Character

While language is being spoken, it changes. All of us, in fact, alter language slightly. We take the sounds we first learn from our parents, brothers, and sisters, and then we add what we hear at school, at work, on the radio, on TV, and in the movies.

Speech and character. Thus, our own particular speech soon becomes as distinctive as the features on our faces. We sometimes can even recognize a person simply by overhearing a single spoken word. When we meet new people for the first time, their speech can tell us about the regions they come from and about their social, economic, and educational backgrounds. For this reason, a writer tries to breathe life into a fictional character by letting us hear *how* the person speaks, as well as *what* the person says.

Regional speech. Suppose a writer is setting a story in a particular region—for instance, the Deep South or a barrio in Los Angeles or the Flatbush section of Brooklyn. The way people in the story speak must persuade us (even if we've never been to these places) that they are using the region's special grammar, expressions, and pronunciations—in other words, that they are speaking its **dialect**.

Having an "ear" for dialect—being able to hear the peculiarities of speech, its rhythm and flow, the words that are emphasized, the contractions, the slang, the pronunciations—is vital for a writer. The writer with a sensitive ear will record Bostonians' broad *a*'s and the way they pronounce *ar* for *ah* and *ah* for *ar* so that "idea" becomes "idear" and "dear" becomes "deah." In a story set in a rural black neighborhood in Arkansas, the writer will hear "ask" become "aks" and "my" become "mah," and will notice how final consonants are dropped so that "don't" becomes "don." The writer will also let the character use the **idioms** of his or her locale. Idioms are expressions that mean something different from the literal meaning of the words. The narrator of this story uses a common idiom when she says "And people just can't stand it" (page 270). What does that idiom mean?

Even in her comment about writing (page 274), Bambara reproduces a dialect with its peculiar pronunciations, its special vocabulary, its special syntax, and its rhythms.

Try It Out

1. Look through the story and find at least five good examples of dialect. Arrange your examples under two headings.

Nonstandard Grammar	Nonstandard Pronunciation

2. Try this experiment: Take one of Granny's speeches or conversations in "Blues Ain't No Mockin Bird," and rewrite it in standard, formal English, without Granny's usual pronunciations and grammar. How much of Granny's character is lost when her dialect is taken away from her?

Students can select from their portfolios a piece of writing that contains dialogue and read the dialogue aloud to a partner. Ask each student to rewrite their dialogue until it sounds more like their own regional dialect. Then have them reread their revised versions to the class for further evaluation.

Try It Out
Possible Answers

1. Nonstandard grammar: "don't never" (p. 268), "their faces swallow up the eager" (p. 270), "flyin into things reckless with crazy" (p. 272), "Granny gonna bust through that screen" (p. 273), "can't neither" (p. 273).
   Nonstandard pronunciation: "nuthin" (nothing), "ole" (old), "woulda" (would've), "whatcha" (what do you), "ya" (your), dropping the *g* on *-ing* forms.

2. Sample speech: Granny's anecdote about the man on the bridge on p. 269: "So here comes . . . this person . . . with a camera, takin pictures of the man and the minister and the woman. Takin pictures of the man in his misery about to jump, cause life so bad and people been messin with him so bad. This person takin up the whole roll of film practically. But savin a few, of course."
   Rewrite: The unhappy man was about to jump because his life was difficult and people had been cruel to him. A person with a camera came along and started shooting pictures and used most of the film but saved a few shots.
   Character: Although the rewrite still reveals Granny's compassion, the loss of the dialect causes much of her personality and all traces of her background to disappear. She seems less real, and it becomes harder for the reader to identify with her.

Resources ——————

Language
- *Grammar and Language Links* Worksheet, p. 25

Language Link Quick Check

Rewrite the following passage from the story in standard English.

"'You woulda done whatcha always do—go cry to Mama, you big baby,' said Tyrone. So naturally Terry starts hittin on Tyrone, and next thing you know they tumblin out the tire and rollin on the ground. But Granny didn't say a thing or send the twins home or step out on the steps to tell us about how we can't afford to be fightin amongst ourselves. She didn't say nuthin." (p. 270)

["You would have done what you always do—go crying to Mama, you big baby," said Tyrone. Naturally Terry starts hitting Tyrone, and the next thing you know they're tumbling out of the tire and rolling on the ground. But Granny didn't say a thing or send the twins home or step out on the steps to tell us that we can't afford to fight among ourselves. She didn't say anything.]

Planning

- **Block Schedule**
  Block Scheduling Lesson Plans with Pacing Guide
- **Traditional Schedule**
  Lesson Plans Including Strategies for English-Language Learners
- **One-Stop Planner**
  CD-ROM with Test Generator

Before You Read

MARIGOLDS

Make the Connection

The Beginning of Compassion

The Depression forms the backdrop for this story, but it is not just a story about economics and how money—or the lack of it—affects families. The story is also about the passage from childhood to adulthood, a passage that is usually marked with conflicts. In fact, negotiating that passage to adulthood can demand as much courage as a struggle with some outside enemy—or with economic hardships.

Quickwrite

Write down your responses to this question before you read: What fears and conflicts do most young people have to deal with as they move into adult life? Keep your notes for use later when you talk about the story.

go.hrw.com
LEO 9-4

Elements of Literature

Internal Conflict

Though there's a violent confrontation in this story, important conflicts also take place inside the mind and heart of fourteen-year-old Lizabeth. Some people would say that Lizabeth is battling her own interior "monsters."

> In **internal conflict,** a character struggles to resolve some personal problem, such as fear, shyness, anger, or anxiety.
>
> *For more on Conflict, see pages 32–33 and the Handbook of Literary Terms.*

Reading Skills and Strategies

Identifying the Key Passages

As you read this story, note key passages in which the writer seems to make an important general statement about life. When you finish reading the story, skim the text and locate other passages that seem to you to be especially important. Be prepared to explain why you think one particular passage is the most important one. You should find that the passage you choose has a direct connection to the story's theme.

Background

In the 1930s a terrible economic depression swept the world. Banks closed their doors. People lost their life savings. The stock market collapsed. Businesses failed all over America, and factories closed their doors. Life was hard for almost every American during those years. As the narrator of this story says, however, the Depression was nothing new to her family—the black workers of rural Maryland were used to hard times.

278 THE SHORT-STORY COLLECTIONS

Preteaching Vocabulary

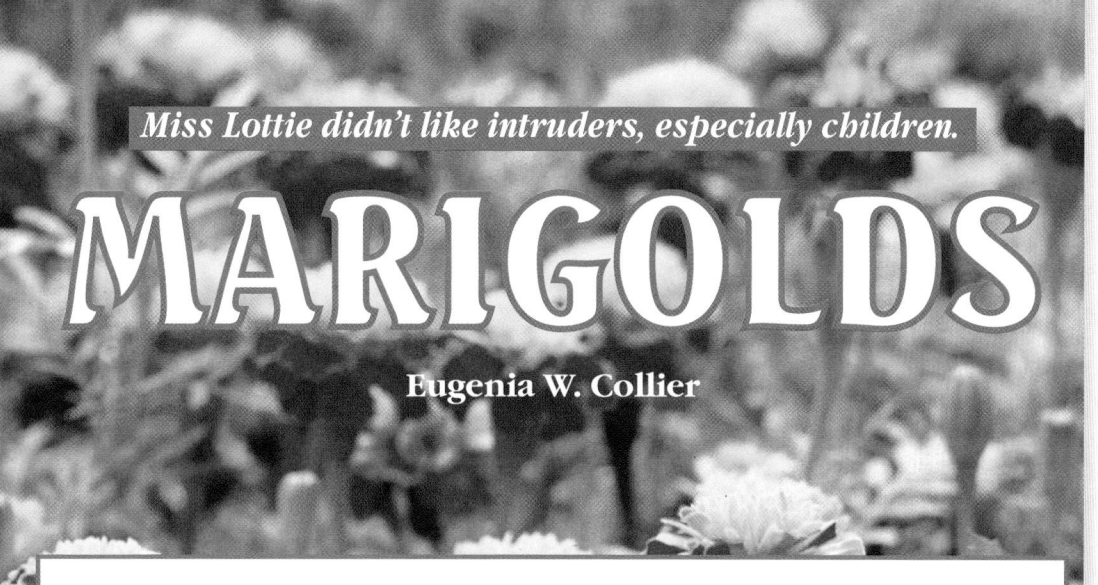

Miss Lottie didn't like intruders, especially children.

MARIGOLDS

Eugenia W. Collier

When I think of the hometown of my youth, all that I seem to remember is dust—the brown, crumbly dust of late summer—arid, sterile dust that gets into the eyes and makes them water, gets into the throat and between the toes of bare brown feet. I don't know why I should remember only the dust. Surely there must have been lush green lawns and paved streets under leafy shade trees somewhere in town; but memory is an abstract painting—it does not present things as they are, but rather as they *feel*. And so, when I think of that time and that place, I remember only the dry September of the dirt roads and grassless yards of the shantytown where I lived. And one other thing I remember, another incongruency[1] of memory—a brilliant splash of sunny yellow against the dust—Miss Lottie's marigolds.

Whenever the memory of those marigolds flashes across my mind, a strange nostalgia comes with it and remains long after the picture has faded. I feel again the chaotic emotions of adolescence, illusive as smoke, yet as real as the potted geranium before me now. Joy and rage and wild animal gladness and shame become

tangled together in the multicolored skein[2] of fourteen-going-on-fifteen as I recall that devastating moment when I was suddenly more woman than child, years ago in Miss Lottie's yard. I think of those marigolds at the strangest times; I remember them vividly now as I desperately pass away the time. . . .

I suppose that futile waiting was the sorrowful background music of our impoverished little community when I was young. The Depression that gripped the nation was no new thing to us, for the black workers of rural Maryland had always been depressed. I don't know what it was that we were waiting for; certainly not for the prosperity that was "just around the corner," for those were white folks' words, which we never believed. Nor did we wait for hard work and thrift to pay off in shining success, as the American Dream promised, for we knew better than that, too. Perhaps we waited for a miracle, amorphous[3] in concept but necessary if one were to have the grit to rise before dawn each day and labor in the white man's vineyard until after dark, or to wander about in the September

1. **incongruency** (in'kän'grōō·ən·sē): inconsistency; lack of agreement or harmony.

2. **multicolored skein** (skān): The writer is comparing her many feelings to a long coiled piece (a skein) of many-("multi-") colored yarn.

3. **amorphous** (ə·môr'fəs): vague, shapeless.

  —⊙— *Resources: Print and Media* — ⊏▭⊐ —

Reading
- *Graphic Organizers for Active Reading*, p. 17
- *Words to Own*, p. 12
- *Audio CD Library*, Disc 10, Tracks 4, 5

Writing and Language
- *Daily Oral Grammar*
  Transparency 17
- *Grammar and Language Links*
  Worksheet, p. 27

Assessment
- *Formal Assessment*, p. 41
- *Portfolio Management System*, p. 122
- *Test Generator (One-Stop Planner* CD-ROM)

Internet
- go.hrw.com (keyword LE0 9-4)

Summary ▪ ▪

The narrator of the story is Lizabeth, a poor African American girl; the setting is rural Maryland during the Depression. One day Lizabeth, her brother, and their friends taunt Miss Lottie, an old woman who lives with her son, who is mentally retarded. Miss Lottie cultivates a spectacular plot of marigolds in her front yard, a bright contrast to her ramshackle house. The children throw stones at the marigolds and chant insults at Miss Lottie. Afterwards, however, Lizabeth develops an internal conflict: she starts to feel ashamed of her behavior. That night, she overhears her parents talking. For the first time, she hears her father weep in despair about his inability to support his family. Her mother comforts her father, but Lizabeth cannot sleep. Finally she rouses her brother, and they return to Miss Lottie's house. Impelled by fear, need, bewilderment, and hopelessness, Lizabeth destroys the remaining marigolds in a bitter, violent rage. When Miss Lottie comes outdoors, Lizabeth looks into the old lady's face and recognizes Miss Lottie's humanity for the first time. The young girl discovers compassion; she has learned to respect people, but had to lose her innocence to do so.

Resources ————

Listening
Audio CD Library
A reading of this story is provided in the *Audio CD Library*:
- Disc 10, Track 4

Ⓐ Critical Thinking
Speculating
❓ Why might it feel scary, even devastating, to move from childhood to adulthood? [Sample response: You can't just play any more but have to take on adult cares and worries.]

Ⓑ Cultural Connections
❓ The narrator describes a situation that civil rights activists in the 1960s worked hard to change. What are five hopes or goals that many Americans might have in common today? [Possible responses: education, job, home, family, security in old age.]

A Elements of Literature

Figurative Language

? The speaker uses two metaphors in this sentence. To what does she compare poverty? [a cage] To what does she compare the hatred of poverty? [the natural instincts of a flamingo bred in captivity] What do the two images have in common? [the feeling of being trapped]

B Elements of Literature

Internal Conflict

? What external conflict is faced by the narrator's father? [He is struggling to find work.] Even though his unemployment is caused by the Depression, how might it also cause an internal conflict? [Sample response: The father must feel torn by his inability to provide for his family.]

C Elements of Literature

Internal Conflict

? What internal conflict is felt by the narrator of the story? [Sample response: She is becoming an adult, and she finds the thought of facing an unpredictable future terrifying.]

dust offering one's sweat in return for some meager share of bread. But God was chary[4] with miracles in those days, and so we waited—and waited.

We children, of course, were only vaguely aware of the extent of our poverty. Having no radios, few newspapers, and no magazines, we were somewhat unaware of the world outside our community. Nowadays we would be called culturally deprived and people would write books and hold conferences about us. In those days everybody we knew was just as hungry and ill clad as we were. Poverty was the cage in which we all were trapped, and our hatred of it was still the vague, undirected restlessness of the zoo-bred flamingo who knows that nature created him to fly free.

As I think of those days I feel most poignantly the tag end of summer, the bright, dry times when we began to have a sense of shortening days and the imminence of the cold.

By the time I was fourteen, my brother Joey and I were the only children left at our house, the older ones having left home for early marriage or the lure of the city, and the two babies having been sent to relatives who might care for them better than we. Joey was three years younger than I, and a boy, and therefore vastly inferior. Each morning our mother and father trudged wearily down the dirt road and around the bend, she to her domestic job, he to his daily unsuccessful quest for work. After our few chores around the tumbledown shanty, Joey and I were free to run wild in the sun with other children similarly situated.

For the most part, those days are ill-defined in my memory, running together and combining like a fresh watercolor painting left out in the rain. I remember squatting in the road drawing a picture in the dust, a picture which Joey gleefully erased with one sweep of his dirty foot. I remember fishing for minnows in a muddy creek and watching sadly as they eluded my cupped hands, while Joey laughed uproariously. And I remember, that year, a strange

4. **chary** (cher'ē): not generous.

280 THE SHORT-STORY COLLECTIONS

restlessness of body and of spirit, a feeling that something old and familiar was ending, and something unknown and therefore terrifying was beginning.

One day returns to me with special clarity for some reason, perhaps because it was the beginning of the experience that in some inexplicable[5] way marked the end of innocence. I was loafing under the great oak tree in our yard, deep in some reverie which I have now forgotten, except that it involved some secret, secret thoughts of one of the Harris boys across the yard. Joey and a bunch of kids were bored now with the old tire suspended from an oak limb, which had kept them entertained for a while.

"Hey, Lizabeth," Joey yelled. He never talked when he could yell. "Hey, Lizabeth, let's go somewhere."

I came reluctantly from my private world. "Where you want to go? What you want to do?"

The truth was that we were becoming tired of the formlessness of our summer days. The idleness whose prospect had seemed so beautiful during the busy days of spring now had degenerated to an almost desperate effort to fill up the empty midday hours.

"Let's go see can we find some locusts on the hill," someone suggested.

Joey was scornful. "Ain't no more locusts there. Y'all got 'em all while they was still green."

The argument that followed was brief and not really worth the effort. Hunting locust trees wasn't fun anymore by now.

"Tell you what," said Joey finally, his eyes sparkling. "Let's us go over to Miss Lottie's."

The idea caught on at once, for annoying Miss Lottie was always fun. I was still child enough to scamper along with the group over rickety fences and through bushes that tore our already raggedy clothes, back to where Miss Lottie lived. I think now that we must have made a tragicomic spectacle, five or six kids of different

5. **inexplicable** (in·eks'pli·kə·bəl): not explainable or understandable.

WORDS TO OWN

clarity (klar'ə·tē) n.: clearness.

Reaching All Students

Southern Limited (1976) by Romare Bearden. Collage.

RESPONDING TO THE ART

Romare Bearden (1914–1988) was an African American artist famous for his colorful collages depicting aspects of black life. A collage contains various materials, cut and pasted on a surface. Bearden often combined photographic images with areas painted in oil or watercolor. Additional collages by Bearden appear on pp. 283 and 284.

Activity. Have students identify what is depicted in the collage. [an African American couple, a train, a bird, a tree, a yard, a farm worker, a ramshackle house or barn] Then ask them to suggest possible interpretations of the title, *Southern Limited*. [Possible responses: The title suggests the name of a railroad; the title recalls the limited futures that were once all that most African Americans could expect.]

ages, each of us clad in only one garment—the girls in faded dresses that were too long or too short, the boys in patchy pants, their sweaty brown chests gleaming in the hot sun. A little cloud of dust followed our thin legs and bare feet as we tramped over the barren land.

When Miss Lottie's house came into view we stopped, ostensibly[6] to plan our strategy, but actually to reinforce our courage. Miss Lottie's house was the most ramshackle of all our ramshackle homes. The sun and rain had long since faded its rickety frame siding from white to a sullen gray. The boards themselves seemed to remain upright not from being nailed together but rather from leaning together, like a house that a child might have constructed from

6. **ostensibly** (ä·sten′sə·blē): seemingly; apparently.

cards. A brisk wind might have blown it down, and the fact that it was still standing implied a kind of enchantment that was stronger than the elements. There it stood and as far as I know is standing yet—a gray, rotting thing with no porch, no shutters, no steps, set on a cramped lot with no grass, not even any weeds—a monument to decay.

In front of the house in a squeaky rocking chair sat Miss Lottie's son, John Burke, completing the impression of decay. John Burke was what was known as queer-headed. Black and ageless, he sat rocking day in and day out in a mindless stupor, lulled by the monotonous squeak-squawk of the chair. A battered hat atop his shaggy head shaded him from the sun. Usually John Burke was totally unaware of everything outside his quiet dream world. But if

MARIGOLDS 281

D Appreciating Language
Descriptive Language
? What words and phrases help create a vivid image of Miss Lottie's house? [Sample responses: "ramshackle," "faded," "rickety frame siding," "leaning together," "like a house … constructed from cards," "gray," "rotting," "a monument to decay."]

E Elements of Literature
Character
? What do you learn about John Burke, Miss Lottie's son? [He is mentally retarded—he lives in a dream world, he is easily angered, his language is strange.] What do you think of the children's "game" of disturbing him? [It is cruel, insensitive, and dangerous.]

Using Students' Strengths

Interpersonal Learners
"Marigolds" presents an opportunity to explore a young person's turbulent emotions and to consider the possible consequences. After students have read the story, have pairs of students spend three to five minutes improvising a possible dialogue between Lizabeth and Miss Lottie, in which an apology is offered and accepted. Ask for volunteers to present their versions to the class.

Auditory/Musical Learners
After students have read the story, suggest that they select music to reflect its mood or to accompany a memorable scene. They might consider, in particular, blues songs. Have them play their choices for the class after reading the scene aloud. Ask students to give two reasons that make their selection appropriate.

Verbal/Linguistic Learners
The narrator describes the children's impressions of Miss Lottie and her son. Ask students to create and deliver a dramatic monologue in which Miss Lottie or John Burke expresses her or his impression of the children. Or students may work in pairs on a dialogue about the children, between Miss Lottie and John Burke.

(A) Reading Skills and Strategies

Making Inferences

? Why did the children think Miss Lottie was a witch? [Possible responses: her stern face, her bent body, her rotting house, the way she kept to herself.]

(B) Reading Skills and Strategies

Identifying the Key Passages

? The narrator says that "old fears have a way of clinging like cobwebs," even when a person knows better. What does she mean by this? [Sample response: Even though there may be a logical reason for not believing something, it is hard to change former beliefs.]

(C) English Language Learners

Dialect

Explain that "Yeh" and "er" capture the children's pronunciation. In standard English, the sentence would read, "Yes, look at her."

(D) Reading Skills and Strategies

Making Inferences

? Why do the children hate the marigolds? [Possible response: They can't understand trying to create a mysterious spot of beauty in such an ugly place.]

(E) Elements of Literature

Internal Conflict

? What would the children gain by destroying the flowers? [Possible response: They would get rid of something they cannot understand.] What conflicts can you see in this situation? [youth versus age; destruction versus creation]

(F) Reading Skills and Strategies

Challenging the Text

? Is this a good explanation for what made the children so destructive? Why or why not? [Possible responses: Yes, the children feel frustrated and take out that feeling on someone else; or no, the speaker is still searching for the real explanation.]

you disturbed him, if you intruded upon his fantasies, he would become enraged, strike out at you, and curse at you in some strange enchanted language which only he could understand. We children made a game of thinking of ways to disturb John Burke and then to elude his violent retribution.

But our real fun and our real fear lay in Miss Lottie herself. Miss Lottie seemed to be at least a hundred years old. Her big frame still held traces of the tall, powerful woman she must have been in youth, although it was now bent and drawn. Her smooth skin was a dark reddish brown, and her face had Indian-like features and the stern stoicism[7] that one associates with Indian faces. Miss Lottie didn't like intruders either, especially children. She never left her yard, and nobody ever visited her. We never knew how she managed those necessities which depend on human interaction—how she ate, for example, or even whether she ate. When we were tiny children, we thought Miss Lottie was a witch and we made up tales that we half believed ourselves about her exploits. We were far too sophisticated now, of course, to believe the witch nonsense. But old fears have a way of clinging like cobwebs, and so when we sighted the tumbledown shack, we had to stop to reinforce our nerves.

"Look, there she is," I whispered, forgetting that Miss Lottie could not possibly have heard me from that distance. "She's fooling with them crazy flowers."

"Yeh, look at 'er."

Miss Lottie's marigolds were perhaps the strangest part of the picture. Certainly they did not fit in with the crumbling decay of the rest of her yard. Beyond the dusty brown yard, in front of the sorry gray house, rose suddenly and shockingly a dazzling strip of bright blossoms, clumped together in enormous mounds, warm and passionate and sun-golden. The old black witch-woman worked on them all summer, every summer, down on her creaky knees, weeding and cultivating and arranging, while the house crumbled and John Burke rocked. For some perverse reason, we children hated those marigolds. They interfered with the perfect ugliness of the place; they were too beautiful; they said too much that we could not understand; they did not make sense. There was something in the vigor with which the old woman destroyed the weeds that intimidated us. It should have been a comical sight—the old woman with the man's hat on her cropped white head, leaning over the bright mounds, her big backside in the air—but it wasn't comical, it was something we could not name. We had to annoy her by whizzing a pebble into her flowers or by yelling a dirty word, then dancing away from her rage, reveling in our youth and mocking her age. Actually, I think it was the flowers we wanted to destroy, but nobody had the nerve to try it, not even Joey, who was usually fool enough to try anything.

"Y'all git some stones," commanded Joey now and was met with instant giggling obedience as everyone except me began to gather pebbles from the dusty ground. "Come on, Lizabeth."

I just stood there peering through the bushes, torn between wanting to join the fun and feeling that it was all a bit silly.

"You scared, Lizabeth?"

I cursed and spat on the ground—my favorite gesture of phony bravado. "Y'all children get the stones, I'll show you how to use 'em."

I said before that we children were not consciously aware of how thick were the bars of our cage. I wonder now, though, whether we were not more aware of it than I thought. Perhaps we had some dim notion of what we were, and how little chance we had of being anything else. Otherwise, why would we have been so preoccupied with destruction? Anyway, the pebbles were collected quickly, and everybody looked at me to begin the fun.

"Come on, y'all."

7. **stoicism** (stō′i·siz′əm): calm indifference to pleasure or pain.

WORDS TO OWN

retribution (re′trə·byo͞o′shən) *n.*: revenge.

intimidated (in·tim′ə·dāt′id) *v.*: frightened.

Getting Students Involved

Cooperative Learning

Literary Scrapbook. Have students work in groups of three or four to create a literary scrapbook for Lizabeth or Miss Lottie. The scrapbook should contain images or items that reflect the character's time, place, circumstances, and personality, as these are described or suggested in the story. Each group member should perform one of the following tasks: lead a brainstorming session, organize items, design the scrapbook pages, or write identifying notes.

"Just Say No." The children in "Marigolds" had nothing to do, so they were perfectly happy to follow Joey's suggestion to go over to Miss Lottie's. Lizabeth thinks about the fun, but not the consequences, and goes along with the other children. Have the class suggest possible strategies for resisting peer pressure to do something destructive or hurtful. Ask a volunteer to list the suggestions on the board.

The Magic Garden (1978) by Romare Bearden. Watercolor and collage (10 ⅛" x 7").

RESPONDING TO THE ART

Romare Bearden (1914–1988) was born in New York City and raised during the intellectual and artistic ferment of the Harlem Renaissance of the 1920s. But he also spent long periods of his youth in the rural South and industrial Pittsburgh. Thus he knew people of all types—intellectuals, artists, musicians, field workers, iron workers. In his art Bearden felt free to combine influences from many sources. He found collage especially apt for conveying both the order and the fragmentation of city life. The collages illustrating this story, however, are drawn from his experience of the rural South. (See also pp. 281 and 284.) But as in his city collages, Bearden emphasizes people: faces dominate the settings.

Activity. Ask students to study the collage and to suggest the kinds of materials Bearden may have pasted together to create it. [blue fabric, photograph of a face, watercolor paints, glue] **How does the collage connect with the story?** [It shows the contrast between a black woman's house and her flower garden.] **Why do you think Bearden titled this work** *The Magic Garden?* [Sample response: The woman in the painting is making her garden a bright, magical place of escape.] **What phrase or sentence from the story could serve as a caption for this collage?** [Sample responses: "dazzling strip of bright blossoms," p. 282; "whatever was of love and beauty and joy . . . had been there in the marigolds," p. 286.]

Skill Link

Using Figurative Language

Figurative language is discussed in the Language Link on p. 291. Figures of speech compare one thing to another thing that is very different. There are many kinds of figures of speech. A **simile** uses words such as *like, as,* or *than* in making the comparison: Miss Lottie's house looks "*like* a house that a child might have constructed from cards" (p. 281). A **metaphor** is a comparison between two unlike things in which one thing becomes another thing without the use of the word *like, as, than,* or *resembles:* "Poverty was the cage in which we all were trapped" (p. 280).

Activity

Ask students to choose a piece of writing from their portfolios. Have them review their writing for descriptive statements such as "The day was hot" or "The night was long," and make a list of these statements. Then have the class brainstorm a list of random nouns and write this list on the board. Finally, have students choose words from the list on the board (or choose new words that come to mind) and use them to construct similes or metaphors that can help transform their original sentences into new, more vivid sentences. [Sample response: *Original description:* The day was hot. *Word from board:* dog. *New sentence:* The day was like a dog panting in the sun.]

RESPONDING TO THE ART

Romare Bearden (1914–1988) studied at the Art Students League in New York City, Columbia University, and the Sorbonne in Paris. He met and was influenced by artists like the German social commentator, George Grosz, and the French proponent of *papier collé* (collage), Georges Braque. Bearden repeated themes based on ritual, music, and family life in many of his collages. *La Primavera,* which means "Springtime," contains elements both from technology (the cogs on the woman's bandanna; the robot-like male figure) and from nature (the green growth).

Activity. Ask students to describe the kinds of experiences the collage calls to mind. [Possible responses: daily life, fieldwork, parents and a child working together.] What elements most strongly suggest springtime? [The dominant color green; the plants in the hands of two of the figures.]

Ⓐ Appreciating Language
Onomatopoeia
❓ The word *zing* mimics the sound the stone makes. What other words do you know that sound like what they mean? [Sample responses: *crunch, wham, plop, buzz, jiggle, sizzle.*]

Ⓑ English Language Learners
Dialect
Help students rewrite Miss Lottie's words in standard English. ["Who's out there?" "You'd better get away from here!"]

Ⓒ Critical Thinking
Speculating
❓ Why do you think Lizabeth is acting like this? [Sample responses: She is taking out her negative feelings on Miss Lottie; she is caught up in group excitement; it makes her feel important to show off in front of the other children.]

La Primavera (1967) by Romare Bearden. Collage, oil on board (44″ x 56″).

We crept to the edge of the bushes that bordered the narrow road in front of Miss Lottie's place. She was working placidly, kneeling over the flowers, her dark hand plunged into the golden mound. Suddenly *zing*—an expertly aimed stone cut the head off one of the blossoms.

"Who out there?" Miss Lottie's backside came down and her head came up as her sharp eyes searched the bushes. "You better git!"

We had crouched down out of sight in the bushes, where we stifled the giggles that insisted on coming. Miss Lottie gazed warily across the road for a moment, then cautiously returned to her weeding. *Zing*—Joey sent a pebble into the blooms, and another marigold was beheaded.

Miss Lottie was enraged now. She began struggling to her feet, leaning on a rickety cane and shouting. "Y'all git! Go on home!" Then the rest of the kids let loose with their pebbles, storming the flowers and laughing wildly and senselessly at Miss Lottie's <u>impotent</u> rage. She shook her stick at us and started shakily toward the road crying, "Git 'long! John Burke! John Burke, come help!"

Then I lost my head entirely, mad with the power of inciting such rage, and ran out of the bushes in the storm of pebbles, straight toward Miss Lottie, chanting madly, "Old witch, fell in a

WORDS TO OWN
impotent (im'pə·tənt) *adj.*: powerless; helpless.

284 THE SHORT-STORY COLLECTIONS

Crossing the Curriculum

History
Have students work in small groups to research the Great Depression and its effects on the state in which they live. If possible, they should interview older community members or relatives in addition to doing research in libraries or museums. If resources are available, have each group present a multimedia report that includes pictures, taped interviews, newspaper clippings, and videos.

Art
Provide the class with a copy of Faith Ringgold's book, *Tar Beach.* It is a work of autobiographical fiction based on her story-quilt painting that is displayed in the Guggenheim Museum in New York City. As students read the book, have them think about how it compares to Lizabeth's experiences in "Marigolds." Have students design and, if possible, create story-quilt paintings that depict Lizabeth's experiences.

ditch, picked up a penny and thought she was rich!" The children screamed with delight, dropped their pebbles, and joined the crazy dance, swarming around Miss Lottie like bees and chanting, "Old lady witch!" while she screamed curses at us. The madness lasted only a moment, for John Burke, startled at last, lurched out of his chair, and we dashed for the bushes just as Miss Lottie's cane went whizzing at my head.

I did not join the merriment when the kids gathered again under the oak in our bare yard. Suddenly I was ashamed, and I did not like being ashamed. The child in me sulked and said it was all in fun, but the woman in me flinched at the thought of the malicious attack that I had led. The mood lasted all afternoon. When we ate the beans and rice that was supper that night, I did not notice my father's silence, for he was always silent these days, nor did I notice my mother's absence, for she always worked until well into evening. Joey and I had a particularly bitter argument after supper; his exuberance got on my nerves. Finally I stretched out upon the pallet[8] in the room we shared and fell into a fitful doze.

When I awoke, somewhere in the middle of the night, my mother had returned, and I vaguely listened to the conversation that was audible through the thin walls that separated our rooms. At first I heard no words, only voices. My mother's voice was like a cool, dark room in summer—peaceful, soothing, quiet. I loved to listen to it; it made things seem all right somehow. But my father's voice cut through hers, shattering the peace.

"Twenty-two years, Maybelle, twenty-two years," he was saying, "and I got nothing for you, nothing, nothing."

"It's all right, honey, you'll get something. Everybody out of work now, you know that."

"It ain't right. Ain't no man ought to eat his woman's food year in and year out, and see his children running wild. Ain't nothing right about that."

"Honey, you took good care of us when you had it. Ain't nobody got nothing nowadays."

8. **pallet**: small bed or cot.

"I ain't talking about nobody else, I'm talking about *me*. God knows I try." My mother said something I could not hear, and my father cried out louder, "What must a man do, tell me that?"

"Look, we ain't starving. I git paid every week, and Mrs. Ellis is real nice about giving me things. She gonna let me have Mr. Ellis's old coat for you this winter——"

"Damn Mr. Ellis's coat! And damn his money! You think I want white folks' leavings? Damn, Maybelle"—and suddenly he sobbed, loudly and painfully, and cried helplessly and hopelessly in the dark night. I had never heard a man cry before. I did not know men ever cried. I covered my ears with my hands but could not cut off the sound of my father's harsh, painful, despairing sobs. My father was a strong man who could whisk a child upon his shoulders and go singing through the house. My father whittled toys for us, and laughed so loud that the great oak seemed to laugh with him, and taught us how to fish and hunt rabbits. How could it be that my father was crying? But the sobs went on, un-stifled, finally quieting until I could hear my mother's voice, deep and rich, humming softly as she used to hum to a frightened child.

The world had lost its boundary lines. My mother, who was small and soft, was now the strength of the family; my father, who was the rock on which the family had been built, was sobbing like the tiniest child. Everything was suddenly out of tune, like a broken accordion. Where did I fit into this crazy picture? I do not now remember my thoughts, only a feeling of great bewilderment and fear.

Long after the sobbing and humming had stopped, I lay on the pallet, still as stone with my hands over my ears, wishing that I too could cry and be comforted. The night was silent now except for the sound of the crickets and of Joey's soft breathing. But the room was too crowded with fear to allow me to sleep, and finally, feeling the terrible aloneness of 4 A.M., I decided to awaken Joey.

"Ouch! What's the matter with you? What you want?" he demanded disagreeably when I had pinched and slapped him awake.

"Come on, wake up."

MARIGOLDS 285

Taking a Second Look

T285

A Elements of Literature
Internal Conflict
❓ What do you think is haunting Lizabeth? [anger; fear about growing up; hopelessness about poverty] What do you predict that she might do? [Some students will predict a destructive act; others may think she means to make amends to Miss Lottie in some way.]

B Reading Skills and Strategies
Finding Details
❓ What emotions combine to impel Lizabeth to act destructively? [neediness, hopelessness, bewilderment, fear]

C Elements of Literature
Plot
❓ What makes this paragraph the climax of the story? [Lizabeth has committed a shocking act. The tension cannot build any further; some kind of resolution must follow.]

D Reading Skills and Strategies

Identifying the Key Passages
❓ What do you think Lizabeth means by "a kind of reality which is hidden to childhood"? [Possible response: She now sees the reality of another adult's life, with its individual hopes and passions, and can never again be unaware of the effects of her actions on another.]

E Reading Skills and Strategies
Identifying the Main Idea
Have students paraphrase the key idea of this passage, and comment on whether or not they agree with the final sentence. [Sample response: Innocence means having only a surface knowledge, but compassion demands seeing below the surface, so you can't be both innocent and compassionate at the same time. I agree because life is more complex than children realize.]

"What for? Go 'way."

I was lost for a reasonable reply. I could not say, "I'm scared and I don't want to be alone," so I merely said, "I'm going out. If you want to come, come on."

The promise of adventure awoke him. "Going out now? Where to, Lizabeth? What you going to do?"

I was pulling my dress over my head. Until now I had not thought of going out. "Just come on," I replied tersely.

I was out the window and halfway down the road before Joey caught up with me.

"Wait, Lizabeth, where you going?"

A I was running as if the Furies[9] were after me, as perhaps they were—running silently and furiously until I came to where I had half known I was headed: to Miss Lottie's yard.

The half-dawn light was more eerie than complete darkness, and in it the old house was like the ruin that my world had become—foul and crumbling, a grotesque caricature. It looked haunted, but I was not afraid, because I was haunted too.

"Lizabeth, you lost your mind?" panted Joey.

B I had indeed lost my mind, for all the smoldering emotions of that summer swelled in me and burst—the great need for my mother who was never there, the hopelessness of our poverty and degradation, the bewilderment of being neither child nor woman and yet both at once, the fear unleashed by my father's tears. And these feelings combined in one great impulse toward destruction.

"Lizabeth!"

C I leaped furiously into the mounds of marigolds and pulled madly, trampling and pulling and destroying the perfect yellow blooms. The fresh smell of early morning and of dew-soaked marigolds spurred me on as I went tearing and mangling and sobbing while Joey tugged my dress or my waist crying, "Lizabeth, stop, please stop!"

And then I was sitting in the ruined little garden among the uprooted and ruined

9. **Furies** (fyōōr′ēz): in Greek and Roman mythology, spirits who pursue people who have committed crimes, sometimes driving them mad.

286 THE SHORT-STORY COLLECTIONS

---

flowers, crying and crying, and it was too late to undo what I had done. Joey was sitting beside me, silent and frightened, not knowing what to say. Then, "Lizabeth, look."

I opened my swollen eyes and saw in front of me a pair of large, calloused feet; my gaze lifted to the swollen legs, the age-distorted body clad in a tight cotton nightdress, and then the shadowed Indian face surrounded by stubby white hair. And there was no rage in the face now, now that the garden was destroyed and there was nothing any longer to be protected.

D "M-miss Lottie!" I scrambled to my feet and just stood there and stared at her, and that was the moment when childhood faded and womanhood began. That violent, crazy act was the last act of childhood. For as I gazed at the immobile face with the sad, weary eyes, I gazed upon a kind of reality which is hidden to childhood. The witch was no longer a witch but only a broken old woman who had dared to create beauty in the midst of ugliness and sterility. She had been born in squalor and lived in it all her life. Now at the end of that life she had nothing except a falling-down hut, a wrecked body, and John Burke, the mindless son of her passion. Whatever verve there was left in her, whatever was of love and beauty and joy that had not been squeezed out by life, had been there in the marigolds she had so tenderly cared for.

Of course I could not express the things that I knew about Miss Lottie as I stood there awkward and ashamed. The years have put words to the things I knew in that moment, and as I look back upon it, I know that that moment marked the end of innocence. Innocence involves an unseeing acceptance of things at face value, an ignorance of the area below the surface. In that **E** humiliating moment I looked beyond myself and into the depths of another person. This was the beginning of compassion, and one cannot have both compassion and innocence.

The years have taken me worlds away from that time and that place, from the dust and squalor of our lives, and from the bright thing that I destroyed in a blind, childish striking out at God knows what. Miss Lottie died long ago

---

Making the Connections

Connecting to the Theme: "Discoveries"
Ask students to list the discoveries Lizabeth makes during the course of the story. [Sample responses: the reality of Miss Lottie's humanity; the streak of cruelty within herself; the worries her parents face; the hopelessness that accompanies poverty; the pain of growing up; the loss of innocence; the complexity of adulthood.]

Cultural Connections
"Marigolds" builds to the climactic event that marks the end of Lizabeth's childhood. Many cultures and religions around the world observe coming-of-age traditions that mark the transition from childhood to adulthood, such as confirmation, a bar mitzvah or bat mitzvah. Ask students to research such a tradition and to share what they learn with the class. Suggest that students answer questions like these:

- What preparation is involved?
- How do young adults seem to feel about the tradition?
- Is the tradition changing or disappearing in the culture?
- What is the young adult expected to gain from the experience?

T286

and many years have passed since I last saw her hut, completely barren at last, for despite my wild <u>contrition</u> she never planted marigolds again. Yet, there are times when the image of those passionate yellow mounds returns with a painful poignancy. For one does not have to be ignorant and poor to find that his life is as barren as the dusty yards of our town. And I too have planted marigolds. **G**

F

WORDS TO OWN

contrition (kən·trish′ən) *n.:* deep feelings of guilt and repentance.

MEET THE WRITER

I Must Have Done My Job Well

Eugenia W. Collier (1928–   ) has taught English at Howard University, Baltimore Community College, and Morgan State College. Collier wrote this about her story "Marigolds":

❝When I talk with people about 'Marigolds,' someone usually asks me whether the story is autobiographical. I am always pleased with the question, because it means that I must have done my job well—convinced the reader that the incidents in the story are actually happening. However, I always end up admitting that Lizabeth and I are two very different people. I was born and bred in the city of Baltimore, and my family never had the economic problems of Lizabeth's. In some ways we are different in temperament: I was never as daring as Lizabeth, never a leader among my peers. However, I hope that through her I have captured an experience which most young people have—the painful passage from childhood to adulthood, a passage which can

be understood only in retrospect. Also, I was tapping into another deeply human experience: hoping desperately for something (planting marigolds) and then having that hope destroyed.

I wrote 'Marigolds' at a time of profound unhappiness. One night I had a tremendous urge to write. I wrote nonstop until the story was finished—about twenty-four hours. Later I sent 'Marigolds' (along with a fee I could hardly afford) to a well-advertised literary agency, which returned the story (not the fee) with a note saying that it had no plot, no conflict, and no hope of publication. Discouraged, I put 'Marigolds' away. Five years later, doing research for a project on black writing of the 1960s, I read stories in *Negro Digest* which were similar in subject matter to 'Marigolds.' I submitted my story, and *Negro Digest* published it. It won the Gwendolyn Brooks Prize for Fiction, it was selected for inclusion in an anthology of black fiction, and since then it has been included in a number of collections. Of all the fiction I have written, 'Marigolds' remains my favorite. ❞

MARIGOLDS **287**

F Critical Thinking

Speculating

? Why do you think Miss Lottie never again planted marigolds? [Possible responses: It was too much work; she was too devastated ever to expose herself to that kind of pain again.]

G Reading Skills and Strategies

Interpreting

? What might Lizabeth mean by this last line? [She has also tried to create beauty amid ugliness.]

BROWSING IN THE FILES

About the Writer. Born in Baltimore, Collier is the daughter of a physician father and an educator mother. Collier has spent most of her adult life teaching English literature at colleges and universities. Her own stories and poems have appeared in a variety of anthologies. Her reflections on African American life appear in her collection *Breeder and Other Stories*. She writes, "The fact of my blackness is the core and center of my creativity. After a conventional Western-type education, I discovered the richness, the diversity, the beauty of my black heritage. This discovery has meant a coalescence of personal and professional goals. It has also meant a lifetime commitment."

Resources

Selection Assessment

Formal Assessment
• Selection Test, p. 41

Test Generator (One-Stop Planner)
• CD-ROM

Assessing Learning

Check Test: Questions and Answers
Answers will vary slightly.
1. What does the author remember most about the place where she lived as a child? [dust and Miss Lottie's marigolds]
2. Why do the children decide to go to Miss Lottie's house? [They are bored and seeking excitement.]
3. What do the children call Miss Lottie? [a witch]
4. What happens one night at home to upset Lizabeth? [She hears her father crying as he talks with her mother about hard times.]
5. In her rage, what does Lizabeth do? [She destroys Miss Lottie's marigolds.]

Peer Evaluation
When you have students discuss each other's projects, have them ask each other these questions: What details of your project show your understanding of the story? What did you hope others would understand about the story through your project?

Standardized Test Preparation
For practice in proofreading and editing, see
• *Daily Oral Grammar,* Transparency 17

Connections

The poem's speaker relates an event from his childhood that still troubles him today. He shot at and broke the wings of two birds. The birds, who could not fly, swam out to sea, and their cries could be heard for days.

Resources

Listening
Audio CD Library
A recording of this poem is provided in the *Audio CD Library:*
• Disk 10, Track 5

A Literary Connections

Robert P. Tristram Coffin (1892–1955) was an American poet whose work focused on New England farm and sea-faring life. He also wrote the novel *Red Sky in Morning* (1935). He saw poetry as a public service that could inspire people. He was awarded the Pulitzer Prize for poetry in 1936 for his collection *Strange Holiness* (1935).

B Reading Skills and Strategies
Summarizing

Play the poem from the *Audio CD Library* or read it aloud in class. Then have students work in pairs to summarize what happens and the effect on the speaker. [Sample response: As a boy, the speaker shot two birds, badly injuring their wings instead of killing them. The guilt of this "sin" remains a part of his life; it still causes him to hear the cries of the injured birds above all other sounds of sorrow.]

RESPONDING TO THE ART

John James Audubon (1785–1851) may be the most famous of all American illustrators of the birds of North America. Tell students that a plover is a shorebird. **Activity.** Have students connect the illustration with the poem. [The illustration depicts two shore-birds; the speaker in the poem shoots two similar birds.]

Connections — A POEM

Forgive My Guilt

A Robert P. Tristram Coffin

Not always sure what things called sins may be,
I am sure of one sin I have done.
It was years ago, and I was a boy,
I lay in the frostflowers with a gun,
5　The air ran blue as the flowers, I held my breath,
Two birds on golden legs slim as dream things
Ran like quicksilver on the golden sand,
My gun went off, they ran with broken wings
Into the sea, I ran to fetch them in,
10　But they swam with their heads high out to sea,
They cried like two sorrowful high flutes,
With jagged ivory bones where wings should be.

B

For days I heard them when I walked that headland
Crying out to their kind in the blue,
15　The other plovers were going over south
On silver wings leaving these broken two.
The cries went out one day; but I still hear them
Over all the sounds of sorrow in war or peace
I ever have heard, time cannot drown them,
20　Those slender flutes of sorrow never cease.
Two airy things forever denied the air!
I never knew how their lives at last were spilt,
But I have hoped for years all that is wild,
Airy, and beautiful will forgive my guilt.

Black-Bellied Plover by John James Audubon.

© Collection of The New-York Historical Society.

Connecting Across Texts

Connecting with "Marigolds"

Ask students to identify events, concepts, or themes of the poem that connect with events, concepts, or themes of "Marigolds." [Possible responses: The speaker in the poem and Lizabeth in "Marigolds" both commit an act of destruction; both feel guilty about what they did; both view the act as a loss of innocence; both events teach a lesson about respecting other living beings.]

Suggest that students create their own poems, modeled after "Forgive My Guilt," using an experience that marked their own loss of innocence. If you plan to ask students to read their poems in class, remind them to choose an experience they are willing to share with their classmates.

MAKING MEANINGS

First Thoughts

[infer] **1.** Why do you think Lizabeth hated the marigolds? Are the reasons for her feelings common? Check your Quickwrite.

Shaping Interpretations

[analyze] **2.** What are Lizabeth's **internal conflicts**—what personal "monsters" are troubling her?

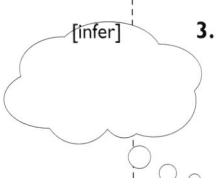

[infer] **3.** Draw a thought bubble like the one shown opposite. Fill it with words that represent Lizabeth's thoughts as she commits her act of cruel destruction. Be prepared to explain why you chose the words you did.

[infer] **4.** Lizabeth says that destroying the marigolds was her last act of childhood. Why does she think of herself as an adult from that moment on?

[interpret] **5.** What does Lizabeth mean at the end when she says that she too has planted marigolds? What do you think the marigolds have come to mean in the story? Consider the feelings that the characters have had about the marigolds throughout the story:

- Miss Lottie loves and cares for them.
- The children do not understand why they are there.
- Lizabeth wants to destroy them.

[identify] **6.** What do you think is the **key passage** in this story—the passage that says something very important about our lives? If you haven't chosen a passage yet, skim the story now and find one. Be sure to compare your passages in class, and be prepared to explain your choice.

Extending the Text

[compare] **7.** Compare Lizabeth's feelings at the end of the story with the feelings of the speaker of "Forgive My Guilt" (see *Connections* on page 288). What did both children discover?

[infer] **8.** The narrator doesn't tell us much about the effect of the destruction on Miss Lottie. From what she *does* tell us, how do you think Miss Lottie was affected?

[interpret] **9.** "The world had lost its boundary lines," Lizabeth writes about her parents' conversation that night. What does she mean? What situations might make a child feel that boundaries have been lost?

Reading Check

a. When and where does this story take place?

b. Who is Miss Lottie and why are the children afraid of her?

c. Describe the children's confrontation with Miss Lottie.

d. What does Lizabeth discover about her parents that night?

e. Years later, what things about Miss Lottie and herself is the narrator able to express?

MAKING MEANINGS

First Thoughts

1. Possible responses: She didn't understand them; she hated them as a symbol of Miss Lottie's hope, when she herself felt hopeless. Many students will connect with Lizabeth's feelings.

Shaping Interpretations

2. Possible conflicts: clinging to childhood versus becoming an adult; taking responsibility versus not being conscious of it; dealing with a sense of despair creatively versus destructively.

3. Sample thoughts: I hate you, I hate these flowers, I've got nothing so now you've got nothing, Why am I doing this?

4. Possible responses: She has learned that actions have meaning and carry responsibility; she can no longer act without considering the effects on someone else.

5. Lizabeth means that she has taken a stand against despair by creating beauty. In the story, marigolds stand for beauty, hope, and the strength of the human spirit.

6. Possible key passages: "The world had lost its boundary lines," p. 285; "I know that that moment marked the end of innocence," p. 286; "And I too have planted marigolds," p. 287.

Extending the Text

7. Both discovered that acts of physical destruction destroy something in the human spirit as well.

8. Possible response: Miss Lottie may or may not have given up her spirit of hope, but she decides that flowers no longer express the message to others.

9. Lizabeth's words might mean that she is confused by role changes. Other situations that might make a child feel this way are moving to a new town or losing a family member.

Reading Check

Answers may vary slightly.

a. The story takes place in rural Maryland during the Great Depression of the 1930s.

b. Miss Lottie is an elderly neighbor who plants colorful marigolds. The children believe she is a witch.

c. The children taunt Miss Lottie and call her a witch; they throw stones that chop the heads off her flowers.

d. Lizabeth learns that her mother is currently the strong one of the family and that her father is overwhelmed with sadness at being unable to find work and support his family as he thinks he should.

e. The narrator regrets the fact that Miss Lottie never replanted the flowers; the narrator says that she has also tried to create beauty.

Rubrics for each Choices assignment appear on p. 122 in the *Portfolio Management System.*

CHOICES: Building Your Portfolio

1. **Writer's Notebook** Direct students' attention to the conflict diagram at the bottom of the page, and suggest that they organize their ideas in the same way. Remind students to save their work. They may use it as prewriting for the Writer's Workshop on p. 332.

2. **Writing a Letter** Remind students that the story does not have to be their favorite. They simply need to show that they understand what the author is trying to say. Encourage students to discuss how effective the author's first-person point of view is.

3. **Conflict Resolution** This is a good activity for small groups. Once students have completed their charts, ask them to reflect on possible solutions and to add that section to their charts. Groups may share their insights with the rest of the class.

4. **Art** After students finish their collages, you might hold a gallery showing. Ask students to display their artworks. Make paper available, and have viewers write a brief comment about what they like best in each of the works.

CHOICES: Building Your Portfolio

Writer's Notebook

1. Collecting Ideas for an Analysis of a Short Story

Conflicts. When you analyze a short story for the Writer's Workshop on page 332, you'll probably want to discuss the story's **conflicts.** Select a story you are interested in, and take notes on its conflicts. Make a diagram like the one below for "The Necklace" (page 221), listing conflicts and their resolutions. If a conflict is internal, write that down. If a conflict is left unresolved, write that down, too. Save your notes.

The Necklace

Conflicts	Resolutions
1. Mme. Loisel struggles with envy. (internal)	She borrows the necklace.
2. Mme. Loisel is disappointed in M. Loisel.	Unresolved
3. Mme. Loisel wants to get into society.	The Loisels end up with less status than before.

Writing a Letter

2. A Personal Response

In Meet the Writer on page 287, Collier recalls that the first agency she sent her story to returned it with a note saying the story had no hope of publication. Write a response to that agency in the form of a letter. You might talk about one or all of these issues:

- how you felt about the story in general
- how you connected with the text
- how you felt about certain passages

Conflict Resolution

3. Resolving Conflicts

An important part of solving problems is understanding the results, or effects, of certain troublesome actions. Using a chart like the one below, focus on Lizabeth's actions and their effects on other people and on herself. Then, focus on a conflict in your school or community. Prepare another chart citing actions or events and the ways they affect other people.

Actions	Effects
1.	1.
2.	2.
3.	3.

Art

4. Imitating Bearden

The collages on pages 281, 283, and 284 are by Romare Bearden. A **collage,** as you can see from the one below, is a collection of images taken from various sources (magazines, newspapers, photographs, even the artist's own drawings). Collages can also include pieces of cloth, words, or even objects like stones or shells or dried flowers. Create a collage of your own showing Miss Lottie's house and her flowers. For your collage, be sure to add some words from the story.

La Primavera (detail) (1967) by Romare Bearden. Collage, oil on board.

LANGUAGE LINK MINI-LESSON

Handbook of Literary Terms
H E L P

See Figure of Speech.

Figures of Speech—Making It Vivid

Collier's story is remarkable for its vivid figures of speech, which make the place and the characters' feelings come alive. In a figure of speech, one thing is compared to another, very different, thing. There are several kinds of figures of speech. A **simile** states the comparison using words such as *like, as,* or *than*:

> "I feel again the chaotic emotions of adolescence, illusive as smoke. . . ." [Emotions are compared to smoke.]

A **metaphor** compares two unlike things without using the words *like* or *as*:

> ". . . memory is an abstract painting" [Memory is directly compared to a painting.]

At times in a metaphor, only one part of the comparison is directly stated; you have to infer the other part:

> "Joy and rage and wild animal gladness and shame become tangled together in the multicolored skein of fourteen-going-on-fifteen. . . ." [A teenager's mixed emotions are compared to a multicolored skein of wool.]

Try It Out

Complete these sentences with imaginative figures of speech. Remember that a figure of speech compares two *unlike* items.

1. The marigolds were _____.
2. The garden looked like _____.
3. The days were as empty as _____.

Figures of speech are most often visual. Select two or three figures of speech from the story, and illustrate them.

A tip for writers: When you create a figure of speech, put it to a test. Ask: "In what specific way are these two unlike things alike?" Ask: "Does this work?"

VOCABULARY HOW TO OWN A WORD

WORD BANK

clarity
retribution
intimidated
impotent
contrition

How Would You Say It?

Read the following sentences from the story. Then reword them as if you were speaking. Use your everyday language.

1. "One day returns to me with special clarity. . . ."
2. "We children made a game of thinking of ways to disturb John Burke and then to elude his violent retribution."
3. "There was something in the vigor with which the old woman destroyed the weeds that intimidated us."
4. "Then the rest of the kids let loose with their pebbles, storming the flowers and laughing wildly and senselessly at Miss Lottie's impotent rage."
5. "Miss Lottie died long ago and many years have passed since I last saw her hut, completely barren at last, for despite my wild contrition she never planted marigolds again."

MARIGOLDS 291

LANGUAGE LINK
Try It Out
Possible Answers

1. gold hubcaps; miniature suns
2. a parking lot; the victim of a bad haircut
3. discarded milk cartons; popped balloons

Figures of speech used for illustration might include those given as examples in the Language Link or any of the following:

"Poverty was the cage in which we all were trapped." (p. 280)
"But old fears have a way of clinging like cobwebs." (p. 282)
"My mother's voice was like a cool, dark room in summer." (p. 285)
"Everything was suddenly out of tune, like a broken accordion." (p. 285)

VOCABULARY
Possible Answers

1. I remember one day very clearly.
2. It was a game for us kids to annoy John Burke and then run away from his violent revenge.
3. The old woman seemed so strong, the way she killed weeds, that she scared us.
4. Everybody threw pebbles, pounding the flowers and laughing wildly at Miss Lottie's powerless anger.
5. Miss Lottie died many years ago, and it's been a long time since I last saw her hut, without any flowers, because in spite of my regrets, she never again planted marigolds.

Resources —————

Language Resource
• *Grammar and Language Links* Worksheet, p. 27

Vocabulary Resource
• *Words to Own,* Worksheet, p. 12

Language Link Quick Check

Complete each sentence by creating a vivid simile or metaphor. Remember that you are comparing two mostly *unlike* items that are still *alike* in some way. Sample answers are provided in brackets.

1. Children's games are _____. [battles]
2. Lizabeth's courage was _____. [a brick wall]
3. Conflict can simmer _____. [like a pot of soup on the stove]
4. Our usual supper of beans and rice tasted _____. [like dust]
5. Innocence is _____. [a sleeping puppy]

T291

OBJECTIVES

1. Read and interpret the story
2. Identify key passages and interpret theme
3. Monitor comprehension
4. Express understanding through critical and creative writing, oral history, or drawing / social studies
5. Identify and use adverb clauses and subordinating conjunctions
6. Understand and use new words

SKILLS

Literary
- Identify key passages and interpret theme

Reading
- Monitor comprehension

Writing
- Take notes on setting
- Write a character sketch
- Write a short essay

Report Writing/Social Studies
- Conduct interviews

Drawing/Social Studies
- Draw symbolic images

Grammar
- Identify and use adverb clauses and subordinating conjunctions

Vocabulary
- Use new words

Viewing/Representing
- Identify images in an artwork (ATE)
- Update images in an artwork (ATE)

Planning

- **Block Schedule**
  Block Scheduling Lesson Plans with Pacing Guide
- **Traditional Schedule**
  Lesson Plans Including Strategies for English-Language Learners
- **One-Stop Planner**
  CD-ROM with Test Generator

Before You Read

AMERICAN HISTORY

Make the Connection

Missed Chances

It seems simple enough. You'd like to be friends with somebody who seems interesting from a distance—nice, smart, talented—but very different from you. Say that person is much older or younger, or is from another country, or speaks a different language. It might not be so easy to start a friendship.

Reading Skills and Strategies

Dialogue with the Text

As you read "American History," jot down your thoughts, questions, and predictions. Be especially sure to record your responses to some of the statements made by adults in the story. Perhaps some of them strike you as biased or unfair, or perhaps you feel they are all true. You might note these passages and your reactions in a double-entry journal.

Elements of Literature

Theme and Key Passages

A writer can reveal theme in many ways. Sometimes theme is directly stated in the text. But in most fiction you have to think about all the story events and then infer, or guess at, the meaning of the whole story for yourself. Very often a key passage in the story helps you discover the theme.

Not everyone sees the same theme in the same story. Some writers say that they themselves don't know the meaning of a story until their characters beg them to reveal it.

> **A** story may contain several passages that reveal the essence of the **theme**.
>
> *For more on Theme, see pages 264–265 and the Handbook of Literary Terms.*

Background

President John F. Kennedy was assassinated on November 22, 1963, while riding in a motorcade in Dallas, Texas. That unforgettable day has become an important piece of American mythology—that is, it has become a part of what we think of ourselves as a nation. Even today, people from all walks of life share stories about where they were and what they were doing when Kennedy was killed. Elena, in this story, has a very personal reason to remember the day Kennedy died.

go.hrw.com
LE0 9-4

"Listen," he repeated, "something awful has happened."

Teach Our Children (1990) by Juan Sanchez. Oil and mixed media on canvas.

Collection of the Museum of Tourism, San Juan, Puerto Rico.

Preteaching Vocabulary

Words to Own

After students have studied the Words to Own on pp. 294–298, have them choose the word that most closely corresponds to the idea in each quotation.

"Only the facts, please." [c]
"Stay awake and be watchful." [e]
"There, there; it's OK." [d]
"Head over heels in love." [b]
"You're in a trance!" [a]

a. enthralled
b. infatuated
c. literally
d. solace
e. vigilant

American History

Judith Ortiz Cofer

I once read in a "Ripley's Believe It or Not" column that Paterson, New Jersey, is the place where the Straight and Narrow (streets) intersect. The Puerto Rican tenement known as El Building was one block up on Straight. It was, in fact, the corner of Straight and Market; not "at" the corner, but *the* corner. At almost any hour of the day, El Building was like a monstrous  jukebox, blasting out salsas from open windows as the residents, mostly new immigrants just up from the island, tried to drown out whatever they were currently enduring with loud music. But the day President Kennedy was shot, there was a profound silence in El Building; even the abusive tongues of viragoes,[1] the cursing of the

1. **viragoes** (vi·rā′gōz): quarrelsome women.

Summary ■■

The story's first-person narrator, Elena, is a fourteen-year-old Puerto Rican girl who lives with her family in an apartment building in Paterson, New Jersey. She develops a crush on a blond-haired boy named Eugene, who lives in a house next door. An external conflict ensues on the day President John F. Kennedy is shot, when her mother is grieving but Elena insists on leaving the apartment in order to go to Eugene's house to study for an American history test. Elena is turned away by Eugene's mother, who says she does not want her son to become close to anyone in the neighborhood. Later that evening, Elena tries to summon up grief for the dead president, but she feels an internal conflict, because her tears are for herself and the loss of her friend. The story ends without resolving the conflict between Elena's personal feelings and what she thinks she should feel about the assassination. Elena discovers that prejudice and personal loss are not put "on hold" even when the country seems united in a great public loss.

Resources

Listening
Audio CD Library
A reading of this story is provided in the *Audio CD Library*:
• Disk 11, Track 2

Viewing and Representing
Videocassette A, Segment 4
Available in Spanish and English. The *Visual Connections* segment "A Shared Memory" provides a historical background for the story; it reviews the events surrounding the Kennedy assassination. For full lesson plans and worksheets, see *Visual Connections Teacher's Manual*.

Ⓐ Appreciating Language
Allusion
The narrator refers to Matthew 7:13–14 in the Bible, which speaks of the "strait" gate and "narrow" way to salvation.

Ⓑ Cultural Connections
The island of Puerto Rico was a significant source of immigrants to the New York City area in the 1950s and 1960s, and still is today.

Resources: Print and Media

Reading
• *Graphic Organizers for Active Reading,* p. 18
• *Words to Own,* p. 13
• *Audio CD Library,* Disc 11, Track 2

Writing and Language
• *Daily Oral Grammar* Transparency 18
• *Grammar and Language Links* Worksheet, p. 29
• *Language Workshop CD-ROM*

Viewing and Representing
• *Visual Connections* Videocassette A, Segment 4

Assessment
• *Formal Assessment,* p. 43
• *Portfolio Management System,* p. 123
• *Test Generator (One-Stop Planner* CD-ROM)

Internet
• go.hrw.com (keyword LE0 9-4)

A Cultural Connections

The "Sacred Heart" is a devotional image of Jesus Christ, consisting of a stylized picture of his heart as a symbol of love. "Spiritist altars," which often feature photographs, reflect the belief that the spirits of the dead can communicate with the living. See also the footnote on the "hierarchy of martyrs." Taken together, these details show the mix of Roman Catholic and Caribbean influences in Puerto Rican spirituality.

B Reading Skills and Strategies

Finding Cause and Effect

❓ Beans, rice, and pork chops are a popular Puerto Rican meal. Why do the girls start chanting about pork chops? [They are making fun of Elena's Puerto Rican heritage.]

C Elements of Literature

Character

❓ What details in this passage provide a description of Elena? [Her glasses fogging up and the chill entering her body tell us that she wears glasses and does not like the cold. Her burning cheeks show that she is shy and easily embarrassed. We also learn that she is skinny, does not like the city, and is less athletic than the other girls.]

D Reading Skills and Strategies

Dialogue with the Text

❓ Do you think Elena is correct in the conclusions she draws from watching the elderly couple while they have their meals? What do her conclusions reveal about her character? [Most students will probably feel that Elena's conclusions are accurate. She is observant, and her conclusions reveal perception and intelligence.]

---

unemployed, and the screeching of small children had been somehow muted. President Kennedy was a saint to these people. In fact, **A** soon his photograph would be hung alongside the Sacred Heart and over the spiritist altars that many women kept in their apartments. He would become part of the hierarchy of martyrs[2] they prayed to for favors that only one who had died for a cause would understand.

On the day that President Kennedy was shot, my ninth-grade class had been out in the fenced playground of Public School Number 13. We had been given "free" exercise time and had been ordered by our PE teacher, Mr. DePalma, to "keep moving." That meant that the girls should jump rope and the boys toss basketballs through a hoop at the far end of the yard. He in the meantime would "keep an eye" on us from just inside the building.

It was a cold gray day in Paterson. The kind that warns of early snow. I was miserable, since I had forgotten my gloves and my knuckles were turning red and raw from the jump rope. I was also taking a lot of abuse from the black girls for not turning the rope hard and fast enough for them.

"Hey, Skinny Bones, pump it, girl. Ain't you got no energy today?" Gail, the biggest of the black girls, had the other end of the rope, **B** yelled, "Didn't you eat your rice and beans and pork chops for breakfast today?"

The other girls picked up the "pork chop" and made it into a refrain: "Pork chop, pork chop, did you eat your pork chop?" They entered the double ropes in pairs and exited without **C** tripping or missing a beat. I felt a burning on my cheeks and then my glasses fogged up so that I could not manage to coordinate the jump rope with Gail. The chill was doing to me what it always did: entering my bones, making me cry, humiliating me. I hated the city, especially in winter. I hated Public School Number 13. I hated my skinny, flat-chested body, and I envied the

---

black girls, who could jump rope so fast that their legs became a blur. They always seemed to be warm, while I froze.

There was only one source of beauty and light for me that school year—the only thing I had anticipated at the start of the semester. That was seeing Eugene. In August, Eugene and his family had moved into the only house on the block that had a yard and trees. I could see his place from my window in El Building. In fact, if I sat on the fire escape I was <u>literally</u> suspended above Eugene's back yard. It was my favorite spot to read my library books in the summer. **D** Until that August the house had been occupied by an old Jewish couple. Over the years I had become part of their family, without their knowing it, of course. I had a view of their kitchen and their back yard, and though I could not hear what they said, I knew when they were arguing, when one of them was sick, and many other things. I knew all this by watching them at mealtimes. I could see their kitchen table, the sink, and the stove. During good times, he sat at the table and read his newspapers while she fixed the meals. If they argued, he would leave and the old woman would sit and stare at nothing for a long time. When one of them was sick, the other would come and get things from the kitchen and carry them out on a tray. The old man had died in June. The last week of school I had not seen him at the table at all. Then one day I saw that there was a crowd in the kitchen. The old woman had finally emerged from the house on the arm of a stocky middle-aged woman, whom I had seen there a few times before, maybe her daughter. Then a man had carried out suitcases. The house had stood empty for weeks. I had had to resist the temptation to climb down into the yard and water the flowers the old lady had taken such good care of.

By the time Eugene's family moved in, the yard was a tangled mass of weeds. The father had spent several days mowing, and when he

---

2. **hierarchy** (hī′ər·är′kē) **of martyrs** (märt′ərz): Martyrs are people who have suffered or died rather than give up their faith or principles; here, the author refers to martyrs who are honored and worshiped by Roman Catholics. *Hierarchy* means "ranking in order of importance."

WORDS TO OWN

literally (lit′ər·əl·ē) *adv.*: actually; in fact.

Reaching All Students

English Language Learners

Like Elena, some students may have experienced feeling like an outsider. After they finish reading the story, suggest that they write a letter from Elena to Eugene's mother, describing what it feels like to be turned away. Have them include everything Elena might have wanted to say, including comments about her feelings. For additional strategies for engaging English language learners, see
• *Lesson Plans Including Strategies for English-Language Learners*

Advanced Learners

A young teenager's first awareness of prejudice is a major theme of this story. You might suggest that students look for this theme in other works of literature, such as Richard Wright's *Black Boy*. Students can audiotape or videotape readings from these works as part of a class presentation on how prejudice affects young people.

finished, from where I sat I didn't see the red, yellow, and purple clusters that meant flowers to me. I didn't see this family sit down at the kitchen table together. It was just the mother, a redheaded, tall woman who wore a white uniform—a nurse's, I guessed it was; the father was gone before I got up in the morning and was never there at dinner time. I only saw him on weekends, when they sometimes sat on lawn chairs under the oak tree, each hidden behind a section of the

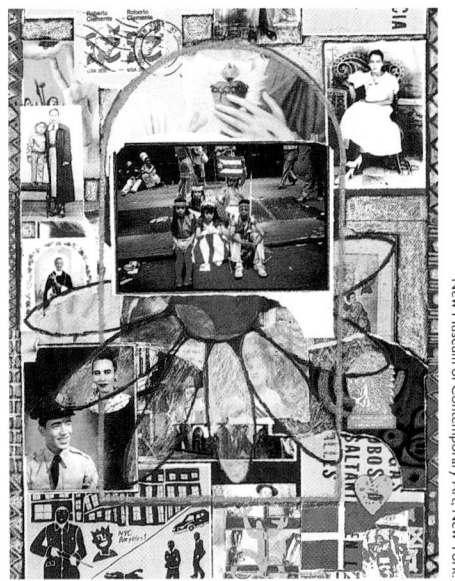

Untitled (1992) by Juan Sanchez.
Mixed media on paper.

Originally commissioned for the Testimonio Exhibit,
New Museum of Contemporary Art, New York.

newspaper; and there was Eugene. He was tall and blond, and he wore glasses. I liked him right away because he sat at the kitchen table and read books for hours. That summer, before we had even spoken one word to each other, I kept him company on my fire escape.

Once school started, I looked for him in all my classes, but PS 13 was a huge, over-populated place and it took me days and many discreet questions to discover that Eugene was in honors classes for all his subjects, classes that were not open to me because English was not my first language, though I was a straight-A student. After much maneuvering I managed to "run into him" in the hallway where his locker was—on the other side of the building from mine—and in study hall at the library, where he first seemed to notice me but did not speak, and finally, on the way home after school one day when I decided to approach him directly, though my stomach was doing somersaults.

I was ready for rejection, snobbery, the worst. But when I came up to him, practically panting in my nervousness, and blurted out: "You're Eugene. Right?" he smiled, pushed his

glasses up on his nose, and nodded. I saw then that he was blushing deeply. Eugene liked me, but he was shy. I did most of the talking that day. He nodded and smiled a lot. In the weeks that followed, we walked home together. He would linger at the corner of El Building for a few minutes, then walk down to his two-story house. It was not until Eugene moved into that house that I noticed that El Building blocked most of the sun and that the only spot that got a little sunlight during the day was the tiny square of earth the old woman had planted with flowers.

I did not tell Eugene that I could see inside his kitchen from my bedroom. I felt dishonest, but I liked my secret sharing of his evenings, especially now that I knew what he was reading since we chose our books together at the school library.

One day my mother came into my room as I was sitting on the windowsill staring out. In her abrupt way she said: "Elena, you are acting 'moony.'" "Enamorada" was what she really said, that is—like a girl stupidly <u>infatuated</u>. Since I had turned fourteen . . . , my mother had been more <u>vigilant</u> than ever. She acted as if I was going to go crazy or explode or something if she didn't watch me and nag me all the time about being a señorita now. She kept talking about virtue, morality, and other subjects that did not

---

WORDS TO OWN

infatuated (in·fach′o͞o·āt′id) *adj.:* carried away by shallow or foolish love.
vigilant (vij′ə·lənt) *adj.:* watchful.

AMERICAN HISTORY 295

RESPONDING TO THE ART
Juan Sanchez combines patriotic and spiritual images in this collage. The arch near the top contains a detail from an image of the Sacred Heart, and the photographs suggest spiritist altars and martyrs (see p. 294).
Activity. Have students identify as many of the images in the collage as possible.

E ## Reading Skills and Strategies
Comparing and Contrasting Characters
? What are some ways Elena and Eugene are alike? [Both wear glasses and like to read.] What is a major way that they differ? [They come from different cultural and ethnic backgrounds.]

F ## Elements of Literature
Theme and Key Passages
? This passage is one of several in the story that reveal the essence of the theme. How does this detail reinforce the theme of prejudice that was suggested earlier in the playground incident? [Denying honors classes to Elena because her first language is not English is unfair, considering her ability.]

G ## Reading Skills and Strategies

Dialogue with the Text
? Do you think Elena should share this fact with Eugene? Why or why not? [Possible responses: Yes, because friends should be honest with one another; no, because he might misinterpret her motives and feel as if she has been spying on him.]

Skill Link

Using Adverb Clauses
Adverb clauses are discussed in the Grammar Link on p. 302. An adverb clause is a dependent clause that tells *where, when, how, why, to what extent,* or *under what conditions* something occurs. Subordinating conjunctions that introduce adverb clauses include *after, although, because, even, even though, if, since, than, until, when,* and *while.*
Activity
Have students practice using adverb clauses by selecting a conjunction from the above list that

expresses the relationship they see between the two sentences. More than one way of combining each set of sentences is possible. Sample responses are provided in brackets.

1. Someone earns straight As. She should be admitted to honors classes. [If someone earns straight As, she should be admitted to honors classes.]
2. President Kennedy was shot. The nation went into shock. [The nation went into shock

when President Kennedy was shot.]
3. Adults everywhere were grieving for President Kennedy. Elena could not. [Although adults everywhere were grieving for President Kennedy, Elena could not.]
4. Something important happens in public life. Private problems do not take a vacation. [Even though something important happens in public life, private problems do not take a vacation.]

T295

interest me in the least. My mother was unhappy in Paterson, but my father had a good job at the bluejeans factory in Passaic and soon, he kept assuring us, we would be moving to our own house there. Every Sunday we drove out to the suburbs of Paterson, Clifton, and Passaic, out to where people mowed grass on Sundays in the summer and where children made snowmen in the winter from pure white snow, not like the gray slush of Paterson, which seemed to fall from the sky in that hue. I had learned to listen to my parents' dreams, which were spoken in Spanish, as fairy tales, like the stories about life in the island paradise of Puerto Rico before I was born. I had been to the island once as a little girl, to Grandmother's funeral, and all I remembered was wailing women in black, my mother becoming hysterical and being given a pill that made her sleep two days, and me feeling lost in a crowd of strangers all claiming to be my aunts, uncles, and cousins. I had actually been glad to return to the city. We had not been back there since then, though my parents talked constantly about buying a house on the beach someday, retiring on the island— that was a common topic among the residents of El Building. As for me, I was going to go to college and become a teacher.

But after meeting Eugene I began to think of the present more than of the future. What I wanted now was to enter that house I had watched for so many years. I wanted to see the other rooms where the old people had lived and where the boy spent his time. Most of all I wanted to sit at the kitchen table with Eugene like two adults, like the old man and his wife had done, maybe drink some coffee and talk about books. I had started reading *Gone With the Wind.* I was <u>enthralled</u> by it, with the daring and the passion of the beautiful girl living in a mansion, and with her devoted parents and the slaves who did everything for them. I didn't believe such a world had ever really existed, and I wanted to ask Eugene some questions since he and his parents, he had told me, had come up from Georgia, the same place where the novel was set. His father worked for a company that had transferred him to Paterson.

His mother was very unhappy, Eugene said, in his beautiful voice that rose and fell over words in a strange, lilting way. The kids at school called him "the Hick" and made fun of the way he talked. I knew I was his only friend so far, and I liked that, though I felt sad for him sometimes. "Skinny Bones and the Hick" was what they called us at school when we were seen together.

The day Mr. DePalma came out into the cold and asked us to line up in front of him was the day that President Kennedy was shot. Mr. DePalma, a short, muscular man with slicked-down black hair, was the science teacher, PE coach, and disciplinarian at PS 13. He was the teacher to whose homeroom you got assigned if you were a troublemaker, and the man called out to break up playground fights and to escort violently angry teenagers to the office. And Mr. DePalma was the man who called your parents in for "a conference."

That day, he stood in front of two rows of mostly black and Puerto Rican kids, brittle from their efforts to "keep moving" on a November day that was turning bitter cold. Mr. DePalma, to our complete shock, was crying. Not just silent adult tears, but really sobbing. There were a few titters from the back of the line where I stood shivering.

"Listen," Mr. DePalma raised his arms over his head as if he were about to conduct an orchestra. His voice broke, and he covered his face with his hands. His barrel chest was heaving. Someone giggled behind me.

"Listen," he repeated, "something awful has happened." A strange gurgling came from his throat, and he turned around and spat on the cement behind him.

"Gross," someone said, and there was a lot of laughter.

"The president is dead, you idiots. I should have known that wouldn't mean anything to a bunch of losers like you kids. Go home." He was shrieking now. No one moved for a minute or

---

WORDS TO OWN
enthralled (en·thrôld') v.: fascinated.

Getting Students Involved

Cooperative Learning

Character Attribute Web. To encourage students to develop an in-depth understanding of the story's narrator, have them, after they finish the first three pages of the story, work in pairs to create a Character Attribute Web for Elena. Ask students to add new attributes to the web as they gain additional insight into her character. Here is a sample graphic students can use:

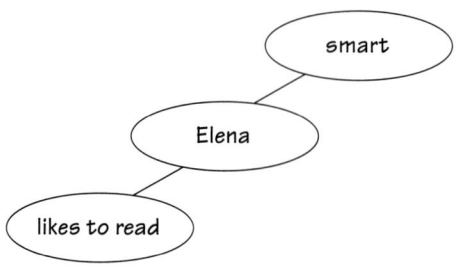

Duologue. After students finish reading the story, divide the class into pairs. Have the partners choose a scene in which a conversation could have taken place between Elena and her mother but did not. Students should role-play the characters and improvise a conversation that might have developed. Remind them that their improvisations must fit what the story tells them about the characters.

two, but then a big girl let out a "Yeah!" and ran to get her books piled up with the others against the brick wall of the school building. The others followed in a mad scramble to get to their things before somebody caught on. It was still an hour to the dismissal bell.

A little scared, I headed for El Building. There was an eerie feeling on the streets. I looked into Mario's drugstore, a favorite hangout for the high school crowd, but there were only a couple of old Jewish men at the soda bar talking with the short-order cook in tones that sounded almost angry, but they were keeping their voices low. Even the traffic on one of the busiest inter-**D** sections in Paterson—Straight Street and Park Avenue—seemed to be moving slower. There were no horns blasting that day. At El Building, the usual little group of unemployed men was not hanging out on the front stoop making it difficult for women to enter the front door. No music spilled out from open doors in the hallway. When I walked into our apartment, I found my mother sitting in front of the grainy picture of the television set.

She looked up at me with a tear-streaked face and just said: "Dios mío," turning back to the set as if it were pulling at her eyes. I went into my room.

Though I wanted to feel the right thing about President Kennedy's death, I could not fight the feeling of elation that stirred in my chest. Today was the day I was to visit Eugene in his house. He had asked me to come over after school to study for an American history test with him. We had also planned to walk to the public library together. I looked down into his yard. The oak tree was bare of leaves and the ground looked gray with ice. The light through the large kitchen

Retroactive I (1964) by Robert Rauschenberg.
Oil on canvas (84″ x 60″).

© Wadsworth Atheneum, Hartford. Gift of Susan Morse Hilles.
© Robert Rauschenberg/Licensed by VAGA, New York, NY.

window of his house told me that El Building blocked the sun to such an extent that they had to turn lights on in the middle of the day. I felt ashamed about it. But the white kitchen table with the lamp hanging just above it looked cozy and inviting. I would soon sit there, across from Eugene, and I would tell him about my perch just above his house. Maybe I should.

In the next thirty minutes I changed clothes, put on a little pink lipstick, and got my books together. Then I went in to tell my mother that I was going to a friend's house to study. I did not expect her reaction.

"You are going out *today*?" The way she said "today" sounded as if a storm warning had been issued. It was said in utter disbelief. Before I

AMERICAN HISTORY **297**

D ### Reading Skills and Strategies
Finding Details

❓ What details demonstrate the shock people felt on hearing that President Kennedy had been shot? [Details include: the "eerie feeling on the streets," the men's low voices, slowness of the traffic, absence of noise and music, tears of Elena's mother, the televised reports.]

Crossing the Curriculum

History

To give students a better understanding of the importance of President Kennedy to the American public, have them research either his role in developing the space program or the controversy surrounding his assassination. Have them report orally to the class in the form of a panel report or a discussion, using visual aids such as maps, diagrams, and magazine and newspaper articles from the 1960s.

Drama

In the story, a disturbing scene takes place between Eugene's mother and Elena. Ask students to act out the scene from the story, and then to improvise a more positive outcome by changing what one of the characters says and does. Remind students that their improvised version must be believable and must be based on what they have learned about the characters.

Theme and Key Passages

? Point out to students that this is a key passage in the story; it is one of several passages that reveal the essence of the theme. What does Elena's mother understand that Elena, as yet, does not? [Elena's mother knows that Eugene's parents may not want him to associate with a Puerto Rican immigrant.] Why does she permit Elena to go to Eugene's house anyway? [Sample response: Perhaps she feels that Elena must live her own life and make her own discoveries.]

B Elements of Literature

Symbols

? Why might green be considered the color of hope? [Green represents new life and spring, the return of the growing season. Many people associate spring with hope and a chance for new beginnings.]

C Reading Skills and Strategies

Dialogue with the Text

? What do you think of Elena's response? How would you feel if you were Elena? Why? [Sample responses: would be angry, hurt, and confused because Eugene's mother is being so mean; I would feel that my mother was right when she said I was heading for humiliation and pain.]

D Historical Connections

The widow and her children are Jacqueline, Caroline, and John Kennedy.

Resources

Selection Assessment
Formal Assessment
• Selection Test, p. 43
Test Generator (One-Stop Planner)
• CD-ROM

---

could answer, she came toward me and held my elbows as I clutched my books.

"Hija,[3] the president has been killed. We must show respect. He was a great man. Come to church with me tonight."

She tried to embrace me, but my books were in the way. My first impulse was to comfort her, she seemed so distraught, but I had to meet Eugene in fifteen minutes.

"I have a test to study for, Mama. I will be home by eight."

"You are forgetting who you are, Niña.[4] I have seen you staring down at that boy's house. You are heading for humiliation and pain." My mother said this in Spanish and in a resigned tone that surprised me, as if she had no intention of stopping me from "heading for humiliation and pain." I started for the door. She sat in front of the TV holding a white handkerchief to her face.

I walked out to the street and around the chain-link fence that separated El Building from Eugene's house. The yard was neatly edged around the little walk that led to the door. It always amazed me how Paterson, the inner core of the city, had no apparent logic to its architecture. Small, neat single residences like this one could be found right next to huge, dilapidated apartment buildings like El Building. My guess was that the little houses had been there first, then the immigrants had come in droves, and the monstrosities had been raised for them—the Italians, the Irish, the Jews, and now us, the Puerto Ricans and the blacks. The door was painted a deep green: verde, the color of hope. I had heard my mother say it: verde-esperanza.

I knocked softly. A few suspenseful moments later the door opened just a crack. The red, swollen face of a woman appeared. She had a halo of red hair floating over a delicate ivory face—the face of a doll—with freckles on the nose. Her smudged eye makeup made her look unreal to me, like a mannequin[5] seen through a warped store window.

---

3. **hija** (ē′hä): Spanish for "daughter."
4. **niña** (nē′nyä): Spanish for "girl."
5. **mannequin** (man′i·kin): life-size model of a person.

"What do you want?" Her voice was tiny and sweet sounding, like a little girl's, but her tone was not friendly.

"I'm Eugene's friend. He asked me over. To study." I thrust out my books, a silly gesture that embarrassed me almost immediately.

"You live there?" She pointed up to El Building, which looked particularly ugly, like a gray prison, with its many dirty windows and rusty fire escapes. The woman had stepped halfway out and I could see that she wore a white nurse's uniform with "St. Joseph's Hospital" on the name tag.

"Yes. I do."

She looked intently at me for a couple of heartbeats, then said as if to herself, "I don't know how you people do it." Then directly to me: "Listen. Honey. Eugene doesn't want to study with you. He is a smart boy. Doesn't need help. You understand me. I am truly sorry if he told you you could come over. He cannot study with you. It's nothing personal. You understand? We won't be in this place much longer, no need for him to get close to people—it'll just make it harder for him later. Run back home now."

I couldn't move. I just stood there in shock at hearing these things said to me in such a honey-drenched voice. I had never heard an accent like hers, except for Eugene's softer version. It was as if she were singing me a little song.

"What's wrong? Didn't you hear what I said?" She seemed very angry, and I finally snapped out of my trance. I turned away from the green door and heard her close it gently.

Our apartment was empty when I got home. My mother was in someone else's kitchen, seeking the solace she needed. Father would come in from his late shift at midnight. I would hear them talking softly in the kitchen for hours that night. They would not discuss their dreams for the future, or life in Puerto Rico, as they often did; that night they would talk sadly about the young widow and her two children, as if

---

WORDS TO OWN
solace (säl′is) *n.*: comfort; easing of grief.

Assessing Learning

Check Test: True-False

1. The story is set in an apartment building in Puerto Rico. [False]
2. Eugene's family lives in the only house on the block that has a yard and trees. [True]
3. Elena manages to meet Eugene in one of her honors classes. [False]
4. Elena finally tells Eugene that she can see into his family's kitchen window. [False]
5. Eugene's mother refuses to let Elena enter the house. [True]

Peer Evaluation: Speaking and Listening

Remind students that they should avoid filler words like "uh" and "you know" when they give an oral presentation. Keep a tally of the types and number of unnecessary words used in presentations during a one-week period, and discuss the results with the class.

Standardized Test Preparation

For practice in proofreading and editing, see
• *Daily Oral Grammar,* Transparency 18

they were family. For the next few days, we would observe *luto* in our apartment; that is, we would practice restraint and silence—no loud music or laughter. Some of the women of El Building would wear black for weeks.

That night, I lay in my bed trying to feel the right thing for our dead president. But the tears that came up from a deep source inside me were strictly for me. When my mother came to

E

the door, I pretended to be sleeping. Sometime during the night, I saw from my bed the street-light come on. It had a pink halo around it. I went to my window and pressed my face to the cool glass. Looking up at the light, I could see the white snow falling like a lace veil over its face. I did not look down to see it turning gray as it touched the ground below.

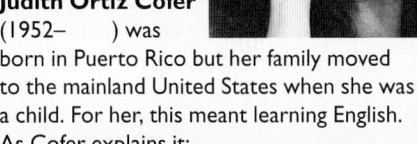
Connections — A POEM

this morning

(For the girls of Eastern High School)

Lucille Clifton F

this morning
this morning
                    i met myself
coming in

5   a bright
       jungle girl
       shining
       quick as a snake
       a tall
10   tree girl a
       me girl
                    i met myself G
       this morning
       coming in

15   and all day
       i have been
       a black bell
       ringing
       i survive
20   survive
       survive

Making the Connections

Connecting to the Theme: "Discoveries"
Ask students to summarize what Elena discovers or learns in the story. [Sample responses: She learns that a person does not always feel what other people are feeling; she learns that prejudice can cause injustice and stand in the way of friendship; she learns that private problems coexist with public problems.]

Cultural Connections
Puerto Rico, an island in the Caribbean Sea, is a self-governing commonwealth in union with the United States. Its people are born citizens of the United States. Since World War II, Puerto Rican immigration has had a significant impact on the economy and culture of the greater New York metropolitan area and other urban areas. In the 1950s and early 1960s, thousands of Puerto Ricans immigrated to the mainland United States in search of economic opportunity.

Connecting Across Texts

Connecting with "American History"
In a word, how does the speaker of the poem "this morning" feel about herself? [Sample responses: self-aware, confident, strong, proud.] If the two girls could meet, what might the speaker tell Elena? [Sample response: The speaker might tell Elena to be proud of who she is and to be strong, to realize that she can survive despite the ignorance and bigotry of other people.]

First Thoughts

1. Sample responses: Elena and Eugene remain friends until they go off to different colleges; Elena and Eugene marry and become teachers; their friendship ends because of Eugene's parents.

Shaping Interpretations

2. Both Elena and Eugene are outsiders who love reading and excel academically.

3. Students may mention the statements by Mr. DePalma or Eugene's mother, or the warning of Elena's mother against going to Eugene's house. Sharing responses to the text helps show that there may be several reasons for a character's words or action.

4. Sample response: President John F. Kennedy was shot on November 22, 1963. In this story, the words "American History" refer to that day's events and its effects on the life of one American. The title also ties in with the subject Elena and Eugene meant to study that day.

5. Eugene's mother does not want him to associate with immigrants. She might also be afraid that if he makes friends in the neighborhood, the family is admitting that their stay might be more than temporary.

6. The statement reveals that Elena does not want to see what is beautiful become unattractive. This ties into a theme of not losing hope over life's disappointments but instead concentrating on positives.

Connecting with the Text

7. Sample responses: I would explain that often people are prejudiced against what they fear or do not understand. I would advise her to continue to be friendly to Eugene at school and to remember that he is not responsible for what his mother says and does.

Extending the Text

8. Experiencing some kind of rejection is a part of most people's lives. Being excluded because of prejudice is a common experience.

9. Possible responses: She may present the same outer facade as always; she may act more withdrawn than usual. The speaker of the poem might tell Elena to

---

First Thoughts

[infer]

1. What do you think happens to Elena and Eugene after the story is over?

Shaping Interpretations

[compare]

2. Eugene, nicknamed "the Hick," and Elena, nicknamed "Skinny Bones," come from very different cultures, yet they have something important in common. What is it?

[respond]

3. Look at the notes you made as you read the story. Which statements in the story seem important or controversial to you? Share the passages and your responses to them in class. Does sharing your reactions to the text change your feelings about it?

[interpret]

4. If someone who hadn't read the story asked you what the **title** means, what would you say?

[infer]

5. Why do you think Elena is turned away from Eugene's house?

[interpret]

6. Look at the last statement in the story. Why do you think Elena doesn't want to see the snow turning gray? Could this statement reveal something important about Elena's character—about how she faces a loss in her life? Think about the whole story and try to state in your own words your interpretation of the story's **theme**.

Connecting with the Text

[connect]

7. What would you say to Elena about her experience with Eugene's mother? What would you advise her to do?

Extending the Text

[extend]

8. Do you think that Elena's rejection is something that others have experienced? Explain.

[infer]

9. Imagine it is the week after Elena's heartbreak and she has to go to school. How do you think she will manage? What does the narrator of Lucille Clifton's poem "this morning" (see *Connections* on page 299) have to say to Elena?

[infer]

10. Eugene disappears from the story after page 297. What do you suppose he thinks that evening, when Elena doesn't show up? Do you think he knows what his mother did?

Reading Check

Imagine that it is fifty years later. Elena now has grandchildren who are studying the 1960s in history class. Their assignment is to interview someone who was alive at that time. Stage the interview with a partner. One of you will play Elena's grandchild and will ask the other (Grandmother Elena) questions about the sixties. Elena will answer by **summing up the main events** that happened on the day Kennedy was killed.

---

acknowledge her own strength and beauty and to remember that she is the same bright, determined girl she was before this incident.

10. Eugene might think that Elena does not come because of the president's assassination, that she has some other reason for not coming, or that her parents would not let her come. He may not know what his mother did, or she may have told him after Elena left.

Reading Check

Elena might first sum up her own experiences on that day: the cold playground, hearing the news from Mr. DePalma, the eerie quiet of the street as she walked home, her determination to study with Eugene, being turned away by Eugene's mother, her inability to mourn the president as adults were doing. She might also add the broader perspective of an adult looking back at the shock that gripped the nation and kept people glued to their television sets.

CHOICES: Building Your Portfolio

Writer's Notebook

1. Collecting Ideas for an Analysis of a Short Story

Focusing on setting. In some stories, time and place are especially important. This is true in "American History"— we know the exact day, month, and year, and we know what buildings the characters live in. Collect notes about the setting of one other story in these collections. Look carefully through the story, and list all the details about setting you can find—the details that help you picture the time and place. How important is setting in that story? Save your notes for the Writer's Workshop on page 332.

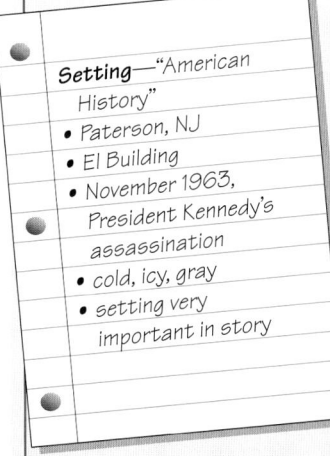

Setting—"American History"
• Paterson, NJ
• El Building
• November 1963, President Kennedy's assassination
• cold, icy, gray
• setting very important in story

Report Writing/Social Studies

2. Oral History: "Where Were You When . . . ?"

At the beginning of the story, the author describes the "profound silence" in El Building the day President Kennedy was shot. Interview at least three people who remember that day. Ask them: "Where were you and what were you doing when you heard the news?" Present your interviews in a question-and-answer format, and include a short introduction to each person you interview. You can add background information about the time period. Use history textbooks, encyclopedias, and the Internet.

Creative Writing

3. Just the One I'm Looking For

Elena is attracted to Eugene for several reasons. Think about the qualities in a person that are attractive to you. Consider appearance, attitudes, values, ways of treating others, interests. (If some of these details are not important, say so.) Then, write a character sketch of your ideal friend—either a boy or a girl.

Drawing/Social Studies

4. La puerta de la esperanza (Door of Hope)

Elena knocks on Eugene's door, which is green, "the color of hope." Draw two green doors that are beginning to open. Under one door, write "Door of Hope for the United States." Under the other door, write "Door of Hope for Me." Fill in the opening with images and words that describe your hopes for this nation and for yourself. You might also draw a third green door, "Door of Hope for the World."

Responding to Art

5. Collages

The collages on pages 292–293, 295, and 297 use images that were drawn from many sources and placed together to make us think about them in a new way. Choose one of the collages, and write a short essay explaining how it relates to "American History." Try to identify all the images represented in the collage. How do they relate to the story? Does the collage help you see issues or events in the story in a new way?

Rubrics for each Choices assignment appear on p. 123 in the *Portfolio Management System.*

CHOICES: Building Your Portfolio

1. **Writer's Notebook** Call students' attention to the details about the setting of "American History."
2. **Report Writing/Social Studies** Tell students that some interviewers provide the person being interviewed with the questions beforehand. This gives the person time to prepare thoughtful responses. If possible, model the interviewing process by inviting a member of the community to answer students' questions about his or her personal experience of the Kennedy assassination. Videotape the interview for use with other classes.
3. **Creative Writing** Students may wish to create a chart with spaces for all of the qualities suggested in the activity or other qualities they think are important. They should next decide the relative importance of each quality. When students write their character sketches, tell them to explain which qualities are most important to them and why.
4. **Drawing/Social Studies** Have a student artist in the class draw a sketch of three doors beginning to open. Make copies of the sketch available for others who wish to use it.
5. **Responding to Art** Give students the information on the art from the notes on pp. T295 and T297. Suggest students also look at pictorial histories of the 1960s. To identify images within each collage, students may find it helpful to use a magnifying glass.

Using Students' Strengths

Auditory Learners
Some students may have difficulty taking notes during the oral interviews for Choice 2. Suggest that they tape the interviews. Students may then use the taped interviews to write their reports.

Verbal/Linguistic Learners
To help students generate images for Choice 4, have them write in a stream-of-consciousness style. They should try not to focus too narrowly, but to let their thoughts and feelings wander as broadly as possible.

Try It Out

Sample Answers

1. *Because* Elena is also a good student, she likes the fact that Eugene reads so much.
2. *Since* Elena is an immigrant and lives in El Building, Eugene's mother will not allow Eugene to study with her.
3. *When* Elena first speaks to Eugene, he blushes.
4. Elena is not invited to Eugene's house *until* the day President Kennedy is shot.

VOCABULARY

Answers

1. *enthralled* (antonyms)
2. *vigilant* (cause and effect)
3. *solace* (synonyms)
4. *infatuated* (antonyms)
5. *literally* (synonyms)

Resources ─────

Language Resource

• *Grammar and Language Links* Worksheet, p. 29

Vocabulary Resource

• *Words to Own,* Worksheet, p. 13

GRAMMAR LINK [MINI-LESSON]

Language Handbook HELP

See Clauses, *page 1009.*

Technology HELP

See Language Workshop CD-ROM. *Key word entry: adverb clauses.*

All for a Good Clause

To avoid writing a series of short, choppy sentences and to show relationships between ideas, writers use adverb clauses.

An adverb clause is a subordinate clause that tells *where, when, how, why, to what extent,* or *under what conditions.* Cofer uses adverb clauses (underlined below) and a variety of subordinating conjunctions (such as *if, because,* and *when*) to make the relationships between her ideas clear. The first sentence in each pair shows how a passage from Cofer's story would look if she did not put one of her ideas in a subordinate clause.

1. I sat on the fire escape. In fact, I was literally suspended above Eugene's back yard.

   Cofer: "In fact, if I sat on the fire escape I was literally suspended above Eugene's back yard."

2. He sat at the kitchen table and read books for hours. I liked him right away.

   Cofer: "I liked him right away because he sat at the kitchen table and read books for hours."

3. I got home. Our apartment was empty.

   Cofer: "Our apartment was empty when I got home."

Try It Out

➤ Jot down four observations about Elena and Eugene's friendship. Then, make those four statements more precise by reshaping them into sentences using any of the subordinating conjunctions from the list below.

• after
• although
• because
• since

• than
• until
• when
• while

➤ When you revise your own writing, experiment with subordinating conjunctions. Find exactly the right conjunction to express your ideas. Notice that in some of the example sentences, other conjunctions could have been used. (Cofer could have written "*When* I sat on the fire escape . . .")

VOCABULARY [HOW TO OWN A WORD]

WORD BANK

literally
infatuated
vigilant
enthralled
solace

Analogies

In an analogy the relationship expressed in the first pair of words is repeated in the second pair. To complete an analogy, look closely at the relationship between the first two words. Is it cause and effect? Are the words synonyms or antonyms? Use a word from the Word Bank to complete each analogy below.

1. *Insult* is to *compliment* as *bored* is to _____.
2. *Mother* is to *loving* as *guard* is to _____.
3. *Ridicule* is to *mockery* as *comfort* is to _____.
4. *Casual* is to *committed* as *indifferent* is to _____.
5. *Ornate* is to *fancy* as *actually* is to _____.

Grammar Link Quick Check

Combine the following sentences by using each of these subordinating conjunctions once: *although, until, after, because.* Sample answers are provided in brackets.

1. Elena is miserable. She has forgotten her gloves. [Elena is miserable *because* she has forgotten her gloves.]
2. School starts. She looks for him in all her classes. [*After* school starts, she looks for him in all her classes.]
3. Elena makes straight A's. She is not allowed to take honors classes. [*Although* Elena makes straight A's, she is not allowed to take honors classes.]
4. Elena has always thought of the future. She meets Eugene. [Elena has always thought of the future *until* she meets Eugene.]

Before You Read

HELEN ON EIGHTY-SIXTH STREET

Make the Connection

Hopes and Dreams

We all have hopes and dreams. Some come true, some don't. What happens when our wishes don't come true, when we have to accept a loss or when we are disappointed in love or friendship?

Quickwrite

Jot down some of your own hopes and dreams. Have any of them come true? What do those hopes and dreams tell you about yourself?

Elements of Literature

Moments of Discovery

Almost every story is about a discovery. Discoveries in fiction usually come at the end of the action. In describing a character's discovery, a writer wants to make us, the readers, discover something too. In fact, at these moments of discovery, we may grasp the **theme**, or the whole meaning, of the story. A discovery happens when a character sees or experiences or does something that brings about a sudden, intense feeling—like a light going on. This discovery usually changes the character in some important way.

> **T**heme in fiction is often revealed by what a character has **discovered** as a result of the action.
>
> *For more on Theme, see pages 264–265 and the Handbook of Literary Terms.*

Reading Skills and Strategies

Monitoring Your Comprehension: Using Resources

When writers use **allusions,** they expect readers to understand their references. Usually allusions refer to features of a culture that people share—literature, for example, and history. This writer presumes that you know something about the Trojan War and Greek mythology. Probably you have already read some mythology; in this book you'll find stories from the great Greek epic the *Odyssey* (page 889).

If some of the story's allusions stop you, you can consult three resources in this text:

1. "The Beautiful Helen," on page 305, which gives a thumbnail sketch of the story behind this story

2. the Meet the Writer on page 311

3. the footnotes

Don't get bogged down in identifying allusions. Sometimes you can just guess what a name or event refers to by looking at the context clues.

go.hrw.com
LEO 9-4

OBJECTIVES

1. Read and interpret the story
2. Interpret theme
3. Monitor comprehension by using resources
4. Express understanding through critical writing or research/ narrative
5. Identify coordinating conjunctions and use them in writing
6. Understand and use new words
7. Recognize word roots and research word etymologies

SKILLS

Literary
- Interpret theme

Reading
- Monitor comprehension by using resources

Writing
- Take notes on a character
- Research a character from mythology and write a first-person narrative from that character's point of view
- Evaluate a character

Grammar
- Identify and use coordinating conjunctions

Vocabulary
- Use new words
- Recognize word roots and research word etymologies

Planning

- **Traditional Schedule**
  Lesson Plans Including Strategies for English-Language Learners

- **One-Stop Planner**
  CD-ROM with Test Generator

Preteaching Vocabulary

Words to Own

After students have studied the meanings of the Words to Own on pp. 304–310, have them match each word with the correct set of the following words. Tell students that some sets offer synonyms for a Word to Own, while others use the same word roots as a Word to Own.

a. embodies
b. enunciate
c. incantation
d. litany
e. odyssey
f. polytheism
g. ramparts
h. scourge
i. stifled
j. supplication

cantor, chant [c]
journey, quest [e]
theology [f]
bodily, bodiless [a]
announce [b]
list, series [d]
suppliant [j]
afflict, chastise [h]
fort, embankment [g]
muffle, suffocate [i]

T303

Summary ∎∎∎

Vita, the first-person narrator, lives in a Manhattan apartment with her mother, a translator of classic literature. Vita misses her father, who left them three years earlier, and writes letters to him every night, although these are never sent. At school her class is mounting a production of the story of Helen of Troy. Vita longs to play Helen, and envies Helen McGuire, who has the role. Helen McGuire, in turn, envies Vita for being cooped inside the Trojan horse with Tommy Aldridge. One day, remembering what her mother told her about the Parthenon where the Greeks offered sacrifices to the goddess Athena, Vita burns three years' worth of letters to her father while chanting Greek words (for food) and asking Athena for three things: the role of Helen of Troy, the return of her father, and the departure of her mother's boyfriend, "Old Farfel." When Helen McGuire comes down with chicken pox, Vita gets the role and believes that her ceremony caused these events. Further, her mother stops seeing Farfel, so Vita fully expects her father to appear the night of the play. But her mother reminds her that people no longer believe in those old gods. By the time Vita delivers her climactic speech as Helen, she is able to insert a quiet, powerful goodbye we know she means for her father. Vita discovers that some losses in life must simply be accepted.

NOTE: You might want to use this story after students have read the *Odyssey* in Collection 14.

Resources ———

Listening
Audio CD Library
A reading of this story is provided in the *Audio CD Library*:
• Disc 11, Track 3

Ⓐ Reading Skills and Strategies
Making Inferences

❓ Who are the Helens in this paragraph on p. 304? What do you know about the speaker? [The first Helen, the one the speaker hates, is her classmate Helen McGuire. The other Helen is the mythical Helen of Troy. We know that the speaker is a sixth grader; she is a girl; she knows mythology; she is jealous.]

Helen on Eighty-sixth Street

I want my father back.

Wendi Kaufman

I hate Helen. That's all I can say. I hate her. Helen McGuire is playing Helen, so Mr. Dodd says, because, out of the entire sixth grade, she most <u>embodies</u> Helen of Troy. Ⓐ Great. Helen McGuire had no idea who Helen of Troy even was! When she found out, well, you should have seen her—flirting with all the boys, really acting the part. And me? Well, I know who Helen was. I am unhappy.

My mother doesn't understand. Not that I expected she would. When I told her the news, all she said was "Ah, the face that launched a Ⓑ thousand ships." She didn't even look up from her book. Later, at dinner, she apologized for quoting Marlowe. Marlowe is our cat.[1]

At bedtime I told my mother, "You should have seen the way Helen acted at school. It was disgusting, flirting with the boys."

Mom tucked the sheets up close around my chin, so that only my head was showing, my body covered mummy style. "Vita," she said, "it sounds like she's perfect for the part."

So, I can't play Helen. But, to make it worse, Mr. Dodd said I have to be in the horse. I can't

---

1. **Marlowe:** The cat is named after Christopher Marlowe, an English dramatist. "The face that launched a thousand ships," referring to Helen of Troy, is from one of Marlowe's plays.

WORDS TO OWN
embodies (em·bäd′ēz) *v*.: conveys the impression of; represents.

304 THE SHORT-STORY COLLECTIONS

 — Ⓞ — *Resources: Print and Media* — 🖳 —

Reading
• *Graphic Organizers for Active Reading*, p. 19
• *Words to Own*, p. 14
• *Audio CD Library*, Disc 11, Track 3

Writing and Language
• *Daily Oral Grammar* Transparency 19

• *Grammar and Language Links* Worksheet, p. 31
• *Language Workshop* CD-ROM

Assessment
• *Formal Assessment*, p. 45
• *Portfolio Management System*, p. 125
• *Standardized Test Preparation*, p. 38
• *Test Generator* (One-Stop Planner CD-ROM)

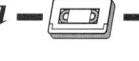

believe it. The horse! I wanted to be one of the Trojan women—Andromache, Cassandra, or even Hecuba. I know all their names. I told Mr. Dodd this, and then I showed him I could act. I got really sad and cried out about the thought of the body of my husband, Hector, being dragged around the walls of my city. I wailed and beat my fist against my chest. "A regular Sarah Heartburn"[2] was all he said.

"Well, at least you get to be on the winning team," my mother said when I told her about the horse. This didn't make me feel any better. "It's better than being Helen. It's better than being blamed for the war," she told me.

Mom was helping me make a shield for my costume. She said every soldier had a shield that was big enough to carry his body off the field. I told her I wasn't going to be a body on the field, that I was going to survive, return home.

"Bring the shield, just in case," she said. "It never hurts to have a little help."

Mom and I live on West Eighty-sixth Street. We have lived in the same building, in the same apartment, my entire life. My father has been gone for almost three years. The truth is that he got struck with the wanderlust—emphasis on "lust," my mother says—and we haven't heard from him since.

"Your father's on his own odyssey," my mother said. And now it's just me and Mom and Marlowe and the Keatses, John and John,[3] our parakeets, or "pair of Keats," as Mom says. When I was younger, when Dad first left and I still believed he was coming back, it made me happy that we still lived in the same building. I was happy because he would always know where to find us. Now that I am older, I know the city is not that big. It is easy to be found and easy to stay lost.

And I also know not to ask about him. Sometimes Mom hears things through old friends—that he has traveled across the ocean, that he is living on an island in a commune with

2. **Sarah Heartburn:** humorous reference to Sarah Bernhardt, a French actress known for her emotional style.
3. **Keatses, John and John:** The parakeets are named after the English Romantic poet John Keats.

LITERATURE AND MYTHOLOGY

The Beautiful Helen

Long ago the god Zeus fell in love with Leda, a mortal woman, and visited her in the form of a swan. Their daughter Helen grew up to be the most beautiful woman on earth. Helen married Menelaus, king of Sparta, but Paris, a handsome young prince, fell in love with her and ran away with her to Troy, his kingdom in Asia Minor. Helen's husband, Menelaus, gathered together other Greek kings and warriors, including his brother, Agamemnon, and they sailed to Troy in a thousand ships to fetch Helen home.

For ten long years the Greeks camped outside the walls of Troy, but they were unable to break down the thick walls of the city. Finally the Greeks tricked the Trojans. They built a huge wooden horse with a hollow belly and hid some soldiers in it. They left the horse on the beach at Troy and pretended to sail away. The Trojans thought that the Greeks had at last retreated and had left the horse as a gift. They wheeled the huge horse into their city. That night the Greeks crept out of the horse, opened the city gate to their comrades, and slaughtered the Trojans. The old king, Priam, was killed. The Trojan women, including Queen Hecuba and her daughter Cassandra, were murdered or dragged into slavery. The queen of Troy had already seen her beloved son Hector killed by Achilles, his bleeding body dragged three times in the dust around the walls of the city.

In the story you are reading, a class reenacts the tale of the beautiful Helen of Troy.

WORDS TO OWN

odyssey (äd′i·sē) *n.:* extended journey marked by wandering, adventure, and changes of fortune.

HELEN ON EIGHTY-SIXTH STREET 305

B **Reading Skills and Strategies**
Monitoring Your Comprehension: Using Resources

? How would you find out what the quotation on p. 304 means and who Marlowe is? [The information is in footnote 1.]

C **Reading Skills and Strategies**
Monitoring Your Comprehension: Using Resources

? How does reading the Literature and Mythology feature and footnote 2 on this page help you understand the content of this paragraph? [The resources explain what the speaker means by being "in the horse," help sort out the Trojan characters she mentions, and explain the pun on the name of a famous actress.]

D **Elements of Literature**
Plot
The narrator changes direction at this point to provide some basic exposition. Have students summarize Vita's home situation. [Vita lives with her mother and their pets in New York City on West 86th Street. Her father left them three years earlier and hasn't been heard from since then.]

E **Reading Skills and Strategies**
Making Inferences
? How can you tell that the narrator's mother is well acquainted with literature? [Earlier, "Helen of Troy" triggered a literary allusion, and their cat is named for the English playwright who wrote the line. The *Odyssey* is a Greek epic. Also, the parakeets are named for a famous poet.]

Reaching All Students

Struggling Readers
Monitoring Comprehension was introduced on p. 303. The many literary and historical allusions in this story might intimidate struggling readers. Reassure them that it is not necessary to understand each allusion fully. They can simply recognize that an allusion has been made, move on, and return to it later.

English Language Learners
Help students who come from non-Western cultures understand the story's many allusions to Greek mythology and English literature. Have them make 3″ x 5″ reference cards or a one-page chart that summarizes each allusion. For additional strategies for engaging English language learners, see
• *Lesson Plans Including Strategies for English-Language Learners*

Advanced Learners
Challenge advanced learners to work as a team to develop their own brief play about Helen of Troy. They will need to research the story, determine the roles needed, decide on the number and content of scenes, and work out basic designs for sets and costumes. If possible, have students actually videotape their play or present it live, perhaps involving additional students as actors and stage hands.

A ⬤ Reading Skills and Strategies

Monitoring Your Comprehension: Using Resources

❓ Where can you get help in understanding details in these paragraphs? [See footnotes 4 and 5.]

B ⬤ Reading Skills and Strategies

Making Inferences

❓ Why does Helen McGuire say, "Lucky you"? [Helen is attracted to Tommy Aldridge.] From the fact that Vita doesn't understand, what can you infer about her? [Possible response: She is not yet romantically attracted to boys; she is young and naive.]

C ⬤ Literary Connections

Shakespearean Allusions

Farfel combines two Shakespearean allusions: "The play's the thing" is from *Hamlet* (Act II, Scene 2) and "Life's but a walking shadow, a poor player / That struts and frets his hour upon the stage" is from *Macbeth* (Act V, Scene 5).

D ⬤ Struggling Readers

Breaking Down Difficult Text

Help students work through this passage until they understand what Vita means by "spinning Argus": her mother is twirling a vase that contains the ashes of the family dog.

E ⬤ Reading Skills and Strategies

Summarizing

Even Vita can have trouble interpreting her mother's comments. Ask students to reread these paragraphs, Literature and Mythology on p. 305, and footnote 8 and then to write a sentence or two summarizing Vita's mother's advice to her daughter. [Sample responses: It's better to follow your head than your heart; truth or knowledge is more important than surface beauty.] Be sure students note that Helen's father was the god Zeus, who took the form of a swan.

---

some people she called "the lotus eaters,"[4] that he misses us.

(A) Once I heard Mr. Farfel, the man who's hanging around Mom now, ask why she stayed in this apartment after my father left. "The rent's stabilized,"[5] she told him, "even if the relationship wasn't."

At school, Helen McGuire was acting weird because I'm going to be in the horse with Tommy Aldridge. She wanted to know what it's like: "Is it really cramped in there? Do you have to sit real close together?"

I told her it's dark, and we must hold each other around the waist and walk to make the horse move forward. Her eyes grew wide at this description. "Lucky you," she said.

(B) Lucky me? She gets to stand in the center of the stage alone, her white sheet barely reaching the middle of her thighs, and say lines like "This destruction is all my fault" and "Paris, I do love you." She gets to cry. Why would she think I'm lucky? The other day at rehearsal, she was standing onstage waiting for her cue, and I heard Mrs. Reardon, the stage manager, whisper, "That Helen is as beautiful as a statue."

At home Old Farfel is visiting again. He has a chair in Mom's department.[6] The way she describes it, a chair is a very good thing. Mom translates old books written in Greek and Latin. She is working on the longest graduate degree in the history of Columbia University. "I'll be dead before I finish," she always says.

Old Farfel has been coming around a lot lately, taking Mom and me to dinner at Italian places downtown. I don't like to be around when he's over.

"I'm going to Agamemnon's apartment to rehearse," I told Mom.

---

4. **lotus eaters:** in the *Odyssey*, people who eat the fruit of the lotus tree, a sort of drug, which causes them to forget forever their homes and families. The Greek soldier Odysseus enters the Land of the Lotus Eaters on his journey home from the Trojan War. (See page 898.)
5. **rent's stabilized:** In New York City, rent stabilization is a form of government-controlled rent regulation. Rent-stabilized apartments are cheap and so are much sought after.
6. **chair in Mom's department:** A "chair" is an important teaching position at a university.

306 THE SHORT-STORY COLLECTIONS

Old Farfel made a small laugh, one that gets caught in the back of the throat and never really makes it out whole. I want to tell him to relax, to let it out. He smells like those dark cough drops, the kind that make your eyes tear and your head feel like it's expanding. I don't know how she can stand him.

(C) "Well, the play's the *thing*," Old Farfel said. "We're all just players strutting and fretting our hour on the stage." Mom smiled at this, and it made me wish Old Farfel would strut his hours at his apartment and not at our place. I hate the way he's beginning to come around all the time.

When I get back from rehearsal, Mom is spinning Argus.[7] It's what she does when she gets into one of her moods. Argus, our dog, died last summer when I was away at camp. My mother can't stand to part with anything, so she keeps Argus, at least his ashes, in a blue-and-white vase that sits on our mantel.

(D) Once I looked into the vase. I'd expected to see gray stuff, like the ash at the end of a cigarette. Instead, there was black sand and big chunks of pink like shells, just like at the beach.

My mother had the vase down from the mantel and was twirling it in her hands. I watched the white figures on it turn, following each other, running in a race that never ends.

"Life is a cycle," my mother said. The spinning made me dizzy. I didn't want to talk about life. I wanted to talk about Helen.

"Helen, again with Helen. Always Helen," my mother said. "You want to know about Helen?"

I nod my head.

(E) "Well, her father was a swan and her mother was too young to have children. You don't want to be Helen. Be lucky you're a warrior. You're too smart to be ruled by your heart."

"And what about beauty? Wasn't she the most beautiful woman in the world?" I asked.

Mom looked at the Greek vase. "Beauty is truth, truth beauty—that is all ye need to know."[8]

---

7. **Argus:** Odysseus' old dog. When Odysseus returns home after twenty years, Argus is the only one who recognizes him. (See page 932.)
8. **Beauty is truth . . . know:** The last two lines of Keats's "Ode on a Grecian Urn" are " 'Beauty is truth, truth beauty,' that is all / Ye know on earth, and all ye need to know."

Getting Students Involved

Cooperative Learning

Reciprocal Teaching. To help the class understand and enjoy this wryly humorous, richly allusive story, divide them into groups of four or five students for reciprocal teaching. One student reads aloud until any group member poses a comment or asks a question. The group stops to respond to the comment or answer the question. The next student in the group then reads aloud until another comment is offered or question is raised, and so on.

Before assigning the entire class to reciprocal teaching groups, it's a good idea to model the technique with a selected group of students. Use the activity with the first three pages of the story, or until readers become accustomed to the writer's style and to checking footnotes to resolve some questions.

T306

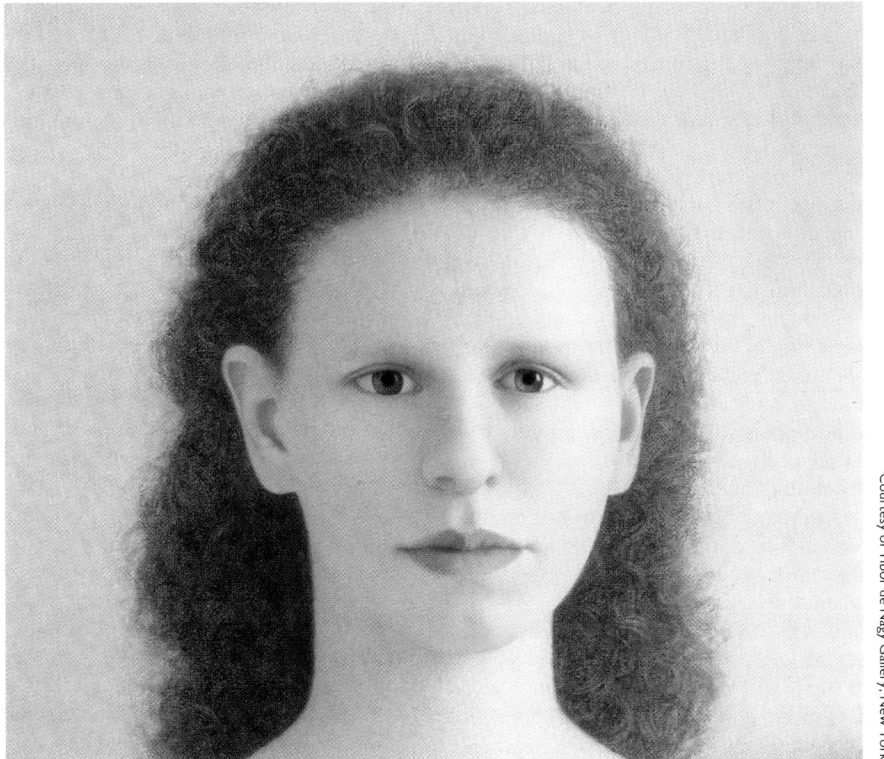

Couch (detail) (1990–1994) by Brett Bigbee. Oil on canvas (72¼" × 51¾").

RESPONDING TO THE ART

Brett Bigbee is a contemporary artist. This painting is called *Couch* because in the full piece of art (this is a detail), the young girl is sitting on a couch.

Activity. It is important for students to learn to evaluate artistic interpretations of characters in literature. Books often have illustrations on their covers, and readers sometimes feel that the depictions of characters are not at all what they had imagined. Ask students to evaluate this image. Is this how they visualize Vita? Why or why not? How do they feel about stories that are illustrated with pictures that are supposed to represent the characters?

She is not always helpful.

"Manhattan is a rocky island," Mom said at dinner. "There is no proper beach, no shore." My mother grew up in the South, near the ocean, and there are times when she still misses the beach. Jones, Brighton, or even Coney Island beaches don't come close for her. I know when she starts talking about the water that she's getting restless. I hope this means that Old Farfel won't be hanging around too long.

Every night I write a letter to my father. I don't send them—I don't know where to send them—but, still, I write them. I keep the letters at the back of my closet in old shoe boxes. I am on my third box. It's getting so full that I have to keep the lid tied down with rubber bands.

I want to write "Mom is talking about the water again. I think this means she is thinking of you. We are both thinking of you, though we don't mention your name. Are you thinking of us? Do you ever sit on the shore at night and wonder what we're doing, what we're thinking? Do you miss us as much as we miss you?"

But instead I write, "I am in a play about the Trojan War. I get to wear a short white tunic, and I ambush people from inside a big fake horse. Even though we win the war, it will be many, many years before I return home. Until I see my family again. In this way, we are the same. I will have many adventures. I will meet giants and witches and see strange lands. Is that what you are doing? I wish you could come to the play."

Old Farfel is going to a convention in Atlanta. He wants Mom to go with him. From my bed, I can hear them talking about it in the living room. It would be good for her, he says. I know

HELEN ON EIGHTY-SIXTH STREET 307

F Background

Jones Beach, Brighton Beach, and Coney Island are beaches in the New York City area.

G Reading Skills and Strategies
Comparing and Contrasting Texts

❓ Compare and contrast the kind of letter Vita *wants* to write to her father with the one she actually *does* write. How are they different? [The first focuses on feelings; the second lists what's happening at school.] **How are the letters similar?** [In both, Vita tries to connect with her father by asking him questions that relate his experiences to hers and her mother's. In both she expresses her wish to see her father.] Note that in the first letter Vita wonders if her father is sitting by the sea thinking of them, just as Odysseus sat by the sea on Calypso's island, weeping for his home. (See p. 892.)

Skill Link

Using Coordinating Conjunctions

Coordinating conjunctions are discussed in the Grammar Link on p. 313. Coordinating conjunctions join words, phrases, or clauses of equal value. Words that function as coordinating conjunctions are: *and, but, for, nor, or, so, yet.* The conjunction *or* joins words of equal value in this sentence from the story: "Jones, Brighton, or even Coney Island beaches don't come close for her" (p. 307). The conjunction *and* joins two parallel phrases in this sentence: "It is easy to be found and easy to stay lost" (p. 305). The conjunction *for* joins clauses in this sentence: "The gods must have envied me my beauty, for now my name is a curse" (p. 309).

Activity

Have students identify the coordinating conjunction in each of the following passages, and state whether it joins words, phrases, or clauses:

1. "I didn't really understand, but it was one of the few times I saw her upset" (p. 308). [*but*; clauses]
2. "Helen nods and looks at him blankly" (p. 308). [*and*; words]
3. "... when Achilles threw up the Tater Tots or when Priam's beard got caught in Athena's hair ..." (p. 309). [*or*; clauses]
4. "... like a big pit, dark and endless" (p. 310). [*and*; words]

A Elements of Literature
Character

❓ What does this passage add to what you already know about Vita's mother? [Her name is Victoria; she doesn't like to travel; she worries about the apartment when she isn't there.]

B Elements of Literature
Metaphor

❓ How does Vita's mother, Victoria, convert the concept of traveling into a metaphor? [She speaks of traveling as a mental activity and uses it as a metaphor for the direction one takes in life.] When Victoria says that sometimes it's easier to look outside than in, what could she mean? [Possible response: She means that sometimes it is easier to look outside for solutions to your problems, rather than to examine yourself to see if you are responsible for your own troubles. In other words, sometimes it is easier to run away from a problem than to look inward and try to solve it.]

C Reading Skills and Strategies
Monitoring Your Comprehension: Using Resources

❓ What does the swan refer to? What resource would help you find out? [The swan refers to the father of Helen of Troy, the god Zeus, who visited Helen's mother, Leda, in the form of a great swan. The feature Literature and Mythology on p. 305 explains this.] Vita refers to the swan often in the story—the swan stands for her own father, whom she so desperately wants to see again.

D Reading Skills and Strategies
Summarizing

Be sure students understand what is happening here. Vita is eating a take-out dinner from a coffee shop. Her mother and Old Farfel have gone out to dinner. Vita looks at the paper cup holding her soup and remembers that she saw a cup like it in a coffee shop one day, and her mother explained that the design on the paper cup showed the Parthenon in Greece where people once made burnt sacrifices to the goddess Athena. (Many coffee shops in New York City do in fact use such cups. At one time many coffee shops in the city were owned by people of Greek ancestry.) Vita gets an idea from the cup; she cuts out the little temple and glues it in her notebook. Be sure students read footnote 9, which explains what the Parthenon is.

---

that Mom doesn't like to travel. She can't even go to school and back without worrying about the apartment—if she turned the gas off, if she fed the cat, if she left me enough money. She tells him that she'll think about it.

"You have to move on, Victoria," he tells her. "Let yourself go to new places."

"I'm still exploring the old places," she says.

He lets the conversation drop.

Mom said once that she traveled inside herself when Dad left. I didn't really understand, but it was one of the few times I saw her upset. She was sitting in her chair, at her desk, looking tired. "Mom, are you in there?" I waved my hand by her face.

"I'm not," she said. "I'm on new ground. It's a very different place."

"Are you thinking about Dad?"

"I was thinking how we all travel differently, Vita. Some of us don't even have to leave the house."

"Dad left the house."

"Sometimes it's easier to look outside than in," she said.

That night I dreamed about a swan. A swan that flies in circles over the ocean. This is not the dark water that snakes along the West Side Highway and slaps against the banks of New Jersey but the real ocean. Open water. Salty, like tears.

At play practice, I watch the other girls dress up as goddesses and Trojan women. They wear gold scarves wound tight around their necks and foreheads. They all wear flowers in their hair and flat pink ballet slippers. I wear a white sheet taken from my bed. It is tied around the middle with plain white rope. I also wear white sneakers. I don't get to wear a gold scarf or flowers. Mr. Dodd wrote this play himself and is very picky about details. Tommy Aldridge, my partner in the horse, was sent home because his sheet had Ninja Turtles on it. "They did not have Ninja Turtles in ancient Greece," Mr. Dodd said.

Mr. Dodd helps Helen McGuire with her role. "You must understand," he tells her, "Helen is the star of the show. Men have traveled great distances just to fight for her. At the end, when

you come onstage and look at all the damage you've caused, we must believe you're really upset by the thought that this is all your fault."

Helen nods and looks at him blankly.

"Well, at least try to think of something really sad."

Old Farfel is taking Mom out to dinner again. It's the third time this week. Mom says it is a very important dinner, and I am not invited. Not that I would want to go, but I wasn't even asked. Mom brought in takeout, some soup and a cheese sandwich, from the coffee shop on the corner.

I eat my soup, alone in the kitchen, from a blue-and-white paper cup. I remember once at a coffee shop Mom held the same type of cup out in front of me.

"See this building, Vita?" she said. She pointed to some columns that were drawn on the front of her cup. It wasn't really a building—more like a cartoon drawing. "It's the Parthenon,"[9] she said. "It's where the Greeks made sacrifices to Athena."

"How did they make sacrifices?" I asked.

"They burned offerings on an altar. They believed this would bring them what they wanted. Good things. Luck."

I finish my soup and look at the tiny building on the cup. In between the columns are the words "Our Pleasure to Serve You." I run my fingers across the flat lines of the Parthenon and trace the roof. I can almost imagine a tiny altar and the ceremonies that were performed there.

It is then that I get an idea. I find a pair of scissors on Mom's desk and cut through the thick white lip of the cup toward the lines of the little temple. I cut around the words "Our Pleasure to Serve You." Then I take the temple and the words and glue them to the back of my notebook. The blue-and-white lines show clearly against the cardboard backing. I get Argus's big metal water bowl from the kitchen and find some matches from a restaurant Old Farfel took us to for dinner.

9. **Parthenon:** temple of Athena, the Greek goddess of wisdom and warfare. She took the Greeks' side during the war. The Parthenon was built in the fifth century B.C.

Using Students' Strengths

Visual/Spatial Learners

Have students make cluster diagrams or character webs to organize what they have learned about Vita, Helen McGuire, Victoria (Vita's mother), Mr. Farfel, or all four. Students should place the character's name in the central circle. Radiating out from the name, they should enter what they know about the appearance, personality, character, abilities, and desires or needs.

Visual Learners

Vita describes in great detail the costumes worn in the play (p. 308) and the items she sets up for her ritual (pp. 308–309). Using these passages, have students create illustrations of the school play or of the scene of Vita's ritual. They should begin by rereading the selected passage closely and listing every item it mentions.

In my room I put on my white sheet costume and get all my letters to Dad out from the back of the closet. I know that I must say something, to make this more like a ceremony. I think of any Greek words I know: *spanakopita, moussaka, gyro.* They're only food words, but it doesn't matter. I decide to say them anyway. I say them over and over out loud until they blur into a litany, my own incantation: *"Spanakopitamoussakaandgyro, Spanakopitamoussakaandgyro, Spanakopitamoussakaandgyro."*

As I say this, I burn handfuls of letters in the bowl. I think about what I want: to be Helen, to have my father come back. Everything I have ever heard says that wishes are granted in threes, so I throw in the hope of Old Farfel's leaving.

I watch as the words burn. Three years of letters go up in smoke and flame. I see blue-lined paper turn to black ashes; I see pages and pages, months and years, burn, crumble, and then disappear. The front of my white sheet has turned black from soot, and my eyes water and burn.

When I am done, I take the full bowl of ashes and hide it in the vase on the mantel, joining it with Argus. My black hands smudge the white figures on the vase until their tunics become as sooty as my own. I change my clothes and open all the windows, but still Mom asks, when she comes home, about the burning smell. I told her I was cooking.

She looked surprised. Neither of us cooks much. "No more burnt offerings when I'm not home," she said. She looked upset and distracted, and Old Farfel didn't give that stifled laugh of his.

It's all my fault. Helen McGuire got chicken pox. Bad. She has been out of school for almost two weeks. I know my burning ceremony did this. "The show must go on," Mr. Dodd said when Achilles threw up the Tater Tots or when Priam's beard got caught in Athena's hair, but this is different. This is Helen. And it's my fault.

I know all her lines. Know them backward and forward. I have stood in our living room,

towel tied around my body, and acted out the entire play, saying every line for my mother. When Mr. Dodd made the announcement about Helen at dress rehearsal, I stood up, white bedsheet slipping from my shoulders, and said in a loud, clear voice, "The gods must have envied me my beauty, for now my name is a curse. I have become hated Helen, the scourge of Troy."

Mr. Dodd shook his head and looked very sad. "We'll see, Vita. She might still get better," he said.

Helen McGuire recovered, but she didn't want to do the part because of all the pockmarks that were left. Besides, she wanted to be inside the horse with Tommy Aldridge. Mr. Dodd insisted that she still be Helen until her parents wrote that they didn't want her to be pressured, they didn't want to *do any further damage,* whatever that means. After that, the part was mine.

Tonight is the opening, and I am so excited. Mom is coming without Old Farfel. "He wasn't what I wanted," she said. "I don't think she'll be seeing him anymore.

"What is beautiful?" I ask Mom before the play begins.

"Why are you so worried all the time about beauty? Don't you know how beautiful you are to me?"

"Would Daddy think I was beautiful?"

"Oh, Vita, he *always* thought you were beautiful."

"Would he think I was like Helen?"

She looked me up and down, from the gold lanyard[10] snaked through my thick hair to my too tight pink ballet slippers.

10. **lanyard** (lan'yərd): here, a decorative cord.

WORDS TO OWN

litany (lit''n·ē) *n.*: repetitive prayer or recitation.
incantation (in'kan·tā'shən) *n.*: chant of words or phrases that is meant to produce a magical result.
stifled (stī'fəld) *v.*: used as *adj.*: smothered.
scourge (skurj) *n.*: cause of serious trouble or great suffering.

E Cultural Connections

Spanakopita is a traditional Greek pie made from thin sheets of dough, spinach, and feta cheese. *Moussaka* (the word comes to us through Greek from Turkish) is a Greek dish of ground meat and sliced eggplant. A *gyro* is a Greek sandwich: lamb or beef, tomato, and onion stuffed in pita bread.

F Reading Skills and Strategies
Summarizing

❓ This is a key moment in the story. What three wishes does Vita make as she burns her letters? [Vita wishes that she will get the part of Helen, that her father will return, and that Old Farfel will leave.]

G Elements of Literature
Irony

❓ In ancient times, "burnt offerings" were meats and grains that were burnt and offered as a gift to the gods. Victoria uses the phrase humorously to refer to Vita's alleged cooking. What is ironically appropriate about her word choice? [She accidentally hits upon exactly what Vita was doing.]

H Critical Thinking
Speculating

❓ Earlier we were told that the dinner between Vita's mother and Farfel was "very important"; now her mother seems upset and Farfel is not his usual self. What do you think happened? [Sample responses: They quarreled; Farfel asked Vita's mother to do something she didn't want to do, like marry him.]

Crossing the Curriculum

Geography

At the beginning of the story, Vita told us that she lives on West Eighty-sixth Street (p. 305); on pp. 307–308, she mentions several locations in the greater New York City metropolitan area. Have students list all of the place references in the story and locate a city map that shows these locations and also tourist attractions, such as the Statue of Liberty. Have them draw and illustrate a simplified map to be posted in the classroom as a "tour guide" to the story.

Social Studies

Some students may wish to research ancient Greek religious rituals. Have them answer these questions: What were the names and attributes of the deities worshiped? What did the worshippers ask for or expect? What kinds of offerings were considered appropriate? Where was the ritual held—in the fields, in homes, or in temples? Who conducted the ceremony? What objects added solemnity to the ritual? Was music an important part of the ritual?

T309

❓ Reread the exchange between Vita and her mother carefully. What discovery is Vita making here? [Vita has pretended that the old gods still exist and that they can help her get her three wishes. Here, with her mother's reminder, Vita is forced to realize that the gods can't help her, though she persists in hoping that Athena will come through. Vita also hopes that since her first two wishes have come true, her third wish—for her father's return—will also come true.]

Ⓑ Critical Thinking
Interpreting

❓ What does Vita's mother mean by her ironic remark? [That some things are finished, and the outcome cannot be changed.]

Ⓒ English Language Learners
Idioms

"Break a leg" is a traditional good-luck wish exchanged by actors. They consider it dangerous to tempt fate by wishing for a hit production, so they make the opposite wish.

Ⓓ Appreciating Language

Note the comic juxtaposition of Mr. Dodd's remarks: "Break a leg" followed by " try not to trip."

Ⓔ Reading Skills and Strategies
Making Inferences

❓ What is the hole, the empty pocket, the absence? [Vita's father is not there.]

Ⓕ Elements of Literature
Theme: Moments of Discovery

❓ What double audience is Vita addressing with these words? [the people attending the play and her absent father] What has she discovered? [Sample responses: She has discovered that she must say goodbye to her expectation that her father will return.]

Resources ━━━━

Selection Assessment
Formal Assessment
- Selection Test, p. 45
Test Generator (One-Stop Planner)
- CD-ROM

T310

"He would think you're more beautiful than Helen. I'm almost sorry he won't be here to see it."

"*Almost* sorry?"

"Almost. At moments like this—you look so good those ancient gods are going to come alive again with envy."

"What do you mean, come alive again? What are you saying about the gods?"

"Vita, Greek polytheism is an extinct belief," she said, and laughed. And then she stopped and looked at me strangely. "When people stopped believing in the gods, they no longer had power. They don't exist anymore. You must have known that."

Ⓐ Didn't I get the part of Helen? Didn't Old Farfel leave? I made all these things happen with my offering. I know I did. I don't believe these gods disappeared. At least not Athena.

"I don't believe you."

She looked at me, confused.

"You can't know for sure about the gods. And who knows? Maybe Daddy will even be here to see it."

Ⓑ "Sure," she said. "And maybe this time the Trojans will win the war."

I stand offstage with Mr. Dodd and wait for my final cue. The dry-ice machine has been turned on full blast and an incredible amount of fake smoke is making its way toward the painted backdrop of Troy. Hector's papier-mâché head has accidentally slipped from Achilles' hand and is now making a hollow sound as it rolls across the stage.

I peek around the thick red curtain, trying to see into the audience. The auditorium is packed, filled with parents and camcorders. I spot my mom sitting in the front row, alone. I try to scan the back wall, looking for a sign of him, a familiar shadow. Nothing.

Soon I will walk out on the ramparts, put my hand to my forehead, and give my last speech. "Are you sure you're ready?" Mr. Dodd asks. I think he's more nervous than I am. "Remember," he tells me, "this is Helen's big moment. Think loss." I nod, thinking nothing.

Ⓒ "Break a leg," he says, giving me a little push

310 THE SHORT-STORY COLLECTIONS

Ⓓ toward the stage. "And try not to trip over the head."

The lights are much brighter than I had expected, making me squint. I walk through the smoky fog toward center stage.

"It is I, the hated Helen, scourge of Troy."

With the light on me, the audience is in shadow, like a big pit, dark and endless. I bow before the altar, feeling my tunic rise. "Hear my supplication," I say, pulling down a bit on the back of my tunic.

"Do not envy me such beauty—it has wrought only pain and despair."

I can hear Mr. Dodd, offstage, loudly whispering each line along with me.

"For this destruction, I know I will be blamed."

I begin to recite Helen's wrongs—beauty, pride, the abdication of Sparta—careful to enunciate clearly. "Troy, I have come to ask you to forgive me."

I'm supposed to hit my fist against my chest, draw a hand across my forehead, and cry loudly. Mr. Dodd has shown me this gesture, practiced it with me in rehearsal a dozen times—the last line, my big finish. The audience is very quiet.

Ⓔ In the stillness there is a hole, an empty pocket, an absence. Instead of kneeling, I stand up, straighten my tunic, look toward the audience,
Ⓕ and speak the line softly: "And to say goodbye."

There is a prickly feeling up the back of my neck. And then applause. The noise surrounds me, filling me. I look into the darkened house and, for a second, I can hear the beating of a swan's wings, and, then, nothing at all.

WORDS TO OWN

polytheism (päl′i·thē·iz′əm): belief in more than one god.

ramparts (ram′pärts′) *n.*: broad embankments surrounding a castle, fort, or city for defense against attack.

supplication (sup′lə·kā′shən) *n.*: humble plea or request.

enunciate (ē·nun′sē·āt′) *v.*: pronounce; articulate.

Assessing Learning

Check Test: Sentence Completion

1. Vita lives with her [mother] in Manhattan.
2. She wants to play the role of [Helen of Troy] in a class production, but is instead assigned to be a warrior inside the [Trojan horse].
3. Every night she writes letters she cannot send to [her father].
4. She sacrifices the letters to [Athena] in an attempt to make her wishes come true.
5. The wish that does not come true is [the return of her father].

Standardized Test Preparation

For practice with standardized test format specific to this selection, see
- *Standardized Test Preparation*, p. 38

For practice in proofreading and editing, see
- *Daily Oral Grammar*, Transparency 19

MEET THE WRITER

"Is Vita Based on Me?"

Wendi Kaufman (1964–) lives in Virginia, but her written "voice" was shaped by her childhood experiences—growing up in a small town in upstate New York. Kaufman is a graduate of George Mason University's MFA program. She currently works for *The Sound of Writing: National Public Radio's Literary Journal of the Airwaves*. Here is what she says about "Helen on Eighty-sixth Street":

66 I was reading the *Odyssey* and thought the stage production of a mythic tale would make a good backdrop for a short story. The *Odyssey* was originally an oral tale, an epic poem recited for hundreds of years before it was finally written down. I wanted to somehow incorporate that incantatory tone, to have my story sound like it was being spoken out loud—that's where the voice of Vita, the narrator, comes from.

Vita is twelve years old. I remember that as a hard age, a time on the cusp, when you're stuck in that middle ground between child and teen and it's difficult to know where you belong, to find your own place. Vita wants to be Helen of Troy because she wants everything that Helen represents: beauty, popularity, adoration. I think these are things that many of us have desired at one time or another. The truth about Vita is that she *is* beautiful. She is warm, funny, knows her own mind, and is capable of great love—what could be more beautiful than that? She just doesn't know it yet.

I grew up in a sleepy town in the Hudson River valley, about an hour from New York City, the kind of place Washington Irving wrote about. I always felt it was a boring town, a place where nothing ever happened. What I didn't realize was that the most important things were happening around me every day, the drama of daily life. As an adult, I have lived all over the country and have had many different experiences, but it is those childhood years, those early memories and discoveries, that I return to and write about most often.

Is Vita based on me? Not really. But as a young girl, I did love reading mythology. Myths are great stories for young writers. The plot twists, the drama—it's all there. Myths run the gamut of human emotion and experience. Love, loss, deceit, regret, betrayal, there's something in there for everybody. I would recommend them to any young writer—and to a few old ones.

For me, writing is an experience of the imagination, that chance to take a kernel of an idea or experience and explore it by becoming anyone or saying anything. That's what I love about writing. As for advice for young writers? Simple: Read, read, read. And, of course, keep writing. There are things that come out on the page, when pen hits paper, that you weren't expecting, that you didn't plan for. Those are the moments we all strive for.

Writing is about possibilities, about the freedom of the blank page. I can remember reading *Little Women* in the fourth grade and crying my eyes out. That was the first time I realized the power of literature. Never underestimate that power. 99

Making the Connections

Connecting to the Theme: "Discoveries"

Vita experiences at least two moments of discovery in the story: when her mother says that the old gods don't exist, and when she is finally able to say goodbye to her father. What does she discover in each of these moments? [She discovers wishes do not necessarily come true; she discovers that some wishes never come true, and reality must simply be accepted.]

Connecting Across Texts

Connecting with "Helen on Eighty-sixth Street"

Have students read and discuss what Wendi Kaufman says in her reflection about writing "Helen on Eighty-sixth Street." What parallels do they find between the life of the author and that of her character, Vita? [Both found twelve a difficult age; both love to read mythology.]

First Thoughts

1. Vita might be thinking that some things cannot be changed, that she is saying goodbye to her beloved father and to her wish for his return.

Shaping Interpretations

2. Sample response: She triumphs in her studies and in the role of Helen, but loses her belief in the old myths and stops believing in the return of her father. The triumphs make her feel good, but it is the losses that help her to change and grow.

3. Possible theme: Vita's experience shows that one must accept some sadness in life and let go of trying to change things.

4. Lists should include but not be limited to: Helen of Troy, Marlowe (p. 304); Trojan horse, Trojan women, Sarah Bernhardt, John Keats (p. 305); lotus eaters, Paris, Agamemnon, "the play's the thing," Argus, the quote from Keats (p. 306); Manhattan, New York beaches (p. 307); West Side Highway, Ninja Turtles, Parthenon, Athena (p. 308). Most students will say that the Literature and Mythology feature on p. 305 and the text footnotes were helpful resources. (The swan wings at the end might be her father's presence. They might also be the mysterious presence of the old myths, still powerful in human life.)

Connecting with the Text

5. Students may feel that there are times when it is more important to follow one's heart than one's head. Encourage them to offer examples.

Grading Timesaver

Rubrics for each Choices assignment appear on p. 125 in the *Portfolio Management System.*

T312

First Thoughts

[respond]

1. What do you think is going through Vita's mind as she stands on the stage reciting Helen's last speech?

Reading Check

What are Vita's three wishes? How does each wish turn out?

Shaping Interpretations

[identify]

2. Describe Vita's triumphs and losses. Which do you think are more important to her—the triumphs or her losses? Explain why.

[interpret]

3. Think of Vita at the story's end and what she has learned. How would you state the **theme** of this story—what truth does Vita's experience reveal to you?

[analyze]

4. Make a list of all the story's **allusions**—to Greek mythology, to literature, even to New York City. In a group, discuss how you figured out the meaning of each one. What resources in the text helped you? Are any of these allusions still puzzling you? (For example, what are those swan wings at the story's end?)

Connecting with the Text

[connect]

5. Vita's mother tells her, "You don't want to be Helen. Be lucky you're a warrior. You're too smart to be ruled by your heart." What do you think of this advice?

CHOICES: Building Your Portfolio

Writer's Notebook

1. Collecting Ideas for an Analysis of a Short Story

Focus on character. What can you say about Vita? What are her most noticeable traits? How does she feel about herself? What does she want? What has she discovered? Use a graphic to gather details about Vita or a character from another story in these collections. Save your notes for the Writer's Workshop on page 332.

Research/Narrative

2. "I Am Helen of Troy…"

Use **resources** (encyclopedias, dictionaries, collections of myths, and on-line sources) to find out more about a character from Greek mythology. You might research one of the characters in the story. What was the judgment of Paris, for instance, and why is Achilles' heel famous? Present your findings in a **first-person report,** speaking as if you *are* the figure you've researched. Tell *who* you are, *why* you're remembered, and *what* you accomplished.

Evaluating a Character

3. Is Vita Real?

Vita is one of many interesting characters you have met in this collection. Did she come alive for you, or did she remain a fictional character? Write a paragraph evaluating Vita's character. Does she seem realistic, like a person you might know? Can you identify with her and her problems? Would you like her? Think about all the things Vita wants. Are her dreams and worries like those of other kids her age? Be sure to check your Quickwrite notes.

Reading Check

Vita wishes for the role of Helen, the departure of Old Farfel from her mother's life, and the return of her father. She gets the role when Helen McGuire comes down with chicken pox; her mother tires of Farfel, and he stops hanging around; but her father does not return.

CHOICES: Building Your Portfolio

1. **Writer's Notebook** Help students create charts, cluster diagrams, or character webs to organize their notes.

2. **Research/Narrative** Suggest Zeus, Hera, Apollo, Aphrodite, Hades, Poseidon, Athena, or Hermes.

3. **Evaluating a Character** Suggest students organize their notes in a chart using the questions posed in Choice 3 as heads.

GRAMMAR LINK   MINI-LESSON

Language Handbook HELP

See Sentence Combining, page 1015.

Technology HELP

See Language Workshop CD-ROM. *Key word entry:* coordinating conjunctions.

Coordinating Conjunctions—Getting It Together

Coordinating conjunctions join words, phrases, or clauses of equal importance. Suppose the following are Kaufman's notes, and she wants to include all of these details in a sentence:

> Told Helen McGuire it's dark. Hold each other around waist. Walk to make horse move forward.

Here is how she puts these notes together in a sentence using coordinating conjunctions to join a series of verbs:

> "I told her it's dark, <u>and</u> we must hold each other around the waist <u>and</u> walk to make the horse move forward."

Here are two other sentences from the story that use coordinating conjunctions to join words, phrases, and clauses of equal importance. Break these sentences into shorter ones to see how many details the writer combined.

1. "I will meet giants <u>and</u> witches <u>and</u> see strange lands."

2. "I change my clothes <u>and</u> open all the windows, <u>but</u> still Mom asks, when she gets home, about the burning smell."

Try It Out

Using each of the coordinating conjunctions listed below, summarize the main events in "Helen on Eighty-sixth Street." Be sure to compare your summaries.

- and
- but
- for
- nor
- or
- so
- yet

VOCABULARY   HOW TO OWN A WORD

WORD BANK

embodies
odyssey
litany
incantation
stifled
scourge
polytheism
ramparts
supplication
enunciate

Word Roots: Core Meanings

A **word root** is the part of a word that carries its core meaning. Word roots are different from prefixes or suffixes because they're not add-ons. Vita's name is an example of a word root; it is the Latin word for "life." The same root is found in *vital, vitality,* and *vitamin.*

Use a good dictionary to research the **etymologies** (word histories) of each word in the Word Bank, and put your information in a graphic like the one below for *polytheism.* (Be sure you check the meanings of the abbreviations that refer to the language the root comes from. For examples, *Gr* usually stands for "Greek" and *L* for "Latin.")

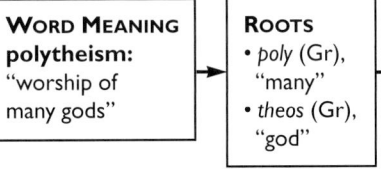

WORD MEANING	ROOTS	RELATED WORDS
polytheism: "worship of many gods"	• *poly* (Gr), "many" • *theos* (Gr), "god"	• polygon • polyp • theology • atheist

HELEN ON EIGHTY-SIXTH STREET   313

GRAMMAR LINK

Try It Out
Answers will vary. Check for correct use of all seven conjunctions.
Sample Answer
Vita wants to play the role of Helen of Troy, *but* Helen McGuire gets the part. Helen McGuire envies Vita, *for* Vita gets to be a warrior. Vita does not know Greek ritual, *nor* does she know the Greek language, *yet* she still manages to create a ceremony. Her wishes for the role of Helen *and* for the departure of "Old Farfel" come true, *so* she believes her third wish will also be granted. She learns that there are some things you cannot change *or* cause to happen.

VOCABULARY
Possible Answers
embodies: "represents"; *em-* (Gr), "within" + *bodig* (Old English), "body"; embodiment, bodily
odyssey: "adventurous journey"; *Odyssey* (Gr), title of epic by Homer; Odysseus
litany: "repetitive prayer"; *litanos* (Gr), "suppliant"; no related words
incantation: "chant meant to produce magical results"; *incantare* (L), "to enchant"; cantor, enchant
stifled: "smothered"; *stuflen* (Middle English), "stifle"; stifling
scourge: "cause of grave suffering"; *corrigia* (L), "whip"; scourger, scourging
polytheism: "belief in more than one god"; *poly* (Greek), "many" + *theos* (Greek), "god"; monotheism, polytechnic
ramparts: "embankments surrounding a fort"; *ante-* (L), "before" + *parare* (L), "to prepare"; prepare
supplication: "humble plea or request"; *supplex* (L), "suppliant"; supplicate, supplicant
enunciate: "pronounce, articulate"; *e-* (Gr), "out, away, forth" + *nuntiare* (L), "to report"; announce, enunciation

Resources

Grammar Resource
- *Grammar and Language Links* Worksheet, p. 31

Vocabulary Resource
- *Words to Own,* Worksheet, p. 14

Grammar Link Quick Check

Combine the following sentences by using an appropriate coordinating conjunction from the following list: *and, but, for, or, so, yet.* Sample responses are provided in brackets.

1. Vita is miserable. Vita is lonely. [Vita is miserable and lonely.]
2. Vita wants the role. Helen McGuire gets it. [Vita wants the role, but Helen McGuire gets it.]
3. Vita writes to her father. Vita loves him. [Vita writes to her father, for she loves him.]
4. Vita's father deserted her. Vita still loves him. [Vita's father deserted her, yet Vita still loves him.]
5. Helen McGuire gets sick. Vita gets the role. [Helen McGuire gets sick, so Vita gets the role.]
6. Vita's mother says the old gods do not exist. The old gods do not answer prayers. [Vita's mother says the old gods do not exist or answer prayers.]

Before You Read

THE SCARLET IBIS

Make the Connection

Southern Exposure

Some people say "The Scarlet Ibis" is a story they will never forget. The story is set in the American South. Its climax takes place in 1918, the year World War I ended in Europe. You'll find references in the story to battles being fought in parts of the world far from this peaceful Southern setting, but the story is not about the wider war. It is about a small but still tragic struggle that takes place between two young brothers.

Reading Skills and Strategies

Dialogue with the Text

Read to the end of the paragraph that starts "It was bad enough" (page 317). Then stop and write down at least three questions that the story-teller has made you wonder about. When you finish the story, see if your questions have been answered.

Elements of Literature

Symbols

We communicate by means of symbols. We use groups of sounds or letters to stand for things in the outer physical world and for ideas in our own inner worlds. The sounds or letters themselves are not the things or ideas; they only symbolize, or stand for, these things or ideas.

In literature a symbol is somewhat different. It's a specific object, person, or event that stands for something more than itself. In the story "Marigolds" (page 279), those sturdy, pungent flowers could stand for hope and endurance. But, as is the way with all symbols, you might have other ideas about what the marigolds stand for. In fact, symbols in literature may have different shades of meaning for each of us.

 go.hrw.com
LE0 9-4

> **A** symbol is an object, a person, or an event that functions as itself but also stands for something more than itself.
>
> *For more on Symbol, see the Handbook of Literary Terms.*

314 THE SHORT-STORY COLLECTIONS

Preteaching Vocabulary

THE Scarlet Ibis

James Hurst

Doodle was just about the craziest brother a boy ever had.

It was in the clove of seasons, summer was dead but autumn had not yet been born, that the ibis lit in the bleeding tree. The flower garden was stained with rotting brown magnolia petals, and ironweeds grew rank[1] amid the purple phlox. The five o'clocks by the chimney still marked time, but the oriole nest in the elm was untenanted and rocked back and forth like an empty cradle. The last graveyard flowers were blooming, and their smell drifted across the cotton field and through every room of our house, speaking softly the names of our dead.

---

1. **rank:** thick and wild. *Rank* also means "smelly" or "overripe."

THE SCARLET IBIS **315**

Summary ■■■

This story's first-person narrator is a boy whose little brother, Doodle, is born physically disabled. Doodle is expected to die, yet lives. The narrator must care for his brother, taking him everywhere in a go-cart. He is often frustrated, but after much effort, succeeds in teaching Doodle to walk. Proud of this success, the narrator works to teach him to run, swim, climb trees, and fight. In a symbolic episode that foreshadows the story's tragic resolution, Doodle buries a fallen bird—the brilliant "scarlet ibis" of the title. Shortly afterwards, the strain of trying to learn physical skills leaves Doodle gravely weakened. In the climactic final scene, Doodle collapses and dies while running to catch up with his brother, who has abandoned him. The conflict between the brothers is unhappily resolved. The narrator feels guilt for his brother's death, and he discovers too late the depth of his feelings.

Resources

Listening
Audio CD Library
A reading of this story is provided in the *Audio CD Library:*
- Disc 12, Track 2

Ⓐ Reading Skills and Strategies
Paraphrasing
Point out that *clove* can also mean a cleft, gap, or ravine. It is also the past tense of *cleave*, which means "split." Also, point out that *bleeding* suggests a vivid red. Ask students to paraphrase the sentence. [Sample response: The ibis settled in the red tree just between summer and fall.]

Ⓑ Appreciating Language
Sensory Detail
❓ What words directly appeal to the senses? [Possible responses: smell—"rotting," "rank"; sight—"brown," "rank"; touch, "rocked"; hearing—"softly."]

Resources: Print and Media

Reading
- *Reading Skills and Strategies*
    MiniRead Skill Lesson, p. 12
    Selection Skill Lesson, p. 19
- *Graphic Organizers for Active Reading,* p. 20
- *Words to Own,* p. 15
- *Audio CD Library,*
    Disc 12, Track 2

Writing and Language
- *Daily Oral Grammar*
    Transparency 20

- *Grammar and Language Links,*
    Worksheet p. 33
- *Language Workshop CD-ROM*

Assessment
- *Formal Assessment,* p. 47
- *Portfolio Management System,* p. 126
- *Standardized Test Preparation,* pp. 40, 42
- *Test Generator (One-Stop Planner CD-ROM)*

Internet
- go.hrw.com (keyword: LE0 9-4)

T315

RESPONDING TO THE ART

Lulu Saxon painted in the late nineteenth century. This painting is 7½ feet tall, making viewers of the original feel as if they can walk right into her *Uptown Street*.

Activity. Ask students to use their imaginations. If they could walk into the picture, what would they see, hear, taste, touch, and smell? What size of town is it? What time of year? What time of day? Are they alone or with someone? Are they in a rush or taking a stroll? How do their surroundings make them feel?

(A) Elements of Literature

Symbols

❓ The adult narrator repeats the word *bleeding* to mean "red." (He first used this word in the opening paragraph of the story.) What associations are triggered by "red"? Think of red objects, expressions like "seeing red," titles of books or movies. [Sample responses: stop sign, valentine, exit sign, matador's cape, red-letter day, red light, *The Red Badge of Courage*, *The Hunt for Red October*, *The Scarlet Letter*.] What qualities does "red" seem to symbolize? [Sample responses: Danger, love, courage, death.] Watch to see what meaning "red" takes on in this story.

(B) Elements of Literature

Style and Tone

❓ Notice the shift in style and tone from that of an adult looking back in time to that of the child who was actually there in that long-ago summer. What differences do you notice between this paragraph and the first two paragraphs of the story? [The sentences become shorter, the vocabulary easier, and the language more conversational.]

Uptown Street (1890) by Lulu Saxon. Oil on canvas (90″ x 68″).

It's strange that all this is still so clear to me, now that that summer has long since fled and time has had its way. A grindstone stands where the bleeding tree stood, just outside the kitchen door, and now if an oriole sings in the elm, its song seems to die up in the leaves, a silvery dust. The flower garden is prim, the house a gleaming white, and the pale fence across the yard stands straight and spruce. But sometimes (like right now), as I sit in the cool, green-draped parlor, the grindstone begins to turn, and time with all its changes is ground away—and I remember Doodle.

Doodle was just about the craziest brother a boy ever had. Of course, he wasn't a crazy crazy like old Miss Leedie, who was in love with President Wilson and wrote him a letter every day, but was a nice crazy, like someone you meet in your dreams. He was born when I was six and was, from the outset, a disappointment. He seemed all head, with a tiny body which was red and shriveled like an old man's. Everybody thought he was going to die—everybody except Aunt Nicey, who had delivered him. She said he would live because he was born in a caul[2] and cauls were made from Jesus' nightgown. Daddy had Mr. Heath, the carpenter, build a little mahogany coffin for him. But he didn't die, and when he was three months old, Mama and Daddy decided they might as well name him. They named him William Armstrong, which was like tying a big tail on a small kite. Such a name sounds good only on a tombstone.

I thought myself pretty smart at many things, like holding my breath, running, jumping, or climbing the vines in Old Woman Swamp, and I wanted more than anything else someone to

2. **caul:** membrane (thin, skinlike material) that sometimes covers a baby's head at birth.

The Ogden Museum of Southern Art, University of New Orleans, Louisiana.

Reaching All Students

Struggling Readers

Dialogue with the Text was introduced on page 314. For a lesson directly tied to this story that teaches students to question as they read by using a strategy called Say Something, see the *Reading Skills and Strategies* binder:
• MiniRead Skill Lesson, p. 12
• Selection Skill Lesson, p. 19

English Language Learners

These students will need prereading help with vocabulary and figurative language. Familiarize them with the definitions of the Words to Own, and point out some of the plant and flower names mentioned in the opening paragraph. Review, also, the techniques of simile and metaphor. For additional strategies for engaging English language learners, see
• *Lesson Plans Including Strategies for English-Language Learners*

Advanced Learners

These students may appreciate the story best through silent reading. Read the first three paragraphs aloud, however, to alert them to the author's metaphorical style and to be sure they absorb the point of view and time frame.

race to Horsehead Landing, someone to box with, and someone to perch with in the top fork of the great pine behind the barn, where across the fields and swamps you could see the sea. I wanted a brother. But Mama, crying, told me that even if William Armstrong lived, he would never do these things with me. He might not, she sobbed, even be "all there." He might, as long as he lived, lie on the rubber sheet in the center of the bed in the front bedroom where the white marquisette³ curtains billowed out in the afternoon sea breeze, rustling like palmetto fronds.⁴

It was bad enough having an invalid brother, but having one who possibly was not all there was unbearable, so I began to make plans to kill him by smothering him with a pillow. However, one afternoon as I watched him, my head poked between the iron posts of the foot of the bed, he looked straight at me and grinned. I skipped through the rooms, down the echoing halls, shouting, "Mama, he smiled. He's all there! He's all there!" and he was.

When he was two, if you laid him on his stomach, he began to try to move himself, straining terribly. The doctor said that with his weak heart this strain would probably kill him, but it didn't. Trembling, he'd push himself up, turning first red, then a soft purple, and finally collapse back onto the bed like an old worn-out doll. I can still see Mama watching him, her hand pressed tight across her mouth, her eyes wide and unblinking. But he learned to crawl (it was his third winter), and we brought him out of the front bedroom, putting him on the rug before the fireplace. For the first time he became one of us.

As long as he lay all the time in bed, we called him William Armstrong, even though it was formal and sounded as if we were referring to one of our ancestors, but with his creeping around on the deerskin rug and beginning to talk, something had to be done about his name. It was I who renamed him.

---

3. **marquisette** (mär´ki·zet´): thin, netlike fabric.
4. **palmetto fronds:** fanlike leaves of a palm tree.

When he crawled, he crawled backward, as if he were in reverse and couldn't change gears. If you called him, he'd turn around as if he were going in the other direction, then he'd back right up to you to be picked up. Crawling backward made him look like a doodlebug⁵ so I began to call him Doodle, and in time even Mama and Daddy thought it was a better name than William Armstrong. Only Aunt Nicey disagreed. She said caul babies should be treated with special respect since they might turn out to be saints. Renaming my brother was perhaps the kindest thing I ever did for him, because nobody expects much from someone called Doodle.

Although Doodle learned to crawl, he showed no signs of walking, but he wasn't idle. He talked so much that we all quit listening to what he said. It was about this time that Daddy built him a go-cart, and I had to pull him around. At first I just paraded him up and down the piazza,⁶ but then he started crying to be taken out into the yard and it ended up by my having to lug him wherever I went. If I so much as picked up my cap, he'd start crying to go with me, and Mama would call from wherever she was, "Take Doodle with you."

He was a burden in many ways. The doctor had said that he mustn't get too excited, too hot, too cold, or too tired and that he must always be treated gently. A long list of don'ts went with him, all of which I ignored once we got out of the house. To discourage his coming with me, I'd run with him across the ends of the cotton rows and careen him around corners on two wheels. Sometimes I accidentally turned him over, but he never told Mama. His skin was very sensitive, and he had to wear a big straw hat whenever he went out. When the going got rough and he had to cling to the sides of the go-cart, the hat slipped all the way down over his ears. He was a sight. Finally, I could see I was licked. Doodle was my brother, and he was going to cling to me forever, no matter what I

---

5. **doodlebug:** larva of a type of insect; also, a shuttle train that goes back and forth between stations.
6. **piazza:** large covered porch.

C English Language Learners
Idioms

Explain that to be "all there" is a colloquial expression that means to be sane, or mentally healthy. Mama is afraid the baby may be impaired mentally as well as physically.

D Reading Skills and Strategies
Making Inferences

? At the age of two, what character traits does the baby begin to show? [Possible responses: determination, perseverance.] Do you think he is "all there"? [Most students will think the baby is fine, mentally, if he works so hard despite his physical limitations.]

E Critical Thinking
Evaluating an Opinion

? What do you think about the narrator's opinion that naming his little brother "Doodle" was a kind act? [Sample responses: The nickname is silly and degrading—I wouldn't want to be called "Doodle"; he may feel that giving Doodle the nickname made him feel more like other people.]

F Reading Skills and Strategies

Dialogue with the Text

Ask students to write in their journals or notebooks about any personal connections they can make with the narrator's feelings about Doodle and with the way the narrator treated him. Many students will have had to take care of younger siblings, and eliciting their feelings will bring them more in touch with the theme of the story.

Getting Students Involved

Cooperative Learning
Hot Seat. After students have read the story, divide the class into small groups. Have each group discuss and answer the following question: Why do you think the narrator begins to run when he hears his brother call out not to leave him? Answering this question gives students an understanding of the motivations and feelings of the story's narrator. Have group members take turns being the adult narrator and responding as that character to questions posed by other group members about events in the story.

A Elements of Literature
Character

❓ What does his reaction to the swamp tell you about Doodle? [Sample response: He is bright, emotional, and sensitive to beauty.]

B Reading Skills and Strategies
Dialogue with the Text

❓ What do you think of the way the narrator treats Doodle? [Sample response: He was cruel, but teasing is a normal part of what happens between brothers.] Do you have any questions about the story at this point? If so, write them down. As you read the story, see if your questions are answered.

C Critical Thinking
Interpreting

❓ What do you think the narrator means by this statement? [Possible responses: Pride can be healthy, because it leads you to accomplish things, but it can also turn into something negative; since he mentions "life and death," perhaps something terrible is going to happen to Doodle.]

---

did, so I dragged him across the burning cotton field to share with him the only beauty I knew, Old Woman Swamp. I pulled the go-cart through the sawtooth fern, down into the green dimness where the palmetto fronds whispered by the stream. I lifted him out and set him down in the soft rubber grass beside a tall pine. His eyes were round with wonder as he gazed about him, and his little hands began to stroke the rubber grass. Then he began to cry.

"For heaven's sake, what's the matter?" I asked, annoyed.

"It's so pretty," he said. "So pretty, pretty, pretty."

After that day Doodle and I often went down into Old Woman Swamp. I would gather wildflowers, wild violets, honeysuckle, yellow jasmine, snakeflowers, and waterlilies, and with wire grass we'd weave them into necklaces and crowns. We'd bedeck ourselves with our handiwork and loll about thus beautified, beyond the touch of the everyday world. Then when the slanted rays of the sun burned orange in the tops of the pines, we'd drop our jewels into the stream and watch them float away toward the sea.

There is within me (and with sadness I have watched it in others) a knot of cruelty borne by the stream of love, much as our blood sometimes bears the seed of our destruction, and at times I was mean to Doodle. One day I took him up to the barn loft and showed him his casket, telling him how we all had believed he would die. It was covered with a film of Paris green[7] sprinkled to kill the rats, and screech owls had built a nest inside it.

Doodle studied the mahogany box for a long time, then said, "It's not mine."

"It is," I said. "And before I'll help you down from the loft, you're going to have to touch it."

"I won't touch it," he said sullenly.

"Then I'll leave you here by yourself," I threatened, and made as if I were going down.

Doodle was frightened of being left. "Don't go leave me, Brother," he cried, and he leaned toward the coffin. His hand, trembling, reached

---

7. **Paris green:** poisonous green powder used to kill insects.

---

out, and when he touched the casket, he screamed. A screech owl flapped out of the box into our faces, scaring us and covering us with Paris green. Doodle was paralyzed, so I put him on my shoulder and carried him down the ladder, and even when we were outside in the bright sunshine, he clung to me, crying, "Don't leave me. Don't leave me."

When Doodle was five years old, I was embarrassed at having a brother of that age who couldn't walk, so I set out to teach him. We were down in Old Woman Swamp and it was spring and the sick-sweet smell of bay flowers hung everywhere like a mournful song. "I'm going to teach you to walk, Doodle," I said.

He was sitting comfortably on the soft grass, leaning back against the pine. "Why?" he asked.

I hadn't expected such an answer. "So I won't have to haul you around all the time."

"I can't walk, Brother," he said.

"Who says so?" I demanded.

"Mama, the doctor—everybody."

"Oh, you can walk," I said, and I took him by the arms and stood him up. He collapsed onto the grass like a half-empty flour sack. It was as if he had no bones in his little legs.

"Don't hurt me, Brother," he warned.

"Shut up. I'm not going to hurt you. I'm going to teach you to walk." I heaved him up again, and again he collapsed.

This time he did not lift his face up out of the rubber grass. "I just can't do it. Let's make honeysuckle wreaths."

"Oh yes you can, Doodle," I said. "All you got to do is try. Now come on," and I hauled him up once more.

It seemed so hopeless from the beginning that it's a miracle I didn't give up. But all of us must have something or someone to be proud of, and Doodle had become mine. I did not know then that pride is a wonderful, terrible thing, a seed that bears two vines, life and death. Every day that summer we went to the pine beside the stream of Old Woman Swamp, and I put him on his feet at least a hundred times each afternoon. Occasionally I too became discouraged because it didn't seem as if

---

Skill Link

Using Figurative Language

Figurative language, specifically the simile, is discussed in the Language Link on p. 327. A simile uses words such as *like*, *resemble*, and *as* to compare two things that are unlike in most ways, yet similar in one startling way. For example, "That child has as many toys as a flower has bees." But if a simile is used too often, it loses its sparkle. For example, most people are tired of hearing, "I'll stick to you like glue." Watch for fresh, creative similes as you continue to read the story.

Activity

Complete the following similes with a word or phrase that creates a fresh, interesting comparison. Sample responses are provided in brackets.

1. Mona is always as fresh as _____. [new bread]
2. Jake is as thin as _____. [a Q-tip]
3. The buckles on his jacket clattered like _____. [lobsters' claws]
4. He walks like _____. [a sick caterpillar]
5. Pete's as tall as _____. [the Statue of Liberty]

he was trying, and I would say, "Doodle, don't you *want* to learn to walk?"

He'd nod his head, and I'd say, "Well, if you don't keep trying, you'll never learn." Then I'd paint for him a picture of us as old men, white-haired, him with a long white beard and me still pulling him around in the go-cart. This never failed to make him try again.

Finally, one day, after many weeks of practicing, he stood alone for a few seconds. When he fell, I grabbed him in my arms and hugged him, our laughter pealing through the swamp like a ringing bell. Now we knew it could be done. Hope no longer hid in the dark palmetto thicket but perched like a cardinal in the lacy tooth-brush tree, brilliantly visible. "Yes, yes," I cried, and he cried it too, and the grass beneath us was soft and the smell of the swamp was sweet.

With success so imminent, we decided not to tell anyone until he could actually walk. Each day, barring rain, we sneaked into Old Woman Swamp, and by cotton-picking time Doodle was ready to show what he could do. He still wasn't able to walk far, but we could wait no longer. Keeping a nice secret is very hard to do, like holding your breath. We chose to reveal all on October eighth, Doodle's sixth birthday, and for weeks ahead we mooned around the house, promising everybody a most spectacular surprise. Aunt Nicey said that, after so much talk, if we produced anything less tremendous than the Resurrection, she was going to be disappointed.

At breakfast on our chosen day, when Mama, Daddy, and Aunt Nicey were in the dining room, I brought Doodle to the door in the go-cart just as usual and had them turn their backs, making them cross their hearts and hope to die if they peeked. I helped Doodle up, and when he was standing alone I let them look. There wasn't a sound as Doodle walked slowly across the room and sat down at his place at the table. Then Mama began to cry and ran over to him, hugging him and kissing him. Daddy hugged him too, so I went to Aunt Nicey, who was thanks-praying in the doorway, and began to waltz her around. We danced together quite well until she came down on my big toe with

her brogans,[8] hurting me so badly I thought I was crippled for life.

Doodle told them it was I who had taught him to walk, so everyone wanted to hug me, and I began to cry.

"What are you crying for?" asked Daddy, but I couldn't answer. They did not know that I did it for myself; that pride, whose slave I was, spoke to me louder than all their voices; and that Doodle walked only because I was ashamed of having a crippled brother.

Within a few months Doodle had learned to walk well and his go-cart was put up in the barn loft (it's still there) beside his little mahogany coffin. Now, when we roamed off together, resting often, we never turned back until our destination had been reached, and to help pass the time, we took up lying. From the beginning Doodle was a terrible liar, and he got me in the habit. Had anyone stopped to listen to us, we would have been sent off to Dix Hill.

My lies were scary, involved, and usually pointless, but Doodle's were twice as crazy. People in his stories all had wings and flew wherever they wanted to go. His favorite lie was about a boy named Peter who had a pet peacock with a ten-foot tail. Peter wore a golden robe that glittered so brightly that when he walked through the sunflowers they turned away from the sun to face him. When Peter was ready to go to sleep, the peacock spread his magnificent tail, enfolding the boy gently like a closing go-to-sleep flower, burying him in the gloriously iridescent,[9] rustling vortex.[10] Yes, I must admit it. Doodle could beat me lying.

Doodle and I spent lots of time thinking about our future. We decided that when we were grown, we'd live in Old Woman Swamp and pick dog's-tongue[11] for a living. Beside the

---

8. **brogans** (brō′gənz): heavy ankle-high shoes.
9. **iridescent** (ir′i·des′ənt): rainbowlike; displaying a shifting range of colors.
10. **vortex:** something resembling a whirlpool.
11. **dog's-tongue:** wild vanilla.

WORDS TO OWN
imminent (im′ə·nənt) *adj.*: near; about to happen.

D Elements of Literature

Symbols

❓ Ask students to identify and explain the symbol for hope. How do the brothers now feel about Doodle's chances of learning to walk? [Hope is symbolized by the cardinal, a bird whose brilliant red plumage suggests a vibrant life force. The brothers now truly believe Doodle will walk.]

E Reading Skills and Strategies

Dialogue with the Text

Ask students to write in their notebooks or journals about a time they had trouble keeping a secret. Remind them to choose a situation they would not mind sharing with others.

F English Language Learners

Cultural Connections

Explain that children make a cross-shaped gesture and say the words "Cross my heart and hope to die" when they want to seal a promise.

G Critical Thinking

Evaluating a Judgment

❓ Do you think the narrator judges himself too harshly? [Sample response: Yes, his motives are not entirely selfish. The scenes he describes show that he truly likes being with Doodle, and that he is willing to work hard at helping Doodle accomplish things.]

H Elements of Literature

Character

❓ Why do you think a boy like Doodle would tell stories ("lies") of this particular type? [Sample response: Since he is physically limited, it is natural that he would tell stories about people who can fly everywhere and who look so magnificent that even sunflowers turn their heads away from the sun to look at them.]

Using Students' Strengths

Intrapersonal Learners
To help introspective students better understand characterization, have them write a letter from Doodle to his brother. This letter should mention Doodle's feelings toward his brother, his feelings about his own successes and failures, and his hopes for the future.

Visual/Spatial Learners
Have students work in groups of three or four to create a collage depicting the swamp as Doodle might see it. Each group should select one student to oversee design and layout, but all students should contribute their ideas. Each student should also contribute at least four objects to the collage—things that are representative of the color, texture, or life forms of the swamp.

Verbal/Linguistic Learners
Ask these students to create a Word Wall for the classroom. They should include the Words to Own from the story and other words that give them (or other students) trouble, such as *ibis*. Have the students add to the wall as the story is read. They can also include pictures to illustrate the words. Discuss the meaning of each new word as it is added to the wall.

A Reading Skills and Strategies

Making Predictions

❓ Do you think that the narrator's goals for Doodle will be realized? Why or why not? [Possible responses: Given enough time, maybe Doodle could learn all of these things, but not in "less than a year"; his colds suggest that he is weaker than the narrator realizes.]

B Elements of Literature

Symbols

❓ If the summer is taken as an omen, or symbol, of what is to come, what do you think may lie in Doodle's future? [If the weather is symbolic, then Doodle is in for a very bad time, and may even die.]

C Cultural Connections

At the time events in this story take place, most Southern farmers were Democrats, and the Republicans were the party of Lincoln and the North— the people at whose hands they had suffered defeat during the Civil War. For the rest of the nineteenth century and into the twentieth, the United States was politically divided along regional lines. The North voted primarily Republican, while the South was solidly Democratic. In the late decades of the twentieth century, political lines shifted, and the Democratic party made significant inroads in the North, and the Republican in the South.

D Appreciating Language

Repetition

❓ In the opening paragraph of the story, the narrator referred to "the clove of seasons." Why does the author repeat his metaphor here? [He is reminding the reader of the time frame he established in the first sentence of the story.]

---

stream, he planned, we'd build us a house of whispering leaves and the swamp birds would be our chickens. All day long (when we weren't gathering dog's-tongue) we'd swing through the cypresses on the rope vines, and if it rained we'd huddle beneath an umbrella tree and play stickfrog. Mama and Daddy could come and live with us if they wanted to. He even came up with the idea that he could marry Mama and I could marry Daddy. Of course, I was old enough to know this wouldn't work out, but the picture he painted was so beautiful and serene that all I could do was whisper yes, yes.

A Once I had succeeded in teaching Doodle to walk, I began to believe in my own infallibility and I prepared a terrific development program for him, unknown to Mama and Daddy, of course. I would teach him to run, to swim, to climb trees, and to fight. He, too, now believed in my infallibility, so we set the deadline for these accomplishments less than a year away, when, it had been decided, Doodle could start to school.

That winter we didn't make much progress, for I was in school and Doodle suffered from one bad cold after another. But when spring came, rich and warm, we raised our sights again. Success lay at the end of summer like a pot of gold, and our campaign got off to a good start. On hot days, Doodle and I went down to Horsehead Landing, and I gave him swimming lessons or showed him how to row a boat. Sometimes we descended into the cool greenness of Old Woman Swamp and climbed the rope vines or boxed scientifically beneath the pine where he had learned to walk. Promise hung about us like leaves, and wherever we looked, ferns unfurled and birds broke into song.

B That summer, the summer of 1918, was blighted.[12] In May and June there was no rain and the crops withered, curled up, then died under the thirsty sun. One morning in July a hurricane came out of the east, tipping over the

12. **blighted** (blīt′id): suffering from conditions that destroy or prevent growth.

---

oaks in the yard and splitting the limbs of the elm trees. That afternoon it roared back out of the west, blew the fallen oaks around, snapping their roots and tearing them out of the earth like a hawk at the entrails[13] of a chicken. Cotton bolls were wrenched from the stalks and lay like green walnuts in the valleys between the rows, while the cornfield leaned over uniformly so that the tassels touched the ground. Doodle and I followed Daddy out into the cotton field, where he stood, shoulders sagging, surveying the ruin. When his chin sank down onto his chest, we were frightened, and Doodle slipped his hand into mine. Suddenly Daddy straightened his shoulders, raised a giant knuckly fist, and with a voice that seemed to rumble out of the earth itself began cursing heaven, hell, **C** weather, and the Republican party.[14] Doodle and I, prodding each other and giggling, went back to the house, knowing that everything would be all right.

And during that summer, strange names were heard through the house: Château-Thierry, Amiens, Soissons, and in her blessing at the supper table, Mama once said, "And bless the Pearsons, whose boy Joe was lost in Belleau Wood."[15]

D So we came to that clove of seasons. School was only a few weeks away, and Doodle was far behind schedule. He could barely clear the ground when climbing up the rope vines, and his swimming was certainly not passable. We decided to double our efforts, to make that last drive and reach our pot of gold. I made him swim until he turned blue and row until he couldn't lift an oar. Wherever we went, I purposely walked fast, and although he kept up, his face turned red and his eyes became glazed.

13. **entrails** (en′trālz): inner organs; guts.
14. **Republican party:** At this time most Southern farmers were loyal Democrats.
15. **Château-Thierry** (sha′tō tē·er′ē), **Amiens** (ä·myan′), **Soissons** (swä·sôn′), **Belleau** (be·lô′) **Wood:** World War I battle sites in France.

WORDS TO OWN

infallibility (in·fal′ə·bil′ə·tē) n.: inability to make a mistake.

Crossing the Curriculum

Art

Have students choose one character, theme, or scene from the story, and create an artwork based on it. Possible art forms include a drawing, a painting, a diorama, a sculpture, or a mobile. Students may work individually or in groups. Have them use lines from the story as captions. Display their works to the class.

Psychology

The narrator in this story resolves his feelings of guilt over the death of his brother by trying to understand the pride, cruelty, and insensitivity that drove him to hurt Doodle. Have students think of effective ways to deal with inner conflicts. They might suggest, for example, that one way to cope with a guilty conscience is to discuss the situation with a friend.

Geography

To enhance students' sense of the time period of the selection, give them a map of Europe, and have them locate the Rhine River and the battle sites the story mentions on p. 320—Château-Thierry, Amiens, Belleau Wood, and Soissons. You might also have them locate the sites of other famous World War I battles such as Verdun and the Somme.

Once, he could go no further, so he collapsed on the ground and began to cry.

"Aw, come on, Doodle," I urged. "You can do it. Do you want to be different from everybody else when you start school?"

"Does it make any difference?"

"It certainly does," I said. "Now, come on," and I helped him up.

As we slipped through the dog days, Doodle began to look feverish, and Mama felt his forehead, asking him if he felt ill. At night he didn't sleep well, and sometimes he had nightmares, crying out until I touched him and said, "Wake up, Doodle. Wake up."

It was Saturday noon, just a few days before school was to start. I should have already admitted defeat, but my pride wouldn't let me. The excitement of our program had now been gone for weeks, but still we kept on with a tired doggedness. It was too late to turn back, for we had both wandered too far into a net of expectations and had left no crumbs behind. **E**

Daddy, Mama, Doodle, and I were seated at the dining-room table having lunch. It was a hot day, with all the windows and doors open in case a breeze should come. In the kitchen Aunt Nicey was humming softly. After a long silence, Daddy spoke. "It's so calm, I wouldn't be surprised if we had a storm this afternoon."

"I haven't heard a rain frog," said Mama, who believed in signs, as she served the bread around the table. **F**

"I did," declared Doodle. "Down in the swamp."

"He didn't," I said contrarily.

"You did, eh?" said Daddy, ignoring my denial.

"I certainly did," Doodle reiterated, scowling at me over the top of his iced-tea glass, and we were quiet again.

Suddenly, from out in the yard came a strange croaking noise. Doodle stopped eating, with a piece of bread poised ready for his mouth, his eyes popped round like two blue buttons. "What's that?" he whispered.

I jumped up, knocking over my chair, and had reached the door when Mama called, "Pick up the chair, sit down again, and say excuse me."

By the time I had done this, Doodle had excused himself and had slipped out into the yard. He was looking up into the bleeding tree. "It's a great big red bird!" he called.

The bird croaked loudly again, and Mama and Daddy came out into the yard. We shaded our eyes with our hands against the hazy glare of the sun and peered up through the still leaves. On the topmost branch a bird the size of a chicken, with scarlet feathers and long legs, was perched precariously. Its wings hung down loosely, and as we watched, a feather dropped away and floated slowly down through the green leaves.

"It's not even frightened of us," Mama said.

"It looks tired," Daddy added. "Or maybe sick."

Doodle's hands were clasped at his throat, and I had never seen him stand still so long. "What is it?" he asked.

Daddy shook his head. "I don't know, maybe it's——" **G**

At that moment the bird began to flutter, but the wings were uncoordinated, and amid much flapping and a spray of flying feathers, it tumbled down, bumping through the limbs of the bleeding tree and landing at our feet with a thud. Its long, graceful neck jerked twice into an S, then straightened out, and the bird was still. A white veil came over the eyes, and the long white beak unhinged. Its legs were crossed and its clawlike feet were delicately curved at rest. Even death did not mar its grace, for it lay on the earth like a broken vase of red flowers, and we stood around it, awed by its exotic beauty.

"It's dead," Mama said.

"What is it?" Doodle repeated.

"Go bring me the bird book," said Daddy.

I ran into the house and brought back the bird book. As we watched, Daddy thumbed

----

WORDS TO OWN

doggedness (dôg′id·nis) *n.*: stubbornness; persistence.
reiterated (rē·it′ə·rāt′id) *v.*: repeated.
precariously (prē·ker′ē·əs·lē) *adv.*: unsteadily; insecurely.

THE SCARLET IBIS 321

Breaking Down Difficult Text
If some readers are finding the similes and metaphors challenging, work through this one as an example. Draw a net or web on the board, discuss how easy it is to get lost in such a pattern, and discuss the allusion to crumbs—trail markers such as those left by Hansel and Gretel in the fairy tale. Finally, have students paraphrase the sentence. [Sample response: We had gone too deeply into our plan to turn back, and we had left ourselves no way out.]

F Cultural Connections
Weather Traditions
The rain frog that Mama mentions serves as an indicator of rain. Point out that many cultures have weather signals. For example, some students may know the rhyme, "Red sky at night, sailors delight. Red sky in morning, sailors take warning."

G Elements of Literature
Symbols
? What details alert you to the fact that the events in this passage are symbolic and extremely significant to the story? [Clues that the scarlet ibis will stand for something beyond itself include the sudden entrance of the bird into the story, the link between the bird's name and the title of the story, and the detailed description of the bird's death.]

Assessing Learning

Observation Assessment: Reading
As students discuss or write about the story, use the following criteria for observing and assessing their reading performances.
1 = Rarely   2 = Sometimes   3 = Often
____ **1.** Makes personal connections
____ **2.** Attends to multiple levels of meaning
____ **3.** Uses the text to verify ideas
____ **4.** Challenges the text
____ **5.** Draws on story elements when making meaning

through its pages. "It's a scarlet ibis," he said, pointing to a picture. "It lives in the tropics—South America to Florida. A storm must have brought it here."

Sadly, we all looked back at the bird. A scarlet ibis! How many miles it had traveled to die like this, in *our* yard, beneath the bleeding tree.

"Let's finish lunch," Mama said, nudging us back toward the dining room.

"I'm not hungry," said Doodle, and he knelt down beside the ibis.

"We've got peach cobbler for dessert," Mama tempted from the doorway.

Doodle remained kneeling. "I'm going to bury him."

"Don't you dare touch him," Mama warned. "There's no telling what disease he might have had."

"All right," said Doodle. "I won't."

Daddy, Mama, and I went back to the dining-room table, but we watched Doodle through the open door. He took out a piece of string from his pocket and, without touching the ibis, looped one end around its neck. Slowly, while singing softly "Shall We Gather at the River," he carried the bird around to the front yard and dug a hole in the flower garden, next to the petunia bed. Now we were watching him through the front window, but he didn't know it. His awkwardness at digging the hole with a shovel whose handle was twice as long as he was made us laugh, and we covered our mouths with our hands so he wouldn't hear.

When Doodle came into the dining room, he found us seriously eating our cobbler. He was pale and lingered just inside the screen door. "Did you get the scarlet ibis buried?" asked Daddy.

Doodle didn't speak but nodded his head.

"Go wash your hands, and then you can have some peach cobbler," said Mama.

"I'm not hungry," he said.

"Dead birds is bad luck," said Aunt Nicey, poking her head from the kitchen door. "Specially *red* dead birds!"

As soon as I had finished eating, Doodle and I hurried off to Horsehead Landing. Time was short, and Doodle still had a long way to go if he

was going to keep up with the other boys when he started school. The sun, gilded with the yellow cast of autumn, still burned fiercely, but the dark green woods through which we passed were shady and cool. When we reached the landing, Doodle said he was too tired to swim, so we got into a skiff and floated down the creek with the tide. Far off in the marsh a rail was scolding, and over on the beach locusts were singing in the myrtle trees. Doodle did not speak and kept his head turned away, letting one hand trail limply in the water.

After we had drifted a long way, I put the oars in place and made Doodle row back against the tide. Black clouds began to gather in the southwest, and he kept watching them, trying to pull the oars a little faster. When we reached Horsehead Landing, lightning was playing across half the sky and thunder roared out, hiding even the sound of the sea. The sun disappeared and darkness descended, almost like night. Flocks of marsh crows flew by, heading inland to their roosting trees, and two egrets, squawking, arose from the oyster-rock shallows and careened away.

Doodle was both tired and frightened, and when he stepped from the skiff he collapsed onto the mud, sending an armada[16] of fiddler crabs rustling off into the marsh grass. I helped him up, and as he wiped the mud off his trousers, he smiled at me ashamedly. He had failed and we both knew it, so we started back home, racing the storm. We never spoke (what are the words that can solder[17] cracked pride?), but I knew he was watching me, watching for a sign of mercy. The lightning was near now, and from fear he walked so close behind me he kept stepping on my heels. The faster I walked, the faster he walked, so I began to run. The rain was coming, roaring through the pines, and then, like a bursting Roman candle, a gum tree ahead of us was shattered by a bolt of lightning. When the deafening peal of thunder had died, and in the moment before the rain arrived, I heard Doodle,

16. **armada** (är·mä′də): group. *Armada* is generally used to mean "fleet, or group, of warships."
17. **solder** (säd′ər): patch or repair. Solder is a mixture of metals melted and used to repair metal parts.

Assessing Learning

Check Test: True-False

1. The narrator's mother wonders whether or not the sickly child is "all there." [True]
2. The narrator nicknames his brother Doodle because Doodle likes the song "Yankee Doodle Dandy." [False]
3. The narrator teaches Doodle to walk because Aunt Nicey insists on it. [False]
4. Doodle buries the dead scarlet ibis by himself. [True]

5. The narrator leaves Doodle behind in a rainstorm and returns to find him dead. [True]

Standardized Test Preparation

For practice with standardized test format specific to this selection, see
• *Standardized Test Preparation*, pp. 40, 42
For practice in proofreading and editing, see
• *Daily Oral Grammar*, Transparency 20

who had fallen behind, cry out, "Brother, Brother, don't leave me! Don't leave me!"

The knowledge that Doodle's and my plans had come to naught was bitter, and that streak of cruelty within me awakened. I ran as fast as I could, leaving him far behind with a wall of rain dividing us. The drops stung my face like nettles, and the wind flared the wet, glistening leaves of the bordering trees. Soon I could hear his voice no more.

I hadn't run too far before I became tired, and the flood of childish spite evanesced[18] as well. I stopped and waited for Doodle. The sound of rain was everywhere, but the wind had died and it fell straight down in parallel paths like ropes hanging from the sky. As I waited, I peered through the downpour, but no one came. Finally I went back and found him huddled beneath a red nightshade bush beside the road. He was sitting on the ground, his face buried in his arms, which were resting on his drawn-up knees. "Let's go, Doodle," I said.

18. **evanesced** (ev'ə·nest'): faded away; disappeared.

He didn't answer, so I placed my hand on his forehead and lifted his head. Limply, he fell backward onto the earth. He had been bleeding from the mouth, and his neck and the front of his shirt were stained a brilliant red.

"Doodle! Doodle!" I cried, shaking him, but there was no answer but the ropy rain. He lay very awkwardly, with his head thrown far back, making his vermilion[19] neck appear unusually long and slim. His little legs, bent sharply at the knees, had never before seemed so fragile, so thin.

I began to weep, and the tear-blurred vision in red before me looked very familiar. "Doodle!" I screamed above the pounding storm, and threw my body to the earth above his. For a long, long time, it seemed forever, I lay there crying, sheltering my fallen scarlet ibis from the heresy[20] of rain.

19. **vermilion** (vər·mil'yən): bright red.
20. **heresy** (her'i·sē): here, mockery. *Heresy* generally means "denial of what is commonly believed to be true" or "rejection of a church's teaching."

Making the Connections

Connections

This short and bittersweet poem reminds the reader that it is important to show one's love.

A Reading Skills and Strategies
Paraphrasing
To find the essential meaning of the poem, read it through at least twice and paraphrase it in your own words. [Sample response: If you grieve, be sorry about things you didn't do or dream or attain, and especially for love you withheld.]

B Critical Thinking
Analyzing
❓ What is the effect of the repetition and visual pattern of these three words? [They lend emphasis to the last lines of the poem, which state the importance of love.]

MEET THE WRITER
Brothers at War

James Hurst (1922–) was born on a farm by the sea in North Carolina. Although he studied singing in New York at the famous Juilliard School of Music, and in Rome, Italy, he eventually became a banker. For thirty-four years he worked in the international department of a large bank in New York. During this time Hurst also published some short stories, including "The Scarlet Ibis." He reminds readers of "The Scarlet Ibis" to think of how the war raging among "brothers" in Europe is related to the conflict between Doodle and *his* brother. Perhaps, he reflects, people always suffer when others try to make them over in their own image.

Hurst finally retired from banking and returned to North Carolina—to New Bern, a town near his birthplace.

Connections   A POEM

A [If There Be Sorrow

Mari Evans

If there be sorrow
let it be
for things undone . . .
B [undreamed
   unrealized
     unattained
to these add one;
Love withheld . . .
. . . restrained

The Kiss (1922–1940)
by Constantin Brancusi.

Musée National d'Art Moderne, Paris. © 1999 Artists Rights Society (ARS), New York/ADAGP, Paris.

Connecting Across Texts

Connecting with "The Scarlet Ibis"
What do the speaker of this poem and the narrator of "The Scarlet Ibis" have in common? [Both realize that when you are sad, it should be for "restraining" or holding back love. The narrator of the story realizes at the end that instead of being cruel to his brother, he should have protected him from harm.]

First Thoughts

[respond]

1. How were the questions you noted answered? You should have stopped when you got to the end of the paragraph on page 317 beginning "It was bad enough." Were you left with unanswered questions when you finished the story?

Shaping Interpretations

[respond]

2. How do you feel about the narrator's behavior at the end of the story? Is he responsible for Doodle's death? Could he be partially responsible? Is his emotion at the very end sorrow, guilt, or something else?

[respond]

3. By the end of the story, whom do you pity more—the narrator or Doodle? Why?

[infer]

4. Do you think the narrator makes any kind of discovery at the story's end, as he cradles his brother's little body?

[interpret]

5. In Meet the Writer (page 324), there is an indication of what Hurst thinks his famous story means. How would you state the **theme** of his story—what truth about our lives do the story's events reveal to you? Find passages from the story to support your response.

[interpret]

6. In the last sentence, the narrator calls his brother his "fallen scarlet ibis." In what ways could the ibis be a **symbol** for Doodle? Consider:
   - how Doodle and the ibis resemble each other
   - how Doodle's and the ibis's deaths are similar
   - how Doodle himself identifies with the bird
   - how both Doodle and the ibis are put in worlds where they can't survive

Connecting with the Text

[connect]

7. Why do you think this story is so popular and is remembered for a long time by many readers? What feelings do you think it taps into?

Extending the Text

[extend]

8. Reread what the storyteller says on page 318 about human pride. What incidents from life could illustrate the good and bad effects of human pride? Does pride lead to the kinds of sorrow that Mari Evans writes about in her poem "If There Be Sorrow" (see *Connections* on page 324)?

THE SCARLET IBIS **325**

Reading Check

a. Whose point of view is the story told from?

b. When does the story about Doodle take place?

c. Why does the narrator teach Doodle to walk, and why does he cry when his family congratulates him for his effort?

d. After Doodle has learned to walk, what does his brother try to teach him, to prepare him for school?

e. How does Doodle respond to the scarlet ibis and to its death?

Reading Check
Answers may vary slightly.

a. The story is told from the first-person point of view by a Southern man who is remembering his boyhood.

b. The story takes place during World War I, 1914–1918.

c. The narrator is embarrassed to have a brother who is not normal. He knows that his motivations for teaching Doodle to walk were shame and pride more than concern for his brother.

d. He tries to teach Doodle to run, to swim, to climb trees, to fight.

e. Doodle responds with love, compassion, and respect; he gives the bird a proper burial.

MAKING MEANINGS

First Thoughts

1. Responses will vary; make sure students cite examples.

Shaping Interpretations

2. Most students will find the narrator at least partly responsible for Doodle's death. His emotions are a mixture of grief and guilt.

3. Some students will pity the narrator more because of the guilt and sorrow he has felt in the years since Doodle's death. While it lasted, Doodle had a much better life than anyone expected.

4. The narrator realizes what he has lost. To him, Doodle becomes a precious being who should have been cherished and protected.

5. Possible themes: No human emotion is entirely pure; our lives are shaped by conflicting emotions. Two passages containing the theme are "There is within me (and with sadness I have watched it in others) a knot of cruelty borne by the stream of love" (p. 318) and "pride is a wonderful, terrible thing, a seed that bears two vines, life and death" (p. 318).

6. Both Doodle and the scarlet ibis are thin and fragile, and both are out of place in their worlds. Doodle's blood reminds the narrator of the redness of the scarlet ibis. Doodle himself seemed to identify with the bird when he took pains to give it a proper burial. Even with help the bird could not survive in the wrong climate, and Doodle is unable to survive his disabilities.

Connecting with the Text

7. Sample response: Readers can identify with the feelings and behavior of the narrator. Many will recall frustrations and joys between themselves and their siblings. The feelings the story taps into are universal: guilt, sorrow, compassion, regret, hurt, joy, love.

Extending the Text

8. Responses will vary. When people are afraid of shame or failure, they often hold their efforts or feelings in check. But pride can also be a great energizer and unifier, as when people excel in academics or sports. Pride can contribute to not doing or loving enough, the sorrows that Mari Evans writes about.

T325

Rubrics for each Choices assignment appear on p. 126 in the *Portfolio Management System*.

CHOICES: Building Your Portfolio

1. **Writer's Notebook** Call students' attention to the graphic organizer at the bottom of the page. It will help them organize their notes about point of view. Remind them to save their work; they may use it as prewriting for the Writer's Workshop on p. 332.

2. **Creative Writing** Remind students that in the third-person limited point of view the pronouns *he* and *she* are used, and the thoughts and feelings are limited to those of one character. After students choose their scene, have them reread it carefully, looking for words and actions that show what Doodle might have been thinking or feeling. Have students follow the action in the story, changing only the point of view from which the events are told. Let them test the success of what they have written by presenting it orally.

3. **Analyzing a Character** Have students brainstorm about the questions with a partner before they begin to write their analyses. To help students generate and organize their ideas, encourage them to make a two-column organizer labeled "Doodle's Stories" and "Doodle's Life." In the first column they should enter things like "His characters want" and "Their world is (3 adjectives)"; in the second column they should enter things like "He wants" and "His world is (3 adjectives)."

4. **Research/Drawing** Have students work with partners to locate all the references to plants in the story.

5. **Expository Writing/Interviewing** To better prepare students to conduct their interviews with tact and sensitivity, have them rehearse asking their questions with a partner.

CHOICES: Building Your Portfolio

Writer's Notebook

1. Collecting Ideas for an Analysis of a Short Story

Whose story is it? By now you have read enough short stories to know how important **point of view** is in a story. When you analyze a story for the Writer's Workshop on page 332, you will want to think about who is telling the story. Did the writer choose the first-person "I"? Or did he or she choose an omniscient narrator, one who knows the thoughts and feelings of all the characters? Or did the writer zoom in on just one character?

Event	Point of View	Reaction
Eugene's mother's rejection of Elena in "American History"	First person (Elena)	I felt sympathy because I could identify with her.
The loss of the Christmas present in "The Gift"	Third-person limited (parents)	I don't feel much for the boy because I don't know what he's thinking.

Using a chart like the one below, list the important events in some of the stories you have read. Take notes about how your reaction to the events was affected by the story's point of view. Save your notes.

Creative Writing

2. Doodle's Point of View

"The Scarlet Ibis" would be a different story if it were told from Doodle's point of view. Pick a key scene from the story and tell it from the third-person limited point of view, through Doodle's senses and feelings. Write a paragraph or two.

Analyzing a Character

3. The Inner Life

Doodle's inner life is revealed in the "lies" he tells. Write a paragraph analyzing these stories. Be sure to review the passage on page 319 where the stories are described. Consider these questions:

- What do Doodle's characters want?
- What kind of world do they live in?
- Why does Doodle tell these stories?
- What do his stories reveal about him?

Research/Drawing

4. Flora of the South

There is a distinct feeling of nature in "The Scarlet Ibis"—the seasons, the drought, the vegetation, the details of Old Woman Swamp. Make a list of all the plants mentioned in the story: trees, flowers, and grasses. In an encyclopedia or botanical reference book, find out what these plants look like and then use them in a series of illustrations that will capture the story's lush setting.

Expository Writing/Interviewing

5. Sibling Rivalry

Siblings can have mixed feelings about each other. They can be the closest of friends and still get on each other's nerves. They can love each other and still be competitive. Interview your own sibling or someone else's as if you were doing research for a book on sibling rivalry. First, ask your subject three or four questions, which you should write out before the interview. Then, get your subject to tell you a story about his or her sibling. After you've gathered your information, write a paragraph on the topic of "Being a Brother or a Sister."

326 THE SHORT-STORY COLLECTIONS

LANGUAGE LINK MINI-LESSON

Figurative Language—Picture This

**Handbook of
Literary
Terms**
H E L P

*See Figure of
Speech.*

". . . like a bursting Roman candle, a gum tree ahead of us was shattered by a bolt of lightning." How is a Roman candle like a tree struck by lightning? That question is not a riddle. James Hurst is using a **simile**—the simplest form of figurative language—to help us see what a tree struck by lightning looks like. In a simile, two dissimilar things are compared by a word such as *like, as,* or *resembles.*

Here are five more sentences from "The Scarlet Ibis" that contain similes.

1. ". . . the oriole nest in the elm was untenanted and rocked back and forth like an empty cradle."

2. "They named him William Armstrong, which was like tying a big tail on a small kite."

3. ". . . the white marquisette curtains billowed out in the afternoon sea breeze, rustling like palmetto fronds."

4. ". . . [the ibis] lay on the earth like a broken vase of red flowers. . . ."

5. ". . . the sick-sweet smell of bay flowers hung everywhere like a mournful song."

Try It Out

1. In each passage at the left, locate the simile and tell what is being compared to what. What exactly do the two things have in common?

2. Reword each passage using new similes. Can you change the whole emotional tone of the passage with a different comparison?

➤ Select a piece of descriptive writing from your Writer's Notebook, and highlight at least two places where you could make your writing more vivid and interesting by using a simile. Rewrite each passage with a fresh comparison.

A tip for writers: When you use figurative language, be sure to avoid trite, or overused, expressions. Try to find new comparisons that say what *you* want to say.

VOCABULARY HOW TO OWN A WORD

WORD BANK

*imminent
infallibility
doggedness
reiterated
precariously*

Don't Mix Them Up!

There is a character in an English play called Mrs. Malaprop who always gets a laugh by using the wrong word. Once Mrs. Malaprop proclaimed, "Lead the way and we'll precede." She meant to use *proceed; precede* means "to go before"—her sentence is a complete blunder. Answer these questions about the words in the Word Bank to be sure you don't commit any malapropisms:

1. How is *imminent* different from *eminent*?
2. How is *infallibility* different from *infantile*?
3. How is *doggedness* different from *doggishness*?
4. How is *reiterated* different from *retaliated*?
5. How is *precariously* different from *precociously*?

THE SCARLET IBIS 327

LANGUAGE LINK
Try It Out
Possible Answers

1. (1) nest = cradle. An empty cradle, like a nest, can rock wildly because no weight secures it.
   (2) long name, tiny baby = big tail, small kite
   (3) sound of billowing curtains = rustling of palmetto fronds. Both make a similar rustling noise in the wind.
   (4) dead ibis = broken vase of red flowers. Both are graceful, red, broken things of beauty.
   (5) sick-sweet smell of bay flowers = mournful song. Both spread into space and evoke feelings of sadness and nostalgia.

2. Answers will vary. Make sure the unlike things are connected by words such as *like, as,* or *resembles.* The tone of a passage can be changed by using a different comparison.

VOCABULARY
Possible Answers

1. *Imminent* means "about to happen, impending, threatening"; *eminent* means "prominent" or "famous."
2. *Infallibility* means "incapability of error"; *infantile* means "childish."
3. *Doggedness* means "stubborn determination"; *doggishness* means "being like a dog" or "stylishness."
4. *Reiterated* means "repeated"; *retaliated* means "repaid an injury in kind."
5. *Precariously* means "unstably" or "dangerously"; *precociously* means "exceptionally early in development."

Language Link Quick Check

Fill in the blanks with an appropriate simile. Sample answers are provided in brackets.

1. Doodle is as fragile as _____. [a delicate crystal]
2. He walks awkwardly, like _____. [a waddling penguin]
3. The heat of summer feels like _____. [the inside of a furnace]
4. He rows as fast as _____. [a high-speed bike]
5. His body lies crumpled like _____. [a tattered rag doll]

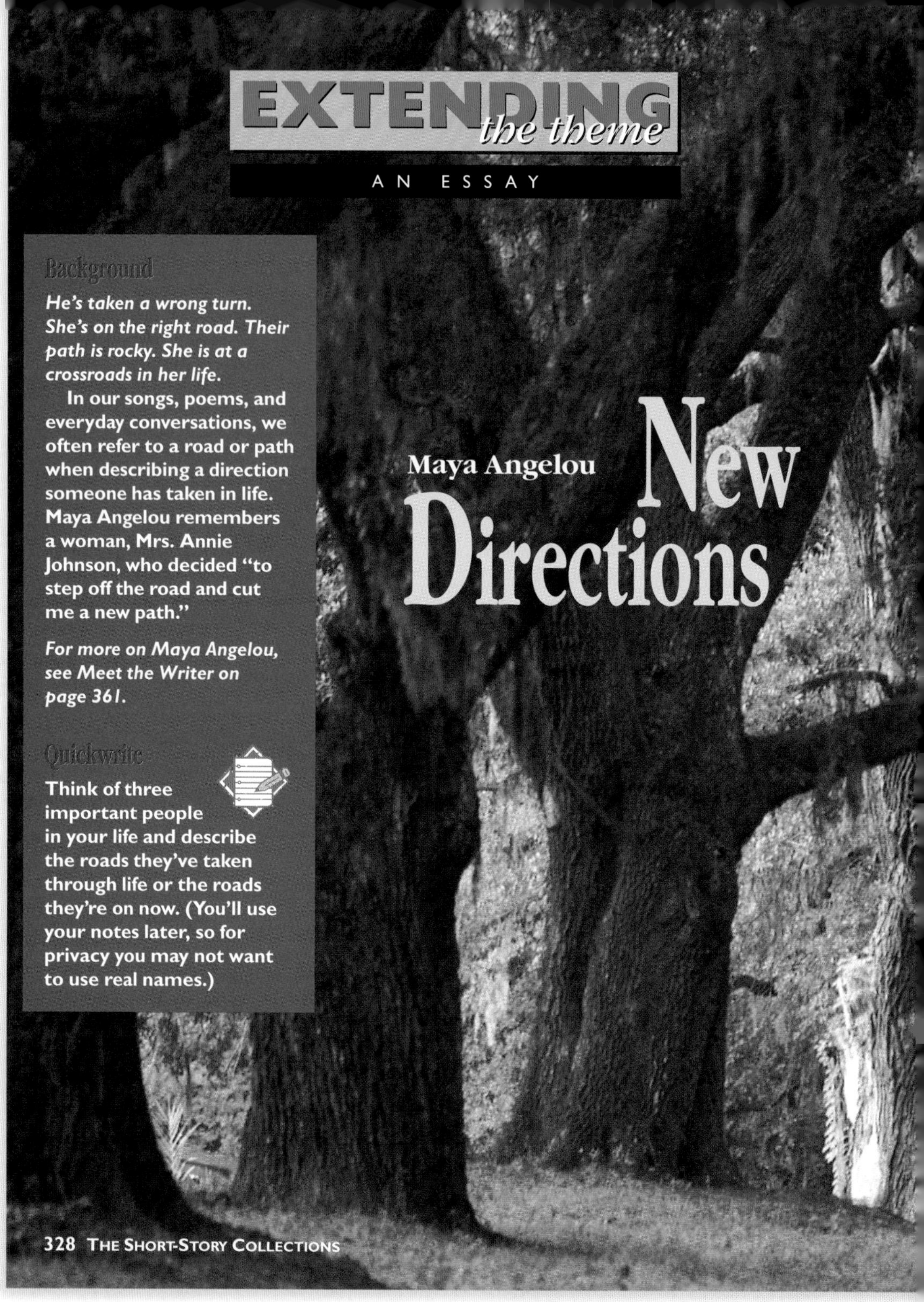

EXTENDING *the theme*

AN ESSAY

Extending the Theme

In this portrait, Maya Angelou presents Mrs. Annie Johnson, a poor African American woman, who is the sole support for two young sons after she and her husband decide to separate. Angelou uses paths and roads as metaphors for a new start in life. Annie becomes an enterprising businesswoman, cooking hot meat pies for the workers of two factories five miles apart. Every workday for the next few years, Annie carries the heavy pies to the workers, never disappointing her customers. Eventually she earns enough to build a stall halfway between the locations, and later a successful store at which she sells additional provisions. Annie discovers that hard work and determination can make one a self-sufficient entrepreneur.

Resources

Listening
Audio CD Library
A reading of this story is provided in the *Audio CD Library:*
• Disc 12, Track 3

Viewing and Representing
Fine Art Transparency
After students have read the selection, a fine art transparency of Willie Birch's sculpture, *Coming Home,* can be used to complement it.
• Transparency 6
• Worksheet, p. 24

Background

He's taken a wrong turn. She's on the right road. Their path is rocky. She is at a crossroads in her life.

In our songs, poems, and everyday conversations, we often refer to a road or path when describing a direction someone has taken in life. Maya Angelou remembers a woman, Mrs. Annie Johnson, who decided "to step off the road and cut me a new path."

For more on Maya Angelou, see Meet the Writer on page 361.

Quickwrite

Think of three important people in your life and describe the roads they've taken through life or the roads they're on now. (You'll use your notes later, so for privacy you may not want to use real names.)

Maya Angelou New Directions

Reaching All Students

Read "New Directions" aloud to the class while students follow along silently. Have students write anonymous questions about the selection on index cards. When you have finished reading, collect and shuffle the cards. Read them to the class and have the class propose answers to the questions.

Getting Students Involved

Cooperative Learning
Character Skits. Have students work in groups to write a skit about a day in the life of Mrs. Johnson. The time frame for their skits could be either the first day she serves meat pies or five or ten years later. Students should include dialogue from characters not mentioned in the narrative: customers, family members, townspeople. All group members should collaborate on the writing, and each member should take a role when the skit is presented.

"I decided to step off the road."

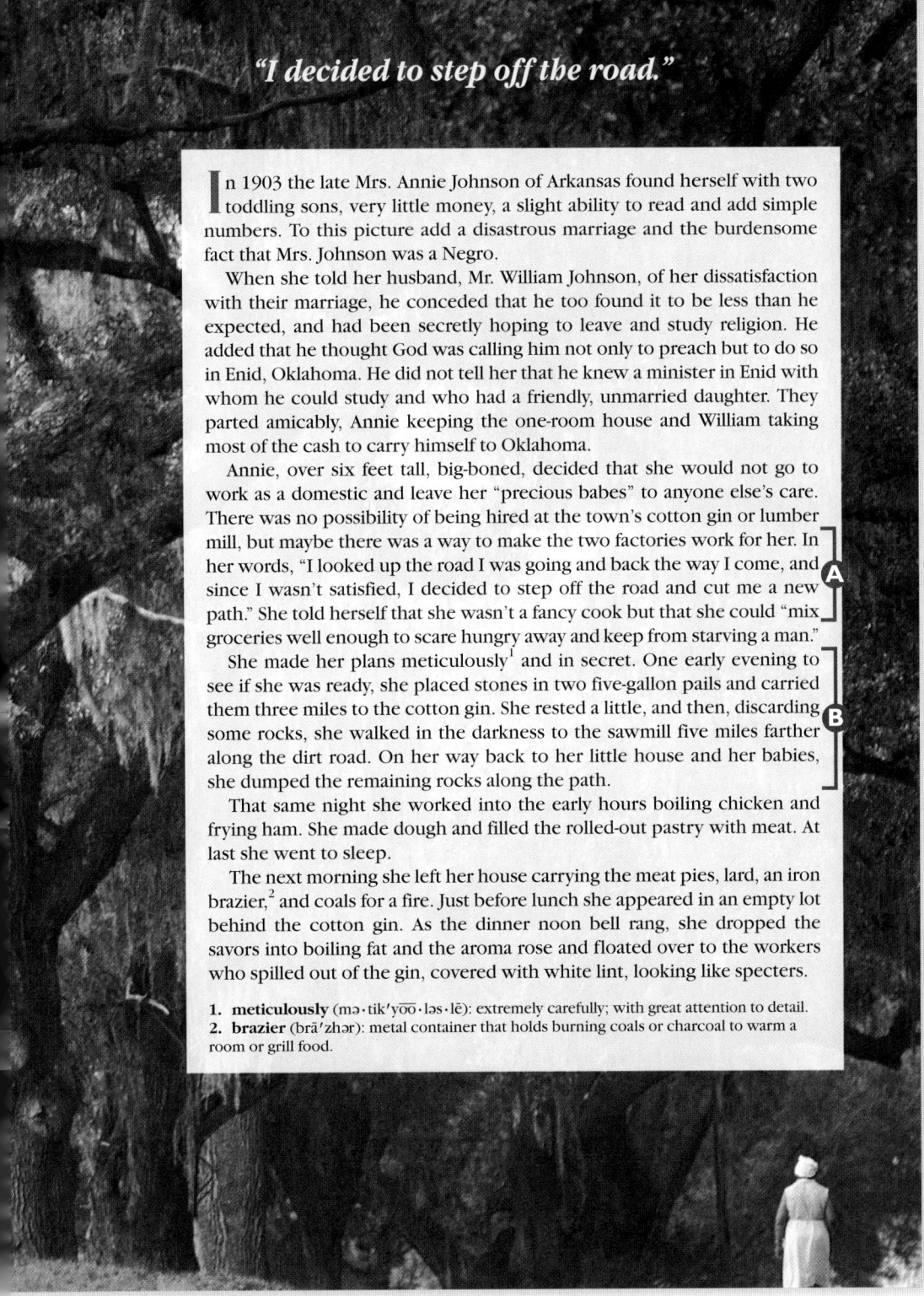

In 1903 the late Mrs. Annie Johnson of Arkansas found herself with two toddling sons, very little money, a slight ability to read and add simple numbers. To this picture add a disastrous marriage and the burdensome fact that Mrs. Johnson was a Negro.

When she told her husband, Mr. William Johnson, of her dissatisfaction with their marriage, he conceded that he too found it to be less than he expected, and had been secretly hoping to leave and study religion. He added that he thought God was calling him not only to preach but to do so in Enid, Oklahoma. He did not tell her that he knew a minister in Enid with whom he could study and who had a friendly, unmarried daughter. They parted amicably, Annie keeping the one-room house and William taking most of the cash to carry himself to Oklahoma.

Annie, over six feet tall, big-boned, decided that she would not go to work as a domestic and leave her "precious babes" to anyone else's care. There was no possibility of being hired at the town's cotton gin or lumber mill, but maybe there was a way to make the two factories work for her. In her words, "I looked up the road I was going and back the way I come, and since I wasn't satisfied, I decided to step off the road and cut me a new path." She told herself that she wasn't a fancy cook but that she could "mix groceries well enough to scare hungry away and keep from starving a man."

She made her plans meticulously[1] and in secret. One early evening to see if she was ready, she placed stones in two five-gallon pails and carried them three miles to the cotton gin. She rested a little, and then, discarding some rocks, she walked in the darkness to the sawmill five miles farther along the dirt road. On her way back to her little house and her babies, she dumped the remaining rocks along the path.

That same night she worked into the early hours boiling chicken and frying ham. She made dough and filled the rolled-out pastry with meat. At last she went to sleep.

The next morning she left her house carrying the meat pies, lard, an iron brazier,[2] and coals for a fire. Just before lunch she appeared in an empty lot behind the cotton gin. As the dinner noon bell rang, she dropped the savors into boiling fat and the aroma rose and floated over to the workers who spilled out of the gin, covered with white lint, looking like specters.

1. **meticulously** (mə·tik′yo͞o·ləs·lē): extremely carefully; with great attention to detail.
2. **brazier** (brā′zhər): metal container that holds burning coals or charcoal to warm a room or grill food.

A **Reading Skills and Strategies**
Drawing Conclusions
? What do Annie's words mean? [Sample answer: She does not like the future that lies ahead of her (work as a domestic) or the past that lies behind her (an unhappy marriage), so she decides to create a new opportunity for herself.]

B **Critical Thinking**
Speculating
? Why do you think Annie carries the rocks in pails to the cotton gin and the sawmill? [She is testing to see whether or not she can manage the weight of the food she plans to carry to those two places.]

Making the Connections

Connecting to the Theme: "Discoveries"

How does the message in Angelou's portrait of Annie Johnson extend the theme of the collection? [Possible responses: Angelou says that people must be open to discoveries at any time in their lives, and that they have "the right and the responsibility" to act on what they discover about their life situations; Angelou points out that by seeking new directions, people will make even more discoveries.]

A Elements of Literature
Character

? What does this paragraph reveal about Annie's character? [She is hard-working, dependable, conscientious, patient, practical, and forward-thinking.] What details support your conclusions? [Sample responses: The fact that no weather conditions keep her from her customers; the way she carefully turns the pies; the fact that she waits to build a stall until her clientele is steady.]

B Critical Thinking
Challenging the Text

? Do you agree with the narrator? Explain. [Sample responses: Yes, because people are in charge of their lives and must be strong enough to make decisions and take chances; no, because sometimes family responsibilities or money problems prevent a person from changing directions.]

FINDING COMMON GROUND

Remind students to choose examples they would not mind sharing with others. To help students get started on the first two activities, have them make a short list of historical, fictional, or media figures who have changed the directions of their lives. After discussing people they do not know, students may find it easier to talk about the lives of people closer to them.

Remind students that for the last activity they may be writing songs or poems about real people and situations, and care should be taken not to include recognizable material that may embarrass someone.

Most workers had brought their lunches of pinto beans and biscuits or crackers, onions and cans of sardines, but they were tempted by the hot meat pies which Annie ladled out of the fat. She wrapped them in newspapers, which soaked up the grease, and offered them for sale at a nickel each. Although business was slow, those first days Annie was determined. She balanced her appearances between the two hours of activity.

So, on Monday if she offered hot fresh pies at the cotton gin and sold the remaining cooled-down pies at the lumber mill for three cents, then on Tuesday she went first to the lumber mill presenting fresh, just-cooked pies as the lumbermen covered in sawdust emerged from the mill.

For the next few years, on balmy spring days, blistering summer noons, and cold, wet, and wintry middays, Annie never disappointed her **A** customers, who could count on seeing the tall, brown-skin woman bent over her brazier, carefully turning the meat pies. When she felt

certain that the workers had become dependent on her, she built a stall between the two hives of industry and let the men run to her for their lunchtime provisions.

She had indeed stepped from the road which seemed to have been chosen for her and cut herself a brand-new path. In years that stall became a store where customers could buy cheese, meal, syrup, cookies, candy, writing tablets, pickles, canned goods, fresh fruit, soft drinks, coal, oil, and leather soles for worn-out shoes.

Each of us has the right and the responsibility to assess the roads which lie ahead, and those over which we have traveled, and if the future road looms ominous or unpromising, and the roads back uninviting, then we need to gather our resolve and, carrying only the necessary baggage, step off that road into **B** another direction. If the new choice is also unpalatable,[3] without embarrassment, we must be ready to change that as well.

Center: *Field Trilogy* (1985) by Viola Burley Leak.
Appliqué, tapestry, and soft sculpture (38" x 25").
Courtesy of the artist.

3. **unpalatable** (un·pal′ə·tə·bəl): unpleasant. *Unpalatable* often means "tasting bad."

FINDING COMMON GROUND

1. Reread your Quickwrite and add new details to your notes if you wish. In a small group, take turns and read your notes about the roads people have chosen.

2. Are there any people you wrote about who might benefit from reading about Mrs. Annie Johnson's new direction? Discuss your responses in your group.

3. With your group, write a song or a poem about traveling the road of life. Tell about the forks in the road that people come to. What choices are available? What might wait at the end of each person's road? What rough places might lie along the way? Share your songs and poems with the class.

Assessing Learning

Check Test: Questions and Answers
Answers may vary slightly.

1. Why does Annie not want to go to work as a domestic? [She does not want to leave her children in someone else's care.]

2. Why does she carry stones in pails to the cotton gin and the sawmill? [She wants to be sure she can carry the heavy food the same distance.]

3. What does Annie sell to the men on their lunch break? [hot meat pies]

4. What does Annie eventually build between the cotton gin and the sawmill? [first a stall and then a store]

5. At the end of the narrative, what responsibility does Angelou say that all people have? [People are in charge of their own lives and must have the courage to step in a new direction if they do not like where they've been or where they are heading.]

READ ON

A Sapling Stands Tall

In Betty Smith's novel, a tree grows in Brooklyn—and so does young Francie Nolan. Living in a poor neighborhood with her parents and brother, Francie finds joys and an assortment of troubles as she comes of age. Her experiences are sometimes painful, but they become the building blocks of wisdom. *A Tree Grows in Brooklyn* (HarperCollins) takes place between 1902 and 1919, but don't be surprised if Francie and the Nolan family remind you of people you know today.

America Has Many Streets

Reading the stories in *America Street* (Persea) is like taking a walk in fourteen neighborhoods. On one street Toni Cade Bambara will introduce you to Squeaky, who's determined to win the neighborhood race if it kills her. On another street you'll meet Gary Soto's Fausto, who's busy scraping pennies together to buy a guitar. Duane Big Eagle will take you to Raoul's neighborhood, where he is boarding a train in search of his mysterious medicine-woman aunt. Why not go for a walk and meet your neighbors?

Be Yourself

When you read the stories, poems, and plays in *American Dragons* (HarperCollins), you'll hear the voices of twenty-five Asian American teenagers expressing their feelings. They are trying to figure out how to fit in and how to be themselves at the same time. Their struggle is expressed in a range of feelings—from rage to sorrow, from worry to wonder.

Not Enough Time

The absence of her father was always painful to Bebe Moore Campbell while she was growing up. She saw him during the summers, but she desperately wished they could have more time together. In *Sweet Summer: Growing Up with and Without My Dad* (Ballantine), the story of her youth, Campbell tells how she learned to deal with the pain of missing him. Read it and find out how her father came to be a constant presence in her life in spite of their separation.

READ ON 331

MAIN OBJECTIVE
Write an analysis of a short story

PROCESS OBJECTIVES

1. Use appropriate prewriting techniques to identify and develop a topic
2. Create a first draft
3. Use evaluation criteria as a basis for determining revision strategies
4. Revise the first draft incorporating suggestions generated by self- or peer evaluation
5. Proofread and correct errors
6. Create a final draft
7. Choose an appropriate method of publication
8. Reflect on progress as a writer

Planning

- **Block Schedule**
  Block Scheduling Lesson Plans with Pacing Guide
- **One-Stop Planner**
  CD-ROM with Test Generator

BUILDING YOUR PORTFOLIO
Writer's Workshop

Technology HELP

See Writer's Workshop 2 CD-ROM. *Assignment: Interpretation.*

ASSIGNMENT

Write an essay analyzing a short story you have read in this textbook.

AIM

To explain; to give information.

AUDIENCE

Your classmates and your teacher or a student publication that accepts literary reviews.

EXPOSITORY WRITING
ANALYZING A SHORT STORY

By now you've become an expert short-story reader. You've read many different kinds of stories in this textbook and on your own, and you've talked about the **elements of fiction**—plot, character, setting, irony, point of view, and theme. In this workshop you'll write an essay analyzing a story you've read. When you **analyze** a story, you examine it—you look at its separate parts (all of them or some of them), and then you see how the parts work together to create the story's meaning.

Remember, there is no single correct analysis, so don't look for one. Even though you and a classmate may write about the same story, your analyses may end up being quite different. Your analysis should be *your* interpretation. As long as you can support everything you say by referring to details in the text, your interpretation—or analysis—will be fine.

Prewriting

1. Choose a Story

Of all the stories you've read, which one intrigues you the most? Which one has given you the most to think about? Which one did you hate? In your Writer's Notebook you've collected some ideas about stories you have read. You can use those notes to choose the focus of your analysis, or you can start with an entirely different story. Be sure to choose a story you feel strongly about.

2. More Than One Close Reading

Reread the story carefully—at least two or three times—taking notes as you go. Keep in mind that while you are examining the literary elements, you are analyzing the writer's craft. You are trying to find out how the writer put the story together to create meaning.

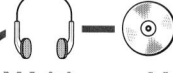 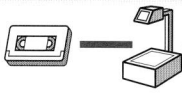 *Resources: Print and Media*

Writing and Language
- *Portfolio Management System*
  Prewriting, p. 128
  Peer Editing, p. 129
  Assessment Rubric, p. 130

- *Workshop Resources*
  Revision Strategy Teaching Notes, p. 19
  Revision Strategy Transparencies 10, 11, and 12
- *Writer's Workshop 2 CD-ROM,* Interpretation

The history
of the written
word is rich and

Page 1

3. One Element at a Time

Now, focus on each element separately. Make a chart as you think about what each element contributes to the story and which elements are the most important ones. Below is a partial chart that might have been prepared for the Student Model on page 334. (What might the writer have said about the story's tone, symbols, and theme?)

Elements	Examples, References	Importance in Story
Suspense	We worry about what will happen to Doodle.	Very important.
Conflict	Narrator's inner conflict—he loves and hates younger brother.	Central to story—everything relates to this problem.
Character	Narrator is motivated by embarrassment and pride, is believable, changes in course of story.	Most important—character is revealed through actions, dialogue, thoughts.
Setting	Tropical, lush—weather is both calm and raging.	Important—the weather reflects narrator's inner conflict. Setting creates mood.
Point of view	Narrator is looking back from years later.	Crucial—only the narrator knows what happened and can reveal the inner conflict.

4. Organize Your Main Ideas

Sift through your notes, and choose your best insights. Plan your paper around three or four main ideas that you know you can support with references to the story. Try stating each main idea in a single sentence.

Language/Grammar Link
H E L P

Dialect: page 277.
Figures of speech: pages 291 and 327.
Adverb clauses: page 302.
Coordinating conjunctions: page 313.

Introducing the Writer's Workshop

- Guide students through an analysis of literary elements—plot, characters, setting, theme—in a movie or fairy tale with which they are familiar. Which element seems most important in a particular movie or fairy tale? How can they tell?
- Lead students to understand that we analyze short stories and novels based on these elements, in terms of both how well a writer expresses them and how well they fit together.

Teaching the Writer's Workshop

Prewriting

Suggest that students review the table of contents of this textbook for stories they have read and would like to analyze. Have them skim the story they have chosen to remind themselves of its plot, characters, theme, and other elements, making notes on these as they do so.

Reaching All Students

Struggling Writers
For students having difficulty deciding which story elements are most important, have them reread the story and put self-sticking notes next to passages, words, or events that provoke an emotional response or are referred to more than once in the story.

English Language Learners
Guide English language learners to analyze a story based on the elements of plot, point of view, and setting, rather than theme or character. The last two are more likely to depend on nuances of speech and on cultural knowledge or values that might be unfamiliar and difficult to interpret.

Drafting

- Have students refer to the student model on pp. 334–335 before beginning to write.
- Remind students to double space when they write their drafts. They should also leave extra space in the right margin. These blank spaces will be used for comments and editing marks.
- Show students how to integrate quotations and examples from stories into their analyses. Model one or two examples of smoothly incorporated quotations or paraphrases that clearly show the importance of a particular element to a story. Note that students should use quotations to illustrate a point or should elaborate on the importance of each quotation used.

Using the Model

After students have completed their drafts, they may benefit from another look at the student model. Have students focus on questions such as these:

? On what short story element(s) does the writer focus?

? How does the writer support her analysis?

? What conclusion does the writer reach about the story? Is this conclusion supported by the evidence she provides?

? What techniques does this writer use that you might incorporate into your own paper?

Signal Where You're Going

Like a good driver, signal where you're going. With your thesis statement, announce where you're headed. Use transitional words and expressions to help your readers follow you.

Words that show transition: first, second, third, finally; for example, for instance; in addition; as a result, because, for, so, since

Drafting

1. One Sentence Says It All

Now, draft a thesis statement of the main ideas in your paper. Your thesis statement doesn't have to be perfect; you can change it later. It will help you keep control of what you'll include in your essay. Instead of trying to write everything possible about the story, you'll focus on the main points.

THESIS STATEMENT
James Hurst's short story "The Scarlet Ibis" is the poignant tale of a boy torn between the love and hate he feels for his younger brother.

2. Elaborate on Each Main Idea

The most important part of your analysis is the support you give each main idea. After all, why should your readers believe you unless you can prove that what you say is true? Your tone should be confident and your presentation logical. If you've chosen your main points well, you'll be able to support them with quotations from the story, references to characters and events, and details and examples from the story.

Student Model

"THE SCARLET IBIS"

James Hurst's short story "The Scarlet Ibis" is the poignant tale of a boy torn between the love and hate he feels for his younger brother. Set in a lush, temperamental environment, the story is similarly mysterious and elusive in tone. Bleakness and optimism reign alternately in the mind of the protagonist as, motivated by embarrassment and pride, he forcefully, sometimes cruelly, pushes his handicapped younger brother to learn to walk and run. Despite his evident affection and concern for his brother, the protagonist feels that Doodle is somehow a disgrace and a burden. Moments of tenderness between the siblings are marred by the protagonist's shame for his brother's inabilities as well as for his own lack of compassion. The traumatic end to the story, in which the protagonist leaves his frail brother behind him during a storm, results in two tragedies: Doodle's death and the protagonist's flood of guilt.

   "The Scarlet Ibis" is very much a character study of the protagonist, the narrator. The story spans eight years, covering the narrator's life between

First sentence identifies author and story and is also thesis statement.

Briefly mentions tone and setting.

Points out pattern of opposites.

Main idea 1: Story is character study of narrator.

Getting Students Involved

Cooperative Learning

Some students might find it helpful to team up with other students who have either chosen the same story or are focusing on the same story element for analysis. As a prewriting activity, they can discuss the various elements of the story or examples of a single element in a variety of stories. They may also serve as well-informed peer editors during the revision stage. Students' familiarity with the story or important elements will help them see problems and offer additional ideas.

ages six and fourteen. The protagonist comes across as very believable because he grows and changes over the course of the story, especially in his attitude toward Doodle. At Doodle's birth, the narrator admits that Doodle was "a disappointment." Having yearned for a younger brother to run and play with, the narrator is understandably let down by the puny, weak child, whom no one expects to live. One day the narrator's anger is replaced by hope when Doodle grins at his older brother. This marks the beginning of the cycle of love and hate that the narrator feels for Doodle. Brotherly affection mingles from then on with shame in the protagonist's mind. An example of this confusion is the renaming of Doodle. The narrator feels that Doodle's given name, William Armstrong, is too "formal" and important sounding, so he renames his baby brother Doodle (explaining, "nobody expects much from someone called Doodle"). This act not only removes the pressure of Doodle's living up to his given name, but also expresses the narrator's belief that Doodle will never amount to anything.

Tells how narrator changes; gives example.

Describes cycle of love and hate; gives example.

The protagonist's mixture of feelings toward Doodle causes an external conflict—between the two brothers—that is never resolved. Doodle, as both a "burden" and playmate, provokes love and cruelty in the heart of his brother. The narrator also experiences an inner conflict, feeling at once justified in disliking his brother (the protagonist defines this as a "cruel streak"), but also feeling shame at his lack of compassion and understanding. Opposites tug inside the narrator, and Hurst places other juxtapositions in the text to accent the confusion. A fancy and fussy name is given to an unpromising child; an exotic South American bird lands in the American South; the weather ranges from calm, warm sunshiny days to raging, furious storms. Conflict and instability prevail in the narrator's mind and also in his surroundings.

Main idea 2: External conflict is never resolved.

Main idea 3: Inner conflict is reflected in instability of weather, from calm to stormy.

Restates main idea 3.

"The Scarlet Ibis" is a moving, well-written story. The author has created a flawed, believable character with whom readers can identify and sympathize. Well-crafted and poignant, "The Scarlet Ibis" is an excellent character study and story.

Concludes with evaluation of story.

—Erin-Elizabeth Tadie
The Potomac School
McLean, Virginia

Reaching All Students

Advanced Learners

In addition to analyzing how several elements are used in their chosen stories, students should identify the one element they consider most important to their story and consider how changing it would affect the story. Can they suggest a change that would improve the story? What changes to the major element would diminish the story's impact?

Struggling Writers and English Language Learners

Students having difficulty translating their thoughts about a story into an essay might dictate their ideas to a teacher, an aide, or another student. Once their initial ideas are on paper, they can more easily clarify these ideas by rewording and revising, either alone or in response to teacher or peer questions.

Evaluating and Revising

- Have students use the Evaluation Criteria provided here to review their drafts and determine needed revisions.
- Have peer editors put a check mark next to sentences where the use of a quotation or example from the story does not fit smoothly into the writing.
- Students should assess the sentence structure in their essays and refer to the Sentence Workshop on p. 337 if they find that they are running sentences together without end punctuation between them.

Proofreading

Have students proofread their own papers first and then exchange them with another student. For this assignment, remind students to be particularly careful of correct comma use with adverb clauses and coordinating conjunctions.

If time permits, students should set the final copy aside for at least a day before proofreading it one last time. Students might also try reading their essays backward, sentence by sentence, to catch fragments, run-ons, and misspellings.

Publishing

Create a book of students' fiction analyses to which students can then refer for deeper understanding of a story they have read in this collection.

Reflecting

If students are adding their analyses to their portfolios, have them date their essays and add a reflection:

1. The thing I did best in my analysis was _____.
2. The writing skills I still need to work on are _____.
3. I'm adding this to my portfolio because _____.

Resources ▬▬▬

Peer Editing Forms and Rubrics
- *Portfolio Management System,* p. 129

Revision Transparencies
- *Workshop Resources,* p. 19

Sentence Workshop
H E L P

Avoiding run-on sentences: page 337.

■ *Evaluation Criteria*

A good essay analyzing a short story

1. *has an introduction identifying the story and writer*

2. *has a thesis statement stating the essay's main idea or ideas*

3. *focuses on three or four elements of the story*

4. *supports each main idea with quotations or examples and details from the story*

5. *uses quotation marks to indicate passages quoted from the story*

6. *uses transitional expressions to help the reader follow ideas*

Communications Handbook
H E L P

See Proofreaders' Marks.

Evaluating and Revising

1. Reading the Essay Aloud

Try reading your draft aloud to yourself. Your sentences should flow smoothly, as if you were talking to your audience. Go back and try to tighten your essay, eliminating all padding. Express each idea as clearly and simply as you can.

2. Peer Editing

Exchange drafts with a partner or members of your writing group, and comment on one another's papers. Ask questions about passages or sentences you don't understand, and check to see that the essay meets the evaluation criteria listed on the left.

Revision Model

	Peer Comments
James Hurst's	*Who wrote it?*
~~The~~ short story "The Scarlet Ibis" ^	
poignant tale the	
is the ~~story~~ of a boy torn between ^ ^	
he feels for his younger brother.	*Love and hate of what?*
love and hate. ~~Set in a semi-exotic,~~ ^	
lush, temperamental environment,	
^ly mysterious and elusive	*Please clarify "similar."*
the story is similar in tone. Bleak- ^	
ness and optimism reign alter-	
nately in the mind of the	*Why does he do this?*
, motivated by embarrassment and pride,	
protagonist as he forcefully, ^	
handicapped	
sometimes cruelly, pushes his ^	
younger brother to learn to walk	
and run.	

Grading Timesaver

Rubrics for this Writer's Workshop assignment appear on p. 130 of the *Portfolio Management System.*

Sentence Workshop

OBJECTIVES
1. Identify and revise run-on sentences
2. Understand the difference between a fused sentence and a comma splice

REVISING SENTENCES: STOPPING IN ALL THE RIGHT PLACES

Sentences that run together with no punctuation or only a comma between them are **run-on sentences**. When the sentences have no punctuation between them, they are **fused**. When the sentences are separated only by a comma, they form a **comma splice**.

EXAMPLES   His brother crawls backward like a doodlebug the narrator calls him Doodle. [fused]

His brother crawls backward like a doodlebug, the narrator calls him Doodle. [comma splice]

Here are strategies for revising run-ons.

1. Separate the sentences with a period.

   EXAMPLE
   His brother crawls backward like a doodlebug. The narrator calls him Doodle.

2. Connect the sentences with a semicolon or with a comma and a coordinating conjunction (*and, but, or, nor, so, for, yet*).

   EXAMPLES
   His brother crawls backward like a doodlebug; the narrator calls him Doodle.

   His brother crawls backward like a doodlebug, so the narrator calls him Doodle.

3. Change one of the sentences into a subordinate clause.

   EXAMPLE
   Because his brother crawls backward like a doodlebug, the narrator calls him Doodle.

Writer's Workshop Follow-up: Revision

An effective way of spotting run-ons is to read your work aloud. Usually, you will naturally pause at the end of a full sentence. Stop and be sure it's punctuated correctly. Warning: Watch the relationships between ideas in run-on sentences. If the ideas are not related, separate the sentences with a period.

Language Handbook HELP

See Run-on Sentences, page 1014.

Technology HELP

See Language Workshop CD-ROM. *Key word entry: run-on sentences.*

Try It Out

Act as an editor and correct the run-ons in this report. Be sure to compare your edited versions.

The first American Indian boarding school was the Carlisle Indian Industrial School it was established in 1879, in the 1880s and 1890s American Indian children were sent to faraway federal boarding schools, many American Indian families hid their children, at school the children were made to wear military uniforms they were punished for speaking their native languages, John Collier was the Commissioner of Indian Affairs from 1933 to 1945, he began reforms, these included bilingual education and day schools instead of boarding schools.

Resources

Workshop Resources
• Worksheet, p. 67

Language Workshop CD-ROM
• Run-on Sentences

Try It Out:
Possible Answer
The first American Indian boarding school was the Carlisle Indian Industrial School; it was established in 1879. In the 1880s and 1890s American Indian children were sent to faraway federal boarding schools, so many American Indian families hid their children. At school the children were made to wear military uniforms, and they were punished for speaking their native languages. John Collier was the Commissioner of Indian Affairs from 1933 to 1945. He began reforms, which included bilingual education and day schools instead of boarding schools.

Assessing Learning

Quick Check: Run-on Sentences

Label the correct sentences with an *S* and the run-ons with an *R*.

1. Elena and Eugene both share the same interest they like to read. [R]

2. The cameramen take pictures of the Cains without asking, so Granddaddy Cain exposes their film. [S]

3. Doodle and his brother spent their summers in Old Woman Swamp; they both thought it was beautiful. [S]

4. At first Lizabeth enjoys destroying the marigolds later she feels ashamed. [R]

5. Mrs. Annie Johnson decides she does not want to have someone else take care of her babies she does not want to work at the sawmill. [R]

Using the Strategies

Possible Answers

1. Silver uses inductive reasoning, and Vega uses deductive reasoning.
2. Silver's argument fails to back up reasons with evidence (a, b) and his conclusion is phrased in absolute terms (c). Because all of the answers to the evaluation questions are *no*, his argument is weak. Vega's argument is better because her general principle sounds plausible (a), the specific case she cites can be verified (b), and her conclusion refers only to her school, not all schools (c). All evaluation question answers are *yes* for Vega's argument.

   Vega's argument is sound, but Silver's argument is flawed in its inductive reasoning. Had he addressed the length of the lunch period only at his school, rather than at all schools, his argument would have been more logical.

Situation

Student council elections are coming up, and you're trying to decide which candidate to support. You can use the following strategies to evaluate the candidates' arguments, which are reproduced on the right.

Strategies

Understand what an argument is.

- **Argument** is a form of persuasion that uses logical reasoning. Strictly speaking, argument does not use emotional appeals, such as loaded words and anecdotes.

Recognize the type of reasoning that is used.

- **Inductive reasoning** moves from specific to general. Someone who reasons inductively presents a series of facts and then draws a general conclusion, or **generalization,** from them.

  EXAMPLE

  Facts: Twenty-four of the thirty computers in the computer lab are outmoded. *Conclusion:* The computer lab does not meet students' needs.

  A conclusion reached inductively is not certain. Additional facts might lead to a different conclusion.

> **Candidate: John Silver**
> Argument re Lunch Periods
> Lunch period is twenty-five minutes. That's enough time to eat, and it leaves no time for socializing, which is important. All schools should provide a forty-five-minute lunch.
>
> **Candidate: Lori Vega**
> Argument re Internet Access
> Students need the Internet to be competitive. Our school has only thirty computers with Internet access. We must have more Internet access.

- **Deductive reasoning** moves from general to specific. Someone who reasons deductively sets forth a general principle, applies it to a specific case, and then draws a conclusion *about that case.* If both the general principle and the specific case are true, then the conclusion is certain.

  EXAMPLE

  General principle: An outmoded computer is not useful. *Specific case:* All the computers in the computer lab are outmoded. *Conclusion:* The computer lab is not useful.

Evaluate the logic.

- For **inductive reasoning,** ask these questions:

  a. Is there enough evidence, and is it reliable?

  b. Does all the evidence support the conclusion?

  c. Does the conclusion avoid absolute terms, such as *all* and *every?*

- For **deductive reasoning,** ask these questions:

  a. Is the general principle true?

  b. Is the specific case true?

  c. Does the conclusion address only the specific case?

Using the Strategies

Answer these questions about the candidates' arguments.

1. Which candidate uses inductive reasoning, and which uses deductive reasoning?

2. Are both arguments sound? If not, which one is flawed, and in what way?

Extending the Strategies

Find an editorial or a political speech, and identify and evaluate its reasoning.

Using Students' Strengths

Visual Learners

Instruct students to create a chart to help them evaluate arguments in a political statement or editorial. They might use one chart to determine whether an argument is inductive or deductive and another to evalute the strength of the argument based on the evaluation criteria taught in the lesson.

Interpersonal Learners

Have students discuss newspaper editorials in small groups. They should determine what type of reasoning is being used and whether the argument is sound. Then each group may present its conclusions about their selected editorial to the class.

Learning for Life

Interviewing Storytellers

OBJECTIVES
1. Document the recollections of older people through oral histories
2. Conduct interviews
3. Choose and complete a project presenting oral histories

Problem

All the short stories in these collections were published, so they are available to a wide audience and will be preserved for years in libraries. But many people have stories in them that are never recorded and so are lost as time passes. What are some ways you can preserve the stories of older people in your community (or even in your own family)?

Project

Interview at least three older people from your community or family and preserve some of their stories (even their brief anecdotes—don't look for full-fledged short stories like the ones in this unit!).

Preparation

1. Think carefully about the people you would like to interview. Ask your teacher or family or friends for suggestions. When you have chosen your subjects, tell them about your project and arrange a meeting with each one.

2. Prepare a list of questions that will encourage each person to recall some stories. You may want to help the person by asking questions like these:

- How did you come to live in this community?
- What was this community or neighborhood like years ago?
- What was your most memorable experience?
- Who is the most unforgettable character you have ever met?
- What is your favorite place in the world?

Procedure

1. Use the questions you prepared as a general guide, but be ready to forget your questions and pursue any interesting memories that your subject mentions.

2. Your interview should be taped. You can take notes immediately after the interview to record anything of interest you noticed about your storyteller (setting, appearance, and so on).

3. Depending on the presentation you choose to make, you might want to take photographs or make drawings of your storyteller.

Presentation

Present your oral history in one of the following formats (or another that your teacher approves):

1. Newspaper Article

Write a feature article for your community or school newspaper about your storytellers and the tales they shared with you. Begin with an introduction that supplies interesting background information on your storytellers. Send photographs, with captions, along with your copy, which should be neatly typed, double-spaced, and carefully proofread.

2. Tape Recording

Edit your stories and present them on tape to your local museum or historical society. You might want to introduce each speaker using your own voice. Design a cover for the tape cassette. On the cover identify your speakers and the places where the stories were recorded.

3. A Display

Plan a storytellers' wall to be set up in some community building—a church, school, town hall, or library. Mount drawings or photographs of the storytellers, and paste their stories under the pictures.

Processing

What did you learn about your community by doing this project? Write a reflection in your portfolio.

Grading Timesaver

Rubrics for this Learning for Life project appear on p. 131 of the *Portfolio Management System*.

Developing Workplace Competencies

Preparation	Procedure	Presentation
• Makes decisions • Works well with people from diverse backgrounds • Acquires data	• Uses resources well • Processes information • Organizes data	• Thinks creatively • Communicates ideas and information

The Nonfiction Collections

340

OBJECTIVES

1. Read nonfiction centered on the topics "We Remember," "A Place Called Home," and "What I Think"
2. Analyze literary elements in nonfiction, with special emphasis on biography and autobiography, essays, the writer's purpose, and persuasive techniques
3. Apply a variety of reading strategies to nonfiction, with special emphasis on critical thinking
4. Respond to the literature using a variety of modes
5. Learn and use new words
6. Plan, draft, revise, edit, proof, and publish an autobiographical narrative, an observational essay, and a persuasive essay
7. Write sentences with prepositional phrases, participial phrases, and clauses
8. Demonstrate the ability to read textbooks, maps, and editorials
9. Learn how to research the law

Selection Readability

This Annotated Teacher's Edition provides a summary of each selection in the student book. Following each Summary heading, you will find one, two, or three small icons. These icons indicate, in an approximate sense, the reading level of the selection.

■ One icon indicates that the selection is easy.
■ ■ Two icons indicate that the selection is on an intermediate reading level.
■ ■ ■ Three icons indicate that the selection is challenging.

*If you believe
in the power of words,
you can bring about
physical changes
in the universe.*

—N. Scott Momaday

Indian petroglyphs,
or rock carvings, on Newspaper Rock,
State Historic Monument, Utah.

Responding to the Quotation

? How can words bring about changes in the universe? [Possible responses: Words communicate thoughts, feelings, and ideas that move people to action; the power of persuasive words can change the way people think and behave.] **What examples can you give of words changing the world?** [Sample responses: Words of the Declaration of Independence began a change in government that has swept the world; words of religious texts have told people how to live and what to value; words of individuals like Martin Luther King, Jr., helped bring about a nonviolent revolution in civil rights.]

RESPONDING TO THE ART

Etched in sandstone, these rock carvings are considered forerunners of writing. Carvings and drawings like these have been found around the world suggesting a universal human impulse behind their creation.

Activity. Have students speculate about the purpose these petroglyphs were meant to serve and who their intended audience may have been. To encourage students to think imaginatively about these creations, ask: What feelings do these carvings evoke in you? What do you think the figures mean? [Possible responses: They might symbolize rituals or successful hunts; they might symbolize life's cycles; the hunters and animals might even have magical significance.]

A Critical Thinking

Expressing an Opinion

[?] Which do you prefer to read—fiction or autobiography? Why? [Some students may prefer fictional stories because they are more imaginative and have more tightly constructed plots and clear-cut resolutions; others may prefer autobiography because it is satisfying to read about real people who endured difficult experiences and survived.]

B Literary Connections

In her memoirs *Coming into the End Zone* and *Extra Innings,* writer Doris Grumbach has addressed the issue of the "truth" of autobiography: "At the moment of retrieval, in the process of recall the initial, observer-limited memory is there, incomplete and biased as it was when first it was stored in the mind. Then it is embroidered and encrusted over time . . . until it is like a barnacle-covered shell, with little of the original shape to be seen.

"Then I write about it, giving the memory a literary shape. I leave out what no longer pleases my view of myself. I embellish with euphony and decorate the prose with some color. I subordinate, giving less importance to some matters, raising others to the weight of coordination. I modify. . . . I persist, driven by the need to record in readable form what I think about and remember, however unreliable."

A Writer on Nonfiction

A CONVERSATION WITH SANDRA CISNEROS

When you begin to read the selections in this collection, you will be entering the world of nonfiction. Before you begin, read what Sandra Cisneros, a writer who writes from her personal experience, has to say about the line between fiction and nonfiction. (You will find selections by Cisneros on pages 183 and 475.)

Q: What would you say nonfiction is?

Cisneros: When I was little and spent a lot of time in the Chicago Public Library, I always had a hard time remembering the difference between the books marked "Fiction" and the books marked "Nonfiction." I think somebody told me the difference once, but I kept forgetting.

The way I made myself remember was like this: *Fiction* means "fake" and *nonfiction* means "nonfake." This definition seemed to satisfy me then.

Q: What about your own writing—is it fiction or nonfiction?

Cisneros: Of course, the question students ask the most is "Is this story real?" In other words, how much of this story is "true" (nonfiction)? Well, all of it is true—kind of. All my fiction stories are based on nonfiction, but I add and cut and paste and change the details to make them "more real"—to make the story more interesting. Does this make sense?

Whenever I read my stories from *The House on Mango Street,* my six brothers and my mother say, "It wasn't like that." Or, "We weren't that poor!" They think I'm writing autobiography (nonfiction) about the real house we once lived in at 1525 N. Campbell Street in Chicago. But I'm doing what every good fiction writer does. I'm taking "real" people and "real" events and rearranging them so as to *create* a better story, because "real" life doesn't have

shape. But real stories do. No wonder they call writers liars.

On the other hand, while writing an article for a magazine the other day, I had to rewrite my essay (nonfiction) and add characters that hadn't really been a part of the true event. It was an essay about my father, but the editor kept asking me, "What about your mother? Where is she? Is she still alive?" Yes, she's very much alive, but she played no part in the story I was telling. However, for the sake of the public that might wonder, "What about your mother?" I had to change the facts a bit and add my mother to the story.

See what I mean? Fiction. Nonfiction. Fake? Nonfake? Such rubbery meanings! What is the difference? Now, *you* tell *me.*

342 THE NONFICTION COLLECTIONS

Connecting Across Texts

Connecting with "Salvador Late or Early" and "Those Who Don't"

Two short selections by Sandra Cisneros appear in students' books. To illustrate and reinforce the points she is making here, have students read these selections now. Her fictional vignette "Salvador Late or Early" begins on p. 183 and her brief autobiographical reflection "Those Who Don't," on p. 475. After students have read these works, have them speculate about what autobiographical details from her own experience Cisneros might have included in

"Salvador." [Possible responses: "a raw wood doorway," "the cigar box of crayons," "cornflakes from a tin cup," a child who must take care of younger siblings, a wrinkled shirt, the children's names.] Then, ask what literary techniques Cisneros might have used to "improve on the facts" in her reflection. [Possible responses: She might have invented the name "Davey the Baby" and "the guy with the crooked eye" to add musical and memorable sound effects.]

Reading Skills and Strategies

READING NONFICTION: CRITICAL THINKING

When we read nonfiction, we are engaged in an active process. We interact with the text just as we do when we read fiction or poetry, but with nonfiction we read more critically. We bring our experiences, knowledge, and memories to nonfiction, but we also bring questions, expectations, and even biases. Here are some of the strategies we use when we read nonfiction.

1. **We ask about the writer.** We don't believe everything we read. We ask if the writer is qualified, if the writer has a bias or a special purpose. Is the writer **informing** or trying to **persuade**?

2. **We try to determine if what we are reading is fact or opinion.** Statements of fact can be verified, but opinions cannot.

3. **We interpret.** It's important that we trust our own knowledge and judgment when we read. We try to figure out the writer's **main idea,** and we decide if we agree with it.

4. **We analyze.** We look to see how convincingly—and how thoroughly—the writer supports the main idea. What facts, examples, incidents, anecdotes, comparisons, and other kinds of information hold up the main idea?

5. **We extend the text.** We put the new information to work. We might want to search for more information or look for another point of view.

6. **We challenge the text.** We reflect on the vision of the world the text offers us, questioning it, perhaps disagreeing with it.

HOW TO OWN A WORD

How do you own a word? For one thing, you start using it. For another thing, you listen to the ways other people use it. You also can ask questions about the word, to try out all the situations in which it is exactly the right word.

Elizabeth Wong, in her memoir about going to Chinese school (page 344), calls Chinatown "chaotic." Below are four questions about the word *chaotic* and some answers.

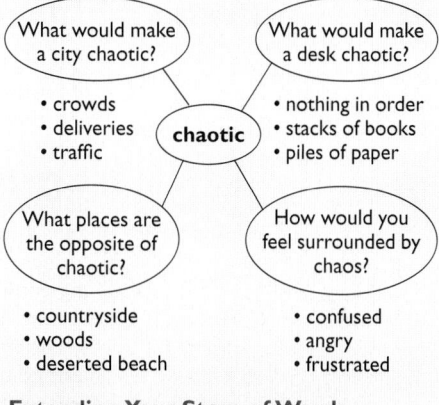

What would make a city chaotic?
- crowds
- deliveries
- traffic

chaotic

What would make a desk chaotic?
- nothing in order
- stacks of books
- piles of paper

What places are the opposite of chaotic?
- countryside
- woods
- deserted beach

How would you feel surrounded by chaos?
- confused
- angry
- frustrated

Extending Your Store of Words

From what you know about *chaotic,* what would you guess about the primeval time that the Greeks called Chaos—the time before the universe was formed? How is chaos worse than mere confusion?

Apply the strategy on the next page.

OBJECTIVES
1. Understand the strategies needed to make meaning from a text
2. Ask questions about a word and use a word to acquire ownership

This feature pays particular attention to the critical thinking skills of questioning, distinguishing fact from opinion, identifying the main idea, extending the text, and challenging the text. These strategies are immediately applied in the following essay, giving students the opportunity to practice the strategies using new material.

Reading Skills and Strategies

This feature focuses on strategies for reading nonfiction, preparing students to use particular critical-thinking skills as they read the selections in this unit.

Mini-Lesson:
Reading Nonfiction—Critical Thinking

After students have read the feature, review its points with the class. You might photocopy a letter to the editor or an editorial from your local newspaper and distribute copies to students. Have students read the piece and then apply these critical thinking questions from the lesson:

1. Who is the writer? Is he or she qualified? biased? Is the writer's purpose to inform or to persuade?
2. Which statements are fact, and which are opinion?
3. What is the main idea? Do you agree with it?
4. What information supports the main idea?
5. What might be another point of view?
6. Do you question the writer's vision? Do you agree or disagree with it?

Mini-Lesson:
How to Own a Word

Sample responses: The Greeks' Chaos must have been a time of total disorder, a state of no form and no boundaries. *Confusion* means things are jumbled and mixed together, suggesting that they can be rearranged in order. *Chaos* means things are out of control.

Summary ▪ ■

As children, the narrator of this memoir and her brother were enrolled by their Chinese mother in an after-school program at a Chinese school. Much more interested in American culture than in her mother's heritage, the narrator rebelled. After two years, she was given a "cultural divorce" and allowed to leave the Chinese school. As an adult, she regrets severing her ties to her mother's culture.

Resources

Listening

Audio CD Library
For a recording of "The Struggle to Be an All-American Girl," see the *Audio CD Library*:
• Disc 13, Track 2

Ⓐ Reading Skills and Strategies

Dialogue with the Text: Interpreting the Text
❓ How does the reader connect her own experience to the text? [Janelle uses her own understanding of emotions to guess at the reason for the narrator's extreme reaction to the principal.]

THE *Struggle* TO BE AN *All-American Girl*

I preferred tacos to egg rolls.

Elizabeth Wong

Dialogue with the Text
The notes that follow show the thoughts of one reader as she read this memoir for the first time. When you read the selection yourself for the first time, cover her responses. Track your own responses on a separate piece of paper, and then compare your responses with Janelle's.

Why did they have to go to school instead of playing with the other children?

Oh, it was to learn Chinese.

Ⓐ She probably saw him in this manner because she was frightened.

It's still there, the Chinese school on Yale Street where my brother and I used to go. Despite the new coat of paint and the high wire fence, the school I knew ten years ago remains remarkably, stoically[1] the same.

Every day at 5 P.M., instead of playing with our fourth- and fifth-grade friends or sneaking out to the empty lot to hunt ghosts and animal bones, my brother and I had to go to Chinese school. No amount of kicking, screaming, or pleading could dissuade my mother, who was solidly determined to have us learn the language of our heritage.

Forcibly, she walked us the seven long, hilly blocks from our home to school, depositing our defiant, tearful faces before the stern principal. My only memory of him is that he swayed on his heels like a palm tree, and he always clasped his impatient, twitching hands behind his back. I recognized him as a repressed maniacal child killer and knew that if we ever saw his hands we'd be in big trouble.

We all sat in little chairs in an empty auditorium. The room

1. **stoically** (stō′ik·lē): indifferently; calmly.

Reaching All Students

Struggling Readers
These students might benefit by tracking details the narrator uses to compare and contrast Chinese culture with American culture. After students have read the selection, have them work with a partner to reread or skim through the selection and create a chart like this one:

Chinese culture	American culture
"pedestrian" sound of Chinese language	"gentle refinement" of Southern speech

English Language Learners
After students have read the selection, have them meet in small groups to discuss what teenage newcomers to the United States might like and dislike about American culture. Suggest that students focus on such things as specific foods, manners, school subjects and activities, shopping, social activities, and holidays. Have groups share their lists with the class and discuss how an adult might feel about the same items.

smelled like Chinese medicine, an imported faraway mustiness. Like ancient mothballs or dirty closets. I hated that smell. I favored crisp new scents. Like the soft French perfume that my American teacher wore in public school.

There was a stage far to the right, flanked by an American flag and the flag of the Nationalist Republic of China,[2] which was also red, white, and blue but not as pretty.

Although the emphasis at the school was mainly language—speaking, reading, writing—the lessons always began with an exercise in politeness. With the entrance of the teacher, the best student would tap a bell and everyone would get up, kowtow,[3] and chant, "Sing san ho," the phonetic for "How are you, teacher?"

Being ten years old, I had better things to learn than ideographs[4] copied painstakingly in lines that ran right to left from the tip of a *moc but,* a real ink pen that had to be held in an awkward way if blotches were to be avoided. After all, I could do the multiplication tables, name the satellites of Mars, and write reports on *Little Women* and *Black Beauty.* Nancy Drew, my favorite book heroine, never spoke Chinese.

The language was a source of embarrassment. More times than not, I had tried to disassociate myself from the nagging loud voice that followed me wherever I wandered in the nearby American supermarket outside Chinatown. The voice belonged to my grandmother, a fragile woman in her seventies who could outshout the best of the street vendors. Her humor was raunchy, her Chinese rhythmless, patternless. It was quick, it was loud, it was unbeautiful. It was not like the quiet, lilting romance of French or the gentle refinement of the American South. Chinese sounded pedestrian. Public.

2. **Nationalist Republic of China:** Republic of China, consisting mainly of Taiwan.
3. **kowtow** (kou′tou′): show respect by kneeling and touching the ground with the forehead.
4. **ideographs** (id′ē·ō·grafs′): written symbols representing objects or ideas. Chinese is written in ideographs.

Dialogue with the Text

It sounds like she would rather try to fit in and be an "All-American" girl rather than a Chinese American girl.

B In this culture the elders and parents are treated with great respect and politeness.

C

She compares everything Chinese with American. American seems to be outweighing Chinese so far.

Her grandmother appears to be overprotective, following her around.

THE STRUGGLE TO BE AN ALL-AMERICAN GIRL 345

Dialogue with the Text

Notice how the narrator structures her essay as a series of comparisons and contrasts.

B Cultural Connections
Showing Respect
❓ Respect for elders is an important aspect of traditional Chinese culture. How did the narrator and her brother show respect to their elders? [They went to the Chinese school even though they did not like it. With the other children, they rose to greet teachers entering the room.] **In what way did they show disrespect?** [They communicated to their mother their defiant feelings about being forced to go to the Chinese school.]

C Reading Skills and Strategies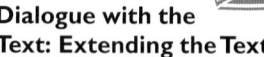
Dialogue with the Text: Extending the Text
❓ What statements by the reader indicate that she is drawing conclusions based on what she reads? [She concludes that the elders and parents in the culture are treated with great respect. She remarks that the narrator seems to prefer the culture of the United States at this point.]

Notice in the student's remarks that she is making many comments about the text. She is involved in her reading.

A Appreciating Language
Word Choice
❓ To what does the narrator compare her break with Chinese culture? ["a cultural divorce"] What does this wording suggest? [Possible responses: a permanent separation; a complete break.]

B Reading Skills and Strategies
Drawing Conclusions
❓ As a child, the narrator chose to turn her back on her Chinese heritage. As an adult, what feelings does she have about her decision? [She regrets having broken her ties to her Chinese heritage.]

C Reading Skills and Strategies

Dialogue with the Text: Challenging the Text
❓ What makes the reader's comment an especially thoughtful concluding observation? [The reader is challenging the text. She is also stating her interpretation of the main idea.]

Dialogue with the Text

She really wants to fit in in America, but everything is holding her back.

She has a lot of potential in the real world, but she is locked up in her own Chinatown world.

This is the complete opposite of what usually happens. Mothers usually correct their children in their English.

Everyone tries to find a scape-goat when they make a mistake.

She fits in now, mostly, but she is still Chinese. She should be proud of the fact that she has a unique heritage.

Janelle Jones
—Janelle Jones
Southeast High School
Bradenton, Florida

In Chinatown, the comings and goings of hundreds of Chinese on their daily tasks sounded chaotic[5] and frenzied. I did not want to be thought of as mad, as talking gibberish. When I spoke English, people nodded at me, smiled sweetly, said encouraging words. Even the people in my culture would cluck and say that I'd do well in life. "My, doesn't she move her lips fast," they would say, meaning that I'd be able to keep up with the world outside Chinatown.

My brother was even more fanatical than I about speaking English. He was especially hard on my mother, criticizing her, often cruelly, for her pidgin speech—smatterings of Chinese scattered like chop suey in her conversation. "It's not 'what it is,' Mom," he'd say in exasperation. "It's 'What *is* it, what *is* it, what *is* it!'" Sometimes Mom might leave out an occasional "the" or "a," or perhaps a verb of being. He would stop her in midsentence: "Say it again, Mom. Say it right." When he tripped over his own tongue, he'd blame it on her: "See, Mom, it's all your fault. You set a bad example."

What infuriated my mother most was when my brother cornered her on her consonants, especially "r." My father had played a cruel joke on Mom by assigning her an American name that her tongue wouldn't allow her to say. No matter how hard she tried, "Ruth" always ended up "Luth" or "Roof."

A After two years of writing with a *moc but* and reciting words with multiples of meanings, I finally was granted a cultural divorce. I was permitted to stop Chinese school.

I thought of myself as multicultural. I preferred tacos to egg rolls; I enjoyed Cinco de Mayo[6] more than Chinese New Year.

B At last, I was one of you; I wasn't one of them.
Sadly, I still am.

5. **chaotic** (kā·ät′ik): completely confused; in total disorder.
6. **Cinco de Mayo** (siŋ′kô de mä′yô): holiday celebrated by Mexicans and Mexican Americans in honor of a Mexican military victory in 1862. *Cinco de Mayo* is Spanish for "May 5."

Assessing Learning

Check Test: True-False
1. The narrator went to Chinese school with her sister. [False]
2. The auditorium at the Chinese school smelled good to the author. [False]
3. At the Chinese school, lessons always started with an exercise in politeness. [True]
4. The narrator regrets losing her connections to her Chinese heritage. [True]

We Remember

Theme

Their Own Stories *The story of someone else's life is fascinating because it gives us the opportunity to see what is ordinarily kept inside. In all of the selections in this collection, writers share their private experiences or observations. In so doing, they give us a chance to know another human being and to identify their hopes and fears with our own.*

Reading the Anthology

Reaching Struggling Readers

The *Reading Skills and Strategies: Reaching Struggling Readers* binder provides materials coordinated with the Pupil's Edition (see the Collection Planner on p. T346B) to help students who have difficulty reading and comprehending text, or students who are reluctant readers. The binder for ninth grade is organized around sixteen individual skill areas and offers the following options:

- **Mini Read** MiniReads are short, easy texts that give students a chance to practice a particular skill and strategy before reading selections in the Pupil's Edition. Each MiniRead Skill Lesson can be taught independently or used in conjunction with a Selection Skill Lesson.

- **Selection Skill Lessons** Selection Skill Lessons allow students to apply skills introduced in the MiniReads. Each Selection Skill Lesson provides reading instruction and practice specific to a particular piece of literature in the Pupil's Edition.

Reading Beyond the Anthology

Read On

Each collection in the grade nine book includes an annotated bibliography of books suitable for extended reading. The suggested books are related to works in the collection by theme, by author, or by subject. To preview the Read On for Collection 5, please turn to p. T385.

HRW Library

The *HRW Library* offers novels, plays, works of nonfiction, and short-story collections for extended reading. Each book in the Library includes a major work and thematically or topically related Connections. Each book in the *HRW Library* is also accompanied by a Study Guide that provides teaching suggestions and worksheets.

FAREWELL TO MANZANAR
Jeanne Wakatsuki Houston
James D. Houston
This memoir of a Japanese American family's years in an internment camp deals with people's responses to conflicts of tradition, culture, and patriotism.

THE GLORY FIELD
Walter Dean Myers
This multi-generational saga depicts key moments in the life of African Americans from 1753 to 1994.

Collection Planner

Collection 5 We Remember

Resources for this Collection

Note: All resources for this collection are available for preview on the *One-Stop Planner CD-ROM 1 with Test Generator.* All worksheets and blackline masters may be printed from the CD-ROM.

Internet Resources
go.hrw.com LE0 9-5

Selection or Feature	Reading and Literary Skills	Vocabulary, Language, and Grammar
Not Much of Me (p. 348) **With a Task Before Me** (p. 350) Abraham Lincoln **Connections: Two Letters** Abraham Lincoln and Grace Bedell (p. 351)	• *Graphic Organizers for Active Reading,* Worksheet p. 21 • *Literary Elements:* Transparency 7 Worksheet p. 22	• *Words to Own,* Worksheet p. 16 • *Grammar and Language Links:* Punctuation, Worksheet p. 35 • *Language Workshop CD-ROM,* Punctuation • *Daily Oral Grammar,* Transparency 21
Elements of Literature: Biography and Autobiography (p. 355)	• *Literary Elements,* Transparency 7	
"When I Lay My Burden Down" *from* **I Know Why the Caged Bird Sings** Maya Angelou (p. 356) **Connections: Sympathy** Paul Laurence Dunbar (p. 362)	• *Graphic Organizers for Active Reading,* Worksheet p. 22	• *Words to Own,* Worksheet p. 17 • *Grammar and Language Links:* Comparisons, Worksheet p. 37 • *Language Workshop CD-ROM,* Comparative and Superlative Forms • *Daily Oral Grammar,* Transparency 22
Choice: A Tribute to Dr. Martin Luther King, Jr. Alice Walker (p. 366) **Connections: No One Ever Told Me Not to Dream** *from* **In My Place** Charlayne Hunter-Gault (p. 371)	• *Reading Skills and Strategies: Reaching Struggling Readers* • MiniRead Skill Lesson, p. 90 • Selection Skill Lesson, p. 96 • *Graphic Organizers for Active Reading,* Worksheet p. 23	• *Words to Own,* Worksheet p. 18 • *Grammar and Language Links:* Emotional Context, Worksheet p. 39 • *Daily Oral Grammar,* Transparency 23
The Talk Gary Soto (p. 375)	• *Graphic Organizers for Active Reading,* Worksheet p. 24	• *Daily Oral Grammar,* Transparency 24
Extending the Theme: Ballad of Birmingham Dudley Randall (p. 383)	The Extending the Theme feature provides students with an unstructured opportunity to practice reading strategies using a selection that extends the theme of the collection.	
Writer's Workshop: Autobiographical Incident (p. 386)		
Sentence Workshop: Prepositional Phrases (p. 391)		• *Workshop Resources,* p. 69 • *Language Workshop CD-ROM,* Prepositional Phrases

Collection Planner

Other Resources for this Collection

- *Cross-Curricular Activities,* p. 5
- *Portfolio Management System,* Introduction to Portfolio Assessment, p. 1
- *Test Generator,* Collection Test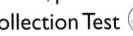

Writing	Listening and Speaking Viewing and Representing	Assessment
• *Portfolio Management System,* Rubrics for Choices, p. 132	• *Audio CD Library,* Disc 13, Tracks 3, 4 • *Viewing and Representing:* Fine Art Transparency 7; Worksheet p. 28 • *Portfolio Management System,* Rubrics for Choices, p. 132	• *Formal Assessment,* Selection Test, p. 56 • *Standardized Test Preparation,* p. 44 • *Test Generator (One-Stop Planner CD-ROM)*
		• *Formal Assessment,* Literary Elements Test, p. 64
• *Portfolio Management System,* Rubrics for Choices, p. 134	• *Audio CD Library,* Disc 13, Tracks 5, 6 • *Portfolio Management System,* Rubrics for Choices, p. 134	• *Formal Assessment,* Selection Test, p. 58 • *Test Generator (One-Stop Planner CD-ROM)*
• *Portfolio Management System,* Rubrics for Choices, p. 135	• *Audio CD Library,* Disc 13, Track 7 • *Portfolio Management System,* Rubrics for Choices, p. 135	• *Formal Assessment,* Selection Test, p. 60 • *Standardized Test Preparation,* pp. 46, 48 • *Test Generator (One-Stop Planner CD-ROM)*
• *Portfolio Management System,* Rubrics for Choices, p. 136	• *Visual Connections:* Videocassette A, Segment 5 • *Audio CD Library,* Disc 13, Track 8 • *Portfolio Management System,* Rubrics for Choices, p. 136	• *Formal Assessment,* Selection Test, p. 62 • *Standardized Test Preparation,* p. 50 • *Test Generator (One-Stop Planner CD-ROM)*
	• *Audio CD Library,* Disc 13, Track 9	

• *Workshop Resources,* p. 25
• *Writer's Workshop 2 CD-ROM,* Autobiographical Incident
		• *Portfolio Management System*
		  • Prewriting, p. 137
		  • Peer Editing, p. 138
		  • Assessment Rubric, p. 139

 Transparency  CD-ROM  Video  Audio CD

Collection Planner

T346C

Skills Focus

Skills Focus

Selection or Feature	Reading Skills and Strategies	Elements of Literature	Language/ Grammar	Vocabulary/ Spelling	Writing	Listening/ Speaking	Viewing/ Representing
Not Much of Me (p. 348) **With a Task Before Me** (p. 350) Abraham Lincoln	Use Prior Knowledge, pp. 348, 352 Identify Main Events, p. 352	Tone, pp. 348, 352 Chronological Order, p. 353	Historical Shifts in Punctuation, Capitalization, and Spelling, p. 354	Cluster Diagram, p. 354	Collect Ideas for an Autobiographical Incident, p. 353 Write a Letter to Lincoln, p. 353 Write a Campaign Appeal for Lincoln, p. 353	Research and Present a Tribute to Lincoln, p. 353	Create a Time Line, p. 353
Elements of Literature: Biography and Autobiography (p. 355)		Biography and Autobiography, p. 355 Diary, p. 355 Objectivity, p. 355 Subjectivity, p. 355					
"When I Lay My Burden Down" *from* **I Know Why the Caged Bird Sings** Maya Angelou (p. 356)	Compare Texts, pp. 356, 363	Imagery, pp. 356, 363 Setting, p. 363 Title, p. 363	Comparisons, p. 365 • Personification • Simile • Metaphor	Semantic Mapping, p. 365 Synonyms, p. 365	Elaborate on an Incident, p. 364 Rewrite a Scene from a Different Perspective, p. 364	Present a Found Poem, p. 364	Design and Illustrate the Set for a TV Show, p. 364
Choice: A Tribute to Dr. Martin Luther King, Jr. Alice Walker (p. 366)	Identify the Main Idea, pp. 366, 372 Make Inferences, p. 366 Identify Key Statements, p. 366 Summarize the Main Idea, p. 373	Main Idea, pp. 366, 372–373 Implied Main Idea, p. 366 Setting, p. 372 Title, p. 372 Motive, p. 372	Emotional Context, p. 374 Connotation, p. 374 Denotation, p. 374	New Words, p. 374	Decide on a Cast of Characters, p. 373 Write about a Place You Love, p. 373 Write a Feature Article, p. 373	Present Alice Walker's Speech on Dr. Martin Luther King, Jr., p. 373	
The Talk Gary Soto (p. 375)	Find the Main Idea, pp. 375, 380	Exaggeration, pp. 375, 380 Tone, p. 380		Analogies, p. 381	Determine an Appropriate Tone, p. 380 Respond to the Author, p. 380		Draw Caricatures of Characters, p. 380
Extending the Theme: Ballad of Birmingham Dudley Randall (p. 383)	Dialogue with the Text, p. 383	Folk Ballads, p. 384 Literary Ballads, p. 384	The Extending the Theme feature provides students with an unstructured opportunity to practice reading strategies using a selection that extends the theme of the collection.				
Writer's Workshop: Autobiographical Incident (p. 386)					Write an Autobiographical Incident, pp. 386–390		Create a Story Map, p. 387
Sentence Workshop: Prepositional Phrases (p. 391)			Prepositional Phrases, p. 391 • Adjective • Adverb		Expand Sentences Using Prepositional Phrases, p. 391		
Reading for Life: Reading Textbooks (p. 392)	Read to Obtain Information, p. 392 • Evaluate Authorship • Preview Book Features • Analyze Graphics						

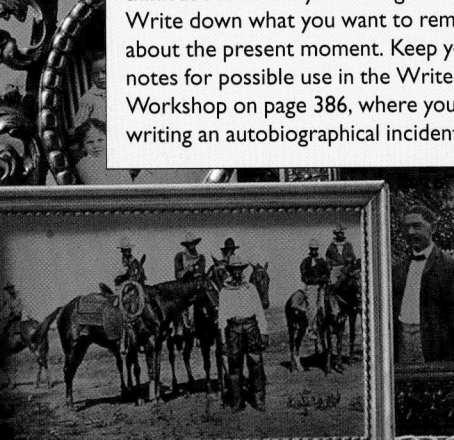

WE REMEMBER

WRITING FOCUS: Autobiographical Incident

Collection 5

Most of us are only half aware of the days we're living through. We barely notice their flavor and their rhythms. We don't realize that gradually these days will transform themselves into memories and will fade into vague shadows in our minds. There we will catch a glimpse of them only occasionally, perhaps when a song brings back, for just a second, the person who sang it long ago, or a scene calls to mind a place we visited long ago. Almost all writers start with memories. A French writer, Marcel Proust, wrote his greatest work after a taste of cake released a flood of childhood memories.

Writer's Notebook

"Life," the saying goes, "is what happens while you're making other plans." What does that mean? Perhaps it means that we don't pay enough attention to the present. Perhaps it means that we lose today because we're thinking about tomorrow—or about what we want instead of what we have. If you're busy making other plans, lay them aside for a few minutes and think about where you are right now. Write down what you want to remember about the present moment. Keep your notes for possible use in the Writer's Workshop on page 386, where you'll be writing an autobiographical incident.

Some memories are realities and are better than anything that can ever happen to one again.

—Willa Cather

OBJECTIVES

1. Read autobiographical incidents centered on the topic "We Remember"
2. Interpret literary elements in nonfiction, with special emphasis on biography and autobiography
3. Apply a variety of reading strategies to the literature, including finding the main idea
4. Respond to the literature using a variety of modes
5. Learn and use new words
6. Plan, draft, revise, edit, proof, and publish an autobiographical narrative
7. Expand sentences with prepositional phrases
8. Demonstrate the ability to read textbooks

Responding to the Quotation

How can memories be realities? Ask volunteers to offer examples of memories that continue to surface in their awareness—memories that are not too private to share with the class. Discuss the fact that some moments from the past are so vivid and unforgettable that replaying them in one's mind can make the present moment vanish from awareness.

RESPONDING TO THE ART

Activity. Discuss with students how photographs, which freeze a moment in time, can trigger vivid memories. Students might compare the photos and frames shown with ones of their own. They might also talk about other memorabilia that help them recapture moments in the past.

Writer's Notebook

Suggest that students focus on the five senses as they write about the present.

Writing Focus: Autobiographical Incident

The following **Work in Progress** assignments build to a culminating **Writer's Workshop** at the end of the collection.

- Not Much of Me / With a Task Before Me — Focusing on important events and places (p. 353)
- "When I Lay My Burden Down" — Focusing on people and places (p. 364)
- Choice: A Tribute to Dr. Martin Luther King, Jr. — Focusing on people (p. 373)
- The Talk — Deciding on tone (p. 380)

Writer's Workshop: Narrative Writing / Autobiographical Incident (p. 386)

Not Much .../With a Task ...
1. Read and interpret the auto-biographical sketch and the speech
2. Analyze tone
3. Use prior knowledge
4. Express understanding through creative writing, research, and speaking
5. Use correct punctuation, capitalization, and spelling
6. Use cluster diagrams to master new words

SKILLS

Literary
- Analyze tone

Reading
- Use prior knowledge

Writing
- Recall past events
- Write a letter
- Write a campaign appeal

Speaking/Listening
- Read a speech or poem

Grammar
- Use correct punctuation, capitalization, and spelling

Vocabulary
- Construct cluster diagrams

Research/History
- Create a time line

Viewing/Representing
- Interpret a caricature (ATE)

Planning

- **Block Schedule**
  Block Scheduling Lesson Plans with Pacing Guide

- **Traditional Schedule**
  Lesson Plans Including Strategies for English-Language Learners

- **One-Stop Planner**
  CD-ROM with Test Generator

Before You Read

NOT MUCH OF ME/WITH A TASK BEFORE ME

Make the Connection

In His Own Words

You probably know a lot about Abraham Lincoln from what biographers and historians have written, from what teachers have said, and from what you've seen on TV. All of this information comes from people other than Lincoln. What do you think you might learn about Lincoln from Lincoln himself—from his own words?

Reading Skills and Strategies

Using Prior Knowledge: What's New?

All the things you have heard or read about Abraham Lincoln are **prior knowledge**. For instance, you probably know that he was president during the Civil War. What else? Do you know anything about his appearance? His family? Using a chart like the one below, record some of the things you know about him. Then, when you have finished reading these autobiographical notes, record the new information Lincoln has given you about himself.

What I Know	New Information

Elements of Literature

Tone: Don't Miss It

In speech, tone is expressed through voice, body language, and word choice. In writing, tone is expressed primarily through the writer's choice of words. In autobiographical writing, tone is especially revealing. The writer can be modest or boastful about accomplishments, satirical or generous about other people, comical or serious about life. When you read any piece of writing, you must be sensitive to the writer's tone. If you misinterpret tone, you've missed the whole point.

> **T**one is the attitude a writer takes toward an audience, a subject, or a character.
>
> *For more on Tone, see pages 586–587 and the Handbook of Literary Terms.*

go.hrw.com
LEO 9-5

Not Much of Me
Abraham Lincoln

Background

Just five months before his nomination to the presidency in 1860, Lincoln wrote this sketch as background for newspaper writers in the eastern United States. "There is not much of it," Lincoln apologized, "for the reason, I suppose, that there is not much of me." It is one of the few things that he ever wrote about himself. It is reproduced here just as Lincoln wrote it—you will find some unusual spellings and punctuation.

   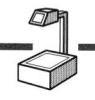

Resources: Print and Media

Reading
- *Graphic Organizers for Active Reading*, p. 21
- *Words to Own*, p. 16
- *Audio CD Library*
  Disc 13, Tracks 3, 4

Elements of Literature
- *Literary Elements*
  Transparency 7
  Worksheet, p. 22

Writing and Language
- *Daily Oral Grammar*
  Transparency 21
- *Grammar and Language Links*
  Worksheet, p. 35
- *Language Workshop CD-ROM*

Viewing and Representing
- *Viewing and Representing*
  Fine Art Transparency 7
  Fine Art Worksheet, p. 28

Assessment
- *Formal Assessment*, p. 56
- *Portfolio Management System*, p. 132
- *Standardized Test Preparation*, p. 44
- *Test Generator (One-Stop Planner CD-ROM)*

Internet
- *go.hrw.com (keyword: LEO 9-5)*

I was born Feb. 12, 1809, in Hardin County, Kentucky. My parents were both born in Virginia, of undistinguished families—second families, perhaps I should say. My mother, who died in my tenth year, was of a family of the name of Hanks, some of whom now reside in Adams and others in Macon counties, Illinois. My paternal grandfather, Abraham Lincoln, emigrated from Rockingham County, Virginia, to Kentucky, about 1781 or 2, where, a year or two later, he was killed by indians, not in battle, but by stealth, when he was laboring to open a farm in the forest. His ancestors, who were quakers, went to Virginia from Berks County, Pennsylvania. An effort to identify them with the New-England family of the same name ended in nothing more definite than a similarity of Christian names in both families, such as Enoch, Levi, Mordecai, Solomon, Abraham, and the like.

My father, at the death of his father, was but six years of age; and he grew up, litterally without education. He removed from Kentucky to what is now Spencer county, Indiana, in my eighth year. We reached our new home about the time the State came in the Union. It was a wild region, with many bears and other wild animals still in the woods. There I grew up. There were some schools, so called; but no qualification was ever required of a teacher, beyond "*readin, writin,* and *cipherin,*" to the Rule of Three. If a straggler supposed to understand latin, happened to sojourn in the neighborhood, he was looked upon as a wizzard. There was absolutely nothing to excite ambition for education. Of course when I came of age I did not know much. Still somehow, I could read, write, and cipher to the Rule of Three; but that was all. I have not been to school since. The little advance I now have upon this store of education, I have picked up from time to time under the pressure of necessity.

I was raised to farm work, which I continued  till I was twenty-two. At twenty-one I came to Illinois, and passed the first year in Illinois—Macon county. Then I got to New-Salem (at that time in Sangamon, now in Menard county), where I remained a year as a sort of Clerk in a store. Then came the Black-Hawk war;[1] and I was elected a Captain of Volunteers—a success which gave me more pleasure than any I have had since. I went the campaign, was elated, ran for the Legislature the same year (1832) and was beaten—the only time I have been beaten by the people. The next, and three succeeding biennial[2] elections, I was elected to the Legislature. I was not a candidate afterwards. During this Legislative period I had studied law, and removed to Springfield to practice it. In 1846 I was once elected to the lower House of Congress. Was not a candidate for re-election. From 1849 to 1854, both inclusive, practiced law more assiduously than ever before. Always a whig[3] in politics, and generally on the whig electoral tickets, making active canvasses.[4] I was losing interest in politics, when the repeal of the Missouri Compromise[5] aroused me again. What I have done since then is pretty well known.

If any personal description of me is thought desirable, it may be said, I am, in height, six feet, four inches, nearly; lean in flesh, weighing, on an average, one hundred and eighty pounds; dark complexion, with coarse black hair, and grey eyes—no other marks or brands recollected. Yours very truly,

A. Lincoln

1. **Black-Hawk war:** war between the United States and the Sauk and Fox tribes in 1832. Black Hawk (1767–1838) was chief of the Sauk people and a leader in the war.
2. **biennial** (bī·en′ē·əl): happening every two years.
3. **whig:** Whigs favored a less powerful presidency than Democrats, but both parties split over the question of slavery.
4. **canvasses:** requests for votes.
5. **Missouri Compromise:** agreement reached in 1820 admitting Maine to the Union as a free state (one where slavery was illegal) and Missouri as a slave state, but limiting the creation of other slave states to the area south of Missouri.

WORDS TO OWN

elated (ē·lāt′id) *v.* used as *adj.*: very happy.
assiduously (ə·sij′oo·əs·lē) *adv.*: industriously; in a careful and hard-working manner.

Preteaching Vocabulary

Words to Own

Ask partners to read the Words to Own and their definitions at the bottom of p. 349. Have them reinforce their knowledge of the words with these exercises:

1. Speak in a tone that expresses an **elated** feeling.
2. Work **assiduously** at your desks.
3. Give a short speech about yourself, a family member, or a friend, using the words *elated* and *assiduously.*

Summary ■■■

In this autobiographical sketch, Lincoln describes his family's humble origins and their westward migrations, as well as his brief schooling in rural Indiana, his service in the Black Hawk War of 1832, his campaigns for the Illinois legislature, and his practice of law. He ends with a humorous physical description of himself.

Resources ——

Listening
Audio CD Library
Lincoln's words come to life on a recording in the *Audio CD Library:*
• Disc 13, Tracks 3, 4

Viewing and Representing
Fine Art Transparency
A Fine Art Transparency of Henry O. Tanner's "An Old Couple Looking at Lincoln" can be used to have students compare their attitudes toward Lincoln with the couple's attitude. See *Viewing and Representing*
• Transparency 7
• Worksheet, p. 28

Elements of Literature
Biography and Autobiography
For more instruction on biography and autobiography, see *Literary Elements*
• Transparency 7
• Worksheet, p. 22

Ⓐ **Reading Skills and Strategies**
Using Prior Knowledge
❓ Up to this point, what have you read that you already knew about Lincoln? What new information have you learned? [Sample responses: Prior knowledge—Lincoln was self-educated; he grew up in a wild area. New information—his mother died when he was ten; he worked as a farmer.]

Ⓑ **Elements of Literature**
Tone
❓ What is Lincoln comparing himself to with the words "marks or brands"? [livestock] What tone does his choice of words reveal? [Possible responses: a humorous tone; a playful tone.]

T349

Summary ■■

Lincoln emotionally bids farewell to the people of Springfield, Illinois, as he prepares to move to Washington as America's newly elected president. Saddened by his departure, he fondly remembers the past and calls on divine guidance to help him.

 Elements of Literature

Tone

❓ How would you describe Lincoln's tone in this address? What words and phrases reveal his tone? [Possible responses: His tone is serious, sad, nostalgic; the details "sadness," "parting," "one is buried," and "whether ever, I may return" reveal his tone.]

B Reading Skills and Strategies

Using Prior Knowledge

❓ What were the tasks that Lincoln and Washington faced? [Washington faced winning the war with England and leading a new nation. Lincoln faced dealing with the threat of civil war and preserving the Union.]

Resources

Selection Assessment
Formal Assessment
• Selection Test, p. 56
Test Generator (One-Stop Planner)
• CD-ROM

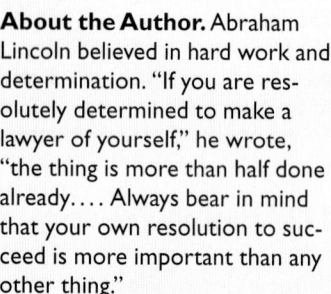

BROWSING IN THE FILES

About the Author. Abraham Lincoln believed in hard work and determination. "If you are resolutely determined to make a lawyer of yourself," he wrote, "the thing is more than half done already.... Always bear in mind that your own resolution to succeed is more important than any other thing."

Background

Elected president in 1860, Lincoln had the sad task of bidding farewell to his home—Springfield, Illinois. He delivered the emotional address "With a Task Before Me" from the back of the train he boarded for the long trip to his new life in Washington. As you read, imagine Lincoln delivering these simple, eloquent words over the noisy chaos of a train depot. There is a particular sadness to this speech. In Washington four years later, Lincoln was assassinated. He was buried in Springfield.

With a Task Before Me
Abraham Lincoln

My friends—No one, not in my situation, can appreciate my feeling of sadness at this parting. To this place, and the kindness of these people, I owe every thing. Here I have lived a quarter of a century, and have passed from a young to an old man. Here my children have been born, and one is buried. I now leave, not knowing when, or whether ever, I may return, with a task before me greater than that which rested upon Washington. Without the assistance of that Divine Being, who ever attended him, I cannot succeed. With that assistance I cannot fail. Trusting in Him, who can go with me, and remain with you and be every where for good, let us confidently hope that all will yet be well. To His care commending you, as I hope in your prayers you will commend me, I bid you an affectionate farewell.

MEET THE WRITER

A Way with Words

Abraham Lincoln (1809–1865) had a way with words and loved to tell stories. People listened to him and people liked him.

When Lincoln ran for the U.S. Senate against Stephen A. Douglas in 1858, he lost the election but won recognition for his brilliant speeches during their now-famous debates. Lincoln's way with words continued after he was elected president in 1860.

His Gettysburg Address (1863), for example, is less than three hundred words in length but is considered one of the greatest speeches by an American political leader. The speech is notable especially for its vision of American democracy: ". . . that this nation, under God, shall have a new birth of freedom—and that government of the people, by the people, for the people, shall not perish from the earth."

Lincoln had four children, all boys; three of his boys died young. The following words are said to have been written on the day one of his sons started school:

❝World, take my son by the hand—he starts to school today. . . .
Try to give my son the strength not to follow the crowd when everyone else is getting on the bandwagon. Teach him to listen to all men, but to filter all he hears on a screen of truth and to take only the good that comes through.
Teach him gently, World, but don't coddle him, because only the test of fire makes fine steel.
This is a big order, World, but see what you can do.
He's such a nice little fellow. . . .❞

Reaching All Students

Struggling Readers

To help these students determine chronological order in Lincoln's life, have them imagine that they are going to create a résumé for Lincoln and are collecting major facts about him. Tell them to outline important information in these areas: his birth, his mother, where he grew up, his education, first work, first major success, positions held, additional studies, a physical description. Students can compare their outlines in a small group.

English Language Learners

Have students read the selections with peer tutors. Ask the partners to identify important facts in each of these categories: (1) family background, (2) early education, (3) career, (4) physical description. For additional strategies for engaging English language learners with the literature, see
• *Lesson Plans Including Strategies for English-Language Learners*

Connections — TWO LETTERS

N Y
Westfield Chatauque Co
Oct 15. 1860

Hon A B Lincoln
Dear Sir
My father has just [come] home from the fair and brought home your picture and Mr. [Hannibal] Hamlin's [Lincoln's running mate]. I am a little girl only eleven years old, but want you should be President of the United States very much so I hope you wont think me very bold to write to such a great man as you are. Have you any little girls about as large as I am if so give them my love and tell her to write to me if you cannot answer this letter. I have got 4 brother's and part of them will vote for you any way and if you will let your whiskers grow I will try and get the rest of them to vote for you you would look a great deal better for your face is so thin. All the ladies like whiskers and they would tease their husband's to vote for you and then you would be President. My father is a going to vote for you and if I was a man I would vote for you to but I will try and get every one to vote for you that I can I think that rail fence around your picture makes it look very pretty. I have got a little baby sister she is nine weeks old and is just as cunning as can be. When you direct your letter dir[e]ct to Grace Bedell Westfield Chatauque County New York
I must not write any more answer this letter right off Good bye

Grace Bedell

PRIVATE

Springfield, Ills.
Oct. 19. 1860

Miss. Grace Bedell
My dear little Miss.
Your very agreeable letter of the 15th. is received.
I regret the necessity of saying I have no daughters. I have three sons—one seventeen, one nine, and one seven, years of age. They, with their mother, constitute my whole family.
As to the whiskers, never having worn any, do you not think people would call it a piece of silly affect[at]ion if I were to begin it now? Your very sincere well-wisher

A. Lincoln.

Presidential candidate Lincoln answered this letter—probably the most famous piece of advice he ever received—with an equally well-known reply.

Connections

When eleven-year-old Grace Bedell wrote a letter of support and advice to Lincoln, he replied personally.

FROM THE EDITOR'S DESK
We thought students would enjoy seeing how Lincoln responded to a letter from an admirer only a few years younger than themselves.

A Historical Connections
Equal Rights
Women finally obtained the right to vote in the United States on August 26, 1920, with the passage of the Nineteenth Amendment to the Constitution.

B Elements of Literature
Tone
❓ How is Lincoln's sense of humor shown here? [In a lighthearted tone ("I regret the necessity . . ."), he makes a gently ironic apology for not having any daughters.]

C Reading Skills and Strategies
Making Inferences
❓ What character trait does Lincoln's question reveal about him? [Possible responses: his modesty; his dislike of artificiality.]

Connecting Across Texts

Connecting with "Not Much of Me"
Discuss with students how Lincoln's letter connects with "Not Much of Me." Ask: What characteristics does Lincoln reveal about himself in both his letter to Grace Bedell and "Not Much of Me"? [Possible responses: his playfulness; his modesty.] What new side of him is revealed in his letter? [Possible responses: his love of family; his concern for people.]

Assessing Learning

Check Test: True-False
"Not Much of Me"
1. Abraham Lincoln's parents were both lawyers. [False]
2. At school, Lincoln was educated in Latin and algebra. [False]
"With a Task Before Me"
3. Lincoln was sorry to leave Springfield, Illinois. [True]
4. Lincoln was confident of his success in the presidency. [False]

Standardized Test Preparation
For practice with standardized test format specific to this selection, see
• *Standardized Test Preparation,* p. 44
For practice in proofreading and editing, see
• *Daily Oral Grammar,* Transparency 21

First Thoughts

1. Possible new information: Lincoln had a good sense of humor; at times, he felt uncertain. Students may feel closer to him.

Shaping Interpretations

2. Possible responses: *humble*—"My parents were both born . . . of undistinguished families"; *serious*—"From 1849 to 1854, both inclusive, practiced law more assiduously than ever before"; *playful*—"No other marks or brands recollected."

3. Lincoln states that he could read, write, and do basic mathematics. Other knowledge he picked up was "under the pressure of necessity." Students may say Lincoln's determination or his ambition or his love of learning led to his success.

4. It means that Lincoln left out what motivated him. Students might wonder why he went into law and politics or how he formed his opinions on slavery.

Extending the Texts

5. Students may say modern presidents might focus on their family life, public or military service, education, aspirations, and achievements. Students may suggest a humorous, solemn, defensive, regretful, or nostalgic tone.

6. Possible responses: Lincoln's humor and humility might have voter appeal; his untelegenic appearance might not. He might run on a platform of honesty in government. The media would be won over by him. His "handlers" might keep him from speaking his mind.

RESPONDING TO THE ART

Frank Bellew (1828–1888) was an American illustrator and caricaturist.

Activity. This caricature appeared when Lincoln was reelected to a second term. Ask students to explain the pun in the caption. [Lincoln's height is exaggerated, or "a little longer" than in reality, and he is to serve "a little longer" in time.]

First Thoughts

[respond]

1. Did these two pieces tell you anything new about Abraham Lincoln? Did they affect the way you feel about him? Be sure to complete the chart you filled in before you read.

Reading Check

What was important about Lincoln's eventful life? Make a list, in **chronological order**, of the **main events** in Lincoln's life up to the time he wrote "Not Much of Me."

Shaping Interpretations

[analyze]

2. People reveal a great deal about themselves when they look back on their lives. Which of the following words would you use to describe Lincoln's **tone** as he writes about himself in "Not Much of Me"? Find details in the selection to support your answers.

bitter	critical	serious
playful	humorous	awed
regretful	affectionate	sad
nostalgic	humble	sarcastic

[infer]

3. How does Lincoln describe his education? What do you think enabled him to achieve so much?

[connect]

4. Someone once said that Lincoln omitted from this thumbnail autobiography all that gave his life direction. What do you think this means—what would you like to ask Lincoln about his life that he failed to tell you?

Extending the Texts

[extend]

5. If someone asked any of the recent presidents to sum up their lives, what might they focus on? What **tone** do you think these modern presidents might take?

[extend]

6. In 1860, when Lincoln ran for president, television was not available. Most of his speeches were delivered to local crowds and then published, sometimes days later, in newspapers or on posters. Suppose Abraham Lincoln were alive today and planned to run for president of the United States. What do you think his chances would be? What kind of platform do you think he would run on? How would the media treat him? How would he do in television campaigning?

From *Harper's Weekly*, November 26, 1864.

Long Abraham Lincoln a Little Longer by Frank Bellew.

Reading Check

Possible list of main events:

1. He was born February 12, 1809.
2. His mother died when he was ten.
3. He had little formal education.
4. He did farm work until he was twenty-two.
5. He was a captain in the Black Hawk War in 1832.
6. He lost a race for the Illinois legislature in 1832 but was later elected and served from 1834 to 1840.
7. He moved to Springfield, Illinois, where he practiced law.
8. He served one term in the House of Representatives, from 1846 to 1848.

CHOICES: Building Your Portfolio

Writer's Notebook

1. Collecting Ideas for an Autobiographical Incident

It happened to you.

When you write your autobiographical incident for the Writer's Workshop on page 386, you'll be writing about an event that happened to *you*—you'll be your own main character. Think about all the important **events** that have happened to you since you were born. Think also of the **places** you've known and perhaps even of your family's **history** before your arrival in their midst. Take notes to see if there is something in your past you'd like to use in your autobiographical incident.

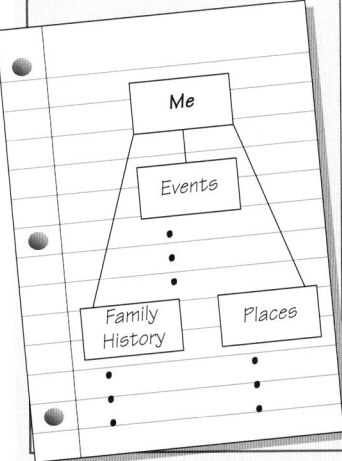

Creative Writing

2. Dear Mr. President

Grace Bedell wrote a letter of advice to Lincoln (see **Connections** on page 351). If you were to write a letter to Lincoln from this century, what would you tell him about equal opportunity in the Union he struggled to preserve? What advice would you ask him for?

Research/History

3. A Life on the Line

Several dates are mentioned in these selections. Use the dates to create a time line showing, in **chronological order,** significant events in Lincoln's life, beginning with his birth in 1809 and continuing to his election to Congress in 1846. Then, using history books and encyclopedias, research the rest of Lincoln's life in Illinois and Washington, and add important dates to the time line. Illustrate the time line, if you wish.

Creative Writing

4. The Campaign Trail

You're Abraham Lincoln's campaign manager. Your job is to convince the public to elect him sixteenth president of the United States. Write an appeal to voters—to be printed in newspapers around the country—urging them to vote for him. "Sell" Lincoln to the public by emphasizing his qualifications: his character, background, achievements, and plans for the country's future.

Research/Speaking

5. A Lincoln Celebration

With a group of classmates, prepare a Lincoln celebration. For your presentations, you should include speeches by Lincoln and a poem or two about Lincoln. Give a brief introduction to each speech and poem to set the scene (time, place, occasion). For some of the selections, you might consider a choral reading. You could include music in your celebration, focusing perhaps on Civil War songs. Here are some ideas:

- The "House Divided" Speech (Abraham Lincoln, 1858)
- The Gettysburg Address (Abraham Lincoln, 1863)
- The Second Inaugural (Abraham Lincoln, 1865)
- "Abraham Lincoln Walks at Midnight" (poem by Vachel Lindsay)
- "O Captain! My Captain!" (poem by Walt Whitman)

Grading Timesaver

Rubrics for each Choices assignment appear on p. 132 in the *Portfolio Management System.*

CHOICES: Building Your Portfolio

1. **Writer's Notebook** With each selection, a Writer's Notebook activity appears as the first option in the Choices section. These brief, work-in-progress assignments build toward the writing assignment presented in the Writer's Workshop at the end of the collection. If students save their work for their Writer's Notebook activities as they move through the collection, they should be able to use some of their notes as starting points for the workshop.

2. **Creative Writing** Before students generate a first draft of their letters, have them work with partners to brainstorm about equal opportunity today and about any questions they would ask Lincoln.

3. **Research/History** Divide the class into groups of three, and assign each group a particular period of Lincoln's life to research. Ask each group to present its research to the class, to add important dates to the time line, and to post helpful illustrations.

4. **Creative Writing** As a variation of the assignment, invite students to write and videotape television campaign spots for Abraham Lincoln as if he were running today. Remind them that most spots are no more than thirty seconds long. Help students determine what speech excerpts, testimonials, and other writings would best convey Lincoln's attributes.

5. **Research/Speaking** Students might also write poems about Lincoln, write words to the music of a song popular during the time period assigned, or create posters promoting the celebration.

Getting Students Involved

Cooperative Learning

Guide four students to work in a small group to create a bulletin-board display headed "A Penny for Your Thoughts." Group members should take on these roles: coordinator, to gather materials and keep members on task; artist, to draw an oversized head of Lincoln modeled on the portrait on a penny; researcher, to contribute quotations about or by Lincoln for display; graphic designer, to plan and, with the others' help, produce the display.

GRAMMAR LINK

After students have completed the Try It Out assignment, ask them to select a piece of writing from their portfolios and have a classmate edit it for punctuation, capitalization, and spelling in the same manner that they edited Lincoln's writing.

Try It Out

Students will choose various parts of the text to edit. In order to use time efficiently, edit a small part of the text and show it to students before they exchange their own edited copies. Reviewing your edited version will enable students to double-check their work, ask questions, and review rules.

VOCABULARY

Sample Answer

elated

How would an elated person feel?
• happy
• overjoyed

What is the opposite of *elated*?
• sad
• depressed

When might someone feel elated?
• winning a sports event
• achieving a goal

What other characteristics might an elated person have?
• optimism
• energy

Resources ─────────

Language
• *Grammar and Language Links* Worksheet, p. 35

Vocabulary
• *Words to Own,* Worksheet, p. 16

GRAMMAR LINK   MINI-LESSON

Language Handbook HELP

See Capitalization, pages 1018-1022; Punctuation, pages 1022-1031; Spelling, pages 1031-1034.

Technology HELP

See Language Workshop CD-ROM. *Key word entry: punctuation.*

Punctuation, Capitalization, Spelling

Our language is always changing. We add new words (such as *camcorder*) and we use old words in new ways (such as *voice mail*). We also adjust the mechanics for writing our language—experts are continually publishing new rules for capitalization, punctuation, and spelling. You can get an idea of how the mechanics of our language have evolved over the years if you compare the following sentence from Lincoln's "Not Much of Me" with the way we would write the sentence today.

> *Lincoln:* "If a straggler supposed to understand latin, happened to sojourn in the neighborhood, he was looked upon as a wizzard."

> *Modern version:* If a straggler supposed to understand Latin [no comma] happened to sojourn in the neighborhood, he was looked upon as a wizard.

Try It Out

Suppose you are an editor and you want to update Lincoln's capitalization, punctuation, and spelling. Write part of the text on a piece of paper, leaving extra space between the lines for your corrections. Then edit the text to make it conform to modern style. Pages 1018–1034 of the Language Handbook and a good dictionary will help you check up-to-date rules on capitalization, punctuation, and spelling. Exchange your edited copy with a classmate. As editors, do you agree on the rules?

VOCABULARY   HOW TO OWN A WORD

WORD BANK

elated
assiduously

What Do You Know About a Word?

This cluster diagram organizes some ideas about the word *sincere*. Try your own cluster diagram with the words *elated* and *assiduously*.

How would a sincere person behave?
• would tell the truth
• would be reliable

How would an insincere person behave?
• might tell lies
• might be two-faced

sincere

When would it be important to know if someone is sincere?
• if you need advice
• if person is a friend

What other characteristics would a sincere person probably have?
• honesty
• directness

Grammar Link Quick Check

Edit the following sentences about Lincoln for modern punctuation, capitalization, and spelling.

1. Lincoln's father litterally was without education. [Delete one t in *litterally.*]
2. At twenty-one Lincoln moved to Illinois and spent the first year in macon county. [Capitalize *Macon* and *County.*]
3. Lincoln, did not consider politics again for a while. [Delete comma.]
4. Lincoln lived in Springfield for a quarter of a century and, was buried there. [Delete comma.]
5. When he wrote back to the girl, Lincoln showd kindness. [Change *showd* to *showed.*]

Elements of Literature

OBJECTIVES
1. Distinguish between biography and autobiography
2. Distinguish between objectivity and subjectivity

BIOGRAPHY AND AUTOBIOGRAPHY *by* Janet Burroway

In Greek the word *bios* means "life" and *graphia* means "writing." A **biography** is therefore a "written life," or the story of a life. *Auto* in the same language means "self," so an **autobiography** is the written story of the writer's own life.

Biography: Someone Else's Life

A biographer who sets out to write the story of someone else's life must do a great deal of study and research. We'd expect someone who is going to write a biography of Anne Frank, for example, to read all about the rise of Nazism in Germany in the 1930s. We'd expect the biographer to find out what kinds of schools Anne went to and what kinds of books and newspapers she read. We'd expect the writer to interview people who knew Anne, people who helped her family hide, and people who were with her in the camp where she died. We'd expect that the biographer would visit the places where Anne lived and

the camp where she died. And then we would expect that all this knowledge would be recorded accurately in a way that would make all the places, people, atmospheres, and events of Anne's life come alive.

Autobiography: Getting Personal

When Anne Frank sat down to write her own diary, she needed no such research. Her "research" was the daily living of her very own life. She already knew which people, places, and events were at the center of her life. Her purpose as a writer was to record the personal reactions and emotions of her experience, day by day.

A **diary** like Anne's is one sort of autobiography. The life is recorded as it is lived, a day or a week at a time. A person may also write an autobiography that is a record from memory of his or her entire life up to the time of writing. In either case, what we expect from autobiography is the kind of personal, internal knowledge that cannot be

> **N**o one can get into another person's mind.

researched, because no one can get into another person's mind.

Objectivity or Subjectivity?

What we usually look for in biography is factual accuracy and **objectivity**. This means that we want an unbiased account of the person the biography deals with—we do not want the account distorted by the writer's own prejudices.

But in autobiography, we look for **subjectivity**—that is, we want this writer to "get personal." We want to know what the writer thinks about her grandmother or how the writer feels about his home-town or why the writer has always been afraid of cats.

The advantage of other kinds of biography is their perspective: An outsider can tell us things about the back-ground, history, influences, and effectiveness of another person—things that this person may not have realized or cared to write about. The advantage of autobiography, on the other hand, is that it reveals the motives, emotions, fears, hopes, doubts, and joys that only the writer can know.

ELEMENTS OF LITERATURE: BIOGRAPHY AND AUTOBIOGRAPHY **355**

Resources

Elements of Literature
Biography and Autobiography
For additional instruction on biography and autobiography, see *Literary Elements:*
- Transparency 7

Assessment
Formal Assessment
- Literary Elements Test, p. 64

Elements of Literature

This feature focuses on the differences between a biography and an autobiography.

Mini-Lesson:
Biography and Autobiography
After students have read the feature, have them quickwrite about something they have accomplished in the past year—something they are willing to share with the class. Encourage students to write about their motives and feelings: Why was the accomplishment important? Then, assign partners to interview each other about the accomplishment and write a brief factual account of it. Finally, have students compare the two accounts and discuss the differences.

Applying the Element
As students read the works in this collection, have them note examples of objectivity and subjectivity. To start, read aloud the biographical material on Maya Angelou on p. 361, and have students list the objective facts they learn about Angelou. Then, have students turn to p. 358 of "When I Lay My Burden Down." Read aloud the paragraph that begins "One summer morning...." Ask students to list subjective feelings Angelou reveals about her family and her home.

Reaching All Students

Struggling Readers
To help students remember the definitions of *biography* and *autobiography,* stress that *auto-* means "self." Have them relate *autobiography* to *autograph* ("self" + "write").

English Language Learners
Pair these students with proficient English speakers. Have the students who are learning English use tape recorders to dictate their ideas and feelings about their accomplishments. Ask each partner to transcribe the tape and then

read the autobiographical incident aloud to the writer. The student learning English can then decide which parts to edit and revise and make these changes with the partner's help.

Advanced Learners
Students might use a video to accompany the factual accounts of a partner that they wrote for the Mini-Lesson. They can videotape their subject performing an accomplishment or displaying records of an achievement and read the factual account as voice-over on the tape.

T355

OBJECTIVES

1. Read and interpret the auto-biographical excerpt
2. Recognize imagery
3. Compare texts
4. Express understanding through creative writing, speaking and listening, or drawing
5. Identify figures of speech and use them in writing
6. Use semantic mapping to master new words

SKILLS

Literary
- Recognize imagery

Reading
- Compare texts

Writing
- Gather sensory details
- Retell an incident

Speaking/Listening
- Create and share a found poem

Language
- Use figures of speech

Vocabulary
- Construct semantic maps

Art
- Design a set

Viewing/Representing
- Use a painting to help understand the selection's setting (ATE)

Planning

- **Block Schedule**
  Block Scheduling Lesson Plans with Pacing Guide
- **Traditional Schedule**
  Lesson Plans Including Strategies for English-Language Learners
- **One-Stop Planner**
  CD-ROM with Test Generator

Before You Read

"WHEN I LAY MY BURDEN DOWN"

Make the Connection

Memories Stay with Us

We all remember people we've admired—people who were wise, funny, or especially kind. We also remember people who were less than perfect—people who were uneasy, demanding, even unkind. All of these memories—good and bad—stay with us and become part of who we are. Here, Maya Angelou reflects on an incident from her childhood, when she witnessed her beloved grandmother's encounter with some mean-spirited children. Why has this experience stayed with her?

Quickwrite

What are some effective reactions to insults or bullying? Could you respond without causing trouble—and still keep your dignity? Suppose you were giving a younger person advice about how to deal with bullying. Write down the advice you would give.

Elements of Literature

Imagery: Make It Real

Angelou uses images to make the people and the places that are so real to her seem just as immediate and real to her readers. Descriptions of "cold, molasses-slow minutes," of an apron so stiff with starch that it could have stood alone, and of children with "greasy, uncolored hair" help us see and experience what Angelou herself saw and experienced as a little girl so many years ago.

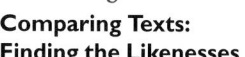

> **I**magery is language that appeals to one or more of our senses—sight, hearing, smell, taste, or touch.
>
> *For more on Imagery, see pages 492–493 and the Handbook of Literary Terms.*

Reading Skills and Strategies

Comparing Texts: Finding the Likenesses

You might wonder about the unusual title of Angelou's autobiography, *I Know Why the Caged Bird Sings*. You'll find the source of the title in a poem called "Sympathy" by Paul Laurence Dunbar (see ***Connections*** on page 362). Angelou's story about her grandmother has specific connections to "Sympathy." To find the ways in which the two texts are alike, read each one twice. After your second read, list all the ways in which they are alike. Consider these questions:
- Is Momma in a "cage"?
- Is the narrator in a "cage"?

- Does Momma sing despite her trials?

Sometimes differences are important, too. Do you find differences between the two works?

Background

"When I Lay My Burden Down" is an excerpt from Maya Angelou's autobiography *I Know Why the Caged Bird Sings*. When Angelou was three years old, her parents divorced and she was sent on a train from Long Beach, California, to live with her grandmother and uncle in the small town of Stamps, Arkansas. Life in this segregated Southern town took some getting used to, but it wasn't long before Maya and her older brother were calling their grandmother Momma and working in her general store. In this selection, Maya is ten years old.

go.hrw.com
LE0 9-5

Preteaching Vocabulary

Words to Own

Call on volunteers to read aloud to the class the Words to Own at the bottom of the selection pages. Have other volunteers suggest synonyms for **appellations** (*names*), **servile** (*submissive*), **impudent** (*rude*), **apparitions** (*ghosts*), and **agitation** (*stirring up trouble or excitement*). Then, ask students the following questions to check their understanding of the words:

1. Describe how **apparitions** might be used in a horror movie.
2. What **appellations** do you use for friends? parents? teachers? officials in your school and community? other adults?
3. How would you describe a **servile** dog? an **impudent** child?
4. What events could cause **agitation** in a classroom?

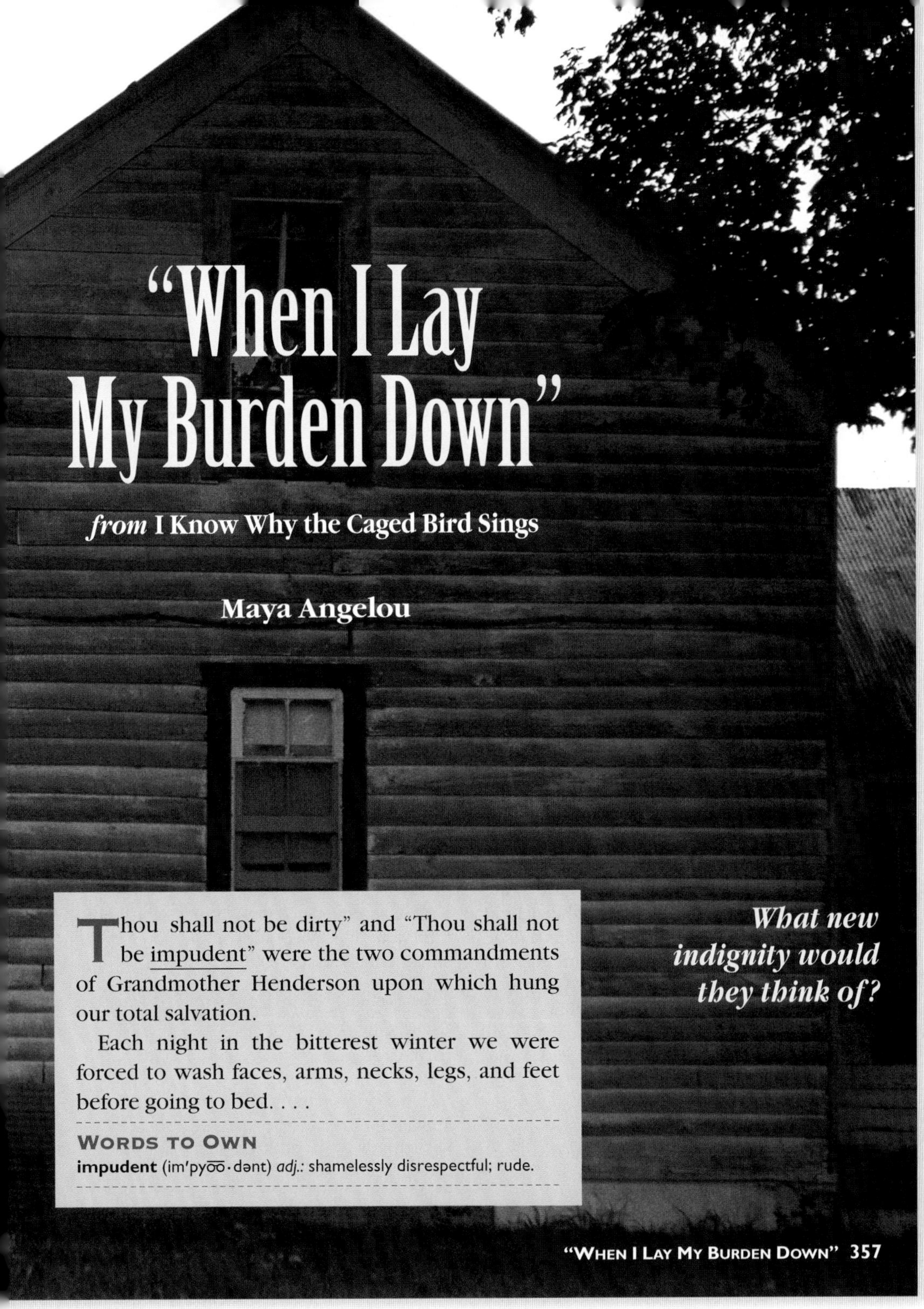

"When I Lay My Burden Down"

from I Know Why the Caged Bird Sings

Maya Angelou

"Thou shall not be dirty" and "Thou shall not be impudent" were the two commandments of Grandmother Henderson upon which hung our total salvation.

Each night in the bitterest winter we were forced to wash faces, arms, necks, legs, and feet before going to bed. . . .

WORDS TO OWN
impudent (im′pyōō·dənt) *adj.*: shamelessly disrespectful; rude.

What new indignity would they think of?

Summary ■ ■

In this episode from her autobiography, Angelou focuses on her grandmother's dignified response to the cruel taunts of white girls who know that she is unable to reprimand them. With vivid imagery, Angelou tells a story about courage and restraint and about the love, loyalty, and protectiveness that bind the generations of a family together in hard times.

Background

Angelou's autobiography is set in Arkansas in the 1930s and 1940s, when "Jim Crow" laws throughout the South maintained racial segregation in public transportation, schools, parks, theaters, and restaurants. The laws, enacted after Reconstruction, remained in effect until the civil rights movement helped bring about federal legislation in the 1960s prohibiting discrimination on the basis of color, race, religion, or national origin.

Resources ————

Listening
Audio CD Library
An engaging reading of this selection is provided in the *Audio CD Library:*
• Disc 13, Tracks 5, 6

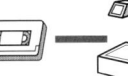

Resources: Print and Media

Reading
• *Graphic Organizers for Active Reading*, p. 22
• *Words to Own*, p. 17
• *Audio CD Library*, Disc 13, Tracks 5, 6

Writing and Language
• *Daily Oral Grammar*
    Transparency 22
• *Grammar and Language Links*
    Worksheet, p. 37
• *Language Workshop CD-ROM*

Assessment
• *Formal Assessment*, p. 58
• *Portfolio Management System*, p. 134
• *Test Generator (One-Stop Planner* CD-ROM)

Internet
• *go.hrw.com* (keyword: *LEO 9-5*)

A English Language Learners

Interpreting Idioms

Explain that the adage "Cleanliness is next to godliness" is a popular folk expression used to encourage children to keep clean. It suggests that being clean is one of the highest virtues. Ask students to share similar admonitions from their first languages.

B Cultural Connections

In the first half of the twentieth century, particularly in the segregated and socially stratified South, titles were one way people showed respect for those considered their social superiors. Race, age, family relationships, and economic level were factors used to determine status. It might be necessary to explain the derogatory term "powhite-trash," which could be offensive to some people. The term probably originated among whites of a higher socioeconomic status.

C Elements of Literature

Imagery

❓ What sensory words and what comparison does Angelou use to help readers imagine the children's voices? ["twanging," "sharp," "like cigar-box guitars"]

D Reading Skills and Strategies

Drawing Conclusions

❓ How would you describe the narrator's feelings toward her uncle and her grandmother? [She feels loving toward and protective of them, even though their behavior around whites causes her shame.]

We would go to the well and wash in the ice-cold, clear water, grease our legs with the equally cold, stiff Vaseline, then tiptoe into the house. We wiped the dust from our toes and settled down for schoolwork, corn bread, clabbered milk,[1] prayers, and bed, always in that order. Momma was famous for pulling the quilts off after we had fallen asleep to examine our feet. If they weren't clean enough for her, she took the switch (she kept one behind the bedroom door for emergencies) and woke up the offender with a few aptly placed burning reminders.

The area around the well at night was dark and slick, and boys told about how snakes love water, so that anyone who had to draw water at night and then stand there alone and wash knew that moccasins and rattlers, puff adders and boa constrictors were winding their way to the well and would arrive just as the person washing **Ⓐ** got soap in her eyes. But Momma convinced us that not only was cleanliness next to godliness, dirtiness was the inventor of misery.

The impudent child was detested by God and a shame to its parents and could bring destruction to its house and line. All adults had to be addressed as Mister, Missus, Miss, Auntie, Cousin, Unk, Uncle, Buhbah, Sister, Brother, and a thousand other appellations indicating familial relationship and the lowliness of the **Ⓑ** addressor.

Everyone I knew respected these customary laws, except for the powhitetrash children.

Some families of powhitetrash lived on Momma's farmland behind the school. Sometimes a gaggle of them came to the Store, filling the whole room, chasing out the air, and even changing the well-known scents. The children crawled over the shelves and into the **Ⓒ** potato and onion bins, twanging all the time in their sharp voices like cigar-box guitars. They took liberties in my Store that I would never dare. Since Momma told us that the less you say to whitefolks (or even powhitetrash) the better, Bailey and I would stand, solemn, quiet, in the displaced air. But if one of the playful apparitions got close to us, I pinched it. Partly out of

1. **clabbered milk:** thickly clotted sour milk.

angry frustration and partly because I didn't believe in its flesh reality.

They called my uncle by his first name and ordered him around the Store. He, to my crying shame, obeyed them in his limping dip-straight-dip fashion.

My grandmother, too, followed their orders, except that she didn't seem to be servile because she anticipated their needs.

"Here's sugar, Miz Potter, and here's baking powder. You didn't buy soda last month, you'll **Ⓓ** probably be needing some."

Momma always directed her statements to the adults, but sometimes, Oh painful sometimes, the grimy, snotty-nosed girls would answer her.

"Naw, Annie . . ."—to Momma? Who owned the land they lived on? Who forgot more than they would ever learn? If there was any justice in the world, God should strike them dumb at once!—"Just give us some extry sody crackers, and some more mackerel."

At least they never looked in her face, or I never caught them doing so. Nobody with a smidgen of training, not even the worst roustabout,[2] would look right in a grown person's face. It meant the person was trying to take the words out before they were formed. The dirty little children didn't do that, but they threw their orders around the Store like lashes from a cat-o'-nine-tails.[3]

When I was around ten years old, those scruffy children caused me the most painful and confusing experience I had ever had with my grandmother.

One summer morning, after I had swept the dirt yard of leaves, spearmint-gum wrappers, and Vienna-sausage labels, I raked the yellow-

2. **roustabout** (roust′ə·bout′): unskilled or temporary laborer.
3. **cat-o'-nine-tails:** whip made of nine knotted cords attached to a handle.

WORDS TO OWN

appellations (ap′ə·lā′shənz) *n.*: names; titles.
apparitions (ap′ə·rish′ənz) *n.*: strange, ghostlike figures.
servile (sur′vəl) *adj.*: humbly submissive; like a slave.

Reaching All Students

Struggling Readers

These students may have difficulty reading the introductory material Angelou uses to set the scene for the episode with the impudent girls. Read aloud the first two pages of the selection, ending with the paragraph that begins "When I was around ten years old. . . ." Help students summarize the important background information Angelou gives to prepare readers for the episode to come.

English Language Learners

Have students share titles of respect from their first languages and explain when each is used. For additional strategies for engaging English language learners with the literature, see

• *Lesson Plans Including Strategies for English-Language Learners*

Advanced Learners

Challenge a small group of advanced readers to research the poetry of Maya Angelou and to find examples of works with themes similar to that of "When I Lay My Burden Down." Invite them to share the works in a poetry reading for the class. They may also wish to explore more of Angelou's prose works and select pertinent passages from them to read aloud as well.

The Hoe Cake (1946) by Horace Pippin. Oil on canvas (14″ × 18″).

New Jersey State Museum Collection, Trenton, New Jersey. Purchase, FA1986.13.

red dirt and made half-moons carefully, so that the design stood out clearly and masklike. I put the rake behind the Store and came through the back of the house to find Grandmother on the front porch in her big, wide white apron. The apron was so stiff by virtue of the starch that it could have stood alone. Momma was admiring the yard, so I joined her. It truly looked like a flat redhead that had been raked with a big-toothed comb. Momma didn't say anything but I knew she liked it. She looked over toward the school principal's house and to the right at Mr. McElroy's. She was hoping one of those community pillars would see the design before the day's business wiped it out. Then she looked upward to the school. My head had swung with hers, so at just about the same time we saw a troop of the powhitetrash kids marching over the hill and down by the side of the school.

I looked to Momma for direction. She did an excellent job of sagging from her waist down, but from the waist up she seemed to be pulling for the top of the oak tree across the road. Then she began to moan a hymn. Maybe not to moan, but the tune was so slow and the meter so strange that she could have been moaning. She didn't look at me again. When the children reached halfway down the hill, halfway to the Store, she said without turning, "Sister, go on inside."

I wanted to beg her, "Momma, don't wait for them. Come on inside with me. If they come in the Store, you go to the bedroom and let me wait on them. They only frighten me if you're around. Alone I know how to handle them." But of course I couldn't say anything, so I went in and stood behind the screen door.

Before the girls got to the porch, I heard their laughter crackling and popping like pine logs in

"WHEN I LAY MY BURDEN DOWN" 359

Using Students' Strengths

Auditory Learners

Remind students that a writer uses imagery to help readers visualize, or form mental images of, sights, sounds, and other sensory impressions. By forming mental images, readers increase their comprehension of the text and become more involved in the events the writer describes. Read aloud the three paragraphs on pp. 358–359 (beginning with "One summer morning…"). Before you start, ask students to close their eyes and try to see and hear a "movie in their minds" as you read. Afterward, have students describe the details they were able to visualize. Then, have pairs of auditory learners take turns reading the rest of the selection to their partners. As one student reads, the other should close his or her eyes and try to see and hear the action.

A Elements of Literature

Imagery

? What vivid detail reminds us that the narrator is observing from inside the house? [She is watching through the "fly-specked screen door."] What details help readers visualize Momma and imagine her feelings? [Her apron ties are jiggling from the vibrations caused by her humming; her knees are "locked as if they would never bend again," suggesting her determination and restraint.]

B Reading Skills and Strategies

Drawing Conclusions

? Why does Momma continue to sing? [Possible responses: to block out painful experiences; to gain inner spiritual strength; to control her temper and keep from saying anything rude.]

C Reading Skills and Strategies

Comparing Texts

After students have read both selections, have them compare the imagery used here to the imagery in Dunbar's poem. [Like a "caged bird," the young narrator is "imprisoned."]

D Reading Skills and Strategies

Comparing Texts

? At this point, how are the narrator and Momma both linked to the caged bird in the poem's last stanza? [Like the bird, Momma is still singing, but her song is really a prayer for strength and release; the narrator, too, is praying.]

E Critical Thinking

Interpreting

? Why do the girls call Momma "Annie"? [Possible responses: to emphasize their disrespect for her; to push her to the limits of her patience.] Why does Momma address each of the girls as "Miz"? [Possible responses: She uses courtesy to show her own moral superiority; she refuses to let their crude behavior influence her own.]

---

a cooking stove. I suppose my lifelong paranoia[4] was born in those cold, molasses-slow minutes. They came finally to stand on the ground in front of Momma. At first they pretended seriousness. Then one of them wrapped her right arm in the crook of her left, pushed out her mouth, and started to hum. I realized that she was aping my grandmother. Another said, "Naw, Helen, you ain't standing like her. This here's it." Then she lifted her chest, folded her arms and mocked that strange carriage that was Annie Henderson. Another laughed, "Naw, you can't do it. Your mouth ain't pooched out enough. It's like this."

I thought about the rifle behind the door, but I knew I'd never be able to hold it straight, and the .410, our sawed-off shotgun, which stayed loaded and was fired every New Year's night, was locked in the trunk and Uncle Willie had the key on his chain. Through the fly-specked screen door, I could see that the arms of Momma's apron jiggled from the vibrations of her humming. But her knees seemed to have locked as if they would never bend again.

She sang on. No louder than before, but no softer either. No slower or faster.

The dirt of the girls' cotton dresses continued on their legs, feet, arms, and faces to make them all of a piece. Their greasy uncolored hair hung down, uncombed, with a grim finality. I knelt to see them better, to remember them for all time. The tears that had slipped down my dress left unsurprising dark spots and made the front yard blurry and even more unreal. The world had taken a deep breath and was having doubts about continuing to revolve.

The girls had tired of mocking Momma and turned to other means of <u>agitation</u>. One crossed her eyes, stuck her thumbs in both sides of her mouth, and said, "Look here, Annie." Grandmother hummed on and the apron strings trembled. I wanted to throw a handful of black pepper in their faces, to throw lye on them, to scream that they were dirty, scummy pecker-

---

4. paranoia (par′ə·noi′ə): mental disorder that often causes people to believe they are being persecuted. The author is using the term in an informal sense, to mean "suspiciousness" or "distrustfulness."

360 THE NONFICTION COLLECTIONS

---

woods,[5] but I knew I was as clearly imprisoned behind the scene as the actors outside were confined to their roles.

One of the smaller girls did a kind of puppet dance while her fellow clowns laughed at her. But the tall one, who was almost a woman, said something very quietly, which I couldn't hear. They all moved backward from the porch, still watching Momma. For an awful second I thought they were going to throw a rock at Momma, who seemed (except for the apron strings) to have turned into stone herself. But the big girl turned her back, bent down, and put her hands flat on the ground—she didn't pick up anything. She simply shifted her weight and did a handstand.

Her dirty bare feet and long legs went straight for the sky. Her dress fell down around her shoulders, and she had on no drawers. . . . She hung in the vacuum of that lifeless morning for only a few seconds, then wavered and tumbled. The other girls clapped her on the back and slapped their hands.

Momma changed her song to "Bread of Heaven, bread of Heaven, feed me till I want no more."

I found that I was praying too. How long could Momma hold out? What new indignity would they think of to subject her to? Would I be able to stay out of it? What would Momma really like me to do?

Then they were moving out of the yard, on their way to town. They bobbed their heads and shook their slack behinds and turned, one at a time:

"'Bye, Annie."

"'Bye, Annie."

"'Bye, Annie."

Momma never turned her head or unfolded her arms, but she stopped singing and said, "'Bye, Miz Helen, 'bye, Miz Ruth, 'bye, Miz Eloise."

I burst. A firecracker July-the-Fourth burst.

---

5. peckerwoods: hostile term for "poor white people."

WORDS TO OWN

agitation (aj′ə·tā′shən) n.: stirring up; disturbance or excitement.

Crossing the Curriculum

Music

Bring in recordings of the gospel songs mentioned in this selection or other gospel songs and spirituals available from your public library. Have students listen to the lyrics to identify common themes and refrains in the songs. List the themes on the chalkboard as students identify them. Ask students to discuss how hearing the songs and spirituals deepens their understanding of the character of Angelou's grandmother.

Economics

Have groups of interested students research state rules and regulations for operating an independent general store like the one Maya Angelou's grandmother worked so long and hard to establish. Ask the groups to pool their findings and to lead a class discussion on the rewards and challenges of being an entrepreneur in a free-enterprise system.

How could Momma call them Miz? The mean, nasty things. Why couldn't she have come inside the sweet, cool store when we saw them breasting the hill? What did she prove? And then if they were dirty, mean, and impudent, why did Momma have to call them Miz?

She stood another whole song through and then opened the screen door to look down on me crying in rage. She looked until I looked up. Her face was a brown moon that shone on me. She was beautiful. Something had happened out there which I couldn't completely understand, but I could see that she was happy. Then she bent down and touched me as mothers of the church "lay hands on the sick and afflicted" and I quieted.

"Go wash your face, Sister." And she went **F** behind the candy counter and hummed, "Glory,

glory, hallelujah, when I lay my burden down."

I threw the well water on my face and used the weekday handkerchief to blow my nose. Whatever the contest had been out front, I **G** knew Momma had won.

I took the rake back to the front yard. The smudged footprints were easy to erase. I worked for a long time on my new design and laid the rake behind the wash pot. When I came back in the Store, I took Momma's hand and we both walked outside to look at the pattern.

It was a large heart with lots of hearts growing smaller inside, and piercing from the outside rim to the smallest heart was an arrow. Momma said, "Sister, that's right pretty." Then **H** she turned back to the Store and resumed, "Glory, glory, hallelujah, when I lay my burden down."

F Cultural Connections

Because communication was restricted, people held in slavery used spirituals and gospel songs as a way of sharing their observations, feelings, and plans.

G Reading Skills and Strategies
Drawing Conclusions
❓ What do you think the "contest" between Momma and the girls was really about? [Possible responses: who was really superior; how much Momma could endure without crumbling or lashing back; answering cruelty and rudeness with dignity.]

H Advanced Learners
Symbol
❓ What might the narrator's final yard design symbolize? [Possible responses: love; emotional pain; the infinite nature of love.] What other symbols could be used to describe the relationship between Grandmother Henderson and the narrator? [Possible responses: a mother bird and a baby bird; a lighthouse and a ship; or other images of shelter, safety, or guidance.]

Resources ———
Selection Assessment
Formal Assessment
• Selection Test, p. 58
Test Generator (One-Stop Planner)
• CD-ROM

MEET THE WRITER
Born Winner

❝ One would say of my life, 'born loser, had to be'—but it's not the truth. In the black community, however bad it looks, there's a lot of love and so much humor. ❞

Maya Angelou (1928–   ) is anything but a loser. After she left Stamps, Arkansas, she won a scholarship to the California Labor School, where she took evening classes in dance and drama. In 1954 and 1955, she toured Europe and Africa in a State Department–sponsored production of the opera *Porgy and Bess*. She later wrote and produced a ten-part television series on Africanisms in American life, wrote songs that were recorded by B. B. King, and published short

stories, magazine articles, and poems. In 1992, she was asked to write a poem for the inauguration of President Clinton. On Inauguration Day of 1993, Maya Angelou presented her eloquent poem "On the Pulse of Morning." Here are the final lines:

❝ Here on the pulse of this new day
You may have the grace to look up and out
And into your sister's eyes,
And into your brother's face,
Your country,
And say simply
Very simply
With hope—
Good morning. ❞

Angelou is an imposing woman, six feet tall, with a gracious, formal manner. She speaks six languages fluently. Although she declares a continuing interest in exploring the character of the black woman, Angelou's focus is not narrow:

❝ I speak to the black experience, but I am always talking about the human condition— about what we can endure, dream, fail at, and still survive. ❞

Making the Connections

Connecting to the Theme: "We Remember"
Point out that this selection presents one of Angelou's most powerful childhood memories. Invite students to consider some of their own childhood memories and to reflect on whether and how those memories change as time goes by. Suggest they freewrite about a particularly vivid memory. Ask them to think about whether they have learned anything new from revisiting this memory.

Assessing Learning

Check Test: True-False
1. Grandmother Henderson encouraged her granddaughter to be rude. [False]
2. In Angelou's family, the children addressed adults with titles showing respect and family relationships. [True]
3. Angelou's family owned property. [True]
4. The narrator enjoys playing with the rude girls. [False]
5. In the end, the narrator has a fistfight with the rude girls. [False]

Standardized Test Preparation
For practice in proofreading and editing, see
• *Daily Oral Grammar*, Transparency 22

The speaker in the poem identifies with the longing for freedom a caged bird expresses in song.

A Critical Thinking
Interpreting
❓ How does this line relate to the title of the poem? [Possible responses: It gives an example of sympathy; the speaker feels sympathy for the caged bird.]

B Elements of Literature
Imagery
❓ What images convey the season of the year? [Images that point to spring include "wind stirs soft," "springing grass," "river flows like a stream of glass," "first bird sings," "first bud opes," "faint perfume from its chalice steals."]

C Appreciating Language
Diction
The archaic word *fain*, meaning "gladly," was once common in literary writing. Point out that *fain* rhymes with the word *pain* in the next line and is a near rhyme with *again* in l. 13.

D Reading Skills and Strategies
Comparing Texts
❓ What do you think the caged bird is praying for? [Possible responses: freedom; to follow his instincts.]

RESPONDING TO THE ART
This painting is one of many by **Jonathan Green** (1955–) that depict life in the isolated Sea Islands off the coast of South Carolina.

Activity. What is the mood of the painting? [Joyful, innocent—the day is fresh and sunny, the young girl pristine in her bright dress.] What details in the painting, including the title, could connect with Dunbar's poem? [Where Dunbar's poem is sad, this painting is joyful, but both works of art deal with communication and birds.]

Resources 🎧
Listening
Audio CD Library
A recording of this poem is provided in the *Audio CD Library*:
• Disc 13, Track 6

Sympathy Paul Laurence Dunbar

A I know what the caged bird feels, alas!
　　　When the sun is bright on the upland slopes;
　　When the wind stirs soft through the springing grass,
B And the river flows like a stream of glass;
5　　　When the first bird sings and the first bud opes,
　　And the faint perfume from its chalice steals—
　　I know what the caged bird feels!

　　I know why the caged bird beats his wing
　　　Till its blood is red on the cruel bars;
10　For he must fly back to his perch and cling
C When he fain would be on the bough a-swing;
　　　And a pain still throbs in the old, old scars
　　And they pulse again with a keener sting—
　　I know why he beats his wing!

15　I know why the caged bird sings, ah me,
　　　When his wing is bruised and his bosom sore,—
　　When he beats his bars and he would be free;
　　It is not a carol of joy or glee,
　　　But a prayer that he sends from his heart's deep core,
20 D But a plea, that upward to Heaven he flings—
　　I know why the caged bird sings!

362

Silence with the Birds (1994) by Jonathan Green. Acrylic on canvas (16" x 20").

Connecting Across Texts

Connecting with *I Know Why the Caged Bird Sings*

Remind students that the title of Angelou's autobiography is *I Know Why the Caged Bird Sings*. Both the Dunbar and the Angelou selections focus on feelings about unjust limitations to freedom. Have students find a word or phrase from the Angelou selection that echoes language from the poem. The word *caged* in the poem, for example, is echoed by the word *imprisoned* in Angelou's text.

MAKING MEANINGS

First Thoughts

[interpret]

1. What does Angelou mean when she says "Whatever the contest had been out front, I knew Momma had won"? Do you agree? Why, or why not?

Shaping Interpretations

[connect]

2. Look back at the advice you wrote in your Quickwrite. Do you think Momma would agree with you? Explain.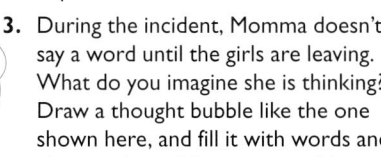

[infer]

3. During the incident, Momma doesn't say a word until the girls are leaving. What do you imagine she is thinking? Draw a thought bubble like the one shown here, and fill it with words and pictures that might represent Momma's thoughts. Be ready to explain your choices.

[draw conclusions]

4. Why do you think the girls mock Momma? Discuss the reasons why people would be so cruel to another person. Why are children occasionally cruel to an innocent adult? (You might think of the story "Marigolds" on page 279.)

[visualize]

5. On page 359, Angelou says that when Momma sees the girls approaching, she sags from the waist down but from the top seems to be pulling for the top of an oak tree. Exactly what does this **image** make you see? What do you think Momma is feeling?

[interpret]

6. Angelou takes some time to tell us about what is considered good behavior and courtesy in her family. What was her purpose for doing this? How does she want you to feel about her family's rules?

Connecting with the Text

[connect]

7. At one point Angelou says that she is afraid of the kids only when Momma is around, and that she knows how to handle them when she's alone. What do you suppose she means? Would you feel the same way?

Extending the Text

[compare]

8. The speaker of Paul Laurence Dunbar's poem "Sympathy" (see **Connections** on page 362) says he knows why the caged bird sings at springtime, when nature is blooming and other birds fly freely. Why do you think Angelou chose Dunbar's image as the **title** of her life story? Look back at the chart you made comparing these two texts. What other similarities and differences did you discover between the poem about the caged bird and Angelou's story about her dignified grandmother?

Reading Check

a. List all the things you know about the **setting** of this incident.

b. How do the "powhitetrash" children behave in the Store?

c. What is the narrator's reaction as the rude girls insult her grandmother?

d. What is Momma's response to the insult?

Reading Check

a. It is set in Stamps, Arkansas, during segregation. It takes place in a store owned by Angelou's grandmother, an African American. The store, which is near a school, has a front porch and a raked yard.

b. They crawl on the shelves and into the vegetable bins, talking loudly and constantly.

c. She is angry, hurt, and frustrated.

d. She continues to hum and is polite and respectful to the girls.

MAKING MEANINGS

First Thoughts

1. Possible responses: Angelou means that her grandmother had lost no dignity or hope, so she won. Some students may agree, because Momma did not allow the girls to see that their rudeness upset her. Some may disagree, saying the girls won because they were not punished for their behavior.

Shaping Interpretations

2. Momma would probably agree with any calm and dignified response to insults or bullies.

3. Words and pictures in the thought bubble might show Momma wishing she could discipline the girls; she might be praying for self-control or freedom or for the girls.

4. Possible responses: They're bored and want excitement; they have low status in society and want to feel superior to someone; they know that society's unwritten rules forbid Momma to lash back. Children may be cruel to adults when they want to feel powerful or lash out at authority or when they have no fear of consequences.

5. Students may see a big, strong oak tree standing tall. Momma may feel fear, sadness, anger, or pity.

6. Possible responses: Angelou describes her family's rules so that readers can understand her shock and anger at the girls' behavior. She wants readers to admire her family's standards of behavior.

Connecting with the Text

7. Possible responses: Angelou means that she fears Momma's disapproval more than she fears the girls; she means that without Momma's restraint she would return the girls' insults or order them off the property. Students may identify with her feelings or find Momma's approach kinder and safer.

Extending the Text

8. Possible responses: Angelou may have identified with the caged bird, feeling trapped by the restrictions and injustices of racism. Both works include images of imprisonment, singing, and praying. The poem describes the natural world, while the story is set in the social world. The poem has a sad, yearning tone, while the story's tone ranges from admiring to angry.

Grading Timesaver

Rubrics for each Choices assignment appear on p. 134 in the *Portfolio Management System*.

CHOICES: Building Your Portfolio

1. Writer's Notebook Remind students to save their work. They may use it as prewriting for the Writer's Workshop on p. 386. The following graphic may help:

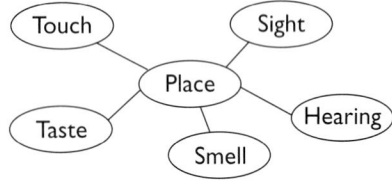

2. Creative Writing To help students get started, read aloud the passage on pp. 358–359 in which Angelou begins describing the specific incident about the rude children. Read from "When I was around ten years old . . . " until Momma tells Maya to go inside. Have students brainstorm ideas about what Momma is thinking and feeling and how she would describe the same events if she were telling the story.

3. Speaking and Listening You might model this found poem created from images on p. 358:

filling the whole room,
chasing out the air,
twanging all the time
like cigar-box guitars,
the grimy, snotty-nosed girls
threw their orders around
like lashes from a cat o'nine tails.

4. Drawing Instead of drawing, students might create shadow boxes or other three-dimensional models, using dollhouse furniture.

CHOICES: Building Your Portfolio

Writer's Notebook

1. Collecting Ideas for an Autobiographical Incident

People and places.
When you write an autobiographical incident for the Writer's Workshop on page 386, you'll want to help your readers visualize people and places, just as Angelou does. Look over your notes: Do you have an incident you would like to elaborate on? Gather notes on the people involved in the incident and on the place where it occurred. Try to find images that will help your readers see the scene, hear it, smell it, maybe even taste it and feel it.

> Incident/I Am 6
> The parking lot was crowded and hot. Waves of heat rose off the pavement. People looked irritable as they wrestled with their grocery carts. I got locked out of the car.

Creative Writing

2. Look Who's Talking

Retell the events of "When I Lay My Burden Down" from Momma's point of view. What is Momma thinking and feeling as the girls taunt her? Be sure to consider why Momma sings when her ordeal is over. Write as "I."

Speaking and Listening

3. A Found Poem

Find a poem in the text of "When I Lay My Burden Down." Meet with two or more classmates and look through the selection for "illuminating" words or phrases—words that you think are especially moving or that create particularly vivid pictures. Take five minutes and create a list of about eight words or phrases. Then narrow your choices to the four you like most. Get together with other groups and read your words aloud. If your group's choices are the same as the others', that's OK; it means the words are important. Read one word or phrase at a time, moving without interruption from group to group. There you have it—a found poem.

Drawing

4. TV Set

Design a set for a TV show based on "When I Lay My Burden Down." Draw a few renderings—color sketches—to show how you visualize the store, inside and outside, including the yard. Label the details in your drawings—furniture, family possessions, the yard. That way the location scouts, carpenters, decorators, and "prop masters" will know exactly what you need to set your scene.

Photograph by Walker Evans (1936).

364 THE NONFICTION COLLECTIONS

Handbook of Literary Terms
H E L P

See Metaphor, Simile, and Personification.

Comparisons—Seeing Unusual Connections

Writers use imaginative comparisons to create striking **images**. These comparisons are "special-effects" language that is not meant to be taken literally. When Maya Angelou says, for example, that "the world had taken a deep breath and was having doubts about continuing to revolve," she doesn't *really* mean that the planet earth was about to stop spinning on its axis. Angelou uses **personification** here, a type of comparison that gives human characteristics to nonhuman things.

Other types of comparisons are similes and metaphors. A **simile** compares two unlike things, using a word like *like* or *as*. A **metaphor**, on the other hand, says that one thing *is* something else, something very different. A metaphor does not use *like* or *as*. Here are some similes and metaphors from Angelou's story:

1. ". . . sharp voices like cigar-box guitars."

2. ". . . threw their orders around the Store like lashes from a cat-o'-nine-tails."

3. ". . . laughter crackling and popping like pine logs in a cooking stove."

4. ". . . I knew I was as clearly imprisoned behind the scene as the actors outside were confined to their roles."

5. "Her face was a brown moon that shone on me."

Try It Out
➤ What two different things is Angelou comparing in each passage to the left? What does each comparison make you see or hear?

➤ Write your own comparisons to describe voices; someone ordering people around; laughter; an observer who feels trapped; a face.

VOCABULARY   HOW TO OWN A WORD

WORD BANK
impudent
appellations
apparitions
servile
agitation

Semantic Mapping
Semantic mapping is a simple strategy that can help you own new words. A semantic map includes (1) the word's definition, (2) its **synonyms**, if any, (3) its use in a sentence, (4) an evaluation of the use of the synonyms in the sentence. A sample is shown here. Make a semantic map for the other words in the Word Bank. Use a thesaurus or a dictionary to locate synonyms.

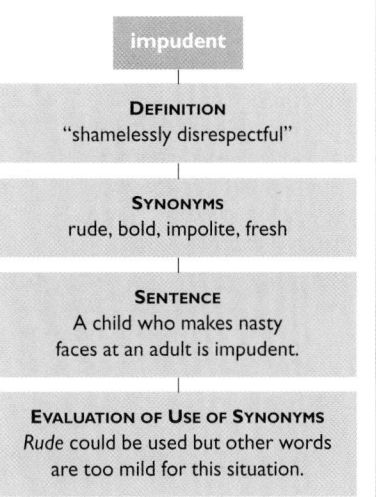

impudent

DEFINITION
"shamelessly disrespectful"

SYNONYMS
rude, bold, impolite, fresh

SENTENCE
A child who makes nasty faces at an adult is impudent.

EVALUATION OF USE OF SYNONYMS
Rude could be used but other words are too mild for this situation.

"WHEN I LAY MY BURDEN DOWN"   365

Ask students to select a page of developed prose from their portfolios. Have students revise sentences or passages to include similes, metaphors, or personifications that make their writing more striking.

Try It Out
Possible Answers
1. voices and guitars; hear: loud, twangy voices
2. thrown orders and whiplashes; hear: noises that make a person cringe
3. laughter and burning pine logs; hear: the pops and hisses of burning wood
4. an actor not allowed on stage and actors limited by a script; see: the backstage area in a theater
5. Momma's face and the moon; see: the brightness and clearness of a full moon

Students' comparisons will vary. Encourage them to generate comparisons from their own experience. Examples: a voice like tinkling glass; laughter as welcome as the sun after a storm; the boy watched his captors as warily as a treed raccoon stares down at barking hounds; her face was a prune of disapproval.

VOCABULARY
Sample Answers
Word: appellations
Definition: "names"
Synonym: titles
Sentence: What are the appellations of those books?
Evaluation: The synonym is better because it sounds less pretentious.

Word: apparitions
Definition: "strange, ghostlike figures"
Synonym: ghosts
Sentence: During the storm, shadows played like apparitions on the wall.
Evaluation: Both words are suitable. The synonym may be better because it is more suggestive.

Resources

Language
• *Grammar and Language Links* Worksheet, p. 37
Vocabulary
• *Words to Own,* Worksheet, p. 17

Language Link Quick Check

Identify each comparison below as personification, metaphor, or simile.
1. Momma was a rock of wisdom. [metaphor]
2. The family store embraced friendly visitors. [personification]

3. The yard designs danced and leapt in the afternoon sun. [personification]
4. The insults pierced her like arrows. [simile]
5. Momma's smile was a beacon of light in the darkest times. [metaphor]

OBJECTIVES
1. Read and interpret the speech
2. Define *main idea*
3. Identify the main idea
4. Express understanding through critical and creative writing or speaking/listening
5. Analyze connotations and denotations
6. Understand and use new words

SKILLS
Literary
• Define *main idea*
Reading
• Identify the main idea
Writing
• List characters in an autobiographical incident
• Describe a favorite place
• Write a feature article
Speaking/Listening
• Deliver and listen to a speech
Language
• Analyze connotations and denotations
Vocabulary
• Use new words
Viewing/Representing
• Research a memorial (ATE)

Planning

• **Block Schedule**
Block Scheduling Lesson Plans with Pacing Guide

• **Traditional Schedule**
Lesson Plans Including Strategies for English-Language Learners

• **One-Stop Planner**
CD-ROM with Test Generator

Before You Read

CHOICE: A TRIBUTE TO DR. MARTIN LUTHER KING, JR.

Make the Connection
Tribute

With eloquence and style Martin Luther King, Jr., brought the message of civil rights to a world television audience. From the mid-1950s until his death in 1968, his voice sounded a call for the elimination of racism in the United States through nonviolent resistance. King became a symbol of the struggle to fulfill at last the century-old promise of emancipation.

As you read, be aware of the setting and the audience for Walker's tribute to King, who was killed by an assassin on April 4, 1968, as he stood on a motel balcony in Memphis, Tennessee.

Quickwrite

Form groups and brainstorm for a few minutes about King. What did he do, and why is he so important? List some positive changes you think have happened as a result of Martin Luther King's work and life. Save your list.

Elements of Literature
Main Idea: What's the Point?

Speeches, essays, and editorials all are focused on a **main idea**—a message, an opinion, or an idea that the writer wants to communicate to the reader. Some writers, especially editorial writers, state their main ideas directly. But in most cases, the main idea is **implied**, or suggested.

> The **main idea** is the message, opinion, or idea that a writer wants to communicate.

go.hrw.com
LE0 9-5

Reading Skills and Strategies

Identifying the Main Idea: How to Find It

When a main idea is directly stated, you almost can't miss it. Look for it somewhere near the beginning, or at the very end, of a speech or an essay. When the main idea is unstated, you can discover it on your own by making **inferences**, or educated guesses, about what all the separate details in the piece of writing add up to. When you read a speech like this one, look for **key statements** that give you clues to the speaker's broader meaning—her main idea. One of the key elements in this speech is a story—why does Walker tell us this story?

Preteaching Vocabulary

Words to Own

Have students work in small groups to preview the vocabulary for this selection. First, have them read the definitions of the Words to Own at the bottom of the selection pages. Then, to reinforce their understanding of the words, ask each group to consider one of the following questions. Afterward, invite groups to share the results of their discussion with the rest of the class.

1. What groups of people in the world today are fighting a history of **dispossession?**
2. How would you describe the average teenager's **sensibility?** as idealistic? cynical? carefree? something else? Give examples to support your views.
3. What values would you like to **embody** in your own life?
4. Name four beautiful things that are **ephemeral.**

This address was given in 1972 at a Jackson, Mississippi, restaurant that had refused to serve African Americans until forced to do so by the civil rights movement a few years earlier.

Choice: A Tribute to Dr. Martin Luther King, Jr.

Alice Walker

Alice Walker's "three greats" grandmother Mary Poole, who was born sometime before 1800 and died in 1921.

He gave us home.

My great-great-great-grandmother walked as a slave from Virginia to Eatonton, Georgia—which passes for the Walker ancestral home—with two babies on her hips. She lived to be a hundred and twenty-five years old and my own father knew her as a boy. (It is in memory of this walk that I choose to keep and to embrace my "maiden" name, Walker.)

There is a cemetery near our family church where she is buried; but because her marker was made of wood and rotted years ago, it is impossible to tell exactly where her body lies. In the same cemetery are most of my mother's people, who have lived in Georgia for so long nobody even remembers when they came. And all of my great-aunts and -uncles are there, and my grandfather and grandmother, and very recently, my own father.

If it is true that land does not belong to anyone until they have buried a body in it, then the land of my birthplace belongs to me, dozens of times over. Yet the history of my family, like that of all

CHOICE: A TRIBUTE TO DR. MARTIN LUTHER KING, JR. 367

Summary ■■

Although six generations of Walkers worked the Georgia soil, racism kept them from truly calling it home. Like so many blacks, Alice Walker's siblings were forced to leave the South in order to improve their lives. Walker recalls her first television glimpse of Martin Luther King, Jr., as he was arrested for courageously claiming his rights. The author uses this incident to convey her main idea: that King's wisdom and fearless courage restored to African Americans their heritage and ancestors—the memories that enable people to call a place home.

Background

In the early 1960s Freedom Riders, groups of both black and white college students, challenged segregation in interstate transportation. The sit-in movement began in 1960, when black students refused to leave a Woolworth's lunch counter in Greensboro, North Carolina, until they were served. Media coverage of the brutal treatment of demonstrators like these helped win support for the civil rights movement. In July 1964, the Civil Rights Act was passed.

Resources

Listening
Audio CD Library
A recording of Walker's speech is available in the *Audio CD Library:*
• Disc 13, Track 7

 Resources: Print and Media

Reading
• *Reading Skills and Strategies*
  MiniRead Skill Lesson, p. 90
  Selection Skill Lesson, p. 96
• *Graphic Organizers for Active Reading*, p. 23
• *Words to Own*, p. 18
• *Audio CD Library*, Disc 13, Track 7

Writing and Language
• *Daily Oral Grammar*
  Transparency 23
• *Grammar and Language Links*
  Worksheet, p. 39

Assessment
• *Formal Assessment*, p. 60
• *Portfolio Management System*, p. 135
• *Standardized Test Preparation*, pp. 46, 48
• *Test Generator (One-Stop Planner* CD-ROM)

Internet
• *go.hrw.com* (keyword: *LEO 9-5*)

T367

Identifying the Main Idea

Explain that two of the many meanings of the prefix *dis-* are "apart" and "take away from." Write the words *dispossession, displaced,* and *disinherited* on the chalkboard, and discuss their meanings by first examining the root words and then adding the prefix *dis-* and the suffixes. Tell students that noticing how these three words are used will help them identify and understand Walker's main idea.

B Critical Thinking

Extending the Text

? What role did television play in the Civil Rights Movement? [Possible responses: People all over the country witnessed and were inspired by the heroic acts; the sight of the demonstrators being cruelly treated won sympathy for their cause.]

C Elements of Literature

Main Idea

? How did seeing Dr. King's resistance change Walker's ideas about her future? [She had thought she would have to leave the South in order to continue loving it. King's resistance gave her the courage to resolve to stay and claim her rights.]

A black Southerners, is a history of <u>dispossession</u>. We loved the land and worked the land, but we never owned it; and even if we bought land, as my great-grandfather did after the Civil War, it was always in danger of being taken away, as his was, during the period following Reconstruction.°

My father inherited nothing of material value from his father, and when I came of age in the early sixties I awoke to the bitter knowledge that in order just to continue to love the land of my birth, I was expected to leave it. For black people—including my parents—had learned a long time ago that to stay willingly in a beloved but brutal place is to risk losing the love and being forced to acknowledge only the brutality.

It is a part of the black Southern <u>sensibility</u> that we treasure memories; for such a long time, that is all of our homeland those of us who at one time or another were forced away from it have been allowed to have.

I watched my brothers, one by one, leave our home and leave the South. I watched my sisters do the same. This was not unusual; abandonment, except for memories, was the common thing, except for those who "could not do any better" or those whose strength or stubbornness was so colossal they took the risk that others could not bear.

B In 1960, my mother bought a television set, and each day after school I watched Hamilton Holmes and Charlayne Hunter as they struggled to integrate—fair-skinned as they were—the University of Georgia. And then, one day, there appeared the face of Dr. Martin Luther King, Jr. What a funny name, I thought. At the moment I first saw him, he was being handcuffed and shoved into a police truck. He had dared to claim his rights as a native son and had been arrested. He displayed no fear, but seemed calm and serene, unaware of his own extraordinary courage. His whole body, like his conscience, was at peace.

°**Reconstruction:** the period after the Civil War, lasting from 1867 to 1877, during which the Southern states were brought back into the Union and the former slaves were granted citizenship and certain other civil and political rights. African Americans were deprived of many of these rights after Reconstruction.

C At the moment I saw his resistance I knew I would never be able to live in this country without resisting everything that sought to disinherit me, and I would never be forced away from the land of my birth without a fight.

He was The One, The Hero, The One Fearless Person for whom we had waited. I hadn't even realized before that we *had* been waiting for Martin Luther King, Jr., but we had. And I knew it for sure when my mother added his name to the list of people she prayed for every night.

I sometimes think that it was literally the prayers of people like my mother and father, who had bowed down in the struggle for such a long time, that kept Dr. King alive until five years ago. For years we went to bed praying for his life and awoke with the question "Is the 'Lord' still here?"

The public acts of Dr. King you know. They are visible all around you. His voice you would recognize sooner than any other voice you have heard in this century—this in spite of the fact that certain municipal libraries, like the one in downtown Jackson, do not carry recordings of his speeches, and the librarians chuckle cruelly when asked why they do not.

You know, if you have read his books, that his is a complex and revolutionary philosophy that few people are capable of understanding fully or have the patience to <u>embody</u> in themselves. Which is our weakness, which is our loss.

And if you know anything about good Baptist preaching, you can imagine what you missed if you never had a chance to hear Martin Luther King, Jr., preach at Ebenezer Baptist Church.

You know of the prizes and awards that he tended to think very little of. And you know of his concern for the disinherited—the American Indian, the Mexican American, and the poor American white—for whom he cared much.

WORDS TO OWN

dispossession (dis′pə·zesh′ən) *n.*: taking away of one's possessions.

sensibility (sen′sə·bil′ə·tē) *n.*: consciousness; awareness. *Sensibility* also means "emotional responsiveness."

embody (em·bäd′ē) *v.*: make real, give form to, or include.

Reaching All Students

Struggling Readers

Identifying the Main Idea was introduced on p. 366. For a lesson that is directly tied to this speech that teaches students to identify the main idea by using a strategy called Most Important Word, see the *Reading Skills and Strategies* binder:

• MiniRead Skill Lesson, p. 90
• Selection Skill Lesson, p. 96

English Language Learners

These students may not be familiar with the history of the American Civil Rights Movement. For their benefit, you may want to screen a short video documentary on the subject or display photos of marches, sit-ins, and other demonstrations. If you have students who are well-informed on the subject, ask them to share their knowledge with the class and to answer any questions other students might have.

Advanced Learners

Dr. King's ideas about nonviolence were influenced by the writings and experiences of Henry David Thoreau, who was jailed for civil disobedience, and of Mohandas Gandhi, who led India to independence through peaceful means. Have these students hold a "teach-in" to inform the class of Thoreau's and Gandhi's ideas about civil disobedience and passive resistance. Ask them to describe ways in which various groups have applied these ideas.

The Civil Rights Memorial in Montgomery, Alabama.

CHOICE: A TRIBUTE TO DR. MARTIN LUTHER KING, JR. **369**

Making the Connections

Connecting to the Theme:
"We Remember"

After students have read the selection, be sure to talk about the theme of remembrance. Discuss the fact that Alice Walker, like Maya Angelou, uses her own personal memories and family history to make important points about family, home, freedom, and fairness. Point out that by sharing their individual memories and experiences, writers help shape readers' understanding of larger events.

Cultural Connections:
"Dispossession"

Students whose families have recently been dispossessed and forced to leave their homelands may have a deep emotional response to this selection. Encourage them to express their feelings, memories, or family stories in writing, in oral histories, or in art projects that memorialize their ancestral homes. Other students may also wish to create memorials to honor their own dispossessed ancestors.

A Reading Skills and Strategies

Identifying the Main Idea

❓ In sentences that begin with the words "He gave us . . . " what link does Walker make between the idea of home and the idea of continuity? [Possible response: A place can never truly be home until you feel free to stay there, where generations of your family have lived and died, leaving you a rich heritage of memories and stories.]

Resources

Selection Assessment

Formal Assessment
• Selection Test, p. 60

Test Generator (One-Stop Planner)
• CD-ROM

BROWSING IN THE FILES

About the Author. Alice Walker became involved in civil rights demonstrations while she was in college. After graduating, she won a fellowship, which she planned to use in West Africa. Instead, in 1966, she decided to work on a voter registration drive of African Americans in Mississippi. She said her decision was based on the realization that she could never live happily in Africa—or anywhere else—until she could live freely in Mississippi.

Writers on Writing. Alice Walker believes that America's South has bequeathed a special heritage to African American writers: "a compassion for the earth, a trust in humanity beyond our knowledge of evil, and abiding love of justice. We inherit a great responsibility . . . for we must give voice to centuries not only of silent bitterness and hate but also of neighborly kindness and sustaining love."

You know that this very room, in this very restaurant, was closed to people of color not more than five years ago. And that we eat here together tonight largely through his efforts and his blood. We accept the common pleasures of life, assuredly, in his name.

But add to all of these things the one thing that seems to me second to none in importance: He gave us back our heritage. He gave us back our homeland; the bones and dust of our ancestors, who may now sleep within our caring *and* our hearing. He gave us the blueness of the Georgia sky, in autumn as in summer; the colors of the Southern winter as well as glimpses of the green of vacation-time spring. Those of our relatives we used to invite for a visit we now can ask to stay. . . . He gave us full-time use of our own woods and restored our memories to those of us who were forced to run away, as realities we might each day enjoy and leave for our children.

He gave us continuity of place, without which community is <u>ephemeral</u>. He gave us home.

WORDS TO OWN

ephemeral (e·fem′ər·əl) *adj.:* short-lived; passing quickly.

370 THE NONFICTION COLLECTIONS

Alice Walker (1944–   ) is a novelist, short-story writer, poet, and essayist. She is best known for her novel *The Color Purple,* which won a Pulitzer Prize in 1983 and was made into a popular movie starring Whoopi Goldberg and Oprah Winfrey. Alice Walker was born in Eatonton, a small town in Georgia. Her father was a sharecropper, and her mother was a maid. Walker was the youngest of eight children.

In a letter Walker wrote this about other heroes:

❝ I stood looking at a picture of Frederick Douglass I have on my wall. And I asked myself: Where is your picture of Harriet Tubman, the General? Where is your drawing of Sojourner Truth? And I thought that if black women would only start asking questions like that, they'd soon—all of them—have to begin reclaiming their mothers and grandmothers—and what an enrichment that would be! ❞

For more on Alice Walker, see page 557.

Assessing Learning

Check Test: True-False

1. Many African American Southerners moved away from their birthplaces. [True]
2. Walker first saw Dr. King when he was preaching a sermon. [False]
3. Because of Dr. King, Walker vowed not to leave her home without a struggle. [True]
4. Dr. King's teachings were easy to follow. [False]
5. Walker says that King's greatest accomplishment was to give back to African Americans their sense of community. [True]

Standardized Test Preparation

For practice with standardized test format specific to this selection, see
• *Standardized Test Preparation,* pp. 46, 48
For practice in proofreading and editing, see
• *Daily Oral Grammar,* Transparency 23

No One Ever Told Me Not to Dream

from In My Place

Charlayne Hunter-Gault

Charlayne Hunter-Gault grew up in a big family in the Deep South. As one of two black students who bravely integrated the all-white University of Georgia, she was a leading civil rights figure. Eventually, she became a national correspondent for PBS.

On January 9, 1961, I walked onto the campus at the University of Georgia to begin registering for classes. Ordinarily, there would not have been anything unusual about such a routine exercise, except, in this instance, the officials at the university had been fighting for two and a half years to keep me out. I was not socially, intellectually, or morally undesirable. I was black. And no black student had ever been admitted to the University of Georgia in its 176-year history. Until the landmark *Brown* v. *Board of Education* decision that in 1954 declared separate but equal schools unconstitutional, the university was protected by law in its exclusion of people like me. In applying to the university, Hamilton Holmes and I were making one of the first major tests of the court's ruling in Georgia, and no one was sure just how hard it would be to challenge nearly two hundred years of exclusive white privilege. It would take us two and a half years of fighting our way through the system and the courts, but finally, with the help of the NAACP Legal Defense and Educational Fund, Inc., and with the support of our family and friends, we won the right that should have been ours all along. With the ink barely dry on the court

order of three days before, Hamilton Holmes and I walked onto the campus and into history.

We would be greeted by mobs of white students, who within forty-eight hours would hurl epithets, burn crosses and black effigies, and finally stage a riot outside my dormitory while, nearby, state patrolmen ignored the call from university officials to come and intervene. Tear gas would disperse the crowd, but not before I got word in my dorm room, now strewn with glass from a rock through my window, that Hamilton and I were being suspended for our own safety. It might have been the end of the story but for the fact that the University of Georgia was now the lead case in a series of events that would become Georgia's entry into the Civil Rights Revolution. And we—like the legions of young black students to follow in other arenas—were now imbued with an unshakable determination to take control of our destiny and force the South to abandon the wretched Jim Crow laws it had perpetuated for generations to keep us in our place.

The newfound sense of mission that now motivated us evolved for me out of a natural desire to fulfill a dream I had nurtured from an early age. With a passion bordering on obsession, I wanted to be a journalist, a dream that would have been, if not unthinkable, at least undoable in the South of my early years. But no one ever told me not to dream, and when the time came to act on that dream, I would not let anything stand in the way of fulfilling it.

CHOICE: A TRIBUTE TO DR. MARTIN LUTHER KING, JR. 371

Connections

Journalist Charlayne Hunter-Gault was one of the two African American students who integrated the University of Georgia in 1961.

A Elements of Literature
Tone
❓ What is Hunter-Gault's tone as she delivers these disturbing facts? [Possible responses: calm, matter-of-fact, understated.] How does the tone affect the reader's response? [Possible responses: The understated tone makes the facts more surprising and disturbing; the contrast between the matter-of-fact tone and the shocking facts jolts the reader into awareness.]

B Advanced Learners
Challenge these students to research the series of events that led to this landmark Supreme Court decision and to trace the effects the case has had. Ask students to share the information on a time line.

C Critical Thinking
Making Connections
❓ How were Hunter-Gault's actions like those of Dr. Martin Luther King, Jr.? [Possible answers: Like King, she claimed her heritage in a peaceful way; she stood up against bigotry and violence with great courage; she served as a role model for those who followed her.]

D Reading Skills and Strategies
Finding the Main Idea
❓ What key statements are clues to the main idea? [Possible answers: We were "imbued with an unshakable determination to take control of our destiny"; "newfound sense of mission"; "no one ever told me not to dream"; "I would not let anything stand in the way."] Express the main idea in your own words. [Possible answer: Given the hope to dream by an older generation, Hunter-Gault was determined to see that African Americans achieved equal rights and to fulfill her own personal dream of being a journalist.]

Connecting Across Texts

Connecting with "Choice"

Both Walker's speech and the excerpt from Hunter-Gault's autobiography recall instances of individuals courageously stepping forward to advocate civil rights in the United States. Ask students how young people denied entry to segregated colleges may have been affected by the actions of Hunter-Gault and Holmes. [They may have been inspired to fight for their own dreams and rights.]

Have students reread what Alice Walker wrote about Charlayne Hunter-Gault and Hamilton Holmes (p. 368). Ask students to imagine how Martin Luther King, Jr., viewed them and their achievements. [Possible responses: He would have seen them as heroes who gave African Americans full use of educational facilities; he would have believed that they helped young people who had been dispossessed and disinherited.]

MAKING MEANINGS

First Thoughts

1. Students may say that they formed a picture of King as a source of sudden hope to African Americans or as a hero the people had longed for.

Shaping Interpretations

2. Students may not have known how greatly King inspired other African Americans to fight for their rights or what a hero he is to so many people.

3. Walker means the free choice of African Americans to remain in the South and pursue their dreams there instead of being forced away.

4. Possible motives: to illustrate that her people have every right to claim the South as home; to present context for the necessity of the changes King inspired.

5. Possible response: She is referring to people who have been deprived of their rights and their sense of belonging.

6. The main idea of Walker's speech is that people deserve the freedom to enjoy a sense of community where they live. Walker's story illustrates how King inspired people to remain in the land of their birth and to claim their rightful sense of belonging.

7. Possible responses: The word *home* also implies heritage, traditions, and culture passed down over time.

Connecting with the Text

8. Some students may bring up their feelings about their places of birth or about ancestral homelands in other countries to which they want to return. Some may express feelings about having family members living nearby or living on property that has been handed down over the generations.

Extending the Text

9. Possible responses: King freed people to be treated as full citizens within the community of their choice. Other deliverers might include Moses, Joan of Arc, George Washington, Mohandas Gandhi, Harriet Tubman, Mother Teresa, and Nelson Mandela.

10. Try to steer discussion toward ordinary people students know, whose heroism has been quiet and has gone unheralded.

MAKING MEANINGS

First Thoughts

[respond]

1. What picture of Martin Luther King, Jr., did Walker's tribute give you?

Shaping Interpretations

[compare]

2. Did Walker's speech tell you anything new about Martin Luther King, Jr., and his effect on American life? Compare your group's list of King's contributions with the lists made by other groups.

[infer]

3. What choice do you think Walker is referring to in the **title** of her speech?

[interpret]

4. In the first eight paragraphs, Alice Walker talks about her own family. What is her **motive,** or intent, in telling you about these memories?

[infer]

5. Alice Walker says that King had concern for "the disinherited" of all ethnic backgrounds. What do you think she means by *disinherited*?

[generalize]

6. How would you state Walker's **main idea**? How does the story she tells support that main idea?

[interpret]

7. What larger meaning do you read into the word *home* in the last sentence?

Connecting with the Text

[connect]

8. Does anything Walker says here about her family and their dreams remind you of your own family and friends and their hopes for the future?

Extending the Text

[extend]

9. Although heroism is never easy to define, few Americans would deny that King is an authentic hero. In literature, heroes are often portrayed as deliverers of their people. How does King qualify as a deliverer? What other people in history do you think of as deliverers?

[extend]

10. Alice Walker tells us what it meant to her to watch Charlayne Hunter and Hamilton Holmes struggle to integrate the University of Georgia in 1961. In the prologue to *In My Place* (see *Connections* on page 371), Charlayne Hunter-Gault describes her walk onto the campus of the university—to be greeted by rocks, mobs, and riots. What other people can you think of—people like Hunter-Gault and Holmes—who are heroes even though they did not lead armies or nations?

Reading Check

a. Identify the **time** and **setting** of Walker's speech. What is the significance of the location?

b. According to Walker, why did African Americans once have to leave the South?

c. How did Walker first learn about Martin Luther King, Jr.? How did this affect her life?

d. According to Walker, what gifts did Martin Luther King, Jr., leave behind? List the things he gave us.

Reading Check

a. The speech was given in 1972 at a Jackson, Mississippi, restaurant that had refused to serve African Americans until the law compelled it to do so. The location symbolizes the success of King's efforts.

b. They had learned that staying in their homeland, where segregation and prejudice caused suffering, meant losing their affection for the place and seeing only its brutality.

c. She first saw him on TV, being arrested for "claim[ing] his rights as a native son." She knew that from then on she would resist all obstacles to claiming her rightful sense of belonging.

d. King gave people a sense of connection to their ancestors, a feeling of belonging to the land itself, and full enjoyment of their memories.

CHOICES: Building Your Portfolio

Rubrics for each Choices assignment appear on p. 135 in the *Portfolio Management System.*

Writer's Notebook

1. Collecting Ideas for an Autobiographical Incident

Cast of characters. When you write your own autobiographical incident in the Writer's Workshop at the end of this collection (page 386), you may find that the other people involved in the incident are as important as the incident itself. Think back to an event that you will always remember. You probably had a major role, but who else was there? What did each person do or say? What feelings did the person have about the incident? About you? Perhaps it was the actions, words, or feelings of another person that changed you or made the event memorable. Make a list like the one shown here, identifying an autobiographical incident and the other people involved in it.

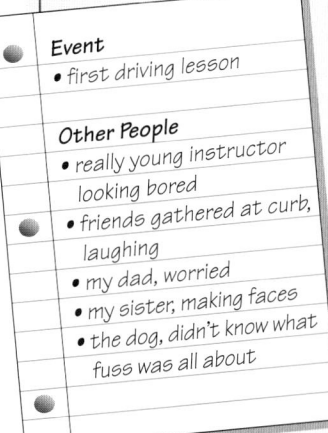

Event
• first driving lesson

Other People
• really young instructor looking bored
• friends gathered at curb, laughing
• my dad, worried
• my sister, making faces
• the dog, didn't know what fuss was all about

Speaking and Listening

2. Telling It Aloud

Read Alice Walker's speech to your class. As you rehearse, decide which words you will emphasize, what tone you will adopt, what gestures you will use. When you are part of the audience for a classmate's presentation, take notes so that you can make helpful suggestions. When the presentations are over, discuss how hearing the speech and delivering it affected the way you feel about it.

Descriptive Writing

3. A Place Called Home

Walker obviously loves the South, the place she and her family call home. She evokes the blueness of the Georgia sky in autumn and summer, the colors of the Southern winter, the green of spring. Write a brief description of a place you love: Tell your readers how you came to know this place, what it looks like and sounds like and feels like. Is it a place connected in your mind with people?

Summarizing an Idea

4. Reporting on the Speech

Suppose you were a reporter who went to the restaurant to hear Alice Walker deliver this speech in memory of Martin Luther King. Write a feature story about the occasion. Summarize the **main idea** of Walker's speech, tell how she supported her idea, and quote any particularly interesting details from the speech. As a feature writer, you will want to present not only objective facts about the occasion but your own subjective feelings as well. If you have any questions about Walker's speech, include them in your feature article.

CHOICE: A TRIBUTE TO DR. MARTIN LUTHER KING, JR. **373**

CHOICES: Building Your Portfolio

1. **Writer's Notebook** Remind students to save their work. They may use it as prewriting for the Writer's Workshop on p. 386.
2. **Speaking and Listening** Before students begin practicing their speeches, write a list of speaking techniques on the chalkboard. Techniques include making eye contact with the audience, pausing, and altering tone of voice and rate of delivery at appropriate times. So that your students can hear and critique themselves, tape-record their presentations.
3. **Descriptive Writing** Have students use a graphic like the one below to generate ideas about a favorite place as the possible setting for an autobiographical incident.

Place:
How I know the place:
Connected to (people):
Looks like:
Smells like:
Feels like:
Sounds like:

4. **Summarizing an Idea** Remind students to begin their feature article with a paragraph that will capture readers' attention and make them want to read about Walker's ideas: a vivid description, fact, or quotation.

T373

LANGUAGE LINK

Ask students to identify words in a piece of their writing that have strong connotations. Have partners share their writing to see if reader reaction is what they intended.

Try It Out
Possible Responses

1. impression: pride; key words: *slave, ancestral home, two babies;* purpose: to stress heroism of the woman
2. impression: awe, reverence; key words: *One, Hero, Fearless;* purpose: to emphasize King's significance
3. impression: gratitude; key words: *homeland, ancestors, caring;* purpose: to convey the importance and meaning of King's gift
4. impression: beauty, contentment, hope; key words: *blueness, sky, autumn, summer, winter, green, spring;* purpose: to show that what King offered people was lasting and to evoke the speaker's deep love for the South

VOCABULARY

Possible Answers

1. A dispossessed person might feel sad, angry, humiliated, frightened, resentful.
2. Memories of childhood joys, family occasions, and natural beauty are part of this sensibility.
3. They might try to solve problems peacefully and work for justice without resorting to force.
4. Most will agree that to have a lasting sense of community, people must feel a sense of permanence in a particular place.

Resources ────────

Language
• *Grammar and Language Links,* Worksheet, p. 39

Vocabulary
• *Words to Own,* Worksheet, p. 18

LANGUAGE LINK 〔 MINI-LESSON 〕

Handbook of Literary Terms
H E L P

See Connotation.

Communications Handbook
H E L P

See Using a Dictionary; Using a Thesaurus.

Connotations: Emotional Context

Many words affect us in powerful ways. The associations and emotional responses that some words call up are their **connotations**. Those same words also have strict dictionary meanings, which are their **denotations**. Consider the name *New York,* which has a dictionary meaning (a city on the Hudson River) but also a whole range of connotations, from negative (overcrowding and noise) to positive (glamour and excitement).

The following passages from Walker's speech carry strong emotional connotations.

1. "My great-great-great-grandmother walked as a slave from Virginia to Eatonton, Georgia—which passes for the Walker ancestral home—with two babies on her hips."

2. "He was The One, The Hero, The One Fearless Person for whom we had waited."

3. "He gave us back our homeland; the bones and dust of our ancestors, who may now sleep within our caring *and* our hearing."

4. "He gave us the blueness of the Georgia sky, in autumn as in summer; the colors of the Southern winter as well as glimpses of the green of vacation-time spring."

> **Try It Out**
>
> ➤ Look at the sentences opposite. Discuss the feeling or impression that each sentence evokes for you. Find the sentence's key words. Think: Why did Walker choose this precise word or phrase? Try asking other people how these sentences make them feel.
>
> ➤ Pull out any of the notes you've taken for an autobiographical incident (for the Writer's Notebook assignments). Now list at least four strong words or phrases you could use to describe a person, a place, or an episode in any of those incidents.

VOCABULARY 〔 HOW TO OWN A WORD 〕

> **WORD BANK**
> *dispossession*
> *sensibility*
> *embody*
> *ephemeral*
>
> ### Back to the Text
>
> 1. Walker states that the history of her family "... is a history of dispossession." How would a victim of dispossession feel?
> 2. Walker says, "It is a part of the black Southern sensibility that we treasure memories. . . ." What sort of memories do you think are part of this sensibility?
> 3. Walker explains King's philosophy as one "... that few people are capable of understanding fully or have the patience to embody in themselves." If people were to embody nonviolent philosophy, how might their behavior change?
> 4. Walker says that King "... gave us continuity of place, without which community is ephemeral." Do you agree?

374 THE NONFICTION COLLECTIONS

Language Link Quick Check

Write two connotations for each word, name, or phrase below. (Possible answers are given.)

1. Martin Luther King, Jr. [heroism, strength]
2. slave [non-person, cruelty, bondage]
3. home [security, happiness]
4. community [neighbors, support]
5. ancestors [heritage, pride]
6. mob [anger, lawlessness]
7. autumn [sadness, beauty]
8. mission [commitment, determination]
9. blood [sacrifice, tragedy]
10. hero [sacrifice, inspiration]

Before You Read

THE TALK

Make the Connection

Do People Like Nice Faces?

In this true story a twelve-year-old boy who is disgusted with his own looks says, "People like people with nice faces." Is he right? How much emphasis does our society place on appearances?

Quickwrite

Write down some of your own thoughts about this boy's statement. Think about the importance of good looks in the media, in your school, and in your own reactions to people.

Elements of Literature

Exaggeration Is a Big Deal

In literature, **exaggeration** is overstating something in order to create some effect: to express a strong emotion, to be funny, to emphasize a point.

Writers have been amusing (and sometimes irritating) readers by making the most of exaggeration for thousands—make that billions—of years.

> **E**xaggeration means overstating something in a big way—make that "in a *colossal* way."

Reading Skills and Strategies

Finding the Main Idea: Supported with a Story

Soto seems to state his main idea—the message that he wants to communicate—in his very first sentence. So what's next? To develop his main idea, he tells us a story. Note how Soto uses his true story to help you share his feelings. Do the boys' exaggerated feelings about their looks seem true to life to you? When you finish the essay, go back and reread the first sentence. Do you think it really states the essay's main idea?

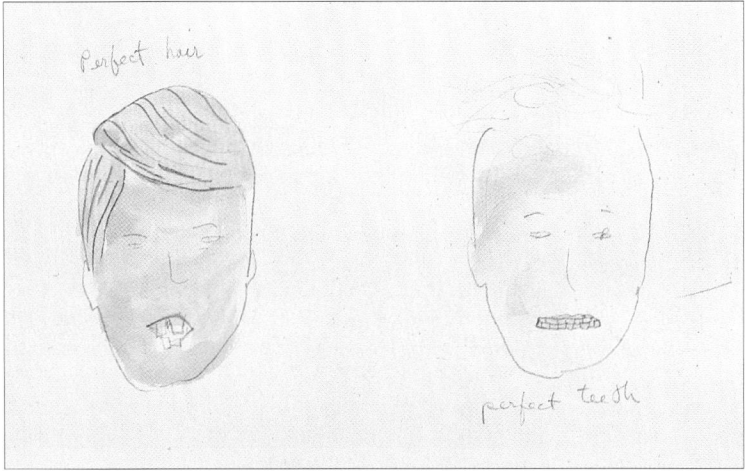

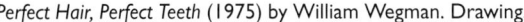

Perfect Hair, Perfect Teeth (1975) by William Wegman. Drawing.

go.hrw.com
LE0 9-5

THE TALK 375

T375

Summary ▪

At age twelve, Gary Soto and his best friend, Scott, have big dreams—of jobs and homes and wives—but believe they are too homely to make their fantasies come true. They bemoan their crooked teeth and odd physiques. When they spot a beautiful girl through a window, her loveliness only plunges them deeper into despair.

Resources

Viewing and Representing
Videocassette A, Segment 5
Available in Spanish and English. This *Visual Connections* segment offers an interview with Gary Soto. For full lesson plans and worksheets, see the *Visual Connections Teacher's Manual.*

Listening
Audio CD Library
A recording of the essay is provided in the *Audio CD Library:*
• Disc 13, Track 8

RESPONDING TO THE ART

Activity. How does the artist draw the viewer's eye to the area of the female figure? [with color (bright red against grays) and a realistic drawing against an abstract background] **What do the abstract areas suggest?** [Possible responses: Shapes in the foreground may be blades of grass or fingers; the area surrounding the window may be a house or an apartment building.] Have students compare the subjects of the painting and the essay. [Sample responses: Both the viewer of the painting and the boys in the essay gaze through a lighted window at a female figure; the boys dream of marrying women who will fulfill traditional female roles, as the woman in the painting appears to be doing.]

Washing a Dish (1986) by Candida Alvarez. Acrylic/gel on paper (44 ¼″ × 30 ¾″).

Reproduced by permission of the artist.

376 THE NONFICTION COLLECTIONS

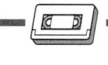 *Resources: Print and Media*

Reading
• *Graphic Organizers for Active Reading*, p. 24
• *Audio CD Library*, Disc 13, Track 8

Writing and Language
• *Daily Oral Grammar*
    Transparency 24

Viewing and Representing
• *Visual Connections*
    Videocassette A, Segment 5

Assessment
• *Formal Assessment*, p. 62
• *Portfolio Management System*, p. 136
• *Standardized Test Preparation*, p. 50
• *Test Generator (One-Stop Planner* CD-ROM)

Internet
• *go.hrw.com* (keyword: *LE0 9-5*)

THE TALK

Gary Soto

My best friend and I knew that we were going to grow up to be ugly. On a backyard lawn—the summer light failing west of the mulberry tree where the house of the most beautiful girl on our street stood—we talked about what we could do: shake the second-base dirt from our hair, wash our hands of frog smells and canal water, and learn to smile without showing our crooked teeth. We had to stop spitting when girls were looking and learn not to pile food onto a fork and into a fat cheek already churning hot grub.

We were twelve, with lean bodies that were beginning to grow in weird ways. First, our heads got large, but our necks wavered, frail as crisp tulips. The eyes stayed small as well, receding into pencil dots on each side of an unshapely nose that cast remarkable shadows when we turned sideways. It seemed that Scott's legs sprouted muscle and renegade veins, but his arms, blue with ink markings, stayed short and hung just below his waist. My gangly arms nearly touched my kneecaps. In this way, I was built for picking up grounders and doing cartwheels, my arms swaying just inches from the summery grass.

We sat on the lawn, with the porch light off, waiting for the beautiful girl to turn on her bedroom light and read on her stomach with one leg stirring the air. This stirred us, and our dream was a clean dream of holding hands and airing out our loneliness by walking up and down the block.

When Scott asked whom I was going to marry, I said a brown girl from the valley. He said that he was going to marry a strawberry blonde who would enjoy Millerton Lake, dirty as it was. I said mine would like cats and the sea and would think nothing of getting up at night from a warm, restless bed and sitting in the yard under the icy stars. Scott said his wife would work for the first year or so, because he would go to trade school in refrigeration. Since our town was made with what was left over after God made hell, there was money in air conditioning, he reasoned.

I said that while my wife would clean the house and stir pots of nice grub, I would drive a truck to my job as a carpenter, which would allow me to use my long arms. I would need only a stepladder to hand a fellow worker on the roof a pinch of nails. I could hammer, saw, lift beams into place, and see the work I got done at the end of the day. Of course, she might like to work, and that would be okay, because then we could buy two cars and wave at each other if we should see the other drive by. In the evenings, we would drink Kool-Aid and throw a slipper at our feisty dog at least a hundred times before we went inside for a Pop-Tart and hot chocolate.

Scott said he would work hard too, but now and then he would find money on the street and the two of them could buy extra things like a second TV for the bedroom and a Doughboy swimming pool for his three kids. He planned on having three kids and a ranch house on the river, where he could dip a hand in the water, drink, and say, "Ahh, tastes good."

But that would be years later. Now we had to do something about our looks. We plucked at the grass and flung it into each other's faces.

Ⓐ Reading Skills and Strategies

Finding the Main Idea

❓ What do the boys consider their biggest problem? [They think they're going to grow up to be ugly.] In the paragraph, how does the author develop this main idea? [He has the boys talk about ideas for improving their appearance—cleaning their hair, washing their hands, smiling without showing their teeth, stopping spitting, eating more slowly.]

Ⓑ Appreciating Language

Figures of Speech

❓ What figures of speech are used to describe the boys' twelve-year-old bodies? [Simile: "our necks wavered, frail as crisp tulips"; metaphor: "eyes . . . receding into pencil dots."]

Ⓒ Elements of Literature

Exaggeration

❓ Do you think the narrator's arms really hung down to his kneecaps? Why does he exaggerate? [Possible responses: The exaggeration suggests how self-conscious he felt about his body when he was twelve; he's poking fun at his gangly adolescent self.]

Ⓓ Reading Skills and Strategies

Connecting with the Text

In their writer's notebooks, have students describe their own ideas of what their adult lives will be like.

Reaching All Students

Struggling Readers

Finding the Main Idea was introduced on p. 375. One good strategy to use with this skill is Most Important Word. For information on using this strategy, see p. 45 in the *Reading Strategies Handbook* in front of the *Reading Skills and Strategies* binder.

English Language Learners

In addition to other challenges of assimilating into American culture, some English language learners may have to deal with the issue of looking "different" from many of their peers. Have students write about this issue in their first language and then translate their ideas into English during a discussion with a trusted partner.

Advanced Learners

In the Quickwrite on p.375, students evaluate the importance of appearance in various segments of society. Advanced students may enjoy developing this idea by studying standards of male and female attractiveness as reflected in newspaper and magazine advertisements. Have them prepare a collage of these images and discuss the messages they convey to teenagers.

A Reading Skills and Strategies

Finding the Main Idea

? Why doesn't Soto give "the beautiful girl" a name? [Possible responses: He doesn't know or remember her name; describing her simply as "beautiful" suggests Soto's main idea—that in adolescence, appearance can seem to be the most important thing in the world.]

B Elements of Literature

Exaggeration

? The phrase "big trouble" exaggerates the problem. Did you find Soto's use of exaggeration funny or sad? [Some students may see the humor in the boys' exaggerated despair; others may still identify too strongly with the boys' insecurity to find the problem anything but sad.]

Resources ———

Selection Assessment

Formal Assessment
• Selection Test, p. 62
Test Generator (One-Stop Planner)
• CD-ROM

"Rotten luck," Scott said. "My arms are too short. Look at 'em."

"Maybe we can lift weights. This would make up for our looks," I said.

"I don't think so," Scott said, depressed. "People like people with nice faces."

He was probably right. I turned onto my stomach, a stalk of grass in my mouth. "Even if I'm ugly, my wife's going to be good-looking," I said. "She'll have a lot of dresses and I'll have more shirts than I have now. Do you know how much carpenters make?"

A Then I saw the bedroom light come on and the beautiful girl walk into the room drying her hair with a towel. I nudged Scott's short arm and he saw what I saw. We flicked the stalks of grass, stood up, and walked over to the fence to look at her scrub her hair dry. She plopped onto the bed and began to comb it, slowly at first because it was tangled. With a rubber band, she

tied it back, and picked up a book that was thick as a good-sized sandwich.

Scott and I watched her read a book, now both legs in the air and twined together, her painted toenails like red petals. She turned the pages slowly, very carefully, and now and then lowered her face into the pillow. She looked sad but beautiful, and we didn't know what to do except nudge each other in the heart and creep away to the front yard.

"I can't stand it anymore. We have to talk about this," Scott said.

"If I try, I think I can make myself better looking," I said. "I read an article about a girl whitening her teeth with water and flour."

B So we walked up the street, depressed. For every step I took, Scott took two, his short arms pumping to keep up. For every time Scott said, "I think we're ugly," I said two times, "Yeah, yeah, we're in big trouble."

MEET THE WRITER

A California Boy

Gary Soto (1952–) grew up in a Mexican American family in Fresno, a city in California's San Joaquin Valley. He went to college planning to major in geography. Then a poem—"Unwanted" by Edward Field—changed his life. The poem helped him discover the power of language. He began to see how he could reach other people by writing about his own experience, and that's exactly what he did—and is still doing today. Soto even called his first book, *The Elements of San Joaquin* (1977), after his birthplace. Much of his award-winning

fiction and poetry draws on childhood memories, the everyday details of Mexican American life. As Soto puts it:

66 I tried to remain faithful to the common things of my childhood—dogs, alleys, my baseball mitt, curbs, and the fruit of the valley. . . . I wanted to give these things life. 99

More Everyday Stories

If you enjoyed "The Talk," take a look at the book it came from: *A Summer Life* (Dell). You might also enjoy Soto's stories in *Baseball in April* (Harcourt Brace) and his collection of poems for young adults, *A Fire in My Hands* (Scholastic).

378 THE NONFICTION COLLECTIONS

Assessing Learning

Check Test: True-False

1. The boys are twelve years old. [True]
2. Both boys are very good looking. [False]
3. The boys observe a girl from a distance. [True]
4. The boys think they are in big trouble because they are late. [False]
5. The narrator is recalling the conversation as an adult. [True]

Standardized Test Preparation

For practice with standardized test format specific to this selection, see
• *Standardized Test Preparation,* p. 50
For practice in proofreading and editing, see
• *Daily Oral Grammar,* Transparency 24

Student to Student

Life's Changes

Adolescence.
For those of you who don't know what adolescence is, it is a time
or period in your life when you're a young teenager.
I know at times it makes us uncomfortable and we don't want to
go through it, but yes it's major.
Oh don't worry you don't have to take a test on it or even study
because it's common sense.

5   I know what I'm talking about because I am 13 myself as we speak.
Adolescence changes you in many ways.
Hips get bigger, you grow taller, shoulders get wider, voices get
deeper, hair grows all over, and zits pop up—sorry to say but
all of this stays.
While you're changing beware, you may feel awkward at times, but
wait and see the finished product, don't be so quick to imagine
yourself as a geek.

But it's really cool not being an adult, not being a child, but our very
own social group of teenage adolescents.
Sometimes we're up, sometimes we're down, sometime we're happy,
10   sometime we frown.

Always remember adolescents have a special beauty of their own.
If it's not found on the outside, it is always found within.
Each adolescent is special from beginning to end.

—Candice Nolan
Sutherland Magnet School
Chicago, Illinois

THE TALK 379

MAKING MEANINGS

First Thoughts

1. Some students will say the tone and content of the conversation remind them of typical conversations they hear every day. They may say teenagers are especially conscious of their changing appearance and of standards of attractiveness set by society and their peers.

Shaping Interpretations

2. Possible exaggerations: "necks . . . frail as tulips," "eyes . . . receding into pencil dots," "nose that cast . . . shadows," "arms nearly touched . . . kneecaps" (p. 377). All the examples reveal how self-conscious the boys feel about their appearance and how unaccustomed they are to their changing and growing bodies.

Extending the Text

3. Answers will vary. Students may point out the mass media's stress on good looks and money but may give high ratings to other important values. Students may enjoy compiling the class results and determining which qualities were rated most and least important.

Grading Timesaver

Rubrics for each Choices assignment appear on p. 136 in the *Portfolio Management System.*

CHOICES: Building Your Portfolio

1. **Writer's Notebook** Remind students to save their work. They may use it as prewriting for the Writer's Workshop on p. 386.

2. **Responding to the Essay** Help students get started by reminding them that the essay is a reflection on the importance of good looks. How important is appearance to the boys? How does the adult Soto seem to view their obsession with looks? Do students agree more with the boys or with the narrator as an adult?

3. **Drawing** Students might create caricatures from magazine cuttings rather than drawing them. Remind students to keep Soto's humorous tone in mind.

T380

MAKING MEANINGS

First Thoughts

[connect]

1. Do any of Soto's characters remind you of yourself—or someone you know? Explain.

Shaping Interpretations

[analyze]

2. Soto uses **exaggeration** to describe himself and his friend Scott. Find two exaggerated statements in the text. What do they tell you about how the boys feel about themselves?

Extending the Text

[extend]

3. Look over the Quickwrite notes you made about the importance of looks in our society. How important *are* good looks? What about other factors—such as good character, honesty, hard work, money? Rate some factors on a scale. Be sure to discuss your ratings in class.

> **Reading Check**
>
> Imagine that in ten years Scott and Gary happen to meet in a restaurant. They reminisce about their talk. With a partner, take the parts of Scott and Gary. Retell what they recall about their talk.

CHOICES: Building Your Portfolio

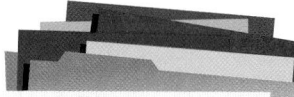

Writer's Notebook

1. Collecting Ideas for an Autobiographical Incident

At the tone. You're going to be writing an autobiographical incident like Soto's in the Writer's Workshop on page 386. Do you want to write humorously like Soto or will you try for some other **tone**? You may want to be serious, sad, sarcastic, or something else altogether. List one or more incidents you might write about (you should have some ideas in your notebook already). Tell why they were important to you, and describe the tone you'd aim for if you wrote about them.

Responding to the Essay

2. What Is Soto Saying?

In a paragraph or two, describe your response to Soto's essay. Open with a statement summing up what you think is Soto's **main idea.** (Does Soto's first sentence really state his main idea?) Then, tell how you responded to the feelings he shares with you. Mention specific details in the essay that made an impact on you.

Drawing

3. Caricatures

Draw caricatures (kar′i·kə·chərz) of what you think Gary and Scott look like. (See page 538 for a caricature of William Shakespeare.) Because a caricature exaggerates certain features, you might want to reread the selection to get ideas. You'll probably find that a cartoon style gives the amusing touch you want. Use a brief passage from the essay as a caption for each caricature.

> **Reading Check**
>
> Students may begin with a dialogue like the following one:
>
> **Gary:** Hey, remember how we talked about our futures that time when we were twelve?
>
> **Scott:** Yeah. You thought you would become a carpenter, and you ended up a writer.
>
> **Gary:** Well, you said you would study refrigeration, and you ended up with your own appliance-repair business.
>
> **Scott:** Remember that girl we used to watch? The one that made us both feel so ugly?

Communications Handbook HELP

See Strategies for Taking Tests.

Analogies

You can reach a better understanding of many words by completing an analogy. An analogy shows the relationship between two pairs of words, stating the relationship in a sentence or expressing the relationship using symbols (: and ::). There are many ways that two things can be related, but the most common types of analogies are shown opposite.

KIND OF RELATIONSHIP	EXAMPLE
Degree	Pink is to red as lavender is to purple. (pink : red :: lavender : purple)
Size	Puddle is to lake as anthill is to mountain.
Parts and wholes	Branch is to tree as petal is to flower.
Cause and effect	Cold is to shiver as danger is to tremble.
Synonyms	Brave is to courageous as friendly is to amicable.
Antonyms	Brave is to cowardly as friendly is to hostile.

Which word is the logical choice? To complete an analogy, you analyze the relationship between the first pair of words and then choose a word to make a second pair with a similar relationship. Here is how you can decide which word fits in the following analogy:

Whacked is to tapped as shoved is to _____.

    flicked   nudged   plucked   plopped

1. The relationship between the first pair of words is one of degree. *Whacked* indicates a strong hit, while *tapped* indicates a light one.

2. In the second pair, *shoved* indicates a rough push. Of the word choices, the one that indicates a gentle push is *nudged*.

Sharpening your reasoning skills. When you use analogies as a vocabulary strategy, you are putting your reasoning and logic abilities to work. Give yourself and your classmates a mental workout by creating analogies. Try coming up with analogies for the following words from "The Talk": *renegade, gangly, feisty, grub.*

GARFIELD © 1990 PAWS, INC. Reprinted with permission of UNIVERSAL PRESS SYNDICATE. All rights reserved.

THE TALK 381

Stress the importance of word order in analogies, and then help students explain in their own words the relationships expressed in each example from the chart. Examples:

Degree: *Pink* is a lighter shade of *red*, just as *lavender* is a lighter shade of *purple.*

Size: A *puddle* is like a tiny *lake*, and an *anthill* is like a tiny *mountain.*

Parts and wholes: A *branch* is part of a *tree*, just as a *petal* is part of a *flower.*

Cause and effect: Exposure to *cold* can make you *shiver*, just as exposure to *danger* can make you *tremble.*

Synonyms: *Brave* equals *courageous*, and *friendly* equals *amicable.*

Antonyms: *Brave* is the opposite of *cowardly*, just as *friendly* is the opposite of *hostile.*

Sharpening Your Reasoning Skills

Have students explain the relationship in each of their analogies.

Sample Answers

1. renegade : turncoat :: warrior : fighter [synonyms]
2. gangly : coordinated :: clumsy : graceful [antonyms]
3. feisty : frenzied :: calm : comatose [degree]
4. hungry : grub :: thirsty : water [cause and effect]

Vocabulary Quick Check

Fill in a word that completes each of the following analogies. Identify the type of relationship each analogy shows. Answers will vary. (Possible responses are given.)

1. Exaggerate is to minimize as bigger is to [smaller]. [antonyms]

2. Elbow is to arm as [knee] is to leg. [parts and whole]

3. Happiness is to laugh as sadness is to [cry]. [cause and effect]

4. Ordinary is to ugly as pretty is to [beautiful]. [degree]

5. Thin is to gangly as tangled is to [twisted]. [synonyms]

T381

In 1993, **Jacob Lawrence** (see p. 272) returned to this work, which he had created in the 1940s, and revised both the text and the title. (The original title of the sixty-panel work was *The Migration of the Negro Northwards*.) The middle figure here might be John the Baptist. The woman at right is probably Mary, the mother of Jesus.

Activity. Ask students in what order their line of vision moves as they view the panel. Discuss the fact that the artist has used diagonals to lead the viewer's eye upward. Then discuss the mood of peace and stillness that the work creates. After students have read Dudley Randall's "Ballad of Birmingham," ask them to compare the mood of the painting with the mood of the ballad. [Students may say that the mood in the ballad is tense, violent, shattering, despairing—opposite to the mood of the artwork.]

The Museum of Modern Art, New York. Gift of Mrs. David M. Levy. Photograph ©2000 The Museum of Modern Art, New York. Courtesy of the artist and the Francine Seders Gallery, Seattle, Washington.

"One of the main forms of social and recreational activities in which the migrants indulged occurred in the church." Panel 54 from *The Migration Series* (1940–1941; text and title revised by the artist, 1993) by Jacob Lawrence. Tempera on gesso on composition board (12" x 18").

Crossing the Curriculum

Social Studies

Martin Luther King, Jr., was a Baptist minister, and many events in the Civil Rights Movement were organized by southern churches with African American ministers. Have students research the role played by clergy and religious organizations in the Civil Rights Movement.

Music

As part of the "We Remember" theme, play for the class recordings of songs that inspired participants in the Civil Rights Movement. For example, protest marchers often sang "We Shall Overcome" and "We Shall Not Be Moved" to keep up their courage. Popular songs of the day such as Marvin Gaye's "What's Goin' On" also reflected the spirit of protest. A moving song about the church bombing is "Birmingham Sunday."

the theme

A BALLAD AND A HISTORY

OBJECTIVES
1. Read a literary ballad
2. Find thematic connections across genres
3. Generate relevant and interesting discussion

Background

On Sunday morning, September 15, 1963, in the midst of the struggle for civil rights for African Americans, a bomb exploded in the Sixteenth Street Baptist Church in Birmingham, Alabama. Four little girls were killed. Dudley Randall responded to the tragic events of that day by writing a ballad, a song that tells a story.

Reading Skills and Strategies

Dialogue with the Text

Keep a record of your responses to this ballad and to the historical account of the bombing that appears on page 384. Respond to details in each account and record any questions you'd like to ask about the explosion.

 go.hrw.com
LEO 9-5

Extending the Theme

Dudley Randall's literary ballad and Taylor Branch's historical account of the 1963 bombing of the Sixteenth Street Baptist Church in Birmingham, Alabama, offer two perspectives on this act of terrorism. Both the ballad and the history, each in its own way, evoke the feelings of despair engendered by an American tragedy.

Ballad of Birmingham

(On the bombing of a church in Birmingham, Alabama, 1963)

Dudley Randall

"Mother dear, may I go downtown
Instead of out to play,
And march the streets of Birmingham
In a Freedom March today?"

5 "No, baby, no, you may not go,
For the dogs are fierce and wild,
And clubs and hoses, guns and jails
Aren't good for a little child."

"But, mother, I won't be alone.
10 Other children will go with me,
And march the streets of Birmingham
To make our country free."

"No, baby, no, you may not go,
For I fear those guns will fire.
15 But you may go to church instead
And sing in the children's choir."

She has combed and brushed her
   night-dark hair,
And bathed rose-petal sweet,
And drawn white gloves on her small
   brown hands,
20 And white shoes on her feet.

The mother smiled to know her child
Was in the sacred place,
But that smile was the last smile
To come upon her face.

25 For when she heard the explosion,
Her eyes grew wet and wild.
She raced through the streets of Birmingham
Calling for her child.

She clawed through bits of glass and brick,
30 Then lifted out a shoe.
"O, here's the shoe my baby wore,
But, baby, where are you?"

BALLAD OF BIRMINGHAM 383

A Historical Connection

A freedom march was an organized protest against racial segregation and for civil rights. The marchers were frequently blasted with high-pressure water from fire hoses, set upon by police dogs, and beaten with nightsticks.

B Elements of Literature

Irony

The mother fears for her child's safety at the march but trusts that the church will be a safe haven. Her trust turns out to be tragically misplaced.

C Elements of Literature

Rhyme

The end rhymes in the second and fourth lines of each stanza produce a soothing sense of regularity in stark contrast with the horror of the unfolding events.

D Reading Skills and Strategies

Dialogue with the Text

❓ What is the impact of the last line of the poem? [Possible responses: It comes as a shock, even though the outcome is known; it makes you hope that the mother's child was not one of the girls killed; it makes you think how awful it would be to have nothing left from a loved one but an article of clothing.]

Using Students' Strengths

Auditory Learners

Select three students to read the parts of mother, daughter, and narrator. Allow them time to practice their speaking parts, encouraging them to interpret the words expressively. Then have readers present their interpretations to the entire class. Consider having several groups give readings so that students can hear various interpretations of the poem.

Visual Learners

Students may not be familiar with the freedom marches of the 1950s and 1960s and the violence the marchers often encountered. Display photos or screen video footage of events from the Civil Rights Movement. You might ask a small group of students to locate relevant visual resources in your school or community library.

A **Reading Skills and Strategies**
Dialogue with the Text

? How did knowing that four young girls died in the bombing affect you as you read this account of events that took place before the explosion? [Possible responses: It gave me a feeling of dread and made me feel helpless to stop the tragedy; it made me wish I could warn the girls or stop them from heading for their Sunday school room.]

B **Critical Thinking**
Analyzing Irony

? What is ironic about the lesson the adults are discussing in their Sunday school class? [Possible responses: The lesson is on forgiveness, but it will be nearly impossible to forgive the cruelty about to occur; people who are striving for high moral character do not deserve to be the objects of hatred.]

FINDING COMMON GROUND

As its name suggests, this activity helps students to work their way to areas of agreement by comparing their responses to two related texts.

1. Students may prefer to work in small groups or with partners to develop the first round of questions and possible answers. Allow students who have strong feelings about their lists of questions to post their work even if it is not the focus reached by consensus.

2. Sample answers follow.
   Historical facts included: the dangers faced by freedom marchers, the little girl's white clothing, the explosion, the finding of a shoe.
   Historical facts omitted: names, details about the other three little girls, the adult meeting upstairs.
   Invented: the dialogue, the daughter's preparations for church, the mother's contentment that her daughter was in a safe place and her race to the church.

The History Behind the Ballad

Taylor Branch

The following account is from Parting the Waters, *a book that won the Pulitzer Prize in history in 1989.*

That Sunday was the annual Youth Day at the Sixteenth Street Baptist Church. Mamie H. Grier, superintendent of the Sunday school, stopped in at the basement ladies' room to find four young girls who had left Bible classes early and were talking excitedly about the beginning of the school year. All four were dressed in white from head to toe, as this was their day to run the main service for the adults at eleven o'clock. Grier urged them to hurry along and then went upstairs to sit in on her own women's Sunday-school class. They were engaged in a lively debate on the lesson topic, "The Love That Forgives," when a loud earthquake shook the entire church and showered the classroom with plaster and debris. Grier's first thought was that it was like a ticker-tape parade. Maxine McNair, a schoolteacher sitting next to her, reflexively went stiff and was the only one to speak. "Oh, my goodness!" she said. She escaped with Grier, but the stairs down to the basement were blocked and the large stone staircase on the outside literally had vanished. They stumbled through the church to the front door and then made their way around outside through the gathering noise of moans and sirens. A hysterical church member shouted to Grier that her husband had already gone to the hospital in the first ambulance. McNair searched desperately for her only child until finally she came upon a sobbing old man and screamed, "Daddy, I can't find Denise!" The man helplessly replied, "She's dead, baby. I've got one of her shoes." He held a girl's white dress shoe, and the look on his daughter's face made him scream out, "I'd like to blow the whole town up!"

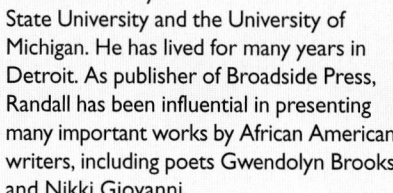

MEET THE WRITER

Poet and Publisher

Dudley Randall (1914–   ), author of "Ballad of Birmingham," was born in Washington, D.C., and educated at Wayne State University and the University of Michigan. He has lived for many years in Detroit. As publisher of Broadside Press, Randall has been influential in presenting many important works by African American writers, including poets Gwendolyn Brooks and Nikki Giovanni.

FINDING COMMON GROUND

1. Look at the notes you made as you read "Ballad of Birmingham" and the selection from *Parting the Waters.* Compare your questions with those of your classmates. See if you can reach a consensus about the questions you'd like to discuss.

2. **Folk ballads** belong to the oral tradition; the songs are passed on through performance, from one singer to another. **Literary ballads,** like the one Randall has written, are composed by known individuals in imitation of folk ballads. Discuss Randall's choice of the ballad as the form in which to relate the events of September 15, 1963. Which historical facts did he include? Which did he omit? Did he invent anything?

Making the Connections

Connecting to the Theme: "We Remember"

You might recommend a Young Adult novel called *The Watsons Go To Birmingham* by Christopher Paul Curtis. The novel, a Newbery Honor Book, is available in the HRW Library. The novel is historical fiction: it uses fictional characters and some fictional situations, but the real setting for the story is Birmingham, Alabama, 1963. The bombing of the church is included in the story. The novel is easy to read. It can provide a springboard for a discussion of the use of real events in fiction. It could also be the start of an investigation into the church bombing. Books and articles have been written about the tragedy, and Spike Lee has produced a film about the bombing, called *4 Little Girls.*

READ ON

A Lost World

Life for young Isaac Bashevis Singer was sometimes treacherous, but as he reveals in *A Day of Pleasure: Stories of a Boy Growing Up in Warsaw* (Farrar, Straus and Giroux), it was also filled with delight. Singer recalls days crowded with fascinating characters—scholars, rabbis, soldiers, panhandlers. Follow him in these autobiographical stories through breezy forests and across filthy gutters, in a world later wiped out forever by the Holocaust.

In Her Mother's Words

Karen was a quiet, well-behaved baby, weighing just under two pounds at birth. She was the delight of family and friends, and when they discovered that she had cerebral palsy, her struggle became their struggle. Karen's mother, Marie Killilea, tells her daughter's story in *Karen* (Dell), sharing special moments in the life of a special child: Karen taking her first shaky steps, Karen writing her first words. This award-winning book has become a classic, touching and inspiring millions of readers.

This Boy's Life

You might already know Roald Dahl's fantasy stories: *James and the Giant Peach,* for starters, or *Charlie and the Chocolate Factory.* Did you ever wonder about the childhood of the writer who created—from scratch—such fantastic worlds? You can read about it in *Boy* (Penguin). Follow Dahl around England, Wales, and Norway, through "sweetshops," magic islands, and public-school days, as he tells of his adventures with all the humor, enchantment, and sometimes even horror, of his fiction.

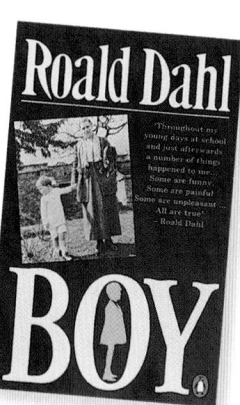

Portfolio Assessment Options

The following projects can help you evaluate and assess your students' reading accomplishments outside class. Videotapes or photographs of completed projects may be included in students' portfolios.

- **A Related Topic** Have students research a particular topic that the book they choose addresses—World War I, children who are physically challenged, or the lives of immigrants, for example. Students' findings should be presented informally to the class with visual aids, such as slides, news clips, illustrations, maps, and photographs.

- **Time Travel** Have students take the class back in time to the year in which one of the books they read took place. Students should create a classroom display including photographs or examples of clothing and hairstyles fashionable at the time. They should list titles of popular songs along with words and phrases spoken during that time, such as "groovy" or "cool" during the 1960s, and should include a synopsis of what was taking place in the world.

- **Hollywood! Hollywood!** Have students make plans for the book they just read to be made into a movie. Students may use a graphic organizer like this to list details.

Title:
Author:
Major Scenes
1. Props:
2. Props:
3. Props:
4. Props:
Main Characters
Name:
Description:
Name:
Description:
Name:
Description:
Name:
Description:

MAIN OBJECTIVE

Write an autobiographical incident

PROCESS OBJECTIVES

1. Use appropriate prewriting techniques to identify and develop a topic
2. Create a first draft
3. Use evaluation criteria as a basis for determining revision strategies
4. Revise the first draft, incorporating suggestions generated by self- or peer evaluation
5. Proofread and correct errors
6. Create a final draft
7. Choose an appropriate method of publication
8. Reflect on progress as a writer

Planning

- **Block Schedule**
  Block Scheduling Lesson Plans with Pacing Guide

- **One-Stop Planner**
  CD-ROM with Test Generator

BUILDING YOUR PORTFOLIO

Writer's Workshop

Technology HELP

See Writer's Workshop 2 CD-ROM. *Assignment: Autobiographical Incident.*

ASSIGNMENT

Write about an incident from your life that is vivid to you—perhaps something that taught you an important lesson or that made you feel something deeply.

AIM

To express yourself; to inform.

AUDIENCE

Your classmates or younger readers or readers of a magazine for teenagers. (You choose.)

NARRATIVE WRITING

AUTOBIOGRAPHICAL INCIDENT

If you wrote down everything that ever happened to you, how many books would your autobiography fill? Of course, some events are more memorable than others. "My mother woke me at 6 A.M. and I got ready to go to school" isn't nearly so interesting as "The earthquake hit at 4:36 A.M. and I heard screams as I found myself falling through the air."

Writing that tells about an incident in your life is a special kind of narrative writing called an **autobiographical incident**.

Prewriting

1. Find a Topic

Narrow your focus to a single incident that happened in a short time—maybe just a few minutes or several hours or a day. Look through your Writer's Notebook for ideas. Or, brainstorm some lists—"Six Memories of Food," "Three Horrible Vacations," "Four School Experiences," "Three Things I Wish I Could Do Again." Write a sentence or two about several incidents and present them to your writing group. Ask for feedback: Which one would they like to read about? Ask yourself which incident gives you most to write about.

2. Jog Your Memory

Once you find a topic, replay the incident in your memory and take notes.

- **Context:** Who was there? How old was I? Where did the incident happen?
- **Sensory details:** What sights, smells, sounds, tastes can I recall?
- **Dialogue/monologue:** Who said what?
- **Events:** Exactly what happened? (List the events in the order they occurred.) What was the most exciting or tense moment?

386 THE NONFICTION COLLECTIONS

 *Resources: Print and Media*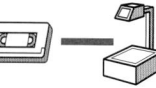

Writing and Language
- *Portfolio Management System*
  Prewriting, p. 137
  Peer Editing, p. 138
  Assessment Rubric, p. 139
- *Workshop Resources*
  Revision Strategy Teaching Notes, p. 25
  Revision Strategy Transparencies 13 and 14

- *Writer's Workshop 2 CD-ROM*
  Autobiographical Incident

T386

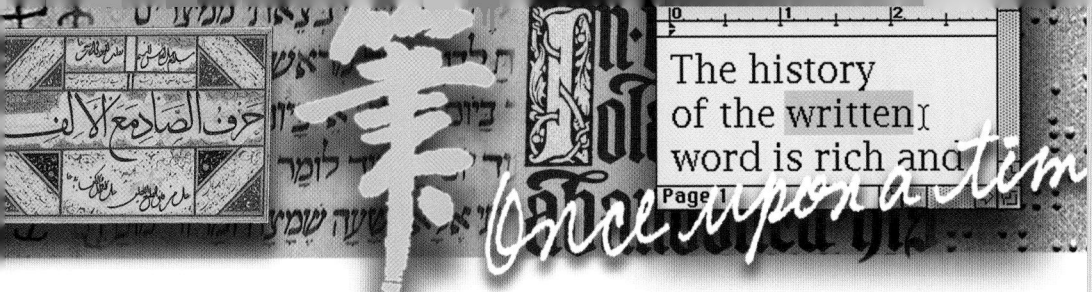

- **Significance:** What did I think or feel about the incident at the time? What do I think or feel about it now?

Here is how a professional writer in this collection uses specific **images** to help us *see* the people and places in her writing:

> One summer morning, after I had swept the dirt yard of leaves, spearmint-gum wrappers, and Vienna-sausage labels, I raked the yellow-red dirt and made half-moons carefully, so that the design stood out clearly and masklike. I put the rake behind the Store and came through the back of the house to find Grandmother on the front porch in her big, wide white apron. The apron was so stiff by virtue of the starch that it could have stood alone.
>
> —Maya Angelou, "When I Lay My Burden Down" (page 358)

A Quickwrite like the one in the margin at the right, below, can help you discover how you feel about an incident and what the incident means to you.

3. Map Your Story

Like other narratives, an autobiographical incident has **characters,** a series of **related events** usually told in chronological order, and a **setting**.

To plan your story, try using a story map (see page 113).

Drafting

There comes a time when you just have to sit down and start writing. The novelist Louise Erdrich remembers that she wrote only poems at first because she couldn't sit still long enough to write prose. Here is her description of how she wrote her first draft:

> One raw and rainy Baltimore evening, in an apartment that smelled of wet wool, I hit upon the solution to my problem and tied myself to my chair. A long scarf, knotted at the waist, allowed me to finish the first piece of prose I'd ever done.
>
> —Louise Erdrich, "What My Mother Taught Me: Nests"

Strategies for Elaboration

Show, Don't Tell
When you elaborate on an autobiographical incident, you want to help the reader imagine your experience. To do this, use words and images—descriptions of people, places, and events—that appeal to the senses. Don't just write, "We ate by the bay, and Mom sang." Tell how the food tasted. How did the air smell? How did Mom's voice sound?

Quickwrite
Visiting the homeless shelter with my mother. Sorry for the sad-looking women—especially the children. But I'm glad to get away, leave, go home. Very very very grateful—for my home and family, for the ordinary, everyday calmness of my life. Security, safety. My cozy, warm room—the good smells of the house.

Introducing the Writer's Workshop

- Have a volunteer read aloud the Student Model on pp. 388–389.
- Discuss with students the side-margin comments. Lead students to see that the successful telling of an autobiographical incident relies on three basics:
  1. a clear sequence of events
  2. the use of descriptive details that give readers a sense of "being there"
  3. an honest expression of the event's significance to the writer
- Be sure students understand the purpose of their writing—to inform readers about an incident and to convey their feelings about it. *Remind students to choose a situation they will not mind sharing with others.*

Teaching the Writer's Workshop

Prewriting
Have students use the techniques suggested on pp. 386–387 (or any others with which they may be comfortable) to generate ideas.

Drafting
Remind students to double-space their drafts. They should also leave extra space in the right margin. These blank spaces will be used for comments and editing marks.

Reaching All Students

Struggling Writers
Students having difficulty may need to replay the event they wish to recall mentally. Have them close their eyes and visualize the scene. They should ask themselves questions like these: What time of day is it? What things or people can be seen most clearly? If photographs of the place, event, or people involved exist, have students study them to pick out details. Or they may be able to interview people who remember the incident.

T387

After students have completed
their drafts, they may benefit from
another look at the student model.
Have them focus on questions such
as these:

❓ What makes the order of events
clear or unclear to you?

❓ What details help you visualize
the event?

❓ Where does the writer explain
what the event meant to him?

❓ This author mixes two tones:
humorous and serious. Is this
effective? Why?

❓ What techniques does this
writer use that you might incorporate into your paper?

Language/Grammar Link
H E L P

Comparisons: page 365.
Connotations: page 374.

Use your story map and the details you've collected to finish your
first draft at one sitting. Here are the steps in that difficult drafting process:

1. **Set the stage.** Choose a few details—just enough to give the
   incident a **context**. Let readers know where and when the
   incident took place and who was there.

2. **Entice the reader.** Try for an opening that catches your
   reader's interest: perhaps a line of dialogue or a quotation or
   an interesting detail, or even one dramatic word.

Student Model

DRIVER'S ED?

The accident was reminiscent of a clip straight out of one of
Mr. Brooks's supposedly enlightening driver's ed movies—
maybe the one I had watched only an hour before.

It was a beautiful day, dry and sunny, not a cloud in the
sky. My half-hour driving lesson with my mother thus far
matched the weather: It was near perfect. I drove at the
speed limit, stopped at all the stop signs, and even landed in
the proper lane after a turn. As I pulled onto my driveway, I
was really proud of myself. But what started out as the
perfect driving lesson ended in a terrible tragedy when I inadvertently pressed down on the accelerator instead of the
brake.

The long driveway lay ahead of me. Unfortunately for my
sake, it was not as long as it originally seemed to be. That
didn't matter because with the help of my mother's 1982
Oldsmobile station wagon, I elongated it, thus decreasing the
length of the garage. But that didn't matter; the car had
shortened also. In those seemingly endless seconds, the
garage door and the corner of my house disappeared.

It was a thunderous crash that brought everyone out as
quick as lightning. My little brother, who had witnessed the
entire catastrophe from two feet away, just stood in awe. My
other brother came running out faster than he does on the
soccer field to see what had happened. My sister, as always,
took pride in pointing out another one of my major mistakes
by screaming about how stupid I was. And unfortunately, my
good friend and next-door neighbor had the foresight to be
playing ball on his driveway at four that afternoon, such an
unlikely occurrence for this nonathletic person. He watched
without commenting. My mother just sat in the car, speechless. As for me, I was out of the car in a dash, cradling my
head in my hands, uttering the same phrase over and over—
"Why me? Why me?"

After what seemed like an eternity, during which time the

*Beginning
generates interest.*

*Here is where the
incident begins.
The stage is set.*

*There is lots of
humor here. He
exaggerates for a
humorous effect.*

*Tells how other
people react to
the incident.*

*Focuses on each
person, then goes
on to the next.*

*Writer tells his own
reaction last.*

Reaching All Students

Struggling Writers

Establishing a strong narrative sequence is
important to this assignment. To help struggling
writers, have them use a graphic like the one
at right to create a master list of events in the
order in which they occurred. When revising,
the student writer should compare his or her
draft to the list to be certain that the sequence
of events is clear and unambiguous.

First, _____

Then, _____

Then, _____

Then, _____

Finally, _____

3. **Tell what happened.** Narrate the events in chronological order, the order in which they happened. If necessary, add a **flashback** to an earlier time to explain something.

4. **Reflect on meaning and feelings.** In your conclusion, tell what the incident means to you, how you feel about it now, and how you felt about it then. Say this as directly and simply as you can.

Sentence Workshop
H E L P

Expanding sentences with prepositional phrases: page 391.

---

initial shock had worn off, I swore I would never drive again and then began to get nervous all over, thinking about my father's anticipated arrival within the next half-hour. The only saving grace was that my family was to immediately leave for a holiday dinner at my grandmother's. My father wouldn't have the nerve to start a scene in front of all those people: He would just give me the eye all night. I made sure to sit at an angle, not conducive to good eye contact. Actually, my father surprised me by saying the accident wasn't completely my fault. It was those cloddy sneakers that he's always despised.

I realized later that this tragedy was a blessing in disguise. The thought of my little brother standing between the car and the garage door rather than a few feet off to the side as he was, kept playing over and over in my mind like a scratched record. Until this day, the thought still terrifies me. Driving is not as easy and carefree as the average sixteen-year-old thinks. I am extra cautious now, realizing that there is no margin for error. A car can truly be a lethal weapon.

My road-training class recently scheduled a field trip past my now infamous garage doors with me as their tour guide: "To the right is the Balsam estate, which is undergoing extensive renovation to the front of the house. . . ."

I have since learned that mine was the most common accident of sixteen-year-olds learning to drive. Because of inexperience, they tend to panic in emergency situations, thus pressing the accelerator. I have learned, however, that I must be responsible for my actions. I cannot rationalize my driving mistakes. Fortunately, my accident was a valuable lesson. Cars are not toys and driving is not a game. Furthermore, accidents don't just happen to the other guy. They can hit home.

—Howie Balsam
Half Hollow Hills High School East
Dix Hills, New York

Suspense—how will the father react?

"Cloddy sneakers" is good. What the incident means to the writer—serious tone here.

A humorous note again.

The conclusion is serious: The writer draws a generalization from the incident.

Reaching All Students

English Language Learners

English language learners may have particular difficulty with using the appropriate verb tenses needed to identify a sequence in time. Have these students map out events in their native languages first. Follow this with a review of the basic tenses in English and a quick survey of words that may be used to indicate chronological order (*after, before, then,* etc.).

Advanced Learners

Have these students search current magazines or books, particularly in their fields of interest, for examples of autobiographical incidents. After assembling an assortment, have students analyze the tone of each narrative.

Evaluating and Revising

Have students use the Evaluation Criteria provided here to review their drafts and determine needed revisions.

Proofreading

Have students proofread their own papers first and then exchange with another student. For this assignment, remind students to be particularly careful of the use of adverbs of time and the consistency of verb tenses. If time permits, the final copy should be put aside for at least a day before it is proofread for the final time by the author.

Remind students who use word-processing programs that the spelling checker cannot detect a misused word. For example, the computer cannot know if the writer meant *its* when the word *it's* was entered.

Publishing

Students may wish to consider expanding this assignment to create a memoir —several autobiographical incidents bound together in a folder. Students might think of these as time capsules, something to be put away for a time and then reread many times in the future. The memoir is really a way to visit with yourself and determine how and why you may have changed over the years.

Reflecting

If students are adding their autobiographical incidents to their portfolios, be sure that they have a date on the top sheet. They should also attach a reflection on the work that they did:

1. I had the most trouble _____
   _____.
2. The easiest part of the writing was
   _____.
3. I'm adding this to my portfolio because _____
4. The next time I write an autobiographical incident, I _____.

Resources

Peer Editing Forms and Rubrics
- *Portfolio Management System*, p. 138

Revision Transparencies
- *Workshop Resources*, p. 25

A good autobiographical incident

1. *deals with a single incident in a limited time*
2. *has an interesting beginning and a clear conclusion*
3. *puts the incident in a context (time, place, other people present)*
4. *has a clear sequence of events, sensory details, and dialogue*
5. *directly states or clearly implies the incident's significance to the writer*

Language/Grammar Link
H E L P

Punctuation, capitalization, spelling: page 354.

Communications Handbook
H E L P

See Proofreaders' Marks.

Proofreading Tip

Here is a tip used by professional proofreaders: Do at least two reads. Read first for sentence structure (check for variety; correct fragments and run-ons). Then, read for errors in spelling, punctuation, and capitalization.

Evaluating and Revising

Look at your draft carefully. Have you used enough details? Have you used images to describe the setting and people so readers can visualize them? Do your sentences flow smoothly? Read your draft to your writing group and ask for specific suggestions. Or ask two peer editors to read your paper and to write their comments in the margin.

Revision Model

> The accident reminiscent of straight out of
> ~~It was like a clip from one of Mr.~~
>
> s   enlightening
> Brooks' supposedly ~~educational~~
>
> driver's ed movies—maybe the one I
>
> had watched only an hour before.
>
>   , dry and sunny, not a cloud
>   beautiful   in the sky.
> ¶ It was a ~~nice~~ day. My half-hour
>
> driving lesson with my mother ~~was~~
>
>   matched
> thus far ~~as good as~~ the weather: It
>
>   near
> was perfect. I drove at the speed limit
>
> ~~that was required~~, stopped at all the
>
> stop signs. . . .

Peer Comments

What is "it"? Can you be more specific?

Say more about the day. Use descriptive words.

Nice comparison. I like the way you link the lesson and the weather. It's a little wordy. Can you simplify?

PEANUTS ® reprinted by permission of UFS, Inc.

Grading Timesaver

Rubrics for this Writer's Workshop assignment appear on p. 139 of the *Portfolio Management System*.

Sentence Workshop

EXPANDING SENTENCES: PREPOSITIONAL PHRASES

A **prepositional phrase** begins with a preposition (a word such as *above, across, behind, between, during, from, in, into, like, of, on, over, to, under, with*) and ends with the object of that preposition. It may also contain words that modify the object of the preposition. Prepositional phrases are usually used the same way as adjectives or adverbs.

A prepositional phrase that modifies a noun or a pronoun is an **adjective phrase.** An adjective phrase tells *what kind* or *which one.*

EXAMPLES
1. "At 7:30 the couple in the next room began to quarrel. . . ." [which one?]

   —O. Henry, "Springtime à la Carte"

2. " The morning of June 27th was clear and sunny. . . ." [which one?]

   —Shirley Jackson, "The Lottery"

An **adverb phrase** is a prepositional phrase that modifies a verb, an adjective, or an adverb. An adverb phrase tells *how, when, where, why,* or *to what extent* (*how long* or *how far*).

EXAMPLES
1. "Her face was gnarled around a beautiful sharp nose." [where?]

   —Louise Erdrich, "Snares"

2. " She had filled the room with magnolia blossoms . . ." [how?]

   —Zora Neale Hurston, "Spunk"

Writer's Workshop Follow-up: Revision

Usually you elaborate on your sentences during the revision process. Look at the autobiographical incident you wrote for the Writer's Workshop on page 386. Find at least three sentences that you can expand with further details supplied by prepositional phrases.

Language Handbook HELP

See Prepositional Phrases, page 1006.

Technology HELP

See Language Workshop CD-ROM. *Key word entry: prepositional phrases.*

Try It Out

Expand these empty sentences by adding prepositional phrases that answer the questions in brackets. Underline the prepositional phrases in your sentences. Be sure to compare your expanded versions in class.

1. The woman waited. [*When* and *where?*]

2. One is missing. [*Which one* and *from where?*]

3. Some cheered. [*Which ones* and *how?*]

4. The driver stopped. [*Which one, how, where,* and *when?*]

5. The couple began to move. [*Which one, where,* and *how?*]

Resources

Workshop Resources
• Worksheet, p. 69

Language Workshop CD-ROM
• Prepositional Phrases

Try It Out
Possible Answers
1. The woman waited at the bus stop until noon.
2. One of the marbles is missing from the box.
3. Some of the fans cheered with enthusiasm.
4. The driver of the bus stopped with a lurch at the ice cream stand at noon.
5. The couple in the park began to move in a leisurely way toward a bench.

Assessing Learning

Quick Check: Prepositional Phrases

What question does each underlined prepositional phrase answer?

1. The girls sauntered down the hill by the store. [Where? Which one?]
2. The best restaurant in Philadelphia is closed on Mondays. [Where? When?]
3. The four boys sat on the ground talking in loud voices. [Where? How?]
4. The two people in the swing fell to the ground. [Which ones? Where?]
5. For five years, that tree has been dropping leaves in our yard. [How long? Where?]

OBJECTIVES
1. Develop strategies for reading a textbook
2. Determine a purpose for reading
3. Evaluate the authorship of the text
4. Preview the presentation
5. Analyze the graphics

Reading for Life
Reading a Textbook

Teaching the Lesson

The day before teaching this lesson, you may wish to ask students to bring a social studies textbook to class. Students not taking a social studies class may pair with another student or bring in a science textbook.

Review the strategies using the graphics provided in the lesson, and then have students write down a research question that could be answered in a social studies (or science) textbook. Students should exchange questions and attempt to answer the questions using the strategies taught in the lesson.

Using the Strategies

Possible Answers
1. Presidential Profiles, Science and Technology, Historical Documents (partially obscured)
2. Yes, the Historical Documents are primary sources. (See Lincoln's First Inaugural Address.) Photographs may also count as primary sources.
3. Coverage begins on p. 548 and ends on p. 617. Although these pages probably cover other topics as well, 70 pages is quite adequate coverage. The topics cited reveal the exact coverage.

Situation

You are taking a school trip to Washington, D.C., and you want to learn more about Lincoln's presidency. You turn to your history textbook. To get the most out of your research, apply these strategies.

Strategies

Focus your research.
- Jot down the questions you want answered.

Evaluate the authorship.
- The author is identified on the book's title page. Look for the author's special qualifications.

Preview the presentation of the textbook.
- To get an overview of the content and organization of the textbook, skim the **table of contents**. Then, search the **index** for key words related to your topic.
- Look for **special features** in your textbook. Usually such features are highlighted in the table of contents.
- Look for **primary sources,** firsthand accounts by people who witnessed an event. Such sources include diaries, speeches, and autobiographies. Primary sources can give you a sense of being there.

CHAPTER **19**
The Civil War (1861–1865) 574
1 The War Begins 575
    Presidential Profiles *Abraham Lincoln* .. 576
5 The Tide of the War Turns ....
    Science and Technology *Photoc...*
    in the Civil War ....
    Historical Docum...
    The Emancipation Pr...
    the Gettysburg Address...

Table of Contents

1863 **1864**

JAN. 1863
The Emancipation Proclamation goes into effect.

NOV. 1863
President Lincoln delivers the Gettysburg Address.

JULY 1863
The Union army wins major victories at Vicksburg, Mississippi, and Gettysburg, Pennsylvania.

Time Line

HISTORICAL DOCUMENTS

1861

Lincoln's First Inaugural Address

In the following excerpt from Abraham Lincoln's first inaugural address, he discussed the nation's greatest crisis.

❝No State, upon its own mere motion, can lawfully get out of the Union . . . acts of violence, within any State or States, against the authority of the United States, are . . . revolutionary. . . .

Primary Source

Lincoln, Abraham, p566, c802; assassination of, 548, 568, 616; Civil War and, 576–577, 580–81, 585, 592; election of 1860, 569–70, m569; Emancipation Proclamation, 589–90, f591, f600–601; first inaugural address, f577; funeral of, p617; Gettysburg Address, 597, f601; Lincoln-Douglas debates, 564–65, p564; Reconstruction plan of, 613; and secession, 570; second inaugural address, f613, 617; Ten-Percent Plan of, 613, 617; Thirteenth Amendment and, 614

Index

From *Call to Freedom* by Sterling Stuckey and Linda Kerrigan Salvucci (Holt, Rinehart and Winston, 2000).

Analyze the graphics.
- Graphics, such as photographs, maps, and charts, may expand on or even substitute for text. Color or special type may highlight important terms, and icons may refer to other parts of the textbook.

Using the Strategies
Answer these questions about the pages above.

1. What special features do you find in the table of contents?
2. Does the book contain primary sources?
3. Judging by the index, how much coverage does the book give Lincoln?

Extending the Strategies
Use these strategies to review *Elements of Literature.* Start with the title page.

392 THE NONFICTION COLLECTIONS

Crossing the Curriculum

Interdisciplinary Studies
Have students bring a variety of textbooks to class, and then group students by types of books: science, math, history, geography, French, etc. Within each group, have students compile a list of features common to the books in their group. Have the groups write their lists on the board and then compare and contrast the textbooks using questions such as the following:

- How are the books in your group organized? How is this organization different from books in other disciplines?
- Which books have glossaries? charts? time lines? maps? Which books do not? Why?
- Are primary sources common in math books? Why not? Which types of books do have primary sources? Why?

- Check the indexes of all the books. What does the index cover? If students are knowledgeable in the subject, have them check the coverage of a particular topic in the index.
- Who are the authors of the books? What are their special qualifications?
- What are the books' copyrights? In which subjects would copyright be most important?

Collection 6

A Place Called Home

Theme

Where Do We Belong? *Most people have a place they call home—a safe and comfortable spot where they can be themselves. The writers in this collection start with that idea and extend it to some surprising views of the places they call home, ranging from the entire earth to a tiny attic garret.*

Reading the Anthology

Reaching Struggling Readers

The *Reading Skills and Strategies: Reaching Struggling Readers* binder provides materials coordinated with the Pupil's Edition (see the Collection Planner, p. T392B) to help students who have difficulty reading and comprehending text, or students who are reluctant readers. The binder for ninth grade is organized around sixteen individual skill areas and offers the following options:

- MiniRead MiniReads are short, easy texts that give students a chance to practice a particular skill and strategy before reading selections in the Pupil's Edition. Each MiniRead Skill Lesson can be taught independently or used in conjunction with a Selection Skill Lesson.

- **Selection Skill Lessons** Selection Skill Lessons allow students to apply skills introduced in the MiniReads. Each Selection Skill Lesson provides reading instruction and practice specific to a particular piece of literature in the Pupil's Edition.

Reading Beyond the Anthology

Read On Each collection in the grade nine book includes an annotated bibliography of books suitable for extended reading. The suggested books are related to works in the collection by theme, by author, or by subject. To preview the Read On for Collection 6, please turn to p. T477.

HRW Library The *HRW Library* offers novels, plays, works of nonfiction, and short-story collections for extended reading. Each book in the Library includes a major work and thematically or topically related Connections. Each book in the *HRW Library* is also accompanied by a Study Guide that provides teaching suggestions and worksheets.

THE YEARLING Marjorie Kinnan Rawlings
The world of Florida's Everglades dominates this story of a young boy and his coming of age.

THE ADVENTURES OF TOM SAWYER Mark Twain
Every part of Tom Sawyer's world is shaped by the Mississippi, a gateway to adventure and a refuge from the constrictions of civilization.

Collection 6 A Place Called Home

Resources for this Collection

Note: All resources for this collection are available for preview on the *One-Stop Planner CD-ROM 1 with Test Generator.* All worksheets and blackline masters may be printed from the CD-ROM.

 **Internet Resources**
go.hrw.com LE0 9-6

Selection or Feature	Reading and Literary Skills	Vocabulary, Language, and Grammar

The Best Gift of My Life *from* **But I'll Be Back Again**
Cynthia Rylant (p. 394)
	• *Reading Skills and Strategies: Reaching Struggling Readers*
	  • MiniRead Skill Lesson, p. 100
	  • Selection Skill Lesson, p. 106
	• *Graphic Organizers for Active Reading,* Worksheet p. 25
		• *Daily Oral Grammar,*
		  Transparency 25

Elements of Literature: Essays (p. 399)	• *Literary Elements,* Transparency 8	

Riding Is an Exercise of the Mind
N. Scott Momaday (p. 400)
	• *Reading Skills and Strategies: Reaching Struggling Readers*
	  • MiniRead Skill Lesson, p. 110
	  • Selection Skill Lesson, p. 117
	• *Graphic Organizers for Active Reading,* Worksheet p. 26
	• *Literary Elements:* Transparency 8
	  Worksheet p. 25
		• *Words to Own,* Worksheet p. 19
		• *Grammar and Language Links:* Showing Time, Worksheet p. 41
		• *Language Workshop CD-ROM,* Verb Tenses
		• *Daily Oral Grammar,*
		  Transparency 26

"Haven't I Made a Difference!" *from* **All Things Bright and Beautiful** James Herriot (p. 406) **Connections: The World Is Not a Pleasant Place to Be** Nikki Giovanni (p. 416)	• *Graphic Organizers for Active Reading,* Worksheet p. 27	• *Words to Own,* Worksheet p. 20 • *Grammar and Language Links:* Description, Worksheet p. 43 • *Daily Oral Grammar,* Transparency 27

The Round Walls of Home *from* **A Natural History of the Senses**
Diane Ackerman (p. 420)
 	
Connections: Prologue
Edward Field (p. 423)
	• *Reading Skills and Strategies: Reaching Struggling Readers*
	  • MiniRead Skill Lesson, p. 121
	  • Selection Skill Lesson, p. 127
	• *Graphic Organizers for Active Reading,* Worksheet p. 28
		• *Words to Own,* Worksheet p. 21
		• *Grammar and Language Links:* Using Commas, Worksheet p. 45
		• *Language Workshop CD-ROM,* Commas
		• *Daily Oral Grammar,*
		  Transparency 28

The Loophole of Retreat *from* **Incidents in the Life of a Slave Girl**
Harriet A. Jacobs (p. 426)
	• *Reading Skills and Strategies: Reaching Struggling Readers*
	  • MiniRead Skill Lesson, p. 131
	  • Selection Skill Lesson, p. 138
	• *Graphic Organizers for Active Reading,* Worksheet p. 29
		• *Words to Own,* Worksheet p. 22
		• *Grammar and Language Links:* Adjective Clauses, Worksheet p. 47
		• *Language Workshop CD-ROM,* Adjective Clauses
		• *Daily Oral Grammar,*
		  Transparency 29

Extending the Theme: The Sacred Stephen Dunn (p. 434)	The Extending the Theme feature provides students with an unstructured opportunity to practice reading strategies using a selection that extends the theme of the collection.	
Writer's Workshop: **Observational Essay** (p. 438)		
Sentence Workshop: **Participial Phrases** (p. 443)		• *Workshop Resources,* p. 71 • *Language Workshop CD-ROM,* Participial Phrases

Other Resources for this Collection

- *Cross-Curricular Activities*, p. 6
- *Portfolio Management System*, Introduction to Portfolio Assessment, p. 1
- *Test Generator*, Collection Test

Writing	Listening and Speaking Viewing and Representing	Assessment
• *Portfolio Management System*, Rubrics for Choices, p. 140	• *Audio CD Library*, Disc 14, Track 2	• *Formal Assessment*, Selection Test, p. 65 • *Standardized Test Preparation*, p. 52 • *Test Generator (One-Stop Planner CD-ROM)*
		• *Formal Assessment*, Literary Elements Test, p. 75
• *Portfolio Management System*, Rubrics for Choices, p. 141	• *Visual Connections:* Videocassette A, Segment 6 • *Audio CD Library*, Disc 14, Track 3 • *Viewing and Representing:* Fine Art Transparency 8; Worksheet p. 32 • *Portfolio Management System*, Rubrics for Choices, p. 141	• *Formal Assessment*, Selection Test, p. 67 • *Standardized Test Preparation*, p. 54 • *Test Generator (One-Stop Planner CD-ROM)*
• *Portfolio Management System*, Rubrics for Choices, p. 142	• *Audio CD Library*, Disc 14, Track 4 • *Portfolio Management System*, Rubrics for Choices, p. 142	• *Formal Assessment*, Selection Test, p. 69 • *Test Generator (One-Stop Planner CD-ROM)*
• *Portfolio Management System*, Rubrics for Choices, p. 144	• *Audio CD Library*, Disc 14, Track 5 • *Viewing and Representing:* Fine Art Transparency 9; Worksheet p. 36 • *Portfolio Management System*, Rubrics for Choices, p. 144	• *Formal Assessment*, Selection Test, p. 71 • *Standardized Test Preparation*, p. 56 • *Test Generator (One-Stop Planner CD-ROM)*
• *Portfolio Management System*, Rubrics for Choices, p. 145	• *Audio CD Library*, Disc 14, Track 6 • *Portfolio Management System*, Rubrics for Choices, p. 145	• *Formal Assessment*, Selection Test, p. 73 • *Standardized Test Preparation*, pp. 58, 60 • *Test Generator (One-Stop Planner CD-ROM)*
	• *Audio CD Library*, Disc 14, Track 7	

• *Workshop Resources*, p. 29
• *Writer's Workshop 2 CD-ROM*, Observational Writing
		• *Portfolio Management System*
		  • Prewriting, p. 146
		  • Peer Editing, p. 147
		  • Assessment Rubric, p. 148

 Transparency    CD-ROM   Video    Audio CD

Collection Planner

T392C

Collection 6 A Place Called Home
Skills Focus

Skills Focus

Selection or Feature	Reading Skills and Strategies	Elements of Literature	Language/ Grammar	Vocabulary/ Spelling	Writing	Listening/ Speaking	Viewing/ Representing
The Best Gift of My Life *from* **But I'll Be back Again** Cynthia Rylant (p. 394)	Compare and Contrast, pp. 394, 398 Summarize, p. 398 Find the Main Idea, p. 398	Objective and Subjective Writing, pp. 394, 398			Choose a Topic, p. 398 Write an Essay on the Best Place to Live, p. 398 Write an Essay Describing a Gift, p. 398		
Elements of Literature: Essays (p. 399)		Essay, p. 399					
Riding Is an Exercise of the Mind N. Scott Momaday (p. 400)	Chronological Order, pp. 400, 405 Flashback, p. 405	Sensory Images, p. 400 Sensory Details, p. 404 Title, p. 404	Verb Tenses, p. 405 Time Words and Phrases, p. 405	Word Play, p. 405	Chart Sensory Details, p. 404 Research and Write About Your Name, p. 404	Research and Record Your Community's Oral History, p. 404	Create a Seasonal Wheel, p. 405
"Haven't I Made a Difference!" *from* **All Things Bright and Beautiful** James Herriot (p. 406)	Cause and Effect, pp. 406, 417 Find the Main Idea, p. 417	Nonfiction Narratives, p. 406	Descriptive Writing, p. 419 • Sensory Details • Vivid Verbs • Precise Nouns and Modifiers	Word Families, p. 419 • Prefix • Suffix	Chart Differences in Settings, Characters, and Objects, p. 418 Create a Glossary of Technical Terms, p. 418 Write a Pet Story, p. 418 State and Support an Opinion, p. 418		Make a Cause-and-Effect Chart, p. 417 Create an Animal Cartoon, p. 418
The Round Walls of Home *from* **A Natural History of the Senses** Diane Ackerman (p. 420)	Identify the Writer's Purpose, pp. 420, 424 Find the Main Idea, p. 424	Exposition, p. 420 Metaphors, p. 424 Title, p. 424	Commas, p. 425	Word Maps, p. 425 Etymology, p. 425	Use Vivid Words, p. 424 Interpret an Essay, p. 424	Debate the Issues, p. 424	
The Loophole of Retreat *from* **Incidents in the Life of a Slave Girl** Harriet A. Jacobs (p. 426)	Draw Upon Background, p. 426 Find the Main Idea, p. 431	Setting, pp. 426, 431 Mood, p. 431 Atmosphere, p. 431 Character, p. 431 Title, p. 431	Adjective Clauses, p. 433 • Essential • Nonessential	Chart and Share New Words, p. 433	Explain Your Feelings about Your Topic, p. 432 Write a Letter to the Author, p. 432	Research and Report on Slavery, p. 432 Research and Report on African American Spirituals, p. 432	Create a KWL Chart, pp. 426, 432
Extending the Theme: The Sacred Stephen Dunn (p. 434)		The Extending the Theme feature provides students with an unstructured opportunity to practice reading strategies using a selection that extends the theme of the collection.					
Writer's Workshop: Observational Essay (p. 438)			Clichés, p. 439	Analogy, p. 438	Write an Observational Essay, pp. 438–442 • Chronological Order • Spatial Order • Order of Importance		
Sentence Workshop: Participial Phrases (p. 443)			Participles, p. 443 • Present • Past • Participial Phrases			Combine Sentences Using Participial Phrases, p. 443	
Reading for Life: Reading a Map (p. 444)	Reading Maps, p. 444 • Title • Key or Legend • Compass Rose • Directions						Map Your Neighborhood, p. 444

A PLACE CALLED HOME

WRITING FOCUS: Observational Essay

Home is where one starts from.

—T. S. Eliot

Much of life seems to be a search for some small place in the world where we fit and feel safe, where we can be comfortably ourselves. When we are young, we need a private place where we can nurse our wounds and dream about the future; and when we are older and the future has come, we want a home of our own, a place that we can shape to fit ourselves. That home we search for is more than just a place to live. It's also a place among people who provide us with friendship and love, and a place in the working world that lets us accomplish something satisfying.

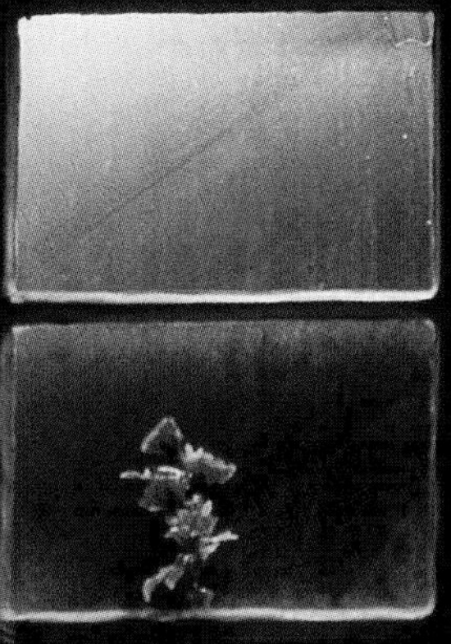

Writer's Notebook

In your Writer's Notebook, jot down some details about a place that makes you feel secure and happy. You might describe your home or some other place. Save your notes for possible use in the Writer's Workshop on page 438.

OBJECTIVES

1. Read essays centered on the topic "A Place Called Home"
2. Identify and interpret literary elements used in nonfiction, with special emphasis on essays
3. Apply a variety of reading strategies to the essays
4. Respond to the essays using a variety of modes
5. Learn and use new words
6. Plan, draft, revise, edit, proof, and publish an observational essay
7. Combine sentences using participial phrases
8. Demonstrate the ability to read a map

Responding to the Quotation

Explain that T. S. Eliot (1888–1965) is a modern American poet. Ask students whether or not they would define the concept of home as Eliot does. To stimulate discussion, you might ask the following question: If home is only "where one starts from," do you stop needing a home after you've started— that is, after you've reached maturity? Have students discuss people's changing ideas of home, and encourage them to formulate their own definitions. To close, you might write on the chalkboard another quotation by Eliot:

> We shall not cease from exploration,
> And the end of all our exploring
> Will be to arrive where we started
> And know the place for the first time.

Ask students what the quote suggests about the enduring importance of "where one starts from."

Writer's Notebook

Invite students to close their eyes before they write, and to imagine all of the sensations they associate with their chosen places: sights, sounds, smells, and textures.

Writing Focus: Observational Essay

The following **Work in Progress** assignments build to a culminating **Writer's Workshop** at the end of the collection.

Planning

- **Traditional Schedule**
  Lesson Plans Including Strategies for English-Language Learners
- **One-Stop Planner**
  CD-ROM with Test Generator

Before You Read

THE BEST GIFT OF MY LIFE

Make the Connection

Somewhere Else

The story you are about to read begins, "I think my idea of heaven when I was a kid was Christy Sanders's home." A quick prediction might lead you to realize that this story was written by someone who, at least at that time in her life, longed to live somewhere else—and to be someone else.

Quickwrite

Write down and complete the following statement. Add reasons for your choice. (Your answer might be "where I live right now.")

If I could live anywhere in the world, it would be . . .

Elements of Literature

Objective and Subjective Writing

A nonfiction writer can be objective or subjective. In **subjective writing,** writers reveal their feelings, their judgments, even their biases. We look for subjective writing in personal essays and autobiographies and in the editorial pages of a newspaper, where writers express opinions about news events. In **objective writing,** writers report just the facts; they reveal no personal emotions, opinions, or judgments. We expect objectivity when we read news reports, encyclopedia articles, and history.

> **S**ubjective writing reveals the writer's feelings, opinions, or biases. **Objective writing** focuses on facts and contains no expression of personal feelings or opinions.

Reading Skills and Strategies

Comparing and Contrasting: Alike or Different?

Cynthia Rylant uses comparison and contrast at the beginning of this excerpt from her autobiography. A **comparison** points out similarities; a **contrast** identifies differences. When you read texts containing comparisons and contrasts, keep these points in mind:

- the subjects that the writer is comparing or contrasting
- how the subjects are alike or different
- the writer's attitude toward the subjects (You can infer an attitude by looking closely at the writer's choice of words and details.)

go.hrw.com
LE0 9-6

The Granger Collection, New York.

394 THE NONFICTION COLLECTIONS

Resources: Print and Media

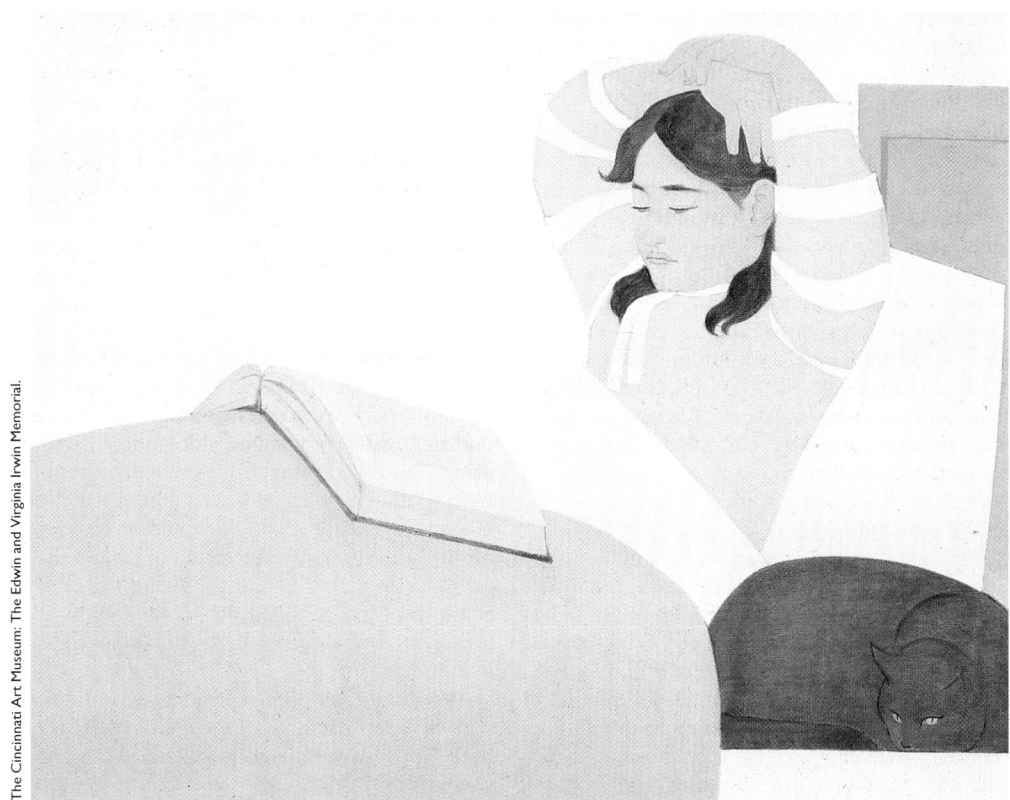

Child Reading—Pink (1966) by Will Barnet. Oil on Canvas.

The Cincinnati Art Museum: The Edwin and Virginia Irwin Memorial.

The Best Gift of My Life

from **But I'll Be Back Again**

Cynthia Rylant

I think my idea of heaven when I was a kid was Christy Sanders's home. She lived in a new brick house with carpeting in it and a bar in the kitchen you could eat on and a picture window in the living room. Her dad wore suits and her mother was queen of the PTA. Christy's house always smelled like those chocolate-covered marshmallow cookies you can get at the grocery. Everything in it was new and it matched and it worked.

I was ashamed of where I lived.

In the apartment my mother and I shared, there were old gas heaters you had to light with a match and which threatened to blow you up every time you did. We didn't have carpet. We

THE BEST GIFT OF MY LIFE 395

Summary ■

In this autobiographical account of her childhood, Rylant recalls the shame she felt whenever she compared her dingy apartment to the bright, modern house of a friend. A concert by a visiting symphony orchestra intensified Rylant's longing to be someone else, a person who would "walk among musicians and artists and writers." She concludes that this longing was both a curse and a gift: a curse because it temporarily kept her from knowing herself, a gift because it later led her to become a writer.

Background

Cynthia Rylant was four years old when her father abandoned the family and she was sent to live with her grandparents in rural Appalachia. Four years later Rylant rejoined her mother, who had found work and an apartment in the small town described in this essay.

Resources

Listening
Audio CD Library
A recording of this essay is included in the *Audio CD Library:*
• Disc 14, Track 2

A **Reading Skills and Strategies**

Comparing and Contrasting

? What two things does Rylant compare and contrast in the first two paragraphs? [Christy's home and her own] What is Rylant's attitude toward each of them? [She idealizes Christy's home, but dislikes her own home.]

RESPONDING TO THE ART
The American artist **Will Barnet** (1911–) uses stylized planes to create evocative portraits.
Activity. Ask students how they think the girl is feeling. What clues in the art suggest this?
[Sample answer: The girl's relaxed posture and peaceful expression and the gentle pastels and softly rounded shapes suggest that the girl is feeling dreamy.]

A. Elements of Literature

Objective and Subjective Writing

? Is Rylant being objective or subjective in the opening four paragraphs? How do you know? [She is being subjective. Her writing expresses emotions (desires, fears, and shame), judgments (unworthiness), and opinions (city kids superior to small-town kids).]

B. Critical Thinking

Making Inferences

? What is Rylant suggesting in these lines? [She suggests that her low self-confidence is a problem.]

C. Appreciating Language

Word Choice

? Which words does Rylant choose to contrast the dull gym with the wondrous musicians? [The musicians are "elegant," "long and fluid, like birds," and their instruments are "marvelous." In contrast, the gym bleachers are "hard" and the curtains "heavy."]

D. Elements of Literature

Objective and Subjective Writing

? Which part of this paragraph is objective? Which part is subjective? [The first sentence objectively describes the conductor. The rest of the paragraph is subjective, drawn from the narrator's imagination.]

had old green-and-brown linoleum with cigarette burns in it. Every morning, there would be at least one spider in the bathtub, and it would take every ounce of nerve I had to look in and check. Once, a really big spider crawled out from under our old couch and I was too scared to step on him; instead I dropped a Sears catalog on his head and left it there for a week, just to make sure he was dead.

If you looked out our front window, you would have seen Todd's warehouse and junkyard. It was a long metal building enclosed by a high chain-link fence, and on the outside were rusting barrels and parts of bulldozers and all manner of rotten equipment. There was some talk that the ghost of Mr. Todd's old father walked around that warehouse at night, but I was too worried about spiders in my bathtub to give it much thought.

Wanting Christy Sanders's brick house was just a symptom of the overall desire I had for better things. I read a lot of magazines, and I wanted to live in houses with yellow drapes and backyard pools. I was ashamed of where I lived and felt the world would judge me unworthy because of it. I wouldn't even go to the library in the nearby city because I felt so unequal to city kids. Consequently, I lived on comic books for most of my childhood, until I moved into drugstore paperback romances as a teenager.

As long as I stayed in Beaver, I felt I was somebody important. I felt smart and pretty and fun. But as soon as I left town to go anywhere else, my sense of being somebody special evaporated into nothing, and I became dull and ugly and poor. This feeling would stick with me for years, and when I went away to college and met students who had grown up in big Northern cities and could breeze through the world talking like they owned it, I realized that no matter how much I studied or how many college degrees I got, there was one thing I might never fully learn: I might never fully learn that it would be all right for me to have a house that smelled like chocolate-covered marshmallow cookies.

One year, the New Orleans Symphony Orchestra came to play in our junior high

school gymnasium. What that orchestra was doing in my little town I cannot imagine, for surely they were all fresh out of London and New York and Los Angeles and didn't need any extra publicity in Beaver, West Virginia.

But the visit of that orchestra was something I have never forgotten. I was not familiar with any real sort of culture. No one I knew played classical records. I had never been to a museum of any kind. In fact, it would not be until I went to college in Charleston, West Virginia, that I set foot in a library or art museum.

The New Orleans Symphony was for me like a visit from God himself, so full of awe and humility was I. We sat on the hard bleachers our bottoms usually warmed for junior varsity games, and we watched these elegant people who seemed long and fluid, like birds, play their marvelous instruments. Their music bounced off the blue-and-gold picture of our school tiger on the wall and the time clock and the heavy velvet curtains we used for school plays, and the gym was transformed into a place of wonder for me.

The conductor was a slender, serious man with a large nose and a lot of dark hair swept back from his forehead. I watched him and I wanted to live in his pink house in New Orleans, surrounded by maids carrying iced tea and peanuts, sleeping each night in a white canopy bed, greeting at the door of our home such notable musicians as Elvis Presley, Paul McCartney, and The Monkees.

Watching the conductor and his beautiful orchestra, I felt something in me that wanted more than I had. Wanted to walk among musicians and artists and writers. Wanted a life beyond Saturdays at G. C. Murphy's department store and Sundays with the Baptist Youth Fellowship.

I wanted to be someone else, and that turned out to be the worst curse and the best gift of my life. I would finish out my childhood forgetting who I really was and what I really thought, and I would listen to other people and repeat their ideas instead of finding my own. That was the curse. The gift was that I would be willing to try to write books when I grew up.

Reaching All Students

Struggling Readers

Comparing and Contrasting was introduced on p. 394. For a lesson directly tied to this selection that teaches students to compare and contrast by using a strategy called Semantic Differential Scales, see the *Reading Skills and Strategies* binder:
• MiniRead Skill Lesson, p. 100
• Selection Skill Lesson, p. 106

English Language Learners

Ask each student to write a new title for the essay. Then have small groups of students discuss which parts of the essay influenced their choices. Invite volunteers to present their new titles to the class. For additional strategies to supplement instruction for English language learners, see
• *Lesson Plans Including Strategies for English-Language Learners*

Advanced Learners

Help students appreciate Rylant's down-to-earth style and wry sense of humor. Examples include the anecdote of the spider and the Sears catalog, and the image of the symphony conductor hobnobbing with fellow musicians Elvis Presley, Paul McCartney, and The Monkees. Encourage students to find other examples and to analyze how humor is created through the writer's choice of words and details.

My Room

I would be willing to sacrifice every other room in the house, if necessary, to salvage my bedroom. My room is a reflection of me. As I grow, my room does too. As I expand, so does my room. When I was little, it was a place of secret kingdoms, faraway lands, and toys. As I grew older, my room became a safe haven where I could escape. . . . I used to sit on my bed with the comforting voice of a friend on the phone. In my room, I ruled. I had a place in this world that was wholly mine. It felt good to know that I would always have a place to which I could escape.

As I got older, so did my room. The toys were put up in the attic, and I got adult furniture. Some of my childhood memories left with the old furniture, but I was glad to have new furniture with which to make new memories.

Now my room has shed its teenage appearance. There are no longer posters on the wall or mismatched furniture. There are no "I love so-and-so's" scrawled on the bedpost or stickers on the side of the dresser. There is matching furniture and a large, simple bed.

Looking into my room, one sees a reflection of me. On the surface it is simple; but on the floor, the bed, the dresser, the entertainment center, and the rocking chair are bits and pieces of my life. They are beautiful things strewn about hopelessly. But that is exactly what I am. A simple person on the outside with beautiful things scattered about within myself, just waiting to be discovered.

—Brooke Olson
Alief-Hastings High School
Houston, Texas

THE BEST GIFT OF MY LIFE 397

MAKING MEANINGS

First Thoughts

1. Sample phrases: a dreamer, sharp observer, self-absorbed, timid and insecure, low self-confidence.

Shaping Interpretations

2. Sample answers: "I was ashamed of where I lived and felt the world would judge me unworthy. . . ." (p. 396); "But as soon as I left town to go anywhere else, my sense of being somebody special evaporated. . . ." (p. 396).

3. Possible answers: It made her realize that she wanted to be among creative people; it gave her new dreams.

4. Christy's house is new; it has carpeting, a breakfast bar, and a picture window; there is the scent of cookies; everything in it is new. In contrast, Rylant's apartment is old; it has green-and-brown linoleum with cigarette burns, spiders in the bathtub, a window that overlooks the junkyard, and old gas heaters. The girls' homes have nothing in common. The details reveal Rylant's feelings of inadequacy.

5. Possible main idea: The desire to be someone else was a curse because it made her imitate others, but it became the best gift of her life because it led her to be a writer. Details: wanting a house like Christy's; feeling unequal to city kids; being impressed by sophisticated college students.

Extending the Text

6. Possible responses: plan to move and start a new life when you graduate; focus on the good in yourself and in your home; explore new places and ideas, but appreciate yourself and your home.

Grading Timesaver

Rubrics for each Choices assignment appear on p. 140 in the *Portfolio Management System*.

CHOICES:
Building Your Portfolio

1. **Writer's Notebook** Encourage students to list subjects from their daily life.

2. **and 3. Creative Writing** Tell students to include specific details, such as anecdotes and sensory images.

T398

MAKING MEANINGS

First Thoughts

[respond]
1. Jot down some phrases that describe your impression of the narrator of "The Best Gift of My Life."

Shaping Interpretations

[analyze]
2. In this very **subjective** excerpt from her autobiography, Rylant is not afraid to let her feelings show. Find some passages that reveal personal details no one else could know.

[infer]
3. Rylant tells a story to show us how she came to be a writer. Why was the concert a peak experience for her?

[analyze]
4. Identify the details Rylant mentions in the first five paragraphs to compare her home with Christy's. How are their homes alike? How are they different? What do the details reveal about Rylant's attitude toward her home and herself?

[interpret]
5. Express Rylant's **main idea** (or ideas, if you think she makes more than one main point) in your own words. What details support your statement of her main idea? (Be sure to use the story's **title** in your statement.)

Extending the Text

[connect]
6. What advice would you give to a young person who is not happy with where he or she lives or who wishes to be someone else?

> **Reading Check**
>
> In three or four sentences, **summarize** Rylant's problem and explain what the best gift of her life was.

CHOICES: Building Your Portfolio

Writer's Notebook

1. Collecting Ideas for an Observational Essay

Choosing a topic. In the Writer's Workshop on page 438, you'll write an essay about a person or place or thing that you can observe directly. (Maybe you'll write about your room or a crowded bus or the ants on the sidewalk building their home.) Brainstorm a list of subjects that interest you, and circle the ones you'd most like to explore. Save your notes.

Creative Writing

2. If I Could . . .

Refer to the notes you took for the Quickwrite. If you had the whole world to choose from, where would you most like to live? Maybe your answer is "right where I am now." Write your answer in a brief essay. Be specific about the reasons for your choice.

Creative Writing

3. The Best Gift . . .

What has been the best gift in your life so far? It might be your family, a teacher, a trip, special lessons. In a brief essay, name the best gift, and tell why you treasure it so much.

> **Reading Check**
>
> Sample answer: As a child, Rylant was ashamed of her home—a rundown apartment in a small town. She felt unequal to other kids. After attending a symphony concert, she realized how much she wished for a different life. Her discontentment had drawbacks but ultimately proved to be a gift because it motivated her to become a writer.

Elements of Literature

ESSAYS: Thoughts About a Subject   by Janet Burroway

Over four hundred years ago, a French lawyer named Michel de Montaigne got tired of his practice, sold it, and retired to his country estate. To amuse himself there, he began to write short prose pieces about various topics that came into his mind—cannibals, smells, names, sleeping, friendship, prayers. Probably he had no intention of publishing these pieces at first, but eventually he published three volumes of what he called his *Essais*. Today, only historians are interested in the fact that Montaigne was at the court of King Charles IX and was mayor of Bordeaux, but his *Essais* are translated, read, and studied in every language of the Western world.

Essais means "tries" or "attempts" in French, and the name too has lasted. *Essays* or *tries* is a good way to describe these short pieces of non-fiction prose, since no essay will ever say everything there is to say about any subject.

> He began to write about various topics that came into his mind—cannibals, smells, names, sleeping, friendship, prayers.

There are as many ways of looking at and writing about cannibals, smells, names, and so forth, as there are people to write about them. Montaigne himself understood that a personal essay presents not only its subject but also its writer's personality. He said about his essays, "I have here only made a small bouquet of flowers and have brought nothing of my own but the thread that ties them together."

The essays in this collection were written many centuries after Montaigne wrote his *Essais*, but each one still reflects a writer's "attempt" or "try" to talk about a subject with the reader. In "Riding Is an Exercise of the Mind," N. Scott Momaday talks about the best home of his childhood. In "The Round Walls of Home," Diane Ackerman writes about the planet we all share. Like Montaigne's essays, these are conversational in style and personal in tone and feeling. In all of them, we hear the voice of one particular writer responding in a personal way to some experience that is part of the real world we live in.

Drawing by W. Miller; © 1987 The New Yorker Magazine, Inc.

ELEMENTS OF LITERATURE: ESSAYS **399**

Resources

Elements of Literature

Essays
For additional instruction on essays, see *Literary Elements:*
• Transparency 8
Formal Assessment
• Literary Elements Test, p. 75

Elements of Literature

This feature examines characteristics of the personal essay and discusses how the genre was first developed.

Mini-Lesson:
Elements of Literature
Use the following activities to reinforce students' understanding after they have read and discussed this feature.
1. Ask students to choose the correct words to complete the sentences.
   a. The term *essay* comes from a French word meaning ("tries," "nonfiction").
   b. A personal essay is (conversational, formal) in style.
   c. A personal essay reveals the writer's (research, personality).
2. Bring in a collection of periodicals. Have students, in small groups, go through them and find two or three examples of personal essays.

Applying the Element
As students read the essays in this collection, have them work individually or in small groups to identify the subject of each essay and to infer what the author's personal feelings are about the subject. Suggest that students fill in charts like the following one:

Essay	"The Best Gift of My Life"	"Haven't I Made A Difference!"
Author		
Subject		
Feelings about Subject		

Reaching All Students

Struggling Readers
Have students take notes as they read the essays in this collection, jotting down words and phrases that reveal the writer's emotions, opinions, and judgments. Afterwards, ask them to review their notes and to draw generalizations about the writer's personality and about his or her biases or attitudes toward the essay's subject.

Advanced Learners
Have students find two personal essays that express different thoughts about the same subject. Then, ask students to write their own brief personal essays on the subject. Invite volunteers to read their essays aloud to the class.

OBJECTIVES

1. Read and interpret the essay
2. Identify sensory images
3. Determine chronological order
4. Express understanding through creative writing or research/oral history
5. Identify and use narrative devices for showing time
6. Understand and use new words

SKILLS

Literary
- Identify sensory images

Reading
- Determine chronological order

Writing
- Make a chart that lists sensory details
- Write a personal essay

Research/Oral History
- Research and prepare an oral history

Grammar
- Identify and use narrative devices for showing time

Vocabulary
- Use new words

Planning

- **Block Schedule**
  Block Scheduling Lesson Plans with Pacing Guide
- **Traditional Schedule**
  Lesson Plans Including Strategies for English-Language Learners
- **One-Stop Planner**
  CD-ROM with Test Generator

Before You Read

RIDING IS AN EXERCISE OF THE MIND

Make the Connection

Surrounded by the Landscape

What's the landscape like where you live? Are there hills or mountains, or is the land basically flat? Do you see buildings and roads or a lot of wide-open space? What kinds of trees and flowers grow? For N. Scott Momaday, remembering "the last, best home" of his childhood is an occasion to reflect on how powerfully its landscape colored his daydreams.

Quickwrite

Describe a landscape that you know well. It might be the landscape of your present home or a place where you once lived or somewhere you visited. Jot down some details to describe what you see, smell, and hear when you imagine that place.

Elements of Literature

Sensory Images

Sensory images add color and life to description, helping readers see, hear, smell, taste, and touch what the writer is describing. Momaday's descrip-

tions show us the caravan of Navajo riders and let us hear their songs; we smell pine and cedar smoke and see the "angles of geese" above the pueblo.

> ensory details are images that appeal to our senses of sight, taste, smell, hearing, and touch.
>
> *For more on Description, see the Handbook of Literary Terms.*

Reading Skills and Strategies

Chronological Order: Organizing Memory

Momaday recalls scenes and events long past. Look for words that help you follow events:

- He begins by anchoring his memory in time: "One autumn morning in 1946." Look for other words and phrases that express time.

- Does Momaday ever flash back to a more distant past? Or does he use straight **chronological order**—that is, does he narrate events in the exact order in which they happened?

Background

N. (Novarro) Scott Momaday grew up on Kiowa and Navajo reservations in the Southwest. In 1946, Momaday's parents began teaching at the two-room Navajo school at Jemez (hā'mās) Pueblo, in the canyon country in the foothills of the Jemez Mountains, fifty miles from Albuquerque.

 go.hrw.com
LEO 9-6

Preteaching Vocabulary

Words to Own

Ask students to read the definitions of the two vocabulary words, **exotic** and **revelry**, at the bottom of p. 402. To reinforce their understanding of the words, have students create an acrostic for each word. The first letters of the words in the acrostic should form the vocabulary word. All the words or phrases in the acrostic should relate in meaning to the vocabulary word. For the letter *x*, students can use words that begin with *ex*. Remind them that a thesaurus can be a source of ideas.

Sample acrostics:

(r) raucous
(e) entertainment
(v) very noisy
(e) excitement
(l) lively
(r) rip-roaring
(y) yippee!

(e) eye-popping
(x) extremely beautiful
(o) out of this world
(t) tantalizing
(i) intriguing
(c) colorful

T400

RIDING
Is an Exercise of the Mind

*I had found
the best home
of my childhood.*

N. Scott Momaday

One autumn morning in 1946 I woke up at Jemez Pueblo.[1] I had arrived there in the middle of the night and gone to sleep. I had no idea of the landscape, no sense of where in the world I was. Now, in the bright New Mexican morning, I began to look around and settle in. I had found the last, best home of my childhood.

1. In the Southwestern United States, pueblos are American Indian communities of flat-roofed, terraced houses made from stone or sun-dried brick.

Summary ▪▪

In this personal essay, Momaday recalls growing up in Jemez Pueblo in New Mexico. He describes his bond with his horse, Pecos, and recounts imaginary adventures that they shared as they explored the canyons. Through the use of sensory detail, the writer brings to life the sweep of the landscape and the Native American peoples who live in the region. They serve as perfect catalysts for the young Momaday's inner journey toward adulthood.

Resources

Viewing and Representing
Videocassette A, Segment 6
This segment explores the landscapes and cultures of the southwestern United States. For full lesson plans and worksheets, see the *Visual Connections Teacher's Manual.*

Listening
Audio CD Library
A reading of this essay is included in the *Audio CD Library:*
• Disc 14, Track 3

Viewing and Representing
Fine Art Transparency
A transparency of John Sloan's *Chama Running Red* can facilitate connection as students read the essay. See the *Viewing and Representing Transparencies and Worksheets:*
• Transparency 8
• Worksheet, p. 32

Elements of Literature
Personal Essay
For additional instruction on the personal essay, see *Literary Elements:*
• Transparency 8
• Worksheet, p. 25

Resources: Print and Media

Reading
• *Reading Skills and Strategies*
   MiniRead Skill Lesson, p. 110
   Selection Skill Lesson, p. 117
• *Graphic Organizers for Active Reading,* p. 26
• *Words to Own,* p. 19
• *Audio CD Library,* Disc 14, Track 3

Elements of Literature
• *Literary Elements* booklet
   Transparency 8
   Worksheet, p. 25

Writing and Language
• *Daily Oral Grammar*
   Transparency 26
• *Grammar and Language Links*
   Worksheet, p. 41
• *Language Workshop* CD-ROM

Viewing and Representing
• *Viewing and Representing*
   Fine Art Transparency 8
   Fine Art Worksheet, p. 32
• *Visual Connections*

Videocassette A, Segment 6

Assessment
• *Formal Assessment,* p. 67
• *Portfolio Management System,* p. 141
• *Standardized Test Preparation,* p. 54
• *Test Generator (One-Stop Planner* CD-ROM)

Internet
• go.hrw.com (keyword: LE0 9-6)

When my parents and I moved to Jemez, I was twelve years old. The world was a different place then, and Jemez was the most exotic corner within it. The village and the valley, the canyons and the mountains, had been there from the beginning of time, waiting for me. So it seemed. Marco Polo in the court of Kublai Khan[2] had nothing on me. I was embarked upon the greatest adventure of all; I had come to the place of my growing up.

The landscape was full of mystery and of life. The autumn was in full bloom. The sun cast a golden light upon the adobe walls and the cornfields; it set fire to the leaves of willows and cottonwoods along the river; and a fresh, cold wind ran down from the canyons and carried the good scents of pine and cedar smoke, of bread baking in the beehive ovens, and of rain in the mountains. There were horses in the plain and angles of geese in the sky.

One November, on the feast of San Diego, Jemez took on all the color of a Renaissance fair. I lived on the southwest corner of the village, on the wagon road to San Ysidro.[3] I looked southward into the plain; there a caravan of covered wagons reached as far as the eye could see. These were the Navajos, coming in from Torreon. I had never seen such a pageant; it was as if that whole proud people, the Diné,[4] had been concentrated into one endless migration. There was a great dignity to them, even in revelry. They sat tall in the wagons and on horseback, going easily with laughter and singing their riding songs. And when they set up camp in the streets, they were perfectly at home, their dogs about them. They made coffee and fried bread and roasted mutton on their open fires.

Gradually and without effort I entered into the motion of life there. In the winter dusk I

heard coyotes barking away by the river, the sound of the drums in the kiva,[5] and the voice of the village crier, ringing at the rooftops.

And on summer nights of the full moon I saw old men in their ceremonial garb, running after witches—and sometimes I saw the witches themselves in the forms of bats and cats and owls on fence posts.

I came to know the land by going out upon it in all seasons, getting into it until it became the very element in which I lived my daily life.

I had a horse named Pecos, a fleet-footed roan gelding, which was my great glory for a time. Pecos could outrun all the other horses in the village, and he wanted always to prove it. We two came to a good understanding of each other, I believe. I did a lot of riding in those days, and I got to be very good at it. My Kiowa ancestors, who were centaurs,[6] should have been proud of me.

Riding is an exercise of the mind. I dreamed a good deal on the back of my horse, going out into the hills alone. Desperadoes were everywhere in the brush. More than once I came upon roving bands of hostile Indians and had, on the spur of the moment, to put down an uprising. Now and then I found a wagon train in trouble, and always among the settlers there was a lovely young girl from Charleston or Philadelphia who needed simply and more than anything else in the world to be saved. I saved her.

After a time Billy the Kid was with me on most of those adventures. He rode on my right

---

2. Marco Polo in the court of Kublai Khan (ko͞o′blī kän): Marco Polo (1254-1324) was one of the first Europeans to visit China, where he served as a government official during the rule of the emperor Kublai Khan.
3. San Ysidro (san ē·sēd′rō).
4. Diné (də·nä′): the Navajos' name for themselves, meaning "the people."

5. kiva (kē′və): underground room in a pueblo, used for ceremonies and other purposes.
6. centaurs (sen′tôrz′): creatures from Greek mythology that are half man and half horse. The Kiowa were great horsemen.

- -

WORDS TO OWN

exotic (eg·zät′ik) *adj.*: fascinating; strangely beautiful. *Exotic* also means "foreign."
revelry (rev′əl·rē) *n.*: noisy, lively celebration.

- -

Reaching All Students

Struggling Readers

Chronological Ordering was introduced on p. 400. For a lesson directly tied to this selection that teaches students to analyze chronological order by using a strategy called Text Reformulation, see the *Reading Skills and Strategies* binder:
- MiniRead Skill Lesson, p. 110
- Selection Skill Lesson, p. 117

English Language Learners

Explain that idioms are expressions particular to a certain region, class, or language. Introduce and discuss the following idioms:
- on the spur of the moment (spontaneously)
- to bear watching (to be unpredictable)
- to get on well together (to enjoy each other)
- in the main (mostly)

For other strategies, see
- *Lesson Plans Including Strategies for English-Language Learners*

Advanced Learners

Have students identify Momaday's historical and mythological allusions: Marco Polo, the court of Kublai Khan, a Renaissance fair, centaurs, and Billy the Kid. Point out that these allusions reinforce Momaday's view of growing up as a universal, timeless journey. Ask students what allusions they would choose to describe the "adventure" of their own adolescence.

side and a couple of steps behind. I watched him out of the corner of my eye, for he bore watching. We got on well together in the main, and he was a good man to have along in a fight. We had to be careful of glory-seeking punks. Incredibly, there were those in the world who were foolish enough to oppose us, merely for the sake of gaining a certain reputation.

When it came time for me to leave home and venture out into the wider world, I sold my horse to an old gentleman at Vallecitos. I like to think that Pecos went on with our games long afterward, that in his old age he listened for the sound of bugles and of gunfire—and for the pitiful weeping of young ladies in distress—and that he heard them as surely as I do now.

E

E Reading Skills and Strategies

Chronological Order

Momaday uses the present tense to describe thoughts and feelings that he has while writing this essay. Have students identify the point in this paragraph where the time frame shifts from the past to the present. [Momaday shifts to the present in the second sentence.]

Resources —————

Selection Assessment
Formal Assessment
• Selection Test, p. 67
Test Generator (One-Stop Planner)
• CD-ROM

MEET THE WRITER

Rock-Tree Boy

When **N. Scott Momaday** (1934–) was six months old, his parents took him to a sacred place—Devils Tower in Wyoming, which the Kiowa people call Tsoai (Rock Tree). There an old storyteller gave Momaday the name Tsoai-talee, which means "Rock-Tree Boy." (If you saw the movie *Close Encounters of the Third Kind,* you know what Devils Tower looks like: a steep-sided volcanic rock tower 865 feet high.)

Momaday says that schooling was a problem at Jemez because there were no high schools nearby. He recalls his mother's influence:

❝ My mother has been the inspiration of many people . . . certainly she was mine at Jemez, when inspiration was the nourishment I needed most. I was at that age in which a boy flounders. I had not much sense of where I must go or of what I must do and be in my life, and there were for me moments of great, growing urgency, in which I felt that I was imprisoned in the narrow quarters of my time and place. I wanted, needed, to conceive of what my destiny might be, and my mother allowed me to believe that it might be worthwhile. ❞

Momaday received his B.A. from New Mexico State University and his Ph.D. in creative writing from Stanford University. While teaching at several universities, he has created novels, memoirs, poems, and paintings that draw upon his American Indian heritage. *House Made of Dawn* (1968), his first novel, won the Pulitzer Prize for fiction. His memoir *The Way to Rainy Mountain* (1969) combines Kiowa legend, history, personal memories, and poetry.

BROWSING IN THE FILES

About the Author. When Momaday was born in the Kiowa and Comanche Indian Hospital in Lawton, Oklahoma, his birth certificate described him as 7/8th degree Indian blood. The son of a Kiowa father and an Anglo-American mother with Cherokee ancestry, he was raised on the Native American reservations of the southwest and grew up speaking English, Kiowa, and Navajo. He identifies especially with his Kiowa heritage.

RIDING IS AN EXERCISE OF THE MIND **403**

Assessing Learning

Making the Connections

Check Test: True-False
1. The narrator dislikes Jemez Pueblo. [False]
2. The narrator has difficulty adjusting to his new community. [False]
3. The narrator's imagination awakens as he rides his horse through the hills. [True]
4. Pecos is lame and slow. [False]
5. The narrator thinks about Pecos long after they part. [True]

Standardized Test Preparation
For practice with standardized test format specific to this selection, see
• *Standardized Test Preparation,* p. 54
For practice in proofreading and editing, see
• *Daily Oral Grammar,* Transparency 26

Connecting to the Theme:
"A Place Called Home"
For Momaday, the concept of "home" involves more than just a house; it encompasses the entire landscape as well. He describes the physical beauty and cultural traditions of the Jemez area as major influences in his development. Ask students if they have ever been attached to a particular landscape in a similar way as Momaday.

T403

MAKING MEANINGS

First Thoughts

1. Possible responses: It would be peaceful; it would be too isolated.

Shaping Interpretations

2. Possible responses: see—gold autumn light on trees along the river; smell—distant rain, bread baking in outdoor ovens; feel—the cold wind from the canyons.

3. The title is the sentence that opens paragraph nine. Possible interpretations: Riding stirs up your imagination; riding gives you a chance to look inward. Possible titles: "Adventures with Pecos" or "Growing Up in Jemez."

4. Possible responses: "Adventure" is the most important word because living in Jemez, riding Pecos, and growing up were all adventures; "an exercise of the mind" is an important phrase because riding, imagining, remembering, reflecting on memories, and writing this essay are all exercises of the mind.

Challenging the Text

5. Possible responses: This mixture of the real and imaginary is an accurate reflection of the way memory works and helps readers relate to Momaday's recollections; this mixture makes the last paragraphs a little confusing.

Grading Timesaver 🕘

Rubrics for each Choices assignment appear on p. 141 in the *Portfolio Management System*.

CHOICES: Building Your Portfolio

1. **Writer's Notebook** You might sketch a sensory details chart on the chalkboard for students to copy.

2. **Creative Writing** Tell students that many dictionaries provide the meanings of common given names.

3. **Research/Oral History** Remind interviewers to ask "how" or "why" questions, rather than "yes" or "no" questions.

T404

MAKING MEANINGS

First Thoughts

[respond]
1. How would you feel about growing up in a place like Jemez Pueblo?

Shaping Interpretations

[analyze]
2. What **sensory details** help you see, smell, and feel the landscape Momaday loves?

[interpret]
3. Find where the **title** is mentioned in the essay. What do you think the title means? What other titles would you suggest for this essay?

[evaluate]
4. Skim the essay again. What word or passage do you think is the most important? Why do you think so?

Challenging the Text

[evaluate]
5. Someone complains: "Momaday writes about imaginary events and real ones mixed up together." How would you respond?

Reading Check

a. In the first three paragraphs, what facts do we learn about Jemez Pueblo?

b. Who was Pecos and why was he important?

c. Why would Momaday's ancestors have been proud of him?

d. Which paragraphs describe imagined events?

CHOICES: Building Your Portfolio

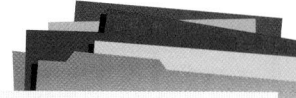

Writer's Notebook

1. Collecting Ideas for an Observational Essay

Sensory details. In the essay you'll write for the Writer's Workshop on page 438, you'll provide **sensory details** to help your readers imagine your subject. Notice how Momaday shows us the Navajos sitting tall in their wagons, helps us smell the coffee and the fried bread and hear the sounds of laugh-ter and singing. Observe a subject closely. Make a chart listing as many sensory details (what you see, hear, smell, taste, and touch) as you can. Your Quickwrite notes might give you a start. Save your chart.

Creative Writing

2. Your Name

What does *your* first name mean, and why was it chosen for you? If you don't already know, do some research to find out about your name. Write a brief essay about it and how you feel about it. (See the details about Momaday's name in Meet the Writer on page 403.)

Research/Oral History

3. Who We Are

Interview relatives or family friends or neighbors, starting with the oldest ones. Take notes or tape-record their answers to questions about who your ancestors are or where people in your community came from or how your town was first settled. You could donate your oral histories to your school library so future students can share your research.

Reading Check

a. It is a village of adobe buildings in New Mexico, set in a valley among cornfields, near a river lined with willows and cottonwoods, and at the base of mountains and canyons.

b. Pecos was Momaday's horse, and he was important because he shared in the boy's imaginary adventures while growing up.

c. They would have been proud of his riding ability.

d. the last three paragraphs

GRAMMAR LINK  MINI-LESSON

Language Handbook HELP

See Tense, page 999.

Technology HELP

See Language Workshop CD-ROM. Key word entry: verb tenses.

Showing Time

Momaday's essay is a journey back in time as well as a journey back to a special place. He uses these devices to capture time in words:

1. **Verb tenses.** The tenses of verbs can show past, present, future, and various shades of continuing action. Most of the verbs in this essay are in the past ("I woke up") and past perfect ("I had arrived there").

2. **Time words and phrases.** When a writer wants to be specific, time can be indicated with words and phrases: "One autumn morning in 1946," "in the middle of the night," "And on summer nights of the full moon."

3. **Chronological order.** Most writers who use the narrative mode write in chronological order, the order in which events happen, from start to finish. (When such writers want to tell us about something that happened in the past, they often use a **flashback**.)

Try It Out

1. Most narratives are told in the past tense, but writers often like to experiment with the present tense. Rewrite one paragraph of Momaday's narrative in the present tense. What parts of the narrative will you have to keep in the past? Does a change of tense change your feeling of participating in the story?

2. Illustrate the events Momaday links with the seasons by describing them in a seasonal "wheel." Note that Momaday misses a season. What events can you supply from your imagination?

3. Do you wish that Momaday had flashed back to an even earlier time to explain anything? What would you like to know?

VOCABULARY — HOW TO OWN A WORD

WORD BANK

exotic
revelry

Word Play

There are only two words in this Word Bank, so take a break and think of some entertaining ways to learn them. Here are two suggestions for starters:

1. You could create two cartoons that use the words *exotic* and *revelry* in captions or in thought bubbles.
2. You might write verses that have words rhyming with *exotic* (hypnotic? periodic?) and *revelry* (celery? bravery?).

Riddles, raps, puns, puzzles—anything goes. Think of some ways to use these two words just for fun and share your ideas with your classmates.

RIDING IS AN EXERCISE OF THE MIND 405

GRAMMAR LINK

Students can apply these devices when they need to convey the passage of time and the chronological order of events in a narrative.

Try It Out
Possible Answers

1. One autumn morning in 1946, I wake up at Jemez Pueblo. Having arrived there in the middle of the night and gone to sleep, I have no idea of the landscape, no sense of where in the world I am. Now, in the bright New Mexican morning, I begin to look around and settle in. I have found the last, best home of my childhood.

2.

SUMMER	FALL
• Sees elders in ceremonies	• Moves to Jemez Pueblo • Feast of San Diego
• Momaday misses this season. Perhaps he sees corn being planted.	• Hears coyotes, ceremonial drums, voice of town crier
	WINTER

3. Students may say they would like to know about Momaday's previous home.

VOCABULARY
Possible Answers

1. Cartoon: Teenager addressing a friend who is dressed in a wild, extreme style: "Exotic? I'd say bizarre is more like it."
2. Please tone down your revelry—The noise is going to level me!

Resources ———

Language
• *Grammar and Language Links* Worksheet, p. 41

Vocabulary
• *Words to Own* Worksheet, p. 19

Grammar Link Quick Check

In each sentence below, underline the word or phrase that indicates time. Then, from the words in parentheses, choose the correct verb tense.

1. The year the narrator turned twelve, he (moves, moved) to Jemez Pueblo. [moved]
2. He (owns, owned) a horse when he was growing up. [owned]
3. Now, as an adult, he still (enjoys, enjoyed) using his imagination. [enjoys]
4. Even today he clearly (recalls, will recall) the details of his imaginary adventures. [recalls]
5. No matter what the future may bring, he always (remembers, will remember) Jemez. [will remember]

T405

1. Read and interpret the memoir
2. Recognize a nonfiction narrative
3. Analyze cause and effect
4. Express understanding through critical and creative writing, interviewing, or drawing
5. Identify and use the techniques of descriptive writing
6. Understand and use new words
7. Use prefixes and suffixes

SKILLS

Literary
- Recognize a nonfiction narrative

Reading
- Analyze cause and effect

Writing
- Chart contrasting details for an observational essay
- Write a pet story
- Write a paragraph supporting an opinion

Art
- Create a cartoon strip

Language
- Interview an expert and compile a glossary of technical terms
- Use descriptive writing techniques

Vocabulary
- Use new words
- Use prefixes and suffixes

Planning

- **Block Schedule**
  Block Scheduling Lesson Plans with Pacing Guide

- **Traditional Schedule**
  Lesson Plans Including Strategies for English-Language Learners

- **One-Stop Planner**
  CD-ROM with Test Generator

Before You Read

"HAVEN'T I MADE A DIFFERENCE"

Make the Connection

Who Cares?

Throughout history and in almost all cultures, pets have made people feel happy. Probably more than fifty thousand years ago, cave dwellers had dogs as household— "cavehold"—pets. Ancient Egyptians tamed baboons and worshiped cats. Before the first Europeans arrived in Mexico, the Aztecs kept pet parrots.

Quickwrite

Why do people make animals part of their homes? Is it because pets seem to care about us, or is it because they give us something to care about? Jot down your ideas about these questions.

Elements of Literature

Nonfiction Narratives

Usually we think of narratives as fiction, but nonfiction writers often tell true stories to make a point. **Nonfiction narratives** are used in news reports, biographies, and histories. The narrative you're about to read tells a lively story that's as entertaining as fiction. The narrator is a veterinarian who uses the pen name James Herriot. Darrowby is a town in Yorkshire, in northeast England.

> **A** nonfiction narrative tells about a series of related events that actually happened.
>
> *For more on Narration, see the Handbook of Literary Terms.*

Reading Skills and Strategies

Cause and Effect: Why Does It Happen?

Events usually happen because of something that has occurred earlier. A **cause** explains *why* something happens, and an **effect** is the *result* of something. Here's how you can discover cause-and-effect relationships:

- Watch for words that signal a cause-and-effect relationship: *because, so, as a result, therefore.*

- Notice how characters or situations change. Ask: *Why do they change? (What event was the cause?)*

 go.hrw.com
LEO 9-6

Preteaching Vocabulary

Words to Own

Have students read the definitions of the Words to Own at the bottom of the selection pages. Then, to reinforce their understanding, ask students to answer the following questions.

1. Name some sights a veterinarian might find **stupefying**.
2. Why might a veterinarian offer **remonstrances** to someone adopting a lion cub?
3. What would **diligent** pet owners do about their pets' fleas?
4. Why might a cat yowl **interminably**?
5. How can the loss of a pet cause **desolation**?
6. What could make a dog's coat **luxuriant**?
7. How would a **callous** person react to a litter of kittens?
8. What is a **dispersing** herd of deer doing?
9. How does a dog show **implicit** faith in its owner?
10. What jobs make use of dogs' **uncanny** sense of smell?

I saw in his eyes only a calm trust.

"HAVEN'T I MADE A DIFFERENCE!"

from **All Things Bright and Beautiful**

James Herriot

Old Mrs. Donovan was a woman who really got around. No matter what was going on in Darrowby—weddings, funerals, house sales—you'd find the dumpy little figure and walnut face among the spectators, the darting, black-button eyes taking everything in. And always, on the end of its lead, her terrier dog.

When I say "old," I'm only guessing, because she appeared ageless; she seemed to have been around a long time but she could have been anything between fifty-five and seventy-five. She certainly had the vitality of a young woman because she must have walked vast distances in her dedicated quest to keep abreast of events. Many people took an uncharitable view of her acute curiosity, but whatever the motivation, her activities took her into almost every channel of life in the town. One of these channels was our veterinary practice.

Summary ■ ■ ■

James Herriot's nonfiction narrative tells the story of Mrs. Donovan, an elderly widow of remarkable vitality who is a self-styled expert on animal care. After Mrs. Donovan's beloved terrier is killed, Herriot suggests that she adopt a young golden retriever that he has found, a victim of abuse. Mrs. Donovan nurses the dog back to health, and the two happily create their own unique version of home.

Resources

Listening
Audio CD Library
A recording of this essay is included in the *Audio CD Library*:
• Disc 14, Track 4

Ⓐ Elements of Literature
Nonfiction Narrative
❓ Characterization is one technique used by narrative writers. How does James Herriot provide readers with an impression of Mrs. Donovan's character? [He describes her looks, actions, and habits.]

Ⓑ Reading Skills and Strategies
Cause and Effect
❓ What are some effects of Mrs. Donovan's acute curiosity? [Possible responses: She walks great distances to keep up on news and gossip; she knows almost everything going on in town; some people resent her nosiness.]

Resources: Print and Media

Reading
• *Graphic Organizers for Active Reading*, p. 27
• *Words to Own*, p. 20
• *Audio CD Library*, Disc 14, Track 4

Writing and Language
• *Daily Oral Grammar*, Transparency 27
• *Grammar and Language Links* Worksheet, p. 43

Assessment
• *Formal Assessment*, p. 69
• *Portfolio Management System*, p. 142
• *Test Generator* (One-Stop Planner CD-ROM)

Internet
• go.hrw.com (keyword: LE0 9-6)

Because Mrs. Donovan, among her other widely ranging interests, was an animal doctor. In fact I think it would be safe to say that this facet of her life transcended all the others.

She could talk at length on the ailments of small animals, and she had a whole armory of medicines and remedies at her command, her two specialties being her miracle-working condition powders and a dog shampoo of unprecedented value for improving the coat. She had an uncanny ability to sniff out a sick animal, and it was not uncommon when I was on my rounds to find Mrs. Donovan's dark Gypsy face poised intently over what I had thought was my patient while she administered calf's-foot jelly or one of her own patent nostrums.[1]

I suffered more than Siegfried[2] because I took a more active part in the small-animal side of our practice. I was anxious to develop this aspect and to improve my image in this field and Mrs. Donovan didn't help at all. "Young Mr. Herriot," she would confide to my clients, "is all right with cattle and suchlike, but he don't know nothing about dogs and cats."

And of course they believed her and had implicit faith in her. She had the irresistible mystic appeal of the amateur and on top of that there was her habit, particularly endearing in Darrowby, of never charging for her advice, her medicines, her long periods of diligent nursing.

Older folk in the town told how her husband, an Irish farm worker, had died many years ago and how he must have had a "bit put away" because Mrs. Donovan had apparently been able to indulge all her interests over the years without financial strain. Since she inhabited the streets of Darrowby all day and every day, I often encountered her and she always smiled up at me sweetly and told me how she had been sitting up all night with Mrs. So-and-so's dog that I'd been treating. She felt sure she'd be able to pull it through.

There was no smile on her face, however, on the day when she rushed into the surgery[3] while Siegfried and I were having tea.

"Mr. Herriot!" she gasped. "Can you come? My little dog's been run over!"

I jumped up and ran out to the car with her. She sat in the passenger seat with her head bowed, her hands clasped tightly on her knees.

"He slipped his collar and ran in front of a car," she murmured. "He's lying in front of the school halfway up Cliffend Road. Please hurry."

I was there within three minutes but as I bent over the dusty little body stretched on the pavement, I knew there was nothing I could do. The fast-glazing eyes, the faint, gasping respirations, the ghastly pallor of the mucous membranes[4] all told the same story.

"I'll take him back to the surgery and get some saline[5] into him, Mrs. Donovan," I said. "But I'm afraid he's had a massive internal hemorrhage.[6] Did you see what happened exactly?"

She gulped. "Yes, the wheel went right over him."

Ruptured liver, for sure. I passed my hands under the little animal and began to lift him gently, but as I did so the breathing stopped and the eyes stared fixedly ahead.

Mrs. Donovan sank to her knees and for a few moments she gently stroked the rough hair of the head and chest. "He's dead, isn't he?" she whispered at last.

"I'm afraid he is," I said.

She got slowly to her feet and stood bewilderedly among the little group of bystanders on the pavement. Her lips moved but she seemed unable to say any more.

3. **surgery:** British term for "doctor's office."
4. **pallor of the mucous membranes:** unnatural paleness of the tissue lining body cavities that connect with outside air, such as those in the nose.
5. **saline** (sā'lĭn): salt solution used in medical treatment.
6. **hemorrhage** (hem'ər·ij'): heavy bleeding.

WORDS TO OWN

uncanny (un·kan'ē) adj.: eerily remarkable.
implicit (im·plis'it) adj.: absolute; unquestioning.
   Implicit is also used to describe something that is implied or suggested but not expressed in words.
diligent (dil'ə·jənt) adj.: careful and hard-working.

1. **patent nostrums** (pat''nt näs'trəmz): trademarked medicines of doubtful effectiveness that can be bought without a doctor's prescription.
2. Siegfried and Herriot are partners in the veterinary practice.

I took her arm, led her over to the car, and opened the door. "Get in and sit down," I said. "I'll run you home. Leave everything to me."

I wrapped the dog in my calving overall and laid him in the boot[7] before driving away. It wasn't until we drew up outside Mrs. Donovan's house that she began to weep silently. I sat there without speaking till she had finished. Then she wiped her eyes and turned to me.

"Do you think he suffered at all?"

"I'm certain he didn't. It was all so quick—he wouldn't know a thing about it."

She tried to smile. "Poor little Rex. I don't know what I'm going to do without him. We've traveled a few miles together, you know."

"Yes, you have. He had a wonderful life, Mrs. Donovan. And let me give you a bit of advice—you must get another dog. You'd be lost without one."

She shook her head. "No, I couldn't. That little dog meant too much to me. I couldn't let another take his place."

"Well, I know that's how you feel just now, but I wish you'd think about it. I don't want to seem callous—I tell everybody this when they lose an animal and I know it's good advice."

"Mr. Herriot, I'll never have another one." She shook her head again, very decisively. "Rex was my faithful friend for many years and I just want to remember him. He's the last dog I'll ever have."

I often saw Mrs. Donovan around the town after this, and I was glad to see she was still as active

as ever, though she looked strangely incomplete without the little dog on its lead. But it must have been over a month before I had the chance to speak to her.

It was on the afternoon that Inspector Halliday of the RSPCA[8] rang me.

"Mr. Herriot," he said, "I'd like you to come and see an animal with me. A cruelty case."

"Right, what is it?"

"A dog, and it's pretty grim. A dreadful case of neglect." He gave me the name of a row of old brick cottages down by the river and said he'd meet me there.

Halliday was waiting for me, smart and businesslike in his dark uniform, as I pulled up in the back lane behind the houses. He was a big blond man with cheerful blue eyes, but he didn't smile as he came over to the car.

"He's in here," he said, and led the way toward one of the doors in the long, crumbling wall. A few curious people were hanging around and with a feeling of inevitability I recognized a gnomelike brown face. Trust Mrs. Donovan, I thought, to be among those present at a time like this.

We went through the door into the long garden. I had found that even the lowliest dwellings in Darrowby had long strips of land at

---

8. **RSPCA:** Royal Society for the Prevention of Cruelty to Animals.

- -

WORDS TO OWN
callous (kal′əs) *adj.*: unfeeling; insensitive.

- -

7. **boot:** British term for "trunk of a car."

"HAVEN'T I MADE A DIFFERENCE!" 409

D **Critical Thinking**
Expressing an Opinion

❓ Do you think the narrator's advice to Mrs. Donovan is good? Why or why not? [Possible responses: It's good, because a new pet will take her mind off her loss; or, it's not good, because people need time to grieve before they try to get over a loss.]

E **Appreciating Language**
British Terms

List on the chalkboard the British terms found in this section; write their American equivalents alongside.

- lead (leash)
- rang (telephoned)
- smart (well-dressed)

Ask students to add to the list, using footnoted British terms from pp. 408–409 and other terms they notice as they continue to read the essay.

F **Elements of Literature**
Nonfiction Narrative

❓ In this passage, where does Herriot use the following elements of narrative: plot, characterization, dialogue, and foreshadowing? [Possible answers: He advances the plot by having Mrs. Donovan enter upon the scene; he uses characterization when describing Halliday and Mrs. Donovan and presenting the narrator's thoughts and feelings; he uses dialogue when Halliday speaks; he uses foreshadowing when he mentions that Halliday is uncharacteristically somber.]

Crossing the Curriculum

Social Studies

Encourage interested students to learn more about the county of Yorkshire and to present their findings to the class. Suggest that they research the following information: the size of the area compared to those of England's other counties; its location and geographic features; its natural resources and industries; lifestyles

in its towns and farms. As part of their presentations, they might play a tape of people speaking in a Yorkshire dialect; one source could be a video from the BBC series *All Creatures Great and Small*, which was based on Herriot's writings.

Getting Students Involved

Cooperative Learning

Herriot Revisited. Divide students into groups of three and have each group choose a different narrative from one of James Herriot's books. Have one member read the narrative aloud to the group. The group should then summarize the main idea and supporting details as the second member takes notes. The third member of the group can write a final draft of the group's summary. Encourage students to read the book in its entirety.

T409

A Struggling Readers

Reading Aloud

Point out the silent *g* in *gnarled*, on this page, and in *gnomelike*, near the bottom of p. 409. Ask students to think of another word starting with silent *g* that means "to chew." [gnaw] Have a volunteer write this word—and any others with a silent *g* that students can think of—on the chalkboard. [gnat, gnash]

B Appreciating Language

Descriptive Writing

? Which descriptive nouns, verbs, and adjectives help to evoke a mood of bleakness? [Possible answers: *wilderness, chilling, desolation, gnarled, rank, forsaken*.]

C Reading Skills and Strategies

Cause and Effect

? How do the details about the dog's surroundings suggest the causes of his condition? [The deep hollow suggests that he has been chained in one place for a long time; the filth suggests that no one cleans his area; the scummy water suggests that he is seldom attended to.]

the back, as though the builders had taken it for granted that the country people who were going to live in them would want to occupy themselves with the pursuits of the soil; with vegetable and fruit growing, even stock keeping[9] in a small way. You usually found a pig there, a few hens, often pretty beds of flowers.

A But this garden was a wilderness. A chilling air of <u>desolation</u> hung over the few gnarled apple and plum trees standing among a tangle of rank grass, as though the place had been forsaken by all living creatures. **B**

Halliday went over to a ramshackle wooden shed with peeling paint and a rusted corrugated-iron roof. He produced a key, unlocked the padlock, and dragged the door partly open.

9. **stock keeping:** raising farm animals.

There was no window and it wasn't easy to identify the jumble inside: broken gardening tools, an ancient mangle, rows of flowerpots, and partly used paint tins. And right at the back, a dog sitting quietly.

I didn't notice him immediately because of the gloom and because the smell in the shed started me coughing, but as I drew closer I saw that he was a big animal, sitting very upright, his collar secured by a chain to a ring in the wall. I had seen some thin dogs but this advanced emaciation[10] reminded me of my textbooks on anatomy; nowhere else did the bones of pelvis, **C**

10. **emaciation** (ē·mā′shē·ā′shən): extreme, abnormal thinness.

WORDS TO OWN

desolation (des′ə·lā′shən) *n*.: loneliness; ruin.

Using Students' Strengths

Naturalist Learners

As students read the essay, encourage them to deepen their understanding of Roy's nature and behavior by exploring the characteristics of the golden retriever breed. They might examine and discuss the needs of golden retrievers, the strengths and weaknesses of the breed, and the ways in which Roy is, and is not, a typical golden retriever.

T410

face, and rib cage stand out with such horrifying clarity. A deep, smoothed-out hollow in the earth floor showed where he had lain, moved about, in fact lived for a very long time.

The sight of the animal had a <u>stupefying</u> effect on me; I only half took in the rest of the scene—the filthy shreds of sacking scattered nearby, the bowl of scummy water.

"Look at his back end," Halliday muttered.

I carefully raised the dog from his sitting position and realized that the stench in the place was not entirely due to the piles of excrement. The hindquarters were a welter of pressure sores which had turned gangrenous[11] and strips of sloughing tissue[12] hung down from them.

---

11. **gangrenous** (gaŋ′grə·nəs): decayed because of blockage of the blood supply caused by disease or injury.
12. **sloughing** (sluf′iŋ) **tissue**: dead skin being shed.

There were similar sores along the sternum[13] and ribs. The coat, which seemed to be a dull yellow, was matted and caked with dirt.

The inspector spoke again. "I don't think he's ever been out of here. He's only a young dog—about a year old—but I understand he's been in this shed since he was an eight-week-old pup. Somebody out in the lane heard a whimper or he'd never have been found."

I felt a tightening of the throat and a sudden nausea which wasn't due to the smell. It was the thought of this patient animal sitting starved and forgotten in the darkness and filth for a year. I looked again at the dog and saw in his eyes only a calm trust. Some dogs would have barked their heads off and soon been discovered, some would have become terrified and vicious, but this was one of the totally undemanding kind, the kind which had complete faith in people and accepted all their actions without complaint. Just an occasional whimper perhaps as he sat <u>interminably</u> in the empty blackness which had been his world and at times wondered what it was all about.

"Well, Inspector, I hope you're going to throw the book at whoever's responsible," I said.

Halliday grunted. "Oh, there won't be much done. It's a case of diminished responsibility. The owner's definitely simple. Lives with an aged mother who hardly knows what's going on either. I've seen the fellow and it seems he threw in a bit of food when he felt like it and that's about all he did. They'll fine him and stop him keeping an animal in the future but nothing more than that."

"I see." I reached out and stroked the dog's head and he immediately responded by resting a paw on my wrist. There was a pathetic dignity about the way he held himself erect, the calm eyes regarding me, friendly and unafraid. "Well, you'll let me know if you want me in court."

---

13. **sternum** (stur′nəm): breastbone.

- -

WORDS TO OWN
stupefying (stoo′pə·fi′iŋ) v. used as *adj.:* paralyzing; numbing.
interminably (in·tur′mi·nə·blē) *adv.:* endlessly.

- -

"HAVEN'T I MADE A DIFFERENCE!" **411**

 **Elements of Literature**
Nonfiction Narrative
Point out that these factual, clinical observations, which might form part of a medical report, have a strong emotional impact. Ask students what they felt as they read this section. [Possible responses: shock; disgust; sympathy; fear that the dog will not survive.]

Ⓔ Reading Skills and Strategies
Cause and Effect
❓ How do the dog's surprising trust and calmness affect the narrator? [Possible responses: He is so filled with pity that he is almost physically ill; he marvels at the dog's patience; he takes a quick liking to the dog.]

Ⓕ Critical Thinking
Expressing an Opinion
❓ Do you think that this is an appropriate punishment for the dog's owner? Why, or why not? [Possible responses: Yes—he didn't know any better, but he shouldn't be allowed to have other animals; no—he shouldn't be fined because he didn't know he was doing wrong; no—the punishment is too lenient in light of the dog's suffering.]

Taking a Second Look

Review: Using Context Clues
Review the use of context clues with students. They should remember that clues to the meanings of unfamiliar words can be found in the surrounding sentences and paragraphs. Clues may include synonyms, antonyms, appositives, or more general content. Tell students they may need to draw inferences in order to interpret context clues. For example, on p. 411, clues to

the word *stench* might be the mention of a bad smell in the preceding and following paragraphs, as well as the mention of "piles of excrement" and gangrenous sores.

Activities
1. Have students identify context clues to understand the meaning of the word *simple* in the next to last paragraph on p. 411.

2. Tell students to scan the narrative for five other words whose meanings they don't know, words that are not footnoted or defined as Words to Own. Have them guess the meaning of each word, listing the context clues they used to formulate their guesses.

B Reading Skills and Strategies

Cause and Effect

❓ Halliday is baffled by the narrator's sudden discourse on shampoos and powders. What effect does the narrator hope that his one-sided conversation with Halliday will have? [He hopes to entice Mrs. Donovan to take the dog.]

C Elements of Literature

Nonfiction Narrative

❓ Point out that Herriot now begins to build suspense about how Roy and Mrs. Donovan fare with each other. Which phrases in this paragraph add to the suspense? [Possible responses: "I scanned the streets"; "anxiously"; "without sighting her"; "I didn't like it"; "Mrs. Donovan was not in evidence"; "she was nowhere to be seen"; "I became seriously worried."]

"Of course, and thank you for coming along." Halliday hesitated for a moment. "And now I expect you'll want to put this poor thing out of his misery right away."

A I continued to run my hand over the head and ears while I thought for a moment. "Yes . . . yes, I suppose so. We'd never find a home for him in this state. It's the kindest thing to do. Anyway, push the door wide open, will you, so that I can get a proper look at him."

In the improved light I examined him more thoroughly. Perfect teeth, well-proportioned limbs with a fringe of yellow hair. I put my stethoscope on his chest and as I listened to the slow, strong thudding of the heart, the dog again put his paw on my hand.

I turned to Halliday. "You know, Inspector, inside this bag of bones there's a lovely, healthy golden retriever. I wish there was some way of letting him out."

As I spoke, I noticed there was more than one figure in the door opening. A pair of black pebble eyes were peering intently at the dog from behind the inspector's broad back. The other spectators had remained in the lane, but Mrs. Donovan's curiosity had been too much for her. I continued conversationally as though I hadn't seen her.

B "You know, what this dog needs first of all is a good shampoo to clean up his matted coat."

"Huh?" said Halliday.

"Yes. And then he wants a long course of some really strong condition powders."

"What's that?" The inspector looked startled.

"There's no doubt about it," I said. "It's the only hope for him, but where are you going to find such things? Really powerful enough, I mean." I sighed and straightened up. "Ah well, I suppose there's nothing else for it. I'd better put him to sleep right away. I'll get the things from my car."

When I got back to the shed, Mrs. Donovan was already inside examining the dog despite the feeble remonstrances of the big man.

"Look!" she said excitedly, pointing to a name roughly scratched on the collar. "His name's Roy." She smiled up at me. "It's a bit like Rex, isn't it, that name."

"You know, Mrs. Donovan, now you mention it, it is. It's very like Rex, the way it comes off your tongue." I nodded seriously.

She stood silent for a few moments, obviously in the grip of a deep emotion, then she burst out.

"Can I have 'im? I can make him better, I know I can. Please, please let me have 'im!"

"Well I don't know," I said. "It's really up to the inspector. You'll have to get his permission."

Halliday looked at her in bewilderment; then he said, "Excuse me, madam," and drew me to one side. We walked a few yards through the long grass and stopped under a tree.

"Mr. Herriot," he whispered, "I don't know what's going on here, but I can't just pass over an animal in this condition to anybody who has a casual whim. The poor beggar's had one bad break already—I think it's enough. This woman doesn't look a suitable person. . . ."

I held up a hand. "Believe me, Inspector, you've nothing to worry about. She's a funny old stick but she's been sent from heaven today. If anybody in Darrowby can give this dog a new life, it's her."

Halliday still looked very doubtful. "But I still don't get it. What was all that stuff about him needing shampoos and condition powders?"

"Oh, never mind about that. I'll tell you some other time. What he needs is lots of good grub, care, and affection and that's just what he'll get. You can take my word for it."

"All right, you seem very sure." Halliday looked at me for a second or two, then turned and walked over to the eager little figure by the shed.

C I had never before been deliberately on the lookout for Mrs. Donovan; she had just cropped up wherever I happened to be, but now I scanned the streets of Darrowby anxiously day by day without sighting her. I didn't like it when Gobber Newhouse got drunk and drove his bicycle determinedly through a barrier into a

---

WORDS TO OWN

remonstrances (ri·män′strən·siz) *n.:* protests.

Getting Students Involved

Cooperative Learning

Script a Scene. Have students turn the dialogue-rich scene on pp. 411–412 (beginning with Halliday saying "I don't think he's ever been out of here" and ending with him saying "All right, you seem very sure") into a screenplay. Tell students to decide whether they will have a narrator or will let the dialogue and action tell the whole story. If necessary, show them an example of a screenplay. Direct them to include information about sets and props, stage directions for the actors, and instructions to the camera crew, such as closeup, pan, zoom in, zoom out, etc. If possible, obtain a video camera and let students stage, tape, and play their video in class.

ten-foot hole where they were laying the new sewer and Mrs. Donovan was not in evidence among the happy crowd who watched the council workmen and two policemen trying to get him out; and when she was nowhere to be seen when they had to fetch the fire engine to the fish-and-chip shop the night the fat burst into flames, I became seriously worried.

Maybe I should have called round to see how she was getting on with that dog. Certainly I had trimmed off the necrotic[14] tissue and dressed the sores before she took him away, but perhaps he needed something more than that. And yet at the time I had felt a strong conviction that the main thing was to get him out of there and clean him and feed him and nature would do the rest. And I had a lot of faith in Mrs. Donovan—far more than she had in me—when it came to animal doctoring; it was hard to believe I'd been completely wrong.

It must have been nearly three weeks and I was on the point of calling at her home when I noticed her stumping briskly along the far side of the marketplace, peering closely into every shop window exactly as before. The only difference was that she had a big yellow dog on the end of the lead.

I turned the wheel and sent my car bumping over the cobbles till I was abreast of her. When she saw me getting out, she stopped and smiled impishly but she didn't speak as I bent over Roy and examined him. He was still a skinny dog but

14. **necrotic** (ne·krät′ik): dead; decayed.

he looked bright and happy, his wounds were healthy and granulating,[15] and there was not a speck of dirt in his coat or on his skin. I knew then what Mrs. Donovan had been doing all this time; she had been washing and combing and teasing at that filthy tangle till she had finally conquered it.

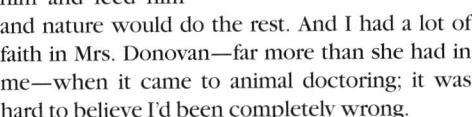

As I straightened up, she seized my wrist in a grip of surprising strength and looked up into my eyes.

"Now Mr. Herriot," she said. "Haven't I made a difference to this dog!"

"You've done wonders, Mrs. Donovan," I said. "And you've been at him with that marvelous shampoo of yours, haven't you?"

She giggled and walked away, and from that day I saw the two of them frequently but at a distance, and something like two months went by before I had a chance to talk to her again. She was passing by the surgery as I was coming down the steps and again she grabbed my wrist.

"Mr. Herriot," she said, just as she had done before. "Haven't I made a difference to this dog!"

I looked down at Roy with something akin to awe. He had grown and filled out and his coat, no longer yellow but a rich gold, lay in luxuriant, shining swaths over the well-fleshed ribs and

15. **granulating** (gran′yo͞o·lāt′iŋ): forming new capillaries, or tiny blood vessels, in the process of healing.

D Reading Skills and Strategies

Cause and Effect

❓ What might have caused Mrs. Donovan and Roy to stay out of sight for so long? [Possible responses: She didn't want anyone to see Roy until she had brought him back to health; Roy was not able to go out for a while and she didn't want to leave him.]

E Elements of Literature

Nonfiction Narrative

❓ This question is becoming Mrs. Donovan's theme song. What might it suggest about her character? [Possible responses: She likes to be right; she likes to be needed; she is happy to have helped Roy; she is proud of her success.]

F Appreciating Language

Descriptive Writing

❓ Which nouns and adjectives that are used to describe Roy's coat also suggest the richness of his new life? [rich gold; luxuriant; shining]

Skill Link

Syntactical Structure: Parts of Speech

To prepare students for the Language Link activities on p. 419, ask them to define the following parts of speech: noun, verb, adjective, and adverb. Explain that strong descriptive writing relies especially on these four parts of speech. Then write the following sentence on the chalkboard and have volunteers label each part of speech. Direct students to ignore articles.

(adj.) (adj.) (n.) (v.) (adv.)
The thin, yellow dog sat quietly.

Activity

Have students label nouns, verbs, adjectives, and adverbs in each of the following sentences that are adapted from the story.

1. A new, brightly studded collar glittered on his neck.
2. His tail, beautifully fringed, fanned the air gently.
3. He reared up, plunked his forepaws on my chest, and gazed calmly and affectionately into my eyes.
4. Roy loped majestically over the grass among a pack of assorted canines.
5. At the cricket match, the old lady glanced keenly around her as Roy gazed placidly out at the field of play, apparently enjoying every ball.

Ⓐ Elements of Literature
Nonfiction Narrative

❓ How do the narrator's words to Mrs. Donovan offer insight into his character? [Possible answer: They show that he is kind and gentle.]

Ⓑ Appreciating Language
Formal and Informal Language

In the first sentence of this section, Herriot uses formal language and complex diction to describe Roy's old life. Herriot then switches to a colloquial voice, using such expressions as "had it quite so good," "absolute pie," and "all go" to describe Roy's new life. Ask students to identify the contrasting tones of these two sentences. [Possible answer: The first sentence is grave and somber; the second is breezy and lighthearted.]

Ⓒ Reading Skills and Strategies
Making Inferences

❓ Mrs. Donovan's kindness to Roy has positive effects on her as well. What moral to the story might be inferred from the mention of Mrs. Donovan's reward? [Possible responses: By giving love, you get love in return; selfless acts bring their own reward.]

Resources ──────

Selection Assessment
Formal Assessment
• Selection Test, p. 69
Test Generator (One-Stop Planner)
• CD-ROM

back. A new brightly studded collar glittered on his neck, and his tail, beautifully fringed, fanned the air gently. He was now a golden retriever in full magnificence. As I stared at him, he reared up, plunked his forepaws on my chest, and looked into my face, and in his eyes I read plainly the same calm affection and trust I had seen back in that black, noisome[16] shed.

Ⓐ "Mrs. Donovan," I said softly, "he's the most beautiful dog in Yorkshire." Then, because I knew she was waiting for it, "It's those wonderful condition powders. Whatever do you put in them?"

"Ah, wouldn't you like to know!" She bridled and smiled up at me coquettishly and indeed she was nearer being kissed at that moment than for many years.

Ⓑ I suppose you could say that that was the start of Roy's second life. And as the years passed, I often pondered on the beneficent providence[17] which had decreed that an animal which had spent his first twelve months abandoned and unwanted, staring uncomprehendingly into that unchanging, stinking darkness, should be whisked in a moment into an existence of light and movement and love. Because I don't think any dog had it quite so good as Roy from then on.

His diet changed dramatically, from odd bread crusts to best stewing steak and biscuit, meaty bones, and a bowl of warm milk every evening. And he never missed a thing. Garden fetes,[18] school sports, evictions, gymkhanas[19]—he'd be there. I was pleased to note that as time went on, Mrs. Donovan seemed to be clocking up an even greater daily mileage. Her expenditure on shoe leather must have been phenomenal, but of course it was absolute pie for Roy—a busy round in the morning, home for a meal, then straight out again; it was all go.

Mrs. Donovan didn't confine her activities to the town center; there was a big stretch of common land down by the river where there were seats, and people used to take their dogs for a gallop and she liked to get down there fairly

16. **noisome** (noi'səm): foul-smelling.
17. **beneficent** (bə·nef'ə·sənt) **providence:** kindly care and protection provided by God or nature; favorable fate.
18. **fetes** (fāts): outdoor parties or festivals.
19. **gymkhanas** (jim·kä'nəz): athletic events.

regularly to check on the latest developments on the domestic scene. I often saw Roy loping majestically over the grass among a pack of assorted canines, and when he wasn't doing that he was submitting to being stroked or patted or generally fussed over. He was handsome and he just liked people; it made him irresistible.

It was common knowledge that his mistress had bought a whole selection of brushes and combs of various sizes with which she labored over his coat. Some people said she had a little brush for his teeth, too, and it might have been true, but he certainly wouldn't need his nails clipped—his life on the roads would keep them down.

Ⓒ Mrs. Donovan, too, had her reward; she had a faithful companion by her side every hour of the day and night. But there was more to it than that; she had always had the compulsion to help and heal animals and the salvation of Roy was the high point of her life—a blazing triumph which never dimmed.

I know the memory of it was always fresh because many years later I was sitting on the sidelines at a cricket match and I saw the two of them; the old lady glancing keenly around her, Roy gazing placidly out at the field of play, apparently enjoying every ball. At the end of the match I watched them move away with the dispersing crowd; Roy would be about twelve then and heaven only knows how old Mrs. Donovan must have been, but the big golden animal was trotting along effortlessly and his mistress, a little more bent, perhaps, and her head rather nearer the ground, was going very well.

When she saw me, she came over and I felt the familiar tight grip on my wrist.

"Mr. Herriot," she said, and in the dark probing eyes the pride was still as warm, the triumph still as bursting new, as if it had all happened yesterday.

"Mr. Herriot, haven't I made a difference to this dog!"

WORDS TO OWN

dispersing (di·spʉrs'iŋ) *v.* used as *adj.*: breaking up; scattering.

Making the Connections

Connecting to the Theme: "A Place Called Home"

James Herriot's essay shows the difference that a good home makes in the life of an abused dog—and the difference that a pet makes in the life of a lonely person. Herriot knows that love and companionship, whether human or animal, are essential to a home. For Mrs. Donovan and Roy in this nonfiction narrative, as for the young N. Scott Momaday in "Riding Is an Exercise of the Mind," the village functions as an extended home. Village events and routines provide social stimulation that keeps Mrs. Donovan and Roy (and, apparently, Herriot himself) "going very well" for many years.

BROWSING IN THE FILES

About the Author. James Alfred Wight was born in England on October 3, 1916, to a father who was a musician and a mother who was a professional singer. Wight borrowed the pen name Herriot from a soccer player when he began to write. Although he expected to produce only one book, he ended up publishing more than fifteen, all dealing with animals and with his life as a veterinarian.

MEET THE WRITER

Tales of a Veterinarian

When he was thirteen, **James Herriot** (1916–1995) read a magazine article about veterinarians and made up his mind to become one, even though he had what he described as a "poor science record." He trained as a vet in Glasgow, Scotland, and took his first job in Yorkshire in northern England. For twenty-five years he talked about writing a book on his work but never wrote a word until his wife challenged him one day: "Who are you kidding? Vets of fifty don't write first books." He bought some paper, chose a pen name (his real name was James Alfred Wight), and began to write.

66 I suppose I started out with the intention of just writing a funny book, because veterinary life was funny in those days, but as I progressed I found that there were so many other things I wanted to say. I wanted to tell about the sad things, too, because they are inseparable from a vet's experiences; about the splendid old characters among the animal owners of that time and about the magnificent Yorkshire countryside . . . [whose] wildness and peace captivated me instantly. **99**

Eager readers made Herriot's entertaining tales best-sellers, and soon there were a TV series and a movie. Four of Herriot's most popular books (all published by St. Martin's Press) take their titles from this nineteenth-century hymn:

> All things bright and beautiful,
>   All creatures great and small,
> All things wise and wonderful,
>   The Lord God made them all.

Assessing Learning

Check Test: Short Answer
Answers may vary slightly.
1. What are Mrs. Donovan's strongest traits? [Possible answers: a desire to be needed; nosiness or curiosity; a talent for animal care.]
2. How long was Roy in the shed before being found? [He'd been there about a year, or almost all his life.]

3. What does Mrs. Donovan do for Roy after adopting him? [She bathes, brushes, doctors, and feeds him.]
4. What does the narrator notice the last time he sees Mrs. Donovan and Roy? [Possible answers: Both are still surprisingly active; she still proudly speaks of the good she has done the dog.]

Standardized Test Preparation
For practice in proofreading and editing, see
• *Daily Oral Grammar,* Transparency 27

Connections

In this free-verse poem, Giovanni muses on the bleakness of life without someone to love. She personifies various elements of nature—a river, a stream, an ocean, and clouds—in order to stress the pervasive and all-encompassing desire to love and be loved in return.

FROM THE EDITOR'S DESK

We actually had too many possibilities to choose from when we were looking for a Connection for this selection. But we chose the poem we did—Nikki Giovanni's "The World Is Not a Pleasant Place to Be"—because it adds another dimension to Herriot's multi-faceted tale. Herriot says that sometimes all it takes to make life worthwhile is "someone" to love; Giovanni believes that without that special someone life comes to a standstill.

The World Is Not a Pleasant Place to Be

Nikki Giovanni

A the world is not a pleasant place
to be without
someone to hold and be held by

5   a river would stop
its flow if only
a stream were there
to receive it

B an ocean would never laugh
if clouds weren't there
10 to kiss her tears

C the world is not
a pleasant place to be without
someone

416 THE NONFICTION COLLECTIONS

A **Critical Thinking**
Interpreting
❓ What do you think the first stanza means? [Possible answer: Life is empty without love.]

B **Elements of Literature**
Personification
❓ Personification is a special kind of metaphor in which a nonhuman thing or quality is talked about as if it were human. How might an ocean "laugh"? How might clouds "kiss her tears"? [Possible answer: An ocean might laugh when it sparkles in the sun and sends up spray; clouds might kiss the ocean's tears when rain falls on the ocean.] How do these natural images illustrate mutual caring? [Possible answer: The ocean and the clouds replenish each other through the cycle of evaporation and rainfall. In the same way, people sustain each other by caring about each other.]

C **Critical Thinking**
Interpreting
❓ Why do you think Giovanni did not repeat the phrase "to hold and be held by"? [Possible answer: Perhaps she did this in order to emphasize the word *someone*.]

Connecting Across Texts

Connecting with "Haven't I Made a Difference!"

The poem and the essay both reveal the necessity, and the reciprocal nature, of love. In "Haven't I Made a Difference!" Roy would have died without Mrs. Donovan's love and care, and her life is enriched—perhaps even prolonged—by caring for him. In Giovanni's poem, the speaker suggests that emotional stagnation can occur ("a river would stop / its flow") when people have no one to love. Point out to students that both the poem and the essay close with the repetition of a key phrase, which serves to highlight the theme and create closure. But in the final stanza of "The World Is Not a Pleasant Place to Be," Giovanni stops short of repeating the entire first stanza, prompting readers to repeat for themselves the phrase "to hold and be held by" or to fill in their own words.

First Thoughts

[respond]

1. List three words that you think describe Mrs. Donovan in Herriot's story. Did you like her? Why or why not?

Shaping Interpretations

[interpret]

2. If Herriot has a **main idea** (or ideas) in mind, he doesn't tell us directly. Brainstorm with a group of students to come up with some statements of what the main idea might be. What details support this main idea?

[analyze]

3. To hook our interest and keep it, Herriot uses many of the elements of fiction you studied in the short-story collections. Examine Herriot's story to find examples of each element of fiction listed in the following chart. What other elements of fiction does Herriot use in this nonfiction narrative?

Elements of Fiction	Examples in Herriot's Story
Characterization	
Dialogue	
Suspense	

Reading Check

Make a **cause-and-effect** chart to map the important events in this story. Begin like this:

Mrs. Donovan's dog is run over by a car. → □ → □

Extending the Text

[connect]

4. One person can make a big difference in the life of a dog. But can one person make a big difference in the life of another person? (People's problems are usually complicated.) Support your opinion with examples, facts, and/or anecdotes.

[synthesize]

5. What do you think James Herriot's response would be to the message of "The World Is Not a Pleasant Place to Be" (see *Connections* on page 416)? Would you count a pet as "someone" (see line 13) who helps make a place home? Check your Quickwrite notes.

[extend]

6. Mrs. Donovan repeats "Haven't I made a difference. . . !" Is it important that you make a difference in the world? What people can you name who *have* made a difference?

First Thoughts

1. Possible words: nosy, caring, active, determined, ageless. Although some students may find Mrs. Donovan an annoying busybody, most will be touched by her desperation and grief over Rex and by her tenderness toward Roy.

Shaping Interpretations

2. Possible main ideas: Animals and people are interdependent; an animal can help transform a person's life. Details include Mrs. Donovan's renewed vigor, exemplified by her giggle (p. 413, paragraph seven), and long daily walks (p. 414, paragraph four), as well as her repeated exclamation, "Haven't I made a difference to this dog!"

3. Possible examples: characterization —"darting, black-button eyes taking everything in" (p. 407); dialogue— "Haven't I made a difference to this dog!" (pp. 413–414); suspense— Mrs. Donovan's temporary disappearance from town events. Other elements of fiction that Herriot uses are plot and foreshadowing.

Extending the Text

4. Some students may feel that it takes more than one person to make a big difference in someone's life; others may feel that one person can be a pivotal force in the life of another. Students may cite mentors, family, or friends.

5. Possible responses: Herriot would agree with Giovanni—he also believes that love makes an important difference in our lives; or, he might disagree with Giovanni—Roy was trusting and friendly despite his isolated life. Some students may feel strongly that a pet is an important part of home life; others may maintain that an animal can't take the place of a person.

6. Some students may believe that it is very important to leave a mark or to make the world a better place; others may feel that personal contentment, rather than achievement, is enough. Students may name historical figures, community workers, friends, or family members who have had an effect either on society or on those close to them.

Reading Check

Mrs. Donovan's dog is run over by a car. → She is lonely without her dog. → She shows up when a badly neglected dog is found. → Mr. Herriot tricks her into taking the dog. → Her care transforms the dog. → She and the dog are happy together for many years.

Rubrics for each Choices assignment appear on p. 142 in the *Portfolio Management System.*

CHOICES: Building Your Portfolio

1. **Writer's Notebook** Encourage students to include specific, sensory details. Remind them to save their work for the Writer's Workshop on p. 438.
2. **Language** Have students write out their questions and practice with a partner before conducting their interviews. Specify that their finished glossaries should contain between ten and fifteen terms.
3. **Creative Writing** Students might work with partners to brainstorm ideas for pet stories. Remind them to use elements of fiction such as characterization, dialogue, plot, suspense, and foreshadowing.
4. **Supporting an Opinion** Encourage students to research current facts and examples to strengthen their paragraphs. The Internet, periodicals, and newspapers are good sources of information. After students have finished their paragraphs, consider holding a debate on the use of animals in research. If possible, videotape the debate and present it to other classes.
5. **Drawing** Tell students to start by rereading the narrative from p. 410, when Roy appears in the story. Have them take notes on the scenes they wish to use for their cartoon strip and direct them to limit their strips to four or five frames.

CHOICES: Building Your Portfolio

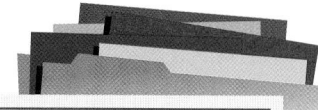

Writer's Notebook

1. Collecting Ideas for an Observational Essay

How is it different?  When you write an observational essay, your subject will be something you know well and can observe easily (a person, place, or thing). To make your subject seem more alive, you might contrast it with something else. Think of a possible topic for an observational essay. (You should have some ideas jotted down in your notebook.) Can you contrast that person, place, or thing with something else? For example, if you are describing your favorite place, you might contrast it with a place you don't like at all. Organizing your notes in a chart like this one may be helpful:

My yard	W's yard
lots of secret places	too neat
	no fence
private	no trees
favorite tree	no grass
three old sheds	concrete

Language

2. Technical Vocabulary: Expert Words

Herriot was a veterinarian, and so he often uses the technical terms of his profession (*respirations, mucous membranes, massive internal hemorrhage, pressure sores*). Every kind of work and hobby has a specialized vocabulary. Interview an expert in order to compile a glossary of terms specific to a job or hobby that interests you (perhaps medicine, teaching, or computer science). You might illustrate your glossary so that the terms can be more readily understood by another user.

Creative Writing

3. A Pet Story

Tell a pet story of your own, using an animal—your own pet or someone else's—as the main character. Try to describe your pet in a way that brings him or her to life. In your narrative, tell what happened to the pet, when and where it happened, and how you felt about it.

Supporting an Opinion

4. Do Animals Have Rights?

What do you think should be done when people mistreat animals? How do you feel about the use of animals for medical research? for psychological research? for testing cosmetics? Choose one of these animal rights issues, and write at least one paragraph stating your opinion. Try to support your opinion with facts and examples.

Drawing

5. Cartoon Chronicle

The comics are full of famous animals, from Snoopy (the dog) to Hobbes (the tiger). You might work with a partner or small group to create a cartoon strip called "Roy." Choose scenes that you think summarize Roy's story, and draw the characters as you imagine them, sketching in background details. Write a caption for each frame or write dialogue in speech balloons, keeping in mind the humor and the drama of Roy's story. Post your cartoon strips on a bulletin board.

"The bidding will start at eleven million dollars."

Assessing Learning

Informal Assessment

After students have worked in pairs or groups on one of the Choices assignments, have them evaluate the experience by completing the following sentences.

1. My group's/partner's ideas are that _____.
2. My ideas differ in that I think _____.
3. We agree that _____.
4. I would evaluate our performance as _____, because _____.
5. I would evaluate my participation as _____, because _____.

LANGUAGE LINK `MINI-LESSON`

Handbook of Literary Terms
HELP

See Description.

Description Makes It Live

Descriptive writing uses sensory details, vivid verbs, and precise nouns and modifiers to help readers form a sharp mental image of a subject. Herriot introduces his animal and human characters with descriptions that appeal to our senses of sight, smell, taste, hearing, and touch. We seem to step along at the doctor's side, seeing what he sees, observing small details. Which specific words in these sentences help you picture Mrs. Donovan and Roy? (What details of your own do you supply?)

1. "... you'd find the dumpy little figure and walnut face among the spectators, the darting, black-button eyes taking everything in."

2. "He had grown and filled out and his coat, no longer yellow but a rich gold, lay in luxuriant, shining swaths over the well-fleshed ribs and back."

3. "I often saw Roy loping majestically over the grass among a pack of assorted canines, and when he wasn't doing that he was submitting to being stroked or patted or generally fussed over."

Try It Out

You're a newspaper reporter. Write two or three sentences describing each of the following characters, who play an important part in the true story you're writing. Use sensory details, vivid verbs, and precise nouns and modifiers.

1. a bus driver
2. a teenage musician
3. an animal
4. someone who lives in your neighborhood

VOCABULARY `HOW TO OWN A WORD`

WORD BANK

uncanny
implicit
diligent
callous
desolation
stupefying
interminably
remonstrances
luxuriant
dispersing

Word Families

By adding **prefixes** (word parts added to the beginnings of words) and **suffixes** (word parts added to the ends of words) or by taking them away, you can create a word family made up of a basic word and its many variations. A word family for *luxuriant* is shown below. For each of the other words in the Word Bank, work with a partner or a small group to make a similar chart. (Some words have small families.) Consult a dictionary for help. Place an asterisk next to the basic word, the one on which the variations are built, and underline all prefixes and suffixes.

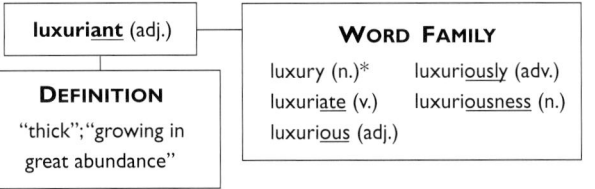

luxuri<u>ant</u> (adj.)

DEFINITION

"thick"; "growing in great abundance"

WORD FAMILY

luxury (n.)*   luxuri<u>ously</u> (adv.)
luxuri<u>ate</u> (v.)   luxuri<u>ousness</u> (n.)
luxuri<u>ous</u> (adj.)

"HAVEN'T I MADE A DIFFERENCE!" **419**

Language Link Quick Check

Underline the descriptive words and phrases in each of the following sentences.

1. <u>Fat</u> seagulls <u>shrieked</u> when the <u>fleet-footed</u> dog <u>raced</u> across the <u>flat stretch</u> of <u>common</u> land <u>down by the river</u>.

2. The <u>golden lab pup blundered up</u> to the <u>snowsuit-clad baby</u> and gave her a <u>slurp</u>.

3. In the vet's office there were <u>two outspoken cockatoos</u> in a <u>gilded cage ten feet tall</u>.

4. <u>Arm outstretched</u>, the <u>police officer</u> in his <u>yellow slicker directed</u> the <u>drenched</u> woman and her <u>golden</u> dog across the street.

LANGUAGE LINK

Students can use these skills when planning and drafting their observational essays for the Writer's Workshop on pp. 438–442.

Try It Out
Possible Descriptions

1. The gray-haired bus driver never takes his pale, sharp eyes off the road. When a passenger climbs aboard, he points his crooked forefinger at the coin box.
2. Her slim fingers fly over the keyboard. Her eyes are clear, and her mind holds a thousand tunes.
3. Perched on the man's shoulder, the monkey looks somewhat like a worried person. It wears a turquoise jacket and cap and an anxious frown.
4. My neighbor darts from the door of his dark house to the door of his battered silver convertible, never looking up.

VOCABULARY
Possible Answers

uncanny (adj.)—"mysterious or unfamiliar"—uncannily (adv.), canny* (adj.), canniness (n.); **implicit (adj.)**—"suggested, but not directly expressed"—imply* (v.), implicitly (adv.), implicate (v.); **diligent (adj.)**—"careful and hard-working"—diligence* (n.), diligently (adv.); **callous* (adj.)**—"unfeeling"—callousness (n.), callously (adv.); **desolation (n.)**—"a wasted state or loneliness"—desolate (v.), desolate* (adj.), desolately (adv.); **stupefying (v.)**—"astounding or making dull"—stupefy* (v.), stupefacient (adj.), stupefaction (n.); **interminably (adj.)**—"endlessly"—terminate (v.), terminal* (adj.), terminable (adj.); **remonstrances (n.)**—"protests or complaints"—remonstrate* (v.), remonstration (n.), remonstrative (adj.); **dispersing (v.)**—"breaking up and scattering in all directions"—disperse* (v.), dispersedly (adv.), disperser (n.)

Resources ———

Language
• *Grammar and Language Links* Worksheet, p. 43

Vocabulary
• *Words to Own,* Worksheet, p. 20

T419

THE ROUND WALLS OF HOME

1. Read and interpret the essay
2. Analyze exposition
3. Determine the writer's purpose
4. Express understanding through critical writing or speaking and listening
5. Identify and use comma rules
6. Understand and use new words
7. Research word origins

SKILLS

Literary
- Analyze exposition

Reading
- Determine the writer's purpose

Writing
- Use vivid verbs to describe a subject
- Interpret an essay

Speaking/Listening
- Choose and debate a topic

Grammar
- Identify and use comma rules

Vocabulary
- Use new words
- Research word origins

Planning

- **Traditional Schedule**
  Lesson Plans Including Strategies for English-Language Learners
- **One-Stop Planner**
  CD-ROM with Test Generator

Before You Read

THE ROUND WALLS OF HOME

Make the Connection

A View from Space

With our feet planted firmly here on earth, it's hard to hold on to the thought that our complicated lives take place on a planet spinning in space. But it's all a matter of perspective. Picture yourself cruising in outer space. What might you think and feel as you looked back at your home on earth?

Quickwrite

List some global problems or issues that affect everyone on earth. When you finish making your list, check the items you think most endanger earth's living things.

go.hrw.com
LEO 9-6

Elements of Literature

Exposition: Informative Writing

Exposition, writing that explains or gives information, is a main ingredient in most kinds of nonfiction. Essayists often combine exposition with description and narration.

> **E**xposition is the kind of factual writing that explains a subject, gives information, or clarifies an idea.
>
> *For more on Exposition, see the Handbook of Literary Terms.*

Reading Skills and Strategies

The Writer's Purpose: What Is the Aim?

To find out if a writer's purpose is **expository** (to give information) or **persuasive** (to persuade), ask these questions:

- Does the writer convey factual information or express opinions?
- Are the facts accurate? Is the information biased (slanted) to support the writer's views?
- Does the writer know what he or she is talking about? That is, how qualified is the writer?
- Is the writer trying to persuade me to do or believe something?

THE ROUND WALLS OF HOME

from A Natural History of the Senses

Diane Ackerman

Picture this: everyone you've ever known, everyone you've ever loved, your whole experience of life, floating in one place, on a single planet underneath you. On that dazzling oasis, swirling with blues and whites, the weather systems form and travel. You watch the clouds tingle and swell above the Amazon and know the weather that develops there will affect the crop yield half a planet away in Russia and

---

WORDS TO OWN

oasis (ō·ā′sis) *n.:* fertile place. *Oasis* may also mean "place or thing offering welcome relief."

Preteaching Vocabulary

Words to Own

Have students, working in pairs, read the definitions of the Words to Own at the bottom of the selection pages. Then, to reinforce understanding of the words, tell each pair of students to write answers to the following questions. Ask each pair to share their answers with the class.

1. In what way is earth an **oasis** in space?
2. Name an object, a place, or an activity that has an **intricate** pattern or design.
3. What **anthems** do you know?
4. If a **petitioner** approached you, what would you expect that person to do?
5. If you were experiencing **euphoria,** how would you feel?

Home is springtime.

China. Volcanic eruptions make tiny spangles below. The rain forests are disappearing in Australia, Hawaii, and South America. You see dust bowls developing in Africa and the Near East. Remote sensing devices, judging the humidity in the desert, have already warned you there will be plagues of locusts[1] this year. To your amazement, you identify the lights of Denver and Cairo. And though you were taught about them one by one, as separate parts of a jigsaw puzzle, now you can see that the oceans, the atmosphere, and the land are not separate at all, but part of an intricate recombining web of nature. Like Dorothy in *The Wizard of Oz,* you want to click your magic shoes together and say three times: "There's no place like home."

You know what home is. For many years, you've tried to be a modest and eager watcher of the skies and of the Earth, whose green anthem you love. Home is a pigeon strutting like a petitioner in the courtyard in front of your house. Home is the law-abiding hickories out back. Home is the sign on a gas station just outside Pittsburgh that reads "If we can't fix it, it ain't broke." Home is springtime on campuses all across America, where students sprawl on the grass like the war-wounded at Gettysburg.[2] Home is the Guatemalan jungle, at times deadly as an arsenal. Home is the pheasant barking hoarse threats at the neighbor's dog. Home is the exquisite torment of love and all the lesser mayhems of the heart. But what you long for is to stand back and see it whole. You want to live out that age-old yearning, portrayed in myths and legends of every culture, to step above the Earth and see the whole world fidgeting and blooming below you.

I remember my first flying lesson, in the doldrums of summer in upstate New York. Pushing the throttle forward, I zoomed down the runway until the undercarriage began to dance; then the ground fell away below and I was airborne, climbing up an invisible flight of stairs. To my amazement, the horizon came with me (how could it not, on a round planet?). For the first time in my life I understood what a valley was, as I floated above one at 7,000 feet. I could see plainly the devastation of the gypsy moth, whose hunger had leeched[3] the forests to a mottled gray. Later on, when I flew over Ohio, I was saddened to discover the stagnant ocher[4] of the air, and to see that the long expanse of the Ohio River, dark and chunky, was the wrong texture for water, even flammable at times, thanks to the fumings of plastics factories, which I could also see, standing like pustules[5] along the river. I began to understand how people settle a landscape, in waves and at crossroads, how they survey a land and irrigate it. Most of all, I discovered that there are things one can learn about the world only from certain perspectives. How can you understand the ocean without becoming part of its intricate fathoms? How can you understand the planet without walking upon it, sampling its marvels

A

---

3. **leeched:** drained. Leeches are worms that suck blood.
4. **stagnant ocher** (stag′nənt ō′kər): foul dark yellow.
5. **pustules** (pus′tyo͞olz′): pimples or blisters.

WORDS TO OWN

intricate (in′tri·kit) *adj.*: elaborately detailed.
anthem (an′thəm) *n.*: song of praise. The writer imagines earth's vivid greenness as a song of praise.
petitioner (pə·tish′ən·ər) *n.*: person seeking favors.

---

1. **plagues of locusts:** swarms of large grasshoppers that eat all plants in their path.
2. **Gettysburg:** town in Pennsylvania where a bloody Civil War battle was fought in 1863. Some 48,000 men were killed or wounded in the battle.

THE ROUND WALLS OF HOME **421**

Summary ■■

In this expository essay, Ackerman explains her belief that the earth is everyone's home. Her viewpoint zooms in and out; she floats above the planet and sees the intricate web that connects water, land, and air and then comes down to earth for a tight closeup on a strutting pigeon. Each of these images is a metaphor for home. She describes polluted landscapes viewed from a small airplane, and then imagines earth from outer space with no fences or political borders. She concludes by calling for people to value and respect the earth—and one another.

A **Elements of Literature**
Exposition
❓ **What information do these lines give the reader?** [Sample answer: They present the ecological damage that has been done to the earth as seen from a plane.] **What descriptive words enliven the exposition?** [forests "leeched . . . to a mottled gray"; " the stagnant ocher of the air"; "dark and chunky" river; factories "standing like pustules"]

Resources ——

Listening
Audio CD Library
A recording of this essay is included in the *Audio CD Library:*
• Disc 14, Track 5

Viewing and Representing
Fine Art Transparency
A transparency of Mitsumasa Anno's *The Shadow of the Earth* complements the images of earth presented in the essay. See the *Viewing and Representing Transparencies and Worksheets:*
• Transparency 9
• Worksheet, p. 36

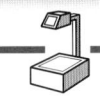

Resources: Print and Media

Reading
• *Reading Skills and Strategies*
    MiniRead Skill Lesson, p. 121
    Selection Skill Lesson, p. 127
• *Graphic Organizers for Active Reading,* p. 28
• *Words to Own,* p. 21
• *Audio CD Library,*
    Disc 14, Track 5

Writing and Language
• *Daily Oral Grammar*
    Transparency 28
• *Grammar and Language Links*
    Worksheet, p. 45
• *Language Workshop* CD-ROM

Viewing and Representing
• *Viewing and Representing*
    Fine Art Transparency 9
    Fine Art Worksheet, p. 36

Assessment
• *Formal Assessment,* p. 71
• *Standardized Test Preparation,* p. 56
• *Portfolio Management System,* p. 144
• Test Generator (*One-Stop Planner* CD-ROM)

Internet
• go.hrw.com (keyword: LE0 9-6)

T421

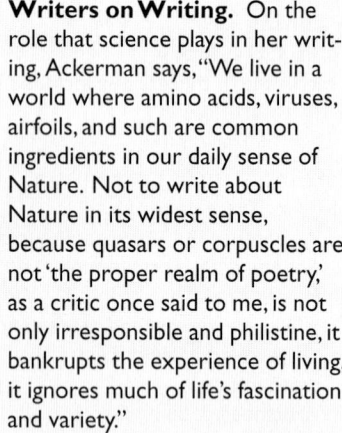
one by one, and then floating high above it, to see it all in a single eye-gulp?

Most of all, the twentieth century will be remembered as the time when we first began to understand what our address was. The "big, beautiful blue, wet ball" of recent years is one way to say it. But a more profound way will speak of the orders of magnitude of that bigness, the shades of that blueness, the arbitrary delicacy of beauty itself, the ways in which water has made life possible, and the fragile <u>euphoria</u> of the complex ecosystem[6] that is Earth, an Earth on which, from space, there are no visible fences, or military zones, or national borders. We need to send into space a flurry of artists and naturalists, photographers and painters, who will turn the mirror upon ourselves and show us Earth as a single planet, a single organism that's buoyant, fragile, blooming, buzzing, full of

6. **ecosystem** (ek′ō·sis′təm): community of animals and plants and their physical and chemical environment.

spectacles, full of fascinating human beings, something to cherish. Learning our full address may not end all wars, but it will enrich our sense of wonder and pride. It will remind us that the human context is not tight as a noose, but large as the universe we have the privilege to inhabit. It will change our sense of what a neighborhood is. It will persuade us that we are citizens of something larger and more profound than mere countries, that we are citizens of Earth, her joy riders and her caretakers, who would do well to work on her problems together. The view from space is offering us the first chance we evolutionary toddlers have had to cross the cosmic street and stand facing our own home, amazed to see it clearly for the first time.

WORDS TO OWN

euphoria (yōō·fôr′ē·ə) *n.:* feeling of well-being.

MEET THE WRITER

"A Great Fan of the Universe"

To gather material for her writing, **Diane Ackerman** (1948–   ) has stood in the midst of millions of bats, straddled alligators, and swum right up to a whale's mouth. Sometimes, she admits, she's been truly frightened.

❝ I try to give myself passionately, totally, to whatever I'm observing, with as much affectionate curiosity as I can muster, as a means of understanding a little better what being human is, and what it was like to have once been alive on the planet. . . . I appear to have a lot of science in my work, I suppose, but I think of myself as a Nature poet, if what we mean by nature is . . . the full sum of creation. ❞

Ackerman grew up in a small Chicago suburb and walked to school through its deep, dark woods instead of staying on the sidewalks, as she was supposed to do. She remembers creating her first metaphor in those forests: Bats hanging from the trees, she told her horrified friends, were "living plums."

Ackerman, an award-winning poet, published four books of poetry before she began writing nonfiction. She has taught at Cornell, Columbia, and New York University and is now a contributor to *The New Yorker.* "The Round Walls of Home," from *A Natural History of the Senses* (1990), reveals her concerns about nature:

❝ I'm a great fan of the Universe, which I take literally: as one. All of it interests me, and it interests me in detail. ❞

The book inspired a PBS television series, which aired in 1995.

Reaching All Students

Struggling Readers

Determining Writer's Purpose was introduced on page 420. For a lesson directly tied to this selection that teaches students to determine writer's purpose by using a strategy called Read, Rate, Reread, see the *Reading Skills and Strategies* binder:
• MiniRead Skill Lesson, p. 121
• Selection Skill Lesson, p. 127

English Language Learners

Students may need definitions or explanations of the following: jigsaw puzzles, Dorothy and her magic shoes in *The Wizard of Oz,* gypsy moths, the expression *joy rider.* For strategies for engaging English language learners with the literature, see
• *Lesson Plans Including Strategies for English-Language Learners*

Prologue

Edward Field

Look, friend, at this universe
With its spiral clusters of stars
Flying out all over space
Like bedsprings suddenly busting free;
5   And in this galaxy, the sun
Fissioning° itself away,
Surrounded by planets, prominent in their dignity,
And bits and pieces running wild;
And this middling planet
10   With a lone moon circling round it.

Look, friend, through the fog of gases at this world
With its skin of earth and rock, water and ice,
With various creatures and rooted things;
And up from the bulging waistline
15   To this land of concrete towers,
Its roads swarming like a hive cut open,
Offshore to this island, long and fish shaped,
Its mouth to a metropolis,
And in its belly, this village,
20   A gathering of families at a crossways,
And in this house, upstairs and through the wide-open door
Of the front bedroom with a window on the world,
Look, friend, at me.

6. **fissioning:** splitting apart.

THE ROUND WALLS OF HOME **423**

MAKING MEANINGS

First Thoughts

1. Some students may find "an intricate recombining web" an interesting metaphor for ecosystems. Some students may believe that "we are citizens of something larger and more profound than mere c... tries" is a controversial st...

Shaping Interpreta...

2. Possible respons... courtyard, hi... sign, spring... Guatem... the fe...

3. Fa...

...ern United States and let them find the open "mouth" and the "belly" of fish-shaped Long Island in New York State.

C Critical Thinking

Speculating

❓ A prologue is an introductory speech. What might this poem be introducing? [Possible responses: a book of poetry; a new way of looking at people and the world.]

Assessing Learning

Check Test: True-False

1. The essay describes the earth's inner layers and core. [False]
2. The narrator took flying lessons. [True]
3. From the air, the Ohio River was a clear, light blue. [False]
4. The narrator wants to send artists into space. [True]
5. The narrator urges readers to be good citizens of the United States. [False]

Standardized Test Preparation

For practice with standardized test format specific to this selection, see
• *Standardized Test Preparation,* p. 56
For practice in proofreading and editing, see
• *Daily Oral Grammar,* Transparency 28

Connecting Across Texts

Connecting with "The Round Walls of Home"

For both Diane Ackerman and Edward Field, the concept of home is extensive. Ackerman describes earth as our home, encouraging readers to protect the planet. Field initally focuses on an image of the universe and then progresses to a picture of himself at a window. He calls the reader "friend"—as if, positioned against the universe's vastness, no two human beings could ever be strangers.

T423

...un-
...atement.

...ions

...s: a pigeon in a
...ories, a gas station
...me on campuses, the
...alan jungle, a pheasant's cry,
...elings associated with love.
...cts: information about weather
patterns in paragraph one, pollution
in paragraph three. Opinion: Everyone needs to know how earth looks
from outer space (paragraph four).
Possible purposes: She wants to
explain how everything is interre-
lated; she urges us to change our
thinking about our relationship to
our home planet.

4. Possible main idea: Seeing earth
   from the broader perspective of
   space can help inspire us to protect
   the ecology and prevent wars.
   Details: Seen from above, the
   oceans, atmosphere, and land form a
   web; earth has a fragile, complex
   ecosystem; earth has no visible
   boundries but is a single organism;
   inhabitants of the earth should work
   together on the planet's problems.

Extending the Text

5. Possible responses: Both texts
   describe earth as vast and fascinating; both place the concept of home
   in a universal context.

Grading Timesaver

Rubrics for each Choices assignment
appear in the *Portfolio Management
System,* p. 144.

CHOICES: Building Your Portfolio

1. Writer's Notebook Remind
students to save their work for the
Writer's Workshop on p. 438.
2 and 3: Encourage students to
develop their own perspectives.

MAKING MEANINGS

First Thoughts

[evaluate]

1. Which statement did you find most
   interesting—or most controversial—
   in Ackerman's essay? Why?

Shaping Interpretations

[analyze]

2. What **metaphors** does Ackerman
   use to say what home is?

[analyze]

3. Find some sentences that convey
   facts and some that express opinions.
   Would you say that Ackerman's
   purpose here is mainly **expository**
   (explaining and informing) or do you
   think she has a different aim? Explain.

[interpret]

4. Try to state Ackerman's **main idea** in one or two sentences. What details in
   the essay lead you to think that is her main idea?

Extending the Text

[compare]

5. How do Ackerman's ideas compare with those in the poem "Prologue"
   (see *Connections* on page 423)?

Reading Check

a. Explain Ackerman's **title**.

b. When Ackerman takes her
   first flying lesson, what does
   she discover?

c. List the global problems that
   Ackerman alludes to or
   mentions directly in
   paragraphs three and four.

d. What new "address" does
   she want us to accept?

CHOICES: Building Your Portfolio

Writer's Notebook

1. Collecting Ideas for an Observational Essay

Say it in a new way.
Ackerman might have written, "I went down the runway. . . ." Instead, she wrote, "I *zoomed* down the runway. . . ." Think of a subject you would like to describe— maybe the view from a bus or airplane. Jot down some fresh, vivid words to describe what you are observing. Focus on your verbs. Save your notes.

Interpreting an Essay

2. Your Interpretation

According to Ackerman, "Learning our full address may not end all wars, but it will enrich our sense of wonder and pride." Focusing on that statement, write an interpretation of her essay. What is her **main idea**? How will changing our perspective—looking at the world from afar—help us enrich our lives? What would happen if everyone took Ackerman's advice? What probably wouldn't happen?

Speaking and Listening

3. Debate the Issues

Refer to your Quickwrite notes and Ackerman's essay to prepare to brain-storm some debatable topics. For each topic, write an affirmative statement, such as "The UN must en-force global rules to limit air pollution." Form opposing teams to challenge or sup-port one of the statements. Let your audience vote to decide which side has won the debate.

Reading Check

Answers may vary slightly.

a. The earth, which is everyone's home, is
   spherical.

b. She discovers how widespread ecological
   damage is; how people affect a landscape
   as they settle it; how a new perspective
   brings new insights.

c. Problems include: gypsy moths, pollution
   from factories, expanding population,
   greed, war, intolerance.

d. planet earth

GRAMMAR LINK | MINI-LESSON

Language Handbook HELP

See Commas, page 1023.

Technology HELP

See Language Workshop CD-ROM. Key word entry: commas.

Communications Handbook HELP

See Proofreaders' Marks.

Using Commas: Keeping It Clear

Here are some comma rules that Ackerman follows:

1. Use commas to separate items in a series:

   "The rain forests are disappearing in Australia, Hawaii, and South America." [Commas separate a series of nouns.]

   "How can you understand the planet without walking upon it, sampling its marvels one by one, and then floating high above it. . . ?" [Commas separate a series of phrases.]

2. When *and* or *or* joins each item in a series, no comma is necessary:

   "For many years you've tried to be a modest and eager watcher of the skies. . . ." [no comma between <u>modest</u> and <u>and eager</u>]

3. Do not use a comma between an adjective and the noun it modifies:

   "You see <u>dust bowls</u> developing in Africa. . . ." [no comma between <u>dust</u> and <u>bowls</u>]

Try It Out

Practice using commas correctly. Be sure to have a partner proofread your work.

1. Ackerman says that "big, beautiful blue, wet ball" is one way to describe earth. Write a sentence containing another series of adjectives describing earth or one of its features.

2. In her last paragraph, Ackerman calls human beings joy riders, caretakers, and evolutionary toddlers. Write a sentence containing a series of verbs that describe what human beings have done to earth.

3. Write a sentence in which you include a series of nouns naming at least four places you'd like to visit someday.

4. Describe yourself to a pen pal, using a series of phrases.

VOCABULARY | HOW TO OWN A WORD

WORD BANK

oasis
intricate
anthem
petitioner
euphoria

Word Maps

You can use a college or unabridged dictionary to discover a word's history, or **etymology.** Etymologies move backward in time: The oldest known origin is given last. Can you "translate" this etymology for *oasis*?

[L < Gr, fertile spot: orig. Coptic]

Here is the "translation": The English word *oasis* comes from a Latin word, which in turn came from a Greek word that means "fertile spot." That word originally came from the Coptic language. Work with a partner to create word maps (see page 93) that show the etymologies of the other four words in the Word Bank. (Look in the front of the dictionary for a key to symbols and abbreviations.)

THE ROUND WALLS OF HOME **425**

GRAMMAR LINK

The information in this lesson will help students as they draft and proofread their essays for the Writer's Workshop on pp. 438–442.

Try It Out
Possible Answers
1. Earth is a giant, blue, spinning top.
2. Human beings have mined natural resources, cleared land, and built cities.
3. I'd like to visit Malaysia, Peru, Russia, and Kenya.
4. I'm a reader of science fiction, a fan of soccer, and an enthusiastic builder of model planes.

VOCABULARY
Sample Answers
1. **intricate:** from a Latin word meaning "to entangle, perplex," from the Latin prefix *in-,* meaning "in" and the Latin word *tricae,* meaning "perplexities"
2. **anthem:** from a Greek word meaning "sounding in answer," from the Greek prefix *anti-,* meaning "over against" and the Greek word *phonē,* meaning "voice"
3. **petitioner:** from a French word meaning "to beg," from the Latin word *petere,* meaning "to request"
4. **euphoria:** from Latin, from the Greek word *euphoros,* meaning "easy to bear" or "healthy"

Resources ——————

Language
• *Grammar and Language Links* Worksheet, p. 45

Vocabulary
• *Words to Own* Worksheet, p. 21

Grammar Link Quick Check

Insert commas as needed.

1. The essay includes exposition description narration and persuasion. [exposition, description, narration,]
2. Ackerman saw gray forests brown air and a flammable river. [forests, air,]
3. Earth has a delicate beauty a fragile ecosystem and no borders visible from space. [beauty, ecosystem,]
4. Ackerman wants to change our concept of home show that we are citizens of one world and remind us of our role as the earth's caretakers. [home, world,]

Before You Read

THE LOOPHOLE OF RETREAT

Make the Connection

Trapped

Imagine a place so small you can't stand up, with little air and no light. You don't see the rats, mice, and bugs crawling on you, but you can feel them. Then imagine that this is a place you've chosen to be in. What could bring you to such a place—and keep you there?

Reading Skills and Strategies

Drawing Upon Your Background

Divide a page of your notebook into three columns for a KWL chart on slavery in America. KWL stands for "what I already *know* [about slavery]," "what I *want* to find out," and "what I've *learned* from reading this selection." Fill in the K and W columns now; save the L column until after you have read "The Loophole of Retreat."

K	W	L

Elements of Literature

Setting: Where and When?

Setting can be crucial in nonfiction. Sometimes, the setting actually *causes* what happens. In the true narrative you're about to read, the narrator's "home" setting is key, and

you should try to picture exactly what it looks like. Another, wider setting is also important: To understand this story, you must also know about the time in history when these events took place.

> **S**etting is the time and place in which specific events occur.
>
> *For more on Setting, see pages 164–165 and the Handbook of Literary Terms.*

Background

In August 1835, in Edenton, North Carolina, a twenty-two-year-old woman held in slavery hid in a swamp and then crept into the crawl space above her grandmother's storeroom. She went into hiding to escape the abuse of her owner (called Dr. Flint in her narrative).

The title of this chapter from Jacobs's autobiography comes from these lines by the English poet William Cowper:

'Tis pleasant, through the
  loopholes of retreat,
To peep at such a world; to see
  the stir
Of the great Babel, and not feel
  the crowd.

 go.hrw.com
LEO 9-6

The rats and mice ran over my bed.

Preteaching Vocabulary

Words to Own

Have students, working in pairs, read the definitions of the Words to Own at the bottom of the selection pages. To ensure familiarity with the words, give students the following acrostic to solve. [Acrostic word order: lacerated, devoid, irascible, abatement, aperture, contaminating, intolerable, impertinent, omen, consolations. Hidden word: liberation.]

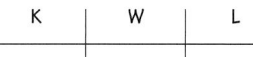

1. _ _ c _ _ _ t _ d
2. _ _ v _ _ _
3. i _ _ _ c _ _ l _
4. _ b _ _ _ m _ n _
5. a _ _ r _ u _ _
6. _ o _ t _ _ i _ _ _ i _ _
7. _ n _ _ l _ r _ _ _ e
8. _ m _ _ _ _ _ n _ _
9. _ _ e _
10. c _ _ _ o _ a _ _ _ n _

from Incidents in the Life of a Slave Girl

The LOOPHOLE of RETREAT

Harriet A. Jacobs

A small shed had been added to my grandmother's house years ago. Some boards were laid across the joists[1] at the top, and between these boards and the roof was a very small garret,[2] never occupied by anything but rats and mice. It was a pent roof,[3] covered with nothing but shingles, according to the Southern custom for such buildings. The garret was only nine feet long and seven wide. The highest part was three feet high and sloped down abruptly to the loose board floor. There was no admission for either light or air. My uncle Phillip, who was a carpenter, had very skillfully made a concealed trapdoor, which communicated with the storeroom. He had been doing this while I was waiting in the swamp. The storeroom opened upon a piazza.[4]

To this hole I was conveyed as soon as I entered the house. The air was stifling; the darkness, total. A bed had been spread on the floor. I could sleep quite comfortably on one side, but the slope was so sudden that I could not turn on the other without hitting the roof. The rats and mice ran over my bed; but I was weary, and I slept such sleep as the wretched may when a tempest[5] has passed over them. Morning came. I knew it only by the noises I heard; for in my small den, day and night were all the same. I suffered for air even more than for light. But I was not comfortless. I heard the voices of my children. There was joy and there was sadness in the sound. It made my tears flow. How I longed to speak to them! I was eager to look on their faces; but there was no hole, no crack, through which I could peep. This continued darkness was oppressive. It seemed horrible to sit or lie in a cramped

1. **joists:** parallel beams.
2. **garret** (gar′it): attic.
3. **pent roof:** roof sloping on only one side.
4. **piazza** (pē·az′ə): large covered porch.
5. **tempest** (tem′pist): violent storm.

THE LOOPHOLE OF RETREAT **427**

Summary ■ ■ ■

In this autobiographical narrative, Harriet Jacobs describes a garret where she hid for seven years after escaping from slavery. Dr. Flint, from whom she escaped, went to great lengths to find her, never guessing that she was right under his nose. Jacobs endured summer heat, winter cold, and vermin. She was fed by relatives and sustained by watching her children (who did not know of her presence) through a peephole. Because of Dr. Flint's abuse, she preferred the intense hardships of this limited freedom to slavery.

Resources

Listening
Audio CD Library
A recording of this essay is included in the *Audio CD Library:*
• Disc 14, Track 6

Ⓐ Elements of Literature
Setting
❓ How would you describe the feeling or mood that the setting creates? [Possible responses: trapped, claustrophobic, nightmarish.]

Ⓑ Reading Skills and Strategies

Drawing Upon Your Background
❓ What can you conclude about the narrator from her words and from your knowledge about slavery? [Possible answers: She is incredibly brave, tough, and determined to have attempted an escape; despite the abuses of slavery, she is educated and loving.]

Resources: Print and Media

Reading
• *Reading Skills and Strategies*
   MiniRead Skill Lesson, p. 131
   Selection Skill Lesson, p. 138
• *Graphic Organizers for Active Reading,* p. 29
• *Words to Own,* p. 22
• *Audio CD Library,*
   Disc 14, Track 6

Writing and Language
• *Daily Oral Grammar*
   Transparency 29
• *Grammar and Language Links*
   Worksheet, p. 47
• *Language Workshop* CD-ROM

Assessment
• *Formal Assessment,* p. 73
• *Portfolio Management System,* p. 145
• *Standardized Test Preparation,* pp. 58, 60
• *Test Generator* (One-Stop Planner CD-ROM)

Internet
• *go.hrw.com* (keyword: LE0 9-6)

Have students work in small groups to research the landmark laws and court decisions regarding the institution of slavery. Have them address the following questions in their reports:

- What event sparked the law or court decision you are researching?
- What were the immediate effects of the law or decision?
- What were the long-term effects of the law or decision?

Ⓐ Reading Skills and Strategies

Writer's Purpose

❓ Jacobs's *Incidents in the Life of a Slave Girl,* from which this autobiographical narrative is excerpted, was published in 1861—the same year the Civil War began. Jacobs's comparison of her life to the lives of other enslaved people has a purpose other than to make her seem fortunate. What might that purpose be? [Possible responses: She wants to show how bad slavery is; her purpose might be to influence readers to oppose slavery.]

Ⓑ Elements of Literature

Setting

❓ How does the setting affect Jacobs's actions? [She can't stand; she can move only by crawling; she can talk with others and receive food only at night.]

LITERATURE AND REAL LIFE

Database: Slavery in America

First Africans to arrive: Dutch ship brings 20 African indentured servants to Jamestown, Virginia, 1619.

First legalization of slavery: Massachusetts becomes the first colony to legalize slavery, 1641.

Number of Africans brought to the Americas as slaves: 10–12 million (estimate)

Percentage of Africans who died during the Middle Passage (from Africa to the West Indies): 10–20 percent

Percentage of Africans who died "in training" in the West Indies: 30 percent (estimate)

Landmark laws and court decisions:

- Fugitive Slave Act of 1793 (Runaway slaves, even in a free state, can be forcibly returned to their owners.)
- Compromise of 1850 (Some new states will be free; some will allow slavery.)
- *Dred Scott* decision, 1857 (Slavery is legal in the territories.)
- Emancipation Proclamation, January 1, 1863 (Slaves in seceded states are freed.)
- Thirteenth Amendment, 1865 (Slavery is abolished in the United States.)
- Fourteenth Amendment, 1868 (African Americans born in the United States are citizens.)
- Fifteenth Amendment, 1870 (African American men have the right to vote.)

---

position day after day, without one gleam of light. Yet I would have chosen this rather than my lot as a slave, though white people considered it an easy one; and it was so compared with the fate of others. I was never cruelly overworked; I was never <u>lacerated</u> with the whip from head to foot; I was never so beaten and bruised that I could not turn from one side to the other; I never had my heel strings[6] cut to prevent my running away; I was never chained to a log and forced to drag it about, while I toiled in the fields from morning till night; I was never branded with hot iron or torn by bloodhounds. On the contrary, I had always been kindly treated and tenderly cared for, until I came into the hands of Dr. Flint. I had never wished for freedom till then. But though my life in slavery was comparatively <u>devoid</u> of hardships, God pity the woman who is compelled to lead such a life!

My food was passed up to me through the trapdoor my uncle had contrived;[7] and my grandmother, my uncle Phillip, and my aunt Nancy would seize such opportunities as they could to mount up there and chat with me at the opening. But of course this was not safe in the daytime. It must all be done in darkness. It was impossible for me to move in an erect position, but I crawled about my den for exercise. One day I hit my head against something and found it was a gimlet.[8] My uncle had left it sticking there when he made the trapdoor. I was as rejoiced as Robinson Crusoe[9] could have been at finding such a treasure. It put a lucky thought into my head. I said to

6. **heel strings:** The writer is referring to her Achilles' tendons, the tough, stiff cords of tissue connecting the back of the heel to the muscles of the calf.
7. **contrived** (kən·trīvd′): constructed skillfully.
8. **gimlet** (gim′lit): hand tool used to bore holes.
9. **Robinson Crusoe:** character in a novel of the same name by Daniel Defoe (1660–1731); Crusoe is shipwrecked on a small tropical island, where he survives for many years.

WORDS TO OWN

lacerated (las′ər·āt′id) *v.*: torn.
devoid (di·void′) *adj.*: empty.

Reaching All Students

Struggling Readers

Drawing Upon Background was introduced on page 426. For a lesson directly tied to this selection that teaches students to draw upon their background by using a strategy called Say Something, see the *Reading Skills and Strategies* binder:

- MiniRead Skill Lesson, p. 131
- Selection Skill Lesson, p. 138

English Language Learners

To familiarize students with the institution of slavery in the United States, have them review the database on this page. Explain that by law, enslaved people were considered property and had no Constitutional rights. Runaways could legally be tortured or killed. For other strategies for engaging English language learners with the literature, see

- *Lesson Plans Including Strategies for English-Language Learners*

Advanced Learners

Have students research and discuss historical or current struggles for equality in the United States. They might focus on women's rights, workers' rights, rights for the disabled, or other struggles. Ask students to speculate about what advice Jacobs would offer to people involved in these struggles.

myself, "Now I will have some light. Now I will see my children." I did not dare to begin my work during the daytime, for fear of attracting attention. But I groped round; and having found the side next the street, where I could frequently see my children, I stuck the gimlet in and waited for evening. I bored three rows of holes, one above another; then I bored out the interstices[10] between. I thus succeeded in making one hole about an inch long and an inch broad. I sat by it till late into the night, to enjoy the little whiff of air that floated in. In the morning I watched for my children. The first person I saw in the street was Dr. Flint. I had a shuddering, superstitious feeling that it was a bad <u>omen</u>. Several familiar faces passed by. At last I heard the merry laugh of children, and presently two sweet little faces were looking up at me, as though they knew I was there and were conscious of the joy they imparted. How I longed to *tell* them I was there!

My condition was now a little improved. But for weeks I was tormented by hundreds of little red insects, fine as a needle's point, that pierced through my skin and produced an <u>intolerable</u> burning. The good grandmother gave me herb teas and cooling medicines, and finally I got rid of them. The heat of my den was intense, for nothing but thin shingles protected me from the scorching summer's sun. But I had my <u>consolations</u>. Through my peeping hole I could watch the children, and when they were near enough, I could hear their talk. Aunt Nancy brought me all the news she could hear at Dr. Flint's. From her I learned that the doctor had written to New York to a colored woman who had been born and raised in our neighborhood and had breathed his <u>contaminating</u> atmosphere. He offered her a reward if she could find out anything about me. I know not what was the nature of her reply; but he soon after started for New York in haste, saying to his family that he had business of importance to transact. I peeped at him as he passed on his way to the steamboat. It was a satisfaction to have miles of land and water between us, even

10. **interstices** (in·tʉrʹstə·siz′): small spaces.

for a little while; and it was a still greater satisfaction to know that he believed me to be in the Free States. My little den seemed less dreary than it had done. He returned, as he did from his former journey to New York, without obtaining any satisfactory information. When he passed our house next morning, Benny was standing at the gate. He had heard them say that he had gone to find me, and he called out, "Dr. Flint, did you bring my mother home? I want to see her." The doctor stamped his foot at him in a rage and exclaimed, "Get out of the way, you little damned rascal! If you don't, I'll cut off your head."

Benny ran terrified into the house, saying, "You can't put me in jail again. I don't belong to you now."[11] It was well that the wind carried the words away from the doctor's ear. I told my grandmother of it, when we had our next conference at the trapdoor, and begged of her not to allow the children to be <u>impertinent</u> to the <u>irascible</u> old man.

Autumn came, with a pleasant <u>abatement</u> of heat. My eyes had become accustomed to the dim light, and by holding my book or work in a certain position near the <u>aperture</u>, I contrived to read and sew. That was a great relief to the tedious monotony of my life. But when winter came, the cold penetrated through the thin shingle roof, and I was dreadfully chilled. The winters there are not so long or so severe as in northern latitudes; but the houses are not built

11. The freedom of Jacobs's two children, Benny and Louisa Matilda, had been bought by their father, a lawyer. The children were living with Harriet Jacobs's grandmother.

WORDS TO OWN

omen (ōʹmən) *n.*: sign; thing or happening believed to foretell an event.
intolerable (in·tälʹər·ə·bəl) *adj.*: unbearable; too painful or severe to be endured.
consolations (kän·sə·lāʹshənz) *n.*: things that comfort.
contaminating (kən·tamʹə·nāt′iŋ) *v.* used as *adj.*: polluting; poisoning.
impertinent (im·pʉrt′′n·ənt) *adj.*: shamelessly disrespectful; rude.
irascible (i·rasʹə·bəl) *adj.*: irritable; easily angered.
abatement (ə·bātʹmənt) *n.*: lessening; reduction.
aperture (apʹər·chər) *n.*: opening; gap.

THE LOOPHOLE OF RETREAT 429

C Reading Skills and Strategies
Drawing Upon Your Background
❓ Drawing on what you know about the treatment of people who attempted to escape slavery, what might have happened to Jacobs if Flint had found her? [Sample answers: He might have tortured, sold, or killed her.]

D Appreciating Language
Adjective Clauses
Point out the adjective clause "that pierced through my skin and produced an intolerable burning." Ask students which noun the clause modifies. [insects] If students need support, use the Skill Link on p. T432.

E Critical Thinking
Extending the Text
Seeing her children is Jacobs's consolation, and Flint's absence makes her grim home seem a little less dreary. How important do you think human relationships are in creating a home? [Sample responses: A place isn't really a home—it's just a place to live—if relationships are bad; good relationships are essential to creating a good home; good relationships are important, but so is a pleasant physical setting.]

F Elements of Literature
Setting
❓ For a black person to speak impertinently to a white person was, in many slave states, illegal. How does this fact about the wider setting help to explain Jacobs's anxiety about her son's behavior? [Sample answer: She realizes that Flint could get Benny thrown into jail or do worse to him for his impertinent remark.]

Getting Students Involved

Cooperative Learning
Economic History. The Industrial Revolution was, to some extent, responsible for the Civil War and its outcome. The South was heavily agricultural and depended on slave labor to run its huge plantations. In contrast, the economy of many Northern states was increasingly fueled by industry; these states could afford to reject the institution of slavery, since they had a steady supply of cheap immigrant labor. The factories of the North also produced armaments during the Civil War. Have students work in small groups to research the Industrial Revolution and the economic impact it had upon the country.

Making the Connections

Connecting to the Theme: "A Place Called Home"
Harriet Jacobs's autobiographical narrative strips the concept of home to its essence. The "home" she describes is physically wretched in every way. Yet it has two overriding advantages: It protects her from the abuses of slavery and it keeps her close to her family, whom she loves. For Jacobs, home is shelter, love, and, above all, freedom.

A Appreciating Language

Adjective Clauses

Ask students to identify the adjective clause in this sentence. ["who, perhaps, were playing near the gate"] If students need support, use the Skill Link on p. T432. Then ask which noun or pronoun the clause modifies. ["children"]

B Elements of Literature

Setting

? How does the narrative's wider setting—a slave state in the pre-Civil War era—make the cramped and miserable crawl space "good"? [Sample answers: Jacobs needs a hiding place no one will suspect, and the garret is such a place; escape often meant losing contact with family members, but Jacobs is cared for by her relatives and can observe her children.]

Resources

Selection Assessment
Formal Assessment
• Selection Test, p. 73
Test Generator (One-Stop Planner)
• CD-ROM

BROWSING IN THE FILES

About the Author. Harriet Jacobs was the daughter of Delilah and Daniel Jacobs. Both her parents were enslaved, but in different North Carolina households. When Jacobs's mistress died, she was willed to her mistress's niece, and thus came into the household of Dr. Norcom, the real name of "Dr. Flint." After years of repulsing his advances, she ran away and hid for seven years in her grandmother's home. She spent the next ten years running from the Norcom family and trying to get her children back. In 1852, she finally gained her freedom.

---

to shelter from cold, and my little den was peculiarly comfortless. The kind grandmother brought me bedclothes and warm drinks. Often I was obliged to lie in bed all day to keep comfortable; but with all my precautions, my shoulders and feet were frostbitten. Oh, those long, gloomy days, with no object for my eye to rest upon and no thoughts to occupy my mind except the dreary past and the uncertain future! I was thankful when there came a day sufficiently mild for me to wrap myself up and sit at the loophole to watch the passers-by. Southerners have the habit of stopping and talking in the streets, and I heard many conversations not intended to meet my ears. I heard slave hunters planning how to catch some

poor fugitive. Several times I heard allusions to **A** Dr. Flint, myself, and the history of my children, who, perhaps, were playing near the gate. One would say, "I wouldn't move my little finger to catch her, as old Flint's property." Another would say, ". . . A man ought to have what belongs to him, even if he *is* a damned brute." The opinion was often expressed that I was in the Free States. Very rarely did anyone suggest that I might be in the vicinity. Had the least suspicion rested on my grandmother's house, it would have been burned to the ground. But it was the last place they thought of. Yet there was no place, where **B** slavery existed, that could have afforded me so good a place of concealment.

Reproduced by permission of Harvard University Press.

MEET THE WRITER

A Horrible System

Harriet A. Jacobs (1813–1897), born into slavery in Edenton, North Carolina, was taught to read, write, and sew by her first mistress. (Reading and writing were forbidden to slaves.) When Jacobs was a teenager, her second owner harassed her repeatedly. Furious at her refusals, he sent her away to hard labor as a plantation slave and threatened to do the same with her two young children.

She ran away from the plantation and hid for seven years in the crawl space she describes in her autobiography. All she ever sought, she said, was freedom and a home for her children and herself. In 1842, Jacobs escaped to New York City, where she found work as a nursemaid.

She began writing the story of her life in 1853 and published it herself in 1861, using the pen name Linda Brent. This quotation, attributed to "A Woman of North Carolina," appears on the title page:

66 Northerners know nothing at all about Slavery. They think it is perpetual bondage only. They have no conception of the depth of *degradation* involved in that word, *slavery*; if they had, they would never cease their efforts until so horrible a system was overthrown. 99

Assessing Learning

Check Test: True-False

1. Jacobs hides in a slave owner's barn. [False]
2. Jacobs describes the cruel conditions of slavery. [True]
3. Jacobs bores a peephole to get fresh air and light and to see her children. [True]
4. Dr. Flint suspects that Jacobs is hiding nearby. [False]
5. If Jacobs were found, her relatives' house would be burned down. [True]

Standardized Test Preparation

For practice with standardized test format specific to this selection, see
• *Standardized Test Preparation*, pp. 58, 60
For practice in proofreading and editing, see
• *Daily Oral Grammar*, Transparency 29

MAKING MEANINGS

First Thoughts

[respond]

1. Jot down some words and phrases that describe your feelings as you read this selection from Jacobs's autobiography.

Shaping Interpretations

[analyze]

2. In a short story a writer sometimes chooses details of **setting** to create a **mood** or **atmosphere**. How would you describe the mood of this selection? Which details of the setting contribute to that mood?

[analyze]

3. Think of some words and phrases you'd use to describe the narrator's **character**. Find details in the text that show us the sort of person she is.

[compare]

4. Compare Jacobs's "loophole of retreat" with William Cowper's "loopholes" (see his three lines of poetry quoted in the Background, page 426). What do you think of Jacobs's **title**? What other titles would you suggest?

[interpret]

5. What **main idea** do you think this selection reveals? Is the main idea directly stated, or is it implied? What details support your interpretation of the main idea?

Extending the Text

[connect]

6. Jacobs faces great hardship but doesn't give up. What do you think keeps some people going in the face of great hardship? Why do others give up?

Reading Check

a. Draw a picture of Jacobs's hiding place as you see it. Show its dimensions. Where is it?

b. Why is she hiding there?

c. Why is the gimlet a lucky find?

d. Who is Dr. Flint, and what news of him does Aunt Nancy bring?

e. Where do people imagine that Jacobs has gone?

Slave Auction, Virginia (19th century) by Lefevre James Cranstone.

Virginia Historical Society, Richmond.

Reading Check

Answers may vary slightly.

a. Students' drawings should show a small, windowless crawl space above a storage shed, which is attached to a house.

b. She is hiding because she has escaped from slavery and is being pursued.

c. The gimlet lets her bore a peephole through which she can watch her children play and get fresh air and light.

d. Dr. Flint is Jacobs's enslaver. Aunt Nancy says that he wrote to a woman in New York, offering her a reward for information about Jacobs, and that he traveled to New York and back, thinking Jacobs was there.

e. Most people think that she is somewhere in the free states.

MAKING MEANINGS

First Thoughts

1. Possible responses: outraged about slavery, impressed by Jacobs's courage, anxious.

Shaping Interpretations

2. Sample answer: mood— oppressive, claustrophobic; details—stifling air, total darkness, low ceiling, Flint's threats, isolation.

3. Sample answers: She is resourceful— exercises by crawling, uses gimlet to bore peephole; she has a powerful will—manages to survive; she is brave—runs away at risk of her life; she is talented—writes this narrative.

4. Cowper's poem suggests that it is refreshing to step back from life and be an observer for a while. Jacobs, on the other hand, watches the world as she hides in her wretched garret. Some students may appreciate the ironic twist Jacobs gives to Cowper's phrase; others may find the title obscure.

5. The main idea is that anything is better than slavery, but it is never directly stated. Jacobs's declaration in the second paragraph "Yet I would have chosen this [the miserable conditions of her hiding place] rather than my lot as a slave . . ." is the closest she comes to a direct statement of the main idea.

Extending the Text

6. Students may say that people who persevere see hardships as challenges rather than as insurmountable obstacles, focus on the positive rather than the negative, have the love and support of family, or look for and take comfort in small pleasures.

RESPONDING TO THE ART

The British artist **Lefevre James Cranstone** toured the eastern United States in 1859–1860, painting scenes of what he saw. **Activity.** Point out that children were often sold away from their mothers at auctions. Ask what emotions and attitudes the women's postures suggest. Some perceptive students might note that the painter has "prettied up" what was a horrifying scene.

Grading Timesaver

Rubrics for each Choices assignment appear on p. 145 in the *Portfolio Management System*.

CHOICES: Building Your Portfolio

1. **Writer's Notebook** Students searching for ways to describe their feelings might try examining the effects of their feelings. For example, Jacobs writes that her children's voices "made my tears flow." Remind students to save their notes for the Writer's Workshop on p. 438.
2. **Creative Writing** Students might exchange their letters with a partner and then write each other notes that they imagine Jacobs might have sent in response.
3. **Research/History/Speaking and Listening** You might divide the class into small groups for this assignment. Assign specific roles: a researcher to locate material that will help answer the group's questions; a person to read aloud relevant material for members to discuss; a person to summarize the group's findings; a person to present the oral report.
4. **Research/Music** As a class, brainstorm a list of keywords that will help students to research spirituals: slavery, music, spirituals, songs, African American, folk, tradition. To present the songs to the class, students might play or sing along with a recording, sing and play their own instruments, or sing a cappella.

CHOICES: Building Your Portfolio

Writer's Notebook

1. Collecting Ideas for an Observational Essay

Feelings. Jacobs lets readers know her feelings  when she describes the crawl space. In the essay you will write for the Writer's Workshop on page 438, you might want to let your readers know how you feel about your topic. Choose a subject from your notes, and try to pinpoint your feelings about it.

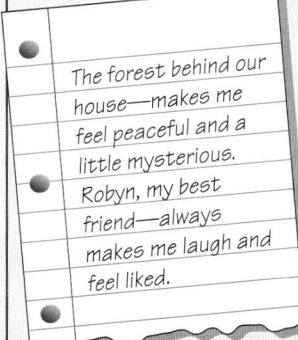

The forest behind our house—makes me feel peaceful and a little mysterious. Robyn, my best friend—always makes me laugh and feel liked.

Creative Writing

2. Letter to the Past

Write a letter to Harriet A. Jacobs, telling what you thought and felt after reading this episode from her true narrative. In your letter include any questions you would like to ask her. Be sure to read Jacobs's biography (page 430).

Research/History/Speaking and Listening

3. Finding More Facts

Go back to the KWL chart you made before you started reading, and fill in the L column. What new facts about slavery did you learn from Jacobs's story? What questions (from your W column) remain unanswered? (Be sure to check the database on page 428.) With a partner or small group, research the questions you still have. Use reference books, histories, books about slavery, the Internet. Present the answers to your own questions in a brief oral report to the class. You might want to present information in the form of a chart or graph.

Research/Music

4. Spiritual Sing-Along

No one knows who first sang the African American spirituals, or "sorrow songs," as W.E.B. Du Bois called them. Many spirituals are based on Biblical stories. Many express faith that one day freedom will come. Others are "signal songs," used to carry messages (about meetings and escapes) that overseers would not understand. Many spirituals are still sung as gospel hymns. Do some research to find other spirituals. Look for anthologies of African American music, or check to see if your library has recordings of spirituals. Present several spirituals to the class. Introduce each song with a commentary.

Swing Low, Sweet Chariot

Swing low, sweet chariot,
Coming for to carry me home,
Swing low, sweet chariot,
Coming for to carry me home.

I looked over Jordan and what did I see
Coming for to carry me home,
A band of angels, coming after me,
Coming for to carry me home.

If you get there before I do,
Coming for to carry me home,
Tell all my friends I'm coming too,
Coming for to carry me home.

Swing low, sweet chariot,
Coming for to carry me home,
Swing low, sweet chariot,
Coming for to carry me home.

Skill Link

Identifying Adjective Clauses

To prepare students for the Grammar Link activities on p. 433, remind them that a clause is a group of words with its own subject and predicate. In adjective clauses, the words *who, which,* or *that* can serve as the subject. Adjective clauses modify nouns or pronouns.

Activity

Underline the adjective clause in each sentence.

1. It was stifling to be in a garret <u>that had no windows</u>.
2. Grandmother was the one <u>who brought herb teas and medicine</u>.
3. Jacobs's children, <u>who meant everything to her</u>, played nearby.
4. A peephole <u>that let her see them</u> was a small source of comfort.
5. Jacobs hid for seven years, <u>which must have been nearly unbearable</u>.

GRAMMAR LINK   MINI-LESSON

Language Handbook HELP

See Clauses, page 1009.

Technology HELP

See Language Workshop CD-ROM. Key word entry: adjective clauses.

Adjective Clauses—Essential or Not?

Adjective clauses, which modify nouns and pronouns, are either essential or nonessential. If an adjective clause is necessary, or **essential,** to the meaning of the sentence, it is not set off with commas. Read these sentences without the underlined essential clauses. Do they make sense?

1. "But though my life in slavery was comparatively devoid of hardships, God pity the woman who is compelled to lead such a life!"

2. For seven years Harriet Jacobs lived in conditions that seem impossible to us.

If an adjective clause gives only extra information and the sentence's sense is not affected when the clause is omitted, then you have a **nonessential** clause, one that should be set off by commas.

3. "My uncle Phillip, who was a carpenter, had very skillfully made a concealed trapdoor...."

Try It Out

Add an adjective clause to each sentence and punctuate it correctly. Begin the clause with the word in parentheses.

1. Harriet Jacobs hid in a crawl space. (which)

2. She was hiding from Dr. Flint. (who)

3. She was eager to see her children. (who)

4. Harriet Jacobs's grandmother, aunt, and uncle were the only people. (who)

VOCABULARY   HOW TO OWN A WORD

WORD BANK

lacerated
devoid
omen
intolerable
consolations
contaminating
impertinent
irascible
abatement
aperture

Word Meanings

Work with a group to find out what you know about the meanings of the Word Bank words. To do this, make up three questions about each word (similar to the questions for *lacerated* below) and organize your answers in a chart. After you have completed charts for all the other words, invite another group to answer some of your questions.

LACERATED	
Questions	**Answers**
What would you do for someone who has been lacerated?	• comfort the person • get medical help for wounds
How might wild animals lacerate something?	• tear with claws • rip with teeth
If your feelings were lacerated, how would you feel?	• hurt (emotionally) • depressed

THE LOOPHOLE OF RETREAT **433**

GRAMMAR LINK

Try It Out
Possible Answers

1. Harriet Jacobs hid in a crawl space, which was above a shed.
2. She was hiding from Dr. Flint, who believed she was in New York.
3. She was eager to see her children, who were living with her grandmother.
4. Harriet Jacobs's grandmother, aunt, and uncle were the only people who saw her for seven years.

VOCABULARY
Possible Questions

1. What could cause a person to be **devoid** of money?
2. What do you consider an **omen** of bad weather?
3. What might you do when the summer heat gets **intolerable?**
4. Under what circumstances would you offer **consolations** to a friend?
5. How might a farmer avoid the use of **contaminating** substances?
6. How would you respond to an **impertinent** person?
7. How do **irascible** children act?
8. How do you cause the **abatement** of a cold?
9. What might a dentist advise about an **aperture** between teeth?

Resources ———————

Language
• *Grammar and Language Links* Worksheet, p. 47

Vocabulary
• *Words to Own* Worksheet, p. 22

Grammar Link Quick Check

In each sentence, underline the adjective clause. Insert commas where they are needed.

1. She stayed in the garret which was a narrow space for seven years. [garret, space,]

2. The garret roof had a steep slope that kept Jacobs from standing. [no commas]

3. Through the peephole she saw Dr. Flint who was her abusive owner. [Flint,]

4. Benny who missed his mother asked about her. [Benny, mother,]

5. Her place of concealment which was in plain sight was never discovered. [concealment, sight,]

T433

OBJECTIVES

1. Read a poem
2. Find thematic connections across genres
3. Generate relevant and interesting discussion

Extending the Theme

In this free-verse poem, a classroom of students resists a discussion about their sacred places until one serious boy describes his car—filled with music, its dashboard lit like an altar. Other students understand "the key / in having a key": freedom to escape from prying questions and to retreat into oneself.

Resources

Listening
Audio CD Library
A recording of this poem is included in the *Audio CD Library*:
• Disc 14, Track 7

RESPONDING TO THE ART

Activity. Ask students to identify what is pictured in the photograph. [the dashboard and part of the steering wheel of a car] Invite students to discuss what the photo leads them to expect from the poem on the next page.

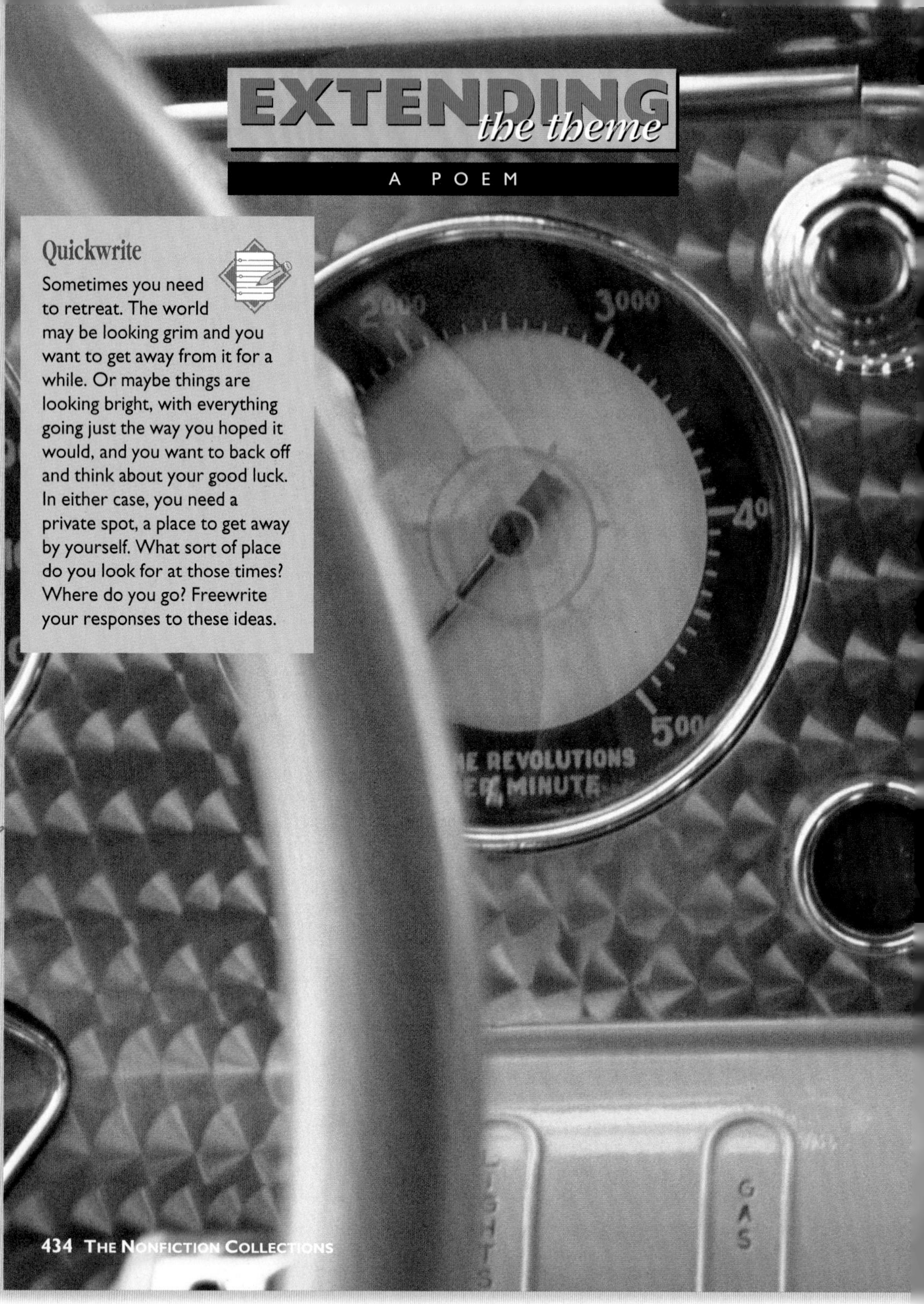

Quickwrite

Sometimes you need to retreat. The world may be looking grim and you want to get away from it for a while. Or maybe things are looking bright, with everything going just the way you hoped it would, and you want to back off and think about your good luck. In either case, you need a private spot, a place to get away by yourself. What sort of place do you look for at those times? Where do you go? Freewrite your responses to these ideas.

434 THE NONFICTION COLLECTIONS

Reaching All Students

Struggling Readers
The lack of end punctuation in this poem might make it slightly difficult for some students. Have them rewrite the poem—breaking it into several sentences. They can add transitional words to make the sentences flow more smoothly.

English Language Learners
To determine how well students have understood the poem, write the following statements on the chalkboard and ask students whether each is true or false. Have them rewrite the false statements in order to make them true.

1. In l. 3, the verb *fidgeted* means the students did not sit still. [True]

2. One student says that his car is a sacred place. [True]
3. There are no references to music in this poem. [False]
4. Only one student speaks about his sacred place. [False]
5. In ll. 16 and 17, the word *key* has more than one meaning. [True]

T434

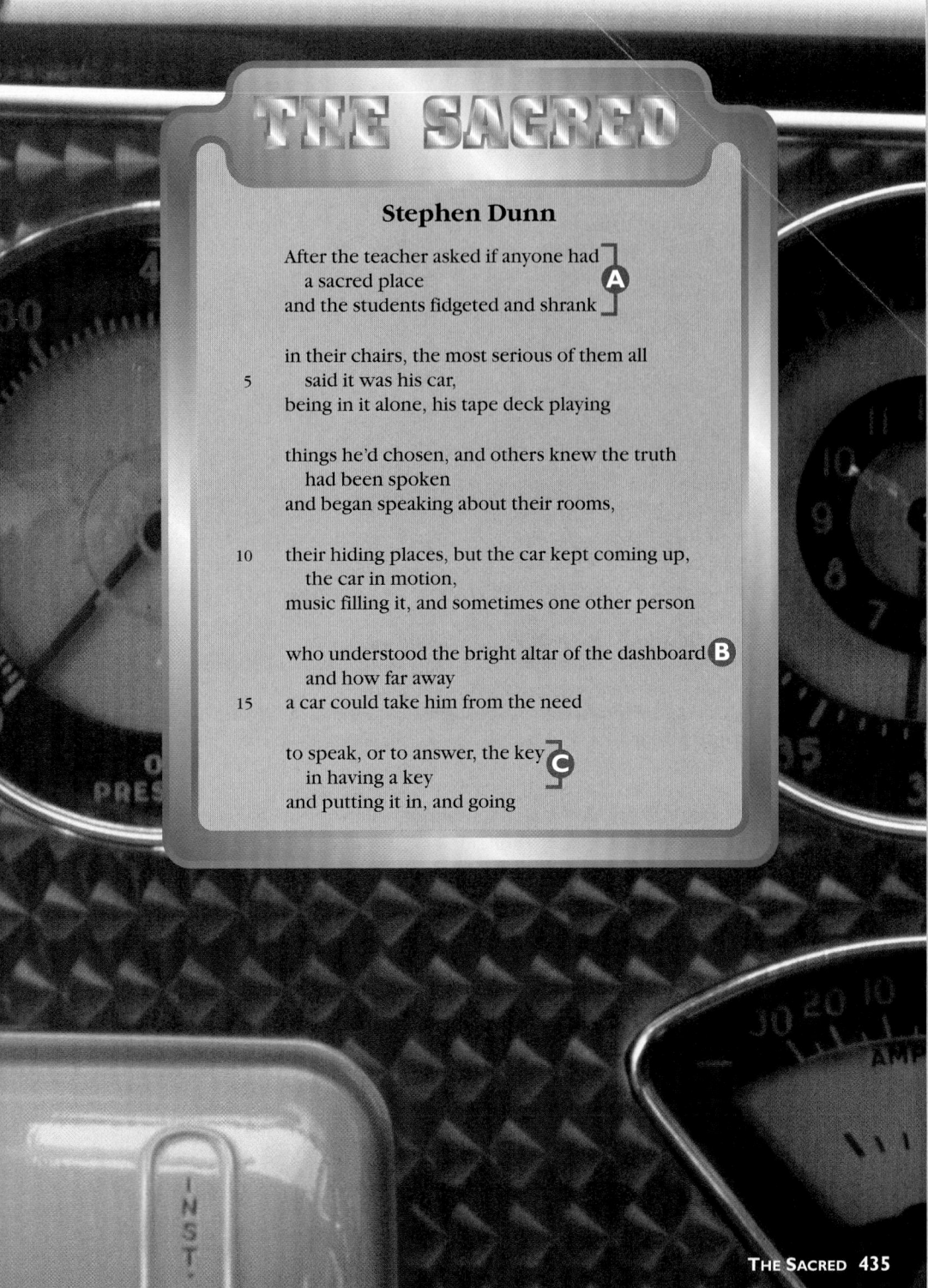

THE SACRED

Stephen Dunn

After the teacher asked if anyone had
   a sacred place
and the students fidgeted and shrank

in their chairs, the most serious of them all
5   said it was his car,
being in it alone, his tape deck playing

things he'd chosen, and others knew the truth
   had been spoken
and began speaking about their rooms,

10   their hiding places, but the car kept coming up,
   the car in motion,
music filling it, and sometimes one other person

who understood the bright altar of the dashboard
   and how far away
15   a car could take him from the need

to speak, or to answer, the key
   in having a key
and putting it in, and going

A Reading Skills and Strategies
Making Inferences
❓ Why are the students hesitant to speak? [Possible responses: They don't know how to answer the question; they don't like prying questions.]

B Elements of Literature
Metaphor
❓ In what ways might a car's dashboard be like an altar? [Possible responses: Dashboards have lights, and many altars have candles; a dashboard is a central control panel, and an altar is the central feature in a place of worship.]

C Appreciating Language
Puns
❓ What is the pun in these lines? [The word *key* is used in two senses, first as a central or crucial idea and second as a thing that opens locks.]

Making the Connections

Connecting to the Theme:
"A Place Called Home"

"The Sacred" describes a student's car as a sacred retreat; it is his "home" in the sense that he is happy and at ease there. The car offers freedom, as does Harriet Jacobs's garret in "The Loophole of Retreat." It allows thoughts and dreams free rein, as does the Jemez area for N. Scott Momaday in "Riding Is an Exercise of the Mind." The music of the tape deck reflects the boy's personality, as Cynthia Rylant wishes that her home could in "The Best Gift of My Life." The car also has room for an understanding companion, a requirement stressed by James Herriot in "Haven't I Made a Difference" and by Nikki Giovanni in "The World Is Not a Pleasant Place to Be." Perhaps most importantly, the car provides solitude, a welcome retreat from life's difficulties.

As its name suggests, this feature is meant to initiate a lively discussion among students in order to discover areas of agreement about something related to the theme, or about controversial issues in the literature.

1. You might suggest that students pause for a moment before freewriting and imagine themselves, or people they know, behind the wheel of the car. They might look again at the photo on p. 434 for inspiration.

2. If students are unable to relate to the metaphor of the dashboard, remind them that freewriting means writing without analyzing or planning. Encourage them to copy the phrase "the bright altar of the dashboard" and then write nonstop for five minutes. If they get stuck, they can use the technique of free association—jotting down whatever ideas or memories come to mind. After five minutes, tell students to read their freewriting and underline the parts that seem most important or meaningful.

MEET THE WRITER

Poet of Everyday Life

When **Stephen Dunn** (1939–   ) graduated from college with a degree in history, his first job was playing professional basketball for the Williamsport (Pennsylvania) Billies for a year. Then he wrote advertising copy for a few years. When he was twenty-five, he went to Spain "to try to change my life and see if I could write poetry." He could and did, becoming an award-winning poet whose many books of poetry celebrate the stuff of everyday life.

66 . . . For the most part, because I'm lucky or unlucky enough to live where and how I do, I'm mostly dealing with local things, like getting through a day, or trying to deal with the demands and failures of relationships, the normal difficulties and pleasures of ordinary living. . . . To get that kind of experience right—to somehow deliver it and also say what it might mean—seems to me a large thing. 99

Dunn teaches at Richard Stockton College of New Jersey.

FINDING COMMON GROUND

Look back at the notes you made for the Quickwrite. Do you identify at all with the feelings of the speaker in "The Sacred"?

Freewrite for a few more minutes about the need to find a place where you can be yourself. Here are some questions to respond to.

1. Dunn's speaker may be both escaping and seeking, both running away *from* something and running *toward* something else. When he pulls out of his driveway, what is he leaving behind—or trying to leave behind—and what is he trying to find?

2. If it were *you* in the poem, what would the "bright altar of the dashboard" represent, and what would be your equivalent of "the need / to speak, or to answer"?

After you've written briefly about these issues, discuss them with other readers. How varied are your responses to the questions and to this poem? Are there any points on which you all agree?

Assessing Learning

Check Test: True-False

1. The poem opens with the teacher asking if anyone in the class owns a car. [False]

2. At first the students are unwilling to answer the teacher's question. [True]

3. The discussion in the poem takes place on a high school football field. [False]

4. The first student to answer the question is a boy. [True]

5. The title of the poem refers to the teacher's car. [False]

READ ON

Searching for Home

Meet Dicey, Maybeth, James, and Sammy—two sisters and two brothers. In Cynthia Voigt's *Homecoming* (Fawcett Juniper), you'll follow their struggle to stay together and look out for one another. They grow up fast because they have to, and their moving story will surprise you.

On the Road in Search of America

Some people say that you don't know what home means until you leave it. Travel along in a camper with the Nobel Prize–winning writer John Steinbeck and Charley, his "gallant" poodle, as they set off to rediscover America. In *Travels with Charley in Search of America* (Penguin), Steinbeck records his adventures as he journeys across America from coast to coast and back home again.

A Home of Her Own

Esperanza (whose name means "hope") wants to change her name to Zeze the X. A young girl growing up in the Latino section of Chicago, she longs to reinvent herself and escape her confining home life. Lyrical and playful, Sandra Cisneros's *The House on Mango Street* (Vintage) captures the rage and the rhythms of a young girl whose imagination has outgrown her environment.

When Home Is Hopeless

What's Eating Gilbert Grape (1993) is a film about life in Endora, Iowa (population 1,091). Gilbert (Johnny Depp) is responsible for taking care of his autistic younger brother, Arnie (Leonardo DiCaprio), and their mother, who hasn't left the house in seven years. When a free-spirited young woman (Juliette Lewis) unexpectedly enters Gilbert's dead-end life, things begin to change.

READ ON **437**

READ ON
Portfolio Assessment Options
The following projects can help you evaluate and assess your students' reading accomplishments outside class. Videotapes or audiotapes of completed projects may be included in students' portfolios.

- **Design an Advertising Poster** Have students design and create an advertising poster to promote the book they have read. A quotation from the book and a visual representing a key character or key scene in the book should appear on the poster. Students can use any medium in their work. Ask students to display their posters and to explain their advertising pitch to the class.

- **Tape a Monologue** Have each student assume the role of a character in the book they have read. Have them tape a three-minute monologue of that character telling about his or her experiences. Students should write a script before taping. After students play their tapes for the class, they should answer any questions class members have.

- **Make a Test** Have students work in small groups to make a test for the book they have read. Students should include ten true-false questions, ten multiple choice questions, and five short answer questions. After writing the test, students should provide answers to the questions. Then, ask other students who have read the book to take the test and to discuss with the group any questions that seem unclear.

- **Videotape a Storytelling** Have students make a tape of themselves retelling the plot of the book they have read to a small child. They should consider how the story might appear in a third-grade reading book. Remind students that the vocabulary they use should be appropriate for that age group. Have students play their videotapes for the class, and ask students to compare the simplified versions to the actual book.

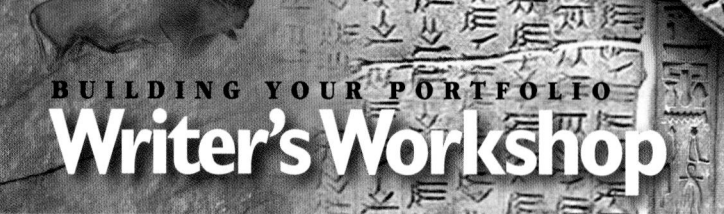

MAIN OBJECTIVE
Write an observational essay

PROCESS OBJECTIVES

1. Use appropriate prewriting techniques to identify and develop a topic
2. Create a first draft
3. Use evaluation criteria as a basis for determining revision strategies
4. Revise the first draft incorporating suggestions generated by self- or peer evaluation
5. Proofread and correct errors
6. Create a final draft
7. Choose an appropriate method of publication
8. Reflect on progress as a writer

Planning

- **Block Schedule**
  Block Scheduling Lesson Plans with Pacing Guide
- **One-Stop Planner**
  CD-ROM with Test Generator

Technology HELP

See Writer's Workshop 2 CD-ROM. *Assignment: Observational Writing.*

ASSIGNMENT

Write a description of a person or place or thing you can observe, so that your reader has the experience of seeing the subject too.

AIM

To re-create an experience; to give information; to express your feelings.

AUDIENCE

Your classmates or readers of a magazine of student writing. (You choose.)

BUILDING YOUR PORTFOLIO
Writer's Workshop

DESCRIPTIVE WRITING
OBSERVATIONAL ESSAY

Observational writing is used in many ways. It can be used in a character profile, a journal entry, a news report, or a firsthand account in a history book. Observational writing is especially important in the field of science.

In the observational essay you'll write here, you'll use **description** (writing that includes sensory details) and perhaps **narration** (writing that tells about a series of related events).

Prewriting

1. Review Your Writer's Notebook

You've already made some Writer's Notebook entries about various subjects. Look over these notes now. You can make changes or add to them.

2. Brainstorm or Cluster or Freewrite

If your notebook entries haven't helped you identify a subject, choose a partner and brainstorm ideas for possible subjects. Or prepare clusters of possible subjects and see which ones offer the best possibilities. Think of **people** you know at home, at school, at work, on the bus, in the store, on the street. Think of **places** you feel strongly about. Think of **animals** or even **events** (a ballgame, a party). If you are interested in science, try describing an **experiment** you performed or a **biological process** you observed.

3. Consider Your Audience

If you are describing a scientific process to someone who is unfamiliar with science, you will have to explain difficult concepts. The best science writers use a kind of comparison called **analogy**—they explain something complex in terms of something familiar. For example, to explain the movement of certain kinds of wave particles, one scientist used this analogy: "When the beams meet, they act like two sets of ripples colliding in a pond."

438 THE NONFICTION COLLECTIONS

  *Resources: Print and Media*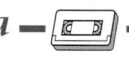

Writing and Language
- *Portfolio Management System*
  Prewriting, p. 146
  Peer Editing, p. 147
  Assessment Rubric, p. 148

- *Workshop Resources*
  Revision Strategy Teaching Notes, p. 29
  Revision Strategy Transparencies
  15, 16, and 17
- *Writer's Workshop 2 CD-ROM.*
  Observational Writing

4. Elaborate

Take notes in your Writer's Notebook as you observe your subject closely. Try to keep all your senses alert at the same time (it's a challenge). Here are the kinds of details that you're looking for:

- specific concrete details about objects, buildings, people, animals, landscapes, and setting
- sensory details about what you see, hear, smell, taste, and touch
- details about actions—how people move, what other events take place, where they take place
- details about the mood or atmosphere of a place
- dialogue—what the person says; what others say

Drafting

1. Show, Don't Tell

General descriptions won't help your reader see your subject. Use some of the concrete, sensory details you collected in your Writer's Notebook. Express those details with precise and vivid nouns, verbs, and modifiers, as in the following passage:

> Mrs. Donovan sank to her knees and for a few moments she gently stroked the rough hair of the head and chest. "He's dead, isn't he?" she whispered at last.
>
> —James Herriot, "Haven't I Made a Difference!" (page 408)

2. Avoid Clichés

If you find yourself about to write a familiar-sounding expression (such as "eyes like stars" or "pretty as a picture"), *stop*! It's probably a wilted, gasping cliché. Clichés are expressions that were once fresh and original but have been worn out by use. Search for new comparisons and figures of speech, like the ones underlined in these sentences:

> We sat on the hard bleachers our bottoms usually warmed for junior varsity games, and we watched these elegant people who seemed long and fluid, like birds, play their marvelous instruments. Their music bounced off the blue-and-gold

---

A Boxful of Descriptive Words

Sight: towering, rusty, jagged, shadowy, silver, fluorescent
Sound: jingling, hoarse, echoing, musical, loud, murmuring
Smell: musty, cut-grass, putrid, garlicky, earthy, lemony
Taste: curried, tart, syrupy, pickled, fiery, salty
Touch: frozen, satiny, splintered, mushy, slimy

Organizing Your Essay

1. **Chronological order.** Put events in the order in which they happened.

2. **Spatial order.** Describe details according to the way they are arranged in space: nearest to farthest, left to right, and so on.

3. **Order of importance.** Start with the most important detail and work toward the least important, or vice versa.

WRITER'S WORKSHOP **439**

Introducing the Writer's Workshop

- Ask students to think about a friend or family member who lives far away. Or students may wish to recall a place that has meaning for them.
- Have them decide how they would describe this person or place to someone who does not know the person or has never seen the place.
- As you discuss the attributes of the person or place to be described, stress that description is more than a list of physical characteristics.

Teaching the Writer's Workshop

Prewriting

Encourage students to apply the following criteria to evaluate their subject choice:

- Do they have sufficient access to the subject?
- Will the subject provide an opportunity for an interesting sensory description?
- Can they easily incorporate specific action or examples of dialogue in their essay?

Drafting

- Before students begin writing their drafts, have them study the Student Model on p. 440.
- Remind students to double-space their drafts. They should also leave extra space in the right margin. These blank spaces will be used for comments and editing marks.

Reaching All Students

English Language Learners

Encourage English language learners to use their native language while prewriting if that is more comfortable for them. If they choose their original language for prewriting, allow them to write their first draft this way, too. Then, have them select two paragraphs from their essay (the introduction and one other) to translate into English. Allow them to complete their entire essay in English as a portfolio option.

Using Students' Strengths

Auditory Learners

Students can work quietly in pairs during several stages of this writing assignment. Allow them to bounce topic ideas off one another, to read aloud their prewriting notes to one another, and to listen to their own drafts read aloud by their partner in order to fix any weak or ineffective descriptions.

picture of our school tiger on the wall and the time clock and the heavy velvet curtains we used for school plays.

—Cynthia Rylant, "The Best Gift of My Life" (page 396)

3. Let Your People Speak

Even if you're writing about a place, people may be part of your description. Let your reader hear how people talk. Perhaps your grandmother, for example, always says goodbye with "God bless you." Adding that detail would reveal something about her.

Using the Model

After reading the model, discuss the side annotations with students. Then, focus discussion on the following:

? What details make you feel as if you are there with the writer? Can you identify specific sensory details the writer uses to make the scene more vivid?

? Can you find transition words or phrases that indicate the essay is organized in chronological order? What makes this organization appropriate for the writer's subject?

? Does the writer's conclusion reveal how she feels about her subject? How does the writer's conclusion make you feel about her subject?

Student Model

A VIETNAM REMEMBRANCE

Looking back on yesterday, November 8, I began to realize how important the Vietnam War was, not only to those who had gone and fought, but also to those who had stayed home and prayed for their loved ones to return safely.

It was an extremely cold morning, that November day. My stepfather, Michael, and I were waiting for the cameraman and Anne Taylor Fleming to arrive. Michael works for the MacNeil/Lehrer NewsHour and was doing a piece on the tenth anniversary of the Wall.

Cold and uncomfortable, I took in the scene around me. I saw veterans standing perfectly still, almost as if they were frozen in time. I had no idea whether they were thinking or not. All I know is that they had the memories of the war.

The cameraman and Anne eventually showed up. However, we weren't able to go straight to shooting the Wall because there was a ceremony going on. Jesse Jackson was leading a prayer service for all the Vietnam vets who had died. He sent a message to them saying that although they were gone, they would not be forgotten. After his prayer, people came up on stage and read off some names of the people who had died during the war. Some people had a list of twenty names and while they recited the names, they would say every once in a while, "I knew that man." Some people would only have one name on their list. There was a lady who had been married the day before who read off her father's name. It seemed as if she wanted her father to be part of her wedding. This calling of names would continue for twenty-four hours a day until the 11th of November. In rain or shine, whether people showed up or not, the litany of names would echo across the Mall.

About half of the people I saw were Vietnam vets. Surprisingly, they were all wearing their uniforms. One vet found a name of a friend or a brother or someone with whom

The writer begins with a powerful event and states its significance. She describes a particular occasion and gives background.

Descriptive details set the scene.

She narrates in chronological order events she observed.

The writer includes specific details to help the reader visualize the scene.

Reaching All Students

Struggling Writers
Students may have difficulty punctuating dialogue. Review the order of punctuation when more than one punctuation mark appears. See the Language Handbook, pp. 1026–1027.

Crossing the Curriculum

Science
Invite a science teacher to discuss with the class the role of observation in science. Talk about field notes, lab notes, and other methods scientists have for recording data. Afterward, invite comparisons between the work of the scientist and the task of writing an observational essay.

4. A Strong Ending

Both Momaday and Ackerman end their essays with strong images: Pecos still riding to the rescue and toddlers waiting to cross the cosmic street. Try to find a strong ending for your essay. You'll know your ending is right when it sounds right and feels like a definite closure. You might want to end with a **reflection** to let your readers know how you feel and what you think about your subject, as in the Student Model below.

Evaluating and Revising
Have students use the Evaluation Criteria on p. 442 to review their drafts and determine needed revisions. In particular, encourage students to look carefully at the method of organization used and its effectiveness. Also, have students give each other feedback on the effect of sensory details used in their essays.

he was close during the war. He simply stood there and cried for a long time. A father saw his son's name imprinted on the wall. I remember seeing him feel the inscription of his son's name while he rested his head on his arm. I also saw a woman who commented to everyone who passed by, saying repeatedly, "This is my husband."

The writer looks at the ceremony from several perspectives. She is very specific in describing what she sees.

Out of this whole wall, one name stood out the most to me. That name was Billy Frank Dodd, an old friend of my mom's. When I saw his name, I fell to my knees. I wasn't crying, however, until a vet came up to me, put his hand on my shoulder, and said, "May he rest in peace." I stayed at this section of the Wall thinking, "My mom knew you. She came here once, but had to leave before she made it to the Wall because she was crying so hard. She misses you." After I was done crying, I gave Billy a kiss goodbye. I can still remember the feel of the smooth marble surface on my lips.

An anecdote illustrates the writer's personal connection to the event.

Another sensory detail.

After I left the Wall, I went to look around and it surprised me that people had left gifts—roses, Tabasco sauce, a teddy bear, even a bottle of whiskey. However, the one gift that touched me the most was a letter written by a man to his brother. In this letter he assured his brother of his love and wished that he could see him just one last time.

A list of specific sights.

Visiting this Wall made me realize many things. I understand what an important event this was in a vet's life. It also made me realize that a war can bring people closer together and yet pull them apart. However, what the Wall made me appreciate the most was that the war still haunts people. Looking back on yesterday, November 8, I began to realize how important the Vietnam War is.

The conclusion summarizes the writer's thoughts; a strong conclusion that echoes the beginning.

—Alicia Guevara
Marymount School
New York, New York

Getting Students Involved

Technology Tip

Encourage students who have word processors to use them even in the prewriting stages. Students can type their thoughts and later, using the cut and paste functions, rearrange, organize, and revise their ideas. If students have access to graphics programs, they can illustrate their essays. You might also ask students to publish their work on your school's Web site. To make their work truly interactive, ask them to write in hypertext, linking key terms and phrases to their definitions and explanations.

You may want to preview any Internet activity that you suggest to students. Because web sites are sometimes public forums, their content can be unpredictable.

Proofreading

Have students proofread their own papers first and then exchange them with another student. Have one partner slowly read aloud the other student's paper, including every punctuation mark. Students should stop and discuss any errors they find in the paper. For this assignment, remind students to be particularly careful of punctuating dialogue.

If time permits, the final copy should be put aside for at least a day before it is proofread one last time by the author.

Publishing

Encourage students to share their essays with their intended audience. Some students may wish to submit their essays to scientific magazines or to electronic magazines on the World Wide Web. Others may wish to give their essays to the person they have written about or that person's family. Still, other students may wish to submit their essays to local newspapers.

Reflecting

Have students reflect upon the following questions:

1. What was the most difficult part of writing their descriptions?
2. What do they like best about their descriptions?
3. What do they want to learn to do better for their next writing assignment?

Resources ——————

Peer Editing Forms and Rubrics
- *Portfolio Management System*, p. 147.

Revision Transparencies
- *Workshop Resources*, p. 29

Language/Grammar Link
H E L P

Time order: page 405.
Description: page 419.
Using commas: page 425.
Adjective clauses: page 433.

Sentence Workshop
H E L P

Combining sentences using participial phrases: page 443.

Communications Handbook
H E L P

See Proofreaders' Marks.

Evaluating and Revising

1. Peer Review

Work with a small group to read and comment on one another's drafts. As you read, ask yourself the following questions:

- Does the writer organize the details clearly?
- What details in the description hold my interest? Are there enough specific details? Does the writer *show* the subject or *tell* about it in a general way? Would dialogue help?
- Does the writer explain difficult concepts?

Peer reviewers should also be sure to comment on details, sentences, and wording that they think are especially good.

2. Self-Evaluation

Consider your writing group's comments as you go over your first draft. Sometimes less is more. Cutting wordy sentences can sharpen your focus.

Revision Model

	Peer Comments
After I left the Wall, I went to	*Can you combine your first two*
and	*sentences so*
look around. ∧It surprised me that	*they're not so choppy?*
⌐roses, Tabasco sauce, a teddy	
⌐bear, even a bottle of whiskey.⌐	*It would be*
people had left gifts. However, the	*nice to know what the gifts*
	were.
that was	*Fragments.*
one gift touched me the most. ∧A	
letter written by a man to his	*Tell us why the gift touched*
In this letter he assured his brother of his	*you so much.*
love and wished that he could see him just	
one last time.	
brother.	
∧	

Grading Timesaver 🕘

Rubrics for this Writer's Workshop assignment appear on p. 148 of the *Portfolio Management System*.

Sentence Workshop

OBJECTIVES
1. Use participial phrases to combine sentences
2. Recognize present and past participles
3. Learn how to punctuate participial phrases

COMBINING SENTENCES: PARTICIPIAL PHRASES

N. Scott Momaday might have written these short sentences:

> These were the Navajos. They were coming in from Torreon. They sat tall in the wagons and on horseback. They went easily with laughter. They sang their riding songs.

Instead, he uses participial phrases to combine ideas and create a smoother-sounding paragraph:

> "These were the Navajos, coming in from Torreon. . . . They sat tall in the wagons and on horseback, going easily with laughter and singing their riding songs." (page 402)

A **participle** is a verb form that can be used as an adjective. Participles come in two varieties: **present participles** (baking bread, running men) and **past participles** (covered wagons, imagined adventures).

A **participial phrase** is made up of a participle and any of its modifiers and objects. Participial phrases, which are always used as adjectives, should be placed close to the noun or pronoun they modify. An introductory participial phrase is always followed by a comma.

> Finding a gimlet, Harriet Jacobs bored a small hole through which she could watch her children.

> Tormented by hundreds of tiny biting insects, Harriet Jacobs suffered for weeks until she got rid of them.

Writer's Workshop Follow-up: Revision

Take another look at the observational essay you wrote for the Writer's Workshop. See if there are short sentences you can combine by using participial phrases. Read both versions aloud (with and without the participial phrases). Which version sounds better?

Language Handbook HELP

See Participles and Participial Phrases, page 1007.

Technology HELP

See Language Workshop CD-ROM. Key word entry: participial phrases.

Try It Out

First, to see how ideas are combined by professional writers, take each sentence that follows and make it into two sentences; one sentence should consist of the information now in the participial phrase. Then, write an original sentence modeled after each professional sentence. Underline the participial phrases in your own sentences.

1. "We watched a hundred-ton shaft plunging down to that place where the water was."
   —Joan Didion, "At the Dam"

2. "We are at our human finest, dancing with our minds, when there are more choices than two."
   —Lewis Thomas, "To Err Is Human"

3. "He sleeps almost as soon as he lies down, relieved to be at last alone."
   —V. S. Naipaul, A Way in the World

Resources

Workshop Resources
• Worksheet, p. 71

Language Workshop CD-ROM
• Participial Phrases

Try It Out
Possible Answers
1. a. We watched a hundred-ton shaft. It was plunging down to that place where the water was.
   b. We saw a blue heron dipping its beak down to where the fish were.
2. a. We are at our human finest when there are more choices than two. This is when we dance with our minds.
   b. We are at our best, laughing in our hearts, when we are at play.
3. a. He sleeps almost as soon as he lies down. He is relieved to be at last alone.
   b. She eats everything on her plate, satisfied to be at home.

Assessing Learning

Quick Check: Participial Phrases

Combine the following sentences using a participial phrase.

1. Cynthia Rylant wanted to live in the conductor's house. She wanted to sleep in a white canopy bed. [Cynthia Rylant wanted to live in the conductor's house, sleeping in a white canopy bed.]

2. Billy the Kid accompanied Momaday on many of his adventures. He rode at Momaday's right side. [Billy the Kid, riding at Momaday's right side, accompanied him on many of his adventures.]

3. Mrs. Donovan made a difference to Roy. She washed and combed his coat every day. [Mrs. Donovan made a difference to Roy, washing and combing his coat every day.]

4. The forests were destroyed by gypsy moths. They had turned gray. [Destroyed by gypsy moths, the forests had turned gray.]

5. She lived in the garret for seven years. She crawled around in the darkness for exercise. [She lived in the garret for seven years, crawling around in the darkness for exercise.]

Reading a Map

OBJECTIVES

1. Develop strategies for reading a map
2. Determine a map's purpose
3. Correctly interpret map symbols using the map's key
4. Determine cardinal directions using the map's compass rose

Teaching the Lesson

If possible, bring in examples of maps to show students, such as a road atlas or a map of bus routes for your city or one nearby. Have students plan an imaginary trip to a destination of their choice using a road atlas. They should calculate mileage, choose a main route and an alternative one, and decide where they want to stop along the way.

Using the Strategies

Answers

1. Jemez is approximately forty miles from Albuquerque. This information can be found by using the scale of miles.
2. northwest
3. the southwestern United States
4. ■ = ancient pueblo site
   ▲ = present-day pueblo

Situation

Your family will be visiting relatives in Albuquerque this summer, and you'd like to see where N. Scott Momaday lived as a child. You use these strategies as you study this map of the area and plan a trip to the canyon country.

Strategies

Take in the title.

• Maps can show much more than just roads. Always read the map title first to determine what the map's specific purpose is and whether it contains the information you need.

Turn to the key.

• The **map key,** or **legend,** explains the symbols on the map. The symbols stand for features or facilities, such as roads or campgrounds.

Locate the compass rose.

• The **compass rose** indicates the four **cardinal directions:** north, south, east, and west. If only north is indicated, use your background knowledge to figure out the three other cardinal directions. Don't assume that the top of the map is north! North may be at an angle or even at the bottom of the map. Also use your background knowledge

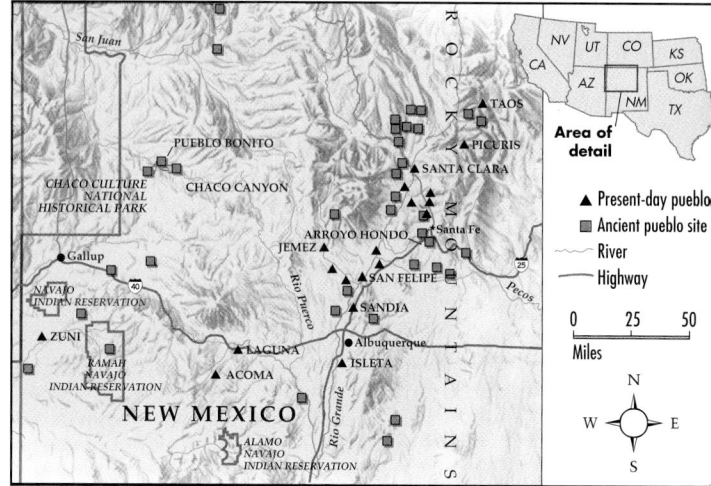

to find **intermediate directions.** Southwest, for example, is midway between south and west.

Get the big picture.

• Some maps contain a smaller map, called a **locator map.** It locates the area shown in the main map within a larger area. The locator map for a map of Chicago, for example, may show where in the state of Illinois the city is located.

Using the Strategies

Use the preceding strategies to answer these questions about the map at the top of the page.

1. About how far is Jemez from Albuquerque? How can you tell?

2. In which direction would you travel to reach Chaco Canyon from Jemez?

3. What larger area does the locator map show?

4. What do these symbols represent: ■ , ▲ ?

Extending the Strategies

Draw or locate a map of your own town, your neighborhood, or the setting of a selection in this book. Make up four questions about the map, trade papers with a partner, and answer each other's questions.

Crossing the Curriculum

Social Studies and Science

Many disciplines have their own type of maps used to convey information specific to that knowledge area. Have students review their textbooks, particularly science and social studies books, and bring samples of different types of maps to class. Have students compare and contrast them. How are weather maps different from battle maps or from electoral maps? How are they alike?

Collection 7

What I Think

Theme

A Matter of Opinion One of the many uses of language is to persuade. On some issues, there are as many opinions as there are people. When writers believe in something strongly enough, they pull out their persuasive techniques. They use humor, compassion, irony, logic, statistics—whatever it takes to convince a reader to see it their way.

Reading the Anthology

Reaching Struggling Readers

The *Reading Skills and Strategies: Reaching Struggling Readers* binder provides materials coordinated with the Pupil's Edition (see the Collection Planner, p. T444B) to help students who have difficulty reading and comprehending text, or students who are reluctant readers. The binder for ninth grade is organized around sixteen individual skill areas and offers the following options:

- **MiniRead** MiniReads are short, easy texts that give students a chance to practice a particular skill and strategy before reading selections in the Pupil's Edition. Each MiniRead Skill Lesson can be taught independently or used in conjunction with a Selection Skill Lesson.

- **Selection Skill Lessons** Selection Skill Lessons allow students to apply skills introduced in the MiniReads. Each Selection Skill Lesson provides reading instruction and practice specific to a particular piece of literature in the Pupil's Edition.

Reading Beyond the Anthology

Read On Each collection in the grade nine book includes an annotated bibliography of books suitable for extended reading. The suggested books are related to works in the collection by theme, by author, or by subject. To preview the Read On for Collection 7, please turn to p. T477.

HRW Library The *HRW Library* offers novels, plays, works of nonfiction, and short-story collections for extended reading. Each book in the Library includes a major work and thematically or topically related Connections. Each book in the *HRW Library* is also accompanied by a Study Guide that provides teaching suggestions and worksheets.

ANIMAL FARM
George Orwell
The animals' revolution doesn't work out the way it was planned. As readers follow the ups and downs of this peculiar society, they must grapple with the issues Orwell believed to be important.

NEVER CRY WOLF
Farley Mowat
Farley Mowat's sympathetic portrayal of the society of wolves helped to stimulate the current interest in reintroducing the wolf to its traditional habitat in America.

Resources for this Collection

Note: All resources for this collection are available for preview on the *One-Stop Planner CD-ROM 1 with Test Generator.* All worksheets and blackline masters may be printed from the CD-ROM.

Internet Resources
go.hrw.com LE0 9-7

Selection or Feature	Reading and Literary Skills	Vocabulary, Language, and Grammar
from **An Indian's Views of Indian Affairs** Chief Joseph (p. 446) **Connections: The Man from Washington** James Welch (p. 449)	• *Reading Skills and Strategies: Reaching Struggling Readers* • MiniRead Skill Lesson, p. 142 • Selection Skill Lesson, p. 149 • *Graphic Organizers for Active Reading*, Worksheet p. 30 • *Literary Elements:* Transparency 9 Worksheet p. 28	• *Words to Own*, Worksheet p. 23 • *Grammar and Language Links:* Connotations, Worksheet p. 49 • *Daily Oral Grammar*, Transparency 30
Elements of Literature: The Writer's Purpose (p. 452) **Persuasive Techniques: Watch for the Tricks** (p. 453)	• *Literary Elements,* Transparency 9	
Darkness at Noon Harold Krents (p. 454)	• *Graphic Organizers for Active Reading*, Worksheet p. 31	• *Words to Own*, Worksheet p. 24 • *Grammar and Language Links:* Euphemisms, Worksheet p. 51 • *Daily Oral Grammar*, Transparency 31
Homeless Anna Quindlen (p. 460)	• *Reading Skills and Strategies: Reaching Struggling Readers* • MiniRead Skill Lesson, p. 153 • Selection Skill Lesson, p. 160 • *Graphic Organizers for Active Reading*, Worksheet p. 32	• *Words to Own*, Worksheet p. 25 • *Grammar and Language Links:* Parallel Structure, Worksheet p. 53 • *Language Workshop CD-ROM*, Improving Sentence Style • *Daily Oral Grammar*, Transparency 32
Misspelling Charles Kuralt (p. 468) **Connections: Hints on Pronunciation for Foreigners** T. S. W. (p. 471)	• *Graphic Organizers for Active Reading*, Worksheet p. 33	• *Grammar and Language Links:* Homonyms, Worksheet p. 55 • *Daily Oral Grammar*, Transparency 33 • *Language Workshop CD-ROM*, Homonyms
Extending the Theme: Those Who Don't Sandra Cisneros (p. 474)	The Extending the Theme feature provides students with an unstructured opportunity to practice reading strategies using a selection that extends the theme of the collection.	
Writer's Workshop: Persuasive Essay (p. 478)		
Sentence Workshop: Clauses (p. 483)		• *Workshop Resources*, p. 73 • *Language Workshop CD-ROM*, Clauses
Learning for Life: You and the Law (p. 485)		

Collection Planner

Other Resources for this Collection

- *Cross-Curricular Activities*, p. 7
- *Portfolio Management System,* Introduction to Portfolio Assessment, p. 1
- *Formal Assessment,* Genre Test, p. 86
- *Test Generator,* Collection Test 💿

Writing	Listening and Speaking Viewing and Representing	Assessment
• *Portfolio Management System,* Rubrics for Choices, p. 149	• *Visual Connections:* Videocassette A, Segment 7 📼 • *Audio CD Library,* Disc 14, Track 9 🎧 • *Viewing and Representing:* Fine Art Transparency 10; Worksheet p. 40 📠 • *Portfolio Management System,* Rubrics for Choices, p. 149	• *Formal Assessment,* Selection Test, p. 76 • *Standardized Test Preparation,* p. 62 • *Test Generator (One-Stop Planner CD-ROM)* 💿
		• *Formal Assessment,* Literary Elements Test, p. 84
• *Portfolio Management System,* Rubrics for Choices, p. 150	• *Audio CD Library,* Disc 14, Track 10 🎧 • *Portfolio Management System,* Rubrics for Choices, p. 150	• *Formal Assessment,* Selection Test, p. 78 • *Standardized Test Preparation,* p. 64 • *Test Generator (One-Stop Planner CD-ROM)* 💿
• *Portfolio Management System,* Rubrics for Choices, p. 151	• *Portfolio Management System,* Rubrics for Choices, p. 151	• *Formal Assessment,* Selection Test, p. 80 • *Test Generator (One-Stop Planner CD-ROM)* 💿
• *Portfolio Management System,* Rubrics for Choices, p. 152	• *Portfolio Management System,* Rubrics for Choices, p. 152	• *Formal Assessment,* Selection Test, p. 82 • *Standardized Test Preparation,* p. 66 • *Test Generator (One-Stop Planner CD-ROM)* 💿
• *Workshop Resources,* p. 35 • *Standardized Test Preparation:* Worksheet pp. 108, 116 📠 Transparencies 1–11 📠 • *Writer's Workshop 2 CD-ROM,* Controversial Issue 💿		• *Portfolio Management System* • Prewriting, p. 153 • Peer Editing, p. 154 • Assessment Rubric, p. 155 • *Standardized Test Preparation:* Worksheet pp. 108, 116 📠 Transparencies 1–11 📠
		• *Portfolio Management System,* Rubrics, p. 156

 Transparency    CD-ROM    Video    Audio CD

T444C

Collection Planner

Skills Focus

Selection or Feature	Reading Skills and Strategies	Elements of Literature	Language/ Grammar	Vocabulary/ Spelling	Writing	Listening/ Speaking	Viewing/ Representing
from **An Indian's Views of Indian Affairs** Chief Joseph (p. 446)	Identify the Techniques of Persuasion, pp. 446, 450 Find the Main Idea, p. 450	Logical and Emotional Appeals, pp. 446, 450	Connotation and Denotation, p. 451 Loaded Words, p. 451 Tone, p. 451	Synonyms, p. 451	Write a Thesis Statement, p. 450	Respond to Chief Joseph's Speech, p. 450	Create a KWL Chart, pp. 446, 450 Design a Poster, p. 450
Elements of Literature: • **The Writer's Purpose** (p. 452) • **Persuasive Techniques: Watch for the Tricks** (p. 453)		The Writer's Purpose, p. 452 Persuasive Techniques, p. 453 • Deduction and Induction • Fallacies • Emotional Appeals					
Darkness at Noon Harold Krents (p. 454)	Find the Main Idea, pp. 454, 458 Summarize an Anecdote, p. 458	Anecdotes, pp. 454, 458 Tone, p. 458 Title, p. 458	Euphemisms, p. 459	Word Origins: Roots, p. 459	Find Anecdotes to Support an Opinion, p. 458 Write a Letter to the Editor, p. 458		
Homeless Anna Quindlen (p. 460)	Analyze Persuasive Techniques, pp. 460, 465 Main Idea and Supporting Details, p. 465	Facts and Opinions, pp. 460, 465 Subjective Writing, p. 460	Parallel Structure, p. 467	Word Maps, p. 467	Find Support for an Opinion, p. 466 Write a Letter to the Author, p. 466	Present an Oral Report, p. 466 Participate in a Group Discussion, p. 466	
Misspelling Charles Kuralt (p. 468)	Summarize the Main Idea, pp. 468, 472	Humor, pp. 468, 472	Homonyms, p. 473	Prefixes and Suffixes, p. 473	Prepare Counterarguments, p. 472 Write a Feature Article, p. 472	Research and Prepare an Oral Report on Some Aspect of English Spelling, p. 472	
Extending the Theme: Those Who Don't Sandra Cisneros (p. 474)	The Extending the Theme feature provides students with an unstructured opportunity to practice reading strategies using a selection that extends the theme of the collection.						
Writer's Workshop: Persuasive Essay (p. 478)		Logical and Emotional Appeals, p. 479			Write a Persuasive Essay, pp. 478–482		Prepare a Pro-Con Chart, p. 479
Sentence Workshop: Clauses (p. 483)			Adjective and Adverb Clauses, p. 483		Combine Sentences Using Adjective and Adverb Clauses, p. 483		
Reading for Life: Reading an Editorial (p. 484)	Read an Editorial, p. 484 • Separate Fact from Opinion • Watch for Fallacies • Recognize Emotional Appeals						
Learning for Life: You and the Law (p. 485)					Write a Letter to an Elected Official, p. 485	Research and Present a Panel Discussion, p. 485	Research and Create a Website, p. 485

Collection 7

WHAT I THINK

WRITING FOCUS: Persuasive Essay

How can I know what I think till I see what I say?

—A little girl, on being told to think before she speaks

We're often advised to think before we speak, but the little girl has a point—we may not *know* what we think until we express the thought, or try to. After all, thoughts aren't objects lying around in the corners of our brains, like old sneakers in a closet, waiting to be dusted off and used whenever the mood strikes. We *make* our thoughts; we don't just *have* them. We know what we think by paying attention to our feelings, looking hard at our experiences, focusing on issues and questions, and finding the words that make sense to us.

Writer's Notebook

WORK IN PROGRESS

The writers in this collection try to persuade readers to see things their way. You'll do the same when you write a persuasive essay for the Writer's Workshop on page 478. Start by listing some ideas and issues you have strong opinions about, especially ones that reasonable people often disagree about. Your list will come in handy when you're looking for a topic for a persuasive essay.

OBJECTIVES

1. Read essays centered on the topic "What I Think"
2. Identify and interpret literary elements used in the literature with special emphasis on the writer's purpose and persuasive techniques
3. Apply a variety of reading strategies
4. Respond to literature using a variety of modes
5. Learn and use new words
6. Plan, draft, revise, edit, proof, and publish a persuasive essay
7. Combine sentences by using clauses
8. Demonstrate the ability to read an editorial
9. Explore how laws affect teenagers in the marketplace and in the workplace through a variety of projects

Responding to the Quotation

? How would you describe the relationship between thoughts and speech? [Possible response: Putting thoughts into words is part of the process of creating ideas.]

RESPONDING TO THE ART

Most teenagers love the telephone, perhaps because they can figure out what they think as they ramble along. Ask students how the act of speaking might help them to articulate their thoughts. Ask volunteers to share their insights.

Writing Focus: Persuasive Essay

WORK IN PROGRESS

The following **Work in Progress** assignments build to a culminating **Writer's Workshop** at the end of the collection.

- An Indian's Views of Indian Affairs   Deciding what you think (p. 450)
- Darkness at Noon   Choosing anecdotes (p. 458)
- Homeless   Supporting your opinion (p. 466)
- Misspelling   Considering opposing views (p. 472)

Writer's Workshop: Persuasive Writing / Persuasive Essay (p. 478)

Writer's Notebook

WORK IN PROGRESS

To help students come up with ideas, have them consider these questions:

- What issues have you argued about with friends or family members?
- What have you seen on television or read in a newspaper that made you angry?
- What would you most like to see change in your school or neighborhood?

T445

OBJECTIVES

1. Read and interpret the speech
2. Identify logical and emotional appeals
3. Recognize persuasive techniques
4. Express understanding through expository writing/speaking or art
5. Identify loaded words and replace them with words that have different connotations
6. Understand and use synonyms

SKILLS

Literary
- Identify logical and emotional appeals

Reading
- Recognize persuasive techniques

Writing
- Brainstorm debatable topics and write a thesis statement for each
- Write a letter or speech

Speaking/Listening
- Deliver a speech

Language
- Identify loaded words

Vocabulary
- Use synonyms

Art
- Create a poster based on the selection

Planning

- **Block Schedule**
  Block Scheduling Lesson Plans with Pacing Guide
- **Traditional Schedule**
  Lesson Plans Including Strategies for English-Language Learners
- **One-Stop Planner**
  CD-ROM with Test Generator

T446

Before You Read

from AN INDIAN'S VIEWS OF INDIAN AFFAIRS

Make the Connection

Exiled

In 1877, when three Nez Percé (nez' pɜrs') braves killed four white settlers, Chief Joseph, their leader, fled the Wallowa Valley in Oregon with some 250 warriors and their families. For more than three months and more than one thousand miles, they outmaneuvered federal troops, finally surrendering thirty miles from the Canadian border.

Exiled to a reservation in Oklahoma, Chief Joseph spent the rest of his life trying to persuade the government to let his people return to their home.

Quickwrite

Make a KWL chart like the one shown below. In the K column, write what you already *know* about "Indian affairs." In the W column, fill in what you *want* to know—some questions you'd like answered. Complete the L column (what you *learned*) after you read Chief Joseph's speech.

K	W	L

Elements of Literature

Appealing to the Head and Heart

When people are trying to persuade, they can use **logical appeals** (reasons, facts, statistics, and examples) and **emotional appeals** (words, phrases, and anecdotes that appeal strongly to their audiences' feelings—their fears, hopes, even prejudices).

> Persuasive writers use **logical** and **emotional appeals** to convince the reader or listener to think or act in a certain way.
>
> *For more on Logical Arguments and Emotional Appeals, see page 453.*

Reading Skills and Strategies

Reading Persuasion: Watch for the Techniques

When you read or listen to a persuasive speech, you should be aware of how the writer or speaker is using language to persuade you to act or think in a certain way. As you read this speech—one of the great pieces of American oration—be aware of how you are responding. Ask yourself
- What is the speaker trying to get me to believe?
- Is there a clear statement of his position?
- What reasons does he give to support his position?
- How is he making me feel?

HRW go.hrw.com
LEO 9-7

Professional Notes

The History Of The Nez Percé. The Nez Percé traditionally lived in villages, each headed by its own civil chief and war leader. When gold was discovered in Nez Percé territory in 1860, prospectors wanted them evicted. In 1863, a warrior who was not a chief signed a treaty with the U.S. government, agreeing to give up the Nez Percé lands in Oregon. Although Chief Joseph refused to recognize this treaty, he reluctantly agreed to move his people to a reservation in Idaho. He was preparing for the move when four white settlers were killed. Fearing retaliation, he attempted to lead his people to Canada. After Chief Joseph's surrender, General Miles, the U.S. officer who captured him, promised that the tribe would be returned to Idaho. But this promise was not kept. Chief Joseph later said: "General Miles had promised that we might return to our country with what stock we had left. I thought we could start again. I believed General Miles, or I never would have surrendered."

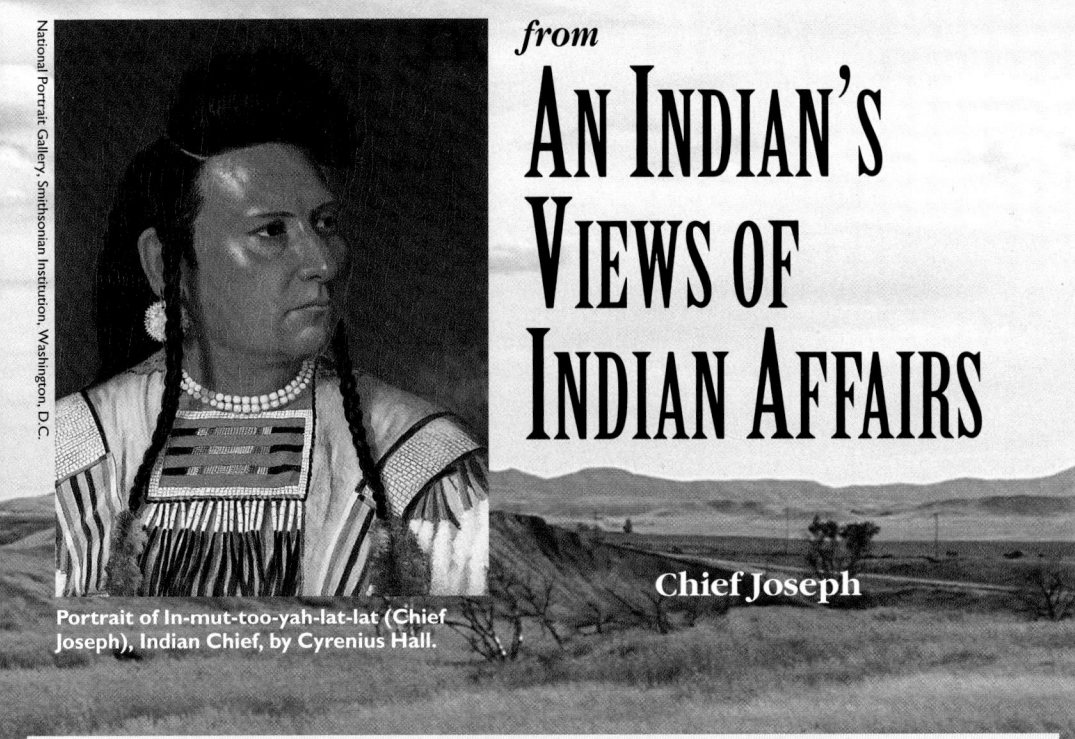
National Portrait Gallery, Smithsonian Institution, Washington, D.C.

Portrait of In-mut-too-yah-lat-lat (Chief Joseph), Indian Chief, by Cyrenius Hall.

from

AN INDIAN'S VIEWS OF INDIAN AFFAIRS

Chief Joseph

Summary ■■

In this speech, Chief Joseph says he is tired of empty words, broken promises, and bloodshed. After years of being persecuted by white men and their government, he defends the right of Native Americans to be treated as equals. He agrees to submit to the laws of the whites, as long as the Nez Percé are granted their freedom. He ends his speech by longing for a time when all people are united and wars cease.

Words do not pay for my dead people.

. . . I have heard talk and talk, but nothing is done. Good words do not last long unless they amount to something. Words do not pay for my dead people. They do not pay for my country, now overrun by white men. They do not protect my father's grave. They do not pay for all my horses and cattle. Good words will not give me back my children. Good words will not make good the promise of your war chief General Miles.° Good words will not give my people good health and stop them from dying. Good words will not get my people a home where they can live in peace and take care of themselves.

I am tired of talk that comes to nothing. It

°**General Miles:** Nelson Appleton Miles (1839–1925), an army officer who led many military campaigns against American Indians. In 1877, he led a campaign against the Nez Percé warriors and captured Chief Joseph.

makes my heart sick when I remember all the good words and all the broken promises. There has been too much talking by men who had no right to talk. Too many misrepresentations have been made, too many misunderstandings have come up between the white men about the Indians.

If the white man wants to live in peace with the Indian, he can live in peace. There need be no trouble. Treat all men alike. Give them the same law. Give them an even chance to live and grow. All men were made by the same Great Spirit Chief. They are all brothers. The earth is the mother of all people, and all people should have equal rights upon it.

You might as well expect the rivers to run backward as that any man who was born a free man should be contented when penned up and denied liberty to go where he pleases. If you tie

AN INDIAN'S VIEWS OF INDIAN AFFAIRS 447

Resources ———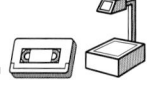

Viewing and Representing
Videocassette A, Segment 7
Available in Spanish and English. The video segment "The Power of Speech" explores the power of persuasive speaking. For full lesson plans and worksheets, see the *Visual Connections Teacher's Manual.*

Viewing and Representing
Fine Art Transparency
Use Howard Terpning's *Chief Joseph Rides to Surrender* to help convey the dramatic impact of the speech. See the *Viewing and Representing Transparencies and Worksheets:*
• Transparency 10
• Worksheet, p. 40

Ⓐ **Reading Skills and Strategies**

Recognizing Persuasive Techniques
❓ Why does Chief Joseph repeat the phrase "Good words will not"? [Possible responses: to make his audience feel his anger at the empty promises he has heard; to emphasize the ironic contrast between what is said by the whites and the suffering they have inflicted upon his people.]

Resources: Print and Media

Reading
• *Reading Skills and Strategies:*
  MiniRead Skill Lesson, p. 142
  Selection Skill Lesson, p. 149
• *Graphic Organizers for Active Reading,* p. 30
• *Words to Own,* p. 23
• *Audio CD Library,* Disc 14, Track 9

Elements of Literature
• *Literary Elements*
  Transparency 9
  Worksheet, p. 28

Writing and Language
• *Daily Oral Grammar*
  Transparency 30
• *Grammar and Language Link*
  Worksheet, p. 49

Viewing and Representing
• *Viewing and Representing*
  Fine Art Transparency 10
  Fine Art Worksheet, p. 40
• *Visual Connections*
  Videocassette A, Segment 7

Assessment
• *Formal Assessment,* p. 76
• *Portfolio Management System,* p. 149
• *Standardized Test Preparation,* p. 62
• *Test Generator (One-Stop Planner CD-ROM)*

Internet
• go.hrw.com (keyword: LE0 9-7)

A Elements of Literature
Logical and Emotional Appeals

❓ What logical appeals does Chief Joseph use here to argue for the tribe's freedom? [He compares placing his people on a reservation to tethering a horse to a stake—neither will prosper in captivity. He asks whites where they get their authority to restrict his people's freedom.]

B Elements of Literature
Logical and Emotional Appeals

❓ Does Chief Joseph appeal to logic, emotion, or both in this passage? Explain. [He appeals to both. The first sentence is a logical appeal for equal treatment. The language of the second sentence—"where my people will not die so fast"—is meant to elicit sympathetic feelings.]

C Appreciating Language
Connotations

❓ What associations are suggested by the words *outlaws* and *animals*? [Possible response: Both words suggest traits of fierceness and uncontrollability.] What point is Chief Joseph making with these words? [White society thinks of Native Americans as being uncivilized and treats them as less than human.]

D Critical Thinking
Speculating

❓ How do you think Chief Joseph's audience reacted to his appeals for equality? [Sample response: Some people in the audience may have been convinced that Native Americans should have the same rights as other citizens and be subjected to the same laws. Others would need more than a speech to change their attitudes.]

---

a horse to a stake, do you expect he will grow fat? If you pen an Indian up on a small spot of earth and compel him to stay there, he will not be contented, nor will he grow and prosper. I **A** have asked some of the great white chiefs where they get their authority to say to the Indian that he shall stay in one place while he sees white men going where they please. They cannot tell me.

I only ask of the government to be treated as **B** all other men are treated. If I cannot go to my own home, let me have a home in some country where my people will not die so fast. . . .

When I think of our condition, my heart is **C** heavy. I see men of my race treated as outlaws and driven from country to country or shot down like animals.

I know that my race must change. We cannot hold our own with white men as we are. We ask **D** only an even chance to live as other men live. We ask to be recognized as men. We ask that the same law shall work alike on all men. If the Indian breaks the law, punish him by the law. If the white man breaks the law, punish him also.

Let me be a free man—free to travel, free to stop, free to work, free to trade where I choose, free to choose my own teachers, free to follow the religion of my fathers, free to think and talk and act for myself—and I will obey every law or submit to the penalty.

Whenever white men treat Indians as they treat each other, then we will have no more wars. We shall all be alike—brothers of one father and one mother, with one sky above us and one country around us, and one government for all. Then the Great Spirit Chief who rules above will smile upon this land and send rain to wash out the bloody spots made by brothers' hands from the face of the earth.

For this time the Indian race is waiting and praying. I hope that no more groans of wounded men and women will ever go to the ear of the Great Spirit Chief above and that all people may be one people.

MEET THE WRITER
An Eloquent Leader

Chief Joseph (c. 1840–1904), whose name In-mut-too-yah-lat-lat means "Thunder Rolling in the Mountains," was about thirty-one when he became leader of the Wallowa band of Nez Percés. "Always remember that your father never sold his country," his dying father told him. "You must stop your ears whenever you are asked to sign a treaty selling your home."

Reaching All Students

Struggling Readers

Reading Persuasion was introduced on p. 446. For a lesson directly tied to this selection that teaches students to read persuasion by using a strategy called Save the Last Word for Me, see the *Reading Skills and Strategies* binder:
• MiniRead Skill Lesson, p. 142
• Selection Skill Lesson, p. 149

English Language Learners

Encourage students to read at a slower, more deliberate pace in order to visualize the images in the text. Demonstrate by reading aloud the fourth paragraph that starts on p. 447 and continues on p. 448. For other strategies for engaging students with the literature, see
• *Lesson Plans Including Strategies for English-Language Learners*

Advanced Learners

Have students locate other examples of well-known speeches by historical figures and read them aloud to the class. For each of the speeches, ask the following questions:
• Why was the speech memorable?
• What was the main point of the speaker?
• Have any lines from the speech become famous?
• What comparisons can be drawn between the speech and Chief Joseph's speech?

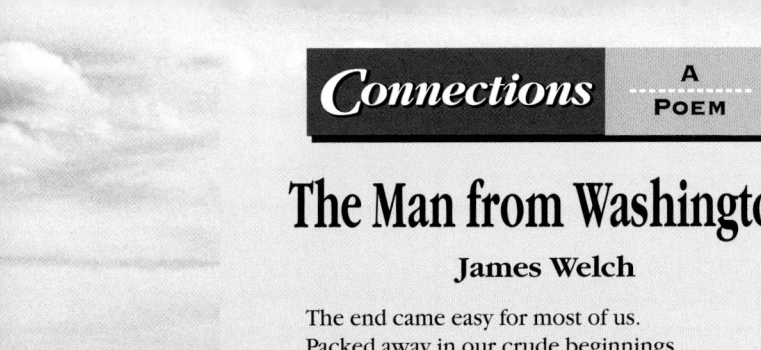

The Man from Washington 🅐

James Welch

The end came easy for most of us.
Packed away in our crude beginnings
in some far corner of a flat world,
we didn't expect much more
5 than firewood and buffalo robes
to keep us warm. The man came down, 🅑
a slouching dwarf with rainwater eyes,
and spoke to us. He promised
that life would go on as usual,
10 that treaties would be signed, and everyone—
man, woman, and child—would be inoculated 🅒
against a world in which we had no part,
a world of money, promise, and disease.°

13. Epidemics of smallpox and chickenpox, caused by contact with white settlers, wiped out whole American Indian villages.

In October 1877, Chief Joseph surrendered his band of Nez Percés, who had refused to sign the latest government treaty, with these now-famous words:

66 I am tired of fighting. Our chiefs are killed. . . . The old men are all dead. . . . It is cold, and we have no blankets. The little children are freezing to death. My people, some of them, have run away to the hills, and have no blankets, no food. No one knows where they are—perhaps freezing to death. I want to have time to look for my children and see how many of them I can find. Maybe I shall find them among the dead. Hear me, my chiefs! I am tired. My heart is sick and sad. From where the sun now stands I will fight no more forever. 99

Chief Joseph continued to fight—not with weapons but with words—traveling twice to the nation's capital to plead for his people's return to their ancestral lands. After eight years 150 surviving Nez Percés (all of Chief Joseph's children had died by then) were allowed to return to the Northwest but not to their beloved Wallowa Valley. When Chief Joseph died on the Colville Reservation in Washington, the doctor said he had died of a broken heart.

AN INDIAN'S VIEWS OF INDIAN AFFAIRS **449**

Connections

The Native American speaker in this poem describes the interaction between his people and a U.S. government official. Although promises are made by the official, the speaker realizes that his people are being treated unfairly.

🅐 Historical Connections

To help students connect with the text, have them research and report on the history of Native Americans in their state. They can either cover a broad time range or concentrate on a particular event or time period that was of special significance. What tribes are (or were) native to the area? (Point out that since European settlers constantly pushed the Indians farther west, many tribes were relocated.) What government policies were established to deal with the Native American population? What is the current economic and legal status of Native tribes?

🅑 Appreciating Language
Word Choice
❓ What does the poet's choice of words reveal about his feelings toward the man from Washington? [Possible response: The phrases "slouching dwarf," and "rainwater eyes" suggest dislike or distrust.]

🅒 Elements of Literature
Irony
❓ What is ironic about the promise of inoculation? [Possible responses: The whites have brought diseases from which Native Americans must be protected; the government's false promises have been as devastating as any disease.]

Resources 💿

Selection Assessment
Formal Assessment
• Selection Test, p. 76
Test Generator (One-Stop Planner)
• CD-ROM

Connecting Across Texts

Connecting with "An Indian's Views of Indian Affairs"
Ask students to think of three adjectives that describe the tone of the poem. [Possible responses: righteous, indignant, wary, defeated, ironic.] Discuss with students which of these adjectives can also apply to Chief Joseph's speech. [Students may say that both the poem and the speech convey indignation, but Chief Joseph's speech conveys more hope for the future than does Welch's poem.]

Assessing Learning

Check Test: True-False
1. Chief Joseph is tired of talk that comes to nothing. [True]
2. Chief Joseph is convinced that his people must be confined in one place. [False]
3. Chief Joseph believes that his people and white people need separate laws. [False]
4. According to Chief Joseph, wars will end when people are treated equally. [True]

Standardized Test Preparation
For practice with standardized test format specific to this selection, see
• *Standardized Test Preparation*, p. 62
For practice in proofreading and editing, see
• *Daily Oral Grammar*, Transparency 30

T449

MAKING MEANINGS

First Thoughts

1. Most students will say the speech persuaded them to feel sorry or angry about the treatment of Chief Joseph's people. Others may remain unpersuaded perhaps because of the lack of statistical information.

Shaping Interpretations

2. Chief Joseph uses both logical and emotional appeals. Logical appeals: He asks whites to recognize Native Americans as people and to treat them equally under the law. Emotional appeals: He describes how his people are "shot down like animals" and expresses a desire to hear "no more groans of wounded men and women." He wants to persuade his audience to treat Native Americans as equals.

3. The man is probably an official from the Bureau of Indian Affairs and the speaker a disillusioned Native American. Students may say that the speaker, unlike Chief Joseph, seems to have no hope that his people will ever achieve equal rights.

Extending the Text

4. Students may say that words without action mean little, citing such examples as empty campaign promises to improve schools.

5. Charts will vary; students may want to learn more about life on reservations, government treaties, or early Native American leaders.

Grading Timesaver

Rubrics for each Choices assignment appear on p. 149 in the *Portfolio Management System*.

CHOICES: Building Your Portfolio

1. **Writer's Notebook**   Remind students to avoid topics about which most people have similar opinions.

2. **Expository Writing/Speaking**   Discuss the importance of tone in students' responses.

3. **Art**   Students can illustrate a single word or phrase rather than a complete sentence.

T450

MAKING MEANINGS

First Thoughts

[connect]

1. Were you persuaded by Chief Joseph? Tell how you responded to his speech.

Shaping Interpretations

[infer]

2. Does Chief Joseph use **logical** or **emotional appeals** or both to persuade his audience? Find some examples. What does he want to persuade his audience to do?

[compare]

3. Who is "The Man from Washington" in the *Connections* poem on page 449, and who is the speaker? Compare this speaker's message with Chief Joseph's.

Extending the Text

[connect]

4. Are actions always more important than "good words"? Support your opinion with examples from history or from your own experience.

[evaluate]

5. Fill in the L column in the KWL chart you made for your Quickwrite. If you have any unanswered questions, do some research and share your findings with the class.

> **Reading Check**
>
> In a chart like the one below, state each **main idea** in the speech and list its supporting details.
>
> | Main Idea |
> |---|
>
> | Supporting Details |
> |---|
> | 1. |
> | 2. |

CHOICES: Building Your Portfolio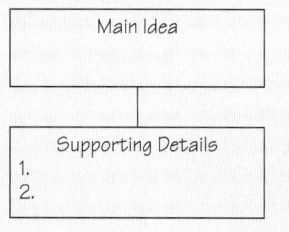

Writer's Notebook

1. Collecting Ideas for a Persuasive Essay

Pinning down what you think. In the persuasive essay you'll write for the Writer's Workshop on page 478, you'll choose a debatable topic, decide what you think about it, and try to convince your audience you're right. With a small group, brainstorm debatable topics (topics that people have opposing opinions about). (A topic might be suggested by Chief Joseph's speech.) Choose two topics that interest you and decide what you think about each one. For each topic, write a **thesis statement**, a sentence that clearly states your opinion. Save your notes.

Expository Writing/ Speaking

2. Dear Chief Joseph

You are one of the members of Congress who listened to Chief Joseph plead his case. Write a letter or deliver a brief speech responding to his statements.

Art

3. Good Words

Choose one sentence from the speech that you found especially powerful, and create a poster based on it. Experiment with different design elements (lettering, color, symbols, images, decorative patterns) to express Chief Joseph's ideas.

Reading Check
Possible Answers:

Main Idea
Empty words have not helped the Nez Percé.

Supporting Details
1. The Nez Percé have lost lives, health, homes, and cattle.
2. Promises have been made and broken by the U.S. government, resulting in distrust.

Main Idea
Human beings must not be denied freedom.

Supporting Details
1. Everyone should be free to travel, work, trade, be educated, practice religion, think, talk, and act as they please.
2. Whites have no authority to restrict the movements of Native Americans.

LANGUAGE LINK MINI-LESSON

**Handbook of
Literary
Terms**
H E L P

See Connotation.

**Communications
Handbook**
H E L P

*See Using a
Dictionary;
Using a
Thesaurus.*

Connotations and Loaded Words

Many English words have **connotations** (feelings and associations) in addition to their **denotations** (strict dictionary definitions). Connotations stir people's feelings in a positive or negative way. When such words are used in persuasive writing or speaking, they're called **loaded words**. For example:

> Senator Blank is <u>rigid</u>.
> Senator Blank is <u>firm</u>.

Both of these sentences really say the same thing (Senator Blank does not change her mind easily). Which sentence uses a loaded word designed to make you approve of her, and which one is meant to make you disapprove?

You should be aware of loaded words in advertisements and political speeches. Someone may be trying to sway your feelings so that you'll buy a product or support a candidate.

Try It Out

1. If you can think of a word to fill each empty space in this chart, you'll have pairs of words that mean more or less the same thing but are loaded positively and negatively.

Positive	Negative
slender	
	cheap
	stubborn
	timid

2. Look for loaded words in Chief Joseph's speech and in line 7 in Welch's poem. Are the words positive or negative? Can you substitute other words that would change the **tone** of each text?

VOCABULARY HOW TO OWN A WORD

Synonyms

Synonyms are words that have the same or nearly the same meaning (*protect/shield, equal/alike*). The English language has few exact synonyms but many words that mean almost the same thing. Choose five words from the speech, and make a diagram like the one here for each. Write the word, one synonym, and a sentence for each. Can the synonyms be used interchangeably, or are there important differences in meaning?

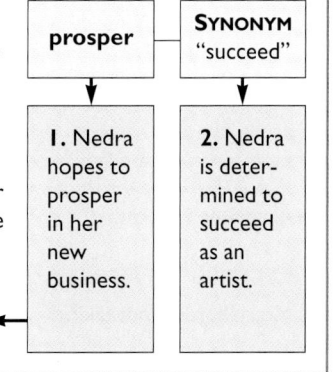

> *Prosper* wouldn't be right in the second sentence unless Nedra wanted to get rich.

prosper → SYNONYM "succeed"

1. Nedra hopes to prosper in her new business.
2. Nedra is determined to succeed as an artist.

AN INDIAN'S VIEWS OF INDIAN AFFAIRS **451**

LANGUAGE LINK

Try It Out
Possible Answers

1.

POSITIVE	NEGATIVE
slender	**scrawny**
thrifty	cheap
determined	stubborn
modest	timid

2. "Slouching dwarf" from l. 7 of the poem is a negative image; *slouching* suggests that the man is not morally upright. A phrase like *small man* would create a different tone. "Overrun" in the first paragraph of Chief Joseph's speech suggests that his land has been trampled or ruined by white men. *Populated by* would be a substitute without negative connotations.

VOCABULARY
Sample Answer

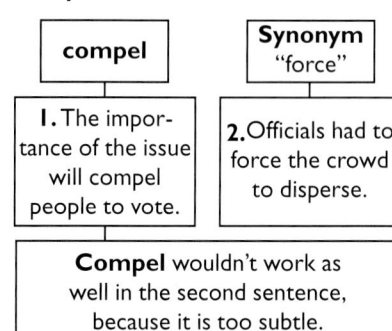

compel | Synonym "force"

1. The importance of the issue will compel people to vote.
2. Officials had to force the crowd to disperse.

Compel wouldn't work as well in the second sentence, because it is too subtle.

Resources ——————

Language
• *Grammar and Language Links* Worksheet, p. 49

Vocabulary
• *Words to Own* Worksheet, p. 23

Language Link Quick Check

Write a plus (+) next to the sentences that have a positive connotation and a minus (–) next to the sentences that have a negative connotation. Have them underline the word that is loaded positively or negatively.

1. The <u>callous</u> boss arrived for the meeting. [–]
2. My friend on the swing was quite <u>serene</u>. [+]
3. The <u>mob</u> raced toward the star's dressing room. [–]
4. The <u>meddling</u> neighbor at long last moved away from us. [–]
5. My <u>conscientious</u> brother wrote his own election speech. [+]

Resources

Elements of Literature

The Writer's Purpose

For more instruction on the writer's purpose, see *Literary Elements*:
• Transparency 9

Elements of Literature

This feature describes various purposes for writing nonfiction and the methods of writing that best accomplish those purposes: exposition, description, narration, and persuasion. It also introduces the specific techniques that are used in persuasive writing: *deduction* and *induction,* fallacies, and emotional appeals.

Mini-Lesson:
The Writer's Purpose

Have students work in groups of four or five to create their own brief examples of each type of writing method. Ask a volunteer from each group to read each example aloud. Have other students name the writing method exemplified.

Next, you may want to discuss the terms *deduction* and *induction* with the class in more detail. The text uses the terms in an organizational sense; it tells where in an essay the writer places his or her conclusion. In general usage, however, the terms refer to the way in which a person draws a generalization or conclusion.

Deductive reasoning moves from the general to the specific; a person begins with a general statement (a generalization), which is then supported by specific details. Here's an example:

Generalization: Although some people see *Gulliver's Travels* as a child's adventure story, it is actually a biting satire.

Detail: There are many parallels between events in Lilliput and events in England.

Detail: The book is directed against follies and excesses wherever they are found.

In a deductive essay, the writer would first state the generalization and then state the details from which it was derived.

T452

THE WRITER'S PURPOSE
by Janet Burroway

Every good writer of nonfiction has a purpose when he or she sits down to write. The purpose may be to explain or inform; to create a mood or stir an emotion; to tell about a series of events; to persuade the reader to believe something or do something. A writer may want to do several of these things in a single essay or report, but he or she will know what the primary purpose of the piece of writing is and will select and arrange words and details that best accomplish that purpose.

Suppose, for instance, that Jim Greene breaks Terry Lewis's arm in the gym on Friday afternoon during a judo workout. Jim says it was an accident; Terry says Jim did it on purpose. Mrs. Jeffords, the judo instructor, wasn't looking. Another student, Stan Jones, was looking. The principal asks each one to write down what he or she knows. Their four accounts are all based on the same facts. What differs in each case is the writer's purpose and the method of writing.

Exposition: Informing

Mrs. Jeffords is not taking sides. She simply wants to explain how such an accident could have happened. Most of her report is **exposition,** the method of writing that explains or informs.

Judo throws require both precise timing and exact balance. At this level (yellow belt) there is always a slight possibility that the participants have insufficient agility or coordination.

Description: Sensing It

Stan Jones, the only witness, writes a more detailed and dramatic piece. He adds a great deal of **description,** the kind of writing that uses images to help us experience something with our senses.

The air conditioner in the gym was broken, and the place was like a giant oven. Jim was sweating heavily after the last throw. Terry lunged for Jim, but his fingers slipped on Jim's glistening skin.

Narration: What Happens

Jim Greene, who feels innocent and wants to appear as reasonable as possible, sticks to a straight **narration**.

This method of writing tells about a series of events, usually in chronological order.

I had just come out of the last throw and had turned toward Terry, who was getting up to come at me from the left. I made a quarter turn and moved my left leg forward when he reached for my neck and his hand slipped.

Persuasion:
Influencing People

Terry's arm hurts and he's angry that he'll miss the spring tournament. His purpose is **persuasion,** so he'll select all the evidence he can to persuade the principal that Jim broke his arm on purpose.

Jim's jealous of me and always has been. I got my yellow belt three meets ahead of him, and I'm the only one who's ever thrown him three out of four.

In general, **exposition** answers "What is it, and how does it work?" **Description** answers "What does it look, sound, smell, feel, taste like?" **Narration** answers "What happened?" **Persuasion** answers "What should I feel or do about it?"

Inductive reasoning moves from the specific to the general; a person draws a conclusion from a range of factual information, individual cases, and experience. Here's an example:

From the news: Report that a scientific study links cholesterol to heart disease.

Statistics: On the average, the diets of Americans contain high amounts of cholesterol.

Conclusion: Americans should limit their consumption of cholesterol in order to combat heart disease.

Finish the discussion by guiding students through the examples of fallacies, or errors in logic. Students can read and discuss the examples on p. 453. Then, ask the class to brainstorm examples of television commercials that use the two types of emotional appeals discussed—the bandwagon approach and the testimonial.

PERSUASIVE TECHNIQUES: Watch for the Tricks

When your purpose is **persuasion,** you'll develop a **logical argument,** a series of statements made up of your opinion supported by reasons and evidence. You'll find step-by-step techniques for developing such an argument in the Writer's Workshop on page 478.

Deduction and Induction— Two Different Approaches

You can present a persuasive argument in one of two ways.

1. The **deductive** approach starts with an opinion (the main idea) and then supports it with reasons and examples. This is the approach in the Writer's Workshop on page 478.
2. The **inductive** approach begins with details (the evidence and the reasons) and ends with a logical conclusion (your opinion).

Fallacies: How Not to Argue

Beware of **fallacies,** which are errors in logical thinking. They'll weaken your argument and make your audience doubt *everything* you say. Suppose, for instance, the school board has announced plans to cut all after-school sports. Here are four fallacies to avoid:

1. Attacking the Person

Mr. McAloo, who proposed these cuts, hates sports and is a penny-pinching meanie.

Don't attack an opponent's character or judgment. Stay focused on the issue.

2. Circular Reasoning

After-school sports are essential because they're a necessary part of school activities.

This may look like a reason, but it's not. What follows *because* just restates the writer's opinion.

3. False Cause and Effect

When after-school sports were dropped at Adams High School, the dropout rate increased immediately.

Just because Event 2 happens *after* Event 1 doesn't mean that Event 1 *caused* Event 2. The two events may be (and usually are) unrelated.

4. Hasty Generalization

Everyone in school agrees that dropping after-school sports is a dumb idea. I know because I asked my friend Chad, and he agrees with me.

You can't generalize about everyone or everything based on only one or two cases. You need a great many observations before you can make a valid generalization.

Emotional Appeals

In a persuasive essay or speech, **emotional appeals** add an extra persuasive push, but they're not a substitute for a logical argument. On page 451, you learned about

loaded words. Here are other emotional appeals that you'll recognize from advertisements and campaign speeches:

1. Bandwagon

Everyone's throwing a Spiro-cylinder, the best thing since a boomerang. Get yours today before they're all gone.

The bandwagon appeal suggests that unless you "jump on the bandwagon" and act right now, you'll be left out, the only one who's different.

2. Testimonial

Carrie, the Most Valuable Player in the soccer league, starts every morning with Brand X cereal.

Entertainers and athletes are paid to endorse products they often know little about. Advertisers hope they'll persuade their fans to "be like me; do what I do."

Check It Out

Find and display examples of these fallacies and emotional appeals. Look for them in television and radio commercials, magazine and newspaper advertisements, editorials, political messages, and campaign speeches. In each case, determine the writer's purpose and the intended audience.

Applying the Element

Use "An Indian's Views of Indian Affairs" to help students review persuasive techniques.

Ask the following questions:

- What is Chief Joseph's purpose? [to persuade his listeners to believe or do something] What method of writing does he choose to accomplish this purpose? [persuasion]
- What type of emotional appeal does he make? Give examples. [He uses loaded words and phrases, such as "protect my father's grave," "give me back my children," "shot down like animals."]
- What is Chief Joseph's opinion or main idea? [If Indians are given the same freedom and legal rights as white men, peace will prevail.]
- Summarize the argument he gives to support his opinion? [Indians have not been treated the same as white men—they have been driven from their homes and confined on reservations. Under these terrible conditions, they cannot survive and prosper. Whites cannot justify their claim to authority over Native Americans. However, Native tribes are realistic and realize they must change. If they are granted freedom and equal rights, they will obey the law.]

As students read other selections in this collection, have them look for the persuasive techniques that each writer uses.

Resources ———

Formal Assessment
- Literary Elements Test, p. 84

Reaching All Students

Struggling Readers

Before students begin the feature, give them a framework like the one below and have them complete it as they read. After they finish, correct and discuss their frameworks.

Purposes of Writing Nonfiction:
- (1) _____
- (2) _____
- (3) _____
- (4) _____

Persuasive Techniques
Two Different Approaches:
- (1) _____
- (2) _____

Fallacies:
- (1) _____
- (2) _____
- (3) _____
- (4) _____

Emotional Appeals:
- (1) _____
- (2) _____

T453

Make the Connection

Seeing What He Means

In this essay the narrator tells some humorous stories about how people have reacted to his blindness. Although he claims to have a "saintlike disposition," some reactions clearly annoy him. As you read this essay, you'll discover how Krents wants to be treated.

Quickwrite

What do you think is the right way to treat a person who has impaired sight or hearing or who uses a wheelchair? Quickwrite for a few minutes.

Elements of Literature

Stories with a Point

Anecdotes are very brief stories that have some of the elements of a short story: characters, plot, and dialogue. In a persuasive essay, anecdotes usually help the writer make some kind of point. Look for anecdotes in "Darkness at Noon."

> **A**n **anecdote** is a brief story used to make a point or provide an example.

Reading Skills and Strategies

Looking for the Main Idea

When you read an essay, you look for the **main idea** expressed in the text, and then you notice how the writer supports or develops it. As you read this essay, look for key statements that seem to point to the main idea. Look also at Krents's anecdotes. What points is he making with these stories?

DARKNESS at NOON

Harold Krents

Blind from birth, I have never had the opportunity to see myself and have been completely dependent on the image I create in the eye of the observer. To date it has not been narcissistic.[1]

There are those who assume that since I can't see, I obviously also cannot hear. Very often people will converse with me at the top of their lungs, enunciating each word very carefully. Conversely,

> *Others know that I can hear, but believe that I can't talk.*

---

1. **narcissistic** (när'sə·sis'tik): here, flattering. Narcissism is an excessive interest in one's self.

 go.hrw.com
LEO 9-7

Preteaching Vocabulary

Words To Own

Ask volunteers to read aloud the definitions of the Words to Own listed at the bottom of the selection pages. Point out that to *mandate* something means to "require it without exception." Then, model for students an *intoned* reading of the appropriate line from the essay. Finally, reinforce students' understanding of the words by having them work with partners to complete the following sentences.

1. Our school rules **mandate** that _____ _____ .

2. It is amusing that *droned* rhymes with **intoned** because _____ _____ .

3. **Invariably**, the clumsy waiter would _____ _____ .

4. Opening the package was **disillusioning** because _____ _____ .

OBJECTIVES

1. Read and interpret the essay
2. Identify purpose of anecdotes
3. Find the main idea
4. Express understanding through persuasive writing
5. Identify euphemisms and replace with more direct terms
6. Understand and use new words
7. Identify and define word roots

SKILLS

Literary
- Identify purpose of anecdotes

Reading
- Find the main idea

Writing
- Collect anecdotes
- Write a letter to the editor of a newspaper

Language
- Identify and analyze euphemisms

Vocabulary
- Use new words
- Define word roots

Planning

- **Block Schedule**
  Block Scheduling Lesson Plans with Pacing Guide

- **Traditional Schedule**
  Lesson Plans Including Strategies for English-Language Learners

- **One-Stop Planner**
  CD-ROM with Test Generator

people will also often whisper, assuming that since my eyes don't work, my ears don't either.

For example, when I go to the airport and ask the ticket agent for assistance to the plane, he or she will invariably pick up the phone, call a ground hostess, and whisper: "Hi, Jane, we've got a 76 here." I have concluded that the word blind is not used, for one of two reasons: Either they fear that if the dread word is spoken, the ticket agent's retina will immediately detach,[2] or they are reluctant to inform me of my condition, of which I may not have been previously aware.

On the other hand, others know that of course I can hear, but believe that I can't talk. Often, therefore, when my wife and I go out to dinner, a waiter or waitress will ask Kit if "he would like a drink" to which I respond that "indeed he would."

This point was graphically driven home to me while we were in England. I had been given a year's leave of absence from my Washington law firm to study for a diploma in law at Oxford University. During the year I became ill and was hospitalized. Immediately after admission, I was wheeled down to the X-ray room. Just at the door sat an elderly woman—elderly I would judge from the sound of her voice. "What is his name?" the woman asked the orderly who had been wheeling me.

"What's your name?" the orderly repeated to me.

"Harold Krents," I replied.

"Harold Krents," he repeated.

"When was he born?"

---

2. **retina** (ret′'n·ə) **will immediately detach:** The retina is the innermost lining of the eyeball. A detached retina can cause blindness.

WORDS TO OWN

invariably (in·ver′ē·ə·blē) *adv.*: always; without exception.

Summary ▪

In this essay Harold Krents, who has been blind since birth, describes with humor his various encounters with people who assume that because he cannot see, he also cannot speak or hear. The worst misconception people have about him, though, is that he is unable to work. Krents is persuasive in demonstrating to readers that people with disabilities are capable of working. Though he is gratified by workplace policies that mandate equal-employment opportunities for people with disabilities, he looks forward to the day when they are considered just as capable as other people.

Resources ———

Listening
Audio CD Library
A recording of this essay is provided in the *Audio CD Library:*
• Disc 14, Track 10

Ⓐ Elements of Literature
Anecdote
❓ What point is the writer trying to make with this brief story? [The writer is trying to show that people are reluctant to use the word *blind*.]

Ⓑ Reading Skills and Strategies
Looking for the Main Idea
❓ Which of the author's main ideas does this anecdote support? [The anecdote supports the author's contention that people often think he is generally incapacitated because he cannot see.]

  — ◎ — *Resources: Print and Media* —  —

Reading
• *Graphic Organizers for Active Reading,* p. 31
• *Words to Own,* p. 24
• *Audio CD Library*
    Disc 14, Track 10

Writing and Language
• *Daily Oral Grammar*
    Transparency 31
• *Grammar and Language Links*
    Worksheet, p. 51

Assessment
• *Formal Assessment,* p. 78
• *Portfolio Management System,* p. 150
• *Standardized Test Preparation,* p. 64
• *Test Generator (One-Stop Planner CD-ROM)*

LITERATURE AND THE LAW

A Time Line of Rights for the Disabled

1971: An episode of Julia Child's *The French Chef* is the first TV show captioned for hearing-impaired viewers. Twenty-two-year-old Judy Heumann, who has quadriplegia, founds Disabled in Action, a rights group.

1975: Education of All Handicapped Children Act guarantees free appropriate public education; final regulations delayed.

1988: Students at Gallaudet University for the hearing-impaired demand and finally get a deaf president; their protests shut down the campus.

1962: Ed Roberts, with quadriplegia, appeals the terms of his acceptance by the University of California at Berkeley. Roberts enters Berkeley, and the disability rights movement is born.

1973: Rehabilitation Act forbids discriminatory practices in employment and requires that federal buildings and federally funded services be accessible to disabled persons.

1977: Activists occupy San Francisco offices of the Department of Health, Education and Welfare for twenty-five days. Result: the 1973 and 1975 acts are more strictly enforced.

1990: President Bush signs the Americans with Disabilities Act, banning discrimination in jobs, transportation, and government services.

"When were you born?"

"November 5, 1944," I responded.

"November 5, 1944," the orderly <u>intoned</u>. This procedure continued for approximately five minutes, at which point even my saintlike disposition deserted me. "Look," I finally blurted out, "this is absolutely ridiculous. Okay, granted I can't see, but it's got to have become pretty clear to both of you that I don't need an interpreter."

"He says he doesn't need an interpreter," the orderly reported to the woman.

The toughest misconception of all is the view that because I can't see, I can't work. I was turned down by over forty law firms because of my blindness, even though my qualifications included a cum laude[3]

---

3. **cum laude** (koom lou′dā): Latin phrase meaning "with praise," used in college or university diplomas to indicate above-average grades.

---

degree from Harvard College and a good ranking in my Harvard Law School class.

The attempt to find employment, the continuous frustration of being told that it was impossible for a blind person to practice law, the rejection letters, based not on my lack of ability but rather on my disability, will always remain one of the most <u>disillusioning</u> experiences of my life.

Fortunately, this view of limitation and exclusion is beginning to change. On April 16, [1978,] the Department of Labor issued

---

WORDS TO OWN

intoned (in·tōnd′) *v.*: said or recited in a dull, unchanging tone.
disillusioning (dis′i·lōō′zhən·iŋ) *v.* used as *adj.*: disappointing; making one feel bitter.

LITERATURE AND THE LAW

Have students work in groups to research one of the events on the time line. Each group can share its research with the class.

A Struggling Readers
Finding Details

Ask students to identify personal details about the author that they have learned up to this point. Explain that some of the details are buried in the narrative. [Possible responses: He was born blind; he travels widely; he is married; he practices law but was on leave to study at Oxford; he was born in 1944.]

B Elements of Literature
Anecdote

? Why is this an amusing end to this anecdote? [Possible response: Although Krents clearly states he doesn't need an interpreter, the orderly continues to interpret anyway.] What three anecdotes has the author included up to this point in the essay? [the scenes at the airport, in the restaurant, and at the hospital]

C Critical Thinking
Drawing Conclusions

? Why do you think the author becomes more serious at this point in the narrative? [Possible responses: While the author is able to joke about some misconceptions about blindness, he finds no humor in misconceptions that restrict employment opportunities; because the author has worked so hard and has ability, he cannot take lightly the "blindness" of those judging him.]

Reaching All Students

Struggling Readers

Looking for the Main Idea was introduced on page 454. One good strategy to use with looking for the main idea is Most Important Word. For information on using this strategy, see p. 45 in the *Reading Strategies Handbook* in front of the *Reading Skills and Strategies* binder.

Advanced Learners

Tell students that Krents assumes first a humorous and then a serious tone in the essay. Have students work in pairs to note details that show tone. While one student reads the humorous first half of the selection aloud, a partner should fill in three or four details on a chart like the following:

Humorous	Serious
1. [people talking loudly]	1.
2.	2.
3.	3.

Partners should discuss the first half of the selection—making sure they agree on each of the listed details—before they switch roles and read the serious conclusion.

regulations that <u>mandate</u> equal-employment opportunities for the handicapped. By and large, the business community's response to offering employment to the disabled has been enthusiastic.

I therefore look forward to the day, with the expectation that it is certain to come, when employers will view their handicapped workers as a little child did me years ago when my family still lived in Scarsdale.

I was playing basketball with my father in our back yard according to procedures we had developed. My father would stand beneath the hoop, shout, and I would shoot over his head at the basket attached to our garage. Our next-door neighbor, aged five, wandered over into our yard

with a playmate. "He's blind," our neighbor whispered to her friend in a voice that could be heard distinctly by Dad and me. Dad shot and missed; I did the same. Dad hit the rim; I missed entirely; Dad shot and missed the garage entirely. "Which one is blind?" whispered back the little friend.

I would hope that in the near future, when a plant manager is touring the factory with the foreman and comes upon a handicapped and a nonhandicapped **D** person working together, his comment after watching them work will be, "Which one is disabled?" **E**

WORDS TO OWN
mandate (man′dāt′) v.: require; formally order.

MEET THE WRITER

Independent and Proud of It

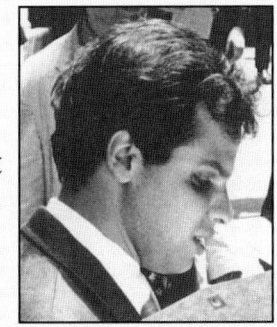

Harold Krents (1944–1987) titled his autobiography *To Race the Wind* (1972) because when he was three, he used to try to run faster than the wind, racing ahead of his mother. Because he was almost totally blind and was running on city sidewalks, he sometimes crashed into lampposts and parking meters. His family raised him to be independent. When Krents was nine, for example, his older brother threw passes at him until Krents could catch the football he couldn't see:

66 It was this confidence, which I received from every member of my family, that gave me the strength to attempt, to fail, and to try again until the goal, whatever it happened to be, was achieved. 99

Playwright Leonard Gershe, who heard Krents being interviewed on the radio, was "bowled over by this boy's humor and healthy attitude about his situation." This inspired Gershe to write *Butterflies Are Free* (1969), a successful play about a visually impaired young man living alone in a city.

Krents practiced law in Washington, D.C., and was a lifelong advocate for the rights of all people with disabilities. He advised presidents and helped establish Mainstream, Inc., an organization that works for legal rights for the disabled.

D **Reading Skills and Strategies**

Looking for the Main Idea

? Remind students that in an essay, the main idea or key elements that point to it can often be found in the first or last paragraphs. What point is the author making here? [He hopes that in the future, blind people will be considered just as capable as others.]

E **Vocabulary Note**
The Prefix *dis–*
On the board write the word *disabled* and explain that *dis–* is a prefix meaning "not." Ask volunteers to define the root word *able*. [capable, having ability] Ask students what effect the prefix has on the root word. [The prefix transforms the root into its opposite; *disabled* means "not able" or "not capable."] Have students name other words with this prefix. [Sample words: disagree, disappear, dislike.]

BROWSING IN THE FILES
About the Author. Krents exhibited extraordinary courage and determination to live a normal life in a world he could not see. In high school, he became president of the student body. As an adult, he took up serious reform issues. Always he impressed people with his wry outlook and quick wit. His 1972 autobiography, *To Race the Wind*, was adapted for a television movie.

Resources ————

Selection Assessment
Formal Assessment
• Selection Test, p. 78
Test Generator (One-Stop Planner)
• CD-ROM

Assessing Learning

Check Test: Questions and Answers
Answers will vary slightly.
1. How do some people alter their voices when responding to the author? [They shout or whisper.]
2. What misconception do the people in restaurants and at the hospital have about Krents? [They believe he cannot speak for himself.]
3. How many firms refused to hire Krents because of his blindness? [over forty]

4. What did the Department of Labor mandate on April 16, 1978? [equal-employment opportunities for the handicapped]

Standardized Test Preparation
For practice with standardized test format specific to this selection, see
• *Standardized Test Preparation,* p. 64
For practice in proofreading and editing, see
• *Daily Oral Grammar,* Transparency 31

MAKING MEANINGS

First Thoughts

1. Possible responses: intelligent, humorous, confident, optimistic, persistent, independent.

Shaping Interpretations

2. Krents's tone is humorous at first and then becomes serious yet optimistic when he discusses his difficulties in finding work. Details that help create a humorous tone include anecdotes and exaggerations; details that create a serious tone include factual information about Krents's job search.

3. Possible responses: The airport anecdote indicates that people with disabilities want to have their limitations dealt with frankly. The hospital anecdote shows that some people's attitudes are absurd. The basketball anecdote demonstrates that people with disabilities and people without physical limitations can perform on an equal basis.

4. Possible main ideas: People can be illogical and thoughtless in the ways they treat people with disabilities; people with disabilities should be treated just like anyone else. Supporting details include the anecdotes about the restaurant, hospital, airport, and basketball game. Possible meanings of the title: Krents lives in darkness no matter what the time of day; the inability of the sighted to acknowledge the blind as equals is true darkness.

Connecting with the Text

5. Students may say a disabled person wants to be treated with frankness, sensitivity, and respect.

Grading Timesaver

Rubrics for each Choices assignment appear on p. 150 in the *Portfolio Management System.*

CHOICES: Building Your Portfolio

1. **Writer's Notebook** Suggest that students browse through the editorial section of their local newspaper to see how writers use anecdotes to persuade their readers.

2. **Persuasive Writing** Have students brainstorm a list of places that are accessible and inaccessible.

T458

MAKING MEANINGS

First Thoughts

[connect]

1. Jot down some words or phrases that describe Harold Krents's character and personality as you see them.

Shaping Interpretations

[analyze]

2. Krents deals with a serious personal issue in a way that's designed to appeal to readers. Describe his essay's **tone**. What details create that tone?

[infer]

3. Tell what point you think Krents is making with each of the **anecdotes** about events at the airport, in the hospital, and in a backyard basketball game.

[interpret]

4. How would you summarize the essay's **main ideas**? What details does Krents use to support these ideas? What do you think the unusual **title** means?

Connecting with the Text

[connect]

5. Look back at your Quickwrite notes. How does a disabled person really want to be treated? Would you want to add anything to Krents's main points?

> **Reading Check**
>
> a. Summarize one **anecdote** that shows how Krents doesn't want to be treated.
>
> b. Which **anecdote** shows how he *wants* to be treated?
>
> c. Describe his job-hunting experience after law school.
>
> d. What rules did the Department of Labor issue about jobs for people with disabilities?

CHOICES: Building Your Portfolio

Writer's Notebook

1. Collecting Ideas for a Persuasive Essay

Anecdotes to persuade. Professional writers often advise: "Write what you know." Review your notebook and find a controversial topic you have firsthand knowledge about. Think of some anecdotes—your own experiences or observations, true stories you've read or heard—that will help convince your readers that your opinion on this issue is correct. List these anecdotes in your notebook. Save your notes for possible use in the Writer's Workshop on page 478.

Persuasive Writing

2. Expressing Your Views

Look around you—at your school and at your community's sidewalks, streets, transportation system, and public buildings. How easily can a person with a disability get around? Write a letter to the editor of your local newspaper expressing your views about what changes need to be made. Be sure you don't use the fallacies mentioned on page 453.

458 THE NONFICTION COLLECTIONS

> **Reading Check**
>
> a. Sample responses: When asking for help at the airport, Krents is referred to as a "76"; in a restaurant, the waiter asks Krents's wife to order for him.
>
> b. The basketball anecdote reveals how Krents wants to be treated.
>
> c. Krents was rejected by more than forty law firms because of his blindness.
>
> d. In 1978, the Department of Labor issued rules requiring equal-employment opportunities for people with disabilities.

Communications Handbook H E L P

See Using a Dictionary; Using a Thesaurus.

Euphemisms—Language That Covers Up

On page 455, Harold Krents suggests two humorous reasons why airline employees might use a code term instead of the straightforward word *blind.* When a less direct word or phrase is used as a substitute for a term some people find offensive or distasteful, it is called a **euphemism** (yo͞o′fə·miz′əm). *Passed away,* for example, is a euphemism for *died;* a *pre-need arrangement* with a funeral home is really a prepaid funeral. Euphemisms aren't used only to spare feelings; sometimes they're used to mislead people or hide the facts. A *pre-owned car,* for instance, is a used car with a classier name.

Use each of the following euphemisms in a sentence, and then substitute the more direct word each one replaces. Do you notice the difference?

Euphemism	Direct Term
house of correction	prison
disinformation	lies
downsizing	firings, layoffs
depressed socio- economic area	slum

Try It Out

➤ For three TV programs in a row, listen carefully to every commercial. Then read your newspaper or newsmagazine very carefully. Pay attention to political speeches and quotes from public officials. List any euphemisms you discover. What, in each case, is the speaker or writer *really* saying? Be sure to share your findings with the class.

➤ Look for euphemisms in your own writing. In the revision stage, or when you review a peer's work, bracket any words or phrases you think are not direct enough. Then go back over your paper and see if you can find clearer, more forceful ways of saying what you mean.

VOCABULARY `HOW TO OWN A WORD`

WORD BANK

invariably
intoned
disillusioning
mandate

Word Origins: Look for the Roots

The **root** of a word is the part that carries the word's core meaning. Roots in English come from several languages because English has been borrowing words from different languages for centuries. Here are some Latin (L) and Greek (Gr) roots found in thousands of English words. How many words can you list that have these roots?

-aud-, "hear" (L)	-mit-, "send" (L)	-dem-, "people" (Gr)
-duc-, "lead" (L)	-chron-, "time" (Gr)	-phone-, "sound" (Gr)

Now, use a dictionary to locate the root of each word in the Word Bank. List at least two other words that share that root. If you like, you can put your information in graphic form.

DARKNESS AT NOON 459

Try It Out
Possible Answers
• Sample responses: *dental hygiene* for *tooth-brushing; digestive upset* for *nausea; public assistance* for *welfare.*
• Responses will vary based on individual student writings and revisions.

VOCABULARY

Possible Answers
−aud−: audacious, audible, auditory
−duc−: ductile, induce, deduce, produce
−mit−: transmit, remit, admit
−chron−: chronological, chronicle
−dem−: democracy, democratic, demographics
−phone−: telephone, xylophone, phonics, symphony
invariably: −var−; "to vary, change" (L); variable, various, variety
intoned: −ton−; "a sound" (L); intonation, monotone, tonality
disillusioning: −illu−; "a mocking" (L); illusion, illustration, illumine
mandate: −man−; "a hand" (L); mandatory, manipulate, manufacture

Resources ━━━━━

Language
• *Grammar and Language Links* Worksheet, p. 51

Vocabulary
• *Words to Own* Worksheet, p. 24

Language Link Quick Check

Match the euphemism with its plain English equivalent:
1. Permanent prehostility
2. Negative gain in test scores
3. Controlled flight into terrain
4. Reutilization marketing yard
5. Unlawful or arbitrary deprivation of life
6. Suboptimal
7. Vegetarian leather
8. Violence processing
9. Sufferer from fictitious disorder syndrome
10. Personnel surplus reduction

A. Junkyard [4]
B. Combat [8]
C. Killing [5]
D. Airline crash [3]
E. Lower test scores [2]
F. Employee layoffs [10]
G. Liar [9]
H. Failed [6]
I. Vinyl [7]
J. Peace [1]

OBJECTIVES

1. Read and interpret the essay
2. Distinguish facts from opinions
3. Analyze persuasive techniques
4. Express understanding through critical writing or social history/speaking and listening
5. Identify parallel structure and use it in writing
6. Understand and use new words
7. Construct word maps

SKILLS

Literary
- Distinguish facts from opinions

Reading
- Analyze persuasive techniques

Writing
- Collect evidence to support an opinion
- Write a letter

Grammar
- Use parallel structure

Vocabulary
- Use new words
- Construct word maps

Social History/Speaking and Listening
- Present an oral report on a social issue
- Discuss solutions for homelessness

Viewing/Representing
- Interpret an art work (ATE)
- Describe images (ATE)

Planning

- **Block Schedule**
  Block Scheduling Lesson Plans with Pacing Guide

- **Traditional Schedule**
  Lesson Plans Including Strategies for English-Language Learners

- **One-Stop Planner**
  CD-ROM with Test Generator

Before You Read

HOMELESS

Make the Connection

The Worst Thing

In this essay, Anna Quindlen takes a new approach to a problem she calls "the thing that seems most wrong with the world." Instead of talking about the problem, gathering statistics, complaining, and hoping it will go away, what does Quindlen want us to do?

Quickwrite

As you read, jot down some of the statements you agree or disagree with (you'll probably find some of each) and any statements you find puzzling.

Statements	My Comments
"You are where you live."	That doesn't sound right to me—people can be better than terrible places they live in.

 go.hrw.com
LEO 9-7

Elements of Literature

More Than Just the Facts

A **fact** is something that can be proved true, so what more do you need to persuade someone? Anna Quindlen does *not* just stick to the facts in this essay. She states her opinions (beliefs and judgments), tells stories, and shares her feelings.

> A **fact** is something that can be proved true. An **opinion** is a personal belief that can't be proved, only supported.

Reading Skills and Strategies

Analyzing Persuasive Techniques: How Does She Do It?

Facts and statistics—even when they're alarming—sometimes leave us cold. Skillful persuaders, however, can work on our feelings by using techniques like these:

- talking about real people instead of abstract issues
- relating issues to our own lives
- writing **subjectively,** that is, revealing their own thoughts and feelings
- viewing issues in a wide, historical context
- defining abstract terms

As you read Quindlen's essay, look for these and other persuasive techniques. How do they affect your reading of the essay?

Home is where the heart is.

Quilt for crib (c. 1885).

Courtesy of America Hurrah Archive, New York.

Preteaching Vocabulary

Words To Own

Call on volunteers to read aloud the Words To Own and their definitions listed at the bottom of the selection pages. Then, have students complete the following exercise.

1. Describe the **legacy** a grandparent might leave a grandchild.
2. Name something you love and would defend with **ferocity**.
3. List three things that might happen when someone becomes **enfeebled**.
4. Describe a **compromise** you have made with a friend or family member.
5. Explain what behavior is **customary** during the lunch period at your school.

Quilt for a crib (detail) (c. 1885).

HOMELESS
Anna Quindlen

Her name was Ann, and we met in the Port Authority Bus Terminal several Januaries ago. I was doing a story on homeless people. She said I was wasting my time talking to her; she was just passing through, although she'd been passing through for more than two weeks. To prove to me that this was true, she rummaged through a tote bag and a manila envelope and finally unfolded a sheet of typing paper and brought out her photographs.

They were not pictures of family, or friends, or even a dog or cat, its eyes brown-red in the flashbulb's light. They were pictures of a house. It was like a thousand houses in a hundred towns, not suburb, not city, but somewhere in between, with aluminum siding and a chain-link fence, a narrow driveway running up to a one-car garage and a patch of back yard. The house was yellow. I looked on the back for a date or a name, but neither was there. There was no need for discussion. I knew what she was trying to tell me, for it was something I had often felt. She was not adrift, alone, anonymous, although her bags and her raincoat with the grime shadowing its creases had made me believe she was. She had a house, or at least once upon a time had had one. Inside were curtains, a couch, a stove, potholders. You are where you live. She was somebody.

I've never been very good at looking at the big picture, taking the global view, and I've always been a person with an overactive sense of place, the <u>legacy</u> of an Irish grandfather. So it

---

WORDS TO OWN

legacy (leg'ə·sē) *n.:* inheritance; something handed down from an ancestor or from the past.

HOMELESS **461**

Summary ■ ■

In her essay, Anna Quindlen uses a personal experience to illustrate her ideas about homelessness. She describes her meeting with Ann, a woman living at the Port Authority Bus Terminal in New York City, who displays photographs of a house, as if to prove she belongs somewhere. Quindlen goes on to characterize her own home as a place of stability, certainty, and privacy. She feels that referring to homeless individuals as a collective group—the homeless—makes the issue more distant and abstract and thus less personal.

(A) Elements of Literature
Fact and Opinion
? What are three facts Quindlen gives in the first three sentences? [The author met a woman whose name was Ann; they met in the Port Authority Bus Terminal; they met several years ago in January; Quindlen was doing a story on homeless people.] **What opinion does Quindlen report?** [Quindlen reports Ann's opinion that their conversation is a waste of the author's time.]

(B) Reading Skills and Strategies
Making Inferences
? Why do you think Ann says she is just passing through? [Possible response: She does not think of her situation as permanent.]

(C) Reading Skills and Strategies
Analyzing Persuasive Techniques
? Which of the persuasive techniques listed on p. 460 has Quindlen used in the second paragraph? [She has used the first three techniques: writing about real people instead of abstract issues; relating issues to our own lives; and writing subjectively.]

Resources: Print and Media

A Elements of Literature

Fact and Opinion

? What opinion about the world does Quindlen state here? [Homelessness is what is most wrong with the world right now.] Do you agree? Why or why not? [Sample responses: Yes, because shelter is a basic human necessity; no, because war and disease kill millions and death is worse than homelessness.]

B Critical Thinking

Analyzing

? According to Quindlen, what makes a home something more than a shelter? [A home is a place you care about, while a shelter merely protects you from the elements.]

RESPONDING TO THE ART

Jasper Johns (1930–) is a self-taught artist, sculptor, and printmaker. With his friend Robert Rauschenberg (see p. 297), he helped to found the Pop Art movement of the 1960s. *Fool's House* reveals his interest in ambiguity.

Activity. Explore with students how viewing a work of art, like reading a written work, involves making meanings. Ask students to interpret the word *fool* in relation to this work; does it mean "a silly person," "a jester," or something else? How does placing the labels, the broom, and the other objects in an artistic context change the viewer's perception of them? How might the homeless woman who longs for "one room, painted blue" respond to this work?

A is natural that the thing that seems most wrong with the world to me right now is that there are so many people with no homes. I'm not simply talking about shelter from the elements or three square meals a day or a mailing address to which the welfare people can send the check— **B** although I know that all these are important for survival. I'm talking about a home, about precisely those kinds of feelings that have wound up in cross-stitch and French knots on samplers[1] over the years.

Home is where the heart is. There's no place like it. I love my home with a <u>ferocity</u> totally out of proportion to its appearance or location. I love dumb things about it: the hot-water heater, the plastic rack you drain dishes in, the roof over my head, which occasionally leaks. And yet it is precisely those dumb things that make it what it is—a place of certainty, stability, predictability, privacy, for me and for my family. It is where I live. What more can you say about a place than that? That is everything.

Yet it is something that we have been edging away from gradually during my lifetime and the lifetimes of my parents and grandparents. There was a time when where you lived often was where you worked and where you grew the food you ate and even where you were buried. When that era passed, where you lived at least was where your parents had lived and where you would live with your children when you became <u>enfeebled</u>. Then, suddenly, where you lived was where you lived for three years, until you could move on to something else and something else again.

And so we have come to something else again, to children who do not understand what it means to go to their rooms because they have never had a room, to men and women whose

---

1. cross-stitch and French knots on samplers: embroidery designs sewn on cloth with sayings like "Home Sweet Home."

WORDS TO OWN

ferocity (fə·räs′ə·tē) *n.*: fierceness.
enfeebled (en·fē′bəld) *adj.*: weakened, usually by old age or illness.

---

462 THE NONFICTION COLLECTIONS

Fool's House (1962) by Jasper Johns. Oil on canvas with objects (72″ x 36″).

Jean Christophe Castelli, New York City. © Jasper Johns/Licensed by VAGA, New York, NY.

Reaching All Students

Struggling Readers

Analyzing Persuasive Techniques was introduced on p. 460. For a lesson directly tied to this selection that teaches students to analyze persuasion by using a strategy called Anticipation Guides, see the *Reading Skills and Strategies* binder:
• MiniRead Skill Lesson, p. 153
• Selection Skilll Lesson, p. 160

English Language Learners

Quindlen's essay contains descriptions of "typical" American homes. You may wish to bring in pictures or have other students describe such objects as "a chain-link fence," "aluminum siding," "a one-car garage," and "a patch of backyard." For other strategies for engaging English language learners with the literature, see
• *Lesson Plans Including Strategies for English-Language Learners*

Advanced Learners

Ask students how important a "sense of place" is in their own lives. Are they greatly attached to a physical home or not? Were they raised in a certain geographic area such as a small town, a suburb, or a city? Encourage each student to write an editorial about a related issue. Have students present their editorials to the class.

fantasy is a wall they can paint a color of their own choosing, to old people reduced to sitting on molded-plastic chairs, their skin blue-white in the lights of a bus station, who pull pictures of houses out of their bags. Homes have stopped being homes. Now they are real estate. **C**

People find it curious that those without homes would rather sleep sitting up on benches or huddled in doorways than go to shelters. Certainly some prefer to do so because they are emotionally ill, because they have been locked in before and they are damned if they will be locked in again. Others are afraid of the violence and trouble they may find there. But some seem to want something that is not available in shelters, and they will not <u>compromise</u>, not for a cot, or oatmeal, or a <u>shower</u> with special soap that kills the bugs. "One room," a woman with a baby who was sleeping on her sister's floor once told me, "painted blue." That was the crux[2] of it: not size or location, but pride of ownership. Painted blue.

This is a difficult problem, and some wise and compassionate people are working hard at

2. **crux** (kruks): basic or deciding point.

it. But in the main I think we work around it, just as we walk around it when it is lying on the sidewalk or sitting in the bus terminal—the problem, that is. It has been <u>customary</u> to take **D** people's pain and lessen our own participation in it by turning it into an issue, not a collection of human beings. We turn an adjective into a noun: the poor, not poor people; the homeless, not Ann or the man who lives in the box or the woman who sleeps on the subway grate.

Sometimes I think we would be better off if we forgot about the broad strokes and concentrated on the details. Here is a woman without a bureau. There is a man with no mirror, no wall to hang it on. They are not the homeless. They are people who have no homes. No drawer that holds the spoons. No window to look out upon the world. My God. That is everything.

WORDS TO OWN

compromise (käm′prə·mīz′) v.: give up something to receive something desired; settle for less than what one wants.

customary (kus′tə·mer′ē) adj.: usual; established by custom.

C Reading Skills and Strategies
Finding the Main Idea
? This passage contains one of the essay's main ideas. What is the difference between a home and a piece of real estate? [Real estate is something physical that can be bought and sold, but a home is a place that evokes feelings of belonging and a sense of family and stability.]

D Reading Skills and Strategies

Analyzing Persuasive Techniques
? Which techniques from the list on p. 460 is Quindlen using in this passage? [She is writing subjectively, revealing her own thoughts and feelings on the subject of homelessness, and talking about real people instead of abstract issues.]

MEET THE WRITER

"The Unknown and the Everyday"

Even before she graduated from Barnard College, **Anna Quindlen** (1953–) sold a story to *Seventeen* magazine and landed a job as a staff reporter at the *New York Post*. In 1977, she moved to *The New York Times*, starting as a reporter and later becoming a columnist. Her columns, "Life in the 30s" and "Public and Private," addressed personal and political issues that affect us all. Quindlen is an avid reader and the mother of three children.

Books and children appear frequently in her writing:

❝ Reading has always been life unwrapped to me, a way of understanding the world and understanding myself through both the unknown and the everyday. If being a parent consists often of passing along chunks of ourselves to unwitting—often unwilling—recipients, then books are, for me, one of the simplest and most sure-fire ways of doing that. ❞

Quindlen's pursuit of "the unknown and the everyday" won her the Pulitzer Prize for commentary in 1992. These days Quindlen is a full-time novelist living in New Jersey.

BROWSING IN THE FILES
About the Author. Anna Quindlen says that writing a column is like having a dialogue with someone she happens not to see. She gained national attention through such "conversations" and proved that essay writing doesn't have to be stuffy and boring.

HOMELESS 463

Assessing Learning

Check Test: True–False
1. Ann showed the author pictures of her family. [False]
2. Quindlen assumed that Ann was homeless because she had been living in the Port Authority Bus Terminal for a while. [True]
3. The thing that seems most wrong with the world, according to Quindlen, is that so many people are without homes. [True]

4. Quindlen is dissatisfied with her home. [False]
5. Quindlen believes that the era has passed in which most families establish a sense of place. [True]

Standardized Test Preparation
For practice in proofreading and editing, see
• *Daily Oral Grammar*, Transparency 32

A young girl describes her visit to a shelter for battered women and their children.

Ⓐ Reading Skills and Strategies

Responding to the Text

❓ If you were in the author's shoes, would you have been reluctant to visit The Haven? Explain. [Sample response: Reluctance is probably a normal reaction; since the people living there have had some harsh experiences, the visit might be disturbing.]

Ⓑ Critical Thinking

Speculating

❓ What kinds of "tales of despair and fear" do you think the trees could tell? [They could tell stories about the women and their children who are staying at The Haven—why they are there and how the families became homeless.]

Resources

Selection Assessment

Formal Assessment
- Selection Test, p. 80

Test Generator (One-Stop Planner)
- CD-ROM

A House Is Not a Home

Several months ago, when the weather was still warm and many people were trying to get the most out of the remaining days of summer, my mother and I volunteered to be part of a group bringing food for a picnic to The Haven. The Haven is **Ⓐ** the only home in Oakland County for battered women and their children. I didn't know what to expect, and I must confess that I was a little reluctant to go.

The Haven is actually a big old house on a heavily shaded street. From the outside it could be any old house. The mighty trees manage to keep the house cool. **Ⓑ** I suspect these tall, full trees have tales of despair and fear to tell, but they, like the residents who stay there, are silent. The yard has been turned into a playground. It is not the colorful state-of-the-art kind you find in the suburbs. Instead it is a grassless area with a few rickety swings and a basketball hoop without a net.

We brought chicken, potato chips, and chocolate chip cookies. We set the food on a picnic table, and the mothers and their children joined us. It was a bit awkward at first, not so much for the children, who didn't seem to care, but for the women, who seemed quiet and self-conscious. They were average-looking women with not-so-average experiences. I wondered about the very young children. I wondered what they must think about the kind of world this is. . . .

—Layne Sakwa
Andover High School
Bloomfield Hills, Michigan

College student volunteers help to clean up a neighborhood.

Connecting Across Texts

Connecting with "Homeless"
Ask students to discuss what the inhabitants of The Haven have in common with the subjects of Quindlen's essay. [Possible responses: Both are without permanent places to live; both have experienced suffering; both must face society's indifference.] **Point out that both authors focus on the idea that a home is much more than a building.**

Crossing the Curriculum

Art
Have students create drawings or collages that illustrate their homes, hometowns, or other favorite personal places. Ask students to try to show how the locations they have chosen reflect their individual identities. Create a "personal places" display with students' finished work.

MAKING MEANINGS

First Thoughts

[connect]

1. Which **facts** or **opinions** in Quindlen's essay did you find most important or significant or disturbing? Look back at your Quickwrite notes.

Shaping Interpretations

[infer]

2. What do you think was Quindlen's motive in writing this essay?

[infer]

3. What do you think Quindlen wants the reader to do or to believe when she says, "It has been customary to take people's pain and lessen our own participation in it by turning it into an issue, not a collection of human beings"?

[analyze]

4. Suppose you were reorganizing the selections in this book. Look at the titles of the collections. Could Quindlen's essay and the student essay (opposite) fit somewhere else? Why or why not?

[analyze]

5. Fill out a chart like the one at the right to show all the **persuasive techniques** Quindlen uses in her essay. Which ones do you think are the most powerful?

States facts	
Quotes statistics	
States opinions	
Talks about real people	
Relates issues to readers' lives	
Reveals feelings	
Shows the historical context	

Challenging the Text

[evaluate]

6. Quindlen believes that homelessness is a major problem. Her source is a series of interviews. Do you think interviews are a credible source? Are they enough, or are statistics also necessary? Give your reasons.

[connect]

7. What do you think of Quindlen's choice of homelessness as "the thing that seems most wrong with the world to me right now"? What seems most wrong in the world to you?

[connect]

8. The media is often criticized for intruding on people's private lives or making news out of people's suffering. What do you think of these criticisms? Do you think journalists like Quindlen perform a public service by writing articles like this one, or do you think people like Ann should be left alone? Share your opinions with other readers.

Reading Check

Using a chart like the one that follows, summarize the **main idea** and the supporting **details** of Quindlen's editorial. Use your own words and as many boxes as you need.

Main Idea

Supporting Details
1.
2.

HOMELESS 465

Reading Check

Responses will vary.

Main Idea:

The thing most wrong with the world today is that there are so many people without homes (p. 462, ll. 1–3).

Supporting Details:

1. We have lost the old notion of home as a place of certainty, stability, predictability, and privacy.

2. The loss of family-oriented communities makes having a home of one's own even more important.

3. A shelter is an inadequate compromise because it is not truly a home.

4. By thinking of the homeless as an impersonal group, we distance ourselves from their pain.

MAKING MEANINGS

First Thoughts

1. Students may cite Ann's situation as a disturbing fact; or they may be upset by the author's opinion that our society treats homes as mere real estate.

Shaping Interpretations

2. Possible motives: She wants her readers to stop depersonalizing the homeless; she feels so strongly about the importance of a sense of place that she needed to tell others her opinions.

3. Quindlen wants readers to see homeless people as individuals rather than as a faceless group with a label attached.

4. They could fit into Collection 6, "A Place Called Home," because they deal with the importance of having a home. They could also fit into Collection 5, "We Remember," because the accounts of Ann and the battered women discuss people that are often forgotten by society.

5. Charts will vary. Quindlen uses all the techniques except quoting statistics. Students may consider Quindlen's most powerful technique her interview with Ann, a real person.

Challenging the Text

6. Some students may feel that if the interviews were backed up by statistics, the scope of the problem would be even more persuasive. Others might think that the individual examples of homelessness collected by the author are more moving than any cold numbers could be.

7. Possible response: Quindlen's choice is justified because a home is a necessity. Other wrongs include hunger, war, poverty, and prejudice.

8. Sample response: Sensitive journalists like Quindlen perform a public service by encouraging people to think about difficult issues. Other journalists are intrusive; they sensationalize people's misfortunes for their own gain. Although homeless people who seem healthy and who cause no problems might be left alone, those who are ill should be helped.

Rubrics for each Choices assignment appear on p. 151 in the *Portfolio Management System*.

CHOICES: Building Your Portfolio

1. **Writer's Notebook** Newspapers and news magazines are good source material for evidence.
2. **Expressing an Opinion** As a class, discuss responses to each question before students begin to write.
3. **Social History/Speaking and Listening** Work with the class to create a chart like the following before they give their reports.

Issue	Opinion	What Should Be Done
violent crimes	too many in our community	**A.** Require community service for offenders. **B.** Organize neighborhood-watch programs.

4. **Social History/Speaking and Listening** If students need help coming up with solutions, encourage them to contact nonprofit organizations, such as the Coalition for the Homeless or Habitat for Humanity, or consult a resource such as *The Kid's Guide to Social Action* by Barbara A. Lewis.

RESPONDING TO THE ART

Sculptor **Michael Lucero** (1953–) works primarily in clay. *White House Dreamer* is one of the works in his series entitled *Dreamers*. The "dreamers" are oversized heads displayed on their sides (turning the textbook sideways will make the head evident). From the tops of their skulls rise a variety of features—here, a cluster of mesas—and landscapes are painted on their faces. Presumably, the figures are "dreaming" about a favorite personal place.
Activity. Ask students to describe images that Anna Quindlen might use if she created a similar sculpture.

CHOICES: Building Your Portfolio

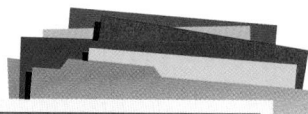

Writer's Notebook

1. Collecting Ideas for a Persuasive Essay

Supporting your opinion.
Remember that you can't *prove* an opinion. The closest you can come is to support your opinion with overwhelmingly convincing evidence. Examples, anecdotes, statistics, and quotations from experts are kinds of evidence that you can use to persuade your readers. You should have a list of possible topics for a persuasive essay for the Writer's Workshop on page 478. Select a topic you have especially strong feelings about and collect some evidence to support your opinion.

Expressing an Opinion

2. This Is Just to Say

How did Anna Quindlen's essay affect you? Did it change your thinking or feelings about homelessness? Will it affect your actions? Let the author know. Write a letter to Quindlen, sharing your thoughts about her essay and the problem of homelessness.

Social History/Speaking and Listening

3. Speaking Up

What problems do you see in this country, in your community, or in your school that you feel people are "working around"? Take a stand on one issue and make notes on what you think should be done. Then present your ideas in a brief, informal report to the class. Be sure to state your opinion clearly and back it up.

Social History/Speaking and Listening

4. What to Do?

Homelessness hasn't gone away; in many cities, it's increased. With a group, brainstorm three possible reasons for homelessness and then discuss possible solutions. See if you can reach a consensus (agreement among everybody). Share your ideas with the class.

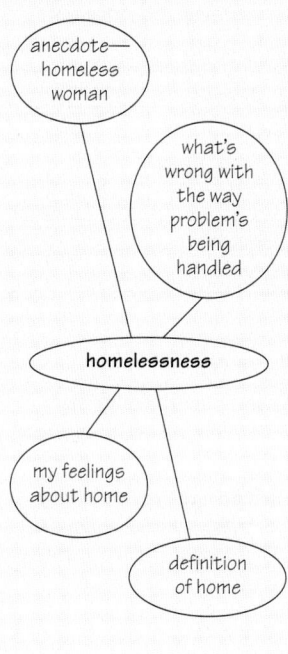

White House Dreamer (1983) by Michael Lucero.

The Metropolitan Museum of Art, New York. Purchase, Marcy and Josef Mittleman Gift, 1983. (1983.587).

Using Students' Strengths

Kinesthetic Learners

For Choice 1, provide index cards for students to use when recording examples, anecdotes, statistics, and quotations. Students can easily manipulate the cards when organizing their ideas.

Visual Learners

Students working on Choice 3 may want to display the main ideas of their reports on poster boards.

GRAMMAR LINK   MINI-LESSON

Language
Handbook
HELP

See Improving Sentence Style, page 1017.

Parallel Structure—Keeping Things Balanced

Related items in a sentence should be expressed in a similar way. Single words should be matched with other single words, phrases with phrases, and clauses with clauses. This kind of balanced writing is called **parallel structure**. Careful writers make sure they use parallel structure when related ideas are doing the same work in a sentence.

FAULTY	She was not adrift, alone, someone without a name.
PARALLEL	"She was not <u>adrift, alone, anonymous</u>. . . ." [three single-word predicate adjectives]
FAULTY	Quindlen writes about her feelings, her impressions, and thinking.
PARALLEL	Quindlen writes about <u>her feelings, her impressions, and her thoughts</u>. [three nouns, all objects of a preposition, modified by pronouns]

Try It Out

Edit the following sentences for parallel structure. There's more than one way to create parallel structure in each sentence. Be sure to compare your revisions in class.

1. Let's solve this problem quickly and to be efficient.
2. Everyone complains that homelessness is serious, urgent, and a problem that's difficult.
3. People who want to solve the problem can't seem to agree about what to do or how it should be done.

VOCABULARY   HOW TO OWN A WORD

WORD BANK

legacy
ferocity
enfeebled
compromise
customary

Mapping an Unfamiliar Word

One trick to owning a word is figuring out what you already know about it. Take *customary*, for example. A word map like the one here, which organizes some ideas about *customary*, will help you get to know a new word better. Fill out this map for *customary* and then make word maps of your own for the other words in the Word Bank.

- meaning
  - •
- things that are customary for me
  - •
  - •
- **customary**
- things that aren't customary for me
  - •
  - •
- sample sentence
  - •

HOMELESS 467

GRAMMAR LINK

Try It Out

Possible Answers

1. Let's solve this problem quickly and efficiently.
2. Everyone complains that homelessness is a serious, urgent, and difficult problem.
3. People who want to solve the problem can't seem to agree about what should be done first or how the problem should be eliminated.

VOCABULARY

Possible Answer

- **meaning**
  - savagery
  - cruelty
  - fierceness
- **things that show ferocity**
  - lion
  - grizzly bear
  - hurricane
- **ferocity**
- **sample sentence**
  We are all amazed at the ferocity of the blizzard.
- **things that do not show ferocity**
  - kitten
  - baby
  - friend

Resources

Grammar
- *Grammar and Language Links* Worksheet, p. 53

Vocabulary
- *Words To Own* Worksheet, p. 25

Grammar Link Quick Check

Underline the parallel constructions in each sentence from "Homeless."

1. "I've never been very good at <u>looking at the big picture, taking the global view</u>. . . ."
2. "I love dumb things about it [home]: <u>the hot-water heater, the plastic rack you drain dishes in, the roof over my head</u>, which occasionally leaks."
3. "And so we have come to something else again, <u>to children who do not understand what it means to go to their rooms . . . to men and women whose fantasy is a wall they can paint, . . .to old people reduced to sitting on molded-plastic chairs</u>. . . ."
4. "Certainly some prefer to do so <u>because they are emotionally ill, because they have been locked in before</u>. . . ."
5. "We turn an adjective into a noun: <u>the poor</u>, not poor people; <u>the homeless</u>, not Ann. . . ."

OBJECTIVES

1. Read and interpret the essay
2. Analyze humor
3. Summarize the main idea
4. Express understanding through creative writing or research/speaking
5. Identify homonyms and use them correctly in writing
6. Understand and use prefixes and suffixes

SKILLS

Literary
- Analyze humor

Reading
- Summarize the main idea

Writing
- Develop opinions and counter-arguments for a persuasive essay
- Write about a place

Language
- Identify and use homonyms

Vocabulary
- Use prefixes and suffixes

Research/Speaking
- Research and report on the history of English spelling

Planning

- **Traditional Schedule**
  Lesson Plans Including Strategies for English-Language Learners
- **One-Stop Planner**
  CD-ROM with Test Generator

Before You Read

MISSPELLING

Make the Connection

Signs of the Times

You've probably heard many times that it's important to spell words correctly, but it isn't always easy. See what Charles Kuralt discovered about spelling "on the road" in the United States.

Quickwrite

Suppose we suddenly toss out all spelling rules, dictionaries, and spelling checkers. You are free to spell words any way you want. Quickwrite for a few minutes about what the results might be.

 go.hrw.com
LE0 9-7

Elements of Literature

Humor

Persuasive writers sometimes use **humor**—to make us laugh, of course, but also to make a point. If we find something funny, we'll keep on reading and maybe think twice about the writer's ideas. How can the topic of correct spelling possibly be funny? See what you think of the signs Kuralt mentions and his wry comments on them.

Reading Skills and Strategies

Summarizing the Main Idea

When you finish reading an essay, such as Kuralt's essay on spelling, you should be able to state the writer's main ideas in your own words. Here is a strategy for monitoring your reading that will help you get a writer's point: Stop at the end of each paragraph and see if you can quickly sum up the meaning of the paragraph. Try doing this with Kuralt's essay as you read.

"How can it be misspelled? I just made it up!"

© 1992; Reprinted courtesy of Bunny Hoest and *Parade* Magazine.

Reaching All Students

Struggling Readers

These students may have difficulty with English spelling. You might want to start by reading aloud the poem on p. 471. Point out that the poet's rhymes help with the pronunciation of end words, e.g.,"lose" and "choose," "ward" and "sword." Ask them to review their own writing and make a list of words that they often misspell.

English Language Learners

The inconsistent spelling conventions of the English language can make learning to spell and pronounce certain words tricky. Ask for volunteers to share their difficulties in trying to master spelling rules and exceptions. Then, reassure students that this essay points out that many people have problems with spelling—not just English language learners. The selection also makes the point that spelling mistakes may not always be that critical and can sometimes be taken lightly.

T468

Misspelling

Charles Kuralt

They say this is an age of conformity, but wherever we go, we keep finding refreshing evidence of individualism, even on the roadside signs. You know that no stuffy conformist painted this sign: PARK HEAR. It is spelled wrong, but it does tell you where to park: "hear"! MACHANIC ON DUTY. FRONT END REPAIRES. This mechanic may not be good at spelling, but he's probably fine at making "repaires." Anything which can be sold, we have found, can also be misspelled . . . ANTIQES . . . anything from "antiques" to "souvenirs" . . . SOUVINERS . . . especially "souvenirs" . . . SOUVENIERS. How *do* you spell "souvenirs"? SOUVENIRES. This is the American answer: just exactly as you please!

We have found our country's spelling to be horrible, and entirely excusable. ACERAGE FOR SAIL—we may excuse this man

Summary ■

In his travels Charles Kuralt has read a lot of roadside signs—and found refreshing evidence of individualism in the unique spellings that are displayed. In this brief essay, Kuralt uses humor to persuade readers to delight in these misspellings, reading them as signs of a lively and diverse society.

Ⓐ Elements of Literature
Humor
❓ How does the author's tone in the first two sentences hint that the essay will not be entirely serious? [Possible responses: The informal "You know," the characterization of good spellers as "stuffy" conformists, and the "PARK HEAR" sign indicate that the essay will be playful or humorous.]

Ⓑ Reading Skills and Strategies

Summarizing the Main Idea
When students are asked to summarize a paragraph, remind them to look at its first and last sentence. Often repeated words or concepts will help them find the main idea. Ask students to summarize the main idea in the opening paragraph. [Possible response: Americans' tendency to misspell words is an expression of nonconformity or individuality.]

Ⓒ Critical Thinking
Challenging the Text
❓ Do you agree that misspellings are excusable? [Possible responses: Yes, people are more concerned about communicating an idea than about proper forms; or no, misspellings are a sign of laziness.]

  *Resources: Print and Media*

Reading
• *Graphic Organizers for Active Reading*, p. 33

Writing and Language
• *Daily Oral Grammar* Transparency 33
• *Grammar and Language Links* Worksheet, p. 55
• *Language Workshop CD-ROM*

Assessment
• *Formal Assessment*, p. 82
• *Portfolio Management System*, p. 152
• *Standardized Test Preparation*, p. 66
• *Test Generator (One-Stop Planner* CD-ROM)

Internet
• go.hrw.com (keyword: LE0 9-7)

A Reading Skills and Strategies

Drawing Conclusions

? What does Kuralt conclude about the man who misspelled *spaghetti,* and why does he draw this conclusion? [Kuralt assumes that the man is a foreigner because of the types of food he is selling.]

B Elements of Literature

Humor

? Kuralt creates humor by emphasizing the size of the lighted sign containing the misspelled word. Do you think Kuralt (and his readers) would find the sign as funny if it were not large and lighted? [Possible answers: Yes, the misspelling itself makes it funny; or no, it's the fact that the misspelling is projected so proudly that makes it funny.]

C Critical Thinking

Determining Author's Purpose

? What do you think is Kuralt's purpose in focusing so much on "No Trespassing" signs? [Possible responses: It's a humorous way of pointing out that individualism can be taken to an extreme—the exclusion of other people; it's a humorous way of pointing out that many Americans are protective of their privacy.]

D Reading Skills and Strategies

Summarizing the Main Idea

The first sentence of this paragraph expresses the main idea of the essay. Have students paraphrase the sentence. [Sample response: Spelling in the United States is weak, but people show individuality and still manage to get their message across.]

A because he's a farmer, not a schoolteacher. RASBERIES—so is this man. SPEGHETTI AND PIZZA—and this man because he's probably from across the sea. BEER AVAILABE HERE—and this man because, like as not, he was sampling his own product while he painted the sign. BAR DRINKS 55¢ ANEYTIME—that can blur anybody's memory of how to spell.

B Some misspellings are quiet and private, like this one in the back room of an Oklahoma diner: BE CURTEOUS AND SMILE. Others are spectacular, like this one in Oregon—(*huge lighted sign*) BAR AND RESTRUANT—and proclaim their error proudly for half a mile in every direction. HUNGARY? MARION'S SNACK SHACK 6 MILES. If you are hungary enough, of course, it doesn't matter much.

C NO TRESSPASSING. We like the snappy, rude signs. NO TRASPASSING. You get the idea. NO TRUSTPASSING. Keep out. NO BOATS ALOUD—silent boats OK, but no boats aloud.

D The point about American spelling is that, however awful, it serves the cause of individualism and serves the purpose. We read this one at a gas station in Tennessee: NO CONGRETATING ON THE DRIVEWAY. VIALTORS WILL BE PROSCUATED. Well, naturally we didn't congretate. Fearing proscuation, we paid for our gas and pulled right out of there and headed on down the road.

MEET THE WRITER

A Roving Reporter

When **Charles Kuralt** (1934–1997) was a boy on his grandparents' North Carolina farm, he "traveled" the world by reading *National Geographic* magazines. As an adult, he spent his life on the road—first as a radio and TV reporter in Europe and Latin America covering political strife, war, and terrorism. In 1967, Kuralt decided to change direction:

66 I got the idea . . . one night in an airplane as I looked down at the lights in the countryside and wondered . . . what was going on down there. There are a lot of Americans who don't live in cities and don't make headlines. I was interested in finding out about them. **99**

He started reporting offbeat, human-interest stories for radio and TV and stayed on the road for the next thirty years. He traveled in a secondhand camper from one end of the country to the other, searching for what he jokingly called unimportant, irrelevant, and even "resolutely insignificant" stories for his program *On the Road.* His wit and unusual perspective on everything from lumberjacks to unicyclists made his audience see an America they never knew existed.

Assessing Learning

Check Test: True-False

1. The author is praising conformity. [False]
2. The author discusses words that are misspelled on signs. [True]
3. The author believes that all spelling rules should be done away with. [False]
4. The author feels that misspellings reflect American individualism. [True]

Standardized Test Preparation

For practice with standardized test format specific to this selection, see
• *Standardized Test Preparation,* p. 66
For practice in proofreading and editing, see
• *Daily Oral Grammar,* Transparency 33

Hints on Pronunciation for Foreigners

T.S.W.

I take it you already know
Of tough and bough and cough and dough?
Others may stumble but not you,
On hiccough, thorough, lough, and through?
5   Well done! And now you wish, perhaps,
To learn of less familiar traps?

Beware of heard, a dreadful word
That looks like beard and sounds like bird,
And dead: it's said like bed, not bead—
10   For goodness sake don't call it "deed"!
Watch out for meat and great and threat.
(They rhyme with suite and straight and debt.)
A moth is not a moth in mother
Nor both in bother, broth in brother,
15   And here is not a match for there
Nor dear and fear for bear and pear,
And then there's dose and rose and lose—
Just look them up—and goose and choose,
And cork and work and card and ward,
20   And font and front and word and sword,
And do and go and thwart and cart—
Come, come, I've hardly made a start!
A dreadful language? Man alive!
I'd mastered it when I was five!

Drawing by Modell; © 1970
The New Yorker Magazine, Inc.

Modell

MISSPELLING 471

First Thoughts
1. Sample responses: The essay fir... because Kuralt presents his ... views on misspellings; the ... not fit because the hu... and tone are not c... those of the ot...

Shaping I...
2. Kural...

...ght have
...een purposefully created to trap people. Can you think of some "traps" that the poet might be referring to? [Answers will vary. Possibilities include *veer* and *seer; sleight* and *weight*.]

B Reading Skills and Strategies
Summarizing the Main Idea
Point out to students that this poem is basically a list. What is the main idea the poet is trying to convey with this list? [English is a difficult language because words that are spelled alike are often pronounced differently.]

Resources
Selection Assessment
Formal Assessment
• Selection Test, p. 82
Test Generator (One-Stop Planner)
• CD-ROM

Skill Link

Listening and Speaking: Pitch and Tone of Voice
Point out that the humor of T.S.W's poem relies on the inconsistent pronunciation of certain similarly spelled words, for example, *heard* and *beard*. An effective reading of the poem would emphasize these words through careful use of pitch and tone. Call on volunteers to read aloud stanzas from the poem, varying the pitch of their voices and using a mock-serious tone to try to make the audience laugh.

Connecting Across Texts

Connecting with "Misspelling"
Discuss with students the similarities between this poem and Kuralt's essay. [They both explore the topic of spelling, and they are both amusing.] Ask students to offer examples of humor from each selection that they particularly liked. What is each author's attitude about the lack of consistency and logic in English spelling? [Both seem to think that this problem should be addressed with humor rather than criticism.]

Ask students what focus each writer has taken in addressing the pitfalls of English. [Kuralt focuses on the casual attitude many Americans have toward spelling; they tend to spell a word according to the way it sounds. T.S.W. focuses on pronunciation; he warns English language learners that spellings are often illogical and inconsistent and that this makes pronunciation difficult.]

T471

personal
e essay does
morous topic
onsistent with
er essays.

...terpretations

...t's attitude is good-natured
...d tolerant. He states his attitude
directly when he says that misspelling shows "refreshing evidence
of individualism" (p. 469).

3. Some students may say that misspellings can lead to misunderstandings and even legal problems. Others
may agree with Kuralt that most
misspellings "serve the purpose."

Extending the Text

4. Students who agree may cite
the way in which television and
other forms of media expose all
Americans to the same images and
messages. Those who disagree may
cite the diversity of hair and clothing
styles as evidence that Americans
care about individuality.

5. Learning to speak English is difficult
because words with similar spellings
are often pronounced differently
and words that are pronounced the
same (homonyms) often have different spellings and meanings. Other
pronunciation problems include *paid*
and *said, daughter* and *laughter*.

Grading Timesaver

Rubrics for each Choices assignment
appear on p. 152 in the *Portfolio
Management System*.

CHOICES:
Building Your
Portfolio

1. **Writer's Notebook** Students
might want to work in pairs—a
partner can help formulate the
counterarguments.
2. **and 3.** Ask students to brainstorm for two minutes about places
or spelling topics they would like to
explore.

MAKING MEANINGS

First Thoughts

[connect]

1. Do you think Kuralt's essay belongs in
a collection called "What I Think"?

Shaping Interpretations

[infer]

2. How do you think Kuralt feels about
misspellings? Does he describe his
attitude directly or let the reader infer
it?

[connect]

3. How do you feel about the need to spell English words correctly? Look back
at your Quickwrite notes.

Extending the Text

[connect]

4. Do you agree that we live in an "age of conformity"? Why, or why not?
Besides the misspellings on roadside signs, how do you think Americans
show "refreshing evidence of individualism"?

[infer]

5. How is the problem described in "Hints on Pronunciation . . ." (see
Connections on page 471) related to English spelling? (Don't miss the
chance to read this poem aloud.) What other pronunciation problems can
you add to this list?

> **Reading Check**
> Summarize the **main idea** of
> this essay. If you find **humor** in
> it, give examples of details you
> smiled at.

CHOICES: Building Your Portfolio

Writer's Notebook

1. Collecting Ideas for a Persuasive Essay

Be prepared for opposing views. You
have your
opinion; others may hold
opposing views. Check your
notebook for topics you've
been considering for the
Writer's Workshop on page
478. Select a topic and
formulate your opinion on it.
Now imagine what people
who disagree with your

opinion might say. How
would they attack your
reasons and evidence? Take
notes for the **counter-
arguments** you could use
to refute your opponents
(attacks on what they say and
further defense of your
position).

Creative Writing

2. Going Places

Using "Misspelling" as a
model, choose a place (your
hometown or a place you've
visited) and write a short
feature about it. What is

unique or unusual about the
place and its residents?

Research/Speaking

3. Spelling's History

Who decides what's correct
and not correct? What's a
lexicographer? Who wrote
the first dictionaries, and how
are they written now? With a
small group, research some
aspect of the history of
English spelling and share
your findings with the class.
You might want to report on
the work of Samuel Johnson
and Noah Webster.

> **Reading Check**
> Sample Answer: The essay is about the
> amusing misspellings Americans create and
> how these can be interpreted as expres-
> sions of individuality. Humorous details
> include the idea that the "No Boats Aloud"
> sign means that only silent boats are per-
> mitted and the huge lighted sign on which
> the word *restaurant* is misspelled.

LANGUAGE LINK `MINI-LESSON`

Technology HELP

See Language Workshop CD-ROM. *Key word entry:* homonyms.

Communications Handbook HELP

See Using a Dictionary; Proofreaders' Marks.

Homonyms—Words That Sound Alike

Some of the spelling mistakes Kuralt discovers are pesky **homonyms** (häm′ə·nimz′), words that are pronounced alike but spelled differently. What homonyms are mixed up in the following signs?

NEWS AND WHETHER
THREE DAZE LEFT
I BREAK FOR ANIMALS

A spelling checker on your computer won't catch these mistakes; the words are spelled correctly, but they're the wrong words.

Another difficulty is that the same sound can be spelled in many ways. The poem on page 471 illustrates these "eye rhymes," words that look as if they're pronounced alike but aren't.

Whenever you write, proofread your work carefully to make sure you've got the right word in the right place and that you've spelled it correctly. Use a dictionary whenever you're in doubt.

> ### Try It Out
>
> 1. Correct all the misspelled signs Kuralt mentions.
>
> 2. Make up a dozen signs, some containing misspellings, and exchange your signs with a partner. You might use some of the following homonyms: *sent/scent, led/lead, course/coarse, peace/piece, plane/plain.* Correct each other's misspellings.
>
> ➤ Which homonyms cause you trouble? Keep a list of trouble-makers in your proofreading log, and refer to it whenever you use these sound-alike words in your writing.

VOCABULARY `HOW TO OWN A WORD`

Powerful Prefixes, Stupendous Suffixes

Prefixes and suffixes can't usually stand alone, but they can totally change the words they're attached to. A **prefix** is a word part that is added to the beginning of a word; a **suffix** is a word part that's added to the end of a word.

1. *Mis-* turns a word into its opposite. Describe a misfortune. Name three things you wouldn't do with someone you mistrusted.
2. *Dis-, non-,* and *un-* also mean "no" or "not." Which of these prefixes can you add to each of these words to give them a negative meaning: likely, appear, important, sense?
3. Don't confuse the look-alike prefixes *ante-* (before) and *anti-* (against). Which prefix would you use to describe someone who is against smoking? What does antedate mean?
4. The suffix *-ist* means "someone who (does a particular action)." Give an example of how two people—a conformist and a nonconformist—might behave at a wedding.
5. The suffixes *-ism* and *-ion* turn words into nouns. They mean "the act or condition of (doing or being something)." How would you turn the verb correct into a noun? What does tourism mean?

MISSPELLING **473**

LANGUAGE LINK

Try It Out
Possible Answers

1. Corrections: Park Here; Mechanic on Duty; Front End Repairs; Antiques; Souvenirs; Acreage for Sale; Raspberries; Spaghetti and Pizza; Beer Available Here; Bar Drinks 55¢ Anytime; Be Courteous and Smile; Bar and Restaurant; Hungry? Marion's Snack Shack 6 Miles; No Trespassing; No Boats Allowed; No Congregating on the Driveway; Violators Will Be Prosecuted.
2. Signs should include homonyms, as well as transposed letters and other common misspellings.

VOCABULARY
Possible Answers

1. It would be a *misfortune* if someone borrowed your bike and you never saw it again. If you *mistrusted* someone, you would not lend that person your car, go into business with him or her, or reveal a secret.
2. *unlikely, disappear, unimportant, nonsense*
3. *antismoker; antedate* means "to come before or to label with a date earlier than the actual date"
4. A *conformist* would probably dress up for a wedding, whereas a *nonconformist* would wear shorts and sandals.
5. *Correction* is the noun form of *correct. Tourism* means "traveling for fun."

Resources ———

Language
• *Grammar and Language Links* Worksheet, p. 55

Language Link Quick Check

Replace the underlined words in the sentences below with appropriate homonyms.

1. The author has a neighbor keep the male while he is on the road. [mail]
2. Kuralt does not say he wants to council people about their misspellings. [counsel]
3. Witch sign did you find the most humorous? [Which]
4. Weather or not you laughed, you will agree the essay is well written. [Whether]
5. Your likely to notice more humorous spelling errors from now on. [You're]

OBJECTIVES

1. Read a brief reflection
2. Find thematic connections across genres
3. Generate relevant and interesting discussion
4. Recognize distinctive and shared characteristics of cultures through reading and discussion

Extending the Theme

The narrator of this reflection describes the way outsiders misjudge her neighborhood. They drive through, feeling tense and scared, because of preconceived ideas and stereotypes about Hispanic neighborhoods. However, the narrator also sees similar attitudes in people from her neighborhood when they venture into unfamiliar places. People have a hard time seeing those in other ethnic groups as individuals, the narrator observes, which is what keeps the cycle of prejudice going round.

RESPONDING TO THE ART

Graffiti is not a modern phenomenon; archaeologists have found similar scrawlings on ancient buildings and monuments in many parts of the world.

Activity. Ask students to speculate about the impulse behind such scrawls. Are the markings simply territorial, or do they serve other purposes? Also discuss how the boy in the photograph may feel about his surroundings. [He seems sure of himself and comfortable in his surroundings.]

Quickwrite

Them and us. We sometimes divide the world that way. What makes people suspicious or even afraid of other people? Is it the way they look, the place they live in, the way they talk, or something else? Write down some of your ideas.

go.hrw.com
LE0 9-7

474 THE NONFICTION COLLECTIONS

Reaching All Students

Struggling Readers
Ask students to record the details in the vignette on two lists, one headed "Us" and the other "Them." Then, have the students summarize the narrator's views of "Us" and "Them." What does she say about each group?

English Language Learners
The short length of "Those Who Don't" makes it perfect for reading aloud. Pair English language learners with partners who are fluent in English and can model the reading before they trade roles. Suggest that the partners also discuss how the author creates a certain tone and rhythm by her use of such words and phrases as "shakity-shake" and "rolled up tight."

Advanced Learners
Remind students that the word *prejudice* is related to the word *prejudging*. As they read the vignette, ask them to concentrate on what Cisneros is implying about prejudice and prejudging. Suggest that they compare and contrast her ideas on the subject with those of other writers. Have them write a paragraph or two to wrap up their thoughts.

Those Who Don't

Sandra Cisneros

Those who don't know any better come into our neighborhood scared. They think we're dangerous. They think we will attack them with shiny knives. They are stupid people who are lost and got here by mistake.

But we aren't afraid. We know the guy with the crooked eye is Davey the Baby's brother, and the tall one next to him in the straw brim, that's Rosa's Eddie V., and the big one that looks like a dumb grown man, he's Fat Boy, though he's not fat anymore nor a boy.

All brown all around, we are safe. But watch us drive into a neighborhood of another color and our knees go shakity-shake and our car windows get rolled up tight and our eyes look straight. Yeah. That is how it goes and goes.

They think we're dangerous.

Making the Connections

Connecting to the Theme: "What I Think"

Sandra Cisneros says a lot about human emotions and reactions in this vignette, as do the other writers in this collection. Ask students to compare the thoughts expressed in the various selections and make a generalization that can be applied to all of them. [Sample response: The writers believe that people of different races, classes, and ethnic groups sometimes view each other with distrust and prejudice, rather than celebrating or accommodating diversity.]

Have students work together to create a bulletin board display titled What I Think. Students may create collages, sketches, lists of rules, posters, and statements of belief, or find quotations, articles, and other items that reflect their opinions about the things they have read about in this collection. Students who are talented in art may design the display.

FINDING COMMON GROUND

As its name suggests, this feature is meant to initiate lively discussion among students in order to discover areas of agreement in response to the literature.

1. Ask students to work with partners to complete a chart like the following, comparing the ideas in their Quickwrites with the narrator's views in "Those Who Don't."

PEOPLE ARE OFTEN SUSPICIOUS ABOUT	NARRATOR IS SUSPICIOUS ABOUT
Those who are unfamiliar	Going into unfamiliar neighborhoods
Anyone who looks dangerous	Knowing others are looking at her and her friends

2. After groups have finished their discussions, have them combine all of their responses into one chart on poster board. They may need to condense two similar ideas into one.

3. Have groups add a column to their charts titled "How to Deal with Suspicion and Fear." Brainstorm with the class to generate some ideas, and remind students to review selections in this collection that address the treatment of other people.

4. Ask each group to form one statement of approximately twenty words about learning tolerance and respect for others. Have the groups write and illustrate their statements and display them in the classroom.

MEET THE WRITER

Sandra Cisneros (1954–   ), poet, essayist, and short-story writer, began writing at the age of ten. "Those Who Don't" is a vignette from her first book, *The House on Mango Street* (Vintage). For a biography of Cisneros, see page 184.

FINDING COMMON GROUND

1. Compare the notes from your Quickwrite with Cisneros's little reflection.

2. In a group, discuss and compare your responses.

3. With your group, talk about ways mutual suspicion and fear can be dealt with. Bring in examples from your own experience and from what you've learned from history and from stories—perhaps from some selections in this book.

4. Write down and present to the class at least one way your group feels people can learn to live together with more tolerance and respect.

476 THE NONFICTION COLLECTIONS

Assessing Learning

Check Test: True-False

1. Some people are scared when they come into the narrator's neighborhood. [True]
2. The narrator says these people are stupid and lost. [True]
3. People who live in the neighborhood are scared of Fat Boy and Davey the Baby's brother. [False]
4. When they are in a strange neighborhood, the narrator and her friends feel comfortable. [False]

READ ON

Ask Andy

If you've ever watched CBS's *60 Minutes* on Sunday night, you've heard Andy Rooney's wry, offbeat observations of the world around him. In his best-selling collection of essays, *Not That You Asked . . .* (Penguin), Rooney tries to persuade you to see things his way. His topics range from textbooks to leftovers, from baseball to holiday cards.

A Seat at the Front of the Bus

When Rosa Parks boarded a bus in Montgomery, Alabama, on December 1, 1955, she was about to play an important role in the civil rights movement. She sat in an empty seat and quietly refused to give it up to a white passenger. *Quiet Strength* (Zondervan) is Parks's own story of the civil rights movement, a story of pride, commitment, and courage.

Everyday Laughs

In *Dave Barry's Greatest Hits* (Fawcett/Columbine), Dave Barry makes fun of TV commercials, mutant fleas, newspaper columnists (like himself), and just about anything else you might encounter.

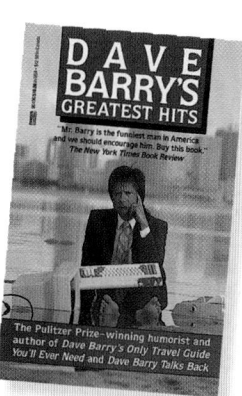

One Woman's Views

In *In Search of Our Mothers' Gardens* (Harcourt Brace), you'll meet Alice Walker up close and personal. In this collection of essays, she writes about her life, her family, her writing, and her political views.

MAIN OBJECTIVE
Write a persuasive essay

PROCESS OBJECTIVES

1. Use appropriate prewriting techniques to identify and develop a topic
2. Create a first draft
3. Use evaluation criteria as a basis for determining revision strategies
4. Revise the first draft incorporating suggestions generated by self- or peer evaluation
5. Proofread and correct errors
6. Create a final draft
7. Choose an appropriate method of publication
8. Reflect on progress as a writer

Planning

- **Block Schedule**
  Block Scheduling Lesson Plans with Pacing Guide
- **One-Stop Planner**
  CD-ROM with Test Generator

BUILDING YOUR PORTFOLIO
Writer's Workshop

Technology HELP

See Writer's Workshop 2 CD-ROM. *Assignment: Controversial Issue.*

ASSIGNMENT

Write a persuasive essay about a debatable issue you feel strongly about.

AIM

To persuade.

AUDIENCE

Your classmates, members of a club, readers of a local newspaper. (You choose.)

PERSUASIVE WRITING
PERSUASIVE ESSAY

Have you ever been sure you were right but you couldn't convince the person you were talking to? You'll sharpen your skills of **persuasion** as you write this essay, and you'll be able to use the same skills with your friends and family (when you're trying to persuade your brother to lend you his car), in school (when you're trying to convince your teacher to give an essay test as a final), and at work (when you're trying to persuade your boss that you deserve a raise).

Prewriting

1. Choose a Topic

Check your Writer's Notebook for topic ideas. If you're still undecided, brainstorm with a small group for more ideas. The topic that you choose should meet these criteria:

- **You care about the issue.** To be convincing, you need to feel strongly about your topic.
- **Reasonable people disagree on the issue.** "War is bad" and "Eating is important" aren't topics that most people have serious disagreements on.
- **You can research the issue.** Choose a current topic so you can easily find evidence to support your views (facts, examples, quotations).

2. What Do You Think?

Before you take a stand on an issue, you may need to do some research. Once you figure out what you think, write a **thesis statement** that clearly states your view.

3. Who's Your Audience?

Tailor your argument to fit your specific audience. What are their main concerns? What are their biases? What do they know about the issue? What reasons will they find most convincing?

478 THE NONFICTION COLLECTIONS

 *Resources: Print and Media*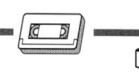

Writing and Language
- *Portfolio Management System*
  Prewriting, p. 153
  Peer Editing, p. 154
  Assessment Rubric, p. 155
- *Workshop Resources*
  Revision Strategy Teaching Notes,
  p. 35

Revision Strategy Transparencies, 18, 19
- *Writer's Workshop 2 CD-ROM,*
  Controversial Issue

Assessment
- *Standardized Test Preparation,* pp. 108, 116

T478

4. Elaborate: Use Logical Appeals

You can elaborate on your thesis statement by developing a **logical argument** step by step. First, draft two or three statements that express your **reasons** for believing that your opinion is the best one possible. Then, use **supporting evidence—facts, statistics, examples, anecdotes,** and **quotations**—to illustrate the validity of your reasons. As you develop your argument, be sure to avoid fallacies (see page 453), or errors in logic—they make your point of view less convincing.

5. Use Emotional Appeals

It helps to appeal to readers' feelings. In both "Homeless" (page 461) and "Darkness at Noon" (page 454), **anecdotes** make the writers' points more powerfully than facts could. **Loaded words** can also influence your audience's emotional response.

6. Plan What You'll Say

- The **introduction** should grab the readers' attention and contain your thesis statement.
- The **body** states your argument point by point and gives reasons in **order of importance**. As in a debate, you'll attack the opposing views in **counterarguments**. A pro-con chart like this one will help you plan your essay.

Con: Against Curfew	Pro: For Curfew	Counterarguments
Innocent teens will be punished.	It will decrease crime and violence.	Are there statistics to prove this?
Teens who work late at necessary jobs will be stopped by police.	Smaller number of teenagers on street means less crime.	Crime occurs at home, in other places.

- The **conclusion** may include a **call to action** that asks your audience to do something specific, like write a letter.

Try It Out

The daily news is a good source of topics for a persuasive essay. Write a thesis statement expressing your opinion on each of these recent laws.

- In an Oregon city parents are held responsible for crimes committed by their children under eighteen. Parents may be fined $1,000 and required to attend classes on parenting and/or alcohol and drug abuse.

- In an Indiana city it's illegal to wear gang colors or emblems in school and to carry a cellular phone or pager to communicate with a gang member.

Find two more news stories and write a thesis statement expressing your opinion of each one.

Language/Grammar Link
H E L P

Connotations and loaded words: page 451. Euphemisms, page 459.

WRITER'S WORKSHOP 479

Drafting

- Before beginning their drafts, have students examine the Student Model on this page. Use the annotations in the pupil's book and the questions below to guide discussion about the techniques the writer has used.
- Remind students to double-space their drafts. They should also leave extra space in the right margin. These blank spaces will be used for comments and editing marks.

Sentence Workshop
HELP

Combining sentences using clauses: page 483.

Using the Model

After reading the model aloud, discuss the side annotations with students. Then, focus discussion on the following questions:

? In the first few paragraphs, what are some of the loaded words the writer has used to evoke an emotional reaction in her readers?

? Does the writer include a thesis sentence in this piece? If so, which sentence is it?

? Why is it a good idea for the writer to include the opposing side's arguments?

? What do you consider the writer's strongest argument in convincing her readers? Why?

Drafting

1. Say It Simply and Clearly

Wordiness weakens your argument by making it hard for your audience to follow your reasoning, so be as clear and direct as Chief Joseph is in the speech on page 447. The repetition of a catchy phrase may be effective because it stays in the reader's mind, but you should cut unnecessary repetition and padding.

2. Watch Your Tone

No one will believe you if you sound unsure of yourself, so eliminate "hedge words" (like *probably, possibly, maybe,* and *perhaps*) and phrases like "I think," "I feel," "I believe," "in my opinion," and "it seems to me."

Student Model

TICK TOCK

Headlines: The *Atlanta Constitution* newspaper reports that an eleven o'clock curfew will be imposed upon persons sixteen years of age and younger who live in the city of Atlanta. Young people who do not comply with this order may be detained by the police. Further, fines may be imposed upon the parent(s). Throughout the ages, youth have had to watch the clock. They have lived under the "Cinderella" beliefs of guardians who seem to think that when the clock strikes twelve, the adolescents' "Air Jordans" will turn into brogans or combat boots, leading them to trouble and shame.

Surely a curfew serves some beneficial purposes. For example, requiring that a youth be in a designated place as expected by his or her parents helps to teach discipline and responsibility. Clearly, there are times when circumstances may necessitate that groups of people obey laws imposed on them for the safety of society. However, this usually occurs when a state of emergency exists, and other means of control have failed. In the case of Atlanta, one may question whether there is a state of emergency, or whether the rights of adolescents are being violated by the city-imposed curfew. One thing is certain, many teens and parents are watching the clock—tick tock. The question is whether the assumption that "early to bed" (or home) results in fewer crimes is fair and therefore should be enforced on adolescents.

Despite the seemingly good intentions of a curfew for Atlanta's urban teens, there are many disadvantages that accompany this approach. For example, as is true with all mass punishments, some innocent teens will be forced to bear the embarrassment and constraints of having to abide

Attention-grabbing introduction.

Fairy tale allusion is clever idea.

Here are two opposing arguments supporting the curfew. Counter-arguments.

Clock sounds repeated throughout the essay, a kind of refrain.

Writer uses deductive approach.

Reason 1 and evidence.

480 THE NONFICTION COLLECTIONS

Using Students' Strengths

Auditory Learners

Some students might benefit from working with a partner on their drafts. You may want to pair each student with another who will ask questions and record responses. Have one student question the other about supporting reasons, opposing arguments, and their refutation. Students can then switch roles.

Visual Learners

Have students complete a graphic like the one below as an informal plan for their essays:

Introduction with thesis

↓

Reasons 1-3 with details to support thesis

↓

Opposing arguments with refutation

↓

Conclusion with call to action

WEAK | There are four reasons that I can think of that explain why I think that the curfew probably isn't a good idea.

STRONGER | The curfew is a bad idea for four reasons.

Evaluating and Revising

1. Peer Review

Read your draft aloud to your writing group or give it to them to read. Ask them for feedback on parts of your essay that concern you. For example: Do you think the anecdote works better at the beginning or at the end of the essay? Is my third reason strong enough? Is there enough supporting evidence?

Publishing Tips

- Turn your essay into a speech.
- Conduct a panel discussion or a debate with students who have written about the same issue.
- Include your main points in a letter to the editor of your local newspaper.

---

by a curfew for which they have no need. The teens who followed the rules given by their guardians and enjoyed a later curfew than is now allowed by the city of Atlanta are being unduly punished. Indeed, such a state of affairs may result in the "good" teen rebelling. Tick tock—parents and teens are watching the clock.

Each paragraph ends with clock sounds.

Many adolescents are gainfully employed, helping pay for such things as their clothes, cars, and entertainment. Some youths are even helping to sustain the family household or pay for their education. Even if these youths are able to verify why they are out past curfew, this does not spare them the humiliation of being stopped and questioned by the police. Nonetheless, tick tock—these youths must watch the clock.

Reason 2 and elaboration.

Many crimes do not occur on the street. Often, crimes are as prevalent in the household, at neighboring residences, or establishments where people congregate. Bringing the adolescent "home" does not necessarily yield the desired "safe and sound" outcome that people concerned about public safety in Atlanta are searching for. In spite of this, tick tock—teens must be off the street at the stroke of the clock.

Reason 3 and logical appeals.

While the leaders of Atlanta may be applauded for good intentions in terms of public safety, the imposition of a curfew on a select group of people based solely on their age, as a means to prevent crime, is questionable. Until it is proven that teens are more likely than any other age group to commit offenses after eleven o'clock, they should not have to be watchful of the ticking of the clock.

Conclusion.

Strong ending with clock sound.

—Ashaki M. Brown
Brookwood High School
Snellville, Georgia

Evaluating and Revising

Have students use the Evaluation Criteria provided on p. 482 to review their drafts and determine needed revisions. Remind students that they should evaluate their papers twice, once for content and organization and once for style. If students are trying to improve their style by varying sentence structures, have them turn to the Sentence Workshop on p. 483 for help with sentence combining.

Proofreading

- Have students proofread their own papers first and then exchange them with another student. For this assignment, remind students to look especially for misspelled words that are homonyms, like there and their, and for problems with parallel structure.
- If time permits, the final copy should be put aside for at least a day before it is proofread one last time by the author.

Publishing

Remind students of the options given on this page. If students choose to write about a school issue, they could prepare their papers for public display on a bulletin board.

Getting Students Involved

Cooperative Learning

Have students work in groups to become advertising analysts. Groups should choose two ads from different media (print, television, radio, direct mail). Then, groups should analyze and give oral reports on the persuasive techniques used in the ads they have selected. The following questions can be used to guide the investigations:

- What product, service, or cause is the ad selling?
- What logical appeals are used? How sound are they?
- How are emotional appeals made? Look at language, visuals (consider content, color, style), music, and the use of celebrity endorsements.
- Does the ad work? Why or why not?

Reflecting

If students add their essays to their portfolios, have them date their papers and attach a brief reflection based on these questions:

- What was difficult for me? What will I do differently next time?
- What is the strongest part of my argument? What is the weakest?
- Why am I including this essay in my portfolio?

Resources

Peer Editing Forms and Rubrics
- *Portfolio Management System,* p. 154

Revision Transparencies
- *Workshop Resources,* p. 35

Language/Grammar Link
H E L P

Homonyms: page 473.
Parallel structure: page 467.

■ *Evaluation Criteria*

A good persuasive essay

1. *has an attention-grabbing introduction and a clear thesis statement*

2. *provides at least two strong reasons that are supported by evidence*

3. *may also contain emotional appeals*

4. *states the opposition's arguments and refutes them*

5. *presents an effective conclusion that may include a call to action*

Communications Handbook
H E L P

See Proofreaders' Marks.

2. Self-Evaluation

As you read your essay to yourself, focus first on content. Are your reasons clearly identified? (You might state them as topic sentences or add transitions, such as *first, second, most important, finally.*) Read your draft a second time for style, paying attention to the way the sentences sound together. Are the ideas smoothly connected? Maybe you can combine some sentences by using participial phrases or adjective or adverb clauses.

Revision Model

	Peer Comments
Many crimes do not occur on the	*Clear topic sentence.*
are as prevalent in the household, at	
street. Often, crimes ~~occur in other~~	
neighboring residences, or establishments	
where people congregate.	
places. Bringing the adolescent	*What places? Be specific.*
"home" does not necessarily yield	
concerned about public	
"safe and sound" *safety in Atlanta*	*What outcome? What people?*
the desired outcome that people are	
In spite of this,	
searching for. Tick tock—teens	*A transition here would help.*
must be off the street at the stroke	
of the clock.	

482 THE NONFICTION COLLECTIONS

Grading Timesaver

Rubrics for this Writer's Workshop assignment appear on p. 155 of the *Portfolio Management System.*

Assessing Learning

Standardized Test Preparation
For practice with standardized test prompts and formats, see
- *Standardized Test Preparation,* pp. 108, 116

Sentence Workshop

OBJECTIVES
1. Combine sentences using adjective and adverb clauses
2. Recognize the functions of adjective and adverb clauses

COMBINING SENTENCES: CLAUSES

When you want to combine two short sentences and make their relationship clearer, you can often make one of them into a subordinate clause.

You can make a sentence into an **adjective clause** by inserting a word like *who, which,* or *that* in place of the subject and moving the clause so that it clearly modifies a noun or pronoun.

They are people. They have no homes.

"They are people <u>who have no homes</u>." (page 463)

An **adverb clause** may modify a verb, an adjective, or another adverb. You can make a sentence into an adverb clause by using a subordinating conjunction like *if, because, until, unless, when,* or *although.*

This point was graphically driven home to me. We were in England.

"This point was graphically driven home to me <u>while we were in England</u>." (page 455)

When you combine sentences using subordination, you usually have many choices. Notice in the sentences above that the subordinate clause could be some other group of words or it might be placed at another spot in the sentence.

1. When the point was graphically driven home to me, we were in England.
2. We were in England when the point was graphically driven home to me.

Writer's Workshop Follow-up: Proofreading

To see how useful clauses are in combining sentences, go back to a piece of writing you are working on. Find at least three sets of sentences you could combine by making one sentence in each set into a subordinate clause. Then, exchange papers. Can your peer reviewer suggest variations?

Language Handbook
HELP

See Clauses, page 1009.

Technology HELP

See Language Workshop CD-ROM. *Key word entry: clauses.*

Try It Out

Act as an editor and combine the following sentences by using adjective or adverb clauses. Be sure to compare your rewritten sentences in class to see if any variations are possible.

1. The Nobel Committee awarded Elie Wiesel the peace prize in 1986. They called him "a messenger to mankind."
2. Mother Teresa began her work in India. Her work to aid the poor has spread all over the world.

SENTENCE WORKSHOP 483

Resources ─────

Workshop Resources
• Worksheet, p. 73
Language Workshop CD-ROM
• Clauses

Try It Out
Possible Answers
1. When Elie Wiesel was awarded the peace prize in 1986, the Nobel Committee called him "a messenger to mankind."
2. Mother Teresa's work to aid the poor, which began in India, has spread all over the world.

Assessing Learning

Quick Check: Combining Sentences with Clauses

Use adjective or adverb clauses to combine each pair of sentences below. Answers will vary.
1. This is the lifeguard. He is in charge of the pool. [This is the lifeguard who is in charge of the pool.]
2. Sue had a great time at the reunion. She saw many family members. [Sue had a great time at the reunion because she saw many family members.]
3. We were on vacation. Someone broke into our house. [When we were on vacation, someone broke into our house.]
4. Jim carries camping supplies. The camping supplies will fit in his backpack. [Jim carries camping supplies that will fit in his backpack.]
5. Mr. Rodriquez is our English teacher. I greatly admire him. [Mr. Rodriquez, whom I greatly admire, is our English teacher.]

T483

OBJECTIVES

1. Develop strategies for critical reading of editorials
2. Distinguish between facts and opinions
3. Recognize logical fallacies
4. Recognize emotional appeals
5. Analyze and evaluate tone
6. Evaluate an author's effectiveness in an editorial

Teaching the Lesson

You may want students to work in small groups to answer the questions listed under Using the Strategies. Before students work on these questions, find an example of an editorial and model the critical thinking necessary to analyze and evaluate an editorial. Put the editorial on a transparency and work through the questions. Advise students that editorialists often put their thesis statement (opinion) in the title of the editorial.

Using the Strategies

Possible Answers

1. The writer wants the reader to support his or her cause and believe that libraries need more money to offer Internet access.
2. Opinions: Computers are a necessary part of life; wisely, the governor has allocated more money to libraries. Facts: 20 percent of school libraries and 60 percent of public libraries offer Internet access; the proposed budget allocates $90.3 million; $11 million more is needed according to the state library association.
3. "*beleaguered* libraries"
4. Yes, the writer was persuasive; Internet access is important, and the facts indicate that libraries do not yet have enough money to meet access demands. No, the writer was not persuasive; he or she seems to exaggerate the necessity of computers and the Internet.

Situation

The headline of this editorial catches your eye because it reminds you of the Quickwrite for "Those Who Don't." Use these strategies as you read and evaluate editorials.

Strategies

Separate fact from opinion.

- Are you reading facts or opinions? Most editorials are a mix of both. **Facts** are statements that can be verified, or proved. **Opinions** are beliefs that can be supported but not proved.
- Does the writer cite reliable sources for the facts and provide convincing support for the opinions? If the writer mentions opposing views, does he or she refute them?

Watch for fallacies.
Some editorials may contain these errors in logic:

- **Attacking the person:** name-calling. Example: *Those who don't agree are dumb.*
- **Circular reasoning:** restating an opinion as though it were a reason. Example: *We need more computers because we don't have enough.*
- **False cause and effect:** looking at two events that occurred in a row and con-

cluding that the first caused the second. Example: *Because the library offers Internet access, fewer books are stolen.*

- **Hasty generalization:** generalizing on the basis of only a few cases. Example: *Most people dislike spinach. I know this because no one in my family likes spinach.*

Recognize emotional appeals.

- Be aware of arguments that are based on loaded words or anecdotes. Such devices are legitimate tools in persuasion, but they shouldn't take the place of logical reasoning.

What do *you* think?

- Finally, decide whether or not you agree with the writer's

position. Why or why not? If the editorial includes a call to action (for example, to vote in a particular way), will you answer it?

Using the Strategies

1. What does the writer of the editorial above want the reader to believe and do?
2. Identify at least two opinions and four facts.
3. Find at least one example of loaded language.
4. Did the writer persuade you? Why or why not?

Extending the Strategies

Use the strategies discussed here to analyze an editorial in your school or local newspaper.

Erase the On-line Line Between Them and Us

Computers have now become a necessary part of life. At the dawn of the electronic age, some critics predicted that libraries would empty as people bought their own computers. Reality check: Libraries offering Internet access have been swamped by people unable to purchase a computer or pay monthly Internet access fees. Yet only 20 percent of the state's school libraries and 60 percent of the public libraries currently offer Internet access. Wisely, the governor's proposed budget allocates $90.3 million for putting beleaguered libraries on-line. But even more money is needed—$11 million more, according to the state library association. As the long waiting lines for existing terminals attest, the need is real. Lawmakers must find the money to ensure that on-line, "them" and "us" truly become "we the people."

—*Dover Hill Times*
February 9, 1999

484 THE NONFICTION COLLECTIONS

Crossing the Curriculum

History

Editorials are a perfect cross-curriculum connection to the study of current events. Have students look for examples of two editorials about a current event, one for each side of the issue. Then, have students use the strategies taught in this lesson to write a short analysis of the editorials. Finally, have students choose which editorial is most effective and explain their choice.

Learning for Life
Researching the Law

Problem

Consumers and laborers are protected by local, state, and federal laws. What about teenagers who work part-time? How about teenagers as consumers? What does the law say about your rights and responsibilities in the workplace and the marketplace?

Project

Find out how local, state, and federal laws affect what you can and cannot do as a teenage consumer and producer.

Preparation

1. Working with a small group, brainstorm to explore what you know about such laws.

2. Develop a list of questions to guide your search for facts. Questions like these will get you started:

   In the workplace. How many hours a week can I work? What should I do if my boss insists that I work more hours? What kinds of machines can I operate? What happens if I get hurt on the job? Is there a minimum-wage law?

   In the marketplace. Is joining a mail-order CD club the same as signing a contract? Can teenagers use layaway plans and get credit cards? If I want to start a business, what laws do I need to know about?

3. Decide which questions your group will tackle and how you'll divide them among the group members.

Procedure

1. Research and take notes on the questions you've chosen. Possible sources:

   • magazine and newspaper articles

   • law guides and handbooks for nonprofessionals

   • interviews with lawyers

   • the Internet

2. As you look for answers, watch for anecdotes as well as facts and figures. They're a good way to clarify and enliven legal jargon.

Presentation

Present your findings in one of these formats (or another that your teacher approves):

1. On-line Q & A

Work with your group to prepare a question-and-answer page for your school's Web site. Be sure to cite the sources you used so that other students will know where to go for more information. Ask the editor of the school paper to print a notice about the new page and the way to access it.

2. Fact Forum

Present a panel discussion explaining your findings. Meet with your group to choose a question for discussion, prepare an outline, and elect a leader. Hold the discussion in front of the rest of the class, at a school-wide assembly, or in a class of eighth-graders. You might convert your research to charts or graphs to use in your presentation.

3. Letter

Write a letter to an elected official who can influence laws that affect teenagers. Express your view of one such law and try to persuade the official to take steps to change the law so that it conforms to your point of view.

Processing

Draw conclusions from the information you have gathered. What did you learn about your own rights and responsibilities by doing this project? What about the rights and responsibilities of others? Write a brief reflection for your portfolio.

Developing Workplace Competencies

Preparation	Procedure	Presentation
• Communicating ideas and information • Working in teams • Making decisons • Leading others	• Acquiring data • Using self-management skills • Organizing and maintaining files for data • Interpreting information • Working well with people • Reasoning	• Thinking creatively • Evaluating data • Communicating ideas and information • Applying technology to specific tasks

OBJECTIVES

1. Read poetry centered on the collection themes "See the Miracles," "Imagine," "The Ways We Are," and "Say It!"
2. Identify literary elements used in poetry with special emphasis on imagery, figures of speech, rhythm, rhyme and other sound effects, and tone
3. Apply a variety of reading strategies to poetry with special emphasis on making a poem the reader's own
4. Respond to poetry using a variety of modes
5. Plan, draft, revise, edit, proof, and publish an essay interpreting a work of art and a comparison-contrast essay
6. Write a poem or group of poems
7. Prepare, plan, rehearse, and perform a poetry reading
8. Revise sentence structure and length
9. Demonstrate the ability to create a topic outline
10. Explore the relationship between popular music and American society through various activities

Responding to the Quotation

❓ Ask students to give some examples of how a word "begins to live" once it is spoken. What effects can a word have on people's lives? What processes can a word set in motion? [Possible responses: The words spoken by a parent to a child can help the child learn lessons that he or she will use throughout life; the words in a speech can inspire people to take action; calming words can prevent violence between angry parties and initiate a process of healing; the words of a poet can inspire people or cause them to see something in a different way.]

Dialogue of Two Poets Disguised as Birds (1988) by Alfredo Castañeda.

Selection Readability

This Annotated Teacher's Edition provides a summary of each selection in the student book. Following each Summary heading, you will find one, two, or three small icons. These icons indicate, in an approximate sense, the reading level of the selection.

■ One icon indicates that the selection is easy.

■ ■ Two icons indicate that the selection is on an intermediate reading level.

■ ■ ■ Three icons indicate that the selection is challenging.

Mary Ann Martin/Fine Art, New York.

Catañeda '88

THE POETRY COLLECTIONS

A word is dead
When it is said,
Some say.
I say it just
Begins to live
That day.

—Emily Dickinson

A Writer on Poetry
A CONVERSATION WITH GLADYS CARDIFF

As you read the poems in these collections, you may wonder what inspired the poets, how they set to work on the poems, or how they got their ideas so clearly and brightly down on paper.

Gladys Cardiff has this to say about her poem "Combing" (page 567).

Q: How did you get the idea for your poem?
Cardiff: As a young mother, I often helped my small daughter comb out the tangles in her bright orange, curly hair after it was washed. My mother used to reminisce about combing *her* grandmother's hair. . . .

Q: How did you set to work on this poem?
Cardiff: When I write, I write alone and where it is quiet. At the time of this poem, that was usually at night when everyone was settled into bed and I was settled at the dining-room table with lots of clean paper and a pen. Several weeks had gone by during which I had sort of rolled the feelings and ideas around in my head. The idea of myself doing something so ordinary, something all of the women on the maternal side of my family had done for each other for generations, was part of what interested me. But it was trying to pinpoint the feelings I had when I stood behind my seated daughter and her clean, lively hair that fascinated me. I realized I felt lucky, and thankful. Lucky to have her, to be able to care for her, and thankful to have learned this kind of love from my own mother. At the dining-room table

that feeling of thanksgiving was called up again. I felt it as I leaned over the page. "Bending, I bow my head. . . ."

Q: Did you revise your poem?
Cardiff: It is very rare for a poem to set itself upon the page as a finished work. This poem did. It is the only poem I have ever written that did not require additional labor and revision. When I look at it now as a writer—and see how the lines all fell into three beats to the line, its three stanzas, and ending triad, how the color orange was true to the facts and also a refrain that, like the experience itself, reverberated down through the poem—I take no conscious credit for its craft.

Q: How does someone become a writer?
Cardiff: People often say writing is a gift. And it is a gift, but not one that you own. I have never successfully forced a poem into being. My experience is that writing is often like playing, sometimes pretty rough playing, as if the poem has a mind of its own. In that sense, poems are gifts, ones which I work hard to prepare myself for so they can be received, and then passed on. Like the braided rug in "Combing," what starts them is often a tangle of rags, dull and colorful, ordinary or special, that want to be put together in some form that is right for them. You try to stay alert for that time when your attention is grabbed— and you've been practicing how to catch what comes your way.

488 THE POETRY COLLECTIONS

Getting Students Involved

Cooperative Learning

Have students work in groups to create a bulletin board display about the process of writing poetry. Ask students to collect material in which writers describe their working methods and how they find ideas for poems. Here are some possible sources for this material:
• introductions to collections of a poet's work
• articles about and interviews with poets in newspapers, magazines, and online journals
• phone interviews with poets who teach at local colleges or universities
• letters to poets, which can be sent to their publishers.

You may want to review interview questions and letters.

Reading Skills and Strategies

Booking space on the Net:

OBJECTIVES
1. Recognize ways of making a poem the reader's own
2. Understand how poets play with words

READING POETRY: MAKING A POEM YOUR OWN

When you read a poem, you respond to it just the way you respond to fiction and nonfiction. You connect it with your own memories and feelings and experiences; you interpret; you shape your own meanings.

Reading poetry, however, also demands certain strategies.

1. **Look for punctuation in the poem telling you where sentences begin and end.** Most poems are written in full sentences.

2. **Do not make a full stop at the end of a line if there is no period, comma, colon, semicolon, or dash there.** If a line of poetry has no punctuation at its end, most poets intend us to read right on to the next line to complete the sense of the sentence.

3. **If a passage of a poem is difficult to understand, look for the subject, verb, and complement of each sentence.** Try to decide what words the clauses and phrases modify.

4. **Be alert for comparisons—for figures of speech.** Try to *see* what the poet is describing for you.

5. **Read the poem aloud.** Poets are not likely to work in silence. The sound of a poem is very important.

6. **After you have read the poem, talk about it and read it again.** This time, the poem's meaning will change, slightly or dramatically. You'll see things in the poem you didn't see before.

7. **Read the poem a third time.** This time, the poem should become "yours."

HOW TO OWN A WORD

Playing with Words

Motto for a Dog House

I love this little house because
   It offers, after dark,
A pause for rest, a rest for paws,
   A place to moor my bark.

— Arthur Guiterman

Many books have been written to explain what poetry is, how it came to be, and how it works. But it is important to remember that poetry is also a form of playing. Just as we all play at games for the pleasure and challenge we find in them, so do poets play with words, rhymes, and rhythms.

The simplest kind of wordplay is **punning**. One kind of punning uses a word that can have two different meanings at once. You'll see one of the puns in Guiterman's little poem if you know two meanings for the word *bark*. Another kind of punning uses words that sound the same but are spelled differently. If you spotted two words that sound alike, you caught the other pun in this poem.

Apply the strategy on the next page.

Reading Skills and Strategies

This feature focuses on the specific strategies students can use to comprehend a poem, placing special emphasis on punctuation, syntax, and figurative language. These strategies are then modeled for them using a poem by Emily Dickinson.

Mini-Lesson:
Making a Poem Your Own
Have students read these strategies silently or read them aloud to the class. Then, using the first stanza of "A Narrow Fellow in the Grass" on p. 490, demonstrate how the strategies can be applied to an actual poem. Be sure students recognize the following:
1. Punctuation divides the stanza into three complete thoughts.
2. Line 1 ends with no punctuation; the thought is completed in l. 2.
3. The verb and subject complement are transposed in l. 4.

Mini-Lesson:
How to Own a Word
Remind students that a pun is a play on words that is usually humorous. They are commonly found in poetry. Note the pun on the words *pause* and *paws* in "Motto for a Dog House." Point out that a small sailing boat is called a bark, and then ask students to explain the pun on the word. [The sound that a dog makes is called a bark; the dog is going to moor (a nautical term meaning "to hold in place or secure") his bark within the doghouse.]

Using Students' Strengths

Visual Learners
Have students make pictorial representations of "Motto for a Dog House" that illustrate the wordplay embodied in the puns. For example, students might draw the dog with the features of a small boat or replace his paws with the hands of a clock that is stopped at an appropriate time. Additionally, work with the class to brainstorm a list of puns and have students work in small groups to create pictorial representations of each.

Auditory Learners
Divide students into groups of three and have them read aloud the poem "A Narrow Fellow in the Grass," p. 490. Assign each complete thought in the first stanza of the poem to one member of the group. The first student reads ll. 1 and 2; the second reads l. 3; the third reads l. 4. Let groups divide and assign the remaining stanzas themselves. Circulate among the groups, listening to each give a final reading.

Summary ■ ■

The speaker describes a boyhood memory of coming upon a snake in a grassy field. He is both exhilarated and terrified—afraid of the snake's quickness and near invisibility, but intrigued by its beauty and alien quality.

Dialogue with the Text

Point out that the student's responses to the poem involve both comments and questions. Note that a second reading might help her answer some of the questions.

Ⓐ Reading Skills and Strategies

Identifying Parts of Speech

❓ Identify the subject, verb, and complement of l. 4 and rearrange the syntax into standard word order. [subject: *His notice*; verb: *is*; complement: *sudden*; standard syntax: His notice is sudden.] **What do you think l. 4 means?** [Possible answers: His appearance is unexpected; both he and the boy are startled to see each other.]

Ⓑ Reading Skills and Strategies

Comparisons

❓ What two things are compared by the author? How does this comparison help the reader imagine the "narrow fellow's" movement? [He compares the path made in the grass to hair parted by a comb. Although readers may be unfamiliar with a snake's movement, they can easily visualize a comb parting hair.]

Ⓒ Critical Thinking

Interpreting

❓ The speaker describes his reaction to a snake as "zero at the bone." What do you think he means? [Sample response: Zero is the intermediate point between positive and negative quantities, and the speaker's feelings are both positive and negative—"cordiality," which refers to a friendly feeling, and "tighter breathing," which indicates fear.]

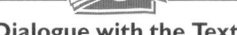
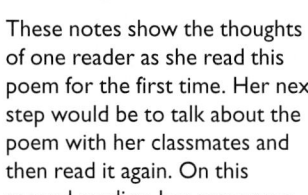

Dialogue with the Text

These notes show the thoughts of one reader as she read this poem for the first time. Her next step would be to talk about the poem with her classmates and then read it again. On this second reading, her responses would probably change.

A Narrow Fellow in the Grass

Emily Dickinson

A narrow fellow in the grass
Occasionally rides;
You may have met him—did you not?
Ⓐ His notice sudden is.

5 Ⓑ The grass divides as with a comb,
A spotted shaft is seen;
And then it closes at your feet
And opens further on.

He likes a boggy acre,
10 A floor too cool for corn.
Yet when a boy, and barefoot,
I more than once, at noon,

Have passed, I thought, a whip-lash
Unbraiding in the sun—
15 When, stooping to secure it,
It wrinkled, and was gone.

Several of nature's people
I know, and they know me;
I feel for them a transport
20 Of cordiality;

Ⓒ But never met this fellow,
Attended or alone,
Without a tighter breathing,
And zero at the bone.

Snake, evil, representing an evil person.

He's quiet, sneaky.

What opens and closes? How can it close at your feet and open further on at the same time?

What does a floor too cool for corn represent?
Isn't Emily Dickinson female? Is she supposed to be writing this from a boy's point of view?
What's a whip-lash unbraiding in the sun?

She loves nature and almost all of its creatures.

She's petrified.
What does zero at the bone mean?

—Erika Cole
Southeast High School
Bradenton, Florida

Reaching All Students

Struggling Readers

Make and distribute copies of the poem to students. Encourage them to mark up the copies as they read the poem a first time. Suggest that students underline words, phrases, or lines they have difficulty understanding. Ask them to record their personal thoughts or questions in the margins on either side of the poem. After students have completed their initial readings, divide them into pairs to discuss their comments and questions. Students can work together to break down difficult sections, rearrange sentences, paraphrase lines, and visualize comparisons and descriptions made by the poet. After discussing the poem, students should read it a second time. They can then talk about their reactions to this second reading.

See the Miracles

Theme

Seeing the World in New Ways *The language of a poem can reintroduce a reader to the miracles of everyday life. Poets don't take the world for granted. They write about ordinary things—a field of daffodils, the night sky, creeping fog—and use language to make us see these things as if for the first time, as if through the eyes of a child.*

Reading the Anthology

Reaching Struggling Readers The *Reading Skills and Strategies: Reaching Struggling Readers* binder includes a Reading Strategies Handbook that offers concrete suggestions for helping students who have difficulty reading and comprehending text, or students who are reluctant readers. When a specific strategy is most appropriate for a selection, a correlation to the Handbook is provided at the bottom of the teacher's page under the head Struggling Readers. This head may also be used to introduce additional ideas for helping students read challenging texts.

Reading Beyond the Anthology

Read On At the end of the poetry collections in the grade nine book, there is an annotated bibliography of books suitable for extended reading. The suggested books are related to works in these collections by theme, by author, or by subject. To preview the Read On for the poetry collections, please turn to p. T613.

HRW Library The *HRW Library* offers novels, plays, works of nonfiction, and short-story collections for extended reading. Each major work in the Library is accompanied by thematically or topically related Connections. The Connections are magazine articles, poems, or other pieces of literature. Each book in the *HRW Library* is also accompanied by a Study Guide that provides teaching suggestions and worksheets. For Collecton 8, the following title is recommended.

READINGS IN WORLD LITERATURE
This anthology offers a representative sampling of poetry from diverse cultures and includes additional examples of haiku.

Collection 8 See the Miracles

Resources for this Collection

Note: All resources for this collection are available for preview on the *One-Stop Planner CD-ROM 2 with Test Generator.* All worksheets and blackline masters may be printed from the CD-ROM.

 **Internet Resources**
go.hrw.com LE0 9-8

Selection or Feature	Reading and Literary Skills	Vocabulary, Language, and Grammar
Elements of Literature: Imagery (p. 492) **Lost** Carl Sandburg (p. 493)	• *Literary Elements,* Transparency 10	
Daily Naomi Shihab Nye (p. 494) **When I Heard the Learn'd Astronomer** Walt Whitman (p. 496)	• *Graphic Organizers for Active Reading,* Worksheet pp. 34, 35 • *Literary Elements:* Transparency 10 Worksheet p. 31	
Haiku Chora, Chiyo, Bashō, Issa (p. 499) **Fog** Carl Sandburg (p. 502) **in Just-** E. E. Cummings (p. 504)	• *Graphic Organizers for Active Reading,* Worksheet pp. 36, 37, 38	• *Daily Oral Grammar,* Transparencies 34, 35
I Wandered Lonely as a Cloud William Wordsworth (p. 509) **Connections: I Never Saw Daffodils So Beautiful** Dorothy Wordsworth (p. 512)	• *Graphic Organizers for Active Reading,* Worksheet p. 39	
Extending the Theme: Return of the Prodigal Son Sister Wendy Beckett (p. 514)	The Extending the Theme feature provides students with an unstructured opportunity to practice reading strategies using a selection that extends the theme of the collection.	
Writer's Workshop: Interpreting Art (p. 516)		

Other Resources for this Collection

- *Cross-Curricular Activities*, p. 8
- *Portfolio Management System*, Introduction to Portfolio Assessment, p. 1
- *Words to Own*, Worksheet p. 26
- *Test Generator*, Collection Test

Writing	Listening and Speaking Viewing and Representing	Assessment
		• *Formal Assessment*, Literary Elements Test, p. 95
• *Portfolio Management System*, Rubrics for Choices, p. 157	• *Audio CD Library*, Disc 15, Tracks 3, 4 • *Portfolio Management System*, Rubrics for Choices, p. 157	• *Formal Assessment*, Selection Test, p. 90 • *Standardized Test Preparation*, p. 68 • *Test Generator (One-Stop Planner CD-ROM)*
• *Portfolio Management System*, Rubrics for Choices, p. 158	• *Visual Connections:* Videocassette B, Segment 8 • *Audio CD Library*, Disc 15, Tracks 5, 6, 7 • *Portfolio Management System*, Rubrics for Choices, p. 158	• *Formal Assessment*, Selection Test, p. 92 • *Standardized Test Preparation*, p. 70 • *Test Generator (One-Stop Planner CD-ROM)*
• *Portfolio Management System*, Rubrics for Choices, p. 160	• *Audio CD Library*, Disc 15, Track 8 • *Viewing and Representing:* Fine Art Transparency 11; Worksheet p. 44 • *Portfolio Management System*, Rubrics for Choices, p. 160	• *Formal Assessment*, Selection Test, p. 94 • *Test Generator (One-Stop Planner CD-ROM)*
	• *Audio CD Library*, Disc 15, Track 9	

• *Workshop Resources*, p. 39
• *Writer's Workshop 2 CD-ROM*, Interpretation
		• *Portfolio Management System*
		  • Prewriting, p. 162
		  • Peer Editing, p. 163
		  • Assessment Rubric, p. 164

 Transparency    CD-ROM    Video    Audio CD

Collection Planner

Skills Focus

Selection or Feature	Reading Skills and Strategies	Elements of Literature	Language/ Grammar	Vocabulary/ Spelling	Writing	Listening/ Speaking	Viewing/ Representing
Elements of Literature: Imagery (p. 492) **Lost** Carl Sandburg (p. 493)	Identify and Interpret an Image, p. 492	Imagery, pp. 492–493					
Daily Naomi Shihab Nye (p. 494) **When I Heard the Learn'd Astronomer** Walt Whitman (p. 496)	Visualize a Scene or Image, p. 498	Catalog Poems, p. 494 Scene, pp. 496, 498 Images, p. 498			Make Notes on a Painting, p. 498 Write a Poem or a Paragraph Imitating Whitman, p. 498 Write a Catalog Poem, p. 498		Research a Constellation and Draw a Diagram of Its Principal Stars, p. 498
Haiku Chora, Chiyo, Bashō, Issa (p. 499) **Fog** Carl Sandburg (p. 502) **in Just-** E. E. Cummings (p. 504)	Paraphrase a Haiku, p. 507	Haiku, pp. 499, 507 Translating Haiku, p. 499 Extended Images, pp. 502, 507–508 Clichés, pp. 504, 508 Refreshed Images, p. 504		Set up a Word Bank, p. 508 Synonym, p. 508 Antonym, p. 508 Use a Dictionary and Thesaurus, p. 508	Write a Haiku, p. 508 Compose a Weather Report, p. 508 Write a Poem Based on a Word Bank, p. 508 Extend an Extended Image, p. 508		Research and Interpret Japanese Screens, p. 508
I Wandered Lonely as a Cloud William Wordsworth (p. 509)	Sketch a Picture of an Image, p. 513	Figures of Speech, pp. 509, 513 • Personification • Simile			Create a Simile, p. 513 Write a Paragraph Comparing Texts, p. 513 Write a Description, p. 513		Contrast Paintings, p. 513
Extending the Theme: Return of the Prodigal Son Sister Wendy Beckett (p. 514)	The Extending the Theme feature provides students with an unstructured opportunity to practice reading strategies using a selection that extends the theme of the collection.						Interpret a Painting, p. 515
Writer's Workshop: Interpreting Art (p. 516)					Write an Essay Interpreting a Work of Art, pp. 516–518		

Collection 8

SEE THE MIRACLES

WRITING FOCUS: Interpreting Art

To me every hour of the light and dark is a miracle,
Every cubic inch of space is a miracle.

—*Walt Whitman*

Every molecule and moment of life is a miracle. Children are good at seeing miracles—but as people grow older, they often stop noticing them. Not so the poet. Noticing miracles is the poet's specialty. Describing them in the right words is the poet's job. How can you do it? First, keep your ears and eyes and heart as open as a child's. Second, work on developing special skills with words and images. A few people seem to be born with these skills—just as some people are "born athletes." But most writers have to learn and practice, just as most ballplayers have to learn to hit grounders and catch fly balls before they can play the game.

Writer's Notebook

Walt Whitman created miracles in words. Miracles are also created by artists— with images and color. Take a minute now to skim this collection and look at the art that accompanies the poems. Note those works of art that especially appeal to you or even those works that puzzle or irritate you. Save your notes for the Writer's Workshop on page 516.

OBJECTIVES

1. Read poetry centered on the collection theme "See the Miracles"
2. Identify literary elements used in poetry with special emphasis on imagery
3. Respond to poetry using a variety of modes
4. Plan, draft, revise, edit, proof, and publish an essay interpreting a work of art

Responding to the Quotation

❓ What does this quotation suggest about the way Walt Whitman views the world? [Possible response: Whitman thinks everything in nature is a miracle; he sees ordinary things as being remarkable.] Why do you think this quotation was chosen to open a collection titled "See the Miracles?" [Sample response: Whitman implies that people only have to look around themselves in order to see miracles.]

Writer's Notebook

Whitman believed that everything around him was a miracle. Point out to students that visual artists often feel the same way, and that they try to capture the wonder of everyday objects and events in their work. Ask students to consider what remarkable things or events the artists who created the works in this collection were trying to represent. Have students glance through the collection and look at each artwork, asking themselves questions such as the following: What did the artist think was special about the moment or object represented? What miracle does the artist want me to see?

Writing Focus: Interpreting Art

The following **Work in Progress** assignments build to a culminating **Writer's Workshop** at the end of the collection.

- Daily / When I Heard the Learn'd Astronomer   Noting the elements of painting (p. 498)

- Haiku / Fog / in Just-   Researching details (p. 508)
- I Wandered Lonely as a Cloud   Contrasting other works (p. 513)

Writer's Workshop: Expository Writing / Interpreting Art (p. 516)

T491

Resources

Elements of Literature

Imagery

For additional instruction on imagery, see *Literary Elements*
• Transparency 10

Formal Assessment
• Literary Elements Test, p. 95

Elements of Literature

This feature focuses on how imagery is used in poetry to evoke feelings and create sensory impressions.

Mini-Lesson:
Imagery

After students have read the feature, use the following questions to initiate a discussion about imagery.

1. What images contribute to a feeling of loneliness in the lines from "The House on the Hill"? [Possible responses: The "broken walls" suggest that no one tends the house; the color gray indicates that there is little light; the winds that "blow bleak and shrill" create a feeling of coldness; "all gone away" emphasizes the sense of desolation.]

2. What images project a feeling of life in "The Black Cottage"? [Possible responses: "Fierce heads" suggest that the insects are ready to fight; "bodies pivoted" emphasizes their energy and movement; "Sunset blazed" captures a flood of light.]

3. How do the images in "Lost" make you feel? What images contribute to that effect? [Sample response: They evoke feelings of sadness and loneliness; "The whistle of a boat/Calls and cries unendingly" makes the boat seem like a sad and troubled person; "some lost child/In tears and trouble" makes the reader feel sad and worried.]

IMAGERY: Seeing Things Freshly

Imagery is one of the elements that give poetry its forcefulness. Images are basically copies of things you can see. But images in poetry can do even more than help us see things. An **image** is a single word or a phrase that appeals to one of our senses. An image can help us see color or motion. Sometimes it can also help us hear a sound, smell an odor, feel texture or temperature, or even taste a sweet, sour, or salty flavor.

Suppose you were an artist and wanted to paint a picture of a house. You would emphasize certain aspects of the house. You might emphasize the age of the house by making its shingles look as worn and wrinkled and cracked as an old shoe. Or you might emphasize the emptiness of the house by painting curtainless windows that reflect the clouds, and doors opening onto empty hallways. In each case, as an artist, you would give the actual image (the house) a certain twist, a particular shading.

Poets do the same thing. Edwin Arlington Robinson in "The House on the Hill" saw an empty house and emphasized its loneliness:

House by the Railroad (1925) by Edward Hopper. Oil on canvas 24″ x 29″.

The Museum of Modern Art, New York. Given anonymously. Photograph © 2000 The Museum of Modern Art, New York.

492 THE POETRY COLLECTIONS

Using Students' Strengths

Naturalist Learners

The emotional power of images drawn from nature perhaps explains their frequent use in poetry. Note that each poem in the feature contains images that describe nature. Invite students to recall a personal experience in which nature played a major role. Have them write a brief description of the experience using words and phrases that appeal to the senses.

Visual Learners

To give students experience in conveying emotions through images, have them draw, paint, sculpt, or build a model of a house. They should first determine how they want the audience to feel when they look at the house—happy, disturbed, angry, amazed, or amused. Then, students should choose the colors and materials that they believe can best achieve this effect.

by John Malcolm Brinnin

Through broken walls and gray
The winds blow bleak and shrill;
They are all gone away.

Robert Frost in "The Black Cottage" saw an empty house and emphasized the new life that had moved in:

"There are bees in this wall."
  He struck the clapboards,
Fierce heads looked out; small
  bodies pivoted.
We rose to go. Sunset blazed
  on the windows.

Imagery is part of a poet's style. It is the product of the poet's own way of seeing the world. Just as we learn to recognize certain painters at once by noticing the colors and shapes that mark their works, so we learn to identify poets by paying attention to their imagery. Of course, the time and place in which poets live influence the kind of imagery they use. Poets who live in cities will usually draw upon the street scenes and industrial landscapes they know so well. Poets who live far from cities will usually draw their images from what they see of country life.

Imagery and Feelings

An image can be so fresh, so powerful, that it can speak to our deepest feelings. An image can be so phrased that it makes us feel joy or grief, wonder or horror, love or disgust.

Here is a poem that uses images to help us see a scene on the Great Lakes and hear the sounds made by a boat lost in the mist. But what readers remember most about this little poem is the way the images make them feel:

> **An image can be so fresh, so powerful, that it can speak to our deepest feelings.**

Lost

Desolate and lone
All night long on the lake
Where fog trails and mist
  creeps,
The whistle of a boat
Calls and cries unendingly,
Like some lost child
In tears and trouble
Hunting the harbor's breast
And the harbor's eyes.
                —Carl Sandburg

The poet . . . should stop and examine what others have missed, whether it be veins on a leaf or the surge of a mob; he should hear what others miss— not just skylarks but the breath of an old man or sleet against the window; he should respond to the feel of a rusted iron railing, a cut, or a gull's feather; he should identify the variety of city smells and country odors and consider what it is that makes an unoccupied house different from one lived in; and he should taste not only food but pine gum and smog.
                —Stephen Minot

ELEMENTS OF LITERATURE: IMAGERY **493**

Reaching All Students

Advanced Learners

Focus students' attention on Stephen Minot's statement that the poet should "taste not only food but pine gum and smog." Pine gum is typically associated with the sense of smell and smog with the sense of sight. But here they are linked to taste. Explain that one way poets create vivid images is by applying individual senses to things with which they are not normally associated. Have students work in small groups to practice creating images using this method. Students in the group can take turns naming ordinary objects (for example, a house, a sunset, a street) while other group members describe the objects using phrases that apply senses not usually associated with them.

Planning

The Grinder (1924) by Diego Rivera. Encaustic on canvas (90 cm x 117 cm).

Courtesy Museo de Arte Moderno (INBA), Mexico City. ©1995 The Detroit Institute of Arts. Photograph by Dirk Bakker.

Before You Read

DAILY

Make the Connection

Days Are Nouns

Since your life is different from everyone else's, your miracles are unique. At any moment nobody is standing exactly where you're standing, and nobody is thinking what you're thinking, feeling what you're feeling, or seeing, smelling, or hearing the way you are.

Quickwrite

Make a list of the sounds, smells, tastes, and sights from your daily life that make you happy. Call your list "Daily," meaning "they happen every day."

Keep your notes. For questions and activities on this poem, see page 498.

Elements of Literature

Catalogs

One of America's greatest poets, Walt Whitman, wrote in catalogs—long, rolling lists of things that he saw and wondered at and wanted to share. One of the interesting things about catalogs is that they can bring together very different items in one list.

A **catalog poem** is built on a list of images. The repetition of items in the list creates a rolling rhythm when the poem is read aloud.

 go.hrw.com
LE0 9-8

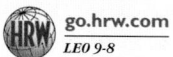 **Resources: Print and Media**

Daily

Naomi Shihab Nye

These shriveled seeds we plant,
corn kernel, dried bean,
poke into loosened soil,
cover over with measured fingertips

5　These T-shirts we fold
into perfect white
squares
These tortillas we slice and fry to crisp strips
This rich egg scrambled in a gray clay bowl

10　This bed whose covers I straighten
smoothing edges till blue quilt fits brown blanket
and nothing hangs out
This envelope I address
so the name balances like a cloud

15　in the center of the sky
This page I type and retype
This table I dust till the scarred wood shines
This bundle of clothes I wash and hang and wash again
like flags we share, a country so close

20　no one needs to name it
The days are nouns: touch them
The hands are churches that worship the world

MEET THE WRITER

Noticing the World

Naomi Shihab Nye (1952–　　), born and raised in St. Louis, Missouri, has written several collections of poems, including *Red Suitcase* (1994) and *Words Under the Words: Selected Poems* (1995). Also a songwriter, she has two albums to her credit—*Rutabaga-Roo* and *Lullaby Raft*. Many of Nye's poems are inspired by childhood memories and by her travels, including visits to her Palestinian grandmother in Jerusalem. Nye lives in San Antonio, Texas, with her husband and her son, Madison Cloudfeather. She regularly reads her poetry in schools, where she also runs workshops to help students find the poetry hiding in their own imaginations. She says:

66 Being alive is a common road. It's what we notice makes us different. 99

Summary ■

In this catalog poem, the speaker lists her daily domestic chores, which range from cooking to doing laundry. Repetition is a key element of the poem's structure and content, but it is ultimately transcendent rather than tedious. The poem's theme—that everyday, hands-on tasks connect a person to the world—is contained in the metaphor of the last line.

Resources

Listening
Audio CD Library
A recording of this poem is provided in the *Audio CD Library*:
• Disc 15, Track 3

Ⓐ Elements of Literature
Catalog Poem
❓ Ask students to identify the repetitive images and language in ll. 16–18. How does this catalog of images affect the poem's rhythm? [Images: typing a page, dusting a table, washing and hanging clothes. Language: *this, I, type, wash, and.* The repetition creates a rolling rhythm.]

Ⓑ Elements of Literature
Metaphors
❓ What might the metaphor in l. 21 mean? [Sample responses: A day can be defined by naming the tasks performed during the course of it; daily tasks are essential to life as nouns are essential to sentences.] What might the metaphor in l. 22 mean? [Sample responses: Hands connect people to the material world as churches connect people to the spiritual world; hands and churches both serve a greater purpose.]

RESPONDING TO THE ART
Mexican artist **Diego Rivera** (1886–1957) is best known for his historical murals. This painting shows a woman grinding *masa harina* for tortillas.
Activity. Ask students how the focus of this painting is similar to that of "Daily." [Both focus on the hands as central to the routines of daily life; both convey a sense of respect for work done by hand.]

Reaching All Students

Struggling Readers
Students often lose confidence in their reading ability when they cannot remember what they have just read. Instruct students to write the heads "First Reading" and "Second Reading" on a piece of paper. Then, ask them to read the poem, concentrating on three images. After reading, students should close their books and list the images in their own words. Have them repeat the process a second time, noticing three additional images.

Advanced Learners
Have students read some of Whitman's catalog poems and choose one to compare to "Daily." (Many of Whitman's poems are available on-line through electronic archives.) Ask students to write a couple of paragraphs comparing the two catalog poems. Have them list the catalog elements in each poem and tell what they like best about each. Also ask them to express their opinion of the form of catalog poetry in general.

Summary ■ ■

This free verse poem begins within the confines of a stuffy lecture room where an astronomer is giving a talk. The repetition in the first four lines captures the boredom of the poem's speaker, who is a member of the audience. Becoming "tired and sick," he wanders outside to contemplate first-hand the awesome beauty of the night skies.

Resources —

Listening
Audio CD Library
A recording of this poem is provided in the *Audio CD Library:*
• Disc 15, Track 4

Elements of Literature
Imagery
For additional instruction on imagery, see *Literary Elements:*
• Transparency 10
• Worksheet, p. 31

Ⓐ Critical Thinking
Analyzing
❓What words or images are repeated in ll. 1–4? [Repetition includes the use of "When I" to begin each line, the phrase "heard the astronomer," and the words "lectured" and "lecture." The image of numbers and charts is also repeated.] How does the repetition help the reader understand the speaker's mood? [Sample responses: The repetition creates a monotonous rhythm, echoing the boredom felt by the speaker; readers can almost hear the astronomer drone on and on.]

Ⓑ Elements of Literature
Scene
❓How does the image of the "mystical moist night air" help the reader identify the external and internal scenes in this part of the poem? [The words *moist, night,* and *air* appeal to the senses of sight and touch and describe the external physical setting; the word *mystical* reveals the speaker's mental state, which is the internal scene.] How does this scene differ from the lecture room? [Sample responses: The night sky has a feeling of expansion and freedom, while the lecture room feels closed and contained; this scene conveys mystery and wonder, while the lecture room seems rigid and dull.]

Before You Read

WHEN I HEARD THE LEARN'D ASTRONOMER

Make the Connection
The Real Thing
If you have ever wanted to be outdoors enjoying a fine spring day instead of wrestling with tenses and equations in school, you will know how the speaker of this poem feels. He sits in a lecture hall and listens to the cold facts of astronomy while outside is the real thing—the beautiful starry night.

To place the poem in its time, remember that astronomy was of great interest to many nineteenth-century Americans, who followed scientific lectures and debates as eagerly as their great-grandchildren would follow television serials.

Quickwrite
Find at least one image from the world of nature that fills you with wonder. Your image could be as big as the starry sky or as small as an ant.

Keep your notes. For questions and activities on this poem, see page 498.

Elements of Literature
Setting the Scene
Images are used to set the scene of a poem. A scene can be an external physical setting—a hillside, a city, a pond. A scene can also be internal—it can take you inside the speaker's mind. In this poem, how many scenes do you see and share?

> **E**very poem has a **scene**, or location. The scene can be internal, external, or both.

HRW go.hrw.com
LE0 9-8

When I Heard the Learn'd Astronomer

Walt Whitman

When I heard the learn'd astronomer,
When the proofs, the figures, were ranged in
    columns before me,
Ⓐ When I was shown the charts and diagrams, to add,
    divide, and measure them,
When I sitting heard the astronomer where he
    lectured with much applause in the lecture room,
How soon unaccountable I became tired and sick,
Till rising and gliding out I wandered off by myself,
Ⓑ In the mystical moist night air, and from time to time,
Looked up in perfect silence at the stars.

Reaching All Students

English Language Learners
Explain that a *proof* is a written demonstration showing the validity of a proposition in logic or mathematics. Show students an example from a math book. You might ask volunteers to draw mathematical figures and formulas on the chalkboard to demonstrate the speaker's vision of the astronomer's lecture. For other strategies, see
• *Lesson Plans Including Strategies for English-Language Learners*

Connecting Across Texts

Connecting with "Daily"
Ask students to speculate about why these two poems, "Daily" and "When I Heard the Learn'd Astronomer," were paired together. [Possible responses: The speaker of each poem finds special significance and a spiritual connection in the ordinary moments of life and in concrete reality; both poems list images and contain repetition; both are written in free verse.]

BROWSING IN THE FILES

About the Author. Whitman extended his compassion to all people and all living things. During the Civil War, he worked as a volunteer in Washington, D.C. hospitals, caring for wounded and dying soldiers. This experience, along with his grief over the assassination of President Lincoln, provided material for subsequent poems.

MEET THE WRITER

An American Treasure

Walt Whitman (1819–1892), born on Long Island, New York, was one of the first world-class poets America ever produced. He transformed the language of literature, especially poetry, forever—by writing it in free verse and using common speech and slang. Nobody would publish his radical book *Leaves of Grass,* so he published it himself in 1855. He even wrote glowing reviews of it himself. In one review he said:

> 66 Very devilish to some, and very divine to some, will appear the poet of these new poems. . . . 99

Whitman left school at the age of eleven and went to work. But on weekends he read Sir Walter Scott, the Bible, Shakespeare, Homer, Dante, and "the ancient Hindoo poems." In his thirties, he described himself as "a Fine Brute." He dressed differently from most people and is said, on one occasion, to have driven a horse-drawn carriage up and down Broadway reciting passages of Shakespeare at the top of his lungs. For years, Whitman kept notebooks of his thoughts and experiences. He drew heavily on these notebooks when he created *Leaves of Grass.*

Rare Books and Manuscripts Division, The New York Public Library, Astor, Lenox and Tilden Foundations.

The great naturalist John Burroughs, who often saw Whitman on the street, wrote: "The first and last impression which his personal presence always made upon one was of a nature wonderfully gentle, tender, and benignant. . . . I was impressed by the fine grain and clean, fresh quality of the man. . . . He always had the look of a man who had just taken a bath."

Certainly, Walt Whitman gave old-fashioned poetry a good, hard scrubbing, but at first not many people thanked him for it. As a poor old man, he was reduced to selling his book out of a basket on the streets of Philadelphia. But he never stopped working on his *Leaves of Grass,* revising and adding to it until his death. Today, Whitman's *Leaves* is one of the treasures of American literature.

WRITERS ON WRITING

In his preface to the first edition of *Leaves of Grass,* Whitman wrote, "The art of art, the glory of expression and the sunshine of the light of letters is simplicity. Nothing is better than simplicity." Discuss with students how "When I Heard the Learn'd Astronomer" expresses this viewpoint. The poem's rejection of astronomy's complex theories and its celebration of the simple beauty of the night sky emphasize simplicity over artifice.

Resources

Selection Assessment
Formal Assessment
• Selection Test, p. 90
Test Generator (One-Stop Planner)
• CD-ROM

Assessing Learning

Check Test: True-False

"Daily"
1. There are no writing activities mentioned in the poem. [False]
2. All of the activities mentioned in the poem are done by hand. [True]

"When I Heard the Learn'd Astronomer"
3. The speaker is astonished at the vast knowledge and brilliance of the astronomer. [False]
4. The audience's reaction to the lecturer is the same as the speaker's. [False]
5. The speaker feels more in touch with the stars when he is outdoors than when he is in the lecture hall. [True]

Standardized Test Preparation
For practice with standardized test format specific to this selection, see
• *Standardized Test Preparation,* p. 68

First Thoughts

1. Responses will vary widely.

Shaping Interpretations

2. Possible responses: Images of planting corn and beans and frying tortillas suggest that Nye lives in the American southwest; images of housework suggest that she has a home and a family to care for; images of typing suggest that she writes.

3. External scenes include a lecture hall and the outdoors under the stars. Internal scenes are the speaker's opposite states of mind: inside, he feels stifled; outside, he feels at peace. Students will probably be familiar with all these scenes.

4. The speaker was sick at heart and unsettled because the astronomer reduced the beauty of the stars to charts and diagrams. Outside, the speaker's mood is restored.

Challenging the Text

5. Some students may feel that the astronomer would be annoyed by Whitman's irreverence and lack of respect for learning. Others may think that the astronomer would disagree with Whitman and claim that astronomy makes people appreciate the night sky all the more.

Grading Timesaver

Rubrics for each Choices assignment appear on p. 157 in the *Portfolio Management System*.

CHOICES: Building Your Portfolio

1. **Writer's Notebook** Bring in other examples of Rivera's work to show students.
2. **and 3. Creative Writing** Have students concentrate on imagery.
4. **Science/Drawing** Students can search the Internet for relevant sites.

MAKING MEANINGS
DAILY
WHEN I HEARD THE LEARN'D ASTRONOMER

First Thoughts

[connect]

1. When you think of **images** in the world that give you joy or that fill you with wonder, do you look at ordinary things, as Nye does, or at cosmic things, as Whitman does? Or do you find wonder in abstractions like math (or astronomy)? Talk over your responses to each poet's source of wonder and joy.

Shaping Interpretations

[interpret]

2. What do Nye's particular **images** tell you about her life and where she lives?

[connect]

3. What **scenes** do you see and share in Whitman's poem?

[interpret]

4. What do you think *sick* means in Whitman's poem—what was bothering the speaker as he listened to the astronomer? At the end of the poem, what part of the speaker has been restored by the "mystical" starry night?

Challenging the Text

[connect]

5. Suppose you, the learn'd astronomer, came upon Whitman's poem a week after your lecture. How would you respond to the poet?

CHOICES: Building Your Portfolio

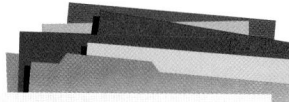

Writer's Notebook

1. Collecting Ideas for Interpreting Art

Starting. Take notes on important elements of Diego Rivera's *The Grinder* (page 494): subject, colors, shapes, the feelings it evokes, the story you see in it. Save your notes.

Creative Writing

2. Looking Up (or Down)

Refer to the notes you made for the Quickwrite on page 496. Expand your notes into a poem or paragraph that imitates the structure of Whitman's poem: A speaker tells where he or she is, how he or she feels, and what he or she does to capture a sense of mystery. Try to set two scenes: one actual place and one inside the speaker's mind.

Creative Writing

3. Daily

Refer to your notes for the Quickwrite on page 494. Expand them into a **catalog poem** or paragraph that lists images of things in your daily life that are miracles or make you happy to be alive.

Science/Drawing

4. Drawing the Stars

A lot of constellations are named after Greek gods or animals. Choose a famous constellation—Ursa Major, Cancer, Orion—and do some research to find out where its name came from. Then, locate your constellation on a star map and draw a diagram of its principal stars. Finally, draw the person or animal it is named after.

Assessing Learning

Observation Assessment: Group Work
Use the following criteria to assess individuals during group discussion.

A = Always
S = Sometimes
R = Rarely
N = Never

Criteria	Rating
Values others' perspectives	
Uses others' ideas to increase interpretative possibilities	
Asks questions	
Seeks help of others to clarify meaning	
Can disagree without disrupting dialogue	

Before You Read

HAIKU

Make the Connection

Snapshot Album

Haiku, the most famous form of Japanese poetry, capture moments of life with all the speed and precision of a snapshot. But haiku are better than snapshots. Cameras don't lie about the outside of people, but they can't tell you what's going on inside them. Haiku are different. To unlock a haiku, read one word or phrase at a time, pausing long enough to let yourself see, hear, smell, taste, or touch that single element of the original moment. In the end you will find yourself standing inside a special moment in someone else's life—whether that experience was captured three minutes ago or three hundred years ago.

Quickwrite

Pick a special day of the year. Write down at least two things you might hear, see, taste, smell, or touch on that day. Try to find images that reveal the way you feel at this moment, on this day.

Keep your notes. For questions and activities on these poems, see pages 507–508.

Elements of Literature

Haiku

Haiku work by suggestion. The scene in the haiku—that special moment of someone else's life—is supposed to serve as a starting-off place for your own thoughts and associations.

Haiku are written as if they were telegrams and each word

cost money. The Japanese language has no articles (*a, an, the*), uses practically no pronouns, and in general does not indicate whether a noun is singular or plural.

> A Japanese **haiku**
>
> 1. has seventeen syllables, five in lines 1 and 3 and seven in line 2
>
> 2. presents images from everyday life
>
> 3. usually contains a seasonal word or symbol (*kigo*)
>
> 4. presents a moment of discovery or enlightenment (*satori*)

go.hrw.com
LE0 9-8

The Original Language

Here, in the original Japanese, with the English translation, is Bashō's haiku from the next page. You might want to try your own version. (*Ya* is a word frequently used in haiku to mean something like "Lo!" Some translators indicate it with a colon, since it suggests a kind of equation.)

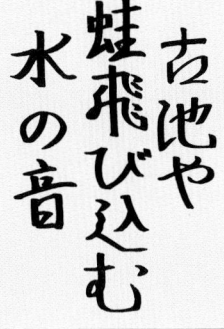

Furu	ike	ya
old	pond	:
Kawazu	tobikomu	
frog	jump in	
Mizu	no	oto
water	sound	

 *Resources: Print and Media*

Reading
- *Graphic Organizers for Active Reading*, pp. 36, 37, 38
- *Audio CD Library*, Disc 15, Tracks 5, 6, 7

Writing and Language
- *Daily Oral Grammar* Transparencies 34, 35

Viewing and Representing
- *Visual Connections* Videocassette B, Segment 8

Assessment
- *Formal Assessment*, p. 92
- *Portfolio Management System*, p. 158
- *Standardized Test Preparation*, p. 70
- *Test Generator (One-Stop Planner* CD-ROM)

Internet
- go.hrw.com (keyword: LE0 9-8)

OBJECTIVES

Haiku / Fog / in Just-
1. Read and interpret the poems
2. Identify characteristics of haiku
3. Recognize an extended image
4. Distinguish clichés from fresh images
5. Express understanding through creative writing and critical thinking

SKILLS

Literary
- Identify characteristics of haiku
- Recognize an extended image
- Distinguish clichés from fresh images

Writing
- Jot down thoughts about an artwork
- Write a haiku
- Compose a weather report using an extended image
- Write a poem imitating the style of Cummings's poem
- Create a word bank
- Further develop an extended image

Viewing/Representing
- Compare images in artworks with those in haiku (ATE)

Planning

- **Block Schedule**
  Block Scheduling Lesson Plans with Pacing Guide
- **Traditional Schedule**
  Lesson Plans Including Strategies for English-Language Learners
- **One-Stop Planner**
  CD-ROM with Test Generator

Summary ■■

These four haiku present images of nature and ambiguous messages that are typical of the genre. Chora's poem expresses the speaker's reaction to the toad that interrupts his work. Chiyo uses the image of a twining flower to suggest the bonds that can grow between neighbors. In Bashō's poem, a frog jumping into a pond transforms silence into sound. Issa sees the larger world reflected in the miniature eyes of a dragonfly.

Background

The form of haiku was developed in seventeenth-century Japan from multi-verse poems called *renga*. Poets detached the first three lines from these longer poems, transforming them into independent structures. The miracle of haiku is that within three brief lines and a strict syllable count an incredibly diverse and expressive range of poems can be produced. Haiku have room only to suggest, not to explain. Matsuo Bashō viewed this as an advantage, saying, "Is there any good in saying everything?"

Resources

Listening
Audio CD Library
A recording of these poems is provided in the *Audio CD Library:*
• Disc 15, Track 5

Viewing and Representing
Videocassette B, Segment 8
Available in Spanish and English. Introduce your students to the traditions of haiku with the *Visual Connections* segment "Images in Haiku." For full lesson plans and worksheets, see *Visual Connections Teacher's Manual.*

Ⓐ Elements of Literature
Haiku

❓ In haiku, comparisons are suggested, but not stated directly. What comparison is suggested in this haiku? [The relationship between neighbors is likened to the way the morning glory wraps itself around the bucket.]

Haiku

Ⓐ
Get out of my road
and allow me to plant these
bamboos, Mr. Toad.
—Miura Chora

Ⓑ
A morning glory
Twined round the bucket:
I will ask my neighbor
for water.
—Chiyo

Ⓒ The old pond;
Ⓓ A frog jumps in:
Sound of water.
—Matsuo Bashō

Ⓔ
A dragonfly!
The distant hills
Reflected in his eyes.
—Kobayashi Issa

Morning Glories by Suzuki Kiitsu (19th century). Japanese Screen, six-fold, one of pair. Color and gold leaf on paper (6' high X 13' wide).

500 THE POETRY COLLECTIONS

Reaching All Students

Struggling Readers
To help students connect to the expressive language of the haiku, have them cut pictures of nature from a magazine. Students can then write phrases or short sentences that capture the mood of the pictures.

Advanced Learners
Many poets have been inspired to write haiku. Ask students to collect haiku from non-Japanese poets and compare them with the Japanese selections.

Using Students' Strengths

Naturalist Learners
Point out that in three of the haiku, the first lines consist solely of a single image from nature ("The old pond," "A morning glory," "A dragonfly!"). Ask students to make lists of ten natural images they might choose for the first line of a haiku. Then have students choose two of the images from their lists and create complete haiku.

MEET THE WRITERS
Captured Moments

Miura Chora (1729–1780), like most writers of haiku, drew his images from the ordinary objects and activities of daily life—in this case, the work of planting bamboo shoots. In Japanese, every haiku has exactly seventeen syllables, but English translators can't always keep to that. Check the number of syllables here and see if this translator has performed a miracle of translation.

The Metropolitan Museum of Art, New York, Seymour Fund, 1954 (54.69.1). Photograph © 1982 The Metropolitan Museum of Art.

Chiyo (1703–1775) is the most celebrated of the women writers of haiku. Some critics say her poems are too explicit and unmysterious to be true haiku. They want their haiku to be more subtle, indirect, and suggestive—like the classical Bashō poem here. But Chiyo's admirers remind us that some people mistake "haziness" in haiku for profound thought.

Matsuo Bashō (1644–1694) is considered the developer of the haiku form as well as its greatest master. Bashō was a deeply spiritual man who became a Zen monk in his later years. His haiku show a zest for every mote and speck of life—a sense that nothing in this world is unimportant.

Kobayashi Issa (1763–1827) had a very sad life. Despite his poverty and the fact that he saw all his beloved children die, Issa's extraordinarily simple poems are full of human tenderness and wry humor.

群鷺

Asian Prints. The Metropolitan Museum of Art, New York, Rogers Fund, 1931 (JIB 81.10).

A Magician Turning Paper into Cranes (1819) (detail) from the *Manga* (a book of humorous sketches), vol. 10, by Katsushika Hokusai.

HAIKU 501

B Critical Thinking
Making Inferences

? Why does the speaker need to get water from the neighbor? [The speaker does not want to disturb the morning glory by moving the bucket.]

C Reading Skills and Strategies
Making Inferences

? What might the speaker be doing? [Possible responses: walking beside a pond; napping, then waking with the sound of the splash.]

D Elements of Literature
Haiku

Traditional haiku contain *kigo,* or words associated with a season. The Japanese would know, for example, that *snow* indicates winter and *evening showers* mean that it is summer. Here, the word *frog* suggests spring.

E Struggling Readers
Reading Aloud

Punctuation in a haiku—colons, dashes, or exclamation marks—indicate a shift in subject or mood. Ask students to practice reading the haiku aloud, capturing the change in the speaker's mood after his surprise at seeing the dragonfly.

RESPONDING TO THE ART

Suzuki Kiitsu (1796–1858) captures the fleeting moment in which the blossoms of morning glories open.

Katsushika Hokusai (1760–1849) presents his own twist on the Japanese art of paper folding, *origami*. He imagines that the sheets of paper actually become living birds.

Activity. Invite students to draw connections between the artworks and the haiku. [Possible responses: The art and the haiku freeze a moment in nature; both highlight simple natural images.]

Making the Connections

Cultural Connections

Writing haiku remains extremely popular in Japan. Newspapers publish haiku columns, and they receive hundreds of new submissions. Magazines and even television shows focus on the haiku form. Increasingly popular is *senryu*, an informal haiku variation that allows writers to express their feelings on just about any topic.

Matsuo Bashō's haiku about the "old pond" has received much critical attention. Share these observations with your students:

- "The Zen monk Hakuin always talked about the sound of one hand clapping. The sound of water in this haiku is also like that: it is there and it is not there."
- There is "a sudden shift from stillness (no sound) to movement (sound), and then a return from movement (sound) to stillness (no sound)."
- The poem is "like a flash of lightning illuminating a quiet corner."

Summary ■

This free verse poem re-creates the appearance and movement of fog over a harbor and city. In an extended image, the poet compares the fog to a cat; he pictures the fog entering "on little cat feet" and silently sitting on its "haunches" before it "moves on." Despite this restless movement, the poem's mood is serene and tranquil.

Resources

Listening
Audio CD Library
A recording of this poem is provided in the *Audio CD Library:*
- Disc 15, Track 6

FROM THE EDITOR'S DESK
We paired "Fog" with the haiku partly because of a little-known connection. We found out that Sandburg was inspired to write this poem on a day when he rediscovered several Japanese haiku he had stuffed into his pocket and forgotten.

Before You Read

FOG

Make the Connection

Images People Treasure

One day a CBS morning weather report began with the words "It's little cat feet out there for large swatches of the country." People listening knew exactly what that meant. Fog. Creeping fog. And they knew because they knew this poem.

Quickwrite

Choose a weather condition—a hurricane, tornado, blizzard, thunderstorm, drought. Write the name of a creature that might serve as an image for that kind of weather. Describe how that weather-animal looks, smells, sounds, and behaves, especially when hungry or angry or moving.

   Keep your notes. For questions and activities on this poem, see pages 507–508.

Elements of Literature

Extended Images

Sandburg never comes right out and says, "The fog is a cat." But after the first line, every line in the poem describes some aspect of a cat's anatomy or behavior. Of course, Sandburg has said all he wants to in these six short lines—but can you think of at least one other thing a cat does that might fit into the extended image of "Fog"?

An **extended image** is an image developed over several lines of a poem or even throughout an entire poem.

For more on Imagery, see pages 492–493 and the Handbook of Literary Terms.

go.hrw.com
LE0 9-8

Reaching All Students

Struggling Readers
Have students work in small groups to brainstorm and discuss other possible weather-animal comparisons.

English Language Learners
Ask students to write short poems about snow, a heat wave, or another type of weather. What animals do they associate with this weather? Have students compose the poems in their native languages and then prepare a summary (*not* a translation) in English.

Advanced Learners
Challenge students to compare and contrast this poem with T.S. Eliot's poem, "The Yellow Fog," which also imagines the descent of fog on an urban landscape in feline terms. Instruct students to pay particular attention to each poet's use of an extended image and the mood this image creates. Have students tell which of the poems they liked better and explain why.

Getting Students Involved

Cooperative Learning
Weather Words Watch. Television and radio weather forecasters use figurative language to describe the weather almost as frequently as poets do. Students can create a class bulletin board that contains the imagery, similes, metaphors, and personification used in area weather reports. Ask students to keep track of examples they hear on the news and then add them to the board. They can illustrate the examples as well.

Fog

Carl Sandburg

The fog comes
on little cat feet.  **A**

It sits looking
over harbor and city **B**
on silent haunches
and then moves on.

MEET THE WRITER

An American Singer

Carl Sandburg (1878–1967) wrote a poem called "Ten Definitions of Poetry." Here are four of the definitions:

> Poetry is a search for syllables to shoot at the barriers of the unknown and the unknowable. . . .
>
> Poetry is the silence and speech between a wet struggling root of a flower and a sunlit blossom of that flower. . . .
>
> Poetry is the synthesis of hyacinths and biscuits. . . .
>
> Poetry is the opening and closing of a door, leaving those who look through to guess about what is seen during a moment.

Sandburg, the son of Swedish immigrants, was born in Galesburg, Illinois. Between the ages of thirteen and nineteen, he worked on a milk wagon, in a barbershop, theater, and brickyard, and as a hotel dishwasher and a harvest hand. He became known as the poet of Chicago in the days when that city was the expanding center of steel mills, stock-yards, and railroads. Sandburg helped change American poetry by insisting that the rhythms of American speech could best be caught in free verse (see pages 554–555). Though he was unknown to the poetry world until he was thirty-six, by the time he died, Sandburg's name was a household word. His sometimes tough, often tender poems about nature and the American people, especially working-class people, were loved by millions. Still a landmark in American musical history is Sandburg's *The American Songbag*—in which, for the first time, are printed more than a hundred songs gathered from people who sing "because they must." Sandburg often gave public recitals of his poems and these songs, accompanying himself on the guitar. Sandburg loved Lincoln, another son of Illinois, and won a Pulitzer Prize for part of his massive lifework: a six-volume biography of the Great Emancipator.

FOG 503

Taking a Second Look

Summary ■ ■ ■

Spring has arrived and children come rushing outside to enjoy nature. Cummings captures their enthusiasm and energy in the rhythm of his poem, alternately running words together and spacing them unusually far apart. In the spirit of childhood, he coins compound words that are fun to pronounce. The flood of youthful emotions, thawed by the warm weather, is the true miracle of spring. But perhaps a somewhat melancholy tone is introduced by the sound of the whistling balloonman, whose cry is repeated at the beginning, middle, and end of the poem.

Resources ———

Listening

Audio CD Library

A recording of this poem is provided in the *Audio CD Library:*
• Disc 15, Track 7

BROWSING IN THE FILES

About the Author. An artist as well as a poet, Cummings used the typography of his poems to enhance their meaning. The look of the poems sometimes makes readers think that they are difficult and abstract, but their subject matter is often simple feelings and basic human relationships. Among the poet's most serious and personal poems are several that express his love and admiration for his parents.

A Critic's Comment. Cummings's poetry is often concerned with the transitory nature of time. About "in Just-," one critic has written, "The very fact of time permitting spring's return also makes inevitable its loss. . . . One thing 'in Just-/spring' says is that it is *only* in spring, which is seasonal and can't last, that such delight can be." In other words, the fleeting nature of something can make it all the more enjoyable or delightful. Ask students to give their opinions about this idea.

Before You Read

IN JUST-

Make the Connection

The Mysterious Stranger

In this poem, E. E. Cummings has given spring a new look. Sure, there's plenty of mud and water. The kids are outdoors playing, and the balloon man is back in town. But just who is this mysterious stranger?

He's lame and goat footed. If you know your Greek mythology, you should be hearing little bells right now. Hephaestus, god of fire, was lame. Here he is—thousands of years later—to throw a little heat on this year's spring. Pan, the remarkably homely god of nature who loved to dance with all the nymphs, was goat footed. Here he is, calling the kids to dance.

By the way, Pan invented the flute. Can you hear its echoes in this poem?

Quickwrite

Make a catalog of all the things you associate with each season of the year where you live. Think of activities, sights, smells, tastes, sounds—even people.

Keep your notes. For questions and activities on this poem, see pages 507–508.

Elements of Literature

Refreshed Images

Part of any good poet's job is to find fresh images, to avoid those old, worn-out phrases called **clichés.** Notice how Cummings combines words to make brand-new images of springtime. "Mud-luscious" and "puddle-wonderful" are refreshed images. They make us remember how much fun it was to play in the mud and splash in puddles when we were kids.

> **A** cliché is an overused, worn-out expression or phrase. Poets want to find **fresh images** that help us see the world in an unusual or original way.
>
> *For more on Imagery, see pages 492–493 and the Handbook of Literary Terms.*

MEET THE WRITER

Nobody-but-Himself

E. E. Cummings (1894–1962) began writing a poem a day when he was eight years old—and kept at it until he was twenty-two. Multiply 365 poems a year by fourteen and see what you get! Many of these poems were very short, and a lot of them weren't very good. But if practice makes perfect, then Cummings must have been perfect—on some days, anyhow.

Cummings once got a letter from a high school editor asking him what advice he had for young people who wanted to become poets. The poet's reply tells us something of what poetry meant to him:

> **66** A poet is somebody who feels, and who expresses his feeling through words. This may sound easy. It isn't . . . [because] the moment you feel, you're nobody-but-yourself. To be nobody-but-yourself—in a world which is doing its best, night and day, to make you everybody else—means to fight the hardest battle which any human being can fight; and never stop fighting. . . . If, at the end of your first ten or fifteen years of fighting and working and feeling, you find you've written one line of one poem, you'll be very lucky indeed. . . . Does this sound dismal? It isn't. It's the most wonderful life on earth. **99**

go.hrw.com
LE0 9-8

Reaching All Students

Struggling Readers

Assist students with the juxtaposition and repetition in Cummings's poem. Distribute photocopies of the poem and have students highlight descriptions of the balloonman in one color, the images of springtime in a second color, and the actions of the children in a third color.

English Language Learners

Ask students from different countries to share the sights and sounds they associate with spring in their native lands.

Using Students' Strengths

Kinesthetic Learners

Divide the class into small groups to create pantomime interpretations of the poem. Ask students to select a director and a stage manager. The director casts the roles and makes suggestions regarding the actors' actions and gestures; the stage manager obtains props and prepares the presentation space. Groups can accompany their presentation with music if they wish.

in Just-

E. E. Cummings

in Just-
spring   when the world is mud-
luscious the little
lame balloonman

5   whistles   far   and   wee

and eddieandbill come
running from marbles and
piracies and it's
spring

10   when the world is puddle-wonderful

the queer
old balloonman whistles
far   and   wee
and bettyandisbel come dancing

15   from hop-scotch and jump-rope and

it's
spring
and
    the

20   goat-footed

balloonMan   whistles
far
and
wee

A Appreciating Language
Style

? Cummings uses spacing, word position, and repetition to give this poem a very musical quality. He also chooses his words with great care. What does the word *Just* mean in this poem? Ask students to consider why the word is capitalized. [Possible answers: *Just* means "barely" since the poem takes place in early spring; *Just* means "only" in the sense that it is only at this time of year, after being cooped up all winter long, that children are so happy and excited to be outside. The capitalization emphasizes the period of time in which the poem takes place.]

B Elements of Literature
Fresh Images

? What do the images "mud-luscious" and "puddle-wonderful" make you think of? [Sample responses: They conjure up early spring when it rains a lot and the ground is moist and full of new life; they remind readers of the childhood joy of jumping in mud puddles.] Why are these images fresh? [Possible answers: These words have been coined by the poet to help the reader experience springtime; these images bestow a magical aura on mud and puddles, which generally have negative associations.]

C Literary Connection

By calling the balloonman "goat-footed," Cummings is alluding to Pan, a Greek deity, who was part animal, with goat's horns and hoofs. Pan was the god of wild animals, forests, and fields, as well as the god of shepherds and goatherds. The word *panic* stems from his name, because he was considered the source of scary noises that emanated from the forest at night. Pan was always chasing after nymphs and always being rejected for his ugliness. Yet he was a wonderful musician. (The musical rhythm of the poem and the association of Pan with the flute also brings to mind the story of the Pied Piper of Hamlin.)

Resources

Assessing Learning

Ongoing Assessment: Response to Literature
Use the following criteria to assess students' written or oral responses to literature.
A = Always
S = Sometimes
R = Rarely
N = Never

Criteria	Rating
Shows enjoyment of and involvement with the literature	
Makes personal and general connections to the literature	
Gets beyond "I like/dislike" the literature	
Considers multiple interpretations	
Analyzes author's control of elements in creating the literature	

Student to Student

Using sensory details and precise, concrete images, a young girl describes her grandmother's house.

Ⓐ Reading Skills and Strategies
Visualizing
❓ Which details help you visualize the family's trip to the grandmother's house and their arrival? [Answers will vary. Students may mention these details: the bridge packed with cars, the seagulls on the bridge posts, the bay, the brown-shingled house, the freshly mowed grass.]

Ⓑ English Language Learners
Popular Culture
Some students may not be familiar with the popular cartoon character Charlie Brown. Bring in some "Peanuts" comic strips to show them. Explain that many American children grow up reading "Peanuts" and watching the animated specials on television, and that products based on the comic strip have been developed and sold.

Ⓒ Elements of Literature
Fresh Images
❓ Which images are fresh and original? Which images are clichés? [Possible fresh images: "flip-flops crunching," "the local bomb." Possible clichés: "smell the bacon," "crashing of the waves," "floor shines brightly."]

Ⓓ Reading Skills and Strategies
Connecting with the Text
❓ Name an important place in your life where every detail creates a strong impression. [Answers will vary. Students may mention a public place or their own homes or their grandparents' homes.]
Why are the details so important?
[Possible answers: The details are what makes a place unique; details make a place familiar and comfortable.]

My Grandmother's House

Ⓐ The car rumbles across the bridge along with the other hundred cars. As usual everyone remarks how beautiful the bay is. Mac says hello to the seagulls that seem to greet us by standing on all the posts of the bridge.

We glance and see what's playing at the movies, and pass through the section which always has the putrid smell of bay mud. There's a quick look at the flume and the amusement park. Then we make the turn, and there is my grandmother's house.

Almost at the same time, my family gives a sigh of relief. The brown-shingled house always makes everyone feel at ease. It looks small from the front, except for the addition which sticks out but still seems to blend in.

We all step out on the freshly mowed grass. The grass is green and lush and has a nice squishy feeling to it. There is an exchange of hugs and kisses and an "Oh my, haven't you grown!"

We kids dash up the stairs that would give you a bad scrape if you stepped on one of the many nails that stick up dangerously. We run down the hall and jump into the Charlie Brown bedroom. It is a small room, so all three of us have a bit of Ⓑ trouble standing side by side, yet it is the most popular room. The Charlie Brown bedspread is on, and the old broken radio is still under the bedside table. The number one plus is that there is a great view of the family-room window. You can have a great time spying on everyone.

As the boys rush down to grab a Coke and I slide out of the room on the hard wooden floor, I glance into my grandmother's room. The two single beds are neatly made, the cats are quietly sleeping on the chaise longue, the weeping willow ruffles its leaves against the window, and the chest of old clothes is still there.

Last of the rooms upstairs is my Aunt Kappy's room. This is my favorite room. For at night you can hear the flip-flops crunching against the sandy sidewalks and the talk of the local bomb playing at the movies. In the morning you can Ⓒ smell the bacon cooking downstairs, and maybe hear the chimes of the church bell and the crashing of the waves.

The kitchen always smells delicious. There is always something being prepared. There are always dishes in the drying rack and the red floor shines brightly.

Ⓓ The house would not be complete if a single detail were taken away. To me, my grandmother's house is perfect.

—Kate Daniel
Radnor Middle School
Wayne, Pennsylvania

506

Connecting Across Texts

Connecting with "in Just-"
Both Cummings and the student writer realize the miraculous quality of ordinary events. Ask students to identify other ways in which "My Grandmother's House" is similar to "in Just-." [Possible responses: Both contain sensory details and descriptions of children's activities; both create an eventful mood.] Then have students discuss ways in which the poem and the prose piece are different. [Possible responses: The prose piece lacks the poem's rhythm and original use of imagery; the poem is full of action and movement while the prose piece is more visual.]

[respond]

First Thoughts

1. All of these poems contain **images** of moments and miracles in nature. What image in the haiku, in "Fog," and in "in Just-" did you find most striking, original, or powerful? Compare your choices with those of your classmates.

Shaping Interpretations

[interpret]

2. One of the characteristics of a **haiku** is that it presents a moment of discovery or revelation. In your own words, describe the moment frozen in each of the haiku on page 500.

[interpret]

3. In Chiyo's haiku, the plant is a "morning glory." How could these words also describe what the poet experienced at her morning encounter?

[interpret]

4. Why do you think Sandburg thought the fog was like a cat? What other cat actions could fit into "Fog"?

[analyze]

5. E. E. Cummings is famous for his unusual punctuation and arrangements of words. What are the children doing in "in Just-" that matches the leaps and jumps of the words? Why do you think Cummings made single words out of the names Eddie and Bill, Betty and Isbel?

[evaluate]

6. Both Pan and Hephaestus, like most other Greek gods, were pretty tricky customers. Do you think Cummings depicts the balloon man as completely harmless and kind? Which of the poem's words and images support your response?

Connecting with the Texts

[connect]

7. Inside each of the haiku there is a person. Put yourself in each person's shoes, one by one. Consider:

   • In the first haiku, do you wait for the toad to move, or do you poke it?

   • In the second haiku, do you ever use that bucket again?

   • In the third haiku, what do you think you were doing the minute before the frog jumped in?

   • In the fourth haiku, how long are you able to see the hills?

[connect]

8. Read Sandburg's "Fog" again. Pretend you are actually standing at the edge of a harbor and watching the fog come in across the water. How do you feel about everything around you disappearing? How does the fog feel against your skin?

Oriental Museum, Durham University, England.

Turquoise frog-shaped snuff bottle, Qing dynasty (18th–19th century), Chinese.

HAIKU, FOG, IN JUST- 507

MAKING MEANINGS

First Thoughts

1. Answers will vary. Students may cite the "mud-luscious," "puddle-wonderful" image of spring, the image of fog creeping in on cat feet, or the image of morning glories entwined around a bucket.

Shaping Interpretations

2. Chora: The speaker discovers a toad on his farm road. Chiyo: The speaker finds a flower that has wrapped itself around a water bucket. Bashō: The speaker hears a frog jump into a pond. Issa: The speaker admires the dragonfly because it can travel to distant places.

3. The words could also describe the glorious moment of discovery when the poet encountered the plant.

4. Sample response: Fog creeps in silently like a cat; cats also move quickly, as can fog.

5. The children are playing hopscotch, jump-rope, marbles, and pirate games—all games that involve movement. The names are probably run together to show they are indistinguishable and represent all children, and also to convey the excitement and rapid speech of children.

6. Possible responses: Words with unflattering connotations, such as "queer" and "goat-footed," suggest that the balloonman is not totally harmless; the image of the children running to him suggests that he is basically kind.

Connecting with the Texts

7. Possible responses:
   • wait and appreciate the moment
   • not until the flower dies
   • watching it rest on a lily pad
   • only until the dragonfly flies away

8. Sample responses: The moment feels mysterious and spooky; the fog feels clammy.

Assessing Learning

Check Test: Multiple Choice

"Haiku"

1. Which of the following is not cited? (a) toad (b) pond (c) leaf (d) frog [c]

2. What does the dragonfly reflect? (a) sky (b) hills (c) colors (d) mood [b]

"Fog"

3. What does the fog do at the end? (a) creep (b) cover (c) thicken (d) move on [d]

"in Just-"

4. The season in the poem is (a) spring (b) fall (c) winter (d) summer [a]

Standardized Test Preparation

For practice with standardized test format specific to this selection, see
• *Standardized Test Preparation*, p. 70
For practice in proofreading and editing see
• *Daily Oral Grammar*, Transparencies 34, 35

Rubrics for each Choices assignment appear on p. 158 in the *Portfolio Management System*.

CHOICES: Building Your Portfolio

1. **Writer's Notebook** Students should pay particular attention to the images that are depicted on Japanese screens as they do their research. Students may reproduce these images or create their own variations.
2. **Creative Writing** Remind students that their haiku should have seventeen syllables, five in ll. 1 and 3 and seven in l. 2.
3. **Creative Writing** Tell students that they should use characteristics that are commonly associated with their animals, not obscure ones. Researching the animal's characteristics and behavior may suggest some ideas to students.
4. **Creative Writing** Be sure students understand that the images, typography, and punctuation of their poems should contribute to the mood, scene, or message of the poem. Have them review Cummings's poem on p. 505 as a model. They should see that the word patterns suggest play, that the children's names are grouped together to de-emphasize their individuality, and that the space around "far" in l. 5 emphasizes distance.
5. **Critical Thinking/Creative Writing** Invite students to present their word banks and explain why they found a word unusual or interesting.
6. **Creative Writing** You may wish to have the class brainstorm a list of cat characteristics that students can work from.

CHOICES: Building Your Portfolio

Writer's Notebook

1. Collecting Ideas for Interpreting Art

Look around. Look again at the Japanese screen on pages 500–501, and jot down your thoughts about it. What do you see? How does it make you feel? Then, do some research in a library or on the Internet. Find out what you can about Japanese screens. What's their history? What are they used for? Save your notes for the Writer's Workshop on page 516.

Creative Writing

2. A Special-Day Haiku

Look at the notes you made for the Quickwrite on page 499. Now, write a haiku about your special day. Keep in mind that a haiku brings two **images** together for comparison, contains a seasonal or weather word, and presents a moment of discovery.

Creative Writing

3. A Weather Change!

Using the notes you made for the "Fog" Quickwrite on page 502, compose a weather report that describes how tomorrow's weather will look, sound, smell, and behave—in terms of the animal you chose.

Creative Writing

4. A Seasonal Salute

Imitate the style of Cummings's poem on page 505 and write a poem presenting **fresh images** that you associate with a particular season. Avoid **clichés** and other overused expressions. Your notes for the Quickwrite on page 504 should give you a start. You might open the way Cummings did: "in Just- . . . when the world is . . ." Play with words and punctuation and typography just as Cummings did.

Critical Thinking/ Creative Writing

5. You Can Bank on It!

Poets are always searching for words. Work as a class to set up a **word bank** in which you enter unusual and interesting words. To get started, tear up an old magazine or newspaper, with each of you taking one page. Then, define and enter in the word bank any unusual or interesting words from your page. Set your words up in a computer file or in a scrapbook. Map each word as shown in the next column. Give its

meaning, a **synonym,** an **antonym,** and an example of the word in a sentence. Use a **dictionary** and a **thesaurus** if you like. Then, using one of the poems in this collection as a model, write a poem of your own. Use as many of the words from your word bank as you can. (If you are inspired, write a poem *about* a word bank.)

Word: *implacable*
Meaning: "relentless"; "can't be satisfied or stopped"
Synonyms: "inflexible"; "rigid"
Antonyms: "flexible"; "easy-going"
Uses: Robert is an <u>implacable</u> force on the Student Council. I am never <u>implacable</u>.

Creative Writing

6. Foggy Weather

Sandburg's poem "Fog" appeals to our sense of motion by comparing the movement of fog to the movement of a cat. Sandburg develops this **extended image** over the six lines of his poem. Extend the image in the poem even further. Write three or four sentences describing other catlike qualities and actions that might be applied to fog.

Using Students' Strengths

Auditory Learners
For Choice 3, students may want to prepare their reports for a simulated radio or television broadcast in which they mimic the style of reporters. To add drama, they might add sound effects, such as the sound of wind, thunder, or rain. Working with partners, students might tape-record their reports and play them for the class.

Visual Learners
Encourage these students to illustrate the poems they write for Choices 2, 4, and 5 or the sentences they write for Choice 6. They might create a drawing or a collage or find a photograph that captures the essence of the poem. Alternatively, a small group of students might create a bulletin board display to showcase the haiku written by the class.

Before You Read

I WANDERED LONELY AS A CLOUD

Make the Connection

Two People, One Miracle

This poem captures with enormous precision a special moment that occurred almost two hundred years ago—on April 15, 1802, to be precise. We *can* be precise because there was another witness to that miracle—the poet's sister, Dorothy, also a wonderful writer—who captured the very same miracle in her journal.

Quickwrite

Remember when you saw some scene that made a big impression on you: the earth from a plane window, the ocean, the desert, a city blackout, a mountain peak, snow blanketing city streets? Close your eyes and be there again. Make notes about what you see.

Keep your notes. For questions and activities on this poem, see page 513.

go.hrw.com
LE0 9-8

Elements of Literature

Figures of Speech

This poem uses two kinds of figures of speech. In a **simile** the writer compares two unlike things using a word such as *like*, *as*, or *resembles*. The first line of this poem has become a famous simile. In **personification** the writer speaks of something nonhuman as if it has human qualities. This poet uses personification when he imagines the daffodils dancing, as if they're in a chorus line.

> **F**igures of speech are words or phrases that describe one thing in terms of another very different thing. Figures of speech are not meant to be taken literally.
>
> *For more on Figures of Speech, see pages 520–521 and the Handbook of Literary Terms.*

Drawing by Donald Reilly; © 1970. The New Yorker Magazine, Inc.

"'I wandered lonely as a cloud.' Hey, wild!"

I WANDERED LONELY AS A CLOUD **509**

OBJECTIVES

1. Read and interpret the poem
2. Identify figures of speech such as similes and personification
3. Express understanding through creative writing and comparing texts

SKILLS

Literary
• Identify figures of speech

Writing
• Contrast two paintings
• Write a poem or paragraph imitating the structure of Wordsworth's poem
• Compare a poem and a journal entry
• Describe a scene

Viewing/Representing
• Compare a poem and a painting (ATE)

Planning

• **Block Schedule**
  Block Scheduling Lesson Plans with Pacing Guide
• **Traditional Schedule**
  Lesson Plans Including Strategies for English-Language Learners
• **One-Stop Planner**
  CD-ROM with Test Generator

Resources: Print and Media

Reading
• *Graphic Organizers for Active Reading*, p. 39
• *Audio CD Library*, Disc 15, Track 8

Viewing and Representing
• *Viewing and Representing*
  Fine Art Transparency 11
  Fine Art Worksheet, p. 44

Assessment
• *Formal Assessment*, p. 94
• *Portfolio Management System*, p. 160
• *Test Generator (One-Stop Planner CD-ROM)*

Internet
• go.hrw.com (keyword: LE0 9-8)

Summary ■ ■ ■

The poem opens with a simile comparing the speaker's solitude to a drifting cloud. But the solitude is broken when the speaker comes upon "a crowd" of daffodils. Personification gives the flowers a life force, and they become "jocund company" for the speaker. In the final stanza the speaker tells how, at a later date, he reexperiences the glory of the daffodils in his imagination.

Resources

Listening
Audio CD Library
For a recording of this poem, see the *Audio CD Library:*
• Disc 15, Track 8

Viewing and Representing
Fine Art Transparency
The fine art transparency of John D. Dawson's *Rivers of Life* will complement students' reading of "I Wandered Lonely as a Cloud."
• Transparency 11
• Worksheet, p. 44

Ⓐ Elements of Literature
Figures of Speech: Simile
❓What kind of figure of speech is used in this line? [simile] What do you think it means to be "lonely as a cloud"? [Sample responses: to be alone and adrift; to have no real sense of purpose.]

Ⓑ Struggling Readers
Using Context Clues
❓Have students use context clues to figure out the meaning of "host" in l. 4. They should note that it is used as a synonym, almost a definition, of "crowd."(l. 3). What other, more common meaning of *host* is implied here? [A *host* is one who greets and entertains guests. The daffodils are the speaker's "hosts" or greeters on this solitary walk by the lake.] Point out that both of these meanings add to the personification of the daffodils.

Ⓒ Elements of Literature
Figures of Speech: Personification
❓What two things are personified in these lines? [the daffodils and the waves on the lake] What human qualities are they given? [Both are portrayed as dancing. The daffodils are also imbued with the human quality of glee.]

I Wandered Lonely as a Cloud
William Wordsworth

Ⓐ I wandered lonely as a cloud
That floats on high o'er vales and hills,
When all at once I saw a crowd,
Ⓑ A host, of golden daffodils,
5   Beside the lake, beneath the trees,
Fluttering and dancing in the breeze.

Continuous as the stars that shine
And twinkle on the Milky Way,
They stretched in never-ending line
10   Along the margin of a bay;
Ⓒ Ten thousand saw I at a glance,
Tossing their heads in sprightly dance.

The waves beside them danced, but they
Outdid the sparkling waves in glee;
15 A poet could not but be gay,
In such a jocund° company;
I gazed—and gazed—but little thought
What wealth the show to me had brought:

For oft, when on my couch I lie
20 In vacant or in pensive mood,
Ⓓ They flash upon that inward eye
Which is the bliss of solitude;
And then my heart with pleasure fills,
And dances with the daffodils.

16. jocund: merry.

Study of Cumulus Clouds (1822) by John Constable. Oil on paper laid on panel (11¼" X 19").

Reaching All Students

English Language Learners
Have these students work with more fluent readers to paraphrase the poem. Partners should paraphrase each stanza rather than the poem as a whole, trying to retain the writer's message as they rewrite his words.

Advanced Learners
Ask students to explore the poetry of Samuel Taylor Coleridge, Wordsworth's collaborator. They should select one of Coleridge's poem and write a brief response to it.

Using Students' Strengths

Naturalist Learners
Encourage students to find pictures of flowers in books, garden catalogs, or magazines, and to identify as many different varieties as they can. If the season permits, students can obtain live specimens. Have students share their examples with the class either in an illustrated report or in a flower collage that they create from the images they obtained.

MEET THE WRITER

Nature: The Best Teacher

> One impulse from a vernal wood
> May teach you more of man,
> Of moral evil and of good,
> Than all the sages can.

The English Romantic poet **William Wordsworth** (1770–1850) believed that nature is the best teacher. And he believed that common, uneducated people who live close to nature have at least as much to teach us as people with college degrees.

Wordsworth's mother died when he was seven. Six years later his father was also dead. William had started writing poems by the time he was fifteen. When he was twenty-eight, he and his close friend Samuel Taylor Coleridge published a collection of poems called *Lyrical Ballads*. This slim

William Wordsworth (1842) by B. R. Haydon.

book contained only twenty-four poems, but it was very different from the fancy, aristocratic poetry that most poets then wrote. Wordsworth and Coleridge used simple people and ordinary experiences as their subjects. They used common speech. They said that the human mind is intimately related to the workings of the natural world. They said that God is revealed in the laws and forces of nature.

According to Wordsworth, poetry begins when we get in touch with a memory and relive the experience:

> . . . poetry is the spontaneous overflow of powerful feelings: It takes its origin from emotion recollected in tranquillity.

"In tranquillity," Wordsworth says, meaning that it's better to write about something later than when you're right in the middle of it. Of course, you can still take notes, as Wordsworth and his sister, Dorothy, regularly did. Then you can take your time to relive what you experienced and put it down on paper exactly the way you want to.

I WANDERED LONELY AS A CLOUD 511

D Elements of Literature

Rhyme Scheme

? Call on students to analyze the rhyme scheme of each stanza. [Each stanza has the same rhyme scheme: ababcc.] Point out that poets often use inverted word order to create rhyme and to emphasize an idea. What idea is emphasized by the inverted word order in l. 23? [By putting "fills" at the end of the line, the poet emphasizes the speaker's happiness.]

BROWSING IN THE FILES

About the Author. Wordsworth, his wife Mary, and his sister Dorothy lived together for many years in England's scenic Lake District. The walk described in the poem and in the journal entry on p. 512 took place there. Dorothy was a prolific journal writer. In his poems, William frequently reflected upon and referred to the entries she made about experiences they had shared.

RESPONDING TO THE ART

John Constable (1776–1837) is considered one of Britain's most important landscape painters. He is known for his innovative use of light. Often he sketched directly from nature, then finished the work in his studio.

Activity. What do Constable's painting and Wordsworth's poem have in common? [Possible answers: Both focus on an image in nature; both capture beauty and reflect upon it.]

Professional Note

Critical Comment: The Poet's World

Matthew Arnold wrote, "Wordsworth's poetry is great because of the extraordinary power with which Wordsworth feels the joy offered us in Nature . . . and because of the extraordinary power with which he shows us this joy." The cottage depicted in the painting by Arthur Claude Strachan (p. 512) offers a sense of the natural beauty and simplicity of rural life that Wordsworth found so appealing. From 1813 to 1850, he lived with his family in a house that had the same idyllic charm as Strachan's cottage (though Wordsworth's home was much more substantial). The poet felt a strong bond of kinship with nature. At first he was laughed at by critics for the simplicity of his poems and ideas, but later he achieved fame and acclaim as poet laureate of England. You might use Strachan's painting to help students bridge the gap between Wordsworth's world and our own more technologically driven society.

Resources

Selection Assessment

Formal Assessment
- Selection Test, p. 94

Test Generator (One-Stop Planner)
- CD-ROM

William Wordsworth's sister, Dorothy, describes in great detail a springtime walk in the Lake District.

Background

Dorothy Wordsworth's journal entry is dated two years before William wrote his poem about the same experience. The poet might have used her journal to help jog his memory when he wrote "I Wandered Lonely as a Cloud."

Ⓐ Critical Thinking

Making Connections

❓ How does the journal entry's introduction of the daffodils differ from the poem's introduction? [Possible responses: The journal entry gives a lot of details about the surroundings while the poem focuses on the daffodils; the journal entry describes the walkers' route, while the poem describes the speaker's mood and emotions.]

Ⓑ Elements of Literature

Figures of Speech: Simile

❓ What two things are being compared here? [Daffodils laying upon stones are compared to weary people resting their heads on pillows.]

Ⓒ Elements of Literature

Figures of Speech: Personification

❓ What words and phrases help to personify the daffodils? [*reeled and danced, laughed, looked so gay, ever glancing*]

Ⓓ Critical Thinking

Making Connections

❓ What is the difference between the way the poem ends and the way the journal entry ends? [Possible responses: The poem ends in a mood of tranquillity while the journal entry ends with a description of a storm; the poem ends with a recollection some time after the walk, while the journal entry ends when the walk is over.]

Resources ⌒🎧

Listening

Audio CD Library

A recording of this poem is provided in the *Audio CD Library*:
• Disc 15, Track 9

I Never Saw Daffodils So Beautiful

Dorothy Wordsworth

April 15, 1802: . . . The wind seized our breath. The lake was rough. There was a boat by itself floating in the middle of the bay below Water Millock. We rested again in the Water Millock Lane. The hawthorns are black and green, the birches here and there greenish, but there is yet more of purple to be seen on the twigs. We got over into a field to avoid some cows—people working. A few primroses by the roadside—wood sorrel flower, the anemone, scentless violets, strawberries, and that starry, yellow flower which Mrs. C. calls pile wort. When we were in the woods beyond Gowbarrow Park, we saw a few daffodils close to the waterside. We fancied that the lake had floated the seeds ashore, and that the little colony had so sprung up. But as we went along there were more and yet more; and at last, under the boughs of the trees, we saw that there was a long belt of them along the shore, about the breadth of a country turnpike road. I never saw daffodils so beautiful. They grew along the mossy stones about and about them; some rested their heads upon these stones as on a pillow for weariness; and the rest tossed and reeled and danced, and seemed as if they verily laughed with the wind that blew upon them over the lake, they looked so gay, ever glancing, ever changing. This wind blew directly over the lake to them. There was here and there a little knot, and a few stragglers a few yards higher up; but they were so few as not to disturb the simplicity, unity, and life of that one busy highway. We rested again and again. The bays were stormy, and we heard the waves at different distances, and in the middle of the water. Rain came on—we were wet when we reached Luff's. . . .

A Worcestershire Cottage (late 19th to early 20th century) by Arthur Claude Strachan.
Courtesy of Julian Simon/Fine Art Photographic Library.

Connecting Across Texts

Connecting with "I Wandered Lonely as a Cloud"

Many things are dissimilar about Dorothy Wordsworth's journal entry and her brother's poem. For one thing, in the journal entry there is the presence of other people; "we" rather than "I" is the pronoun that is repeatedly used. The journal entry also contains many details that the poem does not. But the poem focuses on the lasting spiritual and emotional value that the sight of the daffodils brings. Ask students to discuss possible reasons for the differences between these two descriptions of the same event. [Sample responses: Dorothy wrote right after the experience happened, while William had time to consider its lasting impact; the two writers had different purposes—the journal writer wished to record an actual event, and the poet wanted to create an image that captured a feeling or mood.]

First Thoughts

[visualize] 1. Listen to Wordsworth's poem read aloud, and sketch a picture of what you *see*. Be sure to compare your sketches in class. Did you see different things?

Shaping Interpretations

[identify] 2. What **simile** helps you imagine the number of daffodils the speaker saw?

[identify] 3. Which words in the poem **personify** the daffodils—make them seem like people, even friends and companions, to the lonely speaker?

[interpret] 4. In your own words, how would you explain the "inward eye" in line 21?

[infer] 5. The word *wealth* can mean several things. What kind of wealth is the speaker referring to in line 18? How do people accumulate this kind of wealth?

Extending the Text

[extend] 6. When could people use an "inward eye" to get through difficult times?

CHOICES: Building Your Portfolio

Writer's Notebook

1. Collecting Ideas for Interpreting Art

Contrasting paintings. When you interpret a work of art for the Writer's Workshop on page 516, you might contrast it with another work. Take notes on Constable's *Study of Cumulus Clouds* (pages 510–511) and Strachan's *A Worcestershire Cottage* (page 512). First, write down what you see in each painting. Then, note how the paintings differ. Consider colors, feeling, and style (Romantic art versus Impressionism). Save your notes.

Creative Writing

2. A Change of Mood

Imitate the first verse of this poem and write four lines or a paragraph that opens with a **simile** describing how you once felt and what you saw that changed your mood. Open with the words "I wandered [lonely as? happy as? silly as?]. . . ."

Comparing Texts

3. Journal and Poem

Write at least one paragraph comparing Dorothy Wordsworth's **journal entry** (see *Connections* on page 512) with "I Wandered Lonely as a Cloud." Before you write, identify the similarities and differences between the two accounts. For your comparison, consider the details and the figurative language in the poem and in the journal entry.

Creative Writing

4. Vivid Descriptions

Go back to your Quickwrite notes, and write a description of the scene you visualized. Ask yourself, What time of year is it? What time of day? Is anybody with you? Do you speak? Do you smell anything? hear anything? Why do you remember the scene so well? Your answers will help you add details to your description.

First Thoughts

1. Students might sketch daffodils; or sketch the landscape with a cloud, hills, valleys, a lake, trees, and daffodils; or sketch the speaker recollecting the scene.

Shaping Interpretations

2. Lines 7–8: "Continuous as the stars . . . on the Milky Way."
3. "a crowd," " A host," "dancing in the breeze," "Tossing their heads in sprightly dance," "Outdid the sparkling waves in glee," "a jocund company," "dances with the daffodils"
4. Possible responses: as imagination; as memory; as the ability to visualize.
5. Sample response: He is referring to the riches of the mind or to treasured memories. People can accumulate this wealth by experiencing the wonders of nature.

Extending the Text

6. Possible responses: Memories can provide inner strength and solace during tragic situations, such as a serious illness or the death of a loved one; imagination can be used to overcome a minor disappointment, failure, or rejection.

Grading Timesaver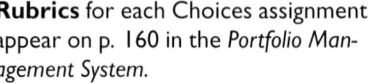

Rubrics for each Choices assignment appear on p. 160 in the *Portfolio Management System*.

CHOICES: Building Your Portfolio

1. and 3. Students might organize their notes in the form of a chart.
2. and 4. Remind students to use similes and images that are fresh.

Assessing Learning

Check Test: Multiple Choice

1. In the opening line, the speaker is (a) lonely (b) sad (c) frightened (d) thoughtful [a]
2. The speaker suddenly sees a great many (a) roses (b) clouds (c) dancers (d) daffodils [d]
3. The setting is beside a (a) hill (b) river (c) forest (d) lake [d]
4. As the speaker recalls the scene, he is filled with (a) longing (b) remorse (c) happiness (d) loneliness [c]

OBJECTIVES
1. Read an essay
2. Find thematic connections across genres
3. Generate relevant and interesting discussion
4. Recognize distinctive and shared characteristics of cultures through reading and discussion

EXTENDING *the theme*

AN ESSAY

Return of the Prodigal Son
Sister Wendy Beckett

Return of the Prodigal Son (1668–1669) by Rembrandt.
Oil on canvas (262 cm x 205 cm).

Scala/Art Resource, NY.

go.hrw.com
LE0 9-8

Extending the Theme

Sister Wendy Beckett discusses Rembrandt's *Return of the Prodigal Son* and the Gospel parable on which it is based. In the parable, a young man asks for his inheritance and then squanders it. He decides to return home and ask his father's forgiveness. However, his father sees him coming and embraces him with open arms, ordering a celebration feast and denying the need for any apology. Sister Beckett believes that everyone in the world would understand and respond to Rembrandt's depiction of parental love. She also thinks the parable may have had special resonance for Rembrandt, who outlived all of his children.

Ⓐ Critical Thinking
Expressing an Opinion
❓ Do you agree with this opening statement? Why or why not? [Possible responses: Yes, the desire for parental love is universal so everyone would respond to this picture; no, ideas about families and parenting vary from culture to culture, and some people may not understand or relate to the painting.]

Ⓑ Reading Skills and Strategies
Making Inferences
❓ Why might Sister Beckett think this is the loveliest part of the story? [Possible answers: It shows that love conquers all; two people who love each other are reunited and all is forgiven.]

Ⓒ Literary Connections
In the painting, the elder brother is present at the reunion of father and son. In written versions of the parable, the elder brother encounters the feast upon returning from the field and becomes angry, complaining that his loyalty and diligence have never earned him such a feast. Have students examine the elder brother's expression in the painting and discuss how Rembrandt portrays emotions.

Making the Connections

Connecting to the Theme: "See the Miracles"
Ask students how the scene depicted in the painting—and described in the essay—fits into the collection's theme. What is the miracle shown in this work? [Possible responses: The miracle of a father's love for his son; the miracle of repentance and forgiveness.] Discuss with students how *Return of the Prodigal Son* is related to the other selections. What connections can be drawn between this painting and the poems in this collection? [Sample responses: The father's welcome of the prodigal son is a moment of wonder and revelation as are the moments described in the poems; the artist captures strong emotions as do the poets; the painting and the poems capture moments of discovery and joy through the use of images.]

T514

You could take this picture anywhere in the world, to the deserts, jungles, or islands, and everybody would immediately understand it and respond.

This is a picture about parental love, and we have all either had a loving father or longed to have one. The story is the Gospel parable about the father who had two sons. The younger was unwilling to wait until his father died and asked for his inheritance in advance. The father gave it, and the son went off and wasted it. Then there was a famine, and the son found he had only fair-weather friends. He kept alive by working on a pig farm, so hungry that he envied the pigs their swill. He came to his senses, remembering how even the servants at home were well fed and housed, and he decided to go back. He composed a little speech confessing that he had been a rotten son, and asking only to be treated as a servant.

Now we come to what I think is the loveliest part of the story. We are told that when he was a long way off, his father saw him coming and ran out to meet him. It is as if the old man, knowing his son's weakness and that he would one day return penniless, had gone out every day to watch for him. When they embraced, the son tried to stammer out his speech of repentance, but the father would not let him. He simply held him tight and rejoiced, summoning the servants to bring out the best garments and to kill the fatted calf, because the true father offers total love, always.

Rembrandt shows them lost in a silent intimacy, the son's face half hidden, his poor, worn-out shoes falling from his calloused feet, his clothes ragged, his exhaustion palpable. The father's cloak swells out in almost womblike protection, enclosing them in that one-to-oneness that is the essence of all relationships and cannot be judged by anyone else. The elder son looms judgmentally at the side, resentful, as stiff as his staff, a man of legal narrowness instead of love. He receives no embrace because he does not seek it, standing aloof from the family and the extended family of servants, all eyes in the background.

This parable may have had a special poignancy for Rembrandt, all of whose children died young, except for one son, Titus, and even he died before his father.

MEET THE WRITER

Art Critic with an "Innocent Eye"

Sister Wendy Beckett (1930–) has earned a reputation as a compelling television personality. Born in South Africa, Sister Wendy now lives on the grounds of an English Carmelite monastery, in a trailer piled high with art books. Before she made her popular TV series, *Sister Wendy's Story of Painting*, she'd never seen a television program.

According to Sister Wendy, everyone should view art with "an innocent eye." Her message is simple: "We must refuse labels and prejudices—just try to see, as a child sees."

FINDING COMMON GROUND

Imitate Sister Wendy, and "just try to see" one of the paintings on page 224, 267, 272, or 537.

1. Make notes about the colors you see. What draws your eye immediately? What other details do you see?

2. What story do the images suggest?

3. What do you think the painting is about?

4. How does it make you feel?

Share your responses with classmates who chose the same work. What similarities and differences do you find?

FINDING COMMON GROUND

Before students begin their notes, point out that responses to art are highly individual. There are no right or wrong ways to look at a painting. Any response is legitimate, as long as they use elements in the painting to defend their responses and interpretations. You might want to divide students into groups, based on the painting they chose. Have each group discuss their responses and draw up a list of ten words or phrases that represent their observations. Each group can present their list to the class or post it on the bulletin board.

BROWSING IN THE FILES

About the Author. Sister Wendy is the author of fifteen books, including *The Mystery of Love*. Through her television shows, she tries to bring artworks to life for everyone. Although she has a degree in English Literature, Sister Beckett taught herself about art by reading books. She scoffs at the idea that she doesn't know enough about art. As she says, "Many people feel I am not really equipped to understand art, that I am not educated enough . . . but, don't you see, that's the point!" Her goal is to help ordinary people understand art and make it a part of their lives.

Assessing Learning

Check Test: True-False

1. In the parable, the older son inherits the entire fortune. [False]
2. The younger son is sent away by his father. [False]
3. The younger son works on a pig farm. [True]
4. The elder son has loving feelings for his brother. [False]
5. Sister Beckett believes that everyone can understand and respond to the painting. [True]

Reaching All Students

English Language Learners
Point out to students that *prodigal* means "spendthrift" or "exceedingly wasteful."

Advanced Learners
The story of the child who strays, then comes back to receive forgiveness for his errors is a classic theme, one found in sources as varied as Shakespeare's plays and made-for-television movies. Have students give examples of other works that are based on this theme.

Writer's Workshop

MAIN OBJECTIVE
Write an interpretive essay

PROCESS OBJECTIVES

1. Use appropriate prewriting techniques to identify and develop a topic
2. Create a first draft
3. Use evaluation criteria as a basis for determining revision strategies
4. Revise the first draft incorporating suggestions generated by self- or peer evaluation
5. Proofread and correct errors
6. Create a final draft
7. Choose an appropriate method of publication
8. Reflect on progress as a writer

Planning

- **Block Schedule**
  Block Scheduling Lesson Plans with Pacing Guide
- **One-Stop Planner**
  CD-ROM with Test Generator

Introducing the Writer's Workshop

- Bring several examples of various periods and types of art to class.
- Number each example and display them at various points in the room. Then, on the board, list a variety of adjectives such as *happy, gloomy, mysterious,* etc. Have students number a paper to match the number of examples on display. As they walk around, have students write the adjective they feel best characterizes the work next to its number. Students should feel free to select adjectives not on the list.
- Discuss with students the range of feelings that art can generate in viewers and begin to develop a list of possible explanations. For example, students may comment on the colors used in a painting and how those colors make them feel.

Technology HELP

See Writer's Workshop 2 CD-ROM. *Assignment: Interpretation.*

ASSIGNMENT

Write an essay explaining your interpretation of a work of art (a painting, drawing, or sculpture).

AIM

To inform; to explain.

AUDIENCE

Your classmates or members of an art class.

You must go absolutely defenseless to the work. And I think if you know something about the artist, you can go defenseless with more confidence, but you must not let any biographical details or others' opinions sway you. You must be prepared to spend time.

—Sister Wendy Beckett

EXPOSITORY WRITING

INTERPRETING ART

In this workshop you'll write an essay interpreting a work of art. This diagram shows the elements to look for. You don't have to be an art critic to interpret art; you just have to learn to look closely, to trust what you see.

Elements of Art

Subject Matter — Colors — Repetition or Contrast — Lines and Shapes — Experience and Feeling

Prewriting

1. Choose Your Subject

You should have some notes about the works of fine art that illustrate the poems in this collection. If you aren't satisfied with using one of those works as your subject, skim this book to find a work of art that does interest you enough to want to examine it closely.

2. Analyze the Work

Get to know the work—it takes time. Take notes on everything you see. Then, take a break, and come back for a second and even a third viewing. You're sure to notice things you didn't see before.

- **Subject matter.** What is happening in the painting? What story, if any, can you read in the images? (Not all art tells a story.) Which image draws your eye immediately? What details do you notice when you take a closer look?
- **Design elements.** Focus on light and shadow, color, line, and shape. What repetition or contrasts do you see?
- **Responses.** Describe what you think the work's mood is and how you think the mood is created. How does the work make you feel? What meaning do you find in it?

3. State Your Claim

Your main idea—your statement about what the work means to you—is your **interpretive claim,** or **thesis statement**. (What is Sister Wendy's interpretive claim about Rembrandt's painting? See page 514.)

 *Resources: Print and Media*

Writing and Language
- *Portfolio Management System*
  Prewriting, p. 162
  Peer Editing, p. 163
  Assessment Rubric, p. 164

- *Workshop Resources*
  Revision Strategy Teaching Notes, p. 39
  Revision Strategy Transparencies 20, 21, and 22
- *Writer's Workshop 2 CD-ROM,* Interpretation

Writing

1. Organize Your Ideas

Even a brief essay needs three parts: a beginning, a middle, and an end. In the first paragraph, identify the work's title and the artist, and then move directly to your interpretive claim. Remember that there is no single right interpretation of any work.

2. Elaborate

The rest of your essay should support your claim. Tie every statement to specific details in the work (images, colors, lines, shapes, repetition, contrast). In a separate paragraph, discuss your feelings and ideas—your responses to the work.

Language Handbook HELP

See Revising for Sentence Variety, page 1009; Varying Sentence Structures, pages 1013 and 1017.

Communications Handbook HELP

See Proofreaders' Marks.

Professional Model

In the following essay the art critic Frank Getlein writes about Mary Cassatt's painting Mother and Child *(see page 518).*

The French title for this picture, <u>Maternité</u>, expresses what a lot of people have thought of it: the summation of motherhood, quiet caring, sheltering love, undivided attention. The quietness is made quieter still by the colors. There is a lot of white, but it never flashes or dazzles. It's all grayed down, or blued down, or browned down—even softened by roses on the mother's dress, as the floral pattern exudes its dominant tone into the surrounding white, an effect of the eye, not of the fabric, and one essential to Impressionist vision. The brightest of the whites is right where it should be, on the baby's chest, to center our attention on the face by reflecting, softly, a little light up there.

The idea of motherhood is expressed here most intently by the utter relaxation of the infant. The child has total confidence in its situation, a confidence beyond feeling confident. Life simply is and is as it should be. The child's hand on its mother's chin is not so much a conscious gesture of love as it is just keeping in touch with the best part of a familiar and totally supportive environment.

States interpretive claim, or thesis.

Describes mood. Describes colors and patterns.

Notes image that draws his eye.

Interprets images.

(continued on next page)

WRITER'S WORKSHOP 517

Teaching the Writer's Workshop

Prewriting

Work through the prewriting steps outlined on p. 516 with students. You may wish to take one of the examples of art and work with the class to develop an example of an interpretive claim.

Drafting

- Before students begin to draft their papers, read aloud the Professional Model provided on pp. 517–518.
- Students should write a clear statement of their interpretive claim before attempting to draft their essays. They should also have notes indicating what aspects of the painting they intend to use to support their views. If students have difficulty with this, it may help them to discuss their interpretation with a partner before starting.

Using the Model

Read through the model with students and discuss the side-margin comments. You may wish to focus the discussion by asking questions such as the following:

❓ What is the subject of Frank Getlein's essay? Where in the essay is this information provided for the reader?

❓ What aspect of the painting is focused on in the first paragraph?

❓ Why do you think Getlein focuses first on color?

❓ What other aspects of the painting does he use to support his opinion?

❓ Which of his supporting arguments do you think is most effective? Why?

Encourage students to model their opening lines on Getlein so that they avoid the clichéd sentence "The painting I'm writing about is ..."

Reaching All Students

Struggling Writers

Students having difficulty developing an interpretive claim may benefit from working at first with two pictures that have similar themes but dramatically different moods: for example, two dance scenes or two landscapes. For example, the heroic painting by Jacques-Louis David of Napoleon contrasts sharply with the scenes of the French army in Spain as painted by Francisco Goya, yet both painters are from the same period and both are dealing with the Napoleonic Wars.

T517

Evaluating and Revising

Have students use the Evaluation Criteria provided here to review their drafts and determine needed revisions. A quick reality check is possible if students show their selected paintings to a small group. Let the group supply the adjectives suggested to them by the works of art. Writers can quickly determine how much evidence they will need to substantiate their interpretation.

Proofreading

Have students scan through their papers and identify critical vocabulary and terms. For example, it would be disastrous to misspell the name of the artist or the work of art. Essential art terms should also be spelled and used correctly. Have students attach a list of the critical words and terms that they have verified to their final draft.

Publishing

Students who are also taking art classes may wish to take their essays to art class and present them for extra credit.

Reflecting

If students are adding their interpretive essays to their portfolios, be sure they date their papers and attach a brief reflection on their writing experiences focusing on questions such as these:

1. Why did I select this piece of art?
2. How are an artist's choices similar to those of a writer?
3. What can art teach me about writing?

Grading Timesaver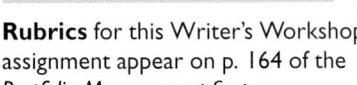

Rubrics for this Writer's Workshop assignment appear on p. 164 of the *Portfolio Management System*.

Resources

Peer Editing Forms and Rubrics
• *Portfolio Management System*, p. 163
Revision Transparencies
• *Workshop Resources*, p. 39

Professional Model (continued)

For all that relaxation, however, the mother and child are fixed in the painting by the pitcher, which matches the line of the mother's head and shoulder, and by the basin at the child's head. The structure of the painting, beneath its glowing softness, is as firm as the two-handed grasp with which the mother holds the child. The diagonal of the rose-strewn dress is equaled and answered by the opposite diagonal of the shadowed skirt and the lighter upper-right background. Like the crockery and the line of the table or counter behind the figures, this centers everything on the two faces and what they say in silence.

—from *Mary Cassatt: Paintings and Prints*

Notes details that repeat shapes.

Describes what he sees the lines doing.

Notes that the lines draw his attention to the faces.

■ *Evaluation Criteria*

An effective essay that interprets art

1. *includes an introduction that identifies the title and artist*
2. *includes a clear thesis statement, or interpretive claim*
3. *supports the claim with details from the work*
4. *is clearly organized*

Revision
STRATEGIES

Ask a writing partner for feedback. Make sure you've provided a satisfying conclusion and have not just trailed off or stopped abruptly. In a final sentence or two, use different words to restate or reword the key ideas in your interpretive claim.

Mother and Child by Mary Cassatt. Oil on canvas.

The Roland P. Murdock Collection, Wichita Art Museum.

518 THE POETRY COLLECTIONS

Using Students' Strengths

Auditory Learners

Students who are primarily auditory learners may need to work with a partner who has stronger visual skills. This assignment is a good one for allowing students to work through the early stages with a partner or in small discussion groups, but each student should create an individual essay.

Visual Learners

If there are students in the class who are talented artists, you may wish to allow them to interpret one of their own works of art for this assignment. Have students explore the creative choices they made and their motivations for making the decisions.

T518

Collection 9

Imagine

Theme

Making Connections *The major element in poetry is figurative language—the use of words to help us see how things in the world are alike, in surprising ways. Some poems create worlds of imagination. What a poet asks is that readers step into this world. . . .*

Reading the Anthology

Reaching Struggling Readers

The *Reading Skills and Strategies: Reaching Struggling Readers* binder includes a Reading Strategies Handbook that offers concrete suggestions for helping students who have difficulty reading and comprehending text, or students who are reluctant readers. When a specific strategy is most appropriate for a selection, a correlation to the Handbook is provided at the bottom of the teacher's page under the head Struggling Readers. This head may also be used to introduce additional ideas for helping students read challenging texts.

Reading Beyond the Anthology

Read On   At the end of the poetry collections in the grade nine book, there is an annotated bibliography of books suitable for extended reading. The suggested books are related to works in these collections by theme, by author, or by subject. To preview the Read On for the poetry collections, please turn to p. T613.

Collection 9 **Imagine**

Resources for this Collection

Note: All resources for this collection are available for preview on the *One-Stop Planner CD-ROM 2 with Test Generator*. All worksheets and blackline masters may be printed from the CD-ROM.

Internet Resources
go.hrw.com LE0 9-9

Selection or Feature	Reading and Literary Skills	Vocabulary, Language, and Grammar
Elements of Literature: **Figures of Speech** (p. 520) **Fork** Charles Simic (p. 521)	• *Literary Elements,* Transparency 11	
I Never Saw a Moor Emily Dickinson (p. 522) **Kidnap Poem** Nikki Giovanni (p. 524) **Southbound on the Freeway** May Swenson (p. 526)	• *Graphic Organizers for Active Reading,* Worksheet pp. 40, 41, 42	• *Words to Own,* Worksheet p. 28 • *Daily Oral Grammar,* Transparency 36
Beware: Do Not Read This Poem Ishmael Reed (p. 530) **Connections:** **Eyeglasses for the Mind** Stephen King (p. 532) **The Secret** Denise Levertov (p. 533)	• *Graphic Organizers for Active Reading,* Worksheet pp. 43, 44	• *Words to Own,* Worksheet p. 28 • *Daily Oral Grammar,* Transparency 37
The Seven Ages of Man William Shakespeare (p. 536)	• *Graphic Organizers for Active Reading,* Worksheet p. 45 • *Literary Elements:* Transparency 11 Worksheet p. 34	• *Words to Own,* Worksheet p. 30
Fire and Ice Robert Frost (p. 540) **All Watched Over by** **Machines of Loving Grace** Richard Brautigan (p. 542)	• *Graphic Organizers for Active Reading,* Worksheet pp. 46, 47	• *Words to Own,* Worksheet p. 28
Extending the Theme: **Claiming Breath** Diane Glancy (p. 546)	The Extending the Theme feature provides students with an unstructured opportunity to practice reading strategies using a selection that extends the theme of the collection.	
Writer's Workshop: Poetry (p. 550)		

Other Resources for this Collection

- *Cross-Curricular Activities*, p. 9
- *Portfolio Management System*, Introduction to Portfolio Assessment, p. 1
- *Test Generator*, Collection Test 💿

Writing	Listening and Speaking Viewing and Representing	Assessment
		• *Formal Assessment*, Literary Elements Test, p. 105
• *Portfolio Management System*, Rubrics for Choices, p. 165	• *Visual Connections:* Videocassette B, Segment 9 📼 • *Audio CD Library,* Disc 15, Tracks 11, 12, 13 🎧 • *Viewing and Representing:* Fine Art Transparency 12; Worksheet p. 48 📽 • *Portfolio Management System*, Rubrics for Choices, p. 165	• *Formal Assessment*, Selection Test, p. 97 • *Standardized Test Preparation*, p. 72 • *Test Generator (One-Stop Planner CD-ROM)* 💿
• *Portfolio Management System*, Rubrics for Choices, p. 167	• *Audio CD Library,* Disc 15, Tracks 14, 15 🎧 • *Viewing and Representing:* Fine Art Transparency 13; Worksheet p. 52 📽 • *Portfolio Management System*, Rubrics for Choices, p. 167	• *Formal Assessment*, Selection Test, p. 99 • *Test Generator (One-Stop Planner CD-ROM)* 💿
• *Portfolio Management System*, Rubrics for Choices, p. 168	• *Audio CD Library,* Disc 15, Track 16 🎧 • *Portfolio Management System*, Rubrics for Choices, p. 168	• *Formal Assessment*, Selection Test, p. 101 • *Test Generator (One-Stop Planner CD-ROM)* 💿
• *Portfolio Management System*, Rubrics for Choices, p. 170	• *Audio CD Library,* Disc 15, Tracks 17, 18 🎧 • *Portfolio Management System*, Rubrics for Choices, p. 170	• *Formal Assessment*, Selection Test, p. 103 • *Test Generator (One-Stop Planner CD-ROM)* 💿
	• *Audio CD Library,* Disc 15, Track 19 🎧	
		• *Portfolio Management System* • Prewriting, p. 172 • Peer Editing, p. 173 • Assessment Rubric, p. 174

 Transparency    CD-ROM    Video    Audio CD

Collection Planner

T518C

Collection 9 Imagine

Skills Focus

Selection or Feature	Reading Skills and Strategies	Elements of Literature	Language/ Grammar	Vocabulary/ Spelling	Writing	Listening/ Speaking	Viewing/ Representing
Elements of Literature: Figures of Speech (p. 520) **Fork** Charles Simic (p. 521)		Figures of Speech, pp. 520–521 • Simile • Metaphor: Direct and Implied • Personification					
I Never Saw a Moor Emily Dickinson (p. 522) **Kidnap Poem** Nikki Giovanni (p. 524) **Southbound on the Freeway** May Swenson (p. 526)	Multiple Meanings of Words, p. 524 Understanding Word Play, pp. 524, 528	Pun, pp. 524, 528 Speaker, pp. 526, 528 Diction, pp. 522, 528 Figures of Speech, p. 528	Using Nouns as Verbs, pp. 528–529		Create Similes, p. 529 Write Lines Imitating Dickinson, p. 529 Create a Riddle, p. 529 Write a "Kidnap" Poem, p. 529 Create a Class Notebook of Figures of Speech, p. 529		
Beware: Do Not Read This Poem Ishmael Reed (p. 530) **The Secret** Denise Levertov (p. 533)	Make Inferences, p. 535	Narration in Poetry, pp. 530, 535 Implied Ideas, p. 533 Personify, p. 535 Speaker, p. 535			Collect Ideas for a Poem, p. 535 Write a Poem, p. 535 Write Another Stanza for a Poem, p. 535 Write a Letter to an Author, p. 535		
The Seven Ages of Man William Shakespeare (p. 536)	Paraphrase a Poem, p. 539 Context, p. 539	Extended Metaphor, p. 536 Images, p. 538 Simile, p. 538 Metaphor, p. 538		Multiple Meanings, p. 539	Adapt a Poem, p. 539	Write and Perform a Short Play Based on a Poem, p. 539	Evaluate Illustrations, p. 539
Fire and Ice Robert Frost (p. 540) **All Watched Over by Machines of Loving Grace** Richard Brautigan (p. 542)		Implied Metaphor, pp. 540, 544 Tone, pp. 542, 544			Collect Ideas for a Poem, p. 545 Write a Paragraph Describing an Imaginary Situation, p. 545 Create Metaphors, p. 545 Evaluate a Poem, p. 545		Compare Art and Text, p. 545
Extending the Theme: Claiming Breath Diane Glancy (p. 546)	Dialogue with the Text, pp. 546, 549	The Extending the Theme feature provides students with an unstructured opportunity to practice reading strategies using a selection that extends the theme of the collection.					
Writer's Workshop: Poetry (p. 550)		Free Verse, p. 551 Rhyme, p. 552 • Rhymed Couplets • Quatrains Meter, p. 552			Write a Poem or Group of Poems, pp. 550–552		

IMAGINE
WRITING FOCUS: Poetry

*Think with your body
And dance with your mind.*

—*Victor Hernandez Cruz*

Can dogs imagine? Can whales imagine? Can cats imagine? Maybe. Maybe not. But you can imagine that they can, even if they can't—and that's what's important. Your imagination is a time-and-space ship more powerful than *Star Trek*'s *Voyager*. Your ship can take you anywhere, any time—backward, forward, upside down and inside out—and you are the captain. Want to visit Mars? China? Win a million dollars? Go on a date? See Timbuktu? You can. For everything we imagine is real—at least as real as our dreams and hopes and fears.

Writer's Notebook

Exercise your imagination. Pick a hungry insect, bird, or animal and put yourself in its shoes (or feet). Close your eyes and picture what time of year it is, what time of day it is, and what the weather is like. Write these down in your Writer's Notebook. Now close your eyes again, look around carefully, make notes on exactly where you—the hungry insect, bird, or animal—are located, and tell what you want, right this minute. Save your notes.

WORK IN PROGRESS

Writing Focus: Poetry

WORK IN PROGRESS

The following **Work in Progress** assignments build to a culminating **Writer's Workshop** at the end of the collection.

- I Never Saw a Moor / Kidnap Poem / Southbound on the Freeway — Creating similes (p. 529)
- Beware: Do Not Read This Poem / The Secret — Finding a subject (p. 535)
- The Seven Ages of Man — Imitating a poem (p. 539)
- Fire and Ice / All Watched Over by Machines of Loving Grace — Writing a first line (p. 545)

Writer's Workshop: Poetry (p. 550)

OBJECTIVES

1. Read poetry centered on the theme "Imagine"
2. Identify and analyze literary elements used in the poems with special emphasis on figures of speech
3. Respond to the literature using a variety of modes
4. Plan, draft, revise, proof, and publish a poem

Responding to the Quotation

? Tell students that the experience of reading a poem can be like taking a trip through time and space. Explain that a poem is a vehicle, created from words, that transports readers away from present-day reality and into a world of imagination. As students read the poems in the collection, remind them to think about how the poets use their own imaginations to stir the imagination of the reader. How do you think dancing with one's mind differs from thinking? [Possible response: *Thinking* suggests using reason, while *dancing* suggests using the imagination and intuition.]

RESPONDING TO THE ART

How does this photograph of a dancer support the collection's theme? [Possible response: Her exuberant pose and uplifted arms and legs suggest joy and spontaneity.] The dancer is the great Judith Jamison (1943–   ), dancing in Alvin Ailey's *Revelations*. A video of one of Judith Jamison's performances is available. It was made in 1982 at New York's City Center.

Writer's Notebook

WORK IN PROGRESS

Point out to students that the word *imagine* is related to the word *image* and suggests the ability to form a mental picture. Encourage students to use their imaginative abilities to create a vivid picture of the hungry insect, bird, or animal in a place that they have never seen.

T519

Resources

Elements of Literature
Figures of Speech
For additional instruction on figures of speech, see *Literary Elements*:
• Transparency 11

Formal Assessment
• Literary Elements Test, p. 105

Elements of Literature

This feature focuses on the most commonly used types of figures of speech: simile, direct and implied metaphor, and personification. It points out that figures of speech are always based on some kind of comparison and explains how this comparison is made in each type.

Mini-Lesson:
Figures of Speech
After students have read the feature, list the terms simile, direct metaphor, implied metaphor, and personification on the board. Ask volunteers to come up with their own examples for each term and write them under the respective head. Have other students explain the connection that is being made in each example.

Next, hand out copies of magazines or newspapers. Have students work in groups to find examples of the different kinds of figurative language. Each group should make a list of the examples they find. Finally, have groups choose their favorite examples and share them with the class.

Applying the Element
After students have read the feature, expand on Brinnin's point that everyday speech contains figures of speech we no longer recognize as such. Have students describe or illustrate the literal meaning of each of the following

(Activity continues on page T521.)

FIGURES OF SPEECH: Seeing Connections

One of the ways that poets play with words is by using figurative language—expressions that put aside literal meanings in favor of imaginative connections. A **figure of speech** is always based on a comparison, and it is not literally true. If someone says to you, "Listen, I'm going to give you a piece of my mind," you don't say, "OK, I'll bring a plate to put it on." You understand that the speaker is using a figure of speech, that he's going to tell you what he's *really* thinking, and that it's not going to be nice.

Figurative language can be a kind of shorthand. It can take a lot of words to express an idea in literal terms. But the same idea can be communicated instantly by a figure of speech. Think of all the words you'd have to use to explain literally what these common expressions say: "Judy's uptight." "The check bounced." "Gilford's laid back." "Cool it."

Figures of Speech in Everyday Language

Many figures of speech that were once fresh and original have been completely absorbed into our everyday language. We use them without realizing that they aren't literally true. When we think about our language, in fact, we realize that figures of speech are the foundation of thousands of expressions.

When we refer to the "roof of the mouth" or the "arm of the chair" or the "foot of the bed," we are using figurative language. In each case, we are imaginatively relating a part of the body to something that has nothing to do with the body.

Even the languages of science and business are based on figures of speech. Dentists talk about "building bridges."

Biologists talk about "the bloodstream." Stockbrokers talk about "the market crash." Even our newest technology, computer science, already has its own figures of speech in terms such as *menu, virus, window,* and *mouse.*

Similes: "X Is Like Y"

A simile is the simplest form of figurative language. In a **simile,** two dissimilar things are compared using a word such as *like, as, than,* or *resembles.* "The moon shines *like* a fifty-cent piece." "Eva's eyes are *as* glassy *as* marbles." "Lucy feels lighter *than* a grasshopper."

Reprinted with special permission of King Features Syndicate.

Using Students' Strengths

Visual Learners
Ask students to choose a poem from their textbooks that they have already read and identify the figures of speech it contains. Then, have students use their imaginations to draw representations of the metaphors, similes, and personification found in the poem. If possible, ask them to integrate the various representations into a single picture. Students can display their representations on the class bulletin board.

Auditory/Musical Learners
Point out that the use of figurative language is as common in song lyrics as it is in poetry. Have students collect examples of figurative language from their favorite songs; they can either transcribe the lyrics or play recordings for the class. (Instruct students to select lyrics suitable for general audiences.) Have the class discuss which lyrics use figurative language most imaginatively and what the effect is upon the listener.

by John Malcolm Brinnin

Here is a poet who looked at an ordinary fork and thought of a simile.

Fork

This strange thing must have
  crept
Right out of hell.
It resembles a bird's foot
Worn around the cannibal's
  neck.
As you hold it in your hand,
As you stab with it into a piece
  of meat,
It is possible to imagine the
  rest of the bird:
Its head which like your fist
Is large, bald, beakless, and
  blind.

— Charles Simic

Metaphors: "X Is Y"

Similes are easily recognized because of their connectives (*like, as, than, resembles*): "You eat like a pig!" When the connective is omitted, we have a metaphor: "You're a pig!" A **metaphor,** then, is a comparison between two unlike things, in which one thing becomes another thing without the use of the word *like, as, than,* or *resembles*. The difference between a metaphor and a simile is a matter of emphasis.

In a simile, the two things remain separate, but in a metaphor they are united.

A metaphor can be direct or implied. A **direct metaphor** directly compares the two things by the use of a verb such as *is*. An **implied metaphor** implies or suggests the comparison between the two things without stating it directly. If we say, "The city is a sleeping woman," we are using a direct metaphor. If we say, "The city sleeps peacefully," we use an implied metaphor. Both metaphors identify a city that has its lights out with a person who has quietly fallen into the darkness of sleep.

Metaphor is the most flexible and suggestive element of figurative language. It is a means by which all experience can be imaginatively connected.

According to an old Hebrew saying, "The world is a wedding"—and in that, we have a single metaphor that defines all metaphors.

Personification: Making the World Human

Personification is a special kind of metaphor in which human qualities are given to something that is not human— an animal, an object, or even an idea. What personifications can you find in these headlines?

- Every Computer "Whispers" Its Secrets
- China Now a Struggling Giant
- White House Digs In Its Heels on Budget Issue

According to an old Hebrew saying, "The world is a wedding"—and in that, we have a single metaphor that defines all metaphors.

Sometimes personification simply involves giving life and feelings to things that are inanimate, or lifeless. When we say that a tooth is angry or a cough is stubborn or a computer is friendly or love is blind, we are using a kind of personification. Personification is yet another example of how we use our imaginations to give meaning to the whole nonhuman world.

ELEMENTS OF LITERATURE: FIGURES OF SPEECH **521**

(*Activity continues from page T520.*)
words or phrases. Then discuss how the word or phrase may have acquired its present meaning.

Nouns	Verbs
• beachcomber	• booby trap
• blind date	• brainwash
• breadwinner	• buttonhole
• disc jockey	• hitchhike
• egghead	• moonlight
• frogman	• pussyfoot
• housewarming	• boot up
• mudslinger	• whitewash
• paydirt	

Help students distinguish similes from metaphors by reading the following sentences aloud and having students write down *S* for simile and *M* for metaphor. Review the answers. If students still have difficulty distinguishing the two, review the list of connecting words that mark similes (p. 521).

1. Love is a red, red rose. [M]
2. Joe is a walking encyclopedia. [M]
3. Chris looks as white as a sheet. [S]
4. Angela blossoms in the spring. [M]
5. Keisha has a mind like a razor. [S]
6. Mitch can be as cold as ice. [S]
7. Happiness is a cuddly kitten. [M]
8. Mona looks as fresh as a daisy. [S]
9. The huge conglomerate was a sleeping giant. [M]
10. The news came like a bolt from the blue. [S]

Note that the five metaphors above can also be used to distinguish implied from direct metaphors. Sentence 4 uses an implied metaphor; 1, 2, 7, and 9 use direct metaphors.

Finally, give students some practice with personification by asking them to complete the following sentences. They should have the subject of each sentence do something that a human being would do. Sample responses are provided in brackets.

1. Mike's jalopy _____ . [sputtered, coughed, and finally died]
2. Fear wrapped its _____ . [cloak around her shoulders]
3. Jealousy _____ . [reared its ugly head]
4. The moon _____ . [smiled down on the newlyweds]
5. The wind _____ . [raced through the forest]

Getting Students Involved

Cooperative Learning

Group Poetry Project. Provide students with poetry collections from the library. Have them work in groups of three to analyze the figures of speech in three poems they choose. The first student should look for similes, the second for metaphors, and the third for personification. Each group member should present his or her findings to the rest of the group. They can then organize and convert this information into a chart.

Animal Similes. Note that people are using figurative language when they compare themselves to animals in similes such as "strong as an ox," "hungry as a horse," or "mad as a bull." Have students work in pairs to brainstorm a list of common similes in which humans compare their attributes, qualities, and feelings to those of animals.

OBJECTIVES

I Never Saw a Moor / Kidnap Poem / Southbound on the Freeway

1. Read and interpret the poems
2. Analyze diction
3. Interpret puns
4. Identify the speaker
5. Express understanding through creative writing or research/ collaboration

SKILLS

Literary
- Analyze diction
- Interpret puns
- Identify the speaker

Writing
- Create similes
- Write a poem that imitates the structure of Dickinson's poem
- Write a paragraph from an alien's point of view
- Write a poem based on Giovanni's poem

Research/Collaboration
- Collect figures of speech

Viewing/Representing
- Improvise a dialogue based on a work of art (ATE)
- Analyze how an artist plays with images (ATE)

Planning

- **Block Schedule**
  Block Scheduling Lesson Plans with Pacing Guide
- **Traditional Schedule**
  Lesson Plans Including Strategies for English-Language Learners
- **One-Stop Planner**
  CD-ROM with Test Generator

Before You Read

I NEVER SAW A MOOR

Make the Connection

Imagining Things Unseen

Every day each of us travels in imagination. (Yes, that includes thinking about running the marathon or dreaming of being a hoop star.) Being a poet means tuning in and paying attention to these journeys—and writing down what they look and feel like as they flash by.

Quickwrite

Name two things that you've never seen firsthand but that you can imagine clearly. Describe what you see, hear, smell, taste, touch.

Keep your notes. For questions and activities on this poem, see pages 528–529.

Elements of Literature

Diction: Words Count

After Emily Dickinson's death, her friends set to work copying her poems (Dickinson's handwriting was often hard to make out) and trying to get them published. In this process, they made changes. In "I Never Saw a Moor" the word *Billow* was changed to *Wave*. The word *Checks* was changed to *Chart.* The changes in diction made a difference.

> **D**iction is a writer's or speaker's choice of words.
>
> *For more on Diction, see the Handbook of Literary Terms.*

 go.hrw.com
LE0 9-9

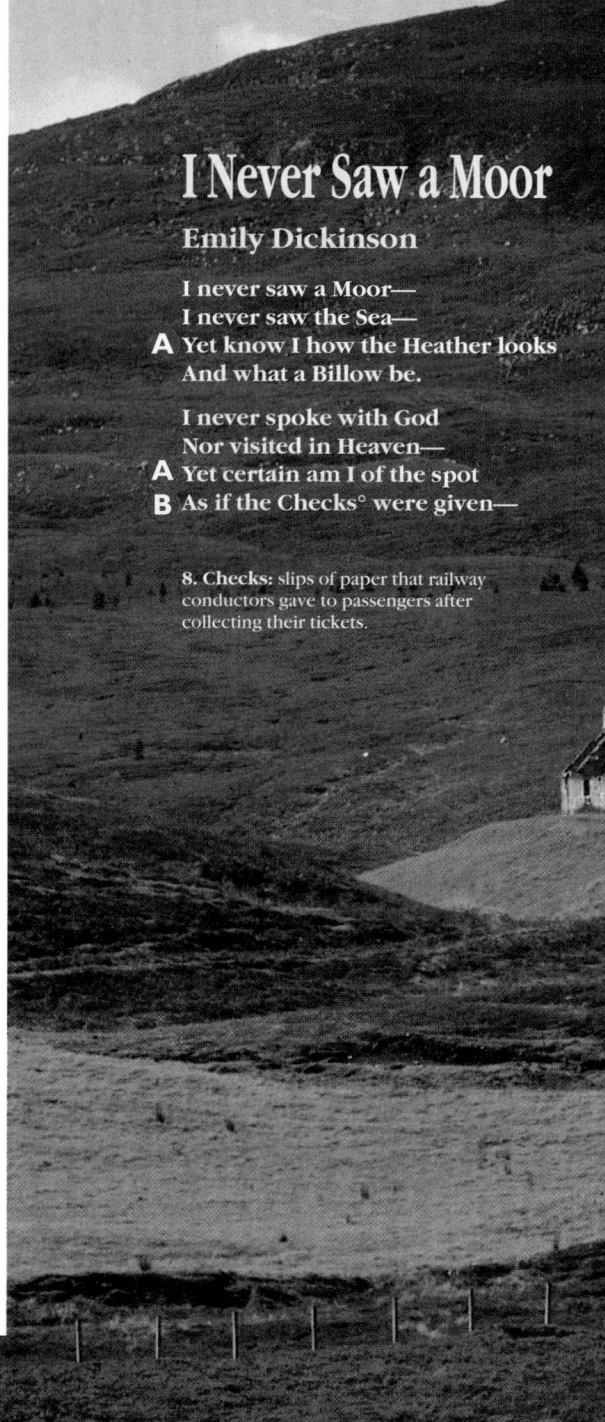

I Never Saw a Moor

Emily Dickinson

I never saw a Moor—
I never saw the Sea—
A Yet know I how the Heather looks
And what a Billow be.

I never spoke with God
Nor visited in Heaven—
A Yet certain am I of the spot
B As if the Checks° were given—

8. Checks: slips of paper that railway conductors gave to passengers after collecting their tickets.

 — *Resources: Print and Media* —

Reading
- *Graphic Organizers for Active Reading,* pp. 40, 41, 42
- *Audio CD Library,* Disc 15, Tracks 11, 12, 13

Writing and Language
- *Daily Oral Grammar,* Transparency 36

Viewing and Representing
- *Viewing and Representing* Fine Art Transparency 12 Fine Art Worksheet, p. 48

- *Visual Connections* Videocassette B, Segment 9

Assessment
- *Formal Assessment,* p. 97
- *Portfolio Management System,* p. 165
- *Standardized Test Preparation,* p. 72
- *Test Generator (One-Stop Planner* CD-ROM)

Internet
- go.hrw.com (keyword: LE0 9-9)

MEET THE WRITER

She Knows Poetry

Unlike most people today, **Emily Dickinson** (1830–1886) was born, lived most of her life, and died in the same house. After she was twenty-six, she rarely went out of that house in Amherst, Massachusetts. But for the next thirty years she traveled to the ends of the earth and the universe in her imagination. She jotted down poems in the margins of newspapers, on brown paper bags, and even on the insides of envelopes.

Dickinson also wrote many letters. In one of them, she defined poetry:

66 If I read a book and it makes my whole body so cold no fire can ever warm me, I know it is poetry. If I feel physically as if the top of my head were taken off, I know that it is poetry. These are the only ways I know it. 99

A famous editor, T. W. Higginson, once asked Emily Dickinson for a photograph of herself. In her reply the poet created a photograph in words.

Amherst College Library.

66 Could you believe me—without? I had no portrait, now, but am small, like the Wren, and my Hair is bold, like the Chestnut Bur— and my eyes like the Sherry in the Glass, that the Guest leaves. 99

While she was alive, only seven of her poems were published—all anonymously. Dickinson died not knowing that she would become recognized as one of the greatest poets who ever wrote in English.

I NEVER SAW A MOOR 523

Summary ■■

The poet declares that even though she has never seen either a moor or the sea, she can imagine what they look like. Similarly, although she has had no firsthand experience of heaven, her faith makes her confident that it exists. The poet's strong and simple faith is mirrored in her diction—she chooses simple nouns and verbs—and in her use of alliteration (l. 2 and 4). Her diction creates a tone of serenity and peaceful certainty. The poem's theme can be inferred from the apparent contradiction that she illustrates: Knowledge is not necessarily based on experience; imagination and faith give people a certainty they would not otherwise possess.

Resources ——

Viewing and Representing
Videocassette B, Segment 9
Available in Spanish and English. This segment provides students with biographical background on the poet. For full lesson plans and worksheets, see *Visual Connections Teacher's Manual.*

Listening
Audio CD Library
A recording of this poem is provided in the *Audio CD Library*:
• Disc 15, Track 11

Ⓐ Struggling Readers
Reading Inverted Sentences
Point out Dickinson's use of inverted word order in l. 3 and 7. Ask struggling readers to rewrite these lines in standard word order. Have them read their revised versions of the poem silently and then aloud. Next, have them reread the poem in its original form and ask them what effect is produced by the inverted syntax. Help them hear the change in emphasis and rhythm in l. 7.

Ⓑ Elements of Literature
Diction
❓ What comparison does the speaker suggest with the word *Checks*? What effect is produced by her diction? [The speaker compares dying and going to heaven with travel on a train. Her choice of words underscores her certainty of her destination.]

Reaching All Students

English Language Learners
For strategies for engaging English language learners with the literature, see
• *Lesson Plans Including Strategies for English-Language Learners*

Advanced Learners
Explain to students that individual faith is the theme of many of Dickinson's poems. Ask students to find other Dickinson poems that present this theme and then share them with the class.

Crossing the Curriculum

Geography
Both moors and heather are characteristic features of the British Isles. A moor is an expanse of open, rolling land. Heather is a low, hardy evergreen shrub with small pinkish flowers; it grows well in the marshy soil of a moor. Ask students to prepare a display that compares the geographical characteristics of the British Isles with those of New England, Dickinson's home. The display might include illustrations, botanical facts, and labeled maps.

Summary ■■

In this free verse poem, Giovanni compares the experience of being swept up by a really great poem to being kidnapped by the poet. She extends the metaphor throughout the poem, listing all the things she wants to do with her kidnapped readers: take them to the beach, take them home, sing to them. She puns with poetic terms, which serve double duty as verbs of movement: for example, "meter" in l. 6 and "dash" in l. 10. Her vision helps the reader imagine the true force of the reading experience—the force of being pulled into another's world.

Resources

Listening
Audio CD Library
A recording of this poem is provided in the *Audio CD Library*:
• Disc 15, Track 12

RESPONDING TO THE ART

For information on the artwork, see p. T281; for information on the artist, see p. T283.
Activity. Ask students to improvise a brief dialogue between the two figures in this work. Have them create puns based on the musical terms suggested by the painting (for example, fret, strings, pick). Students might also compare the composition and mood of *Serenade* with Bearden's *La Primavera* (p. T284), a work he created two years earlier.

Before You Read

KIDNAP POEM

Make the Connection

Taken for a Ride

Poets and children like to play games with words—listen to any four-year-old. In "Kidnap Poem" a poet pretends to abduct you into her world, and she turns nouns into verbs to help her do it. Actually, there's as much kidding around as kidnapping in this poem.

Quickwrite

Imagine a job you'd like to have—jet pilot, teacher, writer, plumber, diver, actor, homemaker, DJ. Anything you want. Then, list all the words you can think of that are associated with that job. If you choose musician, you might start with *symphony, notes, strings, keys, chorus.*

Keep your notes. For questions and activities on this poem, see pages 528–529.

Elements of Literature

Puns for Fun

As you saw on page 489, poets play with words—this poet plays with nouns and makes them verbs, she plays with words that sound the same but are spelled differently, and she plays with words that have several meanings. Read carefully— this poem is like one of those word games that contain hidden tricks.

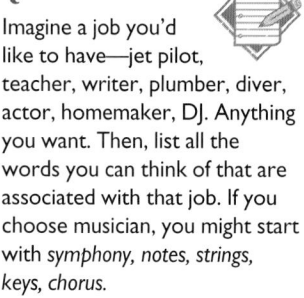

A pun is a play on the **multiple meanings** of a word (*flies, club, kid*) or on two words that **sound alike but have different meanings** (*pause/paws*).

For more on Puns, see the Handbook of Literary Terms.

Serenade (1969) by Romare Bearden. Collage and paint on panel (45¾" × 32½").

go.hrw.com
LE0 9-9

524 THE POETRY COLLECTIONS

Reaching All Students

Struggling Readers

Review the meaning of the terms used in the poem: meter, lyric, alliterate, and ode. Explain that they are used as verbs rather than nouns and are not meant to be taken literally; Giovanni is interested in creating an impression of movement and in collapsing the boundaries between real life and poetry.

Using Students' Strengths

Visual Learners

Ask students which images in the poem they find most striking. Then have students create a visual representation of the whole poem or of one of the specific images they identified. They can choose any medium or, like Bearden, mix different mediums. Students should add captions, either quotations from the text or something they invent, to tie their representations to the poem.

Kidnap Poem

Nikki Giovanni

ever been kidnapped
by a poet
if i were a poet
i'd kidnap you

5   put you in my phrases
and meter you to jones beach  **A**
or maybe coney island
or maybe just to my house

lyric you in lilacs
10   dash you in the rain
alliterate the beach **B**
to complement my see

play the lyre for you
ode you with my love song
15   anything to win you
wrap you in the red Black green
show you off to mama

yeah if i were
a poet i'd kid
20   nap you **C**

MEET THE WRITER

"The Princess of Black Poetry"

Nikki Giovanni (1943–) was born in Knoxville, Tennessee, and grew up in Cincinnati, Ohio. She is affectionately called the Princess of Black Poetry because of the large, enthusiastic crowds she attracts whenever she gives public readings of her work. Behind all of Giovanni's poetry, according to one critic, are "the creation of racial pride and the communication of individual love." Giovanni herself says:

❝ I write out of my own experiences—which also happen to be the experiences of my people. ❞

Not flattered when students who take her classes try to write poems that sound like hers, she says:

❝ I already sound like me. I want my students to hear their own voices. ❞

KIDNAP POEM **525**

A Appreciating Language

Style

❓ What is unusual about the speaker's use of the word *meter*? [It is a noun used as a verb.] How would you describe Giovanni's style based on this usage and on the poem's lack of punctuation? [Sample response: Breaking grammatical patterns is a daring innovation that mirrors the imaginative, free spirit of the speaker.]

B Elements of Literature

Puns

❓ What is the play on words in l. 11? [The word "alliterate" sounds like the word *litter*.] What might Giovanni be suggesting by using this pun? [Possible response: The poet is commenting ironically on the cleverness of her own wordplay.]

C Advanced Learners

Interpreting

❓ How does Giovanni use the word *kidnap* to mean more than one thing? [*Kidnap* literally means "capture"; the capture that the poet threatens, however, is that of the reader's attention. The action of kidnapping is used as an extended metaphor.] Why do you think the poet breaks the word into "kid" and "nap" in l. 19-20? [It creates three levels of meaning: "kid" you (tease); "nap" you (raise a nap, rub you, or put you to sleep); and "kidnap" you (capture).]

BROWSING IN THE FILES

About the Author. Nikki Giovanni once said, "I come from a long line of storytellers. My grandfather was a Latin scholar and he loved the myths, and my mother is a big romanticist, so we heard a lot of stories growing up...I appreciated the quality and the rhythm of the telling of the stories."

Two Critics' Comments. In the *New York Times Book Review,* Nancy Klein wrote that Giovanni's poems "exhibit a combination of casual energy and sudden wit." According to another *New York Times* reviewer, Nancy Rosenberg, Giovanni's poems "are sly and seductive, freewheeling and winsome, tough, sure and proud."

Skill Link

Compare Reviews of Literature with Your Own Response

Ask students to reread the poem and then list three adjectives or phrases that describe Giovanni's poetry. When students are finished, introduce them to the quotations in Two Critics' Comments, reading their remarks aloud and copying these words onto the board: *casual energy, sudden wit, sly, seductive, freewheeling, winsome, tough, sure, proud.* Have students compare the words and phrases on their lists with those used by the critics. Ask students to use details from the poem to defend their own responses. Then have students find details from the poem that support the critics' choice of words.

Summary ■

In an ironic comment on the role of the automobile in our lives, Swenson describes what a tourist from Orbitville, a city in outer space, thinks of earth. The alien, who is the speaker for most of the poem, mistakes cars for living beings and describes them as having metal and glass bodies, round feet, four eyes, and hissing voices. The alien wonders whether the soft shapes inside are the creatures' guts or brains. The poet's humorous imagination raises a serious question: Has the automobile become the most notable "creature" on Earth?

Resources

Listening
Audio CD Library

A recording of this poem is provided in the *Audio CD Library*:
• Disc 15, Track 13

Viewing and Representing
Fine Art Transparency

A fine art transparency of Gary Ruddell's *Hot Air Balloon* can be used with "Southbound on the Freeway." See the *Viewing and Representing Transparencies and Worksheets*:
• Transparency 12
• Worksheet, p. 48

RESPONDING TO THE ART

The artist **James Doolin** (1932–) lives and works in California. He recently completed a series of public murals for the Metropolitan Transit Authority in Los Angeles, which depict the city circa 1870, 1910, 1960, and after 2000.

Activity. Point out the image in the rearview mirror. How does this image suggest that cars are living beings? [Possible response: The lights in the rearview mirror look like a pair of eyes, as suggested in ll. 11–12 of the poem.] Ask: Is anyone driving this car?

Before You Read

SOUTHBOUND ON THE FREEWAY

Make the Connection

Imagination on Location

This poem opens with a long traveling shot, zooms in, hovers, and takes a series of close-ups. If that sounds like making a movie, it is. Just like a movie, the imagination can do long shots, jump-cuts, splices, wide-angle shots, and close-ups. Here's a creature feature about . . . Well, you have to discover that for yourself. As you watch this "movie," you'll have to decide where the poet's imagination is taking you.

Quickwrite

Imagine that you are an extremely intelligent alien from outer space, but you have never seen a human before. For the very first time, you watch a human get out of bed, brush his or her teeth, sing in a chorus, or play softball. Choose a few of these activities (or some others you think of) and jot down how the alien might describe what is going on.

Keep your notes. For questions and activities on this poem, see pages 528–529.

Elements of Literature

Speaker: Who's Talking?

In Emily Dickinson's poem on page 490, we hear a voice that calls himself "I." We know this speaker is a boy because he tells us so in line 11—but the writer of the poem is a female. Poets can imagine anyone or anything as the speaker of their poems. In Don Marquis's poem on page 140, the speaker is a cockroach. When you start to read a poem, ask yourself: Who is speaking to me?

> The **speaker** is the voice talking to us in a poem.

Highway Patrol (1986) by James Doolin. Oil on canvas (72″ x 188″).
Courtesy of Koplin Gallery, Santa Monica, CA.

Reaching All Students

Struggling Readers

Encourage students to draw pictures in order to visualize the view of earth as seen by the alien. Using their pictures as prompts, students can discuss why roads might look like "diagrams" or "measuring tapes."

English Language Learners

For strategies for engaging English language learners with the literature, see
• *Lesson Plans Including Strategies for English-Language Learners*

Crossing the Curriculum

Science

Aerial photographs are taken from above the earth's surface. Shot from cameras mounted on satellites, helicopters, or airplanes, these photos share the visual perspective of the aliens in Swenson's poem. Have students locate examples of aerial photographs and find out why the detailed geographical information they provide is useful to scientists, cartographers, and planners. (There are several sites on the Internet that are devoted to aerial photography.)

Southbound on the Freeway

May Swenson

A tourist came in from Orbitville,
parked in the air, and said:

The creatures of this star
are made of metal and glass.

5 Through the transparent parts
you can see their guts.

Their feet are round and roll
on diagrams—or long

measuring tapes—dark
10 with white lines.

They have four eyes.
The two in the back are red.

Sometimes you can see a 5-eyed
one, with a red eye turning

15 on the top of his head.
He must be special—

the others respect him,
and go slow,

when he passes, winding
20 among them from behind.

They all hiss as they glide,
like inches, down the marked

tapes. Those soft shapes,
shadowy inside

25 the hard bodies—are they
their guts or their brains?

MEET THE WRITER
"You Discover the Answer"

May Swenson (1919–1989) said:

❝ 'Southbound on the Freeway' makes you see, feel, and experience something *before* you know its name. That's why neither the title nor the text specifically states what is being described. *You* discover the answer, solve the poem like a riddle, by reading it. Just as a visitor from a planet different from Earth could mistake our speeding cars for the inhabitants and might suppose the people in them to

© Rollie McKenna

be guts or brains—so we, closely examining something for the first time, might reach imaginative conclusions—ones that contain kernels of symbolic truth. Once you discover what each poem is *about*, and name the subject for yourself, next you might notice what is hinted at beyond that: Haven't cars in our world really become more conspicuous, more important than people? ❞

Born and brought up in Logan, Utah, Swenson often wrote about animal life and about the curiosities of human existence. Like E. E. Cummings, she sometimes used unusual forms and typographical patterns to shape her poems.

SOUTHBOUND ON THE FREEWAY **527**

A Elements of Literature
Speaker
❓ What do you know about the "tourist" from reading the first two lines of the poem? [The visitor is from another planet and is hovering above earth.]

B Critical Thinking
Interpreting
❓ What is the 5-eyed creature? [It's a police car, with its fifth light on the roof.]

C Elements of Literature
Figures of Speech: Simile
❓ What is the effect of the simile that compares the cars to "inches"? [Possible response: The comparison makes the cars seem tiny and insignificant.]

D Reading Skills and Strategies
Responding to the Text
❓ In your opinion, is the alien's question credible? [Possible responses: The question is logical considering the alien's perspective, in which cars are the most visibly active "beings" it sees; or, the question is not believable, because the alien must also see pedestrians.]

Resources ——

Selection Assessment
Formal Assessment
• Selection Test, p. 97
Test Generator (One-Stop Planner)
• CD-ROM

BROWSING IN THE FILES
Writers on Writing. Of her riddle-poems, Swenson wrote: "The aim is not to mystify or mislead but to clarify and make recognizable through the reader's own uncontaminated perceptions. By bringing into play the sensual apparatus of the reader, the poem causes him to realize the content eye-wise, ear-wise, taste, touch, and muscle-wise *before* beginning to cerebralize."

Taking a Second Look

Review: Drawing Inferences
Remind students that drawing inferences means making educated guesses based on details in the text and facts known from their own experience. Readers draw inferences when the author implies something but doesn't state it directly. Swenson does not tell us that the speaker is an alien; this fact must be inferred by the reader.

1. Have students make a two-column chart, with columns labeled "Author's Details" and "Prior Knowledge."

2. Ask students to list details from the poem about the "5-eyed one" in the first column. Examples: "a red eye turning," "the others respect him."

3. In the second column, have students fill in facts known from their own experience that help them figure out what the poet is implying. Possible answers: "emergency vehicles have rotating red lights," "people show respect for the police."

First Thoughts

1. The speaker of "I Never Saw a Moor" imagines places that she has never seen. The speaker of "Kidnap Poem" imagines kidnapping someone with the force of her poetry. The speaker of "Southbound on the Freeway" imagines how an alien from outer space might view cars and highway traffic.

Shaping Interpretations

2. The speaker claims to know how things look even though she has never seen them. The fact that she can visualize what she has not seen is testament to the poet's power of imagination.

3. By using the word *Checks*, Dickinson emphasizes her certainty about going to heaven by comparing it with holding a train ticket to a specific destination. The word *Chart* suggests knowledge of a place, but not the certainty of getting there.

4. The five nouns related to writing or poetry that are used as verbs are: *meter, lyric, dash, complement, ode.*

5. In l. 11, "alliterate" is a pun on *litter.* In l. 12, "see" is a pun on *sea.* In l. 13, "lyre," the musical instrument, is a pun on *liar.* In ll. 19–20, the separation between "kid" and "nap" is a pun on *kid,* as in "kidding around."

6. Knowing this fact unlocks the line's meaning, which can be paraphrased as "I'd make you proud of your African roots."

7. The speaker is an alien from Orbitville.

8. The tourist is looking at cars on a freeway. The clues can be identified as follows: "guts" = people inside cars; "tapes" = highway lanes and the white marker lines; "5-eyed one" = police car; "feet" = tires; "eyes" = headlights and taillights.

Connecting with the Texts

9. Students might describe the shape of the alien craft as a bright second moon or a blazing ball.

10. Some students may agree that cars are so prevalent that they seem to be the planet's dominant life form; others may argue that people are the brains or controllers of automotive technology.

MAKING MEANINGS

I NEVER SAW A MOOR
KIDNAP POEM
SOUTHBOUND ON THE FREEWAY

First Thoughts

[review]

1. What are the poets imagining in "I Never Saw a Moor," "Kidnap Poem," and "Southbound on the Freeway"?

Shaping Interpretations

[analyze]

2. In what ways does the first stanza of "I Never Saw a Moor" appear to be stating a contradiction? How does this contradiction reveal the power of the imagination?

[analyze]

3. Dickinson's editors changed the word *Checks* in "I Never Saw a Moor" to *Chart,* meaning "map." How does this change in **diction**, or word choice, change the sense of lines 5–8?

[identify]

4. "Kidnap Poem" uses terms associated with writing, especially with poetry. See if you can find five nouns connected with writing and poetry that are used as verbs here.

[identify]

5. "Kidnap Poem" is full of word tricks. Can you spot the **puns** in lines 11, 12, 13, and 19–20?

[interpret]

6. Red, black, and green are the colors of the black liberation flag, which originated with Marcus Garvey's African-centered movement early in this century. How could knowing this fact add to your reading of line 16 in "Kidnap Poem"?

[identify]

7. Who is the **speaker** of the poem "Southbound on the Freeway"?

[infer]

8. Each detail in "Southbound on the Freeway" is a clue to the riddle. What *is* the "tourist" looking at? See if you can identify all the clues by completing these "equations": guts = ; tapes = ; 5-eyed one = ; feet = ; eyes =

Connecting with the Texts

[synthesize]

9. Suppose you are driving one of the cars southbound on the freeway. You look up and see this tourist parked in the air. Think of some **figures of speech** you'd use to describe this vision to your skeptical friends.

[respond]

10. Look at what May Swenson said about cars and people in Meet the Writer on page 527. How do you feel about her opinion?

Assessing Learning

Check Test: True-False
"I Never Saw a Moor"
1. The speaker has observed the sea. [False]
2. The speaker is on a train. [False]
"Kidnap Poem"
3. The speaker literally describes a kidnapping. [False]
"Southbound on the Freeway"
4. The speaker is not human. [True]
5. Highways are compared to rivers. [False]

Standardized Test Preparation
For practice with standardized test format specific to this selection, see
• *Standardized Test Preparation,* p. 72
For practice in proofreading and editing, see
• *Daily Oral Grammar,* Transparency 36

Writer's Notebook

1. Collecting Ideas for a Poem

Finding a subject. Poetry is first of all about feelings. Make a list of all the feelings you can think of: hate, love, anger, honesty, grief, joy, and so on. Choose five feelings from this list that could be starting points for a poem. Try making up five **similes** that compare the feelings to an object, an animal, or a person. If you want, try to extend your comparison—in other words, show several ways in which your two things are alike. Save your similes for the Writer's Workshop on page 550.

> Hate is like ice.
> It freezes feelings.
> Makes the eyes like stones.
> Hardens the heart.
>
> Love is like the sun.
> It nurtures life.
> It brings light to darkness.

Creative Writing

2. "I Never Saw..."

Imitate the structure of Dickinson's poem and write at least four lines describing things you can imagine even though you have never seen them, and things you have faith in even though you've never seen or touched them. Your Quickwrite notes should give you a start.

Creative Writing

3. Your Alien Riddle

Using the notes you made in the Quickwrite for "Southbound on the Freeway," write a paragraph that describes some everyday human activities from your alien's point of view. Open with the line "I came in from _____, parked in the air, and saw _____." Before you write, take notes on all the specific features of the human activities your speaker will observe. Try not to give away what the speaker is looking at. See if a classmate can guess.

Creative Writing

4. Your "Kidnap Poem"

Refer to the notes you took for the Quickwrite for "Kidnap Poem" and, using the words and phrases associated with your job, write a "kidnap poem" to someone you like. Use some of your nouns as verbs, if you're inspired:

> Ever been kidnapped by a singer?
> I'd music you to meet my mom
> put you in my chorus...

Research/Collaboration

5. Class Notebook for Figures of Speech

With your classmates, start a group notebook in which you gather striking and original figures of speech—metaphors, similes, and personifications. Start by looking in one issue of a daily newspaper. (The sports and entertainment sections are usually riddled with figures of speech.) Schedule a few minutes each week to read new entries aloud and try to identify the terms of the figures of speech—that is, tell what is compared to what. Just as starters, here are some metaphoric news headlines. If these were taken literally, what would be happening?

"Taxpayers Are Drained"
"Senate Committee Grills President"
"President Puts Lid on News Leaks"

Grading Timesaver

Rubrics for each Choices assignment appear on p. 165 in the *Portfolio Management System*.

CHOICES: Building Your Portfolio

1. **Writer's Notebook** Remind students that in a simile, two dissimilar things are compared by using words such as *like, as, than,* or *resembles*.

2. **Creative Writing** Have students use the following format when writing their poems:
   I never saw a _____
   I never saw a _____
   Yet I know _____
   And _____
   Tell students to fill in the blanks with things they can imagine or things they have faith in.

3. **Creative Writing** Point out to students the number of details included in the alien's description of the "creatures" in "Southbound on the Freeway." Remind students that effective writers like Swenson use specific details. Encourage students to focus on one or two human activities and to brainstorm specific details about those activities.

4. **Creative Writing** Before students write their "Kidnap" poems, have them brainstorm and list ten words associated with a particular job, making sure at least five of the words are nouns. They should then create phrases made from these words to use in their poems.

5. **Research/Collaboration** You might want to divide the class into small groups for this project. Assist groups with selecting their first set of notebook entries.

Assessing Learning

Self-Assessment
Have students use a chart like the following to evaluate their appreciation and understanding of poetry. Ask them to rate themselves using the following key:
1 = yes   2 = somewhat   3 = not sure

1. My understanding of a poem improves with several rereadings.	
2. I find that I understand a poem better if I analyze its use of figurative language.	
3. I appreciate a poem more if I pause to visualize the imagery.	
4. It is helpful to hear other people read a poem aloud.	
5. My appreciation of rhyme and rhythm in a poem has increased.	

Beware .../ The Secret

1. Read and interpret the poems
2. Follow narration in poetry
3. Infer implied ideas
4. Express understanding through creative or critical writing

SKILLS

Literary
- Follow narration in poetry
- Infer implied ideas

Writing
- Collect ideas for a poem
- Write a poem about shoes
- Create another stanza for Reed's poem
- Write a letter explaining a response

Viewing/Representing
- Compare the work of artists and writers (ATE)

Planning

- **Traditional Schedule**
  Lesson Plans Including Strategies for English-Language Learners
- **One-Stop Planner**
  CD-ROM with Test Generator

Before You Read

BEWARE: DO NOT READ THIS POEM

Make the Connection

Swallowed Alive

Mirrors can do many things—in real life or in people's imaginations. This poem is like one of those houses of mirrors in an amusement park, where you don't know where in the world *you* are.

Quickwrite

Write down your first reaction to this poem's unusual title.

Keep your notes. For questions and activities on this poem, see page 535.

Elements of Literature

Narration in Poetry

This unusual poem tells *two* stories. The external story is strange enough: It is about a woman and some other people who disappear into a mirror. But this only sets the stage for the internal story—the tale of what happens to *you*, the reader, as you disappear into the poem. Like all stories, this one is meant to be told aloud.

> **N**arration is any kind of writing or speaking that tells a story—a series of related events.
>
> *For more on Narration, see the Handbook of Literary Terms.*

 go.hrw.com
LE0 9-9

 *Resources: Print and Media*

Reading
- *Graphic Organizers for Active Reading*, pp. 43, 44
- *Audio CD Library*, Disc 15, Tracks 14, 15

Writing and Language
- *Daily Oral Grammar*, Transparency 37

Viewing and Representing
- *Viewing and Representing*
  Fine Art Transparency 13
  Fine Art Worksheet, p. 52

Assessment
- *Formal Assessment*, p. 99
- *Portfolio Management System*, p. 167
- *Test Generator (One-Stop Planner* CD-ROM)

Internet
go.hrw.com (keyword: LE0 9-9)

Beware: Do Not Read This Poem

Ishmael Reed

tonite, *thriller* was
abt an ol woman, so vain she
surrounded her self w/
   many mirrors
5   It got so bad that finally she
locked herself indoors & her
whole life became the
   mirrors

one day the villagers broke
10 into her house, but she was too
swift for them. she disappeared
   into a mirror
each tenant who bought the house
after that lost a loved one to
15   the ol woman in the mirror:
     first a little girl
     then a young woman
     then the young woman/s husband
the hunger of this poem is legendary
20 it has taken in many victims
back off from this poem
it has drawn in yr feet
back off from this poem
it has drawn in yr legs
25 back off from this poem

it is a greedy mirror
you are into this poem. from
   the waist down
nobody can hear you can they?
30 this poem has had you up to here
   belch
this poem aint got no manners
you cant call out frm this poem
relax now & go w/ this poem
35 move & roll on to this poem

     do not resist this poem
     this poem has yr eyes
     this poem has his head
     this poem has his arms
40   this poem has his fingers
     this poem has his fingertips
this poem is the reader & the
   reader this poem

statistic: the us bureau of missing persons reports
45   that in 1968 over 100,000 people disappeared
    leaving no solid clues
       nor trace   only
  a space   in the lives of their friends

MEET THE WRITER

"Writin' Is Fightin' "

Ishmael Reed (1938–   ), as a fellow poet noted, "alters our notion of what is possible." Known for his bold, brash, and blunt style, Reed has written several satiric novels that blend African American vernacular with standard English and hip jargon. As the title of one of his books indicates, Reed believes "writin' is fightin'" and ought to stir up controversy. A native of Tennessee (his daughter is named for her father's home state), Reed lives in Oakland, California. You probably won't be surprised that Reed says:

> ❝ My novels and poems are meant to be read aloud. That's why jazz musicians have been able to adapt my stuff. ❞

Summary ■ ■ ■

This free verse poem opens by telling the story of a greedy mirror that swallows first its vain owner and then those who buy her house. Reed uses the mirror as a metaphor for the reader's experience of being drawn into "this poem." The poem ends with a statistic on missing persons and its final lines include blank spaces—perhaps typographical images of those who have disappeared.

Resources

Listening
Audio CD Library
A dramatic recording of this poem is provided in the *Audio CD Library*:
• Disc 15, Track 14

Viewing and Representing
Fine Art Transparency
Use the fine art transparency of Salvador Dali's *The Persistence of Memory* to discuss the role imagination plays in art. See the *Viewing and Representing Transparencies and Worksheets*:
• Transparency 13
• Worksheet, p. 52

Ⓐ Reading Skills and Strategies
Making Inferences
❓ What kind of TV show do you think a "thriller" is? [It's a horror show.] What does the mention of this show make you expect from the poem? [Sample answer: The poem might be scary or mysterious.]

Ⓑ Critical Thinking
Speculating
❓ What do you think is the writer's purpose for leaving out letters from some words? [Possible answers: It leads the reader to expect strange things from the poem; it reflects the poem's experimental nature; the missing letters have been swallowed by the poem itself and so serve as a warning to the reader.]

Ⓒ Elements of Literature
Narration in Poetry
❓ A shift in the narration occurs here. What has suddenly taken the place of the mirror that swallows its victims? [the poem] Who is threatened now? [the readers]

Reaching All Students

Struggling Readers
Instruct students to make a two-column chart. In the first column, have them list all the words from the poem that have missing apostrophes or unconventional spellings. In the second column they should write the word correctly.

English Language Learners
Explain the idioms "taken in" (l. 20) and "back off" (l. 21) before students begin to read. Also tell students that "w/" (l. 34) is an abbreviation for the word *with* and "yr" for *your*.

Using Students' Strengths

Kinesthetic Learners
Have students work in pairs to pantomime being swallowed up by the poem. While one student reads the lines aloud, the other acts out being drawn into the poem limb by limb. Discuss how Reed's image is a literal interpretation of the way some readers become engrossed or figuratively "swallowed up" by literature.

Stephen King relates an anecdote about an automatic door that was malfunctioning and tells how this incident gave him an idea for a story. He concludes that what sets writers and artists apart from other people is that they retain a childlike perspective.

Ⓐ Elements of Literature

Figures of Speech: Personification

❓ What figurative phrases does King use to personify the door? [He says that the door "was almost pitching a fit" and that it had "the hiccups."]

Ⓑ Critical Thinking

Expressing an Opinion

❓ Do you agree with King that children see things from a different perspective? Why or why not? [Sample responses: Yes, kids have less experience than adults and so look at things more imaginatively; yes, from the perspective of a small child, a door that behaves strangely can seem huge and threatening.]

Ⓒ Reading Skills and Strategies

Connecting With the Text

❓ Have you read any stories or poems about things that come to life? Why did you like or dislike them? [Sample responses: In "Beware: Do Not Read This Poem," the mirror and poem came alive, and I liked that because it was unexpected and exciting; stories like *The Indian in the Cupboard,* about toys coming alive, thrilled me when I was a kid, but now I prefer realistic stories.]

Ⓓ Elements of Literature

Figures of Speech: Metaphors

❓ What two metaphors does King use to express his lack of skills? [He calls himself "excess baggage" and a "dickey bird on the back of civilization."]

Ⓔ Elements of Literature

Figures of Speech: Similes

❓ To explore the comparison, ask students to relate the purpose of eyeglasses to King's title. How does King make "eyeglasses for the mind"? [Glasses help people see things more clearly; they restore lost vision. King helps people look at things from a different perspective; he helps people regain the use of their imaginations.]

Connections — AN INTERVIEW

Eyeglasses for the Mind

from **Feast of Fear: Conversations with Stephen King**

Stephen King

I did the Mike Wallace radio show in New York at the CBS building. We went in and the electric eye had a case of the hiccups. The door was one of these doors where you'd step on the pad and the door would slide open. And this door was almost pitching a fit. It was jerking back and forth, not closing or opening all the way.

Ⓐ And my feeling about that is that somebody else would look at that and say: "Oh, that door has the hiccups." Whereas a little kid would walk up to that door and might very well shrink away from even going near it.

Ⓑ And say: "It wants to eat me, it's alive!" Children see things from a different perspective.

Ⓒ And in that sense I'm childlike. I looked at the door and I thought: "Gee, that would make a good story if that thing came alive and somebody walked up to it and CHUNG!" Which is a very childish sort of fantasy.

People respond to this perspective. It doesn't really die. It atrophies[1] and lies dormant.[2] And I get paid to show people that different perspec-

1. **atrophies** (a′trə·fēz): wastes away.
2. **dormant** (dôr′mənt): inactive.

tive. It's like exercising a muscle, rather than letting it go slack. But I'll tell you a funny thing. There are writers who look like children. They've used this facility so much for so long that they literally look like children.

Ⓓ Ray Bradbury is sixty years old and he has the face of a child. You see it in the eyes a lot of the time. Isaac Singer has the eyes of a child in that old face. They look out of that old face and they're very young.

That's why people pay writers and artists. That's the only reason we're around. We're excess baggage. I can't even fix a pipe in my house when it freezes. I am a dickey bird on the back of civilization.

I have no skill that improves the quality of life in a physical sense at all. The only thing I can do is say: "Look here, this is the way you didn't look at it before. It's just a cloud to you, but look at it, doesn't it look like an elephant?" Somebody says: "Boy! it does look like an elephant!" And for that, people pay because they've lost all of it themselves.

Ⓔ You know, I'm like a person who makes eyeglasses for the mind.

Connecting Across Texts

Connecting with "Beware: Do Not Read This Poem"

Ask students to explain how this interview with Stephen King relates to "Beware: Do Not Read This Poem." [King's description of a writer as someone who is imaginative and who looks at things from a different perspective readily applies to Ishmael Reed, a poet who is able to imagine a poem as a dangerous monster.]

Before You Read

THE SECRET

Make the Connection

The Secret Never Told

If you knew the secret of life, you'd be superhuman. And you're not. But certain poems can put you in touch with matters bigger than yourself. Remember, poems capture bits of life the way plants capture sunlight in their leaves. Once written, those poems wait quietly for some reader to open them so they can release that stored-up light. Of course, poems reveal different things to different people. There is, after all, no one big secret to life, but thousands of little ones.

Quickwrite

Write down what *you* think are some of the secrets of life. Try to say what you feel.

Keep your notes. For questions and activities on this poem, see page 535.

Elements of Literature

Implied Ideas: Speaking Indirectly

Poetry uses the language of suggestion, not the language of direct statement. This means that a good poem never comes right out and says: "This is my main idea." Instead, a good poem lets us, the readers, enter the poem and discover its meanings for ourselves.

Landscape with Two Who Are Lost (1938) by Paul Klee.
Öeffentliche Kunstsammlung Basel Kupferstichkabinett. Photo by Martin Bühler.

THE SECRET 533

Summary ■ ■

In this conversational blank verse poem, Levertov tells the story of two girls who claim to have found the secret of life in one of Levertov's poems. However, the girls neglect to tell the poet the secret or even the line in which they discovered it, so she is unsure what it is. The poet loves them for creating meaning from her poetry. She imagines them in the future, discovering other secrets in other poems. Most of all, the poet loves the fact that the girls think there are such secrets to be found.

Resources ───────

Listening

Audio CD Library

A dramatic recording of this poem is provided in the *Audio CD Library*:
• Disc 15, Track 15

RESPONDING TO THE ART

The artist **Paul Klee** (1879–1940) was born in Berne, Switzerland, but studied in Munich, Germany, and eventually settled there. He was a member of the German Expressionist group known as *Blaue Reiter* ("Blue Rider"). During the 1920s and early 1930s, Klee taught at the Bauhaus school of art and architecture but, sensing the disaster that was to come, returned to Berne when Hitler came to power in Germany. Klee developed a system of pictorial symbolism that in some ways corresponds to the use of notation in music.

Activity. Have students compare the way abstract artists use color, line, and form to communicate meaning with the way poets use imagery, rhythm, and diction to communicate meaning. Students might also compare Levertov's message about poetry in "The Secret" with this statement by Klee: "Art does not reproduce the visible but makes visible."

Ask students to find the "two who are lost." How could this title relate to Levertov's poem? [It might remind us of the two girls in the poem searching for the meaning of life.]

Crossing the Curriculum

Music

Thriller is the generic name for a novel, film, or other work that deals with crime and detection. Both Stephen King's writing and Ishmael Reed's poem (p. 531) have elements of a thriller. In cinematic thrillers, music is often used to prepare viewers for what they are about to see. Have students find examples of suspenseful music. For example, what music do they think would go well with Reed's narrative poem or King's idea for a story about a door that eats people alive (p. 532)?

Social Studies

Have students do research to update Reed's statistics on missing persons (p. 531). What does the Bureau of Missing Persons think happens to people who disappear? To present their findings, students might convert statistical information into a chart or graph and prepare profiles of typical missing persons. Profiles should explain why the person may have disappeared, what was done to find him or her, and what may have been their fate.

A Reading Skills and Strategies
Responding to the Text
? What do you think is the secret of life that the girls discover? [Sample response: The secret could be anything; it is kept mysterious to make readers curious and encourage them to continue reading.]

B Critical Thinking
Speculating
? How could the speaker write about a secret and not know it? [Possible responses: Because of their individual experiences, readers often uncover unique meanings in a text; sometimes we do something without being conscious of it.]

C Elements of Literature
Implied Ideas
? By repeating the words "in other," what connection is the poet making between lines of poetry and life experience? [She is implying that poetry and experience are two places where people discover important ideas.]

Resources

Selection Assessment
Formal Assessment
• Selection Test, p. 99
Test Generator (One-Stop Planner)
• CD-ROM

The Secret
Denise Levertov

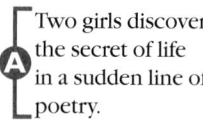

A Two girls discover
the secret of life
in a sudden line of
poetry.

5 **B** I who don't know the
secret wrote
the line. They
told me

(through a third person)
10 they had found it
but not what it was
not even

what line it was. No doubt
by now, more than a week
15 later, they have forgotten
the secret,

the line, the name of
the poem. I love them for
finding what
20 I can't find,
and for loving me
for the line I wrote,
and for forgetting it
so that
25 a thousand times, till death
finds them, they may
discover it again, in other
lines

C

in other
30 happenings. And for
wanting to know it,
for

assuming there is
such a secret, yes,
35 for that
most of all.

534 THE POETRY COLLECTIONS

MEET THE WRITER
"Members of One Another"

66 I believe poets are instruments on which the power of poetry plays . . . it is given to the seer to see, but it is then his responsibility to communicate what he sees, that they who cannot see may see, since we are members of one another. 99

For most of her education, **Denise Levertov** (1923–1997) relied on her mother's reading aloud to the family such writers as Tolstoy, Conrad, Dickens, and Cather. Levertov, who was born in England, served as a nurse during the bombing of London in World War II. Later she was active in antiwar and antinuclear protest movements. On the relationship of poets and poetry to life, she once said:

66 The spring sunshine, the new leaves: [Poets] still see them, still love them; but in what poignant contrast is their beauty and simple goodness to the evil we are conscious of day and night. . . . 99

Taking a Second Look

Review: Drawing Conclusions
Remind students that a conclusion is a type of inference in which you combine information in a text with information you already know to make a judgment that is specific to the text. For instance, in "Beware: Do Not Read This Poem" (p. 531), Reed implies that there is a connection between a mirror and a poem but does not explicitly state what this connection is. Readers must draw their own conclusions.

Activity
After students read the poem, have them draw their own conclusions about the connection Reed sees between a mirror and a poem. Make sure they explain how they reached that conclusion.
1. Have students first list information they know from prior experience and information gathered from the poem. For example:

• information I already know: you see yourself in a mirror
• information in the poem: both the mirror and poem take in the person
2. Then ask students to draw their conclusions. What do they think is the connection between a mirror and a poem? [Sample response: When people look into a mirror or a poem, they see themselves—either their physical selves or their mental selves.]

T534

MAKING MEANINGS

BEWARE: DO NOT READ THIS POEM
THE SECRET

First Thoughts

[respond]

1. Suppose you could ask Reed and Levertov one question each about their poems. What would you ask? Your Quickwrite notes might give you ideas.

Shaping Interpretations

[draw conclusions]

2. Based on the last stanza of "Beware: Do Not Read This Poem," what do you conclude has become of all those missing persons?

[interpret]

3. How is "Beware: Do Not Read This Poem" like a greedy mirror? What words do you think **personify** the poem as some kind of greedy monster?

[evaluate]

4. Can poetry be dangerous? Talk about Reed's ideas.

[identify]

5. Who is the **speaker** of "The Secret"? What can you **infer** about how the speaker feels about the two girls?

[respond]

6. In your own words tell what "The Secret" reveals to *you* about poetry.

CHOICES: Building Your Portfolio

Writer's Notebook

1. Collecting Ideas for a Poem

Finding a subject.

These poets probably found their subjects in something that happened in ordinary life. Perhaps Ishmael Reed read a news article about missing persons. Perhaps Denise Levertov heard about two girls who liked her poetry. Look through the newspaper, or think about what people have said to you today. Take notes on something that might be interesting to express in a poem. Save your notes for the Writer's Workshop on page 550.

Creative Writing

2. A Shoe

To prove that poems can be made out of anything, look at your shoes. If they're new, write a birth-announcement poem for your "twins." Give their names, sex, length, and weight. Don't forget to describe details such as soles, tongues, heels, and laces. Use as many figures of speech as you like. Or, if your shoes are old, write an epitaph poem announcing the end of your shoes and giving highlights of their lives. Or, write a poem in which your shoes take over your life and go wherever they please.

Creative Writing

3. More of the Story

What happens next? Use **narration** to write another stanza for "Beware: Do Not Read This Poem." Write as "I," the reader who has become the poem. If you wish, imitate Reed's typography and spelling.

Explaining a Response

4. Dear Stephen King . . .

Write King a letter telling him how you feel about his ideas in the interview "Eyeglasses for the Mind" (see *Connections* on page 532). What do *you* think writers and artists do for us?

MAKING MEANINGS

First Thoughts

1. Possible response: To Reed—What happened to the woman who disappeared into the mirror? To Levertov—What can you find in your own lines of poetry?

Shaping Interpretations

2. They have disappeared into the poem.

3. The poem is greedy because it envelops the reader or draws the reader into it. Words and phrases like "hunger," "victims," "taken in," "drawn in," "belch," and "no manners" personify the poem as a greedy monster.

4. Sample responses: Poems can be dangerous when they upset or incite their readers with strange ideas; readers can lose themselves in poetry and therefore neglect other important things in life, which can be dangerous.

5. The speaker is the poet. She is flattered by the girls' attention and seems to be glad that they find the secret of life in her poem even though she does not.

6. Possible responses: You can discover truths about life each time you pick up a poem; poetry gives a perspective on life you might never have considered.

Grading Timesaver

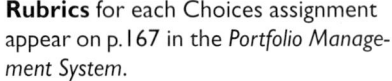

Rubrics for each Choices assignment appear on p. 167 in the *Portfolio Management System*.

CHOICES: Building Your Portfolio

1. **Writer's Notebook** Bring in old newspapers and magazines for the students to look through.

2. and 3. **Creative Writing** Encourage students to let their own voices shine through in their writing.

4. **Explaining a Response** You might want to collect the letters and send them to King's publisher.

Assessing Learning

Check Test: True-False

"Beware: Do Not Read This Poem"

1. The speaker says his poem is a greedy mirror. [True]

2. The poem contains statistics from the U.S. Bureau of Missing Persons. [True]

"The Secret"

3. Two girls discover the secret of life in a poem. [True]

4. The poet hates the idea of a secret hidden in her poem. [False]

Standardized Test Preparation

For practice in proofreading and editing, see
• *Daily Oral Grammar,* Transparency 37

OBJECTIVES

1. Read and interpret the poem
2. Analyze an extended metaphor
3. Express understanding through creative writing, speaking, critical thinking, or evaluating the art
4. Rely on context to determine meanings of multiple-meaning words

SKILLS

Literary
• Analyze an extended metaphor

Writing
• Write an extended metaphor
• Write a dramatic interpretation of the poem
• Paraphrase Jaques' speech

Speaking/Listening
• Perform a dramatic interpretation of the poem

Vocabulary
• Rely on context to determine the meanings of multiple-meaning words

Art
• Evaluate a work of art

Viewing/Representing
• Compare two paintings (ATE)

Planning

• **Block Schedule**
  Block Scheduling Lesson Plans with Pacing Guide

• **Traditional Schedule**
  Lesson Plans Including Strategies for English-Language Learners

• **One-Stop Planner**
  CD-ROM with Test Generator

Before You Read

THE SEVEN AGES OF MAN

Make the Connection

Life in Seven Acts

Seven acts. Yes, that's how long this poet imagines the play of your life is going to be. According to this speaker, you're already in the middle of the second act. See what Jaques (pronounced jā'kwēz) predicts about the rest of your life in this speech from Shakespeare's comedy *As You Like It*.

Quickwrite

Second-guess Shakespeare. Write down what *you* think are the seven stages of a person's life.

Keep your notes. For questions and activities on this poem, see pages 538–539.

Elements of Literature

Extended Metaphor

Jaques opens with one of the most famous metaphors ever written—"All the world's

a stage." Then he extends that metaphor to compare the stages of our lives to seven actors who say their parts and then exit from the stage.

> **A**n extended **metaphor** is a comparison developed over several lines of a poem.
>
> *For more on Metaphors, see pages 520–521 and the Handbook of Literary Terms.*

For a biography of William Shakespeare, see page 726.

The Seven Ages of Man
William Shakespeare

               All the world's a stage,
A And all the men and women merely players;
They have their exits and their entrances,
And one man in his time plays many parts,
5 His acts being seven ages. At first the infant,
Mewling and puking in the nurse's arms;
B And then the whining schoolboy, with his satchel
And shining morning face, creeping like snail
Unwillingly to school. And then the lover,
10 Sighing like furnace, with a woeful ballad
Made to his mistress' eyebrow. Then a soldier,
Full of strange oaths, and bearded like the pard,°   **12. pard:** leopard.
Jealous in honor, sudden and quick in quarrel,
Seeking the bubble reputation
15 Even in the cannon's mouth. And then the justice,°   **15. justice:** judge.
In fair round belly with good capon° lined,   **16. capon:** fat chicken.
With eyes severe and beard of formal cut,
Full of wise saws° and modern instances;   **18. saws:** sayings.
And so he plays his part. The sixth age shifts

Resources: Print and Media

Reading
• *Graphic Organizers for Active Reading*, p. 45
• *Words to Own*, p. 30
• *Audio CD Library*, Disc 15, Track 16

Elements of Literature
• *Literary Elements* Transparency 11 Worksheet, p. 34

Assessment
• *Formal Assessment*, p. 101
• *Portfolio Management System*, p. 168
• *Test Generator (One-Stop Planner* CD-ROM)

Internet
• go.hrw.com (keyword: LE0 9-9)

First Steps (19th century), after Millet by Vincent van Gogh. Oil on canvas (28½" x 35⅞").

The Metropolitan Museum of Art, New York. Gift of George N. and Helen M. Richard, 1964. (64.165.2). Photograph by Malcolm Varon. Photograph ©1982 The Metropolitan Museum of Art.

20	Into the lean and slippered pantaloon,°	**20. pantaloon:** silly old man.
	With spectacles on nose and pouch on side;	
	His youthful hose,° well saved, a world too wide	**22. hose:** stockings.
	For his shrunk shank; and his big manly voice,	
	Turning again toward childish treble, pipes	
25	And whistles in his sound. Last scene of all,	
	That ends this strange eventful history,	
	Is second childishness and mere oblivion,	
	Sans° teeth, sans eyes, sans taste, sans everything.	**28. sans:** without.

THE SEVEN AGES OF MAN 537

MAKING MEANINGS

First Thoughts

1. Possible response: He's left out the more positive aspects of our lives—the carefree, productive, happy, loving aspects.

Shaping Interpretations

2. The infant "mewls" (whimpers) "pukes"; the schoolboy has a ... ing morning face" but whi... creeps to school. The s... ing like snail" captur... tance. Students ... images are tru... happier asp...

3. In ll. 9—... who ... lad...

For additional instruction on figures of speech, see *Literary Elements*:
- Transparency 11
- Worksheet, p. 34

Ⓐ Elements of Literature

Extended Metaphor

❓ What does Shakespeare compare the world and its inhabitants to? How does the poet extend or develop this metaphor? [The world is compared to a stage and people are compared to actors. He develops his metaphor by dividing a man's life into seven ages.]

Ⓑ Reading Skills and Strategies

Making Inferences

❓ What does the description of the infant and the schoolboy indicate about Jaques' attitude toward human life? [Negative words, such as "puking" and "whining," indicate cynicism.]

RESPONDING TO THE ART

Dutch painter **Vincent van Gogh** (1853–1890) painted "copies" of several paintings of Francois Millet (1814–1875). **Activity.** Ask students to describe what is happening in this painting. [A father has put down his spade and reaches out to his child held by its mother. A tree is flowering and sun shines on fresh laundry. The painting suggests great love, symbolized by the widespread arms of the father. Sadly, Van Gogh never had a family like this.]

Reaching All Students

Struggling Readers

You might want to use a strategy called Read, Rate, Reread with this selection. For information on using this strategy, see p. 59 of the *Reading Strategies Handbook* in the front of the *Reading Skills and Strategies* binder.

Getting Students Involved

Cooperative Learning

Students working in groups of three might create a time line for the seven ages. One student can coordinate the project—gather materials, divide the time line into seven segments, and arrange a display of the finished work. The second can illustrate each age. The third can write descriptive captions and paraphrase in modern English the lines from the poem that identify each age.

...and
..."shin-
...mes and
...simile "creep-
...s his reluc-
...ay say that the
...e to life but omit the
...cts of childhood.
...1, Jaques describes a lover
...omposes a ballad about his
...y's eyebrow; Jaques belittles the
...over by imagining him to be fixated
on such a trivial feature. "Sighing like
furnace" (l. 10) describes the lover's
sighs.

4. Reputation is compared to a "bubble." This metaphor makes a reputation seem fragile and transitory; it
can burst or disappear in an instant.
Examples of fame seekers might
include a soldier seeking to earn a
medal for bravery even though he
might be injured or an athlete who
faces danger while seeking to set a
new record.

5. We know that the justice eats well.
The justice assumes an intellectual
look but pronounces judgments that
are merely old sayings illustrated by
modern examples.

6. The changes include weight loss,
silliness, poor sight, ill-fitting clothes,
weakened voice, raspy breathing,
loss of memory and mental awareness, loss of teeth, sight, and taste.

Extending the Text

7. Students may feel that the ages of
the infant and schoolboy are the
most true to life today.

Challenging the Text

8. Possible response: Old age need not
mean oblivion. Free of the worries
of parenting and work, older people
may travel, spend time with their
grandchildren, do volunteer work,
and further their education.

Resources

Selection Assessment
Formal Assessment
• Selection Test, p. 101
Test Generator (One-Stop Planner)
• CD-ROM

First Thoughts

[connect]   **1.** Jaques is a gloomy character, so it's not surprising that he views people
(especially men—he pretty much ignores women) as ridiculous. What
characteristics of our lives has Jaques left out of his speech?

Shaping Interpretations

[identify]   **2.** In the first two acts, what **images** help you picture childhood as Jaques sees
it? What **simile** describes the schoolboy's attitude toward school? How do
you feel about these pictures of childhood?

[identify]   **3.** In Shakespeare's day, it was fashionable to compose serious love poems
celebrating the perfection of a woman's eyes, lips, or complexion. Find the
lines where Jaques makes fun of this type of poetry. What **simile** describes
the sighs of the person who writes it?

[identify]   **4.** In lines 13 and 14, what does Jaques compare "reputation" to? What point
about the permanence of a reputation is he making by using this **metaphor**?
What kind of people might seek reputation "even in the cannon's mouth"?

[infer]   **5.** If the justice's belly is lined "with good capon," what do we know about him?
What details make the justice seem like a ridiculous character?

[identify]   **6.** According to Jaques, what physical and mental changes take place as a man
reaches the sixth and seventh ages?

Extending the Text

[extend]    **7.** These famous lines were
written nearly four hundred
years ago. Of all the
seven ages of man that
Shakespeare characterizes,
which do you think remain
true to life today? How do
they compare with your
Quickwrite?

Challenging the Text

[evaluate]   **8.** Do you find Jaques'
descriptions of old age
horrifying? What other,
equally valid descriptions of
old age can you think of?

William Shakespeare.

David Levine © 1987. Courtesy
of the Forum Gallery, New York City.

go.hrw.com
LEO 9-9

Assessing Learning

Check Test: Fill in the Blanks
1. The speaker begins by comparing the world
to a _____. [stage]
2. The speaker says that a man's life progresses
through _____ ages. [seven]
3. The first stage is the _____. [infant or
baby]
4. He associates poetry-writing with the
_____. [lover]
5. The final stage is a second _____. [child-
hood]

T538

CHOICES: Building Your Portfolio

Writer's Notebook

1. Collecting Ideas for a Poem

An imitation.  Take notes on how you could adapt this poem to focus on women, not men. Stick with seven ages. Extend your metaphor, comparing life to a stage as far as you can logically take it. Save your notes for the Writer's Workshop on page 550.

Speaking/Creative Writing

2. Talking Stages

Suppose each stage of life is assigned to a different actor and each of the seven actors has a chance to deliver one speech as he (or she) occupies the spotlight for a second on the stage of life. Write seven one-line comments and, with a group of classmates, act each player entering and leaving the stages of life. You might add costumes and props (for example, each character could hold something symbolic).

Critical Thinking

3. Paraphrasing a Poem

To **paraphrase** a passage means to restate it in your own words. Because a paraphrase restates complex ideas in plainer words, it is often longer than the original passage (and never as interesting). Write a paraphrase of Jaques' speech. Explain in your own words each figure of speech. Pretend you are writing the paraphrase for a reader who has had trouble understanding Jaques' language.

Evaluating the Art

4. A Good Match?

Select one poem from those you've read in this collection. Reread it, and look at the art that illustrates it. Is the art a good choice? Write two paragraphs. In the first, summarize the poem and describe the piece of art. Be sure to cite titles, author, and artist. In the second, clearly state and explain your evaluation.

VOCABULARY — HOW TO OWN A WORD

WORD BANK
strange
fair
saws
hose

Multiple Meanings

Those very ordinary words in the Word Bank on the left have multiple meanings. Each word is used at least once by Jaques. Find where he uses each word, examine its **context,** and then explore the meaning of the words by drawing a map for each word like the one on the right. You will have to do two maps for *strange*.

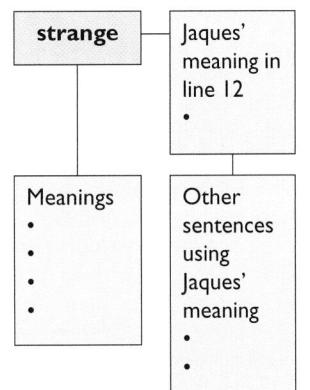

strange → Jaques' meaning in line 12
  •

Meanings
  •
  •
  •
  •

Other sentences using Jaques' meaning
  •
  •

Listening to Music

"Blow, Blow, Thou Winter Wind," by Thomas Arne, lyrics from *As You Like It* by William Shakespeare, performed by the Folger Consort

"Under the Greenwood Tree," by Sir William Walton; lyrics from *As You Like It* by William Shakespeare, performed by Philip Langridge & Felicity Lott

The English composer Thomas Arne (1710–1778) is best remembered for his musical settings of Shakespeare's lyrics and for the British national anthem "Rule, Britannia." Sir William Walton, one of England's finest twentieth-century composers, created operas, orchestral works, and film scores.

Activity

After students read Jaques' speech from *As You Like It,* play these two songs, whose lyrics are from the same play. Have students compare and contrast the worldview presented in each song with Jaques' philosophy.

Grading Timesaver

Rubrics for each Choices assignment appear on p. 168 in the *Portfolio Management System.*

CHOICES: Building Your Portfolio

1. **Writer's Notebook**   Some students might want to write their own poems.
2. **Speaking/Creative Writing**   Encourage students to develop expressions and gestures.
3. **Critical Thinking**   Have students exchange their papers with partners, check each other's work for clarity and plain language, and then revise their paraphrases.
4. **Evaluating the Art**   Work with students to develop the criteria for an evaluation.

VOCABULARY
Possible Answers
Strange. Meanings: foreign, unfamiliar, peculiar, extraordinary. Jaques' meaning 1. 12: foreign, alien. Sentence: Soldiers in combat see many strange sights. Jaques' meaning 1. 26: peculiar, odd. Sentence: The lover's strange behavior worried his friends.
Fair. Meanings: attractive, clean, clear, just, according to the rules, moderately large, average. Jaques' meaning 1. 16: moderately large. Sentence: The judge developed a fair-sized belly.
Saws. Meanings: cutting tools, maxims. Jaques' meaning 1. 18: maxims, sayings. Sentence: Many a judge peppers his advice with old saws.
Hose. Meanings: stockings, flexible tube. Jaques' meaning 1. 22: stockings. Sentence: The old man's hose were too large for him.

Resources

Vocabulary
Words to Own, Worksheet, p. 30

OBJECTIVES

Fire and Ice / All Watched Over ...

1. Read and interpret the poems
2. Interpret implied metaphors
3. Recognize tone
4. Express understanding through creative writing, comparing art and text, or evaluating a poem

SKILLS

Literary
- Interpret implied metaphors
- Recognize tone

Writing
- List ideas for making the world a better place
- Compare a poem and a painting
- Write a paragraph describing life without machines
- Create metaphors that compare human acts with elements of nature
- Evaluate a poem

Art
- Compare a poem with a painting

Viewing/Representing
- Analyze a response to a painting (ATE)
- Describe how an artist might portray Brautigan's vision of the future (ATE)

Planning

- **Block Schedule**
  Block Scheduling Lesson Plans with Pacing Guide
- **Traditional Schedule**
  Lesson Plans Including Strategies for English-Language Learners
- **One-Stop Planner**
  CD-ROM with Test Generator

Before You Read

FIRE AND ICE

Make the Connection

Whose Fault Is It?

From the beginning of time, people have imagined—and often predicted—the end of the world. Today, scientists tell us that the sun will burn itself out in about six billion years. That may be a bit far off to worry about—but what about the hole in the ozone layer? And global warming? What about that meteorite hurtling through space? What about a new ice age?

Quickwrite

What thoughts come into your mind when you hear the words *fire* and *ice*? What characteristics do the two elements share? Take notes on your thoughts.

Elements of Literature

Implied Metaphor

"Fire and Ice" is built around two metaphors, but the comparisons are never directly stated. Use your powers of inference to figure this out:

What emotions do fire and ice stand for?

An implied metaphor does not tell us directly that one thing *is* something else. Instead, it uses words that suggest the nature of the comparison.

For more on Metaphors, see pages 520–521 and the Handbook of Literary Terms.

go.hrw.com
LE0 9-9

MEET THE WRITER

A "Stay Against Confusion"

Robert Frost (1874–1963) lived and wrote in New England most of his life. New England still bears the scars of the Ice Age glacier that stripped the land bare and buried everything in its path. Enormous boulders still litter the landscape where the glacier dropped them millions of years ago.

Indeed, Frost had only to look out his farmhouse window to see the destructive effects of ice—and had only to take a short walk to find the charred clearing and the blackened cellar holes left by lightning fires. And then, like all human beings, he had only to look inside himself to discover the destructive forces of desire and hate.

In his essay "The Figure a Poem Makes," Frost talks about poetry:

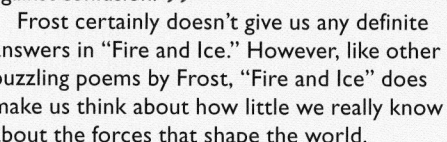

❝ [A poem] . . . begins in delight and ends in wisdom . . . a clarification of life—not necessarily a great clarification, such as sects and cults are founded on, but in a momentary stay against confusion. **❞**

Frost certainly doesn't give us any definite answers in "Fire and Ice." However, like other puzzling poems by Frost, "Fire and Ice" does make us think about how little we really know about the forces that shape the world.

Despite the dark side of his poetry, Robert Frost was the last American poet to achieve the status of a national figure on the order of certain sports or movie stars. As an old man, he recited one of his poems on the cold windy day of John F. Kennedy's inauguration as president in 1961.

  *Resources: Print and Media*

Reading
- *Graphic Organizers for Active Reading,* pp. 46, 47
- *Audio CD Library,* Disc 15, Tracks 17, 18

Assessment
- *Formal Assessment,* p. 103
- *Portfolio Management System,* p. 170
- *Test Generator (One-Stop Planner* CD-ROM)

Internet
- go.hrw.com (keyword: LE0 9-9)

Fire and Ice

Robert Frost

Some say the world will end in fire,
Some say in ice.
From what I've tasted of desire
(A) I hold with those who favor fire.
But if it had to perish twice,
I think I know enough of hate
To say that for destruction ice
Is also great
(B) And would suffice.

The Wreck of the Hope by Caspar David Friedrich (1774–1840).
Kunsthalle, Hamburg / Bridgeman Art Library, London / New York [PHD21401].

FIRE AND ICE **541**

Summary ■ ■

In this poem, Robert Frost uses an implied metaphor to create irony. He equates desire with fire and hate with ice; although these emotions are opposites, they are equally destructive. In a casual voice, he informs the reader that he has experienced both of these emotions and that they have the power to end the world.

Resources

Listening
Audio CD Library
A recording of this poem is provided in the *Audio CD Library*:
• Disc 15, Track 17

(A) Elements of Literature
Implied Metaphor
❓ With what emotion does the speaker indirectly compare fire? [desire] Ice? [hatred] What does the speaker suggest by saying the world may end in either fire or ice? [Fire and ice are implied metaphors for destructive emotions and represent ways humans may destroy the earth.]

(B) Appreciating Language
Word Choice
❓ What is the effect of the word "suffice" at the end of the poem? [The word "suffice" sounds like the word *suffer*, reinforcing the terrible power of hate.]

BROWSING IN THE FILES
About the Author. In Frost's poems, simple things take on deep significance. Describing the trajectory of his writing, the poet remarked that "Poetry begins in trivial metaphors and goes on to the profoundest thinking we have."

Reaching All Students

Struggling Readers
Frost uses colloquial speech to give his poem a conversational voice. However, the idioms in ll. 3–4 might confuse some students. Explain that *tasted* means "to experience" and *hold with* means "agree with." Also make sure you preteach the word *suffice*, meaning "to be adequate."

Advanced Learners
Have students analyze the poem's irony. Its conversational voice masks a darker message: the destructive nature of extreme emotion.

Using Students' Strengths

Auditory/Musical Learners
The wonderful rhythm of "Fire and Ice" and its short length make it perfect for an oral reading. Have pairs take turns reading the poem aloud. Then play the recording of the poem in the *Audio CD Library*. Finally have students compare their renditions with the recorded version. Which sounded the best or most natural? Did reading the poem aloud help them to understand it better?

RESPONDING TO THE ART
Caspar-David Friedrich (1774–1840) was a German painter, who was identified with the Romantic Movement. His work often shows man being overwhelmed by the force of nature.
Activity. Ask students what "story" they can read into this painting.

Summary ■■■

In this free verse poem, the speaker seemingly imagines a futuristic utopia—meadows where mammals and computers coexist peacefully and forests that are "filled with pines and electronics." The speaker refers to this vision as "a cybernetic ecology." Human beings, freed from labor by machines who keep loving watch, are reunited with nature. However, the tone of the poem is ambiguous. Does the speaker look forward to the coming of this new world, or is he warning us of a future dominated by machines?

Resources

Listening
Audio CD Library
A dramatic reading of this poem is provided in the *Audio CD Library*:
- Disc 15, Track 18

FROM THE EDITOR'S DESK

There was a lot of lively discussion among the editors about the pairing of these two poems. Most of us agreed that Frost's vision of the future is a dark one even though his voice is so casual. But we could not agree whether Brautigan's poem was best seen as a contradiction to Frost or a complement. Is Brautigan just being amusing? Does he really believe that machines are gentle? Or is his message as dark as Frost's?

Before You Read

ALL WATCHED OVER BY MACHINES OF LOVING GRACE

Make the Connection

Imagination to the Rescue

Machines free us and improve our incomes and our minds. Machines enslave us, invade our privacy, and are destroying the environment at a rapid rate. Both statements are true. In this poem Richard Brautigan imagines a world like the Biblical vision of a peaceable kingdom (see the art on page 544), where the lion lies down with the lamb. But Brautigan's vision includes technology.

Quickwrite

Name three machines you feel you couldn't live without. Pretend these machines disappear from the face of the earth. Write down quickly what you would miss.

Keep your notes. For questions and activities on this poem, see pages 544–545.

Elements of Literature

Tone: An Attitude

You've read poems in these collections that reveal many tones, from cynical to sincere to playful. It is important to be sensitive to tone: If you are talking to a friend and you mistake a tone of sarcasm for a tone of sincerity, you've made a serious mistake. In speech, tone is revealed by voice and body language. In writing, tone can be revealed only by words.

> **T**one is a writer's or speaker's attitude toward a subject, a character, or an audience.
>
> *For more on Tone, see pages 586–587 and the Handbook of Literary Terms.*

542 THE POETRY COLLECTIONS

Reaching All Students

Struggling Readers
To help students recognize Brautigan's tone, ask them to consider the following: the urgent pleas in parentheses (ll. 10 and 18); the conditional phrase "as if" in l. 15; and the negative connotations of being "watched over."

English Language Learners
Make sure that students know that "programming" (l. 6) involves writing a sequence of coded instructions for a computer.

Advanced Learners
Encourage students to compare the futuristic world of the poem with other futuristic worlds they have read about in works by such authors as Isaac Asimov, Kurt Vonnegut, Ursula K. Le Guin, and George Orwell. Students might also want to make comparisons with futuristic visions they have seen in films such as the *Star Wars* trilogy.

Crossing the Curriculum

Art
Have students look at the utopian painting by Edward Hicks on p. 544. Do they picture the world described in Brautigan's poem as being similar to *The Peaceable Kingdom*? Ask students to draw or paint their vision of the world described in the poem. They can either portray the poem in general or concentrate on a particular image, such as "pines and electronics."

All Watched Over by Machines of Loving Grace

Richard Brautigan

I like to think (and
the sooner the better!)
of a cybernetic° meadow
where mammals and computers
5 live together in mutually
programming harmony
like pure water
touching clear sky.

A

10 I like to think
    (right now, please!)
of a cybernetic forest
filled with pines and electronics
where deer stroll peacefully
past computers
15 as if they were flowers
with spinning blossoms.

I like to think
    (it has to be!)
of a cybernetic ecology
20 where we are free of our labors
and joined back to nature,
returned to our mammal
brothers and sisters,
and all watched over
25 by machines of loving grace.

B

C

3. **cybernetic:** having to do with computers.

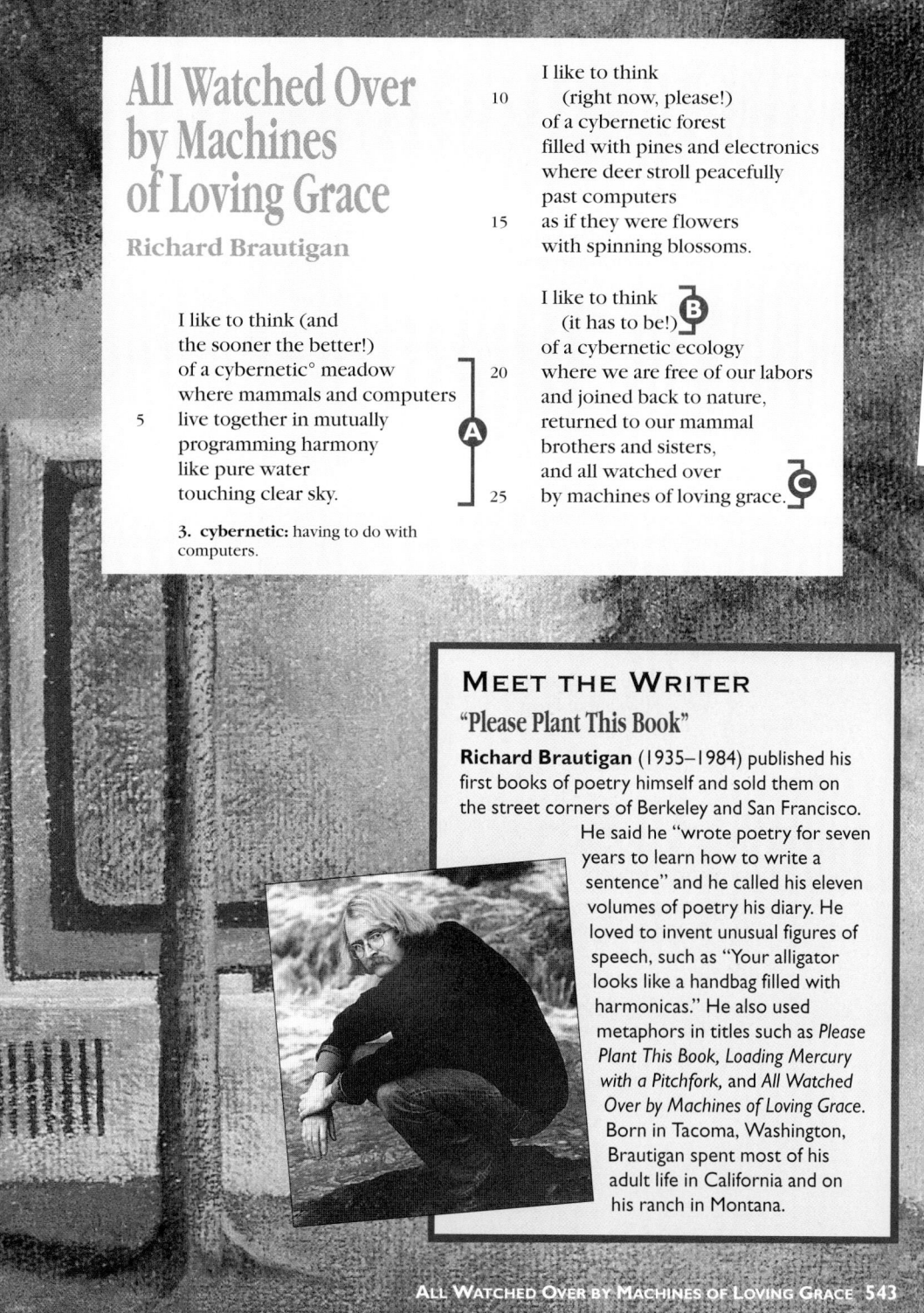

MEET THE WRITER

"Please Plant This Book"

Richard Brautigan (1935–1984) published his first books of poetry himself and sold them on the street corners of Berkeley and San Francisco. He said he "wrote poetry for seven years to learn how to write a sentence" and he called his eleven volumes of poetry his diary. He loved to invent unusual figures of speech, such as "Your alligator looks like a handbag filled with harmonicas." He also used metaphors in titles such as *Please Plant This Book, Loading Mercury with a Pitchfork,* and *All Watched Over by Machines of Loving Grace.* Born in Tacoma, Washington, Brautigan spent most of his adult life in California and on his ranch in Montana.

ALL WATCHED OVER BY MACHINES OF LOVING GRACE 543

Getting Students Involved

Cooperative Learning

"Finding" a Poem. After students have read the poem, have them work in small groups to brainstorm a number of words or phrases that they feel best communicate the essence of the poem. Ask each group to narrow their choices down to the top three. Then have one student from each group write the words on the board. Let each group use these words to create a "found" poem. Have the groups select a reader to present their poems to the class.

Marvelous Machines. Have students work in small groups to brainstorm lists of imaginary machines that might exist in a "cybernetic meadow" or a "cybernetic forest." Groups should work together to create a short description of each machine, explaining what it would do and how it would look.

... autigan's
... for a harmo-
... may see Frost's
... ems as prophetic

... terpretations

... ompares fire to desire and
... hate.
... the poem *desire* refers to a burning, all-consuming passion. A person
can burn with desire and be consumed by it just as by fire.
4. Both ice and hate are hard, cold,
cutting, and painful.
5. A drastic increase (fire) or decrease
(ice) in temperature on earth could
end the world. The conflicts caused
by people's desires and hatreds
could lead to nuclear war and subsequent worldwide destruction.
6. Most machines, such as cars, are
seen as enemies of nature. Brautigan
may perceive machines as friendly or
may be warning readers of a world
overrun by technology.
7. Some students will say that Brautigan's tone is optimistic because he
wishes for harmony between technology and nature. Others may say
that his tone is pessimistic because
he is being sarcastic—machines can
never be loving and will never
coexist peacefully with nature. Most
students will say that Frost's poem is
pessimistic because it only examines
ways that the earth may end.

Extending the Texts

8. We depend on machines for transportation, food, work, and recreation. In addition, computers are
"guardians" in the sense that they
are used to collect all sorts of information about our lives. Students
may say that although machines have
made life easier for people, they
aren't "loving" because this is a quality only living beings can possess.
9. Students may say it is possible for
mammals and computers to live
together harmoniously because they
like this hopeful vision of the future.
Others may reject this vision either
because it seems an impossible
dream or because they find it cold
and unappealing.

MAKING MEANINGS
FIRE AND ICE
ALL WATCHED OVER BY MACHINES OF LOVING GRACE

[connect]

First Thoughts

1. Both Frost and Brautigan think about what is going to happen to us and to the planet. Which view comes closer to yours?

Shaping Interpretations

[identify]

2. Frost uses two **implied metaphors** to make his point. What emotion does he compare to fire? What emotion does he compare to ice?

[interpret]

3. How would you define desire as Frost uses the word in his poem? How is desire like fire?

[infer]

4. Explain why Frost's speaker might feel that hate and ice have something in common.

[draw conclusions]

5. In the Quickwrite you wrote before you read "Fire and Ice," you thought of how fire and ice share some characteristics. How could each of them cause the world to end? How could desire and hate also do the job?

[analyze]

6. Brautigan also has a vision of the future. How are machines usually thought of in relation to nature? As enemies? As guardians? How does Brautigan think of them?

[interpret]

7. Would you call Brautigan's poem optimistic in **tone** or pessimistic or neither? Why? How about Frost's?

Extending the Texts

[extend]

8. Brautigan's poem is a vision of the future, but in what sense do we already live under the guardianship of machines? Do you think of them as "loving" machines? Explain why or why not.

[speculate]

9. Do you think any part of Brautigan's vision of the future can come true? Would you want it to come true—or do you find it unappealing? Explain.

Albright-Knox Art Gallery, Buffalo, New York. James G. Forsyth Fund, 1940.

The Peaceable Kingdom (c. 1848) by Edward Hicks.
Oil on canvas (23⅞″ x 31⅛″).

544 THE POETRY COLLECTIONS

Assessing Learning

Check Test: Questions and Answers
Answers may vary slightly.
"Fire and Ice"
1. What emotion is linked with fire? [desire]
2. What emotion is linked with ice? [hate]
"All Watched Over by Machines of Loving Grace"
3. What kind of meadow does the speaker envision? [a cybernetic one]

4. What are humans freed of in the poet's future world? [labor]
5. To what will people be rejoined in the new ecology? [to nature]

CHOICES: Building Your Portfolio

Writer's Notebook

1. Collecting Ideas for a Poem

A first line. Sometimes it's just a matter of getting started. Use Brautigan's opening line and list some things you like to imagine could happen to make the world a better place. You might want to add "(and the sooner the better!)." Save your lists for the Writer's Workshop on page 550.

> "I like to think..."
> - of factories where they dismantle nuclear weapons
> - of edible chocolate plates
> - of drinking water that cures the common cold
> - of farms on the moon that deliver fresh produce to every home

Comparing Art and Text

2. Two Peaceable Kingdoms

Compare Edward Hicks's portrait of a peaceable kingdom, painted in 1848 (page 544), with Brautigan's written vision, published in 1968. Before you write, make a list of the similarities and the differences in the works:

Characteristic	Hicks	Brautigan
Details		
Tone		

If you wish, go on to transform Hicks's vision into a poem, beginning with "I like to think," and transform Brautigan's vision into art.

Creative Writing

3. A Machine Fantasy

Using your notes from the Quick-write for "All Watched Over by Machines of Loving Grace," write a paragraph about how your life would be different without your favorite machines. Think hair dryer, washing machine, toaster, car, computer, popcorn popper, chain saw, lawn mower, snow blower, water heater, oil furnace, electric lights.

Creative Writing

4. Creating Your Own Metaphors

Add to Frost's list of destructive human acts and qualities. Don't forget jealousy and greed. For each item, choose an element of nature that might express or stand for that human act or quality. Set the items up as equations:

anger	=	volcano
sadness	=	rain

Then make a parallel list of equations for positive and constructive human acts and qualities.

loyalty	=	rock
kiss	=	rain

(Don't be surprised if some of the things on your lists, like rain in the examples, can be both destructive and beneficial. Metaphors are famous for being hard to pin down. That's what makes them interesting.)

Evaluating a Poem

5. Your Choice

0	1	2	3	4	5

We all write best when we feel passionately about a subject. Look back at the poems you've read so far. Select one poem that you would rank high on this scale, or low. Write an evaluation of the poem, explaining your rating. You might want to focus on the poem's message, attitude toward life, language, images, metaphors, or sounds. You can't just say, "I love it" or "I hate it." You have to find at least one reason for your response. (For help in writing an evaluation, see the Writer's Workshop on page 250.)

FIRE AND ICE, ALL WATCHED OVER BY MACHINES OF LOVING GRACE **545**

Grading Timesaver

Rubrics for each Choices assignment appear on p. 170 in the *Portfolio Management System*.

CHOICES: Building Your Portfolio

1. **Writer's Notebook** If students have trouble coming up with ideas, suggest that they glance through newspapers or news magazines.
2. **Comparing Art and Text** If students wish to transform Hicks' vision into a poem, have them first translate the images into phrases.
3. **Creative Writing** Have students use a three-column chart to organize their thoughts; the columns can be labeled Machine, What I Couldn't Do, What I Would Do Differently.
4. **Creative Writing** Brainstorm with the class two lists: one of destructive and one of constructive human acts and qualities. Then have students work individually to create metaphors for these qualities.
5. **Evaluating a Poem** Have students collaborate to think of ways to measure a poem's impact on a reader.

RESPONDING TO THE ART

American folk artist **Edward Hicks** (1780–1849) became an itinerant Quaker preacher and began painting works that expressed his religious beliefs. His best-known works are many versions of *The Peaceable Kingdom*, based on Isaiah 11:6–9 ("The wolf also shall dwell with the lamb . . ."). **Activity.** Ask students to describe how an artist might portray Brautigan's vision of a cybernetic nature.

Using Students' Strengths

Visual Learners

To help students create metaphors for Choice 4, have them work with a partner to draw illustrations that depict emotions and elements of nature. They should then compare the illustrations to see if there are any similarities between the emotions and the natural elements.

Intrapersonal Learners

To help students find a poem that they feel passionate about for Choice 5, ask them to recall the first time they read each of the poems. Did a particular poem make them feel angry, or happy, or confused? Have students review the poem or poems to which they had a strong initial reaction. Then, have students look for reasons for that reaction.

OBJECTIVES

1. Find thematic connections across genres
2. Generate relevant and interesting discussion

Extending the Theme

In this essay, Diane Glancy offers advice for writing poetry: All poets should read a lot, write what they want to say, share their works with others, and revise. Poetry, she suggests, works the same way that a good conversation does—through loose association, one image or idea eliciting another. Poetry, however, should also have some kind of focus and an overall coherence. She believes that experimenting with imagery and figurative language is a good idea. Because writing poetry is a highly individualistic endeavor, a poet must develop a unique voice. Her most important advice, therefore, is to lead an interesting life and to be confident that you have something to say.

Resources ———

Listening

Audio CD Library
A recording of this essay is provided in the *Audio CD Library*:
• Disc 15, Track 19

EXTENDING *the theme*
AN ESSAY

Reading Skills and Strategies

Dialogue with the Text

In this reflection a poet named Diane Glancy writes directly to someone, anyone, who wants to be a poet. She might be writing directly to you. While you read, keep your journal or a piece of paper or some self-sticking notes handy. As Glancy makes her suggestions and even gives orders, write down your responses. Include questions you'd like to ask her. Pretend that Glancy is talking directly to you. What do you want to say back? You should read the essay twice, at least.

HRW go.hrw.com
LEO 9-9

546 THE POETRY COLLECTIONS

Reaching All Students

Struggling Readers
Students may become confused by the many pieces of advice the writer gives in the essay. Direct students to jot down very briefly the main point of each paragraph as they read (such as "write what you know") and then review their notes to find the essay's main ideas.

English Language Learners
Before students read the poem, point out the ampersand (&) in paragraph four, and explain that it is a sign meaning "and." Also tell them that "thru" in paragraph six is a colloquial spelling of *through*. For other strategies for engaging English language learners with the literature, see
• *Lesson Plans Including Strategies for English-Language Learners*

Advanced Learners
Ask students who enjoy writing poetry to reflect upon their own creative processes. Then, have them write a paragraph that answers the question, "How do you begin writing poetry?" You might suggest a specific audience to whom they should direct their writing. Possibilities include a classmate, a friend, or a younger student who is looking for help in how to get started writing poetry.

T546

Claiming Breath

Diane Glancy

How do you begin writing poetry? I would say after all these years I'm not sure. First of all, you read. You have to be aware of what's being written. Poetry is a conversation. Often while I'm reading, I start a poem. An image will set off another image, or I think of something I want to say. It also helps to know the tradition of poetry, though often there's something about it that gets in the way. You strain for a rhyme without thought for the fire, the energy of the poem, the originality of voice. Yet I've heard others say that structure forces them to work in ways they would have missed on their own.

Begin by getting words down. What have you got to say? Even if you want to remain obscure there has to be coherence on some level. I remember hearing Gerald Stern say, if you get your words in order on the first row, you make room for a craziness later on, deeper in the poem, in a more important place.

Work with what you've experienced. I think sometimes, who cares about my ordinary life? But often, that's exactly what matters.

What idea, impression, image, do you want to convey? Why should I listen to you? Again, (1) read, (2) write what you have to say, & (3) read it to someone. Listen to their reaction, their criticism, & write again. So much of writing is rewriting.

Contemporary poetry says what you have to say in whatever way you want to say. Make sure you have a style, a voice, a certain way of expressing yourself. Where's your uniqueness, your individuality? You have a thumbprint different from other thumbprints. You have a way of seeing & a way of expressing what you see that is also different. Develop that difference. Take chances with unusual words & combinations. Writing is a long process. Reveal what it's like to be you.

CLAIMING BREATH 547

A Reading Skills and Strategies
Dialogue with the Text
❓ In your opinion, what does Glancy mean here by "conversation"? [Possible responses: She means that there is a back-and-forth dialogue between what a poet writes and what a poet reads because a text can spark ideas or provide a reference point; for Glancy, writing her own poetry is like speaking to the texts that inspired her.]

B Critical Thinking
Analyzing Sequence
❓ What process does the poet recommend when writing poetry? [Read extensively in order to know what others are thinking about, write what you want to communicate to others, read it to someone else to get their opinion, and rewrite.]

Making the Connections

Connecting to the Theme: "Imagine"
After students have read the essay, discuss with them how it relates to the theme of the collection, which deals with the power and importance of the imagination. Glancy encourages beginning poets to use their imaginations when writing poetry. Although poets should learn from other writers, they should not merely imitate them. Glancy emphasizes that each individual has a unique way of seeing, or imagining. She suggests paying attention to the mental pictures that are created with words—pictures that will encourage one's readers to use their own imaginations. She also suggests experimenting with language and the arrangement of words on the page. The author takes some of the mystery out of the process of using the imagination by saying that poetry is largely based on actual life experiences. The essay, in essence, offers practical advice to beginning poets on how to incorporate their imaginations and their actualities to create a poem.

You may want to have students relate Glancy's ideas on writing poetry to the ideas presented in some of the poems in this collection, as well as in the author biographies. Also encourage students to connect these poems to the collection's theme. What did the students imagine—or picture in their mind's eye—as they read these poems?

A **Appreciating Language**
Style
? Why does the writer use the short-ened form "thru" instead of *through*? [Possible responses: The writer is quickly dashing off her ideas; the unconventional spelling is consistent with the style of the essay, which is informal, conversational, fast-paced, and enthusiastic; the writer's spelling is consistent with her suggestion of finding a unique style of expression.]

B **Critical Thinking**
Challenging the Text
? What do you think of the author's advice to assume responsibility in life? [Sample responses: I am not sure how this can make a difference in the kind of poetry a person might write; I think that being responsible gives you the disci-pline to stick to your writing.]

C **Literary Connections**
Sara Teasdale (1884–1933) was an extremely popular poet during the first half of the twentieth century. Like Emily Dickinson, Teasdale is known for short, simple, intensely personal lyric poems. The note in the upper left-hand corner of the manuscript page reproduced here refers to *Love Songs* (1917), her third published collection of poems. It won Teasdale the 1918 Pulitzer Prize in poetry. You may wish to use the next-to-last line of the poem on the manu-script page as an example of "workshopping" a poem; note how Teasdale replaces the clichéd expres-sion "break your heart" with the more original line "goad you & set you mad."

Do you have something bothering you? Get into it. That will save the trouble of writing boring poems.

A Remember imagery, the mental pictures your writing makes, usually thru metaphor & simile. Make sure they haven't been said before. They have to be new. Tell me something in a way I haven't heard before. Let an image connect with a thought, sometimes a memory. Get rid of weak verbs. Watch tenses; make them consis-tent. Use DETAIL! A cotton dress printed with crocuses is usually better than "a dress." Look for the right word. The inevitable one. Ask what your poem means. What conclusion is drawn from it? Even if not a logical thought, but an im-pression. Good poems are sometimes simple, on at least one level.

What is life like for you? That's what you should begin writing about.

Remember also the richness of language. Make sure there's a lot in your writing. Read your words to yourself. Listen to them on a tape recorder.

The form a poem takes on the page is also inte-gral. Experiment with line breaks, stanzas, the square or prose poem, the words wiggling over the page.

Then workshop a poem. Critiques are usually common sense. Does the poem work? Do you like it? Does it begin at the first stanza or do you really get into the poem several lines later? Do all the parts form a whole? What central thought holds the poem together? What emo-tion or impression is shared? What stays in your

mind after you've heard it? Is it in the form it should be in? Is the poem clear? Have you said the same thing too many times? Is the reader re-warded for reading it?

B Be interested in a lot of things. Be an interesting person; live a responsible life. Start keeping notes.

I think it's also important to know why you write. When I go into a bookstore & see shelves full of books, I think why do I do this? Hasn't it been done better than I can do it? That's when I have to be able to look in myself & decide, I have something to say too—these other books can move over & make room for mine.

C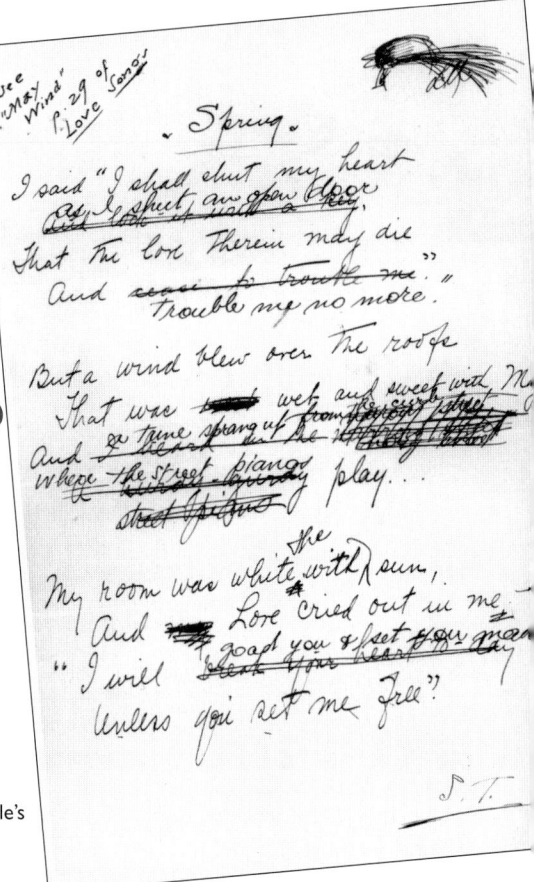

A manuscript page showing Sara Teasdale's revisions of her poem "Spring."
Courtesy, the Lilly Library, Indiana University, Bloomington, Indiana.

Assessing Learning

Check Test: Questions and Answers
Answers may vary slightly.
1. When does the speaker often get an idea for a poem? [The speaker often gets an idea for a poem while she is reading.]
2. Why does the speaker think it is important to write about ordinary life? [It is important to write about ordinary life because that's what really matters.]
3. What four steps does the speaker recom-mend that you follow when writing a poem?

[Read, write what you have to say, share the poem, rewrite.]
4. How should you phrase your thoughts? [You should try to write in your own voice.]
5. What kind of person does the speaker say a writer should be? [She says a writer should be an interesting person who lives a responsible life.]

MEET THE WRITER

"A Pencil Is a Buffalo Migration"

Like the poets of long ago, **Diane Glancy** (1941–   ) has spent much of her life traveling. For years she earned her living by driving through Oklahoma and Arkansas to teach poetry in schools. The prose reflections in *Claiming Breath* (1992) are a diary of one of those years. Now Diane Glancy teaches creative writing and American Indian literature at Macalaster College in St. Paul, Minnesota. Here she talks about being an American Indian woman and a poet:

66 I often write about being in the middle ground between two cultures, not fully a part of either. I write with a split voice, often experimenting with language until the parts equal some sort of a whole. I would say a pencil is a buffalo migration under the sky with its stars turning like a jar-lid poked with holes. Writing affects my life, my Real life, while the rest spins through the lone pines. I write from everyday circumstances, old ordinary life, and the stampede of the past. 99

FINDING COMMON GROUND

1. Referring to the notes you made as you read this essay, quickly write a brief answer to Glancy. Speak directly to her, as if you were talking face-to-face. Ask her questions. Tell her about the problems you have with creative writing. Tell her what you don't understand about her suggestions, and what you especially like. Maybe she says some things you disagree with: Tell her why you disagree.

2. When you finish writing your personal reflections, compare your responses in class. Do you all agree on what's important and interesting about Glancy's reflection? Or do people have very different responses? How do you account for the differences in responses?

3. One thing you must do: talk about her title.

CLAIMING BREATH 549

MAIN OBJECTIVE
Write a poem or group of poems

PROCESS OBJECTIVES

1. Use appropriate prewriting techniques to identify and develop a topic
2. Create a first draft
3. Use evaluation criteria as a basis for determining revision strategies
4. Revise the first draft incorporating suggestions generated by self- or peer evaluation
5. Proofread and correct errors
6. Create a final draft
7. Choose an appropriate method of publication
8. Reflect on progress as a writer

Planning

- **Block Schedule**
  Block Scheduling Lesson Plans with Pacing Guide
- **One-Stop Planner**
  CD-ROM with Test Generator

BUILDING YOUR PORTFOLIO

Writer's Workshop

ASSIGNMENT

> **Write a poem or group of poems.**

AIM

> **To express yourself; to be creative.**

AUDIENCE

> **Yourself, classmates, family, readers of a magazine of student writing. (You choose.)**

I don't look at anything as being insignificant. I think that's another overlooked gift of poetry. Many times people imagine that poets wait for some splendid experience to overtake them, but I think the tiniest moments are the most splendid. This is the wisdom that all these small things have to teach.

—Naomi Shihab Nye

POETRY

Where poems come from is a mystery. All we know is that a poem is a kind of wedding between something in the outside world that can be observed and pointed to, and some feeling inside the poet that lives like an untold secret in the mind and heart. In a sense, all poems are revelations—they help poets and their readers discover connections between inside feelings and the outside world.

Getting Started

1. Check Your Writer's Notebook

You've been collecting ideas for poems and doing exercises on imagery and figurative language as you worked with the poems in Collections 8 and 9. See if any of that work interests you enough to develop it further.

If you still need help, the exercises that follow might give you some ideas. Begin with the confidence that you have feelings that can be expressed in a poem. You just have to find a subject that will urge them into expression.

2. Find an Occasion

Start by listing moments or days in your life that you associate with some feeling. Any one of these moments may provide that spark, that connection between outside events and inside feelings that may lead you to a poem.

a. You learn that your family is moving to another city and you know you'll have to give up friends and neighborhood and everything familiar.

b. Your grandmother has died and you realize you'll never see her face again or open the birthday and Christmas presents she never failed to send.

c. You smile at someone you like a lot, and you see that person looking back and smiling at you.

d. You go back to your old playground and find that all the kids there look so young.

e. You have a wonderful dream.

550 THE POETRY COLLECTIONS

 — *Resources: Print and Media* —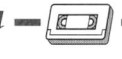

Writing and Language
- *Portfolio Management System*
    Prewriting, p. 172
    Peer Editing, p. 173
    Assessment Rubric, p. 174

3. Look Around

If those occasions won't work for you, there are other ways of finding topics for poems:

a. Look through a newspaper for items that catch your imagination.

b. Pretend you are Cinderella, a rock star, the last dinosaur (or any other figure from a story or a movie or real life).

c. Begin with a question:
- "What kind of house would I have lived in in 1600?"
- "How would I be remembered if I disappeared this very moment?"
- "Twenty years from now, who will I be?"

d. Choose an object or a creature and speak to it as though it were capable of understanding what you say. You might call your poem "A Conversation with a House" or "To a Pizza Pie" or "Words for an Old Dog."

e. Write a poem consisting of a series of images. Its title might be "A Catalog of Sounds" or "A List of Memories." Or its first line might be "I see —" (or "I smell," "I taste," "I touch," "I hear").

f. Write a poem consisting of a series of contrasting metaphors.
- "A cat seems to be _____, but it really is _____."
- "Fog seems to be _____, but it really is _____."
- "An onion seems to be _____, but it really is _____."

Finding a Form

Once you have an idea for a poem, you have to find a form to write it in.

1. Free Verse: Imitate Natural Speech

The simplest form for a beginning poet to use is **free verse**—poetry written in lines that imitate the natural rhythms of speech (see page 555). If you use free verse, take special care in deciding

---

Poetry can do a hundred and one things, delight, sadden, disturb, amuse, instruct—it may express every possible shade of emotion, and describe every conceivable kind of event, but there is only one thing that all poetry must do: It must praise all it can for being and for happening.

—W. H. Auden

How Poetry Comes to Me

*It comes blundering over the
Boulders at night, it stays
Frightened outside the
Range of my campfire
I go to meet it at the
Edge of the light*

—Gary Snyder

Introducing the Writer's Workshop

Introducing the Writer's Workshop

Ask students to think about an event in their past that was particularly emotional. Have them freewrite for a few minutes about the event and the feelings associated with that event. (Caution students not to write about anything too personal.) As students write, ask them to identify the emotions they recall and to think about why this occasion still has the power to move them. Point out that one of the purposes of poetry is to explore feelings and gain understanding of ourselves and others.

Teaching the Writer's Workshop

Prewriting
- Have students use the techniques suggested on pp. 550-51 (or any others with which they may be familiar) to generate ideas.
- Remind students to choose a situation they will not mind sharing with others.

Drafting
- Encourage students to look again at some of the poems in the book. In particular, look at the way the poems are set on the page. Poetry has more options for individual expression than most other forms, and students should experiment with line length and breaks.
- Before beginning to write their poems, students may find it helpful to write a prose version of the event they wish to describe. As they read the paraphrase, they may find clues to the most appropriate mood or feeling, which they should try to capture in the poems they will write.

Crossing the Curriculum

Music
Many songs are similar to poems in the sense that both are means of self-expression; both show the relationship between feelings and the external world, and both are written in a structured format. Have students describe in a brief paragraph a favorite song, and ask them to compare the form of the song to the form of the poem they are writing. Do the poem and song share the same emotion or theme? If their

poems were songs, what would they sound like? Some students may wish to set their poems to music or to choose appropriate background music for a reading of their poems.

History
Poets often lead interesting lives or live in interesting times.
- Have students write a short biography of a poet in Collections 8 or 9 (or another poet they may find interesting).

- Have students include a time line of major personal, historical, and cultural events during the poet's lifetime.
- More advanced students could write a short poem from the perspective of either a famous historical figure or an average person living during the same era.

T551

Evaluating and Revising

1. If students used **free verse**, did they choose natural-sounding line breaks? begin with an attention-catching statement? use interesting punctuation to keep the reader's attention?
2. If students used **rhyme**, have them circle words with similar rhymes in similar colors. Do the patterns follow couplet or quatrain structure?
3. If students used **meter**, ask them to divide between syllables and put check marks above stressed syllables. Did they use either six or eight syllables? an alternating stressed/unstressed pattern?

Proofreading

Poetry, especially free verse, allows for nonstandard grammar and punctuation. Have students proofread their own poems first, circling any intentional "mistakes." Then have students exchange poems with each other to check for unintended mistakes.

Publishing

Have students use the Publishing Tip provided here to review their final draft and determine whether or not it is ready for publication. Encourage students to consider illustrating their poems for a display in the classroom or in a bound booklet that could be distributed to other classes.

Reflecting

If students are adding their poems to their portfolios, be sure that they have a date on the top sheet. They should also attach a reflection on the work that they did.

1. I had the most trouble_____.
2. The easiest part of writing was _____ _____.
3. I'm adding this to my portfolio because _____.

Resources

Peer Editing Forms and Rubrics
- *Portfolio Management System*, p. 173

Publishing Tip

Think about how you want your poem to look on the page. Where will the lines break? Which letters will be capitalized? What typeface will you use? If you publish your poem in a school literary magazine, you may be able to influence its design.

Running
1933
(North Caldwell, New Jersey)

What were we playing? Was it
*   prisoner's base?*
I ran with whacking keds
Down the cart-road past
*   Rickard's place,*
And where it dropped beside the
*   tractor-sheds*

Leapt out into the air above a
*   blurred*
Terrain, through jolted light,
Took two hard lopes, and at the
*   third*
Spanked off a hummock-side
*   exactly right,*

And made the turn, and with
*   delighted strain*
Sprinted across the flat
By the bull-pen, and up the
*   lane.*
Thinking of happiness, I think
*   of that.*

—Richard Wilbur

---

where to break your lines, and be sure that no one line is so long that it almost runs off the page. Begin with a statement to catch the reader's attention. Then keep your reader's interest, not only by what you say, but also by using question marks (?), by using dots (. . .) to continue a thought, by using dashes (—) to add a thought, even by using exclamation marks (!).

2. Try Rhyme

Almost as simple are poems in **rhymed couplets** (two rhyming lines) or **quatrains** (four rhyming lines). If you use couplets, the last words in each line should rhyme:

> I wish I could unlOCK
> The secrets of a clOCK.

If you use quatrains, you can rhyme just two of the four lines, or you can rhyme the last words in every line. Here is a quatrain in which only two lines are rhymed:

> This morning, late for class, I skipped   **a**
> My cornflakes and, gung-ho, departed.   **b**
> Nice timing! I made history   **c**
> Before the Civil War got started.   **b**

For more on rhyme, see pages 559–560.

3. Meter: A Challenge

Perhaps you'll want a challenge and will try to write a poem in **meter**—that is, to give each line a regular pattern of stressed and unstressed syllables. For beginners, one of these two meters is best:

a. Each line has six syllables, alternating an unstressed syllable with a stressed syllable: da/DAH, da/DAH, da/DAH ("The dead began to speak").

b. Each line has eight syllables, also alternating an unstressed syllable with a stressed syllable: da/DAH, da/DAH, da/DAH, da/DAH ("I wandered lonely as a cloud").

If you write in meter, maintain your beat, but at times add a little variation so your verse doesn't become singsong. For instance, you can reverse the beat of the first two syllables in any line without doing serious harm to your pattern (from da/DAH to DAH/da).

For more on meter, see pages 554–555.

Opposite is a poem by a famous American poet who found a feeling, a moment that he associated with that feeling, and a form to write his thoughts in.

Grading Timesaver

Rubrics for this Writer's Workshop assignment appear on page 174 of the *Portfolio Management System*.

Collection 10

The Ways We Are

Theme

Sounds and Sense *The poems in this collection re-create the intimate world of the poet. The focus is on the sounds of language and how sound can be used to reinforce sense.*

Reading the Anthology

Reaching Struggling Readers

The *Reading Skills and Strategies: Reaching Struggling Readers* binder includes a Reading Strategies Handbook that offers concrete suggestions for helping students who have difficulty reading and comprehending text, or students who are reluctant readers. When a specific strategy is most appropriate for a selection, a correlation to the Handbook is provided at the bottom of the teacher's page under the head Struggling Readers. This head may also be used to introduce additional ideas for helping students read challenging texts.

Reading Beyond the Anthology

Read On At the end of the poetry collections in the grade nine book, there is an annotated bibliography of books suitable for extended reading. The suggested books are related to works in these collections by theme, by author, or by subject. To preview the Read On for the poetry collections, please turn to p. T613.

Collection 10 The Ways We Are

Resources for this Collection

Note: All resources for this collection are available for preview on the *One-Stop Planner CD-ROM 2 with Test Generator.* All worksheets and blackline masters may be printed from the CD-ROM.

Selection or Feature	Reading and Literary Skills	Vocabulary, Language, and Grammar
Elements of Literature: The Sounds of Poetry—You've Got Rhythm (p. 554)	• *Literary Elements,* Transparency 12	
Women Alice Walker (p. 556)	• *Graphic Organizers for Active Reading,* Worksheet p. 48	• *Words to Own,* Worksheet p. 31 • *Daily Oral Grammar,* Transparency 38
Elements of Literature: The Sounds of Poetry—Rhyme and Other Sound Effects (p. 559)	• *Literary Elements,* Transparency 13	
My Papa's Waltz Theodore Roethke (p. 561)	• *Graphic Organizers for Active Reading,* Worksheet p. 49 • *Literary Elements:* Transparency 13 Worksheet p. 40	• *Words to Own,* Worksheet p. 31
The Gift Li-Young Lee (p. 564)	• *Graphic Organizers for Active Reading,* Worksheet p. 50	• *Words to Own,* Worksheet p. 31
Combing Gladys Cardiff (p. 566)	• *Graphic Organizers for Active Reading,* Worksheet p. 51 • *Literary Elements:* Transparency 12 Worksheet p. 37	• *Words to Own,* Worksheet p. 31
Fifteen William Stafford (p. 570)	• *Graphic Organizers for Active Reading,* Worksheet p. 52 • *Literary Elements:* Transparency 14 Worksheet p. 43	• *Words to Own,* Worksheet p. 31 • *Daily Oral Grammar,* Transparency 39
American Hero Essex Hemphill (p. 572)	• *Graphic Organizers for Active Reading,* Worksheet p. 53	• *Words to Own,* Worksheet p. 31
The Girl Who Loved the Sky Anita Endrezze (p. 576)	• *Graphic Organizers for Active Reading,* Worksheet p. 54	
Extending the Theme: Americans All Michael Dorris (p. 579)	The Extending the Theme feature provides students with an unstructured opportunity to practice reading strategies using a selection that extends the theme of the collection.	
Speaking and Listening Workshop: Poetry Reading (p. 582)		

Other Resources for this Collection

- *Cross-Curricular Activities,* p. 10
- *Portfolio Management System,* Introduction to Portfolio Assessment, p. 1
- *Test Generator,* Collection Test

Writing	Listening and Speaking Viewing and Representing	Assessment
		• *Formal Assessment,* Literary Elements Test, p. 111
• *Portfolio Management System,* Rubrics for Choices, p. 175	• *Audio CD Library,* Disc 16, Track 2 • *Viewing and Representing:* Fine Art Transparency 14; Worksheet p. 56 • *Portfolio Management System,* Rubrics for Choices, p. 175	• *Formal Assessment,* Selection Test, p. 107 • *Test Generator (One-Stop Planner CD-ROM)*
		• *Formal Assessment,* Literary Elements Test, p. 113
• *Portfolio Management System,* Rubrics for Choices, p. 176	• *Audio CD Library,* Disc 16, Track 3 • *Portfolio Management System,* Rubrics for Choices, p. 176	• *Formal Assessment,* Selection Test, p. 107 • *Standardized Test Preparation,* p. 74 • *Test Generator (One-Stop Planner CD-ROM)*
• *Portfolio Management System,* Rubrics for Choices, p. 177	• *Audio CD Library,* Disc 16, Track 4 • *Portfolio Management System,* Rubrics for Choices, p. 177	• *Formal Assessment,* Selection Test, p. 107 • *Test Generator (One-Stop Planner CD-ROM)*
• *Portfolio Management System,* Rubrics for Choices, p. 177	• *Audio CD Library,* Disc 16, Track 5 • *Portfolio Management System,* Rubrics for Choices, p. 177	• *Formal Assessment,* Selection Test, p. 107 • *Test Generator (One-Stop Planner CD-ROM)*
• *Portfolio Management System,* Rubrics for Choices, p. 179	• *Visual Connections:* Videocassette B, Segment 10 • *Audio CD Library,* Disc 16, Track 6 • *Portfolio Management System,* Rubrics for Choices, p. 179	• *Formal Assessment,* Selection Test, p. 109 • *Test Generator (One-Stop Planner CD-ROM)*
• *Portfolio Management System,* Rubrics for Choices, p. 179	• *Audio CD Library,* Disc 16, Track 7 • *Viewing and Representing:* Fine Art Transparency 15; Worksheet p. 60 • *Portfolio Management System,* Rubrics for Choices, p. 179	• *Formal Assessment,* Selection Test, p. 109 • *Test Generator (One-Stop Planner CD-ROM)*
• *Portfolio Management System,* Rubrics for Choices, p. 181	• *Audio CD Library,* Disc 16, Track 8 • *Portfolio Management System,* Rubrics for Choices, p. 181	• *Formal Assessment,* Selection Test, p. 109 • *Test Generator (One-Stop Planner CD-ROM)*
	• *Audio CD Library,* Disc 16, Track 9	
		• *Portfolio Management System,* Rubrics p. 182

 Transparency    CD-ROM    Video   Audio CD

Collection 10 The Ways We Are

Skills Focus

Skills Focus

Selection or Feature	Reading Skills and Strategies	Elements of Literature	Language/ Grammar	Vocabulary/ Spelling	Writing	Listening/ Speaking	Viewing/ Representing
Elements of Literature: The Sounds of Poetry—You've Got Rhythm (p. 554)		Rhythm, pp. 554–555 Meter, pp. 554–555 • Foot • Iamb • Trochee • Anapest • Dactyl • Spondee Free Verse, p. 555					
Women Alice Walker (p. 556)	Identify Implied Comparison, pp. 556, 558	Metaphor, p. 556 Implied Metaphor, pp. 556, 558			Write a Poem or a Paragraph, Describing Heroes, p. 558	Create a Reader's Script for a Poem, p. 558	
Elements of Literature: The Sounds of Poetry—Rhyme and Other Sound Effects (p. 559)		Rhyme, pp. 559–560 Rhyme Scheme, p. 559 Approximate Rhyme, p. 559 Internal Rhyme, p. 559 Onomatopoeia, p. 560 Alliteration, p. 560					
My Papa's Waltz Theodore Roethke (p. 561)	Identify Positive and Negative Connotations, p. 563	Rhyme, p. 561 Rhyme Scheme, pp. 561, 563 Theme, p. 563 Meter, p. 563		Connotation, p. 563	Write a Poem, p. 563 Write a Brief Essay in Response to a Poem, p. 563	Create a Reader's Script, p. 563	
The Gift Li-Young Lee (p. 564) **Combing** Gladys Cardiff (p. 566)		Free Verse, pp. 564, 569 Repetition, pp. 566, 569 Assonance, p. 566 Alliteration, pp. 566, 569 Onomatopoeia p. 569			Write a Poem, p. 569 Write Sentences Describing Sounds, p. 569	Identify Breath Groupings, p. 564 Practice Diction, p. 569 Read a Poem Aloud, p. 569	Make a Collection of Brand Names Using Sound Effects, p. 569
Fifteen William Stafford (p. 570) **American Hero** Essex Hemphill (p. 572)		External and Internal Conflict, pp. 570, 574 Onomatopoeia, pp. 572, 575 Refrain, p. 574			Write a Letter to a School Newspaper, p. 575 Write a Poem About Sports, p. 575 Write a Personification of a Machine, p. 575 Create a Class Notebook, p. 575	Prepare and Perform a Group Reading of a Poem, p. 575	
The Girl Who Loved the Sky Anita Endrezze (p. 576)	Visualize Images, p. 578	Images, pp. 576, 578			Write a Series of Linked Images, p. 578	Create a Reader's Script, p. 578	Paint or Draw an Illustration for a Poem, p. 578
Extending the Theme: Americans All Michael Dorris (p. 579)	The Extending the Theme feature provides students with an unstructured opportunity to practice reading strategies using a selection that extends the theme of the collection.						
Speaking and Listening Workshop: Poetry Reading (p. 582)						Perform an Oral Reading of a Poem Before an Audience, pp. 582–583	

THE WAYS WE ARE

SPEAKING AND LISTENING FOCUS: Reader's Theater

The people who speak in poems will tell you that they sometimes are afraid, envious, confused, sad. And, oh yes, sometimes suffused with joy and kindness and compassion and gratitude and love. You may feel you don't have much in common with some of the people who speak in poems. Or, you may not like it when one of them hits a nerve or comes too close to home. But whatever happens, when you read a poem, you win. For you get to know people of all kinds, without moving anything (except your brain). All of this may give you a better handle on your own relationships—starting with how you feel about yourself.

Reader's Theater

You already know a lot of poetry. Most of us can recite a nursery rhyme, a prayer, a jump-rope chant, or a football cheer, and we can sing a few songs or hymns. Start preparing for a poetry reading now by finding one poem you like the sound of and memorizing it.

Each of us inevitable;
Each of us limitless—each of us
*   with his or her right upon the earth ...*
Each of us here as divinely as any is here.
                          —Walt Whitman

Speaking and Listening Focus: Reader's Theater

The following **Work in Progress** assignments build to a culminating **Speaking and Listening Workshop** at the end of the collection.

• Women	Looking at rhythm (p. 558)
• My Papa's Waltz	Writing a script (p. 563)
• The Gift / Combing	Practicing diction (p. 569)
• Fifteen / American Hero	Reading with a group (p. 575)
• The Girl Who Loved the Sky	Practicing pauses (p. 578)

Speaking and Listening Workshop: Reader's Theater / Poetry Reading (p. 582)

OBJECTIVES

1. Read poetry centered on the theme "The Ways We Are"
2. Identify and analyze literary elements used in the literature with special emphasis on the sounds of poetry
3. Respond to the literature using a variety of modes
4. Prepare, plan, rehearse, and present a poetry reading

Responding to the Quotation

Write the key words from the quotation—*inevitable, limitless, right,* and *divinely*—on the chalkboard. Ask students to define these words and tell what connotations, or associations, they bring to mind. Then ask a volunteer to read the quotation aloud. Discuss possible interpretations of Whitman's meaning, reminding students to keep in mind the collection title "The Ways We Are."

RESPONDING TO THE ART

? How does this photograph of a ticker-tape parade convey the joy in poetry? [Possible response: The photograph shows partygoers clustered at a window throwing colorful confetti. People seem to be appreciating each other and the occasion.]

Reader's Theater

Challenge students to list nursery rhymes, songs, chants, and cheers they can recite from memory. Ask volunteers to read their lists and recite some of the items. Students may be surprised that they have so many shared items on their lists.

OBJECTIVES
1. Identify metrical units: iamb, trochee, anapest, dactyl, spondee
2. Recognize free verse

Elements of Literature

Resources

Elements of Literature

Rhythm

For additional instruction on rhythm, see *Literary Elements*:
- Transparency 12

Elements of Literature

This feature focuses on rhythm in poetry and explains how rhythmic patterns can be organized as meter or as free verse.

Mini-Lesson:

Rhythm

Read this feature aloud to students or assign an initial reading for homework. Review the different metrical patterns: iamb, trochee, anapest, dactyl, and spondee. To help students remember the name of each type of poetic foot, present the following mnemonic device in which each girl's name begins with the same letter as the name of the foot and also possesses the same stressed syllables:

An-toi-**nette**—anapest
Dor-o-thy—dactyl
I-**rene**—iamb
Says-who—spondee
Tra-cy—trochee

Ask students to scan their own names: for example, **Rob**ert **John**son (trochees) or Chris**tine** Mc**Grath** (iambs).

Reinforce the idea that free verse does contain rhythm, but the rhythm is not expressed in a regular pattern of beats.

THE SOUNDS OF POETRY: You've Got Rhythm

Poetry is not irregular lines in a book, but something very close to dance and song, something to walk down the street keeping time to.
—Northrop Frye

As long as your heart is beating, you've got rhythm. Musicians and poets, perhaps in imitation of that heartbeat, also create rhythm. Rhythm is based on repetition. In poetry, rhythmic patterns can be organized either as meter or as free verse.

Meter: A Pattern of Stressed Syllables

One way to think of meter in poetry is to compare it with a metronome. A metronome is an instrument that often sits on top of a piano. It has an upside-down pendulum that moves back and forth, ticking and tocking like a clock, at whatever speed the musician has chosen.

The metronome gives the musician a basic beat that must be kept—but not exactly. Music that followed the beat of the metronome exactly would be dull and monotonous. Musicians must learn to keep the beat but also to make variations on it. Every musician knows you must be *offbeat*—without ever forgetting that you can't be "off" until you have a sense of what's "on."

The same is true for poets. When a poet chooses to write in a meter, that meter, like the metronome's beat, is "given." The meter sets the basic mechanical beat, around which, and over which, and even against which, the poet's own voice must play.

Poetry that is written in **meter** has a regular pattern of stressed and unstressed syllables in each line.

The following poem is written in meter. The stressed syllables are marked ´; the unstressed syllables are marked ˇ. Read Frost's poem aloud, to feel its steady beat.

> **As long as your heart is beating, you've got rhythm.**

> **If you listen to spoken English, you will find that very often we speak in iambs.**

Dust of Snow
The way a crow
Shook down on me
The dust of snow
From a hemlock tree

Has given my heart
A change of mood
And saved some part
Of a day I had rued.
—Robert Frost

Frost wrote his poem mostly in iambs. An **iamb** (ī′amb′) is an unstressed syllable followed by a stressed syllable (da DAH). (You may think meter is artificial, but if you listen to spoken English, you will find that very often we speak in iambs.)

An iamb is an example of a poetic foot—a **foot** being the basic building block of meter. A foot usually consists of one stressed syllable and one or more unstressed syllables.

English poetry has other kinds of feet. A **trochee** (trō′kē) is a stressed syllable followed by an unstressed syllable (DAH da); it is the

Using Students' Strengths

Logical/Mathematical Learners

Explain that metrical rhythm refers to the total number of feet in every line of a poem. The number is indicated by a prefix placed before the word *meter*. *Pentameter,* for example, means that there are five feet in each line of the poem. Ask students to research other types of metrical rhythm and to organize and convert this information into a chart. Their charts should include the terms for one to five feet and provide an example for each term.

Visual Learners

Students may benefit from seeing the stressed syllables in poetry spelled out in capital letters. Write the following line from "The Raven" on the board: ONCE up-ON a MID-night DREAR-y. Ask students to come up with other techniques to show rhythm, such as using a different color for stressed syllables. Have them choose a poem and create a poster in which they use one of the techniques to diagram the poem's meter.

Auditory/Musical Learners

Ask students with musical knowledge to demonstrate examples of rhythm in music, such as 3/4 time, 4/4 time, and syncopation. Then, challenge them to drum the stress patterns of a trochee, an anapest, a dactyl, and a spondee on a desk or table. Finally, have them beat out these patterns in accompaniment as other students read the examples for each term on pp. 554–555.

T554

by John Malcolm Brinnin

opposite of an iamb. Here is a line from Edgar Allan Poe's famous poem "The Raven" that uses trochees:

Once upŏn ă mídnĭght dreăry

An **anapest** is two unstressed syllables followed by a stressed syllable (da da DAH). Here is a line from Byron's poem "The Destruction of Sennacherib" that uses anapests:

Thĕ Ăssýrĭan came dówn lĭke thĕ wolf ŏn thĕ fóld

A **dactyl** is one stressed syllable followed by two unstressed syllables (DAH da da). Here is the beginning of a nursery rhyme that uses dactyls:

Híckŏrў, díckŏrў, dóck

A **spondee** is two stressed syllables (DAH DAH). Here are some lines from "We Real Cool" by Gwendolyn Brooks that use spondees:

Wé reál coól. Wé léft schoól. Wé Lúrk láte. . . .

When you analyze a poem to show its meter, you are **scanning** the poem. Scanning a poem is like analyzing the construction of a song. You are trying to take the poem apart to see how the poet has created the music.

Free Verse Isn't Free

Until the last century, all poetry in English was written with a strict concern for meter. But eventually, some poets began to rebel against the old poetic "rules." They insisted that new rhythms were necessary to create new moods. Many poets abandoned meter and began writing what is called free verse.

Free verse is poetry that is free of regular meter—that is, free of a strict pattern of stressed syllables and unstressed syllables. This new kind of poetry sounds very close to prose and to everyday spoken language. But free verse is free only in the sense that it is liberated from the formal rules governing meter. Poets writing in free verse pay close attention to the rhythmic rise and fall of the voice, to pauses, and to the balance between long and short phrases.

The poem below by David Ignatow is written in free verse, and so is Walt Whitman's poem on page 496. When you read Whitman's poem aloud, you'll notice how close to ordinary spoken language it sounds at first. But then you'll notice how it soars into the kind of language used by preachers and orators. That's free verse at its most eloquent.

This poem, along with many others, has appeared in New York City subway cars as part of a program called Poetry in Motion.

Applying the Element

First ask students to scan "I Never Saw a Moor" (p. 522) and "Fire and Ice" (p. 541), and identify the meter of these poems. [Both are written in iambs.] Then invite volunteers to read aloud "All Watched Over by Machines of Loving Grace" (p. 543) and "Southbound on the Freeway" (p. 527); ask other students to identify each poem's rhythm. [Both are written in free verse.] As students read the poems contained in this collection, have them identify those that are written in free verse. [All are except "My Papa's Waltz."] Ask them to invent terms that describe the rhythmic effects of these poems.

Resources ———

Elements of Literature
Formal Assessment
• Literary Elements Test, p.111
Test Generator (One-Stop Planner)
• CD-ROM

RESPONDING TO THE ART

"The Bagel" by David Ignatow appeared on New York City subways and buses as part of a program called Poetry in Motion, sponsored by New York City Transit.
Activity. Is this poem written in meter or in free verse? [free verse, which is appropriate to the subject] Why do you think the speaker feels so happy? [Perhaps he feels free. He is experiencing what it is like to become something else—he is transformed.]

Reaching All Students

Struggling Readers

When you introduce meter, be sure students understand the basics of syllabification. Have students use the dictionary to find the stressed syllables in some common words such as *classroom, occupation,* and *discuss.* Let pairs of students take turns sounding out the syllabification of multi-syllable words. Then, read aloud some of the accented poetry lines in the feature, showing students how to lightly emphasize the rhythm as they read. Call on volunteers to read other lines, emphasizing the stressed syllables as they do so.

Assessing Learning

Check Test: True-False
1. Rhythm is based on repetition. [True]
2. Poetry that is written in meter has a regular pattern of stressed and unstressed syllables. [True]
3. A metered poem never varies from the underlying pattern. [False]
4. A foot is a group of syllables that serves as a metrical unit. [True]
5. Free verse does not use regular meter. [True]

Before You Read

WOMEN

Make the Connection

What We Are Given

Very few of us are born into this world with lots of money. Yet every one of us inherits incalculable treasure, for we are the living beneficiaries of every person who has ever lived. What they did with their lives affects ours. If we inherit a polluted planet, they are partially responsible. If they struggled to make the world a better place, that's part of our legacy too.

Quickwrite

Take notes about people who helped you become the person you are today. You'll probably think of relatives, teachers, and religious leaders—but think also about others, even people from the past.

Keep your notes. For questions and activities on this poem, see page 558.

Elements of Literature

Metaphor: Battering Doors

Walker's famous poem is built around a metaphor that is first suggested in lines 12–13 and then extended through line 18. The metaphor is based on a comparison that is never openly stated. After you read the poem, talk about what Walker is comparing her women and their struggle to.

An **implied metaphor** does not directly state that one thing *is* something else. Instead it uses words to suggest the comparison.

For more on Metaphor, see pages 520–521 and the Handbook of Literary Terms.

---

556 THE POETRY COLLECTIONS

Women

Alice Walker

They were women then
My mama's generation
Husky of voice—stout of
Step
5   With fists as well as
     Hands
     How they battered down
     Doors
     And ironed
10   Starched white
     Shirts
A   How they led
     Armies
B   Headragged generals
15   Across mined
     Fields
     Booby-trapped
     Ditches
     To discover books
20   Desks
     A place for us
C   How they knew what we
     Must know
     Without knowing a page
25   Of it
     Themselves.

©1998 Roland L. Freeman.

go.hrw.com
LE0 9-10

   *Resources: Print and Media*

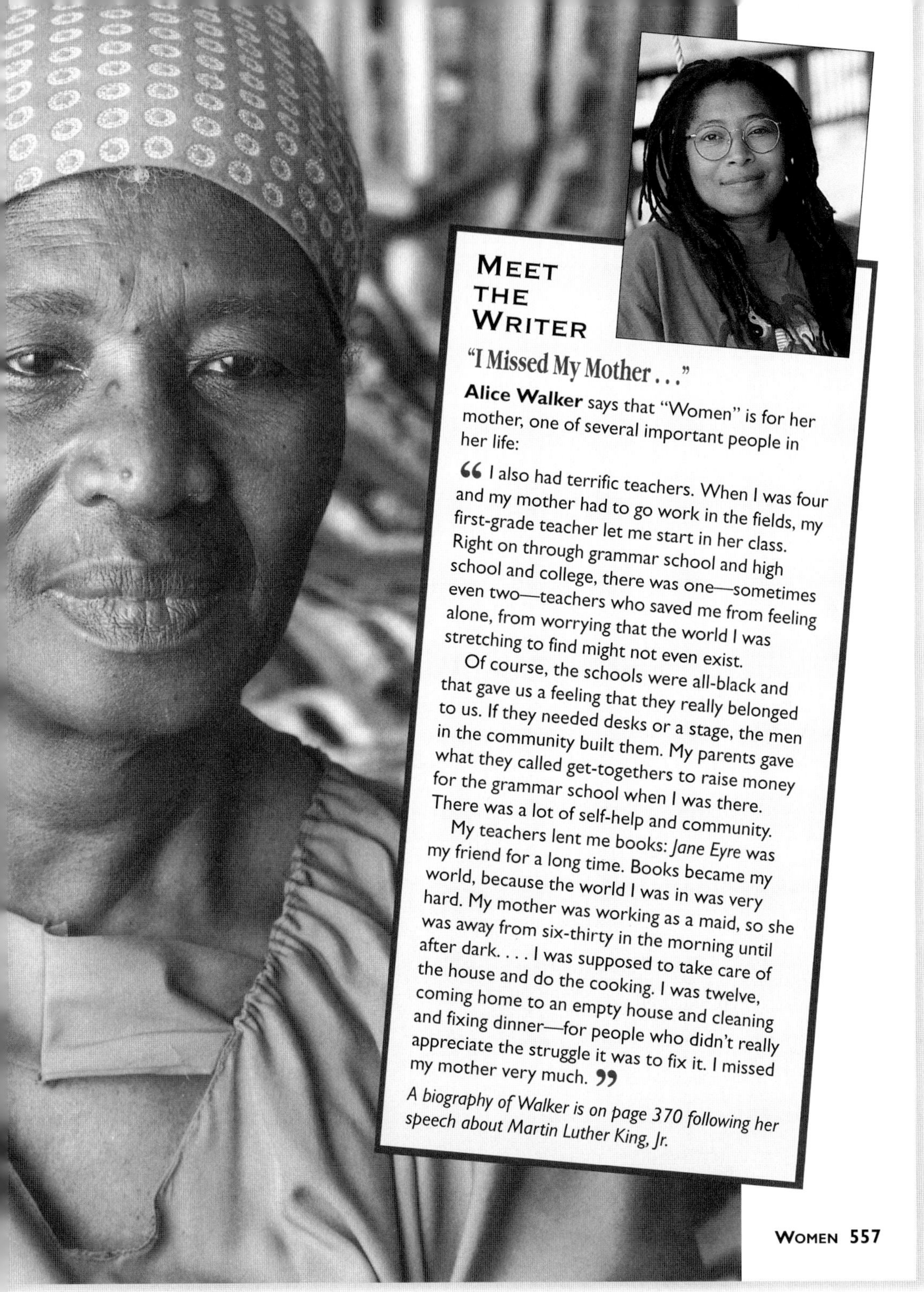

MEET THE WRITER

"I Missed My Mother..."

Alice Walker says that "Women" is for her mother, one of several important people in her life:

66 I also had terrific teachers. When I was four and my mother had to go work in the fields, my first-grade teacher let me start in her class. Right on through grammar school and high school and college, there was one—sometimes even two—teachers who saved me from feeling alone, from worrying that the world I was stretching to find might not even exist.

Of course, the schools were all-black and that gave us a feeling that they really belonged to us. If they needed desks or a stage, the men in the community built them. My parents gave what they called get-togethers to raise money for the grammar school when I was there. There was a lot of self-help and community.

My teachers lent me books: *Jane Eyre* was my friend for a long time. Books became my world, because the world I was in was very hard. My mother was working as a maid, so she was away from six-thirty in the morning until after dark. . . . I was supposed to take care of the house and do the cooking. I was twelve, coming home to an empty house and cleaning and fixing dinner—for people who didn't really appreciate the struggle it was to fix it. I missed my mother very much. 99

A biography of Walker is on page 370 following her speech about Martin Luther King, Jr.

WOMEN 557

Summary ■■

"Women" celebrates the courageous love of mothers who struggle to gain a better life for their children. The poem indirectly compares the mothers' struggle for their children's education with a military operation; battle is suggested by such images as "Headragged generals" and "Booby-trapped/Ditches."

Resources

Listening
Audio CD Library
A recording of this poem is provided in the *Audio CD Library*:
• Disc 16, Track 2

Viewing and Representing
Fine Art Transparency
A transparency of John Biggers's *Shotguns* can be used with the poem. See the *Viewing and Representing Transparencies and Worksheets*:
• Transparency 14
• Worksheet, p. 56

A Elements of Literature
Implied Metaphor
? What comparison is made beginning in ll. 12–13? [The women are compared to generals advancing their armies into enemy territory.] Is the comparison directly stated or only suggested? [It is suggested through words like "Armies."]

B Struggling Readers
Questioning
? Encourage students to monitor their reading strategies by asking themselves questions such as the following: What does the speaker mean by "Headragged generals"? [The speaker compares the women to military officers; instead of helmets, the women wear kerchiefs.]

C Critical Thinking
Interpreting
? Who are the people referred to as "we" in l. 22? [Possible responses: the women's children; future generations.]

Reaching All Students

English Language Learners
For strategies for engaging English language learners with the literature, see
• *Lesson Plans Including Strategies for English-Language Learners*

Advanced Learners
Have students discuss other works by Alice Walker with which they are familiar, including her tribute to Martin Luther King, Jr. (pp. 367–370). Ask them to explain how the theme of this poem fits in with those of her other works.

Getting Students Involved

Cooperative Learning
Finding a Place to Rest. When students begin to work on the first Choices activity on p. 558, point out that the poem lacks punctuation until the final line. Ask students to work in pairs to choose logical breaks or stopping places for reading the poem aloud. Students should consider various factors when they decide where to pause, such as the poem's imagery, its rhythm, and ideas or words that they think are important.

MAKING MEANINGS

First Thoughts

1. Many students will envision a group of strong women literally knocking down doors and marching across minefields. Others may envision civil rights protesters.

Shaping Interpretations

2. She compares the women's struggle to secure a good education for their children to the struggle of generals leading soldiers on the battlefield.

3. The doors represent such barriers to educational opportunity as school segregation, racism, and poverty.

4. Students may mention the hostile actions of politicians and segregationists who opposed equal educational opportunity in the sixties. They may cite other obstacles to equal education, such as the poor quality of schools in black neighborhoods and the fight against racial integration in schools.

5. The women knew that education was the key to their children's success in American society.

Extending the Text

6. Possibilities include Martin Luther King, Jr., Mohandas Gandhi, and Mother Teresa, as well as parents who fight to keep their children out of gangs and off drugs.

Grading Timesaver

Rubrics for each Choices assignment appear on p. 175 in the *Portfolio Management System.*

CHOICES: Building Your Portfolio

1. **Reader's Theater** See the Cooperative Learning activity on p. T557.
2. **Creative Writing** Encourage students to use the cluster technique to organize their ideas before they begin to write.

MAKING MEANINGS
WOMEN

First Thoughts

[respond]
1. What do you *see* happening in this poem? Compare your images in class. Are your mental pictures very different?

Shaping Interpretations

[identify]
2. Alice Walker uses an **implied metaphor** to compare two kinds of actions or struggles. What does she compare the women's struggle to?

[interpret]
3. Think about the historical context of this poem. What doors did these women really batter down?

[interpret]
4. Again, think about American history. What do you think the mined fields and booby-trapped ditches stand for?

[infer]
5. What do you think these women knew their children had to know?

Extending the Text

[extend]
6. What other people in the world could be described as generals leading armies? What do these people fight against?

CHOICES: Building Your Portfolio

Reader's Theater

1. Preparing for a Poetry Reading

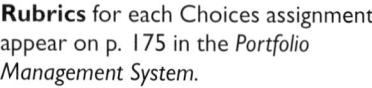

Feeling the rhythm.

Repetition is what gives poetry its rhythm. Walker creates rhythm in her poem by repeating certain words and by alternating long and short lines.

Write Walker's poem on a separate piece of paper. This is your script for oral reading.

On your script, mark the ends of lines where you will pause briefly. Do not put a mark if you will keep right on reading on to the next line without a pause. Underscore the words or phrases in the poem that you will emphasize in your reading.

Practice reading the poem aloud until you feel you are expressing its natural rhythms.

Save your script. You might choose to present this poem in the Reader's Theater discussed on page 582.

Creative Writing

2. Celebrate Other Heroes

How would you describe the heroic women and men of today? What do they struggle for? What do they want for their children? Write a poem or paragraph describing these men and women. What would you compare your heroes to? Use your Quickwrite notes for ideas about who is important to you.

Assessing Learning

Check Test: True-False

1. The women described in the poem are from the same generation as the speaker. [False]
2. The "Headragged generals" led armies during the Civil War. [False]
3. The women in the poem discover books and desks for their children. [True]
4. The women value education even though it has been denied to them. [True]

Standardized Test Preparation

For practice in proofreading and editing, see
• *Daily Oral Grammar,* Transparency 38

Elements of Literature

OBJECTIVES
1. Identify end rhyme, internal rhyme, and approximate rhyme
2. Recognize onomatopoeia and alliteration

THE SOUNDS OF POETRY: Rhyme and Other Sound Effects

Everyone loves rhyme—babies respond to rhyme, and your first books (like Dr. Seuss's *Hop on Pop*) were probably written in rhyme. Rhyme is easy to recognize. **Rhyme** is the repetition of the sound of a stressed vowel and any sounds that follow it within a word: *nails* and *whales; material* and *cereal; icicle* and *bicycle.*

Until very recently, poets thought rhyme was essential, and readers expected it. Today, rhyme is a matter of choice—except for those versifiers who grind out the little singsong messages found on some greeting cards.

Modern poets who use rhyme feel that it not only helps to make a poem sing, but that it also defines the shape of a poem and holds it together. Rhyme enhances the music of a poem with chiming sounds. It sets up in the reader a sense of expectation. We expect that the pattern of sounds

> **M**any poets have turned away from rhyme because they feel that just about all of the words in the English language that can be rhymed have long ago been used up.

introduced in the opening lines of a poem will be skillfully sustained until the poem is concluded. Readers also know that poems with a regular pattern of rhyme, or a **rhyme scheme,** are especially easy to memorize.

Many poets have turned away from rhyme because they feel that just about all of the words in the English language that can be rhymed have long ago been used up. The contemporary poet who would like to continue the practice of using rhyme is faced with having to repeat rhymes that have echoed down the centuries. Or the poet faces the challenge of making new rhymes that might sound strained.

Approximate Rhyme: Not Quite Exact

Some poets have solved this problem by using **approximate rhyme**—that is, words

that repeat some sounds but are not exact echoes. These approximate rhymes are also called half rhymes, off rhymes, or slant rhymes. Readers who dislike them call them imperfect rhymes. In any case, all of them are substitutes for familiar "head-on" rhymes like *June* and *moon* or *hollow* and *follow*. Instead of being an exact echo, approximate rhyme is a partial echo: *moon* and *morn* or *hollow* and *mellow*.

Internal Rhyme: Chimes Inside Lines

Rhymes usually occur at the ends of lines. They are seldom spaced more than four lines apart—an interval longer than that is too long for the chiming sound to be clearly heard. But rhyme can also occur inside the lines. This is called **internal rhyme**. Here are some lines from "The Raven" by Edgar Allan Poe in which two internal rhymes (*remember* and *ember*) chime with *December*:

> Ah, distinctly I remember it
> was in the bleak December;
> And each separate dying
> ember wrought its ghost
> upon the floor.

[Continued on next page]

Resources

Elements of Literature
Rhyme and Other Sound Effects
For additional instruction on rhyme and other sound effects, see *Literary Elements:*
• Transparency 13

Elements of Literature

This feature focuses on the kinds of rhyme that are most commonly found in poetry—end rhyme, internal rhyme, and approximate rhyme. It explores the effect of sound on meaning and introduces students to the techniques of onomatopoeia and alliteration.

Mini-Lesson:
Rhyme and Other Sound Effects
Read this feature aloud to students or assign an initial reading for homework. Review the definitions of the key terms: rhyme, rhyme scheme, approximate rhyme, internal rhyme, onomatopoeia, and alliteration. Note that rhyme is basically a type of repetition—the repetition of sounds rather than words, phrases, or lines. Rhyme can enliven a poem, impose order, and build a sense of expectation in the reader.

Divide students into groups of three or four, and ask them to make up their own examples for each of the terms presented in this feature. After students have completed the assignment, ask each group to choose a spokesperson to present their examples to the class.

Reaching All Students

English Language Learners

Because exact rhyme is characteristic of nursery rhymes, children's poetry, and classical poetry, students from various backgrounds are likely to be familiar with it. Ask volunteers to share examples of nursery rhymes and rhyming children's songs from other languages.

These students may have more trouble, however, identifying approximate rhyme. Write an example of approximate rhyme on the chalkboard and pronounce the words slowly and clearly. You might use ll. 6 and 8 in "I Never Saw a Moor" on p. 522 or offer an example like *now* and *know*. Finally, pair English language learners with more fluent partners and have them work together to create their own examples of approximate rhyme.

Elements of Literature

[Continued from previous page]

by John Malcolm Brinnin

Onomatopoeia: Imitating Sounds

Beyond rhythm and the forms it may take, the most important aspect of sound in poetry is the one with the very unusual name: onomatopoeia (än′ō·mat′ō·pē′ə). **Onomatopoeia** is the use of words that sound like what they mean.

Literally, *onomatopoeia* means "the making of words." Long ago, it came into the English language from the Greek. It eventually came to mean not merely word-making, but word-making by the imitation of sounds. We use onomatopoeia when we say a gun "bangs" or a cannon "booms." We use onomatopoeia when we say that bacon "sizzles."

In its simplest form onomatopoeia is a single word that echoes a natural sound (*hiss, slap, rumble, snarl, moan, drip*) or a mechanical sound (*zing, whack, clickety-clack, putt-putt, toot*).

Alliteration: Repeating Sounds

Alliteration is the repetition of the same consonant sound in several words: *money mad,* hot and heavy, dog days, drip dry, wash and wear, ready and raring to go. Alliteration can also be the repetition of similar, but not identical, sounds: a series of *p*'s and *b*'s, or *s*'s and *z*'s, or *d*'s and *t*'s, or *m*'s and *n*'s. Alliteration can also be used to echo sounds. Here is another example from "The Raven":

The silken sad uncertain
rustling of each purple
curtain

Alliteration (the repetition of rustling *s* sounds in *silken sad uncertain*) and onomatopoeia (the word *rustling*) together imitate the sound wind makes when it blows past heavy silk draperies.

Onomatopoeia comes naturally to us. Suppose we want to describe the movement of a snake through the grass. We wouldn't say it goes "bumping along like a bicycle," because that's not what a snake in the grass sounds like. We are more likely to say the snake "slithers swiftly across the grass." Then we would be imitating in words the sound we might actually hear.

"Griping, greedy, grasping, grotesque, gruesome, grisly— do you know any other good 'grr' words?"

Drawing by Ed Fisher; © 1984 The New Yorker Magazine, Inc.

560 THE POETRY COLLECTIONS

T560

Before You Read

MY PAPA'S WALTZ

Make the Connection

Remembered Feelings

Think of a time when you were little and you felt something intensely. Something may have frightened you or made you so happy you thought you'd burst. You may have just been handed a puppy, or you may have gotten lost in a supermarket. What about this experience do you still remember? Where were you? What were you doing? What were you wearing? Who was with you? What colors or sounds are still real to you?

Quickwrite

Now, think of how you can tell about that experience and express those feelings in words. Jot down some details that will convey the experience and the feelings—but don't name the feelings.

Keep your notes. For questions and activities on this poem, see page 563.

Elements of Literature

Rhyme: Chiming Sounds

Of course nothing in poetry works in isolation. The rhythm, the subject matter, the speaker's attitude, even the length of the poem—all these elements combine to produce effects on us. **Rhyme,** however, is often what we notice first. Rhyme can have widely varying effects. In some poems it may create humor. In some poems it may sound solemn and serious; in others it may sound haunting or songlike. In bad poems, rhyme can seem singsong and mechanical. Listen for Roethke's rhymes. Do they have one syllable or many? Do they appear in a pattern?

> **R**hyme is the repetition of accented vowel sounds, and all sounds following them, in words that are close together. **Rhyme scheme** is the pattern of rhymes in a poem.
>
> *For more on Rhyme, see pages 559–560 and the Handbook of Literary Terms.*

go.hrw.com
LE0 9-10

MEET THE WRITER

Great Tenderness

Theodore Roethke (1908–1963) was a big, bearish man who wrote with delicacy about small creatures and with tenderness about the formative experiences of his life. His poetic themes were the secret and mysterious life of nature and the ways in which nature is reflected in human life.

Born in Michigan to a family of German immigrants, Roethke achieved an outstanding reputation as a teacher at Pennsylvania State University, Bennington College in Vermont, and the University of Washington in Seattle. He was young when he died—and at the height of a much-honored and still-expanding poetic career.

MY PAPA'S WALTZ **561**

OBJECTIVES

1. Read and interpret the poem
2. Understand rhyme and rhyme scheme
3. Express understanding through creative or critical writing

SKILLS

Literary
• Understand rhyme and rhyme scheme

Writing
• Write a poem about a remembered moment
• Write an essay responding to the selection

Speaking/Listening
• Prepare for a poetry reading

Viewing/Representing
• Describe a painting (ATE)

Planning

• **Block Schedule**
  Block Scheduling Lesson Plans with Pacing Guide

• **Traditional Schedule**
  Lesson Plans Including Strategies for English-Language Learners

• **One-Stop Planner**
  CD-ROM with Test Generator

Resources: Print and Media

Reading
• *Graphic Organizers for Active Reading,* p. 49
• *Audio CD Library,*
    Disc 16, Track 3

Elements of Literature: Rhyme
• *Literary Elements*
    Transparency 13
    Worksheet, p. 40

Assessment
• *Portfolio Management System,* p. 176
• *Standardized Test Preparation,* p. 74
• *Test Generator (One-Stop Planner* CD-ROM)

Internet
• go.hrw.com (keyword: LE0 9–10)

Summary ▪

Using a singsong *abab* rhyme scheme, Roethke presents a vivid scene from childhood: a small boy clings "like death" as his father waltzes him around the kitchen in a boisterous romp.

Resources

Elements of Literature

Rhyme
You may wish to use the transparency *Rhyme: Chiming Sounds* with this selection. See *Literary Elements:*
• Transparency 13
• Worksheet, p. 40

RESPONDING TO THE ART

Grant Wood (1892–1942) is famous for his realistic portraits of rural Midwesterners.

Activity. List five adjectives that could describe the young boy in the painting. Which of these words could also describe the poem's speaker? [Sample answers: serious, young, reserved, clean-cut, vulnerable, innocent. All adjectives could also describe the speaker.]

Ⓐ Elements of Literature

Rhythm
Help students hear the trimeter (three-beat) waltz rhythm by orally exaggerating it. For example, ll. 3–4:

But I hung on like death
Such waltzing was not easy

Ⓑ Elements of Literature

Rhyme
❓ What effect does the simple rhyme have on the listener? [Sample response: The listener feels as if he or she is hearing a young child's voice.]

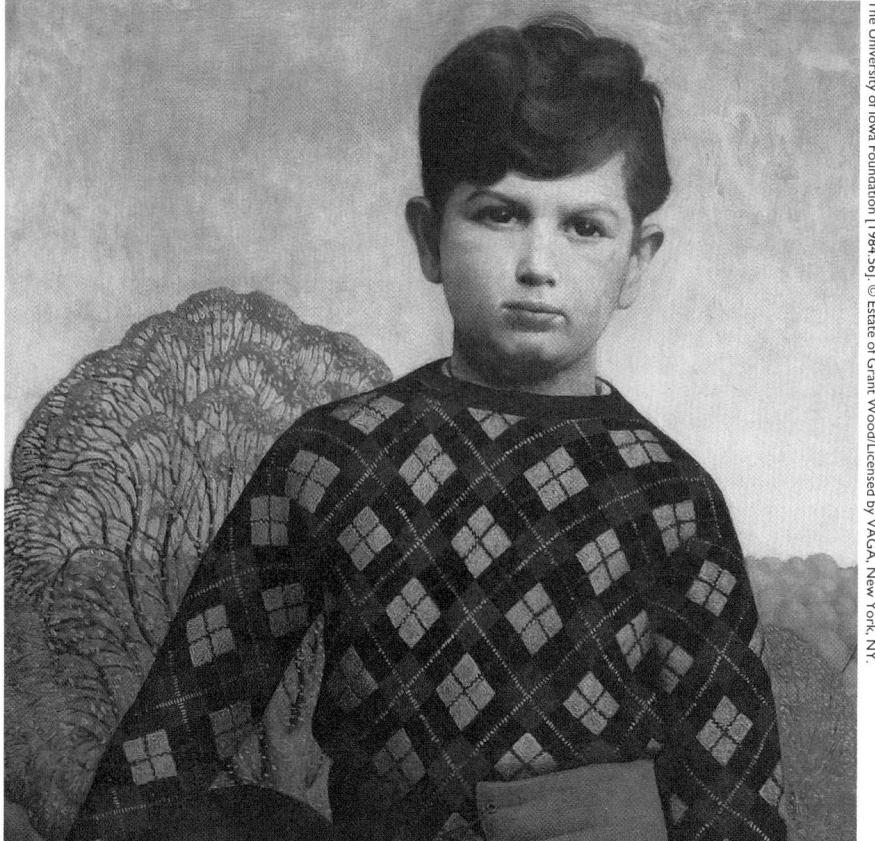

The Plaid Sweater (1931) (detail) by Grant Wood. Oil on masonite (29½″ × 25″).

My Papa's Waltz

Theodore Roethke

The whiskey on your breath
Could make a small boy dizzy;
Ⓐ But I hung on like death:
Such waltzing was not easy.

5 We romped until the pans
Slid from the kitchen shelf;
My mother's countenance
Could not unfrown itself.

10 The hand that held my wrist
Was battered on one knuckle;
At every step you missed
My right ear scraped a buckle.

You beat time on my head
Ⓑ With a palm caked hard by dirt,
15 Then waltzed me off to bed
Still clinging to your shirt.

562 THE POETRY COLLECTIONS

Reaching All Students

Struggling Readers

Tell students that no reader can grasp the full meaning of a poem in a single reading. Urge them to make a note about anything they don't understand; they can return to their notes after they have finished reading the poem. Also encourage them to reread the poem several times.

English Language Learners

Explain that "unfrown" in l. 8 is a word coined by the writer. Roethke simply joined the word *frown* and the prefix *un-*, meaning "not."

Using Students' Strengths

Auditory/Musical Learners

Invite students interested in music to find examples of waltzes or other musical pieces that they feel capture the mood of the scene described in "My Papa's Waltz." Have students play recordings of these pieces for the class and then read the poem aloud with the pieces as musical accompaniment.

T562

First Thoughts

[infer] 1. How do you think the speaker feels about his father and the rough waltz?

Shaping Interpretations

[infer] 2. How does the mother feel about the waltz? How would you explain her reaction?

[interpret] 3. How would you interpret line 3, "But I hung on like death"?

[interpret] 4. *Death* is a word that usually has **connotations** of loss and sadness. Which other words and images in the poem have negative connotations? Which have positive connotations? You could prepare your response by making a chart like the one above.

Negative	Positive

[generalize] 5. How would you express the poem's message, or **theme**? (Hint: Does the poem say anything about love?)

[identify] 6. The title promises music, and Roethke delivers a three-beat waltz rhythm and a regular rhyme scheme. Scan the poem to show its **meter**. What is the **rhyme scheme**? Read the poem aloud. Do you think it sounds happy or sad?

CHOICES: Building Your Portfolio

Reader's Theater

1. Preparing for a Poetry Reading

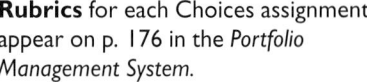

Making a script. Prepare a script for this poem just as a professional actor would. Identify *the speaker, what he is trying to say,* and *his tone of voice.* Note where his tone might change. Mark the *slowest, fastest, softest,* and *loudest* points. Save your script for possible use in a Reader's Theater (see page 582).

Creative Writing

2. A Remembered Moment

Intense moments— when we feel very happy or extremely sad, triumphant or defeated—are probably captured in poetry more effectively than in any other form of writing. Take your Quickwrite notes or make notes about some other moment that seems right, and turn them into a poem. You might open with "I remember_____."

Explaining a Response

3. A Happy or Sad Memory?

Some readers think that the father has scared the little boy with his crazy dancing. Others think that the speaker loves his father and their waltz. What do you think? In a brief essay, state your response to the poem, and then support it with at least three details from the poem. Before you write, refer to the lists you made in response to Making Meanings question 4.

MAKING MEANINGS
First Thoughts

1. Sample responses: The speaker remembers his father and the waltz fondly; the son has mixed feelings of love and fear.

Shaping Interpretations

2. The mother's frown shows that she is disturbed by the waltz. Perhaps she is worried about her kitchen and her son's safety.
3. The boy's grip is unbreakable. He is worried that he might fall if he let go.
4. Positive details: romped, held, waltzed. Negative details: whiskey, death, unfrown, battered, scraped, beat, hard.
5. Possible responses: Love can be expressed in many different ways; sometimes love can be frightening or rough.
6. The poem's regular rhyme scheme is *abab.* Many students will hear the poem's singsong rhythm as a happy one. The meter of the first stanza can be scanned as follows:

The whiskey on your breath
Could make a small boy dizzy;
But I hung on like death:
Such waltzing was not easy.

Grading Timesaver

Rubrics for each Choices assignment appear on p. 176 in the *Portfolio Management System.*

CHOICES: Building Your Portfolio

1. **Reader's Theater** Have students use colored pencils to make performance notes.
2. **Creative Writing** Remind students to develop sensory images for their poems that help convey the requisite emotion.
3. **Explaining a Response** Make sure that students use details from "My Papa's Waltz" in their essays.

Assessing Learning

Check Test: Questions and Answers
Answers may vary slightly.

1. Who is dancing in the poem? [A boy and his father are dancing.]
2. Where are they dancing? [in the kitchen]
3. Who is watching them? [the boy's mother]
4. How does the speaker describe his father's hands? [They are battered and caked hard by dirt.]
5. How does the father keep time? [He beats time on his son's head.]

Standardized Test Preparation
For practice with standardized test format specific to this selection, see
- *Standardized Test Preparation,* p. 74

OBJECTIVES

The Gift / Combing

1. Read and interpret the poems
2. Understand breath groupings in free verse
3. Identify repetition in poetry, including assonance and alliteration
4. Express understanding through critical thinking, creative writing, or research

SKILLS

Literary

- Understand breath groupings in free verse
- Identify repetition in poetry, including assonance and alliteration

Writing

- Chart examples of repetition in poems
- Write a poem about a mystery
- Write sentences using onomatopoeia and alliteration

Speaking/Listening

- Practice diction

Research

- Find poetic sound effects in advertising and popular music

Planning

- **Block Schedule**
  Block Scheduling Lesson Plans with Pacing Guide
- **Traditional Schedule**
  Lesson Plans Including Strategies for English-Language Learners
- **One-Stop Planner**
  CD-ROM with Test Generator

Before You Read

THE GIFT

Make the Connection

Tenderness and Discipline

It seems to be the very intense moments, when things are going wonderfully well or terribly wrong, that give us the sharpest images of people. In moments like these, people show us who they are—and who we may become.

Quickwrite

Try to recall one incident in which the actions of a parent, teacher, or friend were a model for something you would like to become yourself.

Keep your notes. For questions and activities on this poem, see pages 568–569.

Elements of Literature

Breath Groupings

Free-verse poems can create rhythm by organizing words in breath groups. Breath groups are usually defined by punctuation. Watch for punctuation marks in this poem. Pause briefly for breath at commas. Make full stops at periods. Let your voice rise and fall in a natural way, just like the voice of an oral storyteller. Do you feel the rhythm?

> In **free verse**, rhythm can be created by breath groupings, which are signaled by marks of punctuation.
>
> *For more on Free Verse, see pages 554–555 and the Handbook of Literary Terms.*

 **go.hrw.com**
LE0 9-10

564 THE POETRY COLLECTIONS

The Gift

Li-Young Lee

To pull the metal splinter from my palm
my father recited a story in a low voice.
I watched his lovely face and not the blade.
Before the story ended he'd removed
5 the iron sliver I thought I'd die from.

A   I can't remember the tale
but hear his voice still, a well
of dark water, a prayer.
And I recall his hands,
10 two measures of tenderness
he laid against my face,
the flames of discipline
he raised above my head.

B   Had you entered that afternoon
15 you would have thought you saw a man
planting something in a boy's palm,
a silver tear, a tiny flame.
Had you followed that boy
you would have arrived here,
20 where I bend over my wife's right hand.

Look how I shave her thumbnail down
so carefully she feels no pain.
Watch as I lift the splinter out.
I was seven when my father
25 took my hand like this,
and I did not hold that shard
between my fingers and think,
Metal that will bury me,
christen it Little Assassin,
30 Ore Going Deep for My Heart.

C   And I did not lift up my wound and cry,
Death visited here!
I did what a child does
when he's given something to keep.
35 I kissed my father.

Resources: Print and Media

Reading

- *Graphic Organizers for Active Reading,* pp. 50, 51
- *Audio CD Library,* Disc 16, Tracks 4, 5

Elements of Literature

- *Literary Elements* Transparency 12 Worksheet, p. 37

Assessment

- *Portfolio Management System,* p. 177
- *Test Generator (One-Stop Planner* CD-ROM)

Internet

- go.hrw.com (keyword: LE0 9-10)

MEET THE WRITER

"The Winged Seed"

The great-grandfather of **Li-Young Lee** (1957–   ) was the first president of the Republic of China. His father, on whom the character in "The Gift" is based, was personal physician to the revolutionary leader Mao Tse-tung. In the 1950s, the family had to flee the political turmoil of China when the Communist People's Republic was established. They went first to Indonesia; Li-Young Lee was born in Jakarta. But there his father was thrown into jail by the corrupt dictator Sukarno. The father spent nineteen months in prison, seventeen of them in a leper colony. When the family fled again, they went to Hong Kong. When Li-Young Lee was six, they arrived in the United States where his father became a Presbyterian minister.

Li-Young Lee has recorded his family's history in *The Winged Seed: A Remembrance* (1995). His first book of poems, *Rose*, won the 1986 Delmore Schwartz Memorial Poetry Award, and a second book, *The City in Which I Love You*, was the 1990 Lamont Poetry Selection of the Academy of American Poets.

Lee now lives in Chicago with his family.

> 66 I know I am not a poet. How do I know this? Because I know a poet when I read one. There are living poets in the world today. I am not one of them. But I want to be one, and I know only of one path: serious and passionate apprenticeship, which involves a strange combination of awe and argument, with the Masters.
>
> Other than this, I don't know anything about poetry, though if space permitted, I could go on earnestly, and to the boredom and horror of everyone, about all those things I don't know. 99

Summary ■■■

As the speaker removes a splinter from his wife's thumb, he remembers a similar incident from his childhood, when his father pulled a splinter from his palm. The speaker remembers his father's tenderness, rather than the pain. Love transforms the operation—the metal splinter is imagined as a gift planted in the boy's hand by his father. This recollection helps to explain the speaker's own tenderness as he delicately performs a similar operation for his wife.

Resources

Listening

Audio CD Library
A recording of this poem is provided in the *Audio CD Library:*
• Disc 16, Track 4

Ⓐ Advanced Learners

Interpreting Metaphors
Ask students to identify and explain the metaphors in these lines. [The speaker compares his father's voice to a well of dark water and to a prayer.] Have them discuss what these comparisons indicate about the speaker's attitude toward his father. [The speaker trusts his father and finds his voice calm, deep, resonant, and respectful.]

Ⓑ Elements of Literature

Breath Groupings
Point out the punctuation marks in this stanza. Ask a volunteer to read the stanza aloud, pausing at the commas and making full stops at the periods.

Ⓒ Elements of Literature

Breath Groupings
❓ Call attention to the four breath groupings in the last five lines. Read the stanza aloud for the class, letting your voice rise for the line that ends in an exclamation mark and pause significantly before the last line. What effect is produced by the increased number of breath groupings? [They impart a sense of urgency followed by calm.]

Reaching All Students

Struggling Readers
The poem's shifts in time may confuse some students. Help them recognize that only ll. 18–23 pertain to the present, while the lines preceding and following that section pertain to the past.

English Language Learners
For strategies for engaging English language learners with the literature, see
• *Lesson Plans Including Strategies for English-Language Learners*

Using Students' Strengths

Visual Learners
Help students personalize the experience related in this poem by asking them to closely study and then draw, paint, or outline the hand of a friend or family member. They can either fill the page with words or phrases describing what that person does with his or her hands, or create a collage by pasting on bits and pieces of symbolic materials.

Summary ▪▪

A mother who is combing her daughter's hair thinks back to the time when she was young and her mother would do the same for her. She also remembers her mother combing her grandmother's hair with a comb made of bone while the older woman was braiding a cotton rug. There are various forms of repetition in this poem: note the many uses of the words *comb, braid, hair,* and *orange;* the alliteration in ll. 1 and 6; and the assonance in ll. 9 and 20. In the final line of the poem, the repeated image of women preparing each other's hair is transformed into a metaphor for generational love.

Resources

Listening
Audio CD Library
A recording of this poem is provided in the *Audio CD Library:*
• Disc 16, Track 5

Elements of Literature
The Sounds of Poetry: Rhythm
For additional instruction on the sounds of poetry, see *Literary Elements:*
• Transparency 12
• Worksheet, p. 37

FROM THE EDITOR'S DESK

When we were choosing the poems for this collection, we wrote to Gladys Cardiff to ask her about the process of her writing "Combing." (Her answer is on p. 488.) Her response made our choice easy. Cardiff makes the point that poetry is all around us, part of everyday life. That's exactly what we want students to see.

Before You Read

COMBING

Make the Connection

A Portrait in Words

Many families keep an album of photos of family members collected through the years. Maybe your family does this. In "Combing" we are given word portraits of several generations of a family, all connected by the same action that is learned and repeated and passed on. Can you imagine how pleased this poet's grandchildren will be to have this poem-portrait of those who came before them? Perhaps you'll be inspired to plait (braid, or weave) a poem to pass on to the people who come after you.

Quickwrite

Make notes on one or more legacies you have received from the past, including where the legacy came from and why you are glad to have it. Hint: a photograph, jewelry, clothing, a song or poem, a prayer, a recipe, a special way of observing a holiday.

Keep your notes. For questions and activities on this poem, see pages 568–569.

Elements of Literature

Repetition

Repetition is basic to the music you hear in poetry. When you repeat vowel sounds, you get **assonance**. When you repeat consonants, you get **alliteration**. You can also repeat words and phrases. After you read "Combing," go back and read it aloud and count the number of sounds you hear repeated—start with *b.*

> **R**epetition in poetry includes assonance, alliteration, and the repetition of words, phrases, and even entire lines.
>
> *For more on Rhyme and Other Sound Effects, see pages 559–560.*

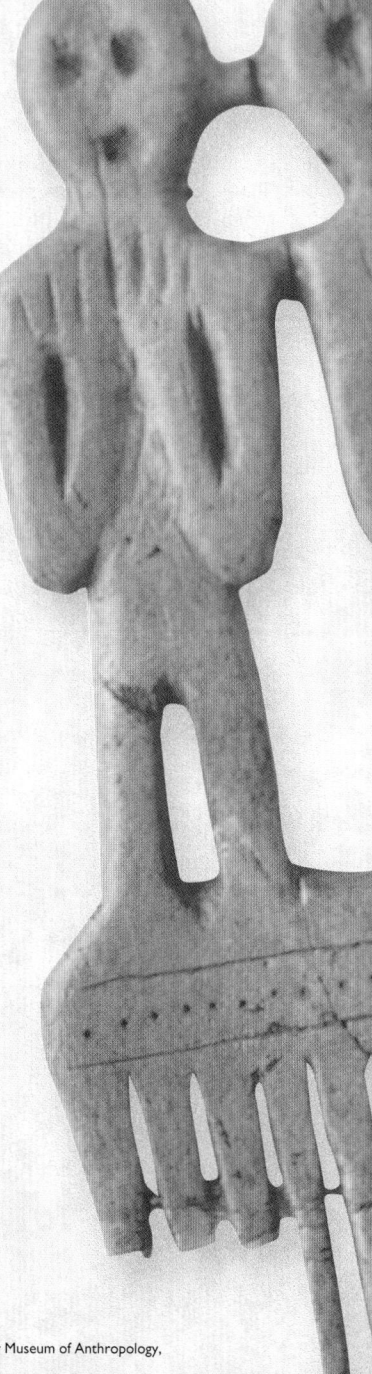

Iroquois bone comb.

Herbert Bigford, Sr., Collection, Longyear Museum of Anthropology, Colgate University, Hamilton, NY.

566 THE POETRY COLLECTIONS

Reaching All Students

Struggling Readers
Review the pronunciation of *comb* and *combing,* reminding students that the *b* is silent. Ask students to provide examples of other words with the silent *b* ending. [Possible responses: bomb, climb, crumb, plumbing, tomb.]

English Language Learners
You might show a picture of a young girl with braids so students from various cultures will understand the concept of plaiting hair. Explain that *plait* is a synonym for *braid.* For other strategies for engaging English language learners with the literature, see
• *Lesson Plans Including Strategies for English-Language Learners*

Getting Students Involved

Cooperative Learning
All in the Family. Ask students to bring photographs of family members or friends to class. Working in pairs, have one student orally describe the people in the photograph while the other student lists the spoken phrases in the form of a rough poem. Then have partners switch roles. When students have finished, they should work with their phrases until an idea for a poem emerges.

Combing

Gladys Cardiff

Bending, I bow my head
And lay my hand upon
Her hair, combing, and think
How women do this for
5   Each other. My daughter's hair
Curls against the comb,
Wet and fragrant—orange
Parings. Her face, downcast,
Is quiet for one so young.

10 I take her place. Beneath
My mother's hands I feel
The braids drawn up tight
As a piano wire and singing,

15 Vinegar-rinsed. Sitting
Before the oven I hear
The orange coils tick
The early hour before school.

She combed her grandmother
20 Mathilda's hair using
A comb made out of bone.
Mathilda rocked her oak-wood
Chair, her face downcast,
Intent on tearing rags
25 In strips to braid a cotton
Rug from bits of orange
And brown. A simple act,

Preparing hair. Something
Women do for each other,
Plaiting the generations.

MEET THE WRITER

"Paths from Every Direction"

On page 488 you'll find a conversation with **Gladys Cardiff** (1942–   ), in which she tells how she came to write "Combing." Gladys Cardiff had a Cherokee father and an Irish/Welsh mother. She was born in Montana, where her parents taught on the Blackfoot Reservation, and she grew up in Seattle, Washington. Cardiff earned a bachelor's degree and a master's degree in creative writing from the University of Washington. She says that writing for her is an art of celebration, and she especially connects her poetry with an old Cherokee blessing and prayer: "Let the paths from every direction recognize each other."

COMBING 567

Ⓐ Elements of Literature
Repetition
Remind students that repetition in poetry can include assonance and alliteration, as well as the repetition of words or phrases. Call on volunteers to point out different examples of repetition in this first stanza. [the *b* in *Bending* and *bow*; the *h* in *head*, *hand*, *Her*, and *hair*; the *k* sound in *curls* and *comb*; the *-ing* in *Bending*, *combing*, and *Parings*; the assonance of *hair* and *Parings* and of *downcast*, *one*, and *young*]

Ⓑ Advanced Learners
Analyzing Shifts in Time
❓ Encourage students to note this switch in time and in the speaker's role. The sentence "I take her place" moves the speaker from the present to the past, from grooming her daughter to being groomed by her own mother. What lines in "The Gift" on p. 564 introduce similar time and role shifts? [ll. 18 and 24]

Ⓒ Elements of Literature
Repetition
Call on volunteers to point out instances of repetition in ll. 18–20. [the repeated forms of a word— *combed*, *comb*; the alliteration of *her* and *hair*; the assonance of *comb* and *bone*]

Ⓓ Critical Thinking
Interpreting
❓ How is Mathilda's activity also an example of connecting the generations? [Possible responses: The rug that she makes can be passed from one generation to another; she is recycling material so that it can be used by the next generation.]

Skill Link

Analyze Text Structures

The speakers in "The Gift" and "Combing" shift between the present and the past. Ask students to chart the time shifts and the linking elements of each poem. They could also use a time line or create their own original graphic organizer. To help them get started, ask the following questions:

1. How many time periods are represented in "The Gift"? [two] What is the action that links the different time periods? [removing a splinter from a hand]

2. How many time periods are represented in "Combing"? [three] What action links them? [combing someone's hair]

3. In what directions do the poems move in time? ["The Gift" moves from the past to the present and then back to the past; "Combing"

moves from the present to the past and then to a more distant past.]

4. Which poem's method of time shifting is more effective? Why? [Possible responses: "The Gift," because it shows how the present can trigger memories of the past; "Combing," because the time shifts are easier to follow.]

T567

Student to Student

A young girl writes about her grandmother. She admires *Abuela* (Spanish for grandmother) for her diverse talents and open mind.

Ⓐ Reading Skills and Strategies
Making Inferences

After students have read the essay, ask them what they think the writer likes best about Abuela. [She likes the way her grandmother treats everyone as an individual.]

MAKING MEANINGS

First Thoughts

1. In "The Gift," discipline and tender caring have been passed from father to son. The gifts in "Combing" are the help a mother gives a daughter in hair grooming and a handmade rag rug that will be handed down through the generations. In both poems the gifts are the bonds created by sharing.

Shaping Interpretations

2. The speaker is talking to the reader when he says *you*. In the present scene, the speaker is removing a splinter from his wife's hand.

3. The speaker did not acknowledge that the metal shard could have seriously injured him or killed him; instead, he kissed his father for tending to his wound.

4. Possible response: The poet means that through the activity of braiding —either caring for one another's hair or making a rug from strips of cloth—women of different generations are also linked together or intertwined.

Extending the Texts

5. Students might mention such activities as caring for the sick, preparing meals according to traditional family recipes, telling family stories, playing sports and games, or sharing family photographs. Parents give children an example of how a life might be lived; they often pass on family traditions and offer advice or support.

Ⓐ An Open Mind

She sits by the window, rocking back and forth in the early morning light. I look at her hands. They are old, rough and wrinkled, not like my hands, which are young and smooth, yet hers are stronger. There's a story behind the left index finger, the one with half a nail. That's where a parrot bit her, on the outskirts of a small Central American village.

I look at her arms, round and firm. They are strong from those nights she would swim with her sisters, proud and graceful as dolphins, in the lake by their country house.

I look now at her face, so much like my own, like my mother's. I'm not fooled by the crow's-feet and deep creases on her forehead, because her eyes are young, alive with a shining vitality.

Who is she? I call her Abuela. She is my grandmother. She knows many things, like how to catch fish with her bare hands, pan for gold, cook a soufflé. She can dance a waltz and climb a cliff.

Born of wealthy Spanish-Arabic parents in Honduras, she traveled far and wide in her childhood, picking up several languages. As an adult, she lived in different countries like India, Norway, France, and even Australia. In each of these places she did not bring preconceived notions of what her particular culture considered "normal." In fact, she never did, and still doesn't, judge people based on their appearance or cultural background, but waits until she knows their personality.

I hope one day I'm as strong and wise as my grandmother.

—Nicole A. Plumail
Stuyvesant High School
New York, New York

MAKING MEANINGS
THE GIFT
COMBING

[interpret]   **First Thoughts**
1. What gifts are given in "The Gift" and "Combing"?

[infer]   **Shaping Interpretations**
2. Whom do you think the speaker of "The Gift" is talking to when he says "you"? What scene is taking place in the present?

[interpret]
3. What does the speaker of "The Gift" say he *didn't* do with that shard, or piece of metal, in his hand? Why, instead, did he kiss his father?

[interpret]
4. What do you think the poet means in "Combing" when she refers in the last line to women "plaiting the generations"?

[extend]   **Extending the Texts**

5. What other things do family members do that tie or braid generations? What other gifts do parents give children? Be sure to check your Quickwrites.

568 THE POETRY COLLECTIONS

Assessing Learning

Check Test: True-False
"The Gift"
1. The speaker tells of an injury to his knee. [False]
2. Both father and son at some time remove a splinter from a hand. [True]
3. The boy kisses his father. [True]
"Combing"
4. A mother recalls the past as she combs her daughter's hair. [True]
5. The speaker braids a rag rug to give to her daughter. [False]

CHOICES: Building Your Portfolio

Reader's Theater

1. Preparing for a Poetry Reading

Practice your diction. All professional actors and singers pay attention to their diction—because they wish to be understood by their audiences. The secret is to *extra*-pronounce every one of your consonants—eX-aGG-eR-aTe! It will feel funny at first, but it will sound just right to the audience. Next time you see singers or actors on TV, listen to them land on their consonants. To practice your diction, chant some tongue twisters. Start slowly, then build up speed. If you begin losing consonants, slow down. Ask for feedback from your listeners. Taping your tongue-twister chant will help you evaluate your own diction.

Critical Thinking

2. Verbal Music

Many poets use **free verse** because it gives them room to create their own individual voices—and make their own rules. Both "The Gift" and "Combing" are written in free verse. Notice that the poets have used all kinds of strategies to create verbal music. Working with a group, make a chart for each poem. Map all the examples of **repetition** you can find—**alliteration, internal rhymes,** and **onomatopoeia**. If a poet uses a strategy repetitively, you can bet it's for a reason. For example, you should be able to find four words in "Combing" that sound like *hair*. Those words evoke an image in the reader's mind and sound musical to the ear. Once your chart is finished, read the poems aloud, emphasizing the verbal strategies you've found in them.

Creative Writing

3. Rhyme Crime

Write a poem about a mystery—a crime that needs solving. Make your poem at least four lines long and use exact rhymes, either from this list or from a list you make up:

begun, done, fun, gun, none, one, outdone, outrun, pun, run, shun, son, spun, stun, sun, ton, undone, won

If there's a rhyming dictionary within reach, don't hesitate to use it.

Creative Writing

4. How Does It Sound?

Write a sentence describing the sounds made by each of the following things. Try to use **onomatopoeia** and **alliteration** to echo the sounds you hear.

- a rainy, windy night
- a cat eating dry pet food
- a drummer practicing
- a city street
- a person eating soup

Research

5. Poetry in Pop Culture

Advertisers know how powerful poetry is: They use the strategies of poetry to fix in our memories the names of their products. Make a class collection of brand names that use **rhyme, alliteration,** or **onomatopoeia**. Next, think of a song that's popular now or any song that you particularly like or know well. How does it use rhyme, alliteration, and onomatopoeia? Add the song to the class "Poetry in Pop Culture" collection.

Rubrics for each Choices assignment appear on p. 177 in the *Portfolio Management System.*

CHOICES: Building Your Portfolio

1. **Reader's Theater** Work with the class as a whole to collect a list of tongue twisters that they can use to practice diction with.
2. **Critical Thinking** Before students begin, have volunteers provide one example for each of the following terms: alliteration, assonance, internal rhyme, and onomatopoeia.
3. **Creative Writing** Encourage students to work with one or two classmates to brainstorm their own lists of rhyming words.
4. **Creative Writing** Suggest that students close their eyes and try to imagine how each thing would sound before they begin writing.
5. **Research** You might extend the research by having students videotape their own television ads for imaginary products. Ads should use rhyme, alliteration, or onomatopoeia.

Connecting Across Texts

Connecting with "The Gift" and "Combing"
Discuss the thematic similarities between the two poems and the student selection. Then, have students compose sentences that express a theme common to all three works. [Possible responses: Family members can feel closely connected to one another through the sharing of daily experiences and memories; no tie is stronger than the deep tenderness and respect family members have for one another.]

After several students share their thematic sentences with the class, ask the class to list other specific features the poems and the student selection have in common, such as mood, imagery, organization, or language. [All three selections comment tenderly on the hands of a beloved family member; the writers evoke the presence of a loved one with great physical detail; the selections all possess a calm, appreciative tone.]

Using Students' Strengths

Verbal Learners For Choice 1, students may enjoy creating their own tongue twisters.

Auditory/Musical Learners For Choice 4, have students tape-record themselves reciting their sentences. Students can replay the tapes to hear the sound effects produced by alliteration and onomatopoeia.

Interpersonal Learners Allow students to work on Choices 1, 2, and 5 in small groups.

OBJECTIVES

Fifteen / American Hero

1. Read and interpret the poems
2. Identify external and internal conflict
3. Understand onomatopoeia
4. Express understanding through critical or creative writing

SKILLS

Literary

- Identify external and internal conflict
- Understand onomatopoeia

Writing

- Write a letter to the school newspaper
- Write a sports report in free verse
- Describe a machine in human terms
- Collect and invent onomatopoetic words

Speaking/Listening

- Prepare for a poetry reading

Planning

- **Block Schedule**
  Block Scheduling Lesson Plans with Pacing Guide
- **Traditional Schedule**
  Lesson Plans Including Strategies for English-Language Learners
- **One-Stop Planner**
  CD-ROM with Test Generator

Before You Read

FIFTEEN

Make the Connection

Coming Close

We sometimes come close to things that we want but can't have. We may not be old enough, strong enough, or brave enough to possess the things yet. Or we may not yet have earned the right to them. Still, coming close to what we long to possess can leave us with strange conflicting feelings.

Quickwrite

When you're young, a great many things seem out of reach. Think of some moment when you were close to something you wanted badly but you couldn't quite achieve or acquire it. What was it? What feelings did you have after the moment passed? Did the incident present you with any choices?

Keep your notes. For questions and activities on this poem, see pages 574–575.

Elements of Literature

Conflict: Two Kinds

Conflict comes in two flavors—external and internal. **External:** You are taking your neighbor to court for planting poison ivy between your houses. You and a large bear have just found a terrific raspberry patch. **Internal:** The ship is sinking, and a mother with an infant begs you to give up your place in the lifeboat. If you tell your buddies what you really think of how they behave, they'll drop you.

> In an **external conflict,** a character struggles against some outside force. An **internal conflict** is a struggle between opposing needs or desires or emotions within a single person.
>
> *For more on Conflict, see pages 32–33 and the Handbook of Literary Terms.*

570 **THE POETRY COLLECTIONS**

     *Resources: Print and Media*

Reading

- *Graphic Organizers for Active Reading,* pp. 52, 53
- *Audio CD Library,*
  Disc 16 Tracks 6, 7

Elements of Literature

- *Literary Elements*
  Transparency 14
  Worksheet, p. 43

Writing and Language

- *Daily Oral Grammar*
  Transparency 39

Viewing and Representing

- *Viewing and Representing*
  Fine Art Transparency 15
  Fine Art Worksheet, p. 60
- *Visual Connections*
  Videocassette B, Segment 10

Assessment

- *Portfolio Management System,* p. 179
- *Test Generator (One-Stop Planner* CD-ROM)

Internet

- go.hrw.com (keyword: LE0 9-10)

Fifteen

William Stafford

South of the Bridge on Seventeenth
I found back of the willows one summer
day a motorcycle with engine running
as it lay on its side, ticking over
5   slowly in the high grass. I was fifteen.

I admired all that pulsing gleam, the
shiny flanks, the demure headlights
fringed where it lay; I led it gently
to the road and stood with that
10 companion, ready and friendly. I was fifteen.

We could find the end of a road, meet
the sky on out Seventeenth. I thought about
hills, and patting the handle got back a
confident opinion. On the bridge we indulged **Ⓐ**
15 a forward feeling, a tremble. I was fifteen.

Thinking, back farther in the grass I found **Ⓑ**
the owner, just coming to, where he had flipped
over the rail. He had blood on his hand, was pale—
I helped him walk to his machine. He ran his hand
20 over it, called me a good man, roared away.

I stood there, fifteen.

MEET THE WRITER

"One of the Great Free Human Activities"

William Stafford (1914–1993), born in Hutchinson, Kansas, of Native American heritage, grew up in several small Kansas towns. The people, animals, and landscapes of his childhood became lifelong subjects for his poetry. Early in his adult life, Stafford worked as a laborer in sugar-beet fields, on construction jobs, and in an oil refinery. He also spent four years in prison during World War II because of his conscientious objection to war. Stafford's poetry is marked by his concern about choices and tough decisions, especially those involving our aggression toward nature and other human beings. He believes that "writing is one of the great free human activities."

Starting in 1948, Stafford taught at Lewis and Clark College in Portland, Oregon. For more than forty years, he instructed and influenced several generations of students. Many of these students went on to make their own reputations as poets. They never forgot William Stafford.

Reaching All Students

Struggling Readers

Remind students that in free verse, sentences don't necessarily end at the end of a line. Urge students to pause only when they see some form of punctuation, such as a comma, a dash, or a period.

Advanced Learners

Cars and motorcycles are often seen as symbols of personal freedom. Ask students to give examples of their symbolic use from music, film, or advertising.

Getting Students Involved

Cooperative Learning

Categorizing Conflicts in Cinema. Ask volunteers to name films that most students might have seen. List these films on the chalkboard. Then divide the class into small groups and assign a film to each group. Have students identify and discuss the external and internal conflicts facing the film's main character. Then have them discuss how the different conflicts move the plot along and keep the audience engaged.

Summary ■■

On a summer day when the speaker is fifteen, he finds a motorcycle lying abandoned, its engine still running. Admiring the bike, the boy personifies it as a "companion" and fantasizes about riding away. But then he searches for the owner, who is recovering from the accident. The man runs his bloodied hand over the machine, calls the boy "a good man," and roars off. Internal conflict is inherent in the choice that the boy is forced to make —a choice that moves him from childhood to adulthood.

Resources

Viewing and Representing
Videocassette B, Segment 10
Available in Spanish and English. You may wish to use the segment "Poetry as Performance" in connection with this poem. For full lesson plans and worksheets, see *Visual Connections Teacher's Manual.*

Listening
Audio CD Library
A recording of this poem is provided in the *Audio CD Library:*
• Disc 16, Track 6

Elements of Literature
Conflict
For additional instruction on conflict, see *Literary Elements:*
• Transparency 14
• Worksheet, p. 43

Ⓐ Elements of Literature
Denotation and Connotation
❓ In ll. 14–15, what literal meaning does the word *tremble* denote? [It refers to the motorcycle's vibration.] What might the word also suggest about the speaker's emotional state? [Possible responses: The speaker is quivering with anticipation and excitement; the speaker wavers between the temptation to ride off on the motorcycle and his responsibility to the bike's owner.]

Ⓑ Elements of Literature
Internal Conflict
❓ Have students reflect on the use of the word *thinking* in l. 16. What is the boy thinking about? [He is conflicted about whether to take the motorcycle or search for its owner.]

Summary ▪

The poem opens with an exhilarating description of a basketball player's star performance. The game's fast pace and immediacy is conveyed through metaphor, alliteration, an accumulation of sensory details, and onomatopoeia. Often these techniques are combined; note the verbs that begin with the letter s and that have a strong sensory appeal. The player is pumped up by the wildly cheering audience, but is quickly deflated when he thinks of less friendly crowds. He realizes that his presence is unwelcome in some neighborhoods, where he is judged on the basis of his race rather than his talent.

Resources ——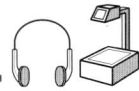

Listening
Audio CD Library
A recording of this poem is provided in the *Audio CD Library:*
• Disc 16, Track 7

Viewing and Representing
Fine Art Transparency
The fine art transparency of Colleen Browning's *Union Mixer* can be used to extend discussion of the poem's message. See the *Viewing and Representing Transparencies and Worksheets:*
• Transparency 15
• Worksheet, p. 60

RESPONDING TO THE ART

Visual Literacy. Discuss the details in the photograph that help to convey a sense of freedom, movement, or excitement. Have students comment on the angle from which the photograph was taken, the exact position of the ball, the backdrop of clouds and sky, and the balletlike position of the athlete. Ask them whether they can easily imagine the sound of the ball going through the hoop.

Before You Read

AMERICAN HERO

Make the Connection

Seeing Stars

We all have expectations of our heroes. We expect firefighters to race at the first sound, police officers to answer every plea for help, sport stars to win every game, movie and television stars to be perfect and beautiful all the time. After all, that is what we see and we can't look inside their heads to know what they are thinking. But what *are* they thinking? How do they see themselves? What thoughts do firefighters have as they rush into a burning building? Or rock stars as the applause rises around them? Or basketball players when they make a three-point shot? Our heroes may be seeing things from a different point of view.

Quickwrite

Before you read this poem, take a few minutes to write down what a hero in action might be feeling. For example, what do you think the player shown here was thinking at the moment he was photographed?

Keep your notes. For questions and activities on this poem, see pages 574–575.

Elements of Literature

Onomatopoeia

It quacks like a duck. It must be a duck. The sounds of certain words tell you unmistakably what is being described. *Racketa-racketa-racketa. Chug-chug. Toot-toot.* It's got to be a train. *Choke, slap, slam, holler.* Those are four of the words Hemphill uses to give us the sound of a basketball game. *Double dribble* would sound great, too. Can you think of others?

> **O**nomatopoeia is the use of a word whose sound imitates or suggests its meaning: *bang, bow-wow, buzz, chug, clack, clang, crash, crunch, glug, honk, moo, murmur, neigh, rat-a-tat, slurp, splat, squeak, thud.*
>
> *For more on Onomatopoeia, see pages 559–560 and the Handbook of Literary Terms.*

Reaching All Students

English Language Learners
Before reading the poem, ask volunteers to explain and demonstrate the basics of playing basketball for the benefit of those not thoroughly familiar with the game. For other strategies for engaging English language learners with the literature, see
• *Lesson Plans Including Strategies for English-Language Learners*

Using Students' Strengths

Visual Learners
If possible, videotape a portion of a basketball game and replay it for the class. Ask students to bring in photographs from newspapers and sports magazines as well. Have students think of onomatopoeic words or descriptive adjectives for each shot. Then discuss the accuracy of the poem's depiction of a game.

American Hero

Essex Hemphill

I have nothing to lose tonight.
All my men surround me, panting,
as I spin the ball above our heads
on my middle finger.
5 It's a shimmering club light
and I'm dancing, slick in my sweat. **A**
Squinting, I aim at the hole
fifty feet away. I let the tension go.
Shoot for the net. Choke it.
10 I never hear the ball
slap the backboard. I slam it
through the net. The crowd goes wild
for our win. I scored
thirty-two points this game **B**
15 and they love me for it.
Everyone hollering
is a friend tonight.
But there are towns,
certain neighborhoods
20 where I'd be hard pressed **C**
to hear them cheer
if I move on the block.

MEET THE WRITER

Writer, Poet, Activist

Essex Hemphill (1957–1995),
born in Chicago and later a
Philadelphian, was a writer, poet, and cultural
activist. Hemphill was the author of two books
of poetry and a collection of prose and poetry.
He received a Fellowship in Literature from the
National Endowment for the Arts in 1986.

A **Elements of Literature**
  Metaphor
  ? The speaker compares playing basketball to what activity? [He compares it to dancing in a nightclub.]

B **Elements of Literature**
  Onomatopoeia
  ? Which words are onomatopoetic in ll. 11–16? [*slap, slam, hollering*] How do these words help suggest the noisy excitement of a winning basket? [Possible response: They create an aural context, making the reader feel immersed in the event.]

C **Critical Thinking**
  Extending the Text
  ? What is the speaker saying about racism? [Sample response: Although some people love you for entertaining them, they don't want you as a neighbor.] Do you agree with the speaker? Why or why not? [Possible responses: Yes, some people like to watch African American athletes, but don't want to live next to them; no, the people who cheer are not the racists.]

Skill Link

Technical Vocabulary

Explain to students that most sports, fields of study, and occupations have their own technical vocabulary, a set of words and phrases that are used to describe things specific to that field. This specialized vocabulary is also referred to as argot (är´ gō). Much as a tourist may have difficulty with the language of a foreign country, someone unfamiliar with a certain field may

have difficulty with its technical vocabulary. Tell students that context can help them understand unfamiliar technical vocabulary. For example, a person unfamiliar with basketball might not know that *hole* (l. 7) means "goal" or "basketball hoop." Using the surrounding sentences, however, a reader can easily determine that the speaker is aiming the ball at the basket.

Activity

1. Ask basketball experts in the class to draw up a short list of basketball's technical vocabulary, terms such as "pick-and-roll," "screen," "the key," and "post-up."

2. Then have the experts take turns describing scenes from a basketball game with sentences that use those terms.

3. Have students who don't know the game try to define the terms using only the context of the sentences.

MAKING MEANINGS

First Thoughts

1. Possible responses: Stafford's portrayal of the emotions of someone facing a moral choice suggests first-hand understanding; Hemphill's powerful writing suggests that he relates strongly both to sports and to racial conflict.

Shaping Interpretations

2. Lines 8–10, 11–12, and 14–15 suggest that the boy thinks of the motorcycle as something that could bring excitement into his life. Students may say that they experienced similar feelings while trying out a state-of-the-art computer, riding in a new car, or buying a new CD player.

3. The phrase means they could ride the open highway toward the horizon. It could also refer to enjoying the rushing air or suggest the possibility of a fatal accident.

4. Since sixteen is the minimum legal age for acquiring a driver's license in most states, fifteen-year-olds are especially eager to attain the freedom that motor vehicles afford. Twelve-year-olds are farther removed from driving status, and eighteen-year-olds may already own a motor vehicle.

5. When tomorrow comes, the mood will be different from the winning mood at the game.

6. The speaker's mood has changed from elated to somber. He feels an internal conflict about enjoying the applause of his fans because he suspects that some would turn on him. These last few lines suggest that the loyalty of his fans is only superficial.

7. The short sentences describe the player's actions as he shoots the ball.

Connecting with the Texts

8. You may be ashamed of what you almost did, yet surprised and pleased that you acted responsibly in the end.

9. Sample responses: The speaker should take pride in his skill and accomplishments and ignore racists; the speaker can be a role model and help some people overcome their biases.

MAKING MEANINGS

FIFTEEN
AMERICAN HERO

First Thoughts

[respond]

1. How do you think the writers of "Fifteen" and "American Hero" felt about the **conflicts** that they made into poems?

Shaping Interpretations

[connect]

2. How does the boy in "Fifteen" feel about the motorcycle? What lines convey that feeling? What have *you* experienced that allows you to understand his emotion?

[infer]

3. What do you think the boy in "Fifteen" means in lines 11–12 when he says that he and the motorcycle could "meet the sky out on Seventeenth"? What else could "meet the sky" mean?

[infer]

4. The writer uses "Fifteen" as the title of the poem, and the phrase "I was fifteen" as a **refrain,** or chorus. What is the significance of that number? Could it as well have been sixteen? How about twelve or eighteen?

[infer]

5. The American hero in Hemphill's poem says he has "nothing to lose *tonight,*" and "Everyone hollering / is a friend *tonight.*" What does this repetition of the word *tonight* suggest about tomorrow?

[interpret]

6. Look at the last five lines of "American Hero." How has the speaker's mood changed? What **conflict** is the speaker feeling now? What is he saying about his fans?

[analyze]

7. Hemphill structured his poem so that it has some long sentences and some short, staccato sentences. Analyze the poem to locate the long and short sentences. What action is described with the short sentences? Read the poem aloud to hear how the short sentences create a kind of tension.

Connecting with the Texts

[connect]

8. Suppose you are the person who finds the motorcycle in "Fifteen." The man who owns it calls you a good man or woman. Given what you were just thinking about doing, how does that make you feel?

[connect]

 9. If you had a chance to speak to the "American Hero," what would you say? Did you predict his thoughts in your Quickwrite?

Basketball Collage (1992) by Josh Falley, Topeka West High School, Topeka, Kansas. Oils, pastels.

Courtesy of the artist.

574 THE POETRY COLLECTIONS

Assessing Learning

T574

CHOICES: Building Your Portfolio

Reader's Theater

1. Preparing for a Poetry Reading

A group reading.  Find a poem from this book that you think would be effective read by more than one voice. (You might try Alice Walker's "Women" on page 556.) To prepare your script, you'll have to make these decisions: How do you *interpret* the mood of the poem—is it sad, happy, bitter, tender? How many readers will you need? Will you have the whole poem read by several voices? Or will you have some lines read by individual voices? Will you need males and females? Mark up your script and rehearse it for presentation to the class.

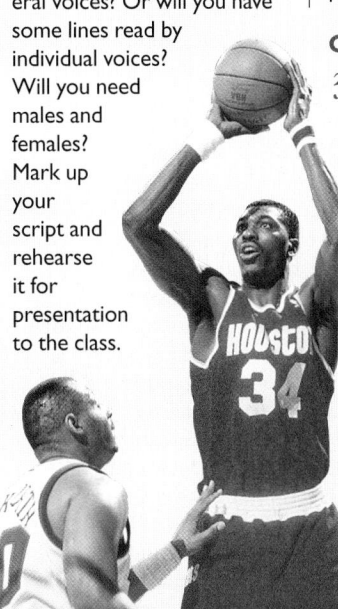

Explaining a Response

2. Moral Dilemmas

If you think one or both of these poems say something important that students in your school should think about, write your ideas in the form of a letter to your school newspaper. Open your letter with a statement telling why you are writing. Be sure to sum up briefly what happens in each poem you write about, before you get into details about why you think the poem is important. Check what you wrote for the Quickwrites before you read these poems.

Creative Writing

3. Poetry in Sports

Hemphill's poem is about more than sports, but you may find the game part as exciting to read as the sports page of your newspaper. Try reporting a game you've watched closely (or better, played in) using free verse and all the musical strategies available to the poet. When you're describing action, use short, fast sentences. Try to find words that sound like the sounds of your game. (Maybe you started a list before you read the poem. See page 572.)

Creative Writing

4. Personify That Machine

Stafford's motorcycle is described as if it's a horse or even a person. Describe a machine you like a lot in terms that make the machine seem human. Before you write, list the parts of the machine and think of how they could seem human. The engine of a car, for example, could be its lungs. The bottom of a boat could be its fat belly. The vacuum cleaner's suction could be its breath. Write three sentences or more.

Creative Writing

5. The Class Onomatopoeia Collection

Establish a class **onomatopoeia** collection on a bulletin board or computer. Collect words you hear or read, but also try to invent new onomatopoetic words or phrases for things such as the sounds of skates, skateboards, computers and computer games, VCRs, copying machines, home appliances, smoke alarms or car alarms, sports sounds, classroom sounds—or any other special or unusual sounds you want to imitate. Inventors should sign their contributions.

Grading Timesaver

Rubrics for each Choices assignment appear on p. 179 in the *Portfolio Management System*.

CHOICES: Building Your Portfolio

1. **Reader's Theater** Help students draw up a list of poems from the textbook that would be effectively read by more than one voice.
2. **Explaining a Response** Ask students to come up with at least three reasons why the issues raised in the poem they chose are important.
3. **Creative Writing** To help students get started, suggest they quickly freewrite a list of words, phrases, and sentences that capture the sounds and images they want to describe. Students can then go over their lists and choose which images and onomatopoetic words to include in their poems.
4. **Creative Writing** Students may wish to make a two-column chart to help them as they create their personifications. In one column, they can list machine parts; in the other, matching human characteristics.
5. **Creative Writing** Encourage students to include visuals—either drawings or pictures from magazines or newspapers—along with their words and phrases.

Crossing the Curriculum

Health

As the rider in "Fifteen" discovered, motorcycles can be hazardous to your health. With little of the protection afforded by a car, motorcyclists are far more susceptible to injury than car drivers and occupants. Per mile driven, motorcyclists are 15 to 20 times more likely to die in a crash. Proper training and wearing a helmet are essential to safety. Ask interested students to create a poster that presents safety tips for riding a motorcycle. This poster should teach riders how not to be a *squid,* a term used to refer to rookie riders who drive recklessly or buy motorcycles that they cannot handle.

Make the Connection

Seeing the World Clearly

The two second-graders in this poem deal in different ways with the lives they've been given. Before you read, you might want to see what the poet says about her poem on page 577.

Quickwrite

Do you know anyone who has felt like an outsider? Maybe you have had that feeling from time to time—most people have. Write down your thoughts about being inside and outside.

Keep your notes. For questions and activities on this poem, see page 578.

Elements of Literature

Images: Sharing Sensations

As you read, let the poet's words create pictures in your mind—pictures that also help you smell, hear, touch, and even taste the vivid world this lonely little girl shared with her best friend.

> **I**mages are words that create sensory impressions.
>
> *For more on Imagery, see pages 492–493 and the Handbook of Literary Terms.*

go.hrw.com
LE0 9-10

The Girl Who Loved the Sky

Anita Endrezze

Outside the second-grade room,
the jacaranda tree blossomed
into purple lanterns, the papery petals
drifted, darkening the windows.
5   Inside, the room smelled like glue.
The desks were made of yellowed wood,
the tops littered with eraser rubbings,
rulers, and big fat pencils.
Colored chalk meant special days.
10 The walls were covered with precise
bright tulips and charts with shiny stars
by certain names. There, I learned
how to make butter by shaking a jar
until the pale cream clotted
15 into one sweet mass. There, I learned
that numbers were fractious° beasts
with dens like dim zeros. And there,
I met a blind girl who thought the sky
tasted like cold metal when it rained
20 and whose eyes were always covered
with the bruised petals of her lids.
She loved the formless sky, defined
only by sounds, or the cool umbrellas
of clouds. On hot, still days
25 we listened to the sky falling
like chalk dust. We heard the noon
whistle of the pig-mash factory,
smelled the sourness of homebound men.
I had no father; she had no eyes;
30 we were best friends. The other girls
drew shaky hopscotch squares
on the dusty asphalt, talked about
pajama parties, weekend cookouts,
and parents who bought sleek-finned cars.
35 Alone, we sat in the canvas swings,
our shoes digging into the sand, then pushing,
until we flew high over their heads,
our hands streaked with red rust
from the chains that kept us safe.

16. **fractious:** hard to manage; rebellious.

 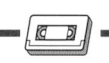 *Resources: Print and Media*

Reading
- *Graphic Organizers for Active Reading*, p. 54
- *Audio CD Library*, Disc 16, Track 8

Assessment
- *Portfolio Management System*, p. 181
- *Test Generator (One-Stop Planner CD-ROM)*

Internet
- go.hrw.com (keyword: LE0 9–10)

40   I was born blind, she said, an act of nature.
      Sure, I thought, like birds born
      without wings, trees without roots.
      I didn't understand. The day she moved
      I saw the world clearly; the sky
45   backed away from me like a departing father.
      I sat under the jacaranda, catching
      the petals in my palm, enclosing them
      until my fist was another lantern
      hiding a small and bitter flame.

MEET THE WRITER

Different from the Rest

Anita Endrezze (1952–   ) bridges the two worlds of visual arts and literary arts. "The Girl Who Loved the Sky" is from her book *At the Helm of Twilight* (1992). Her paintings have been widely shown and have appeared on book covers in the United States and in Europe.

In the early 1980s, Endrezze and her husband lived in a home they built out of logs in the middle of a pine forest. They now live with their two children, Aaron Joseph Sunhawk and Maja Sierra Rose, in Spokane, Washington.

❝ 'The Girl Who Loved the Sky' was written about my early life. My parents divorced when I was very young, in a time when divorce was unusual. Not one other kid in my class came from a divorced family. My situation was also different because my parents were from two different races. My father was Yaqui Indian and my mother is white (European-mixed background). I didn't find it easy to make friends.

We also moved a lot. Finally, I did make friends with a blind girl who was also lonely and not accepted by the other kids. In her case, I don't think they knew how to relate to her. I don't remember them being actively cruel; they just didn't know how to play with someone who could not see. We became friends because we were the only two girls who were left outside the 'circle.' After I got to know her, though, I began to understand her and what her life was like. I tried to imagine myself in her position. Maybe we would have gone on to be great friends, but my family moved again and I no longer saw her.

To write this poem, I needed to remember the smells, sights, feelings, and sounds of my childhood and of elementary school. I tried to use my five senses to evoke images others could identify with. I wanted to express the loneliness of a child who is different from the rest. ❞

THE GIRL WHO LOVED THE SKY **577**

Summary ■■■

This poem creates a nostalgic mood through the use of sensory details and impressions. The speaker, a young girl who has lost her father, identifies strongly with a classmate who cannot see. Lacking sight, the speaker's blind friend comes into contact with the world through her other senses, such as hearing and touch. When the blind girl moves away, the speaker feels loss and disappointment.

Resources ━━━━━━

Listening
Audio CD Library
A recording of this poem is provided in the *Audio CD Library*:
• Disc 16, Track 8

Ⓐ **Elements of Literature**

Images

❓ What images of a second grade classroom does Endrezze create? [Possible responses: the smell of glue; the sight and feel of wooden desks; the classroom litter of eraser rubbings, rulers, pencils, and chalk; walls covered with pictures and charts with metallic star stickers.]

Ⓑ **Reading Skills and Strategies**

Responding to the Text

❓ How might the girl's eyes be like flower petals? [Possible responses: Flowers and eyesight are both delicate; her eyes are beautiful even though she cannot see; the shape of her closed eyelids is like the shape of flower petals.]

Ⓒ **Advanced Learners**

Analyzing Parallelism

❓ Why do you think the poet pairs these two clauses? [Possible response: to emphasize that the speaker's kinship with her friend is intensified by a shared sense of loss.]

Reaching All Students

Struggling Readers
Students may have difficulty with the dense, unbroken text. Have them divide the poem into sections and then paraphrase each section. Encourage them to ask questions about anything they do not understand.

English Language Learners
For the benefit of those unfamiliar with American childhood pastimes, ask other students to describe the game of hopscotch, and to explain a pajama party.

Using Students' Strengths

Naturalist Learners
Invite these students to find pictures and information about the jacaranda tree, including facts about where it is found, its flowers, bark, leaves, size, and ideal growing conditions. Ask them to try to locate pictures of the tree's clusters of purple flowers. Have students share their research with the class and make inferences about the setting of the poem, based on what they've learned.

MAKING MEANINGS

First Thoughts

1. Students might tell her that everyone feels like an outsider at one time or another.

Shaping Interpretations

2. One girl has lost her father; the other has lost her sight. Each also loses a best friend.

3. Students may say that the blind girl taught her friend to experience life through senses other than sight and to enjoy life, despite a loss.

4. Sample responses: the cooling effect of clouds passing overhead, the delicate appearance of the blind girl's eyes, the sound of the factory whistle, and the taste of rain.

5. The chains firmly secure the swings. In the swings, the two friends are safe from feelings of isolation in the schoolyard.

Connecting With the Text

6. With her blind friend, the speaker had learned to enjoy life despite the loss of her father. But now she realizes that she is alone in a vast, unloving world. Students may not like the bitter ending, preferring that the girl cherish memories of good times with her friend.

Grading Timesaver

Rubrics for each Choices assignment appear on p. 181 in the *Portfolio Management System*.

CHOICES: Building Your Portfolio

1. **Reader's Theater** You might provide enlarged photocopies of the poem for students to use as scripts.
2. **Art** Have students research images of a jacaranda tree in print or CD encyclopedias or in botanical reference books.
3. **Creative Writing** Model a few images for students.

T578

MAKING MEANINGS
THE GIRL WHO LOVED THE SKY

[respond]

First Thoughts

1. If you had a chance, what would you say to the little girl who speaks in this poem? (Check your Quickwrite notes.)

Shaping Interpretations

[interpret]

2. What has each girl in this poem lost?

[draw a conclusion]

3. Do you think the girl who was blind taught her friend anything? Is the poem clear on this point? Explain your response.

[identify]

4. What **images** does Endrezze create for you in her poem? What can you *see*? *hear*? almost *taste*?

[infer]

5. How could chains keep the girls safe—safe from what?

Connecting with the Text

[evaluate]

6. What do you think the little girl means in lines 43–44 when she says that the day her friend moved she "saw the world clearly"? Do you agree with her vision of what the world is like? Why, or why not?

CHOICES: Building Your Portfolio

Reader's Theater

1. Preparing for a Poetry Reading

Pauses.
Prepare a script for a reading of "The Girl Who Loved the Sky," either for a group performance or for a single voice (see page 582). Your main challenge will be to decide on places in the text where you must make pauses: full pauses or brief pauses. Punctuation marks will guide you. On your script, write *p* in the places

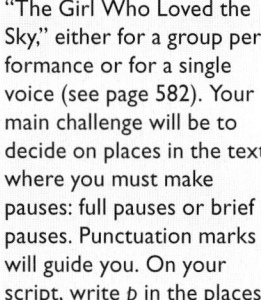

where you'll make a full pause and *b* in the spots where you'll stop briefly for a breath.

Art

2. Views of the Jacaranda

The tree with the odd name opens and closes the poem, shedding both light and darkness on the two little girls. Suppose you are asked to illustrate this poem. Paint or draw the tree as the speaker sees it, but first be sure you know exactly what it looks like yourself. Include in your painting one important line from the poem.

Creative Writing

3. Mixing Senses

The blind girl knew how the sky tasted and how the clouds felt. Write a series of images in which you describe some ordinary object as it would appear to a sense you wouldn't associate with it—just as you probably wouldn't associate the sky with the sense of taste. Here are some ideas:

How does math smell?
How does the sun taste?
How does a pizza sound?

578 THE POETRY COLLECTIONS

Assessing Learning

Check Test: Questions and Answers
Answers may vary slightly.

1. What place is described in the beginning of the poem? [a second-grade classroom]
2. What does the speaker lack? [a father]
3. Who becomes the speaker's best friend? [Her best friend is a blind girl.]
4. What activity do the girls enjoy? [swinging]
5. When does the speaker's perspective of the world change? [It happens the day her friend moves away.]

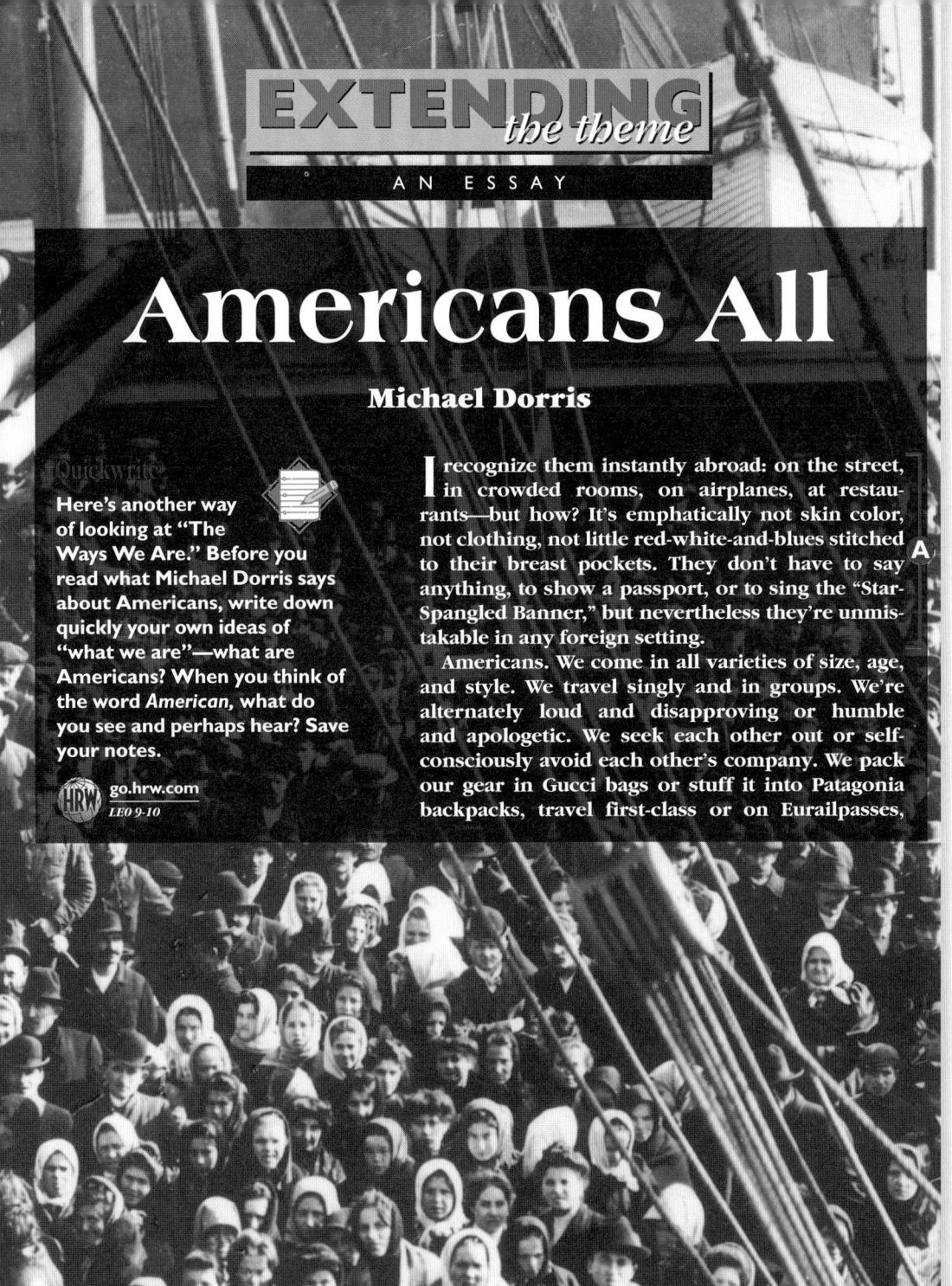

Americans All

Michael Dorris

I recognize them instantly abroad: on the street, in crowded rooms, on airplanes, at restaurants—but how? It's emphatically not skin color, not clothing, not little red-white-and-blues stitched to their breast pockets. They don't have to say anything, to show a passport, or to sing the "Star-Spangled Banner," but nevertheless they're unmistakable in any foreign setting.

Americans. We come in all varieties of size, age, and style. We travel singly and in groups. We're alternately loud and disapproving or humble and apologetic. We seek each other out or self-consciously avoid each other's company. We pack our gear in Gucci bags or stuff it into Patagonia backpacks, travel first-class or on Eurailpasses,

---

Objectives

Extending the Theme

Meditating on what it means to be an American, Michael Dorris reflects on his ability to instantly recognize fellow American tourists whenever he is traveling abroad. It's as if there is a "national homing device" that allows Americans to recognize their compatriots, even though they wear different clothing, travel in different styles, and share no single distinguishing physical characteristic. Dorris discusses the links that connect us—our shared sensibilities and a common body of cultural knowledge—and then questions why a group that shares so much is so fractious when at home. He comes to the conclusion that being different, "not a clone," may be the defining characteristic of an American. Heterogeneous backgrounds and beliefs are an inescapable part of our essence.

Ⓐ Reading Skills and Strategies
Making Inferences

❓ Who are "them" and "they" in the first paragraph? [Americans] What clues led you to this conclusion? [The mention of "red-white-and-blues" and the "Star Spangled Banner" are hints that Dorris is talking about Americans.]

Reaching All Students

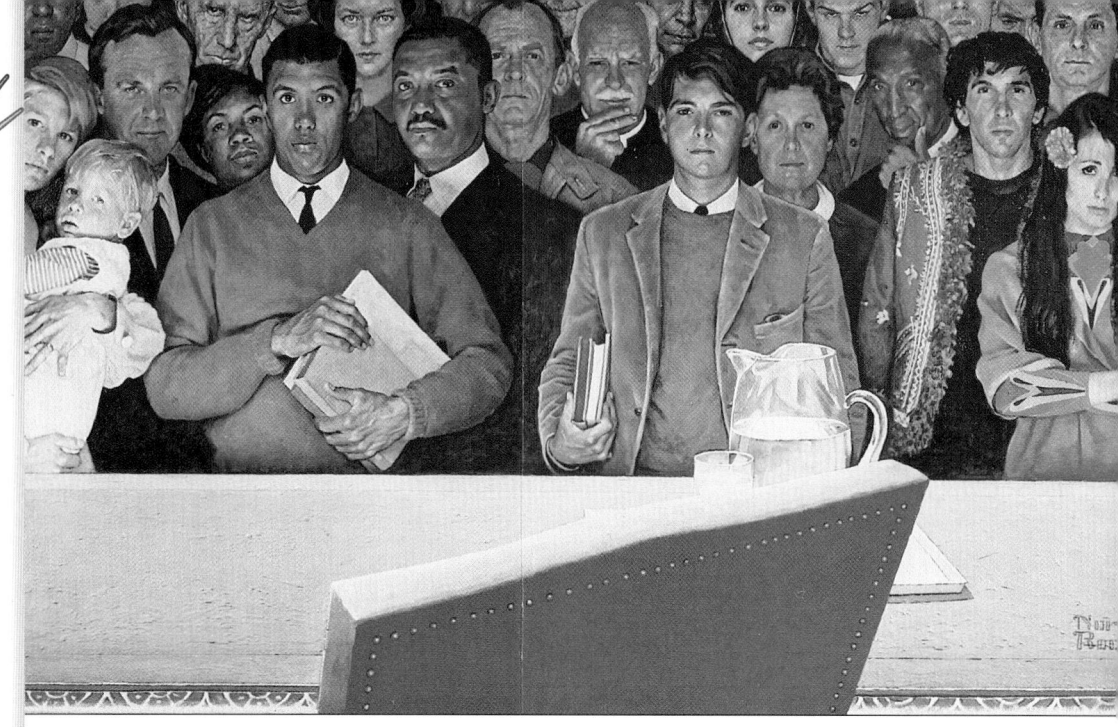

The Right to Know (1968) by Norman Rockwell.
Printed by permission of the Norman Rockwell Family Trust. © 1968 the Norman Rockwell Family Trust.
Photo courtesy of the Norman Rockwell Museum at Stockbridge.

stay in youth hostels or in luxury hotels, but none of that matters. It's as though we're individually implanted with some invisible beeper, some national homing device, that's activated by the proximity of similar equipment.

This common denominator is manifest in shared knowledge (we all know who Mary Tyler Moore is), topics of mutual interest or dispute (guns, the environment, choice), and popular culture (do we or do we not deserve a thousand-calorie break today?). In other words, we take the same things seriously or not seriously, are capable of speaking, when we choose to, not merely a common language but a common idiom, and know the melodies, if not all the words, to many of the same songs.

Why, then, doesn't any of this count when we're *not* overseas? Why, at home, do we seem so different from each other, so mutually incompatible, so strange and forbidding? Do we have to recognize each other in Tokyo or Cairo

in order to see through the distinctions and into the commonalities? How does that "we," so obvious anywhere else in the world, get split into "us" and "them" when we're stuck within our own borders?

The answer is clear: To be Americans means to be not the clone of the people next door. I fly back from any homogeneous country, from a place where every person I see is blond, or black, or belongs to only one religion, and then disembark at JFK. I revel in the cadence of many accents, catch a ride to the city with a Nigerian American or Russian American cabdriver. Eat Thai food at a Greek restaurant next to a table of Chinese American conventioneers from Alabama. Get directions from an Iranian American cop and drink a cup of Turkish coffee served by a Navajo student at Fordham who's majoring in Japanese literature. Argue with everybody about everything. I'm home.

— from *Newsday,* October 1992

Making the Connections

MEET THE WRITER

From Within

Michael Dorris (1945–1997), novelist and nonfiction writer, was the husband and collaborator of poet and novelist Louise Erdrich. A member of the Modocs, a Native American people originally from Lost River Valley on the California-Oregon border, Dorris was a professor of cultural anthropology and Native American studies at Dartmouth College before taking a leave to devote full time to his writing.

One of Dorris's nonfiction books, *The Broken Cord* (1989), is about his adopted son Adam, who was born with fetal alcohol syndrome (FAS). "As with all hard challenges," Dorris said, "motivation must come from within." That's a motto Dorris lived by—in his personal and professional lives. It's also a motto he passed on to his children, his students, and his readers.

Dorris adopted Adam and two other children before he was married to Erdrich. The house-keeping and parenting duties didn't faze him:

66 I have this very rich background of grand-mothers and aunts and a mother, a wonderful extended family who made nothing seem im-possible or out of reach. We were poor when I was growing up, but I never felt it. They could kill me for telling this, but sometimes on Sunday afternoons they'd lock the door to the house, everyone would dress up and we'd sit at the dining-room table and have lunch. If it were later at night, they'd call it the Stork Club. Everything they did was wonderful. When you don't have a lot of things, every event becomes special, like The Adventure of Getting the Deep Fryer. 99

FINDING COMMON GROUND

As its name suggests, this feature is meant to initiate a lively discussion among students in order to discover areas of agreement in their responses to issues in the literature.

Have students use a chart like the following one as they discuss Dorris's article and generate ideas for their own articles.

What I Agree With	What I Question	What I Think

1. Make sure that students pay equal attention to both areas of agree-ment and areas they question.
2. Note that students may use a vari-ety of genres when writing their article; they can structure their responses as a letter to Dorris, an expository essay, or a comparison-contrast essay.
3. As students listen to the readings, have them jot down the types of differences they notice—everything from genre to tone to the kinds of examples that are used.

FINDING COMMON GROUND

1. Review the notes you made in your Quickwrite and then meet with a group of other readers to discuss Dorris's article. What audience do you think Dorris had in mind when he wrote the article? Talk over what you agree with and what you would question in the article.

2. Using your Quickwrite notes and any new ideas you got from Dorris and from your discussion, write your own article about "Americans and the Ways We Are." You can write it as a response to Dorris, or as an independent essay of your own. You can include some reference to poems in this collection, if you think they are relevant.

3. Put aside some class time to read aloud your essays—and Dorris's. Dorris says "We come in all varieties." Do your essays come in all varieties too?

AMERICANS ALL 581

Assessing Learning

Check Test: Questions and Answers

Answers may vary slightly.

1. Who does the writer recognize instantly when traveling abroad? [fellow Americans]
2. What does the writer say Americans have in common? [They share knowledge, topics of mutual interest or dispute, and popular culture.]
3. According to the writer, when do Americans seem very different from each other? [when they are at home in the United States]
4. How does the writer feel about the diversity he encounters when returning to the United States? [He appreciates this diversity.]
5. Where does the writer feel he is when he can "argue with everybody about every-thing"? [He feels he is home.]

Speaking and Listening Workshop

MAIN OBJECTIVE
Perform a Reader's Theater poetry reading

PROCESS OBJECTIVES
1. Select a suitable poem
2. Create an interpretive script
3. Plan movements and the use of props, scenery, and costumes
4. Use evaluation criteria to critique a performance
5. Reflect on personal progress in interpretive reading

Resources

Portfolio Management System
• Performance Rubric, p. 182

Introducing the Speaking and Listening Workshop

Much of the success of poetry reading in Reader's Theater depends on the poem selected. Have students consider the following criteria for choosing a selection appropriate for Reader's Theater.

• Is the poem enjoyable?
• Does the poem's subject matter appeal to most people?
• Does the poem offer new ideas or insights?
• Does the poem offer a variety of creative opportunities for the presenters?
• Does the poem fit the time limits and other requirements of the assignment?

Students may better understand the process of Reader's Theater if they observe examples. If possible, show a videotape of a Reader's Theater poetry reading, such as the Visual Connections video offered with Collection 10.

ASSIGNMENT

Perform at least one of the poems in this collection before an audience.

... poetry readings have moved out of smoky cafes and into libraries, bookstores, and cafes (nonsmoking, of course) around the country. With help from MTV's poetry videos and poetry slams at places like Nuyorican Poets Cafe on East Third Street in the East Village [of New York City], where audiences rate performances like Olympic judges, poetry readings—as opposed to reading poetry—are becoming a staple of the country's cultural scene.

—Diana Jean Schemo,
from *The New York Times*

READER'S THEATER
POETRY READING

©Tribune Media Services, Inc. All rights reserved. Reprinted with permission.

"So what I get from acting is using it for others, using it for people. I find that when I work well, people enjoy it and . . . things happen to them."

—Sidney Poitier

How is "reader's" theater different from "regular" theater? The main difference is the text that the performer shares with the audience. In regular theater, the actor performs a play, which is written in dramatic form with dialogue and stage directions. In reader's theater, one or more actors perform works of nondramatic literature as they were originally written—poems, stories, even whole novels that are read aloud over several performances.

Preparation

Your first job in preparing for a reader's theater performance is to build your private, personal understanding of the poem.

1. Making Your Choice

As you worked through this collection, you might already have chosen a poem you feel a connection with. If you still haven't selected a text, read a few poems from this collection out loud to see which one you'd most enjoy reading in public.

WORK IN PROGRESS

2. Shaping Interpretations

• Make a copy of the poem and use it as a working script. Underline the parts you find most dramatic—words, phrases, images,

Using Students' Strengths

Interpersonal Learners
Suggest that small groups of students work together to generate a list of poems suitable for Reader's Theater. Have a spokesperson from each group explain the group's choices while a recorder adds to a class list on the chalkboard or on kraft paper. To form the Reader's Theater groups, have students write their names next to two or three poems they would be interested in helping present.

Visual/Kinesthetic/Musical Learners
Reader's Theater is well suited to the gifts and needs of a diverse group of students. Since the participants interpret the literature and decide on appropriate action, props, and sound accompaniment, a presentation can be tailored to draw on individual abilities. During the group's initial meeting, have students discuss the kinds of participation they prefer. After agreeing on a poem to be presented, students should determine each group member's contribution.

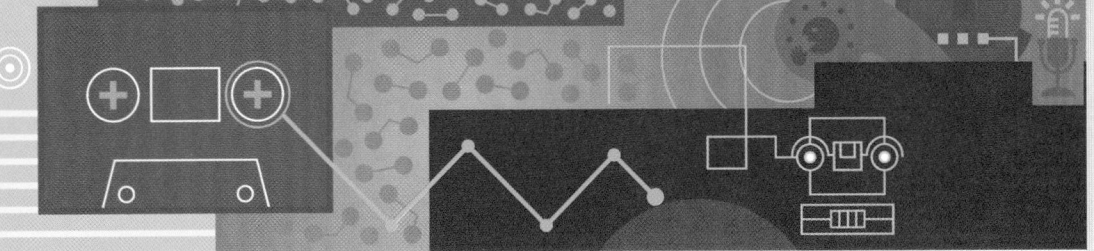

sounds, rhythms. Note places where you want to go slowly or speed up or pause. Be sure to note which lines do *not* end with a punctuation mark. This means that you don't come to a full pause but read on to the next line to complete the thought.

• Make notes describing the speaker in the poem. Is the speaker a particular age? How does the speaker feel in the poem, and do his or her feelings change as the poem goes on?

• What will your own tone or attitude be? Thoughtful? Serious? Sad? Sarcastic? How will you use your voice to convey your tone?

• Complete this statement: If my audience gets just one single impression from my reading, I want them to . . .

Planning and Rehearsing

Now it's time to develop ways to communicate your private, personal, unique experience of the poem to your audience.

1. Memorizing (or Not)

You may or may not decide to memorize the poem. Even if you plan to hold a copy of the poem throughout your reading, you should be extremely familiar with it. And if you choose to memorize your poem, an actors' secret will help you: Thoroughly understanding a text makes it much easier to memorize.

2. Planning Your Movements

You may feel most comfortable standing still and speaking to your audience. Be aware of your posture—stand up straight. Or you may want to move around, to act out parts of the poem. You may want to sit. Make eye contact with your audience: Don't keep your head buried in your script.

FRANK & ERNEST reprinted by permission of Newspaper Enterprise Association, Inc.

Naomi Shihab Nye stood under the bright lights at Waterloo Village [New Jersey] on Thursday night, a television camera hovering around her like a mobile X-ray, to read her work into a microphone. The poet could not hear herself; the wind whipping the tent's plastic walls, the rain's ping-ping drumbeat on the roof and the expanse of empty seats seemed to swallow the sound of her.

I want to be famous in the
    way a pulley is famous,

or a buttonhole, not
    because it did anything
    spectacular,

but because it never forgot
    what it could do.

It was only the anticipation on the faces in the audience and the final applause that made Ms. Nye realize she had struck the right mix of words, gestures, and pauses in performing her poetry, a talent that has become crucial to a poet's success.

—Diana Jean Schemo,
from *The New York Times*

Teaching the Speaking and Listening Workshop

• Remind students that they may move around and act out their parts. However, caution them against making gestures that distract the audience or the other performers.

• Encourage students to be creative in their choice of props, scenery, and costumes. They may also want to use sound effects or background music.

• To make your students' performances come alive, host a poetry day and invite parents and community members. Students may read their favorite poems and their own works. Videotape the event to share with other classes, and give a copy of the tape to the school library. Suggest that students write and submit a press release to the local newspaper.

Reaching All Students

Struggling Learners
Encourage Reader's Theater groups to read through the poems together to gain a full understanding of each stanza. Have groups focus on irregular sentence structures that may be challenging for students. Group members should reach a consensus on how to interpret and impart the meaning of these challenging sentences to an audience.

English Language Learners
Encourage these students to take an active speaking role in their presentations. Remind them that a well-defined role in the poetry reading will provide opportunities to practice their pronunciation and delivery. Demonstrate how intonation can convey emotions, attitudes, and moods. Students who feel less comfortable participating in live performances may choose to work with a small group that plans to videotape their poetry reading for presentation to the class.

Evaluating and Revising

To help students evaluate their progress as they rehearse, provide them with an opportunity to make a practice recording. Students should make individual comments while they listen to their recorded practice session. Ask them to share their comments about what they like in their presentations and what they want to change. Remind students working together to offer constructive criticism only and to articulate what they found effective about one another's efforts before suggesting changes in approach.

When I first gave readings, I had nightmares before the readings; I felt that the hearers were my judges. I had nightmares in which I was way down below and the audience was all the way up behind the judge's bench, and they were all saying, "To the lions!" But I don't feel that way anymore.

—Sharon Olds

■ *Evaluation Criteria*

A good reader's theater performance

1. respects the original literary text

2. reveals the performer's understanding of and feelings about the literature

3. shares that understanding and those feelings with an audience

4. is entirely clear, audible, and understandable to the audience

3. Using Props, Scenery, Costumes

Props—objects that are significant in the poem—can help establish the speaker's identity or setting. For example, if you are reading "American Hero" (page 573), you may want to handle a basketball and then toss it away near the poem's end. During a performance, props can provide a focus for you and help relieve your nervousness. If you use props, however, you should definitely memorize the poem.

You may want to use costumes and even special makeup to bring a speaker to life. Scenery pieces (a bench, a rug, a table) will help define your performing area and give you ideas for movement. If you use music or sound effects (a purring motorcycle for "Fifteen"), keep them subtle and don't let them distract your audience.

4. Rehearsing Your Reading

Make a clean copy of the poem. Across the top write your finished version of the sentence that begins "If the audience gets just one single impression." Add any important interpretive and performance notes. This is your script.

Reflecting: How Did It Go?

If you decide to include a tape of your reading in your portfolio, date the tape and attach a brief reflection:

1. Was my poem a good choice?

2. Do I still need to work on some performance skills?

3. What did I learn about performing for an audience?

4. What did I learn about myself as a public speaker?

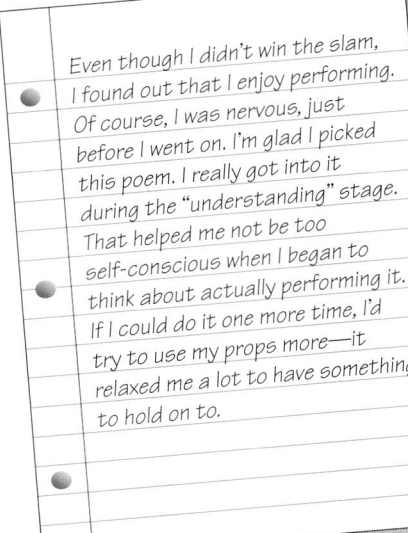

Even though I didn't win the slam, I found out that I enjoy performing. Of course, I was nervous, just before I went on. I'm glad I picked this poem. I really got into it during the "understanding" stage. That helped me not be too self-conscious when I began to think about actually performing it. If I could do it one more time, I'd try to use my props more—it relaxed me a lot to have something to hold on to.

T584

Collection 11

Say It!

Theme

Dare to Say What You Mean *Writers have to learn, from generation to generation, to say what they mean and to say it honestly. It is not always obvious that this is true of poets as well as of prose writers. In this collection, poets express their views and explore their feelings on issues that are important to all of us.*

Reading the Anthology

Reaching Struggling Readers

The *Reading Skills and Strategies: Reaching Struggling Readers* binder includes a Reading Strategies Handbook that offers concrete suggestions for helping students who have difficulty reading and comprehending text, or students who are reluctant readers. When a specific strategy is most appropriate for a selection, a correlation to the Handbook is provided at the bottom of the teacher's page under the head Struggling Readers. This head may also be used to introduce additional ideas for helping students read challenging texts.

Reading Beyond the Anthology

Read On At the end of the poetry collections in the grade nine book, there is an annotated bibliography of books suitable for extended reading. The suggested books are related to works in these collections by theme, by author, or by subject. To preview the Read On for the poetry collections, please turn to p. T613.

Collection 11 Say It!

Resources for this Collection

Note: All resources for this collection are available for preview on the *One-Stop Planner CD-ROM 2 with Test Generator.* All worksheets and blackline masters may be printed from the CD-ROM.

 **Internet Resources**
go.hrw.com LE0 9-11

Selection or Feature	Reading and Literary Skills	Vocabulary, Language, and Grammar
Elements of Literature: Tone (p. 586)	• *Literary Elements,* Transparency 15	
The Puppy Aleksandr Solzhenitsyn (p. 588)	• *Graphic Organizers for Active Reading,* Worksheet pp. 55, 56, 57	• *Words to Own,* Worksheet p. 33
Harlem Langston Hughes (p. 590)	• *Literary Elements:* Transparency 15 Worksheet p. 46	
Connections: Langston Hughes on the IRT Joe Sexton (p. 593)		
"Hope" Is the Thing with Feathers Emily Dickinson (p. 594)		
Legal Alien/Extranjera legal Pat Mora (p. 598)	• *Graphic Organizers for Active Reading,* Worksheet p. 58	• *Words to Own,* Worksheet p. 33 • *Daily Oral Grammar,* Transparency 40
The Road Not Taken Robert Frost (p. 601)	• *Graphic Organizers for Active Reading,* Worksheet p. 59	• *Words to Own,* Worksheet p. 35 • *Daily Oral Grammar,* Transparency 41
Connections: Crossing Paths Robert Frost (p. 603)	• *Literary Elements:* Poetry Transparencies 1–5 Teaching Notes, p. 57	
Lucinda Matlock Edgar Lee Masters (p. 606)	• *Graphic Organizers for Active Reading,* Worksheet p. 60	• *Words to Own,* Worksheet p. 33
Extending the Theme: Ain't I a Woman? Sojourner Truth (p. 610)	The Extending the Theme feature provides students with an unstructured opportunity to practice reading strategies using a selection that extends the theme of the collection.	• *Words to Own,* Worksheet p. 33
Writer's Workshop: Comparison-Contrast Essay (p. 614)		
Sentence Workshop: Revising Sentence Structure and Length (p. 619)		• *Workshop Resources,* p. 75 • *Language Workshop CD-ROM,* Sentence
Learning for Life: Music and Change (p. 621)		

Other Resources for this Collection

- *Cross-Curricular Activities*, p. 11
- *Portfolio Management System*, Introduction to Portfolio Assessment, p. 1
- *Formal Assessment*, Genre Test, p. 120
- *Test Generator*, Collection Test 💿

Writing	Listening and Speaking Viewing and Representing	Assessment
		• *Formal Assessment*, Literary Elements Test, p. 118
• *Portfolio Management System*, Rubrics for Choices, p. 183	• *Visual Connections:* Videocassette B, Segment 11 📼 • *Audio CD Library*, Disc 16, Tracks 11, 12, 13 🎧 • *Viewing and Representing:* Fine Art Transparency 16; Worksheet p. 64 📽 • *Portfolio Management System*, Rubrics for Choices, p. 183	• *Formal Assessment*, Selection Test, p. 115 • *Standardized Test Preparation*, p. 76 • *Test Generator (One-Stop Planner CD-ROM)* 💿
• *Portfolio Management System*, Rubrics for Choices, p. 185	• *Audio CD Library*, Disc 16, Tracks 14, 15 🎧 • *Portfolio Management System*, Rubrics for Choices, p. 185	• *Formal Assessment*, Selection Test, p. 117 • *Test Generator (One-Stop Planner CD-ROM)* 💿
• *Portfolio Management System*, Rubrics for Choices, p. 186	• *Audio CD Library*, Disc 16, Track 16 🎧 • *Portfolio Management System*, Rubrics for Choices, p. 186	• *Formal Assessment*, Selection Test, p. 117 • *Test Generator (One-Stop Planner CD-ROM)* 💿
• *Portfolio Management System*, Rubrics for Choices, p. 187	• *Audio CD Library*, Disc 16, Track 17 🎧 • *Portfolio Management System*, Rubrics for Choices, p. 187	• *Formal Assessment*, Selection Test, p. 117 • *Test Generator (One-Stop Planner CD-ROM)* 💿
	• *Audio CD Library*, Disc 16, Track 18 🎧	
• *Workshop Resources*, p. 45 • *Standardized Test Preparation:* Worksheet p. 132 Transparencies 19–24 📽		• *Portfolio Management System* • Prewriting, p. 189 • Peer Editing, p. 190 • Assessment Rubric, p. 191 • *Standardized Test Preparation:* Worksheet p. 132 Transparencies 19–24 📽
		• *Portfolio Management System*, Rubrics, p. 192

 Transparency  CD-ROM  Video  Audio CD

Collection Planner

Collection 11 Say It!

Skills Focus

Skills Focus

Selection or Feature	Reading Skills and Strategies	Elements of Literature	Language/ Grammar	Vocabulary/ Spelling	Writing	Listening/ Speaking	Viewing/ Representing
Elements of Literature: Tone (p. 586)		Tone, pp. 586–587 Diction, p. 586					
The Puppy Aleksandr Solzhenitsyn (p. 588) Harlem Langston Hughes (p. 590) "Hope" Is the Thing with Feathers Emily Dickinson (p. 594)	Dialogue with the Text, pp. 594, 596	Prose Poem, pp. 588, 597 Simile, pp. 590, 596 Metaphor, pp. 590, 596, 597 Denotation, p. 594 Connotation, pp. 594, 596 Tone, p. 597			Comparing Metaphors, p. 597 Write Two Linked Poems, p. 597 Write a Prose Poem, p. 597	Stage a "Speak-In," p. 597	Create an "I Dream" Collage, p. 597
Legal Alien/ Extranjera legal Pat Mora (p. 598)	Identify Points of View, p. 600	Tone, pp. 598, 600	Adjectives and Tone, p. 600	Multiple Meanings, p. 600	Compare Tone in Two Poems, p. 600 Write a Poem Using a Framework, p. 600		
The Road Not Taken Robert Frost (p. 601)		Verbal Irony, pp. 601, 604 Symbolize, p. 604 Tone, p. 604 Rhyme, p. 605 Meter, p. 605 Free Verse, p. 605	Adjectives and Tone, p. 604	Word Map, p. 605 Antonyms, p. 605	Compare the Structure of Two Poems, p. 605 Write a "Road" Poem, p. 605		
Lucinda Matlock Edgar Lee Masters (p. 606)	Visualize an Image, p. 608	Dramatic Monologue, pp. 606, 609 Tone, p. 608	Adjectives and Tone, p. 608		Compare and Contrast the Speakers in Two Poems, p. 609 Write a Dramatic Monologue, p. 609 Write a Letter to a Character, p. 609 Research the Location of Museums, p. 609	Create a Class Oral History, p. 609	
Extending the Theme: Ain't I a Woman? Sojourner Truth (p. 610)	Create a KWL Chart, pp. 610, 612	The Extending the Theme feature provides students with an unstructured opportunity to practice reading strategies using a selection that extends the theme of the collection.					
Writer's Workshop: Comparison-Contrast Essay (p. 614)	Analyze a Poem, p. 615	Features of a Poem, p. 615			Write a Comparison-Contrast Essay, pp. 614–618		Use a Venn Diagram, p. 615
Sentence Workshop: Revising Sentence Structure and Length (p. 619)			Sentences, p. 619 • Simple • Compound • Complex • Compound-Complex		Vary Sentences by Structure and Length, p. 619		
Reading for Life: Creating a Topic Outline (p. 620)	Skimming, p. 620 Close Reading, p. 620 Scanning, p. 620 Paraphrase, p. 620				Create a Topic Outline, p. 620		
Learning for Life: Investigating Song Lyrics (p. 621)					Write a Found Poem, p. 621	Create a Musical Medley, p. 621	Create a Time-Line Wall Display, p. 621

Skills Focus

T584D

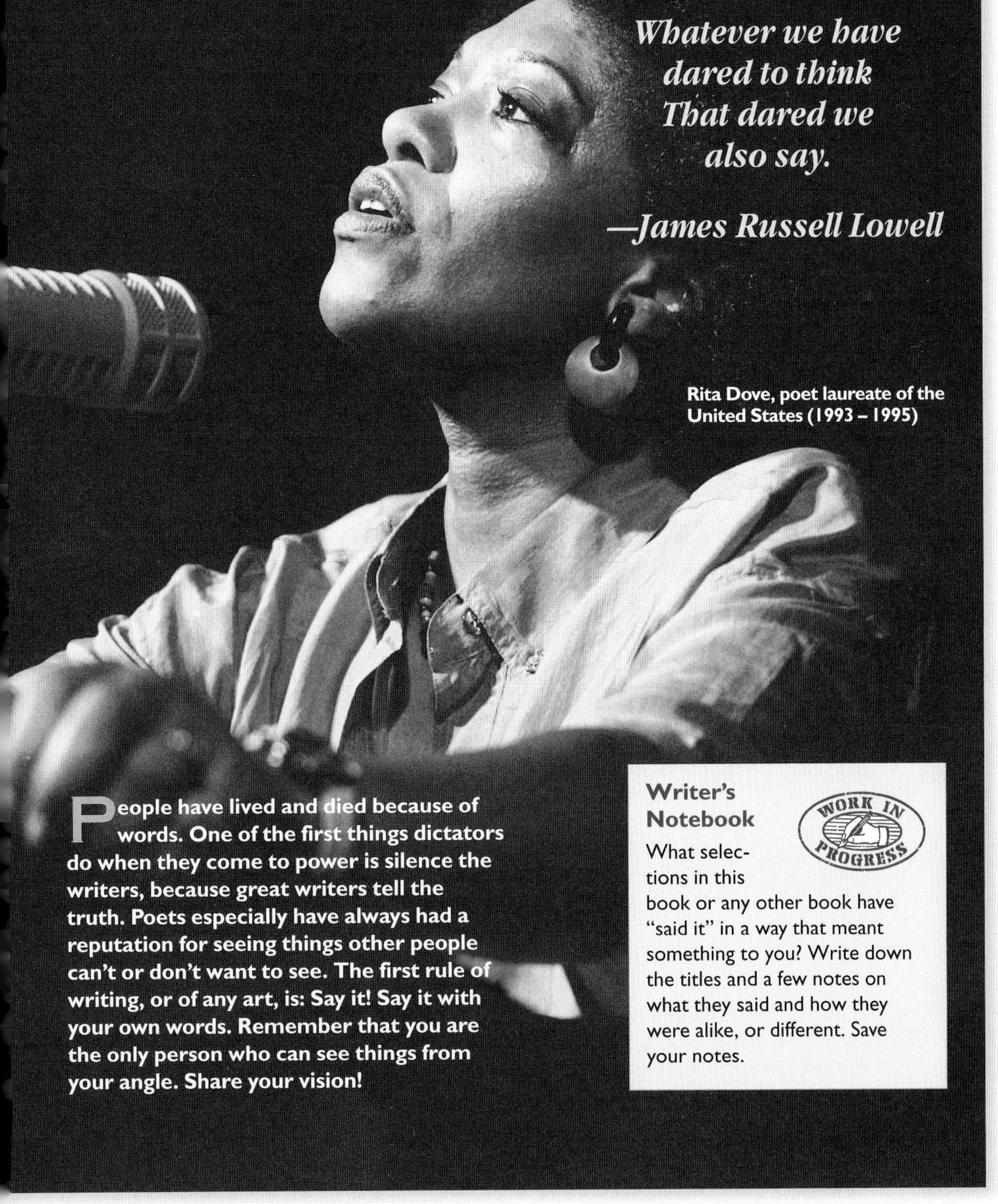

*Whatever we have
dared to think
That dared we
also say.*

—James Russell Lowell

**Rita Dove, poet laureate of the
United States (1993 – 1995)**

Responding to the Quotation

Tell students that James Russell Lowell (1819–1891) was an American author and reformer who spoke out freely on abolition, women's suffrage, the terrible conditions in factories, and capital punishment. Ask students what the quotation advises about speaking out. [Sample responses: Don't be afraid to say what you think; speak the truth.]

People have lived and died because of words. One of the first things dictators do when they come to power is silence the writers, because great writers tell the truth. Poets especially have always had a reputation for seeing things other people can't or don't want to see. The first rule of writing, or of any art, is: Say it! Say it with your own words. Remember that you are the only person who can see things from your angle. Share your vision!

Writer's Notebook

What selections in this book or any other book have "said it" in a way that meant something to you? Write down the titles and a few notes on what they said and how they were alike, or different. Save your notes.

RESPONDING TO THE ART

Rita Dove once said, "I never dreamed of becoming Poet Laureate, but I'm very happy to be who I am." Ask students to do research on the position of poet laureate in the United States. What is the purpose of a poet laureate? [Dove herself said that the poet laureate reminds us of the necessity of a cultural life in America.]

Writing Focus: Comparison-Contrast Essay

The following **Work in Progress** assignments build to a culminating **Writer's Workshop** at the end of the collection.

Writer's Notebook

Students might use a Venn diagram or a chart with the headings Alike and Different to organize their notes.

Resources

Elements of Literature

Tone

For additional instruction on tone, see *Literary Elements:*
- Transparency 15

Formal Assessment
- Literary Elements Test, p. 118

Elements of Literature

This feature defines tone and explains how it is conveyed in poetry—through diction, rhythms, and rhymes.

Mini-Lesson:
Tone

After explaining to students that tone refers to a speaker's attitude, ask students what kinds of tone they might hear in an author's voice. List these tones in the first column of a chart like the one below. Then ask students to think of an adjective or two that describes the mood, or atmosphere, they would expect such a tone to create. List these words in the second column of the chart.

Tone	Mood
sincere	comforting, uplifting
sarcastic	critical, angry
playful	joyous

As you complete this chart on an overhead transparency or on the chalkboard, students may realize that words describing tone are often the same or very close to words describing mood. This similarity suggests the power of an author's tone over the mood of a literary work.

TONE: It's an Attitude

Tone is not easy to define, because it's a quality of language that is suggested, not stated. Tone is a speaker's attitude—toward a subject or toward an audience. Tone can be sarcastic, teasing, critical, serious, playful, angry, admiring, ironic, and so on. (Painters can also reveal tones. The artist whose work is shown below takes a mocking tone toward the poor poet, who counts out his syllables in a leaky attic.)

When we speak out loud, we reveal tone by the way we use our voices and bodies. We use our voices to create emphasis—that is, we give importance to particular words by pausing and by varying our pitch and volume.

Take a simple sentence such as "School starts next week." By emphasizing different words and by varying your pitch, volume, and pauses, you can change your tone. Try it.

- School starts next week. (sincere)
- School starts next week? (disbelieving)
- School starts next week! (excited)
- School starts next week. (disgusted)

When a poem is printed on a page, we can't hear its tone in the way we can hear a tone of voice. But a poem does convey a tone, and until you've heard its tone, you haven't grasped the poet's complete message.

The Poor Poet (1839) by Carl Spitzweg. Oil.
Nationalgalerie, Staatliche Museen, Preussischer Kulturbesitz, Berlin.

Look at the Words

One way tone is revealed is through word choice, or **diction**. If a poet sees a red face and describes it as beefy, the tone is unsympathetic, maybe even sarcastic—no one

Skill Link

Speaking: Literary Interpretation
Getting the tone right is key in any oral literary presentation. Ask students to fill in the chart defining what the purpose, audience, occasion, and tone of their voice might be if they were reading each selection listed. When students have finished, ask them to change some factors. For example, how would the tone change if they were reading "Cinderella" not to children but to a college class?

Title	"Declaration of Independence"	"Cinderella"	an acceptance speech
Purpose			
Audience			
Occasion			
Tone of Voice			

by John Malcolm Brinnin

wants to look like a piece of steak. But if the poet describes the face as rosy or robust, the tone is positive and approving.

If a poet compares the world to a rose, the tone is approving—the world seems beautiful. But if a poet compares the world to a prickly cactus, the world does not seem so beautiful, and we sense a cynical tone.

If the poet describes a gaping wound as a minor scratch, we sense an ironic tone—we know the poet is saying one thing but really means something else.

William Wordsworth's tone was solemn when he said, "A slumber did my spirit seal." If you said, "I blanked out," you'd be saying more or less the same thing, but your tone would be completely different.

William Shakespeare was adoring when he asked his lover, "Shall I compare thee to a summer's day?" But when he stated in another poem, "My mistress' eyes are nothing like the sun," he was mocking

> **U**ntil you have heard a poem's tone, you haven't grasped the poet's complete message.

poets who use such exaggerated comparisons.

Listen to the Sounds

Rhythms and rhymes can also convey tone. If we hear a lively, bouncy rhythm and jingly rhymes, we know the poet is probably not feeling solemn about the subject. If a poem is slow-moving and stately, we figure the poet is not looking at the subject in a light, humorous way.

When Ogden Nash writes: "Any hound a porcupine nudges/Can't be blamed for harboring grudges," we laugh. The bouncy rhythm and jingly rhyme reveal to us at once that Nash is being silly and funny.

When you read a poem, try to hear the poet's tone of voice and what he or she is emphasizing. Look at the words the poet has chosen and listen to the way the poem sounds. Once you catch the poet's tone of voice, you become aware of a particular attitude, and the meaning of the poem will become clearer for you.

" 'Born in conservation,' if you don't mind. 'Captivity' has negative connotations."

Drawing by Handelsman; ©1993 The New Yorker Magazine, Inc.

ELEMENTS OF LITERATURE: TONE 587

Applying the Element

The following lines are excerpted from poems in this collection. Ask students to identify the tone they hear in each of the excerpts.

1. Degenerate sons and daughters,
   Life is too strong for you—
   It takes life to love Life.
   ("Lucinda Matlock")
   [Possible answers: anger, scorn, confidence.]
2. "Hope" is the thing with feathers—
   That perches in the soul—
   And sings the tune without the words—
   And never stops—at all—
   (" 'Hope' is the Thing with Feathers") [Possible answers: praise, happiness, joy.]
3. *Or does it explode?* ("Harlem")
   [Possible answers: anger, threat, despair.]

Tell students that, as they read the poems these lines are excerpted from, they will be better able to judge tone. Point out that tone can also vary within a poem.

Ask students to read the cartoon and to create sentences for the words *conservation* and *captivity*. Then ask students to explain how the choice of words affects the tone of each sentence. [Possible response: *Conservation* suggests and creates a positive tone, whereas *captivity* implies cruelty and exploitation and projects a negative tone.]

RESPONDING TO THE ART

German painter **Carl Spitzweg** (1808–1885) worked as a pharmacist until 1833, when an inheritance freed him to pursue his interest in art. *The Poor Poet* is his best-known work.

Activity. Ask students to list the details in the painting that show the artist is taking a mocking tone toward the poet. [Note the stereotyped view of the poet confined to a garret; the umbrella positioned to protect the poet from the leaking roof; the newspaper used as fuel for the stove. The poet is counting out his meters on his fingers.]

THE PUPPY

Make the Connection

Lesson from a Puppy

The most serious subjects are sometimes presented in a light way. Here the Russian writer Aleksandr Solzhenitsyn (sōl'zhə·nēt'sin) offers a simple description of a puppy who is permitted to play in the snow. Solzhenitsyn spent eight years in a labor camp for criticizing dictator Joseph Stalin, and his writings were banned in Russia for much of his lifetime. Knowing this makes us realize how much more serious than a romping puppy his real subject is.

Quickwrite

Write three metaphors in which you identify freedom with something else. Open with the words "Freedom is." Say what you think.

Keep your notes. For questions and activities on this poem, see pages 596–597.

Elements of Literature

A Prose Poem

Solzhenitsyn has written his light and delicate description in the form of a **prose poem**—a compact composition that creates the rhythms of free verse. Here, the writer uses the sight of a small puppy, unchained for a few moments on a snowy day, to convey a message. See if the words he uses could apply to a bear, the traditional symbol of Russia.

> A **prose poem** is a compact and rhythmic composition written in the form of a prose paragraph. Like any poem, a prose poem often presents its message by means of a vivid figure of speech.

MEET THE WRITER

He Wrote in a Prison Hut

Aleksandr Solzhenitsyn (1918–   ) was sentenced to prison for eight years when he was twenty-six years old because he wrote a letter to a friend criticizing the Russian dictator Joseph Stalin.

Denied writing materials, he managed to compose in his head and commit to memory a verse novel of 10,000 lines and a play of some 2,500 lines in iambic rhymed couplets. The first thing he did when released from prison was to write these compositions down on paper. Here is what he said later about his writing:

66 I myself had learned long ago in the camp to compose and to write as I marched in a column under escort; out on the frozen

OBJECTIVES

The Puppy/Harlem/"Hope" Is the Thing . . .

1. Read and interpret the poems
2. Identify characteristics of a prose poem
3. Analyze figures of speech
4. Distinguish denotations and connotations
5. Monitor comprehension
6. Express understanding through critical and creative writing, speaking/research, or art

SKILLS

Literary
- Identify characteristics of a prose poem
- Analyze figures of speech
- Distinguish denotations and connotations

Reading
- Monitor comprehension

Writing
- Interpret metaphors
- Write two related poems
- Write a prose poem

Speaking/Research
- Find material for an exchange on freedom of speech

Art
- Create a collage

Viewing/Representing
- Compare the subject and setting of a painting (ATE)
- Respond to a painting (ATE)

Planning

- **Block Schedule**
  Block Scheduling Lesson Plans with Pacing Guide
- **Traditional Schedule**
  Lesson Plans Including Strategies for English-Language Learners

Resources: Print and Media

Reading
- *Graphic Organizer for Active Reading,* pp. 55, 56, 57
- *Audio CD Library* Disk 16, Tracks 11, 12, 13

Elements of Literature
- *Literary Elements* Transparency 15 Worksheets, p. 46

Viewing and Representing
- *Viewing and Representing*

Fine Art Transparency 16
Fine Art Worksheet, p. 64
- *Visual Connections* Videocassette B, Segment 11

Assessment
- *Formal Assessment,* p. 115
- *Portfolio Management System,* p. 183
- *Standardized Test Preparation,* p. 76
- *Test Generator (One-Stop Planner CD-ROM)*

Internet
- go.hrw.com (keyword: LE0 9-11)

The Puppy

Aleksandr Solzhenitsyn

translated by Michael Glenny

In our back yard a boy keeps his little dog Sharik chained up, a ball of fluff shackled since he was a puppy.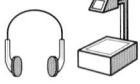

One day I took him some chicken bones that were still warm and smelled delicious. The boy had just let the poor dog off his lead to have a run round the yard. The snow there was deep and feathery; Sharik was bounding about like a hare, first on his hind legs, then on his front ones, from one corner of the yard to the other, back and forth, burying his muzzle in the snow.

He ran toward me, his coat all shaggy, jumped up at me, sniffed the bones—then off he went again, belly-deep in the snow.

I don't need your bones, he said. Just give me my freedom. . . .

steppe; in an iron foundry; in the hubbub of a prison hut. A soldier can squat on the ground and fall asleep immediately; a dog in freezing weather is as snug in his own shaggy coat as he would be by a stove, and I was equipped by nature to write anywhere. **"**

Solzhenitsyn's novel *One Day in the Life of Ivan Denisovich* (1962)—set in a forced-labor camp very much like the one he endured—made him famous. After the fall of Nikita Khrushchev in 1964, however, Solzhenitsyn's writings were banned from publication in the Soviet Union. Awarded the Nobel Prize for literature in 1970, he did not even dare to go to Sweden to accept it, for fear that he would not be allowed back into Russia.

In 1974, Solzhenitsyn was stripped of his Soviet citizenship and exiled. He moved to a small village in Vermont and continued to write and lecture. In 1990, his citizenship was restored, and Solzhenitsyn has returned to the land of his birth.

THE PUPPY **589**

Making the Connections

Cultural Connections

Freedom means different things to different people, but the word has added significance in a country where there is political oppression. When there is also government censorship, as there was in the Soviet Union (1922–1991), the meaning of freedom or the desire for it must be stated in oblique or metaphorical ways, as it is in this prose poem. Because the Soviet government put strict controls on all the arts

beginning in the 1920s, to write about freedom was to risk imprisonment.

The indirect expression of a forbidden desire for freedom is found in many cultures. Have students discuss African American spirituals. Few of these songs explicitly say "we want freedom"; instead, they speak of reaching the "promised land," being carried "home" by sweet chariots, or following the drinking gourd to the North.

T589

Summary ■ ■

In this short and deceptively simple poem, Hughes uses various figures of speech to evoke the feelings of disappointment, frustration, bitterness, and rage that are engendered by racial and social injustice. The poet offers five vivid similes to capture the essence of "a dream deferred." In the last line, he uses an implied metaphor to suggest that repressed rage is as dangerous as a ticking bomb. The poem should be read aloud: Many of the observations are phrased as rhetorical questions, and the final line is italicized for emphasis.

Resources

Viewing and Representing
Videocassette B, Segment 11
Available in Spanish and English. "The Harlem Renaissance" provides a brief introduction to Harlem's glorious past before it became the place reflected in Hughes's poem. For full lesson plans and worksheets, see *Visual Connections Teacher's Manual.*

Listening
Audio CD Library
A dramatic recording of this poem is provided in the *Audio CD Library:*
• CD 16, Track 12

Viewing and Representing
Fine Art Transparency
The fine art transparency of Aaron Douglas's *Aspects of Negro Life: From Slavery Through Reconstruction* connects especially well with Langston Hughes's poem, "Harlem." Have students discuss how art, like poetry, expresses a culture's feelings and concerns. See the *Viewing and Representing Transparencies and Worksheets:*
• Transparency 16
• Worksheet, p. 64

Before You Read

HARLEM

Make the Connection
"A Dream Deferred"
We all have dreams for the future. We all need to believe that these dreams can come true. But what happens when we must keep postponing these dreams? Langston Hughes has written a poem that answers the question "What happens to a dream deferred?"

Quickwrite
What happens when you have to give up or postpone a dream? Freewrite your answers to the question posed in the opening line of the poem. Use the sharpest words and images that you can think of.

Keep your notes. For questions and activities on this poem, see pages 596–597.

Elements of Literature
Figures of Speech
When the playwright Lorraine Hansberry wrote about the hopes and courage and defeats of an African American family, she found her title, *A Raisin in the Sun,* in one of the lines from this poem. By using a figure of speech, Hansberry chose to put aside literal meaning in favor of an imaginative connection.

Figures of speech are always based on comparisons and they are not literally true. A **simile** creates a comparison by using a connective word such as *like, as, than,* or *resembles.* A **metaphor** compares two unlike things without the use of these specific connective words. See if you can find the five similes that Hughes uses to describe a dream deferred. What powerful metaphor tells what the dream might become?

> **A** **figure of speech** is a word or phrase that describes one thing in terms of something very different from it.
>
> *For more on Figures of Speech, see pages 520–521 and the Handbook of Literary Terms.*

go.hrw.com
LE0 9-11

Slum Song (1944) by Hughie Lee-Smith. Oil on canvas.
Courtesy of the Golden State Mutual Life Insurance Company, African American Collection. © Hughie Lee-Smith/Licensed by VAGA, New York, NY.

Reaching All Students

Struggling Readers
The word *deferred* is one key to understanding this poem. Before they read the poem, have students define the word and suggest synonyms. [*Deferred* means "put off until later"; possible synonyms are postponed, delayed, procrastinated.] Struggling readers should have little difficulty with the language and syntax in the rest of the poem. But you may want to note the use of *sugar* as a verb and *sweet* as a noun.

English Language Learners
You may want to tell students that Harlem, a section of New York City established by the Dutch as Niew Haarlem in 1658, became a center of African American culture in the 1920s. After World War II, however, the area became economically depressed, and many young blacks such as those Hughes wrote about in *Montage of a Dream Deferred* (1951) faced futures without opportunity or hope.

Harlem  **A** 5

Langston Hughes

What happens to a dream deferred?

Does it dry up
like a raisin in the sun? **B**
Or fester like a sore—
And then run?
Does it stink like rotten meat?
Or crust and sugar over—
like a syrupy sweet?

10 Maybe it just sags **C**
like a heavy load.

Or does it explode? **D**

A **Cultural Connections**

Harlem

Although Harlem is rich in culture, the name still connotes to many a place where African Americans live with little social or economic opportunity. Hughes warns what might happen in a place where dreams are always out of reach.

B **Elements of Literature**

Figures of Speech: Similes

Ask students to find the similes in ll. 2–5 and tell what words or phrases they associate with each. [Possible answers: for "like a raisin in the sun," students might say "shriveled, dried up, parched, juiceless"; for "like a sore," they might say "a nagging hurt, an infected cut."]

C **Reading Skills and Strategies**

Visualizing

? What images come to your mind when you read these lines? [Sample responses: Someone bent over a heavy load of bricks or laundry; the tires of a truck bulging under the weight of a load of sand.]

D **Elements of Literature**

Figures of Speech: Metaphor

The last line of the poem is an implied metaphor. Students will need your help in understanding that through this metaphor, Hughes is identifying the people who cherish the dream with the dream itself. Ask students what the poet achieves by framing this comparison as a question. [Sample answers: He creates suspense; he suggests the threat of impending violence.]

RESPONDING TO THE ART

In the painting *Slum Song*, **Hughie Lee-Smith** (1915–1999), depicts a young musician playing a flute against a grim wall. The painting suggests the frail but fervent quality of hope that forever rises above a dehumanizing situation. **Activity.** Ask students to imagine the music the musician is playing and compare this sound to the setting of the painting. [Sample response: The music of a flute is clear and bright and contrasts with the bleak setting of the painting.]

Getting Students Involved

Cooperative Learning

Have students first read the poem silently, noting the images, or mental pictures, that form in their minds. Then have someone read the poem aloud. You might have one student read the title, the first line, and the last, and have other students read each of the five similes (ll. 2–3, 4–5, 6, 7–8, and 9–10). Ask students to share their mental pictures and to tell what words and phrases triggered those images.

Using Students' Strengths

Intrapersonal Learners

The ability to understand and express our emotions and goals is an important life skill. Anger or frustration often results from not being able to successfully transfer feelings into words. Have students write briefly in their notebooks about the following: an aspiration or hope that they cherished, how having this "dream" made them feel, whether it was realized or not.

About the Author. As a young man, Hughes was determined to create opportunities for himself that he had only dreamed of in childhood. He was getting ready to sail to Africa as a crew member when he decided to pick up a box of books that he had left behind in Harlem. When Hughes looked through the box, he realized that the books were only reminders of past frustrations and disappointments, and he threw them away. "I wanted to be a man on my own, control my own life, and go my own way. I was twenty-one."

A Critic's Comment. Hughes lived in Harlem, where he viewed broken dreams firsthand. When he composed this poem, which was published in 1951, the tensions that would lead to the civil rights movement were mounting. In the following passage, Arnold Rampersad, Hughes's biographer, describes the circumstances influencing the composition of "Harlem": "From [Hughes's] townhouse at 20 East 127th Street, not far from the steamy intersection of Lenox Avenue and 125th Street, Hughes listened to the rising rhetoric of integration . . . looked out on the detritus of cracked promises and broken dreams, and warned of a coming disintegration."

MEET THE WRITER
Speaking to People's Hearts

Langston Hughes (1902–1967) was voted class poet before he had ever written a single poem. But the position inspired him to write some poems—and he went on to become one of the most important American writers of the twentieth century. Hughes broke barriers in writing and in race relations—bringing the blues, jazz rhythms, and street slang into American literature and gaining an audience of millions of people of every race. In an early collection of his poems, he wrote:

66 . . . I have felt that there has been a distinct lack of rhymed poems dramatizing current racial interests in simple, understandable verse, pleasing to the ear, and suitable for reading aloud. . . . I have felt that much of our poetry has been aimed at the heads of the highbrows, rather than at the hearts of the people. 99

Hughes, in his boldly different poems, lets ordinary people speak for themselves. His poems are often written in slang—his speakers say what is on their minds and they say it in the language they use every day. As might be expected, Hughes had to put up with a lot of scorn: "Langston Hughes's Book of Poems Trash," said a Pittsburgh *Courier* headline long ago.

Just before he died Hughes asked:

66 What is poetry? 99

And then he answered his own question:

66 It is the human soul entire squeezed like a lemon into atomic words. 99

A story by Hughes appears on page 120.

Crossing the Curriculum

History
Direct students to locate and read Martin Luther King, Jr.'s "I Have a Dream" speech. Then pose the following question: "Has King's dream been fulfilled or is it still a dream deferred?" Students should research and identify specific events, such as civil rights marches or legislation, that have enabled African Americans to achieve equal rights. Have them organize and convert this information into a time line and state their conclusions in a short paragraph.

Architecture
Although Hughes paints a grim picture of Harlem in this poem, the neighborhood is both culturally and historically rich. This section of New York contains some of the city's finest examples of row houses. Suggest that students find out what row houses are and sketch what they look like in Harlem or in other areas of the country.

Music
Hughes said this poem was marked by "conflicting changes, sudden nuances, sharp and impudent interjections, broken rhythms, and passages sometimes in the manner of a jazz session, sometimes the popular song, punctuated by the riffs, runs, breaks, and disc-tortions of the music of a community in transition." To test this statement, play jazz music associated with Harlem at that time, including works by Louis Armstrong, Bessie Smith, and Cab Calloway.

Langston Hughes on the IRT

A Poem Arouses Many Feelings.

JOE SEXTON

The New York City Transit Authority's program is called "Poetry in Motion," and on this particular morning eight lines of Langston Hughes rumble along the length of the IRT No. 3 line.

> Sometimes a crumb falls
> From the tables of joy
> Sometimes a bone
> Is flung
> To some people
> Love is given
> To others
> Only heaven.

The poem, titled "Luck," is in the last days of its singular urban life on Car No. 2000, which sits awash in filtered morning sunlight in the outdoor New Lots Avenue station in Brooklyn. It is scheduled to be taken down, replaced by poems No. 26 and 27 in the series that began sixteen months ago in the subways.

Wendy Richards is the first person to glance at the poem poster this morning. She reads it quietly and then both smiles and cries. Ms. Richards is two hours late for work. She had spent the morning attending to the details of the death of a neighbor who used to ride the subway with her. Lois Russell, who had talked with Ms. Richards recently about the Hughes poem, had died in her sleep only hours before. She was forty-five years old.

"She was with me yesterday," Ms. Richards said of her neighbor. "We both loved the poem. It seems full of knowledge, and it's nice to be offered a bit of it."

The No. 3 train courses through the cold. There are stops at Van Siclen Avenue and then Pennsylvania Avenue. The poem is posted above the exit doors in the center of the car, helping to frame a frozen East New York. The car at nearly 11:00 A.M. is crowded, rush hour evidently as free-form as the verse.

Lakiesha McNeil, twenty-two years old, sits across from the poem, along with her husband. She does not read poetry beyond what interrupts her stares on the subway. She re-reads "Luck" and waits a long time before talking.

"I can't express it, but I get it," Ms. McNeil says of the poem. "Everybody has luck, although sometimes you can't be happy. Everything is not good in this world."

The world of the moment for Car No. 2000 changes with each stop. Daylight vanishes as the train descends again under-ground. Above, the neighbor-hoods are shifting, and the population of the car undergoes the constant, arbitrary, oddball integration that happens throughout the city.

Hughes, who died in 1967, lived in New York for significant parts of his life, and "mightily did he use the streets," another poet, Gwendolyn Brooks, once said of him. "He found its multiple heart, its tastes, smells, alarms, formulas, flowers, garbage, and convulsions," she said.

Now on this day, on this train, a construction worker stands under "Luck" and never happens to look up. A man with a briefcase rummages through computer printouts in his lap. A mother and child peer curiously into a black-ened window, each peacefully deciphering the darkness.

—from *The New York Times*
March 2, 1994

HARLEM 593

Connecting Across Texts

Connecting with "Harlem"

After students have read the article by Joe Sexton, ask them to write briefly in their journals about one of the following ideas.

- the ways in which people let their thoughts wander while traveling on a bus, subway, or train
- what people daydream about

Discuss with students how the Transit Authority's program, "Poetry in Motion," might be one solution to the rage and despair depicted in Hughes's poem. Poetry helps people to articulate their emotions. It makes them aware that there are other people who have similar feelings and therefore makes them feel less isolated.

Connections

This article from *The New York Times* focuses on a program called "Poetry in Motion" that was established by the New York City Transit Authority. (See the poem on p. 555.) The aim of this program is to expose more people to poetry. The program posts poems in subway trains, offering tired and busy commuters a chance to read something other than advertisements. The writer interviewed a couple of subway commuters—an older woman on her way to work, a young couple in their 20s—to get their responses to the poem "Luck" by Langston Hughes.

A Critical Thinking
Speculating
❓ Why do you suppose the Transit Authority chose "Poetry in Motion" as the name for its poetry program? [While the phrase is usually used in a fig-urative sense, the Transit Authority has used it in a literal sense—poems being transported on subways.]

B Appreciating Language
Word Choice
❓ What are some synonyms for the word *luck*? [chance, fortune, fate, coinci-dence] *Luck* is a more common word than many of its synonyms. We speak of being lucky in love, lucky in life, lucky at work, etc. Also, the word *luck* car-ries few philosophical or religious overtones; it suggests a totally random influence.

C Struggling Readers
Rereading
If students lose their focus, ask them to go back and reread. Sometimes an arti-cle may seem confusing when it shifts emphasis, as this article does in para-graph three when it zooms in on Wendy Richards. Explain to students that rereading allows them to pinpoint a digression or transition. So when a writer turns in a new direction, stu-dents can make sure that they are following along.

D Reading Skills and Strategies
Finding the Main Idea
After students have read the news feature, ask them what they think the main idea of Sexton's article is. What facts or anecdotes does he supply to support this main idea? [A wide variety of people are able to appreciate poetry; the interviews with commuters support this idea.]

Dickinson gives hope feathers and likens it to a bird whose song never stops. Both are fragile yet able to endure the harshest conditions and warm those who hear their music. Also like the bird, hope gives freely and asks for nothing in return.

Resources

Listening

Audio CD Library

A recording of this poem is provided in the *Audio CD Library:*
• CD 16, Track 13

FROM THE EDITOR'S DESK

The expression of hopes, dreams, and aspirations tie together the three poems in this cluster. The downside of having dreams, though, is that one is often disappointed—the puppy is able to run free for only a brief period, the society that yearns for justice explodes in rage. We chose Dickinson's poem to end the cluster on an upbeat note—even in rough weather, hope lives.

BROWSING IN THE FILES

About the Author. Like most women of her time, Emily Dickinson spent a great deal of time keeping house, a task she defined as "a prickly art." Her work included drawing water, keeping fires lit, sewing, gardening, caring for chickens, filling lamps, and making candles. She drafted some of her poems on paper bags or on the backs of recipes and often stayed up late to continue writing.

A Critic's Comment. The biographer Richard Sewall says that Emily Dickinson "does not tell us how to live . . . so much as what it feels like to be alive." She defines emotions including both joy and longing with metaphors that startle the reader with their clarity. For example, "Exultation is the going of an inland soul to sea" or "Longing is like the Seed/That wrestles in the Ground."

Before You Read

"HOPE" IS THE THING WITH FEATHERS

Make the Connection

On Wings of Hope

Emily Dickinson says that hope doesn't use words. But *she* certainly does—special words, carefully chosen to bring hope alive—perched, feathered, singing—before our very eyes.

"In Extremity," she says in this poem. Her poems are full of extremities—sorrow, grief, loss, death, joy, exaltation, despair, frustration, loneliness, unrequited love, longing—extremities she might not have been able to bear, much less put down on paper, had hope not perched in her soul, as it does in each of ours.

Elements of Literature

Denotation and Connotation: A Way with Words

This poem about hope has a calm tone, at least when it's talking about hope. But wherever hope is, there's got to be trouble to begin with. And there's plenty of trouble here. The words *gale* and *storm* literally mean "a strong wind" and "a disturbance of the atmosphere." These are the dictionary definitions—the **denotations** of the words. But what do you also get with your usual gale and storm? **Connotations,** that's what. Thunder. Lightning. Rain, snow, hail, sleet. Howling wind. Downed trees. Snapped power lines. Sunken ships. Flattened buildings. Flooded fields. Destruction. Death.

Whenever we use a word, we use all its connotations— the associations and feelings that are attached to it. Poets, who know words well, choose them carefully.

> **D**enotation is the literal, dictionary definition of a word. **Connotation** is all the meanings, associations, or emotions suggested by a word.
>
> *For more on Connotation, see the Handbook of Literary Terms.*

For a biography of Emily Dickinson, see page 523.

Reading Skills and Strategies

Dialogue with the Text

As you read this poem, track your responses. Ask questions, note details that match your own experiences, and respond to Dickinson's words as they speak to you.

Keep your notes. For questions and activities on this poem, see pages 596–597.

go.hrw.com
LEO 9-11

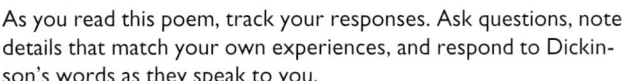

Reaching All Students

English Language Learners

Some students may be confused by Dickinson's use of capital letters. Explain that this is the exact way her poems were written. No one knows if the capitalization was deliberate or if it was at times unintentional. Several common words are capitalized in this poem—*Gale, Bird, Sea, Extremity,* and *Me.* After students have read the poem, discuss why Dickinson might have chosen to draw attention to these words.

Using Students' Strengths

Visual Learners

Ask students to create a collage or montage composed of images suggested by the poem. Students may draw images or cut them out from magazines such as *Discover* or *National Geographic.* They can also paste on various bits of objects such as cloth or dried flowers. Have them use words or lines from the poem in their collage or as captions. Suggest that students make a list of images in the poem before beginning the project.

Bird Singing in the Moonlight (1938–1939) by Morris Graves.
Tempera and watercolor on mulberry paper (26 ¾″ x 30 ⅛″, 68 cm. x 76.5 cm.).

The Museum of Modern Art, New York. Purchase. Photograph © 1997 The Museum of Modern Art, New York.

"Hope"
Is the Thing
with Feathers

Emily Dickinson

"Hope" is the thing with feathers— **A**
That perches in the soul—
And sings the tune without the words—
And never stops—at all—

5   And sweetest—in the Gale—is heard—
And sore must be the storm— **B**
That could abash the little Bird **C**
That kept so many warm—

I've heard it in the chillest land—
10 And on the strangest Sea—
Yet, never, in Extremity, **D**
It asked a crumb—of Me. **E**

"HOPE" IS THE THING WITH FEATHERS **595**

Skill Link

T595

MAKING MEANINGS

First Thoughts

1. Responses will vary. Students may say "The Puppy" describes the exuberance or relief they have felt; "Harlem" describes their sense of dashed hopes; and "Hope" conveys their optimism.

Shaping Interpretations

2. Responses will vary. Students might say that words like *chained, shackled,* and *freedom* are details that suggest the poem is about the loss of liberty during Soviet rule.

3. Possible answers: The dream is equality and justice; the dream is just to be able to realize one's full potential.

4. Hughes compares a dream deferred to a raisin in the sun, a sore, rotten meat, a syrupy sweet, and a heavy load.

5. The final metaphor suggests that unfulfilled dreams generate destructive energy like that of a ticking bomb. Students may say that people who are oppressed for generations could "explode" with rage.

6. The metaphor states that hope is a bird. Student reactions will vary.

7. Possible responses: The word *strangest* brings to mind foreign or exotic locations; the word *chillest* brings to mind physical cold, as well as the ideas of unfriendly places and loneliness. Other words: farthest, deepest; coldest, northernmost.

Extending the Texts

8. Possibilities include Moses, Joan of Arc, Martin Luther King, Jr., Mohandas Gandhi, Nelson Mandela.

9. Some dreams are still postponed for people who lack equal opportunities.

10. Hope keeps up morale during wars, natural disasters, and personal tragedies.

11. Poems might be displayed on fences around construction sites, the walls of school buildings, bulletin boards in public buildings like post offices, places where people wait in line such as fast-food restaurants, or even on the Internet. Suggested poems will vary.

T596

MAKING MEANINGS

THE PUPPY
HARLEM
"HOPE" IS THE THING WITH FEATHERS

First Thoughts

[respond]

1. Which of the three poems comes closest to describing feelings you've had?

Shaping Interpretations

[generalize]

2. Look back at the details in Solzhenitsyn's prose poem. Do you think this is only about a puppy or do you think it refers to a broader subject? Find details to justify your response.

[conclude]

3. The word *deferred* in line 1 of "Harlem" means "delayed," "postponed." What is the dream that is being postponed here?

[identify]

4. What are the five **similes** that Hughes uses to restate the first question—that is, what does he compare a "dream deferred" to?

[interpret]

5. What final **metaphor** is implied when Hughes uses the word *explode*—what are we to understand that the dream might become? Why might a "dream deferred" one day explode?

[identify]

6. What **metaphor** does Dickinson use to speak of hope throughout her poem? What do you think of her metaphor?

[interpret]

 7. Think about why Dickinson chose the word *strangest* to describe the sea and *chillest* to describe the land. What **connotations** do these words have for you? What feelings and associations do they evoke? Check your notes for your first reactions. What other words could Dickinson have chosen—words that would have different connotations for you?

Extending the Texts

[extend]

8. Solzhenitsyn's puppy prefers freedom to food. What people in history might agree with him?

[extend]

9. "Harlem" was published in 1951. What conditions still exist that make this poem relevant to people's lives today?

[connect]

10. Think back on Dickinson's poem: What "extremities" can you think of in which hope keeps people warm?

[extend]

11. Read the article "Langston Hughes on the IRT" (see **Connections** on page 593), about the Langston Hughes poem that was posted in the subway for busy commuters to enjoy. Where else might poems be displayed? Which poems that you've read would you recommend for a public display?

Assessing Learning

Check Test: True-False

"The Puppy"

1. Sharik is usually chained. [True]
2. Sharik prefers food to freedom. [False]

"Harlem"

3. According to the speaker, it is dangerous to defer a dream. [True]
4. The poet predicts what may happen. [True]

"'Hope' Is the Thing with Feathers"

5. The poet compares hope to a bird. [True]
6. The speaker has lost hope. [False]

Standardized Test Preparation

For practice with standardized test format specific to this selection, see:
• *Standardized Test Preparation*, p. 76

CHOICES: Building Your Portfolio

Writer's Notebook

1. Collecting Ideas for a Comparison-Contrast Essay

Finding a topic. The first thing to do when you are preparing to **compare** two texts (see the Writer's Workshop on page 614) is to look at their elements. Look, for example, at the **metaphor** in Hughes's poem "Harlem" and the one in Dickinson's poem on hope. Take notes now on these metaphors: Tell what the poets are basing their comparisons on and how each metaphor makes you feel. Save your notes. (The model below is based on other poems.)

Metaphors
- Hughes's "Mother to Son" uses metaphor of stairways to describe life. Easy life = crystal, hard life = battered.
- Makes me feel awe, admiration.
- Frost's "Road Not Taken" uses road as metaphor for life.
- Makes me feel nervous about making choices.

Creative Writing

2. Your Own Dream, Your Own Hope

Write two poems. One should be about your own dream or dreams and should open with the words "I dream." The other should be about what happens when those dreams are taken away or "deferred." (Be sure to check the notes you made for the Quickwrite on page 590 before you read Hughes's poem.) Before you write your poems, think carefully about your **tone.** Here are some emotions you might want to convey: *anger, gladness, cheerfulness, joy, sorrow, confidence, gratitude, awe.*

Creative Writing

3. Your Own Prose Poem

Solzhenitsyn probably got the idea for his **prose poem** on page 589 when he saw the puppy frolicking in the snow. Write a prose poem of your own about freedom. Base it on something you've observed in everyday life. Be sure to check the notes you made for the Quickwrite on page 588 for ideas.

Speaking/Research

4. A "Speak-in"

Contribute quotations, poems, speeches, and news stories to a class freedom-of-speech collection. Share that collection in a "speak-in," in which you read aloud your selections and then exchange views on the freedom of speech guaranteed to Americans under the First Amendment.

Art

5. "I Dream" Collage

Using lines or ideas from the notes you took for the Quickwrite on page 590, plus drawings or found images as illustrations, create your personal "Dream" collage. Then, with your classmates, contribute to a "We Have Dreams" class poster.

Grading Timesaver

Rubrics for each assignment appear in the *Portfolio Management System,* p. 183.

CHOICES: Building Your Portfolio

1. **Writer's Notebook** Remind students to save their work for the Writer's Workshop on p. 614. Have the class suggest elements that the two poems have in common and ways in which they differ.
2. **Creative Writing** You might have a class discussion on tone. Explain that tone is conveyed through a writer's choice of words and details. Different readers might pick up different tones.
3. **Creative Writing** Help students expand on the ideas in their Quickwrites. Some students might enjoy working with partners.
4. **Speaking/Research** To help develop students' research skills, have them search a CD-ROM encyclopedia for information on the First Amendment. If possible, have them demonstrate their findings to the class as a multimedia electronic presentation. They will need an active matrix LCD panel and a high-intensity overhead projector.
5. **Art** Be sure that all students have access to visual resource materials. Invite students to bring in newspapers and magazines that the entire class can share.

OBJECTIVES
1. Read and interpret the poem
2. Analyze tone
3. Express understanding through critical or creative writing

SKILLS
Literary
• Analyze tone
Writing
• Describe the tone in two poems
• Write a poem modeled on the selection

Planning

• **Block Schedule**
  Block Scheduling Lesson Plans with Pacing Guide
• **Traditional Schedule**
  Lesson Plans Including Strategies for English-Language Learners
• **One-Stop Planner**
  CD-ROM with Test Generator

Before You Read

LEGAL ALIEN/EXTRANJERA LEGAL

Make the Connection

Between Worlds

Each of us belongs to several different worlds—of gender, ethnicity, economic status. The combinations are infinite. The speaker in "Legal Alien" is a Mexican American who lives in two worlds at once—the world of her Mexican ancestry and heritage and the so-called Anglo world all around her. A legal alien is a person who enters the United States via legal channels.

Quickwrite

Think of all the worlds you belong to: worlds of home, family, school, church, sports, friends. Make lists in which you cite at least three ways you feel or behave in two of your worlds. A sample is started below.

My Worlds	
School	Sports
Sometimes feel slow.	Feel special, successful, free.

Keep your notes. For questions and activities on this poem, see page 600.

Elements of Literature

Tone: Look at Word Choice

Bilingual, bicultural. These seem like innocent, OK things to be. But what follows in this poem is anything but calm. Look at the choice of words: *exotic, inferior, definitely different, alien.* These are disturbing words—deliberately chosen by Pat Mora to let you know how passionate she feels.

When you read, you can't see the writer's face or gestures. You can't hear the writer's voice. So writers have to make words do the job of showing you how they feel—of getting across their **tone**. Tone may be simple or complicated—and very changeable.

> **T**one is the attitude a writer takes toward the audience, the subject, or a character. Tone can be conveyed through the writer's choice of words.
>
> *For more on Tone, see pages 586–587 and the Handbook of Literary Terms.*

 go.hrw.com
LEO 9-11

Resources: Print and Media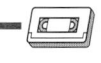

Reading
• *Graphic Organizers for Active Reading,* p. 58
• *Audio CD Library,* Disc 16, Tracks 14, 15

Writing and Language
• *Daily Oral Grammar*
  Transparency 40

Assessment
• *Portfolio Management System,* p. 185
• *Test Generator (One-Stop Planner CD-ROM)*

Internet
• go.hrw.com (keyword: LE0 9-11)

Legal Alien

Pat Mora

Bi-lingual, Bi-cultural, Ⓐ
able to slip from "How's life?"
to *"Me'stan volviendo loca,"*
able to sit in a paneled office
5   drafting memos in smooth English,
able to order in fluent Spanish
at a Mexican restaurant,
American but hyphenated,
viewed by Anglos as perhaps exotic,
10   perhaps inferior, definitely different,
viewed by Mexicans as alien
(their eyes say, "You may speak
Spanish but you're not like me"),
an American to Mexicans
15   a Mexican to Americans
a handy token
sliding back and forth
between the fringes of both worlds Ⓑ
by smiling
20   by masking the discomfort
of being pre-judged
Bi-laterally.

Extranjera legal

Pat Mora

Bi-lingüe, bi-cultural,
capaz de deslizarse de *"How's life?"*
a "Me'stan volviendo loca",
capaz de ocupar un despacho bien apuntado,
5   redactando memorandums en inglés liso,
capaz de ordenar la cena en español fluido
en restaurante mexicano,
americana pero con guión,
vista por los anglos como exótica,
10   quizás inferior, obviamente distinta,
vista por mexicanos como extranjera
(sus ojos dicen "Hablas español
pero no eres como yo"),
americana para mexicanos
15   mexicana para americanos
una ficha servible
pasando de un lado al otro
de los márgenes de dos mundos
sonriéndome
20   disfrazando la incomodidad
del pre-juicio
bi-lateralmente.

MEET THE WRITER

Beyond Borders

Pat Mora (1942–   )
maintains that people's
identities grow out of all
the worlds they inhabit—
the ones they inherit from the past as well as
the ones they encounter as they go through
life. Born and raised in the border town of El
Paso, Texas, Mora has spent her life observing
the interactions between Mexican and Anglo
cultures. While never denying the painful side
of bicultural existence, Mora stresses the
harmonies between the cultures—harmonies
that are the result of centuries of shared
living.

Often inspired by the high-desert
landscape of the Southwest as a source
of renewal and connection, Mora finds
differences between people less important than the things all cultures share—
living, loving, marrying, raising children,
working, growing old, and dying.

The poem "Legal Alien" is from *Chants*
(1984), Mora's first book of poems. Her
other books include *Communion* (1991), a
book of poems; *Tomas and the Library Lady*
(1989) and *A Birthday Basket for Tía* (1992),
both children's books. In 1997, she published
House of Houses, a memoir of her family.

LEGAL ALIEN/EXTRANJERA LEGAL **599**

Reaching All Students

English Language Learners

Invite Spanish-speaking students to read aloud
the Spanish version of the poem. Give students
an opportunity to discuss the advantages of being
familiar with more than one language or culture.

Advanced Learners

If you have any advanced learners who are proficient in Spanish, ask them to cover the English
version, write their own translations of the
Spanish text, and then discuss any areas where
their word choices differ from Mora's.

Summary ▪▪

The speaker describes the difficult position of people like herself, who are both
bilingual and bicultural. Although she
can function effectively in either an
"Anglo" or a Mexican context, she does
not feel fully at home in either of them.
She straddles two worlds that are separate and suspicious of each other, and
both worlds view her, at least to some
extent, with prejudice. The speaker's
bilingual background is reinforced by
the two versions of the poem, one in
English and one in Spanish.

Resources

Listening

Audio CD Library

A recording of this poem is provided in
the *Audio CD Library*:
• Disc 16, Tracks 14, 15

FROM THE EDITOR'S DESK

Since this poem addresses the
issue of belonging, we felt it was
particularly relevant for high
school students. Feeling that one
is part of a group, that one is
accepted is important to everyone. But during the teen years,
cliques and peer groups are an
especial source of both joy and
frustration. Be sure to extend the
issue of belonging beyond the specific situation of this poem.

Ⓐ Appreciating Language
Punctuation

These two words are usually not
hyphenated. Ask students to speculate
why the poet used this unorthodox
punctuation. [Possible answers: She
wanted to accent the word *bi,* meaning
"two"; she wanted to show the separate
parts of the words.]

Ⓑ Elements of Literature
Tone

❓ What does "the fringes" mean? [The
word refers to something that is at the
edges, borders, or margins; something
considered peripheral.] What do you
judge the speaker's tone of voice to be
when she says that she is "between the
fringes of both worlds"? [Possible
responses: Her tone suggests she is discontented; her tone seems critical.]

T599

MAKING MEANINGS

First Thoughts

1. Students may cite experiences in which they also felt out of place.

Shaping Interpretations

2. Anglos view her as exotic, inferior, and different. Mexicans view her with suspicion.
3. The speaker is hiding discomfort at being prejudged.
4. In the sense of "symbol," *token* suggests that the speaker has no individual identity or value; in the sense of "something used in place of money," *token* suggests that the speaker is a medium of exchange between cultures.
5. Sample responses: *Exotic, inferior,* and *alien* (ll. 9–13) suggest a slightly sarcastic or impatient tone; *token, fringes, discomfort,* and *prejudged* (ll. 16–21) suggest an angry tone.
6. *Bi-lingüe, bi-cultural, memorandums, fluido, restaurante mexicano, americana, exótica* and *inferior.*

Connecting with the Text

7. *Hyphenated* means the speaker has a dual cultural background. Self-descriptions may include European-American and African-American.
8. Students may cite cases in which older people dismissed them as "kids."

Grading Timesaver

Rubrics for each assignment appear on p. 185 in the *Portfolio Management System.*

CHOICES: Building Your Portfolio

1. **Writer's Notebook** Remind students to save their work for the Writer's Workshop on p. 614.
2. **Creative Writing** Suggest students use different colored pens or pencils for each cultural perspective.

T600

MAKING MEANINGS
LEGAL ALIEN/EXTRANJERA LEGAL

First Thoughts

[respond]

1. How would you respond to these questions: How am I like or unlike the person in "Legal Alien"? What could we learn from each other?

Shaping Interpretations

[summarize]

2. How do "Anglos" view the speaker? How do Mexicans view her?

[infer]

3. According to lines 20–22, what is the speaker "masking," or hiding?

[identify]

4. *Token* is a word with **multiple meanings**. In line 16, what two meanings of *token* is Mora suggesting?

[interpret]

5. Of the following adjectives, which two best describe the speaker's **tone** in this poem: *sad, impatient, understanding, critical, angry, amused, accepting*? Which particular words and phrases tip you off to the speaker's tone?

[identify]

6. English and Spanish may have more in common than you think. Take a look at the Spanish version of "Legal Alien"—"Extranjera legal." List the words you recognize as similar to English words.

Connecting with the Text

[extend]

7. The speaker says "American but hyphenated." What does she mean? What hyphenated words, if any, might describe your own identity?

[connect]

8. Have you ever been prejudged? In what ways do people prejudge others?

CHOICES: Building Your Portfolio

Writer's Notebook

1. Collecting Ideas for a Comparison-Contrast Essay

Looking at tones. One way to compare two texts is to look at how each uses a common element. Make a list of adjectives to describe the tones you hear in Hughes's poem on page 591 and in Mora's poem. Jot down details from each poem that contribute to that tone. Save your notes.

Creative Writing

2. Use Mora as a Model

Look at the notes you made for the Quickwrite on page 598. Use your notes and any additions as the basis of a poem of your own, about *your* worlds. Here is a framework you might want to use for your poem.

In the world of _____ I am _____.
In the world of _____ I am _____.
Some people think _____
But I am really _____.
Find specific things to say in your poem, as Mora does. Think also of your word choice: What **tone** do you want to give your poem? Create a suitable title for your poem.

Assessing Learning

Check Test: True-False

1. The speaker knows only a little English. [False]
2. The speaker is Mexican American. [True]
3. Most people accept the speaker as an American. [False]
4. When the speaker smiles, it always means she is happy. [False]
5. The speaker thinks of herself as a victim of prejudice. [True]

Standardized Test Preparation

For practice in proofreading and editing, see
• *Daily Oral Grammar,* Transparency 40

Before You Read

THE ROAD NOT TAKEN

Make the Connection

"If Only…"

"If only I'd been born a genius. Or staggeringly beautiful. Or fabulously talented or rich. Or made this decision instead of that one. Or had gone to a different school. Then my life would be different."

Quickwrite

Think of a turning point in your life (or in someone else's life)—moving to a new place, meeting a special person, learning a sport, changing your mind about something, having someone help you at the right time. Go back to that moment and pretend it never happened. Make notes on how you imagine your life might have been different if that turning point had never happened.

Keep your notes. For questions and activities on this poem, see pages 604–605.

Elements of Literature

Verbal Irony

Verbal irony is a contrast between what a writer or a speaker says and what is really meant. Verbal irony can range from gentle to sarcastic. Robert Frost is a master of the subtle uses of irony. Perhaps that's why he called "The Road Not Taken" a tricky poem. Read it several times and try to figure out exactly what Frost's attitude is about life and the choices we make.

> **I**rony is the contrast between expectation and reality. In **verbal irony,** the writer or the speaker says one thing but really means something different.
>
> *For more on Irony, see pages 212–213 and the Handbook of Literary Terms.*

For a biography of Robert Frost, see page 540.

go.hrw.com
LE0 9-11

Summary ■ ■ ■

When the speaker encounters a forked path in the woods, he is undecided about which road to take, for both seem just as fair. After long consideration, the speaker chooses the road less traveled. Reflecting on his decision, the speaker realizes that, someday, this choice will have made all the difference.

Resources ———

Listening
Audio CD Library
A recording of this poem is provided in the *Audio CD Library*:
• Disc 16, Track 16

Ⓐ Struggling Readers
Syntax
Explain that *syntax* is simply the technical term for sentence structure. Words in poetry often appear in a different order than in common, everyday speech. "Long I stood" is an example of this unexpected word order. Ask students if they can explain why the poet may have placed *stood* at the end of the line. [Possible responses: The poet wanted to rhyme *stood* with *wood* (l. 1) and *could* (l. 4); the rhythm of the poem called for a strong beat at the end of the line.]

Ⓑ Elements of Literature
Verbal Irony
❓ What does the speaker really mean in this exclamatory statement? Does the speaker believe he will ever come back? [Possible answers: The speaker means the opposite of what he says and is being ironic; the speaker ironically contrasts youthful expectations with mature knowledge.]

Ⓒ Reading Skills and Strategies
Making Inferences
❓ Why do you think Frost titled this poem "The Road Not Taken," rather than "The Road Taken"? [Possible answers: Perhaps the speaker remains curious about how things would have turned out had he made a different choice; perhaps he regrets his choice.]

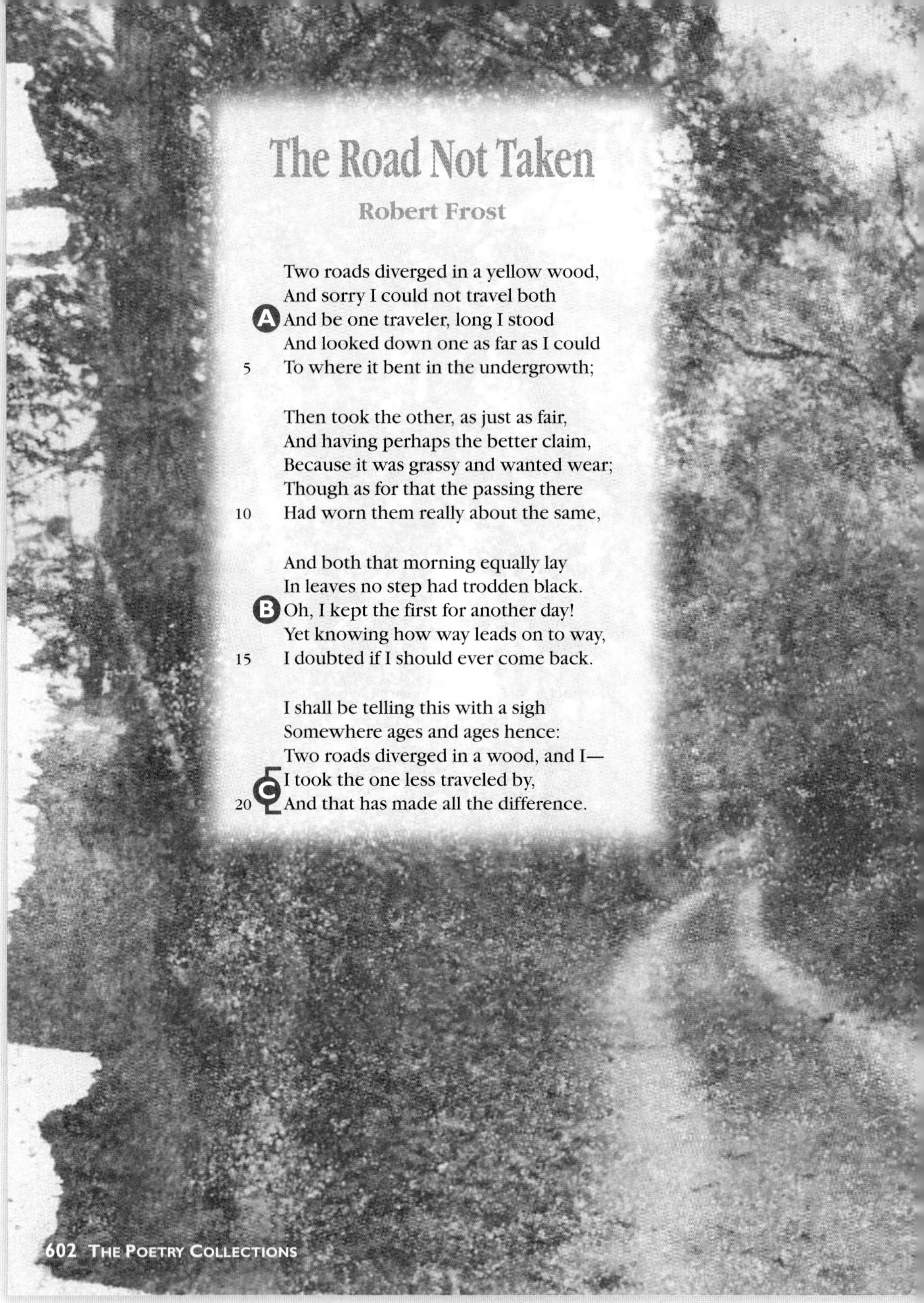

T602

The Road Not Taken
Robert Frost

Two roads diverged in a yellow wood,
And sorry I could not travel both
Ⓐ And be one traveler, long I stood
And looked down one as far as I could
5   To where it bent in the undergrowth;

Then took the other, as just as fair,
And having perhaps the better claim,
Because it was grassy and wanted wear;
Though as for that the passing there
10   Had worn them really about the same,

And both that morning equally lay
In leaves no step had trodden black.
Ⓑ Oh, I kept the first for another day!
Yet knowing how way leads on to way,
15   I doubted if I should ever come back.

I shall be telling this with a sigh
Somewhere ages and ages hence:
Two roads diverged in a wood, and I—
Ⓒ I took the one less traveled by,
20   And that has made all the difference.

602 THE POETRY COLLECTIONS

Taking a Second Look

Review: Monitor Your Reading—Ask Questions

Remind students that successful readers stop occasionally as they're reading to monitor their comprehension of the text. If they have trouble understanding something, one "fix-up" strategy they can use is asking questions. For example, they might ask: "What exactly don't I understand? Is a particular line or phrase confusing?"

Activity

1. Have students stop reading at the end of the first stanza and ask a question about the speaker or what is happening in the poem.

2. Repeat this strategy at the end of each stanza. Remind students, however, that they cannot answer all questions with certainty and that a question can often have more than one answer.

3. After students finish reading, have them discuss how asking and answering questions helped them better understand the poem.

Connections | A LETTER

Crossing Paths

Robert Frost

Robert Frost wrote this letter to the literary editor Susan Hayes Ward.

Plymouth, New Hampshire
10 February 1912

Dear Miss Ward:

. . . Two lonely crossroads that themselves cross each other I have walked several times this winter without meeting or overtaking so much as a single person on foot or on runners. The practically unbroken condition of both for several days after a snow or a blow proves that neither is much traveled. Judge then how surprised I was the other evening as I came down one to see a man, who to my own unfamiliar eyes and in the dusk looked for all the world like myself, coming down the other, his approach to the point where our paths must intersect being so timed that unless one of us pulled up we must inevitably collide. I felt as if I was going to meet my own image in a slanting mirror. Or say I felt as we slowly converged on the same point with the same noiseless yet laborious strides as if we were two images about to float together with the uncrossing of someone's eyes. I verily expected to take up or  absorb this other self and feel the stronger by the addition for the three-mile journey home. But I didn't go forward to the touch. I stood still in wonderment and let him pass by; and that, too, with the fatal omission of not trying to find out by a comparison of lives and immediate and remote interests what could have brought us by crossing paths to the same point in the wilderness at the same moment of nightfall. Some purpose I doubt not, if we could but have made it out. I like a coincidence almost as well as an incongruity. . . .

Nonsensically yours, **B**

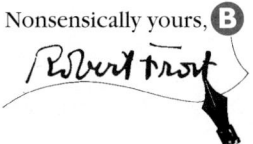

THE ROAD NOT TAKEN **603**

T603

MAKING MEANINGS

First Thoughts

1. Students may say they have often wanted to follow two paths simultaneously. When comparing their feelings to those of the speaker, they might say that they agonize less when making a decision.

Shaping Interpretations

2. The word *woods* suggests a place with lots of trees that keep one from seeing ahead. (Woods are commonly used in fairy tales as places where people are lost or abandoned.) Similarly, decision making is not always orderly or clear.

3. The speaker is telling himself he can return to the same choice and take the other route the next time. But he later realizes (ll. 14–15) that one choice leads to others, so each choice is final.

4. Possible responses: The choice has had a lasting effect; it has influenced other choices along the way.

5. In l. 8 the speaker says the road is not traveled and in ll. 9–10 he says people have passed there. Another contradiction is that in ll. 11–12, the speaker says the paths are equally untrodden, but in l. 19, the path taken is described as "less traveled by."

6. Sample answers: Lines 16–17 have a regretful tone; l. 20 has a positive tone.

Connecting with the Text

7. People who travel less common paths may experience some loneliness or social criticism, but perhaps develop a greater sense of pride or accomplishment. Responses about acquaintances will vary, but stress that people can find happiness on either path.

8. Sample answers: People are often given a second chance in life. Life-altering decisions might include the route taken to school, being early or late, whom they talked with during the day. Decisions that affect others are the hardest to reverse.

Challenging the Text

9. Students might ask Frost if he ever again met his double, or what he liked to think about on his walks.

MAKING MEANINGS
THE ROAD NOT TAKEN

First Thoughts

[respond]

 1. Are this speaker's feelings about the choices he's made in life familiar to you? Compare the speaker's thoughts with your Quickwrite notes.

Shaping Interpretations

[interpret] 2. Instead of roads through a garden or a wide-open plain, why do you think the poet writes about roads that go through a wood? (Think about what *woods* usually **symbolizes,** or stands for, as in the statement "We're not out of the woods yet.")

[infer] 3. What do you think the speaker means when he says that he "kept" the first road for another day? How do we know that he realizes his choice of paths is utterly final?

[conclude] 4. Why do you think the speaker's choice "has made all the difference"?

[interpret] 5. How does Frost's speaker contradict himself in lines 8 through 10? In what other ways does this speaker **ironically** contradict himself?

[interpret] 6. Some adjectives that describe **tone** are listed below. Which adjectives would you choose to describe the tone of this poem? What words, phrases, or lines in the poem make you feel this tone? *Angry, awed, bitter, cynical, fearful, hopeful, ironic, playful, positive, puzzled, regretful, sad.*

Connecting with the Text

[connect] 7. What might happen if someone chooses a "less traveled" road? Do you know people who have made choices like this—and people who have chosen well-traveled roads? What kinds of lives did they have?

[connect] 8. Do you think people ever have a chance to go back and try another road? Talk about your responses. What decisions could you have made since you got up this morning that might have changed the course of your life? Are any life decisions harder to alter or reverse than others?

Challenging the Text

[respond] 9. Talk over your responses to Frost's letter "Crossing Paths" (see **Connections** on page 603). What questions would you ask him if you could?

604 THE POETRY COLLECTIONS

Assessing Learning

Check Test: Questions and Answers

1. Where is the "road not taken"? [in a wood]
2. Why did the speaker choose the path he took? [because it appeared less frequently traveled]
3. Does the speaker think he will get a chance to travel the other road? [no]
4. What was the result of the speaker's choice? [It has made a great difference in his life by influencing later choices.]

Standardized Test Preparation

For practice in proofreading and editing, see
• *Daily Oral Grammar,* Transparency 41

CHOICES: Building Your Portfolio

Writer's Notebook

1. Collecting Ideas for a Comparison-Contrast Essay

Looking at structure. When you compare and contrast poems (see the Writer's Workshop on page 614), you might want to talk about the structure of each poem. Is one **rhymed** and written in **meter**? Is one written in **free verse**? How does the structure affect the way you respond to the poems? Take notes on the

structure of Frost's poem and of one other poem in these collections. Be specific in the details you gather.

> Form of "'Hope' Is the Thing . . ."
> 1. Written in meter.
> 2. Iambic (˘ ′).
> 3. Alternates 3 & 4 stresses a line.
> 4. Some lines rhyme at end.
> 5. Some half rhymes.
> 6. Can sing this poem to "The Yellow Rose of Texas."

Creative Writing

2. Your Own Road Poem

Think of another setting, another traveler (maybe a younger person, maybe a female), and another attitude toward life and all the roads life offers its travelers. Put all these details into your own road poem (maybe it's a Road Taken). Open with "Two roads diverged. . . ."

VOCABULARY HOW TO OWN A WORD

Precise Meanings: A Word Map

Diverge is a key word in Frost's poem. *Diverge* looks like certain other words but has a different meaning. Here is a word map exploring *diverge*—what it means, examples of its use, and examples of its opposites, or **antonyms**. Use this vocabulary strategy to create similar word maps for words that resemble *diverge*: *divert*, *diverse*, *divulge*, and *divest*.

You might add to your word map an illustration for each word.

diverge

meanings
- move in different directions
- become different
- depart from some viewpoint

antonyms
- converge
- meet
- come together
- unite
- intersect

what things diverge?
- roads
- opinions
- careers
- lives
- life styles

THE ROAD NOT TAKEN 605

Grading Timesaver

Rubrics for each assignment appear on p. 186 in the *Portfolio Management System*.

CHOICES: Building Your Portfolio

1. **Writer's Notebook** Have students save their work for possible use in the Writer's Workshop on p. 614. Quickly review poetic terminology such as rhyme, meter, and stanzas.
2. **Creative Writing** Have students brainstorm ideas in small groups or use clusters to help them get started.

VOCABULARY

Sample Answer:

diverse

meanings
- different
- dissimilar
- varied
- diversified

what things are diverse?
- hobbies
- customs
- opinions
- accents

antonyms
- uniform
- consistent
- invariable
- duplicate

Resources

Vocabulary
- *Words to Own*, Worksheet, p. 35

Assessing Learning

Self-Reflection

Ask students to use a chart like the following to evaluate their own appreciation and understanding of poetry.

1=yes 2=somewhat 3=not sure

My understanding of a poem improves with several readings.	
The meaning of a poem is clearer if I examine its figurative language.	
I understand a poem better if I read it aloud to hear its tone.	
I can appreciate a poem more if I stop to think about denotation and connotations of the words in the poem.	
It helps to know that a poet can sometimes use irony, that is, say one thing and yet mean something different.	

Before You Read

LUCINDA MATLOCK

Make the Connection

"It Takes Life"

Here is a message from beyond the grave from a very outspoken old woman. How do you feel about Lucinda's advice?

Quickwrite

Write a short speech for a person who is complaining about "kids today." Think manners, slang, music, grooming, eating habits, cars, video games, attitudes toward money.

Keep your notes. For questions and activities on this poem, see pages 608–609.

Elements of Literature

Dramatic Monologue

"Lucinda Matlock" is one of more than two hundred portraits created by Edgar Lee Masters in *Spoon River Anthology*, a book of **dramatic monologues** spoken by the dead in a small-town cemetery. These housewives, bankers, poets, druggists, losers, ministers, and laborers are "saying it"

to anybody who will listen. And since the book's publication in 1915, hundreds of thousands of readers have listened intently.

> **A dramatic monologue** is a poem in which a character speaks to one or more listeners. The reactions of the listener must be **inferred** by the reader.

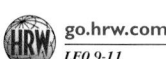

go.hrw.com
LE0 9-11

All Had a Good Time (c. 1910) by anonymous artist. Wool on burlap hooked rug (17½" x 45½").

Shelburne Museum, Shelburne, Vermont. Photograph by Ken Burris.

  *Resources: Print and Media*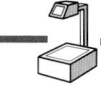

T606

Lucinda Matlock

Edgar Lee Masters

I went to the dances at Chandlerville,
And played snap-out at Winchester.
One time we changed partners,
Driving home in the moonlight of middle June,
5   And then I found Davis.
We were married and lived together for seventy years,
Enjoying, working, raising the twelve children,
Eight of whom we lost
Ere I had reached the age of sixty.
10   I spun, I wove, I kept the house, I nursed the sick,
I made the garden, and for holiday
Rambled over the fields where sang the larks,
And by Spoon River gathering many a shell
And many a flower and medicinal weed—
15   Shouting to the wooded hills, singing to the green valleys.
At ninety-six I had lived enough, that is all,
And passed to a sweet repose.
What is this I hear of sorrow and weariness,
Anger, discontent, and drooping hopes?
20   Degenerate sons and daughters, **B**
Life is too strong for you—
It takes life to love Life.

MEET THE WRITER
Speaker from a Small Town

Edgar Lee Masters (1869–1950) wasn't afraid to look under the surface of small-town American life. His *Spoon River Anthology* was an enormous success but it angered many people. Although Masters lets many good people speak, he also lets us hear from people who are intolerant, small-minded, mean, and hypocritical. But the book outlived its attackers and is now considered a classic of American literature.

Born in Garnett, Kansas, and raised in Petersburg and Lewistown, Illinois, Edgar Lee Masters became a lawyer with a flourishing practice. The idea for *Spoon River Anthology* came to him after a visit from his mother reminded him of the people he grew up with.

By the time Masters died, *Spoon River Anthology* had been translated into at least eight languages, including Arabic, Korean, Czech, and Chinese. It has even been made into an opera.

Masters is now buried next to his grandparents, Squire Davis Masters and Lucinda Masters. "Lucinda Matlock" is based on his grandmother, who represented his ideal of the undaunted pioneer woman. The real Lucinda also gave birth to twelve children and lived a very long life.

Summary ■ ■

In this poem, written in the form of a dramatic monologue, the speaker describes the simple, yet fulfilling country life that she led for ninety-six years—falling in love, marriage, children, household tasks, and the constant inspiration of nature. Her tone runs from joy and pride to nostalgia and culminates in a burst of anger. The speaker's message to "degenerate" younger generations is that a person must take all that life has to offer, sorrow as well as joy, to be fully alive.

Resources ————

Listening
Audio CD Library
A recording of this forceful poem is provided in the *Audio CD Library*:
• Disc 16, Track 17

Ⓐ Elements of Literature
Dramatic Monologue
? What can you infer about Lucinda's ideas of family life? [Sample answers: She looks on it as a hard job that she enjoyed; she thinks of it as a rich time that cannot last forever.]

Ⓑ Elements of Literature
Connotation
? What connotations does the word *degenerate* have? [Possible answers: corrupt, vulgar, vicious, depraved, immoral, wicked.] Ask students what the speaker is really saying to the younger generation in using this word. [Sample responses: She is scolding them and trying to shock them; she is expressing anger at their weakness and lack of moral character.]

Reaching All Students

Struggling Readers
Explain that "snap-out" is a game similar to crack the whip in which people join hands and then try to spin off the individuals at the end of the line.

Also explain to struggling readers that the archaism *Ere* in l. 9 means before and point out the old-fashioned use of *a* in ll. 13–14. Make sure they understand that when Lucinda mentions "sons and daughters" in l. 20, she is referring not to her own children, but to subsequent generations.

English Language Learners
Pair these students with Advanced Learners. Have the peer tutors explain unfamiliar words and read the poem aloud, using their tone of voice to help express the poem's meaning. For additional strategies to supplement instruction for these students, see
• *Lesson Plans Including Strategies for English-Language Learners*

MAKING MEANINGS

First Thoughts

1. Students may agree with the woman's negative view, or, more likely, find it unfair or incorrect.

Shaping Interpretations

2. Possible answers: *proud, joyful, reflective, nostalgic* (ll. 1–17); *scolding, angry, annoyed, judgmental* (ll. 18–22).

3. Hardships: caring for a large family, enduring the deaths of eight children, doing chores. Joys: dancing, marrying, children, enjoying nature, living to an old age. Her life is best described as a mixture of joy and hardship.

4. First *life:* energy, courage, determination. Second *Life:* the richness of human experience. The second *Life* is capitalized because it refers to a general concept.

5. Possible responses: Masters admires her for her love of life; he shows his approval by contrasting this energetic, joyful woman with weary, younger complainers.

6. Possible responses: The sad resignation on the woman's face contrasts with the speaker's joy, energy, and anger.

7. In l. 20 *degenerate* means "inferior" or "lacking moral character." Its use reveals Lucinda's disapproval.

8. Students may name celebrities or ordinary people who have risen above hardships. They may admire these people, or say that such people don't understand what life is like for others.

Challenging the Text

9. Sample responses: Her approach shows a self-centeredness and lack of sensitivity; others should follow her upbeat example.

MAKING MEANINGS
LUCINDA MATLOCK

[respond]

First Thoughts

1. What do you think of this old woman's final words?

Shaping Interpretations

[interpret]

2. What adjectives would you choose to describe Matlock's **tone** in lines 1–17? What different adjectives best describe her tone in lines 18–22?

[identify]

3. Identify the details in the text that describe the hardships Matlock has endured. Then, pick out the details that depict her joys and pleasures. How would you describe Lucinda's life?

[interpret]

4. What two meanings does the word *life* have in "It takes life to love Life"—the last line of the poem? Why do you suppose the second *Life* is capitalized?

[infer]

5. How do you think Masters feels about his outspoken Lucinda?

[compare]

6. Now that you have read about Lucinda, how does your image of her compare with the painting on this page? Explain your responses.

[infer]

7. In line 20, what does the word *degenerate* mean? By calling her neighbors "degenerate," what **feelings** about them does Lucinda reveal?

[connect]

 8. What kinds of Lucindas do you know in life today? Be sure to refer to your Quickwrite responses. What do you admire about these people? Do you have other feelings about them too?

Challenging the Text

[evaluate]

9. How fair is it for Lucinda Matlock to insist that other people deal with sorrow, weariness, anger, and depression the way she has dealt with them in her own life?

Woman with Plants (1929) by Grant Wood. Oil on upsom board.

RESPONDING TO THE ART

Grant Wood (1891–1942) who was born in Iowa and lived most of his life there, painted the farm people and landscapes he knew so well.

Activity. As an exercise in responding to the art, have students write down everything they see in this painting. Then have them write down what this image is *saying* to them.

Assessing Learning

Check Test: Questions and Answers

Answers may vary slightly.

1. What roles did Lucinda Matlock play in life? [She was a wife and mother.]

2. Where does the speaker go for holiday? [She goes to nature—the fields, Spoon River, the hills, the valleys.]

3. How does the speaker describe the younger generation's attitudes toward life? [They are full of anger and disappointment.]

4. What does the speaker say is too strong for subsequent generations? [Life]

CHOICES: Building Your Portfolio

Writer's Notebook

1. Collecting Ideas for a Comparison-Contrast Essay

Looking at speakers. Take notes on the speakers you hear in various poems in these collections. Who are they? What do you think of them? What attitudes do you find in the words they speak? (Notice the strong contrast between Frost's speaker and the bold Lucinda.)

> • *Speakers* in "The Gift" and "Combing": Son/Mother. Loving, tender, caring. Both talk of passing on love from generation to generation.
> • **Supporting details:**
>   • *a childhood memory; speaker remembers his father gently removing a splinter from his hand*
>   • *combing her daughter's hair, remembering her mother combing her hair*

Creative Writing

2. A Dramatic Monologue in Response

What do you think of Lucinda's speech? In a paragraph (or a poem, if you like), respond to this voice from the old Spoon River cemetery. Open your own **dramatic monologue** with *I*. Be sure you make clear who your speaker is and where your speaker lives.

Creative Writing

3. Send a Letter Back

Lucinda Matlock probably died more than a hundred years ago—before there were movies, telephones, television, computers, cars, or antibiotics. Write Lucinda a letter comparing and contrasting the details of her rural life and those of most people's lives today. Hint: Take each part of Matlock's story and think of how it would be different if it were happening today. For instance, it was probably a wagon drawn by horses that was being driven home in line 4. What would it be today? Have many people alive today been married for seventy years? Do many have twelve children? Why would it be unlikely today that eight of Matlock's children would die (as they did) before they were forty or so years old? Talk to Lucinda from your perch in time a hundred years later.

Interviewing

4. Class Oral History Project

With a group, form a class oral history collection. You could contribute a written, taped, or videotaped interview of an older person, possibly a relative or friend. Prepare your questions carefully; in fact, the person might appreciate seeing a copy of your questions in advance. Each interviewer should be sure to ask the subject how life was different in his or her youth from what life is like today. You may want to invite some of your subjects to present their histories directly to the class. Preserve your collection for future classes. You might even donate it to your local library or museum.

Research/Speaking

5. How It Was

Museums around the country have exhibits showing American life as it was many years, even centuries, ago. Probably the most famous is the immigration museum on Ellis Island in New York City. Find out if there is a museum in your area. What does it focus on? How is it funded? Does it need volunteers? If you can, visit the museum and report to the class on what you learn there.

Grading Timesaver

Rubrics for each Choices assignment appear on p. 187 in the *Portfolio Management System*.

CHOICES: Building Your Portfolio

1. **Writer's Notebook** Remind students to save their work for the Writer's Workshop on p. 614. Make sure they support their opinions with details from the poems.

2. **Creative Writing** Be sure students have clearly defined their speakers. The opinions expressed by the speaker should fit with his or her persona.

3. **Creative Writing** Offer students a precise format to use for their letters. For example, in the first paragraph, students can introduce themselves to Lucinda. In successive paragraphs, students can comment on changes that have occurred in specific areas of life, such as medicine and transportation. They should conclude by telling Lucinda what they like about her era and their own.

4. **Interviewing** Have students work together to prepare a list of interview questions. As a group, students can also set up a timetable for the completion of their assignments.

5. **Research/Speaking** If there is no museum in your area that students can easily visit, have them research what American life was like in earlier times. Besides looking through books in the library, they can view antiques in stores or in the collections of local people.

Using Students' Strengths

Auditory Learners

Encourage students interested in activity #2 to consider several possibilities for the speaker in their monologues. Once they choose the speaker and begin drafting their monologues, they should work with a partner to read aloud lines of their work to develop an authentic voice. Have students tape-record their monologues, and have the entire class listen to them.

Spatial Learners

Before beginning activity #3, students might complete a prewriting Venn diagram that shows the differences and similarities between the present and life one hundred years ago.

OBJECTIVES
1. Read a speech
2. Find thematic connections across genres
3. Generate relevant and interesting discussion
4. Recognize distinctive and shared characteristics of cultures through reading and discussion

Extending the Theme

This poem was adapted from a speech made by Sojourner Truth in defense of women's rights. Truth, a former slave, protests the notion that women are physically inferior to men by presenting the harsh facts of her life, during which she worked harder than most men and endured more suffering. She ends by challenging the religious doctrine that denied women equal status with men.

Background

In part, the struggle for women's rights that took place during the nineteenth century grew out of the antislavery movement. Women at the time, in most states, had few political or legal rights, and those who were married were generally regarded as the property of their husbands. Women could not vote, could not serve on juries, and could not hold office.

FROM THE EDITOR'S DESK

Orators, like poets, use the sounds of words as well as their meanings to communicate ideas. Because of the close connection between poetry and oratory, we thought it fitting to close the collection with this famous speech.

RESPONDING TO THE ART

Elizabeth Catlett (1919–   ) captures the dignity and strength of her African American subject in this woodcut.
Activity. Ask students why they think this woodcut was paired with the speech. [Both evoke images of strong women who have worked hard and earned wisdom.]

T610

EXTENDING *the theme*

A SPEECH

Reading Skills and Strategies

What You Know

Before you read this speech, take some time to write down what you know about the history of women's rights in this country. Fill out a KWL chart. K = what you *know*. W = what you *want* to know. L = what you *learn* from the reading. Fill out the chart after you have completed the reading.

K	W	L

Background

In 1851, a women's rights convention was held in Akron, Ohio. Various speakers, many of them members of the clergy, used the Bible to argue that men had superior rights and, moreover, that men held superior principles to those held by women. Sojourner Truth, who had not been invited, stood up and walked to the platform to attack those arguments. This is the speech she made. It is probably the only speech at that event that is still remembered today. Sojourner Truth knew what she wanted to say—and she said it!

610 THE POETRY COLLECTIONS

Sharecropper (1970) by Elizabeth Catlett. Woodcut.
Evans-Tibbs Collection, Washington, D.C. © Elizabeth Catlett / Licensed by VAGA, New York, NY.

Unfortunately, there is no exact copy of the speech in existence today. It has been adapted here in the form of a poem.

go.hrw.com
LEO 9-11

Reaching All Students

Struggling Readers
Encourage these students to work in small groups to prepare oral readings of the speech that they can present to the class.

English Language Learners
Point out to students that this speech attempts to recreate Sojourner Truth's dialect, and that this explains her use of *say* in ll. 1 and 25; *ain't* in ll. 8, 14, 19, 24; and *most all* in l. 21. Have students give examples of dialect or colloquial speech from their native languages.

Getting Students Involved

Cooperative Learning
You Were There. When students have read the speech, assign groups of four or five to role-play various audience types: women's rights advocates, men opposed to women's rights, women opposed to women's rights, news reporters, and clergy. Each group member should script one or two responses their audience member might make to this speech and then come together to act out the scenario.

Ain't I a Woman?

Sojourner Truth

That man over there say **Ⓐ**
    a woman needs to be helped into carriages
and lifted over ditches
    and to have the best place everywhere.
5   Nobody ever helped me into carriages **Ⓑ**
    or over mud puddles
        or gives me a best place. . . .

And ain't I a woman? **Ⓒ**
    Look at me
10   Look at my arm!
    I have plowed and planted
and gathered into barns
    and no man could head me. . . .
And ain't I a woman?
15   I could work as much
and eat as much as a man—
    when I could get to it—
and bear the lash as well
    and ain't I a woman?
20   I have borne 13 children
    and seen most all sold into slavery
and when I cried out a mother's grief
    none but Jesus heard me . . .
and ain't I a woman?
25   that little man in black there say **Ⓓ**
a woman can't have as much rights as a man
    cause Christ wasn't a woman
Where did your Christ come from?
    From God and a woman!
30   Man had nothing to do with him!
    If the first woman God ever made
was strong enough to turn the world **Ⓔ**
    upside down, all alone
together women ought to be able to turn it
35   rightside up again.

AIN'T I A WOMAN? 611

Ⓐ Appreciating Language
Dialect
Note that in the first line, as well as elsewhere, Truth expresses her ideas in dialect, which differs from standard English. An example of this dialect is found in her use of verbs: In standard English, a singular subject *(man)* takes a singular verb *(says)*; but here Truth uses the plural form of the verb *(say)*. Ask students how the use of dialect affects the speech. [Sample responses: It adds a sense of reality, making you feel you are listening to an authentic individual voice; it contributes to the power of the speech.]

Ⓑ Elements of Literature
Allusion
An allusion is an indirect reference. Here, Truth may be referring to the legendary gallantry of Sir Walter Raleigh, who is said to have laid his coat over a puddle so a lady would not wet her feet.

Ⓒ Reading Skills and Strategies
Responding to the Text
? Explain that rhetorical questions are asked only for effect or to emphasize a point—no answer is expected. How does Truth's repeated rhetorical question affect you? [Sample responses: It makes one realize she is sure of her own worth; it makes one feel one wouldn't be able to argue with her about her achievements.]

Ⓓ Critical Thinking
Making Generalizations
? What do you think the speaker wants from her audience or the world in general? [Sample responses: a decent place; equal rights; her children returned; recognition; courtesy.]

Ⓔ Elements of Literature
Allusion
Truth is alluding to Eve in the book of *Genesis*. According to that account, Eve brought sorrow and death into the world by eating the forbidden fruit and encouraging Adam to do likewise. For their disobedience to God's law, they were banished from Eden.

Making the Connections

Connecting to the Theme: "Say It"
Although Truth originally presented her ideas as a speech, her words are full of poetic rhythms and imagery. Her speech also contains a repeated refrain, which is a characteristic of song. These poetic and musical elements combine to give her speech great persuasive power. Ask students to reflect on the importance of the orator's role in society today.
• Who are some famous orators?
• What accounts for their power and influence?

Then, have students reread the Collection opener on p. 585. Point out how well Sojourner Truth's speech serves as an example of a work by a person determined to "say it." Have students comment on the similarity of tone in Truth's speech and the quotation by James Russell Lowell.

MEET THE WRITER
Up and Down the Land

Sojourner Truth (c. 1797–1883) was born in slavery in Ulster County, New York, and was named Isabella. Just before New York State abolished slavery in 1827, she was sold to a man named Isaac van Wagener, who gave her her freedom.

Isabella and her two youngest children moved in 1829 to New York City where she worked as a servant until 1843. Then she had a vision that changed her life. According to her own testimony, God instructed her to take the name Sojourner Truth and "travel up and down the land," spreading a message against slavery and in favor of women's rights.

That's exactly what she did, and her speeches drew huge crowds, whether she was an invited speaker or, as was often the case, a zealous impromptu preacher.

In the 1850s, Sojourner Truth settled in Battle Creek, Michigan. When the Civil War broke out, she gathered supplies for African American volunteer regiments. In 1864, Abraham Lincoln received her at the White House. A painting that records that meeting is below.

FINDING COMMON GROUND

1. Complete your **KWL** chart now that you've finished the reading. Be sure to compare your charts in class. Did the text raise any new questions in your mind?

2. How might Sojourner Truth update "Ain't I a Woman?" for today? Meet in groups to discuss these questions and report on your answers.

   • Who might her audience be? What issues might she choose to address?

   • How do you think she would feel about the lives of women today? Look at your own community and school. What progress would she notice? What would she like to see changed?

   • Rewrite the speech in prose or verse. Use your own words but remember that you are writing as Sojourner Truth, from her point of view.

Schomberg Center for Research in Black Culture.

612 THE POETRY COLLECTIONS

Assessing Learning

Check Test: True-False

1. The speaker agrees that women need to be pampered. [False]
2. The speaker has done heavy farm work. [True]
3. The speaker has seen most of her children sold into slavery. [True]
4. The speaker says no one can straighten out the world. [False]
5. The speaker seems proud to be a woman. [True]

READ ON

Distant Times and Remote Places

Ever read any African chants, European lullabies, or American Indian myths set to verse? If you'd like to, *Talking to the Sun* (The Metropolitan Museum of Art/Henry Holt) is the place to start. The collection is full of art from New York's Metropolitan Museum of Art and poetry from all over the world.

Almost There

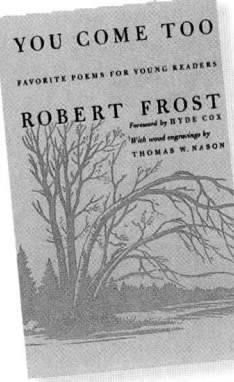

Discover some of the best of Robert Frost's poetry in *You Come Too: Favorite Poems for Young Readers—Robert Frost* (Henry Holt). In poems like "Christmas Tree" and "Hyla Brook," Frost brings to life the trees, mountains, cliffs, dirt roads, old fences, grassy fields, and abandoned houses of his part of New England. Reading his work, you'll almost believe you're there—in the woods or at the edge of the brook.

All Twisted Up

Drumbeats, dreamers, and skyscrapers—those are the stuff of Carl Sandburg's poetry. In *Harvest Poems: 1910–1960* (Harcourt Brace) you'll find everyday subjects described in everyday language—but it all sounds brand new. Sandburg's poems appeal to everyday people but are in no way ordinary.

The Spoken Word

Julie Harris won a Tony Award for her portrayal of Emily Dickinson in the Broadway play *The Belle of Amherst*. You can listen to her interpretation of Dickinson's letters and poems on audiotape. *The Poems and Letters of Emily Dickinson* (HarperCollins/Caedmon) contains forty-eight minutes of Harris as Dickinson—reciting her most famous poems and most personal correspondence.

READ ON 613

T613

MAIN OBJECTIVE
Write a comparison-contrast essay

PROCESS OBJECTIVES
1. Use appropriate prewriting techniques to identify and develop a topic
2. Create a first draft
3. Use evaluation criteria as a basis for determining revision strategies
4. Revise the first draft, incorporating suggestions generated by self- or peer evaluation
5. Proofread and correct errors
6. Create a final draft
7. Choose an appropriate method of publication
8. Reflect on progress as a writer

Planning

- **Block Schedule**
  Block Scheduling Lesson Plans with Pacing Guide

- **One-Stop Planner**
  CD-ROM with Test Generator

ASSIGNMENT
Write an essay comparing and contrasting two poems. Choose any two poems that are alike in at least one important way.

AIM
To give information.

AUDIENCE
Your classmates and teacher, other English classes, readers of a magazine of student writing. (You choose.)

EXPOSITORY WRITING
COMPARISON-CONTRAST ESSAY

How is football like soccer? How are you different from your best friend, and what do you have in common? You answer questions like these all the time. Without being aware of it, you're comparing and contrasting. Your ability to recognize similarities (**compare**) and differences (**contrast**) is what lets you recognize your dog in a roomful of dogs, or define a word, or explain how the Civil War was different from all other American wars. In this workshop you'll compare two poems and write an essay discussing their similarities and their differences. A comparison-contrast essay is one kind of expository writing—writing that explains or gives information. Remember:

- *Comparing* means "seeing similarities."
- *Contrasting* means "seeing differences."
- *Comparing* is often used to mean both comparing and contrasting.

Prewriting
1. Choose Two Poems

You should already have some notes on comparing and contrasting various poems. Pull your notes out now to see if you'd like to develop any of them into an essay. The poems you compare might have similar **subjects** or **themes**. They might have similar **figures of speech**. They might even be written by the same person. The important thing is to find two poems with something in common. The next important thing is to find poems you want to write about.

If you don't feel satisfied with the notes you've been taking, try these strategies:

- Review the poems in these collections. Briefly list the subjects of all the poems you've read. Which poems are about similar subjects?

- Look at the titles of the collections of poems. Under each title you should be able to find poems with similar themes or concerns.

 *Resources: Print and Media*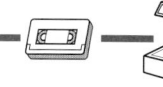

Writing and Language
- *Portfolio Management System*
  Prewriting, p. 189
  Peer Editing, p. 190
  Assessment Rubric, p. 191

- *Workshop Resources*
  Revision Strategy Teaching Notes, p. 45
  Revision Strategy Transparencies 23, 24

Assessment
- *Standardized Test Preparation*, p. 132

ARLO AND JANIS reprinted by permission of Newspaper Enterprise Association, Inc.

- Look at the sections called Elements of Literature. Clustered around these sections you should find poems that make prominent use of the same element.

2. Find the Features

Once you have your poems, look closely at the features you'll compare. A **feature** is a part that you can examine and talk about separately from the whole. If you were a dog breeder, for instance, you might compare dogs by these features: type of breed, size, color of coat, body shape, and special abilities. In this workshop you'll use the elements of poetry (such as **subject, speaker, figures of speech, imagery, sound effects, tone**) as your main features. Your essay will focus on how each poem you choose uses one or more features.

3. Analyze Both Poems and Take Notes

Analysis is the thinking skill that breaks a whole into its parts and examines each part separately. One reading isn't enough to analyze a poem. Reread each poem you're comparing until you feel you understand it and can discuss each of its major elements.

One way to collect details to support your main idea is to use a Venn diagram like the one below. This will help you focus on all the ways the poems are different and on the important features they share.

Differences: Poem 1 — Features They Share — Differences: Poem 2

Feature Focus

EXAMPLES

- Shakespeare's "The Seven Ages of Man" and Dickinson's "'Hope' Is the Thing with Feathers" both begin with a metaphor that extends throughout the poem.

- "Daily" and "When I Heard the Learn'd Astronomer" both express tones of awe and wonder and joy.

- "Lucinda Matlock" and "Women" are both about courageous women.

Communications Handbook HELP

See Checking Your Comprehension; Taking Notes and Documenting Sources.

Introducing the Writer's Workshop

Begin the Writer's Workshop by asking students to think about the poems they have read so far and to jot down the titles of a few that are memorable to them. Then, have students list the topic of each memorable poem. When they discover two poems with the same topic, ask students to jot down ways in which they are similar and ways in which they are different.

Teaching the Writer's Workshop

Read and discuss the information on Prewriting and Drafting (pp. 614–616).

Prewriting

As students search for poems to compare and contrast and prepare their prewriting notes, guide them by providing examples of what they might find in common between two poems. For example, explain that poems might have similar speakers, settings, tones, themes, or main ideas.

Using Students' Strengths

Interpersonal Learners

To help students understand the initial organizational steps for writing this essay, have them work in pairs or small groups to compare and contrast two poems such as "The Gift" and "Combing." Volunteers may present their results on an overhead transparency. Students should then apply the process to poems of their own choice.

Reaching All Students

Struggling Readers

These students may find it difficult to compare and contrast two poems. If your class has done the group work suggested for interpersonal learners, you may wish to allow students with reading problems to write papers based on that group work. Or help these students by first comparing two concrete objects such as a car and a motorcycle. Then guide students to choose two poems that are on the same topic but have distinctive differences in content and tone.

T615

Drafting

- Before students begin to draft their essays, read the model in class with them. Analysis questions are provided on the student's page and on p. T617 of this Teacher's Edition.
- As students write their essays, ask them to label clearly their system of organization in the side margins of their papers. These notes should resemble those in the boxes on p. 616.
- Remind students to double-space when they write their drafts. They should also leave extra space in the right margin. These blank spaces will be used for comments and editing marks.

Block Method
Subject 1: Mrs. Jones
Feature 1: caring, sincere, kind
Feature 2: invites boy to her home, talks honestly
Feature 3: makes kid feel accepted
Subject 2: Sister Zoe
Feature 1: motherly
Feature 2: makes immigrant girl feel accepted
Feature 3: gives private lessons

Point-by-Point Method
Feature 1: kind to young people
Subject 1: Mrs. Jones
Subject 2: Sister Zoe
Feature 2: motherly, teacher
Subject 1: Mrs. Jones
Subject 2: Sister Zoe
Feature 3: makes outsiders feel accepted
Subject 1: Mrs. Jones
Subject 2: Sister Zoe

Language Handbook
H E L P

See Comparison of Modifiers, page 1004.

---

4. Organize Your Information

Think of the details you've collected as building blocks of information. You can build the essay's body in either of two ways.

- **Block method.** First, you say *everything* you have to say about poem 1. Then you say *everything* you have to say about poem 2. Discuss the features in the same order for both poems. (The student model on the next page, which compares and contrasts two stories, uses the block method.)
- **Point-by-point method.** You discuss the *features* one at a time. First, you might talk about sound effects in poem 1; then you talk about sound effects in poem 2. Next, you might discuss imagery in poem 1 and go on to discuss imagery in poem 2. You follow this same neat and tidy organization in discussing each feature.

5. Write a Thesis Statement

Are the two texts more alike than different? In what ways? Write a **thesis statement,** a summary of what you've discovered.

EXAMPLE

Naomi Nye's poem "Daily" and Walt Whitman's poem "When I Heard the Learn'd Astronomer" both communicate tones of awe and wonder and joy, but Nye's poem is very domestic while Whitman goes cosmic.

Drafting

1. A Formula for a Comparison-Contrast Essay

Like all essays, a comparison-contrast essay has three basic parts:

- The **introduction** captures the reader's attention, identifies the two works by title and author, and provides background information if the works are new to the reader. The thesis statement usually appears in the introductory paragraph.
- The **body** discusses at least two features, using either the block method or the point-by-point method of organization. Specific details, facts, examples, and quotations support your statements.
- The **conclusion,** usually a single paragraph, summarizes the essay's main ideas or adds a final thought to close the essay.

2. Elaboration: Details Are Important

To **elaborate** on your essay, you must supply solid examples from the text to prove your main points. Thus, if you say a poem is morbid in tone, you should cite details from the poem that support your point—words, images, and figures of speech. The more details you supply, the more convincing your essay will be.

Reaching All Students

Struggling Writers

Remind students that it is important in expository writing to use transition words to connect sentences in a paragraph and ideas from paragraph to paragraph. Useful connecting words for comparison-contrast essays are *however, instead, but, yet, although,* and *while.* Remind students to check for connecting words when they are peer editing.

English Language Learners

Comparison-contrast papers often require the use of the comparative and superlative forms of adjectives and adverbs. You may wish to review these forms with English language learners using material in the Language Handbook, p. 1004.

CHARACTERS IN "SNOW" AND "THANK YOU, M'AM"

When I first read "Snow" and "Thank You, M'am," I didn't really see any similarities in any of the characters. But after rereading both stories, I realize that there are actually more similarities than differences in the characters.

Identifies the works and makes a general statement about the characters.

Mrs. Luella Bates Washington Jones, a character in "Thank You, M'am," is a very caring and sincere person. When Roger tries to steal her pocketbook, she could have him arrested, but instead she takes him home with her, makes him dinner, and talks to him, which I think is very kind of her. She doesn't ask any embarrassing questions, so he won't feel uncomfortable. She tells him that she can understand how he wanted to steal money to buy shoes. She says that she too wanted things. Because of his talk with Mrs. Jones, I don't think Roger will ever steal again. Mrs. Jones isn't just a person to talk to. She is more than that. She makes Roger feel accepted by inviting him into her home. I know Roger feels comfortable with Mrs. Jones because he has every opportunity to run away but he doesn't.

Introduces first character. Block method.

Supplies supporting details.

The experience Yolanda has with her teacher Sister Zoe in the story "Snow" is similar to Roger's experience with Mrs. Jones. Sister Zoe is very motherly. She tries to make Yolanda feel accepted when she is the only immigrant in her class. She takes the time to tutor Yolanda when she doesn't have to. She also teaches Yolanda new words. Both women have the same basic effect on the children.

Second character is introduced. Supplies supporting details.

Sister Zoe and Mrs. Jones are also different. Though they both make significant differences in the lives of two young people, they go about it in two different ways. In the few hours Mrs. Jones is with Roger, I feel she may have given him a new outlook on life, whereas the change in Yolanda is gradual, over a long period of time. The changes are made in different ways by different people.

Sums up how characters are alike. Shows differences as well as similarities between the characters.

Though Sister Zoe and Mrs. Jones are different, they have many similar traits, and I feel they both changed the lives of two young people. I wonder how different Yolanda's and Roger's lives would have been without Sister Zoe and Mrs. Jones.

Conclusion adds a personal note.

—Jessica Preston
Hamden High School
Hamden, Connecticut

Getting Students Involved

Peer Editing

Peer reviewers often have difficulty framing positive comments on other students' papers and frequently resort to general statements such as "This is a good paper." To help students give more specific positive feedback to their peers, have them complete the following statements after reviewing a paper:

- What I like best about this paper is _____.
- The most effective sentence is _____.
- Good word choices are _____.

Evaluating and Revising

Have students use the Evaluation Criteria provided on p. 618 to review their drafts and determine needed revisions.

Proofreading

Have students proofread their own papers first and then exchange them with another student. For this assignment, remind students to be particularly careful to use the correct forms of comparison and to avoid making double comparisons.

If time permits, the final copy should be put aside for at least a day before it is proofread one last time by the author.

Publishing

- Suggest that students submit their essays to a magazine or web site that publishes student writing.
- Put all the class essays into a Comparison/Contrast folder to share with other English classes or with parents at a Back-to-School Night.
- Publish student essays on a school web site.

Reflecting

If students include these essays in their portfolios, have them write a brief reflection on their writing experience:

1. What do I like best about my essay? What part or parts am I less satisfied with? Why?
2. Did writing the essay increase my understanding of the texts? How?
3. Which part of the writing assignment was easiest for me? Which part was the most difficult? Why?

Resources

Peer Editing Forms and Rubrics
- *Portfolio Management System*, p. 190.

Revision Transparencies
- *Workshop Resources*, p. 45

A Boxful of Transitions

Words that show similarities:
also, too, similarly, in addition, both . . . and

Words that show differences:
in contrast, however, on the other hand, although

Sentence Workshop
H E L P

Revising sentences for structure and length: page 619.

Communications Handbook
H E L P

See Proofreaders' Marks.

■ *Evaluation Criteria*

A good comparison-contrast essay

1. *has an introduction that identifies the works and contains a thesis statement*
2. *has a body that compares and contrasts at least two features*
3. *expresses ideas clearly, using either point-by-point or block method*
4. *supports statements with details and quotations from the texts*
5. *has a concluding paragraph that summarizes the main ideas or adds a final thought*

Evaluating and Revising

Share your paper with your writing group or with a partner. Ask your reader(s) to focus especially on these points:

1. What organization did I use? Is it clear?
2. What are the features I used for comparison? Are they clear?
3. Can you follow everything I've said? Do you have questions?

Revision Model

	Peer Comments
The experience Yolanda has with	
her teacher Sister Zoe in the story	How does this relate to Mrs. Jones?
similar to Roger's experience with Mrs. Jones. "Snow" is interesting, too.	
Sister Zoe is very motherly.	
She tries to make Yolanda feel	These sentences are choppy.
when she is the only immigrant accepted in her class. She takes	
when she doesn't have to. the time to tutor Yolanda.	
also She teaches Yolanda new words.	Add transition?
Both women have the same Sister Zoe has an effect on Yolanda	Can you express this idea more clearly?
basic effect on the children. that is sort of like the way	
Mrs. Jones has an effect on Roger.	

T618

BUILDING YOUR PORTFOLIO
Sentence Workshop

REVISING SENTENCES: STRUCTURE AND LENGTH

Professional writers vary their sentences to create a pleasing rhythm and to keep readers interested. They write short sentences and long ones. They open their sentences with subjects or with modifying phrases and clauses. The possibilities are almost endless. (Writer Jay McInerney says that every sentence is potentially revisable in thirty directions!) Think of sentences as falling into four basic types:

1. **Simple** (one independent clause)
2. **Compound** (two or more independent clauses combined)
3. **Complex** (one independent clause combined with one or more dependent clauses)
4. **Compound-complex** (two or more independent clauses combined with one or more dependent clauses)

Below are examples of sentences from the work of professional writers. (The slash marks divide the clauses.)

1. "Drifting down the river of grass, Billie Wind could see the sun and the water and soils at work." [simple sentence, opens with a participial phrase]
   —Jean Craighead George, *The Talking Earth*

2. "They had won, / but they were weary and bleeding." [compound sentence]
   —George Orwell, *Animal Farm*

3. "When they were arranging him for his last rest, / they found upon his bosom a small, plain miniature-case, opening with a spring." [complex sentence, opens with a dependent clause]
   —Harriet Beecher Stowe, *Uncle Tom's Cabin*

Writer's Workshop Follow-up: Revision

Read aloud your comparison-contrast essay. Do the sentences have a pleasing rhythm? Do they vary or are many of them put together the same way? Try combining some simple sentences to make compound ones. Would a short dramatic sentence add emphasis?

Language Handbook HELP

See Sentence Structure, page 1010.

Technology HELP

See Language Workshop CD-ROM. Key word entry: sentence.

Try It Out

1. Model the professional sentences at the left: That is, write a sentence of your own that imitates the structure of each professional example. When you have completed your own sentences, go back to them and rewrite each one so that it opens in a different way—or becomes two short, punchy sentences. Compare your sentences in class.

2. Rewrite the following paragraph to give it variety.

   I got lost on the way to Corky's shop. She sells magnets at her shop. I wanted to buy a magnet for Grandma Trumble. She has a collection of magnets on her refrigerator. I thought this would be a short trip. It took two hours. I bought a dolphin magnet. Grandma Trumble loves dolphins.

SENTENCE WORKSHOP **619**

Try It Out
Sample Answers

1. Peering out the front window, Lydia could see the neighborhood children at play. Revision: When Lydia peered out the front window, she could see the neighborhood children at play. Or: Lydia peered out the window. She could see the neighborhood children at play.

   They had finished, but they were exhausted and angry. Revision: Although they had finished, they were exhausted and angry.

   After they had set out the last of the flowers, they found in the weeds a pot of begonias, opening into full bloom. Revision: Setting out the last of the flowers, they found in the weeds a pot of begonias, opening into full bloom.

2. Responses will vary. Discuss with students the different effects of various versions. Sample: I got lost on the way to Corky's shop, which sells magnets. I wanted to buy a magnet for Grandma Trumble, who has a collection of magnets on her refrigerator. Although I thought this would be a short trip, it took two hours. I bought a dolphin magnet because Grandma Trumble loves dolphins.

Assessing Learning

Quick Check: Revising Sentences

Examine each of the following sentences and identify its sentence type.

1. Running alongside the hay wagon, the boy soon grew out of breath. [simple]
2. The wind howled and the rain fell. [compound]
3. She guessed who had left the package. [complex]
4. When we heard the news, we offered our congratulations. [complex]
5. The puppy wanted to play, but its mother preferred to nap. [compound]

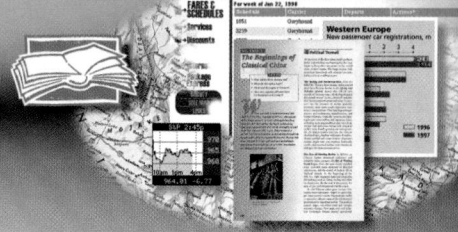

Reading for Life

Creating a Topic Outline

OBJECTIVES
1. Create a topic outline
2. Develop skimming, close reading, and scanning skills
3. Paraphrase ideas
4. Use correct format for a topic outline

Teaching the Lesson

There are two kinds of outline: the **topic outline**, in which the ideas are stated in words or brief phrases (not sentences), and the **sentence outline**, in which the ideas are expressed in complete sentences. The outline on this page is a topic outline—the easier outline to make.

Here are some of the rules for making outlines:

1. Number the main headings with Roman numerals. (In the type font used for the outline on this page, the Roman numerals look like Arabic numbers); letter the subtopics under each main heading with capital letters. Follow with, in descending order of importance, Arabic numbers, small letters, Arabic numerals in parentheses, small letters in parentheses.

2. Never allow a subtopic to stand alone; use two or more subtopics or none at all. Subtopics are divisions of the topic above them, and a topic cannot be divided into fewer than two parts.

3. Begin each topic and subtopic with a capital letter.

4. In a topic outline, do not follow topics with a period.

5. All main topics should be parallel in form.

Using the Strategies

Possible Answers

The outline could be continued as follows:

   B. Internal (inside character's mind)

III. Bare bones of plot

   A. Basic situation

   B. Exposition

   C. Complication

   D. Climax

   E. Resolution or denouement

Situation

You have been asked to work with a group of younger students who have formed a writers' club. Your task is to review with them the basic elements of a plot. To make sure you can explain the elements of a plot clearly, you outline the information found on pages 32–33 in this textbook.

Strategies

Focus on the framework.

• An outline reveals the skeleton of a text: The entries list the main ideas in order, and the indentations and the numbers and letters show their relative importance.

Pace yourself.

As you prepare an outline, adjust your reading rate to suit your note-taking needs.

• **Skimming** is reading quickly to identify main ideas.

• **Close reading** is reading slowly enough to understand not only what the words say but also what they suggest.

• **Scanning** is rapidly searching for key words and then checking the context to make sure you've found what you were looking for. In this book, use headings and boldface words as a guide.

Plot

I. Definition: series of related events

   A. Events connected to one another like links in chain

   B. Reader pulled from one event to next event

II. Conflict: struggle

   A. External

     1. Between two characters

     2. Between one character and a group of characters

     3. Between one character and nonhuman force

   B. Internal

Use your own words.

• As you outline, **paraphrase** the ideas—that is, state them in your own words.

Go formal.

• Use Roman numerals to order the main topics.

• Use letters and numbers to order the subtopics.

• Never include just one subtopic; include two or more or none at all.

• Use parallel forms for parallel entries. For example, if the first item in a series is a noun phrase, make the others noun phrases as well.

Using the Strategies

1. Reread the Elements of Literature feature on plot (pages 32–33), and complete the topic outline.

2. Review your outline. Could you use it to explain the features of a plot to someone? If not, make any needed revisions.

3. Compare your outline with a classmate's. How similar are they? What do you think accounts for any differences?

Extending the Strategies

Use these strategies to create an outline. You might want to outline another Elements of Literature feature in this book or the introduction to the *Odyssey* (pages 878–884).

Using Students' Strengths

Visual Learners

Some students may find it easier to develop a topic outline if they first visualize the structure of a text. Provide students with examples of flow charts or maps that effectively convey a text's organization. Have them create a visual display before attempting the topic outline.

Interpersonal Learners

Have students work in groups. Ask students to decide on the main topics first. Then pull the class together to see if everyone agrees. Arrive at a consensus about the first topic, and then ask the groups to decide what subtopics belong with it. Again, pull the class together long enough to see if everyone agrees. After a brief discussion, let the groups continue working independently to complete the assignment.

Learning for Life

Investigating Song Lyrics

OBJECTIVES
1. Identify social trends expressed in popular song lyrics
2. Conduct research
3. Choose and complete a project, summarizing and presenting research information

Problem

Poetry is in the air—and on the airwaves. Popular music is big business in the United States. What do the lyrics of the twentieth century's popular songs reveal about American society?

Project

With the approval of your teacher, investigate the lyrics of the twentieth century's most popular songs. Determine what these changes reveal about our tastes in music and our changing concerns and values.

Preparation

1. Working with a partner or a small group, decide how you'll divide up these tasks:
   - determining the most popular song of each decade—1901–1910, 1911–1920, and so on
   - finding recordings of the songs
2. Identify possible resources for your project, such as
   - anthologies of popular music
   - songbooks
   - newspapers and magazines

Procedure

1. Find out which song was most popular in each decade. For the early decades of the century, look at sales of sheet music. For later decades, look at sales of records, tapes, and CDs.
2. Find the lyrics and the music of the most popular song of each decade, and make notes. Pay special attention to the songs' use of
   - imagery
   - figures of speech
   - sound effects
   - tone
3. Decide what each song says and why it was so popular at the time. To do this, think about what you know of the decade from other sources, such as
   - books and movies set in the same time
   - history and social studies classes
   - stories you've heard from friends and family

Presentation

Do one of the following activities (or another that your teacher approves).

1. Found Poem

Present your findings in a poem of your own. You could combine snatches of lyrics from each of the songs in chronological order. Give your poem an original title and read it to the rest of the class or submit it to the school paper.

2. Musical Medley

Create a musical medley by combining soundtracks of the songs. Write a brief introduction and conclusion to your soundtrack. Give the tape to a senior citizens' center or a retirement residence.

3. Time-Line Wall Display

With a group of classmates, create a wall display of the hit songs and major events of the century. (Be sure to plan your design before you begin.) Put your display in your school's lobby or a hallway, along with cards on which viewers can write their responses.

Processing

Draw conclusions about twentieth-century American society from the information you have gathered. Write a brief reflection for your portfolio.

Copyright Permissions

The educational fair-use provisions of the copyright laws allow students to make tapes provided that
1. the recordings do not copy a complete work
2. the recordings are not sold

This is a good opportunity to discuss with students the fact that song lyrics, musical compositions, and performances are all protected by copyright. Making copies of complete works, whether or not they are sold, violates the rights of copyright holders.

Resources

Viewing and Representing
HRW Multimedia Presentation Maker

Students may wish to use the *Multimedia Presentation Maker* to create their wall displays.

Grading Timesaver

Rubrics for this Learning for Life project appear on p. 192 of the *Portfolio Management System*.

Developing Workplace Competencies

Preparation	Procedure	Presentation
• Works on teams • Acquires data • Evaluates data	• Interprets information • Evaluates data • Reasons	• Communicates ideas and information • Processes information

OBJECTIVES
1. Read a modern drama centered on the theme "Opening Doors"
2. Identify and analyze literary elements in a modern drama, with special emphasis on character, conflict, and climax
3. Learn how to read a play
4. Respond to drama using a variety of modes
5. Learn and use new words
6. Plan, draft, revise, edit, proof, and publish an interpretive essay
7. Revise sentences to create parallel structure
8. Learn how to read a play or film review
9. Research the efforts being made to improve the lives of people with disabilities

Responding to the Quotation

? Why do you think theater might provide a more intense or pleasurable experience than reading a book or watching a movie? [Possible responses: Unlike a book, theater provides visual stimulation or spectacle; the actors in a play are performing right in front of you, with no chances for retakes, making the experience more immediate and intimate than watching a movie.]

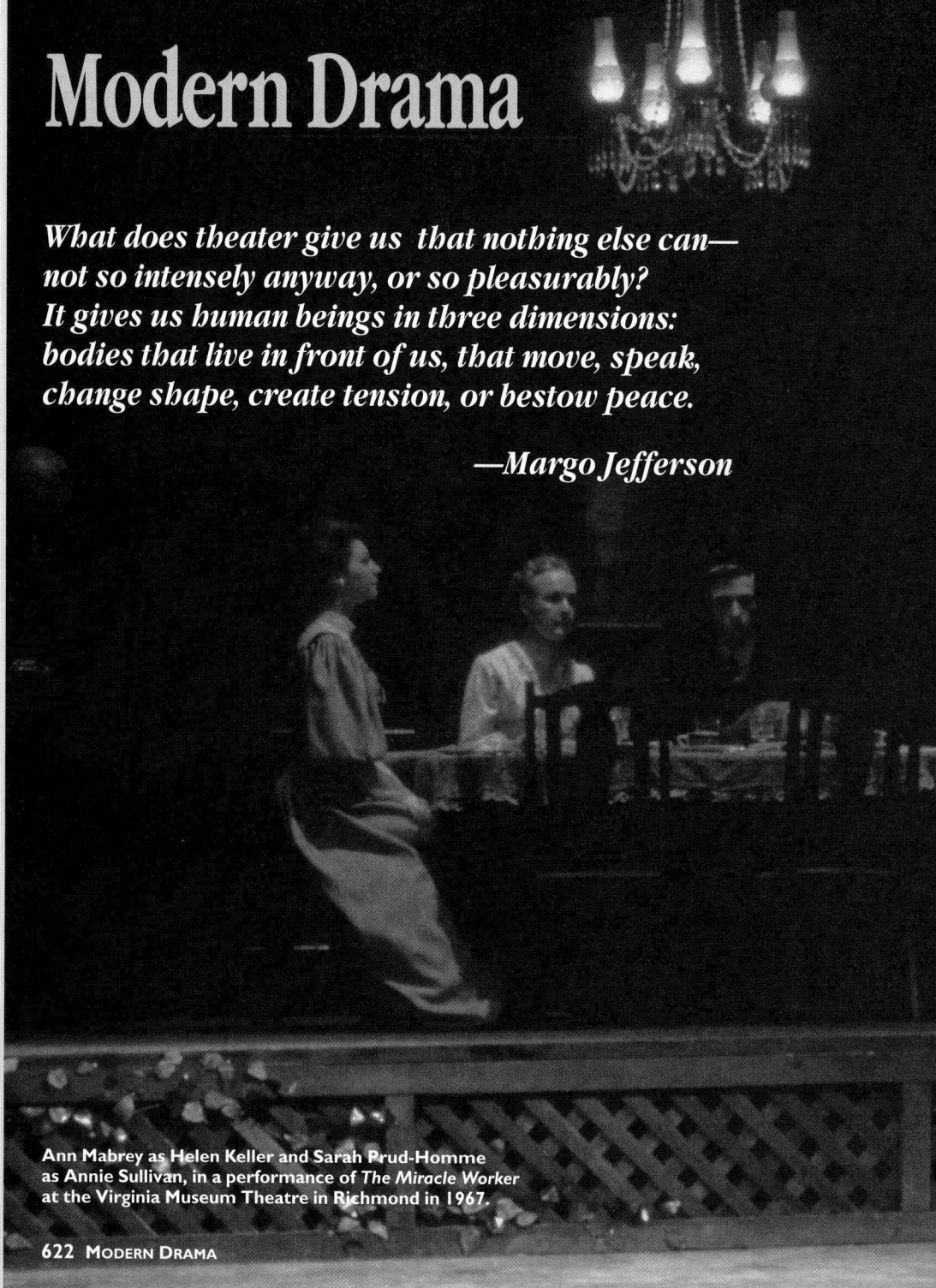

Modern Drama

What does theater give us that nothing else can—not so intensely anyway, or so pleasurably? It gives us human beings in three dimensions: bodies that live in front of us, that move, speak, change shape, create tension, or bestow peace.

—*Margo Jefferson*

Ann Mabrey as Helen Keller and Sarah Prud-Homme as Annie Sullivan, in a performance of *The Miracle Worker* at the Virginia Museum Theatre in Richmond in 1967.

622 MODERN DRAMA

Selection Readability

This Annotated Teacher's Edition provides a summary of each selection in the student book. Following each Summary heading, you will find one, two, or three small icons. These icons indicate, in an approximate sense, the reading level of the selection.

■ One icon indicates that the selection is easy.

■ ■ Two icons indicate that the selection is on an intermediate reading level.

■ ■ ■ Three icons indicate that the selection is challenging.

RESPONDING TO
THE ART

Activity. Ask students to summarize the details in this photograph. [Details: In the right foreground are a girl and a woman wearing old-fashioned dresses; the woman is wearing sunglasses; they stand near an old water pump; a broken dish lies at their feet; behind them is the facade of a house; the light is dim; in the left background are two men and two women sitting at a dining room table on a raised platform beneath a chandelier; along the bottom of the photograph is a strip of latticework.] **What can you infer from these details?** [Possible response: The expressions of the woman and the girl suggest surprise or shock.] **What questions do you have about the photograph?** [Possible questions: Why is the woman wearing sunglasses? Why are the two groups of people separated from each other?] **What clues can you find in the photograph to show that this is a scene from a play and not from a film?** [Possible responses: There is no wall separating the outdoors from the dining room; there is a stark contrast in lighting between the scene in the foreground and the scene in the background.]

A Writer on Writing Plays

WILLIAM GIBSON TALKS ABOUT THE MIRACLE WORKER

The following comments about The Miracle Worker *were made by playwright William Gibson the night that a film version of his famous play was scheduled for a rerun on TV.*

Gibson:

Tonight at eight on **NBC**, *The Miracle Worker* will be broadcast in its second television incarnation. Set in 1887, the play recounts the critical events in the first months of Annie Sullivan's struggle to teach the young deaf, mute, and blind Helen Keller how to communicate with the rest of humanity. Its first telecast was live. I wrote that version twenty-three summers ago when *all* television was live, rehearsal time was scant, unwritten pages were improvised, actors went blank over missing props, cameras photographed each other, and everything was sprightlier. So, for example, our first chance to hear the score was in dress rehearsal, violins sobbing away in another studio piped in to us in the control booth; our director, Arthur Penn, groaned, "This music is killing us!" and an hour later on the air was—unbeknownst to the musicians giving their all—dialing most of it out ad lib. . . .

No such misadventures will occur in tonight's filmed production. This cast rehearsed in Los Angeles for three weeks, played on stage in Palm Beach for two, and went back to the Coast for another month of filming. But one surprise, for audiences who

two decades ago saw Patty Duke as young Helen Keller, may be that she grew up to portray her teacher Annie; her pupil now is played by Melissa Gilbert, at age fifteen, a most familiar figure to viewers of *Little House on the Prairie*.

I never thought much of the play, till last year. My opinion is hardly objective; after opening night, I can't stand any of my plays and do my best to avoid seeing them. With *The Miracle Worker* I got trapped in venality.[1] I wrote it a second time as a stage play, and a third time as a movie; the present teleplay is my fourth trek through it. My favorite editions now are in those exotic languages I can't tell front from back of. Last year I saw it in Afrikaans, couldn't comprehend a word, and for the first time thought it looked like a real play—by somebody else. . . .

What makes for a hit is always an enigma,[2] but one element certainly is common ground between the writer and his audience. The author of *The Miracle Worker* believed in children, was young, energetic, incorrigibly[3] optimistic, no stranger to the "uplifting" in life; these are not objectionable qualities, and they flowed naturally into the script.

Patty Duke and Melissa Gilbert in *The Miracle Worker* on NBC in 1979.

And it was obviously a love letter. To whom, I would learn later. I like to fall a little in love with my heroines, and the title—from Mark Twain, who said, "Helen is a miracle, and Miss Sullivan is the miracle worker"—was meant to show where my affections lay. This stubborn girl of twenty, who six years earlier could not write her name, and in one month salvaged Helen's soul, and lived thereafter in its shadow, seemed to me to deserve a star bow.

1. **venality** (vi·nal′ə·tē): willingness to waste one's talents for financial gain.
2. **enigma** (i·nig′mə): something puzzling.
3. **incorrigibly** (in·kôr′ə·jə·blē): in a way that cannot be corrected.

OBJECTIVES

1. Understand literary forms and terms related to drama, including exposition, conflict, dramatic questions, complications, climax and resolution
2. Identify the protagonist and the antagonist and analyze character
3. Recognize time structures used in drama: linear style, flashbacks, and dream sequences

Resources

Elements of Drama

For additional instruction on the elements of drama, see *Literary Elements*
• Transparency 16

Formal Assessment
• Literary Elements Test, p. 129

Elements of Drama

This feature, written by playwright Robert Anderson, focuses on the elements of drama: character, protagonist, antagonist, exposition, conflict, dramatic question, complication, climax, and resolution.

Mini-Lesson:
Elements of Drama

You may want to begin by having students give definitions in their own words for familiar literary elements. For example, ask students to
• describe the difference between external and internal conflict
• define the four major parts of a plot: exposition (or basic situation), complication, climax, and resolution.
Have students provide examples of each familiar literary element, using selections they have read in other collections. Then focus students' attention on the elements introduced in this collection: protagonist, antagonist, and dramatic question. Have students discuss the protagonists and antagonists in works they are all familiar with. Finally, explore the difference between an ordinary question such as "What time is it?" and a dramatic question such as "What action will my brother take?" Help students understand that a dramatic question always involves conflict.

Elements of Drama
by Robert Anderson

Eugene O'Neill, America's first great playwright, said that a play should reveal the most intense basic human interrelationships. Perhaps this is why, over the years, so many playwrights have written about families. Probably nowhere else do we find such intense feelings as those we find within the family.

Even the happiest families have conflicts, great and small. Parents have dreams for their children. Children have dreams of their own. Children need to belong to the family and to feel its support; they also need to be independent. Families feel the strains from living closely together. Families face the problems of aging. The conflicts in a family range from mild, funny blowups to battles royal which break families apart.

Conflict: The Basis of Drama

Let's imagine a typical family situation:

The Nortons have just finished dinner. Then Sara starts the trouble: She tells her brother that she's going to ask for the family car tonight. Her brother, knowing that Sara disobeyed her parents and kept the car out too late the night before, feels a sense of dread and warns Sara not to ask for it. But Sara is going ahead. It is important to her. She fears she'll lose her friends if she can't drive them—she *promised*.

Here we have all the elements for the beginning of a drama. One character, Sara, expresses a want. ("I want the car.") She is our protagonist. A **protagonist** is generally the person who drives the action, who has the want, who takes the step to get what she (or he) wants. Sara has something at stake (her friends), and there is an obstacle in her way—her parents (the **antagonists**) and their probable refusal to let her have the car.

In dramatic terms, then, we have the **exposition**—the presentation of the characters and their basic situation; we have the foreshadowing, or suggestions, of a **conflict** (Sara's brother has asked her not to ask for the car); and we have a basic **dramatic question**: "Will Sara get what she wants?"

Sara goes to her ally, her mother, and tells her that she wants the car. Her mother says no: The roads are slick with ice. Then, in irritation, the mother adds something else: She doesn't care for Sara's friends.

626 MODERN DRAMA

Using Students' Strengths

Visual Learners

Using a story they've read, have students create a storyboard for the three drama segments—exposition, complication, and climax—described on pp. 626–627. After labeling their storyboards with the appropriate terms, they may wish to develop a concluding scene portraying some resolution of the problem. Ask students to share their storyboards in small groups.

Interpersonal Learners

Have students work in pairs to read Elements of Drama and to rewrite each heading in the form of a question such as "How is conflict the basis of drama?" or "Why are feeling, story, and form important concerns for a playwright?" Then, partners should provide answers to the questions.

T626

The protagonist has now taken her first step and has met an obstacle and an unexpected **complication:** She's discovered that her mother doesn't like her friends.

Sara ignores what her brother and mother say (as the protagonist, she has to, if we're to have a story) and she asks her father.

Now we are moving toward the drama's **climax**—that moment when our tension and emotions are at a peak, when we watch the characters engage in the final struggle that is going to determine the **resolution** of the problem. (In westerns and detective movies this is the moment of the last big shootout.)

Sara makes her request. The battle begins. Her father not only says no because the roads are bad, but he goes on to reveal other feelings; he says that Sara is showing poor judgment and has become irresponsible. Under the pressure of the situation, Mr. Norton, like Mrs. Norton, reveals what he never would have said under other circumstances.

Now an argument may follow. The mother at first sides with the father; then she starts to defend her daughter. The brother may run away from the argument, or join in on Sara's side. "You don't understand her. You don't understand either of us." Blowup. Tears. The pressure-cooker situation has exposed all the characters to themselves and to one another. Sara storms out of the house. The question asked at the beginning of the story is answered: Sara does *not* get the car. In most homes the daughter would return and some compromise would be worked out. In a serious drama Sara might be gone forever.

During the working out of the conflict in this family story, something else has taken place. Relationships have changed. Relationships and what happens to them are one of the main elements of a play. Sara, who always thought her parents trusted her, finds out what they really think.

Characters We Care About

Writing about the family can help the playwright with a basic task—to organize the emotions of the audience, to arouse our interest or sympathy for one or more of the characters. (In the old melodramas, where there were real, detestable villains, writers organized the emotions of the audience very simply: Early in the play they would turn the audience against the villain by having him kick a dog.)

Poster Courtesy of Triton Gallery. © Romare Bearden Foundation/Licensed by VAGA, New York, NY.

ELEMENTS OF DRAMA 627

After students have read the material on pp. 626–630, ask them to make a checklist like the one below. Students can complete the checklist as they read *The Miracle Worker.* Encourage them to revise their responses as they read— changing their first guess at the protagonist, for example, or identifying a second antagonist.

Elements of Drama

- Identify the **protagonist:** _____
  _____

- List **antagonists:** _____
  _____

- Summarize the information presented in the **exposition:** _____
  _____

- Describe a **conflict:** _____
  _____

- Express this play's **dramatic question:** _____
  _____

- Describe a **complication:** _____
  _____

- Identify the **climax:** _____
  _____

- Briefly describe the **resolution:** ____
  _____

- Did you experience the **"shock of recognition"?** If so, identify the scene: _____
  _____

Reaching All Students

Struggling Readers
To help students understand the terms associated with drama, have them write each bold-faced term and its definition on the front of a three- by five-inch note card. Students may refer to these cards as they read *The Miracle Worker* and write examples of each term on the backs of the cards. Also, the cards may be combined into a class reference file.

Advanced Learners
After students have read the material on pp. 626–630, ask them to consider ways in which drama and fiction are similar and different. Have students hypothesize about the varying challenges of writing for the stage and writing for the printed page.

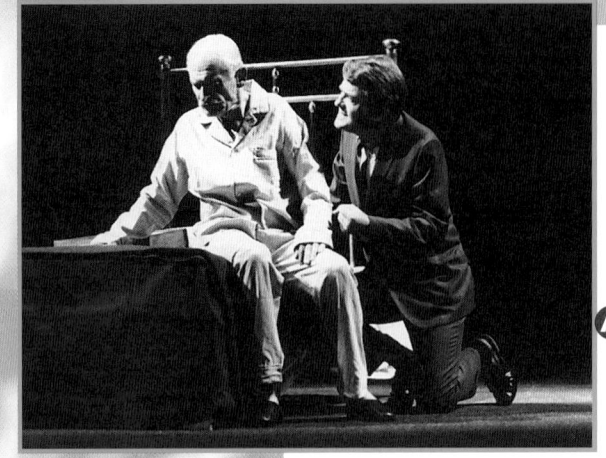

Scene from *I Never Sang for My Father.*

We are all more or less familiar with the "cast of characters" in families. Though these characters are as unique as thumbprints, they are all as similar as thumbs. When my play *I Never Sang for My Father* was produced, I received letters from people asking questions like "How did you know my father?" Of course, I didn't know *their* fathers, but I knew my own. Thus playwrights may write out of feelings for their own particular family, and if they write truly, they sometimes achieve a universality. They may make the audience understand something about all families.

This, of course, is one of the aims of art—to reveal the universal through the particular. The characters in plays may seem larger than life, but they are not bizarre, theatrical creatures. The great plays are able to revitalize the familiar. They help us to see our own lives in perspective—our own parents, our own wives or husbands, our own friends. Play-wrights strike notes from their own feelings and experiences, and they hope for a responsive chord from the audience.

The "Shock of Recognition"

A play, then, actually exists halfway between the stage and the audience. By choosing the familiar ground of the family, the playwright sometimes finds it easier to reach an audience. Spectators in the theater are often doing two things at once: They are watching a play on the stage, and at the same time they are relating to their own experiences. They are feeling what is known as the shock of recognition. *"How did you know my father?"*

The two plays in this book dramatize conflicts within the general framework of the family. They examine easily recognized situations about which hundreds of plays, films, and television dramas have been written. In *The Miracle Worker* there is a family with a severely handi-capped child and an outsider who comes to help. In *Romeo and Juliet* there are the two young lovers who will marry despite all obstacles. In the case of *Romeo and Juliet,* the protagonists' obstacle is an old feud between their families. In more modern plays based on this situation, the obstacles might be race, religion, or class, as in the musical version of Shakespeare's play—the Bernstein-Sondheim-Laurents *West Side Story.*

628 MODERN DRAMA

Taking a Second Look

"Is It True?"

While playwrights write out of what they know, out of what concerns them, probably very little of their work is strictly autobiographical. The Nobel Prize–winning novelist William Faulkner said that a writer needs experience, observation, and imagination. Writers rarely limit themselves to re-creating an actual person as a character in a play. Playwrights may base a character on a person they know, but then they invent and expand to suit the needs of the story. Painters may use models for poses or outlines, but after a while they become more interested in what is on the canvas. Artists develop their paintings so that they may end up scarcely resembling the original model.

An example of a dramatist who expanded and invented to suit the particular aims of each play was Eugene O'Neill. He used his family as the basis for two plays: the comic and sentimental play called *Ah, Wilderness!* and the tragic play called *Long Day's Journey into Night.* The same family—very different plays!

Drama Is a Verb

The dynamic, or drive, of each play in this book is the same: People we care about struggle through crucial situations because they have something important at stake. Note the word *struggle. Drama* is, in a sense, a verb. Drama should involve action, and that action can be verbal or physical. In our Norton family story, the action was verbal, as each person in the family tried to achieve his or her ends with words. (The gunfight in the dusty Western town at high noon would be physical action.)

A Playwright's Concerns: Feeling, Story, and Form

When playwrights sit down to write plays, they have many things to consider. First, they must decide if their feeling about the material is strong enough. Will it hold their interest for the time it takes to write the play— which might be as long as three years? Will they be able to convey their excitement or humor or emotion to an audience? Mildness is a curse in the theater, and playwrights have to decide if the feelings they are communicating will have a strong impact.

Next, playwrights must ask whether the story they want to tell is dramatic. Does it involve interesting people in a conflict which moves to a crisis and a climax?

Finally, playwrights must consider the form in which they'll write. Probably most of us are more aware of form in painting than in

STANLEY KRAMER PRODUCTIONS presents
GARY COOPER
"HIGH NOON"

THERE IS NOTHING UNDER THE SUN
LIKE THE HIGH ADVENTURE OF "HIGH NOON"!

C Literary Connections

New York born Eugene O'Neill (1888–1953) was the first and only American playwright to receive the Nobel Prize in literature. He borrowed freely from his often unhappy family life for dramatic material. His masterpiece, the autobiographical *Long Day's Journey into Night* (1956), details the family conflicts between a once famous actor, his morphine-addicted wife, and their two adult sons. The warm and humorous *Ah, Wilderness!* (1933)—a comedy about a turn-of-the-century middle class family in a small Connecticut town—is a rare exception to the bleak pessimism found in most of O'Neill's works.

D Critical Thinking
Interpreting

? What does Anderson mean by the statement "Mildness is a curse in the theater"? [Possible responses: Compelling plays concern intense, important, life-changing events and themes; actions and emotions are heightened to ensure that the audience will understand and be interested; audiences expect a lot to happen on stage and are bored if the play is too quiet or uneventful.]

? Why do you think a playwright might choose to use flashbacks? [Possible responses: The audience can quickly gain insight into the backgrounds and motivations of characters by being shown their previous experiences; showing past events, rather than having characters talk about them, makes them easier to understand.]

writing. We know that a picture may be painted in the more or less realistic style of a Rembrandt or in the impressionistic style of a Monet or in the cubist style of a Picasso.

A In somewhat the same way, the story of a play can be told in various forms. It can be told in a conventional straightforward way (often called linear style), with a beginning, a middle, and an end, presented in chronological order. Or the story can move back and forth in time, with such devices as flashbacks or dream sequences. One contemporary play, *Betrayal* by Harold Pinter, actually begins at the end of the story and ends at the beginning.

The two plays in this book—*The Miracle Worker* and *Romeo and Juliet*—are more or less conventional in their form. They tell their stories from beginning to end. *The Miracle Worker* uses some memory flashbacks in which we hear the voices that Annie remembers from her childhood. Otherwise, the play moves ahead in a straightforward chronological manner.

Although these two plays are different in style and tone, the shock of recognition awaits you in each. See how these particular characters and their conflicts reveal truths that are still important today. See if you ask: "How did that writer know *my* family?"

Manuscript of *Our Town* by Thornton Wilder, showing author's revisions.

The Yale Collection of American Literature, Beinecke Rare Book and Manuscript Library, Yale University, New Haven.

Assessing Learning

Check Test: Fill-in-the-Blank

1. A(n) _____ is the person who drives the action. [protagonist]

2. A(n) _____ is a person who stands in the way of or opposes the protagonist. [antagonist]

3. The _____ is the presentation of the characters and their basic situation. [exposition]

4. _____ is the basis of drama. [Conflict]

5. The drama's_____ is the most tense and emotional moment. [climax]

Collection 12

Opening Doors

Theme

From Darkness to Light *Focus on drama: A dramatist must create a character who wants something badly enough to take action to get it. Helen Keller's obstacles seem insurmountable, but Annie Sullivan is the character who will not say "no" to life.*

Reading the Anthology

Reaching Struggling Readers

The *Reading Skills and Strategies: Reaching Struggling Readers* binder includes a Reading Strategies Handbook that offers concrete suggestions for helping students who have difficulty reading and comprehending text, or students who are reluctant readers. When a specific strategy is most appropriate for a selection, a correlation to the Handbook is provided at the bottom of the teacher's page under the head Struggling Readers. This head may also be used to introduce additional ideas for helping students read challenging texts.

Reading Beyond the Anthology

Read On

Each collection in the grade nine book includes an annotated bibliography of books suitable for extended reading. The suggested books are related to works in the collection by theme, by author, or by subject. To preview the Read On for Collection 12, please turn to p. T715.

HRW Library

The *HRW Library* offers novels, plays, works of nonfiction, and short-story collections for extended reading. Each book in the Library includes a major work and thematically or topically related Connections. The Connections are magazine articles, poems, or other pieces of literature. Each book in the *HRW Library* is also accompanied by a Study Guide that provides teaching suggestions and worksheets. The two titles shown here will work well to extend the theme of Collection 12.

NARRATIVE OF THE LIFE OF FREDERICK DOUGLASS
The lifelong struggle of Frederick Douglass was to open doors for himself and for other African Americans. His dramatic autobiography recounts his efforts to abolish the dehumanizing practice of slavery.

PYGMALION George Bernard Shaw
Shaw's play centers on the struggle of Dr. Higgins to teach a cockney girl, Eliza Doolittle, to speak the King's English. The doctor's goal is to prove it can be done, but Eliza's goal is to open doors and improve her station in life.

Collection 12 **Opening Doors**

Resources for this Collection

Note: All resources for this collection are available for preview on the *One-Stop Planner CD-ROM 2 with Test Generator.* All worksheets and blackline masters may be printed from the CD-ROM.

Internet Resources
go.hrw.com **LE0 9-12**

Selection or Feature	Reading and Literary Skills	Vocabulary, Language, and Grammar
Elements of Drama (p. 626)	• *Literary Elements,* Transparency 16	
The Miracle Worker William Gibson (p. 632) **Connections: Everything Had a Name** *from* **The Story of My Life** Helen Keller (p. 704)	• *Graphic Organizers for Active Reading,* Worksheet pp. 61, 62, 63 • *Literary Elements:* Transparency 16 Worksheet p. 49	• *Words to Own,* Worksheet pp. 36, 37, 38 • *Daily Oral Grammar,* Transparencies 42, 43
Extending the Theme: Annie *from* **Helen and Teacher** Joseph P. Lash (p. 710)	The Extending the Theme feature provides students with an unstructured opportunity to practice reading strategies using a selection that extends the theme of the collection.	
Writer's Workshop: Interpretive Essay (p. 716)		
Sentence Workshop: Parallel Structure (p. 721)		• *Workshop Resources,* p. 77 • *Language Workshop CD-ROM,* Parallel Structure
Learning for Life: Opening Doors for Others (p. 723)		

Other Resources for this Collection

- *Cross-Curricular Activities*, p. 12
- *Portfolio Management System*, Introduction to Portfolio Assessment, p. 1
- *Formal Assessment*, Genre Test, p. 131
- *Test Generator*, Collection Test 🔘

Writing	Listening and Speaking Viewing and Representing	Assessment
		• *Formal Assessment*, Literary Elements Test, p. 129
• *Portfolio Management System*, Rubrics for Choices, pp. 193–195	• *Visual Connections:* Videocassette B, Segment 12 📼 • *Audio CD Library,* Disc 17, Track 2 🎧 • *Viewing and Representing:* Fine Art Transparency 17; Worksheet p. 68 🖥️ • *Portfolio Management System,* Rubrics for Choices, pp. 193–195	• *Formal Assessment*, Selection Tests, pp. 123, 125, 127 • *Standardized Test Preparation,* pp. 78, 80, 82 • *Test Generator (One-Stop Planner CD-ROM)* 🔘
	• *Audio CD Library,* Disc 17, Track 3 🎧	

• *Workshop Resources*, p. 49
 	
• *Writer's Workshop 2 CD-ROM,* Interpretation 🔘
		• *Portfolio Management System*
		  • Prewriting, p. 197
		  • Peer Editing, p. 198
		  • Assessment Rubric, p. 199

		• *Portfolio Management System*, Rubrics, p. 200

Collection Planner

 Transparency    CD-ROM   Video   🎧 Audio CD

T630C

Collection 12 Opening Doors

Skills Focus

Skills Focus (side tab)

Selection or Feature	Reading Skills and Strategies	Elements of Literature	Language/ Grammar	Vocabulary/ Spelling	Writing	Listening/ Speaking	Viewing/ Representing
The Miracle Worker William Gibson (p. 632) **Act One** (p. 636)	How to Read a Play, pp. 632, 660–661 • Stage Directions • Activity • Action • Mood	Protagonist, p. 660 Antagonist, p. 660 Action, p. 660 Symbols, p. 660 Conflict, p. 660		Semantic Mapping, p. 661	Keep a Double-Entry Journal to Note Key Passages, p. 661 Write a Diary from the Point of View of a Character, p. 661	Perform a Scene from the Play, p. 661	
Act Two (p. 662)		Reversal, p. 686 Internal Conflict, p. 686 Flashback, p. 686 Character Change, p. 686	Sign Language, p. 684	Synonyms, p. 687	Identify Symbols in the Play, p. 687 Add to a Diary, p. 687	Make a Sound-Effects Recording, p. 687	
Act Three (p. 688)		Character Change, p. 707 Reversal, p. 707 Climax, p. 707 Subplot, p. 707 Conflict, p. 707 Message, p. 707 Stage Directions, p. 708		Roots and Affixes, p. 709	Identify Changes in a Character, p. 708 Write a Scene as a Sequel to the Play, p. 708 Write a Short Essay Based on a Topic Sentence, p. 708 Write a Response to a Critical Comment, p. 708 Compare and Contrast Texts, p. 708		
Extending the Theme: Annie from **Helen and Teacher** Joseph P. Lash (p. 710)	Dialogue with the Text, p. 710 Double-Entry Journal, p. 710	The Extending the Theme feature provides students with an unstructured opportunity to practice reading strategies using a selection that extends the theme of the collection.					
Writer's Workshop: Interpretive Essay (p. 716)	Primary and Secondary Sources, p. 718			Punctuate Quotations Correctly, p. 718	Write an Interpretive Essay, pp. 716–720		
Sentence Workshop: Parallel Structure (p. 721)			Parallel Structure, p. 721		Revise Sentences to Correct Parallel Structure, p. 721		
Reading for Life: Reading a Play or Film Review (p. 722)	Compare Critical Viewpoints, p. 722					Develop Criteria for Evaluating a Play or Film, p. 722	
Learning for Life: Opening Doors for Others (p. 723)					Prepare and Tape a Thirty-Second Public Service Announcement, p. 723	Create a Photo Essay, p. 723 Create a Model and Demonstrate Its Use, p. 723	

We come across many doors in a lifetime—doors into relationships, responsibilities, opportunities. If life is easy, the doors all open smoothly. If life is more difficult, we find that some doors require a lot of effort to open—some stay locked and bolted no matter how we pound at them. Often, even with those doors we struggle to open, we aren't really sure what we'll find on the other side.

But sometimes opening a door can change our lives. In this play, which is based on a true story, a young teacher tries to open a door that will give a little girl a fuller life. Behind the door, the little girl is locked out of the world of words. Behind that door, Helen is totally alone.

A journey of a thousand miles must begin with a single step.

—*Laotzu*

Writer's Notebook

In the Writer's Workshop on page 716 you'll write an interpretation of *The Miracle Worker*. Before you start reading the play, think about its title and the theme of this collection: Opening Doors. In a few words, give your first impressions of what the title might mean and how it might relate to "opening doors." Save your notes.

OPENING DOORS **631**

Responding to the Quotation

Laotzu is considered one of China's greatest philosophers. Born around 600 B.C., he is the presumed author of the influential *Tao Te Ching*, or *The Way of Power*.

❓ What does this quotation by Laotzu make you think of? [Sample responses: a baby learning to walk; a person learning a new skill; a person trying to achieve a hard-to-reach goal.] Why do you think the first step is so important? [Students may say that taking the first step may be the hardest part of doing something that a person has never done before. These first steps can be frightening yet extremely rewarding.]

RESPONDING TO THE ART

Activity. What metaphorical door is the teacher helping to open up for the children in the photograph? [the door to schooling or education]

Writer's Notebook

To help students focus their responses, have them consider the following questions:
- What does the last word in the title suggest?
- What are some events that might be considered miraculous?
- What kind of doors might be opened only as a result of a miracle?

Writing Focus: Interpretive Essay

The following **Work in Progress** assignments build to a culminating **Writer's Workshop** at the end of the collection.

- Act One — Focusing on key passages (p. 661)
- Act Two — Looking for symbols (p. 687)
- Act Three — Looking at the characters (p. 708)

Writer's Workshop: Expository Writing / Interpretive Essay (p. 716)

1. Read and interpret the play
2. Analyze character
3. Learn how to read a play
4. Express understanding through creative writing and speaking
5. Understand and use new words
6. Construct semantic maps

SKILLS

Literary
- Analyze character

Reading
- Learn how to read a play

Writing
- Start a double-entry journal
- Write diary entries from a character's point of view

Speaking/Listening
- Prepare and present a scene from the play

Vocabulary
- Use new words
- Construct semantic maps

Viewing/Representing
- Respond to photographs of film and stage productions of the play (ATE)

Planning

- **Block Schedule**
  Block Scheduling Lesson Plans with Pacing Guide

- **Traditional Schedule**
  Lesson Plans Including Strategies for English-Language Learners

- **One-Stop Planner**
  CD-ROM with Test Generator

Before You Read

THE MIRACLE WORKER

Make the Connection

**"She Can't *See!* . . .
She Can't *Hear!* . . ."**

Close your eyes for a few minutes. What can you tell about what's going on around you? Now, keeping your eyes closed, cover your ears. Concentrate on the hum that seems to come from inside your head. What can you tell about what's going on around you? Finally, consider all that we learn through the senses of sight and hearing. Can you imagine what it would be like to live without sight and hearing from infancy?

Quickwrite

Before you read the play, take a few minutes to write down your ideas about what *you* think a child would be like who has lived in a dark and silent world since she was a baby.

Young Helen Keller.

Reading Skills and Strategies

How to Read a Play

A playwright tells a story by letting us see and hear what the characters say and do. Plays are not meant to be read; they are written to be performed before an audience. Dialogue—the words that the characters speak—gives us our best clues to what those characters are like and what they are thinking. Stage directions—descriptions of the setting and of the characters' appearances, personalities, thoughts, and movements—provide another good clue.

We use stage directions to help us understand what the characters are feeling. In plays written for the stage, directions are usually printed in italics and appear in parentheses or brackets. Often stage directions follow a character's name: **Walter** (*tense*). Sometimes they appear in paragraph-sized chunks between characters' speeches.

We use our imagination to see important actions taking place onstage. Two kinds of movements take place on the stage: activity and action. **Activity** is any movement: picking up a cup, closing a door. **Action** is dramatically meaningful activity. Action moves a story forward or deepens our understanding of a character. For example, the stage directions might say, *"Clara closes the door."* We have to read carefully and picture this happening onstage. Is closing the door just an activity that means Clara shuts a door, nothing more or less? Or is this a dramatically meaningful activity, one that means something more, such as the end of Clara's relationship with Ken? When you read *The Miracle Worker,* you must be especially sensitive to the stage directions. Read them carefully, and try to picture what is happening. Some of the action in the play is more important than the dialogue.

We are aware of changes in mood onstage. When a stage direction says *"The room darkens,"* you have to picture the room getting darker. You have to imagine how the set looks. You have to feel the change in mood. When you read a play with your imagination, you stage the play for yourself. You see and hear everything that is happening—just as if you were sitting in a theater on Broadway.

Preteaching Vocabulary

Words to Own

Call on volunteers to locate the Words to Own at the bottom of the pages of Act One. Ask them to read the words and their definitions aloud. Have another volunteer write each word on the board as it is read. The words are: **vivacious, benign, indolent, impudence, inarticulate, resurrection, appraisal, voluminous, caricature,** and **asperity.**

Next, place students in groups of three, and pair the groups. Have the groups take turns pantomiming the meaning of a word and guessing what the word is. Students might find it easier to suggest the meaning of a word through a drawing rather than pantomime. For example, they might draw a picture of a person in a hammock to suggest *indolent.*

Background

William Gibson's play *The Miracle Worker,* a true story, is based on the early life of Helen Keller, blind and deaf from infancy, and her teacher, Annie Sullivan. The play was first presented in 1957 on a CBS television program called *Playhouse 90.*

Gibson later expanded this teleplay into the full-length stage play we have here, which opened on Broadway on October 10, 1959. This play retains the fluid quality of its original television form: Short, highly dramatic scenes flow into one another, each scene developing conflicts and crises and decisions that move the story to the next scene.

Note particularly the arresting opening scene—evidence of the play's original television format. One of the principles of television writing is that the writer must capture the attention of the viewers immediately or they will turn to another channel. Thus, we are immediately hooked by the family crisis. The play plunges us at once into a desperate situation with "She can't *see!* . . . She can't *hear* you!"

Because this play deals with a main character who cannot speak or hear, much of the action must be worked out in activity, which is indicated in the long stage directions. Anyone who reads what Annie and Helen do onstage should not be surprised to learn that the actresses in these roles found their jobs physically exhausting. During the Broadway production, the actresses playing Helen and Annie wore padding under their clothing to protect themselves from each other's blows.

Throughout the play, Annie hears voices from her past. In the stage production these voices were taped and amplified. Speakers placed on the side walls of the theater projected the voices with an echo that sounded otherworldly. The result was that members of the audience heard the echoing voices just as Annie was hearing them.

The Miracle Worker was made into a movie that won several Academy Awards. Later it was turned back into a television play. This time, on television, Patty Duke, who had played Helen onstage and in the movie, played the part of Annie Sullivan.

Annie spelling into Helen's hand, in the movie.

Helen and Annie at the pump, in the NBC television movie.

go.hrw.com
LE0 9-12

THE MIRACLE WORKER 633

Summary ■ ■

Set in Alabama in the 1880s, *The Miracle Worker* tells the true story of the early weeks in the relationship between six-year-old Helen Keller, left deaf and blind by a childhood illness, and twenty-year-old Annie Sullivan, a recent graduate of the Perkins Institution for the Blind in Boston. In struggling to reclaim Helen's future by unlocking her intelligence through language, Annie makes peace with her own tortured past and learns to love again. [See also the summaries provided on the opening page of each act.]

Resources

Viewing and Representing

Videocassette B, Segment 12
Available in Spanish and English. Prepare students for their reading of *The Miracle Worker* by showing them "An Enlightening Life: Helen Keller," the *Visual Connections* segment about Helen Keller's life. For full lesson plans and worksheets, see *Visual Connections Teacher's Manual.*

Listening

Audio CD Library
Look for a recording of Act One of the play in the *Audio CD Library:*
• Disc 17, Track 2

Viewing and Representing

Fine Art Transparency
The fine art transparency of Winslow Homer's *Summer* will complement students' reading of the play. See the *Viewing and Representing Transparencies and Worksheets:*
• Transparency 17 • Worksheet, p. 68

Elements of Literature

The Elements of Drama
See *Literary Elements:*
• Transparency 16 • Worksheet, p. 49

Resources: Print and Media

Reading
• *Graphic Organizers for Active Reading,* p. 61
• *Words to Own,* p. 36
• *Audio CD Library,*
    Disc 17, Track 2

Elements of Literature
• *Literary Elements*
    Transparency 16
    Worksheet, p. 49

Writing and Language
• *Daily Oral Grammar*
    Transparency 42

Viewing and Representing
• *Viewing and Representing*
    Fine Art Transparency 17
    Fine Art Worksheet, p. 68
• *Visual Connections*
    Videocassette B, Segment 12

Assessment
• *Formal Assessment,* p. 123
• *Portfolio Management System,* p. 193
• *Standardized Test Preparation,* p. 78
• *Test Generator (One-Stop Planner* CD-ROM)

Internet
• go.hrw.com (keyword: LE0 9-12)

Responding to the Quotation

❓ **What comparison does the simile in this quotation make?** [Helen is compared to a locked safe that no one can open.] **What is the meaning of this simile?** [Possible responses: Helen's mind is locked up inside her, and no one can understand her; no one knows what is inside Helen because she can't communicate.] **What do you think the "treasure" might be?** [Possible response: Helen's unique thoughts and feelings, which are waiting to be expressed.] **How might the "safe" that is Helen be unlocked?** [Possible response: Someone must provide the "key" or the "combination" that will allow her to communicate.]

"She is like a little safe, locked, that no one can open. Perhaps there is a treasure inside."

634 MODERN DRAMA

Reaching All Students

Struggling Readers

Encourage readers to pay close attention to the information provided in the first scene of the drama. You may wish to pair readers, ask them to reread the scene aloud, and then have them ask each other questions such as the following:
- Where does the first scene take place?
- What characters have been introduced?
- What have we learned about these characters so far?

English Language Learners

Discuss how the dialect of Viney, Martha, and Percy (examples on pp. 638, 647–648) varies from standard English. Point out how Gibson uses spelling and punctuation to reproduce the dialect as a way of bringing even these minor characters to life. For strategies for engaging English language learners with the literature, see
- *Lesson Plans Including Strategies for English-Language Learners*

Advanced Learners

William Gibson worried that Hollywood studios would ruin his play; he feared that a film version "would end up having Helen marry Alexander Graham Bell, or something." Have students consider Gibson's fears as they read the play. How might Hollywood change the story and the staging to appeal to moviegoers? Would such changes ruin the story?

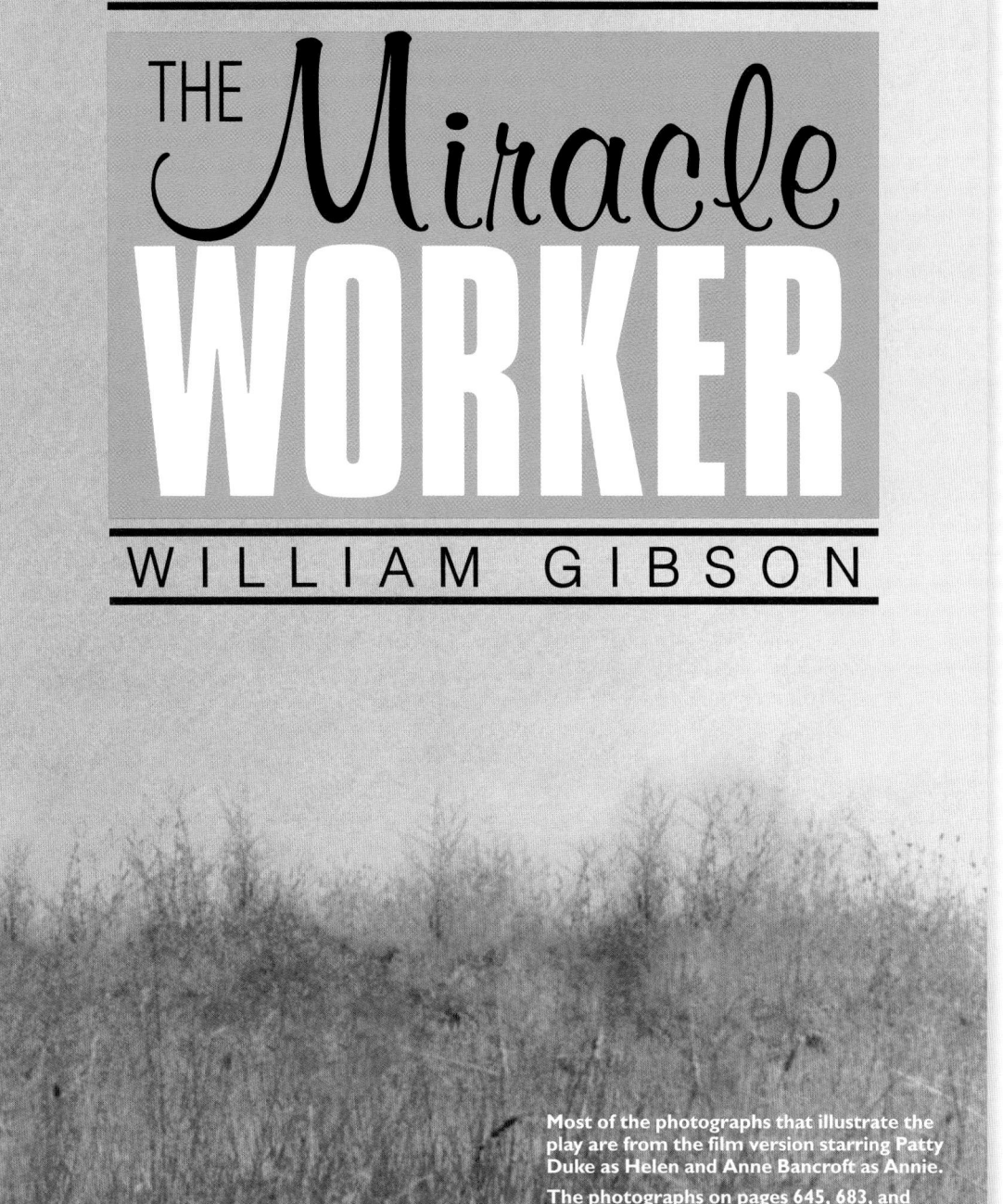

THE *Miracle* WORKER

WILLIAM GIBSON

Most of the photographs that illustrate the play are from the film version starring Patty Duke as Helen and Anne Bancroft as Annie.

The photographs on pages 645, 683, and 702 are from the Broadway production of the play.

Historical Connections

Before students begin the play, have them locate Tuscumbia, Alabama, and Boston, Massachusetts, on a map. Point out that in the 1880s the Civil War (1861–1865) was still fresh in the memories of Americans—particularly those of Southerners, whose way of life had been radically altered. Encourage students to keep an eye out for references to this historical context as they read the play. You might also want to have small groups of students research their state's history in relation to the Civil War. What role did their state play in the war? What was the war's effect on their state?

FROM THE EDITOR'S DESK

It has been many years since most of us read *The Miracle Worker*. It was, after all, written more than four decades ago. But rereading it is always a deeply moving experience. The story is so inspiring, and the drama, particularly during the last scene of the play, is both riveting and heart-wrenching. We are convinced that students encountering the play for the first time today will be as emotionally struck by it as we are.

In additional to its dramatic qualities and its portrayal of a genuine heroine, the play can provide spin offs into several other subject areas. Students interested in history can investigate Irish immigration in the mid-1800s and the existence of poorhouses like Tewksbury. Scientifically oriented students could investigate the prevalence of eye diseases and tuberculosis among the poor in the nineteenth century. They might also investigate the exact cause of Helen's blindness and deafness.

Using Students' Strengths

Kinesthetic Learners

Help students relate to the strategies Helen uses to navigate and make sense of the world. Organize the class into groups. Then, ask each group to find a scene in which Helen must use means other than sight or hearing to accomplish an ordinary task. Each group should write a description of Helen's approach to completing her task and share it with the rest of the class.

Summary ■ ■ ■

Act One

The play opens with a short scene where the Kellers' discover that an illness has left their infant daughter, Helen, unable to hear or see. Scene two takes place five years later. Helen's handicaps threaten the safety of herself and others. Discouraged by the failure of doctors to help Helen and by their own inability to control her, the Kellers hire Annie Sullivan as a governess. Although Helen's mother becomes Sullivan's ally, Helen's father—who distrusts Annie because she is a Northerner—and Helen's half brother, James, challenge the newcomer at every turn. Helen herself proves to be stubborn and rambunctious. Annie tries to make Helen aware of language by tracing out each letter of the words in the child's hand. When Helen locks her new teacher in a bedroom and hides the key, Annie learns to respect Helen's intelligence and strong will.

 **Reading Skills and Strategies**

How to Read a Play

Explain that the terms *downstage* and *upstage* refer to the front and rear of the stage, respectively. *Stage left* and *stage right* identify the two sides of the stage from the point of view of an actor facing the audience. Thus "down left" indicates the area at the front of the stage to the actor's left. The terms *downstage* and *upstage* date to the end of the 19th century, when many stages were raked, or sloped upward, from front to rear.

The playing space is divided into two areas by a more or less diagonal line, which runs from downstage right to upstage left.

The area behind this diagonal is on platforms and represents the Keller house; inside we see, down right, a family room, and up center, elevated, a bedroom. On stage level near center, outside a porch, there is a water pump.

The other area, in front of the diagonal, is neutral ground; it accommodates various places as designated at various times—the yard before the Keller home, the Perkins Institution for the Blind, the garden house, and so forth.

The less set there is, the better. The stage should be free, airy, unencumbered by walls. Apart from certain practical items—such as the pump, a window to climb out of, doors to be locked—locales should be only skeletal suggestions, and the movement from one to another should be accomplishable by little more than lights.

Characters

A Doctor
Kate, *Helen's mother*
Keller, *Helen's father*
Helen
Martha⎫
Percy⎭ *children of servants*
Aunt Ev
James, *Captain Keller's son by his first marriage*
Anagnos, *Director of the Perkins Institution for the Blind, in Boston*
Annie Sullivan
Viney, *a servant*
Blind Girls
A Servant
Offstage Voices

Time: The 1880s.
Place: In and around the Keller homestead in Tuscumbia, Alabama; also, briefly, the Perkins Institution for the Blind, in Boston.

SCENE 1

It is night over the Keller homestead.

Inside, three adults in the bedroom are grouped around a crib, in lamplight. They have been through a long vigil, and it shows in their tired bearing and disarranged clothing. One is a young gentlewoman with a sweet girlish face, KATE KELLER; *the second is an elderly* DOCTOR, *stethoscope at neck, thermometer in fingers; the third is a hearty gentleman in his forties with chin whiskers,* CAPTAIN ARTHUR KELLER.

Doctor. She'll live.
Kate. Thank God.

[The DOCTOR *leaves them together over the crib, packs his bag.]*

Doctor. You're a pair of lucky parents. I can tell you now, I thought she wouldn't.
Keller. Nonsense, the child's a Keller, she has the constitution[1] of a goat. She'll outlive us all.
Doctor (*amiably*). Yes, especially if some of you Kellers don't get a night's sleep. I mean you, Mrs. Keller.
Keller. You hear, Katie?
Kate. I hear.

1. **constitution** (kän'stə·tōō'shən): here, physical makeup.

636 MODERN DRAMA

Reaching All Students

Struggling Readers

Remind students that graphic organizers can be useful tools for comprehending the information presented in a text, particularly in a long work such as *The Miracle Worker.* Readers can construct graphic organizers to organize important facts and details. The pyramid shown here can aid understanding of literary elements such as character, plot, conflict, and setting.

Activity

Have students work in pairs to complete pyramids for each of the five main characters in Act One.

```
              1. _____
            2. _____ _____
          3. _____ _____ _____
        4. _____ _____ _____ _____
      5. _____ _____ _____ _____ _____
    6. _____ _____ _____ _____ _____ _____
```

1. Name of character
2. Two words describing this character
3. Three words describing the setting
4. Four words stating the character's problem
5. Five words describing an event involving the character
6. Six words describing a second event

"She can't see. Look at her eyes. She can't see!"

Keller (*indulgent*). I've brought up two of them, but this is my wife's first, she isn't battle-scarred yet.

Kate. Doctor, don't be merely considerate, will my girl be all right?

Doctor. Oh, by morning she'll be knocking down Captain Keller's fences again.

Kate. And isn't there anything we should do?

Keller (*jovial*). Put up stronger fencing, ha?

Doctor. Just let her get well, she knows how to do it better than we do. (*He is packed, ready to leave.*) Main thing is the fever's gone, these things come and go in infants, never know why. Call it acute congestion² of the stomach and brain.

Keller. I'll see you to your buggy, Doctor.

Doctor. I've never seen a baby with more vitality, that's the truth.

[*He beams a good night at the baby and* KATE, *and* KELLER *leads him downstairs with a lamp. They go down the porch steps and across the yard, where the* DOCTOR *goes off left;* KELLER *stands with the lamp aloft.* KATE *meanwhile is bent lovingly over the crib, which emits a bleat; her finger is playful with the baby's face.*]

Kate. Hush. Don't you cry now, you've been trouble enough. Call it acute congestion, indeed, I don't see what's so cute about a congestion, just because it's yours. We'll have your father run an editorial in his paper, the wonders of modern medicine, they don't know what they're curing even when they cure it. Men, men and their battle scars, we women will have to—— (*But she breaks off, puzzled, moves her finger before the baby's eyes.*) Will have to—Helen? (*Now she moves her hand, quickly.*) Helen. (*She snaps her fingers at the baby's eyes twice, and her hand falters; after a moment she calls out, loudly.*) Captain. Captain, will you come—— (*But she stares at the baby, and her next call is directly at her ears.*) Captain!

[*And now, still staring,* KATE *screams.* KELLER *in the yard hears it and runs with the lamp*

2. **acute congestion** (ə·kyoot' kən·jes'chən): severe blockage (an old-fashioned medical diagnosis).

B Elements of Literature
Character
❓ What do Keller's comments reveal about him? [Possible responses: Keller is self-confident; he has raised two children from an earlier marriage.]

C Struggling Readers
Breaking Down Difficult Text
Since so much of this play's action is physical, you will want to make sure that struggling readers don't just gloss over the stage directions. Have students act out or summarize the stage directions with a partner. Also, point out that sometimes, as in Kate's last words on the page, dialogue is embedded within the italicized stage directions.

D Reading Skills and Strategies
How to Read a Play
Review the difference between an activity and a dramatic action. Then ask students whether Kate's hand movements over Helen's eyes are a dramatic action or an activity. Ask students to explain their reasoning. [Her movements are a dramatic action because they are meaningful activities that move the story forward and deepen the audience's understanding of Kate's and Helen's characters. These movements let us know that the child apparently cannot hear or see and that Kate is sensitive, attentive, and increasingly upset.]

Skill Link

Determining the Meaning of Idioms
Explain that idioms are unique to a specific class, region, or language, and their actual meanings are different from their literal meanings. For example, when Keller says that Helen "has the constitution of a goat" (p. 636), he means that she is physically strong. Sometimes (but not always) an idiom's meaning can be determined from its context.

Activities
1. Have students discuss familiar idioms and their meanings. Ask students learning English to give examples from other languages.
2. Point out the idiom *battle-scarred* on p. 637 (l. 1). Ask volunteers to explain the meaning of the idiom and to contrast that meaning with the literal meaning. [Idiomatic definitions: experienced; wary or proficient as a result of personal experience. Literal definition: marked by an injury suffered in combat.]

Call on volunteers to explain how the context helps them figure out the meaning of the idiom. [The word *but* signals the contrast between Keller's experience and his wife's inexperience.]

3. Have students look for other idioms as they read the play. Examples include *at sixes and sevens* (p. 641), *cooling my heels* (p. 655), *pregnant moment* (p. 670), and *lost my temper* (p. 680).

T637

A Critical Thinking

Analyzing

? Why is this an effective way to end an opening scene? [Possible responses: It is fast-paced and suspenseful; the scene is a cliffhanger, because we don't know what will happen to Helen and her family after this discovery.]

B Reading Skills and Strategies

How to Read a Play

? How does the mood change from the end of Scene 1 to the opening of Scene 2? [The mood changes from horror and fear to calm and playfulness.]

C Reading Skills and Strategies

Making Inferences

? Why do you think Helen pokes her hand into Percy's mouth? What makes her frustrated when she puts her fingers into her own mouth? [She pokes her hand into Percy's mouth because she wants to understand what talking is; she puts her fingers into her own mouth because she wants to imitate Percy's speech and then becomes frustrated when she can't.]

---

back to the house. KATE *screams again, her look intent on the baby and terrible.* KELLER *hurries in and up.*]

Keller. Katie? What's wrong?

Kate. Look. (*She makes a pass with her hand in the crib, at the baby's eyes.*)

Keller. What, Katie? She's well, she needs only time to——

Kate. She can't see. Look at her eyes. (*She takes the lamp from him, moves it before the child's face.*) She can't *see!*

Keller (*hoarsely*). Helen.

Kate. Or hear. When I screamed she didn't blink. Not an eyelash——

Keller. Helen. Helen!

Kate. She can't *hear* you!

Keller. *Helen!*

A [*His face has something like fury in it, crying the child's name;* KATE, *almost fainting, presses her knuckles to her mouth, to stop her own cry. The room dims out quickly.*]

SCENE 2

B [*Time, in the form of a slow tune of distant belfry chimes which approaches in a crescendo and then fades, passes; the light comes up again on a day five years later, on three kneeling children and an old dog outside around the pump.*

The dog is a setter named BELLE, *and she is sleeping. Two of the children are black,* MARTHA *and* PERCY. *The third child is* HELEN, *six and a half years old, quite unkempt, in body a* vivacious *little person with a fine head, attractive, but noticeably blind, one eye larger and protruding; her gestures are abrupt, insistent, lacking in human restraint, and her face never smiles. She is flanked by the other two, in a litter of paper-doll cutouts, and while they speak* HELEN'S *hands thrust at their faces in turn, feeling baffledly at the movements of their lips.*

Martha (*snipping*). First I'm gonna cut off this doctor's legs, one, two, now then——

Percy. Why you cuttin' off that doctor's legs?

Martha. I'm gonna give him a operation. Now I'm gonna cut off his arms, one, two. Now I'm gonna fix up—— (*She pushes* HELEN'S *hand away from her mouth.*) You stop that.

Percy. Cut off his stomach, that's a good operation.

Martha. No, I'm gonna cut off his head first, he got a bad cold.

Percy. Ain't gonna be much of that doctor left to fix up, time you finish all them opera——

C [*But* HELEN *is poking her fingers inside his mouth, to feel his tongue; he bites at them, annoyed, and she jerks them away.* HELEN *now fingers her own lips, moving them in imitation, but soundlessly.*]

Martha. What you do, bite her hand?

Percy. That's how I do, she keep pokin' her fingers in my mouth, I just bite 'em off.

Martha. What she tryin' do now?

Percy. She tryin' *talk.* She gonna get mad. Looka her tryin' talk.

[HELEN *is scowling, the lips under her fingertips moving in ghostly silence, growing more and more frantic, until in a bizarre rage she bites at her own fingers. This sends* PERCY *off into laughter, but alarms* MARTHA.]

Martha. Hey, you stop now. (*She pulls* HELEN'S *hand down.*) You just sit quiet and——

[*But at once* HELEN *topples* MARTHA *on her back, knees pinning her shoulders down, and grabs the scissors.* MARTHA *screams.* PERCY *darts to the bell string on the porch, yanks it, and the bell rings.*]

WORDS TO OWN

vivacious (vī·vā′shəs) *adj.:* very lively.

638 MODERN DRAMA

Crossing the Curriculum

History/Social Studies

The domestic situation in the Keller household may surprise students. Explain that the Keller household is typical of Southern upper-middle-class households of the 1880s, in which a white family had African American domestic servants who lived in the house. Although the Civil War had been over for more than twenty years, African Americans were still among the poorest members of Southern society and were restricted to the most menial jobs. For people like Captain Keller, the South's defeat in the Civil War was a watershed event that they never completely got over—a fact alluded to by William Gibson more than once during the course of *The Miracle Worker.* Invite students to research social conditions in the post–Civil War South. Then have them discuss whether and how their research has affected their view of the characters in *The Miracle Worker.*

Six and a half years old, quite unkempt . . .

THE MIRACLE WORKER, ACT ONE, SCENE 2 **639**

A Advanced Learners

Analyzing the Scene

❓ Discuss with students the fact that a play (unlike a novel) can use silence, or the absence of language, to make a point. Why might Gibson use pantomime, or silent acting, in this particular scene? [The pantomime underscores what the world is like for Helen; although the audience cannot fully experience Helen's condition, this silent scene conveys a little of what deafness is like. Also, the serenity provides a marked contrast to Helen's frenetic behavior and economically conveys a lot of information about these characters.]

B Reading Skills and Strategies

Comparing and Contrasting

Have students compare and contrast Keller's and Kate's attitudes towards Helen's plight. [Sample response: Keller finds it too painful to have his hopes repeatedly dashed, whereas Kate still believes that something can be done for Helen.]

C Elements of Literature

Character

❓ What does Helen's behavior reveal about her character? [Possible response: She is intelligent, curious, and in need of attention and understanding.]

A *Inside, the lights have been gradually coming up on the main room, where we see the family informally gathered, talking, but in pantomime:* KATE *sits darning socks near a cradle, occasionally rocking it;* CAPTAIN KELLER, *in spectacles, is working over newspaper pages at a table; a* benign *visitor in a hat,* AUNT EV, *is sharing the sewing basket, putting the finishing touches on a big shapeless doll made out of towels; an* indolent *young man,* JAMES KELLER, *is at the* window *watching the children.*

With the ring of the bell, KATE *is instantly on her feet and out the door onto the porch, to take in the scene; now we see what these five years have done to her: The girlish playfulness is gone, she is a woman steeled in grief.*

Kate (*for the thousandth time*). Helen. (*She is down the steps at once to them, seizing* HELEN'S *wrists and lifting her off* MARTHA; MARTHA *runs off in tears and screams for momma, with* PERCY *after her.*) Let me have those scissors.

[*Meanwhile the family inside is alerted,* AUNT EV *joining* JAMES *at the window;* CAPTAIN KELLER *resumes work.*]

James (*blandly*). She only dug Martha's eyes out. Almost dug. It's always almost, no point worrying till it happens, is there?

[*They gaze out, while* KATE *reaches for the scissors in* HELEN'S *hand. But* HELEN *pulls the scissors back, they struggle for them a moment, then* KATE *gives up, lets* HELEN *keep them. She tries to draw* HELEN *into the house.* HELEN *jerks away.* KATE *next goes down on her knees, takes* HELEN'S *hands gently, and using the scissors like a doll, makes* HELEN *caress and cradle them; she points* HELEN'S *finger houseward.* HELEN'S *whole body now becomes eager; she surrenders the scissors.* KATE *turns her toward the door and gives her a little push.* HELEN *scrambles up and toward the house, and* KATE, *rising, follows her.*]

Aunt Ev. How does she stand it? Why haven't you seen this Baltimore man? It's not a thing you can let go on and on, like the weather.

James. The weather here doesn't ask permission of me, Aunt Ev. Speak to my father.

Aunt Ev. Arthur. Something ought to be done for that child.

Keller. A refreshing suggestion. What?

[KATE, *entering, turns* HELEN *to* AUNT EV, *who gives her the towel doll.*]

Aunt Ev. Why, this very famous oculist[3] in Baltimore I wrote you about, what was his name?

Kate. Dr. Chisholm.

Aunt Ev. Yes, I heard lots of cases of blindness people thought couldn't be cured he's cured, he just does wonders. Why don't you write to him?

Keller. I've stopped believing in wonders.

Kate (*rocks the cradle*). I think the Captain will write to him soon. Won't you, Captain?

Keller. No.

James (*lightly*). Good money after bad, or bad after good. Or bad after bad——

Aunt Ev. Well, if it's just a question of money, Arthur, now you're marshal you have this Yankee money. Might as well——

Keller. Not money. The child's been to specialists all over Alabama and Tennessee. If I thought it would do good I'd have her to every fool doctor in the country.

Kate. I think the Captain will write to him soon.

Keller. Katie. How many times can you let them break your heart?

Kate. Any number of times.

[HELEN *meanwhile sits on the floor to explore the doll with her fingers, and her hand pauses over the face: This is no face, a blank area of towel, and it troubles her. Her hand searches for features and taps questioningly for eyes, but no one notices. She then yanks*

3. **oculist** (äk′yŏŏ·list): formerly, eye doctor.

WORDS TO OWN

benign (bi·nīn′) *adj.*: good-natured; harmless.
indolent (in′də·lənt) *adj.*: lazy, idle.

Using Students' Strengths

Visual Learners

Assign students, alone or in pairs, scenes from Act One to sketch. These illustrations can be used to create storyboards for display in the classroom. Have students add a quotation from the play to each scene as a caption.

Auditory Learners

Have students tape-record sounds from a particular place, such as home, a city street, a park, a playground, or a barn. As each student plays his or her tape, other class members should close their eyes and try to identify the place and the individual sounds they hear.

After they have listened to the tapes, have students discuss what it might feel like to depend solely on the sense of hearing for impressions of the physical world. The discussion can be extended to what it might feel like to be unable to see, hear, or speak, and how the absence of each ability might change the relative importance of the remaining ones.

at her AUNT'S *dress and taps again vigorously for eyes.*]

Aunt Ev. What, child?

[*Obviously not hearing,* HELEN *commences to go around, from person to person, tapping for eyes, but no one attends or understands.*]  **D**

Kate (*no break*). As long as there's the least chance. For her to see. Or hear, or——
Keller. There isn't. Now I must finish here.
Kate. I think, with your permission, Captain, I'd like to write.
Keller. I said no, Katie.
Aunt Ev. Why, writing does no harm, Arthur, only a little bitty letter. To see if he can help her.
Keller. He can't.
Kate. We won't know that to be a fact, Captain, until after you write.
Keller (*rising, emphatic*). Katie, he can't. (*He collects his papers.*)
James (*facetiously*). Father stands up, that makes it a fact.
Keller. You be quiet! I'm badgered enough here by females without your impudence. (JAMES *shuts up, makes himself scarce.* HELEN *now is groping among things on* KELLER'S *desk and paws his papers to the floor.* KELLER *is exasperated.*) Katie. (KATE *quickly turns* HELEN *away and retrieves the papers.*) I might as well try to work in a henyard as in this house——
James (*placating*). You really ought to put her away, Father.
Kate (*staring up*). What?
James. Some asylum. It's the kindest thing.
Aunt Ev. Why, she's your sister, James, not a nobody——
James. Half sister, and half—mentally defective, she can't even keep herself clean. It's not pleasant to see her about all the time. **E**
Kate. Do you dare? Complain of what you *can* see? **F**
Keller (*very annoyed*). This discussion is at an end! I'll thank you not to broach it again, Ev. (*Silence descends at once.* HELEN *gropes her way with the doll, and* KELLER *turns back for a final word, explosive.*) I've done as much as I

can bear, I can't give my whole life to it! The house is at sixes and sevens[4] from morning till night over the child. It's time some attention was paid to Mildred[5] here instead!
Kate (*gently dry*). You'll wake her up, Captain.
Keller. I want some peace in the house. I don't care how, but one way we won't have it is by rushing up and down the country every time someone hears of a new quack. I'm as sensible to this affliction as anyone else. It hurts me to look at the girl.
Kate. It was not our affliction I meant you to write about, Captain.

[HELEN *is back at* AUNT EV, *fingering her dress, and yanks two buttons from it.*]

Aunt Ev. Helen! My buttons.

[HELEN *pushes the buttons into the doll's face.* KATE *now sees, comes swiftly to kneel, lifts* HELEN'S *hand to her own eyes in question.*] **G**

Kate. Eyes? (HELEN *nods energetically.*) She wants the doll to have eyes.

[*Another kind of silence now, while* KATE *takes pins and buttons from the sewing basket and attaches them to the doll as eyes.* KELLER *stands, caught, and watches morosely.* AUNT EV *blinks, and conceals her emotion by inspecting her dress.*]

Aunt Ev. My goodness me, I'm not decent.
Kate. She doesn't know better, Aunt Ev. I'll sew them on again.
James. Never learn with everyone letting her do anything she takes it into her mind to——
Keller. You be quiet!
James. What did I say now?
Keller. You talk too much.
James. I was agreeing with you!
Keller. Whatever it was. Deprived child, the least she can have are the little things she wants.

4. **at sixes and sevens:** in disorder and confusion.
5. **Mildred:** the Kellers' second child.

WORDS TO OWN
impudence (im′pyŏŏ·dəns) *n*.: disrespect; rudeness.

THE MIRACLE WORKER, ACT ONE, SCENE 3 **641**

Taking a Second Look

T641

? How does this scene show both Helen's positive potential and her disturbing, sometimes dangerous limitations? [Sample response: Helen's determination to give her doll eyes, her joy at achieving that goal, and her empathetic, maternal behavior toward the doll reveal her potential; her inability or unwillingness to distinguish between the welfare of a real baby and that of a doll is alarming and discouraging.]

B Critical Thinking
Interpreting

? Why is Helen so upset? [Sample responses: Helen may sense her mother's sadness and fear; Helen is frustrated because she cannot communicate her own powerful feelings.]

C Reading Skills and Strategies
How to Read a Play

? Why does the playwright have the family members move off in different directions, leaving Kate and Helen together on stage? [Possible responses: The separation emphasizes the different opinions about Helen held by Aunt Ev, James, and Keller; the staging underscores Kate's deeper understanding of Helen as well as the bond between them.]

[JAMES, *very wounded, stalks out of the room onto the porch; he remains here, sulking.*]

Aunt Ev (*indulgently*). It's worth a couple of buttons, Kate, look. (HELEN *now has the doll with eyes and cannot contain herself for joy; she rocks the doll, pats it vigorously, kisses it.*) This child has more sense than all these men Kellers, if there's ever any way to reach that mind of hers.

[*But* HELEN *suddenly has come upon the cradle and unhesitatingly overturns it; the swaddled baby tumbles out, and* CAPTAIN KELLER *barely manages to dive and catch it in time.*]

Keller. Helen!

[*All are in commotion, the baby screams, but* HELEN, *unperturbed, is laying her doll in its place.* KATE *on her knees pulls her hands off the cradle, wringing them;* HELEN *is bewildered.*]

Kate. Helen, Helen, you're not to do such things, how can I make you understand——
Keller (*hoarsely*). Katie.
Kate. How can I get it into your head, my darling, my poor——
Keller. Katie, some way of teaching her an iota of discipline has to be——
Kate (*flaring*). How can you discipline an afflicted child? Is it her fault?

[HELEN'S *fingers have fluttered to her* MOTHER'S *lips, vainly trying to comprehend their movements.*]

Keller. I didn't say it was her fault.
Kate. Then whose? I don't know what to do! How can I teach her, beat her—until she's black and blue?
Keller. It's not safe to let her run around loose. Now there must be a way of confining her, somehow, so she can't——
Kate. Where, in a cage? She's a growing child, she has to use her limbs!

Keller. Answer me one thing, is it fair to Mildred here?
Kate (*inexorably*). Are you willing to put her away?

[*Now* HELEN'S *face darkens in the same rage as at herself earlier; and her hand strikes at* KATE'S *lips.* KATE *catches her hand again, and* HELEN *begins to kick, struggle, twist.*]

Keller. Now what?
Kate. She wants to talk, like—*be* like you and me. (*She holds* HELEN *struggling until we hear from the child her first sound so far, an* inarticulate *weird noise in her throat such as an animal in a trap might make; and* KATE *releases her. The second she is free* HELEN *blunders away, collides violently with a chair, falls, and sits weeping.* KATE *comes to her, embraces, caresses, soothes her, and buries her own face in her hair, until she can control her voice.*) Every day she slips further away. And I don't know how to call her back.
Aunt Ev. Oh, I've a mind to take her up to Baltimore myself. If that doctor can't help her, maybe he'll know who can.
Keller (*presently, heavily*). I'll write the man, Katie. (*He stands with the baby in his clasp, staring at* HELEN'S *head hanging down on* KATE'S *arm.*)

[*The lights dim out, except the one on* KATE *and* HELEN. *In the twilight,* JAMES, AUNT EV, *and* KELLER *move off slowly, formally, in separate directions;* KATE *with* HELEN *in her arms remains, motionless, in an image which overlaps into the next scene and fades only when it is well under way.*]

WORDS TO OWN
inarticulate (in'är·tik'yoo·lit) *adj.:* not expressed clearly enough to be understood.

Connecting Across Texts

Connecting with "Darkness at Noon"
Ask students to think about Harold Krents's essay "Darkness at Noon" (p. 454). Have them recall and discuss Krents's observations on what it is like to be blind in a world of sighted individuals. What does Krents say about how blind people are perceived by some sighted

individuals? [Many sighted individuals have misconceptions about people who are blind.] What does Krents say about how some sighted individuals view the abilities of blind people? [They often think blind people are incapable and underestimate their abilities.] Encourage students to

keep Krents's views in mind as they read *The Miracle Worker.* Invite them to analyze how different characters view Helen. You might suggest that students pay special attention to the characters' estimations of Helen's ability to learn and develop as a human being.

SCENE 4

Without pause, from the dark down left we hear a man's voice with a Greek accent speaking:

Anagnos. —— who could do nothing for the girl, of course. It was Dr. Bell[6] who thought she might somehow be taught. I have written the family only that a suitable governess, Miss Annie Sullivan, has been found here in Boston——

[*The lights begin to come up, down left, on a long table and chair. The table contains equipment for teaching the blind by touch—a small replica of the human skeleton, stuffed animals, models of flowers and plants, piles of books. The chair contains a girl of twenty,* ANNIE SULLIVAN, *with a face which in repose is grave and rather obstinate, and when active is impudent, combative, twinkling with all the life that is lacking in* HELEN'S, *and handsome; there is a crude vitality to her. Her suitcase is at her knee.* ANAGNOS, *a stocky bearded man, comes into the light only toward the end of his speech.*]

Anagnos. ——and will come. It will no doubt be difficult for you there, Annie. But it has been difficult for you at our school too, hm? Gratifying, yes, when you came to us and could not spell your name, to accomplish so much here in a few years, but always an Irish battle. For independence. (*He studies* ANNIE, *humorously; she does not open her eyes.*) This is my last time to counsel you, Annie, and you do lack some—by some I mean *all*—what, tact or talent to bend. To others. And what has saved you on more than one occasion here at Perkins is that there was nowhere to expel you to. Your eyes hurt?

Annie. My ears, Mr. Anagnos. (*And now she has opened her eyes; they are inflamed, vague, slightly crossed, clouded by the granular growth of trachoma,[7] and she often keeps them closed to shut out the pain of light.*)

Anagnos (*severely*). Nowhere but back to Tewksbury, where children learn to be saucy. Annie, I know how dreadful it was there, but that battle is dead and done with, why not let it stay buried?

Annie (*cheerily*). I think God must owe me a resurrection.

Anagnos (*a bit shocked*). What?

Annie (*taps her brow*). Well, he keeps digging up that battle!

Anagnos. That is not a proper thing to say, Annie. It is what I mean.

Annie (*meekly*). Yes. But I know what I'm like. What's this child like?

Anagnos. Like?

Annie. Well—bright or dull, to start off.

Anagnos. No one knows. And if she is dull, you have no patience with this?

Annie. Oh, in grown-ups you have to, Mr. Anagnos. I mean in children it just seems a little—precocious, can I use that word?

Anagnos. Only if you can spell it.

Annie. Premature. So I hope at least she's a bright one.

Anagnos. Deaf, blind, mute—who knows? She is like a little safe, locked, that no one can open. Perhaps there is a treasure inside.

Annie. Maybe it's empty, too?

Anagnos. Possibly. I should warn you, she is much given to tantrums.

Annie. Means something is inside. Well, so am I, if I believe all I hear. Maybe you should warn *them*.

Anagnos (*frowns*). Annie. I wrote them no word of your history. You will find yourself among strangers now, who know nothing of it.

Annie. Well, we'll keep them in a state of blessed ignorance.

Anagnos. Perhaps *you* should tell it?

Annie (*bristling*). Why? I have enough trouble with people who don't know.

---

6. **Dr. Bell:** Alexander Graham Bell, inventor of the telephone, who also developed methods for teaching the deaf.
7. **trachoma** (trə·kōʹmə): eye disease that results in "grainy" scar tissue.

WORDS TO OWN
resurrection (rezʹə·rekʹshən) *n.:* rebirth.

D **Struggling Readers**
Questioning
Remind students to ask themselves questions when they don't understand something they read. Suggest that after asking a question, students reread the text to see if it provides a direct answer or if they can make inferences from the context that they can verify or revise as they continue reading. You may wish to model the process for them, as in the following example: "What does Anagnos mean by 'back to Tewksbury'? What is Tewksbury? After rereading, I can guess from the context that Tewksbury is where Annie was before she came to Perkins; the mention of 'children' leads me to this conclusion. I understand from the way Anagnos says 'back to Tewksbury' and from his comment about 'how dreadful it was there' that it may be another institution of some kind. I'll keep reading to see if my guess is confirmed later on."

E **Critical Thinking**
Evaluating
Remind students that this is the quotation that appears on p. 634. Ask whether they think (having now been introduced to Helen) that the simile is fitting.

F **Critical Thinking**
Speculating
? What do you think Anagnos means by Annie's "history"? [Possible responses: Perhaps he is referring to her problems at Perkins; he may mean her past at Tewksbury before she came to Perkins; perhaps her temper led her to clash with authorities.]

Anagnos. So they will understand. When you have trouble.

Annie. The only time I have trouble is when I'm right. (*But she is amused at herself, as is* ANAGNOS.) Is it my fault it's so often? I won't give them trouble, Mr. Anagnos, I'll be so ladylike they won't notice I've come.

Anagnos. Annie, be—humble. It is not as if you have so many offers to pick and choose. You will need their affection, working with this child.

Annie (*humorously*). I hope I won't need their pity.

Anagnos. Oh, we can all use some pity. (*Crisply*) So. You are no longer our pupil, we throw you into the world, a teacher. If the child can be taught. No one expects you to work miracles, even for twenty-five dollars a month. Now, in this envelope a loan, for the railroad, which you will repay me when you have a bank account. But in this box, a gift. With our love. (ANNIE *opens the small box he extends and sees a garnet ring. She looks up, blinking, and down.*) I think other friends are ready to say goodbye. (*He moves as though to open doors.*)

Annie. Mr. Anagnos. (*Her voice is trembling.*) Dear Mr. Anagnos, I—— (*But she swallows over getting the ring on her finger, and cannot continue until she finds a woebegone joke.*) Well, what should I say, I'm an ignorant, opinionated girl, and everything I am I owe to you?

Anagnos (*smiles*). That is only half true, Annie.

Annie. Which half? I crawled in here like a drowned rat, I thought I died when Jimmie died, that I'd never again—come alive. Well, you say with love so easy, and I haven't *loved* a soul since and I never will, I suppose, but this place gave me more than my eyes back. Or taught me how to spell, which I'll never learn anyway, but with all the fights and the trouble I've been here it taught me what help is, and how to live again, and I don't want to say goodbye. Don't open the door, I'm crying.

Anagnos (*gently*). They will not see.

[*He moves again as though opening doors, and in comes a group of girls, eight-year-olds to seventeen-year-olds; as they walk we see they are blind.* ANAGNOS *shepherds them in with a hand.*]

A Child. Annie?

Annie (*her voice cheerful*). Here, Beatrice.

[*As soon as they locate her voice they throng joyfully to her, speaking all at once;* ANNIE *is down on her knees to the smallest, and the following are the more intelligible fragments in the general hubbub.*]

Children. There's a present. We brought you a going-away present, Annie!

Annie. Oh, now you shouldn't have——

Children. We did, we did, where's the present?

Smallest Child (*mournfully*). Don't go, Annie, away.

Children. Alice has it. Alice! Where's Alice? Here I am! Where? Here!

[*An arm is aloft out of the group, waving a present;* ANNIE *reaches for it.*]

Annie. I have it. I have it, everybody. Should I open it?

Children. Open it! Everyone be quiet! Do, Annie! She's opening it. Ssh! (*A settling of silence while* ANNIE *unwraps it. The present is a pair of smoked glasses, and she stands still.*) Is it open, Annie?

Annie. It's open.

Children. It's for your eyes, Annie. Put them on, Annie! 'Cause Mrs. Hopkins said your eyes hurt since the operation. And she said you're going where the sun is *fierce*.

Annie. I'm putting them on now.

Smallest Child (*mournfully*). Don't go, Annie, where the sun is fierce.

Children. Do they fit all right?

Annie. Oh, they fit just fine.

Children. Did you put them on? Are they pretty, Annie?

Annie. Oh, my eyes feel hundreds of percent better already, and pretty, why, do you know how I look in them? Splendiloquent. Like a racehorse!

Children (*delighted*). There's another present! Beatrice! We have a present for Helen, too! Give it to her, Beatrice. Here, Annie! (*This present is*

Getting Students Involved

Cooperative Learning

Classifying Causes for Conflict. In the play, Annie's and Helen's differing wants and needs form the basis of the conflict between them. Have students in small groups brainstorm and list each character's wants and needs and then prioritize them. A graphic organizer can help students organize their ideas. After groups have filled out their organizers, ask them to pinpoint scenes in the play where conflict occurs.

Helen		Annie	
Needs	Wants	Needs	Wants
1. to know her surroundings 2. 3.	1. to have her own way 2. 3.	1. to make a living 2. 3.	1. to teach Helen how to communicate 2. 3.
Order of Importance to Helen		Order of Importance to Annie	
1. 2. 3.	1. 2. 3.	1. 2. 3.	1. 2. 3.

"It's for Helen. And we took up a collection to buy it."

THE MIRACLE WORKER, ACT ONE, SCENE 4 645

RESPONDING TO THE ART

Activity. Remind students that this photograph is from the Broadway play, not from the Hollywood movie. Have them analyze and discuss differences between this photograph and the ones from the movie. Are there any clues that suggest this image is from a stage production and not from a movie? [Students might note the darkness of the background or the way the people in the photo are lit. They may realize that these details relate to the necessarily more abstract way setting is conveyed in the theater.]

Skill Link

Scanning

Remind students that different reading strategies are appropriate for different reading purposes. Explain that scanning—quickly looking through a text to find specific information or particular words—is a useful strategy for doing research or answering a question about something they have read. For example, if they are researching a topic such as the latest treatments for visual impairments, they might scan magazine and newspaper indexes, the tables of contents of medical books, or electronic databases for terms such as *blindness treatments* or *ophthalmology*. If they are trying to answer a question about a text, scanning will save time, since they won't have to reread the text in its entirety.

Activity

1. Ask each student to come up with several questions about characters in *The Miracle Worker*—questions that can be answered by specific information in the play. Have them write the questions.
2. Have students exchange their questions with partners and scan the play to find the answers.

T645

A Elements of Literature

Character

? What does Annie's interaction with the children reveal about her? [Possible responses: She is warm and loving toward children; she seems to understand them.]

B Reading Skills and Strategies

How to Read a Play

? Why do you think Gibson specifies that the color of the light should change? [This lighting change prepares the audience for a flashback; it's a visual way of indicating a break in the normal time sequence of events.]

C Reading Skills and Strategies

Finding Sequence of Events

This is the first of several flashbacks in the play. Have students identify words and phrases that signal that this conversation between Annie and Jimmie took place in the past. [Students may identify the phrase "into another time" in the stage directions or the phrase "Annie Sullivan, aged nine" spoken by the Man's Voice. Students may also recall that earlier in the scene Annie mentioned that Jimmie was dead, yet here he is speaking.] You might tell students that Jimmie suffered from tuberculosis of the bone. See Joseph Lash's story of Annie's early life on pp. 710–713.

---

an elegant doll, with movable eyelids and a momma sound.) It's for Helen. And we took up a collection to buy it. And Laura dressed it.

Annie. It's beautiful.

Children. So don't forget, you be sure to give it to Helen from us, Annie!

Annie. I promise it will be the first thing I give her. If I don't keep it for myself, that is, you know I can't be trusted with dolls!

Smallest Child (*mournfully*). Don't go, Annie, to her.

Annie (*her arm around her*). Sarah, dear. I don't *want* to go.

Smallest Child. Then why are you going?

Annie (*gently*). Because I'm a big girl now, and big girls have to earn a living. It's the only way I can. But if you don't smile for me first, what I'll just have to do is—— (*She pauses, inviting it.*)

Smallest Child. What?

A **Annie.** Put *you* in my suitcase, instead of this doll. And take *you* to Helen in Alabama!

[*This strikes the children as very funny, and they begin to laugh and tease the smallest child, who after a moment does smile for* ANNIE.]

Anagnos (*then*). Come, children. We must get the trunk into the carriage and Annie into her train, or no one will go to Alabama. Come, come.

[*He shepherds them out, and* ANNIE *is left alone on her knees with the doll in her lap. She reaches for her suitcase, and by a subtle*

B *change in the color of the light, we go with her thoughts into another time. We hear a boy's voice whispering; perhaps we see shadowy intimations*[8] *of these speakers in the background.*]

Boy's Voice. Where we goin', Annie?

C **Annie** (*in dread*). Jimmie.

Boy's Voice. Where we goin'?

Annie. I said—I'm takin' care of you——

Boy's Voice. Forever and ever?

Man's Voice (*impersonal*). Annie Sullivan,

---

8. **intimations** (in'tə·mā'shənz): suggestions or hints.

---

aged nine, virtually blind. James Sullivan, aged seven—— What's the matter with your leg, Sonny?

Annie. Forever and ever.

Man's Voice. Can't he walk without that crutch? (ANNIE *shakes her head and does not stop shaking it.*) Girl goes to the women's ward. Boy to the men's.

Boy's Voice (*in terror*). Annie! Annie, don't let them take me—Annie!

Anagnos (*offstage*). Annie! Annie?

[*But this voice is real, in the present, and* ANNIE *comes up out of her horror, clearing her head with a final shake; the lights begin to pick out* KATE *in the* KELLER *house, as* ANNIE *in a bright tone calls back.*]

Annie. Coming!

[*This word catches* KATE, *who stands half turned and attentive to it, almost as though hearing it. Meanwhile* ANNIE *turns and hurries out, lugging the suitcase.*]

Reaching All Students

Struggling Readers

Explain that the term *flashback* means "an interruption in the chronological time sequence to describe earlier events." Explain that in a flashback a character relives a past event. Tell students that the play is interspersed with flashbacks from Annie's childhood, beginning with the one on this page. Alert students to look for other scenes from Annie's memory, and provide them with the page numbers on which the scenes take place (pp. 655, 674–675, 682, and 694).

SCENE 5

The room dims out; the sound of railroad wheels begins from off left and maintains itself in a constant rhythm underneath the following scene; the remaining lights have come up on the KELLER *homestead.* JAMES *is lounging on the porch, waiting. In the upper bedroom, which is to be* ANNIE'S, HELEN *is alone, puzzledly exploring, fingering and smelling things, the curtains, empty drawers in the bureau, water in the pitcher by the washbasin, fresh towels on the bedstead. Downstairs in the family room* KATE, *turning to a mirror, hastily adjusts her bonnet, watched by a servant in an apron,* VINEY.

Viney. Let Mr. Jimmie go by hisself, you been pokin' that garden all day, you ought to rest your feet.

Kate. I can't wait to see her, Viney.

Viney. Maybe she ain't gone be on this train neither.

Kate. Maybe she is.

Viney. And maybe she ain't.

Kate. And maybe she is. Where's Helen?

Viney. She upstairs, smellin' around. She know somethin' funny's goin' on.

Kate. Let her have her supper as soon as Mildred's in bed, and tell Captain Keller when he comes that we'll be delayed tonight.

Viney. Again.

Kate. I don't think we need say *again*. Simply delayed will do.

[She runs upstairs to ANNIE'S *room,* VINEY *speaking after her.]*

Viney. I mean that's what he gone say. "What, again?"

*[*VINEY *works at setting the table. Upstairs* KATE *stands in the doorway, watching* HELEN'S *groping explorations.]*

Kate. Yes, we're expecting someone. Someone for my Helen. (HELEN *happens upon her skirt, clutches her leg;* KATE, *in a tired dismay, kneels to tidy her hair and soiled pinafore.*)[9] Oh, dear,

---

9. **pinafore** (pin′ə·fôr′): sleeveless, apronlike garment worn by little girls over a dress.

---

this was clean not an hour ago. (HELEN *feels her bonnet, shakes her head darkly, and tugs to get it off.* KATE *retains it with one hand, diverts* HELEN *by opening her other hand under her nose.*) Here. For while I'm gone. (HELEN *sniffs, reaches, and pops something into her mouth, while* KATE *speaks a bit guiltily.*) I don't think one peppermint drop will spoil your supper.

[She gives HELEN *a quick kiss, evades her hands, and hurries downstairs again. Meanwhile* CAPTAIN KELLER *has entered the yard from around the rear of the house, newspaper under arm, cleaning off and munching on some radishes; he sees* JAMES *lounging at the porch post.]*

Keller. Jimmie?

James (*unmoving*). Sir?

Keller (*eyes him*). You don't look dressed for anything useful, boy.

James. I'm not. It's for Miss Sullivan.

Keller. Needn't keep holding up that porch; we have wooden posts for that. I asked you to see that those strawberry plants were moved this evening.

James. I'm moving your—Mrs. Keller, instead. To the station.

Keller (*heavily*). Mrs. Keller. Must you always speak of her as though you haven't met the lady?

*[*KATE *comes out on the porch, and* JAMES *inclines his head.]*

James (*ironic*). Mother. (*He starts off the porch, but sidesteps* KELLER'S *glare like a blow.*) I said mother!

Kate. Captain.

Keller. Evening, my dear.

Kate. We're off to meet the train, Captain. Supper will be a trifle delayed tonight.

Keller. What, again?

Kate (*backing out*). With your permission, Captain?

[And they are gone. KELLER *watches them offstage, morosely. Upstairs* HELEN *meanwhile has groped for her mother, touched her cheek*

D ## Elements of Literature
Character
? Why is Helen "smellin' around"? What does this behavior tell us about her? [Sample responses: Helen uses her sense of smell to compensate for the loss of her sight and hearing; the phrase hints at Helen's curiosity about the changes in the bedroom; it suggests how determined Helen is to connect with her environment.]

E ## Reading Skills and Strategies
Drawing Conclusions
? Why does Kate give Helen candy and then feel guilty? [She gives Helen candy to pacify her and encourage her to behave; she feels guilty because although she knows it is wrong to give candy for this reason, it is easy, and she doesn't know how else to affect Helen's behavior.]

F ## Elements of Literature
Irony
? Why is it ironic when James says "Mother"? [Possible responses: He doesn't actually mean it, because Kate is his stepmother, not his mother; he says the word only because his father chided him for calling Kate "Mrs. Keller."]

T647

in a meaningful gesture, waited, touched her cheek, waited, then found the open door and made her way down. Now she comes into the family room, touches her cheek again; VINEY *regards her.*]

Viney. What you want, honey, your momma? (HELEN *touches her cheek again.* VINEY *goes to the sideboard, gets a tea cake, gives it into* HELEN'S *hand;* HELEN *pops it into her mouth.*) Guess one little tea cake ain't gone ruin your appetite.

[*She turns* HELEN *toward the door.* HELEN *wanders out onto the porch, as* KELLER *comes up the steps. Her hands encounter him, and she touches her cheek again, waits.*]

Keller. She's gone. (*He is awkward with her; when he puts his hand on her head, she pulls away.* KELLER *stands regarding her, heavily.*) She's gone, my son and I don't get along, you don't know I'm your father, no one likes me,

and supper's delayed. (HELEN *touches her cheek, waits.* KELLER *fishes in his pocket.*) Here. I brought you some stick candy, one nibble of sweets can't do any harm.

[*He gives her a large stick of candy;* HELEN *falls to it.* VINEY *peers out the window.*]

Viney (*reproachfully*). Cap'n Keller, now how'm I gone get her to eat her supper you fill her up with that trash?

Keller (*roars*). Tend to your work!

[VINEY *beats a rapid retreat.* KELLER *thinks better of it and tries to get the candy away from* HELEN, *but* HELEN *hangs on to it; and when* KELLER *pulls, she gives his leg a kick.* KELLER *hops about,* HELEN *takes refuge with the candy down behind the pump, and* KELLER *then irately flings his newspaper on the porch floor, stamps into the house past* VINEY, *and disappears.*]

Courtesy George Jenkins.

Set designs by George Jenkins for the movie (above) and Broadway (right) productions of *The Miracle Worker*. In the play, the dining room was placed close to the audience because several important scenes are set there. An unexpected result was that the food hurled about during Act Two often hit the first-row viewers.

Courtesy George Jenkins.

648 MODERN DRAMA

Crossing the Curriculum

Science

New inventions and technology can make life easier for people with visual, hearing, and speech impairments. Alphanumeric pagers that vibrate when receiving a message are especially useful to the hearing-impaired. TTY and TDD telephones allow hearing- and speech-impaired people to communicate with each other by typing messages, and visual-ring signalers can connect these telephones to lamps that blink to

signal incoming calls. Closed-caption decoders place subtitles at the bottom of television screens so that people with hearing impairments can read a show's dialogue or narration. People with visual impairments can use computers with special equipment that converts computer signals into Braille. Text-to-speech software allows people to hear rather than read text documents.

Ask students to research these and other technologies. Or, have them brainstorm changes in everyday objects that would make them easier for people with impairments to use. For example, a recent study recommends different sizes of paper currency to help people with visual impairments. Have students present their research and original ideas to the class in oral reports or in a classroom display of drawings, charts, articles, and models of devices.

SCENE 6

The lights half dim on the homestead, where VINEY *and* HELEN, *going about their business, soon find their way off. Meanwhile, the railroad sounds off left have mounted in a crescendo to a climax typical of a depot at arrival time, the lights come up on stage left, and we see a suggestion of a station. Here* ANNIE *in her smoked glasses and disarrayed by travel is waiting with her suitcase, while* JAMES *walks to meet her; she has a battered paperbound book, which is a Perkins report,[10] under her arm.*

James (*coolly*). Miss Sullivan?
Annie (*cheerily*). Here! At last. I've been on trains so many days I thought they must be backing up every time I dozed off——
James. I'm James Keller.
Annie. James? (*The name stops her.*) I had a brother Jimmie. Are you Helen's?
James. I'm only half a brother. You're to be her governess?
Annie (*lightly*). Well. Try!
James (*eying her*). You look like half a governess. (KATE *enters.* ANNIE *stands moveless, while* JAMES *takes her suitcase.* KATE'S *gaze on her is doubtful, troubled.*) Mrs. Keller, Miss Sullivan.

[KATE *takes her hand.*]

Kate (*simply*). We've met every train for two days.

[ANNIE *looks at* KATE'S *face, and her good humor comes back.*]

Annie. I changed trains every time they stopped. The man who sold me that ticket ought to be tied to the tracks——
James. You have a trunk, Miss Sullivan?
Annie. Yes. (*She passes* JAMES *a claim check, and he bears the suitcase out behind them.* ANNIE *holds the battered book.* KATE *is studying her face, and* ANNIE *returns the gaze; this is a*

---

10. **Perkins report:** report on methods of teaching the blind, prepared by the director of the Perkins Institution for the Blind in Boston.

---

mutual appraisal, Southern gentlewoman and working-class Irish girl, and ANNIE *is not quite comfortable under it.*) You didn't bring Helen, I was hoping you would.
Kate. No, she's home.

[*A pause.* ANNIE *tries to make ladylike small talk, though her energy now and then erupts; she catches herself up whenever she hears it.*]

Annie. You—live far from town, Mrs. Keller?
Kate. Only a mile.
Annie. Well. I suppose I can wait one more mile. But don't be surprised if I get out to push the horse!
Kate. Helen's waiting for you, too. There's been such a bustle in the house, she expects something, heaven knows what. (*Now she voices part of her doubt, not as such, but* ANNIE *understands it.*) I expected—a desiccated[11] spinster. You're very young.
Annie (*resolutely*). Oh, you should have seen me when I left Boston. I got much older on this trip.
Kate. I mean, to teach anyone as difficult as Helen.
Annie. *I* mean to try. They can't put you in jail for trying!
Kate. Is it possible, even? To teach a deaf-blind child *half* of what an ordinary child learns—has that ever been done?
Annie. Half?
Kate. A tenth.
Annie (*reluctantly*). No. (KATE'S *face loses its remaining hope; still appraising her youth.*) Dr. Howe did wonders, but—an ordinary child? No, never. But then I thought when I was going over his reports—(*She indicates the one in her hand.*)—he never treated them like ordinary children. More like—eggs everyone was afraid would break.
Kate (*a pause*). May I ask how old you are?

---

11. **desiccated** (des′i·kāt′id): dried up.

WORDS TO OWN
appraisal (ə·prāz′əl) *n.:* evaluation; sizing up.

D **Reading Skills and Strategies**
Drawing Conclusions
? Why does the name surprise Annie? [The name reminds Annie of her brother Jimmie; and it may make her think of other similarities between Helen and herself.]

E **Critical Thinking**
Speculating
? Why do you think Annie was hoping that Helen would appear at the station along with Mrs. Keller? [Possible responses: Annie is eager to meet her student; she wants to begin teaching Helen as soon as possible.]

F **Historical Connections**
Annie mentions Dr. Samuel Gridley Howe, the founder of the Perkins Institution and Michael Anagnos's father-in-law and mentor. Howe became world famous for teaching Laura Bridgman, a deaf, blind, and mute woman, to communicate with the manual alphabet. When Annie says "Dr. Howe did wonders," she is referring to his work with Laura and other deaf-blind children.

Annie. Well, I'm not in my teens, you know! I'm twenty.
Kate. All of twenty.

[ANNIE *takes the bull by the horns, valiantly.*]

Annie. Mrs. Keller, don't lose heart just because I'm not on my last legs. I have three big advantages over Dr. Howe that money couldn't buy for you. One is his work behind me. I've read every word he wrote about it and he wasn't exactly what you'd call a man of few words. Another is to *be* young, why, I've got **A** energy to do anything. The third is, I've been blind. (*But it costs her something to say this.*)
Kate (*quietly*). Advantages.
Annie (*wry*). Well, some have the luck of the Irish, some do not.

[KATE *smiles; she likes her.*]

Kate. What will you try to teach her first?
B **Annie.** First, last, and—in between—language.
Kate. Language.

Annie. Language is to the mind more than light is to the eye. Dr. Howe said that.
Kate. Language. (*She shakes her head.*) We can't get through to teach her to sit still. You *are* young, despite your years, to have such—confidence. Do you, inside?

[ANNIE *studies her face; she likes her, too.*]

Annie. No, to tell you the truth I'm as shaky inside as a baby's rattle!

[*They smile at each other, and* KATE *pats her hand.*]

Kate. Don't be. (JAMES *returns to usher them off.*) We'll do all we can to help, and to make you feel at home. Don't think of us as strangers, Miss Annie.
Annie (*cheerily*). Oh, strangers aren't so strange to me. I've known them all my life!

[KATE *smiles again,* ANNIE *smiles back, and they precede* JAMES *offstage.*]

SCENE 7

The lights dim on them, having simultaneously risen full on the house; VINEY *has already entered the family room, taken a water pitcher, and come out and down to the pump.* **C** *She pumps real water. As she looks offstage, we hear the clop of hoofs, a carriage stopping, and voices.*

Viney. Cap'n Keller! Cap'n Keller, they comin'! (*She goes back into the house, as* KELLER *comes out on the porch to gaze.*) She sure 'nuff came, Cap'n.

[KELLER *descends and crosses toward the carriage; this conversation begins offstage and moves on.*]

Keller (*very courtly*). Welcome to Ivy Green, Miss Sullivan. I take it you are Miss Sullivan——
Kate. My husband, Miss Annie, Captain Keller.
Annie (*her best behavior*). Captain, how do you do.
Keller. A pleasure to see you, at last. I trust you had an agreeable journey?
Annie. Oh, I had several! When did this country get so big?
James. Where would you like the trunk, Father?
Keller. Where Miss Sullivan can get at it, I imagine.
Annie. Yes, please. Where's Helen?
Keller. In the hall, Jimmie——

Using Students' Strengths

Visual Learners
On p. 638 Gibson describes Helen Keller with these words: "unkempt . . . a vivacious little person with a fine head, attractive, but noticeably blind." On p. 643 he describes Annie Sullivan as having "a face which in repose is grave and rather obstinate, and when active as impudent, combative, twinkling with . . . life." After students have read the play, have them create a portrait of Helen, Annie, or both.

Auditory/Musical Learners
Have students choose a scene from Act One to score with incidental music (music used to heighten the mood). Encourage students to analyze the entire scene closely in order to decide exactly which passages might be accented effectively with music. Then have students compose music or locate recordings that heighten the effect of these passages.

Kate. We've put you in the upstairs corner room, Miss Annie, if there's any breeze at all this summer, you'll feel it——

[*In the house the setter* BELLE *flees into the family room, pursued by* HELEN *with groping hands; the dog doubles back out of the same door, and* HELEN, *still groping for her, makes her way out to the porch; she is messy, her hair tumbled, her pinafore now ripped, her shoelaces untied.* KELLER *acquires the suitcase, and* ANNIE *gets her hands on it too, though still endeavoring to live up to the general air of propertied[12] manners.*]

Keller. *And* the suitcase——

Annie (*pleasantly*). I'll take the suitcase, thanks.

12. **propertied** (präp′ər·tēd): like rich people who own a lot of property.

Keller. Not at all, I have it, Miss Sullivan.

Annie. I'd like it.

Keller (*gallantly*). I couldn't think of it, Miss Sullivan. You'll find in the South we——

Annie. Let me.

Keller. ——view women as the flowers of civiliza——

Annie (*impatiently*). I've got something in it for Helen! (*She tugs it free;* KELLER *stares.*) Thank you. When do I see her?

Kate. There. There is Helen.

[ANNIE *turns and sees* HELEN *on the porch. A moment of silence. Then* ANNIE *begins across the yard to her, lugging her suitcase.*]

Keller (*sotto voce*).[13] Katie——

13. **sotto voce** (sät′ō vō′chē): in a low voice.

Annie turns and sees Helen on the porch.

THE MIRACLE WORKER, ACT ONE, SCENE 7 **651**

D Reading Skills and Strategies
How to Read a Play

Draw students' attention to the way Gibson sets up the dramatic moment when Annie and Helen meet. Point out that Helen's clumsy pursuit of the dog is another in a series of verbal references and stage actions that associate Helen with animals. Without language or discipline, the girl seems less than fully human. However, according to Gibson's stage directions, Annie (unlike the audience) does not see Helen groping for the dog. Her first impression of Helen is of the girl isolated on the porch at center stage. Ask students to review Act One for textual references associating the young Helen with animals. [References include: "the constitution of a goat" (p. 636); "knocking down ... fences" and "emits a bleat" (p. 637); the six-year-old Helen's first appearance, alongside Belle, with gestures that are "abrupt, insistent, lacking in human restraint" and with a face that "never smiles" (p. 638); "paws his papers to the floor" and "henyard" (p. 641); "let her run around loose" and "confining her" and "cage" and "inarticulate weird noise in her throat such as an animal in a trap might make" (p. 642); "smellin' around" (p. 647).]

E Reading Skills and Strategies
Predicting

? What will Annie's relationship with Keller be like? [Possible response: They may not get along, since he sees women as being in need of help, and she is independent and strong-willed.]

Crossing the Curriculum

Geography

In the 1880s, trains were the most common form of long-distance transportation in the United States. Have students use a map of the United States to speculate on Annie Sullivan's journey from Boston to Tuscumbia. First have students locate both places on the map. Then have them review the area in between the two locations, keeping in mind that most big cities and large towns in the East had train service in the 1880s. Ask students to figure out the most direct route between Boston and Tuscumbia. What towns and cities would that route pass through?

Now remind students that Annie took a very long and circuitous trip that involved changing trains many times. Where might she have traveled? In which big cities might she have changed trains? Invite students to come up with three different possible routes for Annie's journey from Boston to Tuscumbia.

A Reading Skills and Strategies

How to Read a Play

❓ Point out that Gibson intends this first encounter between Annie and Helen to occur in near silence at center stage. Why do you think this is so? [Possible responses: Silence makes the scene seem tense, focused, and momentous; silence emphasizes the fact that the two cannot communicate with speech.]

B Struggling Readers

Summarizing

Remind students that summarizing is briefly retelling important events in one's own words. Then ask them to summarize the events described in the stage directions. [Summary: Annie gets Helen's attention. Helen proceeds to explore Annie's hand, arm, and face. Then Annie conveys to Helen the idea that her suitcase should go upstairs. Helen tries to take it by herself, but it is too heavy, so Helen and Annie take it up together.]

C Critical Thinking

Interpreting

❓ What does Keller mean when he describes Annie as "rough"? Does he mean she wasn't gentle enough with Helen? [No, he is referring to her manner and social class; he feels that she is not very elegant or refined.]

A [KATE *silences him with a hand on his arm. When* ANNIE *finally reaches the porch steps she stops, contemplating* HELEN *for a last moment before entering her world. Then she drops the suitcase on the porch with intentional heaviness;* HELEN *starts with the jar and comes to grope over it.* ANNIE *puts forth her hand and touches* HELEN'S. HELEN *at once grasps it and commences to explore it, like reading a face. She moves her hand on to* ANNIE'S *forearm, and dress; and* ANNIE *brings her face within reach of* HELEN'S *fingers, which travel over it,* **B** *quite without timidity, until they encounter and push aside the smoked glasses.* ANNIE'S *gaze is grave, unpitying, very attentive. She puts her hands on* HELEN'S *arms, but* HELEN *at once pulls away, and they confront each other with a distance between. Then* HELEN *returns to the suitcase, tries to open it, cannot.* ANNIE *points* HELEN'S *hand overhead.* HELEN *pulls away, tries to open the suitcase again;* ANNIE *points her hand overhead again.* HELEN *points overhead, a question, and* ANNIE, *drawing* HELEN'S *hand to her own face, nods.* HELEN *now begins tugging the suitcase toward the door; when* ANNIE *tries to take it from her, she fights her off and backs through the doorway with it.* ANNIE *stands a moment, then follows her in, and together they get the suitcase up the steps into* ANNIE'S *room.*]

Kate. Well?
Keller. She's very rough, Katie.
Kate. I like her, Captain.
Keller. Certainly rear a peculiar kind of young woman in the North. How old is she?
Kate (*vaguely*). Ohh—Well, she's not in her teens, you know.
Keller. She's only a child. What's her family like, shipping her off alone this far?
Kate. I couldn't learn. She's very closemouthed about some things.

Annie brings her face within reach of Helen's fingers....

Getting Students Involved

Cooperative Learning

Teaching by Touch. To help students appreciate the interactive process that takes place between Annie and Helen, have them work in pairs to teach each other two signs by touch alone. (Have a copy of the American Sign Language alphabet available in the classroom.) Explain that one student will play the role of teacher and the other the role of learner. The teacher demonstrates a sign to the blindfolded learner, keeping their hands in contact. The learner repeats the sign to the teacher, then guesses what the sign means. Next, have students reverse roles. After all pairs finish the exercise, have the entire class list the difficulties they experienced while learning and teaching the signs.

Vocabulary Challenge. Write the Words to Own for Act One on the board. Call on a volunteer, choose a word, and direct the student to define it or use it in a sentence. That student then repeats the process with another volunteer. The accuracy of a word's definition or usage may be challenged and corrected by any other student. The challenger then provides the student with a second word to define and use.

Keller. Why does she wear those glasses? I like to see a person's eyes when I talk to——

Kate. For the sun. She was blind.

Keller. Blind.

Kate. She's had nine operations on her eyes. One just before she left.

Keller. Blind, good heavens, do they expect one blind child to teach another? Has she experience at least? How long did she teach there?

Kate. She was a pupil.

Keller (*heavily*). Katie, Katie. This is her first position?

Kate (*bright voice*). She was valedictorian——

Keller. Here's a houseful of grown-ups can't cope with the child. How can an inexperienced half-blind Yankee schoolgirl manage her?

[JAMES *moves in with the trunk on his shoulder.*]

James (*easily*). Great improvement. Now we have two of them to look after.

Keller. You look after those strawberry plants!

[JAMES *stops with the trunk.* KELLER *turns from him without another word and marches off.*]

James. Nothing I say is right.

Kate. Why say anything? (*She calls.*) Don't be long, Captain, we'll have supper right away——

[*She goes into the house and through the rear door of the family room.* JAMES *trudges in with the trunk, takes it up the steps to* ANNIE'S *room, and sets it down outside the door. The lights elsewhere dim somewhat.*]

SCENE 8

Meanwhile, inside, ANNIE *has given* HELEN *a key; while* ANNIE *removes her bonnet,* HELEN *unlocks and opens the suitcase. The first thing she pulls out is a* voluminous *shawl. She fingers it until she* perceives *what it is; then she wraps it around her, and acquiring* ANNIE'S *bonnet and smoked glasses as well, dons the lot: The shawl swamps her, and the bonnet settles down upon the glasses, but she stands before a mirror cocking her head to one side, then to the other, in a mockery of adult action.* ANNIE *is amused, and talks to her as one might to a kitten, with no trace of company manners.*

Annie. All the trouble I went to and that's how I look? (HELEN *then comes back to the suitcase, gropes for more, lifts out a pair of female drawers.*) Oh, no. Not the drawers! (*But* HELEN, *discarding them, comes to the elegant doll. Her fingers explore its features, and when she raises it and finds that its eyes open and close,* she is at first startled, then delighted. She picks it up, taps its head vigorously, taps her own chest, and nods questioningly.* ANNIE *takes her finger, points it to the doll, points it to* HELEN, *and touching it to her own face, also nods.* HELEN *sits back on her heels, clasps the doll to herself, and rocks it.* ANNIE *studies her, still in bonnet and smoked glasses, like a* caricature *of herself, and addresses her humorously.*) All right, Miss O'Sullivan. Let's begin with doll. (*She takes* HELEN'S *hand; in her palm* ANNIE'S *forefinger points, thumb holding her other fingers clenched.*) D. (*Her thumb next holds all her fingers clenched, touching* HELEN'S *palm.*) O. (*Her thumb and forefinger extend.*) L. (*Same contact repeated.*) L. (*She puts* HELEN'S *hand to the doll.*) Doll.

WORDS TO OWN

voluminous (və·lōōm'ə·nəs) *adj.*: large and bulky.
caricature (kar'i·kə·chər) *n.*: exaggerated portrait.

THE MIRACLE WORKER, ACT ONE, SCENE 8 653

Ⓓ Reading Skills and Strategies
Comparing and Contrasting
Have students compare and contrast Kate's and Keller's views on Annie Sullivan's aptness for teaching Helen. [Keller is a pessimist and Kate is an optimist; Keller cannot understand how Annie's visual impairment and youth can possibly benefit her as Helen's teacher; Kate is more open to the possibility that Annie will be able to help Helen.]

Ⓔ Reading Skills and Strategies
How to Read a Play
Like many skilled dramatists, Gibson uses comic relief to vary the pace, tone, and intensity of the story. Point out that comic relief refreshes an audience, fortifying them for reentry into the play's conflicts and serious issues. Here, as in much of her dialogue, Annie shows a keen wit and a good sense of humor. Have students analyze the humor of this scene. [It's humorous because Helen unwittingly gets herself up to look like a parody of Annie; Annie is both self-mocking and silly, since she is addressing someone who can't hear her.]

Ⓕ Historical Connections
Annie is beginning to teach Helen finger spelling, which involves using the fingers to trace the spelling of words onto another's hand. The hand movements of traditional American Sign Language (see p. 684) evolved in the 1800s from a combination of signs being used in the United States and signs brought from France early in the century. Finger spelling has a long history. As Annie points out on p. 654, monks who lived in silent communities during the Middle Ages sometimes communicated by finger spelling. Also, some 10th-century Latin Bibles contain drawings of such hand signals.

A Critical Thinking

Speculating

❓ Why would Annie want Helen's fingers to learn the letters if Helen doesn't understand what the letters mean? [This is the first step to learning any language—learning its alphabet; by familiarizing herself with the letters, Helen will eventually understand that they form words that stand for things.]

B Reading Skills and Strategies

How to Read a Play

❓ Is Annie's use of the cake to teach Helen an activity or a dramatic action? [It is a dramatic action, because it deepens the audience's understanding of Helen and Annie: The viewer learns that Annie will use every possible device to teach Helen and that Helen is intelligent, quickly learning to connect the hand signs with something she wants.]

C Critical Thinking

Making Judgments

❓ Who wins this battle of wills—Helen or Annie? [Possible answers: Helen, because she not only gets the doll but also gets away from Annie; Annie, because she gets Helen to spell into her palm and learns more about what a challenge Helen presents.]

James. You spell pretty well. (ANNIE *in one hurried move gets the drawers swiftly back into the suitcase, the lid banged shut, and her head turned, to see* JAMES *leaning in the doorway.*) Finding out if she's ticklish? She is.

[ANNIE *regards him stonily, but* HELEN *after a scowling moment tugs at her hand again, imperious.*[14] ANNIE *repeats the letters, and* HELEN *interrupts her fingers in the middle, feeling each of them, puzzled.* ANNIE *touches* HELEN'S *hand to the doll, and begins spelling into it again.*]

James. What is it, a game?
Annie (*curtly*). An alphabet.
James. Alphabet?
Annie. For the deaf. (HELEN *now repeats the finger movements in air, exactly, her head cocked to her own hand, and* ANNIE'S *eyes suddenly gleam.*) Ho. How *bright* she is!
James. You think she knows what she's doing? (*He takes* HELEN'S *hand, to throw a meaningless gesture into it; she repeats this one too.*) She imitates everything, she's a monkey.
Annie (*very pleased*). Yes, she's a bright little monkey, all right.

[*She takes the doll from* HELEN *and reaches for her hand;* HELEN *instantly grabs the doll back.* ANNIE *takes it again, and* HELEN'S *hand next, but* HELEN *is incensed now; when* ANNIE *draws her hand to her face to shake her head no, then tries to spell to her,* HELEN *slaps at* ANNIE'S *face.* ANNIE *grasps* HELEN *by both arms and swings her into a chair, holding her pinned there, kicking, while glasses, doll, bonnet fly in various directions.* JAMES *laughs.*]

James. She wants her doll back.
Annie. When she spells it.
James. Spell, she doesn't know the thing has a name, even.
Annie. Of course not, who expects her to, now? All I want is her fingers to learn the letters.
James. Won't mean anything to her. (ANNIE *gives him a look. She then tries to form* HELEN'S *fingers*

14. **imperious** (im·pir′ē·əs): demanding.

---

into the letters, but HELEN *swings a haymaker*[15] *instead, which* ANNIE *barely ducks, at once pinning her down again.*) Doesn't like that alphabet, Miss Sullivan. You invent it yourself?

[HELEN *is now in a rage, fighting tooth and nail to get out of the chair, and* ANNIE *answers while struggling and dodging her kicks.*]

Annie. Spanish monks under a—vow of silence. Which I wish *you'd* take! (*And suddenly releasing* HELEN'S *hands, she comes and shuts the door in* JAMES'S *face.* HELEN *drops to the floor, groping around for the doll.* ANNIE *looks around desperately, sees her purse on the bed, rummages in it, and comes up with a battered piece of cake wrapped in newspaper; with her foot she moves the doll deftly out of the way of* HELEN'S *groping, and going on her knee she lets* HELEN *smell the cake. When* HELEN *grabs for it,* ANNIE *removes the cake and spells quickly into the reaching hand.*) Cake. From Washington up north, it's the best I can do. (HELEN'S *hand waits, baffled.* ANNIE *repeats it.*) C, a, k, e. Do what my fingers do, never mind what it means. (*She touches the cake briefly to* HELEN'S *nose, pats her hand, presents her own hand.* HELEN *spells the letters rapidly back.* ANNIE *pats her hand enthusiastically and gives her the cake;* HELEN *crams it into her mouth with both hands.* ANNIE *watches her, with humor.*) Get it down fast, maybe I'll steal that back too. Now. (*She takes the doll, touches it to* HELEN'S *nose, and spells again into her hand.*) D, o, l, l. Think it over. (HELEN *thinks it over, while* ANNIE *presents her own hand. Then* HELEN *spells three letters.* ANNIE *waits a second, then completes the word for* HELEN *in her palm.*) L. (*She hands over the doll, and* HELEN *gets a good grip on its leg.*) Imitate now, understand later. End of the first les—— (*She never finishes, because* HELEN *swings the doll with a furious energy. It hits* ANNIE *squarely in the face, and she falls back with a cry of pain, her knuckles up to her mouth.* HELEN *waits, tensed for further combat. When* ANNIE *lowers her knuckles she looks at blood on them; she works her lips, gets to her feet, finds the mirror, and bares her teeth*

15. **haymaker:** powerful punch, as if to knock someone out.

Crossing the Curriculum

Health

As many as half a million Americans function without any vision. According to the American Foundation for the Blind, an estimated ten million Americans have difficulty seeing.

Cataracts, a clouding of the eye's normally clear lens, are one leading cause of blindness. Two others are glaucoma, a group of disorders in which the pressure within the eye increases, and macular degeneration in which scars form

on the center of the retina as a result of leaking blood vessels. In developing countries, blindness is often caused by infectious diseases. One such disease, trachoma (which Annie Sullivan contracted at age five), affects millions of people around the world, though it is now rare in Europe and North America. River blindness, caused by parasites, is common in parts of Africa, Central America, and South America.

Blindness can also be caused by sports or industrial injuries.

Ask students to research a topic related to blindness or vision. Possible topics include the process of vision, the causes of vision impairment, treatments for vision impairments, and eye safety. Have the researchers form a panel and present their information to the class.

at herself. Now she is furious herself.) You little wretch, no one's taught you *any* manners? I'll—— (*But rounding from the mirror she sees the door slam,* HELEN *and the doll are on the outside, and* HELEN *is turning the key in the lock.* ANNIE *darts over, to pull the knob; the door is locked fast. She yanks it again.*) Helen! Helen, let me out of——

[*She bats her brow at the folly of speaking, but* JAMES, *now downstairs, hears her and turns to see* HELEN *with the key and doll groping her way down the steps;* JAMES *takes in the whole situation, makes a move to intercept* HELEN, *but then changes his mind, lets her pass, and amusedly follows her out onto the porch. Upstairs* ANNIE *meanwhile rattles the knob, kneels, peers through the keyhole, gets up. She goes to the window, looks down, frowns.* JAMES *from the yard sings gaily up to her:*]

James. Buffalo girl, gonna come out tonight,
Come out tonight,
Come out——

[*He drifts back into the house.* ANNIE *takes a handkerchief, nurses her mouth, stands in the middle of the room, staring at door and window in turn, and so catches sight of herself in the mirror, her cheek scratched, her hair disheveled, her handkerchief bloody, her face disgusted with herself. She addresses the mirror, with some irony.*]

Annie. Don't worry. They'll find you, you're not lost. Only out of place. (*But she coughs, spits something into her palm, and stares at it, outraged.*) And toothless. (*She winces.*) Oo! It hurts.

[*She pours some water into the basin, dips the handkerchief, and presses it to her mouth. Standing there, bent over the basin in pain— with the rest of the set dim and unreal, and the lights upon her taking on the subtle color of the past—she hears again, as do we, the faraway voices, and slowly she lifts her head to them; the boy's voice is the same, the others are cracked old crones in a nightmare, and perhaps we see their shadows.*] **E**

Boy's Voice. It hurts. Annie, it hurts.
First Crone's Voice. Keep that brat shut up, can't you, girlie, how's a body to get any sleep in this damn ward?
Boy's Voice. It hurts. It hurts.
Second Crone's Voice. Shut up, you!
Boy's Voice. Annie, when are we goin' home? You promised!
Annie. Jimmie——
Boy's Voice. Forever and ever, you said forever—— (ANNIE *drops the handkerchief, adverts to the window, and is arrested there by the next cry.*) Annie? Annie, you there? Annie! It *hurts!*
Third Crone's Voice. Grab him, he's fallin'!
Boy's Voice. *Annie!*
Doctor's Voice (*a pause, slowly*). Little girl. Little girl, I must tell you your brother will be going on a——

[*But* ANNIE *claps her hands to her ears to shut this out; there is instant silence. As the lights bring the other areas in again,* JAMES *goes to the steps to listen for any sound from upstairs.* KELLER, *reentering from left, crosses toward the house; he passes* HELEN *en route to her retreat under the pump.* KATE *reenters the rear door of the family room with flowers for the table.*]

Kate. Supper is ready, Jimmie, will you call your father?
James. Certainly. (*But he calls up the stairs, for* ANNIE'S *benefit.*) Father! Supper!
Keller (*at the door*). No need to shout, I've been cooling my heels for an hour. Sit down.
James. Certainly.
Keller. Viney!

[VINEY *backs in with a roast, while they get settled around the table.*]

Viney. Yes, Cap'n, right here.
Kate. Mildred went directly to sleep, Viney?
Viney. Oh yes, that babe's a angel.
Kate. And Helen had a good supper?
Viney (*vaguely*). I dunno, Miss Kate, somehow she didn't have much of a appetite tonight——
Kate (*a bit guilty*). Oh. Dear.
Keller (*hastily*). Well, now. Couldn't say the same for my part, I'm famished. Kate, your plate.

Getting Students Involved

Cooperative Learning

There are many Internet resources on Helen Keller, Annie Sullivan, and organizations that work to help people with disabilities. The American Foundation for the Blind, located in New York City, is a good starting point. Students may wish to write to this organization to ask for information or find its Web site on the Internet. Small groups of students might want to work together to gather information. They can present their research to the class orally or create a bulletin board display.

Making the Connections

Connecting to the Theme: "Opening Doors"

After students have finished reading Act One, remind them of the theme of this collection. Invite students to explain how this theme is represented both literally and figuratively in Act One of *The Miracle Worker*. [Possible responses: Anagnos figuratively compares Helen to a "locked safe," and Annie is trying to open the door to that safe; Helen literally locks Annie in her room, and much dramatic action and activity concerns searching for the key to Annie's room.]

Have students make predictions about figurative doors that might open as the play progresses. Suggest that they think about different conflicts that Gibson has set up in Act One. [Students might predict that a door of communication will open between Keller and James or between Kate and Helen. Some students might also think that Annie will open an internal door of some kind as she confronts her past. The main focus of the play, however, will be the use of language as the key to opening the door to communication for Helen.]

Kate (*looking*). But where is Miss Annie?

[*A silence.*]

James (*pleasantly*). In her room.

Keller. In her room? Doesn't she know hot food must be eaten hot? Go bring her down at once, Jimmie.

James (*rises*). Certainly. I'll get a ladder.

Keller (*stares*). What?

James. I'll need a ladder. Shouldn't take me long.

Kate (*stares*). What shouldn't take you——

Keller. Jimmie, do as I say! Go upstairs at once and tell Miss Sullivan supper is getting cold——  **A**

James. She's locked in her room.

Keller. Locked in her——

Kate. What on earth are you——

James. Helen locked her in and made off with the key.

Kate (*rising*). And you sit here and say nothing.

James. Well, everyone's been telling me not to say anything.

[*He goes serenely out and across the yard, whistling.* KELLER, *thrusting up from his chair, makes for the stairs.*]

Kate. Viney, look out in back for Helen. See if she has that key.

Viney. Yes, Miss Kate. (VINEY *goes out the rear door.*)

Keller (*calling down*). She's out by the pump. (KATE *goes out on the porch after* HELEN, *while* KELLER *knocks on* ANNIE'S *door, then rattles the knob, imperiously.*) Miss Sullivan! Are you in there?

Annie. Oh, I'm in here, all right.

Keller. Is there no key on your side?

Annie (*with some* <u>asperity</u>). Well, if there was a key in here, *I* wouldn't be in here. Helen took it. The only thing on my side is me.

Keller. Miss Sullivan. I—— (*He tries, but cannot hold it back.*) Not in the house ten minutes, I don't see *how* you managed it! **B**

"She's out by the pump."

[*He stomps downstairs again, while* ANNIE *mutters to herself.*]

Annie. And even I'm not on my side. **C**

Keller (*roaring*). Viney!

Viney (*reappearing*). Yes, Cap'n?

Keller. Put that meat back in the oven!

[VINEY *bears the roast off again, while* KELLER *strides out onto the porch.* KATE *is with* HELEN *at the pump, opening her hands.*]

Kate. She has no key.

Keller. Nonsense, she must have the key. Have you searched in her pockets?

Kate. Yes. She doesn't have it.

Keller. Katie, she must have the key.

Kate. Would you prefer to search her yourself, Captain?

Keller. No, I would not prefer to search her! She almost took my kneecap off this evening, when I tried merely to—— (JAMES *reappears carrying a long ladder, with* PERCY *running after him to be in on things.*) Take that ladder back!

James. Certainly.

[*He turns around with it.* MARTHA *comes skipping around the upstage corner of the house to be in on things, accompanied by the setter* BELLE.] **D**

Kate. She could have hidden the key.

Keller. Where?

Kate. Anywhere. Under a stone. In the flower beds. In the grass——

Keller. Well, I can't plow up the entire grounds to find a missing key! Jimmie!

James. Sir?

Keller. Bring me a ladder!

James. Certainly.

[VINEY *comes around the downstage side of the house to be in on things; she has* MILDRED *over her shoulder, bleating.* KELLER *places the ladder against* ANNIE'S *window and mounts.* ANNIE *meanwhile is running about making herself presentable, washing the blood off her mouth,*

WORDS TO OWN

asperity (ə·sper′ə·tē) *n.*: sharpness of temper.

THE MIRACLE WORKER, ACT ONE, SCENE 8 **657**

A **Elements of Literature**
Character
? How would you characterize James's behavior? [Possible responses: James is being immature and childish; he is being vindictive, getting back at Keller, Annie, and Kate because he thinks they don't treat him well; his actions are aggressive, arising from his feelings of isolation, anger, and self-pity.]

B **Critical Thinking**
Interpreting
? Why is Keller so upset by the situation? [Possible responses: He is hungry and, therefore, irritable; he is frustrated because no one seems to be able to control Helen; he is embarrassed because the family's inability to control Helen has been exposed to an outsider; he is disappointed because deep down he had hoped that Annie could teach Helen, and now he thinks she can't.]

C **Reading Skills and Strategies**
Making Inferences
? What does Annie mean? [She is upset with herself for allowing Helen to lock her in the room ; she is also making a play on the phrase "my side," meaning both "my side of the door" and "my side of the situation."]

D **Reading Skills and Strategies**
How to Read a Play
Encourage students to visualize the frenetic movements of this scene as you read it aloud to them. Ask them to contrast Keller and James in this scene. [Keller can barely contain his fury; James is terse and very self-controlled.] Point out that conflict underlies the comic as well as the serious scenes in the play.

T657

A ▶ Critical Thinking
Analyzing Humor
❓ What is humorous about this exchange? [Keller's furor over the situation has added to the uproar rather than eased it.]

B ▶ Elements of Literature
Dramatic Irony
❓ When the audience knows something important that a character doesn't know, the audience experiences what is called dramatic irony. Playwrights use dramatic irony to create suspense. What is the dramatic irony in this scene? [Unlike the audience, Helen does not know that Annie is watching her.] Why would this scene be less dramatic if Helen were alone onstage when she disposes of the key? [The stakes of the conflict between Annie and Helen are raised by Annie's seeing Helen's shrewd deception.]

C ▶ Critical Thinking
Making Predictions
❓ What do you think will happen between Annie and Helen as the play progresses? Which person do you think will prevail? [Predictions will vary. Suggest that students write down their predictions and then check them for accuracy after finishing the play.]

D ▶ Reading Skills and Strategies

How to Read a Play
❓ Why is this a good place to end Act One? [Possible responses: It is the end of the first big battle between Helen and Annie; the groundwork of the story has been laid; all the major characters have been introduced and have met and formed opinions about each other; it leaves the audience eager to find out more about what happens between Annie and Helen; it underscores Helen's isolation.]

Resources
Selection Assessment
Formal Assessment
• Selection Test, p. 123
Test Generator (One-Stop Planner)
• CD-ROM

---

straightening her clothes, tidying her hair. Another servant enters to gaze in wonder, increasing the gathering ring of spectators.]

Kate (*sharply*). What is Mildred doing up?
Viney. Cap'n woke her, ma'am, all that hollerin'.
Keller. Miss Sullivan!

[ANNIE *comes to the window, with as much air of gracious normality as she can manage;* KELLER *is at the window.*]

Annie (*brightly*). Yes, Captain Keller?
Keller. Come out!
Annie. I don't see how I can. There isn't room.
Keller. I intend to carry you. Climb onto my shoulder and hold tight.
Annie. Oh, no. It's—very chivalrous of you, but I'd really prefer to——
Keller. Miss Sullivan, follow instructions! I will not have you also tumbling out of our windows. (ANNIE *obeys, with some misgivings.*) I hope this is not a sample of what we may expect from you. In the way of simplifying the work of looking after Helen.
Annie. Captain Keller, I'm perfectly able to go down a ladder under my own——
Keller. I doubt it, Miss Sullivan. Simply hold onto my neck. (*He begins down with her, while the spectators stand in a wide and somewhat awestricken circle, watching.* KELLER *half misses a rung, and* ANNIE *grabs at his whiskers.*) My neck, Miss Sullivan!
Annie. I'm sorry to inconvenience you this way——
Keller. No inconvenience, other than having that door taken down and the lock replaced, if we fail to find that key.
Annie. Oh, I'll look everywhere for it.
Keller. Thank you. Do not look in any rooms that can be locked. There.

[*He stands her on the ground.* JAMES *applauds.*]

Annie. Thank you very much.

[*She smooths her skirt, looking as composed and ladylike as possible.* KELLER *stares around at the spectators.*]

Keller. Go, go, back to your work. What are you looking at here? There's nothing here to look at. (*They break up, move off.*) Now would it be possible for us to have supper, like other people? (*He marches into the house.*)
Kate. Viney, serve supper. I'll put Mildred to sleep.

[*They all go in.* JAMES *is the last to leave, murmuring to* ANNIE *with a gesture.*]

James. Might as well leave the l, a, d, d, e, r, hm?

[ANNIE *ignores him, looking at* HELEN; JAMES *goes in too. Imperceptibly the lights commence to narrow down.* ANNIE *and* HELEN *are now alone in the yard,* HELEN *seated at the pump, where she has been oblivious to it all, a battered little savage, playing with the doll in a picture of innocent contentment.* ANNIE *comes near, leans against the house, and taking off her smoked glasses, studies her, not without awe. Presently* HELEN *rises, gropes around to see if anyone is present;* ANNIE *evades her hand, and when* HELEN *is satisfied she is alone, the key suddenly protrudes out of her mouth. She takes it in her fingers, stands thinking, gropes to the pump, lifts a loose board, drops the key into the well, and hugs herself gleefully.* ANNIE *stares. But after a moment she shakes her head to herself; she cannot keep the smile from her lips.*]

Annie. You *devil.* (*Her tone is one of great respect, humor, and acceptance of challenge.*) You think I'm so easily gotten rid of? You have a thing or two to learn, first. I have nothing else to do. (*She goes up the steps to the porch, but turns for a final word, almost of warning.*) And nowhere to go.

[*And presently she moves into the house to the others, as the lights dim down and out, except for the small circle upon* HELEN, *solitary at the pump, which ends the act.*]

> *"Miss Sullivan, follow instructions! I will not have you also tumbling out of our windows."*

Assessing Learning

Observation Assessment: Reader's Response Groups
Use the following criteria to assess participation in group discussions.
A = Always
S = Sometimes
R = Rarely
N = Never

Criteria	Rating
Values others' perspectives	
Uses others' ideas to increase interpretive possibilities	
Asks questions	
Seeks help of others to clarify meaning	
Can disagree without disrupting dialogue	

RESPONDING TO THE ART

Activity. Why do you think William Gibson specified that Helen sit at the pump during this scene? [Possible responses: Since Helen caused Annie's predicament—and all the events that ensued—it is appropriate that she be in the center of the audience's focus; Helen is excited and upset, and the pump is a favorite, comfortable place for her; she is in position to drop the key down the well when she thinks she is alone. As students will see later, the pump plays a key role in the play.]

Assessing Learning

Check Test: Questions and Answers

Act One

1. When does Kate first realize that Helen can neither hear nor see? [She realizes this after the doctor leaves.]

2. Why is Keller reluctant to send for a specialist to see Helen? [Helen has already been seen by many specialists, without results.]

3. How does Annie travel from Boston? [She travels by train.]

4. Why doesn't Keller trust Annie's abilities as a teacher? [She is young, inexperienced, and visually impaired.]

5. How does Annie become trapped in the bedroom? [Helen locks her in and hides the key.]

Standardized Test Preparation

For practice with standardized test format specific to this selection, see
- *Standardized Test Preparation*, p. 78

For practice in proofreading and editing, see
- *Daily Oral Grammar*, Transparency 42

First Thoughts

1. Some students may say that they dislike Helen or are surprised that she is so difficult. Other students may respect her strong spirit and sympathize with her because of the challenges she faces.

Shaping Interpretations

2. Annie faces internal as well as external obstacles. Internal obstacles include the emotional scars left by her background and the insecurity arising from her inexperience as a teacher. In the Keller household she faces several external obstacles or antagonists. Annie must battle Helen's hostility and inability to communicate, Kate's need to indulge Helen, Captain Keller's distrust and insistence on authority, and James's skepticism.

3. Annie's goal is to unlock Helen's closed world by giving her another kind of key—language.

4. These acts indicate that the family overindulges Helen; because they are unable to communicate with her, they use sweets as a pacifier. Annie's greater emotional distance from Helen may allow her to discipline the girl.

5. Possible questions: Will Annie be able to discipline Helen? How will Annie try to teach Helen to communicate? What kind of relationship will develop between the two?

6. The image of the open door could symbolize communication between people or the necessity of opening up to one another. Doors closed for Annie are the possibility of an easy victory with Helen and a respectful attitude from Keller. Doors that have opened for her are the start of a relationship between Kate and Annie and the introduction of Helen to finger spelling. Doors closed for Helen are speech, hearing, and sight. A door that has opened for her is the possibility of learning language.

Connecting with the Text

7. Possible responses: Annie might feel challenged, determined to teach Helen, and aware that other family members could interfere. Mrs. Keller might feel relieved by Annie's presence, yet scared that Annie will not be able to help Helen.

MAKING MEANINGS   ACT ONE

First Thoughts

[respond]

1. How do you feel about the character Helen? Is she what you expected? Check your Quickwrite notes.

Shaping Interpretations

[analyze]

2. If Annie is the play's **protagonist,** who or what would you say are her **antagonists** or obstacles—the forces that block her from getting what she wants?

[interpret]

3. Helen's **action** of putting her fingers to others' mouths is **symbolic**—it stands for Helen's desire for communication. What would you say is symbolic in the fact that the first thing Annie gives Helen is a key?

[infer]

4. In Scene 5 three people give sweets to Helen. What does this tell you about the way Helen has been treated by her family? What might Annie do for Helen that others cannot?

[infer]

5. By the end of Act One, what questions do you have about what will happen next?

PLAYBILL
a weekly magazine for theatergoers
The Playhouse

THE MIRACLE WORKER

660 MODERN DRAMA

> **Reading Check**
>
> **a.** This play begins with a crisis. What do we learn in the first scene?
>
> **b.** What do Helen's **actions** in Scene 2 indicate about her wants?
>
> **c.** By the end of Scene 3, what decision has been reached about Helen? What **action** will be taken?
>
> **d.** New pressures are introduced in Scenes 6 and 7 when the Kellers meet Annie. How does each family member respond to this addition to their already troubled household?
>
> **e.** You can see **conflicts** developing between Annie and Helen and between Annie and the Kellers. What hints of another conflict do you notice between James and his father?

6. Think of the title of this collection, "Opening Doors." What could the image of the open door **symbolize**? What doors are closed to Annie and Helen in this act? Have any doors opened?

[interpret]

Connecting with the Text

7. If you were Annie or Mrs. Keller, how would you be feeling at this point in the story?

[connect]

Reading Check

a. An illness left Helen unable to see or hear.

b. Helen's actions reveal her desire to communicate.

c. The family has decided that something must be done to prevent Helen from harming herself or others. Captain Keller will write to Dr. Chisholm.

d. James expresses doubt about Annie's abilities and suggests that she will further disrupt the household. After initial doubt, Kate responds warmly and is hopeful that Annie will help Helen. Captain Keller is polite but doubtful that Annie can teach Helen. Helen is at first interested in Annie but then becomes rebellious.

e. James seems to want his father's approval and to resent his second marriage and new family. He is sarcastic when speaking to (and about) Keller—who, in turn, tries to keep James quiet. The two have several angry exchanges during Act One.

Choices: Building Your Portfolio

Writer's Notebook

1. Collecting Ideas for an Interpretive Essay

Finding a topic. When you interpret a work (see the Writer's Workshop on page 716), you need to focus on key passages that illuminate the theme or that reveal something important about the characters. A double-entry journal will help you note these key passages and record your responses to them. Draw a line down the center of a page of your notebook. On the left side, quote directly or summarize the passage you're interested in. On the right, jot down your reactions—what you make of it. Later, when it's time to interpret the play, your double-entry journal will help you locate key passages.

Speaking

2. Act It Out

Form a group interested in acting and prepare a scene from the first act of the play for presentation to the rest of the class. Assign parts and choose a director. Rehearse ways you can bring the scene and the characters to life. If the **stage directions** call for special effects (such as the voices from Annie's past), be sure to assign someone to provide them. Remember to assign someone to find props and to design costumes. If you wish, you can perform your scene as a dramatic reading rather than as an enactment.

Creative Writing

3. Just One Person

Begin a diary for one of the characters in this play and record the events that are taking place from that person's point of view. Start on the day Annie arrives. Your diary can reveal things about the character that are only hinted at in the play. Be sure to date your diary entries.

VOCABULARY

HOW TO OWN A WORD

WORD BANK

vivacious
benign
indolent
impudence
inarticulate
resurrection
appraisal
voluminous
caricature
asperity

Semantic Mapping

Work with a partner to create a semantic map for each word in the Word Bank. Make up your own questions about each word and provide your own answers. Use a thesaurus to help you find appropriate synonyms. A sample map is done for *vivacious*. There are two rules: You have to relate each word to *The Miracle Worker*, and you have to come up with an antonym for each.

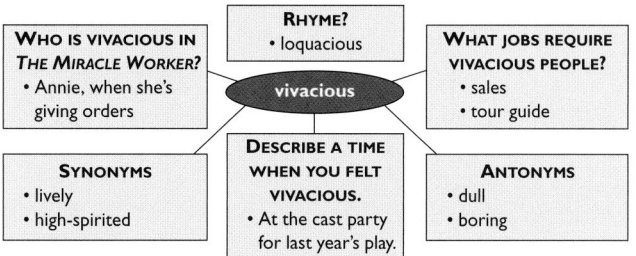

WHO IS VIVACIOUS IN *THE MIRACLE WORKER*?
• Annie, when she's giving orders

RHYME?
• loquacious

WHAT JOBS REQUIRE VIVACIOUS PEOPLE?
• sales
• tour guide

vivacious

SYNONYMS
• lively
• high-spirited

DESCRIBE A TIME WHEN YOU FELT VIVACIOUS.
• At the cast party for last year's play.

ANTONYMS
• dull
• boring

THE MIRACLE WORKER, ACT ONE **661**

Grading Timesaver

Rubrics for each Choices assignment appear on p. 193 in the *Portfolio Management System.*

CHOICES: Building Your Portfolio

1. **Writer's Notebook** At the end of each act, a Writer's Notebook activity appears as the first option in the Choices section. These brief work-in-progress assignments build toward the writing assignment presented in the Writer's Workshop at the end of the collection. Remind students to save their work for the Writer's Notebook activities as they move through the collection; they should be able to use some of their notes as starting points for the workshop.

2. **Speaking** You may want to show students a movie or television version of the scene before they finalize their production.

3. **Creative Writing** If students have trouble getting started, work with the class or with small groups to create a sample diary entry.

VOCABULARY

Possible Answers
Students' maps will vary.

Word	Synonym	Antonym
benign	harmless	harmful
indolent	lazy	active
impudence	rudeness	politeness
inarticulate	tongue-tied	coherent
resurrection	rebirth	extinction
appraisal	sizing-up	dismissal
voluminous	bulky	small
caricature	take-off	likeness
asperity	harshness	gentleness

Resources

Vocabulary
• *Words to Own* Worksheet, p. 36

OBJECTIVES
1. Read and interpret the play
2. Analyze conflict
3. Learn how to read a play
4. Express understanding through creative writing and speaking/listening
5. Understand and use new words
6. Compare synonyms

SKILLS
Literary
- Analyze conflict

Reading
- Learn how to read a play

Writing
- Take notes on symbols
- Write diary entries from a character's point of view

Speaking/Listening
- Make a tape recording

Viewing/Representing
- Respond to photographs of film and stage productions of the play (ATE)

Vocabulary
- Use new words
- Compare synonyms

Planning

- **Block Schedule**
  Block Scheduling Lesson Plans with Pacing Guide

- **Traditional Schedule**
  Lesson Plans Including Strategies for English-Language Learners

- **One-Stop Planner**
  CD-ROM with Test Generator

Act TWO

SCENE 1

It is evening.

The only room visible in the KELLER *house is* ANNIE'S, *where by lamplight* ANNIE *in a shawl is at a desk writing a letter; at her bureau* HELEN *in her customary unkempt state is tucking her doll in the bottom drawer as a cradle, the contents of which she has dumped out, creating as usual a fine disorder.*

ANNIE *mutters each word as she writes her letter, slowly, her eyes close to and almost touching the page, to follow with difficulty her penwork.*

Annie. "... and, nobody, here, has, attempted, to, control, her. The, greatest, problem, I, have, is, how, to, discipline, her, without, breaking, her, spirit." (*Resolute voice*) "But, I, shall, insist, on, reasonable, obedience, from, the, start——" (*At which point* HELEN, *groping about on the desk, knocks over the inkwell.* ANNIE *jumps up, rescues* *her letter, rights the inkwell, grabs a towel to stem the spillage, and then wipes at* HELEN'S *hands;* HELEN *as always pulls free, but not until* ANNIE *first gets three letters into her palm.*) Ink. (HELEN *is enough interested in and puzzled by this spelling that she proffers her hand again, so* ANNIE *spells and* impassively *dunks it back in the spillage.*) Ink. It has a name. (*She wipes the hand clean and leads* HELEN *to her bureau, where she looks for something to engage her. She finds a sewing card, with needle and thread, and going to her knees, shows* HELEN'S *hand how to connect one row of holes.*) Down. Under. Up. And be careful of the needle—— (HELEN *gets it,*

and ANNIE *rises.*) Fine. You keep out of the ink and perhaps I can keep out of—the soup. (*She returns to the desk, tidies it, and resumes writing her letter, bent close to the page.*) "These, blots, are, her, handiwork. I——" (*She is interrupted by a gasp:* HELEN *has stuck her finger and sits sucking at it, darkly. Then with vengeful resolve she seizes her doll and is about to dash its brains out on the floor when* ANNIE, *diving, catches it in one hand, which she at once shakes with hopping pain but otherwise ignores, patiently.*) All right, let's try

WORDS TO OWN

impassively (im·pas'iv·lē) *adv.:* without emotion; calmly.

662 MODERN DRAMA

Preteaching Vocabulary

Words to Own
Have volunteers take turns reading aloud the Words to Own and their definitions at the bottom of the selection pages in Act Two. Then use the following exercises to reinforce students' understanding of the words.

1. Describe possible situations in which a person:
   (a) **retaliates**   (b) shows **compunction**

2. With a partner, role-play reacting **impassively,** behaving in a **deferential** way, and expressing a **feigned** emotion.

3. Tell how the words *temper* and **temperance** are related.

4. Write sentences using these words:
   (a) **siege**   (c) **ominous**
   (b) **interminably**   (d) **paroxysm**

She lets Helen feel the grieved expression on her face. Helen imitates it.

temperance. (*Taking the doll, she kneels, goes through the motion of knocking its head on the floor, spells into* HELEN'S *hand.*) Bad, girl. (*She lets* HELEN *feel the grieved expression on her face.* HELEN *imitates it. Next she makes*

WORDS TO OWN

temperance (tem′pər·əns) *n.:* self-restraint.

HELEN *caress the doll and kiss the hurt spot and hold it gently in her arms, then spells into her hand.*) Good, girl. (*She lets* HELEN *feel the smile on her face.* HELEN *sits with a scowl, which suddenly clears; she pats the doll, kisses it, wreathes her face in a large artificial smile, and bears the doll to the washstand, where she carefully sits it.* ANNIE *watches, pleased.*) Very good girl——

THE MIRACLE WORKER, ACT TWO, SCENE 1 **663**

Summary ■ ■

Act Two
Seeing the family "control" Helen by pacifying her with sweets, Annie realizes that Helen cannot be taught language until she learns obedience. Annie opposes the Kellers over Helen's behavior at mealtime. Left alone, Annie and Helen battle physically and emotionally; at last, after a spectacular battle, Helen eats with a spoon from her own plate and folds her napkin. Annie returns to her room exhausted; she is ready to give up on Helen and leave the Kellers. Then she hears voices from her past, including the sad voice of her dead brother Jimmie. She decides to give Helen another chance. The Kellers finally agree to Annie's proposal: that she and Helen spend two weeks alone in the garden house. At first hostile and terrified, Helen ultimately allows Annie to touch her and is ready to learn—"one word. Everything."

Resources

Elements of Literature
The Elements of Drama
For additional instruction on the elements of drama, see *Literary Elements*:
- Transparency 16
- Worksheet, p. 49

Ⓐ **Elements of Literature**
Conflict
❓ Remind students that conflict—external and internal—is the heart of drama. Ask students to identify this play's central conflict. [the struggle between Helen and Annie] **What other conflicts are going on?** [external conflicts between Keller and James and between Annie and the family; Annie's internal conflict about her past]

Resources: Print and Media

Reading
- *Graphic Organizers for Active Reading*, p. 62
- *Words to Own*, p. 37
- *Audio CD Library*,
    Disc 17, Track 2

Elements of Literature
- *Literary Elements*
    Transparency 16
    Worksheet, p. 49

Writing and Language
- *Daily Oral Grammar*
    Transparency 43

Viewing and Representing
- *Viewing and Representing*
    Fine Art Transparency 17
    Fine Art Worksheet p. 68
- *Visual Connections*
    Videocassette B, Segment 12

Assessment
- *Formal Assessment*, p. 125
- *Portfolio Management System*, p. 194
- *Standardized Test Preparation*, p. 80
- *Test Generator (One-Stop Planner* CD-ROM)

Internet
- go.hrw.com (keyword: LE0 9-12)

T663

A Reading Skills and Strategies
Comparing

❓ What two things is Annie comparing? [Annie is comparing teaching Helen the manual alphabet to teaching a baby spoken language.] What does this comparison suggest? [It suggests that Annie sees Helen as intelligent and capable of learning to communicate rather than as impaired and unteachable.]

B Elements of Literature
Character

❓ What does this exchange tell the audience about Kate? [Possible responses: She is resolved to do whatever she can to help her daughter, as shown by her desire to learn the manual alphabet; she is optimistic about Helen's chances of learning language from Annie.]

C Reading Skills and Strategies

How to Read a Play

Review the difference between dramatic action and activity. Then, ask students whether this sequence is an example of activity or dramatic action, and have them explain why. [The sequence is an example of dramatic action because it sets up the conflict between Annie's and the Kellers' approaches to discipline.]

[*Whereupon* HELEN *elevates the pitcher and dashes it on the floor instead.* ANNIE *leaps to her feet and stands inarticulate;* HELEN *calmly gropes back to the sewing card and needle.*]

ANNIE *manages to achieve self-control. She picks up a fragment or two of the pitcher, sees* HELEN *is puzzling over the card, and resolutely kneels to demonstrate it again. She spells into* HELEN'S *hand.*

KATE *meanwhile coming around the corner with folded sheets on her arm, halts at the doorway and watches them for a moment in silence; she is moved, but level.*]

Kate (*presently*). What are you saying to her?

[ANNIE *glancing up is a bit embarrassed and rises from the spelling, to find her company manners.*]

Annie. Oh, I was just making conversation. Saying it was a sewing card.

Kate. But does that—(*She imitates with her fingers.*)—mean that to her?

Annie. No. No, she won't know what spelling is till she knows what a word is.

Kate. Yet you keep spelling to her. Why?

Annie (*cheerily*). I like to hear myself talk!

Kate. The Captain says it's like spelling to the fence post.

Annie (*a pause*). Does he, now.

Kate. Is it?

Annie. No, it's how I watch you talk to Mildred.

Kate. Mildred.

Annie. Any baby. Gibberish, grown-up gibberish, baby-talk gibberish, do they understand one word of it to start? Somehow they begin to. If they hear it. I'm letting Helen hear it.

Kate. Other children are not—impaired.

Annie. Ho, there's nothing impaired in that head. It works like a mousetrap!

Kate (*smiles*). But after a child hears how many words, Miss Annie, a million?

Annie. I guess no mother's ever minded enough to count.

[*She drops her eyes to spell into* HELEN'S *hand, again indicating the card;* HELEN *spells back, and* ANNIE *is amused.*]

Kate (*too quickly*). What did she spell?

Annie. I spelled card. She spelled cake! (*She takes in* KATE'S *quickness and shakes her head, gently.*) No, it's only a finger game to her, Mrs. Keller. What she has to learn first is that things have names.

Kate. And when will she learn?

Annie. Maybe after a million and one words.

[*They hold each other's gaze;* KATE *then speaks quietly.*]

Kate. I should like to learn those letters, Miss Annie.

Annie (*pleased*). I'll teach you tomorrow morning. That makes only half a million each!

Kate (*then*). It's her bedtime. (ANNIE *reaches for the sewing card,* HELEN *objects,* ANNIE *insists, and* HELEN *gets rid of* ANNIE'S *hand by jabbing it with the needle.* ANNIE *gasps and moves to grip* HELEN'S *wrist; but* KATE *intervenes with a proffered sweet, and* HELEN *drops the card, crams the sweet into her mouth, and scrambles up to search her mother's hands for more.* ANNIE *nurses her wound, staring after the sweet.*) I'm sorry, Miss Annie.

Annie (*indignantly*). Why does she get a reward? For stabbing me?

Kate. Well—— (*Then, tiredly*) We catch our flies with honey, I'm afraid. We haven't the heart for much else, and so many times she simply cannot be compelled.

Annie (*ominous*). Yes. I'm the same way myself. (KATE *smiles and leads* HELEN *off around the corner.* ANNIE *alone in her room picks up things and in the act of removing* HELEN'S *doll gives way to unmannerly temptation: She throttles it. She drops it on her bed and stands pondering. Then she turns back, sits decisively, and writes again, as the lights dim on her. Grimly:*) "The, more, I, think, the, more, certain, I, am, that, obedience, is, the, gateway, through, which, knowledge, enters, the, mind, of, the, child——"

WORDS TO OWN
ominous (äm′ə·nəs) *adj.*: threatening.

Reaching All Students

Struggling Readers
Students may have difficulty with scenes in which much of the action is described in long blocks of stage directions. You may wish to pair students and have them take turns summarizing the action in each paragraph of stage directions.

English Language Learners
Because Annie realizes that she must be able to discipline Helen in order to teach her, *discipline* is a key word in the play. Write *discipline* on the board and have students discuss its meaning. Ask them to describe situations that call for discipline. For other strategies to engage these students, see
• *Lesson Plans Including Strategies for English-Language Learners*

Advanced Learners
As students read Act Two, encourage them to consider how the play might differ if it were set at the end of the 20th century rather than the 19th century. How might modern parents overindulge Helen? What role could technology play in Annie's efforts to break through into Helen's world? What aspects of the drama would probably remain relatively unchanged?

SCENE 2

On the word obedience *a shaft of sunlight hits the water pump outside, while* ANNIE'S *voice ends in the dark, followed by a distant cockcrow; daylight comes up over another corner of the sky, with* VINEY'S *voice heard at once.*

Viney. Breakfast ready!

[VINEY *comes down into the sunlight beam and pumps a pitcherful of water. While the pitcher is brimming we hear conversation from the dark; the light grows to the family room of the house where all are either entering or already seated at breakfast, with* KELLER *and* JAMES *arguing the war.*[1] HELEN *is wandering around the table to explore the contents of the other plates. When* ANNIE *is in her chair, she watches* HELEN. VINEY *reenters, sets the pitcher on the table;* KATE *lifts the almost empty biscuit plate with an inquiring look,* VINEY *nods and bears it off back, neither of them interrupting the men.* ANNIE *meanwhile sits with fork quiet, watching* HELEN, *who at her mother's plate pokes her hand among some scrambled eggs.* KATE *catches* ANNIE'S *eyes on her, smiles with a wry gesture.* HELEN *moves on to* JAMES'S *plate, the male talk continuing,* JAMES *deferential and* KELLER *overriding.*]

James. —no, but shouldn't we give the devil his due, Father? The fact is we lost the South two years earlier when he outthought us behind Vicksburg.[2]

Keller. *Outthought* is a peculiar word for a butcher.

James. Harness maker, wasn't he?

Keller. I said butcher, his only virtue as a soldier was numbers and he led them to slaughter with no more regard than for so many sheep.

James. But even if in that sense he was a butcher, the fact is he——

Keller. And a drunken one, half the war.

---

1. **the war:** the Civil War.
2. **Vicksburg:** On July 4, 1863, at Vicksburg, Mississippi, General Ulysses S. Grant's Northern army won a decisive victory in the Civil War.

James. Agreed, Father. If his own people said he was I can't argue he——

Keller. Well, what is it you find to admire in such a man, Jimmie, the butchery or the drunkenness?

James. Neither, Father, only the fact that he beat us.

Keller. He didn't.

James. Is it your contention we won the war, sir?

Keller. He didn't beat us at Vicksburg. We lost Vicksburg because Pemberton gave Bragg five thousand of his cavalry, and Loring, whom I knew personally for a nincompoop before you were born, marched away from Champion's Hill with enough men to have held them. We lost Vicksburg by stupidity verging on treason.

James. I would have said we lost Vicksburg because Grant was one thing no Yankee general was before him——

Keller. Drunk? I doubt it.

James. Obstinate.

Keller. Obstinate. Could any of them compare even in that with old Stonewall?[3] If he'd been there we would still have Vicksburg.

James. Well, the butcher simply wouldn't give up; he tried four ways of getting around Vicksburg and on the fifth try he got around. Anyone else would have pulled north and——

Keller. He wouldn't have got around if we'd had a Southerner in command, instead of a half-breed Yankee traitor like Pemberton—— (*While this background talk is in progress,* HELEN *is working around the table, ultimately toward* ANNIE'S *plate. She messes with her hands in* JAMES'S *plate, then in* KELLER'S, *both men taking it so for granted they hardly notice. Then* HELEN *comes groping with soiled hands past her own plate, to* ANNIE'S; *her hand goes to it, and* ANNIE, *who has*

---

3. **Stonewall:** General Thomas J. Jackson, nicknamed "Stonewall" by his Southern troops because of his stubborn refusal to give up.

WORDS TO OWN

deferential (def′ər·en′shəl) *adj.:* showing polite respect.

ⒹReading Skills and Strategies
How to Read a Play

❓ How does Gibson link the stage directions for the opening of this scene with Annie's thoughts at the end of Scene 1? [He calls for light to fall on the water pump just as Annie says the word *obedience*.] How does this use of lighting help the audience recall a significant event in Act One? [It focuses the audience's attention on the water pump and the well, where Helen deposited the key to Annie's room; it therefore highlights Helen's *disobedience* and the power struggle between Annie and Helen.]

ⒺHistorical Connections

The real Captain Keller fought for the Confederacy at the Battle of Vicksburg. Perhaps this historical fact led Gibson to use the battle as the focus of this discussion between Keller and his son. Encourage students to examine how the discussions about and references to the Civil War serve as a kind of extended metaphor for conflicts going on in the play. [Possible responses: Annie, a Northerner, is taking on the Southern Kellers in a battle for Helen's future; Annie and Keller are like opposing generals.]

Skill Link

Using Available Technology

Explain that technology can aid in understanding unfamiliar terms or allusions. Point out Keller's statement that begins "He didn't beat us at Vicksburg." Tell students that a CD-ROM encyclopedia or the Internet can help them understand Keller's reference. Using "Vicksburg" or "Pemberton" as search terms on the Internet will yield numerous "hits." For example, in the Encyclopaedia Britannica CD-ROM, under the entry *Pemberton, John Clifford,* are these facts:

"Confederate general during the American Civil War, remembered for his tenacious but ultimately unsuccessful defense of Vicksburg.... Ordered ... to hold Vicksburg at all costs, Pemberton conducted a stubborn defense despite his lack of adequate food, ammunition, and manpower.... On July 4 [1863] Pemberton accepted Grant's terms for unconditional surrender."

Activities

1. After students have reviewed this historical information, ask them what Keller's statement indicates about his character. [Possible responses: He is obstinate; he hates surrender; he refuses to accept defeat.]

2. Have students use technology to help them explain Keller's reference to Pemberton as a "Yankee traitor." [Pemberton was born in Philadelphia.]

Ⓐ **Critical Thinking**
Expressing an Opinion

? What do you think of Helen's behavior and of her family's acceptance of such behavior? [Possible responses: Helen is wild and spoiled; she controls the family, since they have adapted to her behavior; the Kellers are so accustomed to her behavior and so convinced that she cannot be taught that they accept an abnormal situation as normal.]

been waiting, deliberately lifts and removes her hand. HELEN *groves again,* ANNIE *firmly pins her by the wrist and removes her hand from the* Ⓐ table. HELEN *thrusts her hands again,* ANNIE *catches them, and* HELEN *begins to flail and make noises; the interruption brings* KELLER'S *gaze upon them.*) What's the matter there?

Kate. Miss Annie. You see, she's accustomed to

helping herself from our plates to anything she——

Annie (*evenly*). Yes, but *I'm* not accustomed to it.

Keller. No, of course not. Viney!

Kate. Give her something, Jimmie, to quiet her.

James (*blandly*). But her table manners are the best she has. Well.

Annie firmly pins her by the wrist and removes her hand from the table.

Crossing the Curriculum

Health

Almost 30 million Americans have some degree of hearing loss, and the rate of hearing loss has grown by 14 percent over the last two decades. Some of that increase might have been prevented if people had avoided exposure to excessive noise. Two factors are involved in whether sound damages hearing: the loudness of a sound and the duration of exposure to it. The loudness (intensity) of a sound is measured in decibels (db). Normal conversation measures about 60–70 db. Exposure to sound above 90 db over a long period of time is considered dangerous. High-volume music through headphones can exceed 100 db. Machinery such as power saws and mowers can reach levels of 110 db. Since amplified rock music can reach levels over 120 db, it is not surprising that an estimated 13 to 30 percent of rock musicians suffer hearing loss. Ask students to research the loudness of various kinds of sounds, such as city traffic, jet engines, and music at a concert or dance club. Encourage them to display their findings on a poster or chart. Once students have completed their research, ask them to keep a "noise log" tracking the number of times a day they are exposed to potentially dangerous sound levels.

[*He pokes across with a chunk of bacon at* HELEN's *hand, which* ANNIE *releases; but* HELEN *knocks the bacon away and stubbornly thrusts at* ANNIE's *plate.* ANNIE *grips her wrists again. The struggle mounts.*]

Keller. Let her this time, Miss Sullivan, it's the only way we get any adult conversation. If my son's half merits that description. (*He rises.*) I'll get you another plate.

Annie (*gripping* HELEN). I have a plate, thank you.

Kate (*calling*). Viney! I'm afraid what Captain Keller says is only too true. She'll persist in this until she gets her own way.

Keller (*at the door*). Viney, bring Miss Sullivan another plate——

Annie (*stonily*). I have a plate, nothing's wrong with the *plate,* I intend to keep it.

[*Silence for a moment, except for* HELEN's *noises as she struggles to get loose; the* KELLERS *are a bit nonplused,*[4] *and* ANNIE *is too darkly intent on* HELEN's *manners to have any thoughts now of her own.*]

James. Ha. You see why they took Vicksburg?

Keller (*uncertainly*). Miss Sullivan. One plate or another is hardly a matter to struggle with a deprived child about.

Annie. Oh, I'd sooner have a more—(HELEN *begins to kick,* ANNIE *moves her ankles to the opposite side of the chair*)—heroic issue myself, I——

Keller. No, I really must insist you—— (HELEN *bangs her toe on the chair and sinks to the floor, crying with rage and feigned injury;* ANNIE *keeps hold of her wrists, gazing down, while* KATE *rises.*) Now she's hurt herself.

Annie (*grimly*). No, she hasn't.

Keller. Will you please let her hands go?

Kate. Miss Annie, you don't know the child well enough yet, she'll keep——

Annie. I know an ordinary tantrum well enough, when I see one, and a badly spoiled child——

James. Hear, hear.

Keller (*very annoyed*). Miss Sullivan! You would have more understanding of your pupil if you had some pity in you. Now kindly do as I——

Annie. Pity? (*She releases* HELEN *to turn equally annoyed on* KELLER *across the table; instantly* HELEN *scrambles up and dives at* ANNIE's *plate. This time* ANNIE *intercepts her by pouncing on her wrists like a hawk, and her*

---

4. **nonplused** (nän'plust'): puzzled; uncertain what to do next.

WORDS TO OWN
feigned (fānd) *adj.:* pretended or faked.

THE MIRACLE WORKER, ACT TWO, SCENE 2 667

Ⓑ Elements of Literature
Conflict
❓ What two conflicts are going on here? [One conflict is between Annie and Helen, and the other is between Annie and Keller. Both conflicts stem from Helen's lack of manners at the table.]

Ⓒ Critical Thinking
Interpreting
❓ What does James mean by this question? What comparison is he making? [He is comparing Annie's obstinacy to that of General Grant; he is implying that Annie will win this battle, as Grant won the Battle of Vicksburg.]

Ⓓ Vocabulary Note
Idioms
Ask a volunteer to explain what James means. ["Hear, hear" is an idiom used to indicate approval. James is showing his support for Annie's position.]

Ⓔ Elements of Literature
Irony
❓ Why are Keller's words ironic? [Despite his pity, Keller has little understanding of Helen, whereas Annie does understand Helen but does not pity her.]

Getting Students Involved

Cooperative Learning
Producing Pantomime. Have students work in groups of four or five to write a narrative based on a scene from *The Miracle Worker* and to generate a pantomime to accompany this narrative. To assure that each group will make a different presentation, you may wish to make assignments or have groups choose different scenes. Responsibility for writing, finding and organizing props, directing the action, lighting, and performing should be divided among the members of each group. Students may need to accomplish more than one task or perform more than one role. A performance space can be created by hanging a white sheet from ceiling to floor and shining a bright light on the fabric from behind. One group member can then read the narrative as others pantomime the scene behind the fabric, in front of the light.

A Appreciating Language

Euphemisms

Explain that *under the strawberries* is a euphemism for *dead*. **Euphemisms** are substitutions for more direct, less pleasant-sounding terms. Have students suggest other euphemisms they've heard or read. [Possible responses: *sanitation engineer* for *garbage collector*, *correctional institution* for *prison*, *previously owned* for *used*.]

B Elements of Literature

Irony

❓ As the footnote on p. 665 explains, "Stonewall" was General Thomas Jackson's nickname. What is ironic about Annie's statement? [Possible responses: Keller has given up on Helen and so is not at all like old Stonewall; he has never attempted the battle of trying to teach Helen, instead pitying and pacifying her.]

C Reading Skills and Strategies

How to Read a Play

❓ Have students discuss the interaction between James and Kate. How do the stage directions help readers understand what the characters are feeling? [Sample responses: The direction "studies it lightly" indicates that James is challenging Kate to stand up to her husband; Kate's "set" mouth indicates that she is not amused; "not without scorn" and the business with the napkin help readers understand that she is critical of James's cowardly behavior with his father.]

---

temper boils.) For this *tyrant*? The whole house turns on her whims. Is there anything she wants she doesn't get? I'll tell you what I pity, that the sun won't rise and set for her all her life, and **A** every day you're telling her it will. What good will your pity do her when you're under the strawberries, Captain Keller?

Keller (*outraged*). Kate, for the love of heaven will you——

Kate. Miss Annie, please, I don't think it serves to lose our——

Annie. It does you good, that's all. It's less trouble to feel sorry for her than to teach her anything better, isn't it?

Keller. I fail to see where you have taught her anything yet, Miss Sullivan!

Annie. I'll begin this minute, if you'll leave the room, Captain Keller!

Keller (*astonished*). Leave the——

Annie. Everyone, please.

[*She struggles with* HELEN, *while* KELLER *endeavors to control his voice.*]

Keller. Miss Sullivan, you are here only as a paid teacher. Nothing more, and not to lecture——

B **Annie.** I can't *un*teach her six years of pity if you can't stand up to one tantrum! Old Stonewall, indeed. Mrs. Keller, you promised me help.

Kate. Indeed I did, we truly want to——

Annie. Then leave me alone with her. Now!

Keller (*in a wrath*). Katie, will you come outside with me? At once, please.

[*He marches to the front door.* KATE *and* JAMES *follow him. Simultaneously* ANNIE *releases* HELEN'S *wrists, and the child again sinks to the floor, kicking and crying her weird noises.* ANNIE *steps over her to meet* VINEY *coming in the rear doorway with biscuits and a clean plate, surprised at the general commotion.*]

Viney. Heaven sakes——

Annie. Out, please.

[*She backs* VINEY *out with one hand, closes the*

---

door on her astonished mouth, locks it, and removes the key. KELLER *meanwhile snatches his hat from a rack, and* KATE *follows him down the porch steps.* JAMES *lingers in the doorway to address* ANNIE *across the room with a bow.*]

James. If it takes all summer, general.

[ANNIE *comes over to his door in turn, removing her glasses grimly; as* KELLER *outside begins speaking,* ANNIE *closes the door on* JAMES, *locks it, removes the key, and turns with her back against the door to stare ominously at* HELEN, *kicking on the floor.* JAMES *takes his hat from the rack and, going down the porch steps, joins* KATE *and* KELLER *talking in the yard,* KELLER *in a sputter of ire.*]

Keller. This girl, this—cub of a girl—*presumes*! I tell you, I'm of half a mind to ship her back to Boston before the week is out. You can inform her so from me!

Kate (*eyebrows up*). I, Captain?

Keller. She's a *hireling.*[5] Now I want it clear. Unless there's an apology and complete change of manner, she goes back on the next train! Will you make that quite clear?

Kate. Where will you be, Captain, while I am making it quite——

Keller. At the office!

[*He begins off left, finds his napkin still in his irate hand, is uncertain with it, dabs his lips with dignity, gets rid of it in a toss to* JAMES, *and marches off.* JAMES *turns to eye* KATE.]

C **James.** Will you? (KATE'S *mouth is set, and* JAMES *studies it lightly.*) I thought what she said was exceptionally intelligent. I've been saying it for years.

Kate (*not without scorn*). To his face? (*She comes to relieve him of the white napkin, but reverts again with it.*) Or will you take it, Jimmie? As a flag?

---

5. **hireling** (hīr′lin): paid servant. Here, the word shows a lack of respect.

Taking a Second Look

Review: Chronological Order

Understanding the sequence in which major events occur is an important part of analyzing a story. Remind students that when events are narrated in chronological order, they are told in the sequence in which they occurred. With the exception of Annie's flashback scenes, the events in *The Miracle Worker* are presented chronologically. You may wish to use Scene 3 to review chronological order with students.

Activities

1. As students read Scene 3, have them note instances where order is indicated by words such as *now, has begun, when,* and *after.*
2. Have students work in pairs or small groups to answer questions such as the following:
   a. What happens right before Annie first slaps Helen's cheek? [Helen punches Annie.]
   b. When does Annie pour a pitcher of water on Helen? [This happens just after Helen spews her food at Annie's face.]
   c. What happens immediately before Annie spells "Good girl" to Helen? [Annie forces Helen to eat with a spoon.]
   d. What is happening as Scene 3 ends? [Annie and Helen are fighting under the table.]

SCENE 3

JAMES *stalks out, much offended, and* KATE, *turning, stares across the yard at the house; the lights, narrowing down to the following pantomime in the family room, leave her motionless in the dark.*

ANNIE *meanwhile has begun by slapping both keys down on a shelf out of* HELEN'S *reach; she returns to the table, upstage.* HELEN'S *kicking has subsided, and when from the floor her hand finds* ANNIE'S *chair empty she pauses.* ANNIE *clears the table of* KATE'S, JAMES'S, *and* KELLER'S *plates; she gets back to her own across the table just in time to slide it deftly away from* HELEN'S *hand. She lifts the hand and moves it to* HELEN'S *plate, and after an instant's exploration,* HELEN *sits again on the floor and drums her heels.* ANNIE *comes around the table and resumes her chair. When* HELEN *feels her skirt again, she ceases kicking, waits for whatever is to come, renews some kicking, waits again.* ANNIE, *retrieving her plate, takes up a forkful of food, stops it halfway to her mouth, gazes at it devoid of appetite, and half lowers it; but after a look at* HELEN *she sighs, dips the forkful toward* HELEN *in a for-your-sake toast, and puts it in her own mouth to chew, not without an effort.*

HELEN *now gets hold of the chair leg, and half succeeds in pulling the chair out from under her.* ANNIE *bangs it down with her rear, heavily, and sits with all her weight.* HELEN'S *next attempt to topple it is unavailing, so her fingers dive in a pinch at* ANNIE'S *flank.* ANNIE *in the middle of her mouthful almost loses it with startle, and she slaps down her fork to round on* HELEN. *The child comes up with curiosity to feel what* ANNIE *is doing, so* ANNIE *resumes eating, letting* HELEN'S *hand follow the movement of her fork to her mouth; whereupon* HELEN *at once reaches into* ANNIE'S *plate.* ANNIE *firmly removes her hand to her own plate.* HELEN *in reply pinches* ANNIE'S *thigh, a good mean pinchful that makes* ANNIE *jump.* ANNIE *sets the fork down and sits with her mouth tight.* HELEN *digs another pinch into her thigh, and this time* ANNIE *slaps her hand*
D
E
smartly away; HELEN *retaliates with a round-house fist that catches* ANNIE *on the ear, and* ANNIE'S *hand leaps at once in a forceful slap across* HELEN'S *cheek;* HELEN *is the startled one now.* ANNIE'S *hand in compunction falters to her own face, but when* HELEN *hits at her again,* ANNIE *deliberately slaps her again.* HELEN *lifts her fist irresolute for another roundhouse,* ANNIE *lifts her hand resolute for another slap, and they freeze in this posture while* HELEN *mulls it over. She thinks better of it, drops her fist, and giving* ANNIE *a wide berth, gropes around to her mother's chair, to find it empty; she blunders her way along the table upstage, and encountering the empty chairs and missing plates, she looks bewildered; she gropes back to her mother's chair, again touches her cheek and indicates the chair, and waits for the world to answer.*

ANNIE *now reaches over to spell into her hand but* HELEN *yanks it away; she gropes to the front door, tries the knob, and finds the door locked, with no key. She gropes to the rear door and finds it locked, with no key. She commences to bang on it.* ANNIE *rises, crosses, takes her wrists, draws her resisting back to the table, seats her, and releases her hands upon her plate; as* ANNIE *herself begins to sit,* HELEN *writhes out of her chair, runs to the front door, and tugs and kicks at it.* ANNIE *rises again, crosses, draws her by one wrist back to the table, seats her, and sits;* HELEN *escapes back to the door, knocking over her mother's chair en route.* ANNIE *rises again in pursuit, and this time lifts* HELEN *bodily from behind and bears her kicking to her chair. She deposits her and once more turns to sit.* HELEN *scrambles out, but as she passes,* ANNIE *catches her up again from behind and deposits her in the chair;* HELEN *scrambles out on the other side, for the*
F

WORDS TO OWN

retaliates (ri·tal′ē·āts′) *v.:* returns an injury or wrong.
compunction (kəm·puŋk′shən) *n.:* feeling of guilt and regret.

THE MIRACLE WORKER, ACT TWO, SCENE 3 **669**

Using Students' Strengths

? Why is Helen's eating an example of dramatic action rather than merely an activity? [It is dramatic action because it is meaningful. Never before has Helen sat at the table and eaten food from her own plate; it also helps the audience know that Helen can learn and can control her behavior.]

B Advanced Learners

Analyzing the Scene
Have students review the dramatic action that has taken place in this scene so far. Then invite them to compare and contrast this scene with scenes from other plays they are familiar with. Ask students to suggest plays that contain scenes of confrontations between two major characters and to tell how this scene compares to them. [Gibson's play is unusual in its use of strenuous physical action with little or no dialogue. Students may mention fencing or other fighting scenes from Shakespeare that demand physical action, but these scenes often contain dialogue as well.]

---

rear door, but ANNIE, at her heels, catches her up and deposits her again in the chair. She stands behind it. HELEN scrambles out to her right, and the instant her feet hit the floor ANNIE lifts and deposits her back; she scrambles out to her left and is at once lifted and deposited back. She tries right again and is deposited back, and tries left again and is deposited back, and now feints ANNIE to the right but is off to her left, and is promptly deposited back. She sits a moment and then starts straight over the tabletop, dishware notwithstanding; ANNIE hauls her in and deposits her back, with her plate spilling in her lap, and she melts to the floor and crawls under the table, laborious among its legs and chairs; but ANNIE is swift around the table and waiting on the other side when she surfaces, immediately bearing her aloft; HELEN clutches at JAMES's chair for anchorage, but it comes with her, and halfway back she abandons it to the floor. ANNIE deposits her in her chair, and waits. HELEN sits tensed, motionless. Then she tentatively puts out her left foot and hand, ANNIE interposes her own hand, and at the contact HELEN jerks hers in. She tries her right foot, ANNIE blocks it with her own, and HELEN jerks hers in. Finally, leaning back, she slumps down in her chair, in a sullen biding.

ANNIE backs off a step and watches: HELEN offers no move. ANNIE takes a deep breath. Both of them and the room are in considerable disorder, two chairs down and the table a mess; but ANNIE makes no effort to tidy it; she only sits on her own chair and lets her energy refill. Then she takes up knife and fork and resolutely addresses her food. HELEN's hand comes out to explore, and seeing it, ANNIE sits without moving; the child's hand goes over her hand and fork, pauses—ANNIE still does not move—and withdraws. Presently it moves for her own plate, slaps about for it, and stops, thwarted. At this, ANNIE again rises, recovers HELEN's plate from the floor and a handful of scattered food from the deranged tablecloth, drops it on the plate, and pushes the plate into contact with HELEN's fist. Neither of them now moves for a pregnant moment—until HELEN

A

suddenly takes a grab of food and wolfs it down. ANNIE permits herself the humor of a minor bow and warming of her hands together; she wanders off a step or two, watching. HELEN cleans up the plate.

After a glower of indecision, she holds the empty plate out for more. ANNIE accepts it, and crossing to the removed plates, spoons food from them onto it; she stands debating the spoon, tapping it a few times on HELEN's plate; and when she returns with the plate she brings the spoon, too. She puts the spoon first into HELEN's hand, then sets the plate down. HELEN discarding the spoon reaches with her hand, and ANNIE stops it by the wrist; she replaces the spoon in it. HELEN impatiently discards it, and again ANNIE stops her hand, to replace the spoon in it. This time HELEN throws the spoon on the floor. ANNIE, after considering it, lifts HELEN bodily out of the chair and, in a wrestling match on the floor, closes her fingers upon the spoon and returns her with it to the chair. HELEN again throws the spoon on the floor. ANNIE lifts her out of the chair again; but in the struggle over the spoon HELEN, with ANNIE on her back, sends her sliding over her head; HELEN flees back to her chair and scrambles into it. When ANNIE comes after her she clutches it for dear life; ANNIE pries one hand loose, then the other, then the first again, then the other again, and then lifts HELEN by the waist, chair and all, and shakes the chair loose. HELEN wrestles to get free, but ANNIE pins her to the floor, closes her fingers upon the spoon, and lifts her kicking under one arm; with her other hand she gets the chair in place again and plunks HELEN back on it. When she releases her hand, HELEN throws the spoon at her.

ANNIE now removes the plate of food. HELEN, grabbing, finds it missing and commences to bang with her fists on the table. ANNIE collects a fistful of spoons and descends with them and **B** the plate on HELEN; she lets her smell the plate, at which HELEN ceases banging, and ANNIE puts the plate down and a spoon in HELEN's hand. HELEN throws it on the floor. ANNIE puts another spoon in her hand. HELEN throws it on the floor.

Assessing Learning

Ongoing Assessment
Schedule regular conferences with students as they read *The Miracle Worker*. Invite them to discuss their thoughts and feelings about the drama, including points of confusion or identification. To help you evaluate students' understanding, invite them to ask any questions they have so far about the characters, conflicts, setting, plot, or staging. Use this opportunity to assess which students need help and how you might direct their efforts.

She puts the spoon first into Helen's hand. . . .

THE MIRACLE WORKER, ACT TWO, SCENE 3   671

RESPONDING TO THE ART

Activity. What is going on in this picture? How would you describe the scene? [Annie is forcing a spoon into Helen's hand; both Helen and Annie look disheveled and exhausted; the floor is covered with food as though a food fight has broken out.]

A Elements of Literature
Conflict
❓ How has the conflict between Helen and Annie escalated? [Possible responses: Helen has become even more wily, bold, and disrespectful, and Annie has adopted a tough, "take no prisoners" stance; neither seems willing to give in.]

B Reading Skills and Strategies
How to Read a Play
❓ Why do you think Gibson ends the scene before the conflict is resolved? What dramatic impact might this have? [Possible responses: It keeps viewers intrigued; it implies that their struggle is a long way from resolution; it emphasizes how strong-willed both characters are.]

The pain brings Annie to her knees, and Helen pummels her; they roll under the table. . . .

ANNIE *puts another spoon in her hand.* HELEN *throws it on the floor. When* ANNIE *comes to her last spoon, she sits next to* HELEN *and, gripping the spoon in* HELEN'S *hand, compels her to take food in it up to her mouth.* HELEN *sits with lips shut.* ANNIE *waits a stolid moment, then lowers* HELEN'S *hand. She tries again;* HELEN'S *lips remain shut.* ANNIE *waits, lowers* HELEN'S *hand. She tries again; this time* HELEN *suddenly opens her mouth and accepts the food.* ANNIE *lowers the spoon with a sigh of relief, and* HELEN *spews the mouthful out at her face.* ANNIE *sits a moment with eyes closed, then takes the pitcher and dashes its water into* HELEN'S *face,* who gasps astonished. ANNIE, *with* HELEN'S *hand, takes up another spoonful and shoves it into her open mouth.* HELEN *swallows involuntarily, and while she is catching her breath* ANNIE *forces her palm open, throws four swift letters into it, then another four, and bows toward her with devastating pleasantness.*

Annie. Good girl.

[ANNIE *lifts* HELEN'S *hand to feel her face nodding;* HELEN *grabs a fistful of her hair, and yanks. The pain brings* ANNIE *to her knees, and* HELEN *pummels her; they roll under the table, and the lights commence to dim out on them.*]

672 MODERN DRAMA

SCENE 4

Simultaneously the light at left has been rising, slowly, so slowly that it seems at first we only imagine what is intimated in the yard: a few ghostlike figures, in silence, motionless, waiting. Now the distant belfry chimes commence to toll the hour, also very slowly, almost—it is twelve—interminably; the sense is that of a long time passing. We can identify the figures before the twelfth stroke, all facing the house in a kind of watch; KATE *is standing exactly as before, but now with the baby* MILDRED *sleeping in her arms, and placed here and there, unmoving, are* AUNT EV *in her hat with a hankie to her nose, and the two children,* PERCY *and* MARTHA, *with necks outstretched eagerly, and* VINEY *with a knotted kerchief on her head and a feather duster in her hand.*

The chimes cease, and there is silence. For a long moment none of the group moves.

Viney (*presently*). What am I gone do, Miss Kate? It's noontime, dinner's comin', I didn't get them breakfast dishes out of there yet.

[KATE *says nothing, stares at the house.* MARTHA *shifts* HELEN'S *doll in her clutch, and it plaintively says "Momma."*]

Kate (*presently*). You run along, Martha.

[AUNT EV *blows her nose.*]

Aunt Ev (*wretchedly*). I can't wait out here a minute longer, Kate, why, this could go on all afternoon, too.
Kate. I'll tell the captain you called.
Viney (*to the children*). You hear what Miss Kate say? Never you mind what's going on here. (*Still no one moves.*) You run along tend your own bizness. (*Finally* VINEY *turns on the children with the feather duster.*) Shoo!

[*The two children divide before her. She chases them off.* AUNT EV *comes to* KATE, *on her dignity.*]

Aunt Ev. Say what you like, Kate, but that child is a *Keller.* (*She opens her parasol, preparatory to leaving.*) I needn't remind you that all the Kellers are cousins to General Robert E. Lee. I

don't know *who* that girl is. (*She waits; but* KATE, *staring at the house, is without response.*) The only Sullivan I've heard of—from Boston too, and I'd think twice before locking her up with that kind—is that man John L.[6]

[*And* AUNT EV *departs, with head high. Presently* VINEY *comes to* KATE, *her arms out for the baby.*]

Viney. You give me her, Miss Kate, I'll sneak her in back, to her crib.

[*But* KATE *is moveless, until* VINEY *starts to take the baby;* KATE *looks down at her before relinquishing her.*]

Kate (*slowly*). This child never gives me a minute's worry.
Viney. Oh yes, this one's the angel of the family, no question 'bout *that.*

[*She begins off rear with the baby, heading around the house; and* KATE *now turns her back on it, her hand to her eyes. At this moment there is the slamming of a door, and when* KATE *wheels,* HELEN *is blundering down the porch steps into the light, like a ruined bat out of hell.* VINEY *halts, and* KATE *runs in;* HELEN *collides with her mother's knees and reels off and back to clutch them as her savior.* ANNIE *with smoked glasses in hand stands on the porch, also much undone, looking as though she had indeed just taken Vicksburg.* KATE, *taking in* HELEN'S *ravaged state, becomes steely in her gaze up at* ANNIE.]

Kate. What happened?

[ANNIE *meets* KATE'S *gaze and gives a factual report, too exhausted for anything but a flat voice.*]

Annie. She ate from her own plate. (*She thinks a moment.*) She ate with a spoon. Herself. (KATE

6. **John L.:** John L. Sullivan, heavyweight boxing champion of the 1880s.

WORDS TO OWN

interminably (in·tʉr′mi·nə·blē) *adv.:* endlessly.

C Reading Skills and Strategies
How to Read a Play

Draw students' attention to the way Gibson uses light and sound to portray the passage of time. Discuss the differences between a novel, in which an author can write "three hours later," and a play, in which the passage of time must be shown. Ask students what they think has happened between Helen and Annie during this time. [Possible responses: Their struggle has continued; they have made peace and eaten breakfast.]

D Historical Connection

General Robert E. Lee, commander of the Confederate Army during the Civil War, believed that slavery was wrong, but his loyalty to the state of Virginia and his belief in states' rights determined his support of the Confederacy. In 1862 and 1863 he won victories at Fredericksburg and Chancellorsville, but his army was defeated at Gettysburg in July 1863. Lee surrendered to General Grant at the Appomattox Court House, Virginia, in April 1865, ending the war.

E Elements of Literature
Conflict

❓ Are you surprised by the outcome of the conflict in the dining room? Why or why not? [Possible responses: No, because Annie is stubborn and would not have let Helen out of the dining room if she had not obeyed; yes, because Helen is even more stubborn than Annie, and it seemed unlikely that she would do anything she didn't want to do.]

T673

A Elements of Literature

Character

❓ What do you learn about Kate's character from her words and actions here? [Possible responses: She is proud of her daughter and is joyful about her recent accomplishments; she loves Helen very much yet is uncertain of how Helen's becoming independent will alter their relationship; she does not give in to grief easily.]

B Reading Skills and Strategies

How to Read a Play

❓ How does Gibson announce the appearance of people and events from Annie's past? [The color of the lights focused on Annie changes to signify a flashback.]

---

frowns, uncertain with thought, and glances down at HELEN.) And she folded her napkin.

[KATE'S *gaze now wavers, from* HELEN *to* ANNIE, *and back.*]

Kate (*softly*). Folded—her napkin?
Annie. The room's a wreck, but her napkin is folded. (*She pauses, then*) I'll be in my room, Mrs. Keller. (*She moves to reenter the house; but she stops at* VINEY'S *voice.*)
Viney (*cheery*). Don't be long, Miss Annie. Dinner be ready right away!

[VINEY *carries* MILDRED *around the back of the house.* ANNIE *stands unmoving, takes a deep breath, stares over her shoulder at* KATE *and* HELEN, *then inclines her head graciously and goes with a slight stagger into the house. The lights in her room above steal up in readiness for her.*

KATE *remains alone with* HELEN *in the yard, standing protectively over her, in a kind of wonder.*]

Kate (*slowly*). Folded her napkin. (*She contemplates the wild head in her thighs and moves her fingertips over it, with such a tenderness, and something like a fear of its strangeness, that her own eyes close; she whispers, bending to it.*) My Helen—folded her napkin——

[*And still erect, with only her head in surrender,* KATE *for the first time that we see loses her protracted war with grief; but she will not let a sound escape her, only the grimace of tears comes, and sobs that shake her in a grip of silence. But* HELEN *feels them, and her hand comes up in its own wondering, to interrogate her mother's face, until* KATE *buries her lips in the child's palm.*]

SCENE 5

Upstairs, ANNIE *enters her room, closes the door, and stands back against it; the lights, growing on her with their special color, commence to fade on* KATE *and* HELEN. *Then* ANNIE *goes wearily to her suitcase and lifts it to take it toward the bed. But it knocks an object to the floor, and she turns back to regard it. A new voice comes in a cultured murmur, hesitant as with the effort of remembering a text:[7]*

7. **text:** The text is from the writings of Dr. Samuel Gridley Howe, former director of the Perkins Institution, who had died before Annie arrived there. The words that follow refer to a blind, deaf, and mute woman whom Howe visited in an institution in England.

Man's Voice. This—soul—(ANNIE *puts the suitcase down and kneels to the object: It is the battered Perkins report, and she stands with it in her hand, letting memory try to speak.*) This—blind, deaf, mute—woman—(ANNIE *sits on her bed, opens the book, and finding the passage, brings it up an inch from her eyes to read, her face and lips following the overheard words, the voice quite factual now.*) Can nothing be done to disinter[8] this

8. **disinter** (dis′in·tur′): dig up from the grave. Here, the speaker uses the word figuratively to mean "find the soul hidden within a person."

674 MODERN DRAMA

Skill Link

Analyzing the Relevance of the Time Frame

Thinking about the time frame—the historical context in which events take place—is particularly important when reading literature set in the past. Suggest that students take into account *The Miracle Worker*'s 19th-century time frame when considering the play's action and the statements and behavior of its characters.

As an example, have students consider the consequences of Annie's losing her job. How might these consequences be more serious for her than they would be for a woman in a similar situation today? Use the following topics as prompts for a discussion of the relevance of the time frame in *The Miracle Worker.*

- Kate's deference toward her husband
- Keller's distrust of Northerners
- Keller's difficulty dealing with Annie
- the consequences of institutionalization for Helen
- the role of servants in the Keller household

human soul? The whole neighborhood would rush to save this woman if she were buried alive by the caving in of a pit, and labor with zeal until she were dug out. Now if there were one who had as much patience as zeal, he might awaken her to a consciousness of her immortal—— (*When the boy's voice comes,* ANNIE *closes her eyes, in pain.*)

Boy's Voice. Annie? Annie, you there?
Annie. Hush.
Boy's Voice. Annie, what's that noise? (ANNIE *tries not to answer; her own voice is drawn out of her, unwilling.*)
Annie. Just a cot, Jimmie.
Boy's Voice. Where they pushin' it?
Annie. To the deadhouse.
Boy's Voice. Annie. Does it hurt, to be dead?

[ANNIE *escapes by opening her eyes, her hand works restlessly over her cheek; she retreats into the book again, but the cracked old crones interrupt, whispering.* ANNIE *slowly lowers the book.*]

First Crone's Voice. There is schools.
Second Crone's Voice. There is schools outside——
Third Crone's Voice. ——schools where they teach blind ones, worse'n you——
First Crone's Voice. To read——
Second Crone's Voice. To read and write——
Third Crone's Voice. There is schools outside where they——
First Crone's Voice. There is schools——

[*Silence.* ANNIE *sits with her eyes shining, her hand almost in a caress over the book. Then:*]

Boy's Voice. You ain't goin' to school, are you, Annie?
Annie (*whispering*). When I grow up.
Boy's Voice. You ain't either, Annie. You're goin' to stay here take care of me.
Annie. I'm goin' to school when I grow up.
Boy's Voice. You said we'll be together, forever and ever and ever——
Annie (*fierce*). I'm goin' to school when I grow up!
Doctor's Voice (*slowly*). Little girl. Little girl, I must tell you. Your brother will be going on a journey, soon.

[ANNIE *sits rigid, in silence. Then the boy's voice pierces it, a shriek of terror.*]

Boy's Voice. *Annie!*

[*It goes into* ANNIE *like a sword, she doubles onto it; the book falls to the floor. It takes her a racked moment to find herself and what she was engaged in here; when she sees the suitcase she remembers and lifts it once again toward the bed. But the voices are with her, as she halts with suitcase in hand.*]

First Crone's Voice. Goodbye, Annie.
Doctor's Voice. Write me when you learn how.
Second Crone's Voice. Don't tell anyone you came from here. Don't tell anyone——
Third Crone's Voice. Yeah, don't tell anyone you came from——
First Crone's Voice. Yeah, don't tell anyone——
Second Crone's Voice. Don't tell any——

[*The echoing voices fade. After a moment* ANNIE *lays the suitcase on the bed; and the last voice comes faintly, from far away.*]

Boy's Voice. Annie. It hurts, to be dead. Forever.

[ANNIE *falls to her knees by the bed, stifling her mouth in it. When at last she rolls blindly away from it, her palm comes down on the open report; she opens her eyes, regards it dully, and then, still on her knees, takes in the print.*]

Man's Voice (*factual*). ——might awaken her to a consciousness of her immortal nature. The chance is small indeed; but with a smaller chance they would have dug desperately for her in the pit; and is the life of the soul of less import than that of the body?

[ANNIE *gets to her feet. She drops the book on the bed and pauses over her suitcase; after a moment she unclasps and opens it. Standing before it, she comes to her decision; she at once turns to the bureau, and taking her things out of its drawers, commences to throw them into the open suitcase.*]

THE MIRACLE WORKER, ACT TWO, SCENE 5 675

C Elements of Literature
Conflict
? What conflict is evident in this dialogue? [The conflict is in Annie's mind. This is a flashback; both children are in an institution for the poor and insane in Tewksbury, Massachusetts. Jimmie will die soon. In this flashback, Jimmie cries that Annie has promised to take care of him forever; she cannot save him from death. Be sure students read Joseph Lash's account of Annie's tragic early life; see pp. 710–713.]

D Critical Thinking
Making Connections
? How might Jimmie and Helen be linked in Annie's mind? [Possible responses: Annie could not save Jimmie from death, but she might be able to save Helen from a life without communication; Jimmie died, and Helen will not fully live unless she is able to communicate.]

E Critical Thinking
Speculating
? Why is Annie packing her suitcase? [Possible response: She has decided to leave because Helen is too difficult; or, she has a plan for teaching Helen elsewhere.]

Crossing the Curriculum

Social Sciences
Braille is a writing system that uses six raised dots in various combinations to allow blind people to read with their fingertips. The Braille system was developed in the early 19th century by Louis Braille, a blind French teenager. Urge students to work in teams to research different aspects of the history and mechanics of Braille.

Possible topics for research include:
- the struggle by Braille supporters to achieve acceptance for the writing system
- how reading and writing with Braille is taught
- the Braille typewriter
- how technology is changing the way Braille printing is produced
- innovations that allow scientific and mathe-

matical symbols to be translated into Braille
- ways to expand the use of Braille, as on product labels or in mass-transit vehicles.

Have members of each team present their group's findings in oral presentations. Encourage students to supplement their presentations with charts, examples of Braille materials, or other visual aids.

A Reading Skills and Strategies

How to Read a Play

❓ Once again, Gibson uses light and sound to portray the passage of time. What does this stage direction tell us about the time? [It is late at night.]

B Reading Skills and Strategies

Comparing and Contrasting

❓ How would you contrast Keller's and Kate's views of Annie? [Possible response: Kate thinks Annie has made significant progress with Helen, whereas Keller is put off by Annie's manner and methods and cannot see how they are effective.]

C Reading Skills and Strategies

Making Predictions

❓ What do you think will happen in this talk between the Kellers and Annie? [Possible responses: Captain Keller will fire Annie; Annie will defy Keller in order to save Helen; Annie will quit before Keller can fire her.]

A *In the darkness down left a hand strikes a match and lights a hanging oil lamp. It is* KELLER'S *hand, and his voice accompanies it, very angry; the lights rising here before they fade on* ANNIE *show* KELLER *and* KATE *inside a suggestion of a garden house, with a bay window seat toward center and a door at back.*

Keller. Katie, I will not *have* it! Now you did not see when that girl after supper tonight went to look for Helen in her room——

Kate. No.

Keller. The child practically climbed out of her window to escape from her! What kind of teacher *is* she? I thought I had seen her at her worst this morning, shouting at me, but I come home to find the entire house disorganized by her—Helen won't stay one second in the same room, won't come to the table with her, won't let herself be bathed or undressed or put to bed by her, or even by Viney now, and the end result is that *you* have to do more for the child than before we hired this girl's services! From the moment she stepped off the train she's been nothing but a burden, incompetent, impertinent, ineffectual, immodest——

B **Kate.** She folded her napkin, Captain.

Keller. What?

Kate. Not ineffectual. Helen did fold her napkin.

Keller. What in heaven's name is so extraordinary about folding a napkin?

Kate (*with some humor*). Well. It's more than you did, Captain.

Keller. Katie. I did not bring you all the way out here to the garden house to be frivolous. Now, how does Miss Sullivan propose to teach a deaf-blind pupil who won't let her even touch her?

Kate (*a pause*). I don't know.

Keller. The fact is, today she scuttled any chance she ever had of getting along with the child. If you can see any point or purpose to her staying on here longer, it's more than——

Kate. What do you wish me to do?

Keller. I want you to give her notice.

Kate. I can't.

Keller. Then if you won't, I must. I simply will not—— (*He is interrupted by a knock at the back door.* KELLER *after a glance at* KATE *moves to open the door;* ANNIE *in her smoked glasses is standing outside.* KELLER *contemplates her, heavily.*) Miss Sullivan.

C **Annie.** Captain Keller. (*She is nervous, keyed up to seizing the bull by the horns again, and she assumes a cheeriness which is not unshaky.*) Viney said I'd find you both over here in the garden house. I thought we should—have a talk?

Keller (*reluctantly*). Yes. I—— Well, come in. (ANNIE *enters and is interested in this room; she rounds on her heel, anxiously, studying it.* KELLER *turns the matter over to* KATE, *sotto voce.*) Katie.

Kate (*turning it back, courteously*). Captain.

[KELLER *clears his throat, makes ready.*]

Keller. I, ah—wanted first to make my position clear to Mrs. Keller, in private. I have decided I—am not satisfied—in fact, am deeply dissatisfied—with the manner in which——

Annie (*intent*). Excuse me, is this little house ever in use?

Keller (*with patience*). In the hunting season. If you will give me your attention, Miss Sullivan. (ANNIE *turns her smoked glasses upon him; they hold his unwilling stare.*) I have tried to make allowances for you because you come from a part of the country where people are—women, I should say—come from who—well, for whom—(*It begins to elude him.*)—allowances must—be made. I have decided, nevertheless, to—that is, decided I—(*vexedly*) Miss Sullivan, I find it difficult to talk through those glasses.

Annie (*eagerly, removing them*). Oh, of course.

Keller (*dourly*). Why do you wear them? The sun has been down for an hour.

Annie (*pleasantly, at the lamp*). Any kind of light hurts my eyes.

[*A silence;* KELLER *ponders her, heavily.*]

676 MODERN DRAMA

Taking a Second Look

Review: Making Inferences About Character

Remind students that when they make an inference while reading they combine their own knowledge with evidence in the text. To make an inference about a character, they need to pay close attention to the character's speech, appearance, thoughts, and actions, as well as to what other characters say and think about that character. Then they combine this evidence with their knowledge of people to make some decision about the character. Ask volunteers to give examples of the process of making an inference.

Activity

As students read *The Miracle Worker,* ask them to make inferences about Annie, Helen, Keller, Kate, and other characters. Have students make charts like the one shown here to explain how they arrived at their inferences.

Details about the character from the text	
My knowledge of people	
Inference	

"Mrs. Keller, I don't think Helen's worst handicap is deafness or blindness. I think it's your love. And pity."

Keller. Put them on. Miss Sullivan, I have decided to—give you another chance.

Annie (*cheerfully*). To do what?

Keller. To—remain in our employ. (ANNIE'S *eyes widen.*) But on two conditions. I am not accustomed to rudeness in servants or women, and that is the first. If you are to stay, there must be a radical change of manner.

Annie (*a pause*). Whose?

Keller (*exploding*). Yours, young lady, isn't it obvious? And the second is that you persuade me there's the slightest hope of your teaching a child who flees from you now like the plague, to anyone else she can find in this house.

Annie (*a pause*). There isn't.

[KATE *stops sewing and fixes her eyes upon* ANNIE.]

Kate. What, Miss Annie?

Annie. It's hopeless here. I can't teach a child who runs away.

Keller (*nonplused*). Then—do I understand you—propose——

Annie. Well, if we all agree it's hopeless, the next question is what——

Kate. Miss Annie. (*She is leaning toward* ANNIE, *in deadly earnest; it commands both* ANNIE *and* KELLER.) I am not agreed. I think perhaps you—underestimate Helen.

Annie. I think everybody else here does.

Kate. She did fold her napkin. She learns, she learns, do you know she began talking when she was six months old? She could say "water." Not really—"wahwah." "Wahwah," but she meant water, she knew what it meant, and only six months old, I never saw a child so—bright, or outgoing—— (*Her voice is unsteady, but she gets it level.*) It's still in her, somewhere, isn't it? You should have seen her before her illness, such a good-tempered child——

Annie (*agreeably*). She's changed.

[*A pause,* KATE *not letting her eyes go; her appeal at last is unconditional, and very quiet.*]

Kate. Miss Annie, put up with it. And with us.

Keller. Us!

Kate. Please? Like the lost lamb in the parable, I love her all the more.

Annie. Mrs. Keller, I don't think Helen's worst handicap is deafness or blindness. I think it's your love. And pity.

Keller. Now what does that mean?

Annie. All of you here are so sorry for her you've kept her—like a pet, why, even a dog you housebreak. No wonder she won't let me come near her. It's useless for me to try to teach her language or anything else here. I might as well——

Kate (*cuts in*). Miss Annie, before you came we spoke of putting her in an asylum.

[ANNIE *turns back to regard her. A pause.*]

Annie. What kind of asylum?

Keller. For mental defectives.

Kate. I visited there. I can't tell you what I saw, people like—animals, with—*rats,* in the halls, and—— (*She shakes her head on her vision.*) What else are we to do, if you give up?

Annie. Give up?

Kate. You said it was hopeless.

D **Elements of Literature**
Character
❓ What does Annie's response to Keller mean? What does it tell you about her character? [Possible response: She insinuates that it is Keller's manner, not hers, that needs to change; her response shows that she is both quick-witted and courageous.]

E **Reading Skills and Strategies**
How to Read a Play
❓ How do the stage directions help clarify Kate's tone? How else could this line be spoken? [Possible response: The word *appeal* in the stage directions makes clear that the line is a plea; the line could instead be delivered as a command.]

F **Literary Connections**
This Biblical allusion comes from Luke 15:4–7, in which Jesus tells the Parable of the Lost Sheep. It begins, "What man of you, having an hundred sheep, if he lose one of them, doth not leave the ninety and nine in the wilderness and go after that which is lost, until he find it?" Invite students to explain why Helen could be compared to a lost lamb. [Possible responses: Helen is lost to her family because she cannot communicate with them; Kate implies that she loves Helen even more because of Helen's isolation from the family, and she is anxious to "find" Helen and bring her back.]

A Critical Thinking

Expressing an Opinion

? What do you think of Annie's view? Does love sometimes prevent people from helping one another? [Possible responses: Yes, love can make people overprotective, which can prevent the loved ones from becoming independent; no, love is the only way people really connect with each other, so only those who truly care about a person can help him or her.]

B Reading Skills and Strategies

How to Read a Play

Draw students' attention to the masterful way in which Gibson has Annie reveal her past, thereby giving context to the flashbacks. Explain that drama requires that such explanations arise from the situation so that they can be worked into the dialogue without sounding stilted or contrived. Ask students to recall how the script has hinted at the information Annie reveals here. [Possible response: The flashbacks, the references to Tewksbury and Jimmie, and Annie's stubborn, resilient character all hint at a difficult childhood. Be sure, again, that students read Lash's account of Annie, pp. 710–713.]

Annie. Here. Give up, why, I only today saw what has to be done, to begin! (*She glances from* KATE *to* KELLER, *who stare, waiting; and she makes it as plain and simple as her nervousness permits.*) I—want complete charge of her.

Keller. You already have that. It has resulted in——

Annie. No, I mean day and night. She has to be dependent on me.

Kate. For what?

Annie. Everything. The food she eats, the clothes she wears, fresh—(*She is amused at herself, though very serious.*)—air, yes, the air she breathes, whatever her body needs is a—primer,[9] to teach her out of. It's the only way, the one who lets her have it should be her teacher. (*She considers them in turn; they digest it,* KELLER *frowning,* KATE *perplexed.*) Not anyone who *loves* her, you have so many feelings they fall over each other like feet, you won't use your chances and you won't let me.

Kate. But if she runs from you—*to us*——

Annie. Yes, that's the point. I'll have to live with her somewhere else.

Keller. What!

Annie. Till she learns to depend on and listen to me.

Kate (*not without alarm*). For how long?

Annie. As long as it takes. (*A pause. She takes a breath.*) I packed half my things already.

Keller. Miss—Sullivan!

[*But when* ANNIE *attends him he is speechless, and she is merely earnest.*]

Annie. Captain Keller, it meets both your conditions. It's the one way I can get back in touch with Helen, and I don't see how I can be rude to you again if you're not around to interfere with me.

Keller (*red-faced*). And what is your intention if I say no? Pack the other half, for home, and abandon your charge to—to——

Annie. The asylum? (*She waits, appraises* KELLER'S *glare and* KATE'S *uncertainty, and decides to use her weapons.*) I grew up in

9. **primer** (prim′ər): simple book that gives basic information on a subject. Here, Annie is comparing Helen's surroundings to a book she can learn from.

such an asylum. The state almshouse. (KATE'S *head comes up on this, and* KELLER *stares hard;* ANNIE'S *tone is cheerful enough, albeit level as gunfire.*) Rats—why, my brother Jimmie and I used to play with the rats because we didn't have toys. Maybe you'd like to know what Helen will find there, not on visiting days? One ward was full of the—old women, crippled, blind, most of them dying, but even if what they had was catching there was nowhere else to move them, and that's where they put us. There were younger ones across the hall, prostitutes mostly, with T.B.,[10] and epileptic fits, and a couple of the kind who—keep after other girls, especially young ones, and some insane. Some just had the D.T.'s.[11] The youngest were in another ward to have babies they didn't want, they started at thirteen, fourteen. They'd leave afterward, but the babies stayed and we played with them, too, though a lot of them had—sores all over from diseases you're not supposed to talk about, but not many of them lived. The first year we had eighty, seventy died. The room Jimmie and I played in was the deadhouse, where they kept the bodies till they could dig——

Kate (*closes her eyes*). Oh, my dear——

Annie. ——the graves. (*She is immune to* KATE'S *compassion.*) No, it made me strong. But I don't think you need send Helen there. She's strong enough. (*She waits again; but when neither offers her a word, she simply concludes.*) No, I have no conditions, Captain Keller.

Kate (*not looking up*). Miss Annie.

Annie. Yes.

Kate (*a pause*). Where would you—take Helen?

Annie. Ohh—(*brightly*) Italy?

Keller (*wheeling*). What?

Annie. Can't have everything, how would this garden house do? Furnish it, bring Helen here after a long ride so she won't recognize

10. **T.B.:** abbreviation for "tuberculosis," an infectious disease that most often affects the lungs.
11. **D.T.'s:** abbreviation for "delirium tremens," hallucinations and trembling caused by alcoholism.

678 MODERN DRAMA

Skill Link

Researching Word Origins

Focus students' attention on the words *asylum* and *compassion* on p. 678. Explain that the word *asylum* comes from the Greek word *asylon.* The prefix *a-* means "without"; *sylon* means "right of seizure." Thus, the original literal meaning of *asylum* was "a place from which one cannot be seized." *Compassion* derives from the Latin prefix *com-* ("together") and the Latin root *pati-* ("to suffer"). Point out that as many as 75 percent of English words have Greek or Latin

origins. Nearly all scientific words, for example, have their origins in these two classical languages. Remind students that studying Latin and Greek roots is an efficient way to build vocabulary, since learning a single prefix can help them decode the meanings of many words. For example, knowing that *a-* means "without" allows a reader to infer that *apolitical* means "without interest in politics" and *amorphous* means "without form."

Activity

1. Copy the original meaning of *asylum* onto the chalkboard. Demonstrate how to use a dictionary entry to research word origins and to trace the changing usage of a word over time.
2. Have students use dictionaries to compile a list of ten Latin or Greek roots.
3. Ask students to exchange their lists and identify English words that contain these roots.

T678

it, and you can see her every day. If she doesn't know. Well?

Kate (*a sigh of relief*). Is that all?

Annie. That's all.

Kate. Captain. (KELLER *turns his head; and* KATE'S *request is quiet but firm.*) With your permission?

Keller (*teeth in cigar*). Why must she depend on you for the food she eats?

Annie (*a pause*). I want control of it.

Keller. Why?

Annie. It's a way to reach her.

Keller (*stares*). You intend to *starve* her into letting you touch her?

Annie. She won't starve, she'll learn. All's fair in love and war, Captain Keller. You never cut supplies?

Keller. This is hardly a war!

Annie. Well, it's not love. A siege is a siege.

Keller (*heavily*). Miss Sullivan. Do you *like* the child?

Annie (*straight in his eyes*). Do you?

[*A long pause.*]

Kate. You could have a servant here——

Annie (*amused*). I'll have enough work without looking after a servant! But that boy Percy could sleep here, run errands——

Kate (*also amused*). We can let Percy sleep here, I think, Captain?

Annie (*eagerly*). And some old furniture, all our own——

Kate (*also eager*). Captain? Do you think that walnut bedstead in the barn would be too——

Keller. I have not yet consented to Percy! Or to the house, or to the proposal! Or to Miss Sullivan's—staying on when I—(*But he erupts in an irate surrender.*) Very well, I consent to everything! (*He shakes the cigar at* ANNIE.) For two weeks. I'll give you two weeks in this

place, and it will be a miracle if you get the child to tolerate you.

Kate. Two weeks? Miss Annie, can you accomplish anything in two weeks?

Keller. Anything or not, two weeks, then the child comes back to us. Make up your mind, Miss Sullivan, yes or no?

Annie. Two weeks. For only one miracle? (*She nods at him, nervously.*) I'll get her to tolerate me.

[KELLER *marches out, and slams the door.* KATE *on her feet regards* ANNIE, *who is facing the door.*]

Kate (*then*). You can't think as little of love as you said. (ANNIE *glances questioning.*) Or you wouldn't stay.

Annie (*a pause*). I didn't come here for love. I came for money!

[KATE *shakes her head to this, with a smile; after a moment she extends her open hand.* ANNIE *looks at it, but when she puts hers out it is not to shake hands, it is to set her fist in* KATE'S *palm.*]

Kate (*puzzled*). Hm?

Annie. A. It's the first of many. Twenty-six!

[KATE *squeezes her fist, squeezes it hard, and hastens out after* KELLER. ANNIE *stands as the door closes behind her, her manner so apprehensive that finally she slaps her brow, holds it, sighs, and, with her eyes closed, crosses herself[12] for luck.*]

12. **crosses herself:** makes the sign of the cross, touching her forehead, chest, and both shoulders.

- -

WORDS TO OWN

siege (sēj) *n.*: stubborn, continued effort to win or control something.

- -

C Element of Literature
Conflict
❓ Once again, what is Annie's relationship with Helen compared to? [It is compared to a battle.] What does this comparison suggest about the nature of the conflict between the two? [Possible responses: The conflict is extremely difficult; it has a life-and-death intensity.]

D Reading Skills and Strategies
Making Inferences
❓ What does Annie mean by this question? [She is implying that although Keller may love Helen, he does not like her.]

E Critical Thinking
Making Judgments
❓ Do you think Annie is telling the truth here? Why or why not? [Sample responses: Yes, she needed a job and this is the one that was offered to her; no, if she didn't care for Helen, she wouldn't be so upset by Helen's situation.]

F Critical Thinking
Interpreting
❓ What is the significance of this exchange? [Annie's teaching Kate sign language is a further bonding between the two women. They are learning to speak to each other in another way, and Kate is admitting that she must use different means now to reach her daughter.]

Making Connections

Connecting to the Theme: "Opening Doors"

After students have finished reading this act or the entire play, help them explore the play's connection to the collection theme by asking them to freewrite about a time in their own lives when a "door" was opened for them. You might write the following prompts on the chalkboard:

- Has an experience ever made you view something in an entirely different light?

- Has there been a time in your life when a person helped you achieve something you had thought impossible?

- Is there a book you've read or a movie you've seen that has "opened a door" for you?

After students have finished writing, invite them to share and discuss their experiences if they wish.

T679

A Reading Skills and Strategies

How to Read a Play

❓ How do the stage directions convey the mood at the beginning of this scene? What do they imply about Annie's mood? [Carrying in the furniture implies a new beginning, and the mood is hopeful; Annie's rearranging of the furniture makes her seem optimistic.]

B Elements of Literature

Conflict

❓ What conflict is expressed in this passage? [James believes that Helen doesn't have the will or capacity to learn; Annie believes that Helen has not given up and that she can learn.]

C Elements of Literature

Character

❓ From this exchange and from what you already know about him, how would you describe James's character? [Possible responses: He is contrary and angry, especially at his father; he enjoys disagreeing with everyone and mocking people; he seems jealous of the attention and love that Helen gets.]

A *The lights dim into a cool silhouette scene around her; the lamp paling out, and now, in formal entrances, persons appear around* ANNIE *with furniture for the room:* PERCY *crosses the stage with a rocking chair and waits;* MARTHA, *from another direction, bears in a stool,* VINEY *bears in a small table, and the other servant rolls in a bed partway from left; and* ANNIE, *opening her eyes to put her glasses back on, sees them. She turns around in the room once and goes into action, pointing out locations for each article; the servants place them and leave, and* ANNIE *then darts around, interchanging them. In the midst of this— while* PERCY *and* MARTHA *reappear with a tray of food and a chair, respectively—*JAMES *comes down from the house with* ANNIE'S *suitcase and stands viewing the room and her quizzically;* ANNIE *halts abruptly under his eyes, embarrassed, then seizes the suitcase from his hand, explaining herself brightly.*

Annie. I always wanted to live in a doll's house!

[*She sets the suitcase out of the way and continues;* VINEY *at left appears to position a rod with drapes for a doorway, and the other servant at center pushes in a wheelbarrow loaded with a couple of boxes of* HELEN'S *toys and clothes.* ANNIE *helps lift them into the room, and the servant pushes the wheelbarrow off. In none of this is any heed taken of the imaginary walls of the garden house; the furniture is moved in from every side and itself defines the walls.*

ANNIE *now drags the box of toys into center, props up the doll conspicuously on top; with the people melted away, except for* JAMES, *all is again still. The lights turn again without pause, rising warmer.*]

James. You don't let go of things easily, do you? How will you—win her hand now, in this place?

Annie (*curtly*). Do I know? I lost my temper, and here we are!

James (*lightly*). No touching, no teaching. Of course, you *are* bigger——

Annie. I'm not counting on force, I'm counting on her. That little imp is dying to know.

James. Know what?

Annie. Anything. Any and every crumb in God's creation. I'll have to use that appetite too. (*She gives the room a final survey, straightens the bed, arranges the curtains.*)

James (*a pause*). Maybe she'll teach you.

Annie. Of course.

James. That she isn't. That there's such a thing as—dullness of heart. Acceptance. And letting **B** go. Sooner or later we all give up, don't we?

Annie. Maybe you all do. It's my idea of the original sin.

James. What is?

Annie (*witheringly*). Giving up.

James (*nettled*).[13] You won't open her. Why can't you let her be? Have some—pity on her, for being what she is——

Annie. If I'd ever once thought like that, I'd be **C** dead!

James (*pleasantly*). You will be. Why trouble? (ANNIE *turns to glare at him; he is mocking.*) Or will you teach me?

[*And with a bow, he drifts off.*

Now in the distance there comes the clopping of hoofs, drawing near, and nearer, up to the door; and they halt. ANNIE *wheels to face the door. When it opens this time, the* KELLERS—KATE *in traveling bonnet,* KELLER *also hatted—are standing there with* HELEN *between them; she is in a cloak.* KATE *gently cues her into the room.* HELEN *comes in groping, baffled, but interested in the new surroundings;* ANNIE *evades her exploring hand, her gaze not leaving the child.*]

Annie. Does she know where she is?

Kate (*shakes her head*). We rode her out in the country for two hours.

Keller. For all she knows, she could be in another town——

[HELEN *stumbles over the box on the floor and in it discovers her doll and other battered toys, is*

13. **nettled:** irritated. A nettle is a prickly plant that irritates the skin.

Using Students' Strengths

Visual Learners

To help students follow the plot, have them work in groups of three or four to illustrate an episode from Act Two. Each group should first discuss its chosen episode to reach some interpretive agreement. Then, they should divide the episode into several important moments and assign each moment to a member of the group. Group members should create captioned illustrations for their moment. Group drawings can finally be displayed in the classroom.

pleased, sits to them, then becomes puzzled and suddenly very wary. She scrambles up and back to her mother's thighs, but ANNIE *steps in, and it is hers that* HELEN *embraces.* HELEN *recoils, gropes, and touches her cheek instantly.*]

Kate. That's her sign for me.

Annie. I know. (HELEN *waits, then recommences her groping, more urgently.* KATE *stands indecisive and takes an abrupt step toward her, but* ANNIE'S *hand is a barrier.*) In two weeks.

Kate. Miss Annie, I—— Please be good to her. These two weeks, try to be very good to her——

Annie. I will. (KATE, *turning then, hurries out. The* KELLERS *cross back of the main house.* ANNIE *closes the door.* HELEN *starts at the door jar and rushes it.* ANNIE *holds her off.* HELEN *kicks her, breaks free, and careens around the room like an imprisoned bird, colliding with furniture, groping wildly, repeatedly touching her cheek in a growing panic. When she has covered the room, she commences her weird screaming.* ANNIE *moves to comfort her, but her touch sends* HELEN *into a* paroxysm *of rage: She tears away, falls over her box of toys, flings its contents in handfuls in* ANNIE'S *direction, flings the box too, reels to her feet, rips curtains from the window, bangs and kicks at the door, sweeps objects off the mantelpiece and shelf, a little tornado incarnate,[14] all destruction, until she comes upon her doll and, in the act of hurling it, freezes. Then she clutches it to herself, and in exhaustion sinks sobbing to the floor.* ANNIE *stands contemplating her, in some awe.*) Two weeks. (*She shakes her head, not without a touch of disgusted bewilderment.*) What did I get into now?

[*The lights have been dimming throughout, and the garden house is lit only by moonlight now, with* ANNIE *lost in the patches of dark.*]

---

14. **tornado incarnate** (in·kär′nit): tornado in human form.

WORDS TO OWN

paroxysm (par′əks·iz′əm) *n.:* sudden outburst; spasm.

"I'm not counting on force, I'm counting on her. That little imp is dying to know."

THE MIRACLE WORKER, ACT TWO, SCENE 7 **681**

D **Reading Skills and Strategies**
Drawing Conclusions
? Is this tantrum the same as the ones Helen has thrown around her family? [No, Helen's tantrums in the house were angry and manipulative; in this tantrum, Helen appears to be acting out her fear and helplessness.] **How do you think Helen feels?** [Possible responses: sad, scared, alone, confused, abandoned.]

A Critical Thinking

Interpreting

❓ What does Keller realize here? [He realizes that he *does* treat James as harshly as Annie treats Helen.]

B Critical Thinking

Interpreting

❓ What does Kate mean by this question? [Possible response: She is echoing Annie's earlier question to Keller as a way of getting him to examine his feelings for James and to reflect on why he is so hard on his son.]

C Reading Skills and Strategies

How to Read a Play

❓ What do this stage direction and line of dialogue tell you about Annie's state of mind? [Annie was feeling self-pity, but now she is angry at herself and determined to succeed.]

D Reading Skills and Strategies

Drawing Conclusions

❓ Why is Annie so determined to touch Helen? [Annie must be able to touch Helen in order to teach her finger spelling.]

KATE, *now hatless and coatless, enters the family room by the rear door, carrying a lamp.* KELLER, *also hatless, wanders simultaneously around the back of the main house to where* JAMES *has been waiting, in the rising moonlight, on the porch.*

Keller. I can't understand it. I had every intention of dismissing that girl, not setting her up like an empress.

James. Yes, what's her secret, sir?

Keller. Secret?

James (*pleasantly*). That enables her to get anything she wants out of you? When I can't.

[JAMES *turns to go into the house, but* KELLER *grasps his wrist, twisting him half to his knees.* KATE *comes from the porch.*]

Keller (*angrily*). She does *not* get anything she——

James (*in pain*). Don't—don't——

Kate. Captain.

Keller. He's afraid. (*He throws* JAMES *away from him, with contempt.*) What *does* he want out of me?

James (*an outcry*). My God, don't you know? (*He gazes from* KELLER *to* KATE.) Everything you forgot, when you forgot my mother.

Keller. What! (JAMES *wheels into the house.* KELLER *takes a stride to the porch, to roar after him.*) One thing that girl's secret is not, she doesn't fire one shot and disappear! (KATE *stands rigid, and* KELLER *comes back to her.*) Katie. Don't mind what he——

Kate. Captain, *I* am proud of you.

Keller. For what?

Kate. For letting this girl have what she needs.

Keller. Why can't my son be? He can't bear me, you'd think I treat him as hard as this girl does Helen—— (*He breaks off, as it dawns on him.*)

Kate (*gently*). Perhaps you do.

Keller. But he has to learn some respect!

Kate (*a pause, wryly*). Do you like the child? (*She turns again to the porch, but pauses, reluctant.*) How empty the house is, tonight.

[*After a moment she continues on in,* KELLER *stands moveless, as the moonlight dies on him.*]

The distant belfry chimes toll, two o'clock, and with them, a moment later, comes the boy's voice on the wind, in a whisper:

Boy's Voice. Annie. Annie.

[*In her patch of dark* ANNIE, *now in her nightgown, hurls a cup into a corner as though it were her grief, getting rid of its taste through her teeth.*]

Annie. No! No pity, I won't have it. (*She comes to* HELEN, *prone on the floor.*) On either of us. (*She goes to her knees, but when she touches* HELEN's *hand the child starts up awake, recoils,* and scrambles away from her under the bed. ANNIE *stares after her. She strikes her palm on the floor, with passion.*) I *will* touch you! (*She gets to her feet, and paces in a kind of anger around the bed, her hand in her hair, and confronting* HELEN *at each turn.*) How, how? How do I—— (ANNIE *stops. Then she calls out urgently, loudly.*) Percy! Percy! (*She moves swiftly to the drapes, at left.*) Percy, wake up! (PERCY's *voice comes in a thick sleepy mumble, unintelligible.*) Get out of bed and come in here, I need you. (ANNIE *darts away, finds and strikes a match, and touches it to the hanging lamp; the lights come up dimly in the room,*

Getting Students Involved

Cooperative Learning

Father and Son. Many students will be able to relate to the exchange between James and Keller in Scene 8. Ask students (in groups of four) to read this scene aloud and to spend some time sharing their thoughts about it and about the parent-child relationship it reveals. Each group should share with the class their ideas about the nature of the problem between James and his father and an idea for solving it. Groups should assign these roles to their members: moderator, to keep the group on target; recorder, to note down ideas; questioner, to raise issues about clarity; presenter to share the group's ideas with the class.

In the News. Have students work in small groups to create a newspaper article about the events and issues described in *The Miracle Worker.* Each group could be assigned responsibility for a section of the paper: headline story, related stories on the front page, editorial page, advice column (for characters in the play). Each group should choose an editor; the editors then can assign specific jobs to other group members.

and PERCY *stands bare to the waist in torn overalls between the drapes, with eyes closed, swaying.* ANNIE *goes to him, pats his cheeks vigorously.*) Percy. You awake?

Percy. No'm.

Annie. How would you like to play a nice game?

Percy. Whah?

Annie. With Helen. She's under the bed. Touch her hand.

[*She kneels* PERCY *down at the bed, thrusting his hand under it to contact* HELEN'S; HELEN *emits an animal sound and crawls to the opposite side, but commences sniffing.* ANNIE *rounds the bed with* PERCY *and thrusts his hand again at* HELEN; *this time* HELEN *clutches it, sniffs in recognition, and comes scrambling*

out after PERCY, *to hug him with delight.* PERCY, *alarmed, struggles, and* HELEN'S *fingers go to his mouth.*]

Percy. Lemme go. Lemme go—— (HELEN *fingers her own lips, as before, moving them in dumb imitation.*) She tryin' talk. She gonna hit me——

Annie (*grimly*). She *can* talk. If she only knew, I'll show you how. She makes letters. (*She opens* PERCY'S *other hand, and spells into it.*) This one is C. C. (*She hits his palm with it a couple of times, her eyes upon* HELEN *across him;* HELEN *gropes to feel what* PERCY'S *hand is doing, and when she encounters* ANNIE'S *she falls back from them.*) She's mad at me now, though, she won't play. But she knows lots of letters. Here's another, A. C, a. C, a. (*But she is*

Ⓔ
Ⓕ
Ⓖ

Annie rounds the bed with Percy and thrusts his hand again at Helen.

Ⓔ Critical Thinking

Analyzing

❓ Point out to students that Percy's disheveled state, his closed eyes, and his youth mirror Helen's condition. Why might Gibson have inserted this visual parallel? [Possible response: to reinforce Helen's physical helplessness.]

Ⓕ Critical Thinking

Making Connections

❓ Why might this scene seem familiar? [In the second scene of Act One, when Percy, Martha, and Helen are playing at the pump, Helen pokes her fingers into Percy's mouth.]

Ⓖ Elements of Literature

Conflict

❓ Why is Helen mad at Annie? [Possible response: Annie has taken her away from familiar people and surroundings and is making demands on her.]

Assessing Learning

Observation Assessment

Use the following criteria to assess students' written or oral responses to literature.

A = Always
S = Sometimes
R = Rarely
N = Never

Characteristic	Rating
Shows enjoyment of/involvement with the literature	
Makes personal and universal connections to the literature	
Gets beyond "I like/dislike the literature"	
Interprets the literature, showing understanding of multiple meanings	
Discusses author's control of elements in the literature	

LITERATURE AND SCIENCE

Language in Three Dimensions

Sign language is used more often than you might realize. Take a close look at football games on TV: Players and coaches often communicate by sign language.

Annie Sullivan taught Helen Keller to communicate by spelling words into her hand, since Helen was not able to see the hand movements of traditional sign language.

American Sign Language (ASL) is the main way that people with impaired hearing communicate with one another in the United States. Many people think sign language is the same in all countries, but it is not. Users of ASL, for example, cannot easily understand users of Chinese Sign Language. When foreign signers learn ASL, they tend to use it with an "accent." ASL is more closely related to French Sign Language than to British Sign Language, so for hearing-impaired people, communication is easier between Americans and French people than between Americans and British people.

Apart from such differences, is ASL a language in the same way that spoken English is? Or is it a pale reflection of language, a type of broken English on the hands? By studying the way the brain deals with language, scientists have found that ASL *is* a distinct language, not simply a collection of hand pictures. Research suggests that *all* languages, both spoken and signed, are based in the left side of the brain—contrary to the widely accepted theory that visual and spatial relationships are perceived by the brain's *right* side.

Like other languages, ASL has its own distinctive rules, or grammar. Instead of being based on the order and forms of words, however, ASL grammar is based on the shapes and movements of hands and their positions in space. ASL is language in three dimensions.

For example, take the two statements "The girl looks at the boy" and "The girl is looking at the boy." To express the first statement, a signer places the sign for *girl* at one position in space and the sign for *boy* at another, and then moves the *look* sign (two splayed fingers bent horizontally) from the first point to the second. To express the continuous action *is looking,* the signer modifies the *look* sign, moving it like a Ferris wheel from the first position to the second and then back again.

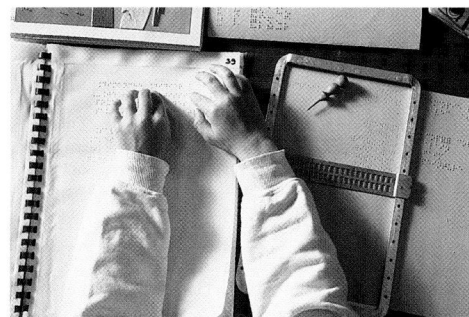

Braille is another way to use language. Here a child reads with his hands.

Crossing the Curriculum

Language

The use of American Sign Language (ASL) is growing among both hearing and hearing-impaired people. We see ASL interpreters at more and more public events like political gatherings and conventions. Knowledge of ASL helps hearing people communicate with members of the deaf community.

Many universities have begun to allow students to fulfill their foreign language requirements with the study of ASL; and some state legislatures have recognized ASL for addition to the high school foreign language curriculum. If you have students who know ASL, you might ask them to demonstrate its use to the class.

Give each student a copy of the American Sign Language alphabet, and have pairs practice its use. Then ask each pair to compose and sign a short message for the class. Class members should try to guess the messages.

watching HELEN, *who comes groping, consumed with curiosity;* ANNIE *makes the letters in* PERCY'S *hand, and* HELEN *pokes to question what they are up to. Then* HELEN *snatches* PERCY'S *other hand, and quickly spells four letters into it.* ANNIE *follows them aloud.*) C, a, k, e! She spells cake, she gets cake. (*She is swiftly over to the tray of food, to fetch cake and a jug of milk.*) She doesn't know yet it means this. Isn't it funny she knows how to spell it and doesn't *know* she knows? (*She breaks the cake in two pieces, and extends one to each;* HELEN *rolls away from her offer.*) Well, if she won't play it with me, I'll play it with you. Would you like to learn one she doesn't know? **Percy.** No'm.

[*But* ANNIE *seizes his wrist and spells to him.*]

Annie. M, i, l, k. M is this. I, that's an easy one, just the little finger. L is this—— (*And* HELEN *comes back with her hand, to feel the new word.* ANNIE *brushes her away and continues spelling aloud to* PERCY. HELEN'S *hand comes back again and tries to get in;* ANNIE *brushes it away again.* HELEN'S *hand insists, and* ANNIE *puts it away rudely.*) No, why should I talk to you? I'm teaching Percy a new word. L. K is this—— (HELEN *now yanks their hands apart; she butts* PERCY *away and thrusts her palm out insistently.* ANNIE'S *eyes are bright, with glee.*) Ho, you're *jealous,* are you! (HELEN'S *hand waits, intractably[15] waits.*) All right. (ANNIE *spells into it,* milk; *and* HELEN *after a moment spells it back to* ANNIE. ANNIE *takes her hand, with her whole face shining. She gives a great sigh.*) Good! So I'm finally back to where I can touch you, hm? Touch and go! No love lost, but here we go. (*She puts the jug of milk into* HELEN'S *hand and squeezes* PERCY'S *shoulder.*) You can go to bed now, you've earned your sleep. Thank you. (PERCY, *stumbling up, weaves his way out through the drapes.* HELEN *finishes drinking and holds the jug out for* ANNIE; *when* ANNIE *takes it,* HELEN *crawls onto the bed and makes for sleep.* ANNIE *stands, looks down at her.*) Now all I have to teach you

15. **intractably** (in·trak′tə·blē): stubbornly.

is—one word. Everything. (*She sets the jug down. On the floor now* ANNIE *spies the doll, stoops to pick it up, and with it dangling in her hand, turns off the lamp. A shaft of moonlight is left on* HELEN *in the bed, and a second shaft on the rocking chair; and* ANNIE, *after taking off her smoked glasses, sits in the rocker with the doll. She is rather happy and dangles the doll on her knee, and it makes its momma sound.* ANNIE *whispers to it in mock solicitude.*) Hush, little baby. Don't—say a word—— (*She lays it against her shoulder and begins rocking with it, patting its diminutive behind; she talks the lullaby to it humorously at first.*)

Momma's gonna buy you—a mockingbird:
If that—mockingbird don't sing——

[*The rhythm of the rocking takes her into the tune, softly, and more tenderly.*]

Momma's gonna buy you a diamond ring:
If that diamond ring turns to brass——

[*A third shaft of moonlight outside now rises to pick out* JAMES *at the main house, with one foot on the porch step; he turns his body, as if hearing the song.*]

Momma's gonna buy you a looking glass:
If that looking glass gets broke——

[*In the family room a fourth shaft picks out* KELLER *seated at the table, in thought; and he, too, lifts his head, as if hearing.*]

Momma's gonna buy you a billy goat:
If that billy goat don't pull——

[*The fifth shaft is upstairs in* ANNIE'S *room and picks out* KATE, *pacing there; and she halts, turning her head, too, as if hearing.*]

Momma's gonna buy you a cart and bull:
If that cart and bull turns over,
Momma's gonna buy you a dog named Rover:
If that dog named Rover won't bark——

[*With the shafts of moonlight on* HELEN, *and* JAMES, *and* KELLER, *and* KATE, *all moveless, and* ANNIE *rocking the doll, the curtain ends the act.*]

THE MIRACLE WORKER, ACT TWO, SCENE 9 **685**

Ⓐ Reading Skills and Strategies
Making Predictions
❓ On the basis of this scene, what do you think will happen next in the conflict between Helen and Annie? [Possible answers: Helen will continue giving in to Annie and allow herself to be taught; or, after this lull, Helen will resume her struggle, and Annie will quit.]

Ⓑ Critical Thinking
Analyzing
❓ Why does Annie sing this song? [Annie has achieved her first objective, to make Helen as dependent on her as an infant is on its mother; savoring this victory, Annie is now happy. The song also underscores Annie's determination to do whatever it takes to get through to Helen. In addition, remember that the song is a lullaby; as such, its poignant tune reminds us of Annie's own losses and of her growing love for Helen.]

Resources ————

Selection Assessment
Formal Assessment
• Selection Test, p. 125
Test Generator (One-Stop Planner)
• CD-ROM

Assessing Learning

Check Test: Questions and Answers
Act Two
1. What does Annie believe she needs to teach Helen first? [discipline]
2. How do the Kellers treat Helen? [They pity her and allow her to do as she pleases.]
3. What does Annie teach Helen during their struggle over the breakfast table? [She teaches Helen to eat from her own plate, to use a spoon, and to fold her napkin.]

4. What word did Helen try to say when she was six months old? [water]
5. At Annie's request, what do the Kellers agree to do? [They agree to let Annie have complete charge of Helen for two weeks and to let Annie and Helen live in the garden house.]

Standardized Test Preparation
For practice with standardized test format specific to this selection, see
• *Standardized Test Preparation,* p. 80
For practice in proofreading and editing see
• *Daily Oral Grammar,* Transparency 43

T685

First Thoughts

1. Students may root for Annie to conquer her demons and break through to Helen, for Helen to find her way out of darkness, for Kate to be happy, or for James to work things out with Keller. Some students may dislike Keller for his bossy, sexist manner or James for his arrogance.

Shaping Interpretations

2. Helen can then understand that everything has a name.

3. Annie's guilt seems to stem from her inability to save Jimmie or keep her promise to stay with him forever.

4. Annie needs to earn a living, and Dr. Howe's report stirs her desire to awaken Helen's soul. Flashbacks reveal that Annie grew up in an institution, that she was blind and did not learn to read and write until her teens, and that her brother Jimmie died at the institution. These details help explain her empathy for Helen and her drive to help the child.

5. Kate grows to trust Annie more. Captain Keller becomes aware that he may be partly responsible for his troubled relationship with James. Helen once again tolerates Annie.

6. Helen wants nothing to do with Annie. The Kellers tolerate uncivilized behavior from Helen and object when Annie insists that Helen behave otherwise. The captain decides to fire Annie and then gives her an ultimatum instead. Helen defies and attacks Annie and refuses to let Annie touch her.

Extending the Text

7. Sample responses: Removing such children might be advisable when a familiar environment impedes their learning. It is difficult because the children may not be equipped to deal with the changes. The risks include the possibility that the children may not get over their fear and shock and that long-term damage may occur.

T686

MAKING MEANINGS   ACT TWO

First Thoughts

[respond]

1. It has been said that in a play we must have someone to root for. So far, whom are you rooting for in this play? Is there anyone you dislike? Explain.

Shaping Interpretations

[infer]

2. Why does Annie feel that if she teaches Helen only one word, she has taught her everything?

[analyze]

3. Annie's voices reveal her **internal conflict**. Why does she feel guilty about her dead brother, Jimmie?

[infer]

4. Why do you think Annie is so determined to teach Helen, no matter what? What does Annie have at stake? Look for clues in the voices of Annie's past that speak in her **flashbacks**.

[analyze]

5. After a while the conflicts in a play wouldn't hold our interest unless the characters involved were also developing and changing. What **changes,** if any, do you see in the main members of the Keller family by the end of Act Two?

[analyze]

6. Someone once said that the art of play writing is to get your character up a tree in Act One, throw stones at him (or her) in Act Two, and get the character down in Act Three. What new "stones," or serious problems, are hurled at Annie in this act?

Extending the Text

[connect]

7. When might taking children like Helen out of their familiar environment be a good way to help them? Why is this a difficult thing to do, and what are the risks?

Reading Check

a. According to Annie's letter and her conversation with Kate Keller in Scene 1, what must be done to help Helen?

b. In contrast, what actions at the breakfast table in Scene 2 reveal the way the Kellers treat Helen?

c. What is Annie's goal in the struggle with Helen in Scene 3?

d. **Reversals** are an important part of drama. We think something is going well, and then suddenly it is going badly. Or something is going badly, and then suddenly it goes well. When Annie packs her suitcase in Scene 5, what does it look as if she intends to do? What does she really intend?

e. What bargain has been struck by Annie and the Kellers by the end of Act Two?

Reading Check
Answers may vary slightly.

a. Annie feels that Helen must be taught discipline and spelled to frequently so that she will learn that everything has a name.

b. The Kellers allow Helen to do anything she wants during meals, even take food from other people's plates, and they object to Annie's attempts to stop the girl's unruly behavior.

c. Annie's goal is to teach Helen to eat food from her own plate with a spoon.

d. The audience may think she is quitting and returning to Boston. In reality, she has decided to take Helen away to prevent family interference.

e. Annie and Helen will live in the Kellers' garden house for two weeks. During that time, the Kellers will not communicate with Helen. In return, Annie must get Helen to "tolerate" her.

CHOICES: Building Your Portfolio

Writer's Notebook

1. Collecting Ideas for an Interpretive Essay

Finding a topic. A **symbol** is  an object or event that stands for itself and for something broader than itself as well. How do you know what the symbols in a work are and what they stand for? One way is to keep track of any object or event that seems to come up in meaningful and interesting ways. Taking notes now on possible symbols in the play will help you draw conclusions later about why they are important. In the Writer's Workshop on page 716, you might use your notes and your tracking of the symbols in an interpretive essay.

Creative Writing

2. What's Happening

If you have started a diary for one of the characters in the play, add to your entries now. Is your character changing in any way? Think about your character's opinions and feelings. What episodes in this act would your character comment on? What else is going on in his or her life?

Speaking/Listening

3. The Sound of Voices

Make a tape recording of the ghostly voices Annie hears from time to time in the play. Will you use additional sound effects? What mood will you aim for? Will you use real children's voices or your own and your classmates'? Be sure to play your tape for an audience and get feedback.

VOCABULARY — HOW TO OWN A WORD

WORD BANK

impassively
temperance
ominous
deferential
feigned
retaliates
compunction
interminably
siege
paroxysm

Synonyms: Nearly the Same

Synonyms are words that mean more or less the same thing. But there are often subtle differences between synonyms, and the words are not always interchangeable. Find the place in Act Two where each word in the Word Bank at left is used. Then find a synonym for each word. Use a chart like the following to indicate if the synonym could be used in place of the word in the play. If you have trouble coming up with synonyms, use a thesaurus.

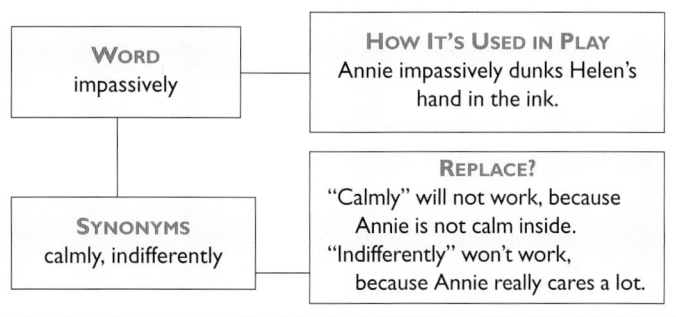

WORD
impassively

HOW IT'S USED IN PLAY
Annie impassively dunks Helen's hand in the ink.

SYNONYMS
calmly, indifferently

REPLACE?
"Calmly" will not work, because Annie is not calm inside. "Indifferently" won't work, because Annie really cares a lot.

THE MIRACLE WORKER, ACT TWO 687

Grading Timesaver

Rubrics for each Choices assignment appear on p. 194 in the *Portfolio Management System*.

CHOICES: Building Your Portfolio

1. **Writer's Notebook** Remind students to save their work. They can use it as prewriting for the Writer's Workshop on p. 716.
2. **and 3.** Students might benefit from a discussion of the relationship between tone of voice and tone in writing.

VOCABULARY

Possible Answers

temperance
How it's used in play: Annie tries temperance.
Usable synonym: restraint

ominous
How it's used in play: Annie speaks with an ominous tone.
Usable synonym: threatening

deferential
How it's used in play: James's attitude is deferential.
Usable synonym: respectful

feigned
How it's used in play: Helen cries with feigned injury.
Usable synonym: pretended

retaliates
How it's used in play: Helen retaliates by hitting Annie.
Usable synonym: takes revenge

compunction
How it's used in play: Annie touches her own face with compunction.
Usable synonym: regret

interminably
How it's used in play: The belfry chimes begin to ring interminably.
Usable synonym: ceaselessly

siege
How it's used in play: Annie is planning a siege.
Usable synonym: sustained effort

paroxysm
How it's used in play: Annie's touch provokes a paroxysm of anger in Helen.
Usable synonym: outburst

Resources

Vocabulary
• *Words to Own* Worksheet, p. 37

SCENE 1

The stage is totally dark, until we see ANNIE *and* HELEN *silhouetted on the bed in the garden house.* ANNIE'S *voice is audible, very patient, and worn; it has been saying this for a long time.*

Annie. Water, Helen. This is water. W, a, t, e, r. It has a *name*. (*A silence. Then:*) Egg, e, g, g. It has a *name*, the name stands for the thing. Oh, it's so simple, simple as birth, to explain. (*The lights have commenced to rise, not on the garden house but on the homestead. Then:*) Helen, Helen, the chick *has* to come out of its shell, sometime. You come out, too. (*In the bedroom upstairs, we see* VINEY *unhurriedly washing the window, dusting, turning the mattress, readying the room for use again; then in the family room a diminished group at one end of the table—*KATE, KELLER, JAMES*—finishing up a quiet breakfast; then outside, down right, the other servant on his knees, assisted by* MARTHA, *working with a trowel around a new trellis and wheelbarrow. The scene is one of everyday calm, and all are oblivious to* ANNIE'S *voice.*) There's only one way out, for you, and it's language. To learn that your fingers can talk. And say anything, anything you can name. This is mug. Mug, m, u, g. Helen, it has a *name*. It—has—a—*name*.

[KATE *rises from the table.*]

Keller (*gently*). You haven't eaten, Katie.
Kate (*smiles, shakes her head*). I haven't the appetite. I'm too—restless, I can't sit to it.
Keller. You should eat, my dear. It will be a long day, waiting.
James (*lightly*). But it's been a short two weeks. I never thought life could be so—noiseless, it went much too quickly for me.

[KATE *and* KELLER *gaze at him, in silence.* JAMES *becomes uncomfortable.*]

688 MODERN DRAMA

Annie. C, a, r, d. Card. C, a——
James. Well, the house has been practically normal, hasn't it?
Keller (*harshly*). Jimmie.
James. Is it wrong to enjoy a quiet breakfast, after five years? And you two even seem to enjoy each other——
Keller. It could be even more noiseless, Jimmie, without your tongue running every minute. Haven't you enough feeling to imagine what Katie has been undergoing, ever since——

[KATE *stops him, with her hand on his arm.*]

Kate. Captain. (*To* JAMES) It's true. The two weeks have been normal, quiet, all you say. But not short. Interminable. (*She rises and wanders out; she pauses on the porch steps, gazing toward the garden house.*)
Annie (*fading*). W, a, t, e, r. But it means *this*. W, a, t, e, r. *This*. W, a, t——
James. I only meant that Miss Sullivan is a boon. Of contention,[1] though, it seems.
Keller (*heavily*). If and when you're a parent, Jimmie, you will understand what separation means. A mother loses a—protector.
James (*baffled*). Hm?
Keller. You'll learn, we don't just keep our children safe. They keep us safe. (*He rises, with his empty coffee cup and saucer.*) There are of course all kinds of separation. Katie has lived with one kind for five years. And another is disappointment. In a child.

[*He goes with the cup out the rear door.* JAMES *sits for a long moment of stillness. In the garden house the lights commence to come up;* ANNIE, *haggard at the table, is*

---

1. **boon. Of contention:** James is making a joke. A boon is a blessing. A bone of contention is a subject that causes an argument or disagreement, like a bone dogs might fight over.

Planning

- **Block Schedule**
  Block Scheduling Lesson Plans with Pacing Guide
- **Traditional Schedule**
  Lesson Plans Including Strategies for English-Language Learners
- **One-Stop Planner**
  CD-ROM with Test Generator

OBJECTIVES
1. Read and interpret the play
2. Analyze the climax of the plot
3. Learn how to read a play
4. Express understanding through critical and creative writing
5. Understand and use new words
6. Chart word roots and affixes

SKILLS
Literary
- Analyze the climax of the plot

Reading
- Learn how to read a play

Writing
- Take notes on a character
- Write a dramatic scene
- Write a short essay supporting an opinion
- Write an essay responding to a character in the play
- Compare and contrast texts

Vocabulary
- Use new words
- Chart word roots and affixes

Viewing/Representing
- Respond to photographs of film and stage productions of the play (ATE)

Preteaching Vocabulary

Words to Own

Call on volunteers to write the Words to Own from Act Three and their definitions on the board. Then have students work in pairs to create five lines of dialogue, each line containing one of these vocabulary words: **simultaneously, consummately, trepidation, mediate,** and **relinquishes.** After students have finished writing, ask the partners to read their lines aloud as other students check to make sure the words are used correctly.

"Helen, it has a name. It—has—a—name."

writing a letter, her face again almost in contact with the stationery; HELEN, apart on the stool, and for the first time as clean and neat as a button, is quietly crocheting an endless chain of wool, which snakes all around the room.]

Annie. "I feel, every, day, more, and, more, in—" (She pauses, and turns the pages of a dictionary open before her; her finger descends the words to a full stop. She elevates her eyebrows, then copies the word.) "—adequate."

[In the main house JAMES pushes up and goes to the front doorway, after KATE.]

James. Kate? (KATE turns her glance. JAMES is rather wary.) I'm sorry. Open my mouth, like that fairy tale, frogs jump out.

Kate. No. It has been better. For everyone. (She starts away, up center.)

Annie (writing). "If, only, there, were, someone, to, help, me, I, need, a, teacher, as, much, as, Helen——"

James. Kate. (KATE halts, waits.) What does he want from me?

Kate. That's not the question. Stand up to the world, Jimmie, that comes first.

THE MIRACLE WORKER, ACT THREE, SCENE 1 **689**

Summary ■ ■

Act Three
At the end of the allotted two weeks, Helen is tidy and obedient but still unable to communicate with language. At her homecoming dinner, Helen deliberately misbehaves; when Annie tries to control her, Helen soaks her with a pitcher of water. As Annie and Helen refill the pitcher at the water pump, Annie spells *water* into Helen's hand, and the "miracle" happens: Helen understands that everything has a name. At the play's conclusion, James has stood up to Keller, Annie and Helen have expressed their love for one another, and Annie has put to rest the voices from her past.

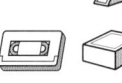

Resources

Viewing and Representing
Videocassette B, Segment 12
Available in Spanish and English. Reinforce students' reading of *The Miracle Worker* by showing them "An Enlightening Life," the *Visual Connections* segment about Helen Keller's life. For full lesson plans and worksheets, see the *Visual Connections Teacher's Manual.*

Fine Art Transparency
The fine art transparency of Winslow Homer's *Summer* will complement students' reading of *The Miracle Worker* and "Annie."
• Transparency 17
• Worksheet, p. 68

Elements of Literature
The Elements of Drama
For additional instruction on the elements of drama, see *Literary Elements*:
• Transparency 16
• Worksheet, p. 49

Resources: Print and Media

Reading
• *Graphic Organizers for Active Reading*, p. 63
• *Words to Own*, p. 38
• *Audio CD Library*,
    Disc 17, Track 2

Elements of Literature
• *Literary Elements*
    Transparency 16
    Worksheet, p. 49

Viewing and Representing
• *Viewing and Representing*
    Fine Art Transparency 17
    Fine Art Worksheet, p. 68
• *Visual Connections*
    Videocassette B, Segment 12

Assessment
• *Formal Assessment*, p. 127
• *Portfolio Management System*, p. 195
• *Standardized Test Preparation*, p. 80
• *Test Generator (One-Stop Planner* CD-ROM)

Internet
• go.hrw.com (keyword: LE0 9-12)

A Critical Thinking

Speculating

? Why might Helen find crocheting so absorbing? [Possible responses: Crocheting allows her to work with her highly developed sense of touch; it provides an outlet for her nervous energy.]

B Critical Thinking

Expressing an Opinion

? Do you agree with what Annie says about language? Why or why not? [Possible responses: Yes, using language is a large part of what makes us human; no, we can't be "born to" do something if we must learn to do it; no, using language is not essential to human survival, as flying is to the survival of birds.]

C Elements of Literature

Climax

? Remind students that complications help develop a play's central conflict until finally we reach the climax—that moment when emotions and tensions are at their peak. What is the play's central conflict? [Annie's attempt to teach Helen language is the main conflict.] What are the most important complications? [Helen's lack of control and stubbornness; the Kellers' lack of discipline] Ask students to speculate about the play's approaching climax.

James (*a pause, wryly*). But the world is him.

Kate. Yes. And no one can do it for you.

James. Kate. (*His voice is humble.*) At least we—— Could you—be my friend?

Kate. I am.

[KATE *turns to wander, up back of the garden house.* ANNIE'S *murmur comes at once; the lights begin to die on the main house.*]

Annie. "—My, mind, is, undisciplined, full, of, skips, and, jumps, and——" (*She halts, rereads, frowns.*) Hm. (ANNIE *puts her nose again in the dictionary, flips back to an earlier page, and fingers down the words;* KATE *presently comes down toward the bay window with a trayful of food.*) Disinter—disinterested—disjoin—dis—— (*She backtracks, indignant.*) Disinterested, disjoin—Where's disipline? (*She goes a page or two back, searching with her finger, muttering.*) What a dictionary, have to know how to spell it before you can look up how to spell it, disciple, *discipline*! Diskipline. (*She corrects the word in her letter.*) Undisciplined.

[*But her eyes are bothering her. She closes them in exhaustion and gently fingers the eyelids.* KATE *watches her through the window.*]

Kate. What are you doing to your eyes?

[ANNIE *glances around; she puts her smoked glasses on and gets up to come over, assuming a cheerful energy.*]

Annie. It's worse on my vanity! I'm learning to spell. It's like a surprise party, the most unexpected characters turn up.

Kate. You're not to overwork your eyes, Miss Annie.

Annie. Well. (*She takes the tray, sets it on her chair, and carries chair and tray to* HELEN.) Whatever I spell to Helen I'd better spell right.

A **Kate** (*almost wistful*). How—serene she is.

Annie. She learned this stitch yesterday. Now I can't get her to stop! (*She disentangles one foot from the wool chain and sets the chair before* HELEN. HELEN, *at its contact with her knee, feels the plate, promptly sets her crocheting down, and tucks the napkin in at her neck, but* ANNIE

690 MODERN DRAMA

---

withholds the spoon. When HELEN *finds it missing, she folds her hands in her lap and quietly waits.* ANNIE *twinkles at* KATE *with mock devoutness.*) Such a little lady, she'd sooner starve than eat with her fingers.

[*She gives* HELEN *the spoon, and* HELEN *begins to eat, neatly.*]

Kate. You've taught her so much, these two weeks. I would never have——

Annie. Not enough. (*She is suddenly gloomy, shakes her head.*) Obedience isn't enough. Well, she learned two nouns this morning, key and water, brings her up to eighteen nouns and three verbs.

Kate (*hesitant*). But—not——

Annie. No. Not that they mean things. It's still a finger game, no meaning. (*She turns to* KATE, *abruptly.*) Mrs. Keller—— (*But she defers it; she comes back, to sit in the bay, and lifts her hand.*) Shall we play our finger game?

Kate. How will she learn it?

Annie. It will come.

[*She spells a word;* KATE *does not respond.*]

Kate. How?

B **Annie** (*a pause*). How does a bird learn to fly? (*She spells again.*) We're born to use words, like wings, it has to come.

Kate. How?

Annie (*another pause, wearily*). All right. I don't know how. (*She pushes up her glasses, to rub her eyes.*) I've done everything I could think of. Whatever she's learned here—keeping herself clean, knitting, stringing beads, meals, setting-up exercises each morning, we climb trees, hunt eggs, yesterday a chick was born in her hands—all of it I spell, everything we do, we never stop spelling. I go to bed with writer's cramp from talking so much!

Kate. I worry about you, Miss Annie. You must rest.

C **Annie.** Now? She spells back in her *sleep*, her fingers make letters when she doesn't know! In her bones those five fingers know, that hand aches to—speak out, and something in her mind is asleep, how do I—nudge that awake? That's the one question.

Reaching All Students

English Language Learners

In Act Three, Scene 1, we learn that Helen has learned to spell twenty-one words. Ask students what they would do if they were responsible for teaching Helen. What five words would they teach her first? Why would they choose those words? For additional instruction for these students, see

• *Lesson Plans Including Strategies for English-Language Learners*

Advanced Learners

After students have read the play and the excerpt on pp. 704–705 from Helen Keller's autobiography, use these questions to initiate a discussion about the literary interpretation of reality: How much of the climactic episode is factual? Where does the playwright take dramatic license? Does it matter whether people know Helen Keller's story from *The Miracle Worker* rather than from her autobiography? Why or why not?

Kate. With no answer.

Annie (*long pause*). Except keep at it. Like this.

[*She again begins spelling—I, need—and* KATE'S *brows gather, following the words.*]

Kate. More—time? (*She glances at* ANNIE, *who looks her in the eyes, silent.*) Here?

Annie. Spell it.

[KATE *spells a word—no—shaking her head;* ANNIE *spells two words—why, not—back, with an impatient question in her eyes; and* KATE *moves her head in pain to answer it.*]

Kate. Because I can't——

Annie. Spell it! If she ever learns, you'll have a lot to tell each other, start now.

[KATE *painstakingly spells in air. In the midst of this the rear door opens, and* KELLER *enters with the setter* BELLE *in tow.*]

Keller. Miss Sullivan? On my way to the office, I brought Helen a playmate——

Annie. Outside please, Captain Keller.

Keller. My dear child, the two weeks are up today, surely you don't object to——

Annie (*rising*). They're not up till six o'clock.

Keller (*indulgent*). Oh, now. What difference can a fraction of one day——

Annie. An agreement is an agreement. Now you've been very good, I'm sure you can keep it up for a few more hours.

[*She escorts* KELLER *by the arm over the threshold; he obeys, leaving* BELLE.]

Keller. Miss Sullivan, you are a tyrant.

Annie. Likewise, I'm sure. You can stand there, and close the door if she comes.

Kate. I don't think you know how eager we are to have her back in our arms——

Annie. I do know, it's my main worry.

Keller. It's like expecting a new child in the house. Well, she *is,* so—composed, so—(*gently*) attractive. You've done wonders for her, Miss Sullivan.

Annie (*not a question*). Have I.

Keller. If there's anything you want from us in repayment tell us, it will be a privilege to——

Annie. I just told Mrs. Keller. I want more time.

Kate. Miss Annie——

Annie. Another week.

[HELEN *lifts her head, and begins to sniff.*]

Keller. We miss the child. *I* miss her, I'm glad to say, that's a different debt I owe you——

Annie. Pay it to Helen. Give *her* another week.

Kate (*gently*). Doesn't she miss us?

Keller. Of course she does. What a wrench this unexplainable—exile must be to her, can you say it's not?

Annie. No. But I——

[HELEN *is off the stool, to grope about the room; when she encounters* BELLE, *she throws her arms around the dog's neck in delight.*]

Kate. Doesn't she need affection too, Miss Annie?

Annie (*wavering*). She—never shows me she needs it, she won't have any—caressing or——

Kate. But you're not her mother.

Keller. And what would another week accomplish? We are more than satisfied, you've done more than we ever thought possible, taught her constructive——

Annie. I can't promise anything. All I can——

Keller (*no break*). ——things to do, to behave like—even look like—a human child, so manageable, contented, cleaner, more——

Annie (*withering*). Cleaner.

Keller. Well. We say cleanliness is next to godliness, Miss——

Annie. Cleanliness is next to nothing. She has to learn that everything has its name! That words can be her *eyes,* to everything in the world outside her, and inside too. What is she without words? With them she can think, have ideas, be reached. There's not a thought or fact in the world that can't be hers. You publish a newspaper, Captain Keller, do I have to tell you what words are? And she has them already——

Keller. Miss Sullivan.

Annie. ——eighteen nouns and three verbs, they're in her fingers now, I need only time to push *one* of them into her mind! One, and everything under the sun will follow. Don't you see what she's learned here is only clearing the

---

D **Critical Thinking**

Analyzing

? Kate has to learn a whole new language to communicate with Helen. How is this a reversal of the usual parent-child relationship? [Most children learn their parents' language simply as a result of hearing it spoken; Kate must make a conscious effort to learn the language Helen herself has not yet learned.]

E **Reading Skills and Strategies**

Making Inferences

? Why is Annie worried about Helen's going back to the Kellers? [Possible responses: The Kellers won't have the willpower to maintain the discipline Annie has taught Helen; Helen will regress, and all Annie's efforts will have been wasted.]

F **Reading Skills and Strategies**

Drawing Conclusions

? What is the "different debt" that Keller mentions? [Helen's absence has made him realize how much he cares for his daughter.]

G **Reading Skills and Strategies**

How to Read a Play

? How do the stage directions make it clear that Helen does need to both give and receive affection? [The stage directions call for Helen to greet Belle with enthusiasm and hug her warmly.]

Getting Students Involved

Cooperative Learning

Freeze in the Action. Have students work in small groups to plan a tableau, or silent frozen-action presentation, inspired by a scene from Act Three in which most of the main characters appear. Students should use posture and facial expressions to show what the characters are thinking. Students without roles in the scene can stage or direct the presentation.

Character Questions. Have student partners choose a scene from Act Three. One student should choose a character from that scene and carefully read through his or her part. The partner should prepare interview questions for that character based on the action in the scene. After the first student answers the questions, the students can switch roles.

A Reading Skills and Strategies

How to Read a Play

❓ Why is Helen's spelling into Belle's paw an example of dramatic action? [The act deepens the audience's understanding of Helen. It underscores the fact that Helen has no more idea than Belle that her hand motions spell a word that stands for a thing.]

B Elements of Literature

Imagery

Draw students' attention to Gibson's repeated use of imagery relating to water. Encourage them to recall that *water* is the word Helen could say before she became ill (Act Two, Scene 6).

C Elements of Literature

Climax

❓ How does this exchange between Annie and the Kellers suggest that the play is building toward its climax? [Possible responses: It seems as if everything Annie has taught Helen will be put to the test when they return to the house; the way the characters have focused on six o'clock suggests that something climactic could happen then.]

D Advanced Learners

Analyzing Stage Directions

Encourage students to consider and explain why the clasping of Annie's and Helen's hands might be symbolic. [Sample responses: The two hands—shining in the light as everything dims around them—symbolize Helen's quest for the light of knowledge, which can come to her only through the contact of her hand with Annie's; the image is a visual representation of Annie's speech about the "light of words."]

---

way for that? I can't risk her unlearning it, give me more time alone with her, another week to——

Keller. Look. (*He points, and* ANNIE *turns.* HELEN *is playing with* BELLE'S *claws; she makes letters with her fingers, shows them to* BELLE, *waits with her palm, then manipulates the dog's claws.*) What is she spelling?

[*A silence.*]

Kate. Water?

[ANNIE *nods.*]

Keller. Teaching a dog to spell. (*A pause*) The dog doesn't know what she means, any more than she knows what you mean, Miss Sullivan. I think you ask too much, of her and yourself. God may not have meant Helen to have the—eyes you speak of.

Annie (*toneless*). I mean her to.

Keller (*curiously*). What is it to you? (ANNIE'S *head comes slowly up.*) You make us see how we indulge her for our sake. Is the opposite true, for you?

Annie (*then*). Half a week?

Keller. An agreement *is* an agreement.

Annie. Mrs. Keller?

Kate (*simply*). I want her back.

[*A wait;* ANNIE *then lets her hands drop in surrender, and nods.*]

Keller. I'll send Viney over to help you pack.

Annie. Not until six o'clock. I have her till six o'clock.

Keller (*consenting*). Six o'clock. Come, Katie.

[KATE, *leaving the window, joins him around back, while* KELLER *closes the door; they are shut out. Only the garden house is daylit now, and the light on it is narrowing down.* ANNIE *stands watching* HELEN *work* BELLE'S *claws. Then she settles beside them on her knees and stops* HELEN'S *hand.*]

Annie (*gently*). No. (*She shakes her head, with* HELEN'S *hand to her face, then spells.*) Dog. D, o, g, dog. (*She touches* HELEN'S *hand to* BELLE. HELEN *dutifully pats the dog's head and resumes spelling to its paw.*) Not water. (ANNIE *rolls to her feet, brings a tumbler of water back from the tray, and kneels with it, to seize* HELEN'S *hand and spell.*) Here. Water. *Water.* (*She thrusts* HELEN'S *hand into the tumbler.* HELEN *lifts her hand out dripping, wipes it daintily on* BELLE'S *hide, and taking the tumbler from* ANNIE, *endeavors to thrust* BELLE'S *paw into it.* ANNIE *sits watching, wearily.*) I don't know how to tell you. Not a soul in the world knows how to tell you. Helen, Helen. (*She bends in compassion to touch her lips to* HELEN'S *temple, and instantly* HELEN *pauses, her hands off the dog, her head slightly averted. The lights are still narrowing, and* BELLE *slinks off. After a moment* ANNIE *sits back.*) Yes, what's it to me? They're satisfied. Give them back their child and dog, both housebroken, everyone's satisfied. But me, and you. (HELEN'S *hand comes out into the light, groping.*) Reach. *Reach!* (ANNIE, *extending her own hand, grips* HELEN'S; *the two hands are clasped, tense in the light, the rest of the room changing in shadow.*) I wanted to teach you—oh, everything the earth is full of, Helen, everything on it that's ours for a wink and it's gone, and what we are on it, the—light we bring to it and leave behind in—words, why, you can see five thousand years back in a light of words, everything we feel, think, know—and share, in words, so not a soul is in darkness, or done with, even in the grave. And I know, I *know*, one word and I can—put the world in your hand—and whatever it is to me, I won't take less! How, how, how do I tell you that *this*——(*She spells.*) ——means a *word*, and the word means this *thing*, wool? (*She thrusts the wool at* HELEN'S *hand;* HELEN *sits, puzzled.* ANNIE *puts the crocheting aside.*) Or this—s, t, o, o, l—means this *thing*, stool? (*She claps* HELEN'S *palm to the stool.* HELEN *waits, uncomprehending.* ANNIE *snatches up her napkin, spells:*) Napkin! (*She forces it on* HELEN'S *hand, waits, discards it, lifts a fold of the child's dress, spells:*) Dress! (*She lets it drop, spells:*) F, a, c, e, face! (*She draws* HELEN'S *hand to her cheek, and pressing it there, staring into the child's responseless eyes, hears the distant belfry begin to toll, slowly: one, two, three, four, five, six.*)

Using Students' Strengths

Verbal Learners

Pair students, and assign each pair two characters from the play; then have pairs create impromptu dialogues between the characters. Allow students ten minutes to prepare their characters' exchange. Have students present their dialogues to the class. If there is time, allow each pair to switch characters and repeat the process.

Intrapersonal Learners

After students finish reading Act Three, ask them to think about how James might later have viewed Annie's stay with his family. Have them write a letter from James to Annie ten years after the play's conclusion. Suggest that they include James's memories of Annie's first few weeks with the Kellers as well as James's feelings about how Annie's presence affected his relationship with Captain Keller.

She makes letters with her fingers, shows them to Belle, waits with her palm. . . .

THE MIRACLE WORKER, ACT THREE, SCENE 1 693

RESPONDING TO THE ART

Activity. How does this photograph support Keller's contention that Helen's capacity to learn language is on a par with Belle's? [Positioned facing each other, Helen and Belle are on the same level and appear to be about the same size; their poses suggest a mirror image.]

Crossing the Curriculum

Social Studies

Helen Keller and Annie Sullivan both made significant contributions to the world. Invite students to write a short biography of another well-known woman. Possible subjects might include Jane Addams, Marian Anderson, Shirley Chisholm, Barbara Jordan, Nina Otero, Jeannette Rankin, Eleanor Roosevelt, Wilma Rudolph, and Harriet Tubman. Alternatively, you might suggest that students profile individuals who have made a difference in the lives of people with disabilities. Profile subjects might include Michael Anagnos, Alexander Graham Bell, Louis Braille, and Samuel Gridley Howe. As a third option, have students work in groups to create a presentation on notable people with physical disabilities. Subjects might include Franklin D. Roosevelt, Christopher Reeve, and Stephen Hawking.

A
Reading Skills and Strategies
Comparing and Contrasting

❓ Before Annie Sullivan arrived at the Keller household, Helen used more than sixty signs to communicate, including stroking her cheek to indicate her mother. What is the difference between Helen's sign for her mother and the word Annie is trying to teach her? [The word is a symbol, part of an accepted system of communication while no one outside Helen's household knows what her sign means.]

B
Reading Skills and Strategies

How to Read a Play

❓ What does the change in lighting mentioned in the stage directions signify? [The change in lighting, as in earlier scenes, is a cue to a flashback to Annie's past.]

C
Critical Thinking

Interpreting

❓ What does Annie mean when she says, "God must owe me a resurrection. . . . And I owe God one"? [In Act One, Scene 4, Annie, speaking to Anagnos, implies that God should "resurrect" Helen in compensation for Jimmie's death; here she suggests that she owes it to God to "resurrect" Helen by bringing her to life through language, as a way of thanking God for her own "resurrection" through education.]

On the third stroke the lights stealing in around the garden house show us figures waiting: VINEY, *the other servant,* MARTHA, PERCY *at the drapes, and* JAMES *on the dim porch.* ANNIE *and* HELEN *remain, frozen. The chimes die away. Silently* PERCY *moves the drape rod back out of sight;* VINEY *steps into the room—not using the door—and unmakes the bed; the other servant brings the wheelbarrow over; leaves it handy, rolls the bed off;* VINEY *puts the bed linens on top of a waiting boxful of* HELEN'S *toys and loads the box on the wheelbarrow;* MARTHA *and* PERCY *take out the chairs, with the trayful, then the table; and* JAMES, *coming down and into the room, lifts* ANNIE'S *suitcase from its corner.* VINEY *and the other servant load the remaining odds and ends on the wheelbarrow, and the servant wheels it off.* VINEY *and the children, departing, leave only* JAMES *in the room with* ANNIE *and* HELEN. JAMES *studies the two of them, without mockery, and then, quietly going to the door and opening it, bears the suitcase out, and houseward. He leaves the door open.*

KATE *steps into the doorway, and stands.* ANNIE, *lifting her gaze from* HELEN, *sees her; she takes* HELEN'S *hand from her cheek and returns it to the child's own, stroking it there twice, in her mother sign, before spelling slowly into it.*

Annie. M, o, t, h, e, r. Mother. (HELEN, *with her hand free, strokes her cheek, suddenly forlorn.* ANNIE *takes her hand again.*) M, o, t, h—— (*But* KATE *is trembling with such impatience that her voice breaks from her, harsh.*) Let her *come!*

[ANNIE *lifts* HELEN *to her feet, with a turn, and gives her a little push. Now* HELEN *begins groping, sensing something, trembling herself; and* KATE, *falling one step in onto her knees, clasps her, kissing her.* HELEN *clutches her, tight as she can.* KATE *is inarticulate, choked, repeating* HELEN'S *name again and again. She wheels with her in her arms, to stumble away out the doorway;* ANNIE *stands unmoving, while* KATE *in a blind walk*

694 MODERN DRAMA

carries HELEN *like a baby behind the main house, out of view.*

ANNIE *is now alone on the stage. She turns, gazing around at the stripped room, bidding it silently farewell, impassively, like a defeated general on the deserted battlefield. All that remains is a stand with a basin of water; and here* ANNIE *takes up an eyecup, bathes each of her eyes, empties the eyecup, drops it in her purse, and tiredly locates her smoked glasses on the floor. The lights alter subtly; in the act of putting on her glasses,* ANNIE *hears something that stops her, with head lifted. We hear it too, the voices out of the past, including her own now, in a whisper:*]

Boy's Voice. You said we'd be together, forever—You promised, forever and—*Annie!*
Anagnos's Voice. But that battle is dead and done with, why not let it stay buried?
Annie's Voice (*whispering*). I think God must owe me a resurrection.
Anagnos's Voice. What?

[*A pause, and* ANNIE *answers it herself, heavily.*]

Annie. And I owe God one.
Boy's Voice. Forever and ever—— (ANNIE *shakes her head.*) ——forever, and ever, and—— (ANNIE *covers her ears.*) —— forever, and ever, and ever——

[*It pursues* ANNIE; *she flees to snatch up her purse, wheels to the doorway, and* KELLER *is standing in it. The lights have lost their special color.*]

Keller. Miss—Annie. (*He has an envelope in his fingers.*) I've been waiting to give you this.
Annie (*after a breath*). What?
Keller. Your first month's salary. (*He puts it in her hand.*) With many more to come, I trust. It doesn't express what we feel, it doesn't pay our debt. For what you've done.
Annie. What have I done?
Keller. Taken a wild thing, and given us back a child.

Skill Link

Using a Glossary

Remind students that if using context clues or other techniques fails to help them determine the meaning of an unfamiliar word, they needn't immediately turn to a dictionary. Point out that many books have built-in minidictionaries called glossaries, normally located at the back of the book. Focus students' attention on the words *inarticulate* and *impassively* on p. 694. Then have them find the entries for those words in the glossary on p. 1042. Discuss how glossary

entries are similar to those in a dictionary: They provide information on pronunciations, parts of speech, and meanings. Note that special-purpose glossaries define technical terms related to specific subjects. Special-purpose glossaries are often available as separate books or electronic documents. Such glossaries can be especially useful for research in an unfamiliar field. Before starting research on how to use the Internet,

for example, a reader might look for a glossary of Web-related terms. Other examples include glossaries of medical, nutritional, or astronomical terms.

Activity

Have students locate examples of special-purpose glossaries. As a class, discuss the information they contain, and identify ways various glossaries could be useful.

Kate, falling one step in onto her knees, clasps her, kissing her.

D Critical Thinking

Interpreting

? What does Annie mean by these statements? How would teaching Helen language be teaching her *yes*? [Possible responses: Teaching Helen language would vastly increase the number of things she is able to do, whereas disciplining her has reduced that number; teaching Helen language would open countless positive aspects in her life.]

E Elements of Literature

Imagery

? Once again Gibson has a character use the word *water* in relation to Helen. What does Annie believe could be inside Helen like underground water? [Language, specifically the mysterious human ability to comprehend and create language, is an internal source of rejuvenation. In this way, it is similar to an underground source of water.]

Annie (*presently*). I taught her one thing, no. Don't do this, don't do that——

Keller. It's more than all of us could, in all the years we——

Annie. I wanted to teach her what language is. I wanted to teach her yes.

Keller. You will have time.

Annie. I don't know how. I know without it to do nothing but obey is—no gift, obedience without understanding is a—blindness, too. Is that all I've wished on her?

Keller (*gently*). No, no——

Annie. Maybe. I don't know what else to do. Simply go on, keep doing what I've done, and have—faith that inside she's—— That inside it's waiting. Like water, underground. All I can do is keep on.

Keller. It's enough. For us.

Annie. You can help, Captain Keller.

Keller. How?

Annie. Even learning no has been at a cost. Of much trouble and pain. Don't undo it.

Keller. Why should we wish to——

Annie (*abruptly*). The world isn't an easy place

Making the Connections

Cultural Connections: Deaf Culture

Deaf Culture is a movement that celebrates the cultural and social identity of deaf people. Many advocates of Deaf Culture dislike the term *hearing-impaired* because they do not consider themselves handicapped. They believe that being deaf is more than a physical condition and that deaf people have a shared cultural and social identity—one with its own languages, stories, and traditions. One unresolved issue in the movement is whether deaf students should be mainstreamed—taught in classrooms alongside hearing students—or are better served in special classrooms for the deaf. Encourage students to research and discuss Deaf Culture in the United States and other current issues involving the deaf community.

A Critical Thinking

Interpreting

❓ What does Annie mean by this question? [She is referring to the resurrection she believes God owes her and wondering why, instead of coming at a scheduled time like a salary, its timing is unpredictable.]

B Elements of Literature

Character

❓ How has Keller changed in regard to Annie? [Possible responses: He is gentler and kinder; he respects her and is grateful to her.]

C Struggling Readers

Summarizing

If students have trouble following the scene between Keller and Annie, have them summarize the events. [Keller gives Annie her salary and compliments her. She expresses her belief that teaching Helen discipline is not enough and asks him to back her up in disciplining Helen at home. He agrees, and they go to dinner.]

D Reading Skills and Strategies

How to Read a Play

❓ What do the stage directions help you understand about Helen? [Helen's checking the doors shows that she remembers being locked in and that she is anxious to make sure it does not happen again.]

---

for anyone. I don't want her just to obey, but to let her have her way in everything is a lie, to *her*, I can't—(*Her eyes fill, it takes her by surprise, and she laughs through it.*) And I don't even love her, she's not my child! Well, you've got to stand between that lie and her.

Keller. We'll try.

Annie. Because *I* will. As long as you let me stay, that's one promise I'll keep.

Keller. Agreed. We've learned something too, I hope. (*A pause*) Won't you come now, to supper?

A **Annie.** Yes. (*She wags the envelope, ruefully.*) Why doesn't God pay his debts each month?

Keller. I beg your pardon?

Annie. Nothing. I used to wonder how I could—— (*The lights are fading on them,*

simultaneously rising on the family room of the main house, where VINEY *is polishing glassware at the table set for dinner.*) ——earn a living.

Keller. Oh, you do.

Annie. I really do. Now the question is, can I survive it!

B [KELLER *smiles, offers his arm.*]

Keller. May I?

C [ANNIE *takes it, and the lights lose them as he escorts her out.*]

WORDS TO OWN

simultaneously (sī′məl·tā′nē·əs·lē) *adv.*: at the same time.

SCENE 3

Now in the family room the rear door opens, and HELEN *steps in. She stands a moment, then sniffs in one deep grateful breath, and her hands go out vigorously to familiar things, over the door panels, and to the chairs around the table, and over the silverware on the table, until she meets* VINEY; *she pats her flank approvingly.*

Viney. Oh, we glad to have you back too, prob'ly.

D [HELEN *hurries, groping, to the front door, opens and closes it, removes its key, opens and closes it again to be sure it is unlocked, gropes back to the rear door and repeats the procedure, removing its key and hugging herself gleefully.*]

AUNT EV *is next in by the rear door, with a relish*

tray; she bends to kiss HELEN'S *cheek.* HELEN *finds* KATE *behind her, and thrusts the keys at her.*]

Kate. What? Oh. (*To* EV) Keys. (*She pockets them, lets* HELEN *feel them.*) Yes, *I'll* keep the keys. I think we've had enough of locked doors, too.

[JAMES, *having earlier put* ANNIE'S *suitcase inside her door upstairs and taken himself out of view around the corner, now reappears and comes down the stairs as* ANNIE *and* KELLER *mount the porch steps. Following them into the family room, he pats* ANNIE'S *hair in passing, rather to her surprise.*]

James. Evening, general.

[*He takes his own chair opposite.*

696 MODERN DRAMA

Getting Students Involved

Cooperative Learning

Character Sociogram. To show the relationships among characters in the play, have students work in groups of three to generate a character sociogram like the one shown here. First, have each group assign members the specific tasks of coordinator, graphic designer, and presenter. All members of the group should work together to choose the main character they wish to analyze, plus three other characters. Since relationships

among characters change, students should also choose a specific time in the play's action. Together group members should then brainstorm a few words that describe the relationship or feelings between the main character and each of the three other characters. Ask each group to make a poster of their character sociogram to be used when they present their ideas to the class.

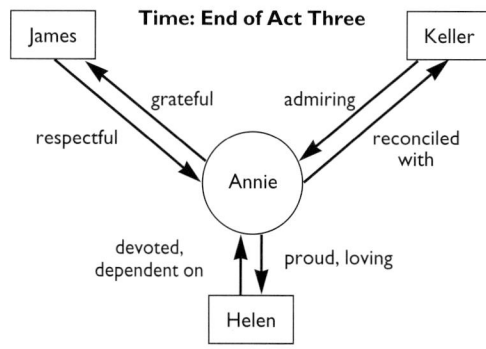

VINEY *bears the empty water pitcher out to the porch. The remaining suggestion of garden house is gone now, and the water pump is unobstructed;* VINEY *pumps water into the pitcher.*

KATE, *surveying the table, breaks the silence.*]

Kate. Will you say grace, Jimmie?

[*They bow their heads, except for* HELEN, *who palms her empty plate and then reaches to be sure her mother is there.* JAMES *considers a moment, glances across at* ANNIE, *lowers his head again, and obliges.*]

James (*lightly*). And Jacob was left alone, and wrestled with an angel until the breaking of the day; and the hollow of Jacob's thigh was out of joint, as he wrestled with him; and the angel said, Let me go, for the day breaketh. And Jacob said, I will not let thee go, except thou bless me. Amen. (ANNIE *has lifted her eyes suspiciously at* JAMES, *who winks expressionlessly and inclines his head to* HELEN.) Oh, you angel.

[*The others lift their faces;* VINEY *returns with the pitcher, setting it down near* KATE, *then goes out the rear door; and* ANNIE *puts a napkin around* HELEN.]

Aunt Ev. That's a very strange grace, James.
Keller. Will you start the muffins, Ev?
James. It's from the Good Book, isn't it?
Aunt Ev (*passing a plate*). Well, of course it is. Didn't you know?
James. Yes, I knew.
Keller (*serving*). Ham, Miss Annie?
Annie. Please.
Aunt Ev. Then why ask?
James. I meant it *is* from the Good Book, and therefore a fitting grace.
Aunt Ev. Well. I don't know about *that.*
Kate (*with the pitcher*). Miss Annie?
Annie. Thank you.
Aunt Ev. There's an awful *lot* of things in the Good Book that I wouldn't care to hear just before eating.

[*When* ANNIE *reaches for the pitcher,* HELEN *removes her napkin and drops it to the floor.*]

ANNIE *is filling* HELEN'S *glass when she notices it; she considers* HELEN'S *bland expression a moment, then bends, retrieves it, and tucks it around* HELEN'S *neck again.*]

James. Well, fitting in the sense that Jacob's thigh was out of joint, and so is this piggie's.
Aunt Ev. I declare, James——
Kate. Pickles, Aunt Ev?
Aunt Ev. Oh, I should say so, you know my opinion of your pickles——
Kate. This is the end of them, I'm afraid. I didn't put up nearly enough last summer, this year I intend to——

[*She interrupts herself, seeing* HELEN *deliberately lift off her napkin and drop it again to the floor. She bends to retrieve it, but* ANNIE *stops her arm.*]

Keller (*not noticing*). Reverend looked in at the office today to complain his hens have stopped laying. Poor fellow, *he* was out of joint, all he could——

[*He stops too, to frown down the table at* KATE, HELEN, *and* ANNIE *in turn, all suspended in mid-motion.*]

James (*not noticing*). I've always suspected those hens.
Aunt Ev. Of what?
James. I think they're Papist.[2] Has he tried——

[*He stops, too, following* KELLER'S *eyes.* ANNIE *now stoops to pick the napkin up.*]

Aunt Ev. James, now you're pulling my—lower extremity,[3] the first thing you know we'll be——

[*She stops, too, hearing herself in the silence.* ANNIE, *with everyone now watching, for the third time puts the napkin on* HELEN. HELEN *yanks it off and throws it down.* ANNIE *rises, lifts* HELEN'S *plate, and bears it away.* HELEN, *feeling it gone, slides down and commences to kick up under the table; the dishes jump.* ANNIE *contemplates this for a moment, then coming*

2. **Papist** (pā'pist): term for "Roman Catholic" that suggests dislike. James jokingly suspects the Papist hens of making trouble for the Protestant reverend.
3. **lower extremity** (ek·strem'ə·tē): leg.

E **Elements of Literature**
Conflict
❓ James's grace is an almost word-for-word quotation from Genesis 32: 24–26. Why would he choose this story? What might it have to do with Annie and Helen's conflict? [This implied analogy of the battles between Annie and Helen and between Jacob and the angel suggests that James realizes that the conflict between Annie and Helen is spiritual as well as physical. In a way, Annie wants Helen to redeem, or "bless," her.]

F **Reading Skills and Strategies**
Making Inferences
❓ Why is Helen behaving this way? [Possible response: She is testing Annie and the Kellers to see whether she can get away with misbehaving again.]

G **English Language Learners**
Interpreting Idioms
Explain to students that the phrase *out of joint* is used in this exchange first literally and then as an idiom. James's reference is to the actual anatomy of Jacob and of the pig (the ham) being served for supper. Keller then uses the phrase *out of joint* to mean "upset, angry." In other words, the Reverend is upset that his hens have stopped laying. Make a class list of other idioms that express being upset or angry, such as *ruffled feathers* or *hot under the collar.*

H **Elements of Literature**
Climax
❓ These repeated actions mark the beginning of the final buildup to the climax of the play. What do you think will happen as a result of Helen's behavior? [Possible responses: Annie will be forced to struggle with Helen again; the Kellers will undermine Annie's authority; Annie will finally break through to Helen.]

T697

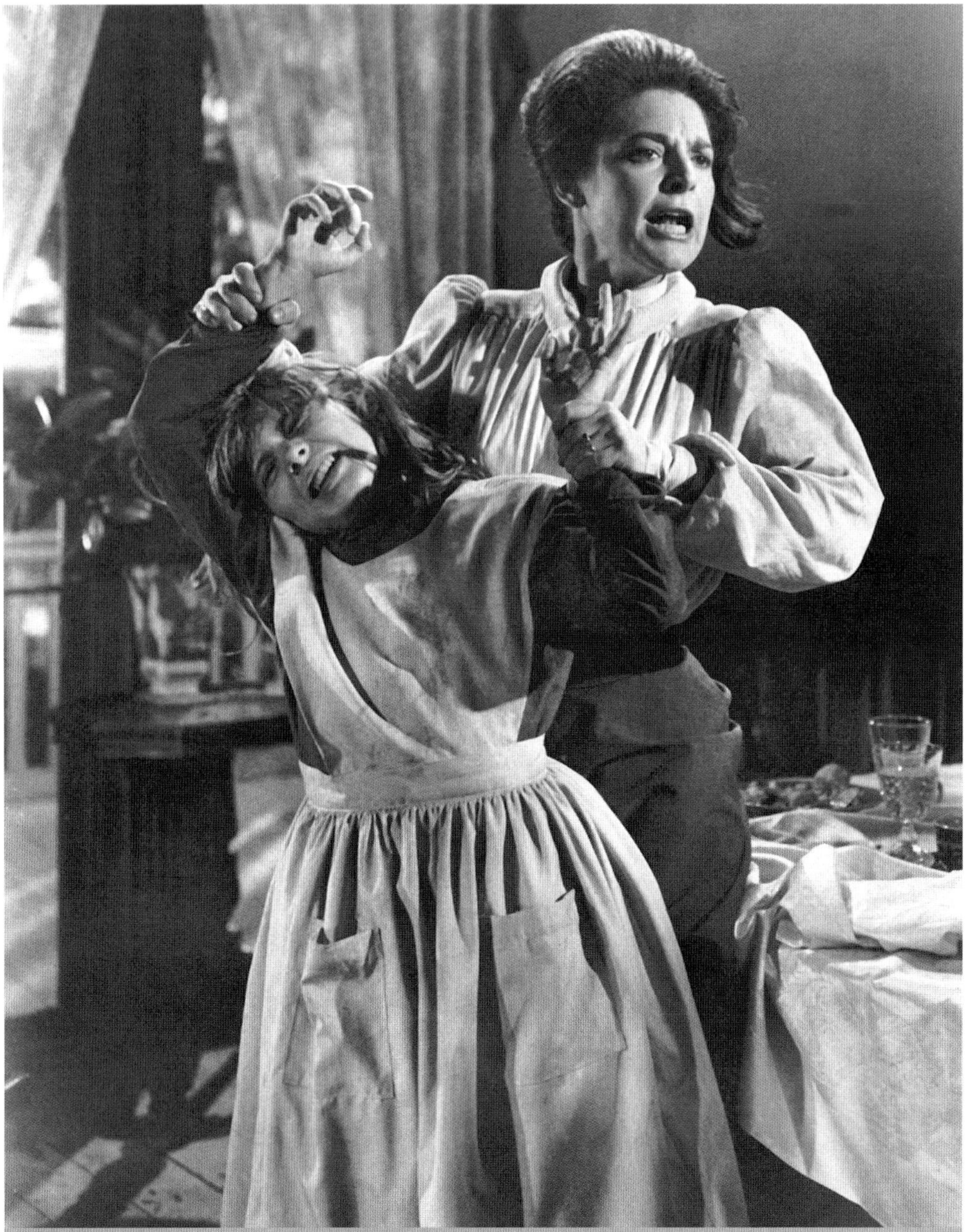

"And ask outsiders not to interfere."

698 MODERN DRAMA

Taking a Second Look

Review: Cause and Effect
Review cause-and-effect relationships with the class. Ask volunteers to describe the difference between a cause and an effect and give examples. Then have them provide examples of causes with multiple effects and effects with multiple causes.

Activities
1. Have students focus on James's relationship with his father. Ask them to identify the causes of the conflict between the two. What effects does this conflict have on James? How does James's standing up to his father affect the relationship?

2. Draw a cause-and-effect chain on the board. Have students copy this graphic organizer and use examples from the story to show linked causes and effects.

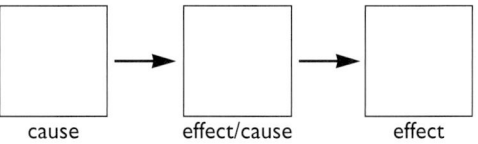

cause   effect/cause   effect

back, takes HELEN'S *wrists firmly and swings her off the chair.* HELEN, *struggling, gets one hand free and catches at her mother's skirt; when* KATE *takes her by the shoulders,* HELEN *hangs quiet.*]

Kate. Miss Annie.
Annie. No.
Kate (*a pause*). It's a very special day.
Annie (*grimly*). It will be, when I give in to that.

[*She tries to disengage* HELEN'S *hand;* KATE *lays hers on* ANNIE'S.]

Kate. Please. I've hardly had a chance to welcome her home——
Annie. Captain Keller.
Keller (*embarrassed*). Oh. Katie, we—had a little talk, Miss Annie feels that if we indulge Helen in these——
Aunt Ev. But what's the child done?
Annie. She's learned not to throw things on the floor and kick. It took us the best part of two weeks and——
Aunt Ev. But only a napkin, it's not as if it were breakable!
Annie. And everything she's learned *is*? Mrs. Keller, I don't think we should—play tug-of-war for her, either give her to me or you keep her from kicking.
Kate. What do you wish to do?
Annie. Let me take her from the table.
Aunt Ev. Oh, let her stay, my goodness, she's only a child, she doesn't have to wear a napkin if she doesn't want to her first evening——
Annie (*level*). And ask outsiders not to interfere.
Aunt Ev (*astonished*). Out—outsi—I'm the child's *aunt*!
Kate (*distressed*). Will once hurt so much, Miss Annie? I've—made all Helen's favorite foods, tonight.

[*A pause.*]

Keller (*gently*). It's a homecoming party, Miss Annie.

[ANNIE *after a moment releases* HELEN. *But she cannot accept it; at her own chair she shakes* ⒶⒷ

her head and turns back, intent on KATE.]

Annie. She's testing you. You realize?
James (*to* ANNIE). She's testing you.
Keller. Jimmie, be quiet. (JAMES *sits, tense.*) Now she's home, naturally she——
Annie. And wants to see what will happen. At your hands. I said it was my main worry. Is this what you promised me not half an hour ago?
Keller (*reasonably*). But she's *not* kicking, now——
Annie. And not learning not to. Mrs. Keller, teaching her is bound to be painful, to everyone. I know it hurts to watch, but she'll live up to just what you demand of her, and no more.
James (*palely*). She's testing *you*.
Keller (*testily*). Jimmie.
James. I have an opinion, I think I should——
Keller. No one's interested in hearing your opinion.
Annie. *I'm* interested. Of course she's testing me. Let me keep her to what she's learned and she'll go on learning from me. Take her out of my hands and it all comes apart. (KATE *closes her eyes, digesting it;* ANNIE *sits again, with a brief comment for her.*) Be bountiful, it's at her expense. (*She turns to* JAMES, *flatly.*) Please pass me more of—her favorite foods. Ⓒ

[*Then* KATE *lifts* HELEN'S *hand, and turning her toward* ANNIE, *surrenders her;* HELEN *makes for her own chair.*]

Kate (*low*). Take her, Miss Annie.
Annie (*then*). Thank you.

[*But the moment* ANNIE, *rising, reaches for her hand,* HELEN *begins to fight and kick, clutching to the tablecloth and uttering laments.* ANNIE *again tries to loosen her hand, and* KELLER *rises.*]

Keller (*tolerant*). I'm afraid you're the difficulty, Miss Annie. Now I'll keep her to what she's learned, you're quite right there—— (*He takes* HELEN'S *hands from* ANNIE, *pats them;* HELEN *quiets down.*) ——but I don't see that we need send her from the table. After all, she's the guest of honor. Bring her plate back. Ⓓ
Annie. If she was a seeing child, none of you would tolerate one——

THE MIRACLE WORKER, ACT THREE, SCENE 3 **699**

Professional Notes

In an essay on language and meaning, Louisiana novelist Walker Percy (1916–1990) notes: "Helen's breakthrough must bear some relation to the breakthrough of the species itself, at that faraway time when our ancestor, having harnessed fire, for the first time found himself seated by the flickering embers, looking into the eyes of his comrades and thinking (not really thinking, of course) about the vivid events of the day's hunt and 'knowing' that the others must be 'thinking' about the same thing: One of them tries to recapture it, to savor it, and so repeats the crude hunting cry meaning *Bison here!;* another, hearing it, knows somehow that the one doesn't mean *get up and hunt now* or do this or do anything, but means something else, means *Remember him, remember the bison,* and as the other waits and sees it, sees the bison, savors the seeing it, something happens, a spark jumps . . .

What happened? . . . "

? Did you expect Helen to act this way, or were you surprised? [Possible responses: I was surprised that she let her father put the napkin around her neck, and she took the fork; I expected her to act up because Annie says (on p. 699) "Take her out of my hands and it all comes apart."]

B **Critical Thinking**
Interpreting

? What does Annie mean when she says "I *expect* her to see"? [Possible responses: She expects of Helen what she would expect of any child, because Helen is intelligent and capable; she expects Helen not only to "see" (understand) how to behave properly but also to "see" how to use language.]

C **Elements of Literature**
Climax

? What is the climax of the conflict between James and his father? [James finally asserts himself and openly challenges his father with strength and authority rather than with sarcasm and hostility. In response, Captain Keller backs down and regards his son with apparent respect.]

Keller. Well, she's not, I think some compromise is called for. Bring her plate, please. (ANNIE'S *jaw sets, but she restores the plate, while* KELLER *fastens the napkin around* HELEN'S *neck; she permits it.*) There. It's not unnatural, most of us take some aversion to our teachers, and occasionally another hand can smooth things out. (*He puts a fork in* HELEN'S *hand;* HELEN *takes it. Genially.*) Now. Shall we start all over?

[*He goes back around the table and sits.* ANNIE *stands watching.* HELEN *is motionless, thinking things through, until with a wicked glee she deliberately flings the fork on the floor. After another moment she plunges her hand into her food and crams a fistful into her mouth.*]

James (*wearily*). I think we've started all over——

[KELLER *shoots a glare at him, as* HELEN *plunges* **A** *her other hand into* ANNIE'S *plate.* ANNIE *at once moves in to grasp her wrist, and* HELEN, *flinging out a hand, encounters the pitcher; she swings with it at* ANNIE; ANNIE, *falling back, blocks it with an elbow, but the water flies over her dress.* ANNIE *gets her breath, then snatches the pitcher away in one hand, hoists* HELEN *up bodily under the other arm, and starts to carry her out, kicking.* KELLER *stands.*]

Annie (*savagely polite*). Don't get up!
Keller. Where are you going?
Annie. Don't smooth anything else out for me, **B** don't interfere in any way! I treat her like a seeing child because I *ask* her to see, I *expect* her to see, don't undo what I do!
Keller. Where are you taking her?
Annie. To make her fill this pitcher again!

[*She thrusts out with* HELEN *under her arm, but* HELEN *escapes up the stairs and* ANNIE *runs after her.* KELLER *stands rigid.* AUNT EV *is astounded.*]

Aunt Ev. You let her speak to you like that, Arthur? A creature who *works* for you?
Keller (*angrily*). No, I don't.

C [*He is starting after* ANNIE *when* JAMES, *on his* feet with shaky resolve, interposes his chair between them in KELLER'S *path.*]

James. Let her go.
Keller. What!
James (*a swallow*). I said—let her go. She's right. (KELLER *glares at the chair and him.* JAMES *takes a deep breath, then headlong.*) She's right, Kate's right, I'm right, and you're wrong. If you drive her away from here it will be over my dead—chair, has it never occurred to you that on one occasion you might be consummately wrong?

[KELLER'S *stare is unbelieving, even a little fascinated.* KATE *rises in trepidation to mediate.*]

Kate. Captain.

[KELLER *stops her with his raised hand; his eyes stay on* JAMES'S *pale face, for a long hold. When he finally finds his voice, it is gruff.*]

Keller. Sit down, everyone. (*He sits.* KATE *sits.* JAMES *holds onto his chair.* KELLER *speaks mildly.*) Please sit down, Jimmie.

[JAMES *sits, and a moveless silence prevails;* KELLER'S *eyes do not leave him.* ANNIE *has pulled* HELEN *downstairs again by one hand, the pitcher in her other hand, down the porch steps, and across the yard to the pump. She puts* HELEN'S *hand on the pump handle, grimly.*]

Annie. All right. Pump. (HELEN *touches her cheek, waits uncertainly.*) No, she's not here. Pump! (*She forces* HELEN'S *hand to work the handle, then lets go. And* HELEN *obeys. She pumps till the water comes, then* ANNIE *puts the pitcher in her other hand and guides it under the spout, and the water, tumbling half into*

WORDS TO OWN
consummately (kən·sum'it·lē) *adv.*: completely.
trepidation (trep'ə·dā'shən) *n.*: fearful uncertainty.
mediate (mē'dē·āt') *v.*: settle a dispute or argument by bringing the two sides together.

Assessing Learning

Peer Assessment
After students working in pairs complete an activity, have them review each other's performance. They should discuss the reviews with each other and then turn them in to you. Reviews may be used in future student-teacher conferences. Students should rate their partners for each of the following characteristics and write a brief comment.
Ratings:　1 = Excellent　　3 = Unsatisfactory
　　　　　　2 = Satisfactory

Comments
Participation: _____

_____

Cooperation: _____

_____

Listening: _____

_____

and half around the pitcher, douses HELEN'S *hand.* ANNIE *takes over the handle to keep water coming, and does automatically what she has done so many times before, spells into* HELEN'S *free palm.*) Water. W, a, t, e, r. Water. It has a—*name*——

[*And now the miracle happens.* HELEN *drops the pitcher on the slab under the spout; it shatters. She stands transfixed.* ANNIE *freezes on the pump handle: There is a change in the sundown light, and with it a change in* HELEN'S *face, some light coming into it we have never seen there, some struggle in the depths behind it; and her lips tremble, trying to remember something the muscles around them once knew, till at last it finds its way out, painfully, a baby sound buried under the debris of years of dumbness.*]

Helen. Wah. Wah. (*And again, with great effort*) Wah. Wah.

[HELEN *plunges her hand into the dwindling water, spells into her own palm. Then she gropes frantically;* ANNIE *reaches for her hand, and* HELEN *spells into* ANNIE'S *hand.*]

Annie (*whispering*). Yes. (HELEN *spells into it again.*) Yes! (HELEN *grabs at the handle, pumps for more water, plunges her hand into its spurt, and grabs* ANNIE'S *to spell it again.*) Yes! Oh, my dear—— (*She falls to her knees to clasp* HELEN'S *hand, but* HELEN *pulls it free, stands almost bewildered, then drops to the ground, pats it swiftly, holds up her palm, imperious.* ANNIE *spells into it.*) Ground. (HELEN *spells it back.*) Yes! (HELEN *whirls to the pump, pats it, holds up her palm, and* ANNIE *spells into it.*) Pump. (HELEN *spells it back.*) Yes! Yes! (*Now* HELEN *is in such an excitement she is possessed, wild, trembling, cannot be still, turns, runs, falls on the porch step, claps it, reaches out her palm, and* ANNIE *is at it instantly to spell.*) Step. (HELEN *has no time to spell back now, she whirls groping, to touch anything, encounters the trellis, shakes it, thrusts out her palm, and* ANNIE, *while spelling to her, cries wildly at the house.*) Trellis. Mrs. Keller! *Mrs. Keller!* (*Inside,*

KATE *starts to her feet.* HELEN *scrambles back onto the porch, groping, and finds the bell string, tugs it; the bell rings, the distant chimes begin tolling the hour, all the bells in town seem to break into speech while* HELEN *reaches out and* ANNIE *spells feverishly into her hand.* KATE *hurries out, with* KELLER *after her;* AUNT EV *is on her feet, to peer out the window; only* JAMES *remains at the table, and with a napkin wipes his damp brow. From up right and left the servants*—VINEY, *the two children, the other servant*—*run in and stand watching from a distance as* HELEN, *ringing the bell, with her other hand encounters her mother's skirt; when she throws a hand out,* ANNIE *spells into it.*) Mother. (KELLER *now seizes* HELEN'S *hand, she touches him, gestures a hand, and* ANNIE *again spells.*) Papa—— She *knows!* (KATE *and* KELLER *go to their knees, stammering, clutching* HELEN *to them, and* ANNIE *steps unsteadily back to watch the threesome,* HELEN *spelling wildly into* KATE'S *hand, then into* KELLER'S, KATE *spelling back into* HELEN'S; *they cannot keep their hands off her, and rock her in their clasp. Then* HELEN *gropes, feels nothing, turns all around, pulls free, and comes with both hands groping, to find* ANNIE. *She encounters* ANNIE'S *thighs,* ANNIE *kneels to her;* HELEN'S *hand pats* ANNIE'S *cheek impatiently, points a finger, and waits; and* ANNIE *spells into it.*) Teacher. (HELEN *spells it back, slowly;* ANNIE *nods.*) Teacher.

[*She holds* HELEN'S *hand to her cheek. Presently* HELEN *withdraws it, not jerkily, only with reserve, and retreats a step. She stands thinking it over, then turns again and stumbles back to her parents. They try to embrace her, but she has something else in mind. It is to get the keys, and she hits* KATE'S *pocket until* KATE *digs them out for her.*

ANNIE, *with her own load of emotion, has retreated, her back turned, toward the pump, to sit;* KATE *moves to* HELEN, *touches her hand questioningly, and* HELEN *spells a word to her.*

D Reading Skills and Strategies
How to Read a Play

❓ What does the lighting change signify here? [Possible responses: The lighting change sets off the climactic moment of the play; the lighting change mirrors the change in Helen's face as the "light" of knowledge comes into it.]

E Elements of Literature
Climax

❓ Why is this scene the climax of the play? [Helen has finally found language: suddenly she knows that a word stands for a thing, that "everything has a name."] What clues in the text have hinted that water might be involved in the play's climax? [Helen spoke the word *water* at six months; the word has been mentioned often throughout the play; much dramatic action has involved water pitchers and the water pump.]

F Critical Thinking
Analyzing

❓ How do Helen's actions show the emotional effect of her discovery of language? How is Helen's discovery different from most other children's? [Possible response: Her intense, demanding, joyous physical actions show how much she has longed to be able to communicate. Most children learn that words stand for things over a period of months. Thus the breakthrough is gradual and does not overcome them with emotion as it does Helen.]

G Elements of Literature
Character

❓ Why does Annie identify herself as Teacher? [The word represents her self-identity as well as her role in Helen's life.]

And now the miracle happens.

702 MODERN DRAMA

Crossing the Curriculum

Science

How does the eye see? How does the ear hear? Ask volunteers to prepare a presentation in which they identify the parts of each organ and explain the processes by which the organs interact with the brain to produce sight and hearing. As an extension, ask students to research and explain how disease or injury can affect the ability of the eye or ear to function properly.

Social Studies

The battle by people with disabilities to gain protection against discrimination—particularly in employment and educational opportunities—took a giant step forward with the passage of the Americans with Disabilities Act (ADA) of 1990. The ADA bans discrimination in jobs, transportation, and housing. Suggest the following activities to students:

1. Have students review and discuss the time line on p. 456 showing legal milestones in the efforts of the disabled to achieve equal opportunity.
2. Research court cases in which people with disabilities challenged barriers to employment; outline the legal principles on which their cases were based.
3. Create a poster that illustrates the provisions of the Americans with Disabilities Act.

KATE *comprehends it, their first act of verbal communication, and she can hardly utter the word aloud, in wonder, gratitude, and deprivation; it is a moment in which she simultaneously finds and loses a child.*]

Kate. Teacher?

[ANNIE *turns; and* KATE, *facing* HELEN *in her direction by the shoulders, holds her back, holds her back, and then* relinquishes *her.* HELEN *feels her way across the yard, rather shyly, and when her moving hands touch* ANNIE'S *skirt she stops. Then she holds out the keys and places them in* ANNIE'S *hand. For a moment neither of them moves. Then* HELEN *slides into* ANNIE'S *arms, and lifting away her smoked glasses, kisses her on the cheek.* ANNIE *gathers her in.*

KATE, *torn both ways, turns from this, gestures the servants off, and makes her way into the house on* KELLER'S *arm. The servants go, in separate directions.*

The lights are half down now, except over the pump. ANNIE *and* HELEN *are here, alone in the yard.* ANNIE *has found* HELEN'S *hand, almost without knowing it, and she spells slowly into it, her voice unsteady, whispering:*]

Annie. I, love, Helen. (*She clutches the child to her, tight this time, not spelling, whispering*

into her hair.) Forever, and—— (*She stops. The lights over the pump are taking on the color of the past and it brings* ANNIE'S *head up, her eyes opening in fear; and as slowly as though drawn she rises to listen, with her hand on* HELEN'S *shoulder. She waits, waits, listening with ears and eyes both, slowly here, slowly there, and hears only silence. There are no voices. The color passes on, and when her eyes come back to* HELEN *she can breathe the end of her phrase without fear.) ——ever.*

[*In the family room* KATE *has stood over the table, staring at* HELEN'S *plate, with* KELLER *at her shoulder; now* JAMES *takes a step to move her chair in, and* KATE *sits, with head erect, and* KELLER *inclines his head to* JAMES; *so it is* AUNT EV, *hesitant and rather humble, who moves to the door.*

Outside HELEN *tugs at* ANNIE'S *hand, and* ANNIE *comes with it.* HELEN *pulls her toward the house, and hand in hand, they cross the yard and ascend the porch steps, in the rising lights, to where* AUNT EV *is holding the door open for them. The curtain ends the play.*]

WORDS TO OWN

relinquishes (ri·lin'kwish·iz) *v.*: surrenders.

MEET THE WRITER

In Love with His Heroines

William Gibson (1914–   ) has also written a light, touching comedy called *Two for the Seesaw* (1958), which starred Henry Fonda and Anne Bancroft. He is also the author of *A Cry of Players* (1968), a play about the young Shakespeare; *Golda* (1977), a play about Golda Meir, who became prime minister of Israel; and *A Mass for the Dead* (1968), a book about his family. In 1982, *Monday After the Miracle*, a sequel to *The Miracle Worker*, had a brief run on Broadway. Gibson's reflections on *The Miracle Worker* appear on page 624.

THE MIRACLE WORKER, ACT THREE, SCENE 3 **703**

Assessing Learning

T703

Connections

In this excerpt from her autobiography, Helen Keller recalls the momentous day when she learned the connection between words and the things they stand for.

Ⓐ Vocabulary Note

Word Origins

Tell students that *cum laude* is a Latin phrase that means "with praise." Students who graduate *cum laude* have earned distinction in their academic work.

Ⓑ Reading Skills and Strategies

Comparing and Contrasting

❓ According to Helen Keller, what can be said about Annie Sullivan's character? [Though she gets frustrated and discouraged, Sullivan doesn't give up.] Is this how Sullivan's character is portrayed in *The Miracle Worker*? Explain. [Yes, in the play Sullivan gets frustrated and discouraged, but she keeps trying. She fights Captain Keller, Kate, James, and Helen to achieve her goal.]

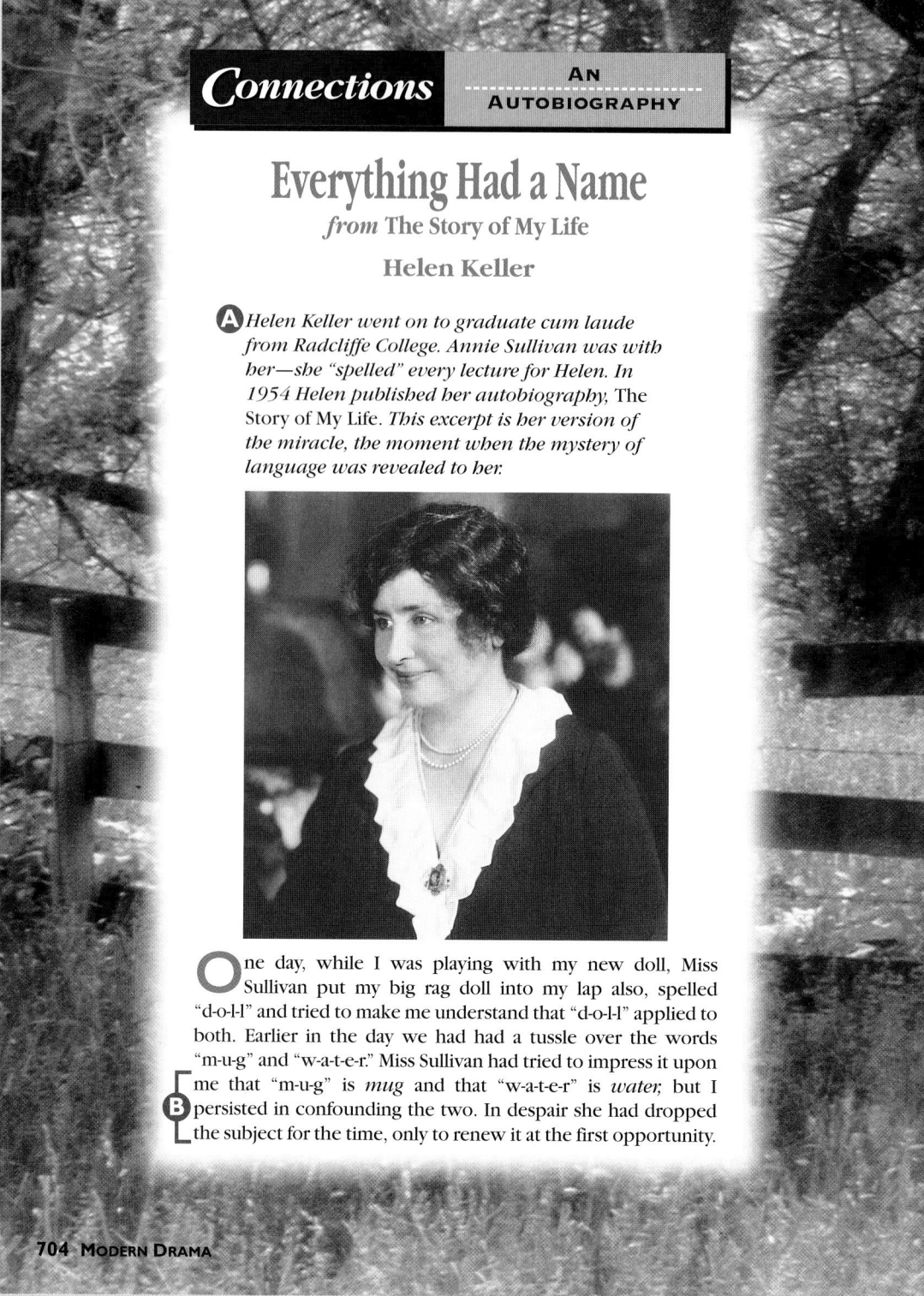

Connections — AN AUTOBIOGRAPHY

Everything Had a Name
from The Story of My Life

Helen Keller

Ⓐ *Helen Keller went on to graduate cum laude from Radcliffe College. Annie Sullivan was with her—she "spelled" every lecture for Helen. In 1954 Helen published her autobiography,* The Story of My Life. *This excerpt is her version of the miracle, the moment when the mystery of language was revealed to her.*

One day, while I was playing with my new doll, Miss Sullivan put my big rag doll into my lap also, spelled "d-o-l-l" and tried to make me understand that "d-o-l-l" applied to both. Earlier in the day we had had a tussle over the words "m-u-g" and "w-a-t-e-r." Miss Sullivan had tried to impress it upon me that "m-u-g" is *mug* and that "w-a-t-e-r" is *water,* but I persisted in confounding the two. In despair she had dropped Ⓑ the subject for the time, only to renew it at the first opportunity.

704 MODERN DRAMA

Connecting Across Texts

Connecting with *The Miracle Worker*

Invite students to discuss how Helen Keller's true story relates to the dramatic version in *The Miracle Worker*. In the play the character of Annie Sullivan believes that any possibility of Helen's leading a productive life is directly linked to her knowing that words stand for things. In "Everything Had a Name" Helen Keller stresses Sullivan's conviction. Discuss with students the changes that occur in Helen after she makes the first connection between a word and the thing it represents. [She is excited about learning other words, and her thinking processes are stimulated. She feels great joy, she begins to sense the consequences of her actions, and she looks forward to what the next day will bring.]

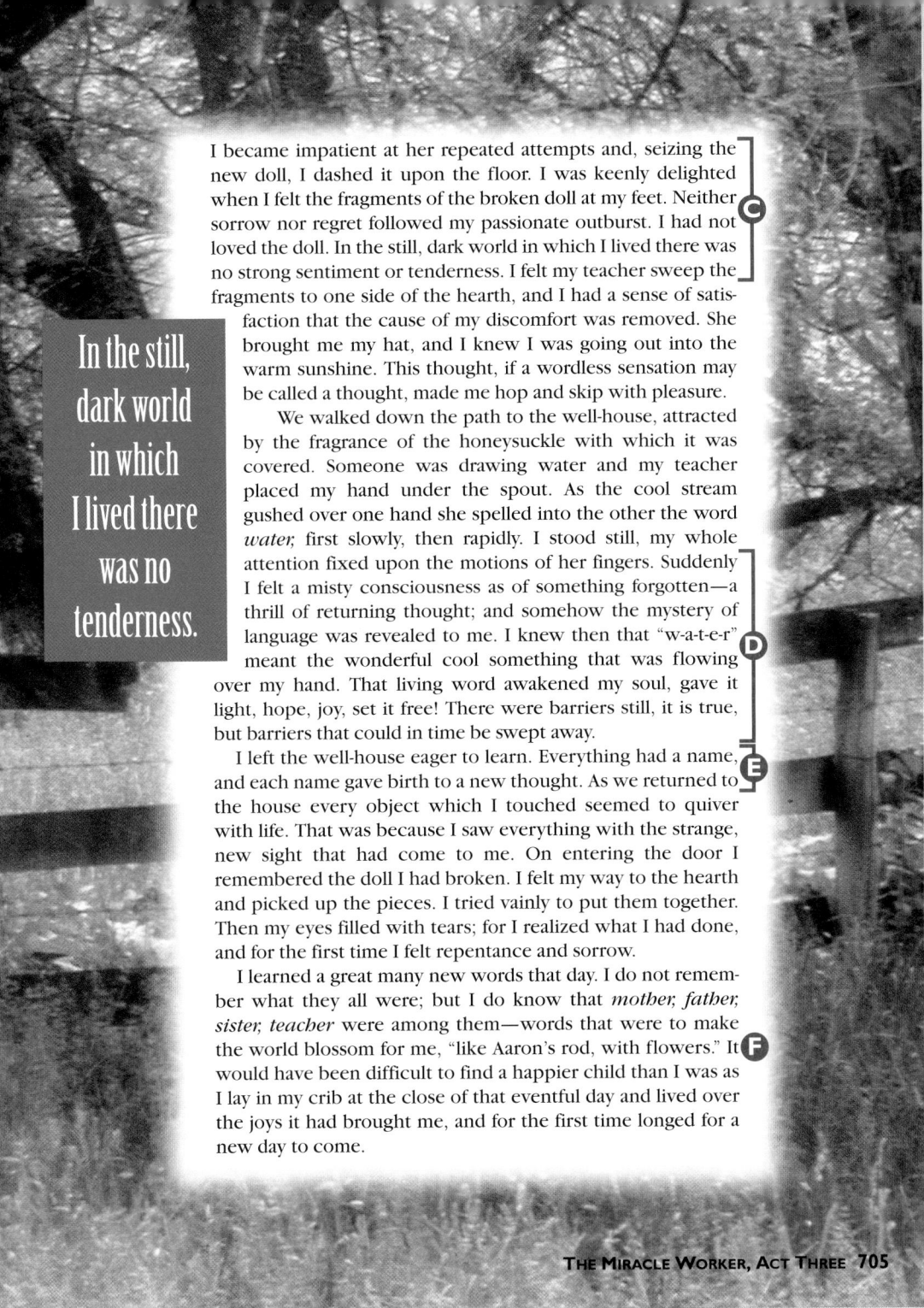

> In the still, dark world in which I lived there was no tenderness.

I became impatient at her repeated attempts and, seizing the new doll, I dashed it upon the floor. I was keenly delighted when I felt the fragments of the broken doll at my feet. Neither sorrow nor regret followed my passionate outburst. I had not loved the doll. In the still, dark world in which I lived there was no strong sentiment or tenderness. I felt my teacher sweep the fragments to one side of the hearth, and I had a sense of satisfaction that the cause of my discomfort was removed. She brought me my hat, and I knew I was going out into the warm sunshine. This thought, if a wordless sensation may be called a thought, made me hop and skip with pleasure.

We walked down the path to the well-house, attracted by the fragrance of the honeysuckle with which it was covered. Someone was drawing water and my teacher placed my hand under the spout. As the cool stream gushed over one hand she spelled into the other the word *water*, first slowly, then rapidly. I stood still, my whole attention fixed upon the motions of her fingers. Suddenly I felt a misty consciousness as of something forgotten—a thrill of returning thought; and somehow the mystery of language was revealed to me. I knew then that "w-a-t-e-r" meant the wonderful cool something that was flowing over my hand. That living word awakened my soul, gave it light, hope, joy, set it free! There were barriers still, it is true, but barriers that could in time be swept away.

I left the well-house eager to learn. Everything had a name, and each name gave birth to a new thought. As we returned to the house every object which I touched seemed to quiver with life. That was because I saw everything with the strange, new sight that had come to me. On entering the door I remembered the doll I had broken. I felt my way to the hearth and picked up the pieces. I tried vainly to put them together. Then my eyes filled with tears; for I realized what I had done, and for the first time I felt repentance and sorrow.

I learned a great many new words that day. I do not remember what they all were; but I do know that *mother, father, sister, teacher* were among them—words that were to make the world blossom for me, "like Aaron's rod, with flowers." It would have been difficult to find a happier child than I was as I lay in my crib at the close of that eventful day and lived over the joys it had brought me, and for the first time longed for a new day to come.

THE MIRACLE WORKER, ACT THREE **705**

C Critical Thinking
Interpreting
❓ What does Helen mean when she claims that she was unable to feel "strong sentiment"? Doesn't dashing her doll to the floor reveal strong sentiment? [Possible responses: The word *or* linking *sentiment* and *tenderness* suggests that Helen equates the two and means that she was unable to feel tenderness; without language, she did not feel the connection with other human beings that would have enabled her to understand that the doll had been given to her as a token of affection.]

D Reading Skills and Strategies
Comparing and Contrasting
❓ Is this version of the "miraculous" moment as moving as the one in the play? Why or why not? [Possible responses: Yes, in both cases the moment is portrayed as the awakening of Helen's soul; yes, because it is told by the person who experienced it; no, in the play it comes after Annie's confrontation with the Kellers, so it has more dramatic impact than it does here; no, Gibson's artful shaping of the story enables the reader to experience the wonder of the moment more fully.]

E Reading Skills and Strategies
Making Inferences
❓ In the play, who says, "Everything has a name"? [Annie] What can you infer about the source of this line from its appearance in both the play and Helen's autobiography? [Possible responses: Gibson used Helen's autobiography as a source for his play; Helen is echoing a phrase that Annie used during their time together.]

F Literary Connections
"Aaron's rod" is an allusion to a Biblical story in Numbers 17, in which Aaron's rod produces buds, blossoms, and almonds as a sign that Aaron's lineage will flourish.

Making the Connections

Connecting to the Theme: "Opening Doors"

Ask students how Annie's gift of language to Helen relates to the collection's theme "Opening Doors." [Possible response: Language is the key to opening the door to a fuller life for Helen. Without it she will be condemned to the isolation of her "still, dark world"; with it she can begin to experience beauty, order, and companionship.]

To prompt further discussion on this theme, share with students what Helen Keller once said about "doors." When one door of happiness closes, she said, another door opens. But we often look so long at the closed door, she goes on to say, that we do not see the new door that has opened.

Angie Erickson was born with cerebral palsy—a motor disorder caused by damage to the central nervous system. In this personal essay Angie relates the challenges she has had to overcome and explains how she has come to terms with her disability by focusing on her abilities.

Ⓐ Reading Skills and Strategies

Drawing Conclusions

❓ Why did Angie's friends begin to shun her when they all started school? [Possible responses: She did not have the muscular control needed to perform school tasks; they may have picked up the negative attitude of some other students who had not known her for years.]

Ⓑ Critical Thinking

Making Judgments

❓ What do you think of Angie's ideas about why some people are mean to those with disabilities? Can you think of any other reasons? [Possible response: Her ideas seem well grounded to me. The fear of the unknown may be another reason for such behavior.]

Ⓒ Reading Skills and Strategies

Connecting with the Text

❓ What do you think of Angie's response to her condition? [Answers will vary. Students may admire Angie for not being full of self-pity, or they may think she is repressing her true feelings.]

It's OK to Be Different

Why me? I often ask myself. Why did I have to be the one? Why did I get picked to be different? Why are people mean to me and always treating me differently? These are the kinds of questions that I used to ask myself. It took more than ten years for me to find answers and to realize that I'm not *more* different than anyone else.

I was born on June 29, 1978. Along with me came my twin sister, Stephanie. She was born with no birth defects, but I was born with cerebral palsy. For me, CP made it so I shake a little; when my sister began to walk, I couldn't. The doctors knew it was a minor case of cerebral palsy. But they didn't know if I'd ever walk straight or do things that other kids my age could do.

At first my disability did not bother me, because when you're a toddler, you do things that are really easy. When it took me a little longer to play yard games, because I couldn't run that well, my friends just thought I was slow. My disability was noticed when other children were learning how to write and I couldn't. Kids I thought were my friends started to stay away from me because they said I was different. Classmates began commenting on my speech. They said I talked really weird. Every time someone was mean to me, I would start to cry and I would always blame myself for being different. . . .

It took a lot of willpower on my part and a lot of love from family and friends to get where I am today. I learned that no one was to blame for my disability. I realize that I can do things and I can do them very well. Some things I can't do, like taking my own notes in class or running in a race, but I will have to live with that. At 16, I believe I've learned more than many people will learn in their whole lives. I have worked out that some people are just mean because they're afraid of being nice. They try to prove to themselves and others that they are cool, but sooner or later, they're going to wish they hadn't said some of those hurtful things. A lot of people will go through life being mean to those with disabilities because they don't know how to act or what to say to them—they feel awkward with someone who's different.

Parents need to teach their children that it's all right to be different and it's all right to be friends with those who are. Some think that the disabled should be treated like little kids for the rest of their lives. They presume we don't need love and friends, but our needs are the same as every other human being's.

There are times when I wish I hadn't been born with cerebral palsy, but crying about it isn't going to do me any good. I can only live once, so I want to live the best I can. I am glad I learned who I am and what I am capable of doing. I am happy with who I am. Nobody else could be the Angela Marie Erickson who is writing this. I could never be, or ever want to be, anyone else.

—Angie Erickson
East Junior High School
Plymouth, Minnesota

[infer]

First Thoughts

1. Now that Helen can communicate, what questions do you think she will want to ask?

Shaping Interpretations

[analyze]

2. What is significant about the fact that Annie no longer hears the voices at the end of the play?

[analyze]

3. Whenever a character announces early in a play that she will never love again, we sense that she will change her mind and we wait to see what will cause the change. Earlier in this play, Annie says she'll never love again. Why does she say this? What happens to change her mind?

[interpret]

4. How is the play's **climax** the resurrection that Annie feels she owes God and God owes her?

[interpret]

5. How has Helen been reborn by the end of the play?

[analyze]

6. The relationship of James to his father has constituted a **subplot,** a smaller story within the major plot. How is James's **conflict** resolved?

[interpret]

7. What do the stage directions mean when they say that Kate has simultaneously found and lost a child?

Connecting with the Text

[connect]

8. What do you think of the methods Annie uses to teach Helen? If someone said Annie is cruel, how would you answer?

Extending the Text

[interpret]

9. Is there a **message** in *The Miracle Worker* that is still important today? What do you think this play reveals about love, disabilities, and courage?

[apply]

10. How many "doors" are opened for people in this play? What people in real life suffer because doors are closed to them? You might refer to "It's OK to Be Different," the Student to Student selection on page 706.

Reading Check

a. The two weeks are now up. (A time limit is always a good way of increasing pressure.) What startling **change** do we see when Helen appears in Scene 1?

b. In Scene 3, at the dining-room table, what surprising **reversal** do we see in Helen's behavior?

c. How does James now reveal a major **change** in his character?

d. The **climax** of the play takes place at the pump—in one of the most moving scenes in the history of the theater. We have been lured into feeling that Helen has gone as far as she can go— that this is good, but still a defeat for Annie *and* Helen. Explain what Helen learns at the pump.

e. Where in Act Two did the playwright establish the word *wahwah,* so that its simple utterance can score in this final scene?

First Thoughts

1. Helen might want to know more about Annie, her own family, her surroundings, and her history.

Shaping Interpretations

2. Annie has been released from guilt about her brother's death and from the fear that love never lasts. She can now put her past to rest.

3. Annie's grief and guilt over the loss of her brother led her to believe she would never love again. Annie's redemption of Helen and Helen's love change her mind.

4. Annie has resurrected Helen by teaching her how to communicate. Annie in turn has been resurrected by being able to love again. This rebirth of love is the resurrection that Annie feels God owes her.

5. When she learns to comprehend that words stand for things, Helen is reborn into the world of human communication. She has reentered the world she left when she became deaf and blind.

6. The conflict is resolved by James's standing up to his father and thus earning his father's respect.

7. Kate has found a child because she and Helen can now communicate. She has lost a child because she will have to share Helen's love with Annie and others.

Connecting with the Text

8. Some may find Annie's methods too harsh; others may agree with Annie that indulging Helen and underestimating her potential is crueler than disciplining her.

Extending the Text

9. Possible messages: One should never give up hope; people can communicate in many different ways; pity can prevent growth; the human spirit can triumph despite great obstacles. Most students will think that the message in the play is still important today.

10. The door to communication opens for Helen; the door to love, for Annie; the door to self-respect, for James; the door to communication with their daughter, for the Kellers. As Angie Erickson shows, in real life disabled people often suffer because doors of acceptance and opportunity are closed to them.

Reading Check

Answers may vary slightly.

a. Clean and neat, Helen sits and quietly crochets. She eats from her own plate and uses a spoon and a napkin.

b. Helen reverts to her old behavior: She drops her napkin and fork, eats with her hands, and throws a temper tantrum.

c. James sides openly with Annie and calls his father wrong. He stands in Captain Keller's way when Keller tries to stop Annie from taking Helen.

d. Helen makes the connection that the water pouring over her hand has a name (*water*), and so does everything else.

e. In Act Two, Scene 6, Kate tells Annie that Helen was a bright baby before her illness; at only six months old, she said *wahwah* in an attempt to say *water*.

CHOICES: Building Your Portfolio

1. **Writer's Notebook** Remind students to save their work. They can use it as prewriting for the Writer's Workshop on p. 716.

2. **Creative Writing** Have students do this activity in groups of four or five. Let each student be responsible for the dialogue of one of the major characters. Before students write, ask each group to discuss possible conflicts and dramatic situations and to choose one by consensus. Remind them that writing a scene also includes writing stage directions.

3. **Supporting an Opinion** After students have chosen a topic sentence, have them find three specific actions or incidents and three lines from the play that support the opinion.

4. **Writing a Response** Students will need to reread Gibson's comments in order to determine whom the love letter is written to. Remind students that they will need to go beyond the events of the play to describe their emotional responses.

5. **Comparing and Contrasting** Have students, working in small groups, use a Venn diagram to organize the differences and similarities in Helen's and Annie's accounts. Students should use one circle for differences in Helen's account and the other for those in Annie's. The overlapping area should be used to list the similarities in both accounts.

CHOICES: Building Your Portfolio

Writer's Notebook

1. Collecting Ideas for an Interpretive Essay

Finding a topic. When you interpret a play, story, or novel (see the Writer's Workshop on page 716), you'll want to look closely at the characters and at how they've changed in the grip of events. What have they learned? Is the change for better or for worse? Take notes now on one of the characters in this play in whom you're particularly interested. Track the character's experiences in chronological order on a time line.

> *Captain Keller*
> **Act 1: Scene 7**
> Thinks Annie too young and inexperienced—"half-blind Yankee schoolgirl"
> **Act 2: Scene 2**
> Furious. Sees Annie as stubborn, rude.
> **Scene 6**
> Wants to fire Annie.
> **Act 3: Scene 1**
> Appreciates her work; thinks she expects too much.
> **Scene 3**
> Falls to knees over Annie's miracle.

Creative Writing

2. What Happens Next?

Write a scene that could be a sequel for *The Miracle Worker*. Begin by thinking of a new conflict that will give dramatic tension to the scene. Do Annie and the Kellers disagree about Helen's education? Will Annie stay with Helen? What will happen to James? In **stage directions,** state the time and setting of the sequel. Gibson called his own sequel *Monday After the Miracle*. What will you call yours?

Supporting an Opinion

3. All You Need Is Love

Love is an important theme in *The Miracle Worker*. Use one of the following opinions as the **topic sentence** of a short essay about the play. Support the opinion with details from the play. Maybe you have another opinion about how love works in the play. If you do, write your essay about that.

- Annie's love for Helen helps her face her past.
- Captain Keller learns that obedience and respect are not proof of love.
- Kate Keller learns that real love can mean letting go of the one you love so much.

Writing a Response

4. Heralding the Heroine

In his comment on page 625, the playwright says that *The Miracle Worker* is a love letter. In an essay, tell which character the love letter is directed to and explain how *you* responded to her.

Comparing and Contrasting Texts

5. Comparing the Miracles

Gibson used the letters of Annie Sullivan and Helen Keller's autobiography as sources for the play. Annie wrote the letter on page 709 on the climactic day that Helen learned that everything has a name. In one paragraph, cite at least four details that the playwright altered in writing the scene at the pump. In a second paragraph, tell how Annie's firsthand version of the miracle compares with Helen's (see **Connections** on page 704). In a final paragraph, tell which you preferred reading, and why: the scene in the play, Annie's letter, or Helen's autobiography.

Using Students' Strengths

Logical Learners

To help students organize their ideas for Choice 3 on p. 708, suggest that they use a graphic organizer like the following one:

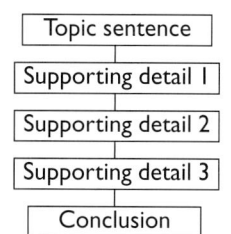

Topic sentence
Supporting detail 1
Supporting detail 2
Supporting detail 3
Conclusion

April 5, 1887

I must write you a line this morning because something very important has happened. Helen has taken the second great step in her education. She has learned that everything has a name, and that the manual alphabet is the key to everything she wants to know.

In a previous letter I think I wrote you that "mug" and "milk" had given Helen more trouble than all the rest. She confused the nouns with the verb "drink." She didn't know the word for "drink," but went through the pantomime of drinking whenever she spelled "mug" or "milk." This morning, while she was washing, she wanted to know the name for "water." When she wants to know the name of anything, she points to it and pats my hand. I spelled "w-a-t-e-r" and thought no more about it until after breakfast. Then it occurred to me that with the help of this new word I might succeed in straightening out the "mug-milk" difficulty. We went out to the pump house, and I made Helen hold her mug under the spout while I pumped. As the cold water gushed forth, filling the mug, I spelled "w-a-t-e-r" in Helen's free hand. The word coming so close to the sensation of cold water rushing over her hand seemed to startle her. She dropped the mug and stood as one transfixed. A new light came into her face. She spelled "water" several times. Then she dropped on the ground and asked for its name and pointed to the pump and the trellis, and suddenly turning around she asked for my name. I spelled "Teacher."

Annie Sullivan

VOCABULARY   HOW TO OWN A WORD

WORD BANK

simultaneously
consummately
trepidation
mediate
relinquishes

Roots and Affixes: Taking Words Apart

Roots are core words with fairly constant meanings. Many word roots have come into English from other languages—often from Greek and Latin. When you know some roots, you can figure out the meanings of many words. Fill out a chart like the one below for each word in the Word Bank at the left. In your chart, show the word's root and any affixes. Affixes may be prefixes (word parts added to the front of a word, such as *mis-* or *anti-*) or suffixes (word parts added to the end of a word, such as *-ation* or *-ment*). In one part of your chart, see if you can list some words that have the same root.

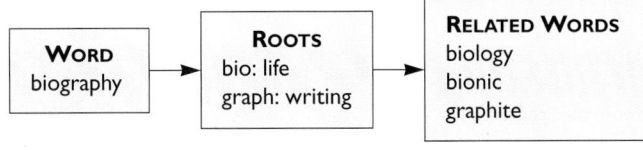

WORD biography	→	**ROOTS** bio: life graph: writing	→	**RELATED WORDS** biology bionic graphite

THE MIRACLE WORKER, ACT THREE **709**

Possible Answers

Answers may vary slightly, depending on the dictionary used.

1. Word: *simultaneously*
   Root: *simul*, at the same time
   Suffixes: *-ous*, characterized by
   -ly, at a (specified) time
   Related words: *simulcast, simulation*

2. Word: *consummately*
   Prefix: *con-*, together
   Root: *summa*, a sum
   Suffixes: *-ate*, characteristic of
   -ly, to a (specified) extent
   Related words: *consummation, summary*

3. Word: *trepidation*
   Root: *trepid*, disturbed
   Suffix: *-ation*, condition of being
   Related word: *intrepid*

4. Word: *mediate*
   Root: *medi*, middle
   Suffix: *-ate*, to arrange for
   Related words: *median, media*

5. Word: *relinquishes*
   Prefix: *re-*, back
   Root: *linquere*, to leave
   Suffixes: *-ish*, do
   -es, (to form the third person singular)
   Related word: *loan*

Resources

Vocabulary

• *Words to Own* Worksheet, p. 38

T709

OBJECTIVES

1. Read an excerpt from a biography
2. Find thematic connections across genres
3. Generate relevant and interesting discussion
4. Recognize distinctive and shared characteristics of cultures through reading and discussion

Extending the Theme

In this excerpt Joseph P. Lash describes Annie's wretched home life, the horrific conditions at the poorhouse, her desolation when her brother Jimmie died, and her ultimately successful efforts to escape the poorhouse and go to school.

Ⓐ Elements of Literature
Biography

❓ Why is "Annie" a biography rather than an autobiography? [A biography is an account of a person's life written by another person; an autobiography is a person's account of his or her own life.]

Ⓑ Struggling Readers
Paraphrasing

Suggest that students use context clues and a dictionary to figure out any unfamiliar words in this challenging sentence and then paraphrase the sentence. [The Sullivans' poverty was even harsher and more extreme than the poverty of their fellow Irish immigrants.]

Ⓒ Reading Skills and Strategies
Distinguishing Fact and Opinion

❓ Does Lash use mostly facts or mostly opinions to describe Annie's parents? [mostly facts] What words indirectly express his opinions? [shiftless, gentle]

Reading Skills and Strategies

Dialogue with the Text

Keep a double-entry journal as you read this account of Annie Sullivan's early years. In the first column, note passages that strike you as interesting. Also note passages that remind you of something that might happen to a child even today. Write your response to each event or passage in the second column.

Passage	My Response

Background

This true story about Annie Sullivan's early years is from the first chapter of *Helen and Teacher* by Joseph P. Lash, a biography of Helen Keller and Annie Sullivan. Annie's young parents, like many other Irish immigrants, fled to the United States to escape the Great Famine that devastated Ireland in the 1840s. When the potato crops failed, a million Irish people died of starvation and two million more fled the country.

When Annie's mother died in Massachusetts in 1876, Annie and her brother were sent to a poorhouse. Poorhouses, or almshouses, were huge institutions for people who were disabled, mentally ill, or diseased. Abandoned or neglected children were also sent to these poorhouses, as were old people who were homeless. Sanitary conditions were very bad and there was little medical care.

EXTENDING *the theme*
Ⓐ A BIOGRAPHY

ANNIE

from **Helen and Teacher**

by **Joseph P. Lash**

Annie was born in April 1866 in Feeding Hills, a village outside of Springfield, Massachusetts, in circumstances of poverty that were not uncommon among Irish immigrants. But the destitution of the Sullivans was starker and more desolate than even that of their compatriots. Annie's father, red-haired Thomas Sullivan, was not only illiterate and unskilled but a drinker and a brawler, and shiftless. Her gentle mother, born Alice Cloesy (spelled Cloahassy on Annie's baptismal certificate), was tubercular and, after a fall when Annie was three or four, was unable to walk again except on crutches. She bore five children. Annie, christened Johanna, was the oldest. The fifth, John, died before he was three months old. A sister, Nellie, had died before that. Her little brother Jimmie was born with a tubercular hip. Only Mary, next to the youngest, did not ail. Annie, although physically robust, contracted trachoma when she was about five. Untreated, this was gradually destroying her vision. One of her earliest memories was a neighbor saying, "She would be so pretty if it were not for her eyes." A woman urged her mother to wash them in geranium water, and Annie remembers thin hands dabbing her "bad" eyes.

Half-blind, hot-tempered like her father, Annie responded to the miseries within and about her by lashing out childishly, throwing things, going into tantrums. "What a terrible child," the neighbors said. "You little devil," her father often shouted and tried to control her by beatings so severe that, to save her, Annie's mother would try to hide her little daughter. Horror followed horror. Her mother, "gentle Alice Cloesy," as her neighbors from Limerick called her, died. . . .

Professional Notes

Joseph P. Lash decided that it was impossible to write a biography of Helen Keller without also writing about Annie Sullivan, and the critics applauded his decision. Reviewer Joseph Featherstone called Lash's work a deeply absorbing portrait of two intertwined lives whose meanings can't be understood separately. Ask students to discuss why it might be difficult to understand Helen's life without understanding Annie's, and vice versa.

Helen Keller, aged thirteen, and Annie Sullivan.

RESPONDING TO THE ART

Activity. Contrast this image of Annie with the depiction of her early life on p. 710. [Sample response: In the photograph, Annie looks like a prosperous, refined lady; the text describes her as an extremely poor, uneducated, hot-tempered child.] **What does this contrast tell you about Annie?** [Possible responses: Annie made drastic changes in her life; Annie learned to put her emotion to good use; for Annie, education was a way out of poverty.]

Crossing the Curriculum

Social Studies/History

The waves of Irish emigration that began with the Great Famine didn't end for over half a century. Ireland's population was about 8 million before the famine began in 1845; by 1851, the island had only 6 1/2 million people. After five more decades, the Irish population had shrunk to just 4 million. This decrease has been described by some historians as the largest and most sustained drop in population in modern European history.

Many of those who left Ireland came to the United States. Today, there are over 40 million people of Irish descent living in the United States. Offer students interested in immigration issues and the famine the following research options:

1. Create a presentation on the Great Famine.
2. Provide an overview of 19th-century immigration to the United States. Students may want to focus on their state as well.
3. Create a graph that compares population shifts between 1850 and 1900 in the United States and in European countries such as Ireland, England, Italy, and Germany.
4. Collect a portfolio of short excerpts from first-person accounts of 19th-century immigrants describing their early experiences in the United States.

A Reading Skills and Strategies

Visualizing

? What are some of the details that help readers visualize Tewksbury? [Possible responses: "isolated," "grimy," "unpainted, overcrowded, peopled with misshapen, diseased, often manic women."]

B Critical Thinking

Making Connections

? How does William Gibson use this information about Jimmie in *The Miracle Worker*? [He creates flashbacks to Annie and Jimmie's time in Tewksbury to show that Annie is so devastated by Jimmie's death that she is afraid to love again.]

There was no money for the funeral, and the town helped to defray the expenses. She was buried in Potter's Field,[1] a kinswoman told Annie years later. She remembered her father saying after the funeral, "God put a curse on me for leaving Ireland and the old folks." Then he would rage wildly against "the landlords" and weep. . . .

On February 22, 1876, Annie and Jimmie, who was on a crutch because of his diseased hip, were delivered in a Black Maria[2] to the state poorhouse in Tewksbury. It was an isolated, forbidding huddle of grimy structures. The attendant who received them proposed to separate them, sending Annie to the women's ward and Jimmie to the men's; but Annie, whose whole childhood had been one abandonment after another, protested with such passionate sobs that the attendant relented and sent them both to a women's ward. No matter that it was unpainted, overcrowded, peopled with misshapen, diseased, often manic women; they were together.

Somehow it all seemed "very homelike" to Annie. The children's cots were next to each other. They had the "dead house," where corpses were prepared for burial, to play in, and old issues of *Godey's Lady's Book* and the *Police Gazette* to cut up. It seemed homelike to Annie, too, because most of the women were Irish, the Catholic priest was always about—and she was no stranger to filth and disease. . . .

Death was a common occurrence, and all her life Annie remembered the clatter of the cots being wheeled over the wooden floor in the dead house. Then the dead house claimed Jimmie. She awoke suddenly in the middle of the night and, sensing the empty space next to her, knew immediately what had happened. She began to tremble. She crept to the dead room and, feeling his cold body under the sheets, began to scream, wakening everyone. As the women dragged her away, she clung to the lifeless body and kicked and screamed. Only when it was light was she permitted to go into the dead room again and sit on a chair beside the bed. Then the sheet was lifted for her, and again she flung herself on the little body "and kissed and kissed and kissed his face—the dearest thing in the world—the only thing I had ever loved." Later the matron allowed her to go outside to pick an armful of flowers. These she placed on the little body. She begged to be allowed to follow the coffin to the burial ground. No priest was there as it was lowered

> **Annie's whole childhood had been one abandonment after another.**

1. **Potter's Field:** public land set aside for burial of very poor or unknown persons.
2. **Black Maria:** police van.

Using Students' Strengths

Logical Learners

Encourage students to picture what the "isolated, forbidding huddle of grimy structures"—the poorhouse—must have been like for Annie. Have them work in small groups to review the descriptions in the selection. Then, have each group pretend to be a team sent to evaluate the conditions of the poorhouse and write a short report, recommending improvements.

into the bare, sandy spot. "When I got back, I saw that they had put Jimmie's bed back in its place. I sat down between my bed and his empty bed, and I hoped desperately to die. I believe very few children have ever been so completely left alone as I was." . . .

Maggie Hogan, the quiet little woman in charge of her ward . . . , took a special interest in her. She introduced Annie to Tewksbury's small library and persuaded a mildly deranged girl, Tilly, to read to Annie books that she selected, mostly by Irish authors. . . .

Annie's overriding ambition was to get out of the almshouse and to go to school. . . . Her chance to escape from Tewksbury came when she heard that an investigating commission headed by Frank B. Sanborn, chairman of the State Board of Charities, had arrived to inspect the institution. Gruesome stories about Tewksbury were rife in the state, even rumors of skins being sold from dead bodies to make shoes. She followed the group from ward to ward, trying to screw up her courage to approach it directly. Finally, as the men stood at the gate, she acted. Without knowing which figure was the exalted Mr. Sanborn, she flung herself into the group, crying, "Mr. Sanborn, Mr. Sanborn, I want to go to school!" "What's the matter with you?" a voice asked. "I can't see very well." "How long have you been here?" She was unable to tell him. The men left, but soon afterward a woman came and told her she was to leave Tewksbury and go to school.

Two calico dresses were found for her. The red one she wore; the blue one, along with a coarse-grained chemise and two pairs of black cotton stockings, was tied up in a newspaper bundle. The women in the ward crowded around her shouting advice as she walked to the Black Maria. "Don't tell anyone you came from the poorhouse." "Keep your head up, you're as good as any of them." "Be a good girl and mind your teachers." When Tim, the driver, handed her over to a state charity official, he added his own bit of advice: "Don't ever come back to this place. Do you hear? Forget this and you will be all right."

In Boston, the charity worker handed her over to another official. When he told her Annie came from Tewksbury, she patted the girl on the head. "Poor child," she said pityingly. Annie's face burned. She had thought the calico dress pretty, but the woman's pity suddenly aroused in her a sense of how poorly dressed she must be. "The essence of poverty," she told Nella Braddy, "is shame. Shame to have been overwhelmed by ugliness, shame to be a hole in the perfect pattern of the universe."

That day—October 7, 1880—she entered the Perkins Institution for the Blind.

> "The essence of poverty," she told Nella Braddy, "is shame."

C Critical Thinking
Expressing an Opinion
❓ Do you think Helen might have understood Annie's feeling of being completely alone? Why or why not? [Possible responses: Yes, because even though Helen lived with her family, she was totally alone in her "still, dark" world; no, because although she was deaf and blind, Helen always had the love of her family, and she was never beaten or left with strangers.]

D Reading Skills and Strategies
Drawing Conclusions
❓ What can you conclude about Annie from her actions here? [Possible responses: She is bold and determined to succeed in life; she is unusually persistent and clear-thinking; she is both desperate and full of inner strength.]

E Literary Connections
Nella Braddy was a close friend of Annie and Helen and the author of the biography *Anne Sullivan Macy*.

Assessing Learning

Check Test: True-False
1. All of the Sullivan children were healthy except Annie. [False]
2. Annie's family had no money for her mother's funeral, and the town helped with the expenses. [True]
3. After their mother's death, Annie and Jimmie were sent to a poorhouse. [True]
4. Tewksbury had a reputation as a model institution. [False]
5. Annie attended a Boston school for the blind. [True]

BROWSING IN THE FILES

About the Author. When he was twenty-nine years old, Joseph Lash was riding the train to Washington, D.C., with a group of friends when Eleanor Roosevelt, then the First Lady, boarded the car. Because she was acquainted with some of Lash's friends, Lash was introduced to her. At a later meeting, Mrs. Roosevelt invited a troubled Lash to spend some time at Hyde Park (the Roosevelts' estate in New York State) while he worked out problems. Lash views that period as a turning point in his life; it was the start of a more than twenty-year friendship with Eleanor Roosevelt that resulted in his writing six books about her after her death. In 1972 he won the Pulitzer Prize for biography for one of those books, *Eleanor and Franklin*.

FINDING COMMON GROUND

As students discuss and discover areas of agreement in their responses to Annie's experiences, you may wish to use the following prompts:

• Before students write, ask them how might the Perkins Institution for the Blind have "opened doors" for Annie?

• After students share their responses, ask them if a particular piece of information was especially memorable. Why?

MEET THE WRITER
Two Biographies in One

Joseph P. Lash (1909–1987) was at work on one of his biographies of Franklin Delano Roosevelt when the president of Radcliffe College asked if he would write a biography of Radcliffe's famous graduate Helen Keller. Lash at first refused, but his wife pointed out to him that it was an unusual honor for a man to be asked by a women's college to write a book about a woman. He read and was enchanted by Helen Keller's autobiography,

The Story of My Life. He decided that it would be good for him "to get away for a time from those power-oriented men, Roosevelt, Churchill, and Stalin."

Lash's research took him from Massachusetts to New York, Washington, Iowa, Illinois, California, and Tuscumbia, Alabama. He read newspapers and letters, studied journals, and interviewed friends and relatives of Helen Keller. He found that it was impossible to write a book about Helen Keller that was not also a book about her teacher. Therefore, his book *Helen and Teacher* starts with Annie.

FINDING COMMON GROUND

1. Get together with a partner or a group and talk about your responses to this true story. Be sure to refer to your journals.

2. Then, on your own, write about your responses to Annie's experiences. Your response might take the form of an essay, or an article that you can publish in your school newspaper. You might even want to write a poem or a short story. Before you write, be sure to check your journal for passages that caught your attention.

3. You might also set up a read-in, in which each final written response to Annie's story is read aloud in class.

Making the Connections

Connecting to the Theme: "Opening Doors"

Although Annie's and Helen's circumstances were distinct in many ways, these two women nevertheless shared many challenges and opportunities. Invite students to use a diagram like the following one to list the similarities and differences in the challenges they faced.

Challenges

Annie — grew up in a poorhouse

visually impaired

Helen — has loving but overly permissive parents

Differences   **Similarities**   **Differences**

Then have students generate another diagram to list Helen's and Annie's opportunities. Discuss with students how the doors that opened for Helen were very much like the opportunities that Annie finally enjoyed.

Read On

A Different Mountain to Conquer

In 1955, Jill Kinmont, beautiful and already famous, was a promising candidate for the U.S. Olympic ski team. Then, in the last qualifying race before tryouts, she crashed. Jill, only eighteen years old, was paralyzed from the shoulders down. She would never stand up again. Here is her story, with photographs: *The Other Side of the Mountain* told by E. G. Valens (HarperCollins).

Doors to Freedom

The underground railroad was really a collection of "safe houses" placed along the perilous route north that was taken by Africans escaping slavery in the South. Born a slave herself, Harriet Tubman made it her personal mission to open the doors of freedom for more than three hundred others. Ann Petry's *Harriet Tubman: Conductor on the Underground Railroad* (Pocket/Simon and Schuster) tells Tubman's story. All her passengers successfully escaped—and Tubman was never caught, though she had a price on her head.

Mission Impossible

Twenty-eight men defied all the odds. Shipwrecked in the Antarctic, the surviving passengers of the H.M.S. *Endurance* made homes out of flimsy tents and battered lifeboats for fourteen months. For company they had circling killer whales, riptides, frostbite—and of course, hunger and thirst. Ernest Shackleton and five others were sent in a small boat through freezing waters to scout for help. What they didn't know was that their rescue mission would make history—and become a classic: F. A. Worsley's *Shackleton's Boat Journey* (Norton).

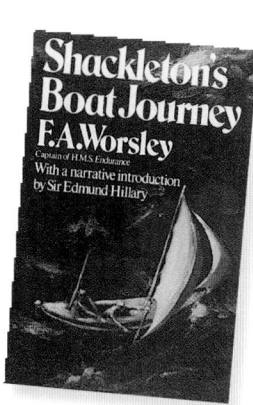
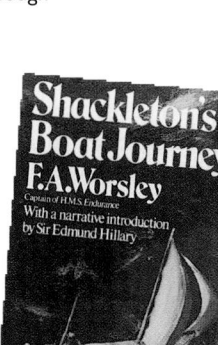

A Struggle to Communicate

In *My Left Foot* (Heinemann), Christy Brown, born with severe cerebral palsy, tells the courageous—and funny—story of his life. Brown grew up with a large and lively family in the slums of Dublin. With fierce discipline, he learned to read and to write, paint, and finally type with the toes of his left foot. His story was made into a motion picture in 1989 starring Daniel Day-Lewis.

READ ON 715

MAIN OBJECTIVE
Write an interpretive essay

PROCESS OBJECTIVES
1. Use appropriate prewriting techniques to identify and develop a topic
2. Create a first draft
3. Use evaluation criteria as a basis for determining revision strategies
4. Revise the first draft incorporating suggestions generated by self- or peer evaluation
5. Proofread and correct errors
6. Create a final draft
7. Choose an appropriate method of publication
8. Reflect on progress as a writer

Planning

- **Block Schedule**
  Block Scheduling Lesson Plans with Pacing Guide
- **One-Stop Planner**
  CD-ROM with Test Generator

BUILDING YOUR PORTFOLIO
Writer's Workshop

Technology HELP

See Writer's Workshop 2 CD-ROM. *Assignment: Interpretation.*

ASSIGNMENT

Write an essay in which you interpret the meaning of some aspect of *The Miracle Worker*. You can focus on the play as a whole or on a single character or symbol.

AIM

To inform, to explain, to persuade.

AUDIENCE

Your classmates and teacher; the Drama Club; readers of a magazine of student writing. (You choose.)

EXPOSITORY WRITING
INTERPRETIVE ESSAY

What is an interpretation? It is a meaning; it's what we make of something. Scientists interpret data. Politicians interpret polls. Historians interpret events. Audiences interpret movies. Readers interpret literature.

When you write an essay of interpretation, you try to show other people a meaning that you see in a work of literature. To do so, you have to think carefully about the text. You have to find passages to support your sense of what the text means.

Prewriting

1. Review Your Writer's Notebook

The first thing you'll decide is your focus—what *you* make of some aspect of the play. To find possible topics, browse through your Writer's Notebook. Make notes about the issues you raised or explored while reading this play.

2. Discuss the Play with a Partner

Talk about the play with a partner or small group, and see where you disagree. You might focus especially on how the elements of **character** and **conflict** contribute to the play's meaning, or **theme**. Zero in on the parts you disagree most strongly about. They may point you toward your own interpretation of the play.

3. Shape an Interpretive Claim

Now, develop a statement or **interpretive claim** about the play based on your discussion and notes (or write several claims and choose the best one). Think of an interesting interpretation that goes beyond the literal facts. Good interpretive statements might deal with the following:

- **Motive.** Why do certain characters behave as they do?
- **Changes.** Which characters change in the course of the play? How do they change, and why?
- **Theme.** What statement about life is the play making?

716 MODERN DRAMA

 *Resources: Print and Media*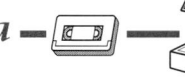

Writing and Language
- *Portfolio Management System*
  Prewriting, p. 197
  Peer Editing, p. 198
  Assessment Rubric, p. 199

- *Workshop Resources*
  Revision Strategy Teaching Notes, p. 49
  Revision Strategy Transparencies 25, 26
- *Writer's Workshop 2 CD-ROM*
  Interpretation

- **Relevance.** How does this play relate to our own lives?
- **Symbols.** What things keep recurring in the play that seem to stand for broad subjects such as life, death, growth, communication?
- **Judgment.** Is the play believable?

Drafting

1. Establish Your Subject and Focus

Start by giving your readers a context. Tell them what literary work you are going to discuss and who wrote it. Tell if you are going to interpret the whole play or just one part. Which part? Try to hook your readers' interest in your opening paragraph.

2. Make Your Claim

Basically, an interpretive essay issues a challenge. It tells the reader: "Here's something that may not be obvious, but it's true and I can prove it." This claim is your **thesis,** the core of your interpretation. Get it on the table early. In fact, you might include a **thesis statement,** which is a sentence that directly states your point. Here, for example, are thesis statements from three essays about Harper Lee's novel *To Kill a Mockingbird*.

- Scout, Jem, and Dill learn valuable lessons from adults in *To Kill a Mockingbird*.
- Though Dill may seem like a minor character in the book, he has great impact on the lives of Jem and Scout.
- Tom Robinson is just one of many victims of the prejudice that runs throughout *To Kill a Mockingbird*.

3. Elaborate

Now back up your claim. Think of yourself as a guide, giving your readers a tour of the play *your* way—a tour in which you point out the details that support your thesis. For every statement you make *about* the play, present **supporting evidence** *from* the play. Remember that your essay must provide enough evidence to convince your audience that your interpretation is correct.

Try It Out

Support each of the following statements with evidence from *The Miracle Worker*. Provide the type of evidence called for in parentheses.

1. As a young child, Helen Keller was a troublemaker. (Report an action.)
2. Annie was torn with doubt. (Provide a direct quotation.)
3. James felt ignored and unloved. (Paraphrase some dialogue.)

WRITER'S WORKSHOP 717

Using Students' Strengths

Visual Learners

As a prewriting activity, have students record their brainstorm ideas using colored markers on large pieces of paper or poster board. Each student should write a topic in the center and write objective information in one color and subjective responses in another color. Students may easily refer to the poster when drafting their essays.

Auditory Learners

To help students clarify any problems they may have interpreting a character or symbol from *The Miracle Worker*, have them write down passages or references they do not understand. Then have them work in small groups to discuss confusing passages. Remind students to listen as other students discuss their responses because the discussion may suggest potential topics for writing.

Introducing the Writer's Workshop

- Bring several examples of abstract or modern art to class, and ask students to write down what they think the artwork depicts and how it makes them feel. Discuss with students the variety of their responses to the same pieces of art.
- Lead students to understand that we interpret literature much as we interpret art, using many of the same techniques for both.
- Explain to students that their assignment will be to write an essay in which they interpret the meaning of some aspect of *The Miracle Worker*.

Teaching the Writer's Workshop

Prewriting

Suggest prewriting techniques such as freewriting, writing responses to the Writer's Notebook activities, and working with a partner to discuss scenes and to write a summary of the discussion.

Drafting

Work with the class to translate prewriting information into organized writing. Remind students to refer to the three drafting steps on p. 717 and to study the student model (pp. 718–719) for ideas about maintaining focus in their essays. As they write a first draft, they should be aware that paragraphs incorporating quoted support material may need revision later on.

Try It Out
Possible Answers
1. Helen takes Annie's key and locks her in the bedroom. (p. 655)
2. Annie says about not having been able to teach Helen the meanings of words: "I don't know how. I know without it to do nothing but obey is—no gift, obedience without understanding is a—blindness, too. Is that all I've wished on her?" (p. 695)
3. In a conversation on p. 682, James asks his father why Annie gets what she wants when he, James, does not. Keller states he does not know what James wants, to which James replies that he wants what he lost when his father forgot his mother.

After students have completed their drafts, they may benefit from another look at the student model. Have students focus on questions such as these:

❓ What theme, or statement about life, does the writer present?

❓ What details does the writer use to support her interpretation?

❓ How does the writer connect her thesis to the world in general?

❓ What techniques does this writer use that you might incorporate into your paper?

Communications Handbook H E L P

See Taking Notes and Documenting Sources.

• Copy **direct quotations** exactly, and punctuate them according to the conventions for including quotations in sentences. For example:

> When Annie says in Act Three, Scene 2, "Obedience without understanding is a—blindness, too," she suggests that without understanding, we are all blind.

• Refer to actions and characters in the play. Use your own words to **paraphrase** the author's words.

• When you write about literature, the text itself is a **primary source.** You may also find evidence in **secondary sources,** such as books and articles about the author or the work. Be sure to credit any secondary sources that you use.

Student Model

HARPER LEE'S TO KILL A MOCKINGBIRD

As children grow older, the beliefs and values of the adults around them help them decide what kind of people they would like to become. These adults serve as examples, so that younger generations can learn from their various experiences. This way children are offered many different perspectives of the world around them.

Throughout Harper Lee's novel To Kill a Mockingbird, Jem and Scout Finch are exposed to the insight and wisdom of loved ones. Yet they are also faced with the ignorance of those who are racially and morally biased. One of the positive influences in their lives is their father, Atticus, a lawyer who has accepted the case of a black man despite the racially explosive times. By standing by Tom, no matter what his color, Atticus shows Jem and Scout what it means to remain steadfast to what they believe in their hearts is right.

During Tom Robinson's trial, however, brother and sister find it isn't always easy to stand up for what you believe. When the Finches' neighbor, Miss Maudie, is publicly berated for working in her garden, Jem and Scout are shown how cruel people can truly be to one another just because they believe different things. But Miss Maudie tries to help them see that even though different races, sexes, and religious denominations can sometimes be unfair to each other, they are all human and therefore are allowed to make mistakes— and be forgiven. Jem and Scout begin to realize that many people make uninformed decisions about others based on prejudices.

General statements elaborate on the essay's thesis.

Interpretive claim: what Jem and Scout learn from loved ones.

First positive influence: Atticus and what Jem and Scout learn from him.

Second positive influence: Miss Maudie and what Jem and Scout learn from her.

Getting Students Involved

Cooperative Learning

Have students work in small groups to help them understand the actions and thoughts of characters in *The Miracle Worker.* Some group members should compose letters or e-mail messages from one character to another. Then, other members should create the responsive message. Remind students that the thoughts and language used should be appropriate to each character.

Interpretive Skit

If students have watched a performance of *The Miracle Worker,* have them work in groups to discuss the director's interpretation of a critical scene. Do they agree or disagree with the director's interpretation? Why? Have the groups explain what they would have done differently.

Evaluating and Revising

1. Peer Review

Your classmates who have read and written about the play make good sounding boards. Trade drafts in groups of three, and write detailed comments and suggestions for one another, keeping in mind the checklist of Evaluation Criteria. (Consider writing your comments on tracing paper laid over your partner's draft, or ask permission to write in the margin with pencil.)

2. Self-Evaluation

Sometimes you can hear problems that don't pop out when you see them. So try reading your essay aloud to yourself and listening for problems (or tape yourself reading and then make notes as you listen to the tape).

Evaluating and Revising
Have students use the Evaluation Criteria provided here to review their drafts and determine needed revisions.

If possible, facilitate students' self-evaluations by allowing them to tape-record their unrevised essays. Listening to their recordings may help students identify weak links in logic or missing details.

Throughout the story, the siblings also face negative influences. They live in an era when racial acceptance isn't common. The two are scared, chased, and hated because of their family's position in the Robinson trial. One night, Scout, Jem, and their friend Dill witness firsthand the danger of hatred when the local "posse" goes to the jail to bring Tom what they consider justice. The group of men threatens Atticus, despite the fact that he is a man once well respected by the entire town. They ignore his reputation and his desire for understanding. As the children discover, people can turn on each other at a moment's notice.

Probably the biggest influence for Jem and Scout turns out to be Boo Radley, the town recluse. Although they feared and misunderstood Boo because he is "different," he comes through for the children when they need somebody most. From Boo they learn not to be afraid of what they do not know, and not to close their hearts to people in need.

These people, both good and bad, serve as guides for the children and the choices they will have to make in life. The influences they provide help teach Jem and Scout the basics of right and wrong, good and bad. These are the influences they will draw upon when they need to make decisions or need support in the future.

—Meg Tracy
Cape Coral High School
Cape Coral, Florida

Negative influences supported by details.

Third and biggest positive influence: Boo Radley and what Jem and Scout learn from him.

Restatement of interpretive claim.

WRITER'S WORKSHOP 719

Proofreading

The proofreading tip provided on p. 720 is an excellent activity for helping students to focus on the basic units of meaning.

If time permits, the final copy should be put aside for at least a day before it is proofread one last time by the author.

Publishing

When submitting a piece of writing for publication be sure to have students do a very thorough job of proofreading and provide a model cover letter for their submissions. Make sure students request that their addresses be withheld if published; any feedback can be routed through the school. Explain to them why having their addresses published could cause trouble ranging from unwanted junk mail to harassment.

Reflecting

If students are adding their interpretive essays to their portfolios, be sure they date their papers and attach a brief reflection on their writing experiences. They should focus on questions such as the following:

1. How did I determine the thesis of my essay?
2. What did I realize about the text that had not occurred to me before?
3. What was the most difficult part of writing this paper?
4. What do I like best about the final version of my essay?

Resources

Peer Editing Forms and Rubrics
• *Portfolio Management System,* p. 198

Revision Transparencies
• *Workshop Resources,* p. 49

Grading Timesaver

Rubrics for this Writer's Workshop assignment appear on p. 199 of the *Portfolio Management System.*

T720

Proofreading Tips
Do at least one reading without thinking about the content. Force yourself to slow down and look for errors in each word and each sentence. Try this: Cut a hole in a piece of paper and proofread your essay through that window.

Sentence Workshop
H E L P

Revising sentences using parallel structure: page 721.

Communications Handbook
H E L P

See Proofreaders' Marks.

Revision Model

	Peer Comments
Throughout To Kill a *(Harper Lee's novel)*	*Give author's name.*
Mockingbird, Jem and Scout	
Finch are exposed to ~~many~~ *(the insight and wisdom of)*	*Can you be more specific?*
~~loved ones.~~ ~~adults' beliefs.~~ Yet they are	
also faced with the ignorance	
of ~~some of the people who~~ *(those who are racially and)*	*Which people?*
~~live in their town.~~ *(morally biased.)* One of	
the influences in their lives *(positive)*	*What kind of influence?*
is their father, Atticus, a	
lawyer who has accepted ~~a~~ *(the)*	
~~case of a black man despite~~ ~~very unpopular case in very~~	*What kind of case? Why is it unpopular?*
~~the racially~~ explosive times.	

Publishing

You might conduct a symposium or gathering of experts on *The Miracle Worker.* Read your essay to your classmates and listen to their essays. Or present your paper to the Drama Club if your school has one. Also, consider sending your essay to a magazine that publishes student writing.

Sentence Workshop

OBJECTIVE
Use parallel structure to balance sentences grammatically

REVISING SENTENCES: PARALLEL STRUCTURE

When you combine several ideas in one sentence, make sure that your combinations are grammatically balanced. For example, you should balance a noun with a noun, a phrase with a phrase, and a clause with a clause. This balance is called **parallel structure**.

FAULTY	I enjoy reading, but I don't like mysteries or reading science fiction. [a noun and a phrase]
PARALLEL	I enjoy reading, but I don't like mysteries or science fiction. [two nouns]
FAULTY	Jason does not have enough time for the piano or to eat dinner or do his homework. [one prepositional phrase, two infinitive phrases]
PARALLEL	Jason does not have enough time to practice the piano, to eat dinner, or to do his homework. [three infinitive phrases]
FAULTY	He promised that he would spend more time studying and to help around the house. [clause and phrase]
PARALLEL	He promised that he would spend more time studying and that he would help around the house. [two clauses]

Some examples of parallel structure are underlined in the following sentences.

1. "I love to <u>sail forbidden seas</u>, and <u>land on barbarous coasts</u>."
   —Herman Melville, *Moby-Dick*

2. "They <u>hugged her</u>, and <u>kissed her</u>, and <u>clapped their hands</u>, and <u>shouted</u>."
   —Harriet Jacobs, *Incidents in the Life of a Slave Girl*

Writer's Workshop Follow-up: Revision

Review your interpretive essay, looking carefully for faulty parallel structure. If you find such problems, decide how to correct them. Make sure that the items that should be parallel are in the same grammatical form.

Technology HELP

See Language Workshop CD-ROM. *Key word entry: parallel structure.*

Language Handbook HELP

See Improving Sentence Style, page 1017.

Try It Out

Write two sentences of your own, modeled on the two numbered sentences at the left. For example, a sentence modeled on number 1 might read: "I try to dunk the basketball and land on my feet." Compare your modeled sentences in class.

Next use parallel structure to correct the following sentences.

1. Gabriel likes playing soccer in summer and to ski in winter.

2. The boss promised Anita more vacation time and that she would work fewer hours.

3. The train was overcrowded, stuffy, and going to arrive behind schedule.

4. I hoped to leave early and that I could catch a taxi.

Resources

Workshop Resources
• Worksheet, p. 77

Language Workshop CD-ROM
• Parallel Structure

Try It Out
Possible Answers
(Modeled sentences)
1. I love to write poems and paint my bedroom.
2. She praised the child, and cared for him, and bought his clothes, and triumphed.

(Corrected sentences)
1. Gabriel likes playing soccer in summer and skiing in winter.
2. The boss promised Anita more vacation time and fewer work hours.
3. The train was overcrowded, stuffy, and behind schedule.
4. I hoped to leave early and to catch a taxi.

Assessing Learning

Quick Check: Parallel Structure

Examine the following sentences and write either *faulty* or *parallel* for each one. Correct those that are faulty.

1. We saw that he tried consistently and worked diligently. [parallel]
2. Young people often like to meet their friends at the mall and watching movies together. [faulty: to watch movies together **or** meeting their friends at the mall]
3. Our puppy likes to be petted, to play fetch, and special dog treats. [faulty: to eat special dog treats]
4. You might prefer doing an art project or to write a story of your own. [faulty: writing a story of your own **or** to do an art project]
5. The balloon seemed to bounce, to spin, and to climb steadily. [parallel]

T721

Situation

You've read *The Miracle Worker,* and you wonder how your opinions compare with those of a critic who reviewed the opening-night Broadway performance. To find out, use the following strategies as you read this excerpt from a review by the critic Walter Kerr.

Strategies

Focus on criteria.

- Note the criteria that the critic uses to judge the work. Is the emphasis on plot, characterization, or message? Is it on the acting, the directing, or special effects? What criteria matter to you, and why?

Scrutinize the support.

- Examine the reasoning. Are opinions backed up by strong reasons and relevant details from the play? Are there any lapses in logic? Look for comments that reveal a bias.

Look for insights and oversights.

- Does the critic offer any new insights into the work? If so, what do you think of them? Did he overlook any points you consider important?

Clarify your own views.

- If you could talk over your response to the play with the critic, what would you say?

First Night Report
WALTER KERR

All reviewers are adjective-happy, and most of us overpraise. Any new show that escapes being dreadful is subsequently described as powerful, hair-raising, spine-tingling, touching, and just plain wonderful.

How, then, are you going to believe me when I tell you that *The Miracle Worker* . . . is really and truly powerful, hair-raising, spine-tingling, touching, and just plain wonderful?

Perhaps you will believe me if I tell you a very simple thing. Author William Gibson has done all of the stirring, frightening, theatrically explosive things that his subject matter suggests. He has shown us the blind, deaf, and mute Helen Keller at the age of five or six, and shown her to us for what she was then: an animal. He has let her claw at the family that would have bestowed tenderness on her, spit in the face of the one woman who might save her, tear a household to tatters—very, very literally—in a manner that is at once factual and dramatically vivid.

He has then turned to the story of nurse Annie Sullivan and extracted from it every last ounce of its heroism, its brisk Irish comedy, and its private pathos. Annie Sullivan, it seems, was herself an abandoned child, herself illiterate, herself once blind. Miss Sullivan's pig-headed and apparently losing battle to tear open the cage in which another soul is confined, and to tear down the protective outer walls that have kept the child a coddled savage, is crackling stuff, round by round. . . .

—*New York Herald Tribune*
October 20, 1959

Using the Strategies

Use the preceding strategies to answer these questions about the opening paragraphs of Walter Kerr's review of *The Miracle Worker.*

1. What criteria do you think Kerr uses in his review?

2. What is his opinion of the play? How does he support it?

3. How does his opinion of the play compare with yours?

4. Did reading the review of the play change your response?

Extending the Strategies

Find a review of a movie you've seen recently, and compare your response with the critic's.

Crossing the Curriculum

Music

Ask students to apply the strategies in this workshop to a magazine review of a popular CD or music video. Have students evaluate the critic's judgment and objectivity. Students may wish to submit their critique of the review to the magazine in which the review was published.

Art

If possible, take students to a local art exhibit or bring to class reproductions of paintings by the Impressionists. Alongside these pictures provide contemporary and historical critiques and ask students to use critical strategies to disagree with or support the critic's comments.

Learning for Life
Opening Doors for Others

OBJECTIVES
1. Identify what society is doing to enable citizens with disabilities to lead full, rewarding lives
2. Conduct research
3. Choose and complete a project summarizing and presenting research information

Problem

Helen Keller suffered from severe disabilities: She could neither hear nor see. Fortunately, Helen's family had the money to hire a special teacher for their child. Today, people who are blind, visually impaired, deaf, or hard of hearing have other options. What are some of the ways society today assists those with disabilities?

Project

Find out what is being done to help people with disabilities lead full, rewarding lives.

Preparation

Using *who, what, where, when,* and *why* questions, brainstorm to find a specific topic that interests you. These ideas will get you started.

People. *Who* provides services to people with disabilities? *Who* is eligible? *What* about children?

Places. *Where* in your community have buildings been modified to comply with the Americans with Disabilities Act (ADA)? *What* services do schools supply?

Things. *What* devices for people with limited sight, hearing, speech, or mobility are available or under development?

Procedure

On your own or with a group of classmates, do one of the following activities or think up an information-gathering activity of your own.

1. Find someone in your community or school who can answer your questions. Arrange a time and place to meet with this expert, and take notes.

2. Take photographs of two public buildings, one that has been modified to make it more accessible to people using wheelchairs or crutches and one that hasn't.

3. Listen for public service announcements (PSAs) on your favorite radio station. Think about the kind of programming the station features and the characteristics of its audience (age, sex, income, etc.).

Presentation

Use one of the following formats (or another that your teacher approves).

1. Photo Essay

Create a photo essay showing the differences between a building that has been modified to

meet the requirements of the ADA and one that hasn't. Write captions explaining what problems the unmodified building presents and how the modifications solve those problems in the other building. Send your photo essay to your community or school newspaper.

2. Public Service Announcement

Prepare and tape a thirty-second PSA to raise public awareness about treating people with disabilities as individuals. Target the PSA to the audience of your favorite radio station and ask the station manager to schedule air time for it.

3. Demonstration

Build or make detailed drawings of a model of a device used by people with a particular disability. With other students who have chosen this option, demonstrate or explain the workings of the device to your classmates.

Processing

Reflect on your work. What conclusions can you draw about what society is doing for citizens with disabling conditions?

Resources ——

Viewing and Representing
HRW Multimedia Presentation Maker
Students may wish to use the *Multimedia Presentation Maker* to create their photo essays or demonstration drawings.

Grading Timesaver

Rubrics for this Learning for Life project appear on p. 200 of the *Portfolio Management System*.

LEARNING FOR LIFE **723**

Developing Workplace Competencies

Preparation	Procedure	Presentation
• Thinks creatively • Reasons • Makes decisions	• Works in teams • Acquires data • Uses resources well	• Evaluates data • Interprets information • Applies technology to specific tasks

William Shakespeare

724 **WILLIAM SHAKESPEARE**

OBJECTIVES

1. Read a Shakespeare play centered on the theme "The Destruction of Innocence"
2. Interpret literary elements used in the play, with special emphasis on the five-part structure of Shakespearean tragedy
3. Apply a variety of reading strategies to the play, with special emphasis on reading Shakespeare's poetry and using paraphrasing and context clues to check understanding of the text
4. Respond to the play using a variety of modes
5. Research word origins
6. Learn about Shakespeare's life and the history of the Globe Theater
7. Stage a scene from the play
8. Plan, draft, revise, edit, proof, and publish a research paper
9. Combine sentences by using appositives
10. Demonstrate the ability to evaluate the credibility of sources
11. Analyze and evaluate a decision-making plan, and use it to solve a real or fictional problem

Selection Readability

This Annotated Teacher's Edition provides a summary of each selection in the student book. Following each Summary heading, you will find one, two, or three small icons. These icons indicate, in an approximate sense, the reading level of the selection.

■ One icon indicates that the selection is easy.

■ ■ Two icons indicate that the selection is on an intermediate reading level.

■ ■ ■ Three icons indicate that the selection is challenging.

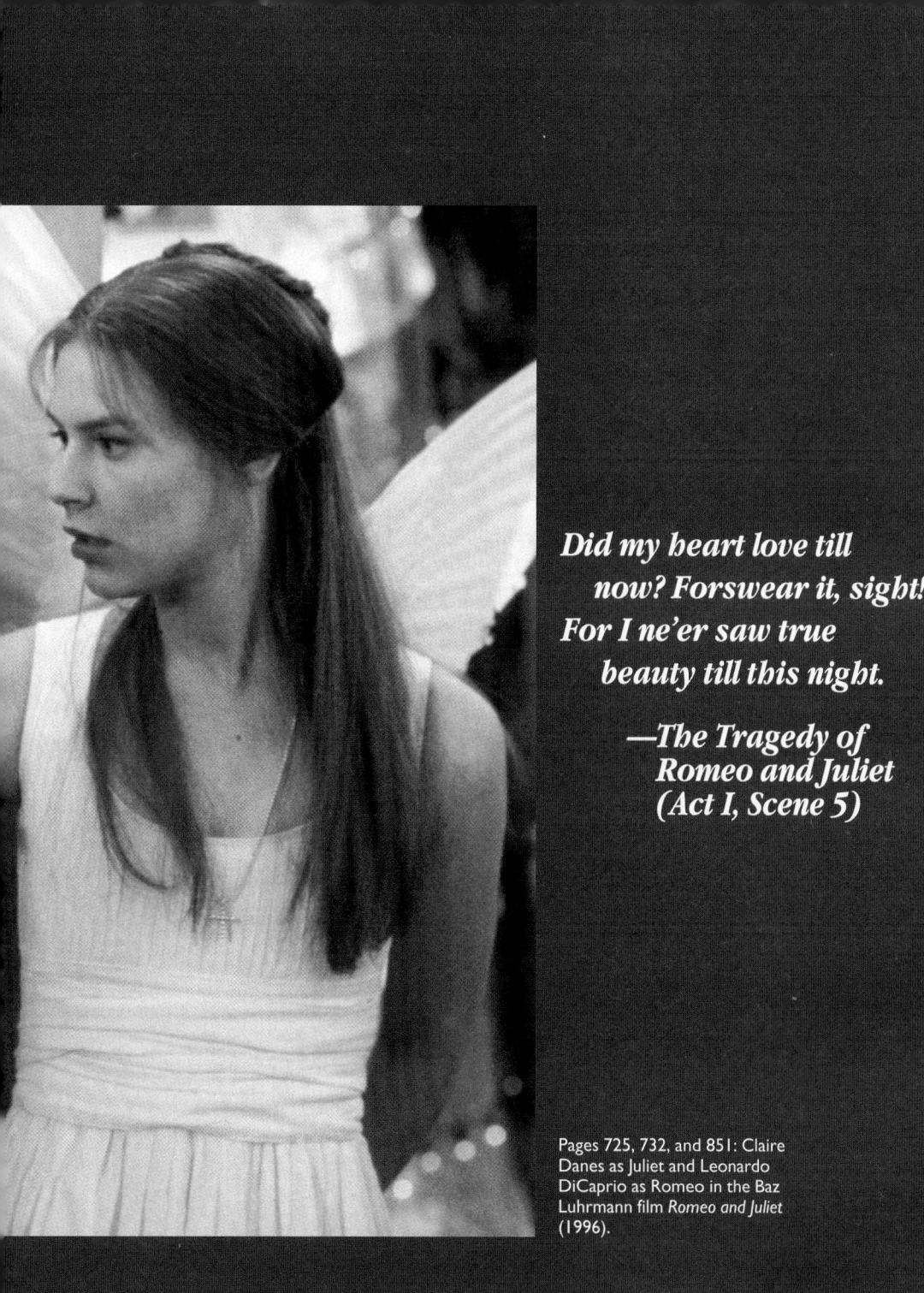

Did my heart love till now? Forswear it, sight! For I ne'er saw true beauty till this night.

—*The Tragedy of Romeo and Juliet (Act I, Scene 5)*

Pages 725, 732, and 851: Claire Danes as Juliet and Leonardo DiCaprio as Romeo in the Baz Luhrmann film *Romeo and Juliet* (1996).

RESPONDING TO THE ART

Activity. Many students have probably seen Baz Luhrmann's film *William Shakespeare's Romeo and Juliet*, which is available on videocassette. Point out that this particular film version of the play has a modern-day Florida setting but that Romeo and Juliet meet at a costume party. Ask students how the costumes add a romantic flavor to the scene in which Romeo and Juliet meet. [Possible responses: Romeo is dressed as a knight, which reminds viewers of romantic stories, such as that of King Arthur and Guinevere; Juliet is dressed as an angel, giving her beauty an unearthly quality and reminding viewers of Cupid, the god of love.]

Responding to the Quotation

Tell students that before he meets Juliet, Romeo thinks he is in love with someone else. Encourage students to discuss whether such a sudden change of heart represents fickleness or the dramatic effects of true love. Point out that they will have a better chance to evaluate Romeo's change of heart as they read the play.

William Shakespeare's Life: A Genius from Stratford

This introductory essay summarizes what is known of Shakespeare's life, stressing his consummate professionalism and placing the writing of *Romeo and Juliet* in context.

Ⓐ Historical Connections

During Shakespeare's time, people saw little need to keep biographical records unless the person was a member of the aristocracy or had a strong connection to either the church or the state. The occupation of playwright was not held in high regard, so information about the life of someone like Shakespeare was generally not reported.

Ⓑ Literary Connections

Critics did write about Shakespeare during his lifetime. In 1598, a critic named Francis Meres compared Shakespeare favorably to the poets of classical antiquity. And Shakespeare's colleague Ben Jonson called Shakespeare "the soul of the age," equal in importance to the ancient Greek playwrights Aeschylus, Euripides, and Sophocles. After Shakespeare's death, however, Jonson complained that Shakespeare should have written less and edited more: "Hee was (indeed) honest, and of an open, and free nature; had an excellent *Phantsie;* brave notions, and gentle expressions: wherein hee flow'd with that facility, that sometime it was necessary he should be stop'd. . . ."

WILLIAM SHAKESPEARE'S LIFE: A GENIUS FROM STRATFORD

BY ROBERT ANDERSON

William Shakespeare (1783). Sketch by Ozias Humphrey.
By permission of the Folger Shakespeare Library, Washington, D.C.

Ⓐ Ⓑ He is the most famous writer in the world, but he left us no journals or letters—he left us only his poems and his plays. What we know about William Shakespeare's personal life comes mostly from church and legal documents—a baptismal registration, a marriage license, and records of real-estate transactions. We also have a few remarks that others wrote about him during his lifetime.

Reaching All Students

Pair students of different abilities and have them read through the introductory pages on Shakespeare and the theater of his time. One student should read a section aloud while the other makes brief notes on interesting new facts in a chart like the following. Partners should take turns reading aloud and taking notes and then complete their individual charts, adding comments about their original observations.

Interesting Facts or Comments	
Shakespeare's Life	Theater of the Time

We know that William was born the third of eight children, around April 23, 1564, in Stratford, a market town about one hundred miles northwest of London. His father, John, was a shopkeeper and a man of some importance in Stratford, serving at various times as justice of the peace and high bailiff (mayor).

William attended grammar school, where he studied Latin grammar, Latin literature, and rhetoric (the uses of language). As far as we know, he had no further formal education.

At the age of eighteen, he married Anne Hathaway, who was eight years older than he was. Sometime after the birth of their second and third children (twins), Shakespeare moved to London, apparently leaving his family in Stratford.

We know that several years later, by 1592, Shakespeare had already become an actor and a playwright. By 1594, he was a charter member of the theatrical company called the Lord Chamberlain's Men, which was later to become the King's Men. (As the names of these acting companies indicate, theatrical groups depended on the support of a wealthy patron—the King's Men were supported by King James himself.) Shakespeare worked with this company for the rest of his writing life. Year after year, he provided it with plays, almost on demand. Shakespeare was the ultimate professional writer. He had a theater that needed plays,

actors who needed parts, and a family that needed to be fed.

Romeo and Juliet was probably among the early plays that Shakespeare wrote, between 1594 and 1596. By 1612, when he returned to Stratford to live the life of a prosperous retired gentleman, Shakespeare had written thirty-seven plays, including such masterpieces as *Julius Caesar, Hamlet, Othello, King Lear,* and *Macbeth.*

Shakespeare's plays are still produced all over the world. During a Broadway season in the 1980s, one critic estimated that if Shakespeare were alive, he would be receiving $25,000 a week in royalties for a production of *Othello* alone. The play was attracting larger audiences than any other nonmusical production in town.

Shakespeare died on April 23, 1616, at the age of fifty-two. He is buried under the old stone floor in the chancel of Holy Trinity Church in Stratford. Carved over his grave is the following verse (the spelling is modernized):

> Good friend, for Jesus' sake forbear
> To dig the dust enclosed here.
> Blessed be the man that spares these stones
> And cursed be he that moves my bones.

These are hardly the best of Shakespeare's lines (if indeed they are his at all), but like his other lines, they seem to have worked. His bones lie undisturbed to this day.

WILLIAM SHAKESPEARE 727

C Cultural Connections
Like other young boys of his social class, Shakespeare probably began grammar school at about age seven. Classes were held for nine hours each day, year-round. Corporal punishment was used to enforce the strict discipline. Students studied Latin because it was needed for careers in medicine, law, or the church and because an educated person was expected to be well versed in Latin.

D Historical Connections
From 1592 to 1594, London authorities repeatedly closed the theaters because of outbreaks of the plague. Since there was little demand for plays, Shakespeare turned his attention to poetry. Two of his long poems, *Venus and Adonis* and *The Rape of Lucrece,* were written during this time.

E Literary Connections
Many critics consider Shakespeare's tragedies to be his greatest plays. Students should also know, however, that Shakespeare wrote comedies— plays that are funny and end happily— and histories—plays about the lives of kings.

F Cultural Connections
Today, burial sites are generally left undisturbed unless the family wishes to have a body moved to another grave site. In Shakespeare's day, however, a body would eventually have been removed from under the church floor and the remains moved into a charnel house (a place where corpses or bones are deposited) to allow room for the burial of another body.

Resources

Viewing and Representing
Videocassette B, Segment 13
Available in Spanish and English.
The *Visual Connections* segment "The Bard" provides an interesting introduction to the life and works of William Shakespeare. For full lesson plans and worksheets, see the *Visual Connections Teacher's Manual.*

Crossing the Curriculum

Social Studies
In Shakespeare's time, the theater was wildly popular but often condemned by government and religious officials. Officials feared not only the spread of contagious diseases but also the moral contagion they believed was spread by such entertainment and mass gatherings. Have students research the causes and effects of attempts to control the theater made by Puritans and government forces in London in the years between 1570 and 1640.

Professional Notes

As producer and director Joseph Papp has explained, Shakespeare's plays were not published until seven years after his death: "Acting companies were violently against the printing of plays. In an age where there were no copyright laws, publishing a popular play meant that rival acting companies could get hold of it and perform it without the fear of legal consequences. An acting company was usually only willing to let a play go to the printer if it was hopelessly out-of-date (and unrevivable) or a total failure."

Shakespeare and His Theater: A Perfect Match

This essay describes the Globe Theater, which was built by Shakespeare's company, and compares and contrasts it with modern theaters. The essay also discusses the differences between the media of theater and film.

Ⓐ Historical Connections

By 1574, playgoers at the inns had become so unruly that the Council of London began to charge innkeepers licensing fees for performances, a fact that probably contributed to Burbage's decision to build a theater. Since public plays were frowned upon by London officials, Burbage's theater was built outside the city limits, south of London Bridge. In 1608, Shakespeare and his colleagues opened an indoor private playhouse at Blackfriars. Shakespeare's company continued to play for part of the year, however, at the "wooden O," the Globe Theater.

Ⓑ Historical Connections

Before he began his theater career, James Burbage was trained as a carpenter. His original theater, called simply The Theater, was built on leased land. Soon after Burbage's death, the lease expired, and the landlord was not eager to renew it. Legally, he could take possession of the building if it was not removed after expiration of the lease. That is why Burbage's sons decided to tear down The Theater while the landlord was away in the country. To help finance the building of the Globe from the old planks of The Theater, the Burbage sons formed a financial partnership with the members of Shakespeare's acting company, the Lord Chamberlain's Men.

SHAKESPEARE AND HIS THEATER: A PERFECT MATCH

BY ROBERT ANDERSON

Sometimes playwrights influence the shape and form of a theater, but more often, existing theaters seem to influence the shape and form of plays. It is important that we understand Shakespeare's theater because it influenced how he wrote his plays. Shakespeare took the theater of his time, and he used it brilliantly.

The Globe Theater (18th century), based on C. J. Visscher's engraved panoramic view of London (published 1616).
British Museum, London. The Granger Collection, New York.

728 WILLIAM SHAKESPEARE

THE "WOODEN O"

In 1576, outside the city walls of London, an actor-manager named James Burbage built the first permanent theater in England. He called it The Theater. Up to that time, touring acting companies had played wherever they could rent space. Usually this would be in the courtyards of inns. There the actors would erect a temporary platform stage at one end of the yard and play to an audience which stood around the stage or sat in the tiers of balconies that surrounded the courtyard. (Normally, these balconies were used as passageways to the various rooms of the inn.) It was natural, then, that the first theater built by Burbage should derive its shape and form from the inns.

In 1599, Burbage's theater was torn down and its timbers were used by Shakespeare and his company to build the Globe Theater. This was the theater for which Shakespeare wrote most of his plays.

Getting Students Involved

Cooperative Learning

Just the Facts, Please. After students have read the introductory essays on Shakespeare and the theater during his lifetime, provide the class with a list of related topics that they may research in the library or media center. Possible topics include Elizabeth I, Stratford-on-Avon, the Globe Theater, the bubonic plague, and dress during the Renaissance. Divide students into small groups. Have each group choose a topic and compile a list of interesting facts relating to it during a set period of time.

When students return to the classroom, ask a presenter from each group to read the list of facts. Remind students to jot down notes as they listen and to save their notes for the Writer's Workshop on p. 868. These notes may later help students decide on topics for their research reports, to be completed after reading *Romeo and Juliet*.

In his play *Henry V*, Shakespeare called his theater a "wooden O." It was a large, round (or polygonal) building, three stories high, with a large platform stage that projected from one end into a yard open to the sky. In the back wall of this stage was a curtained-off inner stage. Flanking the inner stage were two doors for entrances and exits. Above this inner stage was a small balcony or upper stage, which could be used to suggest Juliet's balcony or the high walls of a castle or the bridge of a ship. Trapdoors were placed in the floor of the main stage for the entrances and exits of ghosts and for descents into hell.

C

The plays were performed in the afternoon. Since the stage was open to the sky, there was no need for stage illumination. There were very few sets (scenery, furniture, etc.). The stage was "set" by the language. A whole forest scene is created in one play when a character announces: "Well, this is the Forest of Arden." But costumes were often elaborate, and the stage might be hung with colorful banners and trappings. (The groundlings, those eight hundred or more people who stood shoulder to shoulder around the stage for the price of a penny, loved a good show. Most people still do.)

D

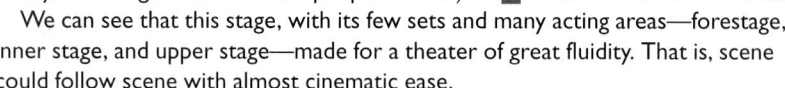

"The Wooden O," the Globe Theater. Drawing by David Gentleman.

We can see that this stage, with its few sets and many acting areas—forestage, inner stage, and upper stage—made for a theater of great fluidity. That is, scene could follow scene with almost cinematic ease.

In one interesting aspect, the theater in Shakespeare's day was very different from the theater we know today. Acting wasn't considered entirely respectable by the English Puritans, so all women's parts were played by boys. Not for many years did women appear on stage in the professional English theater. In Shakespeare's day, Juliet would have been played by a trained boy actor.

E

THE MODERN STAGE:
BACK TO SHAKESPEARE'S THEATER

It has been said that all you need for a theater is "two planks and a passion." Since Shakespeare's time "the planks" (the stage) have undergone various changes. First, the part of the stage which projected into the yard grew narrower, and the

(Background) Panoramic view of London in 1616 (detail) by C. J. Visscher. Globe Theater shown in lower center, page 729.

WILLIAM SHAKESPEARE 729

C **Reading Skills and Strategies**
Using Resources
Use the illustrations to help students imagine the social atmosphere and physical environment of the Elizabethan theater. Playgoers flocked to the Globe in large numbers, and the audience could be rowdy. Help students picture an excited crowd out for an afternoon of entertainment, mesmerized by actors who perform right in their midst on a deep, thrust stage.

D **Historical Connections**
During Shakespeare's time, visitors from abroad wrote in praise of London's theaters. Thomas Platter wrote: "The playhouses are so constructed that they play on a raised platform so that everyone can see the whole spectacle. The actors are most expensively and beautifully dressed. . . ." The German tourist Paul Hentzner wrote: "Without the city are some theaters where English actors almost every day represent tragedies and comedies to very numerous audiences; these are concluded with excellent music, variety of dances, and the great applause of the audience."

E **Reading Skills and Strategies**
Analyzing Cause and Effect
? Some critics contend that since Shakespeare knew that boys would play the women's roles, it affected how he delineated his female characters. For example, a large number of the heroines in Shakespeare's comedies are often disguised as boys and therefore dressed in masculine garb. Do you agree with the cause-and-effect relationship these critics see, or can you think of some other reason for having women disguise themselves as men? [Students may agree with the critics, or may suggest that Shakespeare simply enjoyed creating plot complications by having characters go about in disguise.]

Assessing Learning

Check Test: True-False
1. Shakespeare was the son of a nobleman. [False]
2. Shakespeare's wife and children apparently remained in Stratford when he moved to London. [True]

3. Plays were performed at night, after the end of the workday. [False]
4. There were no actresses on the London stage during Shakespeare's time. [True]

5. The main stage in the Shakespearean theater projected into the audience. [True]

A Historical Connections

The relationship between the play-wright and the theater is important. Robert Anderson tells how stage designer Jo Mielziner invited a number of playwrights to see his model for the Vivian Beaumont Theater, part of the Lincoln Center arts complex in New York City. It was a huge, wide-open space. Mielziner said, "We're going to stretch you all." Anderson points out that no one stretched, and the theater, after struggling for several seasons, had to be closed down and redesigned.

B Critical Thinking

Expressing an Opinion

❓ Ask students who have acting experience to respond to the following questions:

- How does the type of theater affect your acting style and your relationship with the audience?
- What do you like and dislike about a large auditorium? a small, intimate theater? an outdoor performance? [Answers will vary.]

C Literary Connections

For more information on film adaptations of Shakespeare's plays, including *Romeo and Juliet,* see the Literature and the Media feature "Shakespeare in the Video Store" on p. 833.

A cutaway of the Globe, showing the three stage levels and the dressing and prop rooms. Drawing by David Gentleman.

small curtained inner stage grew larger, until there developed what is called the **proscenium stage**. Here, there is no outer stage; there is only the inner stage, and a large curtain separates it from the audience. The effect is like looking inside a window or inside a picture frame. This is the stage most of us know today. It has been standard for well over a hundred years.

But recently, we have seen a reversal of this design. Now, more and more theaters (especially university and regional theaters) are building "thrust" stages, or arena stages. In this kind of theater, the audience once again sits on three or even four sides of the stage.

THE MOVIES AND THE THEATER: WORDS VS. ACTION

Like Shakespeare's stage, this kind of "thrust" stage, with its minimal scenery, allows playwrights (if they want) to move their stories rapidly from place to place. They can establish each new scene with a line like "Well, this is the Forest of Arden." As a result, playwrights have been tempted to write plays that imitate the style of movies. But this imitation rarely works. Theater and movies are two different media. A theater audience does not necessarily want to be whisked from place to place. People who go to plays often prefer to spend a long, long time watching the subtle development of conflicts among a small group of people, all in one setting. For example, all of the action in Lorraine Hansberry's play *A Raisin in the Sun* takes place inside one small apartment on Chicago's South Side.

Movies are basically a *visual* medium and so must chiefly engage and delight the eye, rather than the ear. (One movie director once referred to a dialogue in a movie as "foreground *noise*"!) The theater is much more a medium of *words*. When we go to see a play, it is the movement of the *words* rather than the movement of the scenery that delights us.

This difference between the appeal of a movie and the appeal of a play may account for the failure of some successful plays when they are translated to the screen. The movie producer will say: "Open up the story." In "opening up the story," the producer sometimes loses the concentration, the intensity, which was the prime virtue of the play.

Getting Students Involved

Stage vs. Film. Students who have had limited exposure to plays might have difficulty understanding why a play and a movie of the same story are performed differently. If possible, encourage students to attend a theater performance of *Romeo and Juliet,* or show a taped stage performance in class. Then, show a videotape of a film adaptation. As the class reads the play, work with students to make a chart, like the following, that lists some of the major differences between a play and a movie. Some categories to consider include setting, facial expressions, dialogue, and volume of voices.

Play	Movie
Setting must fit on stage	Camera can pan or zoom
Facial expressions have to be seen from a distance	Camera can shoot close-ups

William Shakespeare: The Destruction of Innocence

Theme

Who Is Responsible? *Focus on tragedy: Conflicts that tear an otherwise civilized city apart also destroy the innocent children that two families hold dearest.*

Reading the Anthology

Reaching Struggling Readers

The *Reading Skills and Strategies: Reaching Struggling Readers* binder provides materials coordinated with the Pupil's Edition (see the Collection Planner, p. T730B) to help students who have difficulty reading and comprehending text, or students who are reluctant readers. The binder for ninth grade is organized around sixteen individual skill areas and offers the following options:

- MiniReads are short, easy texts that give students a chance to practice a particular skill and strategy before reading selections in the Pupil's Edition. Each MiniRead Skill Lesson can be taught independently or used in conjunction with a Selection Skill Lesson.

- **Selection Skill Lessons** Selection Skill Lessons allow students to apply skills introduced in the MiniReads. Each Selection Skill Lesson provides reading instruction and practice specific to a particular piece of literature in the Pupil's Edition.

Reading Beyond the Anthology

Read On

Each collection in the grade nine book includes an annotated bibliography of books suitable for extended reading. The suggested books are related to works in the collection by theme, by author, or by subject. To preview the Read On for Collection 13, please turn to p. T865.

HRW Library

The *HRW Library* offers novels, plays, works of nonfiction, and short-story collections for extended reading. Each major work in the Library is accompanied by thematically or topically related Connections. The Connections are magazine articles, poems, or other pieces of literature. Each book in the *HRW Library* is also accompanied by a Study Guide that provides teaching suggestions and worksheets. The two titles shown here will work well to extend concepts developed in Collection 13.

A MIDSUMMER NIGHT'S DREAM William Shakespeare
This Shakespearean comedy of confused lovers offers an interesting counterpoint to the tragic view of young love in *Romeo and Juliet*.

FAMOUS STORIES FOR PERFORMANCE
Short, easy plays based on myths, folk tales, and famous short stories allow students to experiment with actual performances of various types of plays.

Collection 13 The Destruction of Innocence

Resources for this Collection

Note: All resources for this collection are available for preview on the *One-Stop Planner CD-ROM 2 with Test Generator.* All worksheets and blackline masters may be printed from the CD-ROM.

Internet Resources
go.hrw.com LE0 9-13

Collection Planner

Selection or Feature	Reading and Literary Skills	Vocabulary, Language, and Grammar
The Tragedy of Romeo and Juliet William Shakespeare (p. 732) **How to Read Shakespeare: The Poetry** (p. 740) **Connections: "My Very Dear Sarah"** Major Sullivan Ballou (p. 852) **Your Laughter** Pablo Neruda (p. 853) **How Do I Love Thee?** Elizabeth Barrett Browning (p. 853) **Connections: Dear Juliet** Lisa Bannon (p. 854)	• *Reading Skills and Strategies: Reaching Struggling Readers* • Selection Skill Lesson, p. 164 • *Graphic Organizers for Active Reading,* Worksheet pp. 64, 65, 66, 67, 68 • *Literary Elements:* Transparency 17 Worksheet p. 52	• *Words to Own,* Worksheets pp. 39, 41, 43, 45, 47 • *Grammar and Language Links:* Repetition, Worksheet p. 57; Figures of Speech, Worksheet p. 59 • *Daily Oral Grammar,* Transparencies 44, 45
Extending the Theme: Romeo and Juliet in Bosnia Bob Herbert (p. 860)	The Extending the Theme feature provides students with an unstructured opportunity to practice reading strategies using a selection that extends the theme of the collection.	
Speaking and Listening Workshop: Staging the Play (p. 864)		
Writer's Workshop: Research Paper (p. 868)		
Sentence Workshop: Appositives (p. 873)		• *Workshop Resources,* p. 79 • *Language Workshop CD-ROM,* Appositives
Learning for Life: Making a Decision (p. 875)		

Other Resources for this Collection

- *Cross-Curricular Activities*, p. 13
- *Portfolio Management System*, Introduction to Portfolio Assessment, p. 1
- *Formal Assessment*, Genre Test, p. 147
- *Test Generator*, Collection Test

Writing	Listening and Speaking Viewing and Representing	Assessment
• *Portfolio Management System*, Rubrics for Choices, pp. 201–205	• *Visual Connections:* Videocassette B, Segment 13  • *Audio CD Library,* Disc 17, Tracks 5, 6, 7 • *Viewing and Representing:* Fine Art Transparencies 18, 19 Worksheet pp. 72, 76 • *Portfolio Management System*, Rubrics for Choices, pp. 201–205	• *Formal Assessment*, Selection Tests, pp. 137, 139, 141, 143, 145 • *Standardized Test Preparation*, pp. 84, 86, 88 • *Test Generator (One-Stop Planner CD-ROM)*
	• *Audio CD Library,* Disc 17, Track 8	
		• *Portfolio Management System*, Rubrics p. 208
• *Workshop Resources*, p. 53 • *Writer's Workshop 2 CD-ROM,* Informative Report		• *Portfolio Management System* • Prewriting, p. 209 • Peer Editing, p. 210 • Assessment Rubric, p. 211
		• *Portfolio Management System*, Rubrics, p. 212

 Transparency    CD-ROM    Video    Audio CD

Collection Planner

Skills Focus

Selection or Feature	Reading Skills and Strategies	Elements of Literature	Language/ Grammar	Vocabulary/ Spelling	Writing	Listening/ Speaking	Viewing/ Representing
The Tragedy of Romeo and Juliet William Shakespeare (p. 732) **How to Read Shakespeare: The Poetry** (p. 740) **Your Laughter** Pablo Neruda (p. 853) **How Do I Love Thee?** Elizabeth Barrett Browning (p. 853)	How to Read Shakespeare, pp. 740–741 Paraphrasing, p. 835 Context Clues, pp. 835, 838 Identify Bias, p. 862	Tragedy, p. 732 • Exposition • Rising Action • Crisis or Turning Point • Comedy • Falling Action • Climax • Resolution Blank Verse, p. 740 Iambic Meter, p. 740 Iambic Pentameter, p. 740 Couplets, p. 740 End-Stopped Line, p. 741 Run-On Line, p. 740 Complication, pp. 762, 816 Foil, p. 762 Foreboding, p. 762 Suspense, pp. 762, 816, 834 Foreshadowing, p. 788 Character, pp. 788, 816, 834 Motive, p. 788 Dramatic Irony, pp. 788, 834, 855 Turning Point, p. 816 Blocking Figures, p. 834 Climax, p. 855 Theme, p. 855	Figures of Speech, pp. 858–859 • Similes • Metaphors • Implied Metaphors • Personification • Puns	Archaic Terms, pp. 733, 789 Word Origins, p. 763 The Significance of Names, p. 817	Find a Topic, pp. 763, 789, 817, 834 Write a Newspaper Column, p. 763 Make a Director's Cut, p. 789 Write a Prologue, p. 817 Write from a Character's Point of View, p. 834 Narrow a Topic, p. 856 Plan an Update of *Romeo and Juliet*, p. 856 Write a New Ending, p. 856 Compare Texts, p. 856 Analyze Dramatic Structure, p. 857 Write a Character Analysis, p. 857	Perform a Shakespearean Speech, p. 763 Create a Tableau, p. 817 Make an Oral Report, p. 856 Take Part in a Panel Discussion, p. 857	Create a Chart Analyzing Comic Relief, p. 857 Make a Model of the Globe, p. 857
Extending the Theme: Romeo and Juliet in Bosnia Bob Herbert (p. 860)	The Extending the Theme feature provides students with an unstructured opportunity to practice reading strategies using a selection that extends the theme of the collection.						
Speaking and Listening Workshop: Staging the Play (p. 864)		Tableau, p. 865			Create a Promptbook, p. 866	Stage a Scene from Shakespeare, pp. 864–867	
Writer's Workshop: Research Paper (p. 868)					Write a Research Paper, pp. 868–872		
Sentence Workshop: Appositives (p. 873)			Identify Appositives, p. 873	Combine Sentences Using Appositives, p. 873	Revise Sentences Using Appositives, p. 873		
Reading for Life: Evaluating the Credibility of Sources (p. 874)	Identify Sources, p. 874 Determine the Relevance of Sources, p. 874 Determine the Currency of Sources, p. 874						
Learning for Life: Making a Decision (p. 875)	Identify Options, p. 875 Identify Consequences, p. 875				Write an Advice Column, p. 875	Create and Perform a Soliloquy, p. 875	Make a Chart, p. 875 Create a Cartoon Strip, p. 875

Skills Focus

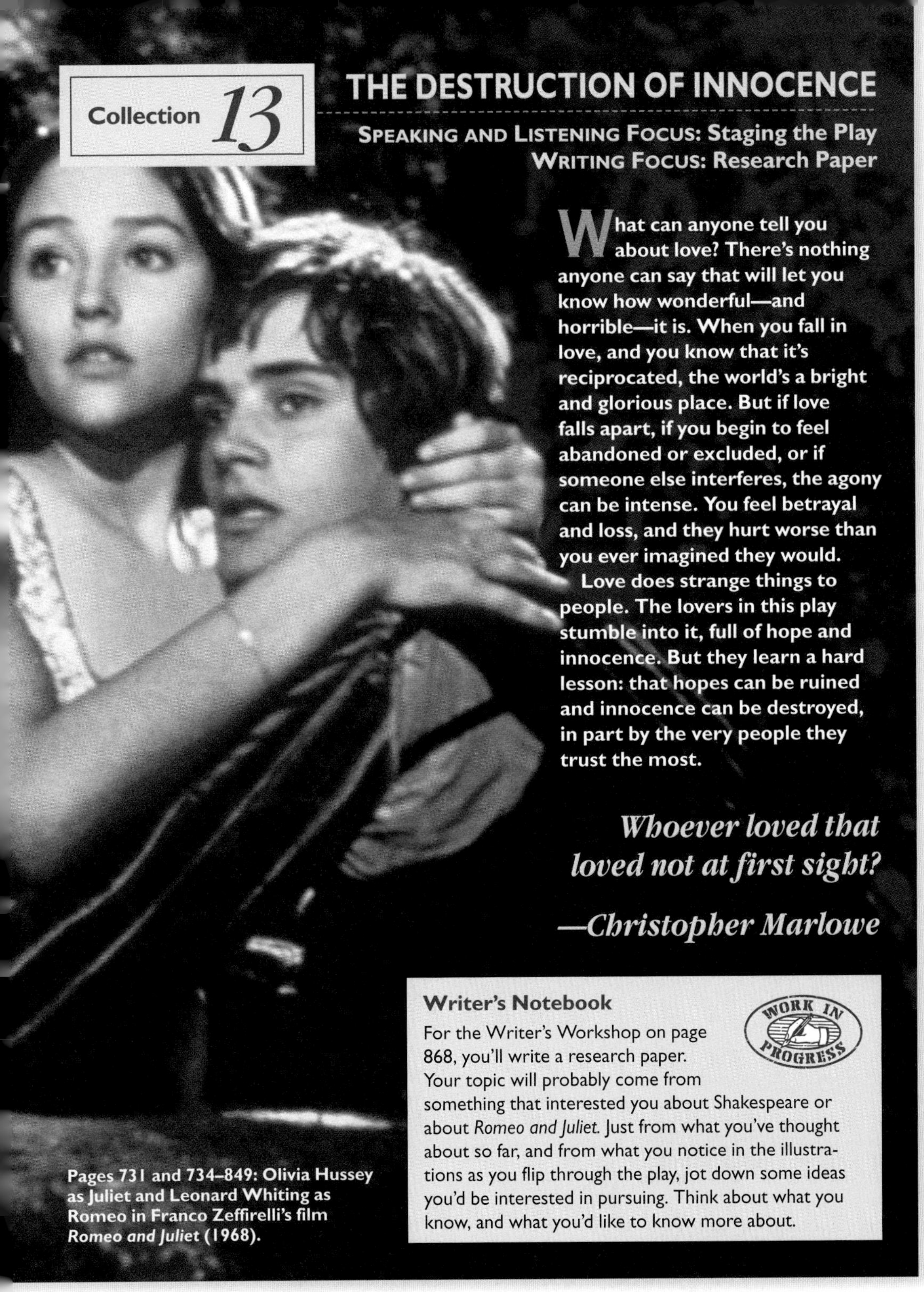

THE DESTRUCTION OF INNOCENCE

SPEAKING AND LISTENING FOCUS: Staging the Play
WRITING FOCUS: Research Paper

What can anyone tell you about love? There's nothing anyone can say that will let you know how wonderful—and horrible—it is. When you fall in love, and you know that it's reciprocated, the world's a bright and glorious place. But if love falls apart, if you begin to feel abandoned or excluded, or if someone else interferes, the agony can be intense. You feel betrayal and loss, and they hurt worse than you ever imagined they would.

Love does strange things to people. The lovers in this play stumble into it, full of hope and innocence. But they learn a hard lesson: that hopes can be ruined and innocence can be destroyed, in part by the very people they trust the most.

Whoever loved that loved not at first sight?

—Christopher Marlowe

Writer's Notebook

For the Writer's Workshop on page 868, you'll write a research paper. Your topic will probably come from something that interested you about Shakespeare or about *Romeo and Juliet*. Just from what you've thought about so far, and from what you notice in the illustrations as you flip through the play, jot down some ideas you'd be interested in pursuing. Think about what you know, and what you'd like to know more about.

Pages 731 and 734–849: Olivia Hussey as Juliet and Leonard Whiting as Romeo in Franco Zeffirelli's film *Romeo and Juliet* (1968).

Responding to the Quotation

? What does the quotation mean? Do you agree with Marlowe's idea? [Possible responses: It means that everyone who has ever been in love has fallen in love at first sight. Yes, because true love is an overpowering emotion that strikes people immediately; no, you can gradually come to love someone as you get to know the person.]

RESPONDING TO THE ART

Activity. Ask students what emotions they think Romeo's and Juliet's faces convey. [Possible responses: fear, sadness, desperation.]

Writer's Notebook

Have students skim through the collection to get some ideas for a topic that they might like to write about later. Tell them to think of aspects of Elizabethan life they'd like to know more about. Suggest that they record their ideas on a KWL chart. Remind students that they should fill in the first two columns now and the last column after they have read the play or done research on a specific topic.

What I Know	What I Want to Know	What I Learned

Writing Focus: Research Paper

The following **Work in Progress** assignments build to a culminating **Writer's Workshop** at the end of the collection.

OBJECTIVES

1. Read and interpret Act I of the play
2. Analyze the structure of Shakespearean tragedy, with special emphasis on exposition and rising action
3. Analyze and read aloud dialogue written in verse
4. Express understanding through creative writing or performance
5. Research word origins

SKILLS

Literary
- Analyze exposition and rising action

Reading
- Analyze and read aloud a verse play

Writing
- Find a topic for a research paper
- Write a society column

Performance
- Prepare and perform a speech from Act I

Vocabulary
- Research word origins

Viewing/Representing
- Respond to photographs of a film production of the play (ATE)

Planning

- **Block Schedule**
  Block Scheduling Lesson Plans with Pacing Guide
- **Traditional Schedule**
  Lesson Plans Including Strategies for English-Language Learners
- **One-Stop Planner**
  CD-ROM with Test Generator

T732

Before You Read

THE TRAGEDY OF ROMEO AND JULIET

Make The Connection

"Kids These Days . . ."

"Kids these days! They think that love conquers all, that nothing matters except how they feel about each other. They have no sense of responsibility to their families, no respect for tradition, no regard for those who are older and wiser. They don't know the problems they're going to have that all the love in the world won't solve for them."

Quickwrite

What do you think of this complaint? Have you heard older people say these things about kids today? How would one of the "kids" respond to this speaker? Write a quick response from the kids' point of view.

732 WILLIAM SHAKESPEARE

A Tragic Pattern: How the Play Is Built

A **tragedy** is a narrative about serious and important actions that end unhappily. Usually a tragedy ends with the deaths of the main characters. In some tragedies the disaster hits totally innocent characters; in others the main characters are in some ways responsible for their downfall. Shakespeare's tragic plays usually follow this five-part pattern:

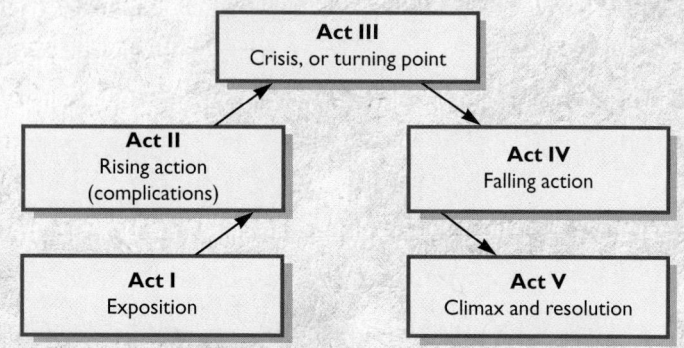

1. The **exposition** establishes the setting, introduces some of the main characters, explains background, and introduces the characters' main conflict.

2. The **rising action** consists of a series of complications. These occur as the main characters take action to resolve their problems.

3. The **crisis,** or **turning point,** is the moment when a choice made by the main characters determines the direction of the action: upward to a happy ending, which would be a **comedy,** or downward to **tragedy.** This turning point is the dramatic and tense moment when the forces of conflict come together. Look for the turning point in Act III.

4. The **falling action** presents events that result from the action taken at the turning point. These events usually lock the characters deeper and deeper into disaster; with each event we see the characters falling straight into tragedy.

5. The final and greatest **climax** occurs at the end of the play—usually, in tragedy, with the deaths of the main characters. In the **resolution** (or **denouement**) the loose parts of the plot are all tied up. The play is over.

go.hrw.com
LEO 9-13

Background

Most of Shakespeare's plays are based on stories that were already well known to his audiences. (He never wrote a play about a contemporary subject.) *Romeo and Juliet* is based on a long narrative poem by Arthur Brooke, which was published in 1562 as *The Tragicall Historye of Romeus and Juliet.* Brooke's popular poem itself was based on older Italian stories.

Romeo and Juliet, a very young man and a nearly fourteen-year-old girl, fall in love at first sight. They are caught up in an idealized, almost unreal, passionate love. They are in love with love. In his Prologue, Brooke preaches a moral, which people of his time expected. He says that Romeo and Juliet had to die because they broke the laws and married unwisely, against their parents' wishes. But Shakespeare does away with this moralizing. He presents the couple as "star-crossed lovers," doomed to disaster by fate.

To understand what *star-crossed* means, you have to realize that most people of Shakespeare's time believed in astrology. They believed that the course of their lives was partly determined by the hour, day, month, and year of their birth—hence, "the star" under which they were born. But Shakespeare may not have shared this belief. In a later play, *Julius Caesar,* Shakespeare has a character question this old idea about astrology and the influence of the stars:

The fault, dear Brutus, is not in
    our stars,
But in ourselves that we are
    underlings.

Although Shakespeare says in the Prologue that Romeo and Juliet are star-crossed, he does not make them mere victims of fate. Romeo and Juliet make decisions that lead to their disaster. More important, other characters have a hand in the play's tragic ending. How important do *you* think fate is in affecting what happens to us? To what degree do you think we control our own destinies?

A Word List

Shakespeare wrote this play about four hundred years ago. It's not surprising, then, that many words are by now **archaic,** which means that they (or their particular meanings) have disappeared from common use. The side notes in the play will help you with these archaic words and with other words and expressions that might be unfamiliar to you. Here are some of the archaic words that are repeatedly used in the play.

blank verse

'a: he.
a': on.
an' or **and:** if.
Anon!: Soon! Right away! Coming!
but: if, or only.
Good-den or **go-den** or **God-den:** Good evening. (This was said in the late afternoon.)

hap or **happy:** luck, or lucky.
humor: mood, or moisture.
Jack: common fellow, ordinary guy.
maid: unmarried girl.
mark: listen to.
Marry!: mild oath, shortened from "By the Virgin Mary!"
nice: trivial, foolish.
owes: owns.

shrift: confession or forgiveness for sins that have been confessed to a priest. After confession a person was said to be **shriven.**
Soft!: Quiet! Hush! Slow up!
Stay!: Wait!
withal: with that, with.
wot: know.

THE TRAGEDY OF ROMEO AND JULIET **733**

Background

Although the feud that dominates the play has struck a familiar chord with audiences in various times and places, it also accurately reflects specific historical conditions in Italy in the thirteenth and fourteenth centuries, when control of cities was divided among rival noble families. The strife between warring factions often led to street brawls.

1200
1300

Resources

Viewing and Representing
Videocassette B Segment 13
Available in Spanish and English. The *Visual Connections* segment "The Bard" provides an introduction to the life and works of William Shakespeare. For full lesson plans and worksheets, see the *Visual Connections Teacher's Manual.*

Listening
Audio CD Library
Students can hear dramatic excerpts from Act I in the *Audio CD Library:*
• Disc 17, Track 5

Viewing and Representing
Fine Art Transparencies
The fine art transparencies *The Lovers (Somali Friends)* and *A Young Couple* can be used for enrichment activities after students have read *Romeo and Juliet.* See the *Viewing and Representing Transparencies and Worksheets:*
• Transparencies 18, 19
• Worksheets, pp. 72, 76

Elements of Literature
Shakespearean Theater
For additional instruction on Shakespearean theater, see *Literary Elements:*
• Transparency 17
• Worksheet, p. 52

Resources: Print and Media

Reading
• *Reading Skills and Strategies*
    Selection Skill Lesson, p. 164
• *Graphic Organizers for Active Reading,* p. 64
• *Words to Own,* p. 39
• *Audio CD Library*
    Disc 17, Track 5

Elements of Literature
• *Literary Elements*
    Transparency 17
    Worksheet, p. 52

Writing and Language
• *Daily Oral Grammar*
    Transparency 44

Viewing and Representing
• *Viewing and Representing*
    Fine Art Transparencies 18, 19
    Fine Art Worksheets, pp. 72, 76
• *Visual Connections*
    Videocasstte B, Segment 13

Assessment
• *Formal Assessment,* p. 137
• *Portfolio Management System,* p. 201
• *Test Generator (One-Stop Planner CD-ROM)*

Internet
• go.hrw.com (keyword: LE0 9-13)

Summary ■ ■ ■

The Prologue

The Chorus, played by a single actor, briefly summarizes the plot of the play. The story is set in Verona, Italy. The recent fighting that has broken out between two feuding noble families dooms a pair of young lovers, each the offspring of one of the families. The unfolding of "their death-marked love" is the play's subject; its tragic climax is their untimely deaths, which cause their respective families to resolve the feud.

Act I, Scene 1

On a street in Verona, Sampson and Gregory, servants of Lord Capulet, provoke a fight with two of Lord Montague's servants, Balthasar and Abram. Benvolio, a relative of the Montagues and a friend of Romeo's, enters and stops the fight; but when Tybalt, a relative of the Capulets, enters and insults Benvolio, a general free-for-all ensues. It is stopped by an officer and several citizens. Lord and Lady Capulet and Lord and Lady Montague enter, and the two men exchange angry words. Prince Escalus enters, warns the lords that any further fighting will be punished by death, and dismisses the crowd.

Left alone on stage, the Montagues and Benvolio discuss Romeo's recent strange and lovelorn behavior. After the Montagues exit, Romeo enters and confesses to Benvolio that he is in despair because he loves a young woman, Rosaline, who has sworn herself to a life of chastity. Benvolio advises his friend to forget her and find someone else, but Romeo says that other women only remind him of his beloved.

CHARACTERS

" A pair of star-crossed lovers "

The Montagues

Lord Montague
Lady Montague
Romeo, son of Montague
Benvolio, nephew of Montague and friend of Romeo
Balthasar, servant of Romeo
Abram, servant of Montague

☆

The Capulets

Lord Capulet
Lady Capulet
Juliet, daughter of Capulet
Tybalt, nephew of Lady Capulet
Nurse to Juliet
Peter, servant to the Nurse
Sampson
Gregory } servants of Capulet
An Old Man of the Capulet family

☆

The Others

Prince Escalus, ruler of Verona
Mercutio, a relative of the Prince and friend of Romeo
Friar Laurence, a Franciscan priest
Friar John, another Franciscan priest
Count Paris, a young nobleman, a relative of the Prince
An Apothecary (a druggist)
Page to Paris
Chief Watchman
Three Musicians
An Officer

Citizens of Verona, Relatives of both families, **Maskers, Guards, Watchmen,** and **Attendants**

☆

Scene: Verona and Mantua, cities in northern Italy

734 WILLIAM SHAKESPEARE

Reaching All Students

Struggling Readers

For teaching suggestions, Blackline Masters and Transparencies including Shakespeare's insults, performances, and cracking the text, see the *Reading Skills and Strategies* binder
• Selection Skill Lesson, p. 164

English Language Learners

Have these students watch one of the film versions of the play before reading it to help them visualize the setting and action and understand the main conflicts. Also, read the summary of each scene aloud before assigning it. For other strategies for engaging English language learners with the literature, see
• *Lesson Plans Including Strategies for English-Language Learners*

Advanced Learners

Ask these students to take notes on Shakespeare's use of contrasting images of light and dark, night and day, young and old, and love and hate throughout the play. Have them meet in small groups to discuss how this imagery relates to the play's themes.

THE TRAGEDY OF ROMEO AND JULIET

William Shakespeare

THE PROLOGUE

Enter CHORUS.

Chorus.

Two households, both alike in dignity,° **Ⓐ**
    In fair Verona, where we lay our scene,
From ancient grudge break to new mutiny,
    Where civil blood makes civil hands unclean.° *alliteration*
5 From forth the fatal loins of these two foes
    A pair of star-crossed lovers take their life;
Whose misadventured piteous overthrows
    Do with their death bury their parents' strife.
The fearful passage of their death-marked love,
10   And the continuance of their parents' rage,
Which, but° their children's end, naught could remove, **Ⓑ**
    Is now the two hours' traffic° of our stage;
The which if you with patient ears attend,
What here shall miss, our toil shall strive to mend. **Ⓒ**

[*Exit.*]

Enter SAMPSON *and* GREGORY, *of the house of Capulet,*

---

1. **dignity:** status.

4. That is, where civilians' passions ("civil blood") make their hands unclean (because they have been used for killing).

11. **but:** unless.
12. **traffic:** business.

? 14. *This Prologue is spoken by a single actor called "the chorus." The Prologue welcomes the audience and gives them a taste of the story. What will the "two hours' traffic" of this stage be about? What will happen to the two lovers?*

Ⓐ Elements of Literature
    Exposition
? Where is the play set? [It is set in Verona, a city in what is now northern Italy.] What previous events does the chorus explain to help the audience understand the play's plot? [The chorus explains that there is an "ancient grudge" between two families and that the feud is being reignited.]

Ⓑ Struggling Readers
    Archaic Language/Inverted Word Order
Help students "translate" this line into contemporary English. Explain that *but* means "except," *end* means "death," and *naught* means "nothing." [A contemporary translation might be "Nothing except their children's deaths could end the feud between the two families."]

Ⓒ Reading Skills and Strategies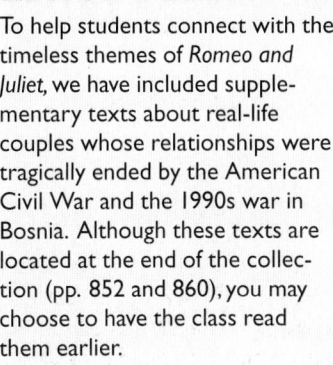
    Reading Shakespeare's Poetry
Point out that the entire prologue is a **sonnet,** a poem of fourteen lines written in rhymed iambic pentameter. The sonnet ends with a couplet and has the rhyme scheme *abab cdcd efef gg*.

Answer to Margin Question
Line 14. The play will be about the continuing conflict between the Montague and Capulet families and the "death-marked love" of Romeo and Juliet. Both Romeo and Juliet will die.

FROM THE EDITOR'S DESK
To help students connect with the timeless themes of *Romeo and Juliet,* we have included supplementary texts about real-life couples whose relationships were tragically ended by the American Civil War and the 1990s war in Bosnia. Although these texts are located at the end of the collection (pp. 852 and 860), you may choose to have the class read them earlier.

Using Students' Strengths

Visual Learners

To help students use prior knowledge in interpreting the play, ask them to share their thoughts on several key words drawn from Act I. List on the board the following words: *feud, parents, infatuation,* and *dreams.* For each word, make a cluster diagram (like the one following) out of the students' responses.

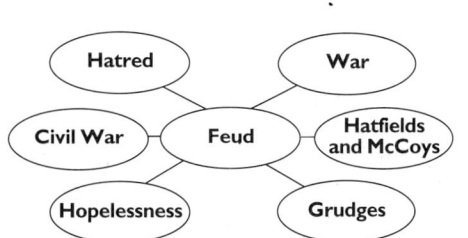

ACT I

Scene 1. *Verona. A public place.*

with swords and bucklers (shields).

Sampson. Gregory, on my word, we'll not carry coals.°
Gregory. No, for then we should be colliers.°
Sampson. I mean, and° we be in choler,° we'll draw.°
Gregory. Ay, while you live, draw your neck out of
5   collar.°
Sampson. I strike quickly, being moved.
Gregory. But thou art not quickly moved to strike.
Sampson. A dog of the house of Montague moves me.
Gregory. To move is to stir, and to be valiant is to stand.
10   Therefore, if thou art moved, thou run'st away.
Sampson. A dog of that house shall move me to stand. I
     will take the wall° of any man or maid of Montague's.
Gregory. That shows thee a weak slave; for the weakest
     goes to the wall.°
15 **Sampson.** 'Tis true; and therefore women, being the
     weaker vessels, are ever thrust to the wall. Therefore I
     will push Montague's men from the wall and thrust his
     maids to the wall.
Gregory. The quarrel is between our masters and us
20   their men.
Sampson. 'Tis all one. I will show myself a tyrant. When
     I have fought with the men, I will be civil with the
     maids—I will cut off their heads.
Gregory. The heads of the maids?
25 **Sampson.** Ay, the heads of the maids or their maiden-
     heads. Take it in what sense thou wilt.
Gregory. They must take it in sense that feel it.
Sampson. Me they shall feel while I am able to stand; and
     'tis known I am a pretty piece of flesh.
30 **Gregory.** 'Tis well thou art not fish; if thou hadst, thou
     hadst been Poor John.° Draw thy tool!° Here comes
     two of the house of Montagues.

[Enter two other servingmen, ABRAM and BALTHASAR.]

Sampson. My naked weapon is out. Quarrel! I will back
     thee.
35 **Gregory.** How? Turn thy back and run?
Sampson. Fear me not.°
Gregory. No, marry. I fear thee!
Sampson. Let us take the law of our sides;° let them

736 **WILLIAM SHAKESPEARE**

A Elements of Literature
Puns
Elizabethans greatly enjoyed puns, especially the rapid-fire exchange of wordplay typical of Shakespeare's comic characters. Have students look for more examples of punning exchanges between characters as they continue to read Act I.

B Elements of Literature
Exposition
? The servants of the house of Capulet are already using insulting language to generalize about members of the Montague family. What does this show about attitudes in the two households? [Even the servants of the two families are ready for a fight.]

Answers to Margin Questions
Stage direction. The servants are probably pretending to fight with imaginary foes, gesturing with their swords and shields.
Stage direction. Instead of attacking, Sampson and Gregory start quarreling with each other; each doubts the other's bravery. Sampson is probably backing away or hiding behind Gregory and pushing him forward.

? **Stage direction:** *The two servants enter, bragging and teasing each other. What actions do you imagine they are engaged in as they cross the city square?*

1. **carry coals:** do dirty work (put up with insults). People often made jokes about men who carted coal.
2. **colliers:** coal dealers (men with dirty jobs). Notice how the servants start making jokes based on words that sound similar (*colliers, choler,* and *collar*).
3. **and:** if. **choler:** anger. **draw:** pull out swords.
5. **collar:** the hangman's noose.

12. **take the wall:** take the best place on the path (which is closest to the wall).
14. **goes to the wall:** is defeated.

31. **Poor John:** kind of salted fish, a poor person's food. **tool:** sword.
? **Stage direction:** *Sampson's and Gregory's swaggering stops when they spy their enemies. How do their next speeches show that they are really cowards? What's Sampson doing when he says "Quarrel! I will back thee"?*

36. **Fear me not:** Do not distrust me.

Professional Notes

The critic Northrop Frye analyzed this scene in his essay "Romeo and Juliet": "The stage direction tells us that servants are on the street armed with swords and bucklers (small shields). Even if you came in late and missed the prologue, you'd know from seeing those servants that all was not well in Verona. Because that means there's going to be a fight. If you let servants swank around like that, fully armed, they're bound to get into fights. So in view of Tudor policy and Queen Elizabeth's personal dislike of duels and brawling, this play would have no trouble with the censor, because it shows the tragic results of the kind of thing that the authorities thoroughly disapproved of anyway.

"The first scene shows Shakespeare in his usual easy command of the situation starting off with a gabble of dialogue that doesn't contribute much to the plot, but gets over the latecomer problem and quiets the audience very quickly because the jokes are bawdy jokes, the kind the audience most wants to hear."

begin.

40 **Gregory.** I will frown as I pass by, and let them take it as
they list.

Sampson. Nay, as they dare. I will bite my thumb° at
them, which is disgrace to them if they bear it.

Abram. Do you bite your thumb at us, sir?

45 **Sampson.** I do bite my thumb, sir.

Abram. Do you bite your thumb at us, sir?

Sampson (*aside to* GREGORY). Is the law of our side if I
say ay?

Gregory (*aside to* SAMPSON). No.

50 **Sampson.** No, sir, I do not bite my thumb at you, sir; but
I bite my thumb, sir.

Gregory. Do you quarrel, sir?

Abram. Quarrel, sir? No, sir.

Sampson. But if you do, sir, I am for you. I serve as good

55 a man as you.

Abram. No better.

Sampson. Well, sir.

[*Enter* BENVOLIO.]

Gregory. Say "better." Here comes one of my master's
kinsmen.

60 **Sampson.** Yes, better, sir.

Abram. You lie.

Sampson. Draw, if you be men. Gregory, remember thy
swashing° blow.

[*They fight.*]

Benvolio.
Part, fools!

65 Put up your swords. You know not what you do.

[*Enter* TYBALT.]

Tybalt.
What, art thou drawn among these heartless hinds?°
Turn thee, Benvolio; look upon thy death.

Benvolio.
I do but keep the peace. Put up thy sword,
Or manage it to part these men with me.

Tybalt.

70 What, drawn, and talk of peace? I hate the word
As I hate hell, all Montagues, and thee.
Have at thee, coward!

[*They fight.*]

C

38. That is, stay on the right side of
the law.

42. bite my thumb: an insulting
gesture.

? **44.** *It takes the Montague
servants some time to speak.
How do their actions show that
these four servants are very wary
of one another?* ③

D

? **58.** *How does Gregory
change when he spots Tybalt
in the distance?* ④

63. swashing: slashing.

? **65.** *What action is Benvolio
involved in here?* ⑤

66. heartless hinds: cowardly
hicks.

E

? **67.** *Sometimes Tybalt's
second line is spoken after
a dramatic silence. Why should
this line demand our attention?* ⑥

? **70.** *This is a key speech.
What is Tybalt's mood? How
is he shown to be opposite in
nature to Benvolio?* ⑦

THE TRAGEDY OF ROMEO AND JULIET, ACT I, SCENE I **737**

C **Reading Skills and Strategies**

Making Inferences

? What are the attitudes of these
characters toward the law? [Possible
response: In spite of their bragging, they
do not want to get into trouble with the
law, which places blame on those who
start fights.]

D **Struggling Readers**

Reading Aloud

To help students follow the escalating
tensions in this section, read the passage aloud. Emphasize the whispered
asides and the fine distinction made by
Sampson between "I do bite my thumb,
sir" and "I do not bite my thumb at
you, sir."

E **Reading Skills
and Strategies**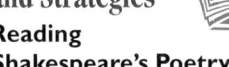

**Reading
Shakespeare's Poetry**

Point out that Shakespeare begins to
use blank verse (unrhymed iambic pentameter) when the aristocratic characters begin to speak. Help students
count the iambs in each line of Tybalt's
and Benvolio's lines. For example, "Pŭt
úp / yoŭr swórds. / Yŏu knów / nŏt
whát / yŏu dó."

Answers to Margin Questions
Line 44. The Montague servants
respond to the weak insults with questions, not with immediate action. The
Capulet servants continue to show
their insecurity in their wary asides
and evasive answers.

Line 58. Tybalt is one of the "master's
kinsmen" referred to here. Assuming
Tybalt will protect them, Gregory now
tells Sampson to issue a real insult
to Abram—that Lord Capulet is a
"better" man than Lord Montague.

Line 65. Benvolio is separating Sampson and Abram, who have started to
fight.

Line 67. Tybalt has drawn his sword
and threatens to kill Benvolio.

Line 70. Tybalt is full of hate and eager
to fight. Benvolio is a peacemaker.

Assessing Learning

Ongoing Assessment

You can use the margin questions in the pupil's
edition as a convenient way to informally monitor students' comprehension of each scene.
After students have read the scene independently, have pairs or small groups work together
to answer the questions or to use the questions
as the basis for discussion.

A Reading Skills and Strategies
Comparing and Contrasting

? How are the responses of Lady Capulet and Lady Montague different?
[Possible response: Lady Capulet is criticizing her husband for not being in good enough physical condition to fight, while Lady Montague is discouraging her husband because she believes he is wrong to go looking for a fight.]

B Reading Skills and Strategies

Reading Shakespeare's Poetry

Have students analyze the Prince's speech to find end-stopped lines and run-on lines. Then, have a student read the speech aloud, pausing only at the end of end-stopped lines.

Answers to Margin Questions

Line 77. Lady Capulet is pointing out to her husband that he is too old and out of shape to fight.

Line 80. Lady Montague is restraining her husband; she does not want him involved in a brawl.

Stage direction. The prince should enter with ceremony and appear to be in control. You can tell he is ignored at first because he asks, "Will they not hear?"

Line 89. The brawlers have thrown down their weapons and are listening to the prince.

Line 104. Three civil disturbances have resulted from the conflict between the Capulets and the Montagues. The prince decrees that the punishment for any future fighting will be death.

[*Enter an* OFFICER, *and three or four* CITIZENS *with clubs, bills, and partisans, or spears.*]

Officer. Clubs, bills, and partisans! Strike! Beat them
75   down! Down with the Capulets! Down with the Montagues!

[*Enter old* CAPULET, *in his gown, and his wife,* LADY CAPULET.]

Capulet.
      What noise is this? Give me my long sword, ho!
Lady Capulet.
      A crutch, a crutch! Why call you for a sword?
Capulet.
      My sword, I say! Old Montague is come
      And flourishes his blade in spite of° me.

[*Enter old* MONTAGUE *and his wife,* LADY MONTAGUE.]

Montague.
80   Thou villain Capulet!—Hold me not; let me go.
Lady Montague.
      Thou shalt not stir one foot to seek a foe.

[*Enter* PRINCE ESCALUS, *with his* TRAIN.]

Prince.
      Rebellious subjects, enemies to peace,
      Profaners of this neighbor-stainèd steel—
      Will they not hear? What, ho! You men, you beasts,
85   That quench the fire of your pernicious rage
      With purple fountains issuing from your veins!
      On pain of torture, from those bloody hands
      Throw your mistempered° weapons to the ground
      And hear the sentence of your movèd prince.
90   Three civil brawls, bred of an airy° word
      By thee, old Capulet, and Montague,
      Have thrice disturbed the quiet of our streets
      And made Verona's ancient citizens
      Cast by their grave beseeming° ornaments
95   To wield old partisans, in hands as old,
      Cankered with peace, to part your cankered° hate.
      If ever you disturb our streets again,
      Your lives shall pay the forfeit of the peace.
      For this time all the rest depart away.
100   You, Capulet, shall go along with me;
      And, Montague, come you this afternoon,
      To know our farther pleasure in this case,
      To old Freetown, our common judgment place.
      Once more, on pain of death, all men depart.

? **77.** *In the midst of the tension over Tybalt, we have a comic touch. Why is Lady Capulet talking about crutches?*
79. in spite of: in defiance of.

? **80.** *Who is holding Montague back?*

? *Stage direction:* *If you were directing this play, how would you stage the entrance of the prince? His dignified procession must contrast with the bloody rioting. How do you know from the next speech that the prince is at first ignored by the brawlers?*

88. mistempered: used with bad temper.
? **89.** *There is a dramatic pause before the next line is spoken. What are the brawlers doing now?*
90. airy: light or harmless.

94. grave beseeming: dignified, as they should be.

96. cankered: The first *cankered* means "rusted" (from lack of use in peaceful times); the second means "diseased," like a canker, a running sore.

? **104.** *What has been happening in Verona? What is the prince's warning?*

Getting Students Involved

Cooperative Learning

Design a Formal Decree. Divide the class into small groups. Ask each group to design and write a formal decree that could have been written by Prince Escalus, warning quarreling factions that those who do not follow his orders will "pay the forfeit of the peace." Each group member can contribute a few lines to the decree. Remind students to imitate Shakespeare's language and style. They can decorate their decrees with official seals and perhaps write them in a decorative script, such as calligraphy.

Organize a Festival. Ask all ninth-grade English classes to sponsor a Shakespeare festival. Participants may wear Elizabethan-inspired costumes and greet one another with appropriate phrases, such as "Good morrow." Assign small groups of students to act out scenes from Shakespeare's plays, provide appropriate music, and prepare food popular in Elizabethan England. Assign pairs of students to greet visitors, decorate the classroom, write invitations, and write press releases publicizing the event. You may also want to invite students from other grades. Videotape the proceeding for evaluation and for future enjoyment.

> ## " Throw your mistempered weapons
> to the ground. . . . "

[*Exeunt all but* MONTAGUE, LADY MONTAGUE, *and* BENVOLIO.]

Montague.
105   Who set this ancient quarrel new abroach?°
       Speak, nephew, were you by when it began?

Benvolio.
       Here were the servants of your adversary
       And yours, close fighting ere I did approach.
       I drew to part them. In the instant came
110   The fiery Tybalt, with his sword prepared,
       Which, as he breathed defiance to my ears,
       He swung about his head and cut the winds,
       Who, nothing hurt withal, hissed him in scorn.
       While we were interchanging thrusts and blows,
115   Came more and more, and fought on part and part,°
       Till the prince came, who parted either part.

Lady Montague.
       O, where is Romeo? Saw you him today?
       Right glad I am he was not at this fray.

Benvolio.
       Madam, an hour before the worshiped sun
120   Peered forth the golden window of the East,
       A troubled mind drave me to walk abroad;
       Where, underneath the grove of sycamore
       That westward rooteth from this city side,
       So early walking did I see your son.
125   Towards him I made, but he was ware° of me
       And stole into the covert of the wood.
       I, measuring his affections by my own,
       Which then most sought where most might not be
           found,°
       Being one too many by my weary self,
130   Pursued my humor not pursuing his,
       And gladly shunned who gladly fled from me.

Montague.
       Many a morning hath he there been seen,
       With tears augmenting the fresh morning's dew,
       Adding to clouds more clouds with his deep sighs;
135   But all so soon as the all-cheering sun

105. new abroach: newly opened.

115. on part and part: some on one side, some on the other.

? **118.** *For the first time, Romeo is mentioned, and by his mother, whose parental concern is accented by a rhyme. Lady Montague does not say anything else in this scene. What do you imagine she is doing while her husband and Benvolio discuss her son?*

(13)

125. ware: aware.

128. He sought a place where no one could be found. (He wanted to be alone.)

THE TRAGEDY OF ROMEO AND JULIET, ACT I, SCENE I   739

C **Critical Thinking**
Making Judgments
? Does Benvolio seem to be telling the truth about what happened? [Possible responses: Yes, he has given an accurate summary of the street brawl; yes, but he is leaving out details that would show how willing most of the Montague people were to fight.]

D **Reading Skills and Strategies**
Drawing Conclusions
? How might you describe Lady Montague's personality at this point? [Possible responses: She seems anxious and worried about her son; she is a concerned mother.]

E **Elements of Literature**
Exposition
? What main character is talked about here for the first time? [Romeo] What do we learn about him? [He is acting strangely; he wants to be alone and is evading his friend.]

Answer to Margin Question
Line 118. Lady Montague might be listening carefully to her husband and Benvolio discuss Romeo, or she might pace behind the two men, looking for Romeo.

Skill Link

Irregular Verbs
Point out that Benvolio's speech on this page contains many irregular verbs, most of the principal parts of which have remained the same since Shakespeare's time. Have students construct a chart that lists the past tense and past participle of the following verbs:

Present Tense	Past Tense	Past Participle
drive	[drove]	[driven]
do	[did]	[done]
make	[made]	[made]
steal	[stole]	[stolen]
seek	[sought]	[sought]
find	[found]	[found]
flee	[fled]	[fled]

For additional practice with irregular verbs, see pp. 998–1000 of the Language Handbook.

T739

Reading Skills and Strategies

How to Read Shakespeare

This feature focuses on strategies for reading a Shakespeare play. It defines the poetic forms and terms that are essential for understanding and appreciating the play: blank verse, iambic meter, iambic pentameter, couplets, and end-stopped and run-on lines. Suggestions are given for reading the play aloud—hearing the play often helps students to understand it better. You might want to play the excerpts provided in the *Audio CD Library*.

Ⓐ Elements of Literature

Imagery

Point out that images of darkness and light play an important part in this love story. At this point, Romeo's yearning for darkness and solitude recalls the Elizabethan stereotype of the courtly lover, whose affection is typically unrequited.

Answer to Margin Question

Line 143. Romeo rises early to walk by himself and then shuts himself in his room at daybreak. He is moody and tearful, and he will not talk to anyone about his sorrow.

The Poetry

Whatever Shakespeare learned of rhetoric, or language, in grammar school, he parades with relish in *Romeo and Juliet*. He is obviously having a fine time here with puns and wordplay and all the other variations he can ring on the English language.

Romeo and Juliet is written in both prose and poetry. Prose is for the most part spoken by the common people and occasionally by Mercutio when he is joking. Most of the other characters speak in poetry.

Blank verse. The poetry is largely written in unrhymed iambic pentameter. In **iambic meter** each unstressed syllable is followed by a stressed syllable, as in the word *prefér*. In **iambic pentameter** there are five of these iambic units in each line. Unrhymed iambic pentameter is called **blank verse**. The word *blank* just means that there is no rhyme at the end of lines.

Read aloud this perfect example of iambic pentameter, spoken by Romeo. The syllables marked (′) should be stressed.

But soft! What light through yonder window breaks?

Couplets. When Shakespeare uses rhymes, he generally uses **couplets,** two consecutive lines of poetry that rhyme. The couplets often punctuate a character's exit or signal the end of a scene. Read aloud Juliet's exit line from the balcony.

Good night, good night! Parting is such sweet sorrow
That I shall say good night till it be morrow.

Reading the lines. We have all heard people ruin a good poem by mechanically pausing at the end of each line, whether or not the meaning of the line called for such a pause. (Maxwell Anderson, who wrote verse plays, had his plays typed as though they were prose, so that actors would not be tempted to pause at the end of

Ⓐ
Should in the farthest East begin to draw
The shady curtains from Aurora's° bed,
Away from light steals home my heavy° son
And private in his chamber pens himself,
140   Shuts up his windows, locks fair daylight out,
And makes himself an artificial night.
Black and portentous must this humor prove
Unless good counsel may the cause remove.
Benvolio.
My noble uncle, do you know the cause?
Montague.
145   I neither know it nor can learn of him.
Benvolio.
Have you importuned° him by any means?
Montague.
Both by myself and many other friends;
But he, his own affections' counselor,
Is to himself—I will not say how true—
150   But to himself so secret and so close,

740 WILLIAM SHAKESPEARE

137. Aurora is goddess of the dawn.
138. heavy: heavy-hearted.

? 143. *Romeo has been described by his father and his friend. What do we know of him so far?*

146. importuned: questioned.

Skill Link

Reading Shakespeare's Poetry

Either before reading the play or after students have read Act I, Scene I, take time to read aloud and discuss the feature at the top of pp. 740–741. It teaches students to recognize, understand, and appreciate the structures of Shakespeare's poetry: iambic pentameter, blank verse, rhymed couplets, end-stopped lines, and run-on lines.

When students have grasped the rhythm of iambic pentameter, point out that this poetic measure is also used in the sonnet form. In the sonnet, there are fourteen lines of iambic pentameter, and they are rhymed in a specific pattern, as in the Prologue on p. 735.

Activity

Have students turn to "The Seven Ages of Man" on p. 536 to analyze another example of Shakespeare's use of blank verse, including end-stopped and run-on lines. (The poem is taken from Shakespeare's comedy *As You Like It.*)

Advanced learners may also wish to locate and analyze examples of modern poems that use blank verse. Suggest some well-known poems of Robert Frost: "Mending Wall," "Birches," and "The Death of the Hired Man." They will find "The Death of the Hired Man" especially relevant because in it Frost, like Shakespeare, uses blank verse in dramatic dialogue.

each line. Consider using this technique when you stage a scene for the Speaking and Listening Workshop on page 864.)

Lines of poetry are either end-stopped lines or run-on lines. An **end-stopped line** has some punctuation at its end. A **run-on line** has no punctuation at its end. In a run-on line, the meaning is always completed in the line or lines that follow.

Try reading aloud this passage from Act II, Scene 2, where Juliet speaks in end-stopped lines—lines ending with punctuation that requires her to pause:

> O, Romeo, Romeo! Wherefore art thou Romeo?
> Deny thy father and refuse thy name;
> Or, if thou wilt not, be but sworn my love,
> And I'll no longer be a Capulet.

But Romeo's speech in the same scene has many run-on lines. Read these lines aloud; where does Romeo pause?

> The brightness of her cheek would shame those stars
> As daylight doth a lamp; her eyes in heaven
> Would through the airy region stream so bright
> That birds would sing and think it were not night.

The glory of *Romeo and Juliet* is its poetry and its theatricality. The play is fast moving, and the poetry suits the story of young people dealing with a matter very important to them— passionate, once-in-a-lifetime love.

"Be but sworn my love . . ."

B **Critical Thinking**

Analyzing Character

? What do these lines reveal about Lord Montague's character? [Sample responses: He wonders what is on his son's mind because he wants to help him; he is an attentive, concerned, and nonjudgmental parent.]

C **Reading Skills and Strategies**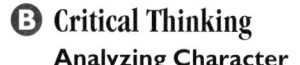

Reading Shakespeare's Poetry

? What purpose do these two sets of couplets serve? [They signal the exit of Romeo's parents and the beginning of a new part of the scene, featuring Romeo and Benvolio.]

Answers to Margin Questions
Stage direction. Romeo should be introverted and distracted, concentrating on his feelings for Rosaline.
Line 161. Romeo should be uninterested in Benvolio's conversation.

> So far from sounding° and discovery,
> As is the bud bit with an envious° worm
> Ere he can spread his sweet leaves to the air
> Or dedicate his beauty to the sun.
> 155 Could we but learn from whence his sorrows grow, **B**
> We would as willingly give cure as know.
>
> [*Enter* ROMEO.]
>
> **Benvolio.**
> See, where he comes. So please you step aside;
> I'll know his grievance, or be much denied.
> **Montague.**
> I would thou wert so happy° by the stay
> 160 To hear true shrift.° Come, madam, let's away. **C**
>
> [*Exeunt* MONTAGUE *and* LADY MONTAGUE.]
>
> **Benvolio.**
> Good morrow, cousin.
> **Romeo.**   Is the day so young?

151. So far from sounding: so far from being sounded out for his mood (as a river is sounded for its depth).
152. envious: evil.

? *Stage direction: Romeo at first doesn't see his parents or Benvolio. How do you think he would be acting as he enters?* (15)

159. happy: lucky.
160. shrift: confession.

? *161. Benvolio is trying to be casual. What attitude should Romeo convey by his answer to Benvolio's cheery greeting?* (16)

THE TRAGEDY OF ROMEO AND JULIET, ACT I, SCENE 1   741

Crossing the Curriculum

Music

Point out that as Renaissance-era English was different from today's English, the music of the Renaissance was quite different from contemporary music. Play recordings of music composed by William Byrd, Renaissance folk songs, or liturgical music of the time. You can play the music as students enter or leave the classroom or as they engage in creative activities related to the collection.

Architecture

Some students may be interested in how Elizabethan theaters looked. Have them work in small groups to research additional information about the Globe Theater. Topics might include outside appearance; seating arrangements; mechanical devices, such as trapdoors; or how sound effects were made. Students should create a visual aid to accompany a report to the class.

Benvolio.
But new struck nine.

Romeo.   Ay me! Sad hours seem long.
Was that my father that went hence so fast?

Benvolio.
It was. What sadness lengthens Romeo's hours?

Romeo.
165   Not having that which having makes them short.

Benvolio. In love?

Romeo. Out——

Benvolio. Of love?

Romeo.
Out of her favor where I am in love.

Benvolio.
170   Alas that love, so gentle in his view,°
Should be so tyrannous and rough in proof!°

Romeo.
Alas that love, whose view is muffled still,°
Should without eyes see pathways to his will!
Where shall we dine? O me! What fray was here?
175   Yet tell me not, for I have heard it all.
Here's much to do with hate, but more with love.°
Why then, O brawling love, O loving hate,
O anything, of nothing first created!
O heavy lightness, serious vanity,
180   Misshapen chaos of well-seeming forms,
Feather of lead, bright smoke, cold fire, sick health,
Still-waking sleep, that is not what it is!
This love feel I, that feel no love in this.
Dost thou not laugh?

> ❝ *Here's much to do with hate,*
> *but more with love.* ❞

Benvolio.   No, coz,° I rather weep.

Romeo.
Good heart, at what?

185   **Benvolio.**   At thy good heart's oppression.

Romeo.
Why, such is love's transgression.
Griefs of mine own lie heavy in my breast,
Which thou wilt propagate,° to have it prest°
With more of thine. This love that thou hast shown
190   Doth add more grief to too much of mine own.

742 WILLIAM SHAKESPEARE

Getting Students Involved

The Varieties of Love. Point out to students that the play contains three different forms of love: (1) Romeo's unrequited love for Rosaline, which follows the convention of courtly love, in which the lover's mistress is proud and cruel and repels all advances; (2) the real love between Romeo and Juliet, the kind of love that culminates in marriage; and (3) a coarse and earthy kind of love, as epitomized by Mercutio and by the nurse. Have students compare Romeo's comments about adult love in this scene with the image of the lover in Shakespeare's "The Seven Ages of Man," on p. 536.

METAPHOR

Love is a smoke made with the fume of sighs;
Being purged, a fire sparkling in lovers' eyes;
Being vexed, a sea nourished with loving tears.
What is it else? A madness most discreet,°
195   A choking gall, and a preserving sweet.
Farewell, my coz.

Benvolio.   Soft!° I will go along.
And if you leave me so, you do me wrong.

Romeo.
Tut! I have lost myself; I am not here;
This is not Romeo, he's some other where.

Benvolio.
200   Tell me in sadness,° who is that you love?

Romeo.
What, shall I groan and tell thee?

Benvolio.   Groan? Why, no;
But sadly tell me who.

Romeo.
Bid a sick man in sadness make his will.
Ah, word ill urged to one that is so ill!
205   In sadness, cousin, I do love a woman.

Benvolio.
I aimed so near when I supposed you loved.

Romeo.
A right good markman. And she's fair I love.

Benvolio.
A right fair mark, fair coz, is soonest hit.

Romeo.
Well, in that hit you miss. She'll not be hit
210   With Cupid's arrow. She hath Dian's wit,°
And, in strong proof° of chastity well armed,
From Love's weak childish bow she lives uncharmed.
She will not stay° the siege of loving terms,
Nor bide th' encounter of assailing eyes,
215   Nor ope her lap to saint-seducing gold.°
O, she is rich in beauty; only poor
That, when she dies, with beauty dies her store.°

Benvolio.
Then she hath sworn that she will still live chaste?

Romeo.
She hath, and in that sparing makes huge waste;
220   For beauty, starved with her severity,
Cuts beauty off from all posterity.
She is too fair, too wise, wisely too fair,
To merit bliss° by making me despair.
She hath forsworn to love, and in that vow

---

194. discreet: discriminating.

? 195. *Romeo refuses to reveal more about his troubles and suggests to Benvolio that he is driven mad by love. What things does he compare love to, before he tries to get away from Benvolio?*

196. Soft!: Wait!

200. sadness: seriousness.

210. Dian's wit: the cunning of Diana, the goddess of chastity, who was not interested in men.
211. proof: armor.
213. stay: submit to.

215. Nor ope . . . gold: In myth, the god Zeus visited Danae in the form of a shower of gold, and Danae bore Zeus a son.
217. when she dies . . . her store: Her store of beauty dies with her, since she'll have no children.

223. bliss: heaven.

THE TRAGEDY OF ROMEO AND JULIET, ACT I, SCENE I   **743**

C Reading Skills and Strategies

Reading Shakespeare's Poetry

? Have a student read aloud Romeo's comments about love. Are the lines written in blank verse or in couplets? [couplets] Are the lines end-stopped or run-on? [end-stopped] Remind students that the reader should pause at the end of end-stopped lines. Ask another volunteer to read the lines aloud so that students can appreciate the poetic elements.

D English Language Learners

Allusions

These students may not be familiar with this allusion to Cupid. Tell them that in Roman mythology, Cupid is the god of love. Usually represented as a winged boy with bow and arrow, Cupid is said to cause people to fall in love by striking them with his arrows. Point out that Cupid's image is commonly used on Valentine's Day.

E Elements of Literature

Exposition

? According to Romeo, why does the young woman he is in love with refuse him? [She has vowed to remain chaste, that is, to refuse all lovers and never marry.]

Answer to Margin Question
Line 195. Romeo uses figurative language to compare love to smoke, fire, the sea, madness, gall (meaning "bile" or "bitterness"), and a sweet.

Reaching All Students

Struggling Readers
To help students develop facility with Elizabethan blank verse, pair strong readers with those who find the reading more difficult. Have the partners read through short segments of the play, stopping to discuss the meaning and significance of each segment before moving on to the next. Have struggling readers take notes on passages that provide significant background information or that move the plot forward.

English Language Learners
You may need to pause for frequent, informal check tests to ensure that English language learners are comprehending the text. Especially after long monologues or dialogues, have them stop to answer these questions:
• Who is speaking?
• What is the character speaking about?
• Whom is the character speaking to?
• What does the monologue or dialogue tell me about the character(s)?

Advanced Learners
These students may wish to explore the problems that scholars encounter when trying to determine the authorship of plays written during this time period. Have them research how the lack of copyright laws in Elizabethan England makes it difficult to determine the original writer of some Elizabethan plays. Have them offer their own suggestions of ways that Shakespeare and other playwrights might have ensured that their work was not plagiarized.

T743

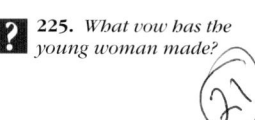

A Reading Skills and Strategies
Drawing Conclusions

? Based on his response, how much time does Romeo spend thinking about the young woman he loves? [He thinks about her all of the time.]

Answers to Margin Questions
Line 225. The young woman, Rosaline, has made a vow of chastity.
Line 237. Romeo says that looking at other women will only remind him of Rosaline's superior beauty.
Line 239. Students might say the audience would feel that Benvolio is a sympathetic, devoted, levelheaded friend who wants to help Romeo forget his unfulfilled love for Rosaline.

Summary ■ ■

Act I, Scene 2
Count Paris asks Lord Capulet for permission to marry his daughter, Juliet. Capulet hesitates because he feels that Juliet, not quite fourteen, is too young for marriage. He relents, however, advising Paris that he must win Juliet's heart, for Capulet has agreed to let his daughter have some degree of choice in choosing the man she will marry. Capulet invites Paris to a feast that he is giving that evening. He hands his servant a list of the names of the people to be invited and exits with Paris. The illiterate servant is at a loss, and when Romeo and Benvolio enter, he asks them for help. Romeo reads the guest list and discovers that Rosaline, Capulet's niece, has been invited. Benvolio, hoping his friend will fall in love with someone else, convinces Romeo that they should "crash" the party.

B Cultural Connections

? At what age does Lord Capulet consider it proper for Juliet to marry? [sixteen] Remind students that attitudes regarding the proper age for marrying and starting a family vary across cultures and throughout history. During Elizabethan times, life expectancy was much shorter than it is today, so people usually married at a younger age.

---

225   Do I live dead that live to tell it now.
Benvolio.
   Be ruled by me; forget to think of her.
A **Romeo.**
   O, teach me how I should forget to think!
Benvolio.
   By giving liberty unto thine eyes.
   Examine other beauties.
Romeo.   'Tis the way
230   To call hers, exquisite, in question° more.
   These happy masks° that kiss fair ladies' brows,
   Being black, put us in mind they hide the fair.
   He that is strucken blind cannot forget
   The precious treasure of his eyesight lost.
235   Show me a mistress that is passing fair:
   What doth her beauty serve but as a note
   Where I may read who passed that passing fair?
   Farewell. Thou canst not teach me to forget.
Benvolio.
   I'll pay that doctrine, or else die in debt.°

                                        [*Exeunt.*]

Scene 2. *A street.*

Enter CAPULET, COUNT PARIS, *and the clown, his* SERVANT.

Capulet.
   But Montague is bound° as well as I,
   In penalty alike; and 'tis not hard, I think,
   For men so old as we to keep the peace.
Paris.
   Of honorable reckoning° are you both,
5   And pity 'tis you lived at odds so long.
   But now, my lord, what say you to my suit?
Capulet.
   But saying o'er what I have said before:
B   My child is yet a stranger in the world,
   She hath not seen the change of fourteen years;
10   Let two more summers wither in their pride
   Ere we may think her ripe to be a bride.

744 WILLIAM SHAKESPEARE

? **225.** *What vow has the young woman made?*

230. call . . . in question: bring her beauty to mind.
231. masks: Women often wore masks to protect their faces from the sun.

? **237.** *Why won't looking at other women help Romeo?*

239. or else die in debt: or die trying.
? **239.** *Benvolio can exit here as if he is running after Romeo. The pair will reenter later, Romeo still being pursued. How would the audience feel about Benvolio?*

1. is bound: is pledged to keep the peace.

4. reckoning: reputation.

Crossing the Curriculum

History
To help students put the writings of William Shakespeare in historical context, ask them to create a time line of notable historical events. Students can use a history textbook or an encyclopedia to locate the dates and descriptions of the following events and place them on a time line in chronological order:

Battle of Hastings [1066]
Marco Polo travels in Asia [1271–1295]
Birth of English poet Geoffrey Chaucer [1340]
Birth of Nicolaus Copernicus [1473]
Birth of Ferdinand Magellan [1480]
Christopher Columbus first sails the Atlantic [1492]
Birth of Galileo Galilei [1564]
Birth of Sir Isaac Newton [1642]

Paris.
Younger than she are happy mothers made.
Capulet.
And too soon marred are those so early made.
Earth hath swallowed all my hopes but she;
15 She is the hopeful lady of my earth.
But woo her, gentle Paris, get her heart;
My will to her consent is but a part.
And she agreed, within her scope of choice°
Lies my consent and fair according° voice.
20 This night I hold an old accustomed° feast,
Whereto I have invited many a guest,
Such as I love; and you among the store,
One more, most welcome, makes my number more.
At my poor house look to behold this night
25 Earth-treading stars° that make dark heaven light.
Such comfort as do lusty young men feel
When well-apparelled April on the heel
Of limping winter treads, even such delight
Among fresh fennel° buds shall you this night
30 Inherit° at my house. Hear all, all see,
And like her most whose merit most shall be;
Which, on more view of many, mine, being one,
May stand in number,° though in reck'ning none.°
Come, go with me.

> **" Earth hath swallowed all my hopes but she;
> She is the hopeful lady of my earth. "**

[*To* SERVANT, *giving him a paper.*]

Go, sirrah, trudge about
35 Through fair Verona; find those persons out
Whose names are written there, and to them say
My house and welcome on their pleasure stay.°

[*Exit with* PARIS.]

Servant. Find them out whose names are written here?
It is written that the shoemaker should meddle with
40 his yard and the tailor with his last, the fisher
with his pencil and the painter with his nets;° but I
am sent to find those persons whose names are here
writ, and can never find° what names the writing

---

12. *Paris is very much at ease with old Capulet and more composed than the lovesick Romeo we just saw. What does Paris want?* (24)

15. *Why doesn't Capulet want his daughter to marry right away? How is Capulet now different from the man who drew his sword in Scene 1?* (25)

18. within her scope of choice: among all she can choose from.
19. according: agreeing.
20. accustomed: traditional.

25. Earth-treading stars: that is, young girls.

29. fennel: an herb. Capulet compares the young girls to fennel flowers.
30. Inherit: have.

33. stand in number: be one of the crowd (of girls). **though in reck'ning none:** though none will be worth more than Juliet is.

34. *Capulet can be played many ways by actors. Some play him here as a loving, considerate father. Other actors interpret him as a man who chiefly wants a socially advantageous marriage for his daughter. How would you play this scene?* (26)
37. stay: wait.
38. *Like the other servants, this one plays for comedy. He can't read or write. How should he show his bewilderment?* (27)
39–41. shoemaker . . . nets: The servant is quoting mixed-up proverbs. He's trying to say that people should attend to what they do best.
43. find: understand.

C Reading Skills and Strategies
Reading Shakespeare's Poetry
? Have a volunteer read Capulet's speech aloud. When does the speech switch from blank verse to couplets? [at l. 16] Point out the run-on lines 26–30 (up to the period), and give several volunteers a chance to read them without pauses so that they sound conversational.

Answers to Margin Questions
Line 12. Paris wants to marry Capulet's daughter, Juliet.
Line 15. Capulet believes that Juliet, not yet fourteen, is too young to marry; she is his only living child, and he fears losing her to Paris.
Capulet shows himself to be reasonable, not quick-tempered, as he was in Scene 1. He is desirous of peace, a loving father, and a sociable, generous man.
Line 34. Responses may vary. Some students may observe that Capulet could have conflicting motives.
Line 38. The servant could use exaggerated gestures, such as shrugging, wringing his hands, and waving his arms.

THE TRAGEDY OF ROMEO AND JULIET, ACT I, SCENE 2 **745**

Getting Students Involved

Youth vs. Age. Explain to students that Act I sets up an opposition between youth and age. Have students write a short essay contrasting Lord Capulet, who embodies the characteristics of older people, and Romeo, who epitomizes the attitudes of youth. Ask students to give examples showing how the actions and statements of each character represent either youth or age. Invite students to read their essays to the class.

? What advice is Benvolio trying to give Romeo here? [Sample responses: If you let yourself fall in love with someone else, you won't feel the pain of your first love; stay lovesick if you want, but pick someone else to concentrate on.]

B Elements of Literature
Rising Action
Point out that this scene brings a new complication to the plot. Through sheer coincidence, the illiterate Capulet servant has come upon two Montagues and asked them to read the list of guests. As a result, Romeo finds out that his beloved, Rosaline, is to be at the Capulet party that evening.

Answers to Margin Questions
Line 45. Romeo speaks sarcastically about medicines used for physical injuries and makes the point that no medicine can assuage his suffering.
Line 57. Romeo mocks the servant, but gently, and offers to help him. Benvolio is no doubt amused, appreciating the wit that the servant cannot.
Line 71. Romeo might read the list of names with mockery or with lack of interest until he gets to Rosaline's name. Then his voice could betray his excitement. Whether he asks the question casually or sharply, Romeo should convey his ulterior motive: He wants to know where Rosaline will be.

---

45   person hath here writ. I must to the learned. In good time!°

[*Enter* BENVOLIO *and* ROMEO.]

Benvolio.
   Tut, man, one fire burns out another's burning;
     One pain is less'ned by another's anguish;
   Turn giddy, and be help by backward turning;°
     One desperate grief cures with another's languish.
50   **A**   Take thou some new infection to thy eye,
   And the rank poison of the old will die.
Romeo.
   Your plantain leaf is excellent for that.—
Benvolio.
   For what, I pray thee?
Romeo.   For your broken° shin.
Benvolio.
   Why, Romeo, art thou mad?
Romeo.
55   Not mad, but bound more than a madman is;
   Shut up in prison, kept without my food,
   Whipped and tormented and—God-den,° good fellow.
   Servant. God gi' go-den. I pray, sir, can you read?
   Romeo.
   Ay, mine own fortune in my misery.
60   **Servant.** Perhaps you have learned it without book. But, I pray, can you read anything you see?
   Romeo.
   Ay, if I know the letters and the language.
   Servant. Ye say honestly. Rest you merry.
B **Romeo.** Stay, fellow; I can read.

[*He reads the letter.*]

65   "Signior Martino and his wife and daughters;
   County Anselm and his beauteous sisters;
   The lady widow of Vitruvio;
   Signior Placentio and his lovely nieces;
   Mercutio and his brother Valentine;
70   Mine uncle Capulet, his wife and daughters;
   My fair niece Rosaline; Livia;
   Signior Valentio and his cousin Tybalt;
   Lucio and the lively Helena."
   A fair assembly. Whither should they come?
75   **Servant.** Up.
   Romeo. Whither? To supper?
   Servant. To our house.
   Romeo. Whose house?
   Servant. My master's.

746 WILLIAM SHAKESPEARE

44–45. In good time!: Just in time!
? **45.** *The servant looks up from the note to see the young gentlemen enter. He now tries to get them to read the note, while one chases the other across the stage. How do Romeo's comments in the next conversation show that he is trying to change the subject?*
48. be help by backward turning: be helped by turning in the opposite direction.

53. broken: scratched.

57. God-den: good evening.
? **57.** *Romeo turns to get away and runs into the servant, who has been listening to them in stupefied silence. How should the two gentlemen treat the servant in this little encounter?*

? **71.** *Rosaline, Capulet's niece, is the woman Romeo is in love with. Some actors read this line to betray to the audience Romeo's secret. How would you have Romeo read this letter? How would he ask his question?*

Crossing the Curriculum

History
Have students research education during the Renaissance, particularly in Elizabethan England. How widespread was the ability to read and write? What differences in education prevailed between the upper and lower classes of society?

Theater Arts
Students particularly interested in the staging of Elizabethan plays may wish to explore how social class and status were revealed by costuming. In this brief scene, for example, how would the clothing of the illiterate servant contrast with that of the two young noblemen, Benvolio and Romeo? At the evening party, how would the dress of female servants contrast with that of female guests?

Romeo.

80 Indeed I should have asked you that before.

Servant. Now I'll tell you without asking. My master is
the great rich Capulet; and if you be not of the house of
Montagues, I pray come and crush a cup of wine. Rest
you merry.

[*Exit.*]

Benvolio.

85 At this same ancient° feast of Capulet's
Sups the fair Rosaline whom thou so loves;
With all the admirèd beauties of Verona.
Go thither, and with unattainted° eye
Compare her face with some that I shall show,

90 And I will make thee think thy swan a crow. *Worships her*

Romeo.

When the devout religion of mine eye
Maintains such falsehood, then turn tears to fires;
And these, who, often drowned, could never die,
Transparent heretics,° be burnt for liars!

95 One fairer than my love? The all-seeing sun
Ne'er saw her match since first the world begun.

Benvolio.

Tut! you saw her fair, none else being by,
Herself poised° with herself in either eye;
But in that crystal scales° let there be weighed

100 Your lady's love against some other maid
That I will show you shining at this feast,
And she shall scant° show well that now seems best.

Romeo.

I'll go along, no such sight to be shown,
But to rejoice in splendor of mine own.

[*Exeunt.*]

---

85. ancient: old; established by
an old custom.

88. unattainted: untainted (by
prejudice).

? **90.** *What does Benvolio say
to lure Romeo to the party?* ㉛

94. Transparent heretics:
His eyes would be easily "seen
through"—they would betray the
truth.

98. poised: balanced (for
comparison).
99. crystal scales: Romeo's eyes.

102. scant: scarcely.

? **104.** *If we know from the letter that Rosaline is to be at
the party and that she is the one
Romeo loves, we know why Romeo
decides to go to Capulet's. Actors
usually say these lines to indicate
that the decision to go is crucial
and fateful. What mood is Romeo
in?* ㉜

**❝One fairer than my love? The
all-seeing sun
Ne'er saw her match since
first the world begun. ❞**

Dramatic Irony
The servant has no idea he is speaking
to the only son of Lord Montague. But
Romeo, Benvolio, and the audience
are aware of the irony of the servant's
revelation.

D **Reading Skills
and Strategies**

**Reading
Shakespeare's Poetry**

? Have a pair of students read aloud
the dialogue between Benvolio and
Romeo. Point out that Benvolio's first
speech begins in blank verse and ends
in a couplet. Romeo's speech has the
rhyme scheme *ababcc*. Benvolio's next
speech is in couplets, as are Romeo's
parting lines. What is significant about
the change from blank to rhymed
verse? [Rhyme usually signals the end of
a scene or a character's exit. It serves
both purposes here.]

Answers to Margin Questions
Line 90. Benvolio claims that other
beautiful young women at the party
will make Rosaline look like a crow in
comparison.
Line 104. Romeo is hopeful, excited,
and optimistic.

THE TRAGEDY OF ROMEO AND JULIET, ACT I, SCENE 2 **747**

Summary ■ ■

Act I, Scene 3

Lady Capulet asks Juliet's nurse to summon Juliet, who subsequently enters. Her initial address to her mother shows that she is submissive and obedient. The nurse rambles on, telling a story about Juliet as a child. Lady Capulet tells the nurse to be quiet and then tells Juliet of Paris's marriage offer, asking her daughter to consider his proposal. Both the mother and the nurse praise Paris's appearance, and Juliet dutifully agrees to her mother's request.

Ⓐ Elements of Literature

Exposition

❓ The nurse's long speech provides background information about Juliet's family and upbringing and about the nurse's position in the family. Why might the nurse feel especially strong affection for Juliet? [Her own daughter, who would have been the same age as Juliet, died, probably making the nurse feel much closer to Juliet.]

Answer to Margin Question
Line 10. The nurse exhibits complete ease with the issue of sexuality. In her earthiness, her bawdiness, and her frankness, she provides a significant contrast to Lady Capulet and reveals her place in the household.

Scene 3. *A room in Capulet's house.*

Enter Capulet's wife, LADY CAPULET, *and* NURSE.

Lady Capulet.
  Nurse, where's my daughter? Call her forth to me.
Nurse.
  Now, by my maidenhead at twelve year old,
  I bade her come. What,° lamb! What, ladybird!
  God forbid, where's this girl? What, Juliet!

[*Enter* JULIET.]

Juliet.
  How now? Who calls?
Nurse.   Your mother.
5 **Juliet.**   Madam, I am here.
  What is your will?
Lady Capulet.
  This is the matter.—Nurse, give leave awhile;
  We must talk in secret. Nurse, come back again.
  I have rememb'red me; thou's° hear our counsel.
10 Thou knowest my daughter's of a pretty age.
Nurse.
  Faith, I can tell her age unto an hour.
Lady Capulet.
  She's not fourteen.
Nurse.   I'll lay fourteen of my teeth—
  And yet, to my teen° be it spoken, I have but four—
  She's not fourteen. How long is it now
  To Lammastide?°
15 **Lady Capulet.**   A fortnight and odd days.
Nurse.
  Even or odd, of all days in the year,
  Come Lammas Eve at night shall she be fourteen.
  Susan and she (God rest all Christian souls!)
  Were of an age.° Well, Susan is with God;
20 She was too good for me. But, as I said,
  On Lammas Eve at night shall she be fourteen;
Ⓐ That shall she, marry; I remember it well.
  'Tis since the earthquake now eleven years;
  And she was weaned (I never shall forget it),
25 Of all the days of the year, upon that day;
  For I had then laid wormwood to my dug,°
  Sitting in the sun under the dovehouse wall.
  My lord and you were then at Mantua.
  Nay, I do bear a brain. But, as I said,

748 WILLIAM SHAKESPEARE

---

3. **What:** impatient call, like "Hey!" or "Where are you?"

9. **thou's:** thou shalt.
❓ 10. *The nurse and Lady Capulet are opposites in nature. Lady Capulet sends the nurse off and then calls her back. Some actresses use this impulsive move to indicate Lady Capulet's reluctance to speak to her daughter about marriage. In contrast, how does the nurse react in this next scene?*
13. **teen:** sorrow.
15. **Lammastide:** church feast, on August 1.

19. **Were of an age:** were the same age.

26. **laid wormwood to my dug:** applied a bitter substance (wormwood) to her breast to wean the baby.

Using Students' Strengths

Kinesthetic Learners

Ask students to think of symbols for key characters, such as Romeo, Juliet, Mercutio, and Tybalt. They should think of objects or animals that connect on more than one level with what they know about each character. For instance, a thunderbolt might suggest both Tybalt's temper and his readiness for violent action. Have students draw, paint, sculpt, or create collages that present their symbols. Have them explain to the class why they chose the symbols they did.

Intrapersonal Learners

As Act I closes with both Romeo and Juliet realizing their love and its dangers, have students think about the thoughts and feelings of either character. Then, as that character, they should write a diary entry or a letter that reveals the character's inner hopes, dreams, and plans for the future.

Spatial Learners

To help them keep track of the characters, ask students to convert the list of characters on p. 734 into a chart or graphic organizer. Like the list, the chart should distinguish between Capulets and Montagues. As students continue reading the play, they should add graphic elements to the chart—such as straight or broken lines, arrows, stars, swords, or lightning bolts—to show how specific characters connect or come into conflict as the plot develops.

*Tell me, daughter Juliet,
How stands your disposition to be married?*

B Reading Skills and Strategies
Drawing Conclusions
? Based on this allusion to her husband, what might the Capulet family have become to the nurse over the years? [Since she has lost both her husband and her child, she probably thinks of the members of the Capulet household as her family.]

30   When it did taste the wormwood on the nipple
      Of my dug and felt it bitter, pretty fool,
      To see it tetchy° and fall out with the dug!
      Shake, quoth the dovehouse!° 'Twas no need, I trow,
      To bid me trudge.
35   And since that time it is eleven years,
      For then she could stand high-lone;° nay, by th'
          rood,°
      She could have run and waddled all about;
      For even the day before, she broke her brow; **B**
      And then my husband (God be with his soul!
40   'A was a merry man) took up the child.
      "Yea," quoth he, "dost thou fall upon thy face?
      Thou wilt fall backward when thou hast more wit;°

32. tetchy: angry.

33. Shake, quoth the dovehouse: The dovehouse shook (from the earthquake).

36. high-lone: alone. **by th' rood:** by the cross (a mild oath).

42. wit: understanding.

THE TRAGEDY OF ROMEO AND JULIET, ACT I, SCENE 3 **749**

Taking a Second Look

Review: Drawing Conclusions

Remind students that drawing conclusions is the process of combining their prior knowledge with evidence from the text in order to decide what is really going on or what characters are really like. Tell them that readers have been drawing their own conclusions about Shakespeare's characters for hundreds of years. Because Shakespeare's characters are dynamic individuals capable of growth and change, readers must often adjust their conclusions about

them as the play continues.

Ask students to jot down their first impressions of the major characters introduced so far. Their lists should, at this point, include Lord and Lady Montague, Romeo, Benvolio, Lord and Lady Capulet, Juliet, the nurse, Tybalt, and Prince Escalus. Have them save their lists and add to or change them as the plot unfolds in the next four acts.

A Reading Skills and Strategies
Responding to the Text

? What are your first impressions of the nurse? [Some students may find her funny and lovable; others may find her tedious, vulgar, and long-winded.]

B Appreciating Language
Word Play

? What double meanings of the word *marry* does Lady Capulet use here? Check the list on p. 733 if you are not sure. [She uses the word as a mild oath, meaning "by the Virgin Mary," as well as the standard meaning "to be wed."]

Answers to Margin Questions
Line 48. Answers will vary, but most students will probably say that Juliet would feel embarrassed at hearing this story of her childhood.
Line 62. Juliet should be serious, reserved, and respectful; perhaps she should be a little frightened, too.

Wilt thou not, Jule?" and, by my holidam,°
The pretty wretch left crying and said, "Ay."
45 To see now how a jest shall come about!
I warrant, and I should live a thousand years,
I never should forget it. "Wilt thou not, Jule?" quoth he,
And, pretty fool, it stinted° and said, "Ay."

Lady Capulet.
Enough of this. I pray thee hold thy peace.

Nurse.
50 Yes, madam. Yet I cannot choose but laugh
To think it should leave crying and say, "Ay."
And yet, I warrant, it had upon its brow
A bump as big as a young cock'rel's stone;
A perilous knock; and it cried bitterly.
55 "Yea," quoth my husband, "fall'st upon thy face?
Thou wilt fall backward when thou comest to age,
Wilt thou not, Jule?" It stinted and said, "Ay."

Juliet.
And stint thou too, I pray thee, nurse, say I.

Nurse.
Peace, I have done. God mark thee to his grace!
60 Thou wast the prettiest babe that e'er I nursed.
And I might live to see thee married once,
I have my wish.

Lady Capulet.
Marry, that "marry" is the very theme
I came to talk of. Tell me, daughter Juliet,
65 How stands your disposition to be married?

Juliet.
It is an honor that I dream not of.

Nurse.
An honor? Were not I thine only nurse,
I would say thou hadst sucked wisdom from thy teat.

Lady Capulet.
Well, think of marriage now. Younger than you,
70 Here in Verona, ladies of esteem,
Are made already mothers. By my count,
I was your mother much upon these years
That you are now a maid. Thus then in brief:
The valiant Paris seeks you for his love.

Nurse.
75 A man, young lady! Lady, such a man
As all the world.—Why, he's a man of wax.°

Lady Capulet.
Verona's summer hath not such a flower.

Nurse.
Nay, he's a flower, in faith—a very flower.

750 WILLIAM SHAKESPEARE

43. by my holidam: by my holy relic (object associated with a saint).

48. stinted: stopped. 34
? **48.** *The nurse must make a strong impression with this speech, which leaves her helpless with laughter. The nurse directs her chatter to Lady Capulet, but Juliet is listening too. How would Juliet react to her fond nurse's memories, which cannot be stifled?*

? **62.** *This short line suggests another dramatic pause. Often, a director will have Juliet rush to the nurse and kiss her. Her fondness for and gaiety with the nurse must contrast with her reserve toward her mother. How should Juliet react when she speaks in line 66?* 35

76. man of wax: man like a wax statue, with a perfect figure.

Crossing the Curriculum

Social Studies/Health
Have students research changes in life expectancy for Europeans since the 1400s. Which centuries showed the most dramatic changes in life expectancy? What social and scientific developments caused these changes? Students might also research family life and child-rearing customs in Elizabethan England. How close were parents and children? How did class affect this relationship? When did children begin to assume adult responsibilities and privileges?

Lady Capulet.

    What say you? Can you love the gentleman?

80   This night you shall behold him at our feast.
    Read o'er the volume of young Paris' face,
    And find delight writ there with beauty's pen;
    Examine every married lineament,°
    And see how one another lends content;°

85   And what obscured in this fair volume lies
    Find written in the margent of his eyes.
    This precious book of love, this unbound lover,
    To beautify him only lacks a cover.
    The fish lives in the sea, and 'tis much pride

90   For fair without the fair within to hide.°
    That book in many's eyes doth share the glory,
    That in gold clasps locks in the golden story;
    So shall you share all that he doth possess,
    By having him, making yourself no less.

Nurse.

95   No less? Nay, bigger! Women grow by men.

Lady Capulet.

    Speak briefly, can you like of Paris' love?

Juliet.

    I'll look to like, if looking liking move;
    But no more deep will I endart mine eye
    Than your consent gives strength to make it fly.

[*Enter* SERVINGMAN.]

100 **Servingman.** Madam, the guests are come, supper
    served up, you called, my young lady asked for,
    the nurse cursed in the pantry, and everything
    in extremity. I must hence to wait. I beseech
    you follow straight.

                          [*Exit.*]

Lady Capulet.

105 We follow thee. Juliet, the county stays.°

Nurse.

    Go, girl, seek happy nights to happy days.

                          [*Exeunt.*]

  ❝ *Go, girl, seek happy nights*
       to happy days. ❞

---

79. *Notice that Juliet isn't answering. How do you suppose she is feeling during the conversation between the nurse and her mother about this man they want her to marry.*

83. married lineament: harmonious feature.

84. how one another lends content: how one feature makes another look good.

90. For fair without the fair within to hide: for those who are handsome outwardly also to be handsome inwardly.

94. *Lady Capulet has made an elegant appeal to Juliet, to persuade her to consider marrying Paris. Which images in this speech compare Paris to a fine book?*

99. *Juliet says she'll look at Paris to see if she likes him (if liking is brought about by looking). How does she show that she is a dutiful daughter?*

100. *Another comical servant enters, speaking breathlessly, but our attention still must be on Juliet. In some productions, we now hear the sounds of music coming offstage, and Juliet exits excitedly, with little dancing motions. Do we really know much about Juliet yet?*

105. the county stays: the count waits.

106. *We meet Juliet for the first time in this scene. What is your first impression of her?*

C Reading Skills and Strategies

Reading Shakespeare's Poetry

Have a student read Lady Capulet's speech aloud, and then have the class analyze its poetic structure. [The speech is written in iambic pentameter. The first four lines are in blank verse; the rest are in rhyming couplets. Most of the lines are end-stopped, except for run-on lines 85 and 89.]

D Elements of Literature

Rising Action

A new complication is being added to the plot. While Romeo will be searching for Rosaline at the party, Juliet is supposed to be looking over Paris to see if she thinks he will make a suitable husband. (Ironically, Romeo and Juliet will find each other instead of the ones they are looking for.)

Answers to Margin Questions

Line 79. Juliet is probably experiencing a mixture of emotions: excitement, happiness, fear, and hope.

Line 94. The images are *fair volume, margent of his eyes, book of love, unbound lover, cover, gold clasps,* and *golden story.*

Line 99. Juliet says she will not, in looking, go beyond what her mother would approve of.

Line 100. Although we don't know a great deal, we might assume Juliet is obedient yet speaks clearly for herself. We also know that she is loving, both from her actions and from the reactions of others.

Line 106. Students' early reactions to Juliet will vary. Some may like and admire her gentle disposition, while others may find her politeness and obedience boring.

Summary ■■

Act I, Scene 4

Romeo, Benvolio, and their friend Mercutio don masks in preparation for attending the Capulets' party. Romeo is still lovesick and tells his friends that a dream has filled him with forebodings about the party. Mercutio, trying to get Romeo to forget his troubles, fancifully explains what happens when a person dreams. In an extended conceit, he describes Queen Mab, who is the fairy in control of the dream world. Romeo chides his friend for prattling on, but Mercutio insists that dreams have no bearing on reality. Romeo, who foresees his own "untimely death" (l. 111), disagrees but decides to confront whatever fate awaits him and sets off for the party with his friends.

Ⓐ Critical Thinking
Making Judgments

❓ Do you think someone truly depressed, as Romeo claims to be, would be so quick with a witty comeback? [Possible responses: Yes, because sometimes people who are upset make jokes to cover their feelings; no, because if he had really lost someone he loved, he would not have the energy to think of quick jokes.]

Answers to Margin Questions

Stage direction. Romeo says he is "heavy" (l. 12), has "a soul of lead" (l. 15), and is so "enpiercèd" with Cupid's arrow that he cannot rise above his woe (ll. 19–22).

Line 13. Romeo feels oppressed by unrequited love and powerless to combat his feelings. Mercutio believes in taking action and being realistic about love: "If love be rough with you, be rough with love" (l. 27).

Line 23. Mercutio enjoys Romeo's intelligence and wit; he shows his friendship by trying to tease Romeo out of his depression. Some students may say that they would want Mercutio for a friend because of his sense of humor and his loyalty; others may say that they would prefer a less teasing friend.

Line 29. Mercutio is selecting and putting on a mask.

Scene 4. *A street.*

Enter ROMEO, MERCUTIO, BENVOLIO, *with five or six other* MASKERS; TORCHBEARERS.

Romeo.
What, shall this speech be spoke for our excuse?°
Or shall we on without apology?

Benvolio.
The date is out of such prolixity.°
We'll have no Cupid hoodwinked° with a scarf,
5 Bearing a Tartar's painted bow of lath,
Scaring the ladies like a crowkeeper;°
Nor no without-book prologue,° faintly spoke
After the prompter, for our entrance;
But, let them measure° us by what they will,
10 We'll measure them a measure° and be gone.

Romeo.
Give me a torch. I am not for this ambling.
Being but heavy, I will bear the light.

Mercutio.
Nay, gentle Romeo, we must have you dance.

Romeo.
Not I, believe me. You have dancing shoes
15 With nimble soles; I have a soul of lead
So stakes me to the ground I cannot move.

Mercutio.
You are a lover. Borrow Cupid's wings
And soar with them above a common bound.

Romeo.
Ⓐ ⌈ I am too sore enpiercèd with his shaft
20 To soar with his light feathers; and so bound
I cannot bound a pitch° above dull woe.
⌊ Under love's heavy burden do I sink.

Mercutio.
And, to sink in it, should you burden love—
Too great oppression for a tender thing.

Romeo.
25 Is love a tender thing? It is too rough,
Too rude, too boist'rous, and it pricks like thorn.

Mercutio.
If love be rough with you, be rough with love;
Prick love for pricking, and you beat love down.
Give me a case to put my visage in.
30 A visor° for a visor! What care I

752 WILLIAM SHAKESPEARE

❓ *Stage direction: It's night. The stage is lit with torches and filled with grotesquely masked young men. The mood is one of excitement—but we are watching Romeo. What does he say in the next speeches to indicate that he is still heavy-hearted?*

1. shall this speech be spoke for our excuse?: Shall we introduce ourselves with the usual speeches? (Uninvited maskers were usually announced by a messenger.)
3. The date is out of such prolixity: Such long-winded speeches are out of fashion now.
4. hoodwinked: blindfolded.
6. crowkeeper: scarecrow.
7. without-book prologue: memorized speech.
9. measure: examine.
10. measure them a measure: dance one dance.

❓ **13.** *Mercutio is a key character. Here he comes out of the crowd and speaks to Romeo. They engage in a verbal duel about love. In the following dialogue, how do Mercutio and Romeo differ in their attitudes toward love?*

21. bound a pitch: fly as high as a falcon.

❓ **23.** *In what ways does Mercutio show that he is a good friend to Romeo? Would you want to be Mercutio's friend?*

❓ **29.** *Mercutio pauses and asks for a mask. What activity would he be engaged in here?*
30. visor: mask.

Taking a Second Look

Review: Comparing and Contrasting

Remind students that when they compare, they show how two or more items are alike. When they contrast, they show how the items are different. Shakespeare's plays are full of contrasting pairs of characters, called **foils,** whose differences strengthen our impression of each character. Differences between characters can be determined by what they say and do, by their outward appearance, and by what others say about them.

Assign different students to compare and contrast different pairs of characters, such as the following:
- Romeo and Mercutio
- the nurse and Lady Capulet
- Benvolio and Tybalt
- the nurse and Mercutio
- Lord Capulet and Tybalt

What curious eye doth quote deformities?°
Here are the beetle brows shall blush° for me.

Benvolio.

Come, knock and enter; and no sooner in
But every man betake him to his legs.°

Romeo.

35 A torch for me! Let wantons light of heart
Tickle the senseless rushes° with their heels;
For I am proverbed with a grandsire phrase,°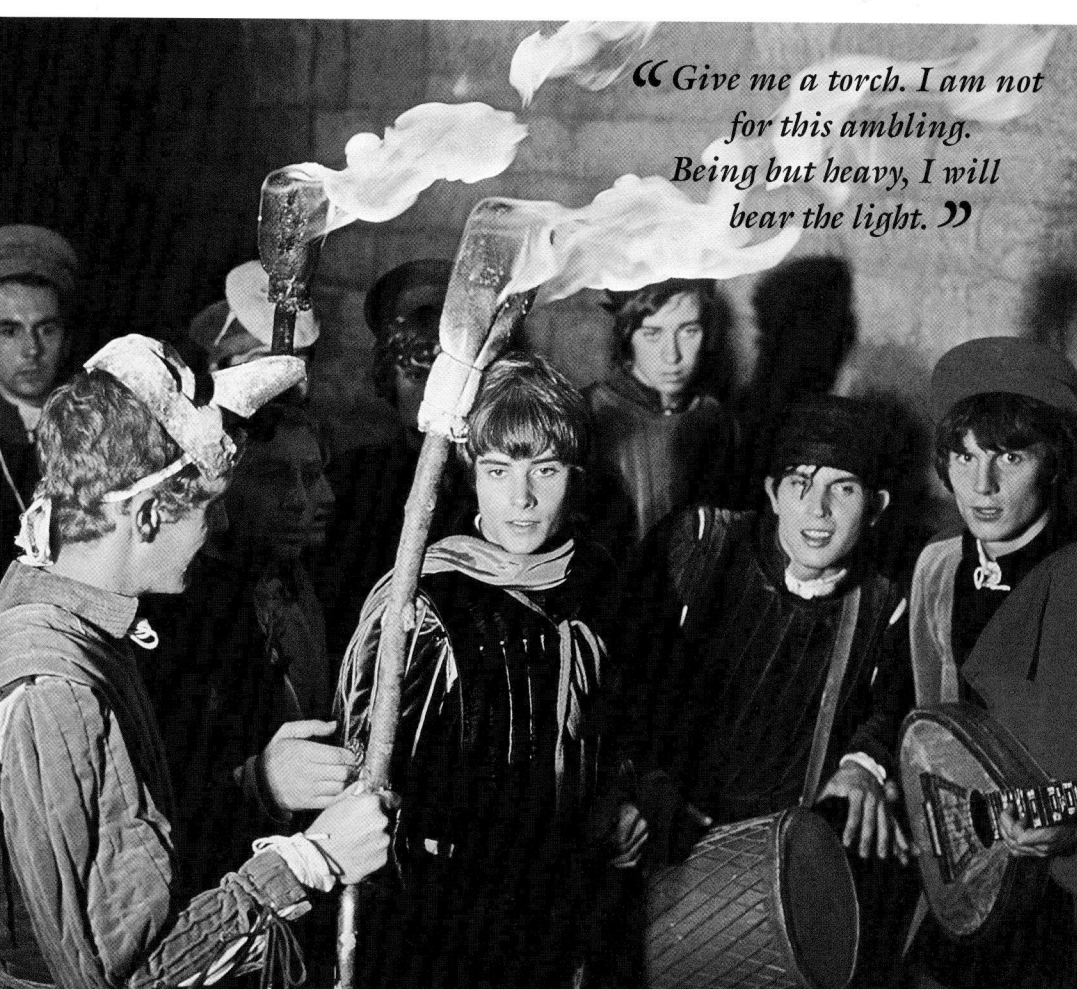
I'll be a candleholder and look on;
The game was ne'er so fair, and I am done.°

31. quote deformities: see imperfections (in the way he looks).
32. Here are the beetle brows shall blush: The mask's heavy eyebrows will blush for him.
34. betake him to his legs: begin dancing.

36. rushes: The dance floor is covered with rushes.
37. grandsire phrase: old man's saying.
39. The game . . . I am done: The game (dancing) was never very good, and I'm exhausted.
? 39. *Despite Mercutio's teasing and Benvolio's urging, what is Romeo determined to do at the dance?*

45

B Struggling Readers
Paraphrasing
Struggling readers may find this combination of archaic vocabulary and figurative language nearly impossible to decipher. Read the passage aloud, and then use the margin notes to help students paraphrase Romeo's words. [Possible paraphrase: Bring me a torch. Let my lighthearted friends dance. As the old men say, I'll be the candlestick and just watch you; the dancing was never that great anyway, and I'm exhausted.]

Answer to Margin Question
Line 39. Romeo will watch, not dance.

« Give me a torch. I am not for this ambling. Being but heavy, I will bear the light. »

Column 1 (Teacher Notes)

A Elements of Literature

Rising Action

Romeo says that he has decided to attend the party despite a warning dream. His fateful decision to attend sets in motion the rest of the plot and seals his fate.

B Reading Skills and Strategies

Reading Shakespeare's Poetry

Point out to students that the beginning of Mercutio's speech contains three run-on lines. Have volunteers take turns reading ll. 53–58 aloud to make them sound conversational. Remind them not to pause at the end of the run-on lines (ll. 54, 55, 57).

C Critical Thinking

Making Connections

? What connection is there between the different visits that Queen Mab makes? [All of the people visited by Queen Mab end up dreaming about what they secretly desire.]

Answers to Margin Questions

Line 50. Romeo is serious, but Mercutio is still joking. Mercutio's wit is always sharp but not necessarily unkind.

Line 53. Through fanciful description, humorous puns, and mockery, Mercutio is trying both to amuse Romeo and to show him the insignificance of dreams.

Mercutio can act out many of his descriptions. He can also use the audience about him, for example, tracing Queen Mab's path down someone's nose (l. 58) and over another's lips (l. 74).

Mercutio says that Queen Mab has brought Romeo's dream and that it is not to be taken seriously.

Column 2 (Play Text)

Mercutio.
40   Tut! Dun's the mouse, the constable's own word!
     If thou art Dun,° we'll draw thee from the mire
     Of this sir-reverence love,° wherein thou stickest
     Upon to the ears. Come, we burn daylight, ho!

Romeo.
     Nay, that's not so.

Mercutio.   I mean, sir, in delay
45   We waste our lights° in vain, like lights by day.
     Take our good meaning, for our judgment sits
     Five times in that° ere once in our five wits.

Romeo.
     And we mean well in going to this masque,
     But 'tis no wit° to go.

A **Mercutio.**   Why, may one ask?

Romeo.
     I dreamt a dream tonight.

50 **Mercutio.**   And so did I.

Romeo.
     Well, what was yours?

Mercutio.   That dreamers often lie.

Romeo.
     In bed asleep, while they do dream things true.

Mercutio.
     O, then I see Queen Mab hath been with you.
     She is the fairies' midwife, and she comes
55   In shape no bigger than an agate stone
B   On the forefinger of an alderman,
     Drawn with a team of little atomies°
     Over men's noses as they lie asleep;
     Her wagon spokes made of long spinners'° legs,
60   The cover, of the wings of grasshoppers;
     Her traces,° of the smallest spider web;
     Her collars, of the moonshine's wat'ry beams;
     Her whip, of cricket's bone; the lash, of film;°
     Her wagoner, a small gray-coated gnat,
65   Not half so big as a round little worm
     Pricked from the lazy finger of a maid;°
     Her chariot is an empty hazelnut,
     Made by the joiner squirrel or old grub,
     Time out o' mind the fairies' coachmakers.
70   And in this state she gallops night by night
     Through lovers' brains, and then they dream of love;
     On courtiers' knees, that dream on curtsies straight;
C   O'er lawyers' fingers, who straight dream on fees;
     O'er ladies' lips, who straight on kisses dream,
75   Which oft the angry Mab with blisters plagues,
     Because their breaths with sweetmeats tainted are.

754 WILLIAM SHAKESPEARE

Column 3 (Glossary Notes)

41. Dun: pun on Romeo's "done"; Dun was the common name used for a horse in an old game called "Dun is in the mire."

42. sir-reverence love: "Save your reverence" is an apologetic expression. Mercutio means, "We'll save you from—pardon me for saying so—love."

45. lights: torches.

47. in that: in our good meaning.

49. no wit: not a good idea.

? 50. *Romeo's mood seems to have changed abruptly, and he has a sense of approaching doom. How would he speak this line about a dream? Would Mercutio's reply be kindly or sharp?*

? 53. *Mercutio is a ringleader and a born entertainer. As he tells this story about Queen Mab, everyone stops and listens in fascinated silence. For the moment, Romeo is in the background. How is Mercutio, in this famous speech, trying to get Romeo's mind off serious thoughts about dreams and their significance? What gestures will he use to embellish his speech? According to Mercutio, what does Queen Mab have to do with Romeo? Be sure to read the speech aloud. (You might want to draw pictures of Mab.)*

57. atomies: tiny creatures.

59. spinners': spiders'.

61. traces: reins and harnesses for a wagon.

63. film: filament, or thread.

66. lazy finger of a maid: Lazy maids were said to have worms breeding in their fingers.

Professional Notes

Critical Comment: Reality and Illusion

Critic Northrop Frye has commented on how Mercutio's speech about Queen Mab reflects ideas about light and darkness, illusion and reality, that are developed throughout the play: "The light and dark imagery comes into powerful focus with Mercutio's speech on Queen Mab. Queen Mab, Mercutio tells us, is the instigator of dreams, and Mercutio takes what we would call a very Freudian approach to dreams. They are primarily wish fulfillment fantasies.... But such dreams are an inseparable mixture of the illusion and a reality profounder than the ordinary realities of the day. When we wake we carry into the daylight world, without realizing it, the feelings engendered by the dream, the irrational and absurd conviction that the world as we want it to be has its own reality, and perhaps is what could be there instead. Both the lovers carry on an inner debate in which one voice tells them that they are embarking on a dangerous illusion, and another says that they must embark on it anyway whatever the dangers, because by doing so they are martyrs, or witnesses, to an order of things that matters more than the sunlit reality."

T754

Sometime she gallops o'er a courtier's nose,
And then dreams he of smelling out a suit;°
And sometime comes she with a tithe pig's° tail

80 Tickling a parson's nose as 'a lies asleep,
Then dreams he of another benefice.°
Sometime she driveth o'er a soldier's neck,
And then dreams he of cutting foreign throats,
Of breaches, ambuscadoes, Spanish blades,

85 Of healths° five fathom deep; and then anon
Drums in his ear, at which he starts and wakes,
And being thus frighted, swears a prayer or two
And sleeps again. This is that very Mab
That plaits the manes of horses in the night

90 And bakes the elflocks° in foul sluttish hairs,
Which once untangled much misfortune bodes.
This is the hag,° when maids lie on their backs,
That presses them and learns them first to bear,
Making them women of good carriage.°
This is she——

95 **Romeo.**   Peace, peace, Mercutio, peace!
Thou talk'st of nothing.

Mercutio.   True, I talk of dreams;
Which are the children of an idle brain,
Begot of nothing but vain fantasy;
Which is as thin of substance as the air,

100 And more inconstant than the wind, who woos
Even now the frozen bosom of the North
And, being angered, puffs away from thence,
Turning his side to the dewdropping South.

Benvolio.
This wind you talk of blows us from ourselves.

105 Supper is done, and we shall come too late.

Romeo.
I fear, too early; for my mind misgives
Some consequence yet hanging in the stars
Shall bitterly begin his fearful date
With this night's revels and expire the term

110 Of a despisèd life, closed in my breast,
By some vile forfeit of untimely death.
But he that hath the steerage of my course
Direct my sail! On, lusty gentlemen!

Benvolio. Strike, drum.

[They march about the stage and retire to one side.]

---

78. suit: person who might want to buy his influence at court.
79. tithe pig's: A tithe is a tenth of one's income given to the church. Farmers often gave the parson one pig as a tithe.
81. benefice: church office that enabled a minister to make a living.

85. healths: toasts to his health.

90. elflocks: locks of hair that were tangled by mischievous elves.

92. hag: nightmare. Nightmares were thought to be spirits who molested women at night.
94. women of good carriage: women who can bear children well.
? **94.** *Mercutio's tone changes here. How are these last details getting into subjects that are more shocking and cynical? Romeo doesn't like this turn of events and cuts Mercutio off.*

? **103.** *Mercutio could be comparing Romeo to the frozen north. If he is, what warning does he give his friend about remaining cold too long?*

? **106.** *Romeo again expresses feelings that something terrible will happen. Does he give any reasons for his fears? Which words in this speech suggest that he is going to the party because he is in the hands of fate?*

D Reading Skills and Strategies

Reading Shakespeare's Poetry
Reading this passage aloud will give students more practice in handling the run-on lines of blank verse. It is especially challenging because it contains four consecutive run-on lines.

Answers to Margin Questions
Line 94. While Mercutio's earlier examples make fun of people's own follies, his example of the "hag" suggests a genuinely evil presence that can harm innocent people.
Line 103. Mercutio warns Romeo that he could lose his friends if he continues to rebuff them. Mercutio uses words that evoke a sense of alienation—*inconstant, frozen, angered.*
Line 106. Romeo expresses his fear as an intuition, a misgiving without logical explanation; however, his phrase "a despisèd life, closed in my breast" (l. 110) suggests that he has always expected tragedy in his life.
    His fatalism is evident in his references to "the stars" and to "he that hath the steerage of my course."

THE TRAGEDY OF ROMEO AND JULIET, ACT I, SCENE 4 **755**

Assessing Learning

Observation Assessment
Use the following criteria to assess students' responses to the literature.

Key: A = Always
      S = Sometimes
      R = Rarely
      N = Never

Characteristic	Date	Rating
Asks questions; seeks help of others to clarify meaning		
Makes reasonable predictions		
Considers multiple interpretations		
Uses text to clarify ideas		

Act I, Scene 5

Three servants enter, bantering with each other as they set up for the Capulets' party. Lord Capulet cheerfully greets his guests, welcomes the maskers, and reminisces about his youth. Romeo sees Juliet and falls in love with her at first sight. Although he inquires about her, he does not learn her identity. Tybalt, recognizing his enemy's voice, prepares for a fight. He is restrained by Capulet, however, who compliments Romeo's manners. Tybalt obeys his uncle's command but swears he will have revenge. Romeo confesses his love to Juliet; their exchange forms a sonnet, which uses religious imagery to describe the passionate devotion of lovers. They kiss but are separated by the nurse, who summons Juliet to her mother. Romeo finds out from the nurse that Juliet is Lord Capulet's daughter, laments his bad fortune, and departs with his friends. Juliet questions her nurse as to Romeo's identity; discovering that he is a Montague, she, too, mourns her bad luck in love.

Ⓐ Reading Skills and Strategies
Connecting with the Text

❓ How would you feel about being welcomed to a party in this way? [Sample responses: I would feel as if the host were really glad to see me and that all the young people could just relax and enjoy themselves; I would expect the host to be a teaser and the party to be a lot of fun.]

Answers to Margin Questions
Stage direction. The first servant speaks in short commands. The mood is excited, hectic, and frantic.
Stage direction. Capulet remembers flirting at masked balls but now can do nothing but sit because he is long past his "dancing days." His comments emphasize Romeo and Juliet's youth.

Scene 5. *A hall in Capulet's house.*

SERVINGMEN *come forth with napkins.*

First Servingman. Where's Potpan, that he helps not to take away? He shift a trencher!° He scrape a trencher!

Second Servingman. When good manners shall lie all in
5   one or two men's hands, and they unwashed too, 'tis a foul thing.

First Servingman. Away with the join-stools,° remove the court cupboard, look to the plate. Good thou, save me a piece of marchpane,° and as thou loves me, let
10   the porter let in Susan Grindstone and Nell, Anthony, and Potpan!

Second Servingman. Ay, boy, ready.

First Servingman. You are looked for and called for, asked for and sought for, in the great chamber.

15 **Third Servingman.** We cannot be here and there too. Cheerly, boys! Be brisk awhile, and the longer liver take all.

[*Exeunt.*]

[*Enter* CAPULET, LADY CAPULET, JULIET, TYBALT, NURSE, *and all the* GUESTS *and* GENTLEWOMEN, *meeting the* MASKERS.]

Capulet.
Ⓐ
Welcome, gentlemen! Ladies that have their toes
Unplagued with corns will walk a bout° with you.
20   Ah, my mistresses, which of you all
Will now deny to dance? She that makes dainty,°
She I'll swear hath corns. Am I come near ye now?
Welcome, gentlemen! I have seen the day
That I have worn a visor and could tell
25   A whispering tale in a fair lady's ear,
Such as would please. 'Tis gone, 'tis gone, 'tis gone.
You are welcome, gentlemen! Come, musicians, play.

[*Music plays, and they dance.*]

A hall,° a hall! Give room! And foot it, girls.
More light, you knaves, and turn the tables up,
30   And quench the fire; the room is grown too hot.
Ah, sirrah, this unlooked-for sport° comes well.
Nay, sit; nay, sit, good cousin Capulet;
For you and I are past our dancing days.
How long is't now since last yourself and I
Were in a mask?

756 WILLIAM SHAKESPEARE

❓ **Stage direction:** *As you read these servants' speeches, note that one speaks in short emphatic sentences and bosses everyone else around. Which one is this? What mood do you think is suggested in this short scene?*
2. **trencher:** wooden plate.

7. **join-stools:** wooden stools made by a carpenter (a joiner).

9. **marchpane:** marzipan.

19. **bout:** dance.

21. **makes dainty:** pretends to be shy.

❓ **Stage direction:** *The dance, slow and stately, takes place at center stage. Old Capulet and his relative reminisce at one side, but our attention is focused on Romeo (in a mask) and Juliet, who is dancing with someone else. How does the following conversation contrast the two old men with Romeo and Juliet?*
28. **A hall:** clear the floor (for dancing).
31. **unlooked-for sport:** He hadn't expected to find some of the dancers masked.

Making the Connections

Cultural Connection

So many of Shakespeare's phrases have entered the English language as common expressions that entire books have been written on the topic, including Michael Macrone's *Brush Up Your Shakespeare!* (Harper & Row). *Cold comfort, crack of doom,* and *milk of human kindness* are but a few of the Shakespearean expressions Macrone presents. Students interested in this phenomenon might use Macrone's book or collections of quotations, such as *Bartlett's Familiar Quotations,* in order to make a list of well-known expressions that come from *Romeo and Juliet* and other Shakespeare plays. Encourage students to compare Shakespeare's use of each phrase with the way it is currently used in ordinary speech.

35   **Second Capulet.** By'r Lady, thirty years.
  Capulet.
    What, man? 'Tis not so much, 'tis not so much;
    'Tis since the nuptial of Lucentio,
    Come Pentecost as quickly as it will,
    Some five-and-twenty years, and then we masked.
  Second Capulet.
40   'Tis more, 'tis more. His son is elder, sir;
    His son is thirty.
  Capulet.   Will you tell me that?
    His son was but a ward° two years ago.
  Romeo (*to a* SERVINGMAN).
    What lady's that which doth enrich the hand
    Of yonder knight?
45   **Servingman.** I know not, sir.
  Romeo.
    O, she doth teach the torches to burn bright!
    It seems she hangs upon the cheek of night   **B**
    As a rich jewel in an Ethiop's ear—
    Beauty too rich for use, for earth too dear!
50   So shows a snowy dove trooping with crows
    As yonder lady o'er her fellows shows.
    The measure° done, I'll watch her place of stand
    And, touching hers, make blessèd my rude° hand.
    Did my heart love till now? Forswear it, sight!   **C**
55   For I ne'er saw true beauty till this night.
  Tybalt.
    This, by his voice, should be a Montague.
    Fetch me my rapier, boy. What! Dares the slave
    Come hither, covered with an antic face,°
    To fleer° and scorn at our solemnity?
60   Now, by the stock and honor of my kin,
    To strike him dead I hold it not a sin.
  Capulet.
    Why, how now, kinsman? Wherefore storm you so?
  Tybalt.
    Uncle, this is a Montague, our foe,
    A villain, that is hither come in spite
65   To scorn at our solemnity this night.
  Capulet.
    Young Romeo is it?
  Tybalt.   'Tis he, that villain Romeo.
  Capulet.
    Content thee, gentle coz, let him alone.
    'A bears him like a portly° gentleman,
    And, to say truth, Verona brags of him   **D**
70   To be a virtuous and well-governed youth.
    I would not for the wealth of all this town

PERSONIFICATION

42. **ward:** minor.

? 43. *In some productions, Romeo puts his torch down here, to draw our attention to his urgent question. Where would Juliet be on stage at this point?* 53

52. **measure:** dance.
53. **rude:** rough or simple.

? 55. *What has happened to Romeo?* 54

? 56. *Why would we feel a sense of fear when we see Tybalt stepping onto center stage again?* 55
58. **antic face:** grotesque mask.
59. **fleer:** jeer.

68. **portly:** well-mannered.

B **Elements of Literature**
Imagery
Point out to students Shakespeare's use of images of light and darkness, particularly in relationship to Romeo and Juliet. You might ask students to record such images in their notebooks from this point on.

C **Reading Skills and Strategies**
Responding to the Text
? What is your response to Romeo's declaration about Juliet's beauty? [Possible responses: It seems as if he falls in love very easily; since he was so attracted to Rosaline before, Juliet must have a truly stunning appearance.]

D **Critical Thinking**
Making Judgments
? Does Lord Capulet seem to have taken seriously the prince's warning about no more feuding? Explain. [Sample answer: Yes, he must sincerely intend to stop the feud, since he is not upset about Romeo's uninvited presence at the party, and he even compliments Romeo.]

Answers to Margin Questions
Line 43. Juliet is dancing and must be downstage from the other couples, or somehow separated from them, so that the audience sees her clearly as Romeo is smitten.
Line 55. Romeo has fallen instantly in love with Juliet, claiming that he knows true love and beauty for the first time.
Line 56. The audience knows Tybalt's hatred of the Montagues and his rash temper. He could kill Romeo or, because of the prince's order, sentence Romeo to death simply by provoking a fight.

A Reading Skills and Strategies
Making Predictions

❓ Tybalt backs away from a confrontation with Romeo here. What do you predict will come of Tybalt's bitterness? [Possible answer: At some later point, he may find an opportunity to confront Romeo about the insult.]

B Reading Skills and Strategies

Reading Shakespeare's Poetry

Point out that this dialogue is actually a sonnet. It consists of fourteen lines of iambic pentameter and has the rhyme scheme *abab cdcd efef gg*. Ask a pair of brave volunteers to read it aloud.

Answers to Margin Questions
Line 78. Capulet says that Romeo is behaving like a gentleman and should be left alone. Capulet is trying to be reasonable and fair, but his pride and temper are also evident in his speeches to Tybalt.

In Scene 1, Capulet automatically assumed that Montague was affronting him, but when Tybalt reacts in a similar way, Capulet is angry and chides him for posturing, childish behavior.

Line 94. Students may wish to work in pairs or in small groups. Advise them to make general sense of each line and then think of how an angry teenager and an angry adult might express the same ideas today.

Line 95. Students should note the following words and phrases: *profane, holy shrine, sin, pilgrims, devotion, saints, palm, holy palmers', prayer, pray, grant, faith.*

Line 98. Juliet says that Romeo has made a "mannerly devotion" and likens their "palm to palm" contact to a kiss.

Here in my house do him disparagement.
Therefore be patient; take no note of him.
It is my will, the which if thou respect,
75   Show a fair presence and put off these frowns,
An ill-beseeming semblance for a feast.

Tybalt.
It fits when such a villain is a guest.
I'll not endure him.

Capulet.   He shall be endured.
What, goodman boy!° I say he shall. Go to!°
80   Am I the master here, or you? Go to!
You'll not endure him, God shall mend my soul!
You'll make a mutiny among my guests!
You will set cock-a-hoop.° You'll be the man!

Tybalt.
Why, uncle, 'tis a shame.

Capulet.   Go to, go to!
85   You are a saucy boy. Is't so, indeed?
This trick may chance to scathe° you. I know what.
You must contrary me! Marry, 'tis time—
Well said, my hearts!—You are a princox°—go!
Be quiet, or—More light, more light!—For shame!
90   I'll make you quiet. What!—Cheerly, my hearts!

Tybalt.
Patience perforce° with willful choler meeting
Makes my flesh tremble in their different greeting.
I will withdraw; but this intrusion shall,
Now seeming sweet, convert to bitt'rest gall.

                          [*Exit.*]

Romeo.
95   If I profane with my unworthiest hand
    This holy shrine, the gentle sin is this:°
My lips, two blushing pilgrims, ready stand
    To smooth that rough touch with a tender kiss.

Juliet.
Good pilgrim, you do wrong your hand too much,
100   Which mannerly devotion shows in this;
For saints have hands that pilgrims' hands do touch,
    And palm to palm is holy palmers'° kiss.

Romeo.
Have not saints lips, and holy palmers too?

Juliet.
Ay, pilgrim, lips that they must use in prayer.

Romeo.
105   O, then, dear saint, let lips do what hands do!
They pray; grant thou, lest faith turn to despair.

Juliet.
Saints do not move,° though grant for prayers' sake.

758 WILLIAM SHAKESPEARE

❓ **78.** *What is Capulet's sensible reply to Tybalt's hostility? What feelings is Capulet revealing in his next speeches? Have Capulet's feelings about the Montagues changed since Scene 1?*

79. goodman boy: a scornful phrase. *Goodman* is below the rank of gentleman; *boy* is insulting. **Go to!:** similar to "Go on!" or "Cut it out!"

83. set cock-a-hoop: start trouble.

86. scathe: hurt.

88. princox: rude youngster.

91. patience perforce: enforced patience.

❓ **94.** *Paraphrase lines 56–94, putting the exchange between Capulet and Tybalt in modern-day language.*

❓ **95.** *In contrast to the raging Tybalt is Romeo, now on center stage with Juliet. Romeo takes Juliet's hand, and in their next 14 lines, the two young speakers' words form a sonnet. Romeo pretends to be a pilgrim going to a saint's shrine. Exactly where do the two young lovers use religious images to talk of their feelings for each other?*

96. the gentle sin is this: this is the sin of a gentleman.

❓ **98.** *Romeo and Juliet bring the palms of their hands together here. What in their words suggests that this is what they are doing?*

102. palmers': pilgrims going to a holy place. They often carried palm leaves to show they had been to the Holy Land.

107. do not move: do not make the first move.

Professional Notes

Critical Comment: The Play's Poetry
The literary critic Phyllis Rackin noted the importance of poetry in *Romeo and Juliet:* "Of all Shakespeare's tragedies, *Romeo and Juliet* depends most upon its poetry. . . . In no other tragedy does Shakespeare use the imagery and the elaborate rhymed verse of lyric poetry to the extent he does in *Romeo and Juliet.* One useful approach to this play is, in fact, to regard it as a poem—a great lyrical, metaphorical definition of romantic love. Imagery of darkness and light, of night and day, pervades the language, and it serves more than anything else to define the nature of the lovers' passion."

For saints have hands
    that pilgrims' hands do touch,
And palm to palm is holy
    palmers' kiss.

Romeo.
    Then move not while my prayer's effect I take.
    Thus from my lips, by thine my sin is purged.

[*Kisses her.*]

Juliet.
110   Then have my lips the sin that they have took.
Romeo.
    Sin from my lips? O trespass sweetly urged!
    Give me my sin again. [*Kisses her.*]
Juliet.   You kiss by th' book.°
Nurse.
    Madam, your mother craves a word with you.
Romeo.
    What is her mother?
Nurse.   Marry, bachelor,
115   Her mother is the lady of the house,
    And a good lady, and a wise and virtuous.
    I nursed her daughter that you talked withal.° **C**
    I tell you, he that can lay hold of her
    Shall have the chinks.°

C **Reading Skills and Strategies**
    Responding to the Text
? How do you feel about the nurse's comment to Romeo about the wealth of the Capulet family? [Possible responses: She is showing a sense of humor about the reasons people marry; she should be a little more cautious about making this comment to a stranger.]

Answers to Margin Questions
Line 109. The audience fears that Tybalt will see the kiss and be unable to restrain his anger.
Line 113. The Capulets want Juliet to marry Paris.

? **109.** *In the midst of the swirling dancers, Romeo and Juliet kiss. All of the audience's attention must be on this kiss. What do you fear as you watch, remembering that Tybalt is nearby?*   60

112. You kiss by th' book: You take my words literally (to get more kisses).
? **113.** *As the nurse interrupts, the dance ends. Juliet runs off, and Romeo is left alone with the nurse. What do we know about the Capulets' plans for Juliet that Romeo does not know?*   61

117. withal: with.

119. chinks: money.

THE TRAGEDY OF ROMEO AND JULIET, ACT I, SCENE 5   759

❝ *Thus from my lips, by thine my sin is purged.* **❞**

RESPONDING TO THE ART

Activity. Have students describe what camera angle this photograph was taken from. [The camera is close up and parallel to the actors.] Ask them what effect this angle has on the viewer and how a different angle might affect the viewer's impression of the scene. [Possible responses: The angle draws the viewer into the scene. If Romeo and Juliet were viewed from far away or from another angle, the scene might not seem as intense.]

Making the Connections

Connecting to the Theme: "The Destruction of Innocence"

Romeo and Juliet deals with several issues beyond that of two young people involved in a passionate, once-in-a-lifetime love. You might discuss these additional, related themes:

- Love can confer integrity upon two very young people.
- Tragedy can occur when older people's rage is carried over to the next generation.

- Humans are often powerless to make the kind of world they would like to live in.
- Innocence, virtue, and beauty can be quickly and thoughtlessly destroyed.
- A disordered and chaotic world can bring disaster down on those who live in it.

Romeo.   Is she a Capulet?

120   O dear account! My life is my foe's debt.°

Benvolio.

    Away, be gone; the sport is at the best.

Romeo.

    Ay, so I fear; the more is my unrest.

Capulet.

    Nay, gentlemen, prepare not to be gone;

    We have a trifling foolish banquet towards.°

125   Is it e'en so? Why then, I thank you all.

    I thank you, honest gentlemen. Good night.

    More torches here! Come on then; let's to bed.

    Ah, sirrah, by my fay,° it waxes late;

    I'll to my rest.

            [*Exeunt all but* JULIET *and* NURSE.]

Juliet.

130   Come hither, nurse. What is yond gentleman?

Nurse.

    The son and heir of old Tiberio.

Juliet.

    What's he that now is going out of door?

Nurse.

    Marry, that, I think, be young Petruchio.

Juliet.

    What's he that follows there, that would not dance?

Nurse.

135   I know not.

Juliet.

    Go ask his name.—If he be marrièd,

    My grave is like to be my wedding bed.

Nurse.

    His name is Romeo, and a Montague,

    The only son of your great enemy.

Juliet.

140   My only love, sprung from my only hate!

    Too early seen unknown, and known too late!

    Prodigious° birth of love it is to me

    That I must love a loathèd enemy.

Nurse.

    What's this? What's this?

Juliet.   A rhyme I learnt even now

    Of one I danced withal.

[*One calls within,* "Juliet."]

145 **Nurse.**   Anon, anon!°

    Come, let's away; the strangers all are gone.

                   [*Exeunt.*]

---

120. My life is my foe's debt: My foe now owns my life.

? **122.** *Romeo stands alone here, horrified. What activity goes on around him?* 62

124. towards: in preparation.

128. fay: faith.

? **130.** *Juliet has moved to the side of the stage. What feelings must she convey in this question? (She is not pointing to Romeo.)* 63

142. Prodigious: huge and monstrous.

? **145.** *What tone of voice would Juliet use here? What has she just realized?* 64

145. anon: at once.

THE TRAGEDY OF ROMEO AND JULIET, ACT I, SCENE 5   761

Ⓐ Critical Thinking
Comparing and Contrasting

? How is this statement different from the first comments Juliet makes about marriage earlier in Act I? [Sample responses: Earlier, she says she has not even thought about marriage, and now she seems to know exactly whom she wants to marry; before the party, she says she will follow her mother's guidance about marrying, and now she says she will die if Romeo is not available.]

Ⓑ Elements of Literature
Rising Action

Have students summarize the plot complications that have occurred by the end of Act I. [Romeo has gone to the Capulet party to see his love Rosaline, but instead has fallen in love, with Juliet, Lord Capulet's daughter, at first sight. Juliet was supposed to look over Paris at the party but instead has fallen in love with Romeo at first sight. Both Romeo and Juliet learn each other's identity after it is too late.]

Answers to Margin Questions

Line 122. Romeo's friends are preparing to leave, and the other guests are going into the banquet hall.

Line 130. While pretending to be idly curious, Juliet must also communicate intense interest and excitement.

Line 145. Juliet could be thoughtful, secretive, and sorrowful. She has just realized that Romeo is a Montague and that therefore her "only love" is a "loathèd enemy."

Assessing Learning

Check Test: Questions and Answers
Answers may vary slightly.

1. Why do the servants argue in the opening scene of Act I? [They are carrying on the feud between their masters, Lord Capulet and Lord Montague.]

2. What warning does Prince Escalus give the feuding families? [He warns the families that the punishment for future fighting will be death.]

3. Why is Romeo acting strangely at the beginning of Act I? [He is distracted and moody because of his unreturned love for Rosaline.]

4. Why does Lady Capulet want Juliet to attend the evening celebration? [She wants Juliet to see Paris, who has asked to marry Juliet.]

5. What realization does Juliet have at the end of Act I? [She realizes that Romeo, the boy she has fallen in love with at first sight, is a Montague and a bitter enemy of the Capulet family.]

Standardized Test Preparation
For practice in proofreading and editing, see
• *Daily Oral Grammar,* Transparency 44

T761

MAKING MEANINGS (ACT I)

First Thoughts

1. Responses will vary. Encourage students to point out specific lines that, in their opinion, are either convincing or unrealistic.

Shaping Interpretations

2. Each episode intensifies the feud.
   - Servants episode: This episode establishes the ongoing quarrel between the Capulets and the Montagues and shows how the feud has infected other household members.
   - Benvolio-Tybalt episode: This episode raises the stakes because Tybalt draws a sword and threatens to kill Benvolio; it also shows how anger can cause people to become irrational.
   - Prince's warning: This episode shows that the feud is creating a public menace, and the prince actually has to threaten the feuders with death.

3. In Scene 2, Lord Capulet approves Paris as a suitor for Juliet, and while he says he will not force her to marry Paris, he makes it clear that he determines her choices (l. 18). In Scene 3, the complication deepens because Juliet desires to be obedient and she pledges not to let her emotions rule her.

4. Possible answers: Mercutio is smart, volatile, creative, loyal and cynical and is a true friend to Romeo. His banter and advice make him believable. Some students may have known people who, like Mercutio, seem confident and lighthearted but are self-critical underneath.

5. Possible responses: Whereas Romeo focuses on his inner life and emotions, Mercutio focuses on his appearance and his "performances" for others; Romeo expects to be a bystander at the party, while Mercutio has a reputation as the life of the party; Romeo is moody and admits to feeling hopeless, while Mercutio displays confidence.

6. In ll. 49–50, he says that he is apprehensive because of a dream. In ll. 106–113, he says he fears the party will set in motion the fated tragedy of his "untimely death."

7. Possible questions: Will the Capulets force Juliet to marry Paris? Will Tybalt get revenge on Romeo? How will Romeo and Juliet manage to see each other again?

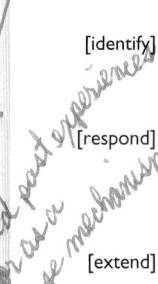

cynical
older
troubled past experiences
humor as a defense mechanism

MAKING MEANINGS   ACT I

[respond]

First Thoughts

1. Did you find the "love at first sight" scene convincing? Why, or why not?

Shaping Interpretations

[analyze]

2. Scene 1 is a brilliant example of how information can be conveyed through theatrical activity. Look at these three segments of the scene: Gregory-Sampson and the Montague servants; Benvolio-Tybalt; and the prince's warning. To examine the scene, use a chart like the following one. List each episode on the left. On the right, explain how the episode clarifies the forces at work in the play (some of them deadly).

Episode	What It Shows

[analyze]

3. Before Romeo and Juliet meet in Scene 4, Shakespeare must set up obstacles to their love, so that when they do meet, we will groan at the problems they are going to face. What problem, or **complication,** is presented in Scenes 2 and 3?

[analyze]

4. Scene 4 introduces us to Mercutio, who will play an important part in the play. How would you **characterize** Mercutio based on what he has said and done? Is he a believable character? Have you known people like him?

[analyze]

5. Mercutio is used as a **foil** to Romeo. The word *foil* in drama means "a character or scene that is set up as a contrast to another so that each will stand out vividly." In what specific ways is Mercutio a foil to Romeo?

[identify]

6. Scene 4 sets up a sense of **foreboding**—a feeling that something bad is about to happen. Identify Romeo's specific expressions of foreboding, as he sets off for the party. *pg. 755*

[respond]

7. By the end of Act I, a lot of **suspense** has been generated. If you were watching this play, what questions would you be asking at this point?

Extending the Text

[extend]

8. Although the action of this play takes place in Italy in the fourteenth century, we can still recognize similarities between the culture of that time and that of our own. Which episodes in Act I could you imagine taking place today? What details would have to change, if any?

135. pg.

Reading Check

a. What does the Prologue say will end the rage between Romeo's and Juliet's families?

b. Who is Tybalt, and why is he dangerous?

c. What warning does the prince give the street brawlers in Scene 1? *pg. 738*

d. In Scene 4, how does Mercutio try to snap Romeo out of his depression?

e. Where do Romeo and Juliet meet?

scene 2 = pg. 744 = scene 3 = pg. 748

Extending the Text

8. Episodes that might take place today include the street fighting, Mercutio's teasing, Romeo and Juliet's falling in love at first sight, and the exchange between Lord Capulet and Tybalt. However, many details—language, dress, and marriage customs—would be different.

Reading Check

a. Romeo's and Juliet's deaths will end the feud.

b. Tybalt is the nephew of Lady Capulet and cousin of Juliet; he hates all Montagues and he is looking for a fight.

c. If they fight again, they'll be put to death.

d. Mercutio urges Romeo to dance and not to take himself, or love, too seriously. He jokes with Romeo and amuses him by describing Queen Mab's exploits.

e. They meet at a party in her parents' home.

CHOICES: Building Your Portfolio

Writer's Notebook

1. Collecting Ideas for a Research Paper

Finding a topic. You'll be writing a research paper for the Writer's Workshop on page 868. The play itself can give you some possible topics.

Shakespeare set his play in Verona, Italy, in the fourteenth century, but the play reflects the attitudes and customs of Elizabethan England at the time Shakespeare lived. The early productions of the play (like Zeffirelli's production illustrated on these pages) used Elizabethan costumes. From looking at the photographs, you can get an idea of how the Elizabethans dressed. From reading about Capulet's party, you can get an idea of what Renaissance parties were like. Study the photos and make a list of questions you have about the period costumes. Or reread Scene 5 and make a list of things you would like to know about Elizabethan music, dancing, and party masks. Keep your notes and add to them as you continue the play.

Creative Writing

2. Society Column

Imagine that you are a columnist for the Verona newspaper. Write a column in which you cover Capulet's party, noting the guests, their outfits, and interesting gossip.

Performance

3. Speak the Speech

Choose a speech from this act and prepare it for performance. Your first step should be to write out or type the speech. Then, read it aloud several times so that you feel the rhythm created by the **blank verse**. Watch for **end-stopped lines** and **run-on lines**. Pay attention to **alliteration** and **rhyme**. Before your performance, read your lines in front of a small audience, and ask for evaluation. If you have a partner you'd like to perform with, do the love "duet" that Romeo and Juliet recite in Scene 5, lines 95–112.

VOCABULARY   `HOW TO OWN A WORD`

Shakespeare's Words and Their Relatives

As you see by the list on page 733, many words in Shakespeare's plays have different meanings today. *Humor,* for example, comes from a Latin word for "moisture" or "fluid." In Shakespeare's time, people believed there were four fluids, or humors, in the body. These regulated a person's temperament. *Humorous* eventually came to refer to a person who can see comedy in situations.

Choose five words from the list on page 733, and use a good dictionary to research their origins. (Which words are very old English words, rooted in Anglo-Saxon, or Old English?) Make a diagram showing their origins, what each word meant in Shakespeare's day, and what it means today.

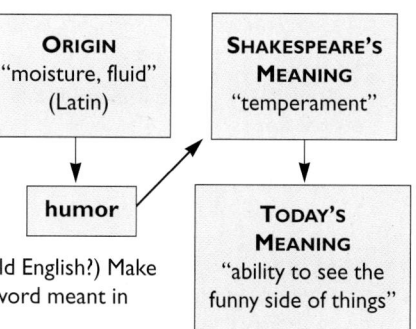

ORIGIN "moisture, fluid" (Latin)

SHAKESPEARE'S MEANING "temperament"

humor

TODAY'S MEANING "ability to see the funny side of things"

THE TRAGEDY OF ROMEO AND JULIET, ACT I 763

Grading Timesaver

Rubrics for each Choices assignment appear on p. 201 in the *Portfolio Management System*.

CHOICES: Building Your Portfolio

1. **Writer's Notebook**   To help spark ideas show students Franco Zeffirelli's film version of *Romeo and Juliet.* Stop the video at the point when Romeo and Juliet meet, and have students discuss details of costume, music, dance, and masks that caught their attention.
2. **Creative Writing**   To help students get started, bring in samples of social or gossip columns from newspapers or magazines. Have students read passages aloud in order to hear the tone of such articles.
3. **Performance**   Students may also choose to perform the Prologue as a choral reading, or partners may choose a dialogue between characters, such as Mercutio and Romeo.

VOCABULARY
Possible Answers
Word: **but**
Shakespeare's meaning: if, only
Today's meaning: except, yet
Origin: without, outside (Old English)
Word: **maid**
Shakespeare's meaning: unmarried girl
Today's meaning: a person whose job is cleaning
Origin: maiden (Middle English)
Word: **nice**
Shakespeare's meaning: trivial, foolish
Today's meaning: agreeable, good
Origin: ignorant, not knowing (Latin)
Word: **owes**
Shakespeare's meaning: owns
Today's meaning: is indebted to
Origin: to own, possess (Old English)
Word: **mark**
Shakespeare's meaning: listen to
Today's meaning: a visible impression on a surface, to set off as distinctive
Origin: borderland (Latin)

Using Students' Strengths

Linguistic Learners
Challenge students to write their column for Choice 2 in Elizabethan English. Remind them that, as in modern English, there will be several ways of expressing the same idea. However, students should attempt to use authentic language conventions of the era, such as *-th* endings *for* the third-person singular, forms of *thou,* and accurate vocabulary, including words from the list on p. 733.

ACT II

Enter CHORUS.

Chorus.
Now old desire doth in his deathbed lie,
    And young affection gapes to be his heir;
That fair° for which love groaned for and would die,
    With tender Juliet matched, is now not fair.
5 Now Romeo is beloved and loves again,
    Alike° bewitchèd by the charm of looks;
But to his foe supposed he must complain,°
    And she steal love's sweet bait from fearful hooks.
Being held a foe, he may not have access
10   To breathe such vows as lovers use to swear,°
And she as much in love, her means much less
    To meet her new belovèd anywhere;
But passion lends them power, time means, to meet,
Temp'ring extremities° with extreme sweet.° [*Exit.*]

3. That fair: Rosaline.

6. Alike: both (both Romeo and Juliet).
7. complain: ask Juliet's father, his foe, for her hand in marriage.

10. use to swear: are used to promising.

14. extremities: difficulties.
extreme sweet: very sweet delights.
? 14. *According to the chorus, what has happened to Romeo's old love? What is his new problem? What line suggests what the love of these young people is based on?*

Scene 1. Near Capulet's orchard.

Enter ROMEO *alone.*

Romeo.
Can I go forward when my heart is here?
Turn back, dull earth, and find thy center° out.

[*Enter* BENVOLIO *with* MERCUTIO. ROMEO *retires.*]

Benvolio.
Romeo! My cousin Romeo! Romeo!
Mercutio.   He is wise
And, on my life, hath stol'n him home to bed.
Benvolio.
5 He ran this way and leapt this orchard wall.
Call, good Mercutio.
Mercutio.   Nay, I'll conjure too.
Romeo! Humors! Madman! Passion! Lover!

2. center: Juliet. The "dull earth" is Romeo, and Juliet is his soul.
? Stage direction: *Though the stage direction says that Romeo "retires," Shakespeare did not mean for him to retire quietly, for a few lines later Benvolio says he was running. Romeo has often been played by actors in middle age, and leaping over the wall has been a problem for them. Many older Romeos have in fact chosen to "retire" behind the wall. How might this wall be arranged on stage so that we continue to see Romeo hiding in Capulet's orchard and Benvolio and Mercutio in the lane?*

764 WILLIAM SHAKESPEARE

Appear thou in the likeness of a sigh;
Speak but one rhyme, and I am satisfied!
Cry but "Ay me!" pronounce but "love" and
10   "dove";
Speak to my gossip° Venus one fair word,
One nickname for her purblind° son and heir,
Young Abraham Cupid,° he that shot so true
When King Cophetua loved the beggar maid!°   **B**
15 He heareth not, he stirreth not, he moveth not;
The ape is dead,° and I must conjure him.
I conjure thee by Rosaline's bright eyes,
By her high forehead and her scarlet lip,
By her fine foot, straight leg, and quivering thigh, **C**
20 And the demesnes° that there adjacent lie,
That in thy likeness thou appear to us!
Benvolio.
And if he hear thee, thou wilt anger him.
Mercutio.
This cannot anger him. 'Twould anger him
To raise a spirit in his mistress' circle°
25 Of some strange nature, letting it there stand
Till she had laid it and conjured it down.
That were some spite;° my invocation
Is fair and honest: in his mistress' name,
I conjure only but to raise up him.
Benvolio.
30 Come, he hath hid himself among these trees
To be consorted° with the humorous° night.
Blind is his love and best befits the dark. **D**
Mercutio.
If love be blind, love cannot hit the mark.
And wish his mistress were that kind of fruit
35 As maids call medlars when they laugh alone.
O, Romeo, that she were, O that she were
An open et cetera, thou a pop'rin pear!
Romeo, good night. I'll to my truckle bed;
This field bed is too cold for me to sleep.
Come, shall we go?
40 **Benvolio.**   Go then, for 'tis in vain
To seek him here that means not to be found.
                             [Exit with others.]

      **❝ Blind is his love and
      best befits the dark. ❞**

---

11. gossip: good friend. Venus is the goddess of love.
12. purblind: blind.
13. Young Abraham Cupid: To Mercutio, Romeo seems the very figure of love—old like Abraham in the Bible and young like Cupid.
14. When . . . maid: from a popular ballad.
16. The ape is dead: Romeo is "playing" dead.

20. demesnes: domains; regions.

? **22.** *What is Benvolio's tone here? Why would Romeo be angry at Mercutio's remarks?*

24. circle: magical place.

27. spite: cause to be angry.

31. consorted: familiar. **humorous:** damp.

THE TRAGEDY OF ROMEO AND JULIET, ACT II, SCENE I **765**

A Reading Skills and Strategies
Reading Shakespeare's Poetry
Have a volunteer read the opening chorus on p. 764 aloud, and ask the class to analyze its rhyme scheme. Then, have them compare the rhyme scheme with that of the Prologue for Act I. [Both are sonnets with the rhyme scheme *abab cdcd efef gg.*]

B Struggling Readers
Reading Aloud
Read this passage aloud to help students appreciate Mercutio's humorous, mocking tone. He is parodying Romeo's earlier flowery speeches about love.

C Elements of Literature
Irony
? What is ironic about this particular taunt by Mercutio? [Mercutio does not realize that Romeo has completely forgotten about Rosaline and is now in love with Juliet.]

D Critical Thinking
Interpreting
? What is meant by the popular saying referred to here, "Love is blind"? [Possible response: When people fall in love, they cannot see any imperfections in the person they love.]

Answers to Margin Questions
Act II, Chorus
Line 14. Romeo's love for Rosaline has died. He now loves Juliet, the daughter of his father's enemy. He will have difficulty even seeing Juliet and cannot expect her father to approve of their marriage. Line 6 of the chorus says that Romeo and Juliet are "Alike bewitchèd by the charm of looks."
Act II, Scene I
Stage direction. The wall could be placed stage right or left, angled so that the side on which Romeo is hiding is visible, and Mercutio and Benvolio are visible on the other side.
Line 22. Benvolio is trying both to subdue and to warn Mercutio. Romeo would be angry because Mercutio is mocking Romeo's passion and making a bawdy joke at Rosaline's expense.

Reaching All Students

English Language Learners
Continue to use videos, audiotaped performances, and reading aloud to help these students follow the play. For other strategies for engaging English language learners with the literature, see
• *Lesson Plans Including Strategies for English-Language Learners*

Advanced Learners
Have students write a love sonnet either from Romeo to Juliet or from Juliet to Romeo. They may use Elizabethan language or contemporary English.

T765

Act II, Scene 2

Romeo glimpses Juliet at her window. Enraptured, he delivers a monologue praising her beauty. Unaware of Romeo's presence, Juliet begins speaking of her love for him, as well as her disregard for the feud that separates their families. Romeo emerges from the shadows, and Juliet recognizes his voice. Aware of the dangerous position Romeo is in, she asks why he is there at all. Romeo says that he would rather be dead than be denied the presence of his love. Juliet is afraid that Romeo will think that her love is not genuine because it has been declared so readily. Romeo begins to swear his love, but Juliet stops his rash declarations, fearful of their intensity. Hearing her nurse call, she withdraws but bids Romeo to wait. When she reappears at the window, she declares that if Romeo really loves her, he will marry her. Juliet says that the next morning she will send a messenger to Romeo, who is to arrange a place and time for their marriage. The nurse calls again, and Juliet withdraws but appears at the window one last time. The lovers are reluctant to part, but they must.

Ⓐ Advanced Learners

Students tracing the play's images of light and darkness will find Romeo's monologue of special interest, since he compares Juliet to both the sun and the stars. He also mocks the moon, symbol of chastity, saying it is envious of Juliet's beauty and urging her to no longer remain under its influence.

Ⓑ Reading Skills and Strategies

Reading Shakespeare's Poetry

Point out how Shakespeare uses a few "tricks" to make his lines fit the rhythmic pattern of iambic pentameter. Accent marks (`) indicate that a syllable or letter should be pronounced, even though it is usually silent. Apostrophes (') indicate that a syllable or letter has been dropped and should not be pronounced.

Answers to Margin Questions

Line 1. Romeo implies that Mercutio has never felt the pain of love. The "wound" is from Cupid's arrow.

Line 25. Romeo says that Juliet is a "bright angel" and "a wingèd messenger of heaven."

Scene 2. *Capulet's orchard.*

Romeo (*coming forward*).
    He jests at scars that never felt a wound.

[*Enter* JULIET *at a window.*]

Ⓐ
    But soft! What light through yonder window breaks?
    It is the East, and Juliet is the sun!
    Arise, fair sun, and kill the envious moon,
5   Who is already sick and pale with grief
    That thou her maid° art far more fair than she.
    Be not her maid, since she is envious.
    Her vestal livery° is but sick and green,°
    And none but fools do wear it. Cast it off.
10 It is my lady! O, it is my love!
    O, that she knew she were!
    She speaks, yet she says nothing. What of that?
    Her eye discourses;° I will answer it.
    I am too bold; 'tis not to me she speaks.
15 Two of the fairest stars in all the heaven,
    Having some business, do entreat her eyes
    To twinkle in their spheres till they return.
    What if her eyes were there, they in her head?
    The brightness of her cheek would shame those stars
20 As daylight doth a lamp; her eyes in heaven
    Would through the airy region stream so bright
    That birds would sing and think it were not night.
    See how she leans her cheek upon her hand!
    O, that I were a glove upon that hand,
    That I might touch that cheek!
Juliet.   Ay me!
25 **Romeo.**   She speaks.
    O, speak again, bright angel, for thou art
    As glorious to this night, being o'er my head,
    As is a wingèd messenger of heaven
Ⓑ Unto the white-upturnèd wond'ring eyes
30 Of mortals that fall back to gaze on him
    When he bestrides the lazy puffing clouds
    And sails upon the bosom of the air.
Juliet.
    O Romeo, Romeo! Wherefore art thou Romeo?°
    Deny thy father and refuse thy name;
35 Or, if thou wilt not, be but sworn my love,
    And I'll no longer be a Capulet.

? **1.** *This begins the balcony scene, one of the most famous scenes in all dramatic literature. In 190 magical lines, the two lovers woo and win each other. (In the wide-open Elizabethan theater, the balcony scene presented no staging problems. In modern theaters, however, it is often difficult to have a balcony high enough and yet still visible to people sitting in the back of the theater.) Romeo has heard all the joking. Whom is he referring to here, and what kind of "wound" is he talking about?*

6. thou her maid: Juliet, whom Romeo sees as the servant of the virgin goddess of the moon, Diana.

8. vestal livery: maidenly clothing. **sick and green:** Unmarried girls supposedly had "greensickness," or anemia.

13. discourses: speaks.

? **25.** *Romeo and Juliet rarely talk of each other in straightforward prose. What are some of the metaphors and images that Romeo uses to express his love here?*

33. In other words, "Why is your name Romeo?" (It is the name of her enemy.)

"O Romeo, Romeo! Wherefore art thou Romeo?"

Using Students' Strengths

Kinesthetic Learners

Ask pairs of students to perform the balcony scene, either in Shakespeare's language, in a modern "translation," or in pantomime. Videotape their performances to share with other classes. Make tapes available for students to share with their families.

Auditory/Musical Learners

As they read the play or work on other assignments, these students may enjoy listening to Tchaikovsky's *Romeo and Juliet* ballet or the soundtrack of Zeffirelli's film version of *Romeo and Juliet.*

Spatial Learners

Following the changes in location in Act II can be difficult. Ask these students to make columns on a sheet of paper with the following headings and then to list events that occur in each location as they read: "Near Capulet's Orchard," "Friar Laurence's Cell," "Street."

A Appreciating Language
Archaic Language

❓ Have students "translate" this famous passage into contemporary English. [Possible response: Does it really matter what name we call something? A rose would still smell as sweet, even if it had a different name. And Romeo would be just as perfect if he had a different name. Give up your name, Romeo, and in exchange, take me.]

B Reading Skills and Strategies
Responding to the Text

❓ Are you surprised by Romeo's immediate willingness to give up being a Montague? [Possible responses: No, because he seems to keep his distance from his family; yes, because he has barely met Juliet.]

C Critical Thinking
Making Connections

Point out that by calling Juliet "dear saint," Romeo is continuing the religious wordplay they started at the party.

Answers to Margin Questions

Line 37. Juliet loves Romeo so much that she is willing to renounce her family for his love.

Line 42. Juliet says that things exist independently from their names: A different name would not change Romeo's appearance or character.

Line 53. Juliet speaks directly to Romeo, asking "What man art thou . . . ?" She is surprised and could be angry, embarrassed, and even frightened, not yet knowing who has overheard her.

Romeo (aside).
    Shall I hear more, or shall I speak at this?
Juliet.
    'Tis but thy name that is my enemy.
    Thou art thyself, though not° a Montague.
40   What's Montague? It is nor hand, nor foot,
    Nor arm, nor face. O, be some other name
    Belonging to a man.
    What's in a name? That which we call a rose
45   By any other word would smell as sweet.
    So Romeo would, were he not Romeo called,
A   Retain that dear perfection which he owes°
    Without that title. Romeo, doff thy name;
    And for thy name, which is no part of thee,
    Take all myself.

> **"** *What's in a name? That which we*
> *call a rose*
> *By any other word would smell*
> *as sweet.* **"**

    Romeo.   I take thee at thy word.
50 B Call me but love, and I'll be new baptized;
    Henceforth I never will be Romeo.
Juliet.
    What man art thou, that, thus bescreened in night,
    So stumblest on my counsel?°
    Romeo.   By a name
    I know not how to tell thee who I am.
55 C My name, dear saint, is hateful to myself
    Because it is an enemy to thee.
    Had I it written, I would tear the word.
Juliet.
    My ears have yet not drunk a hundred words
    Of thy tongue's uttering, yet I know the sound.
60   Art thou not Romeo, and a Montague?
    Romeo.
    Neither, fair maid, if either thee dislike.
Juliet.
    How camest thou hither, tell me, and wherefore?
    The orchard walls are high and hard to climb,
    And the place death, considering who thou art,
65   If any of my kinsmen find thee here.

768 WILLIAM SHAKESPEARE

❓ **37.** *Juliet does not know Romeo is standing beneath her balcony. What has Romeo now learned about her feelings for him?*
39. though not: even if you were not.

❓ **42.** *Short lines like this one usually indicate an interruption or pause. Here, Juliet pauses to think about a question. What does she say in answer to this question about the true significance of a "name"?*
46. owes: owns.

53. counsel: private thoughts.
❓ **53.** *How do you know Romeo has finally spoken aloud to Juliet? What are her feelings in this speech?*

Crossing the Curriculum

Drama
Students interested in theater arts may enjoy researching the different ways that the balcony scene has been staged throughout the play's history. If photographs or illustrations are not available, students can sketch or paint the scene as they imagine it might have looked in performance.

Geography
Students can enhance their understanding of the relationship between geography and culture by exploring a map of Italy, where the action in the play takes place. Ask students to locate Italy on a world map and to note its relationship to the rest of southern Europe and its extension into the Mediterranean Sea. Have students speculate about how trade and the development of a merchant class might have been affected by Italy's being bordered extensively by the sea.

Romeo.

With love's light wings did I o'erperch° these walls;
For stony limits cannot hold love out,
And what love can do, that dares love attempt.
Therefore thy kinsmen are no stop to me.

Juliet.

70   If they do see thee, they will murder thee.

Romeo.

Alack, there lies more peril in thine eye
Than twenty of their swords! Look thou but sweet,
And I am proof° against their enmity.

Juliet.

I would not for the world they saw thee here.

Romeo.

75   I have night's cloak to hide me from their eyes;
And but° thou love me, let them find me here.
My life were better ended by their hate
Than death proroguèd,° wanting of thy love.

Juliet.

By whose direction found'st thou out this place?

Romeo.

80   By Love, that first did prompt me to inquire.
He lent me counsel, and I lent him eyes.
I am no pilot; yet, wert thou as far
As that vast shore washed with the farthest sea,
I should adventure for such merchandise.

Juliet.

85   Thou knowest the mask of night is on my face;
Else would a maiden blush bepaint my cheek
For that which thou hast heard me speak tonight.
Fain would I dwell on form—fain, fain deny
What I have spoke; but farewell compliment.°
90   Dost thou love me? I know thou wilt say "Ay";
And I will take thy word. Yet, if thou swear'st,
Thou mayst prove false. At lovers' perjuries,
They say Jove laughs. O gentle Romeo,
If thou dost love, pronounce it faithfully.
95   Or if thou think'st I am too quickly won,
I'll frown and be perverse and say thee nay,
So thou wilt woo; but else, not for the world.
In truth, fair Montague, I am too fond,°
And therefore thou mayst think my havior° light;
100   But trust me, gentleman, I'll prove more true
Than those that have more cunning to be strange.°
I should have been more strange, I must confess,
But that thou overheard'st, ere I was ware,
My truelove passion. Therefore pardon me,
105   And not impute this yielding to light love,

THE TRAGEDY OF ROMEO AND JULIET, ACT II, SCENE 2   **769**

---

66. **o'erperch:** fly over.

73. **proof:** armored.

? 74. *Juliet is practical. She fears Romeo will be murdered. What is Romeo's tone— is he also fearful and cautious, or is he reckless and elated?*

76. **but:** if only.

78. **proroguèd:** postponed.

? 78. *The two lovers will repeatedly remind us that they prefer death to separation. What does this speech tell us of Romeo's intentions? Do you think he is seriously thinking of death here, or is he being impulsive and exaggerating—as many people are when they've fallen head over heels in love?*

? 85. *Juliet's thoughts race now, and she probably speaks rapidly here. Read this speech aloud. Where does she shift from embarrassment to frankness, to pleading, to anxiety, to doubt? Why is she worried that Romeo will think poorly of her?*

89. **compliment:** good manners.

98. **fond:** affectionate, tender.

99. **havior:** behavior.

101. **strange:** aloof or cold.

D Elements of Literature

Rising Action

? What complication threatens the lovers' happiness? [Their families are enemies, and Romeo could be killed if he were caught under Juliet's window.] Which one of them seems to take this threat more seriously? Explain. [Juliet seems more concerned; she warns Romeo about it twice, but he is so carried away by love that he feels no fear.]

E Appreciating Language

Archaic Language

Have students "translate" this difficult passage into contemporary English. [Possible response: As long as I know you love me, I don't care if I'm caught here. I'd rather die knowing you love me than go on living without your love.]

F Critical Thinking

Challenging the Text

? Do you find it plausible that Romeo found himself beneath Juliet's window at the exact moment she was expressing her love for him? [Possible responses: Romeo's appearance at the right moment is a big coincidence that might strain credibility; we are so caught up in this whirlwind romance, just as the lovers are, that we accept that they are "fated" to be thrown together.]

G Reading Skills and Strategies

Connecting with the Text

? Do you think a teenage girl of today would be just as embarrassed to have the boy she loves overhear her true feelings so early in their relationship? Explain. [Students will probably enjoy discussing how the "rules" for boys and girls in a dating situation have changed in some ways and remained the same in others over the centuries.]

Answers to Margin Questions

Line 74. Romeo is reckless and elated, as though love makes him invulnerable.

Line 78. Romeo intends to risk everything for Juliet's love. The play will eventually prove the truth of Romeo's assertions, but at this point, expect students to debate his seriousness.

Line 85. She shifts from embarrassment to frankness at l. 89, "but farewell compliment"; to pleading at l. 90, "Dost thou love me?"; to anxiety at ll. 91–92, "Yet, if thou swear'st,/ Thou mayst prove false"; to doubt at l. 94. Juliet is worried because she has not been coy but has inadvertently revealed her true feelings.

Listening to the Music ♪♪

"Ah léve-toi, soleil" ("Ah, rise, sun!") from *Roméo et Juliette* by Charles Gounod

"Tonight" from *West Side Story* by Leonard Bernstein, lyrics by Stephen Sondheim

French composer Charles Gounod (shärl' gōō•nō') (1818–1893) won fame with operas inspired by literature, like *Faust* and *Roméo et Juliette*. In the balcony scene of the latter, Romeo sings the aria *"Ah léve-toi, soleil."* *West Side Story* is a musical by the American conductor and composer Leonard Bernstein (1918–1990), with

lyrics by Stephen Sondheim. It is based on the story of *Romeo and Juliet*, but set in 1950s New York, where the lovers, Tony and Maria, are from rival gangs, one white, one Hispanic. The balcony scene is set on a fire escape, where the couple sing "Tonight."

Activity

After students have read Act II, Scene 2, play them the two song adaptations of that scene, and have them consider which composer best captures the lovers' emotions.

" O, swear not by the moon, the inconstant moon,
That monthly changes in her circle orb,
Lest that thy love prove likewise variable. "

Getting Students Involved

Cooperative Learning

Create Summaries of Scenes. Divide the class into small groups, and have each group summarize a different scene that the class has read. Assign a member of each group to take notes and write the finished summary. The summaries should be posted on the bulletin board or copied and passed out to students; they can serve as a handy reference during the reading of subsequent acts.

Analyze Difficult Lines. As students read Act II, ask them to note lines they find difficult to comprehend. After students have finished reading each scene, have group members share their notes with each other. Group members can work together to analyze these lines for meaning.

Write an Advice Letter. Students are likely to suggest that the young couple's plans to be married are impractical. Ask groups to explain, in the form of an advice columnist's response, why the wedding plans are impractical and to offer a more rational solution to the dilemma that Romeo and Juliet face.

Which the dark night hath so discoverèd.°

Romeo.
    Lady, by yonder blessèd moon I vow,
    That tips with silver all these fruit-tree tops——

Juliet.
    O, swear not by the moon, the inconstant moon,
110   That monthly changes in her circle orb,
    Lest that thy love prove likewise variable.

Romeo.
    What shall I swear by?

Juliet.   Do not swear at all;
    Or if thou wilt, swear by thy gracious self,
    Which is the god of my idolatry,
    And I'll believe thee.

115   **Romeo.**   If my heart's dear love——

Juliet.
    Well, do not swear. Although I joy in thee,
    I have no joy of this contract tonight.
    It is too rash, too unadvised, too sudden;
    Too like the lightning, which doth cease to be
120   Ere one can say it lightens. Sweet, good night!
    This bud of love, by summer's ripening breath,
    May prove a beauteous flower when next we meet.
    Good night, good night! As sweet repose and rest
    Come to thy heart as that within my breast!

Romeo.
125   O, wilt thou leave me so unsatisfied?

Juliet.
    What satisfaction canst thou have tonight?

Romeo.
    The exchange of thy love's faithful vow for mine.

Juliet.
    I gave thee mine before thou didst request it;
    And yet I would it were to give again.

Romeo.
130   Wouldst thou withdraw it? For what purpose, love?

Juliet.
    But to be frank° and give it thee again.
    And yet I wish but for the thing I have.
    My bounty° is as boundless as the sea,
    My love as deep; the more I give to thee,
135   The more I have, for both are infinite.
    I hear some noise within. Dear love, adieu!

[NURSE *calls within.*]

    Anon, good nurse! Sweet Montague, be true.
    Stay but a little, I will come again.   [*Exit.*]

THE TRAGEDY OF ROMEO AND JULIET, ACT II, SCENE 2 **771**

---

106. discoverèd: revealed.

? 109. *Why is Juliet afraid of having Romeo swear by the moon? If you were speaking these lines, would you make them comic, or would you make Juliet sound genuinely frightened?*

? 120. *Romeo is quick with vows and promises. Why has Juliet become fearful and cautious?*

131. frank: generous.

133. bounty: capacity for giving.

A Elements of Literature
Rising Action
Have students notice Juliet's interruptions here. Rather than rudeness, the interruptions convey the lovers' excitement, as well as the growing recklessness and urgency they feel about their love. It is this speed and urgency that quickly pushes the plot forward to its tragic conclusion.

B Elements of Literature
Foreshadowing
? How does Shakespeare use images of light and darkness here to hint at dangers to come? [Juliet expresses her fear at the rashness of their love by comparing it to lightning, which flashes briefly and then "doth cease to be." Her description foreshadows the coming deaths of the lovers.]

C Critical Thinking
Analyzing Character
? What does Juliet's response to Romeo reveal about her character? [Possible responses: It shows that Juliet is enjoying the exchange of vows; she is letting herself get carried away with love; she knows true love is a rich feeling.]

Answers to Margin Questions
Line 109. Juliet wants Romeo's vow to be unchangeable, which the moon is not. Most students will not imagine a comic delivery because Juliet has so far been fervent and serious.
Line 120. She fears they are "too sudden" in their vows and believes that time should test their love.

Professional Notes

Critical Comment: Love Tragedy
Advanced learners may wish to compare and contrast *Romeo and Juliet* with *Antony and Cleopatra*. Philip Edwards, writing in the *Oxford Illustrated History of English Literature,* suggests some initial comparisons:

"*Romeo and Juliet* is Shakespeare's love tragedy of youth as *Antony and Cleopatra* is his love tragedy of middle age. To Juliet, a girl of fourteen, hedged around by nurse and parents and a family feud, comes the liberation of first love—which Shakespeare enshrines in a sonnet shared between Romeo and Juliet when they kiss. The plot moves forward by a simple mechanism of ironic reversals which mark the stages of a clear path of 'responsibility' for the tragic outcome. . . . If there is less than full tragedy at the end, it is . . . because, for all their impetuousness, the young lovers in their desperately sad conclusion are simply victims—not of fate, but of their elders and betters. There is nothing of that fatal collaboration in one's own destruction which is so marked in the great later tragedies. Intense pity, little terror. 'Catharsis' there certainly is in *Romeo and Juliet,* however, in our feeling that the lovers, completing their union in death as they could not complete it in life, are at least *safe;* and in our feeling that such love as theirs . . . was a dedication to a higher scale of values than obtained in the violent commerce of the worldly society they lived in."

T771

A Critical Thinking
Making Connections

? How do Romeo's words here echo those of Mercutio in his Queen Mab speech in Act I, Scene 4? [Possible response: Although Romeo and Juliet love the night because it allows them to be together, Romeo also fears that what is happening may be as unreal as a dream. Mercutio described dreams as coming from "vain fantasy" and having no bearing on reality.]

B Critical Thinking
Speculating

? What might have prompted Juliet to talk about marriage upon her return to the balcony? [Possible responses: Seeing her nurse inside reminds Juliet of the talk with her mother about marriage earlier that day; she remembers that plans to engage her to Paris are in the works.]

C Literary Connections

In Greek myth, Echo was a nymph who was deprived of the power of speech as a punishment from the goddess Hera. Afterward, Echo fell in love with Narcissus, but she was unable to declare her love. She went to live in solitary caves, where she died of a broken heart.

Answers to Margin Questions

Line 148. Juliet says that she will give herself to Romeo only through marriage. She shows her fears in ll. 143–144 and 150–151.

Line 154. The similes in ll. 157–158 indicate this movement. Romeo says he is as reluctant to go away from Juliet as a schoolboy is to go toward school.

Romeo.

O blessèd, blessèd night! I am afeard,
140 **A** Being in night, all this is but a dream,
Too flattering-sweet to be substantial.

[*Enter* JULIET *again.*]

Juliet.

Three words, dear Romeo, and good night indeed.
If that thy bent° of love be honorable,
Thy purpose marriage, send me word tomorrow,
145 **B** By one that I'll procure to come to thee,
Where and what time thou wilt perform the rite;
And all my fortunes at thy foot I'll lay
And follow thee my lord throughout the world.

Nurse (*within*). Madam!

Juliet.

150 I come anon.—But if thou meanest not well,
I do beseech thee——

Nurse (*within*). Madam!

Juliet.   By and by I come.—
To cease thy strife° and leave me to my grief.
Tomorrow will I send.

Romeo.   So thrive my soul——

Juliet.

155 A thousand times good night!   [*Exit.*]

Romeo.

A thousand times the worse, to want thy light!
Love goes toward love as schoolboys from their books;
But love from love, toward school with heavy looks.

[*Enter* JULIET *again.*]

Juliet.

Hist! Romeo, hist! O for a falc'ner's voice
160 To lure this tassel gentle° back again!
Bondage is hoarse° and may not speak aloud,
Else would I tear the cave where Echo° lies
C And make her airy tongue more hoarse than mine
With repetition of "My Romeo!"

Romeo.

165 It is my soul that calls upon my name.
How silver-sweet sound lovers' tongues by night,
Like softest music to attending ears!

Juliet.

Romeo!

Romeo.

My sweet?

143. bent: intention.

? 148. *What is Juliet making clear to Romeo here? Where does she show that she still fears he may be false with her?*

153. strife: efforts to win her.

? 154. *With this fervent vow, Romeo swears by his immortal soul. What lines that follow indicate that Romeo turns around and heads away from Juliet's balcony?*

160. tassel gentle: male falcon.
161. Bondage is hoarse: Juliet is in "bondage" to her parents and must whisper.
162. Echo: mythical girl who could only repeat others' final words.

Skill Link

Understanding Inverted Sentences

Tell students that even when we recognize Shakespeare's vocabulary, we often stumble over his sentences because he inverts the standard syntax, or word order, we are used to in English sentences. The patterns we know best are the following:

subject	verb	
The night	fades quickly.	

subject	verb	object
I	kiss	your hand.

But Shakespeare often favors inverted patterns:

verb	subject	
Quickly fades	the night.	

object	subject	verb
Your hand	I	do kiss.

Activity

Have students write the following sentences from the play in standard syntax:

1. "And all my fortunes at thy foot I'll lay." [And I'll lay all my fortunes at thy foot.]
2. "Else would I tear the cave where Echo lies." [Else I would tear the cave where Echo lives.]
3. "How silver-sweet sound lovers' tongues by night." [How silver-sweet lovers' tongues sound by night.]

Juliet. What o'clock tomorrow
Shall I send to thee?

Romeo. By the hour of nine.

Juliet.
170   I will not fail. 'Tis twenty years till then.
  I have forgot why I did call thee back.

Romeo.
  Let me stand here till thou remember it.

Juliet.
  I shall forget, to have thee still stand there,
  Rememb'ring how I love thy company.

Romeo.
175   And I'll still stay, to have thee still forget,
  Forgetting any other home but this.

Juliet.
  'Tis almost morning. I would have thee gone—
  And yet no farther than a wanton's° bird,
  That lets it hop a little from his hand,
180   Like a poor prisoner in his twisted gyves,°
  And with a silken thread plucks it back again,
  So loving-jealous of his liberty.

Romeo.
  I would I were thy bird.

Juliet. Sweet, so would I.
  Yet I should kill thee with much cherishing.
185   Good night, good night! Parting is such sweet sorrow
  That I shall say good night till it be morrow.   *[Exit.]*

Romeo.
  Sleep dwell upon thine eyes, peace in thy breast!
  Would I were sleep and peace, so sweet to rest!
  Hence will I to my ghostly friar's° close cell,
190   His help to crave and my dear hap° to tell.   *[Exit.]*

178. wanton's: careless child's.

180. gyves: chains, like the threads that hold the bird captive.

❓ 184. *What terrible future event does this line foreshadow?*

❓ 185. *Why is parting "sweet" to Juliet? (Is she enjoying this prolonged farewell?)*

189. ghostly friar's: spiritual father's.
190. hap: luck.

" *Parting is such sweet sorrow*
That I shall say good night till it be morrow. "

D 🅓 Critical Thinking
Interpreting
❓ Although Romeo and Juliet have to wait only a few hours to see each other again, Juliet says that it will feel like twenty years. How has Juliet's perception of time changed since she met Romeo? [Possible response: Time is distorted for Juliet; any time away from Romeo seems much longer than it actually is.]

E 🅔 Struggling Readers
Paraphrasing
Have students reread this passage several times, referring to the side notes in the pupil's edition, until they can paraphrase what Juliet is trying to say. [Possible response: I don't want you to go farther than a pet bird on a string that I could pull right back again when it went away from me.]

F 🅕 Reading Skills and Strategies
Reading Shakespeare's Poetry
Ask two students to read these famous farewell speeches aloud. Have students discuss any other lines in the play they have especially enjoyed so far. Encourage them to look for others as they read on and to jot them down in their notebooks.

Answers to Margin Questions
Line 184. Juliet's image foreshadows that her love will be the cause of Romeo's death.
Line 185. Juliet's oxymoron expresses her pleasure in extending her goodbyes, for they allow her to stay with Romeo as long as possible.

Skill Link

Recognizing Elliptical Constructions
Another difficulty students face in reading Shakespeare's archaic language is the playwright's tendency to leave out words. For example, whereas Juliet says, "O for a falc'ner's voice," we would say, "Oh, I wish I had a falconer's voice."

Activity
1. Have students fill in the missing words from the following elliptical sentence:
"Love goes toward love as schoolboys from their books;/But love from love, toward school with heavy looks."
[Love goes toward love as schoolboys go away from their books;/But love goes away from love as schoolboys go toward school—with heavy looks.]

2. Now have students read the completed sentence aloud, and note that filling in all the implied subjects and verbs makes the meaning perfectly clear but destroys the poetry of the lines.

Summary ■ ■

Act II, Scene 3

Early the next morning, Romeo goes to the cell of Friar Laurence, his spiritual adviser. The friar is in his garden, contemplating nature. He soliloquizes that all of nature's creations are beneficial if put to their proper use; if misused, however, the result can be deadly. Men, like nature, are also capable of both good and evil. Romeo greets him, and the friar perceives that there is something amiss, or the young man would not be out so early. Romeo tells of his love for Juliet and asks the friar to perform their wedding. The friar chides Romeo for his change of heart, but agrees to marry them, for he thinks their union will unite their respective families and end the feud.

Ⓐ Reading Skills and Strategies

Reading Shakespeare's Poetry

Point out that Friar Laurence's speech is composed entirely of rhymed couplets. Ask a student to read the speech aloud. Then, have them check the rest of the scene for more speeches in rhymed couplets. [The entire scene is in rhymed couplets.]

Ⓑ Elements of Literature

Foreshadowing

The references to death and the dangers of herbs that are misused foreshadow some of the tragedy to come. Friar Laurence's knowledge of herbs will turn out to be crucial to the plot.

Answers to Margin Questions

Line 1. The friar describes dawn. Romeo said the night was so wonderful he feared it was a dream. Friar Laurence, however, presents night as "frowning" and "dank," a "drunkard" who reels off the path set by the cheering sun.

Line 22. The images of earth as both a tomb and a womb (ll. 10–11) first suggest the duality, which Friar Laurence then details in ll. 17–20. The friar's reminder is "Virtue itself turns vice, being misapplied, / And vice sometime by action dignified" (ll. 21–22).

Line 23. Friar Laurence is saying that like plants, people contain within themselves both creative and destructive powers. The audience is reminded that Romeo and Juliet must handle their passion carefully so that it is enriching, not consuming.

T774

Scene 3. Friar Laurence's cell.

Enter FRIAR LAURENCE *alone, with a basket.*

Friar.

Ⓐ
The gray-eyed morn smiles on the frowning night,
Check'ring the eastern clouds with streaks of light;
And fleckèd darkness like a drunkard reels
From forth day's path and Titan's burning wheels.°
5   Now, ere the sun advance his burning eye
The day to cheer and night's dank dew to dry,
I must upfill this osier cage° of ours
With baleful° weeds and precious-juicèd flowers.
The earth that's Nature's mother is her tomb.
10   What is her burying grave, that is her womb;
And from her womb children of divers kind
We sucking on her natural bosom find,
Many for many virtues excellent,
None but for some, and yet all different.
15   Ⓑ O, mickle° is the powerful grace that lies
In plants, herbs, stones, and their true qualities;
For naught so vile that on the earth doth live
But to the earth some special good doth give;
Nor aught so good but, strained° from that fair use,
20   Revolts from true birth,° stumbling on abuse.
Virtue itself turns vice, being misapplied,
And vice sometime by action dignified.

[*Enter* ROMEO.]

Within the infant rind° of this weak flower
Poison hath residence and medicine° power;
25   For this, being smelt, with that part cheers each part;°
Being tasted, stays all senses with the heart.
Two such opposèd kings encamp them still°
In man as well as herbs—grace and rude will;
And where the worser is predominant,
30   Full soon the canker° death eats up that plant.

Romeo.
Good morrow, father.

Friar.   Benedicite!°
What early tongue so sweet saluteth me?
Young son, it argues a distemperèd head°
So soon to bid good morrow to thy bed.
35   Care keeps his watch in every old man's eye,
And where care lodges, sleep will never lie;
But where unbruisèd° youth with unstuffed° brain
Doth couch his limbs, there golden sleep doth reign.

774 WILLIAM SHAKESPEARE

? **1.** *In the absence of lighting, Shakespeare had his characters "set the stage" in their speeches. What "scene" does the friar set? How are his images of night different from Romeo's images in his "O blessèd, blessèd night" speech in the last scene?*

4. Titan's burning wheels: wheels of the sun god's chariot.

7. osier cage: cage woven of willow branches.

8. baleful: evil or poisonous.

15. mickle: great.

19. strained: turned aside.
20. true birth: true purpose.

? **22.** *What details in the friar's speech casually suggest that these herbs and flowers have qualities that can heal or kill? Where does the friar remind us that good can turn to evil, and evil turn to good?*

23. rind: outer covering.

? **23.** *Romeo enters quietly, unseen by the friar. As the friar talks of the flower he has picked, why might the audience become uneasy about what might happen to Romeo and Juliet?*

24. medicine: medicinal.
25. For . . . part: When the flower is smelled, each part of the body is stimulated.
27. still: always.
30. canker: cankerworm, a larva that feeds on leaves.
31. Benedicite!: Latin for "Bless you!"
33. distemperèd head: troubled mind.
37. unbruisèd: innocent.
unstuffed: untroubled.

Using Students' Strengths

Naturalist Learners

In response to Friar Laurence's soliloquy in ll. 5–30, have students either do research or conduct a field study to collect and classify herbs found in the area. Have them write and illustrate a field guide or give an oral report in which they describe different types of herbs and list their beneficial or harmful qualities.

Crossing the Curriculum

Science

Have students research the medicinal uses of herbs or modern medicines derived from herbs. They might explore, for example, the relationship between aspirin and the folk remedy willow tea.

History

Have students research the role herbs have played in various cultures throughout history—in folklore, religion, food, and medicine.

Therefore thy earliness doth me assure
40 Thou art uproused with some distemp'rature;
Or if not so, then here I hit it right—
Our Romeo hath not been in bed tonight.

Romeo.
That last is true. The sweeter rest was mine.

Friar.
God pardon sin! Wast thou with Rosaline? **C**

Romeo.
45 With Rosaline, my ghostly father? No.
I have forgot that name and that name's woe.

Friar.
That's my good son! But where hast thou been then?

Romeo.
I'll tell thee ere thou ask it me again.
I have been feasting with mine enemy,
50 Where on a sudden one hath wounded me
That's by me wounded. Both our remedies
Within thy help and holy physic° lies.
I bear no hatred, blessèd man, for, lo,
My intercession° likewise steads° my foe.

Friar.
55 Be plain, good son, and homely° in thy drift.
Riddling confession finds but riddling shrift.°

Romeo.
Then plainly know my heart's dear love is set
On the fair daughter of rich Capulet;
As mine on hers, so hers is set on mine,
60 And all combined,° save what thou must combine
By holy marriage. When and where and how
We met, we wooed, and made exchange of vow, **D**
I'll tell thee as we pass; but this I pray,
That thou consent to marry us today.

Friar.
65 Holy Saint Francis! What a change is here!
Is Rosaline, that thou didst love so dear,
So soon forsaken? Young men's love then lies
Not truly in their hearts, but in their eyes.
Jesu Maria! What a deal of brine
70 Hath washed thy sallow cheeks for Rosaline!
How much salt water thrown away in waste
To season° love, that of it doth not taste!
The sun not yet thy signs from heaven clears,
Thy old groans ring yet in mine ancient ears.
75 Lo, here upon thy cheek the stain doth sit
Of an old tear that is not washed off yet.
If e'er thou wast thyself, and these woes thine,
Thou and these woes were all for Rosaline.

❓ 44. *Does the friar approve? If you were playing the friar, how would you speak to Romeo?*

52. holy physic: the friar's healing power (physic) to make Romeo and Juliet husband and wife.
54. intercession: request. **steads:** helps.
55. homely: simple and straight-forward.
56. shrift: forgiveness (in the religious rite of confession).

❓ 56. *As we have seen, the play is basically written in blank verse, but Shakespeare varies his verse forms from time to time. The Prologues are written in sonnet form. The endings of scenes are marked by rhymed couplets. What is the rhyme scheme of this dialogue?*
60. combined: agreed.

❓ 65. *In the early part of the play, Shakespeare keeps Romeo's intense love in some kind of perspective by letting us see how others regard him. We have heard Mercutio's sarcastic "The ape is dead." How does Friar Laurence continue with this scolding and ridicule? What actions do you imagine Romeo is engaged in as he listens to the priest?*
72. season: preserve; keep fresh (food was seasoned with salt to keep it from spoiling).

THE TRAGEDY OF ROMEO AND JULIET, ACT II, SCENE 3 775

C **Reading Skills and Strategies**
Making Inferences
How close a friendship do Romeo and Friar Laurence seem to have? How can you tell? [Possible response: Romeo feels close enough to have confided in the friar about Rosaline when he would not tell his parents and was reluctant to tell his friend Benvolio.]

D **Elements of Literature**
Rising Action
Friar Laurence's startled reaction to Romeo's request for an immediate marriage to Juliet emphasizes the speed at which complications are developing in the plot.

Answers to Margin Questions
Line 44. Friar Laurence cannot approve, and he speaks sharply to Romeo.
Line 56. The dialogue is written in rhymed couplets.
Line 65. Friar Laurence is making fun of Romeo's extravagant behavior when he pined for Rosaline, pretending he can still see Romeo's tears and hear his groans. Different interpretations are possible. Romeo could take the teasing with goodwill, or he could react impatiently, knowing, as the friar cannot, the seriousness of his feelings for Juliet.

Taking a Second Look

Review: Chronology
Remind students that the chronology of a story refers to the sequence of events in the plot and how much time passes from one event to the next. Tell them that the entire plot of *Romeo and Juliet* takes place in just four days. Encourage students to keep track of the passage of time in the play, using clues in the text and their own logic and reasoning.

The following activity offers questions that will start this time-tracking process.
Activity
1. How much time passes in Act I? [It all takes place during the same day and night.]
2. How much time passes in Scenes 1 and 2 of Act II? [It is still the same night as the party in Act I.]

3. How much time has passed between the closing of Act II, Scene 2, and the opening of Scene 3? [It is the next morning. Only one day has passed since the play began.]

As students continue reading, have them note the passage of time and keep track of the events that happen on each of the four days the plot covers.

T775

A And art thou changed? Pronounce this sentence then:
80 Women may fall when there's no strength in men.
Romeo.
Thou chid'st me oft for loving Rosaline.
Friar.
For doting, not for loving, pupil mine.
Romeo.
And bad'st me bury love.
Friar. Not in a grave
To lay one in, another out to have.
Romeo.
85 I pray thee chide me not. Her I love now
B Doth grace° for grace and love for love allow.
The other did not so.
Friar. O she knew well
Thy love did read by rote, that could not spell.°
But come, young waverer, come go with me.
90 In one respect I'll thy assistant be;
For this alliance may so happy prove
To turn your households' rancor to pure love.
Romeo.
O, let us hence! I stand on° sudden haste.
Friar.
Wisely and slow. They stumble that run fast. [*Exeunt.*]

86. **grace:** favor.
88. Romeo recited words of love without understanding them.
? 92. *In these times, it was not at all unusual to form alliances and settle disputes by arranging marriages. How does this explain Friar Laurence's decision to help the young couple?*
93. **I stand on:** I am firm about.
? 94. *Romeo has gotten what he wants and he dashes offstage. But why do the friar's last words leave us with a sense that danger lies ahead?*

❝ *For this alliance may so happy prove*
To turn your households' rancor to pure love. ❞

Scene 4. *A street.*

Enter BENVOLIO *and* MERCUTIO.

Mercutio.
    Where the devil should this Romeo be?
    Came he not home tonight?
Benvolio.
    Not to his father's. I spoke with his man.
Mercutio.
    Why, that same pale hardhearted wench, that
        Rosaline,
5   Torments him so that he will sure run mad.
Benvolio.
    Tybalt, the kinsman to old Capulet,
    Hath sent a letter to his father's house.
Mercutio. A challenge, on my life.
Benvolio. Romeo will answer it.
10 **Mercutio.** Any man that can write may answer a letter.
Benvolio. Nay, he will answer the letter's master, how he
    dares, being dared.
Mercutio. Alas, poor Romeo, he is already dead: stabbed
    with a white wench's black eye; run through the ear
15   with a love song; the very pin° of his heart cleft with
    the blind bow-boy's butt-shaft; and is he a man to
    encounter Tybalt?

> ❝*Alas, poor Romeo, he is already dead . . .*
> *run through the ear with a love song. . . .* ❞

Benvolio. Why, what is Tybalt?
Mercutio. More than Prince of Cats.° O, he's the coura-
20   geous captain of compliments. He fights as you sing
    pricksong°—keeps time, distance, and proportion; he
    rests his minim rests,° one, two and the third in
    your bosom! The very butcher of a silk button, a
    duelist, a duelist! A gentleman of the very first
25   house,° of the first and second cause.° Ah, the immor-

THE TRAGEDY OF ROMEO AND JULIET, ACT II, SCENE 4 777

[?] 7. *Now that the play's love story seems to be heading toward a marriage, Shakespeare turns again to the feuding families. Why is Tybalt looking for Romeo?*

15. pin: center (of a target).

19. Prince of Cats: "Tybalt" is the name of a cat in a fable who is known for his slyness.
21. sing pricksong: sing with attention to every note on a printed sheet of music.
22. minim rests: shortest pauses in a bar of music.
25. first house: first rank. **first and second cause:** dueling terms ("first," offense is taken; "second," a challenge is given).

Summary ■■

Act II, Scene 4
Mercutio and Benvolio, looking for Romeo, reveal that Tybalt will challenge Romeo to a duel. They fear that their lovesick friend is in no state for a fight with Tybalt, who is a talented swordsman. Romeo enters, and Mercutio teases him about his behavior the previous night. Next, the nurse enters. Mercutio, still unaware of the relationship between Romeo and Juliet, insults the nurse, suggesting that she is a bawd for her mistress. Mercutio and Benvolio exit, and the nurse asks Romeo if his love is true. He assures her it is and tells her to have Juliet come to Friar Laurence's cell that afternoon to be married.

Ⓒ Elements of Literature
    Rising Action
For the past two scenes, we have been swept along with Romeo and Juliet's love story. Now we are reminded of another plot complication—Juliet's cousin Tybalt has an angry grudge against Romeo that could doom the couple's love.

Ⓓ Struggling Readers
    Adapting Your Reading Strategies
Read this passage aloud so students can hear Mercutio's humorous, mocking tone. Tell them that Mercutio is a performer who is usually trying to entertain his friends with his quick wordplay and witty observations of people. When he speaks, it's usually more important to catch the tone, tempo, and rhythm of his speeches rather than worry about the meaning of every word.

Answer to Margin Question
Line 7. Tybalt wants to challenge Romeo to a duel; he has harbored a grudge about Romeo's uninvited appearance at the Capulet party.

Using Students' Strengths

Interpersonal Learners
These students may enjoy imagining how Friar Laurence might have ended the feud between the Capulets and Montagues if he had been a skilled pastoral counselor or negotiator. Have students role-play a scene in which Friar Laurence counsels Romeo's and Juliet's parents to make peace based on their children's love for each other.

A Literary Connections

Note that in this speech, Mercutio mocks the conventions of courtly love. A lover in the Renaissance was expected to proclaim his lady superior to women in classical literature who were famous for their beauty, such as Petrarch's Laura, Dido, Cleopatra, Helen of Troy, and Hero. Refer students to the side notes for l. 42 to identify these women.

B Advanced Learners

Challenge these students to write a modern equivalent of this fast-paced, witty dialogue, in which two good friends tease each other and exchange puns at each other's expense.

Answers to Margin Questions

Line 26. Tybalt is an accomplished, if affected, duelist: "one, two and the third in your bosom!" (ll. 22–23). Since Mercutio takes Tybalt's abilities seriously, he probably is fearful for Romeo, even as he acts out Tybalt's showy fencing style. When Mercutio moves on to mock the dandies, he becomes even livelier; even though he's still having fun, he seems truly disgusted with their pretentiousness.
Line 55. Romeo immediately deflects Mercutio's ridicule of his bowing "in the hams" by defining the bow as a curtsy (l. 56) and then continues with a pun, "courteous exposition" (l. 58).
Line 70. Mercutio could be pretending to faint.

T778

---

tal passado!° The punto reverso!° The hay!°

Benvolio. The what?

Mercutio. The pox of° such antic, lisping, affecting
fantasticoes°—these new tuners of accent! "By Jesu,
a very good blade! A very tall° man! A very good
whore!" Why, is not this a lamentable thing, grand
sir, that we should be thus afflicted with these
strange flies, these fashionmongers, these pardon-
me's, who stand so much on the new form° that they
cannot sit at ease on the old bench? O, their
bones,° their bones!

[Enter ROMEO.]

Benvolio. Here comes Romeo! Here comes Romeo!

Mercutio. Without his roe,° like a dried herring. O
flesh, flesh, how art thou fishified! Now is he for the
A ⎡ numbers° that Petrarch flowed in. Laura, to his lady,
⎢ was a kitchen wench (marry, she had a better love
⎢ to berhyme her), Dido° a dowdy, Cleopatra a gypsy,
⎢ Helen and Hero hildings° and harlots, Thisbe
⎣ a gray eye° or so, but not to the purpose. Signior
Romeo, bonjour! There's a French salutation to your
French slop.° You gave us the counterfeit° fairly
last night.

Romeo. Good morrow to you both. What counterfeit did
I give you?

Mercutio. The slip, sir, the slip. Can you not conceive?°

⎡ **Romeo.** Pardon, good Mercutio. My business was great,
⎢ and in such a case as mine a man may strain courtesy.
⎢ **Mercutio.** That's as much as to say, such a case° as yours
⎢ constrains a man to bow in the hams.
⎢ **Romeo.** Meaning, to curtsy.
⎢ **Mercutio.** Thou hast most kindly hit it.
⎢ **Romeo.** A most courteous exposition.
⎢ **Mercutio.** Nay, I am the very pink of courtesy.
B ⎢ **Romeo.** Pink for flower.
⎢ **Mercutio.** Right.
⎢ **Romeo.** Why, then is my pump° well-flowered.°
⎢ **Mercutio.** Sure wit, follow me this jest now till thou hast
⎢ worn out thy pump, that, when the single sole of it is
⎢ worn, the jest may remain, after the wearing, solely
⎢ singular.
⎣ **Romeo.** O single-soled jest, solely singular for the single-
ness!°

Mercutio. Come between us, good Benvolio! My wits
faint.

778 WILLIAM SHAKESPEARE

---

26. passado: lunge. **punto
reverso:** backhand stroke. **hay:**
home thrust.
26. *Mercutio mocks Tybalt's
dueling style, but what do we
also now know about Tybalt's
ability to fight? What do you
picture Mercutio doing as he talks
of duels? Is he also concerned for
Romeo? How do his actions
change in the next speech as he
mocks people who always want to
wear the latest fashions?*
28. pox of: plague on (curse on).
29. fantasticoes: dandies; men
who copy French manners and
fashions.
30. tall: brave.
34. new form: new fashions.
36. bones: pun on their use of the
French *bon* ("good").
38. roe: pun on *roe,* female deer.
Roe also means "fish eggs," so
Mercutio is also suggesting that love
has made Romeo "gutless."
40. numbers: verses. Petrarch was
an Italian poet who wrote verses to
a woman named Laura.
42. Dido: queen of Carthage in
the *Aeneid,* who loved Aeneas.
(The women who follow also were
famous lovers in literature: Cleopatra was the queen of Egypt loved by
Antony; Helen of Troy was loved by
Paris; Hero was loved by Leander;
Thisbe was loved by Pyramus.)
43. hildings: good-for-nothings.
44. gray eye: gleam in the eye.
46. slop: loose trousers then
popular in France. **counterfeit:**
slip.
51. conceive: understand.
54. case: set of clothes.
55. *Romeo is being lured by
Mercutio to match wits. How
can you tell that Romeo soon gets
into the spirit of the game and for
the moment forgets his romantic
problems? In the following verbal
duel, the two friends use puns.*

62. pump: shoe. **well-flowered:**
pun on *well floored.* Men's shoes
were "pinked," or cut with decorations.

68. singleness: pun on "silliness."

70. *What exaggerated action
is Mercutio performing here?*

Romeo. Swits° and spurs, swits and spurs; or I'll cry a
match.

Mercutio. Nay, if our wits run the wild-goose chase, I am
done; for thou hast more of the wild goose in one of
75   thy wits than, I am sure, I have in my whole five. Was I
with you there for the goose?°

Romeo. Thou wast never with me for anything when
thou wast not there for the goose.°

Mercutio. I will bite thee by the ear for that jest.

80 **Romeo.** Nay, good goose, bite not!

Mercutio. Thy wit is a very bitter sweeting;° it is a most
sharp sauce.

Romeo. And is it not, then, well served in to a sweet
goose?°

85 **Mercutio.** O, here's a wit of cheveril,° that stretches from
an inch narrow to an ell broad!°

Romeo. I stretch it out for that word "broad," which,
added to the goose, proves thee far and wide a
broad° goose.

90 **Mercutio.** Why, is not this better now than groaning
for love? Now art thou sociable, now art thou Romeo;
now art thou what thou art, by art as well as by nature. For this driveling love is like a great natu-
ral° that runs lolling up and down to hide his bauble°
95   in a hole.

Benvolio. Stop there, stop there!

Mercutio. Thou desirest me to stop in my tale against the
hair.°

Benvolio. Thou wouldst else have made thy tale large.°

100 **Mercutio.** O, thou art deceived! I would have made it
short; for I was come to the whole depth of my tale,
and meant indeed to occupy the argument no longer.

Romeo. Here's goodly gear!°

[*Enter* NURSE *and her man* PETER.]

A sail, a sail!

105 **Mercutio.** Two, two! A shirt and a smock.°

Nurse. Peter!

Peter. Anon.

Nurse. My fan, Peter.

Mercutio. Good Peter, to hide her face; for her fan's the
110   fairer face.

Nurse. God ye good morrow, gentlemen.

Mercutio. God ye good-den,° fair gentlewoman.

Nurse. Is it good-den?

Mercutio. 'Tis no less, I tell ye; for the bawdy hand of
115   the dial is now upon the prick of noon.

Nurse. Out upon you! What a man are you!

---

71. Swits: switches (a pun on *wits*).

76. Was . . . goose?: Was I right in calling you a goose?

78. goose: here, a woman.

81. bitter sweeting: kind of apple.

84. sweet goose: sour sauce was considered best for sweet meat.
85. cheveril: kid leather (another reference to fashion).
86. ell broad: forty-five inches across.

89. broad: indecent.

94. natural: idiot. **bauble:** liter-ally, trinket or cheap jewel.
? **95.** *What does the loyal Mercutio think he has accomplished for Romeo by this game of wits?*
98. against the hair: against my inclination.
99. large: indecent.

103. gear: matter for play and teasing.
? **104.** *Having established the fact that Tybalt is looking for Romeo, we now return to the love story, with this comic scene involv-ing the nurse and Peter and the young men. The previous scene might well have seemed to drag if we had not in a sense been promised a confrontation between Romeo and Tybalt. Now the young men laugh openly at the nurse as she and her servant "sail" on stage. What does Romeo's comment suggest about her size?*
105. A shirt and a smock: a man (shirt) and a woman (smock).
112. God ye good-den: God grant you a good evening.

C Elements of Literature
Irony
? Point out the irony here. Mercutio still thinks that Romeo's absence the previous night had to do with Rosaline, and now he thinks Romeo has given up on the idea of love. What does the audience know that explains Romeo's better humor? [The audience knows that Romeo and Juliet have exchanged promises of love and that Friar Laurence is ready to conduct a wedding ceremony.]

D Critical Thinking
Interpreting
? The nurse is trying to act dignified and put on airs in front of the young gentlemen by calling for her fan. But the young men mock her pretensions. Why do you think Romeo joins in the teasing (beginning with l. 117 on the next page) when he knows the nurse has come on a very serious mission? [Possible responses: He has gotten car-ried away in his lighthearted teasing with Mercutio and finds it hard to stop; he has to keep up the behavior his friends expect from him so that they don't sus-pect what is really going on.]

Answers to Margin Questions
Line 95. Mercutio thinks he has gotten Romeo's mind off his foolish love for Rosaline and restored him to his usual sociable, clever self.
Line 104. Romeo suggests that the nurse is quite large.

Reaching All Students

Struggling Readers
Have students work in small groups to develop a summary of Act II, Scene 4. Help students see where stage directions mark shifts in the scene—episodes or segments created by the entrances and exits of the characters. Students should then take these episodes one at a time, using the margin notes for help as they discuss what happens in each episode, until they can summarize its action in a sentence or two.

English Language Learners
Show students a single scene from a videotaped film version of the play, such as Act II, Scene 4. Have students focus on the general meaning and action of the scene, rather than individual speeches. Help them draw inferences about the action and the mood. Then, guide them in find-ing textual support for their conclusions.

Advanced Learners
Challenge advanced learners to begin the on-going project of developing a study guide that contains one page for each scene of the play. Each page should include the following: two sig-nificant questions the scene poses and answers (with answers included); two quotes that are sig-nificant for revealing motivation or for advancing the plot; and two symbols or pictures that sug-gest the essence of the scene (such as a balcony and a rose for Act II, Scene 2).

A Struggling Readers
Paraphrasing
❓ How would you paraphrase Romeo's description of Mercutio? [Possible responses: Mercutio is just full of a lot of talk; Mercutio says a lot of things he doesn't really mean.]

B Reading Skills and Strategies
Comparing and Contrasting
❓ How are Mercutio and the nurse similar? How are they different? [Possible responses: Both are very earthy, vulgar, and full of fun; both love to hear themselves speak. Mercutio, however, is bright, well-read, young, and noble, while the nurse is older, of a lower class, and not as quick-witted or educated.]

Answers to Margin Questions
Line 132. Mercutio makes his saucy comment to Benvolio and then may walk around the nurse as he sings, clowning behind her back.
Line 142. Romeo assures her that Mercutio is not to be taken seriously, that he loves to hear himself talk but makes little sense.
Line 159. The nurse is talking to Peter.

Romeo. One, gentlewoman, that God hath made, himself to mar.

Nurse. By my troth, it is well said. "For himself to mar," quoth 'a? Gentlemen, can any of you tell me where I may find the young Romeo?

Romeo. I can tell you; but young Romeo will be older when you have found him than he was when you sought him. I am the youngest of that name, for fault of a worse.°

Nurse. You say well.

Mercutio. Yea, is the worst well? Very well took, i' faith! Wisely, wisely.

Nurse. If you be he, sir, I desire some confidence with you.

Benvolio. She will endite° him to some supper.

Mercutio. A bawd, a bawd, a bawd! So ho!

Romeo. What hast thou found?

Mercutio. No hare,° sir; unless a hare, sir, in a Lenten pie,° that is something stale and hoar° ere it be spent.

[*He walks by them and sings.*]

> An old hare hoar,
> And an old hare hoar,
> Is very good meat in Lent;
> But a hare that is hoar
> Is too much for a score
> When it hoars ere it be spent.

Romeo, will you come to your father's? We'll to dinner thither.

Romeo. I will follow you.

Mercutio. Farewell, ancient lady. Farewell (*singing*) "Lady, lady, lady." [*Exeunt* MERCUTIO, BENVOLIO.]

Nurse. I pray you, sir, what saucy merchant was this that was so full of his ropery?°

Romeo. A gentleman, nurse, that loves to hear himself talk and will speak more in a minute than he will stand to in a month.

Nurse. And 'a speak anything against me, I'll take him down, and 'a were lustier than he is, and twenty such Jacks; and if I cannot, I'll find those that shall. Scurvy knave! I am none of his flirt-gills;° I am none of his skainsmates.° And thou must stand by too, and suffer every knave to use me at his pleasure!

Peter. I saw no man use you at his pleasure. If I had, my weapon should quickly have been out, I warrant you. I dare draw as soon as another man, if I see occasion in a

120
125
130
135
140
145
150
155
160

125. for fault of a worse: for want of a better.

131. endite: invite. Benvolio mocks the nurse, for she said "confidence" but meant "conference."

❓ **132.** *Mercutio, who knows nothing of Romeo's plan to marry Juliet, thinks the nurse has come to arrange a secret date between Romeo and her mistress. He mocks and insults the nurse by suggesting that she is a bawd, or "procurer," for Juliet. Mercutio dominates the stage when he's on it. What do you imagine he's doing here?*
134. hare: slang for "morally loose woman."
135. Lenten pie: rabbit pie, eaten sparingly during Lent, so that it is around for a long time and gets stale. **hoar:** gray with mold (the old nurse has gray hair).
❓ **142.** *Mercutio teases the nurse about being a flirt by singing the chorus from an old song about a "chaste" lady. The nurse is outraged and struggles to keep her fine airs. How does Romeo try to calm her?*
149. ropery: The nurse means "roguery," or vulgar ways.

156. flirt-gills: flirty girls.
157. skainsmates: loose women.

❓ **159.** *Whom is the nurse talking to here?*

Crossing the Curriculum

Music
Have students research humorous madrigals and other Renaissance songs that Mercutio might have enjoyed. Have a group of students learn the parts for one of the madrigals and perform it for the class.

good quarrel, and the law on my side.

Nurse. Now, afore God, I am so vexed that every part
165   about me quivers. Scurvy knave! Pray you, sir, a word;
    and, as I told you, my young lady bid me inquire you
    out. What she bid me say, I will keep to myself; but first
    let me tell ye, if ye should lead her in a fool's paradise,
    as they say, it were a very gross kind of behavior, as
170   they say; for the gentlewoman is young; and therefore,
    if you should deal double with her, truly it were an ill
    thing to be offered to any gentlewoman, and very weak
    dealing.

Romeo. Nurse, commend me to thy lady and mistress. I
175   protest unto thee——

Nurse. Good heart, and i' faith I will tell her as much.
    Lord, Lord, she will be a joyful woman.

Romeo. What wilt thou tell her, nurse? Thou dost not
    mark° me.

180 **Nurse.** I will tell her, sir, that you do protest, which, as I
    take it, is a gentlemanlike offer.

Romeo.
    Bid her devise
    Some means to come to shrift this afternoon;
    And there she shall at Friar Laurence' cell
185   Be shrived° and married. Here is for thy pains.

Nurse. No, truly, sir; not a penny.

Romeo. Go to! I say you shall.

Nurse. This afternoon, sir? Well, she shall be there.

Romeo.
    And stay, good nurse, behind the abbey wall.
190   Within this hour my man shall be with thee
    And bring thee cords made like a tackled stair,°
    Which to the high topgallant° of my joy
    Must be my convoy° in the secret night.
    Farewell. Be trusty, and I'll quit° thy pains.
195   Farewell. Commend me to thy mistress.

Nurse.
    Now God in heaven bless thee! Hark you, sir.

Romeo.
    What say'st thou, my dear nurse?

Nurse.
    Is your man secret? Did you ne'er hear say,
    Two may keep counsel, putting one away?

Romeo.
200   Warrant thee my man's as true as steel.

Nurse. Well, sir, my mistress is the sweetest lady.
    Lord, Lord! When 'twas a little prating thing—O,
    there is a nobleman in town, one Paris, that would
    fain lay knife aboard;° but she, good soul, had as

165. *Which part of this speech is delivered to Mercutio? When does the nurse turn to Romeo? How might her manner change?*

173. *What warning does the nurse give Romeo, and why do you think she does this?*

179. mark: listen to.

185. shrived: forgiven of her sins.

191. tackled stair: rope ladder.
192. topgallant: highest platform on a sailing ship's mast.
193. convoy: means of conveyance.
194. quit: repay.

204. lay knife aboard: take a slice (lay claim to Juliet).

THE TRAGEDY OF ROMEO AND JULIET, ACT II, SCENE 4 781

C English Language Learners
Idioms
Tell students that forms of the expressions *a fool's paradise* and *deal double* are still used in English today. A person living in a fool's paradise thinks everything is perfect but has been sadly misled. The expression *double dealing* refers to an intentional act of deception—pretending to feel or promise something when, in fact, you have no intention of following through on your promise.

D Reading Skills and Strategies
Making Inferences
? What will Romeo use the rope ladder for? [for climbing up the balcony wall to Juliet's room on the night of their wedding]

Answers to Margin Questions
Line 165. The nurse shouts "Scurvy knave!" after Mercutio and turns to Romeo with "Pray you, sir." When she addresses Romeo, she could become respectful, secretive, and even a bit puffed up with her own importance.
Line 173. The nurse warns Romeo not to trifle with Juliet's feelings, not to say he loves her unless he means it. The nurse's motives may be her genuine love for Juliet, her sense that Juliet is too young and inexperienced to take betrayal easily, and her awareness that Juliet indeed loves Romeo.

205 lieve see a toad, a very toad, as see him. I anger her sometimes, and tell her that Paris is the properer man; but I'll warrant you, when I say so, she

Ⓐ looks as pale as any clout° in the versal° world. Doth
210 not rosemary and Romeo begin both with a letter?
Romeo. Aye, nurse; what of that? Both with an R.
Nurse. Ah, mocker! That's the dog's name.° R is for the—no; I know it begins with some other letter;
215 and she hath the prettiest sententious° of it, of you and rosemary, that it would do you good to hear it.
Romeo. Commend me to thy lady.
Nurse. Ay, a thousand times. [*Exit* ROMEO.] Peter!
Peter. Anon.
220 **Nurse.** Before, and apace.   [*Exit after* PETER.]

Scene 5. *Capulet's orchard.*

Enter JULIET.

Juliet.
The clock struck nine when I did send the nurse;
In half an hour she promised to return.
Perchance she cannot meet him. That's not so.
O, she is lame! Love's heralds should be thoughts,
5 Which ten times faster glide than the sun's beams
Driving back shadows over low'ring hills.
Therefore do nimble-pinioned doves° draw Love,
Ⓑ And therefore hath the wind-swift Cupid wings.
Now is the sun upon the highmost hill
10 Of this day's journey, and from nine till twelve
Is three long hours; yet she is not come.
Had she affections and warm youthful blood,
She would be as swift in motion as a ball;

782 WILLIAM SHAKESPEARE

15 My words would bandy her° to my sweet love,
And his to me.
But old folks, many feign as they were dead—
Unwieldy, slow, heavy, and pale as lead. **C**

[*Enter* NURSE *and* PETER.]

O God, she comes! O honey nurse, what news?
Hast thou met with him? Send thy man away.

Nurse.
20 Peter, stay at the gate. [*Exit* PETER.]

Juliet.
Now, good sweet nurse—O Lord, why look'st thou sad?
Though news be sad, yet tell them merrily;
If good, thou sham'st the music of sweet news
By playing it to me with so sour a face.

Nurse.
25 I am aweary, give me leave awhile.
Fie, how my bones ache! What a jaunce° have I!

Juliet.
I would thou hadst my bones, and I thy news.
Nay, come, I pray thee speak. Good, good nurse, speak.

Nurse.
Jesu, what haste! Can you not stay° awhile?
30 Do you not see that I am out of breath?

Juliet.
How art thou out of breath when thou hast breath
To say to me that thou art out of breath?
The excuse that thou dost make in this delay
Is longer than the tale thou dost excuse. **D**
35 Is thy news good or bad? Answer to that.
Say either, and I'll stay the circumstance.°
Let me be satisfied, is't good or bad?

Nurse. Well, you have made a simple° choice; you know
not how to choose a man. Romeo? No, not he. Though
40 his face be better than any man's, yet his leg excels all
men's; and for a hand and a foot, and a body, though
they be not to be talked on, yet they are past compare. **E**
He is not the flower of courtesy, but, I'll warrant him,
as gentle as a lamb. Go thy ways, wench; serve God.
45 What, have you dined at home?

Juliet.
No, no. But all this did I know before.
What says he of our marriage? What of that?

Nurse.
Lord, how my head aches! What a head have I!
It beats as it would fall in twenty pieces.
50 My back a'° t' other side—ah, my back, my back!

THE TRAGEDY OF ROMEO AND JULIET, ACT II, SCENE 5 **783**

---

14. bandy her: send her back and forth, like a tennis ball.

? **17.** *Juliet either has run on stage or is standing on the balcony. What is her mood as she waits for the nurse's return?*

26. jaunce: tiring journey.

29. stay: wait.
? **30.** *The actress playing the nurse can interpret her actions here in several ways. She could be genuinely weary; she could be teasing Juliet; or she could be fearful about the part she has agreed to play in the elopement. How do you think the nurse should play this scene?*
36. stay the circumstance: wait for the details.

38. simple: foolish.
? **38.** *In comedy, a character sometimes has one peculiarity that always can be counted on for a laugh. You push a button and you get the same response. Such a character is sometimes called a jack-in-the-box. What is the nurse's almost inevitable way of responding when she is asked for information?*

50. a': on.

C **Reading Skills and Strategies**
Connecting with the Text
? Do you think this is how most teenagers view older generations? **Explain.** [Possible responses: Yes, especially when they are made to wait for something important; no, because sometimes the older people are the ones in a rush.]

D **Critical Thinking**
Analyzing Character
? What does this line of reasoning show about Juliet? [Possible responses: She is logical and practical; in the throes of love, she has become impatient and inconsiderate with her elders.]

E **English Language Learners**
Interpreting
These students may be confused by the nurse's seemingly nonsensical remarks. Point out that she is being facetious and teasing Juliet, first saying that Juliet has made a bad choice and then listing all of Romeo's good points. She uses words such as *yet, though,* and *but,* as if she is going to offer opposing information, but everything she says about Romeo is positive.

Answers to Margin Questions
Line 17. Juliet is impatient.
Line 30. Ask students to support their answers by referring to the nurse's characterization in earlier scenes.
Line 38. The nurse digresses and rattles on; she is also frequently bawdy.

Assessing Learning

Ongoing Assessment
To check students' reading comprehension and to encourage them to reflect on what they have read, have them respond in writing to one of the following questions near the end of each class period. You might select different students to read their responses each day. Remind students to choose details they would not mind sharing with others.

• Are you like any characters in this work? How?
• Does anyone in this work remind you of someone you know? Why?
• Do you like this work? Why or why not?
• What do you feel is the most important word, phrase, or passage in this scene? Why?
• Were there any parts of this scene that confused you? Which parts? Why?

A Elements of Literature

Rising Action

The plot continues to develop at a breakneck pace as Romeo and Juliet's wedding plans are completed. List some possible complications that could interfere with their happiness. [Possible responses: Paris has asked to marry Juliet; Tybalt is challenging Romeo to a duel; the nurse or the friar could accidentally reveal the secret plans and tip off the warring families.]

B Reading Skills and Strategies

Reading Shakespeare's Poetry

Have a volunteer read the nurse's speech aloud, and ask what is unusual about it. [The nurse's speech is in blank verse (unrhymed iambic pentameter). Usually, the nurse and other common characters do not speak in poetry.]

Answers to Margin Questions

Line 52. "My back a' t' other side—ah, my back, my back!" (l. 50 on p. 783).

Line 61. Responses will vary. Most likely, Juliet is both confused and impatient, wanting to keep the conversation wholly on the subject of Romeo.

Line 69. The nurse says Juliet is blushing, and students might suppose that she hugs the nurse.

Line 78. Elated, Juliet puns on the words *hie* (hasten) and *high* (excellent).

Beshrew° your heart for sending me about
To catch my death with jauncing up and down!
Juliet.
    I' faith, I am sorry that thou art not well.
    Sweet, sweet, sweet nurse, tell me, what says my love?
55 **Nurse.** Your love says, like an honest gentleman, and a
    courteous, and a kind, and a handsome, and, I warrant,
    a virtuous—where is your mother?
Juliet.
    Where is my mother? Why, she is within.
    Where should she be? How oddly thou repliest!
60   "Your love says, like an honest gentleman,
    'Where is your mother?' "
Nurse.   O God's Lady dear!
    Are you so hot?° Marry come up, I trow.°
    Is this the poultice for my aching bones?
    Henceforward do your messages yourself.
Juliet.
65   Here's such a coil!° Come, what says Romeo?
Nurse.
    Have you got leave to go to shrift today?
Juliet.
    I have.
Nurse.
    Then hie you hence to Friar Laurence' cell;
    There stays a husband to make you a wife.
70   Now comes the wanton blood up in your cheeks.
    They'll be in scarlet straight at any news.
    Hie you to church; I must another way,
    To fetch a ladder, by the which your love
    Must climb a bird's nest soon when it is dark.
75   I am the drudge, and toil in your delight;
    But you shall bear the burden soon at night.
    Go; I'll to dinner; hie you to the cell.
Juliet.
    Hie to high fortune! Honest nurse, farewell. [*Exeunt.*]

---

51. Beshrew: shame on.

52. *What line here indicates that Juliet has tried to humor the nurse by rubbing her back?*

61. *Juliet can play this scene in several ways. Do you imagine she is angry here? Or is she bewildered? impatient? Or is she mocking the old nurse?*

62. hot: angry. **Marry come up, I trow:** something like "By the Virgin Mary, come off it, I swear."

65. coil: fuss.

69. *At last, the nurse tells Juliet what she has been waiting for. What do you see Juliet doing as she hears the news?*

78. *Even Juliet puns. What pun does she exit on? What is her mood?*

Scene 6. *Friar Laurence's cell.*

Enter FRIAR LAURENCE *and* ROMEO.

Friar.
So smile the heavens upon this holy act
That afterhours with sorrow chide us not!
Romeo.
Amen, amen! But come what sorrow can,
It cannot countervail° the exchange of joy
5   That one short minute gives me in her sight.
Do thou but close our hands with holy words,
Then love-devouring death do what he dare—
It is enough I may but call her mine.
Friar.
These violent delights have violent ends
10   And in their triumph die, like fire and powder,°
Which, as they kiss, consume. The sweetest honey
Is loathsome in his own deliciousness
And in the taste confounds° the appetite.
Therefore love moderately: long love doth so;
15   Too swift arrives as tardy as too slow.

———————

**" *These violent delights have
violent ends. . . .* "**

———————

[*Enter* JULIET.]

Here comes the lady. O, so light a foot
Will ne'er wear out the everlasting flint.°
A lover may bestride the gossamers°
That idle in the wanton summer air,
20   And yet not fall; so light is vanity.°
Juliet.
Good even to my ghostly confessor.
Friar.
Romeo shall thank thee, daughter, for us both.
Juliet.
As much to him,° else is his thanks too much.
Romeo.
Ah, Juliet, if the measure of thy joy

THE TRAGEDY OF ROMEO AND JULIET, ACT II, SCENE 6 785

---

4. **countervail:** match or equal.

? **8.** *We are continually prepared for the steps Romeo
and Juliet might take if they are
separated. What does Romeo say
here to remind us again of how
desperate their love is?*

10. **powder:** gunpowder.

13. **confounds:** destroys.

? **15.** *What warning does the
friar give about passionate
love? What fear does he express for
the future?*

17. **flint:** stone.
18. **gossamers:** finest spider
threads.

20. **vanity:** fleeting human love.

23. **As much to him:** the same to
him.

Summary ■

Act II, Scene 6
Romeo is at Friar Laurence's cell. The
friar cautions the young man that the
intensity of his love will lead to no
good and advises moderation. When
Juliet enters, Romeo, professing his
own verbal ineptitude, urges her to
describe the extent of their love. Juliet
replies that fancy words are unable to
do justice to the substance of her love.
The friar, fearing their passion, quickly
leads them off to be married.

C Elements of Literature
Theme
Romeo's view of love is one of several
expressed in the play: For Romeo and
Juliet, their intense romantic love is
worth any price—even death.

D Elements of Literature
Foreshadowing
Romeo and Juliet's love is now compared to gunpowder, and a violent,
consuming end is predicted for it.

Answers to Margin Questions
Line 8. Romeo says that marrying
Juliet will be full happiness for him,
even if "love-devouring death" then
claims his life.
Line 15. Friar Laurence warns that
passionate love is so intense that it
may wear itself out quickly. He fears
that love without moderation is all-
consuming and volatile.

Professional Notes

Critical Comment: Self-Defeating Love

Echoing Friar Laurence's warning, critic Derick
Marsh sums up the love of Romeo and Juliet in
the following way: "I think that the play concerns
itself with the nature of a particular kind of love,
first love, that intense sexual attraction that by
its very nature cannot long remain as it is. In the
ordinary course of life, this change is accepted
because it is inevitable; either the love withers
away, or changes into some other kind of love,
of equal or perhaps even greater value, but
different in kind. In this play, it is protected from
change, heightened and intensified by the sense
of doom that pervades the play, but for that very
reason, immune to time's decay, because neither
we nor the lovers are ever allowed to believe
that their love can last long enough to exhaust
its first intensity. In that sense their love wins a
victory over time, but since such a victory can
only be won out of time, the love must end in
death; in this sense it is self-defeating."

A **Reading Skills and Strategies**
Comparing
❓ In what way does Juliet's speech sound like Romeo's style of talking at this point? [Sample responses: She is speaking metaphorically; she says that she cannot express her love in words.]

Answers to Margin Questions
Line 29. Romeo asks Juliet to describe, in eloquent language, their love and happiness.
Line 34. Juliet says that true understanding does not need to be announced with flowery language; indeed, her happiness cannot be fully spoken.
Line 37. Answers may vary. Most students will probably agree that Friar Laurence is both knowing and indulgent; he is hurrying them, but he understands their feelings and is fatherly and affectionate.

25   Be heaped like mine, and that thy skill be more
        To blazon° it, then sweeten with thy breath
        This neighbor air, and let rich music's tongue
        Unfold the imagined happiness that both
        Receive in either by this dear encounter.

Juliet.

30   Conceit,° more rich in matter than in words,
        Brags of his substance, not of ornament.°
     A They are but beggars that can count their worth;
        But my true love is grown to such excess
        I cannot sum up sum of half my wealth.

Friar.

35   Come, come with me, and we will make short work;
        For, by your leaves, you shall not stay alone
        Till holy church incorporate two in one.   [*Exeunt.*]

26. **blazon:** describe.

❓ 29. *What is Romeo asking Juliet to do?*
30. **Conceit:** genuine understanding.
31. **ornament:** fancy language.

❓ 34. *What is Juliet's response to Romeo's request?*

❓ 37. *What do you think the friar's tone is in this last speech? Is there a slight humorous or teasing note here?*

"For, by your leaves, you shall not stay alone Till holy church incorporate two in one."

Making the Connections

Connecting to the Theme: "The Destruction of Innocence"
Of the themes listed on p. T760, Act II brings to the fore the theme that love can confer integrity upon two very young people. As critic Derick Marsh explains, "their discovery of each other gives a sense of purpose and meaning to two young people who have, when the play opens, hardly yet begun to live." Have students discuss all the ways that Romeo and Juliet have changed since the beginning of the play.

Cultural Connections
The end of Act II might be a good time to show the beginning of the film *West Side Story* to your class. Students can then compare and contrast elements of plot and character across cultures: a feud between warring factions, love at first sight in the midst of a party on enemy turf, the balcony scene. Ask students whether a remake of the film could be made today about contemporary teenagers from enemy factions who fall in love.

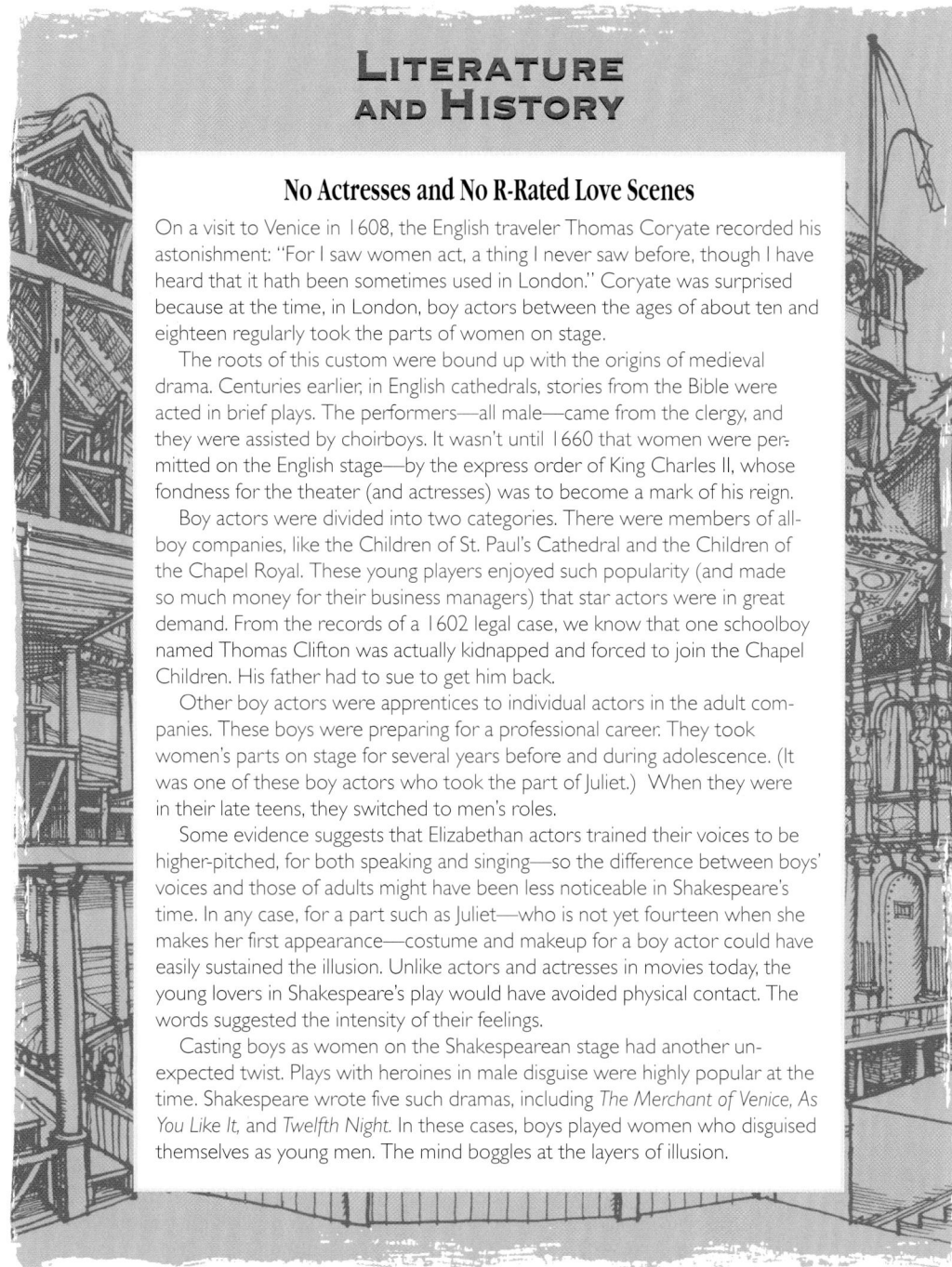

Literature and History

No Actresses and No R-Rated Love Scenes

On a visit to Venice in 1608, the English traveler Thomas Coryate recorded his astonishment: "For I saw women act, a thing I never saw before, though I have heard that it hath been sometimes used in London." Coryate was surprised because at the time, in London, boy actors between the ages of about ten and eighteen regularly took the parts of women on stage.

The roots of this custom were bound up with the origins of medieval drama. Centuries earlier, in English cathedrals, stories from the Bible were acted in brief plays. The performers—all male—came from the clergy, and they were assisted by choirboys. It wasn't until 1660 that women were permitted on the English stage—by the express order of King Charles II, whose fondness for the theater (and actresses) was to become a mark of his reign.

Boy actors were divided into two categories. There were members of all-boy companies, like the Children of St. Paul's Cathedral and the Children of the Chapel Royal. These young players enjoyed such popularity (and made so much money for their business managers) that star actors were in great demand. From the records of a 1602 legal case, we know that one schoolboy named Thomas Clifton was actually kidnapped and forced to join the Chapel Children. His father had to sue to get him back.

Other boy actors were apprentices to individual actors in the adult companies. These boys were preparing for a professional career. They took women's parts on stage for several years before and during adolescence. (It was one of these boy actors who took the part of Juliet.) When they were in their late teens, they switched to men's roles.

Some evidence suggests that Elizabethan actors trained their voices to be higher-pitched, for both speaking and singing—so the difference between boys' voices and those of adults might have been less noticeable in Shakespeare's time. In any case, for a part such as Juliet—who is not yet fourteen when she makes her first appearance—costume and makeup for a boy actor could have easily sustained the illusion. Unlike actors and actresses in movies today, the young lovers in Shakespeare's play would have avoided physical contact. The words suggested the intensity of their feelings.

Casting boys as women on the Shakespearean stage had another unexpected twist. Plays with heroines in male disguise were highly popular at the time. Shakespeare wrote five such dramas, including *The Merchant of Venice, As You Like It,* and *Twelfth Night.* In these cases, boys played women who disguised themselves as young men. The mind boggles at the layers of illusion.

THE TRAGEDY OF ROMEO AND JULIET, ACT II, SCENE 6 787

Literature and History

Male actors stopped playing women's roles in the 1660s, when actresses began to appear regularly in the English theater. Shakespeare's acting company was small, with about fifteen full members. These actors shared in the profits of performances, and Shakespeare often wrote parts tailored to fit the talents and skills of particular company members. *Shakespeare in Love,* a 1998 movie starring Gwyneth Paltrow and Joseph Fiennes, provides an enjoyable look at the acting life in Elizabethan London, especially the custom of using boys to act the parts of women. The story is based on the genesis of *Romeo and Juliet*—a totally unhistorical view but a pleasure to watch all the same. The movie has an R rating.

Assessing Learning

Check Test: Questions and Answers
Answers may vary slightly.
1. Why do Mercutio and Benvolio stop looking for Romeo in the opening scene of Act II? [They think Romeo either has gone home or is hiding.]
2. What does Juliet mean when she says Montague is not a hand, foot, arm, or face? [Romeo's name is not an essential part of him. She loves Romeo for the person he is, regardless of his name.]

3. Why doesn't Juliet want Romeo swearing his love by the moon? [She tells him the moon is not dependable; the moon constantly changes throughout the month.]
4. Why is Friar Laurence skeptical of Romeo's feelings for Juliet? [because Romeo was recently so intent on loving Rosaline]
5. What are Mercutio and Benvolio discussing before Romeo appears in the street? [They are discussing Tybalt's fencing skills and his challenge to Romeo.]

Standardized Test Preparation
For practice with standardized test format specific to this selection, see
• *Standardized Test Preparation*, p. 84

MAKING MEANINGS (ACT II)

First Thoughts

1. Students may cite lines from the passage in which Romeo overhears Juliet. Others may say that later lines where the two exchange vows are more important. Have students explain their choices.

Shaping Interpretations

2. They speak of the intensity, exhilaration, and wonder of love, and they say that they are willing to forsake their families to be together. Juliet is more cautious because she believes that they might be acting impetuously; she urges Romeo to wait, to test their love, but a little later it is she who brings up marriage.

3. Possible responses: Scene 2, ll. 77–78, 118–120, 184; Scene 3, ll. 17–30; Scene 6, ll. 3–8, 9–15.

4. Sample response: The nurse is principled when it comes to love. By taking the coins Romeo offers her (Scene 4, ll. 185–187), she seems to agree to the elopement plans even though she risks losing her job if Juliet's parents find out.

5. He wants to help mend the feud between the two families. This motive shows that the friar truly cares about the well-being of the two families.

6. Possible responses: Mercutio and Benvolio believe that Romeo is still in love with Rosaline when he is actually in love with Juliet; in many of their speeches, Romeo and Juliet look forward to their happiness and profess a readiness to die for love.

7. Some students will be happy that he has agreed to help the lovers. Others might suggest that he could have tried to go to the parents as a mediator for the lovers.

Connecting with the Text

8. Many students will agree that the attitude of the young men is similar to that of boys today; however, they may point out that gang activity today is seldom related to feuding parents. Mercutio's speeches in Scene 1 (ll. 7–21) and Scene 4 (ll. 38–47) and his dialogue with Romeo in Scene 4 (ll. 48–103) use poetic devices to tease Romeo about falling in love.

9. Students may say that real-life Romeos and Juliets include young people who are from different religious, ethnic, or socioeconomic backgrounds.

MAKING MEANINGS ACT II

First Thoughts

[respond]
1. The "balcony scene" (Scene 2) is the most famous love scene in the history of the theater. What lines spoken by Romeo or by Juliet do you think are the most important, the most interesting, or the most beautiful?

Shaping Interpretations

[identify]
2. What different feelings do Romeo and Juliet express in the balcony scene? Which character speaks more cautiously about love, and why?

[identify]
3. Though Act II is a happy act, Shakespeare at times reminds us of the threatening background. He does this by **foreshadowing**—giving clues to what will happen later. Point out lines that foreshadow possible trouble ahead.

[evaluate]
4. The nurse is one of Shakespeare's great comic characters. Do you think the nurse is a principled character, a person with a strong sense of right and wrong? Or does she seem to be easily corrupted, someone who will do whatever people want her to do? Find passages to support your answer.

[analyze]
5. The friar agrees to marry Romeo and Juliet because he wants them to be happy, but he also has another **motive**. What is that motive? What does it reveal about his **character**?

[analyze]
6. When the audience knows something that a character does not know, we feel **dramatic irony**. Since we know how the play will end (the Prologue has told us), we feel this irony when we hear the friar's motives. What other moments of dramatic irony did you feel in this act?

[infer]
7. So far, how do you feel about Friar Laurence's schemes? What else might he have done to help Romeo and Juliet?

Connecting with the Text

[connect]
8. Does Mercutio's teasing of Romeo remind you of the way friends today tease one another? Do the groups of teenagers in this play (some of them looking for trouble) remind you in any way of the gangs that form today? How does Mercutio use tricks of poetry—**rhyme, meter, alliteration, puns**—to tease Romeo?

[extend]
9. Romeo's and Juliet's families hate each other, for reasons that we aren't told about. (Maybe the families themselves have forgotten.) What parallels can you think of from real life—what real-life Romeos and Juliets might be in the world today?

Reading Check

a. What plans do Romeo and Juliet make in Scene 2?

b. What fault does Friar Laurence find in Romeo in Scene 3?

c. We hear in Scene 4 that Tybalt is looking for Romeo. Why does he want Romeo?

d. How does Mercutio feel about Tybalt?

e. What part does the nurse play in Romeo and Juliet's schemes?

Reading Check

a. Juliet will send a messenger to Romeo to find out the time and place for their wedding.
b. He finds Romeo too quick to fall in and out of love.
c. Tybalt wants to challenge him to a duel.
d. Mercutio dislikes Tybalt and, although he ridicules his fencing style, considers him a dangerous opponent.
e. She takes messages between the lovers.

CHOICES: Building Your Portfolio

Writer's Notebook

1. Collecting Ideas for a Research Paper

Finding a topic. Using the play as your guide, brainstorm possible topics for the research paper you'll write for the Writer's Workshop on page 868. Try one of the following exercises:

- Romeo and Juliet swear their love in Act II. Free-write about their love and how it reflects Elizabethan customs of courtship and marriage. For instance, girls often married at the age of twelve or thirteen, and marriages were usually arranged by parents.

- Do some research on any of the literary lovers mentioned in the side note for Scene 4, lines 40–43.

Save your notes.

Critical Thinking

2. Cutting Shakespeare

Many directors of Shakespeare's plays cut some of the lines. Franco Zeffirelli, for example, cut about two thirds of the text for his film version of *Romeo and Juliet.* Imagine that you have been asked to cut Act II, Scene 5, down to twenty lines. How would you do it? Form groups to cut the scene. As you decide what lines to cut and what to keep, think of the director, the actress playing Juliet, and the actress playing the nurse. The director wants to speed up the pace; Juliet and the nurse want to keep the jokes. Work together to decide what to cut, and list your decisions on a chart. In the left-hand column list the lines cut and the reasons for cutting them, and in the right-hand column note any important details you lose by that cut.

GRAMMAR LINK   MINI-LESSON

The Old Problems—Grammar and Vocabulary

Many of Shakespeare's words and expressions are **archaic,** or out of use today, or their meanings have changed. Shakespeare also often omits words. For example, in the Prologue, the speaker says:

> . . . which if you with patient ears attend,
> What here shall miss, our toil shall strive to mend.

Shakespeare has omitted words here, and he depends on your instinct and ear to provide them. He has also used the word *attend* in a way not commonly used today. Here's how we might say the same thing:

> . . . if you listen patiently,
> We'll try to make clear by our work onstage
> What you've missed from the Prologue.

Try It Out

Rewrite each passage below in the kind of English that is spoken today. Check the side notes for help.

1. Scurvy knave! I am none of his flirt-gills; I am none of his skainsmates.

2. Is your man secret? Did you ne'er hear say, Two may keep counsel, putting one away?

3. . . . but she, good soul, had as lieve see a toad, a very toad, as see him.

Rubrics for each Choices assignment appear on p. 202 in the *Portfolio Management System.*

CHOICES: Building Your Portfolio

1. **Writer's Notebook**   If students choose to focus on the literary lovers, suggest that they begin their research by looking up the names in *Benet's Reader's Encyclopedia,* a basic library reference book that will refer them to other sources of information.

2. **Critical Thinking**   As students discuss possible cuts, they might actually assign group members the roles of director and actors. As cuts are suggested, the actors can read the scene aloud without the suggested lines to see if the scene still flows and makes sense.

GRAMMAR LINK
Try It Out
Possible Answers

1. Nasty man! I'm not one of those flirts who like listening to that kind of talk.

2. Are you sure your assistant can keep a secret? Haven't you heard of the saying "Three can keep a secret if two of them are dead"?

3. . . . but she, smart girl, would rather see a toad than look at him.

Grammar Link Quick Check

Have students rewrite these passages from Act II in contemporary English. They should use the scene and line references to place the words in context. Possible answers are given in brackets.

1. "Go then, for 'tis in vain / To seek him here that means not to be found." (Scene 1, ll. 40–41) [Let's go. It's pointless to look for him here. He's hiding, and he doesn't want us to find him.]

2. "I take thee at thy word." (Scene 2, l. 49) [I believe what you're saying.]

3. "What o'clock tomorrow / Shall I send to thee?" (Scene 2, ll. 168–169) [What time tomorrow should I send my messenger to meet you?]

4. "I have forgot that name and that name's woe." (Scene 3, l. 46) [I've forgotten about her and all the troubles she caused me.]

5. "Warrant thee my man's as true as steel." (Scene 4, l. 200) [I swear that my friend is trustworthy.]

OBJECTIVES

1. Read and interpret Act III
2. Analyze the structure of Shake-spearean tragedy, with special emphasis on the crisis, or turn-ing point, and the falling action
3. Analyze and read aloud dialogue written in verse
4. Express understanding through creative writing or speaking
5. Research word origins

SKILLS

Literary
- Analyze the turning point and the falling action

Reading
- Analyze and read aloud a verse play

Writing
- Make notes on aspects of Renaissance life
- Write a prologue

Speaking/Listening
- Present a tableau

Vocabulary
- Research word origins

Viewing/Representing
- Respond to photographs of a production of the play (ATE)

Planning

- **Block Schedule**
  Block Scheduling Lesson Plans with Pacing Guide
- **Traditional Schedule**
  Lesson Plans Including Strategies for English-Language Learners
- **One-Stop Planner**
  CD-ROM with Test Generator

Summary ■ ■ ■

Act III, Scene 1

Benvolio warns Mercutio that they should not be out in public, for if they encounter any of the Capulets, there will be a fight. Mercutio mocks Benvo-lio for giving this advice and, when Tybalt enters, aggressively confronts him. Romeo, who is just returning from his wedding, enters. Tybalt insults Romeo and challenges him to a duel, but Romeo refuses to fight. Mercutio, who thinks that Romeo is a coward, fights Tybalt in his stead. When Romeo intervenes to stop the fight, Tybalt wounds Mercutio and flees. Benvolio helps Mercutio offstage and returns,

(continued on p.T791)

ACT III

Scene 1. *A public place.*

Enter MERCUTIO, BENVOLIO, *and* MEN.

Benvolio.
I pray thee, good Mercutio, let's retire.
The day is hot, the Capels° are abroad,
And, if we meet, we shall not 'scape a brawl,
For now, these hot days, is the mad blood stirring.

5   **Mercutio.** Thou art like one of these fellows that, when he enters the confines of a tavern, claps me his sword upon the table and says, "God send me no need of thee!" and by the operation of the second cup draws him on the drawer,° when indeed there is
10   no need.

Benvolio. Am I like such a fellow?

Mercutio. Come, come, thou art as hot a Jack in thy mood as any in Italy; and as soon moved to be moody, and as soon moody to be moved.

15   **Benvolio.** And what to?

Mercutio. Nay, and there were two such, we should have none shortly, for one would kill the other. Thou! Why, thou wilt quarrel with a man that hath a hair more or a hair less in his beard than thou hast.
20   Thou wilt quarrel with a man for cracking nuts, hav-ing no other reason but because thou hast hazel eyes. What eye but such an eye would spy out such a quarrel? Thy head is as full of quarrels as an egg is full of meat; and yet thy head hath been beaten
25   as addle° as an egg for quarreling. Thou hast quar-reled with a man for coughing in the street, because he hath wakened thy dog that hath lain asleep in the sun. Didst thou not fall out with a tailor for wear-ing his new doublet° before Easter? With another
30   for tying his new shoes with old riband? And yet thou wilt tutor me from quarreling!

Benvolio. And I were so apt to quarrel as thou art, any man should buy the fee simple of° my life for an hour and a quarter.

35   **Mercutio.** The fee simple? O simple!°

[Enter TYBALT *and others.]*

Benvolio. By my head, here come the Capulets.
Mercutio. By my heel, I care not.

790 WILLIAM SHAKESPEARE

2. Capels: Capulets.

? **4.** *Romeo's friends enter the stage. Again, Shakespeare "sets the stage" by having the characters tell us what the weather is like. Why does this weather seem to breed trouble?*

9. draws him on the drawer: draws his sword on the waiter (who "draws" the drink).

? **19.** *Mercutio mocks Benvolio, who is anything but a troublemaker. (Mercutio is the one who can't seem to resist a quarrel.) If you were playing Benvolio, what would you be doing, as Mercutio goes on and on? If you were playing Mercutio, how would you behave as your comments became more and more exaggerated?*
25. addle: rotten.

29. doublet: jacket.

33. buy the fee simple of: buy insurance on.

35. O simple!: O stupid!

  — *Resources: Print and Media* —

Reading
- *Graphic Organizers for Active Reading*, p. 66
- *Words to Own*, p. 43

Writing and Language
- *Daily Oral Grammar*
  Transparency 45

Assessment
- *Formal Assessment*, p. 141
- *Portfolio Management System*, p. 203
- *Test Generator (One-Stop Planner* CD-ROM)

Internet
- go.hrw.com (keyword: LE0 9-13)

Tybalt.
Follow me close, for I will speak to them.
Gentlemen, good-den. A word with one of you.

Mercutio.
40 And but one word with one of us?
Couple it with something; make it a word and a blow.

Tybalt. You shall find me apt enough to that, sir, and you
will give me occasion.

Mercutio. Could you not take some occasion without
45 giving?

Tybalt. Mercutio, thou consortest with Romeo.

Mercutio. Consort?° What, dost thou make us minstrels?
And thou make minstrels of us, look to hear nothing
but discords. Here's my fiddlestick;° here's that shall
50 make you dance. Zounds,° consort!

Benvolio.
We talk here in the public haunt of men.
Either withdraw unto some private place,
Or reason coldly of your grievances,
Or else depart. Here all eyes gaze on us.

Mercutio.
55 Men's eyes were made to look, and let them gaze.
I will not budge for no man's pleasure, I.

[*Enter* ROMEO.]

Tybalt.
Well, peace be with you, sir. Here comes my man.

Mercutio.
But I'll be hanged, sir, if he wear your livery.°
Marry, go before to field,° he'll be your follower!
60 Your worship in that sense may call him man.

Tybalt.
Romeo, the love I bear thee can afford
No better term than this: thou art a villain.°

Romeo.
Tybalt, the reason that I have to love thee
Doth much excuse the appertaining° rage
65 To such a greeting. Villain am I none.
Therefore farewell. I see thou knowest me not.

Tybalt.
Boy, this shall not excuse the injuries
That thou hast done me; therefore turn and draw.

Romeo.
I do protest I never injured thee,
70 But love thee better than thou canst devise°
Till thou shalt know the reason of my love;
And so, good Capulet, which name I tender°
As dearly as mine own, be satisfied.

THE TRAGEDY OF ROMEO AND JULIET, ACT III, SCENE I   791

---

47. Consort: Mercutio pretends to think that Tybalt means a *consort*, or group of musicians.
49. fiddlestick: bow for playing violinlike instruments (referring to his sword).
50. Zounds: slang for "by God's wounds."

[?] Stage direction: *Romeo is returning from his secret marriage—he has no thought about hatred and killing. What would he be doing as he enters? How would he react to the tense situation?*
58. livery: servant's uniform. By *man*, Tybalt meant "target"; but Mercutio uses the word to mean "servant."
59. field: dueling field.

62. villain: boor; clumsy, stupid fellow.

64. appertaining: appropriate.

[?] 68. *What insult does Tybalt use to make Romeo want to draw his sword?*

70. devise: imagine.

72. tender: value.
[?] 73. *Why does Romeo refuse to duel Tybalt?*

(continued from p.T790)

saying he is dead. Romeo, lamenting that his "effeminate" response was the cause of his friend's death, fights with Tybalt when he returns, kills him, and flees. As the Montagues arrive, Benvolio explains what has happened. The prince decrees that Romeo is banished from Verona and will be killed if found in the city.

Ⓐ Reading Skills and Strategies
Drawing Conclusions
[?] What clues tell you that Mercutio really does want to fight? [Possible responses: He dares Tybalt to throw a punch; he engages in a battle of wits to rile Tybalt.]

Ⓑ Struggling Readers
Finding Details
Help students use the side notes to analyze Mercutio's intentional misinterpretation of the word *man*, as used by Tybalt. This misunderstanding helps fuel the violence to come.

Ⓒ Elements of Literature
Dramatic Irony
[?] Dramatic irony occurs when the audience or the reader knows something important that a character in a play does not know. What effect does your knowledge of Romeo and Juliet's wedding have on you during this scene? [Possible responses: It increases my feelings of dread about what is about to happen; it increases my sense of involvement in the scene.]

Answers to Margin Questions
Line 4. The hot weather is making people irritable and testy.
Line 19. Benvolio could be smiling at Mercutio's foolishness, laughing outright, or pretending to ignore it. Mercutio is surely embellishing his description of Benvolio with exaggerated gestures; he might vary his performance by pulling Benvolio's beard (ll. 18–19) or tappng his own head (l. 23).
Stage direction. Romeo, who is buoyant and happy, probably has a bounce in his step and a smile on his face. Because he does not know of Tybalt's intent and is feeling benevolent in general, he may feel removed from the tense situation and be unable to perceive Tybalt's fury.

Reaching All Students

English Language Learners
Continue to use videos, audiotaped performances, and reading aloud to help these students follow the play. For other strategies for engaging English language learners with the literature, see
• *Lesson Plans Including Strategies for English-Language Learners*

Advanced Learners
Act III brings the death of Mercutio, who critic Clifford Leech has claimed is the true tragic hero of *Romeo and Juliet*. Leech says that Mercutio's isolation and anger link him to later Shakespearean heroes, such as Hamlet, Othello, Lear, and Macbeth. Ask advanced students to discuss and write about Mercutio's significance in the play.

A English Language Learners
Cultural Allusions
Remind students that Tybalt is named for a character in a fable who was called the "King of Cats." Tell them that some Western cultures share a folk belief that cats have nine lives. Ask if there are any similar beliefs in their cultures.

B Elements of Literature
Irony
Point out to students that Mercutio says he has a scratch but is really mortally wounded. The ironic banter in spite of dire circumstances is typical of Mercutio's character.

Answers to Margin Questions
Line 77. Mercutio thinks Romeo is cowardly not to meet Tybalt's challenge. Fiery Tybalt is not likely to be afraid, but he could be annoyed or angered.
Stage direction. Interpretations of Mercutio's motivation will vary, but students should see that he must first draw Tybalt away from Romeo so that Romeo can then come between the two swordsmen, attempting to stop the fight. If you show a film of the play, students could enjoy seeing how the director blocks this scene.

Mercutio.
O calm, dishonorable, vile submission!

75   Alla stoccata° carries it away.

[*Draws.*]

Tybalt, you ratcatcher, will you walk?°
Tybalt.
What wouldst thou have with me?

Mercutio. Good King of Cats, nothing but one of your nine lives. That I mean to make bold withal,° and,
80   as you shall use me hereafter, dry-beat° the rest of the eight. Will you pluck your sword out of his pilcher° by the ears? Make haste, lest mine be about your ears ere it be out.
Tybalt. I am for you.

[*Draws.*]

Romeo.
85   Gentle Mercutio, put thy rapier up.
Mercutio. Come, sir, your passado!

[*They fight.*]

Romeo.
Draw, Benvolio; beat down their weapons.
Gentlemen, for shame! Forbear this outrage!
Tybalt, Mercutio, the prince expressly hath
90   Forbid this bandying° in Verona streets.
Hold, Tybalt! Good Mercutio!

[TYBALT *under Romeo's arm thrusts* MERCUTIO *in, and flies.*]

Mercutio.   I am hurt.
A plague a' both houses! I am sped.°
Is he gone and hath nothing?
Benvolio.   What, art thou hurt?
Mercutio.
Ay, ay, a scratch, a scratch. Marry, 'tis enough.
95   Where is my page? Go, villain, fetch a surgeon.

                         [*Exit* PAGE.]

Romeo.
Courage, man. The hurt cannot be much.
Mercutio. No, 'tis not so deep as a well, nor so wide as a church door; but 'tis enough, 'twill serve. Ask for me tomorrow, and you shall find me a grave man.
100   I am peppered,° I warrant, for this world. A plague a' both your houses! Zounds, a dog, a rat, a mouse, a cat, to scratch a man to death! A braggart, a rogue,

75. Alla stoccata: "at the thrust," a fencing term.

76. walk: make a move.

? 77. *Mercutio doesn't know of Romeo's marriage to Juliet (a Capulet). Why is Mercutio so outraged? What feeling should Tybalt express (fear? annoyance?) as he asks Mercutio what he wants?*
79. make bold withal: make free with (take away).
80. dry-beat: thrash.
82. pilcher: scabbard (sword holder).

? Stage direction: *The stage direction above simply says "They fight," but how would you—as director—choreograph the action? Would you have Mercutio challenge Tybalt to protect Romeo? Or would you emphasize Mercutio's dislike of Tybalt? The sword fight can range all over the stage, but where must the three characters be placed when Tybalt stabs Mercutio?*
90. bandying: brawling.
92. sped: wounded.

100. peppered: given a deadly wound ("peppered" food is ready to eat; Mercutio is "ready" to die).

Using Students' Strengths

Visual Learners
To help students visualize the range of powerful emotions affecting the characters in this act, ask them to collect and display pictures that reflect the emotional content of important scenes. For example, students might collect magazine and newspaper photos that suggest hostility and anger among young men, anguish among grieving family members, fear and uncertainty in sweethearts, and anger between parents and children.

Interpersonal Learners
These students may enjoy focusing on aspects of daily life during the Renaissance. For example, some students might research the clothing styles of the period, while others might focus on the forms of entertainment or recreation available to young people. Have students prepare displays or presentations to share their findings with the class.

a villain, that fights by the book of arithmetic!° Why
the devil came you between us? I was hurt under your

105   arm.
  Romeo.
    I thought all for the best.
  Mercutio.
    Help me into some house, Benvolio,
    Or I shall faint. A plague a' both your houses!
    They have made worms' meat of me. I have it,
110   And soundly too. Your houses!

                  [*Exeunt* MERCUTIO *and* BENVOLIO.]

« *A plague a' both your houses!* »

Romeo.
  This gentleman, the prince's near ally,°
  My very friend, hath got this mortal hurt
  In my behalf—my reputation stained
  With Tybalt's slander—Tybalt, that an hour
115   Hath been my cousin. O sweet Juliet,
  Thy beauty hath made me effeminate **C**
  And in my temper soft'ned valor's steel!

[*Enter* BENVOLIO.]

Benvolio.
  O Romeo, Romeo, brave Mercutio is dead!
  That gallant spirit hath aspired° the clouds,
120   Which too untimely here did scorn the earth.
Romeo.
  This day's black fate on more days doth depend;°
  This but begins the woe others must end.

[*Enter* TYBALT.]

Benvolio.
  Here comes the furious Tybalt back again.
Romeo.
  Alive in triumph, and Mercutio slain?
125   Away to heaven respective lenity,
  And fire-eyed fury be my conduct now!
  Now, Tybalt, take the "villain" back again
  That late thou gavest me; for Mercutio's soul
  Is but a little way above our heads, **D**
130   Staying for thine to keep him company.
  Either thou or I, or both, must go with him.

THE TRAGEDY OF ROMEO AND JULIET, ACT III, SCENE 1 **793**

**103. fights by the book of arith-
metic:** fights according to formal
rules for fencing.

? **106.** *How would Romeo say
this pathetic line?*

? **110.** *What curse has Mercutio pronounced four times?
Some actors playing Mercutio
make him seem bitter about his
approaching death and hostile to
Romeo. Other Mercutios are
gallant to the end and extend a
hand to Romeo in friendship. How
would you play this death speech?*

111. ally: relative. Mercutio was
related to Verona's Prince Escalus.

119. aspired: climbed to.

121. depend: hang over.

? **Stage direction:** *Does it
seem unlikely that Tybalt
would return so soon? He must
return, of course, so that Romeo
can avenge Mercutio. An alternative would have been to have
Romeo attack Tybalt as soon as he
stabbed Mercutio, but then Shakespeare would have lost Mercutio's
great dying speech. How would
you stage Tybalt's return so that it
seems believable?*

T793

A Elements of Literature

Turning Point

? What questions might be in the audience's mind during this turning point in the play? [Possible responses: Will Romeo be caught and put to death, or will the prince spare his life? Will Romeo ever see Juliet again? Will Romeo tell everyone about his marriage to Juliet?]

B Reading Skills and Strategies

Making Connections

? Why does the prince choose Benvolio to explain what has happened? [Possible responses: The prince trusts the word of Benvolio; Benvolio showed himself to be capable of objective commentary in Act I.]

Answers to Margin Questions

Line 137. Romeo is standing in amazement (l. 136), apparently immobilized by the shock of having killed Tybalt.

Line 138. He means he is unlucky; by chance, he has been provoked to an action that will further inflame the Capulet-Montague feud and endanger his marriage to Juliet.

Stage direction. The stage would be filled with confusion, with people milling about as they see and react to Tybalt's corpse.

Tybalt.
Thou, wretched boy, that didst consort him here,
Shalt with him hence.

Romeo.   This shall determine that.

[They fight. TYBALT falls.]

Benvolio.
135 Romeo, away, be gone!
The citizens are up, and Tybalt slain.
Stand not amazed. The prince will doom thee death
If thou art taken. Hence, be gone, away!

Romeo.
O, I am fortune's fool!

Benvolio.   Why dost thou stay?

[Exit ROMEO.]

[Enter CITIZENS.]

Citizen.
Which way ran he that killed Mercutio?
140 Tybalt, that murderer, which way ran he?

Benvolio.
There lies that Tybalt.

Citizen.   Up, sir, go with me.
I charge thee in the prince's name obey.

[Enter PRINCE, old MONTAGUE, CAPULET, their WIVES, and all.]

Prince.
Where are the vile beginners of this fray?

Benvolio.
O noble prince, I can discover° all
145 The unlucky manage° of this fatal brawl.
There lies the man, slain by young Romeo,
That slew thy kinsman, brave Mercutio.

Lady Capulet.
Tybalt, my cousin! O my brother's child!
O prince! O cousin! Husband! O, the blood is spilled
150 Of my dear kinsman! Prince, as thou art true,
For blood of ours shed blood of Montague.
O cousin, cousin!

Prince.
B Benvolio, who began this bloody fray?

Benvolio.
Tybalt, here slain, whom Romeo's hand did slay.
155 Romeo, that spoke him fair, bid him bethink
How nice° the quarrel was, and urged° withal
Your high displeasure. All this—utterèd
With gentle breath, calm look, knees humbly bowed—

794 WILLIAM SHAKESPEARE

? **137.** *What details in Benvolio's speech tell us what Romeo is doing and how he is feeling after this second death?*

? **138.** *What do you think Romeo means by calling himself "fortune's fool"? What does he realize will now happen to him and Juliet?*

? *Stage direction: What do you imagine the stage looks like as the prince and his followers enter?*

144. discover: reveal.
145. manage: course.

156. nice: trivial. **urged:** mentioned.

Crossing the Curriculum

Social Studies

The basis for the main conflict of the play lies in the feud between the Capulets and the Montagues. Explain to students that a *feud* is a bitter, long-standing, deadly quarrel that is often passed on from one generation to the next. Ask students to use library resources to find information about a more recent feud—that of the Hatfields and the McCoys in the Appalachian Mountains during the nineteenth century. Ask students to find reasons for the conflict and to discover how the conflict was resolved at last.

Physical Education

Have students research the sport of fencing. Ask them to report on some of the basic moves of the sport, its history, and its current popularity.

Could not take truce with the unruly spleen°
160   Of Tybalt deaf to peace, but that he tilts°
With piercing steel at bold Mercutio's breast;
Who, all as hot, turns deadly point to point,
And, with a martial scorn, with one hand beats
Cold death aside and with the other sends
165   It back to Tybalt, whose dexterity
Retorts it. Romeo he cries aloud,
"Hold, friends! Friends, part!" and swifter than his
      tongue,
His agile arm beats down their fatal points,
And 'twixt them rushes; underneath whose arm
170   An envious° thrust from Tybalt hit the life
Of stout Mercutio, and then Tybalt fled;
But by and by comes back to Romeo,
Who had but newly entertained° revenge,
And to't they go like lightning; for, ere I
175   Could draw to part them, was stout Tybalt slain;
And, as he fell, did Romeo turn and fly.
This is the truth, or let Benvolio die.

Lady Capulet.
He is a kinsman to the Montague;
Affection makes him false, he speaks not true.
180   Some twenty of them fought in this black strife,
And all those twenty could but kill one life.
I beg for justice, which thou, prince, must give.
Romeo slew Tybalt; Romeo must not live.

Prince.
Romeo slew him; he slew Mercutio.
185   Who now the price of his dear blood doth owe?

Montague.
Not Romeo, prince; he was Mercutio's friend;
His fault concludes but what the law should end,
The life of Tybalt.

Prince.   And for that offense **C**
Immediately we do exile him hence.
190   I have an interest in your hate's proceeding,
My blood° for your rude brawls doth lie a-bleeding;
But I'll amerce° you with so strong a fine
That you shall all repent the loss of mine.
I will be deaf to pleading and excuses;
195   Nor tears nor prayers shall purchase out abuses.
Therefore use none. Let Romeo hence in haste,
Else, when he is found, that hour is his last.
Bear hence this body and attend our will.
Mercy but murders, pardoning those that kill. **D**

                    [Exit with others.]

159. spleen: anger.
160. tilts: thrusts.

170. envious: full of enmity or hatred.

173. entertained: thought of.

? **177.** *Is Benvolio's testimony about events fully accurate?*

? **181.** *How does Lady Capulet think Tybalt was killed? Why does she think Benvolio is lying?*

191. My blood: that is, Mercutio, his blood relative.
192. amerce: punish.
? **199.** *The prince has heard arguments from both families and has given judgment in the case. What is Romeo's punishment? Why won't the prince show Romeo mercy?*
    The families exit in two separate processions, with their dead. How does this scene contrast with the fighting that has just taken place?

C Critical Thinking
   Making Judgments
? Do you feel this punishment is fair or unfair? Why? [Possible responses: It is unfair, because the prince originally said that anyone starting another fight would die, so Tybalt would have died anyway; it is fair, because the prince reduced the punishment for fighting (from death to exile) in Romeo's special case.]

D Reading Skills and Strategies
   Reading Shakespeare's Poetry
? Have a volunteer read the prince's speech aloud. Then, ask whether it is written in prose, blank verse, or rhymed couplets. [It is written in iambic pentameter and contains rhymed couplets, or pairs of rhyming lines.]

Answers to Margin Questions
Line 177. In most details it is accurate, but Benvolio does not explain that it was Mercutio who first baited Tybalt and that Romeo fled only at Benvolio's urging.
Line 181. Lady Capulet believes Tybalt was overcome by twenty young men, so that Romeo killed him, in effect, in a cowardly way. She distrusts Benvolio because he is a Montague and Romeo's good friend.
Line 199. Romeo is exiled; if he does not leave Verona, he will be killed. The prince refuses mercy because the feud has now killed one of his own kinsmen, Mercutio.

   In the fighting scene, the youths are spurred to action by their emotions; here the adults use logic to plead their cases.

Summary ■ ■

Act III, Scene 2

Juliet, anxious to consummate her marriage, delivers a soliloquy in which she urges night to hasten its approach. The nurse enters in a distracted state, saying that someone is dead. For some time Juliet believes Romeo is dead. The nurse finally explains that it is Tybalt who is dead and that Romeo, who killed him, is banished. Juliet is torn between conflicting emotions—she is angry at Romeo for having slain her cousin, joyful that Romeo is alive, guilty that she spoke ill of him, and despondent over his exile. Juliet threatens to kill herself, but the nurse comforts her by saying that she will go to the friar's cell and tell Romeo to come to Juliet's chamber that evening, as planned.

Ⓐ Reading Skills and Strategies

Reading Shakespeare's Poetry

Although Juliet's soliloquy is not in strict iambic pentameter, it is a beautiful love poem that offers a moment of respite from the growing sense of doom. The audience feels the dramatic irony as Juliet eagerly awaits her wedding night, unaware of the violence that has just occurred. Divide the soliloquy (ll. 1–31) into several parts, and ask students to read it aloud, paying attention to the run-on lines and end-stopped lines. Then, have the class analyze the soliloquy's imagery.

Ⓑ Critical Thinking

Making Connections

❓ In what way is Romeo like day even during the nighttime? [His very presence lights up the darkness, as he has lit up Juliet's world.]

Answers to Margin Questions

Stage direction. Romeo has killed Tybalt and has been banished from Verona.

Line 24. Possible cluster diagram:

Contemporary associations with night are likely to resemble Juliet's view.

Line 26. Romeo is the mansion. (The image specifically suggests his body.)

Line 31. In ll. 21–25, Juliet mentions Romeo's death as she describes how he brings light to her life.

T796

Scene 2. *Capulet's orchard.*

Enter JULIET *alone.*

Juliet.
Gallop apace, you fiery-footed steeds,°
Towards Phoebus' lodging! Such a wagoner
As Phaethon° would whip you to the west
Ⓐ And bring in cloudy night immediately.
5 Spread thy close curtain, love-performing night,
That runaways' eyes may wink,° and Romeo
Leap to these arms untalked of and unseen.
Lovers can see to do their amorous rites,
And by their own beauties; or, if love be blind,
10 It best agrees with night. Come, civil° night,
Thou sober-suited matron all in black,
And learn me how to lose a winning match,
Played for a pair of stainless maidenhoods.
Hood° my unmanned° blood, bating° in my cheeks,
15 With thy black mantle till strange° love grow bold,
Think true love acted simple modesty.
Come, night; come, Romeo; come, thou day in night;
For thou wilt lie upon the wings of night
Whiter than new snow upon a raven's back.
20 Come, gentle night; come, loving, black-browed night;
Ⓑ Give me my Romeo; and, when he shall die,
Take him and cut him out in little stars,
And he will make the face of heaven so fine
That all the world will be in love with night
25 And pay no worship to the garish sun.
O, I have bought the mansion of a love,
But not possessed it; and though I am sold,
Not yet enjoyed. So tedious is this day
As is the night before some festival
30 To an impatient child that hath new robes
And may not wear them. O, here comes my nurse,

[*Enter* NURSE, *with a ladder of cords.*]

❝ O, I have bought the mansion of a love,
But not possessed it. . . . ❞

---

796 WILLIAM SHAKESPEARE

Stage direction: *What do we in the audience know that Juliet at this point still does not know?*
1. steeds: horses (that pull the sun god Phoebus's chariot across the sky each day).
3. Phaethon: reckless son of Phoebus, who couldn't hold the horses.
6. That runaways' eyes may wink: so that the eyes of the sun god's horses may shut.

10. civil: well-behaved.

14. Hood: cover. **unmanned:** unmated. **bating:** fluttering.
15. strange: unfamiliar.

24. *Work in small groups to make a cluster for the word* night. *Include all the associations, images, and synonyms that you can come up with. How do they compare with Juliet's view of night?*
26. *What is the "mansion of a love" Juliet has bought?*
31. *Where does Juliet, in lines of unconscious foreshadowing, make us think of Romeo's death?*

Crossing the Curriculum

Music

Play an audio or video recording of the song "Tonight" from the movie *West Side Story.* Have students compare the imagery and emotions in the song with those expressed in Juliet's soliloquy in Scene 2. How successfully have the composer and lyricist matched the mood Shakespeare intended for this scene?

And she brings news; and every tongue that speaks
But Romeo's name speaks heavenly eloquence.
Now, nurse, what news? What hast thou there, the
   cords
That Romeo bid thee fetch?

35 **Nurse.**   Ay, ay, the cords.
Juliet.
   Ay me! What news? Why dost thou wring thy hands?
Nurse.
   Ah, weraday!° He's dead, he's dead, he's dead!
   We are undone, lady, we are undone!
   Alack the day! He's gone, he's killed, he's dead!
Juliet.
   Can heaven be so envious?
40 **Nurse.**   Romeo can,
   Though heaven cannot. O Romeo, Romeo!
   Who ever would have thought it? Romeo!
Juliet.
   What devil art thou that dost torment me thus?
   This torture should be roared in dismal hell.
45 Hath Romeo slain himself? Say thou but "Ay,"
   And that bare vowel "I" shall poison more
   Than the death-darting eye of cockatrice.°
   I am not I, if there be such an "Ay,"
   Or those eyes' shot that make thee answer "Ay."
50 If he be slain, say "Ay"; or if not, "No."
   Brief sounds determine of my weal or woe.
Nurse.
   I saw the wound, I saw it with mine eyes,
   (God save the mark!)° here on his manly breast.
   A piteous corse,° a bloody piteous corse;
55 Pale, pale as ashes, all bedaubed in blood,
   All in gore-blood. I swounded° at the sight.
Juliet.
   O, break, my heart! Poor bankrout,° break at once!
   To prison, eyes; ne'er look on liberty!
   Vile earth,° to earth resign; end motion here,
60 And thou and Romeo press one heavy bier!
Nurse.
   O Tybalt, Tybalt, the best friend I had!
   O courteous Tybalt! Honest gentleman!
   That ever I should live to see thee dead!
Juliet.
   What storm is this that blows so contrary?
65 Is Romeo slaught'red, and is Tybalt dead?
   My dearest cousin, and my dearer lord?
   Then, dreadful trumpet, sound the general doom!
   For who is living, if those two are gone?

35. *How does the nurse speak this line?*

37. weraday!: well-a-day! (or alas!)

39. *The nurse rattles on again—but this time, how does she seem to give the* wrong *news, even as she delays it?*

47. cockatrice: legendary serpent that could kill by a glance.

53. God save the mark!: God forbid!
54. corse: corpse.

56. swounded: swooned (fainted).

57. bankrout: bankrupt.

59. Vile earth: Juliet refers to her own body.
60. *This is one of a series of odd scenes in which we cannot share a character's feelings because we know something that the character does not know. What does Juliet think has happened? How does she foreshadow her own death?*

THE TRAGEDY OF ROMEO AND JULIET, ACT III, SCENE 2 **797**

C **Elements of Literature**
Character
❓ Why does Juliet's joy suddenly turn to despair? [Juliet sees the nurse approaching, wringing her hands, and the nurse announces, "He's dead."]

D **Appreciating Language**
Puns
❓ What two homonyms of the word *ay* does Juliet use to make puns? [the pronoun *I* and the noun *eye*] Did you find her wordplay in the face of tragedy inappropriate? Explain. [Possible response: Yes, cleverness is inconsistent with the expression of true, spontaneous emotion, especially sadness; no, her rambling speech emphasizes her confusion and despair.]

E **Vocabulary Note**
Homonyms
Tell students that the word *bier* is pronounced the same way as its homonym *beer*. A *bier* is a coffin; the word can also refer to the supporting platform on which a coffin is placed.

Answers to Margin Questions
Line 35. The nurse speaks distractedly because of her grief.
Line 39. The nurse says only "He's dead," and Juliet assumes she means Romeo.
Line 60. Believing Romeo is dead, Juliet says that she wants to share his "heavy bier."

A Elements of Literature

Figurative Language

? What oxymorons, or pairs of opposites, does Juliet use to express her momentary feeling that Romeo has betrayed her? [*Beautiful tyrant, Fiend angelical, Dove-feathered raven, Wolvish-ravening lamb, damnèd saint, honorable villain*]

B Critical Thinking

Expressing an Opinion

? Do you think the nurse is justified in taking Tybalt's side? Explain. [Possible responses: Yes, because Tybalt is a member of the family whom the nurse serves; no, because she has been a party to the secret wedding between Romeo and Juliet, and she should be loyal to them.]

C Struggling Readers

Paraphrasing

Ask students to paraphrase Juliet's comment. [Possible response: Tybalt died trying to kill Romeo. Romeo was defending himself, and I'm glad he's alive. Then why am I crying?]

Answers to Margin Questions

Line 70. It is unlikely that the nurse is merely "waiting." She seems truly disturbed. Her rambling, disconnected style of speaking, even when she is not upset, has already been established.

Line 73. Possible response: Juliet clenches her fists or runs her hand through her hair as she speaks.

Line 85. Her entire speech is filled with oxymorons that express her internal conflict. She loves Romeo but feels betrayed.

Line 90. The nurse blames Romeo. Perhaps she is not exactly selfish, but she is incapable of reflection or discrimination. The nurse passes judgment too quickly and does not try to analyze events. She is angry because Romeo has hurt Juliet; however, the nurse is not perceptive enough to see that Juliet still loves him or that Tybalt was at fault.

Line 97. Perhaps the nurse's attack on Romeo brings Juliet back to her senses. She decides that, whatever Romeo has done, she must be loyal to her husband.

Nurse.
Tybalt is gone, and Romeo banishèd;
70 Romeo that killed him, he is banishèd.
Juliet.
O God! Did Romeo's hand shed Tybalt's blood?
Nurse.
It did, it did! Alas the day, it did!
Juliet.
O serpent heart, hid with a flow'ring face!
Did ever dragon keep so fair a cave?
75 Beautiful tyrant! Fiend angelical!
Dove-feathered raven! Wolvish-ravening lamb!
A Despisèd substance of divinest show!
Just opposite to what thou justly seem'st—
A damnèd saint, an honorable villain!
80 O nature, what hadst thou to do in hell
When thou didst bower the spirit of a fiend
In mortal paradise of such sweet flesh?
Was ever book containing such vile matter
So fairly bound? O, that deceit should dwell
In such a gorgeous palace!
85 **Nurse.**   There's no trust,
No faith, no honesty in men; all perjured,
All forsworn, all naught, all dissemblers.°
Ah, where's my man? Give me some aqua vitae.°
These griefs, these woes, these sorrows make me old.
Shame come to Romeo!
90 **Juliet.**   Blistered be thy tongue
For such a wish! He was not born to shame.
Upon his brow shame is ashamed to sit;
For 'tis a throne where honor may be crowned
Sole monarch of the universal earth.
95 O, what a beast was I to chide at him!
B **Nurse.**
Will you speak well of him that killed your cousin?
Juliet.
Shall I speak ill of him that is my husband?
Ah, poor my lord, what tongue shall smooth thy name
When I, thy three-hours wife, have mangled it?
100 But wherefore, villain, didst thou kill my cousin?
That villain cousin would have killed my husband.
Back, foolish tears, back to your native spring!
Your tributary drops° belong to woe,
Which you, mistaking, offer up to joy.
105 **C** My husband lives, that Tybalt would have slain;
And Tybalt's dead, that would have slain my husband.
All this is comfort; wherefore weep I then?
Some word there was, worser than Tybalt's death,

798 WILLIAM SHAKESPEARE

? **70.** *Why do you think the nurse waits so long to give Juliet the correct news? Should we feel she is being self-centered here, or is she truly overwhelmed by the news she bears?*

? **73.** *The news that Romeo has killed Tybalt is terrible for Juliet. Try writing stage directions that will help an actress express her horror.*

? **85.** *A moment ago, Juliet thought of Romeo as her very "day in night." Now what does she think of him?*

87. dissemblers: liars.
88. aqua vitae: brandy (Latin for "water of life").

? **90.** *What does the nurse think about these events? Where does she think the blame lies? Do you see her being selfish here, or is she wholly concerned for Juliet?*

? **97.** *Why does Juliet turn against her nurse here?*

103. tributary drops: tears poured out in tribute.

That murd'red me. I would forget it fain;°

110 But O, it presses to my memory
Like damnèd guilty deeds to sinners' minds!
"Tybalt is dead, and Romeo—banishèd."
That "banishèd," that one word "banishèd,"
Hath slain ten thousand Tybalts. Tybalt's death

115 Was woe enough, if it had ended there;
Or, if sour woe delights in fellowship
And needly will be ranked with° other griefs,
Why followed not, when she said "Tybalt's dead," **D**
Thy father, or thy mother, nay, or both,

120 Which modern° lamentation might have moved?°
But with a rearward° following Tybalt's death,
"Romeo is banishèd"—to speak that word
Is father, mother, Tybalt, Romeo, Juliet,
All slain, all dead. "Romeo is banishèd"—

125 There is no end, no limit, measure, bound,
In that word's death; no words can that woe sound.
Where is my father and my mother, nurse?

Nurse.
Weeping and wailing over Tybalt's corse.
Will you go to them? I will bring you thither.

Juliet.
130 Wash they his wounds with tears? Mine shall be spent,
When theirs are dry, for Romeo's banishment.
Take up those cords. Poor ropes, you are beguiled,
Both you and I, for Romeo is exiled.
He made you for a highway to my bed; **E**

135 But I, a maid, die maiden-widowèd.
Come, cords; come, nurse. I'll to my wedding bed;
And death, not Romeo, take my maidenhead! **F**

Nurse.
Hie to your chamber. I'll find Romeo
To comfort you. I wot° well where he is.

140 Hark ye, your Romeo will be here at night.
I'll to him; he is hid at Laurence' cell.

Juliet.
O, find him! Give this ring to my true knight
And bid him come to take his last farewell.

[*Exit with* NURSE.]

THE TRAGEDY OF ROMEO AND JULIET, ACT III, SCENE 2 **799**

---

109. fain: willingly.

117. ranked with: accompanied by.

120. modern: ordinary. **moved:** provoked.
121. rearward: soldiers at the rear of a troop; here, an additional source of injury and pain after the bad news about Tybalt.

? **124.** *Juliet comprehends what has happened. Why does she fix on that one word—banished?*

? **127.** *Juliet pauses before she speaks her last line here. How would you change her tone as she asks the nurse about her father and mother?*

? **137.** *Juliet addresses the rope ladder in this speech. What has she decided to do with the ropes?*
139. wot: know.

D **Struggling Readers**
Paraphrasing
Read Juliet's speech aloud, line by line, and help students paraphrase her meaning. [Hearing that Romeo is banished is worse than hearing that ten thousand Tybalts had been killed. Hearing that Romeo and I must be separated is as bad as if my parents, Tybalt, Romeo, and I myself were all dead.]

E **Reading Skills and Strategies**
Reading Shakespeare's Poetry
Ask a student to read Juliet's speech aloud, and have the class note the rhymed couplets.

F **Elements of Literature**
Turning Point
? How does Shakespeare use the rope ladder as an ironic symbol that the plot has turned from romance to tragedy? [Possible response: The same ladder that Romeo was supposed to use to climb into Juliet's bedroom on their wedding night is now being considered by Juliet as a means of suicide.]

Answers to Margin Questions
Line 124. Romeo's banishment means one thing to Juliet: They will be separated.
Line 127. Juliet must control her grief and begin to seem aware of other people and their concerns.
Line 137. Juliet has decided to kill herself.

Skill Link

Dashes
Explain to students that dashes are used to indicate an abrupt halt or reversal in thought or speech, an unfinished statement or question, or an interruption by another character. In a play, actors can use these punctuation marks as clues for interpreting their lines.

Activity
Have students first read the following lines aloud as if the dashes were not there. Then, have them reinsert the dashes and reread the lines to demonstrate how effective pauses can be used to add dramatic effect.
1. Scene 2, ll. 112–126
2. Scene 3, ll. 74–78
3. Scene 5, ll. 94–103

Summary ■ ■

Act III, Scene 3

At Friar Laurence's cell, the friar tells Romeo of the prince's sentence of banishment. Romeo collapses in despair. Death, he says, would be preferable. When the nurse arrives, she reports that Juliet is also distraught. Feeling responsible for her grief, Romeo tries to stab himself. The nurse prevents him, and Friar Laurence offers a plan: Romeo will go to Mantua while the friar works to reconcile the feuding families, reveal the secret marriage, and obtain the Prince's pardon for Romeo, who will then return to Verona. But first Romeo will visit Juliet. However, the friar cautions him that he must be off to Mantua before the watch is set.

Ⓐ Elements of Literature
Turning Point

❓ How does Shakespeare use personification to signal the turning of the plot from romance to tragedy? [He personifies the words *affliction* and *calamity*, saying that they love Romeo and have married him.]

Ⓑ Vocabulary Note
Multiple Meanings

To help students interpret this line correctly, point out that the word *without* can mean either "lacking" or "outside." Romeo uses the second meaning here: There is no world outside of Verona's walls, that is, away from Juliet.

Ⓒ Reading Skills and Strategies
Making Connections

❓ How does Romeo's response to the news of his banishment compare with Juliet's response to the same news in Scene 2? [Possible responses: Both of them repeat the word *banishèd* several times; both of them consider separation from each other a fate worse than death.]

Answers to Margin Questions

Line 3. The friar says that affliction loves Romeo and that Romeo is "wedded to calamity."

Line 21. For Romeo, Verona is the whole world because it contains Juliet; banishment from her is like death.

Line 28. Romeo ignores the prince's mercy in not sentencing him to death.

Scene 3. *Friar Laurence's cell.*

Enter FRIAR LAURENCE.

Friar.
Romeo, come forth; come forth, thou fearful man.
Ⓐ Affliction is enamored of thy parts,
And thou art wedded to calamity.

[*Enter* ROMEO.]

Romeo.
Father, what news? What is the prince's doom?
5   What sorrow craves acquaintance at my hand
That I yet know not?

Friar.   Too familiar
Is my dear son with such sour company.
I bring thee tidings of the prince's doom.

Romeo.
What less than doomsday° is the prince's doom?

Friar.
10   A gentler judgment vanished° from his lips—
Not body's death, but body's banishment.

Romeo.
Ha, banishment? Be merciful, say "death";
For exile hath more terror in his look,
Much more than death. Do not say "banishment."

Friar.
15   Here from Verona art thou banishèd.
Be patient, for the world is broad and wide.

Romeo.
Ⓑ There is no world without Verona walls,
But purgatory, torture, hell itself.
Hence banishèd is banished from the world,
20   And world's exile is death. Then "banishèd"
Ⓒ Is death mistermed. Calling death "banishèd,"
Thou cut'st my head off with a golden ax
And smilest upon the stroke that murders me.

Friar.
O deadly sin! O rude unthankfulness!
25   Thy fault our law calls death; but the kind prince,
Taking thy part, hath rushed aside the law,
And turned that black word "death" to "banishment."
This is dear mercy, and thou see'st it not.

800 WILLIAM SHAKESPEARE

❓ **3.** *When we last saw Romeo he was speaking of himself as "fortune's fool" (Act III, Scene 1, line 138). Now, in the first lines of this scene, how does the friar remind us again that Romeo seems fated for ill fortune?*

9. **doomsday:** my death.

10. **vanished:** escaped.

❓ **21.** *Romeo, like Juliet, fixes on the word* banished. *What does the word mean to him?*

❓ **28.** *Why is the friar angry at Romeo?*

Taking a Second Look

Review: Cause and Effect

Remind students that a *cause* is an event that brings about another event. The resultant event is called an *effect.* Plots often unfold as a chain of causes and effects, in which each effect then becomes a cause that sets off the next effect. The turning point of a play is an event that causes a chain of increasingly positive or increasingly negative effects. Point out that each cause can have more than one effect, and each effect can have more than one cause.

Activity

As students read the rest of the play, have them complete a cause-and-effect chain that begins with Act III, Scene 1. They can begin like this:

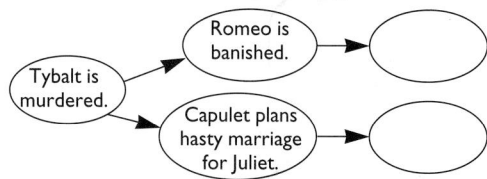

Romeo.

'Tis torture, and not mercy. Heaven is here,
30   Where Juliet lives; and every cat and dog
And little mouse, every unworthy thing,
Live here in heaven and may look on her;
But Romeo may not. More validity,°
More honorable state, more courtship lives
35   In carrion flies than Romeo. They may seize
On the white wonder of dear Juliet's hand
And steal immortal blessing from her lips,
Who, even in pure and vestal modesty,
Still blush, as thinking their own kisses sin;
40   But Romeo may not, he is banishèd.
Flies may do this but I from this must fly;
They are freemen, but I am banishèd.
And sayest thou yet that exile is not death?
Hadst thou no poison mixed, no sharp-ground knife,
45   No sudden mean of death, though ne'er so mean,
But "banishèd" to kill me—"banishèd"?
O friar, the damnèd use that word in hell;
Howling attends it! How hast thou the heart,
Being a divine, a ghostly confessor,
50   A sin-absolver, and my friend professed,
To mangle me with that word "banishèd"?

(D)

33. validity: value.

" Heaven is here,
Where Juliet lives. . . . "

Friar.

Thou fond° mad man, hear me a little speak. (E)

Romeo.

O, thou wilt speak again of banishment.

Friar.

I'll give thee armor to keep off that word;
55   Adversity's sweet milk, philosophy,
To comfort thee, though thou art banishèd. (F)

Romeo.

Yet "banishèd"? Hang up philosophy!
Unless philosophy can make a Juliet,
Displant a town, reverse a prince's doom,
60   It helps not, it prevails not. Talk no more.

Friar.

O, then I see that madmen have no ears.

52. fond: foolish.

? **60.** *It may seem that Romeo goes on too much. But it is important that we get the picture of this "fond mad man" in order to understand the action of the play. None of the other characters can understand Romeo's love. They are more levelheaded (perhaps less lucky in love?). How is Romeo's response to banishment like Juliet's?*

THE TRAGEDY OF ROMEO AND JULIET, ACT III, SCENE 3   **801**

D **Reading Skills and Strategies**

Reading Shakespeare's Poetry

Have students identify the run-on lines in this speech and practice reading them so that the meaning flows smoothly from line to line. Then, ask a volunteer to read Romeo's entire speech aloud.

E **Struggling Readers**

Syntax

Have students rearrange the friar's words in the order we would say them today. [You foolish, nutty man, hear me speak a little.]

F **Reading Skills and Strategies**

Connecting with the Text

? Do you agree with the friar that the pain of life's adversities can be eased through philosophical reflection? Explain. [Answers will vary. Some students may say that philosophical thoughts can distract people from their problems, while others may disagree.]

Answer to Margin Question
Line 60. For both the lovers, banishment is as bad as death, for it means they cannot be together. Both "live" only in each other.

A Elements of Literature

Turning Point

❓ Why are the lovers feeling increasingly isolated? [Possible response: They feel that no one can understand the despair they feel about the banishment; even the nurse and the friar, who know about the marriage, can't understand the depth of the lovers' feelings for each other.] How might this feeling of isolation contribute to the tragedy to come? [Possible response: Because the lovers feel that no one else can really understand what they are going through, it may seem pointless to confide in friends and family and ask for help.]

B Elements of Literature

Suspense

❓ How does Shakespeare create a growing feeling of tension in this scene? [Someone knocks at the door three times. Each time the characters and the audience wonder who is there and whether Romeo is about to be captured as the friar frantically scrambles to convince Romeo to hide.]

Answers to Margin Questions

Line 62. Romeo is talking about Friar Laurence, who cannot "see" what the banishment will mean.

Line 70. In some ways, the friar's response depends on how Romeo delivers his lines. If Romeo is pitiful, Friar Laurence could be moved, even though Romeo's words are unfair and immature. If Romeo is disdainful, the friar could be angry but be restraining himself. He could also be preparing to chastise Romeo for his melodramatic behavior just as the knock comes at the door.

Line 71. Romeo is lying on the floor, weeping. Friar Laurence keeps dashing between the stricken lover and the door; he is trying to force Romeo to his feet while also shouting at the person who is knocking.

Romeo.
How should they, when that wise men have no eyes?
Friar.
Let me dispute with thee of thy estate.°
Romeo.
Thou canst not speak of that thou dost not feel.
65 Wert thou as young as I, Juliet thy love,
An hour but married, Tybalt murderèd,
Doting like me, and like me banishèd,
Then mightst thou speak, then mightst thou tear thy
hair,
And fall upon the ground, as I do now,
70 Taking the measure of an unmade grave.

[*The* NURSE *knocks.*]

Friar.
Arise, one knocks. Good Romeo, hide thyself.
Romeo.
Not I; unless the breath of heartsick groans
Mistlike infold me from the search of eyes.

[*Knock.*]

Friar.
Hark, how they knock! Who's there? Romeo, arise;
75 Thou wilt be taken.—Stay awhile!—Stand up;

[*Knock.*]

Run to my study.—By and by!—God's will,
What simpleness is this.—I come, I come!

[*Knock.*]

Who knocks so hard? Whence come you? What's your
will?

[*Enter* NURSE.]

Nurse.
Let me come in, and you shall know my errand.
I come from Lady Juliet.
80 **Friar.**   Welcome then.
Nurse.
O holy friar, O, tell me, holy friar,
Where is my lady's lord, where's Romeo?
Friar.
There on the ground, with his own tears made drunk.
Nurse.
O, he is even in my mistress' case,°
85 Just in her case! O woeful sympathy!

❓ **62.** *Whom is Romeo talking about?*

63. estate: situation.

❓ **70.** *How do you think the friar responds to these harsh words?*

❓ **71.** *There is a great deal of action in this scene while the knocks are heard at the door. What action is the friar engaged in, and what is Romeo doing?*

84. case: condition.

802 WILLIAM SHAKESPEARE

Piteous predicament! Even so lies she,
Blubb'ring and weeping, weeping and blubb'ring.
Stand up, stand up! Stand, and you be a man.
For Juliet's sake, for her sake, rise and stand!
90   Why should you fall into so deep an O?°
Romeo (*rises*). Nurse——
Nurse.
    Ah sir, ah sir! Death's the end of all.
Romeo.
    Spakest thou of Juliet? How is it with her?
    Doth not she think me an old murderer,
95   Now I have stained the childhood of our joy
    With blood removed but little from her own?
    Where is she? And how doth she? And what says
    My concealed lady to our canceled love?
Nurse.
    O, she says nothing, sir, but weeps and weeps;
100   And now falls on her bed, and then starts up,
    And Tybalt calls; and then on Romeo cries,
    And then down falls again.
Romeo.   As if that name,
    Shot from the deadly level° of a gun,
    Did murder her; as that name's cursèd hand
105   Murdered her kinsman. O, tell me, friar, tell me, **C**
    In what vile part of this anatomy
    Doth my name lodge? Tell me, that I may sack°
    The hateful mansion.

[*He offers to stab himself, and* NURSE *snatches the dagger away.*]

Friar.   Hold thy desperate hand.
    Art thou a man? Thy form cries out thou art;
110   Thy tears are womanish, thy wild acts denote
    The unreasonable fury of a beast.
    Unseemly woman in a seeming man!
    And ill-beseeming beast in seeming both!
    Thou hast amazed me. By my holy order,   **D**
115   I thought thy disposition better tempered.
    Hast thou slain Tybalt? Wilt thou slay thyself?
    And slay thy lady that in thy life lives,
    By doing damnèd hate upon thyself?
    Why rail'st thou on thy birth, the heaven, and earth?
120   Since birth and heaven and earth,° all three do meet
    In thee at once; which thou at once wouldst lose.
    Fie, fie, thou sham'st thy shape, thy love, thy wit,
    Which,° like a usurer, abound'st in all,   **E**
    And usest none in that true use indeed
125   Which should bedeck° thy shape, thy love, thy wit.

90. **O:** fit of moaning ("oh, oh, oh").
❓ 90. *What action is the nurse engaged in as she speaks these lines?*

103. **level:** aim.

107. **sack:** plunder and destroy.
❓ 108. *Romeo is disarmed without a struggle, and probably stands broken as the friar, in this long speech, gradually reestablishes control over him. It is important to remember that to the people in this play, suicide was a mortal sin, which damned one to hell forever. Where does the friar angrily remind Romeo of this?*

120. **birth and heaven and earth:** family origin, soul, and body.

123. **Which:** who (speaking of Romeo).

125. **bedeck:** do honor to.

THE TRAGEDY OF ROMEO AND JULIET, ACT III, SCENE 3 803

C Critical Thinking
Making Connections
❓ In what way do Romeo's words echo Juliet's words in Scene 2? [Possible responses: He, too, contemplates suicide; in Juliet's opening soliloquy, she also refers to Romeo's body as a "mansion" (l. 26).]

D Reading Skills and Strategies
Extending the Text
❓ What effects might this kind of criticism have on a depressed person? [Possible responses: The person can become angry and even more depressed; the person might be shaken out of his feelings of self-pity.]

E Historical Connections
Tell students that a *usurer* is a money-lender who charges high interest rates. In Shakespear's day, the word meant any moneylender who charges interest. In past centuries the Catholic Church condemned usury because it was not considered proper to use money to make more money. Likewise, the friar says, by threatening suicide Romeo is not using his body, mind, and emotions in a proper way.

Answers to Margin Questions
Line 90. The nurse is urging Romeo to stand, probably pulling him up.
Line 108. Friar Laurence says that by committing suicide, Romeo will inflict "damnèd hate" upon himself (l. 118).

Skill Link

Distinguishing Fact and Opinion
Remind students that a *fact* is a statement that can be proved true or false. An *opinion* is a statement that expresses a personal belief or feeling, which cannot be proved. Opinions are often signaled by such words as *should, better,* or *worse.*

Activity
Have students reread ll. 108–145 of Friar Laurence's speech to Romeo. Then, have them make two columns labeled "Fact" and "Opinion" on a sheet of paper. Students should list facts and opinions stated by Friar Laurence regarding Romeo's predicament. Then, ask students which they think Romeo finds more convincing—the facts or the opinions.

T803

Read this passage aloud, and help students summarize Friar Laurence's advice to Romeo. [Possible response: Instead of wallowing in self-pity, you should count your blessings and be grateful for your good luck: Juliet is alive, you're alive, the person who wanted to kill you is dead, and the prince has decided to spare your life.]

B Reading Skills and Strategies
Responding to the Text
❓ Do you think the prince will be willing to forgive Romeo? Explain. [Possible responses: Yes, the prince may reconsider the punishment after Romeo shows extreme remorse for his act; no, the prince has already been lenient about Romeo's punishment and must remain firm about punishing those who continue the feud.]

Answers to Margin Questions
Line 154. "What, rouse thee, man!" (l. 135) suggests that Romeo is listless. The friar begins shaming Romeo immediately with "Art thou a man?" (l. 109) and continues until he begins the appeal to common sense, "Thy Juliet is alive" (l. 135). Beginning with his instructions "Go get thee to thy love" (l. 146), the friar offers hope that Romeo and Juliet can be reunited.
Line 155. The nurse is to tell Juliet to urge the household to go to bed early so that Romeo can come to her.
Line 161. Romeo could rush to the nurse, to hurry her to Juliet.

Thy noble shape is but a form of wax,
Digressing from the valor of a man;
Thy dear love sworn but hollow perjury,
Killing that love which thou hast vowed to cherish;
130   Thy wit, that ornament to shape and love,
Misshapen in the conduct° of them both,
Like powder in a skill-less soldier's flask,
Is set afire by thine own ignorance,
And thou dismembered with thine own defense.°
135   What, rouse thee, man! Thy Juliet is alive,
For whose dear sake thou wast but lately dead.
There art thou happy.° Tybalt would kill thee,
But thou slewest Tybalt. There art thou happy.
The law, that threatened death, becomes thy friend
140   **A** And turns it to exile. There art thou happy.
A pack of blessings light upon thy back;
Happiness courts thee in her best array;
But, like a misbehaved and sullen wench,
Thou pouts upon thy fortune and thy love.
145   Take heed, take heed, for such die miserable.
Go get thee to thy love, as was decreed,
Ascend her chamber, hence and comfort her.
But look thou stay not till the watch be set,
For then thou canst not pass to Mantua,
150   Where thou shalt live till we can find a time
To blaze° your marriage, reconcile your friends,
B Beg pardon of the prince, and call thee back
With twenty hundred thousand times more joy
Than thou went'st forth in lamentation.
155   Go before, nurse. Commend me to thy lady,
And bid her hasten all the house to bed,
Which heavy sorrow makes them apt unto.
Romeo is coming.

Nurse.
O Lord, I could have stayed here all the night
160   To hear good counsel. O, what learning is!
My lord, I'll tell my lady you will come.

Romeo.
Do so, and bid my sweet prepare to chide.

[NURSE *offers to go in and turns again.*]

Nurse.
Here, sir, a ring she bid me give you, sir.
Hie you, make haste, for it grows very late.   [*Exit.*]

Romeo.
165   How well my comfort is revived by this!

131. conduct: management.

134. And . . . defense: Romeo's own mind (wit), which should protect him, is destroying him.

137. happy: lucky.

151. blaze: announce.

❓ **154.** *What line in this speech suggests that Romeo has been standing listlessly? Find where the friar first shames Romeo, then appeals to his common sense, then offers him hope.*
❓ **155.** *The friar turns to the nurse. What are his instructions?*

❓ **161.** *The nurse's amazement at what she calls the friar's "learning" often brings a laugh from the audience and breaks the tension. Romeo thus far has said nothing. How do you imagine he shows that the friar's speech has brought him back to life?*

Professional Notes

Critical Comment: Comic Relief
In her book *An Introduction to Shakespeare*, Marchette Chute makes the following comments about the importance of Mercutio and the nurse as characters in this tragedy: "A lesser writer than Shakespeare might have tried to keep the play to a single note of lyric love. But Shakespeare . . . had no hesitation about putting a couple of cheerful realists into *Romeo and Juliet*. Mercutio and Juliet's nurse do not weaken the tragedy; they enrich it, in the usual astonishing fashion of Shakespeare's comedians. Mercutio is a humorist by intention; he is a subtle and intelligent young man who knows exactly how entertaining he is. . . . The nurse, on the other hand, does not mean to be funny. She feels she is a very sober, sensible, practical woman and she has no idea what actually happens every time she opens her mouth. Shakespeare had no objection to laughter in his tragedies. The two elements combine in real life and they were free to combine in his plays also."

Ask students to evaluate the facts and opinions expressed by this critic.

Friar.
Go hence; good night; and here stands all your state:°
Either be gone before the watch be set,
Or by the break of day disguised from hence.
Sojourn in Mantua. I'll find out your man,
170 And he shall signify from time to time
Every good hap to you that chances here.
Give me thy hand. 'Tis late. Farewell; good night.
Romeo.
But that a joy past joy calls out on me,
It were a grief so brief to part with thee.
175 Farewell.   [*Exeunt.*]

166. **state:** situation.

? **175.** *In spite of Romeo's and Juliet's anguish, the problem at this point seems to be simple. What plans have been made to resolve the young people's difficulties?*

Scene 4. *A room in Capulet's house.*

Enter old CAPULET, *his wife,* LADY CAPULET, *and* PARIS.

Capulet.
Things have fallen out, sir, so unluckily
That we have had no time to move° our daughter.
Look you, she loved her kinsman Tybalt dearly,
And so did I. Well, we were born to die.
5 'Tis very late; she'll not come down tonight.
I promise you, but for your company,
I would have been abed an hour ago.
Paris.
These times of woe afford no times to woo.
Madam, good night. Commend me to your daughter.
Lady Capulet.
10 I will, and know her mind early tomorrow;
Tonight she's mewed up to her heaviness.° **C**
Capulet.
Sir Paris, I will make a desperate tender°
Of my child's love. I think she will be ruled
In all respects by me; nay more, I doubt it not.
15 Wife, go you to her ere you go to bed;
Acquaint her here of my son Paris' love
And bid her (mark you me?) on Wednesday next—
But soft! What day is this?
Paris.   Monday, my lord. **D**

2. **move:** persuade (to marry Paris).

? **7.** *Dramatic irony is felt when the audience knows something that the characters on stage do not know. What intense dramatic irony does the audience feel as this scene unfolds? What do we know that the Capulets and Paris are ignorant of?*

11. **mewed up to her heaviness:** shut away because of her great grief.

12. **desperate tender:** bold offer.

Answer to Margin Question
Line 175. Friar Laurence is to act as a mediator with the prince and the two sets of parents. He will keep in touch with Romeo by messenger and call him back when all is well.

Summary ■

Act III, Scene 4
Lord Capulet explains to the visiting Paris that it is an inappropriate time to woo Juliet because the girl is extremely distraught over her cousin's murder. However, confident of his daughter's obedience, Capulet promises Paris that Juliet will marry him. The marriage day is set for Thursday—three days hence. Lord Capulet tells his wife to go to Juliet's room to tell her the news and prepare her for her wedding day.

C **Critical Thinking**
Interpreting
? How does Lady Capulet interpret the fact that Juliet has shut herself in her room? [Possible responses: She thinks Juliet is overcome with grief over Tybalt; she thinks Juliet is exhausted from crying.]

D **Elements of Literature**
Falling Action
The death of Tybalt causes Lord Capulet to make the decision to have Juliet married to Paris as soon as possible. This decision sets the characters more firmly on a tragic course. There will not be time for Friar Laurence to carry out his plans.

Answer to Margin Question
Line 7. The Capulets and Paris do not know that Juliet is already married to Romeo. Even as this scene unfolds, Romeo is in the house with her.

A Critical Thinking
Expressing an Opinion
? Do you think it is inappropriate for Capulet to plan Juliet's wedding so soon after Tybalt's death? [Possible responses: Yes, because not enough time has passed to mourn Tybalt; no, because the wedding will add some happiness to a family suffering a tragedy.]

Answers to Margin Questions
Line 19. Capulet is at least in part motivated by Tybalt's death and the social status of Juliet's suitor, Paris. His mood as he plans Juliet's wedding is enthusiastic and animated.
Line 32. Lady Capulet may feel that Juliet, distraught over Tybalt's death, should not be forced to marry so soon. (Remember, too, that Juliet did not praise Paris after the party. Lady Capulet may fear Juliet is not interested in him.)
Line 36. For the audience, Romeo and Juliet's happy night is tainted by the complication of her father's plans.
Stage direction. At least by l. 43 (or, some might argue, l. 55), Romeo must be on the ground below the balcony. Juliet claims she hears a nightingale because she wants to delay daybreak, when Romeo must leave.

Summary ■ ■ ■

Act III, Scene 5
Romeo and Juliet have spent the night together. It is now near dawn, and Romeo must leave. The lovers are reluctant to part, but the nurse enters and informs Juliet that her mother is coming to see her. As Romeo climbs from her window, the lovers exchange parting words; Romeo assures Juliet that they will be together again, but Juliet has forebodings. Lady Capulet enters. Thinking that Juliet's tears are for her cousin, Lady Capulet tells her daughter that the murder will be avenged. She then tells Juliet of her father's decision, but Juliet refuses to marry Paris. Lord Capulet enters and is furious when told of Juliet's refusal. He threatens to disown his daughter if she does not comply. Juliet pleads with her mother to postpone the marriage, but Lady Capulet refuses. The nurse advises Juliet to marry Paris and forget the inferior Romeo. Stunned by this last betrayal, Juliet decides never again to confide in her nurse. She resolves to visit Friar Laurence for help, pretending that the purpose of her visit is to seek absolution for her sin of disobedience.

Capulet.
Monday! Ha, ha! Well, Wednesday is too soon.
20   A' Thursday let it be—a' Thursday, tell her,
She shall be married to this noble earl.
Will you be ready? Do you like this haste?
We'll keep no great ado—a friend or two;
For hark you, Tybalt being slain so late,
25   It may be thought we held him carelessly,
Being our kinsman, if we revel much.
Therefore we'll have some half a dozen friends,
And there an end. But what say you to Thursday?
Paris.
My lord, I would that Thursday were tomorrow.
Capulet.
30   Well, get you gone. A' Thursday be it then.
Go you to Juliet ere you go to bed;
Prepare her, wife, against this wedding day.
Farewell, my lord.—Light to my chamber, ho!
Afore me,° it is so very late
35   That we may call it early by and by.
Good night.   [*Exeunt.*]

Scene 5. *Capulet's orchard.*

Enter ROMEO *and* JULIET *aloft.*

Juliet.
Wilt thou be gone? It is not yet near day.
It was the nightingale, and not the lark,
That pierced the fearful hollow of thine ear.
Nightly she sings on yond pomegranate tree.
5   Believe me, love, it was the nightingale.
Romeo.
It was the lark, the herald of the morn;
No nightingale. Look, love, what envious streaks
Do lace the severing clouds in yonder east.
Night's candles are burnt out, and jocund day
10   Stands tiptoe on the misty mountaintops.
I must be gone and live, or stay and die.

806 WILLIAM SHAKESPEARE

? **19.** *Capulet is sometimes played as a foolish old man. Why do you think he wants to get Juliet married as soon as possible? What do you think his mood is here?*

? **32.** *Capulet speaks this line to his wife. Lady Capulet sometimes expresses uneasiness about her husband's plans here. Why would she be uneasy?*
34. Afore me: indeed.
? **36.** *Just as we might feel the situation can be rescued, Shakespeare "raises the stakes" with this short scene. How does this increase our tension in the scene that follows, the wedding-night scene?*

? *Stage direction: This scene was probably played on the upper stage in Shakespeare's time. In movies and modern stage productions, it is often played with varying degrees of frankness in Juliet's bedroom. Perhaps the fact that in Shakespeare's day Juliet was played by a boy dictated the brevity of the scene and the place where it was played. Would any lines not make sense if the scene were played in the bedroom?*

Juliet's first words here alert us to the time: It must be near morning, when Romeo must go to Mantua. We hear the song of a lark, which sings at daybreak. The nightingale, on the other hand, sings at night. Why does Juliet insist she hears the nightingale?

Juliet.
    Yond light is not daylight; I know it, I.
    It is some meteor that the sun exhales°
    To be to thee this night a torchbearer
15   And light thee on thy way to Mantua.
    Therefore stay yet; thou need'st not to be gone.
Romeo.
    Let me be taken, let me be put to death.
    I am content, so thou wilt have it so.
    I'll say yon gray is not the morning's eye,
20   'Tis but the pale reflex° of Cynthia's brow;°
    Nor that is not the lark whose notes do beat
    The vaulty heaven so high above our heads.
    I have more care to stay than will to go.
    Come, death, and welcome! Juliet wills it so.
25   How is't, my soul? Let's talk; it is not day.
Juliet.
    It is, it is! Hie hence, be gone, away!
    It is the lark that sings so out of tune,
    Straining harsh discords and unpleasing sharps.
    Some say the lark makes sweet division;°
30   This doth not so, for she divideth us.
    Some say the lark and loathèd toad change eyes;°
    O, now I would they had changed voices too,
    Since arm from arm that voice doth us affray,°
    Hunting thee hence with hunt's-up° to the day.
35   O, now be gone! More light and light it grows.
Romeo.
    More light and light—more dark and dark our woes.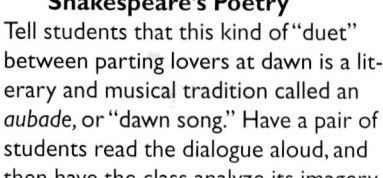

" *More light and light—more dark and dark our woes.* "

[*Enter* NURSE.]

Nurse. Madam!
Juliet. Nurse?
Nurse.
    Your lady mother is coming to your chamber.
40   The day is broke; be wary, look about.   [*Exit.*]
Juliet.
    Then, window, let day in, and let life out.

THE TRAGEDY OF ROMEO AND JULIET, ACT III, SCENE 5 **807**

---

13. exhales: gives off. (It was believed that the sun drew up vapors and ignited them as meteors.)

20. reflex: reflection. **Cynthia's brow:** Cynthia is the moon.

? 26. *What has Romeo said that makes Juliet suddenly practical and aware of danger?*

29. division: literally, a rapid run of notes, but Juliet is punning on the word's other meaning (separation).
31. A fable to explain why the lark, which sings so beautifully, has ugly eyes, and why the toad, which croaks so harshly, has beautiful ones.
33. affray: frighten.
34. hunt's-up: morning song for hunters.

? 41. *What is Juliet doing as she speaks these lines?*

B Reading Skills and Strategies

Reading Shakespeare's Poetry

Tell students that this kind of "duet" between parting lovers at dawn is a literary and musical tradition called an *aubade,* or "dawn song." Have a pair of students read the dialogue aloud, and then have the class analyze its imagery and emotional effect.

C Critical Thinking

Making Connections

? Does the imagery in this passage remind you of other images of light and darkness earlier in the play? [Possible responses: The image of a meteor briefly lighting up the night sky recalls the image of a brief flash of lightning Juliet used in the balcony scene (Act II, Scene 2, ll. 119–120). The image of a torchbearer recalls the beginning of Romeo's soliloquy in Act I, Scene 5, l. 46 ("O, she doth teach the torches to burn bright!"), as well as his volunteering to be a torchbearer for his friends at the party (Act I, Scene 4, ll. 11–12 and 35–39).]

D Elements of Literature

Falling Action

? How are references to light and darkness used ironically here to suggest the tragedy to come? [Possible responses: The image of the sun rising, usually a sign of hope, is contrasted with the reality that the light will separate the lovers. At this moment they have little hope, and the dark despair dominates their future.]

Answers to Margin Questions
Line 26. When Romeo says, "Let me be taken, let me be put to death" (l. 17), Juliet remembers what will happen to Romeo if he is found in Verona.
Line 41. Juliet is opening the window so that Romeo can climb down.

Crossing the Curriculum

Music
Ask students to write lyrics for another *aubade,* or dawn goodbye song of parting lovers, that either Romeo or Juliet might deliver. Students with musical abilities can set the lyrics to music.

« O, think'st thou we shall ever meet again? »

As previously noted, the photographs illustrating the play are taken from the 1968 movie version of *Romeo and Juliet,* directed by Franco Zeffirelli. The editors of *Cinebooks* comment on the making of the film:

"This beautiful version of the Veronese love story was by far the most successful [of all film versions] at the box office, although Zeffirelli took a huge chance casting two unknowns in the leads. Whiting was 17 and Hussey was 15, the closest any screen actors have actually come to the ages of the characters. It's a visually stunning adaptation with much action, broad humor, and eroticism. The Italian director had made *The Taming of the Shrew* the year before with Elizabeth Taylor and Richard Burton. Although that film was not a big hit, his backers felt that his assured direction merited another attempt at Shakespeare, and the project was filmed in Tuscany at Pienza, Gubbio, Artena, and in the palace once owned by the Borgias. In order to take the onus off the relatively inexperienced leads, Zeffirelli trimmed some of the longer speeches, used reaction shots to break matters up, and gave the actors bits of business to do so they wouldn't seem like talking heads. That technique was successful. . . . The sets are magnificent, the supporting actors excellent, and the costumes attractive enough to warrant an Oscar for [Danilo] Donati, beating out another period piece that year, *Oliver!*"

Activity. The caption for this photograph is l. 51. Ask students to evaluate the use of this line as a caption and to suggest alternatives. [Since Romeo has begun his descent from Juliet's room by l. 51, the couple would not be able to embrace when this line is spoken. Some alternatives are l. 23, l. 36, and l. 42.]

Romeo.
   Farewell, farewell! One kiss, and I'll descend.

[*He goes down.*]

Juliet.
   Art thou gone so, love-lord, ay husband-friend?
   I must hear from thee every day in the hour,
45   For in a minute there are many days.
   O, for this count I shall be much in years
   Ere I again behold my Romeo!

Romeo.
   Farewell!
   I will omit no opportunity
50   That may convey my greetings, love, to thee.

Juliet.
   O, think'st thou we shall ever meet again?

Romeo.
   I doubt it not; and all these woes shall serve
   For sweet discourses in our times to come.

Juliet.
   O God, I have an ill-divining soul!
55   Methinks I see thee, now thou art so low,
   As one dead in the bottom of a tomb.
   Either my eyesight fails, or thou look'st pale.

Romeo.
   And trust me, love, in my eye so do you.
   Dry° sorrow drinks our blood. Adieu, adieu!   [*Exit.*]

Juliet.
60   O Fortune, Fortune! All men call thee fickle.
   If thou art fickle, what dost thou with him
   That is renowned for faith? Be fickle, Fortune,
   For then I hope thou wilt not keep him long
   But send him back.

[*Enter Juliet's mother,* LADY CAPULET.]

Lady Capulet.
65   Ho, daughter! Are you up?

Juliet.
   Who is't that calls? It is my lady mother.
   Is she not down so late,° or up so early?
   What unaccustomed cause procures her hither?

Lady Capulet.
   Why, how now, Juliet?

Juliet.   Madam, I am not well.

Lady Capulet.
70   Evermore weeping for your cousin's death?
   What, wilt thou wash him from his grave with tears?
   And if thou couldst, thou couldst not make him live.

---

43. *Where is Romeo now, as Juliet asks him to communicate with her?*

51. *Remember what the Prologue has told you about what will happen to Romeo and Juliet. How do you feel when you hear Juliet speak this line?*

57. *Friar Laurence might have taken Juliet with Romeo, into exile in Mantua. But we must remember that Juliet is not quite fourteen, and at this point in the story, Friar Laurence thinks the situation can be happily resolved. As the lovers part now, where does Juliet foresee Romeo's doom?*

59. Dry: thirsty (sorrow was thought to drain color from the cheeks).

67. down so late: so late getting to bed.

THE TRAGEDY OF ROMEO AND JULIET, ACT III, SCENE 5 809

Ⓐ Struggling Readers
Paraphrasing
Have students reread this passage and try to express Juliet's feelings in their own words. [Possible response: Every minute away from you feels like days, so even if we're apart for just a few days, it will feel like years to me.]

Ⓑ Elements of Literature
Foreshadowing
Ironically, the next time Juliet will see Romeo is when she awakens in her tomb to find him dead beside her.

Ⓒ Elements of Literature
Personification
Point out that Juliet addresses Fortune as if it were a character.

Answers to Margin Questions
Line 43. Romeo is in the orchard beneath her window.
Line 51. Students may wonder whether the young husband and wife will have no more than one night together before they meet in sorrow at their deaths.
Line 57. Looking at Romeo on the ground below her in the gray light of dawn, Juliet has the eerie sensation that she is looking down on him "in the bottom of a tomb."

Skill Link

Using Future-Tense Verbs
Tell students that in this scene Romeo and Juliet express their hopes for the future, using future-tense verbs. Future-tense verbs are made up of the helping verb *shall* or *will,* plus the main verb, as in *shall meet.*

Activities
1. Have students identify the future-tense verbs used on this page. ["shall be" (l. 46), "will omit" (l. 49), "shall (ever) meet" (l. 51), "shall serve" (l. 52), "wilt (not) keep" (l. 63)]
2. Have students write predictions of what they think will happen in Act IV, using future-tense verbs.

Therefore have done. Some grief shows much of love;
But much of grief shows still some want of wit.

Juliet.
75   Yet let me weep for such a feeling loss.°

Lady Capulet.
So shall you feel the loss, but not the friend
Which you weep for.

Juliet.   Feeling so the loss,
I cannot choose but ever weep the friend.

Lady Capulet.
Well, girl, thou weep'st not so much for his death
80   As that the villain lives which slaughtered him.

Juliet.
What villain, madam?

Lady Capulet.   That same villain Romeo.

Juliet (*aside*).
Villain and he be many miles asunder—
God pardon him! I do, with all my heart;
And yet no man like he doth grieve my heart.

Lady Capulet.
85   That is because the traitor murderer lives.

Juliet.
Ay, madam, from the reach of these my hands.
Would none but I might venge my cousin's death!

Lady Capulet.
We will have vengeance for it, fear thou not.
Then weep no more. I'll send to one in Mantua,
90   Where that same banished runagate° doth live,
Shall give him such an unaccustomed dram°
That he shall soon keep Tybalt company;
And then I hope thou wilt be satisfied.

Juliet.
Indeed I never shall be satisfied
95   With Romeo till I behold him—dead—
Is my poor heart so for a kinsman vexed.
Madam, if you could find out but a man
To bear a poison, I would temper° it—
That Romeo should, upon receipt thereof,
100   Soon sleep in quiet. O, how my heart abhors
To hear him named and cannot come to him,
To wreak° the love I bore my cousin
Upon his body that hath slaughtered him!

Lady Capulet.
Find thou the means, and I'll find such a man.
105   But now I'll tell thee joyful tidings, girl.

810 WILLIAM SHAKESPEARE

? **74.** *Actresses playing Lady Capulet have interpreted her character in two ways. Some portray her as loving toward Juliet. Others find in her speeches a signal to play her as distant and strong-willed, to contrast with Juliet's helplessness. What do you think Lady Capulet's tone is here, and how would you play the part?*

75. feeling loss: loss so deeply felt.

? **78.** *All Juliet's lines in this scene have double meanings. Whom is she really grieving for?*

90. runagate: fugitive.

91. unaccustomed dram: unexpected drink (of poison).

? **93.** *This is a hard and fearful threat. How does Juliet reply, and with what hidden emotions does she speak her next words? How does she continue to speak with double meanings?*

? **95.** *How should lines 95–96 be said to indicate that Juliet intends* dead *to refer to* heart?

98. temper: mix (she really means "weaken").

102. wreak: avenge (she really means "express").

? **105.** *Has Juliet convinced her mother that she wants Romeo dead?*

"Would none but I might venge my cousin's death!"

RESPONDING TO THE ART

Activity. Ask students what Juliet and her mother are doing here. [Apparently, they are arguing or disagreeing.] Ask them who is in a position of power and how they know. [Lady Capulet is in control, because she is upright. Juliet appears to be on her knees, pleading.] Ask them how the director would place the actresses if they were equal in power. [They would be in the same position—both standing, for example, or both seated.]

Juliet.
And joy comes well in such a needy time.
What are they, I beseech your ladyship?

Lady Capulet.
Well, well, thou hast a careful° father, child;
One who, to put thee from thy heaviness,
110 Hath sorted out° a sudden day of joy
Ⓐ That thou expects not nor I looked not for.

Juliet.
Madam, in happy time!° What day is that?

Lady Capulet.
Marry, my child, early next Thursday morn
The gallant, young, and noble gentleman,
115 The County Paris, at Saint Peter's Church,
Shall happily make thee there a joyful bride.

Juliet.
Now by Saint Peter's Church, and Peter too,
He shall not make me there a joyful bride!
I wonder at this haste, that I must wed
120 Ere he that should be husband comes to woo.
I pray you tell my lord and father, madam,
Ⓑ I will not marry yet; and when I do, I swear
It shall be Romeo, whom you know I hate,
Rather than Paris. These are news indeed!

Lady Capulet.
125 Here comes your father. Tell him so yourself,
And see how he will take it at your hands.

[*Enter* CAPULET *and* NURSE.]

Capulet.
When the sun sets the earth doth drizzle dew,
But for the sunset of my brother's son
It rains downright.
130 How now? A conduit,° girl? What, still in tears?
Evermore showering? In one little body
Thou counterfeits a bark,° a sea, a wind:
For still thy eyes, which I may call the sea,
Do ebb and flow with tears; the bark thy body is,
135 Sailing in this salt flood; the winds, thy sighs,
Ⓒ Who, raging with thy tears and they with them,
Without a sudden calm will overset
Thy tempest-tossèd body. How now, wife?
Have you delivered to her our decree?

Lady Capulet.
140 Ay, sir; but she will none, she gives you thanks.
I would the fool were married to her grave!

812 **WILLIAM SHAKESPEARE**

Capulet.
>Soft! Take me with you,° take me with you, wife.
>How? Will she none? Doth she not give us thanks?
>Is she not proud? Doth she not count her blest,
>145   Unworthy as she is, that we have wrought°
>So worthy a gentleman to be her bride?

Juliet.
>Not proud you have, but thankful that you have.
>Proud can I never be of what I hate,
>But thankful even for hate that is meant love.

Capulet.
>150   How, how, how, how, chopped-logic?° What is this?
>"Proud"—and "I thank you"—and "I thank you not"—
>And yet "not proud"? Mistress minion° you,
>Thank me no thankings, nor proud me no prouds,
>But fettle° your fine joints 'gainst Thursday next
>155   To go with Paris to Saint Peter's Church,
>Or I will drag thee on a hurdle thither.
>Out, you greensickness carrion! Out, you baggage!
>You tallow-face!

Lady Capulet.   Fie, fie! What, are you mad?

Juliet.
>Good father, I beseech you on my knees,
>160   Hear me with patience but to speak a word.

Capulet.
>Hang thee, young baggage! Disobedient wretch!
>I tell thee what—get thee to church a' Thursday
>Or never after look me in the face.
>Speak not, reply not, do not answer me!
>165   My fingers itch. Wife, we scarce thought us blest
>That God had lent us but this only child;
>But now I see this one is one too much,
>And that we have a curse in having her.
>Out on her, hilding!

Nurse.   God in heaven bless her!
>170   You are to blame, my lord, to rate° her so.

Capulet.
>And why, my Lady Wisdom? Hold your tongue,
>Good Prudence. Smatter with your gossips,° go!

Nurse.
>I speak no treason.

Capulet.   O, God-i-god-en!°

Nurse.
>May not one speak?

Capulet.   Peace, you mumbling fool!
>175   Utter your gravity o'er a gossip's bowl,
>For here we need it not.

Lady Capulet.   You are too hot.

THE TRAGEDY OF ROMEO AND JULIET, ACT III, SCENE 5 813

---

142. Soft! Take me with you: Wait! Let me understand you.

145. wrought: arranged.

149. *How does Juliet show that she knows her father loves her, even though she hates what he has done for her?*

150. chopped-logic: hair-splitting.

152. minion: badly behaved girl.

154. fettle: make ready.

158. *What insulting names does Capulet call Juliet? What would Capulet's actions be, as he speaks these vicious words to his only daughter? Whom is Juliet's mother talking to, in her next line?*

160. *In the midst of this drama, we have a recognizable domestic scene, a family argument, which might have been played out in any century. What is Juliet doing as she talks to her father here? What does she do during her father's next speech?*

170. rate: berate, scold.

172. Smatter with your gossips: chatter with your gossipy friends.

173. God-i-god-en!: Get on with you! ("God give you good evening.")

D Critical Thinking

Expressing an Opinion

❓ Do you think Capulet is overreacting? Explain. [Possible responses: Yes, he is disowning Juliet for refusing to accept a husband she barely knows; no, he has tried hard to cheer up Juliet, and she will not obey him.]

E Reading Skills and Strategies

Making Predictions

❓ Do you think this accusation will have any effect on Capulet? Why or why not? [Possible responses: no, because he is so angry with Juliet that he is beyond rational thought; no, because it comes from a servant who is not supposed to accuse her master.]

Answers to Margin Questions

Line 149. Juliet thanks him for what is "meant love."

Line 158. Capulet calls Juliet "greensickness carrion" (anemia was called *greensickness*), "baggage" (a strumpet), and "tallow-face." He may be making threatening gestures or actually pushing her. Lady Capulet is rebuking her husband.

Line 160. Juliet is on her knees, begging him to listen. During Capulet's speech, she again tries to speak, but he silences her: "Speak not, reply not, do not answer me!" As he threatens her, she is probably weeping and cowering.

Making the Connections

Connecting to the Theme:
"The Destruction of Innocence"

In learning to deceive her parents, Juliet has lost her innocence. Juliet has double meanings in her conversation with her mother regarding her marriage to Paris in Act III, Scene 5. Have students make two columns on a sheet of paper—one labeled "What Juliet Says" and the other "What Juliet Means." Ask them to quote at least four statements Juliet makes to deceive her mother and then to explain Juliet's concealed meanings. Engage students in a discussion about how Juliet has changed from the innocent, obedient daughter she was in her opening scene in Act I.

A Reading Skills and Strategies
Making Predictions

? Do you think Capulet's threats will sway Juliet's thinking? Explain. [Possible responses: Yes, she will give in to her father's wishes because she needs a place to live; no, she will not dishonor her marriage vows to Romeo.]

B Elements of Literature
Falling Action

? What reasons does Juliet have for feeling completely desperate and abandoned at this point in the play? [Possible responses: Her lover has been exiled, her father has threatened to disown her if she doesn't marry Paris, her mother has ignored her threats of suicide, and even her nurse, who helped arrange her marriage to Romeo, now seems to betray her by urging her to marry Paris.]

Answers to Margin Questions
Line 188. Lord Capulet thinks Juliet's reasons are that she doesn't love Paris and that she is too young to marry.
Line 197. Capulet will disown Juliet, force her from his house, and never again acknowledge her existence. Juliet then asks her mother to delay the marriage "for a month, a week" and threatens that otherwise, she will kill herself.
Line 210. The vows can be broken only by death.

Juliet grows up

Capulet.
God's bread!° It makes me mad.
Day, night; hour, tide, time; work, play;
Alone, in company; still my care hath been
180 To have her matched; and having now provided
A gentleman of noble parentage,
Of fair demesnes, youthful, and nobly trained,
Stuffed, as they say, with honorable parts,
Proportioned as one's thought would wish a man—
185 And then to have a wretched puling° fool,
A whining mammet,° in her fortune's tender,°
To answer "I'll not wed, I cannot love;
I am too young, I pray you pardon me"!
But, and you will not wed, I'll pardon you!°
190 Graze where you will, you shall not house with me.
Look to't, think on't; I do not use to jest.
Thursday is near; lay hand on heart, advise.°
A And you be mine, I'll give you to my friend;
And you be not, hang, beg, starve, die in the streets,
195 For, by my soul, I'll ne'er acknowledge thee,
Nor what is mine shall never do thee good.
Trust to't. Bethink you. I'll not be forsworn.°   [*Exit.*]
Juliet.
Is there no pity sitting in the clouds
That sees into the bottom of my grief?
200 O sweet my mother, cast me not away!
Delay this marriage for a month, a week;
Or if you do not, make the bridal bed
In that dim monument where Tybalt lies.
Lady Capulet.
Talk not to me, for I'll not speak a word.
205 Do as thou wilt, for I have done with thee.   [*Exit.*]
Juliet.
O God!—O nurse, how shall this be prevented?
My husband is on earth, my faith in heaven.°
How shall that faith return again to earth
Unless that husband send it me from heaven
210 By leaving earth? Comfort me, counsel me.
Alack, alack, that heaven should practice stratagems
Upon so soft a subject as myself!
What say'st thou? Hast thou not a word of joy?
Some comfort, nurse.
Nurse.   Faith, here it is.
215 **B** Romeo is banished; and all the world to nothing°
That he dares ne'er come back to challenge you;
Or if he do, it needs must be by stealth.
Then, since the case so stands as now it doth,
I think it best you married with the county.

814 WILLIAM SHAKESPEARE

177. God's bread!: oath on the sacrament of Communion.

185. puling: whining.
186. mammet: puppet. **in her fortune's tender:** with all her good fortunes.
? **188.** *What does Lord Capulet think are Juliet's reasons for not wanting to marry Paris?*
189. I'll pardon you!: I'll give you permission to go!
192. advise: consider.

197. forsworn: guilty of breaking my vow.
? **197.** *There is usually a moment of stunned silence onstage after Capulet leaves. What exactly will Lord Capulet do if Juliet refuses to marry Paris? In the next speech, how does Juliet appeal to her mother for help?*

207. my faith in heaven: my wedding vow is recorded in heaven.

? **210.** *Romeo and Juliet constantly remind us that they have taken their marriage vows seriously. According to Juliet here, how can these vows be broken?*

215. all the world to nothing: it is a safe bet.

Making the Connections

Cultural Connections

Students might find the lifestyles, choices, and limitations of Verona's youth to be quite different from the circumstances of modern teenagers. Ask students to identify similarities, as well as differences, between Verona's youth and modern youth by completing a Venn diagram, such as the following:

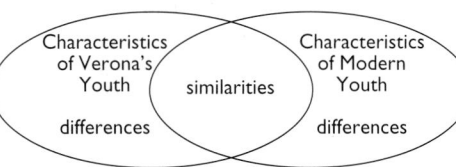

Characteristics of Verona's Youth   similarities   Characteristics of Modern Youth

differences   differences

220   O, he's a lovely gentleman!
       Romeo's a dishclout° to him. An eagle, madam,
       Hath not so green, so quick, so fair an eye
       As Paris hath. Beshrew° my very heart,
       I think you are happy in this second match,
225   For it excels your first; or if it did not,
       Your first is dead—or 'twere as good he were
       As living here and you no use of him.
       Juliet.
       Speak'st thou from thy heart?
       Nurse.
       And from my soul too; else beshrew them both.
230   **Juliet.** Amen!
       Nurse. What?
       Juliet.
       Well, thou hast comforted me marvelous much.
       Go in; and tell my lady I am gone,
       Having displeased my father, to Laurence' cell,
235   To make confession and to be absolved.
       Nurse.
       Marry, I will; and this is wisely done.   [*Exit.*]
       Juliet.
       Ancient damnation!° O most wicked fiend!
       Is it more sin to wish me thus forsworn,
       Or to dispraise my lord with that same tongue
240   Which she hath praised him with above compare
       So many thousand times? Go, counselor!
       Thou and my bosom henceforth shall be twain.°
       I'll to the friar to know his remedy.
       If all else fail, myself have power to die.   [*Exit.*]

221. **dishclout:** literally dishcloth; limp and weak.

223. **Beshrew:** curse.

? 227. *What is the nurse's "comfort" and advice for Juliet? Which line in this speech suggests that Juliet has reacted with shock and that the nurse must pause? Did you expect such advice from the nurse?*

? 235. *In most productions, the nurse embraces Juliet to comfort her. Now Juliet has made a decision. What do you see Juliet doing as she speaks?*
237. **Ancient damnation!:** Damned old woman!

242. **twain:** separate.

? 244. *What has Juliet decided about the nurse? We may wonder why Juliet doesn't just tell her parents why she cannot marry Paris. Why do you think she does not take this easy way out? Is she protecting Romeo, or does she feel abandoned by her parents?*

C Reading Skills and Strategies
Drawing Conclusions

? Do you think Juliet is telling the truth about her reason for going to Friar Laurence? Explain. [Possible responses: No, Juliet has a plan and is pretending to be obedient in order to leave the house; yes, Juliet now feels she has no choice but to beg for forgiveness and go along with her parents' plan.]

D Reading Skills and Strategies

Reading Shakespeare's Poetry

Have students note the end-stopped lines and run-on lines in Juliet's speech, and ask a volunteer to read it aloud.

Answers to Margin Questions
Line 227. The nurse's advice is to commit bigamy. Her comfort is that Romeo probably doesn't dare return to Verona and that Paris is a better man anyway. The dash in l. 226 suggests that Juliet has reacted with shock.

Responses to the nurse's advice will vary. Many students will be shocked that a character they liked can suddenly act with such lack of sensitivity. Remind them that the nurse is, above all, a realist.
Line 235. Juliet will no longer confide in her nurse or trust her. Juliet's manner could suggest her new self-sufficiency, resolution, and distance from the nurse. Juliet could also choose to be affectionate with the nurse, in order to better deceive her.
Line 244. Juliet thinks the nurse is sinful to counsel bigamy and capriciously change her mind about Romeo; she will no longer confide in the nurse or seek her help.

Students will probably feel that both suggested reasons apply.

THE TRAGEDY OF ROMEO AND JULIET, ACT III, SCENE 5 **815**

Assessing Learning

Check Test: Questions and Answers
Answers may vary slightly.
1. Why is Tybalt angry in Scene 1? [He is still angry at Romeo for attending the Capulet party uninvited.]
2. What is Romeo's punishment for killing Tybalt? [He is exiled.]
3. What is Juliet's reaction to the news of Tybalt's death? [She has mixed emotions: She is angry with Romeo but also loves him; she grieves for her cousin.]

4. What is Lord Capulet's reaction to Juliet's insistence that she is not ready to marry Paris? [Lord Capulet tells her that she will either marry Paris or be disowned by her family.]
5. What advice does the nurse finally offer Juliet? [She advises her to forget about Romeo, who is banished, and to go ahead and marry Paris.]

Standardized Test Preparation
For practice in proofreading and editing, see
• *Daily Oral Grammar,* Transparency 45

MAKING MEANINGS (ACT III)

First Thoughts

1. Possible responses: the adults, for feuding and being insensitive; the lovers' own haste; Friar Laurence, Tybalt, or Mercutio, for interfering.

Shaping Interpretations

2. Sample response: If Mercutio had killed Tybalt, Romeo would not have been banished or hated by the Capulets, two factors inflaming the young couple's sense of desperation. Mercutio may not have been able to persuade Romeo, but he might have asked the prince to help reconcile Romeo to his in-laws. The old feud might not have erupted again once the two families learned that their children had married.

3. Romeo is banished for killing Tybalt. Since Tybalt is a Capulet, Romeo and Juliet cannot possibly reveal their marriage now. In response to Tybalt's death, Capulet orders Juliet to immediately marry Paris.

4. Responses include:
Juliet: Scene 2, ll. 45–49, 59–60, 123–124, 135–137; Scene 5, ll. 202–203, 243–244.
Romeo: Scene 3, ll. 12–14, 17–23, 44–46, 69–70, 107–108.

5. The nurse alienates Juliet by advising her to forget Romeo and marry Paris. This adds to the tragedy that follows because Juliet no longer has support within her own home.

6. Sample response: Both Romeo and Juliet, who love each other despite hardships, are loyal and devoted. Romeo learns that people can bring about tragedy, even when they don't mean to. He has not learned to control his rashness, but he overcomes his self-pity for Juliet's sake. Juliet learns that well-meaning adults can cause pain, but she shows courage and determination in going to see Friar Laurence alone.

7. Possible questions: Will Juliet have to marry Paris? Will Friar Laurence tell the families the truth about the marriage? Will Romeo and Juliet see each other alive again?

Extending the Text

8. Responses will vary. Students should see the universality of loving but unreasonable parents and respectful but willful adolescents. Most students will note that parents rarely choose a child's spouse now in the United States.

MAKING MEANINGS   ACT III

First Thoughts

[infer]   1. If you were to assign blame to anyone at this point in the action, who would it be, and why?

Shaping Interpretations

[infer]   2. Suppose Mercutio had killed Tybalt in the sword fight. How might the action of the play have changed? If he had lived, could Mercutio have persuaded Romeo to act differently? Do you think the old feud would still have erupted again? Explain.

[analyze] 3. Romeo's killing of Tybalt is the **turning point** of the play—the point when something happens that will turn the action toward either a happy ending or a tragic one. What actions does the killing set in motion, with possible tragic consequences?

[identify] 4. We already know that the play ends in the deaths of Romeo and Juliet. Their willingness to die comes as no surprise to us, because we have been forewarned. Point out the instances in this act where each young person mentions this willingness to die if they are separated.

[infer]   5. How does the nurse offend Juliet in this act and cease to be her friend? How does this development add to the tragedy of the events that follow?

[analyze] 6. What have the events of this act revealed to you about the **characters** of Romeo and Juliet? Describe how the young lovers are changing. What hard lessons are they learning about life?

[respond] 7. By the end of Act III, we have reached the highest point of suspense. **Suspense** causes us to ask questions, to wonder anxiously "What will happen next?" Write down the questions you are asking at the end of Act III.

Extending the Text

[connect] 8. Does the last scene in this act remind you of encounters between parents and their teenage children that you've seen in movies, TV shows, or novels? Do Juliet and her parents remind you of real-life parents and teenagers today? Explain. Check your Quickwrite notes before you answer.

[extend]   9. Find some lines from this act that could be spoken today—by children, parents, or counselors.

Reading Check

a. What causes the fatal sword fight between Mercutio and Tybalt? How is Mercutio killed?

b. Why does Romeo kill Tybalt?

c. Now the young lovers are in serious trouble. What does Juliet threaten in Scene 2, after hearing of Romeo's banishment?

d. What is the friar's plan to help them in Scene 3?

e. By the end of Scene 4, a new **complication** has come up. What plans do Juliet's parents reveal that they have made for her?

---

9. Possible answers:
Children: "Good father, I beseech you on my knees,/Hear me with patience but to speak a word." (Scene 5, ll. 159–160)
Parents: "Talk not to me, for I'll not speak a word./Do as thou wilt, for I have done with thee." (Scene 5, ll. 204–205)
Counselors: Scene 3, ll. 141–145 (Friar Laurence telling Romeo to look at what's right, not at what's wrong.)

Reading Check

a. Tybalt insults Romeo, and Mercutio challenges Tybalt since Romeo does not. Romeo steps between the two fighting men, blocking Mercutio's line of vision, and Tybalt stabs Mercutio.

b. Romeo kills Tybalt to avenge Mercutio's death and to save his own honor.

c. Juliet threatens to kill herself.

d. The friar hopes to reveal the marriage, reconcile the two families, ask the prince's pardon, and call Romeo home.

e. Juliet is to marry Paris in three days.

CHOICES: Building Your Portfolio

Writer's Notebook

1. Collecting Ideas for a Research Paper

Finding a topic.
Act III is a good place to find a topic for the research paper you'll be writing for the Writer's Workshop on page 868. This act paints a vivid picture of people who have passions just like ours but who live in a society very different from our own. Skim through the act, making notes on one of the following aspects of Renaissance life:

- levels of power, authority, and responsibility assigned to different people: lords, ladies, teenagers, nurses, friars, pages, servants
- ideas of justice, as shown by the prince's instant banishment of Romeo
- relationships between parents and children

Creative Writing

2. Write a Prologue

Did you notice that there is no Prologue for Act III? Yet in this act we have some of the strongest action of the play. Try writing your summary of this act in the form of a sonnet prologue.

Speaking

3. Freeze! Speak!

Work in five groups to create "living pictures" of the key action in each scene of Act III. Each actor should choose one character and search the scene for one of that character's most significant lines. Then the actors should arrange themselves in an appropriate opening tableau and freeze. One at a time each character can come to life, say the line, change position, and then freeze again. Each group should prepare a short opening and closing statement for the presentation.

VOCABULARY

HOW TO OWN A WORD

Word Origins: What's in a Name?

In Act II, Scene 2, Juliet, upset to discover that this handsome young man she has just met is named Montague, delivers these famous lines about the insignificance of names: "What's in a name? That which we call a rose / By any other word would smell as sweet." Names, however, *are* significant in Shakespeare's plays. They are often used to suggest something about a person's character or temperament. Use a dictionary and the side notes to help you research the origins of three important names in *Romeo and Juliet*. Answer the following questions:

1. What chemical element is Mercutio named for?
2. What characteristics of this element match Mercutio's character?
3. What does it mean to say that someone is *mercurial* in temperament?
4. Benvolio's name comes from the same Latin words as the adjective *benevolent*. What do these Latin words mean?
5. How does Benvolio's name match his temperament?
6. How is Tybalt like the cat he is named for?
7. If you were renaming these characters for an updated version of the tragedy, what names would you give them?

Grading Timesaver

Rubrics for each Choices assignment appear on p. 203 in the *Portfolio Management System*.

CHOICES: Building Your Portfolio

1. **Writer's Notebook** Remind students to save their notes for the Writer's Workshop on p. 868.
2. **Creative Writing** Have students study the Prologue for Act I (p. 735) and the opening Chorus of Act II (p. 764) as models. Remind them that a Shakespearean sonnet is written in iambic pentameter and has a rhyme scheme of *abab cdcd efef gg*.
3. **Speaking** Before assigning scenes for tableaus, read the summaries of each scene from your teacher's edition aloud, and list the characters who appear in each.

VOCABULARY

Answers

1. He is named for mercury.
2. He is quick, volatile, and changeable.
3. It means that he or she is quick, changeable, and volatile. It can also mean that the person has the qualities of the god Mercury, who is eloquent, clever, shrewd, and thievish.
4. *Bene* means "well," and *volens* means "wishing"; *benevolent* means "kindly" or "well intentioned." Benvolio is both.
5. Benvolio is a friendly type who is not interested in fighting.
6. He is quick to pounce on his victim.
7. Possible responses: Mercutio— Silver (for quicksilver); Benvolio— Ben (shortened form); Tybalt—Tom (for tomcat) or Tiger (a king of cats).

ACT IV

Scene 1. *Friar Laurence's cell.*

Enter FRIAR LAURENCE *and* COUNT PARIS.

Friar.
  On Thursday, sir? The time is very short.
Paris.
  My father Capulet will have it so,
  And I am nothing slow to slack his haste.
Friar.
  You say you do not know the lady's mind.
5 Uneven° is the course; I like it not.
Paris.
  Immoderately she weeps for Tybalt's death,
  And therefore have I little talked of love;
  For Venus smiles not in a house of tears.
  Now, sir, her father counts it dangerous
10 That she do give her sorrow so much sway,
  And in his wisdom hastes our marriage
  To stop the inundation of her tears,
  Which, too much minded° by herself alone,
  May be put from her by society.
15 Now do you know the reason of this haste.
Friar (*aside*).
  I would I knew not why it should be slowed,—
  Look, sir, here comes the lady toward my cell.

  [*Enter* JULIET.]

Paris.
  Happily met, my lady and my wife!
Juliet.
  That may be, sir, when I may be a wife.
Paris.
20 That "may be" must be, love, on Thursday next.
Juliet.
  What must be shall be.
Friar.   That's a certain text.
Paris.
  Come you to make confession to this father?
Juliet.
  To answer that, I should confess to you.
Paris.
  Do not deny to him that you love me.

5. **Uneven:** irregular or unusual.

13. **minded:** thought about.

 15. *According to Paris, why is Capulet pushing his daughter to marry so quickly?*

818 WILLIAM SHAKESPEARE

Resources: Print and Media

Reading
- *Graphic Organizers for Active Reading,* p. 67
- *Words to Own Worksheets,* p. 45

Assessment
- *Formal Assessment,* p. 143
- *Portfolio Management System,* p. 204

- *Standardized Test Preparation,* p. 86
- *Test Generator (One-Stop Planner CD-ROM)*

Internet
- go.hrw.com (keyword: LE0 9-13)

Juliet.
25   I will confess to you that I love him.
Paris.
    So will ye, I am sure, that you love me.
Juliet.
    If I do so, it will be of more price,
    Being spoke behind your back, than to your face.
Paris.
    Poor soul, thy face is much abused with tears. **B**
Juliet.
30   The tears have got small victory by that,
    For it was bad enough before their spite.°
Paris.
    Thou wrong'st it more than tears with that report.
Juliet.
    That is no slander, sir, which is a truth;
    And what I spake, I spake it to my face.
Paris.
35   Thy face is mine, and thou hast slandered it.
Juliet.
    It may be so, for it is not mine own.
    Are you at leisure, holy father, now,
    Or shall I come to you at evening mass?
Friar.
    My leisure serves me, pensive daughter, now.
40   My lord, we must entreat the time alone.
Paris.
    God shield° I should disturb devotion!
    Juliet, on Thursday early will I rouse ye.
    Till then, adieu, and keep this holy kiss.   [*Exit.*]
Juliet.
    O, shut the door, and when thou hast done so,
45   Come weep with me—past hope, past care, past help!
Friar.
    O Juliet, I already know thy grief;
    It strains me past the compass of my wits.
    I hear thou must, and nothing may prorogue° it,
    On Thursday next be married to this county. **C**
Juliet.
50   Tell me not, friar, that thou hearest of this,
    Unless thou tell me how I may prevent it.
    If in thy wisdom thou canst give no help,
    Do thou but call my resolution wise
    And with this knife I'll help it presently.
55   God joined my heart and Romeo's, thou our hands;
    And ere this hand, by thee to Romeo's sealed,
    Shall be the label° to another deed,°
    Or my true heart with treacherous revolt

? **26.** *In this scene, Juliet's action is to keep up appearances and ward off Paris, who presses his attentions on her. She does this by wittily playing with words. We are fascinated by two things here: by what is being done, and by how it is being done. What double meanings does Juliet intend in the exchange with Paris that follows?*
31. spite: injury or damage (to her face).

? **38.** *Juliet must show here that the tension of keeping up this pretense is unbearable. Where do you think she pauses and changes her tone?*

41. God shield: God forbid.

? **45.** *Paris has gone, and Juliet has endured his "holy kiss." Whom is she talking to now?*

48. prorogue: postpone.

? **54.** *What is Juliet holding in her hand? What is she threatening to do?*

57. label: seal. **deed:** contract (of marriage).

THE TRAGEDY OF ROMEO AND JULIET, ACT IV, SCENE I **819**

Reaching All Students

Struggling Readers
Paraphrasing and Context Clues is introduced in the Reading Skills and Strategies on p. 835. To prepare students for paraphrasing, review the Vocabulary Mini-Lesson at the end of Act I and the Grammar Link activity on archaic grammar and vocabulary at the end of Act II. Also, use the Taking a Second Look lesson on Identifying the Main Idea on p. T821.

Advanced Learners
After students read Act IV through once, have them choose one character who could, at some point, have changed what has happened. They should rewrite the scene from that character's point of view and explain how things would have turned out differently in their version.

A Reading Skills and Strategies
Paraphrasing and Context Clues
Have students work in small groups to paraphrase Paris's speech on p. 818. Then, have them answer the margin question for l. 15. Before students write their paraphrase, encourage them to check the meanings of words such as *immoderately, sway,* and *inundation* by looking them up in the dictionary. Discuss the meaning of the figurative language in l. 8 and the archaic language in ll. 13–14. (You might want to present the Reading Skills and Strategies feature on p. 835 before teaching Act IV.)

B Critical Thinking
Analyzing Character
? What does this statement reveal about Paris's character? [Possible responses: He is concerned about Juliet; he is observant of her grief.]

C Elements of Literature
Falling Action
Juliet's sense of desperation about the planned wedding is causing her to consider any plan, no matter how risky, to avoid marriage to Paris. Her desperation locks her into actions that take her deeper and deeper into disaster.

Answers to Margin Questions
Line 15. Lord Capulet thinks that marriage will help Juliet get over her grief for Tybalt.
Line 26. Juliet says that if she "confesses" her love to the friar, rather than to Paris, it will be more valuable ("of more price") because she would have no reason to speak anything but the truth. When Paris laments that tears have "abused" Juliet's face, she says that they could not much damage an already homely face. Paris then accuses her of slandering her face, but she says the truth can't be slander, particularly when spoken openly "to" (that is, "about") her face. To Paris's claim "Thy face is mine," Juliet agrees "it is not mine own," by which she may mean both that it is Romeo's and that she is dissembling.
Line 38. Juliet probably changes her tone when she changes the topic of conversation at l. 37.
Line 45. Juliet is speaking to the friar.
Line 54. Juliet is holding a knife, threatening to kill herself if Friar Laurence has no way to help her escape from marriage to Paris, a marriage that would be immoral, illegal, and disloyal.

" And I will do it without fear or doubt,
To live an unstained wife to my sweet love. "

RESPONDING TO THE ART

Activity. After students have read Scene 1, ask them which lines of Juliet's they would choose as an alternate caption and why. [Many students will choose l. 121, "Give me, give me! O, tell me not of fear!" It occurs after Friar Laurence has described the effects of his potion, and she appears to be reaching for one of his herbal concoctions.]

Using Students' Strengths

Interpersonal Learners
These students will find paraphrasing easier if they are allowed to role-play scenes of extended dialogue—such as the one between Juliet and Friar Laurence in Scene 1. Assign parts to pairs of students and have them read their dialogue aloud to each other, "translating" it into contemporary English as they go along. Encourage them to act out their "translated" scenes for the class.

Turn to another, this shall slay them both.
60 Therefore, out of thy long-experienced time,
Give me some present counsel; or, behold,
'Twixt my extremes and me this bloody knife
Shall play the umpire, arbitrating that
Which the commission° of thy years and art
65 Could to no issue of true honor bring.
Be not so long to speak. I long to die
If what thou speak'st speak not of remedy.

Friar.
Hold, daughter. I do spy a kind of hope,
Which craves as desperate an execution
70 As that is desperate which we would prevent.
If, rather than to marry County Paris,
Thou hast the strength of will to slay thyself,
Then is it likely thou wilt undertake
A thing like death to chide away this shame,
75 That cop'st° with death himself to scape from it;
And, if thou darest, I'll give thee remedy.

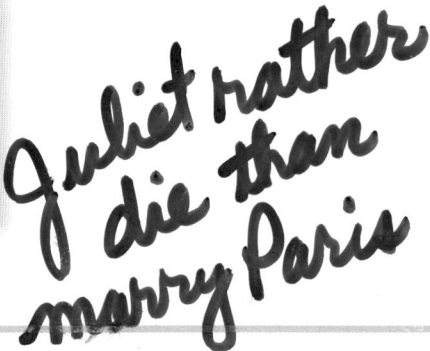

Juliet.
O, bid me leap, rather than marry Paris,
From off the battlements of any tower,
Or walk in thievish ways, or bid me lurk
80 Where serpents are; chain me with roaring bears,
Or hide me nightly in a charnel house,°
O'ercovered quite with dead men's rattling bones,
With reeky° shanks and yellow chapless° skulls;
Or bid me go into a new-made grave
85 And hide me with a dead man in his shroud—
Things that, to hear them told, have made me
    tremble—
And I will do it without fear or doubt,
To live an unstained wife to my sweet love.

Friar.
Hold, then. Go home, be merry, give consent
90 To marry Paris. Wednesday is tomorrow.
Tomorrow night look that thou lie alone;
Let not the nurse lie with thee in thy chamber.
Take thou this vial, being then in bed,
And this distilling° liquor drink thou off;
95 When presently through all thy veins shall run
A cold and drowsy humor;° for no pulse
Shall keep his native° progress, but surcease;°
No warmth, no breath, shall testify thou livest;
The roses in thy lips and cheeks shall fade
100 To wanny° ashes, thy eyes' windows fall
Like death when he shuts up the day of life;
Each part, deprived of supple government,°

THE TRAGEDY OF ROMEO AND JULIET, ACT IV, SCENE I 821

A Reading Skills and Strategies
Paraphrasing and Context Clues
Have students express Friar Laurence's speech in their own words. [Possible response: Wait a minute! I have an idea! It's a desperate plan, but then we are pretty desperate people. If you'd really rather kill yourself than marry Paris, maybe you'd be willing to pretend to be dead. If you're brave enough, I'll tell you my plan.]

B Elements of Literature
Falling Action
? Do you think Friar Laurence's plan is likely to work, or is it locking the characters deeper into disaster? [Possible responses: Yes, it will work because after Friar Laurence and Romeo awaken Juliet, the two lovers can leave for Mantua; no, they are locking themselves into disaster because there are too many uncontrollable factors, such as Romeo's receiving the friar's message in time and Juliet's responding to the drug exactly as Friar Laurence expects.]

Answers to Margin Questions
Line 62. "Be not so long to speak" (l. 66) indicates that Juliet has paused.
Line 77. Juliet is agitated, desperate, and courageous. Rather than marry Paris, she would leap from a tower, become a thief, live with serpents, be chained among bears, live nightly in a charnel house, or be buried alive with a corpse.
Line 89. Juliet is to drink the potion Wednesday night.

? **62.** *The friar has to put up with a good deal of brandishing of knives and daggers from Romeo and Juliet. Now that the nurse is no longer Juliet's friend, the friar has to be the confidant of both Juliet and Romeo. He must listen with patience to their threats of suicide if they cannot be together. What line in Juliet's speech indicates that she has paused and that the friar, for a time, is silent?*
64. commission: authority.

75. cop'st: negotiates.

? **77.** *What would Juliet's mood be as she delivers this speech? What will she do, rather than marry Paris?*

81. charnel house: house where bones from old graves are kept.

83. reeky: damp, stinking. **chapless:** jawless.

? **89.** *Juliet must pay strict attention to the friar's plan, as must the audience. On what day does the friar tell Juliet to take the potion?*

94. distilling: penetrating.

96. humor: fluid.
97. native: natural. **surcease:** stop.

100. wanny: pale.

102. government: control.

Juliet rather die than marry Paris

Taking a Second Look

Review: Identifying the Main Idea
Remind students that the main idea is the most important point a speaker or writer is trying to make. To write a paraphrase of a character's speech, students must first understand the main idea, or gist, of the speech. When a character is making a persuasive speech, as Friar Laurence does in ll. 68–76 of this scene, the main idea is sometimes expressed in the first or last line of the speech. In other speeches, the main idea is

not expressed directly but must be inferred by the speaker or listener of the text.
Activities
1. Have students read ll. 68–76 and identify the main idea that Friar Laurence wants to convey to Juliet. [He has a plan for preventing her marriage to Paris.] Then, ask which lines the main idea is conveyed in. [It is conveyed in l. 68 ("I do spy a kind of hope"), as well as in

l. 76 ("And, if thou darest, I'll give thee remedy").]
2. Have students read the description of Friar Laurence's plan in ll. 89–120 and then explain the main idea, or gist, of his plan. [To prevent her marriage to Paris, Juliet ca... potion that will convince her... dead. Later, she will awaken i... and Romeo will rescue her.]

T822

Answers to Margin Questions

Line 106. At the beginning of Act II, Scene 3, the friar was gathering herbs and discussing their powers—both beneficial and dangerous.

When Juliet takes the drug, she will go into a coma and appear to be dead. She will have no pulse or color and will be stiff, but she will awaken in forty-two hours.

Line 117. Friar Laurence will send a letter to Romeo so that he can join Friar Laurence in waiting at Juliet's side for her awakening. That same night the couple will depart for Mantua.

Line 122. The friar gives her a vial of the sleeping drug, which she is to take Wednesday night. She will be discovered "dead" the next morning, her wedding day, and will be placed uncovered (that is, not enclosed in a coffin) in the Capulets' large burial vault. In the meantime, a friar will take an explanatory letter to Romeo, who will return to Verona, wait for Juliet to awaken, and then take her back to Mantua.

Line 126. The blessing suggests she needs divine protection and highlights the plan's danger.

Summary ■

Act IV, Scene 2

Lord Capulet is making preparations for the marriage when Juliet enters. She appears contrite and tells him that Friar Laurence has told her to apologize to her father. She does so, saying that she will now obey his wishes and marry Paris. Lord Capulet is relieved and decides to move the wedding up to Wednesday, the very next morning.

Answer to Margin Question

Line 1. The happy domestic scene, full of exciting preparations for a celebration, promises new life. The preceding scene, desperate and secretive, was filled with talk of death, conflict, and trouble.

Shall, stiff and stark and cold, appear like death;
And in this borrowed likeness of shrunk death
105 Thou shalt continue two-and-forty hours,
And then awake as from a pleasant sleep.
Now, when the bridegroom in the morning comes
To rouse thee from thy bed, there art thou dead.
Then, as the manner of our country is,
110 In thy best robes uncovered on the bier
Thou shalt be borne to that same ancient vault
Where all the kindred of the Capulets lie.
In the meantime, against° thou shalt awake,
Shall Romeo by my letters know our drift;°
115 And hither shall he come; and he and I
Will watch thy waking, and that very night
Shall Romeo bear thee hence to Mantua.
And this shall free thee from this present shame,
If no inconstant toy° nor womanish fear
120 Abate thy valor in the acting it.

Juliet.
Give me, give me! O, tell not me of fear!

Friar.
Hold! Get you gone, be strong and prosperous
In this resolve. I'll send a friar with speed
To Mantua, with my letters to thy lord.

Juliet.
125 Love give me strength, and strength shall help afford.
Farewell, dear father.   [*Exit with* FRIAR.]

Scene 2. *A hall in Capulet's house.*

Enter father CAPULET, LADY CAPULET, NURSE, *and* SERVING-MEN, *two or three.*

Capulet.
So many guests invite as here are writ.
                              [*Exit a* SERVINGMAN.]
Sirrah, go hire me twenty cunning° cooks.

Servingman. You shall have none ill, sir; for I'll try if they can lick their fingers.

Capulet.
5   How canst thou try them so?

Servingman. Marry, sir, 'tis an ill cook that cannot lick his own fingers. Therefore he that cannot lick his fingers goes not with me.

822 WILLIAM SHAKESPEARE

? **106.** *This may be the most implausible part of the play, but we have been prepared for it. Where have we seen the friar taking care of his herbs and heard him talk of magical potions before? What will happen to Juliet when she takes the drug?*

113. against: before.
114. drift: intentions.

? **117.** *How is Romeo to be told of this plan, and when is he to watch Juliet wake and take her to Mantua?*
119. toy: whim.

? **122.** *What does the friar give Juliet as she exits? What exactly is his plan?*

? **126.** *In some productions, the friar holds Juliet back for just a moment and silently blesses her. Why would this make us more anxious about the outcome of his plan?*

? **1.** *Capulet is sending his servant off to invite guests to Juliet's wedding. How would this comic and busy domestic scene contrast with the previous one?*
2. cunning: skillful.

Skill Link

Synonyms

An important step in writing a paraphrase is to replace difficult words with simple ones. To do so, students must define unfamiliar words and find appropriate synonyms for them. The synonyms should convey the same shade of meaning and the same connotations, or emotional associations, as the original word. To find synonyms, students can look words up in the dictionary; synonyms are often listed at the end of dictionary entries. A college dictionary may even explain the different shades of meaning conveyed by each synonym. Students can also find lists of synonyms by looking up words in a thesaurus.

Activity

Have students use a college dictionary and a thesaurus to find appropriate synonyms for the following words, as they are used on p. 822: "stark" (l. 103), "rouse" (l. 108), "borne" (l. 111), "kindred" (l. 112), "vault" (l. 112), "drift" (l. 114), "hither" (l. 115), "inconstant" (l. 119), "abate" (l. 120), "valor" (l. 120), "resolve" (l. 123).

Capulet. Go, be gone.   [*Exit* SERVINGMAN.]

10   We shall be much unfurnished° for this time.
            What, is my daughter gone to Friar Laurence?
Nurse. Ay, forsooth.
Capulet.
            Well, he may chance to do some good on her.
            A peevish self-willed harlotry it is.

          [*Enter* JULIET.]

Nurse.
15   See where she comes from shrift with merry look.
Capulet.
            How now, my headstrong? Where have you been
                  gadding?
Juliet.
            Where I have learnt me to repent the sin
            Of disobedient opposition
            To you and your behests, and am enjoined
20   By holy Laurence to fall prostrate here
            To beg your pardon. Pardon, I beseech you!
            Henceforward I am ever ruled by you.
Capulet.
            Send for the county. Go tell him of this.
            I'll have this knot knit up tomorrow morning.
Juliet.
25   I met the youthful lord at Laurence' cell
            And gave him what becomèd° love I might,
            Not stepping o'er the bounds of modesty.
Capulet.
            Why, I am glad on't. This is well. Stand up.
            This is as't should be. Let me see the county.
30   Ay, marry, go, I say, and fetch him hither.
            Now, afore God, this reverend holy friar,
            All our whole city is much bound to him.
Juliet.
            Nurse, will you go with me into my closet,°
            To help me sort such needful ornaments
35   As you think fit to furnish me tomorrow?
Lady Capulet.
            No, not till Thursday. There is time enough.
Capulet.
            Go, nurse, go with her. We'll to church tomorrow.
                  [*Exeunt* JULIET *and* NURSE.]
Lady Capulet.
            We shall be short in our provision.
            'Tis now near night.
Capulet.   Tush, I will stir about,
40   And all things shall be well, I warrant thee, wife.

THE TRAGEDY OF ROMEO AND JULIET, ACT IV, SCENE 2   **823**

---

10. **unfurnished:** unsupplied (without food).

? 14. Harlotry *means a "good-for-nothing," a prostitute. Whom is Capulet referring to as "it"?*

? 15. *Do you think Juliet really has a merry look, or is the nurse trying to cover up?*

? 24. *Why do you think Capulet pushes the marriage up to Wednesday?*

26. **becomèd:** proper or becoming.

? 28. *According to this speech, what has Juliet been doing since she first addressed her father?*

33. **closet:** private room.

? 37. *The wedding has been changed to take place on Wednesday. Lady Capulet tries to change her husband's mind, perhaps in consideration of Juliet. But she is not successful. How will this affect the timing of the friar's plans?*

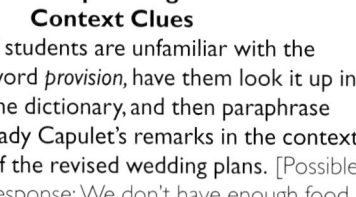

Reaching All Students

T823

Summary ■ ■

Act IV, Scene 3

The nurse has helped Juliet prepare for her wedding tomorrow. At Juliet's request, both the nurse and her mother leave her alone for the night. About to take the sleeping potion, Juliet expresses her last-minute doubts in a soliloquy. What if the potion does not work? (Just in case, she lays a dagger at her ready.) What if the friar, fearing reprisal for marrying Romeo and Juliet, has actually given her poison? What if she should wake in the tomb, among corpses and loathsome odors, before Romeo comes to get her? She especially dreads this last possibility, fearing that she will go mad or that Tybalt's ghost will appear. She recovers her courage and swallows the potion, saying that she drinks to Romeo.

Ⓐ Critical Thinking

Analyzing Plot

❓ Why does Juliet dismiss both the nurse and her mother from her chamber? [Juliet will not be able to drink the potion if anyone sits up with her.]

Ⓑ Struggling Readers

Finding Details

Read aloud Juliet's speech in ll. 14–27. Have students identify Juliet's two worst fears about the potion the friar has given her. [She fears it might not work, in which case she plans to take her own life with a dagger; she fears the friar may poison her in order to retain his reputation.]

Answers to Margin Questions
Line 6. Most students will probably say that Lady Capulet speaks to Juliet with tenderness, love, and concern.
Line 14. Juliet is afraid the potion will not work. She also momentarily fears that the friar has given her poison because he would be "dishonored" to perform a second, false marriage. She fears awakening in the burial vault before Romeo arrives, knowing the foul air could suffocate her. Worst of all, she fears going mad amid the horrors she will encounter there: skeletons, rotting corpses, and loathsome smells.

Juliet brings the vial to her lips and then puts it away; she finds the dagger and places it by her bed; she may pace her room as she describes her visions.

Go thou to Juliet, help to deck up her.
I'll not to bed tonight; let me alone.
I'll play the housewife for this once. What, ho!
They are all forth; well, I will walk myself
45 To County Paris, to prepare up him
Against tomorrow. My heart is wondrous light,
Since this same wayward girl is so reclaimed.
[*Exit with* LADY CAPULET.]

Scene 3. *Juliet's chamber.*

Enter JULIET *and* NURSE.

Juliet.
Ay, those attires are best; but, gentle nurse,
I pray thee leave me to myself tonight;
For I have need of many orisons°
To move the heavens to smile upon my state,
5   Which, well thou knowest, is cross and full of sin.

[*Enter* LADY CAPULET.]

Lady Capulet.
What, are you busy, ho? Need you my help?
Juliet.
No, madam; we have culled such necessaries
As are behoveful° for our state° tomorrow.
So please you, let me now be left alone,
10 And let the nurse this night sit up with you;
For I am sure you have your hands full all
In this so sudden business.
Lady Capulet.   Good night.
Get thee to bed, and rest; for thou hast need.
[*Exeunt* LADY CAPULET *and* NURSE.]
Juliet.
Farewell! God knows when we shall meet again.
15 I have a faint cold fear thrills through my veins
That almost freezes up the heat of life.
I'll call them back again to comfort me.
Nurse!—What should she do here?
My dismal scene I needs must act alone.
20 Come, vial.
What if this mixture do not work at all?

824 WILLIAM SHAKESPEARE

❓ **47.** *Lord Capulet realizes all the servants are gone. What action is he involved in in this speech? What is his new mood?*

3. orisons: prayers.

❓ **6.** *Lady Capulet is sometimes played here as loving and gentle with Juliet, perhaps suggesting that she is uneasy about her daughter's change of heart. What emotions should her next speech show?*
8. behoveful: suitable. **state:** ceremonies.

❓ **14.** *Here is a fine example of the Shakespearean soliloquy, where a character is poised on the edge of action and thinks over its pros and cons. What are the fears and doubts that Juliet must consider before taking the potion?*
Juliet is not standing still as she delivers this speech. What do you think she is doing?

Crossing the Curriculum

Art

Have interested students create a mobile of characters in the play. They might draw an illustration of a character on one side of a piece of cardboard or poster board. On the other side, they could write adjectives that describe that character. From this first tier, students can hang geometrical shapes on which quotations from the character are copied. Encourage variety, and display student work.

Social Studies

Have students research Elizabethan wedding and funeral customs, including the kinds of clothing, food, music, and rituals that were associated with each of these rites of passage. Have students prepare reports of their findings, which they can also illustrate.

"Romeo, Romeo, Romeo, I drink to thee."

RESPONDING TO THE ART

Activity. Ask students to describe the mood in this photograph. [Possible responses: calm, peaceful, serene.] **Ask them to identify specific elements that create this mood.** [Possible responses: the soft, glowing light; the confident manner with which Juliet takes the poison; Juliet's prayer-like pose.]

A Reading Skills and Strategies

Paraphrasing and Context Clues

Have students work in small groups to paraphrase the fears that Juliet expresses here. You might start them off with the following paraphrase of ll. 30–54: What if I wake up alone in the tomb before Romeo comes to get me? There's not much air in the tomb, so I might die of asphyxiation before Romeo arrives. Or if I live, what if I find the tomb—filled with my ancestors' bones, Tybalt's bloody body, ghosts, bad smells, and awful sounds—so scary it drives me mad and I kill myself with an ancestor's bone?

B Cultural and Literary Connections

? Elizabethans tended to be deeply superstitious and believe that ghosts often returned to earth on a specific mission: to warn the living about the future or to avenge their own deaths. Ghosts are dramatically effective and play a prominent role in many of Shakespeare's plays, including *Hamlet, Macbeth,* and *Richard III.* Often the ghosts are visible only to the specific person they are haunting. Why might Juliet fear a visit from Tybalt's ghost? [He might haunt her for betraying her family and loving his murderer.]

Answers to Margin Questions

Line 29. Juliet believes that Friar Laurence is a holy man who always tries to act for the best. But her momentary suspicion in ll. 24–27 suggests that he may be somewhat cowardly: He may fear the censure of the families, both for performing a secret marriage and for seeming to participate in bigamy.

Line 54. Allow students who draw illustrations to display their work.

Shall I be married then tomorrow morning?
No, no! This shall forbid it. Lie thou there.

[*Lays down a dagger.*]

25 What if it be a poison which the friar
Subtly hath ministered to have me dead,
Lest in this marriage he should be dishonored
Because he married me before to Romeo?
I fear it is; and yet methinks it should not,
For he hath still been tried° a holy man.

30 How if, when I am laid into the tomb,
I wake before the time that Romeo
Come to redeem me? There's a fearful point!
Shall I not then be stifled in the vault,
To whose foul mouth no healthsome air breathes in,
35 And there die strangled ere my Romeo comes?
Or, if I live, is it not very like
The horrible conceit of death and night,
Together with the terror of the place—
As in a vault, an ancient receptacle
40 Where for this many hundred years the bones
Of all my buried ancestors are packed;

Ⓐ Where bloody Tybalt, yet but green in earth,°
Lies fest'ring in his shroud; where, as they say,
At some hours in the night spirits resort—
45 Alack, alack, is it not like that I,
So early waking—what with loathsome smells,
And shrieks like mandrakes° torn out of the earth,
That living mortals, hearing them, run mad—
I, if I wake, shall I not be distraught,
50 Environèd with all these hideous fears,
And madly play with my forefathers' joints,
And pluck the mangled Tybalt from his shroud,
And, in this rage, with some great kinsman's bone
As with a club dash out my desp'rate brains?

55 Ⓑ O, look! Methinks I see my cousin's ghost
Seeking out Romeo, that did spit his body
Upon a rapier's point. Stay, Tybalt, stay!
Romeo, Romeo, Romeo, I drink to thee.

[*She falls upon her bed within the curtains.*]

826 WILLIAM SHAKESPEARE

29. **still been tried:** always been proved.
? 29. *Audiences always wonder why the friar has not simply told the families of Romeo and Juliet's secret wedding, rather than involve them in such a dangerous plan. How does Juliet explain the friar's actions?*

42. **green in earth:** newly buried.

47. **mandrakes:** plants resembling the human body, which were said to grow beneath the gallows and to scream when torn up.

? 54. *Draw the mental picture you have of the tomb from Juliet's description of it.*

Juliet's doubt about Friar Laurence

T825

Scene 4. *A hall in Capulet's house.*

Enter LADY CAPULET *and* NURSE.

Lady Capulet.
   Hold, take these keys and fetch more spices, nurse.
Nurse.
   They call for dates and quinces in the pastry.

[*Enter old* CAPULET.]

Capulet.
   Come, stir, stir, stir! The second cock hath crowed,
   The curfew bell hath rung, 'tis three o'clock.
5 Look to the baked meats, good Angelica;
   Spare not for cost.
Nurse.   Go, you cotquean,° go,
   Get you to bed! Faith, you'll be sick tomorrow
   For this night's watching.
Capulet.
   No, not a whit. What, I have watched ere now
10 All night for lesser cause, and ne'er been sick.
Lady Capulet.
   Ay, you have been a mouse hunt° in your time;
   But I will watch you from such watching now.
                    [*Exeunt* LADY CAPULET *and* NURSE.]
Capulet.
   A jealous hood,° a jealous hood!

[*Enter three or four* FELLOWS *with spits and logs and
   baskets.*]
                         Now, fellow,
   What is there?
First Fellow.
15 Things for the cook, sir; but I know not what.
Capulet.
   Make haste, make haste.   [*Exit* FIRST FELLOW.]
                    Sirrah, fetch drier logs.
   Call Peter; he will show thee where they are.
Second Fellow.
   I have a head, sir, that will find out logs°
   And never trouble Peter for the matter.
Capulet.
20 Mass,° and well said; a merry whoreson, ha!
   Thou shalt be loggerhead.°
                    [*Exit* SECOND FELLOW, *with the others.*]
                    Good faith, 'tis day.

THE TRAGEDY OF ROMEO AND JULIET, ACT IV, SCENE 4 **827**

? **1.** *How does this peaceful domestic scene contrast with what has just happened? What is everyone preparing for?*

? **5.** *Angelica is the nurse's name. How does Lord Capulet treat her now, as opposed to how he treated her in Act III, Scene 5? What humor does the nurse add to this scene?*
   6. cotquean: old woman (a man who acts like an old woman).

11. mouse hunt: woman chaser or night prowler.
? **12.** *What is Lady Capulet's tone here?*

13. hood: female.

18. I . . . logs: in other words, "I have a wooden head."

20. Mass: mild oath, "by the Mass."
21. loggerhead: blockhead.
? **21.** *Capulet fusses around and has his nose in everything. What actions do you imagine the old man involved in, in this scene?*

Act IV, Scene 4
Lord and Lady Capulet, amid much jollity, oversee the wedding preparations. Hearing Count Paris approaching, accompanied by musicians, Lord Capulet sends the nurse to waken Juliet.

ⓒ Reading Skills and Strategies
Connecting with the Text
? What emotions are generally associated with the day of a family member's wedding? [Possible responses: excitement about the festivities and ceremony; stress due to the responsibilities of planning and coordinating events.]

Answers to Margin Questions
Line 1. The Capulets and their servants are making jokes and busily preparing for the wedding; meanwhile, the bride-to-be lies in her room in a deathlike state, having risked her life to avoid what her family celebrates.
Line 5. Here Lord Capulet calls the nurse "good Angelica" and treats her with affection and courtesy. In Act III, Scene 5, when Juliet announced that she would not marry Paris, Lord Capulet treated the nurse with harshness, disrespect, and anger. In this scene, the nurse adds to the humor by fondly making fun of her master.
Line 12. Lady Capulet is teasingly affectionate here, poking fun at her husband about the women he used to chase.
Line 21. Capulet is probably tasting food, checking wine flasks, and generally getting in everyone's way.

A Elements of Literature

Suspense

? Even though we know what the nurse will find when she goes to waken Juliet, we still feel a sense of suspense at this point. Why? [Possible responses: We wonder how the nurse will realize that Juliet is "dead," how she will react when she finds out, how she will break the news to the family, and how Juliet's parents and Paris will react.]

Answer to Margin Question
Line 23. The audience knows that Juliet will not be Paris's bride and that the wedding music will give way to a funeral dirge.

Summary ■ ■

Act IV, Scene 5
The nurse goes to wake Juliet but, finding her unresponsive, believes that she is dead. She cries out in alarm, and Juliet's parents rush in and lament the death of their daughter. Friar Laurence and Paris enter and are told the bad news. The friar, who knows that Juliet is not really dead, attempts to comfort the others and tells them that they must prepare Juliet for burial in the family tomb. The scene ends with a comic interlude as Peter and the musicians exchange punning jests.

Answer to Margin Question
Line 1. In l. 14, the nurse discovers that Juliet is "dead."

The county will be here with music straight,
For so he said he would. (*Play music offstage.*)
                    I hear him near.
Nurse! Wife! What, ho! What, nurse, I say!

[*Enter* NURSE.]

25 ⎡Go waken Juliet; go and trim her up.
   ⎢I'll go and chat with Paris. Hie, make haste,
 A ⎢Make haste! The bridegroom he is come already:
   ⎣Make haste, I say.   [*Exit.*]

Scene 5. *Juliet's chamber.*

Nurse.
    Mistress! What, mistress! Juliet! Fast,° I warrant her, she.
    Why, lamb! Why, lady! Fie, you slugabed.
    Why, love, I say! Madam; sweetheart! Why, bride!
    What, not a word? You take your pennyworths° now;
5   Sleep for a week; for the next night, I warrant,
    The County Paris hath set up his rest°
    That you shall rest but little. God forgive me!
    Marry, and amen. How sound is she asleep!
    I needs must wake her. Madam, madam, madam!
10 Ay, let the county take you in your bed;
    He'll fright you up, i' faith. Will it not be?

[*Draws aside the curtains.*]

    What, dressed, and in your clothes, and down again?
    I must needs wake you. Lady! Lady! Lady!
    Alas, alas! Help, help! My lady's dead!
15 O weraday that ever I was born!
    Some aqua vitae, ho! My lord! My lady!

[*Enter* LADY CAPULET.]

Lady Capulet.
    What noise is here?
Nurse.   O lamentable day!
Lady Capulet.
    What is the matter?
Nurse.   Look, look! O heavy day!
Lady Capulet.
    O me, O me! My child, my only life!

828 WILLIAM SHAKESPEARE

? **23.** *The music is bridal music, for the wedding. What irony would the audience sense on hearing this music and knowing what has happened to Juliet?*

1. Fast: fast asleep.
? **1.** *As the nurse speaks to Juliet and to herself, she is busy arranging clothes, opening windows, and doing things around the room. In what line here does she touch Juliet and discover she is cold?*
4. pennyworths: small naps.
6. set up his rest: become firmly resolved.

Professional Notes

Critical Comment: Staging the Scene
Writing in *Shakespeare Bulletin*, critic Justin Shaltz praised the staging of this scene in a 1994 production by the Illinois Shakespeare Festival, directed by Patrick O'Gara: "The portrayal of Juliet's liberation from her family and the feud—through her love for Romeo—is the most memorable sequence of the production.

When she is found 'dead,' the Capulets lift her from her bed, but, once they do, Juliet stands on her own and dances slowly away from them within a spotlight. The men pantomime carrying her corpse away, her body bound, while Juliet dances across the stage, her spirit free."

20   Revive, look up, or I will die with thee!
    Help, help! Call help.

[*Enter* CAPULET.]

Capulet.
    For shame, bring Juliet forth; her lord is come.
Nurse.
    She's dead, deceased; she's dead, alack the day!
Lady Capulet.
    Alack the day, she's dead, she's dead, she's dead! **B**
Capulet.
25   Ha! Let me see her. Out alas! She's cold,
    Her blood is settled, and her joints are stiff;
    Life and these lips have long been separated.
    Death lies on her like an untimely frost
    Upon the sweetest flower of all the field.

> ❝ *Death lies on her like an*
> *untimely frost*
> *Upon the sweetest flower*
> *of all the field.* ❞

Nurse.
    O lamentable day!
30 **Lady Capulet.**   O woeful time!
Capulet.
    Death, that hath ta'en her hence to make me wail,
    Ties up my tongue and will not let me speak.

[*Enter* FRIAR LAURENCE *and* PARIS, *with* MUSICIANS.]

Friar.
    Come, is the bride ready to go to church? **C**
Capulet.
    Ready to go, but never to return.
35   O son, the night before thy wedding day
    Hath Death lain with thy wife. There she lies,
    Flower as she was, deflowerèd by him.   **D**
    Death is my son-in-law, Death is my heir;
    My daughter he hath wedded. I will die
40   And leave him all. Life, living, all is Death's.
Paris.
    Have I thought, love, to see this morning's face,
    And doth it give me such a sight as this?

? **29.** *What actions are taking place on stage as the three actors now find Juliet "dead"?*

B **Reading Skills and Strategies**
Drawing Conclusions
? Why does Lady Capulet repeat herself? [Possible responses: She cannot believe what she has heard; she is in shock over the news.]

C **Elements of Literature**
Dramatic Irony
? What do we know about Friar Laurence that the other characters do not? [Friar Laurence knows Juliet is not ready to go to church as a bride because he is the one who gave her the potion; he is just pretending he doesn't know about Juliet's state.]

D **Elements of Literature**
Personification
? How does Capulet personify death? [Death is personified as a greedy suitor, who has seized Juliet away from Paris, becoming her husband and Capulet's son-in-law.]

Answer to Margin Question
Line 29. Lord Capulet is touching Juliet, checking to see if she is really dead. The other actors may be wandering the room in dazed, erratic patterns, always circling back to check on Juliet one more time.

Using Students' Strengths

Kinesthetic Learners
Read aloud the review in Professional Notes on p. T828 about the staging of this scene, and have students evaluate the idea of having Juliet's spirit dance while her family believes her to be dead. Invite students interested in dance to choreograph a dance for Juliet's spirit and perform it for their classmates.

(A) Vocabulary Note

Synonyms

Have students search these speeches to find as many synonyms as they can for the adjective *sad.* ["unhappy," "wretched," "miserable," "woeful," "lamentable," "black"]

(B) Reading Skills and Strategies

Comparing and Contrasting

? How do these lines contrast with Lord Capulet's earlier threats to dismiss Juliet from his household? [Possible responses: He is filled with grief now rather than anger; he realizes that much of his own happiness was built on his daughter's joy; instead of calling her insulting names, he now calls her "My soul" and "my child."]

Answers to Margin Questions

Line 49. Chief among the lines that indicate Lord Capulet's love for Juliet are ll. 38–40 and 62–64. Lady Capulet's love and grief are evident in ll. 43–48.

Friar Laurence, who could comfort them with the truth, remains silent.

Line 58. Students may suggest extreme grief or a sudden illness. The mourners simply personify death as a villain who has taken Juliet to himself.

Line 64. Because the lines are so repetitive, so exaggerated, and so dependent on apostrophe (addressing things that are not there), they may seem superficial. In addition, the Capulets and Paris concentrate on how cruel death has been to *them* rather than concentrating on Juliet.

Line 65. Friar Laurence offers the consolation that Juliet is now in heaven: "And all the better is it for the maid" (l. 68). He rebukes the adults for their weeping and lack of faith: "O, in this love, you love your child so ill/That you run mad, seeing that she is well" (ll. 75–76).

Line 83. If the Capulets have faith, they must conclude that Juliet is in heaven, happier than she was in her life.

Lady Capulet.
Accursed, unhappy, wretched, hateful day!
Most miserable hour that e'er time saw
In lasting labor of his pilgrimage!
But one, poor one, one poor and loving child,
But one thing to rejoice and solace in,
And cruel Death hath catched it from my sight.

(A) **Nurse.**
O woe! O woeful, woeful, woeful day!
Most lamentable day, most woeful day
That ever ever I did yet behold!
O day, O day, O day! O hateful day!
Never was seen so black a day as this.
O woeful day! O woeful day!

Paris.
Beguiled, divorcèd, wrongèd, spited, slain!
Most detestable Death, by thee beguiled,
By cruel, cruel thee quite overthrown.
O love! O life!—not life, but love in death!

Capulet.
Despised, distressèd, hated, martyred, killed!
Uncomfortable time, why cam'st thou now
(B) To murder, murder our solemnity?
O child, O child! My soul, and not my child!
Dead art thou—alack, my child is dead,
And with my child my joys are burièd!

Friar.
Peace, ho, for shame! Confusion's cure lives not
In these confusions. Heaven and yourself
Had part in this fair maid—now heaven hath all,
And all the better is it for the maid.
Your part in her you could not keep from death,
But heaven keeps his part in eternal life.
The most you sought was her promotion,
For 'twas your heaven she should be advanced;
And weep ye now, seeing she is advanced
Above the clouds, as high as heaven itself?
O, in this love, you love your child so ill
That you run mad, seeing that she is well.°
She's not well married that lives married long,
But she's best married that dies married young.
Dry up your tears and stick your rosemary°
On this fair corse, and, as the custom is,
And in her best array bear her to church;
For though fond nature° bids us all lament,
Yet nature's tears are reason's merriment.

? **49.** *Here again, as with Juliet's bemoaning Romeo's supposed death in an earlier scene, we have Lord and Lady Capulet and the nurse expressing anguish when we, the audience, know that Juliet is not dead. We listen to them, but we are not moved in the way they are. What words of the Capulets here suggest a loving concern for Juliet that seemed to be missing from earlier scenes? Which character enters and plays dumb about the whole situation?*

? **58.** *In your opinion, what might all these people think caused Juliet's death?*

? **64.** *These expressions of grief are by now sounding mechanical and repetitive. Shakespeare might have written them this way to prevent grief at a false death from gaining our sympathy. How could these lines of the parents, of the nurse, and of Paris also suggest that the speakers' feelings might not be very deep?*

? **65.** *The friar, of course, knows that Juliet is drugged, not dead. His words here suggest that there has been great confusion on stage. What consolation does he offer, and what sharp rebuke does he give the adults?*

76. well: that is, she is in heaven.

79. rosemary: herb that stands for remembrance.

82. fond nature: foolish human nature.

? **83.** *Why does the friar say that reason tells us to be merry about death?*

Assessing Learning

Observation Assessment: Discussion

Use the following checklist as you observe and assess student participation in class discussion:

1=Rarely 2=Sometimes 3=Always

__ Actively participates in discussion
__ Articulates responses clearly
__ Listens to what other students say
__ Thinks before speaking
__ Waits to be called upon
__ Gives reasons for responses

Capulet.

> All things that we ordainèd festival
>
> 85   Turn from their office to black funeral—
>
> Our instruments to melancholy bells,
>
> Our wedding cheer to a sad burial feast;
>
> Our solemn hymns to sullen dirges change;
>
> Our bridal flowers serve for a buried corse;
>
> 90   And all things change them to the contrary.

Friar.

> Sir, go you in; and, madam, go with him;
>
> And go, Sir Paris. Everyone prepare
>
> To follow this fair corse unto her grave.
>
> The heavens do lower° upon you for some ill;
>
> 95   Move them no more by crossing their high will.

[Exeunt, casting rosemary on her and shutting the curtains. The NURSE *and* MUSICIANS *remain.]*

First Musician.

> Faith, we may put up our pipes and be gone.

Nurse.

> Honest good fellows, ah, put up, put up!
>
> For well you know this is a pitiful case.   *[Exit.]*

First Musician.

> Ay, by my troth, the case may be amended.

[Enter PETER.*]*

> 100   **Peter.** Musicians, O, musicians, "Heart's ease," "Heart's ease"! O, and you will have me live, play "Heart's ease."
>
> **First Musician.** Why "Heart's ease"?
>
> **Peter.** O, musicians, because my heart itself plays "My
>
> 105   heart is full." O, play me some merry dump° to comfort me.
>
> **First Musician.** Not a dump we! 'Tis no time to play now.
>
> **Peter.** You will not then?
>
> 110   **First Musician.** No.
>
> **Peter.** I will then give it you soundly.
>
> **First Musician.** What will you give us?
>
> **Peter.** No money, on my faith, but the gleek.° I will give you° the minstrel.
>
> 115   **First Musician.** Then will I give you the serving-creature.
>
> **Peter.** Then will I lay the serving-creature's dagger on your pate. I will carry° no crotchets. I'll re you, I'll fa you. Do you note me?

90. *Does Capulet express any guilt? Is he still self-centered?*

94. lower: frown.

98. *These are the nurse's last lines in the play. True to her character, she jokes as she leaves, though she might do this to cover her grief. The musicians are talking about the cases for their instruments. What "case" is the nurse referring to?*

105. dump: sad tune.

113. gleek: jeer or insult.
114. give you: call you (to be called a minstrel was an insult to a musician).

118. carry: endure.

C Elements of Literature

Falling Action

Although Juliet is not really dead, Capulet's words make the audience feel a growing sense of doom about the play's outcome.

D Critical Thinking

Analyzing Character

❓ What motive might Friar Laurence have in speaking these two lines? [Possible response: to suggest to the family that the loss of their daughter might be punishment for the sin of feuding.]

E English Language Learners

Musical Terms

These students may not recognize the words *re* (pronounced "ray") and *fa* (pronounced "fah"), the second and fourth notes of the European eight-tone scale.

Answers to Margin Questions

Line 90. Answers may vary. Students might suggest that because Juliet's father thinks of his preparations for the wedding festivities, he might be considered self-centered, although not necessarily selfish, for he is sad and grieving. However, he expresses no guilt.

Line 98. The nurse is referring to the event of Juliet's death.

Making the Connections

**Connecting to the Theme:
"The Destruction of Innocence"**

Juliet's innocent trust of her father, her mother, and the nurse has been destroyed by Act IV. However, Juliet continues to trust Friar Laurence. Ask students to discuss the progression of Juliet's disassociation from her family and to consider whether she should also distrust Friar Laurence. Students should provide reasons for their opinions.

A **Critical Thinking**

Interpreting

? Are the musicians becoming angry with Peter, or are their insults meant in good humor? [Sample responses: The musicians are in a good humor, planning on eating the food that was meant for the wedding feast; the musicians are enjoying a battle of wits with Peter.]

Answer to Margin Question

Line 144. Peter may be threatening to strike the musicians if they don't play, or he may be giving a mock lecture.

Peter and the musicians are not emotionally involved in Juliet's death; by their joking, they prove that their own lives continue, whether the event is joyful or tragic.

120 **First Musician.** And you re us and fa us, you note us.
Second Musician. Pray you put up your dagger, and put out your wit. Then have at you with my wit!
Peter. I will dry-beat° you with an iron wit, and put up my iron dagger. Answer me like men.
125   "When griping grief the heart doth wound,
         And doleful dumps the mind oppress,
         Then music with her silver sound"—
     Why "silver sound"? Why "music with her silver sound"?
     What say you, Simon Catling?°
130 **First Musician.** Marry, sir, because silver hath a sweet sound.
Peter. Pretty! What say you, Hugh Rebeck?°
Second Musician. I say "silver sound" because musicians sound for silver.
135 **Peter.** Pretty too! What say you, James Soundpost?°
Third Musician. Faith, I know not what to say.
Peter. O, I cry you mercy,° you are the singer. I will say for you. It is "music with her silver sound" because musicians have no gold for sounding.°
140   "Then music with her silver sound
         With speedy help doth lend redress."   [*Exit.*]
A **First Musician.** What a pestilent knave is this same!
Second Musician. Hang him, Jack! Come, we'll in here, tarry for the mourners, and stay dinner.
                                        [*Exit with others.*]

123. **dry-beat:** beat soundly.

129. **Catling:** lute string.

132. **Rebeck:** fiddle.

135. **Soundpost:** peg on violinlike instrument.

137. **cry you mercy:** beg your pardon.

139. **no gold for sounding:** no money to jingle in their pockets.

? 144. *Peter, who was always bossed about by the nurse, here has grabbed at the chance to boss the musicians, who are a step below him socially. Meanwhile, the stage behind them is being cleared of bedroom trappings. What actions do you imagine during this exchange of insults? (Note that they all want to stay for dinner.) How does this scene provide relief for us and remind us that ordinary life goes on amid tragedy?*

Assessing Learning

Check Test: Questions and Answers

1. What is the reason for Paris's visit to Friar Laurence in Scene 1? [Paris wants to make wedding arrangements.]

2. What is Friar Laurence's plan to help Juliet with her dilemma? [The friar gives Juliet a potion that will make her appear to be dead, and while she lies in a cemetery vault, he will get a message to Romeo that he should be there when she awakens.]

3. What event is the Capulet household preparing for at the beginning of Act IV? [the wedding of Juliet to Paris]

4. What are Juliet's fears as she prepares to drink the potion? [that the mixture will not work, that the friar is tricking her, that she will awaken before Romeo finds her, and that the sights, sounds, and smells in the tomb will make her go mad]

5. What main idea does Friar Laurence stress to the Capulets as they grieve over Juliet?

[He tells them that Juliet is in heaven and that they should try to do things that please heaven.]

Standardized Test Preparation

For practice with standardized test format specific to this selection, see
• *Standardized Test Preparation*, p. 86

LITERATURE AND THE MEDIA

Shakespeare in the Video Store

Film and television have brought Shakespeare's plays to millions of viewers and confirmed the playwright's position as a world treasure. *Hamlet* has been by far the most popular of his plays, with forty-seven film versions of all or part of the tragedy (as of 1996). The earliest *Hamlet* movie was made in Paris in 1900. This black-and-white silent film had an interesting reversal of the custom of Shakespeare's time, in which boys took women's roles onstage: The role of Hamlet was played by the great Sarah Bernhardt (1844–1923).

For almost a century, film productions of Shakespeare have showcased some of our most distinguished actors: Laurence Olivier, Vanessa Redgrave, Richard Burton, John Gielgud, Katharine Hepburn, Mel Gibson, Glenn Close, Denzel Washington. Between 1978 and 1985, a partnership between the British Broadcasting Corporation (BBC) and Time Warner completed the ambitious project of filming all of Shakespeare's plays for television. Now Shakespeare is accessible as never before: A performance of one of his plays is as near as your local video store.

But critics have pointed out drawbacks in the performance of these plays on screen. For example, they argue that film controls our perceptions of the plays and deprives us of the tension we feel when seeing the plays live, in the theater. Film and television productions of Shakespearean comedy are at another disadvantage, since the actors can't respond to the feedback of a live audience. Such feedback is unpredictable, but actors say it's critical in comedy.

Not every Shakespeare movie has had celebrity performers. An outstanding example of a director's success with young unknown actors is Franco Zeffirelli's film *Romeo and Juliet* (1968). A comparison between the film script and the play's text shows the great extent to which the camera does in film what dialogue does onstage: Zeffirelli retained only about a third of Shakespeare's lines. He made other changes as well. Some lines are rearranged within scenes, and a few episodes—for example, the apothecary scene and the death of Paris—are dropped altogether.

The changes in the text of *Romeo and Juliet* are controversial, but most critics have agreed that the fiery, youthful passion of Zeffirelli's film faithfully catches the spirit of Shakespeare's play. The film is stunningly beautiful, in part because of the attractive young actors—Leonard Whiting as Romeo and Olivia Hussey as Juliet—and in part because of the dark beauty of the Italian hill towns Zeffirelli used as a setting for the tragedy. Three decades later, Zeffirelli's film is widely acknowledged to represent Shakespeare on screen at its best.

LITERATURE AND THE MEDIA

The film version of *Romeo and Juliet* that students are most likely to be familiar with is Australian director Baz Luhrmann's 1996 production, starring Claire Danes and Leonardo DiCaprio, which received decidedly mixed reviews. Set in present-day Florida, this version features rock music on the soundtrack, the original Elizabethan dialogue spoken by gang members wielding guns, and a balcony scene that is interrupted by the couple's accidental fall into a swimming pool. Many students will feel that the young actors convincingly portray the passion and desperation of young love and bring life to Shakespeare's archaic language. Invite students who have seen this film to share their responses to it and to compare their responses with those of reviewers at the time the film came out. Students can use the *Reader's Guide to Periodical Literature* or the Internet to research movie reviews.

MAKING MEANINGS (ACT IV)

First Thoughts

1. She is relying on the friar's reputation, holy vows, and affection for Romeo. Students may say they would not trust his abilities as a chemist.

Shaping Interpretations

2. Possible responses:
   Scene 2: Lord Capulet is joyful about the good that Friar Laurence has done for Juliet and feels grateful to him when, in fact, the friar has secretly wed Romeo and Juliet and is aiding Juliet in foiling the new wedding plans.
   Scene 3: Lady Capulet urges Juliet to go to bed, unaware that they will be unable to awaken her in the morning.
   Scene 4: Everyone is happily preparing for the wedding, but the audience waits in suspense for what will happen when Juliet is found "dead."

3. Juliet must act without Romeo or the nurse, and she goes alone to the friar's cell to see if he can help her avoid the marriage to Paris. Also, she swallows her pride and avoids further confrontation with her parents by apologizing and pretending to agree to the marriage. Although she is afraid the drug could kill her, she risks taking it so that she might be reunited with Romeo.

4. Possible response: Juliet is a courageous young woman whose love for Romeo is great enough to withstand many obstacles.

5. Although Juliet's parents are unreasonable when she initially refuses to marry Paris, they do love their daughter. Early in the play, for example, Lord Capulet says Juliet should marry a man that she loves when she is ready, and Lady Capulet believes Paris will make a fine husband. When Juliet can't stop grieving, her parents feel that they know what's best for her and arrange the marriage to Paris. Students' feelings about Juliet's parents will vary. Some may not be able to forgive them for the way they treated Juliet in Act III.

Grading Timesaver

Rubrics for each Choices assignment appear on p. 204 in the *Portfolio Management System.*

MAKING MEANINGS   ACT IV

First Thoughts

[connect]   1. Why is Juliet so willing to trust the friar's plan? Would you be willing to?

Shaping Interpretations

[analyze]   2. One of the pleasures of watching a play is knowing something that a character onstage does not know. This use of **dramatic irony** makes us feel **suspense**. We wait anxiously to find out what will happen when the characters discover what we already know. Where do you feel dramatic irony in Scenes 2, 3, and 4?

[infer]   3. What terrible trials does Juliet face in this act? How does she respond to these challenges?

[analyze]   4. What do Juliet's responses tell you about her **character**?

[evaluate]   5. Juliet's parents are the **blocking figures** in the play—their plans for Juliet make it seem impossible for the young couple to stay together. Does Shakespeare present the Capulets as bad characters? Or does he help us see them as complex human beings, not as mere stage villains? Explain your feelings.

> **Reading Check**
>
> a. In Scene 1, what does Juliet threaten to do if the friar cannot help her?
>
> b. What is the friar's plan for getting Romeo and Juliet together?
>
> c. In Scene 2, another major problem comes up: What change does Capulet make in the wedding plans?
>
> d. What is the situation in the Capulet house at the end of Act IV?

CHOICES: Building Your Portfolio

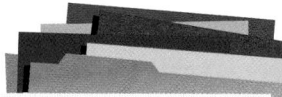

Writer's Notebook

1. Collecting Ideas for a Research Paper

Finding a topic. As you search for a topic for the research paper you'll write for the Writer's Workshop on page 868, you might be inspired by issues in the play that remind you of real-life situations today. Racial or ethnic hatreds often divide people and lead to tragedy.

You might think of problems in places like Northern Ireland, Eastern Europe, the Middle East—even in the United States, where racial animosities still cause tragedy. Jot down some examples of ethnic or racial or religious animosities you're aware of. Could one of these give you a topic for a research paper? Be sure to read "Dear Juliet" (see *Connections* on page 854) and "Romeo and Juliet in Bosnia" (page 860).

Creative Writing

2. Juliet's Thoughts

Write down Juliet's thoughts as you imagine them during this difficult time. (You could write as "I.") Write about her feelings toward her parents, Romeo, her nurse, Paris, and Friar Laurence. Let Juliet describe her feelings about the drug she is about to take and about her horror of being buried alive.

834   WILLIAM SHAKESPEARE

CHOICES: Building Your Portfolio

1. **Writer's Notebook**   Note the cross-references to the Connections feature on p. 854 and Extending the Theme on p. 860. You may want to have small groups of students read and discuss these features now. They may also find ideas in newspapers and news magazines.

2. **Creative Writing**   Students may enjoy recording their entries, perhaps with music playing softly in the background.

> **Reading Check**
>
> a. She threatens to kill herself.
>
> b. He offers Juliet a drug to induce a death-like coma for forty-two hours. During that time, the friar will send a messenger to Mantua, calling Romeo back to Verona so that he can be with Juliet when she awakens in the burial vault.
>
> c. He changes the wedding from Thursday to Wednesday.
>
> d. Everyone is distraught and grieving over Juliet's apparent death.

Reading Skills and Strategies

Booking space on the Net:

PARAPHRASING AND CONTEXT CLUES

Paraphrasing means restating a text in your own words. A restatement, or paraphrase, simplifies a text, but it doesn't necessarily make it shorter. In fact, a paraphrase might be longer than the original passage, and of course it's never as interesting. Paraphrasing is a good way to check on your understanding of the original text. Here is a speech from Act IV of *Romeo and Juliet* and a paraphrase:

> **Paris.**
> My father Capulet will have it so,
> And I am nothing slow to slack his haste.
> —Scene 1, lines 2–3

Paraphrase: My father-in-law Capulet wants it like that, and I'm not going to slow him down.

A Checklist for Paraphrasing

✓ Be sure you understand the main idea of the text.

✓ Look up unfamiliar words.

✓ Replace difficult words with simple ones.

✓ If a word has multiple meanings, be sure to use **context clues** to determine the meaning appropriate to the passage.

✓ Restate figures of speech in your own words, clarifying what's being compared with what.

✓ Try to reproduce the tone or mood of the text. If the text is satiric, the paraphrase should also be satiric.

✓ Be sure your paraphrase has accounted for all details in the original.

Try It Out

The following speeches are from Act IV. Paraphrase each one. Be sure to compare your paraphrases in class. It's almost certain that no two paraphrases will be alike.

1. **Paris.**
   Immoderately she weeps for Tybalt's death,
   And therefore have I little talked of love;
   For Venus smiles not in a house of tears.
   —Scene 1, lines 6–8

2. **Juliet** (*to the Friar*).
   Be not so long to speak. I long to die
   If what thou speak'st speak not of remedy.
   —Scene 1, lines 66–67

3. **Friar Laurence** (*to Juliet*).
   The roses in thy lips and cheeks shall fade
   To wanny ashes, thy eyes' windows fall
   Like death when he shuts up the day of life. . . .
   —Scene 1, lines 99–101

4. **Juliet** (*holding the poison*).
   O, look! Methinks I see my cousin's ghost
   Seeking out Romeo, that did spit his body
   Upon a rapier's point. Stay, Tybalt, stay!
   —Scene 3, lines 55–57

THE TRAGEDY OF ROMEO AND JULIET, ACT IV 835

Reading Skills and Strategies

Paraphrasing and Context Clues

This feature focuses on two reading skills that are essential for understanding and appreciating a Shakespeare play: paraphrasing and using context clues. It includes a list of helpful suggestions for students to use when they paraphrase a passage from the play.

Try It Out
Possible Answers

1. She has been crying so much over Tybalt's death that I haven't talked to her about love. Someone who is grief-stricken doesn't want to think about love.

2. Please say something. I'll just die if you can't help me.

3. You will turn pale, your eyelids will close, and you will appear to be dead.

4. Oh, look! I think I see a vision of my dead cousin Tybalt. He is looking for Romeo because Romeo stabbed him with a rapier. Stop, Tybalt, stop!

Assessing Learning

Quick Check: Paraphrasing

Ask students to paraphrase each of the following lines from Act IV. Answers will vary.

1. "Poor soul, thy face is much abused with tears."—Scene 1, l. 29 [Poor thing, your face is all swollen from crying.]

2. "It strains me past the compass of my wits."—Scene 1, l. 47 [It boggles my mind.]

3. "No warmth, no breath, shall testify thou livest."—Scene 1, l. 98 [You will be cold and breathless and appear to be dead.]

4. "What, I have watched ere now/All night for lesser cause, and ne'er been sick."—Scene 4, ll. 9–10 [Hey, I've stayed up all night before for less important things and never gotten sick.]

5. "The heavens do lower upon you for some ill."—Scene 5, l. 94 [God is punishing you for your sins.]

ACT V

Scene 1. *Mantua. A street.*

Enter ROMEO.

Romeo.
If I may trust the flattering truth of sleep,
My dreams presage° some joyful news at hand.
My bosom's lord° sits lightly in his throne,
And all this day an unaccustomed spirit
5 Lifts me above the ground with cheerful thoughts.
I dreamt my lady came and found me dead
(Strange dream that gives a dead man leave to think!)
And breathed such life with kisses in my lips
That I revived and was an emperor.
10 Ah me! How sweet is love itself possessed,
When but love's shadows° are so rich in joy!

[Enter Romeo's man BALTHASAR, *booted from riding.]*

News from Verona! How now, Balthasar?
Dost thou not bring me letters from the friar?
How doth my lady? Is my father well?
15 How fares my Juliet? That I ask again,
For nothing can be ill if she be well.
Balthasar.
Then she is well, and nothing can be ill.
Her body sleeps in Capel's monument,
And her immortal part with angels lives.
20 I saw her laid low in her kindred's vault
And presently took post° to tell it you.
O, pardon me for bringing these ill news,
Since you did leave it for my office,° sir.
Romeo.
Is it e'en so? Then I defy you, stars!
25 Thou knowest my lodging. Get me ink and paper
And hire post horses. I will hence tonight.
Balthasar.
I do beseech you, sir, have patience.
Your looks are pale and wild and do import
Some misadventure.
Romeo.   Tush, thou art deceived.
30 Leave me and do the thing I bid thee do.
Hast thou no letters to me from the friar?
Balthasar.
No, my good lord.

2. **presage:** foretell.
3. **bosom's lord:** heart.

11. **shadows:** dreams.

 16. *Some actors playing Romeo reveal in this line that they suspect bad news. What, meanwhile, would Balthasar be doing?*

21. **post:** post horse (horse kept at an inn and rented by travelers).

23. **office:** duty.
23. *Balthasar must show that he dreads giving his master the tragic news. What do we know that Balthasar does not know?*
26. *Some actors move away here, or hide their faces in their hands. Romeo could address the stars or fate defiantly or tonelessly, to suggest defeat. What would you say is Romeo's tone here?*
29. *What does Balthasar suggest Romeo looks like, even though he pretends to be calm?*
31. *What letter is Romeo waiting for?*

836 WILLIAM SHAKESPEARE

 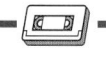 *Resources: Print and Media*

Romeo.   No matter. Get thee gone.
And hire those horses. I'll be with thee straight.

                                   [*Exit* BALTHASAR.]

Well, Juliet, I will lie with thee tonight.
35   Let's see for means. O mischief, thou art swift
To enter in the thoughts of desperate men!
I do remember an apothecary,
And hereabouts 'a dwells, which late I noted
In tattered weeds,° with overwhelming° brows,
40   Culling of simples.° Meager were his looks,
Sharp misery had worn him to the bones;
And in his needy shop a tortoise hung,
An alligator stuffed, and other skins
Of ill-shaped fishes; and about his shelves
45   A beggarly account° of empty boxes,
Green earthen pots, bladders, and musty seeds,
Remnants of packthread, and old cakes of roses
Were thinly scattered, to make up a show.
Noting this penury,° to myself I said,
50   "And if a man did need a poison now
Whose sale is present death in Mantua,
Here lives a caitiff° wretch would sell it him."
O, this same thought did but forerun my need,
And this same needy man must sell it me.
55   As I remember, this should be the house.
Being holiday, the beggar's shop is shut.
What, ho! Apothecary!

> *« O mischief, thou art swift*
> *To enter in the thoughts of desperate men! »*

[*Enter* APOTHECARY.]

Apothecary.   Who calls so loud?
Romeo.
Come hither, man. I see that thou art poor.
Hold, there is forty ducats. Let me have
60   A dram of poison, such soon-speeding gear°
As will disperse itself through all the veins
That the life-weary taker may fall dead,
And that the trunk° may be discharged of breath
As violently as hasty powder fired
65   Doth hurry from the fatal cannon's womb.

THE TRAGEDY OF ROMEO AND JULIET, ACT V, SCENE I   **837**

---

34. *This line is spoken in a still, quiet moment. After a pause, what does Romeo immediately set out to do? Does he hesitate at all to consider his course of action, or does he plunge into it?*
39. weeds: clothes. **overwhelming:** overhanging.
40. simples: herbs.

45. account: number.

49. penury: poverty.

52. caitiff: miserable.

57. *What actions do you imagine Romeo is engaged in as he delivers this speech about the apothecary?*

60. gear: stuff.

63. trunk: body.

A Elements of Literature

Irony and Foreshadowing
Ironically, Romeo has a premonition of good news at the same moment a messenger is arriving to tell him of Juliet's "death." Part of his dream, however, does foreshadow tragic events. Juliet will find Romeo dead and will kiss him —but will not bring him back to life.

B Critical Thinking

Making Connections
By defying the stars, Romeo seems to be resisting the tragic fate that was predicted for the "star-crossed lovers" in the Act I Prologue. In fact, rather than mourn Juliet's death, he is planning to be united with her in death. He sees this union in death as a triumph over fate.

C Reading Skills and Strategies

Drawing Conclusions
? Why might the apothecary be willing to sell the illegal poison to Romeo? [The apothecary is in desperate need of money and has little to lose if caught by the authorities. Note that Romeo's descriptions of the man stress his poverty.]

D Historical Connections

The ducat was a gold coin of considerable value. A fluid dram was equal to one eighth of a fluid ounce. In England the word *dram* came to mean any small drink of alcohol.

E Appreciating Language

Figures of Speech: Simile
This simile compares the speed of death by poison to the speed of a fired cannonball. It also continues the imagery of sudden, brief flashes of light that can be destructive.

Answers to Margin Questions
Line 16. Balthasar, bearing bad news, is reluctant to answer his master; he may be avoiding Romeo's gaze.
Line 23. Juliet is not dead.
Line 26. Some students will favor defiance, based on Romeo's rash vitality. Others will favor subdued defeat, citing the sad death of his dreams.
Line 29. Romeo looks "pale and wild," like a man distraught and out of control.
Line 31. Romeo is hoping for word that he may return to Verona.
Line 34. Romeo sets out to buy poison to kill himself with. He plunges directly into action.
Line 57. Romeo might be walking toward or looking for the apothecary's house.

Reaching All Students

Struggling Readers
Use the Language Link Mini-Lesson on Figures of Speech (pp. 858–859), as well as the side notes in your teacher's edition, to help students interpret Shakespeare's similes, metaphors, personifications, and puns.

English Language Learners
To aid comprehension and convey the atmosphere of Act V, have students view the final scene of Zeffirelli's *Romeo and Juliet* or the end of the film *West Side Story*.

Advanced Learners
These students will be able to appreciate the play's multiple themes and layers of meaning. They may enjoy an extended debate on the First Thoughts question in Making Meanings (p. 855) about the relative importance of fate and free will as causes of the tragedy.

ⒶCritical Thinking
Evaluating

❓ Do you agree with Romeo's argument that a poor man is entitled to break the law in order to survive? [Some students will say that the ends never justify the means. Others will say that desperate people are entitled to use desperate measures to survive.]

ⒷReading Skills and Strategies

Paraphrasing and Context Clues

❓ Judging by the context of this situation, what do you think the words "dispatch you straight" mean? [kill you immediately]

Answers to Margin Questions
Line 74. Romeo argues that the "world's law" is not conducive to the man's well-being; he is poor and almost dead. If the apothecary defies the law, he will have money and live.

Line 79. Romeo could have shown the apothecary the coins in his purse; the apothecary could have taken the poison from a shelf.

Line 83. Romeo says that gold is poison to the soul.

Line 86. Romeo's verbal irony is that the poison, because it will reunite him with Juliet, is really a restorative medicine.

Summary ■

Act V, Scene 2
Friar Laurence learns that his messenger, Friar John, was unable to deliver to Romeo the letter explaining Juliet's coma. The friar sets off for the Capulet tomb, afraid that Juliet, who is to revive within three hours, will awaken alone.

Answer to Margin Question
Line 3. The audience might wonder whether Friar John did reach Romeo or whether the friar perhaps found Romeo after he left the apothecary.

Apothecary.
  Such mortal drugs I have; but Mantua's law
  Is death to any he that utters° them.
Romeo.
  ⎡Art thou so bare and full of wretchedness
  And fear'st to die? Famine is in thy cheeks,
70 Need and oppression starveth in thy eyes,
Ⓐ Contempt and beggary hangs upon thy back:
  The world is not thy friend, nor the world's law;
  The world affords no law to make thee rich;
  ⎣Then be not poor, but break it and take this.
Apothecary.
75 My poverty but not my will consents.
Romeo.
  I pay thy poverty and not thy will.
Apothecary.
  ⎡Put this in any liquid thing you will
Ⓑ And drink it off, and if you had the strength
  ⎣Of twenty men, it would dispatch you straight.
Romeo.
80 There is thy gold—worse poison to men's souls,
  Doing more murder in this loathsome world,
  Than these poor compounds that thou mayst not sell.
  I sell thee poison; thou has sold me none.
  Farewell. Buy food and get thyself in flesh.
85 Come, cordial and not poison, go with me
  To Juliet's grave; for there must I use thee.   [*Exeunt.*]

Scene 2. *Friar Laurence's cell.*

Enter FRIAR JOHN.

John.
  Holy Franciscan friar, brother, ho!

[*Enter* FRIAR LAURENCE.]

Laurence.
  This same should be the voice of Friar John.
  Welcome from Mantua. What says Romeo?
  Or, if his mind be writ, give me his letter.
John.
5 Going to find a barefoot brother out,
  One of our order, to associate° me
  Here in this city visiting the sick,
  And finding him, the searchers° of the town,
  Suspecting that we both were in a house

67. utters: sells.

❓ **74.** *What argument does Romeo use to persuade the apothecary to break the law?*

❓ **79.** *What actions do you think have taken place before the apothecary gives Romeo instructions for taking the poison?*

❓ **83.** *What "poison" has Romeo "sold" the apothecary?*

❓ **86.** *Why does Romeo call the poison a cordial, which is a kind of medicine that restores the heartbeat?*

❓ **3.** *In the previous scene, we learned that Romeo had received no letters from the friar. How would the friar's question immediately put questions in the minds of the audience?*
6. associate: accompany.

8. searchers: health officers.

10   Where the infectious pestilence did reign,
       Sealed up the doors, and would not let us forth,
       So that my speed to Mantua there was stayed.

Laurence.
       Who bare my letter, then, to Romeo?

John.
       I could not send it—here it is again—
15   Nor get a messenger to bring it thee,
       So fearful were they of infection.

Laurence.
       Unhappy fortune! By my brotherhood,
       The letter was not nice,° but full of charge,°
       Of dear import; and the neglecting it
20   May do much danger. Friar John, go hence,
       Get me an iron crow and bring it straight
       Unto my cell.

John.   Brother, I'll go and bring it thee.   [*Exit.*]

Laurence.
       Now must I to the monument alone.
       Within this three hours will fair Juliet wake.
25   She will beshrew me much that Romeo
       Hath had no notice of these accidents;°
       But I will write again to Mantua,
       And keep her at my cell till Romeo come—
       Poor living corse, closed in a dead man's tomb!   [*Exit.*]

Scene 3. *A churchyard; in it, a monument belonging to the Capulets.*

Enter PARIS *and his* PAGE *with flowers and scented water.*

Paris.
       Give me thy torch, boy. Hence, and stand aloof.
       Yet put it out, for I would not be seen.
       Under yond yew trees lay thee all along,°
       Holding the ear close to the hollow ground.
5   So shall no foot upon the churchyard tread
       (Being loose, unfirm, with digging up of graves)
       But thou shalt hear it. Whistle then to me,
       As signal that thou hear'st something approach.
       Give me those flowers. Do as I bid thee, go.

Page (*aside*).
10   I am almost afraid to stand alone
       Here in the churchyard; yet I will adventure.°
                                [*Retires.*]

---

16. *Another accident! Why was the friar's letter never delivered to Romeo?*

18. nice: trivial. **charge:** importance.

26. accidents: happenings.

29. *If we can accept the "accidents of fate," we have here something like a chase scene. We know, but the friar does not, that Romeo also is on his way to the tomb. Why is it essential that the friar get there first?*

3. all along: at full length (on the ground).

9. *Paris is a surprise. He adds an interesting complication, as well as some action, to this scene. He and his servant, probably wearing dark cloaks, enter on the upper stage. Paris makes his way alone into the tomb or vault. Why is Paris here?*

11. adventure: risk it.

THE TRAGEDY OF ROMEO AND JULIET, ACT V, SCENE 3   **839**

C Historical Connections
In the late 1500s, the bubonic plague was the leading cause of death in London. The mayor often closed theaters temporarily to control its spread.

D Reading Skills and Strategies
Making Predictions
Do you think Friar Laurence's adjustments to the plan will work? **Explain.** [Sample responses: Yes, there is still time for him to greet Juliet when she awakens; no, Romeo may get to the tomb first and kill himself before he realizes that Juliet is not truly dead.]

Answers to Margin Questions
Line 16. Friar John was quarantined in someone's house when authorities suspected it of being contaminated by the plague. They would not let the letter be delivered by another messenger.
Line 29. If Romeo arrives and thinks Juliet is dead, he will kill himself.

Summary ■ ■ ■

Act V, Scene 3
Paris, at the Capulet tomb to strew flowers and scented water, sees Romeo and tries to apprehend him. Romeo warns Paris to leave him alone, but Paris ignores him. They fight and Paris is killed. Romeo, who perceives Paris, like himself, as a victim of fortune, lays him in the tomb. Romeo delivers a soliloquy in which he praises Juliet's beauty; he then drinks the poison and dies. The friar arrives, and when Juliet awakens, he tells her that Romeo and Paris are dead. The friar hears the watch approach and leaves, but Juliet will not leave with him. Left alone, she first attempts to kill herself by kissing Romeo, hoping that poison lingers on his lips. When this fails, she picks up Romeo's dagger and stabs herself. The watch enters; they discover the dead bodies, round up the friar and Balthasar, and summon the Capulets, the Montagues, and the prince. The friar explains what has happened. Balthasar presents a letter, given to him by Romeo and addressed to Lord Montague, which confirms the friar's explanation. The prince blames the Montagues and the Capulets for causing their children's deaths, and the repentant families are reconciled.

Answer to Margin Question
Line 9. Paris has come to place flowers and scented water on Juliet's bier. (ll. 9 and 12–14)

Skill Link

Finding Imperative Sentences
Remind students that an imperative sentence is one that makes a request or gives a command. The subject of an imperative sentence is always understood to be *you*, although the word *you* does not usually appear in the sentence.

Activity
1. Have students find six imperative sentences in Paris's speech to his page in ll. 1–9 of Scene 3.

2. Now have students find five imperative sentences in Romeo's orders to Balthasar in ll. 22–39 of Scene 3.
3. Ask students how many imperative sentences they can find in Romeo's speech to Paris in ll. 58–67 of Scene 3.

Paris.

Sweet flower, with flowers thy bridal bed I strew
(O woe! thy canopy is dust and stones)
Which with sweet water nightly I will dew;

15   Or, wanting that, with tears distilled by moans.
The obsequies° that I for thee will keep
Nightly shall be to strew thy grave and weep.

[BOY *whistles.*]

The boy gives warning something doth approach.
What cursèd foot wanders this way tonight

20   To cross° my obsequies and true love's rite?
What, with a torch? Muffle° me, night, awhile.

[*Retires.*]

[*Enter* ROMEO *and* BALTHASAR *with a torch, a mattock, and a crowbar of iron.*]

Romeo.

Give me that mattock and the wrenching iron.
A Hold, take this letter. Early in the morning
See thou deliver it to my lord and father.

25   Give me the light. Upon thy life I charge thee,
Whate'er thou hearest or see'st, stand all aloof
And do not interrupt me in my course.
Why I descend into this bed of death
Is partly to behold my lady's face,

30   But chiefly to take thence from her dead finger
A precious ring—a ring that I must use
In dear employment.° Therefore hence, be gone.
But if thou, jealous,° dost return to pry
In what I farther shall intend to do,

35   **B** By heaven, I will tear thee joint by joint
And strew this hungry churchyard with thy limbs.
The time and my intents are savage-wild,
More fierce and more inexorable far
Than empty tigers or the roaring sea.
Balthasar.

40   I will be gone, sir, and not trouble ye.
Romeo.
So shalt thou show me friendship. Take thou that.
Live, and be prosperous; and farewell, good fellow.
Balthasar (*aside*).
For all this same, I'll hide me hereabout.
His looks I fear, and his intents I doubt.   [*Retires.*]
Romeo.

45   **C** Thou detestable maw,° thou womb of death,
Gorged with the dearest morsel of the earth,

Getting Students Involved

Thus I enforce thy rotten jaws to open,
And in despite° I'll cram thee with more food.

[ROMEO *opens the tomb.*]

Paris.

This is that banished haughty Montague
50 That murd'red my love's cousin—with which grief
It is supposed the fair creature died—
And here is come to do some villainous shame
To the dead bodies. I will apprehend him.
Stop thy unhallowèd toil, vile Montague!
55 Can vengeance be pursued further than death?
Condemnèd villain, I do apprehend thee.
Obey, and go with me; for thou must die.

Romeo.

I must indeed; and therefore came I hither.
Good gentle youth, tempt not a desp'rate man.
60 Fly hence and leave me. Think upon these gone;
Let them affright thee. I beseech thee, youth,
Put not another sin upon my head
By urging me to fury. O, be gone!
By heaven, I love thee better than myself,
65 For I come hither armed against myself.
Stay not, be gone. Live, and hereafter say
A madman's mercy bid thee run away.

Paris.

I do defy thy conjurations°
And apprehend thee for a felon here.

Romeo.

70 Wilt thou provoke me? Then have at thee, boy!

[*They fight.*]

Page.

O Lord, they fight! I will go call the watch.
             [*Exit.* PARIS *falls.*]

Paris.

O, I am slain! If thou be merciful,
Open the tomb, lay me with Juliet.   [*Dies.*]

Romeo.

In faith, I will. Let me peruse this face.
75 Mercutio's kinsman, noble County Paris!
What said my man when my betossèd soul
Did not attend° him as we rode? I think
He told me Paris should have married Juliet.
Said he not so, or did I dream it so?
80 Or am I mad, hearing him talk of Juliet,
To think it was so? O, give me thy hand,
One writ with me in sour misfortune's book!

THE TRAGEDY OF ROMEO AND JULIET, ACT V, SCENE 3 841

48. **in despite:** to spite you.
48. *Whom or what is Romeo talking to here? What is he doing? What "food" is he going to feed this "maw"?*

51. *What was believed to be the cause of Juliet's sudden "death"?*

54. *What does Paris do as he speaks this line?*

67. *Romeo doesn't attempt even to fight Paris. How do his words here show calmness and maturity?*
68. **conjurations:** solemn orders.

70. *What has Paris done to provoke Romeo?*

74. *Whatever we thought of Paris before, we understand now that he loved Juliet. What does Romeo do here?*
77. **attend:** pay attention to.

82. *Remember that Romeo has spoken of himself as "fortune's fool." Why does he see Paris as another victim?*

D Reading Skills and Strategies

Paraphrasing and Context Clues
Ask students to paraphrase Paris's speech. [Possible paraphrase: There's that criminal Romeo who murdered Tybalt. He's also responsible for Juliet's death, since she died of grief for her dead cousin. He's probably come here to desecrate the bodies of Tybalt and Juliet. I'll stop the villain and bring him to justice.]

E Reading Skills and Strategies
Drawing Conclusions
? How do we know that Romeo's reason for killing Paris is not jealousy or retribution for causing Juliet's death? [Romeo doesn't even recognize Paris until after Paris is dead. Only then does Romeo vaguely recall that his messenger told him that Juliet was to have married Paris.]

Answers to Margin Questions
Line 48. Romeo is talking to the tomb as he pries it open, promising to feed it his own body.
Line 51. It is supposed that Juliet died of grief over Tybalt's death.
Line 54. Paris may draw his sword as he commands Romeo to stop digging. He is trying to arrest Romeo, who is a "Condemnèd villain" under the prince's order.
Line 67. Romeo is thinking clearly of the consequences of his actions and tries to reason with Paris, wanting to prevent at least one needless death.
Line 70. Despite Romeo's warning Paris to "tempt not a desp'rate man" (l. 59), Paris tries again to arrest him. Romeo cannot restrain himself.
Line 74. Romeo only now recognizes Paris and recalls, vaguely, that Balthasar said Juliet was to have married Paris. Romeo seizes Paris's hand and promises to lay him with Juliet.
Line 82. Paris had the misfortune of arriving at the tomb at precisely the wrong moment; he has lost both Juliet and his life.

❓ Does this image of light create a positive or negative effect? [Students may say that even in the darkness of the tomb and death, the beauty of love brings a positive note to the tragedy.] Have students refer to the notes they have been keeping on the light and darkness imagery in the play. Ask them to identify each of these images as positive, negative, or a combination of the two.

B **Elements of Literature**

Figures of Speech: Personification

Death is once again personified as a jealous lover who keeps Juliet in the dark tomb because she is so beautiful.

C **Elements of Literature**

Climax

With Romeo's suicide, the climax of the play begins. The tragic deaths of the "star-crossed lovers," announced in the Act I Prologue and foreshadowed throughout the play, are now being realized.

Answers to Margin Questions

Line 87. Romeo says that Juliet's "beauty makes / This vault a feasting presence full of light." Romeo, who is determined to kill himself, is the dead man.

Line 97. Romeo asks forgiveness and offers his own body as a recompense for the murder.

Line 102. Romeo exclaims at Juliet's lifelike beauty in ll. 92–96 and 102.

Line 108. Romeo embraces Juliet (l. 113) and kisses her (l. 114).

Line 120. Students should consider the setting, Romeo's characterization so far, and the punctuation and images in the speech.

I'll bury thee in a triumphant grave.
A grave? O, no, a lanthorn,° slaught'red youth,
85 For here lies Juliet, and her beauty makes
This vault a feasting presence full of light.
Death, lie thou there, by a dead man interred.

[*Lays him in the tomb.*]

How oft when men are at the point of death
Have they been merry! Which their keepers° call
90 A lightning before death. O, how may I
Call this a lightning? O my love, my wife!
Death, that hath sucked the honey of thy breath,
Hath had no power yet upon thy beauty.
Thou art not conquered. Beauty's ensign° yet
95 Is crimson in thy lips and in thy cheeks,
And death's pale flag is not advancèd there.
Tybalt, liest thou there in the bloody sheet?
O, what more favor can I do to thee
Than with that hand that cut thy youth in twain
100 To sunder his that was thine enemy?
Forgive me, cousin! Ah, dear Juliet,
Why art thou yet so fair? Shall I believe
That unsubstantial Death is amorous,
And that the lean abhorrèd monster keeps
105 Thee here in dark to be his paramour?
For fear of that I still will stay with thee
And never from this pallet of dim night
Depart again. Here, here will I remain
With worms that are thy chambermaids. O, here
110 Will I set up my everlasting rest
And shake the yoke of inauspicious stars
From this world-wearied flesh. Eyes, look your last!
Arms, take your last embrace! And, lips, O you
The doors of breath, seal with a righteous kiss
115 A dateless° bargain to engrossing° death!
Come, bitter conduct;° come, unsavory guide!
Thou desperate pilot,° now at once run on
The dashing rocks thy seasick weary bark!
Here's to my love! (*Drinks.*) O true apothecary!
120 Thy drugs are quick. Thus with a kiss I die.

[*Falls.*]

[*Enter* FRIAR LAURENCE, *with lanthorn, crowbar, and spade.*]

Friar.
Saint Francis be my speed! How oft tonight
Have my old feet stumbled at graves! Who's there?

842 WILLIAM SHAKESPEARE

---

84. lanthorn: a windowed dome.

❓ **87.** *Romeo, dragging Paris's body across the stage, now sees Juliet. What words indicate that he sees the tomb transformed? Who is the "dead man" in line 87?*
89. keepers: jailers.

94. ensign: flag (signal).

❓ **97.** *Romeo turns to see Tybalt's body. Is he angry at his enemy, or does he ask forgiveness?*

❓ **102.** *Where in this speech does Romeo see life in Juliet, reminding us that she is not dead?*

❓ **108.** *Romeo has climbed to Juliet's tomb and lies beside her. What other actions do you see him doing here?*

115. dateless: timeless. **engrossing:** all-encompassing.
116. conduct: guide (the poison).
117. desperate pilot: Romeo himself.

❓ **120.** *Actors playing Romeo interpret this last speech in different ways: Some play him as if he is in a dream; others as if he were mad; others as if he is in full control of himself; others as if he is desperate and out of his mind with grief, desire, and fear. What clues would direct the way you'd interpret Romeo's feelings as he gives his final speech?*

Professional Notes

Critical Comment: Antitheses

Director and Shakespeare scholar John Barton says the key to understanding Shakespeare's plays is seeing the ever-shifting pattern of antitheses, or contradictions, in the characters' language and thinking. "If you don't . . . play with the antitheses, a great deal of Shakespeare becomes difficult to follow," he claims. "If you do go with it, he's much easier to follow and enjoy."

The progression of light and darkness imagery is one example of the play of contradictions in the tragedy. Sometimes darkness is the friend of lovers; sometimes it foreshadows death and despair. Love is seen as a brief flash of light in the darkness, but daylight is dull and unromantic.

In Act V, Romeo struggles with the contradictions of fate and free will. By willingly embracing his fate rather than fighting it, Romeo believes he triumphs over fate and is able to "shake the yoke of inauspicious stars" (l. 111).

Balthasar.
　　Here's one, a friend, and one that knows you well.
Friar.
　　Bliss be upon you! Tell me, good my friend,
125　　What torch is yond that vainly lends his light
　　To grubs and eyeless skulls? As I discern,
　　It burneth in the Capels' monument.
Balthasar.
　　It doth so, holy sir; and there's my master,
　　One that you love.
Friar.　　　　　　Who is it?
Balthasar.　　　　　　　　　Romeo.
Friar.
　　How long hath he been there?
130　**Balthasar.**　　　　　　　　Full half an hour.
Friar.
　　Go with me to the vault.
Balthasar.　　　　　　I dare not, sir.
　　My master knows not but I am gone hence,
　　And fearfully did menace me with death
　　If I did stay to look on his intents.
Friar.
135　　Stay then; I'll go alone. Fear comes upon me.
　　O, much I fear some ill unthrifty° thing.

❓ 130. *What feelings must the friar reveal when he hears that Romeo has gotten to the tomb before he has heard of the plan to drug Juliet?*

136. unthrifty: unlucky.

❝ Ah, dear Juliet, Why art thou yet so fair? ❞

Listening to Music

Romeo and Juliet by Sergei Prokofiev

The Russian composer Sergei Prokofiev (1891–1953) excelled in all manner of musical compositions, from orchestral compositions like his *Classical Symphony* and *Violin Concerto No. 1* to the choral work *Alexander Nevsky* to the four part ballet *Romeo and Juliet* to the children's fantasy *Peter and the Wolf.* Prokofiev was still a teenager when he began winning fame as an unconventional pianist and composer. In 1918, with several masterpieces to his credit, he left Russia in the wake of the communist revolution, making America and then France his adoptive homes. By the mid-1930s, however, he reconciled with his homeland and agreed to return. *Romeo and Juliet* premiered soon afterward with Russia's world-famous Bolshoi Ballet.

Activity
Encourage interested students to listen to Prokofiev's ballet and choreograph their own dance or mime show acting out *Romeo and Juliet* to the music.

Ask students to paraphrase the friar's
speech. [Possible paraphrase: I hear the
watch approaching. Juliet, you must leave
this burial vault. It is not a place for living
beings. Our original intentions have not
worked out as planned, but we must
accept what has happened. Your beloved
Romeo and Paris are dead. I will take
you to a convent. You must leave immediately, Juliet. I myself am too frightened
to remain here.]

B Elements of Literature

Climax

With the death of Juliet, the full climax
of the play is realized. The remainder
of the play will depict the resolution, in
which the loose parts of the plot are
all tied up.

Answers to Margin Questions
Line 141. The friar is at the entrance
of the tomb.
Line 147. The friar might feel sad,
guilty, fearful, and trapped by
circumstances.
Line 152. The friar panics; he wants
to leave before he and Juliet are
discovered.
Line 159. The friar wants to take Juliet
to a convent but Juliet refuses to leave.
She may be standing amazed over
Romeo or holding and kissing him.
Line 160. To indicate his distraught
condition, the friar might dash madly
between Juliet and the tomb's entrance
and have a frantic edge to his pleading.

Balthasar.
  As I did sleep under this yew tree here,
  I dreamt my master and another fought,
  And that my master slew him.
Friar.   Romeo!
140 Alack, alack, what blood is this which stains
  The stony entrance of this sepulcher?
  What mean these masterless and gory swords
  To lie discolored by this place of peace?

[*Enters the tomb.*]

145 Romeo! O, pale! Who else? What, Paris too?
  And steeped in blood? Ah, what an unkind° hour
  Is guilty of this lamentable chance!
  The lady stirs.

[JULIET *rises.*]

Juliet.
  O comfortable° friar! Where is my lord?
  I do remember well where I should be,
150 And there I am. Where is my Romeo?
Friar.
  I hear some noise. Lady, come from that nest
  Of death, contagion, and unnatural sleep.
  A greater power than we can contradict
  Hath thwarted our intents. Come, come away.
155 **A** Thy husband in thy bosom there lies dead;
  And Paris too. Come, I'll dispose of thee
  Among a sisterhood of holy nuns.
  Stay not to question, for the watch is coming.
  Come, go, good Juliet. I dare no longer stay.
Juliet.
160 Go, get thee hence, for I will not away.

                              [*Exit* FRIAR.]

  What's here? A cup, closed in my truelove's hand?
  Poison, I see, hath been his timeless° end.
  O churl!° Drunk all, and left no friendly drop
  To help me after? I will kiss thy lips.
165 Haply some poison yet doth hang on them
  To make me die with a restorative.

[*Kisses him.*]

  Thy lips are warm!
Chief Watchman (*within*). Lead, boy. Which way?
B **Juliet.**
  Yea, noise? Then I'll be brief. O happy° dagger!

[*Snatches Romeo's dagger.*]

844 WILLIAM SHAKESPEARE

? **141.** *Where is the friar as he discovers the bloodstains?*

145. unkind: unnatural.

? **147.** *This short line suggests that the friar rushes to Juliet and waits for her to speak. What must his feelings be?*

148. comfortable: comforting.

? **152.** *For the friar, this is a terrible moment. What is his reaction to the noise he hears?*

? **159.** *What does the friar say will become of Juliet? What is Juliet doing, or refusing to do, as the friar repeatedly tries to move her?*

? **160.** *It is hard to believe that after all his concern for these two young lovers, the friar would become a coward at this moment and leave Juliet to harm herself. How must the friar act here to persuade us that he is frantic and not very sensible?*
162. timeless: untimely.
163. churl: rude fellow (spoken teasingly).

169. happy: lucky (to be here when she needs it).

T844

" O happy dagger!
This is thy sheath; there rust, and let me die. "

RESPONDING TO THE ART

Activity. Ask students to compare this photograph with the one on p. 825. Have students point out the similarities and the differences between the photos. [Juliet is in a similar position in both photos—kneeling, with head upturned, and seen in profile. However, she is hopeful in the earlier photograph and full of despair in this one.]

Crossing the Curriculum

Music

Students interested in music can compile a set of songs that have love or lost love as a theme. Students can read excerpts from the play aloud with the music playing softly in the background to create the proper mood.

History

Point out to students that scholars believe that Shakespeare wrote many of his sonnets and other poems while theaters in London were temporarily closed due to outbreaks of bubonic plague. Students can research and report on the plague's effect on European civilization during the Middle Ages and the Renaissance or concentrate specifically on the plague in London during Shakespeare's time.

Art

Students can create a board game by making a playing board with five squares on each side. Several squares can have scenes from the play drawn on them for decoration and reinforcement. Have students write question cards about the events and characters in the play. Each player must draw a card and answer the question before advancing in the game.

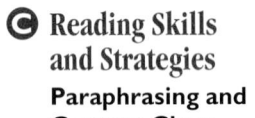

A Critical Thinking
Analyzing Tone
What tone of voice would the chief watchman probably use to make this observation about Juliet? [He would probably sound completely amazed to discover that someone believed to have been dead for two days now appears "bleeding, warm, and newly dead."]

B Elements of Literature
Resolution
Everyone but the audience and Friar Laurence is completely puzzled by this mysterious and tragic turn of events. They are crying out for an explanation.

C Reading Skills and Strategies
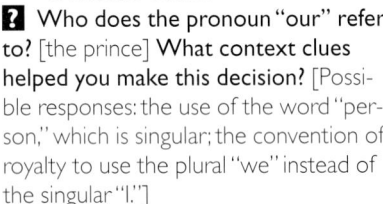
Paraphrasing and Context Clues
❓ Who does the pronoun "our" refer to? [the prince] What context clues helped you make this decision? [Possible responses: the use of the word "person," which is singular; the convention of royalty to use the plural "we" instead of the singular "I."]

Answers to Margin Questions
Stage direction. Students' responses will vary. However, if Juliet is merely crazed, her suicide becomes a weaker statement of her love for Romeo. The audience is well prepared for Juliet's suicide; her death scene is probably best played as the acting out of a conscious decision to achieve her reunion with Romeo, although an actress may be able to portray her as both calm and mad with love.
Line 184. Friar Laurence is distraught and confused, still carrying his tools for opening the tomb.
Line 193. She suggests that the outcry indicates that something terrible involving Romeo, Juliet, and Paris has taken place in the Capulets' tomb.

170 This is thy sheath; there rust, and let me die.

[*She stabs herself and falls.*]

[*Enter Paris's* BOY *and* WATCH.]

Boy.
 This is the place. There, where the torch doth burn.
Chief Watchman.
 The ground is bloody. Search about the churchyard.
 Go, some of you; whoe'er you find attach.
  [*Exeunt some of the* WATCH.]
 Pitiful sight! Here lies the county slain;

175 And Juliet bleeding, warm, and newly dead,
 Who here hath lain this two days buried.
 Go, tell the prince; run to the Capulets;
 Raise up the Montagues; some others search.
  [*Exeunt others of the* WATCH.]
 We see the ground whereon these woes do lie,

180 But the true ground° of all these piteous woes
 We cannot without circumstance° descry.

[*Enter some of the* WATCH, *with Romeo's man* BALTHASAR.]

Second Watchman.
 Here's Romeo's man. We found him in the churchyard.
Chief Watchman.
 Hold him in safety till the prince come hither.

[*Enter* FRIAR LAURENCE *and another* WATCHMAN.]

Third Watchman.
 Here is a friar that trembles, sighs, and weeps.
185 We took this mattock and this spade from him
 As he was coming from this churchyard's side.
Chief Watchman.
 A great suspicion! Stay the friar too.

[*Enter the* PRINCE *and* ATTENDANTS.]

Prince.
 What misadventure is so early up,
 That calls our person from our morning rest?

[*Enter* CAPULET *and his wife,* LADY CAPULET, *with others.*]

Capulet.
190 What should it be, that is so shrieked abroad?
Lady Capulet.
 O, the people in the street cry "Romeo,"
 Some "Juliet," and some "Paris"; and all run
 With open outcry toward our monument.

846 WILLIAM SHAKESPEARE

❓ **Stage direction:** *Do you see Juliet in her last moments as being half-crazed, or calm and purposeful, or something else? Do you think this scene can be played only one way? Or can it be played several ways? How would you play the scene?*

180. **ground:** cause.
181. **circumstance:** details.

❓ **184.** *How do the watchman's words help us picture the state the friar is in?*

❓ **193.** *As the tomb begins to fill up with people, noises and cries are heard offstage. What does Lady Capulet suggest is being "shrieked abroad" in Verona?*

Listening to Music 🎵

Romeo and Juliet Overture by Peter Ilyich Tchaikovsky

Russian composer Peter Ilyich Tchaikovsky (1840–1893) achieved musical greatness despite a highly unstable personality. In fact, several of his compositions, like his famed *Symphonie pathétique,* seem to draw on the mental instability from which he suffered. In 1891, Tchaikovsky made a celebrated trip to America, helping to open New York's Carnegie Hall by conducting his *1812 Overture* there. His other masterpieces include the ballets *The Nutcracker, Swan Lake, Sleeping Beauty,* and *Romeo and Juliet* and the opera *Eugene Onegin.*

Activity
Ask students to try to follow this summary as they listen to Tchaikovsky's overture: After a solemn woodwind introduction describing Friar Laurence, a furious storm of music captures the Capulet-Montague feud. Next comes the love music of Romeo and the response from Juliet, played by the strings. Their love is shattered by the return of the feud music, over which their melodies can at times be heard. The final tragedy, signaled by rumbling kettledrums and a sudden silence, is followed by an epilogue expressing grief over the lovers' death.

Prince.
    What fear is this which startles in your ears?
Chief Watchman.
195   Sovereign, here lies the County Paris slain;
    And Romeo dead; and Juliet, dead before,
    Warm and new killed.
Prince.
    Search, seek, and know how this foul murder comes.
Chief Watchman.
    Here is a friar, and slaughtered Romeo's man,
200   With instruments upon them fit to open
    These dead men's tombs.
Capulet.
    O heavens! O wife, look how our daughter bleeds!
    This dagger hath mista'en, for, lo, his house°
    Is empty on the back of Montague,
205   And it missheathèd in my daughter's bosom!
Lady Capulet.
    O me, this sight of death is as a bell
    That warns° my old age to a sepulcher. **D**

[*Enter* MONTAGUE *and others.*]

Prince.
    Come, Montague; for thou art early up
    To see thy son and heir more early down.
Montague.
210   Alas, my liege, my wife is dead tonight!
    Grief of my son's exile hath stopped her breath. **E**
    What further woe conspires against mine age?
Prince.
    Look, and thou shalt see.
Montague.
    O thou untaught! What manners is in this,
215   To press before thy father to a grave?
Prince.
    Seal up the mouth of outrage for a while,
    Till we can clear these ambiguities
    And know their spring, their head, their true descent;
    And then will I be general of your woes°
220   And lead you even to death. Meantime forbear,
    And let mischance be slave to patience.
    Bring forth the parties of suspicion. **F**
Friar.
    I am the greatest, able to do least,
    Yet most suspected, as the time and place
225   Doth make against me, of this direful murder;
    And here I stand, both to impeach and purge°
    Myself condemnèd and myself excused.

203. house: sheath.

207. warns: summons.

? **215.** *Whom is Montague talking to here?*

219. general of your woes: leader of your mourning.

226. impeach and purge: charge and punish.

THE TRAGEDY OF ROMEO AND JULIET, ACT V, SCENE 3 847

D **Elements of Literature**
Figures of Speech: Simile
? What thought does Lady Capulet express through the use of this simile? [that seeing the corpses of the young Romeo and Juliet makes her feel the approach of her own death]

E **Critical Thinking**
Making Connections
Remind students that Lady Montague tried to keep her husband from participating in the feud in Act I. She may have been more emotionally distressed by the banishment of Romeo than anyone but Juliet.

F **Elements of Literature**
Resolution
The Prince now demands an explanation of how these tragedies came about, and Friar Laurence, the only character still living who knows the whole story, steps forward to explain.

Answer to Margin Question
Line 215. Montague is speaking to Romeo.

❓ Is the friar's summary of the plot both brief and accurate? How might you have improved it? [Answers will vary. The summary is hardly brief, but the friar has a complicated story to explain and hits all the main points the other characters need to know.]

B Elements of Literature

Resolution

❓ Do you think the prince will punish Friar Laurence for his involvement in the tragedy? [probably not] Do you think Friar Laurence deserves punishment? [Possible responses: Yes, because he controlled the fate of Romeo and Juliet and offered misguided advice; no, because he only tried to do what he thought was God's will—he wanted the feuding families to make peace.]

Answers to Margin Questions
Line 230. Students might suggest the families would cry out when they learn that Romeo and Juliet were married and that Juliet threatened to kill herself, as well as when the friar describes Romeo's and Juliet's deaths.
Line 237. The friar is referring to Lord Capulet.
Line 261. Have students identify the "trials" that Romeo and Juliet faced. Then have them identify the impatience of the adults. This question serves as an excellent review of conflict in the play.
Line 269. Friar Laurence says that if the prince decides it was his fault that the plan miscarried, he accepts responsibility and is willing to die as punishment.

Prince.
  Then say at once what thou dost know in this.

Friar.
  I will be brief, for my short date of breath°
230 Is not so long as is a tedious tale.
  Romeo, there dead, was husband to that Juliet;
  And she, there dead, that Romeo's faithful wife.
  I married them; and their stolen marriage day
  Was Tybalt's doomsday, whose untimely death
235 Banished the new-made bridegroom from this city;
  For whom, and not for Tybalt, Juliet pined.
  You, to remove that siege of grief from her,
  Betrothed and would have married her perforce
  To County Paris. Then comes she to me
240 And with wild looks bid me devise some mean
  To rid her from this second marriage,
  Or in my cell there would she kill herself.
  Then gave I her (so tutored by my art)
  A sleeping potion; which so took effect
245 As I intended, for it wrought on her
  The form of death. Meantime I writ to Romeo
  That he should hither come as° this dire night
  To help to take her from her borrowed grave,
A Being the time the potion's force should cease.
250 But he which bore my letter, Friar John,
  Was stayed by accident, and yesternight
  Returned my letter back. Then all alone
  At the prefixèd hour of her waking
  Came I to take her from her kindred's vault,
255 Meaning to keep her closely at my cell
  Till I conveniently could send to Romeo.
  But when I came, some minute ere the time
  Of her awakening, here untimely lay
  The noble Paris and true Romeo dead.
260 She wakes; and I entreated her come forth
  And bear this work of heaven with patience;
  But then a noise did scare me from the tomb,
  And she, too desperate, would not go with me,
  But, as it seems, did violence on herself.
265 All this I know, and to the marriage
  Her nurse is privy;° and if aught in this
  Miscarried by my fault, let my old life
  Be sacrificed some hour before his time
  Unto the rigor of severest law.

Prince.
270 **B** We still° have known thee for a holy man.
  Where's Romeo's man? What can he say to this?

229. date of breath: term of life.
❓ **230.** *All of what the friar says here is known by the audience. In some productions, this long speech is cut entirely, but it is important for us to imagine the effect the speech has on the Montagues, the Capulets, and the prince. This is the moment when they discover what we've known all along. Where do you think the friar must pause as the families cry out and weep?*
❓ **237.** *Whom does the friar mean by "you"?*

247. as: on.

❓ **261.** *This line expresses the friar's view of life. How would the play have been different if both Romeo and Juliet had been able, from the start, to bear their trials "with patience"? How does this also apply to the adults in the play?*
266. to the marriage . . . privy: The nurse knows about the marriage.
❓ **269.** *Does the friar accept responsibility for his part in the tragedy? What does he say?*
270. still: always.

Professional Notes

Critical Comment: Unintended Harm

To critic Bertrand Evans, this play is about the harm people can unknowingly do each other, not realizing the chain of tragic events they perpetuate: "More than any other play of Shakespeare's—even more than *Othello,* as a count of pertinent data shows—*Romeo and Juliet* is a tragedy of unawareness. Fate, or Heaven, as the prince calls it, or the "greater power," as the friar calls it, working out its purpose without the use of either a human villain or a super-natural agent sent to intervene in mortal affairs, operates through the common human condition of not knowing. Participants in the action, some of them in parts that are minor and seem insignificant, contribute one by one the indispensable stitches which make the pattern, and contribute them not knowing; that is to say, they act when they do not know the truth of the situation in which they act, this truth being known, however, to us who are spectators."

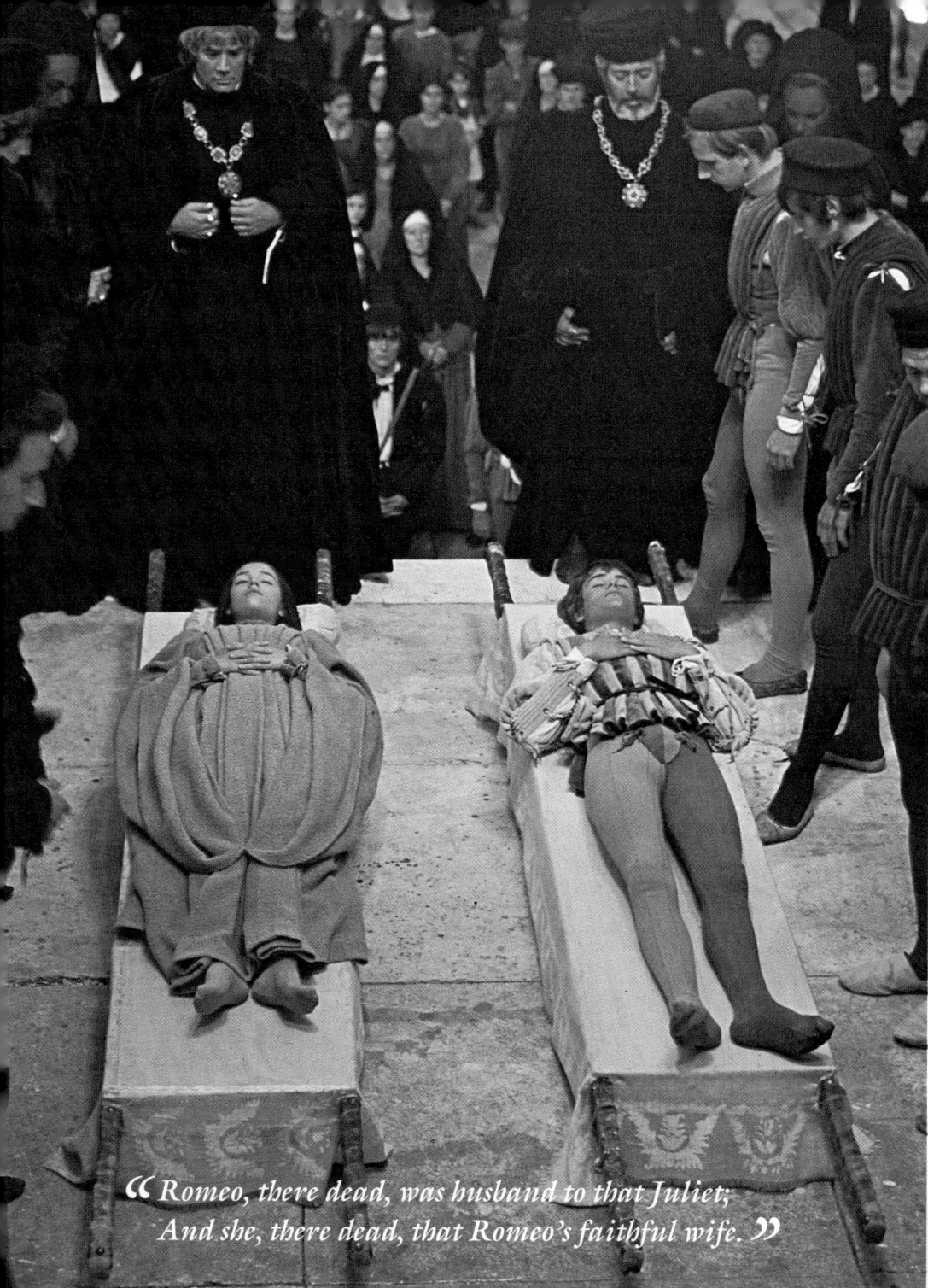

"Romeo, there dead, was husband to that Juliet;
And she, there dead, that Romeo's faithful wife."

RESPONDING TO THE ART

Activity. Ask students to describe their responses to the photograph. [Answers will vary. Most students will feel sadness at seeing the lifeless bodies of the young couple. However, their sadness might be tempered by the fact that the couple is laid out together and that they are finally being shown respect.]

Taking a Second Look

Review: Making Generalizations

Remind students that a generalization is a statement that applies not just to a specific situation, but to all individuals in a similar situation. When students analyze a play's theme, they must think about the general insights about life that the play conveys through its specific characters and events, such as "Love conquers time and space."

Activity

List the following specific lessons the characters in the play might have learned. Then, have students write a generalization based on the specific lesson. This generalization could be one of the play's themes.

Specific Lesson	Generalization
1. Romeo and Juliet shouldn't have gotten married so quickly after their first meeting.	
2. The Capulets and Montagues should have ended their feud before it destroyed their children.	
3. Romeo and Juliet were so in love that they cared about nothing else, and that's why they died.	
4. Romeo and Juliet became much more mature as their love forced them to make difficult decisions.	

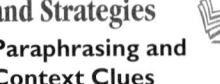
A Reading Skills and Strategies

Paraphrasing and Context Clues

Ask students to paraphrase the prince's view about punishing the Montagues and Capulets. [Sample response: Both families are guilty of continuing the feud after my warnings; with the deaths of your children, both families have already been punished by heaven. I, too, have been punished for letting this feud continue—my relatives Mercutio and Paris are dead.]

B Elements of Literature

Resolution

? What effect do the deaths of Romeo and Juliet have on the feud between their families? [Both Capulet and Montague determine to make peace by honoring each other's children; they are ashamed of the tragic deaths their feud has brought about.]

Answers to Margin Questions

Line 285. The families, perhaps weeping, continue to talk to the boy.

Line 295. The prince admits that he should have put a stop to the enmity earlier, before it cost so many lives. He pardoned the families too many times.

Most students will feel that Mercutio, Juliet, Paris and Romeo did not deserve to lose their lives and that the adults, even if they do deserve punishment, have suffered enough with the loss of their children. The questions of Tybalt's and Friar Laurence's punishment may raise more debate.

Balthasar.
    I brought my master news of Juliet's death;
    And then in post he came from Mantua
    To this same place, to this same monument.
275   This letter he early bid me give his father,
    And threat'ned me with death, going in the vault,
    If I departed not and left him there.
Prince.
    Give me the letter. I will look on it.
    Where is the county's page that raised the watch?
280   Sirrah, what made your master in this place?
Boy.
    He came with flowers to strew his lady's grave;
    And bid me stand aloof, and so I did.
    Anon comes one with light to ope the tomb;
    And by and by my master drew on him;
285   And then I ran away to call the watch.
Prince.
    This letter doth make good the friar's words,
    Their course of love, the tidings of her death;
    And here he writes that he did buy a poison
    Of a poor pothecary and therewithal
290   Came to this vault to die and lie with Juliet.
    Where be these enemies? Capulet, Montague,
    See what a scourge is laid upon your hate,
A That heaven finds means to kill your joys with love,
    And I, for winking at° your discords too,
295   Have lost a brace° of kinsmen. All are punished.

---

285. *What would the families be doing as the prince now pauses to read the letter?*

294. winking at: closing his eyes to.
295. brace: pair (Mercutio and Paris).

295. *We have been repeatedly reminded of the role of fate in this tragedy, but the human characters also admit their responsibility. What does the prince admit? Do you think that some people have been punished too harshly and some not severely enough?*

« *. . . See what a scourge is laid upon your hate,*
That heaven finds means to kill your joys with love. . . . **»**

Capulet.
    O brother Montague, give me thy hand.
B This is my daughter's jointure,° for no more
    Can I demand.

297. jointure: property passed on to a woman after her husband's death.

Making the Connections

Connecting to the Theme: "The Destruction of Innocence"

As students prepare to make generalizations about the play's main theme, remind them of the themes you first discussed after reading Act I. Ask which of the following generalizations—if any— they think best fits the message Shakespeare wanted to convey in *Romeo and Juliet*:

• Love can confer integrity upon two very young people.

• Tragedy can occur when older people's rage is carried over to a new generation.

• Humans are often powerless to make the kind of world they would like to live in.

• Innocence, virtue, and beauty can be quickly and thoughtlessly destroyed.

• A disordered and chaotic world can bring disaster down on those who live in it.

Montague.   But I can give thee more;
     For I will raise her statue in pure gold,

300   That whiles Verona by that name is known,
     There shall no figure at such rate° be set
     As that of true and faithful Juliet.

Capulet.
     As rich shall Romeo's by his lady's lie—
     Poor sacrifices of our enmity!

Prince.

305   A glooming peace this morning with it brings.
       The sun for sorrow will not show his head.
     Go hence, to have more talk of these sad things;
       Some shall be pardoned, and some punishèd;
     For never was a story of more woe

310   Than this of Juliet and her Romeo. [*Exeunt omnes.*]

301. **rate:** value.

? 304. *The central focus onstage now is not the families, but the bodies of Romeo and Juliet. Over the bodies of their children, the families join hands. What words of Capulet's admit his part in the tragedy?*

? 310. *As the actors solemnly file out, the friar is usually the last to exit. Some productions have the fathers leave last. At times, the nurse reappears and makes the final exit. What different effects would be produced by having different characters be the last to leave the stage? Which one would you have exit last?*
    Finally, only the bodies are left onstage. Can you describe how lighting would be used as the action closes?

*« . . . For never was a story of more woe
Than this of Juliet and her Romeo. »*

THE TRAGEDY OF ROMEO AND JULIET, ACT V, SCENE 3 851

This letter, written by an officer in the Civil War to his wife, reinforces many of the themes found in *Romeo and Juliet*.

Ⓐ Reading Skills and Strategies
Comparing and Contrasting

❓ What two wars does Major Ballou compare in this paragraph? [the Civil War and the Revolutionary War] What similarities does he see between them? [In both cases, men are called on to make great sacrifices for the U.S. government and for American civilization.]

Ⓑ Elements of Literature
Figures of Speech: Similes

❓ What does Major Ballou compare his love for Sarah to? [strong cables that can be broken only by God] What does Major Ballou compare his love for his country to? [a wind so strong that it takes him along with it]

Ⓒ Critical Thinking
Evaluating Character

❓ What kind of man does Major Ballou seem to be? Do you admire him? Explain. [Possible responses: He appears to be loving, responsible, sensitive, thankful for his blessings in life, brave, and willing to make sacrifices for things he believes in. Students are likely to admire these qualities.]

Ⓓ Appreciating Language
Word Choice

Point out that from the beginning of the letter, Major Ballou consistently refers to Sarah as *you*. In the last sentence, he refers to her as *thee*. Ask students to suggest reasons that Major Ballou might have switched pronouns. [Possible response: The letter increasingly becomes like a prayer and a poem, and *thee* is often used in prayers and poems.]

Connections · A LETTER

"My Very Dear Sarah"
Major Sullivan Ballou

During the Civil War, 4,500 men were killed, wounded, or captured in a battle in Virginia known as Bull Run or Manassas. A week before the battle, an officer in the Union army, Major Sullivan Ballou, wrote this letter to his wife, Sarah. Their love, like the love of Romeo and Juliet, has survived death and time.

July 14, 1861
Camp Clark, Washington

My very dear Sarah:

The indications are very strong that we shall move in a few days—perhaps tomorrow. Lest I should not be able to write again, I feel impelled to write a few lines that may fall under your eye when I shall be no more. . . .

Ⓐ I have no misgivings about, or lack of confidence in the cause in which I am engaged, and my courage does not halt or falter. I know how strongly American Civilization now leans on the triumph of the Government, and how great a debt we owe to those who went before us through the blood and sufferings of the Revolution. And I am willing—perfectly willing—to lay down all my joys in this life to help maintain this Government and to pay that debt. . . .

Ⓑ Sarah my love for you is deathless, it seems to bind me with mighty cables that nothing but Omnipotence could break; and yet my love of Country comes over me like a strong wind and bears me unresistibly on with all these chains to the battle field.

Ⓒ The memories of the blissful moments I have spent with you come creeping over me, and I feel most gratified to God and to you that I have enjoyed them so long. And hard it is for me to give them up and burn to ashes the hopes of future years, when, God willing, we might still have lived and loved together, and seen our sons grown up to honorable manhood, around us. I have, I know, but few and small claims upon Divine Providence, but something whispers to me—perhaps it is the wafted prayer of my little Edgar, that I shall return to my loved ones unharmed. If I do not my dear Sarah, never forget how much I love you, and when my last breath escapes me on the battle field, it will whisper your name. Forgive my many faults and the many pains I have caused you. How thoughtless and foolish I have often times been! How gladly would I wash out with my tears every little spot upon your happiness. . . .

Ⓓ But, O Sarah! if the dead can come back to this earth and flit unseen around those they loved, I shall always be near you; in the gladdest days and in the darkest nights . . . *always, always,* and if there be a soft breeze upon your cheek, it shall be my breath, as the cool air fans your throbbing temple, it shall be my spirit passing by. Sarah do not mourn me dead; think I am gone and wait for thee, for we shall meet again. . . .

Major Ballou was killed a week after he wrote this letter.

Connecting Across Texts

Connecting with *Romeo and Juliet*
In *Romeo and Juliet*, the lovers are kept apart by their feuding families. In "My Very Dear Sarah," the Civil War is the culprit. Major Ballou pours out his feelings to his wife as he is preparing for battle. Ask students to pretend that they are Romeo and to write a letter to Juliet from his residence in Mantua. How similar to Major Ballou's letter will it be?

Your Laughter

Pablo Neruda

Take bread away from me, if you wish,
take air away, but
do not take from me your laughter.

5 Do not take away the rose,
the lanceflower that you pluck,
the water that suddenly
bursts forth in your joy,
the sudden wave
of silver born in you. **A**

10 My struggle is harsh and I come back
with eyes tired
at times from having seen
the unchanging earth,
but when your laughter enters
15 it rises to the sky seeking me
and it opens for me all
the doors of life.

My love, in the darkest
hour your laughter
20 opens, and if suddenly
you see my blood staining
the stones of the street,
laugh, because your laughter **B**
will be for my hands
25 like a fresh sword.

Next to the sea in the autumn,
your laughter must raise
its foamy cascade,
and in the spring, love,
30 I want your laughter like
the flower I was waiting for,
the blue flower, the rose
of my echoing country.

35 Laugh at the night,
at the day, at the moon,
laugh at the twisted
streets of the island,
laugh at this clumsy
boy who loves you,
40 but when I open
my eyes and close them,
when my steps go,
when my steps return,
deny me bread, air,
45 light, spring,
but never your laughter **C**
for I would die.

How Do I Love Thee?

Elizabeth Barrett Browning

How do I love thee? Let me count the ways.
I love thee to the depth and breadth and
  height
My soul can reach, when feeling out of sight
For the ends of Being and ideal Grace. **D**
5 I love thee to the level of everyday's
Most quiet need, by sun and candle light.
I love thee freely, as men strive for Right;
I love thee purely, as they turn from Praise.
I love thee with the passion put to use
In my old griefs, and with my childhood's
10   faith.
I love thee with a love I seemed to lose
With my lost saints°—I love thee with the
  breath,
Smiles, tears, of all my life!—and, if God
  choose,
I shall but love thee better after death. **E**

12. lost saints: childhood faith.

THE TRAGEDY OF ROMEO AND JULIET **853**

Connecting Across Texts

Connecting with *Romeo and Juliet*
Have students compare the imagery and figures
of speech used by Shakespeare's lovers with
those used by Neruda and Browning. Do these
two poets include light and darkness imagery?
How do the speakers' attitudes toward death
compare with those of Romeo and Juliet? [Possi-
ble response: Neruda uses light and darkness
imagery in ll. 14–15, 18–20, 34–35, and 44–45;
Browning uses imagery of light in ll 5–6. All feel
that their love is impervious to death.]

Connections

These two poems, written by people
who lived in two different centuries
and countries, reflect the universal
inspiration that love provides.

A Elements of Literature
Figures of Speech: Metaphors
❓ What metaphors does the speaker
use to describe his love's laughter? [He
says it is a rose, a lanceflower, a burst of
water, and a wave of silver.]

B Elements of Literature
Irony
❓ What does the speaker want his
love to do if he lies bleeding in the
street? Why? [He wants her to laugh,
because her laughter will renew his
strength "like a fresh sword."] Why is this
ironic? [Laughter is not the response that
a person would expect or consider
appropriate in this situation. The speaker's
cool, detached attitude toward his own
death is ironic.]

C Reading Skills and Strategies
Finding the Main Idea
❓ What main idea about his love does
the speaker want to convey by repeating these images from the first stanza?
[Possible response: His love's laughter is
more important to him than life itself; he
could more easily live without food or
air than without her laughter.]

D Elements of Literature
Sonnet
Point out to students that the Browning poem is an Italian, or Petrarchan,
sonnet. It has a slightly different rhyme
scheme from the Shakespearean sonnet. Have students analyze the poem's
rhyme scheme. [*abba abba cd cd cd*]

E Literary Connections
Tell students that Elizabeth Browning's
relationship with her fellow poet
Robert Browning inspired her to write
this poem. The love affair between the
two poets is told in the play *The Bar-
retts of Wimpole Street,* which has twice
been made into a movie.

Resources
Listening
Audio CD Library
A recording of this poem is available in
the *Audio CD Library:*
• Disc 17, Track 7

T853

This newspaper article relates a phenomenon in modern-day Verona: Hundreds of letters arrive each year addressed to Shakespeare's Juliet. These letters are answered by a retired businessman.

Ⓐ Critical Thinking
Speculating

❓ Why do you think people write to Juliet, a character both fictional and dead? [Possible responses: Sometimes people have no one to listen to them, or they are unable or unwilling to speak to a real person, so they pour out their feelings to an imaginary character who seems real and sympathetic; people might be curious about whether such a letter might be answered.]

Ⓑ Cultural Connections

Point out to students that the author's use of specific examples—a teenage girl in Guatemala, a businessman in Boston, a high school teacher in London—emphasizes that problems with love are common to people from all cultural and social backgrounds.

Ⓒ Reading Skills and Strategies
Responding to the Text

❓ What are the chances that Hala's romance will work out? Explain. [Possible response: The chances of success are not good, because families who have held a grudge for so long are not likely to let it go lightly.]

Connections · A NEWS FEATURE

Dear Juliet

Any man that can write may answer a letter.
—William Shakespeare
Romeo and Juliet, Act II, Scene 4

LISA BANNON

VERONA, Italy—Fate bequeathed a strange legacy to this small city in northern Italy.

As the setting for Shakespeare's sixteenth-century tragedy *Romeo and Juliet,* Verona inherited the curiosity of literary scholars, a celebrated theatrical tradition, and several hundred thousand tourists a year.

In the bargain, the city also became the star-crossed lovers' capital of the world.

"We don't know how it started exactly," explains Giulio Tamassia, the bespectacled city spokesman for matters relating to Romeo and Juliet. "But one day in the thirties, these letters started arriving unprompted—addressed to Juliet. At a certain point somebody decided Juliet should write back."

Juliet's Address

What began sixty years ago as an occasional correspondence has grown into an industry. This year more than one thousand letters from the lovelorn will arrive in Verona, addressed to Shakespeare's tragic heroine. Many of them land on Mr. Tamassia's desk, with no more address than: Juliet, Italy.

"They tend to be sentimental," says Mr. Tamassia, rifling through stacks of musty airmail in the cramped studio that serves as Juliet's headquarters. Inside big pink folders are thousands of sorrowful letters, break-your-heart tales of love and loss. They come from all over—a teenage girl in Guatemala, a businessman in Boston, a high-school teacher in London. Some but not many are written by students in Shakespearean language. About two percent of letters received are addressed to Romeo, but Juliet replies.

"Writing the letter itself is really the first step toward solving the problem," says Mr. Tamassia, a fifty-nine-year-old retired businessman who wants it known at the outset that he himself is not Juliet. He is more her correspondence secretary.

"People express feelings in the letters that they would never admit to the person they love. Juliet's story inspires them," he says.

A Saudi Version

After much rummaging, he pulls out one of his favorites—describing a modern equivalent of the Montague-Capulet family rivalry.

Hala, an eighteen-year-old Saudi Arabian, wrote in March that she had fallen in love with the only son of her family's mortal enemy. Years ago, in Pakistan, her great-grandfather was responsible for the execution of a man who was using his property for smuggling heroin. From that time on, war was declared between the two families.

Now Hala was in love with a descendant of the executed man. "I am torn between the love for my family, which has made me what I am today, and my love for Omer, the man of my dreams," she wrote.

"Please reply quickly . . . my love, my life and future all depend on your answer."

—from *The Wall Street Journal*

Juliet's balcony, Verona, Italy.

Connecting Across Texts

Connecting with *Romeo and Juliet*
Have students imagine that Shakespeare's Juliet can make one last stage appearance before she dies to talk to the people of this century who write to her looking for solutions to their problems in love. What would she say? Would she advise people to stick by their love against all odds, or might her advice be more temperate because of her own tragic experience? Have students write and perform short monologues from Juliet's point of view.

First Thoughts

[infer]

1. In your opinion, what really caused the tragedy of Romeo and Juliet? Was it fate or real human errors? Draw a web showing all the people or forces that might be responsible.

Shaping Interpretations

[infer]

2. What coincidences in Scenes 1 and 2 conspire to wreck the friar's plans? Did any of these coincidences seem unbelievable to you?

[analyze]

3. In which scene of this act did you feel the **dramatic irony** peaked?

[analyze]

4. The **climax** of a play is its most intensely emotional moment, when we know how the conflict will end. In a tragedy it is that moment when we feel overcome with horror, sadness, fear, or regret. The climax of Shakespeare's plays always comes in the final act. When in this act would you say the climax of this play takes place? What were your feelings at this moment?

[generalize]

5. Look back at the prince's speech about love killing the families' joys (Scene 3). It seems ironic that love could kill, but how in this play did love kill joy? In what way is the whole play about the way heaven scourged, or punished, people for hating? Support your generalization with details from the text.

[interpret]

6. What does *Romeo and Juliet* reveal to you about the destructive effects of hatred? In a few sentences, state the **theme** of the play as you see it. Be sure to compare your statements of theme in class.

Extending the Text

[extend]

7. Review your response to the Quickwrite on page 732. What further connections can you see between Romeo and Juliet and their families and people in today's world? What do you think *Romeo and Juliet* has to say to your generation? Be sure to consider "Dear Juliet" (see **Connections** on page 854).

Challenging the Text

[evaluate]

8. Throughout the eighteenth and nineteenth centuries, *Romeo and Juliet* was often rewritten to have a different ending, in which the young lovers do not die but instead live happily ever after. How do you feel about the ending of the play? Would you prefer a happy ending? What changes, if any, would you make in the outcome?

THE TRAGEDY OF ROMEO AND JULIET, ACT V 855

Reading Check

a. What news does Romeo's servant bring him in Scene 1?

b. Why does Romeo buy the poison?

c. Why doesn't Romeo receive the friar's letter explaining the change in plans?

d. What does Romeo find when he enters the tomb?

e. What finally happens to Romeo and then to Juliet?

Reading Check

a. Balthasar tells Romeo that Juliet has died and is buried in the Capulets' tomb.

b. Romeo buys poison so that he can drink it and be reunited with Juliet in death.

c. The friar's messenger was quarantined by health authorities when they thought he might have been exposed to the plague.

d. He finds Juliet's apparently lifeless body.

e. After killing Paris, Romeo poisons himself. When Juliet awakens to find Romeo dead, she fatally stabs herself.

Challenging the Text

8. Some students may feel that a happy ending would dilute the strength of the play's warning about the effects of hatred. Others may say that a happy ending would give people hope about the power of love in the face of adversity.

First Thoughts

1. Some students may cite Romeo's overhearing Juliet declare her love for him or to the chance meeting of Tybalt and Mercutio as evidence that fate was to blame. Others may say such human actions as the feud, Lord Capulet's decision to move up the marriage to Paris, or Friar Laurence's decisions to perform the wedding and to have Juliet pretend to be dead are more to blame.

Shaping Interpretations

2. Balthasar sees Juliet's funeral and reports her death to Romeo at the same time that Friar John is detained by the health authorities and prevented from delivering the message that Juliet is *not* dead. While coincidences happen in life, some students may protest that Balthasar should have been in touch with Friar Laurence (Romeo expected him to bring a letter) and that Friar Laurence should have stressed to Friar John the urgency of the letter's prompt delivery.

3. Possible response: Scene 3, Romeo, wrongly believing Juliet dead, fulfills his suicide pledge, exclaiming before he does that Juliet looks beautiful and alive.

4. The dramatic climax, or most intense emotional moment, is the double suicide of Romeo and Juliet. Students will likely express horror, anger, and sadness.

5. The Montagues and the Capulets love and take joy in their children. Due to the hatred between the families, however, Romeo and Juliet act in secret when they fall in love. The decisions they make to conceal their love lead to their deaths. Ultimately, the parents who perpetuated the feud are punished for doing so.

6. Throughout the play, Shakespeare stresses that hatred breeds violence and death. Possible theme: Hatred can destroy innocence, virtue, beauty, and even love itself.

Extending the Text

7. Students may say that friction between parents and teenagers is still common today. They should see that the play warns us to check the facts, value communication, and live in peace—because ignorance and hatred can destroy the innocent.

T855

Rubrics for each Choices assignment appear on p. 205 in the *Portfolio Management System.*

CHOICES: Building Your Portfolio

1. **Writer's Notebook** Remind students to save their work. They may use their notes for the Writer's Workshop on p. 868. To help students decide whether they want to develop one of their ideas in writing, suggest they make a diagram, like the following, of a topic that they consider a strong possibility.

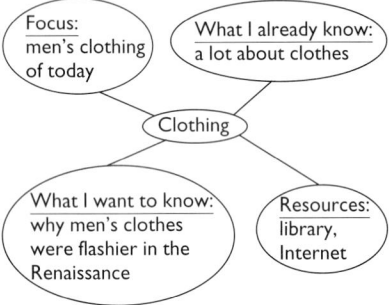

2. **Creative Writing** Remind students that as they plan their updated version, they need to decide how closely to stick to Shakespeare's plot. Students might consider the following issues:
   - Should a family feud be the basis of the crisis?
   - Should fate or self-determination play the larger role?
   - How important should friends be to the plot?
   - Will the lovers die at the end?

3. **Creative Writing** Encourage students to freewrite their endings first without worrying about writing in play form. After they are satisfied with their ideas, tell them to refer to the play as a model for format.

4. **Critical Thinking/Speaking** Ask students what is meant by the term *character type.* [someone who is defined in terms of a specific character trait, a virtue, or a vice] Be sure students recognize that a character type does not grow and change or learn from mistakes. Good examples of character types can be found in TV comedies and soap operas.

CHOICES: Building Your Portfolio

Writer's Notebook
1. Collecting Ideas for a Research Paper

Narrowing your topic. Look over the ideas you have jotted down in your Writer's Notebook. Is there one you would like to research and explore further in a research paper? Ask yourself these questions before you proceed:

- How can I narrow or focus this topic?
- What do I already know about this topic?
- What would I like to know?
- What resources can I use to find more information?

> • Most interested in clothing—especially why men's clothes of Shakespeare's time were so much flashier than ours.
> • I don't know much about topic, but public library has plenty of stuff on fashion.
> • Most of us love clothes, so I could do a report that would interest my classmates.

Creative Writing
2. The Play Today

As a group, prepare a plan for an updated *Romeo and Juliet* that takes place in the United States. The chart below shows how Arthur Laurents and Stephen Sondheim changed the play to make it into a musical, *West Side Story* (1957). When you finish your rough plan, you might map your scenes. You might even write your own new *Romeo and Juliet.*

Romeo and Juliet	West Side Story
Verona, 1300s	New York, 1950s
Feud: Montagues versus Capulets	Gang war: Jets versus Sharks
Lovers: Romeo (Montague); Juliet (Capulet)	Lovers: Tony (Jet); Maria (Shark)
Authority: prince	Authority: NYPD
Friend/confidante: Benvolio (Romeo's); nurse (Juliet's)	Friend/confidante: Riff (Tony's); Anita (Maria's)
Leaders: Mercutio (Montagues); Tybalt (Capulets)	Leaders: Riff (Jets); Bernardo (Sharks)

Creative Writing
3. A New Ending

Suppose Romeo and Juliet survived because the friar's schemes worked. Write a scene showing them twenty years later. In their dialogue, make clear what's happened to the Capulets, the friar, the nurse, and Paris. Use stage directions to tell when and where your scene is set.

Critical Thinking/Speaking
4. Characters Endure

Prepare a report for the class in which you tell how the character types presented in *Romeo and Juliet* are found in movies, novels, and TV sitcoms today. Focus on these types: beautiful girl; handsome boyfriend; socially conscious mother; grumpy father; boyfriend approved by the girl's parents; older confidante; loyal best friend; hotheaded bully; dopey guys who follow the gang leader.

Comparing Texts
5. Words of Love

The words that Romeo and Juliet speak to each other are words of love. "'My Very Dear Sarah,'" "Your Laughter," and "How Do I Love Thee?" (see ***Connections*** on pages 852–853) are about love too, and they are also eloquent. In a

856 WILLIAM SHAKESPEARE

Using Students' Strengths

Kinesthetic Learners

Allow students interested in Choice 3 to collaborate on a new ending to present live or on videotape. Group members should decide on a basic setting and character list for a new final scene and then assign roles before working together to write dialogue and action.

Auditory/Musical Learners

Students working on Choice 2 might enjoy finding a theme song for their updated version of *Romeo and Juliet.* Have them consider various forms of music (rock, country, rap, folk, jazz) before they make their choices. Have each group play the theme song when presenting its plan.

brief essay, compare and contrast these expressions of love. How does love transform each speaker? How does each speaker say that love conquers death and time? Which expression of love speaks most powerfully to you, and why?

Analyzing Structure

6. Tracing the Action

The graphic on page 732 shows the pattern of a typical Shakespearean tragedy. In an essay, analyze the structure of *Romeo and Juliet* according to that pattern. Does the play match the structure? You might provide a graphic with your essay summarizing what happens in each act. You might even add illustrations showing the major action in each act.

Critical Thinking

7. Comic Relief

Playwrights often introduce comic characters or events into intensely emotional or dramatic plays to provide **comic relief**—to ease the tension temporarily. In *Romeo and Juliet* two characters provide comic relief: Mercutio and the nurse. Find at least three instances of comic relief in this tragedy, and make a three-column chart. In the first column, describe the serious events that are interrupted. In the second column, describe

the comic-relief scene. In the third column, tell how long the comedy lasts.

Analyzing a Character/ Supporting a Critical Statement

8. Portrait of Juliet

Write a character analysis of Juliet, using the following comment by a critic as the basis of your thesis statement. Be sure to use details from the play to support what the critic says about Juliet and how the world treated her.

> Shakespeare's real miracle . . . was Juliet, transformed from an adolescent arrogantly eager to outdo her elders to an appealing child-woman, barely fourteen, who learns to mix courage with her innocence, yet falls victim to a world that only briefly and unintentionally, but fatally, treats her as a plaything.
>
> —J. A. Bryant, Jr.

Critical Thinking/ Panel Discussion

9. If Only . . .

Shakespeare doesn't idealize Romeo and Juliet. He is careful to remind us that their love is destructive partly because it fails to see life as it really is.

Romeo and Juliet do not act with caution and patience and wisdom. They act on impulse and in haste—and they get bad advice. Form a panel to discuss these questions: (a) What should Romeo and Juliet have done, instead of what they actually did, at three or more points in the play? (b) Could Romeo and Juliet have triumphed—if they'd had good advice? (Be sure to review the webs you made for question 1.) (c) Would Mercutio have helped them had he lived? Before your panel meets, it should agree on a format.

Research/Art

10. Do-It-Yourself Globe

With a group, find library books that show models of the Globe Theatre and that describe its unique features in detail. You might also search the Internet (Hint: Try spelling *theater* the British way: *theatre*). Then, work together to make your own model of the Globe. Decide what materials you will use for your model and how you will label and describe its parts. (Commercially printed do-it-yourself cardboard models of the Globe are available in some bookstores. Your group might enjoy working on such a kit.) Present your research and finished model to another class or to the Drama Club.

5. **Comparing Texts** Encourage students to work in pairs on this activity. You may wish to have them organize their points for comparison and contrast in a chart that uses the following categories: Time period, Lovers, Main idea, Comparison used, How love transforms, How love conquers, Most powerful/Why.

6. **Analyzing Structure** Encourage students to work in groups, using their notes and any act and scene summaries they have written to help them complete their analysis. Essays must show clearly how *Romeo and Juliet* matches (or does not match) the typical Shakespearean pattern. Encourage inclusion of graphics; make illustrations of the action optional.

7. **Critical Thinking** To help students get started, point out that Mercutio first appears in Act I, Scene 4, as the young Montague men are about to "crash" the Capulet party. Have students reread the scene, and help them fill in their charts. Have them work in small groups to find more incidents of comic relief.

8. **Analyzing a Character** Help students find the main ideas in the thesis statement. [Juliet is transformed from arrogant adolescent to appealing child-woman; Juliet mixes courage with innocence; Juliet falls victim to a world that treats her as a plaything.] Then, have the class brainstorm details in the play that support each main idea of the thesis. Allow students who disagree with part of the thesis statement to develop their own statement.

9. **Critical Thinking/Panel Discussion** As students consider what impact Mercutio might have had on the outcome if he had survived, ask them to consider how Mercutio's family connections might have helped the lovers. (Hint: Mercutio was related to the prince.)

10. **Research/Art** Before they begin their research, students might reread "Shakespeare and His Theater" on pp. 728–730 and study the illustrations.

LANGUAGE LINK

Try It Out
Possible Answers
Similes

1. Juliet, seen at night, is compared to an exotic jeweled earring worn by an Ethiopian. The beauty of both is too great and luxurious for this world.
2. Romeo's relationship with Juliet is compared to schoolboys' attitudes toward books and school. His desire to go to Juliet is the same as the schoolboys' desire to go *away from* their books. His reluctance to go away from Juliet is the same as the schoolboys' reluctance to go *toward* school.
3. Since Juliet is so young, her death is compared to an early frost that kills the sweetest flower.

Metaphors

1. Juliet (or her hand) is compared to a "holy shrine"; Romeo's lips are two "pilgrims" who want to visit the shrine and make amends for their sins.
2. Juliet, appearing at her window, is compared to the sun rising in the east.
3. Romeo and Juliet's love is compared to a bud that will eventually grow into a flower.

Personification

1. April is a well-dressed person, while winter is someone who limps. April is also personified as stepping on winter's heel.
2. A former love is an old man lying on his deathbed; a new love is a young heir waiting to take his place.
3. Night is a well-behaved older woman, dressed in black who can teach Juliet how to play the "game" of love.

LANGUAGE LINK   MINI-LESSON

Figures of Speech

Shakespeare's characters use images and figures of speech so rich and so varied that the play, which has lived now for almost four hundred years, will probably live as long as English continues to be spoken. As you're focusing on Shakespeare's language, you might try to imitate some of his figures of speech.

Similes

The simplest form of figurative language is the **simile,** a clearly stated comparison between two different things. A simile uses a word such as *like* or *as* or *than* in stating its comparison. For example, Romeo, dejected over Rosaline, says of love, "It pricks like thorn." Romeo's simile suggests that love can cause pain, just as a thorn can.

Metaphors

Metaphors omit words such as *like, as,* and *than* and directly equate two different things. When the nurse says of Paris "he's a flower, . . . a very flower," she immediately identifies Paris's good looks with a beautiful blossom. Metaphors may also be **implied**. The prince uses implied metaphors when he angrily accuses the citizens:

> You men, you beasts,
> That quench the fire of
>   your pernicious rage
> With purple fountains
>   issuing from your veins!

The prince compares the anger of the citizens to a fire, and the blood issuing from the wounds to purple water spewing out of fountains.

Personification

Personification is a special kind of metaphor, in which something that is not a person is spoken of as if it were human. When Benvolio says that the sun "peered forth the golden window of the East," he is personifying the sun by saying that it peered, as if it had two eyes.

Puns

Shakespeare's audiences loved **puns,** which are plays on the multiple meanings of words. (Many jokes today are based on puns. Question: "What has four wheels and flies?" Answer: "A garbage truck." This pun is based on two meanings of the word *flies*.) Many of the puns in *Romeo and Juliet* go over our heads today because jokes go out of fashion very quickly and some of Shakespeare's wordplay involves words we don't use today.

Mercutio is the best punster in the play, though Romeo does pretty well in Act II, when he matches wits with his friend. When Mercutio spies Romeo coming down the street, he says Romeo comes "without his roe." *Roe* can refer to a female deer, so if Romeo is without his roe, he's without his girl. *Roe* also refers to fish eggs, so "without his roe" can mean that Romeo's been gutted (we'd say he's "gutless"), as a fish is when its eggs are removed.

If you need help figuring out the examples of figurative language on the next page, go back to the play and see if the **context** helps you.

Try It Out

Similes

In the following quotations, identify the similes and tell what two things are brought together in each. In what way are the two things alike?

1. **Romeo.**
   O, she doth teach the torches to burn bright!
   It seems she hangs upon the cheek of night
   As a rich jewel in an Ethiop's ear—
   Beauty too rich for use, for earth too dear!
   —Act I, Scene 5, lines 46–49

2. **Romeo.**
   Love goes toward love as schoolboys from their books;
   But love from love, toward school with heavy looks.
   —Act II, Scene 2, lines 157–158

3. **Lord Capulet.**
   Death lies on her like an untimely frost
   Upon the sweetest flower of all the field.
   —Act IV, Scene 5, lines 28–29

Metaphors

Here are some passages containing metaphors. Pick out each metaphor and identify the two things that it compares.

1. **Romeo** (*to Juliet*).
   If I profane with my unworthiest hand
   This holy shrine, the gentle sin is this:
   My lips, two blushing pilgrims, ready stand
   To smooth that rough touch with a tender kiss.
   —Act I, Scene 5, lines 95–98

2. **Romeo** (*under Juliet's balcony*).
   But soft! What light through yonder window breaks?
   It is the East, and Juliet is the sun!
   —Act II, Scene 2, lines 2–3

3. **Juliet** (*to Romeo*).
   This bud of love, by summer's ripening breath,
   May prove a beauteous flower when next we meet.
   —Act II, Scene 2, lines 121–122

Personification

Here are some quotations from *Romeo and Juliet* that contain personifications. In each, what nonhuman thing is spoken of as if it were a person? A passage can contain more than one personification.

1. **Capulet.**
   . . . well-appareled April on the heel
   Of limping winter treads . . .
   —Act I, Scene 2, lines 27–28

2. **Chorus.**
   Now old desire doth in his deathbed lie,
   And young affection gapes to be his heir.
   —Act II, Chorus, lines 1–2

3. **Juliet.**
   Come, civil night,
   Thou sober-suited matron all in black,
   And learn me how to lose a winning match. . . .
   —Act III, Scene 2, lines 10–12

Puns

Here are three more puns from the play. If you can explain the plays on meaning, you'll have caught the jokes.

1. **Mercutio** (*after he is stabbed*).
   Ask for me tomorrow, and you shall find me a grave man.
   —Act III, Scene 1, lines 98–99

2. **Romeo.**
   Give me a torch. I am not for this ambling.
   Being but heavy, I will bear the light.
   —Act I, Scene 4, Lines 11–12

3. **Romeo.**
   You have dancing shoes
   With nimble soles; I have a soul of lead
   So stakes me to the ground I cannot move.
   —Act I, Scene 4, lines 14–16

Puns

1. To mortally wounded Mercutio, a "grave man" is both a serious man who ponders matters of great importance and a dead man who lies in his grave.

2. Because Romeo is "heavy," or sad, and not in the mood for dancing (with an additional pun on his being a heavy-footed dancer), he will not participate but will "bear the light," or hold the torch, for the others. "Bear the light" might also mean he will put up with the frivolity of the others.

3. The pun involves *sole* (of a shoe) and *soul* (of a person). Romeo's "soul of lead" is a heavy spirit that won't let him dance.

Resources

Language

- *Grammar and Language Links* Worksheet, p. 59

Language Link Quick Check

Identify and explain the figure of speech used in each of the following passages.

1. Romeo and Mercutio are discussing their dreams.
   Romeo: "Well, what was yours?"
   Mercutio: "That dreamers often lie." (Act I, Scene 4, l. 51)
   [The pun is on the two meanings of *lie*. Dreamers lie in bed, and dreamers often dream things that are not true.]

2. Romeo: "The brightness of her cheek would shame those stars / As daylight doth a lamp." (Act II, Scene 2, ll. 19–20)
   [simile; The glow in Juliet's expression is brighter than starlight, as daylight outshines any lamp.]

3. Nurse: "I think it best you married with the county. / O, he's a lovely gentleman! / Romeo's a dishclout to him." (Act III, Scene 5, ll. 219–221)
   [metaphor; Romeo is compared to a dishcloth.]

4. Romeo: "Night's candles are burnt out, and jocund day / Stands tiptoe on the misty mountaintops." (Act III, Scene 5, ll. 9–10)
   [personification; The day is a high-spirited, lively person who stands on tiptoe, showing first only his or her head—the sun—behind the mountaintops.]

Extending the Theme

This editorial describes the tragic ending of a young couple's relationship by the Bosnian conflict.

Background

Bosnia and Herzegovina is a country in the Balkan Peninsula. From 1918 to 1991, the country was part of Yugoslavia. Muslims, Serbs, and Croats each make up about one third of the population. All three peoples speak the same language, formerly known as Serbo-Croatian. However, most of the Serbs are Eastern Orthodox Christians who use the Cyrillic, or Russian, alphabet. The Croats are Roman Catholics who use the Roman alphabet. The Muslims are descended from Slavs who converted to Islam during the period of Turkish rule, from the fifteenth to seventeenth centuries.

Ⓐ Critical Thinking
Making Connections

❓ In what ways is this opening paragraph similar to the Prologue of the play *Romeo and Juliet*? [Sample responses: It summarizes the story in advance; the reader finds out that a young couple in love died tragically and that the young lovers were from different backgrounds.]

Ⓑ Appreciating Language
Diction

Call students' attention to the word "carnage." Ask them how this word contrasts with the image of a parent grieving for a dead child in the last half of the sentence. [Possible response: The word "carnage" conveys the enormity of mass violence, but it does not convey the individual suffering experienced by each family that has lost loved ones.]

AN EDITORIAL

Romeo and Juliet in Bosnia

Bob Herbert

Quickwrite

Think about the title of this editorial and about the photographs that illustrate it. Based on the title and photographs, predict what the story will be about. As you read, continue to take notes on details in the editorial that you might want to talk about later.

Ⓐ If you watch *Frontline* Tuesday night on PBS, you will see the story of two ordinary young people, Bosko Brkic, an Eastern Orthodox Serb, and Admira Ismic, a Muslim, who met at a New Year's Eve party in the mid-1980s, fell in love, tried to pursue the most conventional of dreams, and died together on a hellish bridge in Sarajevo.

The documentary, called "Romeo and Juliet in Sarajevo,"[1] achieves its power by focusing our attention on the thoroughly human individuals caught up in a horror that, from afar, can seem abstract and almost unimaginable. It's one thing Ⓑ to hear about the carnage caused by incessant[2] sniper fire and the steady rain of mortar shells on a city; it's something quite different to actually witness a parent desperately groping for meaning while reminiscing about a lost daughter.

For viewers overwhelmed and desensitized by the relentless reports of mass killings and mass rapes, the shock of "Romeo and Juliet in

1. **Sarajevo** (sä′rä′ye·vô): capital of Bosnia and Herzegovina, in the former Yugoslavia.
2. **incessant** (in·ses′ənt): never ceasing.

860 WILLIAM SHAKESPEARE

Sarajevo" is that what we see is so real and utterly familiar. We become riveted by the mundane. Bosko and Admira could be a young couple from anywhere, from Queens, or Tokyo, or Barcelona.

Ⓒ We learn that they graduated from high school in June of 1986 and that both were crazy about movies and music. Admira had a cat named Yellow that she loved, and Bosko liked to play practical jokes.

Admira's father, Zijo, speaking amid clouds of cigarette smoke, says, "Well, I knew from the first day about that relationship and I didn't have anything against it. I thought it was good because her guy was so likable, and after a time I started to love him and didn't regard him any differently than Admira."

Admira's grandmother, Sadika Ismic, was not Ⓓ so sanguine. "Yes, I did have something against it," she says. "I thought, 'He is Serb, she is a Muslim, and how will it work?'"

For Admira and Bosko, of course, love was the answer to everything. While Bosko was away on compulsory military service soon after high school, Admira wrote: "My dear love,

Making the Connections

Connecting to the Theme: "The Destruction of Innocence"

As they read *Romeo and Juliet*, many students might suggest that Romeo and Juliet could simply have run away together and lived in some other town. It will likely shock and sadden students to learn that two real-life modern sweethearts, whose innocent hopes rested in the idea of a life together in another place, could have been so heartlessly shot down.

Allow class time for students to discuss this modern tragedy and then time to write quietly about their responses to it.

One of the bridges that span the Miljacka River, which runs through the middle of Sarajevo.

Bosko Brkic and Admira Ismic.

Sarajevo at night is the most beautiful thing in the world. I guess I could live somewhere else but only if I must or if I am forced. Just a little beat of time is left until we are together. After that, absolutely nothing can separate us."

Sarajevo at the time was a cosmopolitan city coming off the triumph of the 1984 Winter Olympics. With a population of Serbs, Croats, Muslims, Jews, and others, the city had become a symbol of ethnic and religious tolerance, a place where people were making a serious attempt to live together in peace.

But civilization is an exceedingly fragile enterprise, and it's especially vulnerable to the primal madness of ethnic and religious hatreds. Simple tolerance is nothing in the face of the relentless, pathetic and near-universal need to bolster the esteem of the individual and the group by eradicating the rights, and even the existence, of others.

When the madness descended on Sarajevo, Bosko Brkic faced a cruel dilemma. He could not kill Serbs. And he could not go up into the hills and fire back down on his girlfriend's people. Says his mother, Rada: "He was simply a kid who was not for the war."

Bosko and Admira decided to flee Sarajevo.

To escape, they had to cross a bridge over the Miljacka River in a no man's land between the Serb and Muslim lines. Snipers from both sides overlooked the bridge.

It has not been determined who shot the lovers. They were about two thirds of the way across the bridge when the gunfire erupted. Both sides blame the other. Witnesses said Bosko died instantly. Admira crawled to him. She died a few minutes later. The area in which they were shot was so dangerous that the bodies remained on the bridge, entwined, for six days before being removed.

Only the times and places change. Bosnia today, Rwanda and Burundi tomorrow. Jews versus Arabs, Chinese versus Japanese, blacks versus whites. There are various ostensible reasons for the endless conflicts—ideological differences, border disputes, oil—but dig just a little and you will uncover the ruinous ethnic or religious origins of the clash.

The world stands helpless and sometimes depressed before the madness. Millions upon millions dead, millions more to die. It is not just the curse of our times. It seems to be the curse of all time.

—from *The New York Times*

ROMEO AND JULIET IN BOSNIA 861

Reaching All Students

FINDING COMMON GROUND

As its name suggests, this feature encourages students to compare their responses to the literature and find areas of agreement. Ask students to share their thoughts on how an awareness of past tragedy might prevent future loss.

Allow students to form their own groups for this discussion, and permit those who wish to respond to questions privately in their writer's notebooks to do so. Students who react strongly to the editorial might be encouraged to exchange their notes with one another rather than participate in a larger group.

Ask students to consider the memorable personal details that Shakespeare and Herbert include in their accounts and to analyze the power of well-chosen language.

MEET THE WRITER

On the Scene

Born in Brooklyn, New York, journalist **Bob Herbert** (1945–   ) earned a Bachelor of Science degree from the State University of New York and has been a reporter ever since. Whether at his first job at *The Star Ledger* in Newark, New Jersey, or on the *NBC Nightly News* or the *Today* show,

Herbert's reporting and commentary on politics, urban affairs, and social trends have been full of valuable information and insights into the stuff communities and nations are made of. He currently covers national and local issues for *The New York Times*. He has taught journalism at Brooklyn College and Columbia University Graduate School of Journalism.

FINDING COMMON GROUND

You know more about Romeo and Juliet than you do about Bosko and Admira; Shakespeare had an entire play to develop their characters, while Bob Herbert had only a short column to portray what happened on the bridge over the Miljacka. Still, there is something powerful in the simple fact that Bosko and Admira lived while we live, dying only a short time ago. Perhaps their story, brief as it is, may be more painful for some readers than Shakespeare's tale.

- Compare and contrast these two stories in a group: Shakespeare's story of Romeo and Juliet and Herbert's story of Bosko and Admira. Which of the two struck you more powerfully? Why?

- What do think were Bob Herbert's motives in writing this editorial? What kind of audience do you think he intended to reach? Herbert's own bias is pretty clear. What are some of the techniques that he uses to persuade his audience to accept his point of view?

- What other observations about the content of the editorial, or about its tone or message, does your group make? Check your Quickwrite notes to see which details in the editorial you wanted to discuss further.

- Assign someone to report to the class on your group's response to the editorial and its relationship to the play. What can you, as a class, agree about? Are there some issues you must agree to disagree on?

862 WILLIAM SHAKESPEARE

Crossing the Curriculum

History

Divide the class into three groups in order to investigate the history of conflict in Bosnia and Herzegovina. Ask one group to research the most recent facts about the conflict, another group to investigate developments in the region from 1900 to 1990, and a third group to report on the earlier history of the region.

Each student might look specifically for two facts that they think are the most significant for understanding the tensions in the region. Ask questions about each historical period, and ask a member from each group to list information in a time line on the chalkboard.

READ ON

In Love and War

"All's fair in love and war." You've heard that before, but Ruth and Adam might disagree. Howard Fast's novel *April Morning* (Bantam) finds young Adam facing the British soldiers who are marching through town on April 19, 1775. Ruth, the girl who loves him, hears the tragic news—that Adam has not survived the battle. Sound fair? Find out what happens by sundown, April 19, 1775.

New Frontiers

Take two cups of love and mix them into the quickly changing batter of the American frontier—and do it all right around the turn of the century. Willa Cather's classic American love story, *My Ántonia* (Houghton Mifflin), describes the product of this mixture. Find out what happens to two young people in a Nebraska landscape you'll never forget.

Wanda and Friends

It's prom night, and Wanda Hickey is aglow—with sweat. That's according to humorist Jean Shepherd. The short stories in Shepherd's collection *Wanda Hickey's Night of Golden Memories and Other Disasters* (Doubleday) uncover what's awkward, weird, even disastrous about growing up—and all for laughs. Join Wanda and friends—like Ollie Hopnoodle, Josephine Cosnowski, and Daphne Bigelow—and follow Shepherd through romance and murder, and of course, to the Junior Prom.

On the West Side

Romeo and Juliet aren't the only "star-crossed" lovers to walk the stage. Their story has been repeated often—in drama, fiction, and real life. In our own century *West Side Story*'s Tony and Maria have been the most famous couple to reenact the tragedy of ill-fated love. *West Side Story* is a musical version of the familiar story—set in a neighborhood of New York City. Tragedy follows when love and two different cultures collide. There's a book that contains both plays, *West Side Story* and *Romeo and Juliet* (Laurel-Leaf).

READ ON 863

READ ON
Portfolio Assessment Options

The following projects can help you evaluate and assess your students' reading accomplishments outside class. Videotapes or audiotapes of completed projects may be included in students' portfolios.

- **Design a Movie Poster** Tell students to imagine that the book or story they have read has been turned into a movie. Have them design a Coming Attractions poster similar to those that hang in the lobbies of movie theaters. The poster not only should depict a scene from the movie but also should list the actors and the names of the characters they play.

- **Create a Time-Travel Brochure** Have students imagine that time travel is possible. Their job as a travel agent is to create a brochure to advertise trips back in time. Ask students to choose a setting from one of the books and to consider how to market the destination best. For example, why would someone want to take a trip back to the Lexington-Concord area during April 1775? Why would someone want to visit Nebraska during pioneer times? Have students illustrate their brochures with pictures to pique a would-be traveler's interest.

- **Participate in a Radio Panel** Students can work in a small group to discuss one of the books. One of the students should be the moderator and prepare questions that panelists can respond to with their opinions. After students have held a practice session, they can tape the discussion as if it were a radio talk show.

- **Make a Plaque** Have students choose a general topic that one of the books deals with, such as love, friendship, war, or fear. Then have them find a quotation from the story that relates to the topic. Students can design a plaque that shows the topic and the quotation, including any artistic embellishments.

Speaking and Listening Workshop

Introducing the Speaking and Listening Workshop

Read the assignment on page 864 aloud. Then, have students consider the following questions before they make their decisions on staging the play:

- How much time will be necessary to prepare and perform a scene? [The time necessary will depend on the content and staging of the scene. You may wish to set some appropriate boundaries.]
- How can suitable props and costumes be obtained? Should each actor be responsible for getting his or her own costume? [Members of an acting group should pool their resources and consider putting one individual in charge of coordinating props and costumes. You may also suggest students read the Reading for Life feature on p. 874 before making costuming decisions.]
- Why is it important to read through a script before one tries to act it? [The actor will have a better understanding of the character and how the character fits into the plot.]

After students have discussed the questions, have them form groups to plan and stage a scene from *Romeo and Juliet*.

Resources

Performance Rubric
- *Portfolio Management System*, p. 208

ASSIGNMENT

Stage a scene from *Romeo and Juliet*.

During the run of Romeo and Juliet, *someone wrote and told me that if the dialogue at the ball could be taken in a lighter and* quicker *way, it would better express the manner of a girl of Juliet's age. The same unknown critic pointed out that I was too slow and studied in the balcony scene. She—I think it was a woman—was perfectly right!*

—Ellen Terry,
British actress

STAGING THE PLAY

Romeo and Juliet has been a favorite with directors, actors, set designers, and costumers for centuries. Present a scene of the play with a group of your classmates. (If you're feeling especially Shakespearean, give your "company" a name, such as the King's Women or the Globe Trotters, or, to bring it up to date, the President's Players.)

Getting Started

1. Select a Scene

Some good possibilities include

- the opening fight scene: Act I, Scene 1 (many characters)
- the party at the Capulets, where Romeo and Juliet first meet: Act I, Scene 5 (lots of people, music, dancing, tension)
- the balcony scene: Act II, Scene 2 (two actors only)
- Mercutio and Benvolio teasing Romeo: Act II, Scene 4
- the fight in the square, when Mercutio dies and Romeo kills Tybalt: Act III, Scene 1 (requires good choreography)
- the scene where Lord Capulet threatens to disown Juliet if she doesn't marry Paris: Act III, Scene 5
- the scene when Juliet says good night to the nurse and her mother and takes the sleeping potion: Act IV, Scene 3 (requires emotional control)

Whichever scene you choose, be sure to watch for commas, periods, and semicolons. Remember what you have learned about end-stopped lines and run-on lines. Pausing in the wrong place can ruin your performance.

2. Assign Tasks

Here are some of the tasks you'll need to take care of (the very same ones Shakespeare's company had to manage):

864 WILLIAM SHAKESPEARE

Reaching All Students

English Language Learners

Encourage English language learners to participate at their level of comfort. For students whose proficiency in English is minimal, this may mean that they will be more at ease speaking as a choral group. This practice in speaking as part of a group helps students develop fluency, correct intonation, and decide on appropriate phrasing.

Using Students' Strengths

Kinesthetic Learners

Many acting roles require the ability to stay motionless for some length of time. Some students may feel more comfortable and productive as active set designers or arrangers. Allow group members enough time to explore the demands of each company task before committing themselves to making a specific contribution; nevertheless, encourage every student to take a performance role, however small.

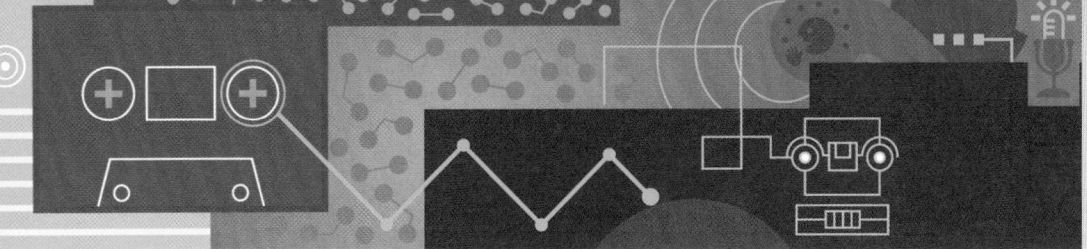

- directing
- lighting
- costuming
- props
- choreography (planning the movement onstage—especially critical in the fight scenes)
- publicity

3. Decide on Your Presentation

Since you are an acting company, you'll want to work as a group to make some of your decisions. Here are some performance possibilities you should consider:

- Assign one role to each group member and act the scene "straight," that is, traditionally, as if you were on a professional stage.

- Create a **tableau,** or frozen moment from the scene. Decide in advance where each character should be situated and what posture, gesture, and facial expression each should have. Once you have created the frozen moment, have a director tap each character in turn, at which point the character can recite his or her most important line in that scene or simply tell, in the language of today, what's going through his or her mind at that moment.

- If you choose a crowd scene, such as the party or the street brawl, some group members can pantomime the action while the rest of the group does a **choral reading** of the dialogue.

- Record your scene as a **radio drama,** using appropriate sound effects. (The fight scene is particularly good for this activity.)

- **Videotape** your scene, trying out different camera shots. Edit your tape to include the best takes, dub in additional sound effects, and replay the film for an audience.

4. Plan Your Costumes, Props, and Lighting

Costume designers use sketches, paper cutouts, or dressed-up dolls to test different effects. Try to think of pieces of clothing that will convey important aspects of your characters' personalities. Remember, you can suggest a lot with types of hats (fancy or plain?), capes, and masks (plain or trimmed with feathers, sequins, or lace?). Vests and baggy, belted shirts make good

"My first love is the theatre, of course, but you're right up there."

Robert Weber © 1986 from The New Yorker Collection. All Rights Reserved.

SPEAKING AND LISTENING WORKSHOP 865

Teaching the Speaking and Listening Workshop

Because the steps of the Workshop are self-explanatory, students may need you less as a teacher and more as a technical adviser as they prepare their scenes. As groups are working, you may wish to make yourself available as a diction or movement coach.

Remind groups that they will need one member to chart and oversee changes in such areas as lighting, volume, setting, and blocking (actor movement). A director who can observe rehearsals and make critical recommendations for improvements is essential. Remind students that negative comments do not help an actor's performance. As students interact with one another, they should frame their comments so that the focus is on what could be done to improve the performance or staging of the scene.

Reaching All Students

English Language Learners

English language learners who wish to memorize parts and attempt the delivery of lines from a scene should be encouraged to practice with a partner. Remind students that all scene presentations will have strengths, as well as weaknesses that could be alleviated with additional experience.

T865

Preparing a Promptbook

If students have access to a computer, they may wish to enter the basic script for their promptbooks in larger print; 14-point type is usually adequate. The larger print will make reading parts during the rehearsal stage easier.

Professional Note

Some students will be interested in performing the fight scenes in *Romeo and Juliet*. Caution students about what types of props will be allowed and how physical the action may be. You might suggest they work with a physical education teacher who knows fencing.

As Juliet made her shy, hurried exit from the ballroom, I chased after her at full speed and, in doing so, trod on one of the hidden chains. The result—a broken bone in my foot. Hobbling with the aid of a cane, which I did my best to hide under my cloak, I managed to struggle through the remaining four performances; though audiences must have been bewildered by this immobile Romeo, particularly in the sword fight with Paris in Juliet's tomb.

—Maurice Evans,
American actor

costumes for the men. Your costumes and props must be carefully chosen to indicate time and place. You might want to set your performance in the present.

Prepare a list of the props you'll need, such as torches, swords, herbs, and vials (for the "poison"). Appoint one person to collect and keep track of these articles. (Avoid using real swords. The fight scenes are fast, and accidents happen even in professional theaters.)

5. Mark Up Your Scripts

Make copies of your scene to use as a script for each group member. Mark up your scripts as you rehearse, recording decisions you make about how to deliver certain lines, about how actors should make their entrances and exits, about facial expressions and movements and use of voice. These marked-up scripts are called promptbooks.

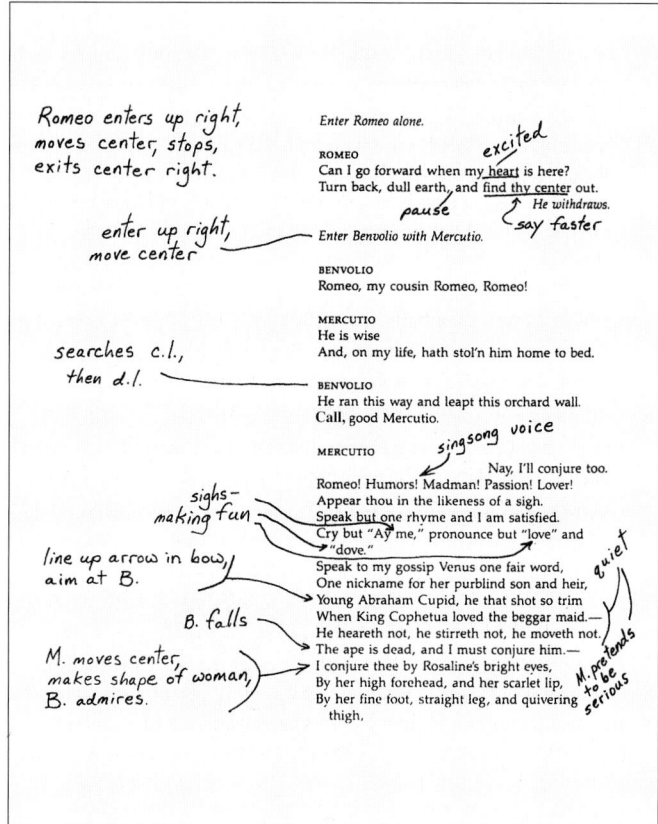

Reaching All Students

Struggling Readers

Students who have difficulty reading Shakespearean language may encounter some challenges in preparing for performance. An essential first step is to ensure that students understand the meaning of the lines they will be speaking. Next, help students to recognize the difference between the end of a line and the end of a sentence. Read through their scenes with them several times and have them mark their promptbooks with colored slashes to indicate correct stopping places.

Rehearsals: Ironing Out the Problems

1. Read It Through

Many directors have their actors read through a play before they ever try to act it. Sit in a circle or onstage in assigned places and read aloud. If you have trouble understanding a passage, paraphrase it (see page 835). Put the paraphrase in your promptbook.

2. Work on the Poetry: A Tip

If you're having trouble with Shakespeare's language, try writing out your speeches as if they are regular prose. Then read them aloud; you'll soon get the sense of the lines and feel their rhythm. You'll also defuse some of your anxiety about Shakespeare.

3. "How Did I Do?"

Devise some means of evaluating your rehearsals. You might prepare a form that each player can fill out after each rehearsal. You might also assign a group of students to be audience critics, and have them fill out evaluation forms after each rehearsal. Be sure to share your evaluations as a group.

4. Players' Journals

Actors, like writers and artists, often keep journals. Performers find it helpful to keep journals of their acting experience. What has acting taught you about yourselves? about Shakespeare's characters? about language?

5. Remember This

In theater tradition a bad dress rehearsal means a good opening night.

> I made a terrible flop as Romeo because they said I couldn't speak verse. It was laughable from my point of view. I couldn't speak? I was brought up speaking; I'd been speaking verse ever since I was eight years old. But I didn't sing it, you see, and the fashion was perhaps to sing it.
>
> —Laurence Olivier, British actor

Grading Timesaver

Rubrics for this workshop appear on p. 208 in the *Portfolio Management System*.

Drawing by Ziegler; © 1993 The New Yorker Magazine, Inc.

Assessing Learning

Check Test: True-False

Each statement is about staging a play. Indicate whether the statement is true or false.

1. A promptbook is usually a marked-up script. [True]
2. A tableau is a frozen moment in a scene. [True]
3. Staging a Shakespearean scene requires elaborate props and costumes. [False]
4. The actor's job is the only really important job in an acting company. [False]
5. A choreographer is needed only for dance scenes. [False]

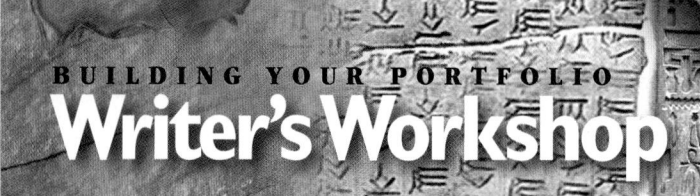

BUILDING YOUR PORTFOLIO
Writer's Workshop

Technology HELP

See Writer's Workshop 2 CD-ROM. *Assignment: Informative Report.*

ASSIGNMENT

Write a research paper based on information gathered from several sources.

AIM

To inform.

AUDIENCE

Your teacher and classmates.

Broad topic: music of the Renaissance

↓

Narrower: music in England in the 1600s

↓

Still narrower: popular musical instruments in Shakespeare's time

go.hrw.com
LE0 Research Paper

EXPOSITORY WRITING

RESEARCH PAPER

When you write a **research paper**, you become a combination detective-reporter. First, you track down the facts of your case and judge their accuracy. Then, like a reporter, you take your information and present it in a clear, well-documented report.

You'll be required to write research papers in many different classes. The research and writing processes remain the same; only the content changes.

Prewriting

1. Explore Topic Ideas

Check your Writer's Notebook for topic ideas on *Romeo and Juliet*. Your own questions about Renaissance life or customs might also be the seeds of a research paper—you're not limited to writing about *Romeo and Juliet*.

Quickly, list some topic ideas: things, people, or concepts you're curious about. For each topic idea, use the *5W-How?* questions (*who, what, where, when, why,* and *how*) to narrow the topic and focus your interest. Say, for example, you're interested in old movies. You might ask who W. C. Fields was, what training a stunt person received, where your favorite black-and-white movie was shot, when the first car-chase scene was filmed, why the film industry developed in Hollywood, or how a particular actor got a start. Write questions like these under each topic you've listed.

2. Choose a Limited Topic

Choose a topic that meets these three criteria: (a) It genuinely interests you, (b) you believe it will interest your readers, and (c) you know you can locate several sources of information on the subject. Don't try to research a topic that's too broad (science fiction movies) or too limited (Princess Leia's costumes in the *Star Wars* films). You'll need to adjust your scope so that you can cover your topic adequately.

868 WILLIAM SHAKESPEARE

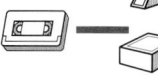

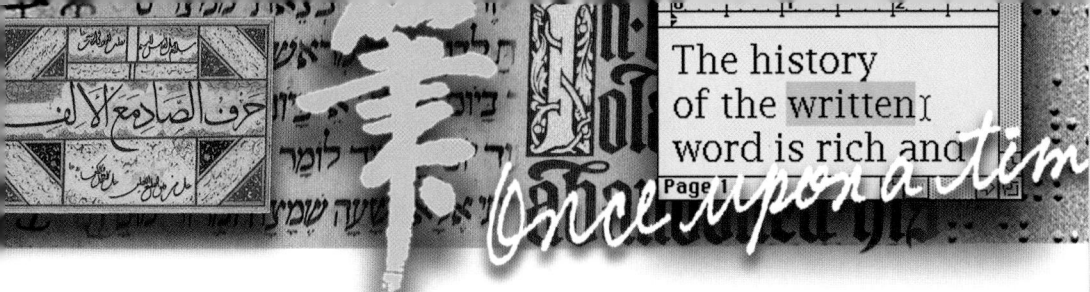

The history of the written word is rich and...

Page 1

Once upon a tim

3. Find Reliable Sources

There are two kinds of sources: **primary sources** (such as literary works, interviews, surveys, letters, journals, autobiographies) and **secondary sources** (such as textbooks, encyclopedia articles, newspaper and magazine articles, biographies, literary criticism).

- **Explore library and community resources.** In a library, you'll find primary and secondary sources. You might visit a museum, government office, or business; or you might interview an expert. For a paper on Renaissance musical instruments, the writer of the model paper on page 870 interviewed a teacher at a local music school.

- **Get on the Net.** Using a search engine, you'll find a lot of information. For example, the key word *rebec* returned 1,365 documents in English. One, *The Rebec,* provides photographs of rebecs and recordings of their sound. Another, *The Rebec Project,* relates the history of the rebec, shows medieval illustrations, and explains how the instrument is built.

As you work, **evaluate** your sources for reliability. Watch for biases, dated facts, and inaccuracies. If possible, verify facts by checking them in several sources.

4. Take Notes and Document Sources

Be sure to take notes in your own words. Make a source card for each source you consult and a note card for each main idea. Enclose direct quotations in highly visible quotation marks, and check to see that you've copied the quotes down word for word.

The MLA (Modern Language Association), preferred by most English teachers, covers two distinct types of documentation:

- **The works cited list at the end of the paper.** This alphabetical listing provides publication information for all sources used to write the paper.

- **Parenthetical documentation within the paper.** Names and page numbers enclosed in parentheses within the text indicate the source of quotations or ideas in the research paper and refer to the works cited list. (See the model paper on the next page.)

Try It Out

For a research report on recent immigration trends, which of these World Wide Web sites would you consider a reliable source? Which would you discard? Why?

1. U.S. Census Bureau

2. Kathy's Green Card Lottery Center

3. U.S. Immigration and Naturalization Service

4. Immigration Lawyers on the Web

5. *The New York Times* on the Web

Communications Handbook HELP

See Research Strategies.

Read the model with students, and discuss the side notes.

❓ How does the writer grab your attention?

❓ What factual support does the writer use?

❓ In paragraph 2, how does the writer handle the introduction of unfamiliar terms, such as *rebec* and *tabor*?

❓ How does the writer incorporate quoted material into the research paper?

Shawm   19

Shawm: double-reed wind instrument, forerunner of the oboe. Has shrill, piercing sound. Of Middle Eastern origin; introduced to Europe during the Crusades.

Subject: A dance band in Shakespeare's time.

Main point: Music in Shakespeare's time was very different from music today. . . .

II. Instruments
   A. Lute
      1. Pear-shaped; stringed
      2. Popular for centuries
   B. Rebec
   C. Tabor
   D. Trombone
   E. Shawm
   F. Spinet
   G. Theorbo
      1. Two sets of strings
      2. Curved neck
      3. Deep sound
      4. High-tech

---

5. Get Organized

Sort your notes into piles. Group together notes that deal with the same idea, and get rid of those that don't apply. Then, arrange your notes in the most logical order. You might choose **chronological order, spatial order, order of importance,** or **cause-and-effect order**. Draft an informal **outline** (see the partial model on the left) to help you plan the arrangement.

6. Elaborate on a Thesis Statement

Your research paper needs a main point, or controlling idea. Read over your notes to see what main point they add up to. You should be able to state it clearly in one sentence, or thesis statement.

THESIS STATEMENT   In Shakespeare's time, tunes and even musical instruments were different from those of today.

Using your notes, elaborate on your main idea with history, direct and indirect quotations, examples, statistics, anecdotes, comparisons. You might add graphics. The writer of the model paper included a drawing of each instrument she describes.

Model

FROM PARTYING WITH THE BARD

[*The following is the introduction and part of the body of a model research paper*]

At the Capulets' party in Act I of <u>Romeo and Juliet</u>, you can be sure the guests were not dancing to heavy metal. What kind of music were they dancing to? What instruments were used to produce popular music in Shakespeare's time? The music and the instruments were very different from those we know today.

A surprising statement and a question catch readers' interest.

Thesis statement.

[*From the body*]

Any band in Shakespeare's time would have included a lute. This pear-shaped stringed instrument had been popular for centuries. Also popular were the violinlike rebec; the tabor, a small drum; an early version of the trombone; and the shawm, ancestor of the oboe (Grove). According to a contemporary pianist, "A band that

Direct quotation from interview.

Drafting

1. Start in the Middle

Start writing the body of your report. (If you get bogged down, a glance at your outline and note cards may help you find your direction.) Be sure to acknowledge the source of quoted or paraphrased ideas. Taking credit for someone else's ideas is plagiarism.

2. Add an Introduction and a Conclusion

Your report should immediately make your readers want to read more. You might start with a striking quotation, a surprising statistic, or an apparent contradiction. End the introduction with your thesis statement. Next, provide any needed background information.

Your conclusion should again focus on your controlling idea. You might explore what your topic means to you, discuss its implications, or refer to your opening lines.

3. Include a Works Cited List

List all the information for every source you refer to in your paper.

---

was really with it might also feature the newly invented, portable keyboard called a spinet." (Karn).

Note parenthetical citation.

Another new Renaissance instrument was the theorbo, a lute with two sets of strings and an S-curved neck. The theorbo sounded deeper than a lute (Grove). With its odd shape and surprising sound, it must have seemed as high-tech as the unusually shaped electric basses in some modern bands. . . .

Comparison to modern instruments.

[*Conclusion*]
Thanks to new instruments and new musical scales, music was changing fast in Shakespeare's time. The changes must have made music as exciting for the people of the Renaissance as modern music is for us today. Maybe the changes also irritated some conservative musicians. After all, rock-and-roll was not accepted for a long time.

Conclusion draws parallels between Renaissance music and modern music.

■ *Evaluation Criteria*

A good research paper

1. *begins with an introduction that contains the **thesis statement**, or **controlling idea***

2. *elaborates on the controlling idea and other general statements with facts, examples, illustrations, quotations, and other kinds of evidence*

3. *is clearly and logically organized*

4. *ends by refocusing on the controlling idea*

5. *presents accurate information from a variety of sources*

6. *uses the writer's own words except with direct quotations*

7. *acknowledges all sources used in the paper*

8. *follows MLA or some other approved style for documenting sources*

Language/Grammar Link
H E L P

Archaic words: page 789.
Figures of speech: page 858.

Drafting

Starting to write a paper with the body rather than the introduction may not work equally well for all students. Explain that the purpose of this suggestion on p. 871 is to promote fluency. Writers often struggle with introductions, and the process of writing the body of the paper may suggest the best type of introduction to pursue. Regardless of where students start to write, however, they should identify their thesis statement—not just their topic—before beginning. Otherwise, the research paper may become a compendium of facts without any focus.

Reaching All Students

Struggling Writers

Some students find it challenging to incorporate research information into a report. They may copy whole passages without citing a source, or they may string together long quotations with few transitional sentences. Have these students read a short informational article. Then, have them give you an oral interpretation of its main points and, together, write a short summary. Compare the summary to the article so students can see how they differ.

Using Students' Strengths

Logical-Mathematical Learners

To help these students, suggest that when they consult a source they copy down and number the bibliographic information. Then, as they gather information from various sources, they should mark each passage with the code number for the book and the page number(s) on which the information was found. For more help, refer students to pp. 986–989 of the Communications Handbook.

Evaluating and Revising

Have students use the Evaluation Criteria on p. 871 to review their drafts and determine needed revisions. In particular, have students highlight the thesis statement and evaluate the supportive evidence for that thesis. Students should also note whether they have any choppy sentences that can be combined. The Sentence Workshop on p. 873 includes instruction in and examples of combining sentences by using appositives.

Proofreading

Have students proofread their own papers first and then exchange them with other students. For this assignment, remind students to be particularly careful about punctuating and citing quotations correctly. Refer students to the section on documenting sources in the Communications Handbook, pp. 986–989, and the section on using quotation marks in the Language Handbook, pp. 1026–1028.

Publishing

Refer students to the Publishing Tips on this page. If your class has access to *HRW Presentation Maker*, encourage students to use this software to prepare their multimedia reports.

Reflecting

Have students consider what they learned about their topics. Are there other aspects of their topics that they would still like to investigate? Encourage them to attach these questions and their answers to their research papers before filing them in their portfolios.

Resources

Peer Editing Forms and Rubrics
• *Portfolio Management System*, p. 211
Revision Transparencies
• *Workshop Resources*, p. 53

Sentence Workshop HELP

Combining sentences by using appositives: page 873.

Publishing Tips

Think of a multimedia approach to presenting your research to your classmates.

• You might include artwork or photographs, an audiotape or a videotape.

• If you are reporting on a historical period, you might dress in period costume.

• If you are reporting on a culture, you might share representative foods and use some expressions common in the language or dialect.

Communications Handbook HELP

See Proofreaders' Marks.

Evaluating and Revising

1. Peer Review

Exchange drafts with a partner. You might use questions like these as you respond to each other's drafts:

• Does the introduction catch your interest? How might it be improved? Is the topic clearly introduced?

• What is the controlling idea?

• Is the controlling idea supported with facts, examples, anecdotes, descriptions, and other kinds of evidence?

2. Self-Evaluation

If you can, put your paper aside for a while. When you're ready, read it as though you were reading it for the first time. Note places where changes might improve it. Think about your readers' comments and suggestions. Then, decide how best to revise it.

Revision Model

Another new Renaissance

~~with two sets of strings and an S-curved neck.~~

instrument was the theorbo, a lute. ∧

deeper than a lute (Grove).

The theorbo sounded different. With ∧

its odd shape and surprising sound,

it must have seemed pretty ∧ *as*

~~as the unusually shaped electric basses in some modern bands.~~

high-tech. ∧

Peer Comments

Give me a clear picture of a lute. Different how?

How do you know this? What's your source?

Maybe compare with a modern instrument?

PEANUTS ® reprinted by permission of United Feature Syndicate, Inc.

872 WILLIAM SHAKESPEARE

Grading Timesaver

Rubrics for this Writer's Workshop assignment appear on p. 211 in the *Portfolio Management System*.

Getting Students Involved

Cooperative Learning

Working together on a broad topic, students can create an informative book rather than separate research papers. For example, the topic of Renaissance parties can be divided among students, with divisions such as entertainment, food, and clothing. While a small group prepares an introduction and conclusion for the book, each of the remaining students should write about one aspect of the topic and illustrate their papers.

T872

Sentence Workshop

COMBINING SENTENCES: APPOSITIVES

Here is an awkwardly written paragraph about *Romeo and Juliet:*

> Two families are feuding. The families are the Montagues and Capulets. Romeo falls in love with Juliet. Romeo is a Montague. Juliet is a Capulet.

The paragraph is made up of five very short sentences. Here is one way you can convey the same information in only two sentences.

> Two families, the Montagues and the Capulets, are feuding. Romeo, a Montague, falls in love with Juliet, a Capulet.

These sentences are combined by the use of appositive phrases (which are underscored). Notice that the appositive phrases are set off by commas.

An **appositive** is a noun or pronoun placed beside another noun or pronoun to identify or explain it. Appositives can also be phrases.

When an appositive is necessary to the sense of the sentence, it is called **restrictive** and it should not be set off by a comma. Benvolio uses a restrictive appositive in Act II:

> Romeo! My cousin Romeo! Romeo!

If Benvolio had only one cousin, the appositive would be nonrestrictive and a comma would be necessary:

> My cousin, Romeo!

Writer's Workshop Follow-up: Revision

When you revise your drafts, look for short sentences that simply identify who someone is or what something is. See if this information can be added to another sentence by making it into an appositive. Watch the use of commas with appositives. Ask yourself if the appositive is necessary for the sense of the sentence. (Omit the appositive to see if the sense of the sentence is still clear.)

Language Handbook HELP

See Appositives and Appositive Phrases, page 1008.

Technology HELP

See Language Workshop CD-ROM. *Key word entry: appositives.*

Try It Out

1. Revise these choppy sentences by combining each pair using an appositive or appositive phrase. Be careful with your commas.

   a. Mercutio is Romeo's friend. He's cynical about love.

   b. Romeo kills Tybalt. Tybalt is Juliet's cousin.

   c. Juliet's father threatens to disown her. Juliet's father is Lord Capulet.

   d. The most famous love scene in drama is the balcony scene. The balcony scene is Act II, Scene 2.

   e. *Romeo and Juliet* was written by William Shakespeare. He is the most famous writer in the world.

2. Be a test writer. Write five sentences to test your partner on the use of commas to set off appositives.

OBJECTIVES
1. Use appositives to combine sentences
2. Identify restrictive and non-restrictive appositives
3. Use correct punctuation for appositives

Resources

Workshop Resources
• Worksheet, p. 79
Language Workshop CD-ROM
• Appositives

Try It Out
Possible Answers
1. **a.** Mercutio, Romeo's friend, is cynical about love.
   b. Romeo kills Tybalt, Juliet's cousin.
   c. Juliet's father, Lord Capulet, threatens to disown her.
   d. The most famous love scene in drama is the balcony scene, Act II, Scene 2.
   e. *Romeo and Juliet* was written by William Shakespeare, the most famous writer in the world.
2. Sentences will vary. Check the corrected sentences for proper comma usage.

Assessing Learning

Quick Check: Appositives
Combine each pair of sentences by using an appositive. (Answers may vary.)
1. Mercutio fought to the death for his friend. His friend was Romeo. [Mercutio fought to the death for his friend Romeo.]
2. Paris is a count. He asks Lord Capulet for Juliet's hand. [Paris, a count, asks Lord Capulet for Juliet's hand.]
3. Shakespeare wrote plays, long poems, and sonnets. He was a prolific writer.

[Shakespeare, a prolific writer, wrote plays, long poems, and sonnets.]
4. My favorite Shakespearean tragedy was written sometime after *Romeo and Juliet. King Lear* is my favorite Shakespearean tragedy. [My favorite Shakespearean tragedy, *King Lear,* was written sometime after *Romeo and Juliet.*]
5. Juliet mourned the death of Tybalt. Tybalt was her cousin. [Juliet mourned the death of Tybalt, her cousin.]

OBJECTIVES

1. Develop strategies for choosing print and electronic sources
2. Analyze the credibility of print and electronic sources
3. Evaluate the relevance of information

Teaching the Lesson

Explain to students that the word *domain* refers to the highest subdivision in the Uniform Resource Locator (URL), the string of characters that precisely identifies an Internet resource's type and location. In the United States, the subdivision is by type of organization. Provide students with the following list:

Domain	Type of Organization
com	commercial
edu	educational
gov	U.S. government
int	international
mil	U.S. military
org	mostly not-for-profit

Using the Strategies

Possible Answers

1. Sources 3, 5, 6, and 7 list helpful books.
2. The web site in source 1 is sponsored by a university; the web site in source 2 is commercial. Source 1 is probably more reliable, since it is an academic site.
3. Phillis Emily Cunnington, who has written three of the books listed in the sources, seems very knowledgeable. C.W. Cunnington, who co-wrote two of these books, also seems to know a great deal about the topic.
4. Possible question: "Can you help me locate reliable sources that document costumes from Shakespeare's plays or from his time period?"

Situation

You plan to go to a costume party as a character from *Romeo and Juliet.* Use these strategies to decide which print and electronic sources are likely to help you create an authentic-looking outfit.

Strategies

Says who?

- Where is the information coming from? Writers with several books on a subject can be expected to have in-depth knowledge. Materials put out by nonprofit organizations, university presses, and established publishers are likely to be trustworthy.

- For sources on the World Wide Web, check the top-level domain in the URL. For example, *gov* usually indicates a government source.

Rate the relevance.

- Examine the title and subtitle (or the URL) of each source. Even without examining the works themselves, you can ignore any whose titles indicate that they deal with subjects other than the one you're interested in.

Check the dates.

- In rapidly changing fields the more recent the source the better. But don't dismiss a

source just because it's older. Some older works remain the standard of excellence.

Go one-on-one.

- Don't hesitate to ask librarians for guidance; they're trained to know which sources can be trusted.

Using the Strategies

Use these strategies to evaluate the sources in the box above.

1. Which books would help you with your costume?

2. What types of organizations sponsor the Web sites? Which site might be more reliable? Why?

3. Which writer seems to know a great deal about the topic? Explain your answer.

4. If you needed help, how would you phrase your question?

Extending the Strategies

Identify at least three sources of information about the new Globe Theatre in London. Evaluate their credibility.

Possible Sources

1. "Production of Romeo & Juliet—October 17, 1935." *Motley Collection of Theatre and Costume Design.* University of Illinois at Urbana-Champaign Library and the Follett Corporation. <http://images.grainger.uiuc.edu/~motley/romeo.htm>.
2. "Shakespeare Web," *dna productions,* May 31, 1997, <http://www.shakespeare.com>.
3. Cunnington, C. W., and P. E. Cunnington. *Handbook of English Costume in the Sixteenth Century.* London: Faber, 1954.
4. Cunnington, C. W., and P. E. Cunnington. *Handbook of English Costume in the Eighteenth Century.* London: Faber, 1972.
5. Cunnington, Phillis Emily. *Costume of Household Servants, from the Middle Ages to 1900.* New York: Barnes and Noble, 1975.
6. Hansen, Henny Harald. *Costume Cavalcade: 685 Examples of Historic Costume in Colour.* London: Methuen, 1956.
7. Peacock, John. *The Chronicle of Western Costume: From the Ancient World to the Late Twentieth Century.* London: Thames and Hudson, 1991.
8. Franco Zeffirelli, director, *Romeo and Juliet,* starring Olivia Hussey and Leonard Whiting. Paramount, 1968.

Crossing the Curriculum

Art

Students may wish to apply the strategies in this lesson and conduct their own research on authentic Shakespearean costumes. Have students who are interested in design create sketches based on their research. Some students may wish to make some part of a costume to use in the scene they stage for the Speaking and Listening Workshop on p. 864.

Learning for Life
Making a Decision

OBJECTIVES
1. Analyze and evaluate a decision-making plan
2. Apply the plan to a real or an imagined problem

Problem

Romeo and Juliet, when faced with horrible choices, made decisions that led to tragedy. In real life the decisions we make also have consequences. How can we learn to make sound decisions?

Project

Analyze and evaluate a decision-making plan, and apply the steps of the plan to a problem, real or imagined.

Preparation

Here is a fairly standard decision-making plan:

1. State all the possible choices that are open to you. If you see only two possible choices, try mixing and matching elements of each, to come up with at least one other possibility.

2. Jot down your thoughts about the possible consequences of each choice, using "If I" statements. ("If I don't try out for the play, I may miss a lot of fun.")

3. What could you gain by making each choice? What could you lose? What's the best thing that could happen if you make each choice? The worst thing?

4. Make a chart of pros and cons for each choice.

5. Imagine someone whose judgment you trust being faced with the same decision. From what you know about the person, what would he or she be likely to do? Why?

6. Weigh the information you've noted on your chart, and make your choice.

Procedure

1. List examples of some choices people must make, based on what you know from literature, the media, or your own experience (use Romeo and Juliet's problem, if you wish). Discuss the ways people approached the problem.

2. Apply one of these problems to the decision-making plan outlined here. What works? What doesn't?

3. Adapt the decision-making plan.

Presentation

Use one of the following formats (or another that your teacher approves).

1. Cartoon Strip

Create a cartoon showing an imaginary character using the decision-making plan. With other students who have chosen this option, display your cartoon in the school media center or lunchroom.

2. Soliloquy

Write a soliloquy (in prose or poetry) for a real or fictional character who is using the plan to make an important decision. Perform your soliloquy in front of the class.

3. Advice Column

Write a letter to an advice columnist as if you were either Romeo or Juliet facing your terrible problem. In a second letter, respond as if you were the columnist. Read the advice you give the young couple and discuss it with a group of classmates. Would following this plan have helped Romeo and Juliet?

Processing

For your portfolio, write a brief reflection answering these questions:

- What conclusions have you drawn from this project?
- What do you think is the strongest feature of the decision-making plan? the weakest? Are there situations where it would not work?

Resources

Viewing and Representing
HRW Multimedia Presentation Maker

Students may wish to use the *Multimedia Presentation Maker,* if available, to help create a cartoon strip.

Grading Timesaver

Rubrics for this Learning for Life project appear on p. 212 in the *Portfolio Management System.*

Using Technology

Explain to students that the process for making personal decisions is similar to the process used in making business decisions. If spreadsheet or personal organizer software packages are available in the school district or community, arrange a demonstration of each to illustrate their use in decision making. With the various software packages, students may organize their notes, make charts and grids, and document their decision-making plans. To complete their presentations —letters, soliloquies, and reflections— students may use computer software to write and publish their final drafts.

Developing Workplace Competencies

Preparation	Procedure	Presentation
• Acquires data • Evaluates data • Reasons	• Works in teams • Solves problems • Processes information • Interprets information	• Thinks creatively • Communicates ideas and information

OBJECTIVES

1. Read and interpret epic poetry
2. Identify and interpret the literary elements and motifs of epic poetry
3. Apply a variety of reading strategies to epic poetry, with special emphasis on monitoring reading comprehension
4. Respond to literature using a variety of modes
5. Learn and use new words
6. Learn about the background of the *Odyssey*
7. Plan, draft, revise, edit, proof, and publish a cause-and-effect essay
8. Revise sentences to eliminate wordiness
9. Demonstrate the ability to compare and evaluate artistic interpretations
10. Identify the qualities that a role model should possess

Responding to the Quotation

No epic has been produced in America, though some people believe Walt Whitman's *Leaves of Grass* comes close to being an American epic, and some would give that honor to Mark Twain's *Adventures of Huckleberry Finn*. You might ask students what manners, customs, and values "bind" American society together. Ask them what they would expect to find in an American epic.

Star Wars   *Superman ?*

Harry Potter   Lord of the Rings
King Arthur = Celtic

THE EPIC

An epic is an encyclopedia of the manners, customs, and values that bind a whole civilization together.

—W. T. Jewkes

Return of Odysseus (5th century B.C., first half).
Relief, believed to be from the island of Melos. Terra cotta.
The Metropolitan Museum of Art, New York. Fletcher Fund, 1930 (30.11.9).
Photograph ©1982 The Metropolitan Museum of Art.

876

Selection Readability

This Annotated Teacher's Edition provides a summary of each selection in the student book. Following each Summary heading, you will find one, two, or three small icons. These icons indicate, in an approximate sense, the reading level of the selection.

■ One icon indicates that the selection is easy.
■■ Two icons indicate that the selection is on an intermediate reading level.
■■■ Three icons indicate that the selection is challenging.

T876

Art used as a wall hanging.
People wanted children to be inspired & reminded of the characters' characteristics, flaws & all; their choices, the consequences, the effects on others

* "Everything in moderation."

- mind, body, spirit connectivity of many ancient cultures such as India, China, Sumerian, Native American
- strive to achieve balance

Heroic / Leadership Qualities:
1. intelligence (not just book smart!)
2. integrity / honesty (integrity = doing the right thing for the right reason even when no one else is around)
3. physically & mentally fit
4. skilled strategist
5. loyal / self sacrificing
6. brave
7. skilled communicator
8. takes ~~initiative~~ initiative / self motivator
9. determined
10. confident

hubris
catharsis

in medias res
rhapsodes

The Odyssey: An Introduction

This introductory essay provides students with a comprehensive background for their reading of the *Odyssey*. It includes a discussion of the epic and its place in Greek culture, a summary of the Trojan War, insight into the roles of the storyteller and the audience in the ancient world, and an overview of the people and places that students will encounter in the *Odyssey*.

Ⓐ Historical Connection

Only in the past hundred years have archaeologists established that Troy was an actual city that met violent destruction about 1200 B.C.—a date very close to 1184 B.C., the traditional date for the climax of the Trojan War. A map of the area is shown on pp. 888–889.

Ⓑ Elements of Literature

Epic

Characteristics of an epic usually include

- a physically impressive hero of national or historical importance
- a vast setting involving much of the known physical world and sometimes the land of the dead as well
- action such as a quest or journey taken in search of something of value
- evidence of supernatural forces at work
- glorification of the hero at the end *overcomes pride*
- a rootedness in a specific culture and society *group of loyal followers*

Ⓒ Literary Connections

The tale of Gilgamesh, which dates back as far as the third millennium B.C., is the earliest extant example of epic poetry. The epic tells about the journeys of a Mesopotamian king in search of immortality.

British Museum, London.

The blind poet Homer (probably 2nd century A.D.). Found near Naples.

These real battles would have taken place as early as 1200 B.C.—a time that was at least as long ago for Homer's audience as the Pilgrims' landing at Plymouth Rock is for us.

THE ODYSSEY
AN INTRODUCTION BY DAVID ADAMS LEEMING

Almost three thousand years ago, people who lived in the starkly beautiful part of the world we now call Greece were telling stories about a great war. The person credited with later gathering all these stories together and telling them as one unified epic is a man named Homer (*Homēros*, in Greek). Homer's great war stories are called, in English, the *Iliad* and the *Odyssey*. (In Greek, the *Iliad* is *Ilias* and the *Odyssey* is *Odysseia*.)

Homer's stories probably can be traced to historical struggles for control of the waterway leading from the Aegean Sea to the Sea of Marmara and the Black Sea. These real battles would have taken place as early as 1200 B.C.—a time that was at least as long ago for Homer's audience as the Pilgrims' landing at Plymouth Rock is for us.

Ⓐ Homer's first epic was the *Iliad*, which tells of a ten-year war fought on the plains outside the walls of a great city called Troy (also known as Ilion). The ruins of Troy can still be seen in western Turkey. In Homer's story the Trojan War was fought between the people of Troy and an alliance of Greek kings (at that time each island and area of the Greek mainland had its own king). The *Iliad* tells us that the cause of the war was sexual jealousy: The world's most beautiful woman, Helen, abandoned her husband, Menelaus, a Greek king, and ran off with Paris, a prince of Troy. (See "The Beautiful Helen," page 305.)

The *Odyssey*, Homer's second epic, is the story of the attempt of one Greek soldier, Odysseus, to get home after the Trojan War. All epic poems in the Western world owe something to the basic patterns established by these two stories.

EPICS AND VALUES

Ⓑ **Epics** are long narrative poems that tell of the adventures of heroes who in some way embody the values of their civilizations. The Greeks for centuries used the *Iliad* and the *Odyssey* in schools to teach Greek virtues. So it is not surprising that later cultures that admired the Homeric epics created their own epics, imitating Homer's style but conveying their own value systems.

Still, for all the epics written since Homer's time and for all the ones composed before it, when we think of the word *epic,* we think primarily of the *Iliad* and the *Odyssey*. Rome's *Aeneid,* France's *Song of Roland,* Italy's *Divine Comedy,* the ancient Sumerian tale of Ⓒ *Gilgamesh,* India's *Mahabharata* and *Ramayana,* Mali's *Sundiata*—all are great stories in the epic tradition. But to discover the heart of that tradition, we need to examine Homer's epics.

Reaching All Students

Struggling Readers

After students read the introduction to the *Odyssey* for the first time, pair them and ask them to create questions for each other. Using at least five note cards each, students should write one question on each card and exchange questions to answer as they reread the introduction. They can then use the questions and answers for review. In creating their questions, students should be encouraged to consider the art also.

English Language Learners

Help build students' confidence by modeling the correct pronunciation of names, and have students repeat the pronunciations several times.

Advanced Learners

Ask each student to become an expert on one of the characters or places mentioned in the introduction and to research that person or place in encyclopedias or in reference books, such as Edith Hamilton's *Mythology*. Experts should also take notes on their subjects as they read the epic. Students can then ask the expert when they want more information about a place or a person.

The *Iliad* is the primary model for the epic of war. The *Odyssey* is the model for the epic of the long journey. The theme of the journey has been basic in Western literature—it is found in fairy tales, in such novels as *The Incredible Journey, Moby-Dick,* and *The Hobbit,* and in such movies as *The Wizard of Oz, Star Wars* (see page 954), *The Lion King,* and *Forrest Gump.* Thus, the *Odyssey* has been the more widely read of Homer's two great stories.

THE WAR-STORY BACKGROUND: VIOLENCE AND BRUTALITY

The background for Odysseus' story is found in the *Iliad,* which is set in the tenth and final year of the Trojan War. According to the *Iliad,* the Greeks attacked Troy to avenge the insult suffered by Menelaus, king of Sparta, when his wife, Helen, ran off with Paris, a young prince of Troy. The Greek kings banded together under the leadership of Agamemnon, the brother of Menelaus. In a thousand ships, they sailed across the Aegean Sea and encircled the walled city of Troy.

The audience of the *Odyssey* would have known this war story. Listeners would have known that the Greeks were eventually victorious, that they gained entrance to Troy, reduced the city to smoldering ruins, and butchered all the inhabitants, except for those they took as slaves back to Greece. They would have known all about the greatest of the Greek warriors, Achilles, who was to die young in the final year of the war. The audience **D** would probably have heard other epic poems (now lost) that told

The Fall of Troy (1974) by Romare Bearden. Collage and mixed media on board (36″ x 48″).

© Romare Bearden Foundation/Licensed by VAGA, New York, NY.

© Romare Bearden Foundation/Licensed by VAGA, New York, NY.

D **Literary Connections**

Achilles is the hero of the Iliad who gives us the term *Achilles' heel.* The term refers to any vulnerable or weak spot. (The worst pitcher in a baseball team's starting rotation might be called the team's "Achilles' heel.") Achilles had been dipped into the river Styx by his mother, Thetis, in order to make him invulnerable, but she forgot the spot on the baby's heel where she held him. Paris killed the great Achilles by shooting a divinely directed poisoned arrow into his heel.

RESPONDING TO THE ART

Romare Bearden (1914–1988), born in North Carolina and educated at Columbia University and the Sorbonne, in Paris, became the premier collagist in the United States in the 1960s. Bearden's collages are pieces of photos and painted paper that often depict aspects of American culture. In this collage, one of a series he did on the Trojan War, Bearden puts the Homeric epic in a black context. Other Beardens are found on pp. 281, 283, 284, 290, and 524. **Activity.** Ask students what events of the Trojan War they can identify in the picture. [Note the wooden horse, the burning towers of Ilium, the ruined city, and the boats taking off.] Note also that the warriors look like African warriors.

Using Students' Strengths

Visual Learners

After students have read the introductory essay, have them create a graphic summarizing what they have read, using the text to verify facts. Post or copy the summaries for the class to use in reviewing the introduction.

Verbal Learners

Have students make a two-column chart to keep track of terms and names from Homer's epics that they come across in everyday use. In the left column, they can list words such as *odyssey, Trojan horse,* and *Achilles' heel.* In the right column, they should record where they found each term (advertisements, news broadcasts, etc.) and the meaning of each reference.

A Literary Connections

In Homer, it is actually Aegisthus, the wife's lover, who kills Agamemnon. But another Greek writer, Aeschylus, wrote a play in which Agamemnon's unfaithful wife, Clytemnestra, is portrayed as the murderer. The name of this play is *Agamemnon,* and it opens the *Oresteia* trilogy.

B Literary Connections

English writer Samuel Butler presented a related theory in his 1897 *The Authoress of the Odyssey.* Although the question of female authorship can never be proved, even today experts disagree on whether the same poet was responsible for both the *Iliad* and the *Odyssey.* The arguments on either side are based primarily on stylistic similarities and differences between the two epics. In ancient times, however, a single poet named Homer was universally credited with the authorship of both epics.

Melancholy = deep sadness

> The *Odyssey* is a story marked by melancholy and a feeling of post-war disillusionment.

> One critic, Robert Graves, was so impressed by the unusual importance of women and home and hearth in the *Odyssey* that he believed Homer must have been a woman.

880 THE EPIC

of the homecomings of the various Greek heroes who survived the war. They would especially have known about the home-coming of Agamemnon, the leader of the Greek forces, who was murdered by his unfaithful wife when he returned from Troy.

Finally, Homer's listeners might well have been particularly fascinated by another homecoming story—this one about a somewhat unusual hero, known as much for his brain as for his brawn. In fact, many legends had already grown up around this hero, whose name was Odysseus. He was the subject of Homer's new epic, the *Odyssey.*

ODYSSEUS: A HERO IN TROUBLE

In Homer's day heroes were thought of as a special class of aristocrats. They were placed somewhere between the gods and ordinary human beings. Heroes experienced pain and death, but they were always sure of themselves, always "on top of the world."

Odysseus is different. He is a hero in trouble. We can relate to Odysseus because we share with him a sense of being somehow lost in a world of difficult choices. Like Odysseus, we have to cope with unfair authority figures. Like him, we have to work very hard to get what we want.

The *Odyssey* is a story marked by melancholy and a feeling of postwar disillusionment. Odysseus was a great soldier in the war, but his war record is not of interest to the monsters that populate the world of his wanderings. Even the people of his home island, Ithaca, seem to lack respect for him. It is as if society were saying to the returning hero, "You were a great soldier once—or so they say—but times have changed. This is a difficult world, and we have more important things to think about than your record."

In the years before the great war, Odysseus had married the beautiful and ever-faithful Penelope, one of several very strong women in the man's world of the Greek epic. (One critic, Robert Graves, was so impressed by the unusual importance of women and home and hearth in the *Odyssey* that he believed Homer must have been a woman.)

Penelope and Odysseus had one son, Telemachus (tə·lem′ə·kəs). He was still a toddler when Odysseus was called by Agamemnon and Menelaus to join them in the war against Troy. But Odysseus was a homebody. He preferred not to go to war, especially a war fought for an unfaithful woman. Even though he was obligated under a treaty to go, Odysseus tried draft-dodging. It is said that when Agamemnon and Menelaus came to fetch him, he pretended to be insane and acted as if he did not recognize his visitors. Instead of entertaining them, he dressed as a peasant and began plowing a field and sowing it with salt. But the "draft board" was smarter than

Getting Students Involved

Cooperative Learning

Have students work in small groups to list words in the introduction that give them trouble. Have groups share their lists with the class. Then, divide the problem words into categories, such as names, literary terms, or social-studies terms. Have each group create an illustrated dictionary page using the words from one of these categories. Each group should be responsible for making copies of the page to share with classmates.

Odysseus. They threw his baby, Telemachus, in front of his oncoming plow. Odysseus revealed his sanity by quickly turning the plow aside to avoid running over his son.

THE WOODEN-HORSE TRICK

Once in Troy, Odysseus performed extremely well as a soldier and commander. It was he, for example, who thought of the famous wooden-horse trick that would lead to the downfall of Troy. For ten years the Greeks had been fighting the Trojans, but they were fighting outside Troy's massive walls. They had been unable to break through the walls and enter the city. Odysseus' plan was to build an enormous wooden horse and hide a few Greek soldiers inside its hollow belly. After the horse was built, the Greeks pushed it up to the gates of Troy and withdrew their armies, so that their camp appeared to be abandoned. Thinking that the Greeks had given up the fight and that the horse was a peace offering, the Trojans brought the horse into their city. That night, the Greeks hidden inside the wooden body came out, opened the gates of Troy to the whole Greek army, and began the battle that was to win the war.

THE ANCIENT WORLD AND OURS

The world of Odysseus was harsh, a world familiar with violence. In a certain sense Odysseus and his men act like pirates on their journey home. They think nothing of entering a town and carrying off all its worldly goods. The "worldly goods" in an ancient city might only have been pots and pans and cattle and sheep. The "palaces" the Greeks raided might have been little more than elaborate mud and stone farmhouses. Yet, in the struggles of Odysseus, Penelope, and Telemachus in their "primitive" society that had little in common with the high Athenian culture that would develop several centuries later, there is something that has a great deal to do with us.

A SEARCH FOR THEIR PLACES IN LIFE

Odysseus and his family are people searching for the right relationships with one another and with the people around them. They want to find their proper places in life. It is this theme that sets the tone for the *Odyssey* and determines the unusual way in which the poem is structured.

Instead of beginning at the beginning with Odysseus' departure from Troy, the story begins with his son, Telemachus. Telemachus is now twenty years old. He is threatened by rude, powerful men

Trojan Horse (16th century) by Niccolò dell' Abbate. Tempera on panel.
Galleria Estense, Modena, Italy.

> Odysseus and his family are people searching for the right relationships with one another and with the people around them.

THE ODYSSEY: AN INTRODUCTION 881

Crossing the Curriculum

A Literary Connections

The phrase "double determination" describes this relationship between gods and mortals. Homer often attributes an event to two causes: the intervention of a god and the act or character of a mortal. Thus, if a hero's arrow strikes a target, the poet may say that Athena helped the hero, but the hero also had to be an excellent archer in the first place.

B Historical Connections

Chios was part of the region called Ionia. The belief that Homer came from Chios arises from the fact that many of the grammatical structures and vocabulary words in the epics are Ionian in origin. In addition, a society of storytellers calling themselves the "sons of Homer" sprang up in Chios in the eighth century B.C.

C Elements of Literature

Rhapsodes

Although written versions of the epics became available in the sixth century B.C., rhapsodes were active for many centuries after Homer. *Rhapsodia,* or oral poetry contests between performers, became common at Greek festivals, and the fourth-century B.C. philosopher Plato describes a rhapsode named Ion who made his living by reciting long passages of epics to music.

Odysseus is in search of a way out of what we might today call his midlife crisis.

Some scholars think Homer was just a legend. But scholars have also argued about whether a man called Shakespeare ever existed. It is almost as if they were saying that Homer and Shakespeare are too good to be true.

swarming about his own home, pressuring his mother to marry one of them. These men are bent on robbing Telemachus of his inheritance. Telemachus is a young man who needs his father, the one person who can put things right at home.

Meanwhile, we hear that his father is stranded on an island, longing to find a way to get back to his wife, child, and home. It is ten years since Odysseus sailed from Troy, twenty years since he left Ithaca to fight in Troy. While Telemachus is in search of his father, Odysseus is in search of a way out of what we might today call his midlife crisis. He is searching for inner peace, for a way to reestablish a natural balance in his life. The quests of father and son provide a framework for the poem and bring us into it as well—because we all are in search of our real identities, our true selves.

RELATIONSHIPS WITH THE GODS

This brings us to mythic and religious questions in the *Odyssey*. **Myths** are stories that use fantasy to express ideas about life that cannot be expressed easily in realistic terms. Myths are essentially religious because they are concerned with the relationship between human beings and the unknown or spiritual realm.

A As you will see, Homer is always concerned with the relationship between humans and gods. Homer is religious: For him, the gods control all things. Athena, the goddess of wisdom, is always at the side of Odysseus. This is appropriate, because Odysseus is known for his mental abilities. Thus, in Homer's stories a god can be an **alter ego,** a reflection of a hero's best or worst qualities. The god who works against Odysseus is Poseidon, the god of the sea, who is known for arrogance and a certain brutishness. Odysseus himself can be violent and cruel, just as Poseidon is.

WHO WAS HOMER?

B No one knows for sure who Homer was. The later Greeks believed he was a blind minstrel who came from the island of Chios. Some scholars feel there must have been two Homers; some think he was just a legend. But scholars have also argued about whether a man called Shakespeare ever existed. It is almost as if they were saying that Homer and Shakespeare are too good to be true. On the whole, it seems sensible to take the word of the Greeks themselves. We can at least accept the existence of Homer as a model for a class of wandering bards or minstrels later called rhapsodes.

C These **rhapsodes,** or "singers of tales," were the historians and entertainers as well as the myth-makers of their time. There was probably no written history in Homer's day. There were certainly no movies and no television, and the Greeks had nothing like a Bible or

882 THE EPIC

Making the Connections

Cultural Connections: The Oral Tradition

The wandering storyteller who keeps history and legend alive through oral recitation is a tradition of many cultures. The *jali* or *griot* of West Africa, for example, is a combination poet, professional musician, cultural historian, and keeper of genealogical information. A griot's repertoire might include records of family lineages to be sung at weddings or other occasions, as well as legends and myths. Griot songs are often accompanied by the *balafon,* a type of xylophone, or the *kora,* a stringed instrument with similarities to the banjo and harp. Traditionally, griots formed a hereditary professional caste, and an apprentice griot might receive his musical education from another family member. The *Sundiata* epic, which tells the story of the thirteenth-century Malian king Sundiata Keita, has been told for centuries by griots. Encourage your students to learn more about the *Sundiata* epic or to find recordings of griot music and griot-influenced music of West Africa to share with the class.

a book of religious stories. So it was that the minstrels traveled about from community to community singing of recent events or of the doings of heroes, gods, and goddesses. It is as if the author of the Book of Kings in the Bible, the writer of a history of World War II, and a famous pop singer were combined in one person. Homer's people saw no conflict among religion, history, and good fun.

A singer with a lyre (Minoan period). Bronze.

Archaeological Museum, Heraklion, Crete, Greece.

HOW WERE THE EPICS TOLD?

Scholars have found that oral epic poets are still composing today in Eastern Europe and other parts of the world. These scholars suggest that stories like the *Iliad* and the *Odyssey* were originally told aloud by people who could not read and write. The stories were composed orally according to a basic story line. But most of the actual words were improvised—made up on the spot—in a way that fit a particular rhythm or meter. The singers of these stories had to be very talented, and they had to work very hard. They also needed an audience that could listen closely. **D**

We can see from this why there is so much repetition in the Homeric epics. The oral storyteller, in fact, had a store of formulas ready in his memory. He knew formulas for describing the arrival and greeting of guests, the eating of meals, and the taking of baths. He knew formulas for describing the sea (it is always "wine-dark") and for describing Athena (she is always "gray-eyed Athena"). **E**

Formulas such as these had another advantage: They gave the

> The oral storyteller, in fact, had a store of formulas ready in his memory. He knew formulas for describing the arrival and greeting of guests, the eating of meals, and the taking of baths.

[handwritten note:] SIMILAR TO MODERN DAY RAPPERS? POETRY SLAM?

THE ODYSSEY: AN INTRODUCTION **883**

D Elements of Literature
Meter
Both the *Odyssey* and the *Iliad* are written in dactylic hexameter, a unit of verse with six metrical feet. The fifth foot is usually a dactyl, with one stressed syllable followed by two unstressed syllables. The last foot is a spondee, with two stressed syllables. The first four feet might be either dactyls or spondees.

E Appreciating Language
Formulaic Repetition
One formula for Odysseus, when his name appears in the nominative case as the subject of a sentence, is *polymetis Odysseus* ("many-counseled Odysseus"). If the poet has a longer stretch of hexameter verse to fill, however, he might use the formula *polytlas dios Odysseus* ("much-enduring, godlike Odysseus"). The concept of a "formula" runs the gamut from a single word to an entire passage. Thus, when the poet has to describe the rigging and departure of a ship, for example, he will ordinarily repeat, with only some minor adjustments, a whole series of suitable lines from his repertoire.

RESPONDING TO THE ART
The Minoan culture flourished in Greece from 2000 B.C. to 1500 B.C. This culture was named for the legendary King Minos, who was said to keep a beast, half man, half bull, in a labyrinth. This sculpture shows a singer playing a lyre, a small stringed instrument similar to our harps today.

Activity. Have students compare this lyre with a kora, the instrument used by the griots of West Africa. They might even find contemporary instruments that are similar.

A Elements of Literature

Homeric Similes

These similes often draw their material from nature (lions, storms, deer, or rivers) or from everyday activities (fishing or herding). Another notable feature of Homeric similes is their length; some, such as the comparison of the blinding of Polyphemus to the actions of a blacksmith (pp. 904–905), continue for many lines.

B Reading Skills and Strategies

Connecting with the Text

? What contemporary situations does the scene described here make you think of? [Possible responses: the expectant audience at a Broadway show, an important concert, or the opening night of a highly anticipated film.]

Imagine a large hall full of people who are freshly bathed, rubbed with fine oils, and draped in clean tunics. Imagine the smell of meat being cooked over charcoal, the sound of voices. Imagine wine being freely poured, the flickering reflections of the great cooking fires, and the torches that light the room.

---

singer and his audience some breathing time. The audience could relax for a moment and enjoy a familiar and memorable passage, while the singer could think ahead to the next part of his story.

A When we think about the audience that listened to these stories, we can also understand the value of the extended comparisons that we call **Homeric** or **heroic similes** today. These similes compare heroic or epic events to simple and easily understandable everyday events—events the audience would recognize instantly. For example, at one point in the *Iliad,* Athena prevents an arrow from striking Menelaus. The singer compares the goddess's actions to an action that every listener would have been familiar with:

> She brushed it away from his skin as lightly as when a mother
> Brushes a fly away from her child who is lying in sweet sleep.

Epic poets such as Homer would come to a city and would go through a part of their repertory while there. A story as long as the *Odyssey* (11,300 lines) could not be told at one sitting. We have to assume that if the singer had only a few days in a town, he would summarize some of his story and sing the rest in detail, in as many sittings as he had time for.

This is exactly what will happen in the selections from the *Odyssey* that are presented here. We'll assume that Homer wants to get his story told to us, but that his time is limited. We'll also assume that the audience, before retiring at the end of each performance, wants to talk about the stories they've just heard. You are now part of that audience.

A LIVE PERFORMANCE

What was it like to hear a live performance of the *Odyssey*? We can guess what it was like because there are many instances in the epic itself in which traveling singers appear and sing their tales. In the court of the Phaeacian king, Alcinous (al·sin′ō·əs), in Book 8, for instance, there is a particularly wonderful singer who must make us wonder if the blind Homer is talking about himself. Let's picture the setting of a performance before we start the story.

B Imagine a large hall full of people who are freshly bathed, rubbed with fine oils, and draped in clean tunics. Imagine the smell of meat being cooked over charcoal, the sound of voices. Imagine wine being freely poured, the flickering reflections of the great cooking fires, and the torches that light the room. A certain anticipation hangs in the air. It is said that the blind minstrel Homer is in the city and that he has new stories about that long war in Troy. Will he appear and entertain tonight?

Assessing Learning

Check Test: Questions and Answers

1. Who is the *Odyssey's* traditionally accepted author? [Homer]
2. How is the *Odyssey* related to the *Iliad*? [The *Odyssey* tells the story of a hero returning from the war described in the *Iliad*.]
3. When and where does the *Iliad* take place? [approximately 1200 B.C. in Troy]
4. Where is Odysseus' home? [in Ithaca]
5. What is a Homeric simile? [an extended comparison between heroic or epic events and everyday occurrences]

PEOPLE AND PLACES C

The following cast of characters includes some of those who take part in the sections of the *Odyssey* included in this book. Note that the Greeks in the *Odyssey* are often referred to as **Achaeans** (ə·kē′ənz) or **Argives** (är′gīvz′). *Achaeans* is the most general term, which also includes the people in Ithaca, the island off the west coast of Greece where Odysseus ruled. The word *Achaeans* is taken from the name of an ancient part of northeastern Greece called Achaea. The name *Argives* usually refers to the Greeks who went to fight at Troy.

THE WANDERINGS: CHARACTERS AND PLACES

Aeaea (ē·ē′ə): home of Circe, the witch-goddess.

Alcinous (al·sin′ō·əs): king of Phaeacia. Odysseus tells the story of his adventures to Alcinous' court.

Calypso (kə·lip′sō): beautiful goddess-nymph who keeps Odysseus on her island for seven years.

Charybdis (kə·rib′dis): female monster who sucks in water three times a day to form a deadly whirlpool (thought to be a real whirlpool in the Strait of Messina).

Cicones (si·kō′nēz): people living on the southwestern coast of Thrace, who battled Odysseus and his men on their journey home.

Circe (sur′sē): witch-goddess who turns Odysseus' men into swine.

Cyclops: See **Polyphemus,** below.

Erebus (er′ə·bəs): dark area of the underworld where the dead reside.

Eurylochus (yoo·ril′ə·kəs): one of Odysseus' loyal crew.

Lotus Eaters: people who feed Odysseus' men with lotus plants to make them forget Ithaca.

Phaeacia (fē·ā′shə): island kingdom ruled by King Alcinous. The Phaeacians are shipbuilders and traders.

Polyphemus (päl′i·fē′məs): the **Cyclops** (sī′kläps′) blinded by Odysseus; the son of the sea god Poseidon. **Cyclopes** (sī·klō′pēz′) are a race of brutish one-eyed giants who live solitary lives as shepherds, supposedly on the island now known as Sicily.

Scylla (sil′ə): female monster with six serpent heads, each head having a triple row of fangs (thought to be a dangerous rock in the Strait of Messina).

Penelope (detail) (1864) by John Roddam Spencer-Stanhope.

The De Morgan Foundation, London.

Circe hands the magic potion to Odysseus (5th century B.C.). Detail from a lekythos, a vase used for oils and ointments.

National Archaeological Museum, Athens.

Ⓐ Literary Connections

As goddess of war and wisdom, Athena allies herself with the brave and intelligent Odysseus and intercedes to aid his return.

Ⓑ Vocabulary Note

Greek Roots

The Greek name *Cronus* is popularly connected with *chronos*, "time." Related English words are *chronic*, *crony*, *chronicle*. The Greek root *helios*, "sun," is apparent in several words; for example, plants whose flowers turn toward the sun are called *heliotropes*. Ask students to find other words that derive from *helios*. [helium; heliograph]

Ⓒ Literary Connections

Poseidon at first supported the Greeks against the Trojans, who had cheated him out of pay for building their city walls. But Poseidon turned against the Greeks when they defiled Athena's temple; he turned, fatally, against Odysseus after Odysseus incurred the curse of the Cyclops Polyphemus, Poseidon's son.

RESPONDING TO THE ART

Athena, who assisted warriors who defended civilized values, is said to have emerged from the head of Zeus, fully grown and dressed for battle.

Activity. You might refer students to the contemporary story "Helen on Eighty-sixth Street" by Wendi Kaufman (p. 303). In that story a young girl acts in a school play about Helen of Troy and becomes particularly fond of Athena. What details in this beautiful sculpture reveal that Athena is associated with warriors? [the helmet] Note that the goddess is mourning one of the great warriors in ancient Greek literature, Achilles.

Poseidon (5th century B.C.). Bronze.

Athens Museum.

Acropolis Museum, Athens.

Athena mourning the death of Achilles at Troy. From a marble stele, or pillar.

886 THE EPIC

Sirens: sea nymphs whose beautiful and mysterious music lures sailors to steer their ships toward the rocks.

Teiresias (tī·rē'sē·əs): famous blind prophet from the city of Thebes. Odysseus meets him in the Land of the Dead.

Thrinakia (thri·nā'kē·ə): island where the sun god Helios keeps his cattle.

ITHACA: THE PEOPLE AT HOME

Antinous (an·tin'ō·əs): one of Penelope's leading suitors; an arrogant and mean young noble from Ithaca.

Eumaeus (yōō·mē'əs): swineherd, one of Odysseus' loyal servants.

Eurycleia (yōō·ri·klī'yə): Odysseus' old nurse.

Eurymachus (yōō·rim'ə·kəs): suitor of Penelope.

Eurynome (yōō·rin'ə·mē): Penelope's housekeeper.

Penelope (pə·nel'ə·pē): Odysseus' faithful wife.

Philoeteus (fi·lœi'tē·əs): cowherd, one of Odysseus' loyal servants.

Telemachus (tə·lem'ə·kəs): Odysseus' son.

THE GODS

Apollo (ə·päl'ō): god of poetry, music, prophecy, medicine, and archery.

Ⓐ **Athena** (ə·thē'nə): favorite daughter of Zeus; the great goddess of wisdom and the arts of war and peace. She favored the Greeks during the Trojan War. She is often called Pallas Athena.

Ⓑ **Cronus** (krō'nəs): Titan (giant god) who ruled the universe until his son Zeus overthrew him.

Helios (hē'lē·äs'): sun god.

Hephaestus (hē·fes'təs): god of metalworking.

Hermes (hʉr'mēz'): messenger god.

Ⓒ **Poseidon** (pō·sī'dən): god of the sea; brother of Zeus. Called Earth Shaker because he is believed to cause earthquakes. Poseidon is an enemy of Odysseus.

Zeus (zyōōs): the most powerful god, whose home is on Olympus.

The Perilous Journey

Theme

The Quest for the Rightful Kingdom *Focus on the epic: Here is the story of a hero who embodies all of a society's ethics and values and who must conquer exterior and interior monsters to be worthy, at last, to reclaim his rightful inheritance. The Odyssey is the story of all our lives.*

Reading the Anthology

Reaching Struggling Readers
The *Reading Skills and Strategies: Reaching Struggling Readers* binder includes a Reading Strategies Handbook that offers concrete suggestions for helping students who have difficulty reading and comprehending text, or students who are reluctant readers. When a specific strategy is most appropriate for a selection, a correlation to the Handbook is provided at the bottom of the teacher's page under the head Struggling Readers. This head may also be used to introduce additional ideas for helping students read challenging texts.

Reading Beyond the Anthology

Read On
Each collection in the grade nine book includes an annotated bibliography of books suitable for extended reading. The suggested books are related to works in the collection by theme, by author, or by subject. To preview the Read On for Collection 14, please turn to p. T957.

HRW Library
The *HRW Library* offers novels, plays, works of nonfiction, and short-story collections for extended reading. Each book in the Library includes a major work and thematically or topically related Connections. The Connections are magazine articles, poems, or other pieces of literature. Each book in the *HRW Library* is also accompanied by a Study Guide that provides teaching suggestions and worksheets. The two titles shown here will work well to extend the theme of Collection 14.

SOUNDER
William Armstrong
Sounder presents the story of a young African American boy whose father has been sentenced to a chain gang for stealing food to feed his hungry family. The son undertakes a perilous journey to find his lost father.

ADVENTURES OF HUCKLEBERRY FINN
Mark Twain
Some mature ninth-graders may be ready for Twain's classic tale of Huckleberry Finn's wanderings on the Mississippi. The book contains language and situations that may be sensitive, particularly at this grade level.

Collection 14 The Perilous Journey

Resources for this Collection

Note: All resources for this collection are available for preview on the *One-Stop Planner CD-ROM 2 with Test Generator.* All worksheets and blackline masters may be printed from the CD-ROM.

Internet Resources
go.hrw.com LE0 9-14

Collection Planner

Selection or Feature	Reading and Literary Skills	Vocabulary, Language, and Grammar

from **The Odyssey**
Homer
translated by Robert Fitzgerald
(p. 888)
 	
Tell the Story (Book 1) (p. 890)
 	
Part One: The Wanderings (p. 891)
• **Calypso** (p. 891)
• **"I Am Laertes' Son ..."** (p. 895)
 	
  Connections: Calypso
  Suzanne Vega (p. 894)
 	
• **The Lotus Eaters** (p. 898)
• **The Cyclops** (p. 899)
 	
  Connections:
  The Cyclops in the Ocean
  Nikki Giovanni (p. 909)
 	
• **The Witch Circe** (p. 911)
• **The Land of the Dead** (p. 914)
• **The Sirens, Scylla and Charybdis** (p. 916)
• **The Cattle of the Sun God** (p. 922)
	• *Graphic Organizers for Active Reading,* Worksheet p. 69	• *Words to Own,* Worksheet p. 49
		• *Grammar and Language Links:* Figures of Speech—Similes, Worksheet p. 61
		• *Daily Oral Grammar,* Transparencies 46, 47

Part Two: Coming Home (p. 928)
• **The Meeting of Father and Son** (p. 929)
• **The Beggar and the Faithful Dog** (p. 932)
• **The Test of the Great Bow** (p. 936)
 	
  Connections:
  An Ancient Gesture
  Edna St. Vincent Millay (p. 940)
 	
• **Death at the Palace** (p. 941)
• **Odysseus and Penelope** (p. 944)
 	
  Connections: Ithaca
  C. P. Cavafy (p. 948)
 	
  Connections: The Sea Call
  Nikos Kazantzakis (p. 949)
	• *Graphic Organizers for Active Reading,* Worksheet p. 70	• *Words to Own,* Worksheet p. 50
		• *Grammar and Language Links:* End Marks, Worksheet p. 63
		• *Language Workshop CD-ROM,* Using End Marks
		• *Daily Oral Grammar,* Transparencies 48, 49

Extending the Theme: Star Wars, A Modern Odyssey (p. 954)	The Extending the Theme feature provides students with an unstructured opportunity to practice reading strategies using a selection that extends the theme of the collection.	
Writer's Workshop: Cause-and-Effect Essay (p. 958)		
Sentence Workshop: Avoiding Wordiness (p. 963)		• *Workshop Resources,* p. 81 • *Language Workshop CD-ROM,* Wordiness
Learning for Life: **Looking at Heroes** (p. 965)		

Other Resources for this Collection

- *Cross-Curricular Activities,* p. 14
- *Portfolio Management System,* Introduction to Portfolio Assessment, p. 1
- *Formal Assessment,* Genre Test, p. 156
- *Test Generator,* Collection Test

Writing	Listening and Speaking Viewing and Representing	Assessment
• *Portfolio Management System,* Rubrics for Choices, p. 213	• *Visual Connections:* Videocassette B, Segment 14  • *Audio CD Library,* Disc 18, Tracks 2, 3  • *Viewing and Representing:* Fine Art Transparency 20; Worksheet p. 80 • *Portfolio Management System,* Rubrics for Choices, p. 213	• *Formal Assessment,* Selection Test, p. 152 • *Standardized Test Preparation,* pp. 90, 92 • *Test Generator (One-Stop Planner CD-ROM)* 
• *Portfolio Management System,* Rubrics for Choices, p. 215	• *Visual Connections:* Videocassette B, Segment 14  • *Audio CD Library,* Disc 18, Track 4  • *Portfolio Management System,* Rubrics for Choices, p. 215	• *Formal Assessment,* Selection Test, p. 154 • *Test Generator (One-Stop Planner CD-ROM)* 

• *Workshop Resources,* p. 57
• *Writer's Workshop 2 CD-ROM,* Cause and Effect 
		• *Portfolio Management System*
		  • Prewriting, p. 218
		  • Peer Editing, p. 219
		  • Assessment Rubric, p. 220

		• *Portfolio Management System,* Rubrics, p. 221

 Transparency    CD-ROM    Video    Audio CD

Collection Planner

Collection 14 The Perilous Journey
Skills Focus

Selection or Feature	Reading Skills and Strategies	Elements of Literature	Language/ Grammar	Vocabulary/ Spelling	Writing	Listening/ Speaking	Viewing/ Representing
from **The Odyssey** Homer translated by Robert Fitzgerald (p. 888) **Tell the Story** (p. 890) **Part One: The Wanderings** (p. 891) • **Calypso** (p. 891) • **"I Am Laertes' Son . . ."** (p. 895) • **The Lotus Eaters** (p. 898) • **The Cyclops** (p. 899) • **The Witch Circe** (p. 911) • **The Land of the Dead** (p. 914) • **The Sirens, Scylla and Charybdis** (p. 916) • **The Cattle of the Sun God** (p. 922)	Monitor Comprehension, p. 888 Strategy Annotations • p. 890 • p. 892 • p. 893 • p. 898 • p. 909 • p. 912 • p. 915 • p. 922 • p. 923 • p. 924 Summarize, p. 925	Foreshadow, p. 925 Personification, p. 926	Figures of Speech, p. 927 • Simile • Homeric Simile	Semantic Map, p. 927	Personify a Force of Nature, p. 926 Describe a Personal Quest, p. 926	Prepare and Deliver an Oral Counter-Argument, p. 926 Dramatize an Episode from the *Odyssey*, p. 926	Create a Cause-and-Effect Chart, p. 926 Draw a Cartoon, p. 926
Part Two: Coming Home (p. 928) • **The Meeting of Father and Son** (p. 929) • **The Beggar and the Faithful Dog** (p. 932) • **The Test of the Great Bow** (p. 936) • **Death at the Palace** (p. 941) • **Odysseus and Penelope** (p. 944)	Strategy Annotations • p. 930 • p. 931 • p. 933 • p. 940 • p. 941 • p. 943 • p. 944 • p. 946 • p. 947	Simile, p. 950 Dramatic Irony, p. 950	Epithet, p. 953	Synonyms, p. 953	Identify Causes and Effects, p. 951 Write an Extension to the Story, p. 951 Write a Movie Proposal to Update the Epic, p. 951 Write a Story Plan for a Version of the *Odyssey* with a Female Hero, p. 951 Analyze an Epic, p. 952	Respond Orally to a Critical Comment, p. 952 Present an Episode as a Play or as a Dramatic Reading, p. 952	Write an Evaluation of a Documentary, p. 952
Extending the Theme: Star Wars, A Modern Odyssey (p. 954)	The Extending the Theme feature provides students with an unstructured opportunity to practice reading strategies using a selection that extends the theme of the collection.						
Writer's Workshop: Cause-and-Effect Essay (p. 958)	Recognize Cause-and-Effect Strategies Used to Persuade, p. 959				Write a Cause-and-Effect Essay, pp. 958–962		
Sentence Workshop: Avoiding Wordiness (p. 963)					Revise Sentences to Correct Wordiness, p. 963		
Reading for Life: Comparing and Evaluating Artistic Interpretations (p. 964)	Compare Literary Sources with Artistic Interpretations, p. 964						Develop Criteria for Judging Artistic Interpretations, p. 964
Learning for Life: Looking at Heroes (p. 965)	Identify a Person who Qualifies as a Hero, p. 965				Write a Personality Profile, p. 965 Write a Personal Essay, p. 965		Create a Collage, p. 965

THE PERILOUS JOURNEY
WRITING FOCUS: Cause-and-Effect Essay

We've always looked at the horizon and wondered what's out there. Today we have ships probing into the outer regions of the solar system, peering with camera and computer through the clouds of distant planets. Centuries ago, when we believed the earth was flat, we stood on the shore and stared out toward the edge where the ocean dropped off into nothing, and speculated about what we'd find if we sailed that far.

We've always journeyed. We've packed up and moved on, to leave something behind or to find something new. The journey isn't always out into the unknown, however—there are also journeys of return, efforts to get home again. . . .

If we are fortunate, if the gods and muses are smiling, about every generation someone comes along to inspire the imagination for the journey each of us takes.

—Bill Moyers

Writer's Notebook

"The journey" is a rich metaphor for life. Think of its many aspects: maps or guides; dangers along the way; chance discoveries; paying for the trip; arriving; returning.

Write briefly about one aspect of your life journey so far. If, for instance, you feel that you've had to work especially hard for something you've accomplished or tried to accomplish, you might write about what you have had to do to get there. If you prefer, don't write about your life so far, but about the journeys you'll take in the next several years. Save your notes.

Responding to the Quotation

❓ Who are these inspiring people? How do they fuel the imagination of others? [Possible responses: those who are exceptionally talented; those who are heroic leaders; those who are willing to take a stand. These people become role models that others can learn from.] Do you think we are so fortunate? If so, name some examples. [Students might name famous athletes, performers, writers, artists, scientists, or political or spiritual leaders.]

Writer's Notebook

To help students focus on an aspect of "the journey," have them brainstorm highlights that are common in people's lives, such as starting school, learning a skill, leaving home, traveling, getting married, and choosing a career.

RESPONDING TO THE ART

Activity. You might discuss the image of the sea here. What other, more modern images could also suggest a "journey"? Think of highways, trains, planes, even the stars themselves.

Writing Focus: Cause-and-Effect Essay

The following **Work in Progress** assignments build to a culminating **Writer's Workshop** at the end of the collection.

- Part One   Looking at the plot (p. 926)
- Part Two   Focusing on cause and effect (p. 951)

Writer's Workshop: Expository Writing / Cause-and-Effect Essay (p. 958)

Planning

• **Block Schedule**
  Block Scheduling Lesson Plans with Pacing Guide
• **Traditional Schedule**
  Lesson Plans Including Strategies for English-Language Learners
• **One-Stop Planner**
  CD-ROM with Test Generator

Before You Read

THE ODYSSEY

Make the Connection

Heroes at Large

We admire them in movies, on TV shows, and in the news; in books, on sports teams, in science labs, and in art studios; and if we look closely, even in our own lives. They're our heroes, female or male, real or fictional. They set off on the journey that we're all on: the quest to discover who we are and what we can do. They encounter challenges, setbacks, and dangers; they make mistakes, lose their way, and find it again. And whether they fail or succeed, they do it on a grand scale, giving us new perspectives on our own lives. As you read these tales of Odysseus' wanderings, notice what he does—and doesn't—have in common with modern heroes.

Quickwrite

What makes a hero? Write down the names of two or three people, real or fictional, whom you consider heroic. Then take a few minutes to list character traits that you think a hero of any time and place should have. Keep adding to your notes as you read the *Odyssey*.

 go.hrw.com
LE0 9-14

888

Reading Skills and Strategies

Monitor Your Comprehension

As you read this epic, stop now and then to ask yourself questions and to sum up what you've read. Ask:
• What has happened so far?
• Why did it happen?
• What are the important events in this episode?
• What might happen next?
• Can I visualize what is being described?

As you read the *Odyssey*, it's especially important to know where you are in time. The questions in the side columns will help you monitor your comprehension. If you can't answer the questions, go back through the text to find the answers.

Preteaching Vocabulary

Words to Own

Have volunteers locate the Words to Own in their text and list them on the chalkboard. Then, have students work in pairs. Each partner should write each of the Words to Own on a separate index card. On the other side of each card, students should draw a picture to illustrate the word. For example, a person sneaking through the bushes might illustrate *stealth*. After they have finished creating cards for each of the words, students should take turns showing the picture side of a card and having their partners guess which of the Words to Own is depicted.

THE ODYSSEY

HOMER

translated by Robert Fitzgerald

Resources

Viewing and Representing
Videocassette B, Segment 14
Available in English and Spanish.
Show the *Visual Connections* segment "Where in the World Did Odysseus Go?" to help students learn more about the geography of Odysseus' journey. For full lesson plans and worksheets, see the *Visual Connections Teacher's Manual.*

Listening
Audio CD Library
Selected readings from the *Odyssey* are available as part of the *Audio CD Library:*
• Disc 18, Track 2

Viewing and Representing
Fine Art Transparency
The transparency of Romare Bearden's *The Land of the Lotus Eaters* can be used to enhance your students' reading of the Lotus Eaters section (p. 898).
• Transparency 20
• Worksheet, p. 80

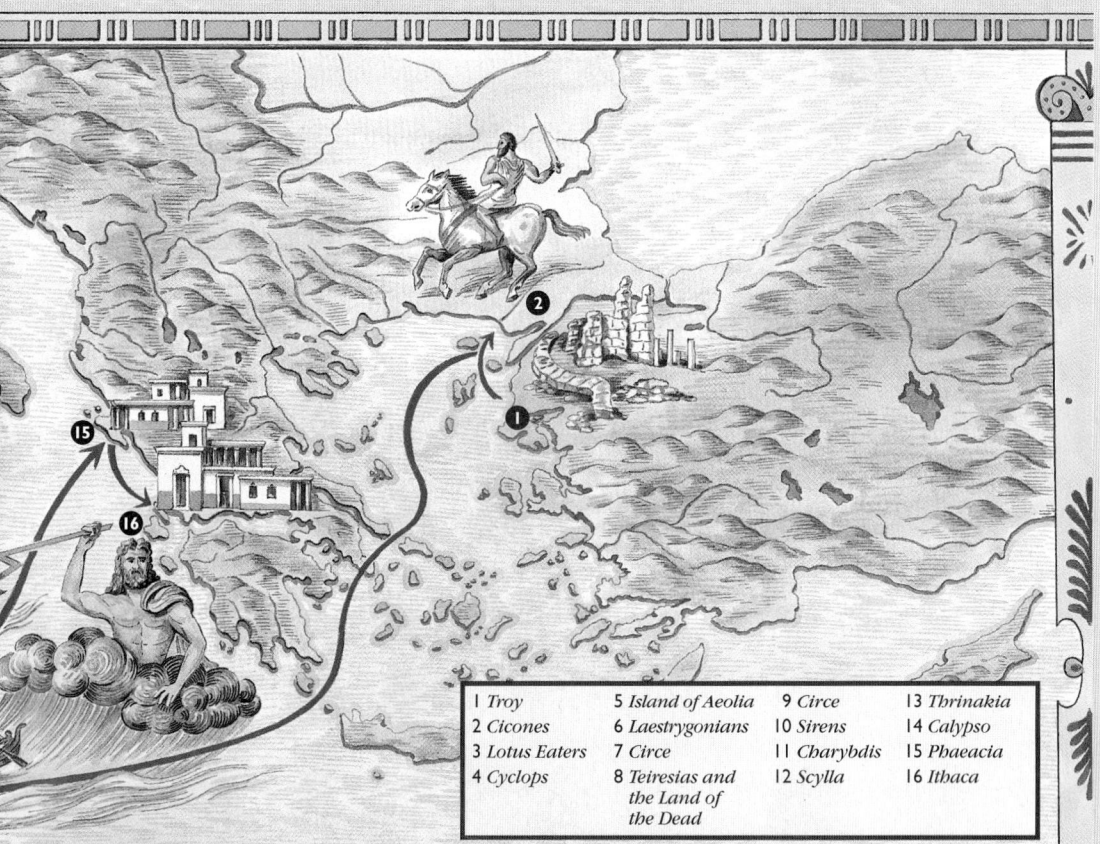

1 Troy	5 Island of Aeolia	9 Circe	13 Thrinakia
2 Cicones	6 Laestrygonians	10 Sirens	14 Calypso
3 Lotus Eaters	7 Circe	11 Charybdis	15 Phaeacia
4 Cyclops	8 Teiresias and the Land of the Dead	12 Scylla	16 Ithaca

Resources: Print and Media

Reading
• *Graphic Organizers for Active Reading,* p. 69
• *Words to Own,* p. 49
• *Audio CD Library,*
    Disc 18, Tracks 2, 3

Writing and Language
• *Daily Oral Grammar*
    Transparencies 46, 47

• *Grammar and Language Links*
    Worksheet, p. 61

Viewing and Representing
• *Viewing and Representing*
    Fine Art Transparency 20
    Fine Art Worksheet, p. 80
• *Visual Connections*
    Videocassette B, Segment 14

Assessment
• *Formal Assessment,* p. 152
• *Portfolio Management System,* p. 213
• *Standardized Test Preparation,* pp. 90, 92
• *Test Generator (One-Stop Planner CD-ROM)*

Internet
• go.hrw.com (keyword: LE0 9-14)

Summary ■ ■ ■

Homer invokes the Muse, asking her to help him tell the story of Odysseus' adventures. Homer mentions Odysseus' hardships, his valor, and his struggle to save his life and bring his shipmates home. He reminds us that the shipmates died because of their own recklessness. He says he will begin his story when all the other warriors had gotten home, but only Odysseus still hungers for home and wife. Odysseus is now held captive to Calypso, who craves him for her own. Homer foreshadows the trials and hungers that lie ahead for Odysseus, though all the gods, except Poseidon, pity him.

Ⓐ Elements of Literature

Epic

❓ The *Odyssey* opens with a convention of epic poetry—the poet's prayer to the Muse. What does the poet ask of the Muse? [He asks her to sing through him and tell the great story once again.]

Answer to Margin Question

The hero is a soldier whose men have all died on the long, terrible voyage from Troy. He longs to return home after all his battles, but he is held captive by the nymph Calypso, who wants him for her own. The gods all pity this soldier—except for Poseidon. Now the time is decreed for him to make his passage homeward.

TELL THE STORY

Homer opens with an invocation, or prayer, asking the Muse° to help him sing his tale. Notice how the singer gives his listeners hints about how his story is to end.

> Sing in me, Muse, and through me tell the story
> of that man skilled in all ways of contending,°
> Ⓐ the wanderer, harried for years on end,
> after he plundered the stronghold
> on the proud height of Troy.
> 5   He saw the townlands
> and learned the minds of many distant men,
> and weathered many bitter nights and days
> in his deep heart at sea, while he fought only
> to save his life, to bring his shipmates home.
> 10 But not by will nor valor could he save them,
> for their own recklessness destroyed them all—
> children and fools, they killed and feasted on
> the cattle of Lord Helios, the Sun,
> and he who moves all day through heaven
> 15 took from their eyes the dawn of their return.
>
> Of these adventures, Muse, daughter of Zeus,
> tell us in our time, lift the great song again.
> Begin when all the rest who left behind them
> headlong death in battle or at sea
> 20 had long ago returned, while he alone still hungered
> for home and wife. Her ladyship Calypso
> clung to him in her sea-hollowed caves—
> a nymph, immortal and most beautiful,
> who craved him for her own.
>   And when long years and seasons
> 25 wheeling brought around that point of time
> ordained for him to make his passage homeward,
> trials and dangers, even so, attended him
> even in Ithaca, near those he loved.
> Yet all the gods had pitied Lord Odysseus,
> 30 all but Poseidon, raging cold and rough
> against the brave king till he came ashore
> at last on his own land. . . .

(from Book 1)

The Greeks believed that there were nine Muses, daughters of Zeus, the chief god. The Muses inspired people to produce music, poetry, dance, and all the other arts.

2. contending: fighting; dealing with difficulties.

Read this prayer to the Muse aloud. (You could read it as a chorus, or you could alternate with single voices.) What does Homer tell you about the hero and about what is going to happen to him?

890 THE EPIC

Reaching All Students

Struggling Readers

To help students keep track of what happens in the epic, have them keep story maps. For each episode, they should summarize the key events and end with a note that tells where Odysseus is at this point. One of the big problems with the *Odyssey* for almost any reader is keeping track of time: The epic is very sophisticated and moves from present to past in subtle ways. The headnotes in the text almost always remind students of who is speaking and where we are.

English Language Learners

Build students' confidence by modeling the correct pronunciation of names such as *Odysseus, Telemachus, Polyphemus,* and *Zeus.* Have students repeat each name several times. For additional strategies to supplement instructions for these students, see

• *Lesson Plans Including Strategies for English-Language Learners*

Advanced Learners

As they read the epic, students could keep a list of motifs, or repeated patterns, that are paralleled in other works. Suggest that they look for similarities between epic and modern stories and films in terms of story lines, situations, characters, and themes. Periodically, ask students to share their lists with the rest of the class.

PART ONE: THE WANDERINGS

CALYPSO, THE SWEET NYMPH

The first books of the epic (Books 1–4) tell about Odysseus' son, Telemachus. Telemachus has been searching the Mediterranean world for his father, who has never returned from the ten-year Trojan War. (Today, Odysseus would be listed as missing in action.)

When we first meet Odysseus, in Book 5 of the epic, he is a prisoner of the beautiful goddess Calypso. The old soldier is in despair: He has spent ten years (seven of them as Calypso's not entirely unwilling captive) trying to get home.

The goddess Athena has supported and helped Odysseus on his long journey. Now she begs her father, Zeus, to help her favorite, and Zeus agrees. He sends the messenger god Hermes to Calypso's island to order Odysseus released. It is important to remember that although Calypso is not described as evil, her seductive charms—even her promises of immortality for Odysseus—threaten to keep the hero away from his wife, Penelope.

Man with a headband
(c. 460–450 B.C.). Bronze.
Museo Archeologico Nazionale,
Reggio Calabria, Italy.

```
         No words were lost on Hermes the Wayfinder
         who bent to tie his beautiful sandals on,
35       ambrosial,° golden, that carry him over water
         or over endless land in a swish of the wind,
         and took the wand with which he charms asleep—
         or when he wills, awake—the eyes of men.
         So wand in hand he paced into the air,
40       shot from Pieria° down, down to sea level,
         and veered to skim the swell. A gull patrolling
         between the wave crests of the desolate sea
         will dip to catch a fish, and douse his wings;
         no higher above the whitecaps Hermes flew
45       until the distant island lay ahead,
         then rising shoreward from the violet ocean
         he stepped up to the cave. Divine Calypso,
         the mistress of the isle, was now at home.
         Upon her hearthstone a great fire blazing
50       scented the farthest shores with cedar smoke
         and smoke of thyme, and singing high and low
         in her sweet voice, before her loom aweaving,
         she passed her golden shuttle to and fro.
         A deep wood grew outside, with summer leaves
```

B

C

D

35. ambrosial: fit for the gods; divine. Nectar and ambrosia are the drink and food that kept the gods immortal.

40. Pieria (pī·ir'ē·ə): place in central Greece not far from Olympus; a favorite spot of Hermes'.

THE ODYSSEY, PART ONE 891

Summary ■■■

Trapped on Calypso's fragrant island, Odysseus has grown weary of her enchantment. Our first glimpse of the hero finds him weeping, scanning the horizon of the sea (ll. 71–74). At Athena's behest, Zeus sends Hermes to order the goddess to release Odysseus. Calypso reluctantly agrees to let him go. Odysseus builds a raft and sets sail. But Poseidon raises a storm and wrecks the raft. Odysseus lands on the island of Scheria and falls asleep in a pile of leaves. (Explain to students that although the textbook has divided the *Odyssey* into two parts for convenience, the epic was not originally separated into parts.)

B Critical Thinking
Speculating

Point out that Book 5 contains many images that appeal to the senses. Ask them why there might be an emphasis on sensory images in this section of the epic. They should reread the notes above. [The abundance of images that appeal to the senses help explain why Odysseus was at first willing to remain on the island as Calypso's captive.]

C Elements of Literature
Homeric Simile

? What is Hermes' flight compared to here? [to a gull skimming just above the white-capped waves, dipping from time to time to catch a fish]

D Elements of Literature
Sensory Images

? What do you see, hear, feel, and smell in this famous description of Calypso's home? [a blazing fire; cedar smoke; thyme; singing; a golden shuttle]

RESPONDING TO THE ART

This beautiful bronze statue of a man was hauled out of the sea at the southern tip of Italy in 1981. The statue, with a companion, had lain at the bottom of the sea for centuries; both statues can be seen in the small museum at Reggio Calabria today. Note that the men are not young, but they are beautiful and heroic. The agates are still in their eyes, the ivory in their teeth, and the pink coral on their lips. Their hair curls like hyacinths, just as described by Homer.

Getting Students Involved

Cooperative Learning

The pantheon of Greek gods, nymphs, and demigods can be likened to a great family filled with complicated relationships and acrimonious feuds. Athena, the goddess of war and wisdom, for example, is the daughter of Zeus; the messenger god, Hermes, is Zeus's son. The sea god, Poseidon, who is the father of the Cyclops Polyphemus, is also brother to both Zeus and Hades. Have groups of students expand on their knowledge of the Greek religious pantheon by creating family trees that illustrate the tangled ties that connect these figures. The trees can be annotated with specific information about each of the deities, their characteristics and histories, the locations in ancient Greece that they are associated with, and what role, if any, they play in the *Iliad* and the *Odyssey*. Within each group, students can be assigned the roles of researcher, graphic artist, editor, and presenter.

A Reading Skills and Strategies

Monitor Your Comprehension

At this point, you might have students check their understanding. Suggest that they ask themselves questions. For example: Why has Hermes arrived on Calypso's island? [At the urging of Athena, Zeus has sent Hermes to tell Calypso that she must free Odysseus.]

B Literary Connections

Greek Gods

Have students note the goddess Calypso's love for Odysseus and her very humanlike desire to take credit for the decision to release him. Unlike other ancient or modern religious figures, Greek gods and goddesses often behave as capriciously as humans. They even display such unsavory human qualities as possessiveness, jealousy, pride, anger, and vindictiveness. This behavior is at the heart of the *Odyssey*, since it is the actions and reactions of the gods that keep Odysseus from returning home to Ithaca.

Answer to Margin Question

The god's flight is described in ll. 41–45. For details appealing to the senses in the description of Calypso's island, see note D on p. 891. In addition, on this page there are pungent cypress, ornate birds, a crooked vine, purple clusters of grapes, bubbling springs, violets, and tender parsley.

Answer to Margin Question

Maybe Calypso is too proud to say she was ordered to free Odysseus. Or perhaps she wants him to think she is kind and generous. Some students will feel her deceit is understandable; others will feel it underscores her selfishness.

---

55   of alder and black poplar, pungent cypress.
    Ornate birds here rested their stretched wings—
    horned owls, falcons, cormorants—long-tongued
    beachcombing birds, and followers of the sea.
    Around the smooth-walled cave a crooking vine
60   held purple clusters under ply of green;
    and four springs, bubbling up near one another
    shallow and clear, took channels here and there
    through beds of violets and tender parsley.
    Even a god who found this place
65   would gaze, and feel his heart beat with delight:
    so Hermes did; but when he had gazed his fill
   he entered the wide cave. Now face-to-face
    the magical Calypso recognized him,
    as all immortal gods know one another
70   on sight—though seeming strangers, far from home.
    But he saw nothing of the great Odysseus,
    who sat apart, as a thousand times before,
    and racked his own heart groaning, with eyes wet
    scanning the bare horizon of the sea. . . .

Hermes tells Calypso that she must give up Odysseus forever. Now we are directly introduced to Odysseus. Notice what this great warrior is doing when we first meet him.

75   The strong god glittering left her as he spoke,
    and now her ladyship, having given heed
    to Zeus's mandate, went to find Odysseus
    in his stone seat to seaward—tear on tear
    brimming his eyes. The sweet days of his lifetime
80   were running out in anguish over his exile,
    for long ago the nymph had ceased to please.
    Though he fought shy of her and her desire,
    he lay with her each night, for she compelled him.
    But when day came he sat on the rocky shore
85   and broke his own heart groaning, with eyes wet
    scanning the bare horizon of the sea.
    Now she stood near him in her beauty, saying:

    "O forlorn man, be still.
    Here you need grieve no more; you need not feel
90   your life consumed here; I have pondered it,
    and I shall help you go. . . ."

Calypso promises Odysseus a raft and provisions to help him homeward without harm—provided the gods wish it. Now Odysseus and Calypso say goodbye.

892 THE EPIC

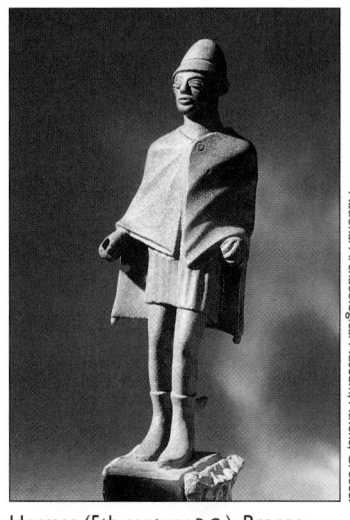

Hermes (5th century B.C.). Bronze.

There is a great deal of nature imagery in this episode. Jot down some of the images that help you see the god's flight. What images describing Calypso's island appeal to your senses of sight, hearing, and smell? How does the natural beauty of Calypso's island compare with the reality of Odysseus' situation?

Zeus ordered Calypso to free Odysseus, but in lines 88–91, the nymph claims that the idea is her own. Why do you think she does this? How do you feel about her deception?

Using Students' Strengths

Kinesthetic Learners

Encourage students to act out or pantomime action scenes from the epic. Students might work with a partner to choose roles and evaluate how their role-playing reflects their understanding of the characters' situations and actions.

Auditory Learners

Pair students and have them use a Think Aloud protocol to explore ideas about Odysseus' journey. Partners can read the epic aloud and pause to express their thoughts about such things as Odysseus' problems, possible resolutions, the connections of the story to real-life people or situations, and students' own problems with the story.

Swiftly she turned and led him to her cave,
and they went in, the mortal and immortal.
He took the chair left empty now by Hermes,
95   where the divine Calypso placed before him
victuals and drink of men; then she sat down
facing Odysseus, while her serving maids
brought nectar and ambrosia to her side.
Then each one's hands went out on each one's feast
100   until they had had their pleasure; and she said:

"Son of Laertes,° versatile Odysseus,
after these years with me, you still desire
your old home? Even so, I wish you well.
If you could see it all, before you go—
105   all the adversity you face at sea—
you would stay here, and guard this house, and be
immortal—though you wanted her forever,
that bride for whom you pine each day.
Can I be less desirable than she is?
110   Less interesting? Less beautiful? Can mortals
compare with goddesses in grace and form?" **C**

To this the strategist Odysseus answered:

"My lady goddess, there is no cause for anger.
My quiet Penelope—how well I know—
115   would seem a shade before your majesty,
death and old age being unknown to you,
while she must die. Yet, it is true, each day
I long for home, long for the sight of home. . . ."

So Odysseus builds the raft and sets sail. But the sea god Posei-
don is by no means ready to allow an easy passage over his
watery domain. He raises a storm and destroys the raft. It is
only with the help of Athena and a sea nymph that Odysseus
arrives, broken and battered, on the island of Scheria
(skē′rē·ə). There he hides himself in a pile of leaves and falls
into a deep sleep.

A man in a distant field, no hearth fires near,
120   will hide a fresh brand in his bed of embers **D**
to keep a spark alive for the next day;
so in the leaves Odysseus hid himself,
while over him Athena showered sleep
that his distress should end, and soon, soon.
125   In quiet sleep she sealed his cherished eyes.

(*from* Book 5)

101. Laertes (lā·ur′tēz′).

Calypso and Odysseus (5th century B.C.).
Detail from a red-figured vase.
Museo Archeologico Nazionale, Naples, Italy.

 What has Calypso
offered Odysseus if he
will stay with her? What
does Odysseus' reply tell you about
his feelings for his wife? How has
Odysseus managed to say no to
Calypso and still not offend her?

THE ODYSSEY, PART ONE **893**

T893

Connections

Suzanne Vega is a contemporary folk singer, and this love song is from her album *Solitude Standing*. The point of adding this song is to show students how eternally current the *Odyssey* is.

A **Elements of Literature**

Tone

❓ What is the tone of the song's first stanza? [sad; nostalgic; accepting; resigned]

B **Critical Thinking**

Analyzing

❓ Why do you think the words "I let him go" are repeated so many times in the song? [The refrain reinforces the sadness of the singer—she let him go of her own free will, and yet she loved him so much.]

C **Critical Thinking**

Making Judgments

❓ Why does the Calypso of the song say that she has a "clean heart"? [She feels she has made an unselfish decision and has a clear conscience; she put Odysseus' happiness ahead of her own, and she knows she has done the right thing, even though it pains her to think of it.] **Does Calypso in the *Odyssey* have an equally "clean heart"?** [Most students will say no, because she was ordered to let Odysseus go.]

T894

Calypso Suzanne Vega

My name is Calypso
And I have lived alone
I live on an island
And I waken to the dawn
5 A long time ago
I watched him struggle with the sea
A I knew that he was drowning
And I brought him into me
Now today
10 Come morning light
He sails away
After one last night
I let him go.

My name is Calypso
15 My garden overflows
Thick and wild and hidden
Is the sweetness there that grows
My hair it blows long
As I sing into the wind
20 I tell of nights
Where I could taste the salt on his skin

Salt of the waves
And of tears
And though he pulled away
25 I kept him here for years
B I let him go.

My name is Calypso
I have let him go
In the dawn he sails away
30 To be gone forever more
And the waves will take him in again
But he'll know their ways now
I will stand upon the shore
C With a clean heart
35 And my song in the wind
The sand will sting my feet
And the sky will burn
It's a lonely time ahead
I do not ask him to return
40 I let him go
I let him go.

Calypso's Island, Departure of Ulysses by Samuel Palmer.

The Whitworth Art Gallery, the University of Manchester.

894 THE EPIC

Connecting Across Texts

Connecting with the *Odyssey*
Human feelings and conflicts don't seem to change. Have students compare the feelings and conflicts in the song "Calypso" with those in the Calypso episode of the *Odyssey*.

• Why would a songwriter of today choose to write about Calypso? [Losing someone you love is a timeless theme.]

• What is the song about? [letting go of a loved one for unselfish motives]

• Does the song help you understand the *Odyssey* in any way? [It makes Calypso and her loss vivid and very sad.]

"I AM LAERTES' SON. . . ."

Odysseus is found by the daughter of Alcinous, king of the Phaeacians. That evening he is a guest at court (Books 6–8).

To the ancient people of Greece and Asia Minor, all guests were godsent. They had to be treated with great courtesy before they could be asked to identify themselves and state their business. That night, at the banquet, the stranger who was washed up on the beach is seated in the guest's place of honor. A minstrel, or singer, is called, and the mystery guest gives him a gift of pork, crisp with fat, and requests a song about Troy. In effect, Odysseus is asking for a song about himself.

Odysseus weeps as the minstrel's song reminds him of all his companions, who will never see their homes again. Now Odysseus is asked by the king to identify himself. It is here that he begins the story of his journey.

Now this was the reply Odysseus made: . . .

"I am Laertes' son, Odysseus.
Men hold me **Ⓐ**
formidable for guile in peace and war:
this fame has gone abroad to the sky's rim.
130 My home is on the peaked seamark of Ithaca
under Mount Neion's windblown robe of leaves,
in sight of other islands—Doulikhion,
Same, wooded Zakynthos—Ithaca
being most lofty in that coastal sea,
135 and northwest, while the rest lie east and south.
A rocky isle, but good for a boy's training;
I shall not see on earth a place more dear,
though I have been detained long by Calypso,
loveliest among goddesses, who held me
140 in her smooth caves, to be her heart's delight,
as Circe of Aeaea, the enchantress,
desired me, and detained me in her hall.
But in my heart I never gave consent.
Where shall a man find sweetness to surpass **Ⓑ**
145 his own home and his parents? In far lands
he shall not, though he find a house of gold:

What of my sailing, then, from Troy?

WORDS TO OWN

formidable (fôr′mə·də·bəl) *adj.*: awe-inspiring in excellence; strikingly impressive.

The passage beginning "I am Laertes' son" in Greek.

Summary ■ ■

Odysseus, at the king's feast, replies to the king, who has asked the stranger to identify himself. Odysseus begins by telling where he is from. He describes how he was detained by Calypso and Circe and tells of the many years he has traveled from Troy, trying to find his way home. He tells of the Cicones and of a storm raised by Zeus, which had his men drifting for nine days.

Ⓐ **Critical Thinking**
Analyzing Character
? What impression do you get of Odysseus from his description of himself? [Students may notice the word *guile* and suggest that Odysseus considers himself cunning. They may consider him boastful. Explain that the ancient Greeks would not have thought this self-identification by an epic hero arrogant.]

Ⓑ **Elements of Literature**
Theme
? What central idea of the poem does Odysseus express in this passage? [He expresses the desire for home that motivates his actions throughout the entire poem. Note that he excuses himself: Though the goddesses loved him, he "never gave consent in his heart."]

Using Students' Strengths

Visual Learners
Have students create cartoon panels of scenes from the *Odyssey* and caption them with relevant quotations.

Verbal Learners
Have students each prepare a two-minute speech that introduces a character from the epic other than Odysseus. Tell students to pretend that they are introducing the character at a dinner at which the character will comment on Odysseus' version of events. After students present their introductions, hold a class discussion. What pictures of the characters do the introductions present? What insights into the characters' feelings and thoughts do they offer?

A Literary Connections

The town of Ismaros was near Troy, and the Greeks may have considered the people no different from the Trojans. Help students follow the events by referring to the map on pp. 888–889.

B Critical Thinking

Expressing an Opinion

❓ Here Odysseus, who considers himself a great leader, blames his men's refusal to obey him for the Cicones' attack. Does their mutiny reflect unfavorably on Odysseus? [Possible answer: Having just successfully destroyed and looted Troy, the men easily got drunk and out of control. However, perhaps Odysseus was expecting too much of them in regard to discipline, and they could not be stopped.]

LITERATURE AND ARCHAEOLOGY

The background etching for this feature shows the ruins of Troy. The man at the left is Schliemann. This feature could provide material for research projects on Troy, Agamemnon (what happened to him when he returned home?), King Priam, and his children Cassandra and Hector. Of course, research could also be done on the digging being carried out in Troy today. What new discoveries have been made, and what light do those discoveries cast on this ancient epic? You might ask students what other great mysteries in history might be solved one day by the work of archaeologists. They might mention places like Stonehenge, Easter Island, the mysterious serpentine mounds in Ohio and Illinois, and Civil War burial grounds. Urban archaeology, a relatively new field, might also be investigated. A very readable book on archaeology is *Gods, Graves, and Scholars* by C. W. Ceram.

> What of those years
> of rough adventure, weathered under Zeus?
> The wind that carried west from Ilion°
> 150 brought me to Ismaros, on the far shore,
> a strongpoint on the coast of the Cicones.
> A I stormed that place and killed the men who fought.
> Plunder we took, and we enslaved the women,
> to make division, equal shares to all—
> 155 but on the spot I told them: 'Back, and quickly!
> Out to sea again!' My men were mutinous,
> fools, on stores of wine. Sheep after sheep
> they butchered by the surf, and shambling cattle,
> B feasting—while fugitives went inland, running
> 160 to call to arms the main force of Cicones.
> This was an army, trained to fight on horseback
> or, where the ground required, on foot. They came

149. **Ilion** (il′ē·än): another name for Troy.

LITERATURE AND ARCHAEOLOGY

Troy: It Casts a Spell

The ancient Greeks and Romans had no doubt that the Trojan War really happened. They believed it took place around 1200 B.C. The Greek historian Thucydides (c. 460–c. 400 B.C.) believed that the causes of the war were really economic and political—he rejected Homer's story of Helen's abduction and the vengeance taken on Troy by the Greeks. By the middle of the nineteenth century, however, most historians had dismissed the Trojan War as a legend.

Enter Heinrich Schliemann (1822–1890). Schliemann was a wealthy German merchant who turned archaeologist when he was middle-aged and archaeology was in its infancy. Armed with a well-thumbed copy of Homer's *Iliad,* Schliemann arrived in northwestern Turkey in 1871. A few miles from the Dardanelles, that narrow and windy sea lane that divides Europe from Asia, Schliemann began excavations at a small hill called Hissarlik, perched about a hundred feet above a wide plain.

After five long years, Schliemann made an electrifying discovery. He unearthed gold cups, bracelets, and a spectacular gold headdress. Homer had called Troy "rich in gold," and Schliemann now told the world he had found the treasure of Priam, the last king of Troy. (The gold's eventful history was not over. Schliemann took the treasure to Berlin, where it disappeared at the end of

896 THE EPIC

Reaching All Students

Struggling Readers

If some students are having trouble, you might encourage them by pointing out that Odysseus could be considered a superhero or action hero, much like today's Superman, Batman, James Bond, or Indiana Jones. Ask students, as they read the epic, to make a comic book that depicts Odysseus' adventures. The activity should be fun and should produce some surprising work.

with dawn over that terrain like the leaves
and blades of spring. So doom appeared to us,
165 dark word of Zeus for us, our evil days.
My men stood up and made a fight of it—
backed on the ships, with lances kept in play,
from bright morning through the blaze of noon
holding our beach, although so far outnumbered;
170 but when the sun passed toward unyoking time, **C**
then the Achaeans, one by one, gave way.
Six benches were left empty in every ship
that evening when we pulled away from death. **D**
And this new grief we bore with us to sea:
175 our precious lives we had, but not our friends.
No ship made sail next day until some shipmate
had raised a cry, three times, for each poor ghost **E**
unfleshed by the Cicones on that field.

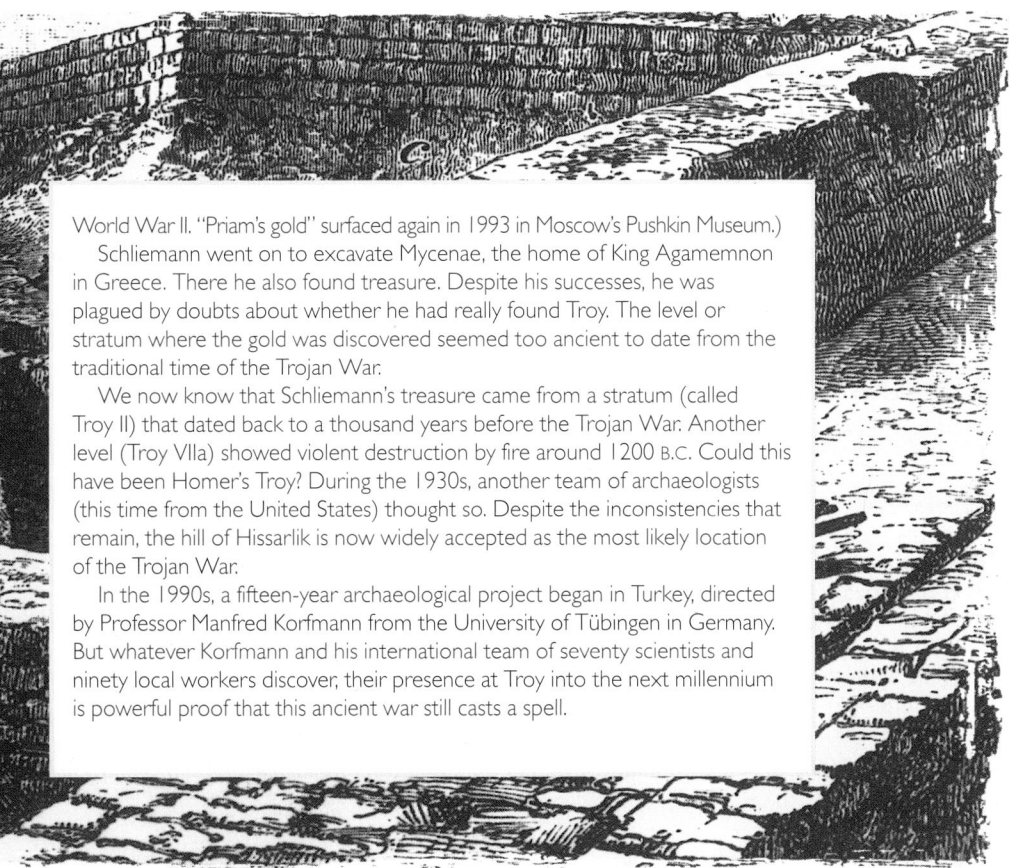

World War II. "Priam's gold" surfaced again in 1993 in Moscow's Pushkin Museum.)

Schliemann went on to excavate Mycenae, the home of King Agamemnon in Greece. There he also found treasure. Despite his successes, he was plagued by doubts about whether he had really found Troy. The level or stratum where the gold was discovered seemed too ancient to date from the traditional time of the Trojan War.

We now know that Schliemann's treasure came from a stratum (called Troy II) that dated back to a thousand years before the Trojan War. Another level (Troy VIIa) showed violent destruction by fire around 1200 B.C. Could this have been Homer's Troy? During the 1930s, another team of archaeologists (this time from the United States) thought so. Despite the inconsistencies that remain, the hill of Hissarlik is now widely accepted as the most likely location of the Trojan War.

In the 1990s, a fifteen-year archaeological project began in Turkey, directed by Professor Manfred Korfmann from the University of Tübingen in Germany. But whatever Korfmann and his international team of seventy scientists and ninety local workers discover, their presence at Troy into the next millennium is powerful proof that this ancient war still casts a spell.

THE ODYSSEY, PART ONE 897

C Reading Skills and Strategies
Drawing Conclusions

❓ What is "unyoking time"? [late afternoon or early evening, the time when yokes were removed from working animals at the end of the day] What conclusions about life in that era can you draw from this phrase? [It was an agrarian society; people did not have clocks and used the sun to tell time.]

D Elements of Literature
Foreshadowing

This tragic episode with the Cicones foreshadows an even worse tragedy that will occur on Thrinakia when Odysseus' men, once again disobeying him, slaughter the sun god's cattle and bring about their own destruction.

E Cultural Connections

Ask students to identify the ritual for the dead mentioned here by Odysseus. [Someone cries out three times for each dead man.] Discuss other rituals of death that students know about. Point out that inclusion of such a ritual in the *Odyssey* underscores just how ancient such human practices are.

Resources ———
Assessment

For practice with standardized test format specific to literature and archaeology, see
• *Standardized Test Preparation*, p. 90

Skill Link

Word Origins: Greek Names

Numerous modern English terms have origins in Greek names found in the *Odyssey*. For example, the Greek word for a place where people could study the arts inspired by the Muses has survived as the word *museum*. The word *music* comes from a Greek word that meant "belonging to or coming from the Muses," and the Muses, all daughters of Zeus and Mnemosyne, the goddess of memory, are especially significant for an oral poet who depended so much on his memory. The silent letter *M* that appears at the beginning of Mnemosyne's name also appears in a modern word that comes from her name: *mnemonic*. Mnemonics are any devices that aid the memory. If the Greek prefix *a-*, meaning "without," is added to the stem of the name Mnemosyne, the words that result mean "without memory." Examples include *amnesia* and *amnesty*.

Activity

Have students look up and list words related to the names they find in the story. Have students keep a running list of terms as they read.

Now Zeus the lord of cloud roused in the north
180   a storm against the ships, and driving veils
of squall moved down like night on land and sea.
The bows went plunging at the gust; sails
cracked and lashed out strips in the big wind.
We saw death in that fury, dropped the yards,
185   unshipped the oars, and pulled for the nearest lee:
then two long days and nights we lay offshore
worn out and sick at heart, tasting our grief,
Ⓐ until a third Dawn came with ringlets shining.
Then we put up our masts, hauled sail, and rested,
190   letting the steersmen and the breeze take over.

I might have made it safely home, that time,
but as I came round Malea the current
took me out to sea, and from the north
a fresh gale drove me on, past Cythera.°
195   Nine days I drifted on the teeming sea
before dangerous high winds."

(from Book 9)

194. Cythera (si·thir′ə).

 Jot down some notes describing your response to the way Odysseus and his men behave toward the Cicones. Do armies behave like this in modern times?

THE LOTUS EATERS

"Upon the tenth
we came to the coastline of the Lotus Eaters,
who live upon that flower. We landed there
200   to take on water. All ships' companies
mustered° alongside for the midday meal.
Then I sent out two picked men and a runner
to learn what race of men that land sustained.
They fell in, soon enough, with Lotus Eaters,
205   who showed no will to do us harm, only
offering the sweet Lotus to our friends—
but those who ate this honeyed plant, the Lotus,
Ⓑ never cared to report, nor to return:
they longed to stay forever, browsing on
210   that native bloom, forgetful of their homeland.
I drove them, all three wailing, to the ships,
tied them down under their rowing benches,
and called the rest: 'All hands aboard;
come, clear the beach and no one taste
215   the Lotus, or you lose your hope of home.'
Filing in to their places by the rowlocks
my oarsmen dipped their long oars in the surf,
and we moved out again on our seafaring. . . ."

(from Book 9)

201. mustered: gathered; assembled.

 Readers have speculated for years on exactly what it was the sailors ate. With a group, make up your own dialogue to dramatize this scene. What do you think really happens here?

898 THE EPIC

THE CYCLOPS

In his next adventure Odysseus describes his encounter with the Cyclops named Polyphemus, Poseidon's one-eyed monster son. Polyphemus may well represent the brute forces that any hero must overcome before he can reach home. Now Odysseus must rely on the special intelligence associated with his name. Odysseus is the cleverest of the ancient Greek heroes because his divine guardian is the goddess of wisdom, Athena.

It is Odysseus' famed curiosity that leads him to the Cyclops's cave and that makes him insist on waiting for the barbaric giant.

Odysseus is still speaking to the court of King Alcinous.

"We lit a fire, burnt an offering, **C**
220   and took some cheese to eat; then sat in silence
around the embers, waiting. When he came
he had a load of dry boughs on his shoulder
to stoke his fire at suppertime. He dumped it
with a great crash into that hollow cave,
225   and we all scattered fast to the far wall.

The Cyclops (detail) (late 19th or early 20th century) by Odilon Redon.

Rijksmuseum Kroller-Muller, Otterlo, the Netherlands.

THE ODYSSEY, PART ONE 899

Summary ■■■

Odysseus and his followers, who have been imprisoned in the Cyclops's cave, watch in horror as two of their number are consumed by the monster each morning and night. The heroic Odysseus conceives of a plan of escape. With his companions, he fashions a sharp wooden stake, which he heats in the fire and stabs into the Cyclops's eye while the monster is sleeping. Odysseus and his men make their escape from the cave by clinging to the underbellies of the Cyclops's sheep, but Odysseus cannot resist taunting the monster, who curses his former captive and implores his father, Poseidon, the sea god, to keep the hero a wanderer on the sea for many years.

C **Reading Skills and Strategies**
Drawing Conclusions
❓ Why do you think Odysseus and his men burn an offering for the gods? [Possible responses: to thank the gods for allowing them to survive the voyage; to appease the gods so that they will be allowed to return home.]

RESPONDING TO THE ART

Odilon Redon (1840–1916), a French painter and graphic artist, wrote that his originality consisted of "bringing to life, in a human way, improbable beings and making them live according to the laws of probability." Drawing on mythology, his own fantasies, and the Bible, Redon painted ethereal, dreamlike scenes of plant and animal life. *The Cyclops* depicts a shy, quiet Polyphemus with a loving eye, unlike the horrible monster described in the *Odyssey*.
Activity. Ask students what elements of the painting help to lessen the ferocious character of the Cyclops. [Possible responses: the pastel colors; the wide-open expanse of the sky; the gentle eye; the blurred outlines.]

Reaching All Students

Struggling Readers
After they finish reading each section, have student partners review the content of what they have just read. Students can work together to write a brief summary of each section. You can collect these summaries to make sure students are comprehending the material.

English Language Learners
Students who are learning English will find the *Odyssey's* structure and vocabulary challenging. You may want to pair these students with native English speakers to read aloud a section of the epic. Have students take turns reading aloud; the more confident reader can coach the English language learner.

A Critical Thinking

Analyzing

? How does Homer help the reader sense what Odysseus is up against with this strange opponent? [Sample responses: The poet shows the brute strength of the Cyclops by having him lift a great rock of unbelievable weight and size; the poet describes the Cyclops's strength as greater than that of twenty-four wagons pulled by teams of horses.]

B Critical Thinking

Interpreting

? What does the phrase "fair traffic" mean? What does the Cyclops mean by these questions? [The phrase "fair traffic" means legitimate business, such as traders or sailors are engaged in. The Cyclops wants to know if the strangers' business in his cave is legitimate or if they have come to take advantage of him in some way.]

C Reading Skills and Strategies

Monitor Your Comprehension

You might suggest that students stop at this point to ask themselves questions. They might ask, for example: What did you learn in an earlier episode that explains why Odysseus gives the Cyclops this warning? [When cast on the island of Scheria, Odysseus was treated as an honored guest. In ancient Greek culture, guests were considered protected by the gods, and they had to be treated with great courtesy.]

Then over the broad cavern floor he ushered
the ewes he meant to milk. He left his rams
and he-goats in the yard outside, and swung
high overhead a slab of solid rock
230 **A** to close the cave. Two dozen four-wheeled wagons,
with heaving wagon teams, could not have stirred
the tonnage of that rock from where he wedged it
over the doorsill. Next he took his seat
and milked his bleating ewes. A practiced job
235 he made of it, giving each ewe her suckling;
thickened his milk, then, into curds and whey,
sieved out the curds to drip in withy baskets,°
and poured the whey to stand in bowls
cooling until he drank it for his supper.
240 When all these chores were done, he poked the fire,
heaping on brushwood. In the glare he saw us.

'Strangers,' he said, 'who are you? And where from?
What brings you here by seaways—a fair traffic?
B Or are you wandering rogues, who cast your lives
245 like dice, and <u>ravage</u> other folk by sea?'

We felt a pressure on our hearts, in dread
of that deep rumble and that mighty man.
But all the same I spoke up in reply:

'We are from Troy, Achaeans, blown off course
250 by shifting gales on the Great South Sea;
homeward bound, but taking routes and ways
uncommon; so the will of Zeus would have it.
We served under Agamemnon, son of Atreus—
the whole world knows what city
255 he laid waste, what armies he destroyed.
It was our luck to come here; here we stand,
beholden for your help, or any gifts
C you give—as custom is to honor strangers.
We would entreat you, great Sir, have a care
260 for the gods' courtesy; Zeus will avenge
the unoffending guest.'

He answered this
from his brute chest, unmoved:

'You are a ninny,
or else you come from the other end of nowhere,
telling me, mind the gods! We Cyclopes

237. withy baskets: baskets made from willow twigs.

253. Agamemnon (ag′ə·mem′nän′). **Atreus** (ā′trē·əs).

WORDS TO OWN
ravage (rav′ij) *v.*: destroy violently; ruin.

---

900 THE EPIC

Taking a Second Look

Review: Making Predictions

Remind students that, as readers, they are like detectives. They follow the trail of clues in a text and combine this evidence with their own knowledge to predict what might happen next. For example, when reading "The Lotus Eaters," they may have predicted that Odysseus would escape from that land, based on evidence in the text of Odysseus' character and on their own knowledge of how people behave.

Activity

Ask students to make four-column charts with the headings "Clues in the Text," "Own Knowledge," "Prediction," and "Actual Outcome" and to fill in the charts as they read. Examples:

1. Read ll. 311–323. Make a prediction about why Odysseus is making the pointed stake, and list the clues in the text and your own knowledge that helped you make this prediction. Read on to learn the outcome.

2. Read ll. 357–361. Predict why Odysseus names himself Nohbdy, and list supporting clues from the text and your own knowledge. Write the outcome on the chart.

Ulysses and His Companions on the Island of the Cyclops by Pellegrino Tibaldi.

Palazzo Poggi, Bologna, Italy.

RESPONDING TO THE ART

Pellegrino Tibaldi (1527–1596) was an Italian painter whose work was greatly influenced by Michelangelo. Starting in 1550, he painted frescoes of the stories of Odysseus in the manner of Michelangelo's Sistine Chapel ceiling. Later he became an architect for the Milan Cathedral and then a court painter for Philip II of Spain.

Activity. How does this depiction of the Cyclops differ from that of Redon on p. 899? [Sample responses: This depiction shows the Cyclops as angry, monstrous, and ferocious, whereas Redon's depiction shows the Cyclops as quiet, sensitive, and dreaming; Tibaldi uses dark colors to highlight the massive muscles and brute strength of the Cyclops, while Redon's painting style highlights the fantastical nature of the creature; Tibaldi's Cyclops has one eye and two eye sockets, but Redon's has one eye.]

Professional Notes

Ancient Architecture

Athena was ancient Athens's most important deity, and the Parthenon, a temple built in her honor during the fifth century B.C., is the most famous example of Athenian architecture. Built on the Acropolis—the oldest and highest area in Athens—the Parthenon was named for the religious epithet *Athena Parthenos* ("Athena the Virgin"). The temple was the brain child of the statesman Pericles. Its construction was part of his goal of making Athens the cultural, political,

and religious center of the world. Built in the Doric and Ionian styles, the Parthenon lived up to the aspirations of its builders. Art historian Thomas Craven said of the temple, "Behold the Parthenon, the only perfect building erected by man." Over the years, the Parthenon has been ravaged by invaders and time. The temple was turned into a church in the sixth century A.D. and later became an Islamic mosque. In the seventeenth century, it was damaged in battles

between the Venetians and the Turks. Lord Elgin, the British Ambassador to Constantinople, stripped the temple of its sculptures and carvings and shipped them to London in the early nineteenth century. Today the "Elgin Marbles" remain the subject of bitter dispute between Great Britain and Greece.

Character

? What is going on here? [Odysseus knows the Cyclops is trying to trick him in order to destroy his ship, so he prepares to reply with a lie.] **What does Odysseus' remark suggest about his character?** [Sample responses: Odysseus is not tricked by the Cyclops's question, which shows how quick-witted the hero is; Odysseus is a practical man and will lie when it is necessary to save his men.]

B Reading Skills and Strategies

Monitor Your Comprehension

Ask which details help readers visualize this gruesome scene. [Possible details: "squirming puppies"; "spattering the floor"; "gaping and crunching like a mountain lion."] Suggest that students pause here to ask themselves questions about this horrifying picture. For example, they might ask: Why does Homer include such gruesome details? [Possible response: He includes these details so that the reader can fully understand the horror of what is happening.]

C Critical Thinking

Analyzing

? What two things are being juxtaposed in this passage? [the Cyclops's horrific eating of men and the ordinary, even peaceful daily routine of his life] **What effect does this juxtaposition have on the reader?** [Possible answers: It makes the episode even more horrific; it emphasizes the Cyclops's inverted value system—he cares more for his sheep than he does for human beings.]

265   care not a whistle for your thundering Zeus
       or all the gods in bliss; we have more force by far.
       I would not let you go for fear of Zeus—
       you or your friends—unless I had a whim to.
       Tell me, where was it, now, you left your ship—
270   around the point, or down the shore, I wonder?'

A He thought he'd find out, but I saw through this,
       and answered with a ready lie:

                         'My ship?

       Poseidon Lord, who sets the earth atremble,
       broke it up on the rocks at your land's end.
275   A wind from seaward served him, drove us there.
       We are survivors, these good men and I.'

       Neither reply nor pity came from him,
       but in one stride he clutched at my companions
       and caught two in his hands like squirming puppies
280 **B** to beat their brains out, spattering the floor.
       Then he dismembered them and made his meal,
       gaping and crunching like a mountain lion—
       everything: innards, flesh, and marrow bones.
       We cried aloud, lifting our hands to Zeus,
285   powerless, looking on at this, appalled;
       but Cyclops went on filling up his belly
       with manflesh and great gulps of whey,
       then lay down like a mast among his sheep.
       My heart beat high now at the chance of action,
290   and drawing the sharp sword from my hip I went
       along his flank to stab him where the midriff
       holds the liver. I had touched the spot
       when sudden fear stayed me: if I killed him
       we perished there as well, for we could never
295   move his ponderous doorway slab aside.
       So we were left to groan and wait for morning.

       When the young Dawn with fingertips of rose
       lit up the world, the Cyclops built a fire
       and milked his handsome ewes, all in due order,
300   putting the sucklings to the mothers. Then,
     C his chores being all dispatched, he caught
       another brace of men to make his breakfast,
       and whisked away his great door slab
       to let his sheep go through—but he, behind,
305   reset the stone as one would cap a quiver.
       There was a din of whistling as the Cyclops
       rounded his flock to higher ground, then stillness.
       And now I pondered how to hurt him worst,

The Cyclops Polyphemus (2nd century B.C.). Marble.

Professional Notes

According to critic Erwin F. Cook, the *Odyssey* portrays a series of contrasts between *metis*, "cunning intelligence," and *bie* (or *bia*), "violent might." Odysseus demonstrates *metis* throughout his adventures, as does his patron, Athena. Poseidon and the various figures who oppose Odysseus represent *bie*. They may be powerful, but their power is savage. Cook argues that in the *Odyssey* and in other works, Poseidon and Athena are opposed to each other. They represent "the Greek polarization of nature and culture. Poseidon embodies the power of nature, [Athena] the ingenuity which renders that power useful or protects us from it." Invite students to keep this comment in mind as they read the different episodes in the *Odyssey*. After they have finished reading, have them discuss whether they agree or disagree with Cook's interpretation.

if but Athena granted what I prayed for.
310   Here are the means I thought would serve my turn:

a club, or staff, lay there along the fold—
an olive tree, felled green and left to season
for Cyclops' hand. And it was like a mast
a lugger° of twenty oars, broad in the beam—
315   a deep-seagoing craft—might carry:
so long, so big around, it seemed. Now I
chopped out a six-foot section of this pole
and set it down before my men, who scraped it;
and when they had it smooth, I hewed again
320   to make a stake with pointed end. I held this
in the fire's heart and turned it, toughening it,
then hid it, well back in the cavern, under
one of the dung piles in profusion there.
Now came the time to toss for it: who ventured
325   along with me? Whose hand could bear to thrust
and grind that spike in Cyclops's eye, when mild
sleep had mastered him? As luck would have it,
the men I would have chosen won the toss—
four strong men, and I made five as captain.

330   At evening came the shepherd with his flock,
his woolly flock. The rams as well, this time,
entered the cave: by some sheepherding whim—
or a god's bidding—none were left outside.
He hefted his great boulder into place
335   and sat him down to milk the bleating ewes
in proper order, put the lambs to suck,
and swiftly ran through all his evening chores.
Then he caught two more men and feasted on them.
My moment was at hand, and I went forward
340   holding an ivy bowl of my dark drink,
looking up, saying:

                    'Cyclops, try some wine.
Here's liquor to wash down your scraps of men.
Taste it, and see the kind of drink we carried
under our planks. I meant it for an offering
345   if you would help us home. But you are mad,
unbearable, a bloody monster! After this,
will any other traveler come to see you?'

WORDS TO OWN
profusion (prō·fyoo′zhən) n.: large supply; abundance.

---

314. lugger: type of sailboat.

Odysseus handing the drink to Polyphemus (1st century A.D.). Relief on Grecian marble sarcophagus.

Museo Archeologico Nazionale, Naples, Italy.

THE ODYSSEY, PART ONE   903

D Reading Skills and Strategies
Predicting
? What do you think Odysseus plans to do with the pointed staff? [Possible responses: He plans to stab the Cyclops with it; he plans to poke out his eye.]

E Critical Thinking
Evaluating
? Since Odysseus is the captain, he could have just chosen the men he wanted for the job rather than drawing lots. Is it smart to "toss" for this job, or is Odysseus foolish in risking the future of the whole group by not just appointing the men he thinks best fit to go with him? [Possible answers: Yes, he is smart, because a toss is fair, thereby ensuring that the men are not resentful about the outcome; no, it is foolish to risk undertaking something dangerous without selecting the best men for the job.]

F Elements of Literature
Foreshadowing
? Odysseus says that the rams may have entered the cave at "a god's bidding." What does this mean, and what does it suggest about the role that the rams will play in the future? [Sample response: It means that the gods may be directing the rams' actions. The rams might play a part in helping Odysseus and his men escape.]

Taking a Second Look

Review: Making Generalizations
Remind students that making a generalization is similar to drawing a conclusion. The reader uses details in the text, as well as prior knowledge, to reach an observation. What is different about making generalizations, however, is that the reader analyzes many different facts, events, or situations. By analyzing a range of information, the reader can make a broad statement that applies not just to one situation, but to other similar situations as well. For example, a reader might examine Odysseus' actions on encountering the Cicones, Polyphemus, and the Sirens before coming to a generalization about how Odysseus tends to respond to dangerous situations.

Activities
1. Ask students to look at the behavior of Athena, Zeus, and Poseidon, recall what they have read about the gods in other Greek myths, and then generalize about the character traits of Greek gods.
2. As students continue to read the *Odyssey*, ask them to think of other generalizations they can make based on what they have read and their prior knowledge. Then, have students discuss the process that they used to reach their generalizations.

A Vocabulary Note

Greek Words

This pun will be more readily appreciated by students if they know that the Greek word for "nobody" is *outis*, which sounds similar to Odysseus.

B Elements of Literature

Irony

? What is ironic about the Cyclops's saying he will eat Nohbdy last? [The Cyclops will indeed eat nobody, because the reader already knows that Odysseus will escape and live to tell the story.]

C Literary Connections

The olive pole used as a weapon here calls to mind Athena, since it is a symbol associated with the goddess. According to Greek myth, Athena and Poseidon once competed to be the patron deity of Athens. To justify their claims on the city, each made a show of power. Poseidon created water in the barren Acropolis. Athena produced an olive tree. The Athenians, preferring Athena's gift, chose the goddess. This myth would have been familiar to contemporary audiences of the *Odyssey*, adding resonance to the fact that Athena's favorite, Odysseus, bests Poseidon's son.

D Elements of Literature

Homeric Simile

? What is the blinding of the Cyclops compared to? [It is compared to plunging a white-hot axhead into a cold tub of water.]

He seized and drained the bowl, and it went down
so fiery and smooth he called for more:

350 'Give me another, thank you kindly. Tell me,
how are you called? I'll make a gift will please you.
Even Cyclopes know the wine grapes grow
out of grassland and loam in heaven's rain,
but here's a bit of nectar and ambrosia!'

355 Three bowls I brought him, and he poured them down.
I saw the fuddle and flush come over him,
then I sang out in cordial tones:

              'Cyclops,
you ask my honorable name? Remember
the gift you promised me, and I shall tell you.
360 My name is Nohbdy: mother, father, and friends,
everyone calls me Nohbdy.'

                    And he said:

'Nohbdy's my meat, then, after I eat his friends.
Others come first. There's a noble gift, now.'

Even as he spoke, he reeled and tumbled backward,
365 his great head lolling to one side; and sleep
took him like any creature. Drunk, hiccuping,
he dribbled streams of liquor and bits of men.

Now, by the gods, I drove my big hand spike
deep in the embers, charring it again,
370 and cheered my men along with battle talk
to keep their courage up: no quitting now.
The pike of olive, green though it had been,
reddened and glowed as if about to catch.
I drew it from the coals and my four fellows
375 gave me a hand, lugging it near the Cyclops
as more than natural force nerved them; straight
forward they sprinted, lifted it, and rammed it
deep in his crater eye, and I leaned on it
turning it as a shipwright turns a drill
380 in planking, having men below to swing
the two-handled strap that spins it in the groove.
So with our brand we bored that great eye socket
while blood ran out around the red-hot bar.
Eyelid and lash were seared; the pierced ball
hissed broiling, and the roots popped.

                        In a smithy°
385 one sees a white-hot axhead or an adze°
plunged and wrung in a cold tub, screeching steam—
the way they make soft iron hale and hard—

385. smithy: blacksmith's shop, where iron tools are made.
386. adze: tool like an ax but with a longer, curved blade.

904 THE EPIC

Getting Students Involved

Cooperative Learning

A Contemporary Epic. Ask students to review the quotation on p. 876 and the introduction that begins on p. 878. Then, have them work in groups to name a film, book, or other story that has the qualities of a modern epic—a work that can be seen as "an encyclopedia of the manners, customs, and values" of our culture. Suggest that students use the following list to assess the works:

What the work tells us about
• our values
• our manners and traditions
• how we respond to adversity
• how we relate to one another
• how we handle problems
• the kinds of behavior we find appropriate or inappropriate

Groups should elect a facilitator to see that all students participate, a recorder to take notes, and a presenter to explain the consensus reached by the group to the class.

A Character's Curiosity. Hold a panel discussion on the extent to which Odysseus' troubles are caused by his own curiosity. Have the panel members find support in the text for their positions.

just so that eyeball hissed around the spike.

390 The Cyclops bellowed and the rock roared round him,
and we fell back in fear. Clawing his face
he tugged the bloody spike out of his eye,
threw it away, and his wild hands went groping;
then he set up a howl for Cyclopes

395 who lived in caves on windy peaks nearby.
Some heard him; and they came by divers° ways
to clump around outside and call:

                                      'What ails you,
Polyphemus? Why do you cry so sore
in the starry night? You will not let us sleep.

400 Sure no man's driving off your flock? No man
has tricked you, ruined you?'

                                Out of the cave
the mammoth Polyphemus roared in answer:

'Nohbdy, Nohbdy's tricked me. Nohbdy's ruined me!'

To this rough shout they made a <u>sage</u> reply:

405 'Ah well, if nobody has played you foul
there in your lonely bed, we are no use in pain
given by great Zeus. Let it be your father,
Poseidon Lord, to whom you pray.'

                                So saying
they trailed away. And I was filled with laughter

410 to see how like a charm the name deceived them.
Now Cyclops, wheezing as the pain came on him,
fumbled to wrench away the great doorstone
and squatted in the breach with arms thrown wide
for any silly beast or man who bolted—

415 hoping somehow I might be such a fool.
But I kept thinking how to win the game:
death sat there huge; how could we slip away?
I drew on all my wits, and ran through tactics,
reasoning as a man will for dear life,

420 until a trick came—and it pleased me well.
The Cyclops's rams were handsome, fat, with heavy
fleeces, a dark violet.

I tied them silently together, twining
cords of willow from the ogre's bed;

425 then slung a man under each middle one

WORDS TO OWN
sage (sāj) *adj.*: wise.

396. **divers:** diverse; various.

Odysseus and his men blinding the Cyclops (530–510 B.C.). Hydria, or water jar.

Three abreast

Collection Villa Giulia, Rome.

THE ODYSSEY, PART ONE 905

E **Elements of Literature**
Irony
Ask students to explain the irony
in these lines. [When Polyphemus tells
the other Cyclopes that Nohbdy has
ruined him, they believe no one has
harmed him.]

F **Critical Thinking**
Expressing an Opinion
❓ Do you think that Odysseus' laughter is wise, since he and his men are
obviously not yet out of danger? [Sam-
ple responses: No, his laughter is premature at this time, since he and his men
are still trapped; no, his laughter may
anger Polyphemus even more; yes, such
a clever trick deserves celebration, and
the Cyclops, who is now blind, cannot
easily find Odysseus.]

G **Elements of Literature**
Character
❓ How would you characterize
Odysseus here? [Possible responses: a
strategist; a trickster; a planner.]

Skill Link

Similes

Remind students that a **simile** is a figure of
speech that makes a comparison between two
very different things and that states the comparison with a word, such as *like* or *as*. You might
write a couple of common examples on the
chalkboard: *skin as smooth as silk, a smile like
sunshine.*

Activities

1. Ask students to complete the following
   sentences by creating similes.

The monstrous giant was _____.
Odysseus' days away from home were _____.
Calypso was _____.

2. Have pairs of students evaluate each other's
   similes. They should ask: In what way or ways
   are these two unlike things alike? Does the
   simile work to make the idea come alive? Is
   the simile fresh and original?

to ride there safely, shielded left and right.
So three sheep could convey each man. I took
the woolliest ram, the choicest of the flock,
A and hung myself under his kinky belly,
430   pulled up tight, with fingers twisted deep
in sheepskin ringlets for an iron grip.
So, breathing hard, we waited until morning.

B When Dawn spread out her fingertips of rose
the rams began to stir, moving for pasture,
435   and peals of bleating echoed round the pens
where dams with udders full called for a milking.
Blinded, and sick with pain from his head wound,
the master stroked each ram, then let it pass,
but my men riding on the pectoral fleece°
440   the giant's blind hands blundering never found.
Last of them all my ram, the leader, came,
weighted by wool and me with my meditations.
The Cyclops patted him, and then he said:

'Sweet cousin ram, why lag behind the rest
445   in the night cave? You never linger so,
but graze before them all, and go afar
to crop sweet grass, and take your stately way
leading along the streams, until at evening
you run to be the first one in the fold.
450   Why, now, so far behind? Can you be grieving
over your Master's eye? That carrion rogue°
and his accurst companions burnt it out
when he had conquered all my wits with wine.
C Nohbdy will not get out alive, I swear. *double negative*
455   Oh, had you brain and voice to tell

439. pectoral fleece: wool on an animal's chest.

451. carrion rogue: rotten scoundrel. Carrion is decaying flesh.

Odysseus escaping the cave of Polyphemus under the belly of the ram (c. 510 B.C.). Detail from a krater, a vessel for holding wine.
Badisches Landesmuseum, Karlsruhe, Germany.

906 THE EPIC

Taking a Second Look

Review: Chronology

Remind students that chronological order is the order in which events happen, from start to finish. Point out that the *Odyssey* is not structured in strict chronological order. Book 5, for example, tells of Odysseus' interactions with Calypso, events that occur later in time than the adventures that Odysseus relates to King Alcinous' court in Books 9–12.

These adventures are themselves told as part of a flashback. Clues in the narrative make it clear that Odysseus is talking about events that have occurred in the distant past. The rhetorical question that Odysseus uses to preface his story is one such clue: "What of those years / of rough adventure, weathered under Zeus?"

Activity

Have students work in groups to create a chronology of the major events that occur in Part One. Students may present their chronology in paragraph form or on a time line.

where he may be now, dodging all my fury!
Bashed by this hand and bashed on this rock wall
his brains would strew the floor, and I should have
rest from the outrage Nohbdy worked upon me.'

460 He sent us into the open, then. Close by,
I dropped and rolled clear of the ram's belly,
going this way and that to untie the men.
With many glances back, we rounded up
his fat, stiff-legged sheep to take aboard,
465 and drove them down to where the good ship lay.
We saw, as we came near, our fellows' faces
shining; then we saw them turn to grief
tallying those who had not fled from death.
I hushed them, jerking head and eyebrows up,
470 and in a low voice told them: 'Load this herd;
move fast, and put the ship's head toward the breakers.'
They all pitched in at loading, then embarked
and struck their oars into the sea. Far out,
as far offshore as shouted words would carry,
475 I sent a few back to the <u>adversary</u>:

'O Cyclops! Would you feast on my companions?
Puny, am I, in a Caveman's hands?
How do you like the beating that we gave you,
you damned cannibal? Eater of guests
480 under your roof! Zeus and the gods have paid you!'

The blind thing in his doubled fury broke
a hilltop in his hands and heaved it after us.
Ahead of our black prow it struck and sank
whelmed in a spuming geyser, a giant wave
485 that washed the ship stern foremost back to shore.
I got the longest boathook out and stood
fending us off, with furious nods to all
to put their backs into a racing stroke—
row, row or perish. So the long oars bent
490 kicking the foam sternward, making head
until we drew away, and twice as far.
Now when I cupped my hands I heard the crew
in low voices protesting:

                              'Godsake, Captain!
Why bait the beast again? Let him alone!'

D
E
F

WORDS TO OWN
adversary (ad′vər·ser′ē) *n.:* enemy; opponent.

Odysseus escaping under a ram (590 B.C.). Detail from a black-figured convex lekythos from Girgenti (now Agrigento), Sicily, Italy (25 cm high).
Antikensammlung, Munich, Germany.

THE ODYSSEY, PART ONE 907

D **Reading Skills and Strategies**
Monitor Your Comprehension
This is a good point for students to stop and make sure they understand what is going on. Have them ask themselves questions, such as these: Why do the "fellows' faces" turn from shining to grief? Why does Odysseus hush his men? [The "fellows" are the shipmates, who have shining faces when they see that Odysseus and his party are safe but who then become mournful when they see that some men are missing. Odysseus hushes them because he does not want the Cyclops to hear them and figure out where they are and what they are doing.]

E **Critical Thinking**
Expressing an Opinion
? Is it wise of Odysseus to taunt Polyphemus? Explain. [Possible responses: No, they have not gotten far enough away to be safe yet; yes, after outwitting the Cyclops, Odysseus deserves a chance to brag.]

F **Elements of Literature**
Irony
? What is ironic about the order that Odysseus gives? [Sample response: It is because of his boasting that the men must "row or perish."]

RESPONDING TO THE ART
In the "black-figured" style of pottery painting, black silhouettes were painted directly onto the red clay. A *lekythos* was a small, cylindrical bottle used for storing oils and perfumes. Note this ram's majestic horn.
Activity. Students might try drawing their own versions of how Odysseus hid under the belly of the ram. You might also ask students to write Odysseus' thoughts as he clings to the ram's wool.

Using Students' Strengths

Naturalist Learners
During the course of the *Odyssey,* Homer lists the abundance of flora and fauna found in the Greek isles. The plants and animals named include horned owls, falcons, cormorants, thyme, olive trees, cedar, and clover. Ask interested students to create a multimedia presentation on the plant and animal life of the Greek isles. Presentations can include photographs, drawings, and written descriptions. Have students concentrate on what a modern-day traveler would encounter on a trip to this region.

Predicting

? How might Odysseus' revelation of his name get him and his men into trouble later on? [Now that he knows who blinded him, Polyphemus can seek revenge through his father, Poseidon.]

B Elements of Literature

Character

Point out to students that Polyphemus's underestimation of his adversary, which is a character flaw, has led to his downfall. He was so sure of his own strength that when his blinding was foretold, he could believe that only another giant would be able to do it. This led him not to be as cautious as he should have been with Odysseus and his men.

C Critical Thinking

Evaluating

? Do you believe Polyphemus's promise? Is he trustworthy? Explain. [No, he has offered false promises before, so there is no reason to believe him now.]

---

495   'That tidal wave he made on the first throw
       all but beached us.'

                     'All but stove us in!'

    'Give him our bearing with your trumpeting,
       he'll get the range and lob° a boulder.'   **498. lob:** toss.

                              'Aye

    He'll smash our timbers and our heads together!'

500   I would not heed them in my glorying spirit,
       but let my anger flare and yelled:

                        'Cyclops,

A   if ever mortal man inquire
       how you were put to shame and blinded, tell him
       Odysseus, raider of cities, took your eye:
505   Laertes' son, whose home's on Ithaca!'

    At this he gave a mighty sob and rumbled:

B   'Now comes the weird° upon me, spoken of old.   **507. weird:** fate.
       A wizard, grand and wondrous, lived here—Telemus,°   **508. Telemus** (tel′ə·məs).
       a son of Eurymus;° great length of days   **509. Eurymus** (yo͞o′rē·məs).
510   he had in wizardry among the Cyclopes,
       and these things he foretold for time to come:
       my great eye lost, and at Odysseus' hands.
       Always I had in mind some giant, armed
       in giant force, would come against me here.
515   But this, but you—small, pitiful, and twiggy—
       you put me down with wine, you blinded me.
       Come back, Odysseus, and I'll treat you well,
       praying the god of earthquake to befriend you—
C   his son I am, for he by his avowal
520   fathered me, and, if he will, he may
       heal me of this black wound—he and no other
       of all the happy gods or mortal men.'

    Few words I shouted in reply to him:

    'If I could take your life I would and take
525   your time away, and hurl you down to hell!
       The god of earthquake could not heal you there!'

    At this he stretched his hands out in his darkness
    toward the sky of stars, and prayed Poseidon:

    'O hear me, lord, blue girdler of the islands,
530   if I am thine indeed, and thou art father:
       grant that Odysseus, raider of cities, never
       see his home: Laertes' son, I mean,

Polyphemus (4th century B.C.). Terra cotta head from Izmir, Turkey.

Department des Antiquites Grecques/Romaines, Louvre, Paris, France.

908 THE EPIC

Making the Connections

Cultural Connections: Homer's World

To a modern reader, Homer's world might appear mysterious but somewhat diminutive. Homer imagined the Earth as a disk with an area only one-third larger than that of the United States. Greece was in the center, and the sanctuary of Delphi, regarded as the center of Greece, came to be referred to as the "navel of the world." A turbulent river bounded Homer's Earth. Beyond this edge were the dark regions that gave access to Erebus, the underground kingdom of the dead where Hades and Persephone reigned. Interested students may research conceptions of the world held by other cultures throughout history. Students can draw maps that illustrate the world views they investigate.

who kept his hall on Ithaca. Should destiny
intend that he shall see his roof again
535 among his family in his fatherland,
far be that day, and dark the years between.
Let him lose all companions, and return
under strange sail to bitter days at home.' . . ."

(*from* Book 9)

Here we will imagine that Homer stops reciting for the night. The listeners would now go off to various corners of the local nobleman's house. The blind poet might take a glass of wine before turning in. The people who heard the poet's stories might ask questions among themselves and look forward to the next evening's installment.

Read *"Welcome: A Religious Duty"* on page 910. *As you continue the story, trace the ways Homer repeatedly dramatizes the importance of mutual respect among people. Think about your own ideas on hospitality today—what are the customs in your family and neighborhood? What about society as a whole?*

Connections

A POEM

The Cyclops in the Ocean E

Nikki Giovanni

Moving slowly . . . against time . . . patiently majestic . . .
the cyclops . . . in the ocean . . . meets no Ulysses . . . **F**

Through the night . . . he sighs . . . throbbing against the
shore . . . declaring . . . for the adventure . . .

5 A wall of gray . . . gathered by a slow touch . . . slash and
slither . . . through the waiting screens . . . separating into
nodules . . . making my panes . . . accept the touch . . .

Not content . . . to watch my frightened gaze . . . he clamors
beneath the sash . . . dancing on my sill . . .

10 Certain to die . . . when the sun . . . returns . . . **G**

Tropical Storm Dennis
August 15–18, 1981, Florida

Connecting Across Texts

Connecting with the *Odyssey*
"The Cyclops in the Ocean" personifies Tropical Storm Dennis by comparing it to the Cyclops. With the class, discuss what traits of the Cyclops are similar to those of a storm. Make a list of similar characteristics or qualities on the chalkboard or on an overhead transparency. Add any other qualities of the Cyclops that students can think of. Then, ask students to make lists of other creatures or natural phenomena that exhibit qualities of the Cyclops. After students have shared their ideas, ask the class to select one creature or phenomenon and to create a class poem comparing it to the Cyclops.

Ask students to think of ways that people from various cultures greet strangers and treat guests. What do these customs show about the cultures' beliefs? Discuss with students how these beliefs emerge in day-to-day life, even in something as simple as the friendly handshake, which demonstrates a certain democratic feeling by showing that both participants are on the same level. You might tell students that originally the custom of a handshake was a protective gesture; it served to prove that neither person was carrying a weapon. Have students share their ideas in a class discussion, and encourage them to be open-minded and attentive to the various beliefs among themselves. Write students' ideas on the chalkboard, and have students compare their customs with those of the ancient Greeks.

Welcome: A Religious Duty

Today's visitors to Greece are often struck by the generous hospitality of the people. An ancient tradition lies behind the traveler's welcome in Greece—and it is a tradition that was fundamentally religious before it became a part of social custom.

Zeus, the king of the gods, demanded that strangers be treated graciously. Hosts had a religious duty to welcome strangers, and guests had a responsibility to respect hosts. The tight interconnections and mutual respect in this host-guest relationship are reflected in the fact that the word *xenos* (zē´näs) in ancient Greek can mean both "host" and "guest." The relationship is often symbolized in the *Odyssey* by the presentation of gifts. Alcinous, the king of the Phaeacians, for example, gives Odysseus a magically swift ship to get him home.

What happens when the host-guest relationship is abused or otherwise breaks down? In Homer's epic songs of the Trojan War, the *Iliad* and the *Odyssey*, this happens at least three times. The first occasion caused the war itself: Paris, prince of Troy, ran off with the beautiful Helen from Sparta while he was the guest of Helen's husband, Menelaus. For the Greeks, this insult to *xenia* (hospitality) was at least as serious as Helen's unfaithfulness, and it meant that Zeus would, in the end, allow the Greeks to triumph in the long war.

The second example of violated hospitality has its humorous and ironic side. In the *Odyssey*, the Cyclops is monstrous not only because of his huge size and brutish appearance. He is set apart from civilized beings precisely because of his barbaric outlook on *xenia*. When Odysseus begs the Cyclops for hospitality and warns that Zeus will avenge an injured guest, the Cyclops replies that he and his kind "care not a whistle for . . . Zeus" (line 265). With dark humor, the Cyclops uses the word *xeineion* (Greek for "guest-gift") when he tells Odysseus that he will have the privilege of being eaten last (lines 362–363). The poetic justice of the Cyclops's blinding would not be lost on Homer's Greek audience.

The final example of a breach in the law of hospitality underlies the entire plot structure of the *Odyssey*: Back in Ithaca, the suitors year after year abuse the hospitality of Odysseus—an absent "host"—and threaten to take away his wife. The bloody vengeance that Odysseus takes on these suitors should be understood in the context of their outrageous violation of religious law. The suitors have turned hospitality into a crude mockery. Perhaps it is not accidental that just before the battle Odysseus invokes the host-guest relationship when he quietly gives his son, Telemachus, the signal to fight (lines 1208–1209):

> "Telemachus, the stranger [*xeinos*]
> you welcomed in your hall has not disgraced you."

Taking a Second Look

Review: Comparing Texts

After students have read "The Cyclops in the Ocean," ask them to recall Carl Sandburg's poem "Fog" from Collection 8 (p. 503). Have a volunteer read the poem aloud for the class. Ask students what the obvious similarity is between the two poems? [In each poem, an extended image is used to describe a weather phenomenon: Sandburg likens fog to a cat; Giovanni compares a storm to the Cyclops.]

Then use questions such as the following to help students compare and contrast the two poems:
- What is similar about the subject of each poem? [Each poem describes a force of nature.]
- What is dissimilar about the subjects? [Giovanni describes a dangerous subject, a tropical storm, whereas Sandburg's subject, fog, is usually a benign phenomenon.]

- Do you think the images chosen by each poet are appropriate to their respective subjects? Why? [Sample response: Yes, the monstrous Cyclops is a fitting metaphor for a fierce tropical storm; the stealthy but harmless cat is equally appropriate for fog.]

THE WITCH CIRCE

After sailing from the Cyclops's island, Odysseus and his men land on the island of Aeolia. There, the wind king, Aeolus (ē'ə·ləs), does Odysseus a favor. He puts all the stormy winds in a bag so that they will not harm the Ithacans. The bull's-hide bag containing the winds is wedged under Odysseus' afterdeck. But during the voyage, the suspicious and curious sailors open the bag, thinking it contains treasure, and the evil winds roar up into hurricanes that blow the ships back to Aeolia. Aeolus drives them away again.

On the island of the Laestrygonians (les·trig·ō'nē·ənz), gigantic cannibals, all the ships but one are destroyed and their crews devoured. Odysseus' ship escapes and lands on Aeaea, the home of the witch Circe. Here, a party of twenty-three men, led by Eurylochus, goes off to explore the island. Odysseus is still telling his story to Alcinous and his court.

> "In the wild wood they found an open glade,
> 540 around a smooth stone house—the hall of Circe—
> and wolves and mountain lions lay there, mild
> in her soft spell, fed on her drug of evil.
> None would attack—oh, it was strange, I tell you—
> but switching their long tails they faced our men
> 545 like hounds, who look up when their master comes
> with tidbits for them—as he will—from table.
> Humbly those wolves and lions with mighty paws
> fawned on our men—who met their yellow eyes
> and feared them.
>   In the entranceway they stayed
> 550 to listen there: inside her quiet house
> they heard the goddess Circe.
>   Low she sang
>
> in her beguiling voice, while on her loom
> she wove ambrosial fabric sheer and bright,
> by that craft known to the goddesses of heaven.
> 555 No one would speak, until Polites°—most
> faithful and likable of my officers—said:
>
> 'Dear friends, no need for stealth: here's a young weaver
> singing a pretty song to set the air
> atingle on these lawns and paven courts.
> 560 Goddess she is, or lady. Shall we greet her?'
>
> So reassured, they all cried out together,
> and she came swiftly to the shining doors

WORDS TO OWN
stealth (stelth) *n.*: secret or sneaky action or behavior.

Pigs, swineherd, and Odysseus (470–460 B.C.) by the Pig Painter. Pelike, or jar.

Fitzwilliam Museum, University of Cambridge.

555. Polites (pō·lī'tēz).

THE ODYSSEY, PART ONE 911

Summary ■ ■

When Odysseus and his men reach the island of the witch Circe, the sailors are beguiled by the sorceress, who turns them into swine and shuts them in a pigsty.

Ⓐ Critical Thinking
Interpreting
❓ What does the sailors' opening of the bull's-hide bag suggest about their relationship with Odysseus? [Possible responses: The sailors don't trust that Odysseus will share a treasure with them; Odysseus does not share information with his sailors.]

Ⓑ Elements of Literature
Simile
❓ To emphasize the strange gentleness of the wild beasts' behavior, what does Odysseus compare them to? [He compares them to domesticated dogs who depend on a master for sustenance.]

Ⓒ Reading Skills and Strategies
Making Inferences
❓ Like Calypso, when we first glimpse her, Circe is at her loom, singing and weaving. Based on this, what inference might you make about women in ancient Greece? [Possible response: Weaving was an important part of women's work in ancient Greece.]

Assessing Learning

Check Test: True-False
1. Odysseus refuses the request of King Alcinous to identify himself. [False]
2. Odysseus and his sailors are welcomed by the Cicones. [False]
3. Odysseus is forced to leave three men behind with the Lotus Eaters. [False]
4. The Cyclops Polyphemus is the son of the god Poseidon. [True]
5. Fellow Cyclopes come to Polyphemus's aid after he is wounded. [False]

Standardized Test Preparation
For practice with standardized test format specific to this selection, see
- *Standardized Test Preparation*, p. 92

For practice in proofreading and editing, see
- *Daily Oral Grammar*, Transparency 47

British Museum, London.

Circe offers the magic potion to Odysseus. Detail of Greek vase from Thebes.

to call them in. All but Eurylochus—
who feared a snare—the innocents went after her.
565 On thrones she seated them, and lounging chairs,
while she prepared a meal of cheese and barley

A and amber honey mixed with Pramnian wine,°
adding her own vile pinch, to make them lose
desire or thought of our dear fatherland.
570 Scarce had they drunk when she flew after them
with her long stick and shut them in a pigsty—
bodies, voices, heads, and bristles, all

B swinish now, though minds were still unchanged.
So, squealing, in they went. And Circe tossed them
575 acorns, mast,° and cornel berries—fodder
for hogs who rut and slumber on the earth.

Down to the ship Eurylochus came running
to cry alarm, foul magic doomed his men!
But working with dry lips to speak a word
580 he could not, being so shaken; blinding tears
welled in his eyes; foreboding filled his heart.
When we were frantic questioning him, at last
we heard the tale: our friends were gone. . . ."

(*from* Book 10)

567. Pramnian wine: strong wine from Pramnios.

575. mast: various kinds of nuts used as food for hogs.

 Note your responses to this horrible experience. What have the men done to deserve being turned into pigs? How did Circe, too, violate the laws of hospitality?

912 THE EPIC

Skill Link

Odysseus leaves the ship and rushes to Circe's ball. The god Hermes stops him to give him a plant that will weaken Circe's power. (Homer calls it a moly; it might have been a kind of garlic.) Protected by the plant's magic, Odysseus resists Circe's sorcery. The witch, realizing she has met her match, frees Odysseus' men. Now Circe, "loveliest of all immortals," persuades Odysseus to stay with her. There Odysseus shares her meat and wine, and she restores his heart. But, after many seasons of feasting and other pleasures, Odysseus and his men beg Circe to help them get home.

She responds to their pleas with the command that Odysseus alone descend to the Land of the Dead, "the cold homes of Death and pale Persephone," queen of the underworld. There, Odysseus must seek the wisdom of the blind prophet Teiresias.

Odysseus pursuing Circe.
Louvre, Paris.

THE ODYSSEY, PART ONE 913

Crossing the Curriculum

Summary ■■■

In the underworld, Odysseus is addressed by the seer Teiresias, who warns him not to raid the cattle of Helios, the sun god. Teiresias tells Odysseus that when he finally arrives home, he will find his household in disarray. Teiresias instructs Odysseus that after slaying his wife's suitors, he must make sacrifices to Poseidon.

Ⓐ Cultural Connections

Ancient Greek beliefs about the concept of life after death covered a broad spectrum. The Greeks believed that a person's soul, which is like a shadow, crosses the river Styx to a dark kingdom called Erebus or Hades, also known as the underworld in English, where existence is generally a pale, cold reflection of life on earth. The idea of eternal punishment for grave misdeeds in life, although rare, appears in two popular Greek myths: the story of Tantalus, who was condemned to be "tantalized" by food and drink that remained out of his reach; and the story of Sisyphus, who had to repeatedly roll a stone up a hillside, only to have it roll back down again each time. In portions of Book 11 not included in the student text, Odysseus encounters both these characters, as well as the heroes Ajax, Achilles, and Heracles (also known as Hercules).

Ⓑ Reading Skills and Strategies
Making Inferences
❓ Whom is Odysseus referring to when he uses the term "sovereign Death?" [Hades, king of the underworld]

Ⓒ Literary Connections

One of the phantoms Odysseus must keep away from the lamb's blood is his own mother, Anticlea. Having been away for so long, Odysseus does not know she died and is surprised and saddened to see her here.

THE LAND OF THE DEAD

In the Land of the Dead, Odysseus seeks to learn of his destiny. The source of his information is Teiresias, the famous blind prophet from the city of Thebes. The prophet's lack of external sight suggests the presence of true insight. Circe has told Odysseus exactly what rites he must perform to bring Teiresias up from the dead. Odysseus continues his story.

> "Then I addressed the blurred and breathless dead,
> 585 vowing to slaughter my best heifer for them
> before she calved, at home in Ithaca,
> and burn the choice bits on the altar fire;
> as for Teiresias, I swore to sacrifice
> a black lamb, handsomest of all our flock.
> 590 Thus to assuage the nations of the dead
> I pledged these rites, then slashed the lamb and ewe,
> letting their black blood stream into the well pit.
> Now the souls gathered, stirring out of Erebus,
> brides and young men, and men grown old in pain,
> 595 Ⓐ and tender girls whose hearts were new to grief;
> many were there, too, torn by brazen lanceheads,
> battle-slain, bearing still their bloody gear.
> From every side they came and sought the pit
> with rustling cries; and I grew sick with fear.
> 600 But presently I gave command to my officers
> to flay° those sheep the bronze cut down, and make
> burnt offerings of flesh to the gods below—
> Ⓑ to sovereign Death, to pale Persephone.°
> Meanwhile I crouched with my drawn sword to keep
> 605 Ⓒ the surging phantoms from the bloody pit
> till I should know the presence of Teiresias. . . .
>
> Soon from the dark that prince of Thebes came forward
> bearing a golden staff; and he addressed me:
>
> 'Son of Laertes and the gods of old,
> 610 Odysseus, master of landways and seaways,
> why leave the blazing sun, O man of woe,
> to see the cold dead and the joyless region?
> Stand clear, put up your sword;
> let me but taste of blood, I shall speak true.'
>
> 615 At this I stepped aside, and in the scabbard
> let my long sword ring home to the pommel silver,
> as he bent down to the somber blood. Then spoke
> the prince of those with gift of speech:

914 THE EPIC

601. flay: strip the skin from.

603. Persephone (pər·sef′ə·nē).

Persephone, queen of the underworld, with her husband, Hades (4th century B.C.).
British Museum, London.

Professional Notes

Moral Education
Homer's epics were required reading for schoolchildren in ancient Greece, where they served as instructional resources for moral and social education. Another Greek storyteller whose works contained moral lessons was Aesop. He was born some one hundred years after Homer, around 700 B.C.

Apparently a slave from a Greek colony in Thrace, Aesop won renown for his storytelling ability after gaining freedom from his master. His fables, which have been told, retold, and adapted for centuries, are distinguished by animal characters who represent different types of people and who display various human traits.

Select several of Aesop's fables, and have students read the fables silently, or ask volunteers to read them aloud to the class. Then, have the class discuss the moral and social lessons that each fable contains. Students can compare and contrast these lessons with those they find in the *Odyssey*.

                                                    'Great captain,
        a fair wind and the honey lights of home
620   are all you seek. But anguish lies ahead;
        the god who thunders on the land prepares it,
        not to be shaken from your track, implacable,°   **D**
        in rancor for the son whose eye you blinded.
        One narrow strait may take you through his blows:
625   denial of yourself, restraint of shipmates.
        When you make landfall on Thrinakia first
        and quit the violet sea, dark on the land
        you'll find the grazing herds of Helios
        by whom all things are seen, all speech is known.
630   Avoid those kine,° hold fast to your intent,
        and hard seafaring brings you all to Ithaca.
        But if you raid the beeves, I see destruction   **E**
        for ship and crew. Though you survive alone,
        bereft of all companions, lost for years,
635   under strange sail shall you come home, to find
        your own house filled with trouble: insolent men   **F**
        eating your livestock as they court your lady.
        Aye, you shall make those men atone in blood!
        But after you have dealt out death—in open
640   combat or by stealth—to all the suitors,
        go overland on foot, and take an oar,
        until one day you come where men have lived
        with meat unsalted, never known the sea,
        nor seen seagoing ships, with crimson bows
645   and oars that fledge light hulls for dipping flight.
        The spot will soon be plain to you, and I
        can tell you how: some passerby will say,
        "What winnowing fan° is that upon your shoulder?"
        Halt, and implant your smooth oar in the turf
650   and make fair sacrifice to Lord Poseidon:
        a ram, a bull, a great buck boar; turn back,
        and carry out pure hecatombs° at home
        to all wide heaven's lords, the undying gods,
        to each in order. Then a seaborne death
655   soft as this hand of mist will come upon you
        when you are wearied out with rich old age,
        your countryfolk in blessed peace around you.
        And all this shall be just as I foretell.' . . ."

                                            (*from* Book 11)

        WORDS TO OWN
        rancor (raŋ′kər) *n.*: bitter hate; ill will.

622. **implacable:** unyielding;
merciless.

630. *Kine* and *beeves* (see line
632) are old terms for "cattle."

648. **winnowing fan:** device used
to remove the useless dry outer
covering from grain. (These people
would never have seen an oar.)

652. **hecatombs:** sacrifices of one
hundred cattle at a time to the gods.

 *What prophecy does
Odysseus receive? Take
notes on how you might
dramatize this important scene in
the underworld. How many actors
would you need? What props
would you use? You might sketch
the scene as you visualize it.*

THE ODYSSEY, PART ONE 915

[handwritten note: BUILD TEMPLE TO POSEIDON — BRING HIS NAME & HIS WORSHIP TO THOSE INLAND]

Getting Students Involved

Summary ■ ■

Odysseus returns to Circe's island. The witch tells him how to avoid the dangers of the Sirens and Scylla and Charybdis. Odysseus is lashed to the mast so that he can hear the Sirens' song without succumbing to it, after he plugs his men's ears with beeswax to prevent their hearing the bewitching voices. Odysseus and his men escape danger, but, passing through the straits of Scylla and Charybdis, they lose six men to Scylla.

(A) Vocabulary
Context Clues

? In l. 663, what is the meaning of the word *innocent*? [any unsuspecting person; someone who would unintentionally, and without being forewarned, hear the Sirens' call]

(B) Reading Skills and Strategies
Predicting

? From what you know of Odysseus, do you think he will take the risk of listening to the Sirens' song? [Possible responses: Yes, Odysseus will listen because he is adventurous and will want to have the experience; no, Odysseus wants to get home too badly and is too clever to be tempted.]

(C) Historical Connections

Many efforts have been made, with varying success, to identify the actual sites of Odysseus' adventures in the Mediterranean. Experts generally agree that the tale of Scylla and Charybdis is a folk legend inspired by the narrow Strait of Messina between mainland Italy and Sicily. Help students locate the Strait of Messina on a map of Europe.

THE SIRENS; SCYLLA AND CHARYBDIS

Odysseus and his men return to Circe's island, where Circe warns him of the perils that await him. The following passage is told by Odysseus, still speaking at Alcinous' court. He is quoting Circe.

'"Listen with care
660   to this, now, and a god will arm your mind.
Square in your ship's path are Sirens, crying
beauty to bewitch men coasting by;
(A) woe to the innocent who hears that sound!
He will not see his lady nor his children
665   in joy, crowding about him, home from sea;
the Sirens will sing his mind away
on their sweet meadow lolling. There are bones
of dead men rotting in a pile beside them
and flayed skins shrivel around the spot.
                    Steer wide;
670   keep well to seaward; plug your oarsmen's ears
with beeswax kneaded soft; none of the rest
should hear that song.
                     But if you wish to listen,
let the men tie you in the lugger, hand
and foot, back to the mast, lashed to the mast,
675 **(B)** so you may hear those Harpies'° thrilling voices;
shout as you will, begging to be untied,
your crew must only twist more line around you
and keep their stroke up, till the singers fade. . . .'"

The next peril lies between two headlands. Circe continues her warning.

'". . . That is the den of Scylla, where she yaps
680   abominably, a newborn whelp's° cry,
though she is huge and monstrous. God or man,
no one could look on her in joy. Her legs—
(C) and there are twelve—are like great tentacles,
unjointed, and upon her serpent necks
685   are borne six heads like nightmares of ferocity,
with triple serried° rows of fangs and deep
gullets of black death. Half her length, she sways

WORDS TO OWN
abominably (ə·bäm′ə·nə·blē) *adv.*: in an extremely unpleasant or disgusting manner.
---

675. Harpies: monsters who are half bird and half woman and are greedy for victims.

680. whelp's: puppy's.

686. serried: crowded together; densely packed.

Making the Connections

Connecting to the Theme: "The Perilous Journey"

Odysseus, the hero of the *Odyssey*, displays many distinguishing qualities as he ably deals with beings of all kinds and with various cultures. Have students think about the qualities of Odysseus that help him successfully interact with the various people and creatures that he meets on his dangerous journey. Ask each student to choose a quality—such as open-mindedness, intelligence, courage, self-confidence, or determination—and to find two examples in the text that show Odysseus using that characteristic to help him deal with a perilous situation. Students can then share their examples with the rest of the class and discuss how these qualities might be useful in facing moments of danger or crisis in today's world.

her heads in air, outside her horrid cleft,
hunting the sea around that promontory°
690 for dolphins, dogfish, or what bigger game
thundering Amphitrite° feeds in thousands.
And no ship's company can claim
to have passed her without loss and grief; she takes,
from every ship, one man for every gullet.

695 The opposite point seems more a tongue of land
you'd touch with a good bowshot, at the narrows.
A great wild fig, a shaggy mass of leaves,
grows on it, and Charybdis lurks below
to swallow down the dark sea tide. Three times
700 from dawn to dusk she spews it up
and sucks it down again three times, a whirling
maelstrom;° if you come upon her then
the god who makes earth tremble could not save you.
No, hug the cliff of Scylla, take your ship
705 through on a racing stroke. Better to mourn
six men than lose them all, and the ship, too. . . .

689. promontory: high land that juts out into a body of water.

691. Amphitrite (am′fi·trīt′ē): goddess of the sea and wife of Poseidon.

702. maelstrom: large, violent whirlpool.

D **Reading Skills and Strategies**
Connecting with the Text
? People sometimes use the expression *caught between Scylla and Charybdis*. What does it mean? [It means having to choose between two undesirable alternatives. A similar expression is *caught between a rock and a hard place*.]

E **Critical Thinking**
Expressing an Opinion
? Do you agree with Circe's advice that it is better to sacrifice six men than to risk losing them all? Explain. [Students may say that her advice is cruel but logical, or that Odysseus ought to try to find a third, better solution.]

RESPONDING TO THE ART
Sir Edward Burne-Jones
(1833–1898) was a devotee of Pre-Raphaelite ideas. The Pre-Raphaelites were English artists who wanted to reform art, claiming that the Italian painter Raphael had ruined art by moving in a classical direction. They believed that in the fifteenth century, before Raphael, art was fresh and spontaneous. Burne, like other Pre-Raphaelites, preferred romantic, medieval themes.
Activity. How does the romantic imagery in this painting contrast with Circe's depiction of the Sirens? [The Sirens are pictured as beautiful and gentle, while Circe compares them to Harpies.]

The Sirens (c. 1875) by Sir Edward Burne-Jones.

National Gallery of South Africa, Cape Town.

THE ODYSSEY, PART ONE **917**

T917

A Critical Thinking

Making Connections

? Who else warned Odysseus to leave Helios's cattle alone? [Teiresias, the blind prophet of Thebes, whom Odysseus visited in the underworld]

B Critical Thinking

Expressing an Opinion

? Do you agree that it is better to know about the dangers you are facing? Explain. [Sample responses: It is better to know about a danger if you can do something to avoid it or if you can protect yourself from it, but otherwise, it doesn't help and may make you feel worse; I think most people would want to know what danger they face, whether they can do anything about it or not, because fear of the unknown is worse than any known fear.]

Then you will coast Thrinakia, the island
where Helios's cattle graze, fine herds, and flocks
of goodly sheep. The herds and flocks are seven,
with fifty beasts in each.
710   No lambs are dropped,
or calves, and these fat cattle never die. . . .

      Now give those kine a wide berth, keep your thoughts
      intent upon your course for home,
A   and hard seafaring brings you all to Ithaca.
715   But if you raid the beeves, I see destruction
      for ship and crew. . . .'"

The Ithacans set off. Odysseus does not tell his men of Circe's last prophecy—that he will be the only survivor of their long journey. Still speaking to Alcinous' court, Odysseus continues his tale.

"The crew being now silent before me, I
addressed them, sore at heart:

                             'Dear friends,
      more than one man, or two, should know those things
720 **B** Circe foresaw for us and shared with me,
      so let me tell her forecast: then we die
      with our eyes open, if we are going to die,
      or know what death we baffle if we can. Sirens
      weaving a haunting song over the sea
725   we are to shun, she said, and their green shore
      all sweet with clover; yet she urged that I
      alone should listen to their song. Therefore
      you are to tie me up, tight as a splint,
      erect along the mast, lashed to the mast,
730   and if I shout and beg to be untied,
      take more turns of the rope to muffle me.'

I rather dwelt on this part of the forecast,
while our good ship made time, bound outward down
the wind for the strange island of Sirens.
735 Then all at once the wind fell, and a calm
came over all the sea, as though some power
lulled the swell.
                        The crew were on their feet
briskly, to furl the sail, and stow it; then,
each in place, they poised the smooth oar blades
740 and sent the white foam scudding by. I carved
a massive cake of beeswax into bits
and rolled them in my hands until they softened—

Listening to Music

"*Sirènes*" ("Sirens"), No. 3 from *Nocturnes for Orchestra* by Claude Debussy.

French composer Claude Debussy (də·bü'sē) (1862–1918) is known for music that attempts to convey a personal emotional impression of a subject instead of trying to capture it more objectively. Among the more famous examples are his three *Nocturnes for Orchestra*, "*Nuages*" ("Clouds"), "*Fêtes*" ("Festivals"), and

"*Sirènes*" ("Sirens"). A *nocturne* is a night piece or night song, usually with a slow, dreamy tempo and a calm, gentle sound. Debussy himself described "*Sirènes*" as music about "the sea and its innumerable rhythms," in the midst of which the wordless "mysterious song of the sirens is heard"; then "they laugh, and the song passes on."

Activity

Have students listen to "*Sirènes*" just after they read the section about the Sirens in the *Odyssey*. Ask them to jot down, while they listen, words and phrases that describe the impressions or feelings that the music conveys. Then, encourage students to explain whether or not they think Debussy effectively captures the Sirens' song.

Odysseus and the Sirens
(c. 490 B.C.).

no long task, for a burning heat came down
from Helios, lord of high noon. Going forward
745   I carried wax along the line, and laid it
thick on their ears. They tied me up, then, plumb°
amidships, back to the mast, lashed to the mast,
and took themselves again to rowing. Soon,
as we came smartly within hailing distance,
750   the two Sirens, noting our fast ship
off their point, made ready, and they sang. . . .

The lovely voices in ardor appealing over the water
made me crave to listen, and I tried to say
'Untie me!' to the crew, jerking my brows;
755   but they bent steady to the oars. Then Perimedes°
got to his feet, he and Eurylochus,
and passed more line about, to hold me still.
So all rowed on, until the Sirens
dropped under the sea rim, and their singing
dwindled away.

C

D

E

746. **plumb:** vertical.

755. **Perimedes** (per·i·mē′dēz).

WORDS TO OWN
ardor (är′dər) *n.:* passion; enthusiasm.

THE ODYSSEY, PART ONE **919**

? Is it necessary for great leaders like Odysseus to inspire their men? **Explain.** [Yes, being able to inspire people is one of the qualities that makes a leader great. Here Odysseus calms and inspires his men by reminding them of how they escaped the Cyclops.]

B **Critical Thinking**

Expressing an Opinion

? What do you think of Odysseus' decision not to tell his men about the danger of Scylla? Is his silence justified? Why or why not? [Possible responses: Some students may agree with Odysseus, because warning the men would just cause a panic; telling the men would not be helpful, since there is nothing the men can do; the men have the right to know that six of them will die.]

C **Elements of Literature**

Character

? What does Odysseus' failure to remember Circe's warning about the uselessness of weapons reveal about his self-image? [Sample responses: It suggests that he continues to think of himself as the clever warrior who solves problems unaided; it suggests that he is not used to situations in which he has no control and must stand by helplessly.]

---

760 My faithful company
rested on their oars now, peeling off
the wax that I had laid thick on their ears;
then set me free.
            But scarcely had that island
faded in blue air when I saw smoke
765 and white water, with sound of waves in tumult—
a sound the men heard, and it terrified them.
Oars flew from their hands; the blades went knocking
wild alongside till the ship lost way,
with no oar blades to drive her through the water.

770 Well, I walked up and down from bow to stern,
trying to put heart into them, standing over
every oarsman, saying gently,
                        'Friends,
A have we never been in danger before this?
More fearsome, is it now, than when the Cyclops
775 penned us in his cave? What power he had!
Did I not keep my nerve, and use my wits
to find a way out for us?
                        Now I say
by hook or crook this peril too shall be
something that we remember.
                        Heads up, lads!
780 We must obey the orders as I give them.
Get the oar shafts in your hands, and lie back
hard on your benches; hit these breaking seas.
Zeus help us pull away before we founder.

You at the tiller, listen, and take in
785 all that I say—the rudders are your duty;
keep her out of the combers° and the smoke;
steer for that headland; watch the drift, or we
fetch up in the smother,° and you drown us.'

That was all, and it brought them round to action.
790 **B** But as I sent them on toward Scylla, I
told them nothing, as they could do nothing.
They would have dropped their oars again, in panic,
to roll for cover under the decking. Circe's
bidding against arms had slipped my mind,
795 **C** so I tied on my cuirass° and took up
two heavy spears, then made my way along
to the foredeck—thinking to see her first from there,

Scylla. Greek bronze.
National Archaeological Museum, Athens.

786. combers: large waves.

788. smother: commotion; violent action or disorder.

795. cuirass (kwi·ras'): armor for the breast and back.

WORDS TO OWN

tumult (too'mult') *n.*: commotion; uproar; confusion.

---

920 THE EPIC

---

the monster of the gray rock, harboring
torment for my friends. I strained my eyes
800 upon that cliffside veiled in cloud, but nowhere
could I catch sight of her.

                                    And all this time,
in travail,° sobbing, gaining on the current,
we rowed into the strait—Scylla to port
and on our starboard beam Charybdis, dire
805 gorge° of the salt sea tide. By heaven! when she
vomited, all the sea was like a caldron
seething over intense fire, when the mixture
suddenly heaves and rises.

                                    The shot spume

soared to the landside heights, and fell like rain.

810 But when she swallowed the sea water down
we saw the funnel of the maelstrom, heard
the rock bellowing all around, and dark
sand raged on the bottom far below.
My men all blanched° against the gloom, our eyes
815 were fixed upon that yawning mouth in fear
of being devoured.

                              Then Scylla made her strike,
whisking six of my best men from the ship.

I happened to glance aft at ship and oarsmen
and caught sight of their arms and legs, dangling
820 high overhead. Voices came down to me
in anguish, calling my name for the last time.

A man surf-casting on a point of rock
for bass or mackerel, whipping his long rod
to drop the sinker and the bait far out,
825 will hook a fish and rip it from the surface
to dangle wriggling through the air;

                                    so these

were borne aloft in spasms toward the cliff.

She ate them as they shrieked there, in her den,
in the dire grapple,° reaching still for me—
830 and deathly pity ran me through
at that sight—far the worst I ever suffered
questing the passes of the strange sea.

                                    We rowed on.

The Rocks were now behind; Charybdis, too,
and Scylla dropped astern.

                              Then we were coasting
835 the noble island of the god, where grazed
those cattle with wide brows, and bounteous flocks
of Helios, lord of noon, who rides high heaven.

802. **travail:** hard, exhausting
work or effort; tiring labor.

805. **gorge:** throat and jaws of a
greedy, all-devouring being.

814. **blanched:** grew pale.

Homeric Simile (handwritten annotation)

829. **dire grapple:** terrible
struggle.

THE ODYSSEY, PART ONE 921

Odysseus warns his men not to touch the sun god's cattle. Storms rage for a month, and their food supply is exhausted. One shipmate, Eurylochus, convinces the others that eating the cattle is preferable to starvation. Odysseus wakes up to discover that his men have feasted on the cattle. He curses the gods for letting him sleep during the feast so that he could not restrain his men.

Ⓐ Critical Thinking
Challenging the Text
❓ Since Odysseus is the captain, shouldn't he have just ordered his men to bypass Thrinakia? Explain your response. [Possible responses: Odysseus probably feared that the men would not obey such an order, because they had just been through a terrible ordeal and were emotionally and physically exhausted; no matter how his men felt, Odysseus had heard the warnings of both Teiresias and Circe and should have insisted on bypassing the island.]

Ⓑ Critical Thinking
Interpreting
❓ What does Odysseus mean when he says that no man can avoid the eye of Helios? [Since Helios is the sun god, he looks down over everyone; no man can escape discovery by the sun god.]

Response to Margin Activity
Main characters may include Odysseus, his men, Circe, the Sirens, Scylla, and Charybdis. Students may suggest the use of music to represent the singing of the Sirens and the sound of Charybdis and a creative visual or costume for Scylla.

From the black ship, far still at sea, I heard
the lowing of the cattle winding home
840 and sheep bleating; and heard, too, in my heart
the words of blind Teiresias of Thebes
and Circe of Aeaea: both forbade me
the island of the world's delight, the Sun. . . ."

(from Book 12)

THE CATTLE OF THE SUN GOD

Ⓐ *Odysseus urges his exhausted crew to bypass Thrinakia, the island of the sun god, Helios. But the men insist on landing. Odysseus makes them swear not to touch the god's cattle. Odysseus is still speaking.*

"In the small hours of the third watch, when stars
845 that shone out in the first dusk of evening
had gone down to their setting, a giant wind
blew from heaven, and clouds driven by Zeus
shrouded land and sea in a night of storm;
so, just as Dawn with fingertips of rose
850 touched the windy world, we dragged our ship
to cover in a grotto, a sea cave
where nymphs had chairs of rock and sanded floors.
I mustered all the crew and said:

'Old shipmates,
our stores are in the ship's hold, food and drink;
855 the cattle here are not for our provision,
or we pay dearly for it.

Fierce the god is
Ⓑ who cherishes these heifers and these sheep:
Helios; and no man avoids his eye.'

To this my fighters nodded. Yes. But now
860 we had a month of onshore gales, blowing
day in, day out—south winds, or south by east.
As long as bread and good red wine remained
to keep the men up, and appease their craving,
they would not touch the cattle. But in the end,
865 when all the barley in the ship was gone,
hunger drove them to scour the wild shore
with angling hooks, for fishes and sea fowl,
whatever fell into their hands; and lean days
wore their bellies thin.

The storms continued.
870 So one day I withdrew to the interior

Suppose you wanted to write a script dramatizing this famous part of the Odyssey—*the crew's struggle against the Sirens and against Scylla and Charybdis. Who would be your main characters? How would you use music and visuals—especially in the Sirens scene? Write down your ideas about a dramatic presentation.*

Palazzo Poggi, Bologna, Italy.

The Companions of Ulysses Slaying the Cattle of the Sun God Helios (16th century) by Pellegrino Tibaldi.

RESPONDING TO THE ART

For information on the artist, see p. T901.

Activity. Point out how the sloping sides of the ship lead the eye upward to the red-cloaked figure and how the outstretched arms of the man to the right lead the eye to the cattle. Ask students to describe the look in the eyes of the animal in the foreground. [Possible responses: imploring; doomed.] What does the soldier in the foreground seem to be signaling? [Sample response: Perhaps he is cautioning the viewer not to tell Odysseus what the men are doing.]

to pray the gods in solitude, for hope
that one might show me some way of salvation.
Slipping away, I struck across the island
to a sheltered spot, out of the driving gale.

875 I washed my hands there, and made supplication°
to the gods who own Olympus, all the gods—
but they, for answer, only closed my eyes
under slow drops of sleep.
                    Now on the shore Eurylochus
made his insidious° plea:

                    'Comrades,' he said,
880 'You've gone through everything; listen to what I say.
All deaths are hateful to us, mortal wretches,
but famine is the most pitiful, the worst
end that a man can come to.
                    Will you fight it?
Come, we'll cut out the noblest of these cattle
885 for sacrifice to the gods who own the sky;
and once at home, in the old country of Ithaca,
if ever that day comes—
we'll build a costly temple and adorn it
with every beauty for the Lord of Noon. **C**

890 But if he flares up over his heifers lost,
wishing our ship destroyed, and if the gods
make cause with him, why, then I say: Better
open your lungs to a big sea once for all **D**
than waste to skin and bones on a lonely island!'

895 Thus Eurylochus; and they murmured 'Aye!'
trooping away at once to round up heifers.
Now, that day tranquil cattle with broad brows
were grazing near, and soon the men drew up
around their chosen beasts in ceremony.
900 They plucked the leaves that shone on a tall oak—
having no barley meal—to strew° the victims,

875. supplication: humble requests; prayers.

879. insidious: crafty; sly.

 What is Eurylochus's "insidious plea" (lines 879–894)? If you were a member of the crew, would you be swayed by this argument, or would you heed Odysseus' warning? Do you think murdering the cattle is justified, or is it sacrilege?

901. strew: scatter about.

THE ODYSSEY, PART ONE 923

C Struggling Readers
Questioning
❓ Who is the "Lord of Noon"? [Helios, the sun god]

D Critical Thinking
Interpreting
❓ What does Eurylochus mean by this comment? [He is talking about drowning.]

Answer to Margin Question
Eurylochus argues that it is better to live and risk Helios's anger by slaughtering his cattle than to die by starvation. Some students might agree. Since the men are facing certain death, why not kill the cattle and try to appease Helios later? It at least gives them a chance of living. Others will feel that the men should explore other alternatives. For instance, the men could wait a little longer or appeal to Helios *before* they kill his cattle.

Assessing Learning

Check Test: Questions and Answers
Answers may vary slightly.
1. Why is Odysseus able to withstand the magical powers of Circe? [Odysseus is protected by a magic herb given him by Hermes.]
2. Whom does Odysseus visit in the Land of the Dead? [Odysseus consults the blind prophet Teiresias.]
3. What prediction does Circe make to Odysseus about his journey home? [Circe prophesies that only Odysseus will survive the trip.]
4. Which two monsters does Odysseus pass between after facing the Sirens? [Odysseus and his crew navigate between Scylla and Charybdis.]
5. What does Odysseus order his men not to do on Thrinakia? [He orders them not to kill the cattle of Helios.]

Standardized Test Preparation
For practice in proofreading and editing, see
• *Daily Oral Grammar,* Transparencies 46, 47

A Elements of Literature

Character

? In the *Odyssey*, Odysseus constantly takes credit when things go well. Now, when a tragedy occurs, he blames the gods for making him fall asleep. What does this reveal about his character? [Sample answers: Odysseus has a big ego and likes to take credit for only the good things; Odysseus cannot accept failure and must find a way of placing the blame elsewhere.]

Answer to Margin Question

Helios is angry because Odysseus' men have slaughtered his cattle. Most students, remembering the prophecies of Teiresias and Circe, as well as the beginning of the epic, will probably say that the men will be brutally punished.

Resources

Selection Assessment

Formal Assessment
• Selection Test, p. 152
Test Generator (One-Stop Planner)
• CD-ROM

MAKING MEANINGS PART ONE

First Thoughts

1. Some students may say that Odysseus is reliable—he cares about his shipmates and takes responsibility for his decisions. Others may cite his taunting of Polyphemus as foolhardy. Some may cite the deaths of the entire crew as evidence of his shortcomings.

Shaping Interpretations

2. Sample answers: The adventure teaches that those who succumb to easy pleasures will forget their ambitions and lose the desire to accomplish anything; the lesson is that taking the easy way out is no solution to problems.

3. Polyphemus lives alone in a crudely furnished cave, in which he also keeps his sheep. He has a strict work routine, but he is otherwise slovenly. According to Greek custom, guests are sacred and must be treated with hospitality, but the Cyclops brutalizes and cannibalizes his guests. Students may say that an

(continued on p.T925)

T924

---

performed the prayers and ritual, knifed the kine
and flayed each carcass, cutting thighbones free
to wrap in double folds of fat. These offerings,
905 with strips of meat, were laid upon the fire.
Then, as they had no wine, they made libation
with clear spring water, broiling the entrails first;
and when the bones were burnt and tripes shared,
they spitted the carved meat.

                              Just then my slumber
910 left me in a rush, my eyes opened,
and I went down the seaward path. No sooner
had I caught sight of our black hull, than savory
odors of burnt fat eddied around me;
grief took hold of me, and I cried aloud:

915 'O Father Zeus and gods in bliss forever,
A you made me sleep away this day of mischief!
O cruel drowsing, in the evil hour!
Here they sat, and a great work they contrived.'

Lampetia° in her long gown meanwhile
920 had borne swift word to the Overlord of Noon:

'They have killed your kine.'

                              And the Lord Helios
burst into angry speech amid the immortals:

'O Father Zeus and gods in bliss forever,
punish Odysseus' men! So overweening,°
925 now they have killed my peaceful kine, my joy
at morning when I climbed the sky of stars,
and evening, when I bore westward from heaven.
Restitution or penalty they shall pay—
and pay in full—or I go down forever
930 to light the dead men in the underworld.' . . .'

                              (from Book 12)

When Odysseus and his men set sail again, they are punished by death—a thunderbolt from Zeus destroys their boat and all the men drown. Only Odysseus survives. Exhausted and nearly drowned, he makes his way to Calypso's island, where we met him originally, in Book 5.

Odysseus has brought us up to date. He can now rest and enjoy the comforts of Alcinous' court—but not for long. Ahead lies his most difficult task—reclaiming his own kingdom.

At this moment of suspense, Homer might have put aside his harp until the next night.

924 THE EPIC

Zeus, seated on his throne, holding thunderbolts (6th century B.C.). Bronze statuette found on Mount Lyceum.

919. Lampetia (lam·pē′shē·ə): daughter of Helios. Lampetia guarded her father's herds of cattle.

924. overweening: excessively proud.

What exactly has happened to cause the god's fury?

First Thoughts

[respond]

1. If you were one of Odysseus' ship-mates, how would you feel about him? Is he foolhardy or a reliable leader? Do you all agree?

Shaping Interpretations

[interpret]

2. The *Odyssey* was used as part of Greek children's education for centuries after the poem was written down. How could the adventure with the Lotus Eaters teach us about the temptation to forget our troubles by dropping out of society?

[contrast]

3. How does Odysseus describe the Cyclopes' way of life? Contrast their customs with those of an ideal human community. (Be sure to think about the significance of the cannibalism.)

[analyze]

4. "Nobody" in Greek is *outis,* which sounds like *Odysseus.* In this episode, how does Odysseus show that he is clever with language? What curse at the end of this adventure **foreshadows** trouble?

[conclude]

5. What conclusions about the deceptive nature of beauty can you draw from the Circe episode?

[identify]

6. What does Odysseus learn about his future from Teiresias in the Land of the Dead?

[evaluate]

7. Evaluate the logical argument that Eurylochus uses to persuade the crew to eat the cattle of the sun god. Do you think the crew had a real choice? Explain.

[compare]

8. Book 5 of the *Odyssey* focuses on Odysseus' captivity on Calypso's island. Suzanne Vega (see **Connections** on page 894) takes Calypso's view of the affair. How does her song compare with Homer's story? Whom do you sympathize with—Odysseus or Calypso?

Extending the Text

[extend]

9. So far, from what you've observed of Odysseus, how would you describe what the Greeks valued in a hero? Do we value these same characteristics today? Check your Quickwrite notes.

Challenging the Text

[evaluate]

10. How many of the monsters or threats to Odysseus in this part of the epic are female? What do you think of the way women are portrayed in the story so far?

THE ODYSSEY, PART ONE **925**

Reading Check

Sum up what happens in each of the episodes you have read so far. What happens to Odysseus in each adventure? Whom does he meet? How does he manage to move on?

Adventure	Summary
Calypso	
Lotus Eaters	
Cyclops	
Circe	
Land of the Dead	
Sirens; Scylla and Charybdis	
Cattle of the Sun God	

(continued from p.T924)

ideal human community should be a place of mutual trust and aid, where people respect one another and work together.

4. Odysseus names himself "Nohbdy," thus ensuring that the other Cyclopes do not rush to help Polyphemus. The Cyclops's curse foreshadows the fact that it will be a long time before Odysseus reaches home and that Odysseus' companions will die.

5. Possible conclusions: Outward beauty does not signify inner virtue; it is unwise to be seduced by outward beauty.

6. Odysseus learns that he will encounter rough seas, caused by Poseidon's wrath; that his men will be killed; that he will be lost for years but eventually return home to chaos; that he will appease Poseidon in a strange land; and that death will come to him from the sea when he is an old man.

7. Some students may say that Eurylochus's argument is valid, since the men might avoid certain death by eating the cattle and then trying to appease Helios. Others may feel that the argument is not valid because it presents only two alternatives—the men might also have appealed to Helios *before* slaughtering his cattle.

8. In the song, Calypso is motivated by love to let Odysseus go; in the epic, she is ordered to do so. The song tells the tale from her point of view; the epic, from his. Some students may sympathize with Calypso and her unrequited love; others may sympathize with Odysseus, who was her prisoner.

Extending the Text

9. Possible Greek values: discipline, loyalty, wit, intelligence, practicality, bravery, love of home, obedience to divine powers. Many students will say that these qualities are still valued today. Others may say that we place less value on home and divinity.

Challenging the Text

10. In this part, all of the threatening beings—except for the Cicones, Polyphemus, and the Laestrygonians—are female. Some students may say that females are unfairly portrayed as selfish and voracious monsters; others may say that the female monsters are balanced by the positive portrayal of Athena.

Reading Check
Possible Summaries

Calypso: Calypso releases Odysseus. Odysseus leaves on a raft. Poseidon raises a storm, and the hero is shipwrecked on Scheria.

Lotus Eaters: Three of Odysseus' men eat the Lotus and lose their desire to leave. Odysseus forces them onto the ship and departs.

Cyclops: Trapped in Polyphemus's cave, Odysseus and his men blind the monster and escape by clinging to sheep. Odysseus taunts the Cyclops, who curses him.

Circe: Circe turns Odysseus' crew into swine.

Odysseus, protected by magic, compels her to restore their human form.

Land of the Dead: In the underworld, Odysseus consults the blind prophet Teiresias.

Sirens; Scylla and Charybdis: Odysseus plugs the crew's ears with beeswax and is tied to the mast to withstand the Sirens' song. Between Scylla and Charybdis, he loses six men.

Cattle of the Sun God: Odysseus' men are starving, and while he is sleeping, they kill and eat Helios's cattle. Zeus sinks their boat. Only Odysseus survives.

Grading Timesaver

Rubrics for each Choices assignment appear on p. 213 in the *Portfolio Management System*.

CHOICES: Building Your Portfolio

1. **Writer's Notebook** Remind students to save their work. They can use it as prewriting for the Writer's Workshop on p. 958. You may wish to remind students that a single cause may have multiple effects and that an effect may have multiple causes.

2. **Persuading an Audience** Students may wish to make a two-column chart to help them prepare their speech. In the left column, they can list the points in Eurylochus's speech. In the right column, they can list the points and techniques that they will use to refute him.

3. **Creative Writing/Art** Suggest to students that before they begin to write, they should make a list of strong verbs and vivid adjectives that describe their chosen forces of nature.

4. **Creative Writing/Performance** Encourage students to be creative with the style of the dialogue that they will use. They can either copy the style of Homer or create one of their own.

5. **Creative Writing** Students may develop storyboards to accompany their journeys.

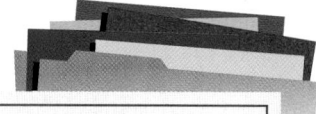

CHOICES: Building Your Portfolio

Writer's Notebook
1. Collecting Ideas for a Cause-and-Effect Essay

Finding a topic. By now you should have noticed that the plot of the *Odyssey* is full of cause-and-effect relationships. For example, think about how Homer explores the effects of disobeying the gods or of acting inhospitably. Choose several episodes from the *Odyssey*, and map out the cause-and-effect relationships that constitute the plot of each one. To do this, list major events, their causes, their effects, or both. You could fill out a cause-and-effect chart like this:

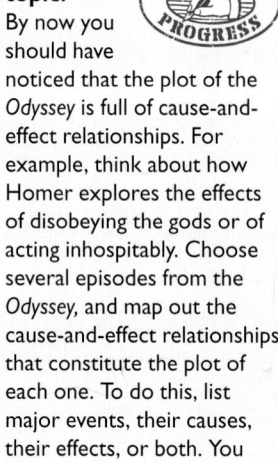

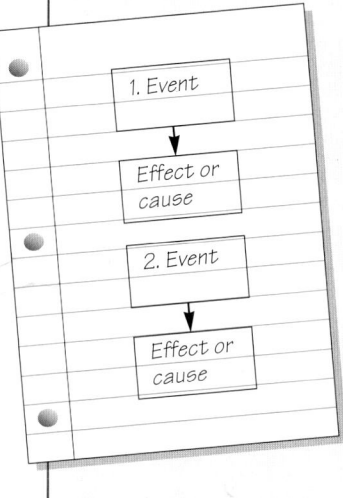

Save your notes for possible use in the Writer's Workshop on page 958.

Persuading an Audience
2. Hold the Beef?

Pretend that you are one of the crew members listening to Eurylochus's speech in Book 12 and you strongly disagree with him. Analyze his speech, and then formulate a counterargument to persuade your fellow shipmates not to kill the forbidden cattle. What persuasive techniques will you use in your speech?

Creative Writing/Art
3. It's Alive!

Homer describes a whirlpool and a dangerous rock as living monsters: Scylla and Charybdis. The whirlpool and the rock are **personified:** They are, in reality, inanimate (nonliving), but the poet describes them as if they have life. In "The Cyclops in the Ocean" (see *Connections* on page 909), the modern poet Nikki Giovanni personifies a tropical storm as a Cyclops. Write a paragraph (or draw a cartoon) personifying some other violent force of nature. Describe how the monster looks and sounds; tell what it hunts and what it does with its prey.

Creative Writing/Performance
4. Make It Real

Choose one of Odysseus' perilous encounters and dramatize it. (You might already have some notes about dramatizing the story.) With classmates, write a script, creating dialogue to show action and reveal character. Then assign roles and rehearse them. Use music and scenery as you wish. Videotape your performance so your teacher can show next year's class *The Odyssey Live.*

Creative Writing
5. Life as a Journey

Before you started the *Odyssey*, you should have taken some notes on life as a journey (see the Writer's Notebook assignment on page 887). Refer to those notes now and describe a meaningful journey or quest in your own life. It may be a journey you have already completed or one just begun. Try to identify the following: What was it that called you? Who were or will be your helpers? What tests, trials, or ordeals did you face or do you expect to face? What did you learn as a result of your journey, or what do you expect to learn?

926 THE EPIC

Reaching All Students

Advanced Learners
To extend Choice 3, after students have written their paragraphs personifying a force of nature, have them rewrite the material as poems. Encourage students to use as much figurative language, including Homeric similes, as possible.

Handbook of Literary Terms
H E L P

See Figure of Speech.

Figures of Speech—Homeric Similes

In a **figure of speech,** a writer compares one thing to something else, something quite different from it in all but a few important ways. For example, Homer compares the army of the Cicones to "the leaves and blades of spring" (lines 163–164). He is saying that enemy soldiers suddenly appeared everywhere, as green grass and leaves do in spring. The comparison is surprising because a fierce army seems very different from the tender leaves and grass of spring.

The **Homeric simile** is an extended comparison between something that the audience cannot have seen (such as Odysseus boring out the Cyclops's eye) and something ordinary that they would have been familiar with (such as a ship-builder drilling a plank; see lines 379–381 on page 904).

Try It Out

1. Reread lines 822–827 on page 921. Explain how this Homeric simile brings the audience into the story by comparing a strange, unfamiliar occurrence with something familiar.

2. Make up three Homeric similes of your own, in which you compare something strange or unfamiliar with something ordinary and familiar. You might consider describing something like the following:

   • a space launch
   • the surface of the moon
   • something you see through a microscope

Try It Out
Answers

1. Scylla is compared to a fisherman, and the men to fish on a line. None of us has ever seen Scylla snatch men from a ship, but most of us can picture a fisherman surf-casting and hauling his wriggling catches out of the sea.

2. Sample answers: With a burst of flame and smoke, the powerful rocket arose like a bird trailing a tail of fire and ascended quickly to take its place as one of the wandering stars of the night. Like the round depressions made by raindrops falling onto a sandy beach, so appear the craters that lie sprinkled across the surface of the moon. Just as insects scurry and jostle against each other, so did the one-celled creatures move about under the lens of the microscope.

VOCABULARY   HOW TO OWN A WORD

WORD BANK
formidable
ravage
profusion
sage
adversary
stealth
rancor
abominably
ardor
tumult

Map It

Work with a partner to create a semantic map for each word in the Word Bank. Make up questions about each word and provide your own answers. A sample map is done for *formidable*. Be sure to compare your maps in class.

Who is formidable in the *Odyssey*?
• Odysseus
• Cyclops
• the gods

formidable

Do I want to be called formidable?
• Yes, I'd like to be formidable as a center forward.

What have I seen that is formidable?
• Josh on football field
• Emma in math class
• volcano

What is not formidable?
• ant
• baby
• peaceful pond

THE ODYSSEY, PART ONE **927**

VOCABULARY

Word Maps will vary. Here is a sample for *stealth*.

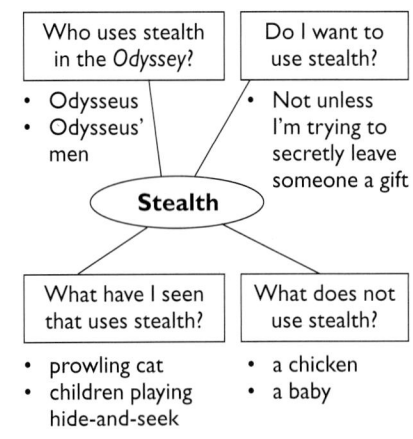

Who uses stealth in the *Odyssey*?
• Odysseus
• Odysseus' men

Do I want to use stealth?
• Not unless I'm trying to secretly leave someone a gift

Stealth

What have I seen that uses stealth?
• prowling cat
• children playing hide-and-seek

What does not use stealth?
• a chicken
• a baby

Resources

Language
• *Grammar and Language Links* Worksheet, p. 61

Vocabulary
• *Words to Own,* Worksheet, p. 49

Language Link Quick Check

The following are Homeric similes from the *Odyssey*. Read the similes, and explain how each simile involves the audience in the story by comparing an unfamiliar occurrence with something familiar.

1. "A man in a distant field, no hearth fires near, / will hide a fresh brand in his bed of embers / to keep a spark alive for the next day; / so in the leaves Odysseus hid himself...." (Book 5) [Odysseus' desire to keep safe by hiding in the leaves is compared to a person saving a spark of fire by burying it in embers.]

2. "Athena lent a hand, making him seem taller, and massive too, with crisping hair in curls like petals of wild hyacinth, but all red-golden. Think of gold infused on silver by a crafts-man...." (Book 23) [The familiar image of a hyacinth and of finely crafted precious metals helps us visualize the radiance of the hero.]

Part 2
told in
3rd person
switch from
1st person in
Part 1

Planning

- **Block Schedule**
  Block Scheduling Lesson Plans with Pacing Guide

- **Traditional Schedule**
  Lesson Plans Including Strategies for English-Language Learners

- **One-Stop Planner**
  CD-ROM with Test Generator

T928

PART TWO: COMING HOME

In Book 13, Odysseus, laden with gifts, is returned in secret to Ithaca in one of the magically swift Phaeacian ships. In Ithaca, Athena appears to the hero. Because his home is full of enemies, she advises him to proceed disguised as a beggar. This new hero of the postwar age must succeed not only by physical power but also by intelligence.

In Book 14, Odysseus, in his beggar's disguise, finds his way to the hut of his old and trusty swineherd, Eumaeus. Eumaeus is the very image of faithfulness in a servant—a quality much admired by Homer's society. The introduction of members of the so-called servant class as important actors is unusual in epic poetry, and it indicates Homer's originality. Odysseus is politely entertained by Eumaeus, but the king remains disguised from his old servant.

In Book 15, Athena appears to Odysseus' son, Telemachus. The young man has gone to Pylos and Sparta to talk to old comrades of his father's to try to discover if Odysseus is alive or dead. Athena advises him to return to Ithaca. His home—the palace of Odysseus—is overrun with his mother's suitors. These arrogant men have taken over Odysseus' house. They are partying with money from the son's inheritance and are demanding that his mother, Penelope, take one of them as a husband. Athena warns Telemachus that the suitors plan to ambush him. Telemachus boards a ship for home, lands secretly on Ithaca, and heads toward the cottage of the swineherd.

As father and son move closer and closer together, the suspense becomes great. Now Homer is ready for what could be the most dramatic moment in the epic. Remember that Odysseus has not seen his son for twenty years. Telemachus has been away from Ithaca for a year.

Penelope at Her Loom (1480–1483) from the series "The Story of Virtuous Women." Wool; tapestry weave.

928 THE EPIC

Preteaching Vocabulary

Words to Own

Introduce the Words to Own by asking volunteers to read the words and their definitions aloud. Then ask students to decide whether each of the following word pairs are antonyms [A], synonyms [S], or neither [N].

1. **adversities**—hardships [S]
2. **disdainful**—contemptuous [S]
3. **adorn**—relish [N]
4. **revelry**—hearsay [N]
5. **restitution**—amends [S]
6. **glowered**—smiled [A]
7. **lavished**—praised [N]
8. **aloof**—reserved [S]
9. **pliant**—rigid [A]
10. **tremulous**—steady [A]

THE MEETING OF FATHER AND SON

But there were two men in the mountain hut—
Odysseus and the swineherd. At first light
blowing their fire up, they cooked their breakfast
and sent their lads out, driving herds to root
in the tall timber.

935   When Telemachus came,
the wolfish troop of watchdogs only fawned on him
as he advanced. Odysseus heard them go
and heard the light crunch of a man's footfall—
at which he turned quickly to say:

                        "Eumaeus,
940 here is one of your crew come back, or maybe
another friend: the dogs are out there snuffling
belly down; not one has even growled.
I can hear footsteps—"

                  But before he finished
his tall son stood at the door.

                       The swineherd
945 rose in surprise, letting a bowl and jug
tumble from his fingers. Going forward,
he kissed the young man's head, his shining eyes
and both hands, while his own tears brimmed and fell.
Think of a man whose dear and only son,
950 born to him in exile, reared with labor,
has lived ten years abroad and now returns:
how would that man embrace his son! Just so
the herdsman clapped his arms around Telemachus
and covered him with kisses—for he knew
955 the lad had got away from death. He said:

"Light of my days, Telemachus,
you made it back! When you took ship for Pylos°
I never thought to see you here again.
Come in, dear child, and let me feast my eyes;
960 here you are, home from the distant places!
How rarely, anyway, you visit us,
your own men, and your own woods and pastures!
Always in the town, a man would think
you loved the suitors' company, those dogs!"

965 Telemachus with his clear candor said:

"I am with you, Uncle.° See now, I have come
because I wanted to see you first, to hear from you
if Mother stayed at home—or is she married
off to someone, and Odysseus' bed
970 left empty for some gloomy spider's weaving?"

Odysseus and Telemachus
(1st century A.D.). Mosaic
(31.5 cm wide).

Kunsthistorisches Museum, Antikensammlung,
Vienna, Austria.

957. Pylos: home of Nestor, one of
Odysseus' fellow soldiers in the
Trojan War. Telemachus had gone to
see if Nestor knew anything about
Odysseus.

966. Uncle: here, a term of
affection.

THE ODYSSEY, PART TWO **929**

Summary ■ ■

After trying to ascertain whether his
father is still alive, Telemachus returns
to Ithaca. He visits Eumaeus, the
swineherd, who explains that Penelope
is besieged by suitors. Still grieving for
her lost husband, she refuses to
remarry. Odysseus, disguised in beggar's rags, is also in the swineherd's hut,
but Telemachus does not recognize his
father. The three men share a meal, and
then the swineherd is sent to tell Penelope about her son's return. Athena
appears and tips her golden wand upon
Odysseus, who is transformed into his
youthful self. Telemachus is incredulous
and suspects a trick, but Odysseus
reassures him. Father and son tearfully
rejoice.

Resources

Viewing and Representing
Videocassette B, Segment 14
Available in English and Spanish.
Show the *Visual Connections* segment
"Where in the World Did Odysseus
Go?" to help students learn more
about the geography of Odysseus'
journey.

Listening
Audio CD Library
Selected readings from the *Odyssey*
and the Connections features are avail-
able as part of the *Audio CD Library:*
• Disc 18, Track 4

Resources: Print and Media

Reading
• *Graphic Organizers for Active Reading,* p. 70
• *Words to Own,* p. 50
• *Audio CD Library*
  Disc 18, Track 4

Writing and Language
• *Daily Oral Grammar*
  Transparencies 48, 49

• *Grammar and Language Links*
  Worksheet, p. 63
• *Language Workshop CD-ROM*

Viewing and Representing
• *Visual Connections*
  Videocassette B, Segment 14

Assessment
• *Formal Assessment,* p. 154
• *Portfolio Management System,* p. 215
• *Test Generator* (*One-Stop Planner* CD-ROM)

Internet
• go.hrw.com (keyword: LE0 9-14)

A Elements of Literature
Theme
? What important Greek value does Telemachus's and Eumaeus's treatment of the unknown beggar reveal? [Their courteous and respectful treatment of him shows how highly the Greeks valued hospitality.]

B Reading Skills and Strategies
Making Inferences
? What does Telemachus's response to Odysseus' transformation suggest about the relationship between the ancient Greeks and their gods? [Possible responses: The gods did not normally appear to mortals, and when they did, it was often to punish them; the ancient Greeks feared their gods and felt they had to be appeased and showered with gifts even if the humans were not aware of having done anything wrong.]

Answer to Margin Question
Students should note that Odysseus is still in disguise during the scene. He might be thinking of how best to reveal his identity to his son and wife and how to oust the suitors. Telemachus and Eumaeus might also be thinking about how to get rid of the suitors.

Gently the forester replied to this:

"At home indeed your mother is, poor lady
still in the women's hall. Her nights and days
are wearied out with grieving."

                                            Stepping back
975 he took the bronze-shod lance, and the young prince
entered the cabin over the worn door stone.
Odysseus moved aside, yielding his couch,
but from across the room Telemachus checked him:

A

980 "Friend, sit down; we'll find another chair
in our own hut. Here is the man to make one!"

The swineherd, when the quiet man sank down,
built a new pile of evergreens and fleeces—
a couch for the dear son of great Odysseus—
then gave them trenchers° of good meat, left over
985 from the roast pork of yesterday, and heaped up
willow baskets full of bread, and mixed
an ivy bowl of honey-hearted wine.
Then he in turn sat down, facing Odysseus,
their hands went out upon the meat and drink
990 as they fell to, ridding themselves of hunger. . . .

Not realizing that the stranger is his father, Telemachus agrees to protect him as best he can. But he says that the beggar cannot stay in the palace hall because he will be abused by the drunken suitors.

The swineherd is sent to Penelope with news of her son's return. Now even Athena cannot stand the suspense any longer. She turns to Odysseus, who is still in beggar's rags:

. . . She tipped her golden wand upon the man,
making his cloak pure white, and the knit tunic
fresh around him. Lithe° and young she made him,
ruddy with sun, his jawline clean, the beard
995 no longer gray upon his chin. And she
withdrew when she had done.

                                            Then Lord Odysseus
B reappeared—and his son was thunderstruck.
Fear in his eyes, he looked down and away
as though it were a god, and whispered:

                                            "Stranger,
1000 you are no longer what you were just now!
Your cloak is new; even your skin! You are
one of the gods who rule the sweep of heaven!
Be kind to us, we'll make you fair oblation°
and gifts of hammered gold. Have mercy on us!"

930 THE EPIC

---

984. trenchers: wooden platters.

We have seen the host-guest relationship played out at several points. Who is still in disguise in this scene? What do you think each of these men is feeling and thinking as he eats?

993. lithe: limber.

1003. oblation: offering of a sacrifice. Telemachus thinks the stranger is a god.

Reaching All Students

Struggling Readers
Pair students with more proficient readers, and have the pairs take turns reading aloud ten lines at a time. Have the listening partner summarize what transpires in the passage before the roles are switched. Paired students should consult each other about any sections that are not clearly understood after the first reading.

English Language Learners
Have student pairs create an illustrated glossary of the Words to Own for the story. Students' illustrations should relate specifically to the *Odyssey*. Students can place their illustrations in the margins beside the words and definitions, or they can make flash cards with the word and definition on one side and the illustration on the other.

Advanced Learners
Most of the selections in Part One are told from the first-person point of view as Odysseus recounts his adventures to the court of King Alcinous, but those in Part Two use third-person. Have students compare and contrast the experience of reading the two parts. How does the change in point of view affect their responses to the characters and events?

1005 The noble and enduring man replied:

"No god. Why take me for a god? No, no.
I am that father whom your boyhood lacked
and suffered pain for lack of. I am he."

Held back too long, the tears ran down his cheeks
as he embraced his son.
1010   Only Telemachus,
uncomprehending, wild
with incredulity,° cried out:

                                    "You cannot

be my father Odysseus! Meddling spirits
conceived this trick to twist the knife in me!
1015 No man of woman born could work these wonders
by his own craft, unless a god came into it
with ease to turn him young or old at will.
I swear you were in rags and old,
and here you stand like one of the immortals!"

1020 Odysseus brought his ranging mind to bear
and said:
                    "This is not princely, to be swept
away by wonder at your father's presence.
No other Odysseus will ever come,
for he and I are one, the same; his bitter
1025 fortune and his wanderings are mine.
Twenty years gone, and I am back again
on my own island. . . ."

                                    Then, throwing
his arms around this marvel of a father,
Telemachus began to weep. Salt tears
1030 rose from the wells of longing in both men,
and cries burst from both as keen and fluttering
as those of the great taloned hawk,
whose nestlings° farmers take before they fly.
So helplessly they cried, pouring out tears,
1035 and might have gone on weeping so till sundown. . . .

                                    (*from* Book 16)

1012. incredulity: disbelief.

Telemachus Sees His Father
(1875) by Friedrich Preller the
Elder. Lithograph.

Archiv f.Kunst and Geschichte, Berlin.

1033. nestlings: young birds that
are not ready to leave the nest.

 *Which part of this recog-
nition scene between
father and son do you
think is most moving or most
dramatic? Sum up the problems
that now face the father and son in
the palace at Ithaca.*

THE ODYSSEY, PART TWO 931

C **Elements of Literature**
Epithet
? What epithet is used to characterize Odysseus here? ["noble and enduring man"]

D **Reading Skills
and Strategies**
**Monitor Your
Comprehension**
Suggest that students stop at this point
to check their understanding of events
and to see what questions they might
ask themselves. For example: Why has
Athena changed Odysseus' appearance? [Possible response: Perhaps she
wants to move events along more
quickly.]

E **Elements of Literature**
Homeric Simile
? To what are the cries of Odysseus
and Telemachus compared? [to the
cries of a hawk whose young have
been stolen from the nest]

Answer to Margin Question
Students should explain their
choice. The problems that now
face Odysseus and Telemachus are
ousting the suitors and restoring
order to the kingdom and, for
Odysseus, renewing his relationship
with Penelope.

Taking a Second Look

Review: Using Prior Knowledge
Before students begin reading Part Two of the
Odyssey, suggest that reviewing what they have
read so far can help them set the stage for the
events to come and enhance their understanding of what they read. Remind them that like
the audiences in Homer's time, they already
know a great deal about what lies ahead in the
epic. You might suggest that they reread
Homer's invocation on p. 890.

Activity
Write a few phrases or sentences describing
what you already know about
• the situation in Odysseus' home
• Penelope
• Telemachus
• the suitors

Summary ▪

Odysseus disguises himself as a beggar once again and heads toward home. Odysseus' old hound, Argos, who lies abandoned outside the gates, recognizes his master's voice. Wagging his tail, the faithful dog greets his master and then expires.

Ⓐ Critical Thinking

Determining Author's Purpose

❓ Why would a great epic concern itself with an old dog? [Possible responses: Perhaps the dog will play a role in the coming events; maybe the dog is a symbol of loyalty; the way a society treats animals can reveal its values.]

Ⓑ Reading Skills and Strategies

Responding to the Text

❓ How does this description of Argos make you feel? [Possible responses: sad about the dog's condition; angry with the people who have neglected it.]

Ⓒ Elements of Literature

Character

❓ What does this scene reveal about Odysseus' character? [Sample response: Odysseus is a sensitive man, but he also has the ability to hide his true feelings; he has self-control.]

Ⓓ Elements of Literature

Irony

❓ Why is this scene ironic? [Eumaeus does not realize, although the reader does, that he is speaking to Odysseus *about* Odysseus.]

THE BEGGAR AND THE FAITHFUL DOG

Telemachus returns to the family compound and is greeted tearfully by his mother and his old nurse, Eurycleia. A sooth-sayer has told his mother, Penelope, that Odysseus is alive and in Ithaca. But Telemachus does not report that he has seen his father. The suspense builds as Odysseus, once again disguised as a beggar, returns to his home, accompanied only by the swineherd. He has been away for twenty years. Only one creature recognizes him.

While he spoke

Ⓐ
1040
an old hound, lying near, pricked up his ears
and lifted up his muzzle. This was Argos,
trained as a puppy by Odysseus,
but never taken on a hunt before
his master sailed for Troy. The young men, afterward,
hunted wild goats with him, and hare, and deer,
but he had grown old in his master's absence.

Ⓑ
1045
Treated as rubbish now, he lay at last
upon a mass of dung before the gates—
manure of mules and cows, piled there until
field hands could spread it on the king's estate.
Abandoned there, and half destroyed with flies,
old Argos lay.

But when he knew he heard

1050
Odysseus' voice nearby, he did his best
to wag his tail, nose down, with flattened ears,
having no strength to move nearer his master.
And the man looked away,
wiping a salt tear from his cheek; but he

Ⓒ
1055
hid this from Eumaeus. Then he said:

"I marvel that they leave this hound to lie
here on the dung pile;
he would have been a fine dog, from the look of him,
though I can't say as to his power and speed

1060
when he was young. You find the same good build
in house dogs, table dogs landowners keep
all for style."

And you replied, Eumaeus:

Ⓓ
1065
"A hunter owned him—but the man is dead
in some far place. If this old hound could show
the form he had when Lord Odysseus left him,
going to Troy, you'd see him swift and strong.
He never shrank from any savage thing
he'd brought to bay in the deep woods; on the scent
no other dog kept up with him. Now misery

Odysseus is recognized by Eurycleia when she washes his feet (Book 19) (1st century A.D.).

Museo Nazionale Romano delle Terme, Rome, Italy.

E Critical Thinking
Challenging the Text
❓ What do you think of Eumaeus's idea about servants? [Possible responses: It's unjust to assume that all servants are lazy and can't think for themselves; being a servant is hard enough, so it's no wonder most servants do only what's required of them; slavery by its very nature keeps human beings from realizing their full potential.]

F Elements of Literature
Character
❓ What qualities does Penelope reveal about herself through her actions here? [Possible responses: her generous hospitality; her discretion; her kindness; her loyalty to her husband.]

Answer to Margin Question
Like Argos, the overall condition of Ithaca, ravaged by the suitors, suggests neglect and abandonment.

1070   has him in leash. His owner died abroad,
and here the women slaves will take no care of him.
You know how servants are: without a master
they have no will to labor, or excel.
For Zeus who views the wide world takes away **E**
1075   half the manhood of a man, that day
he goes into captivity and slavery."

Eumaeus crossed the court and went straight forward
into the megaron° among the suitors;
but death and darkness in that instant closed
1080   the eyes of Argos, who had seen his master,
Odysseus, after twenty years. . . .

(*from* Book 17)

1078. megaron: great hall or central room.

Here again we hear about people who mock the sacred laws of respect and hospitality. In showing us how the old dog is treated, what is Homer telling us about conditions in Ithaca?

In the hall, the "beggar" is taunted by the evil suitors, but Penelope supports him. She has learned that the ragged stranger claims to have news of her husband. Unaware of who the beggar is, she invites him to visit her later in the night to talk about Odysseus.

   In Book 18, Penelope appears among the suitors and reproaches Telemachus for allowing the stranger to be abused. She certainly must have warmed her husband's heart by doing this and by singing the praises of her lost Odysseus. **F**

THE ODYSSEY, PART TWO 933

Crossing the Curriculum

Geography
Have small groups of students research accounts that attempt to explain the geography of Odysseus' voyage. Students can create a map (perhaps using drawings or mapping software) and plot on it all of the stops that Odysseus made on his journey home. Have groups compare their completed work.

Mathematics
Have students build on the information gathered by those working on the geography activity. Using the scale on the source maps, students can figure Odysseus' approximate mileage from one point to another. Once students have totaled the mileage, have them determine how long the voyage would take at various sailing speeds and how long a direct (non-adventure-filled) journey should have taken.

A Reading Skills and Strategies

Making Predictions

? Based on what you know about Odysseus, what do you predict his strategy for dealing with the suitors will be? [Possible responses: He will rally the people of Ithaca to dispel the suitors; he will take the suitors on single-handedly; he will use stealth and cunning to get them to leave.]

B Critical Thinking

Speculating

? Why do you think Odysseus does not reveal his identity to Penelope yet? [Possible responses: He is afraid that she will not believe him; he is worried that she might accidentally spoil the plans he has made for vanquishing the suitors.]

A *In Book 19, the suitors depart for the night, and Odysseus and Telemachus discuss their strategy. The clever hero goes as appointed to Penelope with the idea of testing her and her maids. (Some of the maids have not been loyal to the household and have even slept with the suitors.) The faithful wife receives her disguised husband. We can imagine the tension Homer's audience must have felt. Would Odysseus be recognized?*

The "beggar" spins a yarn about his origins, pretending that he has met Odysseus on his travels. He cannot resist praising the lost hero, and he does so successfully enough to bring tears to Penelope's eyes. We can be sure that this does not displease the beggar.

The storytelling beggar reveals that he has heard that Odysseus is alive and is even now sailing for home. Penelope calls for the old nurse and asks her to wash the guest's feet—a sign of respect and honor. As Eurycleia does so, she recognizes Odysseus from a scar on his leg.

B *Quickly Odysseus swears the old nurse to secrecy. Meanwhile, Athena has cast a spell on Penelope so that she has taken no notice of this recognition scene. Penelope adds to the suspense by deciding on a test for the suitors on the next day. Without realizing it, she has now given Odysseus a way to defeat the men who threaten his wife and kingdom.*

In Book 20, Odysseus, brooding over the shameless behavior of the maidservants and the suitors, longs to destroy his enemies but fears the revenge of their friends. Athena reassures him. Odysseus is told that the suitors will die.

Odysseus is recognized by Eurycleia. Detail from a skyphos, a drinking cup.
Museo Archeologico, Chiusi, Italy.

934

Skill Link

Appositive Phrases

In the *Odyssey*, Homer frequently uses epithets to characterize people. These epithets often consist of adjectives, appositives, or appositive phrases. An appositive is a noun or pronoun placed beside another noun or pronoun to explain or identify it.

"***Father** Zeus, grant our old wish!*" (l. 1135) An appositive phrase consists of an appositive and its modifiers.

"*. . . grant that Odysseus, **raider of cities,** never see his home. . . .*" (ll. 531–532) Appositives and appositive phrases can precede or follow the noun they modify.

Activity

Circle the adjectives in the following epithets. Underline the appositives and appositive phrases.

1. Crooked-minded Cronus
2. Light of my days, Telemachus
3. Agamemnon, son of Atreus
4. Thundering Zeus
5. Telemus, a son of Eurymus
6. Great-hearted Odysseus

T934

Telemachus and Penelope (c. 1509) by Bernadino Pínturícchio.

Penelope to Ulysses

Penelope, distressed by the demands of the suitors that she marry one of them, has thought of a way to trick them. She has set up her weaving in the hall, saying to the suitors that she is weaving a shroud (a cloth used to wrap a body for burial) for Laertes, her father-in-law. She promises that she will choose a husband when she has completed the work. "So every day I wove on the great loom, but every night by torchlight I unwove it. . . ." With this simple trick she has been able to deceive her suitors for three years.

Like a spider committing suicide
each night I unweave the web of my day.
I have no peace.
About me the insistent buzz of flies
5   drones louder every day.
I am starving.
I watch them, always, unblinking stare.
All my dwindling will
I use in not moving, not trying, unweaving.
10 I pull in my empty nets
eating myself, waiting.

—Meredith Schwartz
Highland Park School
Highland Park, New Jersey

THE ODYSSEY, PART TWO 935

RESPONDING TO THE ART

Italian painter **Bernadino Pinturicchio** (1452?–1513) is best known for historical works rendered in the classical style. **Activity.** Ask students to note the domestic details in this busy scene. What might Telemachus be saying to his mother? What does his pose suggest about his state of mind? Has anyone yet noticed the ship outside the window?

Student to Student

This poem is written from the perspective of Penelope and describes her long, lonely wait for Odysseus.

Ⓐ Elements of Literature
Simile
❓ How are Penelope's actions like those of a spider committing suicide? [A spider that destroys its own web cannot catch food and will starve; by unraveling her weaving, Penelope is precluding the possibility of a new marriage, choosing instead to cling to a past that may offer no promise.]

Ⓑ Elements of Literature
Metaphor
❓ What is the "insistent buzz of flies" a metaphor for? [the persistent suitors, who will not leave Penelope alone and each day grow more demanding]

Ⓒ Elements of Literature
Tone
❓ How would you describe the tone of these lines? [Sample response: The tone is determined and weary.]

Connecting Across Texts

Connecting with the *Odyssey*

Ask students to discuss how this student poem connects with Homer's epic. Who is the speaker, and how do you know? [The poem's title makes clear that the speaker is Penelope.] What does Penelope's trick suggest about her character? [She is clever, persistent, totally committed to Odysseus.] What dimension does the student poem add to the portrayal of Penelope presented in the excerpts from the *Odyssey* included in the text? [It shows the depth of her suffering and the toll Odysseus' absence and the presence of the suitors have taken on her.]

Summary ■ ■

Penelope has set an impossible test for her suitors—to string her husband's old bow and shoot an arrow through the sockets of twelve iron ax handles. In his beggar's disguise, Odysseus asks to try the bow. Penelope agrees and then retires inside. Odysseus performs the task, which all of Penelope's suitors have found to be impossible.

Ⓐ Elements of Literature
Sensory Language
❓ What images does Homer use to help his audience visualize even something as ordinary as this scene at the storeroom? [Images of sight include "oaken sill," "sanded clean," "Foursquare," "shining doors," "curving handle," "bright doors," "plank floor," "milk-white arm," and "polished bow case"; of sound, "rasping," "a bellow like a bull's vaunt," and "light footfall"; of scent, "herb-scented robes."]

Ⓑ Reading Skills and Strategies
Making Inferences
❓ Why is Penelope crying? [Possible responses: Seeing Odysseus' bow again after all these years makes her miss him even more; letting others handle his bow seems like a sign that she has given up waiting for him; perhaps she is worried that one of the suitors might actually pass her test.]

Ⓒ Critical Thinking
Determining Author's Purpose
❓ Given that Penelope is carrying a huge bow and arrows capable of inflicting "coughing death," why do you think Homer chooses to mention her beauty here? Does he mean simply her physical attractiveness, or is he suggesting something more? [Possible response: He is suggesting that Penelope's intelligence and strength of character have enabled her to set her own terms and that she has done so with grace and dignity.]

Ⓓ Critical Thinking
Extending the Text
❓ What other contests have you read about that you could compare with this contest for Penelope's hand? [Students may mention fairy tales or folk tales, such as the legend of William Tell or the legend of King Arthur and the sword in the stone.]

THE TEST OF THE GREAT BOW

In Book 21, Penelope, like many unwilling princesses of myth, fairy tale, and legend, proposes an impossible task for those who wish to marry her. By so doing, she causes the bloody events that lead to the restoration of her husband. The test involves stringing Odysseus' huge bow, an impossible feat for anyone except Odysseus himself. Odysseus had left his bow home in Ithaca twenty years earlier.

Now the queen reached the storeroom door and halted.
Here was an oaken sill, cut long ago
and sanded clean and bedded true. Foursquare
1085 the doorjambs and the shining doors were set
by the careful builder. Penelope untied the strap
around the curving handle, pushed her hook
into the slit, aimed at the bolts inside,
and shot them back. Then came a rasping sound
1090 as those bright doors the key had sprung gave way—
a bellow like a bull's vaunt° in a meadow—
followed by her light footfall entering
over the plank floor. Herb-scented robes
lay there in chests, but the lady's milk-white arms
1095 went up to lift the bow down from a peg
in its own polished bow case.
                              Now Penelope
sank down, holding the weapon on her knees,
and drew her husband's great bow out, and sobbed
and bit her lip and let the salt tears flow.
1100 Then back she went to face the crowded hall
tremendous bow in hand, and on her shoulder hung
the quiver spiked with coughing death. Behind, her
maids bore a basket full of ax heads, bronze
and iron implements for the master's game.
1105 Thus in her beauty she approached the suitors,
and near a pillar of the solid roof
she paused, her shining veil across her cheeks,
her maids on either hand and still,
then spoke to the banqueters:
                              "My lords, hear me:
1110 suitors indeed, you recommended this house
to feast and drink in, day and night, my husband
being long gone, long out of mind. You found
no justification for yourselves—none
except your lust to marry me. Stand up, then:
1115 we now declare a contest for that prize.
Here is my lord Odysseus' hunting bow.
Bend and string it if you can. Who sends an arrow

1091. **vaunt:** boast.

Odysseus slaying the suitors (detail) (c. 440 B.C.) by the Penelope Painter. Attic red-figured skyphos, or drinking cup, from Tarquinii.

Antikensammlung Staatliche Museen zu Berlin Preussischer Kulturbesitz.

936 THE EPIC

through iron ax-helve sockets,° twelve in line?
I join my life with his, and leave this place, my home,
1120 my rich and beautiful bridal house, forever
to be remembered, though I dream it only." . . .

*Many of the suitors boldly try the bow, but not a man can even
bend it enough to string it.*

Two men had meanwhile left the hall:
swineherd and cowherd, in companionship,
one downcast as the other. But Odysseus
1125 followed them outdoors, outside the court,
and coming up said gently:

                           "You, herdsman,
and you, too, swineherd, I could say a thing to you,
or should I keep it dark?

                         No, no; speak,
my heart tells me. Would you be men enough
1130 to stand by Odysseus if he came back?
Suppose he dropped out of a clear sky, as I did?
Suppose some god should bring him?
Would you bear arms for him, or for the suitors?"

The cowherd said:

                       "Ah, let the master come!
1135 Father Zeus, grant our old wish! Some courier°
guide him back! Then judge what stuff is in me
and how I manage arms!"

                    Likewise Eumaeus
fell to praying all heaven for his return,
so that Odysseus, sure at least of these,
told them:

1140   "I am at home, for I am he.
I bore adversities, but in the twentieth year
I am ashore in my own land. I find
the two of you, alone among my people,
longed for my coming. Prayers I never heard
1145 except your own that I might come again.
So now what is in store for you I'll tell you:
If Zeus brings down the suitors by my hand
I promise marriages to both, and cattle,

WORDS TO OWN
adversities (ad·vur′sə·tēz) *n.*: great misfortunes; hardships.

THE ODYSSEY, PART TWO 937

1118. An ax helve is an ax handle; a socket is a hollow piece lined with iron at the end of the handle. Shooting an arrow through a line of ax-helve sockets would be a task possible only for a hero like Superman or Odysseus.

1135. courier: guide or messenger.

E Elements of Literature
Conflict
❓ What is the internal conflict that Odysseus faces in these lines? [He doesn't know whether to reveal himself, because he is not sure that he can trust the men and that they will support him.]

F Reading Skills and Strategies
Identifying Cause and Effect
❓ Why does Odysseus decide to reveal his identity to the two men now? [Possible responses: Their prayers to the gods convince him that they are sincere; he needs their help to carry out his plan for the suitors.]

G Critical Thinking
Interpreting
❓ What does Odysseus mean here? [He means that his success in getting rid of the suitors will require the guidance of Zeus.]

Getting Students Involved

Cooperative Learning
Creating a Box Movie. Arrange students in groups of three or four, and have each group choose an episode from the epic to illustrate in a series of same-sized squares on a roll of paper. After each group agrees on an episode, it should illustrate the important scenes in sequence on the squares, with each student making at least two squares. Students should then roll the paper on wrapping-paper tubes. To create a mock TV set, they can cut a frame in the bottom of a box and holes in the sides, extending the tubes through the holes in the sides. Students can then turn the roll to create a movie. Each group should provide narration for its movie, and each student should take part in presenting the movie to the rest of the class.

T937

A Reading Skills and Strategies
Monitor Your Comprehension
Suggest that students pause here to check their understanding of events and to see what questions they might ask themselves. For example: What does Odysseus plan to do to vanquish the suitors? [Possible response: He plans to have Philoeteus lock the suitors in, and then he will string his bow and use it to attack the suitors.]

B Elements of Literature
Irony
❓ Why is Penelope's acceptance of the beggar as a suitor ironic? [The "suitor," Odysseus, is already her husband.]

C Reading Skills and Strategies
Drawing Conclusions
❓ What do Odysseus' actions here suggest about his state of mind? [Possible response: Odysseus is calm and focused under pressure. Even at this suspenseful moment, he is able to concentrate on the task at hand.]

and houses built near mine. And you shall be
1150   brothers-in-arms of my Telemachus.
Here, let me show you something else, a sign
that I am he, that you can trust me, look:
this old scar from the tusk wound that I got
boar hunting on Parnassus° —— . . ."

                              Shifting his rags

1155   he bared the long gash. Both men looked, and knew
and threw their arms around the old soldier, weeping,
kissing his head and shoulders. He as well
took each man's head and hands to kiss, then said—
to cut it short, else they might weep till dark—

1160   "Break off, no more of this.
Anyone at the door could see and tell them.
Drift back in, but separately at intervals
after me.

                      Now listen to your orders:
when the time comes, those gentlemen, to a man,
1165   will be dead against giving me bow or quiver.
Defy them. Eumaeus, bring the bow
and put it in my hands there at the door.
Tell the women to lock their own door tight.
Tell them if someone hears the shock of arms
1170   or groans of men, in hall or court, not one
must show her face, but keep still at her weaving.
Philoeteus, run to the outer gate and lock it.
Throw the crossbar and lash it." . . .

Now Odysseus, still in his beggar's clothes, asks to try the bow. The suitors refuse to allow a mere beggar to try where they have failed, but Penelope insists that the stranger be given his chance. The suspense is very great—by this act, Penelope has accepted her husband as a suitor.

Eumaeus, the swineherd, hands Odysseus the bow and tells the nurse to retire with Penelope and the maids to the family chambers (the harem) and to bolt the doors. Odysseus had earlier told Telemachus to remove the suitors' weapons from the great hall. Now he takes the bow.

                   And Odysseus took his time,
1175   turning the bow, tapping it, every inch,
for borings that termites might have made
while the master of the weapon was abroad.
The suitors were now watching him, and some
jested among themselves:

                          "A bow lover!"

1154. Parnassus (pär·nas′əs): As a young man, Odysseus had gone hunting on Parnassus, his mother's home, and was gored above the knee by a boar.

938 THE EPIC

Reaching All Students

Advanced Learners
Engage students in a discussion of Odysseus' decision to disguise himself upon his return to Ithaca. Ask: Why doesn't he reveal his identity at once to his family members? [Students may say that it is another demonstration of Odysseus' cunning; that he doesn't want to alert the suitors to his presence; or that he is simply obeying Athena.] Then, have students cite examples of other works that use the device of a character in disguise. [Students may mention the legend of Robin Hood; the Biblical story of Jacob disguising himself as Esau; Rosalind in Shakespeare's *As You Like It* disguising herself as Ganymede, a young man; or the Chinese legend and poem of Mu Lan, in which a girl disguises herself as a man to go to war.] Have students name the purposes of the disguises in the tales they mention and discuss the themes the disguises serve.

"Dealer in old bows!"

1180   "Maybe he has one like it
at home!"

     "Or has an itch to make one for himself."  **D**

"See how he handles it, the sly old buzzard!"

And one <u>disdainful</u> suitor added this:

"May his fortune grow an inch for every inch he bends it!"

1185   But the man skilled in all ways of contending, **E**
satisfied by the great bow's look and heft,
like a musician, like a harper, when
with quiet hand upon his instrument
he draws between his thumb and forefinger
1190   a sweet new string upon a peg: so effortlessly
Odysseus in one motion strung the bow.
Then slid his right hand down the cord and plucked it,
so the taut gut vibrating hummed and sang
a swallow's note.

      In the hushed hall it smote the suitors
1195   and all their faces changed. Then Zeus thundered
overhead, one loud crack for a sign.
And Odysseus laughed within him that the son
of crooked-minded Cronus° had flung that omen down.
He picked one ready arrow from his table
1200   where it lay bare: the rest were waiting still
in the quiver for the young men's turn to come.
He nocked° it, let it rest across the handgrip,
and drew the string and grooved butt of the arrow,
aiming from where he sat upon the stool.

        Now flashed **F**
1205   arrow from twanging bow clean as a whistle
through every socket ring, and grazed not one,
to thud with heavy brazen head beyond.

        Then quietly
Odysseus said:

     "Telemachus, the stranger
you welcomed in your hall has not disgraced you.
1210   I did not miss, neither did I take all day
stringing the bow. My hand and eye are sound,
not so contemptible as the young men say."

WORDS TO OWN
disdainful (dis·dān′fəl) *adj.*: scornful; contemptuous.

Suitor hiding behind a table
(380 B.C.). Limestone relief from
Goelbasi-Trysa, Lycia, Turkey
(110 cm × 750 cm).
Kunsthistorisches Museum, Antikensammlung,
Vienna, Austria.

1198. Cronus: father of Zeus,
called crooked minded because of
his schemes to destroy his children.
1202. nocked: fitted to the
bowstring.

D Appreciating Language
Dialogue
Make sure students understand that
each line introduces a new speaker
here. Discuss how the direct quotations make the suitors' scorn more
vivid than a series of indirect quotations would. The directly quoted cat-
calls let readers feel the tense, hostile
atmosphere in the hall.

E Elements of Literature
Epithet
❓ What epithet is used for Odysseus
here? ["the man skilled in all ways of
contending"] Where else has Homer
used this epithet for Odysseus? [In the
invocation at the beginning of the epic,
Homer asks the Muse to help him "tell
the story of that man skilled in all ways
of contending."]

F Elements of Literature
Imagery
❓ How many auditory images can you
find in this passage? [Auditory images
include "hummed and sang a swallow's
note", "hushed hall," "Zeus thundered
overhead, one loud crack," "twanging
bow," and "to thud with heavy brazen
head beyond."]

Crossing the Curriculum

Science/History

Archery was a common sport in many ancient
cultures. The Egyptian pharaohs boasted of
prowess with the bow and arrow, and the
Greeks practiced recreational archery as well.
While Odysseus' bowmanship provides a dramatic moment in the *Odyssey*, archery was not
of major military importance to Greek soldiers
of Homer's time. Early bows were made of
wood and animal sinew; the arrows, also
wooden, were tipped with heads of stone or
flint. Judging by the difficulties the suitors had in
stringing Odysseus' bow, it is possible that the
type of bow described by Homer was Scythian.
Scythian bows were curved in one direction
when strung. When unstrung, the bow would
reverse its shape. Restringing a Scythian bow
required a great deal of force; both arms and
legs were needed to recurve it in the right
direction. Ask interested students to research
and explain the physics behind this early hand-
powered weapon. Students should describe
how energy is accumulated through the pulling
of the bowstring and how the stored energy is
released with the flight of the arrow. As an
extension, students may investigate improvements made in the bow and arrow through the
use of modern composite materials.

Response to Margin Activity

One possible staging of this
scene: Odysseus is center stage
as he examines the bow, strings it, and
shoots the arrow. The suitors, standing
to the side, jest as Odysseus studies
the bow but are stunned into silence as
he strings it. After he shoots the bow,
Odysseus summons Telemachus and
whispers to him.

Connections

The speaker, like Penelope a woman
whose husband has been gone for
years, considers the bond that links all
such women throughout time.

Ⓐ Struggling Readers

**Identifying Pronoun
Antecedents**

? What does the word *this* refer to?
[the "ancient gesture" of the title: wiping
away tears]

Ⓑ Elements of Literature

Metaphor

? What might "weaving" stand for in
this metaphor? [Possible responses:
keeping up a brave front during the day
when with others; any type of repetitive
busywork that helps to pass the long
days of waiting.]

Ⓒ Elements of Literature

Tone

? How does this litany of words and
phrases with positive connotations
alter the tone of the poem? [Possible
responses: The tone changes from one
of weary resignation to one of self-affir-
mation; the speaker seems to be reciting
the positive terms as a way of pulling
herself together.]

Ⓓ Critical Thinking

Challenging the Text

? Is this a fair comment to make
about Odysseus? Explain. [Possible
answers: Yes, because Odysseus is very
preoccupied with his image and often
does things merely for effect; no,
because Odysseus is capable of crying
openly, as he did when he was reunited
with Telemachus (p. 931).]

The hour has come to cook their lordships' mutton—
supper by daylight. Other amusements later,
1215   with song and harping that <u>adorn</u> a feast."

He dropped his eyes and nodded, and the prince
Telemachus, true son of King Odysseus,
belted his sword on, clapped hand to his spear,
and with a clink and glitter of keen bronze
1220   stood by his chair, in the forefront near his father.

(*from* Book 21)

WORDS TO OWN
adorn (ə·dôrn′) v.: add beauty to; decorate.

*This scene and the next
one are well worth
staging. Make notes
about how you visualize these
scenes. Where are various characters placed? How are they reacting?
It might help to draw a picture of
the Great Hall and indicate where
various actions take place.*

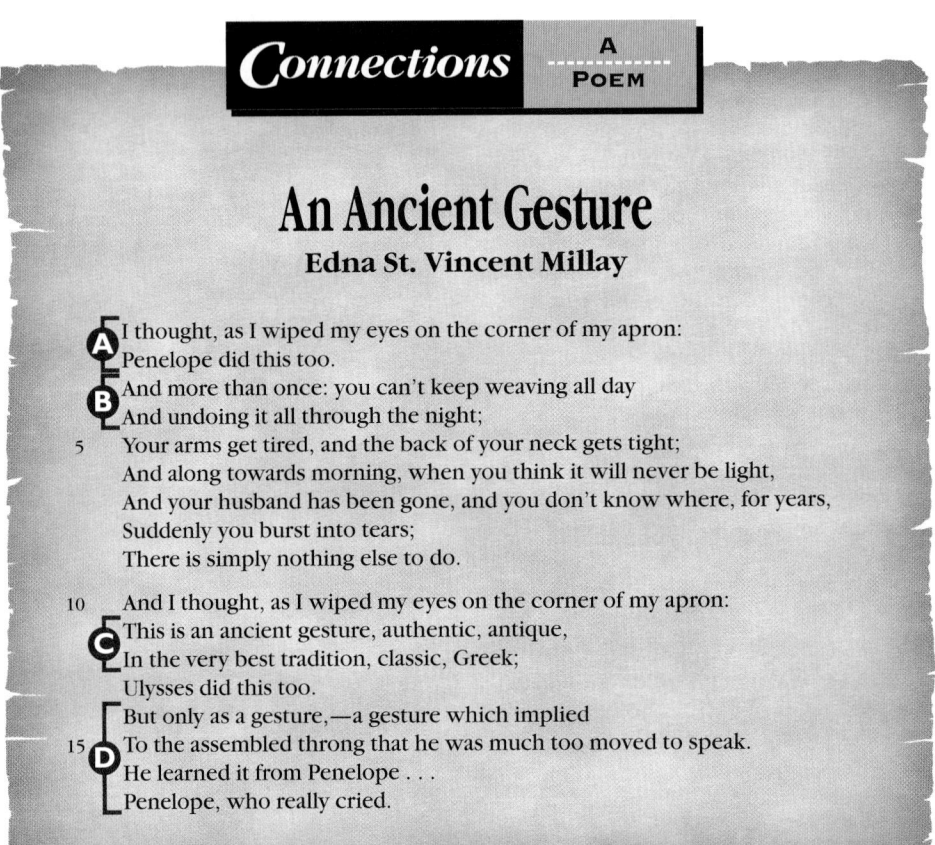

Connections   A POEM

An Ancient Gesture
Edna St. Vincent Millay

Ⓐ⎡ I thought, as I wiped my eyes on the corner of my apron:
 ⎣ Penelope did this too.
Ⓑ⎡ And more than once: you can't keep weaving all day
 ⎣ And undoing it all through the night;
5   Your arms get tired, and the back of your neck gets tight;
       And along towards morning, when you think it will never be light,
       And your husband has been gone, and you don't know where, for years,
       Suddenly you burst into tears;
       There is simply nothing else to do.

10   And I thought, as I wiped my eyes on the corner of my apron:
Ⓒ⎡ This is an ancient gesture, authentic, antique,
 ⎣ In the very best tradition, classic, Greek;
       Ulysses did this too.
   ⎡ But only as a gesture,—a gesture which implied
15 Ⓓ To the assembled throng that he was much too moved to speak.
   ⎣ He learned it from Penelope . . .
       Penelope, who really cried.

940 THE EPIC

Connecting Across Texts

Connecting with the *Odyssey*

Invite students to discuss how Millay's poem
connects with the *Odyssey*. How does the
speaker's situation compare with Penelope's?
Point out that the speaker of the poem seems
to find consolation in knowing that her experience is not unique, but rather timeless and universal. Have students think of other gestures
and situations described in the *Odyssey* that are
similarly timeless and universal.

Write students' ideas on the chalkboard, and
ask for examples from modern life that parallel
those in the epic. You might also ask students to
recall Gladys Cardiff's poem "Combing" (p. 567)
from Collection 10. Students can compare and
contrast the attitude of that poem's speaker
toward an activity that connects women across
generations with the attitude expressed in "An
Ancient Gesture."

DEATH AT THE PALACE

The climax of the story is here, in Book 22. Odysseus is ready to **A** *reclaim his rightful kingdom. But first he must deal with more than a hundred young and hostile suitors. The first one he turns to is Antinous. All through the story, Antinous has been the meanest of the suitors and their ringleader. He hit Odysseus with a stool when the hero appeared in the hall as a beggar, and he ridiculed the disguised king by calling him a bleary vagabond, a pest, and a tramp.*

Now shrugging off his rags the wiliest fighter of the
    islands
leapt and stood on the broad doorsill, his own bow in his
    hand.
He poured out at his feet a rain of arrows from the quiver
and spoke to the crowd:

        "So much for that. Your clean-cut game is over.
1225 Now watch me hit a target that no man has hit before,
if I can make this shot. Help me, Apollo."°

He drew to his fist the cruel head of an arrow for
    Antinous
just as the young man leaned to lift his beautiful drinking
    cup,
embossed, two-handled, golden: the cup was in his
    fingers,
1230 the wine was even at his lips, and did he dream of death?
How could he? In that <u>revelry</u> amid his throng of friends
who would imagine a single foe—though a strong foe
    indeed—
could dare to bring death's pain on him and darkness on
    his eyes?
Odysseus' arrow hit him under the chin
1235 and punched up to the feathers through his throat.

Backward and down he went, letting the wine cup fall
from his shocked hand. Like pipes his nostrils jetted
crimson runnels,° a river of mortal red,
and one last kick upset his table
1240 knocking the bread and meat to soak in dusty blood.
Now as they craned to see their champion where he lay
the suitors jostled in uproar down the hall,
everyone on his feet. Wildly they turned and scanned

B

C

WORDS TO OWN
revelry (rev′əl·rē) *n.*: merrymaking; festivity.

As you read this action scene, imagine it as a film. After you finish reading, draw the scene in your notebook, placing the characters Odysseus, Antinous, and Telemachus. Make a list of the props you would need if you were filming the battle.

1226. Odysseus prays to Apollo because this particular day is one of the god's feast days. Apollo is also the god of archery.

1238. runnels: streams.

THE ODYSSEY, PART TWO **941**

Summary ■ ■

To reclaim his kingdom, Odysseus must fend off Penelope's angry suitors, who have united against the hero, with Antinous as their ringleader. Telemachus and his father, joined by the swineherd and the cowherd, trap the suitors in the hall and defeat them.

A Elements of Literature
Climax
? What is the major question you expect the climax to answer? [Possible response: Will Odysseus succeed in ridding the kingdom of the suitors?]

B Critical Thinking
Analyzing
? What makes this description of Antinous's death especially powerful? [Sample response: The power comes from the juxtaposition of the elaborate description of Antinous drinking his wine, oblivious to his peril, and the stark description of the arrow's impact.]

C Reading Skills and Strategies
Monitor Your Comprehension
At this point you might have students pause in their reading to check their understanding of events and to see what questions they might ask themselves. For example: What has just happened? [Odysseus has killed Antinous.] What will happen next? [Possible responses: Odysseus will kill the rest of the suitors; the suitors will kill Odysseus.]

Response to Margin Activity
The scene might include a long table piled high with plates of food and crowded with people. Props would include bows, arrows, quivers, and wine goblets. Ask students to support their placement of the characters with details or ideas from the text.

Getting Students Involved

Cooperative Learning
The *Ithaca News*. Arrange students in groups of four or five to construct a newspaper that might have come out after Odysseus' return to Ithaca. Direct students to include in their newspapers a factual summary of Odysseus' return and of one or two of his adventures; an eyewitness account of his return; two or three illustrations from the epic; an editorial; and two letters to the editor expressing different opinions about Odysseus' adventures and his return. Each student in a group should have responsibility for an equal share in these tasks. Students can assemble their work by taping together letter-size sheets of paper or using a computer layout program. Have the groups exchange and compare their finished products.

A Critical Thinking

Interpreting

❓ What does Homer mean when he says the suitors "imagined as they wished"? [Possible responses: He means that their initial response to Antinous's death is denial; he means that they can't believe that Odysseus purposely killed Antinous, because if they did, they would realize that their own lives are in danger.]

B Elements of Literature

Character

❓ What does Eurymachus's speech reveal about his character? [Sample response: He is quick-thinking, duplicitous, and wily in trying to save his own life by blaming Antinous for everything.]

the walls in the long room for arms; but not a shield,
not a good ashen spear was there for a man to take and
    throw.

1245

All they could do was yell in outrage at Odysseus:

"Foul! to shoot at a man! That was your last shot!"

"Your own throat will be slit for this!"

      "Our finest lad is down!
You killed the best on Ithaca."

      "Buzzards will tear your eyes out!"

A 1250
For they imagined as they wished—that it was a wild
    shot,
an unintended killing—fools, not to comprehend
they were already in the grip of death.
But glaring under his brows Odysseus answered:

"You yellow dogs, you thought I'd never make it
home from the land of Troy. You took my house to
    plunder,

1255
twisted my maids to serve your beds. You dared
bid for my wife while I was still alive.
Contempt was all you had for the gods who rule wide
    heaven,
contempt for what men say of you hereafter.

1260
Your last hour has come. You die in blood."

As they all took this in, sickly green fear
pulled at their entrails,° and their eyes flickered
looking for some hatch or hideaway from death.
Eurymachus alone could speak. He said:

1262. entrails: guts.

1265
"If you are Odysseus of Ithaca come back,
all that you say these men have done is true.
Rash actions, many here, more in the countryside.
But here he lies, the man who caused them all.
Antinous was the ringleader, he whipped us on

B 1270
to do these things. He cared less for a marriage
than for the power Cronion° has denied him
as king of Ithaca. For that
he tried to trap your son and would have killed him.
He is dead now and has his portion. Spare

1271. Cronion: another name for Zeus, meaning "son of Cronus."

1275
your own people. As for ourselves, we'll make
restitution of wine and meat consumed,

WORDS TO OWN

restitution (res′tə·tōō′shən) n.: compensation; repayment.

942 THE EPIC

Skill Link

Generating Relevant, Interesting, and Researchable Questions

As students read the *Odyssey*, ask them to keep notes about any aspects of ancient Greek culture, mythology, or history that intrigue them and spark interest in further research. After they have finished reading, ask students to examine their notes and decide on a single researchable question to investigate. Discuss with students the kinds of questions that are researchable and the kinds that are not. For example, as interesting as it would be to know what Homer would think of modern adventure stories, this question cannot be answered. After students have posed their initial questions, you might have them work in groups to determine whether the questions are researchable and to brainstorm specific reference sources they could use to find the answers.

Once they have finished their research, have students record their questions and answers on separate index cards. They might also note on the cards the specific section of the *Odyssey* that inspired their curiosity. On the flip side of each card, students should record the source or sources they used to find the answers. Post the cards on an *Odyssey* Q & A bulletin board.

and add, each one, a tithe of twenty oxen
with gifts of bronze and gold to warm your heart.
Meanwhile we cannot blame you for your anger."

1280   Odysseus glowered under his black brows
and said:

> "Not for the whole treasure of your fathers,
> all you enjoy, lands, flocks, or any gold
> put up by others, would I hold my hand.
> There will be killing till the score is paid.
1285   You forced yourselves upon this house. Fight your way out,
or run for it, if you think you'll escape death.
I doubt one man of you skins by." . . .

*Telemachus joins his father in the fight. They are helped by the
swineherd and cowherd. Now the suitors, trapped in the hall
without weapons, are struck right and left by arrows, and
many of them lie dying on the floor.*

At this moment that unmanning thundercloud,
the aegis, Athena's shield,
took form aloft in the great hall.
1290   And the suitors mad with fear
at her great sign stampeded like stung cattle by a river
when the dread shimmering gadfly strikes in summer,
in the flowering season, in the long-drawn days.
After them the attackers wheeled, as terrible as falcons
from eyries° in the mountains veering over and diving
1295   down
with talons wide unsheathed on flights of birds,
who cower down the sky in chutes and bursts along the
        valley—
but the pouncing falcons grip their prey, no frantic wing
        avails,
and farmers love to watch those beakèd hunters.
1300   So these now fell upon the suitors in that hall,
turning, turning to strike and strike again,
while torn men moaned at death, and blood ran smoking
over the whole floor. . . .

                                    (*from* Book 22)

WORDS TO OWN
glowered (glou′ərd) v.: glared; stared angrily.

Ulysses Slaying the Suitors (detail)
(1802) by Henry Fuseli.
Kunsthaus Zurich, Zurich, Switzerland.

1295. eyries (er′ēz): nests built in
high places.

*What does this bloody
scene add to the epic's
theme about the value
of hospitality and about what
happens to people who mock
divine laws?*

THE ODYSSEY, PART TWO 943

Summary ■■

At first Penelope is so shocked by the appearance of her long-lost husband that she is unable to speak or move. Telemachus implores her to show Odysseus some affection, but she wants proof that he is truly her husband. Odysseus bathes and dresses in fresh clothing, yet Penelope is still resistant. Finally, Odysseus proves his identity by revealing the secret of their marriage bed, which is built around the base of a tree. Upon hearing this, Penelope embraces Odysseus, crying tears of joy.

Ⓐ Critical Thinking
Expressing an Opinion
❓ Do you think the maids' punishment fits their crimes, or is it excessive? Explain. [Possible responses: Their punishment does fit their crimes—for the ancient Greeks, betrayals of loyalty were very serious matters; their punishment is excessive—they were coerced by the suitors and thus shouldn't have been held accountable.]

Ⓑ Reading Skills and Strategies
Making Predictions
❓ How do you think Odysseus is likely to react to Penelope's "testing"? [Possible responses: He will be stunned; he will be impatient; he will be angry; he will be hurt.]

Ⓒ Reading Skills and Strategies
Drawing Conclusions
❓ Why does Penelope have so much trouble recognizing Odysseus? [Possible responses: It's been twenty years since she last saw him, and people can change a great deal in that time; she may think the man is an impostor or a test sent by the gods; perhaps she imagined that Odysseus would look different when he returned; doubt and hope are warring within her, clouding her senses and affecting her judgment.]

Answer to Margin Question
Penelope might be thinking that the gods are playing a mean trick on her; she might be thinking that the man really is her husband yet be afraid to let herself hope that he is.

ODYSSEUS AND PENELOPE

Ⓐ *Odysseus now calls forth the maids who have betrayed his household by associating with the suitors. He orders them to clean up the house and dispose of the dead. Telemachus then "pays" them by hanging them in the courtyard.*

Ⓑ *Eurycleia runs to Penelope to announce the return of Odysseus and the defeat of the suitors. The faithful wife—the perfect mate for the wily Odysseus—suspects a trick from the gods and decides to test this stranger who claims to be her husband.*

 Make notes on Penelope as you read this scene. What must she be thinking?

Crossing the doorsill she sat down at once
1305   in firelight, against the nearest wall,
across the room from the lord Odysseus.

                                                            There
leaning against a pillar, sat the man
and never lifted up his eyes, but only waited
for what his wife would say when she had seen him.
Ⓒ 1310   And she, for a long time, sat deathly still
in wonderment—for sometimes as she gazed
she found him—yes, clearly—like her husband,
but sometimes blood and rags were all she saw.
Telemachus's voice came to her ears:

                                                            "Mother,
1315   cruel mother, do you feel nothing,
drawing yourself apart this way from Father?
Will you not sit with him and talk and question him?
What other woman could remain so cold?
Who shuns her lord, and he come back to her
1320   from wars and wandering, after twenty years?
Your heart is hard as flint and never changes!"

Penelope answered:

                                                            "I am stunned, child.
I cannot speak to him. I cannot question him.
I cannot keep my eyes upon his face.
1325   If really he is Odysseus, truly home,
beyond all doubt we two shall know each other
better than you or anyone. There are
secret signs we know, we two."

                                                            A smile
came now to the lips of the patient hero, Odysseus,
1330   who turned to Telemachus and said:

"Peace: let your mother test me at her leisure.
Before long she will see and know me best.
These tatters, dirt—all that I'm caked with now—
make her look hard at me and doubt me still. . . ."

944   THE EPIC

Odysseus orders Telemachus, the swineberd, and the cowberd to bathe and put on fresh clothing.

1335　Greathearted Odysseus, home at last,
　　　was being bathed now by Eurynome
　　　and rubbed with golden oil, and clothed again
　　　in a fresh tunic and a cloak. Athena
　　　lent him beauty, head to foot. She made him
1340　taller, and massive, too, with crisping hair
　　　in curls like petals of wild hyacinth
　　　but all red-golden. Think of gold infused
　　　on silver by a craftsman, whose fine art
　　　Hephaestus taught him, or Athena: one
1345　whose work moves to delight: just so she lavished
　　　beauty over Odysseus' head and shoulders.
　　　He sat then in the same chair by the pillar,
　　　facing his silent wife, and said:

　　　　　　　　　　　　　　　　　"Strange woman,
　　　the immortals of Olympus made you hard,
1350　harder than any. Who else in the world
　　　would keep aloof as you do from her husband
　　　if he returned to her from years of trouble,
　　　cast on his own land in the twentieth year?

　　　Nurse, make up a bed for me to sleep on.
　　　Her heart is iron in her breast."
1355
　　　　　　　　　　　　　　　　　　Penelope

　　　spoke to Odysseus now. She said:

　　　　　　　　　　　　　　　　　"Strange man,
　　　if man you are . . . This is no pride on my part
　　　nor scorn for you—not even wonder, merely.
　　　I know so well how you—how he—appeared
1360　boarding the ship for Troy. But all the same . . .

　　　Make up his bed for him, Eurycleia.
　　　Place it outside the bedchamber my lord
　　　built with his own hands. Pile the big bed
　　　with fleeces, rugs, and sheets of purest linen."

1365　With this she tried him to the breaking point,
　　　and he turned on her in a flash, raging:

　　　"Woman, by heaven you've stung me now!
　　　Who dared to move my bed?

WORDS TO OWN
lavished (lav′isht) *v.:* gave generously.
aloof (ə·lōōf′) *adj.:* at a distance; unfriendly.

Penelope (detail) (1864) by John Roddam Spencer-Stanhope.

The De Morgan Foundation, London.

THE ODYSSEY, PART TWO 945

D Elements of Literature
Homeric Simile
? To what does this simile compare Odysseus? [to a beautiful gold-plated work of art]

E Vocabulary Note
In Greek, the word for "strange woman" is *daimonie*. Odysseus means that Penelope's wits may have been taken away by a *daimon,* or some sort of supernatural force. Amusingly, Penelope echoes the expression back to Odysseus in l. 1356.

F Reading Skills and Strategies
Making Inferences
? What is Penelope implying in these lines? [She is implying that the one claiming to be Odysseus is not a man but a god disguised as a man.]

RESPONDING TO THE ART
John Roddam Spencer-Stanhope (1829–1908) specialized in mythological and allegorical subjects. A Pre-Raphaelite painter, he was influenced by Edward Burne-Jones (see p. 917) but developed his own style.
Activity. Have students compare and contrast this depiction of Penelope with the one by Pinturicchio on p. 935.

Assessing Learning

Group Work Assessment
For cooperative learning to be successful, group members need to reflect on and evaluate how well they worked individually and as a group. Ask students to evaluate their group work by checking the statement that best describes their group efforts. Students should be able to explain their ratings.

1. I thought that the discussion
　____ **a.** gave everyone a chance to participate.
　____ **b.** allowed nearly everyone a chance to participate.
　____ **c.** was dominated by a few.
2. As far as my participation in the discussion is concerned, I

____ **a.** was very involved.
____ **b.** could have been more involved.
____ **c.** was totally uninvolved.
3. The discussion leader
____ **a.** encouraged participation.
____ **b.** selected only a few to participate.
____ **c.** seemed to dominate the discussion.

A Reading Skills and Strategies
Monitor Your Comprehension

Have students pause here to check their understanding of events and to think about what questions they might ask themselves. For example: What was the process by which Odysseus built the bed? [He laid out the bedroom around the trunk of a rooted olive tree, constructing the walls, roof, and doorway. Then, he removed the branches from the olive tree; carved the still-rooted stump into a bedpost; modeled the other posts after it; planed and inlaid all the posts with silver, gold, and ivory; and stretched strips of oxhide thongs between the posts.]

B Reading Skills and Strategies
Drawing Conclusions

❓ What do Penelope's physical sensations suggest she is feeling? [Possible response: Finally convinced that the man before her is Odysseus, she is flooded with relief and joy that her husband has returned and her twenty-year wait is over.]

C Elements of Literature
Irony

❓ What is ironic about Penelope's statement? [Possible response: It is ironic because Penelope has been every bit as cautious as Odysseus.]

Answer to Margin Question

Characteristics that suggest strength are the pillarlike olive trunk and the inlay of silver, gold, and ivory.

No builder had the skill for that—unless
1370 a god came down to turn the trick. No mortal
in his best days could budge it with a crowbar.
There is our pact and pledge, our secret sign,
built into that bed—my handiwork
and no one else's!
                                    An old trunk of olive
1375 grew like a pillar on the building plot,
and I laid out our bedroom round that tree,
lined up the stone walls, built the walls and roof,
gave it a doorway and smooth-fitting doors.
Then I lopped off the silvery leaves and branches,
1380 hewed and shaped the stump from the roots up
into a bedpost, drilled it, let it serve
as model for the rest, I planed them all,
inlaid them all with silver, gold, and ivory,
and stretched a bed between—a <u>pliant</u> web
1385 of oxhide thongs dyed crimson.
                                    There's our sign!
I know no more. Could someone else's hand
have sawn that trunk and dragged the frame away?"

Their secret! as she heard it told, her knees
grew <u>tremulous</u> and weak, her heart failed her.
1390 With eyes brimming tears she ran to him,
throwing her arms around his neck, and kissed him,
murmuring:
                                    "Do not rage at me, Odysseus!
No one ever matched your caution! Think
what difficulty the gods gave: they denied us
1395 life together in our prime and flowering years,
kept us from crossing into age together.
Forgive me, don't be angry. I could not
welcome you with love on sight! I armed myself
long ago against the frauds of men,
1400 impostors who might come—and all those many
whose underhanded ways bring evil on! . . .
But here and now, what sign could be so clear
as this of our own bed?
No other man has ever laid eyes on it—
1405 only my own slave, Actoris, that my father

 This description of Odysseus and Penelope's bed is famous—and complex. You might try drawing a picture of the bed as you visualize it. What characteristics of the bed suggest the strength and endurance of their love?

WORDS TO OWN
pliant (plī′ənt) *adj.*: flexible.
tremulous (trem′yoo·ləs) *adj.*: trembling; shaking.

Making the Connections

Connecting to the Theme: "The Perilous Journey"

Discuss with students how the *Odyssey* embodies the collection theme. Odysseus' struggle to reach home is filled with perils, and his troubles don't end when he reaches home. Penelope and Telemachus, meanwhile, have had to contend with perils of their own. In a sense, every life is a perilous journey, and every person who stays the course is on a quest to discover his or her own Ithaca.

sent with me as a gift—she kept our door.
You make my stiff heart know that I am yours."

Now from his breast into his eyes the ache
of longing mounted, and he wept at last,
1410 his dear wife, clear and faithful, in his arms,
longed for
      as the sun-warmed earth is longed for by a swimmer
spent in rough water where his ship went down
under Poseidon's blows, gale winds and tons of sea.
Few men can keep alive through a big surf
1415 to crawl, clotted with brine, on kindly beaches
in joy, in joy, knowing the abyss behind:
and so she too rejoiced, her gaze upon her husband,
her white arms round him pressed, as though forever. . . .

(*from* Book 23)

The journey ends with an embrace. What simile helps you understand the joy Odysseus feels in the arms of his wife?

Penelope and Her Suitors (1912) by J. W. Waterhouse.

City of Aberdeen Art Gallery and Museums Collection, Scotland.

THE ODYSSEY, PART TWO 947

D Critical Thinking
Interpreting
❓ What does Penelope mean when she refers to her "stiff heart"? [Possible responses: She means her heart is stiff from disuse because she has had no husband to love for so long; she means she has had to harden her heart to protect it from the anguish of accepting that Odysseus might never return.]

Answer to Margin Question
The simile in ll. 1411–1416 compares Odysseus' feelings to the joy a nearly drowning sailor feels on reaching land at last. The simile is especially fitting because Odysseus has had to contend repeatedly with trials brought on by Poseidon, god of the sea.

RESPONDING TO THE ART
English painter **John William Waterhouse** (1849–1917) is best known for his atmospheric treatments of classic myths.
Activity. Ask students to imagine what Penelope is thinking as she concentrates on her weaving, her back turned to the imploring suitors.

Resources
Assessment
Formal Assessment
• *Selection Test*, p. 154
Test Generator (One-Stop Planner)
• CD-ROM

Assessing Learning

Check Test: Questions and Answers
Answers may vary slightly.
1. Why doesn't Telemachus recognize his father right away? [Odysseus arrives disguised as a beggar.]
2. Who is Antinous? [the leader of the suitors assembled in Odysseus' home]
3. What is Odysseus able to do that the suitors cannot do? [He can string the bow.]
4. What signs of approval do the gods give

Odysseus? [Zeus thunders; Athena's shield, a thundercloud, appears.]
5. Who aids Odysseus in his battle with the suitors? [Telemachus, the swineherd, and the goatherd]
6. What is the secret of the marriage bed of Odysseus and Penelope? [One bedpost is carved from the rooted stump of an olive tree.]

Standardized Test Preparation
For practice in proofreading and editing, see
• *Daily Oral Grammar,* Transparencies 48, 49

T947

Connections

In this extended metaphor, the speaker counsels the reader to savor the "marvelous journey" of life.

Ⓐ Reading Skills and Strategies
Making Inferences
❓ What do you think Cavafy is suggesting in the line "pray that your road's a long one"? [Possible responses: He means that you should hope that your life is long and varied; he means that you should not dread getting older but consider each added year a gift.]

Ⓑ Critical Thinking
Interpreting
❓ What does Cavafy mean by these lines? [Possible responses: He means that life is what you make of it; he means that many of our troubles are self-inflicted.]

Ⓒ Critical Thinking
Making Connections
❓ Do you think Odysseus would agree with Cavafy's advice here? [Possible responses: No, Odysseus just wanted to get home as fast as possible; yes, Odysseus relished his adventures, even though he did miss his home.]

Ⓓ Elements of Literature
Symbol
❓ What do you think Ithaca symbolizes in this poem? [Possible responses: heaven; death; one's goal in life; one's ideal place in the world; old age.]

Connections   A POEM

Ithaca

C. P. Cavafy
translated from Greek by Edmund Keeley and Philip Sherrard

Ⓐ   When you set out for Ithaca,
pray that your road's a long one,
full of adventure, full of discovery.
Laistrygonians, Cyclops,
5   angry Poseidon—don't be scared of them:
you won't find things like that on your way
as long as your thoughts are exalted,
as long as a rare excitement
Ⓑ   stirs your spirit and your body.
10   Laistrygonians, Cyclops,
wild Poseidon—you won't encounter them
unless you bring them along inside you,
unless your soul raises them up in front of you.

Pray that your road's a long one.
15   May there be many a summer morning when—
full of gratitude, full of joy—
you come into harbors seen for the first time;
may you stop at Phoenician trading centers
and buy fine things,
20   mother-of-pearl and coral, amber and ebony,
sensual perfumes of every kind,
as many sensual perfumes as you can;
may you visit numerous Egyptian cities
to fill yourself with learning from the wise.

25   Keep Ithaca always in mind.
Arriving there is what you're destined for.
But don't hurry the journey at all.
Better if it goes on for years
Ⓒ   so you're old by the time you reach the island,
30   wealthy with all you've gained on the way,
not expecting Ithaca to make you rich.
Ithaca gave you the marvelous journey.
Without her you wouldn't have set out.
She hasn't anything else to give.

35   And if you find her poor, Ithaca won't have fooled you.
Ⓓ   Wise as you'll have become, and so experienced,
you'll have understood by then what an Ithaca means.

Connecting Across Texts

Connecting with the *Odyssey*
Discuss with students how the journey to Ithaca in Cavafy's poem can be interpreted as the journey that everyone takes in life. This journey may include many of the types of experiences that Odysseus encountered during his journey home: meeting new people, visiting new places, and learning about people different from oneself. Encourage students to analyze Cavafy's poem and to list in their journals the many types of life experiences the poet mentions.

Have them think of examples of such experiences in their own lives so far or in the lives they imagine leading in the future. *Remind students to include only experiences they do not mind sharing.*

Experiences in Cavafy's Poem	Experiences in My Own Life

The Sea Call

Nikos Kazantzakis

translated from Greek by Kimon Friar

When Odysseus met Teiresias in the underworld, the prophet told him that he would reach home but would then take yet another journey to a land where people live who know nothing of the sea. (See pages 914–915.) In this excerpt from a modern sequel to the Odyssey *by the twentieth-century Greek poet Nikos Kazantzakis, Odysseus has returned to Ithaca. Sitting by the hearth with his family, his eyes alight with excitement, he relates his adventures. But then . . .*

Odysseus sealed his bitter lips and spoke no more,
but watched the glowering fire fade, the withering flames,
the ash that spread like powder on the dying coals,
then turned, glanced at his wife, gazed on his son and father,
5 and suddenly shook with fear and sighed, for now he knew
that even his native land was a sweet mask of Death.
Like a wild beast snared in a net, his eyes rolled round
and tumbled down his deep eye-sockets, green and bloodshot.
His tribal palace seemed a narrow shepherd's pen,
10 his wife a small and wrinkled old housekeeping crone,
his son an eighty-year-old drudge who, trembling, weighed
with care to find what's just, unjust, dishonest, honest,
as though all life were prudence, as though fire were just,
and logic the highest good of eagle-mounting man!
15 The heart-embattled athlete laughed, dashed to his feet,
and his home's sweetness, suddenly, his longed-for land,
the twelve gods, ancient virtue by his honored hearth,
his son—all seemed opposed now to his high descent.
The fire dwindled and died away, and the four heads
20 and his son's smooth-skinned calves with tender softness glowed
till in the trembling hush Penelope's wan cries
broke in despair like water flowing down a wall.
Her son dashed and stood upright by his mother's throne,
touched gently with a mute compassion her white arm,
25 then gazed upon his father in the dim light, and shuddered,
for in the last resplendence of the falling fire
he could discern the unmoving eyes flash yellow, blue,
and crimson, though the dark had swallowed the wild body.
With silent strides Odysseus then shot back the bolt,
30 passed lightly through the courtyard and sped down the street.
Some saw him take the graveyard's zigzag mountain path,
some saw him leap on rocks that edged the savage shore,
some visionaries saw him in the dead of night
swimming and talking secretly with the sea-demons,
35 but only a small boy saw him in a lonely dream
sit crouched and weeping by the dark sea's foaming edge.

THE ODYSSEY, PART TWO **949**

Connecting Across Texts

Connecting with the *Odyssey*
In a discussion, guide students in comparing and contrasting the mood of the last episode from the *Odyssey* in the text and of Kazantzakis's poem. You might ask, for example, why does Odysseus weep when Penelope finally accepts that he is her husband? Why does he weep in the poem?

[Possible response: In the epic, Odysseus weeps with joy and relief that he is safe in the warmth and security of his home, surrounded by his family. In the poem, a seemingly dazed Odysseus cowers by the edge of the ocean, weeping because he realizes that he was happier with his adventurous seafaring life or that he will never again feel truly at home in either world.]

Connections

In this excerpt from *The Odyssey: A Modern Sequel,* a Greek poet extends the story to imaginatively portray the hero, home at last, unexpectedly feeling trapped.

Ⓐ Elements of Literature
Imagery
❓ What details does the poet use to help readers visualize the fire? ["glowering fire fade"; "withering flames"; and the "ash that spread like powder on the dying coals"]

Ⓑ Critical Thinking
Speculating
❓ Why might Odysseus feel that his homeland is "a sweet mask of Death"? [Possible responses: He is aware of Teiresias' prophecy that he will leave Ithaca and that death will come to him from the sea; after wandering at will for so long, he finds being in one place claustrophobic; the responsibility of caring for his family is weighing on him; without the invigorating challenges he faced on his journey, he is bored and restless.]

Ⓒ Elements of Literature
Alliteration
❓ Where is alliteration used in these lines? [in l. 19, "dwindled" and "died"; in l. 20, "son's smooth-skinned" and "softness"]

Ⓓ Critical Thinking
Making Connections
❓ Where in the *Odyssey* did Odysseus sit weeping by the water? [In Book 5, when he was held captive by Calypso, Odysseus sat by the water each day "with eyes wet," longing for home (see p. 892, ll. 73–74).] What might Odysseus be longing for here? [Possible responses: for escape from Teiresias' prophecy; for adventure and far-off lands; for the carefree life of his younger days; for relief from this inner conflict between staying home and going to sea.]

T949

MAKING MEANINGS PART TWO

First Thoughts

1. Possible response: Odysseus hasn't changed, for he still slaughters those who cross him; his bravery and cunning make him a hero, although his boasting and bloodlust would not be considered heroic today.

Shaping Interpretations

2. The two men's feelings are compared to those of a hawk whose young have been stolen. Odysseus and Telemachus are probably feeling a mixture of joy at their reunion and grief at their years of separation.

3. The dramatic irony comes when the swineherd greets Telemachus as a father would greet his son after a long absence, while the young man's real father, disguised as a beggar, looks on in silence.

4. Odysseus treats the swineherd and cowherd with affection and respect. Homer may have intended to teach that all humans are worthy of respect.

Connecting with the Text

5. Possible responses: Home and family are still important values, as are courtesy and respect for all people; but today people are expected not to take the law into their own hands.
   Students may identify with Telemachus's need to find his father, with Penelope's loyalty and prudence, or with Odysseus' longing for home and his desire for revenge.

Extending the Text

6. Possible response: The general might suffer from depression or posttraumatic stress syndrome. His or her spouse might not have waited, and the children might have moved far away.

7. Possible responses: reaching a point in life where one feels at home with oneself; attaining wisdom; dying; passing to heaven.

Challenging the Text

8. Possible responses: Yes, because neither Penelope nor Telemachus was physically harmed by the suitors, and the maids might have been coerced into their actions; no, because the suitors abused one of the Greeks' highest values, hospitality. From a modern viewpoint, the rule of law requires that such matters be entrusted to the courts.

T950

MAKING MEANINGS PART TWO

First Thoughts

[respond]

1. Do you think Odysseus has changed since he started on his adventures? Explain your responses to Odysseus as a hero.

Shaping Interpretations

[identify]

2. What **simile** in lines 1031–1032 describes the feelings of Odysseus and his son as they embrace after twenty years? How would you describe exactly what the father and his son are feeling here?

[analyze]

3. **Dramatic irony** refers to a situation in which readers or the audience knows more than the characters. Where in the scene in the swineherd's hut do we get a great sense of dramatic irony?

[infer]

4. It is rare in epics for heroes to have much to do with ordinary people, but in the *Odyssey* servants play important roles. How does Odysseus treat Eumaeus and the cowherd? What values might Homer be trying to teach through that treatment?

Connecting with the Text

[connect]

5. The *Odyssey* is many centuries old. Do you think the feelings and needs shown by the people in the *Odyssey* are still important to people today? Which experiences or people in this story did you most identify with?

Extending the Text

[extend]

6. Suppose Odysseus were a modern general who had fought a war for ten years and was missing for another ten years. What emotional problems might he (or she) have faced after that ordeal? What changes might he (or she) have found in the home and family after twenty years?

[interpret]

7. In "Ithaca" (see **Connections** on page 948), a modern Greek poet reflects on the *Odyssey*. Explain what you think arriving in Ithaca could mean for all of us.

Challenging the Text

[evaluate]

8. Do you think Odysseus' revenge on the suitors and maids is excessive or too brutal? Explore this question from Odysseus' viewpoint (remember he was the rightful king) and from your own modern viewpoint.

950 THE EPIC

Reading Check

a. Describe Argos's condition when Odysseus sees him.

b. What is the test of the bow, and how will Penelope reward the winner of the contest?

c. Just before trying the bow, Odysseus reveals himself to two people. Who are they? Why does he confide in them?

d. List at least five images or events from Odysseus' battle with the suitors.

e. How does Penelope test Odysseus after the battle?

Reading Check

a. The fly-bitten dog lies neglected on a dung pile.
b. The test is to string Odysseus' bow and shoot an arrow through twelve ax-handle sockets. She will marry the winner.
c. Because he needs their help, Odysseus reveals his identity to the swineherd and the cowherd.
d. Events and images include Odysseus casting off his rags (l. 1221), Antinous's "one last kick" (l. 1239), Odysseus' rebuke of the suitors (ll. 1254–1260), the suitors stampeding like cattle (ll. 1290–1293), and blood running "smoking / over the whole floor" (ll. 1302–1303).
e. She tells her servant to move their unmovable bed, provoking him into telling how he built it.

CHOICES: Building Your Portfolio

Writer's Notebook

1. Collecting Ideas for a Cause-and-Effect Essay

Finding a topic. In the Writer's Workshop on page 958, you'll write a cause-and-effect essay. You might already have notes about episodes from the *Odyssey* that you could analyze in terms of causes and their effects. (See the Writer's Notebook activity on page 926.) Instead, you might want to focus on the causes and effects at work in Part Two of the *Odyssey*. Or you might want to map out the entire epic in terms of a series of causes and effects. You might also consider some broader topics: causes and effects of the Trojan War, for example. Review the epic now—including the introduction in this book, the cast of characters, and the side notes—to see if a topic there interests you. Keep your notes.

> Causes of Odysseus' change in character—from a reckless adventurer to a family man
> Effects of the Trojan War on Odysseus' family
> Effects of separation of fathers from their children
> Effects of disobedience to the gods

Creative Writing

2. Prophetic Puzzler

Homer's audiences would have known who Teiresias was and would have realized that his prophecies always came true. In Part One, lines 639–658 (page 915), Teiresias prophesies that Odysseus will make a strange journey. Several writers after Homer have tried to imagine exactly what Teiresias' mysterious prophecy means. (For part of one writer's extension of the story, see "The Sea Call," the *Connections* on page 949.) Write your own extension of Odysseus' story based on this prophecy. Tell what Odysseus does, where he goes, and what happens after he takes over his kingdom again. Be sure to include all the details contained in the prophecy.

Creative Writing

3. And Now—the Movie

Write a proposal suggesting ways for the *Odyssey* to be made into a movie that's set in the present. Imagine that the readers of the proposal will be the producers of the movie. Explain how you would modernize the epic. Use the following chart to organize your ideas.

1200 B.C.	Today
Trojan War is background.	
Hero is soldier who fought in war.	
He travels around Mediterranean and down to underworld.	
He uses ships with oars and sails.	
He meets Lotus Eaters, Sirens, Cyclops, Scylla and Charybdis.	
He is tempted by Calypso and Circe.	
Fortune hunters at home hound his wife.	
Dog lives on garbage heap.	
Son is insulted.	
Gods affect the action.	

Creative Writing

4. Her Odyssey

Write a story plan for an odyssey with a woman as the voyaging hero. (For example, what if Penelope, rather than Odysseus, had been the voyager?) You may set your story in any time and place, from Odysseus' Greece to your present hometown to a distant galaxy in the future.

THE ODYSSEY, PART TWO 951

Grading Timesaver

Rubrics for each Choices assignment appear on p. 215 in the *Portfolio Management System*.

CHOICES: Building Your Portfolio

1. **Writer's Notebook** Remind students to save their work. They can use it as prewriting for the Writer's Workshop on p. 958.
2. **Creative Writing** Before students start to write their extensions, have them work in pairs to explore a detailed interpretation of the prophecy. Students can use a chart like the following one to record their ideas. An example is given.

Teiresias' Advice	Interpretation
["Go overland on foot and take an oar…." (l. 641)]	[Maybe this means he has to humble himself.]

3. **Creative Writing** Have the class brainstorm ideas to complete the first block of the chart. Students can fill out the rest of the chart on their own and then describe the highlights of their film to partners. The partners can help each other evaluate their ideas.
4. **Creative Writing** Encourage students to first write a list of answers for the bulleted list on p. 952. Emphasize to students that they are to write a story plan, not a complete story. Students can organize their plans as a sequence chart using Transparency 12: Sequence Chart in the Transparency Package as a model.

Reaching All Students

Struggling Readers

Allow students interested in Choice 2 to work in pairs or small groups. They should work cooperatively to paraphrase the passage on p. 915 before they attempt to generate their individual story extensions.

T951

5. Analyzing an Epic
Have the class work together to discuss what the *Odyssey* says about one of the bulleted items. Ask students to cite specific lines to support their ideas. Write students' ideas on the chalkboard, and direct them to use the same procedure to continue the activity on their own. Have students use a graphic organizer like the following one.

Value	Example	Lesson

6. Critical Thinking/Speaking
Remind students that both verbal and nonverbal communication skills are involved in an oral presentation. Encourage students to concentrate on the following nonverbal items:
- making eye contact
- limiting unnecessary movement
- maintaining good posture

Students can also keep in mind the following verbal skills:
- speaking clearly
- making concise, logical points
- providing supporting evidence

7. Performance
Have students interested in creating a performance form groups on the basis of whether they want to dramatize a scene conventionally or experiment with a different approach. Have those developing the scene conventionally brainstorm what stage directions they would need, as well as which lines will be read by a narrator and which by characters. The other students can work together to select a setting and create a script.

8. Research/Critical Thinking
Students should cite the name of the documentary, as well as the director, writer(s), and producer. Students' papers might be in the form of a film review.

CHOICES: Building Your Portfolio

As you plan your characters, plot, and action, consider the following:
- occupation of the heroine
- reasons for being away from home
- situation at home
- trials of her journey home
- how she deals with people opposed to her
- how her family responds to her return

Analyzing an Epic
5. Timeless Messages
A work of literature cannot be important to us unless it speaks to us and to our lives. In one or more paragraphs, discuss at least four ways in which the *Odyssey* speaks to you today. You might consider how it says something about these values:
- courtesy and respect for all classes of people
- courage, trust, discipline
- community and law
- home and family
- obedience to the divine world

Be sure to review the notes you took as you read the epic.

Critical Thinking/Speaking
6. Speak Your Mind
Use the following quotation as the basis for a brief talk on the *Odyssey*. Cite specific passages from the epic that you think support the ideas in the quotation. If you disagree with the quotation, cite specific passages from the epic to support your own opinion, which you should make clear in your opening statement.

> . . . what has made Homer for three thousand years the greatest poet in the world is his *naturalness*. We love each other as in Homer. We hate each other as in Homer. We are perpetually being interfered with as in Homer by change and fate and necessity, by invisible influences for good, and by invisible influences for evil. . . .
> —John Cowper Powys

Performance
7. Tell the Story . . .
Select a portion of the epic to present as a play or as a dramatic reading. (Derek Walcott, a Nobel Prize–winning poet from St. Lucia, in the West Indies, wrote a play based on the *Odyssey*. His storyteller is a blind singer called Billy Blue. His Cyclops calls himself The Eye.) Some of the notes you took as you read the epic might give you ideas. Work with a group to decide the form your presentation will take, the episode you'll focus on, and props and costumes you'll need. Where will you set the story?

Research/Critical Thinking
8. Evaluating a Documentary
Documentaries present accounts of actual people and events in a factual way. Some people call documentaries nonfiction films. Libraries, video stores, and museum gift shops are good places to look for documentaries about ancient Greece, the Trojan War, Greek art, Homer, Greek mythology, or other topics related to the *Odyssey*. After you have watched one such documentary, write a brief paper evaluating it. Does the documentary present a particular point of view? Is the documentary factually accurate? Did it hold your interest? Did the information enrich your reading of Homer's epic?

952 THE EPIC

Using Students' Strengths

Visual Learners
For Activity 5, have students use calligraphy to illustrate five lines from the epic that illustrate the values listed in the text. Display students' work, and provide time for students to explain their choices.

Kinesthetic Learners
For Activity 7, students might approach the scene as a pantomime. Suggest that students brainstorm and experiment with ways to convey information and feelings, as well as action, through gesture and facial expression.

LANGUAGE LINK `MINI-LESSON`

Handbook of Literary Terms
H E L P

See Epithet.

Epithets

An **epithet** is an adjective or phrase used to characterize someone. *Catherine the Great, baby boomers, The Refrigerator*—these epithets are used to characterize an empress, a generation, and a football player. Homer uses many epithets as formulas to characterize places and people. When Penelope is referred to as "faithful Penelope," we are instantly reminded of her outstanding character trait.

Try It Out

1. Odysseus is called "versatile Odysseus," "wily Odysseus," "the strategist," and "the noble and enduring man." What does each underlined word mean?

2. Telemachus is called "clear-headed Telemachus." How would you define *clear-headed*? What is its opposite?

3. Dawn is described as "rosy-fingered." What does this epithet help you see?

Make up your own epithets for these characters in the *Odyssey*: Odysseus, Calypso, the Cyclops, Circe, Argos, Penelope, the suitors. Then make up epithets for at least three characters that are popular on TV or in the news today (sports stars? singers?).

A Famous Epithet Mystery

One of Homer's most famous epithets is the descriptive phrase "the wine-dark sea." Since wine is red or white or yellowish, and the sea is none of these hues, the description is puzzling. Some say that the ancient Greeks diluted their wine with water and that the alkali in the water changed the color of the wine from red to blue. Others think the sea was covered with red algae. Still others suggest that the Greeks were colorblind. But Robert Fitzgerald, the great translator of the *Odyssey*, thought about the question when he was sailing on the Aegean Sea:

"The contrast of the bare arid baked land against the sea gave the sea such a richness of hue that I felt as though we were sailing through a bowl of dye. The depth of hue of the water was like the depth of hue of a good red wine."

VOCABULARY `HOW TO OWN A WORD`

WORD BANK
adversities
disdainful
adorn
revelry
restitution
glowered
lavished
aloof
pliant
tremulous

Synonyms

Synonyms are words with similar meanings—like *large* and *big*, *subtract* and *deduct*, or *beast* and *monster*. You have to use synonyms with care. Synonyms do not always mean exactly the same thing. Use a diagram like the one here to map synonyms for each word in the Word Bank. Do the synonyms work when you substitute them in the original sentence in the text?

adversities

SYNONYMS
misfortunes, afflictions, difficulties, troubles

ORIGINAL SENTENCE
"I bore adversities. . . ."

RESPONSE TO SUBSTITUTIONS
Adversities suggests intense troubles. *Afflictions* could work. The other words are too mild to describe what Odysseus suffered. They could refer to problems as minor as troubles with your hair.

THE ODYSSEY, PART TWO 953

LANGUAGE LINK

Try It Out
Answers

1. *versatile:* "adaptable"; *wily:* "crafty, sly"; *strategist:* "one skilled in preparing plans for action"; *enduring:* "lasting"

2. *clear-headed:* "rational, not easily confused or overcome by emotions"; its opposite: "illogical, irrational"

3. Possible answer: The epithet creates an image of pink rays of light streaming up from the horizon.
   Students' epithets will vary. Remind students that their epithet should name or describe outstanding character traits.

VOCABULARY
Possible Answers
Students' responses to various substitutions will vary. Students should try at least two synonyms for each word in the Word Bank.

Word Bank	Synonyms
adversities	hardships, troubles
disdainful	haughty, defiant
adorn	bedeck, beautify
revelry	festivity, pleasure
restitution	compensation, payment
glowered	glared, scowled
lavished	bestowed, gave
aloof	detached, alone
pliant	flexible, docile
tremulous	trembling, fearful

Resources ———

Language
• *Grammar and Language Links* Worksheet, p. 63

Vocabulary
• *Words to Own* Worksheet, p. 50

Language Link Quick Check

Epithets
Identify epithets in the following quotations from Homer's other epic, the *Iliad*.

1. ". . . at last his own generous wife came running to meet him, /Andromache, the daughter of high-hearted Eëtion. . . ." [daughter of high-hearted Eëtion]

2. "Then tall Hector of the shining helm answered her. . . ." [of the shining helm]

3. ". . . where all the other/lovely-haired women of Troy propitiate the grim goddess. . . ." [lovely-haired; grim]

4. "Quick-footed Achilles spoke sternly. . . ." [quick-footed]

5. "Thus they buried Hector, tamer of horses." [tamer of horses]

OBJECTIVES
1. Read a photo essay
2. Compare epic motifs in different media
3. Generate relevant and interesting discussion
4. Collaborate on a presentation

Extending the Theme

This photo essay explores the mythic elements in George Lucas's cinematic trilogy *Star Wars*—the hero's trans-forming journey, the obstacles he faces, his heroine companion, and the strug-gle to the death between good and evil—and concludes that the trilogy, like most myths, opens our hearts to the mystery of life and guides us on our own journeys.

Quickwrite

Suggest that students divide their papers into four blocks, labeled "Hero," "Quest," "Monsters," and "Helpers," and let their minds roam freely as they recall other journeys.

RESPONDING TO THE ART

This photo essay is composed of stills from *Star Wars* that illustrate mythic elements of the movie.
Activity. After students have read the essay, ask them to explain how each still illustrates a motif of the epic form.

EXTENDING *the theme*
A PHOTO ESSAY

STAR WARS
A Modern Odyssey

A long time ago in a galaxy far, far away . . .

Quickwrite

By the end of the *Odyssey,* the hero has returned safely from a journey that kept him from home for twenty years. He and his ill-fated crew fought battles, outsmarted a monster and a witch, and faced a man-eating serpent. Our hero has completed his quest, saved his kingdom, and returned to his faithful Penelope.

Homer's account of this journey has inspired other epics as well as countless films, novels, and television series. Think about the road movies of the 1930s and 1940s, the *Star Trek* series of television and film, and brave Frodo saving the world from darkness in *The Lord of the Rings* trilogy. What else were these but journeys to the unknown to fulfill a quest or brave a new world?

Think about the journeys you have read about or seen in the movies or on television. Jot down notes about the heroes, their helpers, the monsters, and the quest itself. Save your notes.

Reaching All Students

Struggling Readers

Students are not likely to have difficulty with the photo essay—most probably will have seen all the *Star Wars* movies—-but they may be less familiar with other quest stories. You may want to prompt them about movies they have seen with archetypal motifs, such as the *Indiana Jones* series, or provide them with a one-page sum-mary of another quest story.

English Language Learners

Ask students to share with the class myths or stories from their own cultures about quests and to use those stories as examples in the Quickwrite and Finding Common Ground activi-ties. If students have seen one or more of the *Star Wars* movies in another language, encour-age them to watch them again in English and to report on how the two viewings differ or how familiarity with the story helps them to under-stand the English versions better.

Advanced Learners

Encourage students to find quest stories about females in young-adult literature. Possibilities include *The True Confessions of Charlotte Doyle* by Avi or Robin McKinley's *The Hero and the Crown.* Students can consult young-adult bibliographies or on-line sources and either report briefly on two stories or analyze one story in depth in terms of the motifs listed on p. 956.

> Throughout the inhabited world, in all times and under every circumstance, the myths of man have flourished; and they have been the living inspiration of whatever else may have appeared out of the activities of the human body and mind.
>
> —Joseph Campbell, from *The Hero with a Thousand Faces*

Princess Leia, a heroine with ideas of her own, is seen in the shadow of the deadly villain Darth Vader.

The *Star Wars* trilogy captured the imaginations of millions of viewers, and the three films remain among the top box-office hits of all time. George Lucas, *Star Wars'* creator, author, and the director of the first film, combined the universal story of the hero's journey with specific concerns and images from our own times. He dramatized the eternal battle of good versus evil and, by suggesting a way to emerge victorious from that battle, fashioned a tale that has all the elements of myth. . . .

From the beginning, *Star Wars* reveals that good and evil are at war. This first film divides good and evil clearly: The dark side uses the power of the Force for aggression, and the light side for defense. The heroes make the right power choices: They seek independence rather than dominance, and they fight because they must, not because they are consumed by bloodlust. The hero . . . is an ordinary character who is put into an extraordinary situation and rises to the occasion. . . .

Luke's journey through the three films transforms him from a rebellious and impatient teenager itching for adventure into a grown-up hero who has confronted his strengths and weaknesses and found the power to help save the world. Along the way, he encounters ogres and wizards, mazes and traps—the archetypal symbols of the hero's journey. In tracking his voyage, we will identify all the classical elements that help to make a myth of *Star Wars*. . . .

Leia, with her take-charge attitude and gutsy, no-nonsense values, her focus on her career, and her fear of rushing into a romantic commitment, is a most appropriate heroine for her time. . . .

Star Wars fulfills the basic function of myth: to open our hearts to the dimension of mystery in our lives and to give us some guidance on our own hero's journey.

—Mary Henderson, from *Star Wars: The Magic of Myth*

STAR WARS: A MODERN ODYSSEY **955**

Responding to the Quotation

Explore with students why myth-making is such a worldwide phenomenon. Discuss the innate power of the human imagination and the human need to create stories that explain the mysteries of the universe. Also note how often myth has served as the inspiration for visual art, music, drama, poetry, and, in modern times, novels, short stories, and films.

Cultural Connections

Star Wars

The *Star Wars* trilogy includes *Star Wars* (1977), *The Empire Strikes Back* (1980), and *Return of the Jedi* (1983). The original *Star Wars*, once the biggest money-making film ever, and its sequels won numerous awards for their special effects, including a number of Oscars. This trilogy is the second half of a longer cinematic narrative. Another trilogy, which consists of prequels detailing the early lives of Obi-Wan Kenobi and Darth Vader, is in the works. The first episode, titled *The Phantom Menace*, was released in the spring of 1999, and the director, George Lucas, plans to make the second and third episodes in the early years of the twenty-first century.

Cultural Connections

Archetypal Heroes

Explain to students that an *archetype* is a perfect example of a type or group. Luke Skywalker, the hero of the trilogy, like other archetypal folk-tale heroes, does not know his true parentage and begins life as a simple farm boy. In the end, however, he comes face to face with his true father—the evil Darth Vader—and must draw on all he has learned to prevail and become a Jedi knight and an intergalactic hero.

Professional Notes

Critical Comment: The Functions of Myth

"Myth basically serves four functions," says mythologist Joseph Campbell. "The first is the mystical function—that is the one I've been speaking about, realizing what a wonder the universe is, and what a wonder you are, and experiencing awe before this mystery. . . . The second is a cosmological dimension, the dimension with which science is concerned—showing you what the shape of the universe is, but showing it in such a way that the mystery again comes through. . . . The third function is the sociological one—supporting and validating a certain social order. And here's where the myths vary enormously from place to place. . . . But there is a fourth function of myth, and this is the one that I think everyone must try today to relate to—and that is the pedagogical function, of how to live a human lifetime under any circumstances. Myths can teach you that." Ask students to analyze the *Odyssey*, *Star Wars*, or another quest story in terms of how it fulfills each of these functions, especially the fourth.

FINDING COMMON GROUND

As its name suggests, this feature asks students to compare and contrast the *Odyssey* and *Star Wars* or another quest film. As an alternative follow-up to their discussions, allow students to prepare their own photo essays (or one compiled from their own artwork) on one of the archetypal motifs, showing how this feature has been handled in a number of different stories.

Point out to students that both Odysseus and Luke Skywalker face monsters, either earth-centered oddities or exotic extraterrestrials. Monsters are a standard feature or archetype in epics and quest films. These creatures of nightmare have fascinated people since ancient times. Sometimes the monster is a hybrid, like the siren (part woman and part bird) or Darth Vader (an amalgam of man and machine). Sometimes the monster has a deformed or aberrant feature, like the Cyclops's single eye; sometimes the monster is a product of exaggeration, again like the giant Cyclops or like the obese Jabba the Hutt, with his corpulent body and elongated mouth. Students may enjoy compiling a rogues' gallery of monsters: Cyclops, Grendel, dragons, Bigfoot, the Abominable Snowman, the Loch Ness Monster, creatures from contemporary horror stories, or monsters in fine art.

The heroes' helpers come in all forms. This one is the "droid" Artoo-Detoo.

A young, idealistic hero, Luke Skywalker talks with Yoda, the second of the mentors who recognize Luke's destiny and guide him on his journey.

FINDING COMMON GROUND

Think about the ancient Greek epic, which takes place three thousand years ago, and the American *Star Wars* series, which is set in the distant future. (If you are unfamiliar with the *Star Wars* movies, you might want to see one on video.) Get together in a

The heroes meet, and then defeat, a number of monsters. One is the malicious Jabba the Hutt, who once imprisoned Luke's friend Han Solo in a tomb of carbonite.

small group to talk about the similarities between the *Odyssey* and *Star Wars* or another quest film you have chosen. Focus on at least five of these *motifs* or features:
- the journey
- the quest for something of great value
- "monsters" that threaten the quest
- helpers, including monsters
- the role of women
- sons and fathers
- disguises
- descents to the underworld
- returns

Now, look at your Quickwrite notes. With your group, discuss the ways in which other books, television shows, or films are like these quest stories. Consider the burdens the hero takes on, the help he or she gets, the rewards at the journey's end.

With your group, decide on a way to present your findings. You might collaborate on an illustrated article on the persistence of the quest in art and film, or you might present the quest as an illustrated children's book.

Skill Link

Comparing Reviews of Literature, Film, and Performance with One's Own Responses

This would be a good opportunity to discuss the ways in which books, movies, and performances are reviewed on television, in newspapers, in magazines, on the radio, and on the Internet. If possible, bring in some reviews as examples. Explain that critics generally apply a set of evaluation criteria to the productions they are reviewing. Evaluation criteria will vary from critic to critic and will also depend on the type of production being reviewed— for example, criteria applied to a movie will differ from criteria applied to a play. Students should prepare reports in which they compare reviews with their own responses. For their reports, students should choose a book they have read, a film they have seen, or a performance they have attended, such as a concert, dance, or play. They should formulate their own responses to the production before finding and reading a review of it. They should then compare and contrast their own responses with those of the reviewer. Give students an opportunity to present their reports to the class.

READ ON

Another Odyssey at Sea

You've read adventure fiction, and you've seen action movies, but *Kon-Tiki* (Pocket/Simon & Schuster) is a real-life adventure story. Thor Heyerdahl journeyed 4,300 nautical miles across the Pacific Ocean—on a log raft. Read this now-classic tale (it has been translated into sixty-five languages) of Heyerdahl's journey and relive the perils that threatened the Kon-Tiki crew: encounters with strange "monsters," leaks in the raft, and life-and-death struggles with a treacherous sea.

A Space Odyssey

It was a routine journey—the fifth time U.S. astronauts had set out for the moon. But on April 13, 1970, Jim Lovell, Fred Haise, and Jack Swigert felt a strange explosion in their spacecraft. The lights dimmed, and the air got thinner. The three astronauts abandoned ship—for a tiny lunar module with room and supplies for only two. *Apollo 13* (Pocket), co-written by Jim Lovell himself (along with Jeffrey Kluger), tells the story of the epic journey. In 1995, the book was made into a successful movie starring Tom Hanks.

An American Odyssey

How far is too far when it comes to survival? You may know that the Donner party was a group migrating to California over one hundred years ago. It was just a few months from winter and the treacherous Sierra Nevada mountains lay between them and their new homes. George R. Stewart's *Ordeal by Hunger* (Houghton Mifflin) is a compelling, terrifying, and human account of the most horrifying of America's pioneer odysseys.

Odysseys at the Movies

A new kind of hero. Follow an unusual hero on a journey through recent American history in *Forrest Gump* (1994).

A modern epic. Harrison Ford brings the heroism and adventure of the old epics to the modern screen in *Indiana Jones and the Last Crusade* (1989).

READ ON **957**

Writer's Workshop

MAIN OBJECTIVE

Write a cause-and-effect essay based on observations and/or reading

PROCESS OBJECTIVES

1. Use appropriate prewriting techniques to identify and develop a topic
2. Create a first draft
3. Use evaluation criteria as a basis for determining revision strategies
4. Revise the first draft, incorporating suggestions generated by self- or peer evaluation
5. Proofread and correct errors
6. Create a final draft
7. Choose an appropriate method of publication
8. Reflect on progress as a writer

Planning

- **Block Schedule**
  Block Scheduling Lesson Plans with Pacing Guide
- **One-Stop Planner**
  CD-ROM with Test Generator

Technology HELP

See Writer's Workshop 2 CD-ROM. *Assignment: Cause and Effect.*

ASSIGNMENT

Write an essay analyzing the cause or the effect of a trend, a situation, or an event. The topic can come from something you've observed firsthand or from something in the news or from a piece of literature you've read.

AIM

To inform; to persuade.

AUDIENCE

Your teacher and classmates; your family; readers of the school newspaper or readers of your local newspaper. (You decide.)

EXPOSITORY WRITING

CAUSE-AND-EFFECT ESSAY

In this workshop you will write an essay analyzing the causes or the effects of a situation, an event, or a trend. You think about cause and effect in many ways each day, from trying to understand the cause of a friend's upset to imagining the effects of choosing one school over another. The ability to think about cause and effect helps a lawyer imagine how a surprise witness might affect the jury. It helps a naturalist figure out the causes of the growth of the mosquito population. It helps a coach figure out how new strategies will affect a game. It calls for creative thinking as well as careful reasoning.

Prewriting

1. Find a Topic

The main thing to keep in mind as you search for a topic is this: It should be one you feel strongly about or are very interested in.

a. **Look through your Writer's Notebook.** Reread your notebook, as well as the Quickwrites you completed as you worked your way through this book, and look for entries that might give you topics for this workshop. For example, as you read the *Odyssey*, did you take notes on any broad topics that seem to apply to life today? What ideas do you have about their causes or the ways they are affecting life today?

b. **Look around you.** What interests you in school, in your community, or in the world? Here is a list that one writer came up with while brainstorming to find a topic:

What are the causes of

- wars today
- conformity among teenagers
- the football team's string of losses this year
- homelessness
- prejudice
- gang membership

 *Resources: Print and Media*

Writing and Language

- *Portfolio Management System*
  Prewriting, p. 218
  Peer Editing, p. 219
  Assessment Rubric, p. 220

- *Workshop Resources*
  Revision Strategy Teaching Notes, p. 57
  Revision Strategy Transparencies 29, 30
- *Writer's Workshop 2 CD-ROM*
  Cause and Effect

The history
of the written
word is rich and tim

What are the effects of

- allowing women to attend military academies
- illiteracy
- closing a playground
- a good education
- having computers in every classroom
- teaching classics like the *Odyssey*

c. **Think about other works of literature you've read.** Stories, essays, and plays in this book show cause-and-effect relationships relating to a variety of topics—a family feud in *Romeo and Juliet,* time travel in Bradbury's "A Sound of Thunder," homelessness in Quindlen's "Homeless." If a particular selection appealed to you, ask yourself if it would provide a good subject for your cause-and-effect essay.

d. **Focus on fads.** What are your favorite—and least favorite—fads or trends? On your own or with classmates, brainstorm to develop lists showing what's in right now in areas such as slang, clothing, food, music, and recreation. Then, scan the lists for items you love—or hate. You might suggest some reasons for the popularity of a certain fad. You might try to figure out how a trend got started, or you might try to predict how it will affect people's lives over the next few years.

2. Find Causes, Effects, and Supporting Details

Once you've chosen your topic, brainstorm to list all its possible causes or effects. Stretch your imagination, and list all the possibilities that occur to you. Don't worry about logic or even repetition—just write. Then, look over your ideas. Choose strong ones that make the most sense, and find evidence that supports them. This evidence may come from your own experiences, from literature you've read in this book, or from information you've gathered from reliable sources. The following chart shows the details that one writer chose to support an analysis of the possible causes of the dropout rate among high school students:

Cause-and-Effect in Persuasion

Look for cause-and-effect strategies used to persuade audiences in

- political campaigns ("If you vote for me, then . . ." or "If you don't vote for me, then . . .")
- advertisements ("If you buy this product, . . .")
- problems and solutions ("If something isn't done soon, . . ." or "This is the best solution because . . .")
- debate ("The opposing view is ineffective because . . .")

WRITER'S WORKSHOP 959

Introducing the Writer's Workshop

Place the following sentences on the board, and have students label one as *Cause* and one as *Effect.*

- John wrecked his car on Elm St. last night. [Effect]
- The rain was terrible last night. [Cause]

Then, have students consider each of the following bits of information, one by one. How does each new fact affect our understanding of the relationship between the first two sentences?

- John's mechanic told him last week that it was time to adjust his brakes.
- John was going 65 mph in a 35-mph zone.
- A water main burst on Elm St., and the paved street collapsed into a 10-foot hole.

Use this experience to remind students that cause-and-effect relationships are seldom tidy. One effect can have multiple causes, and the reverse is also true. Unless the writer researches all possibilities and thinks logically about the alternatives, the accuracy of his or her judgments will be open to question.

Teaching the Writer's Workshop

Prewriting

Review the prewriting steps outlined for students on pp. 958–961. In particular, stress the false cause-and-effect fallacy described on p. 960. Remind students that a writer who does not do sufficient research is particularly vulnerable to this fallacy.

Getting Students Involved

Cooperative Learning

Ask students to help you tell a story, by responding either "Oh, that's good" or "Oh, that's bad" to a list of events that you relate. For example, begin with "I went to town." They respond, "Oh, that's good." You answer, "No, that's bad, because I forgot my money." The students say, "Oh, that's bad." You respond, "No, that's good, because I couldn't buy anything I didn't really need." Continue creating unexpected, jovial turns in the class story until the students see that causes may produce unexpected effects, that a cause may also be an effect, and that an effect may be the cause of something else. After playing the game as a class, divide the students into groups, if you have time, and have them practice the "That's good; that's bad" sequence. Ask that each member of the group contribute one event to the story.

T959

Read through the model with students and focus on the side-column annotations. Then, discuss the model, using discussion questions such as the following:

❓ Why does the author compare modern values, such as productivity and honesty, with the ancient Greek value of hospitality?

❓ What kind of details does the writer suggest to prove that inhospitable behavior in ancient Greece had disastrous consequences?

❓ How do the last three sentences relate to the opening paragraph of this paper?

❓ What techniques does this writer use that you might incorporate into your paper?

Kinds of Support

- statistics
- examples
- anecdotes
- quotations

Kinds of Sources

- magazine and newspaper articles
- interviews
- World Wide Web sites (Look for the domain suffixes *edu* and *gov.*)

Topic: Dropout rate among high school students	
Possible causes	Supporting details
Repeated failure in school	County, state, and national dropout rates over past ten years, broken down by gender
Lack of involvement in school activities	
Limited educational or work goals	Interviews with dropouts
Immediate need to earn money	Interviews with guidance counselor
Problems at home	

3. Avoid False Causes and Effects

In planning your essay, avoid the **false cause-and-effect fallacy.** (A **fallacy** is an error in logical thinking.) Just because one thing happens after something else doesn't mean that the first event *caused* the second event.

EXAMPLE   Bill wore his green shirt last week and passed his algebra test.

False cause-and-effect thinking: Bill passed a math test because he wore a green shirt.

Model

IGNORING HOSPITALITY: THE EFFECTS

It is difficult for modern audiences to understand just how important hospitality was in ancient Greece. Today we place a casual importance on hospitality; we are more concerned with privacy. For the ancient Greeks the opposite was true. It was more important to welcome guests into their homes or towns than it was to maintain their privacy. A modern equivalent to the value they attached to hospitality might be the value we attach to productivity in the workplace. Lazy, nonproductive workers are likely to be fired. We all know what the cause-and-effect relationship is when it comes to laziness.

States topic in first sentence. Uses a comparison with modern life.

Similarly, the Odyssey demonstrates that the ancient Greeks believed that inhospitable behavior was cause for serious consequences, or effects. Hosts and guests were expected to show each other the utmost respect. When one or the other did not, the consequences could be severe: war, a curse by the gods, the loss of a spouse.

Makes thesis clear early on.

Briefly sums up the consequences of inhospitable behavior.

Reaching All Students

Struggling Writers

Students who rarely consider the causes and effects of events in their world may benefit from considering their personal stake in the topic. For example, instead of the general "effects of cuts in federal/state/district spending for education," encourage them to think, "What will happen to *me* if our school doesn't have enough money for computers (or science lab equipment, or athletics, or band, or art, or choir)."

Advanced Learners

After students have composed a draft of their essays, ask them to exchange papers with a partner. Have them pretend to be a person from another country or from another time period. Direct them to read the essays through the lens of that other culture or other time period and to speculate about the questions they would have about the paper's topic. Have the partners discuss the questions and possible changes they would make in the presentation of their arguments.

4. Consider Your Audience

Ask yourself what your readers probably know about your topic. Then, note information that your readers might need, such as background information or definitions of key terms.

Drafting

1. Make It Clear: State Your Topic

Start by describing the situation, event, or trend you are going to talk about. Provide details and background that will help your readers feel comfortable with your topic. Be sure to include a thesis statement in your introduction. It should briefly identify the causes or effects you will discuss in your essay.

2. Make It Convincing: State Your Support

Provide support for each cause or effect you name. Put your supporting details in an appropriate order. Some writers present possible causes or results in time order; others prefer to open with the least important detail and end with a bang—the most important detail.

Framework for a Cause-and-Effect Essay

Introduction: Identify situation or condition; present thesis statement.

Cause (or effect) 1: Support
Cause (or effect) 2: Support
Cause (or effect) 3: Support

Summary

Drafting

- Remind students to double space when they write their drafts. They should also leave extra space in the right margin. These blank spaces will be used for comments and editing marks.
- Remind students that they are providing reasonable arguments, not necessarily absolute proof of their ideas.
- Encourage students to limit the use of personal anecdotes as support.
- Suggest that students limit the time spent in honing their speculations. Explain that they will evaluate the logic and coherence of their arguments in the revision process.
- Set aside enough class time for individual instruction. Some students may have difficulty with this type of more abstract writing.

There are several examples of inhospitable behavior in the <u>Odyssey</u>, and the effects are always disastrous. Odysseus and his men blind the Cyclops in retaliation for his lack of hospitality. Hermes helps Odysseus diminish Circe's powers of sorcery after she lures some of his men to her house and then turns them into pigs. Finally Odysseus slays Penelope's suitors, who have taken over his home without permission and sought to steal his wife.

The effects of inhospitable behavior are always the same in the <u>Odyssey</u>. When a character fails to observe the codes of hospitality, he or she is punished. One lesson this suggests is that actions always have consequences. In our time, a failure to extend hospitality may cause hurt feelings or even end a friendship, but it is less likely to lead to death or war. That's because our values are not the same as those of the ancient Greeks. The one thing that has remained the same, however, is the fact that for every action there is a consequence, for every cause an effect.

Uses strong examples from the text to support the thesis.

Compares ancient values with present-day values.

Provides a strong conclusion.

Crossing the Curriculum

Art

As an alternative or extension activity, invite students to explore the causes and effects of an issue artistically, using a medium of their choice. Collages and mobiles capture students' speculations, for example, and allow them to be more visually creative. Create a gallery of art when the students finish. If possible, pair some artistic and verbal descriptions of cause-and-effect relationships.

Science

Have groups of three students demonstrate simple cause-and-effect experiments to the class. The groups should explain the planned procedure, then ask the class for speculations about what will happen. Have each group finish its experiment, showing which speculation proved correct. Explain that predicting causes and effects of social issues is often open-ended and usually no "correct" answers emerge.

Evaluating and Revising

Have students use the Evaluation Criteria provided here to review their drafts and determine needed revisions.

- Instruct students first in analyzing the Revision Model on p. 962. Explain how the peer comments pinpoint possible problem areas.
- Encourage students to use both peer and self-evaluations of their drafts. Ask them to comment about the benefits of each method of review.
- Look at the Sentence Workshop on Avoiding Wordiness, p. 963. Ask students to reread their essays, looking for places to use simple words and to eliminate unnecessary words and phrases.

Proofreading

Have students proofread their own papers first and then exchange them with other students. For this assignment, remind students to be particularly careful of unintentional errors. Suggest that they read the essay aloud, sentence by sentence, to catch elusive errors.

If time permits, the final copy should be put aside for at least a day before it is proofread for the final time by the author.

Publishing

- Sources for publishing include the school magazine or a local newspaper.
- Preview any Internet publishing, either on your high school's Web home page or on a Usernet newsgroup page, before assigning students to use such a public forum.
- Members of the community who have more extensive experience or who are involved in an action or a study concerning the student's topic may provide a wider audience.

Reflecting

Ask students to freewrite for ten minutes on what they have discovered about their topic and what they have learned about the process of identifying cause-and-effect relationships.

Language/Grammar Link
HELP

Homeric similes: page 927. Epithets: page 953.

Sentence Workshop
HELP

Avoiding wordiness: page 963.

Communications Handbook
HELP

See Proofreaders' Marks.

■ *Evaluation Criteria*

A good essay analyzing causes or effects

1. *clearly states the topic*

2. *clearly answers at least one of these questions: Why did something happen? What are the results of some situation, event, or trend?*

3. *supports a thesis statement with convincing details*

4. *organizes the evidence so that the content is clear*

5. *shows careful reasoning*

Evaluating and Revising

1. Peer Review

Trade drafts with a partner. Make notes about the parts of your partner's essay that seem strongest. Write questions and suggestions that might help the writer. Be sure to comment on the essay's persuasiveness: Is the writer convincing?

Revision Model		Peer Comments
There are several examples		*Good examples, but how do they relate to the thesis?*
of inhospitable behavior in the		
and the effects are always disastrous. Odyssey, Odysseus and his men		
blind the Cyclops in retaliation for		
his lack of hospitality. Circe is *Hermes helps Odysseus diminish 's powers of sorcery*		*Example is unclear. What exactly are the effects on Circe?*
punished after she lures some of his		
men to her house and then turns		
them into pigs. *Finally* Odysseus slays		*Need a transition before last sentence.*
Penelope's suitors, who have taken		
over his home without permission		
and sought to steal his wife.		

2. Self-Evaluation

Think about your peer reviewer's comments. If a reader is confused, you might include more background information. If a reader disagrees with your conclusions, you might add more evidence or recheck your reasoning. To strengthen your position, you might acknowledge the disagreement and respond to it.

Resources

Peer Editing Forms and Rubrics

- *Portfolio Management System*, p. 219

Revision Transparencies

- *Workshop Resources*, p. 57

Grading Timesaver

Rubrics for this Writer's Workshop assignment appear on p. 220 of the *Portfolio Management System*.

BUILDING YOUR PORTFOLIO
Sentence Workshop

REVISING SENTENCES: AVOIDING WORDINESS

Good writers never use more words than are necessary to get the message across. Read the two sentences below. Notice how the unnecessary words make the first sentence hard to follow.

WORDY   The first part of the long epic, consisting of Books 1, 2, 3, and 4, gives us an introduction to the character called Odysseus, the leader of a band of Greeks who fought against their common enemy in the Trojan War.

CONCISE   The first four books of the epic introduce Odysseus, the leader of a band of Greek veterans of the Trojan War.

Here are some tips for creating sentences that aren't wordy:

- Don't use two or three words to say something that can be expressed in one word. Avoid saying things like "owing to the fact that" (just say "since" or "because") and "the question as to whether" (just say "whether").
- Don't use fancy, difficult words when plain, simple ones will express the same idea.
- Don't repeat words or ideas unless absolutely necessary.

Writer's Workshop
Follow-up: Revision

Read a draft of your cause-and-effect essay to a partner. Ask your partner to note wordy or repetitive passages. Review the essay yourself to see if you can streamline your writing by eliminating unnecessary words.

Language Handbook HELP

See Sentence Structure, page 1010.

Technology HELP

See Language Workshop CD-ROM. *Key word entry: wordiness.*

Try It Out

Revise the following sentences by eliminating unnecessary or repetitive words.

1. The *Odyssey* opens with Odysseus' son, Telemachus, searching every corner of the then-known world, which encompassed all the countries bordering on the coast of the Mediterranean Sea, for his long-lost father, who had been absent, away from home for twenty long years.

2. One of Odysseus' most memorable encounters is his unforgettable meeting with the Cyclops, the deformed monster with one eye, by the name of Polyphemus.

3. The wandering Odysseus is waylaid in his seemingly endless journey home by the powerful charms of the persuasive Circe, who tempts him with the delights of sensual pleasures.

4. Odysseus does not inform his crew of men that Circe has foretold that in the future he alone will live to return alive to his homeland, Ithaca, the place where his wife, Penelope, awaits his coming.

5. Owing to the fact that the suitors swarmed over his home as well as his wife, Odysseus was a man who was cautious.

SENTENCE WORKSHOP 963

OBJECTIVE
Revise sentences to eliminate wordiness

Resources

Workshop Resources
- Worksheet, p. 81

Language Workshop CD-ROM
- Wordiness

Try It Out
Possible Answers
1. The *Odyssey* opens with Telemachus searching all the countries bordering the Mediterranean Sea for his father, who has been away from home for twenty years.
2. One of Odysseus' most memorable encounters is with the Cyclops Polyphemus, a one-eyed monster.
3. In his seemingly endless journey home, Odysseus is waylaid by Circe, who tempts him with sensual pleasures.
4. Odysseus does not inform his crew of Circe's prediction that he alone will live to return to Ithaca, where Penelope awaits.
5. Even though the suitors swarmed over his house and courted his wife, Odysseus was cautious.

Assessing Learning

Quick Check: Avoiding Wordiness
In each of the following sentences, underline the word or phrase that is unnecessary.

1. Epics feature an adventuresome hero <u>interested in bold explorations.</u>
2. Alone and unrecognized, Odysseus experienced a <u>solitary</u> return that was hardly a celebration.
3. The faithful Penelope would not allow her <u>steadfast</u> love to be shaken.
4. Odysseus showed a natural, fatherly trust in <u>his son,</u> Telemachus.
5. The reader wonders <u>with a sense of curiosity</u> what might happen now in Ithaca.

T963

OBJECTIVES
1. Develop strategies for comparing and evaluating artistic interpretations
2. Identify emotional responses to a piece of art
3. Analyze a visual interpretation of a specific passage of literature
4. Recognize how historical context shapes an artist's interpretation
5. Analyze essential elements of art

Teaching the Lesson

Explain to students that comparing and evaluating artistic interpretations helps them appreciate works of art. Point out that Tibaldi shows the interior of the Cyclops's cave, whereas Wyeth shows an exterior scene.

Using the Strategies

Possible Answers
1. Student may express fear or sympathy.
2. Tibaldi's Cyclops has one eye (and two eye sockets) rather than one eye, as described in the story. Wyeth's painting accurately shows the blinded one-eyed Cyclops hurling a stone at Odysseus' ship, but the artist has added another Cyclops in the background. Both artists have interpreted the text fairly accurately.
3. Tibaldi's is more menacing and angry; Wyeth's is more lyrical.
4. The Tibaldi is extremely dramatic, with a central focus on the Cyclops accentuated by sharp contrasts of color, shadow, and texture. The Wyeth achieves its powerful effect by the inclusion of the sea, mountains, and sky, against which the Cyclops appears as another great force of nature, compared to the tiny man-made ship.

Situation

For a mural illustrating the *Odyssey*, you're drawing the Cyclops Polyphemus. As part of your research, you examine two portraits of the monster—the one on this page and the one on page 901. Use these strategies when you compare and evaluate artists' interpretations.

Strategies

Note your emotions.
- Your first response to any visual image will most likely be emotional. Acknowledging an emotional response up front clears the way for a response based on reason.

Check for accuracy.
- Does the art illustrate a specific passage in a literary work? If it does, reread the passage. Look carefully for descriptive details. Is each artist's interpretation consistent with the text?
- What does each image suggest about the way the artist interpreted the details of the text?

Research the historical circumstances and the artist's purpose.
- If you know (or can find out) where, when, and why each work was created, think

about how those factors might have influenced the artist's interpretation. For example, Tibaldi's work (page 901) was commissioned in the sixteenth century for a cardinal's palace in Italy. Wyeth's (on this page) was created in the twentieth century for an American children's book.

Analyze the elements.
- Like works of literature, works of art are built on essential elements. Among the elements of a work of art are placement of the images, color, shape, light, shadow, and perspective. How has each artist handled those elements?

Using the Strategies
1. Describe your first response to each painting, Tibaldi's on page 901 and Wyeth's on this page.
2. Reread the passage each artist illustrated. (See "The Cyclops," pages 899–910.) How accurate is each illustration? Have the artists added any details? What can you say about the way each artist interpreted the text?
3. How do the works differ in mood, or tone?

N.C. Wyeth, *Polyphemus, the Cyclops.* Private Collection.

4. Examine the way the two artists used the elements of art. Point out similarities and differences.

Extending the Strategies
1. Add Odilon Redon's *The Cyclops* (page 899) to your analysis.
2. Compare the artistic depictions of Penelope on pages 928 and 947.
3. Find a children's book, and evaluate its illustrations.

964 THE EPIC

Using Students' Strengths

Auditory Learners
Some students may find it easier to evaluate the accuracy of a painting in relation to a text if they can listen to the text description. Read the description of the Cyclops aloud or play an audio recording of the section. As students listen, have them notice how each artist has presented the Cyclops's features.

Learning for Life

Looking at Heroes

OBJECTIVES
1. Identify the qualities a person must have to serve as a role model for young people
2. Identify the potential audience for a presentation
3. Choose and complete a project that presents a role model or expresses an opinion on why role models are needed
4. Reflect on the project

Problem

Odysseus was a hero of his time, and he embodied the characteristics his society valued. Each year magazines and newspapers print lists of the most admired men and women. In some cases these "heroes" are also good role models—but in other cases they're not. What qualities should a person possess to serve as a role model for young people?

Project

Identify a real person, or describe an imaginary one, who qualifies as a good role model.

Preparation

1. With a group of classmates, brainstorm to develop a list of the qualities a role model should have. You may not need to look any further than your own household: Think of a parent or guardian, an older sibling, or another family member. Then move outward, considering people from your neighborhood, school, place of worship, community, state, and nation. Your group may also want to consider characters in stories, poems, and essays you've read.

2. Work together to list the criteria a role model should meet. Be specific. For example, if one criterion is service to others, is it enough that the service is performed, or must it be done willingly, without a concern for self?

Procedure

1. First decide whether you will focus on a real person or describe an imaginary character. If you choose a real person, take notes on what you already know about him or her. (If you need more information, consider interviewing the person or finding library sources that will give you more background.)

2. Decide what audience you'd like to share your ideas with. This can help you to choose the format you'll use and to adapt your ideas to the audience's needs or interests.

Presentation

Use one of the following formats (or another that your teacher approves).

1. Collage

Create a collage that suggests the person's qualities. Combine a variety of materials and objects—drawings, photo-graphs, scraps of material, words, or anything you find meaningful. Give your collage a catchy title. Exhibit your work at the next open house or meeting of the parent-teacher organization.

2. Personality Profile

Write a one-page profile of the person, using headings such as these: Name, Home, Occupation, Hobbies, Latest Accomplishment, and Goals. If possible, include a statement by the person. Post your profile in the classroom, and if it is about a real person, give him or her a copy.

3. Personal Essay

Write a personal essay express-ing your views on why young people need role models and where they can find them. Submit your essay to the community or school news-paper or to a magazine that accepts student writing. (Your media specialist can help you find a suitable magazine.)

Processing

What did you learn about your own values by doing this project? What was most difficult for you? most reward-ing? Write a reflection for your portfolio that includes answers to these questions.

Resources ——————

Viewing and Representing
HRW Multimedia Presentation Maker
Students may wish to use the *Multime-dia Presentation Maker* to create their presentation of the qualities of a role model.

Grading Timesaver

Rubrics for this Learning for Life project appear on p. 221 of the *Portfo-lio Management System*.

Developing Workplace Competencies

Preparation	Procedure	Presentation
• Works on teams	• Evaluates data	• Communicates ideas and information
• Exhibits sociability	• Interprets information	• Evaluates data
• Thinks creatively	• Makes decisions	• Reasons

RESOURCE CENTER

HANDBOOK OF LITERARY TERMS

For more information about a topic, turn to the page(s) in this book that are indicated on a separate line at the end of the entry. For example, to learn more about *Alliteration,* turn to page 560.

On another line are cross-references to entries in this handbook that provide closely related information. For instance, at the end of *Alliteration* is a cross-reference to *Assonance.*

ALLITERATION **Repetition of the same or very similar consonant sounds in words that are close together in a poem.** In this example the sounds "fl," "t," "n," and "w" are repeated in line 1, and the "s" sound is repeated in line 2:

> Open here I flung the shutter, when with
>   many a flirt and flutter,
> In there stepped a stately Raven of the saintly
>   days of yore.
>
> —Edgar Allan Poe, from "The Raven"

See page 560.
See also *Assonance.*

ALLUSION **Reference to a statement, a person, a place, or an event from literature, history, religion, mythology, politics, sports, science, or pop culture.** In calling one of his stories "The Gift of the

"I think I'll wait for the next elevator."

Drawing by Chas. Addams; © 1988 The New Yorker Magazine, Inc.

Magi" (page 202), O. Henry used an allusion to the wise men from the East called the Magi, who presented the infant Jesus with the first Christmas gifts.

ANALOGY **Comparison made between two things to show how they are alike in some respects.** During the Revolutionary War the writer Thomas Paine drew an analogy between a thief breaking into a house and the king of England interfering in the affairs of the American Colonies (*The Crisis,* No. 1). Similes are a kind of analogy. However, an analogy usually clarifies something, while a simile shows imaginatively how two different things are alike in some unusual way.

ANECDOTE **Very brief account of an incident.** Like parables, anecdotes often point out or illustrate a truth about life. For example, in her essay "Homeless" (page 461), Anna Quindlen uses an anecdote about a homeless woman to introduce a discussion of homelessness.

See pages 454, 458.

ARGUMENT **Form of persuasion that uses reason to try to lead a reader or listener to think or act in a certain way.** Like all persuasive writing, argument is aimed at winning people to the writer's point of view, but argument uses only facts and logical reasoning to achieve its purpose. (Other persuasive writing may use different methods, including an unashamed appeal to the emotions.) Debating societies use arguments to win points. Good arguments may be found in editorials and magazine articles.

See pages 452–453.
See also *Persuasion.*

ASIDE **Words that are spoken by a character in a play to the audience or to another character but that are not supposed to be overheard by the others onstage.** Stage directions usually tell when a speech is an aside. For example, in Shakespeare's *Romeo and Juliet* (page 735), there are two asides in the opening scene. Sampson speaks to Gregory in an aside, and Gregory responds to him in another aside as they pick a fight with the servants of the house of Montague. Sampson and Gregory hear each other's asides, and so do we in the audience, but Montague's servants do not.

See page 768.

HANDBOOK OF LITERARY TERMS 967

ASSONANCE **Repetition of similar vowel sounds that are followed by different consonant sounds, especially in words that are close together in a poem.** The words *base* and *fade* and the words *young* and *love* are examples of assonance. The lines that follow are especially musical because of assonance:

> Seeing the snowman standing all alone
> In dusk and cold is more than he can bear.
> The small boy weeps to hear the wind prepare
> A night of gnashings and enormous moan.
>
> —Richard Wilbur,
> from "Boy at the Window"

See also *Alliteration, Onomatopoeia, Rhyme.*

AUTHOR **The writer of a literary work.**

AUTOBIOGRAPHY **An account of the writer's own life.** An example of a book-length autobiography is *I Know Why the Caged Bird Sings* by Maya Angelou (see page 357). Abraham Lincoln's "Not Much of Me" (page 348) is an example of an autobiographical essay.

See page 355.
See also *Biography.*

BALLAD **Song that tells a story. Folk ballads** are composed by unknown singers and are passed on for generations before they are written down. **Literary ballads,** on the other hand, are composed by known individuals and are written down in imitation of the old folk ballads. "Ballad of Birmingham" by Dudley Randall (page 383) is a modern literary ballad. Ballads usually tell sensational stories of tragedy or adventure. They use simple language and a great deal of repetition and usually have regular rhythm and rhyme schemes, which make them easy to memorize.

BIOGRAPHY **An account of a person's life, written or told by another person.** A classic American biography is Carl Sandburg's multivolume life of Abraham Lincoln. Today biographies are written about movie stars, TV personalities, politicians, sports figures, self-made millionaires, even underworld figures. Biographies are among the most popular forms of contemporary literature. "Annie" (page 710) is an excerpt from Joseph P. Lash's biography of Helen Keller and her teacher, Annie Sullivan.

See page 355.
See also *Autobiography.*

BLANK VERSE **Poetry written in unrhymed iambic pentameter.** *Blank* means the poetry is not rhymed. *Iambic pentameter* means that each line contains five iambs, or metrical feet that consist of an unstressed syllable followed by a stressed syllable ($\smile\,\prime$). Blank verse is the most important poetic form in English epic and dramatic poetry. It is the major verse form in Shakespeare's plays.

See pages 740–741.
See also *Iambic Pentameter, Meter.*

CHARACTER **Person in a story, poem, or play.** Sometimes, as in George Orwell's novel *Animal Farm,* the characters are animals. In myths the characters are divinities or heroes who have superhuman powers, such as Poseidon and Athena and Odysseus in the *Odyssey* (page 889). Most often a character is an ordinary human being, like the grandmother in Toni Cade Bambara's "Blues Ain't No Mockin Bird" (page 267).

The process of revealing the personality of a character in a story is called **characterization.** A writer can reveal a character by

1. letting us hear the character speak
2. describing how the character looks and dresses
3. letting us listen to the character's inner thoughts and feelings
4. revealing what other characters in the story think or say about the character
5. showing us what the character does—how he or she acts
6. telling us directly what the character's personality is like: cruel, kind, sneaky, brave, and so on

The first five ways of revealing a character are known as **indirect characterization.** When a writer uses indirect characterization, we have to use our own judgment to decide what a character is like, based on the evidence the writer gives us. But when a writer uses the sixth method, known as **direct characterization,** we don't have to decide for ourselves; we are told directly what the character is like.

Characters can be classified as static or dynamic. A **static character** is one who does not change much in the course of a story. By contrast, a **dynamic character** changes as a result of the story's events.

Characters can also be classified as flat or round. A **flat character** has only one or two traits, and these can be described in a few words. Such a character has no depth, like a piece of cardboard. A **round character,** like a real person, has many different character traits, which sometimes contradict one another.

The fears or conflicts or needs that drive a character are called **motivation**. A character can be motivated by many factors, such as vengeance, fear, greed, love, even boredom.

See pages 120, 130–131, 144, 627–628.

CLIMAX Moment of great emotional intensity or suspense in a plot. The major climax in a story or play usually marks the moment when the conflict is decided one way or another.

See pages 32–33, 34, 258, 627, 732.

COMEDY In general, a story that ends happily. The hero or heroine of a comedy is usually an ordinary character who overcomes a series of obstacles that block what he or she wants. Many comedies have a boy-meets-girl plot, in which young lovers must face obstacles to their marrying. At the end of such comedies, the lovers marry, and everyone celebrates, as in Shakespeare's play *A Midsummer Night's Dream*. In structure and characterization, a comedy is the opposite of a tragedy.

See also *Comic Relief, Tragedy.*

COMIC RELIEF Comic scene or event that breaks up a serious play or narrative. Comic relief allows writers to lighten the tone of a work and show the humorous side of a dramatic theme. In Shakespeare's tragedy *Romeo and Juliet* (page 735), the nurse and Mercutio provide comic relief.

CONFLICT Struggle or clash between opposing characters or opposing forces. In an **external conflict,** a character struggles against an outside force. This outside force might be another character, or society as a whole, or something in nature. "The Most Dangerous Game" by Richard Connell (page 13) is about the external conflict between the evil General Zaroff and the hunter Rainsford. By contrast, an **internal conflict** takes place entirely within a character's own mind. An internal conflict is a struggle between opposing needs or desires or emotions within a single person. In James Hurst's "The Scarlet Ibis" (page 315), the young narrator struggles with an internal conflict—between love for his brother and hatred of his brother's disabilities. Many works, especially longer ones, contain both internal and external conflicts, and an external conflict often leads to internal problems.

See pages 12, 32–33, 626–627.

CONNOTATION All the meanings, associations, or emotions that a word suggests. For example, *skinny* and *slender* both have the same literal definition—"thin." But their connotations are completely different. If you call someone skinny, you are saying something unflattering. If you call someone slender, you are paying him or her a compliment. The British philosopher Bertrand Russell once gave a classic example of the different connotations of words: "I am firm. You are obstinate. He is a pigheaded fool." Connotations, or the suggestive power of certain words, play an important role in creating **mood**.

See page 451.
See also *Diction, Tone.*

COUPLET Two consecutive lines of poetry that rhyme. Alexander Pope wrote this sarcastic couplet for a dog's collar (Kew is a place in England):

I am his Highness' dog at Kew;
Pray tell me, Sir, whose dog are you?

—Alexander Pope

Couplets work nicely for humor and satire because the punch line comes so quickly. However, they are most often used to express a completed thought. In Shakespeare's plays an important speech or scene often ends with a couplet.

See page 740.

DESCRIPTION Type of writing intended to create a mood or emotion or to re-create a person, a place, a thing, an event, or an experience. Description is one of the four major techniques used in writing. (The others are **narration, exposition,** and **persuasion.**) Description works by creating images that appeal to the senses of sight, smell, taste, hearing, or touch. Writers use description in all forms of fiction, nonfiction, and poetry.

See page 452.
See also *Imagery.*

DIALECT Way of speaking that is characteristic of a particular region or a particular group of people. Dialects may have a distinct vocabulary, pronunciation system, and grammar. In a sense, we all speak dialects; but one dialect usually becomes dominant in a country or culture and becomes accepted as the standard way of speaking. In the United States, for example, the formal

written language is known as standard English. (This is what you usually hear spoken by TV newscasters on the national channels.)

See page 277.

DICTION **A writer's or speaker's choice of words.** Diction is an essential element of a writer's **style**. Some writers use simple, down-to-earth, or even slang words (*house, home, digs*); others use ornate, official-sounding, or even flowery language (*domicile, residence, abode*). The **connotations** of words are an important aspect of diction.

See page 211.
See also *Connotation, Tone.*

DRAMA **Story that is written to be acted for an audience.** The action of a drama is usually driven by a character who wants something and takes steps to get it. The elements of a dramatic plot are **exposition, complications, climax,** and **resolution**.

See pages 626–630.

EPIC **Long story told in elevated language (usually poetry), which relates the great deeds of a larger-than-life hero who embodies the values of a particular society.** Most epics include elements of myth, legend, folk tale, and history. Their tone is serious and their language is grand. Most epic heroes undertake quests to achieve something of tremendous value to themselves or their people. Often the hero's quest is set in both heaven and hell. Homer's *Iliad* and *Odyssey* (page 889) are the best-known epics in Western civilization. The great epic of ancient Rome is Virgil's *Aeneid,* which, like the *Iliad* and *Odyssey,* is based on events that happened during and immediately after the Trojan War.

See pages 878–884.

EPITHET **Adjective or descriptive phrase that is regularly used to characterize a person, place, or thing.** We speak of "Honest Abe," for example, and "America the Beautiful."

Homer created so many epithets in his *Iliad* and *Odyssey* that his name is permanently associated with a type of epithet. The **Homeric epithet** in most English translations consists of a compound adjective that is regularly used to modify a particular noun. Three famous examples are "*wine-dark* sea," "*rosy-fingered* dawn," "the *gray-eyed* goddess Athena."

See page 953.

ESSAY **Short piece of nonfiction that examines a single subject from a limited point of view.** Most essays can be categorized as either **personal** or **formal**.

A **personal essay** (sometimes called an **informal essay**) generally reveals a great deal about the writer's personality and tastes. Its tone is often conversational, sometimes even humorous.

A **formal essay** is usually serious, objective, and impersonal in tone. Its purpose is to inform its readers about some topic of interest or to persuade them to accept the writer's views. The statements in a formal essay should be supported by facts and logic.

See page 399.

EXPOSITION **Type of writing that explains, gives information, defines, or clarifies an idea.** Exposition is one of the four major techniques used in writing. (The others are **narration, description,** and **persuasion**.) We find exposition in news articles, in histories, in biographies (and even in cookbook recipes). In fact, each entry in this Handbook of Literary Terms is an example of exposition.

Exposition is also the term for that part of a plot that gives information about the characters and their problems or conflicts.

See page 452.
See also *Plot.*

FABLE **Very brief story in prose or verse that teaches a moral, or a practical lesson about how to get along in life.** The characters of most fables are animals that behave and speak like human beings. Some of the most popular fables are those attributed to Aesop, who is supposed to have been a slave in ancient Greece.

See page 100.
See also *Folk Tale, Tall Tale.*

FIGURE OF SPEECH **Word or phrase that describes one thing in terms of another and is not meant to be understood on a literal level.** Figures of speech, or **figurative language,** always involve some sort of imaginative comparison between seemingly unlike things.

Some 250 different types of figures of speech have been identified. The most common are the **simile** ("I wandered lonely as a cloud"), the **metaphor** ("Fame is a bee"), and **personification** ("The wind stood up and gave a shout").

See pages 520–521.
See also *Metaphor, Personification, Simile.*

FLASHBACK **Scene in a movie, play, short story, novel, or narrative poem that interrupts the present action of the plot to flash backward and tell what happened at an earlier time.** That is, a flashback breaks the normal time sequence of events in the narrative, usually to give the readers or viewers some background information that helps them make sense of the story. Much of the *Odyssey* (page 889) is told in the form of a flashback, as Odysseus describes his previous adventures to the Phaeacian court of King Alcinous. Flashbacks are extremely common storytelling devices in movies. In fact, the word *flashback* comes from film criticism, and it has spread to the rest of literature.

See page 686.

FOIL **Character who is used as a contrast to another character.** A writer uses a foil to accentuate and clarify the distinct qualities of two characters. The word *foil* is also used for a thin sheet of shiny metal that is placed beneath a gem to intensify its brilliance. A character who is a foil, like the metal behind the gem, sets off or intensifies the qualities of another character. In Shakespeare's *Romeo and Juliet* (page 735), the cynical, sophisticated Mercutio is a foil to the romantic, naive Romeo.

See page 762.

FOLK TALE **Story that has no known author and was originally passed on from one generation to another by word of mouth.** Unlike myths, which are about gods and heroes, folk tales are usually about ordinary people, as in "The Talking Skull" (page 247). Folk tales tend to travel, and you'll often find the same motifs—elements such as characters, images, and story lines—in the tales of different cultures. For example, there are said to be nine hundred versions of the folk tale about Cinderella.

See page 244.
See also *Fable, Tall Tale.*

FORESHADOWING **The use of clues to hint at events that will occur later in a plot.** Foreshadowing is used to build suspense and, sometimes, anxiety in the reader or viewer. In a drama the gun found in a bureau drawer in Act I is likely to foreshadow violence later in the play. In "The Cask of Amontillado" (page 233), Poe uses foreshadowing skillfully. For example, when Montresor produces a trowel from beneath his cloak, he is foreshadowing the means he will use to murder his enemy. When later he begins to build a wall around Fortunato, we remember that trowel.

See page 50.

FREE VERSE **Poetry that does not have a regular meter or rhyme scheme.** Poets writing in free verse try to capture the natural rhythms of ordinary speech. To create its music, free verse may use **internal rhyme, alliteration, onomatopoeia, refrain,** and **parallel structure.** For an example of a poem written in free verse, read "When I Heard the Learn'd Astronomer" (page 496).

See page 555.
See also *Meter, Rhythm.*

HAIKU **Japanese verse form consisting of three lines and, usually, seventeen syllables (five in the first line, seven in the second, and five in the third).** The writer of a haiku uses association and suggestion to describe a particular moment of discovery or enlightenment. A haiku often presents an image of daily life that relates to a particular season.

See page 499.

HYPERBOLE **Figure of speech that uses exaggeration to express strong emotion or to create a comic effect.** Writers often use hyperbole (hī·pur′bə·lē), called **overstatement,** to intensify a description or to emphasize the essential nature of something. If you say that a limousine is as long as an ocean liner, you are using hyperbole.

See page 375.

IAMBIC PENTAMETER **Line of poetry that contains five iambs.** An **iamb** is a metrical foot, or unit of measure, consisting of an unstressed syllable followed by a stressed syllable (⏑ ′). *Pentameter* comes from the Greek

HANDBOOK OF LITERARY TERMS 971

penta (five) and *meter* (measure). Here is one iamb: arı́se. Here is a line measuring five iambs:

But soft! What light through yonder window breaks?

—William Shakespeare,
from *Romeo and Juliet*

Iambic pentameter is by far the most common verse line in English poetry.

See pages 740–741.
See also *Blank Verse, Meter, Rhythm.*

IDIOM Expression peculiar to a particular language that means something different from the literal meaning of each word. "It's raining cats and dogs" and "We heard it through the grapevine" are idioms of American English. One of the difficulties of translating a work from another language is translating the idioms.

IMAGERY Language that appeals to the senses. Most images are visual—that is, they create pictures in the reader's mind by appealing to the sense of sight. Images can also appeal to the senses of sound, touch, taste, or smell or even to several senses at once. Imagery is an element in all types of writing, but it is especially important in poetry. The following lines contain images that make us see, hear, and even smell what the speaker experiences as he travels to meet someone he loves.

Then a mile of warm sea-scented beach;
Three fields to cross till a farm appears;
A tap at the pane, the quick sharp scratch
And blue spurt of a lighted match . . .

—Robert Browning,
from "Meeting at Night"

See pages 492–493.
See also *Description.*

INVERSION Reversal of the normal word order of a sentence. The elements of a standard English sentence are subject, verb, and complement, and in most sentences that is the order in which they appear. (*Ray rowed the boat.*) Writers use inversion for emphasis and variety. They may also use it for more technical reasons—to create end rhymes or to accommodate a given meter. In a

statement about Ulysses S. Grant and Robert E. Lee, the historian Bruce Catton wrote, "Daring and resourcefulness they had too. . . ." Catton inverted the order of the parts of the sentence so that the important words (*daring* and *resourcefulness*) came first.

IRONY Contrast or discrepancy between expectation and reality—between what is said and what is really meant, between what is expected to happen and what really does happen, or between what appears to be true and what is really true.

In **verbal irony,** a writer or speaker says one thing but really means something completely different. If you call a clumsy basketball player "the new Michael Jordan," you are using verbal irony. The murderer in Edgar Allan Poe's "The Cask of Amontillado" (page 233) is using verbal irony when he says to his unsuspecting victim, ". . . your health is precious."

Situational irony occurs when there is a contrast between what would seem appropriate and what really happens or when there is a contradiction between what we expect to happen and what really does take place.

Dramatic irony occurs when the audience or the reader knows something important that a character in a play or story does not know. In Shakespeare's *Romeo and Juliet* (page 735), we know, but Romeo *does not,* that when he finds Juliet in the tomb, she is drugged, not dead. Thus we feel a terrible sense of dramatic irony as we watch Romeo kill himself upon discovering her body.

See pages 202, 212–213.
See also *Satire, Tone.*

LYRIC POETRY Poetry that does not tell a story but is aimed only at expressing a speaker's emotions or thoughts. Most lyrics are short, and they usually imply, rather than directly state, a single strong emotion. The term *lyric* comes from the Greek. In ancient Greece, lyric poems were recited to the accompaniment of a stringed instrument called a lyre. Today poets still try to make their lyrics "sing," but they rely only on the musical effects they create with words (such as **rhyme, rhythm,** and **onomatopoeia**).

See also *Sonnet.*

METAPHOR Figure of speech that makes a comparison between two unlike things, in which one thing becomes another thing without the use of the word *like, as, than,* or *resembles.* The poet

Robert Burns's famous comparison "O my love is like a red, red rose" is a simile. If he had written "O my love *is* a red, red rose" or "O my love bursts into bloom," he would have been using a metaphor.

Notice that the comparison in the second metaphor above is implied, or suggested, rather than directly stated, as it is in the first metaphor. An **implied metaphor** does not tell us directly that one thing *is* something else. Instead, it uses words that suggest the nature of the comparison. The phrase "bursts into bloom" implies that the feeling of love is like a budding flower.

An **extended metaphor** is a metaphor that is extended, or developed, over several lines of writing or even throughout an entire poem.

A **dead metaphor** is a metaphor that has been used so often that we no longer realize it is a figure of speech—we simply skip over the metaphorical connection it makes. Examples of dead metaphors are *the roof of the mouth, the eye of the storm, the heart of the matter,* and *the arm of a chair.*

A **mixed metaphor** is the inconsistent mixture of two or more metaphors. Mixed metaphors are a common problem in bad writing, and they are often unintentionally funny. You are using a mixed metaphor if you say "Put it on the back burner and let it germinate" or "That's a very hard blow to swallow" or "Let's set sail and get this show on the road."

> See pages 520–521, 858.
> See also *Figure of Speech, Personification, Simile.*

METER   Generally regular pattern of stressed and unstressed syllables in poetry. When we want to indicate the metrical pattern of a poem, we mark the stressed syllables with the symbol (′) and the unstressed syllables with the symbol (˘). Indicating the metrical pattern of a poem in this way is called **scanning** the poem, or **scansion** (skan′shən). Notice the pattern of stressed and unstressed syllables in the first four lines of this poem:

> Slowly, silently, now the moon
>
> Walks the night in her silver shoon;
>
> This way, and that, she peers, and sees
>
> Silver fruit upon silver trees. . . .
>
> —Walter de la Mare, from "Silver"

> See pages 554–555.
> See also *Blank Verse, Iambic Pentameter.*

MYTH   Traditional story that is rooted in a particular culture, is basically religious, and usually serves to explain a belief, a ritual, or a mysterious natural phenomenon. Most myths grew out of religious rituals, and almost all of them involve the influence of gods on human affairs. Every culture has its own mythology. For many centuries the myths of ancient Greece and Rome were very influential in the Western world.

> See pages 878–884.

NARRATION   Type of writing or speaking that tells about a series of related events. Narration is one of the four major techniques used in writing. (The others are **description, exposition,** and **persuasion.**) Narration can be any length, from a brief paragraph to an entire book. It is most often found in short stories, novels, epics, and ballads. But narration is also used in any piece of nonfiction that relates a series of events that tell what happened—such as a biography, essay, or news story—and even in a scientific analysis or a report of a business meeting.

> See page 452.
> See also *Point of View.*

NONFICTION   Prose writing that deals with real people, things, events, and places. The most popular forms of nonfiction are **biography** and **autobiography.** Other examples include essays, newspaper stories, magazine articles, historical writing, scientific reports, and even personal diaries and letters.

> See page 342.

NOVEL   Fictional prose narrative usually consisting of more than fifty thousand words. In general, the novel uses the same basic literary elements as the short story (**plot, character, setting, theme,** and **point of view**) but develops them more fully. Many novels have several subplots, for instance. Modern writers often do away with one or more of the novel's traditional elements. Some novels today are basically character studies, with only the barest, stripped-down story lines.

ONOMATOPOEIA   (än′ō·mat′ō·pē′ə)   Use of a word whose sound imitates or suggests its meaning. Onomatopoeia is so natural to us that we begin using it instinctively as children. *Crackle, pop, fizz, click, zoom,* and

HANDBOOK OF LITERARY TERMS 973

chirp are examples of onomatopoeia. Onomatopoeia is an important element in the music of poetry.

> And in the hush of waters was the sound
> Of pebbles, rolling round;
> Forever rolling, with a hollow sound:
>
> And bubbling seaweeds, as the waters go,
> Swish to and fro
> Their long cold tentacles of slimy gray. . . .
>
> —James Stephens, from "The Shell"

See page 560.
See also *Alliteration, Assonance.*

PARADOX **Statement or situation that seems to be a contradiction but reveals a truth.** Paradoxes in literature are designed to make readers stop and think. They often express aspects of life that are mysterious, surprising, or difficult to describe. When O. Henry, in "The Gift of the Magi" (page 202), refers to the impoverished Della and Jim as "one of the richest couples on earth," he is stating a paradox.

PARALLELISM **Repetition of words, phrases, or sentences that have the same grammatical structure or that state a similar idea.** Parallelism, or **parallel structure,** helps make lines rhythmic and memorable and heightens their emotional effect:

> It was the best of times, it was the worst of times, it was the age of wisdom, it was the age of foolishness, it was the epoch of belief, it was the epoch of incredulity, it was the season of Light, it was the season of Darkness, it was the spring of hope, it was the winter of despair, we had everything before us, we had nothing before us, we were all going direct to Heaven, we were all going direct the other way. . . .
>
> —Charles Dickens, from *A Tale of Two Cities*

See pages 467, 721.

PERSONIFICATION **Kind of metaphor in which a nonhuman thing or quality is talked about as if it**

974 HANDBOOK OF LITERARY TERMS

were human. Here are a few lines in which poetry itself is personified—that is, it is described as behaving and feeling the way people do:

> This poetry gets bored of being alone,
> it wants to go outdoors to chew on the
>   winds,
> to fill its commas with the keels of
>   rowboats. . . .
>
> —Hugo Margenat, from "Living Poetry"

See pages 520–521, 858.
See also *Figure of Speech, Metaphor.*

PERSUASION **Type of writing that is aimed at leading the reader or listener to think or act in a certain way.** Examples of persuasive writing are found in newspaper editorials, in speeches, and in many essays and articles. Persuasion can use language that appeals to the emotions, or it can use logic to appeal to reason. When persuasive writing appeals to reason and not to the emotions, it is called **argument.**

See pages 452–453.
See also *Argument.*

PLOT **Series of related events that make up a story or drama.** Plot is what happens in a story, novel, or play. An outline showing the "bare bones" of a plot would include the story's **basic situation,** or **exposition;** the **conflict,** or problem; the **main events** (including **complications**); the final **climax;** and **resolution,** or **denouement.**

See pages 32–33, 626–630.
See also *Exposition.*

POETRY **Type of rhythmic, compressed language that uses figures of speech and imagery to appeal to the reader's emotions and imagination.** The major forms of poetry are the **lyric,** the **epic,** and the **ballad.** Beyond this, poetry is difficult to define, though many readers feel it is easy to recognize. The poet Wallace Stevens, for example, once described poetry as "a search for the inexplicable."

See page 488.
See also *Ballad, Epic, Lyric Poetry.*

POINT OF VIEW Vantage point from which a writer tells a story. In broad terms there are three possible points of view: omniscient, first-person, and third-person limited.

In the **omniscient** (or "all-knowing") **point of view,** the person telling the story knows everything there is to know about the characters and their problems. This all-knowing narrator can tell us about the past, the present, and the future of all the characters. He or she can even tell us what the characters are thinking. The narrator can also tell us what is happening in other places. In the omniscient point of view, the narrator is not in the story at all. In fact, the omniscient narrator is like a god telling the story.

In the **first-person point of view,** one of the characters is actually the narrator telling the story, using the pronoun *I.* We get to know this narrator very well, but we can know only what this character knows, and we can observe only what this character observes. All of our information about the events in the story must come from this one character.

In the **third-person limited point of view,** the narrator, who plays no part in the story, zooms in on the thoughts and feelings of just one character. With this point of view, we observe the action through the eyes and with the feelings of this one character.

See pages 218–219, 220.

PROTAGONIST **Main character in fiction or drama.** The protagonist is the character we focus our attention on, the person who sets the plot in motion. The character or force that blocks the protagonist is the **antagonist.** Most protagonists are rounded, dynamic characters who change in some important way by the end of the story, novel, or play. The antagonist is often but not always the villain in the story. Similarly, the protagonist is often but not always the hero.

See page 626.

PUN **Play on the multiple meanings of a word or on two words that sound alike but have different meanings.** Most often puns are used for their humorous effects; they are used in jokes all the time. ("What has four wheels and flies?" Answer: "A garbage truck.") Shakespeare was one of the great punsters of all time. The servants in *Romeo and Juliet* (page 735) make crude puns as they clown around at the start of the play. Later, Romeo and his friend Mercutio trade wits in a series of more sophisticated puns. Since word meanings change so quickly, some of Shakespeare's puns are barely understandable to us today, just as puns popular today may be puzzling to people a hundred years from now.

See pages 489, 524, 858.

"Does the doctor make mouse calls?"

Drawing by Bernard Schoenbaum; © 1991 The New Yorker Magazine, Inc.

REFRAIN **Repeated word, phrase, line, or group of lines.** Though refrains are usually associated with songs and poems, they are also used in speeches and other forms of literature. Refrains are most often used to build rhythm, but they may also provide commentary or build suspense.

See page 574.

RHYME **Repetition of accented vowel sounds, and all sounds following them, in words that are close together in a poem.** *Choice* and *voice* are rhymes, as are *tingle* and *jingle.*

End rhymes occur at the ends of lines. In this poem the words *defense/tense, know/go,* and *Spain/Maine* are end rhymes:

Old Mary

My last defense
Is the present tense.
It little hurts me now to know
I shall not go
Cathedral-hunting in Spain
Nor cherrying in Michigan or Maine.

—Gwendolyn Brooks

Internal rhymes occur in the middle of a line. This line has an internal rhyme (*dreary* rhymes with *weary*):

> Once upon a midnight dreary, while I
> pondered, weak and weary

> —Edgar Allan Poe, from "The Raven"

When two words have some sound in common but do not rhyme exactly, they are called **approximate rhymes** (or **near rhymes,** or **slant rhymes**). In Brooks's poem on this page, the words *now* and *know* are approximate rhymes.

The pattern of rhymes in a poem is called a **rhyme scheme.** The rhyme scheme of a stanza or poem is indicated by the use of a different letter of the alphabet for each rhyme. For example, the rhyme scheme of Brooks's poem is *aabbcc.*

RHYTHM   Musical quality in language produced by repetition. Rhythm occurs naturally in all forms of spoken and written language. The most obvious kind of rhythm is produced by **meter,** the regular repetition of stressed and unstressed syllables found in some poetry. But writers can also create rhythm by using rhymes, by repeating words and phrases, and even by repeating whole lines or sentences. This stanza by Walt Whitman is written in free verse and so does not follow a metrical pattern. Yet the lines are rhythmical because of Whitman's repeated use of certain sentence structures, words, and sounds.

> Give me the splendid silent sun with all his
>   beams full-dazzling,
> Give me juicy autumnal fruit ripe and red
>   from the orchard,
> Give me a field where the unmowed grass
>   grows,
> Give me an arbor, give me the trellised grape,
> Give me fresh corn and wheat, give me
>   serene-moving animals teaching content,
> Give me nights perfectly quiet as on high
>   plateaus west of the Mississippi, and I
>   looking up at the stars. . . .

> —Walt Whitman, from "Give Me the
> Splendid Silent Sun"

See pages 554–555.
See also *Meter.*

976 HANDBOOK OF LITERARY TERMS

SATIRE   Type of writing that ridicules something—a person, a group of people, humanity at large, an attitude or failing, a social institution—in order to reveal a weakness. Most satires are an attempt to convince us of a point of view or to persuade us to follow a course of action. They do this by pointing out how the opposite point of view or action is ridiculous or laughable. Satire often involves **exaggeration**—the act of overstating something to make it look worse than it is. For example, in the satiric short story "Harrison Bergeron" (page 133), Kurt Vonnegut exaggerates the conditions in his imagined future society so that we can see the flaws in our own society.

See page 132.
See also *Irony, Tone.*

SETTING   The time and place of a story or play. Most often the setting of a narrative is established early in the story. For example, in the fourth paragraph of "The Cask of Amontillado" (page 233), Edgar Allan Poe tells his readers, "It was about dusk, one evening during the supreme madness of the carnival season. . . ." Setting often contributes to a story's emotional effect. In "The Cask of Amontillado" the descriptions of the gloomy Montresor palace, with its damp catacombs full of bones, help create the story's mood of horror. Setting can also contribute to the conflict in a story, as the harsh environment does in Dorothy Johnson's "A Man Called Horse" (page 167). Setting can also be used to reveal character, as it does in Truman Capote's "A Christmas Memory" (page 145).

See pages 164–165, 166.

SHORT STORY   Short, concentrated, fictional prose narrative. Some say Edgar Allan Poe was the first short-story writer. He was also one of the first to attempt to define the short story. He said "unity of effect" is crucial, meaning that a short story ought to concentrate on a single purpose. Short stories are usually built on a plot that consists of these "bare bones": the **basic situation** or **exposition, complications, climax,** and **resolution.** Years ago, most short stories were notable for their strong plots. Today's short-story writers tend to be more interested in character.

See page 2.

SIMILE   Figure of speech that makes a comparison between two unlike things, using a word such

as *like, as, resembles, or than.* Shakespeare, in one of his famous sonnets, uses a simile with an ironic twist, comparing two things that are *not* alike:

My mistress' eyes are nothing like the sun

We would expect a love poem to compare the light in a lover's eyes to the bright sun. But instead, Shakespeare puts a twist into a common comparison—in order to make a point about the extravagant similes found in most love poems of his day.

See pages 520–521, 858, 884, 927.
See also *Figure of Speech, Metaphor.*

SOLILOQUY   An unusually long speech in which a character who is onstage alone expresses his or her thoughts aloud. The soliloquy is a very old dramatic convention, in which the audience is supposedly overhearing the private thoughts of the character. Perhaps the most famous soliloquy is the "To be or not to be" speech in Shakespeare's play *Hamlet.* There are also several soliloquies in *Romeo and Juliet,* including Friar Laurence's soliloquy at the opening of Act II, Scene 3 (page 774); Juliet's at the end of Act IV, Scene 3 (page 824); and Romeo's in Act V, Scene 3 (page 841).

SONNET   Fourteen-line lyric poem that is usually written in iambic pentameter and that has one of several rhyme schemes. The oldest kind of sonnet is called the **Italian sonnet,** or **Petrarchan sonnet,** after the fourteenth-century Italian poet Petrarch. The first eight lines, or **octet,** of the Italian sonnet pose a question or problem about love or some other subject. The concluding six lines, or **sestet,** are a response to the octet. The octet has the rhyme scheme *abba abba;* the sestet has the rhyme scheme *cde cde.*

Another important sonnet form, widely used by Shakespeare, is called the **Shakespearean sonnet**. It has three four-line units, or **quatrains,** followed by a concluding two-line unit, or **couplet.** The most common rhyme scheme for the Shakespearean sonnet is *abab cdcd efef gg.*

See also *Lyric Poetry.*

SPEAKER   Voice that is talking to us in a poem. Sometimes the speaker is identical with the poet, but often the speaker and the poet are not the same. The poet

may be speaking as child, a woman, a man, a whole people, an animal, or even an object. For example, the speaker of "The Lesson of the Moth" by Don Marquis (page 140) is a cockroach.

See page 526.

STANZA   Group of consecutive lines in a poem that form a single unit. A stanza in a poem is something like a paragraph in prose: It often expresses a unit of thought. A stanza may consist of any number of lines. The word *stanza* is Italian for "stopping place" or "place to rest." Emily Dickinson's poem "I Never Saw a Moor" (page 522) consists of two four-line stanzas, or **quatrains,** each one expressing a unit of thought.

STEREOTYPE   Fixed idea or conception of a character that does not allow for any individuality. Stereotypes are often based on racial, social, religious, sexist, or ethnic prejudices. Some common stereotypes are the ideas that all football players are dumb, all New Yorkers are rude, all Texans are rich. Stereotypes are often used in comedies for laughs.

SUSPENSE   Uncertainty or anxiety the reader feels about what is going to happen next in a story. In "The Most Dangerous Game" (page 13) our curiosity is aroused at once when we hear about Ship-Trap Island and sailors' fear of it. When Rainsford lands on that very island and is hunted by the sinister General Zaroff, suspense keeps us on the edge of our seats. We wonder: Will Rainsford be another victim who is hunted down and killed by the evil and weird Zaroff?

See page 80.
See also *Foreshadowing, Plot.*

SYMBOL   Person, place, thing, or event that stands for itself and for something beyond itself as well. For example, a scale has a real existence as an instrument for measuring weights, but it also is used as a symbol of justice. Other familiar symbols are the cross that symbolizes Christianity, the six-pointed star that symbolizes Judaism, and the bald eagle that symbolizes the United States. These are symbols that most people know, but in literature, writers sometimes create new symbols that can be understood only from their context. One of the great symbols in literature is Herman Melville's great

HANDBOOK OF LITERARY TERMS   977

white whale, used as a symbol of the mystery of evil in the novel *Moby-Dick*.

See page 314.

TALL TALE **Exaggerated, far-fetched story that is obviously untrue but is told as though it should be believed.** Most tall tales are humorous. Tall tales are especially popular in the United States. As tall tales are passed on, they often get taller and taller—more and more exaggerated. The tales told about Paul Bunyan, the superheroic logger of the Northern forests, are tall tales. Paul dug the Great Lakes so that his ox, Babe, could have a watering trough. The griddle he used to make his morning pancakes was two city blocks wide. (To grease the griddle, five men skated on it with slabs of bacon on their feet.) And so on and so on. The tales about old Paul get taller and taller each time they are retold!

See also *Folk Tale*.

THEME **Central idea of a work of literature.** A theme is not the same as a subject. The subject of a work can usually be expressed in a word or two: love, childhood, death. The theme is the idea the writer wishes to reveal *about* that subject. The theme is something that can be expressed in at least one complete sentence. For example, one theme of Shakespeare's *Romeo and Juliet* (page 735) might be stated as Love is more powerful than family loyalty. Theme is not usually stated directly in a work of literature. Most often, the reader has to think about all the elements of the work and use them to make an inference, or educated guess, about what its theme is.

See pages 264–265, 266, 292, 303.

TONE **Attitude a writer takes toward the audience, a subject, or a character.** Tone is conveyed through the writer's choice of words and details. For example, Truman Capote's "A Christmas Memory" (page 145) is affectionate and nostalgic in tone. Charles Kuralt's "Misspelling" (page 469) is humorous and lightly mocking in tone.

See pages 586–587.
See also *Connotation, Diction, Irony, Satire*.

TRAGEDY **Play, novel, or other narrative that depicts serious and important events in which the main character comes to an unhappy end.** In a tragedy the main character is usually dignified and courageous. His or her downfall may be caused by a character flaw, or it may result from forces beyond human control. The tragic hero or heroine usually wins some self-knowledge and wisdom, even though he or she suffers defeat, perhaps even death.

See page 732.
See also *Comedy*.

COMMUNICATIONS HANDBOOK

READING STRATEGIES

Whether you're looking for information or reading for pleasure, you can become a more effective reader by practicing the following six strategies.

PREVIEWING AND SETTING A PURPOSE

Before you read, **preview** the text by looking at its title, table of contents, headings, and illustrations. A preview will help you determine the genre of the text (whether it is fiction or nonfiction, for example), whether you should read it carefully or quickly, and whether you should take notes or rely on your memory.

Your **purpose for reading** will help you decide how quickly to read and what to focus on. If, for example, you're reading to be entertained, you might read quickly to find out what happens next. If, however, you're reading to appreciate the writer's craft, to find models for your writing, to make a decision, or to take an action, you will read more carefully. It's important to establish your purpose—whether it is to enjoy, interpret, or learn from the text—before you begin to read. Then you can select the reading rate and strategy that suit your purpose.

A good reader knows that different methods of reading work best in different situations. If, for instance, you want an overview of a nonfiction article, try **skimming,** reading rapidly to identify main ideas. If you're looking for a detail, try **scanning,** searching for specific information by glancing over the text and looking for key words. Skimming and scanning are reading techniques that can save you time and effort. If you're reading to appreciate the writer's craft or absorb information, try **active reading,** interacting with the text by drawing on your background, making predictions and inferences, and monitoring and modifying your reading strategies appropriately.

USING YOUR BACKGROUND

Before they read something, good readers see whether they can draw on their experiences to find a connection to the text. Good readers also use their background knowledge *as* they read. If, for example, you are reading "Choice: A Tribute to Dr. Martin Luther King, Jr." (page 367) and you know something about King, you can use that information as you read. You can keep track of your knowledge on a KWL chart like this one:

K	W	L
What I already **know**	What I **want** to know	What I **learned**

In the K column, list what you already know about King. For example, you might know that he was a civil rights leader. Next, in the W column, list what you want to know. You might want to know how he became involved in civil rights. Then, after you read, fill in the L column with what you learned about King.

MAKING PREDICTIONS

Good readers make predictions by previewing a text and guessing what it is about. As they read, they may even jot down hunches about what will happen next. Then they adjust their predictions as they continue to read. This process makes reading like solving a puzzle. Try plotting your predictions in a chart like this one:

Overall prediction: This selection is about

_____

Prediction 1: _____

   Prediction was correct: _____

   Prediction needs adjustment: _____

[etc.]

MAKING INFERENCES

An **inference** is a guess based on evidence. You make inferences about a literary work based on evidence in the text and your own experiences. In "Thank You, M'am" (page 120), Langston Hughes describes a woman's actions after she is mugged: "The large woman simply turned around and kicked him right square in his blue-jeaned sitter." From this you can infer that the woman is strong and not easily intimidated. When reading, record your inferences in a chart like this one:

> Inference 1: _____
>
>   Evidence in the text: _____
>
>   Personal experience: _____
>
> [etc.]

Here are some clues to look for when making inferences about aspects of literature:

- **Character.** Look at a character's speech, actions, thoughts, and appearance. What do others think and say about the character?
- **Tone (the writer's attitude).** Look at the writer's choice of words and details.
- **Theme.** Look at the turning point in a story. How do the main characters change? What do they learn?

Conclusions and generalizations are types of inferences. A **conclusion** is a judgment based on a consideration of evidence. For example, when you piece together details about an object in a poem and decide that the object is a symbol, you're drawing a conclusion. A **generalization** is a broad statement based on specific examples. When you're talking about a literary theme, you're making a generalization.

MONITORING YOUR READING STRATEGIES

When you're having trouble understanding a text, stop and try one or more of these helpful techniques:

1. **Rereading.** Go back to the last point you understood, and find where you lost the thread.
2. **Reading on.** Keep reading to see whether context clues or additional information clears things up.

3. **Asking questions.** Ask *who, what, where, when, why,* and *how* questions about the material. Questions force you to think about what you are reading.
4. **Using resources.** Use a dictionary or other reference works to figure out difficult passages.

CHECKING YOUR COMPREHENSION

When you finish reading a text, check your understanding by creating a **summary,** a short restatement of the important ideas and details in a work. There are many ways to summarize; the one you choose should depend on the genre of the text. For a short story, use a story map like this one:

Story Map

Basic situation:
Setting:
Main character:
His or her problem:
Main events or complications:
Climax:
Resolution:

For a poem, try a **paraphrase.** In a paraphrase you express every idea line by line in your own words. Here is a paraphrase of "Fire and Ice" (page 541):

Paraphrase of "Fire and Ice"

Some people believe that the end of the world will come in the form of fire; others believe that it will come in the form of ice. The speaker, based on his experience with desire, agrees with those who vote for fire. If, however, the world must end twice, the speaker's experience with hate tells him that ice would also be enough to end the world.

For a work of nonfiction, make an outline that shows the **main ideas** and **supporting details:**

I. Main idea
   A. Supporting detail
      1. Supporting detail
         a. Supporting detail

USING A DICTIONARY

You use a dictionary to find the precise meaning and usage of words. The elements of a typical entry are explained below.

1. **Entry word.** The entry word shows how the word is spelled and divided into syllables. It may also show capitalization and variant spellings.

2. **Pronunciation.** Phonetic symbols and **diacritical marks** show how to pronounce the entry word. A key to these symbols and marks usually appears on every other page.

3. **Part-of-speech label.** This label tells how the entry word is used. When a word can be used as more than one part of speech, definitions are grouped by part of speech. The sample entry shows three definitions of *indulge* as a transitive verb (*vt.*) and one as an intransitive verb (*vi.*).

4. **Other forms.** Sometimes the spellings of plural forms of nouns, principal parts of verbs, and comparative and superlative forms of adjectives and adverbs are shown.

5. **Word origin.** A word's origin, or **etymology** (et′ə·mäl′ə·jē), shows where the word comes from. *Indulge* comes from the Latin *indulgere,* which probably comes from the prefix *in-,* meaning "not," added to the Greek *dolichos,* "long," and the Gothic *tulgus,* "firm."

6. **Examples.** Phrases or sentences show how the entry word is used.

7. **Definitions.** If a word has more than one meaning, the meanings are numbered or lettered.

8. **Special-usage labels.** These labels identify special meanings or special uses of the word. Here, *Archaic* indicates an outdated meaning.

9. **Related word forms.** Other forms of the entry word are listed. Usually these are created by the addition of suffixes.

10. **Synonyms and antonyms.** Synonyms (words similar in meaning) and **antonyms** (words opposite in meaning) may appear at the end of the entry.

A dictionary is available as a book or as part of a word-processing program or Web site (see The World Wide Web, page 984).

Sample Dictionary Entry

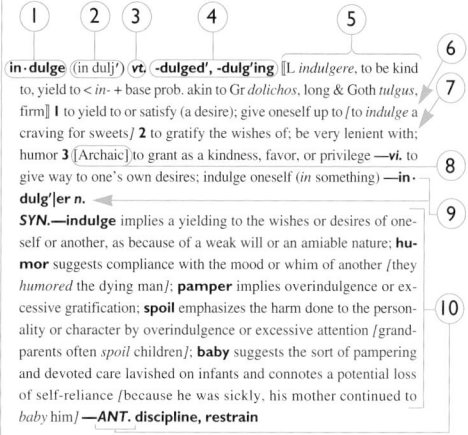

©1996 Webster's New World College Dictionary, Third Edition.

USING A THESAURUS

A **thesaurus** is a collection of synonyms. You use a thesaurus to find a word that expresses a specific meaning. There are two kinds of thesauruses. The first kind, developed by Peter Mark Roget, groups words in categories. Here's how to use it:

- In the index, look up the word that conveys your general meaning. For instance, under *antagonize,* you might find *oppose, provoke,* and *alienate.* Each of these subentries is followed by a number.

- Choose the subentry closest to the meaning you have in mind. In this case, suppose you choose *oppose.*

- In the body of the text, look up the number that follows the subentry *oppose.* There you will find synonyms of *oppose.* The second kind of thesaurus presents words in alphabetical order, as in a dictionary. See below.

Sample Thesaurus Entry

shun, v. —*SYN.* dodge, evade, keep away from, ignore, neglect; see also **avoid.** —*ANT.* accept, ADOPT, take advantage of.

©1997 Webster's New World Thesaurus, Third Edition.

READING MAPS, CHARTS, AND GRAPHS

Types of Maps

Physical maps illustrate the natural landscape of an area, using shading, lines, and color to show landforms and elevation. The map on page 400, showing part of New Mexico, is a physical map. **Political maps** show political units, such as states and nations. They usually show borders and capitals and other major cities. **Special-purpose maps** present specific information, such as the routes of explorers. The special-purpose map below shows agricultural and industrial areas of South Texas.

How to Read a Map

1. **Determine the focus of the map.** The map's title and labels tell you its focus—its subject and the geographical area it covers.
2. **Study the legend.** The **legend,** or **key,** explains the symbols, lines, colors, and shadings used in the map.
3. **Check directions and distances.** Maps often include a **compass rose,** a diagram that shows north, south, east, and west. If there isn't one, assume that north is at the top, west to the left, and so on. Many maps also include a scale that relates distances on the map to actual distances.
4. **Look at the larger context.** The **absolute location** of any place on earth is given by its **latitude** (the number of degrees north or south of the equator) and its **longitude** (the number of degrees east or west of the **prime meridian,** or 0 degrees longitude). Some maps also include **locator maps,** which show the area depicted in relation to a larger area.

Types of Charts and Graphs

Flowcharts show a sequence of events or steps in a process. The flowchart on page 417 is designed to show a cause-and-effect relationship. **Time lines** display historical events in chronological order (the order in which they happened). The time line on page 456 shows events relating to rights for people with disabilities. **Tables** categorize information and organize it in columns and rows so that it is easy to find and compare. A table appears on page 856.

Line graphs generally show changes in quantity over time. In such graphs, dots showing the quantity at certain times are connected to create a line. **Bar graphs** usually compare quantities within categories. **Pie graphs,** or **circle graphs,** like the one on page 516, show proportions by dividing a circle into different-sized sections, like slices of a pie.

How to Read a Chart or a Graph

1. **Read the title.** The title will tell you the subject and purpose of the chart or graph.
2. **Read the headings and labels.** These will help you determine the type of information presented.
3. **Analyze the details.** Read numbers carefully. Note increases or decreases. Look for the direction or order of events and trends and for relationships.

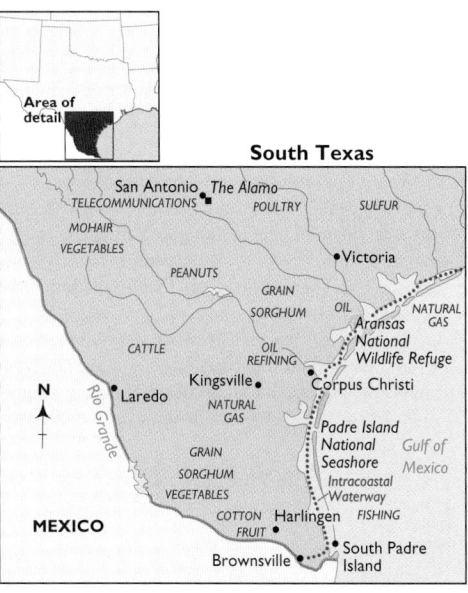

South Texas

When you're looking for information, where should you begin? First you might create a research plan that outlines the topics you want to explore or the questions you want to answer. Then you can begin your search for print and nonprint resources that might be relevant to your plan. When doing research, do not rely solely on one source; instead, consult as many reliable sources as possible. Use the following research strategies when searching for resources in your school's media center, in your local library, or on a home computer that is linked to the Internet.

USING A MEDIA CENTER OR LIBRARY

Library Catalogs

To find information in a library, start by looking in the catalog. Most libraries record their holdings in an **on-line,** or **computer, catalog.**

On-line catalogs vary from library to library. With some you begin by searching for resources by **title, author,** or **subject.** With others you simply enter **key words** relating to the subject you're researching. With either system, when you enter the relevant information in response to the on-screen prompts, a new screen will display a list of materials or subject headings that relate to your request. When you find an item you want to examine, write down the title, author, and **call number,** the code of numbers and letters that shows you where to find the item on the library's shelves.

Some libraries still use **card catalogs.** A card catalog is a collection of index cards arranged in alphabetical order. Every item in the library is cataloged by title and author. Nonfiction is also cataloged by subject.

Other Library Resources

Every library has a **reference section** containing materials you can use only in the library. These materials include encyclopedias; yearbooks; biographical, scien-

tific, and other dictionaries; almanacs; atlases; and **indices,** extensive lists of books, magazines, or newspapers arranged by author, title, and subject. Two useful book indices are *Books in Print* and *The Reader's Catalog.* Many reference works appear in print and various electronic formats.

Electronic Databases   **Electronic databases** are large collections of information that you can access at a computer terminal. Among the types of information stored on databases are statistics, biographical data, museum collections, indices, and back (not current) issues of magazines.

There are two kinds of electronic databases. **On-line databases** are accessed at a computer terminal that is connected to a modem. The modem allows the computer to communicate with other computers via telephone lines. **Portable databases** are available on magnetic tape, diskette, or CD-ROM.

A **CD-ROM** (compact disc–read-only memory) is played on a computer with a CD-ROM player. CD-ROMs can store not only text but also sound, pictures, and video clips. If you were to look up Shakespeare's *The Tragedy of Romeo and Juliet* in a CD-ROM encyclopedia, you might see a clip of Leonard Whiting or Leonardo DiCaprio playing Romeo.

Periodicals   Most libraries have a collection of periodicals and resources for locating information in them. To find up-to-date magazine or newspaper articles on a topic, look in an electronic index such as *InfoTrac* or *EBSCO.* Some electronic indices provide a summary, or **abstract,** of articles. Others provide the entire text, which you can read on screen or print out. The *Readers' Guide to Periodical Literature* is a useful print index of articles that have appeared in hundreds of magazines. Back issues of periodicals may be stored in print form or on **microfilm** (a reel of film), **microfiche** (a sheet of film), or **CD-ROM.**

Audiovisual Resources   Most libraries have collections of books on tape, videos, CDs, and so on.

go.hrw.com
LE0 Research Paper

USING THE INTERNET

The **Internet** is a worldwide electronic network that connects millions of computers and computer networks. The Net can provide up-to-the-minute information on a vast range of topics. Institutions sharing information on the Net include libraries, universities, museums, news media, and government agencies. Resources available on the Net include **e-journals,** periodicals found only on-line. You can reach the Net through Internet service providers (ISPs) or on-line information providers, such as America Online and Prodigy. To use the Internet to do research, explore the options described below.

E-Mail

E-mail is an electronic message sent over a computer network. On the Internet you can use e-mail to contact institutions, businesses, and individuals. When you e-mail institutions such as museums and nonprofit organizations, you may be able to consult **experts** on the topic you're researching. You can also use e-mail to chat about various issues with students around the world.

Electronic Forums

Internet forums, or **newsgroups,** enable you to discuss and debate various subjects. You can post a question to a forum and get a response from someone who may (or may not) know something about the topic.

The World Wide Web

The easiest way to conduct research on the Internet is through the World Wide Web. On the Web, information is stored in colorful, easy-to-access files called **Web pages.** A Web page may contain text, graphics, images, sound, and even video clips.

Using a Web Browser   You view Web pages with a **Web browser,** a program for accessing information on the Web. Every page on the Web has its own address, called a **URL,** or Uniform Resource Locator. If you know the URL of a Web page you want to go to, just enter it in the location field on your browser. See the figure below, in which the browser has pulled up the U.S. Census Bureau Web site.

Hundreds of millions of Web pages are connected by **hyperlinks** that enable you to jump from one page to another. These links are often signaled by underlined or colored words or images, or both, on your computer screen. With hundreds of millions of linked Web pages, how do you find the information you want?

Using a Web Directory   If you're just beginning to look for a research topic, click on a **Web directory,** a list of topics and subtopics created to help you find Web sites. Use a directory as you would a giant index. Begin with a broad category, such as Literature. Then, work your way down through the subtopics, from perhaps Native American: Literature to Native American: Authors, until you find a Web page that looks promising, such as one on N. Scott Momaday.

Sample Web-Browser Screen

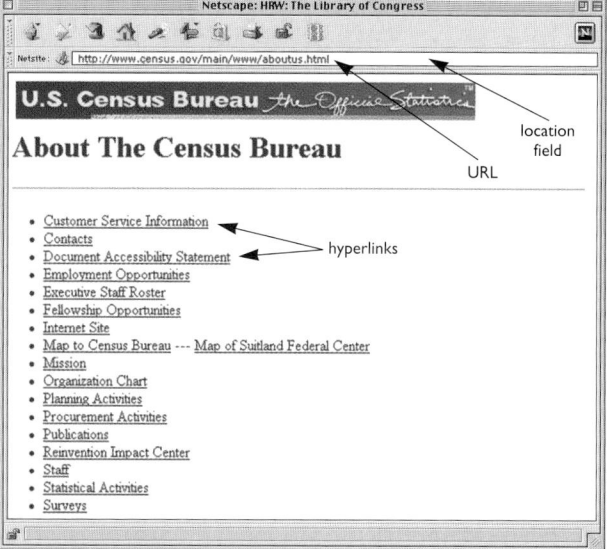

Using a Search Engine   If you already have a well-defined topic and you are looking for specifics, try using a **search engine,** a software tool that locates information on the Web. To use a search engine, enter a **search term,** a keyword or several keywords. The search engine will return a list of Web pages containing your search term. The list will also include the first few lines of each page. A search term like the name *Hughes* can produce thousands of results, or **hits,** including information on the Supreme Court chief justice Charles Evans Hughes, the industrialist Howard Hughes, and his company Hughes Aircraft. If, however, you're looking for material on Langston Hughes, most of these thousands of hits will be irrelevant. It's important, therefore, to refine, or tailor, your search.

Refining a Keyword Search   Searches using more than one keyword generally provide more focused results. Most search engines allow you to use **search operators** to create a string of keywords. Common search operators include the capitalized words AND, OR, NOT, ADJ (adjacent), and NEAR. Use these operators to narrow or broaden the scope of your search. Here's how the operators work. Let's assume, for example, that you're looking for material on Langston Hughes and the time he spent in Harlem. You might use this search term:

`Langston ADJ Hughes AND Harlem`

This more focused search term yields pages that contain the names Langston, Hughes, and Harlem but nothing about Charles Evans Hughes or Howard Hughes. Now, suppose you want to learn about Japanese poetry. If your first search yields only information about haiku, you can expand the range by using OR:

`haiku OR tanka`

The chart below explains various search operators.

Doing a Phrase Search   Exact phrases often produce better results than single words or strings of keywords. If you're looking up prose poems, for example, a search made with the unlinked keywords *prose* and *poems* could yield thousands of pages about prose works and poetry. On the other hand, a search using the exact phrase "prose poems," signaled by quotation marks, will yield only pages containing that phrase.

Knowing Your Search Engine   Not all search engines operate in the same way. Some have rules about using uppercase and lowercase letters. Others require a plus sign or a minus sign between keywords rather than the operator AND or NOT. Others require that you enter exact phrases within quotation marks. Yet others provide a list of options that enable you to search by exact phrases, individual words, and so on. Because the rules governing search engines are constantly changing, read the on-line help information before you begin a search on any engine.

EVALUATING THE CREDIBILITY OF WEB SOURCES

Since anyone can publish a Web page, it's important to evaluate your sources. By examining the top-level domain in the URL of a source, you can learn where the Web site is housed.

COMMON SEARCH OPERATORS AND WHAT THEY DO	
AND	Demands that both terms appear on the page; narrows search
+	Demands that both terms appear on the page; narrows search
OR	Yields pages that contain either term; widens search
NOT	Excludes a word from consideration; narrows search
–	Excludes a word from consideration; narrows search
NEAR	Demands that two words be in proximity; narrows search
ADJ	Demands that two words be in proximity; narrows search
" "	Demands the exact phrase; narrows search

```
                    top-level domain
                        ⌒
┌─────────────────────────────────────────┐
│  http://www.loc.gov                       │
└─────────────────────────────────────────┘
```

Once you know where the Web site is housed (in this case, a government agency), you'll be in a better position to evaluate the information you find there. See the chart below for a list of common top-level domains and what they stand for.

In evaluating any source, also consider the following criteria:

Authority   Who is the author, and what are his or her qualifications? Trust established sources, such as the *Encyclopaedia Britannica*'s Web site or the Library of Congress's, but not an individual's home page.

Accuracy   Is the information reliable? Does the author cite sources? Check information from one site against information from two other sites or print sources.

Objectivity   What is the author's **bias,** or perspective? Does the provider of the information have a hidden motive or a special interest? You don't have to discard information from sources that do, but you should take the bias into consideration.

Currency   How current is the information? At the bottom of a site's home page, look for the date on which the page was created or revised. If you need current information, reject dated sources.

Coverage   How well does a Web site cover the topic? Could you find better information in a reference book?

TAKING NOTES AND DOCUMENTING SOURCES

Whenever you paraphrase someone's ideas or quote a source in a research paper, you must acknowledge that source.

Preparing Source Cards

1. For every source, record the publication data on a 3- × 5-inch index card or in a computer file.
2. Assign each source a number, and note it at the top right of the card or computer entry. Later, when you're taking notes, you can label them by source number instead of author and title.
3. Record the publication data. Specific information about books, videos, Web sites, and other sources appears on pages 987–989. Follow the format of the **works cited** list, which is described on page 987.
4. Note the library call number or the URL.

Sample Source Card

```
                                        3

Shakespeare, William. The Complete Works of
William Shakespeare. World Library.
1990–1993. Project Gutenberg. Jan. 1994.
Illinois Benedictine College. 5 May 1999
<ftp://sailor.gutenberg.org/pub/gutenberg/
etext94/shaks12.txt.>.
```

The criteria opposite have been adapted from the Web site "Evaluating Web Resources" at http://www.widener.edu/libraries.html (select "Evaluating Web Resources"), which complements the book *Web Wisdom: How to Evaluate and Create Information Quality on the Web* by Jan Alexander and Marsha Ann Tate of Widener University, Chester, PA.

COMMON TOP-LEVEL DOMAINS AND WHAT THEY STAND FOR	
.edu	Educational institution. Site may publish scholarly work or the work of elementary, high school, or college students.
.gov	Government body. Information should be reliable.
.org	Usually a nonprofit organization. If the organization promotes culture (as a museum does), information should be reliable; if it advocates a cause, information may be biased.
.com	Commercial enterprise. Information should be evaluated carefully.
.net	Organization offering Internet services. Information should be reliable.

Here's where to find the appropriate publication data, such as the name of the publisher and the copyright date, for different types of sources:

- **Books.** See the title and copyright pages.
- **Portable electronic databases.** Look at the start-up screen, accompanying printed material, such as the package or a package insert, or the disc.
- **On-line sources.** Look at the beginning or end of the document or in a separate electronic file. On a Web page, look for a link containing the word *About.*

Taking Notes

After examining your sources, start taking notes.

1. Use 4- × 6-inch index cards or a separate computer file. Never put notes from more than one source on the same card or on the same page in a file.
2. Write an identifying word or phrase in the upper left and the source number in the upper right of each card or page.
3. **Quote, summarize,** or **paraphrase** your source. If you quote it, be sure to use quotation marks.
4. Note the page number or numbers of the source, if any, in the lower right of the card or page.

Citing Sources

Parenthetical Citations One way to let your readers know what sources you are paraphrasing or quoting is to use **parenthetical citations.** A parenthetical citation consists of the author's last name and a page number enclosed in parentheses. (For unnumbered Web pages, include just the author or, if no author is identified, the title.) If in your text you make clear which work you are referring to—by stating the author's name or the author and title—include only the page number in the parenthetical citation. Here are some rules for the placement of citations and longer quotes:

1. Place a citation as close as possible to the material it documents. If possible, place it at the end of a sentence.
2. Place a citation after closing quotation marks and before the end punctuation mark.

   EXAMPLE   In her book <u>Edgar Allan Poe</u>, Bettina Knapp says that Poe's "inner emotions were encompassed in the mood he created, in the music of the words" (46).

3. If a quotation consists of four lines or more, set it off by indenting each line ten spaces from the left margin. Don't use quotation marks. Insert the citation in parentheses one space after the end punctuation mark.

List of Works Cited A **works cited** list must appear at the end of your report. It should contain a complete citation for every source you used to write your paper. On page 988 are citations of electronic sources based on the Modern Language Association (MLA) style. In the chart on page 989 are sample citations of print and audiovisual sources.

GUIDELINES FOR PREPARING A WORKS CITED LIST

- At the top of a new page, center the title *Works Cited* (or *Bibliography*).
- Alphabetize your sources by authors' last name. If no author is named, alphabetize the source by the first word in the title, ignoring *A, An,* and *The.*
- If two or more sources are by the same author, use the author's full name in the first entry only. For the other entries, type three dashes in place of the name, followed by a period and the rest of the citation.

  EXAMPLE   Poe, Edgar Allan. "The Cask of Amontillado." <u>The Collected Tales and Poems of Edgar Allan Poe</u>. New York: Modern Library, 1992.

  ———. "The Raven." <u>The Collected Tales and Poems of Edgar Allan Poe</u>. New York: Modern Library, 1992.

- Double-space the list, and begin each entry at the left margin. If an entry is longer than one line, indent the succeeding lines five spaces.

Formatting Electronic-Source Citations

Writing entries for electronic sources for a works cited list is not always easy, because on-line sources are constantly changing and many do not provide all the publication information that the format requires. For instance, many Web pages don't identify an author. In such cases, include in your citation whatever relevant publication information is available.

The format for citing electronic sources depends on (1) whether the source is on-line or portable and (2) whether the source has a print version or stands alone.

Listed below are the elements required for the citation of various kinds of electronic sources. Note that most elements likely to be included are listed, but many citations will not include every element (for instance, a source may not have an editor).

Source from a Computer Network, such as the World Wide Web, with a Print Version

Author's Last Name, First Name. "Title of Document, Article, or Part of a Work." Title of Print Source. Print Publication Information. Title of Project, Database, Periodical, or Site. Date of Electronic Publication. Name of Sponsoring Institution. Date Information Was Accessed. <URL> [or] Name of On-line Service or Network.

Note: If an electronic address, or URL, breaks onto a second line, divide the address immediately after one of the slash marks within it. Do not use a hyphen or any other mark of punctuation to divide the address.

EXAMPLE   Shakespeare, William. The Complete Works of William Shakespeare. World Library, 1990–1993. Project Gutenberg. Jan. 1994. Illinois Benedictine College. 5 May 1999. <ftp://sailor.gutenberg.org/pub/gutenberg/etext94/shaks12.txt.>.

Source from a Computer Network, such as the World Wide Web, with No Print Version

Author's Last Name, First Name. "Title of Document, Article, or Part of a Work." Title of Project, Database, Periodical, or Site. Date of Electronic Publi-

cation. Name of Sponsoring Institution. Date Information Was Accessed. <URL> [or] Name of On-line Service or Network.

EXAMPLE   Dirks, Tim. "Romeo and Juliet (1968)." Greatest Films. 1996. 14 Oct. 1999. <http://www.filmsite.org/rome.html>.

Note: In this example, *Romeo and Juliet*, the short work accessed in the *Greatest Films* database, is underlined because it is the name of a full-length film.

CD-ROM with a Print Version and Not Published Periodically

Author's Last Name, First Name. "Title of Document, Article, or Part of a Work." Title of Print Source. Print Publication Information. Database Title. Edition, Release, or Version. Publication Medium [use the term *CD-ROM, Diskette,* or *Magnetic tape*]. City of Electronic Publication: Electronic Publisher, Electronic Publication Date.

EXAMPLE   "Romeo and Juliet." Encyclopaedia Britannica. 15th ed. 1995. Britannica CD. Home ed., version 2.02. CD-ROM. Chicago: Encyclopaedia Britannica, 1995.

CD-ROM with No Print Version and Not Published Periodically

Author's Last Name, First Name. "Title of Document, Article, or Part of a Work." Title of Work. Database Title. Edition, Release, or Version. Publication Medium [use the term *CD-ROM, Diskette,* or *Magnetic tape*]. City of Electronic Publication: Electronic Publisher, Electronic Publication Date.

EXAMPLE   "American Renaissance." The History of American Literature. CD-ROM. Chicago: CLEARVUE/eav, 1995.

Formatting Print and Audiovisual Citations

This chart shows sample entries for various kinds of print and audiovisual sources according to the *MLA Handbook for Writers of Research Papers,* fourth edition.

STANDARD REFERENCE WORKS	
Encyclopedia article	Krutch, Joseph Wood. "Poe, Edgar Allan." Encyclopedia Americana. 1994 ed.
Biographical dictionary	"Poe, Edgar Allan." Merriam-Webster's Biographical Dictionary. 1995 ed.
BOOKS	
Book with one author	Meyers, Jeffrey. Edgar Allan Poe: His Life and Legacy. New York: Scribners, 1992.
Book with two or more authors	Thomas, Dwight, and David K. Jackson. The Poe Log: A Documentary Life of Edgar Allan Poe, 1809–1849. Boston: Hall, 1987.
Book with one editor	Tate, Allen, ed. The Complete Poetry and Selected Criticism of Edgar Allan Poe. New York: New American Library, 1981.
Book with two or more editors	O'Neill, Edward H., and Arthur Hobson Quinn, eds. The Complete Poems and Stories of Edgar Allan Poe. New York: Knopf, 1946.
SELECTIONS FROM BOOKS	
Selection from book of works by one author	Buranelli, Vincent. "The Problem of Poe." Edgar Allan Poe. Boston: Twayne, 1977. 19–21.
Selection from book of works by two or more authors	Bandy, W. T., and Vincent Baudelaire, "Pirates and Plagiarists." Edgar Allan Poe: His Life and Work. Toronto: University of Toronto Press, 1973. xiii–xvi.
Selection from book of works with one or more editors	Poe, Edgar Allan. "The Cask of Amontillado." The Selected Poetry and Prose of Edgar Allan Poe. Ed. T. O. Mabbott. New York: Modern Library, 1951. 323–329.
ARTICLES FROM MAGAZINES, NEWSPAPERS, AND JOURNALS	
Magazine article	Thomas, L. "Mysterious Mr. Poe." Southern Living Apr. 1997: 29.
Newspaper article	O'Donnell, M. "The Tell-Tale Tube." New York Times Magazine 9 Apr. 1995: 92.
OTHER SOURCES	
Telephone interview	Rodriguez, Jorge. Telephone interview. 21 Feb. 1998.
Sound recording	Poe, Edgar Allan. Masterworks and Science Fiction of Edgar Allan Poe. Read by Paul Scofield. Audiocassette. Dove Audio, 1993.
Radio or TV program	NBC Nightly News. NBC. WNBC, New York. 8 July 1991.
Film, filmstrip, or videotape	Edgar Allan Poe: Terror of the Soul. Prod. Film Odyssey. Videocassette. PBS Home Video, 1995.

COMPOSING BUSINESS LETTERS

The ability to write clear and effective letters, memos, and résumés can help you greatly, whatever career you choose. Follow these guidelines whenever you write a business letter:

1. **Use formal, standard English.** The tone of your letter should be polite and respectful.
2. **Be clear.** Explain your purpose clearly. Include all the necessary information, but be as brief as possible.
3. **Use the correct format.** Type, print, or write neatly on white $8\frac{1}{2} \times 11$-inch paper. Follow the **block form** (shown below).

Sample Business Letter (Block Format)

1050 Ocean Parkway, Apt. 25A
Brooklyn, NY 11213

November 11, 1999

Ms. Charmaine M. Stewart
Senior Partner
Stewart, Lyle, Patel, and Associates
150 Joralemon Street
Brooklyn, NY 11201

Dear Ms. Stewart:

In observance of the birthday of Martin Luther King, Jr., Abraham Lincoln High School is planning a Civil Rights Week, January 17–21. We are inviting notable members of the community to share their knowledge of civil rights issues with us.

We would be honored if you would speak on the morning of January 18 on an issue related to civil rights law.

You can reach me at my home address or by phone at 718-555-8306. We would be grateful for your participation.

Sincerely yours,

Carla Ruiz

Carla Ruiz
Chairperson, Civil Rights Week
Abraham Lincoln High School

Heading
Your street address
Your city, state, and ZIP Code
Date you write the letter

Inside Address
Name, title, and address of the person you are writing to. Use a title (for example, *Mr., Ms., Mrs., Dr.*) with the person's name, and put his or her business title after the name.

Salutation (greeting)
Use *Dear* followed by the person's title and last name and a colon. If the letter isn't addressed to a specific person, use a business title.

Body
Your message. If the body contains more than one paragraph, leave a blank line between paragraphs.

Closing
Use *Yours truly* or *Sincerely yours,* followed by a comma.

Signature
Type or print your name, leaving space for your signature. Sign your name in ink.

STRATEGIES FOR TAKING TESTS

When you begin a test, scan it quickly and count the items. Then, decide how to budget your time. Here are some sample questions and specific strategies for answering five common kinds of test questions:

Multiple-choice questions ask you to select a correct answer from a number of choices. For example:

1. **Onomatopoeia** is
   - **A** the repetition of the same consonant sound
   - **B** the use of words that almost rhyme
   - **C** the use of words that sound like what they mean
   - **D** the use of a regular rhythm in poetry

HOW TO COMPLETE MULTIPLE-CHOICE ITEMS

- Make sure you understand the opening part of the question before you examine the choices.
- Look for a **qualifier** (a word that limits a statement), such as *not* or *always,* which might help you eliminate some choices.
- Read all the choices before selecting an answer. Eliminate choices you know are incorrect.
- Think carefully about the remaining choices, and select the one that makes the most sense.

True/false questions require you to decide whether a statement is true or false. For example:

1. T F In a short story the **denouement** comes just before the climax.

HOW TO COMPLETE TRUE/FALSE ITEMS

- Read the statement carefully. If any part of the statement is false, the whole statement is false.
- Check for a qualifier, such as *always* or *never.* A statement is true only if it is always true.

Matching questions require you to match items in one list with items in a second list. For example:

Directions: Match each item in the left-hand column with its definition in the right-hand column.

___**1.** alliteration   **A** a comparison between two unlike things

___**2.** metaphor   **B** repeated vowel sounds

___**3.** assonance   **C** repeated consonant sounds

HOW TO COMPLETE MATCHING ITEMS

- Read the directions carefully. Not all the items in one column may be used, or items may be used more than once.
- Scan the columns. First, match items you are sure of. Then, match items you are less sure of.
- For the remaining items, make your best guess.

Analogy questions require you to recognize the relationship between a pair of words and then identify another pair with a similar relationship. For example:

Directions: Select the pair of words that best completes the analogy.

1. CARROT : VEGETABLE ::
   - **A** flower : tree   **C** rose : flower
   - **B** sentence : paragraph   **D** pea : green

HOW TO COMPLETE ANALOGY ITEMS

- Identify the relationship in the first pair. (In the example a *carrot* is a type of *vegetable.*)
- Express the analogy in a statement or question. ("A *carrot* is a kind of *vegetable.* In what other pair is the first item a kind of the second item?")
- Select the pair of words that have the same relationship. (A *rose* is a kind of *flower.*)

These are some common relationships in analogies: a thing to its cause; a thing to a category it belongs to; a thing to its opposite or a word to its antonym.

Essay questions ask you to think critically about material you have learned and to express your understanding in one paragraph or more.

HOW TO ANSWER ESSAY QUESTIONS

- Scan the questions quickly. If you have a choice of questions, decide which ones you can answer best. See how much time you have to spend on each answer.
- Find the key verb in each question. See the chart below for explanations of what to do in response to different directives.
- Make notes or a simple outline on scratch paper, organize your ideas logically, and write a thesis statement expressing your main idea.
- Revise as you write to tighten and clarify.
- Proofread for mistakes in spelling, mechanics, and usage. See the chart below.

ESSAY QUESTIONS

KEY VERB	TASK	SAMPLE QUESTION
analyze	Take something apart to see how it works.	Analyze the character of Zaroff in "The Most Dangerous Game."
compare/ contrast	Discuss likenesses/differences.	Compare and contrast Helen and Annie in *The Miracle Worker*.
discuss	Examine something in detail.	Discuss how du Maurier builds suspense in "The Birds."
explain	Give reasons for something.	Explain why Odysseus begins his travels.
interpret	Give the meaning or significance of something.	Interpret the symbolism of the ibis in "The Scarlet Ibis."
summarize	Give a brief overview of the main points.	Summarize the plot of Poe's "The Cask of Amontillado."

PROOFREADERS' MARKS

SYMBOL	EXAMPLE	MEANING
≡	Fifty-first street	Capitalize lower-case letter.
/	Jerry's Aunt	Lowercase capital letter.
∧	the capital *of* Ohio	Insert.
ℛ	Where's the the key?	Delete.
∧∨	a close friend ship	Close up space.

SYMBOL	EXAMPLE	MEANING
∿	thier	Change order (of letters or words).
¶	¶ "Hi," he said.	Begin new paragraph.
⊙	Stay well⊙	Add period.
⋏	Of course, you may be wrong.	Add comma.

1 THE PARTS OF SPEECH

Resources
- *Language Handbook Resources,* pp. 1–14
- *Language Workshop CD-ROM,* Chapter 1: Parts of Speech

PART OF SPEECH	DEFINITION	EXAMPLES
NOUN	Names person, place, thing, or idea	captain, swimmers, Maria Tallchief, team, Stratford-on-Avon, stories, "The Scarlet Ibis," justice, honesty
PRONOUN	Takes place of one or more nouns or pronouns	
Personal	Refers to one(s) speaking (first person), spoken to (second person), spoken about (third person)	I, me, my, mine, we, us, our, ours you, your, yours he, him, his, she, her, hers, it, its, they, them, their, theirs
Reflexive	Refers to subject and directs action of verb back to subject	myself, ourselves, yourself, yourselves, himself, herself, itself, themselves
Intensive	Refers to and emphasizes noun or another pronoun	(See Reflexive.)
Demonstrative	Refers to specific one(s) of group	this, that, these, those
Interrogative	Introduces question	what, which, who, whom, whose
Relative	Introduces subordinate clause and refers to noun or pronoun outside clause	that, which, who, whom, whose
Indefinite	Refers to one(s) not specifically named	all, any, anyone, both, each, either, everybody, many, none, nothing
ADJECTIVE	Modifies noun or pronoun by telling *what kind, which one, how many,* or *how much*	**an old, flea-bitten** dog, **a Sioux** custom, **that** one, **the twelve red** roses, **more** water
VERB	Shows action or state of being	
Action	Expresses physical or mental activity	paint, jump, write, know, imagine
Linking	Connects subject with word identifying or describing it	appear, be, seem, become, feel, look, smell, sound, taste
Helping (Auxiliary)	Combines with another verb to form a verb phrase	be, have, may, can, shall, will, would
ADVERB	Modifies verb, adjective, or adverb by telling *how, when, where,* or *to what extent*	drives **carefully, quite** dangerous, **shortly afterward,** arrived **there late**
PREPOSITION	Relates noun or pronoun to another word	across, between, into, near, of, on, with, aside from, instead of, next to
CONJUNCTION	Joins words or word groups	
Coordinating	Joins words or word groups used in same way	and, but, for, nor, or, so, yet

(continued)

PART OF SPEECH	DEFINITION	EXAMPLES
Correlative	A pair of conjunctions that join parallel words or word groups	both . . . and, either . . . or, neither . . . nor, not only . . . but (also)
Subordinating	Begins subordinate clause and connects it to independent clause	as though, because, if, since, so that, than, when, where, while
INTERJECTION	Expresses emotion	hey, oops, ouch, wow

Determining Parts of Speech

The way a word is used in a sentence determines the word's part of speech.

EXAMPLES
The fine feathers of young birds are called **down.**
[noun]
She wore a **down** vest. [adjective]
Did the tackle **down** the ball in the end zone?
[verb]
Her poster fell **down.** [adverb]
My cousin lives **down** the street from my school.
[preposition]

Let's get a drink of **water.** [noun]
Did you **water** the plants? [verb]
Most **water** sports offer good exercise. [adjective]

He promised us **that** he would meet us after the game. [conjunction]
That CD didn't cost much. [adjective]
I never said **that.** [pronoun]

Avoiding Overused Adverbs

The adverbs *really, too, so,* and *very* are often overused. To keep your writing lively, replace those inexact, overused words with more specific adverbs such as *completely, definitely, entirely, especially, extremely, generally, largely, mainly, mostly, particularly, rather,* and *unusually.*

Try It Out

For each of the following sentences, replace the italicized adverb with a more specific adverb.

1. Elie Wiesel's speech was *very* direct.
2. It *really* focused on personal responsibility.
3. People accept injustice *too* easily.
4. One person's actions can be *very* important.
5. The worst part was to be *so* forgotten.

Try It Out
Possible Answers
1. Elie Wiesel's speech was particularly direct.
2. It focused especially on personal responsibility.
3. People accept injustice rather easily.
4. One person's actions can be extremely important.
5. The worst part was to be completely forgotten.

Resources

- *Language Handbook Resources,* pp. 15–26
- *Language Workshop CD-ROM,* Chapter 2: Agreement

2 AGREEMENT

AGREEMENT OF SUBJECT AND VERB

2a. A verb should always agree with its subject in number. Singular subjects take singular verbs. Plural subjects take plural verbs.

SINGULAR   **She searches** for Mme. Forestier's necklace.
PLURAL   **They search** for Mme. Forestier's necklace.

SINGULAR   Miss Lottie's flower **garden was destroyed.**
PLURAL   Miss Lottie's **marigolds were destroyed.**

COMPUTER NOTE   Some word-processing programs can identify problems in subject-verb agreement. If you have access to such a program, you can use it to help you search for errors when you are proofreading your writing. If you are not sure whether a problem identified by the word processor is truly an error, look it up in this section of the Language Handbook.

 For information about identifying subjects and verbs, see pages 1011–1012.

994 LANGUAGE HANDBOOK

2b. The number of the subject is not changed by a phrase following the subject.

SINGULAR	The **sign** near the glass doors **explains** the theme of the exhibit.
PLURAL	Several **paintings** by Emilio Sánchez **were hanging** in the gallery.
SINGULAR	**Romeo**, together with Benvolio and Mercutio, **goes** to Lord Capulet's party.
PLURAL	The **combs** made of pure tortoise shell **were** expensive.

 For information about kinds of phrases, see Part 6: Phrases.

The number of the subject is not changed by a negative construction following the subject.

EXAMPLE
A **human being**, not a tiger nor any other animal, **becomes** the prey hunted by General Zaroff in "The Most Dangerous Game."

2c. The following indefinite pronouns are singular: *anybody, anyone, anything, each, either, everybody, everyone, everything, neither, nobody, no one, nothing, one, somebody, someone, something.*

EXAMPLES
Each of the poems about farm workers **was written** by Gary Soto.
Has anyone else in your study group **read** all of *The Miracle Worker*?

2d. The following indefinite pronouns are plural: *both, few, many, several.*

EXAMPLES
Both of the poems about the San Joaquin Valley **were written** by Gary Soto.
Have many in your study group **read** *The Miracle Worker*?

2e. The indefinite pronouns *all, any, most, none,* and *some* are singular when they refer to singular words and are plural when they refer to plural words.

SINGULAR	**Some** of the show **is** funny.
PLURAL	**Some** of the skits and other acts **are** funny.
SINGULAR	**All** of the house **looks** clean.
PLURAL	**All** of the houses **look** clean.

2f. A *compound subject,* which is two or more subjects that have the same verb, may be singular, plural, or either.

(1) Subjects joined by *and* usually take a plural verb.

EXAMPLE
Both **Leslie Marmon Silko** and **Mari Evans are** poets.

A compound subject that names only one person or thing takes a singular verb.

EXAMPLES
My **pen pal and best friend is** my cousin.
Macaroni and cheese makes a good side dish.

(2) Singular subjects joined by *or* or *nor* take a singular verb.

EXAMPLES
Either the **principal** or the **coach has** to approve it.
Neither **Della** nor **Jim was** disappointed.

(3) When a singular subject and a plural subject are joined by *or* or *nor,* the verb agrees with the subject nearer the verb.

EXAMPLES
Neither the losers nor the **winner was** happy with the outcome of the match.
Neither the winner nor the **losers were** happy with the outcome of the match.

 NOTE If such a construction sounds awkward, revise the sentence to give each part of the subject its own verb.

EXAMPLE
The **losers were** not happy with the outcome of the match, and neither **was** the **winner**.

 For more information about subjects, see pages 1011–1012.

2g. *Don't* and *doesn't* must agree with their subjects.

With the subjects *I* and *you* and with plural subjects, use *don't* (do not).

EXAMPLES
I **don't** know.
You **don't** seem happy.
Some people **don't** care.

With other subjects, use *doesn't* (does not).

EXAMPLES
He **doesn't** drive.
Donna **doesn't** work.
It **doesn't** have one.

2h. A collective noun takes a singular verb when the noun refers to the group as a unit and takes a plural verb when the noun refers to the individual parts or members of the group.

A *collective noun* is singular in form but names a group of persons or things.

SINGULAR   The class **has** elected its officers. [class = a unit]

PLURAL   The class **have** completed their projects on *Romeo and Juliet.* [class = individual students]

Common Collective Nouns

army	club	group	public
assembly	committee	herd	squad
audience	couple	jury	staff
band	crew	majority	swarm
cast	crowd	number	team
chorus	family	pack	troop
class	flock	pair	wildlife

2i. A verb agrees with its subject, not with its predicate nominative.

SINGULAR   The main **attraction is** the marching bands.

PLURAL   The marching **bands are** the main attraction.

2j. A verb agrees with its subject even when the verb precedes the subject, as in sentences beginning with *here* or *there* and in questions.

SINGULAR   Here **is** [*or* here's] my **drawing** of the Cyclops.

PLURAL   Here **are** my **drawings** of the Cyclops.

SINGULAR   When in the program **does** the **skater perform** her triple axel?

PLURAL   When in the program **do** the **fans start** clapping to the music?

 NOTE   Contractions such as *here's, there's,* and *where's* should be used only with subjects that are singular in meaning.

2k. An expression of an amount (a length of time, a statistic, or a fraction, for example) is singular when the amount is thought of as a unit or when it refers to a singular word and is plural when the amount is thought of as many parts or when it refers to a plural word.

SINGULAR   **Twenty dollars is** the amount Della receives for her hair. [*Twenty dollars* is the single amount Della receives.]

PLURAL   **Twenty dollars were stuck** together. [*Twenty individual dollars were stuck together.*]

SINGULAR   **Three fourths** of the barrel **is** full. [*Three fourths* refers to *barrel,* a singular word.]

PLURAL   **Three fourths** of the barrels **have been** loaded. [*Three fourths* refers to *barrels,* a plural word.]

2l. The title of a creative work (such as a book, song, film, or painting) or the name of an organization, a country, or a city (even if it is plural in form) takes a singular verb.

EXAMPLES
"Marigolds" **is** a story by Eugenia W. Collier.
Friends of the Earth was founded in 1969.
The Netherlands has thousands of canals.

2m. A few nouns, although plural in form, take singular verbs.

EXAMPLE
The **news** of the nominee for the Supreme Court **was** a surprise to many observers.

Some nouns that end in –s take a plural verb even though they refer to a single item.

EXAMPLES
The **scissors need** to be sharpened.
Were these **pants** on sale?
The **pliers are** next to the wrench.

AGREEMENT OF PRONOUN AND ANTECEDENT

A pronoun usually refers to a noun or another pronoun. The word that a pronoun refers to is called its *antecedent.*

2n. A pronoun agrees with its antecedent in number and gender. Singular pronouns refer to singular antecedents. A few personal pronouns indicate

gender: feminine, masculine, or neuter. Plural pronouns refer to plural antecedents. No plural pronouns indicate gender.

MASCULINE	he	him	his	himself
FEMININE	she	her	hers	herself
NEUTER	it	it	its	itself

EXAMPLES
Juliet stabs **herself.** [singular, feminine]
General Zaroff thinks that Rainsford has escaped **him.** [singular, masculine]
After eating the Lotus plant, the **men** did not want to return to **their** homeland. [plural]

2o. A singular pronoun is used to refer to *anybody, anyone, anything, each, either, everybody, everyone, everything, neither, nobody, no one, nothing, one, somebody, someone,* or *something.* The gender of any of these pronouns can sometimes be determined by a word in a phrase following the pronoun.

EXAMPLES
Each of the **boys** held some pebbles in **his** hand.
Everyone on the **girls'** tennis team won **her** match.

When the antecedent could be either masculine or feminine, use both the masculine and the feminine pronoun forms connected by *or.*

EXAMPLE
Everybody should choose **his or her** friends carefully.

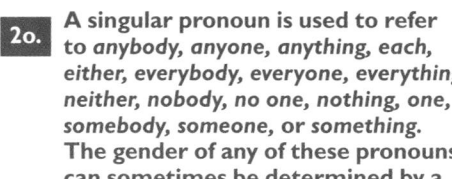

Avoiding the *His or Her* Construction

When an antecedent could be either masculine or feminine, you can avoid the *his or her* construction by using plural nouns and pronouns. You can also change the possessive *his or her* to an article (*a, an, the*) or eliminate it altogether.

ORIGINAL
A person should choose his or her friends carefully.

REVISED
People should choose **their** friends carefully.
A person should choose **a** friend carefully.
People should choose friends carefully.

Try It Out
Revise each of the following sentences to eliminate the *his or her* construction.

1. Each person had to hide his or her talents.
2. Could anyone take off his or her handicap bag?
3. Everybody had to be equal to his or her neighbor.
4. Did Harrison or the dancer realize his or her fate?
5. Neither he nor she wore his or her handicaps.

2p. A singular pronoun is used to refer to two or more singular antecedents joined by *or* or *nor.*

EXAMPLES
Paula or Janet will present **her** interpretation of Denise Levertov's "The Secret."
Neither **Richard nor Bob** has read **his** report on Ray Bradbury.

If a sentence sounds awkward when the antecedents are of different genders, revise it.

AWKWARD Either Ben or Maya will read his or her report on O. Henry.

REVISED Either **Ben** will read **his** report on O. Henry, or **Maya** will read **hers.**

2q. A plural pronoun is used to refer to two or more antecedents joined by *and.*

EXAMPLES
Romeo and Juliet marry despite the feud between **their** families.
Doodle and his **brother** spent much time with each other; **they** became very close.

2r. The number of a relative pronoun (such as *who, whom, whose, which,* or *that*) depends on the number of its antecedent.

EXAMPLES
Aretha is one **friend who** always **keeps her** word. [*Who* refers to the singular noun *friend.* Therefore, the singular forms *keeps* and *her* are used to agree with *who.*]
Many who volunteer find **their** experiences rewarding. [*Who* refers to the plural pronoun *many.* Therefore, the plural forms *volunteer* and *their* are used to agree with *who.*]

 For more about relative pronouns in adjective clauses, see page 1009.

Try It Out
Possible Answers
1. People had to hide their talents.
2. Could anyone take off the handicap bag?
3. Everybody had to be equal to everyone else.
4. Did Harrison and the dancer realize their fate?
5. Neither he nor she wore a handicap.

3 USING VERBS

THE PRINCIPAL PARTS OF VERBS

 3a. The four principal parts of a verb are the *base form*, the *present participle*, the *past*, and the *past participle*. These principal parts are used to form all the different verb tenses.

3b. A *regular verb* forms its past and past participle by adding *–d* or *–ed* to the base form.

3c. An *irregular verb* forms its past and past participle in some other way than by adding *–d* or *–ed* to the base form.

COMMON REGULAR VERBS

BASE FORM	PRESENT PARTICIPLE	PAST	PAST PARTICIPLE
ask	(is) asking	asked	(have) asked
attack	(is) attacking	attacked	(have) attacked
raise	(is) raising	raised	(have) raised
plan	(is) planning	planned	(have) planned
try	(is) trying	tried	(have) tried

COMMON IRREGULAR VERBS

BASE FORM	PRESENT PARTICIPLE	PAST	PAST PARTICIPLE
be	(is) being	was, were	(have) been
begin	(is) beginning	began	(have) begun
bring	(is) bringing	brought	(have) brought
burst	(is) bursting	burst	(have) burst
drink	(is) drinking	drank	(have) drunk
drive	(is) driving	drove	(have) driven
eat	(is) eating	ate	(have) eaten
fall	(is) falling	fell	(have) fallen
find	(is) finding	found	(have) found
freeze	(is) freezing	froze	(have) frozen
go	(is) going	went	(have) gone
keep	(is) keeping	kept	(have) kept
lay	(is) laying	laid	(have) laid
lead	(is) leading	led	(have) led
lie	(is) lying	lay	(have) lain
ride	(is) riding	rode	(have) ridden
rise	(is) rising	rose	(have) risen
set	(is) setting	set	(have) set
shake	(is) shaking	shook	(have) shaken
sing	(is) singing	sang	(have) sung
sit	(is) sitting	sat	(have) sat
steal	(is) stealing	stole	(have) stolen
swim	(is) swimming	swam	(have) swum
tear	(is) tearing	tore	(have) torn

NOTE The examples in the chart at the left include *is* and *have* in parentheses to show that helping verbs (forms of *be* and *have*) are used with the present participle and past participle forms.

 Drop the final silent e in the base form of a verb when adding *–ing* and *–ed* to form the present participle and past participle.

PRESENT PARTICIPLES
share + –ing = shar**ing**
dive + –ing = div**ing**

PAST PARTICIPLES
raise + –ed = raise**d**
receive + –ed = receive**d**

EXCEPTIONS
dye + –ing = dy**eing**
singe + –ing = sing**eing**

For more about correct spelling when adding suffixes to words, see page 1033.

NOTE If you are not sure about the principal parts of a verb, look in a dictionary. Entries for irregular verbs give the principal parts. If no principal parts are listed, the verb is a regular verb.

TENSE

3d. The *tense* of a verb indicates the time of the action or the state of being expressed by the verb. Verbs in English have six tenses: *present, past, future, present perfect, past perfect,* and *future perfect.* The tenses are formed from the verb's principal parts.

(1) The ***present tense*** is used mainly to express an action or a state of being that is occurring now.

EXAMPLES
The car **turns** into the driveway.
They **like** my idea for a science project.

The present tense is also used

- to show a customary or habitual action or state of being
- to express a general truth—something that is always true
- to make historical events seem current (such use is called the **historical present**)
- to discuss a literary work (such use is called the **literary present**)
- to express future time

EXAMPLES
Every November she **bakes** fruitcakes for her friends. [customary action]
The sun **sets** in the west. [general truth]
In 1905, Albert Einstein **proposes** his theory of relativity. [historical present]
Maya Angelou's *I Know Why the Caged Bird Sings* **tells** the story of her childhood. [literary present]
Finals **begin** next week. [future time]

(2) The ***past tense*** is used to express an action or a state of being that occurred in the past but that is not occurring now.

EXAMPLES
Jim **gave** Della a set of combs.
The children **annoyed** Miss Lottie.

A past action or state of being can also be shown with the verb *used* followed by an infinitive.

EXAMPLE
We **used to live** in Chicago.

(3) The ***future tense*** (formed with *will* or *shall* and the verb's base form) is used to express an action or a state of being that will occur.

EXAMPLES
I **shall play** the part of Romeo.
They **will arrive** soon.

A future action or state of being can also be shown in other ways.

EXAMPLES
They **are going to win.**
We **leave** for the theater **in an hour.**

(4) The ***present perfect tense*** (formed with *have* or *has* and the verb's past participle) is used to express an action or a state of being that occurred at some indefinite time in the past.

EXAMPLES
Doodle **has learned** how to walk.
We **have read** the *Odyssey.*

The present perfect tense is also used to express an action or a state of being that began in the past and continues into the present.

EXAMPLE
We **have lived** in the same house for nine years.

(5) The ***past perfect tense*** (formed with *had* and the verb's past participle) is used to express an action or a state of being that was completed in the past before some other past action or event.

EXAMPLES
Lizabeth regretted what she **had done.** [The doing occurred before the regretting.]
When you called, I **had** already **eaten** supper. [The eating occurred before the calling.]

(6) The ***future perfect tense*** (formed with *will have* or *shall have* and the verb's past participle) is used to express an action or a state of being that will be completed in the future before some other future occurrence.

EXAMPLES
By the time Mom returns, I **will have done** my chores. [The doing will be completed before the returning.]
He **will have finished** his Hebrew lessons before his bar mitzvah. [The finishing will be completed before the bar mitzvah.]

Each of the six verb tenses has an additional form called the ***progressive form.*** The progressive form expresses a continuing action or state of being. It consists of the appropriate tense of *be* plus the verb's present participle. For the perfect tenses, the progressive form also includes one or more helping verbs.

Present Progressive	am, are, is giving
Past Progressive	was, were giving
Future Progressive	will (shall) be giving
Present Perfect Progressive	has, have been giving
Past Perfect Progressive	had been giving
Future Perfect Progressive	will (shall) have been giving

LANGUAGE HANDBOOK   999

Try It Out
Possible Answers
1. Before he went away, they had spent much time together.
2. When they have gathered enough nuts, they go shopping.
3. By the time the moon rises tonight, they will have finished.
4. C
5. He was grateful for all they had shared during the past year.

3e. Do not change needlessly from one tense to another.

INCONSISTENT Jim sold his watch and buys Della a set of combs. [change from past to present tense]

CONSISTENT Jim **sold** his watch and **bought** Della a set of combs. [past tense]

Using Appropriate Verb Tenses
Using different verb tenses is often necessary to show the order of events that occur at different times.

NONSTANDARD I regretted that I chose such a broad topic.

STANDARD I **regretted** that I **had chosen** such a broad topic. [Since the action of choosing was completed before the action of regretting, the verb should be *had chosen*, not *chose*.]

Try It Out
For each of the following sentences, change the verb tenses to show the order of events that occur at different times. If a sentence is correct, write *C*.

1. Before he went away, they spent much time together.
2. When they gathered enough nuts, they go shopping.
3. By the time the moon rises tonight, they will finish.
4. She told ghost stories and was superstitious.
5. He was grateful for all they shared during the past year.

ACTIVE AND PASSIVE VOICE

3f. A verb in the *active voice* expresses an action done by its subject. A verb in the *passive voice* expresses an action received by its subject.

A verb in the passive voice is always a verb phrase that includes a form of *be* and the main verb's past participle.

1000 LANGUAGE HANDBOOK

ACTIVE VOICE Rainsford **surprised** General Zaroff. [The subject, *Rainsford*, performs the action.]

PASSIVE VOICE General Zaroff **was surprised** by Rainsford. [The subject, *General Zaroff*, receives the action.]

ACTIVE VOICE William Gibson **wrote** *The Miracle Worker*.

PASSIVE VOICE *The Miracle Worker* **was written** by William Gibson.

3g. Use the passive voice sparingly.

The passive voice is not any less correct than the active voice, but it is less direct, less forceful, and less concise. As a result, a sentence written in the passive voice can often be wordy and can sound awkward or weak.

AWKWARD PASSIVE Mme. Forestier's necklace was borrowed by Mme. Loisel.

ACTIVE Mme. Loisel **borrowed** Mme. Forestier's necklace.

The passive voice is useful, however, in certain situations:

1. when you do not know the performer of the action

EXAMPLE
The Globe Theater **was built** in 1599.

2. when you do not want to reveal the performer of the action

EXAMPLE
Unfounded accusations **were made** against the candidate.

3. when you want to emphasize the receiver of the action

EXAMPLE
Abraham Lincoln **was elected** president of the United States in 1860.

COMPUTER NOTE Some software programs can identify and highlight passive-voice verbs. If you use such a program, keep in mind that it can't tell why you used the passive voice. If you did so for one of the reasons listed under 3g above, you may want to leave the verb in the passive voice.

Resources
- *Language Handbook Resources,* pp. 42–52
- *Language Workshop CD-ROM,* Chapter 4: Using Pronouns Correctly

CASE

Case is the form that a noun or pronoun takes to indicate its use in a sentence. In English, there are three cases: *nominative, objective,* and *possessive*. Most personal pronouns have a different form for each case.

 NOTE The form of a noun is the same for both the nominative and the objective case. For the possessive case, however, a noun changes its form, usually by adding an apostrophe and an s to singular nouns and only an apostrophe to plural nouns.

NOMINATIVE	The **sniper** fired his rifle.
OBJECTIVE	Someone shot the **sniper.**
POSSESSIVE	Who was the **sniper's** enemy?

The Nominative Case

4a. A subject of a verb is in the nominative case.

EXAMPLES
She was glad that **they** were elected. [*She* is the subject of *was; they* is the subject of *were elected.*]

Is **Della** or **he** disappointed? [*Della* and *he* are the compound subject of *is.*]

4b. A predicate nominative is in the nominative case.

A *predicate nominative* follows a linking verb and explains or identifies the subject of the verb.

EXAMPLES
The woman who borrows the necklace is **she.** [*She* follows *is* and identifies the subject *woman.*]

The main characters are **he** and his **brother** Doodle. [*He* and *brother* follow *are* and identify the subject *characters.*]

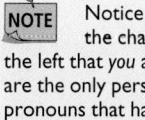 **NOTE** Expressions such as *It's me, That's him,* and *Could it be her?* are informal usage. Avoid such expressions in formal speaking and writing.

The Objective Case

4c. A direct object of a verb is in the objective case.

A *direct object* follows an action verb and tells *whom* or *what.*

EXAMPLES
Lizabeth destroyed **them.** [*Them* tells *what* Lizabeth destroyed.]

Friar Laurence helps **her** and **him.** [*Her* and *him* tell *whom* Friar Laurence helps.]

PERSONAL PRONOUNS			
SINGULAR			
	NOMINATIVE	**OBJECTIVE**	**POSSESSIVE**
FIRST PERSON	I	me	my, mine
SECOND PERSON	you	you	your, yours
THIRD PERSON	he, she, it	him, her, it	his, her, hers, its
PLURAL			
	NOMINATIVE	**OBJECTIVE**	**POSSESSIVE**
FIRST PERSON	we	us	our, ours
SECOND PERSON	you	you	your, yours
THIRD PERSON	they	them	their, theirs

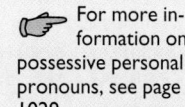 **NOTE** Notice in the chart at the left that *you* and *it* are the only personal pronouns that have the same form in both the nominative case and the objective case.

☞ For more information on possessive personal pronouns, see page 1029.

Try It Out

Possible Answers

1. The girl whom they admired was reading.
2. Do you know boys like the ones of whom he speaks?
3. They talked about the woman whom each of them would marry.
4. The field of carpentry appealed to the boy for whom that kind of work was easy.
5. The other boy of whom Gary Soto wrote said that he would go to school.

4d. **An indirect object of a verb is in the objective case.**

An *indirect object* comes before a direct object and tells *to whom* or *to what* or *for whom* or *for what*.

EXAMPLES

Buddy gave **her** a kite. [*Her* tells *to whom* Buddy gave a kite.]

Molly made **him** and **me** a tape. [*Him* and *me* tell *for whom* Molly made a tape.]

4e. **An object of a preposition is in the objective case.**

An *object of a preposition* comes at the end of a phrase that begins with a preposition.

EXAMPLES

Mme. Loisel borrows a necklace from **her.**
This gift is for **him** and **her.**

SPECIAL PRONOUN PROBLEMS

4f. **The pronoun *who* (*whoever*) is in the nominative case. The pronoun *whom* (*whomever*) is in the objective case.**

NOMINATIVE **Who** wrote *Black Boy*? [*Who* is the subject of *wrote*.]

OBJECTIVE From **whom** did Mme. Loisel borrow the necklace? [*Whom* is the object of the preposition *from*.]

When choosing between *who* and *whom* in a subordinate clause, be sure to base your choice on how the pronoun functions in the subordinate clause.

EXAMPLES

The sniper learned **who** his enemy had been. [*Who* is the predicate nominative identifying the subject *enemy*.]

The sniper learned the identity of the man **whom** he had shot. [*Whom* is the direct object of *had shot*.]

NOTE In spoken English, the use of *whom* is becoming less common. In fact, when speaking, you may correctly begin any question with *who*. In written English, however, you should distinguish between *who* and *whom*.

INFORMAL **Who** did you see at the mall?
FORMAL **Whom** did you see at the mall?

INFORMAL **Who** did you go skating with?
FORMAL With **whom** did you go skating?

Using *Whom* in Formal Situations

Frequently, *whom* is left out of subordinate clauses.

EXAMPLE

The person [whom] I have always admired most is Dr. Margaret Mead. [*Whom* is understood to be the direct object of *admired*.]

Leaving out *whom* in such cases tends to make writing sound more informal. In formal situations, it is generally better to include *whom*.

Try It Out

For each of the following sentences, insert *whom* where appropriate. Make any other changes needed for the sentence to sound correct in a formal situation.

1. The girl they admired was reading.
2. Do you know boys like the ones he speaks of?
3. They talked about the woman each of them would marry.
4. The field of carpentry appealed to the boy that kind of work was easy for.
5. The other boy Gary Soto wrote of said that he would go to school.

4g. **An appositive is in the same case as the noun or pronoun to which it refers.**

An *appositive* is a noun or pronoun placed next to another noun or pronoun to identify or explain it.

EXAMPLES

In the story, the main characters, **Doodle and he,** are brothers. [The appositive, *Doodle and he,* is in the nominative case because it identifies the subject, *characters*.]

Miss Lottie did not say a word to either of the children, **Lizabeth or him.** [The appositive, *Lizabeth or him,* is in the objective case because it identifies an object of a preposition, *children*.]

Sometimes the pronouns *we* and *us* are used with noun appositives.

EXAMPLES

We cast members have a dress rehearsal tonight. [The pronoun *we* is in the nominative case because it is the subject of *have*.]

The principal praised **us** members of the Ecology Club. [The pronoun *us* is in the objective case because it is the direct object of *praised*.]

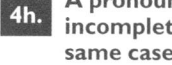

 4h. A pronoun following *than* or *as* in an incomplete construction is in the same case as it would be if the construction were completed.

Notice how the meaning of each of the following sentences is determined by the pronoun form in the incomplete construction.

EXAMPLES

I wrote you more often than **he** [wrote you].
I wrote you more often than [I wrote] **him.**

Did you help Ada as much as **I** [helped Ada]?
Did you help Ada as much as [you helped] **me**?

Clear Pronoun Reference

 4i. A pronoun should refer clearly to its antecedent.

An **antecedent** is the word a pronoun stands for.

(1) Avoid an **ambiguous reference,** which occurs when a pronoun can refer to any one of two or more antecedents.

AMBIGUOUS	Miss Lottie saw Lizabeth when she was in the garden. [*She* can refer to either Miss Lottie or Lizabeth.]
CLEAR	When **Miss Lottie** was in the garden, **she** saw Lizabeth.
CLEAR	When **Lizabeth** was in the garden, Miss Lottie saw **her.**

(2) Avoid a **general reference,** which occurs when a pronoun refers to a general idea rather than to a specific antecedent.

GENERAL	Rainsford had escaped. This annoyed General Zaroff. [*This* has no specific antecedent.]
CLEAR	That Rainsford had escaped annoyed General Zaroff.

(3) Avoid a **weak reference,** which occurs when a pronoun refers to an implied antecedent.

WEAK	Ralph enjoys writing poetry, but he never shows them to anyone else. [*Them* most likely refers to the unstated plural noun *poems,* but the writer has used the singular noun *poetry* instead.]
CLEAR	Ralph enjoys writing poetry, but he never shows his poems to anyone else.

(4) Avoid using an **indefinite reference,** which occurs when a pronoun (such as *you, it,* or *they*) refers to no particular person or thing.

INDEFINITE	In the owner's manual, they explain how to program the VCR. [*They* has no antecedent.]
CLEAR	The owner's manual explains how to program the VCR.

NOTE The indefinite use of *it* is acceptable in familiar expressions such as *It is snowing, It seems as though . . . ,* and *It's late.*

---

5 USING MODIFIERS

WHAT IS A MODIFIER?

A **modifier** is a word or group of words that limits the meaning of another word or group of words. The two kinds of modifiers are *adjectives* and *adverbs.* An **adjective** limits the meaning of a noun or a pronoun. An **adverb** limits the meaning of a verb, an adjective, or another adverb.

Adjective or Adverb?

Although many adverbs end in –*ly,* many others do not. Furthermore, not all words with the –*ly* ending are adverbs. Some adjectives also end in –*ly.* Therefore, you can't tell whether a word is an adjective or adverb simply by looking for the –*ly* ending.

ADVERBS NOT ENDING IN –LY		
arrive **soon**		sit **here**
not angry		run **loose**
walk **home**		**very** hot

ADJECTIVES ENDING IN –LY		
daily diet		**holy** place
curly hair		**silly** joke

In addition, some words can be used as either adjectives or adverbs.

ADJECTIVES	ADVERBS
He is an **only** child.	She has **only** one sister.
I have an **early** class.	I get up **early.**
Tina has a **fast** bicycle.	The baby is **fast** asleep.
We caught the **last** bus.	We left **last.**

Resources

- *Language Handbook Resources,* pp. 53–62
- *Language Workshop CD-ROM,* Chapter 5: Using Modifiers Correctly

COMPARISON OF MODIFIERS

5a. The forms of modifiers change to show comparison.

The three degrees of comparison are *positive, comparative,* and *superlative.*

Regular Comparison

(1) Most one-syllable modifiers form the comparative and superlative degrees by adding *–er* and *–est.*

POSITIVE	COMPARATIVE	SUPERLATIVE
deep	deeper	deepest
gentle	gentler	gentlest
careful	more careful	most careful
slowly	more slowly	most slowly
significantly	more significantly	most significantly
fresh	less fresh	least fresh
common	less common	least common

(2) Some two-syllable modifiers form the comparative and superlative degrees by adding *–er* and *–est.* Other two-syllable modifiers form the comparative and superlative degrees by using *more* and *most.*

(3) Modifiers of more than two syllables form the comparative and superlative degrees by using *more* and *most.*

(4) All modifiers, no matter how many syllables they have, show decreasing degrees of comparison by using *less* and *least.*

 **TIPS FOR SPELLING**

Drop the final silent *e* before adding *–er* or *–est.*

EXAMPLES
strange + –er = strang**er**
noble + –est = nobl**est**

☞ For more information about correct spelling when adding suffixes to words, see page 1033.

Irregular Comparison

(5) Some modifiers form the comparative and superlative degrees in other ways.

POSITIVE	COMPARATIVE	SUPERLATIVE
bad	worse	worst
good/well	better	best
little	less	least
many/much	more	most

NOTE Do not add *–er, –est, more,* or *most* to irregular comparative and superlative forms. Use *worse,* not *worser* or *more worse,* and *best,* not *bestest.*

☞ For information about using *good* and *well,* see page 1036; for information about using *bad* and *badly,* see page 1035.

Use of Comparative and Superlative Forms

5b. Use the comparative degree when comparing two things. Use the superlative degree when comparing more than two.

COMPARATIVE Rainsford was **more resourceful** than Zaroff had expected him to be.

SUPERLATIVE "The Most Dangerous Game" is one of the **most suspenseful** stories I have ever read.

5c. Include the word *other* or *else* when comparing one thing with others in the same group.

ILLOGICAL Ruth is more agile than any member of her gymnastics team. [Ruth is a member of her team. Logically, she cannot be more agile than herself.]

LOGICAL Ruth is more agile than any **other** member of her gymnastics team.

ILLOGICAL Carlos ran faster than everyone. [*Everyone* includes Carlos. Logically, he cannot run faster than himself.]

LOGICAL Carlos ran faster than everyone **else.**

5d. Avoid a *double comparison*—the use of both *-er* and *more* (or *less*) or both *-est* and *most* (or *least*) to modify the same word.

EXAMPLES

William Sydney Porter, **better** [*not* more better] known as O. Henry, wrote "The Gift of the Magi."

This is the **cheapest** [*not* most cheapest] bicycle in the store.

5e. Avoid comparing items that cannot logically be compared.

ILLOGICAL	The average temperature in Dallas is higher than Spokane. [illogical comparison between a temperature and a city]
LOGICAL	The average temperature in Dallas is higher than **the average temperature in** Spokane.
ILLOGICAL	A coral snake's venom is more dangerous than a rattlesnake. [illogical comparison between a snake's venom and a snake]
LOGICAL	A coral snake's venom is more dangerous than a **rattlesnake's** [*or* **rattlesnake's venom**].

State both parts of an incomplete comparison if there is any chance of misunderstanding.

UNCLEAR	I visited her more than Elise.
CLEAR	I visited her more than **I visited** Elise.
CLEAR	I visited her more than Elise **visited her.**

PLACEMENT OF MODIFIERS

5f. Avoid using a *dangling modifier*—a modifying word or word group that does not sensibly modify any word or word group in the same sentence.

DANGLING	Working together, our goal can be attained within a few months.
CLEAR	Working together, we can attain our goal within a few months.
CLEAR	We can attain our goal within a few months by working together.

You may correct a dangling modifier

- by adding a word or words that the dangling modifier can sensibly modify
- by adding a word or words to the dangling modifier
- by rewording the sentence

DANGLING	Peering over the parapet, an armored car was seen. [Who or what was peering over the parapet?]
CLEAR	Peering over the parapet, the **sniper** saw an armored car.
DANGLING	To understand Denise Levertov's poetry, some knowledge of figurative language is necessary. [Who needs to know figurative language?]
CLEAR	To understand Denise Levertov's poetry, the **reader** needs some knowledge of figurative language.
DANGLING	While burying the scarlet ibis, a hymn is sung. [Who or what is burying the scarlet ibis?]
CLEAR	While burying the scarlet ibis, **Doodle** sings a hymn.

 NOTE A sentence may appear to have a dangling modifier when *you* is the understood subject. In such cases, the modifier is not dangling; it modifies the understood subject.

EXAMPLE

To find the correct spelling, [you] look up the word in a dictionary.

☞ For more information about understood subjects, see 8g (4) on page 1012.

5g. Avoid using a *misplaced modifier*—a modifying word or word group that sounds awkward or unclear because it seems to modify the wrong word or word group.

To correct a misplaced modifier, place the modifier as near as possible to the word or word group you intend it to modify.

MISPLACED	Doodle reveals to his family that he has learned to walk on his sixth birthday. [Does Doodle reveal or does he learn on his sixth birthday?]
CLEAR	**On his sixth birthday,** Doodle reveals to his family that he has learned to walk.
MISPLACED	Born eight weeks ago, we adopted one of the puppies. [Were we or the puppies born eight weeks ago?]
CLEAR	We adopted one of the puppies **born eight weeks ago.**

☞ For more information on phrase and clause modifiers, see Part 6: Phrases and Part 7: Clauses.

- *Language Handbook Resources,*
  pp. 63–73
- *Language Workshop CD-ROM,*
  Chapter 6—Lessons 24–28:
  Prepositional Phrases, Verbal
  Phrases, and Appositive Phrases

6 PHRASES

6a. A *phrase* is a group of related words that is used as a single part of speech and that does not contain both a verb and its subject.

EXAMPLES

has been sitting [verb phrase; no subject]
about you and me [prepositional phrase; no subject or verb]

 If a group of words has both a subject and a verb, it is called a clause. For more information, see Part 7: Clauses.

PREPOSITIONAL PHRASES

6b. A *prepositional phrase* begins with a preposition and ends with a noun or pronoun that is called the *object of the preposition.* A prepositional phrase may also contain modifiers of the object of the preposition.

EXAMPLES

The sniper ran **across the street.** [The noun *street* is the object of the preposition *across.*]
In front of him was Fortunato. [The pronoun *him* is the object of the compound preposition *in front of.*]
Kyoko called **to Nancy and me.** [Both *Nancy* and *me* are objects of the preposition *to.*]

(1) A prepositional phrase that modifies a noun or pronoun is called an *adjective phrase.*

An adjective phrase tells *what kind* or *which one.*

EXAMPLES

Lizabeth destroyed Miss Lottie's garden **of marigolds.** [*Of marigolds* modifies the noun *garden,* telling *what kind.*]
All **of them** watched Doodle bury the scarlet ibis. [*Of them* modifies the pronoun *all,* telling *which ones.*]

An adjective phrase usually follows the word it modifies. That word may be the object of another preposition.

EXAMPLE

"Poison" is the title **of a story by Roald Dahl.** [*Of a story* modifies the noun *title. By Roald Dahl* modifies the noun *story,* the object of the preposition *of.*]

More than one adjective phrase may modify the same noun or pronoun.

EXAMPLE

The bottle **of vitamins on the shelf** is almost empty. [*Of vitamins* and *on the shelf* modify the noun *bottle.*]

(2) A prepositional phrase that modifies a verb, an adjective, or an adverb is called an *adverb phrase.*

An adverb phrase tells *when, where, how, why,* or *to what extent.*

EXAMPLES

By his sixth birthday Doodle could walk. [*By his sixth birthday* modifies *could walk,* telling *when.*]
Had a snake crawled **under the sheet?** [*Under the sheet* modifies *had crawled,* telling *where.*]
She answered **with a smile.** [*With a smile* modifies *answered,* telling *how.*]
Everyone remained quiet **because of the snake.** [*Because of the snake* modifies *quiet,* telling *why.*]
Is the water warm enough **for swimming?** [*For swimming* modifies *enough,* telling *to what extent.*]

An adverb phrase may come either before or after the word or word group it modifies.

EXAMPLES

For Christmas, Buddy gave her a kite.
Buddy gave her a kite **for Christmas.**

More than one adverb phrase may modify the same word or group of words.

EXAMPLE

In November she and Buddy bake fruitcakes **for their friends.** [*In November* tells *when* they bake the fruitcakes, and *for their friends* tells *why* they bake them.]

 For more information about placement of modifying phrases, see page 1005.

VERBALS AND VERBAL PHRASES

A *verbal* is a form of a verb used as a noun, an adjective, or an adverb. A *verbal phrase* consists of a verbal and its modifiers and complements. The three kinds of verbals are *participles, gerunds,* and *infinitives.*

Participles and Participial Phrases

6c. A *participle* is a verb form that can be used as an adjective. A *participial phrase* consists of a participle and all the words related to the participle.

(1) *Present participles* end in *–ing*.

EXAMPLES
Doodle collapsed in the **pouring** rain. [The present participle *pouring* modifies the noun *rain.*]
Lying quietly in his bed, Harry told Timber about the snake. [The participial phrase *lying quietly in his bed* modifies the noun *Harry.* Both the adverb *quietly* and the adverb phrase *in his bed* modify the present participle *lying.*]

(2) Most *past participles* end in *–d* or *–ed*. Others are irregularly formed.

EXAMPLES
Lizabeth sat in the **ruined** garden and cried. [The past participle *ruined* modifies the noun *garden.*]
The speaker, **known for her strong support of recycling,** was loudly applauded. [The participial phrase *known for her strong support of recycling* modifies the noun *speaker.* The adverb phrase *for her strong support* modifies the past participle *known.* The adjective phrase *of recycling* modifies *support.*]

Do not confuse a participle used as an adjective with a participle used as part of a verb phrase.

| ADJECTIVE | Fortunato, **struggling** to free himself, begged Montresor to unchain him. |
| VERB PHRASE | Fortunato, who **was struggling** to free himself, begged Montresor to unchain him. |

 For more information about participles, see page 998. For more about the placement of participial phrases, see page 1005.

Gerunds and Gerund Phrases

6d. A *gerund* is a verb form ending in *–ing* that is used as a noun. A *gerund phrase* consists of a gerund and all the words related to the gerund.

EXAMPLES
Violently destroying the marigolds was Lizabeth's last act of childhood. [The gerund phrase is the subject of *was.* The adverb *violently* modifies the gerund *destroying,* and *marigolds* is the direct object of *destroying.*]

They enjoy **making fruitcakes together.** [The gerund phrase is the direct object of *enjoy. Fruitcakes* is the direct object of the gerund *making,* and the adverb *together* modifies *making.*]
His job is **giving the customers their menus.** [The gerund phrase is the predicate nominative explaining the subject *job. Customers* is the indirect object and *menus* is the direct object of the gerund *giving.*]
Rainsford escaped from Zaroff by **leaping into the sea.** [The gerund phrase is the object of the preposition *by.* The adverb phrase *into the sea* modifies the gerund *leaping.*]

Do not confuse a gerund with a present participle used as an adjective or as part of a verb phrase.

EXAMPLE
Following the basketball coach's advice, she was **planning** to go on with her **training.** [*Following* is a present participle modifying *she. Planning* is part of the verb phrase *was planning. Training* is a gerund used as the object of the preposition *with.*]

 NOTE When preceding a gerund, a noun or pronoun should be in the possessive form.

EXAMPLES
Pedro's constant practicing improved **his** playing.

Infinitives and Infinitive Phrases

6e. An *infinitive* is a verb form, usually preceded by *to*, that can be used as a noun, an adjective, or an adverb. An *infinitive phrase* consists of an infinitive and all the words related to the infinitive.

NOUN	**To proofread your writing carefully** is important. [The infinitive phrase is the subject of *is. Writing* is the direct object of the infinitive, *to proofread,* and the adverb *carefully* modifies *to proofread.*]
	Why did she finally decide **to buy that video?** [The infinitive phrase is the direct object of *decide. Video* is the direct object of the infinitive *to buy.*]
	Zaroff's plan was **to hunt Rainsford.** [The infinitive phrase is the predicate nominative identifying the subject *plan. Rainsford* is the direct object of the infinitive *to hunt.*]

ADJECTIVE Friar Laurence's plan **to help Romeo and Juliet** failed. [The infinitive phrase modifies the noun *plan*. *Romeo* and *Juliet* are the direct objects of the infinitive *to help*.]

ADVERB Fortunato was eager **to taste the amontillado.** [The infinitive phrase modifies the adjective *eager*. *Amontillado* is the direct object of the infinitive *to taste*.]

Sometimes the *to* of the infinitive is omitted.

EXAMPLE
You should go [to] get a warmer jacket.

 NOTE Do not confuse an infinitive with a prepositional phrase that begins with *to*.

EXAMPLE
Doodle and he went **to the creek** [prepositional phrase] **to swim.** [infinitive]

 6f. An infinitive may have a subject, in which case it forms an *infinitive clause*.

EXAMPLE
Juliet trusted Friar Laurence and asked **him to help her.** [The infinitive clause is the direct object of *asked*. *Him* is the subject of the infinitive *to help*. *Her* is the direct object of *to help*.]

Notice in the example that a pronoun functioning as the subject of an infinitive clause takes the objective form.

 **Using Verbals and Verbal Phrases**

You can use verbals and verbal phrases to clarify relationships between ideas and to make your writing more interesting and concise.

ORIGINAL Coyotes barked near the river. Momaday heard them at dusk.

REVISED Momaday heard coyotes **barking near the river at dusk.** [present participial phrase]

Try It Out

Combine each of the following pairs of sentences by using the predicate of one sentence to form a verbal or verbal phrase that can be placed in the other sentence. Revise your sentence as needed to make it clear and concise.

1. N. Scott Momaday often rode his horse. For him, this activity was "an exercise of the mind."

2. He rode his horse, Pecos, over the hills of New Mexico. Along the way, he imagined that he was traveling with Billy the Kid.
3. Sometimes he and Billy saved a wagon train in trouble. Such a rescue was one of Momaday's favorite adventures.
4. Pecos could outrun the other horses in Jemez. Momaday was proud of his horse's ability.
5. Scents of pine and cedar smoke filled the air. A fresh, cold wind carried them from the canyon.

APPOSITIVES AND APPOSITIVE PHRASES

6g. An *appositive* is a noun or a pronoun placed beside another noun or pronoun to identify it or explain it. An *appositive phrase* consists of an appositive and its modifiers.

EXAMPLES
Kurt Vonnegut wrote the story **"Harrison Bergeron."** [The appositive *"Harrison Bergeron"* identifies the noun *story*.]
In the movie, Anne Bancroft played the role of Annie Sullivan, **Helen's teacher.** [The appositive phrase *Helen's teacher* explains the noun *Annie Sullivan*.]
Odysseus blinded Cyclops, **the one-eyed giant.** [The appositive phrase *the one-eyed giant* explains the noun *Cyclops*.]

An appositive phrase usually follows the noun or pronoun it refers to. For emphasis, however, it may come at the beginning of a sentence.

EXAMPLE
A noble leader of his people, Chief Joseph spoke with quiet dignity.

Appositives and appositive phrases are usually set off by commas. However, if the appositive is closely related to the preceding noun or pronoun, it should not be set off by commas.

EXAMPLES
My brother **Richard** goes to college. [The writer has more than one brother, and the appositive identifies which brother goes to college. Because this information is essential to the meaning of the sentence, it is not set off by commas.]
My brother, **Richard,** goes to college. [The writer has only one brother; therefore, the appositive is not necessary to identify him. Because the information is nonessential, it is set off by commas.]

Try It Out
Possible Answers
1. For N. Scott Momaday, riding his horse was "an exercise of the mind."
2. Riding his horse, Pecos, over the hills of New Mexico, he often imagined that he was traveling with Billy the Kid.
3. Saving a wagon train with Billy was one of Momaday's favorite adventures.
4. Momaday was proud of Pecos's ability to outrun the other horses in Jemez.
5. Scents of pine and cedar smoke, carried from the canyon by a fresh, cold wind, filled the air.

7a. A *clause* is a group of words that contains a verb and its subject and that is used as part of a sentence.

KINDS OF CLAUSES

7b. An *independent* (or *main*) *clause* expresses a complete thought and can stand by itself as a sentence.

EXAMPLES
Della gives Jim a watch chain, and **Jim gives Della a set of combs.**
When I wrote my report on William Shakespeare, I quoted from *Romeo and Juliet, Hamlet,* **and** *Macbeth.*

7c. A *subordinate* (or *dependent*) *clause* does not express a complete thought and cannot stand alone.

SUBORDINATE CLAUSES
whom you know
because I told him the truth
what the show is about

SENTENCES
Will the player **whom you know** autograph our baseball gloves?
Because I told him the truth, Dad wasn't too angry about the broken window.
Stephanie wants to know **what the show is about.**

7d. An *adjective clause* is a subordinate clause that modifies a noun or pronoun.

An adjective clause, which always follows the word it modifies, usually begins with a *relative pronoun,* such as *who, whom, whose, which,* or *that.* Besides introducing an adjective clause, a relative pronoun has its own function within the clause.

EXAMPLES
In "The Gift of the Magi," Della and Jim, **who are deeply in love,** make sacrifices to buy gifts for each other. [The adjective clause modifies *Della* and *Jim. Who* is the subject of *are.*]
Not all the stories **that Edgar Allan Poe wrote** deal with horror or terror. [The adjective clause modifies *stories. That* is the direct object of *wrote.*]

I read about Sequoyah, **whose invention of a written language aided other Cherokees.**
[The adjective clause modifies *Sequoyah. Whose* modifies *invention.*]

A relative pronoun is sometimes left out of an adjective clause.

EXAMPLES
Was *The Miracle Worker* the first play [that] **William Gibson wrote?**
The mechanic [whom] **you recommended** fixed my stepfather's motorcycle.

Occasionally, an adjective clause begins with the *relative adverb* where or when.

EXAMPLES
We visited the town **where Shakespeare was born.**
Summer is the season **when I feel happiest.**

 **Revising for Sentence Variety**
Although short sentences can be effective, it's a good idea to alternate between shorter sentences and longer ones. To change choppy sentences into smoother writing, revise them into adjective clauses that express the same ideas.

CHOPPY Mary Cassatt was an American painter. I enjoy her works. She was an Impressionist.
SMOOTH I enjoy the works of Mary Cassatt, who was an American Impressionist painter.

Try It Out
Use adjective clauses to combine each of the following pairs of short, choppy sentences.

1. Many people do not have homes. They wander the cities.
2. Ann appears in this article. She is one of these homeless people.
3. At one time, Ann had lived in a house. It had yellow siding.
4. Now she has only a coat. The coat is dirty and creased.
5. People like Ann need help, not labels. Their lives are hard.

Resources ———
• *Language Handbook Resources,* pp. 74–80
• *Language Workshop CD-ROM,* Chapter 6—Lessons 29–32: Clauses

Try It Out
Possible Answers
1. Many people who do not have homes wander the cities.
2. Ann, who appears in this article, is one of these homeless people.
3. At one time, Ann had lived in a house that had yellow siding.
4. Now she has only a coat that is dirty and creased.
5. People like Ann, whose lives are hard, need help, not labels.

7e. An *adverb clause* is a subordinate clause that modifies a verb, an adjective, or an adverb.

An adverb clause, which may come before or after the word it modifies, tells *how, when, where, why, to what extent (how much),* or *under what condition.* An adverb clause begins with a **subordinating conjunction,** such as *although, because, if, so that,* or *when.*

EXAMPLES

Because we students did so well in the discussion of *Romeo and Juliet,* our teacher did not assign any homework. [The adverb clause modifies *did assign,* telling *why.*]

I wrote a poem about war **after I read "The Sniper."** [The adverb clause modifies *wrote,* telling *when.*]

If Harry moves, he may disturb the sleeping snake. [The adverb clause modifies *may disturb,* telling *under what condition.*]

His pitching arm is stronger today **than it ever was.** [The adverb clause modifies *stronger,* telling *to what extent.*]

Doodle's brother was able to run faster **than Doodle could.** [The adverb clause modifies *faster,* telling *how much.*]

7f. A *noun clause* is a subordinate clause used as a subject, a predicate nom-

inative, a direct object, an indirect object, or an object of a preposition.

The words commonly used to begin noun clauses include *that, what, whether, who,* and *why.*

SUBJECT	**What Odysseus did** was clever.
PREDICATE NOMINATIVE	The captains are **who pick the players for their teams.**
DIRECT OBJECT	The sniper discovered **that his brother was the enemy.**
INDIRECT OBJECT	The clerk should tell **whoever calls** the sale prices.
OBJECT OF PREPOSITION	He knew the price of **whatever they requested.**

The word that introduces a noun clause may or may not have a function within the noun clause.

EXAMPLES

Lizabeth regretted **what she had done.** [*What* is the direct object of *had done.*]

Mme. Loisel learned **that the necklace was fake.** [*That* has no function in the clause.]

Sometimes the word that introduces a noun clause is not stated, but its meaning is understood.

EXAMPLE

His mother said [that] **he could go to the concert.**

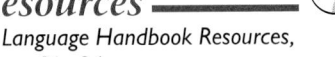

Resources

- *Language Handbook Resources,* pp. 81–94
- *Language Workshop CD-ROM,* Chapter 7—Lessons 33–39: Parts of Sentences and Classifying Sentences

8 SENTENCE STRUCTURE

SENTENCE OR SENTENCE FRAGMENT?

8a. A *sentence* is a group of words that contains a subject and a verb and that expresses a complete thought.

A sentence should begin with a capital letter and end with a period, a question mark, or an exclamation point. A group of words that either does not contain a subject and verb or does not express a complete thought is called a *sentence fragment.*

FRAGMENT	Romeo banished from Verona?
SENTENCE	Why was Romeo banished from Verona?

FRAGMENT	What a clever plan!
SENTENCE	What a clever plan he had!

FRAGMENT	When the Montagues and the Capulets learned of the deaths of Romeo and Juliet.
SENTENCE	When the Montagues and the Capulets learned of the deaths of Romeo and Juliet, they ended their feud.

COMPUTER NOTE

Many style-checking software programs can identify sentence fragments. If you have access to such a program, use it to help you evaluate your writing. Then, revise each fragment to make sure that all your sentences express complete thoughts.

SUBJECT AND PREDICATE

 8b. A sentence consists of two parts: the subject and the predicate. The *subject* tells *whom* or *what* the sentence is about. The *predicate* tells something about the subject.

In the following examples, all the words labeled *subject* make up the **complete subject,** and all the words labeled *predicate* make up the **complete predicate.**

SUBJECT — PREDICATE
Tybalt | was Juliet's cousin.

SUBJECT — PREDICATE
Two of Prince Escalus's kinsmen | died.

SUBJECT — PREDICATE
The setting of the play | is fourteenth-century Italy.

PREDICATE — SUBJECT — PREDICATE
Why did | Juliet | take the sleeping potion?

The Simple Subject

 8c. The *simple subject* is the main word or group of words that tells *whom* or *what* the sentence is about.

EXAMPLES
An **excerpt** from Richard Wright's *Black Boy* appears in this book. [The complete subject is *an excerpt from Richard Wright's* Black Boy.]
The talented **Georgia O'Keeffe** is known for her paintings of huge flowers. [The complete subject is *the talented Georgia O'Keeffe.*]

The Simple Predicate

 8d. The *simple predicate,* or *verb,* is the main word or group of words that tells something about the subject.

A simple predicate may be a single word or a **verb phrase** (a verb with one or more helping verbs).

EXAMPLES
Montresor **led** Fortunato to the catacombs. [The complete predicate is *led Fortunato to the catacombs.*]
Did Mme. Loisel **find** the necklace? [The complete predicate is *did find the necklace.*]

NOTE In this book, the term *subject* refers to the simple subject, and the term *verb* refers to the simple predicate unless otherwise indicated.

The Compound Subject and the Compound Verb

 8e. A *compound subject* consists of two or more subjects that are joined by a conjunction—usually *and* or *or*—and that have the same verb.

EXAMPLES
Does **Rainsford** or **Zaroff** win the game?
Romeo, Benvolio, and **Mercutio** attend the Capulets' party.

 8f. A *compound verb* consists of two or more verbs that are joined by a conjunction—usually *and, but,* or *or*—and that have the same subject.

EXAMPLES
Della **sold** her hair and **bought** Jim a watch chain.
Timber **looked** for the snake but **did** not **find** it.

Finding the Subject of a Sentence

 8g. To find the subject of a sentence, ask "Who?" or "What?" before the verb.

EXAMPLE
The price of those videos seems high. [What seems high? The price seems high. *Price* is the subject.]

(1) The subject of a sentence is never in a prepositional phrase.

EXAMPLES
Her **garden** of marigolds was ruined. [What was ruined? *Garden* was ruined. *Marigolds* is the object of the preposition *of.*]
On the rooftop crouched the **sniper.** [Who crouched? *Sniper* crouched. *Rooftop* is the object of the preposition *on.*]

(2) The subject of a sentence expressing a question usually follows the verb or a part of the verb phrase. Turning the question into a statement may help you find the subject.

QUESTION Did **she** give Buddy a kite?
STATEMENT **She** did give Buddy a kite.

QUESTION Is the ***Odyssey*** an epic?
STATEMENT The ***Odyssey*** is an epic.

(3) The word *there* or *here* is never the subject of a sentence.

EXAMPLES
There are your **keys.** [What are there? *Keys* are.]
Here is your **pencil.** [What is here? *Pencil* is.]

LANGUAGE HANDBOOK 1011

LANGUAGE HANDBOOK

(4) The subject of a sentence expressing a command or request is always understood to be *you*, although *you* may not appear in the sentence.

EXAMPLE
[You] Listen carefully to his question. [Who is to listen? *You* is understood.]

The subject of a command or request is *you* even when the sentence contains a **noun of direct address,** a word naming the one or ones spoken to.

EXAMPLE
Ellen, [you] please read the part of Juliet.

COMPLEMENTS

 8h. **A *complement* is a word or group of words that completes the meaning of a verb.**

Three kinds of complements are the *subject complement,* the *direct object,* and the *indirect object.*

The Subject Complement

 8i. **A *subject complement* is a word or word group that completes the meaning of a linking verb and that identifies or modifies the subject.**

The two types of subject complements are the *predicate nominative* and the *predicate adjective.*

(1) A **predicate nominative** is a noun or pronoun that follows a linking verb and that renames or identifies the subject of the verb.

EXAMPLES
"The Most Dangerous Game" is an exciting **story.** [The noun *story* identifies the subject *"The Most Dangerous Game."*]
The only people in line were **they.** [The pronoun *they* renames the subject *people.*]
The main characters are **Helen Keller** and **Annie Sullivan.** [The nouns *Helen Keller* and *Annie Sullivan* identify the subject *characters.*]

(2) A **predicate adjective** is an adjective that follows a linking verb and that modifies the subject of the verb.

EXAMPLES
The necklace was **inexpensive.** [The adjective *inexpensive* modifies the subject *necklace.*]
Miss Lottie looked **sad.** [The adjective *sad* modifies the subject *Miss Lottie.*]
The corn tastes **sweet** and **buttery.** [The adjectives *sweet* and *buttery* modify the subject *corn.*]

The Direct Object and the Indirect Object

 8j. **A *direct object* is a noun or pronoun that receives the action of a verb or that shows the result of the action. It tells *whom* or *what* after a transitive verb.**

EXAMPLES
The sniper killed his own **brother.** [killed whom? brother]
Although his watch was his most prized possession, Jim sold **it.** [sold what? it]
Shakespeare wrote not only great **plays** but also beautiful **sonnets.** [wrote what? plays and sonnets]

 8k. **An *indirect object* is a noun or pronoun that precedes the direct object and that usually tells *to whom* or *for whom* (or *to what* or *for what*) the action of the verb is done.**

EXAMPLES
Sheila read the **children** a story by Truman Capote. [read to whom? children]
Frank gave the **Red Cross** a donation. [gave to what? Red Cross]
She made her **neighbors** and other **friends** fruitcakes for Christmas. [made for whom? neighbors and friends]

NOTE A complement may precede the subject and the verb.

DIRECT OBJECT   What a good **friend** Buddy has!
PREDICATE ADJECTIVE   How **happy** Della and Jim are!

CLASSIFYING SENTENCES ACCORDING TO PURPOSE

 8l. **Sentences may be classified as *declarative, imperative, interrogative,* or *exclamatory.***

(1) A **declarative sentence** makes a statement. It is followed by a period.

EXAMPLES
One of my favorite stories is "Thank You, M'am**.**"
Jonathan, the CD-ROM you ordered a while back has finally arrived**.**
It's raining**.**

(2) An *imperative sentence* makes a request or gives a command. It is usually followed by a period. A very strong command, however, is followed by an exclamation point.

EXAMPLES

Please open your books to page 3. [request]
Be careful of the undertow. [mild command]
Stop! [strong command]

 NOTE In a command or a request, the understood subject is *you*.

(3) An *interrogative sentence* asks a question. It is followed by a question mark.

EXAMPLES

Did Friar Laurence's plan fail?
What did Romeo do when he found Juliet lying there so still and pale?

(4) An *exclamatory sentence* expresses strong feeling. It is followed by an exclamation point.

EXAMPLES

What a mess we're in now!
The battery is dead!

CLASSIFYING SENTENCES ACCORDING TO STRUCTURE

 8m. **Sentences may be classified as *simple*, *compound*, *complex*, or *compound-complex*.**

(1) A *simple sentence* has one independent clause and no subordinate clauses.

EXAMPLE

Frankenstein and *Dracula* were both written during the nineteenth century.

(2) A *compound sentence* has two or more independent clauses but no subordinate clauses.

EXAMPLES

Rita wanted to see an adventure film, **but** Carlos preferred a comedy. [two independent clauses joined by a comma and the coordinating conjunction *but*]
Harriet Tubman was a leader of the Underground Railroad; she rescued more than three hundred people. [two independent clauses joined by a semicolon]
Romeo killed Tybalt, Juliet's cousin; **as a result,** Romeo was banished from Verona. [two independent clauses joined by a semicolon and the transitional expression *as a result*]

(3) A *complex sentence* has one independent clause and at least one subordinate clause.

EXAMPLES

Juliet declared her love for Romeo before she spoke to him. [The independent clause is *Juliet declared her love for Romeo.* The subordinate clause is *before she spoke to him.*]
On Shakespeare's gravestone is an inscription that places a curse on anyone who moves his bones. [The independent clause is *on Shakespeare's gravestone is an inscription.* The subordinate clauses are *that places a curse on anyone* and *who moves his bones.*]

(4) A *compound-complex sentence* contains two or more independent clauses and at least one subordinate clause.

EXAMPLE

William Golding received the Nobel Prize in 1983; his best-known novel is *Lord of the Flies,* which he published in 1954. [The independent clauses are *William Golding received the Nobel Prize in 1983* and *his best-known novel is* Lord of the Flies. The subordinate clause is *which he published in 1954.*]

 For more on clauses, see Part 7: Clauses.

 **Varying Sentence Structure**

Paragraphs in which all the sentences have the same structure can make for monotonous reading. To help keep your readers interested, evaluate your writing to see whether you've used a variety of sentence structures. If you have not, use revising techniques—add, cut, replace, and reorder—to vary the structure of your sentences.

Try It Out

The following paragraph is composed of simple sentences. Revise the paragraph, using a variety of sentence structures.

[1] "The Most Dangerous Game" begins with a conversation about hunting. [2] Rainsford is the protagonist. [3] He and Whitney are on a yacht in the Caribbean. [4] They're near the eerie Ship-Trap Island. [5] Rainsford loves hunting. [6] According to Rainsford, sympathy for the hunted animal is foolish. [7] Later Rainsford falls overboard and swims to the island. [8] He meets General Zaroff at the general's chateau. [9] Zaroff hunts human beings for sport. [10] Soon Rainsford the hunter becomes the hunted.

Try It Out
Possible Answers

"The Most Dangerous Game" begins with a conversation about hunting. Rainsford, the protagonist, and Whitney are on a yacht in the Caribbean, near the eerie Ship-Trap Island. Rainsford loves hunting and says that sympathy for the hunted animal is foolish. Later Rainsford falls overboard and swims to the island, where he meets General Zaroff at the general's chateau. Zaroff hunts human beings for sport, and Rainsford the hunter soon becomes the hunted.

Resources

- *Language Handbook Resources,*
  pp. 95–101
- *Language Workshop CD-ROM,*
  Chapter 7—Lessons 40 and 41:
  Faulty Sentences

SENTENCE FRAGMENTS

9a. Avoid using a *sentence fragment*—a part of a sentence that has been punctuated as if it were a complete sentence.

Here are two ways to correct a sentence fragment:

1. Add words that will make the thought complete.

FRAGMENT	Shortly after his birth, was baptized in a small church in Stratford. [The verb *was baptized* has no subject. Who was baptized?]
SENTENCE	Shortly after his birth, **Shakespeare** was baptized in a small church in Stratford.
FRAGMENT	Odysseus a great hero of the Greeks. [The verb is missing. What about Odysseus?]
SENTENCE	Odysseus **became** a great hero of the Greeks.
FRAGMENT	For the balcony scene in *Romeo and Juliet.* [The subject and the verb are missing. What about the balcony scene?]
SENTENCE	**The actors are preparing** for the balcony scene in *Romeo and Juliet.*

2. Attach the fragment to a sentence that comes before or after it.

EXAMPLE	One of my favorite stories by Edgar Allan Poe is "X-ing a Paragrab." [sentence] A comic tale of a feud between two newspaper editors. [fragment]
REVISED	One of my favorite stories by Edgar Allan Poe is "X-ing a Paragrab," **a comic tale of a feud between two newspaper editors.** [appositive phrase]
EXAMPLE	When she takes off her coat. [fragment] Mme. Loisel discovers that she is no longer wearing the necklace. [sentence]
REVISED	**When she takes off her coat,** Mme. Loisel discovers that she is no longer wearing the necklace. [subordinate clause]

EXAMPLE	Odysseus figured out a way for his men and him. [sentence] To escape from the Cyclops. [fragment]
REVISED	Odysseus figured out a way for his men and him **to escape from the Cyclops.** [infinitive phrase]

For more information about sentence fragments, see page 1010.

RUN-ON SENTENCES

9b. Avoid using a *run-on sentence*—two or more complete sentences that run together as if they were one complete sentence.

There are two kinds of run-on sentences.

- A *fused sentence* has no punctuation between the complete sentences.
- A *comma splice* has only a comma between the complete sentences.

FUSED SENTENCE	Della sold her hair to buy Jim a chain for his watch Jim sold his watch to buy Della combs for her hair.
COMMA SPLICE	Della sold her hair to buy Jim a chain for his watch, Jim sold his watch to buy Della combs for her hair.

Here are five ways to correct a run-on sentence:

1. Make two sentences.

REVISED	Della sold her hair to buy Jim a chain for his watch. Jim sold his watch to buy Della combs for her hair.

2. Use a comma and a *coordinating conjunction*—*and, but, or, yet, for, so,* or *nor.*

REVISED	Della sold her hair to buy Jim a chain for his watch, **and** Jim sold his watch to buy Della combs for her hair.

3. Use a semicolon.

REVISED	Della sold her hair to buy Jim a chain for his watch; Jim sold his watch to buy Della combs for her hair.

4. Use a semicolon and a *conjunctive adverb,* such as *therefore, instead, meanwhile, still, also,* or *however.* Follow a conjunctive adverb with a comma.

REVISED Della sold her hair to buy Jim a chain for his watch**;** **however,** Jim sold his watch to buy Della combs for her hair.

5. Change one of the complete thoughts into a subordinate clause.

REVISED Della sold her hair to buy Jim a chain for his watch **while Jim sold his watch to buy Della combs for her hair**.

 For more information about combining sentences, see rules 10a–10e on pages 1015–1016.

Style-checking software can help you evaluate your writing for the use of clear, complete sentences. Many such programs can identify and highlight sentence fragments. You can also use the "Search" command offered by computer programs to identify sentences in which you've used a comma and a coordinating conjunction—one search for each different conjunction and the comma in front of it. These searches can help you check to make sure that the ideas you've combined in a compound sentence are complete and are closely related and equally important.

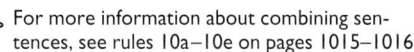

SENTENCE COMBINING

10a. Combine related sentences by taking a key word (or by using another form of the word) from one sentence and inserting it into another.

ORIGINAL Edgar Allan Poe led a short life. His life was tragic.
COMBINED Edgar Allan Poe led a short, **tragic** life.

 **Identifying Run-on Sentences**

One way to spot run-on sentences is to read your writing aloud. A natural, distinct pause in your speech often means that you need to separate sentences in some way. You can also check for run-ons by identifying subjects and verbs. Checking for clauses will help you find where one complete thought ends and another begins.

RUN-ON The family thought that Doodle would die they built him a coffin.
REVISED **Because** the family thought that Doodle would die**,** they built him a coffin.
REVISED The family thought that Doodle would die**, so** they built him a coffin.
REVISED The family thought that Doodle would die**; consequently,** they built him a coffin.

Try It Out

Revise each of the following run-on sentences.

1. Doodle and his brother had an active fantasy world, they created stories and imaginary plans.
2. Doodle was afraid of being left behind, he cried when his brother started to leave.
3. Brother taught Doodle to walk Brother was ashamed of Doodle.
4. Doodle didn't think that he could walk after much help and practice, he did.
5. He could walk perhaps he could run.

WRITING EFFECTIVE SENTENCES 10

ORIGINAL Edgar Allan Poe wrote strange stories. He wrote stories of suspense.
COMBINED Edgar Allan Poe wrote strange, **suspenseful** stories.

 When you change the form of a key word, you often need to add an ending that makes the word an adjective or an adverb. Usually this ending is *–ed, –ing,* or *–ly.*

Try It Out
Possible Answers
1. Doodle and his brother had an active fantasy world. They created stories and imaginary plans.
2. Doodle was afraid of being left behind; he cried when his brother started to leave.
3. Brother taught Doodle to walk because Brother was ashamed of Doodle.
4. Although Doodle didn't think that he could walk, after much help and practice, he did.
5. If he could walk, perhaps he could run.

Resources
- *Language Handbook Resources,* pp. 102–122
- *Language Workshop CD-ROM,* Chapter 7—Lessons 42–45: Writing Effective Sentences

10b. Combine related sentences by taking (or creating) a phrase from one sentence and inserting it into another.

ORIGINAL *A Fire in My Hands* is a collection of poems. The poems were written by Gary Soto.

COMBINED *A Fire in My Hands* is a collection of poems **by Gary Soto.** [prepositional phrase]

ORIGINAL Romeo kills Tybalt. Tybalt is Juliet's cousin.

COMBINED Romeo kills Tybalt, **Juliet's cousin.** [appositive phrase]

10c. Combine related sentences by using a coordinating conjunction (*and, but, or, or nor*) to make a compound subject, a compound verb, or both.

ORIGINAL After lunch Doodle went to Horsehead Landing. His brother went, too.

COMBINED After lunch **Doodle and his brother** went to Horsehead Landing. [compound subject]

ORIGINAL Ernesto Galarza's family immigrated to the United States. They eventually settled in Sacramento, California.

COMBINED Ernesto Galarza's family **immigrated** to the United States **and** eventually **settled** in Sacramento, California. [compound verb]

Using Compound Subjects and Compound Verbs

When you combine sentences by using compound subjects and compound verbs, make sure that your new subjects and verbs agree in number.

ORIGINAL Della has little money. Jim also doesn't have much.

COMBINED **Della and Jim have** little money. [The compound subject *Della and Jim* takes the plural verb *have*.]

Try It Out

Combine each of the following pairs of sentences into one sentence that has a compound subject or a compound verb.

1. Mrs. Johnson's husband moved to Oklahoma. He studied religion.
2. The cotton gin would not hire her. Neither would the lumber mill.
3. She didn't want to become a servant. She saw another possibility.
4. The cotton gin workers walked to her stand and bought lunch. The lumber workers also walked to her stand and bought lunch there.
5. In time, syrup was sold at the store. Canned goods were, too.

10d. Combine related sentences by creating a compound sentence.

You can form a compound sentence by linking two or more independent clauses with a comma and a coordinating conjunction, a semicolon, or a semicolon and a conjunctive adverb.

ORIGINAL Buddy makes his friend a kite. She makes him one, too.

COMBINED Buddy makes his friend a kite**, and** she makes him one, too. [comma and coordinating conjunction]

COMBINED Buddy makes his friend a kite**;** she makes him one, too. [semicolon]

COMBINED Buddy makes his friend a kite**; meanwhile,** she makes him one, too. [semicolon and conjunctive adverb]

10e. Combine related sentences by creating a complex sentence.

You can form a complex sentence by joining one independent clause with one or more subordinate clauses (adjective clause, adverb clause, or noun clause).

ORIGINAL Gwendolyn Brooks often writes about Chicago. She has won a Pulitzer Prize for her poetry.

COMBINED Gwendolyn Brooks, **who has won a Pulitzer Prize for her poetry,** often writes about Chicago. [adjective clause]

ORIGINAL Zaroff turned on the light. He saw Rainsford.

COMBINED **When Zaroff turned on the light,** he saw Rainsford. [adverb clause]

ORIGINAL The snake in "Poison" is just an illusion on Harry's part. Many readers think this.

COMBINED Many readers think **that the snake in "Poison" is just an illusion on Harry's part.** [noun clause]

Try It Out
Possible Answers

1. Mrs. Johnson's husband moved to Oklahoma and studied religion.
2. Neither the cotton gin nor the lumber mill would hire her.
3. She didn't want to become a servant and saw another possibility.
4. The cotton gin workers and the lumber workers walked to her stand and bought lunch there.
5. In time, syrup and canned goods were sold at the store.

For more information about compound and complex sentences, see page 1013.

Varying Sentence Structures

In your writing, try to use a mix of simple, compound, complex, and compound-complex sentences.

EXAMPLE

As the music and the thump of the drums grew louder, the people lined up along the street. [complex] Finally, with a blast of brass, the high school band rounded the corner. [simple] First came the drum major; setting the tempo with her baton, she proudly raised her feet as high as possible. [compound] Behind her, leading the parade of colorful floats, the musicians marched in their bright purple-and-red jackets. [simple sentence]

Try It Out

The following paragraph is composed of simple sentences. Revise the paragraph, using varied sentence structures.

[1] The boy had known hunger before. [2] This hunger was different. [3] It could not be satisfied by just a few bites. [4] It gnawed at his insides and made him weak. [5] His mother got a job. [6] She sent him to the store for groceries. [7] Some boys took his money. [8] She gave him more money and sent him again. [9] Again, the boys took his money. [10] His mother gave him a stick this time and told him to fight.

IMPROVING SENTENCE STYLE

10f. Use the same grammatical form (*parallel structure*) to express equal ideas.

NOT PARALLEL	Buddy and she liked baking fruit-cakes and to fly kites. [gerund phrase paired with infinitive phrase]
PARALLEL	Buddy and she liked **baking fruitcakes** and **flying kites.** [gerund phrase paired with gerund phrase]
PARALLEL	Buddy and she liked **to bake fruitcakes** and **to fly kites.** [infinitive phrase paired with infinitive phrase]

NOT PARALLEL	Harry received help from not only Timber but also from Ganderbai. [noun paired with prepositional phrase]
PARALLEL	Harry received help from not only **Timber** but also **Ganderbai.** [noun paired with noun]
PARALLEL	Harry received help not only **from Timber** but also **from Ganderbai.** [prepositional phrase paired with prepositional phrase]

10g. Avoid using stringy sentences—sentences that have too many independent clauses strung together with coordinating conjunctions like *and* or *but.*

You may revise a stringy sentence in one of two ways.

1. Break the sentence into two or more sentences.
2. Turn some of the independent clauses into subordinate clauses or into phrases.

STRINGY	The fire alarm rang, and everyone started to file out of school, but then our principal came down the hall, and he said that the bell was a mistake, and we went back to our classes.
REVISED	The fire alarm bell rang, and everyone started to file out of school. Then our principal came down the hall to say that the bell was a mistake. We went back to our classes.
REVISED	When the fire alarm bell rang, everyone started to file out of school. Then our principal came down the hall. He said that the bell was a mistake, and we went back to our classes.

 For more information about phrases, see Part 6: Phrases. For more about clauses, see Part 7: Clauses.

COMPUTER NOTE

Whenever you revise your writing on a computer, you can use functions such as "Copy," "Cut," and "Move" to experiment with your sentences. Try a variety of sentence beginnings and structures. Then, decide which ones work best with the other sentences in a particular paragraph.

Try It Out
Possible Answers

The boy had known hunger before, but this hunger was different. Not to be satisfied by just a few bites, it gnawed at his insides and made him weak. When his mother got a job, she sent him to the store for groceries, but some boys took his money. She gave him more money and sent him again; again, the boys took his money. This time his mother gave him a stick and told him to fight.

10h. Avoid using unnecessary words.

Here are three tips for avoiding wordiness.

1. Don't use more words than you need to use.
2. Don't use difficult words where simple ones will do.
3. Don't repeat yourself unless it's absolutely necessary.

WORDY   Fortunato is a wine connoisseur who has much knowledge of and great appreciation for fine wines.

REVISED   Fortunato is a connoisseur of fine wines.

WORDY   In the event that they were able to find the missing necklace belonging to Mme. Forestier by the last day of the month of February, the Loisels could return the other necklace.

REVISED   If they could find Mme. Forestier's necklace by the end of February, the Loisels could return the other necklace.

10i. Use a variety of sentence beginnings.

The basic structure of an English sentence is a subject followed by a verb. The following examples show how you can revise sentences to avoid beginning with the subject every time. Notice that a comma follows the introductory word, phrase, or clause in each revision.

SUBJECT FIRST	Della excitedly opened her present.
ADVERB FIRST	**Excitedly,** Della opened her present.
SUBJECT FIRST	You must study to make good grades.
INFINITIVE PHRASE FIRST	**To make good grades,** you must study.
SUBJECT FIRST	Romeo fell in love with Juliet as soon as he saw her.
ADVERB CLAUSE FIRST	**As soon as Romeo saw Juliet,** he fell in love with her.

Resources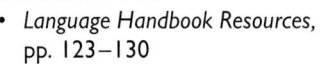

- *Language Handbook Resources,* pp. 123–130
- *Language Workshop CD-ROM,* Chapter 8—Lessons 57 and 58: Rules of Capitalization

11 CAPITALIZATION

11a. Capitalize the first word in every sentence.

EXAMPLES
The two boys in "The Talk" discuss their plans.
Stop!

(1) Capitalize the first word of a direct quotation.

EXAMPLE
Maria asked me, "**H**ave you written your report on Gary Soto?"

(2) Traditionally, the first word of a line of poetry is capitalized.

EXAMPLES
Two roads diverged in a wood, and I—
I took the one less traveled by,
And that has made all the difference.
           —Robert Frost, "The Road Not Taken"

 NOTE   Some writers do not follow these practices. When you are quoting, use capital letters exactly as they are used in the source of the quotation.

 For more information about using capital letters in quotations, see pages 1026–1027.

11b. Capitalize the first word both in the salutation and in the closing of a letter.

EXAMPLES
To Whom It May Concern:
Dear Ann,   **D**ear Sir:
Sincerely,   **Y**ours truly,

11c. Capitalize the pronoun *I* and the interjection O.

EXAMPLES
Mom says that **I** can go this weekend.
Who says "Romeo can, / Though heaven cannot.
    O Romeo, Romeo"?

11d. Capitalize proper nouns and proper adjectives.

A **common noun** is a general name for a person, a place, a thing, or an idea. A **proper noun** names a particular person, place, thing, or idea. A **proper adjective** is formed from a proper noun.

    Proper nouns and proper adjectives are always capitalized. Common nouns are not capitalized unless they begin a sentence, begin a direct quotation, or are part of a title.

1018 LANGUAGE HANDBOOK

COMMON NOUNS	PROPER NOUNS	PROPER ADJECTIVES
poet	Homer	Homeric simile
planet	Mars	Martian landscape

In proper nouns that have more than one word, do *not* capitalize articles (*a, an, the*), prepositions of fewer than five letters (such as *at, for,* and *with*), coordinating conjunctions (*and, but, for, nor, or, so, yet*), or the sign of the infinitive (*to*) unless they are the first word of the proper noun.

EXAMPLES
American Society for the Prevention of Cruelty to Animals
National Campers and Hikers Association
"Writing a Paragraph to Inform"

(1) Capitalize the names of persons and animals.

PERSONS Sandra Cisneros   Langston Hughes
ANIMALS Old Yeller   Brer Rabbit

(2) Capitalize geographical names.

For names with more than one word, capitalization may vary. Always check the spelling of such a name with the person whose name it is, or look in a reference source.

EXAMPLES
Kees van Dongen   Henry Van Dyke

Abbreviations such as *Ms., Mr., Dr.,* and *Gen.* should always be capitalized.

EXAMPLES
Mr. James Thurber   Dr. Mary McLeod Bethune

Capitalize the abbreviations *Jr.* and *Sr.* after a name, and set them off with commas.

EXAMPLE
In 1975, Gen. Daniel James, Jr., became the first African American four-star general in the U.S. Air Force.

TYPE OF NAME	EXAMPLES	
Towns and Cities	San Francisco	St. Charles
Counties, Townships, and Parishes	Hayes Township Union Parish	Kane County Manhattan
States and Territories	Florida Guam	North Carolina Northwest Territory
Countries	Canada	United States of America
Continents	Africa	North America
Islands	Long Island	Isle of Palms
Mountains	Rocky Mountains	Mount McKinley
Other Land Forms and Features	Cape Hatteras Kalahari Desert	Niagara Falls Mammoth Cave
Bodies of Water	Pacific Ocean Cross Creek	Gulf of Mexico Blue Springs
Parks	Yellowstone National Park Cleburne State Recreation Area	
Regions	the North New England	the Middle West the Great Plains
Roads, Streets, and Highways	Route 66 Gibbs Drive	Pennsylvania Turnpike Thirty-first Street

NOTE Words such as *north, west,* and *southeast* are not capitalized when they indicate direction.

EXAMPLES
north of town
traveling southeast

NOTE In a hyphenated number, the second word begins with a small letter.

EXAMPLE
Thirty-first Street

NOTE Words like *city, river, street,* and *park* are capitalized only when they are part of a name.

EXAMPLES
go to the park
go to Central Park

across the river
across the Pecos River

(3) Capitalize the names of organizations, teams, business firms, institutions, buildings and other structures, and government bodies.

TYPE OF NAME	EXAMPLES
Organizations	United Nations National Basketball Association
Teams	Tampa Bay Buccaneers Minnesota Twins
Business Firms	Quaker Oats Company Aluminum Company of America
Institutions	United States Naval Academy Bethune-Cookman College
Buildings and Other Structures	Apollo Theater Taj Mahal Golden Gate Bridge
Government Bodies	Federal Bureau of Investigation House of Representatives

NOTE Capitalize words such as *democratic* or *republican* only when they refer to a specific political party.

EXAMPLES
The new leaders promised **d**emocratic reforms.
The **D**emocratic candidates for mayor held a rally.

The word *party* in the name of a political party may be capitalized or not.

EXAMPLE
Federalist **P**arty *or* **p**arty

(4) Capitalize the names of historical events and periods, special events, holidays, and other calendar items.

TYPE OF NAME	EXAMPLES
Historical Events and Periods	French Revolution Middle Ages Boston Tea Party Mesozoic Era
Special Events	Interscholastic Debate Tournament Kansas State Fair
Holidays and Calendar Items	Labor Day Saturday December Fourth of July National Book Week

NOTE Do not capitalize the name of a season unless it is being personified or used in the name of a special event.

EXAMPLES
I'm on the committee for the **W**inter Carnival.
Soon **A**utumn will begin painting the leaves in bright colors.

(5) Capitalize the names of ships, trains, aircraft, spacecraft, monuments, awards, planets, and other particular places, things, or events.

TYPE OF NAME	EXAMPLES
Ships and Trains	*Mayflower* *Silver Meteor*
Aircraft and Spacecraft	*Spirit of St. Louis* Lockheed C-5A Galaxy *Pioneer 10* Hubble Space Telescope
Monuments and Memorials	Washington Monument Statue of Liberty Vietnam Veterans Memorial
Awards	Pulitzer Prize Congressional Medal of Honor Stanley Cup Key Club Achievement Award
Planets, Stars, and Constellations	Mercury Dog Star Ursa Major Pluto Big Dipper Rigel

NOTE The word *earth* is not capitalized unless it is used along with the names of other heavenly bodies that are capitalized. The words *sun* and *moon* are not capitalized.

EXAMPLES
The **m**oon is a satellite of the earth.
Venus is closer to Earth than Mars is.

(6) Capitalize the names of nationalities, races, and peoples.

EXAMPLES
Greek   African Americans   Hispanic   Cherokee

(7) Capitalize the brand names of business products but not the common nouns that follow the names.

EXAMPLES
Chevrolet van   Teflon pan

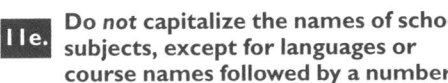

Do *not* capitalize the names of school subjects, except for languages or course names followed by a number.

EXAMPLES
algebra   English   Typing I

11f.   Capitalize titles.

(1) Capitalize the title of a person when it comes before the person's name.

EXAMPLES
President Clinton   Mr. Vonnegut

TYPE OF TITLE	EXAMPLES
Books	*The Pearl* *I Know Why the Caged Bird Sings*
Periodicals	*The Atlantic Monthly* *Field and Stream*
Poems	"The Road Not Taken" "The Girl Who Loved the Sky"
Stories	"The Cask of Amontillado" "The Most Dangerous Game"
Essays and Speeches	"The Death of a Tree" "Work and What It's Worth"
Plays	*The Miracle Worker* *The Phantom of the Opera*
Historical Documents	Declaration of Independence Emancipation Proclamation
Movies	*Dances with Wolves* *Stand and Deliver*
Radio and Television Programs	*All Things Considered* *Nova* *Star Trek: The Next Generation*
Works of Art	*American Gothic* *The Thinker*
Musical Compositions	"The Tennessee Waltz" "The Flight of the Bumblebee"
Cartoons	*Calvin and Hobbes* *The Neighborhood*

Usually, do not capitalize a title that is used alone or following a person's name, especially if the title is preceded by *a* or *the*.

EXAMPLE
Cleopatra reigned as the queen of Egypt between 51 and 30 B.C.

When a title is used alone in direct address, it is usually capitalized.

EXAMPLE
I think, Senator, that the issue is critical.

(2) Capitalize words showing family relationship when used with a person's name but *not* when preceded by a possessive.

EXAMPLES
Aunt Clara   my mother
Harold's grandmother

(3) Capitalize the first and last words and all important words in titles of books, periodicals, poems, stories, essays, speeches, plays, historical documents, movies, radio and television programs, works of art, musical compositions, and cartoons.

NOTE Unimportant words in a title are articles (*a, an, the*), prepositions of fewer than five letters (such as *for* and *from*), and coordinating conjunctions (*and, but, so, nor, or, yet, for*).

NOTE The words *a, an,* and *the* written before a title are capitalized only when they are part of the official title. The official title of a book is found on the title page. The official title of a newspaper or a periodical is found on the masthead, which is usually on the editorial page.

EXAMPLES
The Autobiography of Malcolm X
the *Austin American-Statesman*
A Tale of Two Cities

☞ For information about when to use italics for titles, see page 1026. For information about when to use quotation marks for titles, see page 1028.

(4) Capitalize the names of religions and their followers, holy days and celebrations, holy writings, and specific deities.

TYPE OF NAME	EXAMPLES	
Religions and Followers	Judaism Taoism	Quaker Muslim
Holy Days and Celebrations	Passover Ramadan	Good Friday Lent
Holy Writings	Bible Koran	Upanishads Genesis
Specific Deities	Allah Brahma Zeus	

COMPUTER NOTE Some software programs can identify errors in capitalization. However, even the most complete programs may not include all the terms you need. In addition, the program may be based on rules that vary from the ones you've been given to follow. If your software allows it, modify the capitalization of words already in the program, and add terms that you use frequently.

Resources

- *Language Handbook Resources,* pp. 131–142
- *Language Workshop CD-ROM,* Chapter 8—Lessons 46–50: Punctuating Sentences

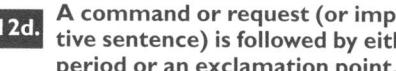

12 PUNCTUATION

END MARKS

Sentences

End marks—*periods, question marks, and exclamation points*—are used to indicate the purpose of a sentence.

 For a discussion of how sentences are classified according to purpose, see pages 1012–1013. For information on using quotation marks with end marks, see page 1027.

12a. A statement (or declarative sentence) is followed by a period.

EXAMPLE
Dorothy M. Johnson wrote "A Man Called Horse."

12b. A question (or interrogative sentence) is followed by a question mark.

EXAMPLE
Did Penelope recognize Odysseus?

 NOTE Be sure to distinguish between a declarative sentence that contains an indirect question and an interrogative sentence, which asks a direct question.

INDIRECT QUESTION	He asked me **what was worrying her.** [declarative]
DIRECT QUESTION	What is worrying her? [interrogative]

1022 LANGUAGE HANDBOOK

A direct question may have the same word order as a declarative sentence. Since it *is* a question, however, it is followed by a question mark.

EXAMPLES
A cat can see color?   The plane was late?

12c. An exclamation is followed by an exclamation point.

EXAMPLE
Wow! What a great play *The Miracle Worker* is!

12d. A command or request (or imperative sentence) is followed by either a period or an exclamation point.

A mild command or an imperative sentence that makes a request is followed by a period. An imperative sentence that shows strong feeling is followed by an exclamation point.

EXAMPLES
Please be quiet. [request]
Turn off your radio. [mild command]
Be quiet! [strong command]

Sometimes a command or request is stated in the form of a question. Because of its purpose, however, the sentence is really an imperative sentence and should be followed by a period or an exclamation point.

EXAMPLES
Could you please send me twenty-five copies.
Will you stop that!

T1022

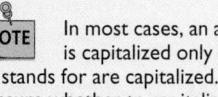

Abbreviations

12e. An abbreviation is usually followed by a period.

TYPES OF ABBREVIATIONS	EXAMPLES
Personal Names	A. E. Housman Eugenia W. Collier
Organizations and Companies	Assn. Co. Inc. Ltd. Corp.
Titles Used with Names	Mr. Mrs. Jr. Dr.
Times of Day	A.M. P.M.
Years	B.C. (written after the date) A.D. (written before the date)
Addresses	Ave. St. Blvd. Pkwy.
States	Calif. Mass. Tex. N. Dak.

 NOTE Two-letter state abbreviations without periods are used only when the ZIP Code is included. Each letter of the abbreviation is capitalized, and no comma separates the abbreviation from the ZIP Code.

EXAMPLE

Cincinnati, OH 45233

NOTE In most cases, an abbreviation is capitalized only if the words it stands for are capitalized. If you are unsure whether to capitalize an abbreviation or to use periods with it, look in a recent dictionary.

If a statement ends with an abbreviation, do not use an additional period as an end mark. However, do add a question mark or an exclamation point if the sentence should have one.

EXAMPLES

Mrs. Tavares will be arriving at 3 P.M.
Can you go to meet her at 3 P.M.?

Abbreviations for government agencies and international organizations and some other frequently used abbreviations are written without periods. Abbreviations for most units of measurement are commonly written without periods, especially in science books.

EXAMPLES

CD, VCR, FM, IRS, TV, UFO
cm, kg, lb, ml

 NOTE Include a period with the abbreviation for *inch* (*in.*) so that it will not be confused with *in,* the word.

COMMAS

12f. Use commas to separate items in a series.

EXAMPLES

Odysseus slays Antinous, Eurymachus, and
  Penelope's other suitors.
We can meet before school, at lunch, or after
  school.

(1) If all items in a series are joined by *and* or *or,* do not use commas to separate them.

EXAMPLE

The names of the characters in "Poison" are Harry **and** Timber **and** Dr. Ganderbai.

Some words—such as *bread and butter, rod and reel,* and *law and order*—are used in pairs and may be considered one item in a series.

EXAMPLE

My favorite breakfast is milk, **biscuits and gravy,** and fruit.

(2) Independent clauses in a series are generally separated by semicolons. Short independent clauses, however, may be separated by commas.

EXAMPLE

The sky darkened, branches swayed, the cold deepened, and snow fell.

12g. Use commas to separate two or more adjectives preceding a noun.

EXAMPLE

Montresor leads Fortunato to the dark, cold vaults below the palazzo.

When the last adjective in a series is thought of as part of the noun, the comma before the adjective is omitted.

EXAMPLE

The Loisels bought an expensive **diamond necklace.**

LANGUAGE HANDBOOK 1023

12h. Use commas before *and, but, or, nor, for, so,* and *yet* when they join independent clauses.

EXAMPLE
General Zaroff was confident he would kill Rainsford, **but** the hunt did not go as he had planned.

You may omit the comma before *and, but, or,* or *nor* if the clauses are very short and there is no chance of misunderstanding.

12i. Use commas to set off nonessential clauses and nonessential participial phrases.

A *nonessential* (or *nonrestrictive*) clause or participial phrase adds information that is not needed to understand the main idea in the sentence.

NONESSENTIAL CLAUSE Langston Hughes, **who was a key figure in the Harlem Renaissance,** often used the rhythms of jazz in his poetry.

Omitting the adjective clause in this example would not change the main idea of the sentence: *Langston Hughes often used the rhythms of jazz in his poetry.*

An *essential* (or *restrictive*) clause or phrase provides information that is needed to understand the sentence, and commas are *not* used.

ESSENTIAL PHRASE Actors **missing more than two rehearsals** will be replaced.

Omitting the participial phrase above would affect the meaning of the sentence: The phrase tells *which actors.*

12j. Use commas after certain introductory elements.

(1) Use a comma after a word such as *next, yes,* or *no* as well as after an introductory interjection such as *why, well,* or *oops.*

EXAMPLES
Yes, I've read "Salvador Late or Early."
Ah, there's nothing like cold water on a hot day!

(2) Use a comma after an introductory participial phrase.

EXAMPLE
Having passed Penelope's last test, Odysseus reclaims his home and his kingdom.

(3) Use a comma after the last of two or more introductory prepositional phrases.

EXAMPLE
Of all of his novels, Charles Dickens liked *David Copperfield* best.

(4) Use a comma after an introductory adverb clause.

EXAMPLE
Until he meets Juliet, Romeo is madly in love with Rosaline.

12k. Use commas to set off elements that interrupt a sentence.

EXAMPLES
Dr. Ganderbai, **in fact,** worked very hard.
The storm, **the worst this winter,** raged for days.

(1) Appositives and appositive phrases are usually set off by commas.

EXAMPLE
My sister gave me a copy of *Gorilla, My Love,* **Toni Cade Bambara's first collection of stories.**

 NOTE An appositive that tells which one(s) of two or more is a *restrictive appositive* and should not be set off by commas.

EXAMPLE
The television special is about Graham Greene the British writer, not Graham Greene the Canadian actor.

(2) Words used in direct address are set off by commas.

EXAMPLE
Linda, please read the part of Juliet.

(3) Parenthetical expressions are set off by commas.

Parenthetical expressions are side remarks that add minor information or that relate ideas to each other.

EXAMPLE
He was not angry and, **on the contrary,** was actually glad that you told him about the error.

A contrasting expression introduced by *not* or *yet* is parenthetical and is set off by commas.

EXAMPLE
It is the spirit of the giver, **not the cost of the gift,** that counts.

12l. Use commas in certain conventional situations.

(1) Use a comma to separate items in dates and in addresses (except between a two-letter state abbreviation and a ZIP Code).

EXAMPLES
My family moved to Oakland, California, on Wednesday, December 5, 1990.
On December 5, 1990, our address became 25 Peralta Road, Oakland, CA 94611.

1024 LANGUAGE HANDBOOK

(2) Use a comma after the salutation of a friendly letter and after the closing of any letter.

EXAMPLES
Dear Ms. Chen,   Yours truly,

(3) Use a comma to set off an abbreviation such as *Jr.*, *Sr.*, or *M.D.*, including after the abbreviation unless it ends the sentence.

EXAMPLE
Dr. Martin Luther King, Jr., delivered that speech.

SEMICOLONS

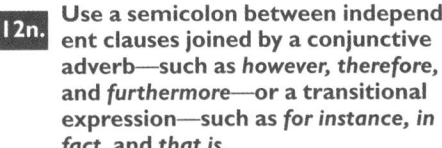 **Use a semicolon between independent clauses if they are not joined by *and, but, or, nor, for, so,* or *yet*.**

EXAMPLE
I enjoyed reading *The Miracle Worker*; it tells what Helen Keller's youth was like.

12n. **Use a semicolon between independent clauses joined by a conjunctive adverb—such as *however, therefore,* and *furthermore*—or a transitional expression—such as *for instance, in fact,* and *that is*.**

EXAMPLES
Sherlock Holmes is a fictional character; however, many people are convinced that he actually did exist.
My parents are strict; for example, I can watch TV only on weekends.

Notice in the two examples above that a comma always follows a conjunctive adverb or a transitional expression that joins independent clauses.

12o. **Use a semicolon (rather than a comma) before a coordinating conjunction to join independent clauses that contain commas.**

EXAMPLE
Doodle's mother, father, and brother went back inside the house; but Doodle remained outside to bury the scarlet ibis.

12p. **Use a semicolon between items in a series if the items contain commas.**

EXAMPLE
I have postcards from Paris, France; Rome, Italy; Lisbon, Portugal; and London, England.

COLONS

12q. **Use a colon to mean "note what follows."**

(1) In some cases a colon is used before a list of items, especially after the expressions *the following* and *as follows*.

EXAMPLE
The reading list includes the following titles: "The Gift," "The Sniper," and "The Necklace."

Do not use a colon before a list that follows a verb or a preposition.

INCORRECT	The list of literary terms includes: *conflict, climax,* and *resolution.*
CORRECT	The list of literary terms includes *conflict, climax,* and *resolution.*
INCORRECT	In the past five years, my family has lived in: Texas, Oregon, Ohio, and Florida.
CORRECT	In the past five years, my family has lived in Texas, Oregon, Ohio, and Florida.

(2) Use a colon before a long, formal statement or a long quotation.

EXAMPLE
O. Henry had this to say about Della and Jim: "But in a last word to the wise of these days, let it be said that of all who give gifts, these two were the wisest."

12r. **Use a colon in certain conventional situations.**

(1) Use a colon between the hour and the minute.
EXAMPLES
9:30 P.M.   8:00 A.M.

(2) Use a colon after the salutation of a business letter.
EXAMPLES
Dear Ms. González: Dear Sir or Madam:
To Whom It May Concern:

(3) Use a colon between chapter and verse in referring to passages from the Bible.
EXAMPLES
Esther 3:5   Exodus 1:6–14

(4) Use a colon between a title and a subtitle.
EXAMPLE
"Shakespeare and His Theater: A Perfect Match"

Resources

- *Language Handbook Resources,* pp. 143–149
- *Language Workshop CD-ROM,* Chapter 8—Lessons 53 and 54: Punctuating Titles and Quotations

ITALICS

When writing or typing, indicate italics by underlining. If your composition were to be printed, the typesetter would set the underlined words in italics. For example, if you typed the sentence

Alice Walker wrote <u>The Color Purple</u>.

it would be printed like this:

Alice Walker wrote *The Color Purple.*

COMPUTER NOTE If you use a computer, you can probably set words in italics yourself. Most word-processing software and many printers are capable of producing italic type.

13a. Use underlining (italics) for titles of books, plays, films, periodicals, works of art, recordings, long musical works, television series, trains, ships, aircraft, and spacecraft.

TYPE OF TITLE	EXAMPLES	
Books	*Black Boy*	*Odyssey*
Plays	*The Miracle Worker* *Romeo and Juliet*	
Films	*The Lion King*	*Jurassic Park*
Periodicals	*Seventeen*	*USA Today*

NOTE The articles *a, an,* and *the* written before a title are italicized only when they are part of the official title. The official title of a book appears on the title page. The official title of a newspaper or periodical appears on the masthead, which is usually found on the editorial page.

EXAMPLE
We subscribe to ***The Wall Street Journal*** and **the** *Austin American-Statesman.*

TYPE OF TITLE	EXAMPLES
Works of Art	*Death of Cleopatra* *Mona Lisa*
Recordings	*Music Box* *Two Worlds, One Heart*
Long Musical Works	*The Magic Flute* *Rhapsody in Blue*
Television Series	*60 Minutes* *The Simpsons*
Trains and Ships	*Orient Express* *U.S.S. Nimitz*
Aircraft and Spacecraft	*Spirit of St. Louis* *Apollo 13*

 For examples of titles that should be placed in quotation marks rather than be italicized, see page 1028.

13b. Use underlining (italics) for words, letters, and figures referred to as such and for foreign words not yet a part of English vocabulary.

EXAMPLES
The word *excellent* has two *l*'s.
The *3* on that license plate looks like an *8.*
The *corrido* is a fast-paced ballad.

QUOTATION MARKS

13c. Use quotation marks to enclose a *direct quotation*—a person's exact words.

EXAMPLES
She asked, "How much does the necklace cost?"
"The Loisels pay thirty-six thousand francs," answered Lamont.

Do not use quotation marks for indirect quotations.

DIRECT QUOTATION	Stephanie said, "I'm going to plant some marigolds." [the speaker's exact words]
INDIRECT QUOTATION	Stephanie said that she was going to plant some marigolds. [not the speaker's exact words]

An interrupting expression is not a part of a quotation and should never be inside quotation marks.

EXAMPLE

"Let's fly our kites," Jennifer suggested, "before the breeze dies down."

When two or more sentences by the same speaker are quoted together, use one set of quotation marks.

EXAMPLE

Brennan said, "I'm making a fruitcake. Do you like fruitcake?"

 13d. A direct quotation begins with a capital letter.

EXAMPLES

Mrs. Perez asked, "**W**ho is Mercutio?"
Charles answered, "**O**ne of Romeo's friends."
[Although this quotation is not a sentence, it is Charles's complete remark.]

 NOTE If a direct quotation is obviously a fragment of the original quotation, it should begin with a lowercase letter.

EXAMPLE

To Romeo, Juliet is like "**a** wingèd messenger of heaven."

 13e. When a quoted sentence is divided into two parts by an interrupting expression, the second part begins with a lowercase letter.

EXAMPLE

"I wish," she said, "**t**hat we went to the same school."

If the second part of a quotation is a new sentence, a period (not a comma) follows the interrupting expression, and the second part begins with a capital letter.

EXAMPLE

"I requested an interview," the reporter said. "**S**he told me she was too busy."

 13f. When used with quotation marks, other marks of punctuation are placed according to the following rules.

(1) A comma or a period is always placed inside the closing quotation marks.

EXAMPLES

"I haven't seen the film version of *Romeo and Juliet*," remarked Jeannette, "but I understand it's excellent."

(2) A semicolon or a colon is always placed outside the closing quotation marks.

EXAMPLES

My mom's favorite poem is Maya Angelou's "Woman Work"; in fact, I can recite it.
Find examples of the following figures of speech in "I Wandered Lonely as a Cloud": simile, personification, and alliteration.

(3) A question mark or an exclamation point is placed inside the closing quotation marks if the quotation is a question or an exclamation; otherwise, it is placed outside.

EXAMPLES

"Where does Romeo first meet Juliet?" asked Mr. Suarez.
"Help me, please!" she exclaimed.
Which of the characters says "Parting is such sweet sorrow"?
It is *not* an insult to be called a "bookworm"!

13g. When you write dialogue (a conversation), begin a new paragraph every time the speaker changes.

EXAMPLE

The gait of my friend was unsteady, and the bells upon his cap jingled as he strode.
"The pipe," said he.
"It is farther on," said I; "but observe the white web-work which gleams from these cavern walls."
—Edgar Allan Poe, "The Cask of Amontillado"

13h. When a quoted passage consists of more than one paragraph, put quotation marks at the beginning of each paragraph and at the end of only the last paragraph.

EXAMPLE

"At nine o'clock this morning," read the news story, "someone entered the Millford Bank by the back entrance, broke through two thick steel doors guarding the bank's vault, and escaped with sixteen bars of gold.

"No arrests have yet been made, but state and local police are confident the case will be solved within a few days.

"FBI agents are due to arrive on the scene later today."

13i. Use single quotation marks to enclose a quotation within a quotation.

EXAMPLE

"Do you agree with O. Henry that Della and Jim 'were the wisest'?" asked Greg.

LANGUAGE HANDBOOK **1027**

13j. Use quotation marks to enclose titles of articles, short stories, essays, poems, songs, individual episodes of TV shows, and chapters and other parts of books and periodicals.

 For examples of titles that should be italicized rather than enclosed in quotation marks, see page 1026.

TYPE OF TITLE	EXAMPLES
Articles	"Computers in the Classroom" "Returning from Space"
Short Stories	"Thank You, M'am" "The Princess and the Tin Box"
Essays	"How to Name a Dog" "The Death of a Tree"
Poems	"The Secret" "Fire and Ice" "who are you,little i"
Songs	"Circle of Life" "Lean on Me"
TV Episodes	"Farewell, Friends" "The Surprise Party"
Chapters and Other Parts of Books and Periodicals	"Life in the First Settlements" "The Talk of the Town" "Laughter, the Best Medicine"

NOTE Neither italics nor quotation marks are used for the titles of major religious texts or for the titles of legal or historical documents.

RELIGIOUS TEXTS
New Testament   Koran   Rig-Veda

LEGAL AND HISTORICAL DOCUMENTS
Declaration of Independence
Code of Hammurabi

EXCEPTION
Names of court cases are usually italicized.

EXAMPLE
Brown v. *Board of Education of Topeka*

Using Italics for Emphasis

Occasionally, writers will use italics (underlining) to emphasize a particular word or phrase. This technique can be especially effective in written dialogue. The italic type helps to show how the sentence is spoken by the character. Read the following sentences aloud. Notice that by italicizing different words, the writer can alter the meaning of the sentence.

EXAMPLES
"Are you *certain* that she said to be here at nine o'clock?" asked Suzanne. [Are you certain, not just guessing?]

"Are you certain that *she* said to be here at nine o'clock?" asked Suzanne. [Did she say so, or did someone else?]

"Are you certain that she said to be here at *nine* o'clock?" asked Suzanne. [Did she say nine o'clock, or was it eight?]

Although italicizing (underlining) words for emphasis is a handy technique, it should not be overused, because it can quickly lose its effectiveness.

Try It Out

Revise the following dialogue by adding commas, end marks, quotation marks, and paragraph breaks where necessary. In addition, underline words you think the speakers would emphasize.

[1] You know what really bothers me about a lot of stories? said Kyle. [2] What? inquired Erin. [3] I can never—well, not never, but often I can't—figure out if a story is fiction or if it really happened, he explained. [4] Yeah she nodded I know what you mean. That reminds me of the story A Man Called Horse. Did it really happen or not? [5] I don't know he answered When I saw the movie, I thought it did, but now I'm not so sure. [6] Erin added, It's the same with stories that don't give the narrator's name. [7] I always wonder whether the narrator is the writer or not. [8] Yes, and the more I like the story, the more I wonder! Kyle agreed. [9] Erin replied Hey let's check the book out again and see if we can find out if Horse was a real person or not. [10] As they read the notes and comments about the story, Kyle said with surprise Wow it says here that Dorothy Johnson also wrote the story The Man Who Shot Liberty Valance!

Try It Out
Possible Answers
"You know what really bothers me about a lot of stories?" said Kyle.

"What?" inquired Erin.

"I can never—well, not <u>never</u>, but <u>often</u> I can't—figure out if <u>a</u> story is fiction or if it really happened," he explained.

"Yeah," she nodded, "I know what you mean. That reminds me of the story 'A Man Called Horse.' Did it really happen or not?"

"I don't know," he answered. "When I saw the movie, I thought it did, but now I'm not so sure."

Erin added, "It's the same with stories that don't give the narrator's name. I always wonder whether the narrator is the writer or not."

"Yes, and the more I <u>like</u> the story, the more I wonder!" Kyle agreed.

Erin replied, "Hey, let's check the book out again and see if we can find out if Horse was a real person or not."

As they read the notes and comments about the story, Kyle said with surprise, "Wow, it says here that Dorothy Johnson also wrote the story 'The Man Who Shot Liberty Valance'!"

14 PUNCTUATION

APOSTROPHES

Possessive Case

The **possessive case** of a noun or pronoun shows ownership or relationship.

| OWNERSHIP | Mme. Forestier's necklace |
| RELATIONSHIP | Buddy's friend |

14a. To form the possessive case of a singular noun, add an apostrophe and an *s*.

EXAMPLES
Miss Lottie's marigolds   a bus's wheel

 **NOTE** For a proper name ending in *s*, add only an apostrophe if adding *'s* would make the name awkward to pronounce.

EXAMPLES
West Indies' island   Mrs. Saunders' class

14b. To form the possessive case of a plural noun ending in *s*, add only the apostrophe. To form the possessive case of a plural noun that does not end in *s*, add an apostrophe and an *s*.

EXAMPLES
birds' feathers   Capulets' party
children's shoes   deer's food

TIPS FOR SPELLING

Do not use an apostrophe to form the *plural* of a noun. Usually an apostrophe shows ownership or relationship.

| PLURAL | Doodle and he are **brothers**. |
| POSSESSIVE | The **brothers'** relationship is special. |

14c. Possessive personal pronouns—*my, mine, your, yours, his, her, hers, its, our, ours, their,* and *theirs*—do not require an apostrophe.

EXAMPLES
This is **our** plant.
This plant is **ours.**

14d. Indefinite pronouns—such as *everybody* and *neither*—in the possessive case require an apostrophe and an *s*.

EXAMPLES
nobody's wish   another's viewpoint

14e. In compound words, names of organizations and businesses, and word groups showing joint possession, only the last word is possessive in form.

EXAMPLES
brother-in-**law's** gift   City **Garage's** tow trucks
United **Fund's** drive   Della and **Jim's** home

14f. When two or more persons possess something individually, each of their names is possessive in form.

EXAMPLE
Poe's and **Dahl's** stories

Contractions

14g. Use an apostrophe to show where letters, words, or numerals have been omitted in a contraction.

EXAMPLES
let us . . . . **let's**   you are . . . . . . **you're**
1991 . . . . **'91**   of the clock . . . **o'clock**

Ordinarily, the word *not* is shortened to *–n't* and added to a verb with no change to the verb's spelling.

EXAMPLES
are not . . . . . . are**n't**   has not . . . . . has**n't**
EXCEPTIONS
will not . . . . . . wo**n't**   cannot . . . . . .ca**n't**

Do not confuse contractions with possessive pronouns.

CONTRACTIONS	PRONOUNS
Who's [Who is] at bat?	**Whose** bat is that?
It's [It is] roaring.	Listen to **its** roar.
You're [You are] late.	**Your** friend is late.
There's [There is] a kite.	That kite is **theirs.**
They're [They are] here.	**Their** bus is here.

LANGUAGE HANDBOOK 1029

Resources
- *Language Handbook Resources,* pp. 150–158
- *Language Workshop CD-ROM,* Chapter 8—Lessons 51 and 52: Punctuating Possessives, Contractions, and Plurals; Lesson 56: Hyphens, Italics, Parentheses, and Dashes

LANGUAGE HANDBOOK

T1029

Plurals

14h. Use an apostrophe and an *s* to form the plurals of all lowercase letters, some capital letters, and some words that are referred to as words.

EXAMPLES

Grandma always tells me to mind my *p*'s and *q*'s.

Those *U*'s look like *V*'s. [Without an apostrophe, the plural of *U* would spell *Us*. An apostrophe and an *s* are used to form the plural of *V* to make the style consistent.]

His *hi*'s are always cheerful. [Without an apostrophe, the plural would spell the word *his*.]

Using Apostrophes

In your reading you may have noticed that some writers do not use apostrophes to form the plurals of numbers, capital letters, symbols, and words used as words.

EXAMPLE

Their music was popular in the **1970s.**

However, using an apostrophe is never wrong. Therefore, it is often best to use the apostrophe.

Try It Out

For each of the following sentences, add an apostrophe wherever it is needed.

1. As in your studies are great, but Bs are good, too.
2. If you use *its*, make sure that they clearly refer to specific words.
3. Try not to include *Is* in the opening paragraph of a business letter.
4. The *10s* in this chart indicate the highest scores.
5. These *hiss* should be *theirss*.

HYPHENS

14i. Use a hyphen to divide a word at the end of a line.

EXAMPLE

"The Most Dangerous Game" is a very suspense-ful story.

When you divide a word at the end of a line, keep in mind the following rules.

(1) Do not divide one-syllable words.

1030 LANGUAGE HANDBOOK

(2) Divide a word only between syllables.

EXAMPLES

fi-an-cé   wor-thy

 NOTE If you need to divide a word and are not sure about its syllables, look it up in a current dictionary.

(3) Words with double consonants may usually be divided between those two consonants.

EXAMPLES

rib-bon   man-ners

EXCEPTION

Words that end in double consonants followed by a suffix are divided before the suffix.

fall-ing   will-ing

(4) Usually, a word with a prefix or a suffix may be divided between the prefix or suffix and the base word (or root).

EXAMPLES

pro-gressive   govern-ment

(5) Divide an already hyphenated word only at a hyphen.

EXAMPLES

man-of-war   daughter-in-law

(6) Do not divide a word so that one letter stands alone.

14j. Use a hyphen with compound numbers from *twenty-one* to *ninety-nine* and with fractions used as adjectives.

EXAMPLES

twenty-four chairs

one-half cup [*One-half* is an adjective.]

one half of the money [*Half* is a noun.]

14k. Use a hyphen with the suffix *–elect* and with all prefixes before a proper noun or proper adjective.

EXAMPLES

president-elect   pre-Revolutionary

14l. Hyphenate a compound adjective that precedes the noun it modifies.

EXAMPLES

a **well-written** book   a **world-famous** skier

Do not use a hyphen if one of the modifiers is an adverb that ends in *–ly*.

EXAMPLE

a **bitterly cold** day

Try It Out
Answers

1. *A*'s in your studies are great, but *B*'s are good, too.
2. If you use *it's*, make sure that they clearly refer to specific words.
3. Try not to include *I*'s in the opening paragraph of a business letter.
4. The *10*'s in this chart indicate the highest scores.
5. These *his*'s should be *theirs*'s.

T1030

NOTE Some compound adjectives are always hyphenated, whether they precede or follow the nouns they modify.

EXAMPLE
an up-to-date dictionary
a dictionary that is up-to-date

If you're not sure whether a compound adjective should be hyphenated, check a recent dictionary.

DASHES

 14m. Use a dash to indicate an abrupt break in thought or speech or an unfinished statement or question.

EXAMPLE
Judy—Ms. Lane, I mean—will be your new coach.

 14n. Use a dash to mean *namely, that is, in other words,* and similar expressions that introduce an explanation.

EXAMPLES
Dr. Ganderbai considered using an anesthetic—ether or chloroform. [namely]
William Sydney Porter—O. Henry—is my favorite writer. [that is]

 NOTE When you type or input your writing on a word processor, you may indicate a dash by using two hyphens. (Do not leave a space before, between, or after the hyphens.) If you are using a computer, you may also find a dash available in your word processing software. When you write by hand, use an unbroken line about as long as two hyphens.

PARENTHESES

 14o. Use parentheses to enclose material that is not considered of major importance in a sentence.

EXAMPLES
Richard Wright (1908–1960) wrote *Black Boy.*
Aunt Constance (Mother's aunt and my great-aunt) will meet us at the airport.

Capitalize and use end punctuation for parenthetical matter that stands alone as a sentence. Do not capitalize and use end punctuation for parenthetical matter contained within a sentence.

EXAMPLES
Complete the form. (Please print or type.)
The protagonist (the author did not give him a name) is a sniper.

15 SPELLING

UNDERSTANDING WORD STRUCTURE

Many English words are made up of roots and affixes (prefixes and suffixes). The **root** of a word is the part that carries the word's core meaning. A **prefix** is one or more letters or syllables added to the beginning of a word or word part to create a new word. A **suffix** is one or more letters or syllables added to the end of a word or word part to create a new word. Learning how to spell commonly used word parts and how to combine them can help you spell thousands of words.

COMMONLY USED ROOTS		
ROOTS	**MEANINGS**	**EXAMPLES**
–aud–, –audit–	hear	audible, auditorium
–bene–	well, good	benefit, benevolent
–chron–	time	chronological, synchronize
–cycl–	circle, wheel	cyclone, bicycle
–dem–	people	democracy, epidemic

(continued)

Resources
• *Language Handbook Resources,* pp. 159–165
• *Language Workshop CD-ROM,* Chapter 9—Lessons 59 and 60: Rules of Spelling

COMMONLY USED ROOTS (continued)

ROOTS	MEANINGS	EXAMPLES
–gen–	birth, kind, origin	generate, generic, generous
–graph–	write, writing	autograph, geography
–hydr–	water	hydrant, hydrate
–log–, –logue–	study, word	logic, mythology, dialogue
–micr–	small	microbe, microscope
–morph–	form	metamorphosis, polymorph
–phil–	like, love	philanthropic, philosophy
–phon–	sound	phonograph, euphony
–port–	carry, bear	export, important
–psych–	mind	psychology, psychosomatic
–verse–, –vert–	turn	reverse, convert
–vid–, –vis–	see	television, evident

COMMONLY USED PREFIXES

PREFIXES	MEANINGS	EXAMPLES
anti–	against, opposing	antipathy, antithesis
bi–	two	bimonthly, bisect
contra–	against	contradict, contrast
de–	away, off, down	defect, desert, decline
dis–	away, off, opposing	dismount, dissent
hemi–	half	hemisphere, hemicycle
hyper–	excessive, over	hyperactive, hypertension
inter–	between, among	intercede, international
mis–	badly, not, wrongly	misfire, misspell
over–	above, excessive	oversee, overdo
post–	after, following	postpone, postscript
re–	back, backward, again	revoke, reflect, reforest
tra–, trans–	across, beyond	traffic, transport
un–	not, reverse of	untrue, unfold

COMMONLY USED SUFFIXES

SUFFIXES	MEANINGS	EXAMPLES
–able	able, likely	capable, changeable
–cy	state, condition	accuracy, normalcy
–er	doer, native of	baker, westerner
–ful	full of, marked by	thankful, masterful
–ic	dealing with, caused by, person or thing showing	classic, choleric, heretic
–ion	action, result, state	union, fusion, dominion
–ish	suggesting, like	smallish, childish
–ist	doer, believer	monopolist, capitalist
–ly	like, characteristic of	friendly, cowardly
–ness	quality, state	softness, shortness
–or	doer, office, action	director, juror, error
–ous	marked by, given to	religious, furious
–tion	action, condition	selection, relation
–tude	quality, state	fortitude, multitude

SPELLING RULES

ie and *ei*

15a. Write *ie* when the sound is long *e*, except after *c*.

EXAMPLES
achieve chief niece **ce**iling de**ce**it re**ce**ive
EXCEPTIONS
either leisure neither seize protein

15b. Write *ei* when the sound is not long *e*.

EXAMPLES
foreign forfeit height heir reign weigh
EXCEPTIONS
ancient conscience friend mischief view

–cede, –ceed, and *–sede*

15c. The only English word ending in *–sede* is *supersede.* The only words ending in *–ceed* are *exceed, proceed,* and *succeed.* Most other words with this sound end in *–cede.*

EXAMPLES
ac**cede** inter**cede** re**cede**
con**cede** pre**cede** se**cede**

Adding Prefixes

15d. When adding a prefix, do not change the spelling of the original word.

EXAMPLES
im + mortal = **im**mortal   mis + step = **mis**step
re + elect = **re**elect   over + run = **over**run

Adding Suffixes

15e. When adding the suffix *–ness* or *–ly,* do not change the spelling of the original word.

EXAMPLES
fair + ness = fair**ness**   sure + ly = sure**ly**
EXCEPTIONS
For most words ending in *y,* change the *y* to *i* before adding *–ness* or *–ly:*
empty—empt**iness**   easy—eas**ily**

However, most one-syllable words ending in *y* follow rule 15e.

EXAMPLES
dry + ness = dry**ness**   sly + ly = sly**ly**

15f. Drop the final silent *e* before a suffix beginning with a vowel.

EXAMPLES
hope + ing = hop**ing**   strange + est = strang**est**
EXCEPTIONS
Keep the final silent *e*

- in words ending in *ce* or *ge* before a suffix that begins with *a* or *o:* knowledg**eable,** outrag**eous**
- in *dye* and in *singe,* before *–ing:* dy**eing,** sing**eing**
- in *mile* before *–age:* mil**eage**

15g. Keep the final silent *e* before a suffix beginning with a consonant.

EXAMPLES
nine + ty = nine**ty**   entire + ly = entire**ly**
EXCEPTIONS
nine + th = nin**th**   awe + ful = aw**ful**
judge + ment = judg**ment**
argue + ment = argu**ment**

15h. For words ending in *y* preceded by a consonant, change the *y* to *i* before any suffix that does not begin with *i.*

EXAMPLES
fifty + eth = fift**ieth**   mystery + ous = myster**ious**

15i. For words ending in *y* preceded by a vowel, simply add the suffix.

EXAMPLES
joy + ful = joy**ful**   boy + hood = boy**hood**
EXCEPTIONS
day + ly = da**ily**   pay + ed = pa**id**
say + ed = sa**id**   lay + ed = la**id**

15j. Double the final consonant before a suffix that begins with a vowel if the word *both* (1) has only one syllable or has the accent on the last syllable *and* (2) ends in a single consonant preceded by a single vowel.

EXAMPLES
drop + ing = dro**pping**
occur + ence = occu**rrence**
strum + ed = stru**mmed**
thin + er = thi**nner**

 NOTE The final consonant in some words may or may not be doubled. Both spellings are equally correct.

EXAMPLES
travel + er = trave**ler** *or* trave**ller**
shovel + ed = shove**led** *or* shove**lled**

Forming Plurals of Nouns

15k. To form the plurals of most English nouns, add –s.

EXAMPLES

boats   houses   nickels   Lincolns

15l. To form the plurals of other nouns, follow these rules.

(1) For nouns ending in *s, x, z, ch,* or *sh,* add –es.

EXAMPLES

glasses   boxes   waltzes   beaches   Bushes

(2) For nouns ending in *y* preceded by a consonant, change the *y* to *i* and add –es.

EXAMPLES

armies   babies   skies   mysteries

EXCEPTION

For proper nouns, add –s: Hardys

(3) For nouns ending in *y* preceded by a vowel, add –s.

EXAMPLES

joys   keys   Momadays

(4) For some nouns ending in *f* or *fe,* add –s. For others, change the *f* or *fe* to *v* and add –es.

EXAMPLES

beliefs   roofs   safes   giraffes
calves   wives   leaves   shelves

EXCEPTION

For proper nouns, add –s: Radcliffs, Rolfes

(5) For nouns ending in *o* preceded by a vowel, add –s.

EXAMPLES

radios   patios   Marios   stereos

(6) For nouns ending in *o* preceded by a consonant, add –es.

EXAMPLES

echoes   heroes   vetoes   tomatoes

EXCEPTIONS

For some common nouns ending in *o* preceded by a consonant, especially musical terms, and for proper nouns, add only –s: tacos, pianos, Sotos

(7) The plurals of a few nouns are formed in irregular ways.

EXAMPLES

children   feet   men   teeth   mice

(8) For a few nouns, the singular and the plural forms are the same.

SINGULAR AND PLURAL

deer   Japanese   Navajo   sheep   trout   series

(9) For a compound noun written as one word, form the plural of only the last word of the compound.

EXAMPLES

iceboxes   blackberries   businesspeople

(10) For a compound noun that is hyphenated or written as separate words, form the plural of the noun that is modified.

EXAMPLES

sisters-in-law   runners-up   music boxes

(11) For some nouns borrowed from other languages, the plurals are formed as in the original languages.

EXAMPLES

crisis—crises   phenomenon—phenomena

A few nouns borrowed from other languages have two plural forms.

EXAMPLES

appendix—appendices *or* appendixes
formula—formulas *or* formulae

(12) For numerals, symbols, some capital letters, and words used as words, add an –s or both an apostrophe and an –s.

EXAMPLES

6—6s *or* 6's   R—Rs *or* R's
&—&s *or* &'s   and—ands *or* and's

To prevent confusion, always use an apostrophe and an –s to form the plurals of lowercase letters, certain capital letters, and some words used as words.

EXAMPLES

Your *i*'s look like *e*'s. [Without an apostrophe, the plural of *i* would look like *is.*]
Ramón got all **A**'s last semester. [Without an apostrophe, the plural of A would look like *As.*]
Her ***and so***'s began to get tiresome. [Without the apostrophe, the plural of *so* would look like *sos.*]

COMPUTER NOTE

Spell-checking software can help you proofread your writing. Even the best spelling checkers aren't foolproof, however. Some accept British and archaic spellings, and most do not identify words that are spelled correctly but are used incorrectly (such as *affect* for *effect*). Always double-check your writing to make sure that your spelling is error free.

LANGUAGE HANDBOOK

Resources
• *Language Handbook Resources,* pp. 166–169
• *Language Workshop CD-ROM,* Chapter 9—Lessons 61 and 62: Words Often Confused; Chapter 10—Lessons 63 and 64: Common Usage Problems

The Glossary of Usage is an alphabetical list of words, expressions, and special terms with definitions, explanations, and examples. Some examples have usage labels. *Standard* or *formal* usages are appropriate in serious writing and speaking, such as in compositions and in speeches. *Informal* words and expressions are standard English usages generally appropriate in conversation and in everyday writing such as in personal letters. *Nonstandard* usages do not follow the guidelines of standard English.

---

accept, except   *Accept* is a verb that means "receive." *Except* may be either a verb or a preposition. As a verb, *except* means "leave out." As a preposition, *except* means "excluding."

EXAMPLES
We **accept** your apology.
All children under age three will be **excepted** from the fee. [verb]
Everyone **except** Bob and me has seen the exhibit. [preposition]

advice, advise   *Advice* is a noun meaning "suggestion about what to do." *Advise* is a verb meaning "offer a suggestion; recommend."

EXAMPLES
He gave me some excellent **advice.**
She **advised** me to finish high school.

affect, effect   *Affect* is a verb meaning "influence." As a verb, *effect* means "accomplish." As a noun, *effect* means "result (of an action)."

EXAMPLES
What he said did not **affect** my decision.
The mayor has **effected** many changes during her administration. [verb]
What **effect** will the new factory have on the environment? [noun]

ain't   Avoid using this word in formal speaking and in all writing other than dialogue; it is nonstandard English.

all together, altogether   *All together* means "everyone or everything in the same place." *Altogether* is an adverb meaning "entirely."

EXAMPLES
When we were **all together,** we voted.
He was **altogether** wrong.

a lot   Do not write the expression *a lot* as one word.

EXAMPLE
In addition to short stories, Edgar Allan Poe also wrote **a lot** [*not* alot] of poetry.

among   See **between, among.**

and etc.   The abbreviation for the Latin phrase *et cetera,* meaning "and other things" is *etc.* Thus, do not use *and* with *etc.*

EXAMPLE
My younger sister collects stickers, bottle caps, string, **etc.** [*not* and etc.]

anyways, anywheres   Use these words (and others like them, such as *everywheres, somewheres,* and *nowheres*) without the final *s.*

EXAMPLES
I have to baby-sit tonight **anyway** [*not* anyways].
The Loisels could not find the necklace **anywhere** [*not* anywheres].

as   See **like, as.**

as if   See **like, as if.**

at   Do not use *at* after *where.*

NONSTANDARD   Where was Romeo at?
STANDARD   **Where** was Romeo?

bad, badly   *Bad* is an adjective. *Badly* is an adverb. In standard English, only *bad* should follow a linking verb, such as *feel, look, sound, taste,* or *smell,* or forms of the verb *be.*

EXAMPLE
The fruitcake doesn't taste **bad** [*not* badly].

being as, being that   Use *since* or *because* instead of these expressions.

EXAMPLE
Because [*not* being as] President Clinton admired Maya Angelou's writing, he invited her to write a poem for his inauguration.

beside, besides   *Beside* is a preposition that means "by the side of" or "next to." As a preposition, *besides* means "in addition to" or "other than." As an adverb, *besides* means "moreover."

EXAMPLES
His rifle lay **beside** him.
Who **besides** Timber tried to help? [preposition]
I don't want to go; **besides,** it's snowing. [adverb]

between, among   Use *between* when you are referring to two things at a time, even though they may be part of a group consisting of more than two.

EXAMPLES

There was a feud **between** the Montagues and the Capulets.

The manager could not decide which of the four players to select, because there was not much difference **between** them. [Although there are more than two players, each one is being compared with the others separately.]

Use *among* when referring to a group rather than to separate individuals.

EXAMPLE

We were able to collect only ten dollars **among** the four of us.

bust, busted   Avoid using these words as verbs. Use a form of either *burst* or *break,* depending on the meaning.

EXAMPLES

The balloon **burst** [*not* busted] loudly.

The firefighters **broke** [*not* busted] a window.

consul, council, counsel   *Consul* is a noun meaning "representative of a foreign country." *Council* is a noun meaning "group called together to accomplish a job." As a noun, *counsel* means "advice." As a verb, it means "give advice."

EXAMPLES

The French **consul** outlined his government's plan.

The city **council** will debate the issue.

I'm grateful for your **counsel.** [noun]

Did the doctor **counsel** her to get more rest? [verb]

could of   See **of.**

discover, invent   *Discover* means "be the first to find, see, or learn about something that already exists." *Invent* means "be the first to do or make something."

EXAMPLES

Marguerite Perey **discovered** the element francium.

The zipper was **invented** in 1893.

double negative   A double negative is the use of two negative words when one is enough. Avoid using double negatives.

Common Negative Words			
barely	never	no one	not (–n't)
hardly	no	nowhere	nothing
neither	nobody	none	scarcely

NONSTANDARD	I had not read none of Emily Dickinson's poems.
STANDARD	I **had not read any** of Emily Dickinson's poems.
STANDARD	I **had read none** of Emily Dickinson's poems.

NONSTANDARD	Doodle couldn't hardly walk.
STANDARD	Doodle **could hardly** walk.

double subject   See **he, she, it, they.**

effect   See **affect, effect.**

etc.   See **and etc.**

everywheres   See **anyways, anywheres.**

except   See **accept, except.**

fewer, less   *Fewer* tells "how many"; it is used with plural nouns. *Less* tells "how much"; it is used with singular nouns.

EXAMPLES

There are **fewer** gypsy moths this year than there were last year.

Reading the *Odyssey* took **less** time than we had thought.

good, well   *Good* is an adjective. *Well* may be used as an adjective or an adverb. Never use *good* to modify a verb; instead, use *well* as an adverb meaning "capably" or "satisfactorily."

EXAMPLE

Sandra Cisneros writes **well** [*not* good].

As an adjective, *well* means "healthy" or "satisfactory in appearance or condition."

EXAMPLES

Lying in his bed, Harry did not look **well.**

Friar Laurence thought that all would be **well** with the Montagues and the Capulets.

NOTE   *Feel good* and *feel well* mean different things. *Feel good* means "feel happy or pleased." *Feel well* means "feel healthy."

EXAMPLES

The news made her feel **good.**

I didn't feel **well,** so I went home.

had ought, hadn't ought   Unlike other verbs, *ought* is not used with *had.*

EXAMPLES

I think Doodle's brother **ought** [*not* had ought] to be more patient; he **ought not** [*not* hadn't ought] to push Doodle so hard.

hardly See **double negative.**

he, she, it, they Do not use an unnecessary pronoun after the subject of a verb. This error is called the **double subject.**

| NONSTANDARD | Miss Lottie she likes to grow marigolds. |
| STANDARD | Miss Lottie likes to grow marigolds. |

hisself, theirselves Do not use these words for *himself* and *themselves.*

EXAMPLE
Romeo unburdens **himself** [*not* hisself] to Friar Laurence.

imply, infer *Imply* means "suggest indirectly." *Infer* means "interpret" or "draw a conclusion (from a remark or an action)."

EXAMPLES
Doug **implied** that he will vote for me.
From Doug's remark, I **inferred** that he will vote for me.

inside of See **of.**

invent See **discover, invent.**

it See **he, she, it, they.**

its, it's *Its* is the possessive form of *it. It's* is the contraction of *it is* or *it has.*

EXAMPLES
The bird stopped **its** singing.
It's [it is] an easy problem.
It's [it has] been raining since noon.

kind of, sort of In formal situations, avoid using these terms to mean *somewhat* or *rather.*

| INFORMAL | Zaroff was kind of surprised to see that Rainsford was still alive. |
| FORMAL | Zaroff was **somewhat** [*or* **rather**] surprised to see that Rainsford was still alive. |

kind of a, sort of a Avoid using *a* after *kind of* and *sort of* in formal situations.

| INFORMAL | What kind of a snake was it? |
| FORMAL | What **kind of** snake was it? |

kind(s), sort(s), type(s) Use *this* or *that* with the singular form of each of these nouns. Use *these* or *those* with the plural form.

EXAMPLES
I like **this kind** of jeans better than any of **those** other **kinds.**

lay See **lie, lay.**

learn, teach *Learn* means "acquire knowledge." *Teach* means "instruct" or "show how."

EXAMPLES
Doodle **learns** to walk.
His brother **teaches** him to walk.

leave, let *Leave* means "go away" or "depart from." *Let* means "allow" or "permit." Avoid using *leave* for *let.*

EXAMPLE
Let [*not* leave] her speak if she insists.

less See **fewer, less.**

let See **leave, let.**

lie, lay The verb *lie* means "rest" or "stay, recline, or remain in a certain position." *Lie* never takes an object. Its principal parts are *lie, lying, lay, lain.* The verb *lay* means "put (something) in a place." Its principal parts are *lay, laying, laid, laid. Lay* usually takes an object.

EXAMPLES
Is there a real snake **lying** on Harry's stomach? [no object]
He **laid** her gift on the table. [*Gift* is the object of *laid.*]

like, as In formal English, use *like* to introduce a prepositional phrase, and use *as* to introduce a subordinate clause.

EXAMPLES
Does Juliet look **like** Rosaline? [The preposition *like* introduces the phrase *like Rosaline.*]
Juliet does **as** Friar Laurence suggests. [The subordinating conjunction *as* introduces the clause *as Friar Laurence suggests.*]

like, as if In formal situations, *like* should not be used for the compound conjunction *as if* or *as though.*

EXAMPLE
Juliet looks **as though** [*not* like] she is alive.

might of, must of See **of.**

moral, morale As an adjective, *moral* means "good; virtuous." As a noun, it means "lesson of conduct." *Morale* is a noun meaning "spirit; mental condition."

EXAMPLES
In Pearl Buck's short story "The Old Demon," Mrs. Wang's **moral** values compel her to help the Japanese pilot. [adjective]
James Thurber's fables end with **morals** quite unlike the ones in traditional fairy tales. [noun]
The employees' **morale** is high.

nowheres   See **anyways, anywheres.**

of   *Of* is a preposition. Do not use *of* in place of *have* after verbs such as *could, should, would, ought (to), might,* and *must.* Also, do not use *had of* for *had.*

NONSTANDARD	You would of enjoyed our production of *The Miracle Worker.*
STANDARD	You **would have** [*or* **would've**] enjoyed our production of *The Miracle Worker.*
NONSTANDARD	If I had of known it was your birthday, I would of given you a card.
STANDARD	If I **had** known it was your birthday, I **would have** given you a card.

Also, do not use *of* after other prepositions such as *inside, off,* or *outside.*

EXAMPLES
The sniper's enemy fell **off** [*not* off of] the roof.
The sleeping Juliet is carried **inside** [*not* inside of] the Capulets' tomb.

off of   See **of.**

ought   See **had ought, hadn't ought.**

ought to of   See **of.**

peace, piece   *Peace* means "calmness; absence of war or strife." *Piece* means "part of something."

EXAMPLES
After the long war, **peace** was welcome.
Do you have a **piece** of paper I can borrow?

principal, principle   As a noun, *principal* means "the head of a school." As an adjective, it means "main or most important." *Principle* is a noun meaning "a rule of conduct" or "a general truth."

EXAMPLES
Ted had a long talk with the **principal.** [noun]
Winning is not our **principal** goal. [adjective]
My friends have high **principles.**
I don't know the **principles** of physics.

rise, raise   The verb *rise* means "go up" or "get up." *Rise* almost never takes an object. Its principal parts are *rise, rising, rose, risen.* The verb *raise* means "cause (something) to rise" or "lift up." *Raise* usually takes an object. Its principal parts are *raise, raising, raised, raised.*

EXAMPLES
Everyone **rose** when the judge entered the room. [no object]
The sniper **raised** his revolver and fired. [*Revolver* is the object of *raised.*]

scarcely   See **double negative.**

set   See **sit, set.**

she   See **he, she, it, they.**

should of   See **of.**

sit, set   The verb *sit* means "rest in an upright, seated position." *Sit* almost never takes an object. Its principal parts are *sit, sitting, sat, sat.* The verb *set* means "put (something) in a place." *Set* usually takes an object. Its principal parts are *set, setting, set, set.*

EXAMPLES
The campers were **sitting** around the fire. [no object]
Ganderbai **set** the bag on a chair. [*Bag* is the object of *set.*]

some, somewhat   In formal situations, do not use *some* to mean "to some extent" or "slightly." Instead, use *somewhat.*

INFORMAL	My spelling has now improved some.
FORMAL	My spelling has now improved **somewhat.**

somewheres   See **anyways, anywheres.**

sort(s)   See **kind(s), sort(s), type(s)** and **kind of a, sort of a.**

sort of   See **kind of, sort of.**

teach   See **learn, teach.**

than, then   *Than* is a conjunction used in comparisons. *Then* is an adverb meaning "at that time" or "next."

EXAMPLES
This box is heavier **than** that one.
Did the sniper know **then** who his enemy was?
First, I read *Romeo and Juliet;* **then,** I watched the film version.

that   See **who, which, that.**

their, there, they're   *Their* is a possessive form of *they.* As an adverb, *there* means "at that place." *There* is also used to begin a sentence. *They're* is the contraction of *they are.*

EXAMPLES
Their daughter, Juliet, was in love with a Montague.
Harry Pope lay **there** quietly.
There is a conflict between Odysseus and the Cyclops.
They're throwing pebbles at Miss Lottie's flowers.

theirs, there's   *Theirs* is a possessive form of the pronoun *they*. *There's* is the contraction of *there is*.

EXAMPLES
Our team was ready to play, and so was **theirs**.
There's a sniper on the rooftop.

theirselves   See **hisself, theirselves.**

them   *Them* should not be used as an adjective. Use *those*.

EXAMPLE
Their unselfish love is symbolized by **those** [*not* them] gifts.

then   See **than, then.**

there   See **their, there, they're.**

there's   See **theirs, there's.**

they   See **he, she, it, they.**

they're   See **their, there, they're.**

this, that, these, those   See **kind(s), sort(s), type(s).**

try and   Use *try to*, not *try and*.

EXAMPLE
Timber and Ganderbai **try to** [*not* try and] keep Harry calm.

type(s)   See **kind(s), sort(s), type(s).**

unless   See **without, unless.**

way, ways   Use *way*, not *ways*, in referring to a distance.

EXAMPLE
Odysseus traveled quite a long **way** [*not* ways] to get back home.

well   See **good, well.**

what   Use *that*, not *what*, to introduce an adjective clause.

EXAMPLE
The poem **that** [*not* what] I wrote about was Naomi Shihab Nye's "Daily."

when, where   Do not use *when* or *where* to begin a definition.

NONSTANDARD	A "bomb" in football is when a backfielder throws a long pass.
STANDARD	A "bomb" in football is a long pass thrown by a backfielder.

Also, do not use *where* for *that*.

EXAMPLE
I read in this book **that** [*not* where] Robert Frost won the Pulitzer Prize four times.

where . . . at   See **at.**

who, which, that   *Who* refers to persons only; *which* refers to things only; *that* may refer to either persons or things.

EXAMPLES
Isn't Walt Whitman the poet **who** [*or* that] wrote *Leaves of Grass*? [person]
They decided to replace Mme. Forestier's necklace, **which** they did not know was fake. [thing]
The necklace **that** the Loisels bought cost thirty-six thousand francs. [thing]

who's, whose   *Who's* is the contraction of *who is* or *who has*. *Whose* is the possessive form of *who*.

EXAMPLES
Who's [who is] the narrator of "A Christmas Memory"?
Who's [who has] been helping Helen?
Whose autobiography is titled *Black Boy*?

without, unless   Do not use the preposition *without* in place of the conjunction *unless*.

EXAMPLE
I will not be able to sing **unless** [*not* without] my cold gets better.

would of   See **of.**

your, you're   *Your* is a possessive form of *you*. *You're* is the contraction of *you are*.

EXAMPLES
What is **your** opinion of General Zaroff?
You're [you are] my best friend.

GLOSSARY

The glossary below is an alphabetical list of some of the words found in the selections in this book. Use this glossary just as you use a dictionary—to find out the meanings of unfamiliar words. (Some technical, foreign, and more obscure words in this book are not listed here but instead are defined in footnotes.)

Many words in the English language have more than one meaning. This glossary gives the meanings that apply to the words as they are used in the selections in this book. For some of these words, an additional meaning is given and the separate meanings are numbered. Words closely related in form and meaning are usually listed together in one entry (for instance, *prosper* and *prosperous*), and the definition is given for the first form.

The following abbreviations are used:

adj.	adjective
adv.	adverb
n.	noun
v.	verb

Each word's pronunciation is given in parentheses. A guide to the pronunciation symbols appears at the bottom of each right-hand glossary page.

For more information about the words in this glossary, or for information about words not listed here, consult a dictionary.

abatement (ə·bāt'mənt) *n.*: lessening; reduction.
abominable (ə·bäm'ə·nə·bəl) *adj.*: extremely unpleasant or disgusting. **—abominably** *adv.*
abscond (ab·skänd') *v.*: go away hastily and secretly.
abyss (ə·bis') *n.*: 1. deep hole in the earth. 2. something beyond understanding or measurement.
accost (ə·kôst') *v.*: approach and speak to, especially in an intrusive way.
accumulate (ə·kyoom'yoo·lāt') *v.*: pile up; collect.
acquiesce (ak'wē·es') **in** *v.*: accept; comply with.
adorn (ə·dôrn') *v.*: add beauty to; decorate.
adversary (ad'vər·ser'ē) *n.*: enemy; opponent.
adversity (ad·vʉr'sə·tē) *n.*: misfortune; hardship.
affable (af'ə·bəl) *adj.*: pleasant and friendly.
affront (ə·frunt') *n.*: insult.
aghast (ə·gast') *adj.*: horrified.
agility (ə·jil'ə·tē) *n.*: quickness of movement.
agitation (aj'ə·tā'shən) *n.*: stirring up; disturbance or excitement.

aloof (ə·loof') *adj.*: distant; unfriendly.
amendment (ə·mend'mənt) *n.*: change; revision.
amenity (ə·men'ə·tē) *n.*: something that comforts; convenience.
annihilate (ə·nī'ə·lāt') *v.*: destroy; wipe out.
anonymous (ə·nän'ə·məs) *adj.*: with no name; not easily distinguished from others.
anthem (an'thəm) *n.*: religious song; song of praise.
aperture (ap'ər·chər) *n.*: 1. opening; gap. 2. opening through which light passes in a camera or telescope.
apparition (ap'ə·rish'ən) *n.*: strange, ghostlike figure.
appellation (ap'ə·lā'shən) *n.*: name; title.
appraisal (ə·prāz'əl) *n.*: evaluation; sizing up.
apprehensive (ap'rē·hen'siv) *adj.*: fearful; uneasy.
arbitrary (är'bə·trer'ē) *adj.*: not fixed by rules.
ardent (ärd''nt) *adj.*: eager.
ardor (är'dər) *n.*: passion; enthusiasm.
asperity (ə·sper'ə·tē) *n.*: sharpness of temper.
assiduous (ə·sij'oo·əs) *adj.*: industrious; careful and hard-working. **—assiduously** *adv.*
atonement (ə·tōn'mənt) *n.*: something done to make up for wrong deeds.
attribute (a'trə·byoot') *n.*: quality; typical way of behaving.

baffle (baf'əl) *v.*: confuse.
bedeck (bē·dek') *v.*: decorate.
beguile (bē·gīl') *v.*: charm or delight, often in order to deceive. **—beguiling** *v.* used as *adj.*
benediction (ben'ə·dik'shən) *n.*: blessing.
benign (bi·nīn') *adj.*: good-natured; harmless.
billow (bil'ō) *v.*: rise or swell like a wave.
bounteous (boun'tē·əs) *adj.*: plentiful.
brandish (bran'dish) *v.*: wave in a threatening way.
bravado (brə·vä'dō) *n.*: pretense of courage or confidence.
brazen (brā'zən) *adj.*: 1. made of brass. 2. bold; showing no shame.
buoyancy (boi'ən·sē) *n.*: 1. ability to keep something afloat. 2. cheerfulness.
burnish (bʉr'nish) *v.*: make shiny; polish.

callous (kal'əs) *adj.*: unfeeling; insensitive.
caper (kā'pər) *v.*: jump about playfully.
caricature (kar'i·kə·chər) *n.*: exaggerated portrait.
carnage (kär'nij) *n.*: slaughter.
cavort (kə·vôrt') *v.*: leap about.
clamor (klam'ər) *n.*: 1. loud outcry. 2. noisy disturbance.

clarity (klar′ə·tē) *n.*: clearness.

commence (kə·mens′) *v.*: begin.

compel (kəm·pel′) *v.*: force.

compromise (käm′prə·mīz) *v.*: 1. give up something to receive something one desires; settle for less than one wants. 2. adjust conflicting viewpoints.

compunction (kəm·puŋk′shən) *n.*: feeling of guilt and regret.

condone (kən·dōn′) *v.*: approve of; forgive.

conformity (kən·fôrm′ə·tē) *n.*: behavior that follows the usual customs.

connoisseurship (kän′ə·sur′ship) *n.*: expert knowledge.

consolation (kän′sə·lā′shən) *n.*: thing that comforts.

consternation (kän′stər·nā′shən) *n.*: fear; bewilderment.

consummate (kən·sum′it) *adj.*: 1. complete or perfect. 2. very skillful. —**consummately** *adv.*

contaminate (kən·tam′ə·nāt′) *v.*: pollute; poison. —**contaminating** *v.* used as *adj.*

contemptuous (kən·temp′choo·əs) *adj.*: scornful.

contrition (kən·trish′ən) *n.*: deep feelings of guilt and repentance.

contrive (kən·trīv′) *v.*: 1. think up; devise. 2. manage cleverly.

converse (kän′vurs) *adj.*: opposite. —**conversely** *adv.*

coordinate (kō·ôr′də·nāt′) *v.*: adjust so that the various parts or people work smoothly together.

covet (kuv′it) *v.*: 1. long for. 2. envy. —**coveted** *v.* used as *adj.*

cower (kou′ər) *v.*: draw back or crouch in fear and helplessness.

customary (kus′tə·mer′ē) *adj.*: usual; established by custom.

decree (dē·krē′) *v.*: 1. give an official order. 2. command or decide beforehand.

deferential (def′ər·en′shəl) *adj.*: showing polite respect.

deft *adj.*: skillful in a quick, sure, and easy way.

deplorable (dē·plôr′ə·bəl) *adj.*: regrettable; very bad.

depreciate (dē·prē′shē·āt′) *v.*: 1. belittle. 2. lower the value of.

desolation (des′ə·lā′shən) *n.*: 1. loneliness. 2. ruin.

desperado (des′pər·ä′dō) *n.*: bold outlaw.

detractor (dē·trak′tər) *n.*: one who makes something seem less important or less valuable.

deviation (dē′vē·ā′shən) *n.*: change from usual behavior.

devoid (di·void′) *adj.*: empty.

dilapidated (də·lap′ə·dāt′id) *adj.*: shabby; falling apart.

diligent (dil′ə·jənt) *adj.*: careful and hard-working.

disarming (dis·ärm′iŋ) *adj.*: removing or lessening suspicions or fears.

discern (di·zurn′) *v.*: see; detect by looking carefully.

disconsolate (dis·kän′sə·lit) *adj.*: very unhappy.

disdainful (dis·dān′fəl) *adj.*: scornful; contemptuous.

disillusion (dis′i·lōō′zhən) *v.*: disappoint; make feel bitter. —**disillusioning** *v.* used as *adj.*

disperse (di·spurs′) *v.*: break up; scatter. —**dispersing** *v.* used as *adj.*

dispirited (di·spir′it·id) *adj.*: depressed; discouraged.

disposition (dis′pə·zish′ən) *n.*: usual frame of mind; personality or temperament.

dispossession (dis′pə·zesh′ən) *n.*: taking away of one's possessions.

diverting (də·vurt′iŋ) *adj.*: amusing; entertaining.

docile (däs′əl) *adj.*: easy to manage; submissive.

doggedness (dôg′id·nis) *n.*: stubbornness; persistence.

droll (drōl) *adj.*: amusing in an odd way.

earnest (ur′nist) *adj.*: serious; sincere. —**earnestly** *adv.*

ecstatic (ek·stat′ik) *adj.*: filled with delight.

elated (ē·lāt′id) *adj.*: very happy.

elude (ē·lōōd′) *v.*: get away from.

embark (em·bärk′) *v.*: 1. go aboard. 2. begin a journey.

embody (em·bäd′ē) *v.*: make real, give form to, or include; represent.

emit (ē·mit′) *v.*: send out.

endeavor (en·dev′ər) *v.*: try.

enfeeble (en·fē′bəl) *v.*: weaken, usually by old age or illness. —**enfeebled** *v.* used as *adj.*

enthrall (en·thrôl′) *v.*: fascinate; hold as if in a spell.

enthusiasm (en·thōō′zē·az′əm) *n.*: eager interest.

enunciate (ē·nun′sē·āt′) *v.*: pronounce clearly.

envelop (en·vel′əp) *v.*: conceal; wrap; surround. —**enveloped** *v.* used as *adj.*

ephemeral (e·fem′ər·əl) *adj.*: short-lived; passing quickly.

euphoria (yōō·fôr′ē·ə) *n.*: feeling of vigor or well-being.

exasperate (eg·zas′pər·āt′) *v.*: annoy greatly.

exhilarate (eg·zil′ə·rāt′) *v.*: gladden; excite.

exorbitant (eg·zôr′bi·tənt) *adj.*: much too high in price or amount.

exotic (eg·zät′ik) *adj.*: fascinating; strangely beautiful; foreign.

---

at, āte, cär; ten, ēve; is, īce; gō, hôrn, look, tool; oil, out; up, fur; ə *for unstressed vowels, as* a *in* ago, u *in* focus; ′ *as in* Latin (lat′'n); chin; she; zh *as in* azure (azh′ər); thin, *the*; ŋ *as in* ring (riŋ)

---

expedient (ek·spē′dē·ənt) *n.:* 1. means; resource. 2. device used in an emergency.

expendable (ek·spēn′də·bəl) *adj.:* worth sacrificing to gain an objective.

expenditure (ek·spen′di·chər) *n.:* payment for expenses.

falter (fôl′tər) *v.:* hesitate; be unsteady.

fanatic (fə·nat′ik) *n.:* person with extreme beliefs.

fathom (fath′əm) *n.:* unit for measuring the depth of the ocean.

feigned (fānd) *adj.:* pretended or faked.

feisty (fīs′tē) *adj.:* high-spirited; lively.

ferocity (fə·räs′ə·tē) *n.:* fierceness.

festoon (fes·tōōn′) *v.:* decorate.

flank (flaŋk) *v.:* be at the side of.

forestall (fôr·stôl′) *v.:* prevent by acting ahead of time.

formidable (fôr′mə·də·bəl) *adj.:* awe-inspiring in excellence; strikingly impressive.

founder (foun′dər) *v.:* fill with water and sink.

frenzied (fren′zēd) *adj.:* wild and frantic.

fretful (fret′fəl) *adj.:* irritable and discontented.

frivolous (friv′ə·ləs) *adj.:* silly; not as serious as the occasion requires.

furtive (fur′tiv) *adj.:* stealthy, as if to avoid being seen or heard. —**furtively** *adv.*

futile (fyōōt′′l) *adj.:* pointless.

gallant (gal′ənt) *adj.:* graciously polite. —**gallantly** *adv.*

gambol (gam′bəl) *v.:* skip about.

gangly (gaŋ′glē) *adj.:* loose and awkward; more commonly spelled **gangling** (gaŋ′gliŋ).

garish (gar′ish) *adj.:* too bright; showy.

gesticulation (jes·tik′yōō·lā′shən) *n.:* movement of hands or arms to express a thought or feeling.

glower (glou′ər) *v.:* glare; stare angrily.

goad (gōd) *v.:* drive; push into action.

grimace (gri·mās′) *n.:* twisting of the face because of pain or distress.

haversack (hav′ər·sak′) *n.:* canvas shoulder bag.

heifer (hef′ər) *n.:* young cow.

hindrance (hin′drəns) *n.:* obstacle; thing that restrains or prevents an activity.

imminent (im′ə·nənt) *adj.:* about to happen.

immobile (im·mō′bəl) *adj.:* not moving.

immolation (im′ə·lā′shən) *n.:* destruction.

impassive (im·pas′iv) *adj.:* showing no emotion. —**impassively** *adv.*

impediment (im·ped′ə·mənt) *n.:* defect that makes doing something difficult.

imperative (im·per′ə·tiv) *adj.:* extremely important; urgent.

imperious (im·pir′ē·əs) *adj.:* arrogant; expecting others to obey one's orders.

impertinent (im·purt′′n·ənt) *adj.:* shamelessly disrespectful; rude.

implicit (im·plis′it) *adj.:* absolute; unquestioning; implied or suggested but not expressed in words.

implore (im·plôr′) *v.:* plead. —**imploringly** *adv.*

impose (im·pōz′) **upon** *v.:* take advantage of.

imposture (im·päs′chər) *n.:* deception.

impotent (im′pə·tənt) *adj.:* powerless; helpless.

impoverish (im·päv′ər·ish) *v.:* make poor. —**impoverished** *v.* used as *adj.*

imprudent (im·prōōd′′nt) *adj.:* unwise.

impudent (im′pyōō·dənt) *adj.:* shamelessly disrespectful; rude. —**impudence** *n.*

impunity (im·pyōō′ni·tē) *n.:* freedom from punishment.

inarticulate (in′är·tik′yōō·lit) *adj.:* not expressed clearly enough to be understood.

inaugurate (in·ô′gyoo·rāt′) *v.:* formally begin.

incantation (in′kan·tā′shən) *n.:* chant of words or phrases that is meant to produce a magical result.

incessant (in·ses′ənt) *adj.:* constant; continual. —**incessantly** *adv.*

incite (in·sīt′) *v.:* stir up.

incredulous (in·krej′oo·ləs) *adj.:* unwilling to believe or unable to believe.

indolent (in′də·lənt) *adj.:* lazy; idle. —**indolently** *adv.*

indomitable (in·däm′i·tə·bəl) *adj.:* unconquerable; not easily discouraged or defeated.

inexorable (in·eks′ə·rə·bəl) *adj.:* unyielding; immovable; unchangeable.

inexplicable (in·eks′pli·kə·bəl) *adj.:* unexplainable; without apparent reason. —**inexplicably** *adv.*

infallibility (in·fal′ə·bil′ə·tē) *n.:* inability to make a mistake.

infatuated (in·fach′ōō·āt′id) *adj.:* carried away by shallow or foolish love.

insolent (in′sə·lənt) *adj.:* boldly disrespectful.

instigate (in′stə·gāt′) *v.:* give rise to; provoke or urge on to some action.

interminable (in·tur′mi·nə·bəl) *adj.:* endless. —**interminably** *adv.*

intermittent (in′tər·mit′′nt) *adj.:* occurring from time to time. —**intermittently** *adv.*

intersect (in′tər·sekt′) *v.:* cross each other.

intimate (in′tə·māt′) *v.:* hint.

intimidate (in·tim′ə·dāt′) *v.:* frighten.

intolerable (in·täl′ər·ə·bəl) *adj.*: unbearable; too painful or severe to be endured.

intone (in·tōn′) *v.*: say or recite in a dull, unchanging tone.

intravenous (in′trə·vē′nəs) *adj.*: directly into a vein. —**intravenously** *adv.*

intrepid (in·trep′id) *adj.*: fearless; brave.

intricate (in′tri·kit) *adj.*: complicated; elaborately detailed.

invalid (in′və·lid) *adj.*: having a long-term illness.

invariable (in·ver′ē·ə·bəl) *adj.*: without exception. —**invariably** *adv.*

irascible (i·ras′ə·bəl) *adj.*: irritable; easily angered.

jostle (jäs′əl) *v.*: bump or shove.

keel (kēl) *v.*: 1. fall over. 2. capsize.

lacerate (las′ər·āt′) *v.*: tear.

languor (laŋ′gər) *n.*: weakness; weariness.

lavish (lav′ish) *v.*: give generously.

leer (lir) *v.*: look sideways in an unpleasant way. —**leering** *v.* used as *adj.*

legacy (leg′ə·sē) *n.*: 1. money or property left to someone in a will. 2. something handed down from an ancestor or from the past.

litany (lit′′n·ē) *n.*: repetitive prayer, utterance, or recitation.

literal (lit′ər·əl) *adj.*: actual. —**literally** *adv.*

loam (lōm) *n.*: rich, dark soil.

lore (lôr) *n.*: knowledge that is passed from person to person, often without being written down.

luxuriant (lug·zhoor′ē·ənt) *adj.*: thick; growing in great abundance.

malicious (mə·lish′əs) *adj.*: spiteful.

mandate (man′dāt′) *v.*: require; formally order.

maneuver (mə·noo′vər) *n.*: skillful movement.

mar (mär) *v.*: spoil; make less attractive.

marauder (mə·rôd′ər) *n.*: someone who roams in search of loot.

mediate (mē′dē·āt′) *v.*: settle a dispute or argument by bringing the opposing sides together.

migrate (mī′grāt′) *v.*: move from one place to another.

mingle (miŋ′gəl) *v.*: mix.

mirage (mi·räzh′) *n.*: scene or object that looks real but isn't actually there.

misconception (mis′kən·sep′shən) *n.*: false idea.

misgiving (mis′giv′iŋ) *n.*: doubt; uneasy feeling.

mockery (mäk′ər·ē) *n.*: imitation, often to make fun of someone or something.

monosyllabic (män′ō·si·lab′ik) *adj.*: one-syllable.

monotony (mə·nät′′n·ē) *n.*: 1. lack of variation. 2. tiresome sameness.

morose (mə·rōs′) *adj.*: gloomy. —**morosely** *adv.*

mottled (mät′′ld) *adj.*: spotted.

murmur (mur′mər) *v.*: speak softly.

nimble (nim′bəl) *adj.*: moving quickly and lightly.

noncommittal (nän′kə·mit′′l) *adj.*: not admitting or committing to any particular purpose or point of view.

oasis (ō·ā′sis) *n.*: fertile place; place or thing offering welcome relief.

obstinate (äb′stə·nət) *adj.*: stubborn; persistent. —**obstinately** *adv.*

obstruction (əb·struk′shən) *n.*: blockage; hindrance.

odyssey (äd′i·sē) *n.*: extended journey marked by wandering, adventures, and changes of fortune.

omen (ō′mən) *n.*: sign; thing or happening believed to foretell an event.

ominous (äm′ə·nəs) *adj.*: suspicious; threatening; suggesting future problems. —**ominously** *adv.*

opiate (ō′pē·it) *n.*: anything that tends to soothe or calm someone; medicine containing opium or a related drug used to relieve pain.

oppressive (ə·pres′iv) *adj.*: heavy; hard to endure.

pageant (paj′ənt) *n.*: 1. elaborate parade. 2. drama celebrating a historic or religious event.

palate (pal′ət) *n.*: sense of taste.

palpable (pal′pə·bəl) *adj.*: easily felt or touched.

paradox (par′ə·däks′) *n.*: something that has or seems to have contradictory qualities.

paraphernalia (par′ə·fər·nāl′yə) *n.*: equipment; gear.

paroxysm (par′əks·iz′əm) *n.*: 1. sudden outburst; spasm. 2. fit of laughter, rage, or sneezing.

pauper (pô′pər) *n.*: very poor person.

peril (per′əl) *n.*: danger.

perplexed (pər·plekst′) *adj.*: puzzled.

perverse (pər·vurs′) *adj.*: rebellious; stubbornly disobedient.

---

at, āte, cär; ten, ēve; is, īce; gō, hôrn, look, tool; oil, out; up, fur; ə *for unstressed vowels, as* a *in* ago, u *in* focus; ′ *as in* Latin (lat′′n); chin; she; zh *as in* azure (azh′ər); thin, the; ŋ *as in* ring (riŋ)

---

petitioner (pə·tish′ən·ər) *n.*: person seeking favors.

pious (pī′əs) *adj.*: 1. showing religious devotion. 2. seemingly virtuous.

piteous (pit′ē·əs) *adj.*: arousing pity or compassion. —**piteously** *adv.*

placid (plas′id) *adj.*: undisturbed; calm; tranquil; untroubled.

pliant (plī′ənt) *adj.*: flexible; adaptable.

plod (pläd) *v.*: trudge; walk heavily.

poignant (poin′yənt) *adj.*: sad; emotionally moving. —**poignantly** *adv.*

polytheism (päl′i·thē·iz′əm) *n.*: belief in or worship of more than one god.

ponderous (pän′dər·əs) *adj.*: 1. very heavy. 2. dull.

potent (pōt′'nt) *adj.*: 1. powerful. 2. convincing; influential.

precarious (prē·ker′ē·əs) *adj.*: unsteady; unstable; unsure. —**precariously** *adv.*

precipitous (prē·sip′ə·təs) *adj.*: very steep.

preclude (prē·klo͞od′) *v.*: make impossible in advance; prevent.

pretext (prē′tekst′) *n.*: excuse.

primeval (prī·mē′vəl) *adj.*: primitive; of the earliest times.

privation (prī·vā′shən) *n.*: 1. hardship. 2. lack of something needed for a happy, healthy life.

procession (prō·sesh′ən) *n.*: formal parade.

proffer (präf′ər) *v.*: offer.

profusion (prō·fyo͞o′zhən) *n.*: large supply; abundance.

prolong (prō·lôŋ′) *v.*: make longer; extend. —**prolonged** *v.* used as *adj.*

proposition (präp′ə·zish′ən) *n.*: suggestion; plan.

prosaic (prō·zā′ik) *adj.*: ordinary.

pummel (pum′əl) *v.*: hit repeatedly.

querulous (kwer′yo͞o·ləs) *adj.*: complaining.

quizzical (kwiz′i·kəl) *adj.*: questioning. —**quizzically** *adv.*

rampart (ram′pärt′) *n.*: broad embankment surrounding a castle, fort, or city for defense against attack.

rancid (ran′sid) *adj.*: spoiled; tasting or smelling bad.

rancor (raŋ′kər) *n.*: bitterness; resentment; ill will.

ravage (rav′ij) *v.*: destroy violently; ruin.

realm (relm) *n.*: 1. kingdom; 2. region; sphere.

recoil (ri·koil′) *v.*: move backward, as if in horror. —**recoiling** *v.* used as *adj.*

recollect (rek′ə·lekt′) *v.*: remember.

recount (ri·kount′) *v.*: describe in detail; narrate.

reiterate (rē·it′ə·rāt′) *v.*: repeat.

relinquish (ri·liŋ′kwish) *v.*: surrender.

remit (ri·mit′) *v.*: cancel payment.

remonstrance (ri·män′strəns) *n.*: protest.

replica (rep′li·kə) *n.*: model or copy.

repose (ri·pōz′) *n.*: rest.

resilient (ri·zil′yənt) *adj.*: 1. elastic; able to return to the original shape quickly after being stretched or compressed. 2. able to recover quickly from misfortune or difficulty.

resound (ri·zound′) *v.*: make a loud echo.

restitution (res′tə·to͞o′shən) *n.*: compensation; repayment.

restive (res′tiv) *adj.*: restless; unsettled.

restriction (ri·strik′shən) *n.*: 1. rule. 2. limitation.

resurrection (rez′ə·rek′shən) *n.*: coming or bringing back to life.

retaliate (ri·tal′ē·āt′) *v.*: cause an injury or wrong in response to one.

retribution (re′trə·byo͞o′shən) *n.*: punishment; revenge.

revelry (rev′əl·rē) *n.*: merrymaking; festivity; noisy, lively celebration.

revert (ri·vurt′) *v.*: go back, as to a former state.

revoke (ri·vōk′) *v.*: cancel; withdraw.

ruse (ro͞oz) *n.*: trick.

ruthless (ro͞oth′lis) *adj.*: without pity.

sacrilegious (sak′rə·lij′əs) *adj.*: disrespectful of religion.

sage (sāj) *adj.*: wise.

scalpel (skal′pəl) *n.*: knife used by surgeons.

scanty (skan′tē) *adj.*: small; only just enough.

scourge (skurj) *n.*: cause of serious trouble or great suffering.

scruple (skro͞o′pəl) *n.*: feeling of doubt or guilt about a suggested action.

scrutinize (skro͞ot′'n·īz′) *v.*: look at carefully.

scrutiny (skro͞ot′'n·ē) *n.*: close inspection.

sensibility (sen′sə·bil′ə·tē) *n.*: capacity for being emotionally responsive.

serum (sir′əm) *n.*: 1. fluid used in medical treatment. 2. clear, yellowish fluid that is part of blood.

servile (sur′vəl) *adj.*: humbly submissive; like a slave.

sever (sev′ər) *v.*: separate; break or cut off.

siege (sēj) *n.*: stubborn, continued effort to win or control something.

silhouette (sil′o͞o·et′) *v.*: show as a dark shape against a light background.

simultaneous (sī′məl·tā′nē·əs) *adj.*: happening at the same time. —**simultaneously** *adv.*

sloop (slo͞op) *n.*: type of sailing ship.

sojourn (sō′jurn) *v.*: 1. stay briefly. 2. live someplace temporarily.

solace (säl′is) *n.*: comfort; easing of grief.

solemnity (sə·lem′nə·tē) *n.*: seriousness.

solicitous (sə·lis′ə·təs) *adj.*: showing concern. —**solicitously** *adv.*

solicitude (sə·lis′ə·tōōd′) *n.:* concern.

somber (säm′bər) *adj.:* 1. solemn; dull. 2. depressed.

sprawl (sprôl) *v.:* spread out in relaxed position.

squalor (skwäl′ər) *n.:* filth or shabbiness.

squander (skwän′dər) *v.:* waste.

staccato (stə·kät′ō) *adj.:* consisting of short, sharp sounds.

stamina (stam′ə·nə) *n.:* ability to keep going.

starboard (stär′bərd) *adj.:* on the right-hand side of a ship.

stealth (stelth) *n.:* secret or sneaky action or behavior.

stifle (stī′fəl) *v.:* 1. smother. 2. hold back; prevent from being expressed. —**stifled** *v.* used as *adj.*

stifling (stī′fliŋ) *adj.:* 1. making breathing difficult; suffocating. 2. too close and confining.

stolid (stäl′id) *adj.:* 1. showing no emotion. 2. unexcitable.

stronghold (strôŋ′hōld′) *n.:* place that is strongly built for protection from enemies.

stupefy (stōō′pə·fī′) *v.:* 1. paralyze; make numb. 2. amaze; bewilder. —**stupefying** *v.* used as *adj.*

stupor (stōō′pər) *n.:* dull or half-conscious state of mind.

suave (swäv) *adj.:* gracious and confident; smoothly polite.

subliminal (sub·lim′ə·nəl) *adj.:* below the level of consciousness.

subservient (səb·sur′vē·ənt) *adj.:* submissive; showing too great a willingness to serve or obey.

succession (sək·sesh′ən) *n.:* series.

succor (suk′ər) *n.:* help given to someone in distress; relief.

suffuse (sə·fyōōz′) *v.:* spread over or through.

sullen (sul′ən) *adj.:* gloomy.

supplication (sup′lə·ka′shən) *n.:* humble plea or request.

surmount (sər·mount′) *v.:* be at the top of.

sustenance (sus′tə·nəns) *n.:* 1. nourishment; food. 2. support.

symmetry (sim′ə·trē) *n.:* balanced arrangement.

synchronize (siŋ′krə·nīz′) *v.:* cause to occur at the same rate or time.

synonymous (si·nän′ə·məs) *adj.:* similar in meaning.

tangible (tan′jə·bəl) *adj.:* able to be touched.

taunt (tônt) *v.:* 1. jeer. 2. mock; reproach.

tawdry (tô′drē) *adj.:* cheap and flashy; sleazy.

teem (tēm) *v.:* swarm; overflow —**teeming** *v.* used as *adj.*

temperance (tem′pər·əns) *n.:* 1. self-restraint. 2. moderation in drinking alcohol.

tentative (ten′tə·tiv) *adj.:* hesitant; uncertain. —**tentatively** *adv.*

terse (turs) *adj.:* using few words. —**tersely** *adv.*

thoroughbred (thur′ō·bred′) *adj.:* carefully bred, or raised, for a special purpose. The term is often used to describe animals such as racehorses.

tremulous (trem′yōō·ləs) *adj.:* trembling; shaking.

trepidation (trep′ə·dā′shən) *n.:* fearful uncertainty.

tress (tres) *n.:* lock of hair.

truant (trōō′ənt) *adj.:* 1. staying away from school. 2. idle. 3. straying.

tumult (tōō′mult′) *n.:* commotion; uproar; confusion.

uncanny (un·kan′ē) *adj.:* eerily remarkable.

undertow (un′dər·tō′) *n.:* current of water that moves beneath and in a different direction from the surface water.

undulate (un′dyōō·lāt′) *v.:* move in waves or like a wave.

unencumbered (un·en·kum′bərd) *adj.:* 1. not blocked or cluttered. 2. free to act.

unperturbed (un·pər·turbd′) *adj.:* untroubled; not upset.

unwieldy (un·wēl′dē) *adj.:* awkward; difficult to handle.

veranda (və·ran′də) *n.:* open porch along the outside of a building.

verification (ver′ə·fi·kā′shən) *n.:* proof of accuracy or truth.

verve (vurv) *n.:* liveliness.

vexation (veks·ā′shən) *n.:* annoyance.

vigilant (vij′ə·lənt) *adj.:* 1. alert for danger or trouble. 2. watchful.

virile (vir′əl) *adj.:* strong.

vitality (vī·tal′ə·tē) *n.:* energy.

vivacious (vī·vā′shəs) *adj.:* very lively.

voluminous (və·lōōm′ə·nəs) *adj.:* large and bulky.

wince (wins) *v.:* move back slightly, as if in pain.

wither (with′ər) *v.:* dry up; lose freshness.

wrench (rench) *v.:* twist sharply.

zealous (zel′əs) *adj.:* enthusiastic and thorough.

---

at, āte, cär; ten, ēve; is, īce; gō, hôrn, look, tōōl; oil, out; up, fur; ə *for unstressed vowels, as* a *in* ago, u *in* focus; ′ *as in* Latin (lat′'n); chin; she; zh *as in* azure (azh′ər); thin, the; ŋ *as in* ring (riŋ)

ACKNOWLEDGMENTS

For permission to reprint copyrighted material, grateful acknowledgment is made to the following sources:

Abbeville Press, Inc.: Description of painting *Emmie and Her Child* from *Mary Cassatt: Paintings and Prints* by Frank Getlein. Copyright © 1980 by Cross River Press, Ltd.

Arte Público Press: "Hate" from *Mainstream Ethics* by Tato Laviera. Copyright © 1988 by Tato Laviera. Published by Arte Público Press—University of Houston, Houston, TX, 1988. "Extranjera legal" (translation of "Legal Alien") and "Legal Alien" from *Chants* by Pat Mora. Copyright © 1984 by Pat Mora. Published by Arte Público Press—University of Houston, Houston, TX, 1984.

Asian American Voices: Untitled essay by Li-Young Lee from *Chinese American Poetry: An Anthology,* edited by L. Ling-chi Wang and Henry Yiheng Zhao. Copyright © 1991 by L. Ling-chi Wang and Henry Yiheng Zhao.

Howard A. Balsam: "Driver's Ed?" by Howard A. Balsam from *Pegasus,* Literary-Arts Publication, vol. XVII, 1990. Copyright © 1990 by Howard A. Balsam. Published by Half Hollow Hills High School East, Dix Hills, NY.

The Estate of Toni Cade Bambara: Adapted from "What It Is I Think I Am Doing Anyhow" by Toni Cade Bambara from *The Writer on Her Work,* edited by Janet Sternburg. Copyright © by Toni Cade Bambara. Published by W. W. Norton & Co., Inc., 1980.

Elizabeth Barnett, Literary Executor: "An Ancient Gesture" from *Collected Poems of Edna St. Vincent Millay.* Copyright © 1954, 1982 by Norma Millay Ellis. Published by HarperCollins Publishers, Inc.

BBC Worldwide: From "Return of the Prodigal Son" from *Sister Wendy's Grand Tour* by Sister Wendy Beckett. Copyright © 1994 by Sister Wendy Beckett.

Susan Bergholz Literary Services, New York: From "My English" by Julia Alvarez. Copyright © 1989 by Julia Alvarez. First published in the *Proceedings of the Ollantay Center Conference.* All rights reserved. "Snow" from *How the García Girls Lost Their Accents* by Julia Alvarez. Copyright © 1991 by Julia Alvarez. Published by Plume, an imprint of Dutton Signet, a division of Penguin Putnam Inc., and originally in hardcover by Algonquin Books of Chapel Hill. All rights reserved. "A Conversation with Sandra Cisneros." Copyright © 1989 by Sandra Cisneros. All rights reserved. "Those Who Don't" from *The House on Mango Street* by Sandra Cisneros. Copyright © 1984 by Sandra Cisneros. Published by Vintage Books, a division of Random House, Inc., and in hardcover by Alfred A. Knopf, 1994. All rights reserved. "Salvador Late or Early" from *Woman Hollering Creek* by Sandra Cisneros. Copyright © 1991 by Sandra Cisneros. Published by Vintage Books, a division of Random House, Inc., and originally in hardcover by Random House, Inc. All rights reserved.

Yogi Berra: Comment "It ain't over till it's over" by Yogi Berra, 1973.

Black Sparrow Press: "Prologue" from *Counting Myself Lucky: Selected Poems 1963–1992* by Edward Field. Copyright © 1992 by Edward Field.

BOA Editions, Ltd., 260 East Ave., Rochester, NY 14604: "this morning" from *good woman: poems and a memoir 1969–1980* by Lucille Clifton. Copyright © 1987 by Lucille Clifton. "The Gift" from *Rose* by Li-Young Lee. Copyright © 1986 by Li-Young Lee.

Brandt & Brandt Literary Agents, Inc.: "The Most Dangerous Game" by Richard Connell. Copyright 1924 by Richard Connell; copyright renewed © 1952 by Louise Fox Connell.

George Braziller, Inc.: "Fork" from *Dismantling the Silence* by Charles Simic. Copyright © 1971 by Charles Simic.

Broadside Press: "Ballad of Birmingham" by Dudley Randall. Published by Third World Press, Chicago.

Gwendolyn Brooks: "Old Mary" and from "We Real Cool" from *Blacks* by Gwendolyn Brooks. Copyright © 1991 by Gwendolyn Brooks. Copyright © 1991 by Gwendolyn Brooks. Published by Third World Press, Chicago.

Gladys Cardiff: "Combing" from *To Frighten a Storm* by Gladys Cardiff. Copyright © 1976 by Gladys Cardiff. Comment on "Combing" by Gladys Cardiff. Copyright © 1997 by Gladys Cardiff.

Eugenia W. Collier: Comment on "Marigolds" by Eugenia W. Collier. Copyright © 1992 by Eugenia W. Collier. Slightly adapted from "Marigolds" by Eugenia W. Collier from *Negro Digest,* November 1969. Copyright © 1969 by Johnson Publishing Company, Inc.

Columbia University Press: English translations of "Art" by Hjalmar Flax and from "Living Poetry" by Hugo Margenat from *Inventing a Word: An Anthology of 20th Century Puerto Rican Poetry* by Julio Marzán. Copyright © 1980 by Columbia University Press.

Don Congdon Associates, Inc.: "A Sound of Thunder" by Ray Bradbury. Copyright © 1952 by the Crowell-Collier Publishing Co.; copyright renewed © 1980 by Ray Bradbury. "The Gift" by Ray Bradbury. Copyright © 1952 by Esquire, Inc.; copyright renewed © 1980 by Ray Bradbury.

The Crisis Publishing Company, Inc.: From "Fanniedell Peeples: A Volunteer of Love" by Denise Crittendon from *The Crisis,* vol. 101, no. 5, July 1994. Copyright © 1994 by The Crisis Publishing Company, Inc.

Crown Publishers, Inc.: From *The Diary of Latoya Hunter* by Latoya Hunter. Copyright © 1992 by Latoya Hunter.

Delacorte Press/Seymour Lawrence, a division of Random House, Inc.: "Harrison Bergeron" from *Welcome to the Monkey House* by Kurt Vonnegut, Jr. Copyright © 1961 by Kurt Vonnegut, Jr.

Doubleday, a division of Random House, Inc.: "The Birds" from *Kiss Me Again Stranger* by Daphne du Maurier. Copyright 1952 by Daphne du Maurier. From *Anne Frank: The Diary of a Young Girl* by Anne Frank. Copyright 1952 by Otto H. Frank. "The Road Block" ("Get out of the road") by Chora from *An Introduction to Haiku* by Harold G. Henderson. Copyright © 1958 by Harold G. Henderson. "The Lesson of the Moth" from *Archy and Mehitabel* by Don Marquis. Copyright 1927 by Doubleday, a division of Random House, Inc. Quotes by Naomi Shihab Nye and Sharon Olds from *The Language of Life: A Festival of Poets* by Bill Moyers. Copyright © 1995 by Public Affairs Television, Inc., and David Grubin Productions, Inc. Quote by Bill Moyers from *The Power of Myth* by Joseph Campbell and Bill Moyers. Copyright © 1988 by Apostrophe S Productions, Inc., and Bill Moyers and Alfred Van der Marck Editions, Inc., for itself and the estate of Joseph Campbell. "My Papa's Waltz" from *The Collected Poems of Theodore Roethke* by Theodore Roethke. Copyright 1942 by Hearst Magazines, Inc. From *Conversations with Isaac Bashevis Singer* by Isaac Bashevis Singer and Richard Burgin. Copyright © 1978, 1980, 1985 by Isaac Bashevis Singer and Richard Burgin.

Stephen Dunn and David Weiss: Response by Stephen Dunn from "Spending More Time on the Turtle's Back," an interview with Stephen Dunn by David Weiss, from *Seneca Review,* vol. XIV, no. 2, 1984. Copyright © 1984 by Hobart & William Smith Colleges, Geneva, NY.

Dutton Signet, a division of Penguin Putnam Inc.: Adapted footnotes by J. A. Bryant, Jr., from *Romeo and Juliet* by William Shakespeare, edited by J. A. Bryant, Jr. Copyright © 1964, 1986 and renewed © 1992 by J. A. Bryant, Jr.

Anita Endrezze: Comment on "The Girl Who Loved the Sky" by Anita Endrezze. Copyright © 1997 by Anita Endrezze. "The Girl Who Loved the Sky" from *At the Helm of Twilight* by Anita Endrezze. Copyright © 1988 by Anita Endrezze. Published by Broken Moon Press, 1992.

Mari Evans: "If There Be Sorrow" from *I Am a Black Woman* by Mari Evans. Copyright © 1970 by Mari Evans. Published by William Morrow & Co.

Farrar, Straus & Giroux, Inc.: From Book XVI, "Father and Son," from *The Odyssey* by Homer, translated by Robert Fitzgerald. Translation copyright © 1961; copyright renewed © 1989 by Benedict R. C. Fitzgerald on behalf of the Fitzgerald children; this edition copyright © 1998 by Farrar, Straus & Giroux, Inc. Prologue from *In My Place* by Charlayne Hunter-Gault. Copyright © 1992 by Charlayne Hunter-Gault. "The Washwoman" from *A Day of Pleasure* by Isaac Bashevis Singer. Copyright © 1969 by Isaac Bashevis Singer. "The Puppy" from *Stories and Prose Poems* by Alexander Solzhenitsyn, translated by

Michael Glenny. Translation copyright © 1971 by Michael Glenny.

Gale Research Inc.: Adapted quote by Judith Ortiz Cofer from "Judith Ortiz Cofer" from *Contemporary Authors: New Revision Series,* vol. 32, edited by James G. Lesniak. Copyright © 1991 by Gale Research Inc. Quotes by Cynthia Rylant from "Cynthia Rylant" from *Something About the Author,* vol. 50, edited by Anne Commire. Copyright © 1988 by Gale Research Inc.

Frances Goldin on behalf of Essex Hemphill: "American Hero" from *Ceremonies: Prose and Poetry* by Essex Hemphill. Copyright © 1992 by Essex Hemphill.

Graywolf Press, Saint Paul, Minnesota: "Fifteen" from *The Way It Is: New & Selected Poems* by William Stafford. Copyright © 1966, 1998 by the Estate of William Stafford.

Grove Press, Inc.: Quote by Denise Levertov from "Statements on Poetics" from *The New American Poetry,* edited by Donald M. Allen. Copyright © 1959 by Denise Levertov.

Alicia Pax Guevara: "A Vietnam Remembrance" by Alicia Guevara from *The Muse,* vol. 1, May 1993. Published by Marymount School, New York, NY.

Harcourt Brace & Company: From "East Coker" from *Four Quartets* by T. S. Eliot. Copyright 1943 by T. S. Eliot; copyright renewed © 1971 by Esme Valerie Eliot. "The Necklace" by Guy de Maupassant from *Adventures in Reading,* Laureate Edition. Copyright © 1963 by Harcourt Brace & Company; copyright renewed © 1991 by Deborah Jean Lodge, Alice Lodge, Jeanne M. Shutes, Jessica Sand, Lydia Winderman, Florence F. Potell, and Mary Rives Bowman. From "Tentative (First Model) Definitions of Poetry" from *The Complete Poems of Carl Sandburg.* Copyright © 1969, 1970 by Lilian Steichen Sandburg, Trustee. "Choice: A Tribute to Dr. Martin Luther King, Jr." and from "To the Editors of Ms. Magazine" from *In Search of Our Mothers' Gardens: Womanist Prose* by Alice Walker. Copyright © 1983 by Alice Walker. "Women" from *Revolutionary Petunias & Other Poems* by Alice Walker. Copyright © 1970 by Alice Walker. From "Boy at the Window" from *Things of This World* by Richard Wilbur. Copyright 1952 and renewed © 1980 by Richard Wilbur. "Running, 1933" from *Walking to Sleep: New Poems and Translations* by Richard Wilbur. Copyright © 1968 and renewed © 1996 by Richard Wilbur.

HarperCollins Publishers, Inc.: "Americans All" from *Paper Trail* by Michael Dorris. Copyright © 1994 by Michael Dorris. Excerpt and quote from *Black Boy* by Richard Wright. Copyright 1937, 1942, 1944, 1945 by Richard Wright; copyright renewed © 1973 by Ellen Wright.

David Higham Associates: "Poison" from *Someone Like You* by Roald Dahl. Copyright 1950 by Roald Dahl. Published by Alfred A. Knopf, Inc.

Hill and Wang, a division of Farrar, Straus & Giroux, Inc.: "Thank You, M'am" from *Something in Common* by Langston Hughes. Copyright © 1963 by Langston Hughes; copyright renewed © 1991 by Arnold Rampersad and Ramona Bass.

Henry Holt and Company, Inc.: From "The Figure a Poem Makes" from *Complete Poems of Robert Frost.* Copyright 1930, © 1967 by Henry Holt and Company, Inc. From "The Black Cottage," "Dust of Snow," and "Fire and Ice" from *The Poetry of Robert Frost,* edited by Edward Connery Lathem. Copyright 1951, © 1958 by Robert Frost; copyright © 1967 by Lesley Frost Ballantine; copyright © 1923, 1930, 1939, © 1969 by Henry Holt and Company, Inc.

Houghton Mifflin Company: "All Watched Over by Machines of Loving Grace" from *The Pill Versus the Springhill Mine Disaster* by Richard Brautigan. Copyright © 1965 by Richard Brautigan. All rights reserved.

Houston Chronicle: Adapted from "Eyeglasses for the Mind," an interview with Stephen King, by George Christian from *Houston Chronicle,* September 30, 1979. Copyright © 1979 by Houston Chronicle.

Phillip Whittington Hughes: "So Much Better Back Then" by Whit Hughes from *Earthwinds 1993,* vol. XXII. Copyright © 1993 by Whit Hughes. Published by Jackson Preparatory School, Jackson, Mississippi.

James R. Hurst: "The Scarlet Ibis" by James R. Hurst from *The Atlantic Monthly,* July 1960. Copyright © 1960 by The Atlantic Monthly.

INTERVIEW Inc.: Quote by Sandra Cisneros from "Why Write Now?" from *INTERVIEW,* vol. XXI, no. 5, May 1991. Copyright © 1991 by INTERVIEW. *INTERVIEW* Magazine is published by Brandt Publications.

Alfred A. Knopf, Inc.: From *Jurassic Park* by Michael Crichton. Copyright © 1990 by Michael Crichton. "Dream Deferred" ("Harlem") from *Collected Poems* by Langston Hughes. Copyright © 1994 by the Estate of Langston Hughes.

Charles Kuralt: Quote by Charles Kuralt from an article by Arthur Ungar from *The Christian Science Monitor.*

Lescher & Lescher, Ltd., on behalf of Paula Fox: From *A Servant's Tale* by Paula Fox. Copyright © 1984 by Paula Fox.

Lescher & Lescher, Ltd., on behalf of the Estate of Isaac Bashevis Singer: Quote by Isaac Bashevis Singer from "Singer: 'Every Encounter Is to Me a Potential Story'" by Edith Gold from *Authors in the News,* vol. 2, edited by Barbara Nykoruk. Originally appeared in the *Miami Herald,* March 7, 1976.

Liveright Publishing Corporation: From "A Poet's Advice to Students" from *A Miscellany Revised* by E. E. Cummings, edited by George J. Firmage. Copyright © 1955, 1965 by the Trustees for the E. E. Cummings Trust; copyright © 1958, 1965 by George J. Firmage. "in Just-" and "who are you,little i" from *Complete Poems, 1904–1962* by E. E. Cummings, edited by George J. Firmage. Copyright © 1976 by George James Firmage; copyright 1923, 1951, © 1963, 1991 by the Trustees for the E. E. Cummings Trust.

Lucasfilm Ltd. and Bantam Books, a division of Random House, Inc.: From *Star Wars®: The Magic of Myth* by Mary Henderson. Copyright © 1997 by Lucasfilm Ltd.

Gretchen R. Lund: "Photo Album" by Gretchen Lund from *Dead Center Literary Magazine,* vol. XVII, 1991. Copyright © 1991 by Gretchen Lund. Published by Highland Park High School, Highland Park, NJ.

Macmillan General Reference USA, a division of Ahsuog, Inc.: From *Webster's New World Dictionary,* Third College Edition. Copyright © 1988, 1991, 1994 by Simon & Schuster, Inc.

The Literary Trustees of Walter de la Mare and the Society of Authors as their representative: From "Silver" from *The Complete Poems of Walter de la Mare.* Published in the United States in 1970.

Marlowe & Company: "The Talking Skull" from *A Treasury of African Folklore* by Harold Courlander. Copyright © 1996 by Harold Courlander.

McIntosh and Otis, Inc.: "A Man Called Horse" by Dorothy M. Johnson. Copyright © 1949 and renewed © 1977 by Dorothy M. Johnson.

Merlyn's Pen, Inc.: "Coward" by Drake Bennett from *Merlyn's Pen,* February/March 1993. Copyright © 1993 by Merlyn's Pen, Inc. First appeared in *Merlyn's Pen: The National Magazines of Student Writing.*

N. Scott Momaday: From *The Names: A Memoir* by N. Scott Momaday. Copyright © 1976 by N. Scott Momaday. "Riding Is an Exercise of the Mind" from *The Strange and True Story of My Life with Billy the Kid* by N. Scott Momaday. Copyright © 1985 by N. Scott Momaday.

John Morgan: "Waiting for the Beep" by John Morgan from *Pegasus,* vol. XVIII, 1991. Copyright © 1991 by John Morgan. Published by Half Hollow Hills High School East, Dix Hills, NY.

William Morrow & Company, Inc.: "The World Is Not a Pleasant Place to Be" from *My House* by Nikki Giovanni. Copyright © 1972 by Nikki Giovanni. "The Cyclops in the Ocean" from *Those Who Ride the Night Winds* by Nikki Giovanni. Copyright © 1983 by Nikki Giovanni. "Kidnap Poem" from *The Women and the Men* by Nikki Giovanni. Copyright © 1970, 1974, 1975 by Nikki Giovanni.

National Geographic Society: Adapted map of pueblo territories from *National Geographic,* vol. 189, no. 4, April 1996. Copyright © 1996 by National Geographic Society.

New Directions Publishing Corp.: "The Secret" from *Poems 1960–1967* by Denise Levertov. Copyright © 1964 by Denise Levertov. "Your Laughter" from *The Captain's Verses* by Pablo Neruda. Copyright © 1972 by Pablo Neruda and Donald D. Walsh.

Newsweek: From "It's OK to Be Different" by Angie Erickson from *Newsweek,* October 24, 1994. All rights reserved.

The New York Times Company: From "First Night Report: 'The Miracle Worker'" by Walter Kerr from *New York Herald Tribune,* October 20, 1959. Copyright © 1959 by The New York Times Company. "Darkness at Noon" by Harold Krents from *The New York*

Times, May 5, 1978. Copyright © 1978 by The New York Times Company. From "Looking Back at 'The Miracle Worker' on TV" by William Gibson from *The New York Times*, October 14, 1979. Copyright © 1979 by The New York Times Company. From "Public & Private; Enough Bookshelves" by Anna Quindlen from *The New York Times*, August 7, 1991. Copyright © 1991 by The New York Times Company. "Langston Hughes on the IRT" by Joe Sexton from *The New York Times*, March 2, 1994. Copyright © 1994 by The New York Times Company. From "In America; Romeo and Juliet in Bosnia" by Bob Herbert from *The New York Times*, May 8, 1994. Copyright © 1994 by The New York Times Company. From "Solzhenitsyn Looks Home, to Russia" by Sara Rimer from *The New York Times*, May 26, 1994. Copyright © 1994 by The New York Times Company. From "After the Beats: A New Generation Raises Its Voice in Poetry" by Diana Jean Schemo from *The New York Times*, September 26, 1994. Copyright © 1994 by The New York Times Company. "While We're Young" by Gregg Easterbrook from *The New York Times*, December 23, 1994. Copyright © 1994 by The New York Times Company. "An Open Mind" by Nicole A. Plumail from *The New York Times*, March 25, 1995. Copyright © 1995 by The New York Times Company. From "Sunday View; Perfectly Tuned Actors Hit a High Note" by Margo Jefferson from "Arts & Leisure" from *The New York Times*, April 23, 1995. Copyright © 1995 by The New York Times Company.

W. W. Norton & Company, Inc.: "The Sacred" from *Between Angels* by Stephen Dunn. Copyright © 1989 by Stephen Dunn.

Naomi Shihab Nye: "Daily" and from "Famous" from *Hugging the Jukebox* by Naomi Shihab Nye. Copyright © 1982 by Naomi Shihab Nye.

Brooke Olson: From "My Room" by Brooke Olson from *Voices of Youth*, September/October 1993. Copyright © 1993 by Voices of Youth: Educational Goals Study Group.

Orchard Books, New York: From *But I'll Be Back Again* by Cynthia Rylant. Copyright © 1989 by Cynthia Rylant.

Simon J. Ortiz: "My Father's Song" from *Woven Stone* by Simon J. Ortiz. Copyright © 1992 by Simon J. Ortiz. Published by the University of Arizona Press.

Pantheon Books, a division of Random House, Inc.: "The Trapper Trapped" from *African Folktales: Traditional Stories of the Black World*, selected and retold by Roger D. Abrahams. Copyright © 1983 by Roger D. Abrahams. "How Poetry Comes to Me" from *No Nature* by Gary Snyder. Copyright © 1992 by Gary Snyder.

Penguin Books Ltd: "Silent, but . . ." by Tsuboi Shigeji (p. 191) from *The Penguin Book of Japanese Verse*, translated by Geoffrey Bownas and Anthony Thwaite. Translation copyright © 1964 by Geoffrey Bownas and Anthony Thwaite. Published by Penguin Books, 1964.

The Peters Fraser and Dunlop Group Limited on behalf of Liam O'Flaherty: "The Sniper" from *The Martyr* by Liam O'Flaherty. Copyright © 1933 by Liam O'Flaherty.

Pocket Books, a division of Simon & Schuster: From *Shakespeare Set Free: Teaching "Romeo and Juliet," "Macbeth," and "A Midsummer Night's Dream"* by The Folger Shakespeare Library, edited by Peggy O'Brien. Copyright © 1993 by The Folger Shakespeare Library.

Prentice Hall, a division of Simon & Schuster: From *Three Genres: The Writing of Poetry, Fiction and Drama*, Second Edition, by Stephen Minot. Copyright © 1965, 1971 by Prentice Hall, Inc.

Princeton University Press: "Ithaca" from *Collected Poems* by C. P. Cavafy, translated by Edmund Keeley and Philip Sherrard. Copyright © 1992 by Princeton University Press.

Publishers Weekly: From "Michael Dorris," an interview by Dulcy Brainard, from *Publishers Weekly*, vol. 236, no. 5, August 4, 1989. Copyright © 1989 by Publishers Weekly.

The Putnam Publishing Group: "Misspelling" from *On the Road with Charles Kuralt* by Charles Kuralt. Copyright © 1985 by CBS Inc.

Random House, Inc.: "The Round Walls of Home" from *A Natural History of the Senses* by Diane Ackerman. Copyright © 1990 by Diane Ackerman. From Chapter 5 (retitled "When I Lay My Burden Down") from *I Know Why the Caged Bird Sings* by Maya Angelou. Copyright © 1969 and renewed © 1997 by Maya Angelou. From "On the Pulse of Morning" from *On the Pulse of Morning* by Maya Angelou. Copyright © 1993 by Maya Angelou. "New Directions" from *Wouldn't Take Nothing for My Journey Now* by Maya Angelou.

Copyright © 1993 by Maya Angelou. "Blues Ain't No Mockin Bird" from *Gorilla, My Love* by Toni Cade Bambara. Copyright © 1971 by Toni Cade Bambara. "A Christmas Memory" story and script from *Breakfast at Tiffany's* by Truman Capote. Copyright © 1956 by Truman Capote. "Poem" from *Mainland* by Victor Hernandez Cruz. Copyright © 1973 by Victor Hernandez Cruz. "Homeless" from *Living Out Loud* by Anna Quindlen. Copyright © 1987 by Anna Quindlen.

Lois Rosenthal: From "Writing as Breathing" by Nikki Giovanni from *Writer's Digest*, February 1989. Copyright © 1989 by Nikki Giovanni.

Russell & Volkening as agents for Wendi Kaufman: Adapted from "Helen on 86th Street" by Wendi Kaufman from *The New Yorker*, November 24, 1997. Copyright © 1997 by Wendi Kaufman. Author's comment on "Helen on 86th Street" by Wendi Kaufman. Copyright © 2000 by Wendi Kaufman.

Layne Sakwa: From "A House Is Not a Home" by Layne Sakwa from *Voices of Youth*, September/October 1993. Copyright © 1993 by Voices of Youth: Educational Goals Study Group.

Meredith Anne Schwartz: "Penelope to Ulysses" by Meredith Schwartz from *Dead Center Literary Magazine*, 1992. Copyright © 1992 by Meredith Anne Schwartz. Published by Highland Park High School, Highland Park, New Jersey.

Louise H. Sclove: "Motto for a Doghouse" from *Lyric Laughter* by Arthur Guiterman.

Scribner, a division of Simon & Schuster: From *The Miracle Worker* by William Gibson. Copyright © 1956, 1957 by William Gibson; copyright © 1959, 1960 by Tamarack Productions, Ltd., and George S. Klein and Leo Garel as trustees under three separate deeds of trust; copyrights renewed by William Gibson. No performance of any kind may be given without permission in writing from Samuel French, Inc., 45 West 25th Street, New York, NY 10010.

Simon & Schuster: "Forgive My Guilt" from *Selected Poems* by Robert P. Tristram Coffin. Copyright © 1946 by Robert P. Tristram Coffin; copyright renewed © 1974 by Richard N. Coffin, Mary Alice Wescott, and Robert P. T. Coffin, Jr. "The Sea Call" from *The Odyssey: A Modern Sequel* by Nikos Kazantzakis, translated by Kimon Friar. Copyright © 1958 by Helen Kazantzakis and Kimon Friar; copyright renewed © 1986 by Simon & Schuster.

Simon & Schuster Books for Young Readers, an imprint of Simon & Schuster Children's Publishing Division: "Southbound on the Freeway" from *The Complete Poems to Solve* by May Swenson. Copyright © 1963 and renewed © 1991 by May Swenson.

Sony/ATV Music Publishing c/o Hal Leonard Corporation: "When I'm Sixty-Four," words and music by John Lennon and Paul McCartney. Copyright © 1967 and renewed © 1995 by Sony/ATV Sony LLC. All rights administered by Sony/ATV Music Publishing, 8 Music Square West, Nashville, TN 37203. International copyright secured. All rights reserved.

Gloria Steinem: Quote by Alice Walker from "Do You Know This Woman? She Knows You: A Profile of Alice Walker" by Gloria Steinem from *Ms.* Magazine, June 1982. Copyright © 1982 by Ms. Foundation for Education and Communication, Inc.

St. Martin's Press, Incorporated: Quotes by Diane Ackerman from *Contemporary Poets*, Fourth Edition, edited by James Vinson and D. L. Kirkpatrick. Copyright © 1985 by James Vinson and D. L. Kirkpatrick. Published by St. Martin's Press, New York, 1985. Excerpt (retitled "Haven't I Made a Difference!") from *All Things Bright and Beautiful* by James Herriot. Copyright © 1973 by James Herriot. From "The Books I Almost Never Wrote" (Introduction) from *The Best of James Herriot* by James Herriot. Copyright © 1982 by James Herriot.

The Literary Estate of May Swenson: Comment from "Southbound on the Freeway" from *The Complete Poems to Solve* by May Swenson. Published by Macmillan in 1993.

Bob Tester: "Local Review: 'Babe,' the Pig, Is a Blast" by Bob Tester from *Great Falls Tribune*, September 9, 1995. Copyright © 1995 by Bob Tester.

Thacher Proffitt & Wood, attorneys for Ishmael Reed: From "Ishmael Reed" from *Conversations with Writers II*, vol. 3. Copyright © 1978 by Ishmael Reed. "Beware: Do Not Read This Poem" from *New and Collected Poems* by Ishmael Reed. Copyright © 1970 by Ishmael Reed. Originally appeared in *Scholastic Voice*.

Rosemary A. Thurber and Barbara Hogenson Agency: "The Princess and the Tin Box" from *The Beast in Me and Other Animals* by James Thurber. Copyright © 1948 by James Thurber; copyright renewed © 1976 by Helen Thurber and Rosemary A. Thurber. Published by Harcourt Brace & Company. "My Fifty Years with James Thurber" from *The Thurber Carnival* by James Thurber. Copyright © 1945 by James Thurber; copyright renewed © 1973 by Helen Thurber and Rosemary A. Thurber. Published by HarperCollins.

Mai Trang: "Childhood" by Mai Trang from *Rites of Passage: A Literary Magazine*, 1991–92. Copyright © 1992 by Mai Trang. Published by Thomas Jefferson High School, Portland, OR.

Charles E. Tuttle Co., Inc., 77 Central Street, Boston, MA: "The old pond" by Matsuo Bashō, "A morning glory" by Chiyo, and "A dragonfly!" by Kobayashi Issa from *Zen Art for Meditation* by Stewart W. Holmes and Chimoyo Horioka. Copyright in Japan © 1973 by Charles E. Tuttle Co., Inc. All rights reserved.

United Press International, Inc.: From "Hundreds of Birds Invade Home in California" by United Press International from *The New York Times*, May 5, 1983. Copyright © 1983 by United Press International, Inc.

The University of Georgia Press: Slight adaptation of "American History" from *The Latin Deli: Prose and Poetry* by Judith Ortiz Cofer. Copyright © 1993 by Judith Ortiz Cofer.

University of Nebraska Press: "Claiming Breath" and untitled poem from *Claiming Breath* by Diane Glancy. Copyright © 1992 by the University of Nebraska Press.

The University of North Carolina Press: "Ain't I a Woman?" by Sojourner Truth, adapted by Erlene Stetson, from *Sojourner Truth: God's Faithful Pilgrim* by Arthur Huff Fauset. Copyright © 1938 by The University of North Carolina Press.

University Press of New England: "The Bagel" from *David Ignatow: Poems 1934–1969* by David Ignatow. Copyright © 1970 by David Ignatow. Published by Wesleyan University Press. "The Talk" from *A Summer Life* by Gary Soto. Copyright © 1990 by University Press of New England.

Suzanne Vega: Lyrics from "Calypso" from *Solitude Standing* by Suzanne Vega. Copyright © 1978 by Suzanne Vega.

Vintage Books, a division of Random House, Inc.: From the *Odyssey* by Homer, translated by Robert Fitzgerald. Copyright © 1961, 1963 by Robert Fitzgerald; copyright renewed © 1989 by Benedict R. C. Fitzgerald.

The Wall Street Journal: From "Juliet of Verona Gets a Lot of Letters from the Lovelorn" by Lisa Bannon from *The Wall Street Journal*, November 10, 1992. Copyright © 1992 by Dow Jones & Company, Inc. All rights reserved worldwide.

Robynn Waterstrat and Young Voices Magazine, subscriptions, guidelines, and sample copies, P.O. Box 2321, Olympia, WA 98507, (206) 943-3711: "The Orca" by Robynn Waterstrat from *Young Voices*, May/June 1993. Copyright © 1993 by Robynn Waterstrat.

The Waterways Project of Ten Penny Players, Inc.: "In the Dark" by Leeann Watkins from *Streams*.

Nancy F. Wechsler for Mrs. Joseph P. Lash: Excerpts from "The Making of Annie Sullivan" (retitled "Annie") from *Helen and Teacher* by Joseph P. Lash. Copyright © 1980 by Joseph P. Lash.

James Welch c/o Elaine Markson Literary Agency: "The Man from Washington" from *Riding the Earthboy 40* by James Welch. Copyright © 1971 by James Welch.

Halley Wheeless: "A Chance Meeting" by Halley Wheeless from *Voices of Youth Magazine*, September/October 1993. Copyright © 1993 by Voices of Youth: Educational Goals Study Group.

Kate Wilkinson: From "Para mi Emilio, señor" by Kate Wilkinson from *Voices of Youth*, April/May 1993. Copyright © 1993 by Voices of Youth: Educational Goals Study Group.

Elizabeth Wong: "The Struggle to Be an All-American Girl" by Elizabeth Wong.

SOURCES CITED

Quote by Truman Capote from "The Private World of Truman Capote" (Part 1), an interview by Anne Taylor Fleming, from *The New York Times Magazine*, July 9, 1978. Published by The New York Times Company.

Quote by N. Scott Momaday from *Ancestral Voice: Conversations with N. Scott Momaday* by Charles L. Woodard. Published by the University of Nebraska Press, Lincoln, NE, 1989.

"The Interlopers" by Saki. Published by Dell Publishing Company, Inc., New York, 1966.

PICTURE CREDITS

The illustrations on the Contents pages are picked up from pages in the textbook. Credits for those illustrations can be found either on the textbook page on which they appear or in the listing below.

Page 2, AP/Wide World Photos; 4, (background) Adam Woolfitt/Woodfin Camp & Associates, (left) ©Charlie Traub; 5, (top left) Louis H. Jawitz/The Image Bank; 6–10, (background) Karin Daher/Gamma Liaison; 11, Larry Mayer/Gamma Liaison; 12–19, © SuperStock, Inc.; 20, Erich Lessing/Art Resource, New York; 22–23, © SuperStock, Inc.; 25, Kaz Mori/The Image Bank; 26–27, © SuperStock, Inc.; 28, (bottom) Brandt & Brandt Literary Agents, Inc.; 40, (background) Roger Ressmeyer/Corbis/Starlight; 44, (bottom) Kenneth Johansson/Outline Press; 45–46, Photofest; 75, Topham/The Image Works; 76, Michael Ventura/Bruce Coleman, Inc.; 78, Photofest; 89, © Nancy Crampton; 90, Tom McHugh/The National Audubon Society Collection/Photo Researchers, Inc.; 104–109, (background) Memphis and Shelby County Room, Memphis/Shelby County Public Library and Information Center. Scruggs Collection; 106, (top left) Costa Manos/Magnum Photos, Inc.; 109, (top center) Corbis-Bettmann; 110, From the Tales of Courage International Art Collection. Photo courtesy of the Children's Hospital at Yale–New Haven; 111, (middle left) From *Stranger with My Face* (jacket cover), by Lois Duncan. Copyright. Used by permission of Dell Publishing, a division of Random House, Inc., (top right) Cover, from *The Hobbit*. Copyright © 1966 J.R.R. Tolkien. Reprinted by permission of Houghton Mifflin Company, HarperCollins in Canada. All rights reserved, (bottom right) From *Roll of Thunder, Hear My Cry*, by Mildred D. Taylor, Puffin cover illustration by Max Ginsburg. Copyright © 1991 by Max Ginsburg, cover illustration. Used by permission of Puffin Books, a division of Penguin Putnam Inc. With additional permission from the American Library Association; 119, ©PhotoDisc, Inc. 1998; 125, Henri Cartier-Bresson/Magnum Photos, Inc.; 126, Scott Thode; 132, Photography by David Allison, New York; 139, Leonard Freed/Magnum Photos, Inc.; 148, Murray Alcosser/The Image Bank; 154, © Nancy Crampton; 155–156, Reproduced with permission of Muky Munkacsi; 157, (left) Photofest, (right) Reproduced with permission of Muky Munkacsi; 158, (left) Photofest, (right) Reproduced with permission of Muky Munkacsi; 159, (left) Reproduced with permission of Muky Munkacsi, (right) Photofest; 164, G. K. Vicki Hart/The Image Bank; 166–167, 170 (center), Photo © David Heald; 178, (bottom) Montana Historical Society; 182, Luis Castenada/The Image Bank; 184, AP/Wide World Photos; 186, Marcel Isy-Schwart/The Image Bank; 191, (top left) The Jewish Museum/Art Resource, New York; 192, (top center) © Nancy Crampton; 193, (middle left) From *Woodsong*, by Gary Paulsen, cover by Neil Waldman. Copyright © 1991 by Neil Waldman for cover illustration. Used by permission of Puffin Books, a division of Penguin Putnam Inc., (bottom left) Cover, from *Autobiography of a Face*, by Lucy Grealy. Copyright © 1994 by Lucy Grealy. Jacket photograph © 1994 Alen MacWeeney. Reprinted by permission of Houghton Mifflin Company. All rights reserved, (top right) Warner Books, Inc., (middle right) Cover illustration

INDEX OF SKILLS

in meter 552, **554–555**, 563, 605, 788, **973**, 976
  refrain as 574, **975**
  repetition as **566**
Rising action 732
Run-on line, in poetry 741, 763, 864
Satire **132**, 141, **976**
Scanning, of poetry 555, 973
Scene, in a poem **496**, 498
Screenplay 148, 155, 162
Sensory details 47, 48, 386, 387, **400**, 404, 419, 439, 452, 494, 499, 504, 513, 515, 522, 576, 578. *See also* Imagery.
Sestet 977
Setting 78, 127, **164–165, 166**, 179, 186, 301, 333, 363, 372, 387, **426**, 431, 763, 952, **976**
Shakespearean sonnet 735, 977
Short story **976**
  basic situation in a 32–33, 976
  character in a 29, 50, 78, 119, **120**, 128, **130–131**, 142, 144, 161, 186, 209, 217, 229, 230, 243, 277, 312, 333, **968–969**
  climax in a 33, **34**, 47, 48, 101, **258**, 263, 974, 976
  complications in a 33, 974, 976
  conflict in a 11, **12**, 29, 30, 32, 77, 91, 94, 141, 264, 275, 290, 333
  denouement in a 33, 974
  exposition in a 32–33, **970**, 976
  plot in a **32–33**, 34, 210, 229, **974**
  point of view in a 132, 141, 161, 209, **218–219**, 220, 230, 242, 276, 325, 326, 333, **975**
  resolution in a 29, 33, 78, 91, 275, 976
  setting in a 78, 127, **164–165, 166**, 179, 186, **976**
  theme in a **264–265**, 266, 275, 276, 278, **292**, 300, 303, 312, 325, 333, **978**
Simile 291, 327, 365, 509, 513, 520–521, 529, 538, 590, 596, 858, 859, 884, 927, 950, 967, 971, **976–977**
Situation, basic 32–33, 976
Situational irony 202, 209, 212–213, 972
Slant rhyme 559, 976
Soliloquy 875, **977**
Sonnet **977**
  Italian (Petrarchan) 977
  Shakespearean 735, 977
Sound effects (sound devices)
  alliteration **560**, 566, 569, 763, 788, **967**, 971
  assonance 566, **968**
  onomatopoeia **560**, 569, **572**, 971, 972, **973–974**
  rhyme 489, 552, **559, 561**, 563, 569, 605, 763, 788, 972, **975–976**
  rhythm **554–555**, 558, 563, 564, 588, 972, **976**
Spatial order 439, 870
Speaker 276, **526**, 528, 535, 536, 561, 568, 609, 615, 857, **977**
Stage directions 632, 661, 707, 708
Stanza **977**
Stereotype 162, **977**
Stock character 162

Story. *See* Short story.
Structure, in poetry 605
Subject 264, 614, 615
Subjective writing **394**, 398, 460
Subjectivity 355
Subplot 707
Surprise ending **94**, 102
Suspense 50, 77, **80**, 91, 333, 417, 762, 816, 834, **977**
Symbol **314**, 325, 333, 604, 660, 687, 717, **977–978**
Tag lines 243
Tall tale **978**
Technical vocabulary 200, 418
Teleplay 148, 155, 162, 633
Testimonial 256, 453
Theme **264–265**, 266, 275, 276, 278, **292**, 300, **303**, 312, 325, 333, 563, 614, 708, 716, **978**, 980
  in drama 708, 716, 855, **978**
Thesis 717
Third-person-limited point of view 219, **220**, 326, 975
Title 29, 91, 166, 209, 263, **266**, 275, 300, 363, 372, 398, 404, 424, 431, 444, 458, 530, 549
Tone 132, 253, 333, 334, **348**, 352, 380, 451, 458, 480, **542**, 544, 563, **586–587**, 597, **598**, 600, 604, 608, 615, 862, **978**, 980
Tragedy 732, **978**
Turning point, in drama 732, 816
Unreliable narrator **232**, 241
Verbal irony 212, **601**, 972
Vignette 187

READING AND CRITICAL THINKING

Active reading 3, 343, 979
  assignments. *See* Dialogue with the Text.
  strategies for 979–980. *See also* Dialogue with the Text.
  student models of 5–10, 344–346, 490
Advertisements, analyzing 256
Analogies, analyzing
  literary 438, 967
  word 163, 302, 381
Analysis 30, 162, 194, 263, 276, 332, 615
Analysis questions (Shaping Interpretations) 3, 29, 47, 77, 91, 101, 127, 141, 161, 179, 186, 209, 217, 229, 241, 263, 275, 289, 300, 312, 325, 343, 352, 363, 372, 380, 398, 404, 417, 424, 431, 450, 458, 465, 472, 498, 507, 513, 528, 535, 538, 544, 558, 563, 568, 574, 578, 582–583, 596, 600, 604, 608, 660, 686, 707, 762, 788, 816, 834, 855, 925, 950
Appeals. *See* Bandwagon appeals; Emotional appeals; Logical appeals.
Argument, analyzing 230, 338, 479, 967, 974
Attacking the person 453
Author's point of view, identifying 132, 141

Author's purpose, identifying 258, 263, 420, 424, 452–453, 465, 862
Background, drawing on. *See* Connecting with the Text; Prior knowledge.
Bandwagon appeals 256, 453
Body, of a memo 200
Brainstorming 92, 112, 230, 232, 250, 366, 386, 398, 417, 424, 438, 450, 466, 478, 485, 723, 789, 958, 959, 965
Cause and effect
  identifying 34, 47, 103, 290, 406, 417, 484, 926, 951
  false 453, 484, 960
Charts
  creating 29, 30, 31, 47, 101, 103, 127, 128, 143, 144, 180, 231, 251, 276, 277, 290, 313, 326, 333, 348, 365, 404, 417, 418, 419, 426, 432, 433, 446, 450, 451, 459, 465, 479, 485, 545, 563, 569, 598, 610, 612, 687, 709, 762, 789, 856, 857, 875, 925, 926, 927, 951, 959–960, 979, 980
  reading 982
  types of 982
Choral reading 353, 865
Chronological order, using 48, 113, 352, 353, 387, 389, 400, 405, 439, 708, 870
Circular reasoning 453, 484
Close reading 620
Cluster diagrams 30, 48, 112, 201, 230, 354, 466
Comparing reviews with one's own responses 344, 722
Comparison 5–10, 142, 303, 365, 394, 450, 513
Comparison and contrast 29, 30, 102, 103, 118, 186, 192, 229, 276, 289, 363, 394, 398, 418, 476, 507, 513, 515, 545, 549, 558, 597, 600, 604, 605, 609, 612, 614–618, 708, 835, 857, 862, 925, 964
Comprehension, checking 980
Comprehension questions (Reading Check) 29, 47, 77, 91, 101, 127, 141, 161, 179, 186, 209, 217, 229, 241, 275, 289, 300, 312, 325, 352, 363, 372, 380, 398, 404, 417, 424, 431, 450, 458, 465, 472, 660, 686, 707, 762, 788, 816, 834, 855, 925, 950
Conclusions, identifying 232, 241, 925
Connecting with the Text 4, 12, 34, 50, 80, 94, 120, 132, 144, 166, 182, 202, 214, 220, 232, 258, 266, 278, 292, 303, 314, 348, 356, 366, 375, 394, 400, 406, 420, 426, 446, 454, 458, 460, 468, 494, 496, 499, 502, 504, 509, 522, 524, 526, 530, 533, 536, 540, 542, 556, 561, 564, 566, 570, 572, 576, 588, 590, 594, 598, 601, 606, 632, 732, 888, 979
Connotations, identifying 374, 451, 563, 594, 596, 969, 970
Context clues 3, 29, 49, 94, 120, 127, 144, 161, 303, 835, 858
Context diagrams 49
Counterargument 472, 479, 926
Craft, writer's. *See specific elements of literature in index of Literary Terms.*

LANGUAGE (GRAMMAR, USAGE, AND MECHANICS)

CROSSING THE CURRICULUM

INDEX OF ART

FINE ART AND CRAFTS

INDEX OF AUTHORS AND TITLES

Page numbers in italic type refer to the pages on which author biographies appear.